D0835648

NATURAL SCIENCES IN AMERICA

THE BIRDS

OF

NORTH AMERICA

Spencer F[ullerton] Baird
John Cassin
George N. Lawrence

Volumes I and II

ARNO PRESS
A New York Times Company
New York, N. Y. • 1974

Reprint Edition 1974 by Arno Press Inc.

Reprinted from copies in The American
    Museum of Natural History and the
    University of Illinois Libraries

NATURAL SCIENCES IN AMERICA
ISBN for complete set: 0-405-05700-8
See last pages of this volume for titles.

Manufactured in the United States of America

Publisher's Note: Pages XIII-XVI in Volume I
were missing from all available copies. The
illustrations in Volume II have been reduced
by 30%.

———◆———

Library of Congress Cataloging in Publication Data

Baird, Spencer Fullerton, 1823-1887.
    The birds of North America.

    (Natural sciences in America)
    Reprint of the 1860 ed. published by Lippincott,
Philadelphia.
    Bibliography: p.
    1. Birds--North America. 2. Birds--Catalogs and
collections. 3. Smithsonian institution. I. Cassin,
John, 1813-1869, joint author. II. Lawrence, George
Newbold, 1806-1895, joint author. III. Title.
IV. Series.
QL681.B138 1974   598.2'97   73-17799
ISBN 0-405-05715-6

THE BIRDS

OF

NORTH AMERICA;

THE DESCRIPTIONS OF SPECIES BASED CHIEFLY ON THE COLLECTIONS

IN THE

MUSEUM OF THE SMITHSONIAN INSTITUTION.

BY

SPENCER F. BAIRD,

ASSISTANT SECRETARY OF THE SMITHSONIAN INSTITUTION,

WITH THE CO-OPERATION OF

JOHN CASSIN,

OF THE ACADEMY OF NATURAL SCIENCES OF PHILADELPHIA,

AND

GEORGE N. LAWRENCE,

OF THE LYCEUM OF NATURAL HISTORY OF NEW YORK.

With an Atlas of One Hundred Plates.

TEXT.

———————

PHILADELPHIA:

J. B. LIPPINCOTT & CO.

1860.

CONTENTS.

ADVERTISEMENT.

THE present work is, in part, a reprint of the General Report on North American Birds presented to the Department of War, and published in October, 1858, as one of the series of "Reports of Explorations and Surveys of a Railroad Route to the Pacific Ocean." In this volume, however, will be found many important additions and corrections, including detailed lists of plates, both numerical and systematic, descriptions of newly-discovered species, &c., not in the original edition.

The Atlas contains one hundred plates, representing one hundred and forty-eight new or unfigured species of North American birds. Of these plates about fifty appear for the first time, having been prepared expressly for this work. The remainder form the ornithological illustrations of the Reports of the Pacific Railroad Survey, and of the United States and Mexican Boundary Survey under Major Emory, and are distributed throughout the numerous volumes composing those series. All have, however, been carefully retouched and lettered for this edition, and quite a number redrawn entirely from better and more characteristic specimens. In fact, the plates of the Atlas have been prepared expressly for the present edition with the utmost care and attention.

In the volume of text will be found a complete account of the birds of North America, brought down to the present time, including accurate descriptions of all known species; their arrangement in the genera and families recognized by modern zoologists; their geographical distribution; and, as far as possible, all other information necessary to a complete summary or manual of North American ornithology. No other work extant gives a complete ornithology of our country; and it has been the especial object of the authors and publishers to adapt it to the wants of the student and lover of nature, and to present in a condensed form, and at a price within the reach of all, a reliable text-book in this favorite department of natural history. Extended bibliographical notices, embracing full references to very nearly all authors on American ornithology, have been added, and will be found to be of high interest to the student and naturalist.

The Atlas, embracing as it does one hundred plates of birds not figured by Audubon, will be found indispensable to the possessor of that distinguished author's "Birds of America," completing it to the present time.

As stated in the preface, the descriptions and figures in the present work have been taken almost entirely from specimens in the museum of the Smithsonian Institution. To the Secretary of the Institution the publishers are under many obligations for facilities in the preparation of this much-extended and greatly-improved edition.

PREFACE.

THE present report is a continuation of a systematic account of the vertebrate animals of North America, collected or observed by the different parties organized under the direction of the War Department for ascertaining the best route for a railroad from the Mississippi river to the Pacific ocean.

The collections of these expeditions having been deposited with the Smithsonian Institution by the War Department, in compliance with an act of Congress, the undersigned was charged by the Secretary of the Institution with the duty of furnishing the series of general reports upon them, as called for by the Department. The account of the mammals having been published in 1857, that of the birds is herewith furnished, prepared according to the plan announced in the preface to that volume.

As in the volume on the mammals, by the insertion of the comparatively few species not noticed by the expeditions, this report becomes an exposition of the present state of our knowledge of the birds of North America north of Mexico. This addition, while rendering the work more valuable to the reader, was absolutely necessary for the proper understanding of the western fauna, the species of which are generally so closely allied to the eastern forms as to require in most cases more minute and detailed descriptions of the latter than have been published.

Certain portions of the report have been prepared by Mr. JOHN CASSIN, of Philadelphia, and Mr. GEORGE N. LAWRENCE, of New York, well known as the leading ornithologists of the United States. Mr. Cassin has furnished the entire account of the *Raptores* from p. 4 to 64, of the *Grallae* from p. 689 to 753, and of the *Alcidae* from p. 900 to 918, in all about 135 pages. Mr. Lawrence has written the article on the *Longipennes*, *Totipalmes*, and *Colymbidae*, from page 820 to 900, making 80 pages.

To Mr. P. L. Sclater, of London, acknowledgments are due for the examination of certain specimens in European museums, and for other valuable aid in determining points of synonymy; some of his notes, received too late for insertion in their proper places, will be found in Appendix A. Much assistance has also been rendered in various ways by Dr. J. G. Cooper.

In the introduction to the general report upon the mammals will be found a detailed account of the different railroad surveying parties from which zoological collections were received, with their respective routes. For the proper understanding of the subject, however, it will be necessary to present a brief recapitulation in this place.

1. LINE OF THE 47TH PARALLEL, UNDER GOVERNOR I. I. STEVENS.—This consisted of two principal parties: one under Governor Stevens, passing from St. Paul, Minnesota, to the Pacific, accompanied by Dr. George Suckley, U. S. A., as surgeon and naturalist; the other under Captain G. B. McClellan, proceeding from Vancouver to the Cascade mountains, accompanied by

Dr. J. G. Cooper. After the termination of their official duties with the survey, Dr. Suckley made a very extensive collection of birds at the Dalles, and on Puget's Sound, and Dr. Cooper at Shoalwater bay, on Puget's Sound, and at Santa Clara, California.

2. 38TH AND 39TH PARALLELS, UNDER CAPTAIN J. W. GUNNISON, AND THE 41ST, UNDER CAPTAIN E. G. BECKWITH.—The duties of naturalist were performed by Mr. Kreuzfeldt until his death; afterwards by Mr. Snyder, of Captain Beckwith's party.

3. 35TH PARALLEL, UNDER CAPTAIN A. W. WHIPPLE.—This party was at first divided into two: one under Captain Whipple, starting from Fort Smith, accompanied by Mr. H. B. Mölhausen, as naturalist; the other under Lieutenant Ives, from San Antonio, Texas, with Dr. Kennerly. Both parties met at Albuquerque, and proceeded together to the Pacific.

4. CALIFORNIA LINE, UNDER LIEUTENANT WILLIAMSON.—This party, with Dr. Heermann as naturalist, explored the country from San Francisco to the Tejon Pass and the Colorado river.

5. 32D PARALLEL WEST, UNDER LIEUTENANT J. G. PARKE.—Lieutenant Parke's party, with Dr. Heermann as naturalist, traversed the route from Fort Yuma to El Paso, and thence through Texas.

6. 32D PARALLEL EAST, UNDER CAPTAIN J. POPE.—From El Paso to Preston, on Red river. Captain Pope's collections include the very extensive series of birds gathered by Dr. T. C. Henry, U. S. A., at Fort Thorn and on the Mimbres.

The preceding lines were organized in 1853; the following were sent out subsequently:

7. CALIFORNIA AND OREGON LINE, UNDER LIEUTENANT WILLIAMSON.—This party explored the Cascade mountains of California and Oregon. The zoological collections were made by Dr. J. S. Newberry, geologist of the expedition.

In addition to the preceding railroad explorations, the results of the following miscellaneous government expeditions, made under the War Department, have been embodied in the report:

8. EXPLORATION OF THE LLANO ESTACADO, in 1854 and 1856, by Captain POPE.

9. EXPLORATION OF THE UPPER MISSOURI AND YELLOWSTONE IN 1856, UNDER LIEUT. G. K. WARREN.—Very large collections of birds were made by this party, of which Dr. F. V. Hayden was surgeon and naturalist.

10. EXPLORATION OF THE NORTH SIDE OF THE PLATTE RIVER AND LOUP FORK IN 1857, UNDER LIEUT. G. K. WARREN.—On this second expedition of Lieut. Warren, (Dr. Hayden, naturalist,) large collections of birds were made, especially on Laramie Peak and Loup Fork.

11. WAGON ROAD FROM FORT RILEY TO BRIDGER'S PASS, UNDER LIEUT. F. T. BRYAN.—This party, with W. S. Wood as collector and naturalist, was in the field two seasons, 1856 and 1857, and made very large collections.

12. SURVEY OF THE COLORADO RIVER IN 1857-'58, UNDER LIEUT. J. C. IVES.—H. B. Mölhausen, zoologist, aided by Dr. J. S. Newberry, geologist.

The following expeditions, under the Department of the Interior, have also furnished important materials:

13. SURVEY OF THE UNITED STATES AND MEXICAN BOUNDARY LINE IN 1851 TO 1855.—The collections of this survey were made while Mr. John R. Bartlett, Mr. R. B. Campbell, and Major W. H. Emory, U. S. A., were commissioners; and Col. J. D. Graham, U. S. A., and Major Emory, U. S. A., were in charge of the scientific department. The collections were made by Messrs. John H. Clark, Arthur Schott, Charles Wright, Dr. T. H. Webb, and Dr. C. B. Kennerly.

14. FORT KEARNEY, SOUTH PASS AND HONEY LAKE WAGON ROAD, EASTERN DIVISION, UNDER W. M. F. MAGRAW.—On this route large collections were made by Dr. J. G. Cooper, surgeon of the party, as far as Fort Laramie, in 1857, and on his return eastward. His assistant, Mr. C. Drexler, visited Fort Bridger, Utah, in March, 1858, and mainly through the countenance of General A. S. Johnston, commander of the United States forces stationed there, was enabled to make a very large collection of the birds of that region. His collections were received too late for mention in their proper places, but are given in Appendix B.

Parties fitted out by the State Department:

15. SURVEY OF THE NORTHWESTERN BOUNDARY, UNDER ARCHIBALD CAMPBELL.—Occasional references will be found to collections received from this party, of which Dr. C. B. Kennerly is surgeon and naturalist, made chiefly at Simeahmoo bay, Puget's Sound, near the mouth of Fraser's river.

The following less official collections from the west and south have been used in the preparation of the report:

FROM THE PACIFIC SLOPE.—The very large private collections of Dr. Suckley, in Washington and Oregon Territories, and of Dr. Cooper, in Washington Territory and California, already referred to.

Also, additional collections of great magnitude made along the whole Pacific coast of the United States by Lieut. W. P. Trowbridge, while engaged on Coast Survey duty; by Mr. E. Samuels, at Petaluma, California, and by Mr. John Xantus de Vesey, at Fort Tejon.

Likewise collections of greater or less extent made by Dr. John Potts, U. S. A., Mr. A. J. Grayson, Dr. John F. Hammond, U. S. A., Mr. Richard D. Cutts, Mr. A. Cassidy, Dr. W. F. Tolmie, Dr. Vollum, U. S. A., and Dr. W. S. King, U. S. A.

FROM THE ROCKY MOUNTAIN REGIONS.—The very complete collection of birds of Fort Thorn and the adjacent regions, made by Dr. T. C. Henry, U. S. A.; also, collection from Fort Massachusetts, New Mexico, made by Dr. D. W. C. Peters, U. S. A.; at Cantonment Burgwyn, New Mexico, by Dr. W. W. Anderson, U. S. A.; and by Captain R. B. Marcy, near Cochetope Pass.

FROM TEXAS AND MEXICO.—The large collection of Lieut. D. N. Couch, U. S. A., in Texas and northern Mexico; of Captain S. Van Vliet, U. S. A., at Brownsville; of Dr. Swift, U. S. A., at Fort Chadbourne, Texas, and of Drs. Foard and Crawford, U. S. A.; also, of Mr. Gustavus Würdemann, of the United States Coast Survey, on the coast of Texas. The further collections of this gentleman on the coast of Louisiana, of Florida, and among the Florida Keys, have contained several new species, and many species new to the fauna of the United States.

FROM NEBRASKA, KANSAS, AND ELSEWHERE.—Collections made in Kansas and Nebraska by Dr. W. A. Hammond, U. S. A., and Mr. John Xantus de Vesey; by Dr. Hayden, Colonel Alfred Vaughan, Indian agent, and Dr. J. Evans. On Red River of the North by Donald Gunn, esq. Also, large collections made in Minnesota and Illinois by Mr. R. Kennicott, partly under the auspices of the Northwestern University of Evanston, Illinois; others made in Wisconsin by Dr. Hoy and Mr. Barry; in Ohio by Dr. J. P. Kirtland; and near Chicago by Mr. Thomas E. Blackney. Also, collections made in Georgia by Professor Joseph Leconte.

A collection of about 150 species received from Mr. John Gould, of London, contains many rare birds from the northwest and Arctic regions, (some of them types of the "Fauna Boreali-

Americana,") as well as others from Mexico and Guatemala.   The latter have proved of great service for comparison with closely allied species of the United States, as have also specimens from Mr. P. L. Sclater, of London, Mr. J. P. Verreaux, of Paris, and Messrs. J. H. Gurney and Alfred Newton, of Norwich, England.

The types of eastern birds have been furnished by the collection of the author deposited in the Smithsonian Institution.   This consists of a full collection of birds of Central Pennsylvania, with sex, date, and measurements before skinning.   It also embraces a large number of Mr. Audubon's typical specimens used in the preparation of his "Birds of America," including many of those from the Columbia river and Rocky mountains, furnished him by Mr. J. K. Townsend.

In addition to the collections just mentioned, with others not enumerated, all in charge of the Smithsonian Institution, and amounting to over 12,000 specimens, types have been supplied for the occasion by Mr. Cassin, Mr. Lawrence, Mr. John G. Bell, Dr. Michener, and others.   The ornithological gallery of the Philadelphia Academy of Natural Sciences, believed to be the richest in the world, has also furnished the means of making many essential comparisons.

The measurements of the specimens have usually been made in hundredths of the English inch,[1] mostly with the dividers.   All the measurements in the list of specimens are as made before the bird was skinned, each collector being responsible for the accuracy of his work.   The comparative tables of measurements show, in many cases, the change of dimensions produced in the dried skin.

S. F. B.

WASHINGTON, *October* 20, 1858.

---

[1] The English inch is about equal to 11.26 French lines, .9383 French inches, or to 25.40 millimetres.

EXPLANATION OF PLATES.*

* Where not otherwise mentioned, the specimens figured are to be considered as in the museum of the Smithsonian Institution, and the numbers refer to the Smithsonian record of birds. The original of each figure is indicated as far as can now be ascertained.

* The figures in parenthesis refer to the numbers of the plates in the Mexican Boundary series.

* *Syrnium occidentale*, XANTUS.—Proceedings Phila. Acad. Nat. Sciences, 1859, 193.

SP. CHAR.—A little smaller than *S. nebulosum*; general color liver brown, the feathers barred everywhere, even on the flanks Axillars and under wing and tail coverts banded transversely with white, the bands towards and on the head are contracted into rounded spots.

General appearance that of *S. nebulosum*. Prevailing color light liver brown, each short feather with two transverse bars of white, the basal one tinged with rufous yellow; the subterminal pure white and not generally extending to the edges of the feathers. These bars have a marginal suffusion of brown darker than the ground color. On the top of the head and neck the subterminal bar exhibits a tendency to contraction into rounded or cordate spots, and in other places to a median

EXPLANATION OF PLATES.

interruption along the shaft. On the scapulars, axillars, and other elongated feathers there are several white bars. The facial disk is grayish, obscurely barred with brown; the posterior margin of the ear is uniform liver brown, then becoming banded with white. The longest quills and tail feathers show about 7 to 9 clouded transverse light bars, one of these at the end of the feather; the bars on the inner and outer margins are quite white, especially towards the base of the feather, elsewhere they are mottled yellowish brown or brownish yellow; the legs are dirty yellowish, with obscure and rather transverse mottlings of brown. The bill is greenish yellow; the iris gamboge; the claws horn color; the toes are thickly feathered to within two scutellæ of the base of the claws. The fourth quill is longest, the fifth and then the third a little shorter, the second between the sixth and seventh; the first rather shorter than the eighth.

Length of male 18 inches; extent 40; wing 13; tail 8½; tarsus about 2.

This species, with a general resemblance to the *Syrnium nebulosum*, is of rather smaller size, and readily distinguished by the entire absence of any of the longitudinal brown stripes so conspicuous on the belly, flanks, and lower tail coverts of the latter species; these regions being barred transversely with white and brown. The white bars on the feathers are much less continuous and regular, and on the neck and head are restricted to rounded spots instead of forming regular zones. The under wing coverts are banded transversely instead of being uniform yellowish white. The bill is less pure yellow.

A single specimen (original number 1858) was collected at Fort Teion, March 6, 1858.

* *Helminthophaga virginiae*, BAIRD.—Similar in general appearance to *H. ruficapilla*. Top and sides of head, back, and wings light ashy plumbeous, with an almost imperceptible wash of olivaceous green; quills and tail feathers brown, edged with pure ashy plumbeous, the latter indistinctly and narrowly margined with whitish internally and at the end. Rump and upper and lower tail coverts bright yellow (with a greenish tint above) in vivid contrast to the rest of the body. Crown with a concealed patch of orange brown. Rest of under parts brownish white with indications of yellow along the median region, (perhaps entirely yellow when mature.) Inside of wings and axillars whitish. A white ring around the eye. Length 5 inches; extent 7¼; wing 2¼. No. 10719. Fort Burgwyn, N. M. Collected by Dr. W. W. Anderson, U. S. A.

† *Ibis guaraúna*, SHAW.—This species differs from *Ibis ordii*, in longer legs, and an entire absence of chestnut red, which is replaced by bronzed green. No specimens in the Smithsonian collection show any gloss on the head and neck.

I. TABLE OF THE HIGHER GROUPS.

Order I. RAPTORES. (Page 3.)

Family.	Page.	Sub-family.	Page.	Section.	Page.	Genus.	Page.	Sub genus.	Page.	Species examined and identified.	Species not examined nor identified.	Extra limital species.	Current number of first species mentioned.
1. Vulturidae	4	Cathartinae	4	....		1. Cathartes, Ill........	4	....	4	3	....	1	1
2. Falconidae.......	7	Falconinae	7	....		2. Falco, Linn.........	7	Falco	7	2	....	....	5
								Hypotriorchis.........	9	3	....	....	7
								Gennaia.	12	1	....	....	10
								Hierofalco...........	13	2	....	....	11
								Tinnunculus.........	13	1	....	....	13
		Accipitrinae	15	....		3. Astur, Lac..........	15	.... .		1	....	....	14
						4. Accipiter, Briss	16	....		3	...	....	15
		Buteoninae	19	....		5. Buteo, Cuv........	19	Buteo	19	3	....	....	18
								Leucopternis	23	2	....	....	21
								Poecilopternis.......	25	6	....	...	23
								Tachytriorchis.......	31	1	....	....	29
						6. Archibuteo, Brehm..	32	....		3	....	....	30
						7. Asturina, Vieill.....	35	....		1	....	....	33
		Milvinae..... ...	36	....		8. Nauclerus, Vig.....	36	....		1	....	....	34
						9. Elanus, Sav	37	....		1	....	....	35
						10. Ictinia, Vieill......	37	....		1	....	....	36
						11. Rostrhamus, Less ...	38	....		1	....	....	37
						12. Circus, Lacep	38	....		1	....	....	38
		Aquilinae..	41	....		13. Aquila, Moehr	41	....		1	....	....	39
						14. Haliaetus, Sav	42	....		4	....	....	40
		Polyborinae......				15. Pandion, Sav......	44	....		1	....	....	44
						16. Polyborus, Vieill.....	45	....		1	....	....	45
						17. Craxirex, Gould....	46	....		1	....	....	46
3. Strigidae	47	Striginae	47	....		18. Strix, Linn	47	....		1	....	....	47
		Buboninae.......	48	....		19. Bubo, Cuv	49	....		1	....	....	48
						20. Scops, Sav.........	51	....		2	....	....	49
						21. Otus, Cuv...... ...	53	....		1	....	....	51
						22. Branchyotus, Gould .	54	....		1	....	....	52
		Syrniinae	55	....		23. Syrnium, Sav........	55	....		2	....	....	53
						24. Nyctale, Brehm.....	57	....		3	....	....	55
		Atheninae........	59	....		25. Athene, Boie........	59	....		2	...	....	58
						26. Glaucidium, Boie....	61	....		1	....	....	60
		Nycteinae	63	....		27. Nyctea, Steph	63	....		1	....	....	61
						28. Surnia, Dum	64	....		1	....	....	62

b 3*

Order II. SCANSORES. (Page 65.)

Family.	Page.	Sub-family.	Page.	Section.	Page.	Genus.	Page.	Sub-genus.	Page.	Species examined and identified.	Species not examined nor identified.	Extra limital species.	Current number of first species mentioned.
4. Psittacidae	66					29. Conurus, Kuhl	66			1			63
						Rhynchopsitta, Bon.	66					1	64
5. Trogonidae	69					30. Trogon, Moehr				1			65
6. Cuculidae	71					31. Crotophaga, Linn	71			2			66
						32. Geococcyx, Wag.	73			1			68
						33. Coccygus, Vieill.	75			3			69
7. Picidae	79	Picinae	79	Piceae	80	34. Campephilus, Gray.	81			1		1	72
						35. Picus, Linn	83	Trichopicus, Bp.	83	4			74
								Dyctiopicus, Bp.	83	2			78
								Phrenopicus, Bp.	83	1			80
								Xenopicus, Bd.	83	1			81
						36. Picoides, Lac.	97			3			82
						37. Sphyrapicus, Bd.	101			5			85
						38. Hylatomus, Baird.	107			1			90
				Centureae	108	39. Centurus, Sw.	108			3			91
						40. Melanerpes, Sw.	112			3			94
				Colapteae	117	41. Colaptes, Sw.	117			3			99

Order III. INSESSORES. (Page 126.)

Sub-order A. STRISORES. (Page 128.)

Family.	Page.	Sub-family.	Page.	Section.	Page.	Genus.	Page.	Sub-genus.	Page.	Species examined and identified.	Species not examined nor identified.	Extra limital species.	Current number of first species mentioned.
10. Trochilidae	129					42. Lampornis, Sw.	130			1			100
						43. Trochilus, L.	131			2			101
						44. Selasphorus, Sw.	133			2			103
						45. Atthis, Reich.	136			2			105
11. Cysselidae	140					46. Panyptila, Cab.	140			1			107
						47. Nephoecetes, Bd.	142			1			108
						48. Chaetura, Steph.	144			2			109
12. Caprimulgidae	146	Caprimulginae	146			49. Antrostomus, Gould.	146			3			111
						50. Chordeiles, Sw.	150			3			114

Sub-order B. CLAMATORES. (Page 156.)

Family.	Page.	Sub-family.	Page.	Section.	Page.	Genus.	Page.	Sub-genus.	Page.	Species examined and identified.	Species not examined nor identified.	Extra limital species.	Current number of first species mentioned.
13. Alcedinidae	157					51. Ceryle, Boie	157	Megaceryle, Rch.	157	1			117
								Chloroceryle, Kaup.	157	1			118
14. Prionitidae	161					52. Momotus, Lath	161			1			119
15. Colopteridae	163	Psarinae	164			53. Pachyrhamphus, Gr.	164			1			120
						54. Bathmidurus, Cab.	165			1			121
		Tyranninae.	166	Tyranni	167	55. Milvulus, Sw.	167			2			122
						56. Tyrannus, Cuv.	170			5		1	124
				Tyrannuli	167	57. Myiarchus, Cab.	177			4			130
						58. Sayornis, Bp.	182			3			134
						59. Contopus, Cab.	186			3			137
						60. Empidonax, Cab.	191			7			140
						61. Pyrocephalus, Gould.	201			1			147

Sub-order C. OSCINES.

Family.	Page.	Sub-family.	Page.	Section.	Page.	Genus.	Page.	Sub-genus.	Page.	Species examined and identified.	Species not examined nor identified.	Extra limital species.	Current number of first species mentioned.
16. Turdidae.	207	Turdinae	207			62. Turdus, L.	208	Turdus, L.	210	7			148
								Planesticus, Bp	210	1			155
								Ixoreus, Bp	210	1			156
						63. Saxicola, Bechst	220			1			157
						64. Sialia, Sw	221			3			158
		Regulinae	226			65. Regulus, Cuv	226			2	1		161
		Cinclinae	229			66. Hydrobata, Vieill	229			1			164
17. Sylvicolidae.	231	Motacillinae	231			67. Anthus, Bechst	232			1			165
						68. Neocorys, Sclater	233			1			166
		Sylvicolinae	234	Mniotilteae	235	69. Mniotilta, Vieill	235			1			167
						70. Parula, Bon	237			1			168
						71. Protonotaria, Bd.	239			1			169
				Geothlypeae	240	72. Geothlypsis, Cab	240			3		1	170
						73. Oporornis, Baird	246			2			174
				Icterieae	248	74. Icteria, Vieill	248			2			176
				Vermivoreae	251	75. Helmitherus, Raf.	251			2			178
						76. Helminthophaga, Cab	253			6			180
				Sylvicoleae	259	77. Seiurus, Sw	259			3			186
						78. Dendroica, Gray	263			20	2		189
				Setophageae	291	79. Myiodioctes, Aud.	291			3	2		211
						80. Cordellina, Dubus.	295					1	216
								Basileuterus, Cab.	296				
						81. Setophaga, Sw.	297			2		1	217
		Tanagrinae	299			82. Pyranga, Vieill	300			4			220
						83. Euphonia, Desm	304					1	224
18. Hirundinidae.	307	Hirundininae	307			84. Hirundo, Linn.	307			4			225
						85. Cotyle, Boie.	312			2			229
						86. Progne, Boie.				1			231
19. Bombycillidae.	316	Bombycillinae	316			87. Ampelis, Linn.	316			2			232
		Ptiliogonidinae	318			88. Phainopepla, Scl.	319			1			234
						89. Myiadestes, Sw.	320			1			235
20. Laniidae.	323	Laniinae	323			90. Collyrio, Moehr.	323			4			236
		Vireoninae	329			91. Vireo, Vieill.	329	Vireosylva, Bp	329	4			240
								Vireo, Vieill	329	4			244
								Lanivireo, Bd.	329	5			248
21. Liotrichidae.	343	Miminae	343			92. Mimus, Boie.	343			2			253
						93. Oreoscoptes, Bd.	347			1			255
						94. Harporhynchus, Cab	348	Harporhynchus	348	3			256
								Methriopterus, Reich.	348	3			259
		Campylorhynchi-nae.	354			95. Campylorhynchus, Spix	354			1			262
						96. Catherpes, Baird	356			1			263
						97. Salpinctes, Cab.	357			1			264
		Troglodytinae	358			98. Thriothorus, Vieill.	359			3			265
						99. Cistothorus, Cab.	364	Telmatodytes, Cab.	364	1			268
								Cistothorus, Cab.	364	1			269
						100. Troglodytes, Vieill.	366	Troglodytes, Vieill.	366	3			270
								Anorthura, Rennie	366	1			273
		Chamaeanae	370			101. Chamaea, Gamb.	370			1			274
22. Certhiadae	372	Certhianae.	372			102. Certhia, Linn	372			2			275
		Sittinae	374			103. Sitta, Linn.	374			5			277
23. Paridae	379	Polioptilinae	379			104. Polioptila, Sclater.	379			3			282
		Parinae	379			105. Lophophanes, Kaup.	383			4			285
						106. Parus, Linn.	387			7		1	289
						107. Psaltriparus, Bon.	395			2		1	297
						108. Paroides, Kaup.	399			1			300

TABLE OF THE HIGHER GROUPS.

Sub-order C. OSCINES—Continued.

Family.	Page.	Sub-family.	Page.	Section.	Page.	Genus.	Page.	Sub-genus.	Page.	Species examined and identified.	Species not examined nor identified.	Extra limital species.	Current number of first species mentioned.
24. Dacnididae......	App	Dacnidinae	App	....	....	109. Certhiola, Sund....	App	....	....	1	....	....	301
25. Alaudidae.......	402		....		....	110. Eremophila, Boie ..	402	....	....	1	....	....	302
26. Fringillidae	406	Coccothraustinae.	406	....	....	111. Hesperiphona, Bon.	408	....	....	1	....	....	303
						112. Pinicola, Vieill....,	409	....	....	1	....	....	304
						113. Carpodacus, Kaup..	411	....	....	4	....	1	305
						114. Chrysomitris, Boie.	418	Chrysomitris, Boie...	418	1	....	2	310
								Astragalinus, Cab....	419	5	....	....	313
						115. Curvirostra, Scop...	426	....	....	2	....	....	318
						116. Aegiothus, Cab.....	428	....	....	1	1	....	320
						117. Leucosticte, Sw....	430	....	....	1	2	....	322
						118. Plectrophanes, Mey.	431	Plectrophanes, Meyer.	....	1	....	....	325
								Centrophanes, Kaup.	....	4	....	....	326
								Rhynchophanes, Bd..	....	1	....	....	330
		Spizellinae	438	....	...	119. Centronyx, Baird...	440	....	....	1	....	....	331
						120. Passerculus, Bon...	441	....	....	5	....	....	332
						121. Pooecetes, Baird...	447	....	....	1	....	....	337
						122. Coturniculus, Bon..	449	....	....	2	1	....	338
						123. Ammodromus, Sw...	452	....	....	3	..	....	341
						124. Chondestes, Sw....	455	....	....	1	....	....	344
						125. Zonotrichia, Sw....	457	....	....	5	....	....	345
						196. Junco, Wagler.. .	464	....	....	4	....	1	350
						127. Poospiza, Cab......	469	....	....	2	....	....	355
						128. Spizella, Bon.......	471	....	....	6	....	....	357
						129. Melospiza, Bd......	476	Melospiza, Bd.......	476	5	....	....	363
								Helospiza, Bd.......	477	2	....	....,	368
						130. Peucaea, Aud......	484	....	....	3	....	....	370
						131. Embernagra, Less..	487	....	....	1	....	.	373
		Passerellinae	487	....	...	132. Passerella, Sw.....	488	....	....	3	....	....	374
		Spizinae.........	490	....	....	133. Calamospiza, Bon...	492	....	....	1	....	....	377
						134. Euspiza, Bon......	493	....	....	2	....	....	378
						135. Guiraca, Sw.......	496	Goniaphœa, Bowd...	497	2	....	....	380
								Guiraca, Sw.........	497	1	....	....	382
						136. Cyanospiza, Bd....	500	....	....	5	....	....	383
						137. Spermophila, Sw...	506	....	....	1	....	....	388
						138. Pyrrhuloxia, Bon..	507	....	....	1	....	....	389
						139. Cardinalis, Bon....	508	....	....	1	....	....	390
						140. Pipilo, Vieill......	510	.. ..	....	8	....	....	391
27. Icteridae........	521	Agelaiinae.......	521	....	....	141. Dolichonyx, Sw.....	522	....	....	1	....	....	399
						142. Molothrus, Sw......	523	....	....	1	....	....	400
						143. Agelaius, Vieill....	525	....	....	3	....	....	401
						144. Xanthocephalus, B.	531	....	....	1	....	....	404
						(145.) Trupialis, Bon...	533	....	....	7	....	(?) 1	405
						146. Sturnella, Vieill....	535	....	....	2	....	....	406
		Icterinae	540	....	....	147. Icterus, Daud......	540	....	....	8	....	1	408
		Quiscalinae... ..	550	....	....	148. Scolecophagus, Sw.	551	....	....	2	....	....	417
						149. Quiscalus, Vieill...	553	....	....	4	....	....	419
28. Corvidae	558	Corvinae	558	....	....	150. Corvus, Linn......	559	....	....	7	....	....	423
						151. Picicorvus, Bon....	572	....	....	1	....	....	430
						152. Gymnokitta, Max...	574	....	....	1	....	....	431
		Garrulinae......,..	575	....	..	153. Pica, Briss........	576	....	....	2	....	....	432
						154. Cyanura, Sw.......	579	....	....	3	....	....	434
						155. Cyanocitta, Str.....	584	....	....	5	..	..	437
						156. Xanthoura, Bp.....	589	....	....	1	....	....	442
						157. Perisereus, Bon....	590	....	....	1	....	....	443
						158. Psilorhinus, Rupp..	591	....	....	1	....	....	444

Order IV. RASORES. (Page 593.)

Sub-Order A. COLUMBAE. (Page 595.)

Family.	Page.	Sub-family.	Page.	Section.	Page.	Genus.	Page.	Sub-genus.	Page.	Species examined and identified.	Species not examined nor identified.	Extra limital species.	Current number of first species mentioned.
29. Columbidae ...	595	Columbinae	596	....	....	159. Columba, L......	596	Columba, L..........	596	2	.	..	445
								Patagioenas, Reich..	596	1	...	...	447
						160. Ectopistes, Sw.....	599	....			1	...	448
		Zenaidinae	600	Zenaideae	600	161. Zenaida, Bon.....	601				1	...	449
						162. Melopelia, Bon....	602				1	...	450
						163. Zenaidura, Bon....	603				1	...	451
				Chamaepelieae ..	....	164. Scardafella, Bon....	605				1	...	452
						165. Chamaepelia, Sw...	606				1	...	453
				Starnoenadeae ...	....	166. Oreopeleia, Reich..	607				1	...	454
						167. Starnoenas, Bon....	608				1	...	455

Sub-Order B. GALLINAE. (Page 609.)

Family.	Page.	Sub-family.	Page.	Section.	Page.	Genus.	Page.	Sub-genus.	Page.	Species examined and identified.	Species not examined nor identified.	Extra limital species.	Current number of first species mentioned.
30. Penelopidae	610					168. Ortalida, Merrem ..	610			1	...	...	456
31. Phasianidae.....	613	Meleagrinae.....	613			169. Meleagris, Linn....	613			2	...	...	457
32. Tetraonidae....	619					170. Tetrao, Linn.......	620			3	...	...	459
						171. Centrocercus, Sw...	624			1	...	...	462
						172. Pedioecetes, Bd....	625			1	...	...	463
						173. Cupidonia, Reich..	627			1	...	...	464
						174. Bonasa, Steph..	629			2	...	...	465
						175. Lagopus, Vieill.....	632			3	1	...	467
33. Perdicidae	638	Ortyginae........	638			176. Ortyx, Steph........	639			2	...	...	471
						177. Oreortyx, Baird	642			1	...	...	473
						178. Lophortyx, Bon	643			2	...	...	474
						179. Callipepla, Wagler..	646			1	...	...	476
						180. Cyrtonyx, Gould...	647			1	...	...	477

Order V. GRALLATORES. (Page 650.)

Sub-Order A. HERODIONES. (Page 651.)

Family.	Page.	Sub-family.	Page.	Section.	Page.	Genus.	Page.	Sub-genus.	Page.	Species examined and identified.	Species not examined nor identified.	Extra limital species.	Current number of first species mentioned.
34. Gruidae	652					181. Grus, Linn........	653			3	...	...	478
35. Aramidae.......	657					182. Aaramus, Vieill....	657			1	...	...	480
36. Ardeidae	659	Ardeinae..... ...	659	Ardeae	659	183. Demiegretta, Blyth.	660			3	...	...	482
						184. Garzetta, Bon......	664			1	...	...	485
						185. Herodias, Boie	666			1	...	...	486
						186. Ardea, Linn.......	667			2	...	...	487
						187. Audubonia, Bp....	670			1	...	...	489
						188. Florida, Bd.....?...	671			1	...	...	490
				Botaureae........	659	189. Ardetta, Gray	672			1	...	...	491
						190. Botaurus, Steph....	674			1	...	...	492
				Nycticoraceae....	660	191. Butorides, Blyth....	676			1	...	1	493
						192. Nyctiardea, Sw.....	678			1	...	...	495
						193. Nyctherodius, Reic.	679			1	...	...	496
37. Tantalidae......	681	Tantalinae.......	681	....	....	194. Tantalus, Linn.....	682			1	...	...	497
		Ibinae...........	681			195. Ibis, Moehr.......	682	Ibis, Moehr.		2	...	...	498
								Falcinellus, Bon......			1	...	500
38. Plataleidae.....	686					196. Platalea, L.........	686			1	...	...	501
39. Phoenicopteridae	687					197. Phoenicopterus, L..	687			1	...	...	502

Order V. GRALLATORES—Continued.

Sub-Order B. GRALLAE.) (Page 688.)

Tribe 1. LIMICOLAE. (Page 688.)

Family.	Page.	Sub-family.	Page.	Section.	Page.	Genus.	Page.	Sub-genus.	Page.	Species examined and identified.	Species not examined nor identified.	Extra liminal species.	Current number of first species mentioned.
40. Charadriidae	690	....	....	....	....	198. Charadrius, L......	690	....		1	.....	.....	503
						199. Aegialitis, Boie....	691	Oxyechus, Reich.....	692	2	.....	.....	504
								Ochthodromus, Reich.	693	1	.....	.....	506
								Aegialeus, Reich....	....	2	.....	.....	507
								Leucopolius, Bon....	....	1	.....	.....	509
						200. Squatarola, Cuv....	696	....	....	1	....	.....	510
						201. Aphriza, Aud.......	698	....	....	1	.....	.....	511
41. Haematopodidae	699	....	....	....	....	202. Haematopus, Linn..	699	....	....	2	1	1	512
						203. Strepsilas, Ill..... .	701	....	....	2	.....	.....	515
42. Recurvirostridae..	703	....	....	....	....	204. Recurvirostra, L....	703	....	....	1	.....	.....	517
						205. Himantopus, Briss. .	704	....	....	1	.....	.....	518
43. Phalaropodidae..	705	....	....	....	....	206. Phalaropus, Br	705	Steganopus, Viell....	705	1	.....	.....	519
								Lobipes, Cuv...... .	706	1	.....	.....	520
								Phalaropus, Brisson..	707	1	.....	.....	521
44. Scolopacidae....	708	Scolopacinae....	708	Scolopaceae .?...	709	207. Philohela, Gray....	709	....	....	1	.....	.....	522
						208. Gallinago, Leach..	710	....	....	1	.....	.	523
						209. Macrorhamphus, Leach............	711	....	....	2	.....	.....	524
				Tringeae	713	210. Tringa, Linn.......	714	Tringa, L...........	714	2	.....	.....	526
								Arquatella, Bd......	714	1	.....	.....	528
								Erolia, Vieill.........	714	1	.....	.....	529
								Schoeniclus, Moehr..	714	1	.....	.....	530
								Actodromas, Kaup...	714	3	.....	.....	531
						211. Calidris, Cuv.....	723	....	....	1	.....	.....	534
						212. Ereunetes, Ill......	724	....	....	1	.....	.....	535
						213. Micropalama, Bd...	726	....	....	1	.....	.....	536
		Totaninae.......	727	Totaneae........	727	214. Symphemia, Raf....	729	....	....	1	.....	.....	537
						215. Glottis, Nilss.......	730	....	....	1	.....	.....	538
						216. Gambetta, Kaup....	731	....	....	2	.....	.....	539
						217. Rhyacophilus, Kp...	733	....	....	1	.....	.....	541
						218. Heteroscelus, Bd...	734	....	....	1	.....	.....	542
						219. Tringoides, Bon... .	735	....	....	1	.....	.....	543
						220. Philomachus, Moeh.	736	....	....	1	.....	.....	544
						221. Actiturus, Bon.....	737	....	...	1	.....	..	545
						222. Tryngites, Cab.....	739	....	....	1	.	.....	546
				Limoseae	727	223. Limosa, Briss.....	740	....	....	2	.....	.....	548
				Numenieae......	742	224. Numenius, Linn....	742	Numenius, Temm...	743	1	.....	.....	549
								Phaeopus, Cuv......	.. .	2	.....	.....	550

Tribe 2. PALUDICOLAE. (Page 745.)

Family.	Page.	Sub-family.	Page.	Section.	Page.	Genus.	Page.	Sub-genus.	Page.	Species examined and identified.	Species not examined nor identified.	Extra liminal species.	Current number of first species mentioned.
45. Rallidae.........	745	Rallinae	746	Ralleae..........	746	225. Rallus, L..........	746	....	....	3	.....	.....	552
						226. Porzana, Vieill.....	748	Porzana, Vieill.....	749	1	.....	.....	555
								Creciscus, Cab.......	749	1	.....	.....	556
								Coturnicops, Bon	750	1	.....	.....	557
						227. Crex, Bechst......	751	....	....	1	.....	.....	558
				Fuliceae........	746	228. Fulica, Linn........	751	....	...	1	.....	.....	559
						229. Gallinula, Briss.....	752	Gallinula, Br........	752	1	.....	.....	560
								Porphyrula, Blyth....	753	1	.....	.....	561

Order VI. NATATORES. (Page 752.)

Sub-order A. ANSERES. (Page 753.)

Family.	Page.	Sub-family.	Page.	Section.	Page.	Genus.	Page.	Sub-genus.	Page.	Species examined and identified.	Species not examined nor identified.	Extra limital species.	Current number of first species mentioned.
46. Anatidae	736	Cygninae	757			230. Cygnus, Linn	757	Olor, Wagler	757	2			561
		Anserinae	759	Ansereae	759	231. Anser, Linn	760	Chen, Boie	757	2			563
								Anser, Linn	757	2			565
						232. Bernicla, Steph	763	Leucoblepharon, Bd.	763	3			567
								Bernicla	763	2			570
								Leucopareia, Rch	763	1			572
						233. Chloephaga, Eyton.	769				1		573
				Dendrocygneae	759	234. Dendrocygna, Sw	769			2			574
		Anatinae	772			235. Anas, Linn	773			2			576
						236. Dafila, Leach	774			1			578
						237. Nettion, Kaup	777			2			579
						238. Querquedula, Steph.	779			2			581
						239. Spatula, Boie	781			1			583
						240. Chaulelasmus, Gray.	782			1			584
						241. Mareca, Steph	783			2			585
						242. Aix, Boie	785			1			587
		Fuligulinae	786			243. Fulix, Sund	790			3			588
						244. Aythya, Boie	793			2			591
						245. Bucephala, Bd.	795			3			593
						246. Histrionicus, Less..	798			1			596
						247. Harelda, Leach	800			1			597
						248. Polysticta, Eyton	801			1			598
						249. Lampronetta, Brdt..	802				1		599
						250. Camptolaemus, Gr.	803			1			600
						251. Melanetta, Boie	804			1			601
						252. Pelionetta, Kaup	804			2			602
						253. Oidemia, Flem.	804			1		1	604
						254. Somateria, Leach	808			2		1	606
		Erismaturinae	811			255. Erismatura, Bon	811			1		1	609
		Merginae	812			256. Mergus, Linn	813			2			611
						257. Lophodytes, Reich..	815			1			613
						258. Mergellus, Selby	817					1	614

Sub-order B. GAVIAE. (Page 818.)

Tribe 1. TOTIPALMI. (Page 819.)

Family.	Page.	Sub-family.	Page.	Section.	Page.	Genus.	Page.	Sub-genus.	Page.	Species examined and identified.	Species not examined nor identified.	Extra limital species.	Current number of first species mentioned.
47. Pelecanidae	868					259. Pelecanus, L	868	Cyrtopelicanus, Rch..	868	1			615
								Onocrotalus, Wagl...	870	1			616
48. Sulidae	871					260. Sula, Br.	871	Sula, Br	871	1			617
								Dysporus, Ill	872	1			618
49. Tachypetidae	873					261. Tachypetes, Vieill.	873			1			619
50. Phalacrocoraci-dae	875					262. Graculus, L	875	Phalacrocorax, Br	876	1	2		620
								Graculus, Bon	877	3			623
								Urile, Bon	880	2			626
51. Plotidae	883	Plotinae	883			263. Plotus, L	883			1			628
52. Phaetonidae	885	Phaetoninae	885			264. Phaeton, Linn	885			1			629

Tribe 2. LONGIPENNES. (Page 819.)

Family.	Page.	Sub-family.	Page.	Section.	Page.	Genus.	Page.	Sub-genus.	Page.	Species examined and identified.	Species not examined nor identified.	Extra limital species.	Current number of first species mentioned.
53. Procellaridae....	820	Diomedeinae	820	....	....	265. Diomedea, L	820	Diomedea, L	821	1	....	....	630
								Phoebastria, Rch.....	822	1	....	....	631
								Thalassarche, Rch. ..	822	1	....	....	632
								Phoebetria, Rch......	823	1	....	....	633
		Procellarinae	824	....	....	266. Procellaria, L......	824	Ossifragus, H. & J....	825	1	....	....	634
								Fulmarus, Leach	825	2	....	....	635
								Thalassoica, Reich...	826	1	....	....	637
								Aestrelata, Bon	827	1	....	....	638
						267. Daption, Steph	828		....	1	....	....	639
						268. Thalassidroma, Vig.	828	Oceanodroma, Rch...	829	1	1	....	640
								Thalassidroma, Vig...	830	1	1	....	642
								Oceanites,Keys.& Blas	831	1	....	..	644
								Procellaria, L........	831	1	....	....	645
						269. Fregetta, Bon.....	832	....	....	1	....	....	646
						270. Puffinus, Briss......	832	Ardenna, Reich......	833	1	....	....	647
								Nectris, Bon..........	834	1	....	....	648
								Puffinus, Br.........	834	2	....	....	649
								Adamastor, Bon	835	1	....	....	651
54. Laridae	837	Lestridinae......	837	....	....	271. Stercorarius, Briss..	838	....	....	4	....	....	652
		Larinae	840	....	....	272. Larus, Linn........	841	....	....	9	1	....	656
						273. Blasipus, Bon	848	....	....	1	....	....	666
						274. Chroicocephalus, Eyton	850		....	5	....	....	667
						275. Rissa, Leach......	853	....	....	2	2	....	672
						276. Pagophila, Kaup....	855	....	....	1	1	....	676
						277. Rhodostethia, Macg	856	....	....	....	1	....	678
						278. Creagrus, Bon......	857	....	....	....	1	....	679
						279. Xema, Leach......	857	....	....	....	1	....	680
		Sterninae	858	....	....	280. Sterna, L...........	858	....	....	14	....	....	681
						281. Hydrochelidon, Boie	864		....	1	....	....	695
						282. Anous, Leach......	865		....	1	....	....	696
		Rhynchopinae....	865	....	....	283. Rhynchops, L......	866		....	1	....	....	697

Tribe 3. BRACHYPTERI. (Page 819.)

Family.	Page.	Sub-family.	Page.	Section.	Page.	Genus.	Page.	Sub-genus.	Page.	Species examined and identified.	Species not examined nor identified.	Extra limital species.	Current number of first species mentioned.
55. Colymbidae.....	887	Colymbinae......	887	....	....	284. Colymbus, L.......	887	....	....	4	....	....	698
		Podicipinae......	891	....	....	285. Podiceps, Lath.....	891	....	....	6	1	....	702
						286. Podilymbus, Less...			....	1	....	....	709
56. Alcidae.........	900	Alcinae...........	900	....	....	287. Alca, Linn........	900	Chenalopex, Moehr ..	900	1	....	....	710
								Utamania, Leach	901	1	....	....	711
						288. Mormon, Ill........	901	Lunda, Pall..........	902	1	....	....	712
								Fratercula, Briss.....	902	3	....	....	713
						289. Sagmatorrhina, Bon.	904	....	....	....	1	....	716
						290. Cerorhina, Bon.....	904	....	....	2	....	....	717
						291. Phaleris, Temm ...	906	Simorhynchus, Merr .	906	1	....	....	719
								Tylerhamphus, Brandt	907	2	....	....	720
								Ciceronia, Reich.....	908	2	....	....	722
						292. Ptychorhamphus, Brandt	910	....	....	....	1	....	724
						293. Ombria, Eschsch...	910	....	....	....	1	....	725
		Urinae...........	911	....	....	294. Uria, Moehring.....	911	Uria, Moehr	911	3	....	....	726
								Cataractes, Moehr ...	913	3	....	....	729
						295. Brachyrhamphus, Brandt	915	Apobapton, Brandt...	915	1	3	....	732
								Synthliborhamphus, Brandt	916	2	....	....	736
						296. Mergulus, Ray....	918	....	....	....	1	....	738

II. LIST OF SPECIES.[1]

[1]When authorities are inclosed in parentheses it shows that the species was first described under a different genus. A second authority (or a single one uninclosed) is that of the name as adopted. Extra limital species have their current number similarly inclosed

b 4 *

b 5 *

Page

b 7*

The following birds are enumerated in the preceding list which are not legitimately entitled to a place in the fauna of North America, (exclusive of Mexico.) Some of them have been described in the report for the purpose of comparison with closely allied species of the United States ; others are mentioned because introduced by previous writers, though probably on erroneous data. Future investigations will doubtless result in the removal of others from the list now retained there:

No.　4. Cathartes burrovianus, *Cassin.*　Mexico.
　　63. Rhynchopsitta pachyrhyncha, *Bon.*　Mexico.
　　71. *Campephilus imperialis, *Gray.*　Mexico.
　　　　Dryotomus lineatus.([1])　Mexico ; South America.
　129. *Tyrannus melancholicus, *Vieill.*　South Mexico.
　132. Myiarchus cooperi, *Baird.*　Mexico.
　171. *Geothlypis velatus, *Cab.*　Southern West Indies and South America.
　216. Cardellina rubra, *Bonap.*　Mexico.
　219. Setophaga miniata, *Sw.*　Mexico.
　224. Euphonia elegantissima, *Gray.*　Mexico.
　244. *Vireo virescens, *Vieill.*([1])　South America.(?)
　292. Parus meridionalis, *Sclater.*　South Mexico.
　297. Psaltriparus melanotus, *Bon.*　Guatemala.
　298. Carpodacus hæmorrhous, *Sclater.*　Mexico.
　311. *Chrysomitris stanleyi, *Bonap.*　South America.

---

[1] No North American specimens seen.

312. *Chrysomitris yarrelli, *Bonap.* South America.
350. Junco cinereus, *Sclater.* Mexico.
405. Trupialis militaris, *Bon.* South America.
408. *Icterus vulgaris, *Daud.*([1]) South America.
410. Icterus melanocephalus, *Gray.* Mexico.
494. Butorides brunnescens, *Baird.* Cuba.
498. *Ibis rubra, *L.*([1]) West Indies, Cuba, and South America.
514. *Haematopus ater, *Vieill.* South America.

Total of species, 23 ; of which one is not mentioned in the list, leaving 22. Of the 23 species, nine marked with an asterisk are given by Mr. Audubon.

The following species, claiming to be actually inhabitants of North America, have not been described from the specimens, none having been procurable for the purpose. Of several of them no specimens are known in any collection :

Haliaelitus washingtonii.
Regulus cuvierii.
Dendroica montana.
    carbonata.
Myiodioctes minutus.
    bonapartii.
Ægiothus canescens.
Leucosticte griseinucha.
    arctous.
Lagopus americanus.
Chloephaga canagica.
Polysticta stelleri.([1])
Oidemia bimaculata.
Somateria v-nigra.
Graculus perspicillatus.
    cincinnatus.

Thalassidroma hornbyi.
    melania.
Larus chalcopterus.
Rissa brevirostris.
    nivea.
Pagophila brachytarsi.
Rhodostethia rosea.
Creagrus furcatus.
Xema sabinni.
Chroicocephalus minutus.([1])
Podiceps auritus.([1])
Sagmatorhina labradoria.
Brachyrhamphus kittlitzii.
    wrangelii.
    brachypterus.
Total—31 species.

The following species are probably accidental visitors only, and are not yet entitled to a permanent place in our fauna :

Milvulus tyrannus.
Saxicola œnanthe.
Chrysomitris magellanicus.
Philomachus pugnax.
Crex pratensis.

Heliornis surinamensis.([2])
Mareca penelope.
Nettion crecca.
Erismatura dominica.
Mergellus albellus.—Total, 10 species.

SUMMARY.

Species enumerated in the list ······· ····························· 738
Of these, extralimital ··· 22

    Total of North American species([3]) ···························· 716

North American birds given by Wilson in 1814 ······················ 283
North American birds given by Bonaparte, 1838 ······················ 471
North American birds given by Audubon in 1844 ···················· 506

---

[1] No North American specimen seen.   [2] Not enumerated in the list.
[3] Of these no specimens at all, of 28 species, were to be procured in this country for examination, and extralimital ones only of 3 others. Many supposed species are referred to in different parts of the report ; some of which may prove genuine.

INTRODUCTORY REMARKS.

THE classification of birds, both in reference to the higher groups and to their subdivisons, is a subject which has engaged the attention of a large number of naturalists, although until within a comparatively short time there has not been any very great difference in the systems adopted by the leading writers on general ornithology. The more commonly received basis has been the character of the bill and the shape and general structure of the feet, as expressed in the terms *Raptores, Insessores, Scansores, Rasores, Cursores, Grallatores,* and *Natatores* of most authors ; the *Insessores* again divided into *Fissirostres, Tenuirostres, Dentirostres,* and *Conirostres,* and, according to some systems, including, also, the *Scansores* as a subdivision, instead of that group being of higher independent rank.

Within a few years, however, a great change has taken place in the methods of ornithological classification, and most continental authorities have abandoned the old arrangement of the non-rapacious land birds, as based on the shape and character of the bill, and substituted a much more natural system. The principal agents in this reform have been Nitzsch,[1] Andreas Wagner, Sundevall,[2] Keyserling and Blasius,[3] J. Müller,[4] Cabanis,[5] Bonaparte,[6] Reichenbach,[7] Hartlaub, Burmeister,[8] and several other systematic writers, all contributing more or less to the final result. The most important step was the discovery announced by Müller in reference to the presence or absence of certain peculiar vocal muscles, which proved the key-note to an entirely new arrangement. In addition to this there has been latterly taken into account the number of primary quills, (or quills on the first joint of the wing,) whether ten or nine, and if ten whether the first be about as long as the second, about half as long, or very rudimentary ; also the character of the feet, whether the toes be three anterior and one posterior, or two anterior and two posterior, (and if so, whether the inner or the outer anterior toe be reversible,) or four more or less anterior. Particular reference is also made to the peculiarities of the scales on the legs, the position of the hind toe in relation to the plane of the others, the extent of feathering on the legs, the amount of webbing between the toes, the number of tail feathers, &c.

In the following report I have followed very closely the outlines given by Cabanis, in the "Ornithologische Notizen," already quoted, although obliged, in most cases, to construct the

---

[1] System der Pterylographie, verfasst von Herm. Burmeister. Halle, 1840.

[2] Konglig. Vetensk. Akad. Handlingar, 1835 and 1843. Stockholm.

[3] Wirbelthiere Europas. Braunschweig, 1842.

[4] Ueber die bisher unbekannten typischen Verschiedenheiten der Stimmorgane der Passerinen. Abhandl. K. Akademie der Wissenschaften zu Berlin, for 1845, 321. Berlin, 1847.

[5] Ornithologische Notizen, I, II, in Wiegmann's Archiv für Naturgeschichte, 1847.

[6] Conspectus generum avium, Leyden, 1850 and 1857, and various papers since 1850, in Comptes Rendus, and elsewhere.

[7] Avium systema naturale, and Handbuch der speciellen Ornithologie.

[8] Systematische Uebersicht der Thiere Brasiliens ; Dritter Theil. (Vögel.) Berlin, 1856.

characters of many of the subdivisions for myself. In the discussion of the higher groups I have however derived invaluable assistance from the work of Burmeister. I have also made constant use of the diagnoses of Keyserling and Blasius, which are pre-eminent for acuteness and precision.

The following synopsis of the orders of birds, taken partly from Keyserling and Blasius, will serve to illustrate the characteristics of the higher groups in American Ornithology.

A.—HIND TOE ON THE SAME LEVEL WITH THE ANTERIOR ONES.

a.—Posterior face or the sides of the tarsus more or less reticulated, granulated, or with scales more numerous or smaller than in front; sometimes naked. Anterior face of the tarsus never in one unbroken plate. Larynx without complex vocal muscles.

Order I.—RAPTORES. Base of the upper mandible with a soft skin or cere. Upper mandible compressed; its point curving down over that of the lower, forming a strong, sharp hook. Claws generally retractile. Toes never two behind. Birds usually of large size, and of powerful frame, embracing the so-called birds of prey.

Order II.—SCANSORES. Toes in pairs; two in front and two behind, the outer anterior being usually directed backwards, (the inner in *Trogonidae.*) Tail feathers eight to twelve.

Order III.—STRISORES. Toes either three anterior and one behind, (or lateral) or four anterior; the hinder one is, however, usually versatile, or capable of direction more or less laterally forward. Tail feathers never more than ten. Primaries always ten, the first long.

Order IV.—CLAMATORES. Toes, three anterior and one posterior, (not versatile.) Primaries always ten, the first nearly as long as the second. Tail feathers usually twelve.

b.—Anterior face of the tarsus in one continuous plate, or divided transversely into large quadrate scales. Plates on either the posterior serface of the tarsus or the sides, without subdivisions, never both divided together; when divided the divisions correspond with the anterior ones. Larynx with peculiar complex singing muscles.

Order V.—OSCINES. Toes, three anterior, one posterior. Primaries either nine only, or if ten the first usually short or spurious.

B.—HIND TOE RAISED ABOVE THE LEVEL OF THE REST.

Order VI.—RASORES. Nostrils arched over by an incumbent thick, fleshy valve. Bill not longer than the head, obtuse anteriorly. Nails broad, obtusely rounded.

Order VII.—GRALLATORES. Legs lengthened, adapted for walking, naked above the knee. Nostrils naked. Thighs usually quite free from the body. Toes not connected by a membrane, or for a short distance only; sometimes with a lobed margin.

Order VIII.—NATATORES. Adapted for swimming. Legs generally short. Toes united by a continuous membrane. Thighs mostly buried in the muscles of the body.

Fuller explanations of the characters of these orders will be found under their proper heads in the following pages.

ORDER I.

RAPTORES.

The peculiarities already given of the order *Raptores* are sufficient to define it among the others mentioned, although many additional features might be named. The order embraces three families, which are characterized by Keyserling and Blasius as follows:

A.—DIURNAL BIRDS OF PREY.

Eyes lateral, with lashes, surrounded by a naked or woolly orbital circle; the feathers above, below, and behind the eyes directed backwards, as on the rest of the head; anterior to the eye the lore imperfectly clothed with a radiating star of bristles, or with scale-like feathers. The inner toe without the nail, shorter, or as long as the outer. Nostrils opening in the cere.

VULTURIDAE. Bill contracted or indented on the anterior border of the cere, so that the culmen is bow shaped, or ascending anterior to it. Eyes lying on a level with the sides of the head. Head sparsely covered with downy feathers only, or partially naked. Claws weak, rather slender, and only moderately curved; the tarsi and bases of the toes reticulated.

FALCONIDAE. The bill not contracted, nor the culmen ascending anterior to the cere. Eyes sunken. The head completely covered with compact, perfect feathers. Claws strong.

B.—NOCTURNAL BIRDS OF PREY.

STRIGIDAE. Eyes directed forwards; more or less completely surrounded by a crown of radiating bristly feathers. Lores and base of bill densely covered with bristly feathers directed forwards. The nostrils opening on the anterior edge of the cere. The inner toe without its claw longer than the outer, which is versatile. A crown of peculiarly formed feathers on the side of the head, and above the throat. Head fully feathered. Plumage very soft and downy.

The different families of *Raptores* have much the same character throughout the world, with the exception of the *Vulturidae*, in which the species of America or *Cathartinae*, are distinguishable from the old world *Vulturinae* by narrow, elongated, and perforate nostrils, those of opposite sides not separated by a partition; the toes are longer, with a greater extent of web between the three anterior ones; the neck shows single patches of perfectly naked skin. The tail consists of but twelve feathers, &c. (Burmeister.)

NOTE.—The following article on the rapacious birds has been prepared by Mr. John Cassin, of Philadelphia.—S. F. B.

Family VULTURIDAE. The Vultures.

CATHARTES, Illiger.

CATHARTES AURA. (Linnaeus.)

The Turkey Buzzard.--The Turkey Vulture.

Vultur aura, LINN, Syst. Nat. I, 122. (1766.)
Cathartes septentrionalis, DE WIED, Reise, I, 162. (1839.)
FIGURES.—Catesby, Nat. Hist. Carolina I, pl. 6; Vieill. Ois. d'Am. Sept. 1, pl. 2; Wilson Am. Orn. IX, pl. 75, fig. 1; Aud. B. of Am. pl. 151 : Oct. ed. I, pl. 2.

Entire plumage brownish black, darkest on the back and tail above, and with a purplish lustre, many feathers having pale borders. Bill yellowish ; head and neck in living bird bright red.

Plumage commencing on the neck with a circular ruff of projecting feathers. Head and upper part of neck naked, or with a few scattering hair-like feathers, and with the skin wrinkled. Nostrils large, oval, communicating with each other ; tail rather long, rounded. .

Total length about 30 inches, wing 23, tail 12 inches.

Hab. All of North America, except the Arctic regions. Spec. in Nat. Mus. Washington, and Mus. Acad. Philadelphia.

Specimens from the States and Territories on the Pacific are quite identical with the common bird of the States on the Atlantic. On the Pacific, and throughout a vast extent of the central parts of this republic, the summer range of this vulture extends northwardly into the British possessions, though in the northeastern States it is rarely seen north of New York. This apparent difference of locality, though at present impossible to be accounted for, may be regarded as fully established by recent observation in the western Territories.

The turkey vulture is, however, well known to be much more of a southern than a northern species. In the present collection, specimens are from California and Nebraska ; and it appears to have been observed in abundance in New Mexico by the surveying party in charge of Captain John Pope, U. S. Army, all the specimens obtained by which are labelled as collected at the junction of the Pecos and Delaware rivers, New Mexico, June, 1855.

List of specimens.

Catalogue number.	Sex and age.	Locality.	When collected	Whence obtained.	Original number.	Collected by—	Point of bill to end of tail.	Between tips of out-stretched wings.	Wing from carpal joint.
							Measurements		
3825	----	Eutaw, Alabama _____	Feb., 1853___	Prof. A. Winchell__	----	_____	_____	_____	_____
8498	----	Bois de Sioux, Minnesota_	_____	Governor Stevens_	17	Dr. Suckley_____	_____	_____	_____
4603	----	Cedar island, Missouri river	May 14, 1856_	Lt. G. K. Warren__	----	Dr. Hayden_____	26. 50	72. 00	20. 50
4983	----	Mouth of Delaware creek, Texas_____	June 14, 1855_	Captain J. Pope ___	98	_____	_____	_____	_____
4981	----	Mouth of Delaware creek, Texas_____	June 14, 1855_	Captain J. Pope ___	99	_____	_____	_____	_____
8497	----	Matamoras, Mexico_____	_____	Lieut. Couch_____	----	Dr. Berlandiere _	_____	_____	_____
8499	----	Fort Steilacoom, W. T___	_____	Governor Stevens_	102	Dr. Suckley ____	_____	_____	_____
:	♂	Petaluma, California_____	January, 1856_	E. Samuels _____	---	_____	27. 00	69. 00	21. 00

¹ *Cathartes*, Illiger, Prodromus, p. 236. 1811.

CATHARTES CALIFORNIANUS, Shaw

The California Vulture.

Vultur californianus, SHAW, Nat. Misc. IX, 1, pl. 301 (1779).
Vultur columbianus, ORD, Guthrie's Geog. II, 315 (1815).
Cathartes vulturinus, TEMM. Pla. col. I, pl. 31 (1820).
FIGURES.—Aud. B. of Am. pl. 411, Oct. ed. I, pl. 1 ; GRAY, Gen. of Birds, I, pl. 2.

The largest rapacious bird of North America. Head and neck bare, with a semicircular spot of short black feathers at the base of the upper mandible, and a few straggling, short, or hair-like feathers on other parts of the head. Plumage commencing on the neck, near the body, with a ruff of long lanceolate feathers continued on the breast.

Entire plumage black, lustrous on the upper parts, duller below ; secondary quills with a grayish tinge ; greater wing coverts tipped with white, forming a transverse band on the wing. Bill yellowish white ; iris carmine ; head and neck in living bird orange yellow and red.

Total length 45 to 50 inches, wing 30 to 35, tail 15 to 18 inches.

Hab. Western North America. Spec. in Nat. Mus. Washington, and Mus. Acad. Philadelphia.

This large vulture is inferior in size only to the gigantic condor of the mountains of South America. It appears to be restricted to the countries west of the Rocky Mountains, where it is occasionally observed in abundance, especially in the vicinity of the rivers. It is represented, however, as more cautious in its disposition than the smaller vultures of North America, though much resembling them in its habits.

A single specimen in the National Museum was collected at the mouth of the Columbia river by J. K. Townsend.

CATHARTES ATRATUS, Bartram.

The Black Vulture--The Carrion Crow

Vultur atratus, BARTRAM, Travels, p. 289. (1791.)
Vultur urubu, VIEILLOT, Ois. d'Am. Septent. I, 53. (1807.)
FIGURES.—Vieill. Ois. d'Am. Sept. I, pl. 2 ; Wilson Am. Orn. IX, pl. 75, fig. 2 ; Aud. B. of Am. pl. 106 : Oct. ed. I, pl. 3.

Entire plumage deep uniform black, frequently with a bluish gloss on the back and wings. Shafts of quills white above and below, quills on their under surface pale, in some specimens nearly white. Head and neck brownish or bluish black ; bill dark, yellowish at the end.

Plumage commencing higher on the back of the neck than on its sides or in front Head and naked portion of the neck warted or corrugated, and with a few hair-like feathers ; bill rather long ; nostrils large and communicating with each other ; tail rather short, truncate or even at the end, legs rather long.

Total length, about 23 inches ; wing, 16½ inches ; tail, 8½ inches.

Hab. Southern North America, Central America, Northern South America, Chile. Spec. in Nat. Mus. Washington, and Mus. Acad. Philadelphia.

Abundant in the Southern States and gregarious at all seasons, congregating in large numbers in the cities, where they are of great service in the destruction of all descriptions of waste or dead animal substances. Found also in Central and Northern South America. On the western coast of North America the occurrence of this vulture is doubtful, and no specimens are in the collections of the surveying and exploring expeditions. The specimens in the National Museum are from the Southern Atlantic States.

CATHARTES BURROVIANUS, Cassin.

Burrough's Vulture.

Cathartes burrovianus, CASSIN, Proc. Acad. Philada. II, 212. (1845.)

The smallest of all vultures. Resembling *C. aura*, but smaller and without a ruff on the neck, as in that species. Plumage on the neck ascending behind, as in *C. atratus*, but rather short, wings long, tail rounded, rather long.

Entire plumage deep uniform black, deeper and more uniform than in *C. aura*, shafts of quills white, head and neck red.

Total length, about 22 inches ; wing, 18 inches ; tail 8½ inches.

Hab. Mexico, Vera Cruz ; Mazatlan, Lower California. Spec. in Mus. Acad. Philadelphia.

This little vulture, the smallest of the entire group of vultures, is an inhabitant of the coasts of Mexico and Lower California, of the former both on the Pacific ocean and the Gulf of Mexico, and very likely extends its range along the shores of the Pacific into the territory of the United States. It can readily be distinguished by its small size, and the ascending feathers on the back of the neck, totally unlike the ruff of *C. aura*, which, in general aspect, it resembles.

The above four species are all the vultures ascertained to inhabit the United States. In addition to them, it is quite likely that the king vulture of South America, *Sarcoramphus papa*, may venture occasionally into the States on the southern frontier, being known to appear at times in Mexico. The sacred vulture of Bartram, *Sarcorhamphus sacer*, is a species described by that author, in the last century, as abundant in Florida, but has not been observed or identified anywhere since his time. This has tended to throw a doubt on its existence, but recent information renders it probable that this, or at least a species different from the vultures just described, is found about Lake Okechobee, in Southern Florida, where it is called king buzzard. The verification of this statement by actual specimens would be one of the most important discoveries yet to be made in North American ornithology. The following is Bartram's description :

"Bill long and straight almost to the point, where it is hooked or bent suddenly down, and sharp ; the head and neck bare of feathers nearly down to the stomach, when the feathers begin to cover the skin, and soon become long and of a soft texture, forming a ruff or tippet, in which the bird, by contracting his neck, can hide that as well as his head ; the bare skin on the neck appears loose and wrinkled, which is of a bright yellow color, intermixed with coral red ; the hinder part of the neck is nearly covered with short stiff hair ; and the skin of this part of the neck is of a dense purple color, gradually becoming red as i approaches the yellow of the sides and fore part. The crown of the head is red ; there are lobed lappets of a reddish orange color, which lay on the base of the upper mandible. The plumage of the bird is generally white or cream color, except the quill feathers of the wings and two or three rows of the coverts, which are beautiful dark brown ; the tail, which is rather large and white, is tipped with this dark brown or black ; the legs and feet of a clear white ; the eye is encircled with a gold colored iris, the pupil black."—*Bartram, Travels in Florida, &c.* 1791, *p.* 150.

Family FALCONIDAE. The Falcons.

Sub-family FALCONINAE.

FALCO, Linnaeus.

Falco, LINNAEUS, Syst. Nat. I, 124, (1766.)

General form robust and compact. Bill short, curved strongly from the base to the point, which is very sharp, and near which is a distinct and generally prominent tooth ; nostrils circular, with a central tubercle. Wings long, pointed, formed for vigorous, rapid, and long-continued flight ; tail rather long and wide ; tarsi short, robust, covered with circular or hexagonal scales ; middle toe long ; claws large, strong, curved, and very sharp.

This genus, as restricted, contains species found in all parts of the world, and easily distinguished from all other birds of this group by the prominent tooth in the upper mandible. They are justly regarded by naturalists as the typical or most highly or completely organized of rapacious birds. They are remarkable for exceedingly rapid flight, and great boldness in the attack and capture of small quadrupeds and birds, on which they subsist.

Sub-genus **Falco**.

FALCO ANATUM, Bonaparte.

The Duck Hawk.

Falco anatum, BONAP. Comp. List, p. 4. (1838.)
" *Falco peregrinus*," WILSON, Audubon and other authors.

FIGURES.—Wils. Am. Orn. IX, pl. 76 ; Aud. B. of Am. pl. 16 : Oct. ed. I, pl. 20 ; Lembeye B. of Cuba, pl. 1, fig. 2 ; De Kay, Nat. Hist. New York, Birds, pl. 3, fig. 8.

Adult.—Frontal band white. Entire upper parts bluish cinereous, with transverse bands of brownish black, lighter on the rump. Under parts yellowish white, with cordate and circular spots of black on the breast and abdomen, and *transverse* bands of black on the sides, under tail coverts and tibiæ ; quills and tail brownish black, the latter with transverse bars of pale cinereous. Cheeks with a patch of black ; bill light blue ; legs and toes yellow. Sexes alike.

Younger.—Entire upper parts brownish black, frontal spot obscure, large space on the cheeks black. Under parts dull yellowish white, darker than in adult, and with *longitudinal* stripes of brownish black ; tarsi and toes bluish lead color.

Total length 18 to 20 inches, wing 14 to 15, tail 7 to 8 inches.

Hab. North America, west of the Rocky mountains. Specimens in National Musuem, Washington, and Museum Academy, Philadelphia.

One specimen of this kind only is in the collections made by the expeditions, the results of which are embraced in the present report.

This species is apparently restricted to that portion of North America east of the Rocky mountains, being replaced in the western countries of our continent by the smaller *Falco nigriceps*. We have never seen the present bird from any locality on the western coast of the United States, though on the eastern it ranges throughout the extent of the coast from Greenland to Cuba.

The specimen now before us is of especial interest, having been obtained at the most western locality yet ascertained for this species, and demonstrating a vast range of longitude, in localities which it never before was known to inhabit. It was obtained on the Vermilion river, in Nebraska T rritory, by Lieutenant Warren's expedition.

List of specimens.

Catalogue No.	Locality.	When collected.	Whence obtained.	Collected by—
5166	Mouth of Vermilion river, Upper Missouri	October 25, 1856.	Lieut. G. K. Warren	Dr. F. V. Hayden

FALCO NIGRICEPS, Cassin.

Falco nigriceps, CASSIN, B. of Cal. and Texas I, p. 87. (1853.)—IB. in Gilliss' U. S. Astron. Exped. II, 1855 pl. xiv.

Resembling the preceding, but smaller and with the bill disproportionately weaker. *Adult.*—Frontal band white, narrow Head and neck above black tinged with cinereous; other upper parts bluish cinereous, with transverse bands of brownish black. Quills brownish black; tail bluish cinereous, with transverse bands of black. Under parts reddish white, with circula$_r$ spots and transverse bands of black. Cheeks with a large space of black.

Younger.—Upper plumage dark brown; tail above brown, barred wi   rufous on the inner webs of the feathers. Under part dull reddish yellow, paler on the throat, and with broad longitudinal tripes of black; flanks and under wing coverts with transverse bars and circular spots of reddish white. Bill bluish, legs and toes yellow.

Total length 15 to 17 inches, wing 11 to 12, tail 6 to 6½ inches.

Hab. Western North and South America. Specimens in National Museum, Washington, and Museum Academy' Philadelphia.

Like its relative of the eastern States of the Union, *F. anatum,* this species does not appear to be abundant on the western coast; or if so, like its eastern congener, it is not easily obtained. Three specimens only are in the collections made by the expeditions.

This is one of the rather numerous species which bear more or less intimate relationship to the *Falco peregrinus* of the old world, and to *Falco anatum* of the United States. It is uniformly smaller than both, though most resembling the former, especially specimens from Asia. This bird is as yet known only as an inhabitant of the western countries of the continent of America from Oregon to Chi e.

List of specimens.

Catalogue number.	Sex and age.	Locality.	When collected.	Whence obtained.	Original number.	Collected by—	Point of bill to end of tail.	Between tips of outstretched wings.
						Measurements.		
4307	♂	Puget's Sound, W. T.	Sept. 26, 1854.	Dr. Suckley	183	Geo. Gibbs	16. 50	39. 00
8501		Shoalwater Bay, W. T	Mar. 21, 1854.	Governor Stevens	63	Dr. Cooper	17. 50	30. 50
8500	♀	Bodega, California	Jan., 1855	Lieut. Trowbridge		T. A. Szabo		
		Chile		Lieut. Gilliss				

Sub-Genus **Hypotriorchis.**

FALCO COLUMBARIUS, L i n n a e u s.

Pigeon Hawk.

Falco columbarius, LINN. Syst. Nat I, 128, (1766.)
Falco intermixtus, DAUDIN, Traite d'Orn. II, 141, (1800.)
Falco temerarius, AUDUBON, Orn. Biog. I, 381, (1831.)
Falco Auduboni, BLACKWALL, Researches, Zool. 1834.

FIGURES —Catesby's Carolina, pl. 3 ; Vieill..Ois. d'Am., Sept. pl. 11 ; Wilson Am. Orn. II, pl. 15, fig. 3 ; Swains. Faun. Bor. Am. Birds, pl 25 ; Aud. B. of Am., pl. 75, 92, oct. ed. I, pl. 21 ; De Kay Nat. Hist., N.Y., Birds, pl. 4, fig. 9.

Adult Male. Entire upper parts bluish slate color, every feather with a black longitudinal line ; forehead and throat white, other under parts pale yellowish or reddish white ; every feather with a longitudinal line of brownish black ; tibiæ light ferruginous, with lines of black. Quills black, tipped with ashy white ; tail light bluish ashy, tipped with white and with a wide subterminal band of black, and with several other transverse narrower bands of black ; inner webs nearly white ; cere and legs yellow ; bill blue.

.Younger. Entire upper plumage dusky brown, quite light in some specimens, and with a tinge of ashy ; head above, with narrow stripes of dark brown and ferruginous, and in some specimens many irregular spots and edgings of the latter color on the other upper parts. Forehead and entire under parts dull white, the latter with longitudinal stripes of light brown ; sides and flanks light brown, with pairs of circular spots of white ; tibiæ dull white, with dashes of brown ; tail pale brown, with about six transverse bands of white. Cere and legs greenish yellow.

Young. Upper plumage brownish black, white of the forehead and under parts more deeply tinged with reddish yellow ; dark stripes wider than in preceding ; sides and flanks with wide transverse bands of brownish black, and with circular spots of yellowish white. Quills black ; tail brownish black, tipped with white, and with about four bands of white ; cere and feet greenish yellow.

Total length. Female, 12 to 14 inches ; wing, 8 to 9 inches ; tail, 5 to 5½ inches. Male, total length, 10 to 11 inches ; wing, 7½ to 8 inches ; tail, 5 inches.

Hab. Temperate North America, Mexico, Central America, Northern South America.　Spec. in Nat. Mus., Washington, and Mus. Acad., Philadalphia.

Specimens in the present collection show that this little hawk inhabits the entire coast of the possessions of the United States on the Pacific ocean. Being, also, one of the most abundant species of its family in the States on the Atlantic, its locality may be stated as the whole of temperate North America.

This bird presents the usual variations in plumage which prevail in nearly all the birds of the family Falconidæ, and render the determining of species frequently perplexing and difficult. There are, however, three well-defined stages exhibited in a large number of specimens now before me, including the specimens in the present collection, as given above, and others from various parts of the United States. Of these the adult is easily distinguished, and is very nearly as figured by Audubon, under the name *Falco temerarius*, but of the other two plumages we cannot at present determine which is the more mature. One of the latter is dull brown, as figured in Fauna Boreali Americana, as above, and the other much darker and nearly black, as in the plates of Wilson Am. Orn., and Aud. B. of Am., as above cited.

The darkest colored specimens that we have ever seen are in this collection, and so different from the adult as to readily suggest doubts of their specific identity. Both males and females are clear brownish black, and in one specimen, a male obtained by Dr. Cooper, at Shoalwater bay, Washington Territory, the tail is without a vestige of the spots usually to be noticed, and there are very few on the primaries. This is probably the youngest plumage.

Another plumage is uniformly dull and frequently pale brown above, with nearly every

2 b

feather edged with rufous. This stage is represented in Swainson's plate in Fauna Boreali—Americana. The adult has the upper parts entirely light bluish slate color; nearly every feather with a black central line, and is even lighter colored and of more delicate and handsome shades than as given by Audubon. Between these well-defined and easily recognized stages there are other intermediate plumages impossible to describe, except in general terms.

List of specimens.

Catalogue number.	Sex and age.	Locality.	When collected.	Whence and how obtained.	Original number.	Collected by—	Point of bill to end of tail.	Between the tips o outstretched wings.	Wing from carpal joint.
							Measurements.		
6909	....	Nelson river, H. B........	....	D. Gunn...........	....	....	......	.....	......
5170	♀	Mouth Vermilion, on Mo..	Oct. 25, 1856	Lt. Warren........	....	Dr. Hayden......	12.75	26.75	9.00
5171	♂	......do......do.......	....do......	......do.......	....	......do........	11.75	23.75	8.00
4130	♀	Tamaulipas, Mexico......	....	Lt. Couch........	....	....	12.00	25.00	8.50
5505	....	El Paso, Texas	....	Major Emory......	....	J. H. Clark	......	.....	......
4476	....	Puget's Sound, W. T	....	Dr. Cooper.......	....	....	......	.....	......
4459	....	Cape Flattery, W. T.....	....	Lt. Trowbridge....	....	....	......	.....	......
4477	....	Shoalwater Bay, W. T....	....	Dr. Cooper	....	....	......	.....	......
5831	....	Fort Steilacoom, W. T. .	Oct. 1, 1856	Dr. Suckley	598	....	......	.....	......
5829	....	......do......do.......	Sept. 1, 1856	......do........	548	....	......	.....	......
5828	....	......do......do.......	....do......	......do........	549	....	12.00	25.50	......
5833	♀	......do......do.......	....do......	......do........	546	....	13.00	26.13	......
5832	....	......do......do.......	....do......	......do........	547	....	13.50	26.25	......
4588	....	......do......do.......	....do......	Dr. Potts........	....	....	......	.....	......
4500	....	San Francisco, Cal	....	Lt. Williamson....	....	Dr. Newberry.....	......	.....	......
6875	♂	California	....	......do........	....	Dr. Heerman	......	.....	......
5483	♂	Petaluma, Cal	....	E. Samuels	....	....	......	.....	......
4475	....	Santa Clara, Cal	....	Dr. Cooper.......	....	....	......	.....	......
4615	....	Colorado river, Cal	....	Major Emory......	53	A. Schott........	......	.....	......
7998	....	Mexico...............	....	J. Gould.........	....	....	......	.....	......

FALCO AURANTIUS, Gm.

Falco aurantius, GM., Syst. Nat. I, 283. (1788.)
Falco rufigularis, DAUDIN, Trait d'Orn. II. 131. (1800.)
Falco thoracicus, DONOVAN, Naturalists' Repository, II, (not paged, 1824.)
Falco cucullatus, SWAINSON, Cab. Cy. p. 340. (1838.)
Falco deiroleucus, TEMMINCK.

FIGURES.—Temm. Pl. Col. 348 ; Donovan, Nat. Rep. II, pl. 45.

About the size of, or rather smaller than *F. columbarius*. Entire upper parts bluish slate color, many feathers having darker centres, and concealed transverse bands of black. Throat, neck before, and breast yellowish white ; body beneath, black, with numerous transverse narrow bands of white ; abdomen, tibiæ, and under tail coverts dark rufous. Under wing coverts black, with numerous transverse bands and circular spots of white ; quills ashy black, with transverse bands of white on their inner webs ; tail black, the two middle feathers tinged with ashy, narrowly tipped with white, and with about seven irregular transverse bands of white ; bill horn color ; legs yellow.

Total length—male—9½ to 10 inches, wing 7½ to 8, tail 4 to 4½ inches. Female larger.

Hab. Mexico, Texas, South America. Spec. in Nat. Mus. Washington, and Mus. Acad. Philadelphia.

This handsome little hawk was noticed by Lieutenant Couch in the State of New Leon, Mexico, on the Rio Grande, and undoubtedly is properly to be regarded as a bird of Texas. It is well known as a South American species, and is diffused over a vast extent of the continent of America, having very probably for the most northerly limit of its range the State just mentioned.

The specimen brought by Lieutenant Couch is in quite mature plumage, and is now in the National Museum.

List of specimens.

Catalogue number.	Sex and age.	Locality.	Whence and how obtained.	Original number.	Nature of specimen.	Between tips of outstretched wings.	Wing from carpal joint.
						Measurements.	
4129	♂	New Leon, Mexico...	Lieutenant Couch	145	Eyes, brown; feet, orange; bill, lead and slate.........	23.00	7.75

FALCO FEMORALIS, Temminck.

Falco femoralis, TMM, Pl. col. I. (liv. 21.)
Falco thoracicus, (ILL.) LICHT. Verz. p. 62, (1823.)

Larger than the preceding, but somewhat resembling it in color. Head above, and entire upper parts light cinereous; darker, and with transverse bars of white on the upper tail coverts; front and line over the eye to the back of the neck white, tinged with orange on the latter; a wide band under and behind the eye, and another short band running downwards from the base of the under mandible, dark cinereous. Throat and breast very pale yellowish white; a wide band across the body, beneath black, with narrow transverse stripes of white; abdomen, tibiæ, and under tail coverts light rufous. Under wing coverts pale yellowish white, spotted with black; primaries ashy black, with numerous transverse bands of white on their inner webs; secondaries light cinereous, tipped with white; two middle feathers of the tail light cinereous, with transverse bands of ashy white; other feathers of the tail brownish black, tipped with white, and having about eight transverse bands of white. Bill yellow at base, tipped with light bluish horn color; legs yellow.

Total length about 15 inches, wing 10½, tail 7½ inches.
Hab. New Mexico, Mexico, South America. Spec. in Nat. Mus. Washington, and Mus. Acad. Philadelphia.

A fine specimen of this species is in the collection made by Dr. A. L. Heermann while attached to the party in charge of Lieutenant J. G. Parke. It is in mature plumage, and is strictly identical with South American specimens.

This bird was obtained in New Mexico. It is a common species of South America.

Sub-Genus Gennaia.

FALCO POLYAGRUS, Cassin.

Falco polyagrus, CASSIN,   B. of Cal. and Texas, I, p. 88. (1853.)
FIGURES.—CASSIN, B. of Cal. and Texas, I, pl. 16.

Narrow frontal band, line over the eye and entire under parts white; stripe from the corner of the mouth running downwards, dark brown; breast and abdomen with longitudinal stripes and spots of brown, which color forms a large and Conspicuous spot on the flank.   Upper parts brown, paler on the rump; tail above pale grayish brown, narrowly tipped with white, and with transverse bands of white; quills dark greyish brown; edge of wing at the shoulder and below white, spotted with brown.   Bill bluish; under mandible yellow at base; space around the eye bare, with a narrow edging of brown on the first plumage around it, the brown of the back extending somewhat on to the breast at the wing.

Younger. Frontal band nearly obsolete; upper parts nearly uniform pale brown, with narrow rufous stripes on the head; under a rts white, tinged with dull yellow, nearly every feather having a longitudinal stripe of dark brown; large spaces on the flanks brown; tarsi and toes lead colored.

Total length 18 to 20 inches, wing 13 to 14, tail 7½ to 8 inches.

Hab. Western North America.   Spec. in Nat. Mus. Washington, and Mus. Acad. Philadelphia.

This is exclusively a species of Western North America, but extending its range east of the Rocky mountains, several specimens having been obtained during the exploration of the upper Missouri and Yellow Stone rivers by the party commanded by Lieutenant G. K. Warren, United States army.   A specimen of this species has, also, been recently procured in western Illinois by Mr. J. D. Sergeant, of Philadelphia.

Adults of both sexes are very similar, in fact not differing except in size, and are almost pre_ cisely as described and figured by us as above.

It is possible that this may be the specices described as *Falco mexicanus* in 1850 by Schlegel, but I have been unable to make a reference to his article.

List of specimens.

Catalogue number.	Sex and age.	Locality.	When collected.	Whence obtained.	Original number.	Nature of specimen.	Collected by—	Point of bill to end of tail.	Between tips of outstretched wings.	Wing from carpal joint.
5169	.....	Mouth of Knife river, Mo. river...	Sept. 10, 1856....	Lieut. Warren......		....	Dr. Hayden....	19.00	45.50	13.50
5168	♀	Knife river, Missouri............	Sept. 16, 1856....	........do.........			....do.......	18.25	42.25	13.75
5167	♀ ○	Fort Randall, Nebraska........	Oct. 17, 1856....	........do.........		Iris dark brown	......do.......	19.00	42.00	13.50
5951	♂ ○	N. Platte, Nebraska............	Aug. 20, 1857....	Lieut. Bryan......	429		W. S. Wood...		......	
8502	○	Fort Thorne, New Mexico.......	....	Dr. T. C. Henry...	.....					
8503		Camp on Little Colorado.........	Winter, 1853–'54 .	Lieut. Whipple....	38		Kennerly and Möllhausen..			
8504	♀	Fort Dalles, Oregon Territory.....	....	Dr. Suckley........	143					
4351	.....	Presidio, California..........	....	Lieut. Trowbridge .						14.50
5482	♀	Petaluma, California............	Jan., 1856........	E. Samuels........	82					......

Sub-Genus **Hierofalco**.

FALCO CANDICANS, Gmelin.

Falco candicans, GM. Syst. Nat. I. 275. (1788.)
Falco groenlandicus, DAUDIN, Traite d'Orn. II, 107. (1800.)
Falco fuscus, FABRICIUS, Fauna Groenlandica, p. 56. (1780)?
Falco arcticus, HOLBOLL, Label in Acad. Mus. Philadelphia.

Adult.—Entirely white; upper parts with irregular confluent transverse bands, and large subterminal hastate or sagittat s ot of ashy brown; under parts with a few longitudinal narrow stripes of brown. Primary quills white, with their tips brownish black ; tail white, with transverse bands of brownish black on the outer webs of the external feathers.

Young.—Upper parts with the brown predominating and of a lighter shade than in the adult, and more or less barred and spotted with white. Under parts white, tinged with ashy, with longitudinal stripes of brown, especially on the abdomen Quills and tail ashy brown, with transverse bands of dull white.

Total length about 24 inches, wing 16, tail 10 inches.
Hab. Northern North America, Greenland. Spec. in Mus. Acad. Philad.

A very handsome falcon, almost entirely pure white in its adult plumage. This bird and the succeeding have been demonstrated by Mr. Holboll and other Danish naturalists to be resident species in Greenland, and inhabit also other countries of the northern regions of the continent of America.

FALCO ISLANDICUS, Gmelin.

The Ger Falcon. The Iceland Falcon.

Falco islandicus, GM. Syst. Nat. I, 275. (1788.)
Falco islandus, FABRICIUS, Faun. Groenl., p. 58. (1780)?

Adult.—Entirely white; upper parts with regular transverse and very distinct bands of brown, becoming somewhat crescent, shaped on the scapulars and rump, and slightly acuminate on the shafts of the feathers. Quills white, brownish black at their tips ; tail white, with about twelve transverse narrow bands of brow . Under parts with a few longitudinal lines of dark brown.

Young.—Upper plumage brown, with transverse bands of dull white. Under parts dull white, with numerous circular and irregular shaped spots of dark brown, largest on the sides, and disposed to form transverse bands. Quills and tail dar   rown with transverse bands of ashy white.

Total length about 24 inches, wing 16½, tail 10 inches.
Hab. Northern North America, Greenland. Spec. in Mus. Acad. Philad.

Nearly allied to the preceding, and only to be distinguished from it by the different shape and pattern of the darker markings on the upper parts of the body. Like the preceding too, it inhabits Greenland ; and specimens that we have seen from that country cannot be distinguished from the well known bird of Iceland and northern Europe.

Sub-Genus **Tinnunculus**.

FALCO SPARVERIUS, Linnaeus.

The Sparrow Hawk.

Falco sparverius, LINN. Syst. Nat. I, 128. (1766.)
Falco dominicensis, GM. Syst. Nat. I, 285. (1788.)
Falco gracilis, cinnamominus and *isabellinus*, Sw. Cab. Cy. p. 281. (183 .)

FIGURES.—Vieill. Ois. d'Am., Sept., pl. 12, 13 ; Catesby's Carolina, pl. 5 ; Wilson Am. Orn. II, pl. 16, fig. 1, and IV, pl. 32, fig. 2 ; Aud. B. of Am., pl. 42, Oct. ed. I, pl. 22 ; Rich. and Swains. Faun. Bor. Am. Birds, pl. 24 ; De Kay, Nat Hist. New York, Birds, pl. 7, fig. 16.

Adult.—Smaller than any of the preceding. Frontal band and space, including the eyes and throat, white, spot on the. neck behind, two others on each side of the neck, and line running downwards from before the eye, black. Spot on the top of the head, the neck behind, back, rump, and tail light rufous or cinnamon color. Under parts generally a paler shade of the same rufous as the back, frequently nearly white, but sometimes as dark as the upper parts, and always with more or less numerous circular or oblong spots of black. Quills brownish black, with white bars on their inner webs. Tail tipped with white, frequently tinged with rufous and with a broad subterminal band of black, outer frequently white, tinged with ashy and barred with black. Bill light blue, legs yellow. Back generally with transverse stripes of black, but frequently with very few, or entirely without ; rufous spot on the head, variable in size, and sometimes wanting.

Younger male.—Upper parts as above ; wing coverts, and tail ferruginous red, with numerous transverse bands of brownish black. Under parts with numerous longitudinal stripes, and on the sides with transverse bands of brownish black, external feathers of the tail palest, broad subterminal band on the tail obscure or wanting.

Young.—All the rufous parts of the plumage with wider transverse bands of brownish black ; wing coverts dark bluish cinereous, with large circular spots of black ; under parts with longitudinal stripes, and large circular spots of black.

Total length 11 to 12 inches, wing 7 to 7½, tail 5 to 5½ inches.

H b. The entire continent of America. Specimens in Nat. Museum, Washington, and Mus. Acad. Philadelphia.

List of specimens.

Catalogue number.	Sex and age.	Locality.	When collected.	Whence.	Original number.	Collected by—	Point of bill to end of tail.	Between tips of outstretched wings.	Wing from carpal joint.	Remarks.
6492	♀	Indian Key, Fla..........	Mar. 20, 1857	G. Wurdemann		....	....	....		....
6918	......	Nelson river, H. B	1857..........	D. Gunn....		....				
8521	♀	Milk river, Neb...........	Aug. 31, 1853	Gov. Stevens...........		Dr. Suckley	10.75	22.50	7.50	
5172	♂	Yellow Stone river.........	....	Lieut. Warren		Dr. Hayden...........	10.38	21.50	7.50	....
5178	.....	Fort Berthold, Neb.......	....	......do...		......do.......	......	......	...	....
5175	♂	Mouth Powder river......	....	......do......		......do........	10.13	22.00	7.38	....
5177	♀	Forty miles up the Yellow Stone river........,....	July 10, 1856	..de...		......do........	......	......	.....	
5172	♀	Farm Island, Neb........	May 30, 1856	......do......		......do........	10.75	23.00	8.00	
6953	♂	Medicine Bow creek, Neb.	....	Lieut. Bryan.......	337	W. S. Wood.......	......	......	....	
5026	♂	Indianola, Texas.........	Feb. 12, 1855	Capt. Pope...........	4	....	9.50	21.00	6.00	Eyes light gray...
5024	......	Fifty miles from Indianola.	April 6, 1855	......do.......	42	....	11.00	22.00	8.00	Eyes black.......
4570	......	San Felipe, Texas	....	Major Emory	19	A. Schott..........	......	......	...	
8518	......	San Elizario, Texas	Dec. 9, 1854	......do.......	6	Dr. Kennerly	10.50	21.00	8.00	
8515	......	Cochetope Pass...........	....	Lieut. Beckwith.....	19	Mr. Kreutzfeld......	......	......	...	
5582	♀	Platte river, Neb........	July 14, 1856	Lieut. Bryan........	103	W. S. Wood.......	10.50	20.00		
6952	♂	Black Hills, Neb........	Aug. 11, 1857	......do...........	389	......do...........	......	......	...	
5027	♂	Fort Clark, Texas.......	April 24, 1855	Capt. Pope........	......	....	......	......	...	
5583	♂	North Platte, Neb........	Aug. 14, 1856	Lieut. Bryan........	......	W. S. Wood.......	9.50	18.50		
5025	......	Doña Ana, N. M..........	Oct. 22, 1855	Capt. Pope	152	....	10.50	22.00	7.50	Eyes brown ; feet and gums yellow.
5580	......	Pole creek, Neb..........	July 28, 1856	Lieut. Bryan..........	168	W. S. Wood.......	10.00	......		
8519	......	Fort Thorn, N. M......	....	Dr. Henry	......	....	......	......	...	
6879	♂	Fort Steilacoom, W. T ...	April —, 1856	Dr. Suckley..........	346	....	......	......	...	
4585	......	......do	....	Dr. Potts....	......	....	......	......	...	
8516	......	Bodega, Cal	Jan. —, 1855	Lieut. Trowbridge ...	......	T. A. Szabo\	......	......	...	
5488	♀	Petaluma, Cal	....	E. Samuels..........	153	....	......	21.58	7.58	
4353	......	Presidio, Cal	July 4, 1853	Lieut. Trowbridge ..	......	....	.. ...	...	......	
4938	......	San José, Cal	....	A. J. Grayson	......	....	......	......	...	
6877	......	Sacramento Valley, Cal..	....	Lieut. Williamson...	......	Dr. Heerman.......	......	......	...	
6880	♂	Tulare Valley, Cal........	....	......do...........	......	......do...........	......	......	...	... ...
8517	......	Camp 105, N. M..........	Jan. 23, 1854	Lieut. Whipple	59	Kennerly and Möll-hausen	......	......		
4420	......	City of Mexico..........	....	J. Potts........		....	......	......	...	
7999		Guatemala	....	J. Gould............						

Sub-Family ACCIPITRINAE.

THE HAWKS.

Form rather long and slender, tail and legs long, wings rather short, bill short, hooked, upper mandible lobed, but not toothed. Very active and vigilant and swift of flight, pursuing their prey, which consists of birds and small quadrupeds, into the woods and forests.

ASTUR, Lac.

Astur, LACEPEDE, Mem. Inst. III, p. 506.

The largest birds of this sub-family. General form strong, but rather long and slender ; wing rather short ; tail long and broad ; tarsi long, covered in front with rather wide transverse scales ; toes and claws moderate, the latter fully curved, sharp. Bill short, curved ; nostrils large, ovate, inserted in the cere. This genus contains about twelve species of all countries.

ASTUR ATRICAPILLUS, Wilson.

The Goshawk.

Falco atricapillus, WILSON, Am. Orn. VI. 80. (1812.)
Falco regalis, TEMM. pl. col. 1. (liv. 84, about 1827.)
Dædalion pictum, LESSON, Traite d'Orn. I, 67. (1831.)
FIGURES.—Wilson Am. Orn. VI, pl. 52, fig. 3 ; Rich. and Sw. Faun. Bor. Am. Birds, pl. 26 ; Jard. and Selby, Ill. Orn. pl. 121 ; Aud. B. of Am. pl. 141, Oct. ed. I, pl. 23 ; Temm. pl. col. 495.

Adult.—Head above, neck behind, and stripe from behind the eye, black, generally more or less tinged with ashy. Other upper parts dark ashy bluish or slate color, with the shafts of the feathers black, and frequently with the feathers narrowly edged with black, presenting a squamate or scale-like appearance. A conspicuous stripe over the eye, and an obscure and partially concealed occipital and nuchal band, white. Entire under parts mottled with white and light ashy brown. Every feather with a longitudinal line of dark brown on its shaft, and with numerous irregular and imperfect transverse lines or narrow stripes of light ashy brown, more distinct and regular on the abdomen and tibiæ. Quills brown, with bands of a deeper shade of the same color, and of ashy white on their inner webs. Tail same color as other upper parts ; under surface very pale, nearly white, an having about four obscure bands of a deeper shade of ashy brown, and narrowly tipped with white ; under tail covert white.

Young.—Entire upper parts, including head, dark brown, with the feathers, especially on the head and neck, behind, edged and spotted with light reddish, or nearly white. Tail light ashy, with about five wide and conspicuous bands of ashy brown, and narrowly tipped with ashy white ; quills brown, with wide bars of a darker shade of the same color, and wide bands of reddish white on their inner webs. Under parts white, genearlly tinged with yellowish and frequently with reddish, every feather with a longitudinal stripe, terminating in an ovate spot of brown. Sides and tibiæ frequently with circular and lanceolate spots, and irregular bands of the same color, the latter (tibiæ) generally very conspicuously marked in this manner. Under tail coverts white, with a few large lanceolate spots of brown.

Total length, female, 22 to 24 inches, wing about 14, tail 10½ to 11 inches. Male, about 20 inches, wing 12½, tail 9½ inches.
Hab. North America, chiefly in the northwestern portions.

All the specimens of this fine species in the collections of the expeditions are from Oregon and Washington Territory, and are of both adults and young birds. It is apparently more abundant in northwestern America than it is known to be in any other portion of the United States.

The adult of this species is well known, and is represented in all the plates cited above. It is one of the most strongly marked and easily recognized of American hawks.

Though confounded with the European goshawk (*Astur palumbarius*) by Audubon, the present species is strongly marked, and easily distinguished. The transverse bands on the under surface of the body in the present bird never assume that degree of regularity which is commonly met with in the European bird, and it is in other respects quite distinct, as pointed out by the distinguished naturalists who have described it, Wilson and Temminck.

List of specimens.

Catalogue number.	Sex and age.	Locality.	When collected.	Whence obtained.	Original number.	Collected by—	Measurements.	
							Length.	Extent of wings.
6906	----	Nelson river, H. B...	--------------	D. Gunn --------------	------	---------------	-------	------
6846	----	Port Townsend, W. T.	Jan., 1857....	Dr. Suckley-----------	------	---------------	22. 00	40. 00
5839	♂	Fort Steilacoom, W. T.	Aug., 1856 ---	------do------------	528	---------------	22. 50	38. 00
8508	♂	----do--------do----	--------------	Governor Stevens -------	101	Dr. Suckley----	-------	------
8509	----	----do--------do----	Mar. 25, 1856.	Dr. Suckley -----------	306	---------------	-------	------
4365	----	----do--------do----	--------------	Dr. Potts-------------	------	---------------	-------	------
4518	----	Shoalwater Bay, W. T.	Jan. 0, 1855 .	Dr. Cooper ------------	120	---------------	-------	------
8507	----	Dalles, O. T	Mar. 5 1854..	Governor Stevens -------	141	Dr. Suckley----	-------	------

ACCIPITER, Brisson.

Accipiter, BRISSON, Orn. I, 310, (1760.)

General form more slender and smaller than *Astur*, but otherwise similar. Wings short, tail long, tarsi long and slender, frequently with the scales in front nearly obsolete. Contains about twenty species of all countries, several of which intimately resemble each other. Colors in North American species very similar to each other, especially in adult specimens, though they differ materially in size.

ACCIPITER COOPERII, Bonaparte.

Cooper's Hawk.

Falco Cooperii, BONAP. Am. Orn. II, 1. (1828.)
Falco Stanleii, AUD., Orn. Biog. I, 186. (1831.)
FIGURES.—Bonap. Am. Orn. I, fig. 1 ; Aud. B. of Am. pl. 36, 141, fig. 3, ct. ed. 1, pl. 24.

Adult.—Head above brownish black, mixed with white on the occiput, other upper parts dark ashy brown, with the shafts of the feathers brownish black ; an obscure rufous collar on the neck behind. Throat and under tail coverts white, the former with lines of dark brown, other under parts transversely barred with light rufous and white. Quills ashy brown, with darker bands, and white irregular markings on their inner webs ; tail dark cinereous, tipped with white, and with four wide bands of brownish black.

Young.—Head and neck behind yellowish white, tinged with rufous, and with longitudinal stripes and oblong spo of brown; other upper parts light amber brown, with large partially concealed spots and bars of white; upper tail coverts tipped with white; under parts white, with narrow longitudinal stripes of light brown, tail as in adult ; bill blueish horn-color ; tarsi yellow.

Dimensions.—Female, total length 18 to 20 inches, wing 10 to 11, tail 8¼ inches ; male, 16 to 18 inches, wing 9½ to 10, tail 8 inches.

Hab.—All of temperate North America. Chile (Gay). Spec. in Nat. Mus., Washington and Mus. Acad. Philadelphia.

This species, rather common on the coast of the Atlantic, is apparently not so abundant in the western countries of the United States. Three specimens only are in the present collection, two of which are from Washington Territory, and one from California. These being, however, in young plumage, may be regarded as very probably showing conclusively that this bird is resident in those localities, and is also, in all probability, throughout the temperate regions of North America. Some authors even, though probably erroneously, assign it to South America also.

List of specimens.

Catalogue number.	Sex and age.	Locality.	When collected.	Whence and how obtained.	Original number.	Collected by—	Point of bill to end of tail.	Between tips of outstretched wings.	Wing from carpal joint.
							Measurements.		
5792	----	Society Hill, S. C	April 30, 1855.	M. A. Curtis........	----	....	......	......	.....
5578	----	Republican fork, K. T ...	Aug. 17, 1856.	Lieut. Bryan........	383	W. S. Wood	18.25	25.00	......
5846	----	Fort Steilacoom, W. T ...	Sept. 1856.	Dr. Suckley	540	....	19.00	30.00	......
8511	♂	......do........do......	Oct. 10, 1856.	......do..........	585	....	......	......	......
8512	----	Yakima river, W. T	Sept. 10, 1856.	Gov. Stevens	585	Dr. Cooper.....	......	......	......
4352	----	Presidio, Cal...........	....	Lieut. Trowbridge.	.....	....	18.00	31.00	......
6876	♀	Sacramento valley, Cal...	....	Lieut. Williamson.	.....	Dr. Heermann ..	......	......	......
4619	----	Colorado river, Cal	Oct. 28, 1854.	Major Emory	53	A. Schott	......	......	......

ACCIPITER MEXICANUS, Swainson.

Accipiter Mexicanus, SWAINS. Faun. Bor. Amer. Birds, p. 45, (1831.)

(Not figured.)

Intermediate between *Accipiter Cooperi* and *Accipiter fuscus* in size, and much resembling both in colors. Form slender and long, wings short, tail long, legs rather long, slender.

Adult.—Head above bluish black ; other upper parts dark brownish black, with a tinge of cinereous, darkest on the back; throat and other under tail coverts white ; other under parts fine light rufous, darkest on the tibiæ, and spotted and barred transversely with white, which bars and spots are nearly obsolete on the breast and tibiæ ; longitudinal dark lines on the shafts of the feathers (conspicuous on the under parts in *A. Cooperi*) only on the breast ; quills dark brown, with their outer edges cinereous, and with bands of dark brown and white on their inner webs ; tail dark cinereous, tipped with white, and having four wide bands of brownish black ; bill bluish black ; cere and tarsi yellow; iris yellow.

Young.—Entire upper parts dark brown, every feather on the head above and neck behind edged with yellowish red, which color predominates on those parts in some specimens ; under parts white, more or less tinged with dull yellow, every feather having a narrow longitudinal stripe of brown, and frequently a transverse band of the same near the base of the feather. The stripes often assume a falchion or imperfectly sagittate shape on the flanks. Under wing coverts yellowish white, with ovate and cordate spots of brown ; tail as in adult ; upper tail coverts frequently tipped with white ; iris, cere, and tarsi, light yellow.

Dimensions.—Male, total length, 15 to 16 inches ; wing 9, tail 8 inches. Female, total length, 17 to 18 inches ; wing 9½ to 10, tail 9 inches.

A western species, but not so exclusively so as has been supposed. In the present collection specimens are from New Mexico and the Yellow Stone river, as well as from Oregon and California, as will be seen in the localities given below.

This bird bears an extraordinary resemblance to both *Accipiter Cooperi* and *Accipiter fuscus*, and, in fact, specimens occasionally occur which cannot be distinguished without difficulty.

3 **b**

The young male of *A. Cooperi* may be mistaken for the young female of the present bird. The three American species of *Accipiter*, however, may be said to be so much alike in color as to almost represent different sizes of one species. It is a group in which size is a specific character.

List of specimens.

Catalogue number.	Sex and age.	Locality.	When collected.	Whence and how obtained.	Original number.	Remarks.	Collected by—	Point of bill to end of tail.	Between tips of outstretched wings.	Wing from carpal joint.
5165	......	Mouth of Yellow Stone river.	Aug. 18, 1856	Lieut. Warren	......	......	Dr. Hayden	......	......	10.25
5164	......	Mouth of White Earth river.	Sept. 6, 1856	....do.	......	......	....do.	......	30.25	10.25
5163	♀	Fort Berthold, Nebraska.	Sept. 16, 1856	....do.	......	Iris light yellow	....do.	17.00	29.95	9.00
5579	......	Bridger's Pass, Nebraska.	Aug. 14, 1856	Lieut. Bryan.	......	......	W. S. Wood.	......	......	......
6849	......	Fort Thorn, New Mexico.	......	Dr. Henry.	......	......	......	......	......	......
5841	......	Puget's Sound, W. T.	Oct. 4, 1856	Dr. Suckley.	574	......	......	......	......	......
5846	......	Port Townsend, W. T.	Aug., 1856	....do.	538	......	......	......	......	......
5847	......	Fort Steilacoom, W. T.	Sept., 1856	....do.	539	......	......	......	......	......
4590	......	....do.	......	Dr. Potts.	......	......	......	......	......	......
6848	......	Bodega, California.	Feb., 1855.	Lieut. Trowbridge.	......	......	T. A. Szabo.	......	......	......
6874	♂	Sacramento valley, California.	......	Lieut. Williamson.	......	......	Dr. Heermann.	......	......	......

ACCIPITER FUSCUS, Gmelin.

Sharp-shinned Hawk.

Falco fuscus et dubius, GM. Syst. Nat. I, 280, 281, (1788.)
Accipiter striatus, VIEILL. Ois. d'Am. Sept. I, 42, (1807.)
Falco velox et pennsylvanicus, WILSON Am. Orn. V, 116, and VI, p. 13, (1812.)
Sparvius lineatus, VIEILL. Ency. Meth. III, 1266, (1823.)
Nisus Malfini, LESSON. Traite d'Orn. I, 58, (1831.)

FIGURES.—Temm. pl. col. 67 ; Vieill. Ois. d'Am. Sept. pl. 14 ; Wilson Am. Orn. V, pl. 45, fig. 1, and VI, pl. 46, fig. 1 ; Aud. B. of Amer. pl. 374, Oct. ed. I, pl. 25.

Adult.—Small, tail rather long ; legs and toes slender ; entire upper parts brownish black, tinged with ashy; occiput mixed with white ; throat and under tail coverts white, the former with lines of black on the shafts of the feathers ; other under parts fine light rufous, deepest on the tibiæ, and with transverse bands of white ; shafts of the feathers with lines of dark brown ; tail ashy brown, tipped with white, and with about four bands of brownish black ; quills brownish black, with bands of a darker shade, and of white on their inner webs ; secondaries and tertiaries with large partially concealed spots of white.

Young.—Entire upper parts dull umber brown, tinged with ashy; neck behind mixed with white ; greater wing coverts and shorter quills, with large partially concealed spots of white ; under parts white, with longitudinal stripes and circular and ovate spots of reddish brown, changing into transverse bands on the flanks and tibiæ ; under tail coverts white ; bill dark bluish horn-color ; cere and tarsi yellow.

Total length, female, 12 to 14 inches ; wing 7½ to 8, tail 6¼ to 7 inches. Male, 10 to 11 inches ; wing 6 to 6½, tail 5 to 5½ inches.
Hab.—Throughout North America and Mexico. Spec. in Nat. Mus. Washington and Mus. Acad. Philadelphia.

Apparently, this handsome little hawk inhabits the whole of North America, from Mexico to the confines of the frigid zone. Numerous specimens, from various localities, are in the collections of the expeditions.

This little hawk, when in adult plumage, much resembles *Accipiter nisus* of Europe ; but the young are quite different, as is the case with nearly all the species of this family inhabiting North America, which resemble species of the Old World.

List of specimens.

Catalogue number.	Sex and age.	Locality.	When collected.	Whence and how obtained.	Original number.	Collected by—	Measurements.	
							Point of bill to end of tail.	Between tips of outstretched wings.
5575	....	Saranac lake, N. Y..................	Aug. —, 1855	S. F. Baird............	....	....	....	....
5990	....	Orange, N. J.....................	Oct. —, 1856	Dr. Cooper...........	....	....	....	....
7599	....	Washington, D. C...................	....	W. Hutton...........	....	....	....	....
8632	♂	Cape Florida, Fla...................	Nov. 2, 1857	G. Würdemann........	....	....	11.50	21.50
6908	....	Nelson river, H. B..................	....	Donald Gunn	....	....	....	....
6907	....	Selkirk Settlement..................	....	......do......	....	....	....	....
6954	♀	Black Hills, Neb...................	Aug. 11, 1857	Lieut. Bryan...........	387	W. S. Wood...........	....	....
5584	♂	Bridger's Pass, Neb	Aug. 14, 1856	......do......	262	......do.............	11.00	18.15
5845	♀?	Fort Steilacoom, W. T.............	Aug. —, 1856	Dr. Suckley...........	544	....	13.00	23.00
5842	♀?	........do..................	Sept. —, 1856	......do......	543	....	13.00	25.00
5844	♀?	........do..................	......do......	......do......	541	....	13.50	25.50
8514	♂	Shoalwater bay, W. T	Sept. 23, 1854	Gov. Stevens	94	Dr. Cooper	11.50	21.50
4198	....	San Francisco, Cal.................	Winter 1853–54	R. D. Cutts...........	....	....	....	....
4512	....	........do...	....	Lieut. Williamson.....	....	Dr. J. S. Newberry.....	....	....
6867	♂	Tejon valley................	....	......do......	....	Dr. Heermann........	....	....
8513	....	Camp Yuma, Cal...................	Dec. —, 1854	Major Emory...........	23	A. Schott............	....	....

Sub-Family BUTEONINAE—T h e B u z z a r d s .

General form heavy, flight vigorous and long continued, but not so rapid as in the preceding sub-families. Subsist mainly on small quadrupeds and reptiles.

BUTEO, C u v i e r .

Buteo, CUVIER, Regne Animal I, 323, (1817.)

Bill short, wide at base ; edges of upper mandible lobed ; nostrils large, ovate ; wings long, wide, fourth and fifth quills usually longest ; tail moderate, rather wide ; tarsi moderate, robust, with transverse scales before and behind, laterally with small circular and hexagonal scales ; toes moderate, or rather short ; claws strong. Contains about thirty species, inhabiting all countries.

Sub-Genus **Buteo.**

BUTEO SWAINSONI, B o n a p a r t e .

Swainson's Buzzard.

Buteo Swainsoni, BONAP. Comp. List, p. 3, (1838.)
"*Buteo vulgaris,*" RICH & SW. Faun. Bor. Am. Birds, p. 47.

The obtaining of this species is one of the most interesting results in ornithology attained by the surveying and exploring expeditions. Previously it was entirely unknown to American naturalists, who for the greater part followed the errors of European ornithologists in mistaking for it quite a distinct and very different bird, (*Buteo montanus,* Nuttall.) It possesses additional interest, too, in being more nearly related to a generic form of the Old World (typical *Buteo*) than any bird hitherto discovered inhabiting the continent of America.

All the specimens in the present collection are apparently of mature size, and the plumage is invariably one or the other of the three stages described below. The tail is never red, but uniformly ashy brown, with transverse dark bars.

The first and apparently most adult female is as follows :

Bill wide at base, compressed towards the tip ; edge of upper mandible lobed ; cere large ; wing long, third quill longest ; tail moderate, rather wide, even at the tip ; tarsus feathered in front for nearly half its length, naked behind, bare portion in front having about twelve transverse scales ; toes rather short ; claws strong.

Entire upper parts dark brown, nearly black in the middle of many feathers, paler on the edges ; quills brownish black, with wide transverse bands of cinereous on their inner webs, becoming paler and nearly pure white towards the base of the quill ; tail brown, tinged with ashy, and having about 10 to 12 narrow transverse bands of a darker shade of brown, the subterminal of which is widest ; tip edged with white.

Throat white, with longitudinal lines of dark brown ; *neck before and breast ashy brown*, nearly the same color as the tail ; some of the feathers edged with reddish ; other under parts white, nearly pure on the under tail coverts, and with transverse irregular bars of rufous on the *tibiæ* and flanks, and of darker brownish rufous on the abdomen ; under wing coverts white, with a few spots and transverse stripes of brown ; bill dark slate color ; tarsi, toes, and cere, yellow.

The color of the abdomen, tibiæ, and inferior tail and wing coverts is very liable to vary in specimens having the preceding plumage. Other specimens, precisely as just described in other respects, have these parts with the rufous color predominating, and with more numerous transverse, irregular, and imperfect bars of a darker shade of rufous, and with some broken bars and arrow-heads of dark brown. Shafts of tail feathers and quills dark above, white beneath.

The second plumage is, apparently, that of the younger female. The upper parts are as decribed above, but darker ; throat white, tinged with yellowish, and with the dark lines scarcely discernible ; *breast dark brown, nearly black ;* other under parts pale rufous, with numerous transverse bars of a darker shade of rufous and of dark brown, the latter more numerous than in the preceding. Specimens with the breast of this color vary mainly in the more or less numerous dark brown transverse stripes of the abdomen and flanks.

The third plumage prevails only in specimens labelled as males.

The upper parts are as first above described, though rather lighter, and with some feathers, especially on the back, edged with rufous ; tail above rather lighter, and more strongly tinged with cinereous ; throat white, with lines of dark brown ; *neck before and breast light rufous*, some of the feathers with lines on the shafts of ashy brown ; other under parts white, nearly pure and unspotted on the lower part of the abdomen and under tail coverts, tinged and irregularly barred with pale rufous on the flanks, tibiæ, and upper part of the abdomen ; under wing coverts nearly pure white. This plumage apparently varies but little, and only in the greater or less number of the stripes of rufous on the abdomen. The bird in this plumage is represented in the plate of Fauna Boreali Americana, cited above and in our plate.

Dimensions.—Female, total length, about 21½ inches ; wing 16, tail 8½ inches ; tarsus 2½ inches. Male, total length, about 19½, wing 15½, tail 8 inches.

In all these specimens the color of the neck before and of the breast may be regarded as forming a wide, uninterrupted transverse belt or band, and is a very conspicuous and apparently constant character. The difference in the color of this belt or band is, as will be observed from the descriptions given above, the principal difference between the specimens before us, and is very probably dependent on age, and perhaps sex.

This handsome and interesting species appears to be exclusively an inhabitant of western and northern North America.

The plates represent this bird in the first and third plumages described above.

List of specimens.

Catalogue number.	Sex and age.	Locality.	When collected.	Whence obtained.	Original number.	Remarks.	Collected by—	Point of bill to end of tail.	Between tips of outstretched wings.	Wing from carpal joint.
5154	♂	Mouth of Yellow Stone river......	July 14, 1856.....	Lieut. Warren. ...			Dr. Hayden....	20.63	48.50	15.50
5156	......	Mouth of White Earth river	Sept. 6, 1856.....	......do.........			....do	19.50	46.50	15.50
5155	♀	Knife river, Missouri.............	Sept. 10, 1856....	......do.........			....do	21.25	50.00	16.00
5157	♀	Heart river, Nebraska	Sept. 21, 1856....	......do.........			. ...	21.25	51.25	15.50
8540	......	Cochetope Pass....................	....	Lieut. Beckwith...	24		Kreutzfeldt. ...	......	......	......
8539	......	......do........................	....	......do...	25		....do	......	......	......
8541	......	San Luis valley	....	......do.........	13		....do	......	......	......
4984	......	Pecos river, Texas................	....	Captain Pope	......	Gums and feet yellow	....	22.50	34.50	16.50

BUTEO BAIRDII, Hoy.

Baird'sBuzzard.

Buteo Bairdii, Hoy, Proc. Acad. Philad. VI, 451, (1853.)

Cassin. B. of Cal. and Texas, pl. 41.

Entire upper parts dark brown, with a purplish bronzed lustre, especially on the wings ; plumage of the head and neck behind edged and tipped with yellowish white ; upper tail coverts yellowish white, with transverse bars of brown ; tail above brownish cinereous, with about ten narrow bands of brownish black, and tipped with white ; under parts pale yellowish white, or fawn color, with a few ovate and sagittate spots of dark brown ; a stripe of dark brown running downwards on each side from the corners of the mouth ; cere, legs, and irides yellow.

Older ?—Upper parts very dark brown, or nearly black, with a purplish lustre ; under parts with almost every feather having a large spot of brownish black, which color predominates on the breast, presenting a nearly uniforn color with the upper parts ; throat with narrow stripes of the same color ; flanks and inferior wing coverts with circular and oval spots of white ; tibiæ dark brown, with transverse bars and circular and oval spots of reddish white ; upper tail coverts reddish white, with their outer edges brown, and with transverse stripes of the same ; under tail coverts yellowish white, with transverse stripes of brown ; forehead white ; cheeks yellowish white ; stripes from the corners of the mouth wide and conspicuous.

Total length, 18 to 20 inches ; wing 15, tail 8 inches.

Hab.—Northern and western North America. Spec. in Mus. Acad. Philadelphia and Nat. Mus. Washington.

In the plumage, first described above, this bird bears some resemblance to the young of *Buteo lineatus*, but has a much more mature appearance, and is easily distinguished by its smaller size. It resembles also in colors only the young of *Buteo pennsylvanicus*, but is much larger. Though discovered in the State of Wisconsin, specimens from various western localities are in the collections of the expeditions.

Specimens recently collected by Lieutenant Warren show that the upper figure of our plate, as cited above, really represents the young plumage. Lieutenant Warren's specimens are scarcely fully fledged, and yet agree precisely with this figure.

List of specimens.

Catalogue number.	Sex and age.	Locality.	When collected.	Whence obtained.	Original number.	Collected by—	Point of bill to end of tail.	Between tips of out-stretched wings.	Wing from carpal joint.
							Measurements.		
5152	♀	Little Missouri river..	Sept. 12, 1856	Lieut. Warren.....	....	Dr. Hayden....	22.00	52.00	16.50
5151	♀	....do.........do....	......do......	......do..........	....	......do......	20.50	46.00	15.75
		Loup Fork, of Platte..	1857	......do..........	....	......do......	....	....	....
8542	....	San Luis valley, Upper Rio Grande........	....	Lieut. Beckwith ...	8	Mr. Kreutzfeldt	....	....	....

BUTEO CALURUS, Cassin.

Red-tailed Black Hawk.

Buteo calurus, Cassin, Proc. Acad. Philada. VII, p. 281, (1855.)

Similar in general form to *Buteo vulgaris* and *Buteo augur*. Bill rather strong ; edges of the upper mandible with distinct rounded lobes ; wings long, fourth and fifth quills longest ; tail moderate, or rather short ; tarsi feathered in front for nearly half their length ; naked behind, naked portion in front having about ten transverse scales ; claws large, strong, fully curved.

Tail bright rufous above, white at base, with about eight to ten irregular and imperfect narrow bands and one wide sub-terminal band of brownish black, and narrowly tipped with reddish white ; beneath silky reddish white.

Entire plumage above and below brownish black, deeper and clearer on the back and abdomen, and paler on the throat and breast. Plumage of the upper parts with concealed transverse bands of white at the base of the feathers, and of the under parts with circular spots and transverse bands of the same also at the base of the feathers ; quills brownish black, with a large portion of their inner webs white, banded and mottled with pale ashy brown ; under tail coverts transversely barred with brownish black and pale rufous.

Total length, female, about 21 inches ; wing 16½, tail 9 inches. Male rather smaller.

This remarkable buzzard bears a greater resemblance to *Buteo augur*, Rüppell, an African species, than to any other with which we are acquainted. It resembles no other American species except *Buteo insignatus*, Cassin, but is much larger, and presents other strong points of difference. To a casual observer this bird would present somewhat the appearance of the black hawk of the United States, *Archibuteo sanctijohannis*, with the tail attached of the common red-tailed buzzard, *Buteo borealis*, a combination hitherto quite unknown in the American falconidæ, but which does exist in the African *Buteo augur*.

This species was described by us, as above, from a single specimen in the collection brought by the party in charge of Captain John Pope, United States army, which was obtained by T. Charlton Henry, M. D., United States army, in the vicinity of Fort Webster, New Mexico. This able and zealous naturalist is the discover of this curious species, and has added a large amount of information to the knowledge of the ornithology of western North America. To the collections of this gentleman we shall have frequent occasions to allude.

One other specimen is in the present collection, and was obtained by Mr. E. Samuels at Peta-luma, Sono-a county, California, who found it breeding, and had the good fortune to obtain the eggs. These have recently been described by Dr. Thomas M. Brewer, in his very valuable work on North American Oology, now in the course of publication by the Smithsonian Institution.

List of specimens.

Catalogue number.	Sex and age.	Locality.	When collected.	Whence and how obtained.	Measurements.		
					Point of bill to end of tail.	Between tips of out-stretched wings.	Wing from carpal joint.
5481	♂	Petaluma, California..........	April 25, 1856	E. Samuels..............	21.00	48.00	16.49
8527	......	Fort Webster, New Mexico	....	Dr. Henry...............	....	....	....

Sub-Genus Leucopternis.

BUTEO INSIGNATUS, Cassin.

Buteo insignatus, CASSIN, B. of Cal. and Texas, p. 102, (1854,) pl. 31.

Adult male.—Under coverts of the wings and tail white ; the former striped longitudinally with pale rufous, and the latter transversely with reddish brown ; edges of wings at the shoulder nearly pure white ; tibiæ rufous irregularly barred with brown ; throat and a few feathers of the forehead white, each feather having a line of dark brown, or nearly black.

Entire other plumage above and below dark brown, every feather having a darker, or nearly black, central line. Quills above brown, with a slight purple lustre ; beneath pale cinereous, with their shafts white, and with irregular transverse bands of white. Tail above dark brown, with an ashy or hoary tinge, and having about ten transverse bands of a darker shade of the same color ; beneath nearly white, with conspicuous transverse bands of brown, the widest of which is subterminal ; tip paler, or nearly white ; bill dark ; cere, tarsi, and toes, yellow.

Female, nearly adult.—Like the preceding, but with the upper plumage darker, and the entire under parts dark rufous chestnut ; darker on the breast, quite uniform on the flanks and abdomen, and every feather having the shaft darker brown, nearly black. Throat, forehead, under wing coverts, and under tail coverts white. Tail as in the preceding.

Young.—Under parts reddish white ; every feather with a large terminal oblong spot of dark brown, and on the abdomen and tibiæ with numerous transverse stripes of the same color.

Entire upper parts dark brown ; on the back of the head and neck white at base, and edged with reddish ; scapulars and greater coverts of the wing with large partially concealed rufous spots. Under wing coverts pale reddish white, with large brown spots ; under tail coverts very pale reddish white, with a few stripes and lines of brown.

Dimensions.—Male adult, total length about 17 inches ; wing 14½, tail 7½ inches. Female, total length about 19½ inches ; wing 16, tail 9 inches.

The preceding are the three stages of plumage which characterize specimens brought by the expeditions. The first is precisely identical with that originally described by us, as above cited, which was obtained in the vicinity of Montreal, Canada.

The second specimen, above described, was obtained on the North Platte river by the party commanded by Lieutenant F. T. Bryan, United States army, while engaged in surveying a route for a wagon road to Bridger's Pass, in the Rocky mountains. In this specimen the under parts of the body are chestnut rufous, as described above, in which respect it differs from the presumed and probable adult.

List of specimens.

Catalogue number.	Sex and age.	Locality.	When collected.	Whence obtained.	Original number.	Collected by—
6955	------	Medicine Bow creek, Nebraska ----	July 26, 1856	Lieut. Bryan--------	333	W. S. Wood-------
6871	♂	Tulare valley, California.---------	---------------	Lieut. Williamson---	------	Dr. Heermann -----

BUTEO HARLANI, Audubon.

Harlan's Buzzard ; The Black Warrior.

Falco Harlani, AUD. Orn. Biog. I, 441, (1831, plate published 1830.)
" *Buteo Borealis*," GRAY, Cat. Brit. Mus. Accipitres, p. 34.
Buteo Harlani, AUD. Lawrence, Annals N. Y. Lyc. Nat. Hist. V, p. 220.

FIGURE.—Aud. B. of Am., pl. 86, Oct. ed. I, pl. 8.

Adult.—About the size of, or rather smaller than, *Buteo borealis*. Robust ; bill rather short, strong ; edges of upper mandible lobed ; wing rather long ; tail moderate ; legs strong ; tarsus feathered in front below the joint, naked behind, in front having about nine or ten transverse scales, and about fifteen behind ; claws very strong, sharp, fully curved. Entire plumage brownish black, with a purplish lustre on the back and wing coverts. Front white, and all the feathers of the head above and occiput white at base, easily observed on the latter. Quills brownish black, with transverse bands of a lighter shade, and with a portion of their inner webs ashy white, giving a nearly uniform ashy white color to the under surface of the wing ; under wing coverts brownish black. Tail mottled with brownish black, ashy and white, the former predominating, a rather wide subterminal band of brownish black above and below, which are tinges of bright rufous ; tip paler ; under surface of the tail ashy white, slightly mottled with ashy brown. Bill dark bluish ; legs greenish yellow.

Young.—Entire upper parts light brown, dull fulvous, and white ; tips of the feathers generally with a large ovoid spot of brown, bordered with dull fulvous, and white at base, the fulvous and white predominating on the head and wing coverts ; rump with nearly regular transverse bands of brown and reddish fulvous ; quills dark brown ; under surface (of quills) white ; under wing coverts white, spotted with brown, and rufous or reddish fulvous ; tail light ashy, tinged with reddish, and with about six or seven irregular and imperfect narrow bands of brownish black, all of which are edged with dark reddish fulvous ; tip white. Under parts white, nearly pure on the throat and breast, with ovate and sagittate large spots on the neck before sides and abdomen ; tibiæ and under tail coverts with nearly regular bands of brown and pale reddish ; under surface of the tail ashy white. Bill dark bluish ; legs greenish yellow.

Total length (adult) about 21 inches ; wing 16, tail 9½ inches.

In the collection brought by the surveying party under the command of Captain John Pope, United States army, are two specimens of the bird which we suppose to be *Buteo Harlani*. These were obtained near Fort Thorne, New Mexico, by T. Charlton Henry, M. D., United States army, and, with that described, as above cited, by Mr. George N. Lawrence, are the only ones yet detected within the limits of the United States. We have seen other specimens of the same species from Mexico. One of the present specimens, like that of Mr. Lawrence, is adult in black plumage ; the other is very probably the young, and in plumage totally different, as described above.

This bird comes very near the description by Mr. Audubon in his Ornithological Biography, I, p. 441, and is the same species decided by Mr. Lawrence to be the *Buteo Harlani* of that author, and first announced by him as a species of western North America in the Annals of the New York Lyceum of Natural History, as above cited. In both size and colors, our present adult specimen agrees sufficiently well with Mr. Audubon's description, though a measurement given in the latter—"tarsus 1¾ inches"—is very probably a misprint, though copied into his octavo edition. A *Buteo*, with the tarsus of this length, would be about the shortest legged species known, and rather deviating from the requirements of the genus. In the present bird the *tarsus* measures about three inches.

The bird now before us being much like the figure and description given by Mr. Audubon as pointed out by Mr. Lawrence, we have no scruple in assenting to such designation as applied to it. The proper identification of the species though can be made only from the original specimen in the British Museum. To Mr. Lawrence we are also indebted for the recognition of the young bird of this species, described above, in the collection of the expeditions.

The specimens in the collection of Captain Pope's party were obtained by Dr. Henry in New Mexico, as above stated. Those described by Mr. Lawrence were from California.

Sub-Genus Poecilopternis.

BUTEO BOREALIS, Gmelin.

The Red-tailed Hawk.

Falco borealis, Leverianus, and *jamaicensis,* GM. Syst. Nat. I, 266, (1788.)

Falco aquilinus, BARTRAM, Trav. p. 290, (1791.)

Buteo ferrugineicaudus, VIEILL. Ois. d'Am. Sept. I, 32, (1807.)

Accipiter ruficaudus, VIEILL. Ois. d'Am. Sept. I, 43, (1807.)

Buteo fulvus and *americanus,* VIEILL. Nouv. Dict. IV, 472, 477, (1816.)

FIGURES.—Vieill. Ois. d'Am. Sept. I, pl. 6, 14; Wilson Am. Orn. VI, pl. 52, figs. 1, 2; Audubon B. of Am., pl. 51, Oct. ed. 1, pl. 7; Gosse B. of Jamaica, pl. 2; Lembeye B. of Cuba, pl. 1.

Adult.—Tail bright rufous, narrowly tipped with white and having a subterminal band of black. Entire upper parts dark umber brown, lighter and with fulvous edgings on the head and neck; upper tail coverts yellowish white, with rufous and brown spots and bands. Throat white, with narrow longitudinal stripes of brown, other under parts pale yellowish white with longitudinal lines and spots of reddish brown tinged with fulvous, most numerous on the breast, and forming an irregular band across the abdomen; under tail coverts and tibiæ generally clear yellowish white unspotted, but the latter frequently spotted and transversely barred with light rufous. Under surface of tail silvery white.

Young.—Tail usually ashy brown, with numerous bands of a darker shade of the same color and narrowly tipped with white, upper tail coverts white with bands of dark brown; other upper parts dark umber brown, many feathers edged with dull white and with partially concealed spots of white. Entire under parts white, sides of the breast with large ovate spots of brownish black, and a wide irregular band on the abdomen composed of spots of the same color. Under tail coverts and tibiæ with irregular transverse stripes and sagittate spots of dark brown.

Total length.—Female, 22 to 24 inches; wing, 15 to 16 inches; tail, 8½ inches. Male, 19 to 21 inches; wing, 14 inches; tail, 7½ to 8 inches.

Hab.—Eastern North America, fur countries, (Swainson,) Cuba, (Lembeye,) Jamaica, (Gosse.)

The range of this well known bird covers an extent of longitude from the Atlantic ocean to the base of the Rocky mountains, and in latitude its locality may be said to be from the West India islands northward to the confines of the frigid zone. In the countries on the Pacific it is supplanted by the nearly allied species immediately succeeding, (*Buteo montanus.*)

In the collections made by the surveying and exploring expeditions, there are specimens of this bird from the Yellow Stone river, Nebraska Territory, and others from the Pecos river, Texas. Specimens in immature plumage are also in Dr. T. Charlton Henry's collection made at Fort Fillmore, New Mexico.

List of specimens.

Catalogue number.	Sex and age.	Locality.	When collected.	Whence and how obtained.	Original number.	Collected by—	Measurements.		
							Point of bill to end of tail.	Between tips of out-stretched wings.	Wing, from carpal joint.
5153	....	80 miles above mouth of Yellowstone.....	Aug. 11, 1856	Lt. G. K. Warren	....	Dr. Hayden...	22. 50	49. 25	14..75
5159	♂	Eau qui Court, Neb..	Oct. 20, 1856	......do.........	....	......do......	23. 00	48. 00	16. 25
5158	♂	Fort Randall, Neb ...	Oct. 11, 1856	......do.........	....	......do......	22. 00	49. 50	16. 00
?? 4617	....	Jamacha Ranch, Cal..	....	Maj. Emory.....	7	A. Schott.....	....	....	....
?? 8530	....	Santa Isabel, Cal.....	....	....	14	......do......	....	....	....

BUTEO MONTANUS, Nuttall.

The Western Red-tailed Hawk.

Buteo montanus, Nutt. Manual Orn. U. S. I, 112, (1840.)
Falco buteo, (Linn.) Aud. Orn. Biog. IV, 508.
Falco buteo, (Linn.) Rich. and Sw. Faun. Bor. Am. Birds.
Buteo borealis, (Gm.) Gray, Gen. I, p. 11.
" *Buteo Swainsonii,* (Br.)" Bonap. Consp. Av. p. 19.
Buteo Swainsonii, Bonap. Cassin B. of Cal. and Texas, 1, p. 98

Figures.—Aud. B. of Am., pl. 372, Oct. ed., I, pl

Adult female.—Throat and neck before dark brown mixed with white ; the brown color more extended and with the abdomen, tibiæ and under tail coverts much more tinged with rufous than in *B. borealis.* Tibiæ distinctly barred transversely with rufous. Size rather larger. General appearance similar to *Buteo borealis,* but rather larger, and with the wings longer ; throat and neck before brown ; breast and abdomen white, with a very pale fulvous or rufous tinge ; sides with numerous narrow lanceolate and oblong spots of dark brown and rufous ; abdomen with a broad transverse band composed of spots of the same description. Tibial feathers pale rufous, with numerous transverse bands of a darker shade of the same color. Under wing coverts pale yellowish white, with brown spots. Tail above bright rufous narrowly tipped with white, with a subterminal band of black, and a few indications of transverse-stripes near the shafts of the feathers. Upper parts of the body dark umber brown, with partially concealed ashy white and pale fulvous spots and transverse bands, especially on the scapulars and shorter quills. Upper tail coverts reddish white, with transverse bands of dark brown. Bill dark bluish ; tarsi and toes yellow.

This plumage can only be distinguished from *B. borealis* by its larger size, the greater extent of the dark color of the throat, and the prevalence of the rufous color of the abdomen and tibiæ. In some specimens, however, the abdomen is nearly pure white. Another plumage of this bird, apparently adult, of both sexes is as follows, and is the most easily recognized of any stage :

Adult male and female.—Like the preceding, but with the under parts pale rufous, lighter on the breast, some feathers, especially on the abdomen, having longitudinal lines and spots of dark brown. Tibiæ rufous, with transverse bars of a darker shade of the same color. Tail bright rufous ; tip paler, with a subterminal band of black. This second plumage, described above, we have never seen in *Buteo borealis.*

Young.—Upper parts dark brown, edged and spotted with white tinged with rufous. Under parts white, with large ovate and sagittate spots of dark brown more numerous on the abdomen. Tibial plumes and under tail coverts white, with transverse bars and spots of dark brown. Tail above ashy brown, with transverse bands of dark brown, nearly black. Bill dark bluish black, or slate color ; tarsi and toes dull greenish.

In this plumage, which is evidently that of the young bird, the dark spots of the under parts are usually much larger and more numerous than in the young of *Buteo borealis*, in which we have never seen the tibiæ and under tail coverts so strongly barred as in the present bird.

Dimensions.—Adult female, total length 23 to 25 inches, wing 16½ to 17, tail 9 to 10 inches. Male, total length 19 to 22 inches, wing 15 to 16, tail 8½ to 9 inches.

This is a species much resembling and nearly related to the red-tailed buzzard (*Buteo borealis*) of the States on the Atlantic, and in the examination of collections like the present made during journeys across the continent, it is not without difficulty that a distinct range of locality can be assigned to the two species. The most strongly characterized specimens of the bird now before us are from the countries west of the Rocky mountains, but it is evident from specimens in this collection that this species is not restricted to those regions. It not only inhabits the mountains, but extends into the countries at their eastern base.

Of this rather difficult and obscure species, we have in the present collection no less than thirty specimens, which, with several others from the collection of the Philadelphia Academy, make a series probably representing all the stages of plumage dependent on age, sex, or season. This series admits of division into the three stages above described.

Our comparisons are made with a series of twenty-eight specimens of *Buteo borealis* from various parts of the United States east of the Rocky mountains ; generally, however, from the vicinity of Philadelphia. The present species appears to be the larger, averaging in total length about 24 inches in adult females, which, so far as can be determined from prepared specimens, is nearly two inches greater than the average of the same sex of *Buteo borealis*. The wing is about 1½ inches longer. There are in the entire series of both species now before us not more than three specimens that we have any difficulty in assigning to one species or the other, though specimens of both constantly occur which cannot be recognized without difficulty, unless series are at hand for comparison.

List of specimens.

Catalogue number.	Sex and age.	Locality.	When collected.	Whence and how obtained.	Original number.	Collected by—	Point of bill to end of tail.	Between tips of outstretched wings.	Wing from carpal joint.
							Measurements.		
5836	♀	Fort Steilacoom, W. T.	Aug. 8, 1856	Dr. G. Suckley	527		23.50	53.00	16.75
5834		........do........	Sept. —, 1856	......do..			24.50	51.00	
4581		........do........		Dr. Potts					
8531	♀	........do........		Gov. I. I. Stevens	99	Dr. Suckley			
8538		........do........		Dr. Suckley	536		23.00	49.00	
4372	♀	........do........	Oct. —, 1854	......do.			24.00	54.00	
8535	♂	Shoalwater bay, W. T.	March 21, 1854	Gov. Stevens		Dr. Cooper	22.00	48.00	
8534		Yakima river, W. T.	Aug. 4, 1853	......do.	8	......do.			
4416		Fort Dalles, O. T.	Dec. —, 1854	Dr. Suckley					
4521		Santa Clara, Cal.		Dr. Cooper					
4611		California		Major Emory		A. Schott			
8536		Laguna	Nov. 23, 1854	......do.	14	......do.			
8533		Camp 149, N. M.	March 16, 1854	Lieut. Whipple	185	Dr. Kennerly			
8549		Camp 114, N. M.	Feb. 6, 1854	......do.	71	......do.			
6957	♂	North Platte	Aug. 1, 1857	Lieut. Bryan	371	W. S. Wood			
6956	♀	........do........	........do.	......do.	369	......do.			
4986		Pecos river, Texas		Capt. Pope			22.50	54.50	18.00
4985		........do........		......do.			25.00	53.00	17.50
8532		Devil's river, Texas	Nov. —, 1855	Major Emory	1	Dr. Kennerly			

BUTEO LINEATUS, Gmelin.

The Red Shouldered Hawk; The Winter Falcon.

Falco lineatus and *hyemalis*, Gm. Syst. Nat. I, 268, 274, (1788.)

Falco buteoides, Nutt. Man. I, 100, (1st edition, 1832.)

Figures.—Vieill. Ois. d'Am. Sept., pl. 5 ; Wilson Am. Orn., pl. 53 fig. 3 ; Aud. B. of Am., pl. 56, 71 ; Oct. ed. I, pl. 9 ; Nat. Hist. New York, Birds, pl. 6, fig. 13.

Adult.—Wing coverts from its flexure to the body fine bright rufous ; breast and other lower parts of the body paler orange rufous, many feathers, with transverse bars and spots of white, which predominate on the abdomen and under tail coverts. Entire upper parts brown ; on the head mixed with rufous, and with white spots on the wing coverts and shorter quills and rump. Quills brownish black, with white spots on their outer webs, and with bars of a lighter shade of brown and of white on their inner webs ; tail brownish black, with about five transverse bands of white and tipped with white.

Young.—Entire under parts yellowish white, with longitudinal stripes and oblong spots of dark brown ; throat dark brown. Upper parts lighter ashy brown, with many partially concealed spots and bars of white ; quills dark brown, with wide transverse bars of rufous and white on both webs. Tail ashy brown, with numerous bands pale brownish and rufous white ; tail beneath silvery white.

Total length, female, 21 to 23 inches, wing 14, tail 9 inches. Male, 18 to 20 inches, wing 12, tail 8 inches.

Hab. Eastern and northern North America.

This is one of the most abundant of the rapacious birds of the eastern and southern States on the Atlantic, and appears to be restricted to the countries east of the Rocky mountains. It presents considerable variation in plumage, the young, as described above, bearing very little resemblance to the adult. The latter is much the more frequently met with, and is *Falco hyemalis* of authors.

In western North America this bird is replaced by the succeeding species, from which it can be easily recognized in the adult by the different shade of color of the under parts, and by the different markings of the young.

List of specimens.

Catalogue number.	Sex and age.	Locality.	When collected.	Whence obtained.	Point of bill to end of tail.	Between tips of out-stretched wings.	Wing from carpal joint.	Remarks.
					Measurements.			
8629	....	Cape Florida.........	Nov. 10, 1857	G. Wurdemann..	17.75	40.00	12.00	
8630	♀	Indian Key, Fla	Aug. 31, 1857	......do........	17.50	37.00	11.20	Iris, light brown ; legs
8631	♂	......do...........	......do......	......do........	17.50	37.00	11.10	and feet, green....
4978	....	Ft. Chadbourne, Tex.	....	Dr. Swift.......	18.00	38.00	11.50	

BUTEO ELEGANS, Cassin.

Buteo elegans, Cassin, Proc. Acad. Philada. VII, 281, (1855.)

Generally resembling *Buteo lineatus*. Bill rather slender ; edges of the upper mandible with a rounded lobe ; wing moderate, fourth quill longest, first quill short ; tail moderate wide, rounded at tip. Tarsus feathered in front slightly below the joint ; naked behind ; in front presenting about twelve transverse scales.

Adult female.—Resembling the adult of *Buteo lineatus*, but with the breast dark rufous unspotted, (nearly brick red,) and other under parts, including the under tail coverts, of the same color, with numerous nearly regular transverse bars of reddish white., Under wing coverts dark rufous, transversely barred with reddish white. Throat brownish black, with a few white feathers. Feathers of the breast having dark lines on their shafts. Upper parts dark brown; on the head and back edged with rufous; upper coverts of the tail narrowly tipped with white. Shoulders dark rufous, every feather having a narrow central stripe of dark brown; superior coverts of the wing dark brown; edged on their inner webs with rufous, and with transverse stripes partially concealed, and with circular spots of white, and tipped with the same. Quills brownish black; primaries and secondaries with numerous irregular transverse bands of white, running obliquely on their inner webs; all the quills tipped with white. Tail brownish black; white at base, with four transverse bands of white, and tipped with the same. Bill bluish black; tarsi and cere yellow.

Young female.—Under parts yellowish white; every feather with wide irregular and confluent bands of dark brown, and at its end a large arrow head of the same color. These bands and sagittate spots giving the predominating color to the breast and sides, but less numerous on the abdomen and under tail coverts. Tibial feathers and under coverts of the wings and tail tinged with pale rufous; shoulders with a few rufous feathers. Throat dark brown, with longitudinal narrow stripes of white. Upper parts dull brown; many feathers edged with reddish white, especially on the back and wing coverts. Quills brownish black, with their inner webs barred with white. Tail brown, tinged with ashy, with about ten to twelve transverse narrow bars of a darker shade of the same color, and tipped with white.

Young male.—Similar to the last described, but with the sagittate spots on the under parts more elongated, and the upper parts and shoulders strongly tinged with rufous. Under wing coverts and tibiæ dark rufous.

Dimensions.—Adult female, total length, about 20 inches; wing, 13; tail, 9 inches. Young male, 18½; wing, 12½; tail, 8 inches.

This very handsome bird is nearly related to *Buteo lineatus*, as stated above; but all the specimens constantly present differences. In the adult of the present species the under parts are of a much darker red and more uniformly presented than in *Buteo lineatus*, in which those parts are orange red, and the abdomen and under tail coverts nearly white.

The young bird of the present species is strongly characterized by the large sagittate spots of the under parts, which we have never seen in the young of *Buteo lineatus*.

The plate represents the adult and young of this handsome hawk. Plate II is the fully mature plumage, and Plate III the young in the plumage invariably presented in all the specimens in the collections of the expeditions.

List of specimens.

Catalogue number.	Sex and age.	Locality.	When collected.	Whence and how obtained.	Original number.	Collected by—
4520	♂	Santa Clara, California		Dr. Cooper		Kennerly, and
8524		Camp on Little Colorado, N. Mexico	Nov. 17, 1853	Lieut. Whipple	32	Mollhausen
4618		Santa Isabel, California	Oct. 29, 1854	Major Emory	23	A. Schott

BUTEO PENNSYLVANICUS, Wilson.

The Broad-winged Hawk.

Falco pennsylvanicus, WILSON, Am. Orn. VI, 92, (1812.)
Falco latissimus, WILSON, Am. Orn. VI, 92, (1812, copies printed later than those containing the preceding name.)
Sparvius platypterus, VIEILL. Ency. Meth. III, 1273, (1823.)
Falco Wilsonii, BONAP. Jour. Acad. Philad. III, 348, (1824.)

FIGURES.—Wilson Am. Orn. VI, pl. 54, fig. 1; Aud. B. of Am., pl. 91, Oct. ed. 1, pl. 10; Nat. Hist. New York, Birds, pl. 5, fig. 11.

Smaller than either of the preceding. *Adult.*—Entire upper parts umber brown, feathers on the occiput and back of the neck white at their bases. Throat white, with longitudinal lines of brown, and with a patch of brown on each side running from the base of the lower mandible ; breast with a wide band composed of large cordate and sagittate spots, and transverse bands of reddish ferruginous tinged with ashy ; other under parts white, with numerous sagittate spots of reddish on the flanks, abdomen, and tibiæ. In some specimens the ferruginous color predominates on all the under parts, except the under tail coverts, and all the feathers have large circular or ovate spots of white on both edges, under tail coverts white. Quills brownish black, widely bordered with white on their inner webs ; tail dark brown, narrowly tipped with white, and with one wide band of white and several narrower bands near the base.

Young.—Upper parts dull umber brown, many feathers edged with fulvous and ashy white ; upper tail coverts spotted with white. Under parts white, generally tinged with yellowish, and having longitudinal stripes and oblong and lanceolate spots of brownish black ; a stripe of dark brown on each side of the neck from the base of the under mandible. Tail brown, with several bands of a darker shade of the same color, and of white on the inner webs and narrowly tipped with white.

Total length, female, 17 to 18 inches ; wing, 11 ; tail, 6¼ to 7 inches. Male, total length, 16 to 16½ inches ; wing, 10 inches ; tail 6 to 6½ inches.

Hab.—Eastern North America. Spec. in Nat. Mus., Washington, and Mus. Acad., Philadelphia.

In adult plumage this is a very handsome little hawk, and quite different in its color from any other American species. It appears to be restricted to the States on the Atlantic slope, more abundant in the north.

List of specimens.

Catalogue No.	Sex and age.	Locality.	When collected.	Whence obtained.	Original No.	Collected by—	Measurements.		
							Length.	Extent.	Carpal joint.
5574	......	Saranac lake, N. Y.	August, 1855 ...	S. F. Baird		......	......	......	......
3844	♂	Prairie Mer Rouge, Louisiana.	....	J. Fairie		......	......	......	......

BUTEO OXYPTERUS, Cassin.

Buteo oxypterus, CASSIN., Proc. Acad. Philad. VII, p. 282, (1855.)

About the size of *Buteo pennsylvanicus*, Wilson. Bill rather long and compressed, edge of upper mandible slightly waved in its outline, but scarcely lobed ; wing long, pointed, third quill longest ; tail moderate or rather short ; legs rather long, tarsus feathered in front for about one-third of its length, naked behind, naked portion in front having about fourteen narrow transverse scales ; claws large, strong, fully curved.

Young bird.—Sex unknown. Entire plumage above dark brown, nearly black on the back. Feathers of the head white at base, and edged laterally with the same ; upper plumage with partially concealed spots and transverse bands of white. Quills nearly black, with the inner webs dark cinereous barred with brown ; tail above ashy brown, white at base and having about ten transverse bands of dark brown, outer feathers ashy white on their inner webs ; tail beneath silky, ashy white, with a bronzed yellowish olive lustre.

Behind and under the eye a stripe of rufous brown. Under parts pale yellowish white ; throat with lines and narrow stripes of brownish black, and on other under parts every feather with a large lanceolate, cordate, or circular spot of dark brown, some feathers on the flanks and sides having also some irregular bands of the same color. Nearly all the feathers on the under parts with lines of dark brown on their shafts. Quills, with their inner webs on the under surface grayish or dark ashy, and near the shafts with a bronzed olive lustre ; shafts white, (on the under surface.) Inferior coverts of the wing white, with sagittate spots of dark brown. Tibial feathers yellowish white tinged with rufous, and having irregular transverse bars of dark brown.

Dimensions.—Total length (sex unknown) about 16 inches ; wing, 13½ inches ; tail, 7 inches.

The adult of this bird is unknown, and the only specimen that we have ever seen is that now described. It is about the size of *Buteo pennsylvanicus*, and bears some resemblance to the young of that species, but has the wings and legs much longer and the bill also longer. The colors, too, are different, and in the present bird the dark cinereous of the inner webs of the quills and the bronzed or silky olive lustre of their inferior surfaces are quite remarkable. The exposed edges and ends of some of the secondaries in the present specimen have a distinct purple lustre. On examination and comparison with some black species from Mexico, we are not without a suspicion that the adult of this bird is of that color.

The only specimen of this species is in the collection made by T. Charlton Henry, M. D., United States army, at Fort Fillmore, New Mexico, and is that which is represented in our plate.

List of specimens.

Catalogue No.	Sex and age.	Locality.	When collected.	Whence obtained.	Original No.	Collected by—	Length.	Extent.	Carpal joint.
							Measurements.		
8550	------	Fort Fillmore, N. M	---------------	Dr. Henry	-------	------	-----------------	------	------	------

Sub-Genus **Tachytriorchis**.

BUTEO COOPERI, Cassin.

Buteo Cooperi, CASSIN, Proc. Acad. Philad. VIII, 253, (1856.)

About the size of *Buteo borealis,* but belonging to the same group as *Buteo erythronotus* of South America, (genus *Tachytriorchis,* Kaup, as restricted by Bonaparte, Conspectus Avium, p. 17.)

Bill strong; edges of upper mandible lobed; wings long; quills very wide and strong, fourth quill longest; tail moderate; legs rather long, tarsus feathered in front slightly below the joint, behind and remaining portion in front naked, with about 13 transverse scales in front and 11 to 13 behind, the latter running into a circular or hexagonal form towards the joint with the tibia; claws long, rather slender, very sharp, and strongly curved.

Tail white at its base; external feathers, with their outer webs cinereous and their inner webs white, mottled with cinereous; other feathers of the tail mottled and striped *longitudinally* with white, bright rufous, dark brown, and cinereous, darker on the outer web. The rufous color most conspicuous on the two middle feathers and on the outer webs of others. A subterminal transverse band of dark brown, tipped with reddish and white.

Head above and neck behind having the feathers white at base, tipped and with longitudinal stripes of brownish black; back and rump brownish black tinged with cinereous; upper tail coverts white, transversely barred with dark brown and tinged with rufous; wing coverts and quills brownish cinereous, lighter on the quills; coverts with concealed spots of white at their bases; inner webs of quills white, mottled, and irregularly banded with light ashy; exposed ends of quills light, nearly white. Under parts white, with narrow stripes of dark brown on the throat, neck and flanks; (breast, abdomen, and under tail coverts pure white.) A large spot of brownish black on the under wing coverts next to the upper edge of the wing; other under wing coverts white, with a few spots of dark brown. Tibial plumes tinged with reddish yellow. Bill dark bluish; tarsi and toes yellow.

Total length, about 21¼ inches; wing, 15 inches; tail, 9 inches.

This is the only species yet discovered within the limits of the United States which belongs to the group above indicated, the species of which, as restricted, are principally South American, and are, for the most part, of light colors, as in the present bird. The present bird may be easily distinguished from any other North American *Buteo* by its light colors.

One specimen only is in the collection, and was obtained at Santa Clara, California, by J. G. Cooper, M. D. It is not in adult plumage, but is very probably sufficiently mature to indicate the adult plumage, except the colors of the tail. The latter is quite remarkable and peculiar in its colors, which are disposed in irregular longitudinal stripes, as above described.

This bird is one of the most interesting and valuable of the ornithological discoveries made by the exploring and surveying expeditions. It is well represented in the plate cited above, but necessarily the figure is much reduced, and is made from the only specimen that has ever come under our notice.

List of specimens.

Catalogue No.	Sex and age.	Locality.	When collected.	Whence obtained.	Original No.	Collected by—	Measurements.		
							Length.	Extent.	Carpal joint.
8525	......	Santa Clara, Cal...	October, 1856...	Dr. Cooper	......	......	......	......	......

ARCHIBUTEO, Brehm.

Archibuteo, Brehm, Isis, 1828, p. 1269.

Tarsi densely feathered to the toes, but more or less naked behind and then covered with scales. Wings long and wide; toes short ; claws moderate ; tail rather short, wide. Other characters very similar to those of *Buteo.*

This genus contains six or seven species, inhabiting Europe, Asia, and North America, all birds of heavy, though robust, organization, subsisting mainly on small quadrupeds and reptiles. The species of this genus are easily recognized by their having the *tarsi* feathered.

ARCHIBUTEO LAGOPUS, Gmelin.

Rough-legged Hawk.

Falco lagopus, Gm. Syst. Nat. I, p. 260, (1788)
Falco plumipes, Daudin, Traite d'Orn. II, p. 163.
Falco pennatus, Cuvier, Reg. An. I, p. 323,(817.)
Archibuteo alticeps, Brehm, Vög Deutsch. I, .40.
Archibuteo planiceps, Brehm, Vög. Deutsch. I, p. 40.

Figures.—Naumann, Vög. Deutsch. I, pl. 34, (adult and young.) Brehm, Vög. Deutsch. pl. IV, fig. 2, (adult.) Reichenbach, Deutschland's Fauna, Birds, pl. XIII, fig. 51, (adult.) Korner, Skandinaviska Foglar, pl. V, fig. 15, (adult.) Gould, B. of Eur. I, pl. 15, (young.) Selby Ill. pl. VII, (young.) Wilson, Am. Orn. IV, pl. XXXIII, fig. 1, (young.) Aud. B. of Am. pl. 422, fig. 2, (adult?)

Tarsus densely feathered in front to the toes, naked behind ; wing long ; tail rather short.

Adult.—Head above yellowish white, with longitudinal stripes of brown tinged with reddish, especially on the occiput. Back, scapular, and shorter quills pale cinereous, with 'partially concealed transverse bands of white and dark brown, the latter frequently predominating and giving the color on the back ; rump dark umber brown ; longer quills, and wing coverts umber brown ; primaries edged externally with ashy, and with a large space on their inner webs at their base, white, with a silky lustre. Under parts white ; throat with longitudinal stripes of dark brown ; breast with large spots and concealed stripes of reddish brown ; abdomen, with numerous transverse narrow bands of brownish black, most conspicuous on the flanks and tinged with ashy ; tibiæ and tarsi barred transversely with white and dark brown, and tinged with reddish ; under tail coverts white. Upper tail coverts white at base and tipped with brownish black ; tail white at base, with a wide subterminal band of black and about two other bands of black alternating with others of light cinereous. Cere and toes yellow. Under wing coverts white, with spots of brownish black, and on the longer coverts with a large space of ashy brown.

Young.—Upper parts light umber brown, many feathers, especially on the head and neck behind, edged with yellowish white and pale reddish. A wide transverse band or belt on the abdomen brownish black ; other under parts yellowish white, with a few longitudinal lines and spots of brownish black. Quills ashy brown, with a large basal portion of their inner webs white ; tail at its base white, with a subterminal band of light umber brown, tip white ; tibiæ and tarsi pale reddish yellow, with longitudinal stripes and spots of dark brown.

Total length, female, 21 to 23 inches ; wing, 16 to 17 inches ; tail, 9 inches. Male, total length, 19 to 21 inches ; wing, 15 to 16 inches ; tail, 8 to 8¼ inches.

Hab.—All of temperate North America and Europe. Spec. in Mus. Acad., Philadelphia, and Nat. Mus Washington.

This is one of the few North American birds which appear to be absolutely identical with a species of Europe. In both adult and young plumage, as described above, there are no characters whatever, so far as we can see, by which this bird can be distinguished from *A. lagopus* of Europe, and this identity is even more perfect in specimens from western North America. We regard the plumage first described above as undoubtedly the adult of this species, though it has never been given as such by any American author. It corresponds precisely, so far as we can see, with specimens from Europe in that stage of plumage well understood to be the adult of *A. lagopus* by all the German ornithologists, though apparently unknown to those of more southern and western Europe, and is figured in their works above cited. The regarding of this species as the young of *A. sancti-johannis*, which has been done to some extent by American naturalists, is assuredly erroneous.

The figure in Audubon's plate, cited above, (B. of Am., pl. 422, fig. 2,) may be regarded as very probably representing the adult of this bird, though so distorted in drawing and exaggerated in color as to be very difficult of recognition. The best figure that we have seen of the adult is that in Nauman's work, above cited. The young is well represented by various authors, American and European, as given above.

List of specimens.

Catal. No.	Sex and age.	Locality.	When collected.	Whence obtained.	Original No.	Collected by—	Length.	Extent	Wing.	Remarks.
6853	......	Fort Steilacoom, W. T....	Oct. 20, 1856	Dr. Suckley.	581	....	21.50	52.50	16.50	Irids yellowish gray; legs and cere yellow; bill black............
8549	......	Shoalwater bay, W. T....	Oct. 31, 1854	Gov. Stevens.......	109	Dr. Cooper.........	22.00	52.00	......	Bill slate............
8545	......	Bodega, Cal. ....:	... .	Lieut. Trowbridge..	......	T. A. Szabo.......	......	......	......	....
8548	......	Near Zuñi, N. M.........	Nov. 9, 1853	Lieut. Whipple.....	25	Kennerly and Möllhausen.......	......	......	......	....
8544	......	Mimbres to Rio Grande..	....	Dr. Henry.......	......	....	......	......	......	....
		Fort Fillmore, N. M......	....	Capt. Pope	......	....	......	......	......	....
		Fort Massachusetts	....	Dr. Peters.........	......	....	......	......	......	....

ARCHIBUTEO SANCTI-JOHANNIS, Gmelin.

The Black Hawk.

Falco sancti-johannis, GM. Syst. Nat. I, p. 273, (1788.)
Falco spadiceus, GM. Syst. Nat. I, p. 273, (1788.)
Falco novæ-terræ, GM. Syst. Nat. I, p. 274, (1788.)
Falco niger, WILSON, Am. Orn. VI, p. 82, (1812.)
Buteo ater, VIEILL. Nouv. Dict. IV, p. 482, (1816.)

FIGURES.—Wilson Am. Orn. VI, pl. 53, figs. 1, 2 ; Aud. B. of Am. pl. 422, fig. 1 ; pl. 166, (young?)

Adult.—Entire plumage glossy black in many specimens with a brown tinge; forehead, throat, and large partially concealed spot on occiput, white. Tail with one transverse well defined band of white, and irregularly marked towards the base with the same color. Quills with their inner webs white, readily seen from below. Cere and toes yellow. Tarsi densely feathered in front ; naked behind. Other specimens are entirely dark chocolate brown, with the head more or less striped with yellowish white and reddish yellow. Tail with several transverse bands of white, more or less imperfect and irregular.

Young.—Upper parts light umber brown, with the feathers more or less edged with dull white and reddish yellow. Abdomen with a broad transverse band of brownish black ; other under parts pale yellowish white, with longitudinal stripes of brownish black, frequently giving the predominating color on the breast and sides ; wings and tail brown, tinged with cinereous, the

5 b

former marked with white on their inner webs, the latter white at its base. Tarsi and tibiæ pale reddish yellow, spotted with brown.

Total length, female, 22 to 24 inches; wing 17 to 17½, tail 9 inches. Male 20 to 22 inches ; wing 16 to 16½, tail 8 to 8½ inches. *Hab.*—Eastern and northern North America. Spec. in Nat. Mus., Washington, and Mus. Acad., Philadelphia.

One of the most abundant of the birds of this family in the eastern States, and in adult plumage very easily recognized, but very variable in colors of plumage. The dark brown or chocolate colored plumage is frequently to be met with, and in that stage this bird appears to be *Falco spadiceus*, Gmelin. In young plumage, as described above, and especially with the wide abdominal band well defined, this bird much resembles the young of *Archibuteo lagopus*, as described immediately preceding, from which it can be distinguished by its larger size and the much more numerous dark spots on the under parts in the present bird.

ARCHIBUTEO FERRUGINEUS, Lichtenstein.

California Squirrel Hawk.

Buteo ferrugineus, LICHT. Trans. Acad. Berlin, 1838, p. 428.
Archibuteo regalis, G. R. GRAY, Gen. Birds, I, pl. 6, (plate only.)
Buteo Californicus, Hutchins' California Magazine, March, 1857.

FIGURES —Gray, Genera of Birds, I, pl. 6 ; Cassin, B. of Cal. and Texas, I, pl. 26.

Adult.—Larger than either of the two preceding ; bill wide at base ; wings long ; tarsi feathered in front to the toes ; naked and scaled behind. Tibiæ and tarsi bright ferruginous, with transverse narrow stripes of black. Entire upper parts dark brown and light rufous, the latter predominating on the rump and wing coverts ; quills ashy brown, with the greater part of their inner webs white ; tail above reddish white, mottled with ashy brown ; beneath pale yellowish white. Under parts of the body white, with narrow longitudinal lines and lanceolate spots on the breast of reddish brown, and narrow irregular transverse lines of the same color and of black on the abdomen ; flanks and axillary feathers fine bright ferruginous.

Young.—Entire upper parts dark umber brown, slightly mixed with fulvous ; upper tail coverts white, spotted with brown ; under parts pure white, with a few longitudinal lines of brown on the breast, and sagittate spots of the same color on the sides and abaomen, larger and more numerous on the flanks ; tibiæ white ; tarsi dark brown, mixed with white ; under wing coverts and edges of wings white.

Total length, female, 23 to 25 inches ; wing 17 to 17⅛, tail 9 inches.
Hab.—Western North America. Spec. in Nat. Mus., Washington, and Mus. Acad., Philadelphia.

This is one of the most handsome of the American Falconidæ, and, though known in Europe for the last twenty years, was unknown to the naturalists of this country until brought to their notice by Mr. Edward M. Kern, who was attached to Colonel Frémont's expeditions. It is one of the largest of its group, somewhat exceeding in size both *Archibuteo sancti-johannis* and *lagopus*.

As usual in this family, the adult and young of the present species are quite different, and in well characterized specimens might readily be regarded as different. Both are described and figured by us, as above.

This bird is apparently exclusively western, but not restricted to the countries west of the Rocky mountains. In the present collection specimens are from Nebraska and New Mexico, as well as from California.

List of specimens.

Catal. No.	Sex and age.	Locality.	When collected.	Whence obtained.	Original No.	Collected by—	Length.	Extent.	Wing.
							Measurements.		
6852	♂	Bodega, Cal.	February, 1855.	Lieut. Trowbridge.		T. A. Szabo			
6883	♀	Los Angeles valley, California.		Lt. R. S. Williamson.		Dr. Heermann			
8543	♂	Fort Fillmore, N. M		Dr. Henry					
9122		Fort Davis, Texas.	Nov., 1854.	Maj. W. H. Emory.	2	Dr. Kennerly	22	54	17
5577	♂	Platte river.	Sept. 16, 1856.	Lieut. Bryan.	338	W. S. Wood	21.00	52 00	
4544	♀	Little Mo. river, Nebraska.	Oct. 12, 1855	Lieut. Warren.			25.00	61.25	

ASTURINA, Vieill.

Asturina, VIEILLOT, Analyse, p. 24, (1816.)

Size.—Smaller than in the preceding two genera. General form compact, and adapted to greater activity of habits and swifter flight. Bill rather thick, strong; cere large, extending somewhat into the feathers of the forehead; wings moderate, third and fourth quills longest; tail rather long; legs rather long; claws strong, fully curved. This genus contains a few species, all of which are South American.

ASTURINA NITIDA, Latham.

Falco nitidus, LATH. Ind. Orn. I, 41.
Asturina cinerea, VIEILL. Anal., p. 68, (1816.)
Astur striolatus, CUV. Règ. An. I, 332.

FIGURES.—Temm. Pl. Col. 87, 294; Vieill. Gal. I, pl.2 .

Adult.—Upper parts light cinereous; darker, and sometimes nearly black on the rump; upper tail coverts white; quills ashy brown, with obscure dark bands, and widely edged with white on their inner webs; tail brownish black, with about three transverse bands of white. Under parts with numerous narrow transverse bands of cinereous and white, the former predominating and darker on the breast; under tail coverts white; cere and legs yellow.

Young.—Entire upper parts umber brown; darker on the rump, and much mixed with white on the head; upper tail coverts white; tail light brown, with about eight bands of brownish black. Under parts white, with longitudinal stripes of umber brown; under wing and tail coverts white; cere and legs yellow.

Total length, female, about 18 inches; wing 10, tail 7¼ inches. Male smaller.

Hab.—Northern Mexico and South America.

This handsome hawk was found in the State of New Leon, one of the most northern provinces of Mexico, by Lieutenant D. N. Couch, United States army, and very probably extends its range northward into the territory of the United States. It is a well known species of South America.

List of specimens.

Catal. No.	Sex and age.	Locality.	When collected.	Whence obtained.	Original No.	Collected by—	Length.	Extent.	Wing.
							Measurements.		
4128	♀	New Leon, Mexico.	1853.	Lt. D. N. Couch.			17.25	34 00	10.50

Sub-Family MILVINAE.—The Kites.

Size various, usually medium or small.   General form usually rather slender and not strong ; wings and tail usually long : bill short, weak, hooked, and acute.   Tarsi and toes usually slender and not strong, sometimes short.   The birds of this group habitually feed on reptiles and other small animals, and are deficient in the strength and courage of the other groups of the falcons.

NAUCLERUS, Vigors.

Nauclerus, Vigors, Zool. Jour. II, p. 386, (1825.)

Wings and tail very long, the former pointed, the latter deeply forked.   Bill short, but moderately strong ; tarsi short ; toes short. Contains three species—two American and one African.

NAUCLERUS FURCATUS, Linnaeus.

The Swallow-tailed Hawk.

Falco furcatus, LINN. Syst. Nat. I, 129, (1766.)

FIGURES.—Catesby Nat. Hist. Carolina, Birds, pl. 4 ; Buffon Pl. Enl. 72 ; Wilson Am. Orn. VI, pl. 51, fig. 3 ; Aud. B. of Am. pl. 72. Oct. ed. I, pl. 18 ; Gould B. of Eur. I, pl. 30 ; De Kay Nat. Hist. New York, Birds, pl. 7, fig. 15.

Wings and tail long, the latter deeply forked. Head and neck, under wing coverts, secondary quills at their bases, and entire under parts, white. Back, wings, and tail black, with a metallic lustre ; purple on the back and wing coverts ; green and blue on other parts.   Tarsi and toes greenish blue ; bill horn color.

Total length, female, 23 to 25 inches ; wing, 16 to 17½ inches ; tail, 14 inches.   Male rather smaller.

Hab.—Southern States on the Atlantic, and centrally northward to Wisconsin. Texas, (Mr. Audubon,) Wisconsin, (Dr. Hoy,) Pennsylvania, (Mr. Krider.) Accidental in Europe. Spec. in Nat. Mus., Washington, and Mus. Acad., Philadelphia.

The most handsome of the North American birds of this group, and possessing very graceful flight. It is abundant in the southern States, and occasionally strays as far north as the vicinity of Philadelphia, a very fine specimen having been obtained this year (1857) near that city by Mr. John Krider.

List of specimens.

Catal. No.	Sex and age.	Locality.	When collected.	Whence obtained.	Original No.	Collected by—	Measurements.		
							Length.	Extent.	Wing.
3754	------	Prairie Mer Rouge, Louisiana.	---------------	James Fairie------	-----	----------------	-----	-----	-----

ELANUS, Savigny.

Elanus, SAVIGNY, Nat. Hist. Egypt I, p. 97, (1809.)

Wings long, pointed ; tail moderate, emarginated ; tarsi short. Bill short, compressed, hooked.   Size medium or small, and general form adapted to the capture of reptiles, insects, and other defenceless animals.

ELANUS LEUCURUS, Vieillot·.

The White-tailed Hawk; the Black-shouldered Hawk.

Milvus leucurus, VIEILL. Nouv. Dict. XX, 563, (1818.)
Falco dispar, TEMMINCK, Pl. Col. I, (liv. 54, about 1824.)
" *Falco melanopterus*, DAUDIN." Bonap. Jour. Acad. Philada. V, 28.
" *Falco dispar*, TEMM." Aud. Orn. Biog. IV, 367.

FIGURES.—Bonap. Am. Orn. II, pl. 11, fig. 1; Temm. Pl. Col. 319; Aud. B. of Am. pl. 352; Oct. ed. I, pl. 16; Gay, Nat. Hist. Chili, Orn. pl. 2.

Adult.—Head and tail and entire under parts white. Upper parts fine light cinereous; lesser wing coverts glossy black, which forms a large oblong patch from the shoulder; inferior wing coverts white, with a smaller black patch. Middle feathers of the tail light ashy, uniform with other upper parts; bill dark; tarsi and toes yellow.

Total length, female, 15½ to 17 inches; wing, 12 inches; tail, 7½ inches. Male smaller.

Hab.—Southern and western States and South America. Spec. in Nat. Mus., Washington, and Mus. Acad., Philadelphia.

Of this very handsome hawk four specimens are in the collection, two of which are from the neighborhood of San Francisco, California. These specimens are labelled as having been collected in the winter of 1853-'54, which fact, with others of a similar character which have come to our knowledge, show that this bird is one of several now known to inhabit a much more northern range of locality on the Pacific than on the Atlantic coast of the United States. Though found in all the States on the southern confines of the United States, the white-tailed hawk has rarely, we believe, been observed north of South Carolina.

List of specimens.

Catal. No.	Sex and age.	Locality.	When collected.	Whence obtained.	Original No.	Collected by—	Measurements.		
							Length.	Extent.	Wing.
4199	------	San Francisco, Cal.	Winter 1854-'55.	R. D. Cutts------	------	------------------	------	------	------
5895	------	Santa Clara, Cal---	-------------	Dr. Cooper ------	------	------------------	------	------	------
6866	------	Tulare valley, Cal--	-------------	Lt. Williamson----	------	Dr. Heermann --	------	------	------

ICTINIA, Vieillot.

Ictinia, VIEILLOT, Analyse, p. 24, (1816.)

General form short and compact. Bill short, tip emarginated; wings long, pointed; tail rather short, emarginated; tarsi short. Contains two species only—one of North and the other of South America.

ICTINIA MISSISSIPPIENSIS, Wilson.

Mississippi Kite.

Falco mississippiensis, WILSON, Am. Orn. III, p. 80, (1811.)
Falco ophiophagus, VIEILL. Nouv. Dict. XI, 103, (1817.)
" *Ictinia plumbea*, GM." AUD. Orn. Biog. II, 108.

FIGURES.—Wilson Am. Orn. III, pl. 25, fig. 1; Aud. B. of Am., pl. 117: Oct. ed. 1, pl. 17.

Adult.—Upper parts of body dark lead color, nearly black on the rump; head and under parts cinereous, darkest on the abdomen; quills and tail brownish black, the latter with a bluish or purplish lustre; tips of secondary quills ashy white; a longitudinal stripe on each web of the primaries, chestnut rufous.

Young.—Upper parts brownish black mixed with dull rufous and white; head and under parts dull yellowish white, with longitudinal stripes of reddish brown, darker and more numerous on the head, lighter and frequently clear rufous on the abdomen.

Total length, female, about 15 inches; wing, 11 to 11½ inches; tail, 6¼ inches. Male, total length, about 14 inches; wing, 11 inches; tail, 6 inches.

Hab —Southern States, Texas, and New Mexico, (Woodhouse.)

Only inhabits the southern States of North America, and probably Mexico and Central America. In the southern division of this continent this bird is represented by another species with which it has been confounded.

ROSTRHAMUS, Lesson.

Rostrhamus, LESSON, Traite d'Orn. I, p. 55, (1831.)

Bill long, very slender, hooked and sharp at the tip; wings long, pointed; tail rather long, emarginated; tarsi and toes rather long; claws very long, slender, acute. The present is the only species.

ROSTRHAMUS SOCIABILIS, Vieillot.

Herpetotheres sociabilis, VIEILL. Nouv. Dict. XVIII, 318, (1817.)
Cymindis leucopygius, SPIX, Av. Bras. I, p. 7, (1824.)
Rostrhamus niger, LESSON, Traite, I, 56, (1831.)
Falco hamatus, ILLIGER.

FIGURES.—Temm. Pl. Col. 61, 231; Spix. Av. Bras. 1, pl. 2.

Adult.—Tail at base and under tail coverts white, all other parts black. Naked space before the eye yellow; bill and claws black; feet yellow. Quills and tail black, the latter narrowly tipped with ashy white.

Younger.—Throat and line over and behind the eye dull yellowish white; all other parts brownish black, mixed with dull yellowish white on the under parts.

Young.—Front stripe behind the eye and throat dull reddish white; upper parts brown; many feathers edged with pale ferruginous; under parts yellowish, with longitudinal stripes of black; tail at the tip and at base and under tail coverts dull yellowish white; tarsi yellowish green.

Total length, female, about 16 inches; wing, 14 inches; tail, 7½ inches. Male rather smaller.

Hab.—Florida, (Mr. Edward Harris, Dr. Heermann.) Spec. in Mus. Acad., Philada.

This is a well known South American bird, first ascertained to inhabit Florida by Mr. Edward Harris, and subsequently by Dr. Heermann and Mr. Krider. It is remarkable for its very slender and hooked bill, unlike that of any other falcon, and can very easily be identified by that character.

This bird undoubtedly breeds in Florida, as young specimens were obtained by Mr. Harris. It has not been ascertained to inhabit any other part of the United States.

CIRCUS, Lacepede.

Circus, LACEPEDE, Mem. d'Inst. Paris, III, CXI, 506, (1803.)

Face partially encircled by a ring or ruff of short projecting feathers, as in the owls. Head rather large; bill short, compressed, curved from the base; nostrils large; wings long, pointed; tail rather long, wide; tarsi long and slender; toes moderate; claws rather slender and weak.

This genus embraces about fifteen species, inhabiting all parts of the world, some of which much resemble each other. One species only is known to inhabit North America.

CIRCUS HUDSONIUS, Linnæus.

The Harrier--The Marsh Hawk.

Falco hudsonius, LINN. Syst. Nat. I, 128, (1766.)
Falco uliginosus, GM. Syst. Nat. I, 278, (1788.)
Falco uropogistus, DAUDIN, Traite d'Orn. II, 110, (1800.)
" *Falco uliginosus*," WILSON, Am. Orn. VI, 67.
" *Falco cyaneus*," AUDUBON, Orn. Biog. IV, 396.

FIGURES.—Vieill. Ois. d'Am. Sept. pl. 9 ; Wilson Am. Orn. VI, pl. 51, fig. 2 ; Bonap. Am. Orn. II, pl. 12 ; Aud. B. of Am. pl. 356 ; Oct. ed I, pl. 26 ; Sw. & Rich. Faun. Bor. Am. Birds, pl. 29.

Adult.—Form rather long and slender ; tarsi long ; ruff quite distinct on the neck in front. Entire upper parts, head and breast, pale bluish cinereous ; on the back of the head mixed with dark fulvous ; upper tail coverts white. Under parts white, with small cordate or hastate spots of light ferruginous ; quills brownish black, with their outer webs tinged with ashy, and a large portion of their inner webs white ; tail light cinereous, nearly white on the inner webs of the feathers, and with obscure transverse bands of brown ; under surface silky white ; under wing coverts white.

Younger.—Entire upper parts dull umber brown, many feathers edged with dull rufous, especially on the neck ; under parts dull reddish white, with longitudinal stripes of brown, most numerous on the throat and neck before ; tibiæ tinged with reddish ; upper tail coverts white.

Young—Entire upper parts dark umber brown ; upper tail coverts white. Under parts rufous, with longitudinal stripes of brown on the breast and sides ; tail reddish brown, with about three wide bands of dark fulvous, paler on the inner webs. Tarsi and toes yellow.

Total length, female, 19 to 21 inches ; wing 15½, tail 10 inches. Male, total length 16 to 18 inches ; wing 14½, tail 8½ to 9 inches. *Hab.*—All of North America and Cuba, (Mr. Lembeye.)

Of this species, well known as one of the most common hawks inhabiting the States of the Atlantic, there are no less than fifty specimens in the collections made by the surveying and exploring expeditions. These were obtained, as will be seen below, at various points in the western States and Territories of the republic, and other localities in North America, and show conclusively that this species is equally abundant on the coasts of the Pacific as on those of the Atlantic ocean. It inhabits also, very probably, the entire intermediate country, and may, therefore, be regarded as diffused over the whole of North America from Mexico to the Arctic regions.

Specimens from all parts of the United States are precisely the same specifically, and constantly present the entirely different colors of the adult and young birds. Several fine specimens of the former are in the present collection, all of which have the under parts nearly pure white, with more or less cordate and sagittate spots of reddish fulvous, varying considerably in size and number. One specimen, No. 5161, has those spots so large and numerous on the breast and sides that they give the predominating color to those parts. This specimen was obtained at Fort Randall, on the Missouri river, in October, 1856, by Lieutenant G. K. Warren, United States army, and is marked as a female. The flanks and under tail coverts have also large cordate spots of the same color.

List of specimens.

Catal. No.	Sex and age.	Locality.	When collected.	Whence obtained.	Original No.	Collected by—	Length.	Extent.	Wing.
8633	------	Cape Florida------	-------------	G. Würdemann----	------	--------------	20.70	43.	14.25
8634	♂?	------do---------	-------------	------do---------	------	--------------	20	45.1	15.
4429	------	Quasquiton, Iowa--	-------------	E. C. Bidwell ----	------	--------------	------	------	------
6911	------	Selkirk Settlement-	-------------	D. Gunn ------	------	--------------	------	------	------
6862	------	Bois de Sioux river-	-------------	Gov. Stevens -----	16	Dr. G. Suckley--	------	------	------
5162	♂	Running Water, Mo.	Oct. 20, 1856 ---	Lieut. Warren-----	------	Dr. Hayden-----	17.50	38.45	13.50
5160	♂	Cedar island, Mo --	Oct. 15, 1856 --	------do---------	------	------do-------	------	------	------
5161	♀	Fort Randall, Neb-	-------------	------do---------	------	------do-------	19.13	42.80	14.45
4502	------	Mouth White river, Nebraska.	-------------	Col. Vaughan-----	------	------do---- --	------	------	------
6958	♂	Med. Bow mountains, Nebraska.	July 27, 1857---	Lieut. Bryan-----	------	W. S. Wood ----	------	------	------
6962	♂	South Platte, Neb-	July 7, 1857----	------do---------	284	------do-------	------	------	------
6960	♂	------do---------	------do-------	------do---------	254	------do-------	------	------	------
6961	♀	------do---------	------ do------	------do---------	256	------do-------	------	------	------
5586	♂	Pole creek, Neb---	July 26, 1856---	------do---------	162	------do-------	20.	37.	------
5585	♂	Bridger's Pass-----	August, 1856 ---	------do---------	275	------do-------	20.25	36.	------
5588	♀	Right fork Laramie river.	August 4, 1856--	------do---------	208	------do-------	19.50	38.	------
6860	------	Fort Conrad, N. M.	October, 1853---	Lieut. Whipple----	------	Dr. Kennerly ---	------	------	------
4126	------	Brownsville, Texas-	-------------	Lieut. Couch-----	------	--------------	------	------	------
4125	------	Matamoras, Texas--	-------------	------do---------	------	--------------	------	------	------
5548	------	San Elizario, Texas-	December, 1854-	Major Emory------	4	Dr. Kennerly ---	19.	42.00	14.00
4990	------	Mouth of Delaware creek.	Sept. 7, 1854----	Captain Pope -----	150	--------------	19.	40.	13.50
6858	------	Mimbres to Rio Grande.	-------------	Dr. Henry-------	------	--------------	------	------	------
6859	------	Rocky mountains--	-------------	E. G. Beckwith ---	4	Mr. Kreutzfeldt-	------	------	------
5851	♀	Fort Steilacoom---	August, 1856 ---	Dr. Suckley-------	551	--------------	21.	47.	------
4373	♂	Ft. Dalles, Oregon-	August 22, 1855-	------do---------	157	--------------	18.50	42.75	13.75
6861	♂	Bodega, Cal------	-------------	Lieut. Trowbridge-	------	T. A Szabo----	------	------	------
6869	------	San Francisco, Cal-	-------------	R. D. Cutts------	------	--------------	------	------	------
6868	♀	Tulare valley -----	-------------	Lieut. Williamson -	------	Dr. Heermann --	------	------	------

Sub-Family AQUILINAE.—The Eagles.

Size large, and all parts very strongly organized. Bill large, compressed, straight at base, curved and acute at tip ; wings long, pointed ; tail ample, generally rounded ; tarsi moderate, very strong ; claws curved, very sharp and strong. There are about seventy species of eagles, of all countries.

AQUILA, Moehring.

Aquila, Moehring, Av. Gen. p. 49, (1752.)

General form large and very strong, and adapted to long continued and swift flight. Bill large, strong, compressed, and hooked at the tip ; wings long, pointed ; tarsi rather short, very strong, feathered to the toes ; claws sharp, strong, curved. This genus includes about twenty species, which are regarded as the true eagles.

AQUILA CANADENSIS, Linnaeus.

The Golden Eagle; The Ring Tailed Eagle.

Falco canadensis, Linn. Syst. Nat. I, 125, (1766.)
Falco niger, Gm. Syst. Nat. I, 259, (1788?)
Aquila nobilis, Pallas, Zoog. Ross. As. I, 338, (1811?)

Figures.—Wilson Am. Orn. pl. 55, fig. 1 ; Aud. B. of Am. pl. 181 ; Oct. ed. I, pl. 12.

Adult.—Large ; tarsi densely feathered to the toes. Head and neck behind light brownish fulvous, varying in shade in different specimens, frequently light orange fulvous, generally darker. Tail at base white, which color frequently occupies the greater part of the tail ; other terminal portion glossy black. All other parts rich purplish brown, frequently very dark, and nearly clear black on the under parts of the body. Primaries shining black ; secondaries purplish brown ; tibiæ and tarsi brownish fulvous, generally mixed with dark ashy ; cere and toes yellow.

Younger.—Entire plumage lighter, and mixed with dull fulvous ; under parts of the body nearly uniform with the upper parts.

Total length, female, 33 to 40 inches, wing about 25, tail about 15 inches. Male, total length 30 to 35 inches, wing 20 to 23, tail 12 to 14 inches.

Hab.—All of North America. Spec. in Nat. Mus., Washington, and Mus. Acad., Philadelphia.

The golden eagle, or ring tailed eagle, as it is more commonly called, inhabits the whole of North America. It has usually been regarded as the same as the European, but presents points of difference, which are very probably sufficient to warrant the original distinctive appellation given by Linnaeus.

List of specimens.

Catal. No.	Sex and age.	Locality.	When collected.	Whence obtained.	Original No.	Collected by—	Measurements.		
							Length.	Extent.	Wing.
9124		Fort Thorn, N. M		Dr. J. C. Henry					
9121[1]	♀	Washington, D. C	Dec. 26, 1857	Benjamin Cross			36.25	86.00	25.00

[1] Weight 9 pounds.

6 b

HALIAETUS, Savigny.

Haliaetus, SAVIGNY, Hist. Nat. d'Egypt, I, p. 85, (1809.)

Size large ; tarsi short, naked, or feathered for a short distance below the joint of the tibia and tarsus, and with the toes covered with scales ; toes rather long ; claws very strong, curved, very sharp. Bill large, very strong, compressed ; margin of upper mandible slightly lobed ; wings long, pointed ; tail moderate. General form very robust and powerful; flight very rapid and long continued.

This genus contains ten or twelve species only, inhabiting various parts of the world, all of which subsist more or less on fishes, and are designated fishing or sea eagles.

HALIAETUS PELAGICUS, Pallas.

The Northern Sea Eagle.

Aquila pelagica, PALL. Zoog. Ross. As. I, p. 343, (1811.)
Falco imperator, KITTLITZ, Kupf. Nat. Vög. I, p. 3, (1832.)
Falco leucopterus, TEMM. Pl. Col. I, (not paged)

FIGURES.—Temm. Pl. Col. I, pl. 489 ; Cassin B. of Cal. and Texas 1, pl. 6.

The largest of all the eagles. Wings rather shorter than usual in this genus ; tail wedge shaped, and containing fourteen feathers. *Adult.*—Large frontal space ; greater wing coverts ; abdomen and tail white. All other parts of the plumage dark brown, or brownish black ; bill and legs yellow.

Younger.—Tail white, more or less marked with brownish black ; quills black ; secondaries and tertiaries white at their bases ; bill and feet yellow. All other parts dull brownish black, lighter on the head and neck.

Total length, female, about 45 inches, wing 26 inches, tail 16 inches.

Hab.—Russian American islands, (Pallas,) Japan, (Temminck & Schlegel.)   Spec. in Mus. Acad., Philadelphia.

The largest of the eagles. This enormous and powerful bird inhabits the Russian American islands and the coasts of the two continents at Behring's straits, and very probably extends its range southward. It is strictly a fishing eagle, mainly deriving its subsistance from the sea, but occasionally capturing birds and quadrupeds. It is stated by Pallas to rear its young in northeastern Asia.

HALIAETUS WASHINGTONII, Audubon.

The Washington Eagle.

Falco Washingtonii, AUD. Orn. Biog. I, 58, (1831.)
Falco Washingtoniana, AUD. Loudon's Mag. I, p. 115, (1828.)

FIGURES.—Aud. B. of Am. pl. 11, (published 1827,) Oct. ed. I, pl. 13.

Rather larger than *H. leucocephalus ;* bill shorter, and more abruptly curved ; wings long. Entire plumage dark brown, mixed with dull fulvous ; quills nearly black ; tail dark brown, more or less mottled with white, especially at the base. Bill dark ; tarsi yellow.

Total length about 43 inches, wing 32, tail 15 inches. " Extent of wings 10 feet 2 inches," (Audubon.)

Hab.—Kentucky. Throughout North America ? Spec. in Mus. Acad., Philad. ?

This eagle is stated by Mr. Audubon to have been discovered by himself in Kentucky, and a figure of the first, and apparently the only, specimen that ever came into his possession is given in his plate, cited above. In this figure the transverse scales on the front of the tarsi are represented in a manner which has never been observed since in any North American eagle. These are continued (in the plate alluded to) without interruption to the toes—a character quite unusual in any rapacious bird.

There are, however, very probably two species of white headed eagles inhabiting North America, one of which is, we suspect, the bird now under consideration. The larger has the bill much the shorter, and very nearly as represented in Audubon's plate. In fact, we have seen several specimens, always of large size, which have agreed precisely with his figure in all respects, except the scales of the tarsi.

Several specimens of the larger bird are now before us, all of which were obtained in New Jersey, and are described above. It is, we suspect, a more southern bird than the common white headed eagle.

HALIAETUS ALBICILLA, Linnæus.

The Gray Sea Eagle; The European Sea Eagle.

Vultur albicilla, LINN. Syst. Nat. I, 123, (1766.)
Falco ossifraga et melanaetos, LINN. Syst. Nat. I, 124, (1766.)
Haliaetus groenlandicus, BREHM, Vög. Deutsch. I, 16, (1831.)

FIGURES.—Selby Ill. Brit. Orn. pl. 3 ; Gould B. of Eur. I, pl. 10.

Large; wings long; tail rather short. *Adult.*—Tail white ; head and neck pale yellowish brown, in some specimens very light ; all other parts of the plumage dark umber brown; quills nearly black ; bill, feet, and irides yellow.

Younger.—Bill brownish black ; entire plumage dark brown, with the tail mottled with white, much varying in extent ; throat paler, frequently nearly white ; irides brown.

Total length, female, 35 to 40 inches ; wing, 25 t o inches ; tail, 12 to 15 inches. Male, total length, 31 to 34 inches ; wing, 22 to 25 inches ; tail, 11½ to 13 inches.

Hab.—Greenland. Europe. Spec. Mus. Acad. Philadelphia.

This eagle, which is common on the coasts of Europe, and rears its young in cliffs on the sea shore, we give as an inhabitant of Greenland. It has never been noticed in any more southern locality on the continent of America. We have had no sufficient opportunity of examining specimens ; in fact, have seen but a single one represented to be from that country, which was, unfortunately, that of a young bird.

HALIAETUS LEUCOCEPHALUS, Linnaeus.

The Bald Eagle ; The White-headed Eagle.

Falco leucocephalus, LINN. Syst. Nat. I, 124, (1766.)
Falco pygargus, DAUDIN, Traite d'Orn. II, 62, (1800.)
Falco ossifragus, WILSON, Am. Orn. VII, 16, (1813.)

FIGURES.—Catesby's Carolina I, pl. 1 ; Vieill. Ois. O'Am. Sept. 1, pl. 3 ; Wilson Am. Orn IV, pl. 36, VII, pl. 55 ; Aud. B. of Am., pl. 31, 126 : Oct. ed. I, pl. 14.

Large, but smaller than either of the preceding eagles. Bill large, strong, straight at base, rather abruptly hooked ; wings long ; tarsi rather short.

Adult.—Head, tail, and its upper and under coverts white. Entire other plumage brownish black, generally with the edges of the feathers paler ; bill, feet, and irides yellow.

Younger.—Entire plumage, including head and tail, dark brown ; paler on the throat ; edges of the feathers paler or fulvous, especially on the under parts ; tail more or less mottled with white, which color in more advanced age extends over a large portion of the tail, especially on the inner webs. Bill brownish black ; irides brown.

Total length, female, about 35 to 40 inches ; wing, 23 to 25 inches ; tail, 14 to 15 inches. Male, 30 to 34 inches ; wing, 20 to 22 inches ; tail, 13 to 14 inches.

Hab.—All of temperate North America. Accidental in Europe. Greenland. Iceland. Spec. in Mus. Acad. Philada. and Nat. Mus. Washington.

This is one of the most handsome birds of the family of eagles and is the best known, especially as it has received the high honor of having been adopted as the heraldic representative of the great confederacy of the United States. This eagle possesses extraordinary swiftness and vigor of flight, and is essentially a fisherman, though not at all exclusively so, preying for much the greater part on living animals. It inhabits all parts of the United States, and is apparently common at more northern localities on the Pacific than on the Atlantic ocean.

List of specimens.

Catal. No.	Sex and age.	Locality.	When collected.	Whence obtained.	Original No.	Collected by—	Measurements.		
							Length.	Extent.	Wing.
9125	......	Fort Steilacoom....	....	Gov. I. I. Stevens .	......	Dr. Suckley.....	......	......	......
9126	♀	......do..........	....	......do..........	58	......do..........	43.50	88.00	24.75
9130	♀	Shoalwater bay.....	....	......do..........	53	Dr. Cooper.......	37.00	87.50	......

PANDION, Savigny.

Pandion, SAVIGNY, Hist. Nat. d'Egypt, I, p. 95, (1809.)

Wings very long; general form heavy and not adapted to vigorous nor swift flight like the preceding eagles. Bill short, curved from the base, compressed; tarsi very thick and strong, and covered with small circular scales; claws large, curved, very sharp; toes beneath very rough; tail moderate or rather short.

This genus contains three or four species only, nearly allied to each other, and inhabiting all temperate regions of the world.

PANDION CAROLINENSIS, Gmelin.

The Fish Hawk; The American Osprey.

Falco carolinensis, GM. Syst. Nat. I, 263, (1788.)
Aquila piscatrix, VIEILL. Ois. d'Am. Sept. I, 29, (1807.)
Pandion americanus, VIEILL. Gal. Ois. I, 33, (1825.)
Falco haliaetus, LINN. WILSON, Am. Orn. V, 14.
Falco haliaetus, LINN. AUD. Orn. Biog. I, 415.

FIGURES.—Catesby's Carolina, I, pl. 2; Vieill. Ois. d'Am. Sept. I, pl. 4; Wilson Am. Orn. V, 37; Aud. B. of Am. pl. 81 : Oct. ed. I, pl. 15; Nat. Hist. New York, Birds, pl. 8, fig. 18.

Wings long; legs, toes, and claws very robust and strong. *Adult.*—Head and entire under parts white; stripe through the eye, top of the head, and upper parts of the body, wings and tail, deep umber brown, tail having about eight bands of blackish brown; breast with numerous cordate and circular spots of pale yellowish brown; bill and claws bluish black; tarsi and toes greenish yellow.

Young.—Similar to the adult, but with the upper plumage edged and tipped with pale brownish nearly white. Spots on breast more numerous and darker colored.

Total length, female, about 25 inches; wing, 21 inches; tail, 10½ inches. Male rather smaller.

Hab.—Throughout temperate North America.

Apparently nearly as abundant on the Pacific as on the Atlantic coast of the United States, but evidently migrating in the summer further north on the former than on the latter. This occurs, however, in numerous species of birds.

One specimen, obtained by George Suckley, M. D., at Fort Steilacoom, Puget Sound, Washington Territory, is that of a young bird, and is of especial interest, showing that this species rears its young and is quite at home at the latitude of that locality. There are no appreciable specific differences between specimens from all parts of North America, and we may be allowed to add, very slight between those of this country and of Europe and Asia.

List of specimens.

Catal. No.	Sex and age.	Locality.	When collected.	Whence obtained.	Original No.	Collected by—	Measurements.		
							Length.	Extent.	Wing.
4366	♂	Ft. Steilacoom, W.T	May, 1855	Mr. Geo. Gibbs	181		23.00	64.50	
5837		do	Oct. 2, 1856	Dr. Geo. Suckley	589		22.25	64.50	19.50
6872		Sacramento, Cal		Lieut. Williamson		Dr. Heermann			
4616		Colorado river, Cal		Major Emory					
6844		Ft. Fillmore, N. M		Dr. Henry					

POLYBORUS, Vieillot.

Polyborus, VIEILLOT, Analyse, p. 22, (1816.)

Smaller than in either of the preceding genera of eagles. Bill rather long, compressed; cere large; wings long, pointed; tail moderate or rather long; tarsi long, rather slender; claws long, rather weak, and but slightly curved; space in front of and below the eye naked.

Two species only form this genus, both of which, in their habits and manners, show an approximation to the vultures. They are well known birds of South America.

POLYBORUS THARUS, Molina.

The Caracara Eagle; The Mexican Eagle.

Falco tharus, MOL. Sagg. Stor. Nat. Chili, (1782.)
Falco cheriway, JACQUIN, Beyt. Gesch. der Vög. p. 17, (1784.)
Falco brasiliensis, GM. Syst. Nat. I, 262, (1788.)
Falco plancus, MILLER, Cimelia Physica.
Polyborus vulgaris, VIEILL. Nouv. Dict. V, 257, (1816.)

FIGURES.—Vieill. Gal. I, pl, 7; Swains. Zool. Ill. I, pl, 2; Gay's Chili, Orn. pl. 1; Aud. B. of Am. pl. 161: Oct. ed. I, pl. 4.

Legs rather long, occipital feathers somewhat elongated. *Adult.*—Head and body above and wide belt on the abdomen and tibiæ brownish black; neck, breast, upper and under tail coverts yellowish white, on the breast with narrow transverse bands of black. Tail white at base, with numerous transverse bands of black and widely tipped with black; bill bluish tipped with yellowish white; legs yellow.

Younger.—Head and body above dull brown, darker on the head, and many feathers having paler edgings; under parts dark brown, with longitudinal stripes of dull yellowish white; throat dull white; tail for the greater part and its coverts above and below white with numerous transverse bands of ashy brown, and tipped with brownish black.

Total length, female, about 25 inches; wing, 17 inches; tail, 10 inches.

Hab.—Southern North America. Florida. Texas. Mexico. Spec. in Nat. Mus. Washington, and Mus. Acad. Philadelphia.

One of the most abundant of the rapacious birds of South America. It is of frequent occurrence also in Mexico and Texas, and is found also in Florida. This bird is more sluggish in its habits than is usual in this family, and may belong more properly to the family of vultures. It subsists mainly on dead animals, and walks on the ground with facility.

List of specimens.

Catal. No.	Sex and age.	Locality.	When collected.	Whence obtained.	Original No.	Collected by—	Measurements.		
							Length.	Extent.	Wing.
4248	......	Calcasieu, La	1854	G. Wurdemann	......	....	.....	......	.....
4122°	......	Monterey, Mexico...	....	Lieut. D. N. Couch..	......	....	23.50	47.25	15.50
9136	......	Texas............	....	Major Emory......	......	A. Schott......	.....	......	.....
9137	......	New Mexico	....	Dr. T. C. Henry...	......	....	.....	......	.....
7994	......	Mexico...........	Sept., 1836	J. Gould	......	J. Taylor......	.....	......	.....

* Iris, light brown ; bill, blue ; feet, yellow.

CRAXIREX, Gould.

Craxirex, GOULD, Voy. Beagle, Birds, p. 22, (1841.)

Size smaller than the preceding ; legs long ; tarsi and toes strong. Bill rather long, abruptly curved at the tip ; edges of upper mandible festooned ; wings and tail long. Tarsi with wide transverse scales in front ; claws moderate.

CRAXIREX UNICINCTUS, Temminck.

Harris' Buzzard.

Falco unicinctus, TEMM. Pl. Col. I, (not paged, liv. 53 about 1827.)
Buteo Harrisii, AUDUBON, Orn. Biog. V, 30, (1839.)
Polyborus taeniurus, TSCHUDI, Fauna Peruana?
Craxirex galapagoensis, GOULD, Voy. Beagle, Birds, p. 23?

FIGURES.—Temm. Pl. Col. 313 ; Aud. B of Am. pl. 392 : Oct. ed. I, pl. 5 ; Tschudi, FaunaPer. Orn. pl. ¿? ; Voy. Beagle, Birds, pl. 2?

Adult.—Shoulders, wing coverts, and tibiæ reddish chestnut ; upper and under tail coverts white, tail white at base and tipped with white, presenting the appearance of a very wide band between of brownish black with a violet tinge. Body above and below dark brown, in some specimens nearly black on the under parts.

Younger.—Upper parts dull umber brown, much mixed with fulvous ; shoulders chestnut red, spotted with dark brown ; entire under parts yellowish white, with large oblong and circular spots of brown ; upper and under tail coverts white ; tail brown, with many bands of a deeper shade of the same color, and with the inner webs yellowish and reddish white ; base and tip of tail yellowish white.

Total length, female, 22 to 24 inches ; wing, 15 inches ; tail, 10 inches. Male, total length, 20 inches ; wing, 13 to 14 inches ; tail, 9 to 9½ inches.

Hab.—Southern States, Mexico, South America. Spec. in Nat. Mus. Washington, and Mus. Acad. Philada.

The observations of naturalists attached to the late expeditions demonstrate this bird to be of common occurrence in Texas, on the Rio Grande. It is a dull and heavy bird in its habits, and subsists for the greater part on dead animals.

This bird appears to belong to the genus *Craxirex,* as given by Mr. Gould, if not identical with his species.

List of specimens.

Catal. No.	Sex and age.	Locality.	When collected.	Whence obtained.	Original No.	Collected by—	Measurements.		
							Length.	Extent.	Wing.
4123	......	Brownsville, Texas.	....	Lieut. Couch......	......	....	......	......	......
9135	......	Oyster Point,Texas.	Sept., 1853.....	Major Emory......	......	....	......	......	......
9134	......	New Mexico	Feb. 27, 1854...	Lieut. Whipple....	179	Kennerly and Möllhausen.	......	......	......

Family STRIGIDAE. The Owls.

Form usually short and heavy, with the head disproportionately large, and frequently furnished with erectile tufts of feathers resembling the ears of quadrupeds. General organization adapted to vigorous and noiseless but not rapid flight, and to the capture of animals in the morning and evening twilight. Eyes usually very large, directed forwards, and in the greater number of species formed for seeing by twilight, or in the night. Bill rather strong, curved, nearly concealed by projecting bristle-like feathers ; wings generally long ; outer edges of primary quills fringed ; legs generally rather short, and in all species, except in one Asiatic genus, (*Ketupa*,) more or less feathered, generally densely. Cavity of the ear very large. Face encircled by a more or less perfect disc of short rigid feathers, which, with the large eyes, gives to those birds an entirely peculiar and frequently cat-like expression. Female larger than the male.

There are about one hundred and fifty species of owls, which are found in all parts of the world, of which about forty are inhabitants of the continent of America and its islands. The larger species subsist on small quadrupeds and birds, but much the majority almost exclusively prey on insects. Though much the larger number are nocturnal, a few species are strictly diurnal, and in their habits seem to approach the birds of the preceding family.

Sub-Family STRIGINAE.—Typical Owls.

Size medium, never very large. Head large ; facial disc perfect; bill rather long ; eyes rather small for this family ; legs rather long, fully feathered to the toes.

STRIX, Linnaeus.

Strix, LINNAEUS, I, p. 131, (1766.)

Head large, without ear tufts ; eyes rather small ; facial disc perfect, and very conspicuous ; wings long; tarsi long ; tail rather short ; toes and claws rather long. This genus contains about twelve species of all parts of the world.

STRIX PRATINCOLA, Bonaparte.

The Barn Owl.

Strix pratincola, BONAP. Comp. List, p. 7, (1838.)
Strix Americana, AUD. Orn. Biog. II, p. 421, (1834, not of Gmelin 1788.)

FIGURES.—Wilson, Am. Orn. VI, pl. 50, fig. 2 ; Aud. B. of Am., pl. 171 :_Oct. ed. I, pl. 34 ; Nat. Hist. New York, Birds, pl. 13, fig. 28.

Entire upper parts pale fawn color, or tawny brownish yellow, frequently very pale, nearly every feather with a small sub-terminal black spot succeeded by another of white.   Under parts generally pale fawn color, but frequently pure white, with small lanceolate and circular spots of brownish black ; under coverts of wings and tail white ; quills fawn colored ; primaries with about five irregular transverse bars of brownish black ; tail with about four or five bands of dark brown.   Face white ; spots of dark chestnut brown around the eyes.   Irides brownish black ; bill, toes, and claws light yellowish.

Total length, female, 16 inches, wing 13, tail 5¼ inches.   Male rather smaller.

Hab.—Throughout temperate North America.   Spec. in Nat. Mus., Washington.

All the specimens in the present collection are from California.   They exhibit the variety in shades of color, especially on the under parts of the body, which is usually to be observed in this species ; some specimens having these parts perfectly white, and others different shades of pale buff or fawn color.   There is, however, no American species of this family more easily recognized.

Some specimens from the western countries of North America which have come under our notice have the greater portion of the quills very pale colored, occasionally nearly white ; and these specimens have, too, usually the under parts white.   This is the case with specimens No. 4349 in Lieutenant Trowbridge's collection, and No. 6885 in that of Lieutenant Williamson.

This bird, in the plumage just referred to, approximates quite closely to *Strix furcata,* (Temminck Pl. Col, 432,) a species from the West India islands, and cannot readily be distinguished from it by any character, except a greater degree of whiteness in the West India bird.   The two species, if such they are, will, however, bear careful comparison.

List of specimens.

Catal. No.	Sex and age.	Locality.	When collected.	Whence obtained.	Original No.	Collected by—	Measurements.		
							Length.	Extent.	Wing.
4349	......	Presidio, Cal......	....	Lieut. Trowbridge .	......	....	......	......	......
4194	......	San Francisco, Cal.	Winter 1853-'54.	R. D. Cutts........	......	....	17.00	35.00	......
4133	♂	Monterey, Mexico .	....	Lieut. Couch......	170	....	17.00	35.00	......
6884	♂	Tejon valley, Cal..	....	Lt. R.S.Williamson.	......	Dr. Heermann...			
4626	......	San Miguel, Cal ...	....	......do...........	......	....	16.75	44.25	12.75
4910	......	San Diego, Cal	....	Dr. J. F. Hammond.	......	....	16.75	44.25	12.75
6885	......	Tejon valley, Cal ..	....	Lt. R.S.Williamson.	......	Dr. Heermann...			
5036	......	Doña Ana, N. M...	Nov. 9, 1855....	Capt. J. Pope......	......	....			
8701	♂	Texas	....	Maj. W. H. Emory.	......	A. Schott			
9132	♂	Texas	....	......do...........	......	J. H. Clark......	15.50	45.00	14.00
8063	......	Mexico............	Sept., 1856.....	John Gould.......	......	John Taylor ...	......	......	......

Sub-Family BUBONINAE.—The Horned Owls.

Head large, with erectile and prominent ear tufts.   Eyes large ; facial disc not complete above the eyes and bill ; legs, feet, and claws usually very strong.

This division contains numerous species, some of which are very large, but the greater number as medium sized or small.   They inhabit all parts of the world, except Australia.

BUBO, Cuvier.

Bubo, Cuvier, Règne Animal, I, p. 331, (1817.)

Size large ; general form very robust and powerful. Head large, with conspicuous ear tufts ; eyes very large ; wings long ; tail short ; legs and toes very strong, densely feathered ; claws very strong ; bill rather short, strong, curved, covered at base by projecting feathers.

This genus includes the large horned owls, or cat owls, as they are sometimes called. These birds are most numerous in Asia and Africa, and there are in all countries about fifteen species.

BUBO VIRGINIANUS, Gmelin.

The Great Horned Owl.

Strix virginiana, Gm. Syst. Nat. I, p. 287, (1788.)
Strix pythaules, Bartram, Travels, p. 289, (1791.)
Bubo ludoviciana, Daudin, Traite d'Orn. II, p. 210, (1800.)
Bubo pinicola, Vieill Ois. d'Am. Sept. I, p. 51, (1807.)
Bubo arcticus, Swains. Faun. Bor. Am. Birds, p. 86, (1831.)
Bubo sub-arcticus, Hoy, Proc. Acad. Philada. VI, p. 211, (1852.)
Bubo septentrionalis, Brehm, Vög. Deutschl. p. 120, (1831?)
Strix scandiaca, Linn. Syst. Nat. I, p. 132, (1766) ?
Strix magellanicus, Gm. Syst. Nat. I, p. 286, (1788) ?
Strix nacurutu, Vieill. Nouv. Dict. VII, p. 44, (1817) ?

Figures.—Edward's Birds II, pl. 60; Vieill. Ois. d'Am. Sept. I, pl. 19 ; Wilson Am. Orn. VII, pl. 50, fig. 1 ; Aud. B. of Am. pl. 61 : Oct. ed. I, pl. 39 ; Nat. Hist. New York, pl. 10, fig. 22 ; Fauna Bor. Am. Birds, pl. 30.

Adult.—Large and very strongly organized ; ear tufts large, erectile ; bill strong, fully curved : wing rather long ; third quill usually longest ; tail short ; legs and toes very robust, and densely covered with short downy feathers ; claws very strong, sharp, curved. Very variable in plumage, from nearly white to dark brown ; usually with the upper parts dark brown, every feather mottled and with irregular transverse lines of pale ashy and reddish fulvous, the latter being the color of all the plumage at the bases of the feathers. Ear tufts dark brown, nearly black, edged on their inner webs with dark fulvous ; a black spot above the eye ; radiating feathers behind the eye, varying in color from nearly white to dark reddish fulvous, usually the latter ; feathers of the facial disc tipped with black. Throat and neck before white ; breast with wide longitudinal stripes of black ; other under parts variegated with white and fulvous, and every feather having transverse narrow lines of dark brown. Middle of the abdomen frequently, but not always, white. Legs and toes varying from white to dark fulvous, usually pale fulvous ; in most specimens unspotted, but frequently, and probably always in fully mature specimens, with transvere narrow bars of dark brown. Quills brown, with wide transverse bands of cinereous, and usually tinged on the inner webs with pale fulvous ; tail the same, with the fulvous predominating on the outer feathers ; iris yellow ; bill and claws bluish black.

Dimensions.—Female, length 21 to 25 inches, wing 14½ to 16, tail 10 inches. Male, 18 to 21 inches, wing 14 to 15, tail 9 inches. The smallest specimen of the variety *Pacificus.*

Hab.—The whole of North America, and probably South America.

Variety.—*Bubo virginianus atlanticus*, Cassin, B. of Cal. and Texas, I, p. 178.

Dark colored, as described above. Feathers of the face behind the eye always bright reddish fulvous, and the entire plumage more marked with that color than in the other varieties below.

This variety is found throughout the temperate regions of North America, and we have never known any other to be noticed in the States on the Atlantic ocean, though the variety *Arcticus* may occur. This is the true *B. virginianus* of authors, and is figured by Wilson, Audubon, and others.

Variety.—*Bubo virginianus pacificus*, Cassin, B. of Cal. and Texas, I, p. 178.

Dark colored, as above. Feathers of the face behind the eye ashy, generally, however, tinged with fulvous. General color less tinged with fulvous than in the preceding variety, and frequently much paler, and approximating to the variety *arcticus.*

7 b

This variety appears to be restricted to western North America, and is represented by the majority of the specimens in the present collection.   So far as can be determined from prepared skins, the average of these specimens would be rather smaller than in the preceding, but there are some quite as large as we have ever seen of that variety.   This variety can readily be distinguished from the preceding by the facial disk being ashy, instead of fulvous.

VARIETY.—*Bubo virginianus arcticus*, CASSIN.

> *Bubo arcticus*, SWAINSON, Faun. Bor. Am. Birds, p. 86. (1831.)
> *Bubo sub-arcticus*, HOY, Proc. Acad. Phila., VI. p. 211. (1852.)
> *Bubo septentrionalis*, BREHM?
> *Strix scandiaca*, LINNAEUS?
> FIGURE.—Faun. Bor. Am. Birds, pl. 30.

Light colored, frequently nearly white. General plumage of a predominating pale yellowish white, or cream color, of various shades, from nearly pure white to nearly the color of the two preceding varieties. Under parts generally lighter than the upper, and always throughout the plumage marked and barred with brown, frequently pale and indistinct, but in the same general manner as in the preceding. Tarsi and toes generally very light, frequently nearly pure white. Size generally about the same as that of variety *atlanticus*, and the plumage with more or less of the same reddish fulvous at the bases of the feathers. Feathers of the face pure white, or pale cream color, sometimes tinged with fulvous and cinereous.

This variety appears to inhabit the northern and western countries of North America, and probably occasionally all other parts of that portion of the continent.   Mr. Swainson's figure, above cited, represents an unusually white specimen, though we have seen such, and from that shade to but slightly lighter than the common variety.   So far as we regard ourselves competent to judge, this variety is better entitled to be regarded as a distinct species than any other.

VARIETY.—*Bubo virginianus magellanicus*, CASSIN.

> *Strix magellanicus*, GM. Syst. Nat. I, p. 286. (1788.)
> *Strix nacurutu*, VIEILL. Nouv. Dict. VII, I, p. 44. (1817.)
> *Bubo ludovicianus*, DAUDIN, Traite d'Orn. II, p. 210.
> FIGURE.—Buffon Pl Enl. 385.

Very variable in color, but generally darker than either of the preceding ; plumage at base fulvous. Feathers of the face usually pale cinereous, more or less tinged with fulvous ; size about the same as the preceding, or rather larger.

This variety inhabits, apparently, South America, and perhaps Mexico, and the extreme south of the United States.   Of this we have seen specimens darker than either of the preceding varieties, and more resembling Mr. Audubon's figures than are usually met with in northern localities.

This fine species is either subject to considerable variety in the color of its plumage, or there are several species, some of which have been named by naturalists, as cited above, in our synonymes.   But with no less than thirty specimens now before us, from nearly all parts of North America, we confess ourselves quite unable to detect characters sufficient to distinguish more than one species.   We have, therefore, to regard them all as *Bubo virginianus*, and to attribute the differences in their colors to variety only, either local or caused by accidental circumstances.   With but a single well characterized specimen each of perhaps four varieties, the inducement would be strong to regard them as distinct species, so different are their colors ; but with an extended series, like the present, all the characters exist in such various degrees of modification, and are so blended that it is to us quite impossible.   We have designated the varieties of this species in Birds of California and Texas, I, p. 178, and have no reason to change our views from the examination of the present collection, except that these varieties are evidently not to be regarded as at all strictly geographical, nor not so much so as intimated in our notice of them alluded to above. We have, for instance, in this collection the variety *Bubo virginianus atlanticus*, from Bodega, California, (in the collection made by the party commanded by Lieutenant W. P. Trowbridge, United States army,) and the variety *arcticus*, from various localities in California and New Mexico. The variety *atlanticus*, from California, we cannot distinguish from the common bird of the States on the Atlantic seaboard.

List of specimens.

Catal. No.	Sex and age.	Locality.	When collected.	Whence obtained.	Original No.	Collected by—	Length.	Extent.	Wing.	Remarks.
							Measurements.			
9155	♂	Steilacoom..................	....	Gov. I. I. Stevens..	135	Dr. Suckley.......				Var. pacificus........
9161	o	....do..................	....	......do............	136	........Do.......				......do............
5854	♀♀	....do..................	August, 1856	Dr. Geo. Suckley ..	535					......do............ ..
9159	♀♀	Okanagan..................	....	Gov. I. I. Stevens..	......	Dr. Cooper......				......do............
4513	♂♂	Fort Reading, Cal.......	....	Lt. R. S. Williamson	......	Dr. Newberry......				......do............
	♀	Bodega, Cal.	January, 1853	Lt. W. P. Trowbridge	......					
		Sacramento..................		Lt. R. S. Williamson	......	Dr. Heermann.....				Var. atlanticus........
8006	......	California..................	....	John Gould........	5006	D. Douglas........				....
4613	......	Colorado river, Cal......	March 31, 1855	Major Emory......	......	A. Schott........				....
4423	♀	San Diego, Cal...........	....	Lt. Trowbridge....	......	A. Cassidy...........				Var. pacificus... ....
	♂	Little Colorado	....	Lt. A. W. Whipple.	......	Kenn. & Möll......				......do............
9154	♂	No. 98..................	....	......do............	46	........Do.				Iris chrome yellow; var. arcticus ......
	♂	New Mexico..................	....	Capt. John Pope....	......					Var. arcticus.........
5181	♂	Fort Union	....	Lt. G. K. Warren ..	......	Dr. Hayden........	20.25	47.04	14.00	Iris yellow; var. arcticus... ....
5180	♀	Fort Union	....	Lt. G. K. Warren..	....	....	21.25	51.50	14.75	......do......do......
5589	......	Medicine Bow Creek	Aug. 25, 1856	Lt. F. T. Bryan	299	W. S. Wood........				......do......do.......
9157	......	Devil's river, Texas	Novemb'r,1854	Major Emory	3	Dr. Kennerly......	19.00	48.00	15.00	....
9172	......	Mimbres to Rio Grande ..	....	Dr. Henry.	......	A. Schott..........				....
9158	......	6th camp, Little Colorado	Dec'r 15, 1853	Lt. Whipple........	37	Kenn. & Moll.				....
4137	......	Monterey, Mexico.	....	Lt. Couch	.....	....	18.00	35.00	9.25	Eyes yellow; var. arcticus............
8007	......	Mexico..................	Sept'r, 1836	John Gould........	......	J. Taylor				....

SCOPS, Savigny.

SAVIGNY, Nat. Hist. Egypt, I, p. 105, (1809.)

Size small; ear tufts conspicuous. Head large; facial disc imperfect in front and about the eyes; bill short, nearly covered by projecting feathers; wings long; tail rather short, and frequently curved inwards; tarsi rather long, more or less fully covered with short feathers; toes long, generally partially covered with hair like feathers; head large.

General form short and compact. This genus contains twenty-five to thirty species of small owls, inhabiting all parts of the world except Australia.

SCOPS ASIO, Linn.

The Mottled Owl; the Screech Owl.

Strix asio, LINN. Syst. Nat. I, p. 132, (1766.)
Strix naevia, GM. Syst. Nat. I, p. 289, (1788.)
Bubo striatus, VIEILL. Ois. d'Am. Sept. I, p. 54, (1808.)

FIGURES.—Catesby's Nat. Hist. Carolina I, pl. 7; Vieill. Ois. d'Am. Sept. I, pl. 21; Temm. pl. col. 80; Wilson Am. Orn. pl. 19, fig. 1, pl. 42, fig. 1; Aud. B. of Am. pl. 97: Oct. ed. I, pl. 40; Nat. Hist. New York, Birds, pl. 12, figs. 25, 26.

Short and compact; ear tufts prominent; tail short; tarsi rather long.

Adult.—Upper parts pale ashy brown with longitudinal lines of brownish black, and mottled irregularly with the same, and with cinereous. Under parts ashy white with longitudinal stripes of brownish black, and with transverse lines of the same color ; face, throat and tarsi, ashy white, irregularly lined and mottled with pale brownish ; quills brown with transverse bands, nearly white on the outer webs ; tail pale ashy brown with about ten transverse narrow bands of pale cinereous ; under wing coverts white, the larger tipped with black ; bill and claws light horn color ; irides yellow.

Younger.—Entire upper parts pale brownish red, with longitudinal lines of brownish black, especially on the head and scapulars ; face, throat, under wing coverts and tarsi, reddish white ; quills reddish brown ; tail rufous, with bands of brown, darker on the inner webs.

Young —Entire plumage transversely striped with ashy white and pale brown ; wings and tail pale rufous.

Total length 9½ to 10 inches, wing 7, tail 3½ inches. Sexes nearly alike in size and color.

Hab.—The whole of temperate North America, Greenland, (Fabricius.) Spec. in Nat. Mus. Washington, and Mus. Acad. Philadelphia.

This is the most abundant of the owls inhabiting the States on the Atlantic, and appears to inhabit the entire territory of the United States and the more northern countries of this continent within the temperate zone. In the present collections we find the first specimens that we have ever seen from western North America. One specimen (No. 4530) from Washington Territory, and others from California, in the collections made by Mr. Cutts and Mr. Samuels, (Nos. 4195, 5847,) are in the mottled or adult plumage; and one from Sacramento Valley, in Lieutenant Williamson's collection, is in the red, or that of the immature bird. These specimens differ in no respect from those of the eastern States.

The two stages of plumage described above have been regarded as characterizing distinct species, and they do present a problem scarcely to be considered as fully solved. This bird pairs, and rears young, while in the red plumage ; and it is not unusual to find a mottled male and red female associated, or the reverse. The two stages of plumage, or varieties, are very similar to those of the *Syrnium aluco* of Europe, and of which there are other instances in this family of birds.

Unlike nearly all other rapacious birds, this owl holds its place throughout the country, notwithstanding the destruction of the forest, or the denseness of the population ; and, though well known to our rural population, and scarcely regarded favorably, is seldom molested. Its food is principally insects.

List of specimens.

Catal. No.	Sex and age.	Locality.	When collected.	Whence obtained.	Original No.	Nature of specimen.	Measurements.		
							Length.	Extent.	Wing.
4530	......	Puget's Sound....	....	Dr. Geo. Suckley..	....	Mottled	9.00	20.50	6.50
5487	♂	Petaluma, Cal.....	....	E. Samuels	....	....	....	....	......
4195	......	San Francisco.....	....	M. R. D. Cutts.....	....	Mottled	....	....	......
6887	......	Sacramento valley.	....	Lieut. Williamson .	....	Red	....	....	......

SCOPS McCALLII, Cassin.

The Western Mottled Owl.

Scops McCallii, Cassin, B. of Cal. and Texas, I, p. 180. (1854.)

In form and general characters much resembling *Scops asio*, but smaller ; form, stout and short ; wing rather long, with the fourth quill longest ; tail short, slightly curved inwards ; tarsi rather long, fully covered ; toes partially covered, with long hair-like feathers.

Adult.—Ashy brown ; darker on the upper parts, and every feather with a longitudinal stripe of brownish black, and with numerous irregular transverse lines and points of the same. Under parts paler or ashy white, with longitudinal stripes of brownish black, and with irregular lines of the same ; flanks and sides, tinged with pale fulvous. Quills brown, with several transverse bands of pale reddish white, assuming the form of quadrangular spots on the outer webs, and pale reddish ashy on the inner webs. Tail ashy brown, with about ten narrow transverse bands on all, except the two central feathers, well defined on the outer webs ; scapular feathers and some of the greater coverts of the wings edged with white ; bill greenish horn color ; tip yellowish ; irides yellow.

Young.—Entire plumage rufous ; darker on the head, with longitudinal stripes of brownish black ; middle of the abdomen, and under tail coverts white ; tarsi rufous.

Dimensions.—Total length 7½ to 8 inches, wing 6, tail 3 inches.

Hab.—Western and Southern North America.

This species is not only related to the common *Scops asio* of North America, but also to *Scops choliba* of South America, and other species of this continent. From *S. asio*, it can readily be distinguished by its smaller size and the different shade of color and style of markings, being darker above, and having the transverse lines on the under surface better defined and more numerous

In the present collection are two specimens only of this interesting species, both from Texas, and in mottled plumage. In the collection made by the Mexican Boundary Commission there is a specimen of this bird in red plumage, like that of *S. asio*, and is that above described. A red specimen from Florida we doubtfully refer to the same species.

List of specimens.

Catal. No.	Sex and age.	Locality.	When collected.	Whence obtained.	Original No.	Collected by—	Measurements.		
							Length.	Extent.	Wing.
5857	......	Indian river, Fla..	....	G. Wurdemann ...	......	....	......	......	......
9171	......	Texas...............	Sept. 9, 1853 ...	Major Emory......	......	A. Schott........	......	......	......
9147	......	Camp 118	Feb. 10, 1854...	Lieut. A. Whipple.	......	Kennerly & Möll.	8.	18.50	6.00

OTUS, Cuvier.

Otus, Cuvier, Règne Animal, 1, p. 327. (1817.)

General form longer and more slender than in the preceding genera. Head moderate ; ear tufts long, erectile ; bill rather short, curved from the base ; facial disc more perfect than in the preceding. Wings long ; tail moderate ; tarsi and toes covered with short feathers ; claws long, curved. Eyes rather small, and surrounded by radiating feathers.

This genus contains ten or twelve species of various countries ; all of which are more handsome birds than are usually met with in this family.

OTUS WILSONIANUS, Lesson.

The Long-Eared Owl.

Otus Wilsonianus, Lesson, Traite d'Orn. I, p. 110. (1831.)
Otus Americanus, Bonap. Comp. List, p. 7. (1838.)
Strix Americana, Gm. Syst. Nat. I, p. 288. (1788?)
Strix perigrinator, Bartram, Travels, p. 289. (1790?)

Figures.—Wilson Am. Orn. VI, pl. 51, fig. 1 ; Aud. B. of Am., pl. 383 : Oct. ed. I, pl. 37 : Nat. Hist. New York, Birds, pl. 11, fig. 24.

Ear tufts long and conspicuous ; eyes rather small ; wings long ; tarsi and toes densely feathered. Upper parts mottled with brownish black, fulvous, and ashy white ; the former predominating. Breast pale fulvous, with longitudinal stripes of brownish black ; abdomen white ; every feather with a wide longitudinal stripe, and with transverse stripes of brownish black ; legs and toes pale fulvous, usually unspotted, but frequently with irregular narrow transverse stripes of dark brown. Eye nearly encircled with black ; other feathers of the face ashy white, with minute lines of black ; ear tufts brownish black, edged with fulvous and ashy white ; quills pale fulvous at their bases, with irregular transverse bands of brown ; inferior coverts of the wing pale fulvous, frequently nearly white ; the larger widely tipped with black ; tail brown, with several irregular transverse bands of ashy fulvous, which are mottled, as on the quills ; bill and claws dark ; irides yellow.

Total length, female, about fifteen inches ; wing 11 to 11½ ; tail 6 inches. Male, rather smaller.

Hab.—The whole of temperate North America. Spec. in Nat. Mus., Washington, and Mus. Acad., Philada.

One of the most numerous of the owls of the Atlantic States, and not much less so on the Pacific. It bears a strong resemblance to the European *Otus vulgaris*, with which it has been considered identical by some American authors. We find nothing unusual in the specimens of the present collection, all being quite identical with the well known bird of the eastern States.

List of specimens.

Catal. No.	Sex and age.	Locality.	When collected.	Whence obtained.	Original No.	Collected by—	Measurements.			Remarks.
							Length.	Extent.	Wing.	
9143	♀	John Day's river, W. T ..	Nov'r 12, 1853	Gov. I. I. Stevens..	19	Dr. Suckley.......				....
	♀	Bodega, Cal............	....	Lt. W. P. Trowbridge		.. ..				
	♂	.....do................	....	......do...........		....				
		Fort Fillmore, N. M......	....	Dr. T. C. Henry....		....				
9144	♂	Cochetope pass, R. M.....	....	Capt. Beckwith....		....				
9145	♀	Rio Grande valley........	....	......do...........		....				Eye with orange border...............
9146	......	Camp 107, New Mexico ..	Jan'y 28, 1854	Lt. Whipple	57	Kennerly and Möllhausen.....				Eyes yellow..........
9142	......	Fort Benton......		Gov. Stevens.......	....	Dr. Suckley.				....
8243	......	100 miles E. Ft. Kearney.	Oct'r 28, 1857	Wm. M. Magraw....	225	Dr. Cooper.........	14.50	37.50	12.00	Iris yellow ; bill bluish ; feet gray..........
4536	♂	White river, Neb........	Oct'r 8, 1855	Lt. Warren........		Dr. Hayden.......			....	....
4538	♂	......do............	....	......do...........		.. ...do.........				....
4537	♀	Fort Pierre	Oct'r 21, 1855	......do...........		....				
6916	......	Selkirk settlement, H.B.T.	....	Donald Gunn		....				
		Racine, Wis...........	....	R. Kennicott.......		....				
8635	......	Cape Florida	....	G. Wurdeman......		....				....

BRACHYOTUS, Gould.

Brachyotus, GOULD, Proc. Zool. Soc. London, 1837, p. 10.

Ear tufts very short and inconspicuous. General form rather strong ; wings long ; tail moderate ; legs rather long, which, with the toes, are fully covered with short feathers ; claws long, very sharp, and rather slender. Head moderate ; eyes rather small, surrounded by radiating feathers ; facial disc imperfect on the forehead and above the eyes ; tail moderate.

This genus contains four or five species only, the two best known of which are the European *Brachyotus palustris* and the succeeding.

BRACHYOTUS CASSINII, Brewer.

The Short Eared Owl.

Brachyotus Cassinii, BREWER, Proc. Boston Soc. N. H.
Strix brachyotus, FORSTER, Phil. Trans. London, LXII, p. 384, (1772.)
Brachyotus palustris americanus, BONAP. Consp. Av. p. 51, (1849.)

FIGURES.—Wilson Am. Orn. IV, pl. 33, fig. 3 ; Aud B. of Am. pl. 410 : Oct. ed. I, pl .38 ; Nat. Hist. New York, Birds, pl. 12, fig. 27.

Ear tufts very short. Entire plumage buff or pale fulvous ; every feather on the upper parts with a wide longitudinal stripe of dark brown, which color predominates on the back. Under parts paler, frequently nearly white on the abdomen, with longitudinal stripes of brownish black most numerous on the breast ; very narrow and less numerous on the abdomen and flanks ; legs and toes usually of a deeper shade of the same color as the abdomen. Quills pale reddish fulvous at their bases ; brown at their ends, with wide irregular bands and large spots of reddish fulvous ; tail pale reddish fulvous, with about five irregular transverse bands of dark brown, which color predominates on the two central feathers ; under tail coverts usually nearly white. Throat white ; eyes enclosed by large spots of brownish black ; ear tufts brown, edged with fulvous ; bill and claws dark ; irides yellow.

Total length, female, about 15 inches ; wing, 12 ; tail 6 inches. Male, rather smaller.

Hab.—The whole of temperate North America, Greenland, (Hollboll,) Cuba, (Lembeye.)   Spec. in Nat. Mus., Washington, and Mus. Acad., Philadelphia.

This owl is of frequent occurrence in the Atlantic States, especially in the winter ; and at that season appears to prefer meadows and marshes in the vicinity of rivers, or other streams of water. In the present collection the specimens tend to demonstrate that it is equally abundant on the Pacific, and we detect no differences in specimens from the opposite coasts of our continent.

List of specimens.

Catal. No.	Sex and age.	Locality.	When collected.	Whence obtained.	Original No.	Collected by—	Length.	Extent.	Wing.	Remarks.
4539	♂	White river, N. T........	Oct'r 9, 1855	Lt. G. K. Warren ..	....	Dr. Hayden.........	15.50	42.25	.....	....
4634	♂	Grindstone creek, N. T...	February, 1855	Dr. Hayden........	......	....	......	......	.....	....
4354	♀	Fort Kearney, Neb.......	....	Dr. Wm. Hammond.	......	....	......	......	.....	....
8791	......	N. fork Platte river.......	August 20, 1857	Wm. F. Magraw....	164	Dr. Cooper.........	14.00	41.50	12.00	Iris yellow...........
9140	♀	Bodega, Cal.	Decemb'r,1854	Lt. Trowbridge ...	......	T. A. Szabo.........	......	......	......	......do...........
9139	♀♀	......do.................	January, 1855	......do............	......	......do............	......	......	......	......do...........
6888	♂	Suisun valley, Cal......	....	Lt. R. S. Williamson	......	Dr. Heermann	......	......	......	....
5485	♀	Petaluma, Cal.	....	M. E. Samuels.....	......	....	16.00	39.00	12.00	....

Sub-Family SYRNINAE.—The Gray Owls.

Head large, with very small and concealed ear tufts, or entirely without. Facial disc nearly perfect ; eyes small for the family of owls ; wings rather short, or not so long as in the preceding ; tarsi and toes generally fully feathered. This group contains some of the largest of owls ; generally, however, the size is medium, and frequently small.

SYRNIUM, Savigny.

Syrnium, SAVIGNY, Nat. Hist. Egypt, I, p. 112, (1809.)

Size usually large ; head large, without ear tufts ; eyes rather small ; facial disc somewhat imperfect in front. Bill strong, curved from its base ; wings moderate, somewhat rounded ; fourth and fifth quills longest ; tail rather long, wide, and usually rounded at the end ; legs moderate, or rather long, which, with the toes, are densely covered with short feathers ; claws long, strong, very sharp.

Species of this genus inhabit principally the northern parts of the world, and are generally characterized by the prevalence of gray or cinereous of various shades in their plumage.

SYRNIUM CINEREUM, Gmelin.

The Great Gray Owl.

Strix cinerea, GM. Syst. Nat. I, p. 291, (1788.)

Strix acclamator, BARTRAM, Travels, p. 289, (1790.)

FIGURES.—Fauna Bor. Am., pl. 31 ; Aud. B. of Am. pl. 351 : Oct. ed. I, pl. 35 ; Nat. Hist. New York, Birds, pl. 13, fig. 29.

The largest owl of North America. Head very large ; eyes small ; tail rather long. Upper parts smoky, or ashy brown, mottled and transversely barred with ashy white ; under parts ashy white, with numerous longitudinal stripes of dark ashy brown predominating on the breast, and with transverse stripes of the same on the abdomen, legs, and under tail coverts. Quills brown, with about five wide irregular bands of ashy white ; tail brown, with five or six wide irregular bands of ashy white, mottled with dark brown. Feathers of the disc on the neck tipped with white ; eye nearly encircled by a black spot ; radiating feathers around the eye, with regular transverse narrow bars of dark brown and ashy white ; bill pale yellow ; claws pale yellowish white, darker at their tips.

Total length, 25 to 30 inches ; wing 18 ; tail 12 to 15 inches.

Hab.—Northern North America. Resident in the vicinity of Montreal, (Dr. A. Hall.) Spec. in Nat. Mus. Washington, and Mus. Acad. Philadelphia.

In the western countries of North America the range of this large owl is not well determined, but the probability is, that it wanders in the winter over nearly the whole of North America. It appears to be a constant resident of Canada and other provinces of British America, and has occasionally been noticed as far south as New Jersey. In the present collection, a single specimen is from Washington Territory. This is the largest owl yet discovered in North America, and is one of the largest birds of this family.

List of specimens.

Catal. No.	Sex and age.	Locality.	When collected.	Whence obtained.	Original No.	Collected by—	Measurements.		
							Length.	Extent.	Wing.
9138*	......	Shoalwater bay, W.T	June 10, 1854....	Gov. I. I. Stevens.	80	Dr. Cooper	25	56.00	......
6917	......	Selkirk Settlement, H. B.	....	Mr. D. Gunn					

* Iris, yellow.

SYRNIUM NEBULOSUM, Forster.

The Barred Owl.

Strix nebulosa, FORSTER, Trans. Philos. Soc. London, LXII, pp. 386, 424, (1772.)

Strix varius, BARTON, Frag. Nat. Hist. Penna. p. 11, (1799.)

FIGURES.—Vieill. Ois. d'Am. Sept. pl. 17 ; Wilson Am. Orn. IV, pl. 33, fig. 2 ; Aud. B, of Am. pl. 46 : Oct. ed I, pl. 36 ; Nat. Hist. New York, Birds, pl. 10, fig. 21 ; Gould B. of Eur. I, pl. 46.

Smaller than the preceding ; head large, without ear tufts ; tail rather long. Upper parts light ashy brown, frequently tinged with dull yellow, with transverse narrow bands of white, most numerous on the head and neck behind, broader on the back. Breast with transverse bands of brown and white ; abdomen ashy white, with longitudinal stripes of brown ; tarsi and toes ashy white, tinged with fulvous, generally without spots, but frequently mottled and banded with dark brown. Quills brown with six or seven transverse bars nearly pure white on the outer webs, and ashy fulvous on the inner webs ; tail light brown, with about five bands of white, generally tinged with reddish yellow. Discal feathers tipped with white ; face ashy white, with lines of brown, and a spot of black in front of the eye ; throat dark brown ; claws horn color ; bill pale yellow ; irides bluish black. Sexes alike.

Total length about 20 inches ; wing 13 to 14 ; tail 9 inches. Sexes nearly of the same size.

Hab.—Eastern North America. Spec. in Nat. Mus. Washington, and Mus. Acad. Philadelphia.

Though of frequent occurrence in the States on the Atlantic, this species has not yet been observed in the countries west of the Rocky mountains. The only specimen in the present collection is from the Territory of Nebraska, and is of especial interest as demonstrating the most western locality yet determined for this bird.

List of specimens.

Catal. No.	Sex and age.	Locality.	When collected.	Whence obtained.	Original No.	Collected by—	Length.	Extent.	Wing.	Remarks.
							Measurements.			
4607	♀	Missouri river.............	....	Lt. G. K. Warren ..	......	Dr. Hayden.........	19.00	40.75	13.50	....
8686	♀	Independence, Mo.......	June 22, 1857	Wm. M. Magraw ...	90	Dr. Cooper.........	17.00	45.50	13.00	Iris brown, bill and feet yellow.........
4357	......	Washington..............	January, 1855	Market	......	....	......	......	......	....

NYCTALE, Brehm.

Nyctale, BREHM, Isis, 1828, p. 1271.

Size small. Head with very small ear tufts, only observable when erected ; eyes small ; bill moderate or not very strong ; facial disc nearly perfect. Wings rather long ; tail short ; legs and toes densely feathered.

Contains five species of small and quite peculiar owls, four of which are American and one European.

NYCTALE RICHARDSONI, Bonaparte.

Nyctale Richardsoni, BONAP. Comp. List, p. 7, (1838.)
" *Strix Tengmalmi*, GM." Aud. Orn. Biog. IV, p. 559, and other American authors.

FIGURES.—*Fauna Boreali Americana*, Birds, pl. 32 ; AUD. B. of Am. pl. 380 : Oct. ed. I, pl. 32.

The largest of this genus, wings long. Upper parts pale reddish brown tinged with olive, and with partially concealed spots of white, most numerous on the head and neck behind, scapulars, and rump. Head in front with numerous spots of white ; face white, with a spot of black in front of the eye ; throat with brown stripes. Under parts ashy white, with longitudinal stripes of pale reddish brown ; legs and toes pale yellowish, nearly white, sometimes barred and spotted with brown. Quills brown, with small spots of white on their outer edges and large spots of the same on their inner webs ; tail brown, every feather with about ten pairs of white spots ; bill light yellowish horn color ; irides yellow.

Total length about 10½ inches ; wing, 7½ inches ; tail, 4½ inches.

Hab.—Northern North America, Canada, (Dr. Hall,) Wisconsin, (Dr. Hoy.) Spec. in Mus. Acad. Philada. and Nat. Mus Washington.

Entirely a northern species, common at Hudson bay, but of rare occurrence within the limits of the United States. The only notice of it as a western species is by Dr. Townsend, who gives it as a bird of Oregon

This species is nearly related to the European *Nyctale funerea*, and both have been called *Strix Tengmalmi* by various authors.

NYCTALE ALBIFRONS, Shaw.

Strix albifrons, SHAW, Nat. Misc. V. (not paged, 1794.)
Strix frontalis, LICHTENSTEIN, Trans. Acad. Berlin, 1838, p. 430.
Nyctale Kirtlandii, HOY, Proc. Acad. Philada. VI, p. 210, (1852.)

FIGURES.—Shaw Nat. Misc. V, pl. 171 ; Cassin B. of Cal. and Texas, I, pl. 11.

Small, wing rather long ; tail short. Head, upper portion of breast, and entire upper parts dark chocolate brown ; forehead and eyebrows white. Throat and a line on each side running downwards from the base of the under mandible white ; other

8 b

under parts of the body reddish ochre yellow. Quills dark brown, with small spots of white on their outer edges and large spots of the same on their inner webs ; tail dark brown, with two transverse bands of white, and narrowly tipped with the same ; bill and claws dark ; irides yellow.

Total length about 8 inches ; wing, 5¼ inches ; tail, 3 inches.

Hab.—Northern North America, Wisconsin, (Dr. Hoy,) Canada, (Dr. Hall,) Western, (Prof. Lichtenstein.) Spec. in Mus. Acad. Philadelphia, and Nat. Mus. Washington.

This is a species lost sight of by naturalists for upwards of half a century, and until brought to light through the researches of Dr. Hoy, of Racine, Wisconsin, who is the only naturalist by whom it has been obtained within the limits of the United States. It has been noticed also by Dr. A. Hall in the vicinity of Montreal, Canada. It is given by Professor Lichtenstein in the Transactions of the Berlin Academy, as above cited, as a bird of California ; but he regards it as identical with *N. acadica,* and with reference to locality may allude only to the latter species.

This bird is about the size of *Nyctale acadica,* but is quite distinct, and, in fact, bears but little resemblance to that species. We have no doubt that it is the true *Strix albifrons,* Shaw, as above cited. It is probably a northern and northwestern species.

NYCTALE ACADICA, Gmelin.

Saw-whet Owl.

Strix acadica, GM. Syst. Nat. I, p. 296, (1788.)
Strix acadiensis, LATH. Ind. Orn. I, pl. 65, (1790.)
" *Strix passerina,* LINN." Wilson, Am. Orn. IV, p. 66.
Strix dalhousiei, HALL, MSS. Macgillivray ed. of Cuvier's Reg. An. Birds pl. 8, fig. 3, name on plate, (Edinburg, 1839.)

FIGURES.—Lath. Gen. Syn. I, pl. 5, fig. 2 ; Wilson Am. Orn. IV, pl. 34, fig. 1 ; Aud. B. of Am. pl. 199 : Oct. ed. I, pl. 33 ; Nat. Hist. New York, Birds, pl. 11, fig. 23.

Small, wings long, tail short. Upper parts reddish brown tinged with olive ; head in front with fine lines of white, and on the neck behind, rump, and scapulars with large partially concealed spots of white. Face ashy white ; throat white ; under parts ashy white, with longitudinal stripes of pale reddish brown ; under coverts of wings and tail white. Quills brown, with small spots of white on their outer edges, and large spots of the same on their inner webs ; tail brown, every feather with about three pairs of spots of white ; bill and claws dark ; irides yellow.

Total length about 7½ to 8 inches ; wing, 5½ inches ; tail, 2¾ to 3 inches ; sexes nearly the same size and alike in colors.

Hab.—The whole of temperate North America. Spec. in Nat. Mus. Washington, and Mus. Acad. Philadelphia.

This is the smallest owl found in the eastern and middle States of North America, and is probably an inhabitant of the entire temperate regions of this division of the continent. Specimens in the present collection are from Texas and from Washington Territory. We have known it to be found also in California, where very probably it is of as frequent occurrence as at the same latitude on the Atlantic.

List of specimens.

Catal. No.	Sex and age.	Locality.	When collected.	Whence obtained.	Original No.	Collected by—	Measurements.			Remarks.
							Length.	Extent.	Wing.	
9152	.....	Fort Vancouver, W. T...	Feb'ry 3, 1854	Gov. I. I. Stevens.	26	Dr. Suckley	......	......	....	Iris yellow...........
9151	.....	Fort Dalles, O. T........	Dec'r 7, 1853	......do............	......	......do........	8.50	20.50	....	......do...............
5039	.....	Texas, near lat. 32°.....	....	Capt. Pope.........	......	....	......	......	....	....

Sub-Family ATHENINAE—The Bird Owls.

Size small ; facial disc very imperfect, or nearly obsolete; tarsi generally partially or but thinly covered with feathers ; head without ear tufts. The birds of this group are generally small, and are not so nocturnal in their habits as those of the preceding divisions.

ATHENE, Boie.

Athene, Boie, Isis, 1822, p. 549.

Small ; head moderate, without ear tufts ; wings rather long ; tail rather short ; facial disc nearly obsolete. Bill short ; legs rather long, thinly covered with short feathers ; toes naked, or with a few hair-like feathers. This genus contains about forty species of small owls inhabiting all parts of the world.

ATHENE HYPUGÆA, Bonaparte.

The Burrowing Owl.

Strix hypugæa, Bonap. Am. Orn., 1, p. 72. (1825.)
Athene socialis, Gambel, Proc. Acad. Philada. III, p. 47. (1846.)
Figures.—Bonap. Am. Orn. I, pl. 7, fig. 2 ; Aud. B. of Am., pl. 432, fig. 1 : Oct. ed. 1, p. 31, (upper figure.)

Tarsi long, slender, thinly covered in front only with short feathers, generally with its lower half nearly bare, and frequently almost entirely naked, and with small circular scales laterally and posteriorly ; toes with a few hairs.

Adult.—Upper parts light ashy brown, with numerous partially concealed circular, cordate, and ovate spots of dull white, which spots are enclosed with a narrow edge of dark brown. Throat white ; a transverse band of dark brown and reddish white on the neck in front, succeeded by a large patch of white ; breast light brown, with large spots of white, like the upper parts ; abdomen yellowish, with transverse narrow bands of reddish brown ; under tail coverts, feathers of the tibia and tarsus, and under wing coverts yellowish white. Quills light brown, with semi-circular spots of reddish white on their outer webs, and with oval or irregular spots of the same on their inner webs. Tail light brown, with about five or six irregular transverse bands of yellowish white. Bill dark blueish at base, yellow at tip and on the ridge of the upper mandible. This is the most mature plumage, and is that represented in Audubon's figure cited above. The most usual plumage is, however. as follows :

Adult.—Upper parts like the preceding, but lighter colored, and much more tinged with dull yellow, having generally a faded or bleached appearance. White spots more numerous and irregular in shape, and frequently giving the predominating color to the head. Rump and tail strongly tinged with reddish. Under parts like the preceding, but lighter, and with the reddish brown of the abdomen assuming the form of semi-circular or hastate spots. This plumage has very nearly the same characters as the preceding, but is lighter and has a faded appearance, and is much the most frequently met with in specimens. This plumage is not figured.

Another plumage is : Upper parts much less tinged with yellow or reddish, being nearly light grayish brown ; white spots very irregular in shape. Abdomen nearly pure white, or tinged with yellowish, with traces only or but few spots of reddish brown. This plumage is given in Bonaparte's plate, cited above ; but it is unusual for the abdomen to be so nearly pure white and unspotted as represented.

Total length, female, (of skin,) about 9½ inches, wing 7, tail 3½ inches. Male, total length, about 9 inches, wing 6½, tail 3 inches.

Hab.—From the Mississippi river to the Rocky mountains. Mexico. Spec. in Nat. Mus. Washington, and Mus. Acad. Philadelphia.

In this species the feathers on the tarsus are restricted to a narrow longitudinal band or stripe in front, generally quite imperfect in the lower half, leaving that portion nearly bare to the toes, though it is quite unusual to find the tarsus so entirely uncovered, as represented in Audubon's figure cited above. This bird is rather smaller than the succeeding, and has the tarsus shorter as well as much less feathered. It inhabits the countries east of the Rocky mountains, while the next species appears to be formed exclusively west of the same range. The two species are not difficult to distinguish, on comparison.

List of specimens.

Catal. No.	Sex and age.	Locality.	When collected.	Whence obtained.	Original No.	Collected by—	Measurements.			Remarks.
							Length.	Extent.	Wing.	
9166	......	Fort Benton	Sept. 20, 1853	Gov. Stevens	....	Dr. Suckley	......	......	......	....
4651	......	Fort Pierre	April 5, 1855	Col. A. Vaughan..	......	Dr. Hayden	......	......	......	
5183	♂	......do	June 25, 1856	Lt. G. K. Warren	......	......do	9.20	23.00	6.25	Iris yellow. ....
5182	♀	......do	June —, 1856	......do	......	......do	9.00	23.50	6.50	......do
5184	♂	......do	......do..	......do	......	......do	9.00	22.50	6.50	......do
5590	♀	Platte river	....	Lt. F. T. Bryan	......	W. S. Wood	9.50	......	......	
5591	♂	......do	....	......do	351	......do	......	......	......	
9065	♂	Running Water	Aug. 14, 1857	Lt. G. K. Warren	......	Dr. Hayden	9.50	24.50	7.25	Iris light yellow ......
9067	o♂	Loup Fork	Aug. 4, 1857	......do	......	......do	9.00	23.25	6.75	......do
9066	o♂	......do	....	......do	......	......do	9.00	22.25	6.00	......do
8767	....	35 miles west of Fort Kearney.	Aug. 3, 1857	Wm. M. Magraw	140	Dr. Cooper	9.00	23.50	6.75	Iris yellow; bill grayish............
9164	♀	Fort Davis	....	Col. Graham	......	J. H. Clark	6.50	9.50	23.50	
5038	......	Pecos river	.. ..	Capt. J. Pope	....					
		Fort Thorn	....	Dr. T. C. Henry			... ...			
		El Paso	....	Col. J. D. Graham..	25	J. H. Clark	......			
4976	......	Fort Chadbourne, Texas.	....	Dr. Swift, U. S. A.						
4136	......	Tamaulipas, Mexico	....	Lt. Couch						
9167	....	Mimbres to Rio Grande ..	....	Dr. Henry						

ATHENE CUNICULARIA, Molina.

Burrowing Owl.

Strix cunicularia, MOLINA, Sagg. Stor. Nat. Chili, (1782.)
Strix californica, AUD. B. of Am. pl. 432, fig. 2, (name on plate.)
Athene patagonica, PEALE, Zool. U. S. Ex. Exp. Vincennes, Birds, p. 78. (1848.)
FIGURES.—Aud. B. of Am. pl. 432, fig. 2 : Oct. ed. I, pl. 31, (lower figure.)

Resembling the preceding, but larger ; tarsus longer, and more fully feathered in front to the toes. Varieties of plumage the same, but that first described most usually met with and more common than in the preceding.

Adult.—Upper parts light ashy brown, with large spots of dull white enclosed in edgings of brownish black. Throat white ; a transverse band of brownish black and reddish white feathers across the neck in front, succeeded by a large patch of white. Breast light brown, with large spots of white like the upper parts ; abdomen yellowish white, with hastate or crescent-shaped spots of reddish brown disposed to form transverse bands ; under tail coverts, tibiæ, and tarsus, and under wing coverts yellowish white ; quills and tail light brown, with spots of reddish white, edged (the spots) with brownish black ; tail with about six transverse bands or pairs of spots of reddish white, enclosed or edged with dark brown. This is the plumage represented in Audubon's plate above cited, and is more commonly met with than the same plumage in the preceding species. It is very probably the mature plumage. Another plumage is : Adult? Like that just described, but much lighter, and tinged with dull yellow, or ochre, having a faded or bleached appearance. This plumage is not so frequent as in the preceding species. Another plumage is : Younger? Upper parts light greyish brown, with white spots very irregular in shape and confused, and frequently predominating on the head. Abdomen nearly unspotted, yellowish white, or with traces only of spots or bands.

Total length, female, about 10½ inches ; wing, 7 to 7½ inches ; tail, 3¼ to 4 inches. Male rather smaller.

Hab.—North America, west of the Rocky mountains, South America. Spec. in Nat. Mus. Washington and Mus. Acad. Philadelphia.

This owl may be immediately distinguished from the preceding by the more full feathering of the tarsus, generally continued without interruption to the toes. The tarsus is also longer, and in size the present bird is rather the larger. All these characters are well given in Audubon's plate, cited above, though it is not very common to find the present bird with the *tarsus* so completely covered, nor the preceding with it so bare as represented, in his figures, which appear, however, to be intended to represent the two species here described.

After careful examination and comparison of the specimens in the present collection with others from various parts of western South America, we can detect no differences whatever, all of them being apparently quite identical. The inspection of specimens of the present bird may have induced the Prince Bonaparte to alter his views respecting the distinctness of the North American from the South American bird, which he does in Annals of the New York Lyceum of Natural History, 11, p. 435, (1826,) when he declares his conviction of their identity, and proposes to withdraw his proposed name, *Strix hypugœa*. This name is, however, applicable to the preceding species, which is distinct, though never before so given by any American author.

Our friend, Colonel George A. McCall, late inspector general in the United States army, has constantly assured us, for several years past, that the two species given above were distinct, and readily distinguished from each other, and he designated the characters of each, and the difference in their localities. In the present large collection we find the views of this very accurate naturalist confirmed in the most conclusive manner.

List of specimens.

Catal. No.	Sex and age.	Locality.	When collected.	Whence obtained.	Original No.	Collected by—	Measurements. Length	Extent	Wing	Remarks.
4396	......	Fort Dalles, Oregon......	....	Dr. Geo. Suckley...	160	....	9.75	26.00	7.75	....
4397	......	......do............	....	..... do............	......	....	......	24.00	7.27	....
5486	♂	Petaluma, Cal.	....	Mr. E. Samuels....	......	....	......	......	......	....
5490	♀	......do............	....	......do...........	79	....	......	......	......	....
4195	......	San Francisco, Cal......	....	Mr. R. D. Cutts....	......	....	......	......	......	....
6681	♂	Sacramento valley....	....	Lt. R. S. Williamson	......	Dr. Heerman.	......	......	......	....
5896	......	Santa Clara, Cal....	....	Dr. J. G. Cooper....	......	....	......	......	......	....
5897	......	......do............	....	......do...........	......	....	......	......	......	....
9168	......	Los Angeles, Cal.........	March 4, 1854	Lt. A. Whipple....	191	Kennerly and Möllhausen..........	......	......	......	Iris yellow...........
4627	......	San Miguel, Cal.........	....	Lt. Trowbridge....	......	....	......	......	......	....
4911	......	San Diego, Cal.........	....	Dr. J. F. Hammond.	......	....	10.00	25.00	7.00	Iris yellow...........
4912	......	......do............	....	......do...........	......	....	10.00	23.50	6.75	....
4350	......	......do............	....	A. Cassidy........	......	....	......	......	......	....
4614	......	......do............	....	Major Emory.......	......	A. Schott...........	......	......	......	....
	......	......do....	....	... ..do...........	......	......do...........	......	......	...	....
9169	......	......do....	Nov'r 9, 1854	......do...........	6	......do...........	......	......	......	....
9168	......	Uncompagre river, Utah..	....	Lt. E. Beckwith....	......	....	......	......	......	....

GLAUCIDIUM, B o i e .

Glaucidium, Boïe, Isis, 1826, p. 970.

Size very small ; head moderate, without ear-tufts ; wings moderate, or rather short ; tail short ; facial disk nearly obsolete ; bill short, rather wide, strong ; tarsi fully feathered ; claws rather long, curved, very sharp.

This genus contains a few species only, amongst which are the smallest of known owls.

GLAUCIDIUM GNOMA, Wagler.

The Pigmy Owl.

Glaucidium gnoma, WAGLER, Isis, XXV, p. 275, (1832.)
" *Strix passerinoides*, TEMM.," AUD. Orn. Biog. V, p. 271.
" *Strix infuscata*, TEMM.," CASSIN, B. of Cal. & Texas, I, p. 189.
Glaucidium Californicum, SCLATER, Proc. Zool. Soc. London, 1857, p. 4.

FIGURES.—Aud. B. of Am., pl. 432, figs. 4, 5 : octavo edition, I, pl. 30.

The smallest owl known to inhabit North America. Wing rather short ; fourth quill longest ; tail rather long ; tarsi densely feathered ; toes partially covered with hairs. Spot before the eye, and extending over it, white. Entire upper parts brownish olive, with small circular spots of dull white or pale rufous numerous on the head, and largest on the scapulars. An irregular and partially concealed band of white on the neck behind, succeeded by another of black. Throat white ; a band of brownish olive across the neck and breast ; other under parts white, with longitudinal stripes of dark olive brown ; quills dark brown, with small spots of dull white on their outer webs, and large circular or oval spots of white on their inner webs ; tail dark brown, with about six or seven pairs of circular or oval spots of white on every feather ; larger on the inner webs. Under wing coverts white, with black spots disposed to form a longitudinal or oblique stripe ; bill light greenish yellow ; claws light horn color ; irides yellow. Sexes nearly alike ; female with rather larger and more numerous spots of white on the upper parts.

Dimensions.—Female, total length about 7 inches ; wing 3¾ ; tail 3 inches. Male, total length about 6¼ inches ; wing 3½ ; tail 2¾ inches.

Hab.—Oregon, California, Mexico. Spec. in Nat. Mus. Washington, and Acad. Sci. Philadelphia.

All the specimens of this rare and curious little owl are from Oregon and Washington Territories, and it does not appear to have been noticed in California by either of the surveying parties. It has, however, previously been obtained in that State, and is also very probably an inhabitant of Mexico.

In our synopsis of North American owls, (in Birds of California and Texas, I, p. 175,) we have noticed this bird, under the name of *Glaucidium infuscatum*, regarding it as the *Strix infuscata*, Temminck. At the suggestion of Mr. Philip Lutley Sclater, a distinguished ornithologist, of London, who alludes to this species in Proceedings of the Zoological Society of London, 1857, p. 4, we find his conclusion quite correct, that the two names *Strix infuscata* and *Strix passerinoides* were applied by Temminck to the same species, which is South American. The name given by Wagler, however, we regard as undoubtedly applicable to this bird, and give it accordingly as *Glaucidium gnoma*, (Wagler,) which had previously cited as a synonyme in our synopsis alluded to above.

This species very much resembles the South American owl, above alluded to. It appears to be, however, lighter colored, and, perhaps, rather smaller. In the present bird the spots on the upper parts of the plumage are smaller and more inclined to be circular, and a black stripe is quite distinct on the under coverts of the wing, which we have found but very obscurely indicated in either of numerous specimens of *G. infuscatum*, (or *G. passerinoides*,) now before us. For the present, we regard the northern and the southern as distinct, but nearly related, species.

This little owl appears to be exclusively western and southern.

List of specimens.

Catal. No.	Sex and age.	Locality.	When collected.	Whence obtained.	Original No.	Collected by—	Measurements.			Remarks.
							Length.	Extent.	Wing.	
4395	♂	Fort Steilacoom, W. T. ..	....	Dr. Geo. Suckley...	189	....	......	......	......	....
5855	♀ ○	......do..........do.....	....	......do............	530	....	7.50	14.00	3.80	....
9162	♀	Shoalwater Bay.........	....	Gov. Stevens	111	Dr. Cooper	7.50	14.00	......	Iris yellow ; bill and feet pale yellow....
4515	♂	Cascade mountains, Or...	....	Lt. R. S. Williamson	......	Dr. J. S. Newberry.	......	......	......	....
8002	♂ ○	California..............	....	John Gould........	34	D. Douglas.........	......	......	......	....

Sub-Family NYCTEININAE—T h e D a y O w l s.

General form compact and robust. Head moderate, without ear tufts; wings and tail rather long ; tarsi strong, which, with the toes, are more densely covered than in any other division of this family.

This division embraces two species only, which inhabit the arctic regions of both continents, migrating southward in the winter.

NYCTEA, S t e p h e n s.

Nyctea, STEPHENS, Cont. of Shaw's Zool. XIII, p. 62, (1826.)

Large ; head rather large, without ear tufts ; no facial disc ; legs rather short, and with the toes covered densely with long hair-like feathers, nearly concealing the claws. Bill short, nearly concealed by projecting feathers, very strong ; wings long ; tail moderate, or rather long, wide ; claws strong, fully curved. Contains one species only.

NYCTEA NIVEA, D a u d i n.

The Snowy Owl; The White Owl.

Strix nivea, DAUD. Traite d'Orn. II, p. 190, (1800.)
Strix nyctea, LINN. Syst. Nat. I, p. 132, (1766.)
Strix candida, LATH. Ind. Orn. Supp. p. 14, (1801.)
Strix erminea, SHAW, Gen. Zool. VII, p. 251, (1809.)
Strix arctica, BARTRAM, Travels, p. 289, (1791, but not of Sparrman, 1789.)

FIGURES.—Wilson Am. Orn. IV, pl. 32, fig. 1 ; Aud. B. of Am., pl. 121: oct. ed. I, pl. 28 ; Nat. Hist. New York, Birds, pl. 9, fig. 20 ; Gould B. of Eur. I, pl. 43.

Bill nearly concealed by projecting plumes ; eyes large. Entire plumage white, frequently with a few spots, or imperfect bands, only on the upper parts, dark brown, and on the under parts, with a few irregular and imperfect bars of the same ; quills and tail with a few spots or traces of bands of the same dark brown. The prevalence of the dark brown color varies much in different specimens ; frequently both upper and under parts are very distinctly banded transversely, and sometimes this color predominates on the back. Plumage of the legs and toes, pure snowy white ; bill and claws dark horn color ; irides yellow.

Total length, 24 to 27 inches ; wing 16 to 17 ; tail 10 inches.

Hab.—Northern regions of both continents, migrating southward in the winter. Resident in Canada, (Dr. A. Hall,) Greenland, (Holboll,) South Carolina, Kentucky, (Audubon,) Bermuda, (Jardine.) Spec. in Nat. Mus. Washington, and Mus. Acad. Philadelphia.

The large size and white plumage of this owl render it a conspicuous species when met with in the woods, or during its winter wanderings, and also when prepared for the museum. It is an abundant species in the northern regions, and has been observed at the highest northern latitude yet attained by voyagers. In the winter it migrates over nearly the whole of Europe and North America, and is frequently to be met with in the Northern and Middle United States, varying greatly in numbers in different years. According to Dr. A. Hall, of Montreal, Canada, this fine species is resident in that province, making its nest on the ground.

This bird presents considerable variety of plumage, according to the greater or less number of the dark transverse bands which are present, to more or less extent, in the majority of specimens, sometimes prevailing on the upper parts of the body. Frequently, however, these bands are so few and indistinct that the bird is almost pure and snowy white. Audubon's plate represents this owl unusually dark; Wilson's figure is, in plumage, more usually met with, and is more truthful.

SURNIA, Dumeril.

Surnia, Dumeril, Zoologie Analytique, p. 34, (1806.)

General form rather long, but robust ; size, medium. Head moderate, without ear tufts ; facial disc obsolete ; bill moderate, curved from the base, covered with projecting plumes ; wings long ; tail long, wide, graduated ; legs rather short, and with the toes densely feathered ; contains one species only, which inhabits the arctic regions of both continents.

SURNIA ULULA, Linnaeus.

The Hawk Owl ; The Day Owl.

Strix ulula, Linn. Syst. Nat. I, p. 133. (1766.,
Strix hudsonia, Gm. Syst. Nat. I, p. 295. (1788.)
Strix doliata, Pallas, Zoog. Ross. As. I, p. 316. (1811.)
" *Strix funerea*, Linn."—Audubon.

Figures.—Wilson Am. Orn. VI, pl. 50, fig. 6 ; Aud. B. of Am., pl. 378 : Oct. ed. I, pl. 27 ; Nat. Hist. New York, Birds, pl. 9, fig. 19 ; Gould B. of Eur. I, pl.

Wings rather long ; first three quills incised on their inner webs ; tail long, with its central feathers about two inches longer than the outer ; tarsi and toes densely feathered. Upper parts fuliginous brown, with numerous partially concealed circular spots of white on the neck behind scapulars and wing coverts. Face grayish white ; throat white, with longitudinal stripes of dark brown ; a large brown spot on each side of the breast ; other under parts with transverse lines or stripes of pale ashy brown ; quills and tail brown, with transverse bands of white ; bill pale yellowish ; irides yellow. Color of upper parts darker on the head, and the white markings more or less numerous in different specimens.

Total length, female, 16 to 17 inches ; wing 9, tail 7 inches. Male rather smaller.

Hab.—Northern regions of both continents ; Canada, (Dr. Hall ;) Wisconsin, (Dr. Hoy ;) Massachusetts, (Dr. Brewer.) Spec. in Nat. Mus., Washington, and Mus. Acad., Philadelphia.

This bird inhabits the arctic regions, and has been noticed as far north as explorers or navigators have penetrated, migrating more southwardly in the winter season. It does not, however, wander so extensively as the snowy owl, (*Nyctea nivea,*) and is rarely seen as far south as Pennsylvania. From the western countries of North America we have never seen this species.

This remarkable bird partakes of the general appearance and habits also of both an owl and a falcon, and is represented as being, to a considerable extent, diurnal in its habits, venturing abroad boldly by daylight. Specimens from northern America and from northern Europe and Asia are quite identical.

List of specimens.

Catal. No.	Sex and age.	Locality.	When collected.	Whence obtained.	Original No.	Collected by—	Measurements.		
							Length.	Extent.	Wing.
6912	......	Nelson river, H.B.T	....	D. Gunn........		......	......	......	......
6913	......	Red river settlem't.	....	....do........		......	......	......	......
6914	......	.........do........	....	....do........		......	......	......	......
8000	......	Saskatchewan......	....	John Gould......	7084	......	......	......	......

The preceding descriptions embrace all the owls known to inhabit North America, and with this family we close the order of rapacious birds.

ORDER II.

SCANSORES.

The essential peculiarities of the *Scansores*, as already stated, are to be found in the arrangement of the toes in pairs, (called zygodactyle,) two of them anterior and two posterior, although one of the latter is sometimes wanting. If we include the parrots among the other zygodactyle birds, there will be found two types of bill: one simple, as in the woodpeckers, the other, as in the parrots, with a soft skin at the base similar to the cere of the *Raptores*. The tail usually consists of twelve feathers, although but ten occur in some forms and eight in others. The primaries are always ten in number.

There is considerable diversity in the scutellation of the feet and legs. In the parrots, the whole tarsus is covered with small reticulated plates; in the other families, however, the anterior half of the tarsus is usually provided with a series of large transverse scutellae, the sides and posterior edge with smaller ones, either reticulated, polygonal, or quadrate.

The vocal muscles are but little developed in the *Scansores*, and the voice, in consequence, is harsh and without melody.

The North American *Scansores* are divisible into four families, having the following characters, as given by Burmeister:

PSITTACIDAE or Parrots.—Bill high, thick, and arched, the tip hooked, and the base with a soft skin or cere, as in the hawks. The tarsi covered with small granulated plates. Tail feathers twelve.

TROGONIDAE or Trogons.—Bill short, broad, and encompassed at the base by long, stiff bristles. Feet very small; the tarsi with broad plates; the inner anterior toe turned backwards. Tail with twelve feathers.

CUCULIDAE or Cuckoos.—Bill thin, usually slender, and rather long; the tip more or less decurved; the base usually without rictal bristles. Tarsi usually rather long, clothed with broad plates anteriorly. The tail feathers usually ten, sometimes eight or twelve, all long.

PICIDAE or Woodpeckers.—Bill straight, rigid, and chisel-shaped at the tip, the base without rictal bristles. The feet are stout, and clothed anteriorly with broad plates. Tail feathers twelve; the exterior very small and concealed.

9 b

Family PSITTACIDAE. The Parrots.

The family of parrots is one so strongly marked as to be familiar to every one. The peculiarities belonging to it are very many, and the differences from other forms so great as almost to warrant its erection into a distinct order, as has been done by Bonaparte, who, in addition, places it at the head of his system, separated from the typical *Scansores* by the rapacious birds.

The parrots are very extensively distributed throughout the warmer portions of America, although the United States includes but a single species, as far as known. A second species, *Rhynchopsitta pachyrhyncha*,[1] inhabits the table land of Mexico, and probably extends to within a hundred miles of our frontier. The other Mexican species, according to Sclater, (Pr. Zool. Soc. 1857, 230,) are *Ara militaris*, *Conurus petzii* and *astec*, *Pionus senilis*, *Psittacula lineolata*, and *Chrysotis autumnalis*, *viridigenalis*, and *ochroptera*. Some of these may extend their range northward, and even occasionally occur within our limits.

CONURUS, Kuhl.

Conurus, KUHL, Consp. Psittac. 4, 1830.—IB. Nova Acta K. L. C. Acad. X, 1830.

Tail long, conical, and pointed ; bill stout; cheeks feathered, but in some species leaving a naked ring round the eye ; cere feathered to the base of the bill.

The preceding diagnosis, though not very full, will serve to indicate the essential characteristics of the genus among the American forms with long pointed tails, the most prominent feature consisting in the densely feathered, not naked, cheeks. But one species belongs to the United States, though, as already stated, two others are found in Mexico, and many more in South and Central America.

[1] The following description of this species, taken from Swainson, will serve to identify it, if ever captured within our limits :

RHYNCHOPSITTA PACHYRHYNCHA, Bon.

Thick-billed Parrot.

Macrocercus pachyrhynchus, Sw. Syn. Birds Mex. in Philos. Mag. I, 1827, 439, No. 79.
Rhynchopsitta pachyrhyncha, BON. Tableau des Perroquets, Rev. et Mag. de Zool. 1854, 149.
Psittacus pascha, WAGLER, Isis, 1831, 524.

SP. CH.—Green front ; eyebrows and ridge of shoulders red ; cheeks plumed ; tail feathers broad and obtuse. Wing 10 inches ; middle tail feathers 5.25 ; curve of upper mandible 2.00 ; depth of under mandible 1 inch. *Hab.*—Table lands of Mex. Sw. Syn. Birds Mex. in Philos. Mag. 1827.

A specimen of this species is in the collection of the Philadelphia Academy of Natural Sciences, labelled Rio Grande, Texas, J. W. Audubon. If really taken within the limits of the United States, it is probably of very rare occurrence.

CONURUS CAROLINENSIS, Kuhl.

Parakeet; Carolina Parrot.

Psittaca carolinensis, Brisson, Ornith. II, 1762, 138.
Psittacus carolinensis, Linn. Syst. Nat. I, 1758, 97; 1766, 141, (nec Scopoli.)—Wilson, Am. Orn. III, 1811, 69
     pl. xxvi, fig. 1.—Aud. Orn. Biog. I, 1832, 135, pl. 26.
Conurus carolinensis, Kuhl, Nova Acta K. L. C. 1830.—Bon. List. 1838.—Pr. Max. Cabanis Journ. für Orn.
     V, March, 1857, 97.
Centurus carolinensis, Aud. Syn. 1839, 189.—Ib. Birds Am. IV, 1842, 306, pl. 278.
Psittacus˷ ludovicianus, Gm. Syst. I, 1788, 347.
Carolina parrot, Catesby, Car. I, tab. xi.—Latham, Syn. I, 227.—Pennant, II, 242.
Orange-headed parrot, Latham, Syn. I, 304.

Sp. Ch.—Head and neck all round gamboge yellow; the forehead, from above the eyes, with the sides of the head, pale brick red. Body generally and tail green, with a yellowish tinge beneath. Outer webs of primaries bluish green, yellow at the base; secondary coverts edged with yellowish. Edge of wing yellow, tinged with red; tibiae yellow. Bill white. Legs flesh color. Length about 13 inches; wing 7.50; tail 7.10. Young with head and neck green.

Hab.—Southern and southwestern States, as far west as the Missouri.

In the specimens before me I have been unable to detect any difference between the sexes; the young I have not had the opportunity of examining, but Audubon states that the head and neck are green.

The description by Linnæus of *Psittacus carolinensis* presents nothing characteristic of this species, being based on a defective figure of Catesby. Brisson's indication is, however, unmistakable. The *P. pertinax* of Linnæus has usually been considered as the young of the Carolina parrot, but it proves to be a distinct South American species, without any red on the head.

This species on the Atlantic slope has been seen, at rare intervals, as far north as Pennsylvania, though rare at the present day even in South Carolina. Westward they occur high up on the Missouri, though none have been collected or seen by any recent expeditions much west of that river. Barton, in his Fragments of the Natural History of Pennsylvania, page 6, says that a very large flock was met with in January, 1780, about twenty-five miles northwest of Albany, and caused great terror in the minds of the Dutch settlers, who imagined that they portended the destruction of the world.

List of specimens.

Catal. No.	Sex.	Locality.	When collected.	Whence obtained.	Original No.	Collected by—	Length.	Extent.	Wing.	Tail.	Tarsus.	Middle toe.	Its claw alone.	Bill above.	Along gape.	Specimen measured.	Remarks.
4935		Florida		J. W. P. Jenks			13.80		7.63	7.00	.68	1.25	.43	1.04	.96	Skin	
1298		Southern States		S. F. Baird												Skin	
3896		Cairo, Ill.		R. Kennicott		H. B. Möllhausen											
5854		Fort Smith, Ark.		Lieut. Whipple													
		Fort Riley, K. T.		Dr. Hammond, U.S.A., and J. X. Vesey			11.62	21.50	7.50							Fresh	
4608		Nebraska	April 24, 1856	Lieut. G. K. Warren	98	Lieut. Warren	13.25	22.25	7.50								
4609		Bald island, Missouri river	April 25, 1856	....do	34	Dr. Hayden	13.25	21.37	7.87								
4610		....do	...do	....do	98	....do	13.12	22.	7.87								
4611		....do	do	....do	30	....do	13.67	22.	7.50								
4612		....do	...do	....do	31	....do	13.50	21.87	7.62								
4613		....do	do	....do	97	....do	13.	21.87	7.87								
4614		....do	do	....do		Lieut. Warren	14.	22.25	7.62								Iris brown.
4615		....do	...do	....do	29	Dr. Hayden	13.50	22.50	7.75								
4616		....do	April 24, 1856	....do		Lieut. Warren	13.12	22.50	8.00							Fresh	
4617		....do	April 25, 1856	....do	33	Dr. Hayden	13.12	22.00	7.62								Skin
4618		....do	...do	....do		....do			6.94		.66	1.22	.44	1.00	.80		

Family TROGONIDAE. The Trogons.

In continuation of the diagnosis already given of this family, it may be stated that the bill is much shorter than the head, broadly triangular, with the tip hooked and dentate. Nasal fossae concealed ; the base of both mandibles with long, stiff bristles directed forwards ; the eyelids, also, with similar bristles. Wings short, rounded ; the quills falcate, much graduated. Tail elongated ; the feathers broad. Legs very feeble ; the tarsus short, and hidden in the plumage. The inner anterior toe is versatile, or directed backwards, instead of the outer, as in all other *Scansores*.

TROGON, Moehring.

Trogon " MOEHRING, Genera Avium, 1752."

Bill broad, both mandibles with the cutting edge serrated ; plumage soft and lax, the upper tail coverts not reaching beyond the middle of the tail and but little beyond the tip of the folded wing. The wing coverts are short ; the lateral tail feathers graduated. Anterior toes united beyond the first joint.

The genus *Trogon*, as above characterized, is distinguished from *Calurus* (*Pharomacrus*) by the short upper tail coverts, which do not project in a long train far beyond the true tail. The even tail feathers distinguish it from *Temnurus*, its other American ally.

TROGON MEXICANUS, Swainson.

Mexican Trogon.

Trogon mexicanus, SWAINSON, Syn. Birds Mex. Taylor's Phil. Mag. I, 1827, 440.—WAGLER, Isis, 1831, 524.— GOULD, Mon. Trogonidae, 1838 ; pl. i, adult male, and pl. ii, female and young male.

SP. CH.—Golden green above and on the neck all around. Forehead, chin, and side of head, black. Under parts carmine red ; a narrow pectoral collar and the edges of the wings white. Outer tail feathers white, their middle portion dotted or barred with black. Middle feathers coppery, with or without a terminal bar of black.
Length, 10.75 ; wing, 5.25 ; tail, 6.75. *Hab.*—Northeastern Mexico to Rio Grande.

4338.—The entire upper parts of this species, with the neck and upper part of the breast, are of a rich lustrous metallic golden green, with occasional coppery reflections, especially on the scapulars. The forehead, sides of the head around the eyes, the chin, and upper part of the throat, are dull black, with perhaps a bluish shade. The wing coverts are finely mottled black and white ; the quills are brown, with the outer webs edged with white. The entire under parts are of a rich carmine red ; the feathers with concealed white just below the red ; a narrow white collar separates the green of the breast from the carmine. The outer three tail feathers are white for most of their length, and dusky towards the base, especially on the inner webs. For about the terminal inch the white is pure, elsewhere it is finely dotted with black. The two middle feathers are greenish coppery, abruptly tipped for about an inch with black ; the remaining ones are similar, but with more of a violet tinge. A second specimen (4339) has rather more white on the breast. The middle tail feathers lack the terminal band of black. The external tail feathers, (except the second,) instead of being finely mottled, are barred transversely with black.

The feathers on the rump of this and probably other species of *Trogon* have the shafts thickened and stiffened. so as even to be spinous, this character perceptible in the feathers on the back, though diminishing towards the head.

According to Gould, fully adult specimens of this species have the three outer tail feathers entirely black, with white tips, the narrow bars being characteristic of immaturity, as are also a greater distinctness of the freckles on the wing and the white edgings to the primaries not found in the adult.

In the female the green tints are said to be replaced by brownish, as also the upper part of the carmine ; the hinder portion of the under parts is as in the male. The white pectoral crescent is also indicated by grayish.

The *Trogon elegans* is somewhat similar to this species, but has a longer tail.

In the monograph of *Trogonidae*, Gould figures his *Trogon ambiguus* from northern Mexico, distinguished by the finer mottling on the wing and the replacing of the narrow bars on the tail feathers by black dottings. This is precisely the character of No. 4338, which would, therefore, if distinct, bear this name. As, however, the other characters are so similar, it would seem as if the *ambiguus* were merely another stage of plumage of *T. mexicanus.* A specimen labelled *Trogon ambiguus*, in the collection of the Philadelphia Academy, differs, however, in having a much greener gloss to the feathers of the body. The black of the forehead extends further on the crown. The middle tail feathers are more green than coppery ; the carmine of the belly is less intense. The mottling of the wings and tail is much the same.

List of specimens.

Catal. No.	Sex.	Locality.	When collected.	Whence obtained.	Orig. No.	L'gth.	Extent.	Wing.	Tail.	Tarsus.	Mid'le toe.	Its claw alone.	Bill above.	Along gape.	Specimen measured.	Remarks.
4338	♂	Boquillo, New Leon, Mex.	April, 1853	Lt. Couch ...	138	10.75	16.25	5.25							Fresh....	Iris br'wn, bill yel'w.
do		.....do				11.50		5.10	6 75	.61	.90	.26	.65	.85		Dry skin.
4339	♂	......do	April, 1853	Lt. Couch ...	145	11.25	14.25	5.00							Fresh....	
do		......do				12.00		5.00	6.75	.60			.70			Dry skin.

Family CUCULIDAE. The Cuckoos.

Bill compressed, gently curved, sometimes attenuated, and generally lengthened. A few bristles at the base of the bill or none. Tarsi lengthened; toes rather short. Tail long and soft, of 8 to 12 feathers.

The preceding diagnosis covers a great variety of forms, although those found within the United States embrace but three genera, which may be indicated as follows, each forming the type of a sub-family :

A. Tail feathers eight ; face naked.

CROTOPHAGA.—Bill shorter than the head. Very high, and much compressed.

B. Tail feathers ten ; face covered with feathers.

GEOCOCCYX.—Bill longer than the head. Loral feathers stiff, bristly. Tarsi much longer than the toes. Live on the ground.

COCCYGUS.—Bill not as long as the head. Loral feathers soft. Tarsi shorter than the toes. Live on trees.

CROTOPHAGA, Linnæus.

Crotophaga, LINNÆUS, Systema Naturæ, 1756.

Bill as long as the head, very much compressed ; the culmen elevated into a high crest, extending above the level of the forehead. Nostrils exposed, elongated. Point of bill much decurved. Wings lengthened, extending beyond the base of the tail, the fourth or fifth quill longest. Tail lengthened, of eight graduated feathers. Toes long, with well developed claws.

The feathers in this genus are entirely black ; those on the head and neck with a peculiar stiffened, metallic or scale-like border. The species are not numerous, and are entirely confined to America.

For a number of years the occurrence of specimens of *Crotophaga* at various points on our sea border has been recorded, but the genus has never been formally introduced into our fauna. There is, however, no reason to doubt its existence as a regular summer visitor on the keys and shores of Florida, as well as at various points on the Gulf of Mexico. In the following pages I describe two species, and it is quite possible that others may occasionally occur within our limits.

CROTOPHAGA RUGIROSTRIS, Sw.

Ani ; Black Parrot, (Florida.)

¶ *Crotophaga rugirostra*, Sw. 2¼ Cent. in Anim. in Menag. 1838, 321, fig. 65, b. (bill ;)—" JARDINE & SELBY, Ill. Orn. pl. 41."

Crotophaga rugirostris, BURMEISTER, Thiere Bras. II, Vögel, 1856, 255.

Bill with faint wrinkles transverse to the culmen, which is gently decurved from a point above, or a little posterior to the nostrils. The highest portion of the crest obtusely angular, rounded ; no portion parallel to the commissure. Nostrils situated nearly in the middle of the lower half of the lateral outline of the upper mandible. Color black, with bluish reflections above. Pointed feathers of the head and neck with a bronzed metallic border. Length about 15 inches ; wing, 6 ; tail, 8.

Hab.—Florida to Brazil.

Bill at the nostrils nearly twice as high as broad ; the nostrils elliptical, a little oblique, situated in the middle of the lower half of the upper mandible. Gonys nearly straight. Indications of faint transverse wrinkles along the upper portion of the bill, nearly perpendicular to the culmen. Legs stout ; tarsus longer than middle toe, with seven broad scutellae anteriorly extending round to the middle of each side; the remaining or posterior portion of each side with a series of quadrangular plates, corresponding nearly to the anterior ones, the series meeting behind in a sharp ridge. The wings reach over the basal third of the tail. The primary quills are broad and acute, the fourth longest; the first about equal to the tertials. The tail is graduated, the outer about one and a half inch shorter than the middle ones.

The color generally is black, with steel blue reflections above, changing sometimes into violet; duller beneath. The pointed feathers of the head, neck, and breast, with a bronzy metallic border, appearing also to some extent on the wing coverts and upper part of back.

The determination of the species of *Crotophaga* is a matter of much difficulty, owing to their close relationship and the uncertainty as to the permanency of the characters usually assigned. The present bird, however, agrees most closely with the *C. rugirostra* of Swainson, in having indication of transverse wrinklings or grooves, although much less than those given in the description of this author. It is much smaller than *C. major*, and lacks the peculiar concavity of the culmen on the anterior extremity of the vertical crest, which, besides, is distinct only on the posterior half of the bill. *C. major* likewise has a long sulcus from the nostril nearly to the tip of the bill, which is but little decurved. The entire absence of longitudinal grooves along the side of the crest distinguishes it from *C. sulcirostris*. In this latter species, also, the nostrils are situated high up, their upper edge on a line midway between the culmen and commissure. In *C. rugirostris* and *ani* they are considerably below this level, or on the inferior third of the side of the bill.

The differences between *C. rugirostris* and *ani* are more difficult of expression. The bill of the latter is, however, entirely smooth, and the profile of the crest is more abrupt. Thus a line from the highest point of the culmen, perpendicular to the culmen, falls considerably anterior to the nostrils, while in *C. rugirostris* this line would fall through, or a little behind, the nostrils.

The *C. rugirostris* of Swainson has usually been considered as the same with *C. casasii* of Lesson. A specimen of the latter, in the collection of the Philadelphia Academy, is, however, very different in a much lower bill, with scarcely any crest. The size is much less.

The *C. rugirostris* probably occurs in other parts of the United States besides Florida. It is an inhabitant of the West Indies, and appears to extend as far south as Brazil.

List of specimens.

Catal. No.	Sex.	Locality.	When collected.	Whence obtained.	Length.	Stretch of wings.	Wing.	Tail.	Tarsus.	Middle toe.	Its claw alone.	Bill above.	Along gape.	Specimen measured.	Remarks.
8639	♂	Tortugas, Florida.	June 24, 1857	G. Würdemann...	13.20	......	6.04	8.30	1.48	1.30	0.36	1.30	1.10	Skin	......
do	......	...do.........	....	...do........	15.00	18.00	6.00	......	......	......	......	......	......	Fresh ...	Iris brown.

CROTOPHAGA ANI, L.

Ani.

Crotophaga ani, L. Syst. Nat. I, 1766, 154.—BURMEISTER, Thiere Bras. Vögel, 1856, 254.

Bill smooth; the culmen abruptly decurved; the highest point anterior to the nostrils. The highest portion of the crest nearly straight, and parallel with the commissure. Length, 12 inches; wing, 6.10; tail, 7.75.

Hab. Maritime parts of the southeastern United States, and south to Brazil.

A *Crotophaga*, killed near Philadelphia, and now in the collection of the Philadelphia Academy, appears to be a typical *C. ani* (as described by Burmeister) in the smoothness of the bill and other peculiarities. It is decidedly smaller than *rugirostris*, the culmen straight at its highest point, the anterior extremities of this nearly straight portion anterior to the nostril. The colors are, however, almost precisely the same with those of *rugirostris*. Length, 12 inches: wing, 6.10; tail, 7.75; tarsus, 1.25; chord of culmen, 1.15.

GEOCOCCYX, Wagl r.

Geococcyx, WAGLER, Isis, 1831, 524.
Leptostoma, SWAINSON, Classification Birds, II, 1837, 325.

Bill long and strong, slightly compressed, and at least as long as the head; head crested; loral feathers, and those at base of bill stiffened and bristly. Nostrils elongated, linear. A naked colored skin around and behind the eye; the eyelids ciliated. Tarsi longer than the toes; very stout. Wings very short and concave; the tertials as long as the primries. Tail longer than the head and body; composed of ten narrow, much graduated feathers.

This remarkable genus is represented in the United States by a single species known as the Paisano, Chapparal Cock, or sometimes Road Runner, on account of its frequenting public highways. Its very long legs enable it to run with very great rapidity, faster even than a very fleet horse. A second species occurs in Mexico, the *G. affinis* of Hartlaub. This is smaller and differently proportioned, as shown by the following table of measurement:

Comparative measurements of species.

Catalogue number.	Species.	Locality.	Sex.	Length.	Wing.	Tail.	Tarsus.	Middle toe.	Its claw alone.	Bill above.	Along gape.	Specimen measured.
6187	G. californianus......	San Diego..........	♂	25.00	6.50	12.55	2.60	1.70	.45	2.00	2.61	Skin........
9081	G. affinis............	Mexico..............	♂	19.20	5.70	11.50	1.80	1.53	.41	1.60	1.93	Skin........

GEOCOCCYX CALIFORNIANUS.

Paisano; Road Runner; Chapparal Cock.

Saurothera californiana, " LESSON, Complem. Buff. VI, 1829, 420.—IB. Ann. du Mus, 1835, 121, Pl. ix."
Geococcyx variegata, WAGLER, Isis, V, 1831, 524.
Saurothera bottae, (BLAINVILLE,) LESSON, Traité d'Orn. I, 1831, 145.
Diplopterus viaticus, (LICHT.) BOIE, Isis, 1831, 541. (No description.)
Geococcyx viaticus, HARTLAUB, Rev. Zool. 1844, 215.—M'CALL, Pr. A. N. Sc. III, July, 1847, 234.—BON. Consp.
    1850, 97.—IB. Consp. Zygod. in Aten. Ital. 1854, 5.—HEERMANN, J. A. N. Sc. Ph. 2d series
    II, 1853, 270.—NEWBERRY, Zool. Cal. and Oregon Route, 91, P. R. R. Rep. VI, 1857.
Saurothera marginata, KAUP, Isis, 1832, 991; tab. xxvi. (Fig. of head and foot.)
Leptostoma longicauda, SWAINSON, Birds, II, 1837, 325.—GAMBEL, Pr. A. N. S. I, 1843, 263.
Geococcyx mexicanus, GAMBEL, J. A. N. Sc. 2d series, I, 1849, 215, (not of GMELIN.)—CASSIN, Ill. I, 1855, 213;
    pl. xxxvi.

SP. CH.—Tail very long; the lateral feathers much shortest. An erectile crest on the head. A bare skin around and behind the eye. Legs very long and stout.

All the feathers of the upper parts and wings of a dull metallic olivaceous green, broadly edged with white near the end. There is, however, a tinge of black in the green along the line of white, which itself is suffused with brown. On the neck the black preponderates. The sides and under surface of the neck have the white feathers streaked centrally with black, next to which is a brownish suffusion. The remaining under parts are whitish, immaculate. Primary quills tipped with white, and with a median band across the outer webs. Central tail feathers olive brown; remaining ones clear dark green, all edged, and (except the central two,) broadly tipped with white. Top of the head dark blackish blue. Length 20 to 23 inches. Wing about 6¼. Tail, 12 to 13.

Hab.—Middle Texas, New Mexico, and California to Central Mexico. Seen as far north as Fort Reading, California, and Fort Chadbourne, Texas.

10 b

This species, in addition to the names cited above, is also sometimes called *Correo camino*. It is common in Texas and California, and always excites attention by its large size and peculiar habits.   In a very large series of this species I find great variations in size, although but little in color.   As a general rule, however, skins from California are considerably larger than those from Northern Mexico and Texas.

The difference between this species and *G. affinis* of Hartlaub are very appreciable. The latter is decidedly smaller ; the bill is much smaller, shorter, and both culmen and commissure are curved almost from the base of the bill, instead of straight nearly to the tip.   The culmen is shorter than the head instead of longer, and the nostril is opposite the middle of the commissure instead of decidedly posterior to the same point.   The tarsi are only about two inches long ; the culmen 1.30 inches.   The tertials and outer surface of the wings are glossed with coppery violet instead of green ; the lateral tail feathers with green instead of blue.   The under parts are nearly uniform brownish yellow or whitish, the sides of the breast alone with a few sharply defined, longitudinal streaks of black, instead of brownish cinnamon ; breast feathers edged with hoary white, and much streaked centrally, though narrowly, with black ; the belly dirty white.   The length is about 18 inches ; the wing 5.50 ; the tail 9.75.

If Hartlaub's quotation of 1829, as the date of the *Saurothera californiana*, Lesson, be correct, this name will take precedence among the more modern ones.   Should this not be the case, then the next in order will probably be that of Wagler.   I am unable to say what the relationships of *G. velox* of Karwinski, (Münchner Gelehrte Anzeigen, III, 1836, 95,) may be, not having this volume at hand for reference.

The *Phasianus mexicanus* of Gmelin, I, 1788, 741, based on the Hoitlallotl of Hernandez, (Nova Anim. 1690, app. 25,) in all probability refers to a species of *Geococcyx*, but it is entirely impossible to say which.   Hernandez was most likely to have met with the southern species, or *affinis*.   Still, in the entire impossibility of ever coming to a decision, either in reference to *Phasianus mexicanus*, or *Upupa mexicana* of Gmelin, it seems much better to drop the consideration of these names and to confine investigations to more modern authors.

List of specimens.

Catal. No.	Sex.	Locality.	When collected.	Whence obtained.	Orig'l No.	Collected by—	Length.	Extent.	Wing.	Remarks.
4973	.....	Fort Chadbourne, Tex..	....	Dr. Swift, U. S. A..	......	....	....	....	....	....
6184	......	Rio Grande, New Mex..	Sep. 20, 1853	Major Emory.......	......	Mr. Schott.....	....	....	7.	....
5068	......	Crossing of Pecos......	Aug. 20, 1856	Captain Pope	119	....	23.50	20.	7.	Bill light brown with dark ridge and tips; eyes light brown, with light blue iris! (pupil); feet, light blue; gums, pink.
5069	......	..........do	Aug. 4, 1855	......do	116	....	24.25	21.	7.	Bill light blue, with dark tips; feet, whitish blue; eyes, light brown; gums, pale blue.
5070	......	..........do	Oct. 20, 1855	......do	148	....	23.	20.	6.50	Feet, gray; eyes blue; gums, white.
6176	......	Ringgold Barracks, Tex.	....	Major Emory	......	Mr. Clark......	....	....	....	....
6177	......	Eagle Pass, Texas	....	......do	......	Mr. Schott.....	....	....	....	....
4053	♀	Tamaulipas, Mexico....	March, 1853	Lieut. Couch.......	87	....	20.	18.	6.	....
4054	♂	..........do	......do	......do	79	....	20.	18.	6.25	Eyes, brownish gray; bill, slate; feet, lead colored.
6178	... ..	El Paso, New Mexico..	....	Lieut. Whipple....	......	Dr. Kennerly...	....	....	....	....
5067	......	Doña Ana, New Mex...	Nov. 22, 1855	Captain Pope	65	....	20.	20.	7.50	Eyes brown, with yellow iris; feet and gums, pale blue.
6182	......	Fort Conrad ....do.....	October, 1853	Lieut. Whipple.....	54	Dr. Kennerly...	....	....	....	....
6179	......	Fort Thorn.....do.....	....	Dr. Henry, U. S. A..	......	....	....	....	....	....
6183	......	Little Colorado river....	Nov. 2, 1853	Lieut. Whipple....	33	....	22.	18.	8.	....
4576	......	Fort Yuma, California..	....	Major Emory	40	Mr. Schott.....	....	....	....	....
4914	......	San Diego..... do.....	....	Dr. J. F. Hammond	......	....	....	....	....	....
6187	......	..........do	....	Lieut. Trowbridge..	......	A. Cassidy.....	....	....	....	....
6188	♂	..........do	....	Dr.W.S.King,U.S.A.	......	....	....	....	....	....
6185	♂	Los Angelos, California.	....	Lieut. Williamson..	......	Dr. Heermann..	....	....	....	....
6186	♀	Tejon valley.....do....	....	......do	......	......do	....	....	....	....
4565	......	San Jose ....do....	....	A. J. Grayson	......	....	....	....	....	....
5946	......	Santa Clara .....do....	....	Dr. J. G. Cooper...	......	....	....	....	....	....
4487	......	Calaveras co.....do....	....	Lieut. Williamson..	......	Dr. Newberry..	....	....	....	....

COCCYGUS, Vieillot.

Coccyzus, VIEILLOT, Analyse, 1816.
Eryth ophrys, SWAINSON, Class. Birds, II, 1837, 322.

Head without crest; feathers about base of bill soft; bill nearly as long as the head, decurved, slender, and attenuated towards the end. Nostrils linear. Wings lengthened, reaching the middle of the tail; the tertials short. Tail of ten graduated feathers. Feet weak; tarsi shorter than the middle toe.

The species of *Coccygus* are readily distinguished from those of *Geococcyx* by their arboreal habits, confining themselves mainly to trees, instead of living habitually on the ground. The plumage is soft, fine, and compact.

The American cuckoos differ from the European cuckoos, (*Cuculus*,) by having lengthened naked tarsi, instead of very short feathered ones. The nostrils are elongated, too, instead of rounded. The habits of the two are entirely different, the American species rearing their own young, instead of laying the eggs in the nests of other birds, like the European cuckoo and the American cowbird (*Molothrus pecoris*).

The following synopsis will serve to distinguish the North American species of *Coccygus*, all of them being of a light greenish color, tinged with ashy towards the head:

A. Beneath nearly pure white.

Under mandible yellow. Tail feathers black, broadly and conspicuously tipped with white; of which color also is the outer web of outer feather. All the quills with the concealed portion orange cinnamon...*C. americanus.*

Under mandible black. Tail feathers beneath greyish, narrowly and indistinctly tipped with white; the outer web of outer feathers not white, nor the concealed portion of the quills orange cinnamon...............................*C. erythrophthalmus.*

B. Beneath strongly tinged with yellowish cinnamon.

Tail feathers black, broadly tipped with white, the outer not margined externally. An elongated patch of brown behind the eye. Under mandible yellow, except at tip.

C. seniculus.

The following table exhibit the comparative proportions of the three species:

Catal. No.	Species.	Locality.	Sex.	Length.	Stretch of wings.	Wing.	Tail.	Tarsus.	Middle toe.	Its claw alone.	Bill above.	Along gape.	Specimen measured.
5623	Coccygus americanus.......	Republican river.	♂	12.00	16.50	......	......	......	......	......	......	......	Fresh ...
do	......do.........do... ...	......do		12.00	....	5.90	6.64	1.06	0.98	0.30	1.00	1.20	Skin ....
1541	......do.........do......	Carlisle, Pa......	♂	11.40	16.50	5.15	......	......	......	......	......	......	Fresh ...
do	......do.........do	......do		10.50	....	5.44	5.64	0.90	1.00	0.46	1.06	1.24	Skin ....
8981	......do...erythrophthalmus.	Platte river......	♂	12.37	16.25	5.75	......	......	......	......	......	......	Fresh ...
do	......do.........do	......do		11.66	... .	5.60	6.70	0.96	0.96	0.28	1.00	1.12	Skin ....
8979	......do.........do	......do	♀	12.00	16.00	5.50	......	......	......	......	......	......	Fresh ...
do	......do.........do	......do		12.00	....	5.60	6.70	0.96	0.96	0.30	1.00	1.20	Skin ....
391	......do.........do	Carlisle	♂	11.30	....	5.12	6.24	0.90	1.00	0.30	1.00	1.12	Skin ....
1854	......do..minor............	Key West.........		12.04	....	5.00	6.88	1.00	1.00	0.30	1.10	1.20	Skin ....

COCCYGUS AMERICANUS, Bonap.

Yellow-billed Cuckoo.

Cuculus americanus, LINN. Syst. Nat. I, 1766, 170, 10.

Coccyzus americanus, BON. Obs. Wilson, 1825, No. 47.—IB. Conspectus, 1850, IV.—AUD. Orn. Biog. I, 1832, 18, V: 520, pl. 2.—IB. Birds Am. IV, 1842, 293, pl. 275.

Erythrophrys americanus, SW. Birds, II, 1837.—BON. List, 1838.

Cureus americanus, BON. List Eur. Birds, 1842.

? *Cuculus dominicensis,* LINN. Syst. Nat. I, 1766, 170, 13.

? *Cuculus dominicus,* LATHAM, Syst. I, 1790, 221, (considered distinct by Bonaparte.)

Cuculus carolinensis, (BRISSON,) WILSON, Am. Orn. IV, 1811, 13, pl. xxviii.

Cuculus cinerosus, TEMMINCK, Man. IV, 1835, 277.

Coccyzus pyrrhopterus, VIEILL. Dict.

SP. CH.—Upper mandible and tip of lower, black; rest of lower mandible and cutting edges of the upper yellow. Upper parts of a metallic greenish olive, slightly tinged with ash towards the bill; beneath white. Tail feathers, (except the median, which are like the back,) black, tipped with white for about an inch on the outer feathers, the external one with the outer edge almost entirely white. Quills orange cinnamon; the terminal portion and a gloss on the outer webs olive; iris brown. Length 12 inches; wing 5.95; tail 6.35.

Hab.—Eastern United States to the Missouri plains.

This species is easily known by the yellow under mandible, the black under surface of the tail feathers with the broad and well defined black tip, and the bright orange brown of the covered portions of the quills. The bill is considerably stouter than in *C. erythrophthalmus*. There is no difference between the sexes, except that of size. It goes as far north in summer as Labrador, according to Mr. Audubon, and stragglers have been occasionally taken in Europe. Although Townsend says it occurs west of the Rocky mountains, it has not been collected by any of the recent expeditions.

List of specimens.

Catal. No.	Sex.	Locality.	When collected.	Whence obtained.	Orig. No.	Collected by—	Length.	Stretch of wings	Wing.	Remarks.
1541	♂	Carlisle, Pa..............	May 17, 1844	S. F. Baird		....	11.25	16.50	5.67	....
1651	♀	......do...............	July 27, 1844	......do...		....	12.00	17.25	5.83	....
1614	♂	......do...	July 3, 1844	......do...		....	11.17	16.00	5.50	....
6527	♀	Tortugas, Fla............	April 26, 1857	G. Wurdemann		....	......	......	......	....
5623	♂	Republican, K. T....	June 30, 1856	Lieut. Bryan, U.S.A..	49	W. S. Wood........	12.00	16.50	8.25	....
5624	♂	Clear creek, K. T........	July 1, 1856	......do...	52	....	11.50	16.50		....
86	♂	Elk Horn river............	....	Lieut. G. K. Warren.	......	Dr. Hayden..........	12.00	16.50	6.50	....
8980	♀	Fifty miles above mouth of Platte river........	....	......do...	......	......do...	11.00	15.50	5.50	Iris brown...
8985	♂	Loup Fork, on Platte riv..	July 3, 1856	......do..	......	......do...	12.00	16.50	5.75	....
8987	♀	Fifty miles above mouth of Platte river.	July 2, 1856	......do...	......	......do...	11.09	17.25	5.75	....
8983	♀	Loup Fork, Platte valley .	July 8, 1856	......do............. ..	......	......do...	12.25	19.50	5.75	....
8980	♀	......do...	....	......do...	......	......do...	12.00	16.50	6.50	Iris brown...
8329	♂	Independence, Missouri..	June 3, 1857	Wm. F. Magraw	82	Dr. Cooper	11.25	16.25	6.00	....
8232	♂	......do...	May 29, 1857	......do...	41	......do...	10.75	14.75	5.75	....
8315	♀	......do...	May 27, 1857	......do...	18	......do...	11.50	16.75	5.75	... .,......

COCCYGUS ERYTHROPHTHALMUS, Bon.

Black-billed Cuckoo.

Cuculus erythrophthalmus, WILSON, Am. Orn. IV, 1811, 16 ; pl. xxviii.
Coccyzus erythrophthalmus, BON. Obs. Wils. 1825, 48.—IB. Consp. 1850, IV.—AUD. Orn. Biog. I. 1832, 170 :
   V. 523, pl. 32.—IB. Birds America, IV, 1842, 300 ; pl. 276.
Erythrophrys erythrophthalmus, BON. List, 1838.
Coccyzus dominicus (LATH.) NUTT. Man. I, 1832, 556, (not of Latham, which belongs rather to *C. americanus*, on
   account of the red quills and white edge of outer tail feather.)

SP. CH.—Bill entirely black. Upper parts generally of a metallic greenish olive, ashy towards the base of the bill ; eneath pure white, with a brownish yellow tinge on the throat. Inner webs of the quills tinged with cinnamon. Under urface of all the tail feathers hoary ash gray. All, except the central on either side, suffused with darker to the short, bluish-white, and not well defined tip. A naked, red skin round the eye. Length about 12 inches ; wing, 5 ; tail, 6.50.
Hab.—United States to the Missouri plains.

This species differs from the *C. americanus* in the black bill, and the absence of black on the tail feathers, the white tips of which are much shorter and less abruptly defined. One specimen (5253) from the Upper Missouri has a much stronger tinge of yellowish cinnamon on the inner webs of the quills than the others. The sexes are quite similar.

List of specimens.

Catal. No.	Sex.	Locality.	When collected.	Whence obtained.	Collected by—	Length.	Extent.	Wing.	Remarks.
391	♂	Carlisle, Pa...................	May 18, 1841	S. F. Baird		......	......	......	No label..........
2660	♀	......do	May 13, 1846	......do	....	12.	16.00	5.50	....
5149	♀	Lightning lake, M. T............	June 4, 1853	Gov. Stevens	....	14.50	16.50	5.50	....
5233	♀	Moreau river, Nebraska Territory.	July 3, 1856	Lt. Warren......	Dr. Hayden......	10.75	14.26	5.25	Eyes, brown ....
5232	♂	Fort Lookout.......do............	May 16, 1856	......do	......do	12.	16.25	5.50	......do...
8980	♂	50 miles above mouth of Platte...	....	......do	......do	11.00	15.50	5.50	......do...
8979	♀	......do...............do.........	....	......do	......do	12.00	16.00	5.50	......do...
8981	♂	Fremont, on Platte..............	July 1, 1857	......do	......do	12.35	16.25	5.75	......do...
8982	♀	Loup Fork...................	August 5, 1857	......do	......do	12.00	16.25	6.00	Iris, yellow.......

COCCYGUS MINOR, Cab.

Mangrove Cuckoo.

? *Cuculus minor*, GMELIN, Syst. Nat. I, 1788, 411.
? *Coccyzus minor*, GUNDLACH, Cab. Journal für Orn. 1856, 104, (Cuba.)
Cuculus seniculus, LATH. Ind. I, 1790, 219.
Coccyzus seniculus, NUTT. Man. I, 1832, 558.—AUD. Orn. Biog. II, 1834, 390 ; pl. 169.—IB. Birds America, IV,
     1842, 303 ; pl. 277.—GOSSE, Birds Jamaica, 281.—BON. Conspectus, 1850, III.
Erythrophrys seniculus, BON. List, 1838.

SP. CH.   mandible yellow, except at the tip. Body above olivaceous, strongly tinged with ashy towards and on the
head. Beneath pale yellowish brown, darkest on the legs and abdomen, becoming lighter to the bill. An elongated spot of
ark plumbeous behind the eye. Inner edges of the quills and under wing coverts like the belly. Tail feathers, except the
central, black, with a sharply defined tip of white for about an inch, this color not extending on the outer web of the quill.
Length, about 12 inches ; wing, about 5¼.
Hab.—Florida Keys to West Indies.

This species is readily distinguishable by its fulvous under parts and dark ear coverts. It
has the yellow bill and dark tail, with broad white tips, of *C. americanus*, although the white
does not extend along the outer web of the feathers.

According to Mr. Audubon, this species is a regular summer visitor to Key West and the
other Florida Keys.

List of specimens.

Catalogue No.	Locality.	Whence obtained.	Collected by—
1854	Florida ? -----------------	S. F. Baird -----------------	E. Harris------- -------------

Family PICIDAE. The Woodpeckers.

The diagnosis already given of the *Picidae* will readily serve to distinguish the family among the *Scansores*, although some characteristic features may be properly dwelt upon in more detail. The wedge-shaped bill is pre-eminently calculated for cutting into bark or wood in search of food or the construction of a nesting place. The wings are long; the primaries ten in number, the first very short; the secondaries vary from 9 to 12. The tail feathers in the typical sub-families are excessively rigid and cuneate, especially the middle ones; the outer one on each side is very short and soft, or without stiffened shaft. It lies concealed between the second (now outer) feather and the third.

The tarsi are covered anteriorly with large plates, posteriorly with small ones, more or less reticulated or polygonal. The claws are high, strong, much curved and very sharp. The tongue is elongated and acute, with short spines or barbs on each side near the point, and capable of great protrusion.

The *Picidae* embrace three distinct forms, which constitute as many sub-families, namely, the *Picinae*, the *Yunginae*, and the *Picumninae*. Of these the *Yunginae* have no representatives in America. The *Picumninae* have soft tail feathers, or without a stiffened shaft, as in the true woodpeckers, and do not occur in the United States.

Sub-Family PICINAE.

Although all the woodpeckers have a certain resemblance to each other, and agree more or less in habits, there are distinctions among them which serve readily for division into sub-genera, genera, or even higher groups. Thus the difference between the ivory-billed woodpecker and the common flicker, which may be taken as representing the extremes of the scale in North American species, will be palpable to any observer.

In the woodpeckers inhabiting the United States there are three distinct groups, which may be taken with some authors as so many sub-families; or if, with Bonaparte, we unite all the *Picidae* with stiffened, acuminate, and pointed tails into a sub-family *Picinae*, they will constitute so many separate sections. They may be severally characterized as follows:

PICINAE or *Piceae*.—Bill more or less long; the outlines above and below nearly straight; the ends truncated; a prominent ridge on the side of the mandible springing from the middle of the base, or a little below, and running out either on the commissure, or extending parallel to and a little above it, to the end, sometimes obliterated or confluent with the lateral bevel of the bill. Nostrils considerably overhung by the lateral ridge, more or less linear, and concealed by thick bushy tufts of feathers at the base of the bill. Outer posterior toe generally longer than the anterior.

MELANERPINAE or *Centureae*.—Bill rather long; the outlines, that of the culmen especially, decidedly curved. The lateral ridge much nearest the culmen, and, though quite distinct at the base, disappearing before coming to the lower edge of the mandible; not overhanging the nostrils, which are broadly oval, rounded anteriorly, and not concealed by the bristly feathers at the base. Outer pair of toes nearly equal; the anterior rather longer.

COLAPTINAE or *Colapteae*.—Bill much depressed, and the upper outline much curved to the acutely pointed (not truncate) tip. The commissure considerably curved. Bill without any ridges. The nostrils broadly oval, and much exposed. Anterior outer toe longest.

The preceding diagnosis will serve to distinguish the three groups sufficiently for our present purposes, the bill being stronger in the *Picinae* and best fitted for cutting into trees by its more perfect wedge shape, with strengthening ridges, as well as by the lateral bevelling of both mandibles, which are nearly equal in thickness at the base, and with their outlines nearly straight. The lateral ridge is prominent, extending to the edge or end of the bill, and overhangs the nostrils, which are narrow and hidden. The *Melanerpinae* and the *Colaptinae* have the upper mandible more curved, (the commissure likewise;) the lower mandible smaller and weaker; the bill with little or no lateral bevelling. The nostrils are broadly oval and exposed. In the *Melanerpinae*, however, there is a distinct lateral ridge visible for a short distance from the base of the bill; while in the other there is no ridge at all, and the mandible is greatly curved.

Section Piceae.

With the common characters, as already given, there are several well marked generic groups in this section of woodpeckers which may be arranged for the United States species, as follows:

A. Posterior outer toe longer than the anterior outer one.

 a. Lateral ridge starting above the middle of the base of the bill and extending to the tip.

  1. CAMPEPHILUS.—Lateral ridge above the middle of the lateral profile of the bill when opposite the end of the nostrils, which are ovate, and rounded anteriorly. Bill much depressed, very long, gonys very long. Posterior outer toe considerably longer than the anterior. Primaries long, attenuated towards the tip. Spurious quill nearly half the second.

  2. PICUS.—Lateral ridge in the middle of the lateral profile opposite the end of the nostrils, which are ovate and sharp pointed anteriorly. Bill moderate, nearly as broad as high. Outer hind toe moderately longer than the outer fore toe. Primaries broad to the tip and rounded. Spurious primary not one-third the second quill.

  3. PICOIDES.—Lateral ridge below the middle of the profile, opposite the end of the ovate acute nostrils, which it greatly overhangs. Bill greatly depressed. Inner hind toe wanting, leaving only three toes. Tufts of nasal bristles very full and long.

 b. Lateral ridge starting below the middle of the base of the bill, and running as a distinct ridge into the edge of the commissure at about its middle; the terminal half of the mandible rounded on the sides, although the truncate tip is distinctly bevelled laterally.

  4. SPHYRAPICUS.—Nostrils considerably overhung by the lateral ridge, very small, linear. Gonys as long as the culmen, from the nostrils. Tips of tail feathers elongated and linear, not cuneate. Wings very long; exposed portion of spurious primary about one-fourth that of second quill.

B. Posterior outer toe considerably shorter than the anterior outer one.

  5. HYLATOMUS.—Bill depressed. Lateral ridge above the middle of the lateral profile near the base. Nostrils elliptical, wide, and rounded anteriorly. Tail as in *Picus*. Color, black.

The arrangement in the preceding diagnosis is perhaps not perfectly natural, although sufficiently so for our present purpose. Thus, *Hylatomus*, in having the lateral ridge extending to the end of the bill, is like *Picus*, but the nostrils are broader, more open, and not acute anteriorly. The tail feathers of *Sphyrapicus* differ greatly from those of the others in being abruptly acuminate, the points elongated, narrow, and nearly linear, instead of being gently cuneate at the ends.

CAMPEPHILUS, Gray.

Campephilus, GRAY, List of Genera? 1840, (typ. *C. principalis.*)
Megapicus, MALHERBE, Mem. Ac. de Metz, 1849, 317.

Bill considerably longer than the head, much depressed, or broader than high at the base, becoming somewhat compressed near the middle and gradually bevelled off at the tip. Culmen very slightly curved, gonys as concave, the curve scarcely appreciable; commissure straight. Culmen with a parallel ridge on each side, starting a little above the centre of the basal outline of the bill, the ridge projecting outwards and downwards, and a slight concavity between it and the acute ridge of the culmen. Gonys considerably more than half the commissure. Nostrils oval below the lateral ridge near the base of the bill; concealed by the bristly feathers directed forward. Similar feathers are seen at the sides, and base beneath the lower jaw.

Feet large; outer hind toe much longest; claw of inner fore toe reaching to middle of outer fore claw; inner hind toe scarcely more than half the outer one; its claw reaching as far as the base of the inner anterior claw, considerably more than half the outer anterior toe. Tarsus rather shorter than the inner fore toe. Tail long, cuneate. Wings long and pointed, the third, fourth, and fifth quills longest. Color continuous black, relieved by white patches. Head with a pointed crest.

This genus embraces the largest known species of woodpecker, and is confined to America. The two usually assigned to the United States may readily be distinguished by the following diagnosis:

Common characters.—Bill ivory white. Body entirely black. A scapular stripe and under wing coverts white. Crest scarlet in the male.

A white stripe on each side of the neck. Bristly feathers at the base of the bill white .... *principalis.*

No white stripe on the sides of the neck. More white on the wings. Bristly feathers at the base of the bill black. .... *imperialis.*

CAMPEPHILUS PRINCIPALIS, Gray.

Ivory-billed Woodpecker.

Picus principalis, LINN. Syst. Nat. I, 1766, 173.—WILSON, Am. Orn. IV, 1811, 20; pl. xxxix, f. 6.—WAGLER,
        Syst. Avium, 1827, No. 1.—AUD. Orn. Biog. I, 1832, 341 : V, 525 ; pl. 66.—IB. Birds America,
        IV, 1842, 214 ; pl. 256.
Dendrocopus principalis, BON. List, 1838.
Campephilus principalis, GRAY, List Genera, 1840.
Dryotomus (Megapicus) principalis, BON. Con. Zyg. Aten. Ital. 1854, 7.
Dryocopus principalis, BON. Consp. 1850, 132.
White-billed woodpecker, CATESBY, Car. I, 16.—PENNANT, LATHAM.

SP. CH.—Fourth and fifth quills equal; third a little shorter. Bill horn white. Body entirely of a glossy blue black, (glossed with green below ;) a white stripe beginning half an inch posterior to the commissure, and passing down the sides of the neck. Under wing coverts, and the entire exposed portion of the secondary quills, with ends of the inner primaries, bristles, and a short stripe at the base of the bill, white. Crest scarlet. Length, 21 inches ; wing, 10.

Female similar, without any red on the head, and with two spots of white on the end of the outer tail feather.

Hab.—Southern Atlantic and Gulf States.

11 b

In the male the entire crown (with its elongated feathers) is black. The scarlet commences just above the middle of the eye, and, passing backwards a short distance, widens behind and bends down as far as the level of the under edge of the lower jaw. The feathers, which spring from the back of the head, are much elongated above; considerably longer than those of the crown.

List of specimens.

Catalogue No.	Sex.	Locality.	When collected.	Whence obtained.
1830	♀	Southern States		S. F. Baird
	♂	Prairie Mer Rouge, La		J. Fairie

CAMPEPHILUS IMPERIALIS.

Imperial Woodpecker.

Picus imperialis, GOULD, Pr. Comm. Sc. Zool. Soc. II, 1832, 140.—AUD. Orn. Biog. V, 1839, 313.—IB. Birds Am.
IV, 1842, 213, (no fig.)—NUTTALL, Man. I, 2d ed., 1840, 667.
Dryocopus imperialis, BON. Consp. 1850, 132.
Megapicus imperialis, BONAP. Consp. Zygod. Aten. Ital. May, 1854, 7.
Dryotomus imperialis, CASSIN, Illust. I, 1855, 285 ; pl. xlix.

SP. CH.—Entirely black ; a short scapular stripe, the whole of the tertiaries, secondaries, and the inner primaries, and the under wing coverts, white. A broad depressed nuchal crest ; red in the male. Bill ivory white ; its bristly feathers black. Length about 24 inches ; wing, 13.25 ; tail, 9.50.

Hab.—Chiefly Central America and southwestern Mexico.

This species, in form and general appearance, is very similar to the ivory bill woodpecker. The bill, feet, wings, and tail are much the same. The principal difference, besides the much greater size, is in the absence of the white line on the side of the neck of *P. principalis*, which starts just behind the commissure, and runs into the scapular stripe common to both. The bristly feathers along the base of the bill are black, instead of white.

The feathers of the crown are black ; the posterior ones elongated, but not reaching back as far as the elongated depressed occipital crest of scarlet. This color commences just above the middle of the eye, (the eyelid being black, however,) and widens behind, so as to embrace the entire back of the head. These feathers are, however, all white just below the scarlet.

I have followed Audubon and Cassin in assigning this species to the United States, but it has really no claim to being considered as one of our birds, no specimen having been actually taken in our limits, nor probably coming within hundreds of miles of our southern border. The *P. lineatus* given by Audubon I have omitted entirely, as being still less entitled to a place.

Measurements.

Locality.	Sex.	Point of bill to end of tail.	Wing.	Tail.	Tarsus.	Middle toe.	Its claw alone.	Bill above.	Along gape.	Remarks.
Mexico[1]	♂	23.50	13.20	9.30	2.00	2.38	.88	3.60	3.70	Mounted.

[1] From specimen in Philadelphia Academy of Natural Sciences.

PICUS, Linnæus.

Picus, Linn. Syst. Nat. 1748.

Bill equal to the head, or a little longer ; the lateral ridges conspicuous, starting about the middle of the base of the bill ; the basal elongated oval nostrils nearer the commissure ; the ridges of the culmen and gonys acute, and very nearly straight, or slightly convex towards the tip ; the bill but little broader than high at the base, becoming compressed considerably before the middle. Feet much as in *Campephilus* ; the outer posterior toe longest ; the outer anterior about intermediate between it and the inner anterior ; the inner posterior reaching to the base of the claw of the inner anterior. Tarsus about equal to the inner anterior toe ; shorter than the two other long toes. Wings rather long, reaching to the middle of the tail, rather rounded ; the fourth and fifth quills longest ; the quills rather broad and rounded.

In the genus *Picus*, as characterized above, are contained several subdivisions more or less entitled to distinct rank, and corresponding with peculiar patterns of coloration. Thus, taking the *P. villosus* as the type, *P. borealis* has proportionally much longer primaries ; the spurious primary smaller ; the bill is considerably more attenuated, and even concave in its lateral outlines. The wings are still longer in *P. albolarvatus.*

The species may be arranged as follows :

A. Black above, and white beneath. Two white stripes on the side of the head, with black ear covers. Wings spotted with white.

TRICHOPICUS, Bp.—Middle of back streaked longitudinally with white. Beneath white, without spots. A narrow red nuchal band.

1. *Outer tail feathers pure white. Length about 10 inches.*

Wing coverts and innermost secondaries conspicuously spotted with white..*P. villosus.*

Wing coverts and innermost secondaries nearly uniform black, without spots...*P. harrisii.*

2. *Outer tail feather white, with black transverse bands. Length about 6¼ inches.*

Wing coverts conspicuously spotted with white....................*P. pubescens.*

Wing coverts and innermost secondaries nearly uniform black..*P. gairdneri.*

DYCTIOPICUS, Bp.—Middle of back banded transversely with white and black. Beneath white, with black spots on the side.

Entire crown and nape of male red, spotted with white. Feathers at the base of bill brown...*P. scalaris.*

Crown black ; nape red ; both spotted with white. Feathers at base of bill white.. *P. nuttalli.*

B. Black above and white beneath. Sides of body with black spots ; sides of head black, with a white auricular patch. Wings lengthened.

PHRENOPICUS, Bp.—Back banded transversely with white.

A narrow lateral line of red above the auricular patch.............*P. borealis.*

C. XENOPICUS, Baird.—Entirely black, with white head. Wings lengthened.

A white patch at the base of the longer primaries............*P. albolarvatus.*

The following table will serve to exhibit the comparative measurements of the different species of *Picus* found in the United States.

Comparative measurements of species.

Catal. No.	Species.	Locality.	Sex & age.	Length.	Stretch of wings.	Wing.	Tail.	Tarsus.	Middle toe.	Its claw alone.	Bill above.	Along gape.	Specimen measured.
806	Picus villosus........	Carlisle, Pa......	♀	8.56	......	4.52	3.72	0.88	0.98	0.40	1.18	1.18	Skin......
do	......do..........	......do..........	.....	9.00	15.00	4.16							Fresh......
1562	......do..........	......do..........	○♂	7.04	......	4.24	2.90	0.84	0.88	0.34	1.00	1.00	Skin......
do	......do..........	......do..........	.....	8.50	14.80	4.50							Fresh......
2803	Picus (audubonii)...	Louisiana?	......	7.28	......	4.06	2.78	0.84	0.84	0.34	0.96	0.96	Skin......
2800	Picus (phillipsii)	Massachusetts ...	......	9.28	......	4.66	3.74	0.94	1.00	0.40	1.26	1.30	Skin......
2798	Picus (martinae)....	Canada..........	♂	8.76	......	4.34	3.88	0.86	0.96	0.38	1.12	1.12	Skin......
6079	Picus harrisii	Little Colorado ..	♂	8.72	......	5.10	4.14	0.90	1.00	0.40	1.40	1.40	Skin......
6078	......do..............	New Mexico.....	......	8.20	......	4.86	4.06	0.84	0.84	0.34	1.12	1.14	Skin ......
6087	......do..............	Vancouver	♂	9.28	......	5.00	3.60	0.98	1.04	0.40	1.40	1.40	Skin ......
do	......do..............	......do..........		9.50	16.50								Fresh......
6690	......do......	Steilacoom	♀	8.76	......	5.00	3.64	0.90	0.92	0.49	1.28	1.28	Skin......
876	Picus pubescens.....	Carlisle, Pa.....	♀	6.14	......	3.86	2.88	0.62	0.70	0.30	0.72	0.74	Skin......
do	......do..............	......do..........	......	6.75	12.25	3.75							Fresh......
1291	......do..............	......do..........	♂	6.00	......	3.74	2.74	0.64	0.72	0.28	0.72	0.74	Skin......
do	......do..............	......do..........		6.15	12.25	3.80							Fresh......
3905	Picus gairdneri.......	California	♀	6.00	......	3.74	2.80	0.68	0.74	0.28	0.70	0.70	Skin......
6098	......do..............	Sacramento val...	......	5.74	......	3.68	2.76	0.68	0.62	0.28	0.70	0.72	Skin......
6101	......do..............	Shoalwater bay..	♂	5.86	......	3.86	2.54	0.64	0.74	0.32	0.74	0.76	Skin......
do	......do..............	......do..........		6.75	11.50								Fresh......
1878	Picus borealis.......	Georgia..........	♂	7.20	......	4.56	3.40	0.74	0.84	0.34	0.90	0.98	Skin......
3057	......do......	......do..........	♀	7.92	......	4.70	3.58	0.80	0.88	0.36	0.90	1.00	Skin......
do	......do..............	......do..........		8.00	15.00	4.14							Fresh......
4482	Picus nuttallii.......	Santa Clara, Cal..	......	6.64	......	3.94	3.08	0.70	0.80	0.32	0.98	0.98	Skin...... ...
5400	......do..............	Petaluma........	♀	6.26	......	4.10	2.90	0.72	0.74	0.32	0.90	0.90	Skin......
6105	Picus scalaris........	Texas............	......	6.24	......	3.90	2.74	0.70	0.84	0.34	0.98	1.00	Skin......
9933	......de..............	......do..........	♀	6.20	......	3.78	2.72	0.50	0.50	0.32	0.84	0.86	Skin......
	Picus albolarvatus....	Spokan river.....	♀	8.58	......	5.14	4.24	0.86	0.86	0.40	1.16	1.06	Skin......

PICUS VILLOSUS, Linnæus.

Hairy Woodpecker; Sapsucker*

Variety major.—Northern and Western regions.

? *Picus leucomelas*, BODDAERT, Tabl. Pl. Enl. 1783, (No. 345, f. 1,) (Gray.)
? *Picus canadensis*, GMELIN, Syst. Nat. I, 1788, 437.
    ? LATHAM, Ind. Orn. I, 1790, 231.
    AUD. Orn. Biog. V, 1839, 188; pl. 417.—IB. Syn. 1839, 177.—IB. Birds America, IV, 1842, 235;
        pl. 258.—BONAP. Consp. 1850, 137.—IB. Aten. Ital. 1854, 8.
Picus villosus, FORSTER, Philos. Trans. LXII, 1772, 383.
Picus (Dendrocopus) villosus, Sw. F. Bor. Am. II, 1831, 305.
Picus phillipsii, AUD. Orn. Biog. V, 1839, 186; pl. 417.—IB. Syn. 1839, 177.—IB. Birds Amer. IV, 1842, 238; pl.
    259, (immature, with yellow crown.)—NUTT. Man. I, 2d ed. 1840, 686.
Picus septentrionalis, NUTTALL, Man. I, 2d ed. 1840, 684.

Variety medius.—Middle States.

Picus villosus, LINN. Syst. Nat. I, 1766, 175.—VIEILLOT, Ois. Am. Sept. II, 1807, 64; pl. cxx.—WILSON, Am. Orn.
    I, 1808, 150; pl. ix.—WAGLER, Syst. Av. 1827, No. 22.—AUD. Orn. Biog. V, 1839, 164; pl. 416.—
    IB. Birds Amer. IV, 1842, 244; pl. 262.—BONAP. Conspectus, 1850, 137.
Picus leucomelanus, WAGLER, Syst. Av. 1827, No. 18, (young male in summer.)
Picus martinae, AUD. Orn. Biog. V, 1839, 181; pl. 417.—IB. Syn. 1839, 178.—IB. Birds Amer. IV, 1842, 240; pl.
    260, (young male, with red feathers on crown.)
Picus rubricapillus, NUTT. Man. I, 2d ed. 1840, 685, (same as preceding.)
Hairy woodpecker, PENNANT, LATHAM.

Variety **minor.**—Southern States.

Picus audubonii, SWAINSON, F. B. A. 1831, 306.—TRUDEAU, J. A. N. Sc. Ph. VII, 1837, 404, (very young male, with crown spotted with yellow.)—AUD. Orn. Biog. V, 1839, 194 ; pl. 417.—IB. Birds Amer. IV, 1842, 259 ; pl. 265.—NUTT. Man. I, 2d ed. 1840, 684.

SP. CH.—Above black, with a white band down the middle of the back. All the larger wing coverts and the quills with conspicuous spots of white. Two white stripes on each side of the head ; the upper scarcely confluent behind, the lower not at all so ; two black stripes confluent with the black of the nape. Beneath white. Three outer tail feathers with the exposed portions white. Length 8 to 11 inches.

Male, with a nuchal scarlet crest covering the white, and interrupted in the middle. Immature bird with more or less of the crown spotted with red or yellow, or both.

Hab.—North America, to the eastern base of the Rocky mountains.

In this species the upper parts are of a glossy black ; the feathers on the middle line of the back white, usually with a little black on the outer edge. This white stripe thus produced extends from the upper part of the back to the rump ; the upper tail coverts and tail feathers black. The under parts are nearly pure white. The scapulars are black ; all the exposed larger wing coverts, however, have each a rounded spot of white. The outer webs of all the quills have numerous spots of white, except the first, which is unspotted, and the second, which has only one spot at the base ; the remaining primaries have six each, except the third and the three innermost, which have five. The secondaries have four on their exposed portions. The inner webs of the quills are similarly spotted.

In the male there is a rather narrow nuchal band of scarlet interrupted a little in the middle. This is about a quarter of an inch long ; all the feathers belonging to it, brown at the base, white in the middle, and scarlet at the end. The white is continuous with a broad patch on each side the crown, commencing a little above the anterior canthus of the eye, (rarely continuous with the brownish white bristly feathers at the base of the bill, the shafts of which are tipped with black.) This white stripe then curves around the occiput to the nape (the two almost meeting behind) and is seen through the red. In the female, where the red is wanting, the white is very conspicuous, sometimes appearing almost continuous across the nape. A second white stripe begins at the commissure, and passing a short distance below the eye, down on the side of the neck, widens in curving round on its back and lower part. The two stripes of opposite sides are separated in the lower neck or upper part of the back by a considerable interval of black.

These two white stripes of nearly equal width on the side of the head leave two black ones— the upper one rather wider, the lower narrower than the white. The upper passes from the forehead through the eye, involving considerably more of the lower eyelid than the upper, and widening behind, passes round into the black of the back of the neck. The lower stripe proceeds from the commissure downwards along the side of the throat, and widens considerably on the sides of the lower neck, sending a short branch on to the side of the breast. The sides of the body under the wings are, however, white, as are the under coverts, except a few black blotches.

The three outer tail feathers appear entirely white. There is, however, a very small blotch at the extreme base of the inner web of the first, which in the second is perhaps an inch long, and on the third leaves only an inch of the end white, with an area extending obliquely from this white across the outer web to the base. The other feathers are black.

As already stated, the female differs in the absence of the red crest.

The bill of the young bird differs considerably from that of the adult. Instead of being nearly straight in its upper and lower outlines, with the tip compressed, truncate, and wedge-shaped, it is shorter, sometimes considerably broader, and with the outlines, the upper especially, much curved to a terminal sharp point, instead of wedge. In the immature male ·(and female also, probably) the entire crown from the base of the bill to the occiput, has the feathers sometimes spotted with white, and tipped with orange red or yellow. Sometimes only the posterior half of the crown is so marked, thus indicating a nearer approach to maturity. The peculiar spotting is like that of *Picus scalaris* or *nuttalli*. The white is sometimes almost wanting. The shade of red varies with specimens from carmine to orange yellow, sometimes more decidedly yellow. This is the case in the original of *Picus aududonii* of Trudeau, now before me, (2803,) which, besides this character, has every other feature of a young bird, as shown by the curved broad bill, the loose, woolly texture of the feathers, &c. It is a little smaller than corresponding specimens from Pennsylvania, a difference perfectly intelligible, in view of its more southern locality, (Louisiana.) No. 1562, from Carlisle, however, is scarcely larger.

Specimens vary a little in having the white streak above the eye continuous with the whitish on each side of the base of the bill. The white of the head and under parts is sometimes more extensive, and brighter.

As a general rule the specimens of this species from the far west and north are appreciably larger than those from the more eastern States, in which again southern specimens are considerably smaller. I can detect no other difference, except size, in the *Picus canadensis*, as established by Mr. Audubon. With his typical specimens before me, I find them not even as large as the majority of the western skins; and while Mr. Audubon describes his male *Picus canadensis* as measuring 10.50 inches, the wing 5.08, the tail 3.50, the specimen given in the P. Bor. Amer., from a still more northern locality, measured 11 inches, the wings 5.38, tail 4.25, and in no other way different either from them or Pennsylvania ones. It is to the larger variety from Canada that both *Picus phillipsii* and *Picus martinae* belong. With the original specimens of Mr. Aububon before me, I find every characteristic of the young bird in the soft bones, the woolly, soft feathers of the under parts, &c. In the *"P. phillipsii"* the characters are precisely as in the young males described from Carlisle. The top of the head is irregularly spotted with orange red in one specimen, and orange yellow in the supposed female. In *"Picus martinae,"* again, there is rather more of a dull orange yellow patch on the crown, the feathers, even the black ones, spotted with white, as in 1562 from Carlisle. The immaturity of the red or yellow markings in all these specimens is clearly shown by their lacking the symmetry seen in known adults, the outlines being all irregular and the colors more or less interrupted and unsymmetrical in places. In one specimen from Carlisle, nearly adult, (2423,) the top of the head or crown is spotted with yellow, the occiput with red.

It may be assumed as a general principle, in reference to the black spotted woodpeckers of North America belonging to the restricted genus *Picus*, that whenever the crown is spotted with red or yellow either partly or entirely, the specimen is immature, and may probably be of either sex, while the red is found only in the adult male, and confined to an occipital line. The only exceptions are in *Picus scalaris*, where the entire upper part of the head is red spotted, and *P. nuttallii*, where the posterior half is thus marked. In the young of this last species, however, the anterior half of the head above is similarly spotted with red.

List of specimens.

Catal. No.	Sex and age	Locality.	When collected.	Whence obtained.	Orig'l No.	Collected by—	Length.	Extent.	Wing.	Remarks.
2798	♂	Toronto, C. W......	....	S. F. Baird	......	J. J. Audubon..	....	....	....	Original of *P. martinae*, Aud.
2799	♀ ?	......do	....	......do	......	......do	....	....	....	......do........ do....
2800	....	Massachusetts......	....	......do	......	......do	....	....	....	Original of *P. phillipsii*, Aud.
2794	♀	......do	....	......do	......	......do	....	....	....	Original of *P. canadensis*, Aud.
2793	♂	......do	....	......do	......	......do	....	....	....	....do........ do....
1583	♂	......do	....	......do	......	T. M. Brewer...	....	....	....	....
1612	○	Carlisle, Pa........	June 24, 1844	......do	......	....	9.17	16.50	4.83	....
1764	♀	......do	January, 1845	......do	......	....	9.	14.75	4.67	....
1132	○ ♂	......do	July 22, 1843	......do	......	....	9.	15.	4.58	....
884	♂	......do	Dec. 3, 1842	..... do	......	... .	9.33	15.17	4.42	....
183	○	......do	June 5, 1839	...... do	......	....	......	......	......	....
1606	○ ♀	......do	June 10, 1844	......do	......	....	8.92	14.83	4.67	....
2423		......do	Sept. 3, 1845	......do	......	....	....	....	....	Crown spotted yellow, occiput with red ......
806	♀	....do	Oct. 17, 1842	......do	......	....	9.	15.	4.58	....
1562	○ ♂	......do	May 22, 1844	......do	......	....	8.50	14.83	4.50	Crown, yellow spotted...
2803	○ ♂	Louisiana?.........	....	....	......	....	....	....	....	Original, *P. audubonii*?..
6075	♀	Ft.Leavenworth,K.T.	Nov. 27,1854	Lieut. Couch	13	....	....	....	....	....
5880	♀	Fort Riley, K. T......	——, 1856	Dr. Hammond and J. X. DeVesey.	......	....	....	....	....	....
6551	♀	......do	——, 1857	Dr. W. A. Hammond	......	....	....	....	....	....
6552	♂	......do	....do	......do	......	....	....	....	....	....
4638	♀	Sioux river, N. T.....	May 3, 1856	Lieut. Warren......	......	Dr. Hayden	....	....	....	....
5227		Fort Lookout, N. T...	July, 1856	......do	......	......do	....	....	....	....
5228	....	......do	....do	......do	......	......do	9.25	14.50	5.25	....
5226	....	Powder river, N. T...	Aug. 3, 1856	......do	......	......do	....	....	....	....
8293	♂	Independence, Mo...	May 26,1857	W. M. Magraw	......	Dr. J. G. Cooper	9.00	14.00	4.75	....
8805	♂	Black Hills, Nebraska	Oct. 1,1857	Lieut. Warren......	......	Dr. Hayden	....	16.25	5.25	....
8806	....	......do	Sept. 7,1857	......do	......	...... do	10.00	17.00	5.25	....

PICUS HARRISII, Aud.

Harris' Woodpecker.

Picus harrisii, AUD. Orn. Biog. V, 1839, 191; pl. 417.—IB. Syn. 1839, 178.—IB. Birds America, IV, 1842, 242; pl. 261, (dark-bellied variety.)—NUTTALL, Man. I, 2d ed. 1840, 627.
? *Picus inornatus*, LICHT. (Bon. Consp.)
Picus (Trichopicus) harrisii, BP. Consp. Zyg. Aten. Ital. 1854, 8.

SP. CH.—Size and appearance of *P. villosus*. Above black, a white stripe down the back. The only white spots on the surface of the folded wings, are seen on the outer webs of the primaries and outer secondaries, (none on tertials.) Beneath whitish, with faint streaks on the side of the body. Two white and two black stripes on each side of the head; the latter confluent with the black of the neck, the upper white stripe nearly confluent. Three outer tail feathers with the exposed portions white. Length, 9½ inches; wing, 5 inches. Male, with a nuchal scarlet crest covering the white of the back of the head. Size and general appearance that of the hairy woodpecker, *Picus villosus*.

Hab.—From the Pacific coast to the eastern slope of the Rocky mountains.

Fourth quill longest; fifth but little shorter. Upper parts black; the feathers down the middle of the back brownish white; the outer web mostly black. Rump, upper tail coverts, tail above, scapulars, wing coverts, and tertiary quills black, the larger coverts with only an occasional white spot. The top of the head is black; the bristly feathers at the base of the bill yellowish or brownish white. A white band commencing above the eye and passing round along the side of the head to the nape, where those of opposite sides are confluent, (sometimes interrupted.) In the male there is a scarlet band on the nape about four-tenths of an inch long, formed by tips of this color to the feathers composing the white band. A light stripe starts from the commissure under the eye, and passing downwards, inclines and curves round towards the back of the neck, where, however, those of opposite sides are separated by an interval half the width of the head. A black stripe is encircled between these two white ones, confluent with the black of the nape, and another passes back from the lower mandible along the sides of the throat and neck, diverging below and confluent with black on the upper part of the back. The under parts are smoky brown, with perhaps a lilac tinge. A few feathers on the side of the breast anteriorly are streaked with black, as also are the central lines of a few feathers on the flanks. There are but few spots visible on the wings, these being only seen on the exposed webs of the primary and secondary feathers. The first spurious feather is unspotted; the second has one spot at the base of the outer web, not exposed, and two on the inner; the third has three external and three or four internal; the fourth and fifth four external; the secondaries have about three external. In all the primaries the terminal half of the inner web is unspotted. The three external tail feathers are mostly white, the first entirely so, except at the extreme base; the second black on the basal half; the third with the inner web black, with a terminal spot, and the tip whitish.

In the specimens before me there are apparently two series, one larger, with the white parts throughout tinged with smoke brown; the flanks faintly streaked with black; the white spots on the wings a little smaller. This is most abundant in Washington and Oregon Territories, and is the typical *P. harrisii.* The other has the white quite pure, the spots on the wing larger, the streaks on the feathers less distinct. These are most abundant in southern California and in New Mexico. The specimens before me, however, exhibit every gradation between the two, and I can find no characters to distinguish the species. The color of the white, too, may have something to do with the character of the trees inhabited.

The smallest specimens I have seen are from Fort Thorn, New Mexico. In some specimens the nuchal white and red are more decidedly confluent than in others.

This species represents the *P. villosus* in the west, and closely resembles it. It may, however, be readily distinguished by the much greater predominance of black above. Thus it is only occasionally that a greater wing covert is spotted, instead of having a white spot on every one. The tertiaries, too, are unspotted, and the longest primaries have only four spots externally instead of six. There is less white on the third tail feather. Both have the same tendency to obsolete streaks on the sides of the belly; and the markings about the head appear precisely the same.

The young of this species exhibit the same differences from the adult as described under *P. villosus.* The feathers of the crown almost to the base of the bill, apparently in both sexes, are tipped with scarlet, with a white spot at the base of the red. In this stage of plumage the bird might readily be mistaken for a different species, as has been the case with corresponding stages of *P. villosus.*

List of specimens.

Catal. No.	Sex.	Locality.	When collected.	Whence obtained.	Orig. No.	Collected by—	Length.	Stretch of wings.	Wing.	Remarks.
5960	.....	Whitby's island, W. T ..	April —, 1855	Dr. J. G. Cooper...	......					
6089	♂	Steilacoom, W. T	....	Dr. Suckley........	85					
6090	♀	...... do	....	......do	96					
6091	♀	...... do	Feb. —, 1856	......do	233	....	10.00	15.50		
6092	♂	.... .. do	..... do.....	......do	236	....				
6093	♂	...... do	Mar. —, 1856	......do	245	....				
6094	♀	...... do	May 1, 1856	......do	352		9.00	15.62		
6095	♀	...... do	Mar. —, 1856	......do	280	....				
6084	♀	Spokane river, W. T ...	Oct. 27, 1853	Gov. Stevens	15	Dr. Cooper......				
6085	♂	...... do	Nov. 1, 1853	......do	18	......do				
6087	♂	Vancouver, W. T......	Dec. 10, 1853	......do	6	....	9.50	16.50		Iris brown.........
6086	♂	...... do	July —, 1853	......do		Dr. Cooper				
6088	♂	Shoalwater bay, W. T...	Sept. 9, 1854	Dr. J. G. Cooper ...	92		9.75	16.00		Iris hazel; bill black; feet bluish.
1869	♀	Columbia river...... ..	Sept. 27, 1834	S. F. Baird		J. K. Townsend .				
6083	♀	Fort Dalles, O. T	Sept. —, 1854	Dr. Suckley	144		9.87	16.00	5.00	
4575	♀	...... do	Mar. 10, 1855	......do	149	....	10.00	16.00	5.00	Iris brown..... ...
4597	♀	St. Helens, O. T........	Jan. 27, 1856	......do	202	....				
5498	♀	Petaluma, Cal........	Aug. —, 1856	E. Samuels	......	....				
5961	♂	Santa Clara, Cal	Nov. —, 1855	Dr. J. G. Cooper...	......	....				
6082	♂	Tulare valley, Cal.....	....	Lieut. Williamson..	......	Dr. Heermann ...				
6081	♂	Tejon valley, Cal	....	......do	......	......do				
4589	♂	Santa Isabel, Cal	Nov. 26, 1854	Major Emory......	17	A. Schott........				
6080	♂	...... do.	...... do.......	......do	17	......do				
6079	♂	Little Colorado River, Nebraska............	Dec. 8, 1853	¶Lieut. Whipple	35	Dr. Kennerly				Eyes black ....
5071	♂	Fort Fillmore, Tex.....	Oct. 15, 1855	Captain Pope......	145	....	10.50	15.00	5.00	Eyes black; feet dark gray; gums yellow.
6076	♂	Rio Grande, N. M......	....	Dr. Henry, U. S. A .	......	....				
6077	♀	...... do.......	....	......do	......					
6078	♀	...... do.......	....	......do	......					
8489	♂	Ft. Massachusetts, N. M.	....	Dr. D. C. Peters....	......					

PICUS PUBESCENS, L.

Downy Woodpecker; Sapsucker.

Picus pubescens, L. Syst. Nat. I, 1766, 15.—VIEILLOT, Ois. Am. Sept. II, 1807, 65 ; pl. cxxi.—WILSON, Am. Orn. I, 1808, 153 ; pl. ix.—WAGLER, Syst. Avium, 1827, No. 23.—AUD. Orn. Biog. II, 1834, 81 : V, 539 ; pl. 112.—IB. Birds Am. IV, 1842, 249 ; pl. 263.

Picus (Dendrocopus) pubescens, Sw. F. B. A. II, 1831, 307.

Picus (Trichopicus) pubescens, BONAP. Consp. Zyg. Aten. and Cal. 1854, 8.

? *Picus medianus*, Sw. F. B. A. II, 1831, 308.

Picus meridionalis, Sw. F. B. A. II, 1831, 308. (Small southern race.)

Picus lecontii, JONES, Ann. N. Y. Lyc. IV, 1848, 489 ; pl. xviii. (Georgia. Three toed variety. Type of *Tridactylia*, Bp.)

SP. CH.—A minature of *P. villosus*. Above black, with a white band down the back. Two white stripes on the side of the head ; the lower of opposite sides always separated ; the upper sometimes confluent on the nape. Two stripes of black on the side of the head, the lower not running into the forehead. Beneath white ; wing much spotted with white ; the larger coverts with two series each ; tertiaries or inner secondaries all banded with white. Two outer tail feathers white, with two bands of black at end ; third white at tip and externally. Length about 6¼ inches ; wing 3¾. Male with red, terminating the white feathers on the nape.

Hab.—Eastern United States, towards the eastern slope of the Rocky mountains.

Third and fourth quills equal and longest, second a little shorter, and then the third. Upper parts black, the middle of the back as far as the rump with a broad stripe of white, the feathers

12 b

along the central line being white, more or less edged externally with black. The scapulars are unspotted, but all the greater coverts have about two spots of white, sometimes two on the outer and one on the inner webs. All the quills except the spurious primary are spotted with white on both webs. A series of four white bands is seen over the outer webs of the secondaries when the wing is folded, (one of them at the end.) There is a white band above the eye, and another below, with two black stripes, all much as in *P. villosus*, the black confluent with the black of the neck, the white interrupted behind, the upper white stripe sometimes extending to the whitish feathers of the base of the bill. In the male the posterior portion of the upper white stripe on the occiput is tipped with scarlet, producing a band about a quarter of an inch long. The under parts are dirty white. The black of the neck comes a little forward in front of the wing, producing a black patch on the side of the breast. The first and second tail feathers are white, their extreme base and the two bands near the end black, the anterior of these bands interrupted in the middle, the inner portion wanting in the second. The third feather has the terminal half-inch, and the posterior half of the outer web white, with a round black spot on the inner web, near the end. The fourth feather is black, with a narrow white edge externally towards the end. The female differs in the absence of the red band.

The young male has the entire crown spotted with red of varying tint, which is never perfectly continuous ; the red is sometimes wanting anteriorly, and sometimes the red is also spotted with white. There is usually more or less of obscure black spots or streaks on the under parts. The young also have the same curvature of bill, and other characteristics of immaturity, as described in *P. villosus*.

In some specimens (as in 860) the white stripe above the eye extends forward, and involves the entire space anterior to the eye. There is little difference in the amount of black on the outer tail feathers. Sometimes the white on the side of the crown is confluent behind, as also the crimson in the male ; in others, again, both are distinctly separated by black. One specimen from Ohio (6698) has the bristly feathers of the bill, with the chin and throat, tinged with reddish. Western specimens are not appreciably different.

This species is much smaller than *P. villosus*. The essential differences in coloration are found in the bands of black on the outer tail feathers, and in having two series of white spots on the larger wing coverts, instead of one. There is less black in front of the eye ; in fact, the lower white stripe extends upwards generally to the antero-inferior corner of the eye, so as to cut off the black behind it from that anterior to it. The wing is spotted near its anterior edge, the amount of white proportionally greater.

The *Picus lecontii* of Dr. Jones appears to be precisely like *P. pubescens*, except that it has but three toes. It is very probable that this is merely an accidental feature in one specimen, one toe on each foot not having been developed. Only one specimen of the supposed species has been seen or obtained ; this was taken near the seacoast of Georgia. The size is rather less than specimens of *P. pubescens* from Pennsylvania, as was to be expected, from the more southern habitat. The missing toe is the short inner posterior one.

List of specimens.

Catal. No.	Sex and age.	Locality.	When collected.	Whence obtained.	Orig'l No.	Collected by—	Length.	Extent.	Wing	Remarks.
184	♂	Carlisle, Pennsylvania....	July, 1839	S. F. Baird........			6.50	12.	3.75	
1610	♂	.........do	June 19, 1844	......do			6.67	12.25	3.88	
1291	♂	.........do	Mar. 11, 1844	......do			6.75	12.25	3.75	
876	♀	.........do	Nov. 25, 1842	......do			6.25	11.67	3.67	
860	♂	.........do	Nov. 17, 1842	......do						
1609	♂	.........do	June 18, 1844	......do			6.67	11.75	3.67	
1588	♂	Boston		T. M. Brewer.....						
1584	♂	.........do		......do						
7048	♂	St. Louis, Missouri	May 8, 1857	Lieut. Bryan	42	W. S. Wood......				
6698	♀	Fort Leavenworth, K.T. ..	Nov. 27, 1854	Lieut. Couch......	12					
7049	♀	Salt creek, K.T.	May 29, 1857	Lieut. Bryan......	111	W. S. Wood......				
5878	♂	Fort Riley, K.T.		Dr. Hammond......						
6550	♀	.........do		......do						
4639	♂	Platte river, K.T.	April 26, 1855	Lieut. Warren		Dr. F. V. Hayden..	6.87	11.50	3.62	
4640	♀	.........do	.....do	......do		.........do	6.50	12.25	3.62	
4641	♂	Bonhomme island, N.T..		......do		.........do	6.87	11.75	3.62	Eyes, black.....
8335	♀	Independence, Missouri..	June 8, 1858	W. M. Magraw.....		Dr. J. G. Cooper...	6.50	12.00	3.75	

PICUS GAIRDNERI, Aud.

Gairdner's Woodpecker.

Picus gairdneri, Aud. Orn. Biog. V, 1839, 317.—Ib. Syn. 1839, 180.—Ib. Birds Amer. IV, 1842, 252, (not figured.)
Picus meridionalis, Nutt. Man. I, 2d ed., 1840, 690, (not of Swainson)

Sp. Ch.—Very similar in size and color to *P. pubescens*; darker. Larger wing coverts, and more exposed tertials, either pure black, or with but occasional spots on the outer web in the latter. Back with a white median stripe. Side of head with two white and two black stripes. Two outer tail feathers white, with two bands of black at the end. Length 6¾ inches; wing 3¾, generally rather less. Male with a scarlet occipital band.

Hab.—With *P. harrisii*, from Pacific coast to eastern base of Rocky mountains.

This species, which is about the size of *P. pubescens*, and represents it on the western half of the continent, is very similar in color and pattern of markings, with certain exceptions hereafter to be pointed out. The upper parts are black, with a white stripe down the middle of the back. A white stripe commencing above the eye margins the crown, and passes round on the nape, sometimes apparently confluent. There is a second white stripe from the forehead below the eye and down on the side of the neck. As in *pubescens*, this reaches upwards to the edge of the eye. A distinct white stripe passes from the lower jaw down on the sides of the neck. The under parts are smoky brownish white, with obsolete short streaks and spots on the sides of the body and abdomen. The wing coverts are almost unspotted; sometimes they are perfectly black, at others there is an occasional, mostly concealed spot. The innermost or exposed tertiaries are sometimes perfectly black, (4374,) usually, however, there are a few spots on them. There are five rows on the outer webs of the longer primaries. The two outer tail feathers are white, with the extreme base and two continuous transverse bars at the end black. The third is obliquely white at the tip and along the terminal portion of the outer web. The white tip has a black spot, and there is a round white spot on the inner web anterior to the white tip.

The male has the occiput crimson, this color terminating the white feathers; the color sometimes continuous, sometimes interrupted.

There are the same series in specimens of *Picus gairdneri* that were indicated under *P. harrisii*. Thus the more northern, from Washington Territory and Oregon, have the under parts more brown, with faint black streaks, the white spots above smaller, and less numerous. In specimens from California and further east the white is purer, the spots more conspicuous.

This species differs chiefly from *P. pubescens* in the considerably smaller size of the spots on the wing, and their restricted number. Thus there are none on the wing coverts except very occasionally, chiefly in the concealed portion. The most exposed tertiaries are entirely black, or with one or two spots on the outer webs only, instead of having two or three conspicuous white bands, or double series of spots. The lowermost black stripe on the cheek is generally better defined ; the bristly feathers at the base of the bill browner ; the black bands on the tail feathers more distinct.

A specimen from Sacramento valley, (6098,) labelled *P. meridionalis,* by Dr. Heermann, is exactly intermediate between *P. pubescens* and *gardneri,* with less white on the wing than the one, and more on the other.

The almost perfect parallelism, with appreciable differences, between the markings of the northwestern and southeastern varieties of *Picus harrisii* and *gairdneri,* and their relationship to the eastern *P. villosus* and *pubescens,* is a remarkable fact in American ornithology, and may possibly indicate the necessity either of dividing the dark ones into a Pacific and Rocky mountain series, or of considering all as varieties of two species, a larger and smaller, changing their character with longitudinal distribution. Many other supposed species are involved in the same consideration ; but a larger number of specimens, in better condition than those before me, and from localities of more equable distribution over the continent, will be necessary to settle the question in the present instance.

List of specimens.

Catal. No.	Sex.	Locality.	When collected.	Whence obtained.	Orig. No.	Collected by—	Length.	Stretch of wings.	Wing.	Remarks.
6101	♂	Shoalwater bay, W. T....	Oct. 9, 1854	Dr. Cooper..........	103	Dr. Cooper	6.75	11.50	....	Iris reddish brown
6100	♂	Steilacoom, W. T........	Oct. —, 1855	Dr. Suckley	132	....	....	....	....	....
4574	♂	Fort Dalles, O. T........	Feb. —, 1855	......do	154	....	....	....	....	....
6099	♀	......do........	Nov. 10, 1854	......do	145	....	7.00	12.00	4.00	....
4593	♀	St. Helen's, O. T........	....	......do	207	Dr. Suckley........	7.00	12.37	3.87	....
4594	♀	......do .	....	......do	204	....	6.75	12.12	3.75	....
4595	♂	......do .	Jan. 27, 1856	......do	206	....	6.75	12.12	3.75	....
4596	♀	......do .	....	......do	203	....	6.75	12.12	3.75	....
4598	♂	......do .	Jan. 27, 1856	......do	205	....	6.50	12.00	3.75	....
5499	.....	Petaluma, Cal .	....	E. Samuels........	162	....	....	....	....	....
6098	.....	Sacramento, Cal........	....	Lieut. Williamson..	....	Dr. Heermann.....	....	....	....	*P. meridionalis,* Heermann.....
6097	♂	San Francisco	....	R. D. Cutts.......	......	....	....	....	....	....
3905	♀	California.........	....	Dr. Heermann	......	....	....	....	....	....
3898	♂♀	......do .	....	......do	......	....	....	....	....	....
5622	♀	Laramie river, K. T......	Aug. —, 1856	Lieut. Bryan	209	W. S. Wood.......	6.37	....	4.40	....
8232	.....	Fort Laramie	Oct. 28, 1857	W. M. Magraw	214	Dr. Cooper	7.25	12.75	4.40	....

PICUS NUTTALLI, Gambel.

Nuttall's Woodpecker.

Picus nuttalli, GAMBEL, Pr. A. N. Sc. I, April, 1843, 259, (Los Angeles, Cal.)
Picus scalaris, (WAGL.) GAMBEL, J. A. N. Sc. Ph., 2d ser. I, Dec. 1847, 55 ; pl. 9, f. 2, 3, (not of Wagler.)
Picus wilsonii, MALHERBE, Rev. Zool. 1849, 529.—BONAP. Conspectus, 1850, 138.
Picus (Trichopicus) wilsonii, BONAP. Consp. Zyg. Aten. Ital. 1854, 8.

SP. CH.—Back black, banded transversely with white ; not, however, as far forward as the neck. Crown black, with white spots. Occiput and nape crimson. Tufts of feathers at the base of the bill white. Sides of the head black with two white stripes, one above the eye and passing down on the side of the neck, the other below and interrupted by the black. Under parts smoky yellowish white, spotted on the sides of the head with black. Predominant character of the three outer tail feathers white, with three, two, or one spots on the outer web near the end. Length about 7 inches ; wing, 4½. Female with the top of the head uniform black.

Hab.—Coast region of California.

Third, fourth, and fifth quills nearly equal and longest ; second intermediate between the seventh and eighth. General color above black, barred transversely with white on the back, rump, and flanks ; the upper surface of tail and tail coverts, and a broad patch on the upper part of the back about half an inch long, pure black. The white bands measure about .12ths of an inch, the black about twice as much. The top of the head is black, each feather with a short streak of white ; on the extreme occiput and the nape is a transverse patch of crimson, each feather having a white spot just below the crimson. The crimson patch is usually as far from the base of the bill above, as this is from its point. The sides of the head may be described as black ; a white stripe commences on the upper edge of the eye, and passing backwards margins the crimson, and extends on down the side of the neck to a patch of white, apparently connected with its fellow on the opposite side by white spots. Another narrow white stripe commences at the nostrils, (the bristles of which are whitish,) and passes as far as the occiput, where it ceases in the middle of the black of the cheeks. There are thus two white streaks on the side of the head bordering a black one passing through the eye. The under parts generally are white, with a dirty yellow tinge. The sides of the breast and body are faintly streaked with black ; the flanks barred with the same. The under coverts are barred with black.

The three outer tail feathers are yellowish white, with two or three interrupted bars of black on the posterior fourth. The other feathers are black.

The female has the crown entirely black, without red or white spots. In one specimen only, (4471,) possibly a young male, the black of the crown is spotted with white. In another, (6116,) doubtless a young male, the whole crown is red, spotted with white.

One specimen (5400,) from Petaluma, has the black of the back and sides of the head much more intense, encroaching very greatly on the white markings, which are much reduced. The spots on the sides of the breast are also larger and darker.

Specimens vary a good deal in the length of the wing.

This species has some resemblance to *Picus borealis*, in the transverse white bands on the back and the black spots of the breast. The latter is, however, much larger ; the sides of the head white, with a black stripe from the bill, the crown pure black, with only a slight trace of crimson on the side of the occiput.

The immature bird, apparently of both sexes, has the feathers of the crown tipped with red, as in most young woodpeckers, with or without white at the base of the red. In this stage of plumage it has much resemblance to *Picus scalaris*, but is otherwise distinct. The light yellowish or whitish color of the bristly frontal feathers, in marked contrast with the forehead, instead of a smoky brown, will readily distinguish them, independently of the loose downy texture of the belly feathers, so characteristic of young woodpeckers.

This species was first described by Dr. Gambel as *P. nuttalli,* who subsequently referred it erroneously to *P. scalaris.* It appears to be confined to the region in California west of the coast range, and extending at least as far south as San Diego. In this distribution it rep_ resents the *P. borealis* of the South Atlantic States.

List of specimens.

Catal. No.	Sex.	Locality.	When collected.	Whence obtained.	Collected by—
3337	♂	California	....	Dr. Wilson...............	Dr. Gambel.............
3338	♀	......do	....	......do	....
4482	♂	Santa Clara, Cal...........	Nov. —, 1855	Dr. J. G. Cooper	....
5965	♀	......do...............	......do......	......do...............	....
6116	♂	San Francisco...............	....	R. D. Cutts...............	....
5400	♀	Petaluma, Cal...............	May —, 1856	E. Samuels	....
6117	♀	Bodega, Cal...............	Jan. —, 1855	Lieut. Trowbridge	Mr. Szabo ....
4472	♂	Yreka, Cal...............	Aug. —, 1855	Lieut. Williamson	Dr. Newberry..........
4471	♀	Umpqua river, O. T...........	......do......	......do...............	......do...............

PICUS SCALARIS, Wagler.

Picus scalaris, WAGLER, Isis, 1829, V, 511. (Mexico.)—BONAP. Consp. 1850, 138.
Picus (Dyctiopicus) scalaris, BON. Consp. Zygod. Aten. Ital. 1854, 8.
Picus gracilis, LESS. Rev. Zool. 1839, 90. (Mexico.)
Picus parvus, CABOT, Boston Jour. N. H. V, 1845, 90. (Sisal, Yucatan.)

SP. CH.—Back banded transversely with black and white to the neck. Crown crimson spotted with white, from the bill to the nape ; tuft of feathers at the base of the bill brown. A white stripe above the eye, continued on the side of the neck ; another under the eye, interrupted by the black of the side of the head. Under parts smoky brownish white, spotted on the sides of the breast, and banded on the flank with black. Predominating color of the three outer tail feathers black, with white bands chiefly on the outer webs. Length about 6¼ inches ; wing 4¼. Female without red on the head.

Hab.—Rocky mountains and its slopes, south of 35th parallel, to Yucatan.

This species is among the smallest of all the North American species, and has been but recently introduced into the fauna of the United States. The wings are long, reaching as far as the short feathers of the tail. The third and fourth quills are longest, the second and then the fifth a little shorter. The upper parts generally are black, on the back, rump, and exposed feathers of the wings, banded narrowly and transversely with white; the primaries spotted with the same on both webs. The upper tail coverts and two inner tail feathers on either side are black. The white bands of the back extend all the way up to the neck, without any interscapular interruption. The under parts are of a pale smoky brownish white, almost with a lilac tinge ; on the sides of the breast and belly are a few scattered short, but elongated spots. The posterior part of the sides under the wing and the under tail coverts are obscurely banded transversely with black. The top of the head, extending from the very base of the bill to a short, broad nuchal crest, is crimson in the male, each feather with a white spot between the crimson and the dark brown of the base of the feather. In the female the top of the head is uniformly black, with a tinge of brownish anteriorly. The side of the head is black, with two white stripes, the latter color predominating. One white stripe begins above the eye, and, margining the crown, passes into a white patch on the lower part of the side of the neck. A second stripe begins at the posterior portion of the upper mandible, and, passing backwards under the eye, appears to stop short in the black. The tuft of feathers and bristles over the nostrils, are dirty brown, scarcely different from the feathers of the crown.

The predominant character of all the tail feathers is black, of which color are the bases of all. The outer feather has four white bands on the inner web, and a fifth and sixth basal ones on the outer. The second feather has the same number on the outer web, (six,) besides a white tip, but only three on the inner on the terminal half. The third has five white spots on the outer web, with a trace of a second one at the end of the inner.

There is a little variation in the size of different specimens of this species, but no other of importance. The black spots of the breast are sometimes darker, and more abundant.

This species is closely related to the *Picus nuttalli*, but may be readily distinguished. Both have the back banded transversely with black and white, and the breast spotted, the pattern of stripes on the side of the head similar, &c. The *Picus scalaris* is, however, smaller; the entire top of the head is crimson, instead of the posterior half only; the tufts of feathers at the base of the bill are brown, scarcely different from that which suffuses the forehead, instead of being clear yellowish white in marked contrast. The white bands of the back come up to the neck, instead of ceasing on the upper part of the back. The white of the side of the head is in much greater proportion. The under parts are browner, the spots smaller. The predominating character of the outer tail feathers is black, with six white bands on the outer webs of the first and second, dividing them nearly equally, and five on the third, and four, three, and one band or spot respectively on the inner webs of the first, second, and third. In *P. nuttalli* these feathers are nearly all white; the outer webs of the first, second, and third feathers respectively with three, two, and one black bar towards the end.

This species is confined to the central portions of the western country, from the Rio Grande to the Colorado, southward along the highlands of Mexico to Yucatan.

List of specimens.

Catal. No.	Sex.	Locality.	When collected.	Whence obtained.	Orig. No.	Collected by—	Length.	Stretch of wings.	Wing.	Remarks.
4217	♀	Chihuahua, Mex.........	Oct. 16, 1854	J. Potts......... ..	......	....	6.50	12.00	....	....
6106	♀	Boca Grande, Mex.......	....	Major Emory	35	Dr. Kennerly	6.50	12.00	....	....
6107	♂	Espia, Mex	....	......do............	52	......do............	6.50	13.00	4.00	....
4594	♀	Colorado river, Cal......	....	......do............	40	A. Schott.........	....	....	....	A brown variety.
4605	♂	Gila river, N. M..........	Dec. 24, 1854	......do............	54	......do............	....	....	....	......do.........
6115	♀	Colorado river, Cal.......	Feb. 15, 1854	Lieut. Whipple	165	Dr. Kennerly	6.50	11.50	4.00	....
6108	♂	Rio Grande, Mex........	....	Dr. T. C. Henry ...	.....	....	....	....	....	....
6110	♂	......do .	....	Capt. J. Pope.......	.....	....	....	....	....	....
6114	♂	Rio Grande, Texas.......	....	Major Emory	27	J. H. Clark........	7.25	13.25	4.00	....
6113	♀	San Pedro, Texas........	Sept. 10, 1853	......do............	......	......do............	....	....	....	....
6103	♂	Texas	....	......do............	19	......do............	7.50	13.00	.3.75	....
6104	♀	Texas	....	Lieut. Parke......	......	Dr. Heermann	....	....	....	....
6105	♂	Tamaulipas, Mex........	....	Lieut. Couch.......	......	....	....	....	....	....
4040	♀	New Leon, Mex.........	....	......do...	76	....	6.00	12.00	4.00	Eyes dark purple, bill slate, feet lead color......
4039	♂	New Leon, Mex........	....	......do............	75	....	6.50	12.00	4.00	......do.........

PICUS BOREALIS, Vieill.

Red-cockaded Woodpecker.

Picus borealis, VIEILLOT, Oss. Am. Sept. II, 1807, 66 ; pl. 122.—STEPHENS in Shaw's Gen. Zool. IX, 1817, 174.
Picus querulus, WILSON, Am. Orn. II, 1810, 103 ; pl. xv, f. 1.—WAGLER, Syst. Av. 1827, No. 21.—IB. Isis, 1829, 510.—AUD. Orn. Biog. V, 1839, 12 ; pl. 389.—IB. Birds America, IV, 1842, 254 ; pl. 264.—BP. Consp. 1850, 137.
Picus (Phrenopicus) querulus, BP. Consp. Zyg. Aten. Ital. 1854, 8.
Picus leucotis, ILLIGER, (fide Lichtenstein in letter to Wagler ; perhaps only a catalogue name.)—LICHT. Verzeich. 1823, 12, No. 81.
Picus vieillotii, WAGLER, Syst. Av. 1827, No. 20.

SP. CH.—Fourth quill longest. Upper parts, with top and sides of the head, black. Back, rump, and scapulars banded transversely with white ; webs of quills spotted with white. Bristles of bill, under parts generally, and a silky patch on the side of the head, white. Sides of breast streaked with black. First and second outer tail feathers white, barred with black. Outer web of the third mostly white. A short, very inconspicuous narrow streak of silky scarlet on the side of the head a short distance behind the eye, along the junction of the white and black ; this is wanting in the female. Length about 7¼ inches : wing, 4½.

Hab.—Southern States.

This species is chiefly confined to the southern Atlantic States, being rarely seen as far north as Pennsylvania.

List of specimens.

Catal. No.	Sex.	Locality.	When collected.	Whence obtained.	Collected by—	Length.	Stretch of wings.	Wing.
1878	♀	Southern States		S. F. Baird				
511	♂	do		do				
3057	♀	Liberty county, Ga	1846	do		8.00	15.00	4.58
2392	♀	Savannah, Ga		do	Jos. Leconte			

PICUS ALBOLARVATUS.

White-headed Woodpecker.

Leuconerpes albolarvatus, CASSIN, Pr. A. N. Sc. V, Oct. 1850, 106. California.
Melanerpes albolarvatus, CASSIN, Jour. A. N. Sc, 2d series, II, Jan. 1853, 257 ; pl. 22.—NEWBERRY, Zool. Cal. and Oreg. Route, 9, Rep. P. R. R. VI, 1857.
Leuconerpes albolarvatus, BONAP. Consp. Zyg. At. Ital. 1854, 10.
Picus (Xenopicus) albolarvatus, BAIRD.

SP. CH.—Fourth and fifth quills equal and longest. Entirely bluish black, excepting the head and outer edges, with the entire basal portion, of the primaries, which are white. Length about 9 inches ; wing, 5¼. Male with a narrow line of red on the nape.

Hab.—Cascade mountains of Oregon and southward into California.

This woodpecker is more simple in its colors than any other North American species. The sixth quill is a little shorter than the fifth ; the third again a little less. The second is intermediate between the seventh and eight. There is no white on the first primary, except on the extreme and concealed basal portion. The white on the outer webs does not extend to within an inch of the end. There is no white whatever on the tail. On the side of the head the black of the occiput appears to extend to the eye in an angle: The white of the head scarcely extends down on the neck.

The *P. albolarvatus* was first described by Mr. Cassin from specimens collected in California by J. G. Bell. It is an exceedingly rare species, not more than three or four skins being known to exist in collections.

List of specimens.

Catal. No.	Sex.	Locality.	When collected.	Whence obtained.	Orig. No.	Collected by—
6041	♀ ?	Spokan river, W. T. -----------	Sept. 28, 1853	Gov. Stevens -------	16	Dr. Cooper ------
4474	♀ ?	Cascade mountains, O. T., fifty miles south of Columbia river.	Sept. 28, 1855	Lieut. Williamson---	--------	Dr. Newberry----

PICOIDES, Lacep.

Picoides, LACEP. Mem. Inst. 1799.
Tridactylia, STEPH. Shaw, Gen. Zool. 1815.
Apternus, Sw. F. B. A. II, 1831, 311.

Bill about as long as the head, very much depressed at the base ; the outlines nearly straight ; the lateral ridge at its base much nearer the commissure than the culmen, so as to bring the large rather linear nostrils close to the edge of the commissure. The gonys very long, equal to the distance from the nostrils to the tip of the bill. Feet with only three toes ; the outer lateral a little longer than the inner, but slightly exceeded by the hind toe, which is about equal to the tarsus. Wings very long, reaching beyond the middle of the tail ; 4th and 5th quills longest. Color black, with a broad patch of yellow on the crown ; transversely banded on the sides. Quills with round spots.

The peculiarities of this genus consist in the absence of the inner hind toe and the great depression of the bill.

The American species of *Picoides* (and to a considerable extent the European) agree in being black above and white beneath ; the crown with a square yellow patch ; a white stripe behind the eye, and another from the loral region beneath the eye ; the quills (but not the coverts) spotted with white ; the sides banded transversely with black. The diagnostic characters (including the European species) are as follows :

A. Middle of back not varied with white.
   Back uniformly black..*P. arcticus.*

B. Middle of back varied with white.
   Back with transverse bands of white. White stripes on side of head narrow, inconspicuous. Crissum but slightly banded with black. Two inner tail feathers black ....*P. hirsutus.*
   Back streaked longitudinally with white. Sides banded with black. Crissum pure white. Two inner tail feathers black...*P. dorsalis.*
   Back streaked longitudinally with white, the sides with black. White lines on the side of head very conspicuous. Three inner tail feathers black. Crissum much varied with black ....*P. tridactylus.*

13 b

Comparative measurements of species.

Catal. No.	Species.	Locality.	Sex.	Length.	Extent.	Wing.	Tail.	Tarsus.	Middle toe.	Its claw alone.	Bill above.	Along gape.	Specimen measured.
483	Picoides, arcticus...	Canada............	♂	9.50	....	5.06	3.78	0.96	0.84	0.40	1.34	1.40	Skin.........
6934	.... do.....	Red river, Ark.....	♀	9.20	....	4.84	3.70	0.90	0.92	0.40	1.34	1.34	Skin.........
9972	.... hirsutus..	Hudson's Bay......	♂	7.58	....	4·20	3.50	0.80	0.74	0.40	1.10	1.26	Skin.........
8809	..........dorsalis..	Laramie Peak	♂	6.74	....	4.80	3.50	0.80	0.72	0.42	1.20	1.20	Skin.........
do	.... do.....	.... do.....	......	9.	15.75	5.	....	....	....	....	....	....	Fresh........

PICOIDES ARCTICUS.

Black Backed Three-toed Woodpecker.

Picus (Apternus) arcticus, Sw. F. Bor. Am. II, 1831, 313.
Apternus arcticus, Bp. List, 1838.—IB. Consp. 1850, 139.—NEWBERRY, Zool. Cal. and Oreg. Route, 91; Rep.
   P. R. R. Surv. VI, 1857.
Picus arcticus, AUD. Syn. 1839, 182.—IB. Birds Amer. IV, 1842, 266; pl. 268.—NUTTALL, Man. I, 2d ed ,
   1840, 691.
Picus tridactylus, BON. Am. Orn. II, 1828, 14; pl. xiv, f. 2.—AUD. Orn. Biog. II, 1834, 198; pl. 132.

SP. CH.—Above entirely uniform glossy bluish black; a square patch on the middle of the crown, saffron yellow, and a few white spots on the outer edges of both webs of the primary and secondary quills. Beneath white, on the sides of the breast longitudinally striped, and on the sides of the belly and on the flanks and tibial region banded transversely with black. A narrow concealed white line from the eye a short distance backwards, and a white stripe from the extreme forehead (meeting anteriorly) under the eye, and down the sides of the neck. Bristly feathers of the base of the bill brown. Exposed portion of two outer tail feathers (1st and 2d) white. Female, without yellow on the head.
Length, about 9½ inches; wing, 5; tail, 3.85. Female, without yellow on the head.
Hab.—Northern portions of the United States to the Arctic regions, from the Atlantic to the Pacific.

This species differs from the other American three-toed woodpeckers chiefly in having the back entirely black. The white line from the eye is usually almost imperceptible, if not wanting entirely.

List of specimens.

Catal. No.	Sex.	Locality.	When collected.	Whence obtained.	Orig. No.	Collected by—
4473	-----	Cascade mountains, O. T	Summer of '55.	Lieut. Williamson......	--------	Dr. J. S. Newberry
483	-----	New York................	------------	S. F. Baird	--------	--------------
6934	♀	Selkirk settlement, H. B. T ..	------------	Donald Gunn	--------	--------------
7973	♂	Hudson's bay	------------	J. Gould	84	--------------
7974	♀	......do	------------	....do...............	84 A	--------------

PICOIDES HIRSUTUS.

Banded Three-toed Woodpecker.

Picus hirsutus, VIEILL. Ois. Am. Sept. II, 1807, 68; pl. cxxiv.—WAGLER, Syst. Av. 1827, No. 102, (mixed up with *undulatus.)* AUD. Orn. Biog. V, 1839, 184; pl. 417.—IB. Birds Am. IV, 1842, pl. 269.—NUTT. Man. I, 2d ed. 1840, 622.
Apternus hirsutus, BON. List. 1838.—IB. Consp. 1850, 129.
Picus (Apternus) tridactylus, Sw. F. Bor. Am. II, 1831, 311; pl. lvi.
Apternus americanus, Sw. Class. Birds, II, 1837, 306.

Sp. Ch.—Black above ; the back with transverse bands of white to the rump. A white line from behind the eye, widening on the nape, and a broader one under the eye from the loral region, but not extending on the forehead ; occiput and sides of head uniform black. Quills spotted on both webs with white. Under parts white ; the sides banded transversely with black. Top of the head spotted with white ; the crown of the male with a yellow patch.

Length, about 9 inches ; wing, 4.45 ; tail, 3.35.

Hab.—Arctic regions of North America.

General color black above, white beneath. The crown with a patch of orange yellow forming the tips of the feathers. The entire top of the head spotted with brownish white, which in the colored portion of the crown is at the base of the yellow. There is a narrow line of white (scarcely appreciable) from the upper border of the eye, and another broader one parallel to it from the loral region below the eye, but not extending on the forehead. The frontal bristly feathers are smoky brown or black, much like the forehead. They are very full, reaching over half the culmen. The whole back from near the nape to the rump is distinctly banded transversely with white, and there is a tendency to a white patch on the nape, although the occiput is black. Both webs of all the quills are spotted with white ; the spots on the external webs small and circular, extending to the tips, those on the inner larger and transverse, and more confined to the basal portion. The exposed inner webs of tertials or inner secondaries show these transverse bands quite distinctly. The under parts, as stated, are white ; the sides of the body banded transversely with black to the tail. There are indications of black bands also on the under tail coverts. The two outer tail feathers are white, the bases obliquely black ; the third feather is black, with the tip obliquely white. The remaining feathers are black.

A specimen from New Caledonia, in the collection of the National Institute, differs in having the white stripes on the side of the head more distinct ; the lower one narrow, and not diffused over the side of the lower jaw. In both, there is a distinct maxillary black stripe. In the New Caledonia specimen the outer three tail feathers (including the rudimentary one) are white, banded with black towards the base ; the median ones black, with faint round spots of white.

This species is readily distinguishable from *P. arcticus* by having the back banded transversely with white to the rump, (but exclusive of the tail coverts,) instead of being uniformly black. There is also more of the white spotting on the inner webs of inner secondaries. There is a narrow, scarcely appreciable line of white in both behind the eye, but it extends much further back in *hirsutus*. The lower white stripe is better defined in *arcticus*, and extends forward on the forehead across the bases of the bristly tufts, (but without meeting on the median line.) This character is not appreciable in *hirsutus*.

The female is said to be similar to the male, but wants the yellow patch on the crown, which, however, is spotted with white.

I have not at hand any good specimen of *P. tridactylus* of Europe, and am unable to state with precision in what the distinctions consist. From the indications of descriptions, however, the differences appear to be that in *P. tridactylus* the white stripes on the side of the head are broader, and embrace between them a narrow black malar stripe, instead of being very narrow, inconspicuous, and less distinct behind. The middle of the back is white, and with the sides streaked, not banded, with black ; the under tail coverts are thickly banded with black. There is more black on the tail, the three innermost feathers on either side being entirely black, and the fourth (from inside) with a little white only at the end ; while in *hirsutus* the two inner only are black, the fourth nearly white.

The specimen described was received from Mr. John Gould, and once formed part of the collection of the London Zoological Society; and it is probably the original of the description and figure of Mr. Audubon, his specimens having been borrowed from the society.

It is with great uncertainty that I admit the name of Vieillot as the proper one for this species. His description and figure apply almost equally well to this and the true *P. tridactylus* of Europe. No mention is made of any white on the back, and but for the amount of white on the side of the head the description would answer almost as well to *P. arcticus*. Vieillot evidently considers the bird described as *P. hirsutus* as the only one inhabiting northern Europe and America, and the question can only be settled by knowing exactly what locality furnished the specimen used in his article.

List of specimens.

Catal. No.	Sex.	Locality.	Whence obtained.	Collected by—	Remarks.
7972	♂	Hudson's bay	J. Gould		Supposed type of Audubon's figures.
	♂	New Caledonia	National Institute	Dr. Leib	

PICOIDES DORSALIS, Baird.
Striped Three-toed Woodpecker.

Black above, white beneath. Crown with a patch of yellow. Back streaked longitudinally with white; upper tail covers spotted with the same. Innermost tail feather black; next one with a white spot; third considerably marked with white. Quills spotted with white. Under tail coverts uniform white; sides of body banded transversely with black.

Length 9 inches; wing, 5 inches; tail, 3.55 inches.

Hab.—Laramie peak, Rocky Mountains.

The only specimen of this species which has hitherto fallen under my notice is in very bad condition, having been shot in the moulting season and at the same time much mutilated. There is, however, no doubt of its specific distinction from any other known American species, although it may be difficult to express all its characters.

The upper parts generally are black, but there is a longitudinal stripe of white down the middle of the back as in *Picus villosus* and *pubescens*. This white in the central feathers occupies the whole of the feather beyond the downy base; in the adjacent ones, however, it forms an elongated terminal patch on the end of the inner web, the remainder being black. It is impossible to say how far forward the white extends, but probably as far as the nape. The upper tail coverts have each a white spot at their tips. The wings are black; the quills with a series of small subcircular white spots on the edges of the outer webs to the tips, (six or seven on the primaries.) The inner webs are marked on their edges with larger and more transverse white blotches, commencing at their bases, but not reaching the tips. On the innermost secondaries these bands are very distinct, and the terminal ones extend nearly to the outer edge of the feathers.

There is a patch of gamboge yellow on the crown; the rest of the head is black, with a distinct white stripe beneath the eye from the angle of the mouth, and extending forward across the bases of the bristly nasal tufts. Its backward extension cannot be ascertained, nor whether there is a second white stripe from behind the eye. The bristly feathers of the nostrils are black, somewhat streaked with white; they do not reach to the middle of the culmen.

The under parts are white ; the sides along the wings and under wing coverts banded transversely with black. The under tail coverts are white without any bands. The two outer (stiff) tail feathers are white, the basal portion black. There is a black spot in the white of the inner, and a white one in the black of the second stiff feather. The next feather is black, spotted terminally with white on the edges ; the next black with a single terminal spot. The middle feather entirely black.

This species requires no comparison with *P. arcticus,* which has the entire back uniformly black. It differs from *P. hirsutus* in having the middle of the back streaked longitudinally with white, instead of banded transversely ; the upper tail coverts spotted with white. The white bands on the inner edges of the inner secondaries are broader, and extend nearly to the outer web instead of being confined to the inner. The under tail coverts are pure white instead of banded with black, and the markings of the tail are somewhat different. The size is rather larger ; the bill longer and narrower.

This species differs from *P. tridactylus* of Europe in the pure white under tail coverts, and the more distinctly longitudinal patch of white on the back. The two middle tail feathers on either side only are black, (and, in fact, the second has a white spot,) while the others are much variegated with white. The exposed portions of the outer feathers are entirely white, instead of being conspicuously banded with black. The sides are banded, not streaked, with black.

In the Conspectus Volucrum Zygodactylorum of Bonaparte, mention is made of *Picoides crissoleucos* of Brandt, "*Kamtschatkensis,* Bp.," which may possibly be the present species, especially as it agrees in the white crissum. I have not been able, however, to find the original description, nor have I at present access to the figures of Reichenbach in Icones avium. It is, however, hardly likely that a summer bird, found breeding as far south as the parallel of 42° in the Rocky mountains, should occur also in Kamtschatka.[1]

List of specimens.

Catal. No.	Sex.	Locality.	When collected.	Whence obtained.	Collected by—	Length.	Extent.	Wing.	Remarks.
8809	♂	Laramie Peak	August 25, 1857	Lt. G. K. Warren..	Dr. F. V. Hayden..	9.00	15.75	5.00	Iris, light gray...........

SPHYRAPICUS, Baird.

Pilumnus, Bon. Consp. Zygod. Ateneo Italiano, May, 1854. (*P. thyroideus.*)

Bill as in *Picus,* but the lateral ridge, which is very prominent, running out distinctly to the commissure at about its middle, beyond which the bill is rounded without any angles at all. The culmen and gonys are very nearly straight, but slightly convex, the bill tapering rapidly to a point ; the lateral outline concave to very near the slightly bevelled tip. Outer pair of toes longest ; the hinder exterior rather longest ; the inner posterior toe very short ; less than the inner anterior without its claw. Wings long and pointed ; the fourth longest. Tail feathers very broad, abruptly acuminate, with a very long linear point.

This genus is very remarkable in the prominence of the lateral ridge, and its termination in the middle of the commissure, with the narrowness and low situation of the nostrils. I do not feel exactly satisfied with the position of *P. williamsoni* in the genus, as, although the bill is

---

[1] As these sheets are passing through the press, I find that *P. crissoleucus* has the under parts entirely white, without bands or streaks. The under wing coverts even are white, while in all the other species they are spotted with black. Reichenbach, Handbuch, VI, 1855, 362.

the same, the outer anterior toe appears decidedly longer than the posterior. The specimen is, however, in such a defective state of preservation as to render it almost impossible to ascertain its true characters.

Picus thyroideus, upon which *Pilumnus* was founded, differs a little from *P. varius* in a longer, more attenuated, and slenderer bill; more curved culmen; and less prominent lateral ridge. The outer toes too are more nearly even.

The genus *Pilumnus,* originally established by Bonaparte, is used in the *Crustacea,* and cannot, of course, be again employed. In supplying a new name, I consider the old *Picus varius* as the type instead of *thyroideus,* which may possibly constitute the type of a distinct genus. Reichenbach takes Mr. Cassin quite severely to task for not recognizing a *Colaptes* in his *Picus thyroideus.* There is, however, nothing of the peculiar features of *Colaptes* in the bill, and but little in the coloration. In the latter respect it is more like *Centurus,* but still sufficiently different to justify Bonaparte in combining it with the *Picus varius* and *ruber.*

The species of *Sphyrapicus,* in respect to coloration, are divisible into two sections, the one with *S. varius* as the type, the other embracing only *S. thyroideus.* The following diagnosis will serve readily to distinguish them. All have the central line of the belly yellow, and the upper tail coverts white.

A. No transverse bars on the body. Middle of the back longitudinally spotted with whitish. Upper tail coverts, outer half of middle and greater wing coverts, and line from the nostrils (including the nasal feathers) under the eye, white; middle line of the belly yellow.

Crown red, bordered all around with black. A post-ocular white stripe; chin and throat broadly red; a patch of black on the breast; outer and inner tail feathers varied with white..*S. varius.*

Head, neck, and sides of breast and body black. A post-ocular white stripe; narrow line of chin and throat red. Tail feathers entirely black. Back scarcely spotted..*S. williamsonii.*

Head, neck, and breast red. No post-ocular white stripe. Innermost tail feathers only varied with white...*S. ruber.*

B. Everywhere, except on the head and neck, upper tail coverts and middle line of belly, transversely banded with black and whitish. No white (or red?) on the head.

Head and neck light brown; a large black pectoral patch....................*S. thyroideus.*

Comparative measurements.

Catal. No.	Species.	Locality.	Sex.	Length.	Stretch of wings.	Wing.	Tail.	Tarsus.	Middle toe.	Its claw alone.	Bill above.	Along gape.	Specimen measured.
2107	S. varius	Carlisle, Pa	♀	7.64	....	4.90	3.50	0.80	0.84	0.34	1.00	1.00	Skin ....
do.	......do.........	......do		8.50	14.75	5.00							Fresh ......
782	.....do...	......do		7.44	....	4.86	3.14	0.86	0.80	0.34	1.00	1.04	Skin ....
2076	......do...	......do	♂	7.52	....	4.80	3.24	0.78	0.84	0.32	0.96	1.04	Skin ....
do.	......do...	......do		8.25	15.25	4.84							Fresh ......
6042	......do...	Fort Thorn, N. M....		7.98	....	5.06	3.56	0.90	0.84	0.32	0.94	0.98	Skin ....
5621	.... do...	Medicine Bow, Cr ...		7.40	....	4.78	3.42	0.84	0.86	0.34	0.90	0.96	Skin ....
6038	S. ruber	Sacramento val., Cal.	♂	8.00	....	4.74	3.48	0.80	0.90	0.36	0.96	0.96	Skin ....
3899	......do...	California.		7.98	....	4.86	3.44	0.88	0.88	0.38	1.00	1.06	Skin ....
8804	S. williamsonii	Laramie Peak	♂	7.64	....	4.92	3.76	0.88	0.88	0.30	0.98	0.98	Skin ....
do.	......do.	......do	♂	9.00	15.25	5.00							Fresh ....
9344	......do...	Klamath lake, O. T..	♀	7.60	....	5.24	3.30	0.88	0.82	0.40	1.06	1.04	Skin ....
3903	S. thyroideus	California...........	♀	8.80	....	5.36	4.06	0.84	0.86	0.30	1.20	1.20	Skin ....
8807	......do.	Laramie Peak	♀	7.10	....	4.32	3.44	0.84	0.84	0.34	0.90	0.96	Skin ....
do.	......do.	......do		8.75	15.25	4.50							Fresh ......

SPHYRAPICUS VARIUS, Baird.

Yellow-bellied Woodpecker. '

Picus varius, L. Syst. Nat. I, 1766, 176.—Vieillot, Ois. Am. II, 1807, 63 ; pl. cxviii, cxix.—Wilson, Am. Orn. I, 1808, 147 ; pl. ix, f. 2.—Wagler, Syst. Av. 1827, No. 16.—Aud. Orn. Biog. II, 1834, 519 : V. 537 ; pl. 190.—Ib. Birds Amer. IV, 1842, 263 ; pl. 267.—Bon. List. 1838.—Ib. Consp. 1850, 138.

Picus (Dendrocopus) varius, Sw. F. B. A. II, 1831, 309.

Pilumnus varius, Bon. Consp. Zygod. Aten. Ital. 1854, 8.

?*Picus atrothorax*, Lesson. Traite d'Ornithologie, I, 1831, 229.—Ib. Pucheran, Rev. Zool. VII, 1855, 21. (Refers it to *Picus varius*.)

Yellow-bellied woodpecker, Pennant, Latham.

Sp. Ch.—Fourth quill longest ; third a little shorter ; fourth considerably shorter. General color above black, much variegated with white. Feathers of the back and rump brownish white, spotted with black. Crown scarlet, bordered by black on the sides of the head and nape. A streak from above the eye, and another from the bristles of the bill, passing below the eye, and into the yellowish of the belly, and a stripe along the edges of the wing coverts white. A triangular broad patch of scarlet on the chin, bordered on each side by black stripes from the lower mandible, which meet behind, and extend into a large quadrate spot on the breast. Rest of under parts yellowish white, streaked on the sides with black. Inner web of inner tail feather white, spotted with black. Outer feathers black, edged and spotted with white. Length 8.25 inches ; wing about 4.75 ; tail 3.30. Female with the red of the throat replaced by white. Young male without black on the breast, or red on top of the head.

Hab.—Atlantic ocean to the eastern slopes of Rocky mountains ; Greenland.

Variety *nuchalis*.—The black occipital transverse band succeeded by a nuchal one of scarlet, instead of brownish white (New Mexico).

The brownish white stripes behind the eye are confluent on the nape, and are separated by a black occipital band from the red of the top of head. It then may be traced downwards in two branches over the scapular region, and meeting on the rump. The feathers involved are whitish, with spots and transverse bands of black. The feathers of the middle of the back are somewhat similar, but with more black. The white of the wing coverts is confined to the outermost middle and greater ones. All the quills are spotted with white on the edges of both webs, quite conspicuously so on the inner edges of innermost secondaries. The under tail coverts are whitish, with concealed V-shaped bands of brown. The rump feathers are white, the lateral ones with outer edges marked with black. The three outer tail feathers (not counting the spurious one) are black, terminally edged and spotted with white ; the fourth has a small white spot ; the fifth or innermost is as described. The white cheek stripe extends along the whole neck, and runs into the yellow of the sides and belly.

There is a very curious variety of this species, which I have only seen from the southern Rocky mountains, in which the nuchal brownish white band formed by the confluence of the two post ocular stripes is red, like the crown, and separated from it by the black occipital band. The yellow bordering the black pectoral patch is also tinged with red. I have never seen more than a trace of this in eastern specimens, as in 4632 and 2101. The name of *nuchalis* may be applied to this variety.

There is an occasional variation in the markings of the tail feathers. Thus in No. 782, from Carlisle, the innermost one is entirely black, while in 4631, from the upper Missouri, the outer web of the same feather has nearly, and in 2107, from Carlisle, it has quite, as much white as the inner web. The outer webs do not appear to vary so much.

With the great variations with age and sex exhibited by this species, it is a little remarkable that it has so few synonyms. The *Picus atrothorax* of Lesson, among these, was first shown to belong to *S. varius*, by Pucheran, in his critical studies of the types of French zoologists contained in the Paris Museum of Natural History.

This species is found throughout the eastern portion of North America, from the Atlantic coast to the eastern slope of the Rocky mountains. The Fort Yuma specimen, (6046,) if no mistake has been made in the locality, is the only far western point on record. The variety *nuchalis* has hitherto only been noticed from New Mexico.

List of specimens.

Catal. No.	Sex.	Locality.	When collected.	Whence obtained.	Orig'l No.	Collected by—	Length.	Extent.	Wing.	Remarks.
6935	○	Selkirk settlement, H.B.T.		Donald Gunn						
		Racine, Wis		Dr. Hoy						
1334	♀	Carlisle, Pennsylvania	April 5,1844	S. F. Baird						
2076	♂	...... do	April —, 1845	...... do			8.33	15.33	4.92	
1342	♀	...... do	April 10,1844	...... do			8.25	15.25	4.83	
2598	♀	...... do	May 8,1846	...... do			8.33	15.50	5.	
2107	♀	...... do	April 15,1845	...... do			8.33	15.25	5.	
1332	♂	...... do	May 5,1844	...... do			6.50	14.75	5.	
782	♂	...... do	October 7,1842	...... do			8.25	15.75	5.	
1333	♂	...... do	April 5,1844	...... do			8.67	15.75	5.	
2101	♂	...... do	April 12,1845	...... do						
4635		Mouth of Platte river,N.T.	April 26,1856	Lt. G. K. Warren..	47					
4632	♂	80 mls. ab. Council Bluffs.	April 29,1856	...... do		Dr. Hayden	7.37	14.	4.87	
4631	♀	Big Sioux river, N. T	May 3,1856	...... do		...... do	7.75	13.	4.75	
4633	♀	.... do	...... do	...... do		...... do	8.37	15.25	5.	
4634	♂	...... do	...... do	..... . do		...... do	7.32	14.75	5.	
4636	♂	Above Council Bluffs		...... do		...... do	7.62	14.	5.	
4637		.... do	May 17,—	...... do			7.75	14.	4.75	
5621	♀	Medicine Bow river, K. T.	August 9,1856	Lieut. Bryan	233	W. S. Wood	7.87	13.87	5.	
8807		Laramie Peak	August 24,1857	Lieut. Warren		Dr. Hayden	8.75	15.25	4.50	Iris, light gray.
6042		Mimbres river, New Mex.		Dr.T.C.Henry,U.S.A.						
6046	♀	? Fort Yuma, California ..		Lieut. Williamson.		Dr. Heermann				

SPHYRAPICUS RUBER, Baird.

Red-breasted Woodpecker.

Picus ruber, GM. Syst. Nat. I, 1788, 429.—WAGLER, Syst. Av. 1827, No. 151.—AUD. Orn. Biog. V, 1839, 179 ; pl. 416.—IB. Birds Amer. IV, 1842, 261 ; pl. 266.

Melanerpes ruber, RICH. List, Pr. Br. Assoc. for 1835.—BONAP. List, 1838.—IB. Consp. 1850, 115.

Pilumnus ruber, BON. Consp. Zyg. Aten. Ital. 1854, 8.

Picus flaviventris, VIEILLOT, Ois. Am. Sept. II, 1807, 67.

SP. CH.—Fourth quill longest ; third intermediate between fourth and fifth. Bill brown wax color. Head and neck all round and breast carmine red. Above black, central line of back from nape to rump spotted with whitish ; rump, wing coverts, and inner web of the inner tail feathers white, the latter with a series of round black spots. Belly sulphur yellow, streaked with brown on the sides. Narrow space around and a little in front of the eye black. A narrow yellowish stripe from the nostrils, a short distance below and behind the eye. Length about 8.50 inches ; wing, 5 inches ; tail, 3.40 inches.

Hab.—Pacific slope of the United States.

The red of the breast and belly extends over half the distance from chin to end of lower tail coverts. The tail feathers are immaculate black, except as described. All the wing quills have both webs spotted with white. The white of the upper tail coverts is streaked with black. The white spots on the back are elongated, mostly on the end of the inner webs of the feathers, and are tinged with red.

Specimens vary considerably in size ; one (5959) from Olympia is much larger than the rest, measuring 9½ inches ; the wing over 5 inches. The colors are unusually bright and pure, but no other difference is noticeable.

The 'shade of red sometimes varies to a more purplish tinge. The white on the wing is confined to the outermost middle and greater coverts; the quills spotted on both webs except the innermost and outermost ones. The under wing coverts are white, slightly spotted (not banded) with black.

List of specimens.

Catal. No.	Sex.	Locality.	When collected.	Whence obtained.	Collected by—	Length.	Stretch of wings.	Wing.	Remarks.
5959	.....	Olympia, W. T............	Mar. —, 1855	Dr. J. G. Cooper......	....	......	......	......	....
6040	.....	Shoalwater bay, W. T....	Oct. —, 1854	......do	....	9.25	15.75	5.37	Iris, bill, and feet pale brown ......
2796	♂	Columbia river	Oct. 28, 1835	S. F. Baird	J. K. Townsend......	....	....	......	....
2797	.....	......do	......do.	......do	......do	....	......	......	....
1938	♀	......do	July 8, 1835	......do	......do	....	......	......	....
3896	......	San Francisco, Cal.......	1853.........	Dr. Heermann	....	....	......	......	....
6038	......	Sacramento, Cal.	....	Lieut. Williamson....	Dr. Heermann.. ...	....	......	......	....
6039	.....	......do	....	......do	......do	....	......	......	....

SPHYRAPICUS WILLIAMSONII, Baird.

Williamson's Woodpecker.

Picus williamsonii, NEWBERRY, Zool. California and Oregon Route, 89 : P. R. R. Repts. VI, 1857 ; pl. xxxiv, fig. 1.
Melanerpes rubrigularis, SCLATER, Annals and Mag. N. H. 3d series, I, Feb. 1858, 127.

SP. CH.—Black ; middle line of belly yellow ; central line of chin and throat above red. A large patch on the wing, rump, and upper tail coverts, a line from the forehead beneath the eye, and another from its upper border, white. Tail entirely black. Exposed surface of wing without any white, except on the outer primaries. Female with the chin white instead of red. Length 9 inches ; wing, 5 inches ; tail, 4.70 inches.

Hab.—Rocky mountains to the Cascade mountains.

Head and neck all round, sides of breast and body, upper parts generally, wings, and tail glossy greenish black. A well defined white stripe from the nostrils, (including the bristly nasal feathers,) passing backwards under the eye; another nearly parallel starting at the upper part of the eye, and nearly meeting its fellow on the occiput. Chin and throat red along their central line. A large patch on the wing, including the exposed portions of the middle and greater coverts, white, although the anterior lesser coverts are black. The inner face of the wings is white, banded transversely with white ; the sides of body behind and under tail coverts white, with broadly V-shaped bands of black, which color on the latter occupies the whole central portion of the feathers. Rump and upper tail coverts pure white ; back with a few indistinct and concealed spots of the same. Quills black; the margins of exterior primaries spotted with white, the inner margins only of the remaining quills, with similar but larger and more transverse blotches. Middle of the body, from the breast to the vent, sulphur yellow. Female similar, but with the chin white instead of red.

This beautiful species of woodpecker was first collected by Dr. Newberry, August 23, 1855, on the shores of Klamath lake, southern Oregon. The specimen—a female—was badly shot, and thrown into alcohol, which extracted the yellow color of the belly, leaving it a dull white. In this state it was figured and published in Dr. Newberry's report, in 1857, made to Lieutenant Abbot. A male in good plumage was, however, taken by Dr. Hayden, on the 24th of August, 1857, on Laramie Peak.

14 b

Mr. Thomas Bridges more recently collected a male specimen in northern California, and sent it to London, where it was described by Mr. Sclater, in February, 1858, as quoted above. As Dr. Newberry's report and plate were published in 1857, and the species there named *P. williamsonii* by him, he has, of course, the priority.

This one species is so entirely different from any other American bird as to require no special comparison. It has as yet only been found in the Rocky mountains, about latitude 40°, and westward.

List of specimens.

Catal. No.	Sex.	Locality.	When collected.	Whence obtained.	Collected by—	Length.	Stretch of wings.	Wing.	Remarks.
9344	♀	Shores of Klamath' lake, O. T.	Aug. 23, 1855	Lieut. Williamson..	Dr. J. S. Newberry.				Dried entire from alcohol.
8804	....	Laramie peak	Aug. 24, 1851	Lieut. Warren	Dr. Hayden........	9.00	15.25	5.00	....

SPHYRAPICUS THYROIDEUS, Baird.

Brown-headed Woodpecker.

Picus thyroideus, CASSIN, Pr. A. N. Sc. V, Dec. 1851, 349, (California.)—HEERMANN, J. A. N. Sc. Ph. 2d ser. II, 1853, 270.
Melanerpes thyroideus, CASSIN, Ill. I, 1854, 201 ; pl. xxxii.
Pilumnus thyroideus, BON. Consp. Zygod. Aten. Ital. 1854, 8.
?? *Picus nataliae*, MALHERBE, Cab. Journ. f. Ornith. 1854, 171.

SP. CH.—About the size of *P. varius*. Head dark ashy brown ; rest of body apparently encircled by narrow transverse and continuous bands crossing the wings, of black and brownish white, except a large, round, black patch on the breast ; and the central line of the body from the crest to the vent, which is the color of roll sulphur. No red on the head. Female with rather duller color. Length about 9 inches ; wing, 5 inches ; tail, 4.10 inches.
Hab.—Cascade and Coast ranges of California and Oregon.

This species, but recently added to our *Fauna*, is quite different in its colors from the other North American species. In addition to the characters already assigned, the crown of the head is obscurely streaked or spotted with black. The transverse and well defined narrow bands on the back, breast, and sides of the body are very peculiar. The rump and upper tail coverts are white, with a few spots of black ; the under coverts are barred with black. The tail feathers are black, the inner and outer barred transversely with white on both webs, the shafts, however, entirely black. The quills are all spotted with white on both webs.

The sexes of the specimens collected have not been indicated sufficiently to show whether the absence of red about the head in all of them applies to the male as well as the female.

List of specimens.

Catal. No.	Sex.	Locality.	When collected.	Whence obtained.	Collected by—	Length.	Stretch of wings.	Wing.	Remarks.
3903	♀	California	....	Dr. Heermann					
6047	......	Rio Grande, N. M.......	....	Dr. Henry, U. S. A.....					
8803	♀	Laramie peak	Aug. 24, 1857	Lieut. Warren.........	Dr. Hayden	9.00	19.00	5.25	Iris dark brown..

HYLATOMUS, Baird.

Dryotomus, MALHERBE, Mem. Ac. Metz, 1849, 322. (Not of Swainson, 1831.)
Dryopicus, BONAP. Consp. Zygod. in Aten. Ital. May, 1854. (Not of Malherbe.)

Bill a little longer that the head ; considerably depressed, or broader than high at the base. Shaped much as in *Campephilus*, except shorter, and without the bristly feathers directed forwards at the base of the lower jaw. Gonys about half the length of the commissure. Tarsus shorter than any toe, except the inner posterior. Outer posterior toe shorter than the outer anterior, and a little longer than the inner anterior. Inner posterior very short ; not half the outer anterior ; about half the inner anterior one.

Tail long, graduated ; the longer feathers much incurved at the tip. Wing longer than the tail, reaching to the middle of the exposed surface of tail ; considerably graduated, though pointed ; the fourth and fifth quills longest.
Color uniform black, with white patches on the side of the head. Head with pointed crest.

This genus is very similar to *Campephilus*, but differs chiefly in the less development of the outer hind toe, which is about exactly intermediate between the outer and inner anterior, the outer largest ; instead of being longest, and having the outer anterior intermediate between it and the inner. The bill is shorter ; the gonys fully half the length of the commissure.

HYLATOMUS PILEATUS, Baird.

Black Wood Cock; Log Cock.

Picus pileatus, LINN. Syst. Nat. I, 1766, 173.—VIEILLOT, Ois. Am. Sept. II, 1807, 58 ; pl. cx.—WILSON, Am. Orn. IV, 1811, 27 ; pl. xxix, f. 2.—WAGLER, Syst. Av. 1827, No. 2.—AUD. Orn. Biog. II, 1834, 74 : V, 533 ; pl. 111.—IB. Birds Amer. IV, 1842, 266 ; pl. 257.
Picus (Dryotomus) pileatus, SW. F. Bor. Am. II, 1831, 304.
Dryotomus pileatus, BP. List. 1838.
Dryocopus pileatus, BONAP. Consp. Av. 1850, 132.
Dryopicus pileatus, BON. Consp. Zyg. Aten. Ital. 1854, 8.
Pileated woodpecker, PENNANT.—LATHAM.

SP. CH.—Fourth and fifth quills equal and longest ; third intermediate between sixth and seventh. Bill blue black. General color of body, wings, and tail dull greenish black. A narrow white streak from just above the eye to the occiput ; a wider one from the nostril feathers (inclusive) under the eye and along the side of the head and neck ; sides of the breast, (concealed by the wing,) axillaries, and under wing coverts, and concealed bases of all the quills, with chin and beneath the head, white, tinged with sulphur yellow. Entire crown from the base of the bill to a well developed occipital crest, as also a patch on the ramus of the lower jaw, scarlet red. A few faint white crescents on the sides of the body and on the abdomen. Length, about 18 inches ; wing, 9½.
Female without the red on the cheek, and the anterior half of that on the top of the head replaced by black.
Hab.—North America from Atlantic to Pacific.

Specimens of this species from the southern States are considerably smaller than Pennsylvania and Oregon ones. The wing of a male (4925) from the St. John's river, Florida, is nearly an inch shorter than the northern average. There is no appreciable difference in western and eastern ones.

List of specimens.

Catal. No.	Sex.	Locality.	When collected.	Whence obtained.	Orig. No.	Collected by—	Length.	Stretch of wings.	Wing.	Remarks.
6931	......	Nelson river, H. B. T.....	....	Donald Gunn........	......	John Isbister	....	....	....	....
174	♂	Carlisle, Pa.............	May —, 1839	S. F. Baird	......	....	17.67	28.83	9.25	....
1723	♀	.....do	Oct. 26, 1844	.....do	......	....	17.50	24.00	8.50	....
4925	♂	St. John's river, Fla......	....	G. Würdemann	......	....	....	....	....	....
		Union county, Ill	....	R. Kennicott.......	......	....	....	....	....	....
5600	♂	Kansas.....	....	Lieut. Bryan	......	W. S. Wood....	....	....	....	....
8379	♂	Independence, Mo.......	June 20, 1857	W. M. Magraw......	......	Dr. Cooper..........	18.00	28.00	9.25	Iris yellow...
6132	♂	Rio Grande, N. M........	....	Dr. Henry, U. S. A...	......	....	....	....	....	....
4792	♂	Columbia river..........	May 9, 1835	S. F. Baird.........	95	J. K. Townsend	....	....	....	....
6130	♀	Fort Steilacoom, W. T ...	April —, 1854	Gov. Stevens........	57	Dr. Suckley..	....	....	....	....
6131	♂	.....do ;	May —, 1855	Dr. Suckley.........	381	....	18.00	29.00	....	....

Section Centureae.

The United States genera of this section are very similar to each other, and may be most easily distinguished by color, as follows :

CENTURUS.—Back and wings banded transversely with black and white. Crown more or less red ; rest of head with under parts greyish, and with red or yellow tinge on the middle of the abdomen. Rump white.

MELANERPES.—Upper parts uniform black, without bands, with or without a white rump ; variable beneath, but without transverse bands.

CENTURUS, S w a i n s o n.

Centurus, Sw. Class. Birds, II, 1837, 310, (type *C. carolinus.*)
Zebrapicus, MALH. Mem. Acad. Metz, 1849, 360, (type *C. carolinus.*)

Bill about the length of the head, or a little longer ; decidedly compressed, except at the extreme base. A lateral ridge starting a little below the culmen at the base of the bill, and angular for half the length of the bill, then becoming obsolete, though traceable nearly to the tip. Culmen considerably curved from the base ; gonys nearly straight. Nostrils very broad, elliptical ; situated about midway on the side of the mandible, near the base ; partly concealed. Outer pairs of toes unequal ; the anterior toe longest. Wings long, broad ; third to fifth primaries equal and longest. Tail feathers rather narrow, stiffened.

The species are all banded above transversely with black and white. The rump white. The head and under parts are brown. The belly with a red or yellow tinge.

The species of *Centurus* may be arranged as follows :
A. Middle of belly red.
>   Crown, nape, and behind the auriculars red. Forehead white, tinged with red. *C. carolinus.*
B. Middle of belly yellow ; a square patch of red in the middle of the crown.
>   Forehead yellow ; nuchal collar orange yellow ; a white band between the red of the crown and the yellow front. Rump white. Middle tail feathers black.—*C. flaviventris.*
>   Entire upper parts of head and nape light brownish, except on the crown ; forehead rather purer. Rump banded with black. Middle tail feathers varied with white and black.. ....*C. uropygialis.*

Comparative measurements.

Catal. No.	Species.	Locality.	Sex.	Length.	Stretch of wings.	Wing.	Tail.	Tarsus.	Middle toe.	Its claw alone.	Bill above.	Along gape.	Specimen measured.
865	Centurus carolinus...	Carlisle, Pa........	♂	8.84	....	5.20	3.74	0.84	0.94	0.44	1.26	1.34	Skin ....
do.	........do	........do	.....	9.75	17.00	5.18							Fresh ......
6118	........do	Leavenworth	♀	8.60	....	5.00	3.70	0.80	0.94	0.44	1.16	1.20	Skin ....
6121	Centurus flaviventris.	San Antonio, Tex..	♂	9.14	....	5.24	3.56	0.90	1.00	0.42	1.44	1.46	Skin ....
9085	........do	Mexico...........	♀	9.00	....	5.02	3.52	0.90	1.04	0.42	1.30	1.32	Skin ....
6124	........do	Ringgold Barracks..	......	8.22	... .	5.00	3.20	0.94	1.02	0.38	1.26	1.32	Skin ....
4036	........do	Matamoras, Mex....	♀	8.90	....	5.12	3.38	0.88	0.94	0.38	1.30	1.32	Skin ....
do.	........do	........do	.....	9.00	15.50	5.00	....	....	....	....	....	....	Fresh ....
1256	Centurus flaviventris	........do	♀	9.20	....	5,40	3.76	0.80	1.08	0.40	1.22	1.30	Skin ....
6129	Centurus uropygialis.	Gila river........	.....	8.16	....	4.82	3.66	0.80	0.99	0.34	1.14	1.14	Skin ....
4568	........do	........do	.....	8.50	....	4.90	3.54	0.88	0.94	0.40	1.18	.1.18	Skin ....
6128	........do	........do	♂	8.84	....	5.20	3.78	0.82	1.04	0.40	.1.30	1.32	Skin ....
9087	Centurus striatus	St. Domingo.......	♂	10.08	....	5.08	4.10	1.00	1.10	0.36	1.40	1.46	Skin ....
9086	........do	........do	♀	9.64	....	4.84	4.00	0.90	0.90	0.42	1.10	1.10	Skin ....
9082	Centurus radiolatus ..	Jamaica	.....	9.08	....	4.70	3.72	0.90	1.12	0.40	1.40	1.40	Skin ....

CENTURUS CAROLINUS, Bon.

Red-bellied Woodpecker.

Picus carolinus, Linn. Syst. Nat. I, 1766, 174.—Wilson, Am. Orn. I, 1808, 113 ; pl. vii, f. 2.—Aud. Orn. Biog.
V, 1839, 169 ; pl. 415.—Ib. Birds Amer. IV, 1842, 270 ; pl. 270.
Centurus carolinus, Sw. Bp. List, 1838.—Ib. Conspectus, av. 1850, 119.
Centurus carolinensis, Sw. Birds, II, 1837, 310 ; (error.)
Picus griseus, Vieill. Ois. Am. Sept. II, 1807, 52 ; pl. cxvi.
? Picus erythrauchen, Wagler, Syst. Avium, 1827
Picus zebra, Boddært, Tabl. pl. enl. (Gray, genera.)

Sp. Ch.—Third, fourth, and fifth quills nearly equal, and longest ; second and seventh about equal. Top of the head and nape crimson red. Forehead whitish, strongly tinged with light red, a shade of which is also seen on the cheek, still stronger on the middle of the belly. Under parts brownish white, with a faint wash of yellowish on the belly. Back, rump, and wing coverts banded black and white ; upper tail covert white, with occasional blotches. Tail feathers black ; first transversely banded with white ; second less so ; all the rest with whitish tips. Inner feathers banded with white on the inner web ; the outer web with a stripe of white along the middle. Length 9¾ inches ; wing about 5.

Female with the crown ashy ; forehead pale red ; nape bright red.

Hab.—North America, from Atlantic coast to the eastern slope of the Rocky mountains.

The quills are all tipped and edged with white, and have a white spot near their base. The white bands on the back are about one-tenth of an inch wide ; the black nearly twice as large. The under tail coverts are white, streaked with black. The red of the crown becomes rather lighter on the nape, where there is sometimes a slight indication of yellowish.

Specimens vary in the depth of color of the red on the belly and its extent. The chin is sometimes tinged with red.

A specimen from Fort Thorn does not differ appreciably, except in being a little smaller, and the belly of rather a brighter red. All the western I have seen have the belly more red than eastern ones.

I do not find any difference in eastern and Missouri specimens, except that none before me from Pennsylvania show so much red as do western ones.

A skin from Amelia island, (4924) Florida, is considerably smaller than more northern ones, the wing measuring barely 5 inches. It differs a little in having the white bands above narrower than usual, the black ones being at least three times the white instead of only twice. I am unable to detect any other difference however. Occasionally the breast is tinged with reddish.

Centurus subelegans, a small species of red bellied woodpecker from Mexico and Lower California, (1257) is quite a miniature of *C. carolinus*, the wing measuring only 4½ inches, the body about 8. The band across the base of the bill is of a purer white ; the white bands of the back narrower ; the rump and upper tail coverts more spotted ; the white stripe on the outer web of the inner tail feather broken up into blotches. The tibial feathers and under tail coverts are strongly banded transversely. The fourth quill is longest ; the third and fifth a little shorter.

List of specimens.

Catal. No.	Sex and age.	Locality.	When collect-ed.	Whence obtained.	Orig'l No.	Collected by—	Length.	Extent.	Wing.	Remarks.
865	♂	Carlisle, Pennsylvania..	Nov. 22,1842	S. F. Baird........		....	9.75	17.	5.17	....
813	♀	........do.............	Oct. 19,1842	........do........		....	9.67	17.	5.33	....
2362	○ ♂	........do.............	July 4,1845	........do........		....	10.25	17.	5.33	....
2802	....	Location unknown......	....	J. J. Audubon.....		....	......	......	......	....
2801	♂	........do...........	....	........do........		....	......	......	......	....
6528	♂	Indian Key, Fla........	— —,1857	G. Wurdemann.....		....	......	......	......	....
4924	....	Amelia Island, Fla.....	....	........do........		....	9.	16.	......	....
7050	....	St. Louis, Mo..........	May 13,1857	Lieut. Bryan.......	71	W. S. Wood.....	......	......	......	....
6118	♀	Ft. Leavenworth,K. T..	Oct. 21,1854	Lieut. Couch......	1	....	......	......	......	....
4623	♂	St. Josephs, Mo........	April 22,1856	Lieut. Warren.....	7	Lieut. Warren...	......	16.50	5.62	Eyes, brownish red.
8290	....	Independence, Mo.....	May 26,1856	W. M. Magraw	3	Dr. J. G. Cooper..	10.75	17.25	5.50	Iris, red..........
8289	♂	........do.............	........do.......	........do........	2	........do.......	10.	15.50	5.25	....do ....
4624	♂	Nemaha Reserve,N. T.	April 23,1856	Lieut. Warren.....	23	Dr. Hayden......	......	......	......	....
5884	....	Fort Riley, K. T.......	— —,1856	Dr. Hammond	.. ....	Mr. De Vesey....	......	......	......	....
5885	....	........do.............	........do.......	........do........		........do.......	......	......	......	....
5620	....	........do.............	June 13,1856	Lieut. Bryan	9	W. S. Wood	......	......	......	....
4621	♂	Platte river, N. T......	April 26,1856	........do........	43	Dr. Hayden	10.12	15.75	5.25	....
4622	♀	........do.............	........do.......	........do........	50	........do.......	8.87	16.	5.12	....
6119	....	Rio Grande, New Mex..	....	Dr. Henry, U. S. A.		....	......	......	......	....
6120	....	Near 32° latitude.......	....	Captain Pope......		....	......	......	......	....

CENTURUS FLAVIVENTRIS, Swainson.

Yellow-bellied Woodpecker.

Centurus flaviventris, SWAINSON, Anim. in Menag., 1838, (2½ centenaries) 354.
Centurus elegans, LAWRENCE, Ann. N. Y. Lyc. V, May, 1851, 116.
Centurus santacruzii, LAWRENCE, Ann. N. Y. Lyc. V, 1851, 123, (not of Bonap.)

SP. CH.—Fourth and fifth quills nearly equal ; third a little shorter ; longer than the fourth. Back banded transversely with black and white ; rump and upper tail coverts pure white. Crown with a sub-quadrate spot of crimson, about half an inch wide and long, and separated from the gamboge yellow at the base of the bill by dirty white ; from the orbit and occiput by brownish ash. Nape half way round the neck orange yellow. Under part generally, and sides of head dirty white. Middle of belly gamboge yellow. Tail feathers all entirely black, except the outer, which has some obscure bars of white. Length about 9½ inches ; wing 5.

Female without the red of the crown.

Hab.—Rio Grande region of the United States, south into Mexico.

This species is nearly as large as the *C. carolinus*, although differing appreciably in the color of the crown and nape, the yellow nape, yellow belly, immaculate inner tail feathers, &c. The bands on the back are of the same size and general character as in *C. carolinus* ; the back has, however, a brownish yellow wash. The orange yellow of the nape is about half an inch long. Along the base of the upper mandible the color is gamboge yellow. The under tail coverts are white with V shaped marks of black.

In the young male the occiput as well as nape are gamboge yellow ; the feathers of the under parts faintly streaked with black. The iris is red.

Specimens of a Lower California or Mexican *Centurus*, in the Smithsonian collection, at one time supposed to be *C. flaviventris*, have the wing considerably longer, (5½ inches) ; the fourth and fifth quills longest ; the third but little less. The white transverse marks on the back are much narrower. The entire crown is crimson red, bordered laterally and behind with orange yellow ; the white band separating the red of the crown from the yellow of the bill is purer and better defined. The white of the under parts is of a more smoky tinge, with a general yellowish shade. The gamboge of the abdomen is darker. The tibia is finely barred transversely with black. The rump and upper coverts are white, the inner web of the inner feather barred with white. The female is similar, but lacks the anterior half of the crimson of the crown.

A skin (No. 9085) labelled *Centurus hypopolius*, (Wagl.) by Verreaux, agrees perfectly with the present species. It is, however, very distinct from the true *hypopolius* of Wagler in the original description in Isis.

List of specimens.

Catal. No.	Sex.	Locality.	When collected.	Whence obtained.	Collected by—	Length.	Stretch of wings.	Wing.	Remarks.
6121	♂	San Antonio, Texas......	....	Lieut. J. G. Parke....	Dr. Heermann.......	....	....	....	....
3708	......	Western Texas	....	J. W. Audubon.......	.,.................	....	......	......	....
6125	......	Eagle Pass Tex.........	....	Major Emory,.,......	A. Schott...........	....	....	....	....
6126	......	......do ....·...........	....	......do...............	......do....	....	....	....	....
6122	......	Ringgold barracks.......	....	......do...............	J. H. Clarke........	10.25	17.50	5.50	....
6123	......	......do	July 5, 1853	......do...............	......do	....	....	....	....
6124	......	......do	July 15, 1853	......do.	......do	....	....	....	....
4036	♂	Matamoras, Mexico......	Mar. 1, 1853	Lieut. Couch.........	. ...	9.00	15.50	5.00	Eyes red, bill dark slate, legs lead color.
4037	♀	......do	....	......do.	....	9.50	16.50	5.00	......do ... .
9085	......	Mexico..................	....	Verreaux...........	....	....	.. ..	....	....

CENTURUS UROPYGIALIS, Baird.

Gila Woodpecker.

Centurus uropygialis, BAIRD, Pr. A. N. Sc. Ph. VII, June, 1854, 120. (Bill Williams' river, N. M.)
Centurus hypopolius, (Bp.) PUCHERAN, Rev. et Mag. 1853, 163. (Not *Picus* (*Centurus*) *hypopolius*, Wagler.)
Zebrapicus kaupii, MALHERBE, 1855?—(Sclater in letter.)
Centurus sulfureiventer, REICHENBACH, Handbuch, vi, Picinae, Oct. 1854, 410, figs. 4411, 4412.

SP. CH.—Third, fourth, and fifth quills longest, and about equal. Back, rump, and upper tail coverts transversely barred with black and white, purest on the two latter. Head and neck all round pale dirty brown, or brownish ash, darkest above. A small sub-quadrate patch of red on the middle of the crown, separated from the bill by dirty white. Middle of the abdomen gamboge yellow ; under tail coverts and anal region strongly barred with black. First and second outer tail feathers banded black and white, as is also the inner web of the inner tail feather ; the outer web of the latter with a white stripe. Length, about 9 inches ; wing, 5.

Female with the head uniform brownish ash, without any red or yellow.

Hab.—Lower Colorado river of the West.

This very distinct species combines the peculiar characteristics of both *C. carolinus* and *flaviventris*. The tail is marked almost precisely like the former, except that the first and second outer feathers are banded across with black and white, instead of this being confined to the outer, and less distinct. It differs in the yellow belly and restricted small patch on the crown. It agrees with *flaviventris* in the color of the abdomen and in the small quadrate patch of red on the crown ; it differs, however, in lacking the orange yellow patch on the nape and the gamboge band before the eyes. The rump and upper coverts are banded white and black, not pure white ; the innermost tail feather is banded and streaked with white, not uniform black. The region about the thighs and arms is much more strongly barred. The head and under parts are more smoky brown in tinge. The bill is considerably more slender.

Specimens do not vary much. Sometimes there is a smoky brown wash on the back. In one female from the Gila river the head is considerably lighter, with a tinge of yellow.

I am informed by Mr. Sclater, by letter, that Malherbe has recently described this species as *Zebrapicus kaupi*. I have not been able to find this description, but it is subsequent to my own. It is again indicated by Pucheran as *Centurus hypopolius* of Wagler ; but a comparison with the description in Isis shows that this is not the case, as there is nothing corresponding to the black superciliary streak there indicated.

List of specimens.

Catal. No.	Sex and age.	Locality.	When collected.	Whence obtained.	Orign'l No.	Collected by—	Length.	Remarks.
------	♂	Bill Williams' Fork, N. M	Feb. 16, 1854	Lt. Whipple---	171	Dr. Kennerly----	9. 50	----------
------	○ ♀	----------do----------	Feb. 13, 1854	-- ----do------	99	Möllhausen -----	9. 50	Eyes, black..
6127	♂	Gila river-----do------	------------	Lt. Parke-----	------	Dr. Heermann---	--------	Eyes, brown.
4568	♀	----do--------do------	------------	Maj. Emory---	22	A. Schott-------	--------	----------
6129	♀	Gila river, Fort Yuma--	------------	------do------	------	------do--------	--------	----------

MELANERPES, Swainson.

Melanerpes, SWAINSON, F. B. A. II, 1831, (type *M. erythrocephalus*.)
Melampicos, (section 3,) MALHERBE, Mem. Ac. Metz, 1849, 365.

Bill about equal to the head ; broader than high at the base, but becoming compressed immediately anterior to the commencement of the gonys. Culmen and gonys with a moderately decided angular ridge ; both decidedly curved from the very base. A rather prominent acute ridge commences at the base of the mandible, a little below the ridge of the culmen, and proceeds but a short distance anterior to the nostrils, (about one-third of the way,) when it sinks down, and the bill is then smooth. The lateral outlines are gently concave from the basal two thirds ; then gently convex to the tip, which does not exhibit any abrupt bevelling. Nostrils open, broadly oval ; not concealed by the feathers, nor entirely basal. The outer pair of toes equal. Wings long, broad ; third and fourth quills longest. Tail feathers broad.

The species all have the back black, without any spots or streaks anywhere.

The species of *Melanerpes* found in the United States all differ from each other very much in color—thus, while the *M. torquatus* has a much more compressed and curved bill than *M. erythrocephalus*, the wings are much longer, reaching to within half an inch of the end of the tail ; the entire under plumage has the fibrils stiffened and separated, except at the base—a feature I have never seen in other species. *M. formicivorus* agrees again with *torquatus* in length of wing, but the bill is even stouter than that of *erythrocephalus*.

The species may be distinguished as follows :

Head and neck all round red ; rump and belly white ; a broad white band across the middle of the wing.................................... ....*M. erythrocephalus*.

Crown red. Forehead and rump white. No white on the wings. Sides of head, chin, and a broad pectoral band black. A collar on the throat, passing up in front of the eyes into the frontal band white, tinged with sulphur yellow.. ....*M. formicivorus*.

Above greenish black. Forepart and sides of the head, with belly, red ; breast hoary gray, extending round on the back of the neck........................ ....*M. torquatus*.

Comparative measurements of species.

Catal. No.	Species.	Locality.	Sex.	Length.	Stretch of wings.	Wing.	Tail.	Tarsus.	Middle toe.	Its claw alone.	Bill above.	Along gape.	Specimen measured.
883	Melanerpes erythrocephalus.	Carlisle........	♀	8.62	....	5.54	3 68	0.84	0.90	0.38	1.12	1.14	Skin .....
do.	...........do	....do	......	9.15	17.50	5.50	....	....	....	....	....	......	Fresh'....
5615	..........do	Fort Riley	♂	9.46	....	5.64	3.58	0.94	1.00	0.34	1.20	1.20	Skin .....:
6150	Melanerpes formicivorus...	California	♀	8.52	....	5.48	3.64	0.90	0.94	0.34	1.19	1.19	Skin .....
5495	....do	Petaluma......	♂	8.60	....	5.70	4.10	0.88	0.98	0.38	1.22	1.24	Skin .....
6138	Melanerpes torquatus	Tulare valley ..	♂	9.48	....	6.72	4.52	0.96	1.02	0.40	1.20	1.28	Skin .....
3934	..........do	California	♀	10.00	....	6.64	4.68	0.98	1.10	0.42	1.16	1.22	Skin .....

MELANERPES ERYTHROCEPHALUS, Swainson.

Red headed Woodpecker.

Picus erythrocephalus, LINN. Syst. Nat. I, 1766, 174.—VIEILLOT, Ois. Am. Sept. II, 1807, 60 ; pl. cxii, cxiii.—
    WILSON, Am. Orn. I, 1810, 142 ; pl. ix, fig. 1.—WAGLER, Syst. Av. 1827, No. 14.—IB. Isis,
    1829, 518, (young.)—AUD. Orn. Biog. I, 1832, 141 : V, 536, pl 27.—IB. Birds America,
    IV, 1842, 274 ; pl. 271.
Melanerpes erythrocephalus, Sw. F. B. A. II, 1831, 316.—BON. List, 1838.—IB. Conspectus, 1850, 115.—GAMBEL, J.
    Ac. Nat. Sc. Ph. 2d ser. I, 1847, 55.

Picus obscurus, GM. I, 1788, 429, (young.)
Red-headed woodpecker, PENNANT, KALM, LATHAM.
White-rumped woodpecker, LATHAM.

SP. CH.—Head and neck all round crimson red, margined by a narrow crescent of black on the upper part of the breast.
Back, primary quills, and tail bluish black. Under parts generally, a broad band across the middle of the wing, and the rump
white. The female is not different. Length about 9¾ inches ; wing, 5½.

Hab.—North America, from the Atlantic coast to the eastern slope of the Rocky mountains. (Coast of California, Gambel.)

The crimson feathers on the head and neck all round have the same bristly texture as
described under *M. torquatus*. The red descends much lower below than above ; its posterior
outline well defined and semi-circular. The white on the wing involves the whole of the
secondaries and tertiaries, except the extreme base ; the shafts are black. There is a yellowish
tinge to the white on the middle of the belly, and the exterior tail feathers are tipped with
whitish. The inside of the wing is white.

I can detect no difference in western specimens. Occasionally the secondaries and tertiaries are
blotched or barred with black near the end, (587.) Immature specimens almost always have this
character. The young lack the red of the head, which is replaced by brown obscurely spotted
and streaked. Dr. Gambel speaks of this species as common in oak timber near the Mission
of San Gabriel, California, but none have been noticed west of the mountains by any one else.

15 b

List of specimens.

Catal. No.	Sex.	Locality.	When collected.	Whence obtained.	Orig. No.	Collected by—	Length.	Stretch of wings.	Wing.	Remarks.
2108	♀	Carlisle, Pa	April 15, 1845	S. F. Baird						
883	♀	.....do.	Dec. 3, 1842	......do....			9.67	17.50	5.50	
589	♀	.....do.	Feb. 12, 1842	......do...						
1018	o ♀	..... do	May 24, 1843	......do..			8.83	17.00	5.33	
4298		Calcasieu, La	1854	G. Würdemann						
7051	♀	St. Louis, Mo	May 8, 1857	Lieut. Bryan	14	W. S. Wood				
8326		Independence, Mo	June 3, 1857	W. M. Magraw	49	Dr. J. G. Cooper	9.00	17.50	5.50	
5610	♂	Fort Riley, K.T.	June 19, 1856	Lieut. Bryan	32	W. S. Wood				
5612	♀	.....do	June 16, 1856	.....do	11					
5614	♂	......do	June 20, 1856	......do	37					
5615	♂	.....do	June 13, 1856	......do	3					
5616	♂	.....do	June 20, 1856	......do	36					
6549		...,..do	1857	Dr. Hammond						
5881		.....do		Dr. Hammond and J. X. de Vesey						
5229	♂	Fort Lookout, N. T	May 31, 1856	Lieut. Warren		Dr. Hayden	9.75	17.50	6.00	
8808	♂	Fremont on Platte	July 1, 1857	......do		....do	9.50	17.00	5.75	
4625	♂	Nemaha river, N. T	April 23, 1856	......do	21	......do				
4627	♀	......do	......do	......do		......do	9.25	18.12	5.75	Eyes dark
4628	♂	.....do	......do	......do		......do	9.00	17.00	5.50	......do
4629	♀	.....do	......do	......do		......do	9.87	17.00	5.87	
4630	♀	.....do	......do	......do		......do	6.00	17.25	5.25	Eyes dark
5230	♀	Above Yellowstone R., N.T	July 25, 1856	......do		......do	9.62	18 00	5.37	
5231	o	.....do	......do	......do		......do				
6036	♂	Milk river, N. T	Aug. 25, 1853	Gov. Stevens		Dr. Suckley				
6037	o	.....do	......do	......do		......do				
5617	♀	Black Hills, N.T	Aug. 3, 1856	Lieut. Bryan	197	W. S. Wood				
5618	♂	North Platte river	Aug. 12, 1856	......do	253	......do				

MELANERPES FORMICIVORUS, Bonap.

California Woodpecker.

Picus formicivorus, Swainson, Birds Mex. in Philos. Mag. I, 1827, 439, (Mexico.)—Vigors, Zool. Blossom, 1839, 23, (Monterey.)—Nuttall, Man. I, 2d ed. 1840.
Melanerpes formicivorus, Bp. Conspectus, 1850, 115.—Heermann, J. A. N. Sc. Phil. 2d series, II, 1853, 270.—Cassin, Illust. II, 1853, 11 ; pl. ii.--Newberry, Zool. Cal. & Oregon Route, 90 ; P. R. R. Surv. VI, 1857.
Picus melanopogon, Temminck, Pl. Color. IV, (1829 ?) pl. 451 —Wagler, Isis, 1829, v, 515.
? *Melampicus flavigula*, Malherbe, Rev. et Mag. Zool. 1849, 542.

Sp. Ch.—Fourth quill longest, third a little shorter. Above and on the anterior half of the body glossy bluish or greenish black ; the top of the head and a short occipital crest red. A white patch on the forehead, connected with a broad crescentic collar on the upper part of the neck by a narrow isthmus, white tinged with sulphur yellow. Belly, rump, bases of primaries, and inner edges of the outer quills, white. Tail feathers uniform black.

Female with the red confined to the occipital crest, the rest replaced by greenish black ; the three patches white, black, and red, very sharply defined. Length about 9 inches ; wing about 5.

Hab.—Coast region of California and south ; in northern Mexico, eastward almost to the Gulf of Mexico ; also on Upper Rio Grande.

In most specimens one or two red feathers may be detected in the black of the breast just behind the sulphur yellow crescent. The white of the breast is streaked with black ; the posterior portion of the black of the breast and anterior belly streaked with white. The white of the wing only shows externally as a patch at the base of the primaries.

Specimens vary in the gloss on the black of the upper parts, which is sometimes green, sometimes bluish.

The young male is exactly like the adult; the only evidence of immaturity being in the shorter and more curved bill, as well as the smaller size.

Specimens from New Leon are much smaller than those from California, as shown by a male, (4033,) in which the wing is half an inch shorter than in California specimens. Many specimens have a few red tipped feathers in the posterior edge of the pectoral collar, but it is not found in all. Specimens from the Coppermines are about the size of Californian.

List of specimens.

Catal. No.	Sex.	Locality.	When collected.	Whence obtained.	Orign'l No.	Collected by—	Length.	Extent.	Wing.
4464		Umpqua valley, O. T.	——, 1855	Lt. Williamson..		Dr. Newberry.			
4463		Suisun village, Cal...	......do......	......do........					
5495	♂	Petaluma, Cal........	May —, 1856	E. Samuels......	156				
5496	♀	......do............	July —, 1856	......do	157				
5497	♂	......do............	......do......	......do........	66				
6153		San Francisco.......		R. D. Cutts					
4211		......do............	Winter '53-'54	......do........					
5955		Santa Clara, Cal	Nov. —, 1855	Dr. Cooper.......					
5956		......do............	......do......	......do........					
6150	♀	......do............		Lt. Williamson..		Dr. Heermann.			
6151	♂	......do....		......do........		......do......			
6152	♂	......do............		......do........		......do......			
4955		San José, Cal........		A. J. Grayson..					
4606		Santa Isabel, Cal.....	Dec. 26, 1854	Major Emory....		Mr. Schott....			
6147		Los Nogales, Mexico .	June —, 1856	......do........		Dr. Kennerly .			
6149		Copper Mines, N. M..		......do........		Mr. Clark			
6148		......do............		......do........		......do......			
6145		Fort Thorn, New Mex.		Dr. S. C. Henry..					
4033	♂	New Leon, Mexico...	——, 1853	Lt. Couch........	162		8.75	16.	5.25
4034	♂	......do............		......do........	196				

MELANERPES TORQUATUS, Bonap.

Lewis's Woodpecker.

Picus torquatus, WILSON, Am. Orn. III, 1811, 31 ; pl. xx.—WAGLER, Syst. Av. 1827, No. 82.—AUD. Orn. Biog. V, 1839, 176 ; pl. 416.—IB. Birds Amer. IV, 1842, 280 ; pl. 272.

Melanerpes torquatus, BP. Consp. 1850, 115.—HEERMANN. J. A. N. Sc. Phil. 2d ser. II, 1853, 270.—NEWBERRY, Zool. Cal. & Or. Route, 90 ; in P. R. R. Surv. VI, 1857.

Picus montanus, ORD, in Guthrie's Geog. 2d Am. ed. II, 1815, 316.

Picus lewisii, DRAPIEZ. (Gray.)

SP. CH.—Feathers on the under parts bristle-like. Fourth quill longest ; then third and fifth. Above dark glossy green. Breast, lower part of the neck and a narrow collar all round hoary grayish white. Around the base of the bill and sides o the head to behind the eyes, dark crimson. Belly blood red, streaked finely with hoary whitish. Wings and tail entirely uniform dark glossy green. Female with the markings more obscure. Length about 10¼ inches ; wing 6¼.

Hab.—Western America from Black hills to Pacific.

This species differs in one respect from any other of our North American woodpeckers in the peculiar character of the feathers of the under surface. The fibres of the feathers are longer than usual, and remarkably stiff. Those on the terminal third of each feather are of the usual character at the base, or provided with fibrillae, those of opposite sides interlocking as in feathers generally. The terminal portion, however, of the stem of the fibre is much enlarged, and expanded laterally to twice or more the diameter at the root, and converted into quite a stiff bristle, nearly smooth, or with very slight indications in places of the fibrillae. It is this portion of the feather that is colored.

In addition to the characters given in the above diagnosis it may be stated that the narrow collar around the lower neck is composed of hoary white feathers of the same texture as those on the belly. On the sides of the neck and throat a black suffusion separates the crimson from the hoary. This is seldom as pure as on the nape, appearing as if soiled with brownish. On the upper part of the belly the bright blood red is confined to the central bristly fibres of each feather, the lateral ones being of a roseate hoary, and imparting the streaked character referred to ; posteriorly the red predominates. The anal region, the under tail coverts, the tibia, and the sides of body and under surface of the wing are pure greenish black. The red and hoary are, therefore, entirely superficial when the wing is closed.

In one specimen there is an occasional feather on the back of a violet tinge. One specimen (6144) has the red of the belly of an orange red shade, this varying, in fact, to a considerable degree with different specimens.

A young specimen (5619) lacks the hoary collar entirely, and the red around the bill is replaced by black. The under parts are dirty grayish, obscurely blotched with greenish brown. There are scattered indications of red.

List of specimens.

Catal. No.	Sex.	Locality.	When collected.	Whence obtained.	Orig. No.	Collected by—	Length.	Stretch of wings.	Wing.	Remarks.
6133	.....	Fort Steilacoom, W. T..	Mar. —, 1856	Dr. Suckley	243					
6134	♂	.........do		..... do	83					
6135	♀	.........do		......do............	84		10.50	20.00	6.75	
5954	.....	.........do	May —, 1855	Dr. J. G. Cooper.....						
5953	....♂	.........do		......do						
5952	.....	.........do		......do						
4376	.....	Fort Dalles, O. T	Jan. 9, 1855	Dr. Suckley						
4377	.....	.........do	... do......	......do			10.62	20.00	6.75	
1909	○♀	Col. river.....	Sept. 22, 1834	S. F. Baird..........		J. K. Townsend....				
2795	♀	Rocky mountains......	July 9, 1834	.....do.......		....do				
4213	.....	San Francisco	Winter, 53,'54	R. D. Cutts.........						
3933	♂	California		Dr. Heermann						
6138	♂	Tulare valley, Cal.....	....	Lieut. Williamson...		Dr. Heermann				
6139	.....	Fort Thorn, N. M......		Dr. Henry, U. S. A...						
5619	♀	Pole Creek, N. T......	Aug. 2, 1856	Lieut. Bryan	190	W. S. Wood				
4668	.....	Cheyenne river, Neb...	Mar. 12, 1855	Dr. Hayden						
8811	.....	Laramie peak..........	Aug. 24, 1857	Lieut. Warren.......		Dr. Hayden	11.25	22.25	7.75	Iris reddish brown
8812	♀	.........do	....do	.....do		....do	10.25	20.50	7.00	
8815	♂	.........do	....do	......do		....do............	11.25	20.50	7.00	
8814	♂	.........do	....do	......do		....do............	10.50	21.00	7.00	
8813	♀	.........do	....do	......do		....do	11.50	20.00	7.00	
8810	♂	.... .do	....do	......do		....do............	10.75	21.50	7.25	

Section Colapteae.

This section, formerly embracing but one genus additional to *Colaptes*, has recently had three more added to it, by Bonaparte. The only United States representative, however, is *Colaptes*.

COLAPTES, Swainson.

Colaptes, Swainson, Zool. Jour. III, Dec. 1827, 353. (type *C. auratus*.)
Geopicos, Malherbe, Mem. A   Metz, 1849, 358. (*G. campestris*.)

Bill slender, depressed at the base, then compressed. Culmen much curved; gonys straight, both with acute ridges, and coming to quite a sharp point with the commissure at the end; the bill, consequently, not truncate at the end. No ridges on the bill. Nostrils basal, median, oval, and exposed. Gonys very short; about half the culmen. Feet large; the anterior outer toe considerably longer than the posterior. Tail long, exceeding the secondaries, the feathers suddenly acuminate, with elongated points.

The only two well defined species found within the limits of the United States are readily characterized. They have, as the common character of Colaptes: the back transversely banded with black and brownish; the head and neck all round nearly uniform grayish or brownish, with a short maxillary stripe, and with or without a nuchal patch; a black crescent on the breast, and the belly marked with round black spots. The most conspicuous features are as follows:

1. Maxillary stripe black; a scarlet nuchal crescent; shafts, and the under surfaces of wing and tail feathers yellow..*C. auratus*.
2. Maxillary stripe red; no nuchal crescent; shafts, and the under surfaces of wing and tail feathers brownish orange red...*C. mexicanus*.

A hybrid between the two occurs on the upper Missouri.

Comparative measurements of species.

Catal. No.	Species.	Locality.	Sex.	Length.	Extent.	Wing.	Tail.	Tarsus.	Middle toe.	Its claw.	Bill above.	Along gape.	Specimen measured.
1886	Colaptes mexicanus..	Columbia river.....	♂	12.50	....	6.60	5.22	1.12	1.20	0.50	1.60	1.64	Skin............
6166	.... do......	Ft. Vancouver,N. T.	♀	12.90	....	6.50	5.90	1.12	1.16	0.50	1.68	1.68	Skin...........
do.	.... do...........	.... do...........		13.75	23.25	......							Fresh ....
8218	.... do...........	Ft. Laramie........	♀	12.50	....	6.26	4.94	....	1.14	0.44	1.46	1.54	Skin,(legs br'kn.)
do.	.... do...........	.... do...........		13.	21.	6.50							Fresh ....
9399	Colaptes mexicano...	Mexico				5.96	5 38	1.10	1.16	0.46	1.64	1.64	Skin ....
1341	Colaptes auratus.....	Carlisle.............	♂	10.96	....	6.10	5.20	1.01	1.12	0.38	1.42	1.46	Skin ....
do.	.... do...........	.... do...........		12.50	19.50	6.08							Fresh ....
5604	.... do...........	South Platte, Mo...	♂	11.50	....	6.06	4.66	1.04	1.20	0.42	1.48	1.48	Skin ....
do.	.... do...........	.... do...........		11.	16.								Fresh ....
4569	Colaptes chrysoides ?.	United States and Mex. boundary sur.		10.30	....	5.38	4.14	1.02	1.16	0.38	1.42	1.44	Skin ....
5214	Colaptes ayresii......	Farm Island, near Fort Pierre.	♂	11.80	....	6.28	5.26	1.10	1.28	0.44	1.52	1.60	Skin ....
do.	.... do...........	.... do...........		13.05	19.50	6.50							Fresh ....

COLAPTES AURATUS, Swainson.

Flicker; Yellow Shafted Woodpecker; High Holder.

Cuculus auratus, Linn. Syst. Nat. ed. x, 1758, I, 112.
Picus auratus, Linn. Syst. Nat. I, ed. xii, 1766, 174.—Forster, Phil. Trans. LXII, 1772, 383.—Vieillot, Ois
    Am. Sept. II, 1807, 66 ; pl. cxxiii —Wilson, Am. Orn. I, 1810, 45 ; pl. iii, f.].—Wagler, Syst.
    Av. 1827, No. 84.—Aud. Orn. Biog. I, 1832, 191 : V, 540 ; pl. 37.—Ib. Birds Amer. IV, 1842,
    282 ; pl. 273.
Colaptes auratus, Sw. Zool. Jour. III, 1827, 353.—Ib. F. Bor. Am. II, 1831, 314—Bon. List, 1838.—Ib. Conspectus,
    1850, 113.

Sp. Ch.—Shafts and under surfaces of wing and tail feathers gamboge yellow. A black patch on each side of the cheek. A
red crescent on the nape. Throat and stripe beneath the eye pale lilac brown. Back glossed with olivaceous green. Female
without the black cheek patch.
    Length, 12½ inches ; wing, 6.

Additional Characters.—A crescentic patch on the breast and rounded spots on the belly black. Back and wing coverts
with interrupted transverse bands of black. Neck above and on sides ashy.

    Hab.—Eastern North America to the eastern slopes of Rocky mountains ; Greenland, (Reinhardt.)

In this species the bill is slightly curved ; a little broader than deep. The first quill is very short ; the third, fourth, and fifth about equal, and longest ; the second intermediate between the seventh and eighth.

The prevailing color of the back of this species is a light olivaceous brown, with a very slight tinge of green ; each feather with a crescentic band of black near the end ; sometimes with more. The top of the head and the upper part of the neck half way round are bluish ash ; the former with a tinge of reddish brown, increasing to the base of the bill. The neck, throat, and sides of the breast are of a pale purplish brown ; the sides of the head from the nostrils to around the eye, and including the ear coverts, are similar, with, perhaps, more of a cinnamon tinge. There is a black patch or whisker on the cheek, commencing at the base of the lower mandible, and of that width, and enlarging as it extends backwards to its truncated posterior extremity, which is nearly twice as high as anteriorly. There is a carmine red crescentic collar on the nape, (in the ash color described,) the branches coming round to such an extent on the side of the head that the eye (in the prepared skin) appears to be intermediate between it and the nostrils. The rump is pure white ; the tail coverts barred transversely with white and black. The lower parts are yellowish white, tinged with brownish ; each feather with a nearly circular spot of black near the end ; these spots larger posteriorly and on the tail coverts.

The under surfaces and shafts of the wing and tail feathers are bright gamboge yellow ; the shafts above yellow on the upper surface. On the outer edges of the secondary quills are some spots of the color of the back, forming a series of bars ; the primaries with only faint traces of the same. The quills are margined near the basal portion of their edges with pale buff yellow, of which color are the under wing coverts. The upper surfaces and tips of the tail feathers are black ; the rest of the under surfaces gamboge yellow. The external tail feather has a few indentations of paler yellow on the outer edge, and all (excepting the central) are slightly tipped with the same.

The female is almost precisely similar, except in lacking the black cheek patches ; this is, however, obscurely indicated. The red nuchal band is persistent.

Specimens vary in size of body and bill, size and exact shape of the spots on the under parts, which are sometimes larger or smaller, sometimes slightly transverse, circular, or somewhat longitudinal. Western specimens are rather paler above ; occasionally purer ash on the head. All, too, have the proportions of the quills a little different. Thus, in one the fourth and fifth quills are equal ; the third shorter than the sixth ; the fifth is, however, in most a little longer. One specimen from Selkirk Settlement has the belly tinged with pale sulphur yellow ; the back with a stronger shade of olivaceous green.

This species in general pattern of coloration resembles the *C. mexicanus*, although the colors are very different. Thus the shafts of the quills, with their under surfaces, are gamboge yellow, instead of orange red. There is a conspicuous nuchal crescent of crimson wanting, or but slightly indicated in *mexicanus*. The cheek patch is pure black, widening and abruptly truncate behind, instead of bright crimson, pointed or rounded behind. The shade of the upper parts is olivaceous green, instead of purplish brown. The top of the head and nape are more ashy. The chin, throat, neck, and sides of the head are pale purplish or lilac brown, instead of bluish ash ; the space above, below, and around the eye of the same color, instead of having reddish brown above and ashy below. The third quill is longest, the fourth and fifth but little shorter, instead of having the fifth longest ; the third shorter than the fourth also.

The young of this species is sufficiently like the adult to be readily recognizable. Sometimes the entire crown is faintly tipped with red, as customary in young woodpeckers.

List of specimens.

Catal. No.	Sex.	Locality.	When collected.	Whence obtained.	Orig. No.	Collected by—	Length.	Stretch of wings.	Wing.	Remarks.
6932	♀	Nelson river, H. B. T.....		Donald Gunn......		John Isbister.......				
6933	♀	Selkirk Settlement.......	......do.	......do.						
1341	♂	Carlisle, Pa.......	April 10, 1844	S. F. Baird			12.50	19.50	6.08	
2051	♀	........do.......	April 3, 1845	......do.			12.00	19.75	6.17	
1627	♀	......do.......	July 12, 1844	......do.			11.67	19.00	6.50	
4435	○	Quasqueton, Iowa.......		E. C. Bidwell.....						
4620		Fort Leavenworth, K. T..	April 21, 1856	Lieut. Warren. ...	2	Dr. Hayden........	11.50	16.50	9.00	
6158		........do.......		Lieut. Couch.....						
5605	○	Kansas		Lieut. F. T. Bryan.		W. S. Wood.......				
5606	○ ♂	Fort Riley, Kansas.......	June 19, 1856	.....do.	33	......do.				
6553	♂	........do.	1856..........	Dr. Hammond and J. X. de Vesey..						Eyes blue black.
6554	♀	........do.	1856..........	......do.						
5609	♀	115 miles W. of Ft. Riley.	July 3, 1856	Lieut. Bryan.......	62	W. S. Wood.......				
5608	♂	South Platte river	July 8, 1856	......do.	78	......do.				
5604		South Platte, Neb........	......do.......	......do.	77	......do.				
5607	○ ♀	Platte river, Kan........	July 14, 1856	......do.	105	......do.				
4619	♂	Upper Missouri.........		Lieut. Warren......	8					
5221	♀	Fort Lookout..... ..	June 19, 1856	......do.	.. ..		12.00	17.50	6.00	
8330	♂	Independence, Mo.......	June 3, 1857	W. M. Magraw.....	53	Dr. Cooper.........	12.00	19.00	6.00	
8346	♀	........do.	June 17, 1857	......do.	73	......do.	12.00	18.50	6.75	
8401	♀	........do.	July 1, 1857	......do.	111	......do.	10.25	17.50	5.25	
8868	♂ ○	50 miles ab. mo. of Platte.	1857.........	Lieut. Warren......		Dr. Hayden....	11.00	18.00	5.00	
8866	♀ ○	Fremont on Platte	July 1, 1857	......do.		......do.	10.75	18.60	5.75	
8867	♂ ○	........do.......	......do.......	......do.		......do.	10.50	18.60	5.50	
8862	♀ ○	Loup Fork.............	July....	......do.		......do.	10.50	16.50	4.50	
8861	♀ ○	........do.	July....	......do.		......do.	11.10	18.00	5.50	
8864	○	...... do.	July 27, 1857	......do.		......do.	11.25	18.50	5.50	
8865	♀ ○	........do.	July 28, 1857	......do.		......do.	10.50	17 50	5.50	

COLAPTES MEXICANUS, Swainson.

Red-shafted Flicker.

Colaptes mexicanus, Sw. Syn. Mex. birds, in Philos. Mag. I, 1827, 440.—Is. F. Bor. Am. II, 1831, 315.—
     NEWBERRY, Zool. Cal. & Or. Route, 91; P. R. R. Rep. VI, 1857.
Picus mexicanus, AUD. Orn. Biog. V, 1839, 174; pl. 416.—Is. Birds America, IV, 1842, 295; pl. 274.
Colaptes collaris, VIGORS Zool. Jour. IV, Jan. 1829, 353.—Is. Zool. Beechey's Voy. 1839, 24; pl. ix.
Picus rubricatus, WAGLER, Isis, 1829, v, May, 516. "(Lichtenstein Mus. Berol.)"
Colaptes rubricatus, BON. Pr. Zool. Soc. V, 1837, 108.—Is. List, 1838.—Is. Conspectus, 1850, 114.
? *Picus cafer*, GMELIN, Syst. Nat. I, 1788, 431.—LATH. Index Ornith. II, 1790, 242.
? *Picus lathami*, WAGLER, Syst. 1827, No. 85 (Cape of Good Hope ?)

SP. CH.—Shafts and under surfaces of wing and tail feathers orange red. A red patch on each side the cheek; nape without red crescent; sometimes very faint indications laterally. Throat and stripe beneath the eye bluish ash. Back glossed with purplish brown. Female without the red cheek patch. Length about 13 inches; wing over 6½ inches.

ADDITIONAL CHARACTERS.—Spots on the belly, a crescent on the breast, and interrupted transverse bands on the back, black. *Hab.*—Western N. America from the Black Hills to Pacific.

In describing this species I have taken as types a very fine pair collected on the Columbia river, by Mr. Townsend, in October, 1834. In size these skins considerably exceed specimens of *C. auratus.* The bill is moderately long, a little broader than high, and gently curved. The wings are long, but do not reach the middle of the tail. The first quill is very short; the fifth longest; the fourth but little shorter; the third intermediate between the fifth and sixth.

The prevailing color of the back, scapulars, and wings is brownish ash, each feather with one, two, or three bars of black. These are sub-crescentic, or nearly straight, short and wide, extending across the feather. The entire head and neck all round may be described as plumbeous ash, glossed with dull cinnamon brown above, darkest towards the base of the bill. There is a decided tinge of cinnamon in an obscure stripe passing from the base of the upper mandible above, and a little behind the eye, and involving the lower eyelid. There is a very distinct whisker-like stripe of bright crimson or carmine red passing from the base of the lower mandible, over and to the posterior extremity of the jaw bone, truncate and rounded behind. This is never mixed with black. There is a large, broad crescentic spot of velvet black on the upper part of the breast. The under parts generally are of a dull brownish white, (palest along the median line,) each feather with a circular sharply defined spot .15 to .20 of an inch in diameter. On the flanks these spots become larger, more transverse, and sub-cordate, several on a feather; on the tail coverts they are more like transverse bars.

The rump is pure white, (in this one specimen with a few short streaks of black on the middle of some of the feathers; in most specimens, however, the rump is immaculate.) The upper tail coverts are white and black in transverse bands, the adjacent black bands sometimes confluent along the midrib so as to interrupt the enclosed white band.

The shafts and under surfaces of all the quills, both of wing and tail, are of a bright orange red, the shafts alone of this color on the upper surface in the wing; in the tail the shafts are black above, except at the base. The wing quills are dark brown, (except in the outer primaries,) spotted with series of blotches like the color of the back, producing bands. The inner webs are similarly spotted, except that here they are more confluent and have an orange tinge. The longer primaries are narrowly tipped with brownish white. The tail feathers are black on their upper surface and extremity, the first and second only with a few slight indentations of whitish. The exposed under surface of the outer feather is orange, tipped with black.

The female is similar in every way, perhaps a little smaller, but lacks the red moustache. This is, however, indicated by a brown tinge over an area corresponding with that of the red of the male.

In the present specimen (1886) there is a slight indication of an interrupted nuchal red band, as in the common Flicker, in some crimson fibres to some of the feathers about as far behind the eye as this is from the bill. A large proportion of males before me exhibit the same characteristic, some more, some less, although it generally requires careful examination for its detection. It may possibly be a characteristic of the not fully mature bird, although it occurs in two out of three male specimens.

There is a little variation in the size of the pectoral crescent and spots ; the latter are sometimes rounded or oblong cordate, instead of circular. The bill varies as much as three or four tenths of an inch. The rump, usually immaculate, sometimes has a few black streaks. The extent of the red whisker varies a little. In skins from Oregon and Washington the color of the back is as described ; in those from California and New Mexico it is of a grayer cast. There is little, if any, variation in the shade of red in the whiskers and quill feathers.

There is some difference in size of this species, not only in the same locality, but, as a general rule, the more southern specimens are smaller.

This species is distinct from the *C. mexicanoides* of Lafresnaye, though somewhat resembling it. This is, however, a smaller bird ; the red of the cheeks deeper ; the whole upper part of head and neck uniform reddish cinnamon without any ash, in marked contrast to that on the sides of the head. The back is strongly glossed with reddish brown, and the black transverse bars are much more distinct, closer and broader.

16 b

List of specimens.

Catal. No.	Sex.	Locality.	When collected.	Whence obtained.	Orig'l No.	Collected by—	Length.	Extent.	Wing.	Remarks.
5948	♂	Straits of Fuca, W. T..	April —,1855	Dr. J. G. Cooper..			13.00	21.00		
5949	♂	......do...............	...... do......	...... do..........			12.75	19.00		
5950	♀	......do...............	...... do......	...... do..........			13.00	20.75		
5951	♀	...... do...............	...... do......	...... do..........						
6167	.....	Fort Steilacoom, W. T..	Feb. 15,1854	Gov. Stevens.....	37	Dr. Suckley......	13.00	17.75	7.	
6168	♂	......do...............	Jan. 15,1854	...... do.	15	...... do........				
6169	♀	......do...............	March —,1856	Dr. Suckley......	242	...... do....				
6170	♂	......do...............	May 10,1856	...... do........	386		12.50	19.75		
6171	♂	......do...............	May 13,1866	...... do........	388	....	13.25	21.		
6165	♂	Fort Vancouver, W. T..	Jan. 9,1854	Gov. Stevens....		Dr. Cooper.......	13.25	21.		
6166	♀	......do...............	...... do........,	...... do........		...... do........	13.25	23.25		Iris brown......
1887	♀	Columbia river........	Oct. 18,1834	S. F. Baird......		J. K. Townsend..				
1886	♂	......do...............	...... do......	...... do........		.........do....				
4454	♂	Fort Reading, Cal.....				Lt. Williamson...				
6164	♂	Bodega, Cal.	Jan. —,1855	Lt. Trowbridge...		Mr. Szabo.......				
4209	♂	San Francisco, Cal.....	Winter of 1853	R. D. Cutts......						
4210	♀	......do...............	...... do......	...... do........						
4453	♂	......do..				Lt. Williamson...				
3902	♀	California............				Dr. Heermann....				
6162	♂	Tejon valley, Cal......		Lt. Williamson...		Dr. Heermann....				
6163	♀	......do...............		...... do..... ..		...... do........				
6160	♀	Camp 134, N. M...		Lt. Whipple......	180	Dr. Kennerly.....	11.	18.50	7.	Young.............
6172	.....	Fort Thorn, N. M....		Dr. T. C .Henry....						
5072	♂	Fort Fillmore, N. M...	Oct. 17,1855	Capt. J. Pope	146	....	14.	18.	6.	Gums light blue ......
5073	♂	......do.........	Nov. 27,1855	...... do.	168	....	12.50	22.	7.	......do.............
5074	♀	......do...............	Oct. 17,1855	...... do........	147	....	13.50	20.	6.50	Eyes brown, feet gray.
6161	♀	El Paso, N.M........		....	28					
6159	♂	San Elizario, Texas....	Dec. —,1854	Maj. Emory.....	16	Dr. Kennerly. ...	11.	18.	6.	
4041	♀	Saltillo, Mexico........	May —,1853	Lt. Couch........			11.	18.	6.	Eyes deep crimson, bill dark slate, feet lead.
5601	♂	Republican F'k of Platte river...	October 1,1856	Lt. F. T. Bryan ...	366	W. S. Wood.....				
5602	♂	Republican F'k of Platte. Kansas.	Sept. 24,1856	Lt. F. T. Bryan...	350	W. S. Wood.....				
8226	♀	Fort Laramie	Sept. 11,1857	W. M. Magraw...		Dr. Cooper.......	12.25	20.50	6.75	
8217	♂	......do..	...... do......	...... do........		...... do........ .	13.00	21.00	7,00	
8218	♀	......do...............	...... do......	...... do........		...... do........	13.00	21.00	6.50	

COLAPTES HYBRIDUS, Baird.

Colaptes ayresii, Aud. Birds Am. VII, 1843, 348 ; pl. 494.
? *Geopicus chrysoides*, Malherbe, Rev. et. Mag. Zool. IV, 1852, 553. (Differs from *C. auratus* in wanting red nape)

Sp Ch.—Yellow shafts or feathers on wing and tail combined with red or red spotted cheek patches. Orange shafts combined with a well defined nuchal red crescent. Ash colored throat combined with black cheek patch, or yellow shafts. Shafts and feathers intermediate between gamboge yellow and dark orange red.

By the above name I intend to cover a remarkable series of woodpeckers from the upper Missouri and Yellowstone, combining the characteristics of the *Colaptes auratus* and *mexicanus* in proportions varying with almost each individual, and leading irresistibly to the conclusion that they are descendants of originals of the species mentioned above, mixed up by inter-breeding of successive generations, to a degree unparalleled in the annals of ornithology. I have, in the two preceeding articles, gone into much detail in respect to the characters of *Colaptes auratus* and *mexicanus*, and under the first named head have shown the particular point of difference.

The first striking deviation from the characters of the *C. auratus* is seen in the variety described by Audubon as *Colaptes ayresii.* Here (5214, Fort Pierre) the general characters are those of *auratus*, the lilac or purplish brown throat, the ashy head, the olivaceous green shade of the back, the gamboge yellow quills, &c. The cheek patch, however, is bright carmine red, and the nuchal crescent of much less extent, though quite conspicuous. The fourth quill is longest ; the fifth and third successively a little shorter. There are, however, faint indications of black spots in the red of the cheeks.

A previous stage, however, is indicated in 5224, from White Earth river, where the only aberration from the *C. auratus* is seen in a faint indication of red in the upper part of the black cheek patch. The fourth quill is longest ; the third and sixth about equal. No. 5603, from the Little Blue, has the black and red of the cheek patch so nearly intermixed as to render it difficult to say which color predominates, the feathers being black, with red tips.

Another variety, but little different, consists in having a bluish ash on the throat and under the eye as in *C. mexicanus*, instead of lilac brown. There is only a trace of red on the nape. (6158, Milk river, Neb.)

In 4639, from Fort Pierre, the nuchal crescent is large, the cheek patch red and black. The approach to *C. mexicanus* is shown by the yellow of the quills having an orange tinge almost intermediate between the two. The throat and under the eye are ash color, not lilac brown. Other specimens of the same general character have the shafts either more yellow or more orange.

The variety nearest the *C. mexicanus* is seen in some specimens, as (5213) from the Yellowstone, where the shafts and quills are of nearly the typical orange, the cheek patches red. The back is, however, that of the *C. auratus ;* the nape has a very distinct band of red ; the red of the cheeks has a few specks of black. No. 5212 has more black in the cheek patch, and the whole top of the head tinged with red.

To illustrate more fully this combination of characters of the two species in the numerous specimens before me, I have prepared the following tables, the first serving as a key to the second. Thus, by *a* I refer, in the second table, to the peculiarities of cheek patches ; by *b* to those of the shafts, &c. Where a letter is found in the column of either species opposite a particular specimen it shows that this has the particular character of the species. Where the letters occur in both columns it shows that both characters co-exist in the specimen. Where figures are combined with the letters it indicates the proportion. Thus 1 *a* under *C. auratus*, and 3 *a* under *C. mexicanus*, show that the specimen has three times as much red in the cheek patches as black.

In a large number of young Flickers, from the upper Missouri, (as 5215, 5216, 5217, 5218, 5220, 5222, 5223) the character of *C. mexicanus* is seen in the entire absence of red on the nape. The cheek patches promise to be black ; the shafts mostly yellowish ; some with orange tinge. In a similar series from Kansas and the Platte (5605 and 5609) the nuchal band and black cheek patch, with the yellow shafts, are very distinct.

Malherbe describes a *Colaptes chrysoides* from America as similar to *C. auratus*, but smaller, and without a nuchal red collar. This is the characteristic of many immature birds of the *hybridus* type from the upper Missouri, and Malherbe's species differs but little from these. If from a remote locality, however, it may be distinct, and it is not improbable that the bird described in the next article belongs to it.

CHARACTERS OF SPECIES.

	C. auratus.	C. mexicanus.
a. Cheek patches	Black	Red
b. Shafts	Gamboge yellow	Orange red
c. Throat and beneath eye	Pale lilac brown	Bluish ash
d. Nape	With red crescent	Without crescent
e. Color of back, with shade of	Olivaceous green	Purplish brown

NUMBER AND LOCALITY OF SPECIMENS.

	C. auratus.	C. mexicanus.
5224. White Earth river, Nebraska. 5225. Fort Pierre. 8863. Loup fork	6a. b. c. d. e ..	a.
5603. Little Blue river, Nebraska	a. b. c. d. e....	a.
5214. Near Fort Pierre	b. c. 2d. e.	a*. d.
6158. Milk river, Nebraska	b. e	a*. c. d.
4638. Fort Pierre, female, ashy throat	a'. b. d. e	a b. c.
5212. Yellowstone	a. b. d. e.	a 5b. c.
5213. Yellowstone	d. e	a⁰. b. c.
5211. Fort Union	a. d. e.	a. b. c. 2d.
8258. Fort Laramie	c. d.	a. b. e.
5601. Fort Laramie	c	a. b. c. d. e....

* The slighest possible trace of black on the cheeks.

List of specimens.

Catal. No.	Sex and age.	Locality.	When collected.	Whence obtained.	Orig. No.	Collected by—	Length.	Stretch of wings.	Wing.
		Yellow predominating on shafts.							
4638	♀	Fifty miles west of Fort Pierre, Nebraska.	April 10, 1855	Dr. Hayden					
4639	♂	........do ....do.	..... do......	Col. A. Vaughan		Dr. Hayden..			
4641	♀	........do ....do.	April 18, 1855	......do		.......do			
5214	♂	Fort Pierre	May 30, 1856	Lieut. Warren		......do			
5225	♂	Near Fort Pierre....	.... do.....	......do		......do	13.12	19.50	6.50
5222	○ ♂	Squaw Butte creek, Nebraska.	July 4, 1856	..... do		......do	12.50	19.50	6.25
5223	○ ♂	........do ....do.	...... do......	......do		......do			
5220	○	........do ....do.	..... do......	......do		......do			
5215	○	Powd.r river, Nebraska	Aug. 1, 1856	......do		......do			
5216	○ ♂	Fort Union	July 23, 1856	......do		......do	13.00	20.50	6.00
5217	♀	Yellowstone river	Aug. 19, 1856	......do		......do			
5218	♂	........do	Aug. 22, 1856	......do		......do			
5219	♀	........do	Aug. 23, 1856	......do		......do			
5217	♀	........do	Aug. 19, 1856	......do		...... do			
5224	♂	White Earth river, Nebraska	Sept. 6, 1856	..... do		...... do	12.25	20.12	6.25
6158	♂	Milk river, Nebraska	Aug. 31, 1853	Gov. Stevens		Dr. Suckley .	12.00	20.50	7.00
5603	♂	Little Blue, Nebraska	July 7, 1856	Lieut. Bryan		W. S. Wood...			
8863	♂	Loup fork, Nebraska	July 27, 1857	Lieut. Warren	73	W. S. Wood...			
8869	○	Fifty miles above mouth of Platte	July 2, 1857	......do		......do	12.00	20.50	6.50
							11.10	17.75	5.50
		Orange predominating on shafts.							
8258	....	Fort Laramie	Sept. 1, 1857	W. M. Magraw		Dr. Cooper			
5601	♂	Republican fork	Oct. 1, 1856	Lieut. Bryan	366	W. S. Wood			
4640	....	Fifty miles west of Fort Pierre	April 10, 1855	Col. A. Vaughan		Dr. Hayden			
5211	♂	Fort Union, Nebraska...	J.ly 19, 1856	Lieut. Warren		.....do	12.50	20.00	6.37
5212	♀	Yellowstone	July 28, 1856	......do		......do	12.37	20.12	6.37
5213	♂	......do	July 25, 1856	..... do		......do	13.00	2.08	6.37

COLAPTES CHRYSOIDES.

Geopicus chrysoides, MALHERBE, Rev. et. Mag. Zool. IV, 1852, 553.

An immature *Colaptes* (4569) with yellow shafts, no nuchal collar, and ash colored throat, was collected somewhere on the Mexican boundary line, by Mr. Schott. The precise locality is not known, and the specimen is not perfect enough to show whether it is a distinct species or a hybrid. It is much smaller than the corresponding age of *C. auratus,* the wing measuring but 5¼ inches. The probabilities are that it is a permanent and perhaps distinct species. It may possibly be the *C. chrysoides* of Malberbe, agreeing with this in the absence of a red nape. There is a slight tinge of orange in the yellow of the shafts.

NOTE.—The preceeding pages embrace all the *Scansores* usually assigned to North America, either as good and distinct species or as synonymes. The only ones not given are : 1st, the *Picus leucurus,* Hartlaub, Naumania, II, 1854, 55. This is a species with entirely white tail, said to have been discovered by Prince Paul of Wurttemberg, in the Rocky mountains. Nothing further is mentioned concerning it than the color of the tail, as stated in a note from the Prince. 2d, the *Dryotomus delattri* of Bonaparte, Comptes Rendus, XXVIII, 1854. This, though assigned to California, appears to be really Central American. 3d, *Picus lineatus.* This is given by Mr. Audubon as sent from the Columbia river by Dr. Gairdner, but there is no evidence that such was really the case, or that it ever comes within many hundred miles of our line. *Campephilus imperialis,* although given in the preceding pages, has really no claim to a place in our fauna.

ORDER II .

INSESSORES.[1]

In accordance with the views of many systematic writers, it may perhaps be as well to retain an order *Insessores*, and to place in it the *Strisores, Clamatores*, and *Oscines* as sub-orders. The characters of the order will then consist chiefly in the possession of three toes in front and one behind, (or at least never with two toes directed backwards,) as in *Scansores*. The claws are not retractile, nor the bill with a cere, as in the *Raptores;* nor is the hind toe situated appreciably above the plane of the others, as in *Rasores, Grallatores*, and *Natatores*.

The hind toe of the *Insessores* corresponds to the thumb or inner toe of the mammals, and is usually quite short. The joints of the anterior toes generally follow the law of number characteristic of birds, namely, two to the hinder, three to the inner, four to the middle, and five to the outer toes ; but a deviation is seen in some *Strisores* where there are sometimes but three joints each to the anterior toes, and sometimes only four in the outer. The tarsi are generally covered anteriorly with plates, and furnished behind with granulations or small scales, or else with two long plates covering the sides, the latter feature especially characteristic of the *Oscines*, or singing birds ; in the latter alone is the tarsus sometimes covered anteriorly with a single plate. Sometimes the tarsus is entirely or partly naked, or destitute of plates altogether.

The carpal joint or the hand part of the wing is in most *Insessores* furnished with ten quills, (primaries,) although the first quill is sometimes very short or even entirely wanting, as in many *Oscines*. The fore arm has from six (in the humming birds) to thirteen quills, the average being eight or nine.

There are certain peculiarities in the arrangement of the wing coverts of the different suborders of *Insessores*, constituting important distinctive features. Some of these will be hereafter referred to.

The tail of the *Insessores* exhibits considerable differences. The number of feathers is usually twelve ; sometimes ten only, as in the *Strisores*.

The different groups of the order *Insessores* are subject to considerable variations in respect to the structure of the lower larynx attached to the trachea or wind pipe just anterior to its division into the two bronchial tubes. Cuvier long since showed that the true singing birds had the larynx provided with a peculiar apparatus for the purpose of effecting a modulation of the voice, composed of five pairs of muscles, of which other birds were destitute in greater part or entirely. The characteristic of the groups *Strisores, Clamatores*, and *Oscines*, and of their sub-divisions, as will be shown hereafter, depend very much on these peculiarities of the larynx.

The tongue of the *Insessores* varies to a considerable degree. In the humming birds it is thread-like and bifurcated. In most other insessorial or perching birds it is long or short, flat,

[1] The following remarks on the general charac rs of the *Insessores* are derived chiefly from Burmeister's Thiere Brasiliens, Vögel, page 305.

and triangular, the posterior extremity bilobed, the anterior usually with the tip horny, serrated, or with fibres; more rarely smooth. These furnish important characteristics for the division into families and even genera, the variations being quite considerable.

In dividing the *Insessores* into *Strisores*, *Clamatores* and *Oscines*, I have followed Cabanis instead of Burmeister, who makes *Clamatores* and *Oscines* the sub-orders, and gives *Strisores* and *Tracheophones* as tribes of the former. The *Strisores* of Burmeister are not exactly coequal with those of Cabanis, as they embrace the *Halcedinidae* and *Prionitidae*, which by Cabanis are placed among the *Clamatores*. I am not able to say which classification is the more natural; that of Cabanis, however, answers all my present purposes, besides having been in my mind while preparing the present report, and before becoming acquainted with Burmeister's valuable work.

STRISORES.

The essential characters of this sub-order are presented in the general table at the beginning of the report. Cabanis divides the *Strisores* into the *Macrochires*, including the *Trochilidae*, the *Cypselidae*, and the *Caprimulgidae*, and into the *Amphibolae*, embracing *Opisthocomidae* and *Musophagidae*. The first division is well represented in the United States, the second not at all. A more recent article by Burmeister includes the *Halcyonidae* and *Prionitidae* with the *Strisores*, taking them from the *Clamatores*, where Cabanis placed them. A division of the American forms might then be made into *Macrochires*, with the wings long and pointed, the fore arm shortened; and into *Orthochires*, with the wings moderate and the fore arm rather long. They agree in having the muscles of the lower larynx thin, flat, or entirely wanting, the voice incapable of modulation, &c. As, however, the precise limits and characteristics, external and internal, of these families have not yet been fully settled, I prefer to use Cabanis' arrangement for the present, at least, and with him shall consider the *Anisodactyli* as *Clamatores* rather than *Strisores*.

Of the three families of *Macrochires*, the *Trochilidae* are easily recognized by the long, subulate, very slender, and acute bill, but little cleft at the base, and the peculiar tongue, as well as by the excessively diminutive size and gorgeously metallic plumage. The remaining families agree in having the bill very short, triangular, and weak ; the gape very long and wide, extending to beneath the eyes, and the culmen much shorter than half the gape ; the nostrils opening upwards ; the outer toe usually with an incomplete number of joints. The *Cypselidae*, however, have the plumage compact, the bill entirely without bristles, the middle toe scarcely longer than the lateral, the claw without any serration, the anterior toes all cleft to the base, the fore arm short, the colors uniform, &c. In the *Caprimulgidae* the plumage is soft, loose, and downy, as in the owls ; the bill with bristles, even around the nostrils ; the middle toe considerably longer than the lateral, and the claw serrated, or at least much extended, on its inner edge ; the toes with a web at the base, the fore arm long, and the colors mottled.

The following schemes of the families are taken from Burmeister ; the common characters of the *Macrochires* being : wings long and pointed, the arm portion more or less shortened, the middle and outer toes not closely united :

A. Bill long and thin. Tongue long, divided, thread-like.

TROCHILIDAE.—Secondaries six in number.

B. Bill short, and very broad at the base. Tongue short, flat, three-sided. Secondaries more than six.

CYPSELIDAE.—Plumage unicolor. Fore arm short.

CAPRIMULGIDAE.—Plumage spotted and marbled. Fore arm moderately long.

Family TROCHILIDAE. The Humming Birds.

There is no group of birds so interesting to the ornithologist or to the casual observer as the humming birds, at once the smallest in size, the most gorgeously beautiful in color, and almost the most abundant in species of any single family of birds. They are strictly confined to the continent and islands of America, and are most abundant in the Central American States, though single species range almost to the Arctic regions on the north and to Patagonia on the south, as well as from the seacoast to the frozen summits of the Andes. The number of known species considerably exceeds 300, and new ones are being constantly brought to light; so that an estimate of 400 species is, perhaps, not too large. Many are very limited in their range; some confined to particular islands, even though of small dimensions.

The bill of the humming bird is awl-shaped or subulate, thin, and sharp pointed; straight or curved; sometimes as long as the head; sometimes much longer. The mandibles are excavated to the tip for the lodgment of the tongue, and form a tube by the close apposition of their cutting edges. There is no indication of stiff bristly feathers at the base of the mouth. The tongue has some resemblance to that of the woodpeckers in the elongation of the cornua backwards, so as to pass round the back of the skull, and then anteriorly to the base of the bill. The tongue itself is of very peculiar structure, consisting anteriorly of two hollow threads closed at the ends and united behind. The food of the humming bird consists almost entirely of insects, which are captured by protruding the tongue into flowers of various shapes without opening the bill very wide.

The wings of the humming birds are long and falcate; the shafts very strong; the primaries usually ten in number, the first always longest; there are six secondaries. The tail has but ten feathers. The feet are small; the claws very sharp and strong.[1]

The species now known to inhabit the United States, though few, are yet nearly twice as many as given by Mr. Audubon. It is probable that additional ones will hereafter be detected, particularly on our southern borders.

The different authors who have made a speciality of the humming birds have named a great many sub-families and genera, but there has as yet been no published systematic description of the higher groups. It is probable that the North American species belong to two different sub-families—the *Lampornithinae* and the *Trochilinae*—and to at least four genera; but the precise character and limits of these I am unable to give. The following remarks, however, may serve to sketch out the characters of the North American species:

A. Edges of mandible serrated near the end. Throat without metallic scale-like feathers.

LAMPORNIS.—Bill depressed, slightly curved. Tail broad, slightly emarginate; the outer feather as broad as the rest. Wings reaching the tip of tail. No metallic feathers on the throat.

B. Edges of mandible nearly even towards the tip, without distinct serrations. Throat with metallic scale-like feathers.

TROCHILUS.—Feathers of throat but little elongated laterally. Lateral tail feathers but little narrower than the others, and lanceolate acute. Tail forked.

[1] Most of the above general remarks are borrowed from Burmeister, (Thiere Brasiliens, Vögel, 311,) to which I would refer for an excellent article on the structure and habits of humming birds.

17 b

SELASPHORUS.—Feathers of the throat much elongated laterally into a ruff. Lateral tail feathers much narrower than the middle ones, and linear in shape, or with the sides parallel to the end, which is rounded. Tail graduated or cuneate. Outer primary attenuated at the tip. Crown without red metallic scales.

ATTHIS.—Similar to the last, but the top of the head with metallic scales like the throat. The outer primary not attenuated. Tail emarginated or deeply forked.

The following table exhibits the comparative measurements of the different North American species of humming bird :

Comparative measurements of species.

Catal. No.	Species.	Locality.	Sex.	Length.	Stretch of wings.	Wing.	Tail.	Tarsus.	Bill above.	Specimen measured.	Remarks.
523	Lampornis mango.	South America.........	♂	4.52	....	2.50	1.70	....	0.90	Skin	....
2697	......do.	......do.	♀	4.46	....	2.64	1.72	....	0.92	Skin	....
1843	Trochilus colubris......	Washington..........	♂	3.14	....	1.56	1.26	....	0.70	Skin	....
997	......do.	Carlisle, Pa............	♀	3.26	....	1.74	1.16	....	0.80	Skin	....
	......do.	......do.	....	3.75	4.17	1.83	....			Fresh	
Orig. 563	Trochilus alexandri	Fort Tejon, Cal........	♂	3.32	....	1.64	1.14	....	0.82	Skin	
2896	Selasphorus rufus......	Columbia, river........	♂	3.46	....	1.54	1.32	....	0.68	Skin	
1943	......do.	......do.	○ ♂	3.54	....	1.78	1.24	....	0.80	Skin	
6058	......do.	Steilacoom, W. T	....	3.24	....	1.60	1.32	....	0.70	Skin	
6057	......do.	San Francisco, Cal....	....	3.24	....	1.52	1.24	....	0.76	Skin	
9007	Selasphorus platycercus	Mexico..............	♂	3.32	....	1.94	1.44	....	0.80	Skin	
Orig. 197	......do.		....	... .						Skin	Bill broken ....
6086	Atthis anna............	San Francisco........	♂	3.64	....	1.92	1.46	....	0.80	Skin	
5501	..... do.	Petaluma, Cal.	♂	3.60	....	1.96	1.50	....	0.82	Skin	
6052	......do.	San Francisco.	♀	3.84	....	1.96	1.31	....	0.82	Skin	
6073	Atthis costae	New Mexico..........	♂	3.15	....	1.76	1.06	0.15	0.70	Skin	
6074	......do.	......do.	♀	3.05	....	1.80	....		0.73	....	....
7967	......do.	Guatemala	♂	3.30	....	1.78	....		0.72	....	....

LAMPORNIS, Swainson.

Lampornis, SWAINSON, Zoological Journal, 1827, 358.

The single species of this genus assigned to the United States is readily distinguished by its generic characters from any other belonging to the same region.

LAMPORNIS MANGO, Swainson.

Black-throated Humming Bird.

Trochilus mango, LINN. Syst. Nat. I, 1766, 171.—AUDUBON, Orn. Biog. II, 1834, 486 ; pl. 184.—IB. Birds America, IV, 1842, 186 ; pl. 251.
Lampornis mango, SWAINSON, Zool. Journal, 1827, 358.

Above and on the sides metallic green and golden. Beneath opaque velvety bluish black, this color narrowed on the breast by the encroachment of the green of the sides. Upper surface of wings and tail purplish black ; the latter with greenish reflections. All the tail feathers except the innermost purplish violet, abruptly margined with blackish. A tuft of downy white feathers under the wings, and around the tibia.

Female quite similar, the black of the under parts replaced by white, with a narrow stripe of black down the middle of the hroat and belly. Length 4 50 inches ; wing 2.60 ; tail 1.7

The female of this species is quite similar to the male, except as described. The tail is much the same, except that the feathers are rather narrower, and less rounded at the tip. They are also margined more broadly with black.

The claim of the Mango humming bird to a place in the fauna of the United States rests on the capture of a specimen at Key West, Florida, by Dr. Strobel, many years ago. The specimens described here are from South America.

TROCHILUS, Linnaeus.

Trochilus, LINNAEUS, Systema Naturae ,1748. (Agassiz.)

I have nothing to add to the diagnosis of the genus *Trochilus* already given on a preceding page, except to remark that in the North American species the female has the outer tail feathers lanceolate, as in the male, though much broader. The outer feathers are broad to the terminal third, where they become rapidly pointed, the tip only somewhat rounded ; the sides of this attenuated portion (one or other, or both) broadly and concavely emarginated, which distinguishes them from the females of *Selasphorus* and *Atthis*, in which the tail is broadly linear to near the end, which is much rounded without any distinct concavity.

The following diagnosis will serve to distinguish the species found in the United States.

COMMON CHARACTERS.—Above and on the sides metallic green. A ruff of metallic feathers from the bill to the breast, behind which is a whitish collar, confluent with a narrow abdominal stripe ; a white spot behind the eye. Tail feathers without light margins.

Tail deeply forked, (.30 of an inch.) Throat bright coppery red from the chin. Tail of female rounded, emarginated.............. ....*T. colubris.*

Larger. Tail slightly forked, (.10 of an inch.) Throat gorget with violet, steel green, or blue reflections behind; anteriorly opaque velvety black. Tail of female graduated; not emarginated..*T. Alexandri.*

TROCHILUS COLUBRIS, Linnaeus.

Ruby-throated Humming Bird.

Trochilus colubris, LINN. Syst. Nat. I, 1766, 191.—WILSON. Am. Orn. II, 1810, 26 ; pl. x.—AUD. Orn. Biog. I, 1832, 248 ; pl. 47.—IB. Birds Amer. IV, 1842, 190 ; pl. 253.
Ornismya colubris, DEVILLE, Rev. et. Mag. Zool. May, 1852, (habits.)

SP. CH.—Tail in the male deeply forked ; the feathers all narrow lanceolate-acute. In the female slightly rounded and emarginate ; the feathers broader, though pointed. Male, uniform metallic green above ; a ruby red gorget with no conspicuous ruff ; a white collar on the throat ; sides of body greenish ;tail feathers uniformly brownish violet. Female, without the red on the throat ; the tail is rounded and emarginate, the inner feathers shorter than the outer ; the tail feathers banded with black, and the outer tipped with white ; no rufous nor cinnamon on the tail in either sex. Length 3.25 ; wing 1.60 ; tail 1.25 ; bill .65.
Hab.—Eastern North America to the high central plains ; south to Brazil.

The bill of this species is slightly depressed, subcylindrical, very little decurved, and conically pointed at the end. Measured along the gape it is about half as long as the wing, which is falcate. In the male the outer tail feathers are all a little curved, the concavity inward ; the feathers are narrow and lanceolate-pointed, especially the exterior, which is only .16 of an inch wide ; the others are successively a little broader. The tail is rather deeply forked ; the exterior a very little shorter than the second ; the rest becoming rapidly shorter. The longest tail feather exceeds the shortest by about .21 of an inch.   The innermost tail feather is very broad; a little longer than the lower coverts.

In the female the tail feathers are still more curved, and considerably broader, and more rounded at the end, but still decidedly lanceolate, not linear. The tail, instead of being deeply forked, is only slightly emarginated ; the outer feather rather shorter than the second. The greatest width of the outer feather is about .26 of an inch.

In the male the entire upper parts, (including the crown,) with the sides of the body along the wings, are of a rich metallic green. The metallic scale-like feathers of the chin and throat are of a bright ruby red. These extend from the base of the bill (where the color is quite dull) over the throat, the posterior lateral ones not projecting more than .15 of an inch behind the middle ones. Immediately posterior to the metallic gorget is a collar of dirty white, which is continued along the median line, where it is tinged with brown, to the tail coverts, the centres of which show a little metallic green, and the exterior a little pale rufous. There is a rather purer white around the legs, and a very indistinct spot of the same just behind the eye. The tail feathers are uniform brownish purple ; the wings are similar, with less purple.

The adult female is similar to the male in the colors of the back and wings, with the white spot behind the eye. The entire under parts are of a dirty white, tinged with brownish on the throat and sides. The outer three tail feathers on either side have their central third of a purplish black ; the terminal portion white. The fourth feather is black at the end, with a very slight white tip. In all, the basal half of the upper surface (and of the lower in the fourth) is green like the back. The innermost has an indistinct subterminal bar of blackish. There is no rufous on any part of the tail feathers in either male or female.

The young male is like the female beneath, except that the throat feathers are spotted in the centre, and some show a trace of the metallic red. The tail is mostly like the male.

List of specimens.

Catal. No.	Sex.	Locality.	When collected.	Whence obtained.	Orig. No.	Collected by—	Length.	Stretch of wings.	Wing.
997	♀	Carlisle, Pa.	May 20, 1843	S. F. Baird			3.75	4.33	1.83
1168	⚲ ♂	do.	Aug. —, 1843	do.			3.67	4.25	1.67
1296	♂	Washington	1843	J. K. Townsend.					
1100	♂	do.	1843	do.					
2713	♂	do.	1843	do.					
1297	♀	do.	1843	do.					
1101	♀	do.	1843	do.					
6968	♂	Salt creek, K. T.	May 25, 1857	Lieut. Bryan	104	W. S. Wood			
5040	♂	Indianola.	Feb. 12, 1855	Capt. Pope					
3962		Brownsville, Texas.		Lieut Couch					
3963		Santa Catarina, Mex.		do.	179				
5041	♀	D. vil's river, Texas.	May 1, 1855	Capt. Pope.					
7985		Guatemala		J. Gould					

TROCHILUS ALEXANDRI, Bourc. & Mulsant.

Black-chinned Humming Bird.

Trochilus alexandri, Bourcier & Mulsant, Ann. de la Soc. d'Agric. de Lyons, IX, 1846, 330.—Heermann, Jour. A.
N. Sc. Phila. 2d ser. II, 1853, 269.—Cassin, Ill. N. Am. Birds, I, v, 1854, 141 ; pl. xxii.—Gould,
Mon. Trochilidae, xiv, Sep. 1857. Plate.

Sp. Ch.—Very similar to *Trochilus colubris*. Tail slightly forked ; the chin and upper part of the throat opaque velvety
black, without metallic reflections, which are confined to the posterior border of the gorget, and are violet, changing to steel
blue or green, instead of coppery red.

Female without the metallic scales ; the tail feathers tipped with white ; the tail graduated, not emarginat d ; the innermost
feather among the longest. Length of male 3.30 ; wing 1.70 ; tail 1.26 ; bill .75.

Hab.—Coast of California, southward.

This species is very similar in color to the common ruby-throated humming bird of the
eastern United States, and represents it on the west coast. The upper parts and sides are of the
same metallic golden green, the gorget of much the same extent, bordered behind by whitish,
which (less pure) extends along the middle of the belly, and involving the crissum, the feathers
of which are greenish in the centre. There is the same white spot behind the eye. *T. alexandri*
is, however, rather the larger of the two ; the bill nearly one-tenth of an inch longer. The tail
is much less deeply forked, in fact the outer feather is a little shorter than the second, and the
innermost broad green one only about .10 of an inch shorter than the longest, instead of
about .30. There is a tinge of metallic green to the tips of the tail feathers much less distinct
in *T. colubris*. The whitish collar behind the metallic feathers of the throat, usually considered
as a specific character, I find to be shared almost equally well by *T. colubris*. The chief distinctions between the two species are to be found in the violet steel blue or steel green reflections of
the hinder part of the gorget, varying with the situation of the feathers and the specimen, as
distinguished from the bright fiery or coppery red of the other. The chin and upper part of
the throat extending beneath the eyes are opaque velvety or greenish black, without metallic
lustre, while in *T. colubris* it is only the extreme chin which is thus dull in appearance.

It is exceedingly difficult to distinguish the female of this species from that of *T. colubris*.
The size is rather larger, and the tail rounded, without any emargination ; the middle feathers
being .15 of an inch longer than the lateral ones, instead of actually shorter. The color is
much the same.

In both species the outer tail feathers, though broader than in the male, are quite acutely
pointed on the terminal third, one side or the other of which is slightly concave, instead of
being linear to near the end, and rounded without any concavity, as in *Selasphorus* and *Atthis*.
The preceding description of this species is taken from specimens belonging to the very
extensive collection of birds of the vicinity of Fort Tejon, made by Mr. John Xantus de Vesey.

SELASPHORUS, Swainson.

Selasphorus, Swainson, Faun. Bor. Amer. II, 1831.

After separating the North American species usually called *Selasphorus*, with red metallic
scales on the crown, and the outer primary not attenuated at the top, there remain but two belonging to the restricted genus. Even in these there are some differences of form, but they may be
considered in the present instance as specific characters.

Tail strongly cuneate, the middle feather much' longest and very broad ; the outer very narrow, one-fifth the width of the middle.   Body chiefly cinnamon colored ; throat feathers a coppery red ; top of head, and an occasional gloss on the back, green......................*S. rufus.*

Tail rounded ; the middle feather a little shorter than the next one ; the outer rather broad, more than one-half the width of the middle one.   Above, and on the sides below, green. Throat feathers purple.   Edges of some tail feathers cinnamon brown...............*S. platycercus.*

SELASPHORUS RUFUS, Swainson.

Red-backed Humming Bird.

Trochilus rufus, GMELIN, Syst. Nat. I, 1788, 497.—AUD. Orn. Biog. IV, 1838, 555 ; pl. 372.
Selasphorus rufus, SWAINSON, F. Bor. Am. II, 1831, 324.—IB. AUD. Birds Am. IV, 1842, 200 ; pl. 254.
? *Trochilus ruber*, L.—ORN, I, 1788, 499.   (Fide Bonaparte.)
Trochilus collaris, LATH. (Bonaparte.)
Trochilus sitkensis, RATHKE. (Bonaparte.)
Ornysmia sasin, LESSON. (Bonaparte.)

SP. CH.—Tail strongly cuneate and wedge-shaped. Upper parts, lower tail coverts, and breast cinnamon. A trace of metallic green on the crown, which sometimes extends over the back ; never on the belly. Throat coppery red, with a well developed ruff of the same ; below this a white collar. Tail feathers cinnamon, edged or streaked at the end with purplish brown.
Female with the rufous of the back covered or replaced with green ; less cinnamon on the breast. Traces only of metallic feathers on the throat. Tail rufous, banded with black and tipped with white ; middle feathers glossed with green at the end. Tail still cuneate. Length of male, 3.50 ; wing, 1.55 ; tail, 1.30.
Hab.—West coast of North America, and across from Gulf of California to the Upper Rio Grande Valley.

This species is about the size of the common ruby-throated humming bird, which it resembles also in many respects.   The bill is rather narrower.   The wings are long and falcate ; the two first primaries elongated and acutely lanceolate, but not attenuated as abruptly as in *platycercus;* the third is also acute.   In most of the other species the first quill is much more linear than the second, and less acute than in this.

The tail is strongly cuneate ; the outer feather .40 of an inch shorter than the middle, which projects .14 of an inch beyond the rest.   The outer feather is very narrow, not exceeding .11 of an inch in width ; the rest widen and lengthen rapidly to the central one, which is very broad, (.35 of an inch ;) the central feathers are all ovate acuminate.

In the female the primaries are less acutely falcate than in the male.   The tail also, though cuneate, is less acutely so than in the male ; the outer feathers broader and less acutely pointed. In the male, in its highest plumage, the entire upper parts, excepting the crown and the wing, (but including the tail,) the sides of the body under the wings, and a broad band across the breast and abdomen, with the lower wing coverts, cinnamon brown, rather paler beneath.   The crown is obscurely golden green, not well defined.   The entire throat, including a short ruff on the side of the neck, (about .40 of an inch long,) is metallic red, of the same shade as in the ruby-throat, although with brassy reflections in some lights.   The sides of the neck beneath the ruff, the upper part of the breast, the anal region, and a small spot behind the eye are dull white.   The wings are violaceous brown, their coverts metallic green.   The tail feathers are cinnamon, with the outer webs near the tips violaceous brown ; this gradually becoming central instead of on the outer side.

In some specimens, probably immature, the back shows spots of metallic green, while in others (as 6059) it is entirely covered with this color, except on the tail.

The female is entirely of a metallic green above, with, however, more or less of a cinnamon shade on the covered edges of the feathers on the lower part of the back and rump. The sides of the body along the wings and the under tail coverts are pale cinnamon; the throat with occasional spots of green and metallic red; the rest of the under surface dull white tinged with brown across the breast. The tail feathers are cinnamon at the base, then violaceous black; all are tipped with white, except the middle one, on either side, which is golden green to near the black tip. There is also an indication of green between the black and cinnamon of the other feathers.

In both male and female there is a concealed tuft of white feathers near the insertion of the leg.

This species is entirely dissimilar from any other North American humming bird, and is perhaps the only one without indication of metallic green on the belly. The rufous feathers of both sexes readily distinguish it from any other North American species. There is, however, a closely allied South Mexican species, *Selasphorus scintilla* of Gould, from Veragua, (Proceedings Zool. Soc. 1850, 162,) which is very similar, differing chiefly in the smaller size.

I cannot discover in the *Trochilus ruber* of Linnaeus the exclusive characters of the present species.

List of specimens.

Catal. No.	Sex and age.	Locality.	When collected.	Whence obtained.	Orign'l No.	Collected by—	Length.	Extent.
6058	♂	Steilacoom, W. T.	April 26, 1856	Dr. Suckley	332			
6059	♀	......do		......do				
6060	♂	......do		......do				
6061	♂	......do	April 21, 1856	......do	333			
6062	♂	......do	April 28, 1856	......do				
6063	♂	......do	......do	......do	331		3.87	3.94
6064	♀	......do	......do	......do	330		3.87	4.69
6065	♂	......do	......do	......do	311		3.92	4.25
1943	o ♂	Columbia river	May 29, 1835	J. K. Townsend				
2896	♂	......do	......do	......do				
1198	♀	......do		......do				
1268	. ♂	California		S. F. Baird				
6057	♂	San Francisco	Winter '53-'54	R. D. Cutts				
....		Fort Tejon, Cal.		J. X. DeVesey.				
6067	....	El Paso, Texas		Maj. Emory		J. H. Clark		
7981	♀	Mexico		J. Gould				

SELASPHORUS PLATYCERCUS, Gould.

Broad-tailed Humming Bird.

Trochilus platycercus, Sw. Philos. Mag. I, 1827, 441, (Mexico.)
Selasphorus platycercus, GOULD, Mon. Trochilid. or Humming Birds, iii, May, 1852.
Ornismia tricolor, LESSON, Colibris, 125, (no date); pl. xiv, (Brazil.)—IB. Trochilidees, 1831, 156; pl. lx, (Mexico.)
　　JARDINE, Nat. Lib. II, 77; pl. xiii.
Ornismya montana, LESSON, Trochilid. 1831, 161; pl. lxiii, adult, and 163; pl. lxiv, young, (Mexico.)

SP. CH.—Outer primaries greatly attenuated at the end. Outer tail feathers nearly linear, but widening a little from the base; its width .20 of an inch. Tail slightly graduated and emarginate. Male above and on the sides metallic green; chin and throat light reddish purple, behind which, and along the belly to the tail, is a good deal of white. Wings and tail dusky purplish; the tail feathers, excepting the internal and external ones, edged towards the base with light cinnamon.

Length, 3.50; wing, 1.92; tail, 1.40. Bill, gape, .80.

Hab.—Mexico, as far north as El Paso, Texas, hitherto the only known locality in the United States.

In this species the metallic scales of the throat extend about as far back as in the *Trochilus colubris*. The tail feathers are all broad ; the outer one is rounded at the end and widens from the base ; the next succeeding feathers have the edges parallel at the base, and the tips rather acute. The innermost feather is a little shorter than the longest (by about .05 of an inch) ; the outermost about .15 shorter ; and the tail is thus moderately graduated and slightly emarginate.

The general appearance of this bird is not unlike that of the common ruby-throated *T. colubris*, although the two are distinguishable by generic peculiarities. *S. platycercus* is the larger bird, although the bill, if anything, is a little smaller. The graduated tail, with the broad, rounded, almost oblanceolate outer feather, is, however, in strong contrast to the deeply forked tail, with the acutely tapering outer tail feather of *T. colubris*.

A remarkable peculiarity in this species (shared by *C. rufus*) is seen in the outermost primary. This is narrower and more linear than in most of our other species, as well as straighter or less falcate. The terminal half inch is abruptly attenuated and linear, so as not to exceed .03 of an inch in width.

The green of the throat in this species is purer and less mixed with golden than in the *T. colubris*. The throat has a violet purple reflection instead of a fiery copper red. The crissum and breast are of a purer white. All the tail feathers, except the innermost, (which is like the back,) have a cinnamon edging on the inner edge, except at the extreme tip ; this is seen on both webs of all, except the first, where it is confined to the inner. This border is very conspicuous on the outer edge of the fourth feather.

I have no female of this species before me, but a specimen in the collection of the Philadelphia Academy, supposed to belong here, has no rufous on the tail.

In comparing specimens in the Philadelphia Academy, as well as that from El Paso, with Gould's figure, this is seen to indicate a much larger bird, (nearly 4½ inches long,) with longer tail and broader feathers, the external more pointed. Whether this would indicate the fact of a confounding of two species I am unprepared to say. His figure of the female shows very distinctly a rufous margin to the tail feathers.

For the determination of this species, now for the first time introduced into the fauna of the United States, I am indebted to Mr. John Gould, who identified it when examining the specimens of Humming Birds preserved in the Smithsonian Institution.

List of specimens.

Catal. No.	Sex.	Locality.	When collected.	Whence obtained.	Original No.	Collected by—
6066	♂	El Paso, Texas	1851	Maj. W. H. Emory		J. H. Clark
9007	♂	Mexico		Verreaux	34873	

ATTHIS, Reichenbach.

Atthis, REICHENBACH, Cab. Journal für Orn. Extraheft für 1853, 1854. App. B. (named only.)

I am not sure that the diagnosis given of this genus is that of its founder, but it will answer to separate a well marked form from the other North American species. It is most like *Selasphorus*, and its species have usually been placed in this genus ; it differs, however, in the absence of attenuated tips to the primaries, and in the presence of metallic scales on the whole top of the head similar in texture and color to those on the throat. The two North American species are quite similar, though different in size. The characters are as follows:

Green above and on the sides beneath, as well as on the middle of under tail coverts. Large. Metallic scales of the head uniform purplish red. Tail quite deeply forked, outer feather about half as wide as the inner...*A. anna.*

Smallest North American species. Metallic scales of the head purplish violet, with steel reflections. Tail emarginated only. Outer feather about one-fourth as wide as the middle.. ....*A. costae.*

ATTHIS ANNA, Reichenbach.

Anna Humming Bird.

Ornismya anna, LESSON, Oiseaux Mouches, 1830, (?) pl. cxxiv.
Trochilus anna, JARDINE, Nat. Lib. Humming Birds, I, 93 ; pl. vi.—AUD. Orn. Biog. V, 1839, 428 ; pl. 428.—IB. Birds America, IV, 1842, 188 ; pl. 252.
Calliphlox anna, GAMBEL, Pr. A. N. Sc. Phil. III, 1846, 3.—IB. Journ. 2d ser. I, 1847, 32.
Trochilus (Atthis) anna, REICHENBACH, Cab. Jour. Extraheft for 1853, 1854, app. 12.
Trochilus icterocephalus, NUTTALL, Manual, I, 2d ed., 1840, 712. (Male with forehead covered with yellow pollen.)

SP. CH.—Tail deeply forked ; external feather narrow, linear. Top of the head, throat, and a moderate ruff metallic red, with purple reflections. Rest of upper parts and a band across the breast green. Tail feathers purplish brown, darkest centrally. In the female the tail is slightly rounded, not emarginate ; the scales of the head and throat are wanting. Tail barred with black, and tipped with white.

Length, about 3.60 inches ; wing, 2.00 ; tail, 1.45.
Hab.—Coast region of California.

This species is considerably larger than the ruby-throated humming bird, but the bill is of much the same shape. The wings are long and considerably falcated ; the first primary much the most so ; its sides are nearly parallel to the end, which is rounded or obtusely pointed. The tail in the male is decidedly forked. The second feather is a little longer than the first, and is about 0.16 of an inch longer than the third, and about 0.32 longer than the fourth. The fifth feather (resembling an upper tail covert) is a little longer than the fourth, (by about 0.03.) The exterior feather is narrow and linear to the end, which is rounded ; it is about 0.12 of an inch wide. The next feather is one-half wider ; the others increasing still more. The feathers are all rather blunt at the end, or obtusely acute, with the point rounded.

In the female the tail feathers are all broader, the outer one especially, although still with parallel sides ; the tail itself is slightly rounded, all the feathers being of nearly the same length, except the lateral, which is about 0.10 of an inch shorter.

In this species the top of the head, the chin, and throat, with a conspicuous, though obtuse, ruff on each side of the throat, (about 0.40 of an inch long,) are of a rich purplish red, with an occasional violaceous shade, and on some scales of the top of the head and in the ruff, with steel blue reflections. The remaining upper parts, except the wings, are metallic green, glossed with gold. The under parts are similar, except that the color is not so continuous, much more so, however, than in the other American species ; even the centres of the under tail coverts are green. The lower part of the throat just behind the collar is dirty whitish. The wings and tail feathers are purplish brown ; the latter darkest centrally, with an occasional gloss of green. The central feather on either side is golden green, like the back.

The female is entirely metallic green above, with a tinge of dull brownish grey on the head. Beneath spotted with green, except on the throat, which is brownish white ; the feathers with

18 b

darker centres. The tail feathers are black in their middle portion and tipped with white, this decreasing until there is none in the median ones.

Two males, apparently not quite mature, (3942, 6050,) have the ruff shorter ; the scale feathers dimmer and more of an orange red. They are also rather smaller than the others.

Sometimes the metallic scales encroach on the sides of the head, so as apparently to cover them. There is, however, always a narrow plain line behind the eye. The ruff varies considerably in length with the specimen. There is no trace of cinnamon or rufous on any of the feathers in either sex.

The only North American species to which the male of this bird bears any resemblance is the *A. costae*, which has the same metallic crown and other generic features. The latter, however, is much smaller ; has the metallic reflections varied chiefly violet, instead of nearly uniform purplish red. The tail is much less deeply forked, the depth being only about 0.10 of an inch, instead of 0.32 ; the outer feather is much narrower. The females of the two, however, appear to be distinguishable only by their relative size. The absence of rufous and the rounded, not graduated, tail always separates the female of *anna* from that of *S. rufus*. The larger size is the chief distinction from the female *A. costae*, while the size and less acutely pointed outer tail feathers distinguish it from the female *T. colubris*.

List of specimens.

Catal. No.	Sex and age.	Locality.	When collected.	Whence obtained.	Orign'l No.	Collected by—
5501	♂	Petaluma, California.........	....	E. Samuels..........	282	....
6051	♂	San Francisco...............	Winter of '53-'54	R. D Cutts.........	......	....
6052	○ ♂	.......do...............	......do........	......do.........	......	....
6054	♀	.......do...............	......do........	......do.........	......	....
6050	♂	Cosumnes river, California....	....	Lt. Williamson......	......	Dr. Heermann ......
3942	....	Fort Tejon, California	1857	John Xantus de Vesey	......	....

ATTHIS COSTAE, Reichenbach.

Ornismyacostae, Bourcier, Rev. Zool. Oct. 1839, 294. (Lower California.)—Ib. Ann. Sc. Phys. et d'Hist. Nat. de Lyon, 1840, 225 ; tab. ii.—Prevost & Des Murs, Voyage de la Venus, Zool. I, 1855, 194. Atlas, tab. ii, f. 1, 2.

Selasphorus costae, Bon. Conspectus Avium, I, 1850, 82.

Atthis costae, Reichenbach, Cab. Jour. für Orn. Extraheft, 1853, 1854.

Calypte costae, Gould, Mon. Humming Birds.

Sp. Ch.—Tail very slightly emarginated and rounded ; exterior feather very narrow, and linear. A very long ruff on each side of the throat. Head above and below, with the ruff, covered with metallic red, purple, violet, and steel green. Remaining upper parts and sides of the body green. Throat under and between the ruffs, side of head behind the eye, anal region and under tail coverts whitish. Female with the tail rounded, scarcely emarginate ; barred with black, and tipped with white The metallic colors of the head wanting.

Length, 3.20 inches ; wing, 1.75 ; tail, 1.10 ; bill, .68.

Hab.—Southern California and Colorado Basin, (Monterey, Neboux.)

Of this beautiful humming bird only a single pair has hitherto been collected by any of the expeditions, and these are not sufficiently perfect to furnish a satisfactory description. The size is about that of the common ruby-throated humming bird. The bill is, however, longer and more slender every way. The wings are falcate ; the first quill especially curved, although its outlines are parallel to near the tip, which is not acuminate. In the male the tail is slightly emarginated ; the first or outer feather very little shorter than the second and third, which are about equal. The middle feathers are about 0.12 of an inch shorter than the second. The outer feather is very narrow and linear, about 0.06 wide ; the next is twice as wide ; all are rather linear rounded, or but little acute at the end. In the female the tail is rounded. The feathers broader.

The top of the head and the occiput of this species, with tne throat and a long ruff on each side, about 0.60 of an inch long, are covered with brilliant metallic scales, having various reflections of light purple, violet, and steel blue, and green, the steel green predominating on the points of the ruff. The rest of the upper parts, with the wing coverts, and the sides of the body and breast, are metallic green. The throat behind the scales and between the ruffs, the sides of the head behind the eye, the upper part of the breast, the middle of the belly, the space around the legs, the vent and under tail coverts, are whitish ; the latter with some green spots. The wings and tail feathers are brown ; the latter darker towards the end. The central ones are green on their upper surface.

The female is green above and on the sides of the body. The under parts are whitish, with brownish spots on the throat. The top of the head is likewise tinged with brown. The tail feathers are black in the middle, all tipped with white, though the amount of white rapidly decreases from the exterior to the centre.

This species is readily distinguished from the others belonging to the fauna of the United States, excepting *A. anna*, by the metallic scales of the tip of the head. It is much smaller than the last mentioned species ; the ruff is much longer, and with the other scales on the head of a different color, being purplish violet, not purple red, and the former species being destitute of the metallic green reflections. The white behind the eye and bordering the ruff is much less distinct in *anna*.

The female of this species differs much from the male in the absence of the metallic scales on the head and throat. It has a close resemblance to the female *T. colubris*, although the bill is smaller and narrower. The tail feathers are narrower, more linear, and less acutely pointed at the tip. The black on the outer tail feathers, instead of extending very nearly to the base, is confined to the terminal half, the basal portion being green. All the tail feathers are terminated by white, although that on the fourth and fifth is very narrow. In *T. colubris* this color is confined to the three outer ones. The much smaller size alone appears to distinguish it from the female of *A. anna*.

The specimen (6073) from New Mexico is decidedly different from others I have seen from California and Guatemala, in the great length of the ruff, which reaches back 1.66 of an inch from the base of the bill, instead of 1.45 or 1.50 ; the tips posteriorly having steel blue and green reflections, instead of being uniform purplish violet. This may, however, be indicative of a greater degree of maturity.

List of specimens.

Catal. No.	Sex.	Locality.	When collected.	Whence obtained.	Orign'l No.	Collected by—
6073	♂	Bill Williams' river, camp 117, N.M	February 9, 1854	Lieut. Whipple......	79	Dr. Kennerly and
6074	♀	......do...... ......do	......do..........	......do............	80	H. B. Möllhausen....
		Fort Tejon, California	....	J. X. De Vesey......		....
7977	......	Guatemala	....	J. Gould	......	....

Family CYPSELIDAE. The Swifts.

Bill very small, without notch, triangular, much broader than high ; the culmen not one-sixth the gape. Anterior toes cleft to the base, each with three joints, (in the typical species,) and covered with skin ; the middle claw without any serrations; the lateral toes nearly equal to the middle. Bill without bristles, but with minute feathers extending along the under margin of the nostrils. Nostrils elongated, superior, and very close together. Plumage compact. Primaries ten elongated, falcate.

The *Cypselidae*, or Swifts, are swallow-like birds, generally of rather dull plumage and small size. They were formerly associated with the true swallows on account of their small, deeply cleft bill, short feet, and long wings. T ey are, however, very different in all the essentials of structure, belonging indeed to a different order, or sub-order. The bill is much smaller and shorter ; the edges greatly inflected ; the nostrils superior, instead of lateral, and without bristles. The wing is more falcate, with ten primaries instead of nine. The tail has ten feathers instead of twelve. The feet are weaker, without distinct scutellae ; the hind toe is more or less versatile, the anterior toes usually lack the normal number of joints, and there are other features which clearly justify the wide separation here given, especially the difference in the vocal organs.

There are some forms of *Cypselidae* in which the usual proportional length of toes and number of their joints is as in other birds; nearly all the typical Old World genera, however, agree with the diagnosis above given. It is exceedingly probable, however, that the American genera have all the normal number of joints to the anterior toes, (3, 4, 5,) *Panyptila*, probably, not even forming an exception ; in this case they will be widely separated from the great majority at least, of the Old World species, which have 3, 3, 3. It may therefore be proper, on account of these and other differences, to divide the family into *Cypselinae*, confined to the Old World, and *Chaeturinae*, American and Asiatic.

The American *Cypselidae* are readily distinguished by characters of the legs, and including the Old World *Cypselus*, which has no true representative in this country, convenient diagnoses of the genera will be as follows, without reference to other features :

A. Legs very thick, more or less feathered. Tail forked. Second primary longest. Hind toe not posterior.

CYPSELUS.—Hind toe directed entirely forward. Legs feathered to the base of the toes.
PANYPTILA.—Hind toe directed laterally. Legs feathered to the base of the claws.

B. Legs slender: naked. Hind toe directed backwards ; first primary longest.

NEPHOCAETES.—Tail forked ; soft.
CHAETURA.—Tail even, the shafts stiffened and projecting as spinous points.

PANYPTILA, Cabanis.

Panyptila, CABANIS, Wiegm. Archiv, 1847, I, 345.—BURMEISTER, Thiere Bras. Vögel, I, 1856, 368.
Pseudoprocne, STREUBEL, Isis, 1848, 357.

Tail half as long as the wings, moderately forked ; the feathers rather lanceolate, rounded at tip, the shafts stiffened but not projecting. First primary shorter than the second. Tarsi, toes, and claws very thick and stout ; the former shorter than the middle toe and claw, which is rather longer than the lateral one ; middle claw longer than its digit. Hind toe very short ; half versatile, or inserted on the side of the tarsus. Tarsi and toes feathered to the claws, except on the under surfaces.

The North American representative of this genus, with a general resemblance to *Cypselus apus* in form, is quite different in the structure of the feet   These are stouter and shorter, feathered to the very claws, instead of to the toes only, and the posterior or inferior surface of the tarsus is naked. The greatest difference is in the hind toe, which, instead of being slender and entirely anterior like the rest, is lateral, and very short and thick. The tail feathers are much more rigid, the fork not so deep, the outer feather equal to, or a little shorter than, the second, instead of being considerably longer. The second quill is longest in both. The bills of both are quite similar.

The feathered legs readily distinguish the genus from the other American swifts.

There appears to be a tendeny on the inner toe to a more naked condition than in the others.

According to Burmeister, the numerical proportion of the joints of the anterior toes in this genus is the same as in most birds, namely, 3, 4, 5, instead of 3, 3, 3. This statement I have not yet been able to veri.y in the case of the North American species.

The South American species of this genus, as *P. cayanensis*, appear to be slenderer in form than *P. melanoleuca*, and the tail more deeply forked, approaching in this respect to *Hirundo rufa*. The feet, however, are very similar.

PANYPTILA MELANOLEUCA, Baird.

White-throated Swift.

Cypselus melanoleucus, BAIRD, Pr. A. N. Sc. Phil. VII, June, 1854, 118. (San Francisco mountains, N. M.)—CASSIN, Illust. I, 1855, 248.

SP. CH.—Wings very long ; tail forked ; tarsi and feet covered with feathers. Black all over, except the chin, throat, middle of the belly as far as the vent, a patch on each side of the rump, the edge of the outer primary, and blotches on the inner webs of the median tail feathers, near the base, which are white, as is also a band across the ends of the secondaries. Length 5.50 ; wing 5.50 ; tail 2.70.

Hab.—Colorado Basin, New Mexico.

The bill of this species is very small and short, though deep and much curved from the base. In shape and size it is somewhat similar to that of *Chaetura pelasgia*. The wings are very long and falcate, extending more than an inch beyond the tail. This excessive development is, however, almost entirely in the primaries, which measure nearly four times the secondaries, starting at the carpal joint. The second quill is longest, the first intermediate between this and the third ; the remaining primaries decrease rapidly to the last, are elongated acute, with the points but little rounded. The tail is composed of ten feathers ; it is acutely and quite deeply forked, the feathers all lanceolate acute, with much stiffer shafts than in the swallows. The outer feather is a very little shorter than the second, which is longest. The greatest depth of the fork is about half an inch.

The tarsi and toes are very thick and strong, though short. The anterior faces of both are covered with broad black feathers. The toes are much united anteriorly. The claws are all thick and much curved.

The prevailing color of the upper parts is of a sooty black, darker than in *Chaetura pelasgia ;* the head is brownish, however, and almost exactly as in the last mentioned species. The whole under parts as far as the breast, and a median line extending to the arms, are white, as is also a patch on each side of the rump, mostly concealed by the wings. The remaining under parts, including the lower coverts, are black like the back. The tail feathers, except the outer, have an elongated and obscure spot of whitish on the inner web near the base, otherwise they are in color like the back. The quills are rather more brown. The ends of the secondary quills are white, forming a conspicuous transverse band. The outer web of the outer primary is also narrowly edged with white.

List of specimens.

Catal. No.	Sex.	Locality.	When collected.	Whence obtained.	Orig. No.	Collected by—	Length.	Wing.	Tail.	Tarsus.	Middle toe.	Claw alone.	Bill alone.	Along gape.	Specimen measured.	Remarks.
6017	....	Camp 123, Bill Williams' river, N. M.	Feb. 16, 1854	Lt. Whipple....	169	Kennerly and Möllhausen.	....	5.25	....	....	....	....	....	....	Fresh .	Eyes black.
6018	♂	New Mexico...............	....	Lt J. G. Parke.	....	Dr. Heermann .	5.50	5.50	2.70	0.40	0.58	0.28	0.24	0.65	Skin...	....

NEPHOCAETES, Baird.

Cʜ.—Tail rather less than half the wings ; quite deeply forked ; the feathers obtusely acuminate ; the shafts scarcely stiffened. First quill longest. Tarsi and toes completely bare, and covered with naked skin, without distinct indications of scutellae. Tarsus rather longer than middle toe ; the three anterior toes about equal, with moderately stout claws. Claw of middle toe much shorter than its digit. Hind toe not versatile, but truly posterior and opposite, with its claw, rather longer than the middle toe without it. Toes all slender ; claws moderate. Nostrils widely ovate, the feathers margining its entire lower edge.

This genus is widely different from *Cypselus* in the slender and elongated toes and tarsi, which are completely bare of feathers. The hind toe is elongated and usually posterior, as in the *Oscines*, instead of being directed forward and by the side of the others. The tail feathers are less deeply forked, the lateral being much less lanceolate and elongated. The bill is more decurved. The anterior toes probably have 3, 4, 5 joints, as in most birds.

The affinities of this genus to *Chaetura*, as restricted, are very close, the feet being very similar. The shafts of the tail feathers, however, are only a little stiffened, and not mucronate. The tail also is deeply forked ; not even nor rounded. The larger *Acanthyli* of the older authors are still more like the present species in generic peculiarities. The tail, however, though sometimes forked, has the feathers more or less mucronate ; the legs stouter. The genus *Pallene*, in which they have been placed, is pre-occupied according to Gray. *Cypselus senex* of Temminck, from Brazil, is very closely allied, the tail feathers not being mucronate. The tail is, however, even or slightly rounded, instead of forked. A genus *Pallenis* established for this species by Reichenbach might, without much violence, be made to include *N. niger;* but as this name is pre-occupied for another genus, there seems nothing left but to establish a new one.

The genus *Macropteryx* of Swainson has naked feet, but the tarsi are excessively short and thick ; much shorter than any of the toes, even without the claws. The lower part of the tibia is partly denuded. The tail is very deeply forked, the outer feather having almost the extension of *Hirundo rufa*, and extending beyond the tips of the wings. It probably belongs to the section of *Cypselidae* with three joints to each of the anterior toes.

NEPHOCAETES NIGER, Baird.

Northern Swift.

? Hirundo nigra, GMELIN, Syst. Nat. I, 1788, 1025.
Cypselus niger, GOSSE, Birds Jamaica, 1847, 63.—Iʙ. Illustrations Birds Jamaica.—GUNDLACH and LAWRENCE, Annals New York Lyceum, VI, 1858, 268.
Cypselus borealis, KENNERLY, Pr. Ac. Nat. Sc. Phila. IX, Nov. 1857, 202.
Hirundo apus dominicensis, BRISSON., II, 1760, 514 ; pl. xlvi, fig. 3.

Sᴘ. Cʜ.—Wing the length of the body. General color rather lustrous dark sooty brown, with a greenish gloss, becoming a very little lighter from the breast anteriorly below, but rather more so on the neck and head above. The feathers on the top of the head edged with light gray, which forms a continuous wash on each side the forehead anterior to the usual black crescent in front of the eye. Some feathers of the under parts behind narrowly edged with gray. Bill and feet black. Length 6.75 ; wing 6.75 ; tail 3.00 ; depth of fork .45.

Hab.—Northwestern America to West India islands.

The coloration of this bird is so simple that there is little to be added in this respect to tho preceeding description, while the peculiarities of form are sufficiently well expressed by the generic indications already given. The appearance of the bird is that of a large chimney bird, (*Chaetura pelasgia.*) The color is much darker, however, nor is there the decided whitening on the chin and throat. The top of the head is similar, but rather lighter, with the gray on the sides of the forehead more distinct. In both, as in all swifts, there is a dusky crescent anterior to the eye formed of feathers standing nearly erect.

This remarkable swift was first indicated as North American by Dr. Kennerly, in the proceedings of the Philadelphia Academy, where it is described as *Cypselus borealis*. It was obtained in the northern part of Puget's Sound, at Simiahmoo bay, the locality of the main camp of the Northwest Boundary Survey. A large flock was seen one day sailing about the camp, but, owing to the height at which the birds flew, only one specimen could be procured.

It seems very remarkable that so large a swift could have remained unnoticed in North America until the present day ; but there is good reason to believe that additional species of Cypselidae will yet be discovered in the far west, (among them the one with white rump, *Acanthylis saxatilis*, seen by Dr. Woodhouse at Inscription rock, New Mexico.) It is possible that it may prove to be the *Hirundo niger* of Gmelin ; but this, as well as the *Hirundo apus dominicensis* of Brisson, applies as well to *Progne* as to any swift, and at any rate would answer for several known species. The *Cypselus niger* of Gosse, Birds Jamaica, 1847, 63, referred to the *Hirundo niger* of Gmelin is quite similar to the *N. borealis*, but, judging from the description, is smaller, has the tail differently shaped, and the colors are somewhat different. If really the same it would be somewhat remarkable to find a species to range from almost the northwestern corner of North America to the West India and eastern South America islands, and never observed east of the Rocky mountains.[1]

List of specimens.

Catal. No.	Sex	Locality.	When collected.	Whence obtained.	Collected by—	Length.	Stretch of wings.	Wing.	Tail.	Tarsus.	Mi'dle toe.	Its claw alone.	Bill above.	Along gape.	Specimen measured.
8412	♂	Simiahmoo bay,W.T.	July, 1857	A. Campbell	Dr. Kennerly..	6.75	17.00	6.75	......	......	......	......	......	......	Fresh
do.	....	........do	.... do....	....do	..... do	6.60	......	6.75	3.00	.59	.65	.25	.30	.70	Skin.
	♂	Cuba.................		Borrowed from G. N. Lawrence ..	Dr. Gundlach..	6.50	......	5.90	2.90	.54	.61	.24	.29	.57	Skin.

[1] NOTE.—Since writing the preceding article I have received from Mr. Lawrence a skin collected in Cuba, by Dr. Gundlach, which is exactly like Dr. Kennerly's bird, except in being smaller, (the wing nearly an inch shorter) and the tail feathers more rounded. The difference in size is easily explained by the difference of latitude, and I see no reason for separating them. This extends the known range of the species very largely, and shows an unusual line of geographical distribution. I have not learned whether Dr. Gundlach's bird is a summer or a winter visitor in Cuba.

The identification of the species, however, with *Hirundo niger* of Gmelin, I still consider as very doubtful, though the probabilities are increased by the similarity of the two specimens. For the present, however, I think it may be best to take the name of Gmelin, leaving *Nephocaetes borealis* to be restored hereafter, if necessary.

CHAETURA, Stephens.

Chaetura, STEPHENS, Shaw's Gen. Zool. Birds, XIII, II, 1825, 76, (type, *C. pelasgia*.)
Acanthylis, BOIE, Isis, 1826, 971, (*A. spinicauda*.)

CH —Tail very short, scarcely more than two-fifths the wings ; slightly rounded ; the shafts stiffened and extending some distance beyond the feathers in a rigid spine. First primary longest. Legs covered by a naked skin, without scutellae or feathers. Tarsus longer than middle toe. Lateral toes equal, nearly as long as the middle. Hind toe scarcely versatile, or quite posterior ; with the claw, less than the middle anterior without it. Toes slender ; claws moderate. Feathers of the base of the bill not extending beyond the beginning of the nostrils.

The spinous processes to the nearly even tail readily distinguish this genus from any other of the North American *Cypselidae*. The two North American species differ chiefly in size.

I have restored the generic name of *Chaetura* to this species as being prior to *Acanthylis*. There is, indeed, a genus *Chaeturus* of earlier date in botany, but for all the practical purposes of synonymy the two names are perfectly distinct ; more so, in fact, than *Picus* and *Pica*, which belong to the same class instead of to different kingdoms.

CHAETURA PELASGIA, Stephens.

Chimney Swallow.

Hirundo pelasgia, LINN. Syst. Nat. I, 1766, 345.—WILS. Am. Orn. V, 1812, 48 ; pl. xxxix, fig. 1.
Cypselus pelasgia, AUD. Orn. Biog. II, 1834, 329 : V, 419 ; p'. 158.
Chaetura pelasgia, STEPHENS. in Shaw's Gen. Zool. Birds, XIII, II, 1825, 76.—IB. Birds America I, 1840, 164 ; pl. 44.
Acanthylis pelasgia, " TEMM."—BON. Consp. 1850, 64.—CASSIN, Ill. I, 1855, 241.
Hemiprocne pelasgia, STREUBEL, Isis, 1848, 363.
Aculeated swallow, PENN. Arc. Zool. II, 1785, 432.

SP. CH.—Tail slightly rounded, of a sooty brown all over, except on the throat, which becomes considerably lighter from the breast to the bill. Above with a greenish tinge ; the rump a little paler. Length, 5.25 inches ; wing, 5.10 ; tail, 2.15.
Hab.—Eastern United States to slopes of Rocky mountains?

The western range of the chimney bird is not well ascertained, the only specimens brought in by the expeditions being one from Bijoux Hill, Nebraska, and several from Independence.

List of specimens.

Catal. No.	Sex.	Locality.	When collected.	Whence obtained.	Orig. No.	Collected by—	Length.	Stretch of wings	Wing.	Tail.	Tarsus.	Middle toe.	Claw alone.	Bill above.	Along gape.	Specimen measured
1010	♀	Carlisle, Pa...............	May 22, 1843	S. F. Baird.....	...	...............…......	5.25	12.50	5.17	....	....	....	....	....	....	Fresh.*..
6485	....	Philadelphia	....	C. Drexler... ..	...	...............4.75	......	5.12	2.20	0.55	0.50	0.20	0.21	0.67	Skin ....
4781	....	Bijoux Hill, N. T.	May 15, 1856	Lt. G. K. Warren	...	Dr. Hayden......	4 87	12.50	5.17	....	....	....	....	....	....	
7526	...	Independence, Mo.	1857.........	W. M. Magraw..	...	Dr. Cooper	......	......	....	....	....	....	....	....	
8317	♂	.....do.	Mar. 29, 1857	......do.	34	..... do.	5.00	12.25	5.25	....	....	....	....	....	....	

* Iris dark brown.

CHAETURA VAUXII, DeKay.

Oregon Swift.

Cypselus vauxii, TOWNSEND, J. A N. Sc. VIII, 1839, 148, (Col. river.)—IB. Narrative, 1839.
Chaetura vauxii, DEKAY, N. Y. Zool. II, 1844, 36.
Acanthylis vauxii, BONAP. Comptes Rendus, XXVIII, 1854 ; notes Delattre, 90.—CASSIN, Ill. I, 1855, 250.—
NEWBERRY, Zool. Cal. and Or. Route, 78 ; P. R. R. Surv. VI, 1857.

SP. CH—Light sooty brown ; rump and under parts paler ; lightest on the chin and throat. Length, 4.50 inches ; wing,
4.75 ; tail, 1.90.
Hab.—Pacific coast, from Puget's Sound to California.

This species bears a very close resemblance to the common chimney birds of the eastern
States, being only readily distinguishable by its much smaller size, less than 4¼ inches instead
of 5¼. The wing, too, is nearly an inch shorter. The tarsus and the middle toe, however,
seem absolutely longer. The rump is a little paler than in *C. pelasgia*, as well as the under
parts, where the chin and throat are lighter, almost dirty white, and gradually becoming a
little darker behind, although even the hinder part of the belly is much lighter than the back,
instead of being of the same color with it.

This species, though probably not rare on the western coast, has only been collected by J. K.
Townsend (his specimen in the Phila. Academy) and by Dr. Kennerly of American explorers.
Delattre, however, brought it from California. It is very closely allied to several small South
American species, and may have been described under another if not a prior name.

List of specimens.

Catal. No.	Sex.	Locality.	When collected.	Whence obtained.	Original No.	Collected by—	Length.	Extent.	Wing.	Tail.	Tarsus.	Middle toe.	Its claw alone.	Bill above.	Along gape.	Specimen measured.
8411	♀	Simiahmoo bay, W. T......	July 5,1857	A. Campbell...	10	Dr. Kennerly...	4.50	10.75	4.50							Fresh....
....		....do..............	.....do.......	.....do........	....	........do........	4.40	.....	4.70	1.70	.50	.61	.25	.20	.56	Skin....
....		Oregon. (Specimen of J. K. Townsend.)	.. ..	...,.............	....	....	4.15	.....	4.75	1.90	.40	....	......	.20	.51	Mounted.

19 b

Family CAPRIMULGIDAE. The Goat-suckers.

Sub-Family CAPRIMULGINAE.

Cн.—Bill very short, triangular, the culmen less than one-sixth the gape. The anterior toes united at the base by a membrane The inner anterior toe with three joints, the others with four ; all with distinct scutellae above. The toe much elongated, its middle claw pectinated on the inner edge. Hind toe directed a little more than half forwards. Tarsi partly feathered superiorly. The bill more or less bristled ; the nostrils separated, rather nearer the commissure than the culmen. Pl mage soft, lax, and owl-like.

The *Caprimulgidae* have quite a close resemblance to the owls in the color and texture of the plumage, as well as in the broad head, although, of course, readily distinguishable by unmistakable characters. The closest relationships are to the *Cypselidae*. The primary quills are ten in number, the secondaries eleven or twelve. The latter are much longer than in the *Cypselidae*, covering more than half the primaries. The middle toe is much longer than in the *Cypselidae*, and its claw is usually provided with a comb-like edge on one side. The anterior toes are united by a membrane, the inner and middle usually more so than the middle and outer. The inner toe is small, and the outer is usually so, having generally only four joints instead of the normal five. The tarsi are covered with short scales anteriorly, their upper portion generally clothed with feathers.

The *Caprimulgidae* are divided into two sub-families, the *Steatorninae* and *Caprimulginae*, the former having the inner edge of the middle anterior claw expanded, but not pectinated. A third sub-family *Podagerinae* is sometimes added. The *Caprimulginae* alone are represented in the United States, and by two genera, *Antrostomus* and *Chordeiles*, which may readily be distinguished as follows :

ANTROSTOMUS.—Bill with conspicuous bristles. Wings short, rounded; tail broad, graduated; plumage very lax.

CHORDEILES.—Bill without bristles ; wings very long and pointed ; tail narrow, forked ; plumage compact.

ANTROSTOMUS, Gould.

Antrostomus, GOULD, Icones Avium, 1838, (Agassiz.)

Cн.—Bill remarkably small, with tubular nostrils, and the gape with long stiff, sometimes pectinated, bristles. Wings long, somewhat rounded, second quill longest, the primaries emarginated. Tail rounded. Plumage loose and soft.

The present genus embraces the North American analogues of the European goat-suckers— namely, the chuck-will's widow and the two species of whippoorwill. Of these, the former, or *A. carolinensis*, is much the largest, with the long stiff bristles of the bill provided with lateral filaments ; these are wanting in the *A. vociferus* and *A. nuttalli*. In *vociferus*, which is much the larger of the two last, the throat has a narrow white collar, and the lower terminal half of the tail is white; the head longitudinally streaked. In *nuttalli* the throat has a large white patch ; the under surface of the tail a small one, and the crown is banded transversely, not longitudinally.

Comparative measurements of species.

Orig. No.	Species.	Locality.	Sex.	Length.	Extent.	Wing.	Tail.	Tarsus.	Middle toe.	Its claw.	Bill above.	Along gape.	Specimen measured.
6493	Antrostomus carolinensis.	Tortugas, Fla......	♂	11.62	....	8.60	6.38	0.68	1.02	0.30	0.50	1.72	Skin........
8636	.....do........do.......	Cape Florida.......	♀	11.04	....	8.30	5.84	0.76	1.00	0.30	0.44	1.72	Skin........
do.	......do ....do.......	........do...........	......	12.	25.	8.50	......	......	......	......	......	......	Fresh.......
2144	Antrostomus vociferus....	Carlisle, Penn......	♂	9.20	....,....	6.34	5.08	0.68	0.84	0.24	0.44	1.24	Skin........
do.	.....do .... do......	.... ..do...........	♂	9.75	19.25	*6.41	......	......	......	......	......	......	Fresh.......
6963	......do ....do.......	St. Louis, Mo......	♀	9.54	....	6.22	5.00	0.60	0.90	0.26	0.44	1.16	Skin........
5491	Antrostomus nuttalli......	Petaluma, Cal......	♂	7.20	....	5.78	3.84	0.76	0.84	0.20	0.44	1.10	Skin........
do.	......do ....do......	Yellowstone	♀	7.10	....	5.62	3.70	0.70	0.90	0.26	0.40	1.12	Skin........

ANTROSTOMUS CAROLINENSIS

Chuck-will's Widow.

Caprimulgus carolinensis, GMELIN, Syst. Nat. I, 1788, 1028—AUD. Orn. Biog. I, 1832, 273; pl. lii, & V, 1839, 401.—IB. Birds Amer. I, 1840, 151; pl. 41.

Antrostomus carolinensis, GOULD, Icones Avium, 1838?—CASSIN, J. A. N. Sc. II, 1852, 119.—IB. Illust. N. Am. Birds, I, 1855, 236.

Caprimulgus rufus, VIEILLOT, Ois. Am. Sept. I, 1807, 57; pl. xxv, (♀.)

Caprimulgus brachypterus, STEPHENS, Shaw's Zool. X, I, 1825? 150.

Short-winged goat-sucker, PENNANT, Arctic Zool. II, 1785, 434.

SP. CH.—Bristles of the bill with lateral filaments. Wing nearly nine inches long. Top of the head reddish brown, longitudinally streaked with black. The prevailing shade above and below pale rufous. Terminal two-thirds of the tail feathers (except the four central,) rufous white; outer webs of all mottled, however, nearly to the tips. Female without the white patch on the tail. Length, 12 inches; wing, 8.50.

Hab.—South Atlantic and Gulf States.

This is the largest of the North American species, and is distinguished from the others by having very strong bristles along the base of the bill, each with lateral filaments. The tail is but slightly rounded; the exterior feathers only about a quarter of an inch shorter than the middle ones. The wing is long; the second quill longest. The tip of the third nearly intermediate between the first and second.

This species is said by Audubon to occur in Texas, but no specimens have been collected west of the Missouri by any of the expeditions.

List of specimens.

Catal. No.	Sex.	Locality.	When collected.	Whence obtained.	Length.	Stretch of wings.	Wing.	Specimen measured.	Remarks.
2383	......	Savannah, Ga......	1845.........	S. F. Baird	12.00	26.00	7.25	Fresh	Light purple legs.
2382	♂	......do..........	1845.........	......do.........	......	......	......	......	......
4916	♂	St. John's river, Fla.	....	G. Wurdeman...	......	......	......	......	......
6493	♂	Tortugas, Fla......	1857.........	......do.........	......	......	......	......	......
8636	♂	Cape Florida.......	Oct. 30, 1857..	......do.........	12.00	25.00	8.50	Fresh	......
8637	♀	......do..........	Oct. 9, 1857..	......do.........	11.00	23.00	8.00	......	......

ANTROSTOMUS VOCIFERUS.

Whippoorwill.

Caprimulgus vociferus, WILSON, Am. Orn. V, 1812, 71 ; pl. xli, f. 1, 2, 3.—AUD. Orn. Biog. I, 1832, 443 : V, 405 ; pl. 85.—IB. Birds Am. I, 1840, 155 ; pl. 42.
Antrostomus vociferus, BONAP. List, 1838.—CASSIN, J. A. N. Sc. II, 1852, 122.—IB, Ill. I, 1855, 236.
Caprimulgus virginianus, VIEILL. Ois. Am. Sept. I, 1807, 55 ; pl. xxv.
" *Caprimulgus clamator,* VIEILLOT, Nouv. Dict. X, 1817, 234," (CASSIN.)

SP. CH.—Bristles without lateral filaments. Wing about 6½ inches long. Top of the head ashy brown, longitudinally streaked with black. Terminal half of the tail feathers (except the four central) dirty white on both outer and inner webs. Length, 10 inches ; wing, 6.50.
Female without white on the tail.
Hab.—Eastern United States to the plains.

In this species the bristles at the base of the bill, though stiff and long, are without the lateral filaments of the chuck-will's widow. The wings are rather short ; the second quill longest ; the first intermediate between the third and fourth. The tail is rounded ; the outer feathers about half an inch shorter than the middle ones.

The colors of this species are very difficult to describe, although there is quite a similarity to those of *A. carolinensis,* from which its greatly inferior size will at once distinguish it. The top of the head is an ashy gray, finely mottled, with a broad median stripe of black ; all the feathers with a narrow stripe of the same along their centres. The back and rump are somewhat similar, though of a different shade. There is a collar of white on the under side of the neck, posterior to which the upper part of the breast is finely mottled, somewhat as on the top of the head. The belly is dirty white, with indistinct transverse bands and mottlings of brown. The wings are brown ; each quill with a series of round rufous spots on both webs, quite conspicuous on the outer side of the primaries when the wings are folded. The terminal half of the outer three tail feathers is of a dirty white.

The female is smaller ; the collar on the throat is tinged with fulvous. The conspicuous white patch of the tail is wanting, the tips only of the outer three feathers being of a pale brownish fulvous.

There is a prevalent impression among the unlearned in many parts of the country that the whippoorwill and the night hawk are identical. They are, however, widely different, both generically and specifically, as will be evident to any one on a comparison of specimens. Thus in the whippoorwill the mouth is margined by enormous stiff bristles more than an inch long ; the wings are short, not reaching the end of the tail, which is very broad and rounded. There are bars of rufous spots on the wing quills, but no white whatever. The tail is white beneath for its terminal half. In the night hawk (*Chordeiles popetue*) the bristles of the bill are scarcely appreciable ; the wings are sharp pointed, longer than the tail, uniformly brown, with a broad spot of white across the middle of the long quills, and without any rufous spots. The tail is rather narrow, forked, or emarginate, and with only a small square blotch of white near the end. The most striking feature next to the difference of the bristles of the bill is, perhaps, the absence of the white wing spot of the one and its presence in the other—characters found in both sexes.

The precise range of this species to the westward is not ascertained. On the upper Missouri and westward it is replaced by the *A . nuttalli.*

The first name of Vieillot for this species, although actually prior to that of Wilson, cannot be made use of, as it heads a description and figure relating to both *Antrostomus* and *Chordeiles.*

List of specimens.

Catal. No.	Sex.	Locality.	When collected.	Whence obtained.	Orig'l No.	Collected by—	Length.	Stretch of wings.	Wing.	Specimen measured.
1410	♂	Carlisle, Pa.............	May 1, 1844	S. F. Baird		....	10.00	19.25	6.42	Fresh ...
2144	♂	.....do	April 26, 1845	......do		....	9.75	19.25	6.42	Fresh ...
2432	♀	.....do	Sept. 6, 1845	......do		....	9.83	18.75	6.25	Fresh ...
6963	♀	St Louis, Mo...........	May 8, 1857	Lieut. Bryan........ ...		W. S. Wood	....	....	....	....
8382	♂	Independence, Mo.......	June 20, 1857	Wm. M. Magraw	86	Dr. Cooper	10.00	18.75	6 50	Fresh ...
	♂	Racine, Wis	....	R. Kennicott............		Dr. Hoy	....	....	....	....

ANTROSTOMUS NUTTALLI, Cassin.

Nuttall's Whippoorwill.

Caprimulgus nuttalli, Aud. Birds America, VII, 1843 ; pl. 495 appendix.
Antrostomus nuttalli, Cassin, J. A. N. Sc. Phila. 2d series, II, 1852, 123.—Ib. Ill. I, 1855, 237.—Newberry, Zool. Cal. and Oregon Route, 77 ; Rep. P. R. R. Surv. VI, iv.

Sp. Ch.—Bristles without lateral filaments ; wing about 5¼ inches ; top of the head hoary gray, with narrow transverse, not longitudinal bands. Tail nearly black on the terminal half, the extreme tip only (in the three outer feathers of each side) being white for nearly an inch. Length 8.00 ; wing 5.50.

Hab.—High central plains to the Pacific coast.

I regret that the materials before me are not such as to admit of a satisfactory description, especially as in the wide range of localities there are indications of differences which may even be of specific value. I shall, therefore, be obliged to copy from Audubon the description of the species as obtained in its original locality—the upper Missouri.[1]

This species is said to have a note somewhat similar to that of the whippoorwill, except that the first syllable is omitted, leaving the sound something like that of "poor-will."

The much smaller size of the *A. nuttalli* will at once distinguish it from the *A. vociferus*. The colors, too, are very different. The general hue is much lighter. The top of the head lacks the median stripe. The white patch of the throat is much larger. The white of the tail is confined to a space of less than one inch at the end, &c.

[1] The following is the original description of the species by Audubon :

Caprimulgus nuttalli, Aud. Birds America, VI, pl. 495, 2 ed.

Male.—Bill black ; iris dark hazel ; feet reddish purple ; scales and claws darker ; general color of upper parts dark brownish gray, lighter on the head and medial tail feathers, which extend ½ inch beyond the others, all which are minutely streaked and sprinkled with brownish black and ash gray. Quills and coverts dull cinnamon color, spotted in bars with brownish black ; tips of former mottled with light and dark brown ; three lateral tail feathers barred with dark brown and cinnamon, and tipped with white. Throat brown, annulated with black ; a band of white across fore neck ; beneath the latter black, mixed with bars of light yellowish gray and black lines. Under tail coverts dull yellow. Length, 7.25 ; wing, 5.75 ; bill, edge, .19 ; second and third quills nearly equal. Tail to end of upper feathers, 3.50 ; tarsus, .63 ; middle toe, .63 ; claw, .25 ; strongly pectinated.

List of specimens.

Catal. No	Sex.	Locality.	When collected.	Whence obtained.	Orig. No.	Collected by—	Length.	Stretch of wings.	Wing.	Specimen measured.	Remarks.
8876	♂	Black hills.............	Sept. 7, 1857	Lt. G. K. Warren.	......	Dr. Hayden......	7.12	17.12	4.50?	Fresh....	Iris brown .....
5200	....	Yellow Stone river.....	Aug. 8, 1856	......do	......	......do	......	......	5.70	......	....
6002	♀	Rio Mimbres, N. M.....	....	Maj. Emory	......	Mr. Clark........	......	......	5.60	......	......
6003	....	......do	......	Dr. T. C. Henry..	......	Dr. Henry........	......	......	5.90	......	......
6000	....	Atanam river, W. T....	Aug. 30. 1853	Gov. I. I. Stevens.	5	Dr. J. G. Cooper..	......	......	5.80	......	......
6001	....	......do	....do	......do	6	......do	......	......	......	......	Body lost ......
5491	♂	Petaluma, Cal........	....	E. Samuels.......	590	E. Samuels.......	......	......	6.10	......	......
5912	....	Santa Clara, Cal.......	Nov. —, 1855	Dr. J. G. Cooper..	......	....	8.00	17.50	5.50	....	Iris brown, bill black, feet gray.
3711	....	California.............	....	W. Hutton	......	....	......	......	5.80	......	......
6004	....	Colorado river, N. M. ..	Feb. 23, 1854	Lt. Whipple......	179	Kennerly & Möllhausen.........	......	......	......	......	......
....	....	Camp 130, N. M........	....do	......do	177	do.	... .	....	5.90	....	Eyes black.....

CHORDEILES, S w a i n s o n.

SWAINSON, Fauna Bor. Amer. II, 1831, 496.

CH.—Bill very small, the gape with very short feeble bristles. Wings very long and pointed, with the first quill nearly or quite equal to the second, and the primaries not emarginated on the inner edge. Tail long ; slightly forked in the North American species ; plumage rather compact. '

The described North American species of this genus are three in number, the smaller readily distinguishable by the rounded rufous spots on the webs of the quills, (*C. texensis.*) The others are larger and more closely related.

Comparative measurements of species.

Catal. No.	Species.	Locality.	Sex.	Length.	Stretch of wings.	Wing.	Tail.	Tarsus.	Middle toe.	Its claw alone.	Bill above.	Along gape.	Specimen measured.	Remarks.
1605	Chordeiles virginianus .	Carlisle, Pa........	♂	8.70	......	8.10	4.72	0.62	0.80	0.28	0.34	0.98	Skin	....
do.	......do	......do	......	9.50	24.50	8.30	......	......	......	......	......	......	Fresh ...	....
1522	..... do	......do	♀	8.66	......	7.80	4.60	0.60	0.74	0.24	0.26	0.94	Skin ...	....
do.	......do	......do	......	9.50	23.60	8.16	......	......	......	......	......	......	Fresh ...	....
5201	......do	Above Fort Pierre..	♂	9.10	......	7.56	4.58	0.52	0.68	0.20	......	0.80	Skin ...	Point of bill broken.
do.	......do	......do	......	9.25	22.25	7.75	......	......	......	......	......	......	Fresh ...	....
6698	Chordeiles henryi	Rio Grande valley..	♀	......	......	7.80	5.18	0.54	0.70	0.20	0.28	1.08	Skin ...	....
6010	Chordeiles texensis	El Paso, Texas.....	○	8.30	......	7.54	4.84	0.50	0.68	0.20	0.24	0.82	Skin ...	....
do.	......do	......do	.....	7.87	19 12	7.87	......	......	......	......	......	......	Fresh ...	....
4578	..... do	Colorado river, Cal.	......	8.30	......	6.90	4.60	0.52	0.64	0.18	0.22	0.84	Skin	Head off ; (very poor specimen.)
do.														
6011	......do	Eagle pass, Texas..	.....	8.30	......	6.50	4.16	0.52	0.74	0.19	0.26	0.70	....	......do ....
3957	......do	Sta. Catarina, Mex.	......	8.22	......	7.00	4.30	0.52	0.74	0.22	0.24	0.80	Skin	....
do.				8.75	19.00	7.00	......	......	......	......	......	......	Fresh ...	

CHORDEILES POPETUE.

Night Hawk; Bull Bat.

Caprimulgus popetue, VIEILLOT, Ois. Am. Sept. I, 1807, 56 ; pl. xxiv. (♀).—BONAP. Obs. Wilson, 1825, 177, from
    J. A. N. Sc. Phila. VI.

Caprimulgus americanus, WILSON, V, 1812, 65 ; pl. cxl. f. 1, 2.

Chordeiles americanus, DE KAY, N. Y. Zool. II, 1844, 34 ; pl. xxvii.

Caprimulgus virginianus, BRISSON, II, 1760, 477. (In part only.)—BONAP. Synopsis, 62.—AUD. Orn. Biog. II,
    1834, 273 ; pl. 147.

Caprimulgus (Chordeiles) virginianus, Sw. F. Bor. Am. II, 1831, 62.

Chordeiles virginianus, BON. List. 1838.—AUD. Birds Am. I, 1840, 159 ; pl. 43.—CASSIN, Ill. I, 1855, 238.—NEW-
    BERRY, Zool. Cal. and Oregon Route, 79; Rep. P. R. R. Surv. VI, 1857.

Long-winged goat-sucker, PENNANT, Arctic Zool. II, 1785, 337.

SP. CH.—Male, above greenish black, with but little mottling on the head and back. Wing coverts varied with grayish ;
scapulars with yellowish rufous. A nuchal band of fine gray mottling, behind which is another coarser one of rufous spots.
A white V-shaped mark on the throat ; behind this a collar of pale rufous blotches, and another on the breast of grayish
mottling. Under parts banded transversely with dull yellowish or reddish white and brown. Wing quills quite uniformly
brown. The five outer primaries with a white blotch midway between the tip and carpal joint, not extending on the outer web
of the outer quill. Tail with a terminal white patch.

Female, without the caudal white patch, the white of the throat mixed with reddish. Length of male, 9.50 ; wing, 8.20.

Hab.—North America generally.

Specimen from Pennsyvania, (1605.)—Wings long and acutely pointed ; within an inch
as long (measured from the carpal joint) as the body itself. First quill longest, the rest
successively shorter. Tail acutely emarginate ; the first outer feather very little longer than the
second ; the remaining ones successively shorter, until the two middle ones are about three
quarters of an inch shorter than the exterior. Bill short ; the bristles simple.

The prevailing color of the upper parts of this species is a lustrous greenish black, with a
little mottling of pale rusty on the head, back, and scapulars, and of gray on the wing coverts.
At first sight the crown seems to have but little mottling, this being apparently confined to
a median line of yellowish rusty edging to the feathers. On raising the ends of these, however,
they are found to be more blotched towards their bases. On the nape the blotches are more
terminal and of a grayish color, forming an indistinct transverse band. Here they are quite
small, and confined to the exterior or extremity of the feathers. Immediately succeeding this,
however, is a second indistinct transverse band in which the blotches are much larger, occupying the median line of the feather, and of a more rusty hue. On the middle of the back again
the blotches are even grayer and less conspicuous than on the nape, while the blotches on the
scapulars are larger and more rusty. The wing coverts are finely mottled with grayish,
especially the innermost ones. The primary coverts have comparatively few blotches.

The sides of the head and lower jaw are like the top, only more blotched, and with yellowish
rusty. There is a pure white V-shaped mark on the throat, commencing about a quarter of an
inch behind the base of the lower mandible, the acute angle anterior, the branches curving
back on each side to a point beneath and posterior to the eye. The angle of this mark is filled
up with rusty tipped black feathers. Behind it on the upper part of the breast, and extending
to the tail, the feathers begin to be banded transversely several times on their terminal half
with dark brown and dirty yellowish white, much less conspicuous on the upper part of the
breast and lower throat, where the predominant color of the feathers is dark brown, with the
ends grayish.

The quills are throughout of a uniform dark brown, with an obscure lightening on the inner
edges of the innermost primaries towards the ends. The ends of the secondaries are quite

white, forming a conspicuous band. There is, however, one very decided mark in a white patch on the five outer primaries situated about half way between the carpal joint and the tip of the wing. This commences on the inner vane of the first primary, without involving or crossing the rib, along which it extends for less than half an inch, widening inwards to three quarters of an inch on the inner edge. On the second primary there is a white blotch on the outer vane, opposite the large spot on the inner, which involves the rib. The third, fourth, and fifth primaries have the blotch passing continuously across from inner to outer edge of the quill.

The tail feathers are dark brown, with about eight or ten transverse and rather irregular bands of mottling, which below are nearly white, above of a light brownish gray. The terminal blotch on all but the two inner feathers (one on each side) is white on both surfaces, larger and more quadrate, and scarcely reaches to the outer edges of the feathers.

The female is similar in general characteristics, except that the V-shaped mark on the throat is yellowish rusty instead of white, the white patch on the wing rather less conspicuous, and the quadrate terminal white spots on the end of the four exterior tail feathers (on either side) are wanting. There is also appreciably more rusty in all the grayish or light tints.

In a large series of skins before me I find considerable geographical differences when compared with the typical Pennsylvania specimens. Thus, in skins from the upper Missouri and Platte, as also from Bridger's Pass, (5594,) the general colors are lighter, owing to the much greater amount of grayish mottling on the back and the wing coverts, as well as the scapulars. The color of the upper parts, in fact, exhibits but little of that decided impression of black previously described. The white spot in the middle of the wing is considerably larger, and in most cases crosses the midrib to the outer edge of the first primary. The feet appear shorter; the wings and tail about the same length. All the eastern specimens before me agree in their dark colors. Specimens from Steilacoom are as dark, however, as those from Pennsylvania, and not distinguishable from them. The same may be said of a pair from the Cosumnes river, California.

Still another series, chiefly from southern Texas and New Mexico, is characterized by a great preponderance of pale rufous spotting on the back. The characters in this respect are much as in *C. texensis*, almost every feather on the back having a reddish spot. The size is rather less than in more northern specimens. There is, however, so imperceptible a gradation into the lighter northern series, and from this into the dark eastern ones, that I confess my inability to define any permanent specific differences. The skin described as *C. henryi* belongs to the most rufous type, and may possibly be distinct. With reference to the others, however, I feel in very great doubt.

It is much to be regretted that the name of Vieillot should be of so barbarous a character, since it is the first one that can be used. The *Caprimulgus virginianus* of Brisson includes both this and *Antrostomus vociferus*, and cannot be retained, and with it fall the names of Gmelin and others based upon it. The mistake was first committed by Catesby, whose figure is an unnatural association of the two species.

In two specimens (8224, 8225,) from Fort Laramie, collected by Doctor Cooper, the wing and tail feathers are not fully grown out; but independently of this, the size appears much less than in any others from the same latitude, smaller even than in *C. texensis*. The middle toe and claw measure but .60 of an inch. The color is very gray, without any conspicuous rufous mottling.

As a summary of the whole subject, I am inclined to think that all the varieties described belong to one species, varying somewhat with the locality, those from the Atlantic and, perhaps, Pacific regions being darkest, without much mottling ; those from the interior province, or from the Missouri to the Rocky Mountains, being much more varied, with a tendency to pale grayish tints in northern localities, and reddish in more southern, the latter of smaller size. In this generalization I would scarcely except the *C. henryi*. The *C. texensis* is, however, quite different.

List of specimens.

Catal. No.	Sex.	Locality.	When collected.	Whence obtained.	Orig'l No.	Collected by—	Length.	Extent.	Wing.	Remarks.
		Dark variety.								
4292	......	Calcasieu, La............	....	G. Wurdeman.....	......	....	....	....	....	....
1522	.....	Carlisle, Pa.............	May 16,1846	S. F. Baird	......	....	9.50	25.67	8.17	....
1605	......	.........do...............	June 10,1844	......do...........	......	... .	9.50	24.50	8.33	....
6964	♀	St. Louis..............	May 13,1857	Lt. Bryan, U.S.A..	74	W. S. Wood	....	....	....	....
5592	......	Kansas	....	......do...........	......	....	....	....	8.00	....
7529	......	Independence, Mo.......	——,1857	W. M. Magraw.....	......	Dr. J. G. Cooper...	10.00	24.25	8.25	....
6006	......	Fort Steilacoom, W. T....	....	Dr. Suckley,U.S.A..	3	....	....	....	8.20	....
6007	......	Cosumnes river, Cal.....	....	Lt. Williamson.....	5	Dr. Heermann. ...	....	....	7.50	....
6008	......	Tulare valley, Cal........	....	......do............	7	......do.......	....	....	7.70	....
		Pale variety.								
6555	......	Fort Riley.............	....	Dr.W.A.Hammond	......	....	....	....	7.70	....
5595	♂	70 miles west of Ft. Riley.	June 30,1856	Lt. F. T. Bryan.....	48	W. S. Wood......	....	....	....	Young.........
5593	♂	85 miles west of Ft. Riley.	June 30,1856	......do...........	51	..... do..........	9.	22.	8.	....
5201	♂	40 miles above Ft. Pierre..	June 30,1856	Lt. Warren, U.S.A..	......	Dr. F. V. Hayden..	9.25	22.25	7.25	Eyes black.....
5202	♂	......do......... do.....	May 30,1856	......do...........	......	....	9.25	23.25	8.25	....
5203	♀	......do......... do.....	.....do.......	......do...........	......	....	9.25	23.	8.25	Iris brown.....
5594	♂	Bridger's Pass...........	August 13,1856	Lt. F. T. Bryan.....	260	W. S. Wood......	9.50	21.	8.25	....
8224	○	Fort Laramie.............	Sept. 16,1857	W. M. Magraw.....	......	Dr. Cooper	8.40	21.50	7.00	Not full grown.
8228	○	......do...............	......do.......	......do...........	208	Dr. Hayden.......	8.50	20.75	7.25	......do........
8877	......	Black Hills ? (Camp 4)....	Sept. 7,1857	Lt. Warren.......	......	....	9.25	23.00	7.50	....
8878	♂	Loup Fork.	July 24,1857	...do..........	......	....	9.25	22.25	....	....
?6013	......	Los Nogales, Sonora......	June ——,1855	Major Emory	83	Dr. Kennerly.......	....	....	7.40	....

CHORDEILES HENRYI, Cassin.

Western Night-Hawk.

Chordeiles henryi, CASSIN, Illustrations, I, Jan. 1855, 233.

Sp. Ch.—Female similar to *C. virginianus*, but the upper parts much more mottled and more rufous.

Hab.—Rocky Mountains of New Mexico.

The specimens hitherto collected of this species are not sufficiently perfect to admit of a satisfactory description. The characteristics can only be given by comparison with *C. virginianus*, as already described.

The skin upon which this species was based by Mr. Cassin is a female in very poor condition (6690,) and much stretched, which may account for its having been described as larger than *C. virginianus*. This is scarcely the case, as shown by the comparative measurements of the two. There is no undoubted specimen of the male bird in the collection before me from Texas, the only large one, with a decidedly white patch on the throat, lacking the white marks on the end of the tail.

This species is conspicuously different from Pennsylvania specimens of *C. virginianus* in the very great amount of mottling on the upper parts, which exhibit nothing of the dark tones prevailing in the last mentioned skins. The predominent tint of the mottling is a yellowish rusty, brightest, and the blotches largest, on the scapulars. The under parts are yellowish

20 b

white, transversely barred with dark brown. The V-shaped mark on the throat is of a rusty tinge, and much obscured by having its feathers tipped or spotted at the end with dark brown. The white patch on the wing is situated nearer the carpal joint than the tip of the primary, and is rather restricted, not crossing to the outer web of the first and second primaries. It extends only over the five outer quills. The tail has about ten transverse bands which are conspicuously yellowish rusty above.

This typical specimen has the second quill rather longest, and all the primaries tipped with pale rusty, an evident indication of immaturity. In other specimens, apparently the same, the first quill is longest, the primaries without any paler tips, and the V-shaped mark on the throat not obscured by the dusky blotches.

As already stated, no undoubted males referable to this species are in the collection before me, none having the white marks on the tail.

Compared with female specimens of *C. virginianus*, the upper parts exhibit much more rufous mottling above, thus excluding almost entirely the dusky shades. The coverts are tipped with a much more extended and continuous shade of pale brownish yellow. The white spot of the wing is smaller and nearer the carpal joint. The tail is much lighter, the dark transverse bars narrower. The toes and middle claw are shorter, (possibly not fully grown.)

I am by no means satisfied as to the right of this specimen to specific distinction from *C. virginianus*, as it is decidedly immature and is very similar in many respects to rufous varieties of the latter species. It is barely possible that these varieties may also belong to *C. henryi*; if so, however, I am at present unable to define the two species in any satisfactory manner. A larger collection, in better condition, may hereafter throw some light on the subject not now attainable.

List of specimens.

Catal. No.	Locality.	When collected.	Whence obtained.	Orig'l No.	Length.	Stretch of wings	Wing.
6698	Rio Grande valley	1853	Capt. Beckwith				8.00
4977	Fort Chadbourne, Tex		Dr. Swift				8.00
5046	Crossing of Pecos	July 11, 1855	Capt. J. Pope	107	9.50	23.50	8.00
5045	do	May 9, 1855	do	73			
6005	Rio Mimbres		Dr. T. C. Henry				8.40

CHORDEILES TEXENSIS, Lawrence.

Texas Night-Hawk.

Chordeiles brasilianus, LAWRENCE, Ann. N. Y. Lyceum, V, May 1851, 114, (Texas,) (not of Gm.
CASSIN, Ill. I, 1855, 238.
Chordeiles sapiti, BON. Conspectus Avium, I, 1849, 63.
Chordeiles texensis, LAWRENCE, Ann. N. Y. Lyc. VI, Dec. 1856, 167.

SP. CH —Much smaller than *C. virginianus*, but similar. White on the wing extending over only four outer primaries, the bases of which, as well as the remaining ones, with other quills, have round rufous spots on both webs. Under tail coverts and abdomen with a strong yellowish rufous tinge. Female more rufous and without the white spot of the tail. Length 8.75; wing 7.
Hab.—Rio Grande Valley and south ; west to Gulf of California.

This species in many respects resembles *C. virginianus*, but some of its markings and its much smaller size will at once serve to distinguish the two.

Selecting a specimen (3957) from Santa Caterina, Mexico, as a type, the prevailing color above may be described as a mixed gray, yellowish rusty, black, and brown in varied mottlings. The top of the head is rather uniformly brown, with a few mottlings of grayish rusty, although the concealed portion of the feathers is much varied. On the nape is a finely mottled collar of grayish and black, not very conspicuously defined, and rather interrupted on the median line. A similar collar is seen on the fore part of the breast. The middle of the back and the rump exhibit a coarser mottling of the same without any rufous. The scapulars and wing coverts are beautifully variegated, much as in some of the waders, the pattern very irregular and scarcely capable of definition. There are, however, a good many large round spots of pale yellowish rusty, very conspicuous among the other markings. There is quite a large blotch of white on the wing, situated considerably nearer the tip than the carpal joint. It only involves four primaries and extends across both outer and inner webs. The four first primaries anterior to the white blotches, and the remaining ones, nearly from their tips, exhibit a series of large round rufous spots not seen in the other North American species. The other wing quills have also similar markings. There is a large V-shaped white mark on the throat, as in *C. virginianus*, though rather larger proportionally. Posterior to this there are some rather conspicuous blotches of rufous, behind which is the obscure finely mottled collar of gray and brown already referred to. The breast and remaining under parts are dull white transversely banded with brown, with a strong tinge of yellowish rufous on the abdomen, about the vent, and on the under tail coverts. The tail is dark brown with about eight transverse bars of lighter ; the last are white and extending across both vanes ; the others less continuous, and yellowish rufous beneath as well as above, especially on the inner vane.

There is some variation in different specimens, especially as to the intensity of the rufous tints. The Santa Caterina specimen is larger than those from the lower Rio Grande, while No. 6010, from El Paso, is considerably larger than either, the wing measuring 7½ inches. There is, however, no other appreciable difference.

The females differ, as far as indicated by the specimens before me, chiefly in lacking the white spot on the tail. The throat spot is rather smaller, but is almost pure white. The rufous markings are rather deeper.

This species is readily distinguished from *C. virginianus* by its much smaller size, four primaries crossed with white, instead of five, the round rufous spots on the wing quills, the rufous tinge on the abdomen, and other characters. It, however, seems to present parallel variations of color and size with those described under *C. virginianus*.

I am unable to say whether the subject of the present article be really distinct or not from *C. sapiti*, of Bonaparte, and *C. brasilianus*, of Gmelin. As Mr. Lawrence has given it a new name, I have adopted it provisionally, leaving the final decision to be made by some one having the proper materials before him.

List of specimens.

Catal. No.	Locality.	When collected.	Whence obtained.	Orig'l No.	Collected by—	Length.	Stretch of wings.	Wing.	Remarks.
3951	Santa Catarina, Mexico...	Aug. —, 1853	Lieut. Couch, U. S. A..	186	....	8.75	19.00	7.00	Eyes blue black ; bill black ; feet purple.
6009	Ringgold barracks, Texas.	July —, 1853	Major Emory, U. S. A..		J. H. Clark			6.80	....
6010	Eagle Pass, Texas	....	......do	1	A. Schott............			6.70	....
6012	........do.............	....	......do	6	.....do.........			6.80	....
6010	El Paso, Texas	....	......do		J. H. Clark			7.70	....
4578?	Colorado river, California.	....	......do		A. Schott.........			6.90	....

CLAMATORES.

In the present state of our knowledge of the subject, it is a matter of some uncertainty whether the North American Anisodactyle birds, viz : the *Alcedinidae* and *Prionitidae*, belong more naturally to the *Strisores* or to the *Clamatores* of Cabanis' arrangement, (*Strisores* and *Tracheophones* of Burmeister.) However, although in some respects of closer affinities to the former, I propose to keep them with the *Clamatores*, in accordance with the views of Cabanis. They may be grouped as *Anisodactyli*, in distinction from the remaining families of the sub-order, or *Tracheophones*, although neither of these names is to be taken in the extended signification given it by Müller and others, but merely as having provisional reference to the North American species alone.

The muscles of the lower larynx, in some families, are weak and simple as in the *Strisores ;* in others again they form a powerful fleshy body, which covers the first bronchial ring. These birds have a harsh voice, capable of but little modulation.

The following schedule will be sufficient to indicate the general characters of the different families of this sub-order found in North America, although there are many others from other parts of the world not taken into account :

ANISODACTYLI.

Outer toe much longer than the inner ; united for half its length to the middle so as to have a common sole to this extent. Sole of the hind toe widened and continuous internally with that of the inner toe. Tail usually with twelve feathers, sometimes with ten.

> ALCEDINIDAE.—Tongue small, rudimentary. Tarsi very short. Edge of bill plain.
> PRIONITIDAE.—Tongue of normal size. Tarsi rather long. Cutting edge of bill dentated.

TRACHEOPHONES.

Feet and wings much as in the lowest *Oscines*. Lateral toes usually nearly equal. Tail generally of twelve feathers.

> COLOPTERIDAE.—Tarsus more or less enveloped by scutellae. Posterior portion of the tarsus with small plates, sometimes partly naked. Wings sometimes with peculiarly abbreviated primaries. Bill short, conical, and usually depressed, the tip sometimes abruptly hooked.

Family ALCEDINIDAE. Kingfishers.

Head large ; bill long, strong, straight, and sub-pyramidal, usually longer than the head. Tongue very small. Wings short ; legs small ; the outer and middle toes united to their middle. Toes with the usual number of joints, (2, 3, 4, 5.)

The gape of the bill in the kingfishers is large, reaching to beneath the eyes. The third primary is generally longest ; the first decidedly shorter ; the secondaries vary from twelve to fifteen in number, all nearly equal. The secondaries cover at least three quarters of the wing. The tail is short, the feathers twelve in number ; they are rather narrow ; the outer usually shorter. The lower part of the tibia is bare, leaving the joint and the tarsus uncovered. The tarsus is covered anteriorly with plates ; behind it is shagreen-like or granulated. The hind toe is connected with the inner, so as to form with it and the others a regular sole, which extends unbroken beneath the middle and outer as far as the latter are united. The inner toe is much shorter than the outer. The claws are sharp ; the middle expanded on its inner edge, but not pectinated.

The North American species of kingfisher belong to the sub-family *Cerylinae*, characterized by the crested head, and the plumage varying with sex and age. The single genus *Ceryle* includes two types, *Megaceryle* and *Chloroceryle*.

CERYLE, Boie.

Ceryle, Boie, Isis, 1828, 316, type *C. rudis?*
Ispida, Sw. Birds, II, 1837, 336, (type *C. alcyon.*)

Sp. Ch.—Bill long, straight, and strong, the culmen slightly advancing on the forehead and sloping to the acute tip ; the sides much compressed ; the lateral margins rather dilated at the base, and straight to the tip ; the gonys long and ascending. Tail rather long and broad. Tarsi short and stout.

This genus is distinguished from the typical *Alcedo* (confined to the Old World) by the longer tail, an indented groove on each side the culmen, inner toe much longer than the hinder instead of equal, &c.

The two species of North American kingfishers belong to two different genera of modern systematists, the one to *Megaceryle*, Reich, the other to *Chloroceryle*, Kaup. The characters of these sub-genera are as follows:

Megaceryle, Reichenbach.—Bill very stout and thick. Tarsus about equal to the hind toe ; much shorter than the inner anterior ; scarcely as long as the lower jaw is deep. Plumage without metallic gloss ; the occipital feathers much elongated, linear, and distinct...*M. alcyon.*

Chloroceryle, Kaup.—Size smaller and shape more slender than in preceding. Bill long, thin. Tarsi longer than hind toe; almost or quite as long as the inner anterior. Plumage with a green metallic gloss above ; the occiput with a crest of rather short, indistinct feathers..*C. americana.*

Comparative measurements of species.

Catal. No.	Species.	Locality.	Sex.	Length.	Stretch of wings.	Wing.	Tail.	Tarsus.	Middle toe.	Its claw along.	Bill above.	Along gape.	Specimen measured.
1640	Ceryle alcyon	Carlisle	♀	11.28		6.16	4.24	0.42	0.84	0.28	2.20	2.60	Skin
do.	do	do		13.25	22.00	6.15							Fresh
617	do	do	♂	13.00	22.00	6.50	4.00	0.40	0.97	0.34	2.16	2.85	Skin
8410	do	Simiahmoo, W. T.	♀	12.36		6.44	4.72	0.42	0.90	0.30	2.20	2.52	Skin
6191	do	Bodega, Cal				6.75	4.25	0.40	1.05	0.40	2.40	3.00	Skin
8638	do	Cape Florida, Fla.	♂	11.18		6.18	4.09	0.40	0.90	0.30	2.42	2.54	Skin
do.	do	do		12.25	20.00	6.25							Fresh
6194	Ceryle americana	Nueces, Texas	♀	8.04		3.42	2.82	0.38	0.70	0.28	1.72	1.82	Skin
7103	do	Western Texas	♂			3.30	2.60	0.38	0.68	9.26			Skin
do.	do	do		8.50	12.00	3.50							Fresh
7987	do	Guatemala		7.80		3.42	2.48	0.38	0.68	0.24	1.98	1.98	Skin

CERYLE ALCYON, Boie.

Belted Kingfisher.

Alcedo alcyon, LINNAEUS, Syst. Nat. I, 1766, 180.—WILSON, Am. Orn. III, 1811, 59.—AUDUBON, Orn. Biog. I, 1831, 394; pl. 77.—IB. Birds America.

Ceryle alcyon, BOIE, Isis, 1828, 316.—CASSIN, Illust. I, 1855, 254.—BREWER, N Am. Oology, I, 1857, 110; pl. iv, fig. 52. (Egg.)

Megaceryle alcyon, REICHENB. Handb. Sp. Orn. I, II, 1851, 25; pl. 412, fig. 3108–'9.

Ispida ludoviciana, GMELIN, Syst. Nat I, 1788, 452.

"*Alcedo jaguacate*, DUMONT, Dict. Sc. Nat. I, 1816, 455," (Cassin.)

"*Alcedo guacu*, VIEILLOT, Nouv. Dict. XIX, 1818, 406," (Cassin.)

SP. CH.—Head with a long crest. Above blue, without metallic lustre. Beneath, with a concealed band across the occiput, and a spot anterior to the eye, pure white. A band across the breast, and the sides of the body under the wings, like the back. Primaries white on the basal half, the terminal unspotted. Tail with transverse bands and spots of white.

Young with the sides of body and a transverse band across the belly below the pectoral one, light chestnut; the pectoral band more or less tinged with the same. Length of adult about 12¾ inches; wing, 6 or more.

Hab.—The entire continent of North America.

The above diagnosis will serve to identify the present species sufficiently for all practical purposes. The length of the bill and the other dimensions vary quite considerably, and, as a general rule, specimens from the Pacific coast are appreciably larger than eastern ones, though I have been unable to detect any difference of coloration. Mr. Bell, of New York, says that the difference in size between living birds of New York and California is very striking. The comparative table of measurements will serve to illustrate these differences.

List of specimens.

Catal. No.	Sex and age.	Locality.	When collected.	Whence obtained.	Orig'l No.	Collected by—	Length.	Stretch of wings.	Wing.	Remarks.
6929	....	Nelson river, H. B. T..	....	Donald Gunn	......	Jno. Isbister....	....	....	....	.. ..
6936	....	Selkirk settlement		...do		....	....	....	....	....
617	○	Carlisle, Pa	April 17, 1842	S. F. Baird	......	....	12.75	22.00	....	....
1640	○	.....do	July 18, 1844	.... do	......	....	13.25	22.00	6.17	....
1641	○	.....do	......do	.... do...	......	....	12.25	20.75	5.92	....
6520	....	Key Biscayne, Fla....	....	G. Wurdeman		....	....	....	....	....
5234	....	Yellowstone river, N.T	July 25, 1856	Lieut. G. K. Warren	......	Dr. Hayden......	....	....	....	....
4657	....	Little Missouri........	....	Col. A. Vaughan....	.. ...do	....	....	....	....	
5867	....	Fort Riley, K. T......	....	Dr. Hammond & J. Xantus de Vesey.	......	....	....	....	....	.. ..
5625	♂	Bryan's fork, 115 miles west of Fort Riley, K.T	July 3, 1856	Lieut. F. T. Bryan.	63	W. S. Wood...	11.00	....	....	....
5626	♀	108 miles west of Fort Riley, K. T	July 2, 1856	.......do..........	59	......do	11.00	....	....	....
5627	♂	.....do	June 16, 1856	.... do	17	......do	11.00	....	....	....
5043	....	Texas	....	Capt. J. Pope		....	....	....	....	....
5044	....	Ojo del Cuerpo, N. M ..	Sept. 30, 1856	.... do..........	......	....	14.50	21.50	6.75	....
3960	....	Tamaulipas, Mexico ...	Mar. —, 1853	Lieut. Couch	......	....	12.25	19.75	6.00	Eyes very dark brown; bill slate; feet dove color.
9932	♀'	Russian America.......	Aug. 17, 1841	S. F. Baird	......	Wosnesjensky...	....	....	....	....
4465	....	Cape Flattery, W. T....	....	Lieut. Trowbridge .		....	....	....	....	....
6192	....	Fort Steilacoom........	Feb. 15, 1854	Gov. Stevens	38	Dr. Suckley ...	11.50	19.00	6.75	....
6193	....	.....do	Jan. 20, 1854	.... do........	16	......do	....	....	....	....
6190	....	Bodega, Cal............	Jan. —, 1855	Lieut. Trowbridge .	......	T. A. Szabo....	....	....	....	....
6191	....	.....do	......do......	.... do........	......	......do	....	....	....	....
6189	....	San Diego, Cal.......	....	.... do........	......	A. Cassidy.....	12.00	....	....	....
4587	....	Colorado river, Cal....	....	Major Emory......	......	A. Schott......	....	....	....	....

CERYLE AMERICANA, Bo e.

Texas Kingfisher.

Alcedo americana, GMELIN, Syst. Nat. I, 1788, 451.
Ceryle americana, BOIE, Isis, 1828, 316.—LAWRENCE, Annals, N. Y. Lyceum, V, 1851, 116. (First introduction into the fauna of United States.)—CASSIN, Illustrations, I, 1855, 255.—BREWER, N. Am. Oology, I, 1857, 3 ; pl. iv, f. 53, (Egg.)
Chloroceryle americana, REICHENB. Handb. Sp. Orn. I, II, 1851, 27 ; pl. 413, f. 3112—'15.
Alcedo viridis, VIEILLOT, Nouv. Dict. XIX, 1818, 413, (Cassin.)

SP. CH.—Head slightly crested. Upper parts with a pectoral and abdominal band of blotches, glossy green, as also a line on each side the throat. Under parts generally, a collar on the back of the neck, and a double series of spots on the quills, white ; a chestnut band across the breast in some skins. Length, about 8 inches ; wing, 3¼.
Hab.—Rio Grande region of Texas and southward.

This species is very much smaller than the common northern kingfisher, the body scarcely exceeding in size that of the downy woodpecker.

The third quill is longest ; the second and fourth scarcely shorter. The fifth is intermediate between the fifth and sixth. The tail is considerably rounded ; the lateral feathers about half an inch shorter than the middle ones.

The general color of the upper parts in this species is a rich glossy or metallic green ; of the lower, white. The white of the throat is continued across the back of the neck, and enlarges somewhat on the upper part of the back. There is a transverse band across the upper part of the breast formed by crescentic spots of green like that of the back ; there is a second transverse band with the spots more distinct and rounded ; similar spots are seen on the side of the body. There is also a line of green commencing on each side of the throat below the eye, and running into the pectoral band.

The wing when folded exhibits four transverse rows of spots on the outer webs of the wing feathers, faint traces of a fifth and sixth being visible on the ends of the primaries. The inner webs of the quills are similarly spotted. The middle tail feathers are like the back ; the rest have the extremities green, the basal portion white, with various white blotches elsewhere, especially on the inner webs. The bill and feet are black. There is a good deal of white on the basal portion of the dorsal and scapular feathers.

The specimens before me do not exhibit much variation. In the most mature the top of the head is uniformly green ; in the others it is faintly spotted with whitish. In one specimen there is an indication of white feathers on the lower eyelid.

There is no appreciable difference in color between sexes, as marked on the labels. Two specimens (7104 and 7102, female) have the bill much shorter than in the adult, the culmen being not much longer than the head, and the lower mandible yellow at the base and tip, instead of black. The green of the head above is much duller, and more spotted with brownish white. I cannot say whether this is indicative of immaturity or of the female.

Of the half dozen specimens before me, only one (7103) has the pectoral chestnut colored band, described as characteristic of the adult. This is about an inch wide, and replaces the anterior band of green spots.

A specimen from Guatemala, without chestnut pectoral band, agrees in every respect with those from Texas.

List of specimens.

Catal. No.	Sex.	Locality.	When collected.	Whence obtained.	Orig'l No.	Collected by—	Length.	Extent.	Wing.	Remarks.
3951	♀	New Leon, Mexico.......	August —, 1853	Lieut. Couch......	134	....	6.75	9.75	3.50	Eyes brown, bill black, feet slate color.
6194	♀	Nueces river, Texas.....	....	Lieut. J. G. Parke..	......	Dr. Heermann.....	....	....	....	
5042	......	Devil's river, Texas......	May 2, 1853	Captain J. Pope....	......	....	7.50	12.00	....	Eyes black, feet green, gums white.
7102	♀	Western Texas..........	— —, 1851	Col. J. D. Graham..	9	J. H. Clark........	8.75	12.00	3.50	....
7103	♂	.....do...................	....do........	......do............	9	......do...........	8.50	12.00	3.50	....
7987	......	Guatemala...............	....	J. Gould.............	......	....	....	....	....	....

Family PRIONITIDAE. The Sawbills.

The sawbills or motmots have by most authors been placed as a sub-family with the *Coracianae* of the *Coraciadae*, but latterly each has been raised to independent family rank. With somewhat similar characters, the serration, or rather dentation, of the cutting edges of the bill and the extent of fusion of the outer and middle toes at once distinguish the *Prionitidae*. The bill is as long as the head; gently decurved near the tip, but not hooked. The nostrils are small, circular, and close to the frontal feathers. The wings are rather short; the inner secondaries in the closed wing reaching the tip of the primaries. Of the ten primaries, the exposed portion of the first is scarcely more than half that of the fourth or longest. The secondaries are tenor twelve in number. The tail consists either of ten or twelve feathers; the middle feathers are frequently spatulate, or with a portion of the lateral web wanting. The feet are large; the middle and outer toes connate for more than half their length, the tip of the inner claw reaching to the base of the outer. The toes have the normal number of joints, (2, 3, 4, 5.) The tarsi are clothed anteriorly with short half rings; the sides with a series of plates, more or less broken up into smaller ones. The middle claw has its inner face extended into a sharp but not pectinated edge.

Of the three genera—*Crypticus, Momotus,* and *Hylomanes*—constituting this family, only one, *Momotus,* has any representative near or within the borders of the United States.

MOMOTUS, Latham.

Momotus, LATHAM, Ind. Orn. I, 1790, 110.
Prionites, ILLIGER, Prodromus, 1811, 224.

Bill as long as the head, a little higher than broad; only moderately broad at the base, and tapering gently to a somewhat rounded tip. Both mandibles with the cutting edges dentated, except at the tip and base. Tail very long.

The preceding diagnosis sufficiently expresses the characters of the genus, although som others might be added. The connate toes and toothed or dentate bill are characters which belong to the family.

MOMOTUS CAERULICEPS, Gould.

Sawbill.

Momotus caeruliceps, GOULD, Pr. Zool. Soc. 1836, 18.—SCLATER, Pr. Zool. Soc. 1857, 253.
Prionites caeruliceps, BP. Consp. 1850, 165.—IB. Consp. Vol. Anisod. 1854, 8.
Prionites caeruleocephalus, JARD. & SELBY, Ill. Orn.; pl. 42.
"*Momotus subhutu,* LESS. Desc. Mammif. et Ois. 1847, 265," (fide Sclater.)

SP. CH.—General color yellowish green. Top of the head and occipital crest bright blue, encircled with black, of which color are also the lores, whiskers, and several elongated narrow feathers on the throat. Length, 15 inches; wing, 5¼.
Hab.—Mexico.

The bill of this species is conical, slightly decurved, the upper edge angular. The cutting edges of the mandibles are provided with rounded notches, except near the tip, which is without any notch. The tarsi are rather long; considerably longer than the middle toe and claw. The anterior three toes are connate at the base; the outer and middle united as far as the penultimate articulation of the latter.

The wings are short, broad, and much rounded when closed; the secondaries as long as the

21 b

primaries. The first quill is scarcely more than two-thirds the fourth, (which is longest,) both measured from the carpal joint. It is more than an inch shorter than the second, which, in urn, is half an inch shorter than the third. The tail is long, but, in the specimen before me, too much mutilated to furnish a satisfactory description.

The body generally is green, with a yellowish or, perhaps, fulvous shade, especially on the anterior half of the body. The lower parts are rather paler. The wings and tail are of a purer green ; the outer webs of the primaries and the ends of the tail feathers with a bluish shade. The top of the head, with the short occipital crest, are bright blue, most vivid posteriorly ; anteriorly paler, and on the front and above the eye tinged with greenish yellow. The forehead along the base of the bill, the lores, region around the eye, and a series of pointed whisker-like feathers below the eye, are black ; the latter margined above and below by greenish blue, like that on the top of the head, and separated from it by the color of the back. The occipital crest is also margined with black. On the middle of the throat are three or four much elongated compact feathers, which are black, with greenish blue margins near the base. The inside of the wing, especially the inner webs of the quills, are strongly tinged with yellowish rufous.

In life the iris was yellow, the bill black, the feet dark chestnut.

List of specimens.

Catal. No.	Sex.	Locality.	When collected.	Whence obtained.	Orig'l No.	Length.	Extent.	Wing.	Tarsus.	Middle toe.	Its claw.	Bill above.	Specimen measured.	Remarks.
4337	♂	Boquillo, New Leon, Mexico.	Ap'l, 1853	Lt. D. N. Couch	141	15.00	16.25	5 50	....	....	....	....	Fresh.	Eyes yellow, bill black, feet dark chestnut.
Do.	......	......do........	....	......do........	......	14.20	....	5.35	1.25	1.00	.40	1.50	Skin	....

Family COLOPTERIDAE. The Flycatchers.

This family, which connects the non-melodious birds with the *Oscines*, or true singers, embraces rather small and even diminutive species, with a bill variously shaped, but generally bent down abruptly at the tip, before which is a slight notch. The small circular nostrils are situated close to the forehead. The gape is usually provided with stiff bristles, which are sometimes highly developed. The wings are of moderate length; the first primary always more than one-half the second, usually nearly as long; some of the primaries often curiously attenuated, sometimes abbreviated. The feet are rather strong; the tarsi covered behind with small plates, or warts, or granulations in several series, sometimes entirely naked, sometimes encircled, except on the inner face, by a single series of plates. The tail always has twelve feathers.

This extensive family contains chiefly genera which have been variously combined with the singing birds, but have been mainly brought together in their present relationships in consequence of the researches of Müller and others. It embraces several sub-families, of which, however, only two have any reference to the fauna of the United States. The characters of the sub-families are given by Burmeister at considerable detail. This author divides the American forms into *Ampelinae, Piprinae, Tyranninae, Platyrhynchinae,* and *Fluvicolinae*, to which Cabanis adds *Todinae, Psarinae, Coracininae,* and *Phytotominae*. It is not necessary to give the characters of all these sub-families here, as we have only to do with the *Tyranninae* and *Psarinae*, united into one by Burmeister on account of their close relationship and numerous common characters, the chief of which are the following:

Common characters.—Bill strong and straight, generally almost as long as the head; the distance from the nostril to the tip of bill usually not more than that to the anterior corner of the eye; bill conical and vaulted, somewhat depressed, the tip abruptly bent down. Nostrils free, round, and open, nearer the gape than the culmen, not concealed by the bristles (usually well developed) which line the rictus and base of the bill. Wing rather long and acute; the primaries often attenuated or abbreviated. Tail usually emarginated; leg rather strong and high, covered behind with several series of granulations, or with plates nearly encircling the leg. Basal joints of outer and middle toes more or less united.

PSARINAE.—Second primary in the male much shorter than the first and third; anterior face of the tarsus with a row of plates, which do not extend more than half round the leg. The posterior half covered with a reticulation of small plates; sometimes naked internally.

TYRANNINAE.—Outer primaries frequently attenuated at the tips, but the second never shorter than both the first and third. Anterior and external face of tarsi covered with plates, which completely encircle the bone, except along or near the central line of the inner face; the intervening space either naked or with small plates, only occasionally a separate series on the posterior face of the tarsi. Toes, especially the inner, cleft to the base.

Sub-Family PSARINAE.

The characters of this sub-family have already been sufficiently indicated in the preceding pages to distinguish it among the other *Colopteridae*. The genera have been variously given by different authors. Cabanis and Burmeister adopt three, *Psaris*, *Pachyrhamphus*, and *Bathmidurus*, while Sclater, in a recent monograph of the sub-family, (Proceedings Zool. Soc. 1857, 67,) recognizes only the two first as genera, giving *Bathmidurus* and other groups as sub-genera. Judging from the North Mexican species before me, however, there appears abundant reason for keeping *Pachyrhamphus* and *Bathmidurus* distinct. These are readily characterized and distinguished by the slightly rounded tail, with broad feathers of the first mentioned genus, the second having the tail much graduated. Both differ from *Psaris* (or *Tityra*) in having the sexes dissimilar; in having bristles at the base of the bill; the lores well covered; the second abbreviated quill in the male broad and notched at tip, instead of narrow and falcate.

PACHYRHAMPHUS, G. R. Gray.

Pachyrhynchus, Spix, Av. Bras. II, 1824, 31. (Pre-occupied in botany.)
Pachyrhamphus, G. R. Gray, List Genera, 1838.

Head crested. Bill a little broader than high just behind the nostrils. Rictus with rather long bristles, two-thirds the length of culmen. Posterior portion of tarsus covered with polygonal plates, largest on the sides; naked inside at the upper end. First primary shorter than the sixth; second (in the male only) about two-thirds as wide as the first; emarginated inside near the end, where it runs out in an acute point. Tail moderately rounded; the feathers broad.

I have constructed the generic characters as given above entirely from a single species, *P. aglaiae*, but they probably apply equally well to all. The bill is strong; the culmen distinct; the bill moderately broad; the rictal bristles long. The difference in length between the longest and shortest tail feather amounts to but about .15 of an inch. The legs do not show the scutellation very clearly, but there appear to be a row of large polygonal scales on each side the posterior half of the tarsus, separated by smaller ones behind, these scales inferiorly being granular and set in naked skin, while the superior portion of the inner face of the tarsus appears to be naked. This genus differs from *Psaris* or *Tityra* in the broader bill, bristled rictus, feathered lores, longer tail, different second primary, &c.

But one species has hitherto been detected near the limits of the United States; the others belong to more southern localities.

PACHYRHAMPHUS AGLAIAE, Lafresnaye.

Rose-throated Flycatcher.

Pachyrhamphus aglaiae, Lafresnaye, Rev. Zool. 1839, 98.—Sclater, Pr. Zool. Soc. 1856, 297.—Ib. 1857, 74.
Psaris aglaiae, Kaup, Pr. Zool. Soc. 1851, 46.

Sp. Ch.—Fourth quill longest; first about equal to the sixth. Tail rounded. Head crested. Above dark plumbeous, becoming lighter to the tail. Top and sides of head with the crest, glossy black; the forehead tinged with brown. Beneath pale ash, tinged with brownish white on the abdomen and crissum. Chin ashy white. Central region of the throat and forepart of breast rose color. Cheeks dark ash, tinged with purple. Scapular feathers white at the base. Wings and tail dark brown, edged externally like the back; the outer primaries and secondaries edged with whitish, the former with a white spot at the base.
Length, 7.50; wing, 3.75; tail, 3.10.
Hab.—Mexico to Rio Grande.

This species, according to Mr. Sclater, (to whom I am indebted for the identification of the present specimens,) is closely allied to *P. pectoralis* of Cayenne and New Grenada, and *P.*

roseicollis of Bolivia. The former, however, is of a nearly uniform sooty brown above and below, with a narrow rosy bar on the throat. The latter also is much darker below, being ashy black (rather lighter than in *P. pectoralis*) instead of rather light ash. The rose color of the throat, too, appears to be narrower. According to Lafresnaye, the *roseicollis* has a longer bill.

The abbreviated second primary has the sides parallel to near the acutely pointed tip, which is internally emarginated. The notch, however, is not so deep as in the figure of *P. viridis*, given by Mr. Sclater. It has a slight trace of white on the outer edge.

According to Mr. Sclater, the female is reddish, the wings black internally; their margins and the entire tail bright rufous; the crown black; the under parts whitish cinnamon; the under wing coverts cinnamon.

The specimens of this species collected by Lieutenant Couch are appreciably larger than those described by Mr. Sclater from southern Mexico.

List of specimens.

Catal. No.	Sex.	Locality.	When collected.	Whence obtained.	Original No.	Length.	Extent.	Wing.	Tail.	Tarsus.	Middle toe.	Its claw.	Bill above.	Along gape.	Specimen measured.	Remarks.
4024	♂	San Diego, New Leon......	....	Lt. D. N. Couch...	126	6.98	......	3.69	3.12	0.82	0.70	0.24	0.68	0.84	Skin.	....
Do.	......	......do...............		.........do.........	..	7.50	11.00	3.75	....	....	....	....	....	....	Fresh.	....
4025	♂	..............do................	March, 1853	........do..........	112	7.50	11.00	3.75	....	....	....	....	....	....	Fresh.	Eyes brown.

BATHMIDURUS, Cabanis.

Bathmidurus, Cabanis, Wiegm. Archiv, 1847, I, 243.

Head crested; bill considerably broader than high just behind the nostrils; rictal bristles short, not half the length of culmen. Posterior half of tarsus covered externally and behind with angular plates, internally entirely naked. First quill (in female) about equal to the fifth. Tail much graduated; the feathers narrow. Male with abbreviated broad second primary.

There are many features in this genus (as far as I have been able to establish its character on the female of the single species,) to distinguish it from the preceding. The most conspicuous of these is the much graduated tail, the outer feathers being .65 of an inch shorter than the inner three on either side which are nearly equal. The feathers, too, are considerably narrower than in *Pachyrhamphus*. The bill is shorter and considerably broader and more depressed at the base; the culmen not quite so acutely marked; the bristles short. The nostrils are very small and much concealed. The edge of the first primary in both genera is emarginated near the end of the inner web; the first quill is much longer than in the preceding, being equal to the fifth, instead of shorter than the sixth. The tarsi are quite different in the complete nakedness of the entire inner face, and almost so on the posterior edge. The outer side behind is covered with polygonal plates; the inferior extremity behind with strong granulations.

BATHMIDURUS MAJOR, Cabanis.

Bathmidurus major, Cabanis, Wiegmann's Archiv, 1847, I, 246.
Psaris marginatus major, Kaup, Pr. Zool. Soc. 1851, 48.
Pachyrhamphus major, Sclater, Pr. Zool. Soc. 1857, 78.

FEMALE.—Above light chestnut brown; the top of the head glossy black mixed with rufous; beneath light yellowish brown; the middle of the belly tinged with greenish yellow. Quills dark brown, edged on both webs with rufous; tail feathers mostly black; the tips, outer edges, and basal portions rufous; the middle feat' ers like the back. Length, 6.25; wing, 3.25; tail, 2.75.

MALE.—" Above ash ; the middle of the back black or mixed with black ; a grayish white collar on the nape. Crown lustrous black, with a frontal whitish line. Scapulars white. Wings black, the coverts and secondaries bordered with white. Beneath white, tinged with ash. Tail black, the lateral feathers broadly tipped with white. Bill plumbeous black ; feet black. Length, 6,00 ; wing, 3.30 ; tail, 2.40."

The preceding description of the male is taken from Mr. Sclater's article, as I have no specimen of that sex before me. The single specimen collected by Lieutenant Couch, was supposed for a time to be the female of *Pachyrhamphus aglaiae*, even by Mr. Sclater, whose authority on these birds is so deservedly high. It is, however, generically distinct in many points of structure.

The lustrous greenish black feathers of the top of the head are much edged with rufous, which predominates on the forehead. The neck above· is much lighter than the back, rump, and tail, which are light rusty, or, perhaps, chestnut. In the unexpanded tail no black is visible from above, except a small dusky speck at the end of the middle feather. The black of the tail feathers fades in intensity anteriorly and passes into reddish; posteriorly, however, it is abruptly bordered by the yellowish rufous tips, (these on the outer feathers are .70 of an inch long.) The outer webs of all the feathers are rufous excepting on the third and fourth, where the black extends nearly across. The inner webs of all the feathers, except the innermost, show much black. There is a strong tinge of greenish yellow on the throat as well as the belly, but the breast appears to be of the same light rufous as the sides.

This bird is readily distinguished from the female *Pachyrhamphus aglaiae* by the black on the graduated tail feathers.

List of specimens.

Catal. No.	Sex.	Locality.	When collected.	Whence obtained.	Orig No.	Length.	Stretch of wings.	Wing.	Tail.	Tarsus.	Middle toe.	Its claw alone.	Bill above.	Along gape.	Specimen measured.	Remarks.
4026	♀	Boquillo, N. Leon..	April —, 1853	Lieut. D. N. Couch.	150	5.25	10.00	3.25	....	....	....	....	....	....	Fresh ...	Eyes brown, bill bluish lead color..
Do.	....	......do...........	.....do......	......do	...	7.00	......	3.30	2.86	0.82	0.75	0.22	0.63	0.80	Skin	....

Sub-Family TYRANNINAE.—Tyrant Flycatchers.

Bill broader than high at the base, much depressed, more or less triangular. Culmen nearly as long as the head, or shorter ; straight to near the tip, then suddenly bent down into a conspicuous hook, with a notch behind it ; tip of lower jaw also notched. Commissure straight to near the notch ; gonys slightly convex. Nostrils oval or rounded, in the anterior extremity of the nasal groove, and more or less concealed by long bristles which extend from the posterior angle of the jaws along the base of the bill, becoming smaller, but reaching nearly to the median line of the forehead. These bristles with lateral branches at the base. Similar bristles mixed in the loral feathers and margining the chin. Tarsi short, generally less than middle toe, completely enveloped by a series of large scales which meet near the posterior edge of the inner side, and are separated either by naked skin or by a row of small scales. Sometimes a second series of rather large plates is seen on the posterior face of the tarsus, these, however, usually on the upper extremity only. Basal joint of middle toe united almost throughout to that of the outer toe, but more than half free on the inner side ; outer lateral toe rather the longer. Wings and tail variable ; first quill always more than three-fourths the second. The outer primaries sometimes attenuated near the tip.

The species of this sub-family may, for our present purposes, be divided into *Tyranni* and *Tyrannuli.* The former are large, generally with bright color, pointed wings, with attenuated primaries and a colored crest in the middle of the crown. The others are plainer, smaller, without crest ; the primaries not attenuated.

The following schedule may serve to illustrate the genera of North American Tyrant fly-catchers :

Tyranni.

Size large ; colors generally brilliant ; crown with a brightly colored crest, usually concealed ; outer primaries abruptly contracted or attenuated near the tip ; upper scales of tarsus usually continuing round on the outside and behind.

MILVULUS.—Tail excessively forked and lengthened ; more than twice as long as the wings.

TYRANNUS.—Tail moderate ; nearly even or forked ; less than the wings.

Tyrannuli.

Size small ; colors usually plain ; crown without any colored crest concealed by the tips of the feathers ; primaries normal ; scales of the upper part of the tarsus usually continuing only to the middle of the outer face, and a second series opposite to them behind.

1. Tail lengthened ; about equal to the wings, which reach scarcely to its middle.

MYIARCHUS.—Tarsus equal to the middle toe, which is decidedly longer than the hinder one. Tail even or rounded.

SAYORNIS.—Tarsus rather longer than the middle toe, which is scarcely longer than the hind toe. Tail slightly forked.

2. Tail decidedly shorter than the wings.

CONTOPUS.—Tarsus shorter than the middle toe ; hind toe much longer than the lateral. Tail considerably forked. Wings long, pointed ; much longer than the tail, reaching beyond the middle of the latter ; first quill about equal to the fourth.

EMPIDONAX.—Tarsus considerably longer than the middle toe ; nearly as long as the head ; hind toe much longer than lateral. Tail nearly even or rounded ; but little shorter than the wings ; first primary much shorter than the fourth.

PYROCEPHALUS.—Tarsus but little longer than the middle toe ; hind toe not longer than the lateral. Tail broad, even ; first quill shorter than the fifth.

MILVULUS, Swainson.

Milvulus, SWAINSON, Zool. Jour. III, 1827, 165.
Despotes, REICHENBACH, Avium Syst. Naturae, 1850, (in part.)

SP. CH.—Bill shorter than the head, and nearly equal to the tarsus. Tail nearly twice as long as the wing, excessively forked ; the middle feathers scarcely half the lateral First primary abruptly attenuated at the end, where it is very narrow and linear. Head with a concealed crest of red.

This group is distinguished from *Tyrannus* by the very long tail, but the two species assigned to North America, although agreeing in most respects, differ in others. Thus, in *M. forficatus*

the tail feathers are narrow linear to near the end, where they are slightly spatulate, while in
M. tyrannus they are broader at the base, and taper gently to the end. The legs of *M. forficatus*
are larger, and the linear attenuation of the primaries confined to the first one, extending over
an inch.

In *M. tyrannus* the outer three primaries share a linear attenuation, but this does not amount
to half an inch in length. The colors are very different, *M. forficatus* being whitish ash above,
the rump black, the tail feathers rose white with black at the tips, the shoulders and belly light
vermilion. *M. tyrannus*, on the other hand, has a black head and tail, the outer edge of the
latter only white, the back olivaceous, the under parts pure white. The two species differ in
some points of structure, and are separated generically by some authors.

Comparative measurements of species.

Catal. No.	Species.	Locality.	Sex.	Length.	Wing.	Tail.	Tarsus.	Middle	Its claw alone.	Bill above.	Along gape.	Specimen measured.
2965	Milvulus tyrannus......	South America.........	....	13.86	4.46	10.00	0.68	0.66	0.23	0.68	0.84	Dry........
7374	Milvulus forficatus.....	San Antonio, Texas....	♀	11.60	4.38	7.40	0.74	0.70	0.24	0.74	0.94	Dry........
7375	......do	......do.	♂	12.90	4.80	8.40	....	....	0.28	0.74	1.00	Dry........

MILVULUS TYRANNUS, Bon.

Fork-tailed Flycatcher.

Muscicapa tyrannus, LINN. Syst. Nat. I, 1766, 325.
Milvulus tyrannus, BONAP. Geog. List, 1838.—AUDUBON, Synopsis, 1839, 38.—IB. Birds Am. I, 1840, 196 : pl. 52.
Despotes tyrannus, BONAP. Comptes Rendus, 1854, 87.
Tyrannus savana, VIEILLOT, Ois. Am. Sept. I, 1807, 72 ; pl. xliii.—SWAINSON, Mon. Ty. Shrikes ; Quarterly Jour.
    XX, Jan. 1826, 282.
Muscicapa savana, BONAPARTE, Amer. Orn. I, 1825, 1 ; pl. i, f. 1.—AUDUBON, Orn. Biog. II, 1834, 387 ; pl. 168.
Milvulus savanus, GRAY, List, 1841.
? Tyrannus violentus, VIEILL. Encyc. Meth. II, 853.—BURMEISTER, Thiere Brasiliens, Vögel, 1856, 467.
? Tyrannus nunciola, STEPHENS, Shaw Gen. Zool, Birds XIII, II, 1826, 133.
Tyrannus milvulus, NUTTALL, Man. 2d ed. I, 1840, 307.
Fork-tailed flycatcher, PENNANT, LATHAM.
Tyran a queue fourchue, BUFFON, pl. enl. 571.

SP. CH.—Outer four primaries abruptly attenuated at the end, the sides of the attenuated portion parallel. Second and third
quills longest ; fourth little shorter, and not much exceeding the first. Tail very deeply forked ; the external feather linear,
and twice as long as the head and body alone. Top and sides of the head glossy black. Rump, upper tail coverts, and tail
almost black ; the outer web of outer tail feather yellowish white for more than the basal half ; rest of upper parts ash gray.
Under parts generally pure white. Wings dark brown ; the outer primary and tertials edged with white. Crown with a concealed patch of yellow. Length 14 inches ; wing 4.75 ; tail 10 inches ; depth of fork 7 inches.

Hab.—South America. Accidental in the United States.

This species claims a place in the fauna of the United States on account of two specimens
captured in New Jersey, at long intervals, and one or two seen by Mr. Audubon in the south-
west.

List of specimens.

Catal. No.	Locality.	Whence obtained.	Collected by—
2965	South America...............	S. F. Baird...............	J. G. Bell ....

MILVULUS FORFICATUS, Sw.

Scissor-tail; Swallow-tailed Flycatcher.

Muscicapa forficata, GMELIN, Syst Nat. I, 1788, 931.—VIEILLOT, Ois. Am. Sept. I, 1807, 71.—STEPHENS, in Shaw', Zool. X, II, 413; pl. iii.—BONAP. Am. Orn, I, 1825, 15; pl. ii, f. 1.—AUDUBON, Orn. Biog. IV 1838, 426; pl. 359, f. 3.

Tyrannus forficatus, SAY, Long's Exped. II, 1823, 224.—NUTTALL's Manual, I, 2d ed. 1840, 309.

Milvulus forficatus, "SWAINS." RICH. List, 1837.—AUDUBON, Synopsis, 1839, 38.—IB. Birds Amer. I, 1840, 197; pl. 53

Tyrannus mexicanus, STEPHENS, Shaw Gen. Zool. Birds XIII, II, 1826, 135.

Moucherolle a queue fourchue du Mexique, BUFFON, Pl. enl. 677.

Bird of Paradise of the Texans.

SP. CH.—Wing with the outer primary only abruptly attenuated, and narrowly linear, (for about .85 of an inch) ; the second but slightly emarginate ; second quill longest ; first and third equal. Tail very deeply forked, the lateral feathers twice as long as the body, all narrow and linear or sub-spatulate. Top and sides of the head very pale ash ; the back a little darker, and faintly tinged with light brick red ; under parts nearly pure white, tinged towards the tail with light vermilion, rather more rose on the under wing coverts ; a patch on the side of the breast and along the fore arm dark vermilion red. Tail feathers rosy white, tipped at the end for two or three inches with black. Rump dark brown, turning to black on the coverts. Wings very dark brown ; the coverts and quills, excepting the primaries, (and including the outer of these) edged with whitish. Crown with a concealed patch of white, having some orange red in the centre.

Length, 13 inches ; wing, 4.75 ; tail, 8.50 ; depth of fork, 5.80.

Hab.—Central Texas to Mexico.

This exquisitely beautiful and graceful bird is quite abundant on the prairies of southern Texas, and is everywhere conspicuous among its kindred species. It is usually known as the scissor-tail from the habit of closing and opening the long feathers of the tail like the blades of a pair of scissors. The adult female is very similar, though rather smaller. The young is not conspicuously different, only lacking the concealed patch of the head.

List of specimens.

Catal. No.	Sex.	Locality.	When collected.	Whence obtained.	Orig. No.	Collected by—	Length.	Stretch of wings	Wing.
5059	....	Head of Devil's river.	May 2, 1855	Capt. Pope	65		13.50	13.00	5.00
4974	....	Ft. Chadbourne, Tex.		Dr. Swift					
4975	....	....do		....do					
7374	♀	San Antonio, Texas		Lt. J. G. Parke		Dr. Heermann			
7375	♂	....do		....do		....do			
7381	....	....do	July —, 1853	Lt. A. W. Whipple	15	Dr. Kennerly	14.00	14.00	
7376	...	Eagle pass, Texas		Major Emory		A. Schott			
7377	....	....do		....do		....do			
7382	♀	Lower Texas		....do	12	J. H. Clark	11.25	14.00	4.25
7383	♂	....do		....do		....do	14.00	15.00	4.25
7384	♂	....do		....do	12	....do	13.00	15.00	4.25
3997	♂	Tamaulipas, Mex.	Mar. —, 1853	Lt Couch	107				
9097	....	Mexico		M. Verreaux	29733				
2964	....	South America		S. F. Baird					

TYRANNUS, Cuvier.

Tyrannus, CUVIER, Leçons Anat. Comp. 1799–1800, (Agassiz.)

Tail nearly even, or moderately forked ; rather short erthan the wings ; the feathers broad, and widening somewhat at the ends. Wings long and pointed ; the outer primaries rather abruptly attenuated near the end, the attenuated portion not linear, however. Head with a concealed patch of red on the crown.

The species of this genus are especially characterized by their long, attenuated primaries, their moderately forked or nearly even tail, and the concealed crest in the crown. Their affinities are nearest to *Milvulus*, from which the tail, shorter than the wings, instead of twice as long, or more, will always serve as a point of distinction. The attenuation of the primary differs in being less abrupt and not truly linear, sloping gradually, and not bounded behind by a notch. I am unable to appreciate any other differences of importance.

The character and extent of the attenuation of the primaries, the depth of the fork of the tail, with the size of the legs and bill, all vary considerably, and may, perhaps, serve as ground for further subdivisions. The bill, in particular, varies much in size in the North American species from that of *T. carolinensis*, where the culmen is but little more than half the head, to that of *T. dominicensis*, where it is decidedly longer than the head, and almost as stout as that of *Saurophagus*, (Genus *Melittarchus* of Cabanis.)

The North American species of *Tyrannus* may be arranged by colors, according as they are white beneath or yellow, in the following manner :

A.—Under parts whitish, without any shade of yellow. A grayish plumbeous pectoral band.

    Tail slightly rounded. Bill much shorter than the head. Above black, shading into dark plumbeous on the back. Tail abruptly and broadly margined and tipped with pure white...*T. carolinensis.*

    Tail moderately forked. Bill longer than the head. Above gray ; the tail and wings brownish. The edges and tips of the tail narrowly margined with soiled white...*T. dominicensis.*

B.—Above ashy olive, becoming purer ash on the head. Tail brown or black. Beneath yellow ; the chin paler ; the breast strongly shaded with olivaceous or ashy.

    a.—Tail nearly black ; the outer edges of the outer webs of the feathers with the fibres united closely throughout, and similarly colored with the rest of the feather.

    Tail slightly forked ; external feather with the entire outer web and the outer half of the shaft abruptly yellowish white. Pectoral band pale ashy, lighter than the back...*T. verticalis.*

    Tail nearly even or slightly rounded ; external feather with the shaft brown ; the outer edge of the outer web only obscurely yellowish white. Throat and breast broadly tinged with dark ashy olive like the back.....................*T. vociferans.*

    b.—Tail brown, scarcely darker than the wings ; outer edges of the outer webs of the tail feathers olivaceous like the back, in contrast with the brown ; the fibres loosened externally ; shafts of tail feathers white beneath.

    Tail quite deeply forked ; (depth .65 of an inch); dark brown; the posterior upper tail coverts nearly similar. Wing feathers edged with yellowish...*T. melancholicus.*

    Tail moderately forked ; (depth .30 of an inch) ; light brown ; posterior upper tail coverts scarcely less olivaceous than the back. Wing feathers edged with grayish white...*T. couchii.*

Comparative measurements of the species.

Catal. No.	Species.	Locality.	Sex.	Length.	Extent.	Wing.	Tail.	Tarsus.	Middle toe.	Its claw.	Bill above.	Along gape.	Specimen measured.
8905	Tyrannus carolinensis ...	Frémont, on Platte.	♂	8.00	....	4.64	3.62	0.72	0.66	0.26	0.74	0.98	Dry.........
1513	........do...............	Carlisle, Pa........	♀	7.52	....	4.52	3.66	0.70	0.74	0.26	0.72	0.94	Dry.........
Do.	........do...............	.....do.............	......	8.40	14.50	4.15	......	......	......	....	....	....	Fresh ......
6518	Tyrannus dominicensis...	Indian Key, Fla....	♂	7.80	....	4.70	4.10	0.72	0.76	0.26	1.14	1.38	Dry.........
5247	Tyrannus verticalis.......	Farm Island, Neb ..	♀	8.66	....	4.92	4.10	0.70	0.70	0.24	0.74	0.94	Dry.........
Do.	........do	.....do.............	♀	8.37	14.50	5.	......	......	......	....	....	....	Fresh ......
5905	........do...............	Steilacoom, W. T..	......	8.90	....	5.30	4 40	0.70	0.70	0.26	0.80	0.92	Dry.........
7390	Tyrannus vociferans......	Tejon valley........	♂	8.80	....	5.24	4.24	0.76	0.78	0.30	0.84	1.00	Dry.........
7389	........do...............	Sac valley.........	♀	8.76	....	4.90	4.08	0.76	0.82	0.36	0.88	1.08	Dry.... .....
7939	........do...............	Mexico	......	8.90	....	5.18	4.08	0.78	0.76	0.28	0.78	1.00	Dry.........
8101	Tyrannus melancholicus..	Vera Cruz..........	♂	8.90	....	4.44	4.22	0.80	0.80	0.32	0.90	1.02	Dry.........
4001	Tyrannus couchii........	New Leon, Mexico.	♂	9.40	....	4.94	4.58	0.72	0.74	0.30	0.98	1.04	Dry.........
Do.	........do...............	......do...........	......	9.00	15.08	5.00	......	......	......	....	....	....	Dry.........

TYRANNUS CAROLINENSIS, Baird.

King Bird; Bee Martin.

Lanius tyrannus, Linn. Syst. Nat. I, 1766, 136. This belongs to the Cuban *T. matutinus*, according to Bonaparte.

Muscicapa tyrannus, (Brisson?) Wilson, Am. Orn. I, 1808, 66 ; pl. xiii.—Aud. Orn. Biog. I, 1832, 403 : V, 1839, 420 ; pl. 79.—Ib. Birds Amer. I, 1840, 204 ; pl. 56.

Lanius tyrannus, var. γ *carolinensis*, δ *ludovicianus*, Gmelin, Syst. Nat. I, 1788, 302.

Muscicapa rex, Barton, Fragments N. H. Penna. 1799, 18.

Tyrannus pipiri, Vieillot, Ois. Am. Sept. I, 1807, 73 ; pl. xliv.—Cab. Journ. Orn. III, 1855, 478.

Tyrannus intrepidus, Vieillot, Galerie Ois. I, 1824, 214; pl. 133.—Swainson, Mon. Ty. Shrikes Quart. Jour. 1826, 274.

Muscicapa animosa, Licht. Verz. Doubl. 1823, No. 558.

Gobe Mouche de la Caroline, Buffon, Ois. V, 281 ; enl. pl. 676.

Tyrannus leucogaster, Stephens, Shaw Gen. Zool. XIII, ii, 1826, 132.

Sp. Ch.—Two, sometimes three, outer primaries abruptly attenuated at the end. Second quill longest ; third little shorter ; first rather longer than fourth, or nearly equal. Tail slightly rounded. Above dark bluish ash. The top and sides of the head to beneath the eyes bluish black. A concealed crest on the crown, vermilion in the centre, white behind, and before partially mixed with orange. Lower parts pure white, tinged with pale bluish ash on the sides of the throat and across the breast; sides of the breast and under the wings similar to, but rather lighter than, the back. Axillaries pale grayish brown tipped with lighter. The wings dark brown, darkest towards the ends of the quills ; the greater coverts and quills edged with white, most so on the tertials ; the lesser coverts edged with paler. Upper tail coverts and upper surface of the tail glossy black, the latter very dark brown beneath ; all the feathers tipped, and the exterior margined externally with white, forming a conspicuous terminal band about .25 of an inch broad. Length, 8.50 ; wing, 4.65 inches ; tail, 3.70 ; tarsus, .75.

Hab.—Eastern North America to Rocky Mountains. West of this seen only in Washington Territory.

The young of the year is similar ; the colors duller ; the concealed colored patch on the crown wanting. The tail more rounded ; the primaries not attenuated.

Specimens vary in the amount of white margining the wing feathers ; the upper tail coverts are also margined sometimes with white.

List of specimens.

Catal. No.	Sex and age.	Locality.	When collected.	Whence obtained.	Orig'l No.	Collected by—	Length.	Stretch of wings.	Wing.	Remarks.
1513	♀	Carlisle, Pa............	May 15, 1844	S. F. Baird	.....	....	8.41	14.50	4 66	....
2600	♀	......do	May 8, 1846	......do ....r..	.....	....	8.33	14.50	4.58	....
1127	○	......do	July 18, 1844	......do	.....	....	8.50	14.50	4.50	....
6482	......	Philadelphia, Pa......	....	C. Drexler...	.....	....	....	....	.....	....
6517	♂	Key Biscayne, Fla.....	April 9, 1844	G. Würdemann ...	.....	....	.....	....	.....	....
6971	... ...	St. Louis, Mo..........	May 12, 1857	Lieut. Bryan.......	53	W. S. Wood	.....	....	.....	....
8392	♂	Independence, Mo.....	June 26, 1857	Wm. M. Magraw...	100	Dr. Cooper.......	8.75	15.25	5.25	Iris brown, bill and feet grayish black.
5629	♂	East of Fort Riley, K. T.	June 16, 1856	Lieut. Bryan	13	W. S. Wood	.....	....	.....	....
5631	♂	.... do ......do.....	June 17, 1856	..... do	25	......do	.....	....	.....	....
8181	....	Shawnee reserve, K. T.	July —, 1857	Wm. M. Magraw...	.....	Dr. Cooper.......	.....	....	.....	Iris brown, bill and feet black.
7081	....	Republican river, K. T.	June 16, 1857	Lieut. Bryan	8	D.W.A. Hammond	.....	....	.....	....
5630	♂	Independence Cr., 130 miles west of Ft. Riley.	July 4, 1857	......do	65	......do	8.00	14.00	.....	....
8905	♂	Frémont, on Platte.....	July 1, 1857	Lieut. Warren	......	Dr. Hayden......	8.50	14.75	4.87	....
5238	♂	Farm Island, Mo river.	May 30, 1856	......do	......	......do	8.75	14.75	4.78	....
5237	......	.....do ....do...	......do.....	......do	......	......do	.....	....	.....	....
4692	♀	Upper Missouri	May 12, 1856	......do	......	......do	8.25	13.62	4.62	....
4695	♂	......do	.... do.....	......do	.....	......do	8.25	13.75	4.75	....
4512	... ...	Cedar island, Mo. river.	May —, 1855	Col. Vaughan.....	......	......do	.....	....	.....	....
5235	♀	40 miles above Ft. Pierre	May —, 1856	Lieut. Warren.....	......	......do	8.50	14.50	4.75	....
5236	♀	......do . ...do.....	......do.....	......do	......	......do	8.00	14.25	4.50	Eye black ....
5239	......	Blackfoot country.....	July —, 1855	Dr. Hayden	......	....	.....	....	.....	....
7504	♀	Milk river, Neb.......	Aug. 28, 1853	Gov. Stevens	......	Dr. Suckley.....	8.00	14.50	4.50	....
8798	♂	Fort Laramie..........	Aug. 27, 1857	Wm. M. Magraw...	7	Dr. Cooper	8.00	14.00	4.50	Iris brown, bill and feet grayish black.
7501	....	Near 32° L. west, Texas.	....	Captain Pope.....	......	....	.....	....	.....	....
5054	......	Indianola, Texas......	Mar. 31, 1857	...do	......	....	.....	....	.....	....
5909	......	Fort Steilacoom	....	Dr. Cooper	......	....	8.75	15.00	.....	....
7507	.....	....do	....	Gov. Stevens.....	.....	Dr. Suckley.....	.....	....	.....	....
7508	... ...	....do	....	......do ....,	.....	......do	.....	....	.....	....

TYRANNUS DOMINICENSIS, Rich.

Gray King-bird.

Tyrannus dominicensis, BRISSON, Ois. II, 1760, 394 ; pl. 38, fig. 2.—RICH. List, 1837.
Lanius tyrannus, var β d-minicensis, GMELIN, Syst. Nat. I, 1788, 302.
Muscicapa dominicensis, AUDUBON, Orn. Biog II, 1834, 392 ; pl. 46.—IB. Birds Amer. I, 1840, 201 ; pl. 55.
Melittarchus dominicensis, CABANIS, Journal für Ornith. III. Nov. 1855 478.
Tyrannus griseus, VIEILLOT, Ois. Am. Sept. I, 1807, 76 ; pl. xlvi.—SWAINSON, Mon Shrikes Quart. Jour. XX, 1826, 276.—BP. C-nsp. 1850, 192. (Bonaparte makes two species.)

SP. CH.—Bill very large and short. Tail conspicuously forked. Wings long ; the first six quills attenuated abruptly, much longer than the seventh. Tertials much developed, nearly intermediate in length between the longest primaries and the shortest secondary. Above, and on the sides of the head and neck, ash gray, shaded in places with brown, which forms the middle portion of each feather. Downy portion at the base of each feather above light ash, then light brown, tipped and edged with darke ash gray. The mottled appearance is caused by the brown showing from under the feathers ; the ear coverts darker. A concealed colored patch on the crown, formed by the base of the feathers, white before and behind, orange in the middle. Lower parts grayish white, tinged with ash across the breast, deepest anteriorly. Sides of the breast similar to, but lighter than, the back. Under wing coverts and axillars pale sulphur yellow. The wings brown, darker to the tips ; the secondaries narrowly, the tertials more broadly edged with dull white. Edges of the coverts paler. Alula dark brown. Tail similar in color to the quills. Upper tail coverts brown. Bill and feet black. Length, eight inches ; wing, 4.65 ; tail, 4 ; tarsus .76.

Hab.—South Carolina coast, accidental ; Florida Keys and West Indies.

This species, though about the same size as the *T. carolinensis*, is much more powerfully built, the bill and feet being much stronger, the former considerably longer than the head, and a large as that of *Saurophagus sulphuratus*, though less compressed.

This species is a constant summer visitor to the maritime portions of Florida, and thence to the West Indies ; and a pair has been observed at Charleston, by Mr. Audubon. It is not well established whether our species is to be considered the true *dominicensis* or the *griseus*, if distinct, as asserted by Bonaparte in his Conspectus Avium. The specimen described is a Florida one.

Cabanis, as quoted above, has instituted a genus *Melittarchus*, with *magnirostris* as type, for the tyrants with very large swollen bills, emarginated tails, and less attenuated outer primaries. The gradations, however, in size of bill of the tyrants are so slight, and the other characters so variable, even in the smaller billed species, that the group seems scarcely of generic value.

List of specimens.

Catal. No.	Sex.	Locality.	When collected.	Whence obtained.	Collected by—	Length.	Stretch of wings.	Wing.	Remarks.
6518	♂	Indian Key, Fla..........	May 12, 1857	G. Würdemann....	....	9.50	15.00	4.70	....
6519	♂	......do.	..... do....:.....	......do.	....	....	....	....	Black eyes and tongue
1881	.....	North America...........	....	S. F. Baird	J. J. Audubon	....	....	....	....
2963	......	......do.	....	......do. ....:.....	......do.	....	....	....	....

TYRANNUS VERTICALIS, Say.

Arkansas Flycatcher.

Tyrannus verticalis, Say. Long's Exped. II, 1823, 60.—Nuttall, Man. II, 2d ed. 1840, 306.
Muscicapa verticalis, Bonap. Am. Orn. I, 1825, 18 ; pl. xi.—Aud. Orn. Biog. IV, 1838, 422 ; pl. 359.—Ib. Birds America I, 1840, 199 ; pl. 54.

Sp. Ch.—The four exterior quills attenuated very gently at the end, the first most so ; third and fourth quills longest, second and fifth successively a little shorter. Tail slightly forked ; bill shorter than the head. Crown, sides of head above the eyes, nape, and sides of neck pale lead color or ash gray ; a concealed crest in the crown, vermilion in the centre, and yellowish before and behind. Hind neck and back ash gray, strongly tinged with light olivaceous green, the gray turning to brown on the rump ; upper tail coverts nearly black, lower dusky ; chin and part of ear coverts dull white ; throat and upper part of breast similar to the head, but lighter, and but slightly contrasted with the chin ; rest of lower parts, with the under wing coverts and axillars, yellow, deepening to gamboge on the belly, tinged with olivaceous on the breast. Wing brown, the coverts with indistinct ashy margins ; secondaries and tertials edged with whitish ; inner webs of primaries whitish towards the base. Tail nearly black above and glossy, duller brownish beneath ; without olivaceous edgings. Exterior feather, with the outer web and the shaft, yellowish white ; inner edge of latter brown. Tips of remaining feathers paler. Bill and feet dark brown.

Female rather smaller and colors less bright. Length of male, 8.25 ; wing about 4.50.

Hab.—Western North America, from the high central plains to the Pacific.

The young bird is, in general, quite similar, with the exception of the usual appearance of immaturity, the colored patch on the crown wanting. In one specimen the first primary only is attenuated, in others none are attenuated.

A specimen of this bird, shot at Moorestown, New Jersey, is in the museum of the Philadelphia Academy, but this locality can only be considered as very exceptional.

List of specimens.

Catal. No.	Sex & age.	Locality.	When collected.	Whence obtained.	Orig'l No.	Collected by—	Length.	Extent.	Wing.	Remarks.
1852	.....	Fort Union............	— —,1843	S. F. Baird........	......	J. J. Audubon......				
5265	.....	Yellowstone river........	....	Lt. G. K. Warren....	.....	Dr. Hayden....				
5263	.....	Yellowstone river, (above 15 miles.)	Jan. —,1856	......do.........	......	.....do........	8.12	15.	4.75	Iris dark brown....
5264	♂	Knife river, on Mo......	Sept. 10,1856	......do...		.....do........	8.25	15.25	4.50	
5262	♂	Fort Lookout............	June 22,1856	......do...		.....do... ...	8.75	15.50	5.	
5258	♀	.....do....		......do...		.....do..	8.75	13.75	4.50	Eyes dark........
5260	♂	.....do..	May —,1856	......do...		.....do........	8.75	16.50	5.25	Eyes black....
5259	♀	.....do..	......do...	.... do...		.....do........	8.50	14.50	5.	
5246	♀	Farm Island............	May 10,1856	......do...		.....do........	8.37	14.50	......	
5240	♂	.....do....	May 30,1856	......do...		.... do....	8.75	15.37	5.50	
5243	♀	.....do....	......do...	......do...		.....do........	8.75	15.25	5.25	
5256	♀	.....do.......	May 31,1856	......do...		.....do........	8.25	15.25	4.50	
5253	♂	.....do..	May 29,1856	......do...		.....do........	8.75	15.25	5.25	
5252	♂	.....do..	June 2,1856	......do...		.....do........	9.	15.25	5.50	Iris yellow ??......
5242	♂	.....do..	May 30,1856	......do...		.....do........	8.75	15.50	5.	
5266	♂	Near mouth of Powder river, Nebraska.	Aug. 1,1856	......do...		.....do........	8.25	14.50	4.75	
5261	♂	.....do ....do......	......do......			.....do........	8.	15.	4.75	
8896	♀	Loup Fork........ ...	Aug. 6,1857	......do..		.....do........	9.	15.75	4.75	Iris gray..........
8599	♀	.....do...	Aug. 16,1857	......do...			8.	15.	4.50	
8898	......	.....do...		......do...			8.50	15.75	4.50	
8797	♂	Fort Laramie, Neb........	Aug. 27,1857	Wm. M. Magraw.....	70	Dr. T. G .Cooper.	8.75	14.75	5.00	Iris brown, bill and feet grayish black.
5633	♂	Pole creek, Neb........ ...	July 29,1856	Lieut. Bryan.........	173	W. S. Wood....				
7082	♀	.....do...	......do...	......do...		.....do...				
5632	♀	.....do...	July 28,1856	......do...	169	.....do......		.50		
5634	○	.....do...	July 29,1856	......do...	177	.....do......	8.			
5056	.....	San Pedro river, Texas...	May 1,1855	Captain Pope........	57	....	9.	14.	5.	
5057	○	Crossing of Pecos........	Sept. 1,1855	......do....	135		8.50	14.50	5.	Eyes brown........
7385	.....	Mimbres to Rio Grande...		Dr. Henry...						
5906	♀	Fort Steilacoom, W. T....		Dr. Cooper.........			8.75	15.00		
5907	♂	.....do....... do......		......do.......			9 50			
5905	♀	.....do... do.......		......do...			9.00	15.50		
5908	......	.....do... do.......		......do...						
4378	.....	Fort Dalles, Oregon.......	May 2,1855	Dr. Suckley......	162		9.	16.	5.37	
5506	♀	Petaluma, California.....		E. Samuels..........	557					
5507	♂	.....do....... do.....		......do...	675					
4214	......	San Francisco.....	— —,1853	R. D. Cutts ...						
4470	.....	Benicia, California......		Lt. Williamson	......	Dr. Newberry..				
	.....	Fort Tejon, California.....		John Xantus de Vesey.						

TYRANNUS VOCIFERANS, Swainson.

Cassin's Flycatcher.

Tyrannus vociferans, SWAINSON, Mon. Tyrant Shrikes in Quarterly Journal Sc. XX, Jan. 1826, 273.—IB. Philos. Mag. I, 1827, 368.

Tyrannus cassinii, LAWRENCE, Ann. N. Y. Lyceum, N. H. V, 1852, 39 ; pl. iii, fig. 2, (Texas.)

SP. CH.—Bill from the forehead about as long as the head. Tail even or slightly rounded. Outer five primaries attenuated ; the first four abruptly and deeply emarginated ; third quill longest, second and fourth a little less, first shorter than the sixth, and half an inch less than the longest. Head and neck above and on the sides rather dark bluish ash ; the throat and breast similar, and only a little paler. Rest of upper parts olive green tinged with gray, mixed with brown on the rump ; the upper tail coverts and surface of the tail nearly black ; the outer web of the external feather and the tips of all pale brown. The chin is white, in strong contrast to the dark ash of the throat ; the rest of the under parts bright sulphur yellow, (the sides olivaceous ;) palest on the under tail coverts and inside of wing. A concealed vermilion patch in the crown, bordered by straw yellow. Wing feathers brown, tinged with olive, becoming paler towards the edge. Length, 8.80 inches ; wing, 5.25 ; tail, 4.25.

Hab.—Valley of Gila, eastward to Pecos river, Texas, and into Mexico, on table lands.

This species bears a close relationship to the *T. verticalis*, although the differences are readily appreciable on comparison. The bill is rather larger; the legs considerably more so; the quills are much more abruptly attenuated, and this near the tip, (within half an inch,) instead of being gradually emarginated. The tail is more even, and in some specimens slightly rounded. In respect to coloration, the ash of the head is considerably darker, that of the throat and breast much more so, making a very conspicuous contrast with the white of the throat and yellow of the belly ; the yellow beneath is brighter. The shoulders are more olivaceous. A very appreciable character is seen in the tail. The whole outer web of the external feather, including the shaft, in *T. verticalis* is purely and abruptly yellowish white, the extreme tips of all a little brownish. In the present species the shaft of the outer tail feather is dark brown, its outer webs and a rather broad band at the end of the other feathers rather light brown, with the extreme edges only of this color of a rather pure yellowish white.

The identification of *Tyrannus vociferans*, Sw., with the present species, rather than with *verticalis*, is rendered necessary by the statement of the author, that the bill is larger than that of the king bird, instead of equal ; the primary quills abruptly pointed, instead of very gradually attenuated ; the head, neck, and breast pure slate, with the chin white, in decided contrast, instead of light ash, and the chin scarcely different. The absence of any mention of the white outer web to the external tail feather is also very conclusive as to the name not being referable to *verticalis*. The tail is said to be even. Mr. Swainson's specimen came from Temiscaltepec, and one from a locality not very remote, presented by Mr. Gould, agrees precisely with skins from the United States. The only discrepancy in Swainson's description is in speaking of the tail and covert as deep black, instead of brownish black.

List of specimens.

Catal. No.	Sex.	Locality.	When collected.	Whence obtained.	Orig. No.	Collected by—	Length.	Stretch of wings.	Wing.	Remarks.
7389	♀	? Sacramento valley	....	Lieut. Williamson..	... ...	Dr. Heermann	....	....	....	. ...
7390	♂	? Fort Tejon..........	.. ..	......do............	......	......do..........	....	....	....	....
4579	......	Colorado river, Cal......	....	Major Emory......	......	A. Schott..........	... ...	....	....	....
7204	......	Los Nogales, Mex........	Jan. —, 1855	......do............	......	Dr. Kennerly	....	....	....	....
7387	......	Fort Thorn, N. M........	....	Dr. T. C. Henry....	......	....	....	....	....	....
5055	......	Pecos, Texas............	April 23, 1856	Capt. Pope	191	....	9.00	15.00	5.00	Eyes brown....
7938	......	Mexico	....	J. Gould..........	......	....	....	....	....	....
7939	.....	........do..............	....	......do..........	......	....	....	....	....	....

TYRANNUS COUCHII, Baird.

Couch's Flycatcher.

SP. CH.—Bill as long as the head. Feet stout. Five outer primaries abruptly attenuated at the end ; the third and fourth longest ; the first a little longer than the sixth. Tail considerably forked ; (depth of fork about .30 of an inch.) Top and sides of the head and neck light bluish ash ; rest of upper parts olivaceous green, tinged with ash, less of the olive on the rump ; a concealed patch of red on the crown. Chin white, passing insensibly into an ashy tinge on the fore part of the breast ; rest of under parts generally bright yellow, almost gamboge on the belly. The quills and tail feathers are of about the same shade of brown, not at all black ; in fact, the primaries are darkest ; the upper tail coverts are lighter brown than the tail ; the edges of the wing feathers, except the primaries, are paler ; of the secondaries and tertials almost white. The tail feathers externally are like the back ; internally and at the tip they are brownish white. The external web of the outer tail feather is like the internal, the extreme edge only paler. The shafts of all are white beneath.

Length 9.00 ; wing, 5.00 ; tail, 4.70.

Hab.—Northeastern Mexico to Rio Grande.

This species, though otherwise similar, is readily distinguished from *T. verticalis* and *vociferans* by the absence of the very dark brown, almost black, of the tail and its upper coverts, as well as by the pale external edges to all the tail feathers. The yellow is much brighter ; the chin and throat with more white, and the ashy tinge on the breast is much lighter than even in *T. verticalis*, and does not extend so far down. The inner surface of the wing is very pure yellow. The red in the crown has more of an orange shade. The bill is much larger and the tail much more deeply forked than in either of the species mentioned. The shafts of the tail feathers are white beneath, not brown. The differences from *T. melancholicus* will be found detailed under that species.

A *Tyrannus sulphuraceus* from Cuba and Hayti is indicated in Naumannia by Hartlaub, from the MSS. of Prince Paul, of Würtemberg, and subsequently referred to by Cabanis, in Journal für Ornith. 1855, 479. The *T. couchii*, however, has no white stripe under the eye ; the crest is not golden yellow ; the tail feathers not pale yellowish beneath, &c.

List of specimens.

Catal. No.	Sex.	Locality.	When collected.	Whence obtained.	Orig. No.	Length.	Stretch of wings.	Wing.	Remarks.
4001	♂	New Leon, Mexico	....	Lt. D. N. Couch	99	9.00	15.00	5.00	Eyes dark brown, bill and feet black..............
-002	....	San Diego, Mexico.......	March —, 1853	......do.	111	9.00	15.00	5.00	......do. ....
4003	♂	......do...............	April —, 1853	..... do.	126	9.50	15.50	5.00	......do. ....

TYRANNUS MELANCHOLICUS, Vieillot.

Tyrannus melancholicus, VIEILLOT, Nouv. Dict. N. H. XXXV, 1819, 84.—TSCHUDI, Fauna Per. 1844–'46, 151.— BURM. Th. Bras. Vögel, 1856, 464.

Muscicapa despotes, LICHT. Verz. Doubl. 1823, No. 567, a.

Muscicapa furcata, SPIX, Av. Bras. II tab. xix.

Tyrannus crudelis, SWAINSON, Mon. Tyrant Shrikes Quart. Jour. XX, Jan. 1826, 275, (Brazil.)

SP. CH.—Bill very large. Quills moderately but abruptly emarginate and attenuated at the end ; the third and fourth longest ; the first rather shorter than the sixth. Tail quite deeply forked, (depth of fork half an inch.) Top and sides of the head and neck light bluish ash ; rest of upper parts bright olive ; browner on the upper tail coverts. Chin whitish, passing gradually into pale ash (considerably lighter than above) on the throat, and on the fore part of breast tinged with olive green ; rest of lower parts bright gamboge yellow. Wing and tail feathers dark brown ; the tips of the primaries and tail almost black ; all, except the primaries, edged with olivaceous gray, which in the secondaries and tertials has a strong tinge of sulphur yellow ; edge of outer tail feathers pale brown, and narrow tips of all brownish white. Crown with a vermilion patch encircled by yellow.

Length, 9.00 ; wing, 4.50 ; tail, 4.20.

Hab —Southern Mexico, Central and South America.

I have described this species, although as yet not found near our territory, for the purpose of aiding in the determination of the species of this most difficult group, by showing the peculiar characteristics of some closely allied species. It has the general appearance of the three species just described, but the tail is much more deeply forked than in either *verticalis* or *vociferans*, although it is almost as black. It differs from both in the laxly fibred olivaceous outer edges to the tail feathers, instead of a compact uniform brownish black, without any colored margin. The ash color does not extend so far on the breast, which is more tinged with olive ; the yellow is more intense ; the light edgings of the wings are olivaceous, instead of grayish white. The bill is much larger ; the attenuation of the primaries less. In reality, however, nothing more is needed to separate it from *T. verticalis* than its brown outer margin to the tail, nor from *vouferans* than its deeply forked tail and paler ash of the throat and olivaceous breast.

Its resemblance to *T. couchii* (4003) is much closer. Both have a deep fork to the tail; bright gamboge yellow belly; the bill of nearly the same size; the shafts of the tail feathers white beneath, &c. The tail is, however, more deeply forked, and much darker, nearly black; the feathers narrower; the upper tail coverts darker; the edgings on the wing yellowish, not grayish white, &c. It is barely possible that the two may be the same, but at present I see sufficient differences to distinguish them.

Among a series of specimens otherwise quite similar, I find some difference in the depth of the fork of the tail, which in one is as much as .80 of an inch. The bills vary considerably, both in size and proportions. All, however, agree well both with the *T. melancholicus* and *T. crudelis*. Should two be distinguished, Swainson's name may be applied to the more northern one. In my description I have taken the specimen from Vera Cruz as the type.

List of specimens.

Catal. No.	Locality.	When collected.	Whence obtained.	Orig. No.
8101	Vera Cruz, Mexico		S. F. Baird	
4524	Panama	Dec. 28, 1855	Dr. Suckley.	198
8102	South America		S. F. Baird	
8103	do		do	
8104	do		do	

MYIARCHUS, Cabanis.

Myiarchus, CABANIS, Fauna Peruana 1844-'6, 152.—BURMEISTER, Thiere Brasiliens, II, Vögel, 1856, 469.

Tarsus equal to or not longer than the middle toe, which is decidedly longer than the hinder one. Bill wider at base than half the culmen. Tail broad, long, even, or slightly rounded, about equal to the wings, which scarcely reach the middle of the tail; the first primary shorter than the sixth. Head with elongated lanceolate distinct feathers. Above brownish olive, throat ash, belly yellow. Tail and wing feathers varied with rufous.

This genus is well marked among the American flycatchers, and constitutes what Bonaparte called *Ultimi Tyrannorum sive Tyrannularum primae.* The type is the *Muscicapa ferox* of Gmelin, which, as identified by Cabanis and Burmeister as above, appears to resemble our species very closely. The following analysis exhibits the peculiarities of the latter, including a closely allied Mexican form :

A. Inner web of tail feathers broadly rufous to the extreme tip. Bill broad; its width at base two-thirds the culmen.

Colors darker. Brown stripe along the inside of shafts of tail feathers very inconspicuous and narrow. Tarsus .84 of an inch......................*M. crinitus.*

Colors paler. Brown stripe on inside of shafts of tail feathers very distinct, and on the outer one broader than the outer web. Tarsus .95 of an inch....*M. cooperi.*

B. Inner web of tail feathers broadly rufous only to near the tip, which is brown.

Colors pale. Tarsus .90 of an inch. Bill at base little more than one-half the culmen...*M. mexicanus.*

23 b

C. Inner web of tail feathers entirely brown, with only a narrow edging of rufous. Ou.er primary edged with rufous. First primary shorter than secondaries. No whitish bands on wing...*M. lawrencii.*

Comparative measurements of the species.

Catal. No	Species.	Locality.	Sex.	Length.	Stretch of wings.	Wing.	Tail.	Tarsus.	Middle toe.	Its claw alone.	Bill above.	Along gape.	Specimen measured.	Remarks.
1449	Myiarchus crinitus.......	Carlisle, Pa..........	♂	7.80	......	4.12	4.06	0.80	0.70	0.26	0.72	0.98	Dry.....	....
do	....do..........do.......	......do.............		8.75	13.66	4.25	......	......	......	......	.....	......	Fresh...	....
1426	...do..........do.......	......do.............	♀	7.38	......	3.90	3.82	0.84	0.64	0.24	0.76	1.06	Dry.....	....
do	....do..........do.	......do.............		8.75	13.25	4.08	......	......	......	......	......	......	Fresh...	....
9100	Myiarchus cooperi.......	Mexico............	...	8.30	......	4.06	4.10	0.90	0.70	0.26	0.80	1.12	Dry.....	....
5509	Myiarchus mexicanus....	Petaluma, Cal	♂	7.80	......	4.00	4.24	0.95	0.70	0.24	0.76	1.00	Dry.....	....
7940	....do..........do.......	Mexico............		.....	......	4.02	4.16	0.86	0.50	0.20	0.70	0.96	Dry.....	Head off; feet broken.
3918	...do..........do.......	California		7.64	......	3.96	4.06	0.90	0.70	0.22	0.74	1.04	Dry.....	....
10028	Myiarchus lawrencii.....	New Leon, Mex., San Diego	♀	6.62	......	3.28	3.50	0.74	0.62	0.24	0.66	0.92	Dry.....	....

MYIARCHUS CRINITUS, Cabanis.

Great Crested Flycatcher.

Muscicapa crinita, Linn. Syst. Nat. I, 1766, 325.—Wilson, Am. Orn. II, 1810, 75 ; pl. xiii.—Licht. Verzeichniss Doubl. 1823, No. 559.—Aud. Orn. Biog. II, 1834, 176 : V, 423 ; pl. 129.—Ib. Birds Amer. I, 1840, 209 ; pl. 57.

Tyrannus crinitus, Swainson, Mon. Tyrant Shrikes in Quarterly Journal, XX. Jan. 1826, 271.—Nuttall, Man. I, 2d ed. 1840, 302.

Myiobius crinitus, Gray, Genera, I, 248.

Tyrannula crinita, Bonap. Consp. 1850, 189.—Kaup, Pr. Zool. Soc. 1851, 51.

Myiarchus crinitus, Cabanis, Journ. für Ornith. III, 1855, 479.

Muscicapa ludoviciana, Gm. Syst. Nat. I, 1788, 934.—Latham Ind.

Tyrannus ludovicianus, Vieillot, Ois. Am. Sept. I, 1807 ; pl. 45.

" Tyrannus irritabilis, Vieillot.*"*

Muscicapa virginiana cristata, Brisson, II, 1760, 412.

Crested flycatcher, Pennant, Latham.

Figure, Buffon Enl. 569, fig. 1.

Sp Ch.—Head with a depressed crest. Third quill longest ; fourth and second successively but little shorter ; first a little longer than seventh ; much shorter than sixth. Tail decidedly rounded or even graduated ; the lateral feather about .25 of an inch shorter. Upper parts dull greenish olive, with the feathers of the crown and to some extent of the back showing their brown centres; upper tail coverts turning to pale rusty brown. Small feathers at the base of the bill, ceres, sides of the head as high as the upper eyelid, sides of the neck, throat, and forepart of the breast bluish ashy ; the rest of the lower parts, including axillaries and lower wing coverts, bright sulphur yellow ; a pale ring round the eye. Sides of the breast and body tinged with olivaceous. The wings brown ; the first and second rows of coverts, with the secondary and tertial quills, margined externally with dull white, or on the latter slightly tinged with olivaceous yellow. Primaries margined externally for more than half their length from the base with ferruginous ; great portion of the inner webs of all the quills very pale ferruginous. The two middle tail feathers light brown, shafts paler ; the rest have the outer web and a narrow line on the inner sides of the shaft brown, pale olivaceous on the outer edge ; the remainder ferruginous to the very tip. Outer web of exterior feather dull brownish yellow. Feet black. Bill dark brown above and at the tip below ; paler towards the base. Length, 8.75 inches ; wing, 4.25 ; tail, 4.10 ; tarsus, .85.

Hab.—Eastern North America to the Missouri and south to eastern Texas, (not yet observed further west.)

The female appears to have no brown on the inner web of the quills along the shaft, or else it is confined chiefly to the outer feathers.

List of specimens.

Catal. No.	Sex.	Locality.	When collected.	Whence obtained.	Orig'l No.	Collected by—	Length.	Stretch of wings.	Wing.
1449	♂	Carlisle, Pa.	May 4, 1844	S. F. Baird			8.75	13.66	4.25
1523	♂	...do...	May 16, 1844	...do...			9.00	13.50	4.25
2634	♂	...do...	May 11, 1846	...do...			9.00	13.16	4.25
2539	♂	...do...	May 5, 1844	...do...			9.00	13.50	4.25
1020	♂	...do...	May 24, 1843	...do...			8.08	13.41	4.00
1426	♀	...do...	May 2, 1844	...do...			8.75	13.25	4.08
7414	.....	Cleveland, Ohio		Dr. Kirtland...					
	♀	South Illinois	May 11, 1844	R. Kennicott...					
6970	♂	St. Louis, Mo.	May 8, 1857	Lieut. F. T. Bryan...	33	W. S. Wood...			
7532	.....	Independence, Mo.		Wm. M. Magraw...		Dr. J. G. Cooper...	8.25	12.50	4.00
8398	♂	...do...	July 1, 1857	...do...	108	...do...	8.60	12.70	4.10
		Red fork of Arkansas...		Capt. Sitgreaves...		Dr. Woodhouse...			
7201	.....	Texas		Capt. Pope...					
7202	.....	...do...		...do...					

MYIARCHUS MEXICANUS, Baird.

Ash-throated Flycatcher

Tyrannula mexicana, KAUP, Pr. Zool. Soc. Feb. 1851, 51.
Tyrannula cinerascens, LAWRENCE, Annals N. Y. Lyc. N. Hist. V, Sept. 1851, 109.

SP. CH.—Bill black, the width opposite the nostrils not half the length of culmen. Head crested. Tail even, the lateral feathers slightly shorter. Second, third, and fourth quills longest ; first rather shorter than the seventh. Above dull greyish olive ; the centres of the feathers rather darker ; the crown, rump, and upper tail coverts tinged with brownish. The forehead and sides of the head and neck grayish ash ; the chin, throat, and fore part of the breast ashy white ; the middle of the breast white ; the rest of the under parts very pale sulphur yellow ; wings and tail brown. Two bands across the wing, with outer edges of secondaries and tertials dull white ; the outer edges of the primaries light chestnut brown (except towards the tip and on the outer feather ;) the inner edges tinged with the same. Whole of middle tail feathers, with the outer webs (only) and the ends of the others brown ; the rest of the inner webs reddish chestnut, the outer web of exterior feather yellowish white. Legs and bill black ; lower mandible brownish at the base. Length about 8 inches ; wing, 4 ; tail, 4.10 ; tarsus, .90.

Hab.—Coast of California, and across by valley of Gila and Rio Grande to northeastern Mexico. Seen as far north in Texas as San Antonio.

In a young specimen the crown is more tinged with brown ; the upper tail coverts and the middle tail feathers are chestnut, and, in fact, all the tail feathers are of this color, except along both sides of the shaft on the central feathers, and along its outer side in the lateral ones.

The relationships of this species are clearly with *M. crinitus*, although the differences are readily appreciable. The size is much the same ; the bill narrower and blacker ; the tarsi much longer ; the wings not so much pointed. The colors of the upper parts are quite the same ; beneath, however, the throat and middle of the fore breast are nearly white (quite white behind) instead of ash, and the sulphur yellow of the remaining under parts is exceedingly pale, instead of very intense. The wings are similar, but the chestnut brown of the inner web is deeper and more abruptly defined in *crinitus*. In the lateral tail feathers of *mexicanus* the brown does not cross the shaft from the outer webs, but is continued rather broadly round the tips ; while in the other the inner side of the shaft is bordered by brown, but the inner web is chesnut to the extreme end.

This species is but briefly described by Kaup, as quoted above, still his comparisons of size, &c., with its allies leave no doubt as to the identity with *Tyrannula cinerascens* of Lawrence. A Mexican specimen is a little larger than usual, but otherwise the same.

List of specimens.

Catal. No.	Sex and age.	Locality.	When collected.	Whence obtained.	Orig. No.	Collected by—	Length.	Stretch of wings.	Wing.	Remarks.
5508	♂	Petaluma, Sonoma Co., Cal............		E. Samuels	681					
5509	♂	......do	April —, 1856	......do .	663					
7207	....	San Francisco, Cal.....		R. D. Cutts........						
7209	....	......do		......do .						
4946	....	San José, Cal........		A. J. Grayson......	2					
3720	♀	Los Angeles, Cal......		W. Hutton........						
7210	○ ♂	Posa creek		Lt. R. Williamson..		Dr. Heermann...				
....		Fort Tejon, Cal.......		John X. de Vesey..						
4608	....	Colorado bottom, Cal...	Mar. 31, 1854	Major Emory	38	A. Schott........				
4588	....	Gila river, N. M........	Dec. 31, 1854	......do .	38					
7208	....	Los Nogales, Mex......	June —, 1853	......do .	.. ...	Dr. Kennerly ..,.				
7211	♂	Frontera, Texas		......do .	32	J. H. Clark......				
....		San Antonio, Texas....		Capt. Sitgreaves...		Dr. Woodhouse..				
7213	....	Eagle pass, Texas......		Major Emory		A. Schott........				
7212	♀	Saltillo, Coahuila, Mex.	May —, 1853	Lt. Couch.........	221	....	8.00	11.50	3.62	Eyes dark brown, bill black, feet dark slate.
7940	....	Mexico................		J. Gould..						

MYIARCHUS COOPERI, Baird.

Tyrannula cooperi, KAUP, Pr. Zool. Soc. 1851, 51, (not of Nuttall.)

SP. CH.—Width of bill above grayish olive. Throat and upper part of breast light ash gray ; rest of under parts pale sulphur yellow. Two light-colored bands on the wings ; the primaries, except the first, margined externally and internally with rufous. Tail feathers rufous, the outer webs, and a stripe on the inner side of the shaft extending in a straight line to the tip, brown. This inner stripe is a little wider than the outer web on the outer feather, but diminishes somewhat to the central ones. Length, 8.50 ; wing, 4 ; tail, 3.90 ; tarsus, .95.

Hab.—Mexico.

This species of flycatcher is very similar to *M. crinitus*, and, in fact, occupies a position intermediate in color between it and *mexicanus*, though larger, perhaps, than either. The superiority in size over *M. crinitus* is chiefly noticeable in the tarsus, which is about .12 of an inch longer, and in the bill ; the wing is, however, shorter. The third quill is longest ; the second and fourth but little less ; the first a little longer than the seventh. The coloration is much the same with *mexicanus*, being considerably paler and grayer than *crinitus*. The yellow of the breast is a little deeper than in *mexicanus*, and the throat a very little darker. The upper parts are like *mexicanus*, and there is a decided pure gray shade on the forehead and on the back of the neck, and to a less extent on the rump.

This species differs from *crinitus*, as stated, in the larger bill and tarsi, and shorter wings, with a much paler tint of coloration. Both have the tail similar in the continuation of the reddish of the tail to the extreme tip, instead of having this tip brown as in *mexicanus*. The tail is more nearly even, however, and the brown stripe on the inside of the shaft is wider than the outer web on the exterior feather, as wide on the second, and gradually diminishing to the fifth, where it is about one-fourth the width of the outer web. In *M. crinitus* the brown stripe on the inner web is scarcely half the width of the outer web, and quite pale. On the fifth feather it does not cross the shaft at all ; while in some specimens this color is scarcely appreciable on the inner webs of any but the exterior feathers. The bill is quite black.

From *mexicanus* this species is distinguished by the larger size and much broader bill although the tarsi are the same length. The most striking feature is found in the continuation of the rufous boundary line on the inner webs of the tail feathers in a straight line to the extreme tip of the tail, instead of having this to curve abruptly to the inner edge of the feather, leaving the entire tips brown.

A specimen of this bird, labelled *Tyrannula crinita*, (to which, indeed, it bears a close resemblance,) was received from Mr. Verreaux. It is probably the species described by Kaup as *Tyrannula cooperi*, though widely different from the real bird. As, however, the two fall in different genera, and, especially, as the name of *cooperi* cannot stand for the other species, I very gladly retain it for the present one.

In all three species the outer primaries are without any rufous, thus distinguishing them from *M. gossii*, which has rufous edging to all the primaries. *M. stolidus* has the black stripe on the inside of the shafts of the tail feathers reaching only to the middle of the feathers.

I am under the impression that Kaup is not the first to apply the name of *cooperi* to the present species, and that it is also found in Chile. It is probable that the real olive-sided flycatcher (*T. cooperi*, Nuttall,) has not been found in South America.

List of specimens.

Catalogue number.	Locality.	Whence obtained.	Original number.
9100	Mexico	M. Verreaux	29827

MYIARCHUS LAWRENCII, Baird.

Lawrence's Flycatcher.

Tyrannula lawrencii, GIRAUD, Sixteen Sp. Texas Birds, 1841, pl. ii.

SP. CH.—First quill shorter than the secondaries. *Female.*—Above olive green ; lightest on the rump ; the head dusky. Throat pale ash ; rest of under parts sulphur yellow. Quills and tail feathers brown, edged externally with brownish rufous ; internally with paler rufous. Bill dark brown ; feet black. Length, (female) 7 inches ; wing, 3.25 ; tail, 3.50.

Hab.—Northeastern Mexico to the Rio Grande.

In this species the wing is short and considerably rounded ; the first quill shorter than the secondaries ; the second intermediate between fifth and sixth. The tail is slightly emarginated. There is a wash of rufous on the wing coverts, especially on their edges, but there are no distinct bands. There is a faint trace of rufous only on the outer first primary, and but little more on the second; it is distinct on the outer edges of all the other quills, but turns to yellowish on the innermost ones. The light reddish buff of the inner webs is much more extended than externally, where the rufous is confined to the extreme edge of the web. The tail feathers are, for the most part, olive brown ; the edges only rufous, this color only extending to near the tip ; internally it occupies about one third of the inner vane ; externally it is a mere border. The outer web of the outer feather is paler than in the rest, but not at all white.

This rare flycatcher is similar in general characters to the *M. crinitus* and *mexicanus*, but readily distinguishable by strongly marked characters. The size is less, and the first primary shorter than the secondaries instead of longer. The shades of coloration are those of *crinitus ;* much darker than in *mexicanus*. It lacks the two white bands of the wings, and the broad sulphur yellow edgings to the innermost quills. All the tail feathers are brown on both webs to the tips, with a narrow edging only of reddish, instead, as in both the other species, of having the entire inner webs of most of these feathers light cinnamon. The bill is shaped as in *crinitus*, but the edges are slightly convex instead of straight; it is broader than in *mexicanus*.

It is probable that the male of this species is somewhat differently colored from the female described above.

It is not improbable that this bird may belong to the genus *Blacicus* of Cabanis (Journal für Ornithologie III, Nov. 1855, 480,) characterized as having the wings shorter than in *Myiarchus*; the bill much depressed, flat, and broad; the tail somewhat emarginated. In this event, and should the genus be considered worthy of retention, the present species will be called *Blacicus lawrencii*.

List of specimens.

Catal. No.	Sex.	Locality.	When collected.	Whence obtained.	Orig'l No.	Length.	Extent.	Wing.	Remarks.
10028	♀	San Diego, New Leon	Spring of 1853	Lt. Couch.........	110	7.00	10.00	3.50	Eyes brown, bill and feet dark slate.

SAYORNIS, Bonaparte.

Sayornis, BONAP. ? Ateneo italiano, 1854.—IB. Comptes Rendus, 1854, Notes Orn. Delattre.
Aulanax, CABANIS, Journal für Orn. 1856, 1, (type *nigricans*.)

CH.—Head with a blended depressed moderate crest. Tarsus decidedly longer than middle toe, which is scarcely longer than the hind toe. Bill rather narrow; width at base about half the culmen. Tail broad, long, slightly forked; equal to the wings, which are moderately pointed, and reach to the middle of the tail. First primary shorter than the sixth.

This genus agrees with the preceding in the length of the broad tail, but has a longer tarsus and a different style of coloration. The species are distinguished as follows:

Sooty black; belly and edge of the tail pure white.........................*S. nigricans.*
Brownish olive above; crown darker; beneath and edge of tail yellowish..*S. fuscus.*
Grayish brown; belly reddish cinnamon.....................................*S. sayus.*

This genus I first find referred to by Bonaparte in the notice of Delattres' collections, in Comptes rendus, 1854, where he names *Sayornis nigricans*. I am, however, inclined to believe that he has given a conspectus of the Tyrants in the Paris Ateneo italiano for 1854, and in it this genus.

Cabanis calls the supposed " *Tyrannula fusca*" of Cuba *Aulanax fuscus*, and claims the " *T. nigricans*" as type if Bonaparte's name be untenable.

Comparative measurements of the species.

Catal. No.	Species.	Locality.	Sex.	Length.	Extent.	Wing.	Tail.	Tarsus.	Middle toe.	Its claw.	Bill above.	Along gape.	Specimen measured.	Remarks.
7226	Sayornis sayus . .	Tejon valley......	♂	6.84	....	4.00	3.46	0.80	0.64	0.22	0.56	0.82	Dry.......	....
7219	Sayornis nigricans	Sac. valley.......	♂	6.82	....	3.64	3.54	0.74	0.60	0.22	0.60	0.82	Dry.......	....
4005	........do........	Cadereita, Mexico	♀	6.60	....	3.32	3.06	0.66	0.54	0.20	0.60	0.80	Dry........	Poor specimen.
do.	... ...do.........	.......do........		6.50	11.75	3.25	......	......	......	......	... ...	....	Fresh.....	....
7943	........do.........	Mexico		6.40	....	3.32	3.22	0.66	0.64	0.24	0.54	0.72	Dry.......	....
957	Sayornis fuscus...	Carlisle, Penn....	♂	6.04	....	3.38	3.24	0.70	0.60	0.20	0.54	0.80	Dry.......	....
do.	........do.........	.......do		7.	11.	3.41	......	......	......	......	....	....	Fresh.....	....
1339	........do.........	.......do	♀	6.40	....	3.26	3.16	0.66	0.54	0.24	0.56	0.82	Dry.......	....
do.	........do.........	.......do........		6.75	10.83	3.33	... ...	......	......	......	....	....	Fresh	....
2451	........do.........	.......do........	♂	5.90	....	3.30	3.16	0.70	0.58	0.22	0.50	0.74	Dry.......	....
9102	........do.........	Mexico		6.86	....	3.22	3.30	0.66	0.56	0.20	0.54	0.80	Dry........	....

SAYORNIS NIGRICANS, Bonap.

Black Flycatcher.

Tyrannula nigricans, SWAINSON, Syn. Birds Mex. Taylor's Phil. Mag. I, 1827, 367—NEWBERRY, Zool. Cal. &
Or. Route, Rep. P. R. R. Surv. VI, IV, 1857, 81.
Muscicapa nigricans, AUD. Orn. Biog. V, 1839, 302 ; pl. 474.—IB. Birds Amer. I, 1840, 218 ; pl. 60.
Tyrannus nigricans, NUTTALL, Man. I, 2d ed. 1840, 326.
Myiobius nigricans, GRAY.
Myiarchus nigricans, CABANIS, Tschudi Fauna Peruan. 1844–'46, 153, (Peru.)
Sayornis nigricans, BONAP. Comptes Rendus XXVIII, 1854, notes Orn. 87.
Aulanax nigricans, CABANIS, Cab. Journal für Ornith. IV, Jan. 1856, 2, (type of genus.)
Muscicapa semi-atra, VIGORS, Zool. Beechey Voy. 1839, 17.

SP. CH.—Wings rounded ; second, third, and fourth longest ; first rather shorter than sixth. Tarsi with a second row of
scales behind. The head and neck all round, fore part and sides of the breast, dark sooty brown ; the rest of the upper parts
similar, but lighter ; faintly tinged with lead color towards the tail. The middle of the breast, abdomen, and lower tail coverts
white ; some of the latter with the shafts and the centre brown. The lower wing coverts grayish brown, edged with white.
Wings dark brown ; the edges of secondary coverts rather lighter ; of primary coverts dull white. Edge of the exterior
vane of the first primary and of secondaries, white. Tail dark brown, with the greater part of the outer vane of the exterior
tail feather white ; this color narrowing from the base to the tip. Bill and feet black. The tail rounded ; rather emarginate ;
feathers broad ; more obliquely truncate than in *sayus.* The bill slender ; similar to that of *S. fuscus.*
Length, nearly 7 inches ; wing, 3.60 ; tail, 3.45.

Hab.—California coast, (Umpqua valley, Oregon, Newberry) and across by valley of Gila and upper Rio Grande to New
Leon, and south.

The female appears to differ only in the smaller size. A young bird from San Francisco has
two bands of rusty on the wing ; the shoulders and hinder part of the back tinged with the
same.

List of specimens.

Catal. No.	Sex.	Locality.	When collected.	Whence obtained.	Orig. No.	Collected by—	Length.	Stretch of wings.	Wing.	Remarks.
7218	......	San Francisco, Cal.....	....	R. D. Cutts.........	......	....	......	......	......	....
7217	......	Sacramento valley.....	....	Lt. R. S. Williamson.	......	Dr. Heermann.....	......	......	......	....
7219	♂	......do	....	......do	......	......do.	......	......	......	....
5911	.....	Santa Clara, Cal.......	....	Dr. Cooper.......	......	....	7.00	11.00	......	....
3996	......	....do	....	Dr. Heermann.....	......	....	......	......	......	....
7214	♀	Espia, Mexico	1855.	Major Emory....	54	Dr. Kennerly	6.12	10.00	......	Eyes black ....
7215	.....	Camp 105, Pueblo creek, New Mexico.	Mar. 19, 1854	Lt. Whipple	189	Kennerly and Möllhausen............	......	......	3.00	Eyes dark brown...
7216	......	Fort Thorn	....	Dr. Henry.....	......	....	......	......	......	....
4004	♂	Cadereita, Mexico	Apl. —, 1853	Lt. Couch.....	......	....	......	......	......	....
4005	♀	......do	......do	......do.	......	....	......	......	......	....
2963	......	Northern Mexico......	....	S. F. Baird.......	......	....	......	......	......	..............., ...
7943	......	Mexico..................	....	J. Gould...........	......	....	......	......	......	....
9106	......	Mexico..................	....	M. Verreaux.......	17422	....	......	... .	......	....

SAYORNIS FUSCUS, Baird.

Pewee; Phœbe Bird.

Muscicapa fusca, GMELIN, Syst. Nat. I, 1788, 931—LATHAM, Index Orn. II, 1790, 483—VIEILLOT, Ois. Am.
    Sept. I, 1807, 68; pl. 40—BONAP. Obs. Wilson, 1825, no. 115.—IB. Synopsis, 68.—AUDUBON,
    Orn. Biog. II, 1834, 122 : V, 1839, 424 ; pl. 120.—IB. Synopsis, 1839, 43.—IB. Birds Amer. I,
    1840, 223 ; pl. 63.—GIRAUD, Birds L. Island, 1844, 42.
Tyrannula fusca, RICH. List, 1837.—BONAP. List, 1838.
Tyrannus fuscus, NUTTALL, Man. I, 2d ed. 1840, 312.
? Aulanax fuscus, CABANIS, Cab. Journ. IV, 1856, 1.
Muscicapa atra, GMELIN, Syst. Nat. I, 1788, 946.—NUTTALL, Man. I, 1832, 278.
Muscicapa phoebe, LATHAM, Index Orn. II, 1790, 489.
Muscicapa nunciola, WILSON, Am. Orn. II, 1810, 78 ; pl. xiii.
Myiobius nunciola, GRAY, Genera, I, 248.
Muscicapa carolinensis fusca, BRISSON, Orn. II, 1760, 367.
Black-headed flycatcher, PENNANT, Arc. Zool. II, 389, 269.
Black-cap flycatcher, LATHAM, Synopsis, I, 353.

SP. CH.—Sides of breast and upper parts dull olive brown, fading slightly toward the tail. Top and sides of head dark brown. A few dull white feathers on the eyelids. Lower parts dull yellowish white, mixed with brown on the chin, and in some individuals across the breast. Quills brown, the outer primary, secondaries, and tertials edged with dull white. In some individuals the greater coverts faintly edged with dull white. Tail brown ; outer edge of lateral feather dull white ; outer edges of the rest like the back. Tibiae brown. Bill and feet black. Bill slender, edges nearly straight. Tail rather broad and slightly forked. Third quill longest ; second and fourth nearly equal ; the first shorter than sixth. Length, 7 inches ; wing, 3.42 ; tail, 3.30.

Hab—Eastern North America.

In autumn and occasionally in early spring the colors are much clearer and brighter. Whole lower parts sometimes bright sulphur yellow; above greenish olive; top and sides of the head tinged with sooty. In the young of the year the colors are much duller; all the wing coverts broadly tipped with light ferruginous, as also the extreme ends of the wings and tail feathers. The brown is prevalent on the whole throat and breast; the hind part of the back, rump, and tail strongly ferruginous.

The tail of this species is quite deeply forked, the external feather being from .35 to .40 of an inch longer than the middle one.

The general appearance of this species resembles that of the small olive flycatchers, but I do not observe any generic character in which it differs from *nigricans*.

List of specimens.

Catal. No.	Sex.	Locality.	When collected.	Whence obtained.	Orig'l No.	Collected by—	Length.	Extent.	Wing.	Remarks.
2707	......	Boston, Mass............	....	S. F. Baird........	... ...		....	....	... ...	....
2925	.	Philadelphia	....	......do...........	......	....	....	....	....	...
957	♂	Carlisle, Pennsylvania....	May 9,1843	......do...........	......	....	7.00	11.00	3.41	....
1339	♀	........do.............	April 5,1844	......do...........	......	....	6.75	10.83	3.33	....
1074	♂	...... do............	June 19,1843	......do...........	......	....	6.00	11.25	3 50	....
6602	♂	Washington, D. C......	March —,1844	Wm. Hutton....	......	....	....	....	....	....
4697	♂	Opposite mouth of Vermillion.	May 7,1856	Lieut. Warren......	......	Dr. Hayden....	7.12	11.00	3.50	....
7517	......	Independence, Mo......		W. M. Magraw....	......	Dr. J. G. Cooper	....	....	....	....
7518	......	............do.......		......do...........	......	......do.......	....	....	....	....
4009	......	Brownsville, Texas.......	Feb. —,1853	Lieut. Couch	22	....	6.12	10.50	3.25	Eyes d'k red brown, bill and feet black.
4008	♀	Tamaulipas, Mexico......	March —,—	......do...........	92	....	6.50	10.00	3.12	........do......
9102	......	Mexico..................	....	M. Verreaux.......	29926	....	....	....	....	....

SAYORNIS SAYUS, Baird.

Say's Flycatcher.

Muscicapa saya, Bonap. Am. Orn. I, 1825, 20 ; pl. xi, fig. 3.—Aud. Orn. Biog. IV, 1838, 428 ; pl. 359.—Ib. Birds
    Amer. I, 1840, 217 ; pl. 59.
Tyrannus saya, Nuttall, Man. I, 2d ed. 1840, 311.
Myiobius saya, Gray, Genera, I, 1844–'9, 249.
Ochthoeca saya, Cabanis, Wiegmann Archiv, 1847, I, 255, (not type.)
Tyrannula saya, Bonap. Conspectùs, 1850.
Aulanax sayus, Cabanis, Journ. Orn. 1856, 2.
Tyrannula pallida, Swainson, Syn. Birds Mex. No. 15, in Taylor's Phil. Mag. I, 1827, 367.
Sayornis pallida, Bonap.

Sp. Ch.—Above and on the sides of the head, neck, and breast, grayish brown, darker on the crown ; region about the eye dusky.
The chin, throat, and upper part of the breast, similar to the back, but rather lighter and tinged with the color of the rest of the
lower parts, which are pale cinnamon.   Under wing coverts pale rusty white.   The wings of a rather deeper tint than the back,
with the exterior vanes and tips of the quills darker.   Edges of the greater and secondary coverts, of the outer vane of the outer
primary, and of the secondaries and tertials, dull white.   The upper tail coverts and tail nearly black.   Edge of outer vane of
exterior tail feather white.   Bill dark brown, rather paler beneath.   The feet brown.   Second, third, and fourth quills nearly
equal ; fifth nearly equal to sixth ; sixth much shorter than the fifth.   Tail broad, emarginate.   Tarsi with a posterior row of
scales.   Length, 7 inches ; wing, 4.30 ; tail, 3.35.
Hab.—Missouri and central high plains westward to the Pacific and south to Mexico.

The young of the year have the upper parts slightly tinged with ferruginous ; two broad
(ferruginous) bands on the wings formed by the tips of the first and second coverts.   The quills
and tail rather darker than in an adult specimen.

The bill of this species is narrow, similar to that of *S. fuscus*.   Legs and feet large, stout ; a
separate row of about eight or ten nearly rectangular scales behind the tarsus, most conspicuous
in a young specimen.   Wings long ; tail nearly square, very little emarginate ; the feathers
broad, the edges nearly parallel ; the tip of the outer one obliquely truncated, with the angles
rounded.

A specimen from California (5510) otherwise similar, has the bill much smaller than the
average, measuring but .43 of an inch from the nostrils, and .75 from the gape.

24 b

List of specimens.

Catal. No.	Sex and age.	Locality.	When collected.	Whence obtained.	Orig. No.	Collected by—	Length.	Stretch of wings.	Wing.	Remarks.
1857	♂	Fort Union, Mex.	1843	S. F. Baird		E. Harris				
1904	○ ♀	....do .	July 18, 1843	....do .		J. Audubon				
5268		Near Fort Union.	Aug. —, 1856	Lt. Warren		Dr. Hayden				
5267	♀	Knife river, on Missouri	Sept. 11, 1856	....do.		....do.	7.00	12.00	4.00	Iris brown.
5269	♀	Cannon Ball river	Sept. 26, 1856	....do.		....do	7.00	12.50	4.25	
8893	♀	Camp 4, Black hills	Sept. 7, 1856	....do.		....do	7.50	13.25	4.12	Iris brown.
8775	.... ..	Divide forks, Platte	Aug. 15, 1857	Wm. M. Magraw ..	148	Dr. Cooper	7.50	13.25	4.75	Iris brown, bill and feet black.
8782	......	North Fork, Platte	Aug. 14, 1857	....do.	155	....do				
5635	♀	Mts near Pole creek	July 24, 1857	Lt. Bryan	147	W. S. Wood	7.50	11.25		
8894	♀	....	July 16, 1857	Lt. G. K. Warren..		Dr. Hayden	7.00	12.50	4.00	Iris brown.
6969	♂	Black hills, N. T.	July 21, 1857	Lt. Bryan	308	W. S. Wood				
7229	....	Western Texas		Capt. Pope		Dr. Henry				
7230		Copper mines, N. M		Major Emory		Mr. Clark				
	....	Zuñi		Capt. Sitgreaves..		Dr. Woodhouse.				
7228	....	Bill Williams Fork	Feb. 10, 1854	Lt. Whipple	88	Kenn. and Müll.	7.00	11.00	4.00	Eyes black
7233	....	....do	Feb. 16, 1854	....do.	170	....do	7.00	13.00	5.00	Eyes black
5510	♂	Petaluma, Cal.	.. ..	E. Samuels.	56					
7225	....	Presidio, Cal.		Lt. Trowbridge.						
7226	♂	Tejon valley		Lt. R. S. Williamson		Dr. Heermann..				
7227	♂	....do . ....:.		....do. ...		....do				
4602	....	Santa Isabella	Dec. —, 1854	Major Emory	18	A. Schott				
3721	....	Los Angeles, Cal.		W. Hutton						
4904	....	San Diego, Cal.	Feb. 7, 1856	Dr. J. F. Hammond.			7.75	13.12	4.25	Iris color of plumage.
4905	....	....do .	Feb. 5, 1856	....do.			7.50	13.37	4.25	Iris color of plumage.
7231	♂	Espia, Mex	Mar. —, 1855	Major Emory	55	Dr. Kennerly	7.00	12.50	4.00	Eyes dark chocolate..
9103	....	Mexico	....	M. Verreaux.	17416					

CONTOPUS, Cabanis.

Contopus, CABANIS, Journal für Ornithologie, III, Nov. 1855, 479. (Type *Muscicapa virens*, L.)

Tarsus very short, but stout ; less than the middle toe and scarcely longer than the hinder. Bill quite broad at the base; wider than half the culmen. Tail moderately forked, much shorter than the wings, (rather more than three-fourths.) Wings very long and much pointed, reaching beyond the middle of the tail ; the first primary about equal to the fourth. All the primaries slender and rather acute, but not attenuated. Head moderately crested. Color, olive above, pale yellowish beneath, with a darker patch on the sides of the breast. Under tail coverts streaked.

This genus is pre-eminently characterized among North American flycatchers by the very short tarsi, and the long and much pointed wings. The species are as follows :

Length, 7.50 inches ; wing, 4.40. A concealed silky white tuft on each side of the rump. No white around the eye or on the wing coverts..*C. borealis.*

Length, about 6 inches ; wing, 3.50. Outer primary edged with whitish. The olive on the sides of breast paler than on the back, less extended, and separated along the median line..*C. virens.*

Length, about 6.25 inches ; wing, 3.65. Outer primary without white edge. Breast olive brown, scarcely paler than the back, not divided in the middle line................*C. richardsonii.*

Comparative measurements of species.

Catal. No.	Species.	Locality.	Sex.	Length.	Stretch of wings.	Wing.	Tail.	Tarsus.	Middle toe.	Its claw alone.	Bill above.	Along gape.	Specimen measured.
942	Contopus borealis	Carlisle, Pa	♂	6.80	....	4.26	3.30	0.54	0.64	0.22	0.64	0.90	Dry ......
	.... do............	..... do		7.50	13.25	4.33	....						Fresh ....
7205	.... do....	Shoalwater bay,WT	.....	6.66	....	4.20	3.06	0.56	0.64	0.22	0.70	0.94	Dry ......
	.... do......	..... do	.....	7.75	13.00	....							Fresh ....
2962	Contopus richardsonii..	Colorado river, O.T.	♀	5.86	....	3.26	2.64	0.50	0.50	0.16	0.48	0.70	Dry ......
5511	.... do............	Petaluma, Cal	♂	5.82	....	3.42	2.70	0.50	0.52	0.20	0.50	0.76	Dry ......
2041	.... do.........	Platte river	♂	6.30	....	3.54	3.00	0.51	0.46	0.18	0.52	0.76	Dry ......
9105	.... do............	Mexico....	.....	6.02	....	3.38	2.76	0.50	0.50	0.16	0.48	0.70	Dry ......
2255	Contopus virens	Carlisle, Pa........	♂	5.50	....	3.38	2.86	0.50	0.50	0.20	0.48	0.70	Dry ......
	... do	..... do	.....	6.16	10.75	3.50	....						Fresh ....
1632	.... do............	......do	♀	5.20	....	3.14	2.66	0.50	0.46	0.16	0.50	0.70	Dry ......
	.... do............	.....do	.....	6.16	10.00	3.17	....						Fresh ....
7247	.... do............	?? Sac. valley	.....	5.80	....	3.34	2.76	0.51	0.46	0.20	0.48	0.68	Dry ......
7944	.... do............	Guatemala	.....	5.90	....	3.36	2.74	0.50	0.46	0.20	0.48	0.72	Dry ......

GENERAL REMARKS.

There is, perhaps, no group in ornithology, certainly none among American birds, the species and genera of which are so difficult to determine as those of the small olivaceous flycatchers. The variations of size, color, and proportions are generally very slight, (though constant,) and only to be appreciated after a close examination and actual comparison of specimens, as well as long familiarity with the subject. Very few of the older authors describe the species so that they can be recognized at all, and the identification is usually made from statement of locality, habit, or common name. Wilson was the first to give accurate and intelligible descriptions of the species inhabiting the United States, and it would have avoided much confusion if they had been actually the first presented to the world.

In comparing the small North American olivaceous flycatchers together, usually known as species of *Tyrannula*, I find two well marked groups worthy of generic separation : one with short legs and pointed wings, the other with longer legs and rounded wings. In this, however, it becomes a question what is to be done with the old name. The type of *Tyrannula*, Swainson, (1827,) is the *Muscicapa barbata* of Gmelin, a species with a yellow spot in the middle of the crown, and the rump yellow, the bill very broad and with the bristles equalling it in length.[1] All these characters, and others, are entirely different from those attaching to our species, and the same generic name cannot be used for them without great impropriety.

The same objections apply to *Myiobius* of Gray, (1838,) this being a simple substitute for the *Tyrannula*, supposed to be nullified from its resemblance in sound to *Tyrannulus* of prior date. The two names, however, are sufficiently distinct to involve no difficulty in their use.

Reichenbach makes numerous species among the *Tyranninae*, (Avium Systema Naturæ, plates 65, 66, 67,) but, as far as I can judge from his figures, none are applicable here. In the

[1] TYRANNULA BARBATA, Swainson.

Muscicapa barbata, Gm. I, 1788, 933.—Latham, Ind. Orn. II, 1790, 488.
Muscipeta barbata, Pr. Max. Beiträge, III, 934.
Tyrannula barbata, Swainson, Zool. Jour. III, Dec. 1827, 359.
Myiobius barbatus, Burmeister, Thiere Bras. II, 1856, 501.
Platyrhynchus xanthopygius, Spix, Av. Bras. II, pl. ix.

Hab.—Coast region of Brazil, according to Burmeister, from whom most of the preceding synonyms and the indications of the species are cited.

invaluable list of genera and sub-genera of birds, by G. R. Gray, 1855, this section is left without a name, with *Muscicapa nunciola*, Wils., ("*Tyrannula fusca*") as type, and with *Tyrannula*, Sw., 1831, not of 1827, and *Myiobius*, Gray, 1847, not 1838, as synonymous. To this section Cabanis has applied the name of *Aulanax*, but in giving "*Tyrannula nigricans*" as the type, his name becomes a synonym of *Sayornis*, Bonaparte.

It is possible that, if Bonaparte has presented a conspectus of the Tyrants in the *Ateneo italiano* or elsewhere, in 1854, or subsequently, he has not overlooked the present groups, but I am unable to determine this point. It only remains for the present to take the names of Cabanis, as quoted, namely, *Contopus* for the short-legged group, with *Muscicapa virens*, L., as type, and including also *Muscicapa cooperi*, Nuttall, *Platyrhynchus cinereus*, Spix, and *Tyrannula ardosiaca*, of Lafresnaye, and *Empidonax* for the other one.

CONTOPUS BOREALIS, Baird.

Olive-sided Flycatcher.

Tyrannus borealis, Sw. & Rich. F. Bor. Am. II, 1831, 141 ; plate.
Myiobius borealis, Gray, Genera, I, 248.
Muscicapa cooperi, Nuttall, Man. I, 1832, 282.—Aud. Orn. Biog. II, 1834, 422: V, 1839, 422 ; pl. 174.—Ib. Synopsis, 1839, 41.—Ib. Birds Amer. I, 1840, 212 ; pl. 58.
Tyrannus cooperi, Bonap. List, 1838.—Nuttall, Man. I, 2d ed. 1840, 298.
Contopus cooperi, Cabanis, Journal für Ornithol. III, Nov. 1855, 479.
Muscicapa inornata, Nuttall, Man. I, 1832, 282.

Sp. Ch.—Wings long, much pointed ; the second quill longest ; the first longer than the third. Tail deeply forked. Tarsi short. The upper parts ashy brown, showing darker brown centres of the feathers ; this is eminently the case on the top of the head ; the sides of the head and neck, of the breast and body resembling the back, but with the edges of the feathers tinged with grey, leaving a darker central streak. The chin, throat, narrow line down the middle of the breast and body, abdomen, and lower tail coverts white, or sometimes with a faint tinge of yellow. The lower tail coverts somewhat streaked with brown in the centre. On each side of the rump, generally concealed by the wings, is an elongated bunch of white silky feathers. The wings and tail very dark brown, the former with the edges of the secondaries and tertials edged with dull white. The lower wing coverts and axillaries greyish brown. The tips of the primaries and tail feathers rather paler. Feet and upper mandible black, lower mandible brown. The young of the year similar, but the color duller ; the feet light brown. Length, 7.50 ; wing, 4.33 ; tail, 3.30 ; tarsus, .60.

Hab.—Rare on the Atlantic and Pacific coasts of the United States. Not observed in the interior, except to the north. Found in Greenland. (Reinhardt.)

This large and powerful "*Tyrannula*" is eminent for the length of its wings, which reach beyond the middle of the tail and the coverts to within a little more than an inch of the tip. The primaries are considerably attenuated, and a little cut out on the inner web, towards the end. The longest quill exceeds the secondaries by about 1.80 inches. The depth of fork in the tail is nearly .30 of an inch.

There is a very narrow edging of whitish to the first primary ; the outer web of the outer tail feather is pale brownish towards the edge.

Specimens sometimes have a little more yellow beneath than that described. In some western skins the third quill is a little longer than the fourth.

Hartlaub, in his list of the birds of Chile, quotes a *Tyrannula cooperi*, supposed to be identical with the present species. If it be the bird described as *Tyrannula cooperi* by Kaup, it is totally distinct and belongs to the genus *Myiarchus*, which see.

List of specimens.

Catal. No.	Sex and age.	Locality.	When collected	Whence obtained.	Length.	Extent.	Wing.	Remarks.
1949	○	United States...............	....	S. F. Baird............	....	....	....	....
942	♂	Carlisle.....................	May 6, 1843	......do...............	7.50	13.25	4.33	....
5910	♂	Steilacoom.................	June —, 1855	Dr. Cooper	7.50	12.75	....	....
7205	....	Shoalwater Bay.............	June —, 1854	......do...............	7.75	13.	....	Iris brown and yellow, bill black.
7206	....	San Francisco...............	....	R. D. Cutts	....	....	....	....
	....	Fort Tejon, California.........	....	John Xantus de Vesey..	....	....	....	....

CONTOPUS RICHARDSONII, Baird.

Short-legged Pewee.

Tyrannula richardsonii, SWAINSON, F. Bor. Am. II, 1831, 146 ; plate.
Muscicapa richardsonii, AUD. Orn. Biog. V, 1839, 299 ; pl. 434.
Tyrannula phoebe, BON. List. 1838, 24.
Muscicapa phoebe, AUDUBON, Synopsis, 1839, 42.—IB. Birds America, I, 1840, 219 ; pl. 61, (not of Latham.)
Tyrannus phoebe, NUTTALL, Man. I, 2d ed. 1840, 319.
Tyrannus atriceps, D'ORBIGNY, (fide G. R. Gray.)

SP. CH.—General appearance of *C. virens*. Bill broad. Wings very long and much pointed ; considerably exceeding the tail ; second quill longest ; third a little shorter ; first shorter than fourth, and about midway between distance from second to fifth, (.60 of an inch.) Primaries 1.20 inches longer than secondaries. Tail moderately forked. Above dark olive brown, (the head darker) the entire breast and sides of head, neck, and body of a paler shade of the same, tinging strongly also the dull whitish throat and chin. Abdomen and under tail coverts dirty pale yellowish. Quills and tail dark blackish brown ; the secondaries narrowly, the tertials more broadly edged with whitish. Two quite indistinct bands of brownish white across the wings. Lower mandible yellow ; the tip brown. Length, 6.20 ; wing, 3.65 ; tail, 3.10.

Hab.—High central dry plains to the Pacific ; Rio Grande valley, southward to Mexico ; Labrador, (Audubon.)

This species has a very close relationship to *C. virens*, agreeing with it in general shape of wings and in color. The wings are, however, still longer and more pointed ; the primaries exceeding the secondaries by nearly 1.25 inches. The proportions of the quills are nearly the same in both ; the primaries too are similarly a little emarginated or attenuated towards the end. The tail is rather more deeply forked ; the feathers broader. The bills are similar ; the feet are larger and stouter.

The general colors are almost precisely the same. The outer primary, however, lacks the decidedly white margin. The under parts are much darker anteriorly, the entire breast being nearly a uniform olive brown ; but little paler than the back ; the throat, too, in some specimens, being scarcely paler. There is little or none of the pale sulphur yellow of *C. virens* on the abdomen, and the under wing coverts and axillaries are much darker olivaceous. In *C. virens* the middle line of the breast is always paler than the sides, or at least the connecting space is short.

The lower mandible is generally yellow ; in a few specimens, however, it is quite dusky, especially on its terminal half.

The young bird has the darker head and broader light edgings, with the ferruginous tinge usually seen in young of the Tyrannulas.

This appears to be the species figured by Audubon as *Muscicapa richardsonii*, based probably on Rocky mountain or Columbia river specimens received from Mr. Townsend, (No. 962, 2042, &c.) The *T. richardsonii* of Swainson, however, differs in the proportions of the wings, &c.,

and in some other points appearing more nearly allied to *S. fuscus*. Not to multiply synonyms unnecessarily, however, I have concluded to adopt the name. The discrepancies in the proportions of the quills may have been caused by their incomplete growth during the moulting season. Richardson's description answers better than the figure, which, with the other on the same plate, is wrongly colored. Bonaparte committed a mistake (in which he was followed by Audubon and Nuttall) in referring this bird to the *Muscicapa phoebe* of Latham, Index Orn. II, 1790, 489. This is certainly the *S. fuscus*, as shown by the references, and the statement that the outer tail feather has the outer web white, which applies only to *fuscus*.

List of specimens.

Catal. No.	Sex and age.	Locality.	When collected.	Whence obtained.	Orig'l No.	Collected by—	Length.	Extent.	Wing.	Remarks.
5272	....	Blackfoot country......	July —,1855	Dr. Hayden	. ....	Dr. Hayden	....	....	....	....
2041	♂	Platte river, (north fork)	June 2,1854	S. F. Baird.........	23	J. K. Townsend	....	....	....	....
2042	....	......do...... do....	...... do......	......do....	......	......do.......	....	....	....	....
8892	♀	Loup Fork of Platte....	Aug. 24,—	Lt. G. K. Warren...	....	Dr. Hayden.....	6.25	9.50	3.25	....
2959½	....	Rocky mountains......	....	S. F. Baird........	....	....	....	....	....	....
7235	....	El Paso, Texas..	....	Col. Graham.......	....	J. H. Clark.....	6.	10.75	3.50	Eyes dark brown...
7245	....	Mimbres to Rio Grande.	....	Dr. T. C. Henry....	....	....	....	....	....	....
2962	♀	Columbia river, O. T...	....	S. F. Baird.........	15	J. K. Townsend	....	....	....	....
5511	♂	Petaluma, Cal..........	April —,1856	E. Samuels.........	696	....	....	....	....	....
7238	○	San Francisco.........	....	R. D. Cutts........	....	....	....	....	....	....
7248	....	......do	....	......do........	....	....	....	....	....	....
7239	....	......do............	....	......do........	....	....	....	....	....	....
	....	Fort Tejon, Cal......	....	J. X. DeVesey.....	....	....	....	....	....	....
7251	♂	Monterey, Mexico......	May —,1853	Lt. D. N. Couch....	212	....	6.25	10.50	3.50	Iris light brown....
9105	....	Mexico............	....	M. Verreaux........	29997	....	....	....	....	....
9098	....	New Granada....	....	......do.......	....	....	....	....	....	....

CONTOPUS VIRENS, Cabanis.

Wood Pewee.

Muscicapa virens, LINN. Syst Nat. I, 1766, 327.—GMELIN, Syst. Nat. I, 1788, 936. LATHAM, Index Orn.—Licht.
Verz. 1823, 563.—NUTTALL, Man. I, 1832, 285.—AUD. Orn. Biog. II, 1834, 93 : V, 1839, 425 ;
pl. 115.—IB. Synopsis, 1839, 42.—IB. Birds Amer. I, 1840, 231 ; pl. 64.—GIRAUD, Birds L.
Island, 1844, 43.
Muscicapa querula, VIEILLOT, Ois. Am. Sept. I, 1807, 68 ; pl. xxxix, (not of Wilson.)
Muscicapa rapax, WILSON, Am. Orn. II, 1810, 81 ; pl. xiii, f. 5.
Tyrannula virens, RICH, App. Back's Voyage.—BONAP. List, 1838.
Myiobius virens, GRAY.
Tyrannus virens, NUTTALL, Manual, I, 2d ed. 1840, 316.
Contopus virens, CABANIS, Journal für Ornithologie, III, Nov. 1855, 479.

SP. CH.—The second quill longest ; the third a little shorter ; the first shorter than the fourth ; the latter nearly .40 longer than the fifth. The primaries more than an inch longer than the secondaries. The upper parts, sides of the head, neck, and breast, dark olivaceous brown, the latter rather paler, the head darker. A narrow white ring round the eye. The lower parts pale yellowish, deepest on the abdomen ; across the breast tinged with ash. This pale ash sometimes occupies the whole of the breast, and even occasionally extends up to the chin. It is also sometimes glossed with olivaceous. The wings and tail dark brown ; generally deeper than in *S. fuscus*. Two narrow bands across the wing, the outer edge of first primary and of the secondaries and tertials dull white. The edges of the tail feathers like the back ; the outer one scarcely lighter. Upper mandible black, the lower yellow, but brown at the tip. Length, 6.15 ; wing, 3.50 ; tail, 3.05.

Hab.—Eastern North America to the borders of the high central plains ; south to New Granada.

The young of the year has the colors duller, edges of the upper feathers paler, the white of the wing tinged with ferruginous ; the lower mandible more tinged with black. The bill of this species is very broad. The tail is moderately forked; the feathers broad, with sides nearly parallel, becoming scarcely dilated from the base to the end. The feet are very short. The wing is very long and pointed, reaching considerably beyond the middle of the tail, and beyond the tail coverts. The proportions of the quills vary, although the second is always a little longer than the third. The first is generally a little shorter than the fourth; sometimes about equal, and .25 of an inch shorter than the second. The under tail coverts are much tinged with brown in their median region.

In No. 1632 the first quill is proportionably shorter; the fourth longer than as described; the third quill slightly longest. The relative proportion of the first to the fourth, in fact, varies a good deal, but the first always considerably exceeds the fifth.

I have seen no specimen of this species from the region west of the Missouri plains, except two in Lieutenant Williamson's collection marked Sacramento valley by Dr. Heermann. All those of the same type belong to a different though closely allied species, and it is most probable that some mistake may have occurred in the locality. Dr. Heermann, in his notes on Birds of California, refers to supposed specimens of *Tyrannula virens* as being all darker than eastern ones, evidently having the *richardsonii* in view.

List of specimens.

Catal. No.	Sex and age.	Locality.	When collected.	Whence obtained.	Collected by—	Length.	Stretch of wings.	Wing.	Remarks.
2969	○	Eastern United States......	....	S. F. Baird	....	....	....	....	....
2635	♂	Carlisle, Pa...............	May 11, 1846	......do	....	6.75	11.00	3.58	....
2657	♂	......do	May 12, 1846	......do ...	....	6.91	11.16	3.54	....
2595	♂	......do	May 6, 1846	......do ...	....	6.50	10.66	3.50	....
979	♀	......do	May 16, 1843	......do ...	....	9.25	....	3.25	....
2294	♂	......do	May 20, 1845	......do ...	....	6.16	10.41	3.41	....
1632	♀	......do	July 12, 1844	......do ...	....	6.16	10.00	3.17	....
2354	♂	......do	May 26, 1845	......do ...	....	6.33	9.66	3.54	....
1540	....	......do	May 17, 1844	......do ...	....	6.66	10.50	3.50	....
1657	○	......do	July —, 1844	......do	....	6.33	10.41	3 41	....
2299	♂	......do	May 21, 1845	......do ...	....	6.16	10.58	3.50	....
2255	♂	......do	May 18, 1845	......do ...	....	6.16	10.75	3.50	....
2711	♀	Washington, D. C..........	July —, 1843	......do	J. K. Townsend	....	....	....	....
7588	....	......do	....	Wm. Hutton...	....	....	....	....	....
2394	....	Savannah, Ga	....	S. F. Baird	....	6.20	10.2	3.20	....
	♂	South Illinois.............	May 11,—	R. Kennicott............	....	....	....	....	....
7519	....	Independence, Mo.........	....	Dr. Cooper.............	....	6.00	10.00	3.50	....
7521	....	......do	....	......do	....	6.00	9.50	3.50	....
	....	Red river, M. T.....	Aug. —, 1857	R. Kennicott	....	....	....	....	Iris very dark.
7246	♂	Sac. valley ?............	....	Lieut. R. S. Williamson.	Dr. Heermann......	....	....	....	....
7247	♂	......do .. ?............	....	......do	....	....	....	....	....
9098	♂	New Grenada...............	....	M. Verreaux.............	....	....	....	....	....
7944	....	Guatemala	....	J. Gould...............	....	....	....	....	....

EMPIDONAX, Cabanis.

Empidonax, CABANIS, Journal für Ornithologie, III, Nov. 1855, 480, (type *Tyrannula pusilla*.)
Tyrannula of most authors.

CH.—Tarsus lengthened, considerably longer than the middle toe, which is decidedly longer than the hind toe. Bill variable. Tail very slightly forked, even, or rounded; a little shorter only than the wings, which are considerably rounded; the first primary much shorter than the fourth. Head moderately crested. Color olivaceous above, yellowish beneath; throat generally gray.

The lengthened tarsi, the short toes, the short and rounded wings, and the plain dull olivaceous of the plumage, readily distinguish the species of this genus from any other North American flycatchers. The upper plates of the tarsi in a good many species do not encircle the outside, but meet there a row on the posterior face.

There are no species of North American birds more difficult to distinguish than the small flycatchers, the characters, though constant, being very slight and almost inappreciable, except to a very acute observer. For remarks concerning the genus and its affinities, see page 187 preceding.

The following synopsis may aid in distinguishing the species:

A. Outer tail feather never abruptly margined with white externally.

    Tarsus moderate; but little longer than the middle toe. Claw of hind toe reaching along the middle of the central anterior claw.

        Above rather pure dark olive, not lighter on the rump. Beneath white, tinged with sulphur behind, and with olive across the breast. Wing bands tinged with yellow olive. Second, third, and fourth quills longest; first between fifth and sixth. Length, 6 inches; wing, 2.90.

trailli.

    Tarsus lengthened; decidedly longer than the middle toe, which is scarcely, if any, longer than the hinder one.

        Above dull greenish olive, with a strong tinge of brown, becoming decidedly lighter on the rump. Throat whitish; a gray olive band across the breast; rest of under parts pale yellow.

            Length 5.50 inches; wing, 2.80; tail, 2.50. Third and fourth quills longest; first shorter than sixth. Culmen .35 of an inch; under mandible yellow..*pusillus.*

            Length about 5 inches; wing, 2.65; tail, 2.50. Second and third quills longest; first shorter than fifth. Culmen .30 of an inch long; under mandible brownish...*minimus.*

    Above clear bright olive green, without any brown on the back.

        Beneath white, tinged with greenish yellow on the sides and behind. Wing bands tinged with reddish yellow. Second, third, and fourth quills much longer than first and fifth. First rather longer than fifth. Wing, 3 inches; tail, 2.75...*acadicus.*

        Beneath olivaceous yellow, purest behind; no white on the under surfaces. Wing bands greenish white. Length about 5 inches; wing, 2.80; tail, 2.45. First quill much shorter that fifth........................*flaviventris.*

        Body olive green above and on the breast; throat gray; rest of under parts sulphur yellow. Wing bands grayish. Length, 5.50; wing, 2.80; tail, 2.50. Third quill longest; first much shorter than fifth. Bill very slender...*hammondii.*

B. Outer tail feather margined abruptly with white externally. Bill very narrow. Tarsi unusually long.

        Tail even or rounded. Tarsus as long as the head. Lower mandible whitish; brown at tip. Body above brownish olive. Beneath whitish, tinged with yellow behind and with olive on the breast. Wing with conspicuous whitish bands. Length, 5.75 inches...................*obscurus.*

Comparative measurements of species.

Catal. No.	Species.	Locality.	Sex.	Length.	Extent.	Wing.	Tail.	Tarsus.	Middle toe.	Its claw.	Bill above.	Along gape.	Specimen measured.
2310	Empidonax traillii........	Carlisle, Pa	♀	4.94	....	2.62	2.38	0.62	0.56	0.20	0.44	0.64	Dry........
do.	....do......do	.....do....		5.91	8.50	2.75	......	......	......	......	......	......	Fresh......
1025	....do......do	.....do.............	♂	5.04	....	2.86	2.62	0.64	0.54	0.18	0.46	0.63	Dry........
do.	....do......do	.....do.............		5.91	9.33	2.91	......	......	......	......	......	......	Fresh......
693	....do......do	.....do.............	♂	5.54	....	2.84	2.68	0.64	0.52	0.20	0.44	0.64	Dry........
7252	Empidonax pusillus.......	River Nueces.......	♂	5.06	....	2.78	2.70	0.64	0.58	0.20	0.50	0.70	Dry....:....
do.	....do......do	....		5.50	....	3.	......	......	......	......	......	......	Fresh......
10077	....do......do	Fort Tejon, Cal....	♂	5.20	....	2.80	2.56	0.68	0.50	0.16	0.50	0.70	Dry ......
do.	....do......do	.....do.............		5.75	8.75	3.75	......	......	.. ..	......	......	......	Fresh......
7244	....do......do	Los Nogales, Mex..	......	5.84	....	2.56	2.54	0.68	0.52	0.20	0.48	0.66	Dry........
495	....do......do	Rocky mountains...	♂	5.10	....	2.64	2.50	0·65	0.52	0.20	0.48	0.68	Dry........
2563	Empidonax minimus......	Carlisle, Pa........	♀	4.46	....	2.40	2.40	0.60	0.44	0.18	.038	0.54	Dry........
do.	....do......do	.....do.............	......	5.41	8.	2.50	......	......	......	......	......	......	Fresh......
1415	....do......do	.....do.............	♂	4.82	....	2.66	2.54	0.64	0.54	0.20	0.40	0.56	Dry........
do.	....do......do	.....do.............		5.58	8.58	2.88	......	......	......	......	......	......	Fresh......
7932	Empidonax acadicus	Pennsylvania.......	......	5.50	....	3.00	2.62	0.58	0.48	0.16	0.42	0.68	Dry........
500	....do......do	Chester county, Pa..	♂	5.48	....	3.82	2.62	0.60	0.50	0.18	0.50	0.66	Dry........
9099	Empidonax flaviventris. ..	Coban, Cent. Am...		5.20	....	2.70	2.38	0.66	0.52	0.16	0.40	0.55	Dry........
do.	....do...... do.........	Racine, Wisconsin..		......	......	2.74	2.42	0.64	0.50	0.18	0.42	0.58	Dry ......
2339	....do...... do	Carlisle, Pa........	♀	4.24	....	2.50	2.18	0.65	0.50	0.18	0.40	0.60	Dry ......
985	....do...... do	.....do.............	♂	4.86	....	2.76	2.42	0.66	0.50	0.18	0.42	0.60	Dry........
do.	....do...... do	.....do.............	......	5.16	8.83	2.83	......	......	......	......	......	......	Fresh......
5920	Empidonax difficilis.......	Ft. Steilacoom,W.T.	......	4.86	....	2.64	·2.44	0.63	0.50	0.18	0.41	0.58	Dry........
10079	Empidonax hammondii...	Fort Tejon.........	♂	4.90	....	2.78	2.50	0.62	0.50	0.18	0.40	0.52	Dry........
do.	....do ...... do	.....do.............		5.50	9.	......	......	......	......	......	......	......	Fresh......
10080	....do...... . do...........	.....do....	♀	4.90	....	2.74	2.50	0.64	0.52	0.18	0.43	0.58	Dry........
do.	....do...... do	.....do.............		5.50	8.	......	......	......	......	......	......	......	Fresh......
7237	Empidonax obscurus.	El Paso, Texas.....	♂	5.14	....	2.83	2.76	0.72	0.54	0.16	0.46	0.60	Dry........
do.	....do... ...do	.....do.............	......	5.37	8.50	2.87	......	......	......	......	......	......	Fresh......

EMPIDONAX TRAILLII, Baird.

Traill's Flycatcher.

Muscicapa traillii, AUDUBON, Orn. Biog. I, 1832, 236 : V, 1839, 426; pl. 45.—IB. Syn. 1839, 43 —IB. Birds Amer. I 1840, 234; pl. 65.

Tyrannula traillii, RICH. List, 1837.—BONAP. List, 1838.
Tyrannus traillii, NUTTALL, Man. I, 2d ed. 1840, 323.

SP. CH.—Third quill longest ; second scarcely shorter than fourth ; first shorter than fifth, about .35 shorter than the longest. Primaries about .75 of an inch longer than secondaries. Tail even. Upper parts dark olive green; lighter under the wings, and duller and more tinged with ash on nape and sides of the neck. Centre of the crown feathers brown. A pale yellowish white ring (in some specimens altogether white) round the eye. Loral feathers mixed with white. Chin and throat white ; the breast and sides of throat light ash tinged with olive, its intensity varying in individuals, the former sometimes faintly tinged with olive. Sides of the breast much like the back. Middle of the belly nearly white ; sides of the belly, abdomen, and the lower tail coverts sulphur yellow. The quills and tail feathers dark brown, as dark (if not more so) as these parts in *C. virens*. Two olivaceous yellow white bands on the wing, formed by the tips of the first and second coverts, succeeded by a brown one ; the edge of the first primary and of secondaries and tertials a little lighter shade of the same. The outer edge of the tail feathers like the back ; that of the lateral one rather lighter. Bill above dark brown ; dull brownish beneath. Length nearly 6 inches ; wing, 2.90 ; tail, 2.60.

Hab.—Eastern United States and south to Mexico.

The young bird is similar, but the colors are duller. The markings on the wings are more ochraceous.

The body in this species is stout ; tail short, very nearly even ; feathers broad, distinctly

25 b

pointed, and acuminate. Differs from *E. minimus* in larger size and proportions of the quills. The middle of the back is the same color in both, but instead of becoming lighter and tinged with ash on the rump and upper tail coverts, these parts very rarely differ in color from the back. The markings on the wings, instead of being dirty white, are decidedly olivaceous yellow. The yellow of the lower parts is deeper. The tail feathers are rather broad, acuminate, and pointed ; in *minima* they are narrow and more rounded. The bill is larger and fuller. The legs are decidedly shorter in proportion.

This species is somewhat like *E. acadicus* in the proportions of the quills, but the wing is considerably shorter. The precise differences will be found detailed in the article on *acadicus*.

The proportions of the quills are generally as detailed under the specific character ; the first quill .30 of an inch less than the longest, and intermediate between the fourth and fifth ; the primaries about .70 of an inch longer than the first secondary. In one specimen the second, third, and fourth are nearly equal ; the other proportions the same.

List of specimens.

Catal. No.	Sex.	Locality.	When collected.	Whence obtained.	Original No.	Length.	Extent.	Wing.
2968	♀	New Hampshire	....	E. Harris	....	....	....	....
1026	....	Carlisle, Pennsylvania...............	May 26,1843	S. F. Baird	....	5.75	8.75	2.66
1025	♂	...........do....... :.............	......do.......	......do.........................	....	5.91	9.33	2.91
2345	♀	...........do.......	May 26,1845	......do.........................	....	5.83	8.41	2.66
433	....	...........do....................	May 31,1841	......do.........	....	5.33	8.00	....
2310	....	...........do...............	May 21,1845	......do.........................	....	5.91	8.50	2.75
2347	♂	.... do....	May 26,1845	......do.........	....	....	....	....
2340	♀	...........do..............	......do.......	......do.........	....	5.91	8.75	2.75
9104	....	Mexico............................	....	M. Verreaux.....................	29928	....	....	....

EMPIDONAX PUSILLUS, Cabanis.

? Platyrhynchus pusillus, SWAINSON, Phil. Mag. I, May, 1827, 366.
Tyrannula pusilla, Sw. F. B. Am. II, 1831, 144 ; pl.—RICH. App. Back's Voyage, 1834–'36, 144.—GAMBEL, Pr. A. N. Sc. III, 1847, 156.
Muscicapa pusilla, AUD. Orn. Biog. V, 1839, 288 ; pl. 434.—IB. Birds Amer. I, 1840, 236 ; pl. 66.
Tyrannus pusilla, NUTTALL, Man. I, 2d ed. 1840.

SP. CH.—Second, third, and fourth quills longest ; first shorter than the sixth. Bill rather broad ; yellow beneath. Tail even. Tarsi rather long. Above dirty olive brown, paler and more tinged with brown towards the tail. Throat and breast white, tinged with grayish olive on the sides, shading across the breast ; belly and under tail coverts very pale sulphur yellow. Wings with two dirty narrow brownish white bands slightly tinged with olive ; the secondaries and tertials narrowly and inconspicuously margined with the same. First primary faintly edged with whitish ; the outer web of first tail feather paler than the inner, but not white   Under wing coverts reddish ochraceous yellow. A whitish ring round the eye. Length, 5.50 inches ; wing, 2.80 ; tail, 2.75.

Hab.—High central plains to the Pacific. Fur countries. Southward into Mexico.

In examining carefully a large collection of skins of the small American flycatchers, I have found it necessary to separate a western series intermediate between *E. traillii* and *minimus*, typical specimens of the two latter species being without any representatives from the region beyond the Missouri plains. Although the differences are quite appreciable in the comparison, I yet find it exceedingly difficult to characterize a species so as to carry the same impression of diversity to others as I have experienced myself. The bird is about the size of *E. traillii*, or a little less, but has more the colors of *minimus*. It agrees with the latter in becoming lighter towards the rump, but this and the upper tail coverts and, indeed, the upper parts generally, are of a soiled brownish tinge, taking considerably from the purity of the olive. The under wing coverts have also a decided shade of brownish ochraceous in the yellow. There is much less white in the wing. The tail feathers are narrow and rounded as in *minimus*. The quills are broad and rounded; the second, third, and fourth about equal; the fifth nearly intermediate between the fourth and sixth; the first shorter than the sixth; the primaries are about .65 longer than the first secondary. The legs are of about the same length as in *minimus*. The bill is much larger than in *minimus*, the ridge of the lower mandible measuring .35 of an inch instead of .30; the color yellow instead of brownish.

From *traillii* it differs in the brownish tinge of the under wing coverts, the browner upper parts, and the less amount of white on the wings; the first primary shorter than the sixth instead of the fifth. The tarsi are longer; the bill appears rather longer.

This species appears to agree rather better than any before me with the *Tyrannula pusilla* of Swainson, in F. Bor. Am., and I have accordingly adopted the name. His figure differs materially from the description, and is certainly improperly colored, as is also that of *richardsonii* of the same plate. In some respects *E. minimus*, Baird, agrees with *T. pusilla* of Swainson, but a female of the species I here describe would answer quite as well in general, and if, in the present monograph, I have succeeded in fixing the species of small *Tyrannulas* with any degree of precision, it may be best to assign the synonymy as I have done. It is not likely that the *E. pusilla* of Cabanis belongs here.

Young birds have a good deal of reddish brown on the rump and upper tail coverts, and two bands of the same across the wings. The inner wing coverts are as in the adult.

List of specimens.

Catal. No.	Sex and age.	Locality.	When collected.	Whence obtained.	Original No.	Collected by—	Length.	Ext...t.	Wing.
7253	....	Fort Steilacoom.	August 1, 1856	Dr. Suckley....................	510	....	....	....	....
7254	....	......do....	....	........do..............	505	....	....	....	....
7242	....	......do....	....	........do..............	105	....	....	....	....
10076	♂	Fort Tejon, Cal...........	—, 1857	J. Xantus de Vesey	277	....	....	....	....
10077	○	... .do....	....	........do......	623	....	....	....	....
7244	....	Los Nogales, Mexico.........	June —, 1855	Major Emory	74	Dr. Kennerly	....	....	....
7252	♂	Rio Nasas, Durango......... .	June —, 1853	Lieut. Couch	240	....	5.50	7.25 ?	3.00 '
495	....	Rocky mountains.............	May —, 1855	S. F. Baird..................	....	Dr. Trudeau.......	....	....	....

EMPIDONAX MINIMUS, Baird.

Least Flycatcher.

Tyrannula minima, Wm. M. and S. F. Baird, Pr. A. N. Sc. I, July 1843, 284.—Ib. Sillim. Am. Jour. Sc. July, 1844.— Audubon, Birds Amer. VII, 1844, 343; pl. 491.

Sp. Ch.—Second quill longest; third and fourth but little shorter; fifth a little less; first intermediate between fifth and sixth. Tail even. Above olive brown, darker on the head, becoming paler on the rump and upper tail coverts. The middle of the back most strongly olivaceous. The nape (in some individuals) and sides of the head tinged with ash. A ring round the eye and some of the loral feathers white; the chin and throat white. The sides of the throat and across the breast dull ash, the color on the latter sometimes nearly obsolete; sides of the breast similar to the back, but of a lighter tint; middle of the belly very pale yellowish white, turning to pale sulphur yellow on the sides of the belly, abdomen, and lower tail coverts. Wings brown; two narrow white bands on wing formed by the tips of the first and second coverts, succeeded by one of brown. The edge of the first primary, and of the secondaries and tertials, white. Tail rather lighter brown, edged externally like the back. Feathers narrow, not acuminate, with the ends rather blunt. In autumn the white parts are strongly tinged with yellow. Length, about 5 inches; wing, 2.65; tail, 2.50.

Hab.—Eastern United States to Missouri plains.

As stated under the head of *E. traillii, E. minimus* differs from it in its smaller size, and more ashy tinge on the sides of the head, the nape, and rump. The tail feathers are narrower, more rounded at the end, and less acuminate. The tarsi are one-tenth of an inch longer, though the bird is considerably smaller; the claws also are larger. The second, third, and fourth quills are generally nearly equal, the latter always considerably exceeding the first, as does the fifth also; in *trailli* the fifth is usually nearly the length of the first, or but slightly different from it.

One of the most appreciable differences between the two species lies in the two bands of the wing. These, with the other edgings of the wings in *minimus*, are dirty grayish white; in *traillii* they are strongly tinged with grayish olive. Both have the outer primary edged with yellowish white, and the first tail feather with its outer web paler brownish than elsewhere, but not approaching to white.

List of specimens.

Catal. No.	Sex.	Locality.	When collected.	Whence obtained.	Collected by—	Length.	Stretch of wings.	Wing.
2709	......	Philadelphia	....	S. F. Baird........	....	....	....	......
2450	......	Carlisle, Pa..........	Sept. 10, 1845	......do.........	....	5. 33	8 25	2. 50
2274	♂	.......do............	May 17, 1845	......do.........	....	5. 33	8. 25	2. 58
2132	......	.......do............	April 23, 1845	......do.........	....	5. 50	8. 25	2. 58
3371	♂	.......do............	May 3, 1847	......do.........	....	5. 50	8. 50	2. 75
1415	♂	.......do............	May 1, 1844	......do.........	....	5. 58	8. 58	2. 66
726	......	.......do............	Sept. 16, 1842	......do.........	....	5. 25	8. 00	......
1486	♂	.......do............	May 8, 1844	......do.........	....	5. 41	3. 50	3. 66
2563	♀	.......do............	May 5, 1846	......do.........	....	5. 41	8. 00	2. 50
2254	♀	.......do............	May 12, 1845	......do.........	....	5. 58	7. 83	2. 41
2348	......	.......do............	May 26, 1845	......do.........	....	5. 16	7. 41	2. 33
2163	......	.......do............	April 29, 1845	......do.........	....	5. 50	8. 25	2. 58
2133	......	.......do,...........	April 23, 1845	......do.........	....	5 50	8. 41	2. 50
2624	......	.......do............	May 11, 1846	......do.........	....	5. 33	8. 25	2. 58
2650	......	.......do............	May 12, 1846	......do.........	....	5. 33	8. 16	2. 50
2649	......	.......do............	......do......	......do.........	....	5. 50	8. 00	2. 50
1672	......	.......do............	Aug. 12, 1844	......do......	....	5. 41	8. 00	2. 41
7415	......	Cleveland, Ohio.....	....	Dr. Kirtland......	....	....	....	......
	......	Chicago, Ill.........	May 2, 1855	R. Kennicott......	....	....	....	......
	......	Racine, Wis	....	Northwestern Univ.	....	....	....	......
7415	......	Cleveland, Ohio.....	....	Dr. Kirtland......	....	....	....	......
5270	♂	Near.Powder river...	Aug. 4, 1856	Lt. Warren........	Dr. Hayden........	5. 00	7. 75	2. 50
4700	♂	Eau qui court.......	May 15, 1856	......do.........	......do..........	5. 50	8. 25	2. 75
4699	♀	......do............	......do......	......do.........	......do..........	5. 25	7. 62	2. 75
4701	♂	......do............	......do......	......do.........	......do..........	5. 25	8. 50	2. 75
4702	♂	Vermilion.	May 6, 1856	......do.........	......do..........	5. 37	8. 00	2. 62
4698	♀	Nebraska...........	May 11, 1856	......do.........	......do..........	4. 87	7. 50	2. 75

EMPIDONAX ACADICUS, Baird.

Small Green-crested Flycatcher.

?Muscicapa acadica, GMELIN, Syst. Nat. I, 1788, 947.—LATHAM, Index Orn. II, 1790, 489.—VIEILLOT, Ois. Am.
Sept. I, 1807, 71, (from Latham).—AUDUBON, Orn. Biog. II, 1834, 256 : V, 1839, 429 ; pl.
144 —IB. Birds Amer. I, 1840, 221 ; pl. 62.—NUTTALL, Man. I, 1832, 208.—GIRAUD, Birds L.
Island, 1844, 40.
Muscicapa querula, WILSON, Am. Orn. II, 1810, 77 ; pl. xiii, f. 3, (not of Vieillot.)
" *Platyrhynchus virescens,* VIEILLOT."
Tyrannula acadica, RICHARDSON, ? Bon. List.
Tyrannus acadica, NUTTALL, Man. I, 2d ed. 1840, 320.

SP. CH.—The second and third quills are longest, and about equal ; the fourth a little shorter ; the first about equal to the fifth, and about .35 less than the longest. Tail even. The upper parts, with sides of the head and neck, olive green ; the crown very little if any darker. A yellowish white ring round the eye. The sides of the body under the wings like the back, but fainter olive ; a tinge of the same across the breast ; the chin, throat, and middle of the belly white ; the abdomen, lower tail and wing coverts, and sides of the body not covered by the wings pale greenish yellow. Edges of the first primary, secondaries, and tertials margined with dull yellowish white, most broadly on the latter. Two transverse bands of pale yellowish across the wings formed by the tips of the secondary and primary coverts, succeeded by a brown one. Tail light brown, margined externally like the back. Upper mandible light brown above ; pale yellow beneath. In autumn the lower parts are more yellow. Length, 5.65 ; wing, 3.00 ; tail, 2.75.

Hab.—Eastern United States to the Mississippi.

In this species the wing is rather long and quite acute, reaching about to the middle of the tail ; the primaries about .90 of an inch shorter than the secondaries. The proportions do not vary much from that described, although the third quill is sometimes longest. The tail is almost exactly even, a little rounded on the sides. The tarsi are rather long, exceeding the middle toe.

There is generally a tinge of reddish in the yellow bands of the wings, although most marked in autumn specimens. The under wing coverts are pale sulphur yellow, and the tertials and secondaries have the basal portion of the inner web entirely sulphur yellow. The yellow edges to the lesser quills do not extend as far as the wing coverts, but leave a well defined band of brown just below the yellowish.

This species is very similar to *E. traillii,* but the upper parts are of a brighter and more uniform olive green, much like that of *Vireo olivaceus.* The feathers of the crown lack the darker centre. There is less of the olivaceous ash across the breast. The bands across the wing are brighter yellow. There is much more yellow at the base of the lesser quills. The wings are longer, both proportionally and absolutely. The primaries exceed the secondaries by nearly an inch, instead of by only about .70 ; the proportions of the quills are much the same.

List of specimens.

Catal. No.	Sex and age.	Locality.	When collected.	Whence obtained.	Collected by—	Length.	Stretch of wings.	Wing.
1824		Philadelphia		S. F. Baird				
1089		do	Spring of 1843	do				
1225		do		do				
500	♂	Chester county, Pa..	1841	do				
7589	♀	Washington, D. C...	April 29, 1845	Wm. Hutton				
2395	○ ♀	Savannah, Ga.	1845	S. F. Baird	J. Leconte	5.60	8.50	2.70
2396	♂	do	1845	do	do	5.90	9.00	2.90
7416		Cleveland, Ohio		Dr. J. P. Kirtland.				

EMPIDONAX FLAVIVENTRIS, Baird.

Yellow-bellied Flycatcher.

Tyrannula flaviventris, Wm. M. and S. F. Baird, Pr. Ac. Nat. Sc. Phila. I, July, 1843, 283.—Ib. Am. Journ. Science,
     April, 1844.—Audubon, Birds Amer. VII, 1844, 341 ; pl. 490.
Tyrannula pusilla, (Swainson) Reinhardt, Vidensk. Meddel. for 1853 1854, 82.—Gloger, Cab. Jour. 1854, 426.
Empidonax hypoxanthus, Baird, (Provisional name for eastern specimens.)
Empidonax difficilis, Baird, (Provisional name for western.)

Sp. Ch.—Second, third, and fourth quills nearly equal ; first intermediate between fifth and sixth. Tail nearly even, slightly
rounded. Tarsi long. Above bright olive green ; (very similar to the back of *Vireo noveboracensis*;) crown rather darker.
A broad yellow ring round the eye The sides of the head, neck, breast and body, and a band across the breast like the back,
but lighter ; the rest of the lower parts bright sulphur yellow ; no white or ashy anywhere on the body. Quills dark brown ;
two bands on the wing formed by the tips of the primary and secondary coverts, the outer edge of the first primary and of the
secondaries and tertials pale yellow, or greenish yellow. The tail feathers brown, with the exterior edges like the back. The
bill dark brown above, yellow beneath. The feet black. In the autumn the colors are purer, the yellow is deeper, and the
markings on the wings of an ochry tint. Length, 5.15 inches ; wing, 2.83 ; tail, 2.45.

Hab.—Eastern United States generally. Probably replaced on the Pacific by a closely allied species.

This species is thick set in form ; the wings long, reaching as far as the middle of the tail,
or to the end of the upper coverts. The relative proportions of the second, third, and fourth
quills vary somewhat ; the third is, however, mostly a little the longest. The first is generally
a very little longer than the sixth ; considerably shorter than the fifth ; it is about .40 shorter
than the longest, which exceeds the secondaries by about .65 of an inch. The tail feathers are
rather narrow, and rather acute ; the lateral ones a little shortest. The bill is rather broad.

This species is about the size of *E. minimus*, though rather stouter. The bill is broader ;
the colors are different, *minimus* not having the bright olive green of the back and yellow of
the under parts, even on the throat, which instead is whitish. In respect to color, *flaviventris*
differs materially from all our North American species.

This species differs from some North American flycatchers in not having the uppermost tarsal
scutellae to envelope the outside of the bone, but reach only half way round, where the edge of
another series is seen opposite the first. The lower scales, however, follow the usual rule.
There is no naked space on the inner face of the tarsus.

Although the specimens from the west coast are not sufficiently perfect to allow of a full
criticism, I am inclined to think that they are really distinct, and that they will not constitute
almost the single exception to the fact that no flycatcher is common to both east and west
coasts. The colors are lighter, and duller ; the olive more yellowish, and the bands and
edges of the wings narrower and less distinct. The forehead has a peculiar hoary appearance.
The first quill is intermediate between the sixth and seventh, and half an inch less than the
longest ; the second considerably shorter than the fourth. In *flaviventris* the first is rather
longer than the sixth ; the second and fourth equal. In view of all these circumstances, therefore, it may be well to give it provisionally a new name, and none would be more appropriate
than that of *Empidonax difficilis*.

The *Muscicapa flaviventris* of Vieillot (Ois. Am. Sept. I, 1807, 70) is clearly distinct in the
larger size, rufous tinge above, absence of yellowish on the throat and breast, &c. What the
species really is is not well ascertained, nor whether it actually belongs to this group. It is
spoken of as inhabiting St. Domingo. Should it prove to be of the same genus the present
species may be called *hypoxanthus* in allusion to the yellow of the under parts.

That this species is not the *T. pusilla* of Swainson is sufficiently evident from the fact that the bands on the wing in the latter are said to be grayish white, the throat ash gray, a whitish ring round the eye, &c.; all these parts in *flaviventris* being strongly tinged with yellowish. The proportions of the quills, too, are different.

I have quoted *Tyrannula pusilla* of Reinhardt and Gloger, a species captured in 1853 in the Godthaab district of Greenland, as coming much nearer to the present species than to *pusilla* of Swainson.

Catal. No.	Sex.	Locality.	When collected.	Whence obtained.	Original No.	Length.	Extent.	Wing.	Remarks.
1951	......	Raynor Sound, Long Island.....	Aug. 4, 1831	S. F. Baird					
2339	♀	Carlisle, Pa..................	May 24, 1845	.....do					
985	♂	.....do	May 18, 1843	.....do		5.16	8.83	2.83	
2972	♀	.....do	May 18, 1846	.....do		5.50	8.25	2.50	
2352	♂	.....do	May 26, 1845	.....do		5.50	9.	2.75	
2351	♀	.....do	.....do......	.....do		5.41	8.08	2.50	
2350	♂	.....do	.....do...	.....do		5.54	8.58	2.75	
2428	......	.....do	Sept. 4, 1845	.....do ...		5.25	8.50	2.58	
2302	♀	.....do	May —, 1845	.....do		5.25	8.	2.58	
......	......	West Northfield, Illinois	May 19, 1855	R. Kennicott..........					
......	......	Racine, Wisconsin...........		.....do ...					
5920	......	Fort Steilacoom		Dr. Cooper.............		5.60	8.50		Iris Brown.......
7243	......	Shoalwater Bay......	July 4, 1854	.....do	84	5.50	8.50		Iris brown.
......	......	Fort Tejon, California		J. Xantus de Vesey........					
7099	......	Coban		M. Verreaux..............	32613				

EMPIDONAX HAMMONDII, Baird.

Tyrannula hammondii, De Vesey, Pr. A. N. Sc. May, 1858.

Sp. Ch.—Tail moderately forked ; the feathers acutely pointed. Third quill longest ; second and then fourth a little shorter. First much shorter than fifth, a little longer than sixth. Bill very slender, dark brown. Above dark olive green, considerably darker on the head. Breast and sides of the body light olive green, the throat grayish white ; the rest of under parts bright sulphur yellow. A whitish ring round the eye. Wings and tail dark brown ; the former with two olivaceous gray bands across the coverts ; the latter with the outer edge a little paler than elsewhere, but not at all white. Length, 5.50 ; wing, 2.80 ; tail, 2.50 ; tarsus, .67.

Hab.—Vicinity of Fort Tejon to Los Angeles.

In this species the olive green on the sides is scarcely distinguishable from that on the back, although becoming more yellow on the middle of the breast. There is a decided ashy shade on the whole head. The only light edging to the quills is seen on the terminal half of the secondaries. The upper mandible and feet are black; the tip of the lower (and in one specimen the whole) dark brown. The fork of the tail measures a quarter of an inch in depth ; the longest quill exceeds the first by .40.

This species is at once distinguishable from all the North American *Tyrannulas*, except *obscurus*, by the extreme narrowness of the bill. This is only .25 of an inch wide at the posterior angle of the mouth, and only .19 at the nostrils. Its colors above are those of *acadicus*, while the general effect is much more that of *flaviventris*, although less brightly olive. The throat is grayish, not of the same yellow with the belly ; the ring round the eye white, not yellow ; the olive of the breast much more continuous and distinct ; the bands on the wings dull grayish instead of clear greenish yellow. The tail, instead of being nearly even, is quite deeply forked. The bill is scarcely half as wide, and brownish, not yellow, beneath. The tarsus has the same peculiar scutellation.

The differences from *T. obscurus* are less easily expressed. It is, however, considerably smaller, and more olivaceous above and below ; the tarsi very much shorter ; the most tangible character is seen in the absence of the white on the outer web of the external tail feather, which is only a little paler brown than elsewhere.

Catal. No.	Sex.	Locality.	Whence obtained.	Orig. No.
7236	......	Monterey, Cal............................	W. Hutton	....
10079	♂	Fort Tejon, Cal.........................	John Xantus de Vesey	803
10080	♀	......do..............................	......do.............................	652

EMPIDONAX OBSCURUS, Baird.

?Tyrannula obscura, SWAINSON, Syn. Mex. Birds, in Philos. Mag. I, 1827, 367.

Sp. Ch.—Bill very narrow. Tarsi long. Second, third, and fourth quills longest ; first shorter than sixth. Tail rounded. Above dull brownish olive, paler on the rump, tinged with gray on the head. Loral region and space round the eye whitish. Throat and fore part of the breast grayish white, slightly tinged with olive across the latter ; the rest of the under parts pale yell)wish. Wings and tail brown ; the former with two conspicuous bands of brownish white ; the outer primary edged, the secondaries and tertials edged and tipped with the same. The outer web of the external tail feather white, in strong contrast. Length, 5.75 ; wing, 2.75 ; tail, 2.55 ; tarsus, .70.

Hab.—Rocky mountains of Texas.

In this species the primaries are about .55 of an inch longer than the secondaries ; the first quill about .35 of an inch shorter than the longest. There is a decided tendency to grayish white edgings to the quill and tail feathers.

The most decided character of this species is seen in the combination of the narrow bill and the white outer margin of the external tail feather, together with the long tarsi. The colors are otherwise much like those of *minimus* and *traillii ;* the yellow beneath is, however, more ochraceous. The bill measured across opposite the middle of the nostrils is less than half its length from the forehead, instead of being considerably more, as in nearly all the other North American species, except *hammondii.*

The only description I can find which applies approximately to this species is that of *T. obscura* of Swainson, Syn. birds Mexico, in Philos. Magazine, 1827, No. 10, which is stated to be : "Above olive gray, beneath yellowish white ; wings short, brown, with two whitish bands ; tail brown, even, with a pale yellow margin. Length, 5.25 ; bill nearly .70 ; wings and tail, 2.50 ; tarsi, .60." The present species agrees in the white margin of the tail, but the under parts are gray anteriorly ; the tail slightly rounded ; the wings 2.75 inches ; the tarsi .70, and thus much longer ; the bill only .50. The differences of measurement may, however, be more accidental and real, and the smaller size the result of the more southern locality on the table lands of Mexico. For the present, therefore, I retain the name *obscurus,* but should this prove distinct, shall claim that of *E. wrightii,* the discoverer, by which I had provisionally designated it.

Catal. No.	Sex.	Locality.	Whence obtained.	Collected by—	Length.	Stretch of wings.	Wing.
7234	♂ ?	El Paso, Texas.........	Col. Graham...........	C. Wright.............	5.75	8 62	2.75
7237	♂	......do..............	......do..............	......do.............	5.37	8.50	2.87

PYROCEPHALUS, Gould.

Pyrocephalus, GOULD, Zool. of Beagle, 1838, 44.

CH.—Tarsus moderate, very little longer than the middle toe; hind toe not longer than the lateral. Bill slender, very narrow at the base. Tail broad, even, considerably shorter than the wings, (about four-fifths,) which reach beyond the middle of the tail. First quill shorter than the fifth. Head with a conspicuous rounded crest. Sexes dissimilar. Male with the crown and beneath red; tail, back, and wings brown.

This genus is shaped something like *Saxicola*. Its single North American species is readily distinguished among other flycatchers by the bright red of the under parts.

PYROCEPHALUS RUBINEUS, Gray.

Red Flycatcher.

" *Muscicapa rubineus*, BODDAERT, Tableau des Pl. Enl. Buffon, 1783, 42."

Pyrocephalus rubineus, GRAY, Genera, I. 250 LAWRENCE, Annals N. Y. Lyc. V, May, 1851, 115 CASSIN, Ill I, IV 1853, 127; pl. xvii.

Muscicapa coronata, GMELIN, Syst. Nat. I, 1788, 932.—WAGLER, Isis, 1831, 529.

Pyrocephalus nanus, WOODHOUSE, Sitgreave's Report, 1853, 75.

SP. CH.—Head with a full rounded or globular crest. Tail even. Crown and whole under parts bright carmine red; rest of upper parts, including the cheeks as far as the bill, dull dark brown; the upper tail coverts darker; the tail almost black ; greater and middle wing coverts and edges of secondaries and tertials dull white towards the edges. Outer web of exterior tail feather and tips of all the tail feathers whitish.

Female similar, without the crest; the crown brown, like the back; the under parts whitish anteriorly, streaked with brown; behind white, tinged with red or ochraceous. Length of male, about 5.50; wing, 3.25; tail, 2.75.

Hab.—Valleys of Rio Grande and Gila southward.

In this species the second, third, and fourth quills are longest; the first intermediate between the fifth and sixth. The red tipped feathers are all white in their middle portion. The shade of red varies with specimens, and in winter the red feathers appear to be tipped with grayish. The shade of red on the belly of the female varies considerably, sometimes being even of an ochraceous yellow.

The specimen collected at Quihi, Texas, by Dr. Woodhouse, and referred to *P. nanus* on account of the very short tail, is moulting, and the tail feathers are not fully grown out.

26 b

Comparative measurements of specimens.

Catal. No.	Sex.	Locality.	When collected.	Whence obtained.	Orig'l No.	Collected by—	Length.	Stretch of wings.	Wing.	Tail.	Tarsus.	Middle toe.	Its claw alone.	Bill above.	Along gape.	Specimen measured.	Remarks.
7224	♂	Fort Yuma, Cal.		Major Emory		A. Schott											
7223	♂	......do ...		Lieut. Williamson		Dr. Heermann											
7222	♂	Boca Grande, Mex.	Mar. —, 1855	Major Emory	44	Dr. Kennerly	5.54		3.00	2.50	0.62	0.54	0.16	0.50	0.62	Dry	
7232	♀	Espia, Mex.	......do ...	......do ...	53	......do ...	5.50	6.50	3.00								
7221	♂	San Bernardino, Mex.	May —, 1855	......do ...	70	......do ...											Eye black
7220	♂	Fort Thorn, N. M		Dr. Henry													
		Quitni, Texas.		Captain Sitgreaves		Dr. Woodhouse.											
4012	♂	Charco Escondido New. Leon, Mex	Mar. —, 1853	Lieut. Couch	70	.....	5.50	9.25	3.25								Eyes dark brown.
4013	♀	Santa Caterina, Mex	April —, 1853	......do ...	181		6.00	10.00	3.25							Fresh	
4347	♂	Chihuahua	Oct. 16, 1854	John Potts			5.44		3.20	2.60	0.54	0.52	0.21	0.50	0.64	Dry	
4481	♂	City of Mexico		......do ...													
7937	♂	Mexico		S. F. Baird													

OSCINES.

Singing Birds.

Cʜ.—Toes, three anterior, one behind ; all at the same level, and none versatile, the outer anterior never entirely free to the base. Tail feathers, twelve. Primaries, either nine only, or else the first is spurious or much shorter than the second, making the tenth. Tail feathers usually twelve. Tarsi feathered to the knee ; the plates on the anterior face either fused into one, or with distinct divisions ; the posterior portion of the sides covered by one continuous plate on either side, meeting in a sharp edge behind, or with only a few divisions inferiorly. Occasionally the hinder side has transverse plates, corresponding in number to the anterior, but there are then usually none on the sides. Larynx provided with a peculiar muscular apparatus for singing, composed of five pairs of muscles.

The preceding diagnosis, mainly derived from Dr. Cabanis, expresses the chief characteristics of such land birds as are provided with a peculiar apparatus for producing song. Birds of other orders may have more or less agreeable notes, but it is among the *Oscines* that we find the delightful and varied melody we are accustomed to consider as the "singing" of birds. It is, indeed, seldom, as Cabanis justly remarks, that so great a change has been produced in the systematic arrangement of a class by the discovery of a single fact, as has been the case in ornithology since the announcement that some birds have a peculiar muscular vocal apparatus, denied to others. It is to Cabanis himself, however, that is chiefly due the merit of having been among the first to discover appreciable external characters corresponding to these anatomical peculiarities, and of defining the boundaries of the families as rearranged.

The most natural arrangement of the *Oscines*, or singing birds, is a matter of much uncertainty, and can only be settled by the careful examination, external and internal, of a great number of types. As the birds of North America lack representatives of many sub-families, and even of families, I have done little more than to follow Dr. Cabanis in his Ornithologische Notizen,[1] and Museum Heineanum, making here and there a slight transposition where it seemed necessary. The characters of some of the families, and of nearly all the sub-families, I have been obliged to work out for myself, owing to the very meagre indications given by the above mentioned author.

According to Cabanis, the fusion of all the scutellae of the tarsus into one continuous envelope without indications of division, (called "boot" by the German ornithologists,) is to be considered as indicating the highest type of ornithological structure, and the position of the different families and genera in the scale, to be mainly regulated by their approach to this character. With this, however, are to be combined the hints afforded by the greater or less development of the first primary, the elevation in rank being also, to a considerable degree, proportional to the tendency to a reduction of this quill in size, and to its gradual suppression entirely.

The families of North American Oscines embrace a large proportion of those that have been established ; but some have no representatives whatever, such as the typical *Muscicapidae*, the *Nectarinidae*, the *Melliphagidae*, the *Ploceidae*, the *Sturnidae*, and the *Paradiseidae*. Many sub-families are wanting, too, of families which have other representatives.

[1] Wiegmann's Archiv für Naturgeschichte 1847, i, 186, 308.

In preparing the following diagnoses and descriptions of the families, sub-families, and genera of American Oscines, I have, as already stated, been mainly obliged to make up the characters for myself by personal examination of the species. Without the time or the immediate opportunity to extend this criticism to the exotic forms, I have not succeeded as well as I could have wished, but it cannot be long before some one will take up the subject on the new basis, and work out the details into an acceptable system. The work of Burmeister on the birds of Brazil, containing many original and important remarks on the subject, did not reach me until too late a period to make the use of it I could have wished, although I have derived many valuable hints from it.

The following synopsis may serve to facilitate the determination of the families, and a consequent reference to the page where they are described in rather more detail.

A. Primaries, nine. Outer primary nearly as long as, or more than half, the next. Legs scutellate anteriorly.

    a. Commissure straight.

        Hirundinidae.—Bill very broad, short, and much depressed; the culmen less than half the commissure, which opens to beneath the eye. Rictus smooth. Wings very long, greatly exceeding the tail; the first primary longest. Tarsi shorter than the lateral toes.

        Sylvicolidae.—Bill usually slender, conical, elongated, and acute; or, if broad and depressed, the culmen more than half the gape or commissure, and the rictus with bristles. Tarsus always longer than the lateral toes. Wings rather short, never much longer than the tail. First primary generally shorter than second.

    b. Commissure angulated at base.

        Fringillidae.—Bill much shorter than the head; thick, conical, the tip usually notched, and the rictus with bristles.

        Icteridae.—Bill nearly as long as, or longer than, the head, without notch or bristles.

B. Primaries, ten. First primary very short, (spurious,) the second nearly as long as the third. Bill, with the culmen gently curved, and the upper mandible notched at tip.

    a. Lateral toes about equal. Basal joint of middle toe mostly free internally.

        Turdidae.—Tarsi encased in one heavy "boot," without scutellae; posterior edge acute; hind claw curved.

        Alaudidae.—Tarsi blunt behind; scutellate anteriorly and posteriorly, but not laterally. Spurious primary sometimes wanting. Hind claw long, nearly straight.

    b. Outer lateral toe much longest. Basal joint of middle united throughout.

        Certhiadae.—Legs scutellate anteriorly. Hind toe very long. Claw curved.

C. Primaries, ten. The first spurious, sometimes wanting, or less than half the second. Bill, with both mandibles, abruptly hooked, and conspicuously notched at the tip, with a tooth behind the notch above.

        Bombycillidae.—Bill broad, depressed, weak, moderately hooked. Tarsi shorter than middle toe.

        Laniidae.—Bill narrow, much compressed, and very powerful, strongly hooked. Tarsus longer than middle toe.

D. Primaries, ten, the first nearly half as long as the second. The bill gently curved and moderately notched, or without notch, at the tip.

    a. Nostrils uncovered by bristly feathers.

        LIOTRICHIDAE.—Bill slender, nearly as long as the head, or much longer, gently or much curved. First quill more than half the second. Basal joint of middle toe usually free nearly to the base internally, and halfway externally.

    b. Nostrils usually covered with bristly feathers.

        PARIDAE.—Base of bill covered with rather broad bristly feathers directed forwards, with the shaft projecting anteriorly in a simple bristle, or the lateral branches elongated. Side of tarsi without any groove. Basal joint of middle toe united to lateral nearly its whole length. Bill mostly without terminal notch. First primary less than half the second.

        CORVIDAE.—Base of bill covered usually with narrow bristly feathers directed forwards, with short branches to the very tip. Middle of sides of tarsi with a groove, usually more or less occupied by a row of small scales. Basal joint of middle toe united halfway only to the lateral. First primary more than half the second. Bill mostly notched.

The preceding arrangement is not entirely natural, a less exceptionable order, perhaps, being that adopted in the succeeding pages, namely, *Turdidae, Sylvicolidae, Hirundinidae, Bombycillidae, Laniidae, Liotrichidae, Certhiadae, Paridae, Alaudidae, Fringillidae, Icteridae,* and *Corvidae.* It must be always borne in mind that one set of characters alone is rarely sufficient to establish zoological rank, but rather the varying combination of several sets. The grouping of the families of *Oscines*, as of other orders, will vary greatly with any change in the points of reference adopted. Thus, as to the character of the tarsus, it is very long in *Turdus* and *Saxicola*, and in most *Liotrichidae;* short in *Bombycillidae*, and excessively short in the swallows. The lateral toes are generally nearly equal, but they are very unequal in the *Certhiadae.* The basal joint of the middle toe is sometimes nearly free internally, and united externally by the basal third, as in *Turdus, Geothlypis,* and the *Bombycillidae.* In *Regulus, Sialia,* and *Cinclus,* the union externally is about one-half, while in *Myiodioctes* and *Icteria* it is nearly complete. In *Toxostoma, Mimus,* and *Troglodytes,* the union of this basal joint externally is about one-half, internally about one-third. In *Campylorhynchus, Catherpes,* and *Thryothorus,* the union is nearly two-thirds on both sides. In *Salpinctes* and *Lanius* it is nearly complete externally. In the *Certhiadae, Paridae,* and, to some extent, in *Vireo,* the union of this basal joint is almost complete on both sides.

As already stated, the tarsus is entirely without scutellae in the thrushes or in *Turdus, Regulus, Sialia, Cinclus,* &c., as also in *Myiadestes.* In all the others it is scutellate or divided into broad plates anteriorly; but in *Icteria, Geothlypis, Myiodioctes,* and *Chamaea,* there are no plates visible on the outer side at all, the division only commencing on the extreme anterior face, or towards its inner edge. The same is the case in *Helmitherus swainsoni,* and *Seiurus noveboracensis,* but in *S. aurocapillus* the plates are more evident. In all the others the scutellae are well defined externally, near the median line of the outer side. The rest of the surface is generally undivided, each side being completed by a single plate, the two uniting behind in a sharp edge. Sometimes there is a tendency to division on the sides of the tarsi below, and in in *Corvidae* there is a row of small scales on the middle of one or both sides. In *Lanius borealis* and *Ampelis garrulus* there is a tendency to scales behind and on the sides, inferiorly, below.   The peculiar condition of the posterior scutellae in *Alaudidae* will be found detailed hereafter.   In none of these deviations from the highest character in the exhibition of lateral or posterior scales, however, is there any approach to the peculiarities of the *Tracheophones*, and the first primary is always either short, spurious, or wanting.

It is unnecessary to follow the bill or the tail through its modifications, as the characters of both are of secondary importance, and only available for purposes of generic distinction.

Family TURDIDAE.

Primaries ten, of which the first is always very short, the second nearly equal to the longest, (except in *Regulinae*.) Wings ather long. Tarsi usually rather long, without scutellae, or else having them indistinctly visible at the lower end alone. Basal joint of middle toe united by its basal two-thirds to the outer, and by basal half to the inner toe. Lateral toes about equal. Bill notched at tip.

The chief characteristics of this family are found in the association of a dentirostral bill, with legs destitute of scutellae or divided scales anteriorly, together with the very short or spurious first, and the rather long second primary. The North American species all have the tail short and rather even, or emarginate.

The following is a synopsis of the sub-families:

TURDINAE.—Nostrils oval. Bristles along the base of the bill from gape to nostrils; those of rictus not reaching beyond nostrils. The loral feathers with bristly points. Second quill longer than sixth. Outer lateral toes longer. Wings long.

REGULINAE.—Nostrils oval. The frontal feathers elongated; their bristl shafts with the rictal bristles extending beyond the nostrils, the former scale-like. Points of loral feathers bristly. Second quill shorter than sixth. Size very small.

CINCLINAE.—Nostrils linear. No bristles whatever about the rictus, nor bristly points to the loral and frontal feathers. Legs longer than head, reaching beyond the tip of the tail. Body stout; the wings and tail very short.

Sub-Family TURDINAE.

The family of *Turdinae*, as constituted in the previous synopsis, entirely excludes the mocking birds belonging to the genera *Mimus, Toxostoma*, &c. The true place of the last mentioned forms is very near the wrens, as insisted upon by Cabanis.

The introduction of *Sialia* and *Saxicola* into this sub-family, instead of among the *Saxicolinae*, is contrary to the usual custom of ornithologists. I, however, am unable to appreciate any differences between it and *Turdus*, other than those of generic value, and, at any rate, they are all sufficiently allied to permit them to be combined.

The genera to be referred to here are *Turdus, Saxicola*, and *Sialia*. The chief diagnostic characteristics of these are as follows:

TURDUS.—Tarsi long, exceeding the middle toe; wings reaching to the middle of the tail; which is about four-fifths the length of the wings. Bill stout; its upper outline convex toward the base. Second quill shorter than fifth.

SAXICOLA.—Tarsi considerably longer than the middle toe, which reaches nearly to the tip of the tail. Tail short, even; two-thirds as long as the lengthened wings, which reach beyond the middle of the tail. Second quill longer than fifth. Bill attenuated; its upper outline concave towards the base.

SIALIA.—Tarsi short; about equal to the middle toe. Wings reaching beyond the middle of the tail. Bill thickened.

TURDUS, Linnæus.

Turdus, Linnæus, Systema Naturae, 1735. (Type *T. viscivorus*, fide G. R. Gray.)

Bill rather stout ; commissure straight to near the tip, which is quite abruptly decurved, and usually distinctly notched ; culmen gently convex from base.   Bill shorter than the head ; both outlines curved.   Tarsi longer than the middle toe. Lateral toes nearly equal ; outer longer. Wings much longer than the tail, pointed ; the first quill spurious and very small—not one-fourth the length of longest. Tail short, nearly even, or slightly emarginate.

The essential characters of the true thrushes appear to consist in the long tarsi, without distinct scutellae ; the long pointed wings, with rather short second quill and the spurious primary ; and the moderately short, even tail.   There are, however, several distinct groups among them, of which these in the following synopsis belong to North America.

The *Turdus naevius* of authors is quite different from the other species in the more slender bill, longer gonys, and absence of any notch in the bill.   The general appearance is, however, so thrush-like that I cannot see any reason for transferring it to a separate family, as Bonaparte has done.   The structure of its bill assimilates it to *Toxostoma ;* but it differs in shorter bill, even tail, booted tarsi, and long wings.   The first primary is shorter also, though longer than in *Turdus*.

There are few species of North American birds the synonymy of which has been in such a state of confusion as the small thrushes.   Of these there may now be considered as well established *T. mustelinus, fuscescens, ustulatus, swainsonii, aliciae, pallasii,* and *nanus,* to which may possibly have to be added *T. silens* of Swainson, coming between *swainsonii* and *pallasii.*   In regard to *mustelinus* there has been no difficulty, the only synonym of note being *melodus* of Wilson.   The case is, however, very different with the rest, and a brief sketch of the history of each species may not be out of place.   It will be well to state, as a preliminary, that *Turdus fuscescens* and *ustulatus* have the upper parts throughout of a uniform reddish brown, without any shade of olive, the throat and breast brownish yellow ; the former species with very obsolete spots in these regions, lighter than the ground color above ; the latter with the spots more distinct, and darker than the back.   *T. swainsonii* has the back uniform olive brown, with a shade of green ; the breast with distinct nearly black spots; the sides of head and the breast yellowish red.   *T. aliciae* similar, but the sides of head gray, the breast white.   *T. pallasii* and *nanus* have the back brown, with a faint tinge of reddish ; but the rump, upper coverts, and tail are quite foxy, considerably different from the back.   The under parts are decidedly spotted.   *T. nanus* is considerably the smaller of the two ; the color beneath purer ; the sides bluish ash, rather than yellowish brown.   *T. silens,* if really distinct from *T. pallasii,* is larger and more olivaceous on the back, with the same contrast of color on the tail.   The *Turdus fuscescens* was described improperly by Wilson as *T. mustelinus.*   Stephens, in 1817, first detected the error, and called the species *T. fuscescens,* which name, however, remained unnoticed until brought to light by Gray in the Genera of Birds.   Bonaparte, in 1824, gave the name of *wilsonii,* by which the species has generally been known.   Swainson, in the Fauna Boreali Americana, calls it *T. minor* after Gmelin, and applies the name *wilsonii* erroneously to *T. swainsonii.*   The *Turdus minor* of Gmelin, in fact, applies in part to this species, but also includes characters of *T. swainsonii,* having been compounded of the descriptions of the little thrush of Latham and the little thrush of Pennant.   He supposed them to be merely two different descriptions of one species, whereas that of Latham belonged to *fuscescens,* ("above reddish brown or clay color, breast yellowish, with dusky spots,") and that of Pennant to *T. swainsonii,* ("above uniform brown, breast with *large brown* spots.'') The large brown spots are not found in *fuscescens*. Gmelin describes *T. minor* as "*spadiceus, pectore flavicante, maculis atris*," (reddish brown, breast yellowish with *black* spots.) His name is, therefore, clearly to be set aside in the further discussion of the question.

I have not now the means of verifying the accuracy of the reference of *Turdus parvus* of Selgimann to this species, made by me many years ago ; but if correct, then this name may have to take precedence, unless a true *Turdus parvus* had been previously described.

Turdus ustulatus of Nuttall has been mentioned alone by him, and has no synonyms, as far as I can ascertain. By a typographical error the name was printed *cestulatus*.

By a remarkable oversight the olive-backed thrush, (*T. swainsonii*,) though well known to all of the more recent school of American ornithologists, was not described by either Wilson or Audubon. It was given by Swainson as *Merula wilsonii*, erroneously supposing it to be the species referred to by Bonaparte under this name. His figure of *M. solitaria* is very probably this same species. The figure given by Wilson to accompany his description of *Turdus solitarius* (*pallasii*) unquestionably belongs to *T. swainsonii*. As previously stated, the *T. minor* of Gmelin applies in part to this species ; that of Vieillot to this species, in conjunction with *T. pallasii*.

In the latter part of 1843 Mr. Giraud, a leading American ornithologist, and author of several important works, published the species as *Turdus olivaceus ;* and Dr. Brewer, without knowing the fact, gave it the same name in 1844. This has really priority, unless the *Turdus brunneus* of Boddaert, based on Pl. enlum. 556, fig. 2, be really and incontestibly the present species, as claimed by Gray in the Genera of Birds. The term *olivaceus*, however, had previously been used by Linnæus and Boddaert, as well as by Lichtenstein and others, in connexion with thrushes, and cannot be retained, unless these are shown to belong to genera other than that of the present species. Not having access at present to the Planches enluminées, I am unable to discuss the value of Boddaert's name.

In Tschudi's Fauna Peruana, published between 1844 and 1846, Cabanis gives accurate diagnoses of the American thrushes, showing their relations to each other, although in this he had been anticipated by Dr. Brewer in the Proceedings of the Boston Society of Natural History for July, 1844. He there applies the name of *T. swainsonii* to the olive-backed species, which, in the present state of our knowledge of the question, must be retained.

The *Turdus pallasii* of Cabanis—*T. solitarius* of Wilson—first received a distinctive name in Wiegmann's Archiv, in 1847. Wilson's name had previously been employed by Linnæus and others for a different thrush. The species was at first called *T. minor* by Bonaparte and Audubon, erroneously supposing it to be the bird referred to by Gmelin ; in their later works, however, these authors took Wilson's name. In the article already referred to in Fauna Peruana, Cabanis identified this species with *Muscicapa guttata* of Pallas, which, however, he afterwards found to be distinct.

The *Merula silens* of Swainson, if really identical with the present species, will take priority over Cabanis' name ; but I am inclined to consider it distinct for reasons named elsewhere.

The remaining species was named and described by Audubon as *Turdus nanus*. In his article in the Fauna Peruana, Cabanis considered the *Turdus aonalaschka* of Gmelin and *Muscicapa guttata* of Pallas as young birds of the *Turdus solitarius* of Wilson. The locality— Russian America—and the small size clearly indicate that the names, if belonging to either, apply to the dwarf rather than to the hermit thrush. In the *Muscicapa guttata* of Pallas it is difficult to recognize even a young bird of this species—in the " body brown above, spotted

27 b

with yellow; beneath pale, variegated with black. Tail rufous. Rump rufous yellow, with transverse brown bands. Wings sparsely dotted. Breast white, with transverse bands of black. Length to the rump, 3¼ inches; tail, 2 inches 7 lines; wing, 3 inches 5 lines. Kodiak."

The *Turdus aonalaschka* of Gmelin, based on a bird the "size of a lark, crown and back brown, marked with obscure dusky spots; breast yellow, spotted with black; wing coverts, prime quills, and tail dusky, edged with testaceous; hab. Aonalaschka, cabinet of Sir Joseph Banks," of Latham and Pennant might possibly refer to a young bird of the present species; but in the entire uncertainty in the case, and the possibility of their having some one of the similarly colored American sparrows before them, it may be best to retain Mr. Audubon's name.

SYNOPSIS OF SUB-GENERA AND SPECIES.

TURDUS.—Tarsi elongated, considerably longer than the middle toe; the scutellae not distinguishable. Tail feathers acuminate. Bill distinctly notched. Above plain olive or reddish, beneath white; the breast spotted.

Rufous brown above, much brightest towards the head, becoming olivaceous on the tail; pure white beneath, thickly spotted on the whole breast and sides with blackish.
mustelinus.

Yellowish olive above, becoming decidedly rufous on the rump and tail. Beneath white, scarcely more yellow anteriorly; breast with well defined spots like the back. Tibiae and sides yellowish olive brown...*pallasii.*

Similar to the last, but smaller; the under parts purer white; the tibiae and sides grayish olive brown..*nanus.*

Similar to *pallasii*, but larger; the back greenish, not yellow olive, passing into reddish on the tail..*silens.*

Above uniform yellowish red; throat and jugulum decidedly yellowish, the latter with very obsolete spots ....*fuscescens.*

Similar to the last, but more yellow olivaceous above, and the jugulum distinctly marked with spots like the back...*ustulatus.*

Above greenish olive, not appreciably lighter on the tail. Sides of the head with the breast and throat strongly tinged with reddish yellow, and a ring of the same round the eye. Breast with very distinct spots of dark brown.........................*swainsonii.*

Above greenish olive, not appreciably lighter on the tail. Sides of the head ashy; ring round the eye, with the throat, and breast white. Breast with very distinct spots of dark brown, almost black...*aliciae.*

PLANISTICUS.—Body stout; tarsi not much longer than the middle toe, the scutellae somewhat visible on the inside below. Tail feathers rather truncate. Bill distinctly notched. Above plain olive; throat and chin alone white, streaked with black; breast rufous.

Above grayish olive; top of head and the tail blackish. Beneath reddish brown; the anal region and crissum, with eyelids, white......................................*migratorius.*

IXOREUS.—Bill slender, elongated, nearly as long as the head; commissure curved; tip without any notch. Scutellae not distinguishable. Claws larger than in *Planisticus*. First primary about one-fourth the longest. Tail feathers acuminate. Throat and under parts entirely unspotted.

Above dark plumbeous; beneath reddish brown, with a pectoral band of black; wings varied with reddish brown, and a stripe of the same behind the eye...............*naevius.*

Comparative measurements of species.

Catal. No.	Species.	Locality.	Sex and age.	Length.	Stretch of wings.	Wing.	Tail.	Tarsus.	Middle toe.	Its claw alone.	Bill above.	Along gape.	Specimen measured.
1569	Turdus mustelinus..	Carlisle, Pa........	♂	7.20	....	4.06	3.06	1.28	1.02	0.24	0.72	1.04	Dry.... ......
do.	..... do...........	...... do...........	....	8.08	13.41	4.25	.....	......					Fresh...........
1570	..... do...........	..... do........	♀	7.10	....	4.30	3.20	1.20	0.98	0.24	0.68	0.98	Dry...........
do.	...... do...........	..... do...........	....	8.08	13.58	4.41	.....						Fresh...........
8388	...... do...........	Independence, Mo..	O	4.31	....	2.96	1.40	1.14	0.90	1.98	0.50	0.68	Dry..... .....
7950	Turdus silens?.....	Mexico		7.14	....	4.02	3.20	1.18	0.90	0.22	0.60	0.78	Dry............
2092	Turdus pallasii	Carlisle, Pa..... ...	....	6.80	....	3.80	3.26	1.16	0.82	0.22	0.58	0.84	Dry............
do.	..... do...........	...... do...........	....	7.50	11.83	3.83	......						Fresh........ .
7591	...... do...........	Washington, D. C..	....	6.20	....	3.70	2.90	1.16	0.88	0.23	0.50	0.80	Dry............
1375	...... do...........	Carlisle, Pa	♀	6.40	....	3.64	3.02	1.16	0.82	0.22	0.54	0.78	Dry ....
do	...... do...........	..... do...........		7.16	11.50	3.66							Fresh............
8170	...... do...........	Frontera...........	♀	6.56	....	3.52	2.90	1.10	0.84	0.24	0.54	0.82	Dry............
do.	...... do.	..... do...........	....	6.50	....	2.56	.....						
8168	Turdus nanus	Sacramento Valley.	♂	6.34	....	3.34	2.90	1.08	0.80	0.22	0.52	0.74	Dry............
2145	Turdus fuscescens .	Carlisle, Pa.....	♂	6.64	....	4.00	3.24	1.21	0.90	0.22	0.60	0.84	Dry............
do.	...... do...........	..... do...........	....	7.50	12.58	4.25							Fresh ....
989	...... do...........	..... do...........	♀	6.50	....	3.68	3.12	1.12	0.78	0.18	0.54	0.80	Dry............
do.	...... do...........	..... do........	....	7.08	11.83	3.75							Fresh............
2040	Turdus ustulatus ..	Columbia river.....		7.20	....	3.70	3.04	1.10	0.98	0.20	0.58	0.82	Dry ....
980	Turdus swainsonii.	Carlisle, Pa	♂	6.54	....	4.00	3.16	1.10	0.84	0.22	0.50	0.76	Dry............
do.	...... do...........	..... do...........	....	7.00	12.50	4.16							Fresh............
981	...... do...........	..... do.	♀	6.06	....	3.60	2.90	1.04	0.80	0.20	0.52	0.76	Dry............
do.	...... do...........	.... do...........	....	6.50	11.50	3 56							Fresh............
5657	...... do...........	Rep. Fork, 40 miles west of Riley.	♂	6.80	....	3.84	2.88	1.06	0.84	0.22	0.44	0.74	Dry ....
do.	...... do......	..... do...........	....	7.00	11.00								Fresh............
7948	...... do...........	Mexico		6.70	....	3.74	2.94	1.04	0.89	0.24	0.52	0.74	Dry............
10084	Turdus aliciæ......	W. Northfield, Cook county, Ill.	....	7.30	....	4.14	3.20	1.20	0.92	0 24	0.50	0.76	Dry............
10083	...... do...........	Kentucky, opposite Cairo, Ill.	......	7.80	....	4.18	3.28	1.10	0.90	0.24	0.56	0.78	Dry ....
4708	...... do...........	Nebraska	♂	7.10	....	4.08	3.28	1.18	0 88	0.22	0.50	0.72	Dry............
do.	...... do...........	..... do...........	....	7.25	12.25	4.25							Fresh ....
8144	Turdus migratorius.	Sac. Valley.	♂	9.04	... .	5.30	4.46	1.30	1.20	0.32	0.84	1.08	Dry............
853	...... do...........	Carlisle, Pa	♂	9.30	....	5.20	4.70	1.24	1.10	0.26	0.78	1.07	Dry............
do.	...... do...........	..... do...........	....	9.75	16.25	5.41							Fresh............
9814	Turdus nævius	Simiahmoo, W. T..	♂	9.30	....	4.92	3.90	1.26	1.16	0.28	0.86	1.04	Dry............
do.	...... do...........	...... do...		9.00	14.50	4.75							Fresh............
8123	...... do...........	California...........	♀?	8.70	....	4.88	3.86	1.26	1.16	0.30	0.88	1.16	Dry ....

TURDUS MUSTELINUS, Gmelin.

Wood Thrush.

Turdus mustelinus, GMELIN, Syst. Nat. I, 1788, 817.—LATHAM, Ind. Orn. II, 1790, 331.—VIEILLOT, Ois. Am. Sept
II, 1807, 6 ; pl. lxii.—NUTTALL, Man. I, 1832, 343.—AUDUBON, Orn. Biog. I, 1832, 372 : V, 1839,
446 ; pl. 73.—IB. Birds Am. III, 1841, 24 ; pl. 144.—BONAP. Conspectus, 1850, 270.

Merula mustelina, RICH. List, 1837.

Turdus melodus, WILSON, Am. Orn. I, 1808, 35 ; pl. ii.

Tawny thrush, PENNANT, Arctic Zool. II, 337.

SP. CH.—Above clear cinnamon brown, on the top of the head becoming more rufous, on the rump and tail olivaceous. The
under parts are clear white, sometimes tinged with buff on the breast or anteriorly, and thickly marked beneath, except on the
chin and throat and about the vent and tail coverts, with sub-triangular, sharply defined spots of blackish. The sides of the
head are dark brown, streaked with white, and there is also a maxillary series of streaks on each side of the throat, the central
portion of which sometimes has indications of small spots. Length, 8.10 inches ; wing, 4.25 ; tail, 3.05 ; tarsus, 1.26.

Hab.—Eastern United States to Missouri river ; south to Guatemala

This species is quite stout in form ; the tail is even or very slightly rounded laterally ; the
feathers acuminate. The third and fourth quills are longest ; the second rather longer than
the fifth. The legs are yellow ; the bill brown, but yellow at the base beneath.
A female specimen has nearly the whole lower parts tinged faintly with buff.

List of specimens.

Catal. No.	Sex and age.	Locality.	When collected.	Whence obtained.	Orig. No.	Collected by—	Length.	Stretch of wings	Wing.	Remarks.
1569	♂	Carlisle, Pa........	May 28, 1844	S. F. Baird...........	......	....	8.08	13.43	4.25	....
1570	♀	......do...........	......do.....	......do...	......	....	8.08	13.25	4.43	....
7286	....	Rockport, Ohio	......do.....	J. P. Kirtland........	......	....	....	....	....	....
8390	♀	Independence, Mo.	June 22, 1857	Wm. M. Magraw.....	96	Dr. Cooper	7.75	12.50	4.50	Iris brown, bill black, feet gray.
8388	o	..... do............	......do.....	......do...........	93	......do............	....	....	....	....
4650	....	Fort Pierre........	May 3, 1855	Col. A. Vaughan	....	Dr. Hayden.........	....	....	....	....
7947	....	Guatemala.........	....	John Gould.......	......	....	....	....	....	....

TURDUS PALLASII, Cabanis.

Hermit Thrush.

Turdus pallasii, CABANIS, Wiegmann's Archiv, 1847, I, I, 205.—IB. Museum Heineanum, 1850–1, 5.

Turdus solitarius, WILSON, Am. Orn. V, 1812, 95, (not of Linnaeus. The figure quoted pl. xliii, fig. 2, belongs to
T. swainsonii.)—AUDUBON, Synopsis, 1839.—IB. Birds Am. III, 1841, 29 ; pl. 146.—BONAPARTE,
List, 1838.—IB. Consp. Av. 1850, 270.—BREWER, Pr. Bost. Soc. N. H. 1844, 191.

Merula solitaria, SWAINSON, F. Bor. Am. II, 1831, 184. (The figure pl. xxxv, probably belongs to *T. swainsonii.*)—
VIEILL. Ois. Am. Sept. II, 1807, 7 ; pl. lxiii, (in part with *swainsonii.*)

Turdus minor, BON. Obs. Wilson, 1825, No. 72.—IB. Synopsis, 1828, 75.—NUTTALL, Man. I, 1830, 346.—AUD.
Orn. Biog. I, 1831, 303 : V, 445 ; pl. 58.

Turdus guttatus, CABANIS, Tschudi Fauna Peruana, 1844, 6, 187, (not *Muscicapa guttata*, Pall.)

? *Turdus minimus*, SELIGMANN, Samml. II, 177 ; pl. lxii.

SP. CH.—Fourth quill longest ; third and fourth a little shorter ; second about equal to the sixth ; about .30 of an inch shorter
than the longest. Tail slightly emarginate. Above light olive brown, with a scarcely perceptible shade of reddish, passing,
however, into decided rufous on the rump, upper tail coverts, and tail, and to a less degree on the outer surface of the wings.
Beneath white, with a scarcely appreciable shade of pale buff across the fore part of the breast, and sometimes on the throat ;
the sides of the throat and the fore part of the breast with rather sharply defined subtriangular spots o. dark olive brown ; the
sides of the breast with paler and less distinct spots of the same. Sides of the body under the wings of a paler shade than the
back. A whitish ring round the eye ; ear coverts very obscurely streaked with paler. Length, 7.50 inches ; wing, 3.84 ; tail,
3.25 ; tarsus, 1.16 ; No. 2092.

Hab.—Eastern North America to the Mississippi river.

Specimens vary somewhat in the intensity of the colors above, but the upper coverts and tail are always conspicuously more rufous than the back, especially at the base of the tail. There is sometimes a faint indication of two lighter bars on the tips of the wing coverts. Sometimes the under coverts are tinged with buff. A specimen from Washington (7591) has the back nearly as bright as in *T. wilsonii*, and the bands on the wing unusually distinct, but the tail is conspicuously brighter, as usual.

A Mexican specimen (No. 7950) received from Mr. Gould, compared with Pennsylvania ones, is a little more olivaceous on the back, although but little more so than is exhibited by skins from Carlisle. The wing is longer, however, measuring a little over four inches; the tail, 3.40; the tarsus, 1.18. The lateral toes are shorter and more unequal. The third quill is longer than the fifth; the second .10 of an inch longer than the sixth. I am not prepared to say whether this is more than an extreme case of *T. pallasii*. Should this at any time prove a distinct species from *solitarius*, as it certainly is from *nanus*, it might bear Swainson's name of *T. silens*[1] as best agreeing with it, in spite of some discrepancies.

List of specimens.

Catal. No.	Sex.	Locality.	When collected.	Whence obtained.	Orig. No.	Length.	Stretch of wings.	Wing.
2092	------	Carlisle ----------------	April 11, 1845	S. F Baird --------------	------	7.50	11.83	3.83
2146	♀	----do----------------	April 26, 1845	----do----------------	------	7.25	11.50	3.75
1375	♀	----do----------------	April 20, 1844	----do----------------	------	7.16	11.50	3.66
93	♂	----do----------------	April 10, 1840	----do----------------	37	--- ----	-------	-----
7591	------	Washington, D. C. ------	----------------	Wm. Hutton---------	------	-------	-------	-----
7292	------	Rockport, Ohio---------	----------------	J. P. Kirtland ---------	------	-------	-------	-----

TURDUS NANUS, Aud.

Dwarf Thrush.

Turdus nanus, Aud. Orn. Biog. V, 1839, 201; pl. 419.—Ib. Birds Amer. III, 1841, 32; pl. 147, (Columbia river.)— Gambel, Pr. A. N. Sc. I, 1843, 262.
? *Turdus aonalaschka*, Gmelin, Syst. Nat. I, 1788, 808.
? ? *Muscicapa guttata*, Pallas, Zool. Rosso. As. II, 1811, 465.
? *Aonalaschka Thrush*, Latham, Synopsis II, i, 1783, 23.—Penn. Arc Zool. II, 1785, 338.

Sp. Ch.—Similar to *T. pallasii*, but smaller. The white of the under parts purer; the sides glossed with bluish ash instead of yellowish olive brown. The tail with a purple tinge. Length, 6.50; wing, 3.30; tail, 2.90; tarsus, 1.10.
Hab.—Pacific coast of North America, and along valley of Gila to El Paso.

This species, if really distinct, is so closely allied to *T. pallasii* as to render a separation of the two exceedingly difficult. There is the same shade of olive on the back, passing into reddish on the upper coverts and tail, and to a less extent on the wings; the pale buff tinge of the fore part of breast and sometimes of throat; the distinctly defined triangular dusky spots on the sides of the throat and across the breast; the less distinct and more rounded spots on the sides of the breast behind. Comparing typical specimens of the eastern series (*T. pallasii*) and the western (*T. nanus*) the differences appear to be as follows:

[1] *Merula silens*, Swainson, Syn. Birds Mex. in Philosophical Magazine I, 1827, 369.—Ib. F. Bor. Amer. II, 1831. Length, 7 inches; bill, .75; wings, 3.75; tail, 3; tarsi, 1.

The shade of the back is the same, perhaps a little more olive in *T. nanus*, in which the centres of the feathers of the crown are a little more dusky. There is also in *nanus* a slight purple tinge in the tail. The under parts show a purer white behind, and the sides, axillaries, and under wing coverts show a bluish gray tinge rather than a pale brownish yellow. The under tail coverts are pure white, without the usual tinge of buff. There is no essential difference in the proportion of the quills. The tail may possibly be more rounded in *nanus*.

List of specimens.

Catal. No.	Sex.	Locality.	When collected.	Whence obtained.	Collected by—	Length.	Wing.
3895	------	California --------------	--------------	Dr. Heermann ------	--------------------	--------	------
4483	------	Santa Clara, Cal--------	--------------	Dr. Cooper----------	--------------------	6. 50	9. 25
5943	------	------do--------------	Nov. 1855----	------do------	--------------------	7. 00	10. 50
8168	♂	Sacramento valley -------	------do------	Lt. Williamson------	Dr Heermann------	--------	------
8169	------	Mimbres to Rio Grande---	--------------	Dr. T. C. Henry-----	--------------------	--------	------
8170	♀	Frontera, Texas ---------	May 8, 1851	C. Wright----------	--------------------	6. 80	2. 56

TURDUS FUSCESCENS, Stephens.

Wilson's Thrush.

Turdus fuscescens, STEPHENS, Shaw's Zool. Birds, X, I, 1817, 182.—GRAY, Genera, 1849.
Turdus mustelinus, WILSON, Am. Orn. V, 1812, 98 ; pl. 43, (not of Gm.)
Turdus wilsonii, BON. OBS. Wils. 1825, No. 73, (not of Swainson.)—IB. Conspectus, 1850, 271.—NUTT. Man. I, 1832, 349.—AUD. Orn. Biog. II, 1834, 362 : V, 446 ; pl. 166.—IB. Birds Am. III, 1841, 27 ; pl. 145.—BREWER, Pr. Bost. N. H. Soc. I, 1844, 191.—CABANIS, in Tschudi Fauna Peruana, 1844-'46, 205.
Turdus minor, GM. I, 1788, 809. (From Pennant and Latham, compounded of this and *T. swainsonii*.)—D'ORBIGNY, De la Sagra's Cuba, Birds, 47 ; pl. v.
Merula minor, SWAINSON, F. Bor. Am. II, 1831, 179, (plate that of *swainsonii*.)
Turdus iliacus carolinensis, BRISSON, II, 1760, 212.
? *Turdus parvus*, (Edw.) SELIGMANN, Samml. VIII, 1775, pl. lxxxvi.
Little Thrush, LATHAM, Synopsis II, I, 1783, 20.

SP. CH.—Third quill longest ; fourth a little shorter ; second nearly a quarter of an inch longer than the fifth. Above, and on sides of head and neck, nearly uniform light reddish brown, with a faint tendency to orange on the crown and tail. Beneath, white ; the fore part of the breast and throat (paler on the chin) tinged with pale brownish yellow, in decided contrast to the white of the belly. The sides of the throat and the fore part of the breast as colored are marked with small triangular spots of light brownish, nearly like the back, but not well defined. There are a few obsolete blotches on the sides of the breast (in the white) of pale olivaceous ; the sides of the body tinged with the same. Tibiae white. The lower mandible is brownish only at the tip. The lores are ash colored. Length, 7.50 ; wing, 4.25 ; tail, 3.20 ; tarsus, 1.20.

Hab.—Eastern North America to the Missouri ; north to fur countries.

This species is well distinguished among the American thrushes by the indistinctness of the spots beneath, and their being confined mainly to the fore part of the breast. In some specimens there is a faint tendency to a more vivid color on the rump, but this is usually like the back, which is very nearly the color of the rump in *T. pallasii*.

One specimen (6992) is quite remarkable for the shortness of the bill, which only measures half an inch above instead of .65 of an inch as in other specimens. I am, however, unable to appreciate any other difference.

List of specimens.

Catal. No.	Sex.	Locality.	When collected.	Whence obtained.	Orig. No.	Collected by—	Length.	Stretch of wings.	Wing.
989	♀	Carlisle, Pa..........	May 18, 1843	S. F. Baird.....	......	....	7.08	11.83	3.75
2145	♂	......do.............	April 16, 1845	......do.........	......	....	7.50	11.58	4.25
90	♂	......do.............	May —, 1840	......do.........	69	....	....	....	.....
6949	....	Red river, H. B.....	....	D. Gunn	......	....	....	....	.....
6992	♀	St. Louis, Mo.	May 13, 1857	Lt. Bryan	75	W. S. Wood	....	....	.....
4713	♂	Mouth Vermilion riv.	....	Lt. Warren	......	Dr. Hayden.....	7.25	11.87	4.00

TURDUS USTULATUS, Nuttall.

Turdus ustulatus, NUTTALL, Man. Orn. I, (2d ed.) 1840, 400. Columbia river ; (printed *cestulatus* by a typographical error.)

SP. CH.—Third and fourth quills longest ; second intermediate between fourth and fifth. Tail nearly even. Upper parts uniform reddish brown, with a faint olivaceous tinge. Fore part of the breast tinged with brownish yellow, becoming paler to the chin ; the remaining under parts are white. The sides of the throat and the fore part of the breast with small distinct triangular spots of well defined brown, much darker than the back ; the sides of the breast more obsoletely spotted, and the sides of the body washed with olivaceous yellow brown. The tibiae are yellowish brown. Nearly the whole of the lower mandible, except the rami, is brown. Length, 7.50 ; wing, 3.75 ; tail, 3.00 ; tarsus, 1.12.

Hab.—Coast region of Oregon and Washington Territories.

This species, in the entire uniformity in color of its upper plumage, is related to *T. swainsonii* and to *T. fuscescens.* The former, however, has the upper plumage of a perfectly uniform dull greenish olive, and the spots in the fore breast are larger and better defined. It has much resemblance to *T. fuscescens.* The upper parts, however, show less red, having this of a faint olive shade. The spots on the sides of the throat and on the breast are darker and well defined instead of being rather obsolete ; they are decidedly darker than the ground color above instead of lighter. The spots on the hinder part of the breast, too, are more distinct ; the axillaries brownish yellow instead of ash. The tibial feathers are yellowish brown instead of whitish ash, and the sides of the body more yellowish brown. The color of the tibiae is a strong feature. The bill and feet are shorter. The olivaceous spots on the hind part of the breast extend nearly to the central line, and are otherwise quite conspicuous, while in *fuscescens* there is little or nothing of this.

List of specimens.

Catal. No.	Locality.	When collected	Whence obtained.	Collected by—	Length.	Stretch of wings.
2040	Columbia river.........	....	J. K. Townsend...........	....	....	....
8171	Shoalwater bay..........	May 31, 1854	Gov. Stevens...........	Dr. Cooper	7.25	11.75
8172	......do................	......do......	......do................	......do............	8.00	12.25
8173	Fort Steilacoom, W. T....	Aug. 2, 1856	Dr Suckley...........	....	7.62	11.00

TURDUS SWAINSONII, Cab.

Olive-backed Thrush.

Turdus swainsonii, Cab. in Tschudi F. Peruana, 1844-'46, 188.—Ib. in V. Homeyer's Rhea, II, 149.—Ib. Mus. Hein. 1850, 5. (Siberia.)

? *Turdus brunneus*, Boddaert, Tab. Pl. enl.)783, according to Gray in Genera. Based on Pl. enl. 556, f. 2.

Turdus minor, Gm. Syst. Nat. I, 1788, 809. (Combined with *T. fuscescens*.)—Vieillot, Ois. Am. Sept. II, 1807, 7 ; pl. lxiii. (Mixed with *T. pallasii*)—Bon. List. 1838.—Ib. Conspectus 1850, 271.

? ? *Turdus fuscus*, Gmelin, Syst. Nat. I, 1788, 817. (Mixed with *T. mustelinus?*)

Turdus solitarius, Wilson, Am. Orn. V, pl. xliii, fig. 2, (figure only)—Sw. F. Bor. Am. II, 1831, pl. xxxvi, (figure only.)

Merula wilsonii, Sw. F. B. A. II, 1831, (not the figure.)

Turdus olivaceus, Giraud, Birds Long Island, 1843-'44, 92, (not of Linn. or Bodd.)—Brewer, Pr. Bost. Soc. N. H. July, 1844, 191.

Little Thrush, Pennant, Arctic Zool. II, 1785, 338.

Sp Ch.—Third quill longest ; second and fourth but little shorter, and much longer than the fifth ; (by .35 of an inch.) Upper parts uniform olivaceous, with a decided shade of green. The fore part of breast, the throat and chin, pale brownish yellow ; rest of lower parts white ; the sides washed with brownish olive. Sides of the throat and fore part of the breast with sub-rounded spots of well defined brown, darker than the back ; the rest of the breast (except medially) with rather less distinct spots that are more olivaceous. Tibiae yellowish brown. Broad ring round the eye. Loral region, and a general tinge on the side of the head, clear reddish buff. Length, 7.00 ; wing, 4.15 ; tail, 3.10 ; tarsus, 1.10.

Hab.—Eastern North America to the Black Hills ; south to Mexico and Peru ; north to Greenland. Accidental in Europe and Siberia.

This species is at once distinguished from the others by the perfectly uniform and pure dull olivaceous shade of its upper parts, most strongly marked and appreciable on the rump and tail. The throat and breast are, perhaps, more reddish than in any of our species, and the tinge in the marking on the side of the head is very much more decided than in any other. The spots on the breast larger than in *T. ustulatus*, and rather more numerous than in *pallasii*.

List of specimens.

Catal. No.	Sex.	Locality.	When collected.	Whence obtained.	Orig. No.	Collected by—	Length.	Stretch of wings.	Wing.	Remarks.
981	♀	Carlisle, Penn.	May 18, 1843	S. F. Baird.... ...	......	....	6.50	11.50	3.75	....
2206	♂	......do...............	May 3, 1845	......do...........	.....	....	7.63	12.08	4.08	....
980	♂	......do...............	May 18, 1843	......do...........	.....	....	7.	12.50	4.16	....
2263	♂	.... do...............	May 16, 1845	......do...........	.....	....	7.25	12.50	4.08	....
2639	♂	......do...............	May 12, 1846	......do...........	.....	....	6.83	11.91	3.91	....
388	♂	......do..	May, 1841	......do...........	.....	....	6.75	12.16		
666	♂	......do..	May 13, 1842	......do...........	.....	....	6.50	12.		
6993	♂	St. Louis, Mo	May 15, 1857	Lt. F. T. Bryan....	......	W. S. Wood.......	....	....	....	
6994	♂	......do	......do...........	......do...........	......	......do,........	....	....	....	
7523	......	Independence, Mo......	May. 26, 1857	Wm. M. Magraw...	......	Dr. Cooper	7.00	11.25	3.75	....
8302	......	......do...	....	......do..	15	......do........	7.50	12.25	3.75	Iris brown; bill black and yellow; feet brown.
4324	......	Calcasieu Pass, La......	1854.........	G. Wurdemann....	.....	....	....	....	....	*
5657	♂	Rep. Fork, 40 miles west of Fort Riley.	Jan. 25......	Lt. F. T. Bryan....	......	W. S. Wood	7.00	....	....	....
4707	♂	Opposite mouth Vermilion	May 8, 1856	Lt. Warren	......	Dr. Hayden........	6.75	11.37	4.12	....
4710	♂	Nebraska.......	....	......do...........	......	......do...........	7.25	11.87	4.25	....
8818	♂	Black Hills	Sept. 18. ...	......do...........	......	......do...........	7.12	11.12	4.12	Iris light brown.
8215	......	Fort Laramie, Nebraska..	Sept. 10, 1857	Dr. J. G. Cooper...	197	....	7.37	12.00	4.00	....
7948	......	Mexico...............	....	John Gould........	.....	....	....	..... .	....	....

TURDUS ALICIAE, Baird.

Gray-cheeked Thrush.

Sp. Ch.—Third quill longest; fourth nearly equal; second not much longer than fifth. Above nearly pure dark olive green; sides of the head ash gray; the chin, throat, and under parts, with ring round the eye, white; purest behind. Sides of throat and across the breast with arrow-shaped spots of dark plumbeous brown. Sides of body and axillaries dull grayish olivaceous. Tibiae plumbeous; legs brown. Length, nearly 8 inches; wing, 4.20; tail, 3.20; tarsus, 1.15.

Hab.—Mississippi region to the Missouri.

In this species the most striking feature next to the uniformly olivaceous back is the grayish ashen character of the head, and the entire absence of any buff tinge of the breast and sides of the neck. These parts are not of as pure white as the belly, having the faintest possible shade of yellowish red, but it is barely appreciable, nor is it any more distinct in raising the feathers. There is the faintest possible shade of reddish in the tail and its coverts above, but this is only to be observed on a close examination.

This species comes much nearest to *Turdus swainsonii*, the olive-backed thrush, agreeing with it in the dark greenish olive of the upper surface. This, however, is decidedly darker, and showing a clearer greenish than usual in the other. The absence of any buff on the throat, breast, and sides of the head, and the predominating ashy shade on the latter, with a white ring instead of reddish yellow round the eye, are strong points of distinction. The slight tinge of reddish yellow in the olivaceous of the sides, the inner surface of the wings, and the axillars of *T. swainsonii*, are here replaced by grayish olive. The under mandible is blacker, and the legs are decidedly dusky instead of yellowish. The bill appears more slender, and the whole bird is larger.

The best specimens of this species before me are from Illinois, but several from the upper Missouri belonging to Lieutenant Warren's collection agree with them, and I find no difficulty in distinguishing them at once from any other North American species by more tangible characters than are usually to be found in the small American thrushes. It is barely possible that it may constitute a variety only of *T. swainsonii*, but if so it is a very strongly marked one.

The description by Cabanis of *T. swainsonii* in Fauna Peruana expressly dwells on the buff of the sides of the head and the breast, and consequently belongs to the preceding species.

List of specimens.

Catal. No.	Sex.	Locality.	When collected.	Whence obtained.	Collected by—	Extent.	Stretch of wing.	Wing.	Remarks.
10084		W. Northfield, Ill.		Alice Kennicott					
10083		Near Cairo, Ill.	April 29, 1857	R. Kennicott					
4708	♂	Upper Missouri		Lieut. Warren	Dr. F. V. Hayden	7.25	12.25	4.25	
4709	♂	Mouth of Vermilion	May 8, 1856	do	do	7.62	12.50	4.12	
4712	♂	do	do	do	do	7.00	12.50	4.00	Eyes brown
4711	♂	Jacques river	do	do	do	7.50	12.62	4.25	Iris brown

28 b

TURDUS (PLANESTICUS[1]) MIGRATORIUS, Linn.

Robin.

Turdus migratorius, Linnaeus, Syst. Nat. I, 1766, 292.—Forster, Philos. Trans. LXII, 1772, 382.—Vieillot, Ois.
Am. Sept. II, 1807, 5; pl. lx, lxi.—Wilson, Am. Orn. I, 1808, 35; pl. ii.—Doughty, Cab.
Nat. Hist. I, 1830, 133; pl. xii.—Brehm, Handbuch Vög. Deutsch. 1831, 388, (European
spec.)—Audubon,Orn. Biog. II, 1834, 190; pl. 131.—Ib. Birds Amer. III, 1841, 14; pl. 142.—
Bonaparte, Conspectus, 1850, 272.—Newberry, Zool. Cal. and Or. Route, 81; Rep. P. R.
R. Surv. VI, 1857.
Merula migratoria, Sw. & Rich, Fauna Bor. Amer. II, 1831, 176.
Planesticus migratorius, Bonaparte. (?)
Turdus canadensis, Brisson, Orn. II, 1760, 225.

Sp. Ch.—Third and fourth quills about equal; fifth a little shorter; second longer than sixth. Tail slightly rounded. Above
olive gray; top and sides of the head black. Chin and throat white, streaked with black. Eyelids, and a spot above the eye
anteriorly, white. Under parts and inside of the wings, chestnut brown. The under tail coverts and anal region, with tibiae
white, showing the plumbeous inner portions of the feathers. Wings dark brown, the feathers all edged more or less with pale
ash. Tail still darker, the extreme feathers tipped with white. Bill yellow, dusky along the ridge and at the tip. Length,
9.75; wing, 5.43; tail, 4.75; tarsus, 1.25.

Hab.—Continent of North America to Mexico.

It is very seldom that specimens exhibit the colors exactly as described. Nearly always in
winter, and in most cases at other times, the rufous feathers are margined with whitish, sometimes quite obscuring the color. The black feathers of the head, too, have brownish edgings.
The white spot above the eye sometimes extends forwards towards the nostrils, but is usually
quite restricted. The white patches on the two eyelids are separated from each other, anteriorly
and posteriorly.

The young bird differs in having the back with transverse blackish bars, the underparts
thickly marked with black in transversely elongated blackish spots. The chin and throat are
white, with a maxillary brown streak only. The shafts of the lesser coverts are streaked with
brownish yellow, and the back feathers with white.

Sometimes, especially in winter specimens, the olive gray of the back is much glossed with
yellowish brown. The shade of rufous beneath varies from light cinnamon to dark chestnut.

I have never seen any approach in any of the many west coast specimens before me to the
Turdus rufopalliatus of Lafresnaye, said to have been collected at Monterey, California, and
suspect that this locality is erroneous, as many of those given for the collections of the "Voyage
de la Venus" certainly are. It probably was really taken at Acapulco or elsewhere, on the
southern Mexican coast.

[1] *Planesticus,* Bonaparte, Comptes Rendus, 1854, Notes Orn. Delattre, 27. According to Gray synonymous with *Cichlopsis,*
Cabanis, 1850. (?)

List of specimens.

Catal. No.	Sex and age.	Locality.	When collected.	Whence obtained.	Orig. No.	Collected by—	Length.	Stretch of wings	Wing.	Remarks.
2084	♂	Carlisle, Pa.........	April 11,1845	S. F. Baird		....	10.58	16.25	5.33	....
853	♂	.....do.............	Nov. 16,1842	......do.............		....	9.75	16.25	5.63	....
1351	♀	.....do..	April 13,1844	......do.............		....	10.25	16.50	5.16	....
1634	○	.....do............	July 15,1844	......do.............		....	9.46	16	5.33	....
7592		Washington, D. C....	....	Wm. Hutton.........		....	....	....	....	....
8383	♂	Independence, Mo...	June 20,1857	Wm. M. Magraw	87	Dr. Cooper...........	9	15.25	5.25	Iris brown, bill and feet black.
6747	....	Fort Riley, K. T.....	....	Dr. Hammond		....	....	....	....	....
5655	....	Republican Fork.....	Oct. 20,1856	Lieut. Bryan.........	386	W. S. Wood	9.50	....	....	....
5656	♀	.....do.............	Oct. 21,1856	......do.............	390	.....do.............	10.12	....	....	....
5281	....	Mo. R. Fort Pierre...	....	Lieut. Warren.......		Dr. Hayden..........	9.50	....	5.50	....
4705	♀	Blackbird Hill	May 20	......do.............		.....do.............	9.12	16	5 25	....
5282	♀	10 miles north of Yel-low Stone.	July —,1856	......do.............		.....do.............	11.75	16.75	5.75	....
5654	♀	Black Hills	Aug. 3,1866	Lieut. Bryan.........	199	W. S. Wood..........	9.50	14	....	....
8492	....	Fort Mass. N. M.....	Mar. 30,1856	Dr. Peters...........	19	....	10	15	....	....
8146	....	Fort Stellacoom......	....	Dr. Suckley	282	....	....	....	....	....
8148	....	.....do.............	....	...... do......	238	....	....	....	....	....
8150	♂	.....do., ...	....	Gov. Stevens......		Dr. Suckley.........	....	....	....	....
8153	....	Fort Vancouver......	Feb. 3,1854	......do.............		Dr. Cooper..........	10.75	16	....	....
8154	....	Bodega, Cal.........	Jan. —,1855	Lieut. Trowbridge....		T. H. Szabo.........	....	....	....	....
5522	○	Petaluma, Cal	....	E. Samuels.........	166	....	....	....	....	....
4215	....	San Francisco	Winter, 1855	R. D. Cutts		....	....	....	....	....
8144	♂	SacramentoValley,Cal	....	Lieut. Williamson...		Dr. Heermann... ..	....	....	....	....
		Fort Tejon, Cal	....	J. Xantus de Vesey..		....	....	....	....	....
8145	....	Fort Yuma, Cal.....	....	Lieut. Williamson...		Dr. Heermann......	....	....	....	....
8155	....	Mimbres to RioGrande	....	Dr. Henry...........		....	....	....	....	....
7947	....	Mexico...............	....	J. Gould............		....	....	....	....	....

TURDUS (IXOREUS[1]) NAEVIUS, Gmelin.

Varied Thrush.

Turdus naevius, GMELIN, Syst. Nat. I, 1788, 817.—VIEILLOT, Ois. Am. Sept. II, 1807, 10 ; pl. lxvi.—AUDUBON, Orn. Biog. IV, 1838, 489 : V, 1839, 284 ; pl. 369 and 433.—IB. Birds Amer. III, 1841, 22 ; pl. 143.— BONAP. Conspectus, 1850, 271.—CABOT, Jour. Bost. Soc. N. H. III, 1848, 17.   (Spec. shot near Boston.)—LAWRENCE, Annals N. Y. Lyc. V, June, 1852, 221. (Spec. shot near New York.)— NEWBERRY, Zool. Cal. and Or. Route, 81 ; Rep. P. R. R. Surv. VI, IV, 1857.

Orpheus naevius, RICH, List, 1837.

Ixoreus naevius, BONAP. Notes Orn. Delattre, in Comptes Rendus, XXVIII, 1854, 269.

Orpheus meruloides, RICH. Fauna Bor. Amer. II. 1831, 187 ; pl. xxxviii.

SP. CH.—Fourth quill longest ; third and fifth a little shorter ; second much longer than sixth. Tail nearly even ; the lateral feather shorter. Above, rather dark bluish slate ; under parts generally, a patch on the upper eyelids continuous with a stripe behind it along the side of the head and neck, the lower eyelids, two bands across the wing coverts and the edges of the quills, in part, rufous orange brown ; middle of belly white. Sides of the head and neck continuous with a broad pectoral transverse band, black. Most of tail feathers with a terminal patch of brownish white. Bill black. Feet yellow. Female more olivaceous above ; the white of the abdomen more extended ; the brown beneath paler ; the pectoral band obsolete. Length, 9.75 inches ; wing, 5.00 ; tail, 3.90 ; tarsus, 1.25.

Hab.—Pacific coast North America. Accidental on Long Island and near Boston.

This strongly marked species in general appearance bears a close resemblance to the American robin, but is readily distinguished by its coloration. In addition to the characters already given, it may be stated that the axillars are plumbeous, with a white patch at the base ; the under wing coverts plumbeous, but broadly tipped with white. There is also an obscure whitish patch

[1] *Ixoreus*, BONAPARTE, Notes Orn. Delattre, 1854, 26. (Comptes Rendus, XXVIII, 1854.)

at the base of the inner webs of all the quills, except the exterior, corresponding and opposite to orange brown patches on the outer webs. The sides are tinged with plumbeous ; many of the feathers margined with this color.

List of specimens.

Catal. No.	Sex.	Locality.	When collected.	Whence obtained.	Orig'l No.	Collected by—	Length.	Stretch of wings.	Remarks.
5998	....	Port Townsend, W. T....	Jan. 8, 1857	Dr. Geo. Suckley ..	597				
5997	....	........do	......do	......do............	596				
5996	....	........do	......do.	......do............	598				
5941	♀	........do	March, 1855	Gov. Stevens	.....	Dr. Cooper			
5940	♂	........do	......do......	......do......	......	......do............	9.00	14.75	Bill black.............
5942		........do	......do......	......do.	......	......do............	9.25	15.25	
8125	....	Fort Vancouver	Jan. 30, 1854	......do............	20	......do............	9.00	12.75	Legs yellow ....
8126	....	........do	Jan. 12, 1854	......do............	14	......do............	9.50	15.00	Iris brown.............
8122	♂	........do	....	......do............	14	......do............	9.50	15.00	Legs yellow. ....
1844	♂	Columbia river...........	Jan. 18, 1836	S. F. Baird........	......	J. K. Townsend....			
1883	♀	.... do.	....	......do............	......	......do............			
4488	... ...	Cascade mountains, W. T.	....	Lieut. Williamson..	......	Dr. Newberry.....			
3916	♂	California	....	Dr. Heermann					
8124	....	Calaveras, Cala..........	....	Lieut. Williamson..	......	Dr. Heermann			
.....	....	Fort Tejon..do...	....	J. Xantus de Vesey.	......	....			

SAXICOLA, Bechstein.

Saxicola, BECHSTEIN, Gemeinnützige Naturg. 1802. (Agassiz.) (Type *S. oenanthe.*)

CH.—Commissure slightly curved to the well notched tip. Culmen concave for the basal half, then gently decurving. Gonys straight. Bill slender, attenuated ; more than half the length of head. Tail short, broad, even. Legs considerably longer than the head ; when outstretched reaching nearly to the tip of tail. Third quill longest ; second but little shorter. Claws long, slightly curved ; hind toe rather elongated.

The genus *Saxicola*, represented in North America by stragglers of a single European species, is usually placed far apart from *Turdus* in ornithological systems, and generally in close association with *Sialia* in a sub-family *Saxicolinae*. As, however, of the numerous other allied genera of *Saxicolinae* in the old world, these two are the only ones found in the new, it will create no confusion to bring them with *Turdus* into one sub-family, *Turdinae*, in view of their really close relationships.

SAXICOLA OENANTHE, Bechst.

Stone Chat.

Motacilla oenanthe, LINN. Syst. Nat. I, 1766.
" *Saxicola oenanthe*, BECHST. Gemein. Naturg. 1802," and of European writers, as of BONAP. Consp. 1850, 303.
? *Saxicola oenanthoides*, VIGORS, Zool. Blossom, 1839, 19, (N. W. coast.)—CASSIN, Illust. I, VII, 1854, 208 ; pl. xxxiv. (Nova Scotia.)

SP. CH.—(Description from European specimen.) Forehead, line over the eye, and under parts generally, white ; the latter tinged with pale yellowish brown, especially on the breast and throat. A stripe from the bill through, below, and behind the eye, with the wings, upper tail coverts, bill and feet black. Tail white, with an abrupt band of black (about .60 of an inch long) at the end, this color extending further up on the middle feather. Rest of upper parts ash gray ; quills and greater coverts slightly edged with whitish. Length, 6.00 ; wing, 3.45 ; tail, 2.50 ; tarsus, 1.05.

Hab.—Greenland. Accidental in northern part of North America. Common in Europe.

The preceding description is taken from a South European skin of this species, which, in all probability, is the same with that considered as peculiar to North America under the name of *S. oenanthoides*. The differences are, as far as indicated, merely those of size, the skin described by Mr. Cassin being 6.50 inches long; the wing 4.12; the tail 3.00; the tarsus 1.25. This is, however, by no means an unusual discrepancy in birds of remote localities, and until better characters can be assigned there would seem little propriety in making two species.

The *Saxicola oenanthe* of Europe is recognized as a regular inhabitant of Greenland, and those found on the main land of America in all probability reach it from that country.

List of specimens.

Locality.	Whence obtained.	Len th	Wing.	Tail.	Tarsus.	Middle toe.	Its claw alone.	Bill above.	Along gape.
Europe	J. Cassin	6.00	3.65	2.50	1.05	0.75	0.20	0.60	0.80

SIALIA, Swanson.

Sialia, SWAINSON, Zool. Jour. III, Sept. 1827, 173. (*S. wilsonii.*)

CH.—Bill short, stout, broader than high at the base, then compressed; slightly notched at tip. Rictus with short bristles. Tarsi not longer than the middle toe. Claws considerably curved. Wings much longer than the tail; the first primary spurious; not one-fourth the longest. Tail moderate; slightly forked.

The species of this genus are all well marked, and adult males are easily distinguishable. In all, blue forms a prominent feature.

Above uniform dark blue; beneath brownish red. Abdomen and crissum white....*sialis*.
General color dark blue above and below; crissum whitish. A broad patch on the scapular region (on either side) and on the sides of the breast, brownish red...*mexicana*.
Everywhere greenish blue, becoming whitish on the abdomen and crissum ....*arctica*.

Comparative measurements of species.

Catal. No.	Species.	Locality.	Sex.	Length.	Stretch of wings.	Wing	Tail.	Tarsus.	Middle toe.	Its claw alone.	Bill above.	Along gape.	Specimen measured.
1289	Sialia sialis	Carlisle, Penn.	♂	6.16		3.96	2.88	0.80	0.80	0.22	0.44	0.70	Dry .....
do.	...do	...do		6.75	12.50	4.08							Fresh....
1283	...do	...do	♀	6.22		3.78	2.72	0.80	0.82	0.21	0.50	0.76	Dry......
do.	...do	...do		6.50	12.00	3.75							Fresh ...
3907	Sialia mexicana	California	♂	6.44		4.22	2.80	0.80	0.76	0.22	0.46	0.70	Dry......
3908	...do	...do	♀	6.40		3.40	2.66	0.76	0.78	0.26	0.40	0.70	Dry......
3706	Sialia macroptera, (Baird) ..	Salt Lake City...		7.16		4.78	3.18	0.86	0.82	0.18	0.50	0.80	Dry......
7604	Sialia arctica	Mimbres to Rio Grande.	♂	6.28		4.46	3.04	0.87	0.76	0.22	0.53	0.76	Dry......
8890	...do	Black Hills	♀	6.80		4.26	3.50	0.78	0.78	0.22	0.50	0.74	Dry*.....
do.	...do	...do		7.00	13.25	4.50							Fresh ...

* Legs broken; poor specimen.

SIALIA SIALIS, Baird.

Blue Bird; Red-breasted Blue Bird.

Motacilla sialis, LINNAEUS, Syst. Nat. ed. X, I, 1758, 187.—GMELIN, Syst. Nat. I, 1788, 989.

Sylvia sialis, LATHAM, Index Orn. II, 1790, 522.—VIEILLOT, Ois. Am. Sept. II, 1807, 40 ; pl. ci, cii, ciii, ($\male \female$ O.)—
            WILSON, Am. Orn. I, 1808, 56 ; pl. iii.—DOUGHTY, Cab. N. H. I, 1830, 135 ; pl.
            xii.—AUDUBON, Orn. Biog. II, 1834, 84 : V, 1839, 452 ; pl. 113.

Saxicola sialis, BONAP. Synopsis, 1828.

Ampelis sialis, NUTTALL, Man. I, 1832, 444.

Rubecula carolinensis caerulea, BRISSON, Orn. III, 1760, 423.   (Speaks of blue spots on throat.)—BUFFON, Ois. VI,
            107 ; pl. enl. 396, f. 1, 2.

Sialia wilsonii, SWAINSON, Zool. Jour. III, 1827, 173.—BONAPARTE, List, 1838.—AUDUBON, Synopsis, 1839, 84.—IB.
            Birds Amer. II, 1841, 171 ; pl. 134.

Erythraca (Sialia) wilsonii, SW. & RICH. F. Bor. Am. II, 1831, 210.

SP. CH.—Entire upper parts, including wings and tail, continuous and uniform azure blue ; the cheeks of a duller tint of the same. Beneath reddish brown ; the abdomen, anal region, and under tail coverts white. Bill and feet black. Shafts of the quills and tail feathers black. Female with the blue lighter, and tinged with brown on the head and back. Length, 6.75 ; wing, 4.00 ; tail, 2.90.

Hab.—Eastern North America to a little west of Missouri river   Fort Laramie.

The female is quite similar to the male, only duller above ; the blue tinged with brown, although the wings, tail, and rump are generally light blue. The young male of the year has the head and interscapular region, with the lesser coverts dull brown, streaked (except the head) with white. The throat and fore breast are reddish brown, the feathers streaked with white ; the remaining colors are much as in the adult male, except that the tertials are edged with brown.

There is much difference in the size and shape of the bill in specimens from the same locality.

List of specimens.

Catal. No.	Sex and age.	Locality.	When collected.	Whence obtained.	Orig'l No.	Collected by—	Length.	Extent.	Wing.	Remarks.
739	♂ O	Carlisle, Pa............	Sept. 21,1842	S. F. Baird		....	6.25	12.16	3.91	....
1285	♂	.....do...........	Mar. 9,1844	..... do.......		....	6.83	12.	3.83	....
1309	♂	.....do...........	Mar. 25,1844	......do........	..	....	6.66	12.50	4.08	....
1289	♂	.....do...........	Mar. 11,1844	......do........		....	6.75	12.50	4.08	....
1283	♀	.....do...........	Mar. 7,1844	......do........		....	6.50	12.	3.75	....
7409	♂	Rockport, Ohio...........	Ap il 19,1851	Dr. Kirtland		....	....	....	.....	....
7408	♀	.....do...........	April 1,1851	......do........		....	....	....	.....	....
3819	....	Eutaw, Ala...........	Jan. —,1853	A. Winchell	10	....	....	....	.....	....
3865	....	Prairie Mer Rouge, La....	....	Jas. Fairie		....	....	....	.....	....
4920	....	Nassau county, Fla......	....	G. Wurdemann....		....	....	....	.....	....
		Racine, Wis...........	....	R. Kennicott......		....	....	....	.....	....
7616	....	Ft. Leavenworth.........	Jan. 20,1855	Lt. Couch........		....	....	....	.....	....
8391	♂	Independence, Mo.......	Jan. 22,1857	W. M. Magraw....	98	Dr. Cooper	6.75	12.25	4.25	....
5636	♂	East of Fort Riley, K. T..	June 17,1856	Lt. F. T. Bryan....	22	W. S. Wood....	....	....	.....	....
6560		Fort Riley, K. T	....	Dr.W.A.Hammond		....	....	....	.....	....
4723	♂	Bald island, Neb........	April 24,1856	Lt. Warren..........		Dr. Hayden......	6.62	11.50	3.75	....
5288	♂	Fort Lookout, Neb.......	May 31,1856	. ....do........		........do......	6.75	11.50	4.	....
5290	♂	.... do...........		.....do........		........do......	6.12	11.50	4.12	....
5289	....	Near mouth of Powder riv	Aug. 1,1856	.....do........		........do..⚬....	6.75	11.87	4.25	....
4722	♂	Nebraska Territory......	May 16,1856	......do........		........do......	6.37	11.75	4.	....
4658	♂	White river, Neb.........	May 11,1855	Col. Vaughan......		........do......	7.50	12.50	4.50	....
8884	♂	5 miles above mo. of Platte.	....	Lt. Warren........		........do......	6.75	11.	3.75	Iris brown......
8880	♂	On Loup Fork, Platte.....	July 8,1855	.....do		........do......	6.	11.	4.	....
8882	♂	Near Loup Fork, Platte...	July 3,1855	......do		........do......	6.12	12.12	4.25	....
7615	....	Texas............	....	Capt. Pope		....	....	....	.....	....

SIALIA MEXICANA, Swainson.

Western Blue Bird.

Sialia mexicana, Sw. F. Bor. Am. II, 1831, 202.
Sialia occidentalis, TOWNSEND, Jour. Ac. Nat. Sc. VII, II, 1837, 188.—IB. Narrative, 1839, 343.—AUD. Synopsis, 1839.—IB. Birds America, II, 1841,.176; pl. 135.—NUTTALL, Man. I, (2d ed.,) 1840, 513.— NEWBERRY, Zool. Cal. & Or. Route, 80; Rep. P. R. R. VI, IV, 1857.
Sylvia occidentalis, AUDUBON, Orn. Biog. V, 1839, 41; pl 393.
Sialia caeruleo-collis, VIGORS, Zool. Beechey's Voyage, 1839, 18; pl. iii.

SP. CH.—Bill slender; head and neck all round, and upper parts generally bright azure blue. Interscapular regions, sides and fore part of the breast, and sides of the belly, dark reddish brown. Rest of under parts (with tail coverts) pale bluish, tinged with gray about the anal region. Female duller above; the back brownish; the blue of the throat replaced by ashy brown, with a shade of blue. Length, 6.50; wing, 4.25; tail, 2.90.

Hab.—Pacific coast North America, and along valley of Gila to upper Rio Grande and south.

In perfectly mature males the blue of the throat is as bright as that on the crown; otherwise it is duller. There is generally a blackish shade on the cheeks. The blue on the belly is always paler. The reddish brown on the back and breast are in the form of lateral patches, meeting more or less narrowly on the central line. Sometimes on the middle of the back it does not meet at all, and at others it is quite broadly continuous; the latter is most frequently seen in Rocky mountains specimens. The quills and tail feathers are light blue; the shafts black. The exposed tips of the folded quills, however, are black. Bill and feet are black.

The female is much duller in colors; the blue most conspicuous on the rump, tail, primaries, and wing coverts. The blue of the head is very dull, and there is a broad scapular and interscapular space strongly overlaid with brownish. The throat and sides of the head are of much this same color, shading very insensibly into the reddish brown of the breast.

The young bird has the tail and wings as in the adult. The head, back, and breast are dull brown; each feather, except on the crown, streaked with white.

The shade of blue in this species is much as in the common eastern species—only brighter and more intense. The bill is more slender, the wings longer; the combination of the blue of the under parts with the brown on the back readily distinguishes it. The females of the two species are very similar. They may be distinguished by the brown tinge on the back and the blue on the belly and under tail coverts, with the bluish shade on the throat, as well as by the slenderer and straighter bill of the western species. The spotted young can only be distinguished by the slender bill and bluish belly and under tail coverts.

Specimens from California occasionally have but little brown on the back, but it is almost always distinctly visible.

List of specimens.

Catal. No.	Sex.	Locality.	When collected.	Whence obtained.	Orig'l No.	Collected by—	Length.	Stretch of wings.	Wing.	Remarks.
7618	♂	Fort Steilacoom, W. T...	April 17, 1856	Dr. Suckley		....	6.75	13.0		
7621	♂	.....do...............		Gov. Stevens......	114	Dr. Suckley........	7.75	12.50	4.00	....
7622	♂	.....do...............	....	.....do..·.........	77	.....do....	....	......	4.00	
7625	......	.....do...............	....	Dr. Suckley........	274	....	6.75	12.00		
7636	......	.....do...............			273	....	7.50	12.	....	
7634	......	Fort Vancouver, W. T..	Dec., 1853.	Gov. Stevens......	......	Dr. Cooper	....	....	....	
1930	♂	Columbia river, O. T....	....	S. F. Baird..........	......	J. K. Townsend....	....	....	....	....
2949	♀	.....do...............	....	.....do............		.....do........	....	....	....	
5512	♂	Petaluma, Cal..	May 9, 1856	E. Samuels........	772	....	....	....	....	
5513	♀	.....do...............	.....do.......	.....do......	170	....	....	....	....	
3907	♂	California	....	Dr. Heermann....		....	....	....	....	·.......
3908	♀	.....do...............		.....do........		....	....	....	....	
5944	......	Santa Clara, Cal...... ..	Nov., 1855....	Dr. Cooper.......		....	6.75	12.00	....	Iris brown.....
4220	......	San Francisco..........	Winter of '55 & '6	R. D. Cutts..........	......	....	....	....	....	
7632	♀	Sacramento Valley......	....	Lt. R. S. Williamson		Dr. Heermann	....	....	....	....
7631	♂	Tejon valley, Cal......	....	.....do........	·	.....do.......	....	....	....	
4575	......	Gila river, New Mexico..	....	Major Emory......	24	Arthur Schott.....	....	....	....	
7633	......	.....do...............		.....do........	24	.....do........	....	....	....	
5051	......	Fort Fillmore, N. Mexico.	Oct. 21, 1855	Captain Pope......	151	....	7.00	12.50	4.50	Bill and eye black; gums yellowish.
7623	.....	Mimbres to Rio Grande ..	....	Dr. Henry		....	....	....	....	
5050	......	Organ Mts., New Mexico.	Mar. 9, 1856	Captain Pope......	178	....	7.00	13.00	4.25	Bill, feet, and eyes black; gums bluish.
7624	......	Near 32° latitude.........	....	.....do........		....	....	....	....	....
7637	......	Camp 110, New Mexico..	Jan. 31, 1854	Lieut. Whipple	60	Kenn & Möll	....	....	4.00	Eyes black.....
7638	......	.....do...............	.....do........			....	....	....	....	
7635	......	Fort Conrad, New Mexico.	Oct., 1853......	Lieut. Whipple	52	Dr. Kennerly	....	....	.75	....
4020	♀	Saltillo, Mexico..........	May, 1853	Lieut. Couch......	......	....	6.75	11.50	4.50	Bill & ft. black.

SIALIA ARCTICA, Swainson.

Rocky Mountain Blue Bird.

Erythraca (Sialia) arctica, SWAINSON, F. Bor. Amer. II, 1831, 209 ; pl. xxxix.
Erythraca arctica, RICH. List, 1837.
Sialia arctica, NUTTALL, Man. II, 1832, 573 ; I, 2d ed., 1840, 514.—BONAP. List, 1838.—AUD. Synopsis, 1839, 84.—
       IB. Birds Amer. II, 1841, 178 ; pl. 136.—McCALL, Pr. A. N. Sc. V, June, 1851, 215.
Sylvia arctica, AUDUBON, Orn. Biog. V, 1839, 38 ; pl. 373.
Sialia macroptera, BAIRD, Stansbury Report Exp. Salt Lake, 1852, 314.

SP. CH.—Azure blue above and below, brightest above ; the belly and under tail coverts white ; the latter tinged with blue at the ends. Female showing blue only on the rump, wings, and tail ; a white ring round the eye ; the lores and sometimes a narrow front whitish ; elsewhere replaced by brown. Length, 6.25 ; wing, 4.36 ; tail, 3.00. (1875.)

Hab.—High dry central plains ; Upper Missouri to Rocky mountains range and south to Mexico. Rare on the coast of California.

In this species there is none of the reddish brown of the two other American blue birds, the color throughout being blue, except as mentioned. The shade of blue is much lighter, with more green in it, or smalts-color, especially on the crown, instead of the purplish blue of the others. The shade on the under parts is paler than above ; it extends entirely along the sides and to the abdomen.

The female has the abdomen and under coverts like the male ; the remaining under parts, with the head, neck and back, are light brown, although a bluish shade is appreciable on separating the feathers. The quills are much edged with paler. The young birds have this brown streaked with white, except on the crown ; indeed, the under parts may be described sometimes as whitish, with narrow brownish edgings to the feathers on the under parts anteriorly.

The bill of this species is much stouter than in *mexicana*, as well as longer than in *sialis*. The wings also are longer in proportion, reaching nearly to the end of the tail, which is more deeply forked than in either of the others. The male birds of the three species are readily distinguishable ; the females are all much alike. The greener blue, the absence of rufous brown on either back or belly, and the longer wings, will serve to separate the latter.

In the zoology of Stansbury's report I characterize a species under the name of *Sialia macroptera* on the ground of the unusually long wings, the weak claws, and the different shade of blue. This specimen (3706, Salt Lake, March 21, 1851) still remains quite unique in these respects. I am, however, now inclined to consider it as only a larger race, because more northern, of the *S. arctica*, strengthening the general proposition of the greater size of resident winter or summer specimens in northern than southern localities. The weak claws may have been an individual peculiarity. All the specimens before me, nearly thirty in number, agree, with scarcely an exception, in the smaller size and shorter wings.

List of specimens.

Catal. No.	Sex and age.	Locality.	When collected.	Whence obtained.	Orig'l No.	Collected by—	Length.	Stretch of wings.	Wing.	Remarks.
1875	♂	Fort Union, Neb.......	July 1, 1843	S. F. Baird..........	......	J. J. Audubon......	......	......	4.75	....
8885	♀	Black Hills	Sept. 19,—	Lt. G. K. Warren ..	....	Dr. Hayden........	7.00	13.75	4.75	Iris dark brown..
8888	♀	......do............	Sept. 13,—	......do............	......	......do............	7.50	13.50	4.25	....
8883	....	......do............	Sept. 21,—	......do	......	......do............	7.00	13.50	4.50	....
	♂	Camp 4................	Sept. 7,—	......do............	......	......do	7.25	13.50	4.50	Iris dark brown..
8890	♀	Black Hills	Sept. 18,—	......do............	......	......do............	7.00	13.25	4.50	......do...
8884	♂	......do...............	......do	......do............	......	......do............	7.00	13.50	4.50	......do...... ....
8889	....	......do..........	Sept. 22,—	......do............	... .	......do............	7.00	13.25	4.50	......do. ....
8886	♂	......do	Sept. 20,—	......do............	......	......do............	7.50	13.50	4.50	....
8887	....	......do	Sept. 14,—	......do............	......	...... do............	6.50	13.25	4.50	....
5640	♂	......do .	Aug. 3,1856	Lieut. F. T. Bryan..	196	W. S. Wood	....	....	......	....
5636	♂ ○	Medicine Bow creek,Neb	Aug. 9,1856	......do............	232	......do............	....	....	......	....
6990	....	Cheyenne pass........ .	July 20,1857	......do............	298	......do............	....	....	......	....
5639	♀	Main Fork,Laramie R..	Aug. 6,1856	......do............	216	......do............	....	....	......	....
5638	♂	Medicine Bow creek....	Aug. 9,1856	......do............	235	......do............	....	....	......	....
6691	♀	Medicine Bow mountains	July 27,1857	......do............	335	......do............	....	....	......	....
7080	♀	Cooper's creek	July 26,1857	......do............	76	Dr. Hammond......	....	....	......	....
3706	♂	Salt Lake City.........	Mar. 21,1851	Capt. Stansbury....	......	....	....	....	......	....
7606	....	Cochetope pass........	....	Lieut. Beckwith....	20	....	....	....	......	. ...
8494	♂	Fort Mass. N. M.......	Mar. 30,1856	Dr. Peters..........	20	....	7.25	10.00	....	Eyes dark........
7609	....	Near lat. 32° W. Texas.	....	Capt. Pope	......	....	....	....	......	....
7612	....	Mimbres to Rio Grande.	....	Dr. Henry	......	....	....	....	......	....
7604	♂	Fort Thorn	....	......do............	......	....	....	....	......	....
7605	♀	......do.....	....	......do....	......	....	....	....	......	....
7607	....	75 miles west of Albuquerque.	Nov. —,1853	Lieut. Whipple	15	Kenn. and Möll....	....	....	......	Eyes black ......
7608	....	Espia, Mex....	Mar. —,1853	Maj. Emory... ...	......	Dr. Kennerly	....	....	......	....
......	....	San Diego, Cal........	....	Lieut. Trowbridge..	......	A. Cassidy.........	....	....	......	....

Sub-Family REGULINAE.

REGULUS.[1] Cuvier.

Regulus, Cuvier, Leçons d'Anat. Comp. 1799—1800, (Agassiz.)   (Type *Motacilla regulus,* Linn., *Regulus cristatus,* Koch.)

Ch.—Bill slender, much shorter than the head, depressed at base, but becoming rapidly compressed ; moderately notched at tip. Culmen straight to near the tip, then gently curved. Commissure straight ; gonys convex. Rictus well provided with bristles ; nostril covered by a single bristly feather directed forwards. Tarsi elongated, exceeding considerably the middle toe, and without scutellae. Lateral toes about equal ; hind toe with the claw longer than the middle one, and about half the toe. Claws all much curved. First primary about one-third as long as the longest ; second equal to fifth or six. Tail shorter than the wings, moderately forked, the feathers acuminate. Colors olive green above, whitish beneath. Size very small.

I am unable to appreciate any such difference between the common North American *Reguli* as to warrant Cabanis in establishing the genus *Phyllobasileus* for the *calendula.* The bristly feather over the nostril is perhaps less compact and close, but it exists in a rudimentary condition.

Crown in adult plain olivaceous, with a concealed patch of crimson...............*calendula*.
Forehead and line over the eye white, bordered inside by black, and within this again is yellow, embracing a central patch in the crown of orange.........................*satrapa*.
Forehead and line through the eye black, bordered inside by whitish, and within this again by black, embracing an orange patch in the centre of the crown...........*cuvieri*.

Comparative measurements of species.

Catal. No.	Species.	Locality.	Sex and age.	Length	Stretch of wings.	Wing.	Tail.	Tarsus.	Middle toe.	Its claw alone.	Bill above.	Along gape.	Specimen measured.
1343	Regulus calendula......	Carlisle, Pa........	♂	4.00	......	2.30	1.90	0.70	0.50	0.15	0.32	0.44	Dry.........
do.	......do............	......do...........		4.50	7.16	2.33							Fresh.......
2573	......do............	......do...........	○ 2 yrs.	3.70	......	2.22	1.84	0.70	0.50	0.14	0.32	0.42	Dry ....
do.	......do............	......do...........		4.25	6.83	2.33							Fresh.......
7180	Regulus satrapa........	Fort Steilacoom....	♀	3.64	......	2.04	1.52	0.66	0.46	0.14	0.33	0.45	Dry.........
1758	. . ....do............	Carlisle, Pa........	♀	3.76	......	2.14	1.90	0.68	0.50	0.15	0.32	0.44	Dry.........
do.	......do............	......do...........		4.16	6.50	2.25							Fresh ......
867	......do............	......do...........	♂	3.76	......	2.32	1.92	0.70	0.54	0.14	0.36	0.50	Dry.........
do.	......do............	......do...........	♂	3.91	7	2.37							Fresh.......

REGULUS CALENDULA, Licht.

Ruby-crowned Wren.

Motacilla calendula, Linn. Syst. Nat. I, 1766, 337.—Forster, Phil. Trans. LXII, 1772, 383.—Gmelin, Syst. Nat. I, 1788, 994.
Sylvia calendula, Latham, Ind. Orn. II, 1790, 549.—Wilson, Am. Orn. I, 1808, 83 ; pl. v, f. 3.—Doughty, Cab. N. H. II, 1832, 61 ; pl. vi.
Regulus calendula, Licht. Verzeich. 1823, Nos. 408–'9.—Nuttall, Man. I, 1832, 415.—Audubon, Orn. Biog. II, 1834, 546 ; pl. 195.—Ib. Birds Amer. II, 1841, 168 ; pl. 133.
Reguloides calendula, Bonap. Conspectus, 1850, 292.
Phyllobasileus calendula, Cabanis, Mus. Hein. 1850–'1, 33.
Regulus rubineus, Vieillot, Ois. Am. Sept. II, 1807, 49 ; pl. civ, cv.
? *Parus griseus,* Gmelin, Latham.
Calendula pennsylvanica, Brisson, III, 1760, 584.

[1] Cabanis makes a genus *Phyllobasileus* for our *R. calendula,* replacing by it *Reguloides* of Blyth.—(Museum Heineanum, 1850, 33.)

Sp. Ch.—Above dark greenish olive, passing into bright olive green on the rump and outer edges of the wings and tail. Crown with a large concealed patch of scarlet feathers, which are white at the base. The under parts are grayish white tinged with pale olive yellow, especially behind. A ring round the eye, two bands on the wing coverts, and the exterior of the inner tertials white. Young without the red on the crown. Length, 4.50 ; wing, 2.33 ; tail, 1.85.

Hab.—United States from Atlantic to Pacific.

The female differs very little in color. It is quite probable that the species does not attain the red patch in the crown until the second year, as the spring migrations of the species always embrace a considerable number with the head perfectly plain.

The autumnal plumage differs from the vernal in a lighter olive tinge to the feathers of the back, while the under parts are of a pale brownish yellow, brightest on the belly.

There is a concealed yellowish bar across the quills immediately beneath the tips of the greater coverts, succeeded by an exposed bar of blackish, more or less conspicuous in different specimens. There is also some concealed white on the feathers of the rump.

I am unable to perceive any tangible difference between eastern and western specimens.

List of specimens.

Catal. No	Sex and age.	Locality.	When collected.	Whence obtained.	Orig. No.	Collected by—	Length.	Stretch of wings.	Wing.	Remarks.
134♂	♂	Carlisle, Pa............	April 10,1844	S. F. Baird........			4.50	7.25	2.33	....
784	♂	.. do......	Oct. 10,1842	......do		....	4.25	7.33	2.25	....
2115		.....do.......	April 15,1845	......do			4.63	6.91	2.25	....
959	♀	......do............	May 3,1843	......do			4.25	6.83	2.25	....
2573	○	......do..	May 5,1846	......do			4.25	6.83	2.33	....
4685	....	Mouth of Big Sioux.......	April 24,1856	Lt. Warren		Dr. Hayden......	4.00	6.62	2.25	Eyes black.....
4683	....	....do............	May 4,1856	......do		......do`.......	4.25	7.37	2.37	....do..... ....
4684	....	......do.......	....do...	......do	...	......do	4.37	6.75	2.25	....do..... ....
4686	♀	Mouth of Vermilion.......	May 5,1856	......do		......do	3.75	6.50	2.25	....
7166	....	Ft. Steilacoom ,.........	Mar. 25,1856	Dr. Suckley......			4.25	6.50	....	
7168	....	......do........	April 8,1856	......do	279	....	4.50	6.75	....	
7169	....	......do.......	April 18,1856	......do	315	....	4.50	7.50	....	
7170	....	......do..	....do......	......do	314	....	4.37	7.25	....	
7171	♂	......do.......	....do......	......do	79	....			....	
7173	♂	......do.......	May 3,1856	......do	361	....	4.37	5.50	....	
7165	....	Ft. Vancouver, W. T... ...	Dec. 29,1853	Gov. I. I. Stevens...	.....	Dr. Cooper......			....	
4391	♀	Ft. Dalles, Oregon.........	May 4,1855	Dr. Suckley......	164	....	....	....	'.. ...	
4389	....	......do.......	May 6,1855	......do	166	....	4.50	7.00	....	
5921	....	Santa Clara.......	....	Dr. Cooper......	.. ..	....	....	....	....	
	....	Fort Tejon.......	....	J. Xantus de Vesey.	.....	....	....	....	....	
4564	....	San Diego, Cal.......	....	....	.....	....	....	....	....	
7172	....	Espia, Mex ,.........	Mar. —, 1855	Maj. Emory........	63	Dr. Kennerly.....	4.00	6.50	2.25	....
7174	....	Boca Grande, Mex....	...do.......	......do	43	......do.......	....	....	....	
7177	....	Camp 105, N. M.......	Jan. 24,1854	Lt. Whipple........	55	Kennerly & Müllhausen........	....	....	....	
7167	....	Camp 116, N. M............	Feb. 8,1854	......do	75	......do	....	....	....	Eyes black.....

REGULUS SATRAPA, Licht.

Golden-crested Wren.

Regulus satrapa, Lichtenstein, Verzeich. Doubl. 1823, No. 410. (Quotes *Parus satrapa*, Illiger, probably a museum name.)—Bonap. List, 1838.—Ib. Conspectus, 1850, 291.—Aud. Synopsis, 1839, 82.—Ib. Birds Amer. II, 1841, 165 ; pl. 132.

Sylvia regulus, Wilson, Am. Orn. I, 1808, 126 ; pl. viii, f. 2. (Not of Latham.)

Regulus cristatus, Vieillot, Ois. Am. Sept. II, 1807, 50 ; pl. cvi. (Not of Ray.) Bonap. Obs. Wilson, 1825.— Ib. Synopsis, 1828, 91.

Regulus tricolor, Nuttall, Man. I, 1832, 420.—Aud. Orn. Biog. II, 1834, 476 ; pl. 183.

Sp. Ch.—Above olive green, brightest on the outer edges of the wing ; tail feathers tinged with brownish gray towards the head. Forehead, a line over the eye and a space beneath it, white. Exterior of the crown before and laterally black, embracing a central patch of orange red, encircled by gamboge yellow. A dusky space around the eye. Wing coverts with two yellowish white bands, the posterior covering a similar band on the quills, succeeded by a broad dusky one. Under parts dull whitish. Length under 4 inches ; wing, 2.25 ; tail, 1.80.

Hab.—Northern parts of United States from Atlantic to Pacific ; on west coast only noticed on Puget's Sound.

The black of the head immediately succeeds the white frontal band as one of about the same width, passing behind on each side. Generally the white line over the eye is separated from the white forehead by a dusky lore. There is also a dusky space beneath the whitish under the eye. The yellow of the crown generally overlies and conceals the orange. The orange is wanting in the female. The young birds always appear to have at least the yellow and black of the crown.

In the specimens before me I am unable to perceive any difference between eastern and western specimens. One from Puget's Sound (9819) is smaller, (wing, 2.20,) the crown redder, and the superciliary stripe more white.

According to Audubon, this species differs from the European *R. cristatus* in being considerably longer, with the bill decidedly shorter ; the flame-colored patch on the head more extended ;[1] with *R. calendula* it agrees very well in markings, except in those of the head, which are very different. It is, however, of decidedly smaller size.

List of specimens.

Catal. No.	Sex.	Locality.	When collected.	Whence obtained.	Orig'l No.	Length.	Stretch of wings	Wing.
828	♂	Carlisle, Pa	Oct. 22, 1842	S. F. Baird		3.91	6.91	2.25
1736	♂	do	Oct. 29, 1844	do		4.16	7.00	2.33
867	♂	do	Nov. 22, 1842	do		3.91	7.00	2.33
758	♀	do	Jan. —, 1845	do		4.16	6.50	2.25
7564		Washington city		W. Hutton				
7179		Fort Steilacoom, W. T.	March 24, 1856	Dr Suckley	294			
7186	♀	do	March 3, 1856	do	367	4.25	6.25	
7184		do		do	289	4.50	6.75	

REGULUS CUVIERI, Audubon.

Cuvier's Golden Crest.

Regulus cuvieri, Audubon, Orn. Biog. I, 1832, 288 ; pl. 55.—Ib. Syn. 1839, 82.—Ib. Birds Amer. II, 1841, 163 ; pl. 131.—Nuttall, Man. I, 1832, 416.

Sp. Ch.—Size and general appearance probably that of *R. satrapa*. A black band on the forehead passing back, through and behind the eye, separated by a grayish band from another black band on the crown, which embraces in the centre of the crown an orange patch. Length, 4¼ inches ; extent of wings, 6.

I have introduced the diagnosis of this species from Audubon for the sake of calling attention to it and of completing the account of the genus. It is only known by the figure and

[1] Since writing the above, I have received a specimen of the European species, and a comparison shows that the wings are rather longer, but the bill considerably shorter. The black border to the bright colors of the top of the head, both laterally and in front, is much more distinct ; indeed it is wanting anteriorly almost entirely in the European bird. There is also less yellow on the back and rump.

description of Audubon, being one of several other species not found in the United States by any one else. It differs mainly from *R. satrapa* in having two black bands (not one) on the crown anteriorly, separated by a whitish one; the extreme forehead being black instead of white, as in *satrapa*. The specimen was killed in June, 1812, on the banks of the Schuylkill river, in Pennsylvania.

Sub-Family CINCLINAE.

HYDROBATA, Vieillot.

Hydrobata, VIEILLOT, Analyse, 1816, (Ag.)
Cinclus, BECHSTEIN, Gemein. Naturg. 1802, (Agassiz. Not of Moehring, 1752.)   (Type *Sturnus cinclus*, L.)

CH.—Bill without any bristles at the base; slender, subulate; the mandible bent slightly upward; the culmen slightly concave to near the tip, which is much curved and notched; the commissural edges of the bill finely nicked. Feet large and strong, the toes projecting considerably beyond the tail; the claws large. Lateral toes equal. Tail very short and even; not two-thirds the wings, which are concave and somewhat falcate. The first primary is more than one-fourth the longest.

The tomia of this genus are nicked on the terminal half, a character I have only noticed in specimens of the robin, and possibly not permanent in the latter. The slightly upward bend of the bill, somewhat as in *Anthus*, renders the culmen concave, and the commissure slightly convex. The maxilla at base is nearly as high as the mandible; the whole bill is much compressed and attenuated. The lateral claws barely reach the base of the middle one, which is broad; the inner face extended into a horny lamina, with one or two notches or pectinations somewhat as in *Caprimulgidae*. The stiffened sub-falcate wings are quite remarkable. The tail is so short that the upper coverts extend nearly to its tip.

If the genera of Moehring are to be retained and used in ornithology, there is no reason why his *Cinclus* should not be used for a grallatorial genus, and that of Bechstein be superseded by *Hydrobata* of Vieillot.

HYDROBATA MEXICANA, Baird.

American Dipper; Water Ouzel.

Cinclus pallasii, BONAP. Zool. Jour. II, Jan. 1827, 52.—IB. Amer. Orn. II, 1828, 173; pl. xvi, f. 1. (not the Asiatic *pallasii*.)
Cinclus mexicanus, SWAINSON, Syn. Mex. Birds, in Phil. Mag. I. May, 1827, 368.
Cinclus americanus, Sw. & RICH. F. Bor. Am. II, 1831, 173.—NUTTALL, Man. II, 1834, 569.—AUD. Orn. Biog. IV,
    1838, 493 : V, 1839, 303 ; pl. 370, 435.—IB. Synopsis, 1839, 86.—IB. Birds Amer. II, 1841,
    182 ; pl. 137.—NEWBERRY, Zool. Cal. & Or. Route 80 ; Rep. P. R. R. Surv. VI, IV, 1857.
Cinclus unicolor, BONAP. List, 1838.
Cinclus mortoni, TOWNSEND, Narrative, 1839, 337.
Cinclus townsendii, "AUDUBON," TOWNSEND, Narr. 1839, 340.

SP. CH.—Above dark plumbeous, beneath paler ; head and neck all round a shade of clove or perhaps a light sooty brown ; less conspicuous beneath. A concealed spot of white above the anterior corner of the eye and indications of the same sometimes on the lower eyelid. Immature specimens usually with the feathers beneath edged with grayish white ; the greater and middle wing coverts and lesser quills tipped with the same. The colors more uniform. Length, 7.50 ; wing, 4.00 ; tail, 2.55.

Hab.—Rocky mountains from British America to Mexico.

With a large number of specimens of the American Dipper before me, I find considerable variations, without being at all satisfied of the existence of more than one species. In all, the white spot above the eye is evident, though its extent varies. Sometimes the brown of the head and neck is but slightly different from the plumbeous of the back.

One specimen, 4469, differs in a decided tendency to white about the throat and neck; the feet are darker, the claws shorter, stouter, and more curved. The specimen is not in sufficiently good order to show whether this whiteness of the throat is characteristic or an indication of a tendency to albinism. It may be proper to remark, however, that most of the Old World species are characterized by the white throat.

Skins from Fort Massachusetts differ from the others in having the bill entirely black; the other characters are very similar; the colors generally are purer, the feathers being less edged with paler.

List of specimens.

Catal. No.	Sex.	Locality.	When collected.	Whence obtained.	Collected by—	Length.	Stretch of wings.	Wing.	Tail.	Tarsus.	Middle toe.	Its claw alone.	Bill above.	Along gape.	Specimen measured.
2841	....	N.W. coast Oregon	....	S. F. Baird.....	J. K. Townsend....	....	.....	...	..	.....	.....	.....	....	....	....
2862	....	........do..............	....	.....do.........	.......do...........	..	.....	..	.....	.....	.....	.....	....	....	....
8121	♀	St. Mary's R. mountains....	Oct. 13,1853	Gov. Stevens..	Dr. Geo. Suckley...	8.50	12.50	3.75	....	.....	.....	.....	....	....	....
7099	....	........do........	......do...	.....do..	....do...	....	.....	....	.....	.....	.....	.....	....	....	....
4469	....	Cascade mountains, O. T...	....	Lt. Williamson.	Dr. Newberry......	....	.....	....	.....	.....	.....	.....	....	....	....
8120	♂	Tejon Pass	....	....do...	....	....	.....	....	.....	.....	.....	.....	....	....	....
8496	♂	Fort Mass. N. M............	Mar. 31,1856	Dr. Peters.....	....	7.50	.....	3.88	2.44	1.18	1.10	0.26	0.74	0.96	Dry.....
8495*	♂	... .do..............	Mar. 27,1856	.......do...	....	8.00	11.00	....	....	....	....	....	....	....	....
8117	....	Fort Thorn...........	....	Dr. Henry	....	7.00	......	3.90	2.40	1.20	1.10	0.28	0.76	1.04	Dry.....

* Eyes light brown.

Family SYLVICOLIDAE.

Primaries nine ; the first quill nearly as long as the second or third. Tarsi distinctly scutellate the whole length ante-riorly. Bill conical, slender, or depressed, usually half the length of head ; more or less bristled or notched. Nostrils oval or rounded. Lateral toes nearly or quite equal, and shorter than the middle ; the basal joint of the middle free nearly to its base, externally; united for about half, internally.

This family is well marked by its scutellate tarsi in front, the absence of any spurious or short first primary, and the rather weak, slender, conical, or depressed, sometimes decurved bill. The base of the bill, with the nostrils, is not covered in any genera by setae, as in *Parus*, *Alauda*, &c. In many respects there is a close relationship to some *Fringillidae*, and there are some forms, such as the *Tanagridae*, which it is difficult to assign to the one family rather than to the other. The chief difference, however, is to be found in the longer, slenderer, and less abruptly conical bill of the *Tanagers*.

The following synopsis will serve to point out the sub-families of the *Sylvicolidae:*

MOTACILLINAE.—Bill slender. Culmen slightly concave at base. Legs long; claws but little curved. Hind toe considerably longer than the middle one; its claw much longer (twice) than the middle claw; all the claws but slightly curved. Tertials elongated; much longer than the secondaries.

SYLVICOLINAE.—Bill rather slender, conical, or depressed. Culmen straight or convex. Hind toe shorter than the middle; the claws all much curved. Hind claw not conspicuously longer than the middle one. When the hind toe is lengthened, it is usually in the digit, not the claw. Tertials generally not longer than the secondaries.

TANAGRINAE.—Bill very stout, conical, as high as broad; or considerably broader than high. Tarsi short, not exceeding the hind toe. Claws much curved; the hinder scarcely larger than the middle anterior.

Sub-Family MOTACILLINAE.

CH.—Bill slender, shorter than the head, notched at tip ; rictus without bristles. Basal joint of middle toe entirely free externally. Tarsi distinctly scutellate, longer than the middle, but nearly equal to the hind toe, which is very long, exceeding all the others ; the claw slightly curved. Wing very long, pointed. First quill almost the longest ; the tertials considerably longer than the secondaries. Tail emarginate.

The colors are dull, generally brownish above, whitish beneath; the breast spotted; the outer tail feather white. The species are readily distinguished from the larks (*Alaudidae*) by the tarsi being acute behind and destitute of scutellae. The bill is longer, slenderer, and more depressed, without any setae covering the base.

ANTHUS.—Bill slender, nearly as long as the head. Toes not reaching the tip of tail. Legs weak ; hind toe rather shorter than the tarsus, its claw more than half the total length. Tertials longer than the fifth primary. Tail feathers broad.

NEOCORYS.—Bill stouter at base and shorter. Toes reaching nearly to tip of tail. Legs stout ; hind toe as long as tarsus, much longer than in *anthus*, its claw half the total length. Tertials rather shorter than the sixth primary. Tail feathers narrow.

ANTHUS, Bechstein.

Anthus, BECHSTEIN, Gemein. Naturg. Deutschl. 1802, (Agassiz.) Type, *Alauda spinoletta*.

CH.—Bill slender, much attenuated, and distinctly notched. A few short bristles at the base. Culmen concave at the base. Tarsi quite distinctly scutellate ; longer than the middle toe ; inner lateral toe the longer. Hind toe rather shorter than the tarsus, but longer than the middle toe, owing to the long attenuated and moderately curved hind claw, which is considerably more than half the total length of the toe. Tail rather long, emarginate. Wing very long, considerably longer than the lengthened tail, reaching to its middle. The first primary nearly equal to the longest. The tertials almost as long as the primaries.

Of this genus but one species is well established as belonging to North America. Others occur in South America, and the rest of the world.

The following table of measurements shows the proportions of the North American species compared with the allied *Neocorys :*

Comparative measurements of species.

Catal. No.	Species.	Locality.	Sex.	Length.	Wing.	Tail.	Tarsus.	Middle toe.	Its claw alone.	Bill above.	Along gape.	Specimen measured.
7926	Anthus ludovicianus	Tulare Valley, Cal.	♂	6.06	3.26	2.76	0.84	0.74	0.16	0.51	0.68	Dry.........
328	........do..	Carlisle, Pa.....	♂	6.58	3.38	2.88	0.91	0.70	0.18	0.51	0.70	Dry.........
10087	........do..	Marion county, Ill	......	6.70	3.30	2.76	0.88	0.76	0.20	0.50	0.70	Dry.........
1884	Neocorys spraguei........	Fort Union, Neb.......	♀	5.44	3.12	2.50	0.89	0.84	0.20	0.48	0.66	Dry.........

ANTHUS LUDOVICIANUS, Licht.

Tit Lark.

Alauda ludoviciana, GMELIN, Syst. Nat. I, 1788, 793.
Anthus ludovicianus, LICHT. Verz. 1823, 37, no. 421.—RICH. List, 1837.—BONAP. List, 1838.—IB. Conspectus,
         1850, 249.—AUDUBON, Synopsis, 1839, 94.—IB. Birds Amer. III, 1841, 40 ; pl. 150.
Alauda rubra, GMELIN, Syst. Nat. I, 1788, 794.
Alauda rufa, WILSON, Am. Orn. V, 1812, 89 ; pl. lxxxix.
Anthus spinoletta, BONAP. Synopsis, 1828, 90, (not of Linnaeus.)—AUD. Orn. Biog. I, 1832, 408 : V, 1839, 449 ;
         pl. 80.—NUTTALL, Man. I, 1832, 450.
Alauda pennsylvanica, BRISSON, Orn.
Anthus pennsylvanicus, ZANDER, Cab. Journ. Orn. Extraheft, I, for 1853, 1854, 63.
Anthus aquaticus, AUD. Name on Pl. x, folioed.
Anthus pipiens, AUD. Orn. Biog. I, 1832, 408 : V, 1839, 449 ; pl. 80. (Young ?)
Anthus rubens, MERREM. (Gray.)

SP. CH.—(*Female*, in spring.) Above olive brown, each feather slightly darker towards the central portion ; beneath pale dull buff, or yellowish brown, with a maxillary series of dark brown spots and streaks across the breast and along sides. Ring round the eye, and superciliary stripe yellowish. Central tail feathers like the back, others dark blackish brown ; the external one white, except at the base within ; a white spot at the end of the second. Primaries edged with whitish, other quills with pale brownish. Length, 6.50 ; wing, 3.45 ; tail, 2.95.

Hab.—North America generally. Greenland, (Reinhardt.) Accidental in Europe.

I have no authentic male of this species from the Atlantic States before me, but I am inclined to think that it is not materially different. It may possibly be paler and more streaked. The second and third quills are longest and equal, the first and fourth little shorter, and about equal to the tertials. The tail varies somewhat as to the amount of white, in one specimen the second feather having nearly as much as the first. Specimens from the west appear smaller and paler than eastern ones, and to have the breast much more streaked, but the materials before me are not sufficient to determine whether we have more than one species.

A specimen (7928) from Shoalwater Bay has a greenish olivaceous gloss, not noticed in others. This species is closely related to the *Anthus spinoletta* and *obscurus* of Europe, but, according to Zander, (Cabanis' Jour. für Ornithologie, 1853, Extra Heft, p. 63,) while it agrees with the former in the black bill, it is distinguished from it by a much darker and more olive green color above, a much greater extent and purity of white in the tail, by the tarsus, one to two lines shorter, and by a different relative proportion of the primaries. From the latter it is known by the darker bill, feet, and upper parts generally, and by the pure lustrous white of the tail feathers. It is smaller than either species, has a proportionally longer tail, yellowish lore, and a totally different coloration beneath ; the ground color being rusty or reddish yellow, with dark brown narrow spots across the breast.

The following diagnosis is given by Zander to distinguish the *A. ludovicianus* from its European analogues :

Sp. Ch.—Bill and feet blackish ; the longest tertial (?) one line shorter than the longest primary. The light marking on the outer tail feathers shining white ; and on the outermost one, involving the half of the feather, its shaft for the most part white. Body above olive green, the superciliary stripe yellowish.

List of specimens.

Catal. No.	Sex.	Locality.	When collected.	Whence obtained.	Orig'l No.	Collected by—	Length.	Stretch of wings.	Wing.	Remarks.
328	♀	Carlisle	May 8, 1841	S. F. Baird			6.50	11.00		
10099	....	Washington, D. C.		J. C. McGuire						
	....	Racine, Wis.		R. Kennicott						
	....	Northern Ill.	Sept. 20	......do						
10087	....	Marion county, Ill.	April 8	......do			6.50	10.75		
8844	♀	Black Hills	Sept. 16	Lieut. Warren		Dr. Hayden	6.00	10.25	3.00	Iris whitish gray..
7927	♀	St. Mary's, Rocky Mount's	Oct. 12, 1853	Gov. Stevens		Dr. Suckley	6.50	10.50	3.50	
7929	....	Shoalwater Bay, W. T	Sept. 12, 1854	......do	95	Dr. Cooper	6.00	10.25		
7928	....	......do	......do	......do	95	......do	6.50	10.00		
5514	♀	Petaluma, Cal.		E. Samuels						
7926	♂	Tulare Valley		Lieut. Williamson		Dr. Heermann				
		Fort Tejon		J. Xantus de Vesey.						
7931	♀	Espia, Mexico	Mar. 1855	Major Emory	57	Dr. Kennerly				
7930	....	Mimbres to Rio Grande.		Dr. T. C. Henry						

NEOCORYS, Sclater.

Neocorys, Sclater, Pr. Zool. Soc. Lond. 1857, 5.

Ch.—Bill half as long as the head ; the culmen concave at the base, slightly decurved at the tip. Rictus without bristles. Legs stout ; tarsi distinctly scutellate, longer than the middle toe. Hind toe very long, equal to the tarsus, much longer than the middle toe ; its claw but slightly curved, and about half the total length. Inner lateral toe rather longer than outer. Wings much longer than the tail ; first quill longest. Tertials considerably longer than secondaries. Tail rather short, emarginate.

This genus is closely related to *Anthus*, but is stouter, with shorter tail, a shorter and stouter bill, larger feet, &c. The hind toe is much larger, the claw larger and less curved, and occupies only half instead of more than half the total length.

The coloration is quite similar, but the edges of the feathers above are lighter, the spots or streaks confined to the breast, and sparser.

The detailed measurements of the single species will be found with *Anthus*.

30 b

NEOCORYS SPRAGUEI, Sclater.

Missouri Skylark.

Alauda spraguei, AUD. Birds Amer. VII, 1843, 335 ; pl. 486.
Agrodoma spraguei, BAIRD, Stansbury's report G. Salt Lake, 1852, 329.—BONAP. Notes Delattre, 1854.
Neocorys spraguei, SCLATER, Pr. Zool. Soc. 1857, 5.

SP. CH.—Above wood brown, all the feathers edged with paler, especially on the neck, where there is a brownish yellow tinge. The under parts are dull white, with a collar of sharply defined narrow brown streaks across the fore part and along the sides of the breast. Lores and a superciliary line whitish. Tail feathers, except the middle ones, dark brown ; the outer one white, the second white, with the inner margin brown. The outer primary is edged with white, and there are two dull whitish bands across the wings. Bill and feet yellow, the former brown above. Length, (female,) 5.75 ; wing, 3.35 ; tail, 2.50.
Hab.—About Fort Union, Nebraska.

This little known species has the general appearance of a titlark, but is readily distinguished from *Anthus ludovicianus* by the purer white of its under parts; the much paler margins to the feathers above, the entirely white external tail feather, the yellow legs and bill, as well as by its general peculiarities. In its song and general habits it approaches nearer the European skylark than any bird belonging to our fauna.

This species has thus far been seen only in the vicinity of Fort Union.

List of specimens.

Catalogue No.	Sex.	Locality.	When collected.	Whence obtained.	Collected by—
1854	♀	Fort Union, Nebraska.........	1843	S. F. Baird	J. J. Audubon........

Sub-Family SYLVICOLINAE.

The characters of this extensive sub-family are sufficiently expressed in the synopsis on page 231. The variety of form is very great, but the transitions are so imperceptible as to render it a matter of much difficulty to define the genera with precision. The entire group appears to be wanting in the Old World. It may be conveniently divided into the following sections :

A.—*Rictus with short bristles or none.*

MNIOTILTEAE.—Bill notched. Hind toe longer than the lateral ones, its claw shorter than the digit. Wings pointed. Tail nearly even, spotted.

GEOTHLYPEAE.—Bill notched. Legs very stout. Hind toe longer than the lateral; its claw equal to the digit. Tail unspotted.

ICTERIEAE.—Bill without notch, very stout, much compressed. Commissure and culmen both much curved.

VERMIVOREAE.—Bill entirely without a notch; conical, slender, weak, acutely pointed.

SYLVICOLEAE.—Bill notched. Wings pointed. Hind toe equal to the lateral.

B.—*Rictus with well developed bristles.*

SETOPHAGEAE.—Bill depressed, broad, notched at tip.

Section Mniotilteae.

Bill slightly notched some distance from the tip. Rictus without bristles. Hind toe considerably developed, longer than the lateral toe ; its claw decidedly longer than its digit. First quill nearly or quite as long as the second. Wings long, pointed ; much longer than the tail, which is nearly even. Tail feathers with white spots.

The following genera belong to this section :

MNIOTILTA.—Bill from the base nearly as long as the skull, compressed. Tarsus rather short, but little longer than the hind toe, which is very long, its digit nearly twice as long as the claw alone; middle toe (and claw) fully as long as the tarsus.

PARULA.—Bill shorter ; depressed at base and attenuated at tip; considerably shorter than the head, or than the middle toe. Hind claw nearly two-thirds its digit; the middle toe and claw nearly as long as the tarsus.

PROTONOTARIA—Bill conical, compressed towards the end. Measured from the extreme base, as long as the head, and longer than the middle toe; hind claw but little shorter than its digit; the middle toe and claw only three-fourths the tarsus.

MNIOTILTA, Vieillot.

Mniotilta, VIEILLOT, Analyse, 1816. (Agassiz.)

CH.—General form sylvicoline ; bill rather long, compressed, shorter than the head, with very short rictal bristles, and a shallow notch. Wings considerably longer than the tail, which is slightly rounded ; first quill shorter than second and third. Tarsi rather short ; toes long, middle one equal to the tarsus ; hind toe nearly as long, the claw considerably shorter than its digit. Color white, streaked with black.

This genus differs from other sylvicolines in the elongation of the toes, especially the hinder one, by means of which the species is enabled to move up and down the trunks of trees, like the true creepers. But one species is recognized as North American, although Nuttall describes a second.

Measurements of species.

Catal. No.	Species.	Locality.	Sex and age.	Length	Stretch of wings.	Wing.	Tail.	Tarsus.	Middle toe.	Its claw alone.	Bill above.	Along gape.	Specimen measured.
7496	Mniotilta varia........	Eastern U. States..	♂ ?	5.00	....	2.88	2.28	0.70	0.64	0.16	0.46	0.60	Dry ....
956	......do	Carlisle, Pa........	♀	4.50	....	2.54	2.12	0.64	0.66	0.18	0.46	0.52	Dry ....
do.	...... do	......do		4.66	8.00	2.58	......						Fresh .....
8672	......do	Florida		4.50	....	2.63	2.14	0.64	0.68	0.18	0.52	0.64	Dry ....
do.	......do	......do		4.75	8.25	2.75	......						Fresh .....

MNIOTILTA VARIA, Vieillot.

Black and White Creeper.

Motacilla varia, LINN. Syst. Nat. I, 1766, 333.
Certhia varia, VIEILLOT, Ois. Am. Sept. II, 1807, 69.—AUD. Orn. Biog. I, 1832, 452 : V, 1839, 471 ; pl. 90.
Mniotilta varia, VIEILLOT, Analyse, 1816.—IB. Galerie Ois. I, 1834, 276 ; pl. 169.—AUDUBON, Synopsis, 1839, 71.— IB. Birds Am. II, 1841, 105 ; pl. 114.—? GOSSE, Birds Jam. 1847, 134.
Sylvia varia, BON. Synopsis, 1828, 81.—NUTTALL, Man. I, 1832, 384.
Sylvicola varia, RICH. List, 1837.
Certhia maculata, WILSON, Am. Orn. III, 1811, 22 ; pl. xix.
? *Mniotilta borealis*, NUTTALL, Man. I, 2d ed., 1840, 704.

Sp. Ch.—Bill with the upper mandible considerably decurved, the lower straight. General color of the male black, the feathers broadly edged with white ; the head all round black, with a median stripe in the crown and neck above, a superciliary and a maxillary one of white. Middle of belly, two conspicuous bands on the wings, outer edges of tertials and inner of all the wing and tail feathers, and a spot on the inner webs of the outer two tail feathers, white. Rump and upper tail coverts black, edged externally with white. Female similar ; the under parts white, obsoletely streaked with black on the sides and under tail coverts. Length, 5 inches ; wing, 2.85 ; tail, 2.25.

Hab.—Eastern North America to Missouri river ; south to Guatemala.

The lores are rather dusky ; the ear coverts black. The black of the chin and throat is continuous, but is streaked on the breast with white. The greater quills and tail feathers are edged externally with lead gray.

The colors of this species are something like those of *Dendroica nigrescens*, although the latter is much less streaked with black, and the crown is without the median white stripe. The same character distinguishes it from *D. striata*, in which the superciliary stripe is wanting.

Specimens vary somewhat as to the amount of black on the throat. The bill also varies materially in length, curvature, and color. I have not been able in a large series of specimens before me to detect any strong indications of a second species, although some have more or less of the characters assigned to *M. borealis* by Mr. Nuttall. A skin, probably female, from Cape Florida, has the bill unusually long (.51) and the under mandibles white, except towards the tip. Another from the same locality has the bill as long, but the under mandible is darker. The specimens from the north and west seem to have the bill shorter, straighter, and blacker, and the claws, perhaps, darker, corresponding with what Nuttall calls *M. borealis*. The only very long billed specimens are from Florida and the vicinity of Washington. I cannot from the skins before me give any other characters, although, if there be two species, it will probably be necessary to consider the shorter billed one as the true *M. varia*.

List of specimens.

Catal. No.	Sex.	Locality.	When collected.	Whence obtained.	Orig'l No.	Collected by—	Length.	Stretch of wings.	Wing.	Remarks.
68	♂	Carlisle, Pa.............	May —, 1839	S. F. Baird......						
956	♀	.........do.............	May 9, 1843	...... do......			4.66	8.00	2.58	
1643	♀?	.........do.............	July 18, 1844	...... do......			5.37	8.33	2.56	
7555	♂	Washington, D. C.......		Wm. Hutton.....						
......	♂	Racine, Wis........		R. Kennicott......						
		South Illinois.......	Sept. —, 1857	...... do......						
8673	......	Cape Florida..........	Sept. 25, 1857	G. Wurdemann..			5.00	8.50	2.50	Dark legs, yellow feet, upper m'd black.
6504	♂	Key Biscayne, Fla.....	April 7, 1857	...... do.......						
4680	......	Mouth of Vermilion....	May 5, 1857	Lt. Warren......		Dr. Hayden......	5.37	8.00	2 75	
4681	♂	.........do.............	...... do.......	...... do......		..... do........	5.12	8.50	2.75	
4677	♂.	.........do.............	May 8, 1857	...... do......		..... do......	5.00	8.50	2.86	Eyes b!ack...........
4679	♂	.........do.............	May 5, 1857	...... do......		..... do........	4.62	8.00	2.75	.....do ....
4676	......	Mouth of Big Sioux.....	May 4, 1856	...... do......		..... do........	4.75	8.50	2.75	.....do ....
4678	......	Nebraska..............	May 15, 1856	...... do......		..... do........			.... ..	
7990	......	Guatemala.............		J. Gould........						

PARULA, Bonap.

Chloris, BOIE, Isis, 1826, 972, (not of Moehring, 1752.) Type, *Parus americanus.*

Sylvicola, SWAINSON, Zool. Journ. III, July, 1827, 169. (Not of Humphrey, Mus. Calonnianum, 1797, 60 ; genus of land mollusks.) Same type.

Parula, BONAP. Geog. & Comp. List, 1838. Same type.

Compsothlypis, CABANIS, Mus. Hein. 1850–51, 20. Same type.

CH.—In the species of this genus the bill is conical and acute ; the culmen very gently curved from the base ; the commissure slightly concave. The notch when visible is further from the tip than in *Dendroica,* but usually is either obsolete or entirely wanting. Bristles very short. The tarsi are longer than the middle toe. The tail is nearly even, and considerably shorter than the wing.

The genus *Sylvicola* of Swainson was established on the *Parus americanus* in 1827, but both this nameand *Chloris* of Boie, 1826, were pre-occupied. *Parula* of 1838 has been changed by Gray and Cabanis onaccount of the similarity in sound to *Parulus* of Spix, 1824 ; but, considering this difference of termination as sufficient for distinguishing the two names, I do not follow these authors in dropping the former.

The species of this genus have somewhat the habits of titmice, one only however is found in the United States. The following synopsis will serve to distinguish them :

Above blue, with a dorsal patch of yellowish green ; yellow beneath.

Patch confined to middle of back. Throat pale yellow, with a brown patch. Rest of under parts white ; lower eyelid white...*P. americana.*

A small dorsal patch. Under parts reddish yellow. No patch on the eyelid...*P. pitiayumi.*[1]

Entire back yellowish green. Throat and breast yellow, with a brown bar across the former. Tail unspotted. Belly and superciliary stripe white.............*P. mexicana.*[2]

Comparative measurements of species.

Catal. No.	Species.	Locality.	Sex.	Length.	Stretch of wings.	Wing.	Tail.	Tarsus.	Middle toe.	Its claw alone.	Bill above.	Along gape.	Specimen measured.
750	Parula americana	Carlisle, Pa....	♂	4.70	....	2.48	2.02	0.66	0.56	0.16	0.38	0.50	Dry ....
do.	......do	......do	.....	4.75	7.66	2.50	......	...	......	....	....	....	Fresh ....
2160	......do	......do	♀	3.94	....	2.38	1.90	0.64	0.50	0.14	0.42	0.50	Dry ....
do.	......do	......do	......	4.50	7.50	2.41	......	......	....	....	....	....	Fresh ....
10155	Parula mexicana......	Mexico............	......	4.80	....	2.58	2.20	0.60	0.50	0.16	0.44	0.51	Dry ....
1819	Parula pitiayumi	Brazil............	......	3.54	....	2.02	1.66	0.60	0.44	0.16	0.40	0.50	Dry ....

[1] PARULA PITIAYUMI, Baird.

Sylvia pitiayumi, VIEILLOT, Nouv. Dict. II, 1816, 276.

Compsothlypis pitiayumi, CAB. Mus. Hein. 1851, 21.

Sylvia venusta, TEMM. pl. col. 293, f. 1.

Sylvia plumbea, SWAINSON, Zool. Ill. II. 1821–'2; pl. cxxxix.

Parula brasiliana, BON. Consp. 1850, 310.

[2] PARULA MEXICANA, Bonap.

Parula mexicana, BONAP. Conspectus, 1850, 21.

Compsothlypis mexicana, CAB. Mus. Hein. 1851, 21.

PARULA AMERICANA, Bonap.

Blue Yellow-backed Warbler.

Parus americanus, LINNAEUS, Syst. Nat. ed. 10, I, 1758, 190.—GM. Syst. Nat. I, 1788, 1007.—LATH. Ind. Orn. II, 1790, 571.

Motacilla americana, GMELIN, Syst. Nat. I, 1788, 960.

Sylvia americana, LATHAM, Ind. Orn. II, 1790, 520.—BONAP. Syn. 1828, 33.—AUD. Orn. Biog. I, 1832, 78 ; pl. 15.

Sylvicola americana, RICH. List, 1837.—AUD. Syn. 1839, 59.—IB. Birds Amer. II, 1841, 57 ; pl. 91.

Parula americana, BONAP. List, 1838.—IB. Consp. 1850, 310.—GOSSE, Jamaica, 1847, 154.

Compsothlypis americana, CABANIS, Mus. Hein. 1850, 20, (Type.)

Ficedula ludoviciana, BRISSON, Orn. III, 1760, 500 ; pl. xxvi.

Motacilla ludoviciana, GMELIN, Syst. Nat. I, 1788, 983.

Motacilla eques, BODDAERT, Tabl. pl. enl. 1783, (Gray.)

Sylvia torquata, VIEILLOT, Ois. Am. Sept. II, 1807, 38 ; pl. xcix.

Thryothorus torquata, STEPHENS, Shaw Zool. XIV, I, 1826, 194.

Sylvia pusilla, WILSON, Am. Orn. IV, 1811, 17 ; pl. xxviii.

Sylvicola pusilla, SWAINSON, Zool. Jour. III, 1827, 169. (Type of genus.)

BUFFON, Pl. enl. 731, f. 1 ; 709, f. 1. (?)

SP. CH.—Above blue, the middle of the back with a patch of yellowish green. Beneath yellow anteriorly, white behind. A reddish brown tinge across the breast. Lores and space round the eye dusky ; a small white spot on either eyelid ; sides of head and neck like the crown. Two conspicuous white bands on the wings. Outer two tail feathers with a conspicuous spot of white. Female similar, with less brown on the breast. Length, 4.75 ; wing, 2.34 ; tail, 1.90.

Hab.—Eastern North America to the Missouri ; south to Guatemala.

MALE IN SPRING.—Upper parts, scapulars, sides of the neck and head, edges of the quills and tail feathers bluish ash. A triangular spot of yellowish green between the wings ; (this is slightly tinged in the middle of each feather with reddish brown.) The tips of the bluish feathers above very faintly tipped with greenish yellow, indicating the changes in the fall. Lore dusky ; a spot on the upper and under eyelids white. Individuals differ in the coloring of the throat. In one the chin is yellowish ; across the throat a band of dark reddish brown ; each feather tipped and edged with yellow. Fore part of the breast lighter reddish brown, approximating to chestnut, this on a ground of yellow ; sides of the breast also with traces of this chestnut. In another individual the dusky of the throat is extended more towards the chin, and more decided. Sides under the wing light bluish ash. Traces of reddish brown under the edge of the wing when closed. Abdomen, lower coverts, and vent white, with occasional traces of pale yellow. Two broad bands of white on the wings. Large patch of white on the inner webs of the outer two feathers near the end ; on the third a white spot on the inner vane, and the inner edge of this and the two next margined with the same. Feet dusky ; upper mandible dark brown, lower yellowish.

FEMALE IN SPRING.—Upper parts similar to the male ; white bands on the wings somewhat narrower. Two specimens differ in the color beneath. One specimen is very similar to the male, with the dark reddish brown across the throat very decided. Lores also blackish. This specimen (No. 628) is marked "female ;" it may possibly be male. Another, certainly a female, No. 338, has the throat, chin, and fore part of breast yellowish, very faintly tinted with brownish red across the throat. Lores not dusky ; eyelids faintly white. Tail with less white, and wanting the white spot on the third feather.

MALE IN FALL.—Similar generally to the male in spring. Chin tinged with brownish ; more yellow on the throat and fore breast. Feathers of the head strongly tinged with greenish; secondaries, or some of them, edged with greenish yellow; sides tinged with brown. FEMALE IN FALL.—Whole upper parts light greenish olive, strongly marked with yellowish green between the wings. Throat, chin, and fore part of breast yellow; across the throat slightly tinged with reddish brown. Lower parts dirty white, passing to pale yellow about the vent; edges of secondaries like the head.

List of specimens.

Catal. No.	Sex.	Locality.	When collected.	Whence obtained.	Orig. No.	Collected by—	Length.	Stretch of wings.	Wing.	Remarks.
2219	♂	Carlisle, Pa............	May 3, 1845	S. F. Baird	......	....	4.75	7.43	2.33	....
750	♂	.....do............	Sept. 23, 1842	......do..	......	....	4.75	7.66	2.50	....
725	......	.....do............	Sept. 16, 1842	..... do...........	......	....	4.50	6.37	......	....
2160	♀	.....do............	April 28, 1845	......do....	......	....	4.50	7.50	2.43	....
10101	♂	Washington, D. C....	....	J. C. McGuire.....	......	....	......	......	......	....
7489	......	Rockport, Ohio	....	J. P. Kirtland	......	....	......	......	......	....
	♂	Cook county, Ill.......	May 14	R. Kennicott.......	......	....	......	......	......	....
	♀	South Illinois..........	May 15	......do	......	....	......	......	......	....
6974	♂	St. Louis, Mo.........	May 8, 1857	Lieut. Bryan.......	46	W. S. Wood...	......	......	......	....
8649	...	Cape Florida	Sept. 27, 1857	G. Wurdemann....	......	....	......	......	......	Upper mandible, black; lower, yellow ; legs, light green.
6497	♂	Key Biscayne, Fla.....	April 10.....	......do...	......	....	......	....	......	....
4671	♀	Mouth of Platte river ..	April 27, 1850	Lieut. Warren....	......	Dr. Hayden....	4.12	6.62	2.00	....
7991	......	Guatemala............	....	J. Gould.........	......	....	......	......	......	....

PROTONOTARIA, Baird.

The diagnosis of this section will be found in the synopsis of the genera under the head of *Mniotilteae*. It is well characterized by its long, distinctly notched bill, and long wings, which are an inch longer than the slightly graduated tail, (the lateral feathers about .12 of an inch shorter.) The under tail coverts are very long, reaching within half an inch of the tip of the tail. The tarsi and hind toe are proportionally longer than in the true warblers. The notch and great size of the bill distinguishes it from the swamp warblers. The only North American species belonging to the group appears to be the old *Sylvia protonotaria* of Gm.

PROTONOTARIA CITREA, Baird.

Prothonotary Warbler.

"*Motacilla citrea*, BODDAERT, Tabl. pl. enl. 704, f. 2, 1783," (G. R. Gray.)
Mniotilta citrea, GRAY, Genera.
Motacilla protonotarius, GMELIN, Syst. Nat. I, 1788, 972.
Sylvia protonotarius, LATHAM, Ind. Orn. II, 1790, 542.—VIEILLOT, Ois. Am. II, 1807, 27; pl.lxxxiii.—WILSON, Am. Orn. III, 1811, 72; pl. xxiv, f 3.—AUD. Orn. Biog. I, 1832, 22: V, 1838, 460; pl. 3.
Sylvia (Dacnis) protonotarius, BON. Obs. Wils. J. A. N. S. IV, 1825, 196.—AUD. Orn. Biog. pl. 3, name on plate.
Vermivora protonotarius, BONAP. List, 1838.
Helinaia protonotarius, AUD. Syn. 1839, 67.—IB. Birds Am. II, 1841, 89; pl. 106.
Helmitherus protonotarius, BONAP. Conspectus, 1850, 314.
Compsothlypis protonotarius, CAB. Mus. Hein, 1850, 20. (Not type.)
Ficedula canadensis major, BRISSON, Ois. III, 1760, 308; pl. xxvi, f. 1.—BUFFON, V, 316 : VI, 191 ; enl. 704, f. 2.

SP. CH.—Bill very large; as long as the head. Head and neck all round, with the entire under parts, including the tibiae, rich yellow, excepting the anal region and under tail coverts, which are white. Back dark olive green, with a tinge of yellow;

rump, upper tail coverts, wings, and tail above, bluish ash color. Inner margin of quills and the tail feathers (except the innermost) white, the outer webs and tips like the back. Length, 5.40 ; wing, 2.90 ; tail, 2.25.

Hab.—South Atlantic and Gulf States to mouth of Ohio north, and the Missouri river west. West Indies.

The wings are long and pointed ; the first quill longest ; the tail is moderately rounded. The outer primary and alula are also edged with white.

The female has the yellow of the head more glossed with olivaceous.

A specimen from South Illinois (10111) has the yellow glossed in patches with red.

List of specimens.

Catal. No.	Sex.	Locality.	When collected.	Whence obtained.	Collected by—	Length.	Wing.	Tail.	Tarsus.	Middle toe.	Its claw alone.	Bill above.	Along gape.	Specimen measured.
1927	......	Southern States	....	S. F. Baird...	....	......	......	......	......	......	......	......	......	....
2393	......	Georgia	....	......do......	J. Leconte.....	......	......	......	......	......	......	......	......	....
10112	......	South Illinois....	May 9.....	N. W. Univ.	R. Kennicott...	......	......	......	......	......	......	......	......	....
10111	......	......do.........	April 23 ...	......do......	...... do........	5.30	2.92	2.12	0.72	·0.62	0.16	0.56	0.64	Dry .....
10110	♂	... do...........	May 15....	......do......	......do........	......	......	......	......	......	......	......	......	....
7516	.....	Independence,Mo	1857.......	W. M. Magraw	Dr. Cooper.....	5.10	2.74	2.04	0.78	0.64	0.20	0.56	0.66	Dry .....

Section **Geothlypeae.**

Bill distinctly notched but without bristles. Hind toe considerably longer than the lateral. Legs long and stout, considerably exceeding the middle toe, and as long or decidedly longer than the skull. Under tail coverts long. Legs yellow ; tail unspotted. Color olive above, belly yellow, unspotted.

The North American genera of this section are as follows :

GEOTHLYPIS.—Wings rounded, scarcely longer than the considerably graduated tail ; first quill shorter than fourth.

OPORORNIS.—Wings pointed, much longer than the nearly even tail. First quill almost longest.

GEOTHLYPIS, Cabanis.

Trichas, SWAINSON, Zool. Journ. III, July, 1827, 167, (not of Gloger, March, 1827, equal to *Criniger,* Temm.)
Geothlypis, CABANIS, Wiegmann's Archiv, 1847, I, 316, 349.—IB. Schomburgk's Reise Guiana, 1848.

Bill sylvicoline, rather depressed, and distinctly notched ; rictal bristles very short or wanting. Wings short, rounded, scarcely longer than the tail ; the first quill shorter than the fourth. Tail long ; much rounded or graduated. Legs stout ; tarsi elongated as long as the head. Olive green above, belly yellow. Tail feathers immaculate. Legs yellow.

The species of this genus all agree in general external appearance, and are more terrestrial than other sylvicolines. They constitute two well marked sections, the first having shorter wings and more graduated tail, (about .40 of an inch,) with longer legs than the second, which is more like the typical sylvicolas.

According to Cabanis, Gloger used the name *Trichas,* in March, 1827, for what Temminck had previously called *Criniger.* As Swainson's name was published in the number of Zoological Journal for April—July, 1827, it of course loses priority. The date of Gloger's article I take on the authority of Cabanis, as I have not been able to find it myself.

The following is a synopsis of the species :

A.—Tail graduated. Throat and breast yellow, sides of the head black.

      A broad frontal band of black, bordered behind by hoary white ; rest of crown

        like the back........ ....*G. trichas.*

      A narrow frontal black band, the crown dark ash...........................*G. velatus.*

B.—Tail rounded. Head all round ash ; the feathers of the chin and throat black with ashy margins.

A black patch on the fore part of breast; lores dusky ; no white about the eye...*G. philadelphia.*

Fore part of breast like throat ; forehead and lores black ; eyelids with a white patch...*G. macgillivrayi.*

Comparative measurements of species.

Catal. No.	Species.	Locality.	Sex.	Length.	Stretch of wings.	Wing.	Tail.	Tarsus.	Middle toe.	Its claw alone.	Bill above.	Along gape.	Specimen measured.
2535	Geothlypis trichas	Carlisle, Penn	♂	4.60	......	2.30	2.30	0.76	0.70	0.20	0.44	0.60	Dry......
do.	......do.	......do.		5.50	7.41	2.41	......	......	......	......	......	......	Fresh....
2363	......do.	......do.	♀	4.50	......	2.10	2.10	0.78	0.68	0.19	0.46	0.54	Dry......
do.	......do.	......do.		5.08	6.83	2.16	......						Fresh....
7922	......do.	Racine		5.22		2.30	2.38	0.78	0.68	0.20	0.40	0.56	Dry......
7918	......do.	Fort Steilacoom	♂	5.00	......	2.16	2.30	0.78	0.68	0.16	0.44	0.52	Dry......
do.	......do.	......do.		5.37	6.75	......							Fresh....
7920	......do.	Tulare valley	♂	4.96		2.20	2.24	0.80	0.67	0.18	0.48	0.54	Dry......
10107	......do.	Washington, D. C.	♂	4.36		2.00	2.24	0.70	0.60	0.16	0.42	0.54	Dry......
689	Geothlypis philadelphia.	Carlisle	♂	4.86		2.38	2.26	0.86	0.70	0.18	0.42	0.56	Dry......
1697	......do.	......do.	♂	4.80		2.42	2.28	0.84	0.70	0.18	0.42	0.56	Dry......
do.	......do.	......do.		5.75	8.00	2.50							Fresh....
1037	......do.	......do.	♀	4.56		2.30	2.14	0.82	0.66	0.20	0.41	0.54	Dry......
do.	......do.	......do.		5.33	9.66	2.17	......	......	......	......	......	......	Fresh....
1861	Geothlypis macgillivrayi	Columbia river	♂	5.04		2.38	2.32	0.78	0.66	0.18	0.42	0.56	Dry......

GEOTHLYPIS TRICHAS, Cabanis.

Maryland Yellow-throat.

Turdus trichas, LINN. Syst. Nat. I, 1766, 293.—GMELIN, Syst. Nat. I, 1788.

Sylvia trichas, LATHAM, Ind. Orn. II, 1790.—VIEILLOT, Ois. Am. Sept. II, 1807, 28 ; pl. xxviii & xxix.—AUD. Orn. Biog. I, 1832, 120 : V, 1838, 463, pl. 23 & 240.

Ficedula trichas, BRISSON, Orn.

Geothlypis trichas, CABANIS, Mus. Hein. 1850, 16.

Ficedula marilandica, BRISSON, Orn. III, 1760, 506.

Sylvia marilandica, WILSON, Am. Orn. I, 1808, 88 ; pl. vi, f. 1.

Trichas marilandica, BON. List, 1838.—IB. Consp. 1850, 310.—AUD. Syn. 1839, 65.—IB. Orn. Biog. II, 1841, 78 ; pl. 102.

Regulus mystaceus, STEPHENS, Shaw, Zool. Birds, XIII, II, 1826, 232.

Trichas personatus, SWAINSON, Zool. Jour. III, 1827, 167.

Sylvia roscoe, AUD. Orn. Biog. I, 1832, 124 ; pl. 24. (Young male.)

Trichas roscoe, NUTTALL, Man. I, 2d ed. 1840, 457.

Trichas brachydactyla, SWAINSON, Anim. in Menag. 1838, 295.

BUFFON, Pl. enl. 709, f. 2.

Sp. Ch.—Upper parts olive green, tinged with brown towards the middle of the crown ; chin, throat, and breast as far as the middle of the body, with the under tail coverts bright yellow. Belly dull whitish buff. Sides of body strongly tinged with light olive brown ; under coverts glossed with the same. A band of black on the forehead, (about .20 of an inch wide in the middle,) passing backward so as to cover the cheek and ear coverts, and extending a little above the eye ; this band bordered behind by a suffusion of hoary ash, forming a distinct line above the eye, and widening behind the ear coverts into a larger patch, with a yellow tinge. In winter dress, and in the female, without the black mask, the forehead tinged with brown, the yellow of the throat less extended, the eyelids whitish, and an indistinct superciliary line yellowish. Length of male, 5.50 ; wing, 2.40 ; tail 2.20.

Hab.—North America from Atlantic to Pacific.

The wings of this species are short and much rounded ; they reach a little beyond the basal third of the tail. This is considerably graduated, the outer feather about .40 of an inch

31 b

shorter than the middle ones. The fourth quill is longest; the first shorter than the fifth. The legs are long and of a yellow color.

I have not found any specimens of this species agreeing with the *Trichas personatus* of Swainson as distinguished from his *T. brachydactylus*. All before me have the short lateral toes distinguishing the latter species. Should, therefore, there be really two, as suggested by Swainson, the new one will be that to which he has assigned the name of *personatus*.

Among the specimens before me are several males in autumnal or winter dress in which the entire crown is pale reddish olive, except a very narrow black frontlet. The black of the cheeks is also considerably obscured. This agrees with the *Sylvia roscoe* of Audubon. There is a slight trace only of the conspicuous white ring round the eye, shown in the figure of *roscoe*, this is characteristic of the female; nor is the olive of the back so dark.

Specimens from the west appear larger than eastern ones, and the hoary suffusion back of the black on the head is more sharply defined and whiter. One skin from Racine has the belly yellower than usual, and thus more like *G. velatus*.

This species is readily distinguishable from *G. macgillivrayi* and *philadelphia* in the adult dress. The female and immature specimens of the latter may be distinguished by the bright yellow of the whole under surface of body and tail coverts, and the gray tinge on the neck and throat without the decided yellow of *G. trichas*.

List of specimens.

Catal. No.	Sex and age.	Locality.	When collected.	Whence obtained.	Orig'l No.	Collected by—	Length.	Stretch of wings.	Wing.	Remarks.
2178	♂	Carlisle, Pa.............	April 30, 1845	S. F. Baird........	.....	....	4.75	6.91	2.25	....
2293	♂	......do................	May 20, 1845	.....do............	.....	....	5.08	6 66	2.25	....
2572	♂	......do................	May 4, 1846	......do...........	......	....	5.16	7.08	2.17	....
2656	♂	......do................	May 12, 1846	......do...........	......	....	5.08	7.08	2.17	....
2535	♂	......do................	April 30, 1846	......do....	......	....	5.50	7.43	2.43	....
2215	♂	......do................	April 3, 1846	......do...........	......	....	5.08	7.25	2.25	. ...
385	♀	......do................	April 15, 1846	......do...........	......	....	5.00	6.91		
2303	♀	......do................	May 21, 1845	......do...........	......	....	5.08	6.91	2.16	....
1105	♀	......do................	July 5, 1843	......do...........	......	....	4.75	6.50	2.00	....
703	♂	Washington, D. C.....	April 25, 1842	......do...........	......	....	4.75	6.50	2.00	
8655		Cape Florida..........	....	G. Wurdemann.....	......	....	5.25	7.00	2.25	....
7370	....	Cleveland, Ohio	....	Dr. J. P. Kirtland ..	......	....				....
7922	♂	Racine, Wis	....	A. C. Barry.......	......	....	....	....	....	....
5825	♀	......do................	....	Dr. P. R. Hoy	......	....	....	....		
10152	♂	West Northfield, Ill.....	May 15, 1857	R. Kennicott......	......	....	....	....		
8313	♂	Independence, Mo	May 27, 1857	Wm. M. Magraw..	30	Dr. Cooper	5.00	6.37	2.12	Iris brown; bill black; feet flesh color.
3990	....	Brownsville, Texas.....	....	Lieut. Couch	......	....	4.50	6.25	2.00	....
3992	....	......do...............	....	......do...........	......	....	4.50	6.50	2.00	....
4674	♂	Nebraska..............	May 15	Lieut. Warren.....	......	Dr. Hayden.....	5.37	7.00	2.50	....
4675	....	......do...............	May 12	......do...........	......	......do........	4.75	7.00		....
8836	♂	Loup Fork......	Aug. 6	......do...........	......	......do........	2.25	7.12	2.25	Iris dark brown......
8834	♂	......do...............	Aug. 3	......do...........	......	......do........	5.25	7.00	2.25	....
8837	♂	......do...............	.... do......	......do...........	......	......do........	5.00	7.00	2.25	Iris dark brown......
8835	♂	......do...............	.... do......	......do...........	......	......do........	4.75	6.75	2.25	......do............
5304		Blackfoot country......	Aug. 1, 1855	......do...........	......	....				
8227	○	Fort Laramie, Neb.....	Sept. 17, 1855	Wm. M. Magraw...	209	Dr. Cooper	4.75	6.75	2.25	Iris brown; feet pale brown.
7915	♂	Fort Steilacoom........	April 25, 1856	Dr. Suckley........	327	....	5.87	7.25	2.50	....
7916	♀	......do...............	April 26, 1856	......do...........	398	....				....
7917	....	Shoalwater bay........	Aug. 30, 1854	Gov. Stevens.......	87	Dr. Cooper.....	5.37	6.75		....
7921	....	......do...............	.... do......	......do...........	......	......do........	5.50	7.25		....
4566		San José, al...........	....	A. J. Grayson......	6	....	....	....		
7920	♂	Tulare valley.........	Winter	R. S. Williamson...	......	Dr. Heermann .	....	....		
		Fort Tejon, Cal.......	....	J. Xantus de Vesey.	......	....	....	....		

GEOTHLYPIS VELATUS, Cab.

Gray-headed Warbler.

Sylvia velata, VIEILLOT, Ois. Am. Sept. II, 1807, 22 ; pl. lxxiv.
Trichas velata, SWAINSON, Class. Birds, II, 1837, 247.—NUTTALL., Man. I, 2d ed. 1840, 458.
Geothlypis velata, CAB. Mus. Hein. 1850, 16.
Sylvia cucullata, LATHAM, Ind. Orn. II, 1790, 528. (Not of Wilson.)
" *Sylvia caniicapilla*, PR. MAXIM."
" *Tanagra caniicapilla*, SWAINSON, Zool. Ill. III, 174."
Sylvia delafieldii, AUD. Orn. Biog. V, 1839, 307.
Trichas delafieldii, AUD. Syn. 1839, 65.—IB. Birds Am. II, 1841, 81 ; pl. 103.
Trichas caniicephala, LESSON, Rev. Zool. III, 1840, 13.

SP. CH.—Upper parts and sides dark olive green. Crown ash color. A narrow frontal band passing backwards on the cheeks and ear coverts, and extending a little above the eye. Beneath bright yellow. Length, 4.75 ; wing, 2.55 ; tail, 2.40.

Hab.—West Indies and South America. Oregon?

It is scarcely certain that the present species really belongs to the fauna of the United States. Its occurrence in the West Indies (where it really belongs) and in Oregon, without being found in any intermediate locality, would seem very improbable. Mr. Audubon received his specimen (No. 2905 of the accompanying list) from Mr. Townsend who probably procured it somewhere else than in the assigned locality.[1]

This species is readily distinguishable from the *Geothlypis trichas* by its larger size, bright yellow of the entire under parts, (without any brown,) and the ashy crown, without any lighter space separating it from the black of the forehead. The tail is broad and much graduated ; the lateral feathers .45 of an inch the shortest. The wings are much rounded ; the first quill shorter than the sixth.

List of specimens.

Catal. No.	Sex.	Locality.	Whence obtained.	Collected by—
2905	♂	Oregon?	S. F. Baird	J. J. Audubon
2367	♂	Trinidad	do	John Cassin
562	♂	Mexico?	do	John G. Bell

[1] Nuttall states that Townsend's specimen was taken near Fort Vancouver, O. T., not in California, as given by Audubon.

GEOTHLYPIS PHILADELPHIA, Baird.

Mourning Warbler.

Sylvia philadelphia, WILSON, Am. Orn. II, 1810, 101 ; pl. xiv.—AUDUBON, Orn. Biog. V, 1839, 78, (not figured.)— NUTTALL, Man. I, 1832, 404.
Trichas philadelphia, JARD. Wilson, 1832.—RICH. List, 1837.—BONAP. List, 1838.—AUDUBON, Synopsis, 1839, 64.— IB. Birds Am. II, 1841, 76 ; pl. 101.—REINHARDT, Vidensk. Meddel. for 1853, 1854, 73. (Greenland.)

SP. CH.—Wings but little longer than the tail, reaching but little beyond its base. Head and neck all round with throat and fore part of breast ash gray, paler beneath. The feathers of the chin, throat, and fore breast in reality black, but with narrow ashy margins, more or less concealing the black, except on the breast. Lores and region round the eye dusky, without any trace of a pale ring. Upper parts and sides of the body clear olive green ; the under parts bright yellow. Tail feathers uniform olive ; first primary, with the outer half of the outer web, nearly white. Female with the gray of the crown glossed with olive ; the chin and throat paler centrally, and tinged with fulvous ; a dull whitish ring round the eye. Length, 5.50 inches ; wing, 2.45 ; tail, 2.25.

Hab.—Eastern North America, as far west as Independence Mo. Greenland, Reinhardt.

In this species the wings are short and broad ; the tertials in the closed wing longer than the secondaries, and about .45 of an inch shorter than the primaries ; the wing considerably rounded, the first quill intermediate between the fourth and fifth, the second longest.   The tail is moderately graduated, the lateral feathers .15 of an inch shorter than the middle one.

It is quite possible that in the full plumaged male the entire throat may be black, as there is a tendency to this in some specimens.   A fall male (1697) shows the black only on the fore breast.

Authors describe the black feathers of the throat as crenulated (margined) with white.   I have never seen any specimens (out of about twenty) in which these margins were other than ash color.

The mourning warbler is very similar to the *Oporornis agilis*, and is only to be distinguished by the smaller size, much shorter, and more rounded wings, longer legs, and shorter toes, and other generic characters.   The adult males are easily separated by the decided black of the throat and absence of white ring round the eye in *G. philadelphia*.   The females are much more closely related, both having the pale ring round the eye.   The longer and more pointed wings of *agilis* will distinguish them ; the relations to *G. macgillivrayi* will be pointed out under that species.

A female (2906) has a strong tinge of buff yellow on the throat.

List of specimens.

Catal. No.	Sex.	Locality.	When collected.	Whence obtained.	Orig. No.	Length.	Stretch of wings.	Wing.	Remarks.
1499	♂	Carlisle, Pa.	May 26, 1844	S. F. Baird		5. 50	7. 75	2. 41	
1697	♂	do	Sept. 6, 1844	do		5. 75	8. 00	2. 50	
1011	♂	do	Sept. 24, 1843	do		5. 33	8. 16	2. 58	
1024	♀	do	May 26, 1843	do		5. 25	7. 75	2. 41	
103?	♀	do	May 30, 1843	do		5. 33	7. 66	2. 16	
2273	♀	do	May 17, 1845	do		5. 16	7. 75	2. 41	
427?	♀	do	May 28, 1841	do		5. 41	7. 66		
	♀	South Illinois	May 11, 1841	R. Kennicott					
7515		Independence, Mo		Dr. Cooper	45	5. 00	6. 00	2. 50	Iris and bill brown, feet pale brown

GEOTHLYPIS MACGILLIVRAYI, B a i r d .

Macgillivray's Warbler.

Sylvia macgillivrayi, AUDUBON, Orn. Biog. V, 1839, 75 ; pl. 399. (*Sylvia philadelphia* on plate.)
Trichas macgillivrayi, AUD. Syn. 1839, 64.—IB. Birds Amer. II, 1841, 74 ; pl. 100.
Sylvia tolmiei, TOWNSEND, J. A. N. Sc. VIII, 1839, 149, 159. (Read April, but the volume really not published till 1840.)
Sylvia tolmiei, TOWNSEND, Narrative, 1839, 343.
Trichas tolmiaei, NUTTALL, Man. I, 2d ed., 1840, 460.

SP. CH.—Head and neck all round, throat and fore part of the breast dark ash color ; a narrow frontlet, loral region and space round the eye (scarcely complete behind) black.   The eyelids above and below the eye (not in a continuous ring) white.   The feathers of the chin, throat, and fore breast really black, with ashy gray tips, more or less concealing the black.   Rest of upper parts dark olive green, (sides under the wings paler ;) of lower, bright yellow.   Female with the throat paler and without any black.   Length of male, 5 inches ; wing, 2.45 ; tail, 2.45.

Hab.—Pacific coast of North America, south to Gulf of California and across to Monterey, Mexico.   In Rocky mountains to Fort Laramie? (Dr. Cooper.)

In this species the wings are short and rounded, about as long as the tail, and reaching only over its basal third. The primaries are about half an inch longer than the tertials, the first quill intermediate between the fifth and sixth. The tail feathers are moderately graduated. This species bears a most remarkable resemblance to the *T. philadelphia*, of which it is the western representative ; the only prominent distinction is in the white spots on the eyelids. The size and general proportions are much the same ; but the ash and black of the breast do not come so far down in the western species, the loral region is much blacker, and the black frontlet is wanting in *philadelphia*. The bill is more slender, the wings more rounded, the legs shorter. The females are only distinguishable by the slenderer bill and more rounded wings of *G. macgillivrayi*, in which the first quill is intermediate between the fifth and sixth, instead of being considerably longer than the fifth.

The peculiarities of wing will serve to distinguish this species from *Oporornis agilis* in autumn and winter. The crown then is probably tinged with olive.

The selection of a specific name for this bird from the two at our command is a matter of much perplexity. Both were apparently published in 1839, and without indication of the month. Mr. Townsend's article was read before the Academy at Philadelphia, April 2, 1839, (Journal VIII, II,) and printed on page 149. The next sheet contains a note dated September 10, 1839, in which he refers to the article and page of Audubon, and claims priority of publication for his Narrative of Travels.

A few pages further on, and on the penultimate page (170) of Part I, is an article on *Fuligula grisea* by Dr. Leib, "read January 7, 1840." This evidently shows that the volume was not issued till 1840, as it could not otherwise have contained a paper read January 7, 1840, only 21 pages later than where Townsend's species is described.

This clearly settles the question of priority in favor of Vol. V of the Ornithological Biography. Although Townsend claims precedence of the description in his Narrative, yet as the one work was published in Edinburgh, and the other in Philadelphia, the former might have been issued first without the knowledge of the latter. The article in the Journal of Academy does not quote the Narrative, while that in the Narrative quotes the volume of the Journal, (not the page, however.) The inference would, therefore, be that the latter appeared first of the two.

Under the circumstances, then, I think it proper to retain the better known name of Audubon, and accordingly adopt that of *G. macgillivrayi*.

List of specimens.

Catal. No.	Sex and age.	Locality.	When collected.	Whence obtained.	Orig. No.	Collected by	Length.	Stretch of wings.	Wing.	Remarks.
7905	♂	Fort Steilacoom, W. T..	May 3, 1856	Dr. Suckley......	356					
7907	♂	........do.............	.....do......	......do.........	385	....	5.50	7.50		
7911	♂	........do.............	Jan. 25, 1855	Dr. Cooper......		....	5.25	7.25		
7910	♀	........do.............	.....do......	......do........		....	5.12	7.00		
2907	○♂	Columbia river.........	May —, 1835	J. K. Townsend..						
1910	♂	........do.............	.....do......	......do.........						
1861	♂	........do.............	May 4, 1836	.... do.........						
4947	....	San José, California....	....	A. J. Grayson....	3					
7912	....	Mimbres to Rio Grande.	....	Dr. Henry........						
7913	♂	Frontera......	May 5, 1852	Chas. Wright.....		....	5.50	7.00	2.50	....
	?	Fort Laramie	Aug. 31, 1857	Wm. M. Magraw..	179	Dr. Cooper.	5.50	7.62	2.62	Iris and bill brown...........
	?	........do.............	......do......	......do.........	180	.....do......	5.25	7.37	2.50	Iris black, feet gray.......
3989	....	Monterey, Mexico......	May —, 1853	Lieut. Couch.....	213	....	5.00	7.00	2.50	Eye brown, feet dull white.
3988	♀	........do.............	......do......	...... do.........	205	....	5.50	7.25	2.50	....

OPORORNIS,[1] Baird.

Ch.—Bill sylvicoline, rather compressed ; distinctly notched at tip ; rictal bristles very much reduced. Wings elongated, pointed, much longer than the tail ; the first quill nearly or quite the longest. Tail very slightly rounded ; tail feathers acuminate, pointed ; the under coverts reaching to within less than half an inch of their tip. Tarsi elongated, longer than the head ; claws large, the hinder one as long as its digit, and longer than the lateral toes. Above olive green ; beneath yellow ; tail and wings immaculate. Legs yellow.

This group of American warblers is very distinct from any other. The typical species is quite similar in color to *Geothlypis philadelphia*, but is at once to be distinguished by much longer wings, more even tail, and larger toes and claws. It is also very similar to *Seiurus*, differing chiefly in the longer wings, larger claws, and absence of spots beneath.

Throat and crown ash color ; a white ring round the eye. No black on the side of the head..*O. agilis*.

Throat and superciliary stripe yellow ; top of the head and a streak beneath the eye black..*O. formosas*.

Comparative measurements of species.

Catal. No.	Species.	Locality.	Sex.	Length.	Stretch of wings.	Wing.	Tail.	Tarsus.	Middle toe.	Its claw alone.	Bill above.	Along gape.	Specimen measured.
2309	Oporornis agilis......	Carlisle, Penn.....	♂	5.20	....	2.86	2.28	0.80	0.76	0.18	0.48	0.69	Dry......
do.	......do...............	.....do............		5.91	9.00	3.00	....	....	....	....	....	....	Fresh....
1239	......do...............	Philadelphia......		5.00	....	2.74	2.30	0.80	0.70	0 16	0.43	0.56	Dry......
	Oporornis formosus	Georgia...........	♂	4.76	....	2.86	2.20	0.82	0.72	0.18	0.40	0.54	Dry......
10153	......do...............	South Illinois.. ...	♀	5.36	....	2.60	2.10	0.93	0.74	0.18	0.44	0.58	Dry......

OPORORNIS AGILIS, Baird.

Connecticut Warbler.

Sylvia agilis, Wilson, Am. Orn. V, 1812, 64 ; pl. xxxix, f. 4.—Bonap. Obs. Wils. 1825, no. 163.—Aud. Orn. Biog. II, 1834, 227 ; pl. 138.

Sylvicola agilis, Jardine ed. Wilson, 1832.—Rich. List, 1837.—Aud. Synopsis, 1839, 63.—Ib. Orn. Biog. II, 1841, 71 ; pl. 99.

Trichas agilis, Nuttall, Man. I, 2d ed. 1840, 403.

Trichas tephrocotis, Nuttall, Man. I, 2d ed. 1840, 462, (Chester county, Penn., adult with whole head ash.)

Sp. Ch.—Upper parts and sides of the body uniform olive green, very slightly tinged with ash on the crown. Sides of the head ash tinged with dusky beneath the eye. (Entire head sometimes ash.) Chin and throat grayish ash, gradually becoming darker to the upper part of the breast, where it becomes tinged with dark ash. Sides of the neck, breast, and body, olive, like the back ; rest of under parts light yellow. A broad continuous white ring round the eye. Wings and tail feathers olive, (especially the latter,) without any trace of bars or spots. Bill brown above. Feet yellow. Length, 6 inches ; wing, 3 ; tail, 2.25.

Hab.—Eastern United States. (Very rarely seen.)

In this species the wings are long and pointed, reaching beyond the middle of the tail or within an inch of the end, (in the fresh specimen.) The primaries are .85 of an inch longer than the secondaries. The primaries become successively and decidedly shorter than the first, which is longest. The tail feathers are broad, acuminate, and slightly graduated.

A second specimen (2939) is similar, but differs in having the crown dark plumbeous ash. Both of these are spring specimens. In fall, when the species is much more frequently seen,

[1] The name is used in reference to the abundance of *O. agilis* in autumn, compared with its excessive rarity in spring.

the ash of the throat is so strongly tinged with brownish (with perhaps a tinge of olive) as to obscure the ash. The crown also is like the back.

The *Trichas tephrocotis* of Nuttall appears to be only an adult in very full plumage, with the entire head above clear bluish ash, (as just referred to in No. 2939,) instead of glossed with olivaceous, as in most specimens.

List of specimens.

Catal. No.	Sex.	Locality.	When collected.	Whence obtained.	Collected by—	Length.	Stretch of wings.	Wing.
2939	......	Eastern U. States..	....	....	J. J. Audubon	......	......	......
2309	♂	Carlisle, Pa.......	May 20, 1845	S. F. Baird	....	5.91	9.00	3.00
1235	......	Philadelphia, Pa...	Oct. 3, 1843	......do..........	....	......	......	......
	♂	South Illinois	May 15, 1855	N. W. University..	R. Kennicott......	......	......	......

OPORORNIS FORMOSUS, Baird.

Kentucky Warbler.

Sylvia formosa, WILSON, Am. Orn. III, 1811, 85 ; pl. xxv, f. 3.—BONAP. Obs. Wils. 1825-6, 156.—NUTTALL, Man. I, 1832, 399.—AUDUBON, Orn. Biog. I, 1832, 196 ; pl. 38.
Sylvicola formosa, JARDINE ed. Wilson, 1832.—RICH. List, 1837.—BONAP. List, 1838.
Myiodioctes formosus, AUD. Syn. 1839, 50.—IB. Birds America, II, 1841, 19 ; pl. 74.—BONAP. Conspectus, 1850, 315.

SP. CH.—Upper parts and sides dark olive green. Crown and sides of the head, including a triangular patch from behind the eye down the side of the neck, black, the feathers of the crown narrowly lunulated at tips with dark ash. A line from nostrils over the eye and encircling it (except anteriorly) with the entire under parts, bright yellow. No white on the tail. Female similar, with less black on the head. Length, 5 inches ; wing, 2.95 ; tail, 2.25.

Hab.—Eastern United States as far west as Fort Riley, south to Guatemala.

The wings of this species are long and pointed ; the first three nearly equal and considerably longer than the rest. The tail is slightly rounded.

List of specimens.

Catal. No.	Sex.	Locality.	When collected.	Whence obtained.	Orig. No.	Collected by—	Length.	Stretch of wings.	Wing.	Remarks.
2373	......	Georgia	....	S. F. Baird	.. ....	....	......	......	......	....
10154	......	Union county, Ill	May 12,——	R. Kennicott.......	......	....	......	......	......	....
10153	♀	South Ill.....	May 15,——	......do............	......	....	......	......	......	....
6985	♂	St. Louis, Mo...........	May 13,1857	Lieut. Bryan.......	79	W. S. Wood.....	......	......	......	....
7520	......	Independence, Mo......	....	Dr. Cooper	25	....	5.50	8.00	3.00	Iris brown, feet flesh.
5889	......	Fort Riley, K. T.........	....	{ Dr. Hammond & { Mr. DeVesey.	......	....	......	......	......	....
7988	......	Guatemala	....	J. Gould...........	......	....	......	......	......	....

Section **Icterieae.**

ICTERIA, Vieillot.

Icteria, VIEILLOT, Ois. Am. Sept. I, 1790, iii and 85.

Bill shorter than the head ; broad at the base, but rapidly becoming compressed or much higher than broad, with the ridge elevated and sharp from the very base of the bill ; the upper outline much curved throughout ; the commissure less curved but strongly concave ; the gonys nearly straight, the upper edge of the lower jaw as convex as the commissure is concave. No notch in the bill and the rictal bristles small. Tarsi longer than the toes, without scutellae, except faint indications on the inner side. Lateral toes about equal ; shorter than the hinder. Wings about equal to the tail, rounded ; the first quill longer than the secondaries. Tail graduated ; above olive ; beneath yellow. Abdomen, eyelids, maxillary patch, and line to the bill, white.

The proper position of this genus has always been a matter of much uncertainty, but I see no reason why it may not legitimately be assigned to the *Sylvicolinae*, possessing, as it does, so many of their characteristics. The bill is stouter and more curved than in the rest, but the other characters agree very well. It cannot properly be placed with the vireos and shrikes on account of the absence of a spurious primary, as well as of a notch in either mandible.

The two species are best distinguished by the relative length of the tail.

Comparative measurements of species.

Catal. No.	Species.	Locality.	Sex.	Length.	Stretch of wings.	Wing.	Tail.	Tarsus.	Middle toe.	Its claw alone.	Bill above.	Along gape.	Specimens measured.
8602	Icteria longicauda*...	California.........	......	8.00	....	3.14	3.92	1.00	0.80	0.21	0.58	0.74	Dry...........
5520	......do	Petaluma, Cal.....	♂	7.04	....	3.14	3.80	1.04	0.86	0.20	0.60	0.72	Dry...........
do.	......do	......do	......	7.50	9.16	3.16	.....	.....	.....	.....	.....	.....	Fresh..........
3978	......do	New Leon, Mex....	♂	6.90	....	3.10	3.70	1.00	0.84	0.24	0.60	0.80	Dry...........
do.	......do	......do	....	6.75	9.75	3.25	.....						Fresh..........
2360	Icteria viridis........	Carlisle, Pa......	♂	6.70	....	3.02	3 28	1.02	0.80	0.22	0.60	0.76	Dry...........
do.	......do	......do	....	7.41	10 00	3.25	.....						Fresh..........
2312	...... do	......do	♀	6.20	....	2.93	3.16	1.00	0.84	0.21	0.58	0.68	Dry...........
do.	...... do	......do	......	7.00	9.50	3.00	.....						Fresh... ......

* The original of Mr. Lawrence's *Icteria longicauda.*

ICTERIA VIRIDIS, Bonap.

Yellow Breasted Chat.

Muscicapa viridis, GMELIN, Syst. Nat. I, 1788, 936.
Icteria viridis, BONAP. Obs. Wilson, 1826, No. 163.—IB. List, 1838.—IB. Consp. 1850, 331.—NUTTALL, Man. I,
1832, 299.—AUD. Orn. Biog. II, 1834, 223 : V, 433 ; pl. 137.—IB. Syn. 1839, 163.—IB. Birds Am.
Icteria dumecola, VIEILLOT, Ois. Am. Sept. I, 1807, 85 ; pl. lv.
Pipra polyglotta, WILSON, Am. Orn. I, 1808, 90.
" *Tanagra olivacea*, DESMAREST, Tangaras, (♂, not the ♀ or ○.)"
" *Ampelis luteus*, SPARRMANN, Mus. Carls. tab. lxx," (Bonap.)
? *Icteria velasquezii*, BONAP. Pr. Zool. Soc. 1837, 117.—IB. Consp. 1850, 331.
Merula viridis carolinensis, BRISSON, II, 1760, 315.
Yellow breasted chat, CATESBY, Carol. I, 1730, tab. l.
Chattering flycatcher, PENNANT, II, 388.—LATHAM, Syn. II, I, 360.

SP. CH.—Third and fourth quills longest ; second and fifth little shorter ; first nearly equal to the sixth. Tail graduated. Upper parts uniform olive green ; under parts, including the inside of wing, gamboge yellow as far as nearly half way from the point of the bill to the tip of the tail ; rest of under parts white, tinged with brown on the sides ; the outer side of the tibia plumbeous ; a slight tinge of orange across the breast. Forehead and sides of the head ash, the lores and region below the eye blackish. A white stripe from the nostrils over the eye and involving the upper eyelid ; a patch on the lower lid, and a short stripe from the side of the lower mandible, and running to a point opposite the hinder border of the eye, white. Bill black ; feet brown. Female like the male, but smaller ; the markings indistinct ; the lower mandible not pure black. Length, 7.40 ; wing, 3.25 ; tail, 3.30.

Hab.—Eastern United States to the Missouri, south to Guatemala.

The graduation of the tail in this species amounts to about .40 of an inch or less. There is the faintest possible trace of a whitish tip to the inner webs of the lateral tail feathers.

The female is smaller than the male, the markings less distinct, and the under mandible, instead of being entirely bluish black, is brownish white, the edges darker. A specimen from Guatemala agrees exactly with females from the Atlantic States, except in having the lower mandible rather purer white than in those before me, but the difference is not very great. This character of bill corresponds with that of *Icteria velasquezii* of Bonaparte, but as the long tailed western species or race has the bill light colored also in the female and young, it is difficult to say to which Bonaparte's species should be referred. It is possible that Guatemala winter specimens belong to *J. viridis*, and Mexican summer ones to *J. longicauda*.

List of specimens.

Catal. No.	Sex.	Locality.	When collected.	Whence obtained.	Orig. No.	Collected by—	Length.	Stretch of wings.	Wing.	Remarks.
2311	♂	Carlisle, Pa............	May 23, 1845	S. F. Baird.........		....	7.33	10.00	3.08	....
2260	......	......do.....	May 14, 1845	......do...........	.....	....	7.41	10.00	3.25	....
2292	♂	......do........	May 20, 1845	......do......... ...		....	7.08	9.66	3.00	....
2312	♀	......do.........	May 23, 1845	......do...........		....	7.00	9.50	3.00	....
7578	......	Washington, D. C......	....	W. Hutton		....	....	....		....
7535	......	West Northfield, Ill.....	May 17, 1855	R. Kennicott.......		....	....	....		....
6997	......	South Illinois..........	May 11, 1855	......do...........		....	.....	....	....	....
......	♂	St. Louis, Mo..........	....	C. Drexler.......		....	... ...	....	...	....
......	......	...... do.....	May —, 1857	Lieut. Bryan.......		W. S. Wood...	....	....		....
8397	♂	Independence, Mo.	Jan. 29, 1857	Wm. M. Magraw ..	107	Dr. Cooper	7.20	9.00	3.00	Iris brown, feet lead....
6998	......	Leavenworth, K. T.....	May 28, 1857	Lieut. Bryan.......		W. S. Wood...	....	....		....
5647	♂	East of Fort Riley......	June 14, 1856	......do...........	10	......do.......	....	....		....
5648	♂	......do.....	June 20, 1856	......do...........	34	......do....... ...	.. ..	......		....
8195	♀	Nemaha river, K. T....	July 16, 1857	Wm. M. Magraw...	131	Dr. Cooper	7.00	9.00	2.75	Iris brown, bill black and white, feet lead ......
7954	♀	Guatemala......	....	J. Gould.........		....	....	....		....

ICTERIA LONGICAUDA, Lawrence.

Long-tailed Chat.

Icteria longicauda, LAWRENCE, Ann. N. Y. Lyc. VI, Ap. 1853, 4.
? *Icteria auricollis*, (LICHT. Mus. Ber.) BONAP. Consp. 1850,¦331.

SP. CH.—Similar to *I. viridis*. Fourth quill longest; third and fifth shorter; first shorter than the seventh. Above ash color, tinged with olive on the back and neck; the outer surface of the wings and tail olive. The under parts as far as the middle of the belly bright gamboge yellow, with a tinge of orange; the remaining portions white. The superciliary and maxillary white stripes extend some distance behind the eye. Outer edge of the first primary white. Length, 7 inches; wing, 3.20; tail, 3.70.

Hab.—High central plains of the United States to the Pacific; south into Mexico.

This *Icteria* appears to differ in some appreciable points from the common species of the United States. The upper parts are less olivaceous, the forehead and even the crown decided ash color, instead of olive. The white marks on the head are more extended, the superciliary stripe broader and extending a quarter of an inch behind the eye. The maxillary white stripe is broader, and reaches back to a distance equal to the length of the lower mandible, instead of little more than half as far. The outer edge of the first primary is pure white instead of olivaceous. The yellow of the breast is more orange. The proportions of the quills are different, in having the fourth quill longest, the first shorter than the seventh. The tail also is nearly half an inch longer.

This description, based on No. 3978, from New Leon, agrees in the main with nearly all the

32 b

specimens from the Missouri plains and westward. Some of these vary, however, and in most cases the characters of wing are more like those of *I. viridis*, from Pennsylvania. The only constant feature is the greater length of tail in western specimens, which prevails throughout. If there be a specific difference, it will be based essentially upon the latter feature, upon which the *Icteria longicauda* of Mr. Lawrence was founded. His specimen, now before me, has the tail rather longer than in any other I have seen, measuring 3.90 inches. A California specimen from Petaluma measures 3.60, or a little less than in No. 3978. Mr. Lawrence's specimen is in other respects much like the eastern ones, having less white about the sides of the head, less gray on the crown, and less white on the outer margin of first primary than in No. 3975.

The determination of the name of this long-tailed species (if it be really one) of *Icteria* is a matter of much uncertainty. There are three from which to choose: *I. velasquezii* of Bonaparte, 1837, *auricollis* of 1850, and *longicauda*, Lawrence, of 1853. Neither *velasquezii* nor *auricollis* are described in a way to indicate any material difference from *I. viridis*. The former is said to have the under mandible white. If this be found to be a constant character in adult males, it is probable that none of the specimens in the Smithsonian collection belong to it. The description of *auricollis*, though not distinctive, will answer very well, especially as the white about the head is mentioned so particularly as to render it probable that it appeared more conspicuous than in the *I. viridis*, which is really the case in the subject of the present article. As based on a Mexican specimen, it in all probability is the same with those from New Leon—3978—and these identical, as far as I can see, with Nebraska and California ones. Still, as Mr. Lawrence's description is positively applicable to the one bird only, and Bonaparte's answers almost equally well for both, I prefer to adopt the name of the former, leaving a further examination of the type of *auricollis* in the Berlin Museum to settle the question.

Specimens from Loup Fork, apparently young, (8841–'2,) differ in having the upper parts of a dull brownish yellow, occasionally touched with olivaceous. The under mandibles are whitish.

List of specimens.

Catal. No.	Sex.	Locality.	When collected.	Whence obtained.	Orig'l No.	Collected by—	Length.	Stretch of wings.	Wing.	Remarks.
8602		California		G. N. Lawrence						
5520		Petaluma, Cal.	April —, 1856	E. Samuels			7.50	9.16	3.16	
		Fort Tejon, Cal		J. Xantus de Vesey						
8175		Frontera	May 10, 1852	Chas. Wright						
8174		Fort Thorn, N. M		Dr. Henry						
4725	♂	Nebraska	May 17, 1856	Lt. Warren		Dr. Hayden	7.75	10.00	3.25	
4724		Mouth White river	May 21, —	......do		......do	7.25	9.75	3.25	
5307	♂	Ft. Lookout, Neb.	May 31, —	......do		......do	7.50	10.00	3.00	Eyes black
5310	♀	......do	June 17, 1856	......do		......do	7.00	9.50	3.25	......do
5011	♂	......do		......do		......do	7.25	9.75	3.25	
5308		......do		......do		......do	7.25	10.00	2.00	Eyes black
5304?	♂	......do	June 21, 1856	......do		......do	7.25	9.50	3.25	......do
4647		Ft. Pierre, Neb.	June 12, 1855	Col. Vaughan		......do				
4648	♂	......do	May 12, 1855	......do		......do				
5306	♀	Little Shyenne	June 1, 1856	Lt. Warren		......do	7.00	9.62	3.00	Eyes black
5649	♂	Platte	Aug. 21, 1856	Lt. Bryan	292	W. S. Wood				
8841	♂	Loup Fork	Aug. 5, —	Lt. Warren		Dr. Hayden	7.00	9.50	2.75	Iris gray
8842	♂	......do	......do	......do		......do	6.75	8.12	3.25	
8778		Forks of Platte river	Aug. 13, 1857	W. M. Magraw	151	Dr. Cooper				
4971		Ft. Chadbourne, Tex.		Dr. Swift						
3978	♂	New Leon, Mex	Mar. —, 1853	Lt. Couch			6.75	9.75	3.25	
3979	♂	......do		......do	121		7.25	9.50	3.25	Bill b'k; ft. dark lead.
9109		Mexico		M. Verreaux	34716					

Section **Vermivoreae.**

Bill entirely without notch, and with no rictal bristles. Legs variable.

The following genera compose this section :

HELMITHERUS.—Bill stout, only moderately acute, nearly as long as the head, and on a line with the forehead. Middle toe as long as the short tarsus. Colors plain ; no white on the tail.

HELMINTHOPHAGA.—Bill slender, excessively acute, shorter than the head. Tarsus considerably longer than the middle toe. Tail feathers sometimes with a white patch.

Comparative measurements of species.

Catal. No.	Species.	Locality.	Sex.	Length.	Stretch of wings.	Wing.	Tail.	Tarsus.	Middle toe.	Its claw alone.	Bill above.	Along gape.	Specimen measured.
2148	Helmitherus vermivorus .	Carlisle, Pa......	♂	4.74	....	2.84	2.30	0.72	0.64	0.20	0.56	0.62	Dry......
do.	.....do.........do......	.....do........	......	5.41	9.25	2.92	....	....	....	....	....	....	Fresh ...
2901	.....do.....swainsoni...	Charleston, S. C..	....	5.50	....	2.74	2.24	0.68	0.62	0.20	0.64	0.68	Dry......
2229	Helminthophaga solitaria.	Carlisle, Pa	♂	4.04	....	2.38	2.00	0.66	0.52	0.16	0.46	0.50	Dry......
408	.....do............do....	......do........	♀	4.50	....	2.30	1.96	0.65	0.50	0.16	0.46	0.50	Dry......
10156	.....do.....chrysopterus.	Union county, Ill.	......	5.08	....	2.54	2.16	0.70	0.52	0.16	0.46	0.50	Dry......
1917	.....do.........do......	....	♀	4.46	....	2.34	1.96	0.60	0.48	0.14	0.42	0.50	Dry......
2903	.....do.....bachmani....	Charleston, S. C.	♂	4.50	....	2.46	2.06	0.70	0.50	0.16	0.46	0.50	Dry......
10158	.....do.....peregrina....	Cairo, Ill	......	4.82	....	2.50	1.83	0.66	0.56	0.14	0.42	0.50	Dry......
2929	.....do.....celata........	Columbia river...	♂	5.06	....	2.48	2.04	0.72	0.58	0.16	0.40	0.48	Dry......
2238	.....do.....ruficapilla....	Carlisle, Pa......	♂	4.04	.. ....	2.46	2.00	0.64	0.52	0.16	0.40	0.46	Dry......
2237	.....do.........do......	.....do........	♀	4.06	....	2.31	1.90	0.63	0.54	0.14	0.39	0.44	Dry......

HELMITHERUS, R a f.

Helmitherus, RAFINESQUE, Journal de Physique, LXXXVIII, 1819, 417. Type *Motacilla vermivora*.
Vermivora, SWAINSON, Zool. Jour. IV, 1827, 170, (not of MEYER, 1822.)
Helinaia, AUD. Synopsis, 1839, 66. Type *Sylvia swainsoni*, Aud.

CH.—Bill large and stout, compressed, almost tanagrine ; nearly or quite as long as the head. Culmen very slightly curved ; gonys straight ; no notch in the bill ; rictal bristles wanting. Tarsi short, but little longer, if any, than the middle toe. Tail considerably shorter than the wings ; rather rounded. Wings rather long, the first quill a little shorter than the second and third.

The birds of this division are very plain in their colors, more so than any other American warblers. There are but two species referrible to the genus, of which the *H. swainsoni* differs from the type in having a considerably longer and more compressed bill, the ridge of which is com- pressed, elevated, and appears to extend backwards on the forehead, as well as to be in a straight line with the upper part of the head. The wings are longer ; the tail forked, not rounded ; the feathers narrower and more pointed ; the tarsi shorter than in the type. It is quite possible that systematic writers may hereafter find it necessary to erect this form into a distinct genus or sub-genus to be called *Helinaia*.

Synopsis of the species.

Colors plain. Above olivaceous, beneath nearly white. No spots or bands on wing or tail.

Above olive green. Head yellowish, with two black stripes above and one behind the eye. Tail rounded...*H. vermivorus.*

Above dull olive green, tinged with brown. Stripes on the head somewhat as in the last, but reddish brown ; the median light stripe on the crown scarcely visible. Tail slightly forked... ....*H. swainsoni.*

HELMITHERUS VERMIVORUS, Bonap.

Worm-eating Warbler.

? Motacilla vermivora, GMELIN, Syst. Nat. I, 1788, 951.

Sylvia vermivora, LATHAM, Ind. Orn. II, 1790, 499.—WILSON, Am. Orn. III, 1811, 74 ; pl. xxiv, f. 4.—BONAP, Obs. WILSON, 1826.—AUD. Orn. Biog. I, 1832, 177 : V, 460 ; pl. xxxiv.

Sylvia (Dacnis) vermivora, NUTTALL, Man. I, 1832, 409.

Sylvicola vermivora, RICH. List, 1837.

Helinaia vermivora, AUD. Syn. 1839, 66.—IB. Birds Am. II, 1841, 86 ; pl. 105.

Helmitherus vermivorus, BONAP. Conspectus, 1850, 314.—CAB. Mus. Hein. 1850, 20.

Ficedula pennsylvanica, BRISSON, Orn. VI, 1760, app. 102.

Vermivora pennsylvanica, "SWAINSON," BONAP. List, 1838.—GOSSE, Birds, Jam. 1847, 150.

Helmitheros migratorius, RAFINESQUE, Jour. de Phys. LXXXVIII, 1819, 417.—HARTLAUB, Rev. Zool. 1845, 342.

Vermivora fulvicapilla, SWAINSON, Birds, II, 1837, 245.

SP CH.—Bill nearly as long as the head ; upper parts generally rather clear olive green. Head with four-black stripes and three brownish yellow ones, namely, a black one on each side of the crown and one from behind the eye, (extending, in fact, a little anterior to it,) a broader median yellow one on the crown, and a superciliary from the bill. Under parts pale brownish yellow, tinged with buff across the breast, and with olivaceous on the sides. Tail unspotted. Female nearly similar. Length, 5.50 ; wing, 3.00 ; tail, 2.35.

Hab.—Eastern United States to Missouri river ; south to Guatemala.

The first three quills are about equal and decidedly longer than the fourth. The tail is slightly rounded. A specimen from Florida is brighter olive above.

List of specimens.

Catal. No.	Sex.	Locality.	When collected.	Whence obtained.	Orig'l No.	Collected by—	Length.	Stretch of wings.	Wing.	Remarks.
2148	♂	Carlisle, Pa............	April 26, 1845	S. F. Baird........	......	....	....	....	......	....
358	♀	......do.........	May 12, 1841	......do...	......	....	....	....	......	....
7565	......	Washington	....	W. Hutton	......	....	....	....	......	....
10106	♂	......do............	....	J. C. McGuire	......	....	....	....	......	....
8670	......	Cape Florida	Sept. 25, 1857	G. Wurdemann....	......	....	5.75	8.75	2.75	Upper mandible blackish, lower black, very light legs.
8309	......	Independence, Mo.....	May 27, 1857	Wm. M. Magraw ..	26	Dr. Cooper.....	5.75	9.00	3.00	Iris brown, bill brown, feet flesh color.
8014	......	Guatemala	....	J. Gould........	......	....	....	....	......	....

HELMITHERUS SWAINSONII, Bonap.

Swainson's Warbler.

Sylvia swainsonii, AUD. Orn. Biog. II, 1834, 563 : V, 462 ; pl. cxcviii.

Sylvicola swainsonii, RICH. List, 1837.

Vermivora swainsonii, BONAP. List, 1838.

Helinaia swainsonii, AUD. Syn. 1839, 66.—IB. Birds Amer. II, 1841, 83 ; pl. civ, (type of genus.)

Helmitherus swainsonii, BONAP. Conspectus, 1850, 314.—CABANIS, Mus. Hein. 1850, 20.

SP. CH.—Bill as long as the head. Upper parts dull olive green, tinged with reddish brown on the wings, and still more on the crown and nape ; a superciliary stripe and the under parts of the body are white, tinged with yellow, but palest on the tail coverts ; the sides pale olive brown. There is an obscure indication of a median yellowish stripe on the forehead. The lores are dusky. No spots or bands on wings or tail. Length, 5.60 ; wing, 2.85 ; tail, 2.20.

Hab.—South Atlantic States.

The bill of this species is on a line with the forehead, the upper outline nearly straight almost to the tip, the lower quite so. The wings are long, the quills attenuated at tip ; the first three longest, (first rather shorter,) and abruptly longer than the fourth. The tail is moderately forked. The tarsi are quite short.

This species is very seldom seen in collections, though probably not rare in Georgia and Florida. It is said to have been shot in Massachusetts, though this seems hardly probable.

List of specimens.

Catalogue number.	Locality.	Whence obtained.	Collected by—
2901	Charleston, S. C.	S. F. Baird	J. J. Audubon
3319	Liberty county, Ga.	do.	W. L. Jones

HELMINTHOPHAGA, Cabanis.

Helminthophaga, CABANIS, Mus. Hein. 1850–1851, 20. Type *Sylvia ruficapilla*.

CH.—Bill elongated, conical, very acute ; the outlines very nearly straight, sometimes slightly decurved ; no trace of notch at the tip. Wings long and pointed ; the first quill nearly or quite the longest. Tail nearly even or slightly emarginate ; short and rather slender. Tarsi longer than the middle toe.

The species of this section are well characterized by the attenuation and acuteness of the bill, and the absence of any notch. There are, however, considerable subordinate differences in the different species. In some the bill is larger and more acute than others ; in one species, the *H. peregrina*, the wings are unusually lengthened, the tail being only about seven-twelfths as long.

The following synopsis will serve to distinguish the species. Their measurements will be found on page 251.

A.—A distinct patch of white on the outer tail feathers ; wings varied with white or yellow.

Olive green above ; forehead, vertex and beneath yellow ; lores black ; wings and tail blue ; two bands on the wing and crissum white...*pinus.*

Above and on sides of body blue ; forehead, vertex, and a large patch on the wings yellow. Throat and cheek patch black. Rest of lower parts and maxillary stripe white..*chrysoptera.*

Above olive green ; throat, fore part of breast, and band across the crown black ; forehead, lesser wing coverts, chin, and under parts yellow..................................*bachmani.*

B.—Tail without any conspicuous patch ; wings not varied. Above olive green.

Crown and nape ash, with a concealed patch of brownish orange. A white ring round the eye. Beneath bright yellow..*ruficapilla.*

Above uniform olive green. Crown with a concealed patch of brownish orange. Eyelids and obscure superciliary line yellowish. Beneath greenish yellow.......*celata.*

Crown ash gray, without any patch. Beneath olivaceous white, as are also the eyelids and a superciliary line...*peregrina.*

HELMINTHOPHAGA PINUS, Baird.

Blue-winged Yellow Warbler.

Certhia pinus, LINN. Syst. Nat. I, 1766, 187.—GMELIN, I, 1788, 478.
Sylvia pinus, LATHAM, Index Orn. II, 1790, 537.—VIEILLOT, Ois. Am. Sept. II, 1807, 44. (Not of Wilson.)
Sylvia solitaria, WILSON, Am. Orn. II, 1810, 109 ; pl. xv.—AUD. Orn. Biog. I, 1832, 102 ; pl. 20.
Sylvia (Dacnis) solitaria, BONAP. Obs. Wils. J. A. N. S. IV, 1826, 490.—AUDUBON (name on plate ,) pl. 20.—
    NUTTALL, Man. I, 1832, 410.
Sylvicola solitaria, RICH. List, 1837.
Vermivora solitaria, "SWAINSON," JARD. ed. Wilson, 1832.—BONAP. List, 1838.
Helinaia solitaria, AUD. Syn. 1839, 69.—IB. Birds Amer. II, 1841, 98 ; pl. 111.
Helmitheros solitarius, BONAP. Conspectus, 1850, 315.
Helminthophaga solitaria, CABANIS, Mus. Hein. 1850–'51, 20.

SP. CH.—Upper parts and cheeks olive green, brightest on the rump ; the wings, tail, and upper tail coverts, in part, bluish gray. An intensely black patch from the blue-black bill to the eye, continued a short distance behind it. Crown, except behind, and the under parts generally, rich orange yellow. The inner wing and under tail coverts white. Eyelids, and a short line above and behind the eye, brighter yellow. Wing with two white bands. Two outer tail feathers with most of the inner web, third one with a spot at the end white. Female and young similar, duller, with more olivaceous on the crown. Length, 4.50 ; wing, 2.40 ; tail, 2.10.

Hab.—Eastern United States to the Missouri ; south to Guatemala.

The bill in this species is conical and very acute, shorter than the head. The first four quills are nearly equal and considerably longest. The tail is emarginate and slightly rounded.

This species is somewhat like *Protonotaria citrea,* though much smaller. The yellow of the head is limited to the fore part of the crown. The black band to the eye and the white on the wing are not found in the other species.

The summer or autumnal plumage of this species agrees quite well with the description of *Sylvia montana* of Wilson, in everything but the streaks on the sides of the body.

As this species is unquestionably *Certhia pinus* of Linnaeus, it becomes necessary to restore his specific name, instead of using *solitaria* of Wilson.

List of specimens.

Catal. No.	Sex & age.	Locality.	When collected.	Whence obtained.	Orig. No.	Collected by—
2229	♂	Carlisle, Pa.	May 6, 1845	S. F. Baird.		
408	♀	do	May 20, 1841	do		
1131	o	do	July 22, 1843	do		
6983	♂	St. Louis	May 12, 1857	Lt. Bryan	61	W. S. Wood
		Creek Nation		Capt. Sitgreaves		Dr. Woodhouse
8015		Guatemala		J. Gould.		

HELMINTHOPHAGA CHRYSOPTERA, Cabanis.

Golden-winged Warbler.

Motacilla chrysoptera, LINNAEUS, Syst. Nat. I, 1766, 333.—GMELIN, Syst. Nat. I, 1788, 971.
Sylvia chrysoptera, LATHAM, Index Orn. II, 1790.—WILSON, Am. Orn. II, 1810, 113 ; pl. xv, f. 5.—BONAP. Am Orn.
    I, 1825, 12 ; pl. i, f. 3. (♀)—IB. Synopsis, 1828, 87.
Sylvicola chrys~ptera, RICHARDSON, List, 1837.
Vermivora chrysoptera, (SWAINSON) BONAP. List, 1838.
Helinaia chrysoptera, AUD. Syn. 1839, 67.—IB. Birds Am. II, 1841, 91 ; pl. 107.
Helmitheros chrysoptera, BONAP. Consp. 1850, 315.
Helminthophaga chrysoptera, CABANIS, Mus. Hein. 1850–'51, 20.
Motacilla flavifrons, GMELIN, Syst. Nat. I, 1788, 976.
Sylvia flavifrons, LATHAM, Ind. Orn. II, 1790, 527.

SP. CH.—Upper parts uniform bluish gray ; the head above and a large patch on the wings yellow. A broad streak from the bill 'through and behind the eye, with the chin, throat, and fore part of the breast, black. The external edge of the yellow crown continuous with a broad patch on the side of the occiput above the auriculars, a broad maxillary stripe widening on the side of the neck, the under parts generally, with most of the inner webs of the outer three tail feathers white ; the sides of the body pale ash color. Female similar, but duller. Length, about 5 inches ; wing, 2.65 ; tail, 2.25.

Hab.—Eastern United States to the Missouri. Bogota. (Sclater.)

The bill is rather shorter than the head, and black ; the feet brown. The edges of the secondaries and tertials are olive green. There is a small white patch on the fourth tail feather. A summer male has the back and belly strongly tinged with olive.

List of specimens.

Catal. No.	Sex.	Locality.	When collected.	Whence obtained.	Collected by—
2365	♂	Carlisle, Pa.	July 8, 1845	S. F. Baird	
1242	♂	Philadelphia		do	
1917	♀	United States.		do	
6982	♂	St. Louis.	May 13, 1857	Lt. Bryan	W. S. Wood
10156	♂	Union county, Illinois.	May 11, 1857	N. W. University	Robt. Kennicott.

HELMINTHOPHAGA BACHMANI, Cabanis.

Bachman's Warbler.

Sylvia bachmani, AUDUBON, Orn. Biog. II, 1834, 483 ;   183.
Sylvicola bachmani, RICH. List, 1837.
Vermivora bachmani, BONAP. List, 1838.
Helinaia bachmani, AUD. Syn. 1839, 68.—IB. Birds Am. II, 1841, 93 ; pl. 108.
Helmitheros bachmani, BONAP. Consp. 1850, 315.
Helminthophaga bachmani, CABANIS, Journ. f. Orn. III, 1855, 475. (Cuba.)

SP. CH.—Above olive green, as also are the sides of the head and neck. Hind head tinged with ash. A broad patch on the forehead, bordered behind by black ; chin, stripe from this along the side of the throat, and the entire under parts deep yellow ; Throat and fore part of breast black. A patch on the inner web of the outer two tail feathers near the end white. Length, 4.50 ; wing, 2.35 ; tail, 2.05.

Hab.—South Atlantic States. Cuba ; (Cabanis.)

The bill of this species is much attenuated and considerably decurved. The tail is nearly even and slightly emarginate. The outer primaries are faintly margined with white. The female is said to have less black on the head and throat.

This species is exceedingly rare, and very seldom seen in collections.

List of specimens.

Catal. No.	Sex.	Locality.	Whence obtained.	Collected by—
2903	♂	Charleston, S. C.	S. F. Baird.	J. J. Audubon ....

HELMINTHOPHAGA RUFICAPILLA, Baird.

Nashville Warbler.

Sylvia ruficapilla, Wilson, Am. Orn. III, 1811, 120 ; pl. xxvii, f. 3.—Aud. Orn. Biog. I, 1832, 450 ; pl. 89.
Sylvia rubricapilla, Wilson, Am. Orn. VI, 1812, 15.   (General Index.)—Bon. Obs. 1826, No. 159
Sylvia (Dacnis) rubricapilla, Nuttall, Man. I, 1832, 412.
Sylvicola rubricapilla, Rich. List, 1837.
Vermivora rubricapilla, Bonap. List, 1838.—Reinhardt, Vid. Med. for 1853, 1854, 82.   (Greenland.)
Helinaia rubricapilla, Aud. Syn. 1839, 70.—Ib. Birds Am. II, 1841, 103 ; pl. 113.
Helmitheros rubricapilla, Bonap. Consp. 1850, 315.
Helminthophaga rubricapilla, Cabanis, Mus. Hein. 1850, 20.
Sylvia leucogastra, Shaw, Gen. Zool. X, ii, 1817, 622.
"Sylvia nashvillei, Vieillot."   (Gray.)
Sylvia mexicana, Holböll.

Sp. Ch.—Head and neck above and on sides ash gray, the crown with a patch of concealed dark brownish orange hidden by ashy tips to the feathers. Upper parts olive green, brightest on the rump. Under parts generally, with the edge of the wing deep yellow ; the anal region paler ; the sides tinged with olive. A broad yellowish white ring round the eye ; the lores yellowish ; no superciliary stripe. The inner edges of the tail feathers margined with dull white. Female similar, but duller ; the under parts paler ; but little trace of the red of the crown. Length, 4.65 ; wing, 2.42 ; tail, 2.05.

Hab.—Eastern North America to the Missouri ; Greenland. (Reinhardt.)

The bill is very acute ; the wings long and pointed ; the tail emarginate, not rounded.

In autumn the entire upper parts are olive green, tinged with yellowish on the rump, sometimes with brownish on the head ; the patch on the crown more or less concealed. The female has the white on the middle of the belly more extended.

This species is distinguished from *celata* by the ash of the head, and the much purer and more vivid gamboge (not greenish) yellow of the under parts. Although a smaller bird the wings are proportionately longer. The continuous yellowish ring round the eye and the absence of the superciliary stripe distinguish the species from both *celata* and *peregrina*. The latter, besides being larger, never has any approach to the bright yellow under parts, and moreover, has no concealed patch on the crown.

List of specimens.

Catal. No.	Sex and age.	Locality.	When collected.	Whence obtained.	Length.	Stretch of wings.	Wing.
2150	♂	Carlisle, Pa.	April 26, 1845	S. F. Baird	4.66	7.50	2.41
958	♂	....do	May 3, 1843	....do	4.66	7.75	2.33
791	♂	....do	Oct. 10, 1842	....do	4.58	7.08	2.33
1699		....do	Sept. 6, 1844	....do	4.83	7.50	2.41
768		....do	Sept. 30, 1842	....do	4.50	7.41	2.33
2237	♀	....do	May 6, 1845	....do			
2457	o	....do	Sept. 12, 1845	....do			
7557	♂	Washington, D. C.		W. Hutton			
		Racine, Wisconsin.		R. Kennicott.			
10157	♂	Cairo, Illinois.	April 29, 1845	....do			

HELMINTHOPHAGA CELATA, Baird.

Orange-crowned Warbler.

Sylvia celata, SAY, Long's Exped. R. Mts. I, 1823, 169.—BONAP. Am. Orn. I, 1825, 45; pl. v, f. 2.—BON. Syn. 1828, 38.—NUTTALL, Man. I, 1832, 413, (*Dacnis.*)—AUD. Orn. Biog. II, 1834, 449; pl. 178.
Sylvicola celata, RICH. List, 1837.
Vermivora celata, (JARDINE,) BONAP. List, 1838.
Helinaia celata, AUD. Syn. 1839, 69.—IB. Birds Am. II, 1841, 100; pl. 112.
Helmitheros celata, BONAP. Conspectus, 1850, 315.

SP. CH.—Above olive green, rather brighter on the rump. Beneath entirely greenish yellow, except a little whitish about the anus; the sides tinged with olivaceous. A concealed patch of pale brownish orange on the crown, hidden by the olivaceous tips to the feathers. Eyelids and an obscure superciliary line yellowish, a dusky obscure streak through the eye. No white spots on wings or tail of female, with little or none of the orange on the crown. Length, 4.70; wing, 2.25; tail, 2.00.

Hab.—Mississippi river to the Pacific; south to northern Mexico.

In some specimens there is a narrow margin of whitish along the inner webs of the tail feathers. Sometimes, too, (3993,) the outer primary is edged with white. Some specimens appear to be without the orange crown. Occasionally there is a faint trace of obsolete olivaceous streaks on the breast.

An immature specimen (10159) from Fort Umpqua, referred to this species, is much duller in plumage, and shows a trace of two brownish bands on the wings.

33 b

List of specimens.

Catal. No.	Sex & age.	Locality.	When collected.	Whence obtained.	Orig'l No.	Collected by—	Length.	Stretch of wings.	Wing.	Remarks.
7925?	♀	Dane county, Wis.....	....	Th. Kümlien.........	......	....	....	....	......	....
4672	......	Bon Homme Island....	May........	Lieut. Warren	......	Dr. Hayden	......	......	......	....
4673	♂	Mouth of Big Sioux....	May 4, 1856	......do......	......	......do.......	5.12	8.00	2.50	Eyes dark, bill blue
7697	......	W. Texas..	....	Captain Pope......	......	....	......	......	......	....
3994	......	Brownsville, Texas	....	Lieut. Couch	......	....	4.50	6.75	2.00	....
3995	......	Tamaulipas, Mexico....	....	......do.............	50	....	......	......	......	....
3993	......	......do..............	Mar., 1853 ...	......do............	41	....	......	......	......	Eyes black; bill lead color.
7692	......	Fort Steilacoom, W. T.	April 28......	Dr. Suckley..........	347	....	4.62	7.00	......	....
7693	......	......do............	May 3........	......do.............	362	....	......	......	......	....
7694	......	......do.............	April 11......	......do.............	300	....	5.00	7.50	......	....
7695	♂	......do.............	May 2, 1856	......do..	355	....	......	......	......	....
7696	......	......do.............	April 25, 1856	......do.............	316	....	5.00	7.37	......	....
2929	♂	Columbia river.	May 15, 1835	S. F. Baird	99	J. K. Townsend .	......	......	....	......
1912	......	......do.............	May 16, 1835	......do..	99	......do.........	......	......	......	....
4392	......	Fort Dalles, Oregon....	May 4, 1855	Dr. Suckley.........	163	....	......	......	......	....
10159?	o	Fort Umpqua, Oregon..	....	Dr. Vollum.........	......	....	7.37	2.50	......	....
4221	......	San Francisco, Cal.....	Winter '53-'4	R. D. Cutts	......	....	......	......	......	....
	......	Fort Tejon............	....	J. X. de Vesey......	......	....	......	......	......	....

HELMINTHOPHAGA PEREGRINA. Cabanis.

Tennessee Warbler.

Sylvia peregrina, WILSON, Am. Orn. III, 1811, 83; pl. xxv, f. 2.—BONAP. Syn. 1828, 87.—AUD. Orn. Biog. II, 1834, 307; pl. 154.

Sylvia (Dacnis) peregrina, BONAP. Obs. Wils. 1826, No. 155.—NUTTALL, Man. I, 1832, 412.

Sylvicola peregrina, RICH. List, 1837.

Vermivora peregrina, BONAP. List, 1838.

Helinaia peregrina, AUD. Syn. 1839, 68.—IB. Birds Am. II, 1841, 96; pl. 110.

Helmitheros peregrina, BONAP. Consp. 1850, 315.

Helminthophaga peregrina, CAB. Mus. Hein. 1851, 20.

" *Sylvia tennessaei*, VIEILLOT," GRAY.

SP. CH.—Top and sides of the head and neck ash gray; rest of upper parts olive green, brightest on the rump. Beneath dull white, faintly tinged in places, especially on the sides, with yellowish olive. Eyelids and a stripe over the eye whitish; a dusky line from the eye to the bill. Outer tail feather with a white spot along the inner edge near the tip. Female with the ash of the head less conspicuous; the under parts more tinged with olive yellow. Length, 4.50; wing, 2.75; tail, 1.85.

Hab.—Eastern United States to the Missouri.

In this species the bill is small and quite acute. The wings are long, reaching beyond the middle of the tail, which is slightly emarginate. The second and third quills are longest; the first but little shorter, and longer than the fourth.

It is very seldom that specimens are found with the gray neck and crown, this being generally, especially in winter dress, of the same olive as the back, and the greenish yellow of the under parts much more conspicuous and extended. In this dress it becomes very difficult to distinguish it from autumnal specimens of *H. celata*. The under parts of the latter species are, however, generally of a brighter yellow, especially on the tail coverts, and the wing is considerably shorter; the superciliary stripe, too, is less distinct.

Specimens from Pennsylvania appear to have the bill larger than more western ones. The *Sylvia bicolor* of Vieillot (Ois. Am. Sept. II, 1807, 32; pl. xc, bis) cannot belong to the *Sylvia peregrina* of Wilson, as intimated by Bonaparte, since the former is stated to have the upper parts, including the rump, pale blue. This is never the case in the latter species, where the rump is always green. The absence of white bands on the wing shows that it is not *S. coerulea* of Wilson. The *Helinaia brevipennis* of Giraud is quite similar, but has a much shorter wing.

List of specimens.

Catal. No.	Sex.	Locality.	When collected.	Whence obtained.	Collected by—	Length.	Stretch of wings.	Wing.
752	♀	Carlisle, Pa.......	Sept. 23, 1842	S. F. Baird	....	4. 50	7. 25	2. 50
412	♀	......do..........	May 21, 1841	......do..........	....	4. 75	7. 50	....
790	♂	......do..........	Oct. 10, 1842	......do..........	....	4. 83	7. 75	2. 50
7399	......	Cleveland, Ohio ...	....	Dr. Kirtland......	....	....	....	....
	......	Cairo, Illinois......	April 22, 1842	N. W. University..	Robt. Kennicott...	....	....	....
1879	♂	Fort Union, Neb ..	1843..........	S. F. Baird.	J. J. Audubon	....	....	....

Section Sylvicoleae.

Bill distinctly notched ; rictal bristles short or small, or wanting. Hind toe short, equal to the lateral ; the claw as long as its digit. First quill scarcely shorter than longest.

The following genera compose this section :

SEIURUS.—Legs stout, elongated ; tarsi longer than the skull. Colors olive above ; streaked beneath. Tail feathers unspotted. Legs yellow.

DENDROICA.—Legs slender ; tarsi scarcely equal to the skull. Bill variable. Colors of body brilliant and varied. Tail feathers always with a white patch on the inner web. Legs usually dusky.

SEIURUS, Swainson.

Seiurus, SWAINSON, Zool. Jour. III, 1827, 171. (Sufficiently distinct from *Sciurus*.) Type *Motacilla aurocapilla*, L. *Henicocichla*, GRAY, List of Genera, 1840.

CH.—Bill rather sylvicoline, compressed, with a distinct notch. Gonys ascending. Rictal bristles very short. Wings moderate, about three-quarters of an inch longer than the tail ; first quill scarcely shorter than the second. Tail slightly rounded ; feathers acuminate. Tarsi about as long as the skull, considerably exceeding the middle toe. Under tail coverts reaching within about half an inch of the end of the tail. Color above olivaceous ; beneath whitish, thickly streaked on the breast and sides. Wings and tail immaculate.

This genus is decidedly sylvicoline in general appearance, although the spots on the breast resemble somewhat those of the thrushes. The three species may be grouped as follows :

A. Middle of crown brownish orange, bordered by blackish. No white superciliary streak...*S. aurocapillus.*

B. Crown like the back. A well defined superciliary light stripe.

Thickly streaked beneath, including crissum. Ground color and superciliary stripe yellowish. Bill small..*S. noveboracensis.*

Sparsely streaked beneath ; throat and crissum immaculate. Ground color and superciliary stripe white. Bill very large...........................*S. ludovicianus.*

Comparative measurements of species.

Catal. No.	Species.	Locality.	Sex and age.	Length.	Stretch of wings.	Wing.	Tail.	Tarsus.	Middle toe.	Its claw alone.	Bill above.	Along gape.	Specimen measured.
1433	Seiurus aurocapillus......	Carlisle, Pa....	♀	5.10	....	2.74	2.22	0.91	0.68	0.16	0.48	0.58	Dry .....
...do..	........do.............. ...	......do,.....	....	5.75	9.16	2.75	....	....	......	....	....	....	Fresh ..
6995	........do..............	St. Louis......	♂	6.02	....	3.06	2.44	0.86	0.71	0.16	0.44	0.54	Dry .....
1502	Seiurus noveboracensis...	Carlisle, Pa....	♂	5.40	....	2.96	2.36	0.82	0.72	0.19	0.46	0.66	Dry .....
...do..	........do..............	......do..	....	6.16	9.75	3.08	....	....	......	.....	....	....	Fresh ...
10169	......do..............	Northern Ill...	....	6.14	....	3.10	2.48	0.82	0.66	0.18	0.50	0.64	Dry .....
964	Seiurus ludovicianus.....	Carlisle, Pa....	♂	5.38	....	3.30	2.38	0.90	0.72	0.16	0.57	0.70	Dry .....
...do..	......:.do..............	......do.......	....	6.33	10.75	3.25	....	....	......	....	....	....	Fresh ...
9108	........do..............	Mexico........	♂	5.40	....	3.26	2.40	0.90	0.74	0.16	0.56	0.72	Dry .....

SEIURUS AUROCAPILLUS, Swainson.

Oven bird ; Golden-crowned Thrush.

Motacilla aurocapilla, LINNAEUS, Syst. Nat. I, 1766, 334.—GMELIN, I, 1788, 982.

Turdus aurocapillus, LATHAM, Ind. Orn. I, 1790, 328.—WILSON, Am. Orn. II, 1810, 88 ; pl. xiv, f. 2.—LICHT. Verzeich. 1823, No. 424.—AUD. Orn. Biog. II, 1834, 253 : V, 1839, 447 ; pl. cxliii.

Sylvia aurocapillus, BONAP. Obs. Wils. J. A. N. S. IV, 1826, 35.

Seiurus aurocapillus, SWAINSON, Zool. Jour. III, 1827, 171.—IB. F. Bor. Am. II, 1831, 247.—BON. List, 1838.— IB. Conspectus, 1850, 306.—AUD. Syn. 1839, 93.—IB. Birds Amer.

Turdus (Seiurus) aurocapillus, NUTTALL, Man. I, 1832, 355.

Accentor aurocapillus, RICH. List, 1837.

Enicocichla aurocapilla, GRAY, List Genera, 1840.

Henicocichla aurocapilla, CABANIS, Mus. Hein. 1851, 15.

Turdus coronatus, VIEILLOT, Ois. Am. Sept. II, 1807, 8 ; pl. lxiv.

SP. CH.—Above uniform olive green, with a tinge of yellow. Crown with two narrow streaks of black from the bill, enclosing a median and much broader one of brownish orange. Beneath white ; the breast, sides of the body, and a maxillary line streaked with black. The female and young of the year are not appreciably different. Length, 6.00 ; wing, 3.00 ; tail, 2.40.

Hab.—Eastern North America to the Missouri.

The sides of the head are olivaceous, paler than the back, with a superciliary band of the same color outside the black. The loral space and a ring round the eye are whitish, the latter with a little yellow. The feet and maxilla are yellow; the mandible brownish. The brownish orange of the crown is usually obscured by olivaceous tips to the feathers, sometimes to such an extent as to hide it almost entirely from view, (4719.)

A specimen of this species (8387) from Independance is larger with longer wings than any others in the collection.

List of specimens.

Catal. No.	Sex and age.	Locality.	When collected.	Whence obtained.	Orig. No.	Collected by—	Length.	Stretch of wings.	Wing.	Remarks.
1419	♂	Carlisle, Pa.....	May 1,1844	S. F. Baird	.....	....	6.00	9.50	3.00	....
1433	♀	.....do................	May 3,1844	......do..........	......	....	5.75	9.16	2.16	....
1134	○	.....do...............	July 24,1843	......do...........	......	....	....	....	....	....
7542	....	Washington, D. C	....	Wm. Hutton.......	......	....	....	....	....	....
	....	Cook county, Ill	August.......	R. Kennicott.......	......	....	....	....	....	....
	♂	Union county, Ill......	May 6........	......do	......	....	....	....	....	....
6995	♂	St. Louis, Mo..........	May 15,1857	Lieut. Bryan	......	W. S. Wood....	....	....	....	....
8665	♀	Cape Florida...........	Sept. 24,1857	G. Wurdemann	.. ....	....	5.75	9.50	3.00	....
8666	....	.....do...............	Sept. 25,1857	......do...........	......	....	6.00	9.50	3.00	....
8387	♀	Independence, Mo....	Jan. 20,1857	Wm. M. Magraw...	83	Dr. Cooper.....	6.50	10.00	3.25	Iris brown; bill brown; feet flesh.
5287	♂	Medicine river, on Mo..	July 3,1856	Lieut. Warren.....	......	Dr. Hayden....	6.25	8.75	2.75	....
4720	♂	Vermilion river, Neb...	May 6	......do...........	......	.....do........	6.25	9.00	3.00	....
4719	♀	.....do...............	May 11	......do...........	......	.....do........	5.87	9.37	2.87	....
4718	♂	.....do...	May 6	......do...........	......	.....do........	5.37	9.50	3.00	....
4716	♂	James river, Neb.......	May 8	......do....	......	.. ...do........	6.00	9.87	3.25	....
4717	♂	Mouth of Platte........	April 27	......do...........	......	.....do........	6.25	9.62	3.12	Eyes blue black.....
4714	♂	.....do...	.. do.......	......do...........	......	.....do........	6.50	9.00	3.00	......do..........
4715	♂	Bald island	April 25,1856	......do...........	......	.....do........	6.00	9.75	3.12	Eyes black........ ...

SEIURUS NOVEBORACENSIS, Nuttall.

Water Thrush.

Motacilla noveboracensis, GMELIN, Syst. Nat. I, 1788, 958.

Sylvia noveboracensis, LATHAM, Ind. Orn. II, 1790, 518.—VIEILLOT, Ois. II, 1807, 26 ; pl. lxxxii.—BON. Syn. 1828, 77.

Turdus (Seiurus) noveboracensis, NUTTALL, Man. I, 1832, 353.

Seiurus noveboracensis, BONAP. List, 1838.—IB. Conspectus, 1850, 306.—AUD. Syn. 1839, 93.

Henicocichla noveboracensis, CABANIS, in Schomburgk's Reise Guiana, III, 1848, 666, (Caraccas, Oct. 20.)—IB. Mus. Hein. 1851, 16.

Mniotilta noveboracensis, GRAY.

? *Sylvia tigrina*, var. *β*, LATHAM, Ind. Orn. II, 1790, 537.

Turdus aquaticus, WILSON, Am. Orn. III, 1811, 66 ; pl. xxii, f. 5.—AUD. Orn. Biog. V, 1839, 284; pl. 433.

Turdus aquaticus, BONAP. Obs. Wilson, J. A. N. S. IV, 1826, 34, (error.)

Sylvia anthoides, VIEILLOT, Nouv. Dict. XI, 1817, 208.

Seiurus tenuirostris, SWAINSON, Philos. Mag. I, 1827, 369.—GAMBEL, Pr. A. N. Sc. I, 1843, 261.

? *Seiurus sulfurascens*, D'ORBIGNY, in De la Sagra Cuba, Ois. 1840, 57 ; pl. vi.

SP. CH.—Bill, from rictus, about the length of the skull. Above olive brown, with a shade of green ; beneath pale sulphur yellow, brightest on the abdomen. Region about the base of the lower mandible, and a superciliary line from the base of the bill to the nape, brownish yellow. A dusky line from the bill through the eye ; chin, and throat finely spotted. All the remaining under parts and sides of the body, except the abdomen, and including the under tail coverts, conspicuously and thickly streaked with olivaceous brown, almost black on the breast. Length, 6.15 ; wing, 3.12 ; tail, 2.40. Bill, from rictus, .64.

Hab.—Eastern United States to the Missouri, and south to Guatemala, perhaps to Brazil.

In this species the second and third quills are about equal, and a little longer than the first, which exceeds the fourth. The tail is slightly rounded, the feathers acuminate-acute. The feathers of the chin and throat have each a small triangular spot, the middle of the abdomen being the only immaculate region.

In nearly all specimens there is a trace of a median light stripe on the crown, visible at the base of the bill ; sometimes this being more or less distinctly traceable half way along the crown,

(2159.) It is especially noticable in No. 8020, from Guatemala. This is also of an unusually dark olive above.

The female differs only in being a little smaller, and perhaps in having the spots beneath more restricted. Autumnal and winter specimens are decidedly more sulphury yellow beneath, and the spots less sharply defined. There is little variation in the size of bill and feet in individuals o fthe sa me sex.

It is somewhat a question whether the *Seiurus sulfurascens* of authors be not merely the winter plumage, as observed in South America. This conclusion can only be avoided by showing that the sulphur-bellied bird breeds in South America in this plumage.

List of specimens.

Catal. No.	Sex and age.	Locality.	When collected.	Whence obtained.	Collected by—	Length.	Stretch of wings.	Wing.	Remarks.
2668	....	arlisle, Pa..............	May 14, 1846	S. F. Baird.......	....	5.25	9.33	3.00	....
2531	♂	......do...............	Apl. 30, 1846	......do.........	....	6.25	9.66	3.50	....
1501	♂	......do...............	May 10, 1844	......do.........	....	6.25	9.83	3.16	....
1502	♂	......do...............	May 10, 1844	......do.........	....	6.16	9.75	3.08	....
2434	♀	......do...............	Sept. 8, 1845	......do.........	....	5.91	9.41	3.00	....
2159	♀	......do...............	Apl. 28, 1845	......do.........	....	5.50	8.75	2.75	....
3317	○	Liberty county, Ga.........	1846.........	......do.........	....	6.00	9.50	3.00	....
4304	....	Calcasieu Pass, La........	1854.........	G. Wurdemann...	....	....	....	....	....
8669	♀	Cape Florida, Fla.........	Sept. 24, 1857	......do.........	....	6.00	10.00	3.00	Black bill...................
8668	....	......do..........	Sept. 25, 1857	......do.........	....	6.00	9.00	3.00	Brown bill, light feet.......
8667	....	...do..........	Sept. 26, 1857	......do.........	....	5.25	9.50	3.00	Light brown legs, black eyes.
7358	....	Lansing, Mich............	....	Charles Fox......	.. ....	....	....	....	....
10169	....	West Northfield, Ill.......	....	R. Kennicott....	.. ..	....	....	....	....
4721	♂	Vermilion river...........	....	Lieut. Warren....	Dr. Hayden...	....	....	....	....
4818	♂	Mouth of Vermilion river..	....	......do.........	.....do.....	6.12	10.50	3.12	Eye bluish black...........
8020	....	Guatemala............	....	J. Gould........	....	....	....	....	....
7639?	....	Brazil........	....	S. F. Baird.......	....	....	....	....	....

SEIURUS LUDOVICIANUS, Bonap.

Large-billed Water Thrush.

?? *Turdus motacilla*, VIEILLOT, Ois. Am. Sept. II, 1807, 9 ; pl. lxv.
Turdus ludovicianus, AUD. Orn. Biog. I, 1832, 99 ; pl. 19.
Seiurus ludovicianus, BONAP. List, 1838.
Seiurus motacilla, BONAP. Consp. 1850, 306. (Not of Vieillot.)
Henicocichla major, CABANIS, Mus. Hein. 1850, 16. (Xalapa.)

SP. CH.—Bill longer than the skull. Upper parts olive brown with a shade of greenish. A conspicuous white superciliary line from the bill to the nape, involving the upper lid, with a brown one from the bill through the eye, widening behind. Under parts white, with a very faint shade of pale buff behind, especially on the tail coverts. A dusky maxillary line ; the fore part of breast and sides of body, with arrow shaped streaks of the same color. Chin, throat, belly, and under tail coverts entirely immaculate. Length, 6.33; wing, 3.25 ; tail, 2.40 ; bill from rictus, .75.

Hab.—Eastern United States to the Missouri. South to Mexico.

This species may be readily distinguished from the *S. noveboracensis* by its larger size, especially of bill and tarsi, which are very conspicuously larger, the former especially. The color above is of perhaps a lighter olivaceous. The stripe over the eye, besides being more conspicuous, is, with the under parts, of a decided white, instead of brownish yellow; the spots beneath are paler and much fewer in number ; the chin and throat, the middle of the posterior portion of the breast, the sides of the body behind, and the under tail coverts, being entirely immaculate instead of conspicuously spotted. In both species there is a trace towards the base of the bill of a median light stripe, varying in extent with the specimen.[1]

The precise name of this large-billed species is a matter of uncertainty. The *Turdus mota-cilla*, of Vieillot, has, as its chief distinguishing feature, a white lateral band from the bill involving the eye, or passing above and below it, and with a dusky island anterior to the eye. This is distinctly indicated both in the figure and description, and is so dissimilar in this respect from specimens of the allied species known in the United States, as to render it almost necessary to pass by Vieillot's species at once. He further mentions that the under parts are whitish anteriorly, reddish posteriorly, and throughout, including the forepart of the throat, spotted with brown. The size of the bill, as given in this figure, and the under parts agree best with the slender-billed species, although differing in the color and character of the eye stripe ; if a synonym of either species, I should rather refer it to the *S. noveboracensis*.

The description, by Cabanis, of *Henicocichla major*, from Xalapa, agrees very well with this species, although I do not exactly comprehend the force of the statement that it has a "broader whitish eyelid" than the other species ; although he probably refers to the superciliary stripe.

There is, however, little doubt that the *Seiurus ludovicianus*, of Audubon, was based on an individual of the same species ; although the description is not very minute, yet the yellowish white colors, instead of pale yellow, the connection of the white superciliary and maxillary stripes behind the ear coverts, and the greater size, show this, as indicated still more satisfactorily by the figure.

List of specimens.

Catal. No.	Sex and age.	Locality.	When collected.	Whence obtained.	Orig. No.	Collected by—	Length.	Stretch of wings.	Wing.	Remarks.
964	♂	Carlisle, Pa........	May 12, 1843	S. F. Baird.......	....	....	6.40	10.75	3.25	....
3318	♀	Liberty county, Ga.	1846..........	.... do.........	....	W. L. Jones.	6.30	10.16	3.20	....
7357	....	Ann Arbor, Mich...	....	C. Fox............	....	....	....	....	....	....
7522	♀	Independence, Mo..	Spring, 1857	Dr. Cooper..	97	....	5.75	9.25	3.75	Iris brown, bill dark brown, feet black.
4051	♀	Tamaulipas, Mex..	March, 1853	Lieut. Couch.....	93	....	5.75	10.00	3.50	Eyes dark, bill dark slate, feet light brown.
9108	♂	Mexico......... ..	....	M. Verreaux.....	34420	....	....	....	....	....

DENDROICA, Gray.

Sylvicola, GRAY, Genera Birds, 2d ed., 1841, 32. (Not of Humphreys nor Swainson.)
Dendroica, GRAY, Genera Birds, Appendix, 1842, 8.
Rhimamphus, HARTLAUB, Rev. Zool. 1845, 342. (Not of Rafinesque, Am. Monthly Mag. 1818 and Jour. de Phys. 1819.)

CH.—Bill conical, attenuated, depressed at the base, where it is, however, scarcely broader than high, compressed from the middle. Culmen straight for the basal half, then rather rapidly curving, the lower edge of upper mandible also concave. Gonys slightly convex and ascending. A distinct notch near the end of the bill. Bristles, though short, generally quite distinct at the base of the bill. Tarsi long ; decidedly longer than middle toe, which is longer than the hinder one ; the claws rather small and much curved ; the hind claw nearly as long as its digit. The wings long and pointed ; the second quil usually a very little longer than the first. The tail slightly rounded and emarginate.

Colors.—Tail always with a white spot ; its ground color never clear olive green.

The name *Sylvicola*, which has until recently been assigned to the present genus, cannot longer

[1] In the present species the bases of the feathers behind the ear coverts are whitish, thus connecting the superciliary stripe with the maxillary white stripe. In *noveboracensis* the dusky line through the eye is continuous with the olive of the side of the neck.

be employed on account of prior use in conchology by Humphreys. In any event, as used first for what was subsequently called *Parula* by Bonaparte, it cannot refer to this section.

Gray, in his "Genera," throws all the American warblers under *Mniotilta*. This, however, belongs to a more restricted group with features very distinct from those of the great majority of the species.

The only selection to be made is between *Rhimamphus* "Rafinesque" of Hartlaub, 1845, and *Dendroica* of Gray. Rafinesque, in Jour. de Physique, makes several generic names for North American birds, two of which, *Helmitheros* and *Symphemia*, as referred to species of Wilson, are readily identified. It is quite otherwise with *Rhimamphus*, which has nothing whatever to do with any known warbler, as may easily be seen by the reference to his article.

The description of *Rhimamphus*, however, was published in the American Monthly Magazine prior to its appearance in Journal de Physique,[1] and in somewhat more detail, and an examination of the diagnosis[2] will sufficiently show that it not only has no relation to the common *D. aestiva*, but that the entire paragraph is a pure fabrication, and the *Rimamphus citrinus* an entirely imaginary bird. Whatever may be the case elsewhere, North America certainly contains no bird five inches long, with the upper mandible curved, not notched, and the lower straight, leaving an opening between them! Neither does the *D. aestiva* have five raised feathers on the bend of the wing, with a tail one and a half inches long and a flesh colored bill. The same article describes one rattlesnake with blue tail, another green above, white beneath; not to mention, in other places, a swallow with scarlet head, black and white striped lemmings, and other wonderful animals, all from Kentucky!!

It only remains, therefore, to use the name given by Gray.

In the examination of a full series of American *Sylvicolinae*, it will be found almost impossible to divide them into well defined groups, based on peculiarities of structure. The precise extent and character of the groups will vary with the point in external anatomy selected as the basis of classification. Thus, we find bills approaching to those of the flycatchers associated with the long pointed sylvicoline wings; short wings with sylvicoline bills; legs sometimes long, sometimes short, other features remaining the same, &c., &c. In some species the rictal bristles are distinct, in others they are scarcely appreciable.

In order to facilitate the determination of the species, I have arranged them in sections, based chiefly on color, with which the other characters range to some extent. There is no very striking difference in form among the first fifteen species; *D. castanea* and *icterocephala* alone having much depressed bills, well provided with bristles as in *Myiodioctes mitratus*, differing, however, in the shorter tarsi, more even tail, longer wings, and different ground color; *D. striata*, on the other hand, has a narrow bill, and almost no bristles at all; the legs and wings long. The *D. kirtlandii* and *palmarum* agree in having short wings, scarcely longer than the tail, (.20 of an inch.) The bills, however, are very different, that of the former, being rather

---

[1] Journal de Physique, LXXXVIII, 1819, 418. Prodrome de 70 Nouveaux Genres d'Animaux découverts dans l'interieur des Etats-Unis d'Amerique, durant l'année 1818. Par C. S. Rafinesque.

[2] American Monthly Magazine, IV, Nov. 1818, 39. Further account of discoveries in Natural History in the western States, by C. S. Rafinesque.

N. G. *Rimamphus*, a bird. Natural family of *Leptoramphous*. Bill subulate, mandibles convex, leaving an opening between them; the lower one straight, the upper one longer, curved, and not notched, nostrils naked, *Rimamphus citrinus*, (Citron Open-bill.) General color of a citron yellow, back rather olivaceous, five brown and raised feathers on the bend of the wings, quills tipped with brown, bill and feet flesh colored. A beautiful little bird, about five inches long; the tail, which is truncate, is one inch and a half; the wings are short. It is a native of the south and was shot near the falls of Ohio, in Indiana, in the month of July; very scarce. It lives on insects, and darts on them from the trees. It does not sing.

broad and depressed at base, the latter compressed and attenuated. The attenuation of the bill is much marked in *D. tigrina*. Here the culmen and commissure are gently decurved; the gonys even slightly concave, instead of convex as in all other species. Both mandibles are exceedingly acute, as in the worm-eating warblers. The wings are long, the first quill longest.

The *Dendroica superciliosa* is quite remarkable for the size of its bill, which, measured from the extreme base, is as long as the head. It is much compressed, or higher than broad, almost from the very base. The legs are rather short, though longer than the middle toe. It is not improbable that this may be the form of *Aegithina*, Vieillot.

The *Sylvia protonotarius* of authors is a peculiarly formed species, characterized by its very large bill, as long as the head. In many respects the bill resembles that of *Helmitherus*, but is less acute, and has a distinct notch. The wings are very long, the first quill longest; the folded wing reaches within an inch of the tip of the tail, which is rounded. The lower coverts are very long, reaching within .30 of an inch of the tip of the tail, as in *Oporornis formosus* and *agilis*, to which there is otherwise quite a resemblance. The tarsi are unusually long, (.85 of an inch,) much longer than the middle toe. This I have placed under *Mniotilteae*.

Synopsis of species.

A. Chin, throat, and fore part of the breast black, bordered by lighter; two white bands on the wing. Back streaked. Outer tail feathers almost entirely white.

  Crown and back olive, forehead, superciliary, and maxillary stripes yellow......*D. virens*.
  Top and sides of head yellow; back ash, conspicuously streaked...........*D. occidentalis*.
  Crown blackish; back olive; superciliary and maxillary stripe yellow......*D. townsendii*.
  Crown black; back ash color; superciliary and maxillary stripe white......*D. nigrescens*.

B. Sides and under parts of the head black.

  Above uniform blue, beneath white; primaries with a white patch at the base. Outer tail feathers with a white patch on the inner web...................... ......*D. canadensis*.

C. Crown with a central longitudinal yellow patch. (In this group only.)

  Throat white; breast blackish; the sides and rump with a yellow patch; white spots of the tail on the terminal half. Slate blue above. A white superciliary stripe and two patches on the wing... *D. coronata*.
  Similar to the last; the throat yellow; no superciliary stripe, and one large white patch on the wing..*D. audubonii*.
  Throat bright orange; back black; a patch on the wing and the outer tail feathers (except at the tip) white..*D. blackburniae*.

D. Throat and sides chestnut; back streaked.

  Crown chestnut; sides of head black; belly white................................*D. castanea*.

E. Throat and under parts white. Back streaked with black. Wings with white bands.

  Crown yellow, encircled with white; sides of head black, enclosing a white patch behind; sides of body chestnut.....................................»..........................*D. pennsylvanica*.
  Blue above and across the breast; sides of crown and of body streaked with black.
  D. cœrulea.
  Crown black; cheeks below the eye white; maxillary stripe and streaks on the sides black..*D. striata*.

34

F. Throat immaculate yellow, cut off from the belly by a series of pectoral streaks. The sides streaked.

Above olive green; beneath yellow. Crissum and belly whitish; two dull white bands and white edgings on the wings. Pectoral and lateral streaks very faint, the former, perhaps, wanting...*D. pinus.*

Above uniform olive green; forehead and beneath all yellow, deepest on the throat. Two white bands on the wings. Breast and belly distinctly streaked with dusky. Two outer tail feathers white from the terminal half of inner web.................*D. montana.*

Yellow, without any white; the back olivaceous; the ventral streaks (and sometimes a tinge on the top of head) brownish red..*D. aestiva.*

Crown uniform blue; rump yellow; back and sides of head black; white spots on the central third of the tail; large white patch on the wing; inferior streaks large, black; crissum white..*D. maculosa.*

Wing scarcely longer than tail. Above blue, streaked with black; inferior streaks black, small, especially across the breast; sides of head black; white tail patch at the end of the tail; crissum white...*D. kirtlandii.*

Wing scarcely longer than tail; crown, sides of head, and inferior streaks rufous; rump greenish yellow; white spot on the end of the tail. A superciliary streak and whole under parts, including crissum, yellow...*D. palmarum.*

Bill acute and decurved; olive above, rump and beneath yellow; crown blackish; sides of head chestnut; breast with narrow streak of black; wings longer than tail.
D. tigrina.

G. Throat immaculate yellow, not separated from the belly by pectoral bands or streaks; sides streaked with black.

Olive green above and on the sides of body, spotted with black; rump and tail lighter; beneath dull yellowish, including a line from the lore over the eye; top of head black; a band on wing and the edge of tail whitish....................................*D. carbonata.*

Belly white; a yellow superciliary stripe changing behind to white; crown and sides of head and neck black; back uniform slate.....................................*D. superciliosa.*

Belly and throat uniform yellow; above olivaceous, the back streaked with red; a yellow superciliary stripe, and a V-shaped black mark on the sides of the head.....*D. discolor.*

As a further analysis of the colors of the species it may be stated, that Section C is the only one with a central patch of yellow on the crown; Sections A and B have the throat black; F and C in part have it white. It is chestnut brown in D; orange red in C in part; yellow with streaks on the breast in F, and yellow without streaks in G. The entire under parts, excepting perhaps the crissum, are yellow in members of F and G.

Comparative measurements of species.

Catal. No.	Species.	Locality.	Sex.	Length.	Stretch of wings.	Wing.	Tail.	Tarsus.	Middle toe.	Its claw alone.	Bill above.	Along gape.	Specimen measured.
941	Dendroica virens.......	Carlisle, Penn......	♂	4.62	......	2.56	2.24	0.70	0.54	0.15	0.43	0.50	Dry......
do.	......do.................	..... do..........		5.00	8.00	2.75	....	....	....	....			Fresh....
5518	Dendroica occidentalis .	Petaluma, Cal......	♂	4.70	....	2.63	2.24	0.70	0.58	0.16	0.40	0.50	Dry......
do.	......do............	......do.........		4.66	7.00	2.66	....						Fresh....
939	Dendroica blackburniae.	Carlisle............	♂	4.60	....	2.76	2.20	0.71	0.54	0.14	0.42	0.55	Dry......
do.	......do.................	......do............		5.50	8.50	2.83	....	....					Fresh....
492	Dendroica townsendii...	Northern Mexico...		5.20	......	2.64	2.32	0.76	0.64	0.18	0.40	0.50	Dry......
2909	Dendroica audubonii...	Columbia river....	♂	5.30	....	3.10	2.47	0.76	0.62	0.16	0.41	0.50	Dry......
3384	Dendroica coronata	Carlisle, Penn......	♂	5.10	....	2.86	2.46	0.76	0.62	0.19	0.38	0.52	Dry......
3419	Dendroica canadensis..	......do.........	♂	4.64	....	2.52	2.16	0.74	0.58	0.16	0.40	0.50	Dry......
1908	Dendroica nigrescens...	Columbia river.....	♂	4.68	....	2.28	2.04	0.66	0.50	0.16	0.40	0.54	Dry......
2231	Dendroica castanea	Carlisle, Penn......	♂	4.82	....	2.98	2.31	0.68	0.58	0.18	0.42	0.56	Dry......
7902	......do.........	......do.........		5.10	....	2.74	2.28	0.68	0.56	0.16	0.38	0.52	Dry......
2459	Dendroica pinus	......do.........	♂	5.10	....	2.94	2.40	0.74	0.70	0.18	0.46	0.60	Dry......
2430	.....do.....	......do.........	♀	4.80	......	2.78	2.28	0.70	0.66	0.19	0.42	0.56	Dry......
2233	Dendroica pennsylvanica	......do.....	♂	4.40	......	2.54	2.08	0.68	0.54	0.18	0.40	0.54	Dry.. ...
976	......do.........	......do.........	♀	4.40	......	2.40	2.14	0.70	0.54	0.16	0.40	0.52	Dry......
do.	......do.........	......do.........		5.00	7.50	2.50	......						Fresh....
10163	Dendroica cerulea......	South Illinois	♂	4.60	....	2.40	1.82	0.64	0.52	0.12	0.40	0.48	Dry......
7349	......do.....	Ohio		4.20	....	2.54	1.96	0.60	0.50	0.14	0.38	0.50	Dry......
10165	Dendroica striata.......	West Northfield, Ill.	♂	6.00	....	3.08	2.32	0.78	0.04	0.19	0.44	0.56	Dry......
1545	......do.....	Carlisle, Penn.....		4.84	....	2.86	2.24	0.74	0.60	0.18	0.44	0.52	Dry......
do.	.. ...do.....	......do.........		5.75	9.00	3.00	......						Fresh....
978	......do.....	......do.........	♀	4.70	......	2.80	2.16	0.74	0.62	0.18	0.38	0.53	Dry......
do.	......do.....	......do.........		5.17	8.33	2.92	......						Fresh....
940	Dendroica aestiva......	......do.........	♂	4.56	......	2.54	2.20	0.72	0.60	0.18	0.46	0.55	Dry......
do.	......do.....	......do.........		5.25	8.17	2.66	....						Fresh....
947	......do.....	......do.........	♀	4.10	....:.	2.36	1.84	0.68	0.54	0.16	0.40	0.52	Dry......
do.	......do.....	......do.........		4.91	7.50	2.33	....						Fresh....
10211	Dendroica erithachoridcs	Carthagena, N. G..	♂	5.00	......	2.72	2.32	0.80	0.66	0.18	0.48	0.62	Dry......
10212	......do.....	......do.........	♀	4.86	....	2.46	↘2.00	0.80	0.64	0.18	0.44	0.56	Dry......
2212	Dendroica maculosa....	Carlisle, Penn.....	♂	4.56	....	2.42	2.10	0.68	0.52	0.16	0.40	0.58	Dry......
do.	......do.....	......do.........		4.75	7.75	2.42	....						Fresh....
2278	......do.....	......do.........	♀	3.94	....	2.24	1.98	0.66	0.50	0.16	0.38	0.48	Dry......
do.	......do.....	......do.........		4.50	7.17	2.25	....						Fresh....
4363	Dendroica kirtlandii....	Cleveland, Ohio....		5.50	......	2.78	2.56	3.82	0.60	0.16	0.44	0.56	Dry......
783	Dendroica palmarum...	Carlisle, Penn......	♂	5.22	......	2.72	2.42	0.78	0.66	0.18	0.42	0.53	Dry......
962	Dendroica tigrina	......do.........	♂	4.60	....	2.60	2.06	0.72	0.62	0.18	0.42	0.50	Dry......
do.	......do.....	......do.........		5.00	8.33	2.66	....						Fresh....
2511	......do.....	......do.........	♀	4.10	....	2.52	2.04	0.70	0.60	0.16	0.38	0.44	Dry......
1091	Dendroica discolor.....	Philadelphia.......	♂	4.30	....	2.20	2.04	0.70	0.58	0.16	0.41	0.52	Dry......
2386	Dendroica pensilis	Savannah, Ga.....		4.94	....	2.66	2.24	0.68	0.58	0.16	0.46	0.56	Dry......
1098	......do.................	Washington, D. C..	♀?	5.32	......	2.56	2.30	0.67	0.52	0.16	0.5?	0.68	Dry......

DENDROICA VIRENS, Baird.

Black-throated Green Warbler.

Motacilla virens, GMELIN, Syst. Nat. I, 1788, 985.

Sylvia virêns, LATHAM, Ind. Orn. II, 1790, 537.—VIEILLOT, Ois. Am. Sept. II, 1807, 33 ; pl. xciii.—WILSON, Am. Orn. II, 1810, 127 ; pl. xxvii, f. 3.—BONAP. Obs. Wils. 1826, No. 146.—NUTTALL, Man. I, 1832, 376 —AUD. Orn. Biog. IV, 1838, 70 ; pl. 399.

Sylvicola virens, "SWAINSON," JARD. ed. Wils. 1832.—BONAP. List, 1838.—AUD. Syn. 1839, 55.—IB. Birds Amer. II, 1841, 42 ; pl. 84 —REINHARDT; Vid. Med. for 1853, 1854, 72, 81.

Rhimanphus virens, CABANIS, Mus. Hein. 1851, 19.—IB. Journ. Orn. III, 1855, 474.

SP. CH.—Male—Upper parts, exclusive of wing and tail, clear yellow olive green, the feathers of the back with hidden streaks of black. Forehead and sides of head and neck, including a superciliary stripe, bright yellow. A dusky olive line from the bill through the eye, and another below it. Chin, throat, and fore part of breast, extending some distance along on the sides, continuous black ; rest of under parts white, tinged with yellow on the breast and flanks. Wings and tail feathers dark brown, edged with bluish gray ; two white bands on the wing ; the greater part of the three outer tail feathers white. Female similar, but duller ; the throat yellow ; the black of breast much concealed by white edges ; the sides streaked with black. Length, 5 inches ; wing, 2.58 ; tail, 2.30.

Hab.—Eastern United States to the Missouri ; south to Guatemala. Greenland. (Reinhardt.)

Nearly all the feathers of the upper parts show dusky centres. The forehead is yellowish, the color extending sometimes along the median line of the crown. There is a dusky spot behind the ear coverts. There is a decided tinge of yellow on the breast just below the black, and on the sides of the anal region. The upper tail coverts are bluish gray streaked with brown. The brown of the three outer tail feathers is confined mainly to the inner portion of the outer web, though extending to the inner web at the tip ; the middle tail feathers are brown, with a narrow internal margin of white. The quills are margined internally with white ; the lesser coverts are like the back. The bill is black, the feet brown.

The male in autumn is quite similar ; the black of the throat and breast obscured by yellowish white tips. The female is pale yellowish white beneath, tinged with grayish towards the tail. There is less white on the tail.

In one specimen of the species the third quill is longest ; next the second ; the first and fourth about equal ; the tail is slightly rounded and emarginate.

A specimen from China, Tamaulipas, is like Pennsylvania ones, but smaller.

List of specimens.

Catal. No.	Sex.	Locality.	When collected.	Whence obtained.	Orig. No.	Collected by—	Length.	Stretch of wings	Wing.
941	♂	Carlisle, Pa.	May 5, 1843	S. F. Baird			5.00	8.00	2.16
2578	♂	do	May 5, 1846	do			5.33	7.83	2.50
789		do	Oct. 10, 1842	do			4.75	8.25	2.50
724		do	Sept. 16, 1842	do			5.16	8.00	
7572		Washington, D. C.		Wm. Hutton					
7500		Cleveland, Ohio.		Dr. Kirtland					
10161		West Northfield, Ill.	May 13.	R. Kennicott					
6975	♂	St. Louis, Mo.	May 12, 1857	Lt. Bryan	49	W. S. Wood.			
3987		China, Tamaulipas, Mex.	Mar. —, 1853	Lt. Couch					
8018		Guatemala		J. Gould					

DENDROICA OCCIDENTALIS, Baird.

Western Warbler.

Sylvia occidentalis, Townsend, J. A. N. Sc. VII, ii, 1837, 190.—Ib. Narrative, 1839, 340.—Audubon, Orn. Biog. V, 1839, 55 ; pl. 55.

Sylvicola occidentalis, Bonap. List, 1838.—Ib. Consp. 1850, 308.—Aud. Syn. 1839, 60.—Ib. Birds Am. II, 1841, 60 ; pl. 93.

Mniotilta occidentalis, Gray, Genera.

Sp. Ch.—Crown, with sides of the head and neck, continuous bright yellow, feathers of the former edged narrowly with black ; rest of upper parts dark brown, edged with bluish gray, so much so on the back and rump feathers as to obscure the brown, and with an olivaceous shade. Chin, throat, and fore part of breast, (ending convexly behind in a sub-crescentic outline,) black ; rest of under parts white, faintly streaked on the sides with black. Two white bands on the wing, two outer tail feathers, and the terminal portion of a third, white, the shafts, and an internal streak towards the end, dark brown. Bill jet black ; legs brown. Length, 4.70 ; wing, 2.70 ; tail, 2.30.

Hab.—Pacific coast.

This species resembles somewhat the *Dendroica virens*, but lacks the continuous olive of the back and crown, the former being greatly streaked with black, the latter yellow all round. The outline black of the breast, instead of extending backwards along the sides, is rounded off on the side, (the convexity posterior,) and transverse on the breast.

The female is said to have the yellow of the head less extended ; the throat white, spotted with black.

List of specimens.

Catal. No.	Sex.	Locality.	When collected.	Whence obtained.	Orig. No.	Length.	Stretch of wings	Wing.
5578	♂	Petaluma, Cal	April 1, 1856	E. Samuels.	703	4. 66	7. 00	2. 66

DENDROICA TOWNSENDII, Baird.

Sylvia townsendii, (" NUTTALL,") TOWNSEND, J. A. N. Sc. Ph. VII, II, 1837, 191.—IB. Narrative, 1839, 341.—
    AUD. Orn. Biog. V, 1839, 36 ; pl. 393.
Sylvicola townsendii, BONAP. List, 1838.—IB. Consp. 1850, 308.—AUD. Syn. 1839, 59.—IB. Birds Am. II, 1841,
    59 ; pl. 92.—NUTTALL, Man. I, 2d ed. 1840, 446.

SP. CH.—Above bright olive green ; the feathers all black in the centre, showing more or less as streaks, especially on the crown. Quills, tail, and upper tail covert feathers dark brown, edged with bluish grey ; the wings with two white bands on the coverts ; the two outer tail feathers white, with a brown streak near the end ; a white streak only in the end of the third feather. Under parts as far as the middle of the body, with the sides of head and neck, including a superciliary stripe and a spot beneath the eye, yellow ; the median portion of the side of the head, the chin and throat, with streaks on the sides of the breast, flanks, and under tail coverts black ; the remainder of the under parts white.   Length, 5 inches ; wing, 2.65 ; tail, 2.25.

Hab.—Pacific coast, North America ; south to Mexico and Guatemala.

I have no full plumaged male before me, all being in autumnal dress, the black of the throat and breast obscured by yellow borders. There is, however, a pure yellow superciliary stripe from the nostrils to the nuchal region, confluent behind with another from the base of the lower jaw ; these embrace between them an elongated patch of black from the commissure to behind the auriculars, broken by a yellow spot beneath the eye. It is probable that the spring male has the entire crown, as well as the chin and throat, black. The greater and median coverts exhibit each a broad bar of white, the feathers, however, with a central black streak. The black appears to be continuous only as far as the breast ; the sides of this streaked only with this color.

A specimen, probably female, is quite uniform greenish yellow above and dull yellow on the throat, without any distinct black beneath.

The tail of this species is rounded, emarginate. The second and third quills are equal, and longest ; the first equal to the fourth.

This species is quite similar in markings to *D. virens*. It is, however, considerably larger, has the yellow on the breast much deeper, and lacks that near the lower tail coverts. It has well defined black markings on the side of the head, instead of obscure olivaceous ones, although the pattern is the same ; has a black head, and black streaks in the white of the wing coverts. *D. occidentalis* is blacker on the back and lacks the dark cheek patch, as well as the yellow of the breast.

List of specimens.

Catal. No.	Sex.	Locality.	When collected.	Whence obtained.	Collected by—
2918	♂	Columbia river_____	Oct. 28, 1835 _____	S. F. Baird_ _____	J. K. Townsend_____
4480[1]	_____	Santa Clara, Cal_____	1855_____	Dr. J. G. Cooper_____	_____ _____
4481[2]	_____	_____do_____	1855_____	_____do_____	_____
492	_____	North Mexico_____	_____,	S. F. Baird _____	_____
8017	_____	Guatemala _____	_____	J. Gould _____	_____

[1]Length. 5.25 ; Extent, 8.12.   [2]Length, 5.12 ; Extent, 7.75. Iris, bill, and feet brown.

DENDROICA NIGRESCENS, Baird.

Black-throated Gray Warbler.

Sylvia nigrescens, TOWNSEND, J. A. N. Sc. Ph. VII, II, 1837, 191. –IB. Narrative, 1839, 341.—AUD. Orn. Biog. V, 1839, 57 ; pl. 395.

Vermivora nigrescens, BONAP. List, 1838.—NUTTALL, Man. I, 2d ed. 1840, 471.

Sylvicola nigrescens, AUD. Syn. 1839, 60.—IB. Birds Amer. II, 1841, 62 ; pl. 94.—BONAP. Consp. 1850, 308.

Rhimanphus nigrescens, CAB. Mus. Hein. 1850, 20.

SP. CH.—Head all round, fore part of the breast, and streaks on the side of the body black ; rest of under parts, a stripe on the side of the head, beginning acutely just above the midd'e of the eye, and another parallel to it, beginning at the base of the under jaw (the stripes of opposite sides confluent on the chin,) and running further back, white. A yellow spot in front of the eye. Rest of upper parts bluish gray. The interscapular region and upper tail coverts streaked with black. Wing coverts black, with two narrow white bands ; quills and tail feathers brown, the two outer of the latter white, with the shafts and a terminal streak brown ; the third brown, with a terminal narrow white streak. Bill black ; feet brown. Length, 4.70 ; wing, 2.30 ; tail, 2.10.

Hab.—Pacific coast, United States ; Fort Thorn, New Mexico.

Winter specimens have the black of the crown obscured by gray ; that of the throat by white. A specimen, supposed to be a female, is smaller, but somewhat similar to this ; the chin and throat white, with slight indications of black ; more of this on the side of the breast.

This species scarcely needs comparison with any other North American one, except, perhaps, *D. striata*, which, however, is entirely distinct ; lacking the black throat, the two white stripes on the side of the head, the yellow spot in front of the eye, &c.

List of specimens.

Catal. No.	Sex.	Locality.	When collected	Whence obtained.	Orig. No.	Collected by—	Length.	Stretch of wings.	Wing.
7686	____	Fort Steilacoom, W. T.	May 6, 1856	Dr. Suckley_____	378	_____	_____	_____	_____
7687	____	_____do_____	_____	_____do_____	74	_____ _____	_____	_____	_____
7688	____	_____do_____	_____	_____do_____	106	_____	_____	_____	_____
7691	♂	_____do_____	May 4, 1856	_____do_____	_____	_____	5.25	7.12	2.50
1908	♂	Columbia river_____	June 16, 1835	S. F. Baird _____	_____	J. K. Townsend.	_____	_____	_____
2915	♂	_____do_____	May 14, 1835	_____do._____	_____	_____do_____	_____	_____	_____
7690	♂	Calaveras river _____	_____	R. S. Williamson_	_____	Dr. Newberry___	_____	_____	_____
7689	____	Fort Thorn, N. M.___	_____	Dr. Henry_____	_____	_____	_____	_____	_____

DENDROICA CANADENSIS, Baird.

Black-throated Blue Warbler.

Motacilla canadensis, LINNAEUS, Syst. Nat. I, 1766, 336.—GMELIN, I, 1788, 991.
Sylvia canadensis, LATHAM, Index Orn. II, 1790, 539.—WILSON, Am. Orn. II, 1810, 115 ; pl. xv, f. 7.—BONAP. Obs.
   1826, No. 145.—NUTT. Man. I, 1832, 398.—AUDUBON, Orn. Biog II, 1834, 309 ; pl. cxlviii,clv
Sylvicola canadensis, "SWAINSON," JARD. Ed. Wilson, 1832—RICH, List, 1837.—BON. List, 1838.—IB. Consp. 1850,
   308.—AUD. Syn. 1839, 61.—IB. Birds Am. II, 1841, 63 ; pl. xcv.
Rhimamphus canadensis, CAB. Journ. Orn. III, 1855, 473.
Motacilla caerulescens, GMELIN, Syst. Nat. I, 1788, 960.
Sylvia caerulescens, LATHAM, Index Orn. II, 1790, 520.—VIEILLOT, Ois. Am. Sept. II, 1807, 25 ; pl. lxxx.
Sylvia pusilla, WILSON, Am. Orn. V, 1812, 100 ; pl. xliii, f. 4, (young.)
Sylvia leucoptera, WILSON, Index and 2d ed. (Hall's ed.) II, 390.
Sylvia palustris, STEPHENS, Shaw Zool. X, II, 1817, 722.
" *Sylvia macropus,* VIEILLOT," Gray.
Sylvia sphagnosa, BONAP. Obs. Wils. 1826, No. 164, (female.)—NUTTALL, Man. I, 1832, 406.—AUD. Orn. Biog. II.
   1834, 279.
Sylvicola pannosa, GOSSE, Birds Jam. 1847, 162, (female.)

SP. CH.—Above uniform continuous grayish blue, including the outer edges of the quill and tail feathers. A narrow frontal
line, the entire sides of head and neck, chin and throat, lustrous black ; this color extending in a broad lateral stripe to the tail.
Rest of under parts, including the axillary region, white. Wings and tail black above, the former with a conspicuous white
patch formed by the bases of all the primaries, (except the first ;) the inner webs of the secondaries and tertials with similar
patches towards the base and along the inner margin. All the tail feathers, except the innermost, with a white patch on the
inner web near the end. Length, 5.50 ; wing, 2.60 ; tail, 2.25.

Female, olive green above and dull yellow beneath. Sides of head dusky olive, the eyelids and a superciliary stripe
whitish. Traces of the white spot at the base of the primaries and of the tail.

Hab.—Eastern United States to the Missouri, south to the West Indies.

The male and female of this beautiful species are very dissimilar, though the species may
always be recognized by the white patch at the base of the primaries, which I do not think
exists in any other *Dendroica.* The extent of this patch, however, in both male and female,
varies considerably. The colors of the female are strikingly similar to those of the female
Spiza ciris, or Nonpareil.

The autumnal or young male has the back clouded with greenish olive, and the black feathers
of the throat much margined with whitish. There is also a white line over the eye, as in the
female.

A skin (10102) from Washington, in high spring plumage, has the feathers in the middle of
the back bluish black, margined with blue, giving rise to conspicuous spots.

List of specimens.

Catal. No.	Sex.	Locality.	When collected.	Whence obtained.	Length.	Stretch of wings.	Wing.
2577	♂	Carlisle, Pa.	May 5, 1846	S. F. Baird.	5.41	8.00	2.58
788	♂	......do.	Oct. 12, 1842	......do.	4.83	7.83	2.58
2305	♀	......do.	Oct. 10, 1842	......do.	5.16	7.83	2.41
2429		......do.	Sept. 5, 1845	......do.	5.00	7.66	2.41
8645		Cape Florida.		G. Wurdemann	4.75	7.75	2.50
8646		......do.		......do.	5.00	7.00	2.50
7307	♂	Cleveland, Ohio.		J. P. Kirtland.			
3795		Racine, Wis.		Dr. Hoy			
	♂	Cook county, Ill.	August 31	R. Kennicott.			

DENDROICA CORONATA, Gray.

Yellow-rumped Warbler.

Motacilla coronata, LINNAEUS, Syst. Nat I, 1766, 333.—GMELIN, Syst. Nat. I, 1788, 974, (male.)

Sylvia coronata, LATHAM, Index Orn. II, 1790, 538.—VIEILLOT, Ois. Am. Sept. II, 1807, 24 ; pl. lxxviii, lxxix.—
    WILSON, Am. Orn. II, 1810, 138 ; pl. xvii, f. 4, (summer)—II, 356 ; pl. xlv, f. 3, (winter.)—
    NUTTALL, Man. I, 1832, 361.—AUD. Orn. Biog. II, 1834, 303 ; pl. cliii.

Sylvicola coronata, SWAINSON, F. Bor. Am. II, 1831, 216.—BONAP. List, 1838.—IB. Conspectus, 1850, 307.—AUD.
    Synop. 1839, 76.—IB. Birds Amer. II, 1841, 23 ; pl. lxxvi.

Dendroica coronata, G. R. GRAY, Genera, 2d ed. Suppl. 1842, 8.

Rhimanphus coronatus, CABANIS, Mus. Hein. 1850, 19.—IB. Journ. Orn. III, 1855, 473, (Cuba.)

Parus virginianus, LINN. Syst. Nat. I, 1766, 342, (winter.)

Motacilla umbra, GMELIN, Syst. I, 1788, 959.

Motacilla cincta, GMELIN, Syst. 1, 1788, 980.

Motacilla pinguis, GMELIN, Syst. I, 1788, 973.

"*Sylvia xanthoroa*, VIEILLOT," (Gray.)

Sp. Ch.—Above bluish ash, streaked with black. Under parts white. The fore part of breast and the sides black, the feathers mostly edged with white. Crown, rump, and sides of breast yellow. Cheeks and lores black. The eyelids and a superciliary stripe, two bands on the wing and spots on the outer three tail feathers, white. Female of duller plumage and browner above. Length, 5.65 ; wing, 3.00 ; tail, 2.50.

Hab.—Eastern North America to the Missouri plains. Stragglers seen on Puget's Sound.

Second quill longest, third scarcely shorter ; first longer than fourth. Tail slightly rounded, emarginate, subspatulate.

Male, in spring.—Upper parts bluish gray, broadly streaked with black on the back, less so on the crown and rump ; middle of crown, rump, and a patch on the side of the breast bright yellow. Secondary and first row of smaller coverts tipped with white, forming two bands on the wings. Quills and tail dark brown, margined with bluish gray ; the latter with the inner webs of the outer three having a white patch near the end, largest on the outer feathers. Eyelids and a superciliary stripe white. Lores and cheeks black. Lower neck and fore part of breast and sides black, the feathers often tipped with white, giving the whole a lunulate appearance. Throat and rest of lower parts white. Bill and feet black.

Female, in spring.—Upper parts dirty light brown, slightly streaked with black. Crown, sides, and rump not so bright a yellow. The other markings as in the male, though much duller, (622.)

Male, in fall.—Upper parts as in the female in spring. Eyelids white. Lores dusky; this color reaching round the lower eyelid. Side of breast dirty yellow. The fore part of breast and throat tinged with pale light brown. Lower parts slightly streaked with brown, very faint, however. (No. 829.)

The superciliary white stripe in the adult male does not always extend continuously from the bill, but is interrupted just above the anterior extremity of the eye; the eye too is only bordered above and below by white, not anteriorly and posteriorly. The feathers of the nostrils, and a very narrow frontal band, are black.

It is possible, in high latitudes and during the breeding season, that the fore breast and anterior portion of sides may be pure black, (except the yellow patch.)

A single but unquestionable specimen of this species (7671) has been found west of the Rocky Mountains ; collected at Steilacoom by Dr. Suckley. Dr. Cooper has also seen specimens in Washington Territory.

List of specimens.

Catal. No.	Sex.	Locality.	When collected.	Whence obtained.	Orig. No.	Collected by—	Length.	Stretch of wings.	Wing.
1460	♂	Carlisle, Pa	May 4, 1844	S. F. Baird			5.66	9.00	3.00
829	♂	...do...	Oct. 22, 1842	...do...			5.25	8.83	2.75
1417	♂	...do...	April 30, 1844	...do...			6.00	9.33	3.00
2550	♀	...do...	May 5, 1846	...do...			5.08	8.83	2.83
2179	♀	...do...	April 30, 1845	...do...			5.08	8.25	2.56
10113	♀	Washington, D. C.		J. C. McGuire					
7440	....	Rockport, Ohio		J. P. Kirtland					
6503	....	Indian Key, Fla	Mar. 20, 1857	G. Wurdemann					
4652	....	Mouth Vermilion riv.	May 5, 1856	Lieut. Warren		Dr. Hayden	4.00	6.62	2.25
4655	♂	...do...		...do...		...do...			
4654	....	Mouth Big Sioux	May 3, 1856	...do...		...do...	5.75	9.00	3.00
4651	♂	Mouth Platte river	April 20, 1856	...do...		...do...			
5300	♂	Medicine creek, Mo.	Oct. 8, 1856	...do...		...do...	5.50	8.87	3.00
5061	♀	Indianola	Feb. 26, 1856	Capt. Pope	26		5.00	8.50	2.50
7650	....	Fort Leavenworth	Dec. 20, 1854	Lieut. Couch	16				
7671	♂	Fort Steilacoom, W. T.	May 1, 1856	Dr. Suckley	351		6.00	9.00	

DENDROICA AUDUBONII, Baird.

Audubon's Warbler.

Sylvia audubonii, Townsend, J. A, N. Sc. Ph. VII, ii, 1837.—Ib. Narrative, 1839, 342.—Aud. Orn. Biog. V, 1839, 52; pl. 395.

Sylvicola audubonii, Bonap. List, 1838.—Aud. Syn. 1839, 52.—Ib. Birds Amer. II, 1841, 26; pl. 77.

Sp. Ch.—Above bluish ash, streaked with black, most marked on the middle of the back; on head and neck bluish ash. Middle of crown, rump, chin, and throat, and a patch on the side of the breast, gamboge yellow. Space beneath and anterior to the eyes, fore part of breast and sides, black; this color extending behind on the sides in streaks. Middle of belly, under tail coverts, a portion of upper and lower eyelids, and a broad band on the wings, with a spot on each of the four or five exterior tail feathers, white; rest of tail feathers black. Female brown above; the other markings less conspicuous and less black. Length, 5.25; wings, 3.20; tail, 2.25.

Hab.—Pacific coast of United States to central Rocky mountains. South to Mexico.

This species is very closely allied to *D. coronata*, the upper parts being almost precisely similar. They may be most readily distinguished, however, by the yellow chin and throat of the one, instead of the white of the other. In *D. audubonii*, the black of the side of the head is confined to the lores, and a suffusion around the eye, especially anteriorly, instead of the conspicuous auricular patch; the only white, too, is the spot on either lid, the interrupted superciliary stripe being wanting. The black on the breast is more uniform and continuous, and there is one broad white patch on the wing formed by white margins to the greater coverts, as well as the tips to these and the lesser ones; in the other species there are two. The white on the tail is more extended, the white edging to the quills is more conspicuous, and the wings are longer. The tail is much blacker.

In a specimen from Janos, Mexico, (7651,) the black of the breast is anteriorly much shaded with the color of the back, and the interscapular feathers are edged with yellow. I am, however, unable to detect any other differences.

35 **b**

As stated, the female is considerably duller, showing traces only of the black on the breast; the upper parts dull brownish, with darker streaks. Young birds are brown above, with dusky streaks; beneath white, the breast and sides streaked with brown; the yellow of the crown and rump distinct, that of the breast barely appreciable. A winter specimen, (7661,) marked male, has the under parts almost pure white, very obsoletely streaked with brown on the breast and sides; the yellow of throat and breast rather distinct; two bands of white on the wings instead of one.

List of specimens.

Catal. No.	Sex & age.	Localtity.	When collected.	Whence obtained.	Orig. No.	Collected by—	Length.	Stretch of wings.	Wing.
2910	♂	Columbia river	April 24, 1836	J. K. Townsend .					
2911	♀	......do..........	......do......	......do.........			5. 12	8. 75	
2909	♂	......do..........	May 31, 1835	......do.........					
7656	♂	Ft.Steilacoom,W.T.	April 20, 1856	Dr. Suckley.....	209		6. 00	9. 00	
7654	♀	......do..........	......do......	......do.........	....		5. 87	9. 00	
7658	o	......do..........	July 28, 1856	......do.........	504				
7670	♂	......do..........	....	Gov. Stevens....	81	Dr. Suckley.....	5. 75	9. 50.	3. 75
7671	♀	......do..........	May 1, 1856	......do.........	351	.....do.........	6. 00	9. 00	
7672	......	Shoalwater bay....	June 20, 1854	Dr. Cooper	82		5. 25	8. 50	
7673	......	......do..........	Aug. 30, 1854	......do.........	86		5. 12	8. 75	
7674	......	......do..........	......do......	......do.........	86		5. 75	9. 00	
7662	♀	California		Dr. Heermann...					
3728	......	......do..........		Wm. Hutton....					
7660	♀	Sacramento valley.	....	Lt. Williamson ..	......	Dr. Heermann...			
7661	♂	......do..........		......do.........		.....do.........			
7651	......	Janos, Mex.	April —, 1855	Maj. Emory	67	Dr. Kennerly ...			
7652	......	Boca Grande, Mex.	Mar. —, 1855	......do.........	34	.....do.........			
7653	......	San Bernardino....		......do.........	69	.....do.........			
7663	......	Cocomongor'ch, Cal	Mar. 19, 1854	Lt. Whipple	190	.....do.........			
8826	......	Laramie peak.....		Lt. Warren	......	Dr. Hayden.....			
8016	......	Mexico............	....	John Gould.....					

DENDROICA BLACKBURNIAE, Baird.

Blackburnian Warbler.

Motacilla blackburniae, GMELIN. Syst. Nat. I, 1788, 977.

Sylvia blackburniae, LATHAM, Index Orn. II, 1790, 527.—VIEILLOT, Ois. Am. Sept. II, 1807, 36; pl. xcvi.—WILSON, Am. Orn. III, 1811, 67; pl. xxiii.—NUTTALL, Man. I, 1832, 379.—AUD. Orn. Biog. II, 1834, 208 : V, 73, pl. 135, 399.

Sylvicola blackburniae, JARDINE, Ed. Wilson, 1832.—RICH. List, 1837.—BON. List, 1838.—IB. Conspectus, 1850, 307.—AUD. Syn. 1839, 57.—IB. Birds Am. II, 1841, 48; pl. 87.

Rhimanphus blackburniae, CABANIS, Mus. Hein. 1850, 19.

Sylvia parus, WILSON, Am. Orn. V, 1812, 114; pl. xliv, f. 3 —AUD. Orn. Biog. II, 1834, 205; pl. 134.

Sylvicola parus, AUD. Syn. 1839, 55.—IB. Birds Amer. II, 1841, 40; pl. 83.

Sylvia lateralis, Steph. Shaw's Zool. XII, 1817, 659.

Blackburnian warbler, PENNANT, Arctic Zool. II, 412.—LATHAM, Synopsis II, 461.

Hemlock warbler, AUTHORS.

Sp. Ch.—Upper parts nearly uniform black, with a whitish scapular stripe and a large white patch in the middle of the wing coverts. An oblong patch in the middle of the crown, and the entire side of the head and neck, (including a superciliary stripe from the nostrils,) the chin, throat, and fore part of the breast, bright orange red. A black stripe from the commissure passing over the lower half of the eye, and including the ear coverts; with, however, an orange crescent in it, just below the eye, the extreme lid being black. Rest of under parts white, strongly tinged with yellowish orange on the breast and belly, and streaked with black on the sides. Outer three tail feathers white, the shafts and tips dark brown; the fourth and fifth spotted much with white; the other tail feathers and quills almost black. Female similar; the colors duller; the feathers of the upper parts with olivaceous edges. Length, 5.50; wing, 2.83; tail, 2.25.

Hab.—Eastern North America to the Missouri. South to Guatemala.

This is, perhaps, the most beautiful of the American warblers; none certainly can show any color to compare with the delicate orange of the throat. The precise shade of this, however, varies a good deal in different specimens.

The black ear patch sends a short branch down on the side of the throat, so as to connect with the series of short black stripes on the sides. The under tail coverts are pure white. The female exhibits a much more striated appearance above, and the orange is much more yellowish; the black of the cheeks is replaced by grayish. An autumnal male is like the female, the single white band on the wing replaced by two; the black stripes on the sides much larger and more conspicuous; the upper parts glossed with yellowish; the throat orange yellow, passing insensibly into purer yellow behind. In this condition it is much like an autumnal *D. townsendii*, the top and sides of the head being exactly the same, except the yellow patch on the crown of the former. The throat, however, is more orange, and with no trace of the black. The pure white bases of the outer tail feathers are a strong distinctive mark of *D. blackburniae*. It is this plumage that I consider to be the *Sylvia parus* of Wilson and Audubon, their descriptions agreeing exactly with specimens before me of summer *D. blackburniae*.

A specimen from Calcasieu, La., (4305,) is considerably smaller, though otherwise similar, the wing measuring only 2.50 inches, instead of 2.80.

List of specimens.

Catal. No.	Sex.	Locality.	When collected.	Whence obtained.	Orig. No.	Collected by—	Length.	Stretch of wings.	Wing.
1693	♂	Carlisle, Pa.	Aug. 30, 1844	S. F. Baird			5.33	8.50	2.75
944	♀	......do	May 6, 1843	......do			4.75		2.58
740		......do	Sept. 21, 1842	......do			4.91	8.41	2.75
1160		......do	Aug. 16, 1843	......do			5.08	8.33	2.83
7350		Cleveland, Ohio		J. P. Kirtland					
3793		Racine, Wis.		Dr. Hoy					
	♀	West Northfield, Ill.	May 3, 1855	R. Kennicott					
6972	♂	St. Louis, Mo.	May 12, 1857	Lt. Bryan	62	W. S. Wood			
6973	♂	......do	May 8, 1857	......do	39	......do			
4305	♂	Calcasieu pass, La.	1854	G. Wurdemann					
8008		Guatemala		J. Gould					

DENDROICA CASTANEA, Baird.

Bay Breasted Warbler.

Sylvia castanea, WILSON, Am. Orn. II, 1810, 97; pl. xiv, f. 4.—BONAP. Obs. Wils. 1826, No. 139.—NUTTALL, Man. I, 1832, 382.—AUDUBON, Orn. Biog. I, 1832, 358; pl. 69.

Sylvicola castanea, "SWAINSON," JARD. ed. Wilson, 1832.—RICH. List, 1837.—BON. List, 1838.—IB. Consp. 1850, 308.—AUD. Syn. 1839, 53.—IB. Birds Amer. II, 1841,34; pl. 80.

Rhimanphus castaneus, CAB. Mus. Hein. 1850, 19.

Sylvia autumnalis, WILSON, Am. Orn. III, 1811, 65; pl. xxiii, f. 3.—BON. Obs. 1826, No. 152.—AUD. Orn. Biog. I, 1832, 447; pl. 88.—NUTTALL, Man. I, 1832, 390.   (Female or young in autumn.)

SP. CH.—*Male.* Crown dark reddish chestnut; forehead and cheeks, including a space above the eye, black; a patch of buff yellow behind the cheeks. Rest of upper parts bluish gray streaked with black, the edges of the interscapulars tinged with yellowish, of the scapulars with olivaceous. Primaries and tail feathers edged externally with bluish gray; the extreme outer ones with white; the secondaries edged with olivaceous. Two bands on the wing and the edges of the tertials white. The under parts are whitish with a tinge of buff; the chin, throat, fore part of breast, and the sides, chestnut brown, lighter than the crown. Two outer tail feathers with a patch of white on the inner web near the end; the others edged internally with the same. *Female* with the upper parts olive, streaked throughout with black, and an occasional tinge of chestnut on the crown. Lower parts with traces of chestnut, but no stripes. Length of male, 5.00; wing, 3.05; tail, 2.40.

Hab.—Eastern United States to the Missouri. South to Guatemala.

The female appears not to be very constant in her markings; sometimes the trace of chestnut on the crown is conspicuous; sometimes it is entirely wanting. The extent, too, of the chestnut beneath is subject to considerable variation.

In the young bird and possibly in the adult in autumn, the upper parts and sides of the head and neck are of a bright though light olive green, obsoletely streaked with black, chiefly in the middle of the back, the rump with an ashy tinge. Beneath buff white, the sides tinged with brown, sometimes showing a trace of the chestnut of spring. Sometimes there is a greenish yellow tinge on the throat and breast. There is a pale line over the eye, and the eyelids are yellowish, the eye cut by a faint dusky bar from the base of the bill.

This species is in many respects very closely allied to *D. striata*, and although the adults in spring are readily distinguishable, it becomes very difficult to separate them when in autumnal or immature plumage. They are of about the same size; the upper parts would be almost precisely the same, if the chestnut crown of *D. castanea* were replaced by black; the back of the neck in *striata* is streaked with white, and the back has a less yellow tinge. The females are still more similar above. The absence of streaks, however, on the under parts of *S. castanea* would separate them in all cases, but for the fact that these sometimes are obsolete in young of *D. striata*. The bill of *D. castanea* is broader at the base and more bristled; the tails are almost precisely the same; the inner borders of the quills of *D. castanea* are abruptly pure white, instead of gradually becoming lighter, as in the other.

A careful comparison of an extensive series of immature specimens of the two species shows that in *castanea* the under parts are seldom washed uniformly on the throat and breast, with yellowish green; but while this may be seen on the sides of the neck and breast, or even across the latter, the chin and throat are nearly white, the sides tinged with dirty brown, even if the (generally present) trace of chestnut be wanting on the sides. There is a buff tinge to the under tail coverts; the quills are abruptly margined with white, and there are no traces (however obsolete) of streaks on the breast. In *D. striata* the under parts are quite uniformly washed with greenish yellow nearly as far back as the vent, the sides of the breast and sometimes of belly with obsolete streaks; no trace of the uniform dirty reddish brown on the sides behind and under tail coverts are pure white. The quills are only gradually paler towards the inner edge, not rather abruptly white.

List of specimens.

Catal No.	Sex.	Locality.	When collected.	Whence obtained.	Length.	Stretch of wings.	Wing.
2231	♂	Carlisle, Pa.	May 6, 1845	S. F. Baird			
950	♀	....do.	May 8, 1843	....do.	5. 25	8. 75	2. 75
748		....do.	Sept. 23, 1842	....do.	5. 25	8. 00	2. 91
993	♀	....do.	May 19, 1843	....do.	5. 00	8. 66	2. 75
949	♀	....do.	May 8, 1843	....do.	5. 08	8. 41	2. 75
7443		Cleveland, Ohio	Autumn	Dr. Kirtland			
	♀	Union county, Ill.	May 12	R. Kennicott			
8013		Guatemala.		J. Gould			

DENDROICA PINUS, Baird.

Pine Creeping Warbler.

Sylvia pinus, WILSON, Am. Orn. III, 1811, 25 ; pl. xix, f. 4. (Not *Certhia pinus*, L ; *Motacilla pinus*, Gm. ; *Sylvia pinus*, Lath.)—BONAP. Obs. Wils. 1826, No. 149.—NUTTALL, Man. I, 1832, 387.—AUD. Orn. Biog. II, 1834, 232 ; pl. 111.

Thryothorus pinus, STEPHENS, in Shaw's Gen. Zool. XIV, I, 194.

Sylvicola pinus, JARD. ed. Wilson, 1832.—RICH. List, 1837.—BONAP. List, 1838.—AUD. Syn. 1839, 54.—IB Birds Amer. II, 1841, 37 ; pl. 82.

Rhimamphus pinus, BONAP. Conspectus, 1850, 311.

Sylvia vigorsii, AUD. Orn. Biog. I, 1832, 153 ; pl. 30. (Young.)

Vireo vigorsii, NUTTALL, Man. I, 1832, 318.

SP. CH.—Upper parts nearly uniform and clear olive green, the feathers of the crown with rather darker shafts. Under parts generally, except the middle of the belly behind, and under tail coverts, (which are white,) bright gamboge yellow, with obsolete streaks of dusky on the sides of the breast and body. Sides of head and neck olive green like the back, with a broad superciliary stripe ; the eyelids and a spot beneath the eye very obscurely yellow ; wings and tail brown ; the feathers edged with dirty white, and two bands of the same across the coverts. Inner web of the first tail feather with nearly the terminal half, of the second with nearly the terminal third, dull inconspicuous white. Length, 5.50 ; wing, 3 ; tail, 2.40. (1356.)

Hab.—Eastern United States to the Missouri.

The markings of this species are not very distinct or well defined ; less so, perhaps, than any of our warblers, except possibly *D. palmarum.* The amount of white on the tail varies somewhat, occasionally the entire outer web of the exterior feather and a larger portion of the inner being of this color. The female is similar to the male, but of duller plumage. In autumn the colors are as in spring, the yellow rather lighter and brighter ; the olive above glossed with reddish brown. The yellow of the under parts is sometimes much obscured by pale margins to the feathers. The young are brown above, whitish beneath, tinged with brown before.

This species appears to differ from the *Sylvia montana,* Wilson, chiefly in the absence of a yellow frontlet, in having a greener back, and less distinct streaks beneath ; as also in the white anal region.

List of specimens.

Catal. No.	Sex and age.	Locality.	When collected.	Whence obtained.	Length.	Stretch of wings	Wing.
1336	♂	Carlisle, Pa	April —, 1844	S. F. Baird	5. 50	9. 00	2. 91
307	♂	......do	April 24, 1841	......do	5. 41	8. 25	
736		......do	Sept. 21, 1842	......do	5. 41	9. 33	3. 00
2430	♀	......do	Sept. 5, 1845	......do			
42	○	......do	June 19, 1840	......do			
6484		Philadelphia		C. Drexler			
699		Washington, D. C.	June 7, 1842	S. F. Baird			
10162		Northern Ill		R. Kennicott			

DENDROICA MONTANA, Baird.

Blue Mountain Warbler.

Sylvia montana, WILSON, Am. Orn. V, 1812, 113 ; pl. xliv, f. 2.—AUD. Orn. Biog. V, 1839, 294.

Sylvicola montana, JARD. ed. Wilson, 1832.—AUD. Syn. 1839, 62.—IB. Birds Am. II, 1841, 69 ; pl. 98.

Sylvia tigrina, VIEILLOT, Ois. Am. Sept. II, 1807, 34 ; pl. xciv.—BONAP. Obs. Wils. 1826, No. 165. (Not of Latham.)

" This species is four inches and three-quarters in length ; the upper parts a rich yellow olive ; front, cheeks, and chin yellow, also the sides of the neck ; breast and belly pale yellow, streaked with black or dusky ; vent plain pale yellow. Wings black ; first and second rows of coverts broadly tipped with pale yellowish white ; tertials the same ; the rest of the quills edged with whitish. Tail black, handsomely rounded, edged with pale olive ; the two exterior feathers on each side white on the inner vanes from the middle to the tips, and edged on the outer side with white. Bill dark brown. Legs and feet purple brown ; soles yellow. Eye dark hazel."—(Wilson.)

Hab.—" Blue mountains of Virginia."

The essential features of this bird, "yellow olive above, front and beneath yellow to the vent, (paler behind,) the breast and belly streaked with dusky or black ; wings and tail black, the former with two white bands, the latter with the outer feathers white within from the middle to near the tip," are not shared by any other known North American species in adult spring plumage. The relationships, however, to the pine creeping warbler are very close, and it is not unlikely that some states of autumnal plumage in this, or even in the black poll warbler, may furnish a clue to the species.

A single specimen was taken in the Blue mountains of Pennsylvania by Wilson, and is the only one described from the limits of the United States. Audubon figures a skin in the Museum of the Zoological Society said to have been brought from California.

DENDROICA PENNSYLVANICA, Baird.

Chestnut-sided warbler.

Motacilla pennsylvanica, Linnaeus, Syst. Nat. I, 1766, 333, No. 19.—Gmelin, Syst. Nat. I, 1788, 971, No. 19.

Sylvia pennsylvanica, Latham, Ind. Orn. II, 1790, 540.—Wilson, Am. Orn. I, 1808, 99 ; pl. xiv, f. 5.

Motacilla icterocephala, Linnaeus, Syst. Nat. I, 1766, 334, 25.—Gmelin, Syst. I, 1788, 980.

Sylvia icterocephala, Latham, Ind. Orn. II, 1790, 538.—Vieillot, Ois. Am. Sept. II, 1807, 31 ; pl. xc —Bon. Obs. Wils. 1826, No. 140.—Aud. Orn. Biog. I, 1832, 306 ; pl. 59.—Nuttall, Man. I, 1832, 380.

Sylvicola icterocephala, "Swainson," Jard. ed. Wilson, 1832.—Rich. List. 1837.—Bonap. List. 1838.—Ib. Conspectus, 1850, 308.—Aud. Syn. 1839, 54.—Ib. Birds Am. II, 1841, 35 ; pl. 81.

Sp. Ch.—*Male.*—Upper parts streaked with black and pale bluish gray, which becomes nearly white on the fore part of the back ; the middle of the back glossed with greenish yellow. The crown is continuous yellow, bordered by a frontal and superciliary band, and behind by a square spot of white. Loral region black, sending off a line over the eye, and another below it. Ear coverts and lower eyelid and entire under parts pure white, a purplish chestnut stripe starting on each side in a line with the black moustache and extending back to the thighs. Wing and tail feathers dark brown, edged with bluish gray, except the secondaries and tertials, which are bordered with light yellowish green. The shoulders with two greenish white bands. Three outer tail feathers with white patches near the end of the inner webs.

Female like the male, except that the upper parts are yellowish green, streaked with black ; the black moustache scarcely appreciable.

Length, 5 ; wing, 2.50 ; tail, 2.20.

Hab.—Eastern United States to the Missouri.

The greenish white of the wing is rather in one band in the male than in two, the greater coverts being edged as well as tipped with this color.

The male (possibly of the first year) in autumn is very different from either male or female in spring. The entire upper parts are of a continuous light olive green ; the under parts white ; the sides of the head, neck, and breast ash gray, shading insensibly into and tinging the white of the chin and throat. No black streaks are visible above nor on the cheeks, and the eye is surrounded by a continuous ring of white, not seen in spring. The wings and tail are much as in the female.

In one specimen from St. Louis (6977) the black completely encircles the eye, and the bill is entirely bluish black, instead of being brown beneath.

List of specimens.

Catal. No.	Sex.	Locality.	When collected.	Whence obtained.	Orig. No.	Collected by—	Length.	Stretch of wings.	Wing.
1694	♂	Carlisle, Pa.........	Sept. 4, 1844	S. F. Baird	......	....	5.25	7.41	2.75
2570	♂	......do.............	May 4, 1844	......do.......	......	....	5.16	8.00	2.08
2664	♂	......do.............	May 18, 1844	......do.......	......	....	5.08	7.83	2.08
943	♂	......do.............	May 6, 1844	......do.......	......	....	5.00	7.75	2.50
976	♀	......do.............	May 16, 1844	......do.......	......	....	5.00	7.50	2.50
7361	....	Cleveland, Ohio.....	....	J. P. Kirtland...	......	....	......	......	......
		West Northfield, Ill..	May 15, 1855	R. Kennicott....	......	....	......	......	......
		South Illinois	May 12......	......do.......	......	....	......	......	......
6976	♂	St. Louis, Mo.	May 12, 1857	Lieut. Bryan.....	64	W. S. Wood	......	......	......
6978	....	......do.............	May —, 1857	......do.......	......	......do.......	......	......	......
6977	♂	......do.............	May 12, 1857	......do.......	58	......do.......	......	......	......
4670	....	Mouth of Platte river.	April 26......	Lieut. Warren...	......	Dr. Hayden......	5.00	7.75	2.50

DENDROICA CÆRULEA, Baird.

Blue Warbler.

Sylvia cærulea, WILSON, Am. Orn. II, 1810, 141 ; pl. xvii, f. 5.
Sylvicola cærulea, "SWAINSON," JARD. ed. Wilson, 1832.—RICH. List, 1837.—BONAP. List, 1838.—IB. Consp. 1850,
  308.—AUD. Synop. 1839, 56.—IB. Birds Amer. II, 1841, 45 ; pl. 86.
Sylvia rara, WILSON, Am. Orn. III, 1811, 119 ; pl. xxvii, f. 2, (young or female.)—BONAP. Obs. 1826, No. 158.—
  AUD. Orn. Biog. I, 1832, 258 ; pl. 49.—NUTTALL, I, 1832, 255.
Vermivora rara, JARDINE, Ed. Wilson, 1832.
Sylvia azurea, STEPHENS, in Shaw's Zool. Birds, X, II, 1817, 653.—BON. Obs. 1826, 148.—IB. Am. Orn. II, 1828 ;
  pl. xxvii, (female.)—AUD. Orn Biog. I, 1832, 255 ; pl. xlviii, xlix.—NUTTALL, Man. I, 1832, 407.
Sylvia bifasciata, SAY, Long's Exped. R. Mts. I, 1823, 170.

SP. CH.—Male—Above bright blue, darkest on the crown, tinged with ash on the rump ; middle of back, scapulars, upper tail coverts, and sides of the crown streaked with black. Beneath white, a collar across the breast, and streaks on the sides dusky blue. Lores, and a line through and behind the eye, (where it is bordered above by whitish,) dusky blue ; paler on the cheeks. Two white bands on the wings. All the tail feathers except the innermost, with a white patch on the inner web near the end. Female greenish blue above, brightest on the crown ; beneath white, tinged with greenish yellow, and obsoletely streaked on the sides ; eyelids and a superciliary line greenish white. Length, 4.25 ; wing, 2.65 ; tail, 1.90.

Hab.—Eastern United States to the Missouri river.

This species is sufficiently dissimilar from any other not to require a more minute description than the above.

List of specimens.

Catal. No.	Sex.	Locality.	When collected.	Whence obtained.	Orig. No.	Collected by—
645	♂	Carlisle, Pa.	May 9, 1842	S. F. Baird.		
7346	♂	Rockport, Ohio	May 15, 1852	J. P. Kirtland.		
7345	♀	Cleveland, Ohio.		......do......		
10163	♀	South Illinois.	May 9.	R. Kennicott.		
10164	♂	......do......	May 9.	......do......		
6980	♀	St. Louis, Mo.	May 15, 1857	Lieut. Bryan.	96	W. S. Wood
6979	♂	......do......	May 12, 1857	......do......	52	......do......

DENDROICA STRIATA, Baird.

Black Poll Warbler.

Muscicapa striata, FORSTER, Philos. Trans. LXII, 1772, 383, 428.—GMELIN, Syst. Nat. I, 1788, 930.
Motacilla striata, GMELIN, Syst. I, 1788, 976.
Sylvia striata, LATH. Ind. Orn. II, 1790, 527.—VIEILLOT, Ois. Am. Sept. II, 1807, 22 ; pl. lxxv, lxxvi.—WILSON, Am.
  Orn. IV, 1811, 40 ; pl. xxx, f. 3 : VI, 1812, 101 ; pl. liv.—BON. Obs. Wils. 1826, No. 162.—NUTTALL,
  Man. I, 1832, 383.—AUD. Orn. Biog. II, 1834, 201 ; pl. 133.
Sylvicola striata, SWAINSON, F. B. Am. II, 1831, 218.—BONAP. List, 1838.—IB. Conspectus, 1850, 308.—AUD. Birds
  Am. II, 1841, 28 ; pl. 78.—REINHARDT, Vid. Med. for 1853, 1854, 73. (Greenland.)
Rhimanphus striatus, CAB. Mus. Hein. 1850, 20.—IB. Journ. für Orn. III, 1855, 475, (Cuba.)

SP. CH.—Male—Crown, nape, and upper half of the head black ; the lower half, including the ear coverts, white, the separating line passing through the middle of the eye. Rest of upper parts grayish ash, tinged with brown, and conspicuously streaked with black. Wing and tail feathers brown, edged externally (except the inner tail feathers) with dull olive green. Two conspicuous bars of white on the wing coverts, the tertials edged with the same. Under parts white, with a narrow line on each side the throat from the chin to the sides of the neck, where it runs into a close patch of black streaks continued along the breast and sides to the root of the tail. Outer two tail feathers with an oblique patch on the inner web near the end; the others edged internally with white. Female similar, except that the upper parts are olivaceous and, even on the crown, streaked with black; the white on the sides and across the breast tinged with yellowish; a ring of the same round the eye cut by a dusky line through it. Length of male, 5.75; wing, 3; tail, 2.25.

Hab.—Eastern North America to the Missouri high plains. Cuba, (Gundlach.) Greenland, (Reinhardt.)

The wings are long and pointed; the second longest; the first a little longer than the third. The tail is slightly emarginate and scarcely rounded. The size of specimens varies considerably; thus, in one (4645) the wing measures .40 of an inch more than the type selected, (1545.) Specimens generally from the Mississippi valley appear larger than more eastern ones.

The young birds in the autumnal dress are very different from the spring. The upper parts are light olive green, obsoletely streaked with brown; beneath greenish yellow, obsoletely streaked on the breast and sides, the under tail coverts pure white, a yellowish ring round the eye, and a superciliary one of the same color. In this dress it is scarcely possible to distinguish it from the immature *D. castanea.* The differences as far as tangible will be found detailed under the head of the latter species.

List of specimens.

Catal. No.	Sex.	Locality.	When collected.	Whence obtained.	Orig. No.	Collected by—	Length.	Stretch of wings.	Wing.	Remarks.
1545	♂	Carlisle, Pa............	May 17, 1844	S. F. Baird.......		....	5.75	9.00	3.00	....
723	♂	.....do	Sept. 16, 1842	......do		....	5.50	8.75	....	....
978	♀	.....do	May 17, 1843	......do		....	5.58	8.33	2.91	....
916	♀	Philadelphia...........	Autumn	......do		....	.. ....	....	....	....
702	♀	Washington	May 23, 1842	......do		Wm. M. Baird...	....	....	....	....
7445	.....	Cleveland, Ohio........	Autumn......	Dr. Kirtland		....	....	....	....	....
		West Northfield, Ill....	May 16, 1855	R. Kennicott.......	34	....	....	....	....	......
8310	♂	South Illinois..........	May 13,——	......do		....	....	....	....	Iris browh; bill bl'k & lead color; feet yel.
8300	.....	.......do	May 27, 1857	Wm. M. Magraw...	27	Dr. Cooper.......	5.50	9.00	3.00	Iris brown; bill black; feet brownish.
		.......do	May 26, 1857	......do	13	.....do	5.50	9.12	3.00	
4648	♂	Nebraska..............	May 12,——	Lt. Warren........		Dr. Hayden......	5.50	9.00	3.12	....
4650	♂	.....do	May 11,——	......do		.....do	5.00	8.62	2.75	....
4644	♂	.....do	..... do......	......do	... .	.....do	5.25	9.00	3.12	....
4646	♂	.....do	.... do......	......do		.....do	5.25	8.75	3.00	....
4649	♂	Mouth of Vermilion....	May 6,——	......do		.....do	5.25	8.37	3.25	....
4647	♂	Cedar Island...........	May 12,——	......do		.....do	5.50	9.25	3.25	....
4645	♂	.....do	May 10,——	......do		.....do	5.75	9.25	3.25	....
6501	♂	Tortugas, Fla	April 26,——	G. Wurdemann....		....	....	....	....	....
6502	♂	.....do	..... do......	......do		....	....	....	....	....

36 b

DENDROICA AESTIVA, Baird.

Yellow Warbler.

Motacilla aestiva, GMELIN, Syst. Nat. I, 1788, 996.

Sylvia aestiva, LATHAM, Index Orn. II, 1790, 551.—VIEILLOT, Ois. Am. Sept. II, 1807, 35 ; pl. xcv.—BONAP. Obs. Wils. 1826, No. 144.—AUD. Orn. Biog. I, 1831, 476 ; pl. 95, 35.—NUTT. Man. I, 1832, 370.

Sylvicola aestiva, SWAINSON, F. Bor. Am. II, 1831, 211.—BONAP. List, 1838.—AUD. Syn. 1839, 57.—IB. Birds Amer. II, 1841, 50 ; pl. 88.

Rhimamphus aestivus, BONAP. Consp. 1850, 311.—CABANIS, Mus. Hein. 1851, 19.—IB. Journ. Orn. III, 1855, 472, (Cuba.)

? *Motacilla albicollis*, GMELIN, Syst. Nat. I, 1788, 983.

? *Sylvia albicollis*, LATHAM, Ind. Orn. II, 1790, 535.

? *Sylvia flava*, VIEILLOT, Ois. Am. Sept. II, 1807, 31 ; pl. lxxxi.

Sylvia citrinella, WILSON, Am. Orn. II, 1810, 111 ; pl. xv. f. 5.

?? *Rhimamphus citrinus*, RAF. Journ. de Phys. LXXXVIII, 1819, 417. (Very doubtful if this or any other existing species be referred to.)

Sylvia childreni, AUD. Orn. Biog. I, 1831, 180 ; pl. 35. (Immature.)

? *Sylvia rathbonia*, AUD. Orn. Biog. I, 1831, 333 ; pl. 65.

? *Sylvicola rathbonia*, AUD. Syn. 1839, 58.—IB. Birds Amer. II, 1841, 53 ; pl. 89.

Motacilla petechia, LINN. Syst. Nat. I, 1766, 334.—GMELIN, I, 1788, 983.

Sylvia petechia, LATHAM, Ind. Orn. II, 1790, 535.—VIEILLOT, Ois. Am. Sept. II, 1807, 32 ; pl. xci.

Motacilla ruficapilla, GMELIN, Syst. I, 1788, 971.

?? *Sylvia ruficapilla*, LATH. Ind. Orn. II, 1790, 540.—STEPHENS, Shaw, Gen. Zool. X, II, 1817, 699.

SP. CH.—Bill lead color. Head all round, and under parts generally bright yellow ; rest of upper parts yellow olivaceous, brightest on the rump. Back with obsolete streaks of dusky reddish brown. Fore breast and sides of the body streaked with brownish red. Tail feathers bright yellow ; the outer webs and tips, with the whole upper surfaces of the innermost one, brown ; extreme outer edges of wing and tail feathers olivaceous like the back ; the middle and greater coverts and tertials edged with yellow, forming two bands on the wings. Female similar, with the crown olivaceous like the back, and the streaks wanting on the back, and much restricted on the under parts. Tail with more brown. Length of male, 5.25 ; wing, 2.66 ; tail, 2.25. (940)

Hab.—United States from Atlantic to Pacific ; south to Guatemala and West Indies.

The first, second, and third quills are successively a little shorter, though nearly equal, and longer than the fourth. The shafts of the wing and tail feathers are white beneath, and brown above. The quills, except as mentioned, are of a darker brown than that of the tail. The inner edges of the quills are yellow. The yellow on the tail is sulphur color, and lighter than that on the rest of the body, which exhibits an almost imperceptible trace of red. There are no markings on the head in the male. In the female, however, the extension of the olivaceous yellow over the crown gives rise to a yellow superciliary line. A young bird of the year is similar to the female, although duller, and lighter beneath.

A female bird (758) killed in autumn is darker olivaceous above, the color extending over the sides of the head, neck, and body. The yellow margins of the wing feathers are much more restricted. There is more brown on the tail, this color invading the inner webs to a considerable extent.

Specimens from the Pacific coast appear rather smaller, with less conspicuous streaks than eastern, but no other differences are appreciable.

The *Sylvia rathbonia* of Audubon is known only by his description of a pair killed in Mississippi. Its essential character seems to be in the nearly even tail, with the feathers brown and edged externally with yellow, instead of yellow edged with brown.

In a number of specimens before me I find considerable variation in the extent of brown on outer tail feathers. In all very young birds this crosses the shaft to the inner webs, which in several cases are almost entirely brown, excepting on the inner edge. Such is the case in 10170, from Fort Tejon, 5295, Yellowstone, and 758, Carlisle, all apparently young of the year. Some adult females, too, have more or less of a brown margin on the inner side of the shaft towards the base.

In nearly all full plumaged males of this species from the Missouri plains there is a strong indication of a brownish orange (like the pectoral spots) on the top of the head, especially along the shafts of the feathers. It is this plumage, with perhaps a little greater intensity of red on the crown, which I consider to be the *Motacilla petechia* of Linnaeus, as stated further under the head of *Dendroica palmarum*, and as the former name has priority over *aestiva*, it is a question whether it should not be used for the present species. By some authors the two states of plumage are considered distinct, in which case both names could be used. I agree with Bonaparte, however, (Notes Orn. Delattre,) in considering them the same, but as indicating a variety, not the average of the species ; and in view of there being after all some doubt as to what *Motacilla petechia* really is, I have retained the name of *aestiva*. The same objections apply to the use of Gmelin's name of *ruficapilla*.

The *Motacilla albicollis* of Gmelin answers tolerably well to this species, and the name would have priority over *aestiva*. As, however, the neck is not white, but yellow, the term *albicollis* would convey a false idea of the species, and to be rejected.

The *Sylvia flava* of Vieillot comes nearer this species than any other North American, but does not exactly agree with it.

There is a South American species to which this is closely related, differing in larger size, and in having the entire head all round of a brownish orange. The quills and tail feathers are much darker, showing a more vivid contrast with the yellow. This is called "*Sylvia ruficapilla*, Latham," by Vieillot, in Nouv. Dict. XI, 1817, 228, but is not Latham's species, nor is it the "*Sylvia ruficapillus*" of Vieillot on a preceding page, (187.) He quotes for it a name of Feuillee in "Observations Physiques, 1714–1725," of *Chloris erithachorides,* and its description, referring evidently to the bird before me. Should the species, therefore, have received no better name it may be called *Dendroica erihtachorides.*

List of specimens.

Catal. No.	Sex and age.	Locality.	When collected.	Whence obtained.	Orig'l No.	Collected by—	Length.	Stretch of wings.	Wing.	Remarks.
940	♂	Carlisle, Pa............	May 5, 1843	S. F. Baird........		....	5.25	8.16	2.66	....
947	♀	......do............	.....do.....	......do............		....	4.91	7.50	2.33	....
758	♀	..... do............	Sept. 29, 1843	..... do............		....	4.58	7.50	2.25	.. ..
1656	♂ ?	......do............	July 30, 1844	......do............		....	5.08	8.00	2.66	....
10104	♂	Washington, D. C.....	....	J. C. McGuire		....	....	....	....	....
10103	♀	......do............	....	......do............		....	....	....	....	....
4300	♂	Calcasieu Pass, La.....	1854........	. G. Wurdemann...		....	....	....	....	....
4301	....	......do............	1854........	......do......		....	....	....	....	....
		West Northfield, Ill....	May 12	R. Kennicott		....	....	....	....	....
8301	♀	Independence, Mo.....	May 26, 1857	Wm. M. Magraw...	14	Dr. Cooper	4.50	7.37	2.00	Iris brown, bill black, feet yellow.
5293	♀	Ft. Lookout, Neb......	June 1, 1856	Lieut. Warren....	......	Dr. Hayden....	4.25	6.75	2.00	Eyes black ....
5291	....	Little Sheyenne river ..	......do......	......do............	......	......do.......	4.50	7.00	2.25	......do............
5295	....	Yellowstone river......	June 25, 1856	......do............	......	......do.......	4.87	7.37	2.25	....
5298	....	Blackfoot country......	July —, 1855	......do............	......	......do.......	....	....	....	....
4665	♂	Near Ft. Lookout......	May 15	. ....do.....	......	......do.......	5.50	7.62	2.75	....
4680	....	Fort Pierre	July 12, 1855	Col. Vaughan	......	......do.......	....	....	....	..
4658	♂	Nebraska......... ...	May 17	Lieut. Warren.....	......	......do.......	4.50	7.50	2.50	....
4661	♂	......do............	May 11	......do............	......	......do.......	4.87	8.25	2.62	Eyes black ....
4656	♂	Mouth of White river...	May 2.	......do............	......	......do.......	4.75	7.75	2.50	....
4668	♂	Nebraska............	May 17	......do............	......	......do.......	4.37	7.50	2.50	....
4662	♂	Mouth of Platte river...	April 27, 1856	......do............	......	......do.......	4.75	7.87	3.50	....
4669	....	Nebraska............	....	......do............	......	......do.......	5.12	7.75	2.75	Eyes black ....
5642	♂	East of Ft. Riley, K. T.	June 17, 1856	Lieut. F. T. Bryan.	21	W. S. Wood...	4.00	....	....	....
5292	♀	Fort Lookout..........	June 4, 1856	Lieut. Warren.....	......	Dr. Hayden....	4.25	7.25	2.25	....
5294	♀	Near mouth of Powder	Aug. 1, 1856	... .do............	......	......do.......	4.50	7.62	2.50	Eyes black .....
8825	♂	Loup Fork	July 29	......do............	......	......do.......	4.75	8.00	1.50	....
7648	....	Ft. Steilacoom, W. T...	July 31	Gov. Stevens......	......	Dr. Suckley....	....	....	....	....
7647	....	......do............	....	Dr. Suckley	512	......do.......	....	....	....	....
7643	♂	......do............	May 3	Gov. Stevens	......	Dr. Suckley....	5.25	7.75	....	....
5519	♂	Petaluma, Cal.........	May 7, 1856	E. Samuels........	......	....	....	....	....	....
7645	♂	Sacramento valley....	....	R. S. Williamson...	......	....	....	....	. .....	....
7646	♀	......do............	....	......do............	......	....	....	....	....	....
4474	....	Shoalwater bay, W. T..	May —, 1854	Dr. Cooper	......	....	5.00	7.25	....	Feet pale lemon ....
7644	....	Frontera, Tex........	May —, 1852	C. Wright........	......	....	....	....	....	....
10170	○	Fort Tejon, Cal.......	....	J. Xantus de Vesey.	......	....	....	....	....	....
8010	....	Guatemala............	....	J. Gould..........	......	....	....	....	....	....

DENDROICA MACULOSA, Baird.

Black and Yellow Warbler.

Motacilla maculosa, GMELIN, Syst. I, 1788, 984.

Sylvia maculosa, LATHAM, Ind. Orn. II, 1790, 536.—VIEILLOT, Ois. Am. Sept. II, 1807; pl. xciii.—BONAP. Obs. Wils. 1826, No. 150.—NUTTALL, Man. I, 1832, 370.—AUD. Orn. Biog. I, 1831, 260.—II, 1834, 145: V, 1839, 458; pl. l, cxxiii.

Sylvicola maculosa, SW. F. Bor. Am. II, 1831.—BONAP. List, 1838.—IB. Consp. 1850, 307.—AUD. Syn. 1839, 61.—IB. Birds Amer. II, 1841, 65; pl. xcvi.

Rhimanphus maculosus, CAB. Mus. Hein. 1851, 20.—IB. Journ. Orn. III, 1855, 474, (Cuba).

Sylvia magnolia, WILSON, Am. Orn. III, 1811, 63; pl. xxiii, f. 3.

SP. CH.—*Male, in spring.*—Bill dark bluish black, rather lighter beneath. Tail dusky. Top of head light grayish blue. Front, lore, cheek, and a stripe under the eye, black, running into a large triangular patch on the back between the wings, which is also black. Eyelids and a stripe from the eye along the head white. Upper tail coverts black, some of the feathers tipped with grayish. Abdomen and lower tail coverts white. Rump and under parts, except as described, yellow. Lower throat, breast, and sides streaked with black ; the streaks closer on the lower throat and fore breast. Lesser wing coverts, and edges of the wing and tail bluish gray, the former spotted with black. Quills and tail almost black ; the latter with a square patch of white on the inner webs of all the tail feathers (but the two inner) beyond the middle of the tail. Two white bands across the wings, (sometimes coalesced into one,) formed by the small coverts and secondaries. Part of the edge of the inner webs of the quills white. Feathers margining the black patch on the back behind and on the sides tinged with greenish. Length, 5 inches ; wing, 2.50 ; tail, 2.25.

Hab.—Eastern United States to the Missouri river ; south to Guatemala.

Second and third quills longest ; first shorter than fourth. Tail rounded, emarginate.

Female, in spring.—In general appearance like the male, but with the corresponding colors much duller. The black on the back reduced to a few large proximate spots. The spots on the under parts much fewer. Upper parts dirty ash, tinged with greenish on the lower back ; on the rump dull yellow.

Male, in autumn.—Bill brown, lighter along the edges and base of lower mandible. Head and hind neck dirty ash, tinged above with green. Back greenish yellow, obsoletely spotted with black. Rump yellow. Throat and breast yellow, obsoletely spotted with black ; strongly tinged with light ash on the lower throat. Eyelids dirty white. Differs from the spring plumage in being without the black on the back, front, sides of the head and cheeks, and in a great degree on the under parts. Much less white on the wing and side of the head. The colors generally also are duller.

Female, in autumn.—Similar, generally, to the male in fall. Back greenish yellow, brighter on the rump ; rest of upper parts deep ash. Lower parts yellow, obsoletely streaked with black ; the light ash on the lower throat decided. The white on the wings reduced to two narrow bands. There is a continuous white ring round the eye. Bill light brown. Basal part of lower mandible dirty white. Feet lighter brown.

Specimens vary somewhat in the amount of black on the under parts.

List of specimens.

Catal. No.	Sex & age.	Locality.	When collected	Whence obtained.	Orig. No.	Collected by—	Length.	Stretch of wings.	Wing.
760	♂	Carlisle, Pa.	Sept. 26, 1842	S. F. Baird			4.88	7.50	2.41
2276	♂	......do	May 17, 1845	......do			5.00	7.50	2.41
2212	♂	......do	May 3, 1845	......do			4.75	7.75	2.41
761	♀	......do	Sept. 26, 1842	......do			4.66	7.25	2.25
2671	♀	......do	May 14, 1846	......do			5.00	7.33	2.33
2278	♀	......do	May 17, 1845	......do			4.50	7.16	2.25
2462	o	......do	Sept. 12, 1845	......do					
7333		Rockport, Ohio		J. P. Kirtland					
		Northern Illinois		R. Kennicott					
10166	♂	Union county, Ill.	May 11	......do					
6981	♂	St. Louis, Mo.	May 12, 1857	Lt. Bryan	68	W. S. Wood			
4643		M'th Vermilion riv.	May 5, 1856	Lt. Warren		Dr. Hayden			
8012		Guatemala		J. Gould					

DENDROICA KIRTLANDII, Baird.

Kirtland's Warbler.

Sylvicola kirtlandii, BAIRD, Annals N. Y. Lyc. V, June 1852, 217 ; pl. vi, (Cleveland, Ohio.)—CASSIN, Illust. I, 1855, 278 ; pl. xlvii. (Both figures from the single specimen here described.)

SP. CH.—Above slate blue, the feathers of the crown with a narrow, those of the middle of the back with a broader streak of black ; a narrow frontlet involving the lores, the anterior end of the eye, and the space beneath it, (possibly the whole auriculars,) black ; the rest of the eyelids white. The under parts are clear yellow, (almost white on the under tail coverts ;) the breast with small spots and sides of the body with short streaks of black. The greater and middle wing coverts, quills, and tail feathers are edged with dull whitish. The two outer tail feathers have a dull white spot near the end of the inner web, largest on the first. Length, 5.50 ; wing, 2.80 ; tail, 2.70, (4363).

Hab.—Northern Ohio.

Of this species but a single specimen is known to be extant. It was killed by Dr. Kirtland, near Cleveland, in May of 1851, and its description kindly entrusted to me. No other has been obtained, though Dr. Hoy is under the impression that he has seen the species at Racine.

The specimen is not quite mature, though the markings would not be materially different in the perfect plumage from that above described. There is a brownish tinge on the upper parts which probably change to pure plumbeous.

In size this species appears to exceed any of its North American congeners, while its other markings prevent its being confounded with any of them.

List of specimens.

Catal. No.	Sex.	Locality.	When collected.	Whence obtained.	Collected by—
4363	♂	Cleveland, Ohio	May —, 1851	S. F. Baird.	Dr. J. P. Kirtland........

DENDROICA TIGRINA, Baird.

Cape May Warbler.

Motacilla tigrina, GMELIN, Syst. Nat. I, 1788, 985.
Sylvia tigrina, LATHAM, Ind. Orn. II, 1790, 537. (Not of Vieillot.)
Sylvia maritima, WILSON, Am. Orn. VI, 1812, 99 ; pl. liv, f. 3.—BONAP. Obs. Wils. 1826, No. 157.—IB. Am. Orn. I, 1825 ; pl. iii, f. 3.—NUTTALL, Man. I, 1832, 156.—AUD. Orn. Biog. V, 1839, 156 ; pl. 414.
Sylvicola maritima, JARDINE, Ed. Wilson, 1832.—BONAP. List, 1838.—IB. Conspectus, 1850, 307.—AUD. Syn. 56.—IB. Birds Amer. II, 1841, 44 ; pl. lxxxv.
Certhiola maritima, GOSSE, Birds Jam. 1847, 81.
Rhimamphus maritimus, CAB. Jour. Orn. III, 1855, 474. (Cuba.)

SP. CH.—Bill very acute, conical, and decidedly curved. Bill and feet black. Upper part of head dull black, some of the feathers faintly margined with light yellowish brown. Collar scarcely meeting behind ; rump and under parts generally rich yellow. Throat, fore part of breast, and sides, streaked with black. Abdomen and lower tail coverts pale yellow, brighter about the vent. Ear coverts light reddish chestnut. Back part of a yellow line from nostrils over the eye, of this same color ; chin and throat tinged also with it. A black line from commissure through the eye, and running into the chestnut of the ear coverts. Back, shoulder, edges of the wing and tail yellowish olive ; the former spotted with dusky. One row of small coverts, and outer bases of the secondary coverts, form a large patch of white, tinged with pale yellow. Tertials rather broadly edged with brownish white. Quills and tail dark brown, the three outer feathers of the latter largely marked with white on the inner web ; edge of the outer web of the outer feathers white, more perceptible towards the base. Length, 5.25 ; wing, 2.84 ; tail, 2.15.

Hab.—Eastern United States to the Mississippi. Cuba. (Gundlach.)

The female in spring differs somewhat from the male in having the upper parts dusky, tinged more or less in different individuals with greenish yellow. Rump decided greenish yellow. Head spotted with black. The yellow line from the nostrils over the eye, and the yellow on the sides of neck and breast faintly indicated. In some individuals the whole lower parts are dirty white, tinged with yellowish on the breast. In others, the throat and breast are more strongly marked with yellowish stripes beneath, as in the male, but fainter. The yellowish red of ear coverts wanting, that part being dirty ashy brown. In two specimens the white on the wings is not at all conspicuous, in another more so. The white spots on the tail are less distinct than in the male.

Male in autumn, (747.) Tail feathers pointed. Tail emarginate, outer feather slightly shorter than the next. Third quill longest, second scarcely shorter, first longer than fourth. It resembles the spring male in the distribution of its coloring, but is duller, and with some colors wanting, in fact, more like the female. Like the female as to the back, head, yellow from nostril over eye and sides of head and throat ; yellowish red of ear coverts wanting, that part being yellowish spotted with light dusky. Lower parts strongly yellow, streaked with brown. Abdomen and tail coverts paler. The white on wing coverts rather duller than in spring. Outer edge of the ends of the primaries margined with whitish. Under part of the base of lower mandible light yellowish brown, (747.)

The *Motacilla tigrina*, of Gmelin, and *Sylvia tigrina*, of Latham, are, without doubt, the same as *Sylvia maritima*, of Wilson. The *S. tigrina*, of Vieillot, appears to be the same as *S. montana*, of Wilson, agreeing in the two white wing bands, (not one,) and other characters.

List of specimens.

Catal. No.	Sex.	Locality.	When collected.	Whence obtained.	Length.	Stretch of wings.	Wing.
962	♂	Carlisle, Pa.	May 12, 1843	S. F. Baird	5. 00	8. 33	2. 66
747	♂	...do...	Sept. 23, 1842	...do...	5. 00	8. 00	2. 91
678	♀	...do...	May 17, 1842	...do...			
10167	♀	Racine, Wis.		R. Kennicott.			

DENDROICA CARBONATA.

Sylvia carbonata, Aud. Orn. Biog. I, 1831, 308 ; pl. lx.—Nuttall, Man. I, 1832, 405.
Sylvicola carbonata, Rich. List, 1837.
Vermivora carbonata, Bonap. List, 1838.
Helinaia carbonata, Aud. Syn. 1839, 68.—Ib. Birds Amer. II, 1841, 95 ; pl. cix.

" Bill brownish black above, light blue beneath. Iris hazel. Feet light flesh color. Upper part of the head black. Fore part of the back, lesser wing coverts and sides dusky, spotted with black. Lower back dull yellowish green, as is the tail, of which the outer web of the outer feather is whitish. Tip of the second row of coverts white, of the first row yellow ; quills dusky, their outer webs tinged with yellow. A line from the lore over the eye ; sides of the neck and the throat, bright yellow. A dusky line behind the eye. The rest of the under parts dull yellow, excepting the sides. Length, 4.75 inches ; bill above, 4.42 ; tarsus, .75." (Audubon.)

Hab.—Kentucky.

Judging from the description, this species is closely related to *D. tigrina*, but seems to be distinct in the pure black of the top of the head, the absence of orange brown on the cheeks, the white of the wing being on the middle coverts instead of the greater, and the tail feathers yellowish green ; the outer web of outer feather white instead of a large spot on the inner web. The back appears more distinctly streaked.

The Carbonated Warbler is only known by the description and figure of Mr. Audubon, taken from two specimens killed at Henderson, Kentucky, in 1811. The indications are not sufficient to show in what particular group of warblers it is to be placed.

DENDROICA PALMARUM, Baird.

Yellow Red Poll.

Motacilla palmarum, GMELIN, Syst. I, 1788, 951.

Sylvia palmarum, LATH. Ind. Orn. II, 1790, 544.—VIEILLOT, Ois. Am. Sept. II, 1807, 21 ; pl. lxxiii.—BONAP. J. A. N. S. V, 1826, 29.—IB. Am. Orn.

Sylvia petechia, WILSON, Am. Orn. VI, 1812, 19 ; pl. xxviii, f. 4, (not of Latham.)—BONAP. Obs. 1826, No. 61.— NUTTALL, Man. I, 1832, 364.—AUD. Orn. Biog. II, 1834, 259, 360 ; pl. 163, 164.

Sylvicola petechia, SWAINSON, F. Bor. Am II, 1831.—AUD. Birds Am. II, 1841, 55 ; pl. 90.

Seiurus petechia, McCULLOH, Bost. Jour. N. H. IV, 406.

Sylvicola ruficapilla, BONAP. List, 1838.—IB. Consp. 1850, 307.   (Not *Motacilla ruficapilla*, Gm.)

Rhimamphus ruficapillus, CABANIS, Journ. für Orn. III, 1855, 473, (Cuba in winter.)

SP. CH.—Head above chestnut red ; rest of upper parts brownish olive gray ; the feathers with darker centres, the color brightening on the rump, upper tail coverts, and outer margins of wing and tail feathers to greenish yellow. A streak from nostrils over the eye, and under parts generally, including the tail coverts, bright yellow ; paler on the body. A maxillary line ; breast and sides finely but rather obsoletely streaked with reddish brown. Cheeks brownish, (in highest spring plumage, chestnut like the head) ; the eyelids and a spot under the eye, olive brown. Lores dusky. A white spot on the inner web of the outer two tail feathers at the end. Length, 5 inches ; wing, 2.42 ; tail, 2.25.

Hab.—Eastern United States to the Mississippi, and Red river of the North.

Without a very good series of specimens before me, I am unable to give a complete description of the species. None are marked for sex, but skins supposed to be females differ chiefly in a less amount of chestnut on the crown. There is no clear indication of any bands on the wing, although the edges of the coverts are slightly paler.

An autumnal male (783) shows a strong tinge of reddish in the olive brown of the back, and the chestnut of the crown is much concealed. The under parts are of a very vivid yellow throughout, obscured by brown. The axillaries are yellow. As in other specimens, the outer web of the first tail feather is whitish on the under surface. In this the tail is nearly even, slightly emarginate ; the second and third quills longest ; the first shorter than the fourth. The size appears unusually large. Length of skin, 5.20 ; wing, 2.75 ; tail, 2.50.

In one specimen there is scarcely any yellow about the head and neck, this color being replaced by dirty white ; the crown streaked with brown.

This species in its immature state bears some resemblance to *D. tigrina*, but is distinguishable by the chestnut crown, browner back, less vivid yellow of the rump, much brighter yellow of under tail coverts, smaller blotches on the tail feathers, absence of white bands on the wings, &c.

It is almost certain that the present species is not the *Motacilla petechia* of Linnaeus, as quoted by authors. The diagnosis of Linnaeus, *M. olivacea, subtus flava rubro guttata, pileo rubro,* applies much better to the red crowned variety of *D. aestiva* than to the present bird. The fuller description of Pennant (Arctic Zool. II, 401) says, " crown scarlet, cheeks yellow, hind part of neck, back, and rump olive green ; wings and tail dusky, edged with yellow ; beneath rich yellow speckled with red, except the vent, which is plain." Vieillot describes *Sylvia petechia* in much the same words, and adds that the tail feathers are brown, margined with yellow, which extends furthest in on the inner web. This totally ignores the white terminal spots. The *S. palmarum* is described in detail by Vieillot, and is undoubtedly the present bird.

Motacilla ruficapilla of Gmelin very probably refers to the same plumage of *D. aestiva.* At any rate, it cannot interfere with *Motacilla palmarum,* which has priority, and is undoubtedly the present bird.

List of specimens.

Catal. No.	Sex.	Locality.	When collected.	Whence obtained.	Length.	Stretch of wings.	Wing.	Remarks.
783	♂	Carlisle, Pa..........	Oct. 7, 1842	S. F. Baird.	5. 12	7. 25	2. 49	....
10100	....	Washington, D. C...	....	J. C. McGuire...	......	......	......	....
7351	....	Rockport, Ohio......	....	J. P. Kirtland...	......	......	......	....
		Red River Settlement.	Sept. 10......	R. Kennicott....	......	......	......	....
		Racine, Wis.........	....	......do........	......	......	......	....
		West Northfield, Ill..	May 4, 1855	......do........	......	......	......	....
	♀	Union county, Ill....	May 12......	......do........	......	......	......	....
8647	....	Cape Florida.........	Oct. 27, 1857	G. Wurdemann...	5. 00	8. 00	2. 50	Black eye, bill, and feet.
6494	♀	Indian Key.........	March 23.....	......do........	......	......	......	....
6496	♀	Tortugas, Fla........	April 30.....	......do........	......	......	......	....

DENDROICA SUPERCILIOSA, Baird.

Yellow-throated Warbler.

Motacilla superciliosa, BODDAERT, Tableau Pl. enl. 686, f. 1, 1783, (fide G. R. Gray.)
Motacilla flavicollis, GMELIN, Syst. Nat. I, 1788, 959, No. 71.
Sylvia flavicollis, LATHAM, Ind. Orn. II, 1790.—WILSON, Am. Orn. II, 1810, 64 ; pl xii, f 6.
Motacilla pensilis, GMELIN, Syst. Nat. I, 1788, 960, 76.
Sylvia pensilis, LATHAM, Ind. Orn. II, 1790, 520.—VIEILLOT, Ois. Am. Sept. II, 1807, 11 ; pl. lxxii.—BON. Obs. Wils. 1826, No. 138.—AUD. Orn. Biog. I, 1831, 434 ; pl. 85.—NUTTALL, Man. I, 1832, 374.
Sylvicola pensilis, RICH. List, 1837.—BON. List, 1838.—IB. Consp. 1850, 307.—AUD. Syn. 1839, 53.—IB. Birds Amer. II, 1841, 32 ; pl. 79.—GOSSE, Birds Jam. 1847, 156.
Rhimamphus pensilis, CABANIS, Journ. Orn. III, 1855, 474, (Cuba in winter.)
Ficedula dominicensis cinerea, BR. III, 1760, 520 ; pl. xxvii, f. 3.
La Gorge Jaune de St. Domingue, BUFFON, Ois. VI, 70 ; pl. enl. 686, f. 1, (Male.)

SP. CH.—Upper parts uniform grayish blue. Chin and throat orange yellow ; under parts white. Forehead and sometimes most of crown, lore and cheeks, sides of the throat, and numerous streaks on the sides of the breast, black. A stripe from the nostrils over and behind the eye, a crescent on the lower eyelid, the sides of the neck behind the black cheek patch, and two conspicuous bands on the wings, white. Terminal half of the outer webs of the outer two, and terminal third of the third tail feathers, white. Female similar, but duller. Length, 5.10 ; wing, 2.60 ; tail, 2.30, (3322.)

Hab.—Eastern United States as far as Pennsylvania and Ohio to the Missouri ; south to Mexico.

This species appears subject to considerable variation. The bill varies greatly in length, curve, and proportion, as does the size of body. Sometimes the forehead alone is black, at others, as in 2386, 2913, almost the entire crown is black. The whole superciliary line is often yellow anterior to the eye ; the forehead is sometimes divided by a short whitish line. In one specimen from Washington, the black of the forehead is wanting ; the upper parts have a brownish shade ; the under surface tinged with brown behind. It is considerably larger than any other I have seen.

As a general rule in the specimens before me, those from Georgia have the superciliary stripe anterior to the eye yellow instead of white, as is the case in those from Ohio and Illinois.

37 b

List of specimens.

Catal. No.	Sex.	Locality.	When collected.	Whence obtained.	Orig. No.	Collected by—	Length.	Strexch of wings.	Wing.
1098	♀?	Washington, D C.	1842	S. F. Baird.		J. C. McGuire.			
2390		Savannah, Ga	1845	do		Jos. Leconte			
2386		do	1845	do		do			
3322	♂	Riceboro', Ga	1846	do		W. L. Jones	5. 10	8. 30	2. 60
7700		Rockport, Ohio		Dr. J. P.Kirtland.		R. Kennicott			
		Union county, Ill	May 5	N. W. University		do			
		Cairo, Ill	April 29	do					
3986	♀	Tamaulipas, Mex	1845	Lt. Couch	74		4. 25	7. 75	2. 50

DENDROICA DISCOLOR, Baird.

Prairie Warbler.

Sylvia discolor, VIEILLOT, Ois. Am. Sept. II, 1807, 37 ; pl. xcviii. (No mention of chesnut of back.)—BON. Obs. Wils. 1826, No. 157.—AUD. Orn. Biog. I, 1831, 76 ; pl. 14.—NUTTALL, Man. I, 1832, 294.
S lvicola discolor, JARD. ed. Wilson, 1832.—RICH, List, 1837.—BONAP. List, 1838.—IB. Conspectus, 1850, 309.—AUD. Syn. 1839, 62.—IB. Birds Amer. II, 1841, 68 ; pl. 97.—GOSSE, Birds Jam. 1847, 159.
Rhimamphus discolor, CABANIS, Journ. Orn. III, 1855, 474. (Cuba in winter.)
Sylvia minuta, WILSON, Am. Orn. III, 1811, 87 ; pl. xxv, f. 4.

SP. CH.—Above uniform olive green ; the middle of the back streaked with brownish red. Under parts and sides of the head, including a broad superciliary line from the nostrils to a little behind the eye, bright yellow, brightest anteriorly. A well defined narrow stripe from the commissure of the mouth through the eye, and another from the same point curving gently below it, also a series of streaks on each side of the body, extending from the throat to the flanks, black. Quills and tail feathers brown, edged with white ; the terminal half of the inner web of the first and second tail feathers white. Two yellowish bands on the wings. Female similar, but duller. The dorsal streaks indistinct. Length, 4.86 ; wing, 2.25 ; tail, 2.10.

Hab.—Atlantic States, as far north as New York.

The streaks on the back appear to be in four series. There is a yellow crescent under the eye, and below this the black one already mentioned. After a slight interval the stripes on the side of the throat begin, in one series on each side ; two, however, starting on the breast. The yellow superciliary stripe extends to the base of the bill, although those of opposite sides do not coalesce. Sometimes there is a black line, bordering the olivaceous of the crown, anteriorly.

In this species the second, third, and fourth quills are longest ; the first rather longer than the fifth. The tail is considerably rounded, in fact, almost graduated. The bill is dark brown.

List of specimens.

Catal. No.	Sex.	Locality.	When collected.	Whence obtained.	Length.	Stretch of wings.	Wings.	Remarks.
6483		Philadelphia		C. Drexler				
1051	♂	Washington, D. C.	May 30, 1843	Wm. M. Baird	4.87	7.00	2.25	
1095	♀	do	June 12, 1843	do	4.62	6.87	2.12	
7374		do		Wm. Hutton				
509		New York		S. F. Baird				
1091	♂	Philadelphia	Spring, 1843	do				
8676		Cape Florida	Sept. 24, 1843	G. Wurdemann	4.75	7.30	2.30	Dark eye, legs and bill brown.
8677	♀?	Indian Key	Sept. 2, 1857	do	4.50	7.00	2.20	Bill and feet blackish, with yellow soles.
8678	♂?	do	do	do	4.50	6.50	2.00	

Section **Setophageae.**

Cʜ.—Bill usually distinctly notched at tip ; decidedly broader than high at the base, though thick. Rictus well provided with bristles, the longest nearly equal to the bill. Tail nearly equal to the wings, or longer. Wings rounded ; first quill nearly equal to fourth.

The following genera compose this section :

MYIODIOCTES.—Bill muscicapine. Feet stout. Tarsus longer than the head. Toes developed; hind toe considerably longer than the lateral. Tail about equal to the wings; slightly rounded.

CARDELLINA.—Bill parine ; as high at base as broad ; scarcely deflected at tip. Tail nearly even ; first quill equal to the sixth. Hind toe longer than the lateral.

BASILEUTERUS.—Bill stout, but rather depressed at base. Wings very short ; the first quill shorter than the secondaries. Tail considerably graduated. Hind toe longer than the lateral.

SETOPHAGA.—Bill muscicapine. Feet slender. Tarsus scarcely equal to the head. Hind toe not longer than the lateral. Tail usually longer than the wings ; considerably rounded, or even graduated.

MYIODIOCTES, Aud.

Myiodioctes, Aud. Syn. 1839, 48. (Type *Motacilla mitrata*.)
Wilsonia, Bonap. List, 1838. (Preoccupied in Botany.)
Myioctonus, Cabanis, Mus. Hein. 1850, 18.

Cʜ.—Bill depressed, flycatcher like ; broader than high at the base ; gape with bristles nearly as long as the bill, which is distinctly notched at tip ; both outlines gently convex. Tarsi longer than the head ; considerably exceeding the middle toe ; claws all considerably curved. Tail decidedly rounded or slightly graduated ; the lateral feathers .20 of an inch shorter. Wing very little longer than the tail ; the first quill decidedly shorter than the fourth ; colors yellow.

The species of this genus are decidedly muscicapine in general appearance, as shown by the depressed bill with bristly rictus. The type *M. mitratus* is very similar in character of bill to *Sylvicola castanea*, but the wings are much shorter ; the tail longer and more graduated ; the legs and hind toe longer, and the first primary shorter than the fourth, (.15 of an inch less than the longest,) not almost equal to the longest. The species are plain olive or plumbeous above, and yellow beneath. They may be grouped as follows :

A. Tail with white patches on the outer feathers.
    Head and neck black. Front, cheeks and under parts yellow. Back olive green.*M. mitratus.*
    Olive above ; yellowish beneath. Two white bands on the wings............? *M. minutus.*
B. Tail without white patch on the outer feathers.
    Crown black. Forehead, cheeks, and under parts, yellow. Back olive ......*M. pusillus.*
    Streaks on the crown, stripe on sides of head and neck, with pectoral collar of streaks, black. Rest of under parts, and line to and around the eye, yellow. Back bluish. (*Euthlypis*, Cab. Mus. Hein. 1850, 18.)..............................*M. canadensis.*

Comparative measurements.

Cat. No.	Species.	Locality.	Sex.	Length.	Stretch of wings.	Wing.	Tail.	Tarsus.	Middle toe.	Its claw alone.	Bill above.	Along gape.	Remarks.
2226	Myiodioctes mitratus....	Carlisle, Pa......	♂	5.00	....	2.70	2.58	0.78	0.64	0.18	0.40	0.55	Dry ....
2245	.... do............	......do..........	♂	4.62	....	2.58	2.42	0.77	0.61	0.19	0.38	0.52	Dry ....
2228	.........do............	......do....	♀	4.70	....	2.50	2.36	0.76	0.61	0.16	0.38	0.52	Dry ....
990	Myiodioctes pusillus....	......do..........	♂	4.60	....	2.24	2.26	0.70	0.56	0.14	0.33	0.44	Dry ....
do.	.... ..do............	......do..........	......	4.75	7.00	2.25	....	....	....	....	....	....	Fresh.......
2325	.........do............	......do..........	♀	4.12	....	2.06	2.06	0.72	0.52	0.14	0.33	0.44	Dry ....
945	Myiodioctes canadensis.	......do..........	♂	4.88	....	2.64	2.50	0.74	0.56	0.16	0.43	0.56	Dry ....
do.	.........do............	......do..........	......	5.33	8.33	2.66	....	....	....	....	....	....	Fresh ....
1021	.........do............	......do..........	♀	4.86	....	2.44	2.34	0.71	0.58	0.17	0.38	0.56	Dry ....
do.	....do............	......do..........	......	5.25	7.75	2.50	....	....	....	....	....	....	Fresh.......

MYIODIOCTES MITRATUS, Audubon.

Hooded Warbler.

Motacilla mitrata, GMELIN, Syst. Nat. I, 1788, 977.

Sylvia mitrata, LATHAM, Ind. Orn. II, 1790, 528.—VIEILLOT, Ois. Am. Sept. II, 1807, 23 ; pl. lxxvii.—BONAP. Obs. 1826, No. 125.—NUTTALL, Man. I, 1832, 373.—AUDUBON, Orn. Biog. II, 1834, 68 ; pl 110.

Sylvania mitrata, NUTTALL, Man. I, 2d ed. 1840, 333.

Setophaga mitrata, JARD. ed. Wilson, 1832.—GRAY, Genera, 28.

Wilsonia mitrata, BONAP. List, 1838.

Myiodioctes mitratus, AUD, Syn. 1839, 48, (type.)—IB. Birds Amer. II, 1841, 12 ; pl. 71.—BONAP. Consp. 1850, 315.

Myioctonus mitratus, CABANIS, Mus. Hein, 1851, 18.   (Type.)—IB. Journ. Orn. III, 1855, 472, (Cuba.)

Muscicapa cucullata, WILSON, Am. Orn. III, 1811, 101 ; pl. xxvi, f. 3.   (Not *Sylvia cucullata*, Lath.)

Muscicapa selbyi, AUD. Orn. Biog. I, 1831, 46 ; pl. 9.   (Young.)

SP. CH.—*Male.*—Bill black ; feet pale yellow. Head and neck all round and fore part of the breast black. A broad patch on the forehead extending round on the entire cheeks and ear coverts, with the under parts bright yellow. Upper parts and sides of the body olive green. Greater portion of inner web of three outer tail feathers white.

Female similar ; the crown like the back ; the forehead yellowish ; the sides of the head yellow, tinged with olive on the lores and ear coverts.

Length, 5 ; wing, 2.75 ; tail, 2.55.   (Skin.)

Hab.—Eastern United States to the Missouri ; south to Guatemala.

The bill, though sylvicoline, is broad at the base and depressed, with prominent bristles. The wings are long and pointed, though the first primary is nearly .15 shorter than the second or longest.   The tail is slightly graduated.

An immature male differs from that described above by having the black of the head restricted to a margin of the yellow on the top and sides, and a faint indication of the same on the throat.

As a general thing the yellow of the under coverts is not so intense as that of the belly, and the feathers of the lores are tipped with black.   The width of the yellow forehead varies, being sometimes nearly equal to the black, sometimes one-half only.

List of specimens.

Catal. No.	Sex.	Locality.	When collected.	Whence obtained.	Orig. No.	Collected by—	Length.	Stretch of wings.	Wing.	Remarks.
2246	♂	Carlisle, Pa...........	May 7, 1845	S. F. Baird.........	......	....	....	....	....	....
2228	♀	St. Louis, Mo..........	May 12, 1857	Lieut. Bryan.......	......	Wm. S. Wood.	....	....	....	....
7924	....	Society Hill, S. C......	....	M. A. Curtis.......	......	....	....	....	....a..	....
7493	....	Rockport, Ohio......	May 20, 1852	Dr. J. P. Kirtland ..	......	....	....	....	....	....
	♂	South Illinois...........	....	R. Kennicott.	......	....	....	....	....	....
6984	♂	St. Louis, Mo..........	May 12, 1857	Lieut. Bryan.......	......	W. S. Wood....	....	....	....	....
	♀	Fort Leavenworth	July 13, 1857	Wm. M. Magraw..	128	Dr. Cooper.....	5.25	8.00	2.62	Iris brown; bill brownish ; feet pale brown.
8025	....	Guatemala............	....	J. Gould.........	......	....	....	....	....	....

?MYIODIOCTES MINUTUS.

Small-headed Flycatcher.

Muscicapa minuta, WILSON, Am. Orn. VI, 1812, 62 ; pl. l, f. 5.—AUD. Orn. Biog. V, 1839, 291 ; pl. 434, f. 3.—IB.
      Syn. 1839, 44.—IB. Birds Amer. I, 1840, 238 ; pl. 67.
Sylvia minuta, BONAP. Obs. Wils. 1826, No. 128.
Wilsonia minuta, BONAP. List, 1838.
Sylvania pumilia, NUTTALL, Man. I, 2d ed. 1840, 334.   (Not *Sylvia pumilia*, Vieillot.)

SP. CH.—" Wings short, the second quills longest. Tail of moderate length, even. General color of upper parts light greenish
brown ; wings and tail dark olive brown, the outer feathers of the latter with a terminal white spot on the inner web ; a narrow
white ring surrounding the eye ; two bands of dull white on the wings ; sides of the head and neck greenish yellow ; the rest
of the lower parts pale yellow, gradually fading into white behind. Male, 5 inches long ; extent 8¼ inches."
Hab.—Eastern Atlantic States.

I have never seen a specimen of the small-headed flycatcher, and copy the preceding description from Audubon. It seems to be a perfectly distinct species from any other I have described,
and evidently belongs to the *Oscines* rather than to the *Tyrannulas* (*Clamatores*.) Audubon
expressly mentions that it has several rather pleasing notes. The white spots on the tail distinguish it readily from any of our true tyrant flycatchers. The introduction of the bird into
the genus *Myiodioctes* is purely conjectural, although its affinities seem nearest to the hooded
warbler.

MYIODIOCTES PUSILLUS, Bonap.

Green Black-cap Flycatcher.

Muscicapa pusilla, WI ON, Am. Orn. III, 1811, 103 ; pl. xxvi, f. 4.
Wilsonia pusilla, BONAP. List, 1838.
Sylvania pusilla, NUTTALL, Man. I, 2d ed. 1840, 335.
Myiodioctes pusillus, BONAP. Conspectus, 1850, 315.
Myioctonus pusillus, CABANIS, Mus. Hein. 1851, 18.
Sylvia wilsonii, BONAP. Obs. Wilson, 1826, No. 127.—NUTTALL, Man. I, 1832, 408.
Muscicapa wilsonii, AUD. Orn. Biog. II, 1834, 148 ; pl. 124.
Setophaga wilsonii, JARD. ed. Wilson, 1832.
Myiodioctes wilsonii, AUD. Syn. 1839, 50.—IB. Birds Am. II, 1841, 21 ; pl. 75.
" *Sylvia petasode*. ? LICHT." (Bonap. Consp.)

SP. CH.—Forehead, line over and around the eye, and under parts generally bright yellow. Upper part olive green ; a
square patch on the crown lustrous black. Sides of body and cheeks tinged with olive. No white on wings or tail. Female
similar ; the black of the crown obscured by olive green.
Length, 4.75 ; wing, 2.25 ; tail, 2.30.
Hab.—United States from Atlantic to Pacific ; south to Guatemala.

The wings are moderate ; the second, third, and fourth quills considerably longest and nearly
equal ; the first longer than the fourth. The tail is rather long and graduated ; the lateral
feathers .25 of an inch shorter than the middle.

Specimens differ in some respects. Thus, among those from the Pacific coast, some, as 7678,
have longer wings than those before me from the Atlantic States. No. 7683, from California,
has a broader frontlet of yellow, a richer yellow beneath, a lighter olive of the back, and a considerably smaller and slenderer bill. Other specimens, however, from the same localities agree
precisely with Pennsylvania ones.

List of specimens.

Catal. No.	Sex.	Locality.	When collected.	Whence obtained.	Orig. No.	Collected by—	Length.	Stretch of wings.	Wing.	Remarks.
990	♂	Carlisle, Pa......	May 18,1845	S. F. Baird........	......	....	4.75	7.00	2.25	....
2307	♀	......do..............	May 20,1845	......do........ .	......	... .	4.75	6.58	2.25	....
2270	♀	......do............	......do......	......do............	......	.. ..	4.50	6.33	2.08	....
7314	. . ....	Cleveland, Ohio.......	....	J. P. Kirtland......	......	....	....	....	....	....
		Racine, Wis.........	....	N. W. University...	......	R. Kennicott...	....	....	....	....
		Union county, Ill	May 12......	......do........	......	......do......	....	....	....	....
7537	....	St. Louis, Mo.......	....	Dr. J. G. Cooper...	......	....	....	....	....	....
8799	... ...	Fort Laramie, Neb	Aug. 27,1857	Wm. M. Magraw ..	172	Dr. Cooper.....	5.00	7.00	2.25	Iris brown; bill brown; feet flesh color.
8210	....	......do........	Sept. 8.......	......do.	192	....	5.00	7.00	2.25	Iris brown; feet yellowish brown.
5052	....	Pecos Crossing........	Sept. 18,1855	Capt. Pope........	136	....	5.00	6.50	2.00	....
7675	♂	Frontera	....	Charles Wright	......	....	4.16	6.37	2.00	....
7676	♂	......do..	....	......do........	......	....	5.12	8.16	2.75	....
7677	♀	......do........	May 5,1852	......do........	......	....	....	....	....	....
7685	♀	......do........	....	Maj. Emory.......	......	J. H. Clark	2.12	5.00	6.87	....
3982	♀	Monterey, Mex	....	Lieut. Couch	207	....	4.25	6.25	2.25	....
3981	♀	......do........	.. ..	......do........	214	....	4.50	7.00	2.50	......
3980	♀	......do........	May —,1853	......do........	......	....	4.75	6.75	2.25	......
7678	♂	Fort Steilacoom.......	April 28,1856	Dr. Suckley.......	......	....	5.19	7.00	2.70	......
7681	♂	......do........	May 3,1856	......do........	360	....	5.25	7.00	....	......
7683	... ...	California............	....	Dr. Heermann......	......	....	....	....	....	......
7684	....	San Francisco	....	R. D. Cutts........	......	....	....	....	....	......
		Fort Tejon, Cal.......	....	J. X. de Vesey....	......	....	....	....	....	......
8023	....	Guatemala............	....	J. Gould....	......	......	....	....	....	......

MYIODIOCTES CANADENSIS, Aud.

Canada Flycatcher.

Muscicapa canadensis, LINNAEUS, Syst. Nat. I, 1766, 327.—GMELIN, Syst. Nat. I, 1788, 937.—WILSON, Am. Orn. III, 1811, 100 ; pl. xxvi, f. 2.—AUD. Orn. Biog. II, 1834, 17 ; pl. 103.

Setophaga canadensis, " SWAINSON," Jard. ed. Wilson, 1832.—RICH. List, 1837.—GRAY, Genera.

Myiodioctes canadensis, AUD. Syn. 1839, 49.—IB. Birds Amer. II, 1841, 14 ; pl. 72.

Euthlypis canadensis, CABANIS, Mus. Hein. 1851, 18.

Sylvia pardalina, BONAP. Obs. Wilson, 1826, No. 126.—NUTTALL, Man. I, 1832, 372.

Sylvicola pardalina, BON. List, 1838.

Myiodioctes pardalina, BONAP. Conspectus, 1850, 315.

" *Setophaga nigricincta*, LAFRESNAYE, Rev. Zool." (Bp.)

SP. CH.—Upper part bluish ash ; a ring around the eye, with a line running to the nostrils, and the whole under part (except the tail coverts, which are white,) bright yellow. Centres of the feathers in the anterior half of the crown, the cheeks, continuous with a line on the side of the neck to the breast, and a series of spots across the fore part of the breast, black. Tail feathers unspotted. Female similar, with the black of the head and breast less distinct. In the young, obsolete.

Length, 5.34 ; wing, 2.67 ; tail, 2.50.

Hab.—Eastern United States to the Mississippi ; south to Guatemala.

The precise extent of the black on the breast varies a good deal in different specimens. The quills vary in length ; sometimes the second is longest, (945,) sometimes the third. In some specimens the outer primary is edged with white.

I cannot find any tangible difference between the young bird or female of this species and the *M. bonapartii* of Audubon. Thus, in No. 2438, (female in autumn,) there is no black on the head, and scarcely any light line over the eye ; the first primary is conspicuously edged with white.   The color of the back, as given in the figure of *bonapartii*, is much more like the usual average of specimens of *canadensis* than as figured for the latter species.

List of specimens.

Catal. No.	Sex.	Locality.	When collected.	Whence obtained.	Length.	Stretch of wings.	Wing.
945	♂	Carlisle, Pa.	May 6, 1843	S. F. Baird.	5.33	8.33	2.66
2155	♀	...do...	April 26, 1845	...do...	5.41	7.75	2.50
1021	♀	...do...	May 24, 1845	...do...	5.25	7.75	2.50
2669	♀	...do...	May 14, 1846	...do...	5.50	8.00	2.16
7558	♂	Washington, D. C.		Wm. Hutton.			
		Union county, Illinois.	May 11	R. Kennicott.			
8022		Guatemala.		J. Gould.			
8024		...do...		...do...			

MYIODIOCTES BONAPARTII, Aud.

Bonaparte's Flycatcher.

Muscicapa bonapartii, AUD. Orn. Biog. I, 1831, 27; pl. 5.
Setophaga bonapartii, RICH. List, 1837.
Wilsonia bonapartii, BONAP. List, 1838.
Myiodioctes bonapartii, AUD. Syn. 1839, 49.—IB. Birds Amer. II, 1841, 17; pl. 73.
Sylvania bonapartii, NUTTALL, Man. I, 2d ed. 1840, 332.

"Bristles longer than in the last, second quill longest; tail very long, nearly even; upper parts light greyish blue; quills dusky brown, their outer webs greyish blue, the two outer margined with white; middle tail feathers and edges of the rest like the back; lower parts and a band on the forehead ochre yellow, with a few faint dusky spots on the lower part of the fore neck.

This species differs from the last chiefly in being of a more elongated form, in having the bristles much longer, the upper parts of a much lighter tint; in wanting the black band down the sides of the neck, and the yellow band over the eye; the bill is straighter and more pointed, and the outer primaries are edged with white.   Male, 5.4 inches."

Hab.—Louisiana.

To complete the history of the species of *Myiodioctes*, I copy the description from Mr. Audubon of the *M. bonapartii;* as already stated, however, it is quite likely that it may prove to be only an immature *M. canadensis*.

CARDELLINA, Dubus.

Cardellina, DUBUS, Bp. Consp. Av. I, 1850, 312.

CH.—Bill short, compressed; higher than broad at the base.   Culmen gently convex; tip not decurved; notch not very prominent.   Tail nearly even, about equal to the wings, which is considerably rounded; the first quill about equal to the sixth, the third longest.   Colors partly red.

This genus, in the shortness and compression of its bill, resembles *Parus* to a considerable degree.   The only species I have occasion to mention is entirely red, with white ear patches.

CARDELLINA RUBRA, Bonap.

Vermilion Flycatcher.

Setophaga rubga, SWAINSON, Syn. Mex. Birds, in Philos. Mag. I, 1827, 368.
Cardellina rubra, BONAP. Conspectus, 1850, 312.—CASSIN, Ill. I, 1854, 266; pl. xliii.
Basileuterus ruber, CABANIS, Mus. Hein. 1851, 18.
Sylvia miniata, LAFRESNAYE, Mag. Zool. 1836, pl. liv. (Not of Swainson.)
Parus leucotis, GIRAUD, Texas Birds, 1841, plate.
" Sylvia argyrotis, LICHT." BONAP. Consp.

SP. CH.—Entirely of a dark crimson red ; darker above and a little brighter on the rump. Quills and tail feathers brown, edged with brownish red. Ear coverts silky grayish white. Length about 5.60 ; wing, 2.45 ; tail, 2.55.
Hab.—Northern Mexico.

The wing is considerably rounded ; the first quill shorter than the sixth ; the fourth quill longest ; the third, second, and fourth, successively shorter. The tail appears nearly even.

The propriety of introducing this species into the fauna of the United States is questionable. No specimens have as yet been found, even as far north as northern Tamaulipas, in Mexico. As one of the birds described in Mr. Giraud's work, however, it is entitled to a notice.

The measurements of the species will be found on the next page.

List of specimens.

Catal. No.	Locality.	Whence and how obtained.	Collected by—
561	Northern Mexico	S. F. Baird	J. G. Bell

BASILEUTERUS, Cabanis.

Basileuterus, CABANIS, Wiegmann's Archiv, 1847, i, 316.—IB. Schomburgh's Reise Brit. Guiana, 1847. Type, Sylvia vermivora, Vieillot.

CH.—Bill stout, triangular ; broader than high ; the vertical outlines considerably convex. Rictus strongly bristled. Wings very short and much rounded ; considerably less than the tail ; first quill shorter than the secondaries. Tail long, much graduated ; the feathers narrow ; the lateral ones about .40 of an inch shorter. Tarsi rather long ; toes short.

This genus bears some resemblance to Geothlypis; the tail is, however, longer, the feathers narrower and more graduated. The wings are much shorter and more rounded ; the bill stouter, deeper, and thicker towards the end ; the rictus with bristles instead of without them. The toes are considerably shorter. Although not represented in the United States, I introduce it here for the fuller illustration of the Setophageae, and because Mr. Giraud describes several species, in his work on Texas birds, which are probably to be referred to here.[1]

[1] The only species of the genus before me is—
BASILEUTERUS RUFIFRONS, Cabanis.

Setophaga rufifrons, SWAINSON, Anim. in Menag. 1838, 294.
Basileuterus rufifrons, "CABANIS," Bonap. Conspectus, 1850, 314.

SP. CH.—Top and sides of the head chestnut ; the rest of upper parts olive green ; the throat and fore part of breast yellow; the rest of under parts white, tinged on the side with brown. A well marked white superciliary stripe from the bill to the nape. Length about 5 inches ; wing, 2.15 ; tail, 2.50. For detailed measurements see next page.

Hab.—Mexico. A specimen (No. —) received from Mr. Gould. An allied species from Nicaragua is given by Bonaparte, (B. delattrii, Comptes Rendus ; Notes Orn. Delattre, 1854, 62,) differing in being entirely yellow beneath.

SETOPHAGA, Swainson.

Setophaga, SWAINSON, Zool. Jour. III, Dec. 1827, 360. Type *Muscicapa ruticilla*, Linn.
Sylvania, NUTTALL, Man. Orn. I, 1832. Type *Muscicapa ruticilla*.

CH.—Bill depressed; broader than high; rictus with long bristles. Wings rounded, equal to or shorter than the tail; first quill shorter than the fourth. Tail long; somewhat graduated, the outer feathers about .20 of an inch or more shorter; all the feathers unusually broad, and widened at the end. Feet short; tarsus shorter than the head. Hind toe equal to the lateral. Coloration embracing more or less of red in northern species.

This genus differs from M*yiodioctes* chiefly in the longer broader tail, and rather shorter tarsi and toes, the hinder especially. The bill is more muscicapine; the culmen nearly straight to the abrubtly decurved and much notched tip; the gonys straight. In *Myiodioctes* the vertical outlines are more convex; the gonys more ascending; the tip gently and but slightly decurved. The species of this genus are all characterized by the brilliant red, yellow, black,. &c., of their plumage, and, according to Kaup, (Pr. Zool. Soc. 1851, 49,) may be divided into geographical groups, characterized by the prevalence of particular colors. The South American species have more or less of yellow. The Mexican are usually black and red, without any pure yellow.

Synopsis of species.

Black: base of the quills and tail, and sides of the breast reddish orange. Abdomen white...*S. ruticilla*
Black: belly red, broad patch on the wings, and outer tail feathers white..........*S. picta*
Ash color: forehead, throat, and tail, black; breast and belly, red; a chestnut spot on the crown. Three outer tail feathers tipped with white........................*S. miniata*

Comparative measurements of species.

Catal. No.	Species.	Locality.	Sex and age.	Length.	Stretch of wings.	Wing.	Tail.	Tarsus.	Middle toe.	Its claw alone.	Bill above.	Along gape.	Specimen measured.
984	Setophaga ruticilla	Carlisle, Pa......	♂	4.78	....	2.59	2.46	0.64	0.52	0.14	0.36	0.46	Dry......
do.	........do..............	......do.....	....	5.25	7.66	2.58	......	......	......	......	......	......	Fresh....
2281	........do..............	......do............	♀	4.50	....	2.50	2.44	0.64	0.55	0.16	0.36	0 50	Dry......
do.	........do..............	......do.........	....	5.16	7.75	2.50	......	......	......	......	......	......	Fresh....
4014	Setophaga picta........	New Leon, Mex..	♂	5.00	....	2.70	2.50	0.62	0.58	0.16	0.39	0.46	Dry*.....
do.	.........do............	......do............	....	5.25	7.25	2.50	......	......	......	......	......	......	Fresh....
558	Setophaga miniata......	Texas	....	5.58	....	2.52	3.00	0.72	0.60	0.16	0.34	0.48	Dry .....
8021	........do..............	Guatemala......	....	4.96	....	2.26	2.50	0.70	0.56	0.16	0.38	0.48	Dry .....
561	Cardellina rubra........	Texas	....	4.86	....	2.40	2.54	0.73	0.53	0.14	0.33	0.44	Dry .....
	Basileuterus rufifrons...	Mexico..........	....	4.92	...	1.90	2.54	0.74	0.56	0.16	0.40	0.50	Dry......

* Very much stretched.

SETOPHAGA RUTICILLA, Swainson.

Red Start.

Muscicapa ruticilla, LINNAEUS, Syst. Nat. I, 1766, 326.—GMELIN. I, 1788, 935.—VIEILLOT, Ois. Am. Sept. I, 1807,
66 ; pl. xxxv, xxxvi.—WILSON, Am. Orn. I, 1808, 103 ; pl vi, f. 6.—BON. Obs. 1826, 118.—
AUD. Orn. Biog. I, 1831, 202 : V, 1839, 428 ; pl xl.
Setophaga ruticilla, SWAINSON, Zool. Jour. III, 1827, 358.—IB. F. Bor. Am II, 1831, 223.—BON. List, 1838.—IB.
Consp. 1850, 312.
Sylvania ruticilla, NUTTALL, Man. I, 1832, 291. (Type of genus.)
Motacilla flavicauda, GMELIN, Syst. Nat. I, 1788, 997. (Female.)

Sp. Ch.--*Male.*—Prevailing color, black. A central line on the breast, the abdomen and under tail coverts white; some feathers in the latter strongly tinged with dark brown. Bases of all the quills, except the inner and outer, and basal half of all the tail feathers, except the middle one, a patch on each side of the breast, and the axillary region orange red, of a vermillion shade on the breast. Female with the black replaced by olive green above, by brownish white beneath; the head tinged with ash; a grayish white lore and ring round the eye. The red of the male replaced by yellow. Length, 5.25; wing, 2 50; tail,2.45

Hab.—Eastern United States to the Missouri plain; West Indies in winter. Fort Laramie, Dr. Cooper.

The second, third, and fourth quills are longest, considerably exceeding the first, which is intermediate between the fourth and fifth. The tail feathers are broad, and widening towards the tip ; considerably graduated laterally.

List of specimens.

Catal. No.	Sex & age.	Locality.	When collected.	Whence obtained.	Collected by—	Length.	Stretch of wings.	Wing.	Remarks.
984	♂	Carlisle, Pa	May 18, 1843	S. F. Baird	....	5.16	7.66	2.58	....
1002	♀	......do.........	May 20, 1843	..... do............	....	5.16	7.50	2.33	....
2281	♀	... do.............	May 17, 1845	......do............	....	5.16	7.75	2.50	....
7575	♀	Washington, D. C....	May 1, 1845	Wm. Hutton...........		....	....	....	....
10114	♂♂	......do...........	....	J. C. McGuire...........		....	....	....	....
5826?	......	Cleveland, Ohio......	May —, 1852	Dr. Kirtland...........		....	....	....	....
		Illinois	....	R. Kennicott...........		....	....	....	....
6986	♀	St. Louis, Mo	May 12, 1857	Lieut. Bryan...	W. S. Wood.	....	.. ..	....	....
4306	♂ ♀	Calcasieu Pass, La...	1854.........	G. Wurdemann....		....	....	....	....
6510	♀ ♀	Key Biscayne, Fla....	April 10	......do...........		....	....	....	....
6511	♀	Indian Key, Fla......	May 12......	......do...........	....	5.25	6.00	2.00	....
6508	♀	......do........	May 12	......do...........	....	5.50	7.50	2.50	. ...
6509	♀	......do.......	May 13......	......do...........	....	5.00	7.00	2.10	....
8653	......	Cape Florida.......	....	......do...........	....	5.75	8.00	2.50	Black legs and bill...........
8651	......	......do........	Sept. 27, 1857	......do...........	....	....	....	....	Bill light brown, feet blackish.
8654	......	......do........	Sept. 27, 1857	......do...........	....	5.25	6.25	2.50	Bill light brown, feet blackish.
6507	♂	Tortugas, Fla........	April 27......	......do...........		....	....	....	....
4691	♂	Nebraska	....	Lieut. Warren........	Dr. Hayden...	4.87	6.50	2.50	....
4687	......	Upper Missouri......	May 13......	......do...........	......do......	5.37	7.87	2.50	....
4688	......	Mouth of Big Sioux ..	....	......do...........	......do......	5.00	7.25	2.62	....
8843	♂	Upper Missouri	....	......do...........	......do......	5.00	7.25	2.50	....
4690	......	......do........	May 12......	......do...	......do......	4.75	7.50	2.50	....
5271	......	Medicine creek	....	......do...........	......do......	5.25	7.00	2.12	Eyes black ....
4689	......	Mouth of Platte river.	April 26	......do...........	......do......	....	....	....	....
5877	......	Fort Riley, K. T......	....	Hammond & DeVesey..	....	....	....	....	....
1863	♂	Trinidad	....	S. F. Baird	....	....	....	....	....

SETOPHAGA PICTA, Swainson.

Setophaga picta, Swainson, Zool. Ill. 2d Series, I, 1829; pl. iii.—Is. Anim. in Menag. 1838, 293.—Bonap. Consp. 1850, 312.

Muscicapa leucomus, Giraud, Texas Birds, 1841 ; pl vi. f. 1.

Sp. Ch.—*Male.*—Above, with the head and neck all round, and sides of the breast black; rest of under parts dark crimson red. The under tail and wing coverts, the outer two, and most of the third tail feathers, and a broad patch on the wing, white. Length, 5.25; wing, 2.50; tail, 2.60.

Hab.—Northern Mexico.

The specimen before me of this beautiful species is not sufficiently perfect to admit of a satisfactory description. The form appears to be much like that of *S. miniata.*

List of specimens.

Catal. No.	Sex.	Locality.	When collected.	Whence obtained.	Original No.	Length.	Stretch of wings.	Wing.	Remarks.
4014	♂	Boquillo, N. Leon, Mex..	April —, 1853	Lt. Couch..........	144	5.25	7.25	2.50	Eyes brown; bill black; feet reddish slate.

SETOPHAGA MINIATA, Swainson.

Setophaga miniata, SWAINSON, Phil. Mag. I, 1827, 368.—IB. Anim. in Menag. (2¼ centenaries,) 1838, 293. (Not of Lafresnaye.)

Muscicapa vulnerata, WAGLER, Isis, 1831, 529.

Setophaga vulnerata, GRAY, Genera.—BONAP. Consp. 1850, 313.—CABANIS, Mus. Hein. 1851, 18.

Setophaga castanea, LESSON, Rev. Zool. 1839, 42.

Muscicapa derhami, GIRAUD, Texas Birds, 1841; pl. iii, f. 2.

SP. CH —Upper parts, with head and neck all round, dark plumbeous ; beneath, carmine red. A dark brownish chestnut patch on the forehead. Throat tinged with black Under wing coverts white. Tail black ; the outer two feathers with the outer web, the four outer, with the tips, white. Length about 5.25 ; wing, 2.55 ; tail, 3.05.

Hab.—Northern Mexico to Guatemala.

This species is larger though somewhat similar in shape to *S. ruticilla*, and has a proportionally broader tail. The wing is much rounded ; the first quill equal about to the seventh.

A specimen from Guatemala differs in having the middle tail feathers narrower, (the others lost.) The black of the throat is purer and more continuous. The crown is occupied by a subquadrate patch of orange chestnut ; the front and sides of the crown quite pure black. The size is considerably less.

List of specimens.

Catal. No.	Sex.	Locality.	Whence obtained.	Collected by—
558	♂	Northern Mexico --------------	S. F. Baird--------------------	J. G. Bell----------------------
8021	♂	Guatemala ---- ---------------	J. Gould ----- ---------------	

Sub-Family TANAGRINAE.

The precise position of the tanagers is a matter of much uncertainty, the relationship to the *Fringillidae* being very close. Both have the nine primaries and the scutellate tarsi, and the bill in some genera resembles that of unquestionable finches; it is, however, usually longer, and though stout at the base is not strictly conical, and lacks the great strength necessary for a hard vegetable instead of soft animal diet, or one of berries and fruits.

Of the large number of known tanagers but two genera are found in the United States— *Pyranga* and *Euphonia*. These may be readily distinguished by the large bill, higher than broad at the base, with a distinct tooth in the middle of the commissure in *Pyranga*, and the broad, short, depressed bill, with a double notch near the tip, of *Euphonia*.

The characters of the genera are chiefly taken from Mr. Sclater's masterly monograph, as more accurately expressing their distinctive features than the examination of the North American species alone can furnish.

PYRANGA, Vieill.

Pyranga, VIEILLOT, Ois. Am. Sept. I, 1807, iv.—IB. Analyse, 1816, 32.—SCLATER, Pr. Zool. Soc. 1856, 123.
Phoenisoma, SWAINSON, Class. Birds, II, 1837, 284.

CH.—Bill somewhat straight; sub-conical, cylindrical, notched at tip; culmen moderately curved; commissure with a median acute lobe. Wings elongated; the four first primaries about equal. Tail moderate, slightly forked. Colors of the male chiefly scarlet, of the female yellowish.

The rictus is well provided with bristles, which bend downwards, but if brought forward would reach the nostrils. These are rounded, and are closely crowded by the frontal feathers. The tarsus is shorter than the middle toe, scutellate anteriorly, and smooth on the sides behind. The lateral toes are about equal; the basal joint of the middle toe united for half its length to the inner toe, and by almost the whole length to the outer.

The species may be distinguished by the following diagnoses, borrowed from Mr. Sclater:

Male. Bright scarlet red. Wings and tail black..*rubra.*

Male. Light red; back a little more dusky. Bill light horn color, the edges and tips paler ....*aestiva.*

Male. Dark scarlet red, tinged with ashy on the back and sides. Bill plumbeous black. Feet brownish black...*hepatica.*

Male. Yellow; the interscapular region, wings, and tail, black. Wings with two whitish bands. Head and throat tinged with scarlet..........................*ludoviciana.*

Comparative measurements of species.

Catal. No.	Species.	Locality.	Sex.	Length.	Stretch of wings.	Wing.	Tail.	Tarsus.	Middle toe.	Its claw alone.	Bill above.	Along gape.	Specimens measured.	Remarks.
1566	Pyranga rubra.	Carlisle, Pa..	♂	6.32	....	3.68	3.00	0 74	0.73	0.22	0.63	0.76	Dry......	....
do.	......do...............	... do........	......	7.41	11.75	3.91	......	......	......	......	......	......	Fresh ...	....
1495	......do...............	....do.... ...	♀	6.08	....	3.70	2.90	0.70	0.72	0.24	0.60	0.73	Dry.....	....
do.	......do...............	....do........	......	7.60	11.25	3.75	......	......	......	......	......	......	Fresh ...	....
8256	Pyranga aestiva........	Texas	♀	6.30	....	3.68	3.20	0.76	0.76	0.22	0 70	0.84	Dry.....	....
do.	......do...............	....do........	......	7.00	11.25	3.75	......	......	......	......	......	......	Fresh ...	....
8267	...... do...............	....do........	♂	7.20	....	3.81	3.38	0.78	0.76	0.22	0.78	0.83	Dry	....
8272	...... do...............	Zuni mts ...	♂	7.60	....	3.96	3.62	0.80	0.72	0.24	0.72	0.81	Dry	Mounted...
8259	Pyranga ludoviciana....	Posa creek...	♂	6.62	....	3.70	3.06	0.80	0.75	0.20	0.63	0.77	....	....
8260	......do...............	Tejon valley..	......	6.54	....	3.50	3.00	0.76	0.76	0.22	0.60	0.68	Dry	....
8272	Pyranga hepatica......	Zuni mts	♂	7.50	....	3.96	3.64	0.82	0.72	0.24	0.72	0.78	Dry	....
560	Euphonia elegantissima.	Texas	......	4.88	....	2.70	1.86	0.54	0.60	0.16	0.27	0.44	Dry	....

PYRANGA RUBRA, Vieillot.

Scarlet Tanager.

Tanagra rubra, LINN. I, 1766, 314.—GMELIN, I, 1788, 889.—WILSON, Am. Orn. II, 1810, 42 ; pl. xi, f. 3, 4.—AUD. Orn. Biog. IV, 1838, 388 ; pl. 354.
Pyranga rubra, VIEILLOT, Ois. Am. Sept. I, 1807, iv ; pl. i, f. 12. (Head.)—SWAINSON, F. Bor. Am. II, 1831, 273.—BON. List. 1838.—IB. Conspectus, 1850.—AUD. Syn. 1839, 136.—IB. Birds Amer. II, 1841, 226 ; pl. 209. SCLATER, Pr. Zool. Soc. 1855, 156.—IB. 1856, 123.
Phoenisoma rubra, Sw. Birds, II, 837, 284.
Phoenicosoma rubra, CAB. Mus. Hein. 1851, 24.
Pyranga erythromelas, VIEILLOT, "Encyc. Meth. 800."—IB. Nouv. Dict. XXVIII, 1817, 293.

Sp. Ch.—Bill shorter than the head. Second quill longest; first and third a little shorter. Tail moderately forked. General color of male bright carmine. Wings and tail velvet black; the quils internally edged with white towards the base. Female olive green above, yellowish beneath. Wing and tail feathers brown, edged with olivaceous. Length, 7.40; wing, 4.00; tail, 3.00.

Hab —Eastern United States to the Missouri river.

The young males are colored like the females, but generally exhibit more or less of red feathers among the greenish ones. Sometimes the full plumage is varied by a few yellow feathers, or by olivaceous edges to the wings. Not unfrequently there is a partly concealed bar of red or yellow (1566) on the wing, across the median coverts. Young males are sometimes seen with the body like the female, the wings and tail like the male.

List of specimens.

Catal. No.	Sex.	Locality.	When collected.	Whence obtained.	Orig'l No.	Collected by—	Length.	Stretch of wings	Wing.	Remarks.
1085	♂	Carlisle, Pa..........	June 30,1843	S. F. Baird........	.. ..	....	7.25	12.00	4.50	....
1493	♂	.....do...,.......	May 10,1844	......do........	.....	....	7.08	11.50	3.83	....
1566	♂	.....do............	May 22,1844	......do.	.....	....	7.41	11.75	3.91	....
1425	♀	.....do....	May 2,1844	......do.......	......	....	7.00	11.25	3.75	....
7463	♀	Ohio.........	....	Dr. Kirtland.....	......	....	.....	....	....	....
	......	Union county, Ill.....	April 30	R. Kennicott.....	.....	....	.... ..	....	....	....
8306	♂	Independence, Mo. ..	May 27,1857	Wm. M. Magraw.	21	Dr. Cooper ..	7.25	11.25	4.00	Iris brown, bill olive, feet gray.
8331	♂	.....do...............	June 3,1857	..... do......	54	..... do......	7.50	12.00	4.00	.... do ....:..do......
8305	♂	.....do...........	May 27,1857	......do.........	20	.... do......	7.25	11.25	4 00	......do.............do......
8283	♂	.... do..........	May 29,1857	..... do.........	44	.... do......	6.75	11.25	4.00	..... do.......... ..do......
8380	♀	.....do.............	June 20,1857	......do.........	84	......do......	7.25	11.50	3.75	......do.............do......
8298	♀	.. ...do...........	May 26,1857	......do.........	11	......do......	7.50	12.00	4.00	......do.............do......
8377	♂	.....do.............	June 20,1857	......do.........	79	......do......	7.12	11.75	4.00	Iris brown, bill black, feet lead.
8304	♂	.....do.............	May 27,1857	......do.........	19	......do......	7.25	12.25	4.25	Iris brown, bill black and yellow, feet gray.... ....
8347	♂	......do........... .	June 18,1857	......do.........	74	..... do......	7.00	11.25	4.00	......do...../......... do......
7026	♂	St. Louis, Mo........	May 8,1857	Lieut. Bryan....		W. S. Wood..	....	....	....	....

PYRANGA AESTIVA, Vieillot.

Summer Red Bird.

Muscicapa rubra, Linn. Syst. Nat. I, 1766, 326.

Tanagra aestiva, Gmelin, I, 1788, 889.—Wilson, 1, 1810, 95; pl. vi, f. 3.—Aud. Orn. Biog. I, 1831, 232; V, 1839, 518; pl. 44.

Pyranga aestiva, Vieill. Nouv. Dict. XXVIII, 1819, 291.—Bon. List. 1838.—Ib. Conspectus, 1850.—Aud. Syn. 1839, 136.—Ib. Birds Amer. III, 1841, 222; pl. 208.—Sclater, Pr. Zool. Soc. 1855, 156.—Ib. 1856, 123.

Phoenisoma aestiva, Sw. Birds, II, 1837, 284.

Phoenicosoma aestiva, Cabanis, Mus. Hein. 1851, 25.

? Loxia virginica, Gmelin, I, 1788, 849. (Male changing.)

? Tanagra mississippiensis, Gmelin, I, 1788, 889.

Tanagra variegata, Lath. Ind. Orn. I, 1790, 422. (Male changing.)

Tangare du Mississippi, Buffon, Ois. V, 63; pl. enl 741.

Sp. Ch.—Bill nearly as long as the head, without any median tooth. Tail nearly even, or slightly rounded. Male, vermillion red; a little darker above, and brightest on the head. Quills brown, the outer webs like the back. Shafts only of the tail feathers brown. Bill light horn color, more yellowish at the edges. Female, olive above, yellow beneath, with a tinge of reddish. Length, 7.20; wing, 3.75; tail, 3.00.

Hab.—South Atlantic and Gulf States, through Texas, and south to Guatemala.

The shade of red varies somewhat in the specimen, the shade being sometimes more rose. It is always quite different from that of *P. rubra*. The female lacks the pure olive and yellow tints of *rubra*, having them duller above, and slightly tinged with reddish beneath.   The bill is much larger than in *rubra*, nearly equalling the head ; quite so in some specimens, varying considerably in size, as it does.   Texas specimens generally appear to have larger bills than those farther east.

The young male is like the female.   Immature males, however, exhibit every gradation between the perfect colors of both sexes.

List of specimens.

Catal. No.	Sex.	Locality.	When collected.	Whence obtained.	Orig'l No.	Collected by—	Length.	Stretch of wings.	Wing.	Remarks.
1050	♂	Washington, D. C	May 31,1843	S. F. Baird..........		W. M. Baird...	....	....	....	....
4285	♂	Calcasieu, La....	1854.........	G. Wurdemann......		....	....	....	....	....
		South Illinois..........	....	N. W. University...		R. Kennicott...	....	....	....	....
8298	♂	Independence, Mo.	May 26,1857	Wm. M. Magraw ..	8	Dr. Cooper....	7.25	10.62	4.00	Iris brown, bill olive, feet gray............
8294	♂	.....do................	.....do......	.....do...........	7	.....do........	7.62	12.00	4.00	...........do.........
8296	♀	.....do........	.....do......	.....do...........	9	.....do.......	7.25	11.00	3.62	... .do.........
8297	♀	.....do........	.....do......	.....do...........	10	.....do	7.00	11.00	3.50	.....do.........
8267	♂	Texas...............	....	Lieut. J. G. Parke..	....	Dr. Heermann.	....	....	....	....
8268	♂	.....do........		.....do...........			....	....	... .	....
8265	......	San Antonio, Texas....	....	Col. Graham.......	....	J. H. Clark ...	....	....	....	....
8266	♀	.....do........		.....do...........	. ...	....	7.00	11.25	3.75	..... • ....
8269	♂	Texas.....	....	Capt. J. Pope	....	....	....	....	....	....
4972	♂	Ft. Chadbourne, Texas.	....	Dr. Swift..	....	....	....	....	....	....
4071	♀	Brownsville, Texas.....	Feb. 11......	Lieut. Couch.......	....	....	6.50	11.00	3.75	....
4073	♂	New Leon, Mexico....		.....do...........	....	....	7.50	11.75	4.00	Eyes light brown, bill olive ....
4072	♀	.....do	April —,1853	.....do...........		....	7.25	11.25	3.75	....
4070	♀	Rio Nasas, Mexico	June —,1853	.....do............		....	7.00	12.00	4.00	....
7956	♂	Guatemala............	....	John Gould........		....	....	....	....	....
7957	♀	.....do...........	....	.....do...........		....	....	....	....	....

PYRANGA HEPATICA, Swainson.

Pyranga hepatica, SWAINSON, Phil. Mag. I, 1827, 124.—SCLATER, Pr. Zool. Soc. 1856, 124.
Phœnicosoma hepatica, CAB. Mus. Hein. 1851, 25.
Pyranga azarae, WOODHOUSE, Sitgreave's Expl. Zuñi, 1853, 82.   (Not of other authors.)

SP. CH.—Bill shorter than the head. Tail nearly even. Above ashy red ; the crown and under parts scarlet ; sides ashy. Bill plumbeous black ; feet brownish black. Female, olive above ; yellow beneath, tinged with olive on the sides ; the forehead tinged with yellow. Wings brown, the olive edges of the quills becoming grayish towards the tips. Young male like the female. Length, 8 inches ; wing, 4.00 . tail, 3.50.

Hab.—Rocky mountains of New Mexico southward.

I have at hand no full plumaged male of this bird, and have been obliged to borrow the description from Sclater, as cited above.   The species is considerably larger than *P. aestiva*, with which it agrees somewhat in characters.   The bill, however, is proportionally smaller, with more of a tooth on the commissure.   The color, too, is bluish black, instead of light horn color, with yellowish margins.   The sides are tinged with ashy instead of being like the belly. The red is of a different shade, duller above, and the forehead conspicuously brighter than the back, instead of a mere shade lighter.

According to Sclater the *P. saira*, (*P. azarae*, Auct.,) to which this bird was referred by Dr. Woodhouse, differs in being smaller, the bill bluer, the feet black, not brown, the red colors different.   The female is also said to have a yellowish superciliary stripe.

List of specimens.

Catal. No.	Sex.	Locality.	When collected.	Whence obtained.	Collected by—
8272	♂	Zuñi mountain, N. M_____	Aug. 31, 1851_____	Capt. Sitgreaves_____	Dr. Woodhouse _ _____
		Fort Thorn _____	_____	Dr. Henry_____	_____

PYRANGA LUDOVICIANA, Bonap.

Louisiana Tanager.

Tanagra ludoviciana, WILSON, Am. Orn. III, 1811, 27 ; pl. xx, f. 1.—BON. Obs. 1826, 95.—AUD. Orn Biog. IV, 1838, 385 : V, 1839, 90 ; pl. 354, 400.

Tanagra (Pyranga) ludoviciana BONAP. Syn. 1828, 105.—NUTTALL, Man. 1, 1832, 471.

Pyranga ludoviciana, RICH. List. 1837.—BONAP. List, 1838.—AUD. Syn. 1839, 137.—IB. Birds Amer. III, 1841, 211 ; pl. 210.—SCLATER, Pr. Soc. 1856, 125.

Pyranga erythropsis, VIEILLOT, Nouv. Dict. XXVIII, 1819, 291.

" *Tanagra columbiana*, JARD. ed. Wilson, I, 317." According to Sclater, but I cannot find such name.

SP. CH.—Bill shorter than the head. Tail slightly forked; first three quills nearly equal. Male, yellow; the middle of the back, the wings, and the tail, black. Head and neck all round strongly tinged with red; least so on the sides. A band of yellow across the middle coverts, and of yellowish white across the greater ones; the tertials more or less edged with whitish. Female, olive green above, yellowish beneath; the feathers of the interscapular region dusky, margined with olive. The wings and tail rather dark brown, the former with the same marks as the male. Length, 7.25; wing, 3.60; tail, 2.85.

Hab —From the Black Hills to the Pacific; south to Mexico.

It is not often that the male of this species is found in the highest state of plumage. Generally the feathers of the back are margined with olive, this color also tinging the yellow of the back, and the edges of the quills. The red of the head varies in intensity. The bill is rather smaller and slenderer than in *P. rubra*, although it varies considerably with the specimen.

The female can always be distinguished from that of *rubra* by the slenderer bill. The bill is much smaller than in *P. aestiva*. From both it differs in the whitish or yellow bands on the wings, and the back being duskier than the remaining upper parts.

A young bird exhibits traces of brown in the yellow, and some faint dusky streaks. Young males have the general plumage of the female.

The black back distinguishes this species from the somewhat similar *P. erythrocephala* and *rubriceps*.

List of specimens.

Catal. No.	Sex and age.	Locality.	When collected.	Whence obtained.	Orig. No.	Collected by—	Length.	Stretch of wings.	Wing.	Remarks.
5658	♂	Black Hills, K T ...	Aug 3, 1856	Lieut. Bryan	195	W. S. Wood.	....	....	......	....
5661	♀	.... do............	Aug 4, 1856	.....do	204	.....do.	....	....	......	....
8822	♀	Black Hills..........	Sept. 13, 1857	Lieut. Warren.....	......	Dr. Hayden ...	7.25	11.75	3.50	Iris brown...........
8823	♀	Laramie peak........	Aug. 24, 1857	......do..........	......	.... do..	7.00	11.00	3.50	Iris dark brown......
8207	♂	Fort Laramie, Neb...	Sept. 8, 1857	Dr. Cooper.........	188	....	7.25	11.50	4.00	Iris brown ; bill black and yellow; feet bl'k.
8229	......	......, do........ ...	Sept. 17, 1857	.....do............	211	....	7 75	11.50	3 50	......do......do. ....
5660	♀	Medicine Bow river..	Aug. 25, 1856	Lieut. Bryan.......	300	W. S. Wood ...	....	....	......	....
8264	......	Mimbres to Rio Grande	....	Dr. T. C. Henry....	......	....	....	....	......	....
5927	♂	Steilacoom, W. T. ..	May —, 1855	Dr. Cooper.........	......	....	7.00	11.25	......	....
5928	♂	.... do......	.......do......	....do.......	......	....	......	....	......	....
5929	♂	.... do......	........do.......	....do.......	......	....	......	....	......	....v.. ..
8262	♂	.... do...........	1856..........	Dr. Suckley	98	....	......	....	......	....
8261	♀	.....do............	Aug. —, 1854	.....do...........	......	....	......	....	......	....
1881	♂	Columbia river......	....	S. F Baird	......	J. K. Townsend	......	....	......	....
5544	♂	Petaluma, Cal........	May 13, 1856	E. Samuels	......	....	......	....	......	....
8260	○	Tejon valley, Cal....	....	Lieut. Williamson.	......	Dr. Heermann..	......	....	......	....
8259	♂	Posa creek, Cal......	....	.....do.......	......	......do...... ..	......	....	......	....
4907	♂	San Diego, Cal......	....	Dr. Hammond	......	....	......	....	......	....

EUPHONIA, Desm.

Euphonia, DESM Hist. Nat. des Tangaras, 1805.—SCLATER, Pr. Zool. Soc. 1856, 271.

CH.—Bill short, widened or depressed; the culmen curved; gonys ascending; commissure notched at tip, and somewhat serrate. Wings long; tail short, quadrate. Colors black, blue, and yellowish

The bill of *Euphonia* is much shorter than the head, and very broad at the base. The two or three toothed lobes near the tip of cutting edge of the upper mandible are very distinct. The rictal bristles are very short. The tarsi are much shorter than the middle toe. The tail is very short, the feathers narrow.

EUPHONIA ELEGANTISSIMA, Gray.

Pipra elegantissima, BONAP. Pr. Zool. Soc. 1837, 112.

Euphonia elegantissima, GRAY, Genera, App. 17.—BONAP. Consp. 1850, 232.—DUBUS, Esq. Orn.—SCLATER, Cont. Orn. 1851, 83.—IB. Pr. Zool. Soc. 1856, 273.

Euphonia coelestis, LESSON, Rev. Zool. 1839, 39

Pipra galericulata, GIRAUD, 16 Sp. Birds Texas, 1841.

SP. CH.—Top of head and a half collar on the neck behind opaque blue. Sides of head and neck, chin, throat, and upper parts generally, steel bluish black. Beneath yellow brownish fulvous, tinged with dark brownish chestnut, especially on the forepart of the breast and towards the tail. Forehead dark chestnut, margined behind by black. Length, 4 70; wing, 2.75 tail, 1.80.

Hab.—Northern Mexico to Guatemala. California ?

This is one of the species (*Pipra galericulata*) described by Mr. Giraud in his "Sixteen New Species of Texas Birds," and the specimen 560 was obtained in the same locality with Mr. Giraud's. It is, however, very probable that the sixteen were actually collected some distance to the south of the Texas border, probably in the southern portion of the State of Tamaulipas. I am informed by Dr. Cooper that the same bird has been captured near San Francisco, and that the specimen is now in the collection of the Academy of Natural Sciences of that city.

The specimens before me differ a little from Mr. Sclater's description of *Euphonia elegantissima*. Thus, the throat is of the same dull steel blue color with the back; the under parts have a strong tinge of chestnut.

According to Mr. Sclater, the female is olive green, paler beneath; the crown blue; the forehead chestnut, margined behind with black, or much like the male.

List of specimens.

Catal. No.	Locality.	Whence obtained.	Collected by—
560	Texas? (Northern Mexico)	S. F. Baird	J. G. Bell
7958	Guatemala	J. Gould	

CONCLUDING REMARKS.

Having thus passed in review the well established species of North American *Sylvicolidae*, it may be well to mention those which claim such a place with greater or less propriety. Chief among these are the species described by Mr. Giraud as having been received from Texas, but which were probably taken in a more southern latitude, possibly about that of Tampico. Most of these doubtless at times wander as far as the Rio Grande, and several are described in the present report as having been taken on or near that river.

1. DENDROICA OLIVACEA, Baird.

> *Sylvia olivacea*, GIRAUD, Texas Birds, 1841; pl. vii.—SCLATER, Pr. Zool. Soc. 1855, 66.
> *Sylvicola olivacea*, CASSIN, Ill. I, 1855, 283; pl. xlviii.
> *Sylvia taeniata*, DUBUS, Bull. Acad. Brux. XIV, 1847, 104.—IB. Rev. Zool. 1848, 245.
> *Sylvicola taeniata*, BONAP. Consp. 1850, 309.

2. AEGITHINA LEUCOPTERA, Vieillot.

> *Sylvia leucoptera*, VIEILLOT, Ois. Am. Sept. II, 1807, 28; pl. lxxxiv, (N. America.)
> *Aegithina leucoptera*, " VIEILLOT," SWAINSON, Birds, II, 1837, 246.—BON. Consp. 1850, 311.
> *Mniotilta leucoptera*, GRAY, Genera.

3. PACHYSYLVIA DECURTATA, Bonap.

> *Sylvia decurtata*, BON. Pr. Zool. Soc. 1837, 118, (Mexico.)
> *Pachysylvia decurtata*, BON. Conspectus, 1850, 309.
> *Helinai brevipennis*, GIRAUD, Ann. N. Y. Lyc. V, 1852, 40; pl. iii, f. 1. Texas? and Mexico.

4. BASILEUTERUS BELLI, Sclater.

> *Muscicapa belli*, GIRAUD, Texas Birds, 1841, pl. iv, f. 1.
> *Basileuterus belli*, SCLATER, Pr. Zool. Soc. 1855, 65.
> *Basileuterus chrysophrys*, BONAP. Consp. 1850, 314.

39 b

5. Basileuterus brasieri, Sclater.

    Muscicapa brasieri, Giraud, Texas Birds, 1841 ; pl. vi, f. 2.
    Basileuterus brasieri, Sclater, Pr. Zool. Soc. 1855, 66.
    "*Basileuterus culicivorus*, Bonap. Consp. 1850, 66," (Sclater.)

6. Cardellina rubrifrons, Sclater.

    Muscicapa rubrifrons, Giraud, Tex. Birds, 1841, pl. vii, f. 1.
    Cardellina rubrifrons, Sclater, Pr. Zool. Soc. 1855, 66.
    Cardellina amicta, Dubus, Esq. Orn. 1850 ; pl. xxv.—Bonap. Consp. 1850, 312,
        (Sclater.)

The following supposed *Sylvicolinae*, described by the older authors as North American, have not been fully identified, although most of them doubtless belong to species already referred to :

1. *Motacilla auricollis*, Gmelin, Syst. I, 984.
    Sylvia auricollis, Latham, Ind. Orn. II, 1790, 536.—Stephens in Shaw's Gen. Zool. X,
        ii, 1817, 735.—Nutt. I, 1832, 380.
    Sylvicola auricollis, Nuttall, Man. I, 2d ed., 1840, 431.

2. *Sylvia carolinensis*, Latham, Ind. Orn. II, 1790, 551.—Stephens in Shaw's Zool. X, ii,
        1817, 752.
    Mniotilta carolinensis, Gray, Genera.
    "*Motacilla rubiginosa*, Pallas."

3. *Motacilla fulva*, Gmelin, I, 1788, 973.
    Sylvia fulva, Latham, Ind. II, 1790, 542.—Stephens in Shaw's Zool. X, ii, 1817, 726.
        (Louisiana.)

4. *Sylvia griseicollis*, Vieillot, Ois. Am. II, 29.—Stephens in Shaw's Zool. X, ii, 1817, 685.

5. *Motacilla incana*, Gmelin, I, 1788, 976.
    Sylvia incana, Latham, Ind. Orn. II, 1790, 527.—Stephens in Shaw's Zool. X, ii, 1817,
        628. (New York.) (*Dendroica Blackburnia ?*)

6. *Motacilla ludoviciana*, Gm. I, 1788, 983.
    Sylvia ludoviciana, Lath. Ind. Orn. II, 1790, 535.—Stephens in Shaw's Zool. X, ii, 1817,
        713. (North America.)

7. *Sylvia ochroleuca*, Vieillot, Nouv. Dict. XI, 1817, 187. United States. Dull olive above,
    golden yellow on throat and side of head ; breast beneath yellowish
    white.

8. *Sylvia pumila*, Vieillot, Ois. Am. II, 1807 ; pl. c.
    Sylvicola pumila, Bonap. Consp. 1850, 308.

9. *Sylvia russeicauda*, Vieillot, Ois. Am. Sept. II, 17 ; pl. 71.—Stephens in Shaw's Gen.
    Zool. X, ii, 1817, 675. (North America.)

10. *Sylvia semitorquata*, Latham, Ind. Orn. II, 1790, 542.—Stephens, Shaw's Zool. X, ii,
      1817, 594. (Louisiana.)

Family HIRUNDINIDAE.

Sub-Family HIRUNDININAE.

Bill triangular, very short and broad, much depressed ; the ridge much less than half the head ; the gonys two-thirds this length; the gape extending to below the eye. Primaries nine ; the first longest, and, with the second, considerably longer than the others ; the secondaries and tertials not reaching the middle of the primaries ; the secondaries deeply emarginate Wings very long, reaching beyond the commencement of the fork of the tail, which is generally more or less deep. Tarsi scutellate, very short, less than the lateral toes, the inner of which is more deeply cleft than the outer.

The feet of the true swallows follow the general insessorial type in having three anterior toes and one posterior, none capable of being moved much from their normal position. This, with the much larger and differently shaped bill, as well as the nine primaries, instead of ten, readily distinguish them from the *Cypselidae.*

Comparative measurements of species.

Catal. No.	Species.	Locality.	Sex.	Length.	Stretch of wings.	Wing.	Tail.	Tarsus.	Middle	Its claw alone.	Bill above.	Along gape.	Specimen measured.
6019	Hirundo horreorum	Sacramento valley .	♂	6.90	....	5.03	4.52	0.44	0 68	0.20	0.36	0.62	Dry.......
2284	Hirundo lunifrons......	Carlisle, Pa........	♀	4.86	....	4.38	2.20	0.50	0.64	0.21	0.26	0.55	Dry.......
2284	......do..............	.....do............	......	5 66	12.25	4.41	....	....	....	....	....	....	Fresh.....
2197	Hirundo bicolor........	....do............	♂	5.48	....	4.92	2 66	0.49	0.63	0.19	0.32	0.54	Dry.......
2197	......do.........	.....do............	......	6.25	12.25	5.00	....	....	....	....	....	....	Fresh...
5494	......do..............	Petaluma, Cal.....	♂	5.00	....	4.75	2.55	.46	....	....	.25	.44	Dry.......
1895	Hirundo thalassina.....	Columbia river.....	♂	4.76	....	4.48	2.08	0.46	0.60	0.18	0.24	0.50	Dry.......
2209	Cotyle serripennis......	Carlisle, Pa........	♂	4.52	....	4.28	2.23	0.40	0.58	0 28	0.50	Dry......
5597	Cotyle riparia..........	E. of Riley's.......	♀	5.04	....	3.96	2.34	0.44	0.62	0.22	0.28	0.46	Dry.......
1692	......do..............	Carlisle, Pa........	......	4.46	....	3.98	2.00	0.41	0.56	0.19	0 27	0.44	Dry......
1692	......do..............	.....do............	......	4.75	10.83	4.00	....	....	....	....	...	...	Fresh.....
1561	Progne purpurea.......	.....do............	♂	7.30	....	5.84	3.40	0.60	0.84	0.25	0.50	0.92	Dry.......
5493	......do..............	Petaluma, Cal	♂	7.44	....	6.04	3.66	0.58	0.92	0.26	0.52	0.90	Dry.......
5493	......do.........	.....do............	......	8.25	15.66	5.54	....	.. ....	....	....	....	....	Fresh....
9112	Progne chalybea?......	Chili	♂	8.20	....	5.48	3.75	0.58	0.92	0.25	0.46	0.84	Dry.......

HIRUNDO, Linnaeus.

Hirundo, Linn. Syst. Nat. 1735.—Gray, Genera, I, 1845.

Ch.—Nostrils basal, small, oblong, and covered partly by a membrane. Tail more or less forked ; the outer lateral feather sometimes greatly lengthened. Tarsi shorter than the middle toe, and scutellated. Tarsi naked. Toes long, slender, the lateral ones unequal. Claws moderate, curved, acute.

Of this genus there are two well marked sections among the United States species—one with the tail excessively forked, owing to the great elongation of the lateral tail feathers; the other with the tail nearly square, or but slightly forked. The species will range as follows :

Hirundo.—Tail excessively forked.

Steel blue above; forehead and throat chestnut brown ; belly reddish white...*H. horreorum.*

Petrochelidon.—Tail nearly even, or moderately forked.

Tail emarginate. Forehead, throat, and rump reddish brown ; throat with a large black spot.................... ....*P. lunifrons.*

Tail moderately forked. Beneath entirely white ; above opaque green ; upper tail coverts purple.. .....*P. thalassina.*

Tail moderately forked. Beneath entirely white. Above uniform lustrous green.

P. bicolor.

Hirundo bicolor has by some authors been placed under *Chelidon*, but is readily distinguished by having the tarsi and toes smooth, instead of feathered.

Cabanis has established a genus, *Tachycineta*,[1] for the violet green swallow, *H. thalassina*, on account of its rather forked tail and small bill, and the entire absence of gloss on the feathers. He, however, includes in it the *H. bicolor*, which is remarkable for the lustre of its dorsal plumage. For the purposes of the present report it will be sufficient to consider them under the same head.

HIRUNDO HORREORUM,[2] Barton.

Barn Swallow.

Hirundo horreorum, BARTON, Fragments N. H. Penna. 1799,17.
Hirundo rufa, VIEILLOT, Ois. Am. Sept. I, 1807, 60 ; pl. xxx. (Not of Gmelin.)—CASSIN, Illust. I, 1855, 243.—
    BREWER, N. Am. Ool. I, 1857, 91; pl. v, f. 63—67, eggs.
Hirundo americana, WILSON, Am. Orn. V, 1812, 34; pl. xxxviii, f. 1, 2. (Not of Gmelin.)—RICH. F. B. A. II,
    1831, 329.
Hirundo rustica, AUDUBON, Orn. Biog. II, 1834, 413; pl. 173.—IB. Syn. 1839, 35.—IB. Birds Am. I, 1840, 181; pl.
    48. (Not of Linnaeus.)

SP. CH.—Tail very deeply forked ; outer feathers several inches longer than the inner, very narrow towards the end. Above glossy blue, with concealed white in the middle of the back. Throat chestnut ; rest of lower part reddish white, not conspicuously different. A steel blue collar on the upper part of the breast, interrupted in the middle. Tail feathers with a white spot near the middle, on the inner web. Female with the outer tail feather not quite so long. Length, 6.90 inches ; wing, 5.00 ; tail, 4.50.

Hab.—North America from Atlantic to Pacific.

Specimens from the far west have the same general appearance as eastern ones, except that one (6619) from the Sacramento valley is the largest I have seen, with the tail half an inch longer than in Carlisle specimens.

There is not much variation in skins of this species, except, perhaps, in the intensity of the coloration on the belly. In some specimens (1452) there is very little difference between the throat and abdomen, the former a little more chestnut. Sometimes the belly is nearly white with a slight tinge of brown. Occasionally the black collar on the throat is continuous across, along a single line of feathers. In one (2191) there is a broad collar across the throat as wide as in the European species, interrupted, however, in its central portion by dull chestnut.

The female is much like the male, but has the external tail feathers less elongated. In the young the tail is simply deeply emarginate, not forked as in the adult.

Specimens from Texas and northern Mexico are smaller than those found further north.

This species resembles the European Barn Swallow; in which, however, the pectoral collar is continuous across and quite broad, and the belly more rufous, with other differences.

The determination of the true specific name of this species is a matter of some uncertainty, depending upon whether the South American bird be distinct from the North American or not.

[1] Museum Heineanum, 1850, 48.

[2] The following synonyms refer to the South American species :
    Hirundo erythrogaster, BODDAERT, Tableau Pl. enl. 724, f. 1, 1783, 45.
    Hirundo rufa, GMELIN, Syst. Nat. I, 1788, 1018.
    Hirundo cyanopyrrha, VIEILLOT, Nouv. D'ct. XIV, 1817, 510.
    Hirondelle a ventre reux de Cayenne, BUFFON, Ois. VI, 607.—IB. pl. enl. 724, f. 1.

The names both of Boddaert and Gmelin appear to have been based chiefly upon the *Hirondelle a ventre roux de Cayenne* of Buffon, Pl. enl. 724, f. 1, the former having priority. Should this species, therefore, as is probable from its much smaller size and more intensely rufous under parts, not be the North American one, the next in order will be Barton's *H. horreorum*. Burmeister (Thiere Brasiliens, Vögel, II, 1856, 149) makes two species, retaining *H. rufa* for the South American one. He is mistaken in saying the North American bird differs in having the belly white, and the tail not so deeply forked. The difference appears to lie in the much larger size, and less uniformly rufous belly. According to Burmeister, the length of a Brazilian species is 5.66 inches, (German); the culmen, .18; the wings, 4.25; the tail, 2.67; differences readily appreciable. He gives *H. americana*, Gmelin, 1017, for the North American bird; but this cannot be the case, since this species is described as having a rufous rump and even tail; locality, the La Plata.

List of specimens.

Catal. No.	Sex and age.	Locality.	When collected.	Whence obtained.	Orig. No.	Collected by—	Length.	Stretch of wings.	Wing.	Remarks.
1163	....	Carlisle, Pa............	Aug. 21,1843	S. F. Baird	......	....	5.92	13	4.67	Iris hazel...............
1192	○	......do...............	July 15......	......do......	......	....	......	......	......	....
2191	♀	......do.............	May 1,1845	......do.......	......	....	6.75	13.25	4.75	....
1452	♂	......do...............	May 4,1846	......do.......	......	....	7.25	12.83	4.83	....
8640	♀	Indian Key, Fla........	Aug. 29,1857	G. Wurdemann ..	......	....	6.10	12.10	4.50	....
5206	....	Yellowstone river, N. T.	July 23,1856	Lt. G. K. Warren.	......	Dr. Hayden..	6.75	12.62	4.75	....
5207	....	....do...............	July 2,1857	......do.......	......	....do......	7.75	12.75	4.50	Eyes black ....
5208	....	......do...............	July —,1856	......do.......	......	....do......	6.50	12.25	4.50	......do...
4965	... .	Fort Chadbourne, Tex .	....	Dr. Swift, U. S. A.	......	....	......	....	....	....
5047	....	Pecos river, Tex	July 11,1856	Capt. J. Pope...	108	....	7	12	4.50	Bill black; gums bluish yellow; eyes brown; feet yellow.
5048	....	......do........	Aug. 20,1855	......do.......	123	....	7	12	4.50	Feet gray; gums yellow..
3956	....	San Diego, New Leon, Texas.	Aug. 1,1853	Lieut. Couch	124	....	....	....	....	Eyes very dark brown; bill black; feet slate color.
6019	♂	Sacramento, Cal......	....	Lt. Williamson..	......	Dr. Heermann	....	......	....	....
6020	♂	Benicia, Cal...........	....	......do.......	......	......do......	....	......	....	....

HIRUNDO LUNIFRONS, Say.

Cliff Swallow.

Hirundo lunifrons, SAY, Long's Exped. R. Mts. II, 1823, 47.—CASSIN, Illust. I, 1855, 243.—BREWER. N. Am. Ool. I, 1857, 94; pl. v, no. 68—73, egg.

Hirundo opifex, DEWITT CLINTON, Ann. N. Y. Lyc. I, 1824, 161.

Hirundo respublicana, AUDUBON, Ann. N. Y. Lyc. I, 1824, 164.

Hirundo fulva, BONAP. Am. Orn. I, 1825, 63; pl. ii. (Not of Vieillot.)—AUDUBON, Orn. Biog. I, 1831, 353; pl. 58.— IB. Syn. 1839, 35.—IB. Birds Am. I, 1840, 177; pl. 47.

Hirundo melanogaster, SWAINSON, Philos. Mag. I, 1827, 366.

Petrochelidon melanogastra, CABANIS, Mus. Hein. 47.

SP. CH.—Crown and back steel blue; the upper part of the latter with concealed pale edges to the feathers. Chin, throat, and sides of the head dark chestnut; breast fuscous; belly white. A steel blue spot on throat. Rump light chestnut; forehead brownish white; a pale nuchal band. Tail slightly emarginate. Length about 5 inches; wing, 4.40; tail, 2.20.

Hab.—North America from Atlantic to Pacific.

Entire crown of the head and the back steel blue, separated more or less broadly by a grayish collar. Chin and throat, with sides of the head below the eyes, dark purplish chestnut, this color extending a short distance around towards the nape. Rump light chestnut. Forehead and middle of belly brownish or dull yellow brownish white; the upper part of the breast and the sides of the body light grayish brown. A large spot on the throat crossing the line of separation between the chestnut and brown, steel blue; this sometimes seen in the chin.

The lores and a very narrow line along the base of the bill are black. The feathers on the middle of the back exhibit whitish edges, more or less conspicuously. Wings and tail brown, the secondaries with lighter margins.

The female is not appreciably different in color.

The young lacks the frontal band, and the gray collar on the nape is only faintly indicated. There is usually a good deal of white on the throat, on the lower part of which the black spot is more extended and less distinct than in the adult.

Specimens vary in the extent of chestnut on the rump, in the width and precise shade of the frontal patch, &c.

This species differs from the true *Hirundo fulva*, Vieillot Encyclop. 527, of the West Indies, in the larger size, lighter colored rump, and in the presence of a black spot on the throat.

List of specimens.

Catal. No.	Sex and age.	Locality.	When collected.	Whence obtained.	Original No.	Collected by—	Length.	Stretch of wings.	Wing.
443	....	Carlisle, Pa....................	Aug. 31, 1841	S. F. Baird.............	....	....	5.75	12.50	....
2358	♂	......do.....................	May 26, 1845	......do....			5.92	12.50	4.50
2284	♀	.......do................	May 17......	......do......			5.67	12.25	4.42
2617	♂	....	May 11, 1846	......do......			5.67	12.25	4.50
1565	♂	....	May 22, 1844	......do......			5.83	12.08	4.92
685	♀	....	Aug. 21, 1842	......do......					
1623	♀	....	July 9, 1844	......do......			5.92	12.92	4.33
2616	♀	... .	May 11, 1846	......do.......			5.75	12.33	4.33
6487	....	Philadelphia....................	....	C. Drexler.........					
	....	Illinois	....	R. Kennicott.......					
4776	♂	Bijoux Hill, N. T.	May 20, 1856	Lieut G. K. Warren ...	....	Dr. Hayden............	5.87	12.25	4.50
4777	... .	......do...............	.... do......	......do......		......do....			
4778	♀	......do...............	.... do......	......do......		......do....	5.50	12.25	4.50
4779	♂	......do...............	May 10	......do......		......do....	5.75	12.25	4.50
4780	♀	......do...............	May 20	......do......		......do....	5.75	12.25	4.50
5598	....	Pole creek, Neb..............	July 26, 1856	Lieut. Bryan..........	159	W. S. Wood	5.50	....	4.75
5599	♂	......do...............	.... do......	......do......	158	......do....	5.50	....	4.50
7079	○	W. Fork, Laramie river........	July 22, 1857	Dr. W. A. Hammond...	58				
4394	♂	Fort Dalles, O. T.	May —, 1855	Dr. Suckley, U. S. A....	178	....	5.62	....	4.37
6021	♂	Benicia, Cal.	....	Lieut. Williamson......	....	Dr. Heermann.........			
6022	♂	......do...............	....	......do......		......do....			
6023	....	San Francisco.............	May 8, 1855	Lieut. Trowbridge					

HIRUNDO BICOLOR, Vieillot.

White-bellied Swallow.

Hirundo bicolor, VIELLIOT, Ois. Am. Sept. I, 1807, 61; pl. xxxi.—AUDUBON, Orn. Biog. 1831, 491; pl. 98.—IB. Syn.
1839, 35.—IB. Birds Amer. I, 1840, 175 ; pl. 46.—CASSIN, Illust. I, 1855, 244.—BREWER, N. Am.
Oology, I, 1857, 100 ; pl. iv, fig. 47. (Egg.)

Tachycineta bicolor, CABANIS, Mus. Hein. 1850–'51, 48.

Herse bicolor, BONAP. Conspectus, 1850, 341.

Hirundo viridis, WILSON, Am. Orn. V, 1812, 49 ; pl. xxxviii.

Hirundo leucogaster, STEPHENS, Shaw, Zool. X, 1817, 105.

SP. CH.—Glossy metallic green above ; entirely white beneath. Female much duller in color. Wing 5 inches.
Length, 6.25 inches ; wing, 5.00 ; tail, 2.65.

Hab.—North America from Atlantic to Pacific.

As a general thing specimens of this species from the extreme south of the United States, as Brownsville, Texas, and those from the western coast are considerably smaller than those from Pennsylvania.

The female is duller in color than the male; the metallic tints of the back much more obscure and less continuous. The shade is rather more violet.

The young male of the year (164,) is entirely of a sooty grayish brown above and on the wings, with the faintest possible trace of purplish reflection on the head and back. The color is somewhat like that on the back of *Cotyle riparia*, but darker.

It is not at all improbable that careful comparisons of many specimens may ultimately prove the existence of distinct species of white-bellied swallows on the two sides of the continent. The difference in size will be shown by the table of measurements. In two California specimens before me, one has the same greenish gloss as Pennsylvania skins; in the other the lustre is more of a steel blue.

List of specimens.

Catal. No.	Sex and age.	Locality.	When collected.	Whence obtained.	Orig. No.	Length.	Stretch of wings.	Wing.
2097	♂	Carlisle, Pa.	April 12, 1845	S. F. Baird		6.25	12.25	5.00
2341	♀	...do...	May 24, 1845	...do...		5.33	12.25	4.25
1164	○♂	...do...	Aug. 22, 1843	...do...		5.83	12.50	4.67
2342	♀	...do...	May 24, 1845					
		Northern Illinois		R. Kennicott				
4663	♂	Matamoras, Mex.		Lieut. Couch				
4664		...do...		...do...				
4665	♂	...do...		...do...				
4666	♂	...do...		...do...				
4667	♂	...do...		...do...				
5913	♂	Steilacoom, W.T.	June, 1855	J. G. Cooper		6.00	12.50	
6016	♂	...do...	1854	Dr. Suckley, U.S.A.	88	5.00	12.50	4.75
6015	♂	Shoalwater bay, W.T.	May 2, 1854	J. G. Cooper	76	5.00	12.50	4.75
5494	♂	Petaluma, Cal.		E. Samuels.	712			
4200		San Francisco, Cal.	Winter, 1854	R. D. Cutts				

HIRUNDO THALASSINA, Swainson.

Violet-Green Swallow.

Hirundo thalassina, SWAINSON, Taylor's Philos. Mag I, 1827, 365.—AUD. Orn. Biog. IV, 1838, 597; pl. 385.— IB. Birds Am. I, 1840, 186; pl. 49.—CASSIN, Illust. I, 1855, 245.—BREWER, N. Am. Oology, I, 1857, 102; pl. v, f. 74. (Egg.)
Chelidon thalassina, Boie, Isis, 1844, 171.
Tachycineta thalassina, CABANIS, Mus. Hein. 1850, 48. (Type.)

SP. CH.—Tail acutely emarginate. Beneath pure white. Above soft velvety green. with a very faint shade of purplish violet concentrated on the nape into a transverse band. Rump rather more vivid green; tail coverts showing a good deal of purple. Colors of female much more obscure.

Length, 4.75; wing, 4.50; tail, 2.

Hab.—Rocky Mountains to Pacific; south to Mexico; east to Saltillo, Mexico.

In examining an extensive series of specimens I find some differences which may be of importance. Thus, in the Columbia river specimens the entire back and scapulars are nearly pure uniform green, with the faintest possible wash of purplish brown. The feathers on the rump are purplish violet, slightly glossed with green. In 6625, from the Copper mines, the back is purplish brown, with only a trace of green; the rump nearly pure bluish green, with the merest trace of violet. In a specimen from Agua Nueva the colors are much as in the last, except that the purplish brown is more confined to the scapulars and the middle of the back, as in the Columbia river specimens. The wing is longer than in any I have seen, (4¾ inches.)

In one specimen from Tejon Pass, apparently immature, the tertials are terminated broadly with pure white.

The female differs in the much less brilliancy of color, especially that on top of head and rump, the former more brown. The under parts are dirty white.

List of specimens.

Catal. No.	Sex and age.	Locality.	When collected.	Whence obtained.	Orig'l No.	Collected by—	Length.	Stretch of wings.	Wing.	Remarks.
3954	♂	Saltillo, Mex	Spring of 1853.	Lt. Couch	229	Lt. Couch	5.00	12.00	4.75	Eyes dark br'n; bill black; feet light chesnut.. ....
3955	♂	..... do.................	..... do......	......do	230	......do	5.00	12.00	4.75	......do ....
6094	♀	Rio Grande, N. M......	....	Dr. Henry, U. S. A.	......	....	....	......	......	....
6025	♂	......do................. .	....	......do	......	....	....	......	......	....*...
6965	♀	Medicine Bow C'k, Neb.	July 25, 1857	Lt. F. T. Bryan....	330	W. S. Wood	....	......	......	....
6966	♀	Bridger's Pass, Utah....	July 29, 1857	......do	354	....	....	......	......	....
6026	○	Tejon Pass, Cal.......	....	Lt. Williamson....	......	....	....	......	......	....
1895	♂	Columbia river.........	July 12, 1835	J. K. Townsend ...	......	....	....	......	......	....
1945	♂	......do.................	...... do......	......do	......	....	....	......	......	....
5914	♂	Steilacoom, W. T......	June —, 1855	Dr. J. G. Cooper...	......	....	5.00	12.25	......	....
6027	♂	......do.................	....	Dr. Suckley, U.S.A.	110	....	....	......	......	....
6028	♂	......do.................	Mar. 1, 1854	......do	43	....	....	......	......	....
6029	♀	....	Aug. 3, 1854	......do	45	....	....	......	......	....

COTYLE, Boi

Cotyle, Boie, Isis, 1822, 550. (Type *H. riparia*.)

Ch.—Bill very flat, extremely broad at the base, and gradually narrowed towards the tip; nostrils prominent and rounded. Tail moderate, nearly straight or somewhat emarginated. Tarsi rather shorter than the middle toe, slender and scutellated. Toes very slender, the claws slightly curved. Colors generally dull brown above, without gloss.

This genus is distinguished from *Hirundo* by the slightly forked tail, rather long tarsi, very slender toes, and extremely dull colors. The two United States species are the smallest we have. Each will form the type of a special division, of at least sub-generic value, with the following characters:

Cotyle, Boie.—Tarsi with a tuft of feathers near the toes, on the posterior face. Edges of outer primaries normal.

Above grayish brown; beneath white, with a well defined pectoral band......*C. riparia.*

Stelgidopteryx, Baird.—Tarsi naked. Edge of outer primary with the fibrillae converted into a series of stiffened recurved hooks.

Above light sooty brown; the under parts brownish ash, fading behind into white.

S. serripennis.

COTYLE RIPARIA, o i e.

Bank Swallow.

Hirundo riparia, LINNAEUS, Syst. Nat. I, 1766, 344.—WILSON, Am. Orn. V, 46 ; pl. xxxviii.—AUDUBON, Orn Biog.
IV, 1838, 584 ; pl. 385.—IB. Syn. 1839.—IB. Birds Am. I, 1840, 187 ; pl. 50.
Cotyle riparia, BOIE, Isis, 1822, 550.—BON. List, 1838.—CASSIN, Illust. I, 1855, 247.—BREWER, N. Am. Ool. I, 1857,
105 ; pl. iv. fig. 49, (egg.)
" Hirundo cinerea, VIEILLOT, Nouv. Dict. XIV, 1817, 526."

SP. CH.—Smallest of American swallows. Tail slightly emarginate. Outer web of first primary soft, without hooks. Lower part of the tarsus with a few scattered feathers. Above grayish brown, somewhat fuliginous, with a tendency to paler margins to the feathers. Beneath pure white, with a band across the breast and sides of the body like the back. Length, 4.75 ; wing, 4.00 ; tail, 2.00.

A specimen collected by Dr. Heermann in the Sacramento valley is rather smaller than Pennsylvania ones, and the brown band across the throat is broader and more continuous. Skins from the Upper Missouri are rather larger than from either side of the continent, and the colors purer and more continuous ; the tail and wing feathers without the white edging.

The young of the year are not conspicuously different from the adults, save in the greater amount of light edging to the feathers on the back. The tail is less emarginate.

This species is supposed by most authors to be identical with the European bank swallow, careful comparisons having hitherto failed to exhibit any tangible difference. It furnishes almost a solitary instance, among land birds, of the same species inhabiting both continents permanently, and not as an accidental or occasional visitor on either.

List of specimens.

Catal. No.	Sex.	Locality.	When collected.	Whence obtained.	Orig. No.	Collected by—	Length.	Stretch of wings.	Wing.	Remarks.
1692	♂	Carlisle, Pa....	Aug. 30,1844	S. F. Baird.........	......	....	4.75	10.83	4.00	....
1165	♀	......do	Aug. 22,1844	......do	......	....	4.67	10.67	3.83	....
1194	.....	......do	July 18,1843	......do	......	....	4.83	10.42	3.83	....
5209	♀	Yellowstone R., N.T.....	Aug. —,1856	Lt. G. K. Warren..	....	Dr. Hayden......	5.00	11.25	4.00	Eyes black.........
5210	......	......do	July 23,1856	......do	....	...do	5.12	10.12	3.37	Eyes black; inside of mouth yellow..
5597	♀	East of Ft. Riley.........	June 13.1856	Lt. F. F. Bryan.....	24	W. S. Wood.....	4.75	8.50	....	....
6030	♂	Sacramento, Cal	....	Lt. Williamson	....	Dr. Heermann....	....	....	....	....

COTYLE SERRIPENNIS, B o n a p .

Rough-winged Swallow.

Hirundo serripennis, AUD. Orn. Biog. IV, 1838, 593.— . Birds America, I, 1840, 193 ; pl. 51.
Cotyle serripennis, BONAP. Consp. 1850, 342.—CASSIN, Illust. I, 1855, 247.—BREWER, N. Am. Oology, I, 1857,
106 ; pl. iv, fig. 50, (egg.)

SP. CH.—Tail slightly emarginate ; first primary with the pennulae of the outer web much stiffened, with their free extremities recurved into a hook very appreciable to the touch. No feathers on the tarsus and toes. Above rather light sooty brown, beneath whitish gray, or light brownish ash, becoming nearly pure white in the middle of the belly and on the under tail coverts. Length, 4.50 ; wing, 4.28 ; tail, 2.23.

Hab.—United States from Atlantic to Pacific.

Specimens vary in having the belly of a purer white, and in the greater or less intensity of the ashy brown of the throat and breast.

40 b

In a female from New Leon the wing is half an inch less than in females from Carlisle. In a specimen from Charleston the colors of the throat and breast extend farther down on the belly. In the young of the year the wing feathers above are edged quite broadly with pale brownish rusty, the throat and breast are also tinged more or less with the same.

List of specimens.

Catal. No.	Sex and age.	Locality.	When collected.	Whence obtained.	Orig'l No.	Collected by—	Length.	Stretch of wings.	Wing.	Remarks.
2116	♀	Carlisle, Pa............	April 16,1845	S. F. Baird		....	5.17	11.50	4.08	....
2621	♀	......do	May 11,1846	....do		....	5.33	11.50	4.08	....
2634	♀	......do	May 24,1845	....do		....	....	....	....	....
2209	♂	......do	May 3,1845	....do		....	....	....	....	....
3370	♀	......do	May 3,1847	....do		....	....	....	....	....
1480	♀	......do	May 8,1844	....do		....	5.58	12.00	4.42	....
2619	♀	....do	May 11,1846	....do		....	5.58	12.50	4.50	....
1120	○	......do	July 15,1843	....do		....	....	....	....	....
2620	♂	......do	May 11,1846	....do		....	5.17	12.50	4.50	....
1638	○	......do	July 16,1844	....do		....	5.42	11.50	4.50	....
	....	Washington, D. C.....	....	J. C. McGuire ..		....				
2899	....	Charleston, S. C......	....	Mr. Audubon...		....	... ...	... ..		....
8385	♂	Independence . Mo.....	June 20,1857	Wm. M. Magraw.	89	Dr. Cooper	5.13	12.00	4.63	Iris brown.......... .....
8384		....do	June 22,1857	..... do..........	88	......do	5.75	12.50	4.62	....do ....
8179	○	Shawnee Mission, Kan.	July 3,1857	..... do..........	115	......do	5.50	12.12	4.50	....do ....
3957	♀	New Leon, Mex........	April —,1853	Lieut. Couch	131	....	5.25	11.00	4.00	Eyes brown ; bill black ; feet reddish slate color...
6033	....	Steilacoom, W. T......	....	Dr. Suckley......	82	....				
6034	....	Shoalwater bay, W. T..	June —,1854	Dr. Cooper	81	... .	5.42	12.50	......	Iris br'n ; bill and feet bl'k.
6035	....	......do.............	..... do......	..... do..........	81	....	5.42	12.50	......	....do..........do ....
6032	♂	Sacramento, Cal......	....	Lt. Williamson..	......	Dr. Heermann ..	....	....	......	....
6031	....	Camp 124..............	Feb. 21,1854	Lt. Whipple.....	176	Dr. Kennerly...	5.25	11.00	4.37	....

PROGNE, Boie.

Progne, Boie, Isis, 1826, 971. Type *Hirundo purpurea,* L.

Ch.—Bill strong, short ; the gape very wide ; the sides gradually compressed, the culmen and lateral margins arched to the tip ; the latter inflected ; the nostrils basal, lateral, open and rounded. Tail considerably forked. Tarsi shorter than the middle toe and claw, about equal to the toe alone. Toes long, strong ; lateral ones equal.

The large size, very stout bill and feet, (for this family,) with the usually uniform black glossy plumage, readily distinguish this genus among the swallows. But one species is well established as North American.

PROGNE PURPUREA, Boie.

Purple Martin.

Hirundo purpurea, Linn. Syst. Nat. I, 1766, 344.—Audubon, Orn. Biog. I, 1831, 115 ; pl. xxiii.—Ib. Birds Am. I, 1840, 170 ; pl. xlv.

Progne purpurea, Boie, Isis, 1826, 971.—Bonap. List, 1838.—Cassin, Illust. J, 1855, 245.—Brewer, N. Am. Oology, I, 1857, 103 ; pl. iv, fig. 47, (egg.)

Hirundo subis, Linnaeus, Syst. Nat. I, 1766, 344, (second year.)

Hirundo violacea, Gm. Syst. Nat. I, 1788, 1026.

Hirundo cærulea, Vieillot, Ois. Am. Sept. I, 1807, 57 ; pl. xxvi.

" *Hirundo versicolor,* Vieillot, Nouv. Dict. XIV, 1817, 509."

" *Hirundo ludoviciana,* Cuvier, R. An. I, 1817, 374."

Sp. Ch.—Largest of N. American swallows. Closed wings rather longer than the deeply forked tail. Tarsi and toes naked. Color, in the old male, everywhere glossy steel blue, with purple and violet reflections. Female and immature male less brilliant above, pale brownish beneath, blotched with darker or with bluish. Length, 7.30 ; wing, 5.85 ; tail, 3.40.

Hab.—North America generally.

Specimens of this species from Petaluma, California, are not appreciably different. The gloss of the upper as well as the lower parts is rather more greenish, and less purple. The bills are the same, as well as the size every way. Specimens from Coahuila, Mexico, are more like Pennsylvania ones. In those from the Upper Missouri the gloss is more like that of the Petaluma specimen. In one from Sacramento city again the colors have the usual purplish gloss.

A female from Petaluma has a very distinct grayish white collar across the nape, and the entire forehead is of a similar color.

I have never seen any specimens from the west coast agreeing with Mr. Cassin's description of *P. chalybea*, in the larger and longer bill and smaller size. An adult *Progne*, from Chili, labelled *P. chalybea*, by Mr. Verreaux, is exactly like the North American *P. purpurea* in size, lustre, &c ; the only difference being, apparently, a narrower bill. Number 4773, from the Upper Missouri, is, however, like it in this respect.

List of specimens.

Catal. No.	Sex & age.	Locality.	When collected.	Whence obtained.	Orig. No.	Collected by—	Length.	Stretch of wings.	Wing.	Remarks.
1561	♂	Carlisle, Penn........	May 22, 1844	S. F. Baird.......						
1596	♂	......do.............	June 5, 1844	.....do..........		....	8.17	16.58	6.	
1607	♂	.....do.............	June 15, 1844	......do..........		....	8.08	16.25	5.83	
1636	○	.....do.............	July 16, 1844	......do..........			7.75	15.75	5.59	
1129	♀	.....do.............	July, 1843....	......do..........			7.83	16.50	5.92	
4505	.....	Cedar Island, Neb....	May, 1854....	Col. A. Vaughan..		Dr. Hayden..				
4506	......	....do.......	...do........	.....do..........		.....do......				
4507	......	.....do.............	...do........	.....do..........		.....do......				
4508	......	.....do....	...do........	.....do..........		.....do......				
4769	♀	.....do.............	May 19, 1854	Lt. G. K. Warren.		.....do......	8.	16.12		
4770	♀	Vermillion River, Neb.	May 8, 1854	......do..........	18	.....do......	7.62	15.37		
4771	♂	Nebraska............	May 15, 1854	.....do..........		.....do......	7.87	15.		
4772	♂	Cedar Island, Neb....	....do........	......do..........		.....do......	8.	16.		
4773	♂	....	April 23......	......do..........		Lt. Warren ..	7.50	16.	5.75	Eyes dark........
4774	♀	....	....do..●......	......do..........	17	.....do......	7.75	15.25	6.	
4775	♀	Iowa point..........	April 23......	......do..........		.....do......	7.50	16.	5.75	Eyes dark.......
5204	♀	Fort Union, Neb.... ..	July, 1856....	......do..........		Dr. Hayden..	8.	16.25	5.25	.....do......
5205	♀	Blackfoot country	July, 1855....	......do..........		.....do......				
5596	♂	Fort Riley, K. T.....	June 20, 1856	Lt. F. T. Bryan..	35	W. S. Wood..	8.25	14.		
5049	♂	Indianola, Texas.....	Mar. 12, 1855	Capt. J. Pope....	28	Capt. Pope...	6.	16.	6.	Eyes dark ; gums rose-colored ; feet black ; bill black.
3952	♂	Coahuila, Mex.......	May, 1853....	Lt. Couch........	231	....				Eyes dark brown ; bill black ; feet very dark chestnut.
3953	♂	.....do.....	....do.........	......do..........	232	....	7.75	15.	5.87	Eyes dark brown ; bill black ; feet very dark chestnut.
5482	♀	Petaluma, Cal.......	April, 1856...	E. Samuels	607	....				
5493	♂	.....do........	....do........	......do..........	576	....	8.25	15.25	5.50	
6014	♂	Sacramento..........	....	Lt. Williamson...		Dr. Heermann				

Family BOMBYCILLIDAE.

Primaries ten ; the first very short or moderate, always less than half the second.   Bill short, broad, triangular, much depressed ; gape opening nearly to the eyes ; twice the length of the culmen.   Both mandibles notched, the upper with a tooth behind the notch.   Tarsi scutel'ate anteriorly, with indications also of scales inferiorly on the sides, (except in *Myiadestes?*) ; shorter than the middle toe.   Outer lateral toe longest.   Toes unequally cleft.   Head generally crested.

The waxwings and their natural allies, the *Ptiliogonidinae*, have been variously placed by different authors, Cabanis constituting them a sub-family of *Muscicapidae*.   The differences from the typical muscicapas are very great however, and as none of the latter are found in the United States I have thought it best to raise them to the rank of a distinct family, for the present at least.

The relationships of the group to the *Laniadae* are very close, and if it be a sub-family merely it would seem to go more appropriately there than in *Muscicapidae*.   Both have the notch at the tip of the lower mandible very distinct.

The two sub-families are known by the long pointed wings, much longer than the even tail ; the very rudimentary first primary and the horny tip to the tertials of *Bombycillinae*, are distinguished from the much longer forked or rounded tail and the shorter wings with longer first primary and plain tertials of *Ptiliogonidinae*.

Sub-Family BOMBYCILLINAE.

Wings very long and pointed, reaching nearly to the tip of the short tail.   First primary excessively rudimentary, scarcely appreciable ; second about the longest.   Rictus without bristles.   The frontal feathers extending forward on the bill beyond the nostrils.

Of this sub-family there is but a single representative in the United States, with the following characters :

AMPELIS.—Tail even.   Tertials with horny appendages, like red sealing wax.

AMPELIS, Linnaeus.

Ampelis, LINNAEUS, Syst. Nat. 1735.   Type *A garrulus*.
Bombycilla, VIEILLOT, Ois. Am. Sept. I, 1807, 88.   Type *B. cedrorum*.

CH.—Head with a broad depressed crest.   Bill very broad, opening nearly to the eye ; a series of short velvety feathers at the base of the bill, with bristles directed forwards and covering the nostrils, but none along the rictus.   Commissure straight. Culmen and gonys curved, convex ; both mandibles notched at tip.   Legs stout ; tarsi shorter than the middle toe ; scutellate anteriorly, and slightly on the lower half on the sides behind ; slightly feathered above.   Hind toe shorter than the lateral, which are equal.   Wings very long, pointed, reaching almost to the tip of the nearly even tail.   First primary so short as to be with difficulty discernible ; the second quill longest.   Tips of secondary quills with horny appendages, like sealing wax.

The most essential characters of the genus are to be found in the short, even tail, and the red horny appendages to the tips of the tertials.   The two species found in North America have the body of a tint approaching to yellowish cinnamon, becoming plumbeous behind ; the tail tipped with yellow ; the chin, forehead, and a band from this above and behind the eye, black. There is also a white maxillary patch.   The specific characters are as follows :

Large ; chin and throat black ; crissum orange brown ; two white bands on the wing, and a white line along the tips of the primaries.. *garrulus*.

Small ; chin only black ; crissum whitish ; no white on the wing.................. ...*cedrorum*.

Comparative measurements of species.

Catal. No.	Species.	Locality.	Sex.	Length.	Stretch of wings.	Wing.	Tail.	Tarsus.	Middle toe.	Its claw alone.	Bill above.	Along gape.	Specimen measured
1617	Ampelis cedrorum.....	Carlisle, Pa........	♂	5.82	....	3.80	2.59	0.68	0.80	0.22	0.44	0.66	Dry......
do.	..........do............	.....do............	......	7.25	12.00	4.00	....	....	....	....	....	....	Fresh....
3958	..........do............	Tamaulipas........	♀	6.10	....	3.64	2.58	0.64	0.70	0.20	0.39	0.64	Dry......
do.	..........do............	.....do	......	6.00	11.00	3.75	....	....	....	....	....	....	Fresh....
5818	Ampelis garrulus	Racine, Wis.......	......	6.78	....	4.68	3.10	0.76	0.90	0.27	0.46	0.76	Dry......

AMPELIS GARRULUS, Linn.

Wax-wing; Bohemian Chatterer.

" *Lanius garrulus*, LINN. Fauna Suecica, 2, No. 82."
Ampelis garrulus, LINN. Syst. Nat. I, 1766, 297.—BONAP. 2d List, 1842.—IB. Conspectus, 1850, 336.
Bombycilla garrula, BONAP. Zool. Jour. III, 1827, 50.—IB. Synopsis, 1828, 438.—IB. Am. Orn. III, 1828, pl. xvi.—
RICH. F. B. A. II, 1831, 237.—AUD. Orn. Biog. IV, 1838, 462 ; pl. 363.—IB. Birds Amer. IV,
1842, 169 ; pl. 246.—KEYS. and BLAS. Wirb. Europas, I, 1840, 167.

SP. CH.—Highly crested. General color brownish ash, with a faint shade of reddish, especially anteriorly ; the forehead,
sides of the head, and under tail coverts, brownish orange ; the hinder parts purer ash ; the region about the vent white.
Primaries and tail feathers plumbeous black, especially towards the tips ; the tail with a terminal band of yellow. A narrow
frontal line passing backward and involving the eye, and extending above and behind it. Chin and upper part of throat black.
Tips of the secondary coverts, and a spot on the end of the outer webs of all the quills, white ; those on the inner primaries
glossed with yellow. Secondaries with red horny tips, like sealing wax. Side of the lower jaw whitish. Length, 7.40 ;
wing, 4.50 ; tail, 3.

Hab.—Northern parts of both continents. Seen in the United States only in severe winters, except along the great lakes.
In the Mississippi valley south to Fort Riley.

This species, with the general appearance of the cedar bird, is readily distinguished by its
superior size ; much larger crest ; black chin and throat, instead of chin alone ; brownish
chestnut under tail coverts, instead of white, and the white marks on the wing not found at all
in the other. In the closed wing, the white on the ends of the primaries forms a continuous
narrow stripe nearly parallel with the outer edge of the wing.

The specimen from Fort Riley is probably the most southwestern one on record in North
America.

I have no authentic skins of the European *Bombycilla garrula* before me, but as many
careful comparisons have been made between specimens from the two continents, they may
be pretty fairly considered as identical.

List of specimens.

Catal. No.	Sex.	Locality.	When collected.	Whence obtained.
5810	♂	Racine, Wis.....................	November 10, 1852......	Dr. P. R. Hoy ....
5791	....	Cleveland, Ohio..................	1856....................	Dr. J. P. Kirtland...............
5875	....	Fort Riley, K. T................	1857....................	Dr. W. A. Hammond.............
1871	....	Europe?..........................	....	S. F. Baird......................

AMPELIS CEDRORUM, Baird.

Cedar Bird.

Ampelis garrulus, Var. β , Linn. Syst. Nat. I, 1766, 297.—Gm. I, 1788, 838.
Ampelis carolinensis, Gosse, Birds Jamaica, 1847, 197.—Bonap. Consp. 1850, 336.
Bombycilla carolinensis, Brisson, Orn. II, 1760, 337.—Aud. Orn. Biog. I, 1831, 227 : V, 494 ; pl. 43.—Ib. Syn. 1839,
    165.—Ib. Birds Amer. IV, 1842, 165 ; pl. 245.—Wagler, Isis, 1831, 528.
Bombycilla cedrorum, Vieillot, Ois. Am. Sept. I, 1807, 88 ; pl. lvii.—Ib. Galerie Ois. I, 1834, 186 ; pl. cxviii.
Ampelis americana, Wilson, Am. Orn. I, 1808, 107 ; pl. vii.

Sp. Ch.—Head crested. General color reddish olive, passing anteriorly on the neck, head, and breast into purplish cinnamon ; posteriorly on the upper parts into ash ; on the lower into yellow. Under tail coverts white. Chin dark sooty black, fading insensibly into the ground color on the throat. Forehead, loral region, space below the eye, and a line above it on the side of the head, intense black. Quills and tail dark plumbeous, passing behind into dusky ; the tail tipped with yellow ; the primaries, except the first, margined with hoary. A short maxillary stripe, a narrow crescent on the infero-posterior quarter of the eye, white. Secondaries with horny tips, like red sealing wax. Length, 7.25 ; wing, 4.05 ; tail, 2.60.
    .—North America generally ; south to Guatemala.

I have found it impossible to describe satisfactorily to myself the peculiar tint of color prevailing on the anterior half of this beautiful bird. Mr. Audubon speaks of it as light grayish brown, passing anteriorly into light brownish red. Immature specimens lack the sealing wax tips. The young have the upper parts more ash above, the lower streaked with dusky reddish ash and white, except on the abdomen and under coverts.

I am unable to discern any differences in specimens from western portions of the United States, California, Mexico, or Guatemala.

List of specimens.

Catal. No.	Sex & age.	Locality.	When collected.	Whence obtained.	Orig'l No.	Collected by—	Length.	Stretch of wings.	Wing.	Remarks.
1617	♂	Carlisle, Pa............	July 5,1844	S. F. Baird........		....	7.25	12.00	4.00	....
2446	○	......do..	Sept. 9,1845	......do........		....				....
7577	......	Washington, D. C........		Wm. Hutton.....		......				
7260	......	Rockport, Ohio.........	... .	J. P. Kirtland....		......				
4918	♂	Amelia Island, Fla.......	....	G. Würdemann..		....	6.50	11.50	3.50	
5318	♂	Yellowstone river, Neb...	July 24,1856	Lt. Warren......		Dr. Hayden...	6.50	11.50	4.25	Bill black, iris dark.....
5319	♀	......do..	......do....	......do........		......do....	7.12	12.12	4.00	.... do.........do......
3958	♀	Tamaulipas, Mex.........	Mar. 20,1853	Lt. Couch........	89	....	6.00	11.00	3.75	Eyes dark, bill and feet black.
3959	......	New Leon, Mex.........	April —,1853	......do....	155	....	7.00	11.25	3.75	.... do.........do......
4236	......	San Francisco, Cal......	Winter, 1853	R. D. Cutts		......				....
7952	......	Guatemala		J. Gould........		......				....
7953	......	......do....		......do........						

Sub-Family PTILIOGONIDINAE.

Rictus with bristles. Tail long. Wings graduated ; the first primary always half or one-third the second, which is considerably less than the third. Nostrils entirely anterior to the frontal feathers.

Ptiliogonys.—Head with a broad short crest. Culmen considerably curved from the base. Bill broad. Tarsi slightly feathered at the upper extremity ; scutellate. Wings shorter than the tail ; the first primary very short ; the second and third much graduated, acuminated. Tail forked, the lateral feather graduated. Feathers narrow, linear.

Cichlopsis.—Head with a long narrow crest. Culmen moderately curved from the base.

Bill rather narrow. Tarsus bare above, scutellate. Wings shorter than the tail; first quill scarcely spurious, half the second, which is much graduated; the third to sixth slightly graduated. Tail rounded, graduated. Feathers broad, widening to the tip. MYIADESTES.—Head scarcely crested. Culmen straight to near the tip. Bill moderately broad. Tarsi without scutellae, (except in the young?) Wings very long, longer than the tail; the first quill very short; the second, but not the third, graduated. Tail forked, the lateral feather graduated; feathers broad, tapering to the tip.

Comparative measurements.

Catal. No.	Species.	Locality.	Sex.	Length.	Wing.	Tail.	Tarsus.	Middle toe.	Its claw alone.	Bill above.	Along gape.	Remarks.
8275	Cichlopsis nitens............	Colorado desert....	♂	7.50	3.63	4.36	0.68	0.70	0.20	0.40	0.64	Dry ....
8274	........do................	......do...........	♀	7.50	3.52	4.04	0.70	0.72	0.20	0.42	0.62	Dry ....
2966	Ptilogonys cinereus........	Mexico.............	......	7.60	3.56	4.15	0.67	0.74	0.20	0.42	0.70	Dry ....
	Myiadestes obscurus.......	¹Orizaba....	......	7.62	3.88	4.10	0.82	0.80	0.20	0.44	0.70	Dry ....
4451	Myiadestes townsendii......	Des Chutes , Oregon	......	8.00	4.60	4.46	0.82	0.84	0.26	0.42	0.70	Dry ....

¹ Belonging to Mr. George N. Lawrence.

PTILOGONYS, Swainson.

Ptilogonys, SWAINSON, Catal. Mex. Museum, 1824.
Ptilogonys, SWAINSON, Philosophical Mag. I, May, 1827, 368.
Ptiliogonatus, SWAINSON, Zool. Jour. III, July, 1827, 164.

CH.—Head with a full though short depressed occipital crest. Bill broad, much depressed; sides nearly straight; greatest width equal to the length of culmen. Rictus with short bristles. Nostrils oval, margined by membrane, except below. Tarsus shorter than the middle toe, scutellate; a few feathers on its upper extremity anteriorly; outer toe a little longer than inner, about equal to the hinder; hind claw not half the total length of the hind toe. Tail longer than the wings; slightly forked, but the lateral feather nearly .20 of an inch shorter than the next; the feathers narrow linear. First primary about one fourth the longest; the second and third much graduated and acuminate; the fourth longest and rounded.

I introduce the description of the genus *Ptilogonys* here to show its relationship to the United States species, especially, too, as the *P. cinereus*, the type, will most ‚probably be found within our own territories.²

CICHLOPSIS, Cabanis.

Cichlopsis, CABANIS, Mus. Hein. 1850–'51. Type *C .leucogenys.*

CH.—Head with an occipital crest of long narrow feathers. Bill weak, depressed, decidedly narrower than the length of culmen. Base of bill with short bristles. Tarsi scutellate, bare above; shorter than the middle toe; outer lateral toe rather the longer; equal to the hinder. Wings and tail rather long; the former shortest; the first quill half the length of the second, and two fifths the fifth, or longest. Tail feathers broad, widening to the rounded tip; the tail moderately graduated; the middle ones longest.

²PTILOGONYS CINEREUS, Swainson.
  " *Ptilogonys cinereus,* SWAINSON, Catal. Mex. Mus. 1824, App. page 4."—BON. Consp. 1850, 335.—CABANIS, Mus. Hein. 1851, 55.
  Ptiliogonatus cinereus, SWAINSON, Zool. Jour. III, July, 1827, 164.—IB. Phil. Mag. I, 1827, 368.—IB. Zool. Ill. ; pl. lxiv.
  Ptiliogonys cinereus, SWAINSON, Zool. Ill. tab. lxii.
  " *Hypothymis chrysorrhaea,* LICHT." TEMM. Pl. Col. 452.

General color light plumbeous grey, becoming whitish on the forehead and chin. Sides of head light smoke brown, with a white ring round the eye. Quills and tail greenish black, edged with plumbeous, the former margined internally with white; the tail feathers with a large white patch on the inner webs on the middle third. Sides of body and belly behind greenish yellow, becoming clear yellow on the under tail coverts. Bill and feet black. Length, 7.60; wing, 3.56; tail, 4.15. (No. 2966, Mexico.)

This genus has a much narrower and more depressed bill than *Ptilogonys*. The feet are similar, but with more curved claws, and with no feathers on the upper part of the tarsus. The first quill is much larger ; indeed it can scarcely be called spurious ; the fourth, fifth, and sixth are successively a little longer than the third ; the outer primaries not acuminate. The tail is much broader, widening to the tip ; it is rounded, or graduated, instead of forked. The head has a crest of narrow linear feathers, instead of a short, broad, and full one.

CICHLOPSIS NITENS, Baird.

Ptilogonys nitens, SWAINSON, Anim. in Menag. 2¼ Cent. 1838, 285.—BONAP. Consp. 1850, 335.—HEERMANN, J. A. N.
　　　　　Sc. II, Jan. 1853, 263.—CASSIN, Illust. I, 1854, 169 ; pl. xxix.
Lepturus galeatus, LESSON, Rev. Zool. 1849, 4 .
" *Hypothymys nitens*, LAFR. "

Sp. Ch.—Head with an elongated occipital crest. Exposed portion of spurious quill about half the length of the second, which equals the secondaries ; sixth quill longest. Tail graduated. Male throughout of a uniform lustrous black, glossed with green. Inner webs of the primaries white, except at the base, tips, and margins. Female, ash color, paler beneath ; the quills, wing, and lower tail coverts and outer tail feathers edged with whitish ; rest of tail feathers blackish. Length of male, 7.75 ; wing, 3.90 ; tail, 4.30.

Hab.—Valley of Gila and southern Colorado to upper Rio Grande ; west to Fort Tejon ; east to Coahuila, Mexico.

There is some difference in the size of specimens, one from the Colorado desert being considerably smaller than 3964 from Coahuila. The female has the crest rather less conspicuous than the male.

List of specimens.

Catal. No.	Sex.	Locality.	When collected.	Whence obtained.	Orig. No.	Collected by—	Length.	Stretch of wings.	Wing.
	♀	Fort Tejon, Cal	....	J. X. DeVesey...	......	....	....	....	......
8273	♀	Fort Yuma...........	Nov. 25......	Major Emory....	27	A. Schott........	....	....	......
8281	....	Camp 120 N. Mexico.	Feb. 12, 1854	Lt. Whipple	96	Kenn. and Möll..	7.00	11.00	5.00
8282	....	Camp 113 N. Mexico.	Feb. 5, 1854	......do.........	69	.......do........	....	....	......
8279	....	Fort Yuma..	....	Major Emory....	......	A. Schott........	....	....	......
8274	♀	Colorado desert......	....	Lt. Williamson..	......	Dr. Heermann ..	....	....	......
8275	♂	......do........	....	......do........	......	......do........	... .	....	......
4591	....	Gila river, N. M.....	....	Major Emory....	27	A. Schott........	....	....	......
8280	....	Los Nogales, Mex....	....	......do........	......	Dr. Kennerly ...	....	....	......
4592	♀	Gila river, N. M.....	....	......do........	22	A. Schott	....	....	......
4564	....	Cook's well, Cal.....	....	......do........	21	......do........	....	....	......
8276	....	Mimbres to Rio Grande	....	Dr. Henry......	......	....	....	....	......
3964	♂	Coahuila, Mex......	....	Lt. Couch	......	....	....	....	......

MYIADESTES, Swainson.

Myiadestes, SWAINSON, Naturalist's Library. Flycatchers, 1838. Type *Muscicapa armillata*, Vieill.

Ch.—Head not crested. Bill rather narrower than the length of the culmen ; much depressed ; somewhat attenuated at the end ; lateral outline rather concave. Tarsi without feathers above or scutellae ; shorter than the middle toe. Hind toe rather shorter than the outer lateral toe, which barely reaches the base of the middle claw. Tail and wings very long; the former shorter, quite deeply forked, but the outer lateral feather abruptly graduated, and a little longer than the innermost ; the feathers all broad at the base, and tapering to the tip. Spurious primary nearly one-fourth the longest, (third ;) the second a quarter of an inch less than the longest.

This genus differs from *Ptilogonys* in having the bill narrower and much more depressed ; the culmen nearly straight to the decurved tip ; the nostrils smaller. The tarsus is without scutellae or feathers. The wings are much longer, more pointed, and much less graduated. The tail well forked, and the lateral feathers is graduated ; all broader at the base, and tapering towards the end.

I describe this genus from *M. townsendii*, which belongs to it according to Cabanis, not having a specimen of the type at hand. Its affinities are with *Ptilogonys* and *Cichlopsis* in many respects. It differs in the tarsi without scales, the very short first, and the long second primary, &c. In many respects it has relationship with the *Turdidae*, but I am not sufficiently familiar with exotic forms of the last mentioned family to come to any conclusion at present on the subject.[1]

MYIADESTES TOWNSENDII, Cabanis.

Townsend's Flycatcher.

Ptilogonys townsendii, Aud. Orn. Biog. V, May, 1839, 206 ; pl. 419, f. 2.—Ib. Syn. 1839, 46.—Ib. Birds Amer. I,
    1840, 243 ; pl. 69.—Townsend, Narrative, 1839, 338.—Nuttall, Man. I, 2d ed. 1840,
    361.—Gambel, Pr. A. N. Sc. I, 1843, 261.
Culicivora townsendii, DeKay, N. Y. Zool. II, 1844, 110.
Myiadestes townsendii, Cabanis, Wiegm. Arch. 1847, i, 208.
? *Myiadestes unicolor*, Sclater, Pr. Zool. Soc. 1856, 299 ; 1857, 5. (Is very closely allied. Cordova, Mexico)

Sp. Ch.—Tail rather deeply forked. Exposed portion of spurious quill less than one-third that of the second ; fourth quill longest ; second a little longer than the sixth. Head not crested. General color bluish ash, paler beneath ; under wing coverts white. Quills with a brownish yellow bar at the base of both webs mostly concealed, but showing a little below the greater coverts and alulae ; this succeeded by a bar of dusky, and next to it another of brownish yellow across the outer webs of the central quills only. Tertials tipped with white] Tail feathers dark brown ; the middle ones more like the back ; the lateral with the outer web and tip, the second with the tip only, white. A white ring round the eye.

Length, 8 inches ; wing, 4.50 ; tail, 3.85. (8234.)

Hab.—United States from Rocky Mountains and Black Hills to the Pacific ; south to the borders of Mexico.

In the series of specimens before me I can find none marked male ; they all, however, agree very well in color, and it is probable that there is but little difference in the sexes.

In some specimens there is a white bar across the ends of the greater wing coverts.

In an immature specimen (8899,) from the Black Hills, the tarsus is distinctly scutellate, but the external scales appear thin and very deciduous. It is quite possible that this species forms no exception to the rule of the family in respect to the possession of scutellate tarsi, but that the scutellae peel off in time, leaving a continuous plate beneath.

This species is referred by Bonaparte, Cabanis, and other authors to the *Myiadestes obscurus* of Lafresnaye. This is, however, a different bird, though closely allied, having a brownish olive wash on the back and wings not seen in *townsendii*, and showing only very faintly the rusty yellowish bases of the quills. The bill is broader and heavier, but the size, as shown in the table of comparative measurements, is considerably smaller.

The *M. unicolor* of Sclater, (Pr. Zool. Soc. 1856, 299, Cordova, Mexico,) is more nearly allied, but is smaller, and appears to lack the rusty yellowish bases of the quills.

[1] Since writing the preceding paragraph I have detected scutellae in a young *M. townsendii*, which peeled off at touch, leaving the tarsi smooth. This fact, therefore, shows the separation from the other genera to be not so great as was supposed.

List of specimens.

Catal. No.	Sex.	Locality.	When collected.	Whence obtained.	Orig. No.	Collected by—	Length.	Stretch of wings.	Wing.
8285	♀	Ft. Steilacoom, W. T.		Dr. Suckley			8.75	12.87	4.50
2922		Colorado river		S. F. Baird		J. K. Townsend			
4451		California		Lt. Williamson		Dr. Newberry			
8286		Near Zuñi		Lt. Whipple		Kenn. and Möll	8.00	13.00	
8287		90 miles west of Albuquerque		....do		......do	8.00	11.50	4.00
8283		Mimbres to Rio Grande		Dr. Henry					
8900		Laramie Peak	Aug 24	Lt. Warren		Dr. Hayden	9.50	14.00	5 00
8234		Fort Laramie	Oct. 5, 1857	Dr. J. G. Cooper	216		8 00	13.25	4.50
8899		Black Hills	Sept. 15	Lt. Warren		Dr. Hayden	8.00	13.75	4.25

Family LANIIDAE.

Bill strong and compressed, the tip abruptly hooked ; both mandibles distinctly notched, the upper with a distinct tooth behind, the lower with the point bent up. Tarsi longer than the middle toe, strongly scutellate Primaries ten ; first primary half the second, or shorter, (occasionally wanting.)

The typical species of this family are provided with a bill almost as formidable as that of the Qaptores themselves. There are many sub-families in various parts of the world, only two of which, however, are found in the United States.

An exception to the usual rule in the *Oscines* is seen in the *Laniinae*, where the lower part of the sides of the tarsi behind is divided into scutellae. In *C. borealis* this same character extends over the whole of the outer side of the tarsus, but not on the inner.

The sub-families of *Laniidae* belonging to the United States are as follows :

LANIINAE.—Bill very powerful, much compressed, and abruptly hooked, with a very prominent tooth behind the notch. Wings considerably rounded. Tail rather long and graduated. Sides of the tarsi scutellate behind.

VIREONINAE.—Bill moderate, cylindrical, somewhat compressed. Wings long, the first primary sometimes wanting. Tail short and nearly even. Sides of the tarsi behind not scutellate.

COLLYRIO, Moehring.

Collyrio, MOEHRING, Genera Avium, 1752, 28. Type *Lanius excubitor*, L.
Lanius, of AUTHORS.

Feathers of forehead stiffened ; base of bill, including nostrils, covered by bristly feathers directed forward. Bill shorter than the head, much compressed, and very powerful. Culmen decurved from base, the mandible abruptly bent down in a powerful hook, what in acute lobe near the tip. Tip of lower mandible bent upwards in a hook ; the gonys very convex. Rictus with long bristles. Legs stout ; the tarsi are rather short, longer than the middle toe ; the lateral equal ; the claws all very sharp and much curved. Wings rounded; the first primary about half the second, which is equal to the sixth or seventh. Tail longer than the wings, much graduated, the feathers broad.

As already stated, the. posterior lateral sides of the tarsus inferiorly exhibit two or three small plates, while in *C. borealis* these occupy the entire outer side, corresponding in number and position with the anterior ones. The inner lateral plate, however, is undivided, except at the lower end.

It is with great reluctance that I adopt another name instead of *Lanius* for the present genus ; but a strict adherence to the law of priority renders this necessary. The genus *Lanius* was first used by Linnaeus in the tenth edition of the Systema Naturae, (1758,) with *L. cristatus* as the type. The twelfth edition has as its type of *Lanius* the *L. forficatus*, now *Edolius forficatus*. According to the rules of synonymy, the name must be kept for the species with which it was first used, which in this case was *L. cristatus*, a form which is not represented in North America.

The name of Moehring is next in order and is based by him on the *"Falconis species"* of the first edition, 1735, and the *Ampelidis species"* of the sixth edition of the Systema Naturae, 1748, genus 78. This has for its type the *Lanius excubitor* of subsequent editions, and includes also the American species. To G. R. Gray is due the merit of first restoring for this, as well as many other names of Moehring, the priority to which they are entitled.

The following is a synopsis of the North American species:

Common characters.—Color above bluish ash. Beneath white ; scapulars whitish along the wing. A black patch from the bill through and behind the eye. A white patch at the base of the primaries, and on the tips of the secondaries. All the tail feathers, except the median, tipped with white, and with a basal patch of the same.

A.—Distinctly banded beneath. Black of eye stripe interrupted below the eye by a white crescent. No black at the base of the bill above.

Above soiled light bluish ash. Upper tail coverts, forehead, and side of crown hoary.
C. borealis.

B.—Uniform white (or very obsoletely banded in the young) beneath. A continuous patch through the eye from the bill. A narrow frontal line of black.

Above dark bluish slate. Forehead, sides of crown, and upper tail coverts nearly uniform with the back..*C. ludovicianus.*

Above light bluish ash. Forehead, sides of crown, and upper tail coverts, hoary white, the latter sometimes glossed with ashy.................................... *C. excubitoroides.*

Comparative measurements of species.

Catal. No.	Species.	Locality.	Sex.	Length.	Stretch of wings.	Wing.	Tail.	Tarsus.	Middle toe.	Its claw alone.	Bill above.	Along gape.	Specimen measured.
907	Collyrio borealis......	Carlisle, Pa............	......	9.20	....	4.36	4.88	1.02	0.83	0.30	0.60	1.10	Dry......
do.	........do............	......do	......	9.83	14.50	4.50	......	......	......	......	......	......	Fresh....
7196	........do............	Shoalwater bay, W. T.	......	9.80	....	4.58	4.88	1.02	0.82	0.30	0.58	1.02	Dry......
do.	........do............	......do............	......	10.75	14.50	......	......	......	......	......	......	......	Fresh....
3054	Collyrio ludovicianus.	Liberty Co., Ga......	......	8.50	....	3.72	4.24	1 04	0.86	0.30	0.62	0.92	Dry......
3050	........do............	......do............	♀	8.20	....	3.76	4.42	1.06	0.86	0.26	0.62	0.92	Dry......
do.	........do............	......do............	......	8.80	12.00	3.75	......	......	......	......	......	......	Fresh....
10172	Collyrio excubitoroides	Marion Co., Illinois..	♂	8.80	....	3.92	4.26	1.05	0.86	0.26	0.63	0.92	Dry......
8720	........do............	Fort Yuma, Cal......	.....	8.64	....	4.08	4.58	1.06	0.86	0.30	0.63	0.92	Dry......

COLLYRIO BOREALIS, Baird.

Great Northern Shrike; Butcher Bird.

Lanius septentrionalis, Bon. Syn. 1828, 72.—Bon. List, 1838.—Ib. Rev. et Mag. Zool. 1853, 294.—Nuttall, Man. I, 1832, 258.—Ib. I. 2d ed. 1840, 285. (Not of Gmelin.)

Lanius borealis, Vieillot, Ois. Am. Sep. I, 1807, 90 ; pl. l.—Sw. F. B. Am. II, 1831, 111.—Aud. Syn. 1839, 157.— Ib. Birds Amer. IV, 1842, 130 ; pl. 236.

Lanius excubitor, Forster, Phil. Trans. LXII, 1772, 382.—Wilson, I, 1808, 74 ; pl. v. f. 1.—Bon. Obs. 1826 —Aud. Orn. Biog. II, 1834, 534 ; pl. 192.

Sp. Ch.—Above light bluish ash, obscurely soiled with reddish brown. Forehead, sides of the crown, scapulars, and upper tail coverts hoary white. Beneath white, the breast with fine transverse lines. Wings and tail black ; the former with a white patch at base of primaries and tips of small quills ; the latter with the lateral feathers tipped with white. Bill blackish brown ; considerably lighter at the base. Black stripe from the bill through and behind the eye, but beneath the latter interrupted by a whitish crescent. *Female* and young with the gray soiled with brownish. Length, 9.85 ; wings, 4.50 ; tail, 4.80 ; its graduation .90.

Hab.—Northern regions from Atlantic to Pacific ; in winter south, through most of the United States.

Upper parts of head and body pure clear bluish ash, soiled in the slightest possible manner ; changing on the rump and scapulars to ashy white ; nearly pure white on the outer edge of the latter, behind. Tips of upper coverts like the back. Forehead, and a stripe from the nostrils over and a little behind the eye, purer whitish and more distinct behind. Spot in front of the eye, narrow ring round it, (interrupted above by the superciliary band,) a narrow line from the side of the mandible beneath the eye, and widening behind it so as to include the ear coverts, the wings and tail black. A whitish crescent immediately below the eye. Lesser wing coverts like the back. Tips of the tertiaries and secondaries, the outer webs of the longer primaries at the base, as also the inner webs opposite the same point, and the terminal portion of the four lateral tail feathers, white ; the entire outer web of the exterior also white, except a narrow strip along the basal portion of the shaft ; the extent of the white tip decreasing from about 1.50 inches on the exterior, to about .35 on the fourth. Under parts generally soiled white ; the feathers on the breast and belly in each faintly marked with two or three narrow crescentic bars of blackish, scarcely appreciable on the throat, and not at all on the abdomen and under coverts.

Younger or more immaturely plumaged birds, and perhaps the females generally, have the upper parts more or less soiled with a wash of rufous brown, the bands beneath more distinct, and extending further forward to the bill ; this rufous sometimes tinges the sides, the rump, the under parts, and the back of the head. A rufous tinge is very decided in nearly all the specimens from the upper Missouri and westward, which are also apparently a little larger than in those from Pennsylvania and New York. It is possible that the former may be a distinct though closely allied species.

The *Lanius septentrionalis* of Gmelin, (Syst. Nat. I, 1788, 306,) based on the Northern Shrike of Latham, (Syn. I, i, 165,) from the northern parts of America, cannot, by any possibility, be referred to the present species. The first distinctive name is that of Vieillot, who apparently describes a female.

List of specimens.

Catal. No.	Sex.	Locality.	When collected.	Whence obtained.	Collected by—	Length.	Stretch of wings.	Wing.	Remarks.
907	....	Carlisle, Pa..............	Nov. —,1842	S. F. Baird............	....	9.10	14.50	4.50	....
540	....	Eastern United States....	Jan. —,1841	......do........	....	....	....	....	....
7199	....	Ohio	....	J. P. Kirtland.....	....	....	....	....	....
4552	♂	Fort Pierre, N. T	Oct. 21,1855	G. K. Warren........	....	....	....	....	....
7195	....	St. Mary's, R. mountains.	Oct. 10,1853	Gov. Stevens	Dr. Suckley.......	11.37	14.75	4.75	....
7197	....	Fort Vancouver, W. T...	Feb. —,——	......do........	Dr. Cooper........	....	....	....	....
7196	....	Shoalwater bay..........	Nov. 18,1854	......do........	......do..........	10.75	14.50	....	Iris brown.......
7198	....	........do..............	....	......do........	......do..........	....	....	....	....

COLLYRIO LUDOVICIANUS, Baird.

Loggerhead Shrike.

Lanius ludovicianus, LINN. Syst. Nat. I, 1766, 134.—IB. GMELIN, I, 1788, 298.—BON. Syn. 1828, 72.—IB. List, 1838.—IB. Consp. Av. 1850, 363.—IB. Rev. et Mag. Zool. V, 1853, 294.—NUTTALL, Man. 1. 261.—AUD. Orn. Biog. I, 1831, 300 : V, 1839, 435 ; pl. 37.—IB. Syn. 1839, 72.—IB. Birds Amer. IV, 1842, 135 ; pl. 237.—? BREHM, Cabanis, Journ. II, 1854, 145. (Not of Latham, whose bird has a black crown.)

Lanius ardosiaceus, VIEILLOT, Ois. Am. I, 1807, 81 ; pl. li.—BON. Obs. Wils. 1825, No. 34.

Lanius carolinensis, WILSON, Am. Orn. III, 1811, 57 ; pl. xxii, f. 5.—LICHT. Verzeichniss, 1823, No. 505.

Louisiana shrike, LATHAM, Syn. I, i, 162.

SP. CH.—Above dark pure bluish ash ; forehead, sides of crown, and upper tail coverts scarcely paler. Scapulars whitish. Beneath plain whitish. Wings and tail black ; the former with a white patch at base of primaries and tips of lesser quills ;

the latter with the lateral feathers broadly tipped with white ; but this color restricted at the base. A continuous black stripe from the bill through and behind the eye. Length, 9.00 ; wing, 3.90 ; tail, 4.20.

Hab.—South Atlantic and Gulf States.

No. 3054 is above rather dark slate blue, almost or quite inappreciably lighter on the rump, the outer scapulars shading behind into whitish on their outer webs. Beneath clear white, purest on the throat ; the sides of the body almost to the median line tinged with bluish ash, much lighter than the back ; the feathers of the breast with the most obsoletely possible indications of narrow transverse bars. The wings and tail are black ; the primaries all white at the base, forming a conspicuous patch ; the secondaries and tertials tipped with the same. The outer four tail feathers tipped with white, (the first for an inch ;) this color extending along the outer web, most so in the outer, where it occupies it almost entirely. The forehead is inappreciably lighter than the crown, which, however, is bordered laterally from the bill to above the eye with whitish. The side of the head, including the border of the upper jaw, the lores, region round the eye, and the ear coverts behind it, black. Axillaries dark plumbeous.

There is some difference in specimens as to the color of the scapulars. Occasionally these are whiter than as described, forming a conspicuous band along the black of the wing, almost from the bend. The upper tail coverts are sometimes of a slightly paler ash than the back, but never whitish ; the difference always very slight. There is frequently no trace whatever of bars on the breast. The axillaries, too, are sometimes for the most part white, sometimes dark ash.

The female is of duller plumage than the male. The young is lighter gray above than the adult; more or less tinged with brown; all the feathers waved obscurely and finely with dusky. The under parts are white, waved obscurely with dusky on the breast and sides.

The unbanded white color beneath, and the continuous black stripe through the eye, as well as the smaller size, distinguish this species from the Northern Shrike, (*C. borealis.*)

List of specimens.

Catal. No.	Sex and age.	Locality.	When collected.	Whence obtained.	Collected by—	Length.	Stretch of wings.	Wing.
3053	o	Georgia ----------	1846--------	S. F. Baird -------	W. L. Jones ------	8.00	11.50	3.70
2420	o	Savannah, Ga.-----	1845--------	------do----------	------do----------	8.80	12.50	3.80
2419	--------	------do----------	1845--------	------do----------	------do----------	--------	--------	------
3050	♀	Liberty county, Ga.	1846--------	------do----------	Jos. L. Leconte ----	8.83	12.00	3.75
3054	--------	------do----------	1846--------	------do----------	------do----------	--------	--------	------

COLLYRIO EXCUBITOROIDES, Baird.

White-rumped Shrike.

Lanius excubitoroides, SWAINSON, F. Bor. Am. II, 1831, 115.—GAMBEL, Pr. A. N. Sc. III, 1847, 200.

SP. CH.—Above rather light pure bluish ash. Forehead, sides of crown, scapulars, and upper tail coverts, hoary whitish Beneath plain whitish. Wings and tail black; the former with a white patch at base of primaries and tips of small quills; the latter with the lateral feathers tipped with white, and this extending broadly at the base. Bill throughout pitch black. A continuous black stripe from the bill through and behind the eye. Length, 8.75 or 9 inches; wing, 3.95; tail, 4.35.

Hab.—Missouri plains and fur countries to Pacific coast. Eastward into Wisconsin, Illinois, and Michigan.(?)

Head and body above ashy blue, the forehead slightly hoary; the lower part of rump and upper tail coverts, with the outer scapulars, almost white. Beneath pure white without bands; the sides very slightly touched with ashy. Wings and tail black; the primaries with a band of white at the base, showing externally as a patch in the wing; the white extending obliquely a little further on the inner than the outer web. The tertiaries and secondaries are paler on the outer portion of the inner web towards the base, but not abruptly white. The secondaries, tertials, and inner primaries tipped with white. All the feathers of the tail, except the innermost, are tipped with white, the amount diminishing from the exterior; the outer feather is, in fact, entirely white, except a patch an inch long on the inner web covered by the tail coverts, and there is a white patch at the base of all the others, except the middle. A narrow band on the forehead, including the feathers along the base of the bill, and passing backwards over the lores, eyes, and auriculars, black, this color involving the upper eyelid. This is bordered above by a hoary tinge in the gray of the crown.

The young differ chiefly in a strong tendency to waved, dark lines in the plumage of the upper and under surfaces. There is also a decided indication of reddish brown in the ground color. The female is smaller, and sometimes has the under mandible paler at the base.

This species is similar in appearance to *C. ludovicianus*, but differs in several points. The ash of the upper parts is decidedly lighter, the rump generally almost white, instead of nearly like the back. The white at the base of the tail feathers is much more extended, reaching within half an inch or less of the tips of the coverts. There is also a good deal of white on the secondaries, visible from below, not seen in *ludovicianus*.

In a large series of specimens I find differences, which, however, I can scarcely consider as specific. There is some variation in the ground color, but this is almost always lighter than in *C. ludovicianus*. The hoary tinge on the forehead and alongside the crown is sometimes entirely wanting; and in the most strongly marked specimen (from Presidio) the under parts are strongly tinged with ash. The amount of black on the outer tail feather is sometimes but little more than in *ludovicianus*. Sometimes the black band across the base of the bill is distinctly visible, at others it is wanting, leaving the hoary bluish of the head.

The specimens before me from Wisconsin and Michigan are all immature and not well characterized; I am, however, inclined to refer them to *C. excubitoroides*. An adult, No. 10172, however, from south Illinois, is exceedingly like specimens from the plains, except that the rump is not quite so whitish.

In the collection of the Philadelphia Academy is a shrike collected in California by Dr. Gambel, which exhibits some peculiarities. The ash color above is darker than in *excubitoroides*, and there is no hoary on the forehead and sides of the crown at all. The tail coverts are very nearly the color of the back, not whitish. The black of the sides of the head extends further down, to a point as far from the eye as this is from the tip of the lower mandible. The under parts are more bluish on the sides. There is a white patch on the inner web of the secondaries at the base, which extends nearer the margin along the inner towards the tip, and is distinctly and sharply visible from above. In *excubitoroides* this is seen on the under surface only ; in *ludovicianus* not at all. The most striking difference is in the much larger bill, which measures .75 of an inch in a straight line from base above to point, instead of .60. The nostril is .60 of an inch from the tip, not .46. This bird has been referred to *L. elegans* of Swainson,[1] but seems to differ in some appreciable points.

The *Lanius mexicanus* of Brehm, (Cabanis' Journal, II, March, 1854, 145,) though similar to the *excubitoroides*, yet appears to differ specifically both from this and *elegans*. *Lanius nootka* (Gmelin, I, 309) has not been identified in later times. It evidently is not a true shrike, however.

List of specimens.

Catal. No.	Sex.	Locality.	When collected.	Whence obtained.	Orig'l No.	Collected by—	Length.	Stretch of wings.	Wing.	Remarks.
10172?	♂	Marion county, Ill.		R. Kennicott						
1664		Michigan...		S. S. Haldeman..						
3782		Racine, Wisconsin....		Dr. Hoy......						
8722		...do......		S. F. Baird			8.62	12.50	4.00	
7512	○	Independence, Mo....		Wm. M. Magraw.		Dr. Cooper ..				
8904	♂	Upper Missouri	Aug. 19, 1857	Lieut. Warren...		Dr. Hayden..	8.50	12.50	4.00	Iris brown. ......
8902	♂	......do...............	...do......	......do........		...do......	8.25	12.25	4.00	Iris light brown...........
5312		Yellowstone...	Aug. 22, 1856	......do........		...do......				
4649		White river	May 8, 1855	Col. Vaughan....		...do......				
8703	♂	Running Water	Aug. 16, 1857	Lt. G. K. Warren.		...do......	9.00	13.50	4.00	Iris dark gray............
8901	♂	......do...............	...do......	......do........		...do......	9.00	12.50	3.75	......do............
8795		15 miles E. of Laramie.	Aug. 26, 1857	Wm. M. Magraw.	168	Dr. Cooper ..	9.25	12.50	4.00	Iris brown, bill bl'k, feet gray
8779	♀	Forks of Platte river...	Aug. 13, 1857	......do......	150	.... do......	8.50	12.00	4.00	
8247		Fort Laramie..........	Sept. —, 1857	......do........		...do......				
8214		......do...............	Sept. 9, 1857	......do........	196	......do......	9.25	12.25	4.00	
8248		......do...............	...do......	......do........		...do......				
7001		North Fork of Platte R.	Aug. 1, 1857	Lieut. Bryan	372	W. S. Wood...				
5065		Crossing of Pecos river.	July 7, 1855	Capt. Pope	105	....	10.00	11.00	4.00	
8718		San Elizario, Texas...	Dec. 15......	Maj. Emory.		J. H. Clark..	9.50	11.00	3.50	Eyes brown, gums light blue.
8716		El Paso, Texas		......do........		...do......	12.25	9.00	4.12	
5066		Dona Aña, N. M.	Nov. 14, 1855	Capt. Pope	159					Bill, feet, and eyes black...
8717		Mimbres to Rio Grande.		Dr. Henry......						
4190	♂	Charco Escondido, N. M.	Mar. —, 1853	Lieut. Couch			8.50	11.00	4.00	Eyes dark brown, feet lead..
8715		Camp 130, N. M.......	Feb. 23, 1854	Lieut. Whipple ..		Kenn & Müll..				
5503	♂	Petaluma, Cal.........	Mar. —, 1856	E. Samuels......						
5505	♀	...do...............	May —, 1856	......do........	743					
8721		Presidio, Cal.........		Lt. Trowbridge...						
5947		Santa Clara, Cal......		Gov. Stevens....		Dr. Cooper ..				
5939		......do...............		...do........		...do......				
4940		San José, Cal.......		A. J. Grayson...	12					
8719	♂	Tulare valley		Lt. Williamson...		Dr. Heermann				
		Fort Tejon		J. X. de Vesey...						
4572		Gila river, N. M.......		Maj. Emory. ...		A. Schott				
8720		Fort Yuma, Cal.......		......do........	25	.do......				

[1] LANIUS ELEGANS, S w .—White-winged Shrike.

Lanius elegans, Sw. F. B., A. II, 1831, 122.—NUTTALL, Man. I, 2d ed. 1840, 287.—GAMBEL, Pr. A. N. Sc. I, 1843, 261.—BONAP. Rev. et Mag. Zool. V, 1853, 295.

Clear bluish gray beneath unspotted white, with a frontlet of the same color with the head ; a broad white band across the wing ; a slender and very cuneiform tail, entirely bordered with white ; the second quill feather longer than the sixth, the fourth the longest ; and tarsi exceeding the length of the bill, (measured from the angle of the mouth.)

Sub-Family VIREONINAE.

The characters of the *Vireoninae*, as already given, will serve to distinguish them from the other North American *Laniidae*. The bill, though slenderer and more cylindrical, has the same abrupt and lengthened hook at the tip.

The association of *Icteria* with *Vireo*, as made by most ornithologists, appears to me highly unnatural, its place being more appropriately among the *Sylvicolidae*.

VIREO. Vieill.

Vireo, VIEILL. Ois. Am. Sept. I, 1807, 83. Type *Muscicapa noveboracensis*, Gm.

CH.—Bill short, strong, straight; the culmen slightly curved; the sides much compressed to the tip, which is rapidly curved and deflected; the gonys long and ascending; the gape with short weak bristles; the nostrils basal, rounded, and exposed, the feathers of the head advancing forward on the bill to the nostril. Wings variable, rather long, and pointed; the first quill sometimes spurious, the larger outer one always graduated a little. Tail nearly even, and rather short. Tarsi longer than the middle toe. Outer toe a little longer than the inner; hind toe rather shorter than the middle one.

I have found it very difficult to arrange the North American *Vireos* satisfactorily by dividing into *Vireo* and *Vireosylvia*, according as there is a spurious first primary or none. This character, though strongly marked, combines species which otherwise appear quite dissimilar, and separates some which seem very closely related. Thus *Vireo gilvus* and *philadelphicus* are in some stages of plumage hardly to be distinguished, except by the spurious primary of the former; while the *V. flavifrons*, without this spurious primary, is in other essentials very near *noveboracensis* and *solitarius*, which possess it.

In the difficulty of establishing any trenchant lines of distinction, I have concluded to consider all the species as *Vireo,* and to divide them into the following sections:

VIREOSYLVIA.—Bill long, rather slender, light horn color. Wings long; no spurious primary. Body slender. Top of the head plumbeous, very different from the back, bordered by a line of black.

> *V. olivaceus, flavoviridis, altiloquus, virescens.* Type *V. olivaceus.*

VIREO.—Bill shorter, rather slender, light horn color, (except in *atricapillus*.) Wings shorter. First primary spurious, except in *philadelphicus*. Body slender. Top of the head scarcely different from the back, (except in *atricapillus*.)

> *V. philadelphicus, gilvus, belli, atricapillus.* Type *V. gilvus.*

LANIVIREO.—Bill rather stout and short, dark plumbeous in color. Wings moderate. Body stout. First primary spurious, except in *flavifrons*.

> *V. noveboracensis, huttonii, solitarius, cassini, flavifrons.* Type *V. flavifrons.*

The following synopsis, though its arrangement is not perfectly natural, may yet aid in a ready identification of the species:

A. NO SPURIOUS QUILL.

Crown ash colored, very different from the neck, bordered on each side by a dusky line within a white superciliary one. No black line on the side of the throat, except in *altiloquus*.

Nearly pure white beneath; the under tail coverts with the faintest tinge of sulphur. First and fourth quills nearly equal...*V. olivaceus.*

Sides greenish yellow; under tail coverts bright gamboge yellow. First quill longer than the fifth and sixth...*V. flavoviridis.*

42 b

Somewhat like *olivaceus*. A short black line on each side the chin...........*V. altiloquus*.

Sides yellowish green ; under tail coverts greenish yellow. First and sixth quills nearly
    equal, the former much shorter than the fifth....................................:. *V. virescens*.

Head scarcely, or not at all, different from the back. No dusky line on the sides of the
crown.

    Above dull olive, tinged with ash on the head. Beneath yellowish white. A white
        superciliary line ....*V. philadelphicus*.

    Bright olive green above; throat and breast yellow; belly white; rump ashy...*V. flavifrons*.

B. FIRST QUILL SPURIOUS ; EXPOSED PORTION ABOUT ONE-FOURTH OF THE SECOND.

Bill stout ; color above olive ; beneath white. A ring round the eye, extending to the bill,
two bands on the wing, and edges of inner secondaries white. Outer tail feathers margined
with white all round ; first primary one-fourth the second.

    Top and sides of head sharply defined ash gray ; beneath pure white, abruptly tinged
        with greenish yellow on the sides and on the under tail coverts..............*V. solitarius*.

    Top and sides of head faintly defined brownish olive ; beneath tinged with pale fulvous.
        Sides obscurely tinged with yellowish green......................................*V. cassinii*.

Bill slender. No white on the wings.

    Above dull olive, tinged with ashy on the crown. Sides brownish white........*V. gilvus*.

C. FIRST QUILL SPURIOUS ; EXPOSED PORTION ABOUT TWO-FIFTHS OF THE SECOND.

Back olive. Beneath white, tinged with yellow on the sides.

    Top of head ashy olive, little different from the back....................................*V. belli*.

    Top of head pure black..*V. atricapillus*.

D. FIRST QUILL SPURIOUS ; EXPOSED PORTION ABOUT ONE-HALF OF THE SECOND.

Above olivaceous. Two white bands on the wings.

    Forehead with sides of the head and breast strongly tinged with yellow...*V. noveboracensis*.

    No decided yellow on the head or sides of body......................................*V. huttonii*.

Comparative measurements of the species.

Catal. No.	Species.	Locality.	Sex.	Length.	Stretch of wings.	Wing.	Tail.	Tarsus.	Middle toe.	Its claw alone.	Bill above.	Along gape.	Specimen measured.
1418	Vireo olivaceus.........	Carlisle, Pa.........	♂	5.52	....	3.28	2.46	0.73	0.66	0.13	0.54	0.80	Dry.......
do..	....do...........	..... do........... ..		6.33	10.25	3.33	......						Fresh....
1440	........do......	......do.............	♀	5.22	....	3.04	2.28	0.68	0.60	0.18	0 48	0.70	Dry......
do..	........do.......	......do.............		6 00	9 75	2.16	......						Fresh....
3976	Vireo flavoviridis.........	Monterey, Mexico...	♂	5.90	....	3.12	2.66	0.70	0.56	0.16	0.58	0.78	Dry.......
do..	........do	........do......		5,75	9 75	3.25	......						Fresh....
8050	Vireo virescens.........	Guatemala...........		5.50	....	2.70	2.40	0.70	0.56	0.16	0.50	0.72	Dry.......
	Vireo altiloquus..........	Florida.............		5.20	....	3.20	2 50	0.70	0.62	0.20	0.60	0.87	Mounted..
4333	Vireo philadelphicus.....	Dane county, Wis....		4.70	....	2.56	1.92	0.66	0.57	0.17	0.33	0.64	Dry......
988	Vireo gilvus.............	Carlisle, Pa.........	♂	5.04	....	2.76	2.28	0.70	0.52	0.16	0.46	0.68	Dry......
do..	.....do..............	.. ...do.............	♂	5.33	8.91	2.83	......						Fr sh....
1017	........do...........	......do.............	♀	4.80	....	2.72	2.22	0.64	0.53	0.16	0.40	0.60	Dry......
do..	........do...........	......do.............		5.33	8.83	2.83	......						Fresh...*
5521	........do. var. swainsoni.	Petaluma, Cal.......	♂	4.64	....	2.71	2.40	0.68	0.54	0.16	0.40	0 60	Dry.......
do..	........do...........	......do.............		5.25	6.08	2.25	......						Fresh....
1926	Vireo belli..,....	Fort Union.........		4.30	....	2.18	1.90	0.74	0.52	0.16	0.30	0.55	Dry.......
8197	........do...........	Nemaha, K. T.......	♂	4.26	....	2.16	1.94	0.73	0.54	0.18	0.40	0.58	Dry.......
do..	........do...........	......do.............		4.87	6.87	2.37	......						Fresh....
8187	........do.......	Shawnee Mission,K T.	♂	4.20	....	2.20	2.00	0.72	0.56	0.16	0.42	0.58	Dry.......
do..	........do...........	......do.............		5.00	7.25	2.50	......						Fresh....
6818	Vireo atricapillus........	San Pedro..........		4.12	....	2.16	1.92	0.75	0.56	0 17	0.44	0.55	Dry.......
do..	........do......	......do.............		4.75	7.25	2.12	......						......
3725	Vireo huttoni............	California		4.70	....	2.40	2.16	0.74	0.52	0.16	0.40	0.54	Dry.......
10229	Vireo cassinii...........	Fort Tejon, Cal.....		4.78	....	2.74	2.28	0.74	0.62	0.20	0.47	0.58	Dry.......
10193	Vireo noveboracensis.....	Union county, Ill....		4.82	....	2.44	2.18	0.74	0.62	0.16	0.47	0.57	Dry.......
929	Vireo solitarius	Carlisle, Pa.........	♀	5.00	....	2.84	2.30	0.70	0.63	0.18	0.42	0.59	Dry... ..
do..	........do...........	......do.............	♀	5.41	9.00	2.41	......						Fresh.....
300	........do...........	......do.............	♂	5.30	....	2.90	2 30	0.69	0.62	0.18	0.44	0.69	......
do..	........do...........	......do.............		5.41	9.00	.....							Fresh.....
2591	Vireo flavifrons........ .	......do.............	♂	4.80	....	3.00	2.00	0.73	0.63	0.16	0.50	0.66	Dry.......
do..	........do...........	......do.............		5.83	9.75	3.16	......						Fresh.....
2217	........do........... ...	....do.............	♀	4.83	....	3.08	2.36	0.72	0.64	0.18	0.48	0.60	Dry.......
do.	........do...........	. ....do.............		5.33	9.50	3.16	......						Fresh.....

VIREO OLIVACEUS, Vieill.

Red-eyed Flycatcher.

Muscicapa olivacea, LINN. Syst. Nat. I, 1766, 327.—GM. I, 1788, 938.—WILSON, Am. Orn. II, 1810, 55 ; pl. xii, f. 3.

Lanius olivaceus, LICHT. Verzeich. 1823, 49, No. 525.

Vireo olivaceus, "VIEILLOT," BON. Obs. Wilson, 1826, No. 124.—SW. F. B. A. II, 1831, 233.—NUTTALL, Man. I, 1832, 312.—AUD. Orn. Biog. II, 1834, 287 : V, 430 ; pl. 150.—IB. Syn. 1839, 162.—IB. Birds Amer. IV, 1842, 155 ; pl. 243.

Vireosylvia olivacea, BON. Geog. & Comp. List, 1838.—IB. Consp. 1850, 329.—REINHARDT, Vid. Med. f. 1853, 1854, 82.

Phyllomanes olivaceus, CAB. Mus. Hein. 1850-'51, 63.

Red-eye flycatcher, PENNANT, CATESBY, LATHAM.

SP. CH.—Second and third quills about equal, and longest ; first a little shorter than the fourth, but considerably longer than the fifth. Back, rump, and edges of wing and tail feathers, bright olivaceous green. Side of head and neck paler. Crown dark ash, sharply defined. A well defined whitish line from the bill over the eye, nearly to the occiput ; a dark line separating it above from the ashy crown. A dusky line through the eye. Beneath white ; under tail coverts pale sulphur yellow. Length, about 6.50 inches ; wing, 3.50. Iris red.

HAB.—Eastern United States to the Missouri ; in Texas to Devil's river ; south to Guatemala. Greenland, (Reinhardt.)

This is among the largest of the North American *Vireos*, and is of very plain colors. The bill is long and nearly straight to the abruptly curved tip. There is no spurious primary ; the second quill is longest; the third, fourth, and first, successively, shorter. The tail is slightly emarginate; the lateral feathers very little shorter. The ash color of the crown does not extend beyond the occiput. The sides of the head and neck are lighter olivaceous than the back. The space around the lower eyelid is very little paler. The sides of the body are light olivaceous green; the under wing coverts and axillaries sulphur yellow. There are no whitish edgings whatever on the wings and tail; externally they are margined with the green of the back; the inner margins of the tail feathers similar, but lighter. There is no indication of a line of black feathers on each side of the chin.

Specimens from Texas are smaller, but otherwise similar. The female is smaller than the male.

There is a slight difference in the colors of the under tail coverts. These, sometimes, are almost entirely white, at other times with decided tinge of greenish yellow, as in 7570. In no North American specimens before me, however, are there any of the characters of *Vireo bartramii*, as given by Swainson. The proportions of the quills vary somewhat; the first quill sometimes equal to and sometimes a little shorter than the fourth, but it is always decidedly longer than the fifth. The second and third quills are generally nearly equal; the former is sometimes the longer.

List of specimens.

Catal. No.	Sex.	Locality.	When collected.	Whence obtained.	Orig. No.	Collected by—	Length.	Stretch of wings.	Wing.
1418	♂	Carlisle, Pa	May 1, 1844	S. F. Baird			6.33	10.25	3.33
1435	♂	....do	May 3, 1844	....do			6.50	10.50	3.50
1440	♀	....do	....do	....do			6.00	9.75	2.17
4325		Calcasieu, La		G. Wurdemann					
6847		Rockport, Ohio		J. P. Kirtland					
5650		Kansas		Lt. Bryan		W. S. Wood			
7510		Independence, Mo		Wm. M. Magraw.	74	Dr. Cooper	6.25	9.90	3.50
7511		....do		....do	106	....do	5.90	9.60	3.00
6814		Western Texas		Capt. Pope					
6815		....do		....do					
6813	♂	Devil's river, Texas		Col. J. D. Graham	16	J. H. Clark	6.00	9.50	2.75
8049		Guatemala		J. Gould					

VIREO FLAVOVIRIDIS, Cassin.

Vireosylvia flavoviridis, Cassin, Pr. A. N. Sc. V, Feb. 1851, 152.—Ib. VI; pl. ii. (Panama.)

Sp. Ch.—Second and third quills decidedly longest—equal; first about intermediate between fourth and fifth, but considerably longer than the latter. Above very light yellowish green. The sides of the body greenish yellow, in strong contrast to the almost pure white of the under parts. The under tail and wing coverts and axillaries bright sulphur yellow. Crown ash color, bordered on either side by a brown line, below which is a bluish gray line from the bill over the eye to the side of the occiput; a dusky line from the bill through and behind the eye. Length, 6 inches; wing, 3.25.

Hab.—Northeastern Mexico to Panama.

This species is of the same size with and somewhat similar to *V. olivaceus*, but may be readily distinguished by the much brighter and more sulphur green colors of the upper parts; the strongly marked greenish yellow of the sides in strong contrast to the white, which, on the breast, is only half an inch wide ; the bright sulphur yellow of the under wing instead of very pale sulphury white ; the color of the tail coverts is also characteristic. The whitish line over the eye has a much grayer cast.

The resemblance to *V. virescens* is closer than to *olivaceus;* it is, however, considerably larger ; the dark and light lines over the eye less sharply defined. The shade of green above is much the same in both. The under parts, from bill to vent, are purer white and more strongly marked against the greenish yellow not yellow green sides. The under wing and tail coverts are bright sulphur yellow, without any tinge of green. The quills are very different.

As in *V. olivaceus*, *virescens*, *philadelphicus*, and *flavifrons*, this species has no spurious primary.

The specimens are marked as having the iris yellow ; the bill lead color.

List of specimens.

Catal. No.	Sex.	Locality.	Whence obtained.	Length.	Stretch of wings.	Wing.	Remarks.
3776	♂	Monterey, Mex.	Lieut. Couch.	5.75	9.75	3.25	Eyes yellow, bill and feet lead.
3977	♂	....do............	......do............	6.00	9.25	3.25	Bill slate, feet lead............

VIREO VIRESCENS, Vieillot.

Bartram's Vireo.

? *Vireo virescens*, VIEILL. Ois. Am. Sept. I, 1807, 84 ; pl. liii.
?? *Sylvia chivi*, VIEILL. " Encyclop. 437"—Nouv. Dict. XI, 1817, 174.
? *Phyll anes chivi*, CABANIS, Mus. Hein. 1850–'51, 63.
Lan. s agilis, LICHT. Doubl. 1823, No. 526.
T amnophilus agilis, SPIX, Av. Bras. II, tab. xxxiv, f. 1.
Phyllomanes agilis, BURM. Th. Bras. Vögel, II, 1856, 108.
Vireo bartramii, SW. F. B. Am. II, 1831, 235.—?? AUD. Orn. Biog. V, 1839, 296 ; pl. 434, f. 4.—IB. Syn. 1839, 161.—
IB Birds Amer. IV, 1842, 153 ; pl. 242.—NUTTALL, Man. Orn. I, (2d ed) 1840, 358.

SP. CH.—Second, third, and fourth quills about equal ; first intermediate between fifth and sixth decidedly shorter than the former. Smaller than *V. olivaceus*. Above bright olive green. Crown ash. A greenish white line from the bill over the eye to the side of the occiput, bordered by a dark brown line above. A dusky line from the bill through and behind the eye. Under parts whitish ; the sides strongly yellowish green ; the under tail coverts greenish yellow. Length, 5.25 ; wing, 2.75.

Hab.—Central and eastern South America ; Atlantic United States?

The specimen before me comes from Brazil, and may, possibly, not be the true *V. bartramius*, although resembling it very closely. The bill is gently curved from the base, not so straight in its upper outline as in *olivaceus*. The second and third quills are longest; the fourth scarcely shorter ; the first considerably shorter than the fifth. There is no spurious primary.

This species is smaller than *V. olivaceus*, but very similar. The colors are much brighter green, however. The ash of the nape has a browner tinge. The light line over the eye is narrower, and more greenish white than white ; the dark line above it more distinctly marked. The white of the under parts is more restricted, and the strongly marked yellow olive of the sides is scarcely seen in *V. olivaceus*. The under coverts and inner edges of the tail feathers are much deeper greenish yellow. The sides of the neck and outer margins of the wings and tail are purer olive greenish.

The upper outlines of the bill is considerably more curved. The first primary is a good deal shorter. The tail feathers are more acuminate, the inner webs slightly concave at the ends.

The differences most strongly insisted on by Swainson are in the wings, which here are shorter and more rounded; the first quill considerably shorter instead of decidedly longer than the fifth.

Specimens labelled *Phyllomanes chivi*, (*Lanius agilis*, Licht.) by Cabanis, and received from him, appear precisely the same in every respect.

This species, if found in the United States, is certainly very rare. I have never seen a specimen, nor do I know of any preserved in any cabinet. It is not impossible, but, on the contrary, very likely, that the "young bird" mentioned by Swainson as found on the banks of the Columbia may have been the *V. gilvus* which occurs there, and which was otherwise unknown to the author. The description is made from his Brazilian specimen.

It is quite difficult to say which is the proper name of the present species, before ascertaining whether more than one species be contained in the synonymy quoted above. The descriptions of neither *V. virescens* nor *chivi* contain any positive specific indications, while *agilis* seems unquestionably the same with the *bartramius*, of Swainson, from Brazil, and in any event will have priority over it.

List of specimens.

Catal. No.	Locality.	Whence obtained.
2034	Brazil	Jas. Taylor
10174	Southern Brazil	Dr. J. Cabanis
10173	Bahia	do
8050	Guatemala	J. Gould

VIREO ALTILOQUUS, Gray.

Whip Tom Kelly.

Muscicapa altiloqua, VIEILL. Ois. Am. Sept. I, 1807, 67; pl. xxxviii.

Vireo altiloquus, GRAY, Genera.—GAMBEL. Pr. A. N. Sc. IV, 1848, 127. (Florida.)

Vireosylvia altiloqua, BONAP. Consp. 1850, 330.—CASSIN, Pr. A. N. S. V, Feb. 1851, 152.—IB. Ill. N. Am. Birds, I, 1853, 8 and 221, pl. xxxvii.

Vireo longirostris, Sw. F. Bor. Am. II, 1831, 237.—NUTTALL, Man. I, 2d ed. 1840, 359.

? *Phyllomanes mystacalis*, CABANIS, Ornith. Not. in Wiegmann's Archiv, 1847, I, 348.

? *Vireosylvia olivacea*, GOSSE, Birds Jam. 1847, 194.

? *Vireosylvia frenata*, DUBUS, Bull. Acad. Belg. XXII, I, 1855, 150.

SP. CH.—Very similar to *V. olivaceus*, but with a short dusky maxillary line. Bill longer.

Hab.—The coast of Southern Florida and the West Indies.

This species is very similar to the *V. olivaceus* in the olivaceous upper parts, and ashy crown bordered on each side by a darker shade along the whitish superciliary stripe; the plumbeous stripe from the bill through and behind the eye; the under parts white, with a faint tinge only of yellow on the under tail coverts, and a stronger tinge of olivaceous on the sides. There is, however, in addition to this, a narrow line of dusky ash or plumbeous, continuous with the under side of the rami of the lower jaw, and extending back as far as the somewhat similar stripe through the eye does. The tail is nearly even; the second quill appears to be the longest The bill is decidedly longer and stouter than that of *V. olivaceus*, measuring above about .61 of an inch instead of .54. It is also narrow towards the end. The size, however, is considerably less, the wings being a quarter of an inch shorter. The ash of the crown is not so well defined.

The *Phyllomanes barbatulus* of Cabanis, from Cuba, (Journal für Ornithologie, 1855, 467,) is very closely allied to the present bird.

VIREO PHILADELPHICUS, Cassin.

Vireosylvia philadelphica, Cassin, Pr. A. N. Sc. Phila. V, Feb. 1851, 153.—Ib. VI ; pl. i, f. 1, Philadelphia.

Sp. Ch.—Without any spurious primary. Second and third quills longest ; fourth a little shorter ; first about .20 of an inch shorter than second, and about equal to the fifth. Above dark olive green, slightly inclining to ashy on the crown ; beneath pale sulphur yellow, brightest on the throat and breast. A white line from the bill over the eye, and an obscure white spot below it. A dusky line from the commissure through and behind the eye. Length about 5 inches ; wing, 2.75 ; tail, 2.10 ; tarsus, .65 .

Hab.—Pennsylvania to Wisconsin.

This rare species resembles very closely in size and general appearance the *V. gilvus*, especially those with a decidedly yellow tinge beneath. It will be, however, at once distinguished by the absence of the spurious primary. The under parts are very strongly sulphur yellow instead of almost white ; the upper are darker and purer green ; the markings about the head are better defined. The bill is smaller.

List of specimens.

Catal. No.	Sex.	Locality.	When collected.	Whence obtained.
4364	_____	Cleveland, Ohio _____	_____	Dr. Kirtland_____
4333	_____	Dane county, Wis____	1854_____	T. M. Brewer. _____
4334	_____	_____do_____	1854_____	_____do_____
6842	_____	_____do_____	_____	_____do_____
6841	♂	_____do_____	_____	Th. Thumlien_____

VIREO GILVUS, Bonap.

Warbling Flycatcher.

Muscicapa gilva, Vieillot, Ois. I, 1807, 65 ; pl. xxxiv.
Vireo gilvus, Bonap. Obs. Wilson, 1825, No. 123.—Nutt. I, 1832, 309.—Aud. Orn. Biog. II, 1834, 114: V. 1839, 433 ; pl. 118.—Ib. Birds Amer. IV, 1842, 149 ; pl. 241.
Muscicapa melodia, Wilson, Am. Orn. V, 1812, 85 ; pl. 42, fig. 2.

Sp. Ch.—Third, fourth, and fifth quills nearly equal ; second and sixth usually about equal, and about .25 of an inch shorter than third ; the exposed portion of spurious quill about one-fourth the third. Above greenish olive ; the head and hind neck ashy, the back slightly tinged with the same. Lores dusky ; a white streak from the base of the upper mandible above and a little behind the eye ; beneath the eye whitish. Sides of the head pale yellowish brown. Beneath white, tinged with very pale yellow on the breast and sides. No light margins whatever on the outer webs of the wings or tail. Length about 5¼ inches ; wings nearly 3. Spurious primary one-fourth the length of second.

Hab.—Atlantic to Pacific coast of the United States.

In this species the bill is slender ; nearly straight to the tip, which is suddenly deflexed. The spurious primary is very short and slender ; its exposed portion about one-fourth that of the second quill. The third quill is longest; the fourth and fifth successively a little shorter; the second a little longer than the sixth, about .25 of an inch shorter than the third, much longer than the secondaries. The tail is slightly emarginate and rounded.

The contrast between the ashy of the head and the ashy olive is very little marked, the colors not separated by any well defined line. The white stripe on the side of the head is not well defined; anteriorly it has a yellowish tinge; the dusky of the lore is not very decided. The dusky of the lore is continued through, and a little behind the eye. The sides of the neck along the throat have rather more yellowish in their brown. There is a brownish tinge in the yellowish on the side of the body. The under tail coverts are faintly tinged with yellowish.

Specimens vary a little in the amount of yellow beneath, which, however, very seldom becomes conspicuous; it is usually brightest on the abdomen.

This species is readily distinguished from all the other American *Vireos* with spurious first primary, by the plain colors and absence of pale margins to the outer webs of the quills. Some *Vireosylvas* have no more white in the wings, but these lack the spurious primary.

While all the specimens of *Vireo gilvus* from the Eastern States have the proportions of the quills nearly as described, all from the Pacific coast (five) agree in having the wings more rounded, the third and fourth about equal, the fifth a little shorter, the second about equal to, or only a little longer than the seventh, .15 of an inch shorter than the sixth, and .30 shorter than the third. The bill is smaller, more depressed, and darker above. It is probably to a specimen of this bird that Swainson alludes in his article on *Vireo bartramii*, as having been taken on the Columbia river by Douglass, but immature and injured by insects. The proportions of the quill are the same, if the spurious quill be taken into the account, which would advance his numbers by one throughout, (second and seventh about equal instead of first and sixth, &c.) The description, however, is really based on the Brazilian specimen referred to, which is entirely distinct.

Should the western specimens really prove distinct, they may appropriately bear the name of *Vireo swainsonii*.

List of specimens.

Catal. No.	Sex.	Locality.	When collected.	Whence obtained.	Orig. No.	Collected by—	Length.	Stretch of wings.	Wing.	Remarks.
1017	♀	Carlisle, Pa	May 21,1843	S. F. Baird			5.33	8.83	2.83	
988	♂	...do...	May 19,1843	...do...			5.33	8.92	2.88	
1082	♂	...do...	May 21,1843	...do...			5.67	9.25	2.92	
1016	♂	...do...	May 24,1843	...do...			5.42	9.17	2.83	
1237		Philadelphia, Pa	May —,1843							
10115	♂	Washington, D. C		J. C. McGuire						
4729	♂	Missouri river	May 9,1857	Lieut. Warren... ..		Dr. Hayden	5	9	3	Iris dark brown....
5305	♀	Fort Lookout	June 15,1856	...do...	.. ..		4.75	8	2.50	Eyes black.........
6825		Mimbres to Rio Grande.		Dr. Henry						
6826		Steilacoom		Gov. Stevens		Dr. Suckley				
5915		...do...		...do...		Dr. Cooper	5.00	8.50		
6824		...do...		...do...	96	Dr. Suckley				
5521	♂	Petaluma, Cal	May —,1856	E. Samuels	747		5.25	6.08	2.25	

VIREO BELLI, Aud.

Bell's Vireo.

Vireo belli, Aud. Birds Amer. (8vo.) VII, 1844, 333 ; pl. 485, (Missouri.)—Cassin, Pr. A. N. Sc. V, Feb. 1851, 150.

Sp. Ch.—Similar to *V. gilvus*, but smaller. Olive green above, tinged with ashy on the top and sides of head. A short line from the bill over the eye, and region around lower eyelid white ; lores dusky. Beneath yellowish white ; on the sides of body and posteriorly, sulphur yellow. Two faint bars of whitish across the wing coverts ; inner tertiaries edged broadly with whitish. Third quill longest ; the rest successively shorter, except the second, which is a little shorter than the seventh. Spurious primary about two-fifths the second, and more than one-third of the third. Length about 4.25 inches; wing, 2.25.

Hab.—Missouri river and eastern Texas.

In this diminutive species the bill is shaped much as in *V. gilvus*. The spurious primary is large, its exposed portion about two-fifths that of the second primary. The third primary is longest ; then the fourth, fifth, and sixth ; the second is a little longer than the seventh, and about .24 of an inch shorter than the third. The tail is slightly emarginate and rounded ; the feathers are quite narrow.

The sulphur yellow is strongest about the tibia and on the under tail coverts. The whitish bands are along the edges of the greater and middle coverts. The outer web of the first tail feather is, however, not lighter than the rest.

Specimens vary somewhat, the more southern ones being rather smaller. Sometimes there is a faint tinge of brown on the breast, and of lilac in the white of the belly. There is a tinge of yellow on almost all the under parts. The third quill is sometimes a little shorter than the fourth. This species is a miniature of *V. gilvus,* but may be readily distinguished by its smaller size, by the much larger spurious primary, the exposed portion of which is two-fifths of that of the second quill, instead of one-fourth. The sides of the belly and under tail coverts are bright, though pale, sulphur yellow, instead of faint sulphury white. The white bands on the wing and that on the tertiaries are absolutely wanting in *V. gilvus*. The external edging to the quills and tail feathers is of a brighter olive green.

List of specimens.

Catal. No.	Sex.	Locality.	When collected.	Whence obtained.	Orig. No.	Collected by—	Length.	Stretch of wings.	Wing.	Remarks.
6816	......	Western Texas.......	....	Capt. Pope.......	......	....	....	....	....	....
6817	♂	..... do.............	....	Col. J. D. Graham.	....	J. H. Clark...	4.50	7.	2.	....
4979	......	Fort Chadbourne, Tex.	....	Dr. Swift	......	....	....	....	....	....
8197	♀	Nemaha river, K. T..	July 16, 1857	W. M. Magraw...	133	Dr. Cooper...	4.90	6.90	2.38	Iris brown ; bill brown ; feet blue.
8196	♂	......do.............	.....do......	......do.........	132	... ..do......	5.00	7.50	2 50	....
8187	♂	Shawnee Mission, K.T.	July 4, 1857	......do.........	123	......do.....	5.00	7.00	2.38	....
1926	......	Fort Union, Nebraska.	1843	S. F. Baird.......	......	J. J. Audubon	....	....	....	....

VIREO ATRICAPILLUS, Woodh.

Black-headed Flycatcher.

Vireo atricapillus, Woodhouse, Pr. A. N. Sc. VI, Ap. 1852, 60, San Pedro, Tex.—Ib. Sitgreave's Report on Zuñi, 1853, 75 ; pl. i, Birds.—Cassin, Ill. I, No. 5, 1854, 153 ; pl. xxiv.

Sp. Ch.—Fourth and fifth quills longest ; second little longer than secondaries. Head and neck above and on the sides black. Back olive green, lighter towards the tail. Beneath white, the sides of body greenish yellow. A white ring round the eye interrupted by the black of the head above, and extending in a broad line to the base of the upper mandible. Two bands of greenish white across the wing coverts. Bill black. Length, 4.75 ; wing, 2.12.

Hab.—Devil's river, Texas.

43 b

In this species the spurious quill is about half as long as the longest primary, both measured from the carpal joint. The fourth and fifth quills are longest ; the third and sixth but little shorter ; the second but little longer than the secondaries, and about .26 of an inch shorter than the third quill.

The bill is slender for a *Vireo*, broad at base, and considerably depressed. The tail feathers are narrow, rounded at the end ; the tail very slightly rounded. The quills and tail feathers are edged externally like the back. The bill appears black, the feet lead color. In its black head this differs so decidedly from any other North American species as to render any comparisons unnecessary.

The only specimens of this species hitherto collected were taken at the same time on the San Pedro or Devil's river, of Texas, by J. H. Clark and Dr. S. W. Woodhouse.

List of specimens.

Catal. No.	Sex	Locality.	Whence obtained.	Orig. No.	Collected by—	Length.	Stretch of wings.	Wing.
6818	♂	San Pedro river, Texas	Col. J. D. Graham	21	J. H. Clark	4.75	7.25	2.12

VIREO NOVEBORACENSIS, Bonap.

White-eyed Vireo.

Muscicapa noveboracensis, GM. Syst. Nat. I, 1788, 947.
Vireo noveboracensis, BON. Obs. Wilson, 1825, No. 122.—AUD. Orn. Biog. I, 1831, 328: V, 431, 433 ; pl. 63.—IB. Birds Am. IV, 1842, 146 ; pl. 240.—NUTT. Man. I, 1832, 306.—GOSSE, Birds Jam. 1847, 192.
Vireo musicus, VIEILL. Ois. Am. Sept. I, 1807, 83 ; pl. 52.
Muscicapa cantatrix, WILSON, Am. Orn. II, 1810, 266 ; pl. 18.
Green flycatcher, PENNANT, Arc. Zool. II, 389, 274.

SP. CH.—Spurious primary about half the second, which is about equal to the eighth quill. Entire upper parts bright olivaceous green ; space around the eyes and extending to the bill greenish yellow, interrupted by a dusky spot from the anterior canthus to the base of the gape. Beneath white ; the sides of the breast and body well defined, almost gamboge, yellow. Edges of greater and middle wing coverts (forming two bands) and of inner tertiaries greenish yellow white. Iris white. Length, 5 inches ; wing, 2.50.

Hab.—Eastern United States to the Missouri and throughout Texas.

The bill is short, thick, and curved, shaped like that of *V. solitarius*. The spurious first primary is large and linear; its exposed portion is half that of the second quill, and about two-thirds the length of the same quill, both measured from the carpal joint. The fourth quill is longest ; the fifth and third successively a little shorter ; the second is about .35 of an inch shorter than the third. The tail is slightly emarginate and rounded.

On the front of the head the olivaceous lightens into a yellowish tinge. The sides of the neck are olivaceous, tinged with ashy, which also occasionally glosses the olivaceous of the back. The yellow on the sides of the breast sometimes exhibits a tendency to meet in the middle. The tips of some feathers on the sides are olive green. The under wing coverts and axillaries are sulphur yellow. The bill is black, the cutting edges abruptly horn white.

One specimen (3972) from Brownsville, Texas, is marked as having the iris black instead of white.

List of specimens.

Catal. No.	Sex.	Locality.	When collected.	Where obtained.	Orig'l No.	Collected by—	Length.	Stretch of wings.	Wing.	Remarks.
1036	♂	Washington, D. C......	May 26, 1843	S. F. Baird.......	......	Wm. M. Baird.	5.00	8.00	2.50	....
1094	♀	......do..............	June 12, 1843	......do	......	......do.......	5.12	9.75	2.50	....
499	....	Chester county, Pa.....		......do	......	....	......	......	......	....
10193	♂	Union county, Ill	April 21, 1857	N. W. University.	......	R. Kennicott ..	......	......	......	....
3972	......	Brownsville, Tex.......		Lt. Couch.......	......	....	4.50	6.50	2.12	Eyes black; bill dark slate...
6837	♂	Western Texas... .... \........		Col. Graham.....	7	J. H. Clark	5.00	7.50	2.25	....
6836	......	Mimbres to Rio Grande.		Dr. Henry.......	....	....	.. ....	......	......	....

VIREO HUTTONI, Cassin.

Hutton's Flycatcher.

Vireo huttoni, CASSIN, Pr. A. N. Sc. Phila. V, Feb. 1851, 150.—IB. VI, pl. i, f. 1.

SP. CH.—Fourth, fifth, and sixth quills about equal and longest; third and seventh equal, and .10 of an inch shorter; second quill not longer than secondaries; spurious primary large, broad, about half the second. Above olive green, becoming considerably darker towards the bill and on sides of head. Beneath dirty greenish white, tinged with greenish yellow posteriorly. A paler ring round the eye. Two broad bands across the wing coverts and edges of inner tertiaries, with greater portion of outer web of the outer tail feather greenish or olivaceous white. Length about 4.75 inches; wing, 2.35.

Hab.—South California, across by valley of Gila, to northeastern Mexico.

The yellowish ring round the eye is very narrow. The space between the upper edge of the eye and the bill is yellowish, but not well defined. The rest of the sides of head and neck are dark olivaceous, like the back. There is no white whatever in the under parts or elsewhere, the lightest tints beneath being yellowish, with a brownish tinge. The sides of the body are olivaceous yellowish.

This species differs from *V. gilvus* in its large first primary, the whitish bands and edgings of the wings and tail, and in the more olivaceous colors generally. It is of rather smaller size. It is about the same size as *V. noveboracensis*, but has a much more slender bill, which is horn color instead of blue black; it lacks the vivid yellow on the forehead and in front of the eye; the head is darker; the outer tail feather paler on its outer edge. It lacks the pure white of the throat and the vivid contrast in color between the sulphur yellow of the sides and the whitish of the middle of the body. Both species have concealed whitish on the rump. It is larger than *V. belli*, although the bill is the same size; it has the sides of the head and neck much darker; there is more whitish on the wing and outer tail feather; the inferior colors are much browner, with less of the vivid sulphur yellow.

The differences between the present species and the closely allied *V. cassinii* will be pointed out in the description of the latter species.

List of specimens.

Catal. No.	Sex.	Locality.	When collected.	Whence obtained.	Length.	Stretch of wings.	Wing.	Remarks.
3725	....	Monterey, Cal....	------------	W. Hutton	-------	-------	-------	---------------------
3724	....	......do..........	June —, 1847	......do........	-------	-------	-------	---------------------
3973	♂	Monterey, Mex....	------------	Lt. Couch	4.25	7.50	2.25	Eyes dark brown; bill and feet lead color.

VIREO SOLITARIUS, Vieillot.

Blue-headed Flycatcher.

Muscicapa solitaria, WILSON, Am. Orn. II, 1810, 143; pl. 17, f. 6.
Vireo solitarius, VIEILL. Nouv. Dict. 1817.—AUD. Orn. Biog. 1, 1831, 147 : V, 1839, 432; pl. 23.—IB. Syn. 1839.—
     IB. Birds Amer. IV, 1842, 144; pl. 239.—NUTT. Man. I, 1832, 305.

SP. CH.—Spurious primary very small, not one-fourth the second, which is longer than the sixth. Top and sides of the head and upper part of neck dark bluish ash ; rest of upper parts clear olive green. A white ring round the eye, interrupted in the anterior canthus by a dusky lore, but the white color extending above this spot to the base of the bill. Under parts white ; the sides under the wings greenish yellow. Two bands on the wing coverts, with the edges of the secondaries, greenish white. Outer tail feather with its edge all round, including the whole outer web, whitish. Length about 5½ inches ; wing, 2.40.

Hab.—United States from Atlantic to the north Pacific, (Washington Territory only ?)

In this species the bill is short, broad, and much curved above. The spurious quill is very short and narrow ; the exposed portion less than half an inch ; less than half the second quill (both measured from the carpal joint) by .30 of an inch. The third quill is longest ; the fourth very little shorter ; the second about .30 of an inch shorter than the third and considerably shorter than the fifth, but much longer than the secondary quills.

The white rings round the eye are not continuous anteriorly ; the extensions of the upper portions to the base of the bill are separated on the forehead by a very narrow interval. The whitish margin to the quills is seen only on the two innermost feathers. The bands on the wing cross the ends of the greater and middle coverts. The wing and tail feathers, except as described, are margined with the color of the back. The back is sometimes tinged with ashy. The under tail coverts are tinged with sulphur yellow. The feathers on the sides of the body are yellow towards the base ; the tips olive green ; lighter than the back.

List of specimens.

Catal. No.	Sex.	Locality.	When collected.	Where obtained.	Orig. No.	Collected by—	Length.	Stretch of wings.	Wing.	Remarks.
741	......	Carlisle	Sept. 20,1842	S. F. Baird........	......	....	......	......	......	....
303	♂	.....do	April 22,1841	.....do	......	....	......	......	......	....
784	.....	.....do	Oct. 7,1842	.....do	....	....	5.50	9.25	......	....
929	♀	.....do	April 28,1843	.....do	......	....	5.41	9.00	2.41	....
300	♂	.....do	April 21,1841	....do	......	....	5.41	9.00	......	....
		Illinois		R Kennicott.......	......	....	......	......	......	....
4727	......	Mouth of Vermilion....	May 6,——	Lt. Warren........	......	Dr. Hayden........	......	......	......	....
4728	......	.....do	May 5,——	.....do	......	....do	5.50	9.00	3.12	Iris reddish hazel.....
5916	......	Ft. Steilacoom, W. T...	May, 1855	Gov. Stevens.......	......	Dr. Cooper.........	5.25	9.00	......	....
6819	......	.....do	May 3,1856	Dr. Suckley.......	357	....	5.75	9.00	......	....
6824	......	.....do	... .	Gov. Stevens.......	126	Dr. Suckley	......	......	......	....
6821	♀	.....do		....do	......	....do	......	......	......	....
6822	♂	.....do	May 13,1856	Dr. Suckley........	382	....	5.50	9.00	......	Iris hazel............
6823	♂	....	May 30,1856	.....do	358	....	5.12	8.25	3.00	....

VIREO CASSINII, De Vesey.

Cassin's Vireo.

Vireo cassinii, DE VESEY, Pr. A. N. Sc. Phila. May, 1858.

SP. CH.—Third and fourth quills nearly equal, fifth shorter, second longer than seventh. Spurious primary very narrow, falcate acute ; less than one-third the second quill, and a little more than one-fourth the third. Above, including edges of wing and tail feathers, clear olive green, becoming dusky ashy on the top and sides of head. Beneath fulvous white, tinged with ill-defined olive green on the sides, (scarcely on the crissum.) Two broad bands on the wing coverts and the outer edges of the innermost secondaries greenish white ; the outer edge of outer tail feather, with a broad ring round the eye, extending to a rontal band, dull white. Length about 5 inches ; wing, 2.75 ; tail, 2.30. Hab.—Fort Tejon, Cal.

The outer primaries are edged externally with grayish white ; the inner and secondaries with yellowish green, (extending fully to the lower wing band,) which gradually changes to broad yellowish white on the innermost quills. The under parts are white, tinged with fulvous, least so on the chin and abdomen. The sides are yellowish olive, lighter than the back, and fading gently into the brownish white under parts ; the under tail coverts have only a trace of greenish. The quills and tail feathers are dark brown ; the outermost of the latter edged externally with white on half the web. The ring round the eye is much broader above than below ; the lores and feathers at the base of the bill also dull whitish.

This species bears so close a relationship to *Vireo huttoni*, Cassin, as to render it quite difficult to distinguish them apart by color alone. The size, however, is considerably greater, the bill much larger, the culmen and commissure much more curved and more equably, the gonys straighter. The most striking difference is in the wing, which is much more pointed ; the primaries .70 of an inch longer than the secondaries, instead of about .45. The spurious primary is very slender and short, not one-third the second, instead of large, broad, and nearly half the second. The second quill is about equal to the sixth, instead of not longer than the secondaries.

The colors are much the same ; the under parts with less olive, none on the breast and under tail coverts, as in *huttoni*. The ring round the eye has none of the greenish yellow tinge of the latter species. The olive green edgings of the secondaries extend to the lower wing band, instead of ceasing below it, leaving a dusky spot.

This species is about the size of *V. noveboracensis*, and has a somewhat similar bill, but larger. The wings are much longer and more pointed, the spurious quill smaller. There is nothing of the sharply defined light greenish yellow of the sides and ophthalmic and frontal region. The outer tail feather is edged with white.

In external form the relationship is closest to *V. solitarius*, which has the wing almost precisely similar. It, however, lacks the pure white of the chin and throat, the clear ash of the top and sides of the head, and the bright, sharply defined light greenish yellow of the sides of body and the under tail coverts. The white bands on the wings, too, are much broader.

List of specimens.

Catal. No.	Locality.	Whence obtained.	Orig. No.	Collected by—
10229	Fort Tejon, Cal.	J. Xantus de Vesey	479	

VIREO FLAVIFRONS, Vieill.

Yellow-throated Flycatcher.

Vireo flavifrons, VIEILL. Ois. Am. I, 1807, 85 ; pl. liv.—AUD. Orn. Biog. II, 1834, 119 : V, 428; pl. 119.—IB. Syn.—IB. Birds Am. IV, 1842, 141 ; pl. 238.

Muscicapa sylvicola, WILS. Am. Orn. II, 1810, 117; pl. vii, f. 3.

SP. CH.—No spurious quill ; the first and fourth equal. From bill to middle of back, sides of head, neck, and fore part of breast olive green ; beneath, from bill to middle of belly, with a ring round the eyes, sulphur yellow. Lores dusky ; rest of under parts white ; of upper, ashy blue, tinged with green. Two white bands on the wing ; tertiaries edged with white, other quills with greenish; outer tail feathers edged with yellowish white ; the outer web of first feather entirely of this color, except near the end. Length, nearly 6 inches ; wing, 3.20.

Hab.—Eastern United States to the Missouri ; south to Central America.

Second and third quills longest ; first and fourth about equal, and almost .20 of an inch shorter.

List of specimens.

Catal. No.	Sex.	Locality.	When collected.	Whence obtained.	Orig. No.	Collected by—	Length.	Stretch of wings.	Wing.	Remarks.
2216	♂	Carlisle, Pa...........	May　3, 1845	S. F. Baird........	......	....	5.50	10.00	3.25	....
2591	♂	.....do................	May　6, 1846	......do..........	.....	....	5.83	9.75	3.16	....
3397	♂	.....do.......	May　7, 1847	......do..........	......	....	......	......	....	....
2217	♀	.....do................	May　3, 1845	......do..........	......	....	5.33	9.50	3.16	....
7571	....	Washington, D. C.	....	W. Hutton........	......	....	......	......	....	....
7423	....	Cleveland, Ohio	....	Dr. Kirtland.......	......	....	......	......	....	....
		Union co., Illinois	....	R. Kennicott	......	....	......	......	....	....
8342	♂	Independence	June 13, 1857	Wm. Magraw......	67	Dr. Cooper	5.12	8.25	2.75	Iris brown; bill and feet lead color.
8340	♂	.....do................	.....do.......	..... do........	65	.....do.....	5.50	9.00	3.00	......do...........
8048	....	Guatemala	....	John Gould.......	......	....	......	......	....	....
9113	♂	Coban................	....	M. Verreaux	32614	....	......	......	....	....

Family LIOTRICHIDAE.

Wings short, concave, and rounded, the outer four or five primaries graduated ; the first usually more than half the second. Tarsi long and generally very strongly scutellate ; the basal joint of the middle toe free nearly to the base internally, and half way externally. Bill slender, straight or curved, generally as long as or longer than the head ; but little notched, or not at all.

This extensive family embraces many forms highly varied in character, and distributed originally very widely in ornithological systems. The credit of rearranging these in a natural series is, in a great measure, due to Dr. Cabanis.

The following sub-families are included in the North American species of this family :

MIMINAE.—Tail long, vaulted at the base ; the feathers more or less graduated. Size large ; general appearance Thrush-like. Rictus with distinct bristles. Frontal feathers normal, directed backwards. Anterior half of outer side of tarsi distinctly scutellate.

CAMPYLORHYNCHINAE.—Size medium. Tail feathers broad, plane ; tail rounded ; rictus without bristles.

TROGLODYTINAE.—Size very small. Tail graduated, convex above. Rictus without bristles.

CHAMAEANAE.—Size small. Tail very greatly graduated, much longer than the wings. Rictus with long bristles ; frontal feathers bristly, directed forward. Whole outer side of tarsi continuous and undivided.

Sub-Family MIMINAE.

The *Miminae* are all of large size, and, as already stated, have a Thrush-like appearance, which has caused them to be placed by most authors among the *Turdidae*. From these, however, they are readily distinguished by the usually much longer, or decurved bill, the short and graduated wings, the long graduated tail, and the strongly scutellate legs. The frontal feathers, and,' to a certain extent, the loral, are all soft, compact, and, like the rest, without any inversion or extension into bristly points. As in the wrens (but not in *Chamaea*,) the entire anterior half of the tarsi is embraced by a succession of scutellae which bend round to the middle of the sides, where their lateral margins are distinctly defined.

It is very difficult to draw the line between this sub-family and the wrens ; the chief difference lies in the larger size and bristled gape. The nostrils are round or broadly oval, with but little of a membrane above them, such as is seen in the wrens, where the nostrils are more linear.

Of the subdivisions of this group, *Mimus* has a bill shorter, or not longer than the head, and distinctly notched ; while in *Harporhynchus* and its sub-genera the bill is longer, more decurved, and without notch. *Oroscoptes* differs from both in the longer and more pointed wings, and much less graduated tail.

MIMUS, Boie

Mimus, BOIE, Isis, Oct. 1826, 972. Type *Turdus polyglottus.*
Orpheus, SWAINSON, Zool. Jour. III, 1827, 167. Same type.

CH.—Bill shorter than the head, decurved from the base ; distinctly notched at tip. Tarsi longer than the middle toe ; lateral toes equal, not reaching the base of the middle claw, and shorter than the hind toe, the claw of which is half the total length. Tail variable ; equal to or longer than the wings, moderately graduated. Wings rounded ; the exposed portion of the first nearly or quite half that of the second, which is considerably shorter than the third.

This genus is distinguished from *Harporhynchus* by the shorter bill, (less than the length of the head,) and with a more distinct notch. The lower jaw is smooth, without the distinct longitudinal ridges seen in most of the species of *Harporhynchus*.   The tail is less graduated and shorter ; the feet appear less stout ; the wings are rather longer.

The sub-genera are as follows :

MIMUS.—Culmen much curved from the base.   Wings considerably shorter than the tail, which is a good deal graduated.   First primary half the second.

Olive gray above ; beneath whitish ; wings and tail black; the base of primaries and the tips of the tail white...*polyglottus*.

GALEOSCOPTES.—Much like *Mimus*.   Wings a little shorter than the tail.

Plumbeous, paler beneath ; crissum brownish orange.   Top of head and tail blackish brown...*carolinensis*.

Comparative measurements of species.

Catal. No.	Species.	Locality.	Sex.	Length.	Stretch of wings	Wing.	Tail.	Tarsus.	Middle toe.	Its claw alone.	Bill above.	Along gape.	Specimen measured.
3867	Mimus polyglottus......	Louisiana	......	9.16	....	4.30	5.14	1.18	1.08	0 28	0.72	0.94	Dry......
8167	....do........do..........	Washington, D.C.	♀	8.76	....	4.00	4.52	1.22	1.08	0.27	0.68	0.96	Dry......
6516	....do........do..........	Indian Key, Fla..	♂	8.10	....	3.90	4.72	1.18	1.04	0.24	0.68	0.90	Dry......
8159	....do........do..........	Los Angeles val..	♂	10.10	....	4.58	5.78	1.30	1.14	0.30	0.72	1.00	Dry......
8129	....do.. montanus.........	San Diego	♂	7.90	....	4.06	4.08	1.13	0.92	0.24	0.68	0.96	Dry......
8143	....do........do..........	Los Angeles val..	♀	8.00	.. ...	3.82	3.80	1.17	0.94	0.24	0.64	0.96	Dry......
2596	....do.. carolinensis.......	Carlisle, Pa	♂	8.06	....	3.62	4.16	1.06	1.00	0.25	0.70	0.92	Dry......
Do..	....do........do..........	......do..........	......	8.83	11.58	3.66	....	....	....	....	....	....	Fresh ...
2243	....do........do....... ..	......do..........	♀	7.50	....	3.40	4.08	1.02	1.00	0.23	0.66	0.91	Dry......

MIMUS POLYGLOTTUS, B o i e .

Mocking Bird.

Turdus polyglottus, LINNAEUS, Syst. Nat. I, 1766, 293.—WILSON, Am. Orn. II, 1810, 14 ; pl. x, f. 1.—BON. Syn. 1828, 76.—AUD. Orn. Biog. I, 1831, 108 : V, 1839, 438 ; pl. 21.

Mimus polyglottus, BOIE, Isis, Oct 1826, 972.—BON. List, 1838.—IB. Conspectus, 1850, 276.

Orpheus polyglottus, SWAINSON, Zool Jour. III, 1827, 167.—AUD. Syn. 1839.—IB. Birds Am. II, 1841, 187 ; pl. 137.

? *Orpheus leucopterus*, VIGORS, Zool. Beechey's Voyage, 1839.

SP. CH.—Third to sixth quills nearly equal ; second shorter than seventh.   Tail considerably graduated.   Above ashy brown, the feathers very obsoletely darker centrally, and towards the light plumbeous downy basal portion, (scarcely appreciable, except when the feathers are lifted.)   The under parts are white, with a faint brownish tinge, except on the chin, and with a shade of ash across the breast.   There is a pale superciliary stripe, but the lores are dusky.   The wings and tail are nearly black, except the lesser wing coverts, which are like the back ; the middle and greater tipped with white, forming two bands ; the basal portion of the primaries white ; most extended on the inner primaries.   The outer tail feather is white ; the second is mostly white, except on the outer web and towards the base ; the third with a white spot on the end ; the rest, except the middle, very slightly tipped with white.   The bill and legs are black.   Length, 9.50 ; wing, 4.50 ; tail, 5.00

Hab.—Southern United States from Atlantic to high central plains.   Perhaps replaced by another species to the Pacific.

This species varies somewhat in color with the specimen.   The white at the base of the quills shows only on the more exterior primaries in the closed wing.   The tertials are sometimes edged with white.   The inner tail feathers are edged externally with the color of the back, but this is not conspicuous.   There are some very obsolete streaks on the sides.

The female bird is distinguished by the less extent of the white at the base of the primaries. In the male the white on the inner primaries occupies more than one-half of the free portion of the quill ; in the female it is much less extensive.

Sometimes there is a strong tinge of brownish yellow on the posterior portion of the body beneath.   One male specimen, probably immature, has faint and obsolete transverse bars on the breast, somewhat as in *Lanius*. The purity of white in the outer tail feather, too, is often impaired by blotchings of brown.

In a considerable series of specimens before me, I find two from California (8159, 8165) which differ from the rest in having a considerably longer tail, measuring 5¾ inches. The graduation is much greater, the lateral feathers being 1.20 inches shorter than the middle, instead of about .75 ; the ends of all the feathers distinctly visible from below. The coloration of the tail differs a little in having the third black, with a dull white tip, and not the elongated spot in the end, running up sometimes as far as the middle of the feather. There is less white in the two bands on the wing coverts ; the bill and feet are larger. I cannot satisfy myself, however, that they are distinct, in the absence of a sufficient series of good specimens from the east, and therefore merely call attention to the facts as stated. It may be that they are only a more northern and larger race than the rest before me. It is probably this variety that Vigors had in view when describing *Orpheus leucopterus* from the west coast of America, (Zool. Beechey, 1839, 18,) although this has the wing 5.75 inches long, instead of 4.50. Should further researches substantiate a specific distinction from both the *polyglottus* and Vigors' bird, the name of *Mimus canadatus* would be very appropriate, in view of the lengthened tail.

Young birds from California, of the long-tailed variety, have the feathers of the breast and the sides of body conspicuously marked terminally with a round dusky spot. There are also faint dusky markings on the sides of the throat.

List of specimens.

Catal. No.	Sex & age.	Locality.	When collected.	Whence obtained.	Orig. No.	Collected by—	Length.	Stretch of wings.	Wing.
8167	------	Washington, D. C.---	Mar. 25, 1842	S. F. Baird -----	----	W. M. Baird ----	-------	-------	-----
6516	♂	Indian Key, Fla.-----	Mar. 17, 1857	G. Wurdemann -	----	----------- ----	-------	-------	-----
3867	------	Prairie Mer Rouge, La.	Sept. —, 1853	J. Fairie-------	----	---------------	-------	-------	-----
6515	♀	Indian Key, Fla.-----	Mar. 20, 1857	G. Wurdemann -	----	---------------	-------	-------	-----
8161	------	Western Texas ------	--------------	Capt. Pope -----	----	---------------	-------	-------	-----
5064	------	Texas . -------------	--------------	-----do--------	----	---------------	-------	-------	-----
5063	------	Pecos river----------	May 22, 1855	------do--------	----	---------------	-------	-------	-----
4961	------	Ft. Chadbourne, Tex.	--------------	Dr. Swift-------	----	---------------	-------	-------	-----
5062	------	Indianola ---- -----	Feb. 21, 1855	Capt. Pope -----	25	---------------	-------	-------	-----
4017	------	Brownsville, Texas --	--------------	Lt. Couch ------	2	---------------	9.00	13.00	4.00
8163	------	Eagle pass, Texas----	1852---------	Major Emory----	----	A. Schott-------	-------	-------	-----
8166	------	-----do----------	--------------	-----do---------	----	-----do--------	-------	-------	-----
8160	------	Fort Thorn ---------	--------------	Dr. T. C. Henry.-	----	---------------	-------	-------	-----
8164	------	Bill Williams' fork --	Feb. 9, 1854	Lt. Whipple ----	83	Kennerly & Möll- hausen--------	9.50	13.50	-----
4561	------	Ft. Yuma, Cal -----	--------------	Major Emory----	26	A. Schott-------	-------	-------	-----
8165?	------	Gila river----------	Dec. —, 1854	-----do--------	----	-----do--------	-------	-------	-----
8158	♂	Posa creek----------	--------------	Lt. Williamson--	----	Dr. Heermann --	-------	-------	-----
8159?	------	Los Angeles valley---	--------------	-----do--------	----	-----do--------	-------	-------	-----
	o	Fort Tejon, Cal. ----	--------------	J. X. de Vesey--	----	---------------	-------	-------	-----

44 b

MIMUS CAROLINENSIS, Gray.

Cat Bird.

Muscicapa carolinensis, LINNAEUS, Syst. Nat. I, 1766, 328.
Turdus carolinensis, LICHT. Verz. 1823, 38.—D'ORBIGNY, in De La Sagra's Cuba, 51.
Orpheus carolinensis, AUD. Syn. 1839, 88.—IB. Birds Amer. II, 1841, 195 ; pl. 140.
Mimus carolinensis, GRAY, Genera, 1844–'49.
Galeoscoptes carolinensis, CABANIS, Mus. Hein. 1851, 82.
Felivox carolinensis, BONAP. Comptes Rendus, XXVIII, 1853 : Notes Orn. Delattre, 39. Type.
Turdus felivox, VIEILLOT, Ois. Am. Sept. II, 1807, 10 ; pl. lxvii.—BON. Obs. Wilson, 1825, J. A. N. S. IV, 30.—
           AUD. Orn. Biog. II, 1831, 171 : V, 1839, 440 ; pl. 128.
Orpheus felivox, SWAINSON, F. Bor. Am. II, 1831, 192.
Mimus felivox, BON. List, 1838.—IB. Conspectus, 1850, 276.
Turdus lividus, WILSON, Am. Orn. II, 1810, 90 ; pl. xiv, f. 3. (Not of Lichtenstein.)
? *Spodesilaura*, REICHENB. Av. Syst. Nat. 1850 ; pl. liii. (According to Gray the figure belongs to the present species,
           which, however, lacks the notch of bill shown in the plate. According to Bonaparte, *Pyrrocheira*,
           Reich. pl. liii, represents *carolinensis*, which seems more probable.)

SP. CH.—Third quill longest; first shorter than sixth. Prevailing color dark plumbeous, more ashy beneath. Crown and
nape dark sooty brown. Wings dark brown, edged with plumbeous. Tail greenish black ; the lateral feathers obscurely tipped
with plumbeous. The under tail coverts dark brownish chesnut. Female smaller. Length, 8.85 ; wing, 3.65 ; tail, 4.00 ;
tarsus, 1.05.

Hab.—Eastern United States to the Missouri.

The tail is considerably graduated ; the lateral feathers .60 of an inch shorter than the middle.

List of specimens.

Catal. No.	Sex.	Locality.	When collected.	Whence obtained.	Orig. No.	Collected by—	Length.	Stretch of wings.	Wing.	Remarks.
1123	♂	Carlisle, Pa	July 15, 1843	S. F. Baird			9.00	11.50	3.50	
1635	♂	......do.	July 16, 1844	......do.			9.00	11.75	3.75	
2596	♂	......do.	May 6, 1846	......do.			8.83	11.58	3.66	
2243	♀	......do.	May 7, 1845	......do.						
10119	♂	Washington, D. C		J. C. McGuire						
6513	♂	Indian Key, Fla	March 24	G. Wurdemann						
6514		Key Biscayne, Fla		......do.					..	Bill black
7450		Rockport, Ohio		J. P. Kirtland						
8344		Independence, Mo.	June 17, 1857	Wm. M. Magraw ..	71	Dr. Cooper	9.00	11.25	3.75	Iris brown, bill black, feet brown.
5285	♂	Fort Lookout	June 4, 1857	Lt. Warren		Dr. Hayden	8.25	11.00	3.50	Eye blue black
5286	♂	...... do.	June 22, 1857	......do.		......do.	8.00	11.00	3.00	
4704	♂	White river		......do.		......do.	8.12	11.37	3.75	

OROSCOPTES, Baird.

CH.—Culmen only slightly curved towards the tip. Bill longer and slenderer than in *Mimus* ; nearly equal to the head.
Wings decidedly longer than the tail ; rather pointed ; the first primary less than half the second, which is a quarter of an inch
shorter than the third. Tail rounded ; scarcely graduated.

In general appearance the species resembles *Toxostoma rufum*, though the longer and
more pointed wings, shorter and scarcely graduated tail, and rather shorter bill, which is
rather more notched, will at once distinguish them. The shape of the bill is almost precisely
the same. In the long, pointed, and little concave wings, with the but slightly graduated tail,
there is an approach to the true thrushes. The notch of the bill, however, is less distinct.

The exposed portion of first primary is two-fifths that of the longest one, and the tarsus is very distinctly scutellate. It is very different from the typical *Mimus* in the tail and wings, as well as the longer, slenderer, and straighter bill. Its characteristic color consists in the following points : Above, grayish brown ; beneath, white, with arrow-shaped brown spots. Tail feathers blotched at the end with white.

OROSCOPTES MONTANUS, Baird.

Mountain Mocking Bird.

Orpheus montanus, TOWNSEND, J. A. N. Sc. VII, II, 1837, 192.—AUD. Synopsis, 1839, 87.—IB. Birds Amer. II, 1841, 194 ; pl. 139.

Turdus montanus, AUD. Orn. Biog. IV, 1838, 437 ; pl. 369, f. 1.

Mimus montanus, BONAP. List, 1838.—IB. Consp. 1850, 276.

SP. CH.—First quill rather shorter than the sixth. Tail slightly graduated. Above brownish ash ; each feather obsoletely darker in the centre. Beneath dull white, thicky marked with triangular spots, except on the under tail coverts and around the anus, which regions are tinged with yellowish brown. Wing coverts and quills edged with dull white. Tail feathers brown ; the outer edged, and all (except, perhaps, the middle) tipped with white. Length, 8 inches ; wing, 4.85 ; tail, 4.00 ; tarsus, 1.21.

Hab.—Rocky mountains ; south to Mexico, and along valley of Gila and Colorado and to San Diego, California.

In this species the lateral tail feathers are about .25 of an inch shorter than the middle ones ; all are rather attenuated and rounded at the tip. The under parts are sometimes strongly tinged with brownish yellow, most visible in raising the feathers of the breast. The spots on the throat are arranged in two maxillary series, being otherwise sparse and small. There is a faint indication of a pale superciliary stripe and of a whitish ring round the eye. The white tip to the outer tail feather is about half an inch long ; in the others less. This white is sometimes quite obscure. All the tail feathers are narrowly edged with the color of the back ; the exterior one with white. The bill is black, the feet dusky.

An immature bird (8821) has the spots beneath larger ; the under parts tinged with brown ; the upper parts quite conspicuously streaked.

List of specimens.

Catal. No.	Sex.	Locality.	When collected.	Whence obtained.	Orig'l No.	Collected by—	Length.	Stretch of wings.	Wing.	Remarks.
8251	......	Fort Laramie, Neb.....	Sept. 23, 1857	Dr. Cooper	213	....	8.75	12.75	4.50	Iris brown, bill br'wn and w'te, feet slate and yellow.
8250	......	........do.......	...... do.......	.... do......		....				....
8821	♀	Black Hills, Neb.......	....	Lt. Warren...........		Dr. Hayden......	8.75	13.25	4.25	....
8134	......	W. Texas, near 32° L ..	....	Capt. Pope		....				....
8131	......	Fort Thorn, N. M.....	....	Dr. T. C. Henry....		....				......
4019	♀	Tamaulipas, Mex	....	Lt. Couch.........	108	....	7.50	11.00	3.75	....
4018	......	........do..	....	...... do...........	88	....	8.00	11.00	3.75	Bill slate, feet greenish lead color.
8136	......	Near Zuñi, N. M.......	Nov. 26, 1853	Lt. Whipple........	31	Kenn. and Möll...				.. ..
8137	......	Bill Williams' Fork, Camp 120............	Feb. 12, 1854	...... do.	93	......do........	8.50	11.50	4.00	....
8138	......	Camp 119..............	Feb. 11, 1854	...... do...........	90	....	8.00	11.50	4.00	....
8132	♀	Espia, Mex...........	March —, 1855	Major Emory.....	50	Dr. Kennerly	8.00	11.75	3.75	Eyes yellow ? ......
8133	♂	........do............	...... do.......	...... do...........	49	......do........	8.00	11.75	3.50	....
4562	......	Gila river, N. M........	.. ..	...... do...........	39	A. Schott........				....
4899	......	San Diego, Cal........	....	Dr. J. F. Hammond.		....	8.75	12.50	3.62	....
8129	♂	........do............	.. ..	Lt. Williamson.....		Dr. Heermann....				....
8143	♀	Los Angelos valley.....	....	...... do...........		......do........				.....

HARPORHYNCHUS, Cabanis.

Harpes, GAMBEL, Pr. A. N. Sc. II, 1845, 264. (Not of Goldfuss, 1839.)
Harporhynchus, CABANIS, Wiegmann's, Archiv, 1848, I, 98. (Type *Harpes redivivus*.)
Toxostoma, WAGLER, Isis, 1831, 528. Type *T. vetula*. (Not *Toxostoma*, Raf. 1816.)
Methriopterus, REICH. Avium Syst. Nat. 1850; pl. lv. (No type mentioned here. *Turdus rufus*, according to Gray.)

Bill from front as long or longer than the head; nearly straight to near the tip, or bow shaped, without any notch. Tarsus as long or longer than the middle toe, conspicuously scutellate; outer lateral toe a little the longer, not reaching the base of the middle claw. Hind toe longer than lateral; its claw equal to its remaining portion. Wings short, rounded; the fourth or fifth longest; the exposed portion of the first about half that of longest. Tail longer than the wings, broad, more or less graduated.

It is very difficult to establish any very precise characters for this genus, as species evidently very closely allied in some features differ considerably in others. The transition from the one extreme of structure in *H. redivivus* to the other in *T. rufus* is so gradual as to render it very difficult to separate them; *T. curvirostris* has a shorter tarsus (about equal to the middle toe) than the others, and the graduation of the tail is less. It is very difficult to say whether it should more properly be assigned to the first section or the second. In the character of the bill there is the most gradual transition from its very long and greatly curved shape in *H. redivivus* to the straight and short one of *H. rufus*.

Synopsis of the species.

HARPORHYNCHUS, Cab.—Bill much longer than the head, with both mandibles greatly decurved, or bow shaped. Tail much longer than the wings, broad, much graduated. No spots on the breast, which is brownish.

Above and on the jugulum olivaceous brown; beneath pale cinnamon, but little darker to the crissum. Cheeks uniform dusky...*redivivus*.

Above very light ash gray; beneath paler, unspotted; sides of head plain. Crissum pale brownish yellow. Tips of tail feathers obsoletely lighter...........................*lecontii*.

Above and below olivaceous brown; lighter on the belly and throat. Crissum abruptly orange brown. Cheeks with a light and a dark stripe.................................*crissalis*.

METHRIOPTERUS, Reich.—Bill about as long as the head, or but little longer; moderately decurved, or nearly straight. Tail somewhat longer than the wings. Breast whitish, spotted.

Above grayish ash; the under parts with obsolete spots of the same. Tail and greater wing coverts tipped with white. Bend of wing white. Gonys much decurved, concave ....*curvirostris*.

Above reddish brown; beneath thickly streaked with black. Two white bands on the wings. Gonys moderately decurved, concave...........................*longirostris*.

Above brownish red; beneath thickly streaked with dark brown tinged anteriorly with reddish. Two white bands on the wings. Gonys quite straight.....................*rufus*.

Comparative measurements of species.

Catal. No.	Species.	Locality.	Sex.	Length.	Stretch of wings.	Wing.	Tail.	Tarsus.	Middle toe.	Its claw alone.	Bill above.	Along gape.	Specimen measured.
3932	Harporhynchus redivivus	California	......	11.50	....	4.20	6.06	1.54	1.38	0.40	1.66	1.78	Dry......
8142	......do	Presidio, (near San Francisco,) Cal.	......	10.90	....	3.68	5.48	1.33	1.16	0.30	1.33	1.50	Dry......
	Harporhynchus lecontii	California	......	10.00	....	3.60	4.86	1.20	1.14	0.30	1.21	1.40	Dry......
8127	Harporhynchus crissalis	Mimbres to RioGrande	.....	10.74	....	3.85	6.12	1.26	1.13	0.28	1.54	1.68	Dry......
8128	Harporhynchus curvirostris.	New Mexico.........	♂	10.80	... .	4.24	5.42	1.30	1.32	0.36	1.26	1.50	Dry......
7200	......do	Ringgold barracks ...	......	10.62	....	4.30	4.84	1.33	1.34	0.32	1.22	1.50	Dry......
do.	......do	......do	......	11.50	14.50	4.50	......	......	......	......	......	......	Fresh....
4023	......do	Brownsville, Texas..	♀	10.30	....	3.94	4.68	1.24	1.20	0.34	1.14	1.36	Dry......
do.	......do	......do	......	10.00	12.50	4.12	......	......	......	......	......	......	Fresh....
1377	Harporhynchus rufus...	Carlisle, Pa..........	♂	9.90	....	3.98	5.30	1.28	1.14	0.30	1.04	1.32	Dry......
do.	......do	......do...............	......	11.16	13.16	4.16	......	......	......	......	......	......	Fresh....
2261	......do	......do...............	♀	9.80	....	4.00	5.30	1.30	1.18	0.30	1.00	1.26	Dry......
do.	......do	......do...............	......	9.75	13.41	4.16	......	......	......	......	......	......	Fresh....
5652	......do	Republican Fork .. .	♂	11.40	....	4.40	5.76	1.30	1.20	0.31	1.08	1.36	Dry......
5651	......do	Republican river.....	♀	11.10	....	4.18	5.50	1.28	1.24	0.28	0.98	1.28	Dry......
do.	......do	......do...............	......	11.50	12.50	......	......	......	......	......	......	......	Fresh....
4016	Harporhynchus longirostris.	Brownsville, Texas ..	♂	10.10	....	3.84	5.20	1.34	1.16	0.26	1.08	1.30	Dry......
do.	......do	......do...............	......	10.25	12.00	4.00	......	......	......	......	......	......	Fresh....

HARPORHYNCHUS REDIVIVUS, Cabanis.

Harpes rediviva, GAMBEL, Pr. A. N. Sc. Phil. II, Aug. 1845, 264.

Toxostoma rediviva, GAMBEL, J. A. N. Sc. Phil., 2d ser. I, Dec. 1847, 42.—BONAP. Conspectus, 1850, 277.—CASSIN, Illust. I, ix, 1855, 260 ; pl. xlii.

Harporhynchus redivivus, CABANIS, Wiegmann's Archiv, 1848, i, 98.—IB. Mus. Hein. 1851, 81.

" *Promerops de la Californie septentrionale*, LA PEYROUSE, Atlas Voyage, pl. xxxvii," Gambel.

SP. CH.—Wing much rounded ; the second quill shorter than the secondaries. Tail much graduated. Bill much decurved, longer than the head. Above brownish olive, without any shade of green ; beneath pale cinnamon, lightest on the throat, deepening gradually into a brownish rufous on the under tail coverts. The fore part of the breast and sides of the body brown olive, lighter than the back. An obscure ashy superciliary stripe, and another lighter beneath the eye. Ear coverts and an indistinct maxillary stripe dark brown ; the shafts of the former whitish. Ends and tips of tail feathers obsoletely paler. Length, 11.50 inches ; wing, 4.20 ; tail, 5.75 ; tarsus, 1.55.

Hab.—Coast of California.

The curvature of the bill of this species is very great, the chord of the lower jaw measuring 1.65 inches ; the ordinate is .25 of an inch. The outer tail feathers are about 1.30 inches shorter than the middle. There is no line of demarkation between the colors of the belly and under tail coverts. There is a slight rufous tinge on the upper tail coverts and outer margins of the tail feathers, which are darker than the back, with, perhaps, a faint purplish tinge. The outer webs and tips of the tail feathers are lighter brown than the remaining portion, though the difference is scarcely appreciable. There are no spots on the breast, but cinnamon edgings to some of the brown feathers on the breast impart a waved appearance.

A specimen (4902) from San Diego, California, has a more rufous tinge in the upper parts. There is a faint indication of paler edges to the tertial and wing coverts, forming bands, but this may be merely an immature condition.

In the entire series the differences in length of the bills amount to as much as half an inch.

Young birds differ only in a duller plumage. The under parts do not exhibit any indications of spots.

List of specimens.

Catal. No.	Age.	Locality.	When collected.	Whence obtained.	Orig. No.	Collected by—	Length.	Stretch of wings.	Wing.
4217,	----	San Francisco, Cal---	Winter 1853-'4	R. D. Cutts-----	------	----------------	--------	--------	------
4218	----	------do------------	------do------	------do--------	------	----------------	--------	--------	------
8142	----	Presidio, Cal--------	---------------	Lt. Trowbridge--	------	----------------	--------	--------	------
3932	----	California ----------	---------------	Dr. Heermann---	------	----------------	--------	--------	------
5966	----	Santa Clara, Cal-----	Oct. 29, 1855	Dr. Cooper------	------	----------------	13	13	------
4478	----	------do------------	------do------	------do--------	------	----------------	--------	--------	------
4562	----	San José, Cal. ------	---------------	A. J. Grayson---	------	----------------	--------	--------	------
4948	----	------do------------	---------------	------do--------	------	----------------	--------	--------	------
8141	----	Sacramento valley- --	---------------	Lt. Williamson--	------	Dr. Heermann --	--------	--------	------
10191	o	Fort Tejon, Cal------	---------------	J. X. de Vesey--	52	----------------	--------	--------	------
4902	----	San Diego, Cal-------	---------------	Dr.J.F.Hammond	------	----------------	12. 25	12. 62	------

HARPORHYNCHUS LECONTII, Bonap.

Toxostoma lecontii, Lawr. Ann. N. Y. Lyc. V, Sept. 1851, 109. (Fort Yuma.)
Harporhynchus lecontii, Bonap. Comptes Rendus, XXVIII, 1854, 57 ; Notes Orn. Delattre, 39.

Sp. Ch.—Bill much curved. Second quill about equal to the tenth ; exposed portion of the first more than half the longest ; outer tail feather an inch shortest. General color above light grayish ash, beneath much paler ; the chin and throat above almost white ; the sides behind brownish yellow or pale rusty yellow ash, of which color is the crissum and anal region. Tail feathers rather dark brown on the under surface, lighter above ; the outer edges and tips of exterior ones obscurely paler. Quills nearly like the back.

Hab.—Frot Yuma, California.

This species in form, shape, and curvature of bill and general appearance, is so much like the *H. redivivus* as to render it extremely likely that it will prove only one of those light races or varieties so often met with in birds of the lower Gila river. The size is smaller, but this might be merely the result of its more southern habitat. The colors above are much lighter than in *H. redivivus.* The contrast between the body of the tail feathers and their obsoletely lighter edges is rather more decided than in the other species. The second quill is longer, and the first is fully half the longest instead of less than half. The bill in curvature and general shape is exactly like that of *H. redivivus.*

List of specimens.

Locality.	Whence obtained.
Fort Yuma, Gila river.................................	George N. Lawrence ....

HARPORHYNCHUS CRISSALIS, Henry.

Harporhynchus crissalis, HENRY, Pr. A. N. Sc. Phil. May, 1858.

SP. CH.—Second quill about as long as the secondaries. Bill much curved; longer than the head. Above olive brown, with a faint shade of gray; beneath nearly uniform brownish gray, much paler than the back, passing insensibly into white on the chin; but the under tail coverts dark brownish rufous, and abruptly defined. There is a black maxillary stripe cutting off a white one above it. There do not appear to be any other stripes about the head. There are no bands on the wings, and the tips and outer edges of the tail feathers are very inconspicuously lighter than the remaining portion. Length, 11 inches; wing, 4.00; tail, 5.80; tarsus, 1.25.

Hab.—Southern Rocky Mountains.

This species in general appearance resembles the *H. redivivus,* but is smaller, and may be at once distinguished by the chestnut under tail coverts in marked contrast with the brownish gray of the under parts. The contrast is nearly as marked as in *Mimus carolinensis,* or the cat bird, and the shade of color only a little lighter. The upper parts are paler than in the other species, and the tail and upper coverts are uniform with the back. There is no pectoral band, but the entire under parts are uniform, without any trace of the cinnamon color. The black maxillary stripe cuts off a white one, which is not the case in the other species, where the whole maxillary space is dusky. The character of margination in the tail is very similar. The bill and feet are black. The lateral tail feathers are about 1.35 inches the shortest.

List of specimens.

Catalogue number.	Locality.	Whence obtained.
8127	Mimbres to Rio Grande	Dr. T. C. Henry U. S. A.

HARPORHYNCHUS CURVIROSTRIS, Cabanis.

Orpheus curvirostris, SWAINSON, Phil. Mag. I, 1827, 369.—M'CALL, Pr. A. N. Sc. IV, May, 1848, 63.
Mimus curvirostris, GRAY, Genera, 1844-'49.
Toxostoma curvirostris, BONAP. Conspectus, 1850, 277.
Harporhynchus curvirostris, CAB. Mus. Hein. 1851, 81.
? *Toxostoma vetula,* WAGLER, Isis, 1831, 528.
? "*Pomatorhinus turdinus,* TEMM. Pl. Col. 441."

SP. CH.—Second quill equal to the eighth; considerably longer than the secondaries. Exposed portion of the bill about as long as the head; considerably decurved. Above uniform grayish brown, or light ash; beneath dull white; the anal region and under tail coverts tinged with brownish yellow. The under parts generally, except the chin, throat, middle of the belly and under coverts, with rounded sub-triangular, quite well defined, spots, much like the back. These are quite confluent on the breast. Two narrow bands on the wing coverts, and the edges of primaries and alulae, are white. The tail feathers, except the middle, are conspicuously tipped with white. Length of female, 10 inches; wing, 4.00; tail, 4.55; tarsus, 1.20.

Hab.—Lower Rio Grande.

This species, with some relationships to the *H. redivivus,* is readily distinguished by its smaller size, shorter tail, and white under parts, with distinct spots; these, anteriorly, are rather arrow-shaped, but become more rounded behind, and exhibit a tendency to confluence on the breast. The sides are tinged with brown. The chin is white. The sides of the head ash color, without stripes, although the feathers of the cheeks and before the eye are whitish. The edge of the shoulder is white. The bands on the wing vary in extent, though that on the lower coverts is generally most distinct. The white tips to the tail feathers are very conspicuous, compared with *H.*

redivivus; the outer tail feather is also narrowly margined with white. The difference in length of the second quill in being decidely longer than the secondaries instead of shorter, is very conspicuous.

In the collection before me is a specimen (8128) which I find it difficult to refer to any of the species here described. The upper parts are most like those of *curvirostris,* being of the same grayish brown; there is, however, a very faint trace of the white bands on the wings. The under parts, however, show more of the decided whitish of *curvirostris,* the breast being strongly tinged with ash as far as the belly, which is lighter, and shows some obsolete rounded spots. The under tail coverts and anal region are darker than in *curvirostris,* but less rufous than in *redivivus.* The tail lacks the white tips of *curvirostris,* although absolutely lighter at the end. The wings are, however, similar, even to the whitish flexure and tips of coverts. It is possible that this specimen may belong to a different species from any I here describe. The bill has the moderate curvature of *T. curvirostris.* In general characters it comes nearest to the *Toxostoma vetula,* of Wagler, Isis, 1831, 528. The diagnosis would be as follows :

> Above ash gray; sides and beneath, similar, but a little paler. Throat whitish. Crissum brownish yellow, becoming lighter on the abdomen. Belly with very obscure spots. Tail with indistinctly lighter tips. Bend of the wing and narrow tips to greater coverts whitish.

List of specimens.

Catal. No.	Sex and age.	Locality.	When collected.	Whence obtained.	Orig. No.	Collected by—	Length.	Stretch of wings.	Wing.	Remarks.
7101	....	Eagle pass, Texas......	....	Maj. Emory	....	A. Schott....	....	....	......	....
7200	♂	Ringgold barracks, Tex.	....	......do..........	....	J. H. Clark ..	11.50	14.50	4.50	....
4023	♀	Brownsville, Texas	Feb. —, 1853	Lieut. Couch.....	24	....	10.00	12.50	4.12	Eyes yellow, bill dark lead, feet lead color.
4022	♀	Tamaulipas, Mexico ...	....	......do..........	....	....	10.00	11.75	3.75	....
? 8128	....	New Mexico...........	....	Lieut. Parke.....	....	Dr. Heermann	....	....	......	....

HARPORHYNCHUS LONGIROSTRIS, Cab.

Orpheus longirostris, LAFRESNAYE, Rev. Zool. I, April, 1838, 55.—IB. Mag. de Zool. 1839; Oiseaux, pl. i.
Toxostoma longirostre, CABANIS, Wiegmann's Archiv, 1847, I, 207.—(*longirostris*) Bonap. Consp. 1850, 277.
Mimus longirostris, GRAY, Genera, 1844–'49.
Harporhynchus longirostris, CABANIS, Mus. Hein. 1851, 81.

SP. CH.—Similar to *H. rufus.* Wings much rounded; second quill shorter than the secondaries. Exposed portion of the bill as long as the head; the lower edge decidedly decurved or concave. Above rather dark brownish rufous; beneath pale rufous white; streaked on the sides of the neck and body, and across the breast, with very dark brownish black, nearly uniform throughout. Two rather narrow white bands on the wings. The concealed portion of the quills dark brown. Length, 10.50; wing, 4.00; tail, 5.00; tarsus, 1.40.

Hab.—Lower Rio Grande. South through Eastern Mexico.

This species is very similar to the *H. rufus,* but may be readily distinguished by well marked characters. The feet and bill are decidedly longer; the latter measuring 1.15 inches instead of about .95; it is also much more curved, the lower edge being concave or bow shaped, instead of straight. The wings and tail, on the other hand, are shorter; the former much more rounded. The rufous of the back is considerably darker; the stripes beneath are larger and almost uniform black, instead of partly rufous. The hinder part of the breast and the central portion of the abdomen are much more unspotted.

A specimen of this species from Xalapa, belonging to Mr. Lawrence, is very similar to those from Brownsville, the bill perhaps a little longer; the white bands on the wings narrower.

List of specimens.

Catal. No.	Sex.	Locality.	Whence obtained.	Orig. No.	Collected by—	Length.	Stretch of wings.	Wing.	Remarks.
4016	♂	Brownsville, Tex..	Lt. Couch	1	....	10.25	12.00	4.00	Eyes br'nish yellow.
8139	....	Lower Rio Grande.	Major Emory....	......	A. Schott.....	....	....	.....	....
		Xalapa, Mexico....	G. N. Lawrence..	......	......	....	....	.....	....

HARPORHYNCHUS RUFUS, Cab.

Brown Thrush.

Turdus rufus, Linnaeus, Syst. Nat. I, 1766, 293.—Vieillot, Ois. Am. Sept. II, 1807, 4 ; pl. lix.—Wilson, Am. Orn. II, 1810, 83 ; pl. xiv.—Aud. Orn. Biog. II, 1834, 102 : V, 1839, 441 ; pl. 116.
Orpheus rufus, Swainson, F. Bor. Am. II, 1831, 187.—Nuttall, Man. I, 1832, 328.—Aud. Syn. 1839, 88.—Ib. Birds Amer.
Mimus rufus, Gray, Genera, 1844–'49.
Toxostoma rufum, Cabanis, Wiegm. Archiv, 1847, i, 207.
Methriopterus, Reichenbach, Av. Syst. Nat. 1850, pl. lv. (Figure taken from this species according to Gray.)
Harporhynchus rufus, Cabanis, Mus. Hein. 1851, 82.
Thrasher ; Sandy Mocker ; French Mocking Bird ; Vulgo.

Sp. Ch.—Fifth quill longest ; the third, fourth, and sixth, little shorter ; second equal to ninth. Exposed portion of the bill shorter than the head. Outline of lower mandible straight. Above light cinnamon red ; beneath pale rufous white with longitudinal streaks of dark brown, excepting on the chin, throat, middle of the belly, and under tail coverts. These spots anteriorly, are reddish brown in their terminal portion. The inner surface of the wing and the inner edges of the primaries are cinnamon ; the concealed portion of the quills otherwise is dark brown. The median and greater wing coverts become blackish brown towards the end, followed by white, producing two conspicuous bands. The tail feathers are all rufous, the external ones obscurely tipped with whitish ; the shafts of the same color with the vanes. Length, 11.15 ; wing, 4.15 ; tail, 5.20 ; tarsus, 1.30.

Hab.—Eastern N. America to Missouri river, and perhaps to high central plains.

Among the series before me are several specimens (5651, 5652, 4703) differing in some noticeable points. They are considerably larger than Pennsylvania ones, with decidedly longer tail and wings. The under parts are more decidedly rufous white ; the white band on the wings tinged with the same. The concealed portion of the quills (including the shafts) is much darker brown, and the shafts of the tail feathers are dark brown, conspicuously different from the vanes. The spots on the breast are considerably darker, showing little, if any, of the reddish brown. Length, 11.50 ; wing, 4.50 ; tail, 5.75 ; tarsus, 1.35.

These specimens are associated with others from the same locality, precisely similar to Pennsylvania ones. They are different from *H. longirostris*, though intermediate between this and *rufus*. Whether it be proper or not to erect them into a different species from the latter, as they certainly are from the former, is a question that I am not prepared to decide. A similar relation between eastern and western races is referred to under the head of the mocking bird, (*Mimus polyglottus*.) As a strongly marked variety, at least, it may be well to call it *H. longicauda*.

Young birds are much as in the adult, the back sometimes streaked obsoletely with dusky.

45 b

List of specimens.

Catal. No.	Sex.	Locality.	When collected.	Whence obtained.	Orig. No.	Collected by—	Length.	Stretch of wings.	Wing.	Remarks.
2261	♀	Carlisle, Pa..........	May 16, 1845	S. F. Baird	.. ...	....	9.75	13.43	4.25	....
1377	♂	......do.............	April 22, 1844	......do	......	....	11.16	13.16	3.16	....
4433	......	Quasqueton, Iowa ...	....	E. C. Bidwell......	......	....	......	......	......	....
6948	......	Red river, H. B	....	Donald Gunn......	......	....	......	......	......	....
8292	......	Independence, Mo...	May 26, 1857	Wm. M. Magraw..	5	Dr. Cooper	12.75	13.00	4.50	Iris orange, feet pale gray.
8231	♂	......do	May 29, 1857	......do	......	......do	......	......	......	......do........ do......
4553	♀	Missouri river	June 8, 1857	Lieut. Warren	......	Dr. Hayden....	......	......	......	....
5284	♂	Fort Lookout........	June 18, 1856	......do	......	......do	11.25	12.25	4.50	Eyes yellow ....
5283	♂	......do.............	June 22, 1856	......do	......	......do	9.75	13.50	4.25	....
4703	......	Running Water.....	May —, 1856	..... do	......	......do	......	......	......	....
8819	......	Loup Forks	Aug. 6, 1857	......do	......	......do	12.00	14.00	4.50	Iris yellow ....
8820	......	......do	..... do.......	......do	......	......do	9.50	12.25	3.50	..... do ....
5652	♂	Republican Fork.....	Sept. 26, 1856	Lieut. Bryan	351	W. S. Wood ...	......	......	......	....
5651	♀	......do	..... do.......	......do	358	......do	......	......	......	....
5653	♀	Independence creek, 130 miles west of Fort Riley, Neb.	July 14, 1856	......do	67	......do	......	......	......	....

Sub-Family CAMPYLORHYNCHINAE.

Tail plane; nearly even or slightly rounded; the first and second feathers slightly graduated; the feathers very broad, the longest with the width about one-fifth the length. Size medium.

The following genera are included in the sub-family:

A.—Hind toe and claw much longer than the outer lateral, shorter than the middle. Feet stout.

    CAMPYLORHYNCHUS.—Bill about equal to the head. Lateral toes nearly equal; their claws reaching to the base of the middle claw. Tarsus longer than the middle toe. Wings as long as the tail. Back brown, streaked with white.

    CATHERPES.—Bill longer than the head. Outer lateral toe much longer than the inner, reaching the base of the middle claw. Tarsus short, equal to the middle toe. Wings a little longer than the tail. Back brown, spotted with white.

B.—Hind toe and claw about equal to the outer lateral, shorter than the middle toe. Feet weak.

    SALPINCTES.—Bill as long as the head. Outer lateral toe considerably longer than the inner. Tarsus longer than the middle toe. Wings rather pointed; decidedly longer than the tail. Back brown, spotted with white.

CAMPYLORHYNCHUS, Spix.

Campylorhynchus, Spix, Av. Bras. 1824. (Agassiz.)

CH.—Bill as long as the head; not notched; compressed. Culmen and commissure both gently decurved; gonys nearly straight. Tarsus longer than middle toe, distinctly scutellate; inner lateral toe a little the longer; hind toe reaching nearly to the middle of the middle claw; shorter than its digit. Wings about as long as tail; exposed portion of first quill about two-thirds that of second, and rather more than half the longest, or fourth. Tail feathers very broad, plane; the longest, nearly even, with the width about one-fifth its length; the two lateral graduated; the outer about five-sixths the middle. Plumage soft and loose. Color brown; streaks on the body. Wings and tail transversely barred.

Of this genus the United States possesses but a single species, as far as known, confined to the southern borders.

Comparative measurements.

Catal. No.	Species.	Locality.	Sex.	Length.	Wing.	Tail.	Tarsus.	Middle toe.	Its claw alone.	Bill above.	Along gape.	Specimen measured.
7149	Campylorhynchus brunneicapillus.	Mohave desert...	♂	7.90	3.24	3.52	1.16	1.00	0.56	0.96	1.20	Skin ....
7150	......do...............do	Los Angelos Val.	♀	7.50	3.30	3.60	1.08	0.92	0.94	0.86	1.02	Skin ....

CAMPYLORHYNCHUS BRUNNEICAPILLUS, Gray.

Picolaptes brunneicapillus, LAFRESNAYE, Guerin Mag. de Zool. 1835, 61 ; pl. xlvii. California.—LAWRENCE, Annals N. Y. Lyc. V, May, 1851, 114. Texas.—HEERMANN, J. A. N. Sc. Ph. 2d ser. II, Jan. 1853, 263.—CASSIN, Illust. I, 1854, 156 ; pl. xxv.
Campylorhynchus brunneicapillus, GRAY, Genera, I, March, 1847, 159.—BONAP. Conspectus, 1850, 223.

SP. CH.—Bill as long as the head. Above brown ; darkest on the head, which is unspotted. Feathers on the back streaked centrally with white. Beneath whitish, tinged with rusty on the belly ; the feathers of the throat and upper parts, and under tail coverts, with large rounded black spots ; those of the remaining under parts with smaller, more linear ones. Chin and line over the eye white. Tail feathers black beneath, barred subterminally (the outer one throughout) with white.
Length, 8 inches ; wing, 3.40 ; tail, 3.55 inches.
Hab.—Valleys of Rio Grande and Gila. Southward.

(7149.) This, the largest wren found in the United States, bears a slight resemblance to the common creeper, *Certhia americana,* but differs greatly in all essential features. The bill, from the base of the skull, is about the length of the latter, and is considerably compressed and slightly decurved. The tail is long and broad, about equal to the wings. The black spotting on the throat is very conspicuous, relieved only slightly by the white edges of the feathers. There is a black maxillary stripe. Each feather on the back, including the wing coverts, may be said to have two whitish spots strung along the white midrib, the light portion bordered by a duskier shade than the extreme margin of the feather.

The outer edges of the quills are indented by triangular spots of whitish ; the basal portion of the inner webs somewhat similarly marked. The two middle tail feathers are brown, somewhat like the crown, but with indistinct bands of darker ; the others are as described.

Specimens vary considerably in the length of the bill, and in the amount of black spotting on the throat. In a female, 7150, the white streaks on the back are somewhat wider. The second tail feather is sometimes banded almost as much as the first, and the inner tail feathers are distinctly and narrowly banded with whitish and black, instead of dark brown, and lighter.

List of specimens.

Catal. No.	Sex.	Locality.	Whence obtained.	Collected by—	Length.	Stretch of wings.	Wing.	Remarks.
7148	......	Ringgold barracks, Texas...	Major Emory..........	Mr. Clark	....	....	......	....
3966	♂	Monterey, Mexico	Lieut. Couch.......	....	8.00	10.75	3.50	Bill slate, eyes reddish yellow, feet lead.
7151	......	Fort Yuma, California......	Major Emory	A. Schott......	....	....	......	....
7150	......	Los Angeles valley.........	Lieut. Williamson	Dr. Heermann.	....	....	....	....
7149	♂	California	...... do......	....	....	....	....	....

CATHERPES, Baird.

Ch.—Bill longer than the head, slender; all the outlines nearly straight to the tip, then gently decurved, gonys least so; nostrils linear; tarsus short, about equal to the middle toe, which reaches to the middle of the middle claw. Outer toe considerably longer than the inner, reaching beyond the base of the middle claw. Wings a little longer than the tail; the exposed portion of the first primary about half that of the fourth and fifth. Tail feathers very broad and perfectly plane; tail nearly even; the two lateral graduated; the outer about eleven-twelfths of the middle.

This genus agrees with *Salpinctes* in the broad, plane tail feathers, but the bill is much longer, the nostrils linear, not oval, the feet much stouter, the outer toe rather longer; the tarsus shorter, being equal to the middle toe, not longer; the hind toe much longer than the outer lateral, instead of equal to it. The wings are but little longer than the tail, and less pointed and shorter than in *Salpinctes*.

Cabanis, in establishing this genus on the broad tail feathers and long wings, includes *S. obsoletus* and *mexicanus*. In this, however, he overlooks the remarkable differences in the feet and wings of the two species. His type being *obsoletus*, the new genus belongs to *mexicanus*.

Comparative measurements of species.

Catal. No.	Species.	Locality.	Sex.	Length.	Stretch of wings.	Wing.	Tail.	Tarsus.	Middle toe.	Its claw alone.	Bill above.	Along gape.	Specimen measured.
3969	Catherpes mexicanus.	New Leon, Mex ...	♂	5.70	....	2.48	2.38	0.74	0.74	0.20	0.92	1.20	Skin ....
do.	........do............	......do............	....	6.50	7.75	2 50	....	....	....	....	....	....	Fresh ..
3968	........do............	Patos,Coahuila,Mex	....	5.00	....	2.36	2.40	0.70	0.70	0.20	0.80	0.96	Skin ....
do.	........do............	......do............	....	5.75	7.37	2.37	....	....	....	....	....	....	Fresh ..
7157	Salpinctes obsoletus..	Tejon Valley	♂	5.76	....	2.74	2.36	0.86	0.76	0.18	0.72	0.92	Skin ....
7158	........do............	El Paso, Mex......	♀	5.74	....	2.78	2.24	0.79	0.70	0.18	0.70	0.86	Skin ....
do.	........do............	......do............	....	5.12	8.00	3.00	....	....	....	....	....	....	Fresh :..

CATHERPES MEXICANUS, Baird.

White-throated Wren.

Thryothorus mexicanus, Swainson, Zool. Illustrations, 2d series, I, 1829, pl. xi. Real del Monte.
Salpinctes mexicanus, Cabanis, Wiegmann's Archiv, 1847, i, 323.—Ib. Mus. Hein. 1851, 78.—Bon. Consp. 1850, 224.
Troglodytes mexicanus, Gray, Genera, I, 1847, 159.—Heermann, J. A. N. Sc. 2d ser. II, 1853, 263.—Cassin, Illust. I, vi, 1854, 173; pl. xxx.
"*Troglodytes albicollis*, Cuvier, Gal. de Paris, Cah. No. 3."—"Lesson, Compl. VI, 1829, 188."
? " *Troglodytes murarius*, Licht. Deppe & Schiede, Preis Verz." (I cannot find that any description was published.)
? *Salpinctes murarius*, Cabanis, Nomenclator Av. Mus. Berol, 1854, 35.
Certhia albifrons, Giraud, 16 Sp. Texan Birds, 1841; pl. viii.
Thryothorus guttulatus, Lafresnaye, Rev. Zool. 1839, 99.

Sp. Ch.—Bill considerably longer than the head; claws large. Head and neck above dark ashy brown, passing gradually into light rusty brown on the rump; the sides of the body, belly, and under tail coverts similar, all these regions marked with small rounded white and dusky spots, the latter in the form of waved bars on the feathers of the back; an obscure white line over the eye. Chin, throat, and upper part of the breast pure white. Tail feathers rusty red on both sides, with six or eight narrow transverse bars of black.

Length, 6.50; wing, 2.50; tail, 2.50. (3969.)

Hab.—Valley of Rio Grande, Colorado, and Gila, (but not on the coast of California?) South into Mexico.

This species, first added to the fauna of the United States by Dr. Augustus L. Heermann, is the most handsomely marked of all the American wrens. In addition to the characters given above, it may be stated that the rufous color of the upper and under tail coverts is of about the same shade; the tail rather lighter; the latter nearly similar on both sides, the bars showing with equal distinctness. The dark spots on the feathers are just anterior to the light ones; sometimes they follow as well as precede the white ones. The reddish outer surface of the wings is about the shade of the middle of the back. There are no transverse dusky bars across the quills, the outer webs only showing an alternation of dusky and reddish spots.

The wing is rather short; the first and second quills are graduated, the latter about equal to the secondaries; the third is but little shorter than the fourth, fifth, sixth, all nearly equal. The tail feathers are very broad (half an inch,) the tail plane, and moderately graduated (on the sides only;) the lateral feathers about .20 of an inch less than the longest.

Different specimens vary a little in the width of the black bars of the tail feathers; those on the inner feathers are usually narrower than on the outer, where they are about .05 of an inch broad.

A specimen, 3968, probably a female, is smaller, with the bill appreciably shorter.

List of specimens.

Catal. No.	Sex.	Locality.	When collected.	Whence obtained.	Orig. No.	Collected by—	Length.	Stretch of wings.	Wing.	Remarks.
3968	....	Patos,Coahuila,Mex.	....	Lieut. Couch....	236	....	5.75	7.62	2.37	Eyes dark brown; bill slate and white. ....
3969	♂	New Leon, Mex....	....	......do....	175	....	6.50	7.75	2.50	Eyes dark brown; bill and feet dark copper ....
7116	....	Camp 112,on BillWilliams' Fork, N. M..	Feb. —, 1854	Lieut. Whipple...	66	Kenn & Möll.	....	....	....	....
	....	Fort Tejon, Cal	....	J. Xant de Vesey.	....	....	....	....	....

SALPINCTES, Cabanis.

Salpinctes, CABANIS, Wiegmann's Archiv, 1847, I, 323.

CH.—Bill as long as the head; all the outlines nearly straight to the tip, then decurved; nostrils oval. Feet weak; tarsi decidedly longer than the middle toe; outer lateral toe much longer, reaching to the base of the middle claw, and equal to the hinder. Wings about one-fifth longer than the tail; the exposed portion of the first primary about half that of the second, and two-fifths that of the fourth and fifth. Tail feathers very broad, plane, nearly even or slightly rounded; the lateral moderately graduated.

Of this genus but one species is hitherto known in the United States, the rock wren of the earlier ornithologists.

SALPINCTES OBSOLETUS, Cab.

Rock Wren.

Troglodytes obsoletus, SAY, in Long's Exped. II, 1823, 4. S. Fork of Platte.—NUTTALL, Man. I, 1832, 435.—AUD. Synopsis, 1839, 73.—IB. Orn. Biog. IV, 1838, 443; pl. 360.—IB. Birds Am. II, 1841, 113; pl. 116.—NEWBERRY, Zool. P. R. R. Rep. VI, IV, 1857, 80.
Myothera obsoleta, BONAP. Am. Orn. I, 1825, 6; pl. i, f. 2.
Thryothorus obsoletus, BONAP. List, 1838.—IB. Rev. Zool. II, 1839, 98.
Salpinctes obsoletus, CABANIS, Wiegmann's Archiv, 1847, I, 323, (type *obsoletus.*)—BONAP. Consp. 1850, 224.
? " *Thryothorus latifasciatus,* LICHT. Preis Verzeichniss."—BONAP.

SP. CH.—Plumage very soft and lax. Bill about as long as the head. Upper parts brownish gray, each feather with a central line and (except on the head) transverse bars of dusky, and a small dull brownish white spot at the end, (seen also on the tips of the secondaries.) Rump, sides of the body, and posterior part of belly and under tail coverts dull cinnamon, darker above. Rest of under parts dirty white; feathers of throat and breast with dusky central streaks. Lower tail coverts banded broadly with black. Inner tail feathers like the back; the others with a broad black bar near the end; the tips cinnamon; the outer on each side alternately banded with this color and black. A dull white line above and behind the eye. Length, 5.70; wing, 2.82; tail, 2.40; (7159.)

Hab.—High central plains through the Rocky mountains to the Coast and Cascade ranges, (but not on the Pacific coast?)

The name *obsoletus* applies well to this species, the feathers all having a faded appearance very difficult to define. Very few specimens in collections possess distinctly the markings mentioned above, especially the small whitish spots of the upper parts, the brown of the back having generally a more reddish appearance, the dark bars and lines more indistinct. In one specimen (1857) from Fort Union there is no reddish on the abdomen and under tail coverts, which are nearly white; the bands on the latter too are much less distinct. This agrees better with Say's description, but appears to be of the same species.

In young or immature specimens, which are much oftener seen in collections than adults, there are neither light spots nor dusky lines above, the color being uniform brownish, passing into pale dull cinnamon on the rump. The breast too is unspotted. The bill does not attain its full length until maturity.

This species has some resemblance in form to the *C. mexicanus;* the bill, however, is considerable shorter, being only equal to the head. The wings are rather longer and perhaps more pointed, and reach nearly to the middle of the tail. The claws are considerably smaller. There is also some similarity in the color, but the reddish is paler in *obsoletus*, and the inner tail feathers are brown like the fore part of the back, with crowded bars; the basal half of all except the exterior, similar, instead of all being uniform reddish brown, with six or eight narrow black bars. The comparative diagnoses of the two species, without reference to their generic distinctions, will be as follows:

C. mexicanus.—Bill considerably longer than the head; claws very large. Throat pure unspotted white; posterior part of body all round dark reddish brown; tail feathers nearly similar, all with equidistant bars of black.

S. obsoletus.—Bill as long as the head. Claws moderate. Throat with dusky streaks. Posterior parts of body pale cinnamon. Middle tail feathers much like the back.

List of specimens.

Catal. No.	Sex and age.	Locality.	When collected.	Whence obtained.	Orig. No.	Collected by—	Length.	Stretch of wings.	Wing.	Remarks.
1857	♂	Fort Union, Neb.......	July 8, 1843	S. F. Baird	.....	J. J. Audubon .	....	....	....	....
1917	o	......do.............	July 18, 1843	......do............	.....	......do.......	....	....	....	....
8830	♂	Running Water, Neb...	Aug. 15, 1856	Lieut. Warren.....	.....	Dr. Hayden....	5.37	9.25	2.50	Iris light gray ....
5277	....	Blackfoot country	July —, 1855	Col. Vaughan.....	.....	......do.......	....	....	....	....
5279	....	Powder river..........	Aug. 4, 1856	Lieut. Warren......	.....	......do.......	....	....	....	....
5278	....	......do.............	.. do.......	......do..........	.....	......do.......	....	....	....	....
8832	....	Black Hills, Neb	Sept. 19, 1857	......do..........	.....	.....do.......	5.75	8.50	2.75	Iris light brown....
8831	♀	......do.............	Aug. 18, ——	......do..........	.. ...	......do.......	5.50	8.50	2.50	....
8780	....	Forks of Platte river...	Aug. 13, 1857	Wm. M. Magraw...	153	Dr. Cooper......	....	....	....	....
8781	....	......do.............	.... do........	......do......	154	......do.......	....	....	....	....
8779	....	......do.............	.. do........	......do..........	152	......do.......	....	....	....	....
5645	♀	Pole creek..........	July 25, 1856	Lieut. Bryan......	153	W. S. Wood....	....	....	....	....
7158	♀	El Paso, Mex..........	Dec. —, 1854	Maj. Emory........	15	Dr. Kennerly ..	5.12	8.00	3.00	Eyes chocolate brown.
7162	♂	......do.............	May —, 1852	......do..........	.....	......do	5.12	8.87	2.75	....
3967	....	Patos, Coahuila.......	....	Lieut. Couch......	238	....	5.50	8.75	2.75	Eyes dark brown; feet lead...... ....
7160	....	Camp 113, Bill Williams' Fork.	Feb. 5, 1854	Lieut. Whipple....	68	Kenn & Müll	....	....	....	Eyes gray...........
7157	♂	Tejon valley........ ...	....	Lieut. Williamson.	......	Dr. Heermann..	....	....	....	....
7159	♂	..... do	....	......do..........	......	......do	....	....	....	....
....	....	Fort Tejon............	....	J. X. de Vesey.....	......	....	....	....	....	....

Sub-Family TROGLODYTINAE.

Tail feathers rather narrow ; the middle ones less than one-sixth as wide as long. Tail more or less vaulted or concave below ; usually considerably graduated. Tarsus longer than the middle toe, which exceeds the hinder ones ; the lateral toes generally equal, and reaching the base of the middle claw. Hind toe much longer than the lateral. Size diminutive.

The sub-divisions are as follows :

THRIOTHORUS.—Wings equal to or shorter than the tail, which is nearly even, the lateral feathers only graduated. Bill nearly equal to the head, decurved. Toes not reaching to the end of the tail. Color uniform brown on the back.

CISTOTHORUS.—Wings longer than the tail, which is short, and all the feathers much graduated. Toes reaching to or beyond the tip of the tail. Feet large ; hind claw at least equal to the rest of the toe. Back black, streaked with white.

Telmatodytes.—Bill nearly as long as the head. Hind claw longer than the rest of the toe.
Cistothorus.—Bill much shorter than the head. Hind claw equal to the rest of the toe.

TROGLODYTES.—Wings longer than the tail or nearly equal. Tail rounded ; the lateral feathers graduated. Hind claw shorter than the rest of the toe. Back brown, obsoletely waved with dusky.

Troglodytes.—Wings about equal to the tail. Toes reaching to the tip of the tail. Bill nearly as long as the head, compressed, decurved.
Anorthura.—Wings much longer than the very short tail. Bill shorter than the head, slender, nearly straight. End of tarsus reaching to the tip of the tail.

THRIOTHORUS, Vieillot.

Thriothorus, VIEILLOT, Analyse, 1816.
Thryothorus, VIEILLOT, Nouv. Dict. XXXIV, 1819, 55.
Thryothurus, SWAINSON, Class. Birds, II, 1837, 319.

CH.—Bill about as long as the head ; nearly straight to near the tip, which is abruptly decurved, with an obsolete notch. Gonys nearly straight. Hind toe nearly equal to the middle ; the lateral toes equal, reaching to the base of the middle claw. Tarsus longer than the middle toe. Wings about equal to the tail, which is arched, and nearly even ; the first or second lateral feathers moderately graduated ; the feathers narrow ; the width of longest about one-tenth its length.

This genus is apparently related to *Campylorhynchus* in almost every respect, the chief difference being in the tail, which is rather shorter, being equal to the tail instead of less, and the feathers much narrower, and more vaulted ; the width of the longest is about one-tenth the length, instead of one-fifth or sixth. The bill is straighter to the tip, which is more abruptly decurved.

In *Thryothorus maculipectus* the inner lateral toe is a little shorter than the outer ; the other characters are much the same.

I have associated in this division the *T. bewickii,* which differs in longer tail, the lateral feathers of which are more graduated. The other differences are not important. It is at any rate more naturally placed here than in *Telmatodytes,* where Cabanis has assigned it.

The precise determination of the section of American wrens to which Vieillot's name should belong is a matter of much uncertainty. I have not Vieillot's Analyse at hand to know what species he considers as type, but Gray quotes as such, *Thryothorus arundinaceus,* Vieillot. In the article on *Thryothorus,* in Nouv. Dict. XXXIV, 1819, 55, Vieillot says that when he established the genus he knew of but one species, the "*Thryothore des roseaux.*" The bird of this name described on page 59, and there called likewise *Thryothorus arundineus*, is the *Certhia palustris* of Wilson. The bird he described in 1807 as "*Troglodyte des roseaux*," or *Troglodytes arundinaceus*, is as certainly *Sylvia ludoviciana* of Latham. Vieillot unquestionably knew the latter species in 1816, as he had described it in 1807, although its biography of that date belonged to the first mentioned bird. For this reason, therefore, in the necessary uncertainty of the case, I am inclined to differ from Gray, and to consider the *Sylvia ludoviciana* as the type, especially as the necessity of a new generic name will thereby be avoided.

Synopsis of species.

Tail feathers light brown, with bars of black. Superciliary stripe extending far back on the neck, and spotted with black. Tail about equal to the wings.

Lateral tail feather a quarter of an inch shorter than longest. Above, reddish brown ; beneath, pale yellowish rusty ; sides plain.................... ....*T. ludovicianus.*

Lateral tail feathers half an inch shorter than longest. Above, reddish brown ; beneath bright reddish brown on the sides and behind ; sides obsoletely barred...*T. berlandieri.*

Lateral tail feathers black, varied with white. Superciliary stripe confined to the neck. Tail longer than the wings..*T. bewickii.*

Comparative measurements of species.

Catal. No.	Species.	Locality.	Sex.	Length.	Stretch of wings.	Wing.	Tail.	Tarsus.	Middle toe.	Its claw alone.	Bill above.	Along gape.	Specimen measured.
7113	Thriothorus ludovicianus .	Philadelphia	......	5.40	....	2.36	2.36	0.80	0.78	0.20	0.66	0.86	Skin.....
10204	........do................	South Illinois ...	......	5.70	....	2.34	2.10	0.84	0.76	0.20	0.64	0.80	Skin.....
7123	Thriothorus berlandieri ..	Boquillo....	♂	4.80	....	2.20	2.14	0.84	0.74	0.22	0.74	0.84	Skin.....
do.	........do...............	.....do.........		5.52	7.25	2.25	......	......	......	......	......	......	Fresh....
7122	.....do................	.....do.........	♀	5.20	....	2.16	2.22	0.78	0.72	0.20	0.64	0.76	Skin.....
do.	........do...............	.....do.........		5.25	7.25	2.25	......	......	......	......	......	......	Fresh....
	Thriothorus maculipectus[1]	Guatemala.......	......	5.54	....	2.34	2.14	0.86	0.76	0.20	0.70	0.78	Skin.....
2047	Thriothorus bewickii.....	Carlisle, Pa......	♂	5.00	....	2.18	2.44	0.71	0.68	0.20	0.56	0.68	Skin.....
do.	........do...............	.....do.........		5.50	7.33	2.25	......	......	......	......	......	......	Fresh....
7132	........do...............	Cosumnes river..	♂	5.10	....	2.08	2.32	0.73	0.66	0.18	0.60	0.74	Skin.....
9119	Thriothorus leucogastra ..	Mexico		4.80	....	2.12	2.22	0.73	0.68	0.18	0.58	0.72	Skin.....
1084	Troglodytes aedon	Carlisle, Pa......	♂	4.50	....	2.00	1.94	0.68	0.64	0.14	0.50	0.64	Skin.....
do.	........do...............	.....do.........		4.92	6.83	2.08	......	......	......	......	......	......	Fresh....
8643	.....do...............	Cape Florida....		4.10	....	1.88	1.90	0.66	0.58	0.15	0.51	0.64	Skin.....
do.	........do...............	.....do.........		4.75	5.75	1.75	......	......	......	......	......	......	Fresh....
7135	Troglodytes parkmanni...	Fort Steilacoom..	○	4.44	....	2.04	2.10	0.66	0.63	0.16	0.44	0.56	Skin.....
7136	........do...............	.....do.........	♂	4.90	....	2.06	2.12	0.66	0.64	0.16	0.54	0.70	Skin.....
do.	........do...............	.....do.........		5.50	7.00	......	......	......	......	......	......	......	Fresh....
2951	Troglodytes americanus..		......	4.56	....	1.92	1.88	0.66	0.62	0.16	0.52	0.62	Skin.....
1379	Troglodytes hyemalis.....	Carlisle, Pa	♀	3.50	....	1.78	1.26	0.64	0.58	0.14	0.42	0.56	Skin.....
do.	........do...............	.....do.........		3.92	5.92	1.66	......	......	......	......	......	......	Fresh....
10206	........do...............	West Northfield,Ill	......	3.98	....	1.76	1.32	0.66	0.60	0.16	0.40	0.55	Skin.....
9216	Troglodytes europaeus ...	Nürnberg	♀	3.70	....	1.82	1.38	0.68	0.62	0.16	0.44	0.54	Skin.....
1556	Cistothorus palustris......	Carlisle, Pa......	♀	4.40	....	1.80	1.74	0.76	0.66	0.20	0.52	0.70	Skin.....
do.	.....do...............	.....do.........		4.92	6.00	1.92	......	......	......	......	......	......	Fresh....
1454	........do...............	.....do.........	♂	4.90	....	2.06	2.00	0.80	0.72	0.21	0.62	0.76	Skin....
do.	.....do...............	.....do.........		5.50	6.75	2.08	......	......	......	......	......	......	Fresh....
1510	Cistothorus stellaris......	.....do.........	○	4.12	....	1.72	1.70	0.64	0.56	0.14	0.40	0.50	Skin.....
do.	........do...............	.....do.........		4.42	5.83	1.75	......	......	......	......	......	......	Fresh....

[1] *Thryothorus maculipectus*, Laffr. Rev. Zool. 1845, 338.

THRIOTHORUS LUDOVICIANUS, Bonap.

Great Carolina Wren.

Motacilla troglodytes, Var. γ, GMELIN, Syst. Nat. I, 1788, 994.
Sylvia ludoviciana, LATHAM, Ind. Orn. II, 1790, 548, No. 150.
Troglodytes ludovicianus, LICHT. Verz. Doubl. 1823, 35.—BON. Obs. Wilson, 1824, No. 65.—AUD. Orn. Biog. I,
    1831, 399 : V, 1839, 466 ; pl. 78.—IB. Syn. 1839, 74.—IB. Birds Amer. II, 1841, 116 ; pl.
    117.
Thryothorus ludovicianus, BONAP. List, 1838.—IB. Consp. 1850, 220.—IB. Comptes Rendus, XXVIII, 1854, 57 : Notes
    Delattre, 41.
Troglodytes arundinaceus, VIEILLOT, Ois. Am. Sept. II, 1807, 55 ; pl. cviii. The habits as detailed are those of *T.*
    palustris. Description certainly refers to the present species.
Thryothorus arundinaceus, LESSON, Rev. Zool. 1840, 263, (but not his synonymes.)
Certhia caroliniana, WILSON, Am. Orn. II, 1810, 61 ; pl. xii, f. 5.
Thryothorus littoralis, VIEILLOT, Nouv. Dict. XXXIV, 1819, 56.
Thryothorus louisianae, LESSON, Rev. Zool. 1840, 262.

SP. CH.—Exposed portion of the bill shorter than the head. Above reddish brown, most vivid on the rump. A whitish streak over the eye, bordered above with dark brown. Throat whitish ; rest of under parts pale yellow rusty, darkest towards the under tail coverts, which are conspicuously barred with black. Exposed surface of the wings and tail (including the upper coverts) barred throughout with brown, the outer edges of tail feathers and quills showing series of alternating whitish and dusky spots. Legs flesh colored. Length, 6 inches ; wing, 2.60 ; tail, 2.45.

Hab.—Eastern United States to the Missouri ; north to Pennsylvania. In Texas to upper Rio Grande.

The bill, measured to the forehead, is about as long as the head ; the culmen moderately curved ; the inferior outline nearly straight. The wings are short, reaching over the posterior third of the tail, but not to the ends of the coverts. The under parts are entirely destitute of any trace of bars except on the tail coverts. The brown of the back assumes rather a grayish shade on the crown. As usual there is a good deal of concealed white on the rump. The tail feathers are all similar in color and uniform close barring, the exterior only having rather more dusky and whitish. The middle and secondary coverts have each a light spot at the end, said to be wanting in the female. The shafts of the interscapular feathers are paler than the remaining portion. The white streak over the eye is very conspicuous, and extends down the side of the neck ; beneath this streak and behind the eye is a patch like the back; the rest of the side of the head is grayish white, streaked with dusky.

Specimens vary considerably in the intensity of color, the under parts being sometimes but little tinged with the pale rusty, except on the sides and towards the tail. The under tail coverts are frequently almost pure white, conspicuously barred with black ; generally, however, they have a rusty tinge. In one specimen (7124) the under coverts are without any bars.

The only specimen I have seen from regions west of the Missouri is that collected at Fort Thorn by Dr. Henry.

46 b

List of specimens.

Catal. No.	Sex.	Locality.	When collected.	Whence obtained.	Collected by—	Length.	Stretch of wings	Wing.
7114	......	Philadelphia	....	John Cassin........	....	....	....	....
1785	......	Maryland............	....	S. F. Baird	John Krider	....	....	....
1097	♂	Washington, D. C....	June 12, 1843	......do............	W. M. Baird	6. 00	8. 25	2. 50
7120	......	Rockport, Ohio.......	Jan. 3, 1852	Dr. Kirtland......	....	....	....	....
10204	♂	South Illinois	May 9.........	R. Kennicott.......	....	....	....	....
7118	♂	Fort Leavenworth ...	Jan. 20, 1855	Lieut. Couch......	....	....	....	....
7119	......	......do.............	Dec. 20, 1854	......do...........	....	....	....	....
7117	......	Fort Thorn, N. M....	....	Dr. T. C. Henry ...	....	....	....	....

THRIOTHORUS BERLANDIERI, Couch.

Sp. Ch.—Exposed portion of bill nearly as long as the head. Above, dark rusty brown, most vivid on the rump. A whitish streak over the eye, bordered above with brown. Chin white ; rest of under parts dark brownish red ; the under tail coverts and sides of the body barred with dusky. Exposed surface of wings and tail barred throughout with dusky. Legs flesh color. Length, 5.25 ; wing, 2.25 ; tail 2.12.

Hab.—Northeastern Mexico towards the Rio Grande.

This species bears a very close resemblance to the *T. ludovicianus.* It is, however, smaller, the bill longer and more slender, the notch more conspicuous. The wings are proportionally shorter and more rounded, the primaries projecting less beyond the secondaries ; the first quill is larger. The tail is shorter and considerably more graduated. The colors above are darker, especially the reddish of the rump. The under parts are of a much deeper reddish brown, nearly as dark as the rump of *ludovicianus* and almost as deep as in *Catherpes mexicanus ;* the sides under the wings in two specimens exhibit distinct, though distant bars of dusky, not seen in any skins of the other species before me.

The lateral tail feathers are nearly half an inch less than the others, nearly twice as great a difference as in *ludovicianus.*

This species has been named by its discoverer, Lieut. Couch, after Dr. Berlandier, late of Matamoras, Mexico.

List of specimens.

Catal. No.	Sex.	Locality.	When collected.	Whence obtained.	Orig'l No.	Length.	Stretch of wings.	Wing.	Remarks.
7122	♀	Boquillo, New Leon, Mexico.	April —, 1853	Lieut. D. N. Couch.	142	5.25	7.25	2.25	Eyes brown, bill slate, feet light brown.
7123	♂	......do.............	......do......	......do............	143	5.25	7.25	2.50	....
7121	......	San Diego, Rio San Juan....	Mar. —, 1853	......do............	123	5.25	7.50	2.50	....

THRIOTHORUS BEWICKII, Bonap.

Bewick's Wren.

Troglodytes bewickii, Aud. Orn. Biog. I, 1831, 96 : V, 1838, 467 ; pl. 18.—Ib. Syn. 1839, 74.—Ib. Birds Amer. II,
1841, 120 ; pl. 118.—Nutt. Man. I, 1832, 434.—Lesson, Rev. Zool. 1840, 264.—Newberry,
Zool. P. R. R. Surv. VI, iv, 1857, 80.
Thryothorus bewickii, Bonap. List, 1838.—Ib. Conspectus, 1850, 221.
Telmatodytes bewickii, Cabanis, Mus. Hein. 1851, 78. (Not type.)
Troglodytes leucogastra, Gould, Pr. Zool. Soc. 1836, 89. (From Tamaulipas, Mex.)
Thryothorus leucogastra, Bon. Consp. 1850, 222.—Ib. Comptes Rendus, XXVIII, 1854, 57 ; Notes Orn. Delattre, 43.
Troglodytes spilurus, Vigors, Zool. Beechey's Voyage, 1839, 18 ; pl. iv. f. 1. (California.)

Sp. Ch.—Bill shorter than the head. Tail longer than the wings ; much graduated. Upper parts rufous brown ; beneath
plumbeous white. A white streak over the eye, the feathers edged above with brown. Exposed surface of the wings and the
innermost tail feathers closely barred with dusky ; the remaining tail feathers mostly black, barred or blotched with white at
the tips, and on the whole outer web of the exterior feather, and on the under tail coverts. Length, 5.50 ; wing, 2.25 ;
tail, 2.50. (2047.)

Var. spilurus, with longer bill ; purer white beneath. Colors more grayish olivaceous above.

Hab.—North America from Atlantic to Pacific ; south to Mexico.

This species is very strongly marked among all the North American wrens by the very long
black tail, varied only on the exterior with whitish. The rump is very little brighter than the
rest of the back. The upper and under tail coverts are conspicuously barred. When the tail
is closed its entire upper surface appears rather grayer than the back, and uniformly barred
from base to tip ; the concealed portion, however, is found to be nearly uniformly black, the
white only visible on the exterior when viewed from below. The sides of the body are
tinged with brown, but no bars are visible ; perhaps an occasional dusky streak.

The color of the under parts varies considerably. In one (2532) it is of a sooty brown,
scarcely lighter along the median line ; the colors above, too, are unusually dark. Generally,
however, it is of a dull soiled plumbeous white, darker, perhaps, across the breast. The female
is smaller than the male, but otherwise not different. The young is obscurely blotched beneath
with dusky.

The tail is so long that the outstretched hind feet do not reach to the end of it. The wings
do not quite reach over the posterior third of the tail, nor to the ends of the coverts. The
outer feathers are about .65 of an inch shorter than the middle ones.

All the western specimens with which I have compared series from Pennsylvania agree in
having a longer and more gently curved bill, the tail feathers apparently broader, and in being
less rufous and more olivaceous above ; the bars on the wings more obsolete. The under parts
are of rather a purer white. I am not prepared to say that these differences are constant or of
specific value ; if this should be established, Vigors' name of *spilurus* would be very appropriate. The skins from the Rio Grande are paler and grayer above ; the belly is still purer
white. It is this plumage which Gould has described as *Troglodytes leucogastra* in Pr. Zool.
Soc. 1836, 89. His specimen from Tamaulipas agrees perfectly with others in the Smithsonian
Museum from the same locality.

List of specimens.

Catal. No.	Sex and age.	Locality.	When collected.	Whence obtained.	Orig'l No.	Collected by—	Length.	Stretch of wings.	Wing.	Remarks.
2562	♂	Carlisle, Pa............	April 30, 1846	S. F. Baird......	.....	....	5.16	7.16	2.32	....
2047	♂	......do............	Mar. 29, 1845	......do.........	......	....	5.50	7.32	2.25	....
1061	♀	......do............	June 14, 1843	......do.........	......	....	4.91	6.75	2.16	....
1104	∞	......do............	July 5, 1843	......do.........	......	....	4.91	6.75	2.08	....
1103	∞	......do............	......do......	......do...... ..	......	....	....	......	......	....
7126	....	Fort Steilacoom.......	Feb. —, 1856	Dr. Suckley.....	253	....	....	......	......	....
7128	....	......do............	....	......do.........	251	....	....	......	......	....
7129	♂	Shoalwater bay, W. T.	June —, 1855	Gov. Stevens....	......	Dr. Cooper	5.50	6.50	......	....
7134	....	Fort Vancouver, W. T.	Dec. 29, 1853	......do.........	......	......do.......	5.25	7.00	....	Iris brown, legs gray, bill black and white.
4541	....	Washington Territory..	Dec. 29, 1856	......do.........	......	Dr. Suckley...	....	......	......	....
5516	♀	Petaluma, Cal.........	May 8, 1856	E. Samuels......	......	....	....	......	......	....
7133	♂	San Francisco.........	....	R. S. Williamson.	......	Dr. Heermann .	4.66	5.25	2.00	....
7132	....	Cosumnes river........	....	......do.........	......	......do.......	... ...	......	......	......
....	....	Fort Tejon............	....	J. X. de Vesey..	......	......	......	......	......	......
7127	....	Los Nogales, Mexico...	Jan. —, 1855	Major Emory	77	Dr. Kennerly...	....	......	......	....
7131	♀	Devil's river, Texas...	....	......do.........	18	J. H. Clark	5.00	6.75	1.75	....
7130	....	Ringgold Barracks, Tex.	Jan. 15, 1853	......do.........	......	......do.......	5.00	6.75	2.12	....
3970	... .	New Leon, Mex.........	April —, 185J	Lieut. Couch	158	....	....	6.50	2.25	Eyes brown, feet light brown.
3971	♀	Santa Rosalia, Mex.....	Mar. —, 1853	......do.........	......	....	4.75	6.50	2.00	Eyes brown, feet lead..
9119	....	Mexico...............	....	M. Verreaux.....	29906	....	....	......	......	....

CISTOTHORUS, Cabanis.

Cistothorus, CABANIS, Mus. Hein. 1850–'1, 77. Type *Troglodytes stellaris*.

Telmatodytes, CABANIS, Mus. Hein. 1850–'1, 78. Type *Certhia palustris*.

Thriothorus, VIEILLOT, Analyse, 1816, according to G. R. Gray. See article on genus *Thriothorus*.

CH.—Bill about as long as the head or much shorter, much compressed, not notched, gently decurved from the middle ; the gonys slightly concave or straight. Toes reaching to the end of the tail. Tarsus longer than the middle toe. Hind toe longer than the lateral, shorter than the middle. Lateral toes about equal. Hind toe longer than or equal to its digit. Wings rather longer than the tail, all the feathers of which are much graduated ; the lateral only two-thirds the middle. The feathers narrow. Back black, conspicuously streaked with white.

The excessive graduation of all the feathers of a tail shorter than the wings, in connexion with stout feet and a hind toe as long as or longer than its digit, appears to characterize this group. I have drawn the characters to include both *Cistothorus* and *Telmatodytes* of Cabanis, as they are very closely related. The characters of these will be found under the sub-family *Troglodytinae*.

CISTOTHORUS (TELMATODYTES) PALUSTRIS, Cabanis.

Long-billed Marsh Wren.

Certhia palustris, WILSON, Am. Orn. II, 1810, 58 ; pl. xii, f. 4.

Troglodytes palustris, BONAP. Obs. Wilson, 1824, No. 66.—SWAINSON, F. Bor. Am. II, 1832, 319.—AUDUBON, Orn. Biog. I, 1831, 500 : V, 1839, 467 ; pl. 100.—IB. Birds Amer. II, 1841, 135 ; pl. 123.—NEW-BERRY, Zool. Cal. & Or. Route ; P. R. R. Rep. VI, IV, 1857, 80.

Thryothorus palustris, NUTTALL, Man. I, 1832, 439.—BON. List, 1838.

Thryothorus arundineus, VIEILLOT, Nouv. Dict. XXXIV, 1819, 58. (Not *Troglodytes arundinaceus*, Vieillot, Ois. Am. II, pl. cviii.)

Thryothorus arundinaceus, BONAP. Consp. 1850, 220.

Telmatodytes arundinaceus, CABANIS, Mus. Hein. 1851, 78. (Type.)

Sp. Ch.—Bill about as long as head.   Tail and wing nearly equal.   Upper parts of a dull reddish brown, except on the crown, interscapular region, outer surface of tertials, and tail feathers, which are almost black : the first with a median patch like the ground color ; the second with short streaks of white, extending round on the sides of the neck : the third indented with brown ; the fourth barred with whitish, decreasing in amount from the outer feather, which is marked from the base, to the fifth, where it is confined to the tips ; the two middle feathers above like the back, and barred throughout with dusky.   Beneath rather pure white, the sides and under tail coverts of a lighter shade of brown than the back; a white streak over the eye. Length, 5.50 ; wing, 2.08 ; tail, 2.00.   (1454.)

Hab.—North America from Atlantic to Pacific ; north to Greenland.   (Reinhardt.)

There is only a slight tendency to paler bars on the under parts, these being broad, very obsolete, and confined to the sides.   The under tail coverts are moderately spotted in a male. In a female (1556) they are immaculate, and the black of the tail is less distinct ; the size is considerably smaller ; the colors of the back brighter and more rufous.

Specimens vary in the greater or less intensity of the lighter patch on the head, the crown sometimes appearing nearly black.   The rump is generally a little brighter than elsewhere ; the upper tail coverts more or less distinctly barred.   There is but little marking on the primaries.

In some western specimens there is a brownish tinge across the breast, but otherwise there is but little difference.   No. 7141, from Shoalwater bay, has a shorter bill than any others in the series before me.

Reinhardt (Vidensk. Meddel. for 1853, 81,) quotes "Troglodytes arundinaceus, Vieillot," as found in Greenland.   Vieillot's species of 1807 is really Thryothorus ludovicianus, but reference is probably meant to his Thryothorus arundineus, which, as stated below, is the present species.[1]

List of specimens.

Catal. No.	Sex.	Locality.	When collected.	Whence obtained.	Orig. No.	Collected by—	Length.	Stretch of wings.	Wing.	Remarks.
1456	♂	Carlisle, Pa..............	May 4, 1844	S. F. Baird........	......	....	5.50	6.75	2.50	....
1555	♀	......do...............	May 20	......do...........	......	....	4.91	6.00	1.91	....
4744	......	Mouth Big Sioux, Neb..	May 4, 1856	Lieut. Warren.....	......	Dr. Hayden....	4.50	6.25	2.00	Iris dark brown........ .....
8838	♀	Sand Hills......	Aug.12	..... do...........	......	......do......	5.00	6.50	2.00	....
7142	......	Texas.................	....	Capt. Pope	......	....	....	....	....	....
7141	......	Shoalwater bay, W. T..	Oct. 31, 1854	Gov. Stevens	110	Dr. Cooper....	5.25	6.75	....	Iris brown..............
7140	♂	Sacramento Valley.....	....	Lieut. Williamson.	......	Dr. Heermann.	....	....	....	.....•.................
		Fort Tejon, Cal........	....	J. Xantus de Vesey.	......	....	....	....	....	....

CISTOTHORUS STELLARIS, Cabanis.

Short-billed Marsh Wren.

Troglodytes stellaris, "Licht." Naumann, Vögel Deutschl. III, 1823, 724.   (Carolina.)
Cistothorus stellaris, Cabanis, Mus. Hein. 1851, 77.   Type.
Troglodytes brevirostris, Nuttall, Trans. Amer. Acad. Arts and Sc. New Ser. I, 1833, 98, with figure. Quoted in Manual, though date of volume is subsequent to 1832.—Ib. Manual, I, 1832, 436.—Aud. Orn. Biog. II, 1834, 427 : V, 1839, 469 ; pl. 175.—Ib. Syn. 1839, 76.—Ib. Birds Amer. II, 1841, 138 ; pl. 124.—Bon. List, 1838.—Ib. Consp. 1850, 220.

Sp. Ch.—Bill very short, scarcely half the length of the head.   Wing and tail about equal.   Hinder part of the crown and the scapular and interscapular region of the back and rump almost black, streaked with white.   Tail dusky, the feathers barred

[1] Most recent authors erroneously refer the Troglodytes arundinaceus of Vieillot in Ois. Am. Sept., to the present species. The Thryothorus arundineus, or " Thryothore des Roseaux" of Vieillot, (Nouv. Dict.,) is really the same ; but on the same page he expressly states that the Troglodytes arundinaceus, or " Troglodyte des Roseaux" of the Ois. Am. Sept., is identical with Sylvia ludoviciana of Latham, as would readily be inferred from the description and figure.   The habits, as indicated, were, however, probably based on palustris.

throughout with brown, (the color grayish on the under surface.) Beneath white, the sides, upper part of breast, and under tail covers reddish brown. Upper parts, with the exceptions mentioned, reddish brown. Length, 4.50 ; wing, 1.75 ; tail, 1.75.
Hab.—Eastern United States to the Loup Fork of Platte.

The series before me is not sufficiently full to say if the sexes differ in color. The dusky bars on the wing and tail are broad and conspicuous. The under tail coverts are faintly barred with lighter. There are also obsolete streaks of whitish on the sides of the neck. The forehead is brownish, not dusky.

This species differs in its white streaks on the back from all other North American wrens, excepting *T. palustris.* In this there are no streaks on the head or rump ; the tail is blacker, the bill much longer, the size much larger every way. I have not yet seen any specimens from the regions beyond the Missouri, except that collected by Lieut. Warren's expedition on the Loup Fork of the Platte, probably near the eastern limit of the high central plains.

List of specimens.

Catal. No.	Locality.	When collected.	Whence obtained.	Collected by—	Length.	Stretch of wings.	Wing.
2510	Carlisle, Pa..........	Sept. 20, 1848	S. F. Baird	....	4.41	5.83	1.75
3073	Liberty county, Ga...	1846..........	......do...........	J. Leconte.......	......	......	......
9217	Loup Fork, Neb......	Aug. 30, 1857	Lieut. Warren.......	Dr. Hayden.........	3.75	5.37	1.50
1916	Unknown	....	S. F. Baird	....	......	......	......

TROGLODYTES, Vieillot.

Troglodytes, VIEILLOT, Ois. Am. Sept. II, 1807, 52, type *T. aedon.*
" *Anorthura,* RENNIE, 1831 ;" (in Montague's Ornithological Dictionary ?)   Type *Motacilla troglodytes.*

The characters of this section will be found sufficiently indicated in the synopsis of the genera on a preceding page. It comes nearest to *Cistothorus,* but is distinguished by weaker feet and much smaller hind claws, which, instead of being equal to or longer than the remaining portion of the toe, is decidedly shorter.

The propriety of keeping the *Troglodytes aedon* in the same section with *T. hyemalis* may, perhaps, be questioned, as the latter differs essentially in the slender and nearly straight bill, and the very short tail, which is surpassed by the whole of the toes when outstretched. These differences I have indicated by the sections mentioned in the synopsis.

Of the first section, *Troglodytes,* there are possibly three species. Two of these have a lighter superciliary line ; one is the well known house wren, *T. aedon.* The other, its western representative, differing in the grayer color, without any rufous beneath. The third species, *T. americanus,* has no superciliary stripe.

In the second section, *Anorthura,* there is but one species in this country, *T. hyemalis,* closely related, however, to the European *T. parvulus.*

TROGLODYTES AEDON, Vieillot.

House Wren.

Troglodytes aedon, VIEILLOT, Ois. Am. Sept. II, 1807, 52 ; pl. cvii, (type of genus.)—IB. Nouv, Dict. XXXIV, 1819, 506.—BONAP. Obs. Wilson, 1825, No. 136.—RICH. F. Bor. Am. II, 1831, 316.—AUD. Orn. Biog. I, 1831, 427 : V, 1839, 470 ; pl. lxxxiii.—IB. Syn. 1839, 75.—IB. Birds Amer. II, 1841, 125 ; pl. cxx.

Sylvia domestica, WILSON, Am. Orn. I, 1808, 129 ; pl. viii.

Troglodytes fulvus, NUTTALL, Man. I, 1832, 422

Troglodytes furvus, RICH. List, 1837. (Not *Motacilla furva*, Gmelin.)

SP. CH.—Tail and wings about equal. Bill shorter than the head. Above reddish brown, darker towards the head, brighter on the rump. The feathers everywhere, except on the head and neck, barred with dusky ; obscurely so on the back, and still less on the rump. All the tail feathers barred from the base ; the contrast more vivid on the exterior ones. Beneath pale fulvous white, tinged with light brownish across the breast ; the posterior parts rather dark brown, obscurely banded. Under tail coverts whitish, with dusky bars. An indistinct line over the eye, eyelids, and loral region, whitish. Cheeks brown, streaked with whitish. Length, 4.90 ; wing, 2.08 ; tail, 2.00.

Hab.—Eastern United States to the Missouri, or to the high central plains.

The bill of this species, even from the extreme base, is shorter than the head. The wing is very nearly equal to the tail, and reaches over its basal fourth. The tail is moderately graduated, the lateral feather about .32 of an inch shorter than the middle. The outstretched feet reach about to the end of the tail.

There are a few whitish spots on the wing coverts.

List of specimens.

Catal. No.	Sex and age.	Locality.	When collected.	Whence obtained.	Collected by—	Length.	Stretch of wings.	Wing.	Remarks.
1084	♂	Carlisle, Pa............	June 14, 1843	S. F. Baird.......	....	4.91	6.83	2.08	....
728	....	......do................	Sept. 16, 1842	......do.........	....	4.91	6.83		....
1655	○	......do................	July 30, 1844	......do.........	....	5.08	6.75	2.00	....
1646	○	......do................	July 23, 1844	......do.........	....	5.00	6.50	2.00	....
2443	♂	......do................	Sept. 9, 1845	......do.........	....	....	....		....
7576	....	Washington, D. C....	....	Wm. Hutton	....	.. ....	....		....
8641	♂	Cape Florida, Fla..........	Oct. 23, 1857	G. Wurdemann...	....	4.50	5.75	1.75	Brown iris and legs, bill bl'k.
8642	....	......do................	Oct. 30, 1857	......do.........	....	4.75	6.75	2.00	Black eyes and bill.
8643	....	... ..do................	Oct. 23....	......do.........	....	4.75	5.75	1.75	Brownish legs, bill and eyes brown.
8644	....	......do................	Oct. 22......	......do.........	... .	4.50	6.25	2.00	....
6512	....	Indian Key, Fla............	....	......do.........	....	.....	....	....	....
8846	♂	Loup Fork, Platte river.....	July 3......	....	Lieut. Warren....	Dr. Hayden..	4.75	6.50	2.00	....

TROGLODYTES PARKMANNI, Aud.

Parkmann's Wren.

Troglodytes parkmanni, AUD. Orn. Biog. V, 1839, 310, not figured.—IB. Syn. 1839, 76.—IB. Birds Amer. II, 1841, 133 ; pl. 122.

SP. CH.—Similar in size and general appearance to *T. aedon*, with light line over the eye, &c ; the colors, however, grayer, the upper parts dark brown, the lower grayish white, with little or none of the rufous tinge of particular regions, as seen in *T. aedon*.

Hab.—Western America, from the high central plains and Upper Missouri, to the Pacific.

All the specimens of the house wren type from the western regions appear to differ from eastern ones in a grayer tinge of coloration, both above and below, the reddish brown of the rump and under parts being little if at all appreciable. There is, perhaps, a stronger tendency to bars on the upper parts and sides. Whether these features should be considered as establishing a distinct species I am not prepared fully to admit, but adopt Audubon's name as a provisional one for the western form.

Audubon compares his *T. parkmanni* with *T. hyemalis*. The differences are, however, very great, and the comparison should be made much rather with *aedon*.

List of specimens.

Cat. No.	Sex & age.	Locality.	When collected.	Whence obtained.	Orig'l No.	Collected by—	Length.	Stretch of wings	Wing.	Remarks.
5275	......	Blackfoot country....	July —, 1855	Lt. Warren......	......	Dr. Hayden....	....	....	......	....
5274	......	......do............	July —, 1855	......do .	......	......do.......	....	....	......	....
4734	♀	Upper Missouri	May 11, 1856	.....do	......	......do.......	4.50	6.50	2.00	....
4737	♂	......do............	May 15, 1856	....do	......	......do.......	4.75	6.87	2.12	....
5276	♂	Fort Lookout, Neb...	July —, 1856	......do........	......	......do.......	4.50	6.00	2.00	Eye brown
4739	♂	Near Council Bluffs..	April 29	. ...do........	......	...... do......	....	....	......	....
4740	......	Bald island, Neb......	Ap il 25, 1856	......do........	......	......do.......	4.87	6.50	2.12	Eye brown ....
4735	......	Upper Missouri......	May 14, 1856	......do........	......	......do.......	5.1ย	6.75	2.25	Iris hazel..........
4741	......	......do............	May 15, 1856	......do........	......	......do.......	5.00	6.50	2 50	....
4738	......	.... do............	May 15, 1856	......do........	......	......do.......	4.37	6.75	2.25	Iris light brown..........
4742	♂	....do............	May 12, 1856	......do........	......	......do.......	4.75	6.75	2.12	....do......
4736	♂	North Platte	April 26, 1856	......do........	......	......do.......	4.25	6.25	2.25	....
8211	......	Fort Laramie......	Sept. 18, 1857	W. M. Magraw...	193	Dr. Cooper	5.00	6.87	2.12	Iris brown, bill flesh, feet light brown.
4743	......	Upper Missouri......	April 24, 1856	Lt. Warren......	......	Dr. Hayden....	4.75	6.50	2.00	Eye light brown. ....
5646	♂	South Platte.........	July 7, 1856	Lt. Bryan..........	......	W. S. Wood ...	....	....	......	....
7139	♂	Charco Escondido, Mx	....	Lt. Couch........	76	....	4.50	6.00	2.00	Bill slate, eyes dark brown..
7135	○	Fort Steilacoom......	....	Dr. Suckley	127	....	....	....	......	....
7136	♂	......do..	May 3, 1856	......do..........	363	....	....	....	......	....
7137	......	......do..	....	......do..........	380	....	....	....	......	....
5517	♂	Petaluma, Cal	May 25, 1856	E. Samuels......	887	....	....	....	......	....
7138	♂	Sacramento Valley ...	....	Lt. Williamson...	......	Dr. Heermann.	....	....	......	....

TROGLODYTES AMERICANUS, Aud.

Wood Wren.

Troglodytes americanus, Aud. Orn. Biog. II, 1834, 452 : V, 1839, 469 ; pl. 179.—Ib. Birds Amer. II, 1841, 123; pl. 119.
Troglodytes sylvestris, Gambel, Pr. A. N. Sc. III, 1846, 113, (actually refers to *T. parkmanni*, though quoting Audubon as above.)

Sp. Ch.—Similar in size and color to the *T. aedon ;* the bill shorter, the tail more graduated. Colors throughout much darker ; no light line over the eye, but the sides of the head and neck much like the crown. The lores and ear coverts with the shafts of the feathers scarcely lighter. Length, 4.50 ; wing, 2.00 ; tail, 1.85.

Hab.—Eastern United States.

If I am correct in the reference of No. 2951 to this supposed species of Mr. Audubon, it is very similar to *T. aedon*, but appears to have a shorter and stouter bill. The size and proportions are very nearly the same, though given by Audubon as considerably larger. The colors generally are considerably darker, with very little reddish ; most distinct on the rump. There is no light line over the eye ; in fact the sides of the head and neck are almost uniform brown, with their upper parts being slightly relieved only by pale shafts to the ear coverts, and perhaps to the loral feathers. The under parts are considerably darker, the throat and breast almost brownish ash, the middle of the belly only whitish.

List of specimens.

Catal. No.	Age.	Locality.	Whence obtained.	Collected by—
2951	-----	Eastern United States ---------	S. F. Baird. -----------------	J. J. Audubon ---------------
1906	-----	------do----------------------	------do---------------------	
7255	○	------do----------------------	J. Cassin -----------------	

TROGLODYTES (ANORTHURA) HYEMALIS, Vieillot.

Winter Wren.

Sylvia troglodytes, WILSON, Am. Orn. I, 1808, 139 ; pl. viii, fig. 6.
Troglodytes hyemalis, VIEILLOT, Nouv. Dict. XXXIV, 1819, 514.—BONAP. List, 1838.—IB. Conspectus, 1850, 222 —
    SW. F. B. Am. II, 1831,°318.—AUD. Orn. Biog. IV, 1838, 430 ; pl. 360.—IB. Syn. 1839,
    76.—IB. Birds. Am. II, 1841, 128 ; pl. 121.
Troglodytes europaeus, BON. Obs. Wils. 1825 ; No. 137.—NUTTALL, Man. I, 1832, 427.

SP. CH.—Bill very straight, slender, and conical ; shorter than the head. Tail considerably shorter than the wings, which reach to its middle. Upper parts reddish brown ; becoming brighter to the rump and tail ; everywhere, except on the head and upper part of the back, with transverse bars of dusky and of lighter. Scapulars and wing coverts with spots of white. Beneath pale reddish brown, barred on the posterior half of the body with dusky and whitish, and spotted with white more anteriorly ; outer web of primaries similarly spotted with pale brownish white. An indistinct pale line over the eye. Length, about 4 inches ; wing, 1.66 ; tail, 1.26.

Hab.—North America generally.

Western specimens of this species appear to be of a darker reddish brown generally than in the eastern, and perhaps a little larger. Northern ones are decidedly largest.

This wren is so exceedingly like the European *Troglodytes parvulus*,[1] that I candidly confess my inability to distinguish the single specimen of the latter before me (9216 from Nürnberg,) from American skins.

List of specimens.

Catal. No.	Sex.	Locality.	When collected.	Whence obtained.	Orig. No.	Collected by—	Length.	Stretch of wings.	Wing.
127	----	Carlisle, Pa.---------	Oct. 13, 1840	S. F. Baird -----	-----	---------------	-------		-----
1379	♀	------do-----------	April 22, 1844	------do--------	-----	---------------	3.83	5.83	1.66
10206		Cairo, Illinois-------	April 24------	R. Kennicott----	-----	---------------	-------		-----
7143	----	West Northfield, Ill.--	---------------	------do--------	-----	---------------	-------		-----
7144	----	Ft. Steilacoom, W. T.	Mar. —, 1856	Gov. Stevens----	267	Dr. Suckley-----	-----		-----
7145	----	------do-----------	Dec. 23, 1853	------do--------		------do--------	-----		-----
7146	----	------do-----------	Feb. — ------	------do--------	254	------do--------	-----		-----
7147	----	------do-----------	Mar. —, 1856	------do--------	264	------do--------	-----		-----
4601	----	Shoalwater bay, W. T.	May, 22, 1854	------do--------	75	Dr. Cooper------	3.08	5.25	-----
		Columbia river-------	Jan. 27, 1856	------do--------	208	Dr. Suckley-----	4.25	6.25	1.91

[1] The synonymes of the European wren are—
TROGLODYTES PARVULUS, Koch.
    Motacilla troglodytes, LINN. Syst. Nat.
    Anorthura troglodytes, RENNIE.
    Troglodytes parvulus, KOCH.
    Troglodytes europaeus, CUV. Vieillot.
    Troglodytes regulus, MEYER.

47 b

The preceding pages include all the wrens assigned by more recent writers to the United States, with the exception of *T. maculosa*, Nuttall, described from a specimen seen in a thicket in Oregon. There is no known species to which this can be assigned, unless the description is erroneous, as might readily be the case under the circumstances of observation.[1]

Sub-Family CHAMAEANAE.

CHAMAEA, Gambel.

Chamaea, GAMBEL, Pr. A. N. Sc. III, 1847, 154. (Type *Parus fasciatus*.)

CH.—Bill shorter than the head, much compressed. Rictus with long bristles. Tarsus much longer than the toes; without well marked scales. Lateral toes equal. Wings short, much rounded; two-thirds the length of the tail, which is much graduated; the lateral feathers two-thirds the longest. Plumage very soft and lax.

In this genus the bill is short and much compressed from the middle, broader than high at the base. The culmen is straight half way, then considerably curved; the gonys nearly straight, but ascending. The bill is not notched; nor are the nostrils concealed by incumbent bristles, though a few of these, of large size, with lateral setae, are directed forward. The nostrils are elongated and narrow, though short and overhung by a scale. The bristles at the base of the bill are quite long and conspicuous, measuring a quarter of an inch. The tarsi are very long, and exhibit no divisions of scutellae (except obsoletely) on the inner side. The claws are moderate the hinder as long as the rest of the toe. The wings are short and much rounded; the first five primaries much graduated; the third scarcely longer than the primaries. The tail feathers are very long and subtruncate.

I am not sure that I have correctly indicated the place of *Chamaea*, though there is no other family to which it could so readily be referred. The strongly bristled rictus separates it widely from the wrens, as does also the broad depressed character of the base of the bill. The bristly character of the frontal feathers is quite peculiar in the group. It has been placed among the titmice, but is easily distinguished from them by the free character of most of the basal joints of the middle toe, the absence of a sheath of bristly feathers around the base of the bill, &c. It is, however, very similar, and probably connects the two families.

Comparative measurements.

Catal. No.	Species.	Locality.	Sex.	Length.	Stretch of wings.	Wing.	Tail.	Tarsus.	Middle toe.	Its claw alone.	Bill above.	Along gape.	Specimen measured.
7163	Chamaea fasciata....	Sacramento valley .	♂	5.90	....	2.20	3.40	0.92	0.70	0.18	0.42	0.52	Skin ....
5924	......do	Santa Clara, Cal....	......	6.20	....	2.34	3.42	1.02	0.76	0.22	0.46	0.54	Skin ....

CHAMAEA FASCIATA, Gambel.

Parus fasciatus, GAMBEL, Pr. A. N. S. II, Aug. 1845, 265.

Chamaea fasciata, GAMBEL, Pr. A. N. S. III, Feb. 1847, 154. (Type of genus.)—IB. J. A. N. S. 2d Series, I, 1847, 34; pl. viii, f. 3.—CABANIS, Wiegmann's Archiv, 1848, I, 102.—BP. Consp. 1850, 206.—CASSIN, Ill. I, II, 1853, 39; pl. vii.

SP. CH.—Wings scarcely two-thirds the length of the tail; both very much graduated. Upper and outer parts generally (including the whole tail) olivaceous brown, tinged with gray on the head; beneath pale brownish cinnamon, with obsolete

[1] *Troglodytes maculosa*, NUTTALL, Man. I, 2d ed. 1840, 492.—Above cinereous gray; side of he throat and breast with whitish spots. Mouth of the Columbia and near Santa Barbara.

streaks of dusky on the throat and breast. Sides and under tail coverts tinged with olive brown. Lores and a spot above the eye obscurely whitish. Tail feathers with obsolete transverse bars. Length, 6 inches; wing, 2.25; tail, 3.50. (5924.)

Hab.—Coast of California.

This curious species is very different in appearance from the North American wrens. The colors are very simple, and the female differs from the above description only in being rather smaller and with the reddish of the under parts less distinct; the whitish spot over the eye scarcely recognisable.

List of specimens.

Catal. No.	Sex.	Locality.	Whence obtained.	Collected by—
3339	......	California	S. F. Baird	Dr. Gambel..................
5924	♂	Santa Clara, Cal...............	Dr. Cooper..................	....
7163	♂	Sacramento valley, Nov. 1855..[1]	Lt. Williamson...............	Dr. Heermann..............
7164	♀	......do.....................	......do...................	......do..................
......		Fort Tejon, Cal...............	John Xantus de Vesey	....

[1] Length, 6.75; Extent, 7.00; Iris, white.

Family CERTHIADAE.

First primary very short, less than half the second ; outer lateral toe much longest ; hind toe exceeding both the middle toe and the tarsus, which is scutellate anteriorly, and very short. Bill slender, as long as or longer than the head, without any notch. Entire basal joint of the middle toes united to the lateral.

This family in the United States embraces but two genera, each the type of a sub-family, and so widely different from each other as not to require any comparison. The characters of the sub-families are as follows :

CERTHIANAE.—Bill much compressed and greatly decurved ; gonys concave. Tail long, cuneate ; the feathers stiffened at the tips.

SITTINAE.—Bill straight ; gonys ascending, convex. Tail short, soft, and even.

Sub-family CERTHIANAE.

CERTHIA, Linnaeus.

Certhia, LINNAEUS, Syst. Nat. 1735, (Gray). Type *C. familiaris*.

CH.—Bill as long as the head, slender, much compressed and decurved from the base ; without notch or rictal bristles. Tarsi distinctly scutellate ; very short ; not longer than the outer lateral toes, which much exceeds the inner, reaching nearly as far as the middle toe. Hind toe longer than the middle one ; its claw more than half the total length. Claws all very"long and acute. Tail rather longer than the wings, arched or vaulted, graduated or cuneate ; the feathers very acute at the tips, the shafts stiffened. First primary rather more than one-third the fourth or longest one. Color above brown, streaked with white ; beneath white.

This genus embraces species which resemble each other so closely as to render it a matter of much uncertainty how many really exist.

Comparative measurements of species.

Catal. No.	Species.	Locality.	Sex.	Length	Stretch of wings	Wing.	Tail.	Tarsus.	Middle toe.	Its claw alone.	Bill above.	Along gape.	Specimen measured.
827	Certhia americana..	Carlisle, Pa..............	♂	5.26	....	2.52	2.84	0.56	0.64	0.22	0.58	0.66	Skin .....
do.	......do	......do...............		5.41	7.83	2.58							Fresh ....
1337	..... do .	.......do.	♀	5.00	....	2.46	2.46	0.56	0.62	0.22	0.54	0.66	Skin .....
do.	......do............	......do .		5.00	7.58	2.50							Fresh ....
7154	Certhia americana?	Camp 110, Pueblo c'k, N.M.		5.00	....	2.42	2.66	0.56	0.62	0.20	0.68	0.76	Skin .....
9520	......do	Similahmoo bay, Puget S'd.		4.80	....	2.62	2.30	0.58	0 66	0.20	0.60	0.68	Skin .....
do.	......do	......do		4.75	7.50	2.75							Fresh ....
8176	Certhia mexicana?.	Mexico.........		5.14	....	2.44	2.73	0.56	0.52	0.20	0.62	0.70	Skin .....

CERTHIA AMERICANA, Bonap.

American Creeper.

Certhia americana, BONAP. Consp. List, 1838.—REICH. Handb. I, 1851, 265 ; pl. dcxv, fig. 4102, 3.
Certhia familiaris, VIEILLOT, Ois. Am. Sept. II, 1807, 70.—WILSON, Am. Orn. I, 1808, 122 ; pl .viii.—AUD. Orn. Biog. V, 1839, 158 ; pl. 415.—IB. Syn. 1839, 73.—IB. Birds Amer. II, 1841, 109 ; pl. 115.
? *Certhia mexicana*, " GLOGER, Handbuch," REICHENBACH, Handbuch Spec. Orn. I, 1851, 265 ; pl. dlxii, fig. 3841, 2.—IB. SCLATER, Pr. Zool. Soc. 1856, 290.

SP. CH.—Bill about the length of the head. Above dark brown, with a slightly rufous shade, each feather streaked centrally but not abruptly with whitish ; rump rusty. Beneath almost silky white ; the under tail coverts with a faint rusty tinge. A white streak over the eye ; the ear coverts streaked with whitish. Tail feathers brown centrally, the edges paler yellowish brown. Wings with a transverse bar of pale reddish white across both webs.
Length, 5.50 ; wing, 2.60 ; tail, 2.90. (No. 827.)
Hab.—North America generally.

The wings of this species are greatly variegated. Thus, when closed, the outer edges and tips are seen to be pale fulvous, with a continuous dark line rnnning along the tips. The two outer primaries are unicolor ; the rest have the band of fulvous white on the middle across both webs ; and there is a similar band on the secondaries, the line continuous in the outstretched wings. There are also two bands of white across the coverts.

The female is quite similar to the male, and I have not seen any American specimens with the strong rufous tinge above, indicated by Audubon. The under parts, excepting the tail coverts, are, in perfect specimens, nearly pure white, with, perhaps, a faint tinge on the breast; in No. 1337, however, the body is strongly plumbeous white beneath.

The tail in 827, from Carlisle, is considerably longer than in any other American specimens I have seen, even from the same locality.

There appears to be very little difference between the American creeper and the European *C. familiaris*, although I have not at hand the means of making the comparison. Reichenbach, in his carefully prepared monograph of the genus *Certhia*, (Handbuch Speciellen Ornithologie, I, 265,) gives nothing tangible on the subject, although referring the American form to Brehm's sub-species, *C. septentrionalis*.

Young birds from Washington Territory, 5945 and 7132, are like the adult, with the markings less distinct.

A *Certhia* from Mexico (8176) differs from Carlisle specimens in being darker above, the rufous of the rump considerably deeper and of a brownish orange shade. The light bars on the wings are narrower and less prominent. The under parts are of a duller white ; the throat is similar. The bill is considerably longer, but shorter than in 7154, from New Mexico, which again is lighter above. No. 10208, from Fort Tejon, is, however, precisely identical in all these features. All the west coast specimens agree in rather darker colors above and a darker rufous on the rump, intermediate in this respect, as well as in length of bill, between 8176 or 10208 and Pennsylvania skins. I can hardly see good grounds, however, for making a second species with the insensible gradations visible in the series. The peculiarities of color correspond to those of *Certhia mexicana* of Gloger, which is said to be darker than the common species, but is also said to be smaller, which is not the case with western skins, and the bill is absolutely longer, instead of shorter, as indicated by Reichenbach's measurements.

List of specimens.

Catal. No.	Sex & age.	Locality.	When collected.	Whence obtained.	Orig. No.	Collected by—	Length.	Stretch of wings.	Wing.
827	♂	Carlisle, Pa.	Oct. 22, 1842	S. F. Baird.			5.41	7.83	2.58
1337	♀	do.	April 5, 1844	do.			5.00	7.58	2.50
1767		do.	Jan —, 1845	do.			5.25	7.58	2.50
		West Northfield, Ill.	April 18	R. Kennicott.					
7152	o	Fort Steilacoom, W. T.	Aug. 2, 1856	Dr. Suckley.	514				
7156		do.		do.	256				
7125		do.		do.					
5945[1]	o	do.		Dr. Cooper.			5.00	7.00	
7155		do.		do.	369				
7153	♂	Sacramento valley		Lt. Williamson.		Dr. Heermann			
10208		Fort Tejon.		J. X. de Vesey.					
7154		Pueblo creek, N. M.	Jan. 22, 1854	Lt. Whipple	47	Kenn. and Möll.			
8176		Mexico.		J. Gould					

[1] Feet white; Iris and bill, brown.

Sub-Family SITTINAE.

SITTA, Linnaeus.

Sitta, LINNAEUS, Syst. Nat. 1735. (Agassiz.)

CH.—Bill subulate, acutely pointed, compressed, about as long as the head; culmen and commissure nearly straight; gonys convex and ascending; nostrils covered by a tuft of bristles directed forward. Tarsi stout, scutellate, about equal to the middle toe, much shorter than the hinder, the claw of which is half the total length. Outer lateral toe much longer than inner, and nearly equal to the middle. Tail very short, broad, and nearly even; the feathers soft and truncate. Wings reaching nearly to the end of the tail, long and acute, the first primary one-third of (or less) the third, or longest.

This genus differs from *Sittella* in having the bill entire, not notched, the tail longer, &c. There are several species in the United States, which may be arranged as follows:

a. Crown black.

Pure white beneath. Bill stout... ....*S: carolinensis.*
Similar. Bill slender...*S. aculeata.*
Brownish rusty beneath, a black stripe through the eye...............................*S. canadensis.*

b. Crown not black.

Crown light brown. Hind toe much longer than the middle one........................*S. pusilla.*
Crown greenish plumbeous. Hind toe about equal to the middle one...............*S. pygmaea.*

Comparative measurements of species.

Catal. No.	Species.	Locality.	Sex.	Length.	Stretch of wings.	Wing.	Tail.	Tarsus.	Middle toe.	Its claw alone.	Bill above.	Along gape.	Specimens measured.
1762	Sitta carolinensis.....	Carlisle, Pa.......	♂	5.40	....	3.56	2.20	0.70	0.86	0.24	0.70	0.88	Skin...........
do.	......do	......do		6.50	....								Fresh...........
1761	......do	......do	♀	5.36	....	3.58	2.02	0.78	0.90	0.26	0.76	0.84	Skin...........
do.	......do	......do		6.00	11.25	3.75							Fresh...........
10209	Sitta aculeata.........	Fort Tejon, Cal....	♂	5.42	....	3.40	2 10	0.69	0.78	0.24	0.76	0.90	Skin...........
10210	..... do	......do	♀	5.32	....	3.43	2.12	0.70	0.80	0.26	0.76	0.93	Skin...........
818	Sitta canadensis......	Carlisle, Pa........	♂	4.20	....	2.68	1.70	0.60	0.68	0.22	0.58	0.64	Skin...........
do.	......do	......do		4.58	8.50	2.66							....
2073	......do	......do	♀	4.10	....	2.60	1.56	0.62	0.70	0.22	0.56	0.66	Skin...........
do.	......do	......do		4.58	8.08	2.58							. ..... Fresh...........
1925	Sitta pusilla.........	Georgia...............		4.00	....	2.60	1.52	0.56	0.64	0.20	0.54	0.68	Skin...... ....
3342	Sitta pygmaea	Upper California...	......	4.00	....	2.40	1.44	0.58	0.62	0.20	0.50	0.62	Skin...........

SITTA CAROLINENSIS, Gmelin.

White-bellied Nuthatch.

Sitta europaea, var. γ, *carolinensis,* GMELIN, I, 1788, 440.
Sitta carolinensis, LATHAM, Ind. Orn. I, 1790, 262.—WILSON, Am. Orn. I, 1808, 40; pl.—BON. Obs. Wils. 1825.—IB. List 1838.—IB. Conspectus, 1850, 227.—NUTTALL, Man. I, 1832, 581.—AUD. Orn. Biog. II, 1834, 299: V, 1839, 473; pl. 152.—IB. Birds Amer. IV, 1842, 175; pl. 247.
Sitta melanocephala, VIEILLOT, Gal. I, 1834, 171; pl. clxxi.

SP. CH.—Above ashy blue. Top of head and neck black. Under parts and sides of head to a short distance above the eye white. Under tail coverts and tibial feathers brown; concealed primaries white. Bill stout.

Length, about 6 inches; wing, about 3¾.

Hab.—Eastern North America to the high central plains. West of this replaced by *S. aculeata.*

Third and fourth quills about equal ; fifth a little shorter ; second intermediate between fifth and sixth.   Top of the head and back of the neck, with upper part of back, lustrous greenish black ; rest of upper parts ashy blue.   Under parts generally, with sides of head and neck, white, this color extending from the base of the upper mandible over the eye ; tibial feathers, with inner webs of under tail coverts, light rufous brown.   Quills white at the extreme base and on the basal portion of the inner webs.   Wing feathers dark brown above, except the coverts, the tertiaries, and the ends of primaries and secondaries, which are nearly black, all edged more or less with the color of the back, which becomes more whitish on the tips of the quills and the edges of the outer primaries.   Under wing coverts black.   Central tail feather like the back ; the rest black, with a broad subterminal band and more or less of the outer web white.

The female differs only in having the black of the head with an ashy gloss.

In comparing a large series of specimens together, (about thirty in each,) from the two sides of the continent, the western, as a general rule, have more slender bills than the eastern.   I can detect no other difference whatever.   This constitutes the character of Mr. Cassin's species, *S. aculeata.*

List of specimens.

Catal. No.	Sex and age.	Locality.	When collected.	Whence obtained.	Orig. No.	Collected by—	Length.	Stretch of wings.	Wing.	Remarks.
1645	....	Carlisle, Pa............	July 18, 1844	S. F. Baird.........	......	....	6.08	10.83	3.58	....
1761	♀	.....do..............	Jan. —, 1845	......do	......	....	6.00	11.25	3.75	....
1762	♂	.....do......	.....do......	......do.	......	....	6.50	......	......	....
6802	....	Ft. Leavenworth, K. T..	......do......	Lieut. Couch	17	....	......	......	......	....
8337	O	Independence, Mo.....	Dec. 24, 1854	Wm. M. Magraw	62	Dr. Cooper	5.90	10.50	3.37	Iris and bill black, feet gray.
8336	♀	.....do............	June 6, 1857	......do.	61	......do........	6.00	10.25	3.75	....
5628	♂	East of Fort Riley.....	.....do......	Lt. Bryan.	28	W. S. Wood...	....	......	......	....
5871	....	Fort Riley, K. T.......	June 18, 1856	Hammond & DeVesey.	......	....	....	......	......	....
5870	....	.....do..............	....	.....do.	......	....	....	......	......	....

SITTA ACULEATA, Cassin.

Slender-bill Nuthatch.

Sitta aculeata, CASSIN, Pr. A. N. Sc. Phila. VIII, Oct. 1856, 254.

SP. CH.—Precisely similar to *S. carolinensis*, but the bill slenderer and more attenuated.
Hab.—Pacific coast, and east towards the Rocky mountains.

It is a very difficult matter to decide whether the western white-breasted nuthatches are to be considered merely as varieties of *S. carolinensis* or as distinct species.   The only difference I can discern is the much slenderer bill, a character, however, which is constant in all before me, (about thirty specimens,) while the stout bill is seen in all east of the Missouri plains.   Thus, the depth of the bill opposite the base above is .14 of an inch ; the width at same point is .17, instead of .17 and .22, respectively.   Specimens from Washington Territory, however, appear to be intermediate in this respect between more southern and eastern ones.

The young bird is similar, but duller, the under parts tinged with reddish brown.

List of specimens.

Catal. No.	Sex.	Locality.	When collected.	Whence obtained.	Orig. No.	Collected by—	Length.	Stretch of wings.
6808	----	Fort Steilacoom, W. T. ----	May 1,1856	Dr. Suckley........	353	....	6.00	10.50
6809	----	......do.................	1854......	Gov. Stevens.	104	Dr. Suckley.......		--------
6810	----	......do.................	----------	Dr. Suckley........		....	4.87?	9.50
6811	----	......do.................	----------	......do...........	258	....		--------
6812	----	......do.................	----------	......do...........	208	....	6.00	10.00
5502	----	Petaluma, Cal....	----------	E. Samuels........	280	....	--------	--------
6806	----	San Francisco...........	----------	R. D. Cutts.......		....	--------	--------
4944	----	San José, Cal.	----------	A. J. Grayson.....		....	--------	--------
4492	----	......do.................	----------	Lt. Williamson....		J. S. Newberry....	--------	--------
10209	♂	Fort Tejon.............	----------	J. X. de Vesey....	1268	....	--------	--------
10210	♀	......do.................	----------		875	....	--------	--------
6807	----	100 miles W. of Al uquerque	----------	Lt. Whipple	26	Kenn. & Möll.....	--------	--------

SITTA CANADENSIS, Linn.

Red-bellied Nuthatch.

Sitta canadensis, LINN. Syst. Nat. I, 1766, 177.—NUTTALL, Man. I, 1832, 583.—AUD. Orn. Biog. II, 1834, 24 : V, 474 ; pl. 108.—IB. Birds Amer. IV, 179 ; pl. 248.—BON. Consp. 1850, 227.

Sitta varia, WILS. Am. Orn. I, 1808, 40 ; pl. ii.

Sitta stulta, VIEILL. Nouv. Dict.(?)

SP. CH.—Above ashy blue. Top of head black ; a white line above and a black one through the eye. Chin white ; rest of under parts brownish rusty. Length about 4½ inches ; wing, 2⅗.

Hab.—North America to the Rocky mountains. Probably also to the Pacific.

Fourth quill longest; third a little shorter, but longer than fifth; second intermediate between sixth and seventh. Above ashy blue. Top of head from bill to occiput deep black ; sides of head and chin white, with a narrow black band from the bill through the eye ; under parts generally yellowish rusty, deepest towards the tail. Under wing coverts tinged with black. Wing feathers brown, edged with the color of the back, and without white or black marking. Tail feathers narrowly tipped with bluish ; central one like the black ; rest of feathers black ; the first and second with a subterminal, the third with a terminal bar of white.

The female has the black of the head tinged with dark ash ; the under surfaces lighter, more of a muddy white.

I am unable to detect any difference between eastern and western specimens. One of the latter (6839) has the bill much stouter than any others I have seen from either side of the continent, being quite as broad at the base as in a much larger *S. carolinensis* from Pennsylvania.

The rusty belly and white streak over the eye, with the black one through it, will readily distinguish this from any other North American species.

List of specimens.

Catal. No.	Sex.	Locality.	When collected.	Whence obtained.	Collected by—	Length.	Stretch of wings.	Wing.
6937	......	Selkirk Settlement.	....	Dr. Gunn	....	....	....	....
818	♂	Carlisle, Pa........	Oct. 19, 1842	S. F. Baird	....	4. 16	8. 50	2. 66
2073	......	......do...........	April 5, 1845	......do..........	....	4. 58	8. 12	2. 58
5280	♂	Cedar island, Mo..	1856.........	Lieut. Warren	Dr. Hayden......	....	....	....
8890	......	Black Hills, Neb ..	Sept. 30, 1857	......do..........	......do..........	4. 50	8. 38	2. 50
8889	......	......do...........	......do......	......do..........	......do..........	4. 25	7. 50	2. 57
6838	......	Sacramento valley.	....	Lieut. Williamson.	Dr. Heermann	....	....	....
6839	......	......do...........	....	......do..........	......do..........	....	....	....

SITTA PUSILLA, Latham.

Brown-headed Nuthatch.

Sitta pusilla, LATH. Index Orn. I, 1790, 263.—WILSON, Am. Orn. II, 1810, 105; pl. xv.—NUTTALL, Man. I, 1832, 584.—AUD. Orn. Biog. II, 1834, 151; pl. 125.—IB. Birds Amer. IV, 1842, 181; pl. 249.—BON. Obs. Wilson, 1825, No. 61.—IB. Conspectus, 1850, 227.

SP. CH.—Above ashy blue; top of head and upper part of neck rather light hair brown, divided on the nape by white. Eye involved in the brown, which is deeper on the lower border. Beneath muddy whitish; sides and behind paler than the back. Middle tail feathers almost entirely like the back. Length of female 4 inches; wing, 2½.

Hab.—South Atlantic (and Gulf?) States.

Third, fourth, and fifth quills nearly equal, although the fourth is longest; second shorter than seventh. Above ashy blue; the top of the head and upper part of nape brown, the middle of the latter interrupted by a large whitish spot; the lower edge of the brown involving the lower edge of the eye, and of a darker color than elsewhere. Chin and sides of head and throat below the brown white. Rest of under parts pale bluish ash, lighter than on the back, and tinged with dirty white on the throat, breast, and middle of abdomen. No white markings on the wings. Feathers of tail tipped with bluish; innermost feather like the back; others black; the two outer with a subterminal bar of pale whitish.

List of specimens.

Catal. No.	Sex.	Locality.	When collected	Whence obtained.	Collected by—	Length.	Stretch of wings.	Wing.
2398	......	Savannah, Ga.......	....	S. F. Baird.	Jos. Leconte	....	....	.....
3086	♀	Liberty county, Ga ..	1846.........	......do..........	W. L. Jones	4. 00	7. 50	2. 50
3090	♂	......do...........	1846.........	......do..........	......do..........	4. 40	8. 00	2. 75
3091	♂	......do...........	1846.........	......do..........	......do..........	4. 20	8. 50	2. 70

48 b

SITTA PYGMAEA, Vigors.

California Nuthatch.

Sitta pygmaea, Vigors, Zool. Beechey's Voyage, 1839, 25 ; pl. iv.—Audubon, Orn. Biog. V, 1839, 63 ; pl. 415.—Ib. Syn. 1839, 168.—Ib. Birds Amer. IV, 1842, 184 ; pl. 250.—Newberry, Zool. Cal. Or. Route ; P. R. R. Rep. VI, iv, 1857, 79.

Sp. Ch.—Above ashy blue ; head and upper part of neck greenish ashy brown, its lower border passing a little below the eye, where it is darker ; nape with an obscure whitish spot. Chin and throat whitish ; rest of lower parts brownish white ; the sides and behind like the back, but paler. Middle tail feather like the back ; its basal half with a long white spot ; its outer web edged with black at the base. Length about 4 inches ; wing, 2.40.

Hab.—Pacific coast and towards Rocky mountains.

Third, fourth, and fifth quills nearly equal and longest. General color above ashy blue. Top of head and nape and sides of head ashy brown, with a greenish tinge, the lower portion (passing through the eye) of a purer brown and darker. Chin, upper part of throat, sides of head, and an obscure spot on the nape dividing the brown, white ; sides of body like the back, but paler ; rest of under parts pale rusty or brownish white. Inner tail feathers like the back, but with a long white spot at the base ; all the feathers tipped with ashy blue ; rest of feathers black ; the first and second with a subterminal oblique bar of white.

This species is closely related to *Sitta pusilla* of the southern States. The brown of the head has, however, an olivaceous green tinge not seen in the other ; the white spot on the nape less distinct. The middle tail feather has its basal half white and the outer web edged with black at the base. This black edging is never seen in the other, and the white patch reduced to a faint trace, only visible in very high plumaged specimens.

List of specimens.

Catal. No.	Locality.	When collected.	Whence obtained.	Orig. No.	Collected by—
3342	California		S. F. Baird.		Dr. Gambel
3729	do		W. Hutton		do
6840	Ft. Colville, W. T.	Oct. —, 1853	I. I. Stevens		Dr. Cooper
6804	Cold Spring, R. Mts.	Nov. 17, 1853	Lieut. Whipple	22	Kennerly and Möllhausen.
6803	San Francisco Mts.	Dec. 27, 1853	do		do

Family PARIDAE.

First primary very short, generally less than half the second, which is considerably less than the third. Tarsus longer than the middle toe, strongly scutellate anteriorly ; hind toe rather shorter than the middle. Entire basal joint of middle toe united to the lateral toes. Bill short, straight, conical, usually without notch. Wings short; tail rather long, rounded, or graduated.

In the limited number of forms of this family in North America, I am unable to define the sub-families with any degree of precision, except to state that *Polioptila* appears to belong to one, and the true titmice to another. In *Polioptila* the bill is long, slender, and distinctly notched, the nostrils open, while in the titmice the bill is shorter, more conical, entirely without notch, and the nostrils concealed by feathers. Other differences will be found mentioned under the respective genera.

POLIOPTILINAE.—Bill slender, elongated, distinctly notched ; nostrils not covered by bristly feathers, but exposed ; nostrils elongated.

PARINAE.—Bill short, conical, without indication of notch ; nostrils rounded, completely concealed by elongated bristly feathers directed forwards.

POLIOPTILA, Sclater.

Polioptila, SCLATER, Pr. Zool. Soc. 1855, 11. Type *Motacilla caerulea*.
Culicivora, SWAINSON, Class. Birds, II, 1837, 243. Type *C. atricapilla*. Not *Culicivora* (type *stenura*) of Swainson's Zool. Jour. III, 1827, 359.

CH.—Bill slender, attenuated, but depressed at the base ; nearly as long as the head, distinctly notched at the tip, and provided with moderate rictal bristles. Nostrils rather elongated, not concealed, but anterior to the frontal feathers. Tarsi longer than the middle toe, distinctly scutellate ; the toes small ; the hinder one scarcely longer than the lateral ; its claw scarcely longer than the middle. Outer lateral toe longer than the inner. First primary about one-third the longest ; second equal to the seventh. Tail a little longer than the wings, moderately graduated ; the feathers rounded.

The species all lead color above ; white beneath, and to a greater or less extent on the exterior of the tail, the rest of which is black. Size very small.

Two species of this interesting genus are now known to belong to the United States in addition to the one described by Wilson and Audubon.

Synopsis of species.

Two outer tail feathers entirely white. A narrow frontal line, extending back over the eye, black...*P. caerulea*.

Outer tail feather, with the whole of the outer web (only) white. No black on the forehead, but a stripe over the eye above one of whitish...*P. plumbea*.

Edge only of outer web of outer tail feather white. Entire top of head from the bill black.
P. melanura.

Comparative measurements of species.

Catal. No.	Species.	Locality.	Sex.	Length.	Stretch of wings.	Wing	Tail.	Tarsus.	Middle toe.	Its claw alone.	Bill above.	Along gape.	Specimen measured.
10214	Polioptila caerulea........	South Illinois....	♂	4.60	....	2.06	2.10	0.62	0.44	0.12	0.38	0.52	Skin.....
616	........do............	Washington, D.C.	♀	4.50	....	2.10	2.38	0.68	0.46	0.14	0.43	0.54	Skin.....,
	.........do.....	.....do..........	♂	4.60	6.50	2 10	2.26	0.67	0.48	0.14	0.42	0.56	Fresh....
7191	Polioptila melanura........	San Diego	♂	4.16	....	1.84	2.04	0.70	0.44	0.13	0.38	0.50	Skin.....
7192	........do............	Fort Yuma......	♀	4.20	....	1.80	2.18	0.71	0.47	0.12	0.42	0 52	Skin.....
7187	Polioptila plumbea........	Boca Grande,Mex	.....	4.50	....	1.83	2.20	0.64	0.43	0.13	0 40	0.46	Skin.....
do.	.........do............	.....do	.....	5.00	8.00	2.00	......	......	....	....	....	....	Fresh....
71 9	.........do............	Camp 119........	.....	4.40	....	1.80	2.14	0.65	0.44	0.12	0.38	0.45	Skin.....
do.	.........do............	..... do	○	4.00	5.00	2.00	......	......	....	....	....	....	Fresh....
9110	Polioptila bilineata........	Mexico.....	.....	4.44	....	1.91	1.97	0.71	0.47	0.11	0.44	0.56	Skin.....

POLIOPTILA CAERULEA, Sclater.

Blue-Gray Flycatcher.

Motacilla caerulea, LINNAEUS, Syst. Nat. 1, 1766, 43.—GMELIN, I, 1788, 992.

Sylvia caerulea, LATH. Ind. Orn. II, 1790.—VIEILLOT, Ois. Am. Sept. II, 1807, 30; pl. lxxxviii.—BON. Obs. Wils. 1825, No. 119.

Muscicapa caerulea, WILSON, Am. Orn. II, 1810, 164; pl. xviii, f. 3.—AUD. Orn. Biog. I, 1831, 431; pl. 84.—NUTTALL, I, 1832, 297.

Culicivora caerulea, BON. List, 1838.—IB. Consp. 1850.—AUD. Syn. 1839, 42.—IB. Birds Amer. I, 1840, 244 ; pl. 70.

Sylvania caerulea, NUTTALL, Man. I. 2d ed. 1840, 337.

Polioptila caerulea, SCLATER, Pr. Zool. Soc. 1855, 11.

Motacilla cana, GMELIN, Syst. Nat. I, 1788, 973.

Sylvia cana, LATHAM, Ind. Orn. II, 1790, 543.

? *Culicivora mexicana*, BONAP. Consp. 1850, 316. Female. (Not of Cassin.)

SP CH.—Above grayish blue, gradually becoming bright blue on the crown. A narrow frontal band of black extending backwards over the eye. Under parts and lores bluish white tinged with lead color on the sides. First and second tail feathers white except at the extreme base, which is black, the color extending obliquely forward on the inner web ; third and fourth black, with white tip, very slight on the latter ; fifth and sixth entirely black. Upper tail coverts blackish plumbeous. Quills edged externally with pale bluish gray, which is much broader and nearly white on the tertials. Female without any black on the head. Length, 4.30 ; wing, 2.15 ; tail, 2.95. (Skin.)

Hab.—United States from Atlantic to Missouri, and on the southern border from the Gulf of Mexico to the coast mountains of California. South to Guatemala.

In addition to the above characters there is a narrow white ring round the eye. The lores are rather paler than the cheeks. The black above the eye runs out into a point a little behind it.

The exposed portion of the first or spurious quill is less than half that of the second. This is intermediate between the seventh and eighth. The fourth quill is rather longer than the third and fifth. The narrow tail feathers are long and linear. They are moderately graduated; the outer about a quarter of an inch less than the middle.

Specimens vary somewhat in the amount of black on the forehead, as well as the purity of the whitish on the tertiaries. All the white feathers of the tail have black shafts, sometimes the white tip of the fourth feather is wanting. The feathers of the rump are decidedly whitish towards their base, though this is not visible except when they are separated. Some entirely white are concealed by the others.

Specimens from Tamaulipas differ in a more attenuated bill, and in having the black superciliary line bordered below on the lores and before and above the eyes by bluish white, rather more conspicuous than in eastern specimens, although some from Illinois come quite near to it. Skins from the Mimbres, however, appear precisely similar to eastern ones. Occasionally, especially in winter skins, (7194,) the black advances further along the inner web of the second tail feather, and has a more transverse outline. This is the case in one specimen from Fort Thorn, while another is like eastern ones. The same is the case in Nos. 7193 and 7194, from the Organ mountains. These specimens are smaller than usual, with shorter wings; but I am unable to observe any other characters of difference.

In the collection before me is a specimen from the Colorado river, California, (4593,) which is very similar to eastern specimens, although it is of large size, and has rather more black on the tail. It is, however, in too imperfect condition (in addition to being probably a female) to exhibit its complete characteristics.

A female *Polioptila*, probably *P. bilineata* of Bonaparte,[1] labelled, by Mr. Verreaux, *P. mexicana*, Bonap., and *atricapilla*, Vieill., and received from him, is very similar to the female of *P. caerulea*, but differs in having the sides of the head as white as the throat; this color seen above the eye as a well marked line. Nothing like it is seen in the female of the other species, where there is a narrow whitish ring round the eye but no superciliary white, the whole sides of the head plumbeous, nearly as dark as the crown. The outer two tail feathers are white, as in *caerulea*. The spurious primary is much larger than in *caerulea*, being more than half the second quill. It is unquestionably distinct from any of the known species of the United States. It differs from *P. melanura* and *plumbea* in the white outer tail feathers, and from *caerulea* in the white cheeks and large first primary. It agrees pretty well with *C. bilineata* of Bonap.

Gundlach describes a *Culicivora* (*Polioptila*) *lembeyi* from Cuba, (Annals N. Y. Lyc. Feb. 1858,) differing from the *caerulea*, in having a black line extending from behind the eye around the ear coverts. The outer tail feathers have more black on them.

List of specimens.

Catal. No.	Sex.	Locality.	When collected.	Whence obtained.	Orig'l No.	Collected by—	Length.	Stretch of wings.	Wing	Remarks.
616	♀	Washington, D. C.....	April 5, 1842	S. F. Baird............	......	Wm. M. Baird...				
615	♂	..... do...............	..... do......	......do.........						
7563	......	..... do...............	....	Wm. Hutton.....						
10213	......	Union county, Ill......	April 20, 1857	N. W. University.....	......	R. Kennicott....				
10214	♂	South Illinois	May 15, 1857	......do........						
2401	♂	Savannah, Ga.	1845	S. F. Baird	......	Jos. Leconte.....				
8671	♂	Indian Key, Fla...... ..	Aug. 27, 1857	G. Wurdemann	......		5.50	6.50	2.00	Black eyes & legs; bill blackish....
4682	♂	Bald island, Neb........	April 25, 1856	Lieut. Warren	......	Dr. Hayden	4.50	6.50	2.25	Eyes black ......
5641	♂ ?	East of Fort Riley.....	June 16, 18 6	Lieut. Bryan.........	15	W. S. Wood.....				
7193	♀	Organ mountains, Tex.	....	Major Emory...	......	J. H. Clark	5.00	6.50	2.01	
7194	♀	......do................	....	......do...........	......	......do..........	5.00	6.50	2.04	
7188	.....	Fort Thorn, N. M......	....	Dr. T. C. Henry.....						
5985	♂	Tamaulipas, Mex......	1853	Lieut. Couch						
3984	♀	......do................	1853..... ..	......do...........	......		4.00	....	2.00	Eyes dark brown.
4593	♀	Colorado river, Cal.....	....	Major Emory.........	......	A. Schott......				
......	......	Fort Tejon.............	....	J. X. de Vesey.......						
9223	.....	Mexico...............		John Gould....... ..						
9222	......	Guatemala	...	..... do...........						

[1] POLIOPTILA BILINEATA, Sclater.

Culicivora bilineata, BONAP. Consp. 1850, 316.

Polioptila bilineata, SCLATER, Pr. Zool. Soc. 1855, 12.

POLIOPTILA PLUMBEA, Baird.

Culicivora plumbea, BAIRD, Pr. A. N. Sc. VII, June, 1854, 118.

SP. CH.—Above bluish gray; the forehead uniform with the crown. Eyelids white. A pale grayish white line over the eye; above which is another of black, much concealed by the feathers, and which does not reach to the bill. Under parts dull white, tinged with bluish on the sides, and with brownish behind. Tail feathers black; the first and second edged and tipped with white; involving the entire outer web of the first, and most of that of the second; the third with only a very faint edging of the same. Female without the black superciliary line. Length, 4.40; wing, 1.80; tail, 2.30. (7189.)

Hab.—Valley of Colorado and Gila.

The tail of this species is considerably graduated, the outer feather being nearly .40 of an inch shorter than the middle one. The bill is rather short and broad at the base. The wings are short; the exposed portion of the first primary more than half as long as the second, which is rather shorter than the secondary quill; the third quill is about equal to the sixth, and considerably shorter (.14 inch) than the fourth and fifth, which are equal.

There is a good deal of brown in the bluish of the back; the quills are all margined with paler blue, which becomes whitish on the tertiaries.

This species is about the size of *P. caerulea*, but rather larger. The bluish above is not so pure, having a dirty olivaceous tinge. Both have the black streak over the eye; but this in *caerulea* is continuous with a black frontal band, while in *plumbea* the forehead is like the crown, and the superciliary line does not extend over the lores. The light superciliary line is also more distinct. The under parts are of about the same color in both species. The tail is very different, the feathers being entirely black, the exterior edged only with white instead of having the two outer almost entirely white, as in *caerulea*.

From *P. melanura* this species differs in lacking the black crown. It is larger, the under parts are purer white. The tails are somewhat alike, but the entire outer web of the first and generally the second feather in *plumbea* are white, instead of being only narrowly edged with this color.

List of specimens.

Catal. No.	Sex & age.	Localtity.	When collected.	Whence obtained.	Orig. No.	Collected by—	Remarks.
7189	♂	Camp 119, Bill Williams' Fork.	Feb. 11, 1854	Lt. Whipple	91	Kenn. and Möll .	Eye black ..
	♂	Camp 113	Feb. 5, 1854	......do.........	70	......do.........	....
7187	♀	Boca Grande, Mex............	Mar. —, 1855	Maj. Emory	38	Dr. Kennerly ...	....

POLIOPTILA MELANURA, Lawrence.

Culicivora atricapilla, LAWRENCE, Ann. N. Y. Lyceum, V, Sept. 1851, 124. Not of Swainson.
Culicivora mexicana, CASSIN, Illust. I, vi, 1854, 164; pl. xxvii. Not of Bonaparte.
Polioptila melanura, LAWRENCE, Ann. N. Y. Lyc. VI, Dec. 1856, 168.

SP. CH.—Above ashy blue; whole crown to bill and eyes, and tail feathers lustrous greenish black. Beneath pale bluish gray, almost white in the middle of the belly; the sides behind, with anal region and under coverts tinged with brown. Edge of eyelids and the margin and tip of the outer web of first and second tail feathers white. Female without the black head. Length, 4.15; wing, 1.85; tail, 2.10.

Hab.—Valley of the Rio Grande and Gila. West to San Diego.

The tail feathers of this species are entirely black except as stated, and exhibit a crimped appearance. The size of the species is decidedly less than in *P. caerulea.* The tail is more graduated, the outer feathers being about .35 of an inch shorter than the middle. The wings, are more rounded; the second quill considerably shorter than the secondaries, the third scarcely longer; very different from *caerulea.* The exposed portion of the first primary is half that of the second.

The edges of the quills are paler than the ground color, but the tertials do not have the decided white of *caerulea.*

The synonymy of Swainson's species will be found in the accompanying foot note.[1]

List of specimens.

Catal. No.	Sex and age.	Locality.	Whence and how obtained.	Collected by—
7191	♂	San Diego, Cal	Lieut. Williamson	Dr. Heermann
7192	♀	Fort Yuma, Cal	do	do

Sub-Family PARINAE.

LOPHOPHANES, Kaup.

Lophophanes, KAUP, Entw. Gesch. Europ. Thierwelt, 1829, (Agassiz.) Type *Parus cristatus.*
Baeolophus, CABANIS, Mus. Hein. 1850–'51, 91. Type *Parus bicolor.*

CH.—Crown with a conspicuous crest. Bill conical; both upper and lower outlines convex. Wings graduated; first quill very short. Tail moderately long and rounded.

Of this genus there are several North American species, all agreeing in general characters. One of these, the *L. wollweberi,* is given by Cabanis as typical, while he separates the *L. bicolor* generically under the name of *Baeolophus,* as having a rather different form of crest, stouter bill and feet, and longer wings. All of our species, however, vary in these characters, each one showing a different combination, so that I prefer to consider all as belonging to the same genus with *P. cristatus.*

The species, all of which have the under parts uniform whitish, may be arranged as follows :

Above plumbeous ; forehead black ; crown much like the back......................*L. bicolor.*

Above plumbeous ; forehead whitish ; crown black.............................*L. atricristatus.*

Above olivaceous ; forehead and crown like the back...............................*L. inornatus.*

Sides of head banded black and white ; crown ash ; throat black.............*L. wollweberi.*

---

[1] The following is the synonymy of Swainson's species which has the two outer tail feathers white :
POLIOPTILA LEUCOGASTRA, Sclater.

    Sylvia leucogastra, MAXIM. Beiträge, III, 1830, 710.
    Polioptila leucogastra, SCLATER, Pr. Zool. Soc. 1855, 12.
    Culicivora leucogastra, BURMEISTER, Th. Bras. Vögel, 1856, 111.
    Culicivora atricapilla, SWAINSON, Zool Ill. N. Ser. pl. lvii. (Not of Lawrence.)
    Culicivora dumecola, BP. Conspectus, 1850, 316. Not *Sylvia dumecola* of Vieillot.

Comparative measurements of species.

Catal. No.	Species.	Locality.	Sex.	Length.	Stretch of wings.	Wing.	Tail.	Tarsus.	Middle toe.	Its claw alone.	Bill above.	Along gape.	Specimen measured.
823	Lophophanes bicolor.....	Carlisle, Pa.....	♂	5.92	....	3.12	3.20	0.82	.0.76	0.24	0.46	0.52	Skin ....
do.	......do.................	......do	.....	6.25	10.00	3.16	......	....	....	....	......	......	Fresh ...
10118	......do..	Washington, D. C......	♀	5.60	....	3.00	2.90	0.80	0.66	0.20	0.46	0.50	Skin ....
6752	......do................	Fort Leavenworth......	......	6.60	....	3.32	3.30	0.82	0.74	0.24	0.49	0.54	Skin ....
6757	Lophophanes atricristatus	Fort Clarke, Texas.....	.....	5.30	....	2.80	2.80	0.76	0.66	0.22	0.46	0.52	Skin ....
5515	Lophophanes inornatus..	Petaluma, Cal.........	♂	5.00	....	2.55	2.46	0.80	0.74	0.22	0.44	0.46	Skin ....
do.	......do..	......do	.....	5.54	7.00	2.75	......	....	....	....	......	......	Fresh ...
3340	do................	California..............	......	5.04	....	2.56	2.52	0.78	0.70	0.23	0.42	0.48	Skin.....
9220	Lophophanes cristatus ...	Europe.................	♂	4.70	....	2.52	2.20	0.71	0.52	0.16	0.36	0.40	Skin ....
9221	Lophophanes wollweberi.	Mexico.................	.....	.4.80	....	2.54	2.48	0.63	0.50	0.18	0.35	0.37	Skin ....
6797	......do	Fort Thorn.............	......	*4.40	....	2.52	2.43	0.67	0.53	0.18	0.34	0.35	Skin ....

LOPHOPHANES BICOLOR, Bon.

Tufted Titmouse.

Parus bicolor, LINN. Syst. Nat. I, 1766, 340.—WILSON, Am. Orn. I, 1808, 137; pl. viii, f. 5.—BONAP. Obs. Wils. J. A. N. S. IV, 1825, 225.—IB. List, 1838.—AUD. Orn. Biog. I, 1831, 199 : V, 1839, 472; pl. 301.—IB. Birds America, II, 1841, 143; pl. 125.

Lophophanes bicolor, BP. List Birds Europe, 1842.—IB. Conspectus, 1850, 228.—CASSIN, Illust. I, 1853, 18.

Baeolophus bicolor, CABANIS, Mus. Hein. 1851, 91.   Type.

SP. CH.—Above ashy black; a frontal band. Beneath dull whitish; sides brownish chestnut, of more or less intensity. Length, 6.25 inches; wing, 3.17.

Hab.—Eastern North America to the Missouri river.

Feathers of the crown elongated into a flattened crest, which extends back as far as the occiput.   Bill conical; lower edge of upper mandible nearly straight at the base.   Fourth and fifth quills equal; third a little shorter than seventh; second rather shorter than the secondaries. Tail nearly even, the outer about .20 of an inch shorter than the longest.   Upper parts ash color, with a tinge of olivaceous.   Forehead dark sooty brown.   The feathers of the upper part of the head and crest obscurely streaked with lighter brown.   Under parts of head and body, sides of head, including auriculars, and a narrow space above the eye, dirty yellowish white, tinged with brown; purest on the side of head, the white very distinct in the loral region, and including the tuft of bristly feathers over the nostrils, excepting the tips of those in contact with the bill, which are blackish.   The sides of the body and the under tail coverts are tinged with yellowish brown.   The quills and tail feathers are edged with the color of the back, without any whitish.   Bill black.   Feet lead color.

Specimens from the west differ from eastern ones almost enough to constitute distinct species. They are considerably larger; the crest longer.   The bill is blacker and more sinuate along the cutting edge of the upper mandible.   The black of the forehead is deeper and more sharply defined.   The brownish rusty of the sides is much more conspicuous, while the under tail coverts are much lighter, almost pure white.   Should these be considered as sufficiently distinctive characters by ornithologists, the species might bear the name of *Lophophanes missouriensis*, from the river on or near which all the specimens before me were collected.

List of specimens.

Catal. No.	Sex.	Locality.	When collected	Whence obtained.	Orig. No.	Collected by—	Length.	Stretch of wings.	Wing.
7579	....	Washington, D. C....	.. ..	Wm. Hutton....	......	....	......	......	......
823	♂	Carlisle, Pa.........	Oct. 2, 1842	S. F. Baird	......	....	6. 30	10. 00	3. 17
1292	♀	......do.............	Mar. 11, 1844	......do........	......	....	5. 67	9. 67	3. 08
6987	♂	St. Louis, Mo.	May 13, 1857	Lt. F. T. Bryan ..	83	W. S. Wood.....	......	......	......
4731	....	St. Joseph, Mo......	April 22, 1856	Lt. Warren......	....	....	6. 37	10. 50	3. 25
4730	....	Fort Leavenworth...	April 21, 1856	Lieut. Couch....	5	....	......	......	......
6752	....	......do.............	Jan. 20, 1855	......do........	......	....	......	......	......
7514	....	Independence, Mo ...	June —, 1857	W M. Magraw ..	60	Dr. Cooper	6. 25	10. 00	3. 25
		Northern Illinois....	Winter........	R. Kennicott....	......	....	......	......	......
	♂	Union county, Ill....	April 8, 1857	N. W. University	......	R. Kennicott....	......	......	......

LOPHOPHANES ATRICRISTATUS, Cassin.

Black-crested Tit.

Parus atricristatus, Cassin, Pr. Ac. Nat. Sc. Phila. V, Oct. 1850, 103 ; pl. ii. Texas.
Lophophanes atricristatus, Cassin, Illust. I, 1853, 13 ; pl. iii.

Sp. Ch.—Crest very long and pointed, (1.25 inches). Above ash colored. A broad band on the forehead dirty white, rest of head above, with crest, black, tinged with ash on the sides. Color of the back shading insensibly into the dull ashy white of the under parts. Sides of body pale brownish chestnut. Female with the crest duller black. Iris dark brown. Length, about 5.25 inches ; wing, 3.00.

Hab.—Valley of the Rio Grande and south.

This species is smaller than *L. bicolor*, but the ashy of the back is of much the same shade. The frontal white band is quite conspicuous. The tail is a little rounded. The bill is a good deal sinuated on the edge of the upper mandible ; its color is black ; the legs dark plumbeous. This species is easily distinguished from *L. bicolor* by the white forehead and black crest. It has the same rusty sides. *L. inornatus* differs in the plain crest, and less conspicuous frontal light band, the more olivaceous tinge above, and the absence or mere trace of the brownish rusty of the sides. The crest of *atricristatus* is much longer, narrower, and more pointed than in the other two species. The bill is black, not horn color.

As usual the southernmost specimens are smallest.

List of specimens.

Catal. No.	Sex.	Locality.	Whence obtained.	Orig'l No.	Collected by—	Length.	Stretch of wings.	Wing.	Remarks.
3974	♂	New Leon, Mex	Lieut. Couch..........	96	....	5.25	8.00	3.00	Eyes dark br'n ; bill black.
3975	♀	......do.................	......do	97	....	4.75	7.50	2.50	......do..........do.....
6"56	.....	Fort Clarke, Tex.......... ..	Lieut. Paike............	......	Dr. Heermann	....	....	....	....
6757	.....	......do.................	......do	......	......do	....	....	....	....
9111	.....	Mexico..................	M. Verreaux..........	29713	....	....	....	....	....

49 b

LOPHOPHANES INORNATUS, Cassin.

Parus inornatus, GAMBEL, Pr. A. N. Sc. Phila. II, Aug. 1845, 265, (Upper California.)—IB. III, Feb. 1847, 154.—IB. Jour. Ac. N. Sc. Phila. 2d Series, I, Dec. 1847, 35; pl. viii.
Lophophanes inornatus, CASSIN, Ill. I, 1853, 19.

SP. CH.—Crest elongated. Color above olivaceous ashy, beneath whitish. Sides of body and under tail coverts very faintly tinged with brownish, scarcely appreciable. Sides of head scarcely different from the crown. Forehead obscurely whitish. Length, 5 inches; wing, 2.55.

Hab.—Coast of California and southern Rocky Mountains.

The bill and feet of this species are lead color. The third, fourth, and fifth quills are longest; the third and eighth about equal; the second is shorter than the shortest primaries. The lateral tail feathers are a little shorter than the others.

A specimen from Fort Thorn has the crest longer than in other specimens before me, measuring 1.35 inches from base of bill to its tip. This may be a characteristic of the male, the sexes being otherwise alike.

This species differs from *L. bicolor* in having a whitish instead of black front, a more olivaceous back, and in lacking the ferruginous tint of the sides. The size is considerably less.

List of specimens.

Catal. No.	Sex.	Locality.	Whence obtained.	Orig. No.	Collected by—
3923	....	California	Dr. Heermann		
3340	....	......do	S. F. Baird		Dr. Gambel
5515[1]	♂	Petaluma, Cal	E. Samuels		
5925[2]	....	Santa Clara, Cal	Gov. Stevens		Dr. Cooper
5923	....	......do	......do		......do
4951	....	San José, Cal	A. J. Grayson	18	
6754	....	Tejon valley	Lt. Williamson		Dr. Heermann
		Fort Tejon	John Xanthus de Vesey		
6755	♂	Sacramento valley	......do		
6753	....	Mimbres to Rio Grande	Dr. Henry		

[1] Shot October, 1855. Length, 5.12; extent, 8.50.   [2] Length, 5.60; extent, 8.50. Feet pale blue.

LOPHOPHANES WOLLWEBERI, Bon.

Lophophanes wollweberi, BON. Comptes Rendus, XXXI, Sept. 1850, 478.—WESTERMANN, Bijdragen tot de Dierkunde, III, 1851, 15, Plate.—CASSIN, Ill. I, 1853, 19.
Parus annexus, CASSIN, Pr. A. N. Sc. Phila. V, Oct. 1850, 103; pl. i. (Texas.)
Lophophanes galeatus, CABANIS, Mus. Hein. 1850–'1, 90.

SP. CH.—Central portion of crest ash, encircled by black, commencing as a frontal band, and passing over the eye. Chin, throat, and a line from behind the eye and curving round the auriculars to the throat, (bordered behind by white,) as also some occipital feathers, black. A white line from above the eye margining the crest, with the cheeks below the eye and under parts generally white. A black half collar on the nape. Upper parts of body ashy. Length, about 4.50; wing, 2.50.

Hab.—Southern Rocky mountains, and south into Mexico on the Table lands.

This is the most variegated species of its genus in North America, and is readily distinguished from the others. I regret, however, that none of the specimens before me exhibit the bird in its perfect plumage.

The elongation of the feathers of the head extends quite to the occiput. The feathers on the anterior half of the crown are ashy; their extreme base black. The feathers composing the black frontal band, too, have a few of these short, pale, ashy white tips. The posterior elongated feathers of the crown and the short feathers of the occiput are black. The lateral feathers behind, however, are white, in continuation of the streak over the eye. In most specimens the black crescentic line behind the eye is much broken by white. There does not appear to be any rusty tinge on the sides, as in *L. bicolor*.

The black post-auricular crescent is bordered behind by white, running into a whitish collar just behind the black of the throat. The nape below the crest is black, this dividing and passing around the upper half of the neck as a half collar posterior to the white.

The bill is very short and conical. The second primary quill is longer than the secondaries; the third is intermediate between the eighth and ninth.

The upper parts are of much the same tinge of olivaceous as in *L. inornatus*.

The young birds differ in having the black less intense, especially on the throat.

Poor specimens have a slight resemblance to *Parus montanus*. This, however, lacks the crest; the forehead is white, not black; the middle of the crown is black, not ash colored; the white of the cheeks is not bordered behind by a black crescent, connecting the stripe behind the eye with the throat.

This species is much more like the European *L. cristatus* than any other American titmouse. It differs in the much stouter bill, absence of rufous on the sides, more black on the throat, the feathers of the crown ash, like the back, instead of being black, edged with whitish. The black crescent behind the eye runs into the black of the throat, instead of stopping in the white cheeks. The posterior cervical half collar of black is cut off from that of the throat, instead of being continuous with it. The resemblance of the two species would be much strengthened if the posterior black collar were made to run into the neck, and the crescent on the cheeks interrupted below.

Cabanis, in Mus. Heineanum, places this species in the same genus with the typical *L. cristatus*, and separates the *L. bicolor*, as type of a new genus, on account of the stouter bill, difference in character of crest, longer wings, &c. The other American crested titmice, however, exhibit a very gentle gradation between the two, while the bill of *L. wollweberi* is even stouter in proportion than in *L. bicolor*.

List of specimens.

Catal. No.	Sex.	Locality.	When collected.	Whence obtained.	Orig. No.	Collected by—	Length.	Stretch of wings.	Wing.
6794	♀	Copper mines.		Col. Graham . .	3	J. H. Clark.	5. 00	8. 00	2. 50
6796	....	.....do.		.....do.					
6797	....	Mimbres to R. Grande		Dr. Henry.					
6795	....	Pueblo creek, N. M..	Jan. 22, 1854	Lt. Whipple	50	Kenn. and Möll .			
		Mexico.		J. Gould.					

PARUS, Linnaeus.

Parus, LINNAEUS, Syst. Nat. 1735. (Agassiz.) Type *P. major.*

CH.—Head not crested. Body and head stout. Tail moderately long, and slightly rounded. Bill conical, not very stout; the upper and under outlines very gently and slightly convex. Tarsus but little longer than middle toe. Crown and throat generally black.

In the group, as defined above, are embraced several genera of modern systematists. Thus the true black-capped American titmice are placed under *Poecile* of Kaup, where possibly they belong. The species may be arranged as follows :

A. Head and neck above and below entirely black ; their sides white. (*Poecile.*)

Outer tail feathers and the tertiaries conspicuously edged with white. Outer edges of greater wing coverts also nearly white.

Largest. Wing, 2.70 inches; tail much rounded, or even graduated, exceeding 3.00, or longer than wings...*P. septentrionalis.*

Wing and tail about 2.50 inches, and nearly equal. Tail nearly even. Body beneath white, tinged on the sides with brownish yellow..........*P. atricapillus.*

Size and shape much like the last. Tail more rounded. Beneath pale yellowish rufous brown, lighter only along the median line...................*P. occidentalis.*

Outer tail feathers and the tertiaries pale grayish, not white. Greater wing coverts without paler edges. Tail nearly even, shorter than the wing.

Wing, about 2.60 inches ; tail, 2.45. Beneath plumbeous; similar to the back, only paler..*P. meridionalis.*

Smaller. Beneath white, faintly tinged with reddish brown, conspicuously different from the back...*P. carolinensis.*

B. Crown and throat black, with white frontal and superciliary stripe.

Above plumbeous ; beneath white...*P. montanus.*

C. Throat sooty brownish ; sides of body bright reddish brown.

Back and wing coverts chestnut brown ; crown not very different from the throat ....*P. rufescens.*

Back grayish olive brown. Crown similar.............................*P. hudsonius.*

Comparative measurements of species.

Catal. No.	Species.	Locality.	Sex.	Length.	Stretch of wings.	Wing.	Tail.	Tarsus.	Middle toe.	Its claw alone.	Bill above.	Along gape	Specimen measured.
3704	Parus septentrionalis...	Salt Lake city......	......	5.40	....	2.72	2.96	0.68	0.58	0.18	0.34	0.40	Skin.....
6766	.......do........,......	New Mexico..........	......	5.80	....	2.52	3.00	Legs	broken.	....	0.40	0.42	Skin*....
8827	.... do.....	Black Hills, Neb ...	......	5.30	....	2.64	2.86	0.61	0.60	0.22	0.33	0.46	Skin.....
do.	........do............	.......do...........	......	5.75	8.25	2.75	......	....	....	....	....	....	Fresh....
6493	........do............	Fort Mass., N. M...	♀	5.32	....	2.62	2.98	0.64	0.58	0.18	0.34	0.40	Skin.....
830	Parus atricapillus	Carlisle, Pa........	♀	4.80	....	2.50	2.50	0.62	0.55	0.18	0.36	0.40	Skin.....
do.	........do............	......do...........	......	5.00	7.75	2.50	......	....	....	....	....	....	Fresh....
803	........do............	......do...........	......	4.74	....	2.50	2.44	0.60	0.56	0.20	0.36	0.42	Skin.....
do.	........do............	......do...........	......	4 91	7.75	2.41	....	....	....	....	....	....	Fresh....
6762	Parus occidentalis	Fort Vancouver....	......	5.00	....	2.46	2.50	0.61	0.56	0.20	0.36	0.42	Skin.....
do.	........do	......do...........	......	4.50	7.50	....	....	....	....	....	....	....	Fresh..
6763	........do.:...........	Shoalwater bay	......	5.00	....	2.42	2.52	0.66	0.60	0.20	0.36	0.44	Skin.....
do.	....do...........	......do...........	......	5.00	7.50	....	....	....	....	....	....	....	Fresh ...
10203	Parus meridionalis	Mexico.............	......	5.00	....	2.60	2.54	0.68	0.56	0.18	0.36	0.42	Skin.....
706	Parus carolinensis.....	Washington, D. C..	♂	4.60	....	2.50	2.50	0.60	0.54	0.20	0.32	0.38	Skin.....
do.	........do............	......do...........	......	4.62	7.00	....	....	....	....	....	....	....	Fresh....
5643	Parus montanus........	Medicine Bow cr'k	♀	5.50	....	2.90	2.90	0.78	0.58	0.20	0.44	0.50	Skin.....
3894	........do............	California	......	2.58	2.44	2.58	2.44	0.61	0.64	0.21	0 42	0.42	Skin.....
962	........do............	Fort Tejon	♀	4.80	....	2.70	2.58	0.72	0.60	0.22	0.42	0.44	Skin.....
do.	........do............	......do...........	......	5.00	8.00	....	....	....	....	....	....	....	Fresh ...
6786	Parus rufescens........	Fort Vancouver....	......	4.46	....	2.36	2.16	0.64	0.60	0.18	0.35	0.40	Skin....
do.	........do............	......do...........	......	4.75	7.50	....	....	....	....	....	....	....	Fresh....
6784	........do............	San Francisco	......	4.44	...:...	2.42	2.30	0.64	0.56	0.18	0.40	0.44	Skin.....
2926	Parus hudsonicus	Canada?	......	5.14	....	2.40	2.66	0.70	0.55	0.19	0.38	0.44	Skin.....

* Very poor specimen.

PARUS SEPTENTRIONALIS, Harris.

Long-tailed Chickadee.

Parus septentrionalis, HARRIS, Pr. A. N. Sc. Phila. II, 1845, 300.　(Upper Missouri.)—CASSIN, Illust. I, I, 1853, 17.—IB. I, III, 1852, 80 ; pl. xiv.

SP. CH.—Length, about 5.50 inches ; wing, 2.70 ; tail, about 3 inches.　Head above and below black, separated by white on the sides of the head ; back brownish ash.　Beneath white, tinged with pale brownish white on the sides.　Outer tail feathers, primaries, and secondaries broadly edged with white, involving nearly the whole outer web of outer tail feather.　Tail much graduated ; the outer feather about .30 of an inch shorter than the middle.　Second quill about as long as the secondaries.

Hab.—Missouri river to the Rocky mountains.

This species is similar in general characters to the *P. atricapillus*, but is considerably larger, with proportionately longer tail.　The fifth and sixth quills are equal, the fourth scarcely shorter, the third about equal to the seventh, the second about the length of the secondaries. The tail is long, considerably rounded ; the outer abruptly shorter than the second.　The greatest difference in the length of the tail feathers is .30 of an inch ; in some specimens almost half an inch.　The difference between primaries and secondaries amounts to .41 of an inch.

The top of the head and nape, with the chin and throat, are black ; the space between the two white.　The middle of breast and belly are dirty white.　The sides strongly tinged with yellowish brown, as are also the under tail coverts.　The upper parts, except as described, are grayish ash, washed with yellowish brown, especially on the rump.　The third to the seventh primaries and the inner secondaries are edged with ashy white ; the latter conspicuously so. The outer webs of the outer three tail feathers edged with whitish, almost white on the first one, where the line of demarkation is quite distinct.　All the tail feathers, indeed, have more or less of a light edging, which on the outermost edge of the inner is plumbeous.

In a considerable series of specimens before me of this species, all agreeing very nearly in size, there is one (6776) from New Mexico possessing all the characteristics of the species in an exaggerated degree, even more so than Mr. Harris' typical specimen.　It is larger ; the tail more graduated ; the upper parts are more yellowish ; the black of head and neck is less extensive.　The white margins of the primaries and secondaries are very conspicuous, and the entire outer web of the exterior tail feather is white, except towards the base.

This species is very similar to the *P. atricapillus*, but differs from it somewhat as *atricapillus* does from *carolinensis*.　Its size is much greater ; the tail proportionately longer, and much more graduated ; the white of wing and tail purer and more extended.　The bill appears to be stouter and more conical.　The back has, perhaps, a little more yellowish.　The spurious or first primary is larger.

A specimen from Fort Massachusetts (8193) agrees in general characteristics of form, but differs in having a sooty tinge in all the white parts, above and below.　This is analogous to conditions frequently seen in other species, and may be either an actual tendency to melanism, or the result of actual soiling of the feathers with the carbonaceous matter of burnt trees, or from other causes.

List of specimens.

Catal. No.	Sex.	Locality.	When collected.	Whence obtained.	Orig'l No.	Collected by—	Length	Stretch of wings.	Wing.	Remarks.
......	......	Racine, Wis	....	N. W. University..	......	Dr. Hoy	......	.. ..	....	....
7513	♂	Independence	June, 1857...	Dr. Cooper	43	....	5.50	8.00	....	Feet black...........
4732	......	Fort Leavenworth........	April 21, 1856	Lieut. Warren.....	......	Dr. Hayden....	5.50	7.50	2.75	...
6765	.....	......do.........	Nov. 27, 1854	Lieut. Couch......	......	......	......	....	......	....
5574	.....	Fort Riley, K. T.......	....	Dr. Hammond	......	......	......	....	......	....
5873	.....	......do......	1856.........	Hammond & Vesey.	......	......	......	......	......	......
5872	.....	......do......	1856.........	Dr. Hammond ...	......	......	......	....	......	. ...
5644	♂	East of Fort Riley........	June 18, 1856	Lieut. F. T. Bryan.	29	W. S. Wood....	......	......	......	......
4733	♂	Mouth of Big Nemaha....	April 2, 1856	Lieut. Warren	......	Dr. Hayden....	4.37	8.00	2.75	......
6766	.....	New Mexico...............	....	R. H. Kern	......	......	......	....	......	....
6769	....	Western, Texas	....	Capt. Pope	......	......	......	......	......	....
88.8	.....	Black Hills, Neb..... ..	Sept. 15, 1857	Lieut. Warren. ...	......	Dr. Hayden....	5.50	7.75	2.75	......
88.7	.....	......do......	... do......	......do...........	......	......do....	5.75	8.37	2.75	Iris dark brown......
8493	♀	Fort Massachusetts, N. M.	....	Dr. Peters	......	......	......	......	......	.. ..
......	......	Salt Lake City...........	....	Capt. Stansbury...	......	......	......	......	......	......

PARUS ATRICAPILLUS, Linn.

Black-cap Titmouse.

Parus atricapillus, LINN. Syst. Nat. I, 1766, 341.—GM. I, 1788, 1008.—FORSTER, Philos. Trans. LXII, 1772, 383.—
WILSON, Am. Orn. I, 1808, 134 ; pl. viii, f. 4.—BON. Obs. Wilson, J. A. N. S. IV, 1825, 254.
(Differences from *P. palustris*.)—AUDUBON, Orn. Biog. IV, 1838 ; pl. 353, f. 3.—IB. Birds Amer.
II, 1841, 146 ; pl. 126.—CASSIN, Ill. I, i, 1853, 17.
Poecila atricapilla, BON. Consp. 1850, 230
Parus palustris, NUTT. Man. I, 1832, 79)

SP. CH.—Second quill as long as the secondaries. Tail very slightly rounded ; lateral feathers about .10 shorter than middle.
Back brownish ashy. Top of head and throat black, sides of head between them white. Beneath whitish ; brownish white
on the sides. Outer tail feathers, some of primaries, and secondaries conspicuously margined with white.
Length, 5 ; wing, 2.50 ; tail, 2.50.
Hab.—Eastern North America along the Atlantic border.

In this species the first quill is spurious ; the fourth quill is longest ; the fifth and sixth
successively a little shorter ; the third is about equal to or a little shorter than the eighth ; the
second is a very little longer than the secondaries. The tail is a little rounded, the innermost
feather longest, the rest successively a little shorter. The greatest difference in length of tail
feathers amounts to .10 of an inch.

The entire crown, from the bill to the upper part of the back, coming down on the sides to
the lower level of the eye, is pure black, although the edge alone of the lower eyelid is of this
color. A second black patch, begins at the lower mandible and occupies the entire under
surface of the head and throat, but not extending as far back within a quarter of an inch as
that on the upper part of the neck. The space between these two patches, on the sides of the
head and neck, white, this color extending along the black of the back of the neck as far as its
truncated extremity, but not bordering it behind. The middle of the breast and belly, as far
as the vent, are dull white, that immediately behind the black of the throat a little clearer.
The sides of the breast and body under the wings, with the under tail coverts, are pale, dull
brownish white. The back, rump, and upper tail coverts are of a dirty bluish ash, washed with
yellowish brown, especially on the rump. The wings are brown ; the outer edges of the third
to the seventh primaries narrowly edged with whitish ; the innermost secondaries more broadly

and conspicuously edged with the same; larger coverts edged with dirty whitish. Outer webs of tail feathers edged with white, purest and occupying half the web in the external one, narrowing and less clear to the central feathers, the basal portions, especially, assuming more the color of the back.

List of specimens.

Catal. No.	Sex.	Locality.	When collected.	Whence obtained.	Length.	Stretch of wings	Wing.
830	♀	Carlisle, Pa.	Oct. 22, 1842	S. F. Baird.	5.00	7.75	2.50
803		do	Oct. 14, 1842	do	4.92	7.75	2.42

PARUS OCCIDENTALIS, Baird.

Western Titmouse.

Sp Ch.—Tarsi lengthened. Tail graduated; outer feather about .25 of an inch shorter than the middle.

Above dark brownish ash; head and neck above and below black, separated on the sides by white; beneath light dirty, rusty yellowish brown, scarcely whiter along the middle of body. Tail and wings not quite so much edged with whitish as in *P. atricapillus.*

Length, about 4.75; wing, 2.40; tail, 2.40.

Hab.—North Pacific coast of United States.

This species is of the same size as *P. atricapillus*, and resembles it in its markings; the ashy of the back is, however, washed with a darker shade of yellowish brown. The brown of the under parts is so much darker as to cause the predominant color there to be a pale yellowish brown, instead of brownish white. The fourth quill is longest; the fifth and sixth a little shorter than the third; the second is about as long as the secondaries. The tail is rounded, rather more so than in *atricapillus*, the difference in the lengths of the feathers amounting to about .25 of an inch. The amount of light margining to the quills and tail feathers is much as in *atricapillus*, but rather less, perhaps, on the tail.

It is rather a hazardous undertaking to add another to the list of North American black-capped and throated titmice; but if we have three good species now, instead of one, then the present is equally entitled to specific distinction with *carolinensis* and *septentrionalis*. In external form it resembles the typical *atricapillus*, as to average size, length of wing and tail, and general amount of white, differing in all these appreciably from *septentrionalis*. It is, however, more different from it, in its dark colors, almost brown beneath, than any of the others are among themselves, while the tarsi are even larger than in *septentrionalis*.

This species seems to be the Pacific representative of the American black-capped titmice, as *septentrionalis* belongs to the middle region.

List of specimens.

Catal. No.	Locality.	When collected.	Whence obtained.	Orig'l No.	Collected by—	Length.	Stretch of wings	Wing.	Remarks.
6763	Shoalwater bay	Sept. 12, 1854	Dr. Suckley		Dr. Cooper	5.00	7.50		
6768	do	do	Gov. Stevens		do	5.12	7.62		Iris brown.
6762	Fort Vancouver, W. T.	Feb. 4, 1854	do	25	do	4.50	7.50		Iris black.
4538	Washington Territory		Dr. Suckley						
6767	St. Helen's, Columbia river	Jan. 27, 1856	do	209		5.25	7.50	2.50	
9219	California		J. Gould		D. Douglas				

PARUS MERIDIONALIS, Sclater.

Mexican Titmouse.

Parus meridionalis, SCLATER, Pr. Zool. Soc. 1856, 293.—IB. 1857, 81. (El Jacale, Mex.)

SP. CH.—Generally similar to *P. atricapillus.* Tail nearly even ; second quill rather shorter than the secondaries ; first not quite half as long as second. Head and neck above and below black ; their sides white ; rest of upper parts soiled ash ; beneath a rather paler tint of the same ; lighter, almost whitish, along the middle of the belly, and behind the black of the throat. No whitish on the wing coverts or tail feathers. The quills edged externally with dull bluish white, most conspicuous on the innermost. Length, 5.00 ; wing, 2.60 ; tail, 2.45.

Hab—Eastern Mexico.

This species appears to be perfectly distinct from any of the North American titmice, as shown by the examination of the typical specimen, received from Mr. Gould. The size of body and character of wing and tail are much as in *P. atricapillus*, from which it differs in the entire absence of whitish edgings on the coverts and tail feathers. The extreme outer edge of the outer tail feather indeed is of a very dull whitish, but even this is not seen on the others. There is almost no white on the under parts, which are of the same shade with the back, only paler, and with a lightening along the median line. There is nothing of the reddish brown or rusty whitish wash on the side seen in nearly all the North American titmice. The second and third quills are decidedly shorter than in *atricapillus*.

In the absence of light edgings to the wing coverts, and in their reduction to a minimum on the quills and tail feathers, there is a close resemblance to *P. carolinensis.* This, however, has more whitish on the edges of quills and tail feathers, and the under parts are tinged with a very pale reddish brown, instead of the decided soiled ash of the other. The proportions of the quills are similar.

From *P. occidentalis* this species differs in the ashy tinge of the under parts, instead of the rather deep reddish brown, these colors in both encroaching greatly on the median whitish so conspicuous in the other species. The tail feathers are not so black, nor have they nor the quills edgings quite so light. The tail is more nearly even.

List of specimens.

Catal. No.	Locality.	Whence obtained.	Collected by—
10203	El Jacalo, Mexico	John Gould, (type specimen)	A. Sallé

PARUS CAROLINENSIS, Audubon.

Carolina Titmouse.

Parus carolinensis, AUD. Orn. Biog. II, 1834, 341 : V, 474 ; pl. 160.—IB. Birds Am. II, 1841, 152 ; pl. 127.—CASSIN, Illust. I, 1853, 17.
Poecila carolinensis, BP. Consp. Av. 1850, 230.

SP. CH.—Second quill appreciably longer than secondaries. Tail very little rounded. Length about 4.50 inches ; wing less than 2.50 ; tail 2.40. Back brownish ash. Head above, and throat, black, separated on sides of head by white. Beneath white ; brownish white on sides. Outer tail feathers, primaries, and secondaries, not edged with white.

Hab.—South Atlantic States to Washington.

This species is very similar to the *P. atricapillus*, but is smaller. The first quill, as in all the titmice, is spurious ; the fourth and fifth are equal ; the sixth a little shorter than the third and seventh, which are equal ; the second quill is appreciably longer than the longest second-aries. The tail is slightly rounded, the greatest difference in length of the feathers being .15 of an inch.

The top of the head and upper part of the neck are black, this color coming down to the lower edge of the eye. The under part of the head and the anterior part of the throat are also black, this color not extending as far back below as above. The space between the black patches is white, which borders the upper one obscurely on the posterior portion of the side, but not on the posterior extremity. It also suffuses the posterior portion of the black of the throat. The under parts are dirty white, on the sides and posteriorly tinged with pale brownish. The upper parts are of a dirty bluish ash, tinged with yellowish brown, especially on the rump. The quills are all margined with bluish ash, like the back, which is a little paler on the inner-most secondaries, and third to seventh primaries, but not conspicuously so ; not at all white. Outer webs of tail feathers all edged with the color of the back, becoming rather lighter from the central to the external ones ; never white, however, nor with a well defined line of demark-ation on the outer web of the outer tail feather.

This species is very similar to the *P. atricapillus*, and were they to be separated by a wide interval of locality it might be a question whether it might not be a mere variety. As, however, both are found together in the middle States, and preserving their characteristics, there will be little risk in considering them distinct.

This species is, in general, rather smaller than *P. atricapillus*, although the tail and wing appear of much the same size. The body and feet are, however, smaller, the extent of wing three-quarters of an inch less. The bill is apparently shorter and stouter. The difference in size is, perhaps, even greater than that given by the measurement, as, without a male *P. atri-capillus* or female *carolinensis* before me at the time of writing, I am obliged to compare males of the smaller kind with the female of the larger.

The primaries are proportionally and absolutely considerably longer than the secondaries in the present species, the difference being .55 of an inch, instead of .45. The tail is rather more rounded, the feathers narrower.

The only difference in color appreciable in the specimens before me is the absence of the strongly whitish edgings to the outer tail feathers, the third to the seventh primaries, and the secondaries, the latter especially. There is a lighter shade on these parts, but never of the almost white and well defined character seen in *P. atricapillus*.

List of specimens.

Catal. No.	Sex.	Locality.	When collected.	hence obtained.	Collected by—	Length.	Stretch of wings.
607	♂	Washington, D. C.	Feb. 22, 1842	S. F. Baird.	Wm. M. Baird	4. 25	6. 50
706		do	April 5, 1842	do	do	4. 62	7. 00

50 b

PARUS MONTANUS, Gambel.

Parus montanus, GAMBEL, Pr. A. N. Sc. I, April, 1843, 259, (Santa Fé.)—IB. Pr. A. N. Sc. III, Feb. 1847,
155.—IB. Jour. A. N. Sc. 2d series, I, Dec. 1847, 35; pl. viii, f. 1.—CASSIN, Illust. I, 1853, 18.

SP. CH.—Head and neck above, with under part of head and throat, glossy black; forehead, line above the eye and one
below it, involving the auriculars, white. These stripes embracing between them a black line through the eye and confluent
with the black of the head. Above ashy; beneath similar, but paler; the upper part of breast and middle line of belly white.
Length about 5 inches; wing, 2.60; tail, 2.40.

Hab.—Pacific coast of United States, probably to the Rocky mountains.

In this species the tail is nearly square; the outer feather a very little shorter. The fourth,
fifth, and sixth quills are equal; the third less than the seventh; the second rather shorter
than the secondaries. The whole side of the head from the bill is whitish; this color margins
the black of the neck all the way to its extremity on the upper part of the back, where it is
duller. A black line commences within the white just anterior to the eye, in a line below with
the lower eyelid and above a little above the upper lid. The quills and tail feathers are
margined paler, but there is no white, especially on the secondaries.

This species may be very readily distinguished from P. atricapillus by the white front and
the white line over the eye cutting off a black one through it. The general colors above are
purer ash; below the sides are ashy instead of yellowish brown white. The white on the head
has rather a bluish tinge.

A specimen, apparently of this species, from Medicine Bow creek, (5643,) though marked
female, is larger than those from California, as shown by the measurements. I can detect no
other difference, except that the black on the neck appears more restricted. A female from
Fort Tejon lacks the whitish of the forehead, the black of the crown coming down to the bill.

List of specimens.

Catal. No.	Sex.	Locality.	When collected.	Whence obtained.	Orig. No.	Collected by—
4390	....	Fort Dalles, Oregon	Feb. —, 1855	Dr. Suckley	171	
3894	....	California		Dr. Heermann		
6800	♂	Tejon pass		Lieut. Williamson		Dr. Heermann
6801	♂	...do		...do		
		Fort Tejon		J. X. de Vesey		
6798	....	Mimbres to Rio Grande		Dr. T. C. Henry		
6799	....	...do		...do		
5643	♀	Medicine Bow creek, Neb.	Aug. 7, 1856	Lieut. Bryan	222	W. S. Wood

PARUS RUFESCENS, Towns.

Chestnut-backed Tit.

Parus rufescens, TOWNSEND, J. A. N. Sc. Phil. VII, II, 1837, 190.—AUDUBON, Orn. Biog. IV, 1838, 371; pl.
353.—IB. Birds Am. II, 1841, 158; pl. 129.—CASSIN, Illust. I, 1853, 18.
Poecila rufescens, BON. Consp. 1850, 230.

SP. CH.—Whole head and neck above, and throat from bill to upper part of breast, sooty blackish brown. Sides of head
and neck, upper part of breast, and middle of body, white; back and sides dark brownish chestnut. Length, 4.75 inches;
wing, 2.36; tail, 2.16.

Hab.—Pacific coast of the United States.

The brown cap passes through the lower eyelid as far as can be detected, and its lateral edge and the throat are darker than the top of the head. The third, fourth, and fifth primaries have their edges rather whiter than elsewhere. The female has the colors rather duller.

List of specimens.

Catal. No.	Sex.	Locality.	When collected.	Whence obtained.	Orig'l No.	Collected by—	Length.	Stretch of wings.	Remarks.
6778	....	Fort Steilacoom, W. T...	March, 1856	Dr. Suckley........	283	....	5.00	7.50	....
6779	... .	........do................	April 16, 1856	......do............	310	....	5.00	7.75	....
6789	♂	........do........	May 2, 1856	......do............	354	....	5.00	8.00	....
6790		........do................	....	......do............	295	....	5.00	7.50	....
6791		........do.	March, 1856	......do............	263	....		....	....
6792		........do................	....	......do............	248	....	4.50	6.50	....
2931	....	Columbia river...........	....	S. F. Baird........		J. K. Townsend....	....	....	....
1924		........do................	....	......do............		........do........	....	....	....
1926	....	Fort Vancouver, W. T...	Dec. 29, 1853	Gov. Stevens	41	Dr. Cooper.........	4.75	7.50	Iris brown, legs gray, bill black.
1927			....	Dr. Suckley........	252	....	4.50	6.50	....
1924		San Francisco...........	....	Lt. R. S. Williamson.		Dr. Heermann.....	....	....	....
1925	♀	........do................	....	......do............					....

PARUS HUDSONICUS, Forster.

Parus hudsonicus, FORSTER, Philos. Trans. LXII, 1772, 383, 430.—LATHAM, Index Ornith. I, 566.—"MILLER, Cimel. Phys. 1796; pl. xxi, A," (Gray.)—AUD. Orn. Biog. II, 1834, 543; pl. 194.—IB. Birds Amer. II, 1841, 155; pl. 128.—CASSIN, Ill. I, 1853, 18.

SP. CH.—Above yellowish olivaceous brown; top of head purer brown, not very different in tint. Chin and throat dark sooty brown. Sides of head white. Beneath white; sides and anal region light brownish chestnut. No whitish on wings or tail. Tail nearly even, or slightly emarginate and rounded. Lateral feathers about .20 shortest. Length about 5 inches; wing, 2.40; tail, 2.66.

Hab.—Northeastern portions of North America to the north Atlantic States.

This species is quite different from the other North American titmice, though most resembling *P. rufescens*.

List of specimens.

Catal. No.	Locality.	Whence obtained.	Collected by—
2926............	Eastern North America..........	S. F. Baird	J. J. Audubon ....

PSALTRIPARUS, Bon.

Psaltriparus, BONAP. Comptes Rendus, XXXI, 1850, 478. Type *P. melanotis*.
Ægithaliscus, CABANIS, Museum Heineanum, 1851, 90. Type *Parus erythrocephalus*.
Psaltria, CASSIN, Ill. N. Am. Birds, 1853, 19.

CH.—Size very small and slender. Bill very small, short, compressed, and with its upper outline much curved for the terminal half. Upper mandible much deeper than under. Tail long, slender, much graduated; much longer than the wings; the feathers very narrow. Tarsi considerably longer than the middle toe. No black on the crown or throat.

This group of titmice is very well marked among the American species, and is closely allied to the genus *Psaltria* of Temminck. A comparison with a typical specimen of *P. exilis* from

Java, in the collection of the Philadelphia Academy, shows that the bill in the last mentioned genus is much shorter, deeper, and with the vertical outlines more curved. The wings are longer, being nearly equal to the tail. The hind toe is a little longer than the middle anterior one, not shorter; the outer lateral claw reaches to the middle of the central one instead of only to its base. The legs are yellow instead of black. *P. exilis* is much smaller than any American titmice, measuring but little over three inches. The American species of *Psaltriparus* are, however, the smallest of our *Parinae*.

The species may be arranged as follows:

a. Head striped with black on the sides.

The stripes passing under the eye and uniting on the occiput....................*P. melanotis.*

b. No stripes on the head.

Back ashy; crown light brown..*P. minimus.*

Back and crown uniform ashy..*P. plumbeus.*

The first mentioned species differs in longer and more compressed bill from the others, and may stand alone in the genus, and the others be referred to *Psaltria* or elsewhere.

Comparative measurements of species.

Catal. No.	Species.	Locality.	Length.	Stretch of wings	Wing.	Tail.	Tarsus.	Middle toe.	Its claw alone.	Bill above.	Along gape.	Specimens measured.
	Psaltriparus plumbeus.....	Little Colorado........	4.20	....	2.08	2.62	0.66	0.44	0.14	0.26	0.32	Skin.....
6774	.........do...............	Camp 120.............	4.44	....	1.92	2.50	0.64	0.44	0.14	0.26	0.33	Skin.....
5922	Psaltriparus minimus.....	Santa Clara	4.00	....	1.86	2.26	0.60	0.46	0.13	0.27	0.30	Skin.....
6758	.........do...............	Fort Steilacoom.....	4.10	....	1.84	2.36	0.60	0.44	0.12	0.28	0.32	Skin.....
3718	.........do...............	California	3.62	....	1.76	1.98	0.66	0.44	0.12	0.29	0.32	Skin.....
	Psaltriparus melanotis.....	Texas.................	4.25	....	1.95	2.40	.61	.43	....	....	....	....
	........do...............	Guatemala..........	3.52	....	1.90	2.30	.56	.47	.14	.19	....	....

PSALTRIPARUS MELANOTIS, Bonap.

Black-cheeked Tit.

Parus melanotus, SANDBACH, Pr. Brit. Ass. VI, 1837, (1838,) 99, (only named.)—*P. melanotis,* HARTLAUB, Rev. Zool. 1844, 216.

Poecila melanotis, BP. Consp. Av. 1850, 230.

Aegithaliscus melanotis, CAB. Mus. Hein. 1850–1, 90.

Psaltria melanotis, WESTERMANN, Bijdragen tot de Dierkunde, 1851.—CASSIN, Ill. I, 1853, 20.

Psaltriparus melanotis, BONAP. Comptes Rendus, XXXIII, 1854.

Psaltriparus personatus, BP. Comptes Rendus, XXXI, Sept. 1850, 478.

Psaltria personata, WESTERMANN, Bijdragen tot de Dierkunde I, 1851, 16; plate.

SP. CH.—A black patch on each cheek nearly meeting behind. Crown and edges of the wing and tail ash gray; rest of upper parts yellowish brown, lighter on the rump. Beneath whitish; anal region tinged with yellowish brown. Length about 4 inches; wing, 1.90; tail, 2.30.

Hab.—Eastern Mexico to the Rio Grande.

In this species the bill is moderately long and considerably compressed; the culmen straight at the base, then rapidly curving to the tip which slightly overhangs the lower jaws; the gony also is decidedly curved, less so than the culmen. The tarsus is much longer than the middle toe; the outer lateral toe rather the longer, and reaching the base of the middle claw; the hind toe nearly or quite equal to the middle. The wings are short; the primaries, however, considerably exceeding the other quills; the exposed portion of the first quill nearly half that of the second, which is shorter than the secondaries; the outer primaries much graduated to the fifth, (longest.) The tail is long (much longer than the wings) and considerably graduated laterally; the outer feather about half an inch shortest.

The back and rump with tail coverts of this species are of a dirty yellowish brown. The sides of the head starting at the base of the bill, passing through and a little above the eyes, and passing backwards around on the nape, where it narrows to a line and almost or quite meets its fellow, are of a lustrous greenish black. The crown as enclosed by the black, the edges of the quills and tail feathers are ash gray, the forehead rather lighter. The whole under parts, including the lower tail coverts, are dirty white; the region back of the thighs and about the anus tinged with yellowish brown. The outer tail feather is edged with whitish. Bill and feet black.

The species is described from specimens in the Museum of the Philadelphia Academy, from Guatemala. It should really be credited to Hartlaub, 1844.

PSALTRIPARUS MINIMUS, Bonap.

Least Tit.

Parus minimus, TOWNSEND, Jour. A. N. Sc. Phila. VII, ii, 1837, 190.—AUD. Orn. Biog. IV, 1838, 382; pl. 353, fig. 5, 6.—IB. Birds Amer. II, 1841, 160; pl. 130.

Poecila minima, BONAP. Conspectus, 1850, 230.

Psaltria minima, CASSIN, Illust. I, 1853, 20.

Psaltriparus minimus, BONAP. Comptes Rendus, XXXVIII, 1854 ; Notes Orn. Delattre, 45.

SP. CH.—Tail long, feathers graduated. Above rather dark olivaceous cinereous; top and sides of head smoky brown. Beneath pale whitish brown, darker on the sides. Length, about 4 inches; wing, 1.90; tail, 2.25.

Hab.—Pacific coast of United States.

The bill of this species is slender, the upper mandible not twice as large as the lower; gently but considerably curved to the tip without any notch. The wings are short and concave, the exposed part of the first or spurious quill about half as long as that of the second primary, which is shorter than the secondaries. The wing is much rounded, the primary quills increasing successively to the sixth, the seventh a little shorter, the fourth longer than the eighth. The tail is long, the feathers very narrow; it is considerably rounded or wedge-shaped, a little emarginate in the middle, the exterior feather abruptly shorter than the second, the rest increasing gradually to the fourth, which is longest. The greatest difference in the length of the feathers is about .45 of an inch. The tarsi appear unusually long compared with those of other titmice.

The upper parts are of an ashy gray, with a dull olivaceous tinge. The top and sides of the head are of a pale smoky brown, almost with a purplish tinge; the head in decided contrast to the back. The under parts generally are whitish brown, or brownish white with a tinge of yellowish on the abdomen, the sides more strongly of a pale smoky brown, somewhat similar to that on top of the head, but paler. The tail and wing feathers are edged with the color of the back except the third to the seventh primaries, which are margined whitish ash. Bill and legs blackish in the dried specimen.

There is quite an appreciable difference between specimens of this species from Washington Territory and California; the latter are smaller, the under parts paler. In the specimens before me, however, I see no grounds for specific distinction.

List of specimens.

Catal. No.	Sex.	Locality.	Whence obtained.	Orig. No.	Collected by—
6761	......	Fort Steilacoom, W. T..........	Dr. Suckley..................	302	....
6758	♂	......do.................	......do..................	336	....
6759	......	......do.................	......do..................	327	....
3924	......	California..................	Dr. Heermann.............	......	....
5922¹	......	Santa Clara, Cal.............	Gov. Stevens..............	......	Dr. Cooper..............
6760	♂	Sacramento valley...........	Lt. R. S. Williamson	......	Dr. Heermann..........
3715	......	Los Angeles, Cal...........	Wm. Hutton.............	......	....
		Fort Tejon, Cal.............	J. X. de Vesey.............	......	....

¹ Length, 4.25; extent, 5.75. Iris brown; bill black; feet lead color.

PSALTRIPARUS PLUMBEUS, Baird.

Psaltria plumbea, BAIRD, Pr. A. N. Sc. Phil. VII, June 1854, 118. Little Colorado.

SP. CH.—Tail long, feathers graduated. Above rather light olivaceous cinereous. Top of head rather clearer; forehead, chin, and sides of head, pale smoky brown. Beneath brownish white, scarcely darker on the sides. Length, about 4.20 inches; wing, 2.15; tail, 2.50.

Hab.—Southern Rocky mountains.

This diminutive species has the bill slender, the point of the upper mandible elongatee and gently curved. The tail is long, slightly emarginate, but graduated on the sides; the exterior abruptly shorter than the rest, which are rounded more regularly. The greatest difference between the longest and shortest feathers is .45 of an inch. The fifth quill is longest, the sixth and fourth barely and successively shorter; the third and eighth about equal; the second shorter than the secondaries. The entire upper parts are of a bluish ash with an olivaceous shade, rather clearest on the head. The sides of the head and the chin are pale smoky brown; the forehead is tinged with the same. The under parts are dirty brownish white, lightest on the throat, a little more brown on the sides of the body. The tail feathers and quills are edged externally with the color of the back; the edges of the third and seventh primaries slightly paler.

Specimens vary somewhat in the clearness of their tints, which are sometimes a little darker, sometimes lighter.

This species is very similar to the *Psaltriparus minimus* of the west coast, which it represents in the Rocky mountain region. It is, however, appreciably larger, the wings and tail proportionally longer. The top of the head is plumbeous, uniform with the back, instead of smoky brown. The back is a paler ash, the under parts darker.

The specimens collected by Messrs. Kennerly and Möllhausen are labelled differently as respects the color of the iris, some being marked as yellow, others as black. I find no other appreciable difference, however, between them.

List of specimens.

Catal. No.	Locality.	When collected.	Whence obtained.	Orig'l No.	Collected by—	Length.	Stretch of wings	Wing.	Remarks.
6770	Fort Thorn, N.M...........	....	Dr. Henry	......	....	....	....	....	....
	Little Colorado, N. M.......	Nov. —, 1853	Lieut. A. Whipple....	40	Kennerly and Möllhausen	....	....	....	....
6775	..........do............. ..	Dec. 18, 1853	......do.............	......	......do...................	4.50	5.50	....	....
6776	Camp 111, Bill Williams' fork	Feb. 1, 1854	......do.............	62	......do...................	....	....	....	....
6777	.........do.................	Feb. 1, 1854	......do.............	63	......do...................	4.12	6	....	Eyes black...
6774	Camp 120, Bill Williams' fork	Feb. 12, 1854	..... do......	94	......do...................	....	....	....	Eyes yellow .
	..........do.....	Feb. 12, 1854	......do.............	95	......do...................	....	....	....	..... do.......

PAROIDES, Kaup.

Paroides, KAUP, Entw. Gesch. Europ. Thierw. 1816. (Gray.) Type *P. pendulinus.*
Aegithalus, BOIE, Isis, 1822, 556. Same type.

CH.—Form sylvicoline. Bill conical, nearly straight, and very acute; the commissure very slightly and gently curved. Nostrils concealed by decumbent bristles. Wings long, little rounded; the first quill half the second; third, fourth, and fifth quills nearly equal, and longest. Tail slightly graduated. Lateral toes equal, the anterior united at the extreme base. Hind toe small, about equal to the lateral. Tarsus but little longer than the middle toe.

This genus differs from all other North American titmice in the greater length of the quills, the third being the longest, or very nearly so, instead of the fourth or fifth. The hind toe is rather short, the claw scarcely larger than that of the middle toe. In this respect, and the shorter tarsi, it differs from *Psaltriparus,* (*minimus,*) and its bill is much more straight and acute than this, or any other United States species.

Comparing the single American species with the type of *Paroides,* (*pendulinus,*) the bill, though much elongated, is not quite so conical and acute, the upper outline being slightly convex instead of perfectly straight, or even concave. The legs are much longer, the tarsus measuring (the skins of nearly the same size) .60 of an inch instead of .54. The claws are much smaller and more delicate, which makes the lateral toes shorter as well as the hinder one, which does not exceed the middle toe without the claw, instead of being almost as long as middle toe and claw together. The tail is slightly graduated, instead of nearly even. The spurious primary is longer; the second quill shorter.

While it is thus similar to *Paroides,* it is totally distinct from *Psaltria,* (with *exilis* as the type.) This differs entirely in the much shorter and more curved bill, longer legs, shorter wings, longer and more graduated tail, and dull plumage generally.

Although different from *Paroides,* as shown above, I prefer to continue it in this genus where it was originally placed, being unwilling to create a new one for it, in my ignorance as to whether some one already constructed upon foreign types may not include it.

Comparative measurements of species.

Catal. No.	Species.	Locality.	Length.	Stretch of wings.	Wing.	Tail.	Tarsus.	Middle toe.	Its claw alone.	Bill above.	Along gape.	Specimen measured.
6764	Paroides flaviceps.............	El Paso, Mex......	4.60	....	2.19	2.20	0.62	0.50	0.16	0.35	0.34	Skin........
do.	..........do.....................	......do............	4.25	6.00	....	....	....	....	....	....	....	Fresh........
10216	Paroides pendulinus.............	Europe......... ..	4.42	....	2.23	1.94	0.56	0.50	0.20	0.36	0.40	Skin........

PAROIDES FLAVICEPS, Baird.

Aegithalus flaviceps, SUNDEVALL, Ofversigt af Vet. Ak. Förhandl. VII, v, 1850, 129. " Sitka or California."

Psaltria flaviceps, SCLATER, Pr. Zool. Soc. XXIV, Mar. 1856, 37.

    Conirostrum ornatum, LAWRENCE, Ann. N. Y. Lyceum, V, May, 1851, 113 ; pl. v, fig. 1. Texas. (First introduction into fauna of U. S.)

SP. CH.—Above, cinereous ; head, all round, yellow : lesser wing coverts chestnut ; beneath brownish white. Length, 4.50 inches ; wing, 2.16 ; tail, 2.35.

Hab.—Rio Grande. Valleys of Texas and Mexico.

In this species the bill is conical ; the outlines of the upper mandible very gently and uniformly curved from the base, with an almost inappreciable downward bend near the tip.   In one specimen the lower edge of the lower jaw is curved slightly downward ; in another it is still curved, but almost straight.   The ridge is rounded ; the nostrils covered with superincumbent feathers.   The feet are stout and strong, but rather short ; the hind claw is short.   The wings are moderate ; the exposed part of the first or spurious quill is contained about two-and-a-half times in the second primary, which is considerably longer than the secondary quills, and barely shorter than the second primary ; the third, fourth, and fifth quills are equal, and longest. The tail is rather short, slightly rounded ; the feathers moderately broad.

The upper parts in this bird (excepting the head) are of a light brownish plumbeous, tinged with greenish yellow ; this color quite distinct at the junction of the downy and hairy portions of the feathers, or across their middle line.   This yellow is most evident on the rump, but here, as elsewhere, is only appreciable when the feathers are raised.   The head all round, and the upper part of the throat, are greenish yellow ; the feathers on the crown more olivaceous green at their tips ; those on the front with a tendency to orange at their bases.   The under parts are dull brownish white, slightly tinged with greenish yellow on the abdomen.   The wings and tail are brown, edged with the color of the back ; the edges of the outer tail feathers and of the primaries, rather paler.   The lesser wing coverts are chestnut.

The specimen described is a winter specimen ; the spring plumage may be brighter.   A specimen from Saltillo, Mexico, is smaller than one from El Paso.

This bird differs very much in external form from *Psaltriparus minimus*, and if the latter really belong to *Psaltria*, then the subject of the present article is erroneously assigned to *Psaltria* by Mr. Sclater.   In form it is much more like the sylvicolas, or even the typical titmice ; the bill is broader, longer, more conical, and much less curved above than in *P. minimus ;* the outline of the lower jaw also is slightly concave, instead of convex.   The wings are larger ; the secondary and tertials more nearly of a length ; the outer primaries much less graduated ; the spurious first primary smaller.   The tail feathers are proportionally broader, shorter, and more nearly of a length ; the greatest difference being .16 of an inch instead of .45.   The tarsi, toes, and claws are shorter and stouter.

In reality this species has a close resemblance of form to the species of black-capped *Parus*, with graduated tails, as *P. septentrionalis*.   It differs from them, however, in a more elongated and pointed bill, less curved above ; the outline of the lower mandible concave below ; the claws, especially the hinder one, shorter.   The primaries are less graduated, the third being longest, (with the fourth and fifth,) instead of being nearly .15 of an inch shorter than the fourth.

List of specimens.

Catal. No.	Locality.	When collected.	Whence obtained.	Orig'l No.	Collected by—	Extent.	Stretch of wing.	Wing.	Remarks.
6764	El Paso, Mex............	Dec. 26, 1854	Major Emory......	24	Dr. Kennerly......	4.25	6.00	....	....
4015	Saltillo, Mex............	....	Lieut. Couch	218	....	3.50	6.00	2.12	Eyes dark brown, feet bluish, bill dark slate.
	Matamoras, Mex........	....	......do............	......	Dr. Berlandiere.....	....	....	....	....

51 b

Family ALAUDIDAE.

First primary very short or wanting. Tarsi scutellate anteriorly and posteriorly, with the plates nearly of corresponding position and number. Hind claw very long and nearly straight. Bill short, conical, frontal feathers extending along the side of the bill; the nostrils usually concealed by a tuft of bristly feathers directed forwards. Tertials greatly elongated beyond the secondaries.

Of the family of *Alaudidae* but a single genus, *Eremophila*, is found in North America. The most characteristic feature of the larks, among the other Oscines is seen in the structure of the tarsus. The anterior half of this is covered by divided scales lapping round on the sides, but instead of the two plates which go one on each side of the posterior half, and uniting ultimately behind as an acute ridge, there is but one which laps round on the sides anteriorly, and is divided into scales like the anterior ones, but alternating with them. The posterior edge of the tarsus is as obtuse as the anterior, instead of being very acute. There is a deep separating groove on the inner side of the tarsus, and there may really be but one plate divided transversely, the edges meeting at this place.

The other characters of the *Alaudidae*, the long, straight, or slightly curved hind claw, the elongated tertials, and, to some extent, the shape of the bill, are shared by the *Anthinae* or *Motacillinae*. Here, however, the posterior edge of the tarsus is sharp and undivided transversely, the toes more deeply cleft, the bill more slender, &c.

There are two very distinct groups among the larks, possibly entitled to rank as sub-families. In the one the bill is stout, short, and conical. The nasal fossae transverse and completely filled by the thick tuft of bristly feathers, and perforated anteriorly by a circular nasal opening. In the other the bill is broader, more depressed, and straighter at the base. The nasal fossae are large, elongated, their axis parallel to the commissure, with rather linear nasal openings, not covered by feathers, but with merely a few bristles which do not conceal the nostrils. The type of the former may be considered as the European skylark, to which our *Neocorys spraguei* bears so much resemblance in habit, but there is no American representative in form, the species all belonging to the other group, the *Calandritinae* of Cabanis, as distinguished from the *Alaudinae*.[1]

EREMOPHILA, Boie.

Eremophila, BOIE, Isis, 1828, 322. Type *Alauda alpestris*. Sufficiently distinct from *Eremophilus*, Humboldt, (Fishes,) 1805.

Phileremos, BREHM, Deutschl. Vögel, 1831.

" *Otocoris*, BONAPARTE, 1839. Type *Alauda alpestris*." (Gray.) I am unable to find where the genus is named.

CH.—First primary wanting ; bill scarcely higher than broad ; nostrils circular, concealed by a dense tuft of feathers ; the nasal fossae oblique. A pectoral crescent and cheek patches of black.

This genus differs from *Melanocorypha* in having no spurious first primary, although the other characters are somewhat similar. *Calandritis* of Cabanis, with the same lack of first primary, has a much stouter bill. The spurious primary, more depressed bill, and differently constituted nostrils and nasal fossae of *Alauda* are readily distinctive.

[1] The *Melanocorypha calandra* of Boie, (*Alauda calandra*,) is doubtfully referred to by Richardson, F. B. Am. II, 244, as found in the fur countries.

Comparative measurements of species.

Catal. No.	Species.	Locality.	Sex.	Length.	Stretch of wings.	Wing.	Tail.	Tarsus.	Middle toe.	Its claw.	Bill above.	Along gape.	Specimen measured.
1190	Eremophila cornuta......	Carlisle, Pa........	♂	7.00	....	4.35	3.34	0.93	0.80	0.28	0.52	0.65	Skin ......
do.	......do.................	......do.............	....	7.75	14.75	4.50	....	....	....	....	....	....	Fresh ....
8491	Eremophila occidentalis?.	Fort Massachusetts.	♂	7.20	....	4.32	3.30	0.82	0.81	0.34	0.45	0.62	Skin ......
do.	......do	......do.............	......	7 50	....	....	....	....	....	....	....	....	Fresh .....
3702	......do..........	Salt Lake City	......	6.60	....	4.10	2.84	0.88	0.76	0.30	0.40	0.54	Skin ......
8726	......do (chrysolaema)	Frontera	......	6.40	....	4.00	2.92	0.84	0.66	0.23	0.50	0.56	Skin ......
8728	......do.................	Near Zuñi	......	5 80	....	3.83	2.80	0.80	0.72	0.28	0.40	0.52	Skin ......
do.	......do.............	......do.............	......	7.00	11.00	4.00	....	....	....	....	....	....	Fresh .....
9115	......do.................	Mexico............	♂	6.76	....	3.98	3.08	0.86	0.66	0.22	0.48	0 69	Skin ......
8732	......do.............	Fort Steilacoom....	♀	6.70	....	3.58	2.70	0.78	0.73	0.24	0.44	0.66	Skin ......

EREMOPHILA CORNUTA, Boie.

Sky Lark; Shore Lark.

Eastern and Northern variety.

Alauda cornuta, WILSON, Am. Orn. I, 1808, 85, (in text.)—RICH. F. Bor. Am. II.—MAXIM. Reise Nord. Am. I, 1839, 367.

Eremophila cornuta, BOIE, Isis, 1828, 322.

Phileremos cornutus, BONAP. List, 1838.

Otocoris cornutus, of authors.

Alauda alpestris, FORSTER, Phil. Trans. LXII, 1772, 383.—WILSON, Am. Orn. I, 1808, 85 ; pl. v, f. 4.—BON. Obs. 1825, No. 130.—NUTTALL, Man. I, 1832, 455.—AUD. Orn. Biog. II, 1834, 570; V. 448 ; pl. 200.— IB. Syn. 1839, 97.—IB. Birds Amer. III, 1841, 44 ; pl. 151.—JARDINE, Br. Birds, II, 329, (Am. sp.)

Western and Southern variety.

Alauda chrysolaema, WAGLER, Isis, 1831, 350.—Bp. Pr. Zool. Soc. 1837, 111.

Alauda minor, GIRAUD, 16 sp. Texas Birds, 1841.

Alauda rufa, AUD. Birds Amer. VII, 1843, 353 ; pl. 497.

Otocoris occidentalis, M'CALL, Pr. A. N. S. Phil. V, June 1851, 218, Santa Fe.—BAIRD, Stansbury's Report, 1852, 318.

SP. CH.—Above pinkish brown, the feathers of the back streaked with dusky. A broad band across the crown, extending backwards along the lateral tufts ; a crescentic patch from the bill below the eye and along the side of the head ; a jugular crescent, and the tail feathers, black ; the innermost of the latter like the back. A frontal band extending backwards over the eye, and under parts, with outer edge of wings and tail white. Chin and throat yellow.

Length of Pennsylvania specimens, 7.75 ; wing, 4.50 ; tail, 3.25 ; bill above, .52.

VAR. *chrysolaema*, smaller and lighter colored.

Hab.—Everywhere on the prairies and desert plains of North America. Atlantic States in winter.

Second quill longest ; first and third a little shorter. Above pinkish brown, brightest on the back of the neck, the wing coverts, and rump ; a brownish tinge on the interscapular region, each feather obscurely dusky centrally. There is a black band from the nostrils, to and beneath the eye, curving down towards the throat a short distance behind the eye. A broad band of black across the forehead extending backwards over the tufts alongside the vertex. A short, broad jugular collar ; the rest of the under parts white, with a brownish tinge behind the black of the breast ; the sides, especially along the thighs and breast, like the back. A frontal band, superciliary stripe from the bill, and throat anterior to the pectoral collar, yellow in winter. Tail black, the outer feather edged with white, the innermost colored like the back and resembling an elongated upper tail covert. Wing quills brown, darker at the tips, the outer edged with white.

In summer the yellow tints disappear in great measure, leaving a white frontal band succeeded by a black one of about the same length which extends over the lateral tufts. The white of the forehead, however, is continued through the upper half of the eye and under the black tuft. The side of the head and neck behind the black is white, interrupted by a crescentic patch of brownish ash bordering the ear coverts behind. The throat, however, usually remains yellow.

The very young bird is dusky brown, spotted with whitish above; beneath white, with an indication of the black pectoral and cheek patches.

The preceeding description is taken from specimens collected in Pennsylvania and Wisconsin, the former being winter visitors only in that State. They breed in Wisconsin and, perhaps, further south on the same meridian.

After a protracted examination of a large number of specimens, I have found it impossible to detect any tangible differences between the shore larks of the east and the west, and am very much inclined to consider them as the same species. There are the same proportions, the same colors, and nearly the same size; in fact, the differences which exist are not more than might readily be found in the same species. As a general rule, western specimens are paler in color, with the exception of those from Washington Territory, and those from New Mexico and Texas are smaller than Pennsylvania ones. There is, perhaps, a longer, slenderer bill with the smaller size, and the frontal white band is narrower, the black band on the crown broader than in some Wisconsin summer skins, though No. 4329 agrees with them in this respect. The quills and middle tail feathers are lighter brown. They vary among themselves, however, and specimens are occasionally found as large and dark as eastern ones. The skins from California, in reality, are of a darker shade of reddish above than in eastern ones, decidedly more than in the Texan.

Specimens from Washington Territory differ again from all other western ones in having the feathers of the back conspicuously streaked with dark brown, instead of the usual obsolete tinge of this color. The same difference, however, is seen in eastern specimens, as 7429, from Cleveland.

Upon the whole, therefore, in the absence of perfect spring specimens of the eastern form, I must confess my inability to give reliable distinctive characters of two or more species, the differences being only such as might be found in a wide range of the same species. The question as to the much more southern breeding range of the bird westward than to the east, may be answered by the suggestion of Dr. Cooper, that they there alone find the peculiar prairies or the desert region which they frequent.

The difference insisted on by Mr. Audubon, in reference to the tail feathers of two species, has no real existence in nature.

There is a great diversity of plumage in the western shore larks, varying with the sex, age, and season.

Without specimens at hand, I am unable to state the difference between the American *Eremophila cornuta* and the European *E. alpestris*.

List of specimens.

Catal. No.	Sex and age	Locality.	When collected.	Whence obtained.	Orig. No.	Collected by—	Length.	Stretch of wings.	Wing.	Remarks.
1190	♂	Carlisle, Pa..............	Nov. 4, 1844	S. F. Baird.........		....	7.75	14.75	4.50	....
845	....	do.....	Oct. 29, 1842	......do		....	6.75	13.08	4.00	....
7427	....	Cleveland, Ohio	April 1, 1851	Dr. Kirtland.....		....	....	....	... ...	....
10217	....	W. Northfield, Ill....	March 30	R. Kennicott.....		....	....	....	... ...	....
3780	....	Racine	....	Dr. Hoy.........		....	....	....	.....	....
4329	....	Dane county, Wis..........	Spring '54..	T. M. Brewer......		Th. Kumlien......	....	....	.....	....
8191	♀	Near Fort Leavenworth....	July 12, 1857	Wm. M. Magraw ..	121	Dr. Cooper.......	7.50	13.25	4.37	Feet gray......
6562	....	Fort Riley, K. T...........	....	Dr. W. A. Hammond		....	....	....	.....	....
5318	....	Yellowstone river	....	Lt. Warren	...	Dr. Hayden......	7.50	12.75	3.87	....
5313	♂	Fort Pierre, Nebraska.....	....	......do		......do.........	7.25	13.00	4.12	....
5317	....	Blackfoot country.........	....	......do		......do	....	....	..... .	....
9246	♂	Black Hills, Nebraska......	Sept. 29, 1857	......do		......do	6.75	12.25	3.75	Iris light brown.
9242	♀	......do...............	Sept. 14, 1857	......do	... ..	......do.........	7.50	12.50	4.00	......do..... ....
9241	♀	......do...............	Sept. 2?, 1857	......do		......do.........	6.50	12.50	3.12	......do..... ....
9245	♀	......do...............	.....do..........	......do		......do	6.50	13.50	4.00	......do............
9244	♂	......do...............	.....do..........	......do		......do	7.75	13.00	4.12	......do............
9243	....	Near Bear Bute...........	Oct. 3, 1857	......do		......do	6.75	12.75	4.50	......do............
9240	....	......do...............	Oct. 2, 1857	......do		......do	6.50	12.00	4.00	......do............
9239	....	......do...............	....do	......do		......do	6.50	12.50	4.00	......do............
8241	....	30 miles east of Ft. Kearney.	Oct. 24, 1857	Wm. M. Magraw...	223	Dr. Cooper.......	8.00	14.00	4.75	....
8242	....	......do...............	...do.......	......do	224	......do	7.25	13.25	4.50	....
8198	....	Big Blue river	July 19, 1857	......do	134	......do	7.50	13.00	4.50	Feet gray ......
8199	....	......do...............	......do.......	......do	135	......do	6.75	12.25	4.00	......do.......
5696	♀	Pole creek................	July 28, 1856	Lt. Bryan..........	171	W. S. Wood......				
5699	♀	Platte river..............	July 16, 1856	......do..........	114	......do			....	....
5698	♂	......do...............	....do.......	......do...........	90	......do				....
5697	....	W. Branch Medicine Bow creek...............	August 9...	......do.......	234	......do			....	....
7091	○	505 miles from Fort Riley...	July 15, 1856	......do.........	41	......do			....	....
5314	♀	Medicine creek	June 24, 1856	Lt. Warren...........		Dr. Hayden	6.87	12.00	4.00	
3702	. ...	Salt Lake City	Mar. 18, 1850	Capt. Stansbury....		....	....	....		....
8491	♂	Fort Mass., N. M..........	Mar. 15, 1856	Dr. Peters........	13	....	....	....	.	....
8724	....	Mimbres to Rio Grande.....	....	Dr. Henry		....	....	....		....
8726	....	Frontera...............	May, 1852..	Maj. Emory		C. Wright	....	....		....
8727	....	Near Zuñi, N. M...........	Nov. 19, 1853	Lt. Whipple.........	27	Kenn. & Möll.....	6.50	11.00	....	....
8728	....	......do...............	....do.......	......do	26	......do	7.00	11.00	....	....
8729	....	Ft. Steilacoom	Mar. 31, 1854	Gov. Stevens.......	39	Dr. Suckley......	6.50	11.75	4.50	....
8732	....	......do...............	....do.......	......do...........	4	......do		.?.....	....	....
8733	....	......do...............	....do.......	Mar. 31, 1856	Dr. Suckley......	285			....	....
8734	....	......do..	April 15, 1856	......do...........	299	....	....	....		....
8730	....	Shoalwater Bay, W. T.....	Sept. 8, 1854	Gov. Stevens......	90	Dr. Cooper.	7.25	12.75	....	....
8735	....	Presidio, California........	....	Lt. Trowbridge		....	6.00	10.00	5.50	....
8736	♂	Sacramento valley.........	....	Lt. Williamson		Dr. Heermann ..		....		....
4906	....	San Diego, Cal.......	Feb. 5, 1856	Dr. J. F. Hammond..		....	....	12.12	3.87	....
4097	♂	Saltillo, Mexico..........	May, 1853....	Lt. Couch		....	....	....		....
5034	.. ..	Indianola, Texas	Feb. 14, 1855	Capt. Pope........		....	9.50	11.00	4.00	....
9115	♂	Mexico.......	....	M. Verreaux.......		....	....	....		....

Family FRINGILLIDAE.

Primaries nine. Bill very short, abruptly conical and robust. Commissure strongly angulated at base of bill. Tarsi scutellate anteriorly, but the sides with two undivided plates meeting behind along the median line, as a sharp posterior ridge.

The systematic arrangement of the fringilline birds of the United States is more difficult than that of any other group, owing to the large number of species closely related to each other and exhibiting endless though minute variations in structure and form. Nearly all authors regularly avoid committing themselves by an attempt at the definition of their different divisions, giving only the names of types as indicative of their meaning. I have, therefore, been able to derive no aid from ornithological publications in arranging the species, and have been obliged to work out the whole subject anew from the beginning, as far as North American species are concerned.

In the system adopted I do not claim any very natural combination of species into genera, nor of genera into sub-families; all I have aimed at is to present a convenient artificial scheme by which the determination of the species may be facilitated. The means at my command are manifestly insufficient for the satisfactory solution of a problem which has puzzled the best ornithologists of the day, with all possible resources at their command in the way of specimens and books.

I divide all the United States species into four sub-families, briefly characterizable as follows :

COCCOTHRAUSTINAE.—Bill variable, from enormously large to quite small; with the base of the upper mandible almost always provided with a close pressed fringe of bristly feathers (more or less conspicuous) concealing the nostrils. Wings very long and pointed, usually one-half to one-third longer than the forked or emarginate tail. Tarsi short.

SPIZELLINAE.—Embracing all the plain colored sparrow-like species marked with longitudinal stripes. Bill conical, always rather small; both mandibles about equal. Tarsi lengthened. Wings and tail variable. Lateral claws never reaching beyond the base of the middle claw.

PASSERELLINAE.—Sparrow-like species with triangular spots beneath. Legs, toes, and claws very stout; the lateral claws reaching nearly to the end of the middle ones.

SPIZINAE.—Brightly colored species usually without streaks. Bill usually very large and much curved; lower mandible wider than the upper. Wings moderately long. Tail variable.

Sub-Family COCCOTHRAUSTINAE.

Wings very long and much pointed; generally one-third longer than the more or less forked tail; first quill usually nearly as long, or longer than the second. Tertiaries but little longer, or equal to the secondaries, and always much exceeded by the primaries. Bill very variable in shape and size, the upper mandible, however, as broad as the lower; nostrils rather more lateral than usual; and always more or less concealed by a series of small bristly feathers applied along the base of the upper mandible; no bristles at the base of the bill. Feet short and rather weak. Hind claw usually considerably longer than the middle anterior one; sometimes nearly the same size.

In the preceding paragraph I have combined a number of forms, all agreeing in the length and acuteness of the wing, the bristly feathers along the base of the bill, the absence of conspicuous bristles on the sides of the mouth, and in the shortness of the feet. They are all strongly marked and brightly colored birds, and usually belong to the more northern regions.

The species of the genera all vary remarkably in the shape and size of the bill, which here is of secondary importance to the character of the wing, tail, and feet. Indeed, I am inclined to think that this is the case throughout the *Fringillidae*. Thus, in the genus *Carpodacus*, one species, *C. frontalis*, has the bill so short and much curved as to resemble *Pinicola* or *Pyrrhula*, while the *C. cassinii* has a bill which, in its elongation, size, and general shape, is nearer to that of *Hesperiphona* than any other of our birds, except, perhaps, *Cardinalis*. The same is true of *Plectrophanes*, *Chrysomitris*, &c.

None of the species of *Plectrophanes*, excepting *P. nivalis*, exhibit the peculiar series of feathers along the base of the upper mandible, or else in very limited extent; but, as the other characters are as described, I have thought it best to continue them in their present association, notwithstanding this deviation in one character. As already stated, I do not pretend to any thing more than a convenient artificial arrangement by which the species may be found, and at present see no more eligible place for the species without dividing *P. nivalis* from all the rest, which I am not willing to do.

At the head of the series I place *Hesperiphona*, as combining the most typical features of the insessorial conirostres, in the enormous bill, long wings, and perching feet, &c. The other genera may be arranged in groups, as follows:

SYNOPSIS OF GENERA.

A.—Bill enormously large and stout; the lateral outline as long as that of the skull. Culmen gently curved.

      HESPERIPHONA.—First quill equal to the second. Wings one-half longer than the tail. Lateral claws equal, reaching to the base of the middle claw. Claws much curved, obtuse; hinder one but little longer than the middle. Colors green, yellow and black.

B.—Bill smaller, with the culmen more or less curved; the lateral outline not so long as the skull. Wings about one-third longer than the tail or a little more; first quill shorter than the second. Claws considerably curved and thickened; hinder most so, and almost inappreciably longer or even shorter than the middle anterior one. Tarsus shorter than the middle toe. Lateral toes unequal.

a. Colors red.

      PINICOLA.—Bill short, much curved above. Tail nearly even. Middle fore claw much straighter, and decidedly longer than the hinder. Outer lateral toe, with its claw, reaching beyond the base of the middle claw; a little longer than the hind toe.

      CARPODACUS.—Bill variable, more or less curved above. Tail forked. Middle fore claw scarcely longer than hinder one. Outer lateral toe with its claw, falling short of the base of the middle claw; equal to the hinder toe.

b. Colors black and yellow.

      CHRYSOMITRIS.—Bill nearly straight. Hind claw stouter and more curved, but scarcely longer than the middle anterior one. Outer lateral toe reaching a little beyond the base of the middle claw; shorter than the hind toe. Wings longer and more pointed. Tail quite deeply forked.

C.—Hind claw considerably longer than the middle anterior one, with about the same curvature; claws attenuated towards the point and acute. Lateral toes about equal. Wings usually almost one-half longer than the tail, which is deeply forked.

a. Points of mandibles overlapping.

CURVIROSTRA.—Tarsi shorter than middle toe. Bill much compressed, elongate falcate, with the points crossing like the blades of scissors. Claws very large; lateral extending beyond the base of the middle. Tarsi shorter than the middle toe. Colors red.

b. Points of mandibles not overlapping.

AEGIOTHUS.—Tarsi equal to the middle toe. Bill very acutely conical; outlines with commissure perfectly straight. Lateral toes reaching beyond the base of the middle one. No ridge on the side of the lower mandible. Colors reddish.

LEUCOSTICTE.—Culmen slightly decurved; commissure a little concave. Bill obtusely conical; not sharp pointed. A conspicuous ridge on the side of the lower mandible. Claws large; the lateral not reaching beyond the base of the middle one. Colors red and brown.

D.—Hind claw much the largest; decidedly less curved than the middle anterior one. Tarsi longer than the middle toe. Lateral toes equal; reaching about to the base of the middle claw. Hind toe as long or longer than the middle one. Bill very variable; always more or less curved and blunted. Tail slightly emarginate or even. Wings one-half longer than the tail. First quill as long as the second.

PLECTROPHANES.—Colors black and white. With or without rufous nape or elbows.

HESPERIPHONA, Bonaparte.

Hesperiphona, BONAP. Comptes Rendus, XXXI, Sept. 1850, 424. Type *Fringilla vespertina.*

CH.—Bill largest and stoutest of all the United States fringilline birds. Upper mandible much vaulted; culmen nearly straight, but arched towards the tip; commissure curved. Lower jaw very large, but not broader than the upper, nor extending back, as in *Guiraca;* considerably lower than the upper jaw. Gonys unusually long. Feet short; tarsi less than the middle toe; lateral toes nearly equal, and reaching to the base of the middle claw. Claws much curved, stout, and compressed. Wings very long and pointed, reaching beyond the middle of the tail. Primaries much longer than the nearly equal secondaries and tertial; outer two quills longest; the others rapidly graduated. Tail slightly forked; scarcely more than two-thirds the length of the wings.

The essential character of the genus among its allied North American forms consists, chiefly, in the enormous vaulted bill, .85 of an inch long and half of an inch broad. The wings lack the curious expansion of the tertiaries seen in the European *Coccothraustes.* The secondaries are emarginated at the end, and in some of them there is seen a short thread projecting from the bottom of the notch. This, at first, appears like the mucronate tip of the shaft, but it is, really, a supplementary pennule springing from the under surface of the wing, a short distance from the end.

Species of the genus are said to occur in Asia.

Comparative measurements of species.

Cat'l No.	Species.	Locality.	Sex.	Length.	Stretch of wings	Wings.	Tail.	Tarsus.	Middle toe.	Its claw alone.	Bill above.	Along gape.	Specimens measured.
6371	Hesperiphona vespertina ...	Fort Vancouver..	♀	7.20	....	4.68	2.86	0.84	0.88	0.24	0.80	0.76	Skin ....
do.	..........do..............	......do...........		7.25	12.75								Fresh ...
1874	..........do......	Columbia river ..		7.10	....	4.25	2.76	0.80	0.88	0.24	0.79	0.82	Skin ....

HESPERIPHONA VESPERTINA, B o n a p .

Evening Grosbeak.

Fringilla vespertina, Cooper, Annals New York Lyceum N. H. I, ɪɪ, 1825, 220. (Sault St. Marie.)—Aud. Orn.
Biog. IV, 1838, 515 : V, 235 ; pl. 373, 424.

Fringilla (Coccothraustes) vespertina, Bon. Syn. 1828, 113.—Ib. Zool. Jour. IV, 1828, 2.—Ib. Am. Orn. II ; pl. xv.

Coccothraustes vespertina, Sw. F. Bor. Am. II, 1831, 269.—Aud. Syn. 134.—Ib. Birds Amer. III, 1841, 217 ; pl. 207.

Hesperiphona vespertina, Bon. Comptes Rendus, XXXI, Sept. 1850, 424.—Ib. Conspectus, 1850, 505.

Coccothraustes bonapartii, Lesson. Illust, de Zool. 1834 ; pl. xxxiv.

Sp. Ch.—Bill yellowish green, dusky at the base. Anterior half of the body dark yellowish olive, shading into yellow to the rump above, and the under tail coverts below. Outer scapulars, a broad frontal band continued on each side over the eye, axillaries, and middle of under wing coverts, yellow. Feathers along the extreme base of the bill, the crown, tibiae, wings, upper tail coverts, and tail, black ; inner greater wing coverts and tertiaries white. Length, 7.30 ; wing, 4.30 ; tail, 2.75.

Hab.—Pacific coast to Rocky mountains ; northern America east to Lake Superior.

In this species the bill is very large and thick at the base ; the upper outline nearly straight, most curved at the tip. The bill resembles that of *Cardinalis virginianus* more than *Quiraca*. The wing is very long and much pointed ; the outer three primaries nearly equal, and the others graduating rapidly to the secondaries. The tail is short and slightly emarginate ; the feathers narrow.

The female differs in having the head of a dull olivaceous brown, which color also glosses the back. The yellow of the rump and other parts is replaced by a yellowish ash. The upper tail coverts are spotted with white. The white of the wing is much restricted. There is an obscure blackish line on each side of the chin.

List of specimens.

Catal. No.	Sex.	Locality.	When collected.	Whence obtained.	Collected by—	Length.	Stretch of wings.
1874	....	Columbia river....	....	S. F. Baird	J. K. Townsend .	....	....
6371	♀	Ft. Vancouver,W.T	Jan. 13, 1854	Gov. Stevens..............	Dr. Cooper......	7.25	12.75
6372	♂	......do..........	......do......	......do........	......do........	7.50	13.00
6373	♀	......do..........	......do......	......do........	......do........	7.25	12.75
6374	♂	Ft. Thorn, N. M....	....	Dr. T. C. Henry..........	....	....	....
6375	♂	......do..........	....	......do........	....	....	....

PINICOLA, V i e i l l o t .

Pinicola, Vieillot, Ois. Am. Sept. I, 1807, page iv; pl. i, f. 13.

" *Strobilophaga*, Vieillot, Analyse, 1816."

" *Corythus*, Cuvier, R. An. 1817."

Ch.—Bill short, nearly as high as long ; upper outline much curved from the base ; the margins of the mandibles rounded ; the commissure gently concave, and abruptly deflexed at the tip ; base of the upper mandible much concealed by the bristly feathers covering the basal third. Tarsus rather shorter than the middle toe ; lateral toe short, but their long claws reach the base of the middle one, which is longer than the hind claw. Wings moderate ; the first quill rather shorter than the second, third, and fourth. Tail rather shorter than the wings ; nearly even.

But one species of this genus belongs to the American fauna, and is closely allied to if not identical with that belonging to the northern portions of the Old World.

52 b

Comparative measurements of species.

Catal. No.	Species.	Sex.	Length.	Wing.	Tail.	Tarsus.	Middle toe.	Its claw alone.	Bill above.	Along gape.	Specimens measured.
543	Pinicola canadensis.............	....	8.00	4.36	4.06	0.88	0.96	0.34	0.56	0.60	Skin ....
1208	........do......................	♂	9.00	4.52	4.08	0.86	0.94	0.34	0.58	0.56	Skin ....

PINICOLA CANADENSIS, Cabanis.

Pine Grosbeak.

Coccothraustes canadensis, Brisson, Orn. III, 1760, 250 ; pl. xii, f. 3.
" *Corythus canadensis*, Brehm, Vögel Deutschlands," (1831 ?)
Pinicola canadensis, Cabanis, Mus. Hein. 1851, 167.
Pinicola americana, (Cab. MSS.) Bp. Consp. 1850, 528.
Loxia enucleator, Forst. Phil. Trans. LXII, 1772, 383.—Wils. Am. Orn. I, 1808, 80 ; pl. v.
Pyrrhula enucleator, Aud. Orn. Biog. IV, 1838, 414 ; pl. 358.
Corythus enucleator, Bonap. List, 1838.—Aud. Syn. 127.—Ib. Birds Amer. III, 1841, 179 ; pl. 199.

Sp. Ch.—Bill and legs black.. General color carmine red, not continuous above, however, except on the head ; the feathers showing brownish centres on the back, where, too, the red is darker. Loral region, base of lower jaw all round, sides and posterior part of body, with under tail coverts, ashy, whitest behind. Wing with two white bands across the tips of the greater and middle coverts ; the outer edges of the quills also white, broadest on the tertiaries.

Female ashy, brownish above, tinged with greenish yellow beneath ; top of head, rump, and upper tail coverts, brownish gamboge yellow. Wings as in the male. Length about 8.50 ; wing, 4.50 ; tail, 4.00.

Hab.—Arctic America. South to United States in severe winters.

In comparing an American specimen of the Pine grosbeak (1208) with a European, (*P. enucleator,*) in the collection of the Philadelphia Academy, I find the former considerably larger, (wing 4.76, instead of 4.40,) the bill much stouter and more bulging at the sides, the tip of the upper mandible much less decurved and less projecting over the lower. The tail feathers are much broader. The legs are black, the bill dark brown, instead of both being horn color. There is little difference in the character of the red ; there is, however, much more white on the wing in very broad and sharply defined pure white external edgings of the quills, especially on the tertials, secondaries, and greater coverts, instead of having these narrower, less conspicuous, and tinged with rose. Without being sure that these differences of the two skins are either constant or characteristic, I think it proper to quote such references only as belong to American specimens.

List of specimens.

Catal. No.	Sex.	Locality.	Whence obtained.
543	....	New York...........	S. F. Baird ....
554	....	......do............	......do...........
2866	....	Unknown	......do...........
1208	♂	Philadelphia	......do...........

CARPODACUS, Kaup.

Carpodacus, KAUP, "Entw. Europ. Thierw. 1829." Type *Loxia erythrina*, Pall.

Erythrospiza, BONAPARTE, Saggio di una dist. met. 1831.

Haemorrhous, SWAINSON, Class. Birds, II, 1837, 295. Type *Fringilla purpurea*, Gmelin.

CH.—Bill short, stout, vaulted ; the culmen decurved towards the end ; the commissure nearly straight to the slightly decurved end. A slight development of bristly feathers along the sides of the bill, concealing the nostrils. Tarsus shorter than the middle toe ; lateral claws reaching to the base of the middle one. Claw of hind toe much curved, smaller than the middle one, and rather less than the digital portion. Wings long and pointed, reaching to the middle of the tail, which is considerably shorter than the wing, and moderately forked. Colors red, or red and brown.

The genus *Carpodacus*, including the American purple finches, is composed of species, the males of which are more or less red in full plumage, while the females are brown. They are spread over North America, and species also occur in considerable numbers in northern Europe and Asia.

In addition to the generic names mentioned above, there have been proposed for the group *Erythrina*, Brehm. 1828, pre-occupied in Botany, *Erythrothorax*, Brehm, 1831, and *Pyrrhulinota*, Hodgson, 1844. Should it become necessary to subdivide the genus, there will be no difficulty in finding names already established for the different sections.

The following diagnoses may serve to distinguish the North American species of *Carpodacus*.

A. Tail and wing feathers edged with reddish.

Quite uniformly crimson on the head, neck, breast, and upper parts ; darker across the back. Wing coverts and quills margined with reddish. Belly white, faintly streaked with black. First quill longer than fourth.....................................*C. purpureus*.

Similar to last. Purple of head and rump darker. A light purple supraorbital line. First quill shorter than fourth...*C. californicus*.

Bill very long. Crown continuously crimson ; chin, throat, upper part of breast, and rump, rose red. Back grayish brown, streaked conspicuously with dark brown. Belly white, scarcely streaked...*C. cassinii*.

B. Tail and wing feathers edged with grayish white.

Bill short, very convex. Forehead, superciliary stripe, chin, throat, breast, and rump crimson. Back brown, not streaked. Wings brown. Belly white, strongly streaked ; outlines of red not very sharply defined...*C. frontalis*.

Bill very convex. Forehead, superciliary stripe, chin and throat, with rump, all uniform bright crimson. Back dull brown, not streaked. Breast and belly white, much streaked. All the colors very sharply defined.....................*C. haemorrhous*.

Comparative measurements of species.

Catal. No.	Species.	Locality.	Sex.	Length.	Stretch of wings.	Wing.	Tail.	Tarsus.	Middle toe.	Its claw alone.	Bill above.	Along gape.	Specimen measured.
......	Carpodacus purpureus..	....	.....	5.80	....	3.20	2.56	0.62	0.72	0.20	0.44	0.48	Skin*.......
796	.........do.............	Carlisle, Pa....	♂	5.52	... .	3.10	2.50	0.65	0.72	0.20	0.40	0.50	Skin ....
do.	.........do.............	......do...	......	5.83	9.83	3.16							Fresh.......
1380	.........do.............	......do............	♀	5.50	....	3.25	2.52	0.72	0.79	0.24	0.45	0.56	Skin........
do.	.........do.............	......do............	.....	6.41	10.33	3.16							Fresh.......
10230	Carpodacus californicus..	Fort Tejon	♂	5.50	....	3.20	2.66	0.70	0.76	0.19	0.43	0.48	Skin........
10231	.........do.............	......do............	♀	5.44	....	3.00	2.46	0.72	0.77	0.20	0.46	0.50	Skin ....
6420	Carpodacus cassini.......	Camp 104, Pueblo creek, N. M.	♂	6.02	....	3.56	2.52	0.74	0.76	0.20	0.50	0.58	Skin ....
do.	.........do.............	......do............	......	5.50	10.00	7.00							Fresh ......
6421	.........do.............	......do............	......	6.10	....	3.56	2.72	0.74	0.76	0.20	0.50	0.56	Skin ......
do.	.........do.............	......do............	......	5.50	9.00	3.00	...						Fresh ......
6422	.........do.............	16 miles west of Albuquerque.	♀	5.10	... ...	3.36	2.40	0.68	0.78	0.20	0.48	0.53	Skin........
4568	Carpodacus haemorrhous.	Mexico............	.....	5.60	....	3.10	2.78	0.68	0 68	0.16	0.40	0.50	Skin†.......
5547	Carpodacus frontalis.....	Petaluma, Cal.....	♂	5.40	....	3.08	2.74	0.68	0.60	0.18	0.38	0.50	Skin........
8548	.........do.............	......do............	♂	5.50	....	3.10	2.78	0.68	0.74	0.18	0.39	0.48	Skin ....
6429	.........do.........	Sacramento valley..	♀	5.40	....	2.92	2.54	0.69	0.68	0.18	0.40	0.47	Skin ......
2886	.........do.............	Mexico............	♂	6.00	... .		3.14	0.68	0.72	0.17	0.41	0.50	Skin‡.......

* No label.   † Mounted.   ‡ Mounted; wings broken off.

CARPODACUS PURPUREUS, Gray.

Purple Finch.

Fringilla purpurea, GMELIN, Syst. Nat. I, 1788, 923.—LATH. Ind. I, 1790, 446.—WILSON, Am. Orn. I, 1808, 119 ; pl. vii, f. 4.—IB. V, 1812, 87 ; pl. xlii, f. 3.—AUD. Orn. Biog. I, 1831, 24 : V, 200 ; pl. 4.

Haemorrhous purpurea, SWAINSON, Birds, II, 1837, 295.

Erythrospiza purpurea, BP. List, 1838.—AUD. Syn. 1839, 125.—IB. Birds Amer. III, 1841, 170 ; pl. 196.

Carpodacus purpurea, GRAY's Genera, 1844–'49.—BP. Conspectus, 1850, 533.—BON. & SCHLEGEL, Mon. of Loxiens, 14, tab. xv.

? Loxia violacea, LINN. Syst. Nat. 1766, 306, 43. (Very uncertain.)

Purple finch, CATESBY, PENNANT, LATH. *Hemp-bird*, BARTRAM.

SP. CH.—Second quill longest ; first shorter than third ; considerably longer than the fourth. Body crimson, palest on the rump and breast, darkest across the middle of back and wing coverts, where the feathers have dusky centres. The red extends below continuously to the lower part of the breast, and in spots to the tibiae. The belly and under tail coverts white, streaked faintly with brown, except in the very middle. Edges of wings and tail feathers brownish red ; lesser coverts like the back. Two reddish bands across the wings, (over the ends of the middle and greater coverts.) Lores dull grayish. Length, 6.25 inches ; wing, 3.34 ; tail, 2 50 ; bill above, .46.

Female olivaceous brown ; brighter on the rump. Beneath white. All the feathers everywhere streaked with brown, except on the middle of the belly and under coverts a superciliary light stripe.

Hab.—North America, from Atlantic to the high central plains.

List of specimens.

Catal. No.	Sex.	Locality.	When collected.	Whence obtained.	Collected by—	Length.	Stretch of wings	Wing.
1353	♂	Carlisle, Pa	April 13, 1844	S. F. Baird		6.17	10.50	3.33
796	♂	do	Oct. 14, 1842	do		5.83	9.83	3.17
1380	♀	do	April 22, 1844	do		6.42	10.33	3.17
2138	♂	do	April 23, 1845	do		6.17	9.83	3.17
797		do	Oct. 14, 1842	do		5.83	10.17	3.17
2139	♂	do	April 23, 1845	do		6.42	10.17	3.17
309	♂	do	April —, 1841	do		6.00	10.00	
931	♀	do	April 28, 1843	do				
7040	♂	St. Louis, Mo	May 15, 1857	Lieut. Bryan	W. S. Wood			
4853	♀	Vermilion river, Neb.	May 8, 1856	Dr. Hayden	Lt. Warren	6.00	10.00	3.62

CARPODACUS CALIFORNICUS, Baird.

Western Purple Finch.

Sp. Ch.—Similar to *purpureus.* Third quill longest; first shorter than the fourth. Purple of head and rump much darker than in *C. purpureus;* the head with a broad supraorbital lateral band of lighter purple. Length, 6.25 ; wing, 3.20 ; tail, 2.60.

Hab.—Pacific coast of United States.

In the examination of a large series of skins (over sixty in number) of the western purple finch, I have found differences which indicate either a decided geographical variety, or a distinct species from the typical eastern *C. purpureus.* The size appears somewhat less. The upper mandible appears lower in proportion to the inferior one, and is darker than in eastern specimens. The culmen is more curved, and lacks the gentle concavity on the basal portion. The male is of a considerably darker purple, especially on the head and the rump ; that on the former in quite strong and abrupt contrast to the back, instead of fading gently into it. The sides of the crown are of a lighter purple than elsewhere, giving rise to quite a conspicuous supraorbital stripe, scarcely or not at all appreciable in eastern skins.

The female of the western type differs from that of the eastern in being more olivaceous above, and in having the streaks below rather larger, and not so well defined. There appears to be a difference in the marking of the wings. In eastern *C. purpureus* there is usually a well marked whitish band across the ends of the middle coverts, while the greater coverts, though margined externally by paler, have a still lighter bar across the posterior extremity, which is not seen in the western bird.

The wing formula of the two species differs very greatly, the third quill in the western bird being generally longest, instead of the second ; the first shorter than the fourth, instead of much longer, and shorter than the third.

List of specimens.

Catal. No.	Sex and age.	Locality.	When collected.	Whence obtained.	Orig'l No.	Collected by—	Length.	Stretch of wings.	Remarks.
4488	♀	Straits of Fuca, W. T..	March, 1855	Dr. J. G. Cooper....			6.00	9.50	
4489	♂	......do.........	......do......	......do............			6.25	9.75	
4490	♀	......do...............	......do......	......do..........					
6412	♂	Fort Steilacoom........	April, 1854...	Dr. G. Suckley. ...	72				
6413	♂	..... do..........	......do......	......do...........	66				
6414	♀	......do..............	......do......	......do..........	80				
6415	♀	......do...............	April 10, 1856	......do...........	291		6.50	10.00	
6416	♂	......do...............	......do......	......do...........	294		6.93	10.12	
6417	....	......do...............	Aug. 1, 1856	......do........	516				
4536	♂	W. Territory...........	1856.........	...... do.......					
4537	♂	......do...............	......do......	...... do.......					
4535	♂	......do...............	......do......	...... do.......					
6411	♂	Fort Vancouver, W. T..	Jan. 18, 1854	Gov. Stevens....	13	Dr. Cooper.....	6.50	9.50	Iris brown, bill and feet paler.
6418	♂	Calaveras, Cal......		Lt. Williamson....		Dr. Heerman...			
6419	♀	Cosumnes river, Cal....		......do.......		......do...			
4491	....	Santa Clara............	Nov. 1855....	Dr. J. G. Cooper...					
4492	....	......do............	......do......	......do.......					
4493	....	......do............	...... do......	......do.......					
4494	....	......do............	......do......	......do.......					
4495	....	......do............	......do......	......do.......					
4496	....	......do............	......do......	......do.......					
3731	♂	Monterey, Cal..........	Jan. 22	W. Hutton					
		Fort Tejon, Cal........		J. X. de Vesey. ...					

CARPODACUS CASSINII, Baird.

Cassin's Purple Finch.

Carpodacus cassinii, BAIRD, Pr. Ac. Nat. Sc. Phila. VII, June, 1854, 119.   Colorado River.

SP. CH.—Larger than *C. purpureus*. Bill .55 of an inch above. Second and third quills longest ; first longer than fourth. Above pale grayish brown, the feathers streaked with darker brown, and with only an occasional gloss of reddish, except on the crown, which is uniform deep crimson, and on the rump. Sides of the head and neck, throat and upper part of breast with rump, pale rose color ; rest of under parts white, very faintly and sparsely streaked with brown. Female without any red, and streaked on the head and under parts with brown. Length, 6.50 ; wing, 3.60 ; tail, 2.60.

Hab.—Rocky mountains and valley of the Colorado.

This is the largest of the American purple finches, and is conspicuously different from the others in the size and unusual elongation of the bill. This is very nearly straight above to within one-third or fourth of the end, and then curves gently to the tip ; the cutting edge of the mandible is sinuated in the middle. The proportions of the quills, as given above, are pretty constant, although sometimes the second quill is longest, and sometimes the first as long as the second. The tail is moderately forked ; the feathers broad.

There is rather more of red on the nape than on the back, where this color is only occasionally visible. The rose of the breast is not abruptly defined, but passes gradually into the white of the belly.

This species is more like *C. purpureus* than the other North American purple finches, but is larger and otherwise easily distinguished. The bill is much larger, and longer proportionally. The proportions of the quills are different; the tail less deeply forked, and the feathers broader. The crimson of the head is brighter ; there is much less red on the back, although the crown and rump patches are not abruptly defined. The streaks on the back are darker and more conspicuous. The red of the throat and breast is much paler and does not extend so far back ; there is no red at all on the belly. The under tail coverts are white, with narrow dark streaks. There are two pale bands across the wings, rather more distinct than in *purpureus*. The loral region is grayish.

The females of the two species are very similar, that of *C. cassinii* only to be readily distinguished by the larger size and larger and longer bill. The streaks on the breast appear to be rather narrower and better defined.

List of specimens.

Catal. No.	Sex.	Locality.	When collected.	Whence obtained.	Orig. No.	Collected by—	Length.	Stretch of wings.	Wing.
6420	♂	Pueblo creek, N. M..	Jan. 22, 1854	Lt. Whipple	48	Dr. Kennerly ...	5.50	10.00	......
6421	♂	......do...........	....do.	......do........	52	......do.......	5.50	9.00	......
6422	....	Alberquerque, N. M..	Nov. 15, 1855	......do........	16	......do.......	....	....	......
6423	....	Fort Thorne, N. M. ..	....	Dr. T. C. Henry.	......	....	....	....	......
6424	....	......do...........	....	......do........	......	....	....	....	......
6425	....	......do...........	....	......do........	......	....	... .	....	......

CARPODACUS FRONTALIS, Gray.

Burion ; House Finch.

Fringilla frontalis, Say, Long's Exped. Il, 1824, 40.—(?) Aud. Orn. Biog. V, 1839, 230 ; pl. 424.
Pyrrhula frontalis, Bon. Am. Orn. I, 1825, 49 ; pl. vi.
Erythrospiza frontalis, Bon. List, 1838.—Ib. Pr. Zool. Soc. 1837, 112.—?Aud. Syn 1839, 125.—Ib. Birds Amer. III, 1841, 175 ; pl. 197.—Gambel, Jour. A. N. S. 2d Series, I, 1847, 53.
Fringilla (Pyrrhula) frontalis, Gambel, Pr. A. N. Sc. I, 1843, 262.
Carpodacus frontalis, Gray, Genera, 1844–'49.—M'Call, Pr. A. N. Sc. V, 1851, 219.
? *Carpodacus obscurus,* M'Call, Pr. A. N. Sc. V, June 1851, 220. Sante Fé.
Carpodacus familiaris, M'Call, Pr. A. N. Sc. VII, April 1852, 61 . Santa Fé.

Red-breasted variety.

? *Pyrrhula cruentata,* Lesson, Rev. Zool. 1839, 101.
? *Carpodacus rhodocolpus,* Cab. Mus. Hein. 1851, 166.—Sclater. Pr. Zool. Soc. 1856, 304.
Carpodacus frontalis, Bon. & Schlegel, Mon. of Loxiens, 1850, tab. xvi, f. 1.—Ib. Consp. 1850, 533.

Sp. Ch.—6426.—Bill short, much curved. Forehead for nearly the length of the bill, a broad superciliary stripe extending to the nape, side of lower jaw, chin, throat, and upper part of the breast, crimson red ; rump, paler. Rest of upper parts with sides of neck grayish brown, with an occasional gloss of red externally on the crown, and with scarcely appreciable darker brown towards the centres of the feathers. Belly, under tail coverts, and sides, whitish, conspicuously streaked with light brown ; sometimes red to the middle of the former. Length, 5.75 ; wing, 3.25 ; tail, 2.80.

Hab.—Rocky mountains to the Pacific.

This species is quite remarkable for the very great variation in the shade of red in the different regions of the body. Thus the specimen selected as the basis of the description (6426, May 4, El Paso) has this color a bright crimson red ; the rump scarcely different ; the throat and breast almost as bright as the head. The lower part of the red on the breast is tinged with orange—a character seen also in 6431. The red does not extend beneath the closed wings, (the entire sides of body being like the belly,) and fades rather gradually into the white belly ; it extends about as far as the end of the breast bone. The upper tail coverts are like the back ; the back cannot at all be called streaked, the feathers being merely brown, fading very slightly to the exterior. There is no indication of red on the edges of wing and tail, which are pale whitish brown. There is a faint trace of narrow lightish bands across the wings. The streaks on the belly, sides, and under tail coverts are narrow, long, and well defined. The red gloss on the back is confined to the middle of the interscapular region; the middle of the crown and the nape have the feathers tipped with crimson like the crown, obscuring the outline of the frontal and superciliary band. The loral region, space immediately around and under the eye, the ear coverts, and thence along the sides of the neck, are grayish brown, the lores lighter. The red extends for about .15 of an inch along the upper edge of the lower jaw, then passes obliquely to the throat, leaving the ear coverts untouched.

In 6432 the red on the rump is wanting; the superciliary stripe better defined, owing to the greater lack of red tips to the feathers of the crown. In 6434 the shade of red in the crown is the same, that on the throat paler, that on the rump entirely different, being more of a rose color. In 6433 the red on the head and throat is much more orange. In No. 4085 (Monterey, Mexico, April 16, spring plumage) the red, instead of being bright crimson, is almost a dark purple red; every where of the same tint. No. 5547, from Petaluma, California, is precisely similar in color.

In some full winter specimens the rump is more rosy; the crown more mixed with red; the back considerably glossed with the same.

I have been a good deal perplexed in the determination of the small California *Carpodaci* in the series before me. These, as a general rule, have the middle of the crown rather more thickly filled with red; in one, indeed, (6428, from Los Angeles,) this color is almost as continuous as in *C. purpureus.* No. 5547, from Petaluma, California, is somewhat similar in this respect, but the red is much more purple. In both there is a strong tendency to red on the side of the head and neck. In one specimen (5548) there is a very close resemblance to *C. purpureus* in the shade of red, and this extends to the upper part of the belly. The middle of the crown is strongly tinged with red; the entire sides of the head, too, are as red as in *C. purpureus.* The bill, wings without any reddish, &c., are those of *C. frontalis.* Other specimens, from Santa Clara, California, are similar, but the red does not extend as far on the belly; nor is it seen on the sides of the head.

It would seem very probable that in the gradual transition in California specimens from the peculiar characters of *C. purpureus* or *C. californicus* to those of *C. frontalis*, we may have hybrids between the two, where they are associated, like those of *Colaptes auratus* and *mexicanus*, on the Upper Missouri and Yellowstone. If there be a third permanent species, I am unable to fix its characters.

The *Erythrospiza frontalis* of Audubon seems larger than that from the upper Rio Grande, and I am inclined to think that his figure and description were taken from a specimen now before me, (2886,) marked as received from Mr. J. Gould, probably from Mexico. This lacks the wings, but the tail is much longer, measuring 3.30 inches instead of less than three; the feathers, too, are considerably broader. It resembles California more than New Mexican skins.

A specimen from the city of Mexico (2706) is larger than New Mexican ones, and has the red more restricted to the upper part of the breast. The red of the frontal and superciliary stripes is better defined, as also that of the rump, which is unusually extended. A skin (4568) received from Dr. Hartlaub, of Bremen, as the *Fringilla haemorrhous* of Lichtenstein, from Mexico, has the red of the crown, throat, and rump, much brighter, deeper, and very sharply defined and restricted. That on the throat is confined to it, and does not extend at all on the breast. The under parts are much more streaked. These two specimens I am inclined to consider as distinct from *C. frontalis*, and probably entitled to the name of *haemorrhous*, Wagler.[1]

The *Carpodacus rhodocolpus* of Cabanis resembles very closely some of those California specimens mentioned as so similar to *C. purpureus*. Should they be distinct, Cabanis' name might with propriety be applied to them. I scarcely think, however, that the name can stand.

The *Carpodacus frontalis* of New Mexico is readily distinguished from *C. purpureus*, by the fact that the middle of the crown is not continuously red, the ear coverts and under the eye brown, not red ; the back and wings are uniform brown, the feathers with lighter edges, the red of the rump quite sharply defined, instead of having the red over the back and wings The belly is strongly streaked with brown, instead of being nearly white. The size is considerably less ; the bill shorter, broader, and considerably more convex and curved.

C. cassinii has the back more glossed with red and strongly streaked with dark brown, instead of being nearly uniform ; the belly is very little streaked, instead of strongly so. The size is much larger ; the bill larger, and straighter.

NOTE.—A series of *Carpodacus frontalis* recently collected at Fort Tejon, by Mr. Vesey, strengthens the impression that there is really but one species from the Rocky Mountains to the Pacific, and that this varies greatly in the tint and extent of the red with age and season. Thus, in the most highly colored specimen, 10219, the back is so much tinged with red as to connect that on the head and rump, the centre of the crown being scarcely less intense than the sides and front. Beneath, the bright red extends to the middle of the belly, and farther back on the sides. In 10220 the back has only the faintest possible gloss of red ; the middle of the crown less deeply colored. No. 10221 has the red of the under parts restricted rather abruptly to the fore part of the breast. In 10222, a young male, the red extends further behind, but there is none on the rump. All these are summer skins. No. 10223, an autumnal skin, has the same distribution of red as in 10219, but it is as uniform and continuous to the middle of the belly as in the purple finch. The colors are duller, however, and the whole plumage has a softened character ; 10224 has the red on the belly more restricted, and almost none on the rump.

---

[1] CARPODACUS HAEMORRHOUS, Sclater.

Fringilla haemorrhoa, "LICHT." WAGLER, Isis, 1831, 525. LICHT. Preis-Verzeich. 1831, sp. 57.
Pyrrhulinota haemorrhoa, BP. Comptes Rendus, 1856.
Carpodacus haemorrhous, SCLATER, Pr. Zool. Soc. 1856, 304.

Several specimens of *Carpodacus* in the collection of the Philadelphia Academy, probably from Mexico or Lower California, although labelled North America, agree with numbers 2706 and 4568 in the very precise and sharp definition of the red colors. The forehead for less than the length of the bill, a broad superciliary stripe extending as far behind the eye as the tip of the bill is in front of it, the base of the lower jaw, and the chin and throat, but not the breast, with the rump but not the upper tail coverts, are crimson. And no where else (in five specimens) is there any indication of a reddish gloss, not even in the middle of the crown, on the neck, or back. The width of the red on the throat is scarcely one-fourth the circumference of the neck.

Upon a re-examination of the subject, I am by no means sure that the bird just referred to is the true *Fringilla haemorrhous* of Wagler, which seems nearer to the true *frontalis*. It may possibly not yet have received a name.

53 b

List of specimens.

Catal. No.	Sex.	Locality.	When collected.	Whence obtained.	Orig. No.	Collected by—	Length.	Stretch of wings.	Wing.	Remarks.
5038	......	Doña Ana, N. M...	Nov. 20, 1855	Capt. J. Pope.. .	163	....	6.25	9.50	3.00	Bill light br'n ; eyes dark br'n ; feet brown... ....
6430	....	Fort Thorn, N. M.	....	Dr. T. C. Henry..	.....	... .	....	....	......	....
6426	·♂	Frontera, Mex.....	May 6, —	Maj. Emory.....	......	C Wright...	5.75	8.75	2.25	......
6427	....	Camp 118, N. M. ..	Feb. 10, 1854	Lieut. Whipple..	86	Dr. Kennerly	5.50	9.00	3.50	Eyes gray (?) ....
4084	♀	Monterey, Mex.....	April —, 1853	Lieut. Couch	186	....	6.00	9.00	3.00	Eyes brown ; bill and feet light brown............
4085	♂	......do............	..... do.....	......do.........	169	....	5.50	9.00	3.00	.... do.........do...........
6428	♂	Los Angeles, Cal...	....	Lt. Williamson..	... ..	Dr. Heermann	....	....	....	......
6429	♀	Sacramento, Cal...	....	......do.......	......	......do	....	....	....	......
4484	♂	Santa Clara, Cal...	Nov. —, 1855	Dr. J. G. Cooper..	......	......	6.25	9.75	....	....
4485	♂	......do............	..... do.....	......do.........	......	......	6.00	9.38	....	....
4486	♀	......do............	..... do.....	......do.........	......	......	....	....	....	....
4487	♀	. ...do............	..... do.....	......do......'...	......	......	....	....	....	....
5547	♂	Petaluma, Cal	....	E. Samuels......	473	......	....	....	....	....
5548	♂	......do.....?......	April —, 1856	......do.........	469	......	....	....	....	....
10219(o) 10224	....	Fort Tejon, Cal....	... .	J. X. de Vesey...	......	......	... ...	....	....	....

CHRYSOMITRIS, Boie.

Chrysomitris, Boie, Isis, 1828, 322. Type *Fringilla spinus*, Linn.
Astragalinus, Cab. Mus. Hein. 1851, 159. Type *Fringilla tristis*, Linn.
Hypacanthus, Cabanis, Mus. Hein. 1851, 161. Type *Carduelis spinoides*, Vig.

Ch.—Bill rather acutely conic, the tip not very sharp ; the culmen slightly convex at the tip ; the commissure gently curved. Nostrils concealed. Obsolete ridges on the upper mandible. Tarsi shorter than the middle toe ; outer toe rather the longer, reaching to the base of the middle one. Claw of hind toe shorter than the digital portion. Wings and tail as in *Aegiothus*.
The colors are generally yellow, with black on the crown, throat, back, wings, and tail, varied sometimes with white.

This genus differs from *Aegiothus* in a less acute and more curved bill, a much less development of the bristly feathers at the base of the bill, the claw of hind toe shorter than its digital portion, the claws shorter and less curved and attenuated, and the outer lateral toes not extending beyond the base of the middle claw.

The species exhibit many differences among themselves, especially in the size and shape of the bill, which have been made the basis of generic distinctions.

The North American species of *Chrysomitris* are all readily distinguishable from each other. Setting aside the *Ch. pinus*, in which all the feathers have brown centres, those of the head and crown included, we find the crown in all is black. They may, however, be first arranged into those with white bands or edgings on the wings, and those with yellow.

Top of head more or less black.

A. Chrysomitris—Bill very large.   Entire bases of tail feathers and of quills yellow.
    Head all round black.   Edges of greater wing coverts and of tertials yellow..*C. magellanicus.*
    Head all round black.   Wing coverts and tertials black..............................*C. notatus.*
    Crown and throat black.................. ....*C. stanleyi.*
    Crown alone black...... ....*C. yarrelli.*

B. ASTRAGALINUS, Cabanis.—Wings black ; the bases of the primaries and edgings white ; tail white, blotched. No black on throat.

Body entirely yellow above ; lesser wing coverts white...................................*C. tristis.*
Body olivaceous above ; lesser wing coverts black........................ ....*C. psaltria.*
Body entirely black above; lesser wing coverts black. Tail with white spots..*C mexicanus.*
Similar to the last ; the tail without white spots................................*C. columbianus.*

C. Wings black, edged with yellow, but none at the base of the quills. Tail spot white. Crown, chin, and throat black...*C. lawrencii.*

No black on the head.

D. Feathers of the head and body all streaked with brown. Bases of the quills and tail feathers yellow............... ....*C. pinus.*

Comparative measurements of species.

Catal. No.	Species.	Locality.	Sex.	Length.	Extent.	Wing.	Tail.	Tarsus.	Middle toe.	Its claw.	Bill above.	Along gape.	Specimen measured.
2883	Chrysomitris magellanicus	America............	♂	4.60	....	2.73	1.96	0.54	0.59	0.21	0.40	0.42	Skin ....
9226	Chrysomitris notatus....	Guatemala.........		4.22	....	2.50	1.86	0.48	0.58	0.20	0.42	0.43	Skin ....
2035	Chrysomitris stanleyi	California	♂	4.70	....	2.82	2.10	0.64	0.72	0.22	0.42	0.44	Skin ....
2036	.........do.............	.....do......	♀?	4.60	....	2.84	2.24	0.64	0.72	0.20	0.42	0.42	Skin ....
2037	Chrysomitris yarrelli.....	.....do.............	♂	3.86	....	2.40	1.62	0.50	0.54	0.18	0.36	0.50	Skin ....
8339	Chrysomitris tristis.......	Independence, Mo.	......	4.44	....	2 88	2.24	0.52	0.58	0.20	0.40	0.42	Skin ....
8339	.........do....	......do.............		5.25	8.75	3.00	......	......	......	......	......	......	Fresh ......
1521	.........do.............	Carlisle, Pa........	♀	4.30	....	2.84	2.13	0.52	0.60	0.20	0.38	0.40	Skin ....
1521	.........do.............			5.25	8.82	2 90	......	....	....	....	......	....	Fresh ......
6401	Chrysomitris psaltria.....	Cosumnes river....	♂	4.02	....	2.54	1.90	0.48	0.50	0.18	0.36	0.38	Skin ....
3930	.........do.............	California..........	♀	4.20	....	2.48	1.78	0.49	0.52	0.18	0.34	0.40	Skin ....
4077	Chrysomitris mexicanus..	New Leon, Mex ...	♂	4.00	....	2.40	1.76	0.48	0.54	0.18	0.38	0.34	Skin ....
4077	.........do.............	......do.............		4.00	7.50	2.50	.....	....	....	......	......	......	Fresh ......
6396	.........do.............	Coahuila............	♀	3.90	....	2.45	1.77	0.50	0.51	0.17	0.34	0.36	Skin ....
6396	.........do.............	......do.............		4.00	6.75	2.36	......	....	....	......	......	......	Fresh ......
1818	Chrysomitris columbianus	South America.....	......	4.37	... ...	2.46	1.74	0.46	0.54	0.18	0.40	0.38	Skin ....
6405	Chrysomitris lawrencii ..	Cosumnes river....	♂	4.40	....	2.68	2.22	0.50	0.60	0.20	0.32	0.36	Skin ....
3928	.........do.............	California..........	♀	4.40	....	2.54	2.08	0.48	0.56	0.18	0.32	0.33	Skin ....
836	Chrysomitris pinus.......	Carlisle, Pa........	♂	4.80	....	2.90	2.06	0.56	0.60	0.20	0.42	0.48	Skin ....
836	.........do.............	......do.............		4.80	9.00	2.80	......						Fresh ......
837	.... .do.............	......do.............	♀	4.60	....	2.70	1.95	0.56	0.61	0.17	0.40	0.42	Skin ....
837	.........do.............	......do.............		4.66	8.50	2.75	......	....	....	.. ....	......	....	Fresh ......
9524	.........do.............	Simiahmoo bay,W.T.	......	4.82	....	2.80	2.12	0.56	0.63	0.18	0.42	0.46	Skin ....

CHRYSOMITRIS MAGELLANICUS, Bonap.

Black-headed Goldfinch.

Fringilla magellanica, VIEILL. Dict. XII, 1819, 168.—AUD. Orn. Biog. V, 1839, 46 ; pl. 394.
Carduelis magellanicus, AUD. Syn. 1839, 116.—IB. Birds Am. III, 1841, 133 ; pl. 182.
Chrysomitris magellanica, BONAP. Consp. 1850, 516.—CAB. Mus. Hein. 1851, 160.
Fringilla icterica, LICHT. Verz. Doubl. 1823, 26.
" ? *Fringilla campestris*, SPIX. Av. Bras. II, , tab. lxi, f. 3."

SP. CH.—Head all round and extending below over the lower throat, wings, and tail, (except as hereafter described,) black. Lower part of neck, back to the rump, scapulars, and lesser wing coverts, olive green. Under surfaces generally of the body, rump and upper tail coverts, basal half of all the tail feathers, bases of all the wing feathers, except inner tertials and outer web of first primary, with ends of greater coverts and edges of tertials towards the end, yellow, tinged with greenish below. Bastard feathers black. Length, 4.50 ; wing, 2.75 ; tail, 2.

Hab.—South America. Accidental in the United States, (Kentucky.)

In the preceding diagnosis I have described a specimen from Mr. Audubon's cabinet, and probably one of those mentioned by him as having been obtained at Henderson, Kentucky. There is no authentic instance on record of its having been obtained elsewhere in the United States. Its black head will readily distinguish it from the other species. The first and second quills are equal and longest; the third very little shorter.

The *C. notatus* of Dubus differs in having a slender and more attenuated bill, the black of the throat coming further on the breast. The wing coverts entirely black, excepting a band of yellowish on the tips of the greater ones, and the secondaries without any yellowish edging.

List of specimens.

Catalogue number.	Sex.	Locality.	Whence obtained.
2883	♂	United States_____	J. J. Audubon _____

CHRYSOMITRIS STANLEYI, Bonap.

Stanley's Goldfinch.

Carduelis stanleyi, AUD. Synop. 1839, 118.—IB. Birds Am. III, 1841, 137; pl. 185. (Not given in Orn. Biog.)
Chrysomitris stanleyi, BP. Consp. 1850, 515.
Hypacanthus stanleyi, CAB. Mus. Hein. 1851, 161.

SP. CH.—Above, with scapulars and ends of lesser wing coverts dark olive green, brightening on the rump ; the feathers of the back obscurely streaked with brown. Posterior upper tail coverts dusky. Crown and chin black. Forehead, sides of head, under parts generally and sides, greenish yellow, turning to white posteriorly. Wings and tail dark brown ; the tail feathers, excepting the central, yellow at the base, as are the quills, excepting the first two primaries and the inner tertiaries. The edges and tips of the greater coverts are also yellowish.

Female without the black on head and throat. Length of male, 5.75 ; wing, 2.80 ; tail, 2.20.

Hab.—California,(?) probably western Mexico.

This species is so similar in all essential features to the *C. magellanicus* as almost to indicate that it is only an immature stage of plumage. The crown and chin only are black, instead of the entire head all round ; the black of the chin, however, is edged with yellowish, and there are indications of black on the sides of the head near the bill, showing an immature condition. The upper parts are similar in their shade of green ; the rump is not nearly so bright yellow, and the longer upper tail coverts are not yellow but brown. The middle of belly and thence to the tail coverts are whitish, the latter streaked with brown instead of uniform unspotted yellow. The markings on the wing are very similar, except that the bases of the first two primaries are not marked with yellow as they are in the other, excepting on the outer web of the first. The middle tail feather appears to be brown to the very base instead of yellow.

The feet are, however, much larger ; the toes longer. The bill is larger and more curved above. The proportions of the two quills are much the same.

The pair I here describe are from Mr. Audubon's collection. The draggled appearance of the wings and tail appear to indicate that they had at one time been kept alive in a cage.

This species has somewhat the appearance of *Ch. psaltria*, but is much larger ; has a black chin ; the quills and tail with yellow instead of white markings, &c.

List of specimens.

Catal. No.	Sex.	Locality.	Whence obtained.
2035	♂	California?	J. J. Audubon ......
2036	♀?	......do.............	......do............

CHRYSOMITRIS YARRELLI, Bonap.

Yarrell's Goldfinch.

Carduelis yarrelli, AUD. Syn. 1839, 117.—IB. Birds Am. III, 1841, 136 ; pl. 184.
Fringilla mexicana, AUD. Orn. Biog. V, 1839, 283 ; pl. 433, fig. 4. (Not of Swainson.)
Chrysomitris mexicana, BP. List, 1838. (Not of Conspectus.)

SP. CH.—Bill very large. Head above to middle of eyes and to the rictus, black. Body generally bright yellow ; back and wing coverts olive green. Wings and tail black ; the bases of the tail feathers and of quills, except the inner tertials and outer web of first primary, yellow. Length, 4 inches ; wing, 2.40 ; tail, 1.65.

Hab.—California,(?) probably from western Mexico.

The bill of this species is enormously large and full for the genus. The second quill is longest ; the first and third but little shorter. The markings of the wings and tail are almost exactly as in *C. magellanicus;* the difference between the two is in the smaller size, brighter nape, and black crown only, instead of an entirely black head.

The specimen described is Mr. Audubon's original, and appears to have been kept for a time in a cage.

List of specimens.

Catal. No.	Sex.	Locality.	Whence obtained.
2037	♂	California	J. J. Audubon ......

CHRYSOMITRIS TRISTIS, Bon.

Yellow Bird; Thistle Bird.

Fringilla tristis, LINN. Syst. Nat. I, 1766, 320.—GM. I, 907.—WILS. Am. Orn. I, 1808, 20 ; pl. i, f. 2.—AUD. Orn. Biog. I, 1831, 172 : V, 510 ; pl. 33.
Carduelis tristis, BON. Obs. Wils, 1825, No. 96.—AUD. Syn. 1839, 116.—IB. Birds Amer. II, 1841, 129 ; pl. 181.
Chrysomitris tristis, BON. List, 1838.—IB. Conspectus, 1850, 517.—NEWBERRY, Zool. Cal. & Or. Route ; Rep. P. R. R. Surv. VII, IV, 1857, 87.
Astragalinus tristis, CABANIS, Mus. Hein. 1851, 159, (type.)
Carduelis americana, (EDWARDS,) SW. & RICH. F. B. A. II, 1831, 268.
Golden Finch, PENNANT.—*American Goldfinch,* EDWARDS.—*Chardonneret jaune ; Chardonneret du Canada.—Tarin de la Nouvelle Yorck,* BUFFON.—IB. Pl. enl., pl. 202, f. 2 ; pl. 292, f. 1, 2.

SP. CH.—Bright gamboge yellow ; crown, wings, and tail black. Lesser wing coverts, band across the end of greater ones, ends of secondaries and tertiaries, inner margins of tail feathers, upper and under tail coverts, and tibia, white. Length, 5.25 inches ; wing, 3.

Hab.—North America generally.

In winter the yellow is replaced by yellowish brown ; the black of the crown wanting ; that of wings and tail browner. The throat is generally yellowish ; the under parts ashy brown, passing behind into white.

In No. 8339 the white on the inner edge of the tail feathers, instead of passing obliquely in a straight outline to the inner edge of the feather, constitutes a quadrate blotch in the terminal fourth. There is less white on the wing coverts.

List of specimens.

Catal. No	Sex.	Locality.	When collected.	Whence obtained.	Orig. No.	Collected by—	Length.	Stretch of wings.	Wing.	Remarks.
1349	♂	Carlisle, Penn........	April 12, 1844	S. F. Baird.......		....	5.08	9.00	3.00	....
1644	♂	.....do............	July 18, 1844	.....do.........		....	4.92	8.75	2.83	....
1591	♀	.....do............	May 14, 1844	......do.........		....	5.25	8.83	2.92	....
1637	♂	.....do.	July 16, 1844	.....do......		....	4.92	8.67	2.75	....
2205	♀	.....do............	May 2, 1845	.....do.........		....	4.83	8.50	2.75	....
868	♀	.....do............	Nov. 22, 1842	......do.......		....	4.75	8.50	2.75	....
119	♂	.....do....	Jan. 27, 1841	.....do..... ...		....				....
1348	....	.....do............	April 12, 1844			....	4.75	8.42	2.75	....
7041	♂	St. Louis............	May 15, 1857	Lt. Bryan.......	36	W. S. Wood...				....
6390	......	Ft. Leavenworth, K. T.	Oct. 23, 1824	Lt. Couch.......	8	....				....
6391	......	.....do......	Jan. 20, 1855	......do.........	23	....				....
8339	......	Independence, Mo....	June 6, 1857	W. M. Magraw...	64	Dr. Cooper...	5.25	8.75	3.00	Iris, bill, and feet dark brown.
5876	......	Fort Riley, K. T....	....	Dr. Hammond...		Mr. De Vesey				....
4824	♂	Running Water, Neb..	May 14, 1856	Lt. Warren		Dr. Hayden..	5.00	8.50	2.87	Eyes black ?.................
4825	♂	.....do............	May 16, 1856	.....do.....		.....do....	4.75	8.75	3.25	Iris ash color................
5391	♂	Fort Lookout, Neb....	June 20, 1856	.....do......		.....do...	4.75	8.75	2.50	....
4659	♂	Fort Pierre, Neb	June 12, 1856	......do.........		.....do...				....
5392	......	Blackfoot country, Neb	....do.........	......do.........		do.....	4.75	8.75	2.50	....
8209	......	Fort Laramie.........	Sept. 8, 1857	W. M. Magraw...	191	Dr. Cooper...	4.50	8.58	2.87	Iris, bill, and feet dark brown.
4470	......	Shoalwater Bay, K. T.	....	Dr. J. G. Cooper..		....	5.00	8.75	....	Bill black, feet flesh color.
6392	......	San Francisco........	....	R. D. Cutts.......		....				....
6393	....	.....do............		......do.........		....				....
6394	♂	Sacramento, Cal......	....	Lt. Williamson...		Dr. Heermann				....
6395	♂	.....do............	....	.....do.........		.....do...				....
......	......	Fort Tejon, Cal.......	....	J. X. de Vesey...		......				....

CHRYSOMITRIS PSALTRIA, Bonap.

Arkansas Finch.

Fringilla psaltria, SAY, Long's Exped. R. Mts. II, 1823, 40.—AUD. Orn. Biog. V, 1839, 85 ; pl. 394.
Fringilla (Carduelis) psaltria, BON. Am. Orn. I, 1825, 54 ; pl. 6, f. 3.
Carduelis psaltria, AUD. Syn. 1839, 117.—IB. Birds Am. III, 1841, 134 ; pl. 183.
Chrysomitris psaltria, BP. List, 1838.—IB. Consp. 1850, 516.—GAMBEL, Jour. A. N. S. 2d series I, 1847, 52. (Female.)

SP. CH.—Upper parts and sides of head and neck olive green. Hood, upper tail coverts, wings, and tail black. Beneath bright yellow. A band across the tips of the greater coverts, the ends of nearly all the quills, the outer edges of the tertiaries, the extreme bases of all the primaries, except the outer two, and a long rectangular patch on the inner webs of the outer three tail feathers near the middle, white. Female with the upper parts generally, and sides, olive green ; the wings and tail brown, their white marks as in the male. Length, 4.25 ; wing, 2.40 ; tail, 1.85.

Hab.—Southern Rocky mountains to the coast of California.

This goldfinch is more like *C. tristis* than any other of our species. The upper parts are, however, olive green, instead of yellow. The whole under parts are yellow, even including the under tail coverts. There is no white on the lesser wing coverts. The bill is slenderer and more curved. The third quill is longest ; the first, second, and fourth successively a little shorter. The tail is less deeply forked than in *C. tristis*.

List of specimens.

Catal. No.	Sex.	Locality.	Wen collected.	Whence obtained.	Orig'l No.	Collected by—	Length.	Stretch of wings	Wings.	Remarks.
6397	......	Williams' river, N. M..	Feb. 12, 1854	Lt. Whipple...	97	Dr. Kennerly..	4	5.50	2	....
6398	......	......do................	Feb. 8, 1854	......do........	78	......do........	......	....	....	Eyes gray (?) ....
6399	......	......do................	......do......	......do........	74	......do........	4	7	2.50	....
6400	......	......do................	......do......	......do........	76	......do........	4	6	2.50	....
3122	♂	Monterey, Cal.	June 20, 1848	Wm. Hutton...	......	... .	....	....	... ...	Iris very dark, bill and feet flesh color, dark gray above
6401	♂	Cosumnes river.......	....	Lt. Williamson	.....	Dr. Heermann.	....	....	......	....
6402	♀	Calaveras river	....	......do........	......	....	....	....	......	....
3929	♂	California.............	....	Dr. Heermann..	.....	....	....	....	......	....
3930	♀	......do.....	....	......do........	......	....	....	....	......	....
	......	Fort Tejon, Cal........	....	J. X. de Vesey.	......	....	....	....	......	....

CHRYSOMITRIS MEXICANA, Bonap.

Black Goldfinch; Mexican Goldfinch.

Carduelis mexicanus, SWAINS. Syn. Birds Mex. Phil. Mag. 1827, 435.—WAGLER, Isis, 1831, 525.
Chrysomitris mexicanus, BP. Consp. Av. 1850, 516. (Quotes Aud. tab. 427.)
Astragalinus mexicanus, CAB. Mus. Hein. 1851, 159.
Fringilla melanoxantha, (LICHT.) WAGLER, Isis, 1831, 525.
? *Fringilla catotol*, GM Syst. Nat. I, 1788, 914.
Fringilla texensis, GIRAUD, 16 Sp. Birds Tex. 1841; pl. v, f. 1. (Gives white belly.)

SP. CH.—Upper parts continuously and entirely black; the feathers of the rump white subterminally, and showing this through the black; a few of the feathers with greenish yellow between the white and black; a few, perhaps, without black tips. The bases of the third to seventh primaries, and the ends of the tertiaries externally white. The tail is black, except the outer three feathers, in which the outer webs and tips only are this color; the rest white. Inside of wing black. Under parts of body pale yellow. Female with the black of the head and body replaced by olive green. Length, 4.12 inches; wing, 2.25; tail, 2.00.

Hab.—Mexican side of the valley of the Rio Grande, southward; Copper Mines of the Gila.

All our *Chrysomitris* have the concealed white on the rump, but it is more hidden; where the black tips are wanting, the greenish is broader, and comes to the surface. There is a little black on the side of the breast under the wings; the axillaries also are mostly black. The black of the nape and neck is first greenish and then whitish within the black tip. There is a yellow spot below the eye.

The bill of this species is stouter than in *C. tristis*, the wing shorter and more rounded, the tail less deeply forked. The third quill is longest; then the second and fourth; the first is appreciably shorter.

The female of this species resembles very closely that of *C. psaltria*; the bill is shorter and more obtuse, however; the white spot at the base of the primaries more conspicuous. In the imperfect character of the specimens before me I am not prepared to state the differences in coloration, although the under parts appear of a brighter yellow.

There is a closely allied species from South America (*C. columbianus*[1]) which is larger, the bill especially. There is, however, no white on the tail nor on the wing, except at the base of the primaries. The yellow of the under parts is much deeper.

[1]CHRYSOMITRIS COLUMBIANUS, Baird.
    Astragalinus columbianus, CAB. Mus. Hein. 1851, 159.
    Chrysomitris xanthogastra, DUBUS, Bull. Acad. Belg. XXII, I, 1855, 150.

A specimen from the Copper Mines (6404) differs in having the feathers of the back olive green, tipped occasionally with black. Instead of the one or two spots of white on the tips of the greater wing coverts there is a continuous band. The axillaries are olive green, instead of black. None of these differences, however, are inconsistent with a not quite mature specimen of the *C. mexicanus.*

List of specimens.

Catal. No.	Sex.	Locality.	When collected.	Whence obtained.	Orig'l No.	Collected by—	Length.	Stretch of wings.	Wings	Tail.	Remarks.
4077	♂	Santa Catarina, New Leon, Mex.	April —,'53	Lt. Couch..	183	....	4	7.50	2.50	......	Eyes dark brown, bill bluish lead color, feet light brown or slate.
6396	♀	Agua Nueva, Coahuila, Mex.	May —,'53	....do......	234	....	....	4	6.37	2.37	Bill olive, feet lead............
4078	♂	Parras, Mex.................	June 1,'53	....do.....	......	....	....	4.12	7.25	2.25	....
6403	......	Texas	....	J. G. Bell..	......	....	....	......	......	......	....
6404	......	Copper Mines, N. Mex.....	....	Maj. Emory	......	Mr. Clark	....	....	......	......	....

CHRYSOMITRIS LAWRENCII, Bonap.

Carduelis lawrencii, Cassin, Pr. A. N. Sc. V, Oct. 1850, 105 ; pl. v, (California.)
Chrysomitris lawrencii, Bon. Comptes Rendus, Dec. 1853, 913.

Sp. Ch.—Hood, sides of head anterior to the middle of the eye, chin, and upper part of throat, black. Sides of head, neck, and body, upper part of neck and the back, and upper tail coverts, ash color. Rump and lesser wing coverts yellowish green. Throat below the black, breast, and outer edges of all the quills, (except the first primary, and passing into white behind,) bright greenish yellow. Wings black. Tail feathers black, with a white square patch on the inner web, near the end ; outer edges grayish ; quills black. Female similar, with the black of the head replaced by ash. Length, about 4.70 ; wing, 2.75 ; tail, 2.30.

Hab.—Coast of California.

In this species the second quill is longest; the first intermediate between the third and fourth. The tail is quite deeply forked. There is a slight tendency to olive green in the middle of the back. The yellowish green may be said to cover the whole wing coverts, although the black bases of the greater coverts are somewhat exposed ; the green on these passes into yellowish ; their extreme tips grayish. The axillaries and under wing coverts are white.

The young bird is like the female, with obscure blotches beneath ; the yellow margins of the wing coverts and secondaries brownish.

List of specimens.

Catal. No.	Sex.	Locality.	Whence obtained.	Collected by—
3927	♂	California	Dr. Heermann	....
3928	♀	......do.....................	......do..................	....
6405	♂	Cosumnes river...............	Lieut. Williamson...........	Dr. Heermann..........
10225	....	Fort Tejon, Cal................	J. X. de Vesey............	....

CHRYSOMITRIS PINUS, Bonap.

Pine Finch.

Fringilla pinus, WILSON, Am. Orn. II, 1810, 133 ; pl. xvii, f. 1.—AUD. Orn. Biog. II, 1834, 455 : V, 509 ; pl. 180.
Fringilla (Carduelis) pinus, BON. Obs. Wils. 1825, No. 103.
Linaria pinus, AUD. Synopsis, 1839, 115.—IB. Birds Amer. III, 1841, 125 ; pl. 180.
Chrysomitris pinus, BONAP. Consp. 1850, 515.
? ? Chrysomitris macroptera, DUBUS, Esq. Orn. tab. 23, (Mexico.)—BP. Conspectus, 1850, 515.

SP. CH.—Tail deeply forked. Above brownish olive. Beneath whitish, every feather streaked distinctly with dusky. Concealed bases of tail feathers and quills, together with their inner edges, sulphur yellow. Outer edges of quills and tail feathers yellowish green. Two brownish white bands on the wing. Length, 4.75 ; wing, 3.00 ; tail, 2.20.

Hab.—North America from Atlantic to Pacific.

The lower part of the belly is less spotted than elsewhere.

In winter the yellow colors are much less distinct, scarcely appreciable on the body, in fact ; the brown streak less sharply defined. In young specimens it is scarcely appreciable, even on the wings and tail.

The extent of the yellow at the base of the quills and tail feathers varies with the individual. Sometimes it is visible more or less distinctly beyond the wing coverts and spurious quills. Sometimes the streaks beneath are less distinct, leaving the under parts almost white. Sometimes the upper parts, the rump especially, are tinged with yellow.

I do not find before me any North American specimens differing from types in the greater length of quills and tarsus, as is said to be the case in *C. macroptera*, Dubus, (Bonap. Consp. 1850, 515.) The yellow of the wings and tail given as peculiar to *macroptera* is found in all full plumaged specimens of *pinus*.

List of specimens.

Catal. No.	Sex.	Locality.	When collected.	Whence obtained.	Orig. No.	Collected by—	Length.	Stretch of wings.	Wing.	Remarks.
2523	♂	Carlisle, Penn..........	Oct. 16, 1845	S. F. Baird........		....				.. ..
426	♀	......do..............	May 28, 1841	....do..............		....	4.83	8.50	....	....
838	♂	......do..............	Oct. 26, 1842	....do..............		....	4.75	9.	2.83	....
837	♀	......do..............	....do........	....do..............		....	4.67	8.50	2.75	....
425	♂	......do..............	May 28, 1841	...do..............		....	4.83	9.25	....	....
836	♂	....do..............	Oct. 26, 1842	....do..............		....	4.83	9.	2.83	....
2887	......	Unknown........		S. F. Baird........		J. J. Audubon....	....	....	...	....
6783	......	Rockport, Ohio.........	July, 1849....	Dr. Kirtland.......		....	....	...	...	....
5393	......	Lit. Missouri river, Neb.	Sept. 15, 1856	Lt. Warren...........		Dr. Hayden	....	....	. ...	....
5394	......	......do..............	....do........	....do............		....do........	....	....	...	....
6410	......	Fort Thorne, N. M.....	....	Dr. T. C. Henry....		....	....	....	...	....
10225	......	Fort Tejon, Cal.......	....	J. X. de Vesey.....	727	....	....	....	...	....
6409	♂	Sacramento, Cal.......	....	Lt. Williamson.		Dr. Heermann ...	....	....	...	....
6406	......	Shoalwater Bay, W. T.	Oct., 1854....	Dr. J. G. Cooper....		....	....	....	...	....
6407	......	..... do........	....do........	...do........		....	.....	....	...	....
6408	......	......do..............	....do........	....do..............		....	5.25	8.50	....	Iris, bill, and ft. brown.

54 **b**

CURVIROSTRA, Scopoli.

Loxia, LINNAEUS, Syst. Nat. 1758. Type *Loxia curvirostra*,L. Not of 1735, which has for type *Loxia coccothraustes*, L. *Curvirostra*, " SCOPOLI, 1777." Type *L. curvirostra*.

CH.—Mandibles much elongated, compressed and attenuated ; greatly curved or falcate, the points crossing or overlapping to a greater or less degree. Tarsi very short ; claws all very long, the lateral extending beyond the middle of the central ; hind claw longer than its digit. Wings very long and pointed, reaching beyond the middle of the narrow, forked tail.

Colors reddish in the male.

The elongated, compressed, falcate-curved and overlapping mandibles, readily characterise this genus among birds.

The United States species of *Curvirostra* are readily distinguished by the presence of white bands on the wing in *leucoptera* and their absence in *americana*.

As *Loxia* was first assigned by Linnaeus, in 1735, to his *L. cocothraustes*, I do not understand why G. R. Gray and Cabanis have not retained the genus for the last named type.

Comparative measurements of species.

Catal. No.	Species.	Locality.	Sex.	Length.	Stretch of wings.	Wing.	Tail.	Tarsus.	Middle	Its claw alone.	Bill above.	Along gape.	Specimen measured.
5801	Curvirostra leucoptera..	Philadelphia.......	♀	5.80	....	3.34	2.56	0.62	0.68	0.24	0.64	0.64	Skin .....
1215	..... do	......do	♂	6.80	... .	3.70	2.76	0.64	0.72	0.32	0.64	0.66	Skin .....
5803	Curvirostra americana.	......do	♂	5.34	....	3.26	2.32	0.62	0.78	0.24	0.58	0.54	Skin .....
6441	......do...............	Shoalwater bay....	♀	5.10	....	3.22	2.28	0.62	0.78	0.25	0.54	0.56	Skin .....
do.	......do	......do		5.75	10.25	....	....	....	....	....	....	....	Fresh.....
3727	......do	California	......	5.70	... ...	3.66	2.56	0.70	0.88	0.30	0.70	0.70	Skin .....
8962	......do	Laramie Peak.....	......	6.00	....	3.66	2.50	0.70	0.82	0.30	0.82	0.76	Skin .....
6440	......do	Shoalwater bay....	......	5.50	....	3.50	2.38	0.70	0.86	0.30	0.62	0.64	Skin .....
4485	......do	Des Chutes basin...	......	6.16	....	3.38	2.30	0.64	0.74	0 26	0 63	0.64	Skin .....

CURVIROSTRA AMERICANA, Wilson.

Red Crossbill.

Curvirostra americana, WILS. Am. Orn. IV, 1811, 44 ; pl. xxxi, f. 1, 2.

Loxia americana, BON. List, 1838 —IB Conspectus, 1850, 527.—BON. & SCHLEGEL., Mon. Loxiens, 5, tab. vi.—
NEWBERRY, Zool. California and Oregon Route, P. R. R. Rep. VI, IV, 1857, 87.

Loxia curvirostra, FORSTER, Phil. Trans. LXII, 1772, No. 23.—AUD. Biog. II, 1834, 559: V, 511 ; pl. 197.—IB. Birds
Amer. III, 1841, 186 ; pl. 200.

" *Loxia pusilla*, ILLIGER." (Bp.)

" *Loxia fusca*, VIEILLOT." (Bp.)

SP. CH.—Male dull red ; darkest across the back ; wings and tail dark blackish brown.

Female dull greenish olive above, each feather with a dusky centre ; rump and crown bright greenish yellow. Beneath grayish ; tinged, especially on the sides of the body, with greenish yellow. Young entirely brown ; paler beneath.

Male about 6 inches ; wing, 3.30 ; tail, 2.25.

Hab.—North America generally, coming southward in winter. Resident in the mountains of Pennsylvania.

The immature and young birds exhibit all imaginable combinations of the colors of the male and female. They all agree in the entire absence of white bands on the wings.

I have not enough materials before me to determine whether western specimens differ from eastern. One (4476) has a larger bill and longer, more pointed wings than any eastern skin I have at hand, (wing 3.65 inches.) No. 8962 has a still larger bill. In fact, there appears to be a great difference in the size of the bill in different specimens, and this indiscriminately in both eastern and western skins.

The difference between the European and American Crossbills appears to consist chiefly in the larger size, with larger and stouter bill of the former.

A *Loxia mexicana*, described by Strickland, is said by Bonaparte to have the same relationship to the *americana* that *pytiopsittacus* has to *curvirostra*, namely, a larger bill. I cannot now lay my hand on Mr. Strickland's article, but I doubt whether the characters furnished by a comparison of a small number of specimens will lead to very satisfactory results, in view of the great differences observable in size of bill in specimens from the same locality.

List of specimens.

Catal. No.	Sex.	Locality.	When collected.	Whence obtained.	Orig'l No.	Collected by—	Length.	Stretch of wings.	Wing.	Remarks.
		Liberty co., Ga	....	Prof. Jos. Leconte..	......	....	....	....	....	....
6702	......	Carlisle, Pa...........	June 18, 1848	S. F. Baird	......	....	....	....	....	....
3574	.....	.......do............	........do........	......do..........	......	....	....	....	....	....
5803	♂	Philada., Pa...........	Jan. —, 1856	Acad. Nat. Sciences	......	C. Drexler.......	....	....	....	....
5804	♂	......do............	......do........	......do..........	......	.....do...........	....	....	....	....
5805	♀	......do............	......do........	......do..........	......	.....do...........	....	....	....	....
508	......	New York?...........	....	....	......	....	....	....	....	....
507	○	....	....	....	......	....	....	....	....	....
6435	......	Fort Steilacoom, W. T.	Aug. 1, 1856	Dr. G. Suckley	573	....	....	... .	....	....
6436	......	.....do............	Mar. 30, 1854	......do..........	58	....	....	....	....	....
6437	......	.....do............	April 1, 1854	......do..........	56	....	6.25	9.50	3.37	....
6438	......	.....do........ ...	......do........	..... do..........	64	....	....	....	....	....
6439	......	.....do............	......do........	..... do..........	75	....	....	....	....	....
6440	♂	Shoalwater bay, W. T..	Mar. 4, 1854	Dr. J. G. Cooper...	......	....	6.00	10.50	....	....
6441	......	......do............	......do........	......do..........	......	....	5.75	10.25	....	Iris bill and feet brown.
6442	......	......do............	......do........	......do......	......	....	5.75	10.25	....	....
4476	......	Des Chutes river, O. T..	1855...........	Lieut. Williamson..	......	Dr. Newberry....	....	....	....	....
4485	......	....	Mar. —, 1854	......do..........	......	......do...........	....	....	....	....
3727	......	California	....	W. Hutton	......	....	....	....	....	....
8962	......	Laramie peak, Neb?. ...	1857...........	Lieut. Warren.....	......	Dr. Hayden......	... .	....	....	....
8963	......	......do............ ...	1857...........	......do..........	......	....	....	....	....	....

CURVIROSTRA LEUCOPTERA, Wilson.

White-winged Crossbill.

Loxia leucoptera, GM. Syst. Nat. I, 1788, 540.—AUD. Orn. Biog. IV, 1838, 467; pl. 364.—IB. Birds Amer. III, 1841, 190; pl. 201.—BONAP. Conspectus Av. 1850, 527.—BON. & SCHL Mon. Loxiens, 1850, 8; pl. ix.

Curvirostra leucoptera, WILS. Am. Orn. IV, 1811. 48; pl. xxxi, f. 3.

Crucirostra leucoptera, BREHM, Naumannia, I, 1853, 254, fig. 20.

Loxia falcirostra, LATH. Index Orn. I, 1790, 371.

SP. CH.—Bill greatly compressed, and acute towards the point. Male carmine red, tinged with dusky across the back; the sides of body under the wings streaked with brown; from the middle of belly to the tail coverts whitish, the latter streaked with brown. Scapulars, wings, and tail black; the broad bands on the wings across the ends of greater and median coverts; white spots on the end of the inner tertiaries.

Female brownish, tinged with olive green in places; feathers of the back and crown with dusky centres; rump bright brownish yellow.

Length, about 6.25; wing, 3.50; tail, 2.60.

Hab.—Northern parts of North America generally

Immature and young specimens are intermediate in color.

The bill of this species is much more compressed and slenderer than in *C. americana.* The wings are more pointed ; the claws larger. The white bands on the wing distinguish the two in all stages.

List of specimens.

Catal. No.	Sex.	Locality.	When collected.	Whence obtained.	Collected by—	Length.	Stretch of wings.	Wing.
5793	♂	Philadelphia, Pa	Jan. —, 1856	Acad. Nat. Scien.	C. Drexler			
5802	♀	do		do	do			
2882	♀	Pennsylvania	November	do				
10228		Nelson river, H. B. T.		Donald Gunn				
8965		Laramie peak, Neb.	Aug. 25, 1857	Lt Warren	Dr. Hayden	6.50	10.25	3.38
8964		Laramie peak ?		do	do			

AEGIOTHUS, Cabanis.

Acanthis, BONAP. Conspectus, 1850, not of Bechstein, 1802, nor Keys. & Blas. 1840.
Aegiothus, CABANIS, Mus. Hein. 1851, 161. Type *Fringilla linaria,* Linn.

Bill very short, conical, and acutely pointed, the outlines even concave ; the commissure straight ; the base of the upper mandible and the nostrils concealed by stiff, appressed bristly feathers ; middle of the mandible having several ridges parallel with the culmen. Inner lateral toe rather the longer, its claw reaching the middle of the middle claw ; the hind toe rather longer, its claw longer than the digital portion. Wings very long, reaching the middle of the tail ; second quill a little longer than the first and third. Tail deeply forked.

The specimens before me do not indicate more than one species, *A. linaria,* although the *A. canescens* of Greenland, in all probability, is found in Northern America.

Comparative measurements of species.

Catal. No.	Species.	Locality.	Sex.	Length.	Stretch of wings.	Wing.	Tail.	Tarsus.	Middle toe.	Its claw alone.	Bill above.	Along gape.	Specimen measured.
9224	Leucosticte arctous?	Siberia		6.20		4.50	3.36	0.84	0.82	0.24	0.46	0.54	Skin
3701	Leucosticte tephrocotis.	Salt Lake city		7.10		4.28	3.04	0.80	0.82	0.24	0.44	0.54	Skin
900	Aegiothus linaria	Carlisle, Pa	♂	5.20		3.04	2.72	0.55	0.56	0.22	0.34	0.44	Skin
do.	do	do		5.50	9.00	3.08							Fresh
7109	do	Philadelphia, Pa		5.12		2.94	2.49	0.58	0.56	0.24	0.36	0.44	Skin
962	do	Carlisle, Pa	♀	4.90		2.72	2.38	0.54	0.50	0.21	0.35	0.42	Skin
do.	do	do		5.00	8.42	2.75							Fresh
821	do	do	♂	4.92		2.82	2.58	0.54	0.50	0.20	0.33	0.38	Skin
do.	do	do		5.50	8.50	2.83							Fresh
8883	do	Ann Arbor, Mich		5.00		2.86	2.58	0.60	0.50	0.20	0.38	0.40	Skin

AEGIOTHUS LINARIA, Cabanis.

Lesser Red Poll.

Fringilla linaria, LINN. Syst. Nat. I, 1766, 322.—AUD. Orn Biog. IV, 1838, 538 ; pl. 375.
Fringilla (Acanthis) linaria, KEYS. & BLAS. Wirb. Europ. 1840, No. 115, page 161.
Acanthis linaria, BP. Conspectus, 1850, 541.
Aegiothus linaria, CABANIS, Mus. Hein. 1851, 161.
Linaria minor, SW. F. Bor. Am. II, 1831, 267.—AUD. Syn. 1839, 114.—ID. Birds Amer. III, 1841, 122 ; pl. 179.

SP. CH.—Above light yellowish, each feather streaked with dark brown. Crown dark crimson. Upper part of breast and sides of the body tinged with a lighter tint of the same ; the rump and under tail coverts also, similar, but still less vivid, and with dusky streaks. Rest of under parts white, streaked on the sides with brown. Loral region and chin dusky ; cheeks, (brightest over the eye,) and a narrow front, whitish. Wing feathers edged externally, and tail feathers all round with white. Two yellowish white bands across the wing coverts ; secondaries and tertiaries edged broadly with the same. Bill yellowish, tinged with brown on the culmen and gonys ; the basal bristles brown, reaching over half the bill. Length, 5 50; wing, 3.10 ; tail, 2.70.

Hab.—Throughout eastern North America, coming south in winter. Washington Territory.—(Cooper.)

The specimen described above is a male, (900) in winter dress. The spring plumage has much more of the red. The female winter specimens lack the rose of the under parts and rump ; the breast is streaked across with dusky.

I have not met with any specimens apparently indicative of more than one North American species, although the *A. canescens*, of Greenland, may possibly be found within our limits. This is much larger, has the tail 3¼ inches long instead of 2¼ ; the rump never with dusky streaks. The *A. rufescens*, of Europe differs in the smaller size, the tail scarcely two inches long, the rump tinged with rufous. The *A. holbölli*, of Europe, has a very large yellow bill, a large gular patch and the lores, black.

List of specimens.

Catal. No.	Sex.	Locality.	When collected.	Whence obtained.	Length.	Stretch of wings.	Wing.
902	♀	Carlisle, Pa.	Dec. 6, 1842	S. F. Baird .	5.00	8.42	2.75
821	♂	----do----	Oct. 20, 1842	----do----	5.50	8.50	2.83
900	♂	----do----	Dec. 6, 1842	----do----	5.50	9.00	3.08
494		New York		----do----			
1588		Boston .		T. M. Brewer			
7419		Cleveland, Ohio.		Dr. J. P. Kirtland.			
5824		Racine, Wis.	1852	Dr. P. R. Hoy			
9225		England .		S. F. Baird			

AEGIOTHUS CANESCENS, Cabanis.

Mealy Red Poll.

Linaria canescens, GOULD, "Birds Europe, Tab. 193."
Linota canescens, BONAP. List, 1838.
Acanthis canescens, BON. Conspectus, 1850, 541.—BON. & SCHLEGEL, Mon. Loxiens, Tab. li.
Aegiothus canescens, CABANIS, Mus. Hein. 1851, 161.
"*Fringilla borealis*, TEMMINCK, 1835. Not of Vieillot." Bonaparte.
? *Fringilla borealis*, AUD. Orn. Biog. V, 1839, 87 ; pl. 400.
? *Linaria borealis*, AUD. Birds Amer. III, 1841, 120 ; pl. 178.
"*Linaria hornemanni*, HOLBÖLL, Kroyer Nat. Tidskr. 1843."

SP. CH.—Size large. Bill short. Claws elongated. Rump white, (in the spring male tinged with rose,) never streaked ; the quills broadly margined with white. Tail lengthened. Length, 6 inches ; tail, 3.17.

Hab.—Greenland.

The preceding description, taken chiefly from Bonaparte, is of a species which doubtless occurs in the northern portion of our continent, and is introduced for the purpose of completing the history of the genus, though I have never seen a specimen. It differs from the other in the larger size, generally hoary appearance, and the pure white or rosy rump, never with dusky streaks, as in the female and young of *A. linaria*.

LEUCOSTICTE, Swainson.

Leucosticte, SWAINSON, Fauna Bor. Amer. II, 1831, 265. Type *Linaria tephrocotis,* Sw.

CH —Bill conical rounded, rather blunt at the tip ; the culmen slightly convex ; the commissure slightly concave ; the nostrils concealed by depressed bristly feathers ; a depressed ridge extending about parallel with the culmen above the middle of the bill. Another more conspicuously angulated one, extending forward from the lower posterior angle of the side of the lower mandible, nearly parallel with the gonys. Tarsus about equal to the middle toe. Inner toe almost the longer, its claw not reaching beyond the base of the middle one. Hind toe rather longer, its claw longer than the digital portion. Wings very long ; first quill longest. Tail forked.

This genus differs from *Aegiothus* in the more obtuse and curved bill, the ridge on the lower mandible, the lateral toe not reaching beyond the base of the middle one, and possibly a longer hind toe. The measurements will be found with *Aegiothus*.

Several species are indicated as North American ; only one, however, *L. tephrocotis*, seems to have been found in the United States. The others belong to the Aleutian Islands, but without specimens I cannot introduce them here.[1]

LEUCOSTICTE TEPHROCOTIS, Sw.

Gray-crowned Finch.

Linaria (Leucosticte) tephrocotis, Sw. F. Bor. Am. II, 1831, 255 ; pl. l.
Leucosticte tephrocotis, Sw. Birds, II, 1837.—BON. Consp. 1850, 536.—BAIRD, Stansbury's Salt Lake, 1852, 317.
Erythrospiza tephrocotis, BON. List. 1838.—AUD. Syn. 1839.—IB. Birds Amer. III, 1841, 176 ; pl. 198.
Fringilla tephrocotis, AUD. Orn. Biog. V, 1839, 232 ; pl. 424.

SP. CH.—Head above and nape bounded below by a line from the commissure a little below the eyes, light ashy ; dusky in the loral region. Crown with a distinct patch of sooty black, reaching nearly to the base of the bill. Lesser wing coverts and axillaries, outer edges of primaries and tail feathers, with ends of the feathers of the posterior half of body all round, pale rose red. Rest of body dark umber brown, tinged with dusky on the chin and throat. Wings and tail feathers blackish. The greater coverts are tipped, and the secondaries edged, with white. Length, 7.10 inches ; wing, 4.30 ; tail, 2.90.

Hab.—Northern Rocky mountains. Vicinity of Salt Lake City in winter.

---

[1] The following are the diagnoses of the species said to belong to the northwest coast of America :

LEUCÓSTICTE GRISEINUCHA, Bonap.—Russian America and the Aleutian Islands.

Linaria griseinucha, BRANDT, "Orn. Ross. 1842 "
Leucosticte griseinucha, BONAP. Consp. 1850, 537.
Leucosticte griseogenys, GOULD, Pr. Zool. Soc. July, 1843, 104.—IB. Voyage of Sulphur, I, 1844, 42 ; pl. xxii.

SP. CH.—" Brown. Forehead and throat blackish. Nasal feathers always whitish. Cheeks and back of the neck gray. Interscapular region and breast chestnut brown, the feathers narrowly bordered with ferruginous. Feathers of sides and abdomen, wing coverts and tail, broadly margined with rose. Bill yellow ; blackish at tip.

" Female entire olivaceous ferruginous. Quills and tail feathers brown, bordered with pale rosy. Wing coverts and scapulars with a broad ferruginous margin.

" Similar to *L. tephrocotis*, but duller, and beneath more tinged with rosy. Cheeks and neck above distinctly gray. Length, 7.66 inches."—Bonaparte.

LEUCOSTICTE ARCTOUS, Bonap.—Kurile Islands and Kamtschatka. Russian America. (Cabanis.)

Passer arctous, var. a, Pallas, Zoog. Rosso-As. II, 1811, 21.
Leucosticte arctoa, BON. Consp. 1850, 537.—CAB. Mus. Hein. 1851, 154.—BON. & SCHLEGEL, Mon. Loxiens, 1850, tab. xlv.

SP. Ch.—"Dusky purplish. Neck above pale yellowish. Forehead and nasal feathers blackish (scarcely tinged with purple). Outer web of the quills and greater wing coverts, the tail feathers, the feathers of the rump and crissum, silvery gray, with a very narrow outer margin of rosaceous, and the shafts black. Bill small, blackish at tip. Length, 6 inches."—Bonaparte.

The only specimen before me of this excessively rare species was taken in winter, when the colors may be less brilliant than in spring. The wing is very much pointed ; the first three primaries considerably longer than the fourth.

List of specimens.

Catal. No.	Locality.	When collected.	Whence obtained.
3701	Salt Lake City, Utah	March 21, 1850	Captain Stansbury

PLECTROPHANES, Meyer.

Plectrophanes, MEYER, " Taschenbuch, 1810." Agassiz. Type *Emberiza nivalis*.

Centrophanes, KAUP, " Entw. Gesch. Europ Thierwelt, 1829," Agassiz. Type *E. lapponica*.

CH.—Bill variable ; conical ; the lower mandible higher than the upper ; the sides of both mandibles (in the typical species) guarded by a closely applied brush of stiffened bristly feathers directed forwards, and in the upper jaw concealing the nostrils ; the outlines of the bill nearly straight, or slightly curved ; the lower jaw considerably broader at the base than the upper, and wider than the gonys is long. Tarsi considerably longer than the middle toe ; the lateral toes nearly equal, (the inner claw largest,) and reaching to the base of the middle claw. The hinder claw very long ; moderately curved and acute ; considerably longer than its toe ; the toe and claw together reaching to the middle of the middle claw, or beyond its tip. Wings very long and much pointed, reaching nearly to the end of the tail ; the first quill longest, the others rapidly graduated ; the tertiaries a little longer than the secondaries. Tail moderate, about two-thirds as long as the wings ; nearly even, or slightly emarginated.

In this group there is considerable diversity in the species as respects the size and shape of the bill and claws. In the *P. nivalis* the bill is very small and short, the lower mandible higher than the upper, the sides of the bill conpicuously margined by appressed bristly feathers ; the hind toe with its claw is rather shorter than the middle one. In *P. lapponicus* the bill is larger and longer ; the hind claw much longer than its toe, and with it reaching beyond the middle claw. *P. ornatus* has the hind toe (without the claw,) proportionally longer than in the last ; the claw rather shorter ; the two together, however, longer than the middle toe and claw. In *P. maccownii* again the bill is much larger and stouter ; the hind toe and claw rather shorter than in the latter, and about as long as the middle one. Unless all be thrown into one genus, it will be difficult to get along with less than three, instead of the two hitherto adopted by systematic writers.

The males of the species are all strongly marked, but the females resemble the streaked sparrows very closely. They are either white, with black back, as in *P. lapponicus*, or else streaked on the back ; the head striped with white and black ; the under parts white with a large black patch on the throat or breast. All have the outer tail feathers white. The species may be arranged as follows :

A. PLECTROPHANES, Meyer.—Bill very small. Hind toe not longer than the middle one.

White ; middle of back, inner tail feathers, and ends of wing quills, black....*P. nivalis*.

B. CENTROPHANES, Kaup.—Bill more elongated but rather slender. Hind toe longer than the middle one. Neck with a chestnut collar behind ; hood black.

Chin and throat black ; belly white ; legs black..................................*P. lapponicus*.

Entirely buff beneath ; legs flesh color..*P. pictus*.

Bill slenderest ; chin and throat white ; entire breast black ; shoulders brown..*P. ornatus*.

Similar to the last ; shoulders black...*P. melanomus*.

C. RHYNCHOPHANES, Baird.[1]—Bill very large at the base; hind claw shorter.   No rufous nuchal collar.

Crown black; shoulders chestnut; beneath white, with a black pectoral crescent.

P. maccownii.

The essential characters of the genus, as usually understood, consist in the very long and pointed wings; the moderate, nearly even tail; the very long, little curved, hind claw. Whether the elongated and nearly straight hind claw be not an arbitrary character embracing species otherwise dissimilar I do not pretend to decide.   Bonaparte considers the *P. maccownii,* so totally distinct from the other species, as to warrant a place in a different family.

Comparative measurements of species.

Catal. No.	Species.	Locality.	Sex and age.	Length.	Strech of wings.	Wing.	Tail.	Tarsus.	Middle toe.	Its claw alone.	Hind toe and claw.	Hind claw alone.	Bill above.	Along gape.	Specimen measured.
1889	Plectrophanes nivalis ..	North America		6.70	.... 4.24	3.07	0.81	0.75	0.25	0.58	0.34	0.43	0.43	Skin ......
7107	... .do..	Philadelphia..........		6.10	.... 4.14	2.84	0.79	0.86	0.28	0.66	0.36	0.40	0.51	Skin ......
6701	Plectrophanes lapponicus	Dane county, Wis..	♂	6.20	.... 3.81	2.73	0.86	0.80	0.26	0.76	0.44	0.44	0.52	Skin ......
8246	........do......	50 miles west Fort Leavenworth		5.60	.... 3.78	2.85	0.85	0.85	0.29	0.79	0.46	0.43	0.49	Skin ......
8246	........do..	.... do.............. ...		6.12	10.75	3.75								Fresh .....
1941	Plectrophanes pictus...	Fort Union, N. M	○	5.50	.... 3.40	2.50	0.85	Feet	broke n off..			0.45	0.50	Skin ......
10254	........do..	Pembina, Minn		6.60	.... 3.42	2.73	0.81	0.78	0.20	0.64	0.33	0.40	0 47	Skin ......
1907	Plectrophanes ornatus..	Fort Union	♂	5.10	.... 3.14	2.14	0.76	0.74	0.19	0.72	0.36	0.44	0.46	Skin ......
48`7	........do....	Bijou Hill............	♂	5.10	.... 3.26	2.59	0.73	0.72	0.21	0.72	0.39	0.39	0.54	Skin .. ....
9218	Plectrophanes melano- mus................	Mexico....		5.50	.... 3.26	2.58	0.73	0.74	0 23			0.41	0.44	Skin .....
6292	........do.......	New Mexico.........	♂	5.42	.... 3.27	2.36	0.73	0.64	0.16	0.68	0.36	0.40	0.48	Skin ......
6290	........do..	Mimbres to RioGrande	.....	5.32	.... 3.40	2.62	0.75	0.74	0.20	0.65	0.32	0.37	0.41	Skin ......
6293	........do..	New Mexico.........	♀	5.40	.... 3.24	2.41	0.74	0.71	0.18	0.66	0.32	0.40	0.45	Skin ......
6282	Plectrophanes maccow- nii................	......do..	♂	5.50	..... 3.58	2.47	0.81	0.74	0.20	0.60	0.26	0.44	0.62	Skin ......
6283	.....do..	....do..	♀	5.42	.... 3.36	2.27	0.76	0.69	0.18	0.64	0.35	0.43	0.53	Skin ......

PLECTROPHANES NIVALIS, Meyer.

Snow Bunting.

Emberiza nivalis, L. Syst. Nat. I, 1766, 308. (Not *Fringilla nivalis,* L.)—FORSTER, Phila. Trans. LXII, 1772, 403.-
    WILSON, Am. Orn. III, 1811, 86; pl. xxi.—AUD. Orn. Biog. II, 1834, 575 : V, 1839, 496; pl. 189.
Emberiza (Plectrophanes) nivalis, BON. Obs. 1825, No. 89.
" *Plectrophanes nivalis,* MEYER."—BON. List, 1838.—AUD. Syn. 1839, 103.—IB. Birds Amer. III, 1841, 55; pl. 155.
Emberiza montana, GMELIN, Syst. I, 1788, 867, 25.
Emberiza mustelina, GMELIN, Syst. I, 1788, 867, 7.
Emberiza glacialis, LATHAM, Ind. Orn. I, 1790, 398.

SP CH.—Colors, in full plumage, entirely black and white. Middle of back between scapulars, terminal half of primaries and tertiaries, and two innermost tail feathers, black; elsewhere pure white. Legs black at all seasons. In winter dress white beneath; the head and rump yellowish brown, as also some blotches on the side of the breast; middle of back brown, streaked with black; white on wings and tail much more restricted. Length, about 6.75; wing, 4.35; tail, 3.05; first quill longest.

Hab —Northern America from Atlantic to Pacific; south into the United States in winter.

This species varies much in color, and the male in full plumage is seldom if ever seen within the limits of the United States.

[1] It is my impression that Bonaparte has proposed a name for this section in removing it to another family, but I am unable to find it.

List of specimens.

Catal. No.	Locality.	When collected.	Whence obtained.	Collected by—
1889	Unknown	....	S. F. Baird	J. J. Audubon. ....
7107	Philadelphia, Pa........	....	John Cassin.............	....
7425	Cleveland, Ohio.	....	Dr. Kirtland............	....
	Illinois................	....	R. Kennicott............	....
9530	Simiahmoo bay, W. T.....	November 9, 1857.......	A. Campbell	Dr. Kennerly ....

[PLECTROPHANES LAPPONICUS, Selby.

Lapland Longspur.

" *Fringilla lapponica*, LINN. Fauna Suecica, 1761, sp. 235 "—IB. Syst. Nat. I, 1766, 317.—FORSTER, Phil. Trans. LXII, 1772, 404.

Emberiza (Plectrophanes) lapponica, Sw. F. B. Am. II, 1831, 248 ; pl. xlviii.

Emberiza lapponica, AUD. Orn. Biog. IV, 1838, 473 ; pl. 365.

Plectrophanes lapponicus, "SELBY." BON. List, 1838.—AUD. Syn. 1839, 98.—IB. Birds Amer. III, 1841, 50 ; pl 152

"*Centrophanes lapponicus*, KAUP, Entw. Gesch. Europe Thierw. 1829,"—CABANIS, Mus. Hein. 1851, 127.

" *Fringilla calcarata*, PALL. Itin. 710, Sp. 20."—French ed. III, 1793, 464 ; pl. i.

Centrophanes calcaratus, GRAY, List, Gen. 1841, app. 1842, 11.

SP. CH.—First quill longest. Legs black. Head all round black, this extending as a semicircular patch to the upper part of breast ; sides of lower neck and under parts white, with black streaks on the sides, and spots on the side of the breast. A short brownish white streak back of the eye. A broad chestnut collar on the back of the neck. Rest of upper parts brownish yellow streaked with dark brown. Outer tail feathers white, except on the basal portion of the inner web. Length, about 6.25 inches ; wing, 3.90 ; tail, 2.8 .

Hab.—Eastern Northern America into the United States in winter. Not found much west of the Missouri.

This species is very seldom seen in full spring plumage in the United States. In perfect dress, the black of the throat probably extends further down over the breast. In winter the black is more or less concealed by whitish tips to the feathers beneath, and by yellowish brown on the crown. Some fall specimens, apparently females, show no black whatever on the throat, which, with the under parts generally are dull white, with a short black streak on each side of the throat.

List of specimens.

Catal. No.	Sex.	Locality.	When collected.	Whence obtained.	Orig. No.	Collected by—	Length.	Stretch of wings.	Wing.	Remarks.
4345	......	Racine, Wis	Spring......	A. C. Barry...	......	....	....	....	....	....
6701	♂	Dane county, Wis......	....	Th. Kumlien	......	....	....	....	.....	....
2714	......	Boston	....	S. F. Baird	......	S. Cabot............	....	....	....	....
536	......	New York.............	....	......do...	... ..	G. N. Lawrence ...	....	....	......	
	♂	Pembina, Minn	Sept. 26, 1857	N. W. University ..	......	R. Kennicott.......	....	....	......	
8245	......	50 miles west of Leavenworth, K.	Nov. 5, 1857	Dr. J. G. Cooper ...	227	....	6.12	10.75	3.75	Iris brown, bill pale brown, feet black.
8246	......	........do..............	......do.......	......do...........	......	....	6.12	10.75	3.75	....

55 b

PLECTROPHANES PICTUS, Swainson.

Smith's Bunting.

Emberiza (Plectrophanes) picta, Sw. F. B. Am. II, 1831, 250 ; pl.   , (spring.)—Nutt. Man. II, 589.

Plectrophanes pictus, Aud. Syn. 1839, 99.—Ib. Birds Amer. III, 1841, 52 ; pl. 153, (Richardson's specimen.)

Emberiza picta, Aud. Orn. Biog. V, 1839, 91 ; pl. 400.

Centrophanes pictus, Cab. Mus. Hein, 1851, 127.

Plectrophanes smithii, Aud. Birds Amer. VII, 1844, 337 ; pl. 487, (winter.)

Sp. Ch.—Hood black ; a line passing over the eye, a small spot on the nape, another on the ears, and a large patch on the wings, white ; nuchal collar and the whole under plumage brownish buff yellow. Legs flesh color. Length, 5.50 inches ; wing, 3.50 ; tail, 2.75 ; bill, 45.

Hab.—Prairies of Il'inois in winter ; in summer north to the Saskatchewan.

In the absence of fully plumaged specimens of this bird, I have borrowed the above diagnosis from the *Fauna boreali-americana*, based on Saskatchewan specimens. As far as I know, none in this plumage have ever been taken in the United States, although immaturely marked ones are not unfrequent in early spring throughout Illinois.

The specimen before me has the bill of the size and shape of that of *P. lapponica ;* the hind claw is, however, considerably smaller. The upper parts are yellowish brown, broadly streaked with dark brown ; there is a trace of a light line on the middle crown, and another on each side of it, as of a light spot on the nape ; the light spot on the ear covers is also obscurely indicated. There is also a trace of a light line along the scapular region. There is a maxillary row of spots ; the under parts generally are pale brownish yellow, streaked on the breast and sides with brown. The lesser wing coverts have the feathers partially tipped with white. The tail feathers are brown, except the outer, the exposed portion of which is white, with a brown streak on the outer web towards the end, and a narrow edging on the inner web at the base ; the second has a long narrow stripe of white along the inner border of the shaft. This character will distinguish the species from *P. ornatus* and *maccownii*, although something similar is seen in *P. lapponicus*. Its relationships generally are much closest to the latter species. The hind claw, however, is scarcely more than half as long ; the others also shorter. The bill is smaller. The covered portions of the jugular feathers show no black whatever ; the sides of the throat and the breast show short streaks of brown ; the under parts are more fulvous. The outer tail feathers show more white, there being as much on the second of *pictus* as on the first of *lapponicus*, the second of *lapponicus* having almost none at all, instead of most of the feathers being white. The light brownish flesh color of the legs instead of nearly black, is an important feature.

List of specimens.

Catal. No.	Locality.	When collected.	Whence obtained.	Collected by—
1941	Edwardsville, Illinois ----	1843-----------------	S. F. Baird------------	J. J. Audubon ----------
1862	------do------------	1843----------------		Ed. Harris------ --------
10254	Salem, Illinois----------	April 7, 1857-----------	Northwestern University--	R. Kennicott-----------
10255	Pembina, Minn----------	Sept. —, 1857-----------	------do-----------------	------do----------------

PLECTROPHANES ORNATUS, Towns.

Chestnut-collared Bunting.

Plectrophanes ornatus, Townsend, J. Ac. Nat. Sc. VII, 1837, 189.—Ib. Narrative, 1839, 344.—Aud. Syn. 1839, 99.—Ib. Birds Amer. III, 1841, 53 ; pl. 154.—Nutt. Man. I, 2d ed. 1840, 537.

Emberiza ornata, Aud. Orn. Biog. V, 1839, 44 ; pl. 394, f. 1.

Centrophanes ornatus, Cabanis, Mus. Hein. 1851, 127.[2]

Sp. Ch.—Bill dark plumbeous. Crown, a narrow crescent on the side of the head, with a line running into it from behind the eye, entire breast and upper part of belly all round, black ; throat and sides of the head, lower part of belly and under tail coverts, with bases of the tail feathers, white. The white on the tail feathers runs forward as an acute point. A chestnut band on the back of the neck extending round on the sides. Rest of upper parts grayish brown, streaked with darker. Lesser wing coverts like the back. Length about 5.25 inches ; wing, 3.20 ; tail, 2.30 ; tarsus, .75.

Hab.—Plains of the Upper Missouri.

In this species the line of demarcation between the white of the throat and the black of the breast is very strongly marked. The black of the crown is margined on the sides by the white of the head, and in some specimens there is an indication as if a narrow white line were continued round on the occiput so as to margin the black ; the black crescent may possibly be continued forward to near the base of the lower jaw, making the markings of the head very similar to those of *P. pictus*. There is a very faint indication of a white band along the edges of the lesser coverts, which, towards the elbow joint, increases considerably, but by its position is more or less concealed. There is, however, no tendency to black. The first and second tail feathers are entirely white, the latter with a faint trace only of brownish near the end externally ; the third, fourth, and fifth have the tips and sides near the end brown ; the innermost feather is white only near the basal portion of the inner edge. The white runs out to an elongated acute point in the feather. The wing feathers are edged with paler, but there is no white.

Specimens not in full breeding plumage have the black feathers margined more or less with brownish white.

A young bird probably of this species has the top of the head streaked like the back, and concealed traces only of the black of the breast. The female shows no black ; this is replaced below by brown streaks on brownish yellow ; there is a row of streaks on each side the throat. The top of the head is streaked like the back.

The black breast, white throat, and chestnut collar sufficiently distinguish this species from its congeners, except *P melanomus*.

List of specimens.

Catal. No.	Sex.	Locality.	When collected.	Whence obtained.	Collected by—	Length.	Stretch of wings.	Wing.
1907	♂	Fort Union, Neb	June 21, 1843	S. F. Baird	J. J. Audubon			
4827	♂	Bijou Hills, Neb	May 14, 1856	Lt. Warren	Dr. Hayden			
5917	♀	Fort Pierre	June 26, 1856	do	do	5. 50	10. 12	5. 00
5378	♂	Medicine Hill	June 23, 1856	do	do	5. 75	9. 87	3. 25
5377	♂	Medicine Butte	do	do	do	5. 37	10. 00	3. 12
5379	♂	Medicine creek, Neb	June 12, 1856	do	do	6. 25	10. 50	3. 25

PLECTROPHANES MELANOMUS, Baird.

Sp. Ch.—Bill yellowish, dark brown along the culmen. Crown, a short stripe behind the eye, and a short crescent behind
the ear coverts, entire breast as far back as the thighs, and the lesser wing coverts, black. The black on the breast margined
with dark cinnamon. Sides of head, chin, throat, and region behind the black of the belly, white. A broad half collar of dark
cinnamon brown on the back of the neck. Tail feathers mostly white; the innermost tipped with dark brown; the white ending
in an acute angle. Length, 5.30; wing, 3.40; tail, 2.60. (No. 6290.)
        Hab.—Eastern slope of the Rocky mountains, Mexico, on the table lands.

This species is exceedingly similar in size and color to the *Plectrophanes ornatus*, although
readily distinguished by certain characteristics. The bill, though slender, is rather short; the
culmen and gonys gently curved. The tarsi are considerably longer than the middle toe; the
hind claw is gently curved, and rather longer than its toe; the two about equal to or even a
little longer than the middle toe. The wings are long and pointed, and reach about to the
middle of the exposed portion of the tail; the second quill is longest; the first about equal to
the fourth. The tail is considerably shorter than the wings and very nearly even; the
feathers rather acute towards the ends, but rounded off at the tips.

In addition to the colors already mentioned, there is a square white spot on the back of the
head in the middle of the posterior edge of the black of the crown, as in most *Plectrophanes*.
The white on the sides of the head is interrupted by the dark line behind the eye and the short
crescent behind or a little below the ear coverts. There is a tinge of dirty brownish yellow on
the white of the chin and upper part of the throat; on the lower part, however, the color is
more pure, and occupies the inferior half of the neck, the chestnut half collar completing the
zone. The black feathers on the middle region of the under surface of the body are all much
margined and tipped with dark cinnamon brown, darker than that on the back of the neck;
the external black feathers all round are more or less margined with whitish, though this may
be indicative of immaturity. There is a whitish patch on the side of the breast, covered by
the bend of the wing. The lesser and middle wing coverts are black, although the posterior
row of the former is white internally, or towards the back; some of the innermost of the middle
coverts, too, are edged with white. The general color of the upper parts is dirty brownish
yellow, streaked centrally with dark brown. A considerable portion of the inner webs of the
tertiaries and inner secondaries, with their tips, is white; the outer edges of the primaries, with
nearly the whole outer web of the first quill, are sharply white; the tertials just beyond the
greater wing coverts are pale rufous. The outer two tail feathers on each side are entirely
white, with a faint trace of dusky along the midrib near the end, most distinct on the upper
surface. The rest are margined terminally and tipped with brown, the amount of this increasing
towards the innermost feathers.

As already stated, this species is very similar ot *P. ornatus*. It is, however, a very little
larger, or, at any rate, with considerably longer wings. The bill, however, is shorter and
stouter; the hind claw decidedly longer. The chestnut of the back of the neck is darker. The
white on the outer web of the tertiaries and secondaries is much purer and wider. The
rufous margins of the pectoral feathers I have never seen in *ornatus*. The most striking
peculiarity, however, is in having the shoulders black, instead of brown like the rest of the wing

feathers, edged with paler. Both have the white posterior row of lesser wing coverts. The color of bill differs in each.

An immature male (6291) has the black of the head mixed with brown, and a maxillary series of spots on each side the throat.   A female has a similar series of spots ; the under parts generally being brownish white, the shafts across the breast and along sides streaked with brown, the concealed portions of the feathers light brown, fading out to the whitish exterior. There is no black on the shoulder, nor chestnut on the nape.

List of specimens.

Catal. No.	Sex and age.	Locality.	When collected.	Whence obtained.	Orig. No.	Collected by—	Length.	Stretch of wings.	Win	Remarks.
9115	....	Mexico..................................	....	M. Verreaux........	29951	....	....	....	....	....
9218	....	.....do................	....	....	......	....	....	....	....	....
6290	....	Fort Thorn	....	Dr. Henry	......	....	....	....	....	....
6292	♂	New Mexico............	1854..........	Lieut. Parke.	......	Dr. Heermann...	....	....	....	....
6293	♀	.....do................	1854...........	......do.............	......	....	....	....	....	....
5717	♂	Pole creek.............	Aug. 1,1856	Lieut. Bryan.......	187	W. S. Wood.....	....	....	3.50	Iris dark brown....
8924	....	Black Hills	Sept. 20,1857	Lieut. Warren....	.....	Dr. Hayden......	6.00	10.75	3.50	......do............
8926	....	.....do......... ....do......	....do......	......do.............	......	......do..........	6.50	10.50	3.50	......do............
8925	○	Running water.........	Aug. 14,1857	......do.............	......	......do..........	6.00	10.50	3.25	Iris gray ....

PLECTROPHANES MACCOWNII, Lawrence.

Plectrophanes maccownii, LAWRENCE, ANN. N. Y. Lyc. V, Sept. 1851, 122.   Western Texas.—CASSIN, Illust. I, VIII, 1855, 228 ; pl. xxxix.

SP. CH.—Bill very stout and large. Head above, a sharply defined semi-lunar crescent on the upper part of the breast, and probably a short maxillary line on each side of the chin and throat, black ; rest of under parts, with a superciliary stripe, white; shoulders chestnut. Rest of upper parts yellowish brown, streaked with darker. External tail feather white ; the rest white, tipped and margined externally with brown, the white line of separation going almost transversely across the whole of the inner web, instead of running forward in an acute point. The innermost feather like the back.

Length, about 5.50 ; wing 3.60 ; tail, 2.50 ; bill above .46.

Hab.—Eastern slopes of Rocky Mountains ; from Fort Thorn, N. M., as far east as the Black Hills north of Platte.

In this species the bill is considerably larger and stouter than in any other I have seen. It measures .46 of an inch above, and the distance between the basal portions of the upper and under outlines amounts to .31 of an inch. The tail is quite deeply forked. The claws appear to be straighter than in the other species ; the hinder one unusually short, measuring only .36 of an inch.

The most perfect specimen before me does not appear to be quite mature, although the markings are pretty well indicated. There is only a faint trace of a black maxillary line. There is no trace of the chestnut or rufous collar seen in all the other North American species, excepting *P. nivalis*. The loral region and line over the eye are brownish white, purer behind. The upper rows of lesser coverts immediately along the edge of the wing are like the back, not chestnut, like the rest of these coverts. The peculiarity of the transverse termination of the white in the exterior tail feathers, I have seen in no other species. The innermost feather has no white at its base ; the next has the outer web and tip brown ; in all the rest the whole feather is white, the terminal half, or three quarters of an inch, alone being brown, this color extending furthest back on the outer web.

A female specimen agrees in the characters of bill and tail. The black crown and pectoral crescent, with the chestnut shoulders, are wanting. The whole upper parts are brownish yellow, streaked with darker. There is a short maxillary stripe of brown dots. The chin, throat, and upper part of the breast are tinged in places with brownish. There are no brown streaks on the breast.

The combination of the black pectoral crescent and crown, with the absence of a chestnut collar, and the chestnut shoulders will readily distinguish this species from any other. The female will be best known by the stout bill and transverse outline of the white on the tail feathers.

The *Plectrophanes maccownii* is quite different from the other species of the genus in the enormously large bill and much shorter hind claw, so much so, in fact, that Bonaparte places it in an entirely different family. As, however, many of the characteristics are those of *Plectrophanes*, and the general coloration especially so, I see no objection to keeping it in this genus for the present.

List of specimens.

Catal. No.	Sex.	Locality.	When collected.	Whence obtained.	Orig'l No.	Collected by—	Length.	Stretch of wings.	Wing.	Remarks.
5039	♂	Organ mountains, N. M.	....	Capt. J. Pope....	179	....	6.25	11.50	3.50	Bill light br'n, eyes gray, f't reddish gray, gums yellow.
6282	♂	New Mexico............	... .	Lt. J. G. Parke ..	......	....	....	......	....	....
6283	♀	......do.........		......do.........		....	....	....	....	....
6284	.....	Fort Thorne, N. M.....	....	Dr. T. C. Henry.	......	....	....	....	....	....
6288	♂	......do.........	....	......do.........		....	....	....	....	....
8237	......	40 miles west of Fort Kearney.	Oct. 19, 1857	Wm. M. Magraw.	219	Dr. Cooper.....	6.25	11.50	3.75	Iris brown, bill brown and white, feet dark brown.
8954	......	Eastern Black hills.....	Sept. 29, 1857	Lt. Warren, U S.A.	....	Dr. Hayden....	5.12	11.75	3.50	Iris brown..............
8955	......	......do............	Sept. 20, 1857	......do.........	......	....	6.00	11.75	3.50	......do.... ....
8956	......	......do.........	....,..do.......	......do.........		....	6.50	12.00	3.75	....

Sub–Family SPIZELLINAE.

Ch.—Bill variable, usually almost straight ; sometimes curved. Commissure generally nearly straight, or slightly concave. Upper mandible wider than lower. Nostrils exposed. Wings moderate ; the outer primaries not much rounded. Tail variable. Feet large ; tarsi mostly longer than the middle toe.

The species are usually small, and of dull color. Nearly all are streaked on the back and crown ; often on the belly. None of the United States species have any red, blue, or orange, and the yellow, when present, is as a superciliary streak, or on the elbow edge of the wing.

In the arrangement of this sub-family, as of the others belonging to the *Fringillidae*, I do not profess to give anything like a natural system. The species belonging to it at my command are too few, and my knowledge of exotic forms too limited to permit anything more than an attempt at a convenient artificial scheme by which the determination of the genera may be facilitated.

A.—Tail small and short ; wings considerably or decidedly longer than the tail, owing either to the elongation of the wing or the shortening of the tail. Lateral toes shorter than the middle without its claw. Species streaked above and below.

a. Thickly streaked everywhere above, on the sides, and across the breast. Wing pointed; longest primaries considerably longer than the secondaries. Tail forked.

> CENTRONYX.—Hind claw very large ; rather longer than its digit. The hind toe and claw, together, as long or longer than the middle toe and claw. Other toes as in *Passerculus.* Claws gently curved. Tertials shorter than the secondaries. Tail forked, but the lateral feathers shorter.

> PASSERCULUS.—Hind claw as long as its digit; the toe equal to the middle one without its claw; lateral toes falling considerably short of the middle claw. Wings very long; first primary longest. Tertials as long as the primaries. Tail forked ; feathers acute.

> POOCÆTES.—Hind claw shorter than its digit; the whole toe less than the middle toe without its claw. Lateral toes nearly equal to the middle one, without its claw. Tertials but little longer than secondaries. Tail stiffened, forked ; feathers acute, outer ones white.

b. Moderately streaked above, on the sides, and on the breast; the dorsal streaks broader, the others fainter than in the last. Wings short, reaching a little beyond the base of the tail. Not much difference between the primaries and secondaries. Tail short, graduated, and the feathers lanceolate, acute.

> COTURNICULUS.—Bill short; thick. Tertials almost equal to the primaries ; truncate at the end. Claws small, weak; hinder one shorter than its digit. Outstretched feet not reaching the tip of the tail. Tail feathers not stiffened. (In one species tail nearly equal to the wing.)

> AMMODRAMUS.—Bill slender, small at base, and elongated. Tertials not longer than the secondaries ; rounded at the tip. Claws large, hinder one equal to its digit. Outstretched toes reaching considerably beyond the end of the stiffened, almost scansorial tail.

B.—Tail longer and broader ; nearly or quite as long, sometimes a very little longer than the wings, which are rather lengthened. The primaries considerably longer than the secondaries. None of the species streaked beneath, and the back alone streaked above.

a. Tail rounded or slightly graduated.

> CHONDESTES.—Tail considerably graduated, not emarginated. Lateral toes considerably shorter than the middle toe, without its claw. Wings very long, decidedly longer than the tail, reaching the middle of the tail. First quill longest. Head striped. Back streaked. White beneath. A white blotch on the end of the tail feathers.

> ZONOTRICHIA.—Tail moderately graduated. Wings moderate, about as long as the tail, reaching about over the basal fourth of the tail ; first quill less than the second to fourth. Feet large. Head striped with black and white. Back streaked.

JUNCO.—Tail very nearly equal.to the wings, slightly emarginate, and decidedly rounded. Outer toe rather longer than inner, reaching the middle claw. No streaks anywhere; black or ash color above; belly white; with or without a rufous back and sides. Outer tail feathers white.

POOSPIZA.—Tail lengthened, slightly graduated; the feathers unusually broad to the end. Bill slender. Wings about as long as the tail, reaching but little beyond its external base. Tertials broad, and, with the secondaries, rather lengthened. Second to fifth quills nearly equal, and longest. Bill dark lead color. Tail black. Uniform brown above; white beneath. Sides of head with stripes of black and white.

b. Tail decidedly forked; a little shorter than the wing, sometimes a little longer.

SPIZELLA.—Size rather small. Wings long. Lower mandible largest. Uniform beneath, or with a pectoral spot or black chin.

C.—Tail lengthened and graduated; decidedly longer than the wings, which are very short, scarcely extending beyond the external base of the tail. Feet reaching but little beyond the middle of the tail. Species all streaked above; streaked or nearly unicolor beneath. No white on wings or tail. Outer lateral toe the longer. First quill not the shortest of the primaries.

MELOSPIZA.—Culmen and commissure nearly straight. Claws stout; hinder one as large as its digit. Tail feathers rather broad. Body streaked beneath.

PEUCAEA.—Culmen and commissure curved. Claws weak; hinder one not much curved, decidedly shorter than its digit. Tail feathers narrow. Without streaks beneath, excepting a narrow maxillary stripe.

D.—Tail rather short, and much graduated; longer than the wings; the midrib more median. Culmen curved. Tarsus considerably longer than middle toe. Outer toe longer. But little difference in the length of the quills; the outer ones much rounded; even the second quill is shorter than any other primary except the first.

EMBERNAGRA.—Color, olive green above.

CENTRONYX, Baird.

CH.—Bill elongated; the lower mandible smaller; outlines nearly straight. Tarsus lengthened, considerably exceeding the middle toe. Lateral toes equal, not reaching the base of the middle claw. Hind toe very large; the claw rather longer than its digit, and in its elongation resembling *Plectrophanes*, but more curved; the digit and claw together rather longer than the middle toe and claw. Wings very long, reaching beyond the middle of the tail, and beyond the end of the coverts. Tertials shorter than the primaries, and but little longer than the secondaries. Tail short, much less than from the carpal joint to end of secondaries; little more than two-thirds the entire wing. It is slightly forked, and moderately rounded laterally; the feathers all acute. Color somewhat as in *Passerculus*.

This genus differs from *Passerculus*, as stated in the description of the species further on. It would be taken for *Plectrophanes* on account of its lengthened hind claw, which, however, is more curved than in that genus; the tarsi are much longer, the tertials less elongated, and the coloration different, though closely resembling that of the female *Plectrophanes*.

CENTRONYX BAIRDII, Baird.

Emberiza bairdii, Audubon, Birds Amer. VII, 1843, 359 ; pl. 500.
Coturniculus bairdii, Bon. Syn. 1850, 481.

Sp. Ch.—Somewhat similar in general appearance to *Passerculus savanna*. Back grayish, streaked with dusky. Crown nearly covered by black streaks, but divided by a broad median band of brownish yellow. Eyelids and a faint superciliary stripe yellowish white. Beneath white, with a maxillary blackish stripe and some narrow streaks on the upper part of the breast, and sides of the throat and body. Outer edges and tips of tail feathers white ; the two outer feathers obsoletely white. Bend of wing white. Length, 4.75 ; wing, 2.80 ; tail, 2.20.

Hab.—Mouth of the Yellowstone.

This species has somewhat of the general appearance of *Passerculus savanna*, but with important differences both of form and color. The bill is much longer, and more slender in proportion. The wings are quite unusually long ; the primaries more than half an inch longer than the tertiaries ; the first quill as long as the fourth, and but little less than the second and third. The tail is very short ; the feathers narrow and pointed. The feet are large ; the hind claw very long, and considerably curved, as are the other claws generally.

The yellow patch on the crown ; the longer bill, hind claw, and wings ; the absence of yellow over the eye and on the wing ; the much less amount of spotting on the breast ; the white of the outer tail feathers, &c., all distinguish this species very readily from *P. savanna* and its allies.

This species appears closely related to some *Plectrophanes* in the lengthened wings and very long hind claw. This, however, as well as all the claws, are considerably curved ; the legs are much larger and stouter, and the tertials and inner secondaries are shorter. The coloration is that of female *Plectrophanes*, especially *P. pictus*.

List of specimens.

Catal. No.	Locality.	When collected.	Whence obtained.	Collected by—	Length.	Wing.	Tail.	Tarsus.	Middle toe.	Its claw alone.	Hind toe and claw.	Hind claw alone.	Bill above.	Along gape.	Specimen measured.
1885	Fort Union, Neb.	1843.......	S. F. Baird	J. J. Audubon..	4.64	2.77	2.10	0.84	0.73	0.18	0.72	0.34	0.49	0.50	Skin ....

PASSERCULUS, Bonaparte.

Passerculus, Bonap. Comp. List Birds, 1838. Type *Fringilla savanna*.

Bill moderately conical ; the lower mandible smaller ; both outlines nearly straight. Tarsus about equal to the middle toe. Lateral toes about equal, their claws falling far short of the middle one. Hind toe much longer than the lateral ones, reaching as far as the middle of the middle claw ; its claws moderately curved. Wings unusually long, reaching to the middle of the tail, and almost to the end of the upper coverts. The tertials nearly or quite as long as the primaries ; the first primary longest. The tail is quite short, considerably shorter than the wings ; as long as from the carpal joint to the end of the secondaries. It is emarginate, and slightly rounded ; the feathers pointed and narrow.

Entire plumage above, head, neck, back, rump streaked. Thickly streaked beneath.

The essential characters of this well marked genus lie in the elongated wings, longer than the tail, the tertiaries equal to the primaries, the first quill almost longest. The legs are long, the outstretched toes reaching to the end of the tail ; the lateral considerably shorter than the middle, which is not much longer than the hinder. The tail is short, narrow, and emarginate ; the feathers acute.

I have, with some hesitation, referred the *Emberiza rostrata* of Cassin to this genus. It agrees in most respects, but the bill is much larger, the upper outline decidedly convex throughout, the commissure concave and slightly sinuated, the gonys straight.   The claws are straighter, or less curved.   In other respects of form, &c., there is a very close relationship.

Synopsis of the species.

Back with well defined dark brown streaks.   A yellowish superciliary streak from the bill, and a distinct median light line along the top of the head.   Bill moderate.

Superciliary stripe decided yellow throughout.

Fore part of breast only streaked.   Bill above, .40 ; wing, 2.65......*P. savanna.*

Similar to last, but larger and darker.   Bill above, .50 ; wing, 2.95.

P. sandwichensis.

Breast and fore part of belly thickly streaked.   Under parts with a reddish tinge. Bill, attenuated, .42 ; wing, 2.66..*P. anthinus.*

Superciliary stripe pale, with little or no yellow.

Fore part of breast sparsely streaked.   Bill slender, elongated.......*P. alaudinus.*

Back grayish brown, with very obsolete and rather darker streaks.   No distinct median light line on the crown.   Bill enormously large..*P. rostratus.*

Comparative measurements of species.

Catal. No.	Species.	Locality.	Sex.	Length.	Stretch of wings.	Wing.	Tail.	Tarsus.	Middle toe.	Its claw alone.	Hind toe and claw.	Hind toe alone.	Bill above.	Along gape.	Specimen measured.
6339	Passerculus rostratus.....	San Diego...........	♂	5.30	.....	2.62	2.27	0.85	0.79	0.20	0.60	0.29	0.50	0.54	Skin......
6340	......do ....do........	......do............	♂	5.30	.....	2.82	2.36	0.89	0.84	0.20	0.61	0.28	0.52	0.56	Skin......
10145	......do......savanna....	Washington, D. C.....	♂	5.40	.....	2.77	2.29	0.84	0.80	0.19	0.64	0.30	0.40	0.48	Skin......
10260	......do ....do.......	South Illinois.......	♀	5.40	.....	2.65	2.13	0.78	0.76	0.21	0.61	0.30	0.41	0.46	Skin......
780	......do .. ...do........	Carlisle, Pa..........	♀	4.84	.....	2.53	2.14	0.76	0.73	0.17	0.60	0.30	0 39	0.44	Skin.......
780	......do ....do........	......do......	.....	5.25	8.57	2.64	.....	.....	.....	.....	.....	.....	.....	.....	Fresh ......
781	......do ....do........	......do.............	♂	5.06	.....	2.65	2.12	0.78	0.78	0.18	0.62	0.28	0.40	0.56	Skin......
10263	......do....sandwichensis	Russian America......	.....	5.30	.....	2.89	2.37	0.83	0.78	0.18	0.66	0.29	0.39	0.52	Skin......
6343	......do ....do.......	Shoalwater bay......	♂	5.60	.....	2.80	2.33	0.86	0.86	0.24	.....	.....	0.50	0.52	Skin......
6343	......do ....do.......	......do.............	.....	6.12	9.25	.....	.....	.....	.....	.....	.....	.....	.....	.....	Fresh .....
6345	......do ....do.......	Fort Steilacoom	.....	5.64	.....	2.95	2.57	0.85	0.82	0.22	0.66	0.34	0.43	0.48	Skin......
6345	......do ....do.......	...... do.	.....	6.12	9.37	.....	.....	.....	.....	.....	.....	.....	.....	.....	Fresh .....
4311	......do....alaudinus	Tamaulipas, Mex....	♂	5.00	.....	2.76	2.30	0.81	0.78	0.22	0.62	0.31	0.42	0.44	Skin......
4241	......do .. do...........	......do............	.....	5.25	9.00	2.25?	.....	.....	.....	.....	.....	.....	.....	.....	Fresh .....
5554	......do ....do.......	Petaluma, Cal	♂	5.14	.....	2.90	2.37	0.84	0.77	0.18	0.63	0.30	0.40	0.45	Skin......
4342	......do ....do.......	Tamaulipas, Mex	.....	5.00	.....	2.50	2 03	0.77	0.72	0.19	0.59	0.28	0.40	0.44	Skin......
4342	......do ....do.......	......do............	.....	5.00	8.50	2.50	.....	.....	.....	.....	.....	.....	.....	.....	Fresh .....
5555	......do....anthinus	Petaluma, Cal	♂	5.00	.....	2.66	2.24	0.79	0.76	0.20	0.62	0.30	0.42	0.45	Skin......
6330	......do......do?........	Benicia, Cal	♂	4.90	.....	2.56	2.00	0.80	0.78	0.20	0.62	0.27	0.42	0.50	Skin......

PASSERCULUS SAVANNA, Bonap.

Savannah Sparrow.

Fringilla savanna, WILSON, Am. Orn. III, 1811, 55 ; pl. 22, f. 2.—IB. IV, 1811, 72 ; pl. 34, f. 4.—AUD. Orn. Biog. II, 1834, 63 : V, 1839, 516 ; pl. 109.

Passerculus savanna, BON. List, 1838.—IB. Conspectus, 1850, 480.—CAB. Mus. Hein. 1851, 131.

Emberiza savanna, AUD. Syn. 1839, 103.—IB. Birds Amer. III, 1841, 68 ; pl. 160.

? *Fringilla hyemalis,* GM. I, 1788, 922.—LICHT. Verzeichniss, 1823, No. 250.   Gmelin's description, based on Pennant Arctic Zool. II, 376, (winter finch,) applies equally well to a large number of species.

Linaria savanna, RICHARDSON, List, 1837.

Sp. Ch.—Feathers of the upper parts generally with a central streak of blackish brown; the streaks of the back with a slight rufous suffusion laterally; the feathers edged with gray, which is lightest on the scapulars. Crown with a broad median stripe of yellowish gray. A superciliary streak from the bill to the back of the head, eyelids, and edge of the elbow, yellow. A yellowish white maxillary stripe curving behind the ear coverts, and margined above and below by brown. The lower margin is a series of thickly crowded spots on the sides of the throat, which are also found on the sides of the neck, across the upper part of the breast, and on the sides of body. A few spots on the throat and chin. Rest of under parts white. Outer tail feather and primary edged with white. Length, 5.50; wing, 2.70; tail, 2.10.

Hab.—Eastern North America to the Missouri plains.

In this species the bill is rather short; the tarsus and middle toe with its claw about equal. The wing is acute; the first quill longest; the tertiaries as long as the primaries. The tail is short and somewhat forked; the feathers narrow and rather acute, but rounded at the tips.

The spots on the under parts of the body have a rufous suffusion externally, scarcely appreciable on the breast in spring specimens. The outside edges of all the wing feathers, excepting the primary quills have a yellowish rufous tinge more conspicuous than elsewhere on the body. There is sometimes a tinge of greenish on the smaller wing coverts.

With a considerable number of specimens from the western coast at hand I have been much puzzled to decide how many species there are, and upon their relationship to *P. savanna*. One series from Oregon and Washington Territory is much the largest, considerably exceeding the *P. savanna* of the east. These agree exactly with a specimen from Sitka, collected by Wosnessjensky, the taxidermist of the St. Petersburg Academy, and labelled *Zonotrichia chrysops*, Pallas, probably by Brandt. Another series is composed of specimens that are smaller, though varying considerably in size, and the bill is generally slenderer. In one (5554) the superciliary stripe has only a faint tinge of yellow, and the colors are rather paler than common. The spots on the breast are rather sparser than usual. The bill is rather slenderer than in eastern specimens, but instead of being shorter is actually longer. This agrees with specimens from Northeastern Mexico in Lieutenant Couch's collection. Other specimens have the yellow as bright, that on the axillaries even brighter, than in any eastern ones; the spots blacker and more numerous, extending over the whole breast. In another, otherwise similar, the bill is unusually long, and the spots on the middle of the breast are aggregated into a larger one.

Without feeling assured of an actual specific difference I shall follow Bonaparte in referring the large billed series to *P. chrysops* of Pallas, (*sandwichensis;*) that with the gray colors, few pectoral spots, whitish superciliary stripe, and attenuated bill to *P. alaudinus;* and that with dark colors, yellow superciliary stripe, and numerous pectoral spots to *P. anthinus.*

List of specimens.

Catal. No.	Sex.	Locality.	When collected.	Whence obtained.	Collected by—	Length.	Stretch of wings.	Wing.	Remarks.
10241	....	Liberty county, Ga........	....	Prof. Jos. Leconte....	....	....	....	....	....
10145	♂	Washington, D. C.........	....	J. C. McGuire	....	....	....	....	....
946	♂	Carlisle, Pa...............	May 6, 1843	S. F. Baird	....	....	....	....	....
780	♀	.....do................	Oct. 6, 1842	......do...........	....	5.50	9.17	2.83	....
781	♂	.....do................	Oct. 7, 1842	......do...........	....	5 25	8.58	2.67	....
449	....	.....do................	Sept. 18, 1841	......do...........	....	....	....	....	....
448	....	.....do................	.....do......	......do...........	....	5.25	8.75	....	....
7108	....	Philadelphia...........	....	....	....	....	....	....	....
4323	....	Calcasieu, La.......	1854........	G. Würdemann....	....	....	....	....	....
10260	♀	South Illinois............	May 13, 1857	N.W. University	R. Kennicott....	....	....	....	....
10261	....	North Illinois...........	April 22, 1855	......do...........	......do.....	....	....	....	....
10262	....	Red River settlement...	Sept. 10, 1857	......do...........	......do.....	....	....	....	....
6556	....	Fort Riley, K. T	1857........	Dr. W. A. Hammond.	....	....	....	....	....
4807	♂	Vermilion river, Neb....	May 8, 1856	Lieut. G. K. Warren .	Dr. Hayden.....	....	....	....	....
4808?	....	Mouth of Big Sioux, Neb...	May 3, 1856	......do...........	......do.....	5.50	....	2.50	....
*8956?	....	Black Hills, Neb........	Sept. 20, 1857	......do...........	......do.....	5.25	8.50	2.50	Iris brown........
8957?	....	.....do...........	Sept. 11, 1857	......do...........	......do.....	5.50	9.00	3.00	......do........
8968?	....	.....do...........	Sept. 10, 1857	......do...........	......do.....	5.00	8.50	2.50	....
8786?	....	North fork of Platte....	Aug. 19, 1857	W. M. Magraw......	Dr. J. G. Cooper.	5.25	9.00	2.75	....

* These specimens, in autumnal plumage, scarcely admit of an accurate determination.

PASSERCULUS SANDWICHENSIS, Baird.

Emberiza sandwichensis, Gm. I, 1788, 875.

Emberiza arctica, Latham, Ind. Orn. I, 1790, 414.

Fringilla arctica, Vigors, Zool. of Blossom, 1839, 20, (perhaps one of the smaller species.)—"Brandt, Icon. Ross. 2, 6."

Euspiza arctica, Bp. Conspectus, 1850, 469.

Emberiza chrysops, Pallas, Zoog. Rosso-As. II, 1811, 45 ; tab. xlviii ; fig. 1, (Unalaschka)

Sandwich Bunting, Lath. Syn. II, 1783, 202.

Unalascha Bunting, Pennant, Arctic Zool. II, 363, 320, No. 229. (Not of p. 364, No. 233.)

Sp. Ch.—Almost exactly like *P. savanna*, but half an inch larger, with much larger bill. Length, 6.12 inches : wing, 3.00 ; tail, 2 55.

Hab.—Northwestern coast from the Columbia river to Russian America.

This species is extremely similar to the *P. savanna*, and is only distinguishable by its greater size, and more western locality. The tail feathers also are rather more acutely pointed. There is also a greenish yellow shade on the top and sides of the head, brighter than that seen in *P. savanna*. The bill is considerably larger and longer, measuring .51 of an inch above instead of .44.

The Sandwich Bunting of Latham (Synopsis of birds) and the Unalascha Bunting of Pennant (page 363, No. 229) seem to belong unquestionably to this species, and as Gmelin bases his *sandwichensis* upon these descriptions, it must be retained. The name has no reference to the Sandwich Islands but to Sandwich Sound, on the northwest coast. The Unalascha Bunting of Pennant, page 364, No. 233, is a different species.

The "*temporibus atris*" is not a very accurate expression in the species, but sufficiently near not to be inconsistent with it. At any rate, as the descriptions of *sandwichensis*, *arctica*, and *chrysops*, all seem to apply equally well, it will be best to take the oldest name as a provisional one at least.

List of specimens.

Catal. No.	Sex.	Locality.	When collected.	Where obtained.	Orig'l No.	Collected by—	Length.	Stretch of wings.	Remarks.
10263	♂	Russian America	Mar. 12, 1842	S. F. Baird	......	Wosnessjensky.	....	....	....
6345	......	Fort Steilacoom, W. T..	April —, 1856	Dr. G. Suckley...	308	....	6.12	9.37	....
6342	♀?	Shoalwater bay, W. T..	May 15, 1854	Dr. J. G. Cooper.	73	....	6.12	9.25	Iris brown; feet brownish white..
6343	♂?	..........do............	......do......	........do........	73	....	6.12	9.25	......do............do...........
6344	.....	..........do............	Oct. 15, 1854	........do........	......	....	,.....	....	....

PASSERCULUS ANTHINUS, Bonap.

Passerculus anthinus, BONAP. Comptes Rendus, XXVII, Dec. 1853, 919, Russian America.—IB. Notes Ornith. Delattre, 1854, 19.

SP. CH.—Similar to *P. savanna*, but smaller. Beneath tinged with reddish. Breast and upper part of belly thickly spotted with sharply defined sagittate brown spots, exhibiting a tendency to aggregation on the middle of the belly. Superciliary stripe and one in the middle of the crown decided greenish yellow, the head generally tinged with the same; as also the back and sides of the neck. Length, 5.00; wing, 2.66; tail, 2.24.

Hab.—Coast of California, near San Francisco; Russian America; Kodiak. (Bonaparte.)

This species is the smallest of its group, and differs from all in the much greater amount of spotting on the under parts. The streaks, indeed, extend over the whole breast and upper part of the abdomen, instead of being mainly confined to the jugulum. They are dark brown, well defined, and unusually sagittate. The superciliary stripe is bright greenish yellow, as is also a stripe along the median line of the head above. The feathers on the sides of the head behind the auriculars, are strongly tinged with the same color. There is an indication of a brown tinge around the lower part of throat, as in Lincoln's finch. The feathers in the middle of the back are darker than usual.

This species differs from *alaudinus* in the strong shade of yellow on the head, the much darker tints above, and the thick crowding of larger and better defined spots beneath, with a faint tinge of reddish. The under tail coverts are more distinctly streaked.

List of specimens.

Catal. No.	Sex.	Locality.	When collected.	Whence obtained.	Orig. No.	Collected by—
6331	------	San Francisco, Cal. ------	May 8, 1854 ..	Lt. Trowbridge---------	------	-------------------
6331	♀	Benicia, Cal. -----------	----do--------	Lt. Williamson-----------	------	Dr. Heermann. ---------
5555	♀	Petaluma, Cal.----------	March, 1856 ..	E. Samuels. -----------	143	-------------------

PASSERCULUS ALAUDINUS, Bonap.

Passerculus alaudinus, Br. Comptes Rendus, XXXVII, Dec. 1853, 918, California.—Is. Notes Ornithologiques Delattre, 1854, 18. (Reprint of preceding.)

Sp. Ch.—Similar to *P. savanna,* but smaller ; the bill rather slenderer and elongated. Little of yellow in the superciliary stripe, (most distinct anteriorly); the rest of the head without any tinge of the same. General color much paler and grayer than in *P. savanna.* Breast with only a few spots. Length, 5.25 ; wing, 2.75 ; tail, 2.30.

Hab.—Coast of California, and Lower Rio Grande of Texas and Mexico.

This species, if really distinct from *P. savanna,* differs in the rather smaller size, although the difference is not great, and in the considerably paler colors. The superciliary stripe shows a very faint trace of yellow, especially anteriorly, near the bill. In some specimens, as 4342, there is none at all. The spots on the fore part of the breast are rather few and not large. The bill is slenderer and more attenuated.

List of specimens.

Catal. No.	Sex.	Locality.	When collected.	Whence obtained.	Orig. No.	Length.	Stretch of wings.	Wing.	Remarks.
6332	.....	Shoalwater bay, W. T..	Aug. 30, 1854	Dr. J. G. Cooper.	88	5.50	8.50	......	Iris brown ; bill and feet brownish flesh color.
5554	♂	Petaluma, Cal.	1856	E. Samuels.. ...	124	......	....	......	....
4340	......	Brownsville, Texas	Feb. —, 1853	Lieut. Couch....	....	4.75	7.75	2.50	Eyes dark brown ; bill and legs light brown..
4341	♂	Tamaulipas, Mexico....	Mar. —, 1853	......do	80	5.25	9.00	2.25	Eyes dark brown ; bill slate ; feet whitish ...
4344	......	.... .do.............	.....do......	......do	——	5.00	8.50	2.50	Eyes dark brown.......... ... .

PASSERCULUS ROSTRATUS, Baird.

Emberiza rostrata, Cassin, Pr. A. N. Sc. VI, 1852, 348.
Ammodramus rostratus, Cassin, Ill. I, 1855, 226 ; pl. xxxviii.

Sp. Ch.—Bill very long, (.55 of an inch above). Whole upper parts and sides of ead and neck pale grayish brown, nearly every feather with a darker central blotch, darkest along the shaft. A scarcely appreciable central stripe in the crown, and an obscure yellowish white superciliary, and a whitish maxillary one. Under parts pure white ; streaked on the breast and the sides of throat and body with dark brown, (the streak paler externally). Under tail coverts unspotted white. Tail and wing feathers and wings margined with the color of the back ; the edges of tertiaries rather paler. Length, 5.30 ; wing, 2.90 ; tail, 2.30.

Hab.—Coast of California, near San Diego.

The bill of this species is very long and conical, the cutting edge nearly straight. The wings are rather long, the tertiaries nearly as long in the closed wing as the primaries ; the second, third, and fourth quills longest, the first rather longer than the fifth. The tail is short and emarginate, the feathers narrow, acute, and moderately stiff. The tarsi are long ; the claws little curved.

This species resembles the *Passerculus savanna* rather more than any of the other sparrows with spotted breasts ; the bill is, however, very much longer and larger, exceeding any of our American species of its size. Its colors are much paler, and it lacks the yellow on the head and wing. The much shorter tail and entire absence of rufous distinguish it from the spotted *Melospizas.* The shape of the bill is like that of *Ammodramus caudacutus,* but larger ; the head lacks the yellow, &c.

List of specimens.

Catal. No.	Sex.	Locality.	Whence obtained.	Collected by—
6339	♂	San Diego, Cal.............	Lt. Williamson.................	Dr. Heermann........ ....
6340	♂	......do......................	......do........................	......do.......\.............

POOCÆTES, Baird.

Сн.—Bill rather large ; upper outline slightly decurved towards the end, lower straight; commissure slightly concave. Tarsus about equal to the middle toe ; outer toe a little longer than the inner, its claw reaching to the concealed base of the middle claw ; hind toe reaching to the middle of the middle claw. Wings unusually long, reaching to the middle of the tail, as far as the coverts, and pointed ; the primaries considerably longer than the secondaries, which are not much surpassed by the tertiaries; second and third quills longest; first little shorter, about equal to the fourth, shorter than the tail ; the outer feathers scarcely shorter ; the feathers rathers stiff ; each one acuminate and sharply pointed ; the feathers broad nearly to the end when they are obliquely truncate. Streaked with brown above everywhere ; beneath, on the breast and sides. The lateral tail feather is white.

The essential character of the genus consists in the long and pointed wings, longer than the tail and without long tertials ; and the rather stiff, forked tail, with its acute feathers.

In the long wings and short forked tail this form differs from our other plainly colored and streaked sparrows. It comes nearest to *Passerculus*, but the tail is stiffer and more forked ; the feathers more acute. The tertiaries are but little longer than the secondaries, instead of nearly or quite equal to the primaries. The middle toe is considerably shorter.

Comparative measurements.

Catal. No.	Species.	Locality.	Sex.	Length.	Stretch of wings.	Wing.	Tail.	Tarsus.	Middle toe.	Its claw alone.	Hind toe and claw.	Hind toe alone.	B above.	Along gape.	Specimen measured.
10147	Poocætes gramineus...	Washington, D. C. ..	♂	5.74	....	3.07	2.58	0.82	0.70	0.18	0.53	0.23	0.45	0.47	Skin ......
10146	........do...............	......do	♀	5.78	....	3.10	2.64	0.81	0.76	0.20	0.56	0.25	0.43	0.45	Skin ......
8945	.......do....,.......	Loup Fork	♀	5.81	....	3.37	3.10	0.89	0.79	0.24	0.55	0.26	0.49	0.50	Skin ......
8945	........do.............	......do	......	6.75	10.75	3.75	......	......	......	......	......	......	......	......	Fresh......

POOCÆTES GRAMINEUS, Baird.

Grass Finch ; Bay-winged Bunting.

Fringilla graminea, Gm. Syst. Nat. I, 1788, 922.—Aud. Orn. Biog. I, 1831, 473 : V. 502 ; pl. 90.
Emberiza graminea, Wilson, Am. Orn. IV, 1811, 51 ; pl. xxxi, f. 5.—Aud. Syn. 1839, 102.—Ib. Birds Amer. III, 1841, 65 ; pl. 159.
Fringilla (*Zonotrichia*) *graminea*, Swainson, F. B. Am. II, 1831, 254.
Zonotrichia graminea, Bon. List, 1838.—Ib. Conspectus, 1850, 478.

Sp. Сн.—Tail feathers rather acute. Above light yellowish brown ; the feathers everywhere streaked abruptly with dark brown, even on the sides of the neck, which are paler. Beneath yellowish white ; on the breast and sides of neck and body streaked with brown. A faint light superciliary and maxillary stripe ; the latter margined above and below with dark brown ; the upper stripe continued around the ear coverts, which are darker than the brown color elsewhere. Wings with the shoulder light chestnut brown, and with two dull whitish bands along the ends of the coverts ; the outer edge of the secondaries also is white. Outer tail feather, and edge and tip of the second white. Length, about 6.25 ; wing, 3.10.

Hab.—United States from Atlantic to the Pacific ; or else one species to the high central plains, and another from this to the Pacific

In autumn the dark streaks are less sharply defined, and there is a tinge of very pale cinnamon on the breast.

The form of this species differs considerably from that of *Melospiza melodia*. The bill is less sinuated along the edge of the mandible. The wing is much longer, and more pointed; the first quill nearly as long as the fourth; the second and third equal, and longest. The tail feathers are acuminate, pointed, and quite stiff; the toes are shorter; the claws rather straighter.

I find a good deal of difference in specimens before me, but I am unable to say how important these are for want of a sufficient number of eastern skins to determine the limits of variation in the species. Western specimens, however, appear larger, grayer, and with fewer and narrower streaks on the breast; the legs in some appear longer; the bill more slender. The colors generally are more gray. Young birds of the western variety are marked almost exactly like the adults, except that they are paler above; the feathers edged broadly with light grayish. Without being assured that there is a difference of species, it may be as well to recognize a western variety *confinis*, characterised as grayer than the eastern species, legs and wings longer, bill more slender and straighter, streaks on the breast narrower.

List of specimens.

Catal. No.	Sex and age.	Locality.	When collected.	Whence obtained.	Orig'l No.	Collected by—	Length.	Stretch of wings.	Wing.	Remarks.
......	....	Red river, Min.........	....	N. W. University..	....	R. Kennicott.....	....	....	......	....
10264	....	Union county, Illinois..	April 20, 1857	......do.........	......	...do........	....	....	......	....
713	♀	Carlisle, Pa...........	Sept. 8, 1842	S. F. Baird........	....	....	......	....	......	....
1047	∞♀	......do...........	June 3, 1843	......do........	......	......do........	....	....	......	....
19	♀	Washington	April 15, 1842	Wm. M. Baird	....	J. C. McGuire ...	....	....	......	....
10147	♂	......do	......do......	......do........	......	......do........	....	....	......	....
10146	♀	......do	......do......	......do........	......	o........	....	....	......	....
5408	....	Yellowstone, Neb.....	July 19, 1854	Lt. G. K. Warren...	....	Dr. Hayden.....	....	....	... ...	....
5407	♂	......do	......do.. ...	......do..........	....	......do........	4.50	9.90	2.87	....
6219	....	Fort Union, Neb......	Aug. 11, 1853	Gov. Stevens........	....	Dr. Suckley.....	....	....	......	....
5406	♀	......do	July 19, 1856	Lt. G. K. Warren..	....	Dr. Hayden	6.00	10.37	3.25	Iris dark brown....
5404	♂	...... do	...... do........	......do..........	....	......do........	6.50	10.87	3.50	....
5405	♂	Yellowstone river, Neb.	...... do........	......do..........	....	......do........	6.00	10.50	3.25	Iris dark brown....
5714	♀	Pole creek, K. T......	Aug. 4, 1856	Lt. Bryan..........	191	W. S. Wood......	....	....	......	....
5713	♀	......do..	......do......	......do..........	260	......do	....	....	......	.. ..
5712	♀	Medicine Butte c'k, K.T.	Aug. 7, 1856	......do..........	223	......do........	....	....	......	....
5711	♂	......do...........	Aug. 25, 1856	......do..........	303	......do........	6.25	....	......	....
7085	....	Black Hills	July 21, 1857	Dr. W. A. Hammond	54	....	....	....	......	....
8943	....	Black Hills, Neb.....	Sept. 24, 1857	Lt. Warren........	....	Dr. Hayden......	6.25	11.50	3.25	Iris brown........
8944	♀	......do...........	Aug. 18, 1857	......do..........	....	......do........	6.75	10.50	2.75	...do ....
8945	♀	Loup fork of Platte...	July 29, 1857	......do..........	......	......do........	6.75	10.75	3.75	....
8942	♂	......do..	...... do......	......do..........	....	......do........	6.00	10.25	3.25	....
8947	♀	......do...........	...... do......	......do..........	......	......do........	6.40	10.75	3.25	....
8796	....	Near Laramie	Aug. 26, 1857	W. M. Magraw	169	Dr. J. G. Cooper.	6.50	10.50	3.50	Iris br'n; bill black and flesh color; feet gray.........
8208	....	Fort Laramie	Sept. 8, 1857	......do	190	......do	7.25?	10.12	3.25	Iris brown; bill and feet flesh color.
4343	♂	Tamaulipas, Mex	Aug. —, 1853	Lt. Couch..........	56	....	5.75	9.00	3.00	Eyes dark; upper mandible slate color; lower lighter; feet light brown..
4344	♀	......do	Mar. —, 1853	......do	44	....	5.00	8.75	3.75	...do.......do ....
6220	....	Boca Grande, Mex.....	Mar. —, 1855	Major Emory.....	37	Dr. Kennerly	....	....	......	....
6221	....	Espia, Mex.	..... do.........	...do............	61	......do	....	....	......	....
6222	....	Tejon Valley, Cal.....	....	Lt. Williamson.....	....	Dr. Heermann..	....	....	......	....
6223	....	...do	....	...do............	....	......do	....	....	......	....
6224	....	Fort Steilacoom, W. T.	....	Dr. G. Suckley.....	....	....	....	....	......	....

COTURNICULUS, Bonaparte.

Coturniculus, BONAPARTE, Geog. List, 1838.   Type *Fringilla passerina*, Wils.

Bill very large and stout ; the under mandible broader, but lower than the upper, which is considerably convex at the basal portion of its upper outline.   Legs moderate, apparently not reaching to the end of the tail.   The tarsus appreciably longer than the middle toe ; the lateral toes equal, and with their claws falling decidedly short of the middle claw ; the hind toe intermediate between the two.   The wings are short and rounded, reaching to the base of the tail ; the tertiaries almost as long as the primaries ; not much difference in the lengths of the primaries, although the outer three or four are slightly graduated. The tail is short and narrow, decidedly shorter than the wing, graduated laterally, but slightly emarginate ; the feathers all lanceolate and acute, but not stiffened, as in *Ammodromus*.

The upper parts generally are streaked ; the blotches on the interscapular region very wide.   The breast and sides are generally streaked more or less distinctly.   The edge of the wing is yellow.

This genus agrees with *Passerculus* in the short and narrow tail.   The wings are much shorter and more rounded ; the feet shorter, especially the middle toe, which is not as long as the tarsus.   The tail feathers are more lanceolate.   The bill is much larger, and more swollen at the base.

The essential characters of this genus consist in the swollen convex bill ; the short toes compared with the tarsus ; the short and rounded wings ; and the very small, narrow, slightly graduated tail, with its lanceolate acute feathers.

In some respects there is a resemblance to *Ammodromus*, in which, however, the bill is very much more slender ; the wings still shorter, and more rounded ; the tail feathers much stiffer, and even more lanceolate ; the toes extending beyond the tip of the tail ; the middle toe rather longer than the tarsus, instead of considerably shorter.

Synopsis of species.

Head without a median stripe above ; body beneath whitish ; the sides and across the breast light brownish, without any streaks.   Sides of head ashy...*C. manimbe.*[1]

Head with a median light stripe.   Breast and sides of head and body yellowish brown, with obsolete streaks of darker.   Neck above streaked with rufous..........................*C. passerinus.*

Head with a median light stripe.   Under parts reddish white, conspicuously streaked on the breast and sides with black.   Head and neck above tinged with greenish yellow.....*C. henslowi.*

Head with a median light stripe.   Under parts fine buff, with a yellowish white median line. Sides streaked, but not the breast.   Above light yellowish red, streaked with brownish black..*C. lecontii.*

Comparative measurements of the species.

Catal. No.	Species.	Locality.	Sex.	Length.	Stretch of wings.	Wing.	Tail.	Tarsus.	Middle toe.	Its claw alone.	Hind toe and claw.	Hind claw alone.	Bill above.	Along gape.	Specimen measured.
1807	Coturniculus manimbe...	South America	......	5.52	......	2.27	2.03	0.77	0.69	0.18	0.58	0.24	0.44	0.49	Skin ......
731	Coturniculus passerinus..	Carlisle, Pa..........	♂	5.09	......	2.51	2.13	0.71	0.68	0.14	0.50	0.22	0.42	0.48	Skin ......
do.	......do	......do	......	4.37	8.00	2.62	......	......	......	......	......	......	......	......	Fresh....
1728	......do	......do	♀	4.80	......	2.34	1.96	0.74	0.66	0.14	0.57	0.24	0.43	0.49	Skin ......
do.	......do	......do	......	5.16	8.16	2.42	......	......	......	......	......	......	......	......	Fresh......
10242	Coturniculus henslowi ...	Liberty county, Ga...	......	4.78	......	2.05	2.14	0.63	0.64	0.12	0.67	0.23	0.46	0.43	Skin ......
1897	......do	Washington, D. C....	?	4.92	......	2.22	2.29	0.66	0.73	0.14	0.60	0.25	0.47	0.48	Skin ......

[1] COTURNICULUS MANIMBE, Cabanis.—South America, Brazil.
Fringilla manimbe, LICHT. Verz. 1823, 25.
Coturniculus manimbe, CABANIS, Mus. Hein. 1851, 133.

COTURNICULUS PASSERINUS, Bonap.

Yellow-winged Sparrow.

Fringilla passerina, WILSON, Am. Orn. III, 1811, 76 ; pl. xxvi, f. 5.—AUDUB. Orn. Biog. II, 1834, 180 : V, 497 ; pl. 130.

Fringilla (Spiza) passerina, BON. Obs. Wils. 1825, No. 111.

Coturniculus passerina, BONAP. List, 1838.—IB. Conspectus, 1850, 481.

Emberiza passerina, AUD. Syn. 1839.—IB. Birds Amer. III, 1841, 73 ; pl. 162.

Fringilla savanarum, (GM.) NUTTALL, Man. I, 1832, 494.—IB. 2d ed. 1840, 570.—(An GMELIN, Syst. Nat. I, 1788, 921.)

?? *Fringilla caudacuta*, LATH. Ind. Orn. I, 1790, 459.—NUTT. Man. I, 1832, 505.

? *Passerina pratensis*, VIEILLOT.

SP. CH.—Feathers of the upper parts brownish rufous, margined narrowly and abruptly with ash color ; reddest on the lower part of the back and rump ; the feathers all abruptly black in the central portion ; this color visible on the interscapular region where the rufous is more restricted. Crown blackish, with a central and superciliary stripe of yellowish tinged with brown, brightest in front of the eye. Bend of the wing bright yellow ; lesser coverts tinged with greenish yellow. Quills and tail feathers edged with whitish ; tertiaries much variegated. Lower parts brownish yellow, nearly white on the middle of the belly. The feathers of the upper breast and sides of the body with obsoletely darker centres. Length, about 5 inches ; wing, 2.40 ; tail, 2.

Hab.—Eastern United States to the High Central plains, (Loup Fork.) Also, along the valley of Gila and Colorado.

The young of this species has the upper part of the breast streaked with black, much more distinct than in the adult, and exhibiting a close resemblance to *C. henslowi*.

Specimens from the far west have the reddish of the back considerably paler ; the light stripe on the head, with scarcely any yellow ; a decided spot in front of the eye quite yellow.

This species is not dissimilar in general appearance to *Peucaea bachmani ;* it is, however, smaller, tail much shorter, &c.; the marking also differs considerably. It is distinguished from *henslowi* by the absence of distinct spots on the breast. *C. manimbe*, of South America, lacks the red of the rump, and the median stripe on the head ; the sides of the head are more ashy ; the breast is tinged with brownish ash, but there are no indications whatever of even obsolete streaks.

The Savannah finch, of Latham, II, 270, from Jamaica, (upon which Gmelin's *Fringilla savannarum* is based,) answers in a general way, and may, possibly, be the same species, but in the great uncertainty on the subject I do not follow Nuttall in adopting the name. The *Fringilla caudacuta*, of Latham, also has some relationship to this species, but is equally indefinite.

List of specimens.

Catal. No.	Sex and age.	Locality.	When collected.	Whence obtained.	Orig'l No.	Collected by—	Length.	Stretch of wings.	Wing.	Remarks.
731	♂	Carlisle, Pa...........	Sept. 20, 1842	S. F. Baird..... .	......	....	4.37	8.00	2.62	....
1728	♀	......do...............	Oct. 23, 1844	......do..........	......	....	5.16	8.16	2.43	....
1121	○	... ..do.....	July 15, 1843	......do..........	......	....	....	....	......	....
8183	♂	Shawnee Mission, K. T.	July 3, 1857	Wm. M. Magraw..	119	Dr. Cooper ..	5.25	8.25	2.62	Iris brown ; bill slate and flesh; feet brown......
8188	♂	......do...............	July 4, 1857	......do..........	122	..... do... ..	5.00	8.25	2.62	......do........do ......
8184	♂	.... do...............	July —, 1857	Lieut. Warren ...	120	Dr. Hayden..	5.25	7.87	2.25	......do........do ......
8972	♂	Loup Fork	July 27......	......do..........	......	..... do......	5.25	8.50	2.50	....
8971	♀	......do...............	July 21	......do..........	......	..... do......	5.12	8.25	2.37	....
8974	......	......do...............	Aug. 3.......	......do..........	......	..... do......	4.67	7.75	2.75	Iris light brown..........
8973	♀	......do...............	July 27	......do..........	......	..... do......	4.75	8.25	2.50	....
8978	♀	......do...............	July 24	......do..........	......	..... do......	5.50	9.00	2.50	....
8969	♂	......do...............	Aug. 3.......	......do..........	......	..... do......	5.12	8.37	2.50	....
8970	♂	......do...............	July 3	......do..........	......	..... do......	4.87	8.00	2.50	Iris brown................
8977	♂	......do...............	July 27	......do..........	......	..... do......	4.75	8.50	2.62	....
8966	♂	......do...............	July 28	......do....	......	..... do......	4.75	8.00	2.50	....
8976	♂	......do...............	July 3	......do..........	......	..... do......	5.12	8.62	2.62	....
8975	♀	......do............	July 27	......do..........	......	..... do......	4.87	8.25	2.25	....
6334	....	Bill Williams' Fork, N.M.	....	Lieut. Whipple..	175	Dr. Kennerly.	......	....	....	Eyes black............
6333	....	Los Nogales, Mexico...	June —, 1855	Major Emory.....	85	..... do......	....	....	....	....

COTURNICULUS HENSLOWI, Bonap.

Henslow's Bunting.

Emberiza henslowi, Aud. Orn. Biog. I, 1831, 360 ; pl. 77.—Ib. Syn. 1839, 104.—Ib. Birds Amer. III, 1841, 75 ; pl.
163.—Nuttall, Man. I, 1832. App.
Coturniculus henslowi, Bon. List, 1838.—Ib. Conspectus, 1850, 481.
Fringilla henslowi, Nuttall, Man. I, (2d ed.) 1840, 571.

Sp. Ch.—Upper parts yellowish brown. The hood, neck, and upper parts of back tinged with greenish yellow. Interscapular feathers dark brown, suffused externally with bright brownish red ; each feather with grayish borders. Tertiaries, rump, and tail feathers abruptly dark brown centrally, the color obscurely margined with dark red. Crown with a broad black spotted stripe on each side ; these spots continued down to the back. Two narrow black maxillary stripes on each side the head, and an obscure black crescent behind the auriculars. Under parts light brownish yellow, paler on the throat and abdomen. The upper part of the breast, and the sides of the body, conspicuously streaked with black. Edge of wing yellow. A strong tinge of pale chestnut on the wings and tail. Length, 5.25 ; wing, 2.15 ; tail, 2.15.

Hab.—Eastern United States as far north as Washington ; westward to the Loup Fork of Platte.

There are few birds whose colors are more difficult to describe than those of *Coturniculus henslowi* and *passerinus.* Far from having exhausted all the varied patterns and tints of the present species, I have, however, given enough to show the principal differences from its allies.

The bill is very thick and large ; the wings very short ; the tertiaries as long as the primaries ; the first five primaries nearly equal. The tail feathers are stiff, very narrow, and acute ; pointed on both webs ; the tail itself considerably graduated.

A specimen from Kansas (5716) has the under part dirty white ; the spots smaller, fewer, and more sharply defined. The distinct spots on the breast, and the yellowish head and neck above, without ashy margin, will readily distinguish this species from *C. passerinus;* the reddish being also confined to the interscapular region. The form of the two is, however, much the same.

Western specimens are paler in tint, with the streaks on the under parts smaller and narrower.

List of specimens.

Catal. No.	Sex.	Locality.	When collected.	Whence obtained.	Orig. No.	Collected by—	Length.	Stretch of wings.	Wing.	Remarks.
10243	....	Liberty county, Ga.....	Dec. —, 1848	Prof. Jos. Leconte.	......	....	......	....	......	....
1897	....	Unknown	....	S. F. Baird	......	....	......	....	......	....
1111	♂	Prince-George's, Md....	July 4, 1843	......do	......	W. M. Baird	5.25	7.12	2.17	....
5716	♀	East of Fort Riley, K. T.	June 13, 1856	Lieut. F. T. Bryan.	7	W. S. Wood......	......	....	......	....
8968	....	Loup Fork of Platte ...	June 10, 1857	Lieut. Warren.....	......	Dr. Hayden......	4.75	6.88	2.12	Iris brown..........

COTURNICULUS LECONTII, Bonap.

Leconte's Bunting.

Emberiza lecontii, Aud. Birds Amer. VII, 1843, 338; pl. 488.
Coturniculus lecontii, Bon. Conspectus, 1850, 481.

Sp. Ch.—" Bill much more slender than in *Emberiza henslowi*. First quill the longest, the rest diminishing rapidly. Tail emarginate and rounded, with the feathers acute. Upper parts light yellowish red, streaked with brownish black; the margins of the feathers and scapulars pale yellowish white. Tail feathers dusky, margined with light yellowish. Lower parts, with the cheeks and a broad band over the eyes, fine buff. Medial line yellowish white. The buff extending to the femorals and along the sides, streaked with brownish black. Throat, neck, and upper parts of the breast without any streaks, and plain buff."

Hab.—Mouth of Yellowstone.

" Length, 4.40; wing, 2.13, first quill longest; tail, 1.90; bill along ridge, .37, along edge, nearly .50; both mandibles dark blue, lighter along the edges. Eyes brown. Legs, feet, and claws dull flesh color. Tarsus, .56; middle toe, .50; its claw, .12; hind toe, .24, its claw rather more than .25."

I am obliged to copy the description of this rare sparrow from Mr. Audubon, as I have no skin at hand. The type of the species was presented to me many years ago by Mr. Audubon, but it has somehow been mislaid. I do not feel sure that it is not an *Ammodramus* rather than a *Coturniculus*.

AMMODROMUS, Swainson.

Ammodramus, Swainson, Zool. Jour. III, 1827. Type *Oriolus caudacutus*, Gm.

Ch.—Bill very long, slender, and attenuated, considerably curved towards the tip above. The gonys straight. The legs and toes are very long, and reach considerably beyond the tip of the short tail. The tarsus is about equal to the elongated middle toe; the lateral toes equal, their claws falling considerably short of the base of the middle one; the hind claw equal to the lateral one. Wings short, reaching only to the base of the tail; much rounded; the secondaries and tertials equal, and not much shorter than the primaries. The tail is short, and graduated laterally; each feather stiffened, lanceolate, and acute.

Color.—Streaked above and across the breast; very faintly on the sides.

The essential characters are the slender and elongated bill, more so than in any other North American sparrows; the long legs reaching considerably beyond the tail, with the lateral claws falling considerably short of the middle one; the very short rounded wings, and the cuneate tail, with its stiffened and lanceolate feathers.

A species, *A. samuelis*, is closely related, although more densely streaked below, and with less stiffened and lanceolate tail feathers. It is, in some points, more like *Fringilla palustris*.

Synopsis of species.

Bill blue; a yellow spot in front of the eye; above nearly uniform olivaceous; a white maxillary stripe, with a black one below it; breast with obsolete plumbeous streaks....*A. maritimus.*

Under mandible yellowish ; a superciliary and maxillary stripe light chestnut, the latter bordered below by black ; feathers of back sharply edged with yellowish ; breast and sides tinged with brownish yellow with very distinct streaks ....*A. caudacutus.*

Back with distinct dusky streaks, but without well defined light edges; beneath white ; sides of neck and body, and across the breast, with black streaks; maxillary stripe white; wing coverts orange rufous, and no yellow on the edge of the wing...........................*A. samuelis.*

Comparative measurements of species.

Catal. No.	Species.	Locality.	Sex.	Length.	Stretch of wings.	Wing.	Tail.	Tarsus.	Middle toe.	Its claw alone.	Hind toe and claw.	Hind toe alone.	Bill above.	Along gape.	Specimen measured.
7111	Ammodramus maritimus...	Philadelphia.........	......	5.74	......	2.47	2.55	0.90	0.90	0.20	0.66	0 30	0.57	0.60	Skin ......
609	Ammodramus caudacutus ..	Cape May, N. J....	♂	4.94	......	2.30	2.07	0.80	0.79	0.19	0.58	0.26	0.50	0.56	Skin ......
7098	Ammodramus samuelis	Petaluma, Cal......	♂	5.30	......	2.42	2.56	0.82	0.76	0.20	0.58	0.26	0.50	0.54	Skin ......
do.	.........do	.......do	......	5.50	6.75	2.50	......	......	......	......	......	......	......	......	Fresh......
5553	.........do	.......do	♂	5.08	......	2.20	2.50	0.76	0.74	0.18	0.52	0.25	0.51	0.52	Skin ......

AMMODROMUS CAUDACUTUS, Swainson.

Sharp-tailed Finch.

Oriolus caudacutus, GMELIN, I, 1788, 394.—LATHAM, Ind. Orn. I, 1790, 186. (Not *Fringilla caudacuta,* LATH.)
Fringilla caudacuta, WILSON, Am. Orn. IV, 1811, 70 ; pl. xxxiv, f. 3.—AUD. Orn. Biog. II, 1834, 281 : V, 499 ; pl. 149.
Fringilla (Spiza) caudacuta, BON. Syn. 1828, 110.
Passerina caudacuta, VIEILLOT.
Ammodromus caudacutus, SWAINSON, Birds, II, 1837, 289.—AUD. Synopsis, 1839, 111.—IB. Birds Amer. III, 1841, 108 ; pl. 174.—BONAP. Conspectus, 1850, 482.
Fringilla littoralis, NUTTALL, Man. I, 1832, 504. (2d ed. 1840, 590.)
Sharp-tailed oriole, PENNANT, Arctic Zool. II, 261. New York.

SP. CH.—Upper parts brownish olivaceous. Head brownish, streaked with black on the sides, and a broad central stripe of ashy. Back blotched with darker. A broad superciliary and maxillary stripe, and a band across the upper breast buff yellow. The sides of the throat with a brown stripe ; the upper part of the breast, and the sides of the body streaked with black ; rest of under parts white. Edge of wing yellowish white. Length, 5 inches ; wing, 2.30.

Hab.—Atlantic coast of the United States.

The young is of a more yellowish tinge above and below ; the streaks on the back more conspicuous ; the scapular feathers without the whitish edging.

List of specimens.

Catal. No.	Sex and age.	Locality.	When collected.	Whence obtained.	Collected by—
1954	o	Rayner S. Long Island ...	Aug. 4, 1831......	S. F. Baird	G. N. Lawrence..........
496	....	New York............	....	.......do	John G. Bell............
609	♂	Cape May, N. J..........	June —, 1840.....	.......do	W. M. Baird...........

AMMODROMUS MARITIMUS, Swainson.

Sea-side Finch.

Fringilla maritima, WILSON, Am. Orn. IV, 1811, 68 ; pl. xxxiv, f. 2.—AUD. Orn. Biog. 1, 1831 ; pl. 93.
Ammodramus maritimus, Sw. Zool. Jour. III, 1827, 328. (*Type.*)—BONAP. List, 1838.—IB. Consp. 1850, 482.—AUD.
          Synopsis, 1839, 110.—IB. Birds Am. III, 1841, 103 ; pl. 172.
Fringilla (Ammodramus) maritima, NUTT. Man. I, (2d ed.) 1840, 592.
Fringilla macgillivrayi, AUD. Orn. Biog. II, 1834, 285 : IV, 1838, 394 : V, 1839, 499 ; pl. 355.
Ammodramus macgillivrayi, BON. List, 1838.—IB. Conspectus, 1850, 482.—AUD. Syn. 1839.—IB. Birds Amer. III,
          1841, 106 ; pl. 173.
Fringilla (Ammodramus) macgillivrayi, NUTTALL, Man. I, 2d ed. 1840, 593.

SP. CH.—Above olivaceous brown ; beneath white ; the breast and sides of body yellowish brown, obsoletely streaked with
plumbeous. Sides of head and body, a central stripe on the head above, a maxillary stripe, and indistinct longitudinal streaks
on the breast, ashy brown ; the sides and the breast tinged with yellowish. The maxillary stripe cuts off a white one
above it ; a superciliary stripe is bright yellow anterior to the eye, and plumbeous above and behind it. Edge of wing
yellow ; bill blue. Length, about 6 inches ; wing, 2.50.
Hab.—Atlantic coast as far at least as Long Island.

The appearance of streaks on the breast is caused by the feathers being plumbeous, and edged
with dirty brownish yellow. The scapular feathers are edged with grayish, the wing coverts
and tertial with rufous. The region around the eye is dark brown ; the sides of the head above,
and the back of the neck faintly streaked with blackish.

A bird in the collection of the Philadelphia Academy, labelled *Ammodramus macgillivrayi*,
has much the appearance of a young bird of *A. maritimus*. The bill, feet, wings and tail
are almost exactly the same. The chief differences are in the less distinctness of the yellow at
the base of the bill, the edge of the wing being white, instead of yellow ; the under parts dirty
white, with sharply defined narrow dusky streaks across the breast, instead of the obscure
dusky broad centres of *maritimus*. This, however, is common in young sparrows, even where
the adults are unspotted beneath, and the looseness of the plumage, and its downy character
are such as to render it very probable that the full plumage has not been attained. It is
different from *A. caudacutus* in the larger size, especially of the bill, and the lack of the brownish
yellow on the sides of the head, as of the light edges of the dorsal feathers. Another specimen,
(4362,) from Beesley's Point, New Jersey, and unquestionably very young, as the bill is not
fully grown, has the back and head conspicuously streaked with dark brown, without lighter
edges ; the streaks on the breast and sides as well defined as those of *A. caudacutus*.

List of specimens.

Catal. No.	Sex & age.	Locality.	When collected.	Whence obtained.	Collected by—	Length.	Stretch of wings.	Wing.
1153	♂	Cape May, N. J.	July 20, 1843	S. F. Baird	W. M. Baird	5.75	8.17	2.42
608	♂	......do............	June —, 1840	....do.	.......do.			
2894	o	Unknown		....do.				
4362	o	Beesley's point, N. J.	Aug. —, 1856	....do.				
7497	......	New Jersey		Acad. Nat. Sciences.				

AMMODROMUS SAMUELIS, Baird.

Ammodromus samuelis, BAIRD, Pr. Boston Soc. N. H. for June, 1858.

Sp. Ch.—Somewhat like *Melospiza melodia*, but considerably smaller and darker. Bill slender, attenuated, and acute. Tarsus not longer than middle toe and claw. Above streaked on the head, neck, and rump with dark brown, the borders of the feathers paler, but without any rufous. Beneath bluish white ; the middle of the breast, with sides of throat and body, spotted and streaked with blackish brown. Wings above nearly uniform dark brownish rufous. Under tail coverts yellowish brown, conspicuously blotched with blackish. An ashy superciliary stripe, becoming nearly white to the bill, and a whitish maxillary one ; the crown with faint grayish median line. Length, 5 inches ; wing, 2.20 ; tail, 2.35.

This species is somewhat similar in pattern of coloration to the *Melospiza melodia*, but is readily distinguished on comparison. It is much smaller, the bill longer and much more slender, attenuated and acute. The wing is more rounded ; the first primary is shortest of all, and less than the secondaries. The middle toe appears unusually long. The colors throughout are much darker than in *Melospiza melodia*, the streaks blacker, more abrupt and numerous, and without the light reddish brown margins. The rump, and upper and under tail coverts are strongly streaked with blackish, instead of being nearly immaculate. The wings appear more conspicuously and darkly rufous.

The abrupt blackish spots and streaks will readily distinguish this species from the Californian spotted *Melospizas*, except *hermannii*, but it is smaller, with much shorter wings and slenderer bill.

There is a considerable difference in the proportions of the feet compared with *M. melodia*. Thus the middle toe is so much elongated that, with its claw, it is as long or even longer than the tarsus, instead of shorter.

The precise position of this species in the series is a matter of uncertainty. It appears to connect *Ammodromus* and *Melospiza*. The bill and wings are those of the former, while in general coloration it is most like the *Melospiza melodia*. It is not unlikely, in fact, that it may be quite properly placed in the latter genus, and be called *M. samuelis*.

The spots on the breast appear farther back than in other spotted species, leaving a greater extent of throat without marking. The pectoral spots exhibit a tendency to aggregation in the middle of the breast.

List of specimens.

Catal. No.	Sex.	Locality.	When collected.	Whence obtained.	Length.	Stretch of wings.	Wing.
5523	♂	Petaluma, Cal.	May 9, 1856	E. Samuels			
7098	♂	......do........	......do........	......do........	5.50	6.75	2.50

CHONDESTES, Swainson.

Chondestes, SWAINSON, Phil. Mag. I, 1827, 435.—IB. Fauna Bor. Amer. II, 1831. Type *Chondestes strigatus*, Sw., equal to *Fringilla grammaca*, Say.

Ch.—Bill swollen ; both outlines gently curved ; the lower mandible as high as the lower ; the commissure angulated at the base, and then slightly sinuated. Lower mandible rather narrower at the base than the length of the gonys ; broader than the upper. Tarsi moderate, about equal to the middle toe ; lateral toes equal and very short, reaching but little beyond the middle of the penultimate joint of the middle toe, and falling considerably short of the base of the middle claw. Wings long, pointed, reaching nearly to the middle of the tail ; the tertials not longer than the secondaries ; the first quill shorter than the second and third, which are equal. The tail is moderately long, considerably graduated, the feathers rather narrow, and elliptically rounded at the end.

Streaked on the back. Head with well defined large stripes. Beneath white, with a pectoral spot.

But one species of this genus is at present known. The comparative measurements of different specimens are as follows :

Comparative measurements.

Catal. No.	Species.	Locality.	Sex.	Length.	Wing.	Tail.	Tarsus.	Middle toe.	Its claw alone.	Hind toe & claw.	Hind toe alone.	Bill above.	Along gape.	Specimen measured.
1903	Chondestes grammaca .	Fort Union.......	♀	5.40	3.25	2.69	0.81	0.80	0.19	0.54	0.24	0.48	0.53	Skin ....
10267	......do...............	North Illinois	♂	6.84	3.69	3.54	0.77	0.77	0.20	0.51	0.24	0.48	0.53	Skin ....
1902	......do...............	Fort Union, Neb..	♂	5.70	3.25	2.80	0.78	0.78	0.22	0.56	0.25	0.46	0.53	Skin ....
5557	......do..............	Petaluma, Cal.....	♂	6.10	3.37	3.23	0.80	0.80	0.22	0.56	0.26	0.49	0.52	Skin ....

CHONDESTES GRAMMACA, Bonap.

Lark Finch.

Fringilla grammaca, SAY, in Long's Exped. R. Mts. I, 1823, 139.—BON. Am. Orn. I, 1825, 47 ; pl. v, f. 3.—AUD. Orn. Biog. V, 1839, 17 ; pl. 390.

Chondestes grammaca, BON. List, 1838.—IB. Conspectus, 1850, 479.

Emberiza grammaca, AUD. Synopsis, 1839, 101.—IB. Birds Amer. III, 1841, 63 ; pl. 158.

Chondestes strigatus, SWAINSON, Philos. Mag. I, 1827, 435.

SP. CH.—Hood chestnut, tinged with black towards the forehead, and with a median stripe and superciliary stripe of dirty whitish. Rest of upper parts pale grayish brown, the interscapular region streaked with dark brown. Beneath white, a round spot on the upper part of the breast, a maxillary stripe and a short line from the bill to the eye, continued faintly behind it, black. A white crescent under the eye, bordered below by black and behind by chestnut. Tail feathers dark brown, tipped broadly with white. Length, 6 inches ; wing, 3.30.

Hab.—From Wisconsin and the prairies of Illinois (also in Michigan ?) to the Pacific coast ; south to Texas and Mexico.

The black maxillary stripe does not reach quite to the base of the bill ; it cuts off above a white band, that curves round back of the chestnut colored auriculars, which turn into black anteriorly under the eye. The entire outer web of the first tail feather and about an inch of the tip are white ; the white of the other feathers decreases to the one next the innermost, which is like the back. The outer edges of the primaries are white, the color widening towards the base. The other wing feathers also have paler margins. There are two whitish bands across the coverts.

The colors of the female are duller than in the male ; the black markings very indistinct.

The young bird has the breast and throat with a good many spots of dark brown instead of the single large one on the breast. The other markings are more obscure.

Specimens vary considerably in size, as will be seen by reference to the table of measurements.

List of specimens.

Catal. No.	Sex.	Locality.	When collected.	Whence obtained.	Orig. No.	Collected by—	Length.	Stretch of wings.	Wing.	Remarks.
10267	......	West Northfield, Ill.....	April 28, 1855	N. W. University...	......	R. Kennicott...	......	......	......	......
10266	......	Cairo, Ill..............	May 9, 1857	......do...........	......	......do.......	......	......	......	......
4820	♂	Upper Missouri	May 14, 1856	Lt. G. K. Warren..	......	Dr. Hayden....	6.50	11.00	3.50	Iris light brown; pupil black.
4821	♂	......do..............	......do.....	......do...	......	......do.......	6.37	9.75	3.50	......do..............
4822	♂	Big Sioux river........	......do......	......do...........	......	......do.......	6.50	11.00	3.50	......
4823	♂	......do........	May 14.......	......do...........	......	......do.......	6.37	10.62	3.75	......
5384	♂	Fort Lookout, Neb.....	June 22	......do...........	......	......do.......	6.50	11.12	3.62	Iris light brown; pupil black.
5385	♂	......do........	..... do.....	......do...........	......	......do.......	6.75	11.00	2.75	...do........
5382	♂	Powder river, Neb......	Aug. 1, 1856	......do...........	......	......do.......	6.50	10.75	3.50	......do.......
5383	♂	......do........	Aug. 4, 1856	......do...........	......	......do.......	6.50	11.00	3.00	......do..... .....
1902	♂	Fort Union, Neb.......	June —, 1843	S. F. Baird........	......	J. J. Audubon...	......	......	......	......
1903	♀	......do.......	....	......do...........	......	......do.......	......	......	......	......
5890	......	Fort Riley, K. T........	....	Dr. Hammond.....	......	Mr. De Vesey ...	......	......	......	......
5701	♀	Repub. Fork, K. T.....	Oct. 18, 1856	Lt. Bryan..........	385	W. S. Wood...	......	......	......	......
5700	♀	Platte river, K. T.... ..	July 19, 1856	......do...........	123	......do.......	......	......	......	......
8333	♂	Independence, Mo......	May 6, 1857	Wm. M. Magraw ...	56	Dr. Cooper.....	6.75	11.00	3.50	Iris brown; bill black; feet grayish.
8328	♀	......do...:...........	June 3, 1857	......do...........	51	......do.......	6.75	11.25	3.25	;.....do....
8376	♂	......do........	Jan. —, 1857	......do...........	......	......do.......	7.00	10.50	3.25	......do....
7531	......	......do........	....	......do...........	......	......do.... ..	......	......	......	......
9228	♂	Loup Fork............	August 5.....	Lt. Warren........	......	Dr. Hayden	7.12	11.25	3.75	Iris dark brown ....
9229	♀	......do............	August 4.....	......do.......•....	......	......do.......	5.75	10.25	3.25	,Iris gray?.............
9238	♀	......do............	......do.....	......do...........	......	......do.......	7.00	10.75	3.50	Iris brown ....
9234	♂	......do............	July 30, 1857	......do...........	......	......do.......	6.75	10.75	3.50	Iris gray?.............
9230	♀	......do............	August 6.....	......do...........	......	......do.......	7.00	......	3.50	Iris brown ....
9233	♂	......do........ ..	July 28.......	..... do	......	......do.......	6.25	10 50	3.25	......
9236	♀	......do............	August 5.....	......do...........	......	......do.......	6.75	10.75	3.50	Iris brown ....
9235	♀♂	......do............	July 27.......	......do...........	......	......do.......	6.75	11.00	3.50	......
9231	♂♂	......do.	August 4.....	......do...........	......	......do.......	6.50	11.25	3.75	Iris dark brown........
9232	♂	Fremont, on Platte.....	July 1........	......do...........	......	......do.......	6.75	10.25	3.25	......
9237	♀	Sand Hills............	August 12.....	......do...........	......	......do.......	7.00	11.00	3.50	Iris brown ....
5031	......	Western Texas........	....	Capt. J. Pope .,....	......	......	......	......	......	......
4968	......	Fort Chadbourne, Texas.	....	Dr. Swift, U. S. A..	......	......	......	......	......	......
4083	♀	New Leon, Mexico	....	Lt. Couch..........	147	....	6.00	10.00	3.25	Eyes brown; bill bluish lead color; feet dark flesh color.
6295	......	Fort Thorne, N. M	....	Dr. T. C. Henry....	......	......	......	......	......	......
4590	......	Colorado river, Cal.....	Dec. 30, 1854	Major Emory	31	A. Schott	......	......	......	......
6299	♂	Tejon Valley, Cal......	....	Lt. Williamson....	......	Dr. Heermann....	......	......	......	......
5557	♂	Petaluma, Cal...:.....	....	E. Samuels........	289	......	......	......	......	......
5558	♀	......do......	April —, 1856	......do...........	674	......	......	......	......	......
4393	♀	Fort Dalles, O. T.......	May 21, 1855	Dr. G. Suckley. ...	176	....	6.75	10.87	3.50	Iris hazel ....

ZONOTRICHIA, Swainson.

Zonotrichia, SWAINSON, Fauna Bor. Am. II, 1831. Type *Emberiza leucophrys*.

CH.—Body rather stout. Bill conical, slightly notched, somewhat compressed, excavated inside; the lower mandible rather lower than the upper; gonys slightly convex; commissure nearly straight. Feet stout; tarsus rather longer than middle toe; the lateral toes very nearly equal. Hind toe longer than the lateral ones; their, claws just reaching to base of middle one. Inner claw contained twice in its toe proper; claws all slender and considerably curved. Wings moderate, not reaching to the middle of the tail, but beyond the rump; secondaries and tertials equal and considerably less than longest primaries; second and third quills longest; first about equal to the fifth, much longer than tertials. Tail rather long, moderately rounded; the feathers not very broad.

Back streaked. Rump and under parts immaculate. Head black, or with white streaks, entirely different from the back.

This genus embraces the most beautiful of American sparrows, all of the largest size in their sub-family.

June 15, 1858.

58 b

Synopsis of the species.

Feathers of interscapular region blackish centrally, passing into rufous brown and edged with paler. Rump and upper tail coverts uniform olivaceous ashy brown. Two white bands on the wings; the tertials edged with rufous. Beneath without streaks. Head above marked with black, and generally with white. Cheeks plumbeous.

a. Median light stripe on the top of the head.

Chin, throat, and breast nearly uniform ashy. Head above black. Median and superciliary stripe pure white. A narrow black line from the black lores, through and behind the eye, cutting off the superciliary stripe anteriorly. .... Z. leucophrys.

Similar to the last, but the lores ashy and continuous with the white superciliary stripe.. Z. gambelii.

Chin ashy like throat and breast. Top of the head black; the median stripe yellow anteriorly, ashy posteriorly. A little yellow above the eye...........Z. coronata.

Chin abruptly white; median head stripe white. A broad superciliary stripe, yellow anteriorly, white behind... Z. albicollis.

b. Head above entirely black.

Head all round, neck above and throat, black. Cheeks behind gray. Breast and belly pure white, with a few black streaks on the sides of the breast..Z. querula.

Comparative measurements of species.

Catal. No.	Species.	Locality.	Sex.	Length.	Stretch of wings.	Wing.	Tail.	Tarsus.	Middle toe.	Its claw alone.	Hind toe and claw.	Hind toe alone.	Bill above.	Along gape.	Specimen measured.
1506	Zonotrichia leucophrys.	Carlisle, Pa..........	♂	6.50	....	3.12	3.23	0.91	0.88	0.24	0.64	0.30	0.46	0.50	Skin ......
do..	......do.......do	......do...............	......	7.08	10.50	3.25	......	......	......	......	......	......	......	......	Fresh .....
6199	.....do.......do	Mimbres to RioGrande	......	5.70	....	3 29	3.33	0.97	0.92	0.24	0.63	0.31	0.47	0.47	Skin ......
6205	......do.....gambelii ..	Sacramento valley ...	♂	6.24	....	2.83	3.08	0.86	0.80	0.21	0.53	0.25	0.43	0.45	Skin ......
6198	......do.......do	Mimbres to RioGrande	......	5.60	....	2.90	3.02	0.83	0.81	0.24	0.58	0.29	0.42	0.42	Skin ......
2780	......do....coronata ..	Columbia river.....	♂	7.06	....	3.26	3.52	0.94	0.89	0.24	0.64	0.31	0.46	0.49	Skin ......
1940	......do....querula	Kickapoo Country	......	6.80	....	3.36	3.32	0.95	0.90	0.24	0.60	0.31	0.50	0.56	Skin ......
1434	......do....albicollis....	Carlisle, Pa..........	♂	6.30	....	3.01	3.13	0.90	0.90	0.25	0.60	0.30	0.45	0.50	Skin ......
do..	......do.......do	......do...............	......	7.00	9.75	3.08	......	......	......	......	......	......	......	......	Fresh ....

ZONOTRICHIA LEUCOPHRYS, Swainson.

White-crowned Sparrow.

Emberiza leucophrys, FORSTER, Philos. Trans. LXII, 1772, 382, 426.—GMELIN, Syst. Nat. I, 1788, 874.—WILSON, Am. Orn. IV, 1811, 49; pl, xxxi, f. 4.

Fringilla (Zonotrichia) leucophrys, Sw. F. B. Am. II, 1831, 255.

Zonotrichia leucophrys, BON. List, 1838.—IB. Consp. 1850, 478.

Fringilla leucophrys, AUD. Orn. Biog. II, 1834, 88: V, 515; pl. 114.—IB. Syn. 1839, 121,—IB. Birds Amer. III, 1841, 157; pl. 192.

White-crowned Sparrow, PENNANT.

Figured in BUFFON, Ois. IV, 192, pl. 223, f. 2. Winter.

Sp. Ch.—Head above, upper half of loral region from the bill, and a narrow line through and behind the eye to the occiput, black ; a longitudinal patch in the middle of the crown, and a short line from above the anterior corner of the eye, the two confluent on the occiput, white. Sides of the head, fore part of breast, and lower neck all round, pale ash, lightest beneath and shading insensibly into the whitish of the belly and chin ; sides of belly and under tail coverts tinged with yellowish brown. Interscapular region streaked broadly with dark chestnut brownish. Edges of the tertiaries brownish chestnut. Two white bands on the wing.

Female similar, but smaller ; immature male with the black of the head replaced by dark chestnut brown, the white tinged with brownish yellow.

Length, 7.10 inches; wing, 3.25.

Hab.—United States from Atlantic to the Rocky mountains, where they become mixed up with Z. gambelii. Greenland, Reinhardt.

The white of the crown separates two black lines on either sides, rather narrower than itself. The black line behind the eye is continued anterior to it into the black at the base of the bill. The lower eyelid is white. There are some obscure cloudings of darker on the neck above. The rump is immaculate. No white on the tail, except very obscure tips. The white crosses the ends of the middle and greater coverts.

Eastern specimens of this species vary considerably in size, while the smallest are from southern Texas and California. Even here, however, specimens are occasionally as large as those from Pennsylvania. Oregon skins are generally as large as those from the last mentioned State.

The only difference I can detect between eastern and western skins is, that in the former there is a short black line from the upper side of the anterior canthus of the eye to the black stripe on each side of the crown, the white superciliary stripe being cut off by this from the whitish gray of the lores, while in all from the Pacific coast the superciliary white is continuous with the grayish lores. Whether this is constant throughout I cannot say. The specimens from Texas and east of the Rocky Mountains are like those from Pennsylvania. Of two specimens from the Mimbres, one (6199) has this line ; the other (6198) is without it. A specimen from San Elziario, Texas, is also without it. Some California specimens appear to have the tarsus yellower, and a little longer.

The specific name of gambelii has been assigned to the western white-crowned sparrow, on the strength of its inferior size, and will answer very well for it, if really distinct.

Note.—Since writing the preceding paragraph, the examination of many additional specimens has substantiated the indications of differences between eastern and western birds. Of fifty specimens from the west, all have the superciliary stripe continuous from the bill, while all the eastern have it interrupted. Immature specimens, however, can only be distinguished by the more hoary lores.

List of specimens.

Catal. No.	Sex.	Locality.	When collected.	Whence obtained.	Orig. No.	Collected by—	Length.	Stretch of wings.	Wing.	Remarks.
817	♂	Carlisle, Pa..........	Oct. 19, 1842	S. F. Baird......	......	....	6.75	10	3.17	....
1506	♂	.....do..............	May 11, 1844	.....do.........	......	....	7.08	10.50	3.25	....
1507	♂	.....do..............	.....do...	.....do.........	......	....	7	10.42	3.33	....
2643	♂	.....do..............	May 12, 1846	.....do.........	......	....	7.17	10.33	3.17	....
7397	......	East Rockport, Ohio...	....	Dr. Kirtland	......	....	......	......	......	....
6196	......	Fort Leavenworth......	Oct. 23, 1854	Lt. Couch	7	....	......	......	......	....
6197	......	.....do..............	Oct. 21, 1854	.....do.........	5	....	......	......	......	....
4794	♂	Vermilion river, Neb...	May 8, 1856	Lt. G. K. Warren.	......	Dr. Hayden......	7	9.75	3.50	Iris hazel............
5403	♀	Knife river, Neb......	....	.....do.........	......	....	6.87	9.87	3.25	....
5709	♂	Republican river, Neb..	Sept. 20, 1856	Lt. F. T. Bryan...	359	W. S. Wood.....	......	......	......	....
9283	......	Black Hills, Neb.......	Sept. 19, 1857	Lt. Warren......	......	Dr. Hayden......	6.00	9.25	3.00	Iris brown............
5708	♂	Pole creek, Neb........	July 28, 1856	Lt. F. T. Bryan..	170	W. S. Wood.....	......	......	......	....
7034	♂	Cheyenne Pass.........	July 20, 1857	.....do.........	300	.....do.....	......	......	......	....
4080	♂	Tamaulipas, Mex.. ...	....	Lt. Couch	48	....	6.25	9.50	3.25	Eyes dark brown, bill and feet reddish brown.
4082	......	.....do..............	....	.....do.	68	....	6	9	3	........do............
4081	♀	Brownsville, Texas.....	....	.....do.........	4	....	6.75	10	3.25	........do............
6195	♂	Frontera, Texas........	May 4, ——	Maj. Emory	......	....	6.50	9.50	3.25	....
6199	......	Fort Thorne, N. M.....	....	Dr. T. C. Henry..	......	....	......	......	......	....

ZONOTRICHIA GAMBELII, Gambel.

Fringilla gambelii, NUTT. Man. (I, 2d ed.) 1840, 556.—GAMBEL, Pr. A. N. Sc. Phila. I, 1843, 262. (California.)
Zonotrichia gambelii, GAMBEL, J. A. N. Sc. 2d series, I, Dec. 1847, 50.
Zonotrichia leucophrys, NEWBERRY, Zool. Cal. & Or. Route : Rep. P.R.R, VII, IV, 1857, 87.

SP. CH.—Precisely similar to Z. *leucophrys,* but rather smaller ; the lores are gray throughout, this color continuous with a white superciliary stripe along the side of the head.
Length, 6.25 ; wing, 2.83 ; tail, 3.08.
Hab.—Rocky Mountains to the Pacific coast.

As stated in the previous article, the only appreciable and constant difference between this species and the preceding is found in the character of the black stripe on the side of the crown. In *leucophrys* the black passes down over the upper half of the lores, and in front of the eye, to a line continuous with the cutting edge of the bill, and sends back a short branch to the eye which cuts off the white superciliary stripe.   In *gambelii* the superciliary stripe passes continuously forward to the ashy lores, cutting off the black from the eye.   The lower edge of the black anteriorly is much higher than in *leucophrys,* and nearly on a line with the nostrils.

The difference of size, supposed to establish this species, is hardly characteristic, but depends mainly on the latitude of the specimen.

List of specimens.

Catal. No.	Sex & age.	Locality.	When collected.	Whence obtained.	Orig. No.	Collected by—	Length.	Stretch of wings.	Wing.	Remarks.
? 4795	.....	Opposite Vermillion river.	May 7, 1856	Lt. Warren	......	Dr. Hayden........	7.00	10.12	3.25	Iris hazel........
? 4793	.....	Durion's Hill, Nebraska ..	May 9, 1856	......do............	......	......do........ ...	6.37	9.12	3.00	....
6200	.....	San Elizario, Texas......	Dec. —, 1854	Major Emory	9	Dr. Kennerly	6.	9.50	3.25	....
6198	.....	Fort Thorn, N. M........	......do......	Dr. Henry.........	......	....	6	9	3	....
6201	.....	White Cliff Creek........	Feb. —, 1854	Lt. A. W. Whipple.	65	Kenn. & Möllh	.....	....	......	....
6202	.....	......do........	......do......	......do...........	64	......do........	....	....	......	....
6203	.....	......do........	......do......	......do...........	61	......do........	....	....	......	....
	.....	Fort Tejon..............	....	J. X. de Vesey.....	......	....	....	....	......	....
6204	○	Tejon Valley, California..	....	Lt. Williamson....	......	Dr. Heermann	.. ..	....	......	....
6205	♂	Sacramento, California...	....	....	....	......do........	....	....	......	. ...
3341	♀	California	Winter '53-4	Dr. Wilson	......	Dr. Gambel........	....	....	......	....
4234	.....	San Francisco..........	Jan., 1853...	R. D. Cutts	......	....	....	....	......	....
6206	.....	......do........	May, 1853....	Lt. Trowbridge....	......	....	....	....	......	....
6207	... ..	......do........	May, 1855....	......do.......	......	....	....	....	......	....
5551	♂	Petaluma, California	.... do......	E. Samuels	293	....	....	....	......	....
5552	♀	......do........	April 27, 1855	......do...........	608	....	7.17	10	3.25	....
4387	.....	Fort Dalles, O. T........	....	Dr. Suckley.......	158	....	6.75	9.50	3	....
6208	♂	Fort Steilacoom, W. T. ..	March, 1856..	..... do...........	87	....	....	....	......	....
6209	.....	......do........	..... do......	......do...........	278	....	....	....	......	....
6211	.....	......do........	April 19, 1856	......do...........	313	....	6.50	10.75	......	....
6210	.....	......do........	March, 1856..	......do...........	284	....	....	....	......	....
6212	.....	Shoalwater Bay, W. T. ..	June 16, 1854	Dr. Cooper	76	....	6.62	9.37	....	Bill yellow, tipped with brown ; iris brown : legs yellow.
6213	.....	......do........	.....do......	......do...........	......	....	6.25	9	....	The same ....
5978	.....	Straits of Fuca, W.T.....	April, 1855...	......do...........	......	....	....	....	......	....
5979	.....	......do........	....	......do......	......	....	....	....	......	....

ZONOTRICHIA CORONATA, Baird.

Golden-crowned Sparrow.

Emberiza coronata, PALLAS, Zoog. Rosso-Asiat. II, 1811, 44 ; plate.

Emberiza atricapilla, AUD. Orn. Biog. V. 1839, 47 ; pl. 394 ; (not of Gmelin.)

Fringilla atricapilla, AUD. Synopsis, 1839, 122.—IB. Birds Amer. III, 1841, 162 ; pl. 193.

Fringilla aurocapilla, NUTTALL, Man. I, (2d ed.) 1840, 555.

Zonotrichia aurocapilla, BON. Consp. 1850, 478.—NEWBERRY, Zool. Cal. & Or. Route, Rep. P.R.R.VI, IV, 1857, 88.

Emberiza atricapilla, GM. I, 1788, 875, in part only.—LATH. Ind. 415.

Black-crowned Bunting, PENNANT, Arc. Zool. II, 364.—LATH. II, I, 202, 49 ; tab. lv.

SP. CH.—Hood, from bill to upper part of nape, pure black, the middle longitudinal third occupied by yellow on the anterior half, and pale ash on the posterior. Sides and under parts of head and neck, with upper part of breast, ash color, passing insensibly into whitish on the middle of the body ; sides and under tail coverts tinged with brownish. A yellowish spot above the eye, bounded anteriorly by a short black line from the eye to the black of the forehead. This yellow spot, however, reduced to a few feathers in spring dress. Interscapular region, with the feathers, streaked with dark brown, suffused with dark rufous externally. Two narrow white bands on the wings.

Length, about 7 inches ; wing, 3.30.

Hab.—Pacific coast from Russian America to southern California ; Black Hills of Rocky Mountains.?

In the Oregon specimen described above, (2780) and which served as the original of Mr. Audubon's description and figure, the black stripes on the crown extend down as far as the posterior canthus of the eye, obliterating any black line behind it. In 5550, from Petaluma, California, however, there is an ashy streak above the eye bordering the black, similar to the pattern in *Z. leucophrys*, which, like the median stripe of the crown, is yellow anteriorly. There is a dusky line back of the eye. The dark stripes on the crown are more brownish than black, and considerably narrower. An immature specimen (5980) has each feather of the crown streaked with blackish; the forehead blackish; the whole anterior portion of the crown yellowish, brightest over the eye.

This species is very closely related to the *Z. leucophrys*, which it slightly exceeds in size. It is a little more rufous on the back, and has less ash on the nape. The pattern of coloration of the Petaluma specimen is precisely the same, the median stripe on the head being yellow anteriorly and grayish posteriorly, instead of pure white; in the one from Columbia river, the black on the sides of the crown passes outward so as to obliterate the light superciliary stripe, except in its anterior yellowish portion, as also the dark line behind the eye. This, however, is, I suspect, rather a question of coloration with season, the black in full spring dress being broader and purer, extending down to the eye, while in other seasons it is narrower, leaving a superciliary ashy streak. This is the case with all the California specimens before me, (amounting to over thirty, all in summer or fall dress,) while all those from Washington Territory have the purer and more extended black.

In Lieutenant Bryan's collections are two young sparrows (7032, 7033,) which I am inclined to refer to this species. The back is more broadly streaked with black, the throat, breast, and sides beneath with distinct dusky streaks. The head above shows an obscure median whitish stripe and another superciliary one from above the eye; the rest of the head above is spotted with blackish and brown.

Latham (Synopsis II, 202,) describes a *black-crowned Bunting* from the Sandwcih Islands, and incidentally mentions the present species as a variety from Nootka Sound. Gmelin bases an *Emberiza atricapilla* upon that name, and includes both original and variety. If his name can be retained for either one, however, it must be for the Sandwich Island species, which is very different from ours.

List of specimens.

Catal. No.	Sex and age.	Locality.	When collected.	Whence obtained.	Orig. No.	Collected by—	Length.	Stretch of wings.	Wing.	Remarks.
6216	♂	Fort Steilacoom, W. T.....	....	Dr. Suckley	90	....	7.00	16.50	3.25	....
6217	....	......do...	April 26, 1856	......do........	344	....	......	......	.....	....
2780	♂	Columbia river............	April —, 1836	S. F. Baird	......	J. K. Townsend..	....	....	......	....
4388	♀	Fort Dalles, O. T........	May 11, 1855	Dr. Suckley......	174	....	7.00*	9.75	3.25	Iris dark hazel...
5550	♂	Petaluma, Cal,...........	....	E. Samuels	281	....	....	....	......	....
6214	♂	Sacramento, Cal	....	Lt. Williamson...	......	Dr. Heermann....	....	....	......	....
6215	♂	......do....	....	......do.........	......	......do........	....	....	......	....
5980	○	Santa Clara, Cal	Nov. —, 1855	Dr. J. G. Cooper.	......	....	7.25	9.75	......	{ Bill, brown and { flesh color.
		Fort Tejon, Cal	....	J. X. de Vesey...	......	....	....	....	......	....
7032?	○	W. Fork Med. Bow mount's.	Aug. 5, 1857	Lt. F. T. Bryan..	377	W. S. Wood. ...	....	.. ..	......	....
7033?	○	......do..............	...do......	......do.........	378	......do......	....	....	......	....

ZONOTRICHIA QUERULA, Gambel.

Harris's Finch·

Fringilla querula, NUTTALL, Man. I, (2d ed.) 1840, 555. (Westport, Mo.)
Zonotrichia querula, GAMBEL, J. A. N. Sc. 2d Ser. I, 1847, 51.—BONAP. Consp. 1850, 478.
Fringilla harrisii, AUD. Birds Amer. VII, 1843, 331, pl. 484.
Fringilla comata, PR. MAX. Reise II, 1841.
Zonotrichia comata, BP. Consp. 1850, 479.

Sp. Ch.—Hood and nape, sides of head anterior to and including the eyes, chin, throat, and a few spots in the middle of the upper part of the breast and on its sides, black. Sides of head and neck ash gray, with the trace of a narrow crescent back of the ear coverts. Interscapular region of back, with the feathers reddish brown streaked with dark brown. Breast and belly clear white. Sides of body light brownish, streaked. Two narrow white bands across the greater and middle coverts. Length, about 7 inches ; wing, 3.40 ; tail, 3.65.

Hab.—Missouri river, above Fort Leavenworth.

The bill of this species appears to be yellowish red. More immature specimens vary in having the black of the head above more restricted. The nape and sides of the head to the bill pale reddish brown, lighter on the latter region. Others have the feathers of the anterior portion of the hood edged with whitish. In all there is generally a trace of black anterior to the eye. This species has a considerably larger bill than *Z. leucophrys,* the mandible especially.

List of specimens.

Catal. No.	Sex.	Locality.	When collected.	Whence obtained.	Orig. No.	Collected by—	Length.	Stretch of wings.	Wing.	Remarks.
6218	♂	Fort Leavenworth,K.T.	Oct. 21, 1854	Lt. Couch........	2	....	7.50	10.25	3.37	Eye hazel...... ....
4797	......	......do...........	April 21, 1856	Lt. Warren.... ..	......	Dr. Hayden ..				
4798	......	Upper Missouri.......	....	......do......	......	......do......	7.25	10.37	3.12	Iris brown..................
1940	♂	Kickapoo Co., Mo. R.	May 5, 1843	S. F. Baird	......	J. J. Audubon				
4799	......	Bald Island...........	April 24, 1856	L . Warren.......	......	Dr. Hayden ..				
5400	♂	Medicine Creek, K.T.	Oct. 8........ ...	.do...........	......	......do......	7.50	10.75	3.25	....

ZONOTRICHIA ALBICOLLIS, Bonap.

White-throated Sparrow.

Fringilla albicollis, Gmelin, Syst. Nat. I, 1788, 926.—Wilson, Am. Orn. III, 1811, 51 ; pl. xxii, f. 2.—Licht. Verz. Doubl. No. 247, (1823.)

Zonotrichia albicollis, Bp. Consp. 1850, 478.—Cab. Mus. Hein. 1851, 132.

Passer pennsylvanicus, Brisson, 1760. Appendix 77.

Fringilla pennsylvanica, Lath. Index, I, 1790, 445.—Aud. Orn. Biog. I, 1831, 42 : V. 497 ; pl. 8.—Ib. Syn. 1839, 121.—Ib. Birds Amer. III, 1841, 153 ; pl. 191.

Fringilla (Zonotrichia) pennsylvanica, Sw. F. B. Am. II, 1831, 256.

Zonotrichia pennsylvanica, Bon. List, 1838.

Sp. Ch.—Two black stripes on the crown separated by a median one of white. A broad superciliary stripe from the base of the mandible to the occiput, yellow as far as the middle of the eye and white behind this. A broad black streak on the side of the head from behind the eye. Chin white, abruptly defined against the dark ash of the sides of the head and upper part of the breast, fading into white on the belly, and margined by a narrow black maxillary line. Edge of wing and axillaries yellow. Back and edges of secondaries rufous brown, the former streaked with dark brown. Two narrow white bands across the wing coverts. Length, 7 inches ; wing, 3.10 ; tail, 3.20.

Hab.—Eastern United States to the Missouri.

Female smaller, and the colors rather duller. Immature and winter specimens have the white chin patch less abruptly defined ; the white markings on the top and sides of the head tinged with brown. Some specimens, apparently mature, show quite distinct streaks on the breast and sides of throat and body.

As Brisson's nomenclature is not binomial, and his names merely literal translations into Latin from the French vernacular, consisting usually of three or more words, rather than two, I have followed Cabanis, Bonaparte, and most modern authors in rejecting them altogether.

List of specimens.

Catal. No.	Sex.	Locality.	When collected.	Whence obtained.	Orig. No.	Collected by—	Length.	Stretch of wings	Wing.	Remarks.
1434	♂	Carlisle, Penn........	May 3, 1844	S. F. Baird			7.00	9.75	3.08	
1388	♂	..... do.............	April 24, 1844	......do............			6.25	9.42	2.92	
765	♂	......do.............	Sept. 28, 1842	......do............			6.42	9.50	3.00	
310	♂	.....do.............	April 26, 1841	......do............			6.80	9.42		
859	♂	......do.............	Nov. 15, 1842	......do............			6.67	9.17	2.67	
7544		Washington, D. C.....		W. Hutton						
5893		Prairie Mer Rouge, La.		J. Fairie						
7291		Cleveland, Ohio.....		Dr. Kirtland						
4790	♂	Big Nemaha R., Neb..	April 23, 1856	Lt. G. K. Warren....		Dr. Hayden..........	6.75	9.62	2.87	Iris brown ....
4791	♂	......do.............	......do.........	......do..........		......do..........	6.75	9.62	2.87	......do.........
4788	♂	Wood's Bluff, Neb....	May 1, 1856	......do..........		.... do..........	6.50	9.50	3.12	
4787	♂	Black Bird Hill, Neb..	May 2, 1856	......do..........		......do..........	6.50	9.50	3.25	
4785	♂	.... do	May 2, 1856	......do..........		......do..........	6.00	10.00	3.25	
4782	♂	Big Sioux river, Neb..	May 3, 1856	......do..........		...do..........	7.37	9.75	3.25	
4783	♂	Vermilion river, Neb..	May 8, 1856	......do..........		......do..........	6.50	7.50	3.00	Iris hazel........
4789	♂	......do.............	....do.........	.... do		......do..........	6.87	9.50	3.00	
4784	♂	Big Sioux river, Neb..	....do.........	......do		......do..........	7.00	9.62	2.87	
4786	♂	Vermilion river, Neb..	....do.........	......do..........		......do..........	7.62	9.50	3.00	
4796		Big Sioux river, Neb..	....do.........	......do..........		......do..........	7.37	9.50	3.00	
5402	♀	Cedar Island	Oct. 14.......	......do..........		......do	7.50	8.25	3.00	Iris gray ....
5401		White Earth river....	Sept. 6.......	......do..........		......do..........	6.50	9.	2.75	Iris brown ....

JUNCO, Wagler.

Junco, WAGLER, Isis, 1831. Type *Fringilla cinerea*, Sw.
Niphoea, AUDUBON, Syn. 1839. Type *Emberiza hyemalis*, Gm.

Bill small, conical ; culmen curved at the tip ; the lower jaw quite as high as the upper. Tarsus longer than the middle toe ; outer toe longer than the inner, barely reaching to the base of the middle claw ; hind toe reaching as far as the middle of the latter : extended toes reaching about to the middle of the tail. Wings rather short ; reaching over the basal fourth of the exposed surface of the tail ; primaries, however, considerably longer than the nearly equal secondaries and tertials. The second quill longest, the third to fifth successively but little shorter ; first longer than sixth, much exceeding secondaries. Tail moderate, a little shorter than the wings ; slightly emarginate and rounded. Feathers rather narrow ; oval at the end. No streaks on the head or body ; color above uniform on the head, back, or rump, separately or on all together. Belly white ; outer tail feathers white.

The essential characters of this genus are the middle toe rather shorter than the short tarsus ; the lateral toes slightly unequal, the outer reaching the base of the middle claw ; the tail a little shorter than the wings, slightly emarginate. In *Junco cinereus* the claws are longer ; the lower mandible a little lower than the upper. The species have the upper parts ashy or plumbeous, the belly and lateral tail feathers white.

SYNOPSIS.

A.—Interscapular region, greater wing coverts, and tertials reddish.

Head and neck all round black, the color not extending along the sides.. ......*J. oregonus.*
Head light plumbeous above. Lores abruptly black. Beneath very pale ashy, much lighter than the head. Whitish on the belly..................................*J. cinereus.*

B.—Interscapular region alone reddish.

Above light plumbeous ; beneath nearly white tinged with ash. Lores abruptly black..*J. dorsalis.*

Above darker plumbeous, this continued around the head and neck, and extending along the sides, although a little paler than above. Lores darker......................*J. caniceps.*

C.—Interscapular region without any red.

Body throughout nearly uniform dusky plumbeous, the belly and crissum beneath abruptly white. Claws rather shorter...*J. hyemalis.*

Comparative measurements of species.

Catal. No.	Species.	Locality.	Sex.	Length.	Stretch of wings.	Wing.	Tail.	Tarsus.	e toe.	Its claw alone.	Hind toe and claw.	Hind claw alone.	Bill above.	Along gape.	Specimen measured.
8060	Junco cinereus.....	Mexico...........	......	6.40	......	3.15	3.26	0.82	0.76	0.23	0.58	0.30	0.45	0.45	Skin.......
1947	Junco oregonus	Columbia river......	♂	6.33	......	2.95	2.76	0.79	0.80	0.21	0.56	0.27	0.44	0.50	Skin.......
3920	..... do	California..................	♂	5.60	......	3.04	2.85	0.82	0.75	0.19	0.53	0.26	0.46	0.46	Skin.......
3921	......do	......do	♀	5.60	......	2.79	2.78	0.78	0.72	0.18	0.52	0.26	0.43	0.46	Skin.......
9270	Junco dorsalis	Fort Thorn, N. M.......	......	6.00	......	3.00	3.02	0.85	0.76	0.20	0.62	0.30	0.48	0.48	Skin.......
9272	......do	......do		6.30	......	3.35	3.53	0.86	0.78	0.22	0.60	0.28	0.46	0.49	Skin.......
9281	Junco caniceps	San Francisco mountains...	♀	5.94	......	3.12	3.03	0.79	0.70	0.17	0.50	0.23	0.40	0.40	Skin. .....
7036	......do	Black Hills..............	......	6.00	......	3.23	3.04	0.84	0.74	0.17	0.59	0.28	0.44	0.48	Skin.......
1287	Junco hyemalis	Carlisle, Pa............	♂	5.80	......	3.12	2.94	0.84	0.73	0.20	0.56	0.25	0.43	0.46	Skin.......
do.	......do	......do................	.....	6.25	9.25	3.08	......	......	......	......	......	......	......	......	Fresh .....

JUNCO CINEREUS, Cabanis.

Fringilla cinerea, Sw. Syn. Birds Mex. in Phil. Mag. I, 1827, 435.
Junco cinereus, CABANIS, Mus. Hein. 1850, 134.
" *Fringilla rufidorsis,* LICHT." BONAPARTE ; probably a catalogue name.
Junco phaeonotus, WAGLER, Isis, 1831, 526.—BONAP. Comptes Rendus, XXXVII, 518.

SP. CH.—Bill black above, bright yellow below. Feet yellow. Above, including the outer edges of the primary and secondary quills, grayish ash or plumbeous. Entire interscapular region, scapulars, greater wing coverts, and outer webs of tertials reddish chestnut. Lores abruptly blackish. Under parts generally pale ashy white ; purest on the middle of the belly. Two outer tail feathers white, the basal portion dark brown ; the third with a white spot at the end. Length, 6.40 ; wing, 3.15 ; tail, 3.26.

Hab.—Mexico.

In this species the bill is quite elongated and rather slender. The outer tail feather is brown for the basal third, this color extending obliquely forward along the inner edge. The brown is more extended on the second feather, and it covers the entire outer web. The white of the third feather is confined to a stripe on the end.

Although the *Junco cinereus* has not yet been found within the limits of the United States, it yet occurs on the table lands of Mexico. I describe it here, however, chiefly to serve as an illustration of the other closely allied species of the United States. The specimens before me are both Mexican ; one, No. 8060, received from Mr. John Gould ; the other, 9117 ♂ , from Mr. Verreaux.

June 16, 1858.

59 b

JUNCO OREGONUS, Sclater.

Oregon Snow Bird.

Fringilla oregona, Townsend, J. A. N. Sc. VII, 1837, 188.—Ib. Narrative, 1839, 345.—Audubon, Orn. Biog. V, 1839, 68; pl. 398.

Struthus oregonus, Bon. List, 1838.—Ib. Consp. 1850, 475.—Newberry, Zool. Cal. & Or. Route; Rep. P. R. R. VI, iv, 1857, 88.

Niphoea oregona, Audubon, Synopsis, 1839, 107.—Ib. Birds Amer. III, 1841, 91; pl. 168.—Cab. Mus. Hein. 1851, 134.

Junco oregonus, Sclater, Pr. Zool. Soc. 1857, 7.

Fringilla hudsonia, Licht. Beit. Faun. Cal. in Abh. Akad. Wiss. Berlin, for 1838, 1839, 424. (Not *F. hudsonia*, Forster.)

" *Fringilla atrata*, Brandt, Icon. Rosso-As. tab. ii, f. 8." (Cab.)

Sp. Ch.—Head and neck all round sooty black; this color extending to the upper part of the breast, but not along the sides under the wings. Interscapular region of the back and exposed surface of the wings dark rufous brown. A lighter tint of the same on the sides of breast and belly. Rump brownish ash. Outer two tail feathers white; the third with only an obscure streak of white. Length, about 6.50 inches; wing, 3.00.

Hab.—Pacific coast of the United States to the eastern side of the Rocky mountains. Stragglers as far east as Fort Leavenworth in winter and Great Bend of Missouri.

In this species the wing is rather pointed; the second and third quills equal, and longest; the fourth appreciably shorter; the first intermediate between the fourth and fifth.

Oregon specimens have the back of a darker rufous than California ones, in which this region, as well as the sides of the body are considerably paler.

Immature, and most winter specimens do not have the black of the head and neck so well defined, but edged above more or less with the color of the back; below with light ashy.

The Oregon snow bird in full plumage is readily distinguishable from the eastern species by the purer white of the belly; the more sharply defined outline of the black of the head passes directly across the upper part of the breast, and is even convex in its posterior outline, without extending down the side of the breast, with its posterior outline strongly concave, as in *hyemalis*. The absence of black or ashy brown under the wings, with the rufous tinge, are highly characteristic of *oregonus*. The head and neck are considerably blacker; the rufous of the back and wings does not exist in the other. The wings and quills are more pointed; the second quill usually longest, instead of the third, &c. The dusky of the throat reaches in *S. oregonus* only to the upper part of the breast; to its middle region in *hyemalis*.

List of specimens.

Cat. No.	Sex.	Locality.	When collected.	Whence obtained.	Orig'l No.	Collected by—	Length.	Stretch of wings	Wing.	Remarks.
6251	.....	Fort Steilacoom	Jan. —, 1854	Gov. Stevens ...	23	Dr. Suckley ...				
6252	.....	....do	Feb. —, 1854	....do		....do				
6253	.....	....do		Dr. G. Suckley...	95		5.75	9.25	3.25	
6254	.....	....do		....do	250					
6255	.....	....do	Mar. —, 1856	....do	261		6.00	9.00		
6256	.....	....do		....do	234		6.00	9.00		
6257	.....	....do	Feb...	....do	270		6.00	9.00		
6259	.....	....do	Mar. —, 1856	...do	273		6.00	9.00		
6261	♂	Fort Vancouver, W.T.	Dec. 29, 1853	Gov. Stevens	1	Dr. Cooper	6 00	9.00		Bill flesh color; iris and legs brown.
6262	♂?	....do	....do	....do		....do	6.00	9.00		
1948	.....	Columbia river	Oct. 16, 1834	S. F. Baird		J. K. Townsend				
1947	♂	....do	Oct. 5, 1834	....do		....do				
4592	.....	St. Helens, O. T....	Jan. 26, 1856	Dr. Suckley	200		6.50	9.87	3.25	
6263	.....	San Francisco	Winter 1854..	R. D. Cutts						
3920	♂	California		Dr. Heermann						
3921	♀	....do		....do						
6264	♂	Sacramento, Cal		Lt. Williamson		Dr. Heermann				
6265	♀	Tejon Pass, Cal		....do		....do				
	.....	Fort Tejon		J. X. De Vesey						
6266	.....	Zuñi, N. M		Lt. Whipple	30	Dr. Kennerly				
6250	.....	Fort Thorne, N. M...		Dr. Henry						
5888	.....	Fort Riley, K. T.		Dr. Hammond		Mr. De Vesey				
6564	.....	....do		....do						
6249	♀	Fort Leavenworth ...	Oct. 21, 1854	Lt. Couch						
5372	♂	Medicine Creek, Neb.	Oct. 8, 1856	Lt. G. K. Warren		Dr. Hayden	5.87	8.50	3	Iris brown
5374	♂	Great bend of Mo. river	....do	....do		....do	5.62	9.	3.25	

JUNCO DORSALIS, Henry.

Junco dorsalis, HENRY, Pr. A. N. Sc. X, May, 1858, 117.

SP. CH.—Bill black above; light brownish below. Above, including the entire upper surface of the wings and scapulars, light grayish ash; the interscapular region reddish chestnut brown. Beneath ashy white; the middle of the belly almost pure white. Lores abruptly black; quills and tail feathers nearly black. Three outer tail feathers white; two entirely so, the third with brown on the inner edge. Length, 6.25; wing, 3.05; tail, 3.10.

Hab.—Fort Thorn, New Mexico.

In this species the wing is rounded; the third and fourth quills longest; the second and fifth very little shorter; the first about equal to the sixth. The tail is very slightly rounded.

The bill of this species is considerably larger than that of *Junco hyemalis,* and is black above, instead of red; the claws, too, are larger.

This species differs from *Junco cinereus* in having the chestnut of the back restricted to the interscapular region, instead of having it to extend over the scapulars, wing coverts and outer webs of the tertials.

The closest relationships are to *J. caniceps.* The plumbeous of the back is, however, much lighter; the under parts generally are nearly white, instead of plumbeous anteriorly this color extending backwards on the sides in marked contrast with the white belly. The lores are much more abruptly blackish. The bill is larger; the upper mandible black instead of yellowish; the white of the tail is much the same.

The only specimens yet known of this species are those collected at Fort Thorn by Dr. Henry.

List of specimens.

Catal. No.	Locality.	Whence obtained.
9270	Fort Thorn, New Mexico	Dr. T. C. Henry

JUNCO CANICEPS, Baird.

Struthus caniceps, Woodhouse, Pr. A. N. Sc. Phila. VI, Dec. 1852, 202. (New Mexico and Texas.)—Ib. Sitgreave's
Report Zuñi & Colorado, 1853, 83 ; pl. iii.

Sp. Ch.—Bill yellowish ; black at the tip. Above dark plumbeous, the head and neck all round of this color, which extends
(paling a little) along the sides, leaving the middle of the belly and crissum quite abruptly white. Lores conspicuously, but
not very abruptly darker. Interscapular region abruptly reddish chestnut brown, which does not extend on the wings, except
perhaps a faint tinge on some of the greater coverts. Two outer tail feathers entirely white ; third with a long white terminal
stripe on the inner web. Length, 6.00 ; wing, 3.23 ; tail, 3.04.

Hab.—Rocky mountains ; from Black Hills to San Francisco mountains, New Mexico.

This species is very similar to the common *J. hyemalis* in color, except that the plumbeous of
the under parts and sides is not quite so dark and less abruptly defined against the white. The
conspicuous chestnut patch on the back will distinguish them. The outer web of the third tail
feather is brown, not white. It differs from *oregonus* and *cinereus* in having no chesnut on the
wings, especially the tertials, and from the former in the extension of the ash of the neck along
the sides. It is darker above than *J. dorsalis*, which also lacks the distinct plumbeous of the
throat and sides, has the bill blacker, the lores more abruptly darker, &c.

List of specimens.

Catal. No.	Sex.	Locality.	When collected.	Whence obtained.	Collected by—	Length.	Stretch of wings.	Wing.
7036	♂	Black Hills, Cheyenne riv.	July 21, 1857	Lt. F. T. Bryan	W. S. Wood			
8960		Laramie peak	Aug. 25, 1857	Lt. Warren	Dr. Hayden	6.25	9.00	2.75
8961		do	do	do	do			
9281		San Francisco mountains	Oct. 14, 1857	Capt. Sitgreaves	Dr. Woodhouse			

JUNCO HYEMALIS, Sclater.

Snow Bird.

Fringilla hyemalis, Linn. Syst. Nat. I, 10th ed. 1758, 183. (Not of Gmelin or Latham.)—Aud. Orn. Biog. I, 1831,
72 : V, 505 ; pl. 13.

Fringilla (Spiza) hyemalis, Bon. Syn. 1828, 109.

Emberiza hyemalis, Linn. Syst. Nat. I, 1766, 308.

Struthus hyemalis, Bon. List, 1838.—Ib. Consp. 1850, 475.

Niphoea hyemalis, Aud. Synopsis, 1839, 106.—Ib. Birds Amer. III, 1841, 88 ; pl. 167.

Junco hyemalis, Sclater, Pr. Zool. Soc. 1857, 7.

Fringilla hudsonia, Forster, Philos. Trans. LXII, 1772, 428.—Gmelin, I, 1788, 926.—Wilson's Index, VI, 1812,
p. xiii.

Fringilla nivalis, Wilson, II, 1810, 129 ; pl. xvi, f. 6.

Sp. Ch.—Everywhere of a grayish or dark ashy black, deepest anteriorly ; the middle of the breast behind and of the belly,
the under tail coverts, and first and second external tail feathers, white. The third tail feather white, margined with black.
Length, 6.25 ; wing, about 3.

Hab.—Eastern United States to the Missouri, and as far west as Black Hills.

The wing is rounded ; the second quill longest, the third, fourth, and fifth, successively, a little shorter ; the first longer than the sixth. Tail slightly rounded, and a little emarginate. In the full spring dress there is no trace of any second color on the back, except an exceedingly faint and scarcely appreciable wash of dull brownish over the whole upper parts. The markings of the third tail feather vary somewhat in specimens. Sometimes the whole tip is margined with brown ; sometimes the white extends to the end ; sometimes both webs are margined with brown ; sometimes the outer is white entirely ; sometimes the brownish wash on the back is more distinct.

List of specimens.

Catal. No.	Sex.	Locality.	When collected.	Whence obtained.	Orig. No.	Collected by—	Length.	Stretch of wings.	Wing.	Remarks.
1287	♂	Carlisle, Pa..............	Mar. 9, 1844	S. F. Baird		....	6.25	9.25	3.08	....
276	♂	......do................	Mar. 1, 1841	......do.........						
10138	♂	Washington, D. C......	....	J. C. McGuire						
6248	♂	Fort Leavenworth.....	Oct. 21, 1854	Lieut. Couch	3					
4816?	......	Vermilion river, Neb...	May 6, 1856	Lieut. G. K. Warren	......	Dr. Hayden....	5.50	9.50	3.25	
5706	♂	Repub. Forks, K. T....	Oct. 20, 1856	Lieut. F. T. Bryan..	389	W. S. Wood....				
5707	♀	......do...............	......do....	......do............	387	......do.......				
8959?	......	Black Hills............	Sept. 14, 1857	Lieut. Warren. ...	......	Dr. Hayden....				
5373	.....	Cannon Ball river......	....	..... do..........		......do.......				

POOSPIZA, Cabanis.

Poospiza, Cabanis, Wiegmann's Archiv, 1847, i, 349. (Type *Emberiza nigro-rufa*, Orb., or *Pipilo personata*, Sw.)

Ch.—Bill slender, conical, both outlines gently curved. Under jaw with the edges considerably inflected ; not so high as the upper. Tarsi elongated, slender ; considerably longer than the middle toe. Toes short, weak ; the outer decidedly longer than the inner, but not reaching to the base of the middle claw. Hind toe about equal to the middle without its claw. All the claws compressed and moderately curved. Wings rather long, reaching about over the basal fourth of the exposed portion of the rather long tail. Tertiaries and secondaries about equal, and not much shorter than the lengthened primaries ; the second to fifth about equal and longest ; the first considerably shorter, and longer than the seventh. Tail long, slightly emarginate, graduated ; the outer feather abruptly shorter than the others. Feathers broad, linear, and rather obliquely truncate at the ends, with the corners rounded.

Color.—Uniform above, without streaks. Beneath white, with or without a black throat. Black and white stripes on the head.

In the selection of Cabanis's genus *Poospiza*, for the present group, I follow Mr. Sclater. One of the species has the throat white, the other black.

Comparative measurements of species.

Catal. No.	Species.	Locality.	Sex.	Length.	Stretch of wings.	Wing.	Tail.	Tarsus.	Middle toe.	Its claw alone.	Hind toe and claw.	Hind claw alone.	Bill above.	Along gape.	Specimen measured.
6338	Poospiza belli........	Cosumnes river, Cal......	♂	5.74	......	2.77	3.05	0.82	0.75	0.22	0.53	0.28	0.41	0.44	Skin.......
do.	......do............	Camp 6, Little Colorado..	......	6.20	......	3.13	3.25	0.84	0.74	0.20	0.57	0.30	0.40	0.45	Skin.......
6324	Poospiza bilineata....	New Mexico.............	♂	5.30	......	2.67	2.83	0.70	0.66	0.17	0.50	0.24	0.43	0.50	Skin.......
6318	......do.............	Frontera................	♀	5.20	......	2.55	2.50	0.74	0.65	0.16	0.47	0.20	0.40	0.48	Skin.......
do.	......do.............	......do..............	......	5.12	8.00	2.75									Fresh.......
6320	......do.............	Ringgold Barracks	......	4.30	......	2.33	2.30	0.68	0.62	0.16	0.43	0.21	0.40	0.43	Skin.......

POOSPIZA BILINEATA, Sclater.

Black-throated Sparrow.

Emberiza bilineata, CASSIN, Pr. A. N. Sc. Ph. V, Oct. 1850, 104, pl. iii, Texas.—IB. Illust. I, v, 1854, 150 ; pl xxiii.
Poospiza bilineata, SCLATER, Pr. Zool. Soc. 1857, 7.

SP. CH.—Above uniform unspotted ashy gray, tinged with light brown ; purer and more plumbeous anteriorly. Under parts white, tinged with plumbeous on the sides, and with yellowish brown about the thighs. A sharply defined superciliary and maxillary stripe of pure white, the former margined internally with black. Loral region black, passing insensibly into dark slate on the ears. Chin and throat between the white maxillary stripes black, ending on the upper part of the breast in a rounded outline. Tail black, edged externally with white. Bill blue. Length, 5.40 ; wing, 2.75 ; tail, 2.90.

Hab.—Valley of Rio Grande and of Gila. (As far west as Janos and the Mohave villages.)

This species in external form is very similar to *P. belli*, and will probably fall in the same genus. The cutting edges of the bill are much inflexed. The first quill is shorter than the sixth. The tail is a good deal rounded ; the feathers broad.

The white maxillary stripe does not come quite to the base of the under jaw, which there is black. There is a hoary tinge on the forehead. The white superciliary stripes almost meet on the forehead.

In the immature bird the throat is white, the upper part of the breast streaked with brown.

List of specimens.

Catal. No.	Sex and age.	Locality.	When collected	Whence obtained.	Orig'l No.	Collected by—	Length.	Stretch of wings.	Wing.	Remarks.
4088	♀	Tamaulipas, Mexico....	Mar. —, 1853	Lieut. Couch .. .	77	J. H. Clark	5.25	7.50	2.50	Eyes dark brown; bill black ; feet lead color.
6320	....	Ringgold Barracks, Tex.	July —, 1853	Major Emory.....	.....	J. H. Clark....	....	....	....	....
6321	♂	Texas.......	....	Lieut. J. G. Parke	.....	Dr. Heermann .	....	....	....	....
6322	....	......do........	....	......do......	.....	... .do...	....	....	....	....
6317	....	Frontera, Texas.......	....	Major Emory	.....	J. H. Clark	....	....	....	....
6318	♀	......do........	May 5, 1852	......do......	.....	......do.......	5.12	8.00	2.75	....
6319	○	......do........	......do......	......do......	.....	......do.......	5.00	7.62	2.50	....
6323	....	New Mexico......	......do......	......do......	.....	Lieut. J. G. Parke	.....	Dr. Heermann.		....
6324	♂	......do........	....	......do......	.....	......do......	....	....	....	....
6316	♂	El Paso, N. M.	Dec. —, 1854	Major Emory	17	J. H. Clark	5.50	8.00	2.50	Eyes black. (?)........
6315	....	Boca Grande, N. M	Mar. —, 1855	......do.........	42	Dr. Kennerly .	....	....	....	....

POOSPIZA BELLI, Sclater.

Bell's Finch.

Emberiza belli, CASSIN, Pr. A. N. Sc. Phila. V, Oct. 1850, 104 ; pl. iv. San Diego, Cal.
Poospiza belli, SCLATER, Pr. Zool. Soc. 1857, 7.

SP. CH.—Upper parts generally, with sides of head and neck, uniform bluish ash, tinged with yellowish gray on the crown and back, and with a few obsolete dusky streaks on the interscapular region. Beneath pure white, tinged with yellowish brown on the sides and under the tail. Eyelids, short streak from the bill to above the eye, and small median spot at the base of bill, white. A stripe on the sides of the throat and spot on the upper part of the breast, with the loral space and region round the eyes, plumbeous black. Tail feathers black ; the outer edged with white. Wing feathers all broadly edged with brownish yellow ; the elbow joint tinged with yellowish green. Bill and feet blue. Length, 6.25 ; wing, 2.90.

Hab.—Southern California and valley of Gila and Colorado to Fort Thorn.

This remarkable sparrow needs comparison with no other known North American species for its identification. The tail is very long and considerably emarginated, and the outer feather quite abruptly shorter; the feathers are unusually broad to near the end. The wings are short and considerably rounded; the second, third, fourth, and fifth nearly equal; the first rather shorter than the sixth. The bill is rather small.

List of specimens.

Catal. No.	Sex.	Locality.	When collected.	Whence obtained.	Collected by—
6237	......	Posa creek, Cal..........	....	Lt. Williamson..........	Dr. Heermann ....
6338	♂	Cosumnes river..........	....	......do...............	......do...............
6335	......	Fort Thorn, N. M........	....	Dr. T. C. Henry........	....
6336	......	Colorado river..........	Dec. 15, 1853 ...	Lt. Whipple	Kennerly and Möllhausen..

SPIZELLA, Bonaparte.

Spizella, BONAP. Geog. and Comp. List, 1838. Type *Fringilla canadensis*, Lath.
Spinites, CABANIS, Mus Hein. 1851, 133. Type *Fringilla socialis*, Wils.

CH.—Bill conical, the outlines slightly curved; the lower mandible decidedly lower than the upper; the commissure gently sinuated; the roof of the mouth not knobbed. Feet slender; tarsus rather longer than the middle toe; the hinder toe a little longer than the outer lateral, which slightly exceeds the inner; the outer claw reaching the base of the middle one, and half as long as its toe. Claws moderately curved. Tertiaries and secondaries nearly equal; wing somewhat pointed, reaching not quite to the middle of the tail. First quill a little shorter than the second and equal to the fifth; third longest. Tail rather long, moderately forked, and divaricated at the tip; the feathers rather narrow. Back streaked; rump and beneath immaculate. Hood generally uniform.

This genus differs from *Zonotrichia* in the smaller size and longer and forked, instead of rounded tail.

Synopsis of the species.

Interscapular region with the feathers streaked centrally with black. Rump and back of the neck without streaks. No spots or streaks beneath.

A. Head above and back chestnut. Two white bands on the wings. A light superciliary stripe.

    A chestnut streak behind the eye, and a dull rufous spot in the middle of the breast. Rump yellowish brown. Tail feathers edged with white. Bill black above; under mandible chiefly yellow...*S. monticola.*

    Smaller; a chestnut streak behind the eye. No spot on the breast. Rump yellowish brown. Tail feathers edged with ash. Bill red.............*S. pusilla.*

    Forehead and a line from the bill through and behind the eye black. Superciliary streak white. Rump bright ash. Bill black..............................*S. socialis.*

B. Head above streaked with black and gray, a light superciliary stripe. Beneath dirty white.

    Head above with a broad median light stripe and a conspicuous superciliary one...*S. pallida.*

    Head above without median stripe...*S. breweri.*

C. Body generally plumbeous, except the wings and interscapular region; becoming paler on the middle of the belly. Forehead, lores, chin, and throat, black. Bill red.

                                      S. atrigularis.

Comparative measurements of species.

Catal. No.	Species.	Locality.	Sex.	Length.	Stretch of wings.	Wing.	Tail.	Tarsus.	Middle toe.	Its claw alone.	Hind toe and claw.	Hind claw alone.	Bill above.	Along gape.	Specimen measured.
871	Spizella monticola	Carlisle, Penn	♂	5.80	......	3.02	3.04	0.79	0.74	0.20	0.54	0.24	0.35	0.41	Skin.......
do.	......do	......do		6.25	9.66	3 08	......	......	......	......	......	......	......	......	Fresh......
10151	Spizella pusilla	Washington, D. C.	♂	5 30	......	2.61	2.93	0.67	0.66	0.18	0.48	0.21	0.39	0.40	Skin.......
824	......do	Carlisle, Penn	♀	5.16	......	2.43	2.66	0.69	0.67	0.18	0.43	0.20	0.35	0.36	Skin.......
do.	......do	......do		5.25	7.75	2.42	......	......	......	......	......	......	......	......	Fresh......
10150	Spizella socialis	Washington, D. C.	♂	5.14	......	2.71	2.41	0.65	0.60	0.15	0.46	0 20	0.36	0.40	Skin.......
5556	......do	Petaluma, Cal	♂	5.14	......	2.74	2.60	0.62	0.62	0.17	0.44	0.20	0.48	0.42	Skin.......
10269	......do........ (?)	Red river, Pembina		5.70	......	2.90	2.69	0.64	0 65	0.16	0.44	0.21	0.38	0.44	Skin.......
1937	Spizella pallida	Fort Union, Neb		4.90	......	2.46	2.53	0 67	0.67	0.16	0.46	0.20	0.36	0.40	Skin.......
2890	Spizella breweri	Rocky Mountains	♂	5.10	......	2.46	2.64	0.69	0.63	0 16	4.40	0.18	0.32	0.39	Skin.......
1905	......do	......do	♀	5.04	......	2.53	2.62	0.70	0 60	0.14	0.42	0.17	0.35	0.34	Skin.......
4335	Spizella atrigularis	Agua Nueva, Coahuila	♂	5.50	....	2.51	3.07	0.76	0.72	0.18	0.48	0.22	0.38	0.46	Skin. ...
do.	......do	......do		5.42	7.75	2.50	......	......	......	......	......	......	......	......	Fresh......

SPIZELLA MONTICOLA, Baird.

Tree Sparrow.

Fringilla monticola, Gm. Syst. Nat. I, 1788, 912.

Zonotrichia monticola, Gray, Genera.

Spinites monticolus, Cabanis, Mus. Hein. 1851, 134.

Passer canadensis, Brisson, Orn. III, 1760, 102.

Fringilla canadensis, Lath. Index, I, 1790, 434.—Aud. Orn. Biog. II, 1834, 511 : V, 504 ; pl. 188.

Emberiza canadensis, Sw. F. B. Am. II, 1831, 252.—Aud. Syn. 1839.—Ib. Birds Amer. III, 1841, 83 ; pl. 166.

Spizella canadensis, Bon. List, 1838.—Ib. Conspectus, 1850, 480.

Fringilla arborea, Wils. Am. Orn II, 1810, 12 ; pl. xii, f. 3.

Moineau du Canada, Buffon, Pl. Enl. 223, f. 2.

"*Mountain Finch*, Lath. Syn. II, i, 265."

Sp. Ch.—Middle of back with the feathers dark brown centrally, then rufous, and edged with pale fulvous, (sometimes with whitish.) Hood and upper part of nape continuous chestnut ; a line of the same from behind the eye. Sides of head and neck ashy. A broad light superciliary band. Beneath whitish, with a small circular blotch of brownish in the middle of the upper part of the breast. Edges of tail feathers, primary quills, and two bands across the tips of the secondaries, white. Tertiaries nearly black ; edged externally with rufous, turning to white near the tips. Lower jaw yellow ; upper black. Length, 6.25 inches ; wing, 3.

Hab.—Eastern North America to the Missouri ; also on Pole creek and Little Colorado river, New Mexico.

This species varies in the amount of whitish edging to the quills and tail.

List of specimens.

Catal. No.	Sex.	Locality.	When collected.	Whence obtained.	Orig. No.	Collected by—	Length.	Stretch of wings.	Wing.	Remarks.
1280	♂	Carlisle, Pa	Feb. 28, 1844	S. F. Baird	... ...	....	6.25	9.50	3.00	....
866	♀	......do	Nov. 22, 1842	......do	......	....	6.00	8.83	2.75	....
871	♂	......do	..... do......	......do	......	....	6.25	9.67	3.08	....
7561	......	Washington, D. C.	....	Wm. Hutton						....
1591	......	Boston, Mass	....	T. M. Brewer						
10230	......	Sherburne, Mass	....	A. S. Babcock						
6352	......	Fort Leavenworth	Nov. 27, 1854	Lieut. Couch	11	....				
6353	......	......do	Jan. 20, 1855	......do	22	....				
5409	......	Cedar Island, Neb	Oct. 15, 1856	Lieut. Warren	......	Dr. Hayden	5.87	8.50	3	....
5410	♂	Medicine river	Oct. 8, 1856	..... do	......	......do	6.12	9.25	3.25	Eyes brown...............
5710	♂	Pole Creek, K.T	Aug. 2, 1856	Lieut. F. T. Bryan	192	....	6.	9.		
6354	......	Little Col'do river, N.M	Dec. 18, 1853	Lieut. Whipple	......	Kennerly and Mölhausen	5.50	8.50	3	....
6355	......	......do	Dec. 20, 1853	......do	39	..... do	5.50	8.50	3	....

SPIZELLA PUSILLA, Bonap.

Field Sparrow.

Fringilla pusilla, Wilson, Am. Orn. II, 1810, 121 ; pl. xvi, f. 2.—Licht. Verzeichn. Doubl. 1823, No. 252.—Aud. Orn. Biog. II, 1834, 299 ; pl. 139.

Spizella pusilla, Bonap. List, 1838.—Ib. Conspec. 1850, 480.

Emberiza pusilla, Aud. Syn. 1839, 104.—Ib. Birds Amer. III, 1841, 77 ; pl. 164.

Spinites pusillus, Cab. Mus. Hein. 1851, 133.

Fringilla juncorum, Nutt. Man. I, 1832, 499 ; 2d ed. 1840, 577. (Supposed by him to be *Motacilla juncorum*, Gmelin, I, 952 ; *Sylvia juncorum*, Latham, Ind. II, 511 ; *Little Brown Sparrow*, Catesby, Car. I, 35.)

Sp. Ch.—Bill red. Crown continuous rufous red. Back somewhat similar, streaked with blackish. Sides of head and neck (including a superciliary stripe) ashy. Ear coverts rufous. Beneath white, tinged with yellowish anteriorly. Tail feathers and quills faintly edged with white. Two white bands across the wing coverts. Length, about 5.75 ; wing, 2.34.

Hab.—Eastern North America to the Missouri river.

This species is about the size of *S. socialis*, but is more rufous above ; lacks the black forehead and eye stripe ; has chestnut ears instead of ash ; has the bill red instead of black ; lacks the clear ash of the rump ; has a longer tail, &c. It is more like *monticola*, but is much smaller ; lacks the spot on the breast, and the predominance of white on the wings, &c. The young have the breast and sides streaked.

Although it is quite possible that the " little brown sparrow," of Catesby, refers to the present bird, yet "small sparrow, entirely brown," is scarcely a sufficient diagnosis upon which to found a species.

List of specimens.

Catal. No.	Sex.	Locality.	When collected.	Whence obtained.	Orig'l No.	Collected by—	Length.	Stretch of wings.	Wing.	Remarks.
436	♂	Carlisle, Pa..	May 31, 1841	S. F. Baird			5.25	8.00		
1378	♀	....do.	April 22, 1844	......do.			5.17	7.75	2.33	
824	♀	......do.	Oct. 20, 1842	.. ...do.			5.25	7.75	2.42	
1374	♂	.....do.	April 19, 1844	......do.			5.75	8.17	2.33	
730	♀	..... do.	Sept. 20, 1842	..... do.			5.25	7.50		
10151	♂	Washington...			J. C. McGuire ..					
1592	......	Boston, Mass			S. F. Baird		T. M. Brewer			
8234	♂	Independence, Mo..	June 6, 1857	W. M. Magraw...	57	Dr. Cooper	5.75	8.50	2.75	
4802	......	Fort Leavenworth.	April 21, 1856	Lt. G. K. Warren.		Dr. Hayden		8.25		
4800	......	Big Sioux river, Neb.	May 3, 1856	......do.		......do.	5.87	8.25	2.75	Eyes dark
4801	......	..... do.	May 24, 1856	......do.		......do. ...	5.50	8.12	2.50	
5413	♀	Fort Lookout, Neb.	June 21, 1856	......do.		......do.	5.50	8.00	2.75	Eye black (?)
5412	♂	Knife river, Neb	Sept. —, 1856	......do.		......do.	5.25	8.50	2.75	

SPIZELLA SOCIALIS, Bonap.

Chipping Sparrow.

Fringilla socialis, Wilson, Am. Orn. II, 1810, 127 ; pl. xvi, f. 5.—Aud. Orn. Biog. II, 1834, 21 : V, 517 ; pl. 104.

Spizella socialis, Bon. List, 1838.—Ib. Conspectus, 1850, 480.

Emberiza socialis, Aud. Syn. 1839.—Ib. Birds Amer. III, 1841, 80 ; pl. 165.

Spinites socialis, Cabanis, Mus. Hein. 1851, 133. (Type.)

Sp. Ch.—Rump, back of neck, and sides of neck and head, ashy. Interscapular region with black streaks, margined with pale rufous. Crown continuous and uniform chestnut. Forehead black, separated in the middle by white. A white streak over the eye, and a black one from the base of the bill through and behind the eye. Under parts unspotted whitish, tinged with ashy, especially across the upper breast. Tail feathers and primaries edged with paler, not white. Two narrow white bands across the wing coverts. Bill black. Length, 5.75 ; wing, nearly 3.00.

Hab.—North America, from Atlantic to Pacific.

June 17, 1858.

60 b

The young have the chestnut of the crown varied with narrow blackish lines, sometimes the chestnut little appreciable. The upper part of the breast and sides streaked with brown.

This species is readily distinguished from *S. monticola* by its black bill and forehead; black line behind the eye instead of chestnut; absence of black spot on the breast, and of white on the tail, &c., as also by the much smaller size.

List of specimens.

Catal. No.	Sex and age.	Locality.	When collected.	Whence obtained.	Orig. No.	Collected by—	Length.	Stretch of wings.	Wing.	Remarks.
10150	♂	Washington, D. C.....	....	J. C. McGuire.....	......	....				....
1424	♂	Carlisle, Pa..........	May 2, 1844	S. F. Baird.......	......	....	5.67	8.75	2.92	....
721	♂	......do............	Sept. 16, 1842	......do........			5.50	8.50		
1106	○ ○	......do............	July 5, 1843	......do........						
10269?	....	Pembina...........	Sept. 26, 1857	N. W. University..		R. Kennicott...				
4805	....	Bald Island, Neb......	April 25, 1857	Lt. G. K. Warren..		Dr. Hayden....	5.00	8.00	2.62	Eyes dark.......
5411	♂	Fort Lookout, Neb.....	June —, 1856	......do........		.....do.........	5.25	8 50	2.75	......do....
5715?	....	Pole creek...........	Aug. —, 1856	Lt. Bryan..........		W. S. Wood...				
6348	♂	Fort Steilacoom, W.T..	1854	Dr. Suckley.......	92					
6349	♀	......do............	1854	......do........	93					
6350	♀	......do............	1854	......do........	94					
6351	....	......do............	April —, 1856	......do......	298		5.50	9.00		
5981	....	......do............	May —, 1855	Dr. J. G. Cooper ..			5.50	8.50		
4417	♀	Fort Dalles, O. T.....	May 5, 1855	Dr. Suckley...	165½					
4883	♂	......do............	May 2, 1855	......do........	161		5.87	9.00	2.83	
4384	♂	......do............	May 4, 1855	......do........	165		5.62	8.75		
5556	♂	Petaluma, Cal........	May 24, 1855	E. Samuels........	889					
6346	....	Sacramento, Cal.......	....	Lt. Williamson......		Dr. Heermann .				
6347	....	Tejon Pass, Cal.......	....	......do........		.... do........				
		Fort Tejon...........	....	J. X. de Vesey.....						
8054	....	Mexico...........	....	J. Gould........						

SPIZELLA PALLIDA, Bonap.

Clay-colored Bunting.

Emberiza pallida, Sw. F. Bor. Am. II, 1831, 251. (Not of Audubon.)
Spizella pallida, BONAP. List, 1838.
Spinites pallidus, CABANIS, Mus. Hein. 1851, 133.
Emberiza shattuckii, AUD. Birds Am. VII, 1843, 347 ; pl. 493.
Spizella shattuckii, BONAP. Conspectus, 1850, 480.

SP. CH.—Smaller than *S. socialis*. Back and sides of hind neck ashy. Prevailing color above pale brownish yellow, with a tinge of grayish. The feathers of back and crown streaked conspicuously with blackish. Crown with a median ashy and a lateral or superciliary ashy white stripe. Beneath whitish, tinged with brown on the breast and sides, and an indistinct narrow brown streak on the edge of the chin. Ear coverts brownish yellow, margined above and below by dark brown. Length, 4.75 ; wing, 2.55.

Hab.—Upper Missouri river and High Central plains to the Saskatchewan country.

The ashy collar is quite conspicuous, and streaked above with brown. The rump is immaculate. The streaks on the feathers of the crown almost form continuous lines, about six in number. The brown line above the ear coverts is a post ocular one. The brown line on the side of the chin forms the lower border of a white maxillary stripe which widens and curves around behind the ear coverts, fading into the ashy of the neck. The wing feathers are all margined with paler, and there is an indication of two light bands across the ends of the coverts.

The young of this species is thickly streaked beneath over the throat, breast, and belly, with brown, giving to it an entirely different appearance from the adult. The streaks in the upper parts, too, are darker and more conspicuous. The margins of the feathers rather more rusty.

This species is readily distinguishable from the other American *Spizellas*, excepting *S. breweri*, (which see,) in the dark streaks and median ashy stripe on the crown, the paler tints, the dark line on the side of the chin, &c.

List of specimens.

Catal. No.	Sex.	Locality.	When collected.	Whence obtained.	Orig. No.	Collected by—	Length.	Stretch of wings.	Wing.	Remarks.
1858	......	Fort Union, Neb.....	1843..........	S. F. Baird..	......	Ed. Harris	....	......	.....	....
1937	......	....do............	1843........	......do............	......	J. J. Audubon...	....	......	.....	....
5414	......	......do............	July 18, 1843	Lt. G. K. Warren..	......	Dr. Hayden	5.00	7.50	2.50	....
5415	......	Blackfoot country....	......do......	.....do............	......	......do........	......	......	......	....
894	......	Cheyenne river	Sept. 10, 1857	......do............	......	......do........	5.00	7.00	......	Iris dark brown ....
4804	......	Bijoux Hills..........	May 14, 1857	......do............	......	......do........	5.62	7.75	2.50	Iris hazel ....
4803	♂	Nebraska	......do......	......do............	......	......do........	5.37	7.50	2.25	....
5715	♂	Pole Creek, K. T.....	Aug. 1, 1856	Lt. F. T. Bryan.....	184	W. S. Wood....	......	......	......	....
6359	......	Texas.....	....	Capt. Pope.........	......	....	......	......	......	....
4091	......	Tamaulipas, Mex....	Mar. —, 1855	Lt. Couch..........	73	....	4.75	7.25	2.25	Eyes dark brown; feet light brown; bill slate.

SPIZELLA BREWERI, Cassin.

Brewer's Sparrow.

Emberiza pallida, AUD. Orn. Biog. V, 1839, 66 ; pl, 398, f. 2.—IB. Synopsis, 1839.—IB. Birds Amer. III, 1841, 71 ; pl. 161. (Not of Swainson, 1831.)

Spizella breweri, CASSIN, Pr. A. N. Sc. VIII, Feb. 1856, 40.

SP. CH.—Similar to *S. pallida;* the markings more obsolete ; no distinct median and superciliary light stripes. The crown streaked with black. Some of the feathers on the sides with brown shafts. Length, 5 inches ; wing, 2.50.

Hab.—Rocky mountains of United States to the Pacific coast.

This species, if really distinct, is so very similar to the *S. pallida* as to require very close and critical comparison to separate it. One feature is the more obsolete character of the markings, which have not the sharpness and definition of *pallida*. The streaks on the back are narrower, and the central ashy and lateral whitish stripes of the crown are scarcely, if at all, appreciable. The clear ash of the back of the neck, too, is mostly wanting. The feathers along the sides of the body, near the tibia, and occasionally elsewhere on the sides, have brownish shafts, not found in the other.

List of specimens.

Catal. No.	Sex.	Locality.	When collected.	Whence obtained.	Orig. No.	Collected by—	Length.	Stretch of wings.	Wing.
2890	♂	Rocky mountains....	June 15, 1834	S. F. Baird......	......	J. K. Townsend.	....	....	......
1905	♀	......do............	....	......do........	......	......do........	....	....	......
6361	♂	Tejon valley........	....	Lt. Williamson..	......	Dr. Heermann ..	....	....	......
6360	♂	......do............	....	......do........	......	......do........	....	....	......
6357	....	Boca Grande, Mex....	Mar. —, 1855	Major Emory....	40	Dr. Kennerly ...	....	....	......
6358	....	Camp 127, N. M., Bill Williams' Fork....	Feb. 26, 1854	Lt. Whippple ...	174	......do........	....	....	......
6356?	♀	El Paso, Texas........	May 4, 1852	Col. Graham....	......	C. Wright......	5.25	7.25	2.25

SPIZELLA ATRIGULARIS, Baird.

Black-chinned Sparrow.

Spinites atrigularis, CABANIS, Mus. Hein. 1851, 133.
Struthus atrimentalis, COUCH, Pr. A. N. Sc. Phil. VII, April, 1854, 67.

SP. CH.—Tail elongated, deeply forked and divaricated. General color bluish ash, paler beneath, and turning to white on the middle of the belly. Interscapular region yellowish rusty, streaked with black. Forehead, loral region, and side of head as far as eyes, chin, and upper part of throat black. Quills and tail feathers very dark brown, edged with ashy. Edges of coverts like the back. No white bands on the wings. Bill red. Length, 5.50 ; wing, 2.50 ; tail, 3.00.

Hab.—Mexico just south of the Rio Grande.

This species is about the size of S. pusilla and socialis, resembling the former most in its still longer tail. This is more deeply forked and divaricated with broader feathers than in either. The wing is much rounded ; the fourth quill longest ; the first almost the shortest of the primaries.

List of specimens.

Catal. No.	Sex.	Locality.	When collected.	Whence obtained.	Length.	Stretch of wings.	Wing.	Remarks.
4335	♂	Agua Nueva, Coahuila, Mex.	May, 1853....	Lieut. D. N. Couch.....	5.62	7.75	2.50	Eyes and feet dark brown ; bill light red brown.

MELOSPIZA, Baird.

CH.—Body stout. Bill conical, very obsoletely notched, or smooth ; somewhat compressed. Lower mandible not so deep as the upper. Commisure nearly straight. Gonys a little curved. Feet stout, not stretching beyond the tail ; tarsus a little longer than the middle toe ; outer toe a little longer than the inner ; its claw not quite reaching to the base of the middle one. Hind toe appreciably longer than the middle one. Wings quite short and rounded, scarcely reaching beyond the base of the tail ; the tertials considerably longer than the secondaries ; the quills considerably graduated ; the fourth longest ; the first not longer than the tertials, and almost the shortest of the primaries. Tail moderately long, and considerably graduated ; the feathers oval at the tips. Crown and back similar in color and streaked ; beneath thickly streaked. Tail immaculate.

This genus differs from Zonotrichia in shorter, more graduated tail, rather longer hind toe, much more rounded wing, which is shorter ; the tertiaries longer ; the first quill almost the shortest, and not longer than the tertials. The under parts are spotted ; the crown streaked and like the back.

I have placed in this section, which has the *Fringilla melodia* as its type, the *Fringilla palustris* of Wilson. This differs in the uniform rufous crown of the male, streaked, however, in the female, and in having only obsolete streaks on the breast. The *Fringilla lincolnii* is more aberrant ; it is spotted beneath, but the wing and first primary are a little longer. These two might form a separate section, *Helospiza*, agreeing in the narrower and shorter tail, smaller and more slender bill, more slender toes, &c., with the *Fringilla palustris* as type.

SYNOPSIS OF SPECIES.

Melospiza, Baird.

A. Beneath uniform whitish from chin to anus, thickly streaked on the breast and sides. Head streaked.

Streaks of back and under parts distinctly black in the central portion. Bill stout.

Prevailing color light reddish gray. Feathers of back edged with gray. Stripes of breast with distinct rufous suffusion externally. Wing 2.68 inches..*melodia*.

Prevailing color above olivaceous gray. Stripes of breast purer black, with little or no rufous suffusion externally. Wing 2.50 inches.....................*heermanni*.
Similar to the last but much smaller. Wing 2.10 inches...............**Var.** *gouldii*.
Streaks above and below dark rufous, without black centres. Bill slender.
Above decidedly rufous brown, the streaks very obsolete, without gray edges. Beneath thickly streaked..*rufina*.
Above brownish gray. Streaks distinct ; feathers with gray edging. Beneath rather sparsely streaked...*fallax*.

Helospiza, Baird.

B. Under parts white ; breast reddish yellow, with distinct, well defined streaks. Head streaked ....*lincolnii*.
C. Head above uniform reddish. Beneath white, without streaks, or with very obsolete ones, except on sides of breast. Breast tinged with plumbeous.............................*palustris*.

Comparative measurements of species.

Catal. No.	Species.	Locality.	Sex.	Length.	Stretch of wings.	Wing.	Tail.	Tarsus.	Middle toe.	Its claw alone.	Hind toe and claw.	Hind claw alone.	Bill above.	Along gape.	Specimen measured.
1590	Melospiza melodia ...	Boston, Mass............		6.42	......	2.62	3.08	0.84	0.80	0.20	0.54	0.26	0.47	0.45	Skin.......
808	......do............	Carlisle, Penn...........	♀	5.70	......	2.50	2.76	0.83	0.85	0.23	0.58	0.28	0.44	0.50	Skin.......
do.	......do............	......do................		6.08	8.33	2.43	......	......	......	......	......	......	......	......	Fresh ......
2637	......do............	......do................	♂	5.20	......	2.68	2.88	0.80	0.77	0.20	0.56	0.26	0.48	0.54	Skin.......
do.	......do............	......do................		6.16	8.84	2.75	......	......	......	......	......	......	......	......	Fresh ......
9528	Melospiza rufina	Puget Sound............	♀	6.40	......	2.60	2.93	0.89	0.83	0.20	0.60	0.30	0.47	0.51	Skin.......
6227	Melospiza heermanni.	Tejon Valley............	♂	6.22	......	2.54	2.94	0.92	0.87	0.23	0.66	0.30	0.49	0.50	Skin.......
10274	......do............	Fort Tejon, Cal..........	♂	5.00	......	2.42	2.78	0.86	0.82	0.24	9.64	0.31	0.44	0.51	Skin.......
8053	Melospiza gouldii....	California..............		4.70	......	2.10	2.38	0.79	0.79	0.18	0.54	0.26	0.44	0.50	Skin.......
10281	Melospiza fallax......	Camp 106, Pueblo cr.,N.M.		6.46	......	2.76	3.18	0.78	0.78	0.20	0.62	0.28	0.40	0.44	Skin.......
6225	......do............	Mimbres to Rio Grande ..		5.50	......	2.71	3.24	0.86	0.82	0.22	0.58	0.26	0.44	0.46	Skin.......
934	Melospiza palustris...	Carlisle, Penn............	♂	5.26	......	2.33	2.54	0.82	0.78	0.18	0.62	0.28	0.44	0.47	Skin.......
do.	......do............	......do................		5.66	8.93	2.42	......	......	......	......	......	......	......	......	Fresh ......
375	......do............	......do................	♀?	5.30	......	2.20	2.41	0.79	0.74	0.17	0.56	0.25	0.41	0.44	Skin.......
do.	......do............	......do................		5.50	9.50	......	......	......	......	......	......	......	......	......	......
937	Melospiza lincolni....	......do..	♂	5.24	......	2.60	2.42	0.76	0.82	0.20	0.58	0.26	0.44	0.48	Skin.......
do.	......do............	......do................		5.58	8.35	2.58	......	......	......	......	......	......	......	......	Fresh ......
972	......do............	......do................	♀	4.84	......	2.34	2.32	0.80	0.74	0.18	0 52	0.25	0.43	0.48	Skin.......
do.	......do............	......do................		5.57	8.00	2.33	......	......	......	......	......	......	......	......	Fresh .. ...

MELOSPIZA MELODIA, Baird.

Song Sparrow.

Fringilla melodia, WILSON, Am. Orn. II, 1810, 125 ; pl. xvi, f. 4.—LICHT. Verz. 1823, No. 249.—AUD. Orn. Biog. I, 1832, 126 : V, 507 ; pl 25.—IB. Syn. 1839, 120.—IB. Birds Amer. III, 1841, 147 ; pl. 189.
Zonotrichia melodia, BON. List, 1838.—IB. Conspectus, 1850, 478.
?? *Fringilla fasciata*,[1] GMELIN, Syst. Nat. I, 1788, 922.—NUTTALL, Man. I, 2d ed. 1840, 562.
?? *Fringilla hyemalis*, GMELIN, Syst. Nat. I, 1788, 922.

SP. CH.—General tint of upper parts rufous brown, streaked with dark brown and ashy gray. The crown is rufous, with a superciliary and median stripe of dull gray, the former lighter ; nearly white anteriorly, where it has a faint shade of yellow ; each feather of the crown with a narrow streak of dark brown. Interscapulars dark brown in the centre, then rufous, then grayish

[1] The *fasciated sparrow* of Pennant, Arctic Zool. II, 375, upon which Gmelin's name is based, answers pretty well for our species, but the tail is said to be crossed by numerous dusky bars, which is not the case with *melodia*. The winter sparrow of Pennant, II, 376, *Fringilla hyemalis*, Gmelin, is equally uncertain.

on the margin. Rump grayer than upper tail coverts, both with obsolete dark streaks. There is a whitish maxillary stripe, bordered above and below by one of dark rufous brown, with a similar one from behind the eye. The under parts are white ; the breast and sides of body and throat streaked with dark rufous, with a still darker central line. On the middle of the breast these marks are rather aggregated so as to form a spot. No distinct white on tail or wings. Length of male, 6.50 ; wing, 2.58 ; tail, 3.

Hab.—Eastern United States to the High Central Plains.

Specimens vary somewhat in having the streaks across the breast more or less sparse ; the spot more or less distinct. In autumn the colors are more blended, the light maxillary stripe tinged with yellowish, the edges of the dusky streaks suffused with brownish rufous.

The young bird has the upper parts paler, the streaks more distinct ; the lines on the head scarcely appreciable. The under parts are yellowish ; the streaks narrower and more sharply defined dark brown.

List of specimens.

Catal. No.	Sex and age.	Locality.	When collected.	Whence obtained.	Orig. No.	Collected by—	Length.	Stretch of wings.	Wing.	Remarks.
1294	♂	Carlisle, Penn......	Mar. 9, 1844	S. F. Baird.......		.....	6.08	8.25	2.58	....
192	....	......do............	Oct. 13, 1840	......do.........						....
2637	♂	......do............	May 11, 1846	......do.........			6.17	8.83	2.75	.............? ....
1080	○	......do............	June 2, 1843	......do.........						....
808	♀	......do......	Oct. 17, 1842	......do.........			6.08	8.33	2.42	....
1147	○♂	Cape May, N. J....	July 19, 1843	......do.........		W. M. Baird..				....
1590	....	Boston............	....	T. M. Brewer....						....
4817	♀	Bald I., Neb.......	April 25, 1856	Lt. G. K. Warren.		Dr. Hayden..	6	8.50	2.50	Iris brown; pupil bluish ....
8750?	○	Loup Fork of Platte.	Sept. 11, 1857	......do.........		......do......				....
6226?	....	Boca Grande, Mex.	Mar. —, 1855	Major Emory.....	39	Dr. Kennerly.	5.50	7.50	2.50	....

MELOSPIZA HEERMANNI, Baird.

Heermann's Song Sparrow.

Sp. Ch.—Somewhat like *melodia*. The streaks on the back and under parts blacker, broader, more distinct, and scarcely margined with reddish, except in winter plumage. General shade of coloration olivaceous gray rather than rusty. Length, 6.40 ; wing, 2.56 ; tail, 3.

Hab.—Tejon Pass, California.

In the collection of sparrows before me is a *Melospiza* from the Tejon valley (6227) (winter) labelled *Zonotrichia guttata* by Dr. Heermann, and resembling it somewhat, but differing very appreciably from a large number of specimens from Washington and Oregon Territories. It differs in having the bill considerably larger, broader, and more convex, and bulging laterally at the base; the commissure more sinuated; the tarsus shorter. The under parts are of a purer white; the streaks are less numerous, but larger and more sharply defined, being blackish brown anteriorly, with a slightly rufous edging in places. The sides and under tail coverts are yellowish brown, as in *rufina*, but with darker streaks. The ground color of the upper parts is nearly the same, (darker than in *melodia*,) but the streaks and blotches, instead of being obsolete, are strongly marked. The blotches on the upper surface are even darker than in *melodia* and more extended; they are margined with darker and more brownish rufous, and lack the well defined grayish edges to the feathers. The spots on the under parts, too, are blacker and larger than in *melodia*, with less rusty brown on the sides; the sides of body and under tail coverts are darker and more blotched. The black blotches on the breast distinguish this species from *Z. fallax.*

Although it is very difficult to express the characters of this sparrow by an absolute diagnosis, yet it will most probably prove permanently and specifically different from the more northern and typical *guttata*. The latter appears to be a northern species, several of the specimens having been collected on the Columbia river and northward in January and February, and consequently winter residents, while the locality of the other at Tejon Pass is nearly twelve degrees (or more than eight hundred miles) further south, with no intermediate localities recorded.

After carefully considering the circumstances of the case, I have come to the conclusion that the species is worthy of specific separation, and have accordingly named it *Melospiza heermanni*, after its accomplished collector and discoverer.

Since writing the preceding article, I have had the opportunity of examining a large collection of this same species made at Fort Tejon by Mr. De Vesey, and am still better satisfied of its claim to a specific separation. A spring bird has the spots on the breast and sides entirely black, without any rufous edging, as is also the case with those on the back. The feet are larger and the claws longer than in *melodia*. The tail feathers are much darker, and the tints above, instead of being light rufous, are decidedly grayish olivaceous. The differences from *rufina* consist in the much stouter and thicker bill, and the very distinct dark, usually black, streaks, instead of rufous brown.

The colors of the winter specimens have the usual soft blended appearance peculiar to this season, but the spots still retain their well defined blackness, with only a slight tendency to passing externally into dark rufous.

List of specimens.

Catal. No.	Sex.	Locality.	Whence obtained.	Orig. No.	Collected by—
6127	♂	Tejon valley, Cal..........	Lt. Williamson..............	....	Dr. Heermann ....
10274	♂	Fort Tejon.................	J. X. de Vesey..............	38	....
10273	♀	......do...................	......do	....	....

MELOSPIZA GOULDII, Baird.

Sp. Ch.—Similar to *M. melodia*, still more so to *M. heermanni*, but very much smaller. Breast and sides conspicuously streaked with black ; back and head above distinctly streaked. Length, 4.70 ; wing, 2.10 ; tail, 2.38.
Hab.—California.

In a collection of birds presented by Mr. John Gould to the Smithsonian Institution is a perfectly adult specimen (No. 8053) marked "California," which has a certain resemblance to the song sparrow, but differs in being very much smaller, much less, in fact, than any other known species of the group. The difference in size is much greater than is usually allowed to exist in the same species. The wing measures only 2.10 inches, or less than in *Ammodromus samuelis*.

The bill is a little more slender than in *melodia*, the legs much the same size, the wings and tail much shorter. The sides of the throat and body with the breast are distinctly streaked with black, which has a slightly rufous suffusion externally. The black streaks on the back are also well defined as in *M. heermanni*. The bill and feet are nearly as large as in this species, but the wings and tail are very much shorter. This disproportion of feet, with the difference in size, leads me to consider the species as a good one, as, if it were merely a smaller race of another species, the general proportions would be retained.

MELOSPIZA RUFINA, Baird.

" *Emberiza rufina*, BRANDT, Desc. Av. Rossic. 1836, tab. ii, 5, Sitka." Bonaparte.

Passerella rufina, BONAP. Conspectus, 1850, 477.

Fringilla cinerea, (GM.) AUD. Orn. Biog. V, 1839, 22; pl. 390.—IB. Syn. 1839, 119.—IB. Birds America, III, 1841, 145; pl. 187.

Passerella cinerea, BP. List, 1839.—IB. Conspectus, 1850, 477.

? Zonotrichia cinerea, BP. Conspectus, 1850, 478.

?? Fringilla cinerea, GMELIN, I, 1788, 922.

Fringilla (Passerella) guttata, NUTTALL, Man. I, 2d ed. 1840, 581.

Zonotrichia guttata, GAMBEL, J. A. N. Sc. I, Dec. 1847, 50.

SP. CH.—Bill slender. Similar in general appearance to *M. melodia*, but darker and much more rufous, the colors more blended. General appearance above light rufous brown, the interscapular region streaked very obsoletely with dark brownish rufous, the feathers of the crown similar, with still darker obsolete central streaks. A superciliary and very obscure median crown stripe, ashy. Under parts *brownish* whitish; the breast and sides of throat and body broadly streaked with dark brownish rufous; darker in the centre. A light maxillary stripe. Sides of the body tinged strongly with the colors of the rump, and leaving only a narrow space of the belly white. Under coverts brown. Length, 6.75 ; wing, 2.70 ; tail, 3.00.

Hab.—Pacific coast of the United States to Russian America.

This species appears larger than *M. melodia*, and will be readily distinguished by the absence of the blackish brown centres to the brown streaks, and of any marked contrast of color in different parts of the feathers, as well as by the general dark rufous shades of color. There are no grayish edges to the feathers of the back, nor blackish streaks. The spots beneath are broader, more blended, and more thickly crowded ; the sides and under tail coverts much darker. The bill is smaller and considerably more slender and conical. The light and dark markings about the head are less strongly contrasted.

The color of the spots on the breast is much as in *M. fallax ;* they are broader and much more numerous, however ; the sides and under tail coverts much darker. The upper parts, too, are much darker and more rufous ; the feathers lacking the grayish edges, so conspicuous in *fallax* as well as in *melodia*. In fact, the upper parts are frequently so uniform as almost to resemble *Passerella townsendii*, there being only a faint trace of darker centres.

The bill is more slender and attenuated than in any of our large song sparrows.

The young has the head above olivaceous rufous without any streaks ; the feathers of the back are brownish rufous with obsolete central blotches. The spotting is thus much less than in *melodia*.

I do not agree with Nuttall in considering *Fringilla cinerea* of Gmelin so far removed from the present species; in fact, it is quite possibly the same, as based on the cinereous finch of Pennant.—(Arctic Zool. II, 378.) Still, as the species is not cinereous and there is yet much uncertainty about it, it may be best not to take Gmelin's name.

The next name in order appears to be *rufina* of Brandt, which I identify from Bonaparte's description, not having the original reference at hand.

There is yet much to be done in the determination and identification of the numerous spotted sparrows from the northwest coast, described by Pennant, Gmelin, and other authors.

List of specimens.

Catal. No.	Sex and age.	Locality.	When collected.	Whence obtained.	Orig. No.	Collected by—	Length.	Stretch of wings.	Wing.	Remarks.
5977	....	Straits of Fuca, W. T..	Mar. —, 1855	Dr. J. G. Cooper...	......	....	......	......	......	....
4540	....	Washington Territory..	———, 1856	Dr. G. Suckley.....	......	....	......	......	......	....
4599	....	Steilacoom, W. T.....	Feb. 5, 1856	......do..........	218	....	6.50	8.75	2.62	....
6231	....	......do......	....	......do..........	247	....	7.00	9.00	......	....
6232	....	......do......	....	......do..........	249	....	7.00	9.00	......	....
6233	....	......do......	....	......do..........	255	....	7.00	9.00	......	....
6234	....	......do......	Mar. —, 1856	......do..........	259	....	7.00	9.00	......	....
6235	....	......do......	....	......do..........	262	....	......	......	......	....
6228	....	Shoalwater bay, W. T..	July 5, 1854	Dr. J. G. Cooper...	85	....	6.75	8.75	......	Iris brown ......
6229	....	......do......	......do......	......do..........	......	....	6.75	8.75	......	......do......
6230	♂	......do......	Sept. —, 1854	......do..........	......	....	6.75	8.75	......	Iris brown, bill and feet the same.
1860	♀	Columbia river........	Jan. 18, 1836	S. F. Baird........	59	J. K. Townsend.....	......	......	......	....
1942	♀	......do......	....	......do..........	......	......do.......	......	......	......	....
10275?	♀	Fort Tejon, Cal........	....	J. X. de Vesey.....	861	....	......	......	......	....

MELOSPIZA FALLAX, Baird.

Zonotrichia fallax, BAIRD, Pr. A. N. Sc. Ph. VII, June, 1854, 119. (Pueblo creek, New Mexico.)
? *Zonotrichia fasciata,* (GM.) GAMBEL, J. A. N. Sc. Ph. 2d Series, I, 1847, 49.

SP. CH.—Similar to *Z. melodia,* but with wings and tail longer, and bill smaller. Dark centres to the brownish streaks of the feathers of upper and under surfaces obsolete or wanting. Superciliary light stripe ash color anteriorly. Length, 6.65 ; wing, 2.75 ; tail, 3.36.

Hab.—Rocky mountain region from Fort Thorn to the Colorado. Fort Tejon?

Although this species is very similar to the *M. melodia,* yet, when specimens are compared with an extensive series of the last mentioned species, an impression of difference will at once be conveyed. The bird is rather larger, especially the tail, as shown by the accompanying table, while the feet and especially the bill are smaller. The line above the eye is grayish ash throughout, without the whitish immediately at the base of the bill. The dark brown centres in the brownish rufous streaks of the head, back, and under parts, are almost entirely wanting or very obsolete ; the color of the rufous streaks, too, is paler.

I do not, however, feel sure that this species will stand as perfectly satisfactory, as there is a specimen (6226) from Boca Grande, Mexico, before me which has all the dark markings of eastern specimens, with a decidedly inferior bill. At any rate, I consider it as less strongly established than any of the others before me. It has certain relationships of coloration to the *M. guttata,* but is much grayer.

As far as I can judge the middle toe and claw are proportionally longer than in *M. melodia.*

List of specimens.

Catal. No.	Locality.	When collected.	Whence obtained.	Orig. No.	Collected by—
	Pueblo creek, Camp 106, N.M.	Jan. 22, 1854	Lieut. Whipple----------	51	Kennerly and Möllhausen.
6225	Fort Thorn, N. M---------	---------------	Dr. T. C. Henry --------	-------	---------------------------
10271?	Fort Tejon, Cal----------	---------------	J. X. de Vesey----------	656	---------------------------

June 17, 1856.

61 b

MELOSPIZA LINCOLNII, Baird.

Lincoln's Finch.

Fringilla lincolnii, Aud. Orn. Biog. II, 1834, 539, pl. 193.—Nutt. Man. I, 2d ed. 1840, 569.
Linaria lincolnii, Rich. List, 1837.
Passerculus lincolnii, Bonap. List, 1838.
Peucaea lincolnii, Aud. Synopsis, 1839, 113.—Ib. Birds Amer. III, 1841, 116, pl. 177.—Bonap. Consp. 1850, 481.—
        Ib. Comptes Rendus XXVII, 1854, 920.
Passerculus zonarius, (Bp.) Sclater, Pr. Zool. Soc. 1856, 305.

Sp. Ch.—Crown chestnut, with a median and two lateral or superciliary ash colored stripes ; each feather above streaked centrally with black. Back with narrow streaks of black. Beneath white, with a maxillary stripe curving round behind the ear coverts, a well defined band across the breast, extending down the sides, and the under tail coverts, brownish yellow. The maxillary stripe margined above and below with lines of black spots. The throat, upper part of breast, and sides of the body, with streaks of black, smallest in the middle of the former. There is a chestnut stripe back of the ear, streaked with black. The pectoral bands are sometimes paler. Length, 5.60 ; wing, 2.60.

Hab.—United States from Atlantic to Pacific, and south through Mexico to Guatemala.

This species is easily known among the American sparrows by the well marked yellowish band across the breast and the maxillary stripe of brownish yellow relieved against the white of the under parts generally. *Ammodromus caudacutus* has these stripes somewhat similar ; but the superciliary stripe is also yellowish, not ash color, and the middle of the throat is unspotted. The bill is much longer, and the generic characters otherwise different.

List of specimens.

Catal. No.	Sex.	Locality.	When collected.	Whence obtained.	Orig. No.	Collected by—	Length.	Stretch of wings.	Wing.	Remarks.
937	♂	Carlisle, Pa............	May 4, 1843	S. F. Baird		....	5.58	8.33	2.58	....
972	♀	......do............ ..	May 16, 1843	......do.......		....	5.58	8.00	2.33	
4811	......	Iowa Point, Neb	April 23, 1856	Lt. G. K. Warren.	16	Dr. Hayden......	5.37	7.62	2.37	Iris very dull brown....
4898	......	Bald island, Neb......	April 25, 1856	...... do.......		......do.......	5.50	8.00	2.62	
4809	♂	Platte river, Neb.......	April 26, 1856	......do.......	52	......do....... .	5.75	8.37	2.62	
4814	♂	Big Sioux river, Neb...	April 5, 1856	......do.......		......do.......	5.50	9.50	3.00	
4815	♂	Vermilion river, Neb...	April 8, 1856	......do.......		......do .	5.37	8.00	2.50	
4812	♂	......do....	May 8, 1856	......do.......		......do.......	6.00	8.00	2.50	Iris brown............ .
4813	♂	......do............	May 6, 1856	......do.......		......do.......	5.50	8.12	2.75	......do...
4810	♂	......do............	May 8, 1856	......do.......		......do.......	6.00	9.50	3.12	
5416	......	Blackfoot country, Neb.	July —, 1855	......do....... .		......do.......	....	....	....	
1864	......	Upper Missouri	1843........	S. F. Baird......		J. J. Audubon....	....	....	....	
8218	......	Fort Laramie	Sept. 10, 1857	W. M. Magraw...	198	Dr. Cooper...	5.25	7.50	2.50	....
3703	......	Salt Lake city..........	Mar. 21, 1850	Capt. Stansbury ..		....	....	....	....	
4090	♂	Tamaulipas, Mex	Mar. —, 1853	Lt. Couch	55	....	5.50	7.50	2.50	Eyes dark br'n, bill slate color, yellow at base.
4089	......	Brownsville, Texas....	....	......do.......	7	....	4.87	8.00	2.50	Eyes dark brown.......
4090	......	......do........ ..	....	......do.......	9	....	4.75	6.50	2.50	
6325	......	New Mexico,(Camp 121)	Feb. —, 1854	Lt. Whipple	100	Kenn. and Möll...	....	....	....	
6700		Tejon Pass............	....	Lt. Williamson...		....	....	....		
		Fort Tejon............	....	J. X. de Vesey ...						
3904	......	California	....	Dr. Heermann ...				....		
6326	♂	......do............	....	Lt. Williamson.......		Dr. Heermann ...	....	....		
8051	......	Mexico..........	....	John Gould......						
8052	......	Guatemala............	....	......do........						....

MELOSPIZA PALUSTRIS, B a i r d.

Swamp Sparrow.

Fringilla palustris, WILSON, Am. Orn. III, 1811, 49; pl. xxii, f. 1.—AUDUBON, Orn. Biog. I, 1831, 331 : V, 508; pl. 64.
Fringilla (Spiza) palustris, BONAP. Obs. Wilson, 1825, No. 105.
Passerculus palustris, BONAP. List, 1838.—IB. Conspectus, 1850, 481.
Ammodromus palustris, AUD. Syn. 1839.—IB. Birds Amer. III, 1841, 110 ; pl. 175.
? Fringilla georgiana, L'ATH. Index Orn. I, 1790, 460. (May *Peucæa aestivalis*.)—LICHT. Verz. 1823, No. 251.
Fringilla (Ammodromus) georgiana, NUTT. Man. I, 2d ed. 1840, 588.

SP. CH.—Middle of the crown uniform chestnut ; forehead black ; superciliary streak, sides of head and back and sides of neck, ash. A brown stripe behind the eye. Back broadly streaked with black. Beneath whitish, tinged with ashy anteriorly, especially across the breast, and washed with yellowish brown on the sides. A few obsolete streaks across the breast, which become distinct on its sides. Wings and tail strongly tinged with rufous ; the tertials black, the rufous edgings changing abruptly to white towards the end. Length, 5.75 ; wing, 2.40 inches.

Female with the crown scarcely reddish streaked with black, and divided by a light line.

Hab.—Eastern United States from the Atlantic to the Missouri.

In autumn the male of this species has the feathers of the crown each with a black streak ; and the centre of the crown with an indistinct light stripe, materially changing its appearance. The forehead is usually more or less streaked with black.

A supposed young of this species from the Missouri plains has the head above nearly uniform blackish ; the back pale yellowish brown streaked conspicuously with black, the under parts dirty white, the breast and sides distinctly streaked with black.

In the uncertainty whether the *Fringilla georgiana* of Latham be not rather the *Peucaea aestivalis* than the swamp sparrow, I think it best to retain Wilson's name. It certainly applies as well to the latter, which has the black sub-maxillary streak, and the chin and throat more mouse colored than in *palustris*.

List of specimens.

Catal. No.	Sex.	Locality.	When collected.	Whence obtained.	Collected by—	Length.	Stretch of wings.	Wing.
809	------	Carlisle, Pa..	Oct. 17, 1842	S. F. Baird.	-----------------	5. 25	7. 75	2. 33
375	♀	......do.............	May 13, 1841	......do..........	-----------------	5. 50	7. 50	......
810	♂	......do.........	Oct. 17, 1842	......do..........	-----------------	6. 00	8. 00	2. 42
776	------	......do.........	Oct. 3, 1842	......do..........	-----------------	5. 58	8. 00	2. 42
934	♂	-----------------	May 2, 1843	......do..........	-----------------	5. 67	8. 83	2. 42
10277	------	Union county, Ill....	April 20, 1857	N. W. University..	R. Kennicott....	-------	-------	------
4806	o	Vermilion river, Neb..	-------------	Lt. G. K. Warren ..	Dr. Hayden.......	5. 62	7. 75	2. 50

PEUCAEA, Audubon.

Peucaea, AUDUBON, Synópsis, 1839. Type *Fringilla aestivalis.*

CH.—Bill moderate. Upper outline and commissure decidedly curved ; gonys nearly straight. Legs and feet small ; the tarsus about equal to the middle toe ; the lateral toes equal, their claws falling considerably short of the middle one ; the hind toe reaching about to the middle of the latter. The outstretched feet reach only to the middle of the tail. The wing is very short, reaching only to the base of the tail ; the longest tertials do not exceed the secondaries, while both are not much short of the primaries ; the outer three or four quills are graduated. The tail is considerably longer than the wings ; it is much graduated laterally ; the feathers, though long, are peculiarly narrow, linear, and elliptically rounded at the ends.

Color beneath plain whitish or brownish, with a more or less distinct dusky line each side of the chin. Above with broad obsolete brown streaks or blotches. Crown uniform, or the feathers edged with lighter. Inner tail feathers with obsolete transverse dusky bars.

This is a very well defined group, with a curved upper mandible ; short toes ; very short and much rounded wings, less than the tail ; a long, much graduated tail, with the feathers narrow, linear, and elliptical at the end. This character of the tail, with that of the unspotted under parts and black streak on each side of the chin, and the yellow edge to the wings in two of the species, are all strong distinctive features.

Synopsis of species.

A. Maxillary black streak narrow ; edge of wing yellow (inconspicuously.) Head above streaked.

Feathers above with the central portion dark chestnut ; those of the back with broad streaks of brown. Throat, breast, and sides tinged with yellowish ash....*P. aestivalis.*

Feathers above paler ; those of back with narrow central streaks of brown, or else wanting. Beneath paler ; throat nearly white...............................*P. cassinii.*

B. Maxillary stripe very distinct. Head above nearly uniform reddish. Edge of wing grayish white...*P. ruficeps.*

Comparative measurements of species.

Catal No.	Species.	Locality.	Sex.	Length.	Stretch of wings.	Wing.	Tail.	Tarsus.	Middle toe.	Its claw alone.	Hind toe and claw.	Hind claw alone.	Bill above.	Along gape.	Specimen measured.
3531	Peucaea ruficeps	California		5.48		2.30	2.80	0.77	0.72	0.17	0.50	0.23	0.42	0.47	Skin
6328	Peucaea cassinii	Texas	♂	5.82		2.64	3.05	0.73	0.69	0.17	0.56	0.26	0.46	0.50	Skin
6327	......do......	Los Nogales, Mex.		6.10		2.56	3.12	0.84	0.79	0.18	0.64	0.28	0.49	0.48	Skin
3070	Peucaea aestivalis	Georgia	♀	5.10		2 24	2.50	0.72	0.70	0.16	0.55	0.24	0.45	0.50	Skin
do.	......do......	......do......		5.70	7.50										Fresh
10244	......do......	Liberty county, Ga.	♂	6.00		2.36	2.78	0.76	0.74	0.14	0.60	0.24	0.44	0.52	Skin
do.				6.50	8.00	2.50									

PEUCAEA AESTIVALIS, Cabanis.

Bachman's Finch.

Fringilla aestivalis, LICHT. Verz. Doubl. 1823, 25, No. 254.—BONAP. Conspectus, 1850, 481.
Peucaea aestivalis, CABANIS, Mus. Hein. 1850, 132.
Fringilla bachmani, AUD. Orn. Biog. II, 1834, 366 ; pl. 165.
Ammodromus bachmani, BON. List, 1838.
Peucaea bachmani, AUD. Syn. 1839.—IB. Birds Am. III, 1841, 113 ; pl. 176.—BON. Consp. 1850, 481. (Type.)
Fringilla aestiva, NUTT. I, 2d ed. 1840, 568.
" *Summer finch,* LATHAM, Synopsis, 2d ed. VI, 136." Nuttall.

Sp. Ch.—Feathers of the upper parts rather dark brownish red or chestnut, margined with bluish ash, which almost forms a median stripe on the crown. Interscapular region and upper tail coverts with the feathers becoming browner in the centre. An indistinct ashy superciliary stripe (yellowish anteriorly?) Under parts pale yellow brownish, tinged with ashy on the sides, and with darker brownish across the upper part of the breast. A faint maxillary dusky line. A few obsolete small spots across the breast. Edge of wing yellow ; lesser coverts tinged with greenish.

Length, 6.25 ; wing, 2.30 ; tail, 2.78.

Hab.—Georgia.

The female does not differ, except in the smaller size. Specimens, probably not quite mature, have the breast and sides distinctly streaked with dark brown. The maxillary dark line is very distinct.

List of specimens.

Catal. No.	Sex.	Locality.	When collected.	Whence obtained.	Collected by—	Length.	Stretch of wings.	Wing.
10245	♂	Indian Springs, Ga...	----------	Prof. Jos. Leconte.	----------	-------	-------	-----
10244	♂	Savannah, Ga......	----------	S. F. Baird	Jos. Leconte	-------	-------	-----
2404		......do...........	----------	......do..........	......do.........	-------	-------	-----
2407	♂	......do...........		......do..........	......do.........	6.25	7.75	2.30
3311	----	Liberty county, Ga...	1846	......do..........	W. L. Jones......	5.70	7.80	2.03
3062	♂	......do...........	1846	......do..........	......do.........	5.80	8.00	2.50
3310	♂	......do...........	1846	......do..........	......do.........	5.70	7.60	2.50
3316	♀	......do...........	1846	......do..........	......do.........	5.30	7.80	2.30
3065	♂	......do...........	----------	......do..........	......do.........	5.70	7.80	2.40
3071	----	......do...........	1846	W. L. Jones	......do.........	-------	-------	-----
3068	♂	......do...........	1846	......do..........	......do.........	6.00	8.00	2.30
3070	♀	......do...........	1846	......do..........	......do.........	5.70	7.50	2.00
3314	♂	......do...........	1846	......do..........	......do.........	5.80	7.80	2.20
3066	♂	......do...........	1846	......do..........	......do.........	5.62	7.50	2.25
3316	♀	......do...........	1846	......do..........	......do.........	5.30	7.80	2.30

PEUCAEA CASSINII, Baird.

Zonotrichia cassinii, WOODHOUSE, Pr. A. N. Sc. Ph. VI, April 1852, 60. (San Antonio.)

Passerculus cassinii, WOODHOUSE, Sitgreaves' Rep. Zuñi and Colorado, 1853, 85 ; Birds, pl. iv.

(Apparently related to *Zonotrichia botteri*, Sclater, Pr. Zool. Soc. 1857, 214, Orizaba?)

Sp. Ch.—Similar to *P. aestivalis*, but paler ; wings and tail longer. Above light chestnut, all the feathers margined and tipped with bluish gray. Interscapular and crown feathers with a narrow streak of brown. Beneath white, tinged with ash across the breast, and with brown towards the tail. An obsolete light superciliary, and narrow dusky maxillary stripe. Tail feathers obsoletely blotched with bluish white at the end. Bend of wing yellow ; lesser coverts tinged with greenish yellow.

Length, 6 inches ; wing, 2.65 ; tail, 2.75.

Hab.—San Antonio, Texas, to Los Nogales, Sonora.

This species has a considerable resemblance to *P. aestivalis*, but differs in some appreciable points. The brown of the upper parts is paler, and the ashy edging to the feathers appears rather more extensive. The dark brown blotches on the back are of much less extent, being confined to a mere streak along the shaft, widening a little at the end, instead of occupying nearly all the feather. The upper tail coverts have a distinct subterminal black bar, and are tipped with bluish white ; the tertiaries are margined all round with white, much lighter than in *aestivalis*. The middle tail feathers are dusky in the centre, with obsolete dentations of the same color on either side. This I have not noticed in the other species. The sides of the head are lighter, the superciliary stripe scarcely appreciable. The under parts are much whiter and without any of the yellowish brown ; the breast tinged with pale ash. The obsolete blotches at the tip of the tail feathers are more distinct. The wing appears a good deal longer.

A skin from Los Nogales (6327) is still more similar to *P. aestivalis*, and if of the same species as those first described, is probably considerably older. The back is, however, lighter than in *aestivalis*, the interscapular blotches narrower and more restricted to the very middle of the back. The under parts are paler. The resemblance is, however, so close, that if the specimen were from Georgia it would be considered merely as a slight variation from the type. This specimen measures 6.20 inches ; the tail, 3.15 ; the wing, 2.60. It has a certain resemblance to the *Zonotrichia botteri* of Sclater, Pr. Zool. Soc. 1857, 214, from Orizaba, but is probably sufficiently distinct.

List of specimens.

Catal. No.	Locality.	When collected.	Whence obtained.	Orig'l No.	Collected by—	Length.	Stretch of wings.	Wing.	Remarks.
......	San Antonio..............	... .	Capt. Sitgreaves....	......	Dr. Woodhouse	....	....	....	....
6328	Texas	....	Lt. J. G. Parke.....	......	Dr. Heermann.	....	....	....	....
5035	Camp on Pecos river, Tex..	July 7, 1855	Capt. J. Pope......	104	....	6.00	7.50	2.50	Eyes brown ; feet yellow..
6327	Los Nogales, Mex.........	June —, 1855	Major Emory	84	Dr. Kennerly ..	....	....	....	....

PEUCAEA RUFICEPS, Baird.

Ammodromus ruficeps, Cassin, Pr. A. N. Sc. VI, Oct. 1852, 184. (California.)—Ib. Illust. I, v, 1854, 135 ; pl. xx.

Sp. Ch.—Above brownish ashy. The crown and nape uniform brownish chestnut. The interscapular region and neck with the feathers of this color, except around the margins. A superciliary ashy stripe, whiter at the base of the bill. Beneath pale yellowish brown, or brownish yellow, darker and more ashy across the breast and on the sides of body ; middle of belly and chin lighter ; the latter with a well marked line of black on each side. Under tail coverts more rufous. Length, 5.50 ; wing, 2.35 ; tail, 2.85.

Hab.—Coast of California.

This plainly-colored species has the bill rather slender ; tail rather long, and considerably rounded ; the outer feathers .40 of an inch shorter than the middle ; the feathers soft, and rounded at the tip. The wing is short ; the primaries not much longer than the tertials ; the second, third, fourth, and fifth, nearly equal ; the first scarcely longer than the secondaries.

There is a blackish tinge on the forehead, separated by a short central line, as in *Spizella socialis*. The eyelids are whitish, and there is a short black line immediately over the upper lid. There is a faint chestnut streak back of the eye. The chestnut of the nape is somewhat interrupted by pale edgings. The blotches on the back melt almost insensibly into the colors of the margins of the feathers. The outer edges of the secondaries and tertials, and the outer surface of the tail, are yellowish rusty. The middle tail feathers show obsolete narrow transverse dusky bars.

List of specimens.

Catal. No.	Sex.	Locality.	Whence obtained.	Collected by—
3831	......	California	Dr. Heermann	....
6341	♂	Calaveras county, Cal..........	Lieut. Williamson...........	Dr. Heermann ....
47296	......	San Francisco, Cal.............	R. D. Cutts................	....
....	......	Fort Tejon, Cal..............	J. X. de Vesey.............	....

EMBERNAGRA, Lesson.

Embernagra, LESSON, Traité d'Ornith. 1831. (Agassiz.) Type *Saltator viridis*, Vieillot.

CH.—Bill conical, elongated, compressed ; the upper outline considerably curved, the lower straight ; the commissure slightly concave, and faintly notched at the end. Tarsi lengthened ; considerably longer than the middle toe. Outer toe a little longer than the inner, not reaching quite to the base of the middle claw. Hind toe about as long as the middle without its claw. Wings very short, and much rounded ; the tertials nearly equal to the primaries ; the secondaries a little shorter ; the outer four primaries much graduated, even the second shorter than any other quill. The tail is moderate, about as long as the wings, much graduated ; the feathers rather narrow, linear, and elliptically rounded at the end ; the outer webs more than usually broad in proportion to the inner, being more than one-third as wide. The upper parts are olive green, the under whitish.

The position of this genus is a matter of considerable uncertainty. On some accounts it would be better placed among the *Spizinae*.

EMBERNAGRA RUFIVIRGATA, Lawrence.

Embernagra rufivirgata, LAWRENCE, Ann. N. Y. Lyc. V, May, 1851, 112; pl. v, f. 2. Texas.—SCLATER, Pr. Zool. Soc. 1856, 306.

SP. CH.—Above uniform olivaceous green. Sides of the hood, and a stripe behind the eye, dull brownish rufous, not very conspicuous ; an ashy superciliary stripe rather yellowish anteriorly. Under parts brownish white, tinged with yellowish posteriorly, and with olivaceous on the sides ; white in the middle of the belly. Edge of wing, under coverts, and axillaries, bright yellow. Length, 5.50 ; wing, 2.60 ; tail, 2.70.

Hab.—Valley of the Rio Grande, and probably of Gila, southward ; Mazatlan, Mexico.

In this species the bill is rather long ; the wings are very short, and much rounded ; the tertials equal to the primaries ; the secondaries rather shorter ; the first quill is .65 of an inch shorter than the seventh, which is longest. The tail is short ; the lateral feathers much graduated ; the outer half an inch shorter than the middle.

A specimen of this species from Mazatlan, in the collection of the Philadelphia Academy, has the bill rather stouter at the base, and the stripes on the head much better defined. Those on the crown are continued, though less distinctly, down the back of the neck to the upper part of the back. This is probably a male, and No. 6246 a female.

List of specimens.

Catal. No.	Locality.	Whence obtained.	Collected by—	Length.	Stretch of wings.	Wing.
6246	New Leon, Mexico	Lieut. Couch		5.50	8.00	2.75
6247	Ringgold barracks, Texas	Major Emory	J. H. Clark	6.25	8.50	2.62

Sub-Family PASSERELLINAE.

CH.—Toes and claws very stout ; the lateral claws reaching beyond the middle of the middle one ; all very slightly curved.

Bill conical, the outlines straight; both mandibles equal ; wings long, longer than the even tail, reaching nearly to the middle of its exposed portion. Hind claw longer than its digit ; the toe nearly as long as the middle toe ; tarsus longer than the middle toe. Brown above, either uniformly so or faintly streaked ; triangular spots below.

This section embraces a single North American genus, chiefly characterized by the remarkable elongation of the lateral toes, as well as by the peculiar shape and great size of all the claws ; the lateral, especially, are so much lengthened as to extend nearly as far as the middle. The only approach to this, as far as I recollect, among United States *Conirostres*, is in *Pipilo megalonyx*, and *Agelaius icterocephalus*.

PASSERELLA, Swainson.

Passerella, Swainson, Class. Birds, II, 1837, 288. Type *Fringilla iliaca*, Merrem.

Ch.—Body stout. Bill conical, not notched, the outlines straight ; the two jaws of equal depth ; roof of upper mandible deeply excavated, and vaulted ; not knobbed. Tarsus scarcely longer than the middle toe ; outer toe little longer than the inner, its claw reaching to the middle of the central one. Hind toe about equal to the inner lateral ; the claws all long, and moderately curved only ; the posterior rather longer than the middle, and equal to its toe. Wings long, pointed, reaching to the middle of the tail ; the tertials not longer than secondaries ; second and third quills longest ; first equal to the fifth. Tail very nearly even, scarcely longer than the wing. Inner claw contained scarcely one-and-a-half times in its toe proper.

Color.—Rufous or slaty ; obsoletely streaked or uniform above ; thickly spotted with triangular blotches beneath.

The following species constitute the known members of the genus from the United States :

Back, breast, and sides of neck and body streaked distinctly with light brownish red ; of which color are the wings and tail ....*P. iliaca.*

Wings and tail dark brownish rufous ; rest of upper parts uniform olivaceous rufous. Under parts with thickly crowded, more or less confluent, spots of the same................*P. townsendii.*

Wings and tail dark brownish rufous ; rest of upper parts uniform slate gray. The under parts with distinct triangular spots of the same...*P. schistacea.*

Comparative measurements of species.

Catal. No.	Species.	Locality.	Sex.	Length.	Stretch of wings.	Wing.	Tail.	Tarsus.	Middle toe.	Its claw alone.	Hind toe and claw.	Hind claw and toe.	Bill above.	Along gape.	Specimen measured.
831	Passerella iliaca	Carlisle, Pa.............	♀	6.34	......	3.32	3.00	0.89	0.90	0.28	0.70	0.34	0.42	0.53	Skin ......
do.	.......do...............	......do		6.82	11.00	3.42									Fresh ......
1323	........do.............	......do	♂	6.50	......	3.46	3.10	0.96	0.92	0.28	0.70	0.36	0.47	0.50	Skin ......
do.	........do.............	......do		7.42	11.25	3.50									Fresh ......
2874	Passerella townsendii..	Columbia river.....	♀	6.70	......	2.94	3.04	0.91	0.95	0.32	0.78	0.42	0.46	0.51	Skin ......
6241	.......do...............	Sacramento valley....	♂	6.76	....	3.28	3.24	1.00	1.01	0.38	0.83	0.47	0.50	0.61	Skin ......
10277	Passerella schistacea? .	Fort Tejon, Cal.......	♂	6.90	......	3.46	3.38	1.02	1.00	0.35	0.79	0.42	0.50	0.60	Skin ......
10280	Passerella schistacea...	.......do...............	♀	6.82	......	3.26	3.66	0.90	1.00	0.40	0.83	0.50	0.50	0.56	Skin ......
10279	........do...............	....do	♂	6.80	......	3.08	3.40	0.94	0.87	0.26	0.73	0.38	0.50	0.56	Skin ......

PASSERELLA ILIACA, Swainson.

Fox-colored Sparrow.

Fringilla iliaca, Merrem. " Beitr. zur besond. Gesch. der Vögel, II, 1786-'87, 40 ; pl. x."—Gm. Syst. Nat. I, 1788, 923.—Aud. Orn. Biog. II, 1834, 58 : V, 512 ; pl. 108.—Ib. Syn. 1839.—Ib. Birds Amer. III, 1841, 139 ; pl. 186.
Passerella iliaca, Sw. Birds, II, 1837, 288.—Bon. List, 1838.—Ib. Conspectus, 1850, 477.
Fringilla rufa, Wilson, Am. Orn. III, 1811, 53 ; pl. xxiv, f. 4.—Licht. Verz. 1823, No. 248.
Fringilla ferruginea, Wilson, Catalogue, VI, 1812.—Hall's ed. Wilson, II, 255.
" *Emberiza pratensis*, Vieill." Gray.

Sp. Ch.—Middle of the back dull ash, each feather with a large blotch of brownish red ; top of head and neck, with rump similar, but with smaller and more obsolete blotches. Upper tail coverts, with exposed surface of wings and tail, bright rufous.

Beneath white, with the upper part of the breast and sides of throat and body with triangular spots of rufous, and a few smaller ones of blackish on the middle of the breast. Inner edges of quills and tail feathers tinged with rufous pink. No light lines on the head, but a patch of rufous on the cheeks. First quill rather less than the fifth. Hind toe about equal to its claw. Length, about 7.50 ; wing, 3.50.

Hab.—Eastern United States to the Mississippi.

Sometimes the entire head above is reddish like the back.

List of specimens.

Catal. No.	Sex.	Locality.	When collected.	Whence obtained.	Length.	Stretch of wings.	Wing.
1323	♂	Carlisle, Pa	April 2, 1846	S. F. Baird	7.42	11.25	3.08
846		do	Oct. 29, 1842	do	7.17	11.58	3.42
831	♀	do	Oct. 22, 1842	do	6.83	11.00	3.42
10134	♂	Washington, D. C.		J. C. McGuire			
10133	♀	do		do			
7276		Cleveland, Ohio	May —, 1852	J. P. Kirtland			

PASSERELLA TOWNSENDII, Nuttall.

Fringilla townsendii, Aud. Orn. Biog. V, 1839, 236 ; pl. 424, f. 7.—Ib. Syn. 1839.—Ib. Birds Amer. III, 1841, 43 ; pl. 187.

Fringilla (Passerella) townsendii, Nutt. Man. I, 2d ed. 1840, 533.

Passerella townsendii, Bon. Conspectus, 1850, 477.

Fringilla meruloides, Vig. Zool. Blossom, (Monterey,) 1839, 19.

Emberiza unalaschensis, Gm. I, 875, probably has some relation to the present species. It is based on the *Unalascha Bunting* of Pennant Arctic Zool. II, 364.

Sp. Ch.—Above very dark olive brown, with a tinge of rufous, the color continuous and uniform throughout, without any trace of blotches or spots ; the upper tail coverts and outer edges of the wing and tail feathers rather lighter and brighter. The under parts white, but thickly covered with approximating triangular blotches like the back, sparsest on the middle of the body and on the throat ; the spots on the belly smaller. Side almost continuously like the back ; tibiae and under tail coverts similar, the latter edged with paler. Claws all very large and long ; the hinder longer than its toe. First and sixth quills about equal. Length, about 7 inches ; wing, about 3.00.

Hab.—Pacific coast of United States as far south as Sacramento. Fort Tejon??

This species differs a good deal in form from *P. iliaca*. The claws are much larger and stouter, the wing a good deal shorter and more rounded. The differences in color are very appreciable, the tints being dark olivaceous brown instead of red, and perfectly uniform above, not spotted ; the under parts much more thickly spotted.

List of specimens.

Catal. No.	Sex.	Locality.	When collected.	Whence obtained.	Orig'l No.	Collected by—	Length.	Extent.	Wing.	Remarks.
5975		Straits of Fuca,W.T.	March, 1855	Dr. J. G. Cooper			7.00	10.12		Bill bl'k and yellow.
5976		do	April, 1855	do			7.25	10.38		
6236		Fort Steilacoom	February, 1856.	Dr. Suckley, U.S.A.	235					
6237		do	April, 1856	do	296		7.50	9.50		
6238		do		do	317		7.00	9.00	3.00	
2874	♀	Columbia river	Feb. 15, 1836	S. F. Baird		J.K.Townsend.				
6239		Ft. Vancouver,W.T.	January, 1854	Gov. Stevens	12	Dr. Cooper	7.50	11.00		Feet and iris brown.
6240		do	do	do	15	do	7.25	9.50		do
6241		Sacramento, Cal		Lt. Williamson		Dr. Heermann.				

June 17, 1858.

62 b

PASSERELLA SCHISTACEA, Baird.

Sp. Ch.—Bill very thick ; the upper mandible much swollen at the base ; under yellow. Above and on the sides uniform slate gray ; the upper surface of wings, tail feathers, and upper coverts dark brownish rufous ; ear coverts streaked with white. Beneath pure white, with broad triangular arrow-shaped and well defined spots of slate gray like the back everywhere, except along the middle of the belly ; not numerous on the throat. A hoary spot at the base of the bill above the loral region. Length, 6.80 ; wing, 3.08 ; tail, 3.40.

Hab.—Head waters of Platte to Fort Tejon, California.

This species is readily distinguished from *P. iliaca* by the slate back and spots on the breast, without any streaks above. The bill is much stouter and the claws longer. From *townsendii* it differs in having the head, back, sides, and spots beneath slate colored, instead of dark reddish brown. The spotting beneath is much more sparse, the spots smaller, more triangular, and confined to the terminal portion of the feathers, instead of frequently involving the entire outer edge. The bill is stouter. The wings and tail are the same in both species.

The essential characters of the preceding diagnosis are based on a specimen (5118) from the head of the Platte, and collected by Lieutenant Bryan, in 1856. Since then I have had the opportunity of examining a large number of *Passerellas* collected at Fort Tejon, by Mr. Vesey, and among them skins in the pure slate colors just described. Others, however, have this tinged, both above and on the spots below, with reddish brown, and there is a gentle gradation to what appears to be the true *P. townsendii*. I still think, however, that the species as described is distinct, even though in some stages of plumage it is difficult to draw the line, as in a large number of specimens, both of winter and summer, from Washington Territory, there is not the very slightest trace of the slate, the entire upper parts being of a uniform reddish brown, only a little brighter on the tail.

One specimen, No. 10279, is remarkable for the unusual shortness of the claws, as shown in the table of measurements.

List of specimens.

Catal. No.	Sex.	Locality.	When collected.	Whence obtained.	Orig. No.	Collected by—
5718	♀	Platte river, K. T.	July 19, 1856	Lt. F. T. Bryan	131	W. S. Wood
10278	♂	Fort Tejon, Cal		J. X. de Vesey	1408	
10279	♂	do		do	1299	
10280	♀	do		do	1397	

Sub-Family SPIZINAE.

Ch.—Bill variable, always large, much arched, and with the culmen considerably curved ; sometimes of enormous size, and with a great development backwards of the lower jaw, which is always appreciably, sometimes considerably broader behind than the upper jaw at its base ; nostrils exposed. Tail rather variable. Bill generally black or red. Wings shorter than in the first group. Gape almost always much more strongly bristled. Few of the species sparrow-like or plain in appearance ; usually blue, red, or black and white ; seldom (or never ?) streaked beneath.

The preceding diagnosis is intended to embrace the brightly colored passerine birds of North America different in general appearance from the common sparrows. It is difficult to draw the line with perfect strictness so as to separate the species from those of the preceding group, but the bill is always more curved and larger, and the colors brighter. The shorter wings, and the absence of the stiff bristly feathers concealing the nostrils distinguishes them from the first section. The rictus, however, is almost always very strongly bristled.

The species may be conveniently divided, however artificially, by the proportional length of the tail, as follows:

A.—*Tail decidedly shorter than the wings; nearly even.*

a. Bill elongated ; upper mandible rather deeper, or as deep as the lower. Feet large and strong.

CALAMOSPIZA.—Bill moderate; slightly convex above. Outer lateral toe rather longer, but falling considerably short of the middle claw. Hind toe large ; equal to the middle, without its claw. Claws large, with an indented groove on each side. Outer four primaries equal and abruptly larger than the rest ; tertials as long as the primaries. Color black, with white on the wings.

EUSPIZA.—Bill rather more slender ; commissure distinctly sinuated. Tertials little longer than secondaries ; first quill longest, the others regularly graduated. Lateral toes reaching nearly to the base of the middle claw. Back streaked. Crown and rump nearly uniform. No streaks below, where the colors are white, black, and yellow.

b. Bill stouter, and more curved above; upper mandible generally not so deep as the lower. Feet smaller.

GUIRACA.—Bill enormously large ; the lower mandible wider at base than the length of gonys. Outer web of external tail feather considerably expanded towards the end. Tail even. Hind claw much curved; decidedly longer than the middle anterior one. Second quill longest. Wings reaching to middle of the tail. Size large. Color blue, or with black head.

CYANOSPIZA.—Size very small. Outer web of external tail feathers narrow ; but little expanded at the end. Claws all about equal. Both culmen and commissure gently curved. Color more or less blue.

B.—*Wings and tail of the species about equal in size.*

SPERMOPHILA.—Smallest of American *Conirostres*. Bill greatly curved above and very short, scarcely longer than high. Tail feathers widened at the end ; acuminate, mucronate. Wing broad, short ; quills all nearly equal. Claws long, not much curved ; hinder considerably longer than anterior. Color black, or brown and white.

C.—*Wings much shorter than the tail, which is broad and graduated ; primaries graduated ; the first seldom longer than the secondaries.*

a. Head crested. Prevailing color red. Bill red.

PYRRHULOXIA.—Bill pyrrhuline, very short, and greatly convex; shorter than high. Hind claw less than its digit ; not much larger than the middle anterior one. Tarsus equal to the middle toe.

CARDINALIS.—Bill coccothraustine, very large ; culmen very slightly convex. Wings more rounded. Feet as in the last, except that the tarsus is longer than the middle toe.

b. Head not crested.   No red.   Bill dusky.

PIPILO.—Bill moderate ; culmen and commissure curved.   Hind claw very large and strong ; longer than its digit.   Tarsus less than the middle toe.

CALAMOSPIZA, Bonaparte.

Calamospiza, BONAP. List, 1838.   Type *Fringilla bicolor,* Towns.
Corydalina, AUDUBON, Synopsis, 1839.   Same type.

CH.—Bill rather large, much swollen at the base ; the culmen broad, gently but decidely curved ; the gonys nearly straight ; the commissure much angulated near the base, then slightly sinuated ; lower mandible nearly as deep as the upper, the margins much inflected, and shutting under the upper mandible.   Nostrils small, strictly basal.   Rictus quite stiffly bristly. Legs large and stout.   Tarsi a little longer than the middle toe ; outer toe rather longer than the inner, and reaching to the concealed base of the middle claw ; hind toe reaching to the base of the middle claw ; hind claw about as long as its toe.   Claws all strong, compressed, and considerably curved.   Wings long and pointed ; the first four nearly equal, and abruptly longest ; the tertials much elongated, as long as the primaries.   Tail a little shorter than the wings, slightly graduated ; the feathers rather narrow and obliquely oval rounded at the end.
Color.—Black, with white on the wings.

This genus is well characterized by the large swollen bill, with its curved culmen ; the large strong feet and claws ; the long wings, a little longer than the tail, and with the tertials as long as the primaries ; the first four quills equal, and abruptly longest ; the tail short and graduated.

The only group of N. American *Spizellinae,* with the tertials equal to the primaries in the closed wing, is *Passerculus.*   This, however, has a differently formed bill, weaker feet, the inner primaries longer and more regularly graduated, the tail feathers more acute and shorter, and the plumage streaked brownish and white instead of black.

Comparative measurements of species.

Catal. No.	Species.	Locality.	Sex.	Length.	Wing.	Tail.	Tarsus.	Middle toe.	Its claw alone.	Bill above.	Along gape.	Hind toe and claw.	Hind claw alone.	Specimen measured.
2869	Calamospiza bicolor..	Rocky mountains	♂	....	3.43	2.95	1.00	0.98	0.24	0.56	0.58	0.72	0.32	Skin.....
6305	..........do.........	New Mexico.....	♂	6.40	3.55	2.96	0.92	0.90	0.20	0.54	0.58	0.66	0.32	Skin.....
6306	..........do.........	......do.........	♀	6.24	3.36	2.96	0.98	0.88	0.19	0.54	0.56	0.62	0.28	Skin.....

CALAMOSPIZA BICOLOR, Bonap.

Lark Bunting ; White-winged Blackbird.

Fringilla bicolor, TOWNSEND, J. A. N. Sc. Ph. VII, 1837, 189.—IB. Narrative, 1839, 346.—AUD. Orn. Biog. V, 1839, 19 ; pl. 390.
Calamospiza bicolor, BONAP. List, 1838.—IB. Conspectus, 1850, 475.
Corydalina bicolor, AUD. Synopsis, 1839, 130.—IB. Birds Am. III, 1841, 195 ; pl. 201.
Dolichonyx bicolor, NUTTALL, Manual, I, 2d ed. 1840, 203.

SP. CH.—*Male* entirely black ; a broad band on the wing, with the outer edges of the quills and tail feathers, white.
Female pale brown, streaked with darker above ; beneath white, spotted and streaked rather sparsely with black on the breast and sides.   Throat nearly immaculate.   A maxillary stripe of black, bordered above by white.   Region around the eye, a faint stripe above it, and an obscure crescent back of the ear coverts, whitish.   A broad fulvous white band across the ends of the greater wing coverts.   Tail feathers with a white spot at the end of the inner web.   Length, about 6.50 ; wing, 3.50 ; tail, 3.20 ; tarsus, 1.00 ; bill above, .60.
Hab.—High Central Plains to the Rocky mountains ; southwesterly to valley of Mimbres and Sonora.

In this species the bill is large and much swollen. The tail is slightly emarginate, and a good deal rounded. The second quill is longest; the third, fourth, and first are scarcely shorter. The tertiaries are much elongated, within a quarter of an inch as long as the primaries. The claws are large; moderately curved. The tarsi are large and strong.

The white patch on the wing is confined to the greater and middle coverts. The elongated tertiaries are conspicuously edged with white. Some of the feathers on the posterior part of the body have white margins.

A young male is similar to the female, but the chin and quills, with the lesser wing coverts, as also the tail, are black. There is also a tendency to black in the anterior part of the belly. Very young birds have the characters of the female, the white patch on the wing usually quite distinct, sometimes wanting.

List of specimens.

Catal. No.	Sex.	Locality.	When collected.	Whence obtained.	Orig. No.	Collected by—	Length.	Stretch of wings.	Wing.	Remarks.
2869	♂	Missouri Plains.........	....	S. F. Baird..........	......	J. K. Townsend	....	.....	.....	....
5376	♀?	Medicine Butte.........	June 30, 1856	Lt. G. K. Warren..	......	Dr. Hayden....	7.25	12.00	4.00	Iris dark brown ....
5375	♂?	70 miles above Yellowstone River, Neb......	July 29, 1856	......do............	......	......do........	6.75	11.00	3.37	......do..............
5794	♂	Platte river	July 19.......	Lt. Bryan...........	127	W. S. Wood ...	....	....	.....	....
5728	♀	......do................	....	......do............	......	......do........	....	....	.....	....
5722	♀?	S. Fk. Platte.............	July 19.......	......do............	129	......do........	....	....	.....	....
8929	♂	Loup Fork	Aug. 6.......	Lt. Warren........	146	Dr. Hayden	7.50	12.00	3.50	Iris brown ....
8928	♂	......do................	Aug. 1.......	......do............	......	......do........	8.75	12.00	3.25	....
8931	♀	......do................	Aug. 17.....	......do............	......	......do........	7.00	10.75	5.00	....
8773	♂	Divide Fks. Platte	Aug. 13, 1857	Wm. M. Magraw ..	146	Dr. Cooper.....	7.00	11.25	3.50	Iris brown; bill black; feet pale.
8990	♀?	N. Fk. Platte river......	Aug. 20, 1857	......do............	163	......do........	7.25	12.00	4.00	Iris brown; bill brown & white; feet brown.
5720	♂	Pole creek, K. T........	July 25.......	Lt. Bryan...........	152	W. S. Wood....	....	....	.....	....
7038	♀	Black Hills........	July 21, 1857	......do............	......	......do........	....	....	.....	....
5721	♂?	Bridger's Pass..........	Aug. 13, 1856	......do............	258	......do........	7.00	11.50	.....	....
6313	......	Texas	....	Capt. Pope........	......	....	7.00	11	3.50	Eyes black; feet gray;
5032	♂	Pecos, Texas............	May 13, 1855	......do............	80	....	....	....	.....	....
6305	♂	New Mexico	....	Lt. J. G. Parke.....	......	Dr. Heermann..	....	....	.....	....
6306	♀	......do................	....	......do............	......	......do........	....	....	.....	....
6307	♂	Fort Thorn, N. M.......	....	Dr. T. C. Henry....	......	....	....	....	.....	....
6301	......	Sonora, Mexico	....	Major Emory.......	....	Dr. Kennerly ..	....	....	.....	....
6302	......	......do................	....	......do............	......	......do........	....	....	.....	....
6303	♂	Espia, Mexico..........	March, 1855..	......do............	......	......do........	....	....	.....	....
6304	♀	......do................	......do......	......do............	......	......do........	....	....	.....	....

EUSPIZA, Bonaparte.

Euspiza, BONAPARTE, List, 1838. Type *Emberiza americana*, Gmelin.
Euspina, CABANIS, Mus. Hein. 1851, 133. Same type.

CH.—Bill large and strong, swollen, and without any ridges; the lower mandible nearly as high as the upper; as broad at the base as the length of the gonys, and considerably broader than the upper mandible; the edges much inflexed, and shutting much within the upper mandible; the commissure considerably angulated at the base, then decidedly sinuated. The tarsus barely equal to the middle toe; the lateral toes nearly equal, not reaching to the base of the middle claw; the hind toe about equal to the middle one without its claw. The wings long and acute, reaching nearly to the middle of the tail; the tertials decidedly longer than the secondaries, but much shorter than the primaries; first quill longest, the others regularly graduated. Tail considerably shorter than the wings, though moderately long; nearly even, although slightly emarginate; the outer feathers scarcely shorter. Middle of back only striped; beneath without streaks.

This genus comes nearer to *Calamospiza*, but has shorter tertials, more slender bill, weaker and more curved claws, &c.

Synopsis of species.

Top and sides of head light slate; forehead tinged with greenish yellow. A superciliary stripe, a maxillary spot, sides of breast, and middle line of breast and belly, yellow. Chin white, throat black, shoulders chestnut. Female with the black of the throat replaced by a crescent of spots...*E. americana.*

Body throughout, (including the jugulum,) dark ash, tinged with brownish on the back and wings. Superciliary and maxillary stripe, chin, throat, and middle of belly, white. A maxillary line and a pectoral crescent of black spots. No chestnut shoulders.............*E. townsendii.*

Under the head of *Cyanospiza*, page 500, will be found some remarks upon the genera *Euspiza* and *Spiza*, of Bonaparte. The name of *Spiza* was first used in connexion with the *Emberiza americana*, but so mixed up with types of several other modern genera as to render it uncertain whether to apply it to one rather than another. Under the circumstances, therefore, it may be best to retain *Euspiza*, although if *Spiza* pointed more unmistakeably to the *E. americana* it might, perhaps, be necessary to adopt it.

Comparative measurements of species.

Catal. No.	Species.	Locality.	Sex.	Length.	Stretch of wings.	Wing.	Tail.	Tarsus.	Middle toe.	Its claw alone.	Hind toe and claw.	Hind claw alone.	Bill above.	Along gape.	Specimen measured.
1459	Euspiza americana	Carlisle...............	♂	6.06	.....	3.26	2.80	0.90	0.90	0.26	0.67	0.30	0.53	0.60	Skin ......
do..	........do...............	......do..............	.....	6.66	10.75	3.42	......	......	......	......	......	......	......	......	Fresh .....
9266	........do...............	Frémont on Platte....	♂	5.84	.....	3.34	2.68	0.90	0.90	0.24	0 66	0.30	0.57	0.66	Skin ......
do..	........do...............	......do..............	.....	6.50	10.50	3.50	......	......	......	......	......	......	......	......	Fresh .....
10133	........do.........	Washington, D. C	♀	5.52	.....	2.98	2.50	0.80	0.80	0.23	0.60	0.28	0.52	0.56	Skin ......
10282	Euspiza townsendii......	Chester county, Pa....	♂	5.40	.....	2.86	2.56	0.80	0.80	0.23	0.53	0.24	0.48	0.56	Skin ......
do..	........do...............	......do..............	.....	5.75	9.00	......	......	......	......	......	......	......	......	......	Fresh .....

EUSPIZA AMERICANA, Bonap.

Black-throated Bunting.

Emberiza americana, GMELIN, Syst. Nat. I, 1788, 872.—WILSON, Am. Orn. III, 1811, 86; pl. iii, f. 2.—AUDUBON, Orn. Biog. IV, 1838, 579; pl. 384.—IB. Syn. 1839, 101.—IB. Birds Amer. III, 1841, 58; pl. 156.

Fringilla (Spiza) americana, BONAP. Obs. Wils. 1825, No. 85.

Euspiza americana, BONAP. List. 1838. (Type.)—IB. Conspectus, 1850, 469.

Euspina americana, CABANIS, Mus. Hein. 1851, 133. (Type.)

Fringilla flavicollis, GMELIN, Syst. Nat. I, 926.

"*Emberiza mexicana*, LATHAM," Syn. 1, 1790, 412. (Gray.)

Passerina nigricollis, VIEILLOT.

Yellow-throated finch, PENNANT, Arc. Zool. II, 374.

Sp. Ch.—*Male.* Sides of the head, and sides and back of the neck ash; crown tinged with yellowish green and faintly streaked with dusky. A superciliary and short maxillary line, middle of the breast, axillaries, and edge of the wing yellow. Chin, loral region, spots on sides of throat, belly, and under tail coverts white. A black patch on the throat diminishing to the breast, and a spot on the upper part of the belly. Wing coverts chestnut. Interscapular region streaked with black; rest of back immaculate. Length, about 6.70; wing, 3.50.

Female with the markings less distinctly indicated; the black of the breast replaced by a black maxillary line and a streaked collar in the yellow of the upper part of the breast.

Hab.—United States from the Atlantic to the border of the High Central Plains.

In specimens from the border of the plains the black on the throat is restricted to the upper portion, immediately under the head. The streaks on the back are broader and less distinct. The first quill is longest, as in most specimens.

In a young male, from Carlisle, the tail feathers are all acute and acuminately pointed.

List of specimens.

Catal. No.	Sex.	Locality.	When collected.	Whence obtained.	Orig'l No.	Collected by—	Length.	Stretch of wings.	Wing.	Remarks.
1169	♂	Carlisle, Pa............	Aug. 22,1843	S. F. Baird	......	....	6.75	11.00.	3.42	....
1067	♀	.....do...............	Jan. 19,1843	.....do..........	......	....	6.08	8.33	3.00	....
1459	♂	.....do...............	May 6,1844	......do..........	......	....	6.66	10.75	3.42	....
		West Northfield, Ill....	May 19	N. W. University	.....	R. Kennicott	....	....	......	....
		Union co., Ill.........	April 29	......do........	......	.....do.........	....	....	......	....
8332	♂	Independence, Mo.....	May 6,1857	Wm. M. Magraw.	55	Dr. Cooper	7.00	10.50	3.37	Iris brown, bill and feet grayish.
8178	♂	Shawnee mission, K. T.	July —,1857	......do..	114	..... do.........	6.75	10.62	3.50	Iris br'n, bill bl'k, and flesh color, feet brown.
8182	♀	.....do...............	July 3,1857	......do..	118	.....do.........	6.25	9.75	3.25	....
5380	♂	Fort Pierre, Neb.......	June 18,1856	Lieut. Warren...	....	Dr. Hayden	6.00	9.75	3.37	Iris light brown. ......
5381	♂	Fort Lookout, Neb.....	June 11,1856	......do..........	......	.....do.........	6.25	10.00	3.00	....
9268	♂	.....do...............	July 10	......do..........	......	.....do.........	6.25	9.75	3.00	....
9261	♂.	Loup Fork of Platte....	Aug. 30	......do..........	......	.....do.........	7.00	10.50	3.37	....
9265	♂	.....do...............	Aug. 3	......do..........	......	.....do.........	6.75	10.25	3.25	....
9258	♀	.....do...............	July 29	......do..........	......	.....do.........	6.00	10.00	3.25	....
9263	♂	.. ...do...............		......do..........	......	.....do.........	6.75	10.00	3.50	....
9260	♂	.....do...............	July 10	......do..........	......	.....do.........	7.00	10.25	3.37	....
9254	♂	.....do...............	....do.......	......do..........	......	.....do....... ..	6.37	10.00	3.25	....
9248	♀	.....do...............	July 24	......do..........	......	.....do.........	6.00	9.75	3.00	....
9270	♀	.....do...............	July 3	......do..........	......	.....do.........	6.37	9.50	3.00	Iris dark brown....;.....
9269	♂	.....do...............	July 1	......do..........	......	.....do.........	6.62	10 50	3.50	....
9256	♂	Elk Horn river.........	June 30	......do..........	......	.....do.....	6.62	10.87	3.50	Iris dark brown........
9262	♂	.....do...............	...do.......	......do..........	......	.....do.........	6.75	10.62	3.37	....
9264	......	.....do............ ...	....do.......	......do..........	......	.....do.........	6.37	10.75	3.50	....
9249	♂	.....do...............	...do.......	......do..........	......	.....do.........	6.37	10.50	3.37	Iris dark brown........
9257	......	Frémont on Platte	July 1	......do..........	......	.....do.........	6.12	10.50	3.37	....
5702	♂	East of Fort Riley, K. T.	June 16,1856	Lieut. Bryan	14	W. S. Wood......	....	....	......	....
5704	♂	Republican Fork	July 2,1856	.....do..........	54	.....do..........	....	....	......	....
7087	♂	.....do...............	June 12,1857	Dr. Hammond...	1	....	....	....	......	....
5705	♀	Platte river	July 19	Lieut. Bryan.....	124	W. S. Wood	....	....	......	....
6281	♂	Texas	....	Capt. J. Pope....	......	....	....	....	......	....

EUSPIZA TOWNSENDII, Bonap.

Townsend's Bunting.

Emberiza townsendii, Aud. Orn. Biog. II, 1834, 183: V, 90 ; pl. 400.—Ib. Syn. 1839.—Ib. Birds Amer. III, 1841, 62; pl. 157.—Nuttall, Man. I, 2d ed. 1840, 528.

Euspiza townsendii, Bon. List, 1838.

Sp. Ch.—*Male.* Upper parts, head and neck all round, sides of body and fore part of breast slate blue ; the back and upper surface of wings tinged with yellowish brown ; the interscapular region streaked with black. A superciliary and maxillary line, chin and throat, and central line of under parts from the breast to crissum, white ; the edge of the wing, and a gloss on the breast and middle of belly, yellow. A black spotted line from the lower corner of the lower mandible down the side of the throat, connecting with a crescent of streaks in the upper edge of the slate portion of the breast.

Length, 5.75; wing, 2.86; tail, 2.56.

Hab.—Chester county, Pennsylvania. But one specimen known.

This curious bird has long been a puzzle to ornithologists in the uncertainty whether it is only a variety of the *Euspiza americana* or a distinct species. Thus far but one specimen is known, the one before me, kindly lent to the Smithsonian Institution by Doctor Michener, and previously figured and described by Mr. Audubon. I do not feel able to decide the question of its true relationships to *E. americana*, but will merely remark that the fact of the original of Mr. Audubon's description being unique is no argument against its being a true species, as several other unquestionable species of even the best known portions of the United States, as *Dendroica kirtlandii* and *carbonata*, *Regulus cuvieri*, &c., are in the same category, while several others are not much better known.

The first quill is longest, the others successively shorter. The plumbeous of the rump and upper coverts is glossed with yellowish brown like the back. The streaks on the back are very narrow and inconspicuous, much less distinct than in *americana*.

The peculiarities of this bird, compared with *E. americana*, consist in an extension of the slate of the sides and back of the neck over the entire head above, and to a less degree on the back, across the breast, and along the sides. The yellow of the head is wanting entirely ; the superciliary stripe narrower, not passing so far backward, and white. The white maxillary stripe is very distinct, and linear, for a greater distance than in the other species. There is none of the chestnut red on the shoulders, these parts being yellowish brown like the rest of the wing.

The pattern of coloration in this bird (though marked male,) is much like that of the female *americana* in the black maxillary line, the spots across the breast, and the absence of black on the throat. The female *americana*, however, never has the pure slate of the sides and top of the head, as well as across the breast ; the maxillary light stripe is much less distinct, and, with the superciliary, is strongly tinged with yellow.[1]

GUIRACA, Swainson.

Guiraca, SWAINSON, Zool. Jour. III, Nov. 1827, 350.   Type *Loxia cærulea*, L.
Coccoborus, SWAINSON, Class. Birds, II, 1837, 277.   Same type.
? *Goniaphea*, BOWDICH, "Excursions in Madeira, 1825," Agassiz.   Type *Loxia ludoviciana*, L. according to Gray.
Habia, REICHENBACH, Av. Syst. Nat. 1850 ; plate xxviii.   Type *Loxia ludoviciana*, L.; not *Habia*, Lesson, 1831.
Hedymeles, CABANIS, Mus. Hein. 1851, 153.   Same type.

Bill very large, nearly as high as long ; the culmen curved, with a rather sharp ridge ; the commissure conspicuously angulated just below the nostril, the posterior leg of the angle nearly as long as the anterior, both nearly straight.   Lower jaw deeper than the upper, and extending much behind the forehead ; the width greater than the length of the gonys, considerably wider than the upper jaw.   A prominent knob in the roof of the mouth.   Tarsi shorter than the middle toe; the outer toe a little longer, reaching not quite to the base of the middle claw ; hind toe rather longer than to this base.   Wings long, reaching the middle of the tail ; the secondaries and tertials nearly equal ; the second quill longest ; the first less than the fourth.   Tail very nearly even, shorter than the wings.

[1] The following extract from a letter received from Doctor Michener, dated December 23, 1857, contains some interesting details respecting this species :

"The accompanying paragraph, taken from my note-book, contains the information you desire respecting Townsend's bunting. The bird was killed by Mr. Townsend himself, in an old field grown up with cedar bushes, near New Garden, Chester county, within half a mile of the New Garden meeting house :

"*May* 11, 1833.—This morning J. K. Townsend, in company with John Richards, shot a bunting in Wm. Brown's cedar bushes, which is believed to be a *nondescript*.   We have given it the provisional name (until further examined) of *Emberiza albigula*, or *White-throated Bunting*.   The following brief description was drawn up from the recent bird :

"*Male*.—Upper mandible black, middle edge white, lower light blue with a longitudinal stripe extending from the point half way to the base ; head dark plumbeous, cheeks and breast lighter plumbeous, line over the eye white ; back varied with black and brown ; wings brown, the first and second primaries equal and longest, the two lesser coverts edged with paler ; the throat white, margined with black extending down upon the breast, beneath which is a small spot of ochreous ; sides light plumbeous ; belly and vent brownish white.   Length, 5¾ inches ; extent, 9 inches."

The essential character of the genus, as here established, lies in the very thick, slightly arched bill, the pointed wings, longer than the even tail, and the tarsi shorter than the middle toe.

Taking *G. cœrulea* as the type of the genus, it differs from *ludoviciana* and *melanocephala* in having a larger and deeper lower jaw, in proportion to the upper ; the commissure more abruptly angulated ; a more distinct ridge ; the lateral toes rather shorter.   The *Cyanoloxia parellina* of Bonaparte, assigned to the same genus by him, is radically different, the bill being more like *Cyanopiza* in the comparative weakness of the lower jaw ; the feet are much more slender, the tail shorter and much more rounded.   According to G. R. Gray, the genus *Goniaphea* of Bowdich, has the *Loxia ludoviciana* as type.

The species may be grouped as follows :

GUIRACA.

Blue ; wings banded with chestnut brown...*G. cœrulea.*

GONIAPHEA.

Black ; breast rose colored ; belly white.   Under wing coverts of female saffron yellow or fulvous...*G. ludoviciana.*

Black ; median band on the crown, nuchal collar, rump and under parts yellowish cinnamon ; central line of belly yellow.   Under wing coverts of female clear lemon yellow...*G. melanocephala.*

Comparative measurements of species.

Catal. No.	Species.	Locality.	Sex.	Length.	Stretch of wings.	Wing.	Tail.	Tarsus.	Middle toe.	Its claw alone.	Hind toe and claw.	Hind claw alone.	Bill above.	Along gape.	Specimens measured.
1496	Guiraca ludoviciana....	Carlisle, Pa............	♂	7.20	......	4.13	3.48	0.87	0.92	0.28	0.61	0.36	0.64	0.73	Skin ......
do.	....do......... do......	......do	......	8.41	13.08	4.16	......	......	......	......	......	......	......	......	Fresh .....
7018	....do......... do......	St. Louis............	♀	7.10	......	3.82	3.21	0.87	0.91	0.25	0.60	0.24	0.60	0 66	Skin ......
1867	Guiraca melanocephala.	Fort Union, Mo........	♂	7.40	......	4.14	3.64	0.96	0.94	0.28	0.65	0.28	0.73	0.76	Skin ......
1868	....do......... do......	......do	♀	7.20	......	4.10	3.46	0.91	0.94	0.25	0.60	0.26	0.64	0.75	Skin ......
1484	Guiraca caerulea.......	Carlisle, Pa............	♂	6.20	......	3.33	2.79	0.80	0.84	0.20	0.57	0.23	0.63	0.69	Skin ......
do.	....do......... do......	......do	......	7.16	11.32	3.50	......	......	......	......	......	......	......	......	Fresh .....
10139	....do......... do	Washington, D. C...,..	♀	5.90	......	3.15	2.75	0.80	0.90	0.30	0.60	0.28	0.59	0.60	Skin ......

GUIRACA LUDOVICIANA, Swainson.

Rose-breasted Grosbeak.

Loxia ludoviciana, LINN. Syst. Nat. I, 1766, 306.—WILSON, Am. Orn. II, 1810, 135 ; pl. xvii, f. 2.

Guiraca ludoviciana, SWAINSON, Phil. Mag. I, 1827, 438.—BONAP. List, 1838.—IB. Consp. 1850, 501.

Fringilla ludoviciana, AUD. Orn. Biog. II, 1834, 166 : V, 513 ; pl. 127.

Pyrrhula ludoviciana, SAB. Zool. App. Franklin's Narr.

Coccothraustes ludoviciana, RICH. List, Pr. Br. Ass. 1837.

Coccoborus ludovicianus, AUD. Syn. 1839, 133.—IB. Birds Am. III, 1841, 209 ; pl. 205.

" *Goniaphea ludoviciana,* BOWDICH."

Hedymeles ludoviciana, CABANIS, Mus. Hein. 1851, 153.

Fringilla punicea, GMELIN, Syst. Nat. I, 1788, 921.   (Male.)

Loxia obscura, GMELIN, I, 1788, 862.

Loxia rosea, WILSON, Am. Orn. pl. xvii, f. 2.

Coccothraustes rubricollis, VIEILLOT, Galeri des Ois. I, 1824, 67 ; pl. lviii.

SP. CH.—Upper parts generally, with head and neck all round, glossy black.   A broad crescent across the upper part of the breast, extending narrowly down to the belly, axillaries, and under wing coverts, carmine.   Rest of under parts, rump and upper tail coverts, middle wing coverts, spots on the tertiaries and inner great wing coverts, basal half of primaries and secondaries, and a large patch on the ends of the inner webs of the outer three tail feathers, pure white.

June 19, 1858.

63 b

Female, without the white of quills, tail, and rump, and without any black or red. Above yellowish brown streaked with darker ; head with a central stripe above, and a superciliary on each side, white. Beneath dirty white, streaked with brown on the breast and sides. Under wing coverts and axillars saffron yellow. Length, 8.50 inches ; wing, 4.15.

Hab.—Eastern United States to the Missouri plains, south to Guatemala.

In the male the black feathers of the back and sides of the neck have a subterminal white bar. There are a few black spots on the sides of the breast just below the red.

The young male of the year is like the female, except in having the axillaries, under wing coverts, and a trace of a patch on the breast, light rose red.

The tint of carmine on the under parts varies a good deal in different specimens.

List of specimens.

Catal. No.	Sex and age.	Locality.	When collected.	Whence obtained.	Orig. No.	Collected by—	Length.	Stretch of wings.	Wing.	Remarks.
6945	♂	Selkirk Settlem't, H.B.T.	....	Donald Gunn......	......	....	......	....	......	......
2425	♀	Carlisle, Pa............	Sept. 3,1845	S. F. Baird	......	....	......	....	......	......
135	♂	......do............	Sept. —,1840	......do.........	......	....	......	....	......	......
722	○	......do............	Sept. 16,1842	......do.........	......	....	8.00	12.75	......	......
2157	♂	......do............	April 28,1845	......do.........	......	....	8.00	12.75	4.00	......
1496	♂	......do............	May 10,1844	......do.........	......	....	8.42	13.08	4.17	......
8348	♂	Independence, Mo.....	June 18,1857	Wm. M. Magraw.....	......	Dr. Cooper.....	8.00	12.25	4.25	......
8318	♂	......do............	May 29,1857	......do.........	35	......do........	7.37	12.00	4.00	Iris brown ; bill black and white; feet gray.
7013	♂	St. Louis, Mo	May 12,1857	Lieut. F. T. Bryan..	....	W. S. Wood	......	....	......	....
4849	♂	Vermilion river.......	Sept. 8,1856	Lieut. G. K.Warren	Dr. F V.Hayden	7.37	12.12	3.12	....
4848	♂	Ponka Island, Neb.....	May 10,1856	......do.........	......	......do........	7.87	12.50	3.87	....
4851	♀	Running Water.......	May 12,1856	......do.........	......	......do........	8.12	12.50	3.50	....
4852	♀	Bijou Hill, Neb.........	May 16,1856	......do.........	.. ....	......do........	8.25	12.62	4.13	....
8061	....	Guatemala............	....	J. Gould.......	......	....	....	....	....	....

GUIRACA MELANOCEPHALA, Sw.

Black-headed Grosbeak.

Guiraca melanocephala, Sw. Syn. Mex. Birds, Philos. Mag. I, 1827, 438.—Bon. List, 1838.—Ib. Consp. 1850, 502.
Coccothraustes melanocephala, Rich. List, Pr. Brit. Ass. for 1836, 1837.
Fringilla melanocephala, Aud. Orn. Biog. IV, 1838, 519 ; pl. 373.
Coccoborus melanocephalus, Aud. Synopsis, 1839, 133.—Ib. Birds Amer. III, 1841, 214 ; pl. 206.
Goniaphea melanocephala, Sclater ?
Hedymeles melanocephala, Cabanis, Mus. Hein. 1851, 153.
Fringilla xanthomaschalis, Wagler, Isis, 1831, 525.
Pitylus guttatus, Lesson, Rev. Zool. II, 1839, 102.
? Guiraca tricolor, Lesson, Rev. Zool. II, 1839, 102.

Sp. Ch.—Head above and on the sides, with chin, back, wings, and tail, black. A broad median stripe on the crown, a stripe behind the eye, a well marked collar on the hind neck all round, edges of interscapular feathers, rump, and under parts generally pale brownish orange, almost light cinnamon. Middle of belly, axillaries, and under wing coverts, yellow. Belly just anterior to the anus, under tail coverts, a large blotch at the end of the inner webs of first and second tail feathers, a band across the middle and greater wing coverts, some spots on the ends of the tertiaries, the **basal portions** of all the quills, and the outer three primaries near the tips, white.

Female similar, with less black ; wings and tail more olivaceous, the latter **unspotted** ; the black of the head anteriorly replaced by whitish. The under wing coverts bright yellow. Length of male, **nearly 8 inches** ; wing, 4.25 ; tail, 3.50.

Hab.—High Central Plains from Yellowstone to the Pacific. Table lands of Mexico.

This species has the bill similar to that of *G. ludoviciana*, a little more swollen, perhaps, and of a blackish color. The second quill is longest, then the third, fourth, and first. The tail is slightly emarginate and rounded.

The female is readily distinguishable from that of *G. ludoviciana* by the shade of light cinnamon brown beneath, without streaks or spots, (or else very obsolete,) and the existence of the same color on the back. The tail is more olive green, and the quills are white at their bases. An unmistakeable character is found in the under wing coverts and axillaries, which, in the female *ludoviciana*, are saffron or orange yellow instead of the clear lemon or gamboge yellow of *melanocephala*.

List of specimens.

Catal. No.	Sex & age.	Locality.	When collected.	Whence obtained.	Orig'l No.	Collected by—	Length.	Stretch of wings.	Wing.	Remarks.
1867	♂	Fort Union, Neb.........	June 26,1843	J. J. Audubon ...						
1868	♀	......do	1843.........	......do		... .				
5586	♂	Powder river, Neb.	Aug. 1,1856	Lt. G. K. Warren.		Dr. Hayden....	7.87	12.75	4.37	
4850	....	....	....	....		......do	8.25	12.75	4.25	
2873.	♂	Columbia river...........	July 28,1835	S. F. Baird......		J. K. Townsend	....			
4851	♀	Bijou Hills, Neb.........	May 17,1856	Lt. G. K. Warren.		Dr. Hayden....	8.87	12.50	3.25	Iris dark brown........
4550	♂	......do	...... do......	... ..do........		......do......	8.25	12.75	4.25	
4852	♀	......do	May 16,1856	......do.........		......do......	8.25	12.62	4.12	Eyes dull brown........
8205	♂	Fort Laramie............	Sept. 8,1857	Dr. Cooper.......	187	....	8.50	12.75	4.75	Iris brown ; bill brown.
8206	......	......do	... do......	......do.........	188	....	8.00	12.00	4.00	Feet lead color.........
8251	. ...	......do	... do......	......do		....				
6378	....	Fort Thorn, N. M.......	....	Dr. T. C. Henry.		....		...	...	
6379	♂	California	....	Dr. Heermann...		....		...	...	
6380	○	Posa Creek, Cal.........	....	Lt. Williamson ..		Dr. Heermann .				
5545	♂	Petaluma, Cal...........	May 11,1856	E. Samuels......	842	....	8.00	11.00	4.00	
5546	♂	......do	May 24,1856	......do	888	....				

GUIRACA CAERULEA, Swainson.

Blue Grosbeak.

Loxia caerulea, LINN. Syst. Nat. I, 1766, 306.—WILSON, Am. Orn. III, 1811, 78 ; pl. xxiv, f. 6.—? WAGLER, Isis, 1831, 525.

Guiraca caerulea, SWAINSON, Birds Mex. in Phil. Mag. I, 1827, 438.

Fringilla caerulea, AUD. Orn. Biog. II, 1834, 140 : V, 508 ; pl. 122.

Coccoborus caeruleus, Sw. Birds II, 1837, 277.—AUD. Syn. 1839.—IB. Birds Amer. III, 1841, 204; pl. 204.—CABANIS, Mus. Hein. 1851, 152.

Cyanoloxia caerulea, BP. Conspectus, 1850, 502.

Goniaphoea caerulea, BP.

Blue grosbeak, PENNANT, Arc. Zool. II, 1785, 351.

SP. CH.—Brilliant blue ; darker across the middle of the back. Space around base of the bill and lores, with tail feathers, black. Two bands on the wing across the tips of the primary and secondary coverts, with outer edges of tertiaries, reddish brown. Feathers on the posterior portion of the under surface tipped narrowly with grayish white.

Female yellowish brown above, brownish yellow beneath ; darkest across the breast, and lightest on the throat. Wing coverts and tertials broadly edged with brownish yellow. A faint trace of blue on the crown. Length of male 7.25 ; wing, 3.50 ; tail, 2.80.

Hab.—More southern United States from Atlantic to Pacific, south to Mexico.

This species exhibits but little variety of coloration, except in the purity and intensity of its blue.

List of specimens.

Catal. No.	Sex & age	Locality	When collected	Whence obtained	Orig'l No.	Collected by—	Length	Stretch of wings	Wing	Remarks
1484	♂	Carlisle, Pa..........	May 8, 1844	S. F. Baird	......	....	7.25	11.50	3.50	....
969	♀	......do..............	May 16, 1843	......do........	......	....	6.50	10.37	3.17	....
135	♂	......do..............	Aug. 29, 1840	......do	......	....	....	....	....	....
671	♀	......do..............	May 17, 1842	......do........	......	....	....	....	....	....
1400	♀	......do..............	April 29, 1844	......do........	......	....	6.50	10.50	3.17	....
2417	♀	Savannah..........	1845..........	......do........	......	Jos. Leconte.	....	....	....	....
4092	♂	New Leon, Mexico	April —, 1853	Lieut. Couch.....	146	....	7.25	11.25	3 75	Eyes brown; bill slate color and blue; feet slate col'd.
4093	♀	......do..............	......do.....	......do........	187	....	6.00	10.00	3.25	Eyes brown; feet lead color; bill lead and dove color.
6384	♂	Eagle Pass, Texas	....	Major Emory	......	A. Schott....	....	....	....	....
5033	♂	Pecos, Texas..........	May 2, 1855	Capt. J. Pope	93	....	8 00	11.00	3.00	....
6382	♂	Frontera, Mexico	May —, 1853	Major Emory.....	......	....	....	....	....	....
6385	♂	Fort Thorne, N. M......	....	Dr. T. C. Henry...	......	....	....	....	....	....
6383	♀	Zoquito, Mexico	....	Major Emory.....	......	J. H. Clark...	....	....	....	....
6381	♂	Los Nogales, Mexico...	June —, 1855	......do	80	Dr. Kennerly.	....	....	....	....
6388	♂	Posa creek, Cal......	....	Lt. Williamson ..	......	Dr. Heermann	....	....	....	....
6389	○	......do..............	....	......do........	......	......do......	... .	....	....	....
4467		Pit River valley, Cal....	....	......do........	......	Dr. Newberry.	....	....	.....	....
9285	♂	Loup Fork, Platte......	Aug. 5, 1857	Lt. Warren	......	Dr. Hayden .	7.50	11.50	......	Iris dark brown............
9286	♂	......do..............	Aug. 4, 1857	......do........	......	......do......	7.25	11.50	3.75	......do............
9289		......do..............	......do.....	......do........	......	......do.......	7.12	10.75	3.25	......do............
8062	♂	Mexico..............	Sept. —, 1836	J. Gould..........	......	J. Taylor	....	....	....	....

CYANOSPIZA, Baird.

Passerina, VIEILLOT, Analyse, 1816. Not of Linnaeus, used in Botany.
Spiza, BONAPARTE, Synopsis, 1828. Not of 1825.
Cyanospiza, BAIRD. Type *Tanagra cyanea*, L.

CH.—Bill deep at the base, compressed; the upper outline considerably curved; the commissure rather concave, with an obtuse, shallow lobe in the middle. Gonys slightly curved. Feet moderate; tarsus about equal to middle toe; the outer lateral toe barely longer than the inner, its claw falling short of the base of the middle; hind toe about equal to the middle without claw. Claws all much curved, acute. Wings long and pointed, reaching nearly to the middle of the tail; the second and third quills longest. Tail appreciably shorter than the wings; rather narrow, very nearly even.

The species of this genus are all of very small size and of showy plumage, usually blue, red, or green, in well defined areas.

The species usually associated in this genus vary somewhat in certain points. Thus, in *C. amoena*, the bill is moderately curved, and distinctly sinuated; the tertials not longer than the secondaries, the first primary a little shorter that the fourth; the lateral claws falling considerably short of the base of the middle one. In *C. cyanea*, with the bill somewhat similar, the tertials are much longer than the secondaries, equal to the sixth primary, the lateral toes rather longer. In *C. ciris* the bill is larger and more curved, the lateral toes reaching nearly to the base of the middle claw; the wing more rounded, the first primary shorter than the fifth; the tertials a little longer than the secondaries.

In the so called *Spiza versicolor* the upper mandible, the commissure especially, is more curved; the latter without any sinuation; the wings are shorter; the first primary shorter than the seventh; the tertials a little longer than the secondaries.

The *Cyanoloxia parellina* of Bonaparte is sufficiently similar to species of *Cyanospiza* to be placed among or at least near them. The bill, larger, more swollen, and much curved, though differing from *Guiraca* in having the under jaw much weaker, shorter, and scarcely wider than the upper. The three first quills are considerably graduated, the second a little longer than the sixth, the first about equal to the secondaries. The wing is but little longer than the tail. The hind claw is not longer than the middle anterior, but a little stouter. The tail feathers are as in *Guiraca*. Bonaparte places this species under *Cyanoloxia* or *Guiraca*, and it may be entitled to generic separation both from this and *Cyanospiza*, but I prefer retaining it with the latter, which it connects with *Guiraca*.

The following sketch may serve to distinguish the species of *Cyanospiza*, as far as color is concerned :

Dark dull indigo blue; brightest on the forehead, rump, and elbow...........*C. parellina*.

Rump, forehead, and beneath towards the tail, blue. Back part of crown, back, throat, and breast, reddish. Forehead and lores, black...............................*C. versicolor*.

Head and neck (except below) blue; back green; rump and beneath, red..........*C. ciris*.

Bright ultramarine blue, darkest on head and belly....................................*C. cyanea*.

Head and neck all round, and back blue; breast rusty; belly white; a white band on the wing...*C. amoena*.

It is with much reluctance that I find it necessary to abandon the name of *Spiza* for this group, after it had been so well established by general consent, but a strict adherence to the rules of ornithological systematists renders this necessary. The usual date given for *Spiza*, Bonaparte, is 1828, as published in the Annals of the New York Lyceum, with the *Emberiza amoena* of Say as type. His first mention of it, however, is in his observations on the nomenclature of Wilson's ornithology, published in Vol. IV, I, August, 1824, Journal Philadelphia Academy of Natural Sciences, under the head of *Emberiza americana*, Gmelin, No. 85. Here he states that "the *americana* (*Euspiza americana* of 1838) is certainly not an *Emberiza*, and is evidently congeneric with some of Wilson's FRINGILLAE; such as *F. melodia, savanna, socialis, passerina,* &c. For these birds I was about to propose the adoption of a new genus under the name of SPIZA, (Greek appellation of the FRINGILLA *coelebs*,) intermediate between FRINGILLA and EMBERIZA, but much more closely allied to the former. After an attentive examination of the intermediate species, I shall, however, consider it a sub-genus under FRINGILLA." * * * "The bird under consideration must, according to this innovation, be ranged under the sub-genus *Spiza*, and be called FRINGILLA *americana*."

None of the species of modern *Spiza* are mentioned on this page. On a subsequent one, No. 90, speaking of *Emberiza ciris*, he says: "This bird and the one that Wilson so accurately called *Fringilla cyanea* belong not only to the same genus, but are very closely allied, and may be placed under the sub-genus *Spiza*, if they will not constitute a small one of themselves."

In the American Ornithology, vol. I, 1825, 61, in the article on *Fringilla amoena*, after referring to his remarks on the nomenclature of Wilson's Ornithology, published the previous year, Bonaparte says: "As a species it (*Fringilla amoena*) is more intimately allied to *Fringilla ciris* and *F. cyanea*, which I stated in that paper (observations on Wilson) to differ so much from their congeners, (*i. e.*, the sub-genus *Spiza*,) particularly in the greater curvature of the upper mandible, as to deserve perhaps a separation into a small sub-genus by themselves, (*i. e.*, distinct from *Spiza*); this would unite *Fringilla* to *Tanagra*, as *Spiza*, on the other hand, shows its transition to *Emberiza*."

I do not know what species Vieillot gives as type for his *Passerina* in "*Analyse*," but in the Nouv. Dict. XXV, 1817, 3, the first species mentioned is *P. oryzivora* (*Dolichonyx*).

For these reasons, whatever may be the propriety of restoring the name of *Spiza* to *Euspiza*, there seems little doubt that the former name cannot be retained for the present group. *Passerina* of Vieillot, if otherwise applicable, is preoccupied in Botany.

Comparative measurements of species.

Catal. No.	Species.	Locality.	Sex.	Length.	Stretch of wings.	Wing.	Tail.	Tarsus.	Middle toe.	Its claw alone.	Hind toe and claw.	Hind claw alone.	Bill above.	Along gape.	Specimen measured.
4076	Cyanospiza parellina...	Sierra Madre, N. Leon .	♂	5.00	......	2.76	2.43	0.73	0.66	0.19	0.44	0.20	0.42	0.44	Skin ......
do..	......do ......do......	......do..............		5.00	8.00	2.75	......	......	......	......	......	......	......	......	Fresh .....
4075	......do....versicolor ..	Boquillo...............	♂	5.00	......	2.64	2.38	0.60	0.67	0.18	0.44	0.20	0.40	0.43	Skin ......
do..	......do ......do......	......do..............		5.50	8.25	2.75	......	......	......	......	......	......	......	......	Fresh .....
2645	......do....cyanea.....	Carlisle, Pa............	♂	4.80	......	2.77	2.36	0.69	0.69	0.20	0.46	0.21	0.41	0.44	Skin ......
do..	......do ......do......			5.66	9.08	2.90	......	......	......	......	......	......	......	......	Fresh .....
416	......do ......do......	......do..............	♀	4.74	......	2.52	2.12	0.69	0.69	0.17	0.46	0.18	0.40	0.45	Skin ......
	......do....ciris........	San Antonio, Texas....	♂	5.40	......	2.79	2.37	0.73	0.70	0.20	0.46	0.20	0.40	0.44	Skin ......
3085	......do ......do.......	Georgia...............	♂	5.30	......	2.70	2.41	0.73	0.70	0.20	0.50	0.20	0.40	0.40	Skin ......
do..	......do ......do.......	......do..............		5·50	8.60	3.80	......	......	......	......	......	......	......	......	Fresh .....
1898	......do....amoena......	Fort Union, Neb......	♂	5.00	......	2.90	2.41	0.69	0.69	0.19	0.46	0.18	0.43	0.46	Skin ......
6267	......do ......do.......	Posa creek............	♀	5.10	......	2.69	2.32	0.68	0.68	0.19	0.44	0.20	0.43	0.48	Skin ......

CYANOSPIZA PARELLINA, B a i r d .

Cyanoloxia parellina, BONAP. Conspectus, 1850, 502.
? Pitylus lazulus, LESSON, Rev. Zool. 1842, 174. Speaks of chestnut.

SP. CH.—General color dark blue, almost ultramarine, brightest on the rump, lesser wing coverts and top of head, shading on the hood to whitish blue on the forehead. Sides of head, including lores, and chin, with tail black. A few blue feathers on the lower jaw below the eye. Bill black. Length 5 inches; wing, 2.50; tail, 2.50; tarsus, .75; bill about .45.

Hab.—Northeastern Mexico to the Rio Grande.

The bill of this species though full and turgid, is not as deep as that of *Guiraca coerulea*, the lower not larger than the upper. The wing is much rounded; the fourth quill longest, the third and fifth little shorter; the second and sixth about equal; the first not longer than the secondaries. In *Guiraca coerulea* the second is longest, the first rather shorter than the fourth. The tail is nearly even; very slightly emarginate and rounded.

A specimen received from Mr. Gould has the bill longer and not so black as that of Lieut. Couch.

This species connects *Cyanospiza* with *Guiraca*, and may possibly be entitled to separate generic rank.

List of specimens.

Catal. No.	Locality.	When collected.	Whence obtained.	Orig. No.	Length.	Stretch of wings.	Wing.	Remarks.
4076	Sierra Madre, New Leon, Mexico.	April —, 1853	Lt. Couch	154	5.00	8.50	2.75	Eyes br'wn, bill bl'k, feet slate color.
8059	Tamaulipas, Mex	....	J. Gould					

CYANOSPIZA VERSICOLOR, Baird.

Spiza versicolor, Bon. Pr. Zool. Soc. 1837, 120.—Ib. Conspectus Av. 1850, 475.—Cab. Mus. Hein. 1851, 148.
Carduelis luxuosus, Lesson, Rev. Zool. 1839, 41.

Sp. Ch.—Posterior half of hood, with throat dark brownish red; interscapular region, similar but darker. Fore part of hood, lesser wing coverts, back of the neck, and rump, purplish blue; the latter purest blue; the belly reddish purple, in places tinged with blue, more obscure posteriorly. Feathers of wing and tail dark brown, edged with dull bluish. Loral region and narrow frontal band black. Length, 5.50; wing, 2.75; tail, 2.38.

Hab.—Northeastern Mexico, probably to the Rio Grande. Peru, Bonaparte.

This beautiful *Spiza* is sufficiently distinct from the other North American species not to require any comparison between adult males; the female I have never seen. The bill is stouter and more swollen to the end, and the mandible is much more curved than that of *C. cyanea*, and its perfectly concave commissure, without any shallow lobe in the middle, and the much more arched ridge, would almost separate the two generically. The wing is shorter and more rounded, the fourth quill longest, then the third, second, and fifth. The first is only a little longer than the seventh. The tail is decidedly rounded; rather more so than in *C. cyanea*.

List of specimens.

Catal. No.	Sex.	Locality.	Whence obtained.	Orig. No.	Length.	Stretch of wings.	Wing.	Remarks.
4075	♂	Boquillo, New Leon, Mexico.	Lt. Couch _____	151	5.50	8 25	2.75	Eyes br'n, bill dark purplish, feet very dark purple.

CYANOSPIZA CIRIS, Baird.

Nonpareil--Painted Bunting.

Emberiza ciris, Linn. Kong. Sv. Vet. Akad. Hand. 1750, 278; tab. vii, f. 1.—Ib. Syst. Nat. I, 1766, 313.—Wilson, Am. Orn. III, 1811, 68; pl. xxiv, f. 1, 2.
Passerina ciris, Vieillot, Gal. Ois. I, 1824, 81; pl. lxvi.
Fringilla ciris, Aud. Orn. Biog. I, 1832, 279: V. 517; pl. 53.
Spiza ciris, Bon, List, 1838.—Ib. Conspectus, 1850, 476.—Aud. Syn. 1839, 108.—Ib. Birds Amer. III, 1841, 93; pl. 169.
Painted finch, Catesby, Pennant.

Sp. Ch.—*Male.* Head and neck all round ultramarine blue, excepting a narrow stripe from the chin to the breast, which, with the under parts generally, the eyelids, and the rump, (which is tinged with purplish,) are vermilion red. Edges of chin, loral region, greater wing coverts, inner tertiary and interscapular region, green; the middle of the latter glossed with yellow. Tail feathers, lesser wing coverts, and outer webs of quills, purplish blue. Length, about 5.50 inches; wing, 2.70.

Female.—Clear dark green above; yellow beneath. Young, intermediate.

Hab.—South Atlantic and Gulf States to the Pecos river, Texas. South into Mexico.

Tail very slightly emarginate and rounded; second, third, and fourth quills equal; first rather shorter than the fifth.

The female is readily distinguishable from that of *C. cyanea* by the green instead of dull brown of the back, and the yellow of the under parts.

Specimens from southern Texas are smaller than those of Georgia.

List of specimens.

Catal. No.	Sex & age.	Locality.	When collected.	Whence obtained.	Orig. No.	Collected by—	Length.	Stretch of wings.	Wing.
1953	♂	Southern States		S. F. Baird		Jos. Leconte			
2409	♂	Savannah, Ga.	1845	do		do			
2413	♀	do	1845	do		W. L. Jones			
3080	♀	Liberty county, Ga.	1846	do		do	5.40	8.00	2.80
3077	♂	do	1846	do		do	5.80	8.50	2.80
3081	♂	do	1846	do		Jos. Leconte	5.62	8.30	2.70
3075	♂	do	1846	do		W. L Jones	5.50	8.75	2.75
3324	♂	do	1846	do		Jos. Leconte	5.60	8.50	2.30
3083	♀	do	1846	do		do	5.25	8.37	2.75
3085	○	do	1846	do		do	5.50	8.60	2.80
4310	♀	Calcasieu, La.	Spring of 1854	G. Wurdemann					
6271	♂	San Antonio, Tex.		Lt. J. G. Parke		Dr. Heermann			
6272	♂	do		Col. Graham		J. H. Clark	5.25	9.00	3.00
6273	♀			do	10	do	5.50	8.25	2.25
6277	♂	San Antonio, Tex.	July —, 1853	Lt. Whipple	14	Dr. Kennerly			
6278	♀	do	do	do	17	do			
6279	♂	Texas		Capt. Pope					
6280	♂	do		do					
5034	♂	River Pecos	May 25, 1855	do	94		6.25	9.00	2.50
6274	♀	San Pedro, Tex.		Col. Graham	20	J. H. Clark	2.50	6.00	8.50
6275	♀			do		do			
6276	♂	San Elizario, Tex.	May	Maj. Emory		do	5.87	8.50	2.12
6270	♀	Monterey, Mex.	May —, 1853	Lt. Couch	204		4.75	8.00	2.50

CYANOSPIZA AMOENA, Baird.

Lazuli Finch.

Emberiza amoena, SAY, Long's Exped. II, 1823, 47.
Fringilla (Spiza) amoena, BONAP. Am. Orn. I, 1825, 61 ; pl. vi, f. 5.
Fringilla amoena, AUD. Orn. Biog. V, 1839, 64, 230 ; pls. 398 and 424.
Spiza amoena, BONAP. List, 1838.—AUD. Syn. 1839, 109.—IB. Birds Am. III, 1841, 100 ; pl. 171.

SP. CH.—*Male.* Upper parts generally, with the head and neck all round, greenish blue ; the interscapular region darker. Upper part of breast pale brownish chestnut, separated from the blue of the throat by a faint white crescent ; rest of under parts white. A white patch on the middle wing coverts, and an obscurely indicated white band across the ends of the greater coverts. Loral region black. Length, about 5.50 ; wing, 3.90 ; tail, 2.60.

Female. Brown above ; whitish beneath, with a trace of a buff pectoral band.

Hab.—High Central Plains to the Pacific.

This species is about the size of *C. cyanea ;* the bill exactly similar. The females of the two species are scarcely distinguishable, except by the faint traces of one or two white bands on the wings in *amoena.* Sometimes both the throat and upper part of the breast are tinged with pale brownish buff.

List of specimens.

Catal. No.	Sex and age.	Locality.	When collected.	Whence obtained.	Orig'l No.	Collected by—	Length.	Stretch of wings.	Wing.	Remarks.
1898	♂	Fort Union, Neb.......	June 26, 1843	S. F. Baird..........	......	J. J. Audubon....	...	....	....	....
5399	♂	Fort Pierre, Neb.... ..	June 26, 1856	Lt. G. K. Warren..	....	Dr. Hayden......	....	... ..	....	....
5395	♂	Fort Lookout...........	June 22......	......do..	......	......do..........	5.50	8.75	2.50	....
5396	♂	......do................	...do.........	......do..........	......	......do..........	....	....	....	Eyes black .. ....
5397	♀	......do................	...do.........	......do..........	......	......do..........	5.00	9.00	2.75	......do...........
5398	♂	......do................	...do.........	......do..........	......	......do..........	5.75	9.00	3.00	....
8948	....	Laramie Peak	Aug. 24......	......do............	......	......do.	5.50	8.25	2.75	....
5982	♂	Fort Steilacoom, W. T..	May 15, 1855	Dr. J. G. Cooper...	.....	....	5.60	8.75	....	Bill bluish below...
2870	♀	Columbia river.........	June 3, 1836	S. F. Baird	......	J. K. Townsend..	....	....	....	....
4385	♂	Fort Dalles, W. T......	....	Dr. Suckley........	173	....	6.25	9.50	2.92	....
3897	♂	California	....	Dr. Heermann.....	......	....	....	....	....	....
5549	♂	Petaluma, Cal	....	E. Samuels........	896	....	....	....	....	....
6269	♀	San Francisco, Cal.. ..	....	R. D. Cutts.......	......	....	......	....	....	....
6267	♀	Posa creek, Cal.......	....	Lt. Williamson....	......	Dr. Heermann ..	......	....	....	....
6268	○	......do................	....	......do..........	......	......do..........	....	....	....	....

CYANOSPIZA CYANEA, Baird.

Indigo Bird.

Tanagra cyanea, LINN. Syst. Nat. I, 1766, 315.

Emberiza cyanea, GM. Syst. Nat. I, 1788, 876.

Fringilla cyanea, WILSON, I, 1810, 100 ; pl. vi, f. 5.—AUD. Orn. Biog. I, 1832, 377 : V, 503 ; pl. 74.

Passerina cyanea, VIEILL. Dict.

Spiza cyanea, BON. List, 1838.—IB. Consp. 1850, 474.—AUD. Syn. 1839, 109.—IB. Birds Amer. III, 1841, 96 ; pl. 170.

? *Emberiza cyanella*, GM. I, 1788, 887.

? *Emberiza caerulea*, GM. Syst. Nat. I, 1788, 876.

Indigo bunting, and *Blue bunting*, PENNANT and LATHAM.

SP. CH.—*Male.* Blue, tinged with ultramarine on the head, throat, and middle of breast ; elsewhere with verdigris green. Lores and anterior angle of chin velvet black. Wing feathers brown, edged externally with dull bluish brown.

Female. Brown above ; whitish, obscurely streaked or blotched with brownish yellow, beneath. Immature males similar, variously blotched with blue.

Length, about 5.75 inches ; wing, nearly 3.00.

Hab.—Eastern United States to the Missouri ; south to Guatemala.

In this species, which may be considered the type of the genus, the tail is slightly emarginate ; the second quill is longest, the first shorter than the fourth.

One specimen before me has the primary quills white. This is, however, merely an indication of albinism.

June 19, 1858.

64 b

List of specimens.

Catal. No.	Sex.	Locality.	When collected.	Whence obtained.	Orig. No.	Collected by—	Length.	Stretch of wings.	Wing.
7538	....	St. Louis, Mo........	May, 1857....	W. M. Magraw ..	....	Dr. Cooper			
5738	♂	E. of Ft. Riley, K. T.	June 16, 1856	Lt. Bryan	12	W. S. Wood....			
7024	♂	St. Louis	May 12, 1857	....	60	......do........	5.50		
2645	♂	Carlisle, Pa........	May 12, 1846	S. F. Baird......	.....	....	5.67	9.50	2.92
1479	♂	......do..........	May 8, 1844	......do........			5.42	9.00	2.67
429	♂	......do..........	May 28, 1841	......do........			5.42	8.50	......
1040	♀	......do..........	May 30, 1843	......do........			5.42	8.33	2.67
777		......do..........	Oct. 3, 1842	......do........			5 33	8.00	2.33
732	♂	......do......	Sept. 20, 1842	......do........			5.00	8.25	2.75
8057	....	Guatemala.....	....	J. Gould.					

SPERMOPHILA, Swainson.

Spermophila, Swainson, Zool. Jour. III, Nov. 1827, 348.   Type *Pyrrhula falcirostris,* Temm.   (Sufficiently distinct from *Spermophilus,* F. Cuv. 1822.

Sporophila, Cabanis, Mus. Hein. 1851, 148.   Type *Fringilla hypoleuca,* Licht.

Ch.—Bill very short and very much curved, as in *Pyrrhula,* almost as deep as long ; the commissure concave, abruptly bent towards the end. Tarsus about equal to middle toe ; inner toe rather the longer, (?) reaching about to the base of the middle one ; hind toe to the middle of this claw. Wings short, reaching over the posterior third of the exposed part of the tail ; the tertiaries gradually longer than the secondaries, neither much shorter than. the primaries which are graduated, and but little different in length, the first shorter than the sixth, the second and fourth equal. The tail is about as long as the wings, rounded, all the feathers slightly graduated, rather sharply acuminate and decidedly mucronate. Smallest of American passerine birds.

The essential characters of this genus are the small, very convex bill, as high as long ; the short broad wings, with the quills differing little in length, the outer ones graduated ; the tail as long as the wings, widened towards the end, and slightly graduated, with the acuminate and mucronate tip to the feathers.

As the name of *Spermophila* is sufficiently distinct from *Spermophilus,* of prior date, I see no necessity for the change of name with Cabanis to *Sporophila.*

Comparative measurements of species.

Catal. No.	Species.	Locality.	Sex.	Length.	Stretch of wings.	Wing.	Tail.	Tarsus.	Middle toe.	Its claw alone.	Hind claw alone.	Hind claw alone.	Bill above.	Along gape.	Specimen measured.
4095	Spermophila moreletii	Monterey, Mex..........	♂	4.00	......	1.93	1.96	0.60	0.60	0.20	0.45	0.20	0.33	0.30	Skin .... .
do.	........do...........	......do..............	.....	4.50	6.25	2.00	......	.....							Fresh .....
4096	........do...........	New Leon, Mex........	♂	4.00	......	2.05	2.00	0.62	0.60	0.19	0.45	0.21	0.32	0.30	Skin ......
do.	........do...........	......do..............	......	3.75	5.00	2.00	.....	.....							Skin ......
	........do...........	Honduras..............	......	4.04	......	2.04	1.98	0.60	0.64	0.21	0.50	0.43	0.33	0.32	Skin ......

SPERMOPHILA MORELETII, Pucheran.

Spermophila moreletii, (Pucheran,) Bonap. Conspectus, 1850, 497.—Sclater, Pr. Zool. Soc. 1856, 302.

Sporophila moreletii, Cab. Mus. Hein. 1851, 150.

Spermophila albigularis, (Spix,) Lawrence, Ann. N. Y. Lyceum, V, Sept. 1851, 124.   Texas.   (Not of Spix.)

Sp. Ch.—The top and sides of the head, back of the neck, a broad band across the upper part of the breast extending all round, the middle of the back, the wings and tail, with the posterior upper coverts, black. The chin, upper throat and neck all round, but interrupted behind, the rump, with the remaining under and lateral portions of the body, white ; the latter tinged with brownish yellow. Two bands on the wing, across the greater and middle coverts, with the concealed bases of all the quills, also white. Length, about 4 inches ; wing, 2.05 ; tail, 1.90.

Female, dull yellow ; olivaceous above, brownish yellow beneath. Wings and tail somewhat as in the male.

Hab.— Rio Grande of Texas ; south to Honduras.

The specimen upon which the preceding description of the male has been based is the only one in full plumage I have seen, and was kindly lent by Mr. P. L. Sclater. It was collected in Honduras. Some of the feathers of the back have grayish tips. The specimen described by Mr. Lawrence as *S. albogularis,* though male, is, in most respects, like the female, except that the wings and tail are darker, the color of the upper part grayer, and the interscapular feathers blotched with black. The black of the head is strongly indicated, the feathers, however, all with gray margins. In this and another, a little further advanced, from San Diego, Mexico, (4096,) there is a very faint indication of the black pectoral band, and there is no trace of the whitish of the rump.

List of specimens.

Catal. No.	Sex.	Locality.	When collected.	Whence obtained.	Original No.	Length.	Stretch of wings.	Wing.	Remarks.
4096	♂	Texas...................... San Diego, N. Leon,Mex.	Mar. —, 1853	G. N. Lawrence .... Lt. D. N. Couch.......	113	3.75	5.00	2.00	Bill black; feet brownish slate....
4095	♂ ?	Monterey, Mex.........	April —, 1853	......do................	163	4.50	6.25	2.00	Bill reddish slate, lighter beneath; eyes brown.
9118	......	Mexico...................	....	M. Verreaux............					

PYRRHULOXIA, Bonaparte.

Pyrrhuloxia, Bonaparte, Conspectus, 1850, 500. Type *Cardinalis sinuatus,* Bonap.

Ch.—The bill is very short and much curved, the culmen forming an arc of a circle of 60 degrees or more, and ending at a right angle with the straight gonys ; the commissure abruptly much angulated anterior to the nostrils in its middle point ; the lower jaw very much wider than the upper, and wider than the gonys is long ; anterior portion of commissure straight. Tarsus longer than middle toe ; outer lateral toes longer, not reaching the base of the middle ; wing considerably rounded, first quill longer than secondaries. Tail much longer than the wing, graduated ; the feathers broad, truncate. Head crested.

Color.—Gray, with red feathers and patches.

The essential character of this genus lies in the greatly curved, very short, and broad bill, something like that of *Pyrrhula.* In other respects like *Cardinalis,* but with less graduated wing, and longer and broader tail.

Comparative measurements of species.

Catal. No.	Species.	Locality.	Sex.	Length.	Stretch of wings.	Wing.	Tail.	Tarsus.	Middle toe.	Its claw alone.	Hind toe and claw.	Hind claw alone.	Bill above.	Along gape.	Specimen measured.
6370	Pyrrhuloxia sinuata...	Texas	♂	8.00	......	3.79	4.66	1.00	0.98	0.27	0.64	0.29	0.62	0.52	Skin ......
6369	........do...........	El Paso, Texas...........	♀	7.70	......	3.66	4.34	0.96	0.94	0.30	0.64	0.30	0.59	0.55	Skin ......
10283	Cardinalis virginianus.	Union co., Ill...........	♂	8.90	......	3.76	4.68	0.97	0.90	0.22	0.60	0.26	0 68	0.74	Skin ......
4030	........do...........	Brownsville, Texas.......	♂	7.70	......	3.54	4.24	0.99	0.80	0.24	0.60	0.26	0.66	0.74	Fresh......
do.	........do...........	......do................		8.50	11.25	3.50	......	......	......	......	......	......	......	......	Skin ......
4032	........do...........	......do................	♀	8.60	....	3.59	4.49	0.84	0.90	0.26	0.58	0.28	0.70	0.72	Skin ......
do.	........do.	......do.............. .	......	7.75	10.00	3.50?	......	......	......	......	......	......	......	......	Fresh......

PYRRHULOXIA SINUATA, Bonap.

Cardinalis sinuatus, Br. Pr. Zool. Soc. Lond. V, 1837, 111. (Mexico.)—LAWRENCE, Ann. N. Y. Lyc. V, 1851, 116.— CASSIN, Illust. I, VII, 1854, 204 ; pl. xxxiii.

Pyrrhuloxia sinuata, BON. Consp. 1850, 500.

SP. CH.— Head with an elongated, pointed crest, springing from the crown. Upper parts generally pale ashy brown ; hood, sides of neck, and under parts of body, rather paler. Long crest feathers, bill all round including lores and encircling the eye, wing and tail dark crimson. Chin and upper part of throat, breast, and median line of the belly, under tail coverts, tibia, edge and inner coverts of the wings, bright carmine red. Bill yellowish.

Female similar with the under part brownish yellow ; middle of belly and throat only tinged with red.

Length about 8.50 ; wing, 3.75 ; tail, 4.50.

Hab.—Valley of the Rio Grande of Texas.

In this species the bill is very short and greatly curved, much higher than long. The upper outline almost forms the quadrant of a circle, the commissural outline abruptly bent at an angle of about sixty degrees in its middle. In this respect it differs greatly from *Cardinalis virginianus*, in which the bill is much longer, straighter, and with the angle of the commissural outline much further back.

The wing is considerably rounded, the fourth and fifth quills longest; the first as long as the secondaries, the second longer than the seventh. The tail is long, graduated on the sides ; the outer about half an inch shorter than the middle. The feathers are very broad to the end and obliquely truncate. They are rather broader than in *Cardinalis virginianus*. The crest is narrower and longer, confined to the middle of the crown; it extends back about 1.80 inches from the base of the bill.

The carmine of the breast is somewhat hidden by grayish tips to the feathers ; that of the throat is streaked a little with darker. The exposed surfaces of the wing coverts and of secondaries and tertials are like the back. The tail feathers are tipped with brownish.

List of specimens.

Catal. No.	Sex.	Locality.	When collected.	Whence obtained.	Orig'l No.	Collected by—	Length.	Stretch of wings.	Wing.	Remarks.
4027	♂	New Leon, Mexico.....	May —, 1853	Lt. Couch........	209	....	8.00	11.50	3.50	Eye brown ; bill orange ; feet dove color.
4028	♂	.....do...............	Mar. —, 1853	......do..........	47	Not here.......	7.50	10.50	3.50	Eye brown ; bill dull yellow ; feet lead.
4029	♀	......do..............	......do......	......do.........	59	....	8.75	10.50	3.25	The same...............
6366	♀	Ringgold Barracks, Tex.	July —, 1853	Major Emory.....	......	A. Schott......	....	....	....	
6367	......	....	....	......do.........	......	......do.......	....	....	....	
6368	......	El Paso, Texas.	Jan. —, 1855	......do........	26	Dr. Kennerly...	....	....	....	
6369	♀	......do............	....	Lt. J. G. Parke..	......	Dr. Heermann...	....	....	....	
6370	♂	Texas	....	......do.........	......	......do.... ...	....	....	....	
8056	......	Mexico	....	......do..........	..	J. Gould.......	......	.... .	....	

CARDINALIS, Bonaparte.

Cardinalis, BONAPARTE, Saggio di una distribuzione metod. dei Animagli Vertebrati, 1831, (Agassiz). Type *Loxia cardinalis*, Linn.

CH.—Bill enormously large ; culmen very slightly curved, commissure sinuated ; lower jaw broader than the length of the gonys, considerably wider than the upper jaw, about as deep as the latter. Tarsi longer than middle toe ; outer toe rather the longer, reaching a little beyond the base of the middle one ; hind toe not so long. Wings moderate, reaching over the basal third of the exposed part of the tail. Four outer quills graduated ; the first equal to the secondaries. Tail long, decidedly longer than the wings, considerably graduated ; feathers broad, truncated a little obliquely at the end, the corners rounded. Colors red. Head crested.

The essential characters of this genus are the crested head; very large and thick bill extending far back on the forehead, and only moderately curved above; tarsus longer than middle toe; much graduated wings, the first primary equal to the secondary quills; the long tail exceeding the wings, broad and much graduated at the end.

CARDINALIS VIRGINIANUS, Bonap.

Red Bird; Cardinal.

Coccothraustes virginiana, BRISSON, Orn. III, 1760, 253.
Loxia cardinalis, LINN. Syst. Nat. I, 1766, 300.—WILSON, Am. Orn. II, 1810, 38; pl. vi, f. 1, 2.
Coccothraustes cardinalis, VIEILL. Dict.
Fringilla (Coccothraustes) cardinalis, BON. Obs. Wils. 1825, No. 79.
Fringilla cardinalis, NUTT. Man. I, 1832, 519.—AUD. Orn. Biog. II, 1834, 336: V, 514; pl. 159.
Pitylus cardinalis, AUD. Syn. 1839, 131.—IB. Birds Amer. III, 1841, 198; pl. 203.
Cardinalis virginianus, BON. List, 1838.—IB. Consp. 1850, 501.
Grosbec de Virginie, BUFF. Pl. enl. 37.

SP. CH.—A flattened crest of feathers on the crown.   Bill red.   Body generally bright vermilion red, darker on the back, rump, and tail.   Narrow band around the base of the bill, with chin and upper part of the throat black.

Female of a duller red, and this only on the wings, tail, and elongated feathers of the crown.   Above light olive; tinged with yellowish on the head; beneath brownish yellow, darkest on the sides and across the breast.   Black about the head only faintly indicated.

Length,.8.50; wing, 3.75; tail, 4.50.

Hab.—More southern portions of the United States to the Missouri.   Probably along valley of Rio Grande to Rocky mountains.

The bill of this species is very large and shaped much like that of *Guiraca ludoviciana*. The central feathers of the crest of the crown are longer than the lateral; they spring from about the middle of the crown and extend back about an inch and a half from the base of the bill.   The wings are much rounded, the fourth longest, the second equal to the seventh, the first as long as the secondaries.   The tail is long, truncate at the end, but graduated on the sides; the feathers are broad to the end, truncated obliquely at the end.

Some males, probably immature, have the vermilion replaced by a pale rose color, the back strongly tinged with olivaceous.

List of specimens.

Catal. No	Sex.	Locality.	When collected.	Whence obtained.	Orig'l No.	Collected by—	Length.	Stretch of wings.	Wing.	Remarks.
6479	♂	Philadelphia	....	C. Drexler.....	......	....	......	......	......	....
2690	♂	......do....	... .	S. F. Baird.....	......	....	......	......	......	....
1096	♂	Washington	June 12, 1843	......do........	......	Wm. M. Baird	8.50	12.00	3.75	....
610	♂	.... do............	Feb. —, 1842	......do........	.. ...	...do......	......	......	......	....
613	♀	....do	Mar. 26, 1842	......do........	....	...do......	......	......	......	....
4919	♂	Amelia Island, Fla.	....	G. Würdemann	......	....	7.50	11.50	3.50	....
6526	♂	Key Biscayne, Fla..	May 9, 1856	.....do.........	......	....	......	......	......	....
4854	♂	Iowa Point, Neb...	April 23, 1856	Lieut. Warren..	14	Dr. Hayden..	7.37	14.50	4.50	Eye dull brown ....
4855	♂	Ft Leavenworth,K.T	April 21, 1856	Lieut. Couch ..	1	....	8.50	12.00	3.87	......do....
6365	♂	......do	Nov. —, 1854	.....do........	9	....	......	......	......	....
8381	.....	Independence, Mo.	June 2, 1857	W. M. Magraw.	......	Dr. Cooper..	9.00	12.25	4.00	....
5731	♂	Kansas	1856..........	Lt. F. T. Bryan.	......	W. S. Wood.	......	......	......	....
7031	♂	St. Louis	•May 8, 1857	....do........	23	.... do......	......	......	......	....
5029	♀	Indianola, Texas...	Mar. —, 1855	Capt. J. Pope...	......	....	......	......	......	....
3947	♂	Brownsville, Texas.	....	Capt. Van Vliet.	......	....	......	......	......	....
4030	♂	......do..........	Feb. —, 1853	Lieut. Couch ..	23	....	8.50	11.25	3.50	Bill light scarlet, feet reddish brown.
5028	♂	Rio Seco, Texas....	April 19, 1855	Capt. J. Pope..	44	....	9.00	12.50	4.00	Eyes dark, feet dark gray.......
4032	♀	Brownsville, Texas.	....	Lieut. Couch ..	12	....	7.75	10.00	3.50	Bill light scarlet, eye reddish brown.
4031	.....	New Leon, Mexico.	April —, 1853	....do........	127	....	9.00	11.00	3.75	Bill scarlet, feet light brown, eye brown.
4364	♂	Fort Thorne, N. M.	....	Dr. T. C. Henry.	......	....	......	......	......	....

PIPILO, Vieillot.

Pipilo, VIEILLOT, Analyse, 1816, (Agassiz.) Type *Fringilla erythrophthalma*, Linn.
Kieneria, BONAP. Comptes Rendus, XL, 1855, 356. In part.

CH.—Bill rather stout ; the culmen gently curved, the gonys nearly straight ; the commissure gently concave with a decided notch near the end ; the lower jaw not so deep as the upper ; not as wide as the gonys is long ; but wider than the base of the upper mandible. Feet large, the tarsus as long or a little longer than the middle toe ; the outer lateral toe a little the longer, and reaching a little beyond the base of the middle claw. The hind claw about equal to its toe ; the two together about equal to the outer toe. Claws all stout, compressed, and moderately curved. Wings reaching about to the end of the upper tail coverts ; short and rounded, though the primaries are considerably longer than the nearly equal secondaries and tertials ; the outer four quills are graduated ; the first considerably shorter than the second, and about as long as the secondaries. Tail considerably longer than the wings ; moderately graduated externally ; the feathers rather broad ; most rounded off on the inner webs at the end.

The colors vary ; the upper parts are generally uniform black or brown ; the under white or brown ; no central streaks on the feathers. The hood sometimes differently colored.

The essential characters of the genus are in the curved culmen and commissure ; the strong feet; the outer toe rather longer than the inner ; the wings rounded, but the primaries decidedly longer than the others ; the outer four quills considerably graduated, but the first usually not shorter than the secondaries. The graduated tail longer than the wings.

Of this genus there are three sections well marked by color in the United States species.

In the examination of a large series of specimens of *Pipilo*, belonging to section A, from different parts of North America, I found it very difficult to assign all of them satisfactorily to their respective species. It was quite possible to select typical specimens of the four black ones described, but there were intermediate forms which connected the extremes. I am, however, satisfied that we have these four, and am inclined to believe that many of the uncertain specimens are really hybrids, as appears to be certainly the case with No. 8193.

In the following synopsis I have been obliged to go into more detail than usual with section A, in order to show the exact relationship of the new *P. megalonyx* to its allies.

A. First primary nearly equal to the secondaries. Tail moderately graduated, outer feather about a quarter of an inch shortest. Above, with head and neck, black; middle of belly white; sides chestnut brown. Tail feathers with white patches.

Hind claw scarcely longer than its digit, the toe and claw as long as the middle toe without its claw. Inner lateral claw reaching the base of the middle one. Middle toe and claw as long as the tarsus.

White of tail occupying nearly the terminal half. Outer web of exterior tail feather almost entirely white, a black streak usually at the end. No white on the wing coverts and scapulars. Outer primaries edged with white throughout, this sometimes interrupted in the middle.................*P. erythrophthalmus*.

Wing coverts with rounded, and scapulars with elongated oval spots of white on the tip of outer webs of the feathers, the white rarely extending to the edge of the feather. Outer web of exterior tail feather entirely black; the terminal white inner spot short. Primaries without white edges towards the base. Throat feathers without concealed white spot.............................*P. oregonus*.

Hind claw a little longer than its digit; the toe and claw together a very little longer than the middle toe without it. Inner lateral toe and claw reaching a very little beyond the base of the middle claw. Middle toe and claw a little longer than the tarsus.

Wing coverts and scapulars with spots at the ends of outer webs extending to the tip, and without black border on the edge. Outer web of external tail feather white, this entirely confluent with the extended terminal spot. Outer primaries broadly edged with white throughout. Throat feathers with concealed white spots.. ....*P. arcticus*.

Hind claw much larger than its digit; hind toe and claw reaching nearly as far as the middle of its middle claw; the inner lateral claw reaching nearly as far; the middle toe and claw longer than the tarsus.

Wing coverts and scapulars with large sub-rounded and elliptical white spots. Scapular spots with a narrow edging of black externally; the covert spots generally white to the edge, but not extending to the extreme end of the outer web. Primaries edged externally with white towards the end. Throat feathers with concealed white spots........................ ....*P. megalonyx*.

B. Tail more graduated; outer feather half an inch shortest. First primary mostly less than the secondaries. Above light brown; beneath similar but lighter. No white on wings or tail.

Hood tinged with chestnut. Middle of belly white; a dusky spot on the middle of the breast. Chin and throat lighter, encircled by spots.........*P. mesoleucus*.

Hood almost like the back. Beneath uniform light brown, without the spot. Chin and throat much as in the last...*P. fuscus*.

Nearly uniform yellowish brown, paler beneath. Lores and chin dusky.*P. aberti*.

C. Tail intermediate. First quill longer than the secondaries. Upper parts, with wings and tail olive green.

Hood chestnut. Chin and throat abruptly white, surrounded by dark ash.

P. chlorurus.

I do not venture to give names to sections B and C in my ignorance of the numerous allied genera of South America and Mexico. Bonaparte makes a genus, *Kieneria*, (Comptes Rendus,

XL, 1855, 356,) with *Pyrgisoma kieneri*, of Conspectus, 186, as type (*Pyrgisoma* is based upon *Arremon biarcuatus*, of Lafresnaye, figured in Voyage de la Venus, tab. vi, and erroneously assigned to California.) The other species given as belonging to the genus are *Pipilo rufipileus*, (*chlorurus*) *torquatus, rufescens, fuscus*, and *aberti*. It is probable that the *P. chlorurus* would be our North American type of *Kieneria*. I am not prepared to suggest a name for section B.

Gray gives *Melozone* (not *Meloxene*) of Reichenbach, Av. Syst. Nat. pl. lxxix, 1850, as antedating *Pyrgisoma* of Pucheran, 1851. The name, however, is given in Conspectus Avium, 20 July, 1850, although according to the title page, pl. 79 of Reichenbach was published June 1, 1850.

Comparative measurements of species.

Catal. No.	Species.	Locality.	Sex & age.	Length.	Stretch of wings.	Wing.	Tail.	Tarsus.	Middle toe.	Its claw alone.	Hind toe and claw.	Hind claw alone.	Bill above.	Along gape.	Specimen measured.
2135	Pipilo erythrophthalmus	Carlisle, Pa	♂	7.70	....	3.54	4.30	1.08	1.12	0.30	0.76	0.40	0.54	0.69	Skin
do.	......do............	....do		8.75	11.50	3.75	......	......	......	....	......	......	......	......	Fresh
8194	......do............	Fort Leavenworth, K.T.	♀	6.84	......	3.08	3.70	1.07	1.01	0.30	0.71	0.36	0.56	0.62	Skin
do.	......do............	....do........		7.25	10.25	3 37	......	......	......	....	......	......	......	......	Fresh
8193	......do............	....do........	♂	7.50	......	3.45	4.14	1.00	1.02	0.30	0.72	0.35	0.58	8.68	Skin
do.	......do............	....do........		8.25	11.25	3.56	......	......	......	....	......	......	......	......	Fresh
1944	Pipilo arcticus	Fort Union	♂	7.50	......	3.39	3.99	1.05	1.08	0.31	0.74	0.39	0.55	0.66	Skin
5736	......do............	Republican Fork.	♂	8.00	......	3.36	4.44	1.06	1.06	0.31	0.74	0.41	0.55	0.66	Skin
do.	......do............	....do........		8.25	10.25	......	......	......	......	....	......	......	......	......	Fresh
4845	......do............	Bon Homme island.....	♀	7.20	......	3.08	3.86	1.04	1.06	0.30	0.74	0.38	0.55	0 61	Skin
do.	......do...	....do........		7.75	10.00	3.25	......	......	......	....	......	......	......	......	Fresh
2867	Pipilo oregonus	Colorado river.........	♂	8.00	......	3.32	4.04	1.10	1.02	0.27	0.74	0.37	0.56	0.70	Skin
3910	Pipilo megalonyx	California	♀	7.52	......	3.24	4.14	1.08	1.06	0.36	0.86	0.50	0.60	0.68	Skin
10284	......do............	Fort Tejon	♂	7.62	......	3.39	4.24	1.08	1.10	0.38	0 90	0.53	0.56	0.68	Skin
6717	......do............	Fort Thorn	♂	8.00	.. ...	3.46	4.46	1.08	1.12	0.30	0.86	0.40	0.54	0.69	Skin
5559	Pipilo fuscus	Petaluma, Cal.........	♂	8.90	......	3 86	4.90	1.10	1.12	0.30	0.79	0.40	0.62	0.67	Skin
3710	......do............	Monterey..............	♀	7.84	......	3.42	4.38	1.12	1.09	0.32	0.80	0.44	0 56	0.63	Skin
6830	Pipilo mesoleucus	Los Nogales, Mex......		8.60	......	3.77	4 58	1.01	1.00	0.30	0.70	0.32	0.64	0.66	Skin
6245	Pipilo chlorurus	T·jon valley, Cal......	♂	6.72	......	3.00	3.70	0.96	0.90	0.28	0.66	0.37	0.44	0.48	Skin
1896	......do............	Rocky mountains	○♂	6.80	....	3.05	3.30	0.96	0.92	0.28	0.66	0.36	0.47	0.54	Skin

PIPILO ERYTHROPHTHALMUS, Vieillot.

Ground Robin; Towhee; Chewink.

Fringilla erythrophthalma, LINN. Syst. Nat. I, 1766, 318.—AUD. Orn. Biog. I, 1832, 151 : V, 511 ; pl. 29.

Emberiza erythrophthalma, GM. Syst. Nat. I, 1788, 874.—WILSON, Am. Orn. VI, 1812, 90 ; pl. liii.

Pipillo erythrophthalmus, VIEILL. Gal. Ois. I, 1824, 109 ; pl. lxxx.

Pipilo erythrophthalmus, BON. List, 1838 —IB. Conspectus, 1850, 487.—AUD. Syn. 1839, 124.—IB. Birds Amer. III, 1841, 167 ; pl. 195.

Pipilo ater, VIEILL. Nouv. Dict. XXXIV, 1819, 292.

Towhee Bird, CATESBY, Car. I, 34. —*Towhee Bunting*, LATHAM, Syn II, I, 1783, 199.—PENNANT, II, 1785, 359.

SP. CH.—Upper parts generally, head and neck all round, and upper part of the breast, glossy black, abruptly defined against the pure white which extends to the anus, but is bounded on the sides and under the wings by light chestnut. Under coverts similar to sides, but paler. Edges of outer six primaries with white at the base and on the middle of the outer web ; inner two tertiaries also edged externally with white. Tail feathers black ; outer web of the first, with the ends of the first to the third white, decreasing from the exterior one. Iris red. Length, 8.75 ; wing, 3.75 ; tail, 4.10.

Female with the black replaced by brown.

Hab.—Eastern United States to the Missouri river.

In this species the cutting edge of the mandible is slightly concave, and not sinuated. The wing is short and rounded ; the fourth quill longest ; the first about equal to the secondaries.

The tail feathers are only moderately graduated on the sides ; the outer about .40 of an inch shorter than the middle. The outer tail feather has the terminal half white, the outline transverse ; the white of the second is about half as long as that of the first; of the third half that of the second. The chestnut of the sides reaches forward to the black of the neck, and is visible when the wings are closed.

A young bird has the prevailing color reddish olive above, spotted with lighter ; beneath brownish white, spotted thickly with brown.

In most western specimens the white of the base of primaries is connected with that on the middle so as to have the entire edge of these quills white. One specimen, 8193, from Fort Leavenworth, has a few white spots on the scapulars only, the wing coverts without them, exhibiting an approach to *P. arcticus*. This is probably a hybrid between the two.

List of specimens.

Catal. No.	Sex & age.	Locality.	When collected.	Whence obtained.	Orig'l No.	Collected by—	Length.	Stretch of wings.	Wing.	Remarks.
6938	♂	Selkirk Settlem't,H.B.T.	....	Donald Gunn	......	....	....	....	......	....
820	♂	Carlisle, Penn.	Oct. 19, 1842	S. F. Baird.......	......	....	8.50	11.50	3.33	....
3374	♂	......do..	May 4, 1847	.....do...........	......	... .	7.75	10.07	3.33	....
2135	♂	....'.........	April 23,1845	.....do....	......	.. ..	8.75	11.50	3.58	....
1652	O	Carlisle, Penn.	July 27,1844	......do...........	......	....	8.42	11.00	3.42	....
4835	......	St. Joseph's, Mo.......	April 22,1856	.....do...........	10	Dr. F.V.Hayden	8.12	10.75	3.37	....
4833	......	Bald Island, Mo. river..	April 25,1856	.....do...........	......	.....do.........	8	11.00	3.50	....
4832	......	......do...........	......do......	.....do...........	90	.....do.........	8.75	11.50	3.87	Eye reddish brown.......
4828	♂	......do...............	April 24,1856	.....do...........	......	.....do.........	7.75	10.50	3.25	....
4836	......	......do...............	April 25,1856	.....do...........	41	.....do.........	10.62		3.75	....
4829	......	......do...............	......do......	.....do...........	42	.....do.........	8.02	11.00	3.50	....
4832	......	Iowa Point............	April 23,1856	.....do...........	17	..... do.........	7.50	10.75	3.12	....
4834	♂	Wood's Bluff.........	....	.....do...........	......	..... do.........	7.75	11.00	3.62	....
4835	♀	......do............	May 8.	.....do...........	......	.....do.........	... ...	....	....	....
5735	♂	Wood's Creek.........	....	Lt. F. T. Bryan...	60	W. S. Wood.....	....	....	....	....
8350	O	Independence, Mo.	June 18,1857	W. M. Magraw..	77	Dr. Cooper.....	... .	10.75	3.50	Iris brown ; bill brown and yellow ; feet flesh color.
8349	O	......do............	......do......	.....do...........	76	......do......	....	11.00	3.75	......do........do.......
8327	......	......do............	June 3, 1857	......do...........	56	......do.........	8.00	11.25	3.50	Iris red; bill bl'k; ft. brown.
8174	♀	Leavenworth...........	July 13, 1857	......do...........	130	......do.........	....	....	....	Iris red; bill bl'k; ft. brown.
8193?	♂	......do...............	......do......	...... do	129	......do.........	8.25	11.25	3.87	? Hybrid, with *arcticus*.

PIPILO OREGONUS, Bell.

Oregon Ground Robin.

Pipilo oregonus, BELL, Ann. N. Y. Lyc. V, 1852, 6. Oregon.—BONAP. Comptes Rendus, XXXVII, Dec. 1853, 922.—IB. Notes Orn. Delattre, 1854, 22, (same as prec.)

Fringilla arctica, AUD. Orn. Biog. V, 1839, 49 ; pl. 394.

Pipilo arctica, AUD. Syn. 1839, 123.—IB. Birds Am. III, 1841, 164 ; pl. 194, (not of Swainson.)

SP. CH.—Upper surface generally, with the head and neck all round to the upper part of the breast, deep black ; the rest of lower parts pure white, except the sides of the body and under tail coverts, which are light chestnut brown ; the latter rather paler. The outer webs of scapulars (usually edged narrowly with black) and of the superincumbent feathers of the back, with a rounded white spot at the end of the outer webs of the greater and middle coverts ; the outer edges of the innermost tertials, white ; no white at the base of the primaries. Outer web of the first tail feather black, occasionally white on the extreme edge ; the outer three with a white tip to the inner web. Length, 8.25 ; wing, 4.40 ; tail, 4. Female with the black replaced by brownish.

Hab.—Coast of Oregon and Washington Territories.

June 19, 1858.

65

This species is readily distinguished from *P. erythrophthalmus* by the white on the scapulars and wing coverts. Its relationships to *arcticus* are much closer. There is not much difference between the two in the white of the scapular region, except that the white marks here, as elsewhere on the wing, are rounded, the extreme end of the outer web of the feather being black instead of running out acutely white to the very tip of the outer webs of the feathers. This gives rather less extension to the white. In fact, most of the white marks are edged externally with black, converting them into spots. There is no white whatever at the exposed base of the outer web of the second to fifth primaries, and there is only a trace of white near the end, instead of having a conspicuous white edging from base to near the tip.

The outer web of the outer tail feather, instead of being entirely white for the exposed portion, is only very slightly edged with white; usually entirely black. The white at the end of the feathers is much more restricted, and extends only over the three outer feathers; usually not reaching to the shaft.

List of specimens.

Catal. No.	Sex.	Locality.	When collected.	Whence obtained.	Orig'l No.	Collected by—	Length.	Extent.	Wing.	Remarks.
8416	......	Simiahmoo Bay.........	Sept. 17, 1857	A. Campbell	......	Dr. Kennerly	....	....	....	....
5973	......	Whitby island, W. T.....	....	Gov. Stevens ...	......	Dr. Cooper.......	8.00	10.25	....	Iris red, bill slate. ....
5974	♀	........do.....	....	Dr. J. G. Cooper .	......	......do.........	8.60	10.50	....	....
4532	.....	Washington Territory....	1856..........	Dr. Suckley	......	......	....	....	....	....
5974	♀	.... do...............	....	Gov. I. I. Stevens.	......	Dr. Suckley	....	....	....	Iris olive brown......
6739	......	Steilacoom	June 25, 1856	Dr. Cooper	......	....	8.00	9.75	....	Iris red ....
4531	......	Washington Territory.....	1856..........	Dr. Suckley	......	......	....	....	....	....
4553	......	........do...............	1856..........	......do.......	......	......	....	....	....	....
2867	♂	Columbia river..........	May 27, 1835	S. F. Baird	......	J. K. Townsend..	....	....	....	....
6737	......	Fort Vancouver, W. T...	Jan. 19, 1854	Gov. Stevens ...	......	Dr. Cooper.......	8.25	10.25	....	Iris red ....
4386?	.....	Fort Dalles, Oregon	....	Dr. Suckley	156	....	8 25	10.00	3.50	Iris orange, bill black.

PIPILO ARCTICUS Swainson.

Pyrgita (Pipilo) arctica, Sw. F. Bor. Am. II, 1831, 260.
Pipilo arcticus, NUTTALL, Man. I, 1832, 589.--IB. 2d ed. 1840, 610.—BELL, Ann New York Lyc. V, 1852, 7.

Sp. Ch —Upper parts generally, with head and neck all round to the upper part of the breast, black. Middle of breast and of belly white; sides chestnut; under tail coverts similar, but paler. Outer webs of scapulars and of dorsal feathers immediately above them, ends of primary and secondary coverts, (on the outer web,) outer edges of three innermost tertials, and of the second to fifth primaries, conspicuously white. Outer web of the first and ends of the first to the fourth tail feathers, white, the amount diminishing not very rapidly. Length about 8 inches; wing, 2.40; tail, 4.10; hind toe and claw, .74.

Female brown instead of black.

Hab.— High Central Plains of Upper Missouri, Yellowstone, and Platte.

This species is similar in form to the *P. erythrophthalmus*, which, however, is readily distinguished by the entire absence of white on the scapulars and wing coverts. The amount of white on the tail decreases much less rapidly. The differences between it and *P. oregonus* will be found detailed under the head of the latter species.

One specimen (8193) from Fort Leavenworth, with a few white spots only on the scapulars, may perhaps be considered a hybrid between *arctica* and *erythrophthalmus*.

List of specimens.

Catal. No.	Sex.	Locality.	When collected.	Whence obtained.	Orig'l No.	Collected by—	Length.	Stretch of wings	Wing.	Remarks.
1944	♂	Fort Union, Neb....	....	S. F. Baird	......	J. J. Audubon....	....	......	....	....
5389	... ..	Yellowstone	August, 1856	Lt. G K. Warren.	......	Dr. Hayden......	....	......	....	....
5388	♀	Fort Lookout.............	June 22, 1856	......do...........	.....	......do........	7.50	10.25	3.50	....
5390	♂	......do............	....do.......	......do...........	......	......do	8.25	11.25	4.00	Eyes red.............
4847	♀	Bijou Hills...............	May 1......	......do	......	......do........	7.37	10 50	3.50	....
4846	♀	......do...............	May 15......	......do...........	......	......do	8.00	10.75	3.50	Iris red.... ....
4843	♀	......do...............	....do.......	......do...........	......	.... do........	8.00	10.37	3.25	....
4842	....	......do...............	May 14......	......do	14	......do........	7.62	11.25	3 50	....
4839	♂	Bon Homme island.......	May 9.......	......do...........	......	......do........	8.00	10.25	3.75	Iris dark red........
4840	♂	...... do............ ...	....do.......	......do.........	......	......do	7.62	9.75	3.50	....
4845	♀	......do...............	....do......	......do...........	......	......do........	7.75	10.00	3.25	Iris red........ ...
4838	♂	......do...... ...	....do.. ...	......do...........	......	......do........	8.62	11.50	3.50	Eyes red........ ....
5736	♂	Republican Forks	Sept. 25....	Lt. F. T. Bryan ..	355	......do	8.25	10.00	....	....
8219	♀	Fort Laramie	Sept. 12, 1857	Dr. Cooper......	......	......do........	8.75	11.25	3.75	Iris chestnut.........
		Variety *sub-arcticus.*								
5387?	♂	Fort Pierre...........	June 26, 1856	Lt. G. K. Warren.	.....	Dr. Hayden	5.37	9.37	2.87	Iris dark brown.......
4844?	......	Bijou Hills...............	May 15......	...... do...........	.....	......do.........	8.25	10.87	3.87	....
4841?	♂	The Tower...	May 11......	......do...........	....	......do........	8.12	10.75	3.50	....
5736?	♂	Republican Fork........	Sept. 25, 1856	Lt. F. T. Bry..n...	356	W. S. Wood	8 25	10.25	....	....

PIPILO MEGALONYX, Baird.

Sp. Ch.—Similar to *P. arcticus* in amount of white on the wings and scapulars, though this frequently edged with black. Outer edge of outer web of external tail feather white, sometimes confluent with that at tip of tail. Concealed white spots on feathers of side of neck. Claws enormously large, the hinder longer than its digit; the hind toe and claw reaching to the middle of the middle claw, which, with its toe, is as long, or longer, than the tarsus. Inner lateral claw reaching nearly to the middle of middle claw. Length, 7.60; wing, 3.40; tail, 4.25; hind toe and claw, .90.

Hab.—Southern coast of California and across through vallies of Gila and Rio Grande.

This form, if not a distinct species, constitutes so strongly marked a variety as to be worthy of particular description. The general appearance is that of *P. arcticus*, which it resembles in the amount of white spotting on the wings. This, however, does not usually involve the whole outer web at the end, but, as in *oregonus*, has a narrow border of black continued around the white terminally and sometimes externally. There is not quite so much of a terminal white blotch on the outer tail feather, this being but little over an inch in length, and the outer web of the same feather is never entirely white, though always with an external white border, which sometimes is confluent with the terminal spot, but usually leaves a brown streak near the end never seen in *arcticus,* which also has the whole outer web white except at the base. From *oregonus* the species differs in the much greater amount of white on the wings and the less rounded character of the spots. *Oregonus*, too, has the whole outer web of external tail feather black, and the terminal white spot of the inner web less than an inch in length. I have never seen in *oregonus* any of the concealed white spotting on the sides of the head.

The greatest difference between this species and the two others is in the stout tarsi and enormously large claws, as described, both the lateral extending greatly beyond the base of the middle one, the hinder toe and claw nearly as long as the tarsus. The only North American Passerine birds having any approach to this length of claw are those of the genus *Passerella.*

A *Pipilo macronyx* of Swainson appears to have a similar development of claws, but is described as olive with black head and throat, the light marks on the wings and tail yellow. The *P maculatus* has the body olivaceous; the head and throat black.

The specimens exhibiting the highest development of claw are from Fort Tejon, but the other localities mentioned illustrate the same peculiarity very readily. Specimens frequently occur, however, which it is difficult to refer positively to any one of the three species with spotted scapulars; some of them may possibly be hybrids.

List of specimens.

Catal. No.	Sex.	Locality.	When collected.	Whence obtained.	Orig'l No.	Collected by—	Length.	Stretch of wings.	Wing.	Remarks.
6736	......	San Francisco.........	....	R. D. Cutts.........	......	....	......	....	......	....
4235	......	Francisco county, Cal..	Winter, 1853	.....do.......	......	....	......	....	......	....
6740	......	Presidio, Cal...........	April 25, 1854	Lt. Trowbridge.......	......	....	......	....	......	....
6734	......	Benicia...............	....	Lt. R. S. Williamson.	......	Dr. Heermann..	......	....	......	....
5972	......	Santa Clara.........	....	Dr. J. G. Cooper	......	....	8.25	10.50	......	....
5971	♀	......do........	....	..... do.......	......	....	......	....	......	....
6730	......	......do........	....	..... do.......	......	....	......	....	......	....
6731	......	Sacramento valley.. ...	....	Lt. R. S. Williamson.	......	Dr. Heermann ..	......	....	......	....
6738	......	Cosumnes river	....	.....do..........	......	....do......	......	....	......	....
3910	♀	California............	....	Dr. Heermann	......	....	......	....	......	....
3909	♂	......do............	....	.....do.........	......	....	......	....	......	....
4603	......	Heights of San Pasqual	....	Major Emory.........	12	A. Schott.........	......	....	.....	....
6741	......	San Diego, Cal........	....	Dr. J. F. Hammond...	......	....	8.75	10.75	3.00	Iris scarlet.......
	......	Fort Tejon, Cal.......	....	J. X. de Vesey......	......	....	......	....	......	....
4042	♀	Saltillo, Mex...........	....	Lieut. Couch.........	.....	....	7.50	10.25	3.25	....
5036	♂	New Mexico............	....	Capt. Pope...........	......	....	......	....	......	Eyes dark; bill b'k; feet dark brown.
5037	......	Organ mountains, N. M.	Mar. 10, 1855	.....do............	181	....	......	....	......	....
6732	♀	Copper mines, Min.....	....	Col. Graham.........	......	J. H. Clark	8 50	10.12	2.37	....
6717	......	Fort Thorn	....	Dr. T. C. Henry	......	....	......	....	.	....
	.....	......do............	....	..... do............	......	....	......	....	......	....
6719	.....	.....do............	....	.....do............	......	....	......	....	......	....
6720	.....	...do. ,.....	....	.....do............	......	....	......	....	......	....
6733	......	Pueblo ck, Cp. 104, N. M.	Jan. 22, 1854	Lieut. Whipple	49	Kenn. & Möllhaus	......	.....	.....	Eyes reddish yel.

PIPILO ABERTII, Baird.

Pipilo abertii, BAIRD, Stansbury's Rep. Great Salt Lake, Zoology, June 1852, 325. (New Mexico.)
Kieneria abertii, BONAP. Comptes Rendus, XL, 1855, 356.

SP. CH.—General color of upper parts pale brownish yellowish red; beneath brighter, especially on the under coverts, palest on the middle of the belly. Sides of head anterior to eyes, and chin dark brown. Bill yellowish.

Length, 9 inches; wing, 3.70; tail, 4.85.

Hab.—Base of Rocky Mountains in New Mexico. Valley of Gila and Colorado.

This plainly colored bird is among the largest of the North American species, and is without any blotches, spots, or variations of importance from one color, except on the chin and sides of the head. The bill is similar to that of *P. erythrophthalmus*, but the cutting edge is less concave and more sinuated. The tail is more graduated; the claws thicker and stronger. The wings are short and much rounded; the first quill shorter than the secondaries.

List of specimens.

Catal. No.	Sex.	Locality.	When collected	Whence obtained.	Orig. No.	Collected by—
		Mew Mexico		Lt. Abert		
6751		Camp 120, Bill Williams' Fork, N. M.	Feb. 12, 1854	Lt. Whipple	92	Kenn. and Möll
6750		Camp 114, N. Mexico	Feb. 6, 1854	do	72	do
6749		do	Feb. 13, 1856	do	101	do
6747	♂	Gila river, N. M.		Lt. J. G. Parke		Dr. Heermann
6748	♂	do		do		do
4604		Fort Yuma, Cal.		Major Emory	30	A. Schott
4578		Colorado river, Cal.		do		do

PIPILO FUSCUS, Swainson.

Pipilo fusca, Sw. Philos Mag. I, 1827, 434.—? Ib. Anim. in Menag 1838, 347.—Bonap. Conspectus, 1850, 487.—
    Cassin, Illust. I, iv, 1853, 124; pl. xvii. (The figure seems to be of the California species, the
    description more like *mesoleucus.*)—Newberry, Zool. Cal. & Or. Route, Rep. P. R. R. VI, iv, 1857, 89.
Kieneria fusca, Bonap. Comptes Rendus, XL, 1855, 356.
Fringilla crissalis, Vigors, Zool. Blossom, 1839, 19.

Sp. Ch.—Above dark olive brown, the crown with a very slight tinge of scarcely appreciable dark rufous. Under parts with
the color somewhat similar, but of a lighter shade, and washed with grayish; middle of the belly ashy white; the under tail
coverts pale rufous, shading into lighter about the vent and sides of lower belly; chin and upper part of throat well defined pale
rufous, margined all round by brown spots, a few of them scattered within the margin. Eyelids and sides of head, anterior to
the eye, rufous like the throat. One or two feathers on the lower part of the breast with a concealed brown blotch. Outer
primary not edged with white.
Length, 9 inches; wing, 4; tail, 5.
Hab.—Coast region of California.

In this species the bill is sinuated as in *P. abertii,* differing from that of *P. erythrophthalmus.*
The wing is much rounded; the fourth quill longest; the first shorter than the secondaries.
The tail is considerably graduated; the feathers broad; the outer about .70 of an inch shorter
than the middle ones.

This species is much darker than *P. abertii,* and lacks the black on chin and side of head;
the chin and throat are abruptly different from the breast; the light patch margined with
black spots.

I do not feel sure that this species is really the *P fuscus* of Swainson. His description of
" Gray, beneath paler; throat obscure fulvous, with brown spots; vent ferruginous. Length, 8;
bill, .70; wings, 3.50; tail, 4; tarsi, .90; hind toe and claw, .70," as given in 1827, differs
from that of 1838. "Grayish brown above; beneath white; chin and throat fulvous, with
dusky spots; under tail coverts fulvous; tail blackish brown, unspotted. Bill and legs pale,
the latter smaller, and the claws more curved than in any other known species; crown with a
pale rufous tinge. Length, 7.50; wings, 3.50; tail, 4; tarsus, .90; middle toe and claw the
same; hinder toe, .65." These proportions are certainly quite different from those of the
California species, nor are the colors of either paragraph the same. It is possible that the first
description is that of the present bird, and the second that of a species allied to *P. mesoleucus,*
but it is quite as likely that both of these are entirely different from Swainson's *P. fuscus.*

List of specimens.

Catal. No.	Sex.	Locality.	When collected.	Whence obtained.	Orig. No.	Collected by—
6744	......	San Francisco, Cal.	....	R. D. Cutts.	....	....
6745	......	......do............	....	......do............	....	....
6742	......	Presidio, Cal............	....	Lt. Trowbridge...........	....	....
5559	♂	Petaluma, Cal............	April —, 1856...	E. Samuels.	653	....
4943	......	San José, Cal.	....	A. J. Grayson...........	4	....
5970[1]	......	Santa Clara, Cal.........	....	Gov. Stevens...........	....	Dr. Cooper...... .....
5968	......	......do.........	....	......do............	....	......do...........
5967	......	......do.........	....	......do............	....	......do...........
6746	♂	Sacramento valley.	....	Lt. Williamson...........	....	Dr. Heermann.....
3710	♀	Monterey...............	June 22, 1848...	Wm. Hutton...........	....	....
		Fort Tejon, Cal..........	....	J. Xantus de Vesey......	....	....
6743	♂	Tejon valley............	....	Lt. Williamson...........	....	Dr. Heermann.....
3911	......	California	....	Dr. Heermann...........	....	....

[1] Length, 9.00 ; extent, 12.50 ; iris, reddish brown.

PIPILO MESOLEUCUS, Baird.

Pipilo mesoleucus, BAIRD, Pr. A. N. Sc. Ph. VII, June, 1854, 119.   (Rocky Mountains.)

SP. CH.—Above olivaceous brown, with a grayish tinge; hood dull chestnut, conspicuously different from the back. Sides beyond the edge of the wing like the back, but paler ; posteriorly, and about the vent and under tail coverts, pale brownish red. The ashy olive brown of the sides scarcely meeting across the breast, the lower portion of which, with the upper belly, is rather pure white. The chin, throat, and upper part of the breast pale yellowish rufous, spotted on the sides and across the breast with brown ; an obscure spot in the middle of the breast ; edge of outer primary white.

Length, 8.50 inches ; wing, 3.80 ; tail, 4.70.

Hab.—Valley of upper Rio Grande and across to the Gila river   East to Santa Caterina, New Leon.

This species is similar in general appearance to the *P. fuscus*, but the olive brown and rufous are both of a lighter shade.   The crown is of a decided chestnut, conspicuously different from the back, instead of nearly the same tint.   The light reddish under the head is wider throughout and extends down to the upper part of the breast, blending with the colors of the breast and belly, instead of being narrower, more sharply defined, and restricted to the chin and throat. The isolated larger spot on the breast is more conspicuous ; the breast and belly are quite pure white, shaded with obsolete brownish blotches, instead of being uniform grayish brown, with only an approach to whitish in the very middle.   The edges of the wing and tail feathers are a good deal lighter, the outer web of the first primary being sharply edged with pure white, instead of obscure grayish brown.   The size generally is rather smaller.

List of specimens.

Catal. No.	Sex.	Locality.	When collected.	Whence obtained.	Orig. No.	Collected by—	Length.	Stretch of wings.	Wing.	Remarks.
6834	♂	Sta. Caterina, Mex ..	April —, 1853	Lt. Couch	......	....	7.50	10.50	3.50	Bill slate and white, feet dark flesh.
6835	♀	Copper mines, N. M..	....	Col. Graham	5	J. H. Clark	8.00	11.00	3.62	....
6828	....	......do.....	....	Maj. Emory.........	......	......do.........	....	....	.....	....
6831	......	Fort Thorn, N. M....	....	Dr. Henry	......	....	....	....	.....	....
6832	......	......do...........	....	......do.........	......	....	....	....	.....	....
6827	.....	Bill Williams' Fork..	Feb. 5, 1854	Lt. A. W. Whipple.	67	Kenn. and Möll..	....	....	.....	....
6830	......	Los Nogales, Mex....	June —, 1855	Maj. Emory ,......	......	Dr. Kennerly	....	....	.....	....
6829	♂	Gila river....	....	Lt. J. G. Parke	......	Dr. Heermann....	....	....	.. ..	....

PIPILO CHLORURUS, Baird.

Blanding's Finch.

Fringilla chlorura, (TOWNSEND,) AUD. Orn. Biog. V, 1839, 336. (Young.)
Zonotrichia chlorura. GAMBEL, J. A. N. Sc. Ph. 2d Series, I, 1847, 51.
Embernagra chlorura, BONAP. Conspectus, 1850, 483.
Fringilla blandingiana, GAMBEL, Pr. A. N. Sc. Ph. I, April, 1843, 260.
Embernagra blandingiana, CASSIN, Illus. I, III, 1853, 70 ; pl. xii.
Pipilo rufipileus, LAFRESNAYE, Rev. Zool. XI, June 1848, 176.--Bp. Conspectus, 1850, 487.
Kieneria rufipileus, BON. Comptes Rendus XL, 1855, 356.

SP. CH.—Above dull grayish olive green. Crown uniform chestnut. Forehead with superciliary stripe, and sides of the head and neck, the upper part of the breast and sides of the body, bluish ash. Chin and upper part of throat abruptly defined white, the former margined by dusky, above which is a short white maxillary stripe. Under tail coverts and sides of body behind brownish yellow. Tail feathers generally, and exterior of wings bright olive green, the edge and under surface of the latter bright yellow ; edge of first primary white. Length, about 7 inches ; wing, 3.20 ; tail, 3.65.

Hab.—Valley of Rio Grande and Gila ; Rocky mountains north to the South Pass ; south to Mexico.

In this species the wing is considerably rounded, the tertials considerably shorter than the primaries, and not exceeding the secondaries ; the fourth quill longest, the first shorter than the sixth, the second and fifth quills considerably longer than the rest. The tail is long and considerably graduated, the outer feather half an inch shortest ; the feathers broad and obtusely pointed, the corners rounded.

The extent of the chestnut of the crown varies somewhat ; more extended probably in the males. The region on the side of the head, adjoining the nostrils, is whitish ; the small feathers under the eye are spotted with the same. The posterior outline of the ash of the breast is much less sharply defined than the anterior.

Specimens vary in the brightness of the olive above, which is never as pure as that of the wings and tail. The olive of the tail, too, is darker than that of the wings.

A very young bird (1896) has the whole under parts dull white, streaked and spotted on the sides of the throat, and on the breast, with dark brown. The crown and back are also thickly spotted. In 5734 the ash of the breast has made its appearance ; the middle of the belly is white, spotted ; the chin white, encircled by spots. The spots above are restricted to near the head, and there is a small central patch of chestnut on the crown.

No. 1896 is the original green-tailed sparrow killed July 12, 1834, by Townsend, and described in an extract of a letter to Mr. Audubon, published page 336 of volume V, Orn. Biog. It is unmistakeably the *Pipilo* here described, and settles the question in favor of the priority of the name *chlorurus*.

List of specimens.

Catal. No.	Sex and age.	Locality.	When collected.	Whence obtained.	Orig'l No.	Collected by—	Length.	Stretch of wings.	Wing.	Remarks.
6745	♂	? Tejon Valley, Cal...	....	Lieut. Williamson..	......	Dr. Heermann.	....	....	....	....
4609	....	Colorado river, N. M.	April 10, 1855	Major Emory	60	A. Schott.......	....	....	....	
6242	....	San Elizario, Texas..	Dec. 16, 1854	......do......	23	Dr. Kennerly ..	....	....	....	Eyes chocolate brown.
6243	....	Eagle Pass, Texas....	Fall of 1852	......do......	......	A. Schott......	....	....	....	
6244	♂	New Mexico.........	....	Lieut. J. G. Parke..	......	Dr. Heermann .	....	....	....	
7086	○○	Black Hills..........	July 21, 1857	Dr. W. A. Hammond	55	....	....	....	....	
5732	♂	Medicine Bow Creek.	Aug. 25, 1856	Lieut. F. T. Bryan.	264	W. S. Wood...	....	....	....	
5734	♂	.....do.......	... ..do	......do......	301	......do.......	....	....	....	
5733	♀	Bridger's Pass, K. T.	Aug. 15, 1856	......do......	264	.....do......	....	....	....	....
1896	○♂	Rocky Mountains....	July 12, 1834	S. F. Baird	......	J. K. Townsend	....	....	....	Type of *Fr. chlorura.*
9278	♂	Laramie Peak........	Aug. 24, 1856	Lieut. G. K. Warren.	......	Dr. Hayden....	7.50	9.25	2.75	Iris brown ....
9277	♀	......do............	Aug. 2, 1856	......do......	......	......do.......	7.00	9 25	2.25	......do........
9270	♀	......do...........	Aug. 24, 1856	......do......	......	......do...... ..	7.50	10.00	3.50	......do...... ......
9276	....	Mexico.....	....	J. Gould	......	....	....	....	....	

Family ICTERIDAE.

Cʜ.—Primaries nine. Tarsi scutellate anteriorly ; plated behind. Bill long, generally equal to the head or longer, straight or gently curved, conical, without any notch, the commissure bending downwards at an obtuse angle at the base. Gonys generally more than half the culmen. Basal joint of the middle toe free on the inner side ; united half-way on the outer. Tail rather long, rounded. Legs stout.

This family is strictly confined to the New World, and is closely related in many of its members to the *Fringillidae*. Both have the angulated commissure and the nine primaries ; the bill is, however, usually much longer ; the rictus is completely without bristles, and the tip of the bill without notch.

The affinities of some of the genera are still closer to the family of *Sturnidae* or Starlings, of which the *Sturnus vulgaris* may be taken as the type. This family is, however, exclusively Old World, and readily distinguished by the constant presence of a rudimentary outer primary, making ten in all.

There are three sub-families of the *Icteridae*—the *Agelainae*, the *Icterinae*, and the *Quiscalinae*.

Sub-Family AGELAINAE.

Cʜ.—Bill stout, conical, and acutely pointed, not longer than the head ; the outlines nearly straight, the tip not decurved. Legs adapted for walking, longer than the head. Claws not much curved. Tail moderate, shorter than the wings ; nearly even.

The *Agelainae*, through *Molothrus* and *Dolichonyx*, present a close relation to the *Fringillidae* in the comparative shortness and conical shape of the bill, and, in fact, it is very difficult to express in brief words the distinctions which evidently exist. *Dolichonyx* may be set aside as readily determinable by the character of the feet and tail. The peculiar sub-family character-istics of *Molothrus* will be found under the generic remarks respecting it.

The following diagnosis will serve to define the genera :

A. Bill shorter than the head.

   Dᴏʟɪᴄʜᴏɴʏx.—Tail feathers with rigid stiffened acuminate points. Middle toe very long, exceeding the head.

   Mᴏʟᴏᴛʜʀᴜs.—Tail with the feathers simple ; middle toe shorter than the tarsus or head.

B. Bill as long as the head. Feathers of crown soft. Nostrils covered by a scale which is directed more or less downwards.

   Aɢᴇʟᴀɪᴜs.—First quill shorter than the second and third. Outer lateral claw scarcely reaching to the base of middle ; claws moderate.

   Xᴀɴᴛʜᴏᴄᴇᴘʜᴀʟᴜs.—First quill longest. Outer lateral claw reaching nearly to the tip of the middle. Toes and claws all much elongated.

C. Bill as long as, or longer than, the head. Feathers of crown with the shafts prolonged into stiffened bristles. Nostrils covered by a scale which stands out more or less horizontally.

   Sᴛᴜʀɴᴇʟʟᴀ.—Tail feathers acute. Middle toe equal to the tarsus.

   Tʀᴜᴘɪᴀʟɪs.—Tail feathers rounded. Tarsus longer than the middle toe.

June 24, 1858.

66 b

DOLICHONYX, Swainson.

Dolichonyx, Swainson, Zool. Journ. III, 1827, 351. Type *Emberiza oryzivora*, L.

Ch.—Bill short, stout, conical, little more than half the head ; the commissure slightly sinuated ; the culmen nearly straight. Middle toe considerably longer than the tarsus (which is about as long as the head) ; the inner lateral toe longest, but not reaching the base of the middle claw. Wings long, first quill longest. Tail feathers acuminately pointed at the tip, with the shafts stiffened and rigid, as in the woodpeckers.

The peculiar characteristic of this species is found in the rigid scansorial tail and the very long middle toe, by means of which it is enabled to grasp the vertical stems of reeds or other slender plants. The color of the known species is black, varied with whitish patches on the upper parts.

In coloration, this genus bears a close relation to *Calamospiza*, although the other differences are very decided. Both are black, with white patches on the wings. *Dolichonyx* has, in addition, a white patch on the rump and a yellowish one on the nape.

But one species is at present known to naturalists.

Comparative measurements.

Catal. No.	Species.	Locality.	Sex and age.	Length.	Stretch of wings.	Wing.	Tail.	Tarsus.	Middle toe.	Its claw alone.	Hind toe and claw.	Hind claw alone.	Bill above.	Along gape.	Specimen measured.
977	Dolichonyx oryzivorus.	Carlisle, Pa.........	♂	6.70	....	3.76	3.12	1.03	1.10	0.29	0.84	0.40	0.59	0.60	Skin......
do.	......do............	......do......	......	7.25	12.00	3.90									Fresh......
6522	......do..........	Indian Key, Fla......	♂	6.30	....	3.90	3.10	1.02	1.07	0.30	0.85	0.42	0.60	0.62	Skin......
do.	......do..........	......do............	......	7.08	12.00	4.00									Fresh......
6524	......do..........	......do............	♀	6.00	....	3.52	2.96	0.94	1.00	0.26	0.78	0.40	0.56	0.60	Skin......
do.	......do......	......do............	.....	7.50	10.50	3.50									Fresh......
4582	Molothrus pecoris......	Colorado river, Cal...	♂	6.90	....	4.02	3.18	0.94	0.89	0.28	0.75	0.34	0.66	0.64	Skin......
6486	......do..........	Philadelphia.........	♂	6.84	....	4.34	3.38	1.02	0.90	0.22	0.72	0.31	0.66	0.69	Skin......
611	......do......	Carlisle, Pa...........	♀	6.60	....	3.70	2.98	0.94	0.86	0.24	0.65	0.30	0.58	0.61	Skin......

DOLICHONYX ORYZIVORUS, Swainson.

Boblink; Reed Bird; Rice Bird.

Emberiza oryzivora, Linn. Syst. Nat. I, 1766, 311.—Gm. I, 1788, 850.—Wilson, Am. Orn. II, 1810, 48 ; pl. xii ; f. 1, 2.

Passerina oryzivora, Vieillot, Nouv. Dict. XXV, 1817, 3.

Dolichonyx oryzivora, Swainson, Zool. Jour. III, 1827, 351.—Ib. F. Bor. Am. II, 1831, 278.—Bon. List, 1838.—Ib. Conspectus, 1850, 437.—Aud. Syn. 1839, 139.—Ib. Birds Amer. IV, 1842, 10 ; pl. 211.—Gosse, Birds Jam. 1847, 229.

Icterus agripennis, Bonap. Obs. Wils. 1824, No. 87.—Aud. Orn. Biog. I, 1831, 283 : V, 1839, 486 ; pl. 54.—Nutt. Man. I, 1832, 185.

Icterus (Emberizoides) agripennis, Bon. Syn. 1828, 53.

Dolichonyx agripennis, Rich. List, 1837.

Psarocolius caudacutus, Wagler, Syst. Av. 1827, 32.

Sp. Ch.—General color of *male* in spring black ; the nape brownish cream color ; a patch on the side of the breast, the scapulars and rump white, shading into light ash on the upper tail covers and the back below the interscapular region. The outer primaries sharply margined with yellowish white ; the tertials less abruptly ; the tail feathers margined at the tips with pale brownish ash.

Female yellowish beneath ; two stripes on the top of the head, and the upper parts throughout, except the back of the neck and rump, and including all the wing feathers generally, dark brown, all edged with brownish yellow, which becomes whiter near the tips of the quills. The sides sparsely streaked with dark brown, and a similar stripe behind the eye. There is a superciliary and a median band of yellow on the head.

Length of male, 7.70 ; wing, 3.83 ; tail, 3.15.

Hab.—Eastern United States to the high central plains. Seen 50 miles east of Laramie.

This well known bird varies considerably in color, with differences in the maturity of plumage. Sometimes the black feathers generally have yellowish margins both above and below. The bill is generally bluish black, but in the specimens from Florida the lower mandible is white. The male maintains the black plumage for a comparatively short time. Shortly after mid-summer the female dress is assumed and kept until the ensuing spring.

List of specimens.

Catal. No.	Sex.	Locality.	When collected.	Whence obtained.	Orig. No.	Collected by—	Length.	Stretch of wings.	Wing.	Remarks.
1477	♂	Carlisle, Pa............	May 8, 1844	S. F. Baird			7.66	12.41	3.91	
977	♂	......do..	May 17, 1843	......do......			7.25	12.00	3.91	
1517	♂	.....do..............	May 15, 1844	......do..........			7.33	12.25	3.83	
1174	♀	.....do..............	Sept. 8, 1843	......do........			6.58	11.00	3.41	
6521	♂	Indian Key, Fla........	May 9, 1857	G. Würdemann			7.50	12.00	4.00	
6522	♂	.....do..............	......do..	......do.........			7.08	12.00	4.00	
6523	♀	.....do..........	......do..	......do......			7.50	10.50	3.50	
6524	♀	.....do..............	......do..	......do......			7.50	10.50	3.50	
	♂	North Illinois..........	Spring.......	R. Kennicott						
5360	......	Fort Pierre............	June 25, 1856	Lieut. Warren		Dr. Hayden......	7.12	12.12	3.75	
		Red river, Minn........		N. W. University..		R. Kennicott				
8951	♂	Loup fork of Platte....	July 11. ...	Lieut. Warren		Dr. Hayden........	7.00	12.00	4.00	Iris brown.........
8952	♂	.....do..............	July 20	......do........		......do........	7.25	13.00	3.75	....do.............
8990	....	50 miles E of Ft.Laramie	Aug. 20	Wm. M. Magraw ..	163	Dr. Cooper	7.25	12.00	4.00	

MOLOTHRUS, Swainson.

Molothrus, SWAINSON, F. Bor. Am. II, 1831, 277; supposed by Cabanis to be meant for *Molobrus.* Type *Fringilla pecoris,* GM.

CH.—Bill short, stout, about two-thirds the length of head; the commissure straight, culmen and gonys slightly curved, convex, the former broad, rounded, convex, and running back on the head in a point. Lateral toes nearly equal, reaching the base of the middle one, which is shorter than tarsus; claws rather small. Tail nearly even; wings long, pointed, the first quill longest.

The genus *Molothrus* has the bill intermediate between *Dolichonyx* and *Agelaius.* It has the culmen unusually broad between the nostrils, and it extends back some distance into the forehead. The difference in the structure of the feet from *Dolichonyx* is very great.

The genus *Molothrus* resembles some of the *Fringillidae* more than any other of the *Icteridae.* The bill is, however, more straight, the tip without notch; the culmen running back further on the forehead, the nostrils being situated fully one-third or more of the total length from its posterior extremity. This is seldom the case in the American families. The entire absence of notch in the bill and of bristles along the rictus are strong features. The nostrils are perfectly free from any overhanging feathers or bristles. The pointed wings, with the first quill longest, and the tail with its broad rounded feathers, shorter than the wings, are additional features to be specially noted.

Of several species of the genus found in the New World, but one belongs to the United States. This, the well known cow bird, never incubates, but deposits its eggs in the nests of others, usually smaller birds, to be hatched out by them, as is done also by the European cuckoo. One at least of the South American species is known to possess the same habit, and it is probably the same with all of them.

The measurements of *M. pecoris* will be found with *Dolichonyx.*

MOLOTHRUS·PECORIS, Swainson.

Cow Black bird; Cow bird.

Fringilla pecoris, GMELIN, Syst. Nat. I, 1788, 910, (female).—LATH. Ind. Orn. I, 1790, 443.—LICHT. Verzeich. 1823, Nos. 230, 231.

Emberiza pecoris, WILS. Am. Orn. II, 1810, 145; pl. xviii; f. 1, 2, 3.

Icterus pecoris, BONAP. Obs. Wilson, 1824, No. 88.—AUD. Orn. Biog. I, 1831, 493 : V, 1839, 233, 490; pl. 99 and 424.

Icterus (Emberizoides) pecoris, BON. Syn. 1828, 53.—IB. Specchio comp. No. 41.—NUTT. Man. I, 1832, 178; 2d ed. 190.

Passerina pecoris, VIEILL. Nouv. Dict. XXV, 1819, 22.

Psarocolius pecoris, WAGLER, Syst. Av. 1827, No. 20.

Molothrus pecoris, SWAINSON, F. Bor. Am. II, 1831, 277.—RICH. List, 1837.—BON. List, 1838.—IB. Consp. 1850, 436 —AUD. Syn. 1839, 139.—IB. Birds Amer. IV, 1842, 16; pl. 212.—CABANIS, Mus. Hein. 1851, 193.

? *Oriolus fuscus,* GMELIN, Syst. Nat. I, 1788, 393.

? *Sturnus obscurus,* GMELIN, Syst. Nat. I, 1788, 804. Evidently a *Molothrus,* and probably, but not certainly, the present species.

"*Icterus emberizoides,* DAUDIN.''

? *Sturnus junceti,* LATH. Ind. I, 1790, 326, (same as *Sturnus obscurus,* GM.)

? *Fringilla ambigua,* NUTTALL, Man. I, 1832, 484, (young).

SP. CH.—Second quill longest ; first scarcely shorter. Tail nearly even, or very slightly rounded. Male with the head, neck, and anterior half of the breast, light chocolate brown, rather lighter above; rest of body lustrous black, with a violet purple gloss next to the brown, of steel blue on the back, and of green elsewhere. Female light olivaceous brown all over, lighter on the head and beneath. Bill and feet black. Length 8 inches; wing, 4.42; tail, 3.40.

Hab.—United States from the Atlantic to California; not found immediately on the coast of the Pacific ?

The young bird of the year is brown above, brownish white beneath ; the throat immaculate. A maxillary stripe and obscure streaks thickly crowded across the whole breast and sides. There is a faint indication of a paler superciliary stripe. The feathers of the upper parts are all margined with paler. There are also indications of the light bands on the wings. These markings are all obscure, but perfectly appreciable, and their existence in adult birds may be considered as embryonic, and showing an inferiority in degree to the species with the under parts perfectly plain.

The *Fringilla pecoris* of Gmelin, from which the specific name of the bird is usually derived, is based essentially on the *Fringilla virginiana* of Brisson. The description is "brown, beneath paler, tail sub-bifurcated.'' This is scarcely a satisfactory diagnosis, although the descriptions of Pennant and Latham, likewise quoted by Gmelin, are very accurate. The *Sturnus obscurus* of Gmelin is evidently a *Molothrus,* but described from Mexico, and may possibly not be the present species, although the chances are in its favor. The *Oriolus fuscus* of Gmelin is probably the present bird, but may be a *Scolecophagus.* Under the circumstances, therefore, it may be as well to retain the name of *pecoris,* about which, from the context there can be no doubt, in preference to using any of the really prior names of *fuscus* or *obscurus.*

List of specimens.

Catal. No.	Sex and age.	Locality.	When collected.	Whence obtained.	Orig'l No.	Collected by—	Length.	Stretch of wings.	Wing.	Remarks.
1405	♂	Carlisle, Pa............	April 30, 1844	S. F. Baird	......	....	8.00	13.66	4.41	....
1559	♂	......do........	May 20, 1844	...... do...........	......	....	8.00	13.50	4.41	....
611	♀	......do........	April 2, 1842	...... do........	......	....	......	....	....	....
6486	♂	Philadelphia........	....	C. Drexler.........	......	....	.. ....	....	....	....
8341	♂	Independence, Mo.....	June 30, 1857	Wm. M. Magraw...	66	Dr. Cooper	8.00	13.75	4.50	....
8378	o	......do..	June 20, 1857	...... do...........	81	......do	7.75	13.00	4.25	....
5808	♂	Fort Riley, K. T.......	....	Dr. Hammond and J. X. de Vesey.	......	....	....	....	....	....
9337	♀	Loup fork	Aug. 3, 1857	Lt. Warren........	......	Dr. Hayden....	7.50	13.75	4.25	Iris dark brown......
9336	♀	......do........	......do.....	...... do.........	......	......do	6.75	12.62	3.87	......do.........
9334	♂	......do........	Aug. 1, 1857	...... do.........	......	......do........	7.12	12.25	4.00	......do.........
4365	♂	Mouth of Yellowstone	July 23, 1856	...... do.........	......	......do.........	8.00	13.50	4.37	......do.... ....
5368	♀	......do........	July 22, 1856	...... do.........	......	......do.........	....	....	....	....
4655	♂	Fort Pierre	May 2, 1855	Col. Vaughan	......	......do........	....	....	....	....
5327	♀	Medicine Hill..........	June 24, 1856	Lt. Warren........	......	......do.........	7.75	12.75	4.00	....
5684	♂	Platte river............	July 16, 1856	Lt. Bryan..........	117	W. S. Wood....	....	....	....	....
5681	♂	......do........	......do......	...... do.........	115	......do.........	....	....	....	....
5678	♂	Pole creek, Neb. T.....	July 24, 1856	...... do.........	149	......do.........	....	....	....	....
5011	♂	Pecos crossing, Texas..	May 8, 1855	Capt. Pope	106	....	....	....	....	Eyes dark br'n; gums yellow; feet gray.
5009	♂	Devil's river, Texas....	May 4, 1855	...... do.........	69	....	....	....	....	Eyes bl'k; gums blue; feet gray.
5013	♀	Rio Frio, Texas	April 21, 1855	...... do....... ...	49	....	....	....	....	....
4967	♀	Fort Chadbourne, Texas	....	Dr. Swift.........	......	....	....	....	....	....
4966	♂	......do........	....	...... do.........	......	....	....	....	....	....
8759	....	Eagle pass, Texas......	....	Major Emory......	...	A. Schott......	....	....	....	....
8761	....	Los Nogales, Mexico...	....	...... do.........	82	Dr. Kennerly..	....	....	....	....
8763	♂	Fort Yuma, Cal.......	....	Lt. Williamson.....	......	Dr. Heermann .	....	....	. ...	....
4580	....	......do........	....	Major Emory	......	A. Schott......	....	....	....	....
4585	....	...... do........	Jan. 28, 1855	...... do.........	43	......do........	....	....	....	....
4582	....	......do........	......do......	...... do.........	42	......do........	....	....	....	....
do.	....	Colorado river, Cal.....	....	...... do.........	42	......do........	....	....	....	....
4584	....	Gila river, N. M.......	Dec. 6, 1854	......do.........	28	......do........	....	....	....	....
8764	♀	Sacramento valley.....	....	Lt. Williamson	......	Dr. Heermann.	....	....	....	....

AGELAIUS, Vieillot.

Agelaius, VIEILLOT, "Analyse, 1816." Type *Oriolus phoeniceus*, L.

Ch.—First quill shorter than second; claws short; the outer lateral scarcely reaching the base of the middle. Culmen depressed at base, parting the frontal feathers; length equal to that of the head, shorter than tarsus. Both mandibles of equal thickness and acute at tip, the edges much curved, the culmen, gonys, and commissure nearly straight or slightly sinuated; the length of bill about twice its height. Tail moderate,r ounded, or very slightly graduated. Wingspointed, reaching to end of lower tail coverts. Colors black with red shoulders in North American species.

The nostrils are small, oblong, overhung by a membranous scale. The bill is higher than broad at the base. There is no division between the anterior tarsal scutellae and the single plate on the outside of the tarsus.

The *Agelaius icterocephalus* of North America (type of genus *Xanthocephalus*) differs from true *Agelaius* in a nearly even tail. The claws are considerably larger, and the inner lateral reaches to the middle of the middle claw. The first primary is longest.

Comparative measurements of the species.

Catal. No.	Species.	Locality.	Sex.	Length	Stretch of wings.	Wing.	Tail.	Tarsus.	Middle toe.	Its claw alone.	Hind toe and claw.	Hind claw alone.	Bill above.	Along gape.	Specimen measured.
5531	Agelaius gubernator	Petaluma, Cal.	♂	8.70	.....	4.96	4.00	1.20	1.15	0.34	0.89	0.43	0.85	0.86	Skin ......
5530	.....do..........	.....do..........	♀	7.00	.....	4.16	3.26	1.04	1.00	0.30	0.80	0.38	0.73	0.76	Skin ......
do.	.....do..........	.....do..........		7.75	11.50	4.75	......	......	......	......	......	......	......	......	Fresh......
1386	Agelaius phoeniceus	Carlisle, Pa	♂	8.60	.....	4.84	4.06	1.14	1.08	0.31	0.84	0.38	0.94	0.94	Skin ......
do.	.....do..........	.....do..........		9.50	15.50	5.00	......	......	......	......	......	......	......	......	Fresh......
7002	.....do..........	St. Louis, Mo	♀	7.40	.....	3.83	3.18	1.02	0.96	0.28	0.74	0.34	0.74	0.78	Skin ......
2174	.....do..........	Carlisle, Pa.	♀	7.10	.....	3.96	3.40	1.05	1.00	0.29	0.80	0.40	0.76	0.80	Skin ......
2836	Agelaius tricolor	Santa Barbara, Cal...	♂	9.04	.....	4.82	3.78	1.18	1.10	0.34	0.87	0.40	0.94	0.96	Skin ......
8596	.....do..........	Sacramento Valley...	♀	7.20	... ..	4.24	3.44	1.04	0.98	0.28	0.76	0.34	0.80	0.88	Skin ......
3912	Agelaius icterocephalus ..	California	♂	9.80	.....	5.58	4.46	1.36	1.30	0.41	1.04	0.48	0.98	1.00	Skin ......
8555	.....do..........	Jano, Mexico		10.30	.....	5.50	4.56	1.40	1.32	0.38	1.04	0.50	0.89	0.88	Skin ......
6557	.....do..........	Fort Riley, K. T.		7.20	.....	4 49	3.60	1.16	1.14	0.38	0.86	0.44	0.70	0.72	Skin ......

SYNOPSIS OF SPECIES.

Tail rounded, or graduated; height of bill half or more than its length. Shoulders and lesser coverts bright crimson.

Median wing coverts brownish yellow to the end. Bill with longitudinal wrinkles on both mandibles..*A. phoeniceus.*

Median wing coverts black for the exposed portion, brownish yellow at the base. Lower jaw with transverse wrinkles...*A. gubernator.*

Tail nearly even; height of· bill at base less than half its length. Shoulders and lesser coverts dark brownish orange ; median coverts white.......................................*A. tricolor.*

AGELAIUS PHOENICEUS, Vieillot.

Swamp Blackbird ; Red-wing Blackbird.

Oriolus phoeniceus, LINN. Syst. Nat. I, 1766, 161.—GMELIN, I, 1788, 386.—LATH. Ind. Orn. I, 1790, 428.

Agelaius phoeniceus, "VIEILLOT, Anal. 1816."—SWAINSON, F. Bor. Am. II, 1831, 280.—BONAP. List, 1838.—IB. Consp. 1850, 430.—AUD. Syn. 1839, 141.—IB. Birds Amer. IV, 1842, 31 ; pl. 216.

Icterus phoeniceus, LICHT. Verz. 1823, No. 188.—BON. Obs. Wils. 1824, No. 68.—AUD. Orn. Biog. I, 1831, 348 : V, 1839, 487 ; pl. 67.

Psarocolius phoeniceus, WAGLER, Syst. Nat. 1827, No. 10.

Icterus (Xanthornus) phoeniceus, BONAP. Syn. 1828, 52.—NUTTALL, Man. I, 1832, 167 ; 2d ed. 179.

Sturnus praedatorius, WILSON, Am. Orn. IV, 1811, 30 ; pl. xxx.

Red-winged oriole, PENNANT, Arctic Zool. II, 255.

SP. CH.—Tail much rounded ; the lateral feathers about half an inch shorter. Fourth quill longest ; first about as long as the fifth. Bill large, stout ; half as high, or more than half as high as long.

Male.—General color uniform lustrous velvet black, with a greenish reflection. Shoulders and lesser wing coverts of a bright crimson or vermilion red. Middle coverts brownish yellow, and usually paler towards the tips.

Female.—Brown above, the feathers edged or streaked with rufous brown and yellowish ; beneath white, streaked with brown. Fore part of throat, superciliary, and median stripe strongly tinged with brownish yellow. Length of male, 9.50 ; wing, 5 ; tail, 4.15.

Hab.—United States from Atlantic to Pacific.

The bill is nearly straight in its outlines ; the commissure, except at base, perfectly so ; the thickness of both mandibles the same, measured at the bend of the commissure, and perpendicular to the upper and lower outlines. There are faint indications of striae on the bill proceeding from the nostrils and parallel with the upper outline, as well as at the base of the lower jaw nearly parallel with the gonys. The greatest depth of the bill, measured at the base of, and perpendicular to the lower outline, is just half the length of the culmen, which is about as long as the skull. The third and fourth quills are longest; the first about equal to the fifth. The tail is considerably rounded, the lateral ones about .30 to .50 of an inch shorter. The tarsus is about equal to the middle toe.

The female differs greatly in appearance. The prevailing color above is brownish black, all the feathers margined with reddish brown ; some of those on the back with brownish yellow, which on the median and greater wing coverts forms two bands. The under parts are dull whitish, each feather broadly streaked centrally with dark brown ; the chin and throat yellowish and but little streaked. There is a distinct whitish superciliary streak alongside the head tinged anteriorly with brownish yellow, and another less distinct in the median line of the crown. There is usually no indication of any red on the wing, but in one specimen, (2174,) marked barren female, the plumage generally is darker and approximating to that of the male; the shoulders red, streaked with black ; the light markings about the head tinged with rose color. The immature males exhibit every possible condition of coloration between that of the old male and of the female.

There is some variation in the shade of red on the shoulders, which is sometimes of the color of arterial blood or bright crimson. It never, however, has the haematitic tint of the red in *A. tricolor*. The middle coverts are sometimes uniform brownish yellow to the very tips ; sometimes some of these middle coverts are tipped at the end with black, but these black tips are usually of slight extent.

There is some variation in the size and proportions of the bill. The most striking is in a series of three from the Red River settlement, decidedly larger than more southern ones, (wing, 5.15 ; tail, 4.40.) The bill is about as long as that of Pennsylvania specimens, but much stouter, the thickness at the base being considerably more than half the length of the culmen. One specimen from San Elizario, Texas, has the bill of much the same size and proportions.

A specimen (4050) from Saltillo has the lobe in the commissure larger, and the terminal portion of the commissure much emarginated.

List of specimens.

Catal. No.	Sex.	Locality.	When collected.	Whence obtained.	Orig. No.	Collected by—	Length.	Stretch of wings.	Wing.	Remarks.
1367	♂	Carlisle, Pa	April 17, 1844	S. F. Baird			8.91	14.66	4.66	
1386	♂	.....do	April 24, 1841	..... do			9.50	15.50	5.00	
816	♀	.....do	Oct. 19, 1842	..... do			7.50	12.50	3.75	
10138	♂	Washington, D. C.		J. C. McGuire						
6941		Red river, H. B. T.		D. Gunn						
6942		.....do		..... do						
8589		Sauk Ford, Min	1853	Gov. Stevens		Dr. Suckley.				
8590		.....do	1853	..... do		.do				
		Union county, Ill.	April 23,—	N. W. University		R. Kennicott				
7002	♀	St. Louis, Mo.	May 8, 1857	Lt. Bryan	40	W. S. Wood.				
8338	♂	Independence, Mo	June 6, 1857	Wm. M. Magraw.		Dr. Cooper...	9.25	14.75	5.12	
4644	♂	Ft. Pierre	April 27, 1855	Col. Vaughan ...		Dr. Hayden.				
5325		Medicine creek		Lt. Warren		...do	9.25	15.75	5.00	
5326	♀	Medicine Hill	June 25, 1856	..... do		...do	7.25	12.50	4.00	
4757	♂	Big Nemaha, K. T.	April 23, 1856	..... do		...do	9.25	15.00	4.75	
9332	♂	Frémont, on Platte	July 1,—	..... do		...do	8.37	15.12	5.00	Iris dark brown.....
9331	♂	Sand Hills of Platte	Aug. 1,—	..... do		...do	8.75	15.00	4 75	
9329	♂	.....do	Aug. 10,—	..... do		...do	9.25	15.25	4.87	
9330	♂	Loup Fork of Platte	July 3,—	..... do		...do	9.50	15.25	5.00	
9333	♂	.....do	July 1,—	..... do		...do	8.50	15.75	5.00	
5670	♂	Platte river	July 14, 1856	Lt. Bryan	104	W. S. Wood.				
8244	♂	100 miles E. of Ft. Kearney	Oct. 25, 1857	Wm. M. Magraw.	226	Dr. Cooper...	9.62	15.75	5.25	
7092	♂	Republican river, K. T.	June 12, 1857	Lt. Bryan..... ...	34	W. Hammond				
5000	♂	Indianola	Mar. 29, 1855	Capt. Pope	40		9.50	13.50	4.50	
4048	♀	Brownsville, Tex	Feb. 11, 1853	Lt. Couch	20		7.00	11.75	4.00	
4049	♂	New Leon, Mex	Mar. —, 1851	..... do	170		8.50	13.50	4.75	
4047	♀ ?	.....do	April —, 1853	..... do	182		6.50	11.50	3.75	
4050	♂	Saltillo, Mex	May —, 1853	..... do	17		8.00	13.00	4.75	
8591		San Elizario	Dec. —, 1854	Maj. Emory	7	Dr. Kennerly.				
5004	♂	Doña Ana, N. Mex	Nov. 11, 1855	Capt. Pope	155		9.00	15.50	5.00	
5003	♂	.. ..do	Nov. 3, 1855	..... do	153		9.25	16.00	5.25	
8579		Fort Thorn, N. M		Dr. Henry						
8574	♂	Fort Conrad, N. M.	Oct. —, 1853	Lt. Whipple		Dr. Kennerly.				
8576		Cold Spring, N. M.	Nov. 17,—	..... do	23	...do				
8578		C'p 150, Cocomongo ranch, Cal.	Mar. 19, 1854	... do	187	...do	8.50	15.00	5.50	
8573		Espia, Mex		Maj. Emory	45	...do				
4952?		San José, Cal		A. J. Grayson	14					
8582	♀	Ft. Vancouver, O. T.	Jan. 20, 1854	Gov. Stevens	19	Dr. Cooper.	8.25	12.75		
8583	♀	Ft. Steilacoom, W. T.	April	Dr. Suckley	342		8.00	12.00		
8584	♂	.....do	April 25, 1856	..... do	341		10.00	14.00		
8585	♂	.....do	..... do	..... do	339		9.50	14.00		
8586	♂	.....do	..... do	..... do	340		9.50	13.00		

AGELAIUS GUBERNATOR, Bon.

Red-shouldered Blackbird.

Psarocolius gubernator, WAGLER, Isis, 1832, IV, 281.
Agelaius gubernator, BON. List, 1838.—IB. Conspectus, 1850, 430.—AUD. Syn. 1839, 141.—IB. Birds Amer. IV, 1842,
    29 ; pl. 215.—NEWBERRY, P. R. R. Rep. VI, IV, 1857, 86.
Icterus (Zanthornus) gubernator, NUTTALL, Man. I, 2d ed. 1840, 187.

SP. CH.—Bill rather shorter than the head, without any longitudinal sulci, but with faint traces of transverse ones at the
base of the lower jaw. Tail rounded. First quill nearly equal to the fourth.

Male.—Throughout of a lustrous velvety black, with a greenish reflection. The shoulders and lesser coverts rich crimson ;
the middle coverts brownish yellow at the base, but the exposed portion black.

Female.—Dusky, varied with paler. Length, 9 ; wing, 5 ; tail, 3.80.

Hab.—Pacific coast of the United States. Colorado river?

The bill of this species is rather small, being scarcely as long as the head. It is about half
as high at the base as long, and exhibits no sulci on the upper mandible. At the base of the
lower jaw are some sulci or wrinkles perpendicular to the commissure. The second, third, and
fourth quills are nearly equal ; the first between the fourth and fifth. The tail is considerably
rounded ; the lateral feather about .30 of an inch shortest. The feet are rather slender.

A female is throughout of a dark brownish black, scarcely varied at all, except on the chin
and throat, which are reddish white streaked with brown. There is a rather distinct superciliary stripe of reddish white. The shoulder feathers are edged with darkish rose color.

I find it exceedingly difficult to distinguish satisfactorily this species from the *A. phoeniceus*
in certain stages of plumage. The bill is a little smaller, with a tendency to transverse
sulcations on the lower mandible ; the proportions are much the same ; stouter than in *tricolor*.
The tail is almost as much rounded ; much more so than in *A. tricolor*. The red on the
shoulder is of much the same brilliant crimson, but it is confined to the lesser coverts ; the
bases of the middle row of coverts are brownish yellow, but the exposed portion is black instead
of being brownish yellow as in *phoeniceus*, or white as in *tricolor*. Sometimes, however, by the
elongation of the yellowish basal portion, some of this color shows beyond the red as in
phoeniceus. Wherever, however, these middle coverts were all tipped with black, even if
not very broadly, I have referred the species to *gubernator*, as in a large series of *phoeniceus* I
have seen but one or two with a black tip to even some of these coverts.

The females are scarcely to be distinguished from those of *A. tricolor*, except possibly by the
more rounded tail, and stouter, shorter bill. It was at one time supposed that the female of
gubernator was the darker, but there are three specimens before me, (4598—4600,) which, in
the amount of light color beneath, approximate to *A. phoeniceus*. It is quite possible that there
may be another species mixed in with the supposed *tricolor* and *gubernator*, and distinct from
phoeniceus, but the specimens before me are not sufficient to decide the question.

The transverse striae or wrinkles at the base of the lower jaw, and the absence of any on the
upper, appear in most cases to be quite characteristic and appreciable, (in the adult males at
least,) as compared with the longitudinal wrinkles on both mandibles of *A. phoeniceus* and
tricolor.

The females of both *A. tricolor* and *gubernator* appear to lack the trace of a median stripe on
the crown seen in *phoeniceus*.

June 25, 1858.

67 b

List of specimens.

Catal. No.	Sex.	Locality.	When collected	Whence obtained.	Orig. No.	Collected by—	Length.	Stretch of wings	Wing.
2835	♂	Columbia river		S F. Baird		J. K. Townsend			
5531	♂	Petaluma, Cal.	Feb. —, 1856	E. Samuels	195				
5526	♂	...do		...do	183				
5530	♀	...do	May 14, 1856	...do	839		7.75	11.54	4.33
8599	....	San Francisco, Cal.		R. D. Cutts					
5933	♂	Santa Clara, Cal.		Gov. Stevens		Dr. Cooper	8.00	13.00	
5935	♀	...do		...do		...do	8.12	13.50	
8601	....	Sacramento valley		Lt. Williamson		Dr. Heermann			
8597	....	Camp 150, Cocomongo ranch, Cal.	May 19, 1854	Lt. Whipple	188	Kenn. & Moll.			
4599?	....	Colorado river, Cal.		Major Emory	50	A. Schott			
4600?	....	...do		...do		...do			
4598?	....	...do	Mar. —, 1854	...do	50	...do			

AGELAIUS TRICOLOR, Bon.

Red and white-shouldered Blackbird.

Icterus tricolor, "NUTTALL," AUD. Orn. Biog. V, 1839, 1 ; pl. 388.—NUTTALL, Man. I, 2d ed. 1840, 186.
Agelaius tricolor, BON. List, 1838.—AUD. Syn. 1839, 141.—IB. Birds Amer. IV, 1842, 27 ; pl. 214.

SP. CH.—Tail nearly even. Second and third quills longest ; first a little shorter than the fourth. Bill slender, not half as high as long.

Male.—General color uniform lustrous velvet black, with a decided greenish reflection. Shoulders and lesser wing coverts brownish red, of much the color of venous blood ; the median coverts of a well-defined and nearly pure white, with sometimes a brownish tinge.

Female.—Dark brown, variegated with dark grayish ash. No median stripe on the crown, nor any maxillary one, and scarcely a superciliary.

Length, 9.20 ; wing, 4.85 ; tail, 3.90.

Hab.—Coast of California. Colorado river ?

The bill of this species is about the length of that of *A. phoeniceus,* it is, however, lower ; the greatest height perpendicular to the base of the gonys being considerably less than half the culmen. There are distinct wrinkles or striae extending from the nostrils parallel with the culmen, and sometimes on the lower jaw nearly parallel with the gonys. Tail very nearly even, or slightly rounded. Tarsus about equal to the middle toe. The second and third quills are longest ; the first much longer than the fifth.

The female of this species is dark brown above, the feathers margined with brownish gray ; the under parts dark gray, the feathers broadly streaked with dark brown. The throat is conspicuously streaked, its ground color lighter than on the belly. There is a faint indication of a paler superciliary stripe, most distinct behind the eye. In one specimen there is no red on the wing ; in another it is quite distinct. The under surface of the wing and the axillaries are sooty plumbeous brown.

Immature males sometimes have the white on the wing tinged with brownish yellow, as in *A. phoeniceus.* The red, however, has the usual brownish orange shade so much darker and duller than the brilliantly scarlet shoulders of the other species. The relationships generally between the two species are very close, but the bill, as stated, is slenderer and more sulcate in *tricolor,* the tail much more nearly even ; the first primary longer, usually nearly equal to or longer than the fourth instead of the fifth.

The female of *A. tricolor* is much grayer than *phoeniceus*, lacking the yellow and reddish brown margins to the feathers of the latter. The light margins beneath are gray, not white; besides, being narrower. There is no median stripe on the head; and the superciliary stripe is scarcely visible. There is none of the yellow about the head seen in *phoeniceus;* the throat is more streaked, and there is no light maxillary stripe cut off by an inferior one of black.

The relationships of the female to that of *A. gubernator* are, however, very close; so much so that, in the absence of a sufficiently large series of well established specimens, I can only refer to the usually slenderer and longer bill and more even tail of *tricolor*, to distinguish them.

List of specimens.

Catal. No.	Sex.	Locality.	When collected.	Whence obtained.	Orig. No.	Collected by—
4601	------	Colorado river, Cal.....	Dec. —, 1854...	Major Emory	19	Dr. Kennerly ....
2836	♂	Santa Barbara, Cal.....	-------------	S. F. Baird.............	-------	Thomas Nuttall (Type).
5934	------	Santa Clara, Cal.......	-------------	Governor Stevens	-------	Dr. Cooper ....
5936[1]	♀?	......do............	-------------	........do.............	-------	......do..............
8595	♂	Sacramento valley	-------------	Lieut. Williamson	-------	Dr. Heermann ....
8596	♀	......do............	-------------	........do.............	-------	......do..............
8593	------	Presidio, Cal..........	July 9, 1853....	Lieut. Trowbridge	147	-------------------
5532	♀	Petaluma, Cal.........	-------------	E. Samuels	-------	-------------------

[1] Length, 8.00; Extent, 13 inches.

XANTHOCEPHALUS, Bonap.

Xanthocephalus, BONAP. Conspectus, 1850, 431. Type *Icterus icterocephalus*, Bonap.

CH.—Bill conical, the length about twice the height; the outlines nearly straight. Claws all very long; much curved; the inner lateral the longest, reaching beyond the middle of the middle claw. Tail narrow, nearly even, the outer web scarcely widening to the end. Wings long, much longer than the tail; the first quill longest.

This genus differs from typical *Agelaius* in much longer and more curved claws, even tail, and first quill longest, instead of the longest being the second, third, or fourth. The yellow head and black body are also strong marks. The measurements will be found in the table with *Agelaius*.

XANTHOCEPHALUS ICTEROCEPHALUS, Baird.

Yellow-headed Blackbird.

Icterus icterocephalus, BONAP. Am. Orn. I, 1825, 27; pl. iii.—NUTT. Man. I, 1832, 176.—IB. 2d ed. 187. Not *Oriolus icterocephalus*, Linn.
Agelaius icterocephalus, CABANIS, Mus. Hein. 1851, 188.
Icterus (Xanthornus) xanthocephalus, BONAP. J. A. N. Sc. V, II, Feb. 1826, 222.—IB. Syn. 1828, 52.
Icterus xanthocephalus, AUD. Orn. Biog. V, 1839, 6; pl. 388.
Agelaius xanthocephalus, SWAINSON, F. Bor. Am. II, 1831, 281.—BON. List, 1838·—AUD. Syn. 1839, 140.—IB. Birds Amer. IV, 1842, 24: pl. 213.—NEWBERRY, Zool. Cal. and Or. Route; Rep. P. R. R. Surv. VI, IV. 1857, 86.
Agelaius longipes, SWAINSON, Phil. Mag. I, 1827, 436.
Psarocolius perspicillatus, "LICHT." WAGLER, Isis, 1829, VII, 753.
Icterus perspicillatus, "LICHT. in Mus." WAGLER, as above.
Xanthocephalus perspicillatus, BONAP. Consp. 1850, 431.
Icterus frenatus, LICHT. Isis, 1843, 59.—REINHARDT, in Kroyer's Tidskrift, IV.—IB. Vidensk. Meddel. for 1853, 1854, 82. Greenland.

SP. CH.—First quill nearly as long as the second and third, (longest,) decidedly longer than the third. Tail rounded, or slightly graduated. General color black, including the inner surface of wings and axillaries, base of lower mandible all round, feathers adjacent to nostrils, lores, upper eyelids, and remaining space around the eye. The head and neck all round; the fore part of the breast, extending some distance down on the median line, and a somewhat hidden space round the anus, yellow. A conspicuous white patch at the base of the wing formed by the spurious feathers, interrupted by the black alula.

Female smaller, browner; the yellow confined to the under parts and sides of the head, and a superciliary line. A dusky maxillary line. No white on the wing. Length of male, 10.00 inches; wing, 5.60; tail, 4.50.

Hab.—Western America from Texas, Illinois, Wisconsin, and North Red river, to California, south into Mexico. Greenland, Reinhardt.

The color of the yellow in this species varies considerably; sometimes being almost of a lemon yellow, sometimes of a rich orange. There is an occasional trace of yellow around the base of the tarsus.

The female differs considerably in appearance, as above mentioned. Sometimes the superciliary stripe is broader, and involves much of the side of the neck. The feathers on the middle of the breast are sometimes edged with whitish. The young male of the year is like the female, but larger, and likewise lacks the white of the wing. Immature males of more adult condition have the yellow of the head and neck variously clouded with black margins, especially on the upper surface.

A very young bird has the head and back brownish yellow, the wing coverts with a broad bar of white.

This species is very widely distributed throughout the North American continent, having even been found in Greenland. Its eastern limit in the United States appears to be Illinois. It is essentially a prairie bird.

List of specimens.

Catal. No.	Sex and age.	Locality.	When collected.	Whence obtained.	Orig'l No.	Collected by—	Length.	Stretch of wings.	Wing.	Remarks.
......	o	Racine, Wis....	April..	N. W. University.	......	Dr. Hoy......				
4332	o	Dane county, Wis	1854	T. M. Brewer						
6943	......	Red River, H. B. T		D. Gunn						
1873	♀	Fort Union, Neb		S. F. Baird		J. J. Audubon				
1872	♂	......do		....do		...do...				
2840	♂	Plains of Missouri R		....do		E. Harris				
4653		Fort Pierre, Neb	April 25, 1855	Col. Vaughan		Dr. Hayden				
5323	♂	15 miles below Ft. Pierre	June 28, 1856	Lieut. Warren		...do				
7003	♂	South Platte River	Aug. 25, 1857	Lieut. Bryan	435	W. S. Wood				
8220	♂	Fort Laramie, Neb	Sept. —, 1857	Wm. M. Magraw	203	Dr. Cooper ...	10.50	17.25	5.50	Feet black...
8221	♀	......do	Sept. 12, 1857	...do	204	... do	10.00	17.00	5.50	
5674	♂	Forks of Platte River	July 15, 1856	Lieut. Bryan	113	W. S. Wood				
8792	......	North Fork Platte	Aug. 20	Wm. Magraw	65	Dr. Cooper				Iris brown; bill and feet black...
8794		15 miles east Ft. Laramie	Aug. 26, 1857	...do	167	...... do	10.50	17.25	6.00	......do......do......
5671	♂	Republican River	Sept. 25, 1856	Lieut. Bryan	354	W. S. Wood				
6556	♂	Fort Riley, K. T		Dr. Wm. A. Hammond.						
4962	......	Fort Chadbourne, Tex		Dr. Swift						
4045	♂	New Leon, Mex	May —, 1853	Lieut. Couch						
4046	♀	......do	...do	...do						
4996	......	Del. Creek and Pecos	July 16, 1856	Capt. Pope	109		10.00	15.50	5.00	Eyes dark brown; gums yellow.
4997	......	Pecos R, Texas	April 26, 1856	...do	193		10.00	16.50	5.25	Bill and feet black...
4998	♀	Devil's River, Texas	May 2, 1855	...do	63					Bill brown; feet gray.
8564		Mimbres to Rio Grande		Dr. Henry						
8570	♂	El Paso		Major Emory		A. Schott				
8554	......	Sawatch Pass		Lieut. Beckwith	15	Mr. Kreutzfeldt				
4594		Colorado River, Cal		Major Emory	55	A. Schott				
		Fort Tejon		J. X. de Vesey.						
8572	♂	Los Angelos Valley		Lieut. Williamson		Dr. Heermann				
4561	......	San José, Cal		A. J. Grayson						
8571	......	Presidio, Cal		Lt. Trowbridge						
5534	♂	Petaluma, Cal	April, 1856	E. Samuels	466					
4475	......	Rhett Lake, Cal		Lieut. Williamson		Dr. Newberry				

TRUPIALIS, Bonaparte.

Trupialis, Bonap. Conspectus, 1850, 429. Type *Sturnus militaris,* L.
Pezites, Cabanis, Mus. Hein. 1851, 191. Type *Sturnus loyca,* Mol.

Ch.—Form of *Sturnella.* Bill elongated ; length about two and a half times the height. Feathers on top of head with bristly shafts. Tail feathers broad, widening at the ends ; the inner corner rounded off. Hind toe nearly as long as the middle. Above banded ; throat and beneath red, without any crescent.

This genus, formerly united with *Sturnella,* is very similar, having the same general appearance The bill is higher at the base, and more like *Agelaius;* it is longer than the head, and about equal to the tarsus. The tarsus is longer than the middle toe, which is scarcely longer than the hinder. The toes are much shorter, the claws sharper and more curved, than in *Sturnella.* The tail is differently formed, being rather broad and rounded, with feathers widening externally at the tip, instead of being formed of narrow, lanceolate, acute feathers, with the outer web the same throughout.

Comparative measurements of species.

Catal. No.	Species.	Locality.	Sex.	Length.	Stretch of wings.	Wing.	Tail.	Tarsus.	Middle toe.	Its claw alone.	Hind toe and claw.	Hind toe alone.	Bill above.	Along gape.	Specimen measured.
1303	Sturnella ludoviciana ..	Carlisle, Pa..........	♂	9.10	......	4.79	3.60	1.60	1.46	0.32	1.22	0.54	1.32	1.48	Skin ......
do.	.........do............	......do	......	10.58	16.08	4.91	......	.....	......	......	......	......	......	......	Fresh......
1555	.........do	......do	♀	7.60	......	4.28	2.80	1.57	1.38	0.33	1.12	0.47	1.12	1.21	Skin ......
do.	.........do	......do	......	9.00	14.50	4.41	......	.....	......	......	......	......	......	......	Fresh. ...
8614	Sturnella neglecta......	Espia, Mexico........	♂	9.50	......	4.81	3.28	1.47	1.40	0.33	1.13	0.46	1.38	1.46	Skin ......
do.	..........do............	......do	......	10.00	15.50	4.75	......	.....	......	......	......	......	......	......	Fresh......
5336	...........do...........	Mouth of Yellowstone	♀	8.00	......	4.36	2.79	1.45	1.18	0.32	1.07	0.47	1.12	1.23	Skin ......
do.	..........do...........	......do	......	8.50	14 50	4.50	......	.....	......	......	......	......	......	......	Fresh.....
10292	..........de..	Fort Tejon, Cal.....	♂	8.70	....	4.88	3.88	1.58	1.20	0.26	1.00	0.40	1.32	1.40	Skin ......
10316	..........do...........	Pembina, Minn.........	......	9.00	....	4.96	3.33	1.46	1.36	0.33	1.09	0.48	1.28	1.40	Skin ......
9693	Sturnella hippocrepis...	Mexico...............	......	7.50	....	4.16	2.95	1.66	1.45	0.38	1.28	0.55	1.16	1.15	Skin ......
1950	Sturnella meridionalis..	Brazil...............	......	8.90	....	4.29	3.21	1.62	1.40	0.38	1.22	0.53	1.58	1.66	Skin ......
4230	Trupialis militaris......	San Francisco, Cal...	......	9.30	....	4.74	3.98	1.40	1.16	0.32	1.18	0.46	1.27	1.24	Skin ......
1794	Trupialis brevirostris...	Mexico?............	......	8.62	....	4.22	2.80	1.22	1.28	0.32	1.00	0.43	1.13	1.10	Skin ......

TRUPIALIS MILITARIS, Bonap.

Red-breasted Lark.

Sturnus militaris, Linn. Mantissa, 1771, 527.—Gmelin, Syst. Nat. I, 1788, 803. (Falklands.)
Trupialis militaris, Bonap. Consp. 1850, 429.
Pezites loyca, Cabanis, Mus. Hein. 1851, 191.

Sp. Ch.—Bill longer than the head ; shaped like *Sturnella.* First quill between fourth and fifth in length. Tail slightly graduated ; the lateral feathers about .20 of an inch shorter. Above dark brown, each feather edged with yellowish brown ; the exposed surfaces of wings, tail coverts, and tail almost an olive brown ; the rump grayer ; all banded narrowly and transversely with dark brown, of which color are the concealed portions of wing and tail. A spot in front of the eye, bend of wings, extreme shoulder, with the under parts, red. The sides of the head, neck, and body, with the hinder part of the abdomen and under tail coverts, black, the feathers edged with gray, and showing indistinct transverse bands. The red of the chin passing up on the side of the lower jaw. A faint median, and conspicuous superciliary stripe, with the under wing coverts, white. Tibia brown. Length, 9.50 ; wing, 4.90 ; tail, 4.10.

Hab.—West coast of South America, around to Falkland Islands. Perhaps in Brazil. Coast of California ?

In this species the blackish on the side of the neck extends inwards so as to leave a very narrow streak of red just on the upper part of the neck. The red extends nearly as far back as the anus. There is a strong shade of gray on the feathers of the sides of the body and the rump. The exposed surface of the closed wing and tail exhibits transverse bars going entirely across the web of the feathers; most distinct on the upper tail coverts. The bars on the tail are mainly confined to the two median feathers, but may be seen on the tips of the others. The outer edge of the first primary is broadly white; a less pure shade of the same on the others. The white superciliary stripe on the side of the head and nape is very distinct, and changes anteriorly to red. The lower eyelid and a small maxillary spot are white.

A single specimen of this species (4230) was obtained in San Francisco by Mr. R. D. Cutts of the Coast Survey, from a collector, who asserted positively that it had been shot by him in San Francisco county. It is mentioned in the " Voyage de la Venus" (Zoologie, I, 1855, 203) as having been shot at Monterey by Dr. Neboux, surgeon of the expedition. There is still some uncertainty, however, as to whether it be really entitled to a place in the fauna of the United States, as Mr. Cutts may have been deceived by his informant, and the indications of the Zoologists of the Venus as to the existence of other species of *Vertebrata* in California are certainly erroneous, owing doubtless to accidental transposition of labels.

The specimen sent in by Mr. Cutts agrees perfectly with those collected in Chile by Lieutenant Gillis, and which are considered by some to be the true *Sturnus loyca* of Molina. Cabanis considers the *S. militaris* of Linnaeus to be the *S. defillippii* of Bonaparte, a species found in Brazil, Paraguay, Montevideo, &c., similar in other respects, but with the under wing coverts blackish, not white. Another species from Brazil, Chile, and Mexico, (?) (1794,) has the bill much shorter and higher at the base, (nearly half as high as long, and more like that of an oriole.) The red of the breast does not pass on to the belly at all, nor that of the chin on the side of the jaw. The white on the inside of the wing is purer. There is no median stripe on the crown. There are no transverse bars on the tail and its upper coverts, except faint indications on the edges and tips. The tibia are pure white instead of brown, and the black of the under parts is clearer. This is described by Cabanis as *Pezites brevirostris*, and referred by him in part to the *Trupialis loyca* of Bp. Conspectus, 429. Cabanis also considers the true *S. militaris* of Linnaeus to be the one with the black under wing coverts. It is difficult to say whether Cabanis or Bonaparte be correct in their determinations, but there is no question that the subject of the present article is found as far north on the east coast of South America as the Rio Negro, whence specimens were brought by the United States Exploring Expedition. There is no evidence that the black-winged species occurs as far south as the Falkland Islands or the Magellan region, from which it appears that the specimens of Linnaeus and of Buffon were obtained. The short-billed species is also found in Chile, as shown by the collections of the United States Exploring Expedition. The bird described by Gay as Chilian, under the name of *Leistes americanus* (on the plate as *Sturnus militaris*) is said to have black under wing coverts, and thus referrible to *S. defillippii* of Bonaparte. As, therefore, all three species appear to be found in Chile, it is impossible to say what is the true *S. loyca* of Molina, and it may be best to follow Bonaparte in his identification.

List of specimens.

Catal. No.	Sex.	Locality.	When collected.	Whence obtained.
4230	......	San Francisco, Cal...............	1853–'54	R. D. Cutts ....
8627	♂	Chile	....	Lieut. Gillis...............
8628	♀	..do...............	....	........do...............

STURNELLA, Vieillot.

Sturnella, VIEILLOT, Analyse, 1816. Type *Alauda magna*, L.

CH.—Body thick, stout; legs large, toes reaching beyond the tail. Tail short, even, with narrow acuminate feathers. Bill slender, elongated; length about three times the height; commissure straight from the basal angle. Culmen flattened basally, extending backwards and parting the frontal feathers; longer than the head, but shorter than tarsus. Nostrils linear, covered by an incumbent membranous scale. Inner lateral toe longer than the outer, but not reaching to basal joint of middle; hind toe a little shorter than the middle, which is equal to the tarsus. Hind claw nearly twice as long as the middle. Feathers of head stiffened, and bristly; the shafts of those above extended into a black seta. Tertials nearly equal to the primaries. Feathers above all transversely banded. Beneath yellow, with a black pectoral crescent.

The two species will be best distinguished by the following diagnoses :

Yellow of chin and throat not extending on the side of the lower jaw. Tail feathers and tertials with the centres dusky, and sending out scollops or dentations of the same color towards the margins ....*S. magna.*

Yellow of chin and throat extending on the side of the lower jaw. Tail feathers and tertials with a tendency to transverse isolated bands............ ....*S. neglecta.*

STURNELLA MAGNA, Sw.

Meadow Lark; Old Field Lark.

Alauda magna, LINN. Syst. Nat. I, 1758, 167, ed. 10; (based on *Alauda magna*, Catesby, tab. 33.)—IB. 12th ed. 1766, 289.—GM. I, 1788, 801.—WILSON, Am. Orn. III, 1811, 20; pl. xix.—DOUGHTY, Cab. I, 1830, 85; pl. v.
Sturnella magna, SWAINSON, Phil. Mag. I, 1827, 436.
Sturnus ludovicianus, LINNAEUS, Syst. Nat. I, 1766, 290.—GM. I, 802.—LATH. Ind. I, 1790, 323.—BON. Obs. Wils. 1825, 130.—LICHT. Verz. 1823, No. 165.—AUD. Orn. Biog, II, 1834, 216: V, 1839, 492; pl. 136.
Sturnella ludoviciana, SWAINSON, F. Bor. Am. II, 1831, 282.—NUTTALL, Man. I, 1832, 147.—BON. List, 1838.— IB. Conspectus, 1850, 429.—AUD. Syn. 1839, 148.—IB. Birds Am. IV, 1842, 70; pl. 223.— CABANIS, Mus. Hein. 1851, 192.
Sturnella collaris, VIEILL. Analyse, 1816.—IB. Galerie des Ois. I, 1824, 134; pl. xc.
Sturnus collaris, WAGLER, Syst. Av. 1827, 1.—IB. Isis, 1831, 527.
" *Cacicus alaudarius*, DAUDIN," Cabanis.

SP. CH.—The feathers above dark brown, margined with brownish white, and with a terminal blotch of pale reddish brown. Exposed portions of wings and tail with transverse dark brown bars which on the middle tail feathers are confluent along the shaft. Beneath yellow, with a black pectoral crescent, the yellow not extending on the side of the maxilla; sides, crissum, and tibiae pale reddish brown, streaked with blackish. A light median and superciliary stripe, the latter yellow anterior to the eye; a black line behind.

Length, 10.60; wing, 5; tail, 3.70; bill above, 1.35.

Hab.—Eastern United States to the High Central Plains. South to Mexico? Cuba?

In this species all the feathers of the upper parts have a border of brownish white tinged with yellow in moderately distinct contrast, (except on the sides of the head,) a broad stripe from the bill along side the head, (yellow anterior to the eye,) and a median stripe on top of the head, which are entirely of this color. The feathers of the back are dark brown, passing rather abruptly through reddish brown to the light margins described; they are also tipped with the same, or, perhaps, barred subterminally. The primary quills are ashy brown externally, plain brown on the inner web, this color entering the pale tints of the outer web in obtuse dentations not quite reaching to the outer margin. The secondaries and tertials are somewhat similar; the ground color of the outer web rather more rufous, the intrusion of the brown more linear. In many of these feathers there are corresponding, but very obsolete, indentations of dark brown in an obscure shade of reddish brown, but this is evident only in the uppermost quills towards the inner margin, the central portion inside the rib being continuously brown. The dentations on the outer web are connected also by a narrow stripe of brown along the outer edge of the shaft.

The outermost tertials and the exposed tips of the others have dark bands going entirely across, and separated entirely by broader ones of dull light rufous brown. The tail feathers are somewhat similarly marked with the wings, but the brown is always continuous on both sides the shaft, extending outward in toothed angular lobes, but not reaching the margin ; the inner webs, except on the innermost feathers, being continuously brown, except near the tip, where are some obsolete fasciae. The shafts of the four outer feathers are white and bordered throughout the whole length with white, which, though narrow on the fourth feather, widens successively on the rest until the outer feather is entirely white, with a small dusky streak at the end. The upper tail coverts are streaked centrally with black, with indistinct bands at the ends.

The under parts are bright yellow (much like the yolk of an egg) from the bill to the anus ; the sides, under tail coverts, and tibiae are dull brownish rufous white, the two former broadly streaked with blackish brown. The larger blotches on the sides have a terminal spot of lighter. There is a rather broad crescent of black, the horns of which go half way up the side of the neck ; there is also a black stripe behind the eye, and a fine streak above it caused by the black eyelashes. The yellow on the chin and upper throat is confined strictly within the rami of the lower jaw and does not pass round on the side of the maxilla. The bill is blue, becoming almost black on the ridge, and towards the tips ; the legs are yellowish.

The edge of the shoulder is yellow ; the axillars white ; the under wing coverts grayish white. There is a strong shade of bluish ash on the lesser coverts.

The specimen which I have described above is a very perfect male from Carlisle, Pennsylvania, (1303) in which the continuity of the transverse bars on the exposed surface of the tertials is remarkably distinct. It is more the rule that these brown bars are confluent along the shaft. The female is similar, but smaller.

A young bird, likewise from Carlisle, (1629,) has the under parts yellowish, tinged with brownish on the sides and across the breast ; the pectoral crescent entirely wanting, and the sides of the breast thickly streaked with blackish, with a slight pectoral band of the same. The feathers above are brownish, with a well defined and continuous border of brownish yellow, and with one rather large terminal spot on the back and a series on each web of the tertials of dull light reddish brown, all within the brownish ground color. In the larger quills and tail feathers these light spots are confluent externally and extend entirely to the lighter exterior. The yellow spot in front of the eye is wanting.

Specimens vary considerably in the extent and intensity of the dark markings above, as well as in size and length of bill.

Through the kindness of Dr. Hartlaub, of Bremen, I have had the opportunity of examining a specimen of *Sturnella hippocrepis*, Wagler, from Cuba. According to Wagler, this differs from *S. magna* in smaller size, different tail, more curved bill, and absence of the black streak behind the eye. The skin at my command is not perfect enough to admit of a very just comparison, but I see little that is different from continental specimens, except a narrower pectoral collar.

A skin from Brasil (1956) differs in having a longer bill than in any other that has fallen under my notice, measuring above 1.60 inches. The size is smaller, the color darker above.

In other respects there is a great similarity. The species may, however, prove to be distinct. The American meadow lark was first named by Linnaeus in the tenth edition of Syst. Nat. 1758, and called *Alauda magna*, after Catesby's unmistakeable figure. In the twelfth edition "*Sturnus ludovicianus*" makes its appearance from Brisson. The second description is absolutely inaccurate, ("throat black,") and there is no mention of the yellow under parts. As there is a decided priority for the name of *magna*, therefore, and the description accompanying it is sufficiently accurate, while that of *ludoviciana* is not so, I restore the former, as used by Wilson and Swainson.

List of specimens.

Catal. No.	Sex.	Locality.	When collected.	Whence obtained.	Orig. No.	Collected by—	Length.	Stretch of wings.	Wing.	Remarks.
1303	♂	Carlisle, Pa............	Mar. 21, 1844	S. F. Baird........	.....	....	10.58	16.08	4.91	....
1613	♂	......do...	June 24, 1844	......do	.....	....	9.75	15.50	4.66	.....
1555	♀	......do...	May 20, 1844	......do...	.....	....	9.00	14.50	4.41	.....
4545	♀	Washington, D. C......	Winter......	......do.......	.....	....	7.25	14.00	4.58	.....
7584	......	......do...	....	Wm. Hutton...						
......	......	Salem, Ill............	April 7......	N. W. University...	......	R. Kennicott....				
......	......	Racine, Wis...........		......do.....	.....	......do...				
2689	♂	Illinois	Mar. —, 1844	S. F. Baird						
4294	......	Calcasieu Pass, La.....	1854........	G. Würdemann ...						
8190	♂	Fort Leavenworth......	July 12, 1857	W. M. Magraw....	126	Dr. Cooper......	9.75	....	4.75	Feet brown........
8177	♂	Shawnee Mission, K. T.	July 3, 1857	......do...	113	......do...	10.25	16.00	4.87	Feet flesh......
8180	♂	......do...	......do......	......do...	116	......do...	10.00	15.25	4.75	......do......
5687	♂	East of Fort Riley, K. T.	June 13, 1856	Lieut. Bryan......	5	W. S. Wood......				....
6555	......	Fort Riley, K. T	....	Dr. Hammond.....						
9327	♂	Loup Fork............	July........	Lieut. Warren.....		Dr. Hayden......	10.25	16.00	5.00	Iris dark brown....
9326	♂	......do...		......do.....		......do...	10.00	15.50	4.50	Iris light yellow....
9325	♂	......do...	Aug. 13.....	......do...		......do...	9.75	15.75	4.75	Iris dark brown.....
8621?	......	Fort Thorn		Dr. Henry........						

STURNELLA NEGLECTA, Aud.

Western Lark.

Sturnella neglecta, Aud. Birds Amer. VII, 1843, 339 ; pl. 487.—Newberry, Zool. Cal. & Or. Route ; Rep. P. R. R. Surv. VI, iv, 1857, 86.

? *Sturnella hippocrepis*,)Wagner,) Heermann, J. A. N. Sc. Ph. 2d series, II, 1853, 269, Suisun.

Sp. Ch.—Feathers above dark brown, margined with brownish white, with a terminal blotch of pale reddish brown. Exposed portion of wings and tail with transverse bands, which, in the latter, are completely isolated from each other, narrow and linear. Beneath yellow, with a black pectoral crescent. The yellow of the throat extending on the side of the maxilla. Sides, crissum, and tibia very pale reddish brown, or nearly white, streaked with blackish. Head with a light median and superciliary stripe, the latter yellow in front of the eye ; a blackish line behind it. The transverse bars on the feathers above (less so on the tail) with a tendency to become confluent near the exterior margin. Length, 10 inches ; wing, 5.25 ; tail, 3.25 ; bill, 1.25.

Hab.—Western America from High Central Plains to the Pacific ; east to Pembina, and perhaps to Wisconsin.

This species is so very closely related to the *S. magna* as to render it very difficult to distinguish them. The same description as to pattern, colors, size, &c., will apply almost equally well to both. The prevailing shade of color is, however, decidedly paler in *neglecta*, the light margins to the feathers being purer, the intervals of the dark markings being not reddish brown so much as olivaceous, with a faint trace only of chestnut. As a general rule where the dark brown in *S. magna* margins the shaft of the feather and sends off angular dentations towards the exterior, in *S. neglecta* it is thrown into separate narrow transverse bands going entirely across, and not connected by brown along the shafts. This is most

June 25, 1858.

68 b

particularly the case on the outer webs of the tertials and of the middle tail feathers, and to a less marked extent on the inner webs. In some specimens of *S. magna* the dark bands are entirely transverse on the exposed part of the tertials, but in the concealed portions they are more or less confluent, and in all cases they are broader. The tip of the middle tail feathers of *S. magna* very rarely shows a few completely transverse bands, but they become confluent towards the middle, and exhibit a general tendency to angularity, whereas in *S. neglecta* the sides of the bands are more or less parallel and, in fact, often widen at the exterior, and become nearly or quite confluent.

There is no difference observable in the under parts, except that, as a general thing, the sides, tibia, and crissum are whiter, although this is not constant. There is, however, a slight tinge of reddish in the white of *S. magna* scarcely found in *neglecta*. The yellow is rather lighter. There seems to be a constant tendency in *neglecta* to an extension of the yellow of the throat over on to the side of the lower mandible, instead of being confined strictly to the inferior surface of the head and neck.

To sum up the preceding remarks it may be stated that the real difference between the species lies in the greater tendency to narrow transverse bands on the upper surfaces, especially of the middle tail feathers. Although there is an average difference in the paler tone of color above and below, yet there are specimens, especially from Washington Territory, in which such difference does not exist.

The yellow on the side of the lower mandible appears to be a pretty good mark. It is not to be denied, however, that the difficulties of separating the specimens of the two species are exceedingly great, and that in many cases it is necessary to take an average of characters, no single one furnishing a sufficiently permanent peculiarity, and for quite a number of western specimens, as 8621, from Fort Thorn, 8604, 8608, 8610, from Fort Steilacoom, and 8624, from Presidio, California, I am entirely at a loss which name to assign. No. 8608, in fact, agrees in every respect with eastern specimens.

In discussing the question of specific distinction between the two birds, the remarkable difference in their notes, as attested by all observers from Lewis and Clarke down to the present day, must be kept in mind.

List of specimens.

Catal. No.	Sex and age.	Locality.	When collected.	Whence obtained.	Orig'l No.	Collected by—	Length.	Stretch of wings.	Wing.	Remarks.
		Pembina, Minn	Sept. 24	N. W. University		R. Kennicott				
1939	♂	Fort Union, Neb	June 30, 1843	S. F. Baird		J. J. Audubon				
5338	♂	...do		Lt. Warren		Dr. Hayden	9.25	14.00	4.50	
5334		.....do		...do		...do	8.50	14.50	4.50	
5341		Yellowstone	July 25, 1856	...do		...do	8.62	13.00	4.37	
5336	♂	...do	July 23, 1856	...do		...do	8.50	14.50	4.50	
8603		Fort Benton	Sept. 5, 1853	Gov. Stevens		Dr. Suckley				
5235	♂	Fort Pierre, Neb	Oct. 4, 1856	Lt. Warren		Dr. Hayden	9.50	14.50	4.50	
4749		Ile Tower	May 11	...do		...do	10.00	15.62	5.00	
5339	♂	Fort Pierre	June 25, 1856	...do		...do	9.62	16.37	5.25	
5329		Little Cheyenne, Mo	July 1, 1856	...do		...do	8.37	13.75	4.50	Eyes brown..
5330	♀	Fort Lookout	July 17, 1856	...do		...do	9.25	15.50	4.50	
4748	♂	Nebraska	May 15, 1856	...do		...do	9.87	16.12	5.25	
4752		...do	...do	...do		...do	10.12	16.25	4.75	
4751	♂	......do				...do	9.25	15.25	5.25	
5688	♂	Little Powder	Sept. 4	Lt. Bryan	320	W. S. Wood				
9322	♀	50 miles above mouth of Platte		Lt. Warren		Dr. Hayden	9.00	13.75	4.12	
9321	♂	Loup Fork		...do		...do	9.50	17.00	5.00	
9316	♂	.....do	July 11	.....do		...do	9.75	16.75	5.00	
9314	♂	...do	....do	...do		...do	10.00		5.00	
9318	♀	...do	July 28	...do		...do	8.50	13.50	4.25	
9319	♀	...do	Aug. 3	...do		...do	8.75	14.00	4.25	
9307	♀	...do	July 3	...do		...do	9.00	14.25	4.00	
9317	♀	...do	Aug. 3	...do		...do	9.75	15.50	4.00	
9315	♀	...do	July 22	...do		...do	8.50	14.50	4.50	
9312	♀	...do	July 13, 1857	...do		...do	9.25	14.50	4.50	
5689	♀	Platte river	July 12, 1856	Lt. Bryan	25	W. S. Wood				
7094		Pole creek, Neb	July 18, 1857	...do	48	...do				
5690	♂	W. Fork Medicine Bow	Aug. 25, 1856	...do	298	...do	10.00	13.00	4.25	
5020		Indianola, Tex	Feb. 19, 1855	Capt. Pope	19	Berlandier				
8611		Matamoras		Lt. Couch			8.50	13.50	4.50	
4064	♀	Coahuila, Mex		...do						
5016		Pecos Crossing	June 22, 1855	Capt. Pope	100					
5018		Guadaloupe Mountains	Sept. 27, 1855	...do	138					
8613		San Elizario, Texas	Dec., 1855	Major Emory	19	Dr. Kennerly				
8616		Fort Conrad, N. M	Oct., 1853	Lt. Whipple		...do				
5015		Fort Fillmore, N. M	Oct. 11, 1855	Capt. Pope	144					
3705		Salt Lake, Utah	Mar. 21, 1857	Capt. Stansbury						
8611		Camp 117, N. M	Feb. 9, 1854	Lt. Whipple		Kenn. & Möll				
8612		Camp 126, N. M	Feb. 19, 1854	...do	173					
8614	♂	Espia, Mex	March, 1855	Major Emory		Dr. Kennerly				
8615		Fort Yuma, Cal	Nov., 1854	...do		A. Schott				
		Fort Tejon, Cal		J. X. de Vesey						
4573		San Diego, Cal		Major Emory		A. Schott				
8624	♂	Tulare valley		Lt. Williamson		Dr. Heermann				
8625		Sacramento valley		...do		...do				
4939		San José, Cal		A. J. Grayson	19					
4455		Vacaville, Cal		Lt. Williamson		Dr. Newberry				
8620		San Francisco		R. D. Cutts						
8623??		Presidio, Cal		Lt. Trowbridge		T. A. Szabo				
8618		Bodega, Cal	Dec., 1854	...do						
5537		Petaluma, Cal	April 19, 1856	E. Samuels			8.33	11.16	4.33	Eyes brown..
8609	♀	Ft. Vancouver, W. T	Jan. 30, 1854	Gov. Stevens	22	Dr. Cooper	10.00	16.00		
8605		Shoalwater bay, W. T	Sept. 23, 1854	...do	97	...do	11.25	16.75		
8604		Fort Steilacoom	May 13, 1856	Dr. Suckley	387					
8606		...do		...do			10.50	15.00		
8610	♂	.....do	May 3	...do	365		9.87	16.00		
5937	♂	Whitby's island, W. T	March, 1855	Gov. Stevens			10.00	16.25		
9324		N. W. America		J. Gould		Capt. Beechey				

Sub–Family ICTERINAE.

Ch.—Bill slender, elongated, as long as the head, generally a little decurved, and very acute. Tarsi not longer than the middle toe, nor than the head ; claws short, much curved ; outer lateral toe a little longer than the inner, reaching a little beyond base of middle toe. Feet adapted for perching. Tail rounded or graduated. Prevailing colors yellow or orange, and black.

The species of this sub-family are all as strikingly characterized by diversity and brilliancy of plumage as the others are (with few exceptions) for their uniform sombre black, scarcely relieved by other colors. In certain respects there is a decided resemblance to some of the *Sylvicolidae*, from which, in fact, the much larger size is, in some cases, the chief apparent distinction.

In studying the North American Orioles I have found it exceedingly difficult to arrange them in any sharply defined sections, as whatever characters be taken as the basis of classification, the other features, will not correspond. Thus, species with the bill of the same proportions and amount of curvature differ in the shape and graduation of the tail, while tails of the same form are accompanied by entirely dissimilar bills and wings. The bill is sometimes much attenuated and decurved, as in *I. cucullatus*, while in *melanocephalus* and *baltimore* it is stouter and straighter. The tail is usually much graduated ; in *I. baltimore* and *bullocki* it is only moderately rounded. These last mentioned species constitute the genus *Yphantes*. Many of the species have a naked space round the eye ; very evident in *I. vulgaris*, less so in *melanocephalus*. *I. vulgaris* is peculiar in having the feathers of the throat pointed and lanceolate as in the ravens.

In view of the difficulties attendant upon the definition of subordinate groups among the United States *Icterinae*, I propose to consider them all under the single genus *Icterus*, leaving it for some one with a fuller series of specimens at his command to establish satisfactory divisions into genera.

The colors of the *Orioles* are chiefly black and yellow, or orange, the wing sometimes marked with white. The females are much duller in plumage, and the young male usually remains in immature dress till the third year. In all the North American species the rump is of the same color with the belly ; the chin, throat, and tail, black.

The following synopsis may serve to distinguish the species as far as color is concerned.

A. *Head and neck all round black.*

Back black, separated from that of the head by the color of the belly.

Orange, yellow, and black. Greater wing coverts and edges of secondaries, white ; lesser coverts and tail black, the latter white at the extreme base.....................*I. vulgaris*.

Back greenish yellow ; wings and tail black ; the lesser coverts yellow. Colors yellow and black.

Greater coverts and quills edged with white..*I. audubonii*.

No white edges whatever on the wings and tail. Smaller size and stouter bill.

I. melanocephalus.

Back black, continuous with that of the neck. Lesser coverts like the belly.

Yellowish orange and black. Entire tail, with ends of upper and lower coverts, black.
No white on the wings...*I. wagleri*.

Yellow and black. Edges of greater coverts and of quills white. Tail yellow ; middle feathers and terminal third, with all of upper and under coverts, black...*I. parisorum*.

Chestnut and black. Tail black, except at extreme base ; a slight edging of white on the quills and greater coverts..*I. spurius.*

Brilliant orange, red, and black. Greater coverts and quills edged with white. Tail orange ; the middle feathers, and basal half of all the rest, black............*I. baltimore.*

B. *Sides of head and neck like the belly.*

Orange and black. Forehead, sides of the throat, and tail, orange ; the innermost tail feathers, and median spots on the others, black. Coverts continuously white ; edges of quills white...*I. bullockii.*

C. *Top of head and neck like the belly.*

Forehead, lores, and whole throat, with the interscapular region, black.

Orange and black. Lesser wing coverts and tail, except at extreme base, black. Two bands on wing, and edges of quills, white....................................*I. cucullatus.*

Yellow and black. Lesser and middle coverts, and tail, yellow ; middle tail feathers, and bases of the rest, black ; quills slightly edged with white..............*I. mesomelas.*

Comparative measurements of species.

Catal. No.	Species.	Locality.	Sex and age.	Length.	Stretch of wings.	Wing.	Tail.	Tarsus.	Middle toe.	Its claw alone.	Hind toe and claw.	Hind toe alone.	Bill above.	Along gape.	Specimen measured.
2527	Icterus vulgaris	Cage bird............	♂	9.10	....	4.86	4.43	1.36	1.30	0.38	0.96	0.42	1.37	1.35	Skin........
4063	Icterus audubonii......	Tamaulipas, Mex	♂	9.00	....	3.96	4.54	1.10	1.01	0.29	0.76	0.32	0.97	0.96	Skin........
do.	......do..............	......do............		9.25	12.25	4.00	......	......	......	......	......	......	......	......	Fresh .....
10202	.....do......	Mexico............		9.34	....	4.04	4.45	1.03	1.00	0.29	0.77	0.30	1.06	1.04	Skin ......
6713	......do......	Ringgold barracks....	♂	8.70	....	3.90	4.46	1.06	0.95	0.30	0.73	0.32	0.86	0.90	Skin ......
do.	......do..............	......do............		9.37	12.25	4.00	......	......	......	......	......	......	......	......	Fresh .....
4062	......do..............	Tamaulipas..........	♀	8.70	....	3.84	4.51	1.04	1.00	0.30	0.78	0.35	1.02	1.00	Skin .. ...
do.	......do..............	......do............		8.75	11.50	3.75	.... .	......	......	......	......	......	......	......	Fresh .....
10201	Icterus melanocephalus.	Mexico............		7.70	....	3.75	4.18	1.00	0.90	0.24	0.66	0.30	0.92	0.88	Skin ......
10293	Icterus parisorum......	Pecos?............		8.50	....	4.20	4.12	0.90	0.90	0.26	0.67	0.29	0.89	0.90	Skin ......
4056	......do..............	New Leon, Mex......	♂	7.70	....	4.02	3.70	0.93	0.92	0.24	0.67	0.31	0.85	0.92	Skin ......
do.	......do..............	......do............		8.25	11.75	4.00	......	......	......	......	......	......	......	......	Fresh .....
4057	......do..............	......do............	♀♂	7.20	....	3.90	3.54	0.92	0.94	0.26	0.66	0.31	0.90	0.93	Skin .. ...
do.	......do..............	......do............		8.00	12.00	4.00	......	......	......	......	......	......	......	......	Fresh .....
4058	Icterus wagleri......	Coahuila..........	♂	8.80	....	4.16	4.60	1.02	0.96	0.27	0.72	0.35	0.96	1.02	Skin .. ...
do.	......do..............	......do............		9.50	12.00	4.50	......	......	......	......	......	......	......	......	Fresh .....
8089	......do..............	Guatemala..........		8.20	....	3.75	4.40	0.98	0.82	0.22	0.62	0.25	0.87	0.85	Skin .. ...
1542	Icterus spurius........	Carlisle, Pa..........	♂	6.50	....	3.22	3.23	0.88	0.80	0.22	0.57	0.25	0.71	0.75	Skin .....
do.	......do..............	......do............		7.25	11.33	3.25	......	......	......	......	......	......	......	......	Fresh .....
150	......do..............	......do............	♀	6.40	....	2.98	2.92	0.86	0.80	0.22	0.62	0.26	0.70	0.75	Skin........
4286	.....do	Calcasieu Pass, La...	♂	6.20	....	3.00	3.13	0.86	0.84	0.24	0.62	0.30	0.67	0.70	Skin ......
6711	......do..............	San Antonio, Tex....	♂	6.12	....	2.93	2.86	0.79	0.75	0.21	0.56	0.23	0.64	0.69	Skin ......
6708	......do..............	......do............	♀	5.92	....	2.88	2.80	0.80	0.73	0.20	0.56	0.24	0.62	0.67	Skin ......
4066	Icterus cucullatus......	Tamaulipas, Mex.....	♂	7.60	....	3.42	4.06	0.87	0.81	0.21	0.60	0.27	0.77	0.86	Skin ......
4066	......do..............	......do............		7.50	10.00	3.25	......	......	......	......	......	......	......	......	Fresh .....
do.	......do..............	......do............	♀	6.90	....	3.19	3.74	0.89	0.83	0.26	0.61	0.29	0.72	0.80	Skin ......
4069	......do..............	......do............		7.50	10.00	3.25	......	......	......	......	......	......	......	......	Fresh .....
do.	Icterus mesomelas.....	Mexico............	♂	7.40	....	3.49	4.32	1.10	0.90	0.27	0.68	0.30	0.81	0.83	Skin ......
6721	Icterus baltimore......	Carlisle, Pa..........	♂	7.00	....	3.82	3.26	0.92	0.85	0.27	0.66	0.28	0.73	0.76	Skin ......
7596	......do..............	Washington, D. C....	♀	7.30	....	3.64	3.17	0.90	....	0.64	0 26	0.72	0.80		Skin ......
9092	Icterus bullockii	Mexico............	♂	8.06	....	4.02	3.55	0.94	0.87	0.25	0.66	0.31	0.78	0.84	Skin . ...
5354	......do..............	Farm Island, Neb....	♂	7.70	....	4.10	3.54	1.00	0.80	0.23	0.63	0.27	0.74	0.78	Skin ......
do .	......do..............	......do............		7.62	13.00	4 25	......	......	......	......	......	......	......	......	Fresh .....
5524	......do..............	Petaluma, Cal.......	♂	7.34	....	3.84	3.42	0.96	0.80	0.21	0.65	0.28	0.75	0.77	Skin ......
3900	......do..............	California............	♀	6.90	....	3.58	2.96	0.92	0.84	0.25	0.60	0.27	0.71	0.78	Skin ......

ICTERUS VULGARIS, Daudin.

Troupial.

Oriolus icterus, LINN. Syst. Nat. I, 1766, 161.
Icterus vulgaris, "DAUDIN."—AUD. Birds Amer. VII, 1844, 357 ; pl. 499.—BP. Conspectus Av. 1850, 434.
Le troupiale vulgaire, BUFFON, Pl. enl. " 532." (535, Bp.)

SP. CH.—Bill curved. Throat and chin with narrow pointed feathers. A naked space around and behind the eye. Tail feathers graduated. Head and upper part of neck all round, and beneath from tail to upper part of breast, interscapular region of back, wings, and tail, black. Rest of under parts, a collar on the lower hind neck, rump, and upper tail coverts, yellow orange. A broad band on the wing and outer edges of secondaries, white. Length, 10 inches ; wing, 4.50 ; tail, 4.50 ; bill above, 1.35.

Hab.—Northern South America and West Indies. Accidental on the southern coast of the United States.

This is the largest of the *Orioles* found in the United States, and differs from the rest in its longer bill, and pointed, elongated feathers on the throat. The bill is attenuated and somewhat decurved. The third quill is longest ; the first quill almost the shortest of all the primaries. The outer tail feather is about .60 of an inch less than the middle.

There is only a trace of whitish on the edges of the primaries. The broad white edges to the secondaries are continuous in the folded wing with the white on the greater coverts, the lowest row of which, however, is black. The extreme and concealed base of the tail is white.

One specimen has the light markings yellow instead of orange.

This species is given by Mr. Audubon as North American, on the strength of occasional stragglers from the West Indies to the southern coast. One of the specimens described was received from Mr. Audubon, (2842,) and is, possibly, North American ; the other was a cage bird.

List of specimens.

Catal. No.	Sex.	Locality.	When collected.	Whence obtained.	Remarks.
2842	--------	Unknown ----------- ------------------	S. F. Baird ------------	--------------------
2527	♂	------do-------------	April —, 1846 ----	------do-----------------	Cage bird ----------
---------	--------	Laguayra-----------------------------		C. W. Welch ----------	In alcohol ----------

ICTERUS AUDUBONII, Giraud.

Audubon's Oriole.

Icterus audubonii, GIRAUD, sixteen new species Texas birds, 1841. (Not paged.)
Xanthornus melanocephalus, BON. Consp. 1850, 434. (Not the description of the young.)
Icterus melanocephalus, CASSIN, Ill. I, v, 1854, 137 ; pl. xxi. (The description, but perhaps not the figure.)

SP. CH.—Bill stout ; upper and lower outlines very little curved downwards. Tail much graduated. Head and neck all round, (this color extending down on the throat,) tail, and wings, black ; rest of body, under wing coverts, and middle and lesser upper coverts, yellow ; more olivaceous on the back. An interrupted band across the ends of the greater wing coverts, with the terminal half of the edges of the quills, white.

Supposed female similar, but the colors less vivid.

Length, 9.25 ; wing, 4.00 ; tail, 4.65 ; tarsus, 1.10.

Hab.—Valley of the Lower Rio Grande of Texas, southward.

The bill of this species is shaped very much as in *I. baltimore*, a little more attenuated at the tip, but not more decurved. The tail is long and much graduated; the outer feather 1.10 of an inch shorter than the inner.

In this species there is no yellow below the black of the feathers of the head, the basal portion being plumbeous. The outline of the black on the upper neck is at the same distance from the bill all round, except on the throat, where it extends three quarters of an inch further back as a semicircular patch on the upper part of the breast. There is a slight orange tinge on the breast; the sides under the wings, and back, more greenish. The tail feathers are entirely black to their bases; some of them tipped with whitish. Females and immature males have, sometimes, an elongated patch of dusky greenish yellow on the exterior of some of the tail feathers. The white outer edges of the wings are seen only on the terminal half of the primaries and secondaries; the band across the wing is scarcely continued to its external edge.

The third quill is longest; the fourth and fifth, successively, a very little shorter than the second; the first shorter than the seventh.

From an examination of the description of Wagler it is, I think, clearly evident that he had in view the smaller species of the Black-headed Oriole. (See the next article.) The measurements are exactly the same, and the narrow grayish margins of the quills and the greenish edges of the tail feathers, are merely indicative of immaturity. No mention is made of the broad white or yellowish white borders of the coverts and quills. The dimensions given, (Length, 8 inches; bill from forehead, .75; tail, 3.88; wings, 3.38; tarsi, 1.00,) allowing for the larger size of the German inch, will be almost exactly those of the smaller bird, and necessarily much inferior to that from the Rio Grande.

As far as I can judge, the *Icterus graduacauda* of Lesson, (*alis caudaque nigerrimis,*) belongs to the smaller bird. The *I. audubonii* of Giraud, on the other hand, has the white edges of the wings and is large enough to belong to the more northern species, which, accordingly, should take its name.

The *Xanthornus melanocephalus* of Bonaparte probably refers to the northern bird, but the description of the young is probably that of true *melanocephalus.*

List of specimens.

Catal. No.	Sex.	Locality.	When collected.	Whence obtained.	Orig'l No.	Collected by—	Length.	Stretch of wings.	Wings	Remarks.
4063	♂	Charco Escondido, Tamaulipas, Mex.	May.......	Lt. Couch	64	....	9.25	12.25	4.00	Eyes dark brown; bill dark slate.
4062	♀	........do	....	.....do	63	....	8.75	11.50	3.75	Eyes dark brown; bill black; lower mandible light blue, lead colored at base ....
4059	......	Matamoras, Mex...........	....	.....do........	......	Berlandier.	....	....	......	....
6713	......	Ringgold barracks, Tex.....	....	Maj. Emory...	......	J. H. Clark	9.37	12.25	4.00	....
10202	.... .	Mexico................	....	P. L. Sclater...	......	....	....	....	......	....

ICTERUS MELANOCEPHALUS, Gray.

Psarocolius melanocephalus, WAGLER, Isis, 1829, 756.
Icterus melanocephalus, GRAY, Genera.—SCLATER, Pr. Zool. Soc. 1858, 97.
Xanthornus melanocephalus, BON. Consp. 1850, 434. Description of young only.
? *Icterus graduacauda*, LESSON, Rev. Zool. 1839, 105.

SP. CH.—Similar to *J. audubonii*, but without any white whatever on the wing. Head and neck all round, wings, scapulars, and tail, uniform pure black. Rest of body, including beneath the wing and tibia and the lesser wing coverts, orange yellow;

clouded with olivaceous green on the back, less so on the rump. Bill and legs plumbeous, the former whitish at base. Length 7.70 ; wing, 3.75 ; tail, 4.80.

Hab.—Warm parts of Mexico.

A specimen of this species, (No. 10201), a native of the warmer parts of Mexico, was presented to the Smithsonian Institution by Mr. Sclater, and I introduce it here to show its near relationship to the *I. audubonii.* It is very like the *audubonii*, but is smaller, the bill much stouter, shorter, and the culmen more curved. The third quill is longest ; the fourth, fifth, and second successively a little shorter ; the first and seventh about equal. The black of the head and neck comes further behind and on the sides than in *audubonii.* The wings are totally destitute of the white edges of quills and coverts as seen in *audubonii.* The tail, too, is entirely black.

A criticism of the different names applied conjointly to this species and the *I. audubonii* will be found in the preceding article.

ICTERUS PARISORUM, B o n a p .

Icterus parisorum, (" Bon. Acad. Bonon. 1836.") Bp. Pr. Zool. Soc. V, 1837, 109.

Xanthornus parisorum, Ib. Conspectus, 1850, 434.

Icterus melanochrysura, Lesson, Rev. Zool. 1839, 105.

Icterus scottii, Couch, Pr. A. N. Sc. Phil. VII, April 1854, 66. (Coahuila.)

Sp. Ch.—Bill attenuated ; not much decurved ; tail moderately graduated. Head and neck all round, breast, interscapular region, wings, and tail, black. Under parts generally, hinder part of back to the tail, middle and lesser upper, and whole of lower wing coverts, and base of the tail feathers, gamboge yellow ; a band across the ends of the greater coverts, with the edges of the inner secondaries and tertiaries, white. Length 8.25 ; extent, 11.75 ; wing, 4 ; tail, 3.75 ; tarsus, .95.

Hab.—Valley of the Rio Grande ; south to Guatemala. In Texas, found on the Pecos.

The bill is slender and attenuated, very little decurved, much less than in *I. cucullatus*, slenderer and a little more decurved than in *I. baltimore.* The tail is moderately graduated, the outer feather .45 of an inch less than the middle.

In this species the black feathers of the neck, except below, have a subterminal bar of yellow ; elsewhere it is wanting. The black of the breast comes a little posterior to the anterior extremity of the folded wing. The posterior feathers in the yellow patch on the shoulders are tinged with white. The white in the bar across the ends of the greater coverts is confined mainly to the terminal quarter of an inch of the outer web. In the full plumage, there is only a faint trace of white on the edges of the primaries. The yellow of the base of the tail only extends on the middle feather as far as the end of the upper tail coverts ; on the three outer it reaches to within an inch and a quarter of the end of the tail.

An immature male has the yellow more tinged with green, the black feathers of the head and back olivaceous with a black spot.

In this species the second and third quills are equal and longest ; the first intermediate between the fourth and fifth.

A specimen of this species collected in western Texas by Captain Pope, and the only one yet found within the limits of the United States, differs from those of Lieutenant Couch in being considerably larger ; the black feathers of the neck lacking entirely any subterminal yellow. The outer tail feather is proportionatelly a little longer. There is, however, nothing upon which to found a specific distinction, the difference in size being in accordance with what is usually seen between specimens of the same species from northern and southern breeding localities.

List of specimens.

Catal. No.	Sex & Age.	Locality.	When collected.	Whence obtained.	Orig. No.	Length.	Stretch of wings.	Wing.	Remarks.
4056	♂	Sta. Catarina, New Leon, Mex.	April —, 1853	Lt. D. N. Couch.	185	8.25	11.75	4.00	Eyes brown, bill black and blue, feet blue lead.
4057	○ ♂	.....do.........	....do.........	......do.........	191	8.00	12.00	4.00	....
10293	......	Pecos river, Tex...	1856.........	Capt. J. Pope ...					....

ICTERUS WAGLERI, Sclater.

Icterus wagleri, SCLATER, Pr. Zool. Soc. 1857, 7.
Psarocolius flavigaster, WAGLER, Isis, 1829, 756. (Not of Vieillot.)
Pendulinus domincensis, Bp. Consp. 1850, 432. (Not of Linn.)

SP. CH.—Bill much attenuated and considerably decurved. Tail considerably graduated. Head and neck all round, back, (the color extending above over the whole interscapular region,) wings, and tail, including the whole of the lower coverts and the tips of the upper, black. Lesser and middle upper, with lower wing coverts, hinder part of back, rump, and under parts generally, (except tail coverts,) orange yellow. Length 9.50 inches; extent, 12; wing, 4.50; tail, 4.25; tarsus, 1.15.

Hab.—Northeastern Mexico to Rio Grande valley; south to Guatemala.

In this species the bill is slender, and very similar to that of *I. cucullatus.* The tail is long, much graduated; the outer feather an inch shorter than the inner. The feathers are very broad, measuring three-quarters of an inch; the difference in this respect, when compared with *I. audubonii,* is very striking.

There is no yellow on the black tipped feathers. The orange yellow varies very little in different parts of the body. The quills and tail feathers are entirely black to their bases. The whole outer surface of the wing is pure black, except the yellow coverts. The tips of the posterior upper tail coverts are black; the whole of the lower are black except for a short distance behind the anus.

This species is quite similar in external form and size to *Icterus audubonii,* but the bill is much more slender and decurved.

The third and fourth quills are longest; the second longer than the fifth; the first intermediate between the fifth and sixth.

A specimen from Guatemala (8089) is considerably smaller than that described, though otherwise similar.

The rectification of synonymy, as quoted above, I borrow from Mr. Sclater's article.

List of specimens.

Catal. No.	Sex.	Locality.	When collected.	Whence obtained.	Orig. No.	Length.	Stretch of wings.	Wing.	Remarks.
4058	♂	Saltillo, Coahuila, Mex.	May —, 1853	Lieut. Couch....	3	9.50	12.00	4.50	Eyes dark brown.
8089	......	Guatemala	....	J. Gould.........					....

June 25, 1858.

69 b

ICTERUS CUCULLATUS, Swainson.

Hooded Oriole.

Icterus cucullatus, Swainson, Philos. Mag. I, 1827, 436 —Lawrence, Ann. N. Y. Lyc. V, May, 1851, 116, (first introduced into fana of United States.)—Cassin, Ill. I, ii, 1853, 42 ; pl. viii.

Pendulinus cucullatus, Bon. Consp. 1850, 433.

Sp. Ch.—Both mandibles much curved. Tail much graduated. Wings, a rather narrow band across the back, tail, and a patch starting as a narrow frontal band, involving the eyes, anterior half of cheek, chin, and throat, and ending as a rounded patch on the upper part of breast, black. Rest of body orange yellow. Two bands on the wing and the edges of the quills white.

Female without the black patch of the throat ; the upper parts generally yellowish green, browner on the back.

Length, 7.50 ; wing, 3.25.

Hab.—Valley of Lower Rio Grande, southward.

In this species the bill is slender towards the attenuated acute tip ; both mandibles considerably curved downwards. Third and fourth quills longest ; fifth scarcely shorter ; first less than the sixth. Tail rather long, cuneate, the feathers much graduated ; the outer an inch shorter than the inner.

The orange color varies in different parts of the body, being much redder on the head and breast ; the orange feathers are white towards the base, and pass through yellow to the tints at the tip. The tibia and under wing coverts are yellow. The tail feathers are black, though their extreme concealed bases are light yellow ; each one has a slight brownish white tip. The upper white band on the wing is formed by the lower series of secondary covert feathers, which are white to their bases ; the second band across the edges of the greater coverts is much narrower. The quills are entirely black. The black mark on the head has the eye in its posterior upper corner. The black band on the back is about an inch long. The bill is black, but plumbeous at the base of the lower mandible. The eye is said to be brown.

This species somewhat resembles *I. mesomelas*, (*Psarocolius mesomelas*, Wagler, Isis, 1829, 755) ; the latter, however, has a much stouter bill ; the colors clear yellow instead of orange, except on the head ; the wing coverts yellow, not black, and the wings without white ; the tail feathers chiefly yellow, not black, &c.

List of specimens.

Catal. No.	Sex & age.	Locality.	When collected	Whence obtained.	Orig. No.	Length.	Stretch of wings.	Wing.	Remarks.
4067	♂	Charco Escondido, Tamaulipas, Mex.	Mar. —, 1853	Lt. Couch	83	8.00	10.00	3.25	Eyes dark brown.
4066	♂	Tamaulipas	....do.........	......do.........	91	7.50	10.00	3.25	----------------
4068	○ ♂	......do.........	April	......do.........	159	7.75	9.75	3.00	----------------
4069	♀	......do.........	Mar. —, 1853	......do.........	90	7.25	10.00	3.25	----------------
9091	♂	Mexico	----------------	M. Verreaux....	......	......	....	......	----------------

ICTERUS SPURIUS, Bon.

Orchard Oriole.

Oriolus spurius, Linn. Syst. Nat. I, 1766, 162.—Gm. I, 1788, 389. (Very inaccurate description ; only identified by the references.)

Icterus spurius, Bon. Obs. on Nom. Wils. 1825, No. 44.—Aud. Orn. Biog. I, 1831, 221 : V, 485 ; pl. 42.—Ib. Birds Amer. IV, 1842, 46 ; pl. 219.

Oriolus varius, Gmelin, Syst. Nat. I, 1766, 390.

Turdus ater, Gm. Syst. 1788, I, 1788, 831.

Oriolus castaneus, Latham, Ind. Orn. I, 1790, 181. (Same citations as *O. varius,* Gm.)

Turdus jugularis, Latham, Ind. Orn. I, 1790, 361. (Same citations as *Turdus ater,* Gm.)

Yphantes solitaria, Vieill. ♂.

"*Pendulinus nigricollis,* Vieill. O.—*viridis,* Ib."

Oriolus mutatus, Wilson, Am. Orn. I, 1808, 64 ; pl. 4, f. 1—4.

Xanthornus affinis, Lawrence, Ann. N. Y. Lyc. N. H. V, May, 1851, 113. (Small race from Texas.)

Sp. Ch.—Bill slender, attenuated, considerably decurved ; tail moderately graduated.

Male.—Head and neck all round, wings, and interscapular region of back, with tail feathers, black. Rest of under parts, lower part of back to tail, and lesser upper wing coverts, with the lower one, brownish chestnut. A narrow line across the wing, and the extreme outer edges of quills, white.

Female.—Uniform greenish yellow beneath, olivaceous above, and browner in the middle of the back ; two white bands on the wings. Young male like the female, with a broad black patch from the bill to the upper part of the breast, this color extending along the base of the bill so as to involve the eye and all anterior to it to the base of the bill.

Length of Pennsylvania male specimens, 7.25 ; wing, 3.25.

Hab.—United States from the Atlantic to the High Central Plains, probably throughout Texas ; south to Guatemala.

In this species the bill is slender, attenuated, and a good deal decurved to the tip. The second and third quills are longest ; the first intermediate between the fourth and fifth. The tail is rather long ; the feathers moderately graduated, the greatest difference in length amounting to half an inch.

The black of the throat extends backwards as far as the bend of the wing, and ends as an obtuse angle. The tail feathers are entirely black, with dull whitish tips when not fully mature.

Specimens are found in all stages between the characters given above. When nearly mature, some yellowish feathers are found mixed in with the chestnut ones.

As in most birds with an extensive summer range, the specimens from southern limits are smaller than from northern. The difference is more strongly marked between skins from the lower Rio Grande of Texas and New York or Pennsylvania, and upon the former Mr. Lawrence has founded his *Xanthornus affinis.* The difference is not greater, however, than in nearly every other species of similar habits as to summer range. The table of measurements of species will illustrate the variations in size.

The pattern of coloration in this species resembles that of *I. baltimore,* but the orange red is replaced by dark chestnut ; there is less white on the wing, and the tail is entirely black. The bill is considerably slenderer and more attenuated and curved. The tail also is more graduated.

List of specimens.

Catal. No.	Sex and age.	Locality.	When collected.	Whence obtained.	Orig'l No.	Collected by—	Length.	Stretch of wings.	Wing.	Remarks.
4286	♂	Calcasieu, La.........	1854.........	G. Würdemann	.....	... .	.....	.....	.....	....
3813	♂	Eutaw, Ala...........	....	A. Winchell	.....	....	.....	.....	.....	....
1542	♂	Carlisle, Pa..........	May 17, 1844	S. F. Baird	.....	....	7.25	11.33	3.25	....
1626	○	......do...	July 9, 1844	......do...	.....	....	7.00	9.75	3.17	....
150	♀	......do...........	Sept. 7, 1840	......do....	.....	....	.....	.....	.....	....
1475	♂	......do...........	May 8, 1844	......do....	.....	... .	7.25	10.33	3.33	....
1437	♂	......do...........	May 3, 1844	......do....	.....	....	6.83	10.08	3.83	....
7012	♂	St. Louis, Mo	May 15, 1857	Lieut. Bryan.....	72	Wm. S. Wood	.....	.....	.....	....
5695	♂	East of Fort Riley, K. T.	June 14, 1856	Lieut. F. T. Bryan.	9	...do.....	.....	.....	.....	....
5351	♂	Farm Island, Mo.....	June 21, 1856	Lieut. Warren...	....	Dr. Hayden..	6.50	9.25	3.25	....
5348	♂	......do...........	May 29, 1856	... ..do...........	.....	......do....	6.50	9.75	2.25	....
5349	....	... ..do...........	June —, 1856	......do...........	.....	......do....	.....	.....	.....	....
5356	....	......do...........	May 29, 1856	......do...........	.....	......do....	6.75	9 50	3.25	Eyes dark brown...... ..
5352	♂	......do...........	May 30, 1856	......do...........	.....	......do....	6.75	9.50	3.00	....
5344	♂	......do...........	....	......do...........	.....	....do....	6.75	9.50	3.00	Iris dark brown...........
5353	....	......do...........	1856...........	......do...........	.....	......do....	6.75	9.50	.....	....
5345	♂	Fort Lookout, Neb....	June 15, 1856	......do...........	.....	......do....	5.50	9.50	3.00	Eyes brown.........
5347	♂	......do...........	June 21, 1856	......do...........	.....	......do....	7.25	9.50	3.00	...do.........
5346	♂	......do...........	...do...........	......do...........	.....	......do....	6.00	9.50	3.00	...do.........
5343	....	......do...........	June —, 1856	......do...........	.....	...do....	6.00	9.50	3 25	......do.........
5694	♂	Woods Creek	July 2, 1856	Lieut. Bryan.....	58	W. S. Wood.	5.50	6.50	.....	....
9339	♂	Loup Fork...........	Aug. 5, 1857	Lieut. Warren.....	.....	Dr. Hayden..	6.50	9.25	2 75	....
4957	....	Ft. Chadbourne, Texas .	....	Dr. Swift.......	.....	....	.....	.....	.....	....
6706	....	San Antonio, Texas....	July —, 1855	Lt. A. W. Whipple	.....	Dr. Kennerly.	.....	.....	.....	....
6711	....	......do...........	....	Lt. J. G. Parke...	.....	Dr. Heermann	.....	.....	.....	....
6707	♀	Western Texas	....	Col. Graham...	.....	J. H. Clark...	6.50	9.00	2.50	....
6708	♀	......do...........	....	......do...........	.....	...do...........	.....	.....	.....	....
6712	♂	......do...........	....	......do...........	.....	...do....	6.75	9.25	2.75	....
6710	....	......do...........	....	......do...........	.....	....	6.75	9.62	3.75	....
6709	....	Mimbres to Rio Grande.	....	Dr. T. C. Henry,.	.....	....	.....	.....	.....	....
6704	....	Texas...............	....	Capt. Pope......	.....	....	.....	.....	.....	....
5033	....	Pecos River...........	May 12, 1855	......do...........	78	....	6.75	9.50	3.00	Gums and feet yellow ; bill black.
8090	....	Guatemala...........	....	J. Gould........	.....	....	.....	.....	.....	Eyes dark brown.........

ICTERUS BALTIMORE, Daudin.

Baltimore Oriole; Golden Robin; Hang Nest.

Oriolus baltimore, LINN. Syst. Nat. I, 1766, 162.—WILSON, Am. Orn. I, 1808, 23 ; pl. i.—IB. VI, 1812 ; pl. liii.

" *Icterus baltimore*, DAUD."—AUD. Orn. Biog. I, 1831, 66 : V, 1839, 278 ; pl. 12 and 423.—IB. Birds Am. IV, 1842, 37 ; pl. 217.

Yphantes baltimore, VIEILLOT, Gal. des Ois. I, 1824, 124 ; pl. 87.

Psarocolius baltimore, WAGLER, Syst. Av. 1825, No. 26.

Le Baltimore, BUFF. Pl. Enl. 506, f. 1.

SP. CH.—Tail nearly even. Head all round and to middle of back, scapulars, wings, and upper surface of tail, black ; rest of under parts, rump, upper tail coverts, and lesser wing coverts, with terminal portion of tail feathers, (except two innermost,) orange red. Edges of wing quills, with a band across the tips of the greater coverts, white. Length, 7.50 inches ; wing, 3.75.

Hab.—From Atlantic coast to the High Central Plains, and in their borders, south to Guatemala.

The female is much less brilliant in color ; the black of the head and back generally replaced by brownish yellow, purer on the throat ; each feather with a black spot.

List of specimens.

Catal. No.	Sex and age.	Locality.	When collected.	Whence obtained.	Orig. No.	Collected by—	Length.	Stretch of wings.	Win .	Remarks.
1529	....	Carlisle, Pa..........	....	S. F. Baird........	......	....	......	......	......	....
877	♂	......do............	Nov. 28, 1842	......do...........	......	....	7.50	12.00	3.75	....
1443	♂	......do............	May 4, 1844	......do...........	......	....	7.92	12.50	4.00	....
1653	o	......do........	July 27, 1844	......do...........	......	....	7.50	12.00	3.58	....
7005	♂	St. Louis, Mo.....	May 8, 1857	Lieut. Bryan...	28	W. S. Wood.....	......	......	......	....
5355	♂	Farm island	May 31, 1856	Lt. G. K. Warren...	......	Dr. Hayden......	8.25	11.75	3.75	....
5356	♂	......do............	....	......do...........	......	......do..........	7.37	11.50	4.00	....
4745	♀	....	May 17	......do...........	......	......do..........	8.00	12.25	4.25	....
6715	♀	Fort Lookout..........	....	......do...........	......	......do..........	8.25	12.12	4.00	Iris very dark br'wn.
5357	....	Mouth Powder river....	....	......do......	......	......do..........	8.00	12.00	4.00	....
5358	♂	Near Powder river.....	....	......do...........	.. ....	......do..........	7.25	11.50	3.12	....
5359	♀	Yellowstone.	Aug. 4	......do...........	......	......do..........	......	......	......	....
5692	♂	East of Fort Riley	June 17, 1856	Lieut. F. T. Bryan.	23	W. S. Wood	......	......	......	....
5693	♂	Clear creek, K. T......	June 31, 1856	......do...........	50	......do..........	7.62	11.50	....	....
9342	♂	Elkhorn river...... ...	June 30, 1857	Lieut. Warren	......	Dr. Hayden	7.75	11.75	....	....
9341	♂	Loup fork, Platte	July 25, 1857	......do...........	......	......do..........	7.50	11.75	3.50	....
8307	....	Independence, Mo......	May 27, 1857	W. M. Magraw....	23	Dr. Cooper	7.75	11.75	4.00	Iris brown ....
6714	....	San Antonio, Texas....	....	Col. Graham......	......	J. H. Clark	7.62	11.50	....	....
8091	....	Guatemala	....	J. Gould...........	......	....	....	....	....	....

ICTERUS BULLOCKII, Bon.

Bullock's Oriole.

Xanthornus bullockii, Sw. Syn. Mex. Birds, Taylor's Phil. Mag. I, 1827, 436.
Agelaius bullockii, Rich. Rep. Brit. Assoc. 1837.
Icterus bullockii, Bon. List, 1838.—Aud. Orn. Biog. V, 1839, 9 ; pl. 388 and 433.—Ib. Birds Amer. IV, 1842, 43 ;
    pl. 218.—Newberry, Rep. P. R. R. VI, iv, 1857, 87.
Psarocolius auricollis, Maxim. Reise Nordam. I, 1839, 367. (Fort Pierre, Neb.)

Sp. Ch.—Tail very slightly graduated. Upper part of the head and neck, back, wings, two central tail feathers, line from
base of bill through the eye to the black of the nape, and a line from the base of the bill running to a point on the throat,
black. Under parts generally, sides of head and neck, forehead and line over the eye, rest of tail feathers, rump, and upper
tail coverts, yellow orange. A broad band on the wings, involving the greater and middle coverts, and the outer edges of the
quills, white. Young male with the black replaced by greenish yellow, that on the throat persistent ; female without this.
Length, about 7.50 inches ; wing, 3.80.

Hab.—High Central Plains to the Pacific ; rare on upper Missouri ; south into Mexico.

The subterminal portion of all the feathers in the black of the head above and back, (except
on the posterior portion of the latter) is yellow. The black on the throat is as wide as the base
of the bill, and extends along the sides of the bill to the black in the loral region. The rump
is olivaceous yellow, the tail feathers brighter yellow. All the tail feathers are yellow at the
base ; the exposed portions of the two inner are black ; the rest with a blackish tip, diminishing
from the fourth to first. The shafts of all are black above towards the base. The under surface
of the wings is orange yellow.

In the female and young male the upper surface is olivaceous yellow, browner on the middle
of the back. The black band through the eye is faintly indicated. Nearly mature males have
a much broader orange frontal band ; the top of head is much spotted with the same.

The bill and tail are shaped very much as in *I. baltimore*. It is a larger species, and is
readily distinguished by the yellow of the front and sides of the head and neck, with a black
line through the eye, instead of having the whole head and neck black ; lesser wing coverts
black, not yellow ; a much broader white band on the wing, &c.

The *Pendulinus abeillii* of Lesson, according to Bonaparte, differs from *bullockii* in having the flanks black; it is stated to occur in California.

List of specimens.

Catal. No.	Sex.	Locality.	When collected.	Whence obtained.	Orig. No.	Collected by—	Length.	Stretch of wings.	Wing.	Remarks.
5930	....	Fort Steilacoom, W. T.....	....	Dr. Cooper.......	......	....	7.25	12.00	......	....
6726	....	......do..................	June 5, 1855	......do.........	......	....	7.25	12.00	......	....
6728	♀	......do..................	June 6, 1855	......do.........	......	....	7.12	11.50	......	....
4379	♂	Fort Dalles, O. T..........	May 7, 1855	Dr. Geo. Suckley.	168	....	8.08	12.25	4.00	....
3900	......	California	....	Dr. Heermann ...	......	....	......	......	......	....
3901	♂	......do..................	....	......do.........	......	....	......	......	......	....
1253	......	......do..................	....	S. F. Baird	......	J. J. Audubon.......	......	......	......	....
1891	....	......do..................	....	......do.........	......	....	......	......	......	....
5525	♀	Petaluma, Cal...........	May 11, 1856	E. Samuels	815	....	......	......	......	....
5524	♂	......do..................	April —, 1856	......do.........	591	....	......	......	......	....
5523	♂	......do..................	....	......do.........	......	....	......	......	......	....
6724	......	Sacramento, Cal..........	....	Lt. Williamson ..	......	Dr. Heermann	......	......	......	....
2844	......	Rocky Mountains.........	....	S. F. Baird	......	J. K. Townsend.......	......	......	......	....
2843	♂	.... .do..................	....	......do.........	......	....	......	......	......	....
6727	....	Guadalupe cañon	1855.........	Major Emory	68	Dr. Kennerly.......	......	......	......	....
6725	....	Fort Thorn.............	....	D. T. C. Henry...	......	....	......	......	......	....
6723	....	Eagle Pass.............	....	Major Emory ..	......	A. Schott........	......	......	......	....
5354	♂	Farm Island, Neb..........	1856..........	G. K. Warren.....	......	Dr. Hayden	7.62	13.00	4.25	Iris brown.....
9092	♂	Mexico................	....	M. Verreaux	29891	....	......	......	......	....

The following *Icterinae*, not embraced in the preceding pages, are said, though probably without foundation, to occur in the United States.

1. *Xanthornus mexicanus*, (Brisson) VIGORS, Zool. of Blossom, 1839.   Pacific coast of (North?) America.

2. *Pendulinus abeillii*, LESSON, Rev. Zool. Bonap. Comptes Rendus, 1853, 834.   California. Said to differ from *Icterus bullockii* in black flanks, and to be the *Oriolus costototl* of Gmelin.

3. *Icterus californicus*, LAFRESNAYE.

  Pendulinus californianus, LESSON, Rev. Zool. VII, Dec. 1844, 436, California.—BONAP.
   Conspectus, 1850, 433.

4. *Icterus pustulatus*, LICHT. Bonaparte, Comptes Rendus, XXXVII, 1853, 835.   Notes Delattre, 12.

Sub–Family QUISCALINAE.

CH.—Bill rather attenuated, as long or longer than the head.   The culmen curved, the tip much bent down.   The cutting edges inflected so as to impart a somewhat tubular appearance to each mandible.   The commissure sinuated.   Tail longer than the wings, usually much graduated.   Legs longer than the head, fitted for walking.

The bill of the *Quiscalinae* is very different from that of the other *Icteridae*, and is readily recognized by the tendency to a rounding inward along the cutting edges, rendering the width in a cross section of the bill considerably less along the commissure than above or below.   The culmen is more curved than in the *Agelainae*.

The only genera in the United States are as follows :

SCOLECOPHAGUS.—Tail shorter than the wings ; nearly even.   Bill shorter than the head.

QUISCALUS.—Tail longer than the wings ; much graduated.   Bill as long as or longer than the head.

SCOLECOPHAGUS, Swainson.

Scolecophagus, SWAINSON, F. Bor. Am. II, 1831. Type *Oriolus ferrugineus*, Gmelin.

CH.—Bill shorter than the head, rather slender, the edges inflexed as in *Quiscalus*, which it otherwise greatly resembles ; the commissure sinuated. Culmen rounded, but not flattened. Tarsi longer than the middle toe. Tail even, or slightly rounded.

The above characteristics will readily distinguish the genus from its allies. The form is much like that of *Agelaius*. The bill, however, is more attenuated, the culmen curved and slightly sinuated. The bend at the base of the commissure is shorter. The culmen is angular at the base posterior to the nostrils, instead of being much flattened, and does not extend so far behind.

Comparative measurements.

Catal. No.	Species.	Locality.	Sex.	Length.	Stretch of wings.	Wing.	Tail.	Tarsus.	Middletoe.	Its claw alone.	Hind toe and claw.	Hind toe alone.	Bill above.	Along gape.	Specimen measured.
1322	Scolecophagus ferrugineus	Carlisle, Penn..	♂	8.60	....	4.62	4.03	1.24	1.11	0.25	0.80	0.34	0.78	0.94	Skin ....
[do.	.........do..............	.....do		9.32	14.75	4.72	......	......	......	......	......	......	......	......	Fresh....
5322	......do..............	Twenty miles below Sioux City.	♂	8.20	....	4.58	3.72	1.20	1.11	0.28	0.82	0.36	0.80	0.89	Skin ....
do.	.........do..............	.....do		9.12	15.25	4.25	......	......	......	......	......	......	......	......	Fresh....
1358	.........do..............	.....do	♀	8.10	....	4.26	3.65	1.16	1.10	0.28	0.74	0.40	0.78	0.92	Skin ....
do.	.........do..............	.....do		9.00	13.75	4 25	......	......	......	......	......	......	......	......	Fresh ...
8706	Scolecophagus cyanocephalus.	Fort Vancouver, W.T.	♂?	9.26	....	5.23	4.46	1.30	1.06	0.27	0.85	0.38	0.84	0.90	Skin.....
do.	.........do..............	.....do		9.75	16.25	......	......	......	......	......	......	......	......	......	Fresh ...
3915	.........do..............	California............	♀	8.64	....	4.68	3.90	1.22	1.06	0.27	0.82	0.38	0.70	0.80	Skin ....
10294	.........do..............	Pembina, Minn......		8.52	....	4.66	3.94	1.19	1.05	0.28	0.80	0.40	0.75	0.78	Skin ....

SCOLECOPHAGUS FERRUGINEUS, Swainson.

Rusty Blackbird.

Oriolus ferrugineus, GMELIN, Syst. Nat. I, 393, No. 43.—LATH. Ind. I, 1790, 176.
Gracula ferruginea, WILSON, Am. Orn. III, 1811, 41; pl. xxi; f. 3.
Quiscalus ferrugineus, BON. Obs. Wils. 1824, No. 46.—NUTTALL, Man. I, 1832, 199.—AUD. Orn. Biog. II, 1834, 315 :
 V, 1839, 483; pl. 147.—IB. Synopsis, 1839, 146.—IB. Birds Amer. IV, 1842, 65; pl. 222.
Scolecophagus ferrugineus, SWAINSON, F. Bor. Am. II, 1831, 286.—BON. List, 1838.
?? *Oriolus niger*, GMELIN, I, 1788, 393, No. 4, 5, (perhaps *Quiscalus*.)
Scolecophagus niger, BONAP. Consp. 1850, 423.—CABANIS, Mus. Hein. 1851, 195.
?? *Oriolus fuscus*, GMELIN, Syst. I, 1788, 393, No. 44, (perhaps *Molothrus*.)
Turdus hudsonius, GMELIN, Syst. Nat. I, 1788, 818.—LATH. Ind.
Turdus noveboracensis, GMELIN, I, 1788, 818.
Turdus labradorius, GMELIN, Syst. Nat. I, 1788, 832.—LATH. Ind. I, 1790, 342, (*labradorus*).
" *Pendulinus ater*, VIEILLOT, Nouv. Dict.''
Chalcophanes virescens, WAGLER, Syst. Av. (Appendix *Oriolus* 9).
? *Turdus* No. 22 from Severn river, Forster, Phil. Trans. LXII, 1772, 400.

SP. CH.—Bill slender ; shorter than the head ; about equal to the hind toe ; its height not quite two-fifths the total length. Wing nearly an inch longer than the tail ; second quill longest ; first a little shorter than the fourth. Tail slightly graduated ; the lateral feathers about a quarter of an inch shortest. General color black, with purple reflections ; the wings, under tail coverts, and hinder part of the belly, glossed with green. Female dull brown. Length 9.50 ; wing, 4.75 ; tail, 4.00.

Hab.—From Atlantic coast to the Missouri.

The female of this bird is of a dull plumbeous brown beneath, blacker above, the feathers faintly margined with brownish rusty; the wings and tail purer. In autumn both sexes have the black on the body, and on the edges of the wings more or less concealed (sometimes entirely so) by yellowish brown margins to the feathers; the shade lighter below. There is also a lighter superciliary stripe over the eye and a darker one through it.

The *Oriolus niger* of Gmelin is based upon the *Icterus niger* of Brisson, from Jamaica, and the *Black oriole* of Pennant, from North America. The latter two are probably distinct and possibly refer to *Quiscali*, but to different species; the one to *baritus*, the other to *versicolor;* possibly, however, to *Sc. ferrugineus.*

A specimen of this bird in the collection of the exploring expedition is labelled Columbia river, Oregon. This is the only one I have ever seen said to be from the Pacific coast.

Catal. No.	Sex.	Locality.	When collected.	Whence obtained.	Collected by—	Length.	Stretch of wings.	Wing.
1322	......	Carlisle, Penn...........	April —, 1844	S. F. Baird	....	9.33	14.75	4.75
1314	♂	......do...............	Mar. 28, 1844	......do.........	....	9.17	14.50	4.75
1369	♂	......do...............	April 17, 1844	......do.........	....	9.25	14.00	4.50
1358	♀	......do...............	April 13, 1844	......do.........	....	9.00	13.75	4.25
1356	♀	......do...............	......do......	......do.........	....	8.75	13.58	4.25
2081	♀	......do...............	April 8, 1845.	......do.........	....	9.08	14.00	4.33
5322	......	20 miles below Sioux City.	Oct. 28	Lieut. Warren	Dr. Hayden ..	9.12	15.25	4.25

SCOLECOPHAGUS CYANOCEPHALUS, Cab.

Brewer's Blackbird.

Psarocolius cyanocephalus, WAGLER, Isis, 1829, 758.
Scolecophagus cyanocephalus, CABANIS, Mus. Hein. 1851, 193.
Scolecophagus mexicanus, SWAINSON, Anim. in Men. 2¼ cent. 1838, 302.—BON. Conspectus, 1850, 423.—NEWBERRY,
    Zool. Cal. and Or. Route; Rep. P. R. R. Surv. VI, IV, 1857, 86.
Quiscalus breweri, AUD. Birds Amer. VII, 1843, 345; pl. 492.

SP. CH.—Bill stout, quiscaline, the commissure scarcely sinuated; shorter than the head and the hind toe; the height nearly half the length above. Wing nearly an inch longer than the tail; the second quill longest; the first about equal to the third. Tail rounded and moderately graduated; the lateral feathers about .35 of an inch shorter. General color of male black, with lustrous green reflections everywhere except on the head and neck, which are glossed with purplish violet. *Female* much duller, of a light brownish anteriorly; a very faint superciliary stripe. Length about 10 inches; wing, 5.30; tail, 4.40.

Hab.—High Central Plains to the Pacific; south to Mexico. Pembina, Minn.

There are considerable differences in the bills of different specimens of this bird. The culmen is sometimes much curved from the very base, sometimes quite straight; the size of the bill varies considerably. The third quill is sometimes longest, the first nearly equal to or shorter than the fourth. The graduation of the tail, too, differs by a quarter of an inch in specimens.

The females and immature males differ from the adult males in much the same points as *S. ferrugineus*, except that the "rusty" markings are less prominent. The differences generally between the two species are very appreciable. Thus, in *S. cyanocephalus*, the bill, though of the same length, is much higher and broader at the base, as well as much less linear in its upper outline; the point, too, is less decurved. The size is every way larger. The purplish gloss, which in *ferrugineus* is found on most of the body except the wings and tail, is here confined to the head and neck, the rest of the body being of a richly lustrous and strongly marked green, more distinct than that on the wings and tail of *ferrugineus*. In one specimen only, from Santa Rosalia, Mexico, is there a trace of purple on some of the wing and tail feathers.

List of specimens.

Catal. No.	Sex.	Locality.	When collected.	Whence obtained.	Orig'l No.	Collected by—	Length.	Stretch of wings.	Wing.	Remarks.
10296	.....	Pembina, Minn	Sept. 20, 1857	N. W. University.	......	R. Kennicott..	....	....	....	....
4754	♂	Mouth of Big Nemaha..	April 23, 1856	Lieut. Warren...	......	Dr. Hayden....	10.00	16.37	5.25	....
5320	♂	Fort Randall, on Mo....	Oct. 18, 1856	......do...........	......	....do.........	10.25	16.50	5.37	....
4753	......	Upper Missouri	....	......do...........	......	....do.........	9.25	14.87	5.25	....
4755	♂	.......do.............	....	......do..	......	....do.........	9.00	15.87	5.25	....
4756	......	.......do.............	....	......do..........	24	....do.........	....	....	....	....
5666	♂	Platte river	July 22, 1856	Lieut. Bryan	138	W. S. Wood...	....	....	....	....
8253	♂	Fort Laramie, Neb.....	Sept. —, 1857	W. M. Magraw...	157	Dr. Cooper....	....	....	....	....
8222	♀	.......do.............	Sept. 12, 1857	......do........ .	205	....do.........	9.25	14.50	....	Iris brown.............
8255	♀	.......do.............	....do......	......do........	......	....do.........	9.15	14.50	5.00	.........do.............
8254	♂	.... .do.............	....do......	......do........	517	....do.........	10.50	16.75	5.50	....
8256	♂	.......do.............	. ....do.....	.... do........	37	....do.........	....	....	....	Iris yellow, bill and feet black.
8212	♂	.......do.............	Sept. 8, 1857	......do........	194	....do.........	10.00	16.00	5.50	.........do.............
8257	♀	.......do.............	..... do.....	......do........	157	....do.........	....	....	....	....
8704	......	Fort Riley, K. T.......	....	Dr. Hammond...	.....	....	....	....	....	....
5006	......	Gaudaloupe bottom, Tex.	....	Capt. Pope	41	....	10.50	15.50	5.00	Iris yellow
5007	......	Devil's river, Texas....	April 29, 1855	......do........	......	....	.....	.... ..	....	....
8712	......	Eagle Pass, Texas	....	Maj. Emory	......	A. Schott......	....	....	....	....
8713	......	Santa Rosalia, Mexico..	Mar. —, 1853	Lieut. Couch	......	....	10.25	16.25	5.50	....
5005	......	Doña Ana, N. Mexico..	Nov. 10, 1855	Capt. Pope	156	....	9.50	16.00	5.50	....
8705	♀	Los Angeles, Cal......	....	Lt. Williamson..	......	Dr. Heermann..	....	....	....	....
4942	......	San José, Cal.........	....	A. J. Grayson....	......	....	....	....	....	....
8711	......	San Francisco, Cal.....	....	Lt. Williamson ..	......	Dr. Heermann..	....	....	....	....
8709	......	Presidio, Cal.........	....	Lt. Trowbridge..	......	....	....	....	....	....
5538	♂	Petaluma, Cal........	....	E. Samuels......	125	....	11.00	15.00	5.00	....
8710	♀	.......do.	Feb. —, 1856	......do........	173	....	5.66	12.54	4.54	....
5539	......	.......do.............	May 10, 1856	......do........	797	....	....	....	....	....
4381	♀	Fort Dalles, O. T......	May 9, 1855	Dr. Suckley	172	....	9.62	14.83	4.75	Iris hazel
4382	......	.......do.............	Dec. 29, 1854	......do........	148	....	9.50	15.50	5.25	Iris light yellow.........
8706	♂	Fort Vancouver, W. T..	Jan. 23, 1854	Gov. Stevens....	17	Dr. Cooper	9.75	16.25	....	....
8707	♀	.......do.	Jan. 20, 1854	......do........	18	....do.........	9.50	14.75	....	....
8708	♀	.......do.............	....do.....	......do.	18	....do.........	9.50	14.75	....	....

QUISCALUS, Vieillot.

Quiscalus, VIEILLOT, Analyse, 1816. (Gray.) Type *Gracula quiscala*, L.

CH.—Bill as long as the head, the culmen slightly curved, the gonys almost straight; the edges of the bill inflected and rounded; the commissure quite strongly sinuated. Outlines of tarsal scutellae well defined on the sides; wings shorter than the tail, sometimes much more so; tail long, the feathers conspicuously and decidedly graduated. Colors black.

The excessive graduation of the long tail, with the perfectly black color, at once distinguish this genus from any other in the United States. The species are best known by the comparative size and length of the tail, as shown in the following table of measurements.

June 28, 1858.

70 b

Comparative measurements of species.

Catal. No.	Species.	Locality.	Sex.	Length.	Stretch of wings.	Wing.	Tail.	Tarsus.	Middle toe.	Its claw alone.	Hind toe and claw.	Hind toe alone.	Bill above.	Along gape.	Specimen measured.
3948	Quiscalus macrourus...	Brownsville, Texas ..	♂	18.20	....	7.48	9.26	1.92	1.80	0.45	1.30	0.55	1.58	1.74	Skin ....
do.	......do.............	.... .do.............		18.00	21.50	7.50									Fresh ...
8088	......do.............	Mexico..............	♀?	16.00	....	6.96	8.10	2.03	1.88	0.48	1.44	0.62	1.60	1.76	Skin ....
3949	......do...........	Fort Brown, Texas ..	♀	12.80	....	5.68	6.32	1.54	1.59	0.47	1.13	0.56	1.26	1.46	Skin ....
do.	......do.............	......do.............		13.00	17.00	5 50									Fresh ...
4923	Quiscalus major	Amelia Island, Fla...	♂	14.10	....	6.94	7.34	1.98	1.82	0.46	1.34	0.59	1.52	1.64	Skin ....
do.	......do.............	......do.............		15 00	22.00	7.00									Fresh ...
2104	Quiscalus versicolor ...	Carlisle, Penn.	♂	11.10	....	5.70	5.72	1.34	1.30	0.37	0.98	0.46	1.24	1.36	Skin ....
do.	......do.............	......do.............		13.00	18.00	6.00									Fresh ...
1363	......do.............	......do.............	♂	11.40	....	5.60	5.54	1.46	1.32	0.34	1.00	0.48	1.24	1.31	Skin ....
1364	......do.............	......do.............	♀	10.04	....	4.96	4.86	1.28	1.14	0.30	0.88	0.42	1.12	1.22	Skin ....
6529	Quiscalus baritus......	Key Biscayne, Fla...	♂	10.40	... ...	5.08	5.24	1.38	1.27	0.38	0.98	0.45	1.35	1.48	Skin ....

QUISCALUS MACROURUS, Sw.

Great-tailed Grakle.

Quiscalus macrourus, SWAINSON, Anim. in Menag. 2¼ centen. 1838, 299, fig. 51, a.
Chalcophanes macrourus, CAB. Mus. Hein. 1851, 196.

SP. CH.—Bill longer than the head, edge slightly sinuated. Feathers of the crown short, close, and velvet-like. Tail very long, equaling the head and body, the lateral feathers 3½ inches the shortest. Wing considerably shorter than the tail; third quill longest; first longer than the fifth. General color a lustrous black; the head and neck, fore part of back, and under parts with a purple violet gloss; the rest of back, wings, and tail, including under coverts, glossed with green, the colors blending insensibly. Length 18 inches; wing, 7.50; tail, 9.30; bill above, 1.70.

Hab.—Valley of the lower Rio Grande of Texas, southward.

The graduation of tail in this species is very great, the distances between the tips of the outer tail feather and the next being 1.30 inches, and decreasing successively with the rest. There is something quite peculiar in the softness and closeness of the feathers on the head, which stand almost erect like the pile of velvet.

The female is much smaller and of a dark olive brown, lightest on the head and beneath. There is a strong tinge of brownish yellow in the throat; rather less of it on the side of the head, where there is a faint indication of a dusky streak behind the eye.

This species is somewhat like the *Quiscalus major* of the southern States, but is much larger; the tail especially is more highly developed, being nearly two inches longer than the wing instead of nearly the same size. The soft velvety feathers of the head are quite peculiar. The feet are of nearly the same size. The first primary is shorter in proportion. The color is quite different; the purple gloss extending further down the back, and the entire under parts being purple instead of green.

List of specimens.

Catal. No.	Sex.	Locality.	When collected.	Whence obtained.	Orig'l No.	Collected by—	Length.	Stretch of wings	Wing.	Remarks.
3948	♂	Brownsville, Tex....	Mar. 28,1853	Capt. Van Vliet......	23	....	18.00	21.50	7.50	Eyes yellow .
3949	♀	Ft. Brown, Tex......	..... do	....do.............	24	....	13.00	17.00	5.50	....
8553	......	Texas.............	....	Maj. Emory..........	......	A. Schott...............				
8551	......	Eagle Pass, Tex......	....	....do.............	.....	....do.............				
8552	......	......do........... ..	....	..... do......	.....	....do.............				
8088	......	Mexico..............	Sept. —,1836	John Gould.....	......	John Taylor...........				

QUISCALUS MAJOR, Vieill.

Boat-tailed Grakle; Jackdaw.

Gracula barita, WILSON, Index Am. Orn. VI, 1812, (not of Linnaeus.)
Gracula quiscala, ORD. J. A. N. Sc. I, 1818, 253, (not of Linnaeus.)
Quiscalus major, VIEILLOT, NOUV. Dict. XXVIII, 1819, 487.—BON. Am. Orn. I, 1825, 35 ; pl. iv.— IB. List, 1838.—
    IB. Consp. 1850, 424.—AUD. Orn. Biog. II, 1834, 504 : V, 1838, 480 ; pl. 187.—IB. Syn. 1839,
    146.—IB. Birds Amer. IV, 1842, 52 ; pl. 220.
Chalcophanes major, " TEMM." CABANIS, Mus. Hein. 1851, 196.

SP. CH.—Bill longer than the head. Feathers of the crown stiff and coarse. Tail moderate, about equal to the wing, much
graduated, the lateral feathers about 2.50 inches shortest. General color lustrous black ; the head, neck, and fore part of the
breast glossed with purple, passing insensibly on the rest of the body to green.

Length, about 15 inches ; wing, 7 ; tail, 7.25. Bill above 1.55.

Hab.—Southern Atlantic and Gulf coast. Mouth of Rio Grande, Texas.

A specimen from Brownsville, Texas, though associated there with *M. macrourus*, appears to
possess all the characters of *major*. The loral region and space around the eye are quite bare of
feathers.

List of specimens.

Catal. No.	Sex.	Locality.	When collected.	Whence obtained.	Orig. No.	Length.	Stretch of wings.	Wing.	Remarks.
1932	------	Southern U. S. ----	--------------	S. F. Baird -----	------	------	------	------	----------------
2381	♂	Savannah, Ga. -----	1845 --------	------do --------	------	------	------	------	----------------
4923	♂	Amelia island, Fla.	--------------	G. Wurdemann..	------	15.00	22.00	7.00	----------------
4044?	------	Brownsville, Tex. --	--------------	Lt. Couch ------	6	13.00	19.50	6.75	Iris yellow -----

QUISCALUS VERSICOLOR, Vieillot.

Crow Blackbird; Purple Grakle.

Gracula quiscala, LINN. Syst. Nat. I, 1766, 165.—GMELIN, I, 1788, 397.—LATHAM, Ind. I, 1790, 191.—WILSON,
    Am. Orn. III, 1811, 44 ; pl. xxi, f. 4.
Chalchophanes quiscalus, WAGLER, Syst. Av. 1827, (*Gracula*.)—CAB. Mus. Hein. 1851, 196.
? ? *Oriolus ludovicianus*, GMELIN, Syst. Nat. I, 1788, 387 ; albino var.
? ? *Oriolus niger*, GMELIN, Syst. Nat. I, 1788, 393.
? *Gracula purpurea*, BARTRAM, Travels, 1791, 290.
Quiscalus versicolor, VIEILLOT, Analyse? 1816.—IB. Nouv. Dict. XXVIII, 1819, 488.—IB. Gal. Ois. I, 171 ; pl.
    cviii.—BON. Obs. Wils. 1824, No. 45.—IB. Am. Orn. I, 1825, 45 ; pl. v.—IB. List, 1838.—
    IB. Conspectus, 1840, 424.—SW. F. Bor. Am. II, 1831, 485.—NUTTALL, Man. 1, 1832, 194.—
    AUD. Orn. Biog. I, 1831, 35 : V, 1838, 481 ; pl. vii.—IB. Syn. 1839, 146.—IB. Birds Amer.
    IV, 1842, 58 ; pl. 221.
Gracula barita, ORD, J. A. N. Sc. I, 1818, 253.
" *Quiscalus purpureus*, LICHT."
Quiscalus nitens, LICHT. Verz. 1823, No. 164.
Quiscalus purpuratus, SWAINSON, Anim. in Menag. 1838, No. 55.
Purple Grakle, PENNANT, Arctic Zool. II.

SP. CH.—Bill above, about as long as the head, more than twice as long as high ; the commissure moderately sinuated and
considerably decurved at tip. Tail a little shorter than the wing, much graduated, the lateral feathers 1.10 inches shorter.
Third quill longest ; first between fourth and fifth. Head and neck all round well defined steel blue ; the rest of the body with

varied reflections of bronze, golden, green, copper, and purple, the latter most conspicuous on the tail, the tail coverts, and wings. The edges of primaries and of tail greenish. Female similar, but smaller and duller, with, perhaps, more green on the head.

Length, 13 inches ; wings, 6 ; tail, 5.80 ; bill above, 1.25.

Hab.—From Atlantic to the High Central Plains.

In No. 2104, as in other Pennsylvania specimens, there is a strong shade of violet just above the steel blue on the feathers of the neck. Specimens from the west have a more brassy shade on the blue of the neck, and the back is of a nearly uniform shade of greenish bronze. These differences appear to be nearly constant with the two localities. One specimen from Carlisle has the steel blue on the head replaced, in a great measure, by purple and violet, owing to the extension of this latter color to the tips of the feathers. It is probably to a specimen of this variety that Swainson applied the name of *Quiscalus purpuratus.*

In a series of about thirty specimens there are two males, the bills of which are much shorter than in the majority, measuring barely over an inch, and shorter than the head, (Nos. 6558, 4763.) I find a somewhat similar condition in a specimen from Carlisle, (833,) and as the difference is unaccompanied by any other tangible character, I see no ground for specific distinction.

The young of the year are throughout of a dull brown.

List of specimens.

Catal. No.	Sex.	Locality.	When collected.	Whence obtained.	Orig'l No.	Collected by—	Length.	Stretch of wings.	Wing.
2104	♂	Carlisle, Pa....................	April 12, 1845	S. F. Baird............		....	13.00	18.00	6.00
1363	♂	......do........................	April 16, 1844	......do....		....	12.75	18.00	5.65
1364	♀	......do........	......do....	......do....		....	....	....	....
833	....	......do........	Oct. 24, 1842	......do....		....	11.40	16.00	5.00
7581	.....	Washington, D. C	1857........	W. Hutton		....	....	....	....
4432	......	Quasquiton, Iowa.............		E. C. Bidwell			....	....	....
6944	..	Red river, H. B. T.............		D. Gunn............			....	....	....
4761	♂	Big Nemaha.............	April 23, 1856	Lieut. Warren..............		Dr. Hayden..............	12.75	18.12	5.75
4762	♂	Bald Island, Missouri river.....	April 25, 1856	......do....	39	......do....	12.50	17.12	....
4766	♀	......do...... ......do	......do......	......do....		......do....	11.12	16.00	5.25
4758	♂	......do...... ......do	......do......	......do....		......do....	12.25	17.25	....
4760	♂	......do...... ......do	April —, 1856	......do....	36	......do....	....	....	....
4767	......	......do...... ......do	April —, 1856	......do....		......do....	11.50	16.50	5.25
4513	......	Cedar Island.............		Col. Vaughan......		......do....	....	....	....
8312	♂	Independence	May 27, 1857	Wm. M. Magraw.........	29	Dr. Cooper	12.50	18.00	5.75
6558	......	Fort Riley, K. T................		Dr. W. A. Hammond ..,...			......	......	....
5666	♂	Little Blue river, K. T	July 4, 1846	Lieut. Bryan..............	68	W. S. Wood	....	....	....
5665	♀	Jenny Cr. of Republican	July 2, 1856	......do..............		......do....	....	....	....

QUISCALUS BARITUS, Vieillot.

Gracula barita, LINN. Syst. Nat. I, 1766, 165, (based on *Icterus niger,* Br)—GMELIN, I, 1788, 396.—LATH. Ind. I, 1790, 191.

Quiscalus baritus, VIEILLOT, Nouv. Dict. XXVIII, 1819, 487.—D'ORB. De la Sagra Cuba, Aves, 95.

Chalcophanes baritus, WAGLER, Systema Avium, 1827, Gracula Expos. No. 4.—CABANIS, Mus. Hein. 1851, 197.

? *Quiscalus crassirostris,* SWAINSON, Anim. in Menag. 1838, 355.—GOSSE, Birds Jamaica, 1847, 217.

SP. CH.—Bill about three times as long as high, much longer than the head or the tarsus ; the commissure scarcely sinuated ; the tip lengthened and decurved. Tail about as long as the wing, considerably graduated ; the lateral feathers about .85 of an inch shorter. The second quill longest ; first shorter than the fourth. The head steel blue, passing on the neck into decided purplish ; the body, wings, and tail bronze green, with a purplish violet shade on the tertials and rump.

Length, 10.60 ; wing, 5 ; tail, 5 ; bill above, 1.40 ; tarsus, 1.40.

Hab.—Florida coast and West Indies.

This species, now for the first time introduced into the fauna of the United States, from specimens collected at Key Biscayne by Mr. Wurdemann, in of April 1857 and '58, is the smallest ofthe genus within our limits. The wing and tail each are about an inch shorter than in *Q. versicolor*. The bill, however, is much longer and more slender, and the tip considerably more produced and decurved. The feet are stouter and much coarser, the pads of the toes very scabrous as if to assist in holding slippery substances, a feature scarcely seen in *versicolor*.

The second and third quills are longest ; the first a little shorter only than the fourth.

The colors are quite dissimilar to those of *versicolor*, a purplish violet predominating on the neck. The green of the back and belly is more decided as well as duller and darker than even in western specimens of *versicolor*. The gloss on the tail and most of the wings is green, not purplish violet. The general style of coloration is most like that of *Quiscalus major*, although the bird is much smaller.

This species does not appear to be the *Quiscalus baritus* of the earlier authors, which is stated by Latham to be 13 inches long, the bill 1½ inches, consequently much larger. The colors, too, are chiefly purple, not green. *Q. lugubris* is smaller, the bill especially ; the lustre purple, not green. *Q. minor* of Cabanis is smaller still, with a violet blue lustre. The *Quiscalus baritus* of Vieillot comes nearer to it in size of body and bill, but is also said to have the body purplish instead of greenish, the wing coverts greenish instead of steel blue.

It is possible that the species may really be the *Q. crassirostris* of Swainson, (2¼ cent. 355,) but I cannot identify it from his description. The size is considerably smaller, while the bill is larger than in the Florida bird.

The female is smaller and rather duller in plumage.

List of specimens.

Catal. No.	Sex.	Locality.	When collected.	Whence obtained.	Collected by—	Length.	Stretch of wings.	Wings.	Remarks.
6529	♂	Key Biscayne, Fla.....	April 8,1857	G. Wurdemann	G. Wurdemann....	....	....	....	....
10335	♂	Cape Florida	Mar. 31,1858	......do	....	11.50	16.00	5.50	Bill and feet black ; iris light yellow......... ....
10336	......	......do	April 15,1858	......do	....	11.50	15.25	5.00	....
10337	♂	......do	..... do	......do	....	12.00	15.50	5.00	....
10340	♂	......do	April 22,1858	......do	....	12.00	16.50	5.12	....
10341	♂	......do	April 9,1858	......do	....	11.06	15.25	5 25	....
10342	♂	......do	May 18,1858	......do	....	11.75	16.25	5.00	....
10339	♀	......do	Mar. 31,1858	......do	....	10.25	13.75	4.75	....
10338	♀	......do	April 22,1858	......do	....	11.12	14.50	4.75	....

Family CORVIDAE.

Cн.—Primaries ten ; the first short, generally about half as long as the second (or a little more) ; the outer four sinuated on the inner edge. The nasal fossae and nostrils usually more or less concealed by narrow stiffened bristles, (or bristly feathers,) with short appressed lateral branches extending to the very tip, all directed forwards. Tarsi scutellate anteriorly, the sides undivided (except sometimes below) and separated from the anterior plates by a narrow naked strip, sometimes filled up with small scales. Basal joint of middle toe united about equally to the lateral, generally for about half the length. Bill generally notched.

The preceding characters distinguish the family of crows quite markedly from all others. In some respects there is a resemblance to the *Paridae* or Titmice, especially among the garruline birds ; the nature of this relationship will hereafter be adverted to. The features of the bristles of the bill, and the separation of the lateral and anterior scales by a narrow interval, are worthy of particular attention. The commissure is without the obtusely angular bend near the base, seen in the *Icteridae*.

There are some genera of *Corvidae* with the nostrils not covered by bristly feathers, such as *Psilorhinus*, *Gymnorhinus*, *Gymnokitta*, &c.

There are two sub-families of *Corvidae* represented in America, one embracing the true crows, the other the jays. They pass very insensibly into each other, and it is difficult to mark the dividing line. We may, perhaps, restrict the *Corvinae* to such forms as have a long bill, equal to the head ; the tail short, and nearly even ; the wings long and pointed, considerably longer than the tail, the tip formed by the third, fourth, and fifth quills. The *Garrulinae* are birds of smaller size, shorter wings, which do not exceed the graduated tail, and are sometimes much shorter ; the tip of the wing formed by the fourth, fifth, and sixth quills. Where *Gymnokitta* should come is a little uncertain, but probably among the true crows.

In most genera of *Corvidae* the inner lateral claw is a little larger than the outer, and projects beyond it ; in the true crows they reach about to the same point ; generally the lateral claws extend as far as the base of the middle one ; the hinder is longer.

The row of small scales is usually present on both sides of the tarsi in the *Corvinae*, but in the jays is generally restricted to the inner face.

Sub-Family CORVINAE.

Cн.—Wings long and pointed ; longer than the tail, and, when closed, reaching nearly to its tip, extending far beyond the under tail coverts ; the third, fourth, and fifth quills forming the tip of the wing.

The character given by Swainson of lateral toes equal in *Corvinae* and unequal in *Garrulinae*, is subject to much uncertainty of determination. The features mentioned above, if not defining a natural sub-family, at least apply well to three genera of North American *Corvidae*. The following diagnosis may serve to distinguish them.

A. Nostrils large, covered by bristly feathers ; wings reaching the tip of the rounded tail.

  CORVUS.—Color throughout black. Bill thickened ; culmen very much curved. Bristly feathers at base of bill half as long as culmen.

  PICICORVUS.—Color, grayish. Wnigs and tail above, black; lateral feathers white. Bill slender, attenuated, decurved. Bristly feathers at base of bill one-fourth the culmen.

B. Nostrils small, completely exposed ; wings reaching to the posterior fourth of the nearly even tail.

  GYMNOKITTA.—Color, nearly uniform dull blue.

CORVUS, Linnaeus.

Corvus, LINNAEUS, Syst. Nat. 1735. Type *Corvus corax*, L.

CH.—The nasal feathers lengthened, reaching to or beyond the middle of the bill. Nostrils large, circular, overhung behind by membrane, the edges rounded elsewhere. Rictus without bristles. Bill nearly as long as the tarsus, very stout ; much higher than broad at the base ; culmen much arched. Wings reaching to or nearly to the tip of the tail. Tarsi longer than the middle toe, with a series of small scales on the middle of each side separating the anterior scutellate portion from the posterior continuous plates. Side of the head occasionally with nearly naked patches. Tail graduated or rounded ; the outer four primaries sinuated internally.

The true crows are readily distinguished from the other *Corvidae* by the characters assigned above, the *Garruline* forms, with long wings, being distinguishable by other characters. The feathers at the base of the bill completely conceal the nostrils, and extend over the basal half of the bill, or even more. The lateral toes are equal, and reach nearly to the base of the middle claw ; the hind toe a little further. The hind claw is a little shorter than its digit, but larger than the middle anterior claw. The lower parts of the postero-lateral plates of the tarsus exhibits a few transverse scutellate divisions.

The determination of the species of crows is a matter of much uncertainty, owing to the uniformity of their plumage, and the fact that it is difficult to find them with the feathers all fully developed at the same time. Nearly one half of all the specimens in the collection before me have some of the quills only partly grown out. There also appears to be much variation in size with age and with locality, as well as in proportions, and I am inclined to think that, contrary to what has been observed to be the case in other families, the *Corvidae* of the same species in southern localities are larger than those from points further north. Should this be substantiated it may tend materially to reduce the number of North American species. Thus the *Corvus cacalotl* may be only a large southern *carnivorus*, the *caurinus* a northern, and var. *floridanus* a southern *americanus*. Four species are certainly permanently distinct : *C. carnivorus*, *C. cryptoleucus*, *C. americanus*, and *C. ossifragus*, whatever be the fate of the others.

The following diagnosis may serve to distinguish the American crows from each other.

A. RAVENS.—Feathers of the chin and throat stiffened, elongated, narrow, lanceolate, and with their outlines very distinct.

Length about 24.50 inches ; wing about 17 ; tail, 10. Outer tail feathers about 1.60 to 1.90 inches shorter than the central one ....*C. carnivorus.*

Length about 24 inches ; wing near 18 ; tail, 10.50. Outer tail feather about 2.30 inches shorter than the central..*C. cacalotl.*

Length about 21 inches ; wing, 14 ; tail, 8.50. Outer tail feather about 1.25 inches shorter than the middle one. Feathers of the neck and breast pure snowy white at the base..*C. cryptoleucus.*

B. CROWS.—Feathers of the chin and throat short, soft, broad, obtuse, and with the webs blended.

Middle toe and claw rather shorter than the tarsus measured from the beginning of scutellae. Inner lateral claw reaching to the base of the middle. Black, with violet reflection on the belly. Length, 19.20 inches ; wing, 13 to 13.50 ; tail, 8 inches.

C. americanus.

Similar to the preceding, but smaller. Length, 16 to 17 inches ; wing, 11 to 11.50 ; tail about 8 inches...*C. caurinus.*

About the size of *C. americanus* of the north ; the tarsus much longer ; bill larger.

C. var. *floridanus.*

Middle toe and claw decidedly longer than tarsus measured from the beginning of the scutellae. Inner lateral claw not reaching to the base of the middle. Black, with greenish reflection on the belly. Length 14 to 15 inches ; wing, 10.50 ; tail, less than 7 inches...*C. ossifragus.*

CORVUS CARNIVORUS, Bartram.

American Raven.

Corvus carnivorus, BARTRAM, Travels in E. Florida, 1793, 290
Corvus corax, WILSON, Am. Orn. IX, 1825, 136 ; pl. lxxv, f. 3.—BONAP. Obs. Wils. 1825, No. 36.—IB. Syn. 1828, 56.—DOUGHTY, Cab. N. H. I, 1830, 270 ; pl. xxiv.—RICH. F. B. Am. II, 1831, 290.—
   NUTTALL, Man. I, 1832, 202.—AUD. Orn. Biog. II, 1834, 476 ; pl. 101.—IB. Syn. 1839, 150.—
   IB. Birds Amer, IV, 1842, 78 ; pl. 224.
Corvus cacalotl, "WAGLER," ? BONAP. Pr. Zool. Soc. 1837, 115. (Perhaps true *cacalotl*.)—IB. List, 1838. Probably
   not of Wagler.—IB. Conspectus, 1850, 387.—MAXIMILIAN, Reise innere Nord Amer. II, 1841,
   289. Does not consider it different from European.—NEWBERRY, P. R. R. Rep. VI, IV, 1857, 82.
Corvus lugubris, AGASSIZ, Pr. Bost. Soc. N. H. II, Dec. 1846, 188.

SP. CH.—Fourth quill longest ; third and fifth about equal ; second between fifth and sixth ; first nearly equal to the eighth. Length, about 24 or 25 inches ; extent, 50 to 51 ; wing, about 17 ; tail, 10. Tail moderately graduated ; the outer about 1.60 to 1.90 of an inch less than the middle. Entirely glossy black, with violet reflections.

Hab.—Entire continent of North America. Rare east of the Mississippi.

In this species the feathers of the head above and body are compact and blended ; those of the back of the neck are very smooth and even, but do not show the outlines of each separately as elsewhere. On the chin and throat the feathers are elongated and lanceolate, each one more or less pendent or free, with the outlines distinct to near the base. The bill is very long, (3 inches,) and considerably curved, the upper mandible extending considerably over the upper at the end.

The feet appear very short and stout ; the tarsi with but seven scutellae ; rather longer than the middle toe and claw ; the lateral claws about equal, and extending to a little beyond the base of the middle claw. The fourth quill is longest ; the third about equal to the fifth ; the second considerably longer than the sixth ; the first about equal to the eighth primary. The distances in inches from the end of the longest primary to the tips of the others are as follows :

		1st.	2d.	3d.	4th.	5th.	6th.	7th.	8th.	9th.
5186	Upper Missouri	5.65	1.60	.25	--------	.25	2.80	4.35	5.45	6.40
5865	Riley	5.30	1.50	.25	--------	.29	2.30	3.85	5.00	5.70

The tail is quite considerably graduated, the ends of all the feathers being visible from below. The outer is about 1.66 inches shorter than the inner, in one specimen, (5865,) in another, it is 1.90, (5186.)

The color is everywhere lustrous black, dullest on the belly and top of the head. There is generally a strong violet reflection on the lustrous feathers, more greenish on the outer primaries.

In the series before me I find considerable variation in size and proportions, even in specimens from adjacent localities. Thus No. 5865, from Fort Riley, has the bill 1.08 inches high or deep, while 5186, from the upper Missouri, has it only .97 of an inch. The amount of graduation in the tail varies from 1.60 to 1.90 inches.

A male bird, 5543, from Petaluma, California, compared with 5186, from Fort Randall, has a shorter wing, (one inch,) the first quill a little longer (equal to instead of a little shorter than the eighth.) In 5185, from the upper Missouri, however, the first quill is nearly a quarter of an inch longer than the eighth; 6857, again, from Utah, has the first quill but little shorter than the seventh. In 4563, from Jamacha Ranch, California, the first quill is equal to the seventh. In fact, very few specimens exhibit precisely the same proportions of the quills.

The southern specimens, upon the whole, appear smaller than northern, as will be seen by the table of measurements.

No. 6856, from Steilacoom, has a curious attachment to the chin in the form of a curved horn, about an inch long, pendent from the middle of the chin between the rami of the maxilla, and about 1¾ inches from its point.

As a general thing the thickness of the bill varies considerably; the stoutest before me is from Fort Riley. Sometimes it is quite slender, especially in specimens from Oregon, where the upper mandible is more decurved, and its inferior edge much more concave than usual. This feature, however, is not seen in all, some being like the average of eastern specimens. I find it impossible to detect any tangible differences between the Pacific coast series and those from the Missouri, though it should be remarked that no comparisons are made with any from the Atlantic States, owing to the want of specimens, and that it is quite possible that the latter may be entirely distinct.[1]

In the next article I have separated a raven from Bill Williams' Fork of the Colorado of the west on account of its longer wings and more graduated tail. I am not very decided in the opinion that this is really distinct, and wait for further material to settle the question.

In the accompanying table of measurements of the three ravens here described are columns numbered, successively, one to eight, and showing the progression of size of the different quills. Where two are in the same column it indicates that they are about equal. Thus No. 5185 has the third and fourth quills equal and longest, then, successively, come the fifth, second, sixth, seventh, first, and eighth. The second is thus shorter than the fifth, but longer than the sixth; the first shorter than the seventh, but longer than the eighth. The measurements of tarsus and middle toe cannot be regarded as very precise, the stiffness of the dried leg and the shortness of the basal joint of the toe, with its large overlapping scales rendering it very difficult to say where the tarsus ends and the toe begins.

According to Prince Maximilian the only difference discernable to him between the European and American ravens is in the more slender bill of the latter. He finds the size, proportions, notes, and habits quite the same.

I have not at hand specimens of the European raven for the purpose of making a critical comparison with our own, but most recent authors agree in considering them distinct, although Mr. Audubon maintained the contrary opinion.

Bonaparte (though possibly with a Guatemala skin before him) states that in *cacalotl* the first quill is shorter than the seventh, the second and sixth equal, the third shorter than the

[1] Since writing the preceding remarks I have had the opportunity of examining a skin of a raven from the coast of New Jersey, belonging to Mr. Lawrence. This is not in high plumage, the feathers without much lustre, and the indications generally are that it is a young bird just attaining maturity. Under the circumstances a fair comparison cannot readily be made. The first primary appears to be longer in proportion to the others; the primaries generally broader, and more acutely pointed at the end.

June 28, 1858.

Comparative measurements of species.

Original number.	Species.	Locality.	Sex.	Length.	Stretch of wings.	Wing.	Tail.	Tarsus.	Middle toe.	Its claw alone.	Bill along curve.	In straight line.	Gape.	Height at base.	1	2	3	4	5	6	7	8	Specimens measured.
5185	Corvus carnivorus.	Egg Harbor, N. J.		24.30		16.00	10.30	2.50	2.39	0.76	3.05	2.70	2.92	1.06	4	3,5	2	6	7	1	8	8	Dry
do.	......do......	L'eau qui Court, Neb.	♂	24.00		16.69	10.60	2.66	2.60	0.83	3.00	2.78	3.00	1.02	3,4	5	2	6	7	1	8	9	Dry
10259	......do......	......do......		24.00	56.00	17.00	9.75	2.34	2.34	0.79	3.00	2.70	3.13	1.01	4	3,5	2	6	7	1	8	9	Fresh
5786	......do......	Ft. Steilacoom, W.T.	♂	23.80		15.80	10.94	2.55	2.35	0.72	2.82	2.66	2.97	0.99	4	3,5	2	6	7	1,8		9	Dry
do.	......do......	Ft. Randall.		24.65	51.50	16.90																	Fresh
do.	......do......	......do......		25.50		17.50																	Fresh
6857	......do......	San Rafael, Utah		22.94		16.50	9.76	2.57	2.29	0.66	2.76	2.45	2.73	0.96	4	3,5	2	6	7	1	9	9	Dry
5865	......do......	Ft. Riley, K.T.		24.00		16.54	10.16	2.40	2.38	0.73	2.74	2.62	2.90	1.10	4	3,5	2	6	7	8,1	9	9	Dry
10298	......do......	Espia, Mex.		22.50		16.46	9.70	2.54	2.40	0.72	2.54	2.34	2.66	0.99	4	3,5	2	6	7	8,1	9	9	Dry
do.	......do......	......do......		22.00	46.50	16.50	9.55	2.50	2.24	0.71	2.40	2.36	2.60	0.90	4	3,5	2	6	7,1	8	8	9	Fresh
4563	......do......	California.		22.30		16.10	10.36	2.66	2.44	0.72	2.75	2.52	2.70	1.10	4	3,5	2	6	7	1,8	9	9	Dry
5543	......do......	Petaluma, Cal.		24.00		15.90	9.08	2.61	2.14	0.64	2.44	2.38	2.55	0.90	3	4,5	2	6	7	1,8	9	9	Dry
9083	......do......	Mexico.		21.40		15.46	10.10	2.65	2.22	0.68	2.72	2.50	2.83	0.90	3,4	5	2	6	7	1	8	8	Dry
6886	......do......	Ft. Tejon.	♂	23.94		16.30	10.06	2.60	2.34	0.82	2.78	2.58	2.90	1.07	4	3,5	2	6	7	1	8	9	Dry
do.	......do......	Ft. Steilacoom.		24.00		16.10	9.06	2.56	2.33	0.68	2.50	2.39	2.60	0.91	4	3,5	2	6	7	1	8	9	Dry
do.	......do......	California, (G. N. L.)		23.84		15.50	10.50	2.70	2.36	0.82	3.30	2.92	3.10	1.16	4	3,5	2	6	7	.	8	9	Dry
6855	Corvus nobilis?	Texas.	♀	24.68		18.50	10.50	2.44	2.50	0.85	2.80	2.70	2.87	1.00	4	3,5	2	6	7	1	8	9	Dry
10397	Corvus cacaloti?..	Bill Williams' Fk., N. M.		24.50		18.00	10.16	2.53	2.19	0.80	2.62	2.47	2.65	0.94	3	4	2	5	6	1,8	7	8	Dry
10300	......do......	......do......		22.16		15.80	8.10	2.46	2.17	0.64	2.34	2.30	2.48	0.87	4	3,5	2	6	7	1	8	9	Dry
4118	Corvus cryptoleucus	Janos, Mex.	♀	20.60		14.38	8.40	2.27	2.06	0.65	1.91	1.87	2.05	0.88	4	3,5	2	6	7	1	8	9	Dry
do.	......do......	Charco Escondido, Mex.		17.90		13.00																	Fresh
do.	......do......	......do......		18.75	33.00	13.50	8.23	2.19	1.94	0.65	1.94	1.92	2.08	0.78	4	3,5	2	6	7	1	8	9	Fresh
4993	......do......	Pecos river, Tex.		19.40		13.50																	Dry
do.	......do......	......do......		19.00	36.50	13.00																	Fresh

* This wing was probably defective.

fifth, the fourth longest, the second much shorter than the fourth, which is longer than the third and fifth. In the European bird the second quill is longer than the fourth, the third longest of all.

The first distinctive name for the common North American raven seems to be that of Bartram. The *C. cacalotl* of Wagler, from Mexico, is probably a different species, as described further on. Prof. Agassiz named our bird *C. lugubris* in 1846.

List of specimens.

Catal. No.	Sex.	Locality.	When collected.	Whence obtained.	Orig. No.	Collected by—	Length.	Stretch of wings.	Wing.	Remarks.
		Great Egg Harbor, N. J.		G. N. Lawrence...						
5865	......	Fort Riley, K. T.......	1857	Dr. W. A. Hammond						
5186	♂	Fort Randall, K. T.....	Oct. 18, 1856	Lieut. Warren		Dr. Hayden......	25.50	51.50	17.50	....
4546	♀	Head of Little Mo......	Oct. 18, 1855	......do...........						1ˢ primary, not grown out.
5787	♂	Fort Pierre, Neb.......	Oct. 5, 1856	......do...........		Dr. Hayden......	25.50	50.00	17.50	....do. ....do....
5785	♂	L'eau qui Court, Neb..	Oct. 20, 1856	......do...		......do..........	24.00	50.00	17.00	....
8213	......	Ft. Laramie......	Sept. 13, 1857	W. M. Magraw ...		....	25.00	46.00	16.25	Iris brown ....
10296	......	St. Mary's, Rocky mts..	Oct. 15, 1853	Gov. Stevens......		Dr. Suckley......				1ˢ primary not grown out.
6857	......	San Rafael, Utah	....	Capt. Beckwith...	29	Mr. Kreuzfeldt...				....
0	.. ...	Fort Steilacoom	Mar. 20, 1856	Dr. G. Suckley	305					With horn on chin...
6856	.. ...	......do...............	April —, 1854	......do...........	51	....				....
5543	♂	Petaluma, Cal	....	E. Samuels	299					....
4563	......	Jamacha Ranch, Cal...	....	Maj. Emory	9	A. Schott........				....
10298	♂	Espia, Sonora..........	....	......do...........	51	Dr. Kennerly....	22.00	46.50	16.50	Eyes black ... .
9083?	.....	Mexico.............	....	J. Verreaux..... ...	17212					....

CORVUS CACALOTL, Wagler.

Colorado Raven.

?*Corvus cacalotl*, WAGLER, Isis, 1831, 527, Mexico.

SP. CH.—Wing formula as in the other species. Length about 25 inches; wing, 18; tail, 10.50. Tail much graduated; outer feather about 2.30 inches shorter than the middle. Color glossy black, with violet reflections. Tarsus rather shorter than the middle toe and claw?

Hab.—Colorado river of California, (southward?)

In this beautiful raven, which is very similar to the common species (the bill very much so), the fourth quill is longest, then the third, fifth, second, sixth, and seventh. The first and eighth are about equal. The distances from the tip of the longest quill to that of the others is as follows:

	1st.	2d.	3d.	4th.	5th.	6th.	7th.	8th.	9th.
No. 6855, Camp 115..............	5.30	1.30	.15	0.	.20	2.20	4.40	5.60	6.50
No. 10297, Camp 110	4.76	1.26	0.	.50	3.80	4.20	5.10	6.	--------

The tail is rather long, and the feathers more graduated than in the other species, obtusely acuminated, or mucronate, the outer 2.26 inches shorter than the middle. They are also rather broader than in the other species.

The feet are short and stout; the tarsus a little longer than the middle toe and claw; the lateral claw reaching to the base of the middle one.

A second specimen of this species is a good deal smaller and has the third quill longest. This I am, however, inclined to consider a monstrosity, as I can find but eight primaries, the fourth, at least, probably wanting. In this skin the outer tail feather is 2.30 inches shorter than the middle.

Number 10295, from the Colorado desert, I am inclined to consider the same, although the very great amount of graduation in the tail is owing partly to the fact that the feathers have not fully grown out. The tail feathers are very broad; the inner ones fully two inches wide.

In comparing a skin of this species (No. 6855) with a typical one of *C. carnivorus* from Fort Randall, 5186, almost no difference is appreciable in the bill; the wing is a little longer, with much the same proportion of quills, the first intermediate between the seventh and eighth, instead of equal to the seventh, (a proportion rather peculiar to 5186.) The tail is much more graduated, the difference amounting to near half an inch. The colors of the two, as far as I can judge, are precisely the same. It is, perhaps, a question, whether it be really different from the eastern bird, but as the wings are longer, the tarsi shorter, and the tail rather more graduated, I shall, for the present, separate them.

In looking out for a name to give this more southern species, if really distinct, I find that of *Corvus cacalotl*, Wagler,[1] to answer best. This is described as being $25\frac{1}{2}$ inches long; the wing, 17; the tail, nearly 10; the tarsus, $2\frac{1}{2}$; bill along the rictus, $3\frac{1}{3}$; circumference of bill in the middle, $2\frac{1}{3}$; height, 11 lines. "It is similar, in general, to the European ravens, but with longer, more slender tarsi, more compressed and slender bill, and longer, more cuneate tail, &c." Allowing for the greater size of the German foot, the description would come sufficiently near to that of the skin from Bill Williams' fork, and I shall therefore adopt this name.

The *Corvus sinuatus* of Wagler is said to have the tomia sinuated and bent outwards, the nostrils concealed posteriorly only; the region beneath the eye somewhat naked, &c. The length, 25 inches; wing, $16\frac{2}{12}$; tarsi, $2\frac{1}{2}$; middle tail feather, $9\frac{1}{2}$; outer, almost 7; bill from forehead, $3\frac{1}{4}$. Hab., Mexico.

I owe to Mr. Lawrence the opportunity of examining a raven from Texas, which is even larger than that from the Colorado. It is unfortunately moulting some of its quills and tail feathers and its full characters cannot be ascertained. The bristly feathers of the nostrils are growing out, their basal portion still enveloped in its sheath, leaving the nostrils exposed. This may have been the case in the specimen of *Corvus sinuatus* described by Wagler.

The general appearance is that of the Colorado raven, although it is rather larger, and the middle toe is shorter in proportion. The lustre is much the same. The size is every way greater than that of the North American raven.

In the uncertainty as to what limits of variation may be allowed to the North American *Corvidae*, and in the imperfect condition of Mr. Lawrence's specimen, I shall not venture to make it distinct from *cacalotl*, which itself is perhaps very uncertain. Should it be different, it may properly be called *C. nobilis*, Gould, unless the *C. sinuatus* of Wagler should prove to be

Other references to Mexican species of ravens are as follows:

Corvus sinuatus, WAGLER, Isis, 1829, VII, 748.   Mexico.

Corvus cacalotl, WAGLER, Isis, 1831, 527.   Mexico.

Corvus nobilis, GOULD, Pr. Zool. Soc. 1837, 79.—Bon. Conspectus, 1850, 386.

Corvus splendens, "GOULD."—Bon. Pr. Zool. Soc. 1837, 115.   (Not of Vieillot.)   An erroneous quotation of Gould, by Bonaparte.

the same. The *Corvus nobilis*, according to Gould, is distinguished from both the European bird and that of the United States by more metallic lustre of plumage, more lengthened and slender bill, longer primaries, and more cuneate tail. The length is given at 25 inches; wing, 18; tail, 11; tarsi, 3; bill, 3¼.

List of specimens.

Catal. No.	Locality.	When collected.	Whence obtained.	Orig. No.	Collected by—
6855	Bill Williams' fork, Camp 115, N. M.	Feb. 7, 1854	Lieut. Whipple	73	Kennerly and Möllhausen.
10297?	Camp 110	Jan. 31, 1854	......do	54	......do
10295?	Colorado Desert		Lieut. Williamson		Dr. Heermann

CORVUS CRYPTOLEUCUS, Couch.

White-necked Crow.

Corvus cryptoleucus, COUCH, Pr. A. N. Sc. VII, April, 1854, 66. Tamaulipas, Mexico.

SP. CH.—The fourth quill is longest; the third and fifth equal; the second longer than the sixth; the first about equal to the seventh. Glossy black, with violet reflections; feathers of neck all round, back, and breast, snow white at the base. Length, about 21 inches; wing, 14.00; tail, 8½. Feathers of throat lanceolate; bristly feathers along the base of the bill covering it for nearly two-thirds its length.

Hab.—Valley of Rio Grande and Gila. Abundant on the Llano Estacado.

In describing this curious raven, the smallest of our North American species with pointed feathers on the throat, I have selected a specimen (10300) which is rather larger than the Texan ones, but is otherwise much the same. Considerably smaller than the common raven, the bill is also smaller; the incumbent feathers of the nostrils reach over the basal two-thirds of the bill instead of over one-half only as in the other species. The tarsus is a very little longer than the middle toe and claw; there are eight scutellae in front.

The porportions of the quills are expressed in the following table of distances from the tip of the longest to the tip of each primary:

	1st.	2d.	3d.	4th.	5th.	6th.	7th.	8th.	9th.
No. 10300	4.45	1.10	.05	0.	.50	2.30	3.90	4.70	5.25

The first primary is thus intermediate between the seventh and eighth.

The tail is moderately long, and not much graduated; the outer feathers about 1¼ inches shorter than the inner. The middle feathers have nearly parallel outlines. The lanceolate feathers on the throat are quite distinct, though possibly not so long proportionately as in the common raven.

The general color of this raven is a lustrous black, with violet reflections, almost exactly as in the common species. Its most striking distinctive feature, however, is seen in the feathers of the neck all round, upper part of the back, and the whole breast, which are pure snowy white for about their basal half. The feathers of the head are plumbeous at the base ; the greatest intensity of white is on the lower part of the neck; the color fades out on the back and belly into plumbeous. In no other North American crow is there any approach to this cottony whiteness.

This character, with its smaller size, will at once serve to distinguish this species from any other ravens in the United States.

As already stated, No. 10300 is rather larger than skins from Texas, the largest of which (4995) measures a little less in the body; the bill, too, is smaller, measuring 2.20 inches from the rictus. The others are all decidedly smaller.

The *Corvus jamaicensis* of Gmelin is said to have the downy portion of the feathers white. The size is much less, however; the measurements, as given by Gosse, being: Length, 16.50; extent, 28 ; wing, 9.50 ; tail, 5.75 ; rictus, 2 ; tarsus, 2 ; middle toe, 1.50. Bonaparte, in notes on Delattre's Collection, page 7, says that *C. leucognaphalus* of Vieillot likewise has white down ; but that the skin is naked at the angle of the bill, and the nostrils but little covered, very different in this from *C. cryptoleucus.*

List of specimens.

Catal. No.	Sex.	Locality.	When collected.	Whence obtained.	Orig'l No.	Collected by—	Length.	Stretch of wings.	Wing.	Remarks.
10300	....	Janos, Mex.............	April —, 1855	Maj. Emory	64	Dr. Kennerly ..	....	43.00	12.50	Eyes dark brown...
4995	....	Pecos river, Tex........	April 14, 1856	Capt. J. Pope......	190	....	21.00	40.50	14.00	Eyes brown........
4994	....	........do........	May 23, 1855	......do............	90	....	20.00	40.50	14.00	......do........
4993	....	........do..............	May 25, 1855	......do............	92	....	19.00	36.50	13.00	......do ....
4118	♀	Charco Escondido	May —, 1853	Lieut. Couch......	......	....	18.75	33.00	13.50	....

CORVUS AMERICANUS, Aud.

Common Crow.

Corvus corone, Wilson, Am. Orn. IV, 1811, 79 ; pl. xxv, f. 3.—Bon. Obs. Wils. 1824, No. 37.—Ib. Syn. 1828, 56.— Rich. F. B Am. II, 1831, 291.—Nuttall, Man. I, 1832, 209. Not *Corvus corone* of Linn.
Corvus americanus, Aud. Orn. Biog. II, 1834, 317 : V, 477 ; pl. 156.—Ib. Syn. 1839, 150.—Ib. Birds Amer. IV, 1842, 87 ; pl. 225.—Bon. List, 1838.—Ib. Consp. 1850, 385.—Nuttall, Man. I, 2d ed. 1840, 221.— Maxim. Reise, I, 1839, 140.—Newberry, Zool. Cal. & Or. Route, P. R. R. Rep. VI, iv, 1857, 82.

Sp. Ch.—Fourth quill longest ; second shorter than sixth ; first shorter than ninth. Glossy black with violet reflections, even on the belly. Length, 19 to 20 inches ; wing, 13 to 13.50 ; tail about 8. Tarsus longer than the middle toe and claw.

Hab.—North America to the Missouri region ; also on the coast of California. (Not found on the High Central Plains?)

(4538 ♂ Washington, D. C.) The bill of this species is considerably narrower than high or much compressed. It is gently curved from the very base ; rather more rapidly towards the tip. The incumbent feathers of the nostril reach half the distance from the base of the bill to the end of the lower jaw, and not quite half way to that of the upper.

The tarsus has eight scutellae anteriorly, and is rather longer than the middle toe and claw ; the lateral toes are very nearly equal ; the inner claw the larger, and reaching to the base of the middle claw.

The webs of the throat feathers are a little loose, but lie quite smoothly, without the pointed lanceolate character seen in the ravens.

The wings are elongated; the fourth quill is longest; then the fifth and the fourth, which are successively a little shorter; the fifth to the ninth are graduated rapidly, the diminution in length becoming successively less. The second quill is, however, about intermediate between the sixth and seventh; the first is about the length of the first secondary, shorter than the last primary. The comparative lengths of the quills will be expressed by the following table of distances from the tip of the longest primary to each one in succession :

Catal. No.	Sex.	Locality.	Longest primary.	1st.	2d.	3d.	4th.	5th.	6th.	7th.	8th.	9th.	Secondary.
4358	♂	Washington _ _	4	5. 85	1. 75	. 35	0.	. 15	. 90	2. 40	3. 40	4. 05	4. 60

The tail is rounded, the feathers graduated; the lateral 1.20 of an inch shorter than the middle one. They are rather truncate at the end; the outer webs most rapidly rounded; the outer and inner webs of the innermost feathers very nearly equal.

The color everywhere is black; lustrous above; duller on the head and beneath. There is a violet gloss above, except on the primaries, where it is green.

Specimens vary somewhat in the length of the bill and other dimensions. California skins appear to have the tail rather less graduated; the middle toe proportionately shorter, the size less. In a skin from the Upper Missouri (5191) the bill is rather more slender and less high, although this is probably an indication of immaturity.

According to Mr. Audubon, the chief difference between the European *Corvus corone* and American crow consists, in the first place, in the smaller size of the latter, measuring 18 instead of 20 inches; the wings 12 instead of 13¼. This difference, however, is not very decided, as will be seen from the table of measurements, where some skins are as large as in *C. corone*. The bill and feet are also said to be weaker. The most important feature of distinction appears to lie in the structure of the feathers of the head and neck, which in *C. corone* are narrow, with the tips distinct, while in the American bird these tips are blended together and do not maintain their individuality. The feathers on the fore neck in *corone* are also lanceolate and distinct, showing the outline of each one as in the raven, while in the American crow they are three times as broad, rounded, and entirely blended. Mr. Audubon further remarks, that the neck of the European bird is glossed with green and blue, while that of the American has a decided purplish brown tinge.

Prince Maximilian states, in addition, that the note differs in the two species.

Detailed measurements of species.

Catalogue number.	Locality.	Sex.	Length.	Stretch of wings.	Wing.	Tail.	Tarsus.	Middle toe.	Its claw alone.	Bill—Along curve.	On straight line.	Gape.	Height of base.	1.	2.	3.	4.	5.	6.	7.	8.	Specimen measured.
10092	Washington, D. C.	♂	18.80	......	12.60	7.81	2.38	2.04	0.57	1.97	1.89	2.09	0.83	4	3,5	6	2	7	8	9	1	Dry...
4358	......do.........	♂	18.50	......	12.90	8.38	2.32	1.99	0.62	1.97	1.87	2.10	0.78	4	3,5	6	2	7	8	9	1	Dry...
do.	......do.........	....	20.00	39.50	11.00	......	......	......	......	......	......	......	......									Fresh.
9994	Trémont, Ill.......	....	18.20	......	11.70	7.96	2.42	2.12	0.60	1.97	1.82	2.06	0.78	4	3,5	6	2	7	8	9	1	Dry...
6559	Fort Riley, K. T..	....	19.10	......	13.30	8.28	2.44	2.02	0.54	2.02	2.04	2.24	0.74	4.5	3	6	2	7	8	9	1	Dry...
5191	Fort Union, Neb..	....	17.20	......	12.40	7.83	2.34	1 93	0.56	1.84	1.72	2.04	0.68	....	....	....	....	....	....	....	....	Dry...
do.	......do.........	....	19.50	36.00	13.00	......	......	......	......	......	......	......	......									Fresh.
10305?	Tulare Valley.....	♂	18.30	......	12.72	7 83	2.33	1.86	0.54	2.10	2.02	2.08	0.80	4	3,5	6	2	7	8	9	1	Dry...
10303?	Ft. Vancouver,W.T.	....	17.10	......	12.10	7.74	2.25	1.90	0.56	1.80	1.73	1 99	0.72	4.5	3	6	2	7	8	9	1	Dry...
10304?	Presidio, Cal.......	....	18.20	......	11.64	7.48	2.18	1.82	0.60	1.80	1.76	2.08	0.75	4	3,5	6	2	7	8	9	1	Dry...

List of specimens.

Catal. No.	Sex and age.	Locality.	When collected.	Whence obtained.	Orig'l No.	Collected by—	Length.	Stretch of wings.	Wing.
4358	♂	Washington, D. C.............	Feb. 13, 1855	Market............	......	....	20	39.50	....
10092	....	........do.............	....	J. C. McGuire......					
9994	....	Trémont, Ill............	....	W. J. Shaw.......					
6919	....	Nelson river, H. B. T........	....	Donald Gunn......					
6559	....	Fort Riley, K. T........	1857........	Dr. W. A. Hammond......					
5192	♀	Vermilion river, Neb..........	Oct. 25, 1856	Lieut. G. K. Warren	......	Dr. Hayden	19	37.00	12.50
5191	....	Fort Union, Neb..............	July 19, 1856	......do............	......	.......do.........	19.50	36.00	13.00
5190	○	........do.............	....do....	....do....		....do....			
5189	○	........do.............	....do....	....do....		....do....			
5188	○ ♂	Mouth Powder river, Neb	Aug. 1, 1856	......do............		....do....			
10305	♂	Tulare Valley, Cal............	....	Lieut. R. S Williamson........		Dr. Heermann........			
10304	....	Presidio, Cal................	June 6, 1853	Lieut. Trowbridge					
6854?	....	Fort Vancouver, W. T..........	July 15, 1853	Gov. I. I. Stevens......	1	Dr. J. G. Cooper........			

CORVUS AMERICANUS, var. FLORIDANUS, Baird.

Florida Crow.

Sp. Ch —About the size of *C. americanus*, but bill and feet larger. Tail less rounded. Third, fourth, and fifth quills nearly equal ; third rather longer than fifth. Color less violet above. Length, 19.50 ; wing, 12; tail, 7.70 ; tarsus, 2.60.

Hab.—Southern peninsula of Florida.

The reception of this bird, as the article on *Corvus* is going through the press, prevents any very elaborate criticism of its characters, but there are so many peculiarities in it as clearly to show that it is, if not a distinct species from the common crow, at least a very remarkable variety. Although perhaps rather smaller than the *U. americanus*, the bill and feet, especially the latter, are very considerably larger. The nasal feathers extend over the basal two-fifths of the bill instead of the half. The proportions of the bill are about the same; in the Florida bird it is rather the longer. The greatest difference is in the feet. The tarsal joint of the tibia is bare, the feathers scarcely coming below it, even anteriorly, instead of projecting some distance. The tarsus is almost a quarter of an inch longer ; covered anteriorly by nine scutellae instead of eight. The outer lateral toe is shorter, not reaching the base of the middle claw. The middle toe and claw are considerably shorter than the tarsus; the middle claw is shorter than in the northern bird.

The wings formula differs somewhat; the third, fourth, and fifth quills are nearly equal, the third even longer than the fifth instead of shorter. The tail is short and very nearly even, the difference in length of feathers being less than half an inch instead of an inch. This, however, may in part be owing to the absence of the middle pair.

The colors differ somewhat from those of the common crow. There is less violet, and the feathers of the back have almost a brassy gloss on their margins, as in *Crotophaga*.

The specimen upon which these remarks are based, though apparently perfectly mature, is changing some of its feathers, such as the inner primaries, the middle tail feathers, and the greater coverts. The long primaries and ten tail feathers, however, are of full length. It is possible that the bird is really as large as the northern crow, although this is hardly probable. It was killed on the main land of the extreme southern portion of Florida, not far from Fort Dallas.

No comparison of this bird is required with the fish crow, which has the middle toe and claw longer than the tarsus, not shorter, and the proportions much less. It is much larger than the curious little *Corvus minutus* of Cuba, a specimen of which has been supplied by Mr. Lawrence. The *Corvus minutus*[1] is, of course, still smaller than the *C. americanus*, the bill stouter at the base; the third, fourth, and fifth quills nearly equal and longest. The chin is more bristly, the feathers of the throat more distinctly defined. Although about the size of the fish crow, it has much stouter bill and legs, and the tarsus is much longer than middle toe and claw, not shorter. The *Corvus minutus* and var. *floridanus* are more nearly allied in every respect than either is to *C. americanus*. Their measurement will be found in the accompanying table, the first specimen referring to the Florida bird, the second to the *minutus*.

Bartram, in his list of North American birds, (Travels in Florida,) mentions a "*Corvus maritimus*, Great Seaside Crow," but without specifying locality or giving any description. If a Florida bird, it quite probably refers to the present species, which is doubtless quite maritime in its habits.

Detailed measurements of species.

Catalogue number.	Locality.	Sex.	Length.	Stretch of wings.	Wing.	Tail.	Tarsus.	Middle toe.	Its claw alone.	Bill—				Succession of quills from longest.								Specimen measured.
										Along curve.	In straight line.	Gape.	Height at base.	1.	2.	3.	4.	5.	6.	7.	8.	
10374	Florida (*floridanus*)	♂	.....	.....	12.30	7.68	2.60	1.90	0.52	2.10	1.94	2.22	0.80	4	3.5	....	2	7	8	1	9	Dry ...
do.	....do............	....	19.50	36.00	12.00	.....	.....	.....	.....	.....	.....	.....	.....	...	...	....	....	....	....	....	....	Fresh..
	Cuba, (*minutus*) .	♂	15.10	.....	10.00	6.56	2.12	1.70	0.52	1.90	1.76	1.86	0.76	4	3.5	.6	2	7	8	9	1	Dry....

CORVUS CAURINUS, Baird.

Northwestern Fish Crow.

Sp. Ch.—Fourth quill longest; fifth and third about equal; second longer than sixth; first shorter than ninth. Color black, glossed with purple. Tail nearly even. Tarsus longer than middle toe and claw. Length about 16.50 inches; wing about 11; tail about 7.

Hab.—Washington Territory and northwestern coast.

By the above name I wish to indicate a small crow from the northwest coast, which, though

[1] *Corvus minutus*, GUNDLACH, Cabanis Journal für Ornithologie, IV, March, 1856, 97. Cuba.

June 29, 1858.

72 b

not much like the eastern fish crow, appears to possess its peculiar habits. In all essential features it is like the common *Corvus americanus;* so much so, indeed, that but for the slight difference in size it would be difficult to tell skins of the two apart. According to Drs. Cooper and Suckley, they are maritime, feeding on the sea beach at low tide, and coming about the settlements with considerable familiarity, being much less shy and suspicious than the common crow. The note, too, is said to be a little different.

The species is readily distinguished from the eastern fish crow by the larger size, the absence of green gloss on the belly ; the tarsi longer than the middle toe and claw instead of shorter, and the second quill being generally shorter than the sixth instead of longer. It is so much like the *Corvus americanus* as to be only distinguishable by its inferior size and habits. Indeed, it is almost a question whether it be more than a dwarfed race of the other species.

Crows from California and one from Vancouver (10303) agree, by their larger size, with the eastern *Corvus americanus,* and may thus be distinguished from the *C. caurinus.*

Detailed measurements.

Catalogue number.	Locality.	Sex.	Length.	Stretch of wings.	Wing.	Tail.	Tarsus.	Middle toe.	Its claw alone.	Bill— Along curve.	In straight line.	Gape.	Height at base.	1.	2.	3.	4.	5.	6.	7.	8.	Specimen measured.
9811	Puget Sound		17.70		11.32	7.06	2.01	1.80	0.50	1.84	1.80	2.03	0.82	4	5.3	6	2	7	8	9	1	Dry....
10310	Fort Steilacoom		16.00		11.33	7.08	2.13	1.84	0.50	1.59	1.53	1.73		4	3.5	6	2	7	8	9	1	Dry....
10211	.......do		17.00		11.00	6.92	2 06	1.75	0.52	1.72	1.58	1.81	0.62	4	3.5	6	2	7	8	9	1	Dry....
10309	.......do		16.30		10.92	6.82	2.00	1.78	0.53	1.68	1.60	1.90	0.66	4	3.5	6	2	7	8	9	1	Dry....
10315	.......do	♂			10.90	6.70	2.10	1.88	0.53	1.78	1.70	1.98	0.70	4	3.5	6	2	7	8	9	1	Dry....
do.	.......do		16.50	32.00																		Fresh..
10306	Shoalwater bay		16.10		10.72	6.80	2.12	1.98	0.56	1.60	1.56	1.90	0.64	4	3.5	6	2	7	8	9	1	Dry....
do.	.......do		16.50	33 00																		Fresh..
10308	Fort Steilacoom		16.40		10.90	7.34	1.96	1.71	0.52	1.85	1.69	2.00	0.66	4	3.5	6	2	7	8	9	1	Dry....
10307	.......do		17.20		10.70	6.78	1.96	1.72	0.51	1.80	1.69	1.95	0.70	4	3.5	6	2	7	8	9	1	Dry....

List of specimens.

Catal. No.	Sex.	Locality.	When collected.	Whence obtained	Orig. No.	Collected by—	Length.	Stretch of wings.
9811	------	Simiahmoo bay, W. T.	Dec. 20, 1857	A. Campbell......	87	Dr. Kennerly	....	....
10310	------	Steilacoom, W. T....	Feb. —, 1856	Dr. Suckley.......	230	....	....	....
10311	------	.......do.........	April 25, 1856	.......do.........	322	....	....	....
10308	------	.......do.........	March	.......do.........	241	....	....	....
10309	------	.......do.........	February	.......do.........	231	....	....	....
10307	------	.......do.........	April 25, 1856	.......do.........	324	....	....	....
10312	♂	.......do.........	.......do......	.......do.........	324	....	16.50	32.00
10306	------	Shoalwater bay, W. T.	Sept. 14, 1854	Dr Cooper........	96	....	16.50	33.00

CORVUS OSSIFRAGUS, Wilson.

Fish Crow.

Corvus ossifragus, Wilson, Am. Orn. V, 1812, 27 ; pl. xxxvii, f. 2.—Bon. Obs. Wils. 1825, No. 39.—Ib. Syn. 1828, 57.—Ib. Conspectus, 1850, 385.—Wagler, Syst. Avium, 1827, *Corvus*, No. 12.—Nuttall, Man. I, 1832, 216.—Aud. Orn. Biog. II, 1834, 268 : V, 479 ; pl. 146.—Ib. Syn. 1839, 151.—Ib. Birds Amer. IV, 1842, 94 ; pl. 226.

Sp. Ch.—Fourth quill longest ; second rather longer than seventh ; first shorter than the ninth. Glossy black, with green and violet reflections ; the gloss of the belly greenish. Length, about 15.50 inches ; wing, 10.50 ; tail, less than 7 inches ; tarsus shorter than the middle toe and claw.

Hab.—South Atlantic (and Gulf?) coast.

In this species the bill is shaped much as in the common crow, the upper outline perhaps a little more convex. The bristly feathers at the base of the bill reach nearly halfway to the tip. I find no bare space at the base of the lower mandible, although the feathers are not quite so thick there as in the common crow. The tarsus has eight transverse scutellae, and is decidedly shorter than the middle toe with its claw. The lateral claws do not reach within one tenth of an inch of the base of the middle claw.

The wings are long and acute ; the fourth is longest ; next the third, fifth, second, and sixth ; the first is about as long as the secondaries. The distances from the tip of the longest quill to each primary are as follows :

		Longest quill.	1st.	2d.	3d.	4th.	5th.	6th.	7th.	8th.	9th.
4515	Washington ...	4th.	3.55	1.05	.15	0.	.25	1.10	2.10	2.85	3.00

The four outer primaries are cut out on the inner web as in *C. americanus*.

The tail of the fish crow is nearly even, or only slightly rounded, the outer feathers about .40 of an inch less than the middle ones. The innermost tail feather has the webs on both sides nearly equal.

This species is everywhere lustrous black, with a partly violet and partly green gloss on the back ; a decidedly green gloss on the belly.

The fish crow of the Atlantic States is readily distinguishable from the common crow by the much smaller size, (16 inches instead of 20 ; wing about 11 inches instead of 13 ;) the bill is broader at the base and tapers more rapidly to the end ; the middle toe and claw are longer than the scutellate portion of the tarsus, not shorter, the inner claw not reaching to the base of the middle one. The tail is less rounded. The gloss on the belly is green instead of violet ; that on the back is mixed with green, not entirely violet.

Audubon and Wilson describe the fish crow as having a space bare of feathers at the base of the bill. This I have not found in any of the specimens before me, (all adult,) and am inclined to consider it a feature of the young, as shown in Mr. Audubon's plate. In these adults the face is quite as fully feathered as ever in our common crow, which itself sometimes has the feathers in front of the eye, thickened and sparse.

Detailed measurements.

Catalogue number.	Locality.	Sex.	Length.	Stretch of wings.	Wing.	Tail.	Tarsus.	Middle toe.	The claw alone.	Bill—Along curve.	Bill—On straight line.	Bill—Gape.	Bill—Height at base.	1.	2.	3.	4.	5.	6.	7.	8.	Specimen measured.
4515	Washington, D. C.	♂	15.50	......	10.58	6.88	1.84	1.84	0.53	1.52	1.42	1.61	0.56	4	3.5	6.2	7	8	9	1	....	Dry ...
do.	......do...........		15.56	31.50	10.50	......								...	...							Fresh .
10314	New Jersey.......	....	14.50	......	10.30	6.72	1.86	1.93	0.59	1.64	1.56	1.80	0.59	3	4.5	2	6	7	8	1	9	Dry ...
10313	......do...........	....	14.80	......	10.70	6.45	......	1.84	0.58	1.73	1.60	1.80	0.57	3.4	5	2	6	7	8	9	1	Dry ...
3049	Liberty county, Ga	....	15.60	......	10.44	6.42	1.82	1.90	0.63	1.76	1.60	1.78	0.58	4	3.5	2	6	7	8	9	1	Dry ...
2849	......do...........	♀	14.10	......	9.90	6.00	1.71	1.84	0.54	1.50	1.42	1.66	0.57	3.4	5	2	6	7	8	9	1	Dry ...
6530	Indian Key, Fla..	♂	15.20	......	10.40	6.73	1.80	1.94	0.64	1.66	1.58	1.90	0.57	4	3.5	2	6	7	8	9	1	Dry ...
do.	......do...........		......	33.00	10.00	......								...	...							

List of specimens.

Catal. No.	Sex.	Locality.	When collected.	Whence obtained.	Stretch of wings.	Wing.
4515	♂	Washington, D. C. -----------	Feb. —, 1855...	Market.............		
10313	♂	New Jersey -------------------		J. Cassin		
10314	......	------do-------------------------		------do-------------------		
3049	......	Liberty county, Ga		S. F. Baird		
2849	♀	......do-------------------------		------do-------------------		
6530	♂	Indian Key, Florida.. ---------	Feb. 3. 1857....	G. Wurdemann..............	33.00	10.00

PICICORVUS, Bonaparte.

Picicorvus, BONAPARTE, Consp. Av. 1850, 384. Type *Corvus columbianus,* Wils.

CH.—Lead color. with black wings and tail. Bill longer than the head, considerably longer than the tarsus, attenuated, slightly decurved ; tip without notch. Culmen and commissure curved ; gonys straight or slightly concave, as long as the tarsi. Nostrils circular, completely covered by a full tuft of incumbent white bristly feathers. Tail much shorter than the wings, nearly even or slightly rounded. Wings pointed, reaching to the tip of tail. Third, fourth, and fifth quills longest. Tarsi short, scarcely longer than the middle toe, the hind toe and claw very large, reaching nearly to the middle of the middle claw, the lateral toe little shorter. A row of small scales on the middle of the sides of tarsus.

Without a specimen of *Nucifraga* conveniently at hand I cannot express exactly the difference between it and the present genus. Judging from descriptions, however, the bill is more curved, the culmen being decidedly convex ; the nasal feathers are longer ; the wings extending only to the middle of the tail, instead of near the tip. The very long wings distinguish it from all other American genera, except *Corvus,* which has a much thicker bill, &c., and is entirely black. The short tarsi and lengthened lateral and hinder toes are quite remarkable. The hind claw is rather longer than its digit. The sides of the tarsi exhibit the row of small scales seen in *Corvus.* The commissure is considerably curved, more convex than the culmen, which bends very gently throughout from the very base. There is a general approximation to the *Sturnella*-like bill more decidedly visible in *Gymnokitta.* The nostrils are small, with the anterior portion less deeply bevelled off than in *Corvus.*

Comparative measurements of species.

Catal. No.	Species.	Locality.	Sex.	Length.	Stretch of wings.	Wing.	Tail.	Tarsus.	Middle toe.	Its claw alone.	Hind toe and claw.	Hind claw alone.	Bill above.	Along gape.	Specimen measured.
4461	Picicorvus columbianus .	Cascade mountains ..	......	12.60	......	7.70	5.16	1.36	1.34	0.51	1.73	1.80	1.03	0.56	Skin......
8895	......do..........do.	Rawhide peak, Neb..	♀	11.30	......	7.03	4.73	1.42	1.46	0.52	1.68	1.73	1.06	0.60	Skin.......
do.	......do..........do.	......do...........	......	12.50	21.50	7.12	......	......	......	......	......	......	......	......	Fresh......
8468	Gymnokitta cyanocephala	75 miles west of Albuquerque.	......	9.66	......	5.88	4.70	1.46	1.12	0.36	1.34	1.40	0.84	0.44	Skin.......
do.	......do........ ..do.	.........do............	......	10.00	18.00	6.00	......	......	......	......	......	......	......	......	Fresh......

PICICORVUS COLUMBIANUS, Bon.

Clarke's Crow.

Corvus columbianus, WILSON, Am. Orn. III, 1811, 29 ; pl. xx.—BON. Obs. Wilson, 1824, No. 38.—IB. Syn. 1828,
57.—NUTTALL, I, 1832, 218.
Nucifraga columbiana, AUD. Orn. Biog. IV, 1838, 459 ; pl. 362.—IB. Syn. 1839, 156.—IB. Birds Amer. IV, 1842,
127 ; pl. 235.—BON. List, 1838.—NUTTALL, Man, I, 2d ed 251.
Picicorvus columbianus, BONAP. Consp. 1850, 384.—NEWBERRY, P. R. R. Rep. VI, iv, 1837, 83.
" *Co*rvus megonyx, WAGLER.''

SP. CH.—Tail rounded or moderately graduated, the closed wings reaching nearly to its tip. Fourth quill longest ; secon
considerably shorter than the sixth. General color bluish ash, changing on the nasal feathers, the forehead, sides of head,
(especially around the eye,) and chin, to white. The wings, including their inner surface, greenish black, the secondaries and
tertials, except the innermost, broadly tipped with white ; tail white, the inner web of the fifth feather and the whole of the sixth,
with the upper tail coverts, greenish black. The axillars plumbeous black. Bill and feet black.
Length of male, (fresh,) 12 inches ; wing, 7 ; tail, 4.30 ; tarsus, 1.20.
Hab.—From Rocky mountains to Pacific. East to Fort Kearney.

The tail of this species is nearly even, or but slightly rounded, the lateral feathers being
about .20 of an inch shorter than the other white ones. Sometimes, however, the middle black
feathers project beyond the rest for nearly half an inch.

There is considerable variation in the size of this species, as well as a striking difference in the
length of the bill. Thus, in 4460, from the Cascade mountains, the bill is nearly two inches long,
slender and attenuated, exceeding by half an inch that of 8239. The length is 12.50 inches ;
wing, 7.50 ; tail, 4.65. The general color is sometimes quite pale bluish ash, becoming appreciably lighter on the head. The female is quite similar.

List of specimens.

Catal. No.	Sex.	Locality.	When collected.	Whence obtained.	Orig'l No.	Collected by—	Length.	Stretch of wings.	Wing.	Remarks.
8472	♂	Milk river, Up. Mo.........	Sept. 2, 1853	Gov. Stevens......	......	Dr. Suckley......	11.75	21.50	7.12	....
8240	♀	30 miles east of Ft. Kearney.	Oct. 24, 1857	W. M. Magraw...	222	Dr. Cooper	12.25	22.00	7.75	Bill and feet black.
8239	♂	.....do................	......do......	......do......	221	......do.........	12.00	22.00	7.75	.....do...........
8878	......	Black Hills, Neb............	Sept. 15......	Lt. Warren............	......	Dr. Hayden.......	11.00	20.00	7.00	....
8870	......	..... do.............	......do......	......do......	......	......do.........	11.00	21.50	7.00	....
8871	......	.... do.............	June 29.....	......do......	......	......do.........	11.25	21.50	7.25	....
8872	♂	.... do.............	Sept. 12.....	......do......	......	... ..do.........	12.00	24.00	7.50	Iris brown.........
8874	......	... ..do.............	Sept. 14.....	......do......	......	......do.........	......	......	......	....
8875	♀	Raw Hide Peak, Neb.......	Sept. 6......	......do......	......	......do.........	12.50	21.50	7.12	Iris gray.........
1929	♂	Rocky mountains........	June 16, 1834	S. F. Baird...........	......	J. K. Townsend..	......	......	......	....
6999	♀	Medicine Bow, Neb.........	July 26, 1857	Lt. Bryan...........	334	W. S. Wood....	......	......	......	....
8473	......	Mimbres to Rio Grande.....	......	Dr. Henry......	......	......	......	......	......	....
8475	......	75 miles west of Albuquerque	Nov. 15, 1853	Lt. Whipple......	......	Kennerly & Müll.	......	......	......	....
8474	......	95......do............	Nov. 16, 1853	......do.........	......	......do.........	......	......	......	....
4460	......	Cascade mountains, O.T	....	Lt. Williamson...	......	Dr. Newberry.....	......	......	......	....
4461	......	......do..........	......	......do........	......	......do.........	......	......	......	....
8470	......	Yakima river, W. T.......	Aug. 5, 1853	Gov. Stevens....	29	Dr. Cooper.......	......	......	......	....
8471	......	......do............	Sept. 1, 1853	......do......	10	......do.........	......	......	......	....

GYMNOKITTA, Pr. Max.

Gymnorhinus, Pr. Max. Reise Nord. Amer. II, 1841, 21.   Type *G. cyanocephala.*
Gymnokitta, Pr. Max. " 1850," Gray.
Cyanocephalus, Bonap. " 1842," Preoccupied in Botany.

Ch.—Bill elongated, depressed, shorter than the tarsus, longer than the head, without notch, similar to that of *Sturnella* in shape. Culmen nearly straight ; commissure curved ; gonys ascending. Nostrils small, oval, entirely exposed, the bristly feathers at the base of the bill being very minute. Tail short, nearly even, much shorter than the pointed wings, which cover three-fourths of the tail. Tarsi considerably longer than the middle toe.

This is a very remarkable genus of *Corvidae*, and is readily distinguished among North American forms by the naked nostrils, and short, even tail. The nostrils are small and oblong, not circular, the anterior wall scooped out. There is a striking likeness in the shape of the bill to that of *Sturnella ludoviciana*, even to the depressed culmen at the base, extending back into the forehead. With a general resemblance to *Picicorvus* in the attenuation of the bill, the culmen is nearly straight to near the tip ; the gonys convex at the base, then straight, and ascending ; the tip of the bill in both is broad, flat, and without notch. The edges of the bill are not inflected towards the base, as in *Picicorvus*. The tarsi are proportionately longer, the lateral toes shorter.

In both genera there is a slight indication of a row of small scales along the posterior edge of the tarsi on the inner edge.

The proper generic name for this species is a matter of some uncertainty. In the first edition of Gray's list of genera, in 1840, *Gymnorhina* was proposed for a genus of *Corvidae*, which, according to his views, prevented the subsequent use of *Gymnorhinus* of Prince Maximilian. The year quoted for the latter name is 1843, but this is the date of the French translation, the original German work bearing the imprint of 1841. It is a question whether both names cannot be used, as I have contended in other instances. In the present case, however, as the new appellation for the group is by the same author as the old one, and the conflicting names are in the same family, it may, perhaps, be as well to accept *Gymnokitta*. I have not been able to lay my hand on the place where this genus is first introduced.

GYMNOKITTA CYANOCEPHALA, Pr. Max.

Maximilian's Jay.

Gymnorhinus cyanocephalus, Pr. Maximilian, Reise in das innere Nord Amerika, II, 1841, 21.—Is. Voyage dans Am. du Nord, III, 1843, 296.
Gymnokitta cyanocephala, " Pr. Max." 1850," Bp. Conspectus, 1850, 382.—Cassin, Illust. I, vi, 1854, 165 ; pl. xxviii.— Newberry, Rep. P. R. R. VI, iv, 1857, 83.

Psilorhinus cyanocephalus, Gray, Genera.
Cyanocorax cassinii, M'Call, Pr. A. N. Sc. V, June, 1851, 216.

Sp. Ch.—Wings considerably longer than the tail, and reaching to within an inch of its tip. Tail nearly even. General color dull blue, paler on the abdomen, the middle of which is tinged with ash ; the head and neck of a much deeper and more intense blue, darker on the crown. Chin and fore part of the throat whitish, streaked with blue. Length, 10 inches ; wing, 5.90 ; tail, 4.50 ; tarsus, 1.50.

Hab.—Rocky mountains to Cascades of California and Oregon. Not on the Pacific coast.?

The bill of this species is longer than the head. The wings are long and pointed ; the third, fourth, and fifth quills nearly equal, the second a little longer than the seventh, but half an inch less than the longest ; the exposed portion of the first about half that of the longest.

Specimens vary considerably in size. Thus No. 8488, from Fort Massachusetts, marked female, is 11.50 inches long; the wing 6; the tail 4.80. The color, too, is of a more intense blue throughout.

List of specimens.

Catal. No.	Sex.	Locality.	When collected.	Whence obtained.	Orig. No.	Collected by—	Length.
8488	♀	Fort Mass. N. M	Mar. 28, 1856	Dr. Peters	14		11. 25
8466	....	Mimbres to Rio Grande.		Dr. T. C. Henry			
8468	....	95 mls.W.Albuquerque.	Nov. 16, 1853	Lt. Whipple		Kenn. & Möll	
4466	....	Des Chutes basin, O. T..		Lt. Williamson		J. S. Newberry	

Sub-Family GARRULINAE.

Cн.—Wings short, rounded; not longer or much shorter than the tail, which is graduated, sometimes excessively so. Wings reaching not much beyond the lower tail coverts. Bristly feathers at base of bill variable. Bill nearly as long as the head, or shorter. Tarsi longer than the bill or than the middle toe. Outer lateral claws rather shorter than the inner.

The preceding diagnosis may perhaps characterise the garruline birds, as compared with the crows. The sub-divisions of the group are as follows:

A. Nostrils moderate, completely covered by incumbent feathers.

a. Tail very long.

Pica.—Tail excessively graduated; nearly twice as long as the wings. First primary attenuated, falcate. Head without crest.

b. Tail about as long as the wing, or a little longer.

Cyanurus.—Head crested. Colors of wing and tail blue, banded with black.

Cyanocitta.—Head without crest. Color above blue, with a grey patch on the back.

Perisoreus.—Bill scarcely half the head, with white feathers over the nostrils. Plumage dull.

Xanthoura.—Head without crest. Color above greenish; the head blue; lateral tail feathers yellow.

B. Nostrils very large, naked, uncovered by feathers.

Psilorhinus.—Head smooth; tail broad; wings two-thirds as long as the tail.

Calocitta.—Head with a recurved crest; wings less than half as long as the tail. .

There is a very close relationship between the jays and the titmice, the chief apparent difference being scarcely anything else than in the size. The feathers at the base of the bill, however, in the jays are bristly throughout, with lateral branches reaching to the very tip. In *Paridae* these feathers are inclined to be broader, and the shaft projecting considerably beyond the basal portion, or the lateral branches confined to the basal portion, and extended forwards There is no naked line of separation between the scutellae on the outer side of the tarsi. The basal joint of the middle toe is united almost or quite to the end to the lateral, instead of half way. The first primary is usually less than half the second, instead of rather more; the fourth and fifth primaries nearly equal and longest, instead of the fifth being longer than the fourth.

PICA, Brisson.

Coracias, LINNAEUS, Syst. Nat. 1735. Gray.
Pica, BRISSON, Ornithologia, 1760, and of Cuvier, (Agassiz.) Type *Corvus pica*, L.
Cissa, BARRÈRE, "Orn. Spec. novum, 1745."
Cleptes, GAMBEL, J. A. N. Sc. 2d Ser. I, 1847, 47.

CH.—Tail very long, forming much more than half the total length ; the feathers much graduated ; the lateral scarcely more than half the middle. First primary falcate, curved, and attenuated. Bill about as high as broad at the base ; the culmen and gonys much curved, and about equal ; the bristly feathers reaching nearly to the middle of the bill. Nostrils nearly circular. Tarsi very long ; middle toe scarcely more than two-thirds the length. A patch of naked skin beneath and behind the eye.

The peculiar characteristic of this genus, in addition to the very long graduated tail, lies in the attenuated, falcate first primary. *Calocitta*, which has an equally long or longer tail, has the first primary as in the jays generally, (besides having the nostrils exposed.)

A specimen of *P. nuttalli* has the lateral tarsal plates with two or three transverse divisions, on the lower third. This does not occur in *P. hudsonica*.

The bill of *Pica*, in every respect, is very similar to that of *Corvus*, except that it is shorter. The bristly feathers are also alike. The nostrils are smaller, more nearly circular ; the axis not oblique, nor the anterior margin scooped out, as in *Corvus*.

The two North American species are readily distinguished by the black bill in *hudsonica*, and the yellow one of *nuttalli*.

The first distinct name applied to the magpies is *Coracias*, LINNAEUS, in 1735. Both this and *Cissa*, of Barrère, appear to have been proposed before *Pica*, of Brisson. Why Mr. Gray has passed by both these names I do not know, but presume he had some good reason for so doing. He rejects *Pica*, on account of its similarity to *Picus*, and takes Dr. Gambel's name of *Cleptes*, 1847.

Without the original references before me, I follow Mr. Gray in passing over *Coracias* and *Cissa*, but retain *Pica*, as sufficiently dissimilar from *Picus*.

Comparative measurements of species.

Catal. No.	Species.	Locality.	Length.	Stretch of wings.	Wing.	Tail.	Tarsus.	Middle toe.	Its claw alone.	Hind toe and claw.	Hind claw alone.	Bill above.	Along gape.	Specimen measured.
3938	Pica nuttallii	California	17.30	....	7.42	10.26	1.95	1.43	0.45	1.00	0.49	1.26	1.53	Skin
1922	Pica melanoleuca	Europe	16.90	....	6.97	9.20	1.93	1.42	0.40	1.02	0.50	1.28	1.50	Skin
4547	Pica hudsonica	Fort Pierre	18.50	....	8.08	11.20	1.90	1.42	0.46	0.97	0.50	1.30	1.54	Skin
do.	...do...	...do...	18.75	24.25	8.50	......	......	......	......	......	......	......	......	Fresh

PICA HUDSONICA, Bonap.

Magpie.

Corvus pica, FORSTER, Phil. Trans. LXXII, 1772, 382.—WILSON, Am. Orn. IV, 1811, 75 ; pl. xxxv.—BON. Obs. Wils. 1825, No. 40.—IB. Syn. 1828, 57.—NUTTALL, Man. I, 1832, 219.—AUD. Orn. Biog. IV, 1838, 408 ; pl. 357. Not of Linnaeus.
Corvus hudsonica, JOS. SABINE, App. Narr. Franklin's Journey, 1823, 25, 671.
Picus hudsonica, BONAP. List, 1838.—IB. Conspectus, 1850, 383.—MAXIM. Reise Nord. Amer. I, 1839, 508.—IB. Cabanis' Journ. 1856, 197.—NEWBERRY, Zool. Cal. & Or. Route, Rep. P. R. R, VI, IV, 1857, 84.
Cleptes hudsonicus, GAMBEL, J. A. N. Sc. 2d Ser. I, Dec. 1847, 47.
Pica melanoleuca, "VIEILL." AUD. Syn. 1839, 157.—IB. Birds Amer. IV, 1842, 99 ; pl. 227.

Sp. Ch —Bill and naked skin behind the eye, black. General color black. The belly, scapulars, and inner webs of the primaries white ; hind part of back grayish ; exposed portion of the tail feathers glossy green, tinged with purple and violet near the end ; wings glossed with green ; the secondaries and tertials with blue ; throat feathers spotted with white. Length, 19.00 ; wing, 8.50 ; tail, 11.00.

Hab.—The Arctic regions of North America. The United States from the High Central Plains to the Pacific, north of California.

The tail feathers are brilliant lustrous green, interrupted, however, a few inches from the tip by a shade of golden, which passes into violet, then into bluish, the extreme tip greenish again. This prevails on both webs of the middle feathers, but on the others is confined to the outer ; the inner webs dull blackish, with a shade of indigo. On the wings the prevailing shade is a beautiful blue on the exposed surfaces, this color margining the greenish of the secondaries rather abruptly.

Bill and feet black. Head and neck all round, fore part of breast, interscapular region, rump, base of the tail all round, under wing coverts, axillars, and tibia, dull black, with a shade of very dark blue, except the interscapular patch, which is greenish. Feathers of the hood stiffened, and tipped with metallic greenish. Under parts, inner web of primaries, (except at tips,) scapulars, and tips of the feathers on the hind part of the back, white. Bases of the feathers on the middle of the throat with a spot of white. Wings and tail glossy green, the latter tinged subterminally with purple, violet, and golden, the latter glossed with blue.

Exposed portion of the first primary falcate, half as long as that of the second ; fifth quill longest ; second between eighth and ninth. Tail much graduated ; lateral feather rather more than half the longest, 5.25 inches shorter than the longest ; the tips about equidistant, except that of the terminal one, which is about one and a half times more remote from the penultimate.

The American magpie is very closely related to the European, but differs in a much longer tail, and in the white spots on the feathers of the throat. The voice and habits are said to be entirely different.[1]

[1] In an elaborate article on the American magpie in Cabanis' Journal für Ornithologie, Prince Maximilian takes strong ground in relation to its specific distinction from the European species, and sums up the argument as follows :

1. The American magpie is the larger.

2. Its iris has a grayish blue outer ring, while that of the European magpie is altogether dark.

3. The bill of the American bird is proportionally larger and thicker.

4. The feathers on the lower neck are spotted with white in the American bird, while they are entirely black in the European.

5. The voice is totally distinct in the two.

6. The American bird has but two young.

7. The eggs are differently formed, and a little differently colored.

June 30, 1858.

73 b

List of specimens.

Catal. No.	Sex	Locality	When collected	Whence obtained	Orig. No.	Collected by—	Length	Stretch of wings	Wing	Remarks
8477	.....	Milk river, Neb..........	....	Gov. Stevens......	......	Dr. Suckley ...	18.75	23.25	8.00	....
5198	♂	Fort Berthold, Neb.......	....	Lieut. Warren.....	...	Dr. Hayden...	19.00	24.50	7.50	....
4547	.....	Fort Pierre	Oct. 27, 1856	......do........	.....	......do.......	18.75	24.25	8.50	....
5193	♀	Running Water, Mo......	Oct. 20, 1856	......do........	.....	......do.......	19.50	25.00	8.37	....
5197	♂	Great Bend of Missouri.....	Oct. 10, 1856	......do........	.....	......do.......	18.50	24.50	9.75	....
5196	......	12 miles below Ft. Pierre....	Oct. 8, 1856	......do........	.....	.. ...do.......	21.25	25.25	8.25	....
5194	♂	Ft. Randall, on Missouri...	Oct. 15, 1856	......do........	19	......do.......	23.25	....	7.75	....
5195	♂	........do......	Oct. 16, 1856	......do........	.....	......do.......	20.00	25.75	8.50	Eye black ....
5199	.....	........do......	Oct. 17, 1856	......do........	.....	......do.......	19.75	25.25	7.75	
9060	......	N. branch Fork of Cheyenne	Oct. 3, 1856	......do........	.....	......do.......	19.00	24.00	8.00	
9058	......	Black Hills, Neb	Sept. 24, 1856	......do........	.....	......do.......	16.50	23.75	8.50	....
9063	......	........do............	....	......do........	.....	......do..				
9057	.....	........do............	Sept. 25, 1856	......do........	.....	......do.......	18.00	22.75	7.50	
9059	♂	........do....	Sept. 13, 1856	......do........	.....	......do.......	20.50	24.75	8.75	
9062	......	........do............	....	......do........	.....	......do......				
9067	......	........do..	Sept. 29, 1856	......do....	.....	......do.......	20.50	25.00	8.50	
8233	......	Fort Kearney...........	Oct. 5, 1857	Dr. Cooper........	215	....	18.50	23.50	8.50	Bill and feet black..
8238	......	30 miles west of Ft. Kearney	Oct. 20, 1857	......do.........	87	....	21.00	26.00	8.50	......do...
5663	♂	North Platte	Aug. 12, 1857	Lieut. Bryan......	255	W. S. Wood...	....	....	....	
5564	♀	Medicine Bow creek.	Aug. 9, 1857	......do.........	231	......do.....	....	....	....	
8485	......	Fort Massachusetts, N. Mex.	Feb. 4, 1856	Dr. Peters	3	....	....	....	....	
8481	......	.... do......	....	Lieut. Beckwith...	7	Mr. Kreutzfeldt	....	....	....	
7100	......	Cochetope Pass..........	....	......do.......	14	....	....	....	....	
8480	......	4th camp, Little Colorado...	Dec. 8, 1853	Lieut. Whipple.....	.....	Kenn. and Müll.	17.00	19.00	6.00	
8478	......	St. Mary's, Rocky mount's.	Oct. 12, 1853	Gov. Stevens......	.....	Dr. Suckley ...	21.50	25.50	....	
8483	......	Fort Steilacoom	Aug. —, 1856	Dr. Suckley......	533	....	....	....	....	
8479	......	Yakima river, W. T......	Aug. 4, 1853	Gov. Stevens	7	Dr. Cooper......	....	....	....	
8482	......	Bellingham Bay.....	Sept. —, 1856	Dr. Suckley.......	534	....	....	....	....	
8417	......	Puget Sound.....	Aug. 2.......	A. Campbell	.....	Dr. Kennerly...	....	....	....	

PICA NUTTALLI, Aud.

Yellow-billed Magpie

Pica nuttalli, Aud. Orn. Biog. IV, 1838, 450; pl. 362.—Ib. Syn. 1839, 152.—Ib. Birds Amer. IV, 1842, 104; pl. 228.—Bon. List, 1838.—Ib. Conspectus, 1850, 383.—Nuttall, Man. I, 2d ed. 1840, 236.—Newberry, Rep. P. R. R. VI, iv, 1857, 84.

Cleptes nuttalli, Gambel, J. A. N. Sc. Ph. 2d Series, I, 1847, 46.

Sp. Ch.—Bill, and naked skin behind the eye, bright yellow; otherwise similar to *P. hudsonica*. Length, 17; wing, 8; tail, 10.

Hab.—California.

This species, in every appreciable respect, is precisely similar to the common magpie, with the exception of the bill and naked skin around and behind the eye, which are bright yellow. Sometimes this is rendered darker from the fact that the transparency of the horny covering of the bill allows the bone to be seen through it. The size is rather smaller, but this may be the result of its more southern locality. It is a very serious question, whether the bird is anything more than a permanently yellow-billed variety of the common bird. It is well known that in *Psilorhinus morio*, and other garruline birds, the bill may be either yellow or black, almost in the same brood of young; and if magpies with these differences were habitually associated throughout the continent, there would probably be no hesitation in combining them. The restriction of the yellow billed magpie to the coast region of California, where it is unmixed with black billed individuals, except in the northern portion of the State, is an interesting fact.

List of specimens.

Catal. No.	Locality.	When collected.	Whence obtained.	Collected by—
8476	San Francisco, Cal.......	....	R. D. Cutts.............	....
5899	Santa Clara, Cal..........	1855.....................	Dr. Cooper..............	....
2845	Santa Barbara, Cal.......	....	S. F. Baird.	J. J. Audubon ....
4937	San José, Cal.	....	A. J. Grayson............	....
4567	San Diego, Cal	....	Dr. Hammond.............	....

CYANURA, Swainson.

Cyanurus, SWAINSON, F. Bor. Am. II, 1831, 495, Appendix. Type *Corvus cristatus*, Linn.
Cyanocitta, CABANIS, Mus. Hein. 1851. Not of Strickland, 1845.

CH.—Head crested. Wings and tail blue, with transverse black bars ; head and back of the same color. Bill rather slender, somewhat broader than high at the base ; culmen about equal to the head. Nostrils large, nearly circular, concealed by bristles. Tail about as long as the wings, lengthened, graduated. Hind claw large, longer than its digit.

The culmen is straight to near the tip, where it is gently decurved ; the gonys is convex at the base, then straight and ascending. The bill has a very slight notch at the tip. The nostrils are large, nearly circular, or slightly elliptical. The commissure is straight at the base, then bending down slightly near the tip. The legs present no special peculiarities. The crest on the head consists of a number of elongated, narrow, lanceolate occipital feathers.

The *C. cristata* differs from *C. stelleri*, and still more from *C. macrolophus*, in having a shorter, stouter, and more convex and curved bill ; the nasal bristly feathers with black shafts, and the lateral branches ash color, instead of the whole being black. The tarsi are shorter, the colors quite different.

Synopsis of species.

Common characters.—Wings and tail blue, conspicuously banded with black. Head with a prominent crest.

Bill short. Lateral tail feathers tipped with white. Under parts whitish ; breast with a crescent of black connected with a half collar on the neck above...............*C. cristata.*

Bill longer. Body blue. Head, neck, and upper part of back dull sooty black.

Occipital crest rather short. Frontal feathers slightly glossed with dull blue. No white about the eyes..*C. stelleri.*

Occipital crest very long. Frontal feathers conspicuously streaked with bluish white. A white streak above the eye................................*C. macrolophus.*

Comparative measurements of species.

Catal. No.	Species.	Locality.	Sex & age.	Length.	Stretch of wings.	Wing.	Tail.	Tarsus.	Middle toe.	I claw alone.	Hind toe and claw.	H claw alone.	Bill above.	Along gape.	Specimen measured.
1407	Cyanura cristata........	Carlisle, Pa........	♀	10.12	....	5 02	5.22	1.22	1.04	0.34	0.80	0.40	1.01	1.12	Skin ......
do	........do........	......do....		11.00	16.00	5.17	......	......	......	......	......	......	......	......	Fresh .....
1423	.........do........	.........do........	♂	11.02	....	5.62	5.84	1.36	1.16	0.36	0.86	0.40	1.18	1.20	Skin ......
do	.... do........	......do....		12.25	17.75	5.66	......	......	......	......	......	......	......	......	Fresh .....
8376	Cyanura stelleri..	California	......	10.90	....	5.34	5.18	1.60	1.18	0.36	0.88	0.43	1.13	1.18	Skin ......
8372	........do........	Fort Steilacoom ...	......	12.80	....	5.71	6.10	1.82	1.36	0.44	1.02	0.50	1.18	1.40	Skin ......
8486	Cyanura macrolophus..	Fort Mass, N. M...	♀	11.30	....	5.92	5.90	1.65	1.16	0.32	0.90	0.46	1.10	1.25	Skin ......
8352	........do........	Camp 105, N. M..	.....	11.70	....	6.00	6.10	1.66	1.28	0.38	0.96	0.46	1.24	1.38	Skin ......
do	... .do........	... ..do........	......	12.00	17.00	......	......	......	......	......	......	......	......	......	Fresh .....
4419	........do........	City of Mexico	......	11.20	....	5.46	5.70	1.58	1.10	0.38	0.90	0.47	1.10	1.26	Skin ......
1919	Cyanocitta floridana....			10.30	....	4.43	5.91	1.44	1.10	0.30	0.83	0.34	0.98	1.10	Skin ......
5903	Cyanocitta californica ..	Santa Clara, Cal...	......	11.26	....	4.75	5.65	1.52	1.24	0.40	0.84	0.44	1 14	1.20	Skin ......
8455	........do........	Tejon Pass	♂	10.44	....	4.65	5.64	1.60	1.20	0.37	0.90	0.41	1.10	1.22	Skin ......
9345	........do........	San Francisco......	♀	10.70	....	4.82	5.54	1.47	1.16	0.33	0.72	0.30	1.10	1.25	Skin *.....
8465	........do...... ...	Mexico...	......	11.10	....	5.31	5.96	1.60	1.12	0.34	0.80	0.38	0.94	1.08	Skin ......
8484	Cyanocitta woodhousii .	Fort Thorn, N. M ..	......	11.70	....	5.20	6.08	1.64	1.16	0.34	0.77	0.40	1.10	1.21	Skin ......
9095	Cyanocitta sordida	Mexico	♂	12.80	....	6.54	6.54	1.70	1.28	0.41	0.94	0.44	1.12	1.32	Skin ......
8469	........do........	Copper Mines, N. M	o ♂	12.10	....	6.33	6.28	1.64	1.30	0.36	0.90	0.44	1.10	1.30	Skin ......
do	........do........ ..	......do........	......	13.00	19.00	6.50	......	......	......	......	......	......	......	......	Fresh .....
4112	Cyanocitta ultramarina.?	Monterey, Mex....	♂	10.70	....	5.82	5.43	......	1.22	0.43	0.94	0.47	1.15	1.33	Skin ......
do	........do........	......do........	......	11.50	18.00	6.00	......	......	......	......	......	......	......	......	Fresh .....
9096	Cyanocitta unicolor	Mexico	♂	13.10	....	6.52	6.94	1.59	1.27	0.40	1.00	0.48	1.10	1.33	Skin ......
8452	Perisoreus canadensis..	Sangre Cristo Pass	......	10.90	....	5.78	5.94	1.32	0.98	0.34	0.74	0.40	0.87	0.94	Skin ......
4052	Xanthoura luxuosa....	New Leon, Mex...	♂	10.50	....	4.71	5.62	1.60	1.12	0.36	0.89	0.41	1.06	1.16	Skin ......
do	........do...	......do........	......	11.00	14.25	4.75	......	......	......	......	......	......	......	......	Fresh .....
9094	........do............	Mexico	......	10.90	....	4.58	5.12	1.48	1.12	0.35	0.85	0.41	1.04	1.16	Skin ......

* Mounted.

CYANURUS CRISTATUS, Swainson.

Blue Jay.

Corvus cristatus, LINN. Syst. Nat. I, 10th ed. 1758, 106; 12th ed. 1766, 157.—GMELIN, Syst. Nat. I, 1788, 369.—WILSON, Am. Orn. I, 1808, 2; pl. i. f. 1.—BON. Obs. Wilson, 1824, No. 41.—DOUGHTY, Cab. N. H. II, 1832, 62; pl. vi.—AUD. Orn. Biog. II, 1834, 11 : V, 1839, 475; pl. 102.

Garrulus cristatus, "VIEILLOT, Encyclop. 890."—IB. Dict. XI, 477.—BON. Syn. 1828, 58.—SW. F. Bor. Am. II, 1831, 293.—VIEILLOT, Galerie, I, 1824, 160; pl. cii.—AUD. Birds Am. IV, 110; pl. 231.

Pica cristata, WAGLER, Syst. Av. 1827. *Pica*, No. 8.

Cyanurus cristatus, SWAINSON, F. Bor. Am. II, 1831, App. 495.

Cyanocorax cristatus, BON. List, 1838.

Cyanocitta cristata, STRICKLAND, Ann. Mag. N. H. 1845, 261.—CABANIS, Mus. Hein. 1851, 221.

Cyanogarrulus cristatus, BON. Consp. 1850, 376.

SP. CH.,—Crest about one-third longer than the bill. Tail much graduated. General color above light purplish blue; wings and tail feathers ultramarine blue; the secondaries and tertials, the greater wing coverts, and the exposed surface of the tail, sharply banded with black, and broadly tipped with white, except on the central tail feathers. Beneath white; tinged with purplish blue on the throat, and with bluish brown on the sides. A black crescent on the fore part of the breast, the horns passing forward and connecting with a half collar on the back of the neck. A narrow frontal line and loral region black; feathers on the base of the bill, blue like the crown. Female rather duller in color and a little smaller. Length, 12.25; wing, 5.65; tail, 5.75.

Hab.—Eastern North America, west to the Missouri.

In addition to what has been already stated, there is a narrow black line behind the eye running into the cervical collar, which is overhung by the feathers of the crest; the posterior concealed ones of these also black. The amount of white on the tail decreases from the exterior.

List of specimens.

Catal. No.	Sex.	Locality.	When collected.	Whence obtained.	Orig. No.	Collected by—	Length.	Stretch of wings.	Wing.	Remarks.
1582	.....	Washington, D. C.....	....	Wm. Hutton.........	.....	....	......	....	......	....
1407	♀	Carlisle, Penn.........	April 30, 1844	S. F. Baird	.....	....	11.00	16.00	5.16	....
1423	♂	......do................	May 2, 1844	......do............	.....	....	12.25	17.75	5.65	....
7000	♀	St. Louis.....	May 8, 1857	Lieut. Bryan.........	......	W. S. Wood...	......	....	......	....
	.....	Racine, Wis.	....	Robert Kennicott	......	....	......	....	......	....
6946	.....	Red River, H. B....	....	D. Gunn............	......	....	......	....	......	....
8450	.....	Fort Leavenworth.....	Oct. 23, 1854	Lieut. Couch	6	....	......	....	......	....
8324	♂	Independence, Mo....	May 27, 1857	W. M. Magraw	47	Dr. Cooper.....	12.50	16.50	5.50	Iris brown; bill and feet black.
8325	......	....do........	May 29, 1857	......do.............	48	....do..........	12.50	16.50	5.50	......do........do. ..
5866	.....	Fort Riley, K. T......	....	Hammond & DeVesey	......	....	......	....	......	....

CYANURA STELLERI, Swainson.

Steller's Jay.

Corvus stelleri, GMELIN, Syst. Nat. I, 1788, 370.—LATH. Ind. Orn. I, 1790, 158.—PALLAS, Zoog. Rosso-As. I, 1811,
393.—BONAP. Zool. Jour. III, 1827, 49.—IB. Suppl. Syn, 1828, 433.—AUD. Orn. Biog. IV, 1838,
453 ; pl. 362.

Garrulus stelleri, VIEILLOT, Dict. XII, 1817, 481.—BONAP. Am. Orn. II, 1828, 44 ; pl. xiii.—NUTTALL, Man. I,
1832, 229.—AUD. Syn. 1839, 154.—IB. Birds Amer. IV, 1842, 107 ; pl. 230. Not of Swainson, F. Bor. Amer.?

Cyanurus stelleri, SWAINSON, F. Bor. Am. II, 1831, 495, App.

Pica stelleri, WAGLER, Syst. Av. 1827, Pica, No. 10.

Cyanocorax stelleri, BON. List, 1838.

Cyanocitta stelleri, CAB. Mus. Hein. 1851, 221.—NEWBERRY, P. R. R. Rep. VI, IV, 1857, 85.

Cyanogarrulus stelleri, BONAP. Conspectus, 1850, 377.

Steller's crow, PENNANT, Arctic Zool. II, Sp. 139.—LATH. Syn. I, 387.

SP. CH.—Crest about one-third longer than the bill. Fifth quill longest ; second about equal to the secondary quills. Tail graduated ; lateral feathers about .70 of an inch shortest. Head and neck all round, and fore part of breast, dark brownish black. Back and lesser wing coverts, blackish brown, the scapulars glossed with blue. Under parts, rump, tail coverts, and wing, greenish blue ; exposed surfaces of lesser quills dark indigo blue ; tertials and ends of tail feathers rather obsoletely banded with black. Feathers of the forehead streaked with greenish blue. Length, about 13 inches ; wing, 5.85 ; tail, 5.85 ; tarsus, 1.75, (1921).

Hab.—Pacific coast of North America ; east to St. Mary's Mission, Rocky mountains.

In many specimens there is an appearance of greyish on the chin, owing to the exposed bases of the feathers. There is a faint gloss of bluish gray on the blackish or dark brown of the back, but it is scarcely appreciable. The shafts of the quills and tail feathers are black. The upper surfaces of the tail feathers are blue, not so dark as the secondaries and tertials ; the inferior surfaces brownish black. Bill and feet black. The wings reach about to the end of the upper tail coverts.

There is some difference in specimens as to the shade of blue, which sometimes has much less of green in it than as described. The black bands on the wings and tail also vary in extent and intensity. The sexes do not differ appreciably in color.

The specimens in the collection before me are all from the regions of the Pacific towards the coast, except one procured at the Catholic Mission of St. Mary's, among the Flatheads. This, however, is on the western slope of the mountains. The bird figured by Richardson appears to be the *C. macrolophus*, as shown by the whitish on the forehead and over the eye; the description, however, answers sufficiently well to *C. stelleri*.

The *Pica cyanochlora* of Wagler, Syst. Av. 1827, No. 9, *Pica*, and the *Graculus* (error for *Garrulus*) *melanogaster*, Vieillot, Nouv. Dict. XII, 1817, 478, referred to this species by authors, do not answer at all to it.

List of specimens.

Catal. No.	Sex.	Locality.	When collected.	Whence obtained.	Orig. No.	Collected by—	Length.	Stretch of wings.	Wing.
844	♂	Russian America..............	1841	S. F. Baird.................		Wosnesjensky...........			.. ..
4448	......	Cape Flattery, W. T..........	....	Lieut. Trowbridge.. ...		....	......	......	......
5901	......	Straits of Fuca, W. T.........	....	Dr. Cooper................		....	......	......	......
8369	......	Fort Steilacoom, W. T........	Dec. 26, 1854	Gov. Stevens	.....	Dr. Suckley................			......
8370	......	... .do.....	Feb. —, 1854	......do....	39	......do....	13.00	19.00	6.50
8373	♂	........do.....	April 28, 1856	Dr. Suckley	350	....	12.00	17.00	
8374	......	........do.....	March	......do....	244	....	13.00	17.50	
8375	....	........do.....	April 25, 1856	......do....	326	....			
4583	.. .	........do.....	....	Dr. Potts.................		....			
8366	....	Fort Vancouver, W. T........	....	Gov. Stevens	.....	Dr. Cooper....			
8367	......	........do.....	Jan. 31, 1854	......do....	23	......do....	12.25	18.00	..
8368	......	........do.....	Jan. 30, 1854	......do....	21	......do....	12.25	18.00	
1921	♂	Columbia river..............	1834....	S. F. Baird.................	.....	J. K. Townsend...........			
4380	......	Fort Dalles, Oregon	Jan. 7, 1855	Dr. Suckley	167	....			
4449	......	Cascade mountains	....	Lieut. Williamson.........		Dr. Newberry....			
4447	......	Willamette valley............	....	......do....		......do....			
5541	♂	Petaluma, Cal...............	....	E. Samuels........... .	680	....			
4223	......	San Francisco county, Cal	Winter '53–54	R. D. Cutts		....			
3717	♂	Carmel, Redwoods, Cal.......	Sept. 4......	W. Hutton		....			
3718	♀	Monterey, Cal...	May 12, 1847	......do....		....	......	......	....
		Fort Tejon................	....	J. X. de Vesey............		....			
8371	......	St. Mary's Mission, R. mountains	....	Gov. Stevens	.....	Dr. Suckley..............	13.00	18.00	5.75

CYANURA MACROLOPHUS, Baird.

Long-crested Jay.

Cyanocitta macrolopha, BAIRD, Pr. A. N. Sc. Phila. VII, June, 1854, 118. Albuquerque.
? *Garrulus stelleri*, SWAINSON, F. Bor. Am. II, 1831, 294; pl. liv. The plate, probably, if not the description. Head waters of Columbia. Not *Corvus stelleri* of Gmelin.

SP. CH.—Crest nearly twice the length of the bill. Tail moderately graduated; the lateral feathers about .60 of an inch shorter than the middle. Fourth and fifth quills longest; second shorter than the secondaries. Head all round, throat and fore part of the breast, black, the crest with a gloss of blue; rest of back dark ashy brown with a gloss of greenish. Under parts, rump, tail coverts, and outer surfaces of primaries, greenish blue; greater coverts, secondaries, and tertials, and upper surface of tail feathers, bright blue, banded with black; forehead streaked with opaque white, passing behind into pale blue; a white patch over the eye. Chin grayish. Length, 12.50; wing, 5.85; tail, 5.85; tarsus, 1.70, (8351.)

Hab.—Central line of Rocky mountains to table lands of Mexico.

This species is very similar to the *C. stelleri*, but is readily distinguishable on comparison The most striking peculiarities are the much longer and fuller crest, the streaks on the forehead white, not blue; and the white patch over the eye, not found at all in *stelleri*. The head is much blacker; the crest feathers having also a gloss of blue, instead of opaque dark brown. The back is dusky bluish ash, not opaque brown. The chin is more gray; the blue of the breast extends further forward and is much less abruptly defined. The black bands on the wing feathers are more distinct, especially those on the greater coverts, which, obsolete in *stelleri*, are very conspicuous in the other.

In addition to the peculiarities of coloration, the bill is much more slender, and the tail less rounded.

The bird figured by Richardson in Fauna Boreali Americana appears to be this species, from the white forehead and patch above the eye; the description, on the contrary, applies pretty well to *stelleri*.

Recognizing fully the close relationship which the present species bears to *C. coronata*[1] of Swainson, I am yet inclined to consider it as distinct, notwithstanding a previous impression to the contrary. Swainson's species appears to have the same long crest and the white superciliary patch, but it is described by him as blue, the sides of the head blackish, the wing coverts and tertials with blackish lines. As no mention is made of such lines on the tail, it is presumed that they are wanting. Bonaparte says the bird is entirely blue, the head duller, but with a bluer crest, the quills and tail feathers obsoletely banded. He adds that the adult has the head blackish; the young with the head blue. Cabanis says that the crest is blackish blue, the rest of the head and fore neck more or less blackish according to age. In the present bird the head and neck all round are black, and the crest having only a gloss of blue, scarcely appreciable, and the tail is very distinctly banded with black.

There seems to be a regular succession of jays of the present group between two extremes of color. Thus, the *C. stelleri* has the head and neck opaque black, with a frontal wash of dark blue. *C. macrolophus* has the head even blacker, the crest only glossed with blue terminally, the frontal wash and a superciliary spot whitish; the tail and wings strongly banded with black. *C. diademata*, Bonap., from southern Mexico, apparently lacks the superciliary white spot, the general color is ashy, the rump and abdomen blue. The quills and tail feathers are conspicuously banded. It differs from *macrolophus* in having the crest only black, and the color more ashy. *C. coronata* has the head and neck with the crest bluish, the sides of the head black, a whitish frontal and superciliary spot; and finally *C. galeata*, Cab., (Mus. Hein, 222,) from Bogota, has the head entirely blue, the borders of the crest only blackish.

The *Garrulus stelleri* of the F. B. A. appears to be the present species, and one strong reason for believing it distinct from the *coronata* is the fact, that Swainson did not identify his supposed *stelleri* with the bird he had described only a few years before as *Garrulus coronatus*.

List of specimens.

Catal. No.	Sex and age.	Locality.	When collected.	Whence obtained.	Orig. No.	Collected by—	Length.	Stretch of wings.	Wing.	Remarks.
8856	♂	Laramie Peak...................	Aug. 27......	Lt. Warren.........	......	Dr. Hayden	12.00	18.25	6.25	....
8857	....	......do......................	Aug. 26......	......do........	......	......do........	11.75	21.75	7.00	
8486	♀	Fort Mass., N. M..............	Feb. 9,1856	Dr. Peters.........	6	....	11.75			....
8487	♂	......do......................	......do......	......do.........	4	....	11.75			
8356	....	Fort Thorn, N. M.............		Dr. T. C. Henry....	......	....				
8351	....	100 miles west of Albuquerque..	Nov. 17,1853	Lt. Whipple.......	20	Kenn. & Möll..	11.00	18.00	7.00	Eyes black...
8352	....	Camp 105...................	Jan. 23,1854	......do........	53	......do........	12.00	17.00	7.00	....do.......
4419	....	City of Mexico	....	J. Potts...........	......	....	....	....		....

[1] CYANURA CORONATA, Swainson.

Garrulus coronatus, SWAINSON, Phil. Mag. I, 1827, 437. Table lands Mex.—JARDINE & SELBY, Ill. tab. lxiv.
Pica coronata, WAGLER, Isis, 1829, 750. Possibly *C. macrolophus*.
Cyanurus coronatus, SWAINSON, F. Bor. Am. II, 1831, 495.
Cyanocorax coronatus, BONAP. Pr. Zool. Soc. V, 1837, 115.
Cyanogarrulus coronatus, BON. Conspectus, 1850, 377.
Cyanocitta coronata, CAB. Mus. Hein, 1851, 222.

CYANOCITTA, Strickland.

Cyanocitta, STRICKLAND, Annals and Mag. N. H. XV, 1845, 260. Type, *Garrulus californicus*, Vigors.
Aphelocoma, CABANIS, Mus. Hein. 1851, 221. Same type.

CH.—Head without crest. Wings and tail blue, without any bands. Back with a gray patch, different from the head. Bill about as broad as high at the base, and the culmen a little shorter than the head. Nostrils large, nearly circular, and concealed. Tail shorter or nearly equal to the wings, lengthened, graduated.

This genus has much the general character of *Cyanura* or the blue jays, but is readily distinguished by the absence of a crest and of black bars on the wings and tail. The wings generally are shorter ; the general characteristics, however, appear much the same.

The *C. ultramarina* differs from the other species in having the wings considerably longer, or fully equal to the tail, which also is nearly even, instead of considerably graduated.

Synopsis of species.

Blue of sides of head extending over the sides of the breast to its middle. Chin, throat, and breast white ; the feathers of the latter margined with blue. Interscapular gray patch conspicuously different from the head. A superciliary streak of white.

Belly and under tail coverts dull white. Forehead blue. A well marked superciliary stripe..*C. californica.*

Belly light brownish ash ; under tail coverts blue. Forehead blue like the crown. Interscapular region glossed with blue. Superciliary stripe distinct......*C. woodhouseii.*

Belly brownish ash ; under tail coverts blue. Forehead and sides of crown bluish hoary, conspicuously different from the blue crown, the superciliary stripe not well marked.
C. floridana.

Under parts without any bluish edges to the pectoral feathers ; breast bluish ash ; belly and crissum pure white. Interscapular region scarcely different from the remaining upper surfaces.

Tail nearly even, considerably shorter than the wing...........................*C. ultramarina.*

Tail rounded, nearly as long as the wings ....*C. sordida.*

CYANOCITTA CALIFORNICA, Strickland.

California Jay.

Garrulus californicus, VIGORS, Zool. Beechey's Voyage, 1839, 21 ; pl. v.
Cyanocitta californica, STRICKLAND, Ann. Mag. XV, 1845, 342.—GAMBEL, J. A. N. Sc. 2d series, I, Dec. 1847, 45.—BON. Conspectus, 1850, 377.—NEWBERRY, P. R. R. Rep. VI, IV, 1857, 85.
Cyanocorax californicus, GAMBEL, Pr. A. N. Sc. III, Ap. 1847, 201.
Aphelocoma californica, CABANIS, Mus. Hein. 1851, 221.—BON. Comptes Rendus, XXXVII, Nov. 1853, 828 ; Notes Orn. Delattre.
Corvus ultramarinus, AUD. Orn. Biog. IV, 1838, 456 ; pl. 362. Not *Garrulus ultramarinus*, Bon.
Garrulus ultramarinus, AUD. Syn. 1839, 154.—IB. Birds Amer. IV, 1842, 115 ; pl. 232. Not of Bonaparte.
Cyanocitta superciliosa, STRICKLAND, Ann. Mag. XV, 1845, 260. Type of genus *Cyanocitta.*
" *Corvus palliatus*, DRAPIEZ," BONAP.

SP. CH.—Width of bill at base of lower mandible rather more than half the length of culmen. Lateral tail feathers about an inch shortest. Tail an inch longer than the wings. General color above, including the surface of the wings, bright blue, without any bars. The whole back, including to some extent the interscapulars, brownish ash, very faintly glossed with blue in the adult. A streaked white superciliary line from a little anterior to the eye as far as the occiput. Sides of the head and neck blue, the region around and behind the eye, including lores and most of ear coverts, black. The blue of the sides of the neck extends across the fore part of the breast, forming a crescent, interrupted in the middle. The under parts anterior to the crescent, white streaked with blue; behind it dull white; the sides tinged with brown. Length, 12.25; wing, 5; tail, 6.15; tarsus, 1.55. (2841.)

Hab.—Pacific coast from Columbia river south. Not in the interior.

The forehead and nasal feathers are uniform blue with the crown. The blue extends on the fore part of the back; it is scarcely found on the rump, although the upper tail coverts are like the crown. There is no trace of blue on the belly, although a very faint wash is perceptible on the lower tail coverts. The blue streaks on and anterior to the pectoral collar are on the edges of the feathers, not the centres.

I find considerable differences in size in different specimens of this bird. Thus, No. 8456, from San Francisco, measures nearly 14 inches; the wing, 5.25; the tail, 6.40. No. 8455, (male,) from Tejon Pass, on the contrary, measures 10.40 inches; the wing, 4.65; the tail, 5.50. The more southern specimens are smaller, and have the ashy brown of the back less glossed with blue. In most specimens the tail feathers are nearly truncate; in 2841, however, they are quite acute.

In young birds the head is generally like the back, with only a faint shade of blue. There is a brownish pectoral collar, but no streaks of blue.

List of specimens.

Catal. No.	Sex.	Locality.	When collected.	Whence obtained.	Orig. No.	Collected by—
2641	♂	Columbia river, O. T.	Oct. 11, 1834	S. F. Baird		J. K. Townsend
8458		Bodega, Cal	Jan. —, 1855	Lt. Trowbridge		T. A. Szabo
5542	♂	Petaluma, Cal		E. Samuels	169	
4225		San Francisco, Cal.	Wint. 1853-'4	R. D. Cutts		
5902		Santa Clara, Cal		Dr. Cooper		
5903		...do		...do		
4949		San José, Cal		A. J. Grayson	6	
8457		Presidio, Cal	July 27, 1853	Lt. Trowbridge		
3716		Monterey, Cal	Aug. 24, 1857	W. Hutton		
4565		San Pasqual, Cal		Major Emory	13	A. Schott
8455	♂	Tejon pass		Lt. Williamson		Dr. Heermann
		Fort Tejon, Cal		J. X. de Vesey		
8461		San Felipe, Cal		Major Emory		A. Schott
8462		Camp 149, Cal	Mar. 16, 1854	Lt. Whipple	186	Kenn. and Möll

CYANOCITTA WOODHOUSEII, Baird.

Woodhouse's Jay.

Sp. Ch.—Size and general appearance of *C. californica.* Graduation of tail one inch. Blue, with a very obscure ashy patch on the back. Sides of the head and neck and incomplete pectoral collar, blue; throat streaked with the same. Breast and belly uniform brownish ash glossed with blue; under tail coverts bright blue. Sides of head, including lores, black, glossed with blue below; a streaked white superciliary line. Length, 11.50; wing, 5.35; tail, 6.10; tarsus, 1.60.

Hab.—Central line of Rocky mountains to table lands of Mexico.

This species has so close a relationship to *C. californica* that it may not seem proper to separate them, but the differences are readily perceptible in large series. All of the Rocky mountain

July 1, 1858.

74 b

specimens have common characters in which they differ from California jays. The most striking of these differences is in the much darker shade of the under parts, in which there is no white at all, except perhaps immediately around the anus. The under tail coverts are of a clear blue, almost as bright as that on the upper coverts, and there is a general faint gloss of blue beneath, especially along the middle of the body, while in *californica* there is only a faint trace of blue on the under coverts. The back is more strongly glossed with blue; so much so as almost to take away the impression of any gray patch at all. The lores are quite black, without the mixture of hoary, seen in *californica*. The wing is rather longer in proportion; the tail rather less graduated. The bill is more slender.

A specimen, 8465, from Mexico, doubtfully referred here, is quite similar to those from the Rocky mountains; the tail is, however, rather less graduated, and the under tail coverts are white. There is little or no trace of the superciliary line of white spots. The bill is much shorter, broader, and more obtuse.

List of specimens.

Catal. No.	Sex.	Locality.	When collected.	Whence obtained.	Orig'l No.	Collected by—	Extent.	Stretch of wing.	Wing.	Remarks.
5035	......	Independence Springs, N. M.	Sept. 27, 1855	Capt. J. Pope....	137	....	13.00	15.00	5.00	Bill and feet black; eye dark brown............
8484	.... .	Fort Thorn, N. M......	....	Dr. Henry.........		....	....	....	....	....
9345	♀	San Francisco Mts., N.M	Oct. 11, 1851	Capt. Sitgreaves..	....	Dr. Woodhouse.	....	....	....	....
8465?	......	Mexico..............	Sept. —, 1836	John Gould......	......	John Taylor...	....	....	....	....

CYANOCITTA FLORIDANA, Bonap.

Florida Jay.

Corvus floridanus, BARTRAM, Travels, 1791, 291.—AUD. Orn. Biog. I, 1831, 444; pl. 87.

Garrulus floridanus, BON. Am. Orn. II, 1828, 11; pl. xi.—NUTTALL, Man. I, 1832, 230.—AUD. Syn. 1839, 154.—IB. Birds Amer. IV, 1842, 118; pl. 233.

Cyanurus floridanus, SWAINSON, F. B. A. II, 1831, 495.

Cyanocorax floridanus, BON. List, 1838.

Cyanocitta floridana, BON. Consp. 1850, 377.

Aphelocoma floridana, CABANIS, Mus Hein. 1851, 22.

Garrulus cyaneus, VIEILLOT, Nouv. Dict. XII, 1817, 476. (Not described.)

? *Garrulus caerulescens*, VIEILLOT, Nouv. Dict. XII, 1817, 480.—ORD. J. A. N. Sc. I, 1818, 347.

Pica caerulescens, WAGLER, Syst. Av. 1827, Pica, No. 11.

SP. CH.—Tail much graduated; lateral feathers more than one inch shortest. Tail an inch longer than the wings. Above blue; middle of the back brownish ash. Forehead and sides of the crown, including the nasal feathers, hoary white. Sides of head and neck, blue; the former tinged with blackish, the latter sending a streaked collar of the same across the breast; region anterior to this collar dirty white streaked on the edges of the feathers with blue; rest of under parts dirty whitish brown; under tail coverts blue, the tibia tinged with the same. Length, 10.50; wing, 4.40; tail, 5.70; tarsus, 1.45.

This species is very similar to the Rocky mountain *C. woodhouseii* in the color of the under parts, including the brown belly, the blue crissum, the pectoral band, &c. The back, however, is much lighter and better defined grey, more so even than in *C. californica*. It differs from both species in the hoary on the forehead and sides of the crown, and in the absence of the superciliary line of white spots, as also in being considerably smaller.

List of specimens.

Catal. No.	Locality.	Whence obtained.
1919	Florida............	S. F. Baird ....

CYANOCITTA SORDIDA, Baird.

Garrulus sordidus, Swainson, Philos. Mag. I, June, 1827, 437.—Ib. Zool. Ill. N. S. tab. lxxxvi.
Cyanogarrulus sordidus, Bonap. Consp. 1850, 378.
Aphelocoma sordida, Cab. Mus. Hein. 1851, 221.
Pica sieberi, Wagler, Syst. Avium 1827, *Pica*, No. 23.

Sp. Ch.—Bill short ; thick ; half as high as long. Wings about as long or but little longer than the tail, which is graduated .85 of an inch. Above and on sides of head and neck bright blue, scarcely duller in the middle of the back. Beneath white ; the throat and breast tinged with very faint bluish, especially across the latter. Tibial feathers dull bluish ash ; crissum white, the tips of posterior feathers very faintly tinged with bluish grey. Length, 13 inches ; wing, 6.60 ; tail, 6.60 ; tarsus, 1.65 ; culmen, 1.00 ; height of bill at base .45.

Hab —Mimbres region of Rocky mountains, and south to table lands of Mexico.

Fourth and fifth quills longest, sixth little shorter ; second quill a little longer than the secondaries. Tail lengthened, about equal to or a little shorter than the wings. Lateral feathers about .85 of an inch shorter than the middle.

This species is very much like the *C. ultramarina*, having precisely the same coloration, except that the upper surface of the tail is more blue, and the middle of the back more like the rest of the upper surface. The form is, however, very different ; the bill is much thicker at the base and the gonys curved nearly as much as the culmen, instead of much less. The size is larger, and while the wings are nearly the same length, the tail is an inch longer, and is decidedly graduated by almost an inch, instead of not more than one-fourth as much.

The adult specimen described above is from Mexico, kindly furnished by Mr. Jules Verreaux, the only government skin before me being an immature bird from Fort Webster. This measured when fresh 13 inches; extent, 19 ; wing, 6.50 ; the tail about the same. The general style of coloration when mature is doubtless that of *C. ultramarina*, in the continuous blue of the upper surface, slightly duller on the back. The under parts are equally destitute of a pectoral collar or stripes ; but the entire anterior half gives promise of being light blue, passing behind into pale ashy blue, more whitish about the anus. It differs from *C. ultramarinus* in the more graduated tail, the lateral feathers .75 of an inch shorter, larger size, especially of the tail ; which is equal to the wing instead of shorter. There is more blue on the throat and breast, and a decided tinge of the same behind and under the wings. The lower mandible is yellowish at the base, bluish toward the tip.

This bird appears to be the same with that described by Swainson as *Garrulus sordidus*, and by Wagler as *Pica sieberi*, apparently from the same specimen. I do not understand why the latter name should be preferred by some authors, as the date of publication is the same (1827 ;) while Swainson made his description from the specimen while in Bullock's Museum of Mexican curiosities, before its dispersion, and Wagler after the collection in question had been broken up, and the specimen passed into Mr. Leadbeater's hands.

List of specimens.

Catal. No.	Sex.	Locality.	When collected.	Whence obtained.	Orig. No.	Collected by—	Length.	Stretch of wings.	Wing.
8469	♂	Copper Mines, N. M..	1851..........	Col. Graham....	8	J. H. Clark......	13.00	19.00	6.50
9095	♂	Mexico.............	....	M. Verreaux	17237	....	......	....	.....

CYANOCITTA ULTRAMARINA, Strickl.

Ultramarine Jay.

Garrulus ultramarinus, BONAP. J. A. N. Sc. IV, 1825, 386. Not of Audubon.
Cyanocitta ultramarina, STRICKLAND, Ann. & Mag. XV, 1845, 260.—GAMBEL, J. A. N. Sc. 2d Ser. I, 1847, 45.
Cyanogarrulus ultramarinus, BON. Consp. 1850, 378 ; quotes Pl. Col. 439.

SP. CH.—Tail rounded, but little graduated ; lateral feather about a quarter of an inch shortest. Wings longer than the tail, when closed reaching nearly to its middle. Above and on sides of head and neck bright blue ; the lores blackish ; the middle of the back slightly duller, the tips of some of the feathers dark brown. Beneath brownish ash, paler on the chin and towards the anal region, which, with the crissum, is white. No trace of white or black on the sides of the head, nor of any streaks or collar on the breast. Length, (fresh,) 11.50 ; wing, 6 ; tail, (dried,) 5.40 ; tarsus, 1.50.

Hab.—South side of valley of Rio Grande, near the coast, and southward.

This well marked species is quite different in form from the *C. californica*, having a shorter, more even tail, much longer wings, and stouter feet. The absence of any collar or streaks on the breast and throat, of black or white on the side of the head, and of decided ash on the back, are very well marked features. There is also much more green in the blue of the head.

I am in considerable doubt whether this is the original *Garrulus ultramarinus* of Bonaparte, as the latter appears to be much larger than Lieut. Couch's bird ; the length amounting to 13 inches ; the tail, 7 inches ; the bill, 1.50 inches. The closed wings reach almost to the middle of the tail, which is perfectly even at the tip. Gambel says the wing is 7 inches long ; the tail, 6.75 ; tarsus, 1.75. The measurements given in Conspectus Avium, of length 11 inches, wing 5¾, answer much better to the species here described. Should there be two species, therefore, and the smaller be not named, I shall propose to call it *C. couchii*, in honor of its indefatigable discoverer, Lieut. D. N. Couch, of the United States army, who, at his own risk and cost, undertook a journey into northern Mexico when the country was swarming with bands of marauders, and made large collections in all branches of zoology, which have furnished a great amount of information respecting the natural history of our borders and the geographical distribution of the vertebrata generally.

List of specimens.

Catal. No.	Sex.	Locality.	When collected.	Whence obtained.	Orig. No.	Length.	Stretch of wings.	Wing.	Remarks.
4112	♂	Monterey, Mex....	....	Lt. Couch	156	11.50	18.00	6.00	Eyes dark brown ; bill and feet bl'k.
4113	♂	......do..........	April —, 1853	......do........	157	11.50	18.00	6.60	....

XANTHOURA, Bonaparte.

Xanthoura, BONAPARTE, Consp. Av. 1850.   Type *Corvus peruvianus*, GM.

CH.—Head without crest.   Throat black.   Lateral tail feathers bright yellow.   Bill very stout ; rather higher than broad ; culmen curved from the base.   Nostrils rather small, oval, concealed.   Tail longer than the wings ; graduated.   The wings concave, rounded ; the secondaries nearly as long as the primaries.   Legs very stout ; hind claw about half the total length of the toe.

This genus is most easily to be recognized by the prevailing green color of the body, the blue head, black throat, and yellow outer tail feathers.   The bill is stouter and larger than in any of our other jays, and the culmen more curved.   The chief peculiarity of form is seen in the wings, in which the primaries are remarkably short, scarcely longer than the longest secondaries and tertials.   They thus reach only about as far as the end of the upper tail coverts instead of much beyond them, a character quite peculiar among American *Corvidae*, except approximately in *Psilorhinus*.

XANTHOURA LUXUOSA, Bonap.

Rio Grande Jay.

Garrulus luxuosus, LESSON, Rev. Zool. April 1839, 100.
Cyanocorax luxuosus, DUBUS, Esquisses Ornithologiques, IV, 1848 ; pl. xviii.—CASSIN, Illust. I, 1853, I ; pl. 1.
Xanthoura luxuosa, BON. Consp. 1850, 380.—CABANIS, Mus. Hein. 1851, 224.
Pica chloronota, WAGLER, Isis, 1829, 750.   Young male.   Name belongs to *Corvus peruvianus*, Gm.
Cyanocorax cyanicapillus, CABANIS, Fauna Peruana, 1844-'46, 233.   (Note.)
Cyanocorax yucas, " BODDAERT," Lawrence, Ann. N. Y. Lyc. V, April, 1851, 115.   First added here to fauna o United States.   Name belongs to the *C. peruvianus*.

SP. CH.—Wings shorter than the tail, which is much graduated, the lateral feathers 1.25 inches shorter.   Above green ; beneath yellow, glossed with green ; inside of wings and outer four tail feathers straw yellow ; rest of tail feathers green, glossed with blue.   Sides of the head, and beneath from the bill to the fore part of the breast, velvet black.   Crown, nape, and a short maxillary stripe running up to the eye and involving the upper eyelid, brilliant blue ; the nostril feathers rather darker ; the sides of the forehead white.   Bill black ; feet lead color.   Length, 11 inches ; wing, 4.75 ; tail, 5.40 ; tarsus, 1.65.

Hab.—Valley of Rio Grande, of Texas, and southward.

The blue maxillary patch is broadly truncated behind.   The feathers of the forehead are yellowish at base.   The green of the back is not uniform, but is glossed in the middle of the back with blue ; not so deep as that of the middle tail feathers.   The feathers of the under parts are all yellow at base, which shows through the green, and is particularly distinct on the middle of the belly, and just below the black of the jugulum.   The tibia are chiefly yellow. The white of the forehead borders the black as far as above the eye ; that of opposite sides meets along the middle of the forehead, but is there less conspicuous.

Another specimen, 8365, is of a bright yellowish green above, with less blue on the tail. The blue of the head is much lighter, without any purplish shade ; the light frontal bar is yellowish rather than white.   There is more yellow visible beneath.   In all the specimens I have seen, however, the green of the under parts is very decided.

The description of *Garrulus luxuosus* by Lesson omits mention of the white frontal band.

This species is closely related to *Xanthoura peruviana*, which, however, is pure yellow beneath, has a white patch on the crown, and is, besides, considerably larger.   The *X. guatemalensis*, with a somewhat similar crown, has the abdomen bright yellow.

List of specimens.

Catal. No.	Sex.	Locality.	When collected.	Whence obtained.	Orig. No.	Length.	Stretch of wings	Wing.	Remarks.
8365	....	Rio Grande, Tex....	Oct. 2, 1855	A. Schott......	......	......	......	......	......
8357	....	Matamoras........	......	L. Berlandier ...	......	......	......	......	......
4052	♂	N. Leon, San Diego.	Mar. —, 1853	Lt. Couch	118	11.00	14.25	4.75	Eyes dark brown ; feet lead color.
9094	....	Mexico..........	......	M. Verreaux....	29883	......	......	......	......

PERISOREUS, Bonap.

Perisoreus, BONAP. Saggio di una dist. met. 1831.   Type *Corvus canadensis ?*
Dysornithia, SWAINSON, F. B. Am. II, 1831, 495.   Same type.

CH.—Feathers lax and full, especially on the back, and of very dull colors, without any blue. Head without distinct crest. Bill very short ; broader than high. Culmen scarcely half the length of the head ; straight to near the tip, then slightly curved ; gonys more curved than culmen. Bill notched at tip. Nostrils round, covered by bristly feathers. Tail about equal to the wings ; graduated. Tarsi rather short ; but little longer than the middle toe.

This genus includes the species of dullest colors among all of our jays. It has, too, the shortest bill, and with this feature bears a very strong resemblance in many respects to some of the titmice.

The dates of the two names mentioned above are the same, but as Gray finds *Perisoreus* to possess actual priority I follow him in this, not having a copy of the "Saggio" at hand.

PERISOREUS CANADENSIS, Bonap.

Canada Jay.

Corvus canadensis, LINN. Syst. Nat. I, 1766, 158.—FORSTER, Phil. Trans. LXII, 1772, 382.—WILSON, Am. Orn. III,
      1811, 33 ; pl. xxi.—BON. Obs. 1824, No. 42.—AUD. Orn. Biog. II, 1834, 53 : V, 1839, 208 ;
      pl. 107.
Garrulus canadensis, BON, (Saggio, 1831?) Syn. 1828, 58.—SWAINSON, F. Bor. Am. II, 1831, 295.—NUTTALL, Man.
      I, 1832, 232.—AUD. Syn. 1839, 155.—IB. Birds Amer. IV, 1842, 121 ; pl. 234.
Dysornithia canadensis, SWAINSON, F. Bor Am. II, 1831.   Appendix.
Perisoreus canadensis, BON. List, 1838.—IB. Conspectus, 1850, 375.—CAB. Mus. Hein. 1851, 219.—NEWBERRY, Rep.
      P. R. R. Surv. VI, IV, 1857, 85.
Garrulus fuscus, VIEILLOT, Nouv. Dict. XII, 1817, 479.
Pica nuchalis, WAGLER, Syst. Av. 1827.   Pica No. 14.
Garrulus trachyrrhynchus, SWAINSON, F. Bor. Am. II, 1831, 296 ; pl. lv.   Young.
" *Coracias mexicanus*, TEMMINCK," GRAY.

SP. CH.—Tail graduated ; lateral feathers about one inch shortest. Wings a little shorter than the tail. Head and neck, and fore part of breast white. A plumbeous brown nuchal patch, becoming darker behind, from the middle of the crown to the back, from which it is separated by an interrupted whitish collar. Rest of upper parts ashy plumbeous ; the outer primaries margined, the secondaries, tertials, and tail feathers obscurely tipped with white. Beneath smoky gray. Crissum whitish. Bill and feet black. Length, 10.70 ; wing, 5.75 ; tail, 6.00 ; tarsus, 1.40.

Hab.—Northern America into the northern parts of United States from Atlantic to Pacific ; more south in Rocky mountains.

The young of this species are everywhere of a dull sooty brown, lighter on the middle of the belly, and more plumbeous on the wings and tail. With increasing age the region about the base of the bill whitens, and this color gradually extends backwards until the whole head, excepting the occiput and nape, is white. The under parts are sometimes whiter than in the typical specimens.

List of specimens.

Catal. No.	Sex and age.	Locality.	When collected.	Whence obtained.	Orig. No.	Collected by—	Length.	Stretch of wings.	Wing.	Remarks.
530	....	Northern United States.....	....	S. F. Baird......	......	....	......	......	......	....
1920	○	......do.........	....	......do........	......	....	......	......	......	....
	....	Minnesota................	Oct. 6......	N. W. University.......	......	R. Kennicott...	......	......	......	....
8850	♀	Black Hills.............	Sept. 13...	Lt. Warren.....	......	Dr. Hayden....	10.25	16.25	5.50	Iris brown.........
8854	♀	....do..........	Oct. 1......	......do........	......	......do.......	10.25	17.00	5.50	
8848	♀	......do............	Sept. 13...	......do........	......	......do.......	11.25	18.50	6.00	Iris brown.........
8852	....	......do......	Sept. 27....	......do........	......	......do.......	11.00	16.50	5.50	Eye black.........
8849	....	......do............	Oct. 1......	......do........	......	......do.......	11.00	17.12	5.75	....
8851	....	......do............	Sept. 27....	......do........	......	......do.......	11.25	17.50	5.50	....
8855	....	......do............	Oct. 1......	......do........	......	......do.......	10.75	15.50	5.50	....
8858	....	......do............	....	......do........	......	......do.......	......	......	......	....
8847	♂	Laramie Peak..	....	......do........	......	......do.......	12.00	18.50	6.00	....
8452	....	Sangre del Cristo Pass, Utah.	....	Capt. Beckwith..	5	....	......	......	......	....
8451	....	Port Townsend, W. T...	Aug. 26,1856	Dr. Suckley......	554	....	11.25	17.25	......	....
8453	....	Shoalwater bay............	Mar. 10, 1854	Gov. Stevens.....	61	Dr. Cooper.....	10.50	16.50	......	Bill and feet black.
8454	....	......do............	....do......	......do........	61	......do.......	10.50	16.75	......	......do........
5904	....	......do............	....	Dr. Cooper......	......	....	......	......	......	....
4462	....	Cascade mountains, W. T..	....	Lt. Williamson...	......	Dr. Newberry..	......	......	......	....

PSILORHINUS, Rüppel.

Psilorhinus, Rüppel, Mus. Senck. 1837, 188· Type *Pica morio*, Wagler.

Ch.—Color very dull brown above. Bill very stout, compressed, without notch ; higher than broad at the nostrils ; culmen curved from the base. Nostrils rounded ; the anterior extremity rounded off into the bill ; not covered by bristles, but fully exposed. Tail rather longer than the wings, graduated ; the lateral feather three-fourths the longest ; secondaries and tertials nearly as long as the primaries. Legs stout and short, not equal to the head, and little longer than the bill from base.

This genus embraces jays of large size and very dull plumage. The thick bill, with the much curved culmen, the moderate tail, and the open nostrils, may serve to distinguish it from its allies. The nostril is very large, and its anterior portion is bevelled off to a greater degree than in any genus, except in *Calocitta*. This last mentioned genus has the same form of bill and of nostrils, but the head has a long recurved crest; the tail is twice as long as the wings; the lateral feather nearly half the middle; the lateral tarsal plates scutellate for the inferior half, &c.

In the shape of the bill and the shortness of the primaries, compared with the broad tertials and secondaries, there is much resemblance to *Xanthoura*. The nostrils are, however, uncovered, the legs much stouter and shorter, being shorter than the head instead of longer; the tail feathers are broader, &c.

Comparative measurements of species.

Catal No.	Species.	Locality.	Sex.	Length.	Stretch of wings.	Wing.	Tail.	Tarsus.	Middle toe.	Its claw alone.	Hind toe and chw.	Hind claw alone.	Bill above.	Along gape.	Specimen measured.
4114	Psilorhinus morio......	China, New Leon......	♀	15.50	.....	7.16	8.53	1.80	1.48	0.44	1.42	1.48	1.20	0.56	Skin ......
do.	........do........	........do........	.....	15.17	22.00	7.12	.....	.....	.....	.....	.....	.....	.....	.....	Fresh .....
4116	........do........	Boquillo, Mexico	♂	16.60	.....	7.70	8.37	1.81	1.50	0.46	1.47	1.50	1.24	0.56	Skin ......
do.	........do........	........do........	.....	16.00	24.00	8.00	.....	.....	.....	.....	.....	.....	.....	.....	Fresh .....
4115	........do........	San Diego, New Leon..	.....	15.70	.....	7.56	8.54	1.82	1.50	0.46	1.46	1.48	1.17	0.56	Skin ......
1254	Calocitta bullockii*	Lower California......	.....	20.20	...	7.23	12.50	1.72	1.56	0.52	1.45	1.60	1.14	0.54	Skin ......

* Not of Audubon.

PSILORHINUS MORIO, Gray.

Pica morio, WAGLER, Isis, 1829, VII, 751.—IB. Isis, 1831, 527.—VOYAGE de la Favorite, V, 1839, 54.   Said to have
been killed at San Francisco, Cal. by Botta.

Psilorhinus morio, GRAY, List, genera, 1841, 51.—BONAP. Consp. 1850, 381.—CAB. Mus. Hein. 1851, 226.

" *Pica fuliginosa*, LESSON, Traite d'Orn. 1831, 333."

Psilorhinus mexicanus, RÜPPELL, Mus. Senck. 1837 ; pl. xi, f. 2.

SP. CH.—Tail much graduated ; the lateral feathers about two inches shortest.   Second quill equal to the secondaries ; third
and fourth longest.   General color dark smoky brown, becoming almost black on the head ; the breast brownish gray ; nearly
white about the anus ; under tail coverts tinged with brown ; the exposed portion of the tail with a decided gloss of blue ; bill
and feet, in some specimens, yellow, in others black.   Length, 16.00 inches ; wing, 8.00 ; tail, 8.25 ; tarsus, 1.80.

Hab.—Rio Grande valley of Texas southward.

The difference in the color of the bill appears to be independent of sex.   The feet of the
yellow-billed birds are not of the same pure yellow.

The *Psilorhinus mexicanus* of Rüppel is described as having white tips to the tail feathers ;
of these there is no trace in the adult specimens, male and female, before me.   He speaks of a
supposed young bird sent from Tamaulipas, by Lindheimer, as being without these white tips.

List of specimens.

Catal. No.	Sex.	Locality.	Whence obtained.	Orig No.	Length.	Stretch of wings.	Wing.	Remarks.
4116	♂	Boquillo, Mex.	Lieut. Couch					
4117	♀	do	do	140	16.75	24.00	7.75	Bill and feet yellow
4118		San Diego, Cal	do	109				
4114	♀	China, N. Leon, Mex.	do	98	15.25	22.00	7.25	Eye black, bill slate, feet slate.

The following species of jay have been improperly assigned a place in the fauna of the United
States.

1. CALOCITTA COLLIAEI, Gray.

Pica colliaei, VIGORS, Zool. Jour. IV, Jan. 1829, 353.—IB. Zool. of Blossom, 1839, 22 ;
pl. vi.

Corvus bullockii, AUD. Orn. Biog. I, 1831, 483 ; pl. xcvi.   Not *Pica bullockii* of Wagler.
Pica bullockii, AUD. Syn. 1839, 152.—IB. Birds Am IV, 1842, 105 ; pl. 229.

This species belongs to the west coast of Mexico, and is erroneously credited to California and
Oregon.

2. CYANOCORAX GEOFFROYI, Bonap.

Cyanocorax geoffroyi, BON. Rev. et Mag. Zool. II, 1850, 564.   California.   Not of United
States.

3. CISSILOPHA SANBLASIANA, Bon.

Garrulus sanblasianus, LAFR. Mag. Zool. 1842, Ois. tab. xxviii.   Voyage de la Venus.
Cissilopha sanblasiana, BON. Consp. 1850, 380.   Belongs to San Blas, Mexico.

4. CYANOCITTA BEECHEYII, BON.

Pica beecheyii, VIGORS, Zool. Jour. IV, Jan. 1829, 352.—IB. Zool. of Blossom, 1839, 22 ;
pl. vi.—Voyagede la Favorite, V, 1839, 52 ; pl. xx.   Said to have
been collected in California by Botta.

Cyanocitta beachii, BON. Consp. 1850, 378.   Collected on the west coast of Mexico.
(Montereale.)

ORDER IV.

RASORES.

Cʜ.—Bill not longer than the head; the terminal portion more or less vaulted, hard, with or without a soft skin intervening between it and the head. Nostril with an overlapping fleshy or leathery scale or valve extending over its upper edge.

In the table on page 2 of the present report I have given a synoptical view of such orders as belong to the United States, borrowed chiefly from Keyserling and Blasius. This, however, will be found to contain several important errors, especially in reference to the position of the hind toe. This is stated to be raised above the level of the rest in *Rasores, Grallatores,* and *Natatores,* and such is generally the case; but in the *Columbae* and *Penelopidae,* of the first order, and the *Ardeadae,* of the second, it is inserted either nearly or quite opposite the others. This is only one of the many illustrations of the difficulty of expressing the characters of the primary groups in ornithology by a single concise phrase, the transition from one to the other being so gradual as to render it almost impossible to say where one ends and another begins.

In the table just referred to, and in the arrangement and succession of the higher divisions of the volume, I have not pretended to follow the more recent ideas of Bonaparte and others. My object was merely to indicate the North American species of birds, especially those collected by the government expeditions, with their range and distribution, and not to attempt any of the higher generalizations. For this reason I have followed the older division into orders, although that of Bonaparte in many respects is more philosophical. This author arranges birds into two sub-classes, called *Altrices* and *Praecoces,* accordingly as their young require to be brought up in the nest, or are able to run about immediately after birth and gather food for themselves.

Each of these sub-classes is divided into orders, which range in parallel series, as shown in the accompanying table, taken from volume XXXVII of Comptes Rendus, for October 31, 1853. It will be seen from the table that the *Inepti* (dodo, &c.,) of the *Altrices* represent the *Struthiones* (ostriches) of the *Praecoces;* the *Gyrantes,* or true doves, the gallinaceous birds; the *Herodiones,* or herons, &c., the *Grallae* (sandpipers, snipes, &c.); the *Gaviae,* or gulls, pelicans, &c., the *Anseres,* (ducks, grebes, penguins, &c.) The parallelism in this case corresponds, to a certain degree, with that which prevails in the mammals between the *Marsupiata* and the *Placentalia,* and the time will probably come when naturalists will as little think of mixing up the *Altrices* and *Praecoces* in the same order, as they now do a similar combination of the marsupial and non-marsupial mammals.

The position of the hind toe seems to have a direct relationship to the mode of life of the bird. Those species which live on or among trees, and especially which nest and bring up their young there, have the hind toe elongated, and placed low down more or less on a level with the anterior ones, apparently to facilitate prehension. Such we see to be the case in the herons, and a few other arboricole waders, and in the *Penelopidae* and *Megapodidae* of the gallinaceous birds. Some of the doves exhibit a tendency to an elevation of the hind toe; this, at any rate, appears to be the case in *Starnoenas.*

July 1, 1858.

75 b

As already remarked, however, I shall not attempt to introduce any special innovation in the usual arrangement of the orders of American birds, but merely indicate what has been done by more modern writers. The combination of *Columbae* and *Gallinae* in one order, (after Keyserling and Blasius,) is an unnatural one in some respects, but it makes little difference in the present case. Both have a peculiar character of plumage ; the feathers large and coarse, the shafts thickened, and inserted by a fine point, so as to be easily detached. Both have the short bill ; the hard vaulted apex of the bill, with its blunt point, and the nostril protected by a fleshy or leathery, sometimes tumid, scale, projecting over its upper edge, except in the *Crypturidae* and *Megapodidae*, where the nostrils are elongated and open. This latter exception is another instance of the difficulty of expressing the peculiarities of a group by a single character.

The following characters will serve, in a general way, to distinguish the *Columbae* from the *Gallinae*.

COLUMBAE.—Hind toe on the same level with the rest, and short. Toes free, or the membrane, when present, extending only between the middle and outer toes. Legs weak. Nasal valve and skin at base of bill soft. Feathers of forehead extending in a point on the base of bill along the culmen.

GALLINAE.—Hind toe usually elevated above the level of the rest ; when on the same level much lengthened. Toes generally connected at base by a membrane. Legs very stout, and sometimes greatly lengthened. Nasal valve and base of bill hard. Feathers of forehead parted by the backward extension of the culmen.

Table of orders of birds, with their parallelism, according to Bonaparte.

ALTRICES.	PRAECOCES.
I. PSITTACI.	
American, ... Old World.	
II. ACCIPITRES.	
III. PASSERES.	
Oscines, ... Volucres.	
IV. COLUMBAE.	
Inepti.	VII. STRUTHIONES.
Gyrantes.	VIII. GALLINAE.
	Passeripedes, ... Grallipedes.
	IX. GRALLAE.
V. HERODIONES.	Cursores, ... Alectorides.
	X. ANSERES.
VI. GAVIAE.	
Totipalmi, ... Longipennes.	Lamellirostres, Urinatores, Ptilopteri.

SUB–ORDER

COLUMBAE.

Ch.—The basal portion of the bill covered by a soft skin, in which are situated the nostrils, overhung by an incumbent fleshy valve, the apical portion hard and convex. The hind toe on the same level with the rest ; the anterior toe without membrane at the base. Tarsi more or less naked ; covered laterally and behind with hexagonal scales.

The preceding diagnosis expresses sufficiently the chief characters of this sub-order, or rather order, divided by Bonaparte into two tribes, one *Pleiodi*, including *Didunculus*, of Peale, the other *Gyrantes*, or true doves. The *Gyrantes* are divided by the same author into *Treronidae*, *Columbidae, Caloenidae,* and *Gouridae,* characterized as follows :

TRERONIDAE.—Bill robust, tumid ; rictus ample. Feet short, thick, half feathered ; toes fleshy ; claws strong, hooked. Tail feathers, 14. Feathers soft, without metallic lustre ; prevailing color green ; wing with a yellow band. The species are frugivorous and arboreal. They are confined entirely to the old world, and are especially abundant in the islands of the Pacific.

COLUMBIDAE.—Bill horny at the tip. Tail feathers 12 ; only occasionally 14. Head smooth. Universally distributed.

CALOENIDAE.—Bill lengthened ; cere swollen ; cervical feathers elongated, acute, pendulous. Dorsal accuminate. Tail feathers 12. The single species, *Caloenas nicobarica,* confined to the East India islands.

GOURIDAE.—Head conspicuously crested ; tail feathers 16. The two species confined to New Guinea.

The bill of the *Columbae* is always shorter than the head, thinnest in the middle ; the basal half covered by a soft skin ; the apical portion of both jaws hard ; the upper very convex, blunt, and broad at the tip, where it is also somewhat decurved. There is a long nasal groove, the posterior portion occupied by a cartilaginous scale, covered by a soft cere-like skin. The nostrils constitute an elongated slit in the lower border of the scale. The culmen is always depressed and convex. The bill is never notched in the true doves, though *Didunculus* shows well defined serrations. The tongue is small, soft, and somewhat fleshy.

The wing has ten primaries, and eleven or twelve, rarely fifteen, secondaries, the latter broad, truncate, and of nearly equal length. The tail is rounded or cuneate, never forked.

The tarsus is usually short, rarely longer than the middle toe, scutellate anteriorly, and with hexagonal plates laterally and behind ; sometimes naked. An inter-digital membrane is either wanting entirely, or else is very slightly indicated between the middle and outer toes.[1]

The valuable monograph of Bonaparte in the second part of Conspectus Avium renders the task of arranging the American *Columbae* in proper sequence and of determining their synonomy comparatively easy. He divides the family *Columbidae,* the only one with representatives in the new world, into *Lopholaeminae, Columbinae, Turturinae, Zenaidinae,* and *Phapinae,* the second and fourth alone occurring in North America. They may be briefly distinguished as follows :

COLUMBINAE.—Tarsi shorter than the lateral toe ; feathered above.

ZENAIDINAE.—Tarsi stout, lengthened, longer than the lateral toes ; entirely bare of feathers.

[1]The preceding general remarks are taken chiefly from Burmeister, Thiere Brasiliens, Vögel, II, 289.

Sub-Family COLUMBINAE.

Tarsi stout, short, with transverse scutellae anteriorly ; feathered for the basal third above, but not at all behind. Toes lengthened, the lateral decidedly longer than the tarsus. Wings lengthened and pointed. Size large. Tail feathers 12.

This section of doves embraces the largest North American species, and among them the more arboreal ones. The genera are as follow :

COLUMBA.—Head large ; tail short, broad, and rounded.

Columba.—Lateral toes equal ; bill rather short, stout.

Patagioenas.—Inner lateral toe the longer ; bill lengthened, compressed.

ECTOPISTES.—Head very small ; tail much lengthened, cuneate.

Comparative measurements of species.

Cat'l No.	Species.	Locality.	Sex.	Length	Stretch of wings	Wings.	Tail.	Tarsus.	Middle toe.	Its claw alone.	Bill above.	Along gape.	Specimens measured.
8423	Columba fasciata	Simiahmoo bay	♂	14.40	....	8.58	6.56	1.04	1.61	0.44	0.76	1.06	Skin.....
do.	.........do..............	.......do..............	......	14.00	25.00	8.50	......	....	....	....	....	....	Fresh....
8421	.........do..............	.......do..............	......	15.30	....	8.26	6.23	1.10	1.70	0.46	0.78	1.04	Skin.....
do.	.........do..............	.......do..............	......	....	25.00	8.25	......	....	....	....	....	....	Fresh....
8739	.........do..............	Mimbres to Rio Grande	......	12.64	....	8.20	6.14	1.01	1.57	0.42	0.72	1.01	Skin.....
8741	.........do..............	Los Nogales, Mexico .	......	12.80	....	7.76	6.16	1.04	1.61	0.43	0.72	1.06	Skin. ••••
4111	Columba flavirostris....	New Leon, Mexico...	♂	12.80	....	7.66	5.32	0.98	1.62	0.40	0.66	0.80	Skin.....
do.	....do..............	.......do..............	......	14.00	22.00	8.00	......	....	....	....	....	....	Fresh ...
8662	Columba leucocephala..	Indian Key, Fla.......	♂	12.00	....	7.55	5.44	1.02	1.56	0.39	0.76	1.09	Skin.....
do.	.........do..............	.......do..............	......	13.50	22.50	7.50	......	....	....	....	....	....	Fresh....
8664	.........do..............	.......do..............	♀	12.00	......	7.36	5.52	1.00	1.60	0.40	0.74	1.10	Skin.....
do.	.........do..............	.......do..............	......	13.00	20.00	6.50	......	....	....	....	....	....	Fresh....
7115	Ectopistes migratorius..	Pennsylvania	♂	15.30	....	8.04	8.42	1.08	1.42	0.36	0 63	0.99	Skin.....
1319	.........do..	Carlisle, Pa.........	♀	14.40	....	8.06	8.18	1.06	1.30	0.32	0.70	1.02	Skin.....
do.	.........do..	.......do..............	......	16.00	23.50	8.00	......	....	....	....	....	....	Fresh....

COLUMBA, Linnaeus.

Columba, LINNAEUS, Syst. Nat. 1735. Type *Columba livia,* L.

The characters of the genus are sufficiently indicated in the preceding paragraph for my present purposes. The two sub-genera represented in the United States are as follows :

COLUMBA.—Bill stout and rather short ; culmen from the base of the feathers about two-fifths the head. Lateral toes and claws about equal, reaching nearly to the base of the middle claw ; the claws rather long and not much curved. Tail rather short, rounded, or nearly even ; as long as from the carpal joint to the end of secondaries in the closed wing. Second and third quills longest.

Ashy above. Head and under parts purplish violet. A white half collar on the back of the neck. Tail with a subterminal band of dusky. Feathers on the sides of the neck metallic golden green. Bill yellow, the tip black................................*C. fa ciata.*
Head and neck chocolate red ; back olive ; remaining portion of body slate blue. Bill and lore purple in life; yellow in the skin. No metallic scales on the neck..*C. flavirostris.*
PATAGIOENAS.—Bill slender, elongated. Culmen measured from the base of the frontal feathers about one-half the head. Inner lateral toe with its claw longer than the outer, and reaching

to the base of the middle claw ; the outer falling short of it. Second and third quills longest. Tail much as in *Columba*.

Dark slaty blue. Top of the head white. Sides of neck with golden green scales. Bill dusky in the skin..*P. leucocephalus.*

The sub-genus *Columba*, as characterized above, includes the *C. livia*, or domestic pigeon, the differences between it and the American forms being very slight. Reichenbach and Bonaparte separate the North American birds from *Columba*, under the name of *Chloroenas.*

COLUMBA FASCIATA, Say.

Band-tailed Pigeon.

Columba fasciata, SAY, Long's Exped. R. Mts. II, 1823, 10.—BON. Amer. Orn. I, 1825, 77 ; pl. viii.—IB. Syn. 1828, 119.—IB. List, 1838.—WAGLER, Syst. Av. 1827, *Columba*, No. 47.—NUTTALL, Man. 1, 1832, 624.—AUD. Orn. Biog. IV, 1838, 479 ; pl. 367.—IB. Syn. 1839, 191.—IB. Birds Amer. IV, 1842, 312; pl. 279.—TSCHUDI, Fauna Peruana, 1844–'6, No. 261.—NEWBERRY, Zool. Cal. & Or. Route, Rep. P. R. R. VI, IV, 92.

Chloroenas fasciata, BONAP. Conspectus, II, 1854, 51.

Columba monilis, VIGORS, Zool. Beechey's Voyage, 1839, 26 ; pl. x.

Chloroenas monilis, REICH. Icones Av. ccxxvii, fig. 2481.

SP. CH.—Above olivaceous tinged with ash, changing on the wing coverts to bluish ash, of which color are the hinder part of the back, rump, and basal portion of the tail. The terminal third of the tail is whitish brown, with a tinge of ash, succeeding a narrow bar of dusky. Head all round, sides of neck and under parts, including tibia, purplish violet ; the middle of the abdomen, anal region, and crissum, whitish. Tibia and throat tinged with blue. Quills brown, narrowly margined with white. A conspicuous narrow half collar of white on the nape ; the feathers below this to the upper part of the back metallic golden green. Bill and feet yellow ; the former black at tip.

Female similar, with less purple ; the nuchal collar of white, obsolete or wanting.

Length about 15 inches; wing, 8.80 ; tail, 6.10.

Hab.—From Rocky mountains to Pacific coast ; south to New Leon, Mexico.

There is a strong tinge of bluish in the purplish violet around the base of the bill. The sides of body and inside of the wings are bluish ash like the rump. The outer edges of the greater wing coverts change to whitish. The subterminal band of blackish on the tail is about an inch wide, and some two inches from the tip. It is scarcely appreciable on the under surface. The whitish ash at the end of the tail is often much soiled with brownish.

The female sometimes has a distinct nuchal collar, but without extending as far round the neck.

This species was at one time supposed to occur in Chile, but it is there represented by a distinct though closely allied species.

List of specimens.

Catal. No.	Sex.	Locality.	When collected.	Whence obtained.	Orig. No.	Collected by—	Length.	Stretch of wings.	Wing.
8740	......	Fort Steilacoom, W. T.	Sept. 25	Dr. Suckley......	555				
8738	♀	Shoalwater bay......		Gov. Stevens		Dr. Cooper......			
8734	♂	......do............		......do.........		......do.......			
8733	♀	Fort Vancouver	July —, 1853	......do.........	13	......do.......			
8736	......	......do............	July 10.....	......do.........		......do.......			
1933	♂	Columbia river......	July 30, 1835	S. F. Baird.....		J. K. Townsend..			
2825	♀	......do.......	May 16, 1835	......do.........		......do.......			
.4468	......	North California....		Lt. Williamson..		Dr. Newberry			
		Fort Tejon, Cal.....		J. X. de Vesey...					
8741	......	Los Nogales, Mex....	July —, 1855	Maj. Emory......	86	Dr. Kennerly			
8739	......	Mimbres to Rio Grande		Dr. Henry.......					
4109	♀	New Leon, Mex.		Lt. Couch					

COLUMBA FLAVIROSTRIS, Wagler.

Red-billed Dove.

Columba flavirostris, WAGLER, Isis, 1831, 519.—LAWRENCE, Annals N. Y. Lyc. V, May, 1851, 116.
Chloroenas flavirostris, BONAP. Consp. Av. II, 1854, 52.
? *Columba solitaria*, McCALL, Pr. A. N. Sc. Phila. III, July, 1847, 233. Rio Grande, Texas. Description referring probably to the female of this species.

SP. CH.—Second and third quills equal, and decidedly longer than the first and fourth, also nearly equal. Tail truncate, slightly rounded. Head and neck all round, breast, and a large patch on the middle and lesser wing coverts, light chocolate red, the latter deeper and more opaque red ; the middle of the back, scapulars, and tertials olive ; the rest of body, wings, and tail very dark slaty blue ; the inferior and concealed surfaces of the latter black. Bill and legs yellow in the dried skin, said to be purple in life ; eyes purple. Length, 14 inches ; wing, 8 ; tail, 5.70.

Hab.—Lower Rio Grande.

There is no trace of any metallic scale-like feathers on the neck of this species. The wing feathers, including the greater coverts, are whitish on their external border. There is a tinge of the red on the inside of the wing.

The *Columba solitaria* of McCall appears to be closely related to this species, but, judging from the description, appears to differ in having the head and neck bluish rather than red. It may possibly be the female of *C. flavirostris*, as this sex usually has bluish instead of red ; the smaller size, too, would favor this supposition.[1]

---

[1] *Columba solitaria*, McCALL, Pr. A. N. Sc. Phila. III, July, 1847, 233. "Length, 13 inches 9 lines, &c. Alar extent 23 inches. Wing, from the flexure, 7 inches 5 lines. Tarsus 1 inch ; middle toe 1 inch 2 lines ; first toe 9 lines, and longer than the third ; nails light flesh color ; feet and legs deep red. Iris dark orange. Bill above, 1 inch 1 line, but feathered to within 5 lines of the tip ; reddish near the base, whitish near the tip. Head, chocolate blue. Throat, chocolate white. Neck and breast, bluish chocolate with brilliant reflections. Back, belly, flanks, under wing coverts, and greater exterior wing coverts, light red color, the last faintly bordered with white. Lesser wing coverts chocolate red, forming a bright shoulder spot of elliptical shape. Quill feathers dusky, tinged with lead color on the outer vanes. Third primary longest. Upper and under tail coverts bluish lead color. Tail, 5 inches, slightly rounded, of twelve feathers dusky."

List of specimens.

Catal. No.	Sex and age.	Locality.	When collected.	Whence obtained.	Collected by—	Length.	Stretch of wings.	Wing.
¹4111	♂	New Leon, Mex	Mar. —, 1853	Lt. Couch		14.00	22 00	8.00
7098	o	Rio Grande, Tex		Major Emory	A. Schott			

¹ Eyes, bill, and feet purple.

COLUMBA LEUCOCEPHALA, Linn.

White-headed Pigeon.

Columba leucocephala, LINN. Syst. Nat. I, 1766, 281.—GM. I, 772.—LATH. Ind. 1790, 594.—BONAP. J. A. N. S. Ph. V, 1825, 30.—IB. Syn. 119.—IB. Am. Orn. II, 1828, 11 ; pl. xv.—IB. Geog. List, 1838.—NUTT. Man. I, 1832, 625.—AUD. Orn. Biog. II, 1834, 443 : V, 557 ; pl. 177.—IB. Birds Amer. IV, 1842, 315 ; pl. 280.—TEMM. Pig. et Gallin. I, 459.—GOSSE, Birds Jam. 1847, 299.

Patagioenas leucocephalus, REICHENB. Syst. Avium, 1851, p. xxv.—IB. Icones Av. tab. 223 and 255.—BONAP. Consp. Av. II, 1854, 54.—GUNDLACH, Cabanis Jour. 1856, 107.

Sp. CH.—Tail rounded. Second quill longest ; first equal to fourth. General color very dark slaty blue ; the quills an tail feathers darker above ; black beneath. Upper half of head from bill to nape pure white, not reaching the edge of the eyelids ; margined behind by bluish, which, however, on the back of the neck, passes into rich purplish brown ; the lower part and sides of the neck scaled with metallic golden green, each feather margined with black. In life the bill purple, the tip light blue. Iris white. Legs deep dark red. Length, 13.50 ; wing, 7.50 ; tail, 5.80.

Hab.—Indian key and other southern keys of Florida. Not on main land ? West-Indies generally.

The female of this species appears precisely similar to the male. In the dried skin the red of the bill and legs appear much the same ; the tip of the former whitish.

List of specimens.

Catal. No.	Sex.	Locality.	When collected.	Whence obtained.	Collected by—	Length.	Stretch of wings	Wing.
1934		Florida ?		S. F. Baird.	J. J. Audubon			
¹8662	♂	Indian Key, Fla	July 23, 1857	G. Wurdemann		13.50	22.50	7.50
8664	♀	do	do	do		13.00	20.00	6.50
²8663	♂	Tortugas, Fla.	do	do		13.00	21.50	7.50

¹ Purple bill, with light blue end ; feet red, iris whitish. ² Black eyes and whitish iris, bill purple, with light blue end.

ECTOPISTES, Swainson.

Ectopistes, SWAINSON, Zool. Jour. III, 1827, 362. Type *Columba migratoria,* L.

CH.—Head very small. Bill short, black ; culmen one-third the rest of the head. Tarsi very short, half covered anteriorly by feathers. Inner lateral claw much larger than outer, reaching to the base of the middle one. Tail very long and excessively cuneate ; about as long as the wings. First primary longest.

This genus is readily distinguished from the other *Columbinae* by the excessively lengthened and acute middle feathers. It formerly included the *Columba carolinensis,* but this, with more propriety, has been erected into a different genus, and will be found in the next section.

The *Ectopistes migratoria* is blue above, purplish red beneath, passing into whitish behind. The wing above is spotted with bluish black ; the sides of the neck with metallic gloss.

ECTOPISTES MIGRATORIA, Swainson.

Wild Pigeon ; Passenger Pigeon.

Columba migratoria, LINNAEUS, Syst. Nat. I, 1766, 285.—GM. I, 389.—FORSTER, Phil. Trans. LXII, 1772, 398.— WILSON, Am. Orn. I, 1808, 102 ; pl. xliv.—BON. Obs. Wils. 1825, No. 179.—WAGLER, Syst. Av. 1827, No. 91.—AUD. Orn. Biog. I, 1831, 319 : V, 561 ; pl. 62.

Ectopistes migratoria, SWAINSON, Zool. Jour. III, 1827, 355.—IB. F. Bor. Am. II, 1831, 363.—BON. List, 1838.—IB. Consp. Av. II, 1854, 59.—AUD. Syn. 1839, 194.—IB. Birds Amer. V, 1842, 25 ; pl. 285.— " REICH. Icones Av. tab. 249, figs. 1377, 1379."

Columba canadensis, LINNAEUS, Syst. Nat. I, 1766, 284.—GM. I, 1788, 785. Female or young. (Prior name?)

Columba americana, " KALM, It. II, 527."

Passenger Pigeon, PENNANT, II, 322.—LATT. Syn. II, II, 661.

SP. CH.—Tail with twelve feathers. Upper parts generally, including sides of body, head, and neck, and the chin, blue. Beneath, purple brownish red, fading behind with a violet tint. Anal region and under tail coverts, bluish white. Scapulars, inner tertials, and middle of back, with an olive brown tinge; the wing coverts, scapulars, and inner tertials, with large oval spots of blue-black on the outer webs, mostly concealed, except on the latter. Primaries blackish, with a border of pale bluish tinged internally with red. Middle tail feathers brown ; the rest pale blue on the outer web, white internally ; each with a patch of reddish brown at the base of the inner web, followed by another of black. Sides and back of neck richly glossed with metallic golden violet. Tibia bluish violet. Bill black. Feet yellow.

The female is smaller ; much duller in color ; more olivaceous above ; beneath, pale blue instead of red, except a tinge on the neck ; the jugulum tinged with olive, the throat whitish.

Length of male, 17 inches ; wing, 8.50 ; tail, 8.40.

Hab.—North America to High Central Plains.

The blue of the side of the head extends to the throat and chin. The upper part of the back and lesser coverts are of a darker blue than the head and rump. The inner primaries are more broadly margined with light blue, which tapers off to the end. The axillars and under surface of the wing are light blue. The longest scapulars have the black on both webs. There is no blue on the outer web of the first tail feather, which is white, and the inferior surface of the tail generally is white.

In some specimens the entire head all round is blue.

The immature male varies in having most of the feathers of the head and body margined with whitish.

List of specimens.

Catal. No.	Sex.	Locality.	When collected.	Whence obtained.	Collected by—	Length.	Stretch of wings.	Wing.
1182	♂	Carlisle, Pa.	Sept. 25, 1843	S. F. Baird		17.00	24.00	8.50
1319	♀	......do......	April 1, 1844	......do......		16.00	23.50	8.00
1603	♂	......do......	June 8, 1846	......do......		14.87	23.75	8.16
7115	......	Philadelphia, Pa.		Ph. Acad. Nat. Sc.				
4547	♂	Washington, D. C.	April —, 1856	Market		17.00	24.00	
4857	♂	Mouth of Big Sioux.	May 3, 1856	Lieut. Warren	Dr. Hayden.	17.16	23.75	8.50
14856	♂	......do......	......do......	......do......	......do......	16.87	23.75	8.25
5418	♂	Above mouth Yellowstone.	Aug. 8, 1856	......do......	......do......	16.25	23.50	8.00

¹ Iris red.

Sub-Family ZENAIDINAE.

Cн.—Tarsi stout, lengthened ; always longer than the lateral toes, and entirely without feathers ; the tibial joint usually denuded. Tarsus sometimes with hexagonal scales anteriorly. Tail feathers sometimes 14.

This sub-family is readily distinguished from the preceding by the longer and more denuded tarsi, the feet much better fitted for a terrestrial life. The following sections belong to it :

ZENAIDEAE.—Size moderate. Wings lengthened, acute; primaries much longer than the tertials ; secondaries short. Tarsus shorter than the middle toe and claw, but longer than the lateral ; scutellate anteriorly.

MELOPELIA.—Tail short, rounded ; orbits naked.

ZENAIDA.—Tail short, rounded ; orbits feathered.

ZENAIDURA.—Tail excessively lengthened, cuneate, of fourteen feathers ; orbits naked.

CHAMAEPELIEAE.—Size very small. Secondaries lengthened. Tertials nearly as long as primaries. Primaries dark chestnut internally.

CHEMAEPELIA.—Tail short, rounded.

SCARDAFELLA.—Tail very long, cuneate.

STARNOENADEAE.—Legs very stout ; tarsi decidedly longer than the middle toe, covered anteriorly with small hexagonal scales or transverse scutellae. Wings short, very broad, and much rounded. Tail short, very broad.

STARNOENAS.—Legs very stout ; tarsi covered with hexagonal scales.

GEOTRYGON.—Legs moderate ; tarsi covered with transverse scutellae anteriorly.

Comparative measurements of species.

Catal. No.	Species.	Locality.	Sex & age.	Length.	Stretch of wings.	Wing.	Tail.	Tarsus.	Middle toe.	Its claw alone.	Bill above.	Along gape.	Specimen measured.
1935	Zenaida amabilis.........	West Indies............	......	10.40	1	6.00	4.66	0.91	1.14	0.26	0.60	0.92	Skin. ......
4107	Melopelia leucoptera......	Tamaulipas, Mex...	♀	....	....	6.02	4.30	0.94	1.17	0.26	0.76	0.90	Skin ....
do.	........do.................	......do............	......	11.00	18.25	6.00	....	......	......	......	......	......	Fresh ......
6531	Zenaidura carolinensis ...	Key Biscayne, Fla..	♀	....	....	5.50	5.08	0.76	0.94	0.18	0.62	0.76	Skin ....
1180	........do.................	Carlisle, Penn......	♂	12.50	....	5.66	6.58	0.85	1.03	0.22	0 56	0.70	Skin ....
do.	........do.................	......do............	......	12.82	18.00	5.75	....	......	......	......	......	......	Fresh ......
720	........do.................	......do............	♂♂	10.00	.....	5.50	4.82	0.84	0.97	0.21	0.53	0.80	Skin ....
do.	........do.................	......do............	......	10.75	17.50	......	....	......	......	......	......	......	Fresh ......
4560	........do.................	Colorado river, Cal.	♂	11.40	....	6.13	6.16	0.92	1.02	0.23	0.52	0.75	Skin ....
5560	........do.......	Petaluma, Cal.....	♀	10.70	....	5.32	5.50	0.78	1.00	0.21	0.58	0.76	Skin ....
do.	........do.................	......do............	......	12.00	15.00	5.48	....	......	......	......	......	......	Fresh ......
10320	Zenaidura (type of *marginata*—Woodh.)	North fork Canadian river.	♂	8.50	....	5.38	4.33	0.84	0.95	0.21	0.57	0.72	Skin .....
10328	....do.................	Georgia.............	♂	10.90	....	5.66	5.76	0.69	0.96	0.20	0.59	0.80	Skin ....
do.	........do.................	......do............	......	11.70	17.20	5.70	....	......	......	......	......	......	Fresh ......
2827	Starnoenas cyanocephala .	Florida ?............	......	10.70	....	5.43	4.34	1.32	1.24	0.30	0.58	1.04	Skin ....
2826	Geotrygon martinica......	Key West, Fla......	......	10.60	....	5.91	4.58	1.12	1.20	0.26	0.75	1.00	Skin ....
1936	........do...... ...*+*....	Florida	......	11.20	....	6.14	4.20	1.13	1.20	0.25	0.73	0.95	Skin ....
2828	Chamaepelia passerina....	....	......	6.30	....	3.36	2.78	0.61	0.73	0.16	0.50	0.60	Skin ....
4103	........do.·..............	Tamaulipas, Mex..	♂	......	....	3.39	2.68	0.62	0.74	0.16	0.50	0.60	Fresh ......
do.	........do.................	......do............	......	6.50	10.50	3.24	....	......	......	......	......	......	Skin ....
1191	........do.................	Washington, D. C..	♀	6.30	....	3.26	2.59	0.58	0.70	0.17	0.50	0.60	Skin ....
10318	Chamaepelia albivitta? ...	Carthagena, N. G..	......	5.80	....	3.06	2.53	0.62	0.73	0.18	0.47	0.61	Skin ....
10319	........do.................	......do............	......	5.80	....	3.00	2.62	0.59	0.72	0.18	0.48	0.57	Skin ....
4110	Scardafella squamosa.....	Cadereita, N. Leon.	♀	8.20	....	3.60	4.17	0.61	0.78	0.20	0.54	0.63	Skin ....
do.	....	....	......	8.00	11.00	3.75	....	......	......	......	......	......	Fresh ......

July 1, 1858.

ZENAIDA, Bon.

Zenaida, BONAPARTE, Geog. & Comp. List, 1838.   Type *Columba zenaida*, Bp.

Ch.—Bill black ; the culmen about two-fifths the rest of the head.   Tarsi a little shorter than the middle toe and claw, but considerably longer than the lateral toes.   Tarsus with broad scutellae anteriorly, those on the lower half bifid, making two hexagonal series.   Inner lateral toe a little longer.   Hind toe and claw as long as the inner lateral without claw.   Wings lengthened ; second and third quills longest.   Tail short, about two-fifths the wings, rounded or a little graduated.   Orbits feathered, especially anterior to the eye ; the lids bare.

But one species of this genus belongs to our fauna, and this probably is ▁▁t an occasional visitor.   The *Zenaida martinicana*, of Bonaparte, from Martinique and the Bermudas, may sometimes reach Florida.[1]

ZENAIDA AMABILIS, Bonap.

Zenaida Dove.

Columba zenaida, BONAP. J. A. N. Sc. V, 1825, 30.—IB. Am. Orn II, 1828 ; pl. xv.—IB. Syn. 1828, 119.—WAGLER, Isis, 1829, 744.—NUTTALL, Man. I, 1832, 625.—AUD. Orn. Biog. II, 1834, 354 : V, 558 ; pl. 162.—IB. Syn. 191.—IB. Birds Am. V, 1842, 1 ; pl. 281.

Zenaida amabilis, BON. List, 1838.—IB. Consp. II, 1854, 82.—GOSSE,. Birds Jam. 1847, 307.—REICHENBACH, Icones Av. "tab. 255."—GUNDLACH, Cabanis' Journ. 1856, 111.

Zenaida aurita, GRAY, not *Columba aurita*, of Lichtenstein, (*Z. maculata*,) nor of Temminck, (*Z. martinicana*,) fide Bonaparte.

Sp. Ch.—Wings very long, reaching to the terminal third of the tail.   Above reddish olive, variously glossed with gray ; the top of the head and the under parts violet-purplish red, paler on the chin and throat.   Inside of wings, and sides of body, blue ; greater wing coverts tinged with the same.   Quills dark brown ; the secondaries tipped with white.   Inner tail feathers like the back ; the others blue above ; all with a subterminal bar of black, beyond which the blue is lighter, assuming a whitish tint on the exterior feathers.   Wing coverts with concealed spots of black, which are more visible on the tertials ; a spot of the same below the ear.   Bill black.   Feet yellowish.   Length, 10 inches ; wing, 6.00 ; tail, 4.00.

Hab.—Florida Keys.   Chiefly on or near Indian Key, and the West Indies.

The only specimen of this species I have at my command is one from Mr. Audubon's collection, probably procured in Florida.   It is more seldom seen now than formerly on the Keys, as a collection of birds from Indian Key did not contain any specimens of it.

List of specimens.

Catalogue number.	Locality.	Whence obtained.	Collected by—
1935.	Florida ?	S. F. Baird	J. J. Audubon

MELOPELIA, Bonaparte.

Melopelia, BONAP. Consp. II, Dec. 1854, 81.   Type *Columba leucoptera*, L.

Ch.—Similar to *Zenaida* ; the orbital region naked ; the bill longer ; the middle toe longer ; the hinder shorter.   Tarsal scutellae in a single series anteriorly.   First quill nearly as long as the second and third.

This genus, like nearly all the North American ones, is represented by but a single species in the United States.

[1] *Zenaida martinicana*, Bon. Conspectus II, 1854, 82.   (*Columba aurita*, Temminck, *castanea*, Wagler ; *Zenaida bimaculata*, Gray.)   Similar to *Z. amabilis*, but with the spots on the tertiary quills margined behind with white ; the abdomen and lower tail coverts vinaceous white ; the tips of the outer tail feathers white.

MELOPELIA LEUCOPTERA, Bonap.

White-winged Dove.

Columba leucoptera, Linn. Syst. Nat. I, 1766, 281. (Not the locality—Asia.)—Gm. Syst. Nat. I, 1788, 773.—Wagler, Syst. Av. 1827, *Columba*, No. 71.—M'Call, Pr. A. N. Sc. IV, 1848, 64.

Zenaida leucoptera, Gray, Gen.

Turtur leucopterus, Gosse, Birds Jam. 1847, 304.

Melopelia leucoptera, Bonap. Consp. Av. II, 1854, 81.

? *Columba hoilotl*, Gmelin, Syst. Nat. I, 1788, 777.

Columba trudeaui, Aud. Birds Amer. VII, 1843, 352; pl. 496.

Sp. Ch.—Tail moderately graduated on the sides. Second and third quills longest; first a little shorter; fourth considerably shorter. In the female the upper parts generally are light olive brown; the head and neck above purplish, with a black spot below the ear; the lower part of the neck with scale feathers of metallic golden green. Forehead and under parts light bluish gray; more blue on the sides. Tail feathers, except the middle, bluish above, black beneath, broadly terminated with white; the upper surface with a bar of black in the end of the blue. Quills (except inner tertials) black, margined or tipped with white; a broad white patch along the exterior of the greater wing coverts and alular feathers. Bill black; bill pinkish purple. Iris purple. Length, (female,) 11 inches; wing, 6.00; tail, 4.75.

Hab.—Valley of Rio Grande, southward. California, Dr. Cooper. West Indies.

The preceding description is that of a female, no male being accessible to me. The differences between the sexes are probably much like those in *Ectopistes*, the blue of the breast and under parts of the female, doubtless purplish cinnamon in the male.

List of specimens.

Catal. No.	Sex.	Locality.	When collected.	Whence obtained.	Length.	Stretch of wings.	Wing.	Remarks.
4107	♀	Tamaulipas	Mar. —, 1853	Lieut. Couch	11.00	18.25	6.00	Eyes purple, bill black, feet pinkish purple.

ZENAIDURA, Bonap.

Zenaidura, Bonap. Consp. Avium, II, 1854, 84. Type *Columba carolinensis*, L. Probably named previously in Comptes Rendus.

Perissura, Cab. Jour. für Orn. IV, 1856, 111.

Ch.—Bill weak, black; culmen from frontal feathers, about one-third the head above. Tarsus not quite as long as middle toe and claw, but considerably longer than the lateral ones; covered anteriorly by a single series of scutallae. Inner lateral claw considerably longer than outer, and reaching to the base of middle. Wings pointed; second quill longest; first and third nearly equal. Tail very long, equal to the wings; excessively graduated and cuneate, of fourteen feathers.

The fourteen tail feathers render this genus very conspicuous among the North American doves. It was formerly placed with the Passenger Pigeon in *Ectopistes*, but has nothing in common with it but the lengthened tail, as it belongs to a different sub-family.

ZENAIDURA CAROLINENSIS, Bonap.

Carolina, or Common Dove.

Columba carolinensis, LINNAEUS, Syst. Nat. I, 1766, 286, No. 37.—GMELIN, I, 787.—LATHAM, Ind. II, 1790, 613.—
WILSON, Am. Orn. V, 1812, 91 ; pl. xliii.—BON. Obs. 1825, No. 159.—AUD. Orn. Biog. I,
1831, 91 : V, 1839, 555 ; pl. 17.—NUTTALL, Man. I, 1832, 626.

Turtur carolinensis, BRISSON, I, 110 ; pl. viii.

Ectopistes carolinensis, RICH. List, 1837.—BONAP. Geog. List, 1838.—AUD. Syn. 1839, 195.—IB. Birds Amer. V,
1842, 36 ; pl. 286.

Zenaidura carolinensis, BONAP. Consp. Av. II, 1854, 84. Type.

Perissura carolinensis, CABANIS, Cab. Jour. 1856, 111, 112. Type.

Columba marginata, LINNAEUS, Syst. Nat. I, 1766, 286, No. 40, (best description.)—GMELIN, I, 1788, 791.—WAGLER,
Syst. Av. 1827, No. 91.—IB. Isis, 1831, 519.

Ectopistes marginata, GRAY, List, Br. Mus.

? *Ectopistes marginellus*, WOODHOUSE, Pr. A. N. Sc. VI, June, 1852, 104.—IB. Expl. Zuñi & Color 1853, 93 ; Birds,
pl. v. Canadian river, Ark. Immature bird.

? *Zenaidura marginella*, BONAP. Consp. Av. II, 1854, 85.

SP. CH.—Tail feathers 14. Above bluish, although this is overlaid with light brownish olive, leaving the blue pure only on the top
of the head, the exterior of the wings, and the upper surface of the tail, which is even slightly tinged with this color. The entire
head, except the vertex, the sides of the neck, and the under parts generally, light brownish red, strongly tinged with purple on
the breast, becoming lighter behind, and passing into brownish yellow on the anal region, tibia, and under tail coverts. Sides
of the neck with a patch of metallic purplish red. Sides of body and inside of wings clear light blue. Wing coverts and
scapulars spotted with black, mostly concealed, and an oblong patch of the same below the ear. Tail feathers seen from below
blackish, the outer web of outermost white, the others tipped with the same, the color becoming more and more bluish to the
innermost, which is brown. Seen from above there is the same gradation from white to light blue in the tips ; the rest of the
feather, however, is blue, with a bar of black anterior to the light tip, which runs a little forward along the margin and shaft of
the feather. In the sixth feather the color is uniform bluish, with this bar ; the seventh is without bar. Bill black ; feet yellow.
Female smaller, and with less red beneath. Length of male, 12.85 ; wing, 5.75 ; tail, 6.70.

Hab.—Throughout United States from Atlantic to Pacific. Cuba, Gundlach.

This species resembles the wild pigeon, *E. migratoria*, but is much smaller; has the tail
much longer than the wings, instead of equal to them, and consisting of fourteen feathers
instead of twelve. These feathers are much less acutely pointed. The sides of the head, the
front, and the chin are reddish, instead of blue. The quills lack the broad white and red
border ; the tail feathers the reddish patch. The black spot beneath the ear is not found in *E.
migratoria*.

In comparing a large series of specimens of doves from various localities in North America
I can perceive no differences of moment, except that the more southern are smaller. There is a
purer blue on the tail and upper parts of Pennsylvania skins, the olive brown shade above
being more conspicuous in those from the west.

The young of the year is much duller in general appearance than the adult, and is of a
decided brownish cast, with streaks of blackish on the head, breast, and elsewhere. Nearly all
the feathers are tipped with paler, forming bands. The *Ectopistes marginellus* of Woodhouse is
of this character. It is certainly a young bird, and has nothing to distinguish it from th
common eastern species, whatever may be the case with the adult.

List of specimens.

Catal. No.	Sex & age.	Locality.	When collected.	Whence obtained.	Orig. No.	Collected by—	Length.	Stretch of wings.	Wing.	Remarks.
2427	.....	Carlisle, Pa..............	Sept. —, 1845	S. F. Baird	.....	....	....	....	......	....
1180	♂	.....do..............	Sept. 20, 1843	......do.......	.....	....	12.82	18.00	5.75	....
720	○♂	.....do..............	Sept. 16, 1842	......do.......	.....	....	10.75	17.50	......	....
8750	.....	Rockport, Ohio	....	J. P. Kirtland.....	.....	....	....	....	......	....
7044	.....	St. Louis, Mo.	May 8, 1857	Lieut. Bryan..	25	W. S. Wood	....	....	......	....
6531	♀	Key Biscayne, Fla.	....	G. Wurdemann	.....	....	....	....	......	....
6532	.....	Indian Key, Fla...........	Feb. 5, —	......do...........	.....	....	....	....	......	....
4915	.....	Calcasieu pass, La.......	1854	......do...........	.....	....	....	....	......	....
4291	.....	......do..............	1854	......do... ...	.....	....	....	....	......	....
4858	.....	Cedar Island.......	....	Lieut. Warren	.....	Dr. Hayden......	11.12	16.75	......	Eyes black ....
5740	♂	South Platte	July 7, 1856	Lieut. Bryan	75	W. S. Wood	....	... ...	......	....
7528	.....	Independence, Mo.	....	Dr. Cooper........	.....	....	....	....	......	....
5739	♂	East of Fort Riley, K. T..	June 13, 1856	Lieut. Bryan......	6	W. S. Wood.....	10.75	14.50	......	....
4102	♂	Tamaulipas, Mex.......	....	Lieut. Couch	42	....	11.25	17.00	5.75	Eyes very dark brown.
8754	.....	Ringgold barracks........	July —, 1853	Major Emory	.....	....	....	....	......	....
5077	.....	Texas..............	....	Capt. Pope	.....	....	....	....	......	....
4960	.....	Fort Chadbourne........	....	Dr. Swift, U. S. A...	.....	....	....	....	......	....
5078	.....	Pecos, Tex....	May 15, 1855	Capt. Pope........	82	....	13.00	17.00	6.00	Bill black, gums and feet red...........
5076	.....	Perm. camp, Pecos Riv..	Aug. 21, 1855	......do...........	124	....	12.00	17.00	6.00	Feet red, bill dark and purple, eyes black..
5080	.....	Howard Springs, Tex.....	May 9, 1855	......do...........	.....	....	....	....	......	....
5079	.....	Fort Clark, Tex..........	1855......	......do...........	.....	....	....	....	......	....
8757	.....	San Elizario, Mex.......	Dec. 14, 1854	Maj. Emory........	8	Dr. Kennerly.....	12.00	17.12	......	....
8758	.....	Mimb. to Rio Grande.....	....	Dr. Henry........	.....	....	....	....	......	....
8748	.....	Bill Williams' Fork, N. M.	Feb. 28, 1854	Lieut. Whipple	181	Kenn. and Moll...	....	....	......	....
4560	.....	Colorado river, Cal......	....	Maj. Emory.......	.....	A. Schott......	....	....	......	....
4559	.....	......do..............	....	......do...........	47	......do........	....	....	......	....
5561	.....	Petaluma, Cal.	May 13, 1856	E. Samuels........	838	....	....	....	......	....
5560	♀	......do..............	May 10, 1856	......do...........	.....	....	12.00	15.00	5.50	....
8749	.....	San Francisco...........	....	R. D. Cutts	.....	....	....	....	......	....
8751	.....	Presidio, Cal.............	June 2, 1853	Lieut. Trowbridge..	.....	....	....	....	......	....
8755	.....	Fort Steilacoom........	....	Gov. Stevens......	111	Dr. Suckley.....	....	....	......	....
8756	.....	......do..............	....	......do.......	112	......do........	....	....	......	....

SCARDAFELLA, Bonaparte.

Scardafella, BONAP. Conspectus Av. II, 1854, 85. Type *Columba squamosa*, Temm.

CH.—Bill lengthened ; culmen more than half the length of head measured from the frontal feathers. Feet as in *Chamaepelia*. Wings with the tertials nearly as long as the primaries ; shorter, however, than the first primary. Tail considerably longer than the wings ; much graduated, (of fourteen feathers?) ; the feathers narrow, linear, or tapering towards the end.

This remarkable type is a miniature of *Ectopistes* or *Zenaidura* in respect to the tail, which is even longer compared with the wings. The only specimen before me appears to have had fourteen tail feathers, but of this I cannot speak with certainty.

SCARDAFELLA SQUAMOSA, Bonap.

Scaly Dove.

Columba squamosa, (TEMMINCK,) WAGLER, Isis, 1831, 519.
Chamaepelia squamosa, GRAY, Genera.—CABANIS, (fide Bp.)
Oena squamosa, " REICH. Icones Av. tab. 253, fig. 3381."
Scardafella squamosa, BONAP. Consp. II, 1854, 85. Type.

Female.—Above ashy olive, changing to purer ashy on the wings. Beneath ashy white, changing on the breast and throat to pale violaceous. All the feathers on the head and body abruptly margined with dark brown, except on the forehead and chin.

All the quills except the innermost tertials orange brown ; the outer margins and tips dusky brown ; the under coverts orange brown ; the axillars strongly tinged with sooty. Tail feathers blackish, tinged with gray above ; all (except the innermost) broadly tipped with white ; the exterior with the white extending backwards on the outer web. Iris purple ; bill black ; feet flesh color. (Female.) Length, 8 inches ; wing, 3.75 ; tail, 4.10.

Hab.—South side of valley of Rio Grande, southward.

I regret that no males of this diminutive dove were before me in describing the species. The single female specimen is in rather poor condition also.

List of specimens.

Catal No.	Sex.	Locality.	When collected.	Whence obtained.	Orig. No.	Length.	Stretch of wings.	Wing.	Remarks.
4110	♀	Cadereita, New Leon, Mexico.	April 18, 1853	Lt. Couch _____	128	8.00	11.00	3.75	Eyes purple, bill black, feet flesh.

CHAMAEPELIA, Swainson.

Chamaepelia, SWAINSON, Zool. Jour. III, 1827, 361. Type *Columba passerina*, L.

Сн.—Size very small. Bill slender, elongated. Culmen more than half the head measured from frontal feathers. Legs stout. Tarsi longer than lateral toes ; equal to the middle without its claw ; covered anteriorly by a single series of scutellae. Wings broad ; the tertials excessively lengthened ; nearly as long as the primaries ; quite equal to the first primary. Tail nearly as long as the wings ; rounded laterally.

This group embraces the most diminutive doves known to naturalists. A single species is found abundantly in the southern United States.

CHAMAEPELIA PASSERINA, Swainson.

Ground Dove.

Columba passerina, LINNAEUS, Syst. Nat I, 1766, 285.—GMELIN, I, 1788, 787.—LATHAM, Ind. Orn. II, 1790, 611.— WILSON, Am. Orn. IV, 1811, 15 ; pl. xlvi.—WAGLER, Syst. Av. *Columba*, No. 88.—AUD. Orn. Biog. II, 1834, 471 : V, 1839, 558 ; pl. 182.—IB. Syn. 192.—IB. Birds Amer. V, 1842, 19 ; pl. 283.

Columba (Goura) passerina, BONAP. Obs. Wils. 1825, No. 181.—IB. Syn. 1828, 120.—NUTTALL, Man. I, 1832, 635.

Chaemepelia passerina, SWAINSON, Zool. Jour. III, 1827, 358.

Chamaepelia passerina, BONAP. List, 1838.—IB. Conspectus, II, 1854, 77.—GOSSE, Birds Jamaica, 1847, 311.

Sp. Сн.—Back, rump, exposed surface of tertials, and tail above, uniform grayish olive ; neck above and occiput tinged with bluish ; forehead, sides of head, and neck, under parts generally and lesser upper wing coverts, light purplish red, tinged with dusky towards the tail. Feathers of the head, neck, and fore breast, margined with a darker shade of the ground color, the forehead and chin, only, nearly uniform. Feathers of the breast dusky brown in the centre, this most conspicuous on the jugulum. Under wing coverts, axillars, and quills, brownish orange ; the latter margined externally and tipped with dusky brown, the tertials almost entirely of this color. Middle tail feathers like the back ; the others mostly black, the outer one edged towards the tip with white. The exposed surface of the wing variously marked with blotches exhibiting black, steel blue, and violet. Bill and feet yellow ; the former tipped with brown.

Female with little or none of the purplish red.

Length, 6.30 ; wing, 3.50 ; tail, 2.80.

Hab—South Atlantic and Gulf coasts. Lower California. Accidental near Washington, D. C.

The female of this dove is without the purplish red of the male, this being replaced by pale brownish ash, more anteriorly by white. The forehead feathers have the darker margins as well as the rest of the head. There is also a more ashy tinge on the back. The under tail coverts are brown, conspicuously margined with whitish.

I am unable to detect any material difference between specimens from Florida, the lower Rio Grande, and Lower California.

List of specimens.

Catal. No.	Sex.	Locality.	When collected.	Whence obtained.	Orig. No.	Collected by—	Length.	Stretch of wings.	Wing.
1191	♀	Washington, D. C.	Sept. —, 1844	S. F. Baird		J. C. McGuire			
3045	....	Liberty county, Ga.	1846	....do		W. L. Jones	6.50	10.20	3.50
8660	♀	Cape Florida	Oct. 30, 1857	G. Wurdemann			6.50	10.50	3.50
8661	....	Indian Key, Fla.	Aug. 28, 1857	....do			6.00	11.00	3.50
4921	....	Amelia island, Fla.		....do					
4922	♀	....do		....do					
4105	....	Matamoras, Mex.		Lieut. Couch		Dr. Berlandier			
4104	♀	Tamaulipas, Mex		....do	57				
4103	♂	....do		....do	68		6.50	10.50	3.36
3726	....	La Paz, L. Cal		W. Hutton					

OREOPELEIA, Reichenbach.

Oreopeleia, REICHENBACH, Handbuch der Speciellen Ornithol. I, i, 1851, page xxiv. Type *Columba martinica*, L.

CH.—Bill lengthened, slender; culmen half the rest of the head from the frontal feathers. Feet large, stout; tarsi longer than the middle toe and claw, covered anteriorly by transverse scutellae. Inner lateral claw longer than outer; reaching beyond the base of the middle one, the outer falling short of it. Hind toe and claw more than half the middle do. Quills and tail feathers very broad; the wings rounded; second and third quills longest, the first intermediate between the fourth and fifth. Tail sub-orbicular, the shafts convex outwardly; the feathers rounded, a little graduated.

This genus is placed by Bonaparte as a sub-genus of *Geotrygon* of Gosse.

OREOPELEIA MARTINICA, Reich.

Key West Pigeon.

Columba martinica, GMELIN, I, 1788, 781. Not of Temminck.
Geotrygon martinica, BONAP. Consp. Av. II, 1854, 74.—CAB. Jour. IV, 1856, 108.
Oreopeleia martinicana, REICH. Syst. Av. 1851, page xxv.—IB. "Icones Avium, tab. 257, fig. 1431."
Columba montana, AUD. Orn. Biog. II, 1834, 382; pl. 167.—IB. Syn. 1839, 191.—IB. Birds Amer. V, 1842, 14; pl. 282.—NUTTALL, Man. I, 2d ed. 1840, 756. Not of Linnaeus.
Zenaida montana, BONAP. Geog. & Comp. List, 1838.
"*Columbigallina montana*, TEMMINCK."
"*Columba mystacea*, LEMBEYE." Bonap. (Not of Temminck.)

SP. CH.—Ground color of the upper parts, including wing (both surfaces) and tail feathers brownish orange; the upper part of head and neck with metallic reflections of green and purple; the back, rump, and wing coverts, with reflections of metallic light purplish or violet. There is a white band from the lower mandible along side of the head, bordered below by purplish red, like the forehead, and a similar band through the eyes, which are without metallic lustre. The breast is very light purplish red, fading to white towards the tail and chin. The feathers of the under tail coverts are dusky brown at the base. Length, 10.70; wing, 6.00; tail, 5.75.

Hab.—Key West, Florida, and West Indies.

I am not aware whether there is any difference between the sexes of this species.   It has been referred by Audubon to the *Columba montana*, L., but this appears to differ in lacking the white bridle along the cheeks, &c.

List of specimens.

Catal. No.	Locality.	Whence and how obtained.	Nature of specimen.
2628	Key West, Florida	S. F. Baird	J. J. Audubon
1936	do	do	do

STARNOENAS, Bonaparte.

Starnoenas, BONAPARTE, Geog. & Comp. List, 1838. Type *Columba cyanocephala*, L.

CH.—Bill short; culmen about one-third the rest of head measured from the frontal feathers. Legs very stout and large; tarsi bare on the entire tibial joint, and covered with hexagonal scales, largest anteriorly; it is longer than the middle toe and claw. Inner lateral claw the larger; reaching the base of the middle claw; all the claws short, thick, and blunt. Hind toe and claw short, half the middle do.; wings short, broad, and concave; much rounded. Tail short, broad, nearly even, but slightly vaulted.

The single species of dove, composing the genus, in many respects resembles the partridges or quails, both in external appearance and in manners.

STARNOENAS CYANOCEPHALA, Bon.

Blue-headed Pigeon.

Columba cyanocephala, LINN. Syst. Nat. I, 1766, 282.—GMELIN, Syst. I, 1788, 778.—WAGLER, Syst. Avium, 1827, *Columba*, No. 112.—AUD. Orn. Biog. II, 1834, 441 : V, 1839, 557; pl. 172.

Starnoenas cyanocephala, BONAP. List, 1838.—IB. Consp. II, 1854, 69.—AUD. Syn. 1839, 193.—IB. Birds Amer. V, 1842, 23; pl. 284.—GUNDLACH, Cab. Journ. IV, 1856, 108.

Sternoenas cyanocephala, REICHENBACH, Systema Av. 1851, p. xxv, pl. xxiii.—IB. Icones Av. tab. 260 and 266.

Geophilus ? cyanocephala, SELBY, Pigeons, Jard. Nat. Lib. V, 216, pl. xxvii.

Columba (Lophyrus) cyanocephala, NUTTALL, Man. I, 2d. ed. 1840, 769.

Columba tetraoides, (SCOPOLI,) GMELIN, I, 772.

Blue-headed turtle, LATHAM, Syn. II, ii, 651.

SP. CH.—Bill blue, the fleshy part at the base carmine. Iris brown, scales of feet carmine, the interspaces white. Above and on sides glossy dark olivaceous chocolate; beneath brownish red, lighter centrally. Chin and throat black, with a narrow border of white below. A white line begins in the chin and passes under the eye to the occiput. Sides of head above this and forehead black; crown blue. Length, 10.70; wing, 5.40; tail, 4.35.

Hab.—West India Islands; occasionally at Key West, Florida, and other southern keys.

The axillars and under surface of the wings are like the belly.   The crissum is most like the back.   The outer tail feathers have a bluish tinge above.

The hind toe in this species is not strictly in the same plane with the others, but placed a little above their point of insertion.

SUB–ORDER

GALLINAE.

C<small>H</small>.—Bill usually rather short and stout, and less than the head. Basal portion hard, generally covered with feathers, and not by a soft naked skin. Legs lengthened ; the hind toe generally elevated above the level of the rest, and short ; when lower down, it is longer. Toes connected at the base by a membrane. The feathers of forehead not extending on the culmen in a point, but more restricted, and parted by the backward extension of the culmen.

As already stated, it is difficult to define the two sub-orders of *Rasores* so sharply as to cover all the numerous occasional exceptions in regard to the bill, legs, and other points of external anatomy. The case would be very simple if North American forms only were in question, but in giving an account of higher divisions in ornithology, it becomes necessary to take into account the many varied groups belonging to the world at large.

According to Keyserling and Blasius there is an important difference between *Columbae* and *Gallinae* in the outline of the feathers on the forehead. In the former these feathers extend forward on the culmen in a point, and those on the sides pass directly but obliquely across from the angle of the mouth to the base of this point and behind the scale. In the *Gallinae* with feathered heads, on the contrary, the frontal feathers are more restricted, and are actually parted by the backward extension of the culmen; the feathers on the side of the head extending forward on the bill to an appreciable extent. The cutting edges of the bill, too, are said in *Columbae* to be inflexed, and not overlapping, while in *Gallinae* they are more vertical, the upper overlapping and embracing the lower. The valve covering the nostril, and the base of the bill, are hard, not soft, and the nasal fossae frequently more or less filled with small feathers. The marked elevation and diminutive size of the hind toe, except in a few families, is an important character.

Synopsis of families.

A. Hind toe lengthened and nearly on same plane with the anterior, so as to be in contact throughout with the ground in walking.

P<small>ENELOPIDAE</small>.—Tail feathers 12. Sides of head usually naked.

B. Hind toe short, elevated considerably above the level of the rest, but the end usually touching the ground. Tail feathers generally more than 12.

P<small>HASIANIDAE</small>.—Very large. Tarsi, toes, and nasal valve naked. Tarsi generally in the male, with spurs. Head with naked spaces, or entirely bare.

T<small>ETRAONIDAE</small>.—Of middle size. Tarsi, and sometimes toes feathered. Nasal fossae and valve entirely filled in and concealed by feathers. Head usually closely feathered, except immediately round the eye and on the superciliary region.

P<small>ERDICIDAE</small>.—Size small. Tarsi long, bare. The nasal fossae not filled by feathers, the valve bare, the head well feathered.

July 3, 1858.

77 b

Family PENELOPIDAE.

CH.—Bill lengthened and rather slender; the end vaulted and hooked, covered by a horny plate, which extends backwards along the commissure; the bill posteriorly, with a membrane, which covers the nasal fossae, the lores, and the orbital region, leaving a broad, oval, free nasal aperture in the anterior portion of the nasal groove, without any peculiar scale above it. Plumage coarse. Wings much rounded, reaching to, or a little beyond, the base of the tail; the outer four or five primaries much graduated, pointed, sometimes attenuated and emarginate; secondaries lengthened. Tail of twelve feathers, lengthened, broad, even, or somewhat rounded. Legs moderately stout, the tarsus not very high, covered anteriorly by two rows of scutellae, behind by small oval scales in several series; sometimes reticulated. Toes long and thin, the hinder one long, inserted low down on the heel, scarcely elevated above the plane of the others. The claws narrow, acute, and gently curved.[1]

The preceding characters, borrowed from Burmeister, refer to a family of birds peculiar to Central and South America, many of them of very large size. They replace in these countries the *Phasianidae* of the Old World, which are there entirely wanting, and, where abundant, furnish an important and excellent article of food. They are chiefly arboreal, living and nesting among, and in most cases on, the trees, usually moving about in large flocks.

The family, as defined above, embraces three sub-families, the *Cracinae*, the *Penelopinae*, and the *Oreophasinae*, the first with the bill usually elevated, the culmen curved from the base. The sides of the head are generally well feathered, and the birds are of large size. The genera *Crax* and *Pauxi*, or Curassows and Hoccos, are known by the longitudinal open exposed nostrils, much anterior to the feathers, and rather low bill of the first, and the very much elevated bill, with the nostrils more vertical, basal, and concealed, of the other.

The sub-family *Penelopinae* is the only one represented in our fauna, and by a single genus and species. In this the bill is weak, slender, longer than high, straight at the base above; the portion covered with skin longer than the horny part, and the nostrils oval, elongated, and in the anterior portion of the groove, or extending to or beyond the middle of the bill. The sides of the head and the throat are more or less naked, with occasional feathers or hairs. The legs are as long as the middle toe without the claw.

Of the sub-family *Oreophasinae* but a single species is known, the *Oreophasis derbianus*. In this the nasal groove is filled with feathers throughout, and there is an elevated truncated knob above the eyes.

Of the *Penelopinae*, the typical genera, according to Gray, have the following characters:

ORTALIDA.—Throat without wattles, but with two naked narrow streaks. Outer primaries broad to and at the ends. Hind toe two-thirds the lateral ones.

PENELOPE.—Front of throat naked and wattled. Outer three primaries much attenuated and falcate, linear towards the end. Hind toe nearly equal to the lateral.

Other genera are indicated by Reichenbach and Bonaparte, but these are sufficient to illustrate the characters of the single one belonging to the United States.

ORTALIDA, Merrem.

Ortalida, MERREM, Av. rar. Icones et Desc. II, 1786, 40, (Gray.) Type *Phasianus motmot*, L.

There is little to add in the way of characteristics to the diagnosis of this genus just given. But one species belongs to the United States, though several are found in Mexico and further south.

---

[1] Burmeister, Thiere Brasiliens, Vögel, II, 1856, 335.

Comparative measurements of species.

Catal. No.	Species.	Locality.	Sex.	Length.	Stretch of wings.	Wing.	Tail.	Tarsus.	Middle toe.	Its claw alone.	Bill above.	Along gape.	Specimen measured.
......	Ortalida McCalli.......	New Leon, Mex...	♂	....	....	8.30	10.84	2.34	2.48	0.54	1.06	1.12	Skin ....
......	........do	......do.............	......	23.50	26.25	8.50	....	......	....	....	....	....	Fresh ...

ORTALIDA McCALLI, Baird.

Chiacalacca.

Ortalida vetula, LAWRENCE, Ann. N. Y. Lyc. V, 1851, 116. (Not *Penelope vetula*, WAGLER, Isis, 1830, 1112, and 1831, 517.)

Ortalida poliocephala, CASSIN, Illust. I, IX, 1855, 267; pl. xliv. (Not *Penelope poliocephala*, WAGLER, Isis, 1830, 1112.)

SP. CH.—Body above dark greenish olive; beneath brownish yellow, tinged with olive. Head and upper part of neck plumbeous. Tail feathers lustrous green, all tipped with white, except the middle one. Feathers along the middle of the throat black; outer edge of primaries tinged with gray. Eyes brown. Bill and feet lead colored. Length, 23.50; wing, 8.50; tail, 11.

The bill of this species is rather long and considerably decurved anterior to the nasal groove; the commissure curved almost as much as the culmen. The tarsus is about equal to the middle toe; the anterior half covered by a series of large transverse scutellae, with another series on each side meeting behind in a sharp ridge, except superiorly. These lateral series are separated from the anterior by a narrow strip of skin. The outer toe is rather longer than the inner; the claw falling considerably short of the middle claw. Hind toe without its claw about one-third the middle toe and claw; it is situated on the same level with the others.

The feathers of the head are lengthened and pointed, producing a decided full crest. The side of the head is naked to behind the eyes; the chin is naked, with rather more than the central third longitudinally covered by black feathers, with stiffened shafts and abbreviated vanes. The tail is longer than the wings, broad and graduated; the lateral feather about three-fourths the middle. The secondary quills are long and broad, fully as long as the primaries. The wing is concave and much graduated; the first and second quills much shorter than the secondaries.

I feel considerable uncertainty as to the specific name of the subject of the present article. The *O. vetula*[1] is said to be olivaceous; the head and ears slaty gray; the flanks, crissum, and tibia, brownish; the epigastrium and belly somewhat rufous; the tail feathers above bronze green, with white tips. The length, 18 inches; longest tail feathers, 9.17; the shortest, 6.50. The adult *O. poliocephala*[2] is olive gray; the head and upper part of neck slate color; the epigastrium, middle of belly, and tibia, white; the flanks and crissum fulvous; the tail feathers bronzed black, tipped with fulvous. The young has the head and occiput slate gray; epigastrium, belly, and tibia brownish rufous; the tail like the adult, (tipped with fulvous.) Length, 23 inches; tail, 11 inches.

The specimen before me agrees with neither species as described by Wagler. It is most like the young of *O. poliocephala* as to size and general color, but the tail is tipped with white in all

[1] *Penelope vetula*, WAGLER, Isis, 1830, 1112, No. 14. Mexico.
[2] *Penelope poliocephala*, WAGLER, Isis. 1830, 1112, No. 15, Mexico.

ages instead of the fulvous, so strongly insisted on by Wagler as occurring in both old and young. The size is considerably larger than that of *O. vetula;* the flanks, tibia, and crissum are more fulvous than brownish, and the entire head and upper part of the neck are slaty instead of the head and ears only.

More adult specimens than the one before me are said to be generally of a brownish olive, darker on the head, (probably somewhat slaty;) the breast and belly light rufous, with longitudinal whitish pencillings; as nothing is said of the tibia, they are probably not white, but like the flanks. The irids are dark hazel; the naked skin of the chin orange red and loose.

Upon the whole, I am inclined to believe that this bird is distinct from both *vetula* and *poliocephala*, and therefore propose for it the name of *McCallii*, after Colonel McCall, late inspector general of the United States army, whose admirable biographies of the animals of Texas and New Mexico have added so much to our knowledge of their natural history. His notes on the present species in Cassin's Illustrations (I, 268) furnish all on record of its habits, and from his description has been derived the preceding account of the colors of the adult.

List of specimens.

Catal. No.	Sex.	Locality.	When collected.	Whence obtained.	Orig. No.	Length.	Stretch of wings.	Wing.
¹4106	♂	Boquilla, New Leon......	Spring of 1853	Lieut. Couch.............	137	23.50	26.25	8.50

¹ Eyes brown ; bill blue, lead color, and slate ; feet lead color.

Family PHASIANIDAE.

Cʜ.—Bill moderate ; the legs, toes, and nasal fossae, bare ; the tarsus usually with one or more spurs, in the male. The hind toe elevated above the level of the others. Tail feathers more than twelve. Faci generally more or less naked.

Of the entire family of *Phasianidae*, as above described, but a single genus, *Meleagris*, belongs to America, the others being found entirely in the Old World. It includes the different pheasants, Jungle fowl, the domestic chicken, the turkeys, the peacocks, and other well known birds, among them by far the most important and interesting species domesticated by man.

The precise limits of the family vary with different authors, Gray making five sub-families, *Pavoninae, Phasianinae, Gallinae, Meleagrinae,* and *Lophophorinae;* while Bonaparte has quite à different arrangement.

The family *Numidinae* of Reichenbach is equivalent to *Meleagrinae* of Gray, with the addition, however, of almost another entire family, *Tinamidae,* of the same author, the members all South American. It is not my place to attempt a reconciliation of these differing views of classification, although the association of *Meleagris* with *Tinamus* and others of this group seems not very unnatural.

Sub-family MELEAGRINAE.

Cʜ.—Tail moderate, truncate. Head and neck nearly naked, and more or less carunculated or with fleshy lobes.

The preceding diagnosis is quite sufficient to distinguish the *Meleagrinae* of Gray from his other sub-families, the *Pavoninae* having the tail and its coverts much developed and depressed, but broad and rounded ; the *Phasianinae* have the tail greatly lengthened and attenuated, cuneate, compressed ; the *Gallinae* have the tail moderate, arched, and compressed, the sides of the head only naked; and the *Lophophorinae* have the head feathered, except immediately around the eye ; the tail moderate, broad, and rather depressed.

The two principal genera of this sub-family, as described by Gray, are as follows:

Mᴇʟᴇᴀɢʀɪs.—Head and neck without feathers, but with scattered hairs. An extensible fleshy process on the forehead, but no development of the bone. Tarsi of the male provided with spurs. Tail nearly as long as the wing.

Nᴜᴍɪᴅᴀ.—Frontal bone much developed, producing a vertical crest. Lower jaw with two fleshy lobes. No spur on the tarsi in the male. Tail very short.

The domestic turkey is the type of *Meleagris*, while the Guinea fowl or Pintado represents *Numida*, (*N. meleagris.*) The latter genus embraces five or six species, nearly every one the type of a distinct genus of some author, and all inhabitants of Africa.

MELEAGRIS, Linnaeus.

Meleagris, Lɪɴɴᴀᴇᴜs, Syst. Nat. 1735. Type *Meleagris gallopavo*, Linn.

Cʜ.—Legs with transverse scutellae before and behind ; reticulated laterally. Tarsi with spurs. Tail rounded, rather long, usually of eighteen feathers. Forehead with a depending fleshy cone. Head and the upper half of the neck without feathers. Breast of male in most species with a long tuft of bristles.

The above diagnosis will be sufficient to distinguish the true turkeys from their allies, the nearest being *Numida*, according to most authors. In this, besides the differences already mentioned, the tarsi have two series of scutellae before, instead of one; the posterior and lateral surfaces reticulated. The tail is very short, and concealed by its coverts.

The species of turkey have usually been considered as two, the North American wild bird, from which the domestic turkey was supposed to have descended, and the ocellated turkey, *M. ocellata*, of Honduras, and other portions of Central America. The latter is one of the most beautiful of known birds, with numerous small fleshy tubercles on the head, different from those of the domestic turkey. The feathers exhibit reflections of metallic bronze, gold, green, and blue, while the tail coverts and tail exhibit four series of large ocellated spots. The tail is said to have but fourteen feathers.

The question has been recently agitated whether the supposed single species of common turkey, tame and wild, is not really divisible into two or even three, and in the following pages the reasons will be presented upon which an opinion of the kind may be based. In the mean time, the following diagnoses will serve to show the differences which really appear to exist in the series of wild turkeys of the type of the North American bird.

Common characters.—Head livid blue, legs red, general color copper bronze, with copper and green reflections, each feather with a velvet black margin; all the quills brown, closely barred with white. Tail feathers chestnut, narrowly barred with black; the tip with a very broad, subterminal black bar.

Tail coverts dark purplish chestnut throughout, with the tips not lighter. Tip of tail feathers scarcely paler chestnut than the ground color.........................*M. gallopavo*.

Tail coverts chestnut, the tips much paler, sometimes almost white. Tip of tail feathers light brownish yellow; sometimes with the coverts broadly whitish........*M. mexicanus*.

Comparative measurements of species.

Catal. No.	Species.	Locality.	Sex & age.	Length.	Stretch of wings.	Wing.	Tail.	Tarsus.	Middle toe.	Its claw alone.	Bill from nostril.	Along gape.	Specimen measured.
5148	Meleagris mexicana..	Llano Estacado, Texas .	♂	*48.50	....	19.00	14.60	6.46	4.08	0.90	1.04	2.31	Skin .....
10030	.........do	Near 32° S.............	♀	*37.00	....	17.30	15.30	4.95	3.45	0.84	0.98	1.96	Skin .....
5147	.... do	Llano Estacado........	♀	*42.00	....	17.00	14.00	5.68	3.68	0.91	0.97	2.14	Skin .....
10029	Meleagris gallopavo..	Red Fork of Arkansas..	♂	*44.70	....	20.00	15.50	6.54	4.50	0.80	1.05	2.23	Skin .....
5748	.........do	Republican River	○♂	*34.80	....	18.80	14.00	6 45	4.00	0.84	1.06	1.90	Skin .....
do.	.........do	.........do	......	41.00	57.50	....	....	....	....	....	....	....	Fresh ....
1196	.........do	Washington, D. C.	♂	47.00	....	21.00	17.50	6.00	4.28	0.90	1.05	2.16	Skin .....
do.	.........do	.........do	......	50.00	64.50	20.00	....	....	....	....	....	....	Fresh ....
10322	.........do	.........do	♂	42.00	....	20.00	16.50	6.24	4.16	1.04	1.06	2.10	Skin .....

* About.

MELEAGRIS GALLOPAVO, L.

Wild Turkey.

Meleagris gallopavo, LINNAEUS, Syst. Nat. I, 1766, 268.—GMELIN, I, 1788, 732.—LATHAM, Ind. Orn. II, 1790, 618.—
WILSON, Index, VI, 1812.—STEPHENS, in Shaw's Zool. XI, I, 1819, 156, (domestic bird.)—
BONAP. Am. Orn. 1, 1825, 79; pl. ix.—IB. Syn. 122.—IB. List, 1838.—AUD. Orn. Biog. I, 1831,
1 and 33: V, 1839, 559; pl. 1.—IB. Syn. 1839.—IB. Birds Amer. V, 1842, 42, pl. 287, 288.—
NUTTALL, Man. I, 1832, 630.—REICHENBACH, Systema Av. 1851, pl. xxvi.—IB. Icones Av.
tab. 289.

Meleagris americana, BARTRAM, Travels, 1791, 290.

Meleagris sylvestris, VIEILLOT, Nouv. Dict. IX, 447.

Gallopavo sylvestris, LECONTE, Pr. A. N. Sc. Phil. 1857, 179.

Meleagris fera, VIEILLOT, Galerie Ois. II, 1824, 10; pl. x.

Wild turkey, CLAYTON, Philos. Trans. XVII, 1693, 992.—PENNANT, Philos. Trans..LXXI, 1781, 67.—IB. Arctic
Zool. No. 178.

American turkey, LATHAM, Syn. II, II, 676.

Gallopavo sylvestris, Novae angliae, RAY, Syn. 51.

Gallopavo sylvestris, CATESBY, Carol. I, 1730, App. p. xliv.—BRISSON, Orn. V, 1760, 162.

Bill elongated, slender; culmen rising a little at the base, then gently and equally convex to the tip. Commissure concave from the base. Nostrils elliptical, linear, much overhung by an incumbent scale; about two-fifths its distance from the tip of the bill. Head and upper part of neck all round, as well as the whole throat, bare of feathers, and covered sparsely with short fleshy processes, placed transversely, scarcely to be seen on the under side. The feathers of the lower neck extend narrowly along the median line to the nape. The bare portion thinly covered with short, black hairs, or hair-like feathers. At the point of junction of the bill and head is a long fleshy process, capable of much erection and distension, and well covered with hairs. The jugulum of the male is provided with a close tuft of bristles six or eight inches long.

The tarsus is long and stout, much longer than the middle toe and claw. It is entirely bare of feathers, including the superior joint of the tibia. Anteriorly it is covered by a double row of about eighteen pentagonal scales from tibial joint to the toes, embracing the anterior half, the lateral edges of these rows being straight. There is also a double row behind, the external extending nearly to the hind toe; the inner reaching to the spur. The space between these four rows of scales, and not occupied by them, is covered by small subhexagonal scales. There is in the male a large spur, its centre situated about four-tenths the length of the tarsus from its lower edge. It stands nearly perpendicular to the tarsus, directed postero-internally, is about an inch long, conical, and slightly curving upwards. The lateral toes are about equal, the claws not reaching the base of the middle. There is a membrane extending between the bases of the anterior toes, and slightly continuous between the inner and posterior. The hinder toe is situated about its length (excluding the claw) above the inferior edge of the tarsus.

The wings are moderate; when closed reaching nearly to the middle of the tail. They are rather rounded; the first primary shorter than the tenth; the sixth longest. The secondaries and tertials are long and broad; the longest reaching to the tip of the eighth primary, and much longer than the first.

The tail is about as long as from the carpal joint to the end of the secondaries; it is broad, the feathers all graduated quite evenly, and diminishing successively about half an inch. The feathers are eighteen in number, nearly truncate at tip; or obtusely angular, the corners rounded.

The naked skin of the head and neck is blue; the excrescences purplish red. The legs are red. The feathers of the neck and body generally are very broad, abruptly truncate, and each one well defined and scale-like; the exposed portion coppery bronze, with a bright coppery reflection in some lights, in the specimens before me chiefly on the under parts. Each feather is abruptly margined with velvet black, the bronze assuming a greenish or purplish shade near the line of junction, and the bronze itself sometimes with a greenish reflection in some lights. The black is opaque, except along the extreme tip, where there is a metallic gloss. The feathers of the lower back and rump are black, with little or no copper gloss. The feathers of the sides behind, and the coverts, upper and under, are of a very dark purplish chestnut, with purplish metallic reflections near the end, and a subterminal bar of black; the tips are of the opaque purplish chestnut referred to. The concealed portion of the coverts is dark chestnut barred rather finely with black; the black wider than the interspaces. The tail feathers are dark brownish chestnut, with numerous transverse bars of black, which, when most distinct, are about a quarter of an inch wide and about double their interspaces; the extreme tip for about half an inch is plain chestnut, lighter than the ground color; and there is a broad subterminal bar of black about two inches wide on the outer feathers, and narrowing to about three-quarters of an inch to the central ones. The innermost pair scarcely shows this band, and the others are all much broken and confused. In addition to the black bars on each feather, the chestnut interspaces are sprinkled with black. The black bands are all most distinct on the inner webs; the interspaces are considerably lighter below than above.

There are no whitish tips whatever to the tail or its coverts. The feathers on the middle of the belly are downy, opaque, and tipped obscurely with rusty whitish.

The wing coverts are like the back; the quills, however, are blackish brown, with numerous transverse bars of white, half the width of the interspaces. The exposed surfaces of the wing, however, and most of the inner secondaries, are tinged with brownish rusty, the uppermost ones with a dull copper or greenish gloss.

The female differs in smaller size, less brilliant colors, absence generally of bristles on the breast and of spur, and a much smaller fleshy process above the base of the bill.

The position of the spur in the male varies somewhat in different specimens, and even at times in the two legs of the same bird.

The wild turkey of eastern North America differs in several points, both of structure and manners, from the domesticated bird, as recently insisted on by Major Leconte. I have not at hand a skin of the barn yard turkey for comparison, and owing to the season they are not to be found in our markets; but according to Major Leconte, there is a great difference, in the possession by the latter of an enormous dewlap, extending from the base of the lower mandible to the large caruncles on the lower part of the neck, not found in the other. The color of the skin of the head and neck is not livid blue, but more of a fleshy tint, which in the breeding season of the male becomes fiery red, owing to the turgidity of the caruncles. This skin, too, appears to be more destitute of hairs. According to Bonaparte, the domestic turkey, even in those which have the closest resemblance to the wild bird, may always be distinguished by a whitish tip to the tail, and the tail coverts edged with whitish, never seen in the other.

Major Leconte states furthermore, that the wild turkey has never been so domesticated as to propagate its race in confinement, notwithstanding the many efforts made to accomplish this result.

The difference in the color of the flesh of the two birds when cooked is quite appreciable, that of the wild bird being much darker.

It is upon the whole exceedingly probable that the two birds are specifically distinct. Whether the domestic species be descended from the one recently described by Mr. Gould, or not, remains to be ascertained. In the next article I describe skins which appear to be referable to Gould's *M. mexicana*, and this certainly indicates a near approach to the tamed turkey in the whitish bars of the tail coverts and the tail. The skin of the head, however, appears to be of the same color, and no difference in the carunculation of the throat was noticed, although this may have been obscured by drying. The skin of the head appeared more pilose, but there was the same caruncle at the base of the bill.

If the dewlap be characteristic of a species at present only known in captivity, then, as Major Leconte remarks, it should bear the name of *M. gallopavo*, as based by Linnaeus essentially upon the description by Brisson of *Gallopavo sylvestris*, in which this dewlap is particularly mentioned. In this event our wild bird will be entitled to a new name, which might be that of Bartram, in 1791, *Meleagris americana*. Should the *M. mexicana* be the original of the domestic species, Gould's name will become a synonym, if it be proved that *gallopavo* refers to the same bird.

In conclusion I venture to suggest the following hypothesis, which, however, is not original with myself: That there are really three species of turkey, besides the *M. ocellata*, a fourth species from Central America, entirely different from the rest. That one of these, *M. americana*, is, probably, peculiar to the eastern half of North America; another, *M. mexicana*, belongs to Mexico, and extends along the table lands to the Rocky mountains, the Gila, and the Llano Estacado, and a third is the *M. gallopavo*, or domesticated bird. That it is not at all improbable that the last was originally indigenous to some one or more of the West India islands, whence it was transplanted as tamed to Mexico and other parts of America, and from Mexico taken to Europe about A. D. 1520. Finally, that the wild turkeys were probably completely exterminated by the natives, as has been the case with equally large birds in other islands, as the dodo and solitaire.

This hypothesis will explain the fact of our meeting nowhere at the present day any wild turkeys resembling the domestic one. I have an indistinct recollection of a statement that our barn yard turkey came originally from Bermuda or Jamaica, but I cannot speak positively in regard to it.

The entire subject is one of much interest, and deserves to be investigated thoroughly. It is quite possible that a careful examination of the external form and habits of the New Mexican bird may do much to throw full light on the whole question.

July 3, 1858.

78 b

List of specimens.

Catal. No.	Sex.	Locality.	When collected.	Whence obtained.	Orig. No.	Collected by—	Length.	Stretch of wings.	Wing.
10322	♂	Washington, D. C.	Mar. —, 1855	Wash. market					
1196	♂	......do........	Dec. —, 1843	S. F. Baird			50.00	64.50	20.00
10029	♂	Red fork of Arkansas.	July —, 1850	Capt. Sitgreaves		Dr. Woodhouse			
5748	♂	Republican river	Oct. 16, 1856	Lieut. Bryan	381	W. S. Wood			

MELEAGRIS MEXICANA, Gould.

Mexican Turkey.

Meleagris mexicana, GOULD, Pr. Zool. Soc. 1856, 61.

In the series of turkey skins before me, I find that all from the vicinity of the Rocky mountains differ strikingly from those east of the Mississippi in the feathers of the sides of the body behind, and in the upper and under tail coverts. These are all tipped with light brownish yellow for about half an inch, more or less, with the region, and the tail is tipped with the same. The chestnut ground of the tail and coverts is also considerably lighter. The gloss on the feathers of the rump is green, not purple. The coverts, too, lack in a measure the purple shade in the chestnut. The metallic reflections generally have rather more green than in the eastern bird.

In one specimen (female, 10030, from Fort Thorn) the light edgings are almost white, and so much extended as to conceal the entire rump. All the feathers of the under parts of the body are edged broadly with white, and the tail is tipped with the same for more than an inch. This specimen also has the head considerably more hairy than in the eastern skins, but the others from the same region do not differ so much in this respect from eastern ones.

Whether these differences can be considered as establishing a second species for the United States is a question yet to be decided. It is certain that these peculiarities are constant in all before me, while the eastern skins all agree precisely in their characteristics as described. The New Mexican turkeys, with white tips to the tail feathers and coverts, correspond, in a very striking degree, with the *M. mexicana* of Gould.

List of specimens.

Catal. No.	Sex.	Locality.	Whence obtained.
10030	♀ ?	Fort Thorn, New Mexico	Dr. T. C. Henry
5147		Llano Estacado	Capt. Pope
5148		......do	......do

Family TETRAONIDAE. The Grouse.

As already stated, the *Tetraonidae* are pre-eminently characterised among gallinaceous birds by their densely feathered tarsi, and by the feathers of the nasal fossa or groove, which fill it completely, and conceal the nostrils. The toes are usually naked, (feathered to the claws in the ptarmigans,) and with pectinations of scales along the edges. The tail feathers vary from sixteen to eighteen and even twenty in number ; the tail is rounded, acute, or forked. The orbital region is generally somewhat bare, with a naked stripe above the upper eyelid, beset by short fringe-like processes.

The following synoptical table will give a general view of the North American *Tetraonidae*, although the arrangement is probably much more artificial than natural. The species of *Tetrao* and *Bonasa* inhabit wooded regions ; *Lagopus* belongs to the more arctic portions of the continent and the snowy ridges of the Rocky mountains, while the others are found in the great prairies of the west, *Centrocercus* being confined to the sterile plains covered with sage or wormwood.

Synopsis of genera.

A. Legs feathered to and on the basal membrane of the toes. No ruff on the side of the neck, which, however, has an extensible bare space.

TETRAO.—Tail broad, nearly even, or truncate, and rounded laterally ; two-thirds the wing. Nasal fossae scarcely half the culmen.

CENTROCERCUS.—Tail excessively lengthened and cuneate ; longer than the wings. Nasal fossae two-thirds the culmen. Shafts of feathers on the lower throat very spinous.

PEDIOCAETES.—Tail very short, but graduated, and with the two middle feathers (perhaps tail coverts) lengthened beyond the rest, and two-thirds as long as the wing ; the next longest, half the wing. Nasal fossae not half the length of culmen. Shafts of throat feathers normal.

B. Legs scarcely feathered to the extreme base of tarsus, the lower joint of which is bare, with large transverse scutellae.

CUPIDONIA.—Tail very short, truncate, but laterally graduated ; half the wings. Sides of neck with long, pointed, or lanceolate, stiff feathers. Nasal fossae scarcely one-third the culmen.

C. Legs feathered to the claws.

LAGOPUS.—Tail about two-thirds the wing, truncate ; of sixteen to eighteen feathers. Most species becoming white in winter ; none of the other genera exhibiting this peculiarity.

D. Lower half of tarsi bare, with two rows of scutellae anteriorly.

BONASA.—Sides of neck with a ruff of broad, truncate, soft feathers. Tail very broad, square, as long as the wings.

TETRAO, Linnaeus.

Tetrao, Linnaeus, Syst. Nat. 1744.   Type *T. urogallus*, L.   (Gray.)

Ch.—Tail lengthened, slightly narrowed to the square or somewhat rounded tip ; about two-thirds the wing ; the feathers with stiffened shafts. Tarsus feathered to and between the bases of the toes. No unusual feathers on the side of throat. Culmen between the nasal fossae nearly half the total length. Color mostly black.

Inhabit wooded regions.

The American wood-grouse do not belong strictly to the genus *Tetrao,* as defined by later writers, with *T. urogallus* for type. This species differs chiefly in the pointed feathers of the chin, but in other respects comes quite close to *T. obscurus.* A genus, *Canace,* has been made for the American birds, but I see no special occasion to adopt it here.

The following diagnosis will distinguish the species :

Tail of twenty feathers. General color plumbeous above, with fine mottling. Chin and throat white and black. Tail uniform black, with slaty tip..............................*T. obscurus.*

Tail of sixteen feathers. Above banded with plumbeous. Beneath black, with some white on jugulum and sides of belly. Tail tipped with brownish orange. Upper coverts not tipped with white ....*T. canadensis.*

Similar to last. Tail without orange tip. Upper tail coverts banded terminally with white...*T. franklini.*

Comparative measurements of species.

Catal No.	Species.	Locality.	Sex.	Length.	Stretch of wings.	Wing.	Tail.	Tarsus.	Middle toe.	Its claw alone.	Bill above.	Along gape.	Specimen measured.
4505	Tetrao obscurus	Cascade mountains....	♂	20.50	....	9.40	7.45	1.65	2.19	0.46	0.96	1.19	Skin.....
4398	........do..........	Fort Steilacoom	♂	18.60	....	8.90	6.86	1.66	2.26	0.56	0.80	1.05	Skin.....
do.	........do........ ..	........do......	......	19.75	30.00	9.75	....	....	....	....	....	....	Fresh.....
5746	........do..........	Black Hills............	♂	19.30	....	9.00	7.46	1.62	2.16	0.52	1.04	1.20	Skin.....
10013	........do..........	Fort Steilacoom, W. T.	♀	18.50	....	8.34	5.90	1.62	2.06	0.44	1.00	1.06	Skin.....
do.	........do........	........do....	......	19.00	27.00	8.75	....	....	....	....	....	....	Fresh.....
7046	........do........	Black Hills	♀	17.64	....	8.40	6.16	1.61	2.06	0.46	0.92	1.14	Skin.....
478	Tetrao canadensis...	Nova Scotia...........	♂	16.20	....	6.70	5.44	1.54	1.86	0.48	0.85	0.98	Skin.....
do.	........do...........	........do...........	......	19.70	....	6.60	4.56	1.40	1.76	0.42	0.74	0.82	Skin.....
10025	Tetrao franklini*...	St. Mary's, R. mts	♂	....	....	7.35	5.62	1.38	1.83	0.45	0.84	0.92	Skin.....
10026	........do.*.........	........do.......	♀	....	....	6.90	4.52†	Feet and head wanting			....	....	....

* Very poor specimen.

TETRAO OBSCURUS, Say.

Dusky Grouse.

Tetrao obscurus, Say, Long's Exped. R. Mts. II, 1823, 14.—Bon. Syn. 1828, 127.—Ib. Mon. *Tetrao*, Am. Phil. Trans.
III, 1830, 391.—Ib. Am. Orn. III, 1830 ; pl. xviii.—Sw. F. Bor. Am. II, 1831, 344 ; pl. lix, lx.—
Nuttall, Man. I, 1832, 666.—Aud. Orn. Biog. IV, 1838, 446 ; pl. 361.—Ib. Syn. 1839, 283.—
Ib. Birds Amer. I, 1842, 89 ; pl. 295.—Newberry, Rep. P. R. R. Surv. VI, iv, 1857, 93.

Canace obscura, Bonap. Comptes Rendus, XLV, 1857, 428.

Tetrao richardsonii, Douglas, Trans. Linn. Soc. XVI, 1829, 141.

Sp. Ch.—Sexes dissimilar. Tail of twenty feathers. Above bluish black ; plumbeous or black beneath. Tail uniform black, and finely and obscurely mottled above. Tail broadly tipped with light slate. Beneath uniform plumbeous. A dusky half collar on the throat. The chin and throat above white, varied with black. Tail about two-thirds the length of the wings, broad, rounded, composed of twenty broad, even, and truncated feathers. Tarsi feathered to the toes, the feathers extending along the sides of the basal half of the first joints of the toes. Pectinations on the sides of the toes very short. Length, 20.50 ; wing, 9.40 ; tail, 7.45.

Hab.—Black Hills of Nebraska to Cascade mountains of Oregon and Washington.

The prevailing color of this species is dark brown above, with fine mottlings of plumbeous; beneath nearly uniform plumbeous; the sides, however, under the wings, the scapulars, and the outer surface of the wings are like the back, but also mottled finely with brown, with a tendency to light ashy towards the tips of the feathers, those of the sides streaked centrally, and terminated with white; the chin and upper part of throat have the feathers white, barred terminally with black, and the loral feathers similarly marked; there is, however, a dark brown stripe from the bill beneath the eye and over the ear coverts, as well as a half collar on the lower part of the throat, of a dark plumbeous black. The tail feathers are lustrous black beneath; slaty black above, with a terminal bar of ashy plumbeous, varying considerably in width. The under tail coverts are dark plumbeous, broadly tipped with white. All the feathers on the lower part of the neck are white, except at the tip.

The female is somewhat similar, except that the feathers of the neck and fore part of the back have conspicuous transverse bars of brownish yellow. The outlines of the dark transverse pectoral collar are indistinct, and the dark streak beneath the orbits appears to be wanting. The plumbeous of the under parts is duller, and more obscured with white. The upper tail coverts and inner tail feathers are banded with grayish.

There are considerable differences in different specimens of this species, varying with age and sex. In one specimen, 4505, from the Cascades, much the largest of all, the back is quite uniformly black, with scarcely any mottling, except on the rump and wings; the under parts are dark continuous slate color, passing insensibly into the darker collar of the throat. The white of the chin is much obscured. In another male (5746) the feathers beneath are all edged with whitish. This specimen (of August 3,) has the tarsi nearly bare. One specimen (2859) has the tail entirely black, without slaty tip.

List of specimens.

Catal. No.	Sex and age.	Locality.	When collected.	Whence obtained.	Orig'l No.	Collected by—	Length.	Stretch of wings.	Wing.	Remarks.
5747	♂	Black Hills, Neb.	Aug. 2, 1856	Lieut. Bryan	193	W. S. Wood				Head
5746	♂	do	Aug. 3, 1856	do	194	do	19.00	27.00		
7047?	o	do	Aug. 9, 1857	do	385	do				
7046	♀	do	do	do		do				
8919		Laramie Peak, Neb.	Aug. 24	Lt. Warren		Dr. Hayden	19.12	28.00	8.50	Iris brown
8918		do	Aug.	do		do	18.50	27.00	8.75	
8917		do		do		do				
8920		do		do		do	18.00	28.00	9.00	
8915		do	Aug. 25	do		do	20.00	29.50	9.50	
8916		do	Aug. 29	do		do	17.50	24.12	8.00	Iris brown
10015		St. Mary's Pass, R. mts	Oct. 8, 1853	Gov. Stevens		Dr. Suckley				
10017		Rocky mountains		do		do				
4505	♂	Cascade mountains		Lt. Williamson		Dr. Newberry				Head
10008		Fort Dalles, Oregon		Dr. Suckley	387	do	19.00	26.12		
10010		Clickatat, W. T.	Aug. 4, 1853	Gov. Stevens	22	Dr. Cooper				
10011		Fort Steilacoom	July —, 1856	Dr. Suckley	532	do				
10013	♀	do	Aug. —, 1854	Gov. Stevens	63	Dr. Suckley	19.00	27.00	9.75	
10009		do	Aug. —, 1856	Dr. Suckley	525	do	18.00	28.00		
10012		do		Gov. Stevens	67	Dr. Suckley				
4398	♂	do	April 18, 1855	Dr. Suckley	194	do	19.75	30.00	9.75	
10014	♂	do	May 3, 1856	do	368	Dr. Suckley	20.00	30.00		
10027	♂	do	April —, 1854	Gov. Stevens	69	do	19.75	39.00	9.75	

TETRAO CANADENSIS, Linn.

Spruce Partridge; Canada Grouse.

Tetrao canadensis, LINN. Syst. Nat. 1, 1766, 274.—FORSTER, Phil. Trans. LXII, 1772, 389 —GMELIN, I, 1788, 749.—
SABINE, Zool. App. Franklin's Exped. 683.—BONAP. Syn. 1828, 127.—IB. Amer. Orn. III, 1830;
pl. xxi, f. 2, ♀.—IB. Am. Phil. Trans. III, N. S. 1830, 391.—RICH. F. Bor. Amer. II, 1831,
346; pl. lxii, female.—NUTTALL, Man. I, 1832, 667.—AUD. Orn. Biog. II, 1834, 437 : V, 1839,
563; pl. 176.—IB. Syn. 203.—IB. Birds Amer. V, 1842, 83 ; pl. 294.

Canace canadensis, REICH. Av. Syst. Nat. 1851, p. xxix. Type.—BONAP. Comptes Rendus, XLV, 1857, 428.

Tetrao canace, LINN. Syst. Nat. I, 1766, 275.

Black Spotted Heathcock, EDWARDS, Glean. pl. cxviii.

Spotted Grouse, PENNANT.

SP. CH.—Tail of sixteen feathers. Feathers above distinctly banded with plumbeous ; beneath uniform black, with a pectoral band of white, and white on the sides of the belly. Chin and throat above, black. Tail with a broad brownish orange terminal band. Length, 16.20 ; wing, 6.70 ; tail, 5.44.

Hab.—Spruce forests and swamps of the northern United States to the Arctic seas ; west nearly to Rocky mountains.

Bill rather slender. Eyebrows with the usual papillae. Tarsi densely feathered, the posterior edge bare ; the feathers extending along the sides of the toes for half the basal joint. Pectination on the sides of the toes very conspicuous. Tail as long as the wing from elbow to ends of secondaries ; nearly even ; the lateral feathers slightly graduated, (three quarters of an inch less than the longest ;) the feathers truncate, rounded laterally, and sixteen in number. Middle toe and claw longer than the tarsus ; lateral equal, the claws not reaching the base of middle toe ; the claws long and sharp.

Prevailing color in the male black ; each feather of the head, neck, and upper parts generally, having its surface waved with plumbeous gray. This is in the form of two or three well-defined concentric bars parallel to each other, one along the exterior edge of the feather, the others behind it. The sides of the body, the scapulars, and outer surface of the wings are mottled like the back, but more irregularly, and with a browner shade of gray, the feathers with a central white streak expanding towards the tip, (on the wing these streaks seen only on some of the greater coverts.) There is no white above except as described. The under parts are mostly uniform black, the feathers of the sides of the belly and breast broadly tipped with white, which sometimes forms a pectoral band. There is a white bar across the feathers at the base of the upper mandible, usually interrupted above ; a white spot on the lower eyelid, and a white line beginning on the cheeks and running into a series of white spots in the feathers of the throat, the lower feathers of this are banded terminally with whitish. The feathers at the base of the bill, and the head below the eyes and beneath, are pure black. The quills are dark brown, without any spots or bands, the outer edges only mottled with grayish. The tail feathers are similar, but darker, and the tail is tipped with a band of orange chestnut, nearly half an inch wide, obscured on the central feathers. The under tail coverts are black, broadly barred and tipped with white ; the feathers of the legs mottled brown and whitish ; dirty white behind the tarsi. The bill is black.

The female is smaller but somewhat similar, the black bars above broader, the inner gray bars of each feather, including the tail, replaced by broader ones of brownish orange. The under parts have the feathers black, barred with the brownish orange, which, on the tips of the belly feathers, is pure white. The clear continuous black of the head and breast are wanting. The scapulars, greater coverts, and sides, are streaked as in the male.

List of specimens.

Catal. No.	Sex.	Locality.	Whence obtained.
478	♀	Nova Scotia?.........	S. F. Baird ....
479	♂	......do.............	......do.............
6921	♀.	Selkirk settlement...	D. Gunn............
6920	♂	......do.............	......do.............

TETRAO FRANKLINII, Douglas.

Franklin's Grouse.

Tetrao franklinii, DOUGLAS, Trans. Linn. Soc. XVI, 1829, 139.—RICH. F. Bor. Am. II, 1831, 348 ; pl. lxi.

Tetrao canadensis, var. BONAP. Am. Orn. III, 1830, 47 ; pl. xx.

? *Tetrao fusca*, ORD, Guthrie's Geog. 2d Am. ed. II, 1815, 317. Based on small brown pheasant of Lewis & Clark, II, 182, which very probably is this species.

SP. CH.—Similar to *T. canadensis*, but with the tail feathers entirely black, without orange brown terminal band ; the upper tail coverts broadly tipped with white. Wing, 7.35 ; tail, 5.62.

Hab.—Northern Rocky mountains, and west.

The only specimens of this species before me are so much mutilated as to preclude any accurate description. The difference from *canadensis*, however, even in these, is sufficiently appreciable. This consists chiefly in the rather longer tail with broader feathers, which are pure black instead of very dark brown, and entirely without the orange terminal band. The white streaks on the scapulars are larger terminally and much more conspicuous, and the upper tail coverts are conspicuously barred terminally with white, not seen in the other. The female differs from that of *canadensis* in the white bars at the ends of the tail coverts, and in having the tail feathers tipped with whitish instead of orange brown.

The male of this bird is described and figured by Bonaparte as that of the Canada grouse, *T. canadensis*.

Middendorff, in his Sibirische Reise, speaks of a grouse as occurring on the southern shores of the Sea of Ochotsk, which he considered the same as the North American *Tetrao franklini*. Hartlaub, however, naturally disbelieving a statement so much at variance with what had been found to be the law in the distribution of the *Gallinacea*, made special efforts to procure specimens, and, on comparing them with skins of the American *T. canadensis* and description of *T. franklini*, found that there was a very great difference in the primaries of the Siberian bird, to which, in consequence, he gave the name of *T. falcipennis*. In this the outer five primaries are emarginate internally and greatly falcate ; the second and third most so, a character scarcely found elsewhere among *Gallinacea*, except in *Penelope*. There are many differences in color, such as the upper parts being black, spotted finely with brown, and the shafts streaked with lighter in *falcipennis*, instead of plain gray banded with black. Other differences might readily be indicated, but those just mentioned are quite sufficient to substantiate Dr. Hartlaub's position.

List of specimens.

Catal. No.	Sex.	Locality.	Whence obtained.	Orig. No.	Collected by—
10026	♀	St. Mary's, Rocky mountains..	Gov. Stevens................	142	Lt. Mullen, U. S. A..........
10025	♂	......do....................	......do....................		......do...................

CENTROCERCUS, Swainson.

Centrocercus, SWAINSON, F. Bor. Am. II, 1831, 496.   Type *Tetrao urophasianus,* Bon.

CH.—Tail excessively lengthened, cuneate, longer than the wings, the feathers all lanceolate. Tarsi feathered to the joint and between the bases of the toes. Lower throat and its sides with stiffened spinous feathers. Nasal fossae extending very far forward ; the length of culmen between them two-thirds the total length. Color mottled yellowish above, with large black patches beneath.

The single species of this genus inhabits exclusively the high and almost desert sage plains of the far west, feeding on the *Artemisia* or wild sage which characterises those regions.

Comparative measurements.

Catal. No.	Species.	Locality.	Sex.	Length.	Stretch of wings.	Wing.	Tail.	Tarsus.	Middle toe.	Its claw alone.	Bill above.	Along gape.	Specimen measured.
10018	Centrocercus urophasianus.	....	......	......	......	12.60	12.20	2.14	2.52	0.58	1.64	1.34	Skin........
10023	...........do..............	....	♂?	29.00	......	11.30	11.50	2.03	2.34	0.46	1.42	1.20	Skin........
5419	....do............	90 miles ab. mo. Yellowstone.	♀	......	......	11.20	9.00	1.96	2.10	0.40	1.42	1.22	Skin........
do.	...........do..............	.........do...............	......	25.00	37.50	11.50	......	......	......	......	......	......	Fresh........
10021	...........do..............	Spokan Plain..............	......	......	......	......	12.42	......	......	......	1.58	1.40	Head and tail.

CENTROCERCUS UROPHASIANUS, Swainson.

Sage Cock; Cock of the Plains.

Tetrao urophasianus, BONAP. Zool. Jour. III, Jan. 1828, 214.—IB. Am. Orn. III, 1830 ; pl. xxi, f. 1.—IB. Mon. Tetrao, in Trans. Am. Phil. Soc. N. S. III, 1830, 390.—DOUGLAS, Trans. Linn. Soc. XVI, 1829, 133.—NUTTALL, Man. I, 1832, 666.—AUD. Orn. Biog. IV, 1838, 503 ; pl. 371.—IB. Syn. 205.—IB. Birds Amer. V, 1842, 106 ; pl. 297.—NEWBERRY, Zool. Cal. & Or. Route, Rep. P. R. R. Surv. VI, IV, 1857, 95.

Tetrao (Centrocercus) urophasianus, Sw. F. Bor. Am. II, 1831, 358 ; pl. lviii.

Centrocercus urophasianus, JARDINE, Game birds, Nat. Lib. Birds, IV, 140 ; pl. xvii.

?? *Tetrao phasianellus,* ORD. Guthrie's Geog. 2d Am. ed. II, 1815, 317, based on Lewis & Clark, II, 181.

Cock of the plains, LEWIS & CLARK, II, 180, sp. 2.

SP. CH.—Tail feathers twenty. Above varied with black, brown, and brownish yellow ; coverts having all the feathers streaked with the latter. Beneath black ; the breast white ; the upper feathers with spiny shafts ; the lower streaked with black ; tail coverts with white tips ; the sides also with much white. Length, 29 ; wing, 11.30 ; tail, 11.50.

Hab.—Sage plains of the northwest.

Tarsi feathered to the toes, the feathers extending along the sides of the toes at the base. Tail elongated, longer than the wings, and excessively cuneate ; of twenty feathers, all lanceolate acute and much graduated ; the lateral feathers about four and a half inches shorter than the middle (or about two-thirds) and exceeded in length by the under coverts. The feathers on the fore part of the breast, and especially on its side, are excessively rigid and spinous, with the webs much worn down. The bill is lengthened, and the nasal fossa with its feathers extends very far forwards to a point more than half the length of the culmen.

The upper parts in this species are greatly variegated, with a mottling of black, brownish yellow, and whitish. On the neck and fore part of the back the feathers are blackish, with several broad, zigzag transverse bars of light brownish yellow. On the back and wings the feathers have, in addition, longitudinal streaks of the same, the transverse bars concealed and the terminal portions coarsely mottled. The tertials, in addition, have a terminal bar of brownish yellow, the much elongated upper coverts and the tail feathers are quite similarly mottled.

The under parts, from the breast to the tail, are pure continuous black, the under coverts black tipped with white. The lower part of the throat, with the sides of the neck, have a half collar of black. Below this the throat is lighter; the shafts of the feathers stiff and black. There is a white band behind the eye curving down and crossing the throat; the rest of the neck is mottled with black, white, and gray. The sides beneath the wings are like the scapulars, but the black of the belly is bordered laterally by white, somewhat blotched with black.

Specimens vary somewhat, and it is probable that in full dress the male shows no transverse bars on the back and neck above. The females before me are much like the males, only smaller, more banded above; the black of the belly more restricted; the chin, throat above, and cheeks dull brownish white. The feathers of the neck have stiffened shafts, but these are not conspicuous.

List of specimens.

Catal. No.	Sex.	Locality.	When collected.	Whence obtained.	Orig. No.	Collected by—	Length.	Stretch of wings.	Wing.	Remarks.
8922	♀	Loup Fork	Sept. 9	Lt. Warren		Dr. Hayden	24.50	41.00	12.00	Iris yellow.
5743	♂	North Platte	Aug. 12,1856	Lt. Bryan	256	W. S. Wood				
5419	♀	90 miles above mouth Yellowstone	July 28,1856	Lt. Warren		Dr. Hayden	25.00	37.50	11.50	
8923	♂	Cheyenne river	Sept. 9	...do...		...do...	25.00	41.50	11.50	Iris yellow.
8921	♂	...do...		...do...		...do...	21.00	33.50	10.00	...do...
5745	♀	Medicine Bow creek	Aug. 8,1856	Lt. Bryan	226	W. S. Wood				
5742	♀	W. Branch Medicine Bow Cr	Aug. 10,1856	...do...	238	...do...				
7045	♀	Bridger's Pass	July 30,1857	...do...	390	...do...				
10023	♀	Cochetopee Pass			21	Capt. Beckwith				
10020	♀	Near Snake river, Blue mountains	Oct. 5	Gov. Stevens	139	Mr. Kreutzfeldt.				
10021	♀	Spokan Plain, W T		...do...		Dr. Cooper				
10019		Yakima river, W. T	Sept. 16,1853	...do...	13	...do...				
10022		...do...	Sept. 14,1853	...do...	12	...do...				
4506		Des Chutes, O. T		Lt. Williamson		Dr. Newberry				

PEDIOCAETES, Baird.

Cʜ.—Tail short, graduated; exclusive of the lengthened middle part, (perhaps tail coverts,) half the full rounded wing. Tarsi densely feathered to the toes and between their bases. Neck without peculiar feathers. Culmen between the nasal fossae not half the total length.

But one species of this genus is known to naturalists, most of whom associate it with *Centrocercus*, from which, however, it seems to differ in well marked characters.

July 7, 1858.

79 b

Comparative measurements.

Catal. No.	Locality.	Sex.	Length.	Wing.	Tail.	Tarsus.	Middle toe.	Its claw alone.	Bill above.	Along gape.	Specimen measured.
4543	Fort Pierre	♂	15.30	8.50	5.24	1.74	2.02	0.55	0.94	1.12	Skin....
9999	Spokan river, W. T...	....	16 50	7.90	4.98	1.70	1.98	0.48	0.92	1.00	Skin....

PEDIOCAETES PHASIANELLUS, Baird.

Sharp-tailed Grouse.

Tetrao phasianellus, LINNAEUS, Syst. Nat. I, ed. 10, 1758, 160. (Not in 12th edition.)—FORSTER, Phil. Trans. LXII, 1772, 394, 495.—GMELIN, Syst. Nat. I, 747.—LATHAM, Ind. Orn. II, 635.—?? ORD. Guthrie's Geog. 2d Amer. ed. II, 1815, 317.—BON. Syn. 1828, 127.—IB. Amer. Orn. III, 1828, 37; pl. xix.—NUTTALL, Man. I, 1832, 669.—AUD. Orn. Biog. IV, 1838, 569; pl. 382.—IB. Syn. 1839, 205.—IB. Birds Amer. V, 1842, 110; pl. 298.—NEWBERRY, Zool. Cal. & Or. Route; Rep. P. R. R. Surv. VI, IV, 1857, 94.

Tetrao (Centrocercus) phasianellus, SWAINSON, F. Bor. Am. II, 1831, 361.

Centrocercus phasianellus, JARDINE, Game Birds, Nat. Lib. Birds, IV, 136; pl. xvi.—BONAP. Comptes Rendus, XLV, 1857, 428.

Tetrao urogallus, Var. β. LINN. Syst. Nat. I, ed. 12th, 273.

? *Phasianus columbianus*, ORD, Guthrie's Geog. 2d Am. ed. II, 1815, 317; based on the Columbia pheasant of Lewis & Clark, II, 180.

? *Tetrao urophasianellus*, DOUGLAS, Trans. Lin. Soc. XVI, 1829, 136. Supposed by Richardson to be young in ferruginous plumage.

Long-tailed grouse, EDWARDS; *Sharp-tailed grouse*, PENNANT.

SP. CH.—Tail of eighteen feathers. Colors, white, black, and brownish yellow. Above with transverse bars; the wings with round white spots. Beneath pure white, with dark V-shaped blotches on the breast and sides. Length, 18.00; wing, 8.50; tail, 5.24.

Hab.—Northern prairies and plains, from Wisconsin to Cascades of Oregon and Washington.

Neck without the tuft of elongated feather of *C. cupido*, but with a bare space on each side. A papillose naked skin along the superciliary region, bordered externally by feathers. Tarsus very densely feathered, but with a narrow bare space behind; the feathers extending on the sides of the toes for nearly half the length of the basal joint. Middle toe and claw a little longer than the tarsi, the sides of the toes extended and provided with a conspicuous pectination of linear processes. Tail long, cuneate, the feathers eighteen in number and all graduated; the central pair elongated considerably beyond the rest, (one to one and a half inches.) The tail coverts reach nearly as far as the tips of the third innermost pair of tail feathers; the whole tail is about two-thirds the length of wings.

In form this species differs from *cupido* in the absence of the pointed feathers of the neck. The tail is of much the same shape, but the feathers more abruptly graduated; the outer about one-third the eighth and one-fourth the ninth; this may possibly prove to be an extended tail covert. The bill is much stouter, the culmen more convex and rising at the base. The pectinated processes of the toes are much longer, forming a broader base to the toes. The tarsi are more densely plumose, the feathers not stopping at the base of the toes, but extending beyond them.

The general color above is light brownish yellow, varied with black; the wings with rounded spots of white. The under parts are pure white, the feathers on the breast and sides with a brown V-shaped mark, the legs of which are nearly parallel with the outline of the feather. The feathers of the sides of the belly have concealed marks of the same character. The feathers on the back are blackish brown, variously spotted with brownish yellow, without any decided indication of transverse bars. A usual marking towards the tip of the feathers is an undulating transverse yellowish bar, two opposite U-shaped brown bars, the convexities resting on the shaft and more or less confluent, the spaces between these and the tips of the feathers whitish. The wings are brownish grey, the coverts all with large spots of white; both webs of the secondaries with conspicuous transverse bars, the outer webs of the primaries with spots of the same. The sides of the head and beneath are brownish yellow with a whitish superciliary band; there is a curved dusky line below the eye parallel with the orbits, and a dusky spot below this. The tail feathers are dotted brownish grey, becoming pure white externally and to the tip. The central elongated feathers (or coverts) are like the back.

Specimens vary in the amount of black on the back, and in the extent of brownish yellow on the flanks.

This species differs totally from the *T. cupido* in the V-shaped marks on the breast and sides, instead of transverse bands; the pure white belly; the transverse white bands on the secondaries; the white spots on the wings; the lighter quills, and tail, independently of the more pointed tail, more feathered tarsi, absence of pointed feathers of the neck, stouter bill, &c.

The tibial feathers are soiled white.

Catal. No.	Sex.	Locality.	When collected.	Whence obtained.	Orig. No.	Collected by—	Length.	Stretch of wings	Wing.	Remarks.
10001	......	North Red river......	....	N. W. University....	......	R. Kennicott...	....	......	....	....
10000	......	Red river, Minn......	Sept. 25	......do...............	......	......do.......	....	......	....	....
1969	......	Fort Union, Neb.	...........:.....	S. F. Baird	......	J. J. Audubon..	....	......	....	....
5420	......	......do......	....	Lieut. Warren..........	......	Dr. Hayden....	18.00	26.00	8.25	....
4543	♂	Fort Pierre	Oct. 23, 1855	......do...............	......	......do.......	....	......	....	Eyes black ....
4542	......	......do..	Oct. 21, 1855	......do.	......	......do.......	....	......	....	....
5422	♀	Mo. Vermilion river..	Oct. 25, 1856	......do...............	......	......do.......	18.00	28.75	8.25	Iris yellowish brown....
5421	♀	......do......	Oct. 20, 1856	......do....	......	......do.......	16.75	26.50	8.00	Iris dark ....
10002	.....	Snake river, Oregon..	Oct. 5	Gov. Stevens........	140	Dr. Buckley....	....	.. ....	....	....
9999	......	Spokan river, W. T...	Oct. 30, 1853	......do.............	21	Dr. Cooper.....	....	......	....	....

CUPIDONIA, Reichenbach.

Cupidonia, REICHENBACH, Av. Syst. Nat. 1850, p. xxix. Type *Tetrao cupido*, L.

CH.—Tail short, half the lengthened wings; the feathers stiffened and more or less graduated. Bare space of the neck concealed by a tuft of lanceolate feathers. Tarsi feathered only to near the base, the lower joint scutellate. Culmen between the nasal fossae scarcely one-third the total length.

This genus, as far as known, is entirely peculiar to North America. Its single species, *C. cupido*, is the well known prairie chicken, or prairie hen, of the west, a bird in its abundance and importance as an article of food representing, in the prairies of the United States, the ptarmigan or snow grouse of the north.

Comparative measurements.

Catal. No.	Locality.	Sex.	Length.	Wing.	Tail.	Tarsus.	Middle toe.	Its claw alone.	Bill above.	Along gape.	Specimens measured.
10006	Tremont, Illinois	♂	16.60	8.80	4.70	2.02	2.35	0.62	0.87	1.09	Skin ....
10003	......do.........................	♀	14.00	8.10	4.30	1.86	2.03	0.42	0.84	1.09	Skin ....
10007	Near 32° L, Texas	♂ ?	14.50	8.30	4.18	1.66	1.78	0.40	0.88	1.08	Skin ....
10005	......do.........................	♀ ?	14.80	7.80	3.42	1.59	1.76	0.34	0.90	1.14	Skin ....

CUPIDONIA CUPIDO, Baird.

Prairie Hen; Prairie Chicken; Pinnated Grouse.

Tetrao cupido, LINN. Syst. Nat. I, 1766, 274.—GM. I, 751.—LATH. Ind. Orn. II, 1790.—WILSON, Am. Orn. III, 1811,
104, pl. xxvii —BON. Obs. Wils. 1825, No. 183.—IB. Mon. *Tetrao*, Am. Phil. Trans. III, 1830, 392.—
NUTTALL, Man. I, 662.—AUD. Orn. Biog. II, 1834, 490 : V, 1839, 559 ; pl. 186.—IB. Birds Amer.
V, 1842, 93 ; pl. 296.—KOCH, Wiegmann's Archiv, 1836, I, 159.
Bonasa cupido, STEPHENS, Shaw's Gen. Zool. XI, 299.
Cupidonia americana, REICH. Av. Syst. Nat. 1850, p. xxix.—BONAP. Comptes Rendus, XLV, 1857, 428.

SP. CH.—Tail of eighteen feathers. Varied with whitish brown, and brownish yellow. Almost everywhere with well defined
transverse bars of brown on the feathers. Length, 16.50 inches ; wing, 8.80 ; tail, 4.70.

HAB.—Western prairies and plains within the limits of the United States, east of Rocky mountains ; southeast to Calcasieu,
Louisiana ; east to Pocono mountains, Pennsylvania; Long Island, and eastern coast.

Body stout, compact. A tuft of long pointed lanceolate feathers on each side of the neck,
covering a bare space capable of much inflation. Tail short, truncate, much graduated,
composed of eighteen feathers ; the lateral feathers about two-thirds the middle ; the feathers
stiffened, nearly linear and truncate. The tail is scarcely longer than the coverts, and about
half the length of the wing. Tarsi covered with feathers anteriorly and laterally to the toes,
but bare, with hexagonal scutellae behind. The middle toe and claw longer than the tarsus ;
the toes margined by pectinated processes. A space above the eye provided with a dense pectinated process in the breeding season ; sometimes separated from the eye by a superciliary space
covered with feathers.

Bands on the body transverse throughout. Lanceolate feathers of the throat black ; the
upper ones with a central yellowish stripe. Eyelids and a stripe from the nostril alongside the
head, (interrupted above the eye,) brownish yellow; the sides of the head below a dusky infra-
ocular stripe, with the chin and throat above, similar. Feathers of the body above and below
brown, with a terminal and two transverse bands of well defined white; the brown almost
black and the white tinged with rufous above. The scapular feathers sometimes showing more
black. Wings banded like the back ; the primaries grayish brown, marked only on the outer
webs with light spots ; the shafts black. Tail feathers sometimes uniform brown ; sometimes
with rufous transverse bars. Under coverts marked like the back, with more white ; sometimes
(10006) entirely white. The membrane above the eye said to be scarlet, that of the sounding
bladder dusky orange.

The female lacks the pectinations of the space above the eye, and has but a short cervical tuft
and naked space, but is similar in general markings.

There is considerable variation in the colors of different specimens. In most cases there is an
elongated dusky spot on the side of the lower jaw, separated from the dusky infra-orbital streak.
Sometimes the colors are much darker. Texas specimens have the back more finely and
uniformly barred, without any of the dorsal black spaces.

A summer skin, from Calcasieu, Louisiana, has the tarsal feathers much reduced ; and the
tarsus bare all round for about half an inch from the toes.

The range of this species was once much wider than at the present time. It scarcely seems to
occur north of the United States line, nor, perhaps, beyond the beginning of the High Central
Plains. Eastward it probably was once abundant through the open country to the Atlantic

coast, but at the present day it is only found, and that very sparsely, on the Pocono mountains of Pennsylvania, on Long Island, and on various other tracts of sea coast and island as far east as Maine.

List of specimens.

Catal. No.	Sex and age.	Locality.	When collected.	Whence obtained.	Collected by—	Length.	Stretch of wings.	Wing.	Remarks.
4250	♀	Calcasieu Pass, La.........	1854..........	G. Würdemann..	....	......	......	......	....
4249	♂	......do	1854..........	......do	....	......	......	......	....
10317	....	Missouri..............	....	S. F. Baird......	....	......	......	......	....
10003	....	Tremont, Ill.	....	W. J. Shaw.....	....	......	......	......	....
10006	....	......do	....	......do	....	......	......	......	....
5423	♀	Mouth of Running Water...	Oct. 20, 1856	Lieut. Warren...	Dr. Hayden......	17.50	28.00	8.75	Iris deep yellow...... ..
4541	o♂	Big Sioux..................	Nov. 7, 1856	......do	......do.....	18.00	29.00	9.00	.......f......
4540	♂	......do	.....do......	......do	......do..........	19.00	30.00	9.00	....
10007	....	Texas................	....	Capt. Pope.......	....	......	......	......	....

BONASA, Stephens.

Bonasa, STEPHENS, Shaw's Gen. Zool. XI, 1819. Type *Tetrao bonasia*, L.

Tetrastes, KEYS. & BLAS. Wirb. Europ. 1840, p. lxiv.

CH.—Tail widening to the end, its feathers very broad, as long as the wings; the feathers soft, and eighteen in number. Tarsi naked in the lower half; covered with two rows of hexagonal scales anteriorly, as in the *Ortyginae*. Sides of toes strongly pectinated. Naked space on the side of throat covered by a tuft of broad soft feathers. Portion of culmen between the nasal fossae about one third the total length. Top of head with a soft crest.

This genus, in its partly naked tarsi, with two rows of scutellae anteriorly, indicates a close approach to the American partridges, or quails. It has a single European representative.

There seems a strong probability that the Pacific coast species is different from the Atlantic. The diagnosis will be as follows:

Common characters.—Sexes nearly similar. Colors reddish or gray, white and black. Tuft on the sides of neck velvety black. Tail with a sub-terminal brown bar. Sides banded transversely with brown; back with cordate spots of grey.

Colors pale. Bands on the sides of body obscure brown. Under tail coverts white. Middle toe without claw shorter than tarsus..*B. umbellus.*

Colors very dark. Bands on the sides sharply defined dark brown. Under tail coverts rufous, with terminal white spots. Middle toe without claw apparently longer than tarsus.................. ....*B. sabini.*

Comparative measurements of species.

Catal. No.	Species.	Locality.	Sex.	Length.	Stretch of wings.	Wing.	Tail.	Tarsus.	Middle toe.	Its claw alone.	Bill above.	Along gape.	Specimen measured.
844	Bonasa umbellus...	Carlisle, Pa.............	♂	15.50	....	7.21	6.92	1.66	1.85	0.43	0.84	1.06	Skin ....
do.	......do............	....do.................	......	18.00	23.00	7.24	....	....	....	....	....	....	Fresh ....
0330	......do............	Georgia................	♀	14.60	....	7.00	5.50	1.62	1.90	0.46	0.80	0.90	Skin ....
do.	......do............	....do.................	......	16.50	23.00	7.00	....	....	....	....	....	....	....
8424	Bonasa sabini...	Puget's Sound..........	......	16.50	....	7.30	6.71	1.74	2.42	0.50	0.94	1.00	Skin ....
9996	......do............	Ft. Vancouver, W. T....	♂	16.30	....	7.30	6.66	1.70	2.10	0.59	0.95	1.00	Skin ....
do.	......do........ ...	....do.................	......	18.00	23.00	....	....	....	....	....	....	....	Fresh ...

BONASA UMBELLUS, Stephens.

Ruffed Grouse; Partridge; Pheasant.

Tetrao umbellus, Linn. Syst. Nat. I, 1766, 275, 6.—Gmelin, I, 782.—Wilson, Am. Orn. VI, 1812, 46 ; pl. xlix.—Bon. Obs. Wils. 1825, 182.—Doughty, Cab. N. H. I, 1830, 13 ; pl. ii.—Aud. Orn. Biog. I, 1831, 211 : V, 560 ; pl. 41.—Ib. Syn. 1839, 202.—Ib. Birds Amer. V, 1842, 72 ;. pl. 293.

Tetrao (Bonasia) umbellus, Bonap. Syn. 1828, 126.—Ib. Mon. Tetrao, Am. Phil. Trans. III, 1830, 389.—Nuttall, Man. I, 1832, 657.

Bonasa umbellus, Stephens, Shaw, Gen. Zool. XI, 1824, 300.—Bonap. List, 1838.—Ib. Comptes Rendus, XLV, 1857, 428.

Tetrao togatus, Linn. I, 1766, 275, 8.—Forster, Philos. Trans. LXII, 1772, 393.

Tetrao tympanus, Bartram, Travels in E. Florida, 1791, 290.

Ruffed Grouse, and *Shoulder-knot Grouse*, Pennant and Latham.

?Tetrao umbelloides, Douglas, Trans. Linn. Soc. XVI, 1829, 148.

Sp. Ch.—Tail of eighteen feathers. Reddish brown or grey above ; the back with cordate spots of lighter. Beneath whitish, transversely barred with dull brown. Tail tipped with gray, and with a subterminal bar of black. Broad feathers of the ruff black. Length, 18 inches ; wing, 7.20 ; tail, 7.00.

Hab.—Wooded portions of eastern United States towards the Rocky mountains.

Tail lengthened ; nearly as long as the wing ; very broad, and moderately rounded ; the feathers very broad and truncate ; the tip slightly convex ; eighteen in number. Upper half of tarsus only feathered ; bare behind and below, with two rows of hexagonal scutellae anteriorly. A naked space on the side of the neck, concealed by an overhanging tuft of broad, truncate feathers. There are no pectinated processes above the eye, where the skin instead is clothed with short feathers.

The prevailing color of this species above is sometimes grey, sometimes reddish. In one specimen, (344,) the prevailing color is chestnut, each feather of the back and rump with an elongated sub-cordate terminal large spot of reddish grey, and mottled finely with brown, most distinct in the cordate spot. The scapulars and coverts are streaked with light brownish yellow. The under parts are light brownish yellow, nearly white on the belly ; the feathers with transverse sub-terminal broad bars of obsolete brown ; the sides under the wings, however, streaked like the wing coverts. The broad cervical feathers are uniform dark brown, with a terminal gloss of metallic green. The quills are brown, the outer webs of secondaries mottled with rufous ; of the primaries pale brownish yellow, with bars of brown. The tail feathers are tipped with grey, and have a broad sub-terminal bar of black ; within this is a series of eight or ten narrow waved transverse bars, grey posteriorly, and black anteriorly. The entire feather is, besides, finely mottled. The upper tail coverts are marked like the tail feathers, except in lacking the sub-terminal black. There is an indication of a darker jugular band, owing to the deeper shade of brown in the sub-terminal bars of the feathers. The feathers on the side of the neck adjacent to the cervical tufts are tipped with white, and there is an approach to a whitish scapular band. The under tail coverts are almost clear immaculate in the exposed portion.

Douglas speaks of a smaller and lighter variety of the ruffed grouse, found in the valleys of the Rocky mountains north, near 54° north latitude. This is of "a light mixed speckled grey, the ruffle consisting invariably of only twenty feathers, the crest feathers few and short." It is difficult to say whether this is identical with either of the others or distinct.

List of specimens.

Catal. No.	Sex and age.	Locality.	When collected.	Whence obtained.	Length.	Stretch of wings.	Wing.
6922	....	Red river, H. B. T........	....	Donald Gunn	....	....	....
844	♂	Carlisle, Pa.............	Oct. 29, 1842......	S. F. Baird	18.00	23.00	7.25
1661	o	Columbia, Pa..	....	......do........	....	....	....
10330	♀	Georgia	....	Prof. Jos. Leconte	16.50	23.00	7.00

BONASA SABINII, B a i r d .

Oregon Grouse.

Tetrao sabinii, DOUGLAS, Trans. Linn. Soc. XVI, 1829, 137.—RICH. F. Bor. Am. II, 1831, 343.

? *Tetrao umbellus*, RICH. F. Bor. Am. II, 1831, 342.—NEWBERRY, Zool. Cal. & Or. Route, Rep. P. R. R. Surv. VI, IV, 1857, 94.

SP. CH.—Similar to *B. umbellus*, but much darker. Middle toe longer. Length, about 18 inches ; wing, 7.30 ; tail, 6.70.

Hab.—Rocky mountains to Pacific coast of Oregon and Washington.

The specimens of ruffed grouse from the Pacific coast differ very greatly in much darker tints of coloration, although the pattern is apparently the same. There is no shade of grey anywhere. The upper parts are dark orange chestnut, mottled with black, the cordate light spots very distinct. The feathers of the breast are strongly tinged with reddish yellow ; those of the sides marked with broad and conspicuous bars of black, instead of the obsolete brown. The under tail coverts are orange chestnut, with indistinct bars of black, and an angular terminal blotch of white. All the light brown blotches and edgings of the eastern variety are here dark brown or black. The jugular band between the ruffles is very conspicuously black. The greatest difference is seen in the middle toe, which is much longer than in *umbellus*, and even without its claw, exceeding the tarsus, instead of being shorter.

I am inclined to consider this as a good species of grouse, and distinct from *B. umbellus*, on account of the difference in the length of the middle toes, although this elongation may sometimes be found in *B. umbellus*. When Richardson found no difference between his *T. umbellus* and the *T. sabini* of Douglas, it is not improbable, judging from the measurements, that he had *sabini* before him instead of the other species.

List of specimens.

Catal. No.	Sex.	Locality.	When collected.	Whence obtained.	Orig. No.	Collected by—	Length.	Stretch of wings.
8424	....	Simiahmoo, W. T........	Sept. 16, 1857	A. Campbell......	......	Dr. Kennerly....	....	....
9997	....	Fort Steilacoom, W. T....	April —, 1856	Dr. Suckley........	349	....	....	....
¹9996	♂	Fort Vancouver, W. T....	Jan. 13, 1854	Gov. Stevens......	11	Dr. Cooper.......	18.00	23.00
8087	....	Columbia river, O. T.....	....	J. Gould	......	D. Douglas	....	....
4443	....	Willamette valley	....	Lt. Williamson....	......	Dr. Newberry...	....	....
4439	....	Cascade mountains, O. T..	....	......do........	......	......do........	....	....
4441	....	.....do........	....	......do........	......	......do........	....	....
4446	...	Callapooya mountains....	....	......do........	......	......do........	....	....

¹ Iris brown.

LAGOPUS, Vieillot.

Lagopus, VIEILLOT, Analyse, 1816. Type *Tetrao lagopus*, L.

CH.—Nasal groove densely clothed with feathers. Tail of sixteen or eighteen feathers. Legs closely feathered to the claws. Species snow white in winter.

The ptarmigans inhabit the northern regions of both hemispheres, and with the arctic fox and hares, the lemmings, and a few other species, characterize the Arctic zone. They are of rare occurrence within the limits of the United States, though further north they become abundant. The species all become more white in winter, but in summer they are varied with brown, black, and gray, most of the wing remaining white. There is, generally, considerable difference between the male and female, the former having the mottling finer and the colors more blended; and in some species having a peculiar black stripe through the eye.

As in most grouse there is a naked stripe above the eye, which is generally colored red, and exhibiting a series of fringed processes.

There is some uncertainty as to the name proper to be used for this genus. Gray sets aside *Lagopus* of Vieillot, 1816, as not the same with *Lagopus* of Brisson, 1760. If, however, Brisson be no authority for species, he may not be for genera; and, his name being disregarded, Vieillot's *Lagopus* would retain its position.

The study of the American ptarmigans is rendered very difficult by the extreme difficulty of procuring specimens in summer plumage, and with accurate indications of sex. European naturalists, many of whom live among the ptarmigan, have not yet come to a positive conclusion as to the number of species to be counted, whether two, three or more, while the investigation of our own species is complicated by the extreme rarity of good skins in collections, the imperfect notice of locality and sex, and the remoteness from the localities where these birds abound.

In the collection before me, made up chiefly of specimens kindly presented to the Smithsonian Institution by Mr. John Gould, and of others received from Mr. Audubon, some of them apparently types of his descriptions, are various stages of plumage and structure, which might throw considerable light on the subject, but for the unfortunate uncertainty, in some cases, as to whether they are European or American. There are in this series certainly three species, and indications of a fourth, possibly of a fifth, but I do not venture here to do more than indicate three. I find none which correspond with what Mr. Audubon has called *L. americanus.*

The specimens vary considerably in the precise character of bill, which is more or less convex, but there is a decided difference in the average of the willow and the rock grouse. The size of the two species differs also. Both have the tail feathers black, and differing in this respect from the *L. leucurus*, in which they are white.

I give the accompanying descriptions of North American ptarmigans, without much assurance of even approximate accuracy, in respect to the number, characters, and synonymy of the species. Their chief characters are expressed in the following synopsis :

Tail feathers black.

Bill stout, convex, broad at tip; the distance from the nasal groove to the tip of bill equal to or less than the greatest height of both mandibles together. No black loral stripe in the male...*L. albus.*

Size smaller. Bill slender, rather compressed at tip. The distance from the nasal groove to the tip of bill decidedly greater than the height of the bill. Male with a black stripe through the eye..*L. rupestris.*

Tail feathers entirely white.

No black whatever in the winter bird..*L. leucurus.*

Comparative measurements of species.

Catal. No.	Species.	Locality.	Sex.	Length.	Stretch of wings.	Wing.	Tail.	Tarsus.	Middle toe.	Its claw alone.	Bill above.	Along gape.	Specimen measured.	Remarks.
2852	Lagopus albus ...	Labrador?..............	♂	16.10	......	8.10	5.02	1.56	1.74	0.52	6.86	0.86	Skin	Summer...........
8080	... ..do..	Hudson's Bay.........		16.60	......	7.50	5.07	1.42	1.80	0.75	0.88	0.87	Skin	Spring........
1968	......do..	America....				7.70	5.34	1 50	1.52	0.35	0.80	0.86	Skin	Summer. Very much stretched.
8084	......do..	Hudson's Bay..........		16.50	.....	7.74	5.58	1.52	1.88	0.74	0.87	0.88	Skin.....	Winter...........
3887	......do..	Trois Rivières, between Montreal and Quebec.		14.00	.....	7.80	5.33	1.49	1.86	0.68	0.76	0.83	Skin.....	September.........
4520	......do..	St. John's, N. F..... ..		14.80	.....	7.60	5.14	1.62	1.90	0.68	0.76	0.84	Skin.....	February ....
4518	......do..	.....do..			.....	7.90	5.35	1.56	1.93	0.62	0.88	0.80	Skin.....	....do............
do.	......do..	.....do..		15.20	24.50	7.50	......	......	......	......	......	......	Fresh	...do............
4519	......do..	.....do..		13.00	.....	7.16	4.76	1.40	1.76	0.58	0.75	0.78	Skin.....	...do............
do.	......do..	.....do..		14.40	24.00	7.25	......	......	......	......	......	......	Fresh	...do............
2031	......do..	America.		16.00	.....	8.20	5.48	1.57	1.80	0.66	0.77	0.80	Skin.....	Winter...........
6923	......do..	Red river, Minn........		17.80	.....	8.50	5.90	1.57	1.90	0.74	0.77	0.84	Skin.....	Very much stretched
6924	......do..	Nelson river, H. B......		16.20	.....	7.60	5.02	1.42	1.88	0.85	0.76	0.84	Skin.....	....
8081	Lagopus alpinus?	Norway? perhaps N.Am.		15.00	.....	8.10	5.05	1.30	1.52	0.60	0.70	0.80	Skin.....	Spring...........
8085	.....do..	Norway......		14.90	.....	7.50	4.50	1.30	1.50	0.60	0.67	0.80	Skin.....	....do........
8086	......do..	Europe..........			.....	7.70	4.60	1.25	1.32	0.44	0.70	0.84	Skin.....	....
2494	......do..	Norway	♂	14.00	.....	7.70	4.64	1.25	1.25		0.70	0.84	Skin.....	Mid. claw wanting.
8083	Lagopus rupestris?	N. W. coast America...		14.50	.....	7.50	4.86	1.36	1.62	0.66	0.68	0 88	Skin.....	....
8082	......do..	.....do..		13.60	.....	7.70	5.43	1.34	1.50	0.64	0.70	0.86	Skin.....	....
2854	......do..	America?.............		12.80	.....	7.80	4.82	1.10	1.37	0.64	0.66	0.80	Skin.....	Winter.......
2853	......do..	.....do..		13.00	.....	7.60	4.48	1.16	1.30	0.43	0.70	0.80	Skin.....	Summer.......
2855	......do..	....		13.50	.....	7.00	4.50	.....	1.32	0.50	0.70	0.78	Skin.....	...do.......
10082	Lagopus leucurus.	W. side Rocky mts.....			.....	7.10	4.20	1.23	1.48	0.52	0.70	0.79	Skin.....	Very poor specimen.
10081	...do..	.....do..			.....	7.30	4.24	1.16	1.42	0.46	0.70	0.82	Skin.....	....
do.	......do..	.....do..		13.00	21.00	7.00	.....	......	......	......	......	......	Fresh	....
1269	Lagopus mutus..	Scotland...............		15.00	.....	7.54	5.00	1.28	.....		0.66	0.84	Skin.....	Summer. Claws wanting.

LAGOPUS ALBUS, Aud.

Willow Grouse; White Ptarmigan.

Tetrao albus, GMELIN, I, 1788, 750. (Hudson's Bay.)

Lagopus albus, AUD. Syn. 1839, 207.—IB. Birds Amer. V, 1842, 114 ; pl. 299.

Tetrao (Lagopus) albus, NUTTALL, Man. I, 2d ed. 1840, 816.

? *Tetrao lagopus*, FORSTER, Phil. Trans. LXII, 1772, 390.

Tetrao saliceti, SABINE, App. Franklin's Narr. 681.—RICH, App. Parry's 2d Voyage, 347.—AUD. Orn. Biog. II, 1834, 528 ; pl. 191.

Tetrao (Lagopus) saliceti, SWAINSON, F. Bor. Am. II, 1831, 351.

White Grouse, PENNANT.

SP. CH.—Bill very stout. Bill as high as the distance from the nasal groove to its tip. In summer, rufous or orange chestnut on the head and neck ; the feathers of back black, barred rather closely with yellowish brown and chestnut. In winter, white ; the tail black, but no black through the eye. Length, 15.50 ; wing about 8.00 ; tail about 5.00.

Hab.—Northern America. Rare in northern parts of United States.

July 7, 1858.

Bill very stout and convex, much curved from the nostrils ; the distance from nostrils to the tip of bill a little less than the greatest depth of both mandibles taken together ; gonys a little less than the width of the lower mandible at the base ; upper mandibles depressed at the end, the gape considerably inflected. Claws very long; broad to near the end, where they are rapidly narrowed ; the middle one as long as the culmen. Toes feathered to the claws ; the feathers with rigid shafts. Upper tail coverts nearly as long as the median coverts, like tail feathers ; lower reaching to the white tips of tail feathers. Wings convex ; the first quill between sixth and seventh ; the third and fourth longest. Tail about two-thirds the wing, slightly rounded laterally ; the feathers of nearly uniform width.

Color in winter pure white, without black loral stripe ; the bill black ; the tail feathers, except the two innermost, brownish black ; the exterior with a very narrow tip of white, which increases to nearly a quarter of an inch to the inner ones ; the innermost incumbent pair is entirely white; the latter, however, may really be coverts. The primaries have the shafts brown on the upper surface, except along the extreme edges, which are white.

Summer. I have at hand no summer specimens which I can assert positively to be American ; but two before me, received from Mr. Audubon, I have no doubt are part of his Labrador collection, and the originals of his plate. In one of these, corresponding to the male figure, (2852,) the head and neck all round are nearly uniform rufous chestnut; the back of the head and neck, with the feathers blackish, except on the margins. The rest of the upper plumage has each feather black, barred with a slightly varying shade of yellowish brown or chestnut, (different from the head,) and narrowly margined terminally with white. The subterminal yellowish brown bar is continuous across, the others are more or less broken up, mixed, or interrupted towards the shafts. The jugulum is somewhat like the back, the bands less distinct ; the sides of the body are similar to the back, the bands coarser. The wings, excepting some of the middle coverts, and the inferior surface of the body, except on the sides of the breast and the legs, are white. The toes are bare of feathers, except towards the base, as is also the posterior edge of the tarsus. There is only a trace of white at the tip of the tail feathers.

The supposed female (1968) is quite similar, the mottling rather lighter, and the light bands rather broader. The head and neck have not the uniform rufous chestnut color of the other specimen, those parts being varied more like the back, or with spots of black; the throat, however, is rufous chestnut, with black spots, and no white edges. The colored feathers cover the whole belly, mixed with a good deal of white along the median line and behind. The tibial feathers are white, barred with brown; the tarsi and toes dirty white. The under tail coverts are like the breast.

The coarsely mottled feathers of the breast are mixed with others more like those of the male, being more rufous, with the barring more broken, finer, and more obsolete.

I find a considerable difference in different specimens of the large Ptarmigan before me. Those from eastern Labrador and Newfoundland appear to have decidedly broader, stouter, and more convex bills than those from the Hudson's Bay and more northern countries. I think it not improbable that there may be two species, but without summer specimens I cannot pretend to determine the question.

In the entire uncertainty as to the true character of the American ptarmigans, I can quote only those descriptions that are based on American specimens. I have not at hand the means of settling the synonymy of the different species, and can only call this one *Lagopus albus* as a provisional appellation. Bonaparte, in his list of *Tetraonidae*, in Comptes Rendus XLV, Sept. 1857, 428, assigns to America three species : *L. rupestris*, Lath., with *L. americanus*, Aud., and *lagopus* of American writers as synonyms ; *L. groenlandicus*, Brehm., with *L. reinhardtii?* Brehm, as synonyms, and *L. leucurus*. The European white ptarmigans are given as *L. albus*, *L. mutus*, and *L. islandorum*, Faber, the latter differing from *albus* in the stouter bill. It will be noted that this difference of bill appears to characterise the Newfoundland ptarmigan as compared with those from Hudson's bay. As, however, the original *Tetrao albus* of Gmelin is based primarily on descriptions of American specimens, such as *Lagopede de la Baie de Hudson* of Buffon, *White partridge* of Ellis, &c., it will be proper to use it here, whatever be its relationship to European forms.

List of specimens.

Catal. No.	Sex.	Locality.	When collected.	Whence obtained.	Collected by—	Length.	Stretch of wings.	Wing.
4520	------	St. John's, N. F......	Feb. —, 1856	Dr. Stabb.........	------------------	------	------	------
4519	------	......do...........	......do......	......do.........	------------------	14. 40	24. 00	7. 25
4518	------	......do...........	......do......	......do.........	------------------	15. 20	24. 20	7. 50
1968?	♂	Labrador	Summer.......	S. F. Baird......	J. J. Audubon.....	------	------	------
2852?	♀?	......do...........	......do......	......do.........	......do.........	------	------	------
3887	------	Trois Rivières, Can....	Winter.........	......do.........	T. Broome.........	------	------	------
6923	------	Red river, H. B. T....	-------------	Donald Gunn.....	------------------	------	------	------
6924	------	Nelson river, H. B. T..	-------------	......do.........	------------------	------	------	------
8084	------	Hudson bay	Winter........	John Gould......	------------------	------	------	------
8080	♂	......do...........	Summer......	......do.........	------------------	------	------	------

LAGOPUS RUPESTRIS, Leach.

Rock Ptarmigan.

Tetrao rupestris, GMELIN, Syst. Nat. I, 1788, 751. Based on rock grouse of Pennant.—LATHAM, Ind. Orn. II, 1790, 312.—SABINE, Supplem. Parry's First Voyage, page cxcv.—RICHARDSON, Append. Parry's Second Voyage, 348.—AUD. Orn. Biog. IV, 1838, 483 ; pl. 368.

Lagopus rupestris, LEACH, Zool. Misc. II, 290.—BON. List, 1838.—AUD. Syn. 208.—IB. Birds Amer. V, 1842, 122 ; pl. 301.

Tetro (Lagopus) rupestris, SWAINS, F. Bor. Am. II, 1831, 354 ; pl. lxiv.

Attagen rupestris, REICH. Av. Syst. Nat. 1851, page xxix.

Rock grouse, PENNANT, Arctic Zool. II, 312.

SP. CH.—Bill slender ; distance from the nasal groove to tip greater than height at base. In summer the feathers of back black, banded distinctly with yellowish brown and tipped with white. In winter white, the tail black ; the male with a black bar from bill through eye. Size considerably less than that of *L. albus*. Length about 14.50 inches ; wing, 7.50 ; tail, 4.50.

Hab.—Arctic America.

Bill from the nasal groove considerably longer than the greatest depth of both mandibles taken together. Gonys about equal to width of lower mandible below. First quill intermediate between sixth and seventh. Claws very large and broad, equal to the culmen. Tail of fourteen black feathers and four middle white ones. Tail about two-thirds the length of wings.

The male bird in winter is pure white throughout, except fourteen tail feathers, which are black, narrowly tipped with white, and a black line through and behind the eye. The shafts of the larger primaries are browne xternally, except along the edges.

The female is said to be similar, but without the black stripe through the eye.

A supposed summer specimen of this species, probably a female, has the feathers of the back black, with narrow transverse bars of yellowish brown and terminated by white. The brown bars are largest on the basal half; the terminal ones are usually interrupted towards the shaft; the last of all sometimes continuous, and separated from the white tip by black. Much the greater exposed portion of the feather is black. Beneath and to some extent on the head the brownish bars are lighter and much broader, imparting a yellowish tint. The chin is whitish, spotted with black. There is no trace of the black lore. The entire wing, excepting the middle coverts and tertials, are white, as is also the middle lore of the belly. The outer web of external tail feather is white towards the base.

A specimen from the northwest coast of America, (8082,) presented by Mr. Gould, and perhaps a male of the rock grouse, has the feathers of a chestnut color mottled with black, and with little or no white edging. This may, however, be a distinct species, different, as it certainly is, from the common willow grouse.

The differences between the American rock grouse and the willow grouse are to be found in the smaller size of the latter, and its slenderer, more elongated bill. The black stripe through the eye of the male is not found in the willow grouse in either sex.

List of specimens.

Catal. No.	Age.	Locality.	When collected.	Whence obtained.	Collected by—
8082	......	Northwest coast America	....	John Gould	....
8083	......	......do........	....	......do......	....
2853	......	America?	Summer	S. F. Baird	J. J. Audubon
2854	......	......do?	Winter	......do......	......do......
2855	o	......do?	Summer	......do......	......do......
2856	o	......do?	....do	......do......	......do......

LAGOPUS LEUCURUS, Swainson.

White-tailed Ptarmigan.

Tetrao (Lagopus) leucurus, SWAINSON, Fauna Bor. Amer. II, 1831, 356; pl. lxiii.—NUTTALL, Man. II, 1834, 612.—
    IB. I, 2d ed. 1840, 820.
Tetrao leucurus, AUD. Orn. Biog. V, 1839, 200; pl. 418.
Lagopus leucurus, AUD. Syn. 1839.—IB. Birds Amer. V, 1842, 125; pl. 302.

SP. CH.—Bill slender. Plumage in summer barred with brownish yellow. In winter pure white, including the tail feathers.
Length, 13 inches; wing, 7; tail, 4.25.

Hab.—Northern America to the west. Southward along Rocky mountains to Cochetope Pass in latitude 39o.

Bill rather slender; the length from the nasal groove considerably greater than the height of both mandibles together. Gonys longer than the width of lower jaw at the end of the lateral feathers; the lower jaw with a prominent ridge on the sides below.   Tail rather short, scarcely more than half the wings.   First quill intermediate between sixth and seventh.

Color in winter pure white with a faint rosy tint, even including the tail feathers.   The shafts of the larger primaries brown.

The only specimens I have seen are in winter dress.   The summer plumage is said by Richardson to be varied with blackish brown and ochraceous.

The two skins of this bird before me, and probably the only ones in any American museum, were collected in January, 1858, by Captain R. B. Marcy, on his march from Fort Bridger across the Rocky mountains to Santa Fé, in search of provisions and animals for the Utah army, under Colonel Johnston.   They were met with near the summit of the mountains, probably near the Cochetope Pass.

List of specimens.

Catal. No.	Locality.	When collected.	Whence obtained.	Collected by—	Length.	Stretch of wings.	Wing.
10081	West side Rocky mts., near Cochetope pass, lat. 39°..	Jan. —, 1858	Capt. Marcy, U. S. A.	Dr. Anderson - -----	13. 00	21. 00	7. 00
10082	------do------------------	-----------------	------do----------				

LAGOPUS AMERICANUS? Aud.

American Ptarmigan.

?" Tetrao lagopus, Sabine, E., Suppl. Parry's 1st Voyage, p. cxcvii.—Sabine, J., Franklin's Jour. 682.—Rich. App. Parry's 2d Voyage, 350."

Tetrao (Lagopus) mutus, Rich. F. Bor. Am. II, 1831, 350.

Tetrao mutus, Aud. Orn. Biog. V, 1839, 196.

Lagopus americanus, Aud. Syn. 1839, 207.—Ib. Birds Amer. V, 1842, 119 ; pl. 300.

A ptarmigan, supposed by some authors to be the *Lagopus mutus* or *alpinus* of Europe, is mentioned by authors as found on Baffin's bay and Churchill river.   Mr. Audubon, on an examination of specimens brought from those countries, considers them distinct, but gives no appreciable characters to separate them.   The differences are probably very slight, if they really exist.   The European or Scotch ptarmigan has the bill slenderer than in *L. albus,* though the size is scarcely less.   The summer plumage, however, is very different, the tints being mottled gray, without any of the reddish brown or yellow of the other.   The winter dress is white ; the male with a black line from the bill through the eye.

It is quite probable that some of the specimens enumerated under the head of *L. rupestris* really belong here.

Family PERDICIDAE. The Partridges.

Ch.—Nostrils protected by a naked scale. The tarsi bare and scutellate.

The *Perdicidae* differ from the grouse in the bare legs and naked nasal fossae. They are much smaller in size and more abundant in species. They are widely distributed over the surface of the globe, a large number belonging to America, where the sub-families have no old world representatives whatever. The head seldom if ever shows the naked space around and above the eye, so common in the *Tetraonidae*, and the sides of the toes, scarcely exhibit the peculiar pectination formed by a succession of small scales or plates.

The various species of *Perdicidae* have been divided by Bonaparte into four sub-families, *Perdicinae, Coturnicinae, Turnicinae,* and *Ortyginae,* while Gray unites the first two into one. The common gray partridge or English partridge, (*Perdix cinerea,*) with several other European species, belong to the first sub-family ; the common European quail (*Coturnix dactylisonans*) to the second ; the third embraces the bush quails of the old world, while the *Ortyginae* are entirely peculiar to the new world, which has no representatives in the other sub-families.

Sub-Family ORTYGINAE.

Ch.—Bill stout, the lower mandible more or less bidentate on each side near the end.

The *Ortyginae* of Bonaparte, or *Odontophorinae* of other authors, are characterized as a group by the bidentation on either side of the edge of lower mandible, usually concealed in the closed mouth and sometimes scarcely appreciable. The bill is short, and rather high at base ; stouter and shorter than what is usually seen in Old World partridges. The culmen is curved from the base ; the tip of the bill broad, and overlapping the end of the lower mandible. The nasal groove is short. The tail is rather broad and long.

The species are quite numerous, the number known to naturalists being about forty. They occur mostly in Central America and Mexico, though the genus *Odontophorus* is chiefly composed of South American species.

All the more important genera are represented within the limits of the United States, excepting *Odontophorus.* The following synopsis will convey a general idea of their character:

SYNOPSIS OF GENERA.

a. Head without crest.

ORTYX.—Tail not much more than half the wings; outstretched feet reaching beyond the tail.

b. Head with a crest of a few long narrow, keel-shaped feathers.

OREORTYX.—Crest feathers very long, linear; tail scarcely more than half the wings; bill stout; claws blunt, the lateral not reaching the base of the middle claw. Toes of the outstretched foot reaching beyond the tail.

LOPHORTYX.—Crest feathers widening much at the ends. Tail nearly or quite as long as wings. Bill rather small. Claws acute, the lateral reaching to the base of middle one. Toes not reaching the tip of tail.

c. Crest soft, full and tufted; composed of short, broad and depressed feathers.

CALLIPEPLA.—Crest springing from the crown. Wing coverts normal. Tail stiffened, nearly as long as the wings. Claws small, acute, outstretched feet not reaching the tip of tail.

CYRTONYX.—Crest occipital. Wing coverts greatly developed. Tail very small and soft; half as long as the wings. Toes short; claws very long, blunted; outstretched feet reaching much beyond the tip of the tail.

All the North American quails, except *Cyrtonyx massena*, have the inner tertiaries edged internally with whitish or buff, forming a conspicuous line on the back when the wings are closed.

Comparative measurements of species.

Catal. No.	Species.	Locality.	Sex.	Length.	Stretch of wings	Wing.	Tail.	Tarsus.	Middle toe.	Its claw alone.	Bill above.	Along gape.	Specimens measured.
1714	Ortyx virginianus	Carlisle, Pa.	♀	8.64	... .	4.62	3.02	1.21	1.47	0.34	0.55	0.56	Skin.....
do..	........do....	.....do........		10.50	15.16	4.64	......						Fresh....
1715	......,..do........	.....do......	♂	8.60	....	4.68	2.98	1.25	1.47	0.34	0.57	0.58	Skin.....
do.	........do........ ..	.....do......		10.00	15.50	4.64							Fresh....
2385	........do......	Savannah, Ga.	♂	8.00	....	4.44	2.70	1.24	1.40	0.30	0.55	0.56	Skin.....
9350	Ortyx texanus	Devil's river, Tex	♂	8.70	....	4.35	2.97	1.20	1.30	0.27	0.56	0.50	Skin.....
do..	........do......	.....do......		9.00	14.00	4.00							Fresh...
9354	........do....	.....do........	♀	9.00	....	4.50	2.86	1.22	1.40	0.29	0.54	0.66	Skin.....
do..	........do....	.....do........		9.50	14.00	4.00							Fresh...
9348	........do........	San Antonio, Tex	♂	7.76	....	4.35	2.73	1.20	1.38	0.27	0.55	0.60	Skin.....
9347	........do........	Fort Clark, Tex	♀	7.75	....	4.20	2.66	1.08	1.40	0.32	0.54	0.58	Skin.....
4099	........do......	New Leon, Mex	♂	7.70	....	4.34	2.88	1.10	1.28	0.27	0.53	0.57	Skin.....
do..	........do......	.....do........		9.00	13.50	4.50							Fresh...
3935	Oreortyx pictus	California....	♂	10.00	....	4.91	3.32	1.35	1.56	0.36	0.66	0.57	Skin.....
10321	........do....	Fort Tejon, Cal.	♂	10.70	....	5.36	3.75	1.39	1.63	0.40	0.55	0.58	Skin.....
9390	Lophortyx californicus	Tulare valley	♂	9.50	....	4.32	4.12	1.16	1.50	0.40	0.55	0.60	Skin.....
3936	........do......	California	♀	9.80	....	4.26	3.79	1.16	1.45	0.37	0.50	0.56	Skin.....
9378	Lophortyx gambelii	New Mexico	♂	9.74	....	4.54	4.48	1.27	1.46	0.38	0.56	0.56	Skin.....
9361	........do......	Gila river	♀	9.10	....	4.36	4.08	1.16	1.36	0.23	0.54	0.54	Skin.....
9386	Callipepla squamata	New Mexico	♂	9.30	....	4.74	3.82	1.20	1.37	0.37	0.50	0.56	Skin.....
9387	........do......	.....do....		9.40	....	4.69	3.86	1.20	1.42	0.42	0.50	0.54	Skin.....
3999	........do......	New Leon, Mex.	♂	9.00	....	4.44	3.75	1.20	1.34	0.30	0.54	0.57	Skin.....
do..	........do......	.....do......		9.50	13.50	4.50							Fresh...
3998	Cyrtonyx massena	New Leon, Mex	♂	7.80	....	4.66	2.54	1.14	1.41	0.50	0.60	0.58	Skin.....
.....	........do......	.....do......		8.75	16.25								Fresh....
10258	........do......	Fort Davis, Tex.	♂	8.80	....	4.68	2.48	1.10	1.43	0.56	0.60	0.58	Skin.....
10256	........do......	.....do......	♀	9.00	....	4.82	2.60	1.04	1.40	0.52	0.62	0.58	....

ORTYX, Stephens.

Ortyx, STEPHENS, Shaw's Gen. Zool. XI, 1819. Type *Tetrao virginianus*, L.

CH.—Bill stout. Head entirely without any crest. Tail short, scarcely more than half the wing, composed of moderately soft feathers. Wings normal. Legs developed, the toes reaching considerably beyond the tip of the tail; the lateral toes short, equal, their claws falling decidedly short of the base of the middle claw.

The genus *Ortyx* embraces numerous species, more or less resembling the well known Bob-white of the United States. They are chiefly confined to Mexico, Central America, and the West India Islands. An *Ortyx cubanensis*, from Cuba, is said by Cabanis to resemble *O. texanus* much more than *virginianus*.

The two United States species resemble each other so closely as to require a more extended comparison than usual to distinguish them. They can, however, be generally identified by the following diagnoses:

Synopsis of species.

Size large. Prevailing color above brownish red, especially on the wing coverts; the feathers of the upper part of the back tinged with grey and obscurely mottled with dusky; transverse bars on the edges only, and to a still less degree on the wing coverts. No distinct light spots on the upper parts, except as transverse bars on outer webs of secondaries and tertials. Inner edges of tertials rufous white...*O. virginianus.*

Small. Prevailing color above greyish, with a slight indication of brownish red on the fore part of the back and upper wing coverts, which are conspicuously barred transversely with brownish in zigzag, (from edge to edge,) especially the latter, the feathers of the upper parts all variously edged and spotted with light brownish yellow. Inner edge of tertials dirty yellowish...*O. texanus.*

ORTYX VIRGINIANUS, Bonap.

Quail; Partridge; Bob-white.

Tetrao virginianus, LINNAEUS, Syst. Nat. I, 1766, 277, 16, (female?)—GMELIN, I, 1788, 761.

Perdix virginiana, LATH. Ind. Orn. II, 1790, 650.—WILSON, Am. Orn. VI, 1812, 21; pl. xlvii.—DOUGHTY's Cab. I, 1830, 37; pl. iv.—AUD. Orn. Biog. I, 1831, 388: V, 1839, 564; pl. 76.

Perdix (Ortyx) virginiana, BONAP. Obs. Wils. 1825, No. 203.

Ortyx virginiana, JARDINE, Nat. Library Birds, IV, Game birds, 101; pl. x.—BON. List, 1838.—AUD. Syn. 1839, 199.—IB. Birds Amer. V, 1842, 59; pl. 289.—GOULD, Mon. Odont. pl. 1.

Perdix (Colinia) virginiana, NUTTALL, Man. I, 1832, 646.

Tetrao marilandicus, LINN. Syst. Nat. I, 1766, 277, 18.—GMELIN, I, 1788, 761, 17.

Perdix marilandica, LATHAM, Ind. Orn. II, 1790, 650.

Tetrao minor, BARTRAM, Travels, 1791, 290 bis.

Perdix borealis, VIEILLOT, Nouv. Dict.—IB. Galerie, II, 44, pl. ccxiv.

Ortyx borealis, STEPH. Shaw's Zool. XI, 1819, 377.

Virginia partridge, LATHAM, Syn. II, II, 777.

SP. CH.—Forehead and line through the eye and along the side of the neck, with chin and throat white. A band of black across the vertex, and extending backwards on the sides, within the white, and another from the maxilla beneath the eye, and crossing on the lower part of the throat. The under parts are white, tinged with brown anteriorly, each feather with several narrow, obtusely V-shaped bands of black. The fore part of back, the side of the breast and in front just below the black collar, of a dull pinkish red; the sides of body and wing coverts brownish red; the latter almost uniform, without indication of mottling. Scapulars and upper tertials coarsely blotched with black, and edged internally with brownish yellow. Top of head reddish; the lower part of neck, except anteriorly, streaked with white and black. Primary quills unspotted brown. Tail ash.

Female with the white markings of the head replaced by brownish yellow; the black wanting.

Length, 10 inches; wing, 4.70; tail, 2.85.

Hab.—Eastern United States to the High Central Plains, Devil's river, Texas?

This species is subject to considerable variations both of size and color, the more northern being considerably the larger. Southern specimens are darker, with more black about the head, on the wings, and the middle of the back. There is also a more appreciable mottling on the wings, and the feathers of the back are streaked with black.

In No. 2516, from Carlisle, the ground tint of the upper parts, excepting the fore part of back and the head, is a brownish cream color, the black markings both above and below more distinct than usual. There is also more white about the head. But for the fact of its having been shot near Carlisle, Pennsylvania, in a flock of normally colored birds, it might readily be taken for a different species.

Specimens from the southern States not unfrequently have the white throat feathers margined with black, which sometimes almost conceals the white. A skin, 9350, from Devil's river, Texas, is doubtfully referred to this species, on account of its size and redder color.

The *Ortyx virginianus* is the bird about which there has been so much controversy as to the name it should bear. In New York and New England, as well as in many of the western States, it is called the quail, while in Pennsylvania and further south it is known as the partridge. Where this bird is called quail, the Ruffed Grouse is generally called partridge; and where it is called partridge, the larger species is known as the pheasant. In reality, however, no one of these names can be correctly applied to any American species, though to call our grouse a partridge is, perhaps, a worse misnomer than to apply the same name to our *Ortyx*. It would be much better, however, to select names for the American birds which have not been used for other species; such, perhaps, as Bob white for the *Ortyx*, and Mountain Grouse, or Ruffed Grouse, for the other species.

List of specimens.

Catal. No.	Sex.	Locality.	When collected.	Whence obtained.	Orig. No.	Collected by—	Length.	Stretch of wings.	Wing.	Remarks.
1715	♂	Carlisle, Pa.............	....	S. F. Baird	......	....	....	....	....	....
1714	♀	......do..............	....	......do........	......	....	....	....	....	....
	......	Liberty county, Ga.....	....	......do.........	......	W. L. Jones...	....	....	....	....
4434	......	Quasqueton, Iowa.....	....	E. C. Bidwell......	......	....	....	....	....	....
4859	♂	Iowa Point, Neb.......	April 23, 1856	Lieut. Warren....	......	Dr. Hayden....	8.25	11.75	3.75	....
9350?	.. ...	Devil's River, Texas....	Nov. —, 1854	Major Emory	17	Dr. Kennerly ..	....	....	....	Eyes dull brown ....

ORTYX TEXANUS, Lawrence.

Ortyx texanus, LAWRENCE, Ann. N. Y. Lyc. VI, April, 1853, 1.

SP. CH.—General appearance that of *O. virginianus*. Chin, throat, forehead, and stripe over the eye white. Stripe behind the eye, continuous with a collar across the lower part of the throat, black. Under parts white, with zig-zag transverse bars of black. Above pale brownish red, strongly tinged with ash, the feathers all faintly though distinctly mottled with black; the lower back, scapulars, and tertials much blotched with black, the latter edged on both sides, and, to some extent, transversely barred with brownish white. Secondaries with transverse bars of the same on the outer web. Wing coverts coarsely and conspicuously barred with blackish. Lower part of neck, except before, streaked with black and white.

Female with the white of the head changed to brownish yellow; the black of the head wanting.

Length, 9 inches; wing 4.35; tail, 2.85.

Hab.—Southern Texas and Valley of the Rio Grande.

This species is very similar, in general appearance and markings, to *O. virginianus*, the common quail of the United States, being, perhaps, of smaller size, though some specimens seem almost as large as the other species. The chief difference is seen in a much grayer shade of coloration and a more extended and conspicuous mottling of the feathers. The under parts and head are much the same, except that in *O. texanus* the black collar on the throat is narrower,

July 8, 1858.

81 b

and the reddish of the jugulum is paler. The stripe behind the eye has more black; the feathers on top of the head are black, margined with brownish yellow, instead of being reddish and black. There are distinct transverse bars of dusky in every feather of the upper surface, (except the head,) and in addition there are obscure light brownish yellow spots or bars on the back and wings, the coverts especially, not found in *virginianus*. This light mottling is, perhaps, more distinct in the female than the male. The light margins to the tertials are brownish white, not brownish yellow.

List of specimens.

Catal. No.	Sex.	Locality.	When collected.	Whence obtained.	Orig'l No.	Collected by—	L'gth.	Stretch of wings.	Wing	Remarks.
9348	......	San Antonio.........	....	Capt. Pope ..	......	....	......	......	......	....
5082	......	Nueces, Tex.........	April 21, 1855	......do......	46	....	9.50	14.00	4.50	Feet gray...................
9354	......	Devil's river, Tex....	Nov. —, 1854	Maj. Emory..	20	Dr. Kennerly	9.50	14.00	4.00	....
5083	......	Nueces to Fort Clark.	April 27, 1855	Capt. Pope ..	53	....	9.50	12.00	4.25	....
5081	......	Pecos river..........	May 15, 1855	......do......	83	....	9.50	13.00	4.50	Bill bl'k, feet and gums yellow........
9347	♀	Fort Clark, Tex......	....	......do......	......	....	......	......	......	....
9349	♂	Laredo, Tex.........	....	Maj. Emory.	......	J. H. Clark ..	9.75	14.25	4.25	....
4101	......	Matamoras	....	Lt. Couch...	......	....	......	......	......	....
4099	♂	New Leon, Mex.....	....	......do......	......	....	9.00	13.50	4.50	Eyes dark brown, bill black ....
4098	.....	........do............	May —, 1853	......do......	208	....	9.00	13.75	4.50	....

OREORTYX, Baird.

Cн.—Body stout, broad ; bill large ; crest as in *Lophortyx* ; tail short, broad, scarcely more than half the wing, rounded, the longest feathers not much exceeding the coverts. Legs developed, the claws extending beyond the tip of the tail ; the lateral toes short, the outer claw falling considerably short of the base of the middle. Very similar to *Ortyx*, except in the crest.

I do not find any genus already established for this bird, which appears to me worthy of generic rank, and differing in marked characters both from *Lophortyx* and *Callipepla*. I am unable to say whether more than one species can be included in it.

OREORTYX PICTUS, Baird.

Plumed Partridge ; Mountain Quail.

Ortyx picta, Douglas, Trans. Linn. Soc. XVI, 1829, 143.
Callipepla picta, Gould, Mon. Odont. pl. xv.—Newberry, Rep. P.R.R. VI, iv, 1857, 93.
Ortyx plumifera, Gould, Pr. Zool. Soc. V, 1837, 42.—Aud. Syn. 1839, 200.—Ib. Birds Amer. V, 1842, 69 ; pl. 291.
Perdix plumifera, Aud. Orn. Biog. V, 1839, 220 ; pl. 422.
Lophortyx plumifera, Nuttall, Man. I, 2d ed. 1840, 791.

Sp. Ch.—Head with a crest of two straight feathers, much longer than the bill and head. Anterior half of the body grayish plumbeous ; the upper parts generally olivaceous brown with a slight shade of rufous, this extending narrowly along the nape to the crest. Head beneath the eyes and throat orange chestnut, bordered along the orbits and a short distance behind by black, bounded anteriorly and superiorly by white, of which color is a short line behind the eye. Posterior half of the body beneath white, a large central patch anteriorly (bifurcating behind,) with the flanks and tibial feathers orange chestnut brown, the sides of body showing black and white bands, the former color tinged with chestnut. Under tail coverts black, streaked with orange chestnut. Upper tertials margined internally with whitish.

Length, 10.50 inches ; wing, 5 ; tail, 3.25.

Hab.—Mountain ranges of California and Oregon towards the coast.

The forehead is of a whitish ashy, fading into the plumbeous of the head above. The white mark in front of the eye completely encircles the base of the lower jaw, cutting off the chestnut.

The concealed feathers of the flanks have an oblique bar of white on the outer edges, the chestnut suffused with black towards the abrupt white edge. The feathers on the sides of the body are banded very regularly and transversely with white and black, or white and chestnut, the colors becoming more or less suffused. The region around the anus is fulvous white without any markings.

A specimen, collected at Fort Tejon by Mr. Vesey, differs in lacking the olive wash on the fore part of back and the neck which are pure plumbeous ; there is also much more of the dark chestnut on the belly. The crest is much longer, measuring 3½ inches. This is probably a male. The female appears to exhibit very little difference, except in the rather shorter crest.

List of specimens.

Catal. No.	Locality.	When collected.	Whence obtained.	Orig. No.	Collected by—
4490	Cascade mountains, O. T.		Lieut. Williamson		Dr. Newberry
4309	Near Fort Jones, Cal	Spring of 1855	Dr. Suckley	192	
5935	California		Dr. Heermann		
	Fort Tejon, Cal		J. X. de Vesey		

LOPHORTYX, Bonaparte.

Lophortyx, BONAP. Geog. & Comp. List, 1838. Type *Tetrao californicus*, SHAW.

CH.—Head with a crest of lengthened feathers springing from the vertex, the shafts in the same vertical plane, and the webs roof-shaped, and overlapping each other ; the number varies from two to six or more ; they widen to the tip, where they are slightly recurved. Tail lengthed and graduated ; nearly as long as the wing, composed of twelve stiff feathers. Wings with the tertials not as long as the primaries ; the coverts without any unusual development ; claws rather short ; the lateral reaching to, but scarcely beyond the base of the middle ; the outstretched toe not reaching the tip of the tail.

The two North American species of the genus have the anterior half of the body, and the upper parts generally, plumbeous ; the feathers of neck above, and on the sides, pointed and margined with black. There is a white bar across the head above, between the eyes, which, passing backwards, is bordered behind and internally by black ; a second commences at the posterior border of the eye and then borders the black of the chin and throat laterally and behind, the black reaching up to the eye and bordered anteriorly by a white line from eye to bill ; belly pale buff, with a large spot in the centre ; the flanks streaked with white. The diagnoses of the species are as follows :

Vertex and occiput light smoky olive brown ; forehead whitish ; spot in the middle of the belly orange chestnut ; feathers of breast with narrow black edges ; sides of body olivaceous plumbeous..*L. californicus.*

Vertex and occiput clear chestnut brown ; forehead blackish ; spot in middle of belly black ; none of the belly feathers with black edges ; sides of body orange chestnut............*L. gambelii.*

LOPHORTYX CALIFORNICUS, Bonap.

California Quail.

Tetrao californicus, SHAW, Nat. Misc. pl. 345, (prior to 1801.)

Perdix californica, LATHAM, Suppl. Ind. Orn. II, App. 1801, p. lxii.—AUD. Orn. Biog. V, 1839, 152 ; pl. 413.

Ortyx californica, STEPHENS in Shaw's Zool. XI, 1819, 384.—JARDINE, Game Birds, Nat. Libr. IV, 104, pl. xi.— CUV. R. An. Illust. ed. Oiseaux, pl. lxiv.—BENNETT, Gardens & Menag. Zool. Soc. II, 29, woodcut.—AUD. Syn. 1839, 199.—IB. Birds Amer. V, 1842, 67 ; pl. 290.

Perdix (Ortyx) californica, BONAP. Syn. 1828, 125.

Lophortyx californica, BONAP. List, 1838.—NUTTALL, Man. I, 2d ed. 1840, 789.

Callipepla californica, GOULD, Mon. Odont. pl. xvi.—REICHENBACH, Av. Syst. 1850, pl. xxvii.—NEWBERRY, Rep. P. R. R. VI, IV, 1857, 92.

SP. CH.—Crest black. Anterior half of body and upper parts plumbeous ; the wings and back glossed with olive brown. Anterior half of head above brownish yellow, the shafts of the stiff feathers black ; behind this is a white transverse band which passes back along the side of the crown ; within this white, anteriorly and laterally, is a black suffusion. The vertex and occiput are light brown. Chin and throat black, margined laterally and behind by a white band, beginning behind the eye. Belly pale buff anteriorly, (an orange brown rounded patch in the middle,) and white laterally, the feathers all margined abruptly with black. The feathers on the sides of body like the back, streaked centrally with white. Feathers of top and sides of neck with the margins and shafts black. Under tail coverts buff, broadly streaked centrally with brown.

Female similar, without the white and black of the head ; the feathers of the throat brownish yellow, streaked with brown. The buff and orange brown of the belly wanting. The crest short.

Length, 9.50 inches ; wing, 4.32 ; tail, 4.12.

Hab.—Plains and lowlands of California and Oregon towards the coast. Mohave river.

The white band across the middle of the head above bends abruptly at a right angle and passes back to the occiput ; the second white stripe begins just at the posterior corner of the eye. The imbricated pointed feathers on the neck are streaked centrally and margined with black, although the tip of the shaft is white, producing an indentation of the black border. There is also a tendency to a whitish subapical spot just within the black. In many specimens there is a short white line from the anterior corner of the eye to the commissure. There is no mottling in the feathers of the back, or else but slight indication of it. The inner tertials are margined internally with buff.

This species supplies in western California and Oregon the place of the Bob white of the eastern States, inhabiting the open lowlands and thriving in the vicinity of the settlements. It appears to be confined chiefly to the coast regions, the only specimens from the Colorado basin in the collection before me having been taken near the head of the Mohave river, and consequently close to the limits of the region assigned.

List of specimens.

Catal. No.	Sex.	Locality.	When collected.	Whence obtained.	Orig. No.	Collected by—
4477	-----	Willamette valley, O. T.	-----------	Lt. Williamson	-----	Dr. Newberry
4476	-----	......do	-----------	......do	-----	......do
4481	-----	Fort Jones, Cal.	-----------	......do	-----	......do
9395	-----	Bodega, Cal.	Jan. —, 1855	Lt. Trowbridge	-----	T. A. Szabo
5563	♀	Petaluma, Cal.	-----------	E. Samuels	165	-----
5562	♂	......do	-----------	......do	-----	-----
4483	-----	San Francisco, Cal.	-----------	Lt. Williamson	-----	Dr. Newberry
4239	♂	......do	Wint. 1855–'6	R. D. Cutts	-----	-----
4945	-----	San José, Cal.	-----------	A. J. Grayson	9	-----
4936	♀	......do	-----------	......do	5	-----
9390	♂	Tulare valley	-----------	Lt. Williamson	-----	Dr. Heermann
9392	♀	Tejon valley	-----------	......do	-----	......do
		Fort Tejon	-----------	J. X. de Vesey	-----	-----
9394	-----	San Diego, Cal.	-----------	Lt. Trowbridge	-----	-----
9396	♂	Near San Diego	-----------	Major Emory	-----	A. Schott
9388	-----	Mohave river	Mar. 14, 1854	Lieut. Whipple	183	Kenn. and Möll.

LOPHORTYX GAMBELII, Nuttall.

Gambel's Partridge.

Lophortyx gambelii, "Nuttall," Gambel, Pr. A. N. Sc. Phil. I, 1843, 260.—McCall, Pr. A. N. Sc. V, June, 1851, 221.

Callipepla gambelii, Gould, Mon. Odont. pl. xvii.—Cassin, Illust. I, ii, 1853, 45 ; pl. ix.

Callipepla venusta, Gould, Pr. Zool. Soc. XIV, 1846, 70.

Sp. Ch.—Head with a crest of five or six purplish black feathers, about as long as the bill and head together, or a little longer. Upper parts, with the neck all round, and the breast, plumbeous gray ; the shafts of the feathers brown ; those on the neck above and on the sides edged with same. Anterior half of head all round, with the chin and upper part of throat, and a large spot on the belly, black ; the forehead streaked with hoary gray. Top of the head chestnut, bordered anteriorly and laterally by black, immediately succeeded by an abruptly defined white stripe. A second stripe starts from the posterior corner of the eye and borders the black on the side of head and on the throat all round. Belly pale brownish yellow ; the sides of the body dark orange brown, broadly streaked centrally with white. Inner edges of tertials light brownish yellow. Tail light plumbeous.

Female without the black and white of the head and the black of the belly, and only a slight trace of the chestnut crown ; the crest shorter and of fewer feathers.

Length, 9.50 inches ; wing, 4.50 ; tail, 4.25.

Hab.—Upper Rio Grande and Gila to the Colorado of California.

In many specimens there is a fine mottling on the outer surface of the wings, and an appearance of the same on the gray of the breast and back, but this latter is merely an optical illusion.

The feathers on the forehead are stiff and bristly, their central portions or shafts are black ; the lateral filaments hoary gray, although the general effect is nearly black.

This fine species belongs chiefly to the Rocky mountain region, from the Upper Rio Grande to the Colorado river. It is found as far north on this river as the parallel of 36°, and is very abundant in Sonora. In the limits assigned it appears to replace the *L. californicus*, which is peculiar to the western slope.

List of specimens.

Catal. No.	Sex.	Locality.	When collected.	Whence obtained.	Orig. No.	Collected by—	Length.	Stretch of wings.	Wing.	Remarks.
9362	......	San Elizario, Texas....	Dec. —, 1855	Major Emory	14	Dr. Kennerly..	......	......	......	......
9363		......do......	......do......	......do......	13	......do.......	10.00	13.50	4.00	......
9364	♀	......do.........	Dec. —, 1854	......do......	5	......do..... ...	9.50	13.00	4.00	......
5086	♀	Fort Fillmore, N. M...	Oct. 20, 1855	Capt. Pope........	150	......	11.75	14.25	4.75	Bill black; feet gray....
5085		......do..........	......do......	......do......	149	......	......	......	......	......
9372	......	Mimbres to Rio Grande.	......	Dr. Henry........	......	......	......	......	......	......
5084	......	Doña Ana, N. M.......	Nov. 27, 1855	Capt. Pope	167	......	11.00	15.00	5.00	Bill and eyes black; feet gray; gums pale blue.
9373	♀	Rio Grande.		......do......	26	......	10.25	14.25	4.50	......
9360	♂	Camp 97, N. M........	Jan. 10, 1854	Lieut. Whipple....	44	Kenn. & Möll..	10.00	13.00	5.00	......
9360*	♀	......do.............	......do......	......do......	65	......do.......				......
9361	♀	Gila river.-	......	Lt. Parke	......	Dr. Heermann.	......	......	......	......
9369	♀	Colorado river, Cal....	......	Major Emory	......	A. Schott.....	......	......	......	......
9370	♂	......do.........	......	......do......	......	Dr. Kennerly ..	9.50	13.00	4.00	......

CALLIPEPLA, Wagler.

Callipepla, WAGLER, Isis, 1832.   Type *Ortyx squamata*, Vig.

CH.—Head with a broad short depressed tufted crest of soft thick feathers springing from the vertex.   Other character as in *Lophortyx*.

The single United States species is of a bluish tint, without any marked contrast of color. The feathers of the neck, breast, and belly, have a narrow edging of black.

CALLIPEPLA SQUAMATA, Gray.

Scaled or Blue Partridge.

Ortyx squamatus, VIGORS, Zool. Jour. V, 1830, 275.—ABERT, Pr. A. N. Sc. III, 1847, 221.

Callipepla squamata, GRAY, Gen. III, 1846, 514.—M'CALL, Pr. A. N. Sc. V, 1851, 222.—CASSIN, Ill. I, v, 1854, 129; pl. xix.—GOULD, Mon. Odont. pl. xix.

Callipepla strenua, WAGLER, Isis, XXV, 1832, 278.

Tetrao cristata, DE LA LLAVE, Registro trimestre, I, 1832, 144.   (Cassin.)

SP. CH.—Head with a full broad flattened crest of soft elongated feathers.   Prevailing color plumbeous gray, whitish on the belly, the central portion tinged with brownish ; the exposed surface of the wings tinged with light yellowish brown, and very finely and almost imperceptibly mottled.   Head and throat without markings, light grayish plumbeous, throat tinged with yellowish brown.   Feathers of neck, upper part of back and under parts generally, except on the sides and behind, with a narrow but well defined margin of blackish, producing the effect of imbricated scales.   Feathers on the sides streaked centrally with white.   Inner edge of inner tertials, and tips of long feathers of the crest, whitish.   Crissum rusty white, streaked with rusty.   Female nearly similar.   Length, 9.50 ; wing, 4.80 ; tail, 4.10.

Hab.—Valley of Rio Grande of Texas.   Not yet detected farther west.   Most abundant on the high broken table lands and mezquite plains.

In this species the elongated tertials reach nearly to the tip of the tail, which is long and graduated, the lateral feathers much narrower and an inch shorter than the middle.   The white inner margins to the inner tertials constitute a straight line down the rump, and are bordered on the side next the shaft by a dusky line.   The rump, tail coverts, and upper surface of tail are of a less pure lead color than the fore back, and absolutely mottled like the tertials.   The pale reddish brown tinge along the middle of the belly, also pervades the scale-like margins of the feathers. Those on the neck are light brown, not black. The crest is tinged with brown next to the whitish. Feathers of the breast and belly with the shafts dark brown, occupying the centre of a dark V-mark, the apex pointing backwards, and the branches divaricating more and more posteriorly.

In one specimen of this bird from New Leon, 3999, there is a large brownish chestnut spot on the middle of the belly, quite conspicuously different from what is seen in other skins.

List of specimens.

Catal. No.	Sex.	Locality.	When collected.	Whence obtained.	Orig. No.	Length.	Stretch of wings.	Wing.
9385	......	Mimbres to Rio Grande..........	....	Dr. Henry.........	......	....	....	....
9387	♀	New Mexico	....	Capt. Pope	......	....	....	....
9386	♂	......do.....................	....	......do...........	......	9.50	13.50	4.50
5102	......	Solidad cañon, Organ mts., N. M.	Mar. 10, 1856	......do...........	182	12.00	14.50	5.00
¹5104	......	Permanent camp, Pecos, N. M...	Sept. 5, 1855	......do...........	128	12.00	16.00	5.00
¹5105	......	Pecos, N. M.....................	June 6, 1856	......do...........	198	10.00	14.50	4.50
¹5103	......	Permanent camp on Pecos, N. M.	May 22, 1855	......do...........	115	11.00	15.00	5.00
9381	♀	San Pedro	....	Mr. Clark	22	10.50	14.12	4.50
3999	♂	New Leon, Mexico	....	Lt. Couch	106	....	....	....

¹ Bill and eyes brown, feet flesh-colored.

CYRTONYX, Gould.

Cyrtonyx, GOULD, Mon. Odontoph.? 1845. Type *Ortyx massena*, Lesson.

CH.—Bill very stout and robust. Head with a broad soft occipital crest of short decumbent feathers. Tail very short, half the length of the wings, composed of soft feathers, the longest scarcely longer than the coverts; much graduated. Wings long and broad, the coverts and tertials so much enlarged as to conceal the quills. Feet robust, extending considerably beyond the tip of the tail. Claws very large, the outer lateral reaching nearly to the middle of the central anterior. The toes without the claws, however, are very short.

This genus differs very much from its North American allies in the great development of the feathers composing the wing coverts, the very short and soft tail, and the very short toes and long claws. It is almost worthy of forming the type of a distinct sub-family, so many and great are its peculiarities. The single North American representative is the only one of our species with round white spots on the lower surface and black ones above. A second species, *C. ocellatus*, is found in Mexico.

CYRTONYX MASSENA, Gould.

Massena Partridge.

Ortyx massena, LESSON, Cent. Zool. 1830, 189.
Cyrtonyx massena, GOULD, Mon. Odont. 1850, 14; tab. vii.—M'CALL, Pr. A. N. Sc. V, 1851, 221.—CASSIN, Illust. I, i, 1853, 21; pl. xxi.—REICHENB. Syst. Av. 1850, pl. xxvii.
Ortyx montezumae, VIGORS, Zool. Jour. V, 1830, 275.
Odontophorus meleagris, WAGLER, Isis, XXV, 1832, 279.
Tetrao guttata, DE LA LLAVE, Registro trimestre, I, 1832, 145. (Cassin.)

Sp. Ch.—Head striped with white, black, and lead color ; chin black. Feathers above streaked centrally with whitish, those on the outer surface of the wings, with two series of rounded black spots. Central line of breast and belly dark chestnut ; the abdomen, thighs, and crissum, black ; the sides of breast and body lead color, with round white spots. Legs blue. Length, 8.75 ; wing, 7 ; tail, 2.50.

Hab.—Chiefly on the upper Rio Grande from the high plains of the Pecos.

It is scarcely possible to describe this beautiful quail so as to exhibit an accurate idea of its markings and coloration. It is, however, so different from any other known species as to require mention of its more prominent features only.

Head with a broad depressed and full occipital crest. The sides of the head are striped white, plumbeous, and black. The lead color forms a streak above and below the eye, the latter one widening behind and with a crescent of black parallel to it on the sides of the neck. The chin and middle of the throat, (bounded laterally and behind by white,) with two spots on the upper eyelids and a stripe behind, starting below the middle of the eye, are also black. The forehead is black, with two white streaks on each side, the vertex is likewise black but the feathers are tipped with brownish yellow, of which color is the crest. The under parts are dark bluish ash, each feather with two series of round white spots ; the central line of breast and belly dark orange chestnut ; the thighs, anal region, and beneath the tail, sooty or velvety black. The feathers above are all streaked centrally with brownish white or yellow, bordered with black ; the back and scapulars reddish brown, barred transversely with black ; the exposed surfaces of the wings with two series of black spots on each feather. Primary quills brown spotted with white.

A skin, probably of a young male, is without the black and plumbeous of the head and throat ; the white, however, is speckled with brown.

The female is something like the male on the back, except that the wings lack the round black spots. The under parts are totally different, the ground color being of a light purplish cinnamon, the feathers of the breast and sides streaked centrally and narrowly on each side the (light colored) shafts with black. The throat and median line of belly and anal region are dull purplish white, without markings. The head shows none of the black and white markings.

List of specimens.

Catal. No.	Sex.	Locality.	When collected.	Whence obtained.	Orig. No.	Collected by—	Remarks.
4418	♂	Chihuahua		John Potts			
10356	♀	Fort Davis, Tex		Dr. Foard, U. S. A			
10357	♂	......do		......do			
10358	♂	......do		......do			
9358		Turkey creek, Tex	Nov. —, 1854	Major Emory	25	Dr. Kennerly	
9359		Las Moras, Texas	1853	Dr. Crawford			
9356		Mimbres to R. Grande.		Dr. T. C. Henry			
5106		Western Texas		Capt. Pope			
9355		Laredo, Texas		Major Emory		J. H. Clark	
3998	♂	New Leon, Mex	April —, 1853	Lt. Couch			Eyes dark, bill black.

The preceding species of *Perdicidae* are all that are known with certainty to inhabit the United States. The following are stated to occur in California, but none have been seen there by reliable observers. They probably all belong to Lower California, or to the western coast of Mexico.

EUPSYCHORTYX CRISTATUS, Gould.

> *Tetrao cristatus*, LINN. I, 1766, 277.
> *Eupsychortyx cristatus*, GOULD, Mon. Odont. pl. ix.
> *Ortyx temminckii*, STEPHENS, Shaw's Zool. XI, 1819, 381.
> *Ortyx neoxenus*, VIGORS, Pr. Comm. Sc. Zool. Soc. I, 1830, 3.—BENNETT, Gardens and Menag. II, 1838, 311, cut.—AUD. Synopsis, 1839, 200.—IB. Birds Amer. V, 1842, 71; pl. 292.
> *Perdix neoxenus*, AUD. Orn. Biog. V, 1839, 226; pl. 422.
> *Lophortyx neoxenus*, NUTTALL, Man. I, 2d ed. 1840, 792.

LOPHORTYX ELEGANS, Nuttall.

> *Ortyx elegans*, LESSON, "Traité d'Ornith. 1831."—IB. Cent. Zool. pl. 61.
> *Lophortyx elegans*, NUTTALL, Man. I, 2d ed. 1840, 792.
> *Callipepla elegans*, GOULD, Mon. Odont. pl. xviii.
> *Ortyx spilogaster*, VIGORS, Pr. Comm. Sc. Zool. Soc. II, 1832, 4.   Mexico.

LOPHORTYX DOUGLASSII, Bonap.

> *Ortyx douglassii*, VIGORS, Zool. Jour. IV, 1829, 354.—IB. Zool. Beechey's Voyage, 1839, 27, pl. xi.—DOUGLASS, Linn. Trans. XVI, 1829, 145.[1]—JARD. & SELBY, Ill. pl. cvii.
> *Lophortyx douglassii*, BON. List, 1838.—NUTTALL, Man. I, 2d ed. 1840, 793.

ORTYX FASCIATUS, Natterer.

> *Ortyx fasciatus*, NATTERER, MSS.—GOULD, Pr. Zool. Soc. XI, 1843, 133.   California.

---

[1] *Ortyx douglasii.*—Bill brown; crest linear, black, one inch long. Irides hazel red. Body fuscous-brown, with a mixture of lead color and rusty or yellow streaks. Throat whitish, with brown spots. Belly foxy red or tawny white, spotted. Quill feathers eighteen. Scapulars and outer coverts bright brown. Under coverts light reddish brown. Tail of twelve unequal, rounded feathers. Legs reddish. Length nine inches. Girth twelve inches. Weight ten ounces. Flesh pleasant, dark colored.

July 21, 1858.

82 b

ORDER V.

GRALLATORES.

Сн.—Legs, neck, and usually the bill, much lengthened. Tibia bare for a certain distance above the tarsal joint. Nostrils exposed. Tail usually very short. The species live along or near the water, more rarely in dry plains, wading, never swimming habitually, except perhaps in the case of the phalaropes.

The bill of the *Grallatores* is usually in direct proportion to the length of legs and neck. The toes vary, but are usually connected at the base by a membrane, which sometimes extends almost or quite to the claws.

Under the head of the *Rasores* I have already called attention to the inaccuracy of the table of higher groups on page 2 of the present volume, in reference to the position of the hind toe. In the present order nearly the whole of the *Herodiones*, instead of having this toe elevated and reduced, have it lengthened, and on or near the same level with the anterior ones. This is especially the case with the *Ardeidae*, which nest on trees and spend much of their time there.

The *Grallatores*, like the *Rasores* and *Natatores*, are divisible into two sub-orders, according as the species rear and feed their young in nests, or allow them to shift for themselves. The following diagnoses express the general character of these sub-divisions:

HERODIONES.—Face or lores more or less naked, or else covered with feathers different from those on the rest of the body, except in some *Gruidae*. Bill nearly as thick at the base as the skull. Hind toe generally nearly on same level with the anterior. Young reared in nests and requiring to be fed by the parent.

GRALLAE.—Lores with feathers similar to those on the rest of the body. Bill contracted at base, where it is usually smaller than the skull. Hind toe generally elevated. Young running about at birth and able to feed themselves.

SUB-ORDER

HERODIONES.

Cʜ.—Bill generally thick at the base and much longer than the head. Frontal feathers with a rounded outline ; lores and generally the region round the eye (sometimes most of the head) naked.

In following Bonaparte's arrangement of water birds, as sketched out in his Conspectus Avium, vol. II, and elsewhere, I find great difficulty in constructing the diagnoses of his higher groups, which he has generally left undefined. His sub-order *Herodiones* corresponds very nearly with the *Ardeidae* of Gray, except perhaps in including *Aramus* and its allies, which Gray places in the *Rallidae.* It would be easy enough to characterize the North American forms by themselves, but it becomes necessary, of course, to avoid the introduction of any phrase which would be nullified by the consideration of materials from a wider range.

The primary characteristic of the *Herodiones*, though physiological rather than zoological, is of the highest importance. The young are born weak and imperfect, and are reared in the nest, being fed directly by the parent until able to take care of themselves, when they are generally abandoned. In the *Grallae*, on the contrary, the young run about freely, directly after being hatched, and are capable of securing food for themselves under the direction of the parent.

The chief zoological character (not, however, entirely without exception) is to be found in the bill, which is generally very large, much longer than the head, and thickened at the base so as to be nearly or quite as broad and high as the skull. The lores are almost always naked, or if covered it is with feathers of a different kind from those on the rest of the body. The hind toe in most genera is lengthened and on a level with the anterior, so as to be capable of grasping ; sometimes, however, it is elevated and quite short.

I have not the material at hand for working out the different members of this sub-order, so as to present their characteristics in an intelligible manner. I follow Bonaparte in placing in it of North American forms *Gruidae, Aramidae, Ardeidae, Tantalidae, Plataleidae,* and *Phoenicopteridae.* These all agree pretty well with the characters already assigned, except *Aramidae*, the type of which, *Aramus*, has the head feathered to the bill, as in the *Grallae.* In other respects its affinities to *Grus* are very close, which itself may belong to the *Grallae·* *Phoenicopterus* should probably go with the *Anseres*, especially if the young take to the water immediately on being hatched.

Synopsis of families.

A. Bill contracted opposite the nostrils, much compressed ; the culmen curved at the end, sinking down opposite the nostrils and then rising again. Nasal groove broad ; the nostrils widely open and placed nearly at the middle of the bill.

GRUIDAE.—Head usually with spaces bare of perfect feathers, and warty or papillose ; the tertials elongated and pendent or decurved. Toes connected by a basal membrane. Hind toe short and much elevated.

ARAMIDAE.—Head feathered to the bill. Tertials not unusually elongated nor pendent. Toes cleft to the base. Hind toe long and not much elevated.

B. Bill with the culmen straight to near the tip, or else gently decurving from the base. Nostrils nearer the base of the bill ; not very open.   Middle claw serrated only in *Ardeidae*.

ARDEIDAE.—Middle claw finely pectinated or serrated.   Bill conical, angular, with the commissure nearly straight.   Forehead feathered.

TANTALIDAE.—Bill rounded, very long, large at the base, and then becoming rapidly attenuated and decurved.   Forehead bare.

PLATALEIDAE.—Bill entirely depressed and flattened, very broad, and widening at the end into a spoon shape.

C. Bill with the edges provided internally with transverse lamellae like the ducks, bent abruptly downwards about the middle.

PHOENICOPTERIDAE.—Legs and neck excessively lengthened ; the toes webbed to the claws.

Family GRUIDAE.

The diagnosis of this family has already been given on a preceding page. The species are all very large, and inhabit dry plains rather than marshes. The bill is moderately long; the nostrils broad and pervious, the nasal groove extending but little beyond them. The legs are long, but the toes are short; the hind toe is very short and much elevated; the claw scarcely touching the ground.

The genera are few in number, but one, *Grus*, belonging to North America.

GRUS, Linnaeus.

Grus, LINNAEUS, Syst. Nat. 1735. Type *Ardea grus*, L. (Gray.)

CH.—Bill lengthened, straight, the upper mandible only slightly decurved at the extreme tip; the commissure and other outlines straight. Nasal groove very large and open, extending over the basal two-thirds of the bill. Nostrils broadly open, pervious; the anterior extremity half way from the tip of bill to eye. The upper half of the head naked, warty, but with short hairs.

Legs much lengthened; toes short, hardly more than one-third the tarsus. Inner toe rather longer, its claw much larger than the outer. Hind toe elevated, short. Toes connected at base by membrane. Tarsi broadly scutellate anteriorly. Tertials longer than primaries, decurved; first quill not much shorter than second. Tail of twelve feathers.

The precise number of species of this genus in North America and their character has been a matter of much uncertainty, and the subject cannot even now be said to be well settled. Audubon admits but one, considering the brown sand-hill crane to be the young of the white whooping crane. This, however, is erroneous, the species being perfectly distinct. Mr. Cassin has detected what he considers a third species among the Smithsonian collections, to which he gives the name of *G. fraterculus*. He thinks also that in the same collection are specimens which may even point a fourth species very similar to, if not identical with, *G. longirostris*, Temm.

Synopsis of species.

A. Adult plumage white; primaries black. Bill much longer than middle toe.
　Bill very thick; the gonys convex, ascending; warty portion of head extending in a point backward on top of head, and behind the cheeks below the eye; concealed by black hairs..*G. americanus.*
B. Adult plumage plumbeous.
　Bill slender, longer than middle toe. Gonys straight; in line with lower edge of bill. Warty space of head not extending below eyes, and bifurcated behind by the extension forward in an angle of occipital feathers. Primaries brown with white shafts.
　　　　　　　　　　　　　　　　　　　　　　　G. canadensis.
　Much smaller. Bill shorter than middle toe. Gonys straight, but ascending. Head in young feathered to bill. Primaries black, with brown shafts..............*G. fraterculus.*

Comparative measurements of species.

Catal. No.	Species.	Locality.	Sex & age.	Length.	Stretch of wings.	Wing.	Tail.	Tarsus.	Middle toe.	Its claw alone.	Feather from tibia.	Height of bill at base.	Bill above.	Along gape.	Specimen measured.
10384	Grus americanus	Illinois...........	....	52.00	....	24.00	9.18	11.80	4.86	0.86	6.00	1.30	5.60	6.02	Mounted.
... .do..........		Texas	O									1.22	6.00	5.70	Head....
5786	Grus canadensis	Medicine Bow.......	♂			22.80	8.78	10.01	4.16	0.80	4.82	1.20	5.40	5.48	Skin ....
do.	..........do....	............do........		46.00	82.00										Fresh ...
9493	..........do.........	Mimbres to RioGrande	....			22.20	8.80	9 90	4.10	0.82	4.22	1.20	5.62	5.98	Skin ....
10379	..........do.........	California				22.50	9.00	9.25	4.26	0.84	4.52	1.24	5.62	5.76	...do....
8914	..........do.........	Sand Hill.......										1.26	5.80	6.06	Head....
9492	..........do.........	Takh Plain, W. T....										1.18	5.74	5.74	...do....
9483	..........do....... ..	Oregon...........	O			20 50	8.54	8.88	3.80	0.80	4.34	1.10	5.00	5.10	Mounted.
	..........do.........	Salt Lake......				20 50	8.50	9.70	4.00	0.80	4.34	1.06	4.92	5.50	...do....
	..........do.........	............do.......		51.00		22.00	9.82	10.00	4.00	0.84	4.16	1.06	5.10	5.20	...do....
9483	..........do.........	Steilacoom	O			21.50	9.46	9.50	3.96	0.70		1.12	4.36	4.72	Skin ....
4623	..........do....	Colorado river, Cal...	O			20.00	8.10	9.10	3.80	0.70	3.82	1.08	4.70	4.90	...do....
10378	Grus fraterculus......	Albuquerque, N. M...				17.50	6.80	7.50	3.36	0.50	2.70	0.74	3.04	3.16	...do....
	Grus australasianus..	Australia		50.00		21.00	9.50	10.00	3.78	0.66	5.48	1.34	5.80	6.10	Mounted.

GRUS AMERICANUS, Ord.

White Crane; Whooping Crane.

Ardea americana, LINN. Syst. Nat. I, 1766, 234, No. 5.—GMELIN, I, 621.—FORSTER, Phil. Trans. LXII, 1772, 382, No. 37. (York Fort.)—WILSON, Am. Orn. VIII, 1814, 20 ; pl. lxiv.

Grus americana, ORD's ed. Wils. VIII, 1825.—BON. Obs. Wils. 1825, No. 195.—IB. Conspectus, II, 1855, 99.— SWAINSON, F. Bor. Am. II, 1831, 372.— NUTT. Man. II, 1834, 34.—AUD. Orn. Biog. III, 1835, 202 ; pl. 226.—IB. Syn. 219.—IB. Birds Amer. V, 1842, 188 ; pl. 313.

Grus clamator, BARTRAM, Travels in E. Florida, 1791.

Grus struthio, WAGLER, Syst. Av. 1827, Grus, No. 6.

Grus hoyanus, DUDLEY, Pr. A. N. Sc. Ph. VII, April, 1854, 64. Wisconsin.—HARTLAUB, Cab. Journ. III, 1855, 336 ; considers it the young of *Grus americanus.*

Grue blanche, BUFFON, Ois. VIII, 158.

" *Grue d' amerique,* Pl. enl. 889."

Whooping crane, PENN. Arc. Zool. II, 442, 339.—CAT. Car.—LATHAM.

SP. CH.—Bill deep, compressed. Lower mandible as deep along the gonys as the upper opposite to it. Gonys convex, ascending, not in the same straight line with the lower outline of bill. Commissure straight to very near the tip, where it is a little decurved and crenated. Color pure white ; primary and spurious quills, with their shafts, black. Space in front of the eyes, and extending backward between them to a point on the occiput, and below them (involving the whole cheeks) to a point behind the ears, blackish ; this space having the feathers reduced to stiff hairy black shafts, but concealing the warty and granulated skin. Feathers on middle of nape above plumbeous dusky. Length, 52 inches ; wing, 24 ; tarsus, 12 ; commissure, 6.02.

Hab.—Florida and Texas. Stragglers in the Mississippi valley.

The central line of the head above in 10384 exhibits a series of rather large excrescences, which may, however, be abnormal.

Immature specimens have the entire head covered with perfect feathers to the bill ; the feathers with black shafts on the regions which in adults are covered only with black hairs. Color of head and neck pale grayish chestnut.

The differences of form between the *Grus americanus* and *canadensis* are sufficiently marked to leave no doubt as to their specific distinctness, independently of the entire diversity of color. The former is a much larger bird ; the bill much stouter and higher, with a more convex and deeper apex to the lower jaw. The gony is convex, ascending, and far from being in a straight line with the basal inferior outline, as in *canadensis*. The elongated tertials are more vertical and curved, with more flowing plumes.

The young in some ages may resemble the *G. canadensis*, but the difference in size of body, in the thickness of bill, and in the feathers of the head, will serve to distinguish them. The color is probably much redder, judging from the single head and neck I have had an opportunity of examining. The *Grus hoyanus* of Dudley appears to be, without doubt, as suggested by Hartlaub, the young *G. americanus*.

The *G. americanus*, though common in Texas and Florida, is yet one of the rarest birds in collections. There are none in any of the public museums of the United States, as far as I have been able to ascertain, and for the opportunity of describing the species I am indebted to Mr. Thomas E. Blackney, of Chicago, who generously relinquished the possession of his specimen to the Smithsonian Institution.

According to Wilson this species in his time was occasionally found in the marshes of New Jersey, especially near Beesley's Point.

List of specimens.

Catalogue number.	Locality.	When collected.	Whence and how obtained.	Prepared by—
10384	Chicago, Illinois	June, 1858	Thomas E Blackney	F. Kaempfer
	Texas		Mr. Cassin	

GRUS CANADENSIS, Temm.

Sand-hill Crane; Brown Crane.

Ardea canadensis, LINN. Syst. Nat. I, 1766, 234, No. 3.—GMELIN, I, 1788, 620.—FORSTER, Phil. Trans. LXII, 1772, 382, No. 36. Severn river.
Grus canadensis, "TEMMINCK." Sw. F. Bor. Am. II, 1831, 273.—NUTTALL, Man. II, 1834, 38.—BON. Consp. II, 1855, 98.—GUNDLACH, Cab. Jour. IV, 1856, 339.
Grus pratensis, BARTRAM, Travels in Florida, 1791.
Grus fusca, VIEILLOT, Dict.
Grus poliophaea, WAGLER, Syst. Av. 1827, *Grus*, No. 7.
Grus americana, AUD. Orn. Biog. III, 1835, 441 ; pl. 261.—IB. Birds Amer. V, 1842, 188 ; pl. 314. (Supposed young.)
Brown Crane, PENNANT, Arc. Zool. II, 443.—LATH. Syn. III, I, 43.

SP. CH.—Bill compressed. Lower mandible not as deep towards the tip as the upper. Gonys nearly straight ; in the same ine with the basal portion of bill. Commissure decidedly curving from beyond the middle to the tip, where it is even, not crenated. Color bluish gray ; the primaries and spurious quills dark plumbeous brown ; the shafts white. Cheeks and chin whitish. Entire top of head (bounded inferiorly by a line from commissure along the lower eyelid) bare of feathers, warty and granulated, thinly beset with short scattered black hairs. Feathers of occiput advancing forward in an obtuse angle ; the grey feathers along this point, and over the auricular region, tinged with plumbeous. Length, 48 ; wing, 22 ; tarsus, 10 ; commissure, 6.

Hab.—Whole of western regions of United States. Florida.

The young *Grus canadensis* differs from the adult, in having the ashy feathers washed more or less with light rusty, especially on the wings, scapulars, occiput, and nape. The feathers of the occiput appear to extend along the central line of the crown towards the bill, and, possibly, in the very young, cover the entire head. One specimen, 9483, at least, has the entire head feathered, and in another, 4623, these extend further along the occiput than in the adults. These are smaller than typical *G. canadensis*, but otherwise quite similar. Mr. Cassin suggests that, in case they be distinct from *G. canadensis*, they may possibly be referred to *Grus longirostris* of Temminck and Schlegel, in Fauna Japonica, Birds, pl. 72.

There is much variation in size of different specimens of this species with age ; the bill, feet, and whole body apparently growing considerably, long after the perfect feathers have been attained.

There is an essential difference between *G. canadensis* and *americanus* in the shape of the granulated portion of the head. In *americanus* this extends backwards in a point to the occiput, and beneath the eye to behind the ear, involving the side of the entire lower jaw. In *G. canadensis* it does not extend below a line from the centre of the eye to the gape, and posteriorly it is bifurcated by the anterior extension of the occipital feathers, instead of running back in a point. The granulation, too, is much more conspicuous, and not concealed by black hairs, as in the other.

List of specimens.

Catal. No.	Sex & Age.	Locality.	When collected	Whence obtained.	Orig. No.	Collected by—
5786	-----	Medicine Bow creek. -----	Aug. 7, 1856	Lieut. Bryan -----------	224	W. S. Wood -----------
8914	-----	Sand Hills-------------	Aug. 9, 1856	Lieut. Warren ----------	-----	Dr. Hayden-----------
9493	-----	Mimbres to Rio Grande---	--------------	Dr. Henry--------------		
9394	-----	Rio Grande valley ------	--------------	Capt. Beckwith --------	-----	
4623	-----	Colorado river, Cal------	Feb. 19, 1855	Major Emory-----------	46	A. Schott--------------
10379	-----	California ---- ---------	--------------	Commodore Perry -------	-----	W. Heine ------ ------
9492	-----	Takh Plain, W. T -------	Aug. 13, 1853	Governor Stevens--------	4	Dr. Cooper ---- ---------
9483	o	Fort Steilacoom ---------	Oct. 1, 1853	Dr. Suckley-----------	579	--------------------

GRUS FRATERCULUS, Cassin.

Sp. Ch.—Size small. Bill very short ; its gape less than middle toe. Gonys straight, but bent upwards. Generally similar to the *G. canadensis*, but much smaller. Color light bluish grey. Primaries entirely black ; the shafts dark brown without white.

Young, with the head feathered to the bill ; the feathers generally above marked with pale rusty. Cheeks and chin grayish white ; the middle of crown and occiput reddish. Wing, 17.50 ; tarsus, 7.50 ; commissure, 3.16.

Hab.—New Mexico.

This species, although in many respects similar to the young *G. canadensis*, differs in much smaller size, proportionally shorter and more slender bill, and much darker primaries, which are quite black, with dark brown shafts, instead of their being plumbeous brown with white shafts. The single specimen is immature, though perhaps nearly grown ; the adult probably has the top of the head granulated and without perfect feathers.

List of specimens.

Catal. No.	Locality.	When collected.	Whence obtained.	Collected by—
10378	Albuquerque, New Mexico-------	October, 1853	Lieut. Whipple.----------------	H. B. Möllhausen------

Family ARAMIDAE.

The *Aramidae* of Bonaparte embrace a single genus, *Aramus*, which most authors place in the *Rallidae*.

ARAMUS, Vieill.

Aramus, VIEILL. Analyse, 1816. Type *Ardea scolopacea*, Gm. (G. R. Gray.)

CH.—Bill elongated, much compressed, both mandibles decurved at tip. Gonys very long. Bill of equal width nearly from base to tip ; nostrils pervious, in the basal fourth of the bill. Head feathered to bill ; eyelids only naked. Legs lengthened ; tibia half bare ; tarsus longer than middle toe ; toes without basal membrane ; outer lateral rather longer than inner ; middle claw not pectinated. The tarsi are broadly scutellate anteriorly.

The wings are broad and rounded ; the tertials equal to the primaries. The first quill is scarcely longer than the tenth, and subfalcate. The tail is composed of twelve feathers.

Two species are at present known to naturalists, until recently supposed to be one. Cabanis was the first to point out the differences between them and to insist that they were distinct, and not merely adult and young.

Comparative measurements of species.

Catal. No.	Species.	Locality.	Length.	Stretch of wings.	Wing.	Tail.	Tarsus.	Middle	Its claw alone.	Bill above.	Along gape.	Specimen measured.
8692	Aramus giganteus	Indian Key, Fla......	24.00	....	12.80	5.88	5.03	4.26	0.69	5.04	5.28	Skin .....
do.	........do...................	......do.............	27.50	44.00	13.00	....	....	....	....	....	....	Fresh ....
	Aramus scolopaceus	Brazil	31.00	....	14.20	7.60	5.10	4.22	0.74	4.86	5.18	Mounted..

ARAMUS GIGANTEUS, Baird.

Carau; Crying Bird ; Courlan.

Rallus giganteus, BON. J. A. N. Sc. V, 1825, 31.
Aramus scolopaceus, BON. Am. Orn. III, 1828, 111 ; pl. xxvi.—IB. Conspectus, II, 1855, 104. (Young only.)—IB. Syn. 309.—NUTTALL, Man. II, 1834, 68.—AUD. Orn. Biog. IV, 1838, 543 ; not pl. 377, which is *A. scolopaceus*.—IB. Syn. 219.—IB. Birds Amer. V, 1842, 181 ; not pl. 312, which is *A. scolopaceus*.
Notherodius holostictus, CABANIS, Jour. IV, 1856, 426.

SP. CH.—General color olive chocolate brown, each feather except the quills streaked centrally with white, as a lanceolate spot ; the colors becoming lighter towards the bill ; the chin and upper part of the throat whitish. The under tail coverts and rump almost chocolate brown and unspotted. Length, 27.50 ; wing, 13 ; tarsus, 5.03 ; gape of bill, 5.28.

Hab.—Florida and West Indies.

With a general resemblance to the typical *Aramus scolopaceus*[1] of Brazil, the species

[1] ARAMUS SCOLOPACEUS, Vieillot.

Ardea scolopacea, GMELIN, Syst. Nat. I, 1788, 647.
Aramus scolopaceus, VIEILLOT, Dict.—IB. Gal. des Ois. II, 134 ; pl. 252.—BONAP. Consp. II, 1855, 103, adult, not the supposed young, nor of Am. Orn.—AUD. Orn. Biog. IV ; pl. 377.—IB. Birds Am. V ; pl. 312.— BURMEISTER, Thiere Bras. II, 1856, 380.
Rallus ardeoides, SPIX. Av. Bras. II, 72 ; pl. xci.
Rallus gigas, LICHT. Verz. Doubl. 1823, 79.
Notherodius guarauna, WAGLER, Syst. Av. 1827.—IB. Isis, 1829, vi.

July 24, 1858.

83 b

inhabiting North America is readily distinguishable by its smaller size, although the bill is of the same length. There is much more of the white streaks throughout. These in *scolopaceus* are confined to the head and neck, and indeed not seen at all on the crown and the lower part of throat. A few concealed streaks may be found on the jugulum and middle line of the belly, but they are not conspicuous. In the other bird, all the small feathers show streaks of white, except on the lower part of back, rump, and crissum, and including the jugulum and top of head. The dark colors of the Florida bird are lighter, with less of the chocolate brown shade. Mr. Audubon appears to figure the true South American species, *A. scolopaceus*, although describing *A. giganteus* as the young. There is nothing to show that the original of his figure was taken in Florida.

Measurements.

Catalogue No.	Sex and age.	Locality.	When collected.	Whence and how obtained.	Point of bill to end of tail.	Between tips of outst'ched wings.	Wing from carpal joint.	Remarks.
8691	♂	Indian Key, Fla....	August 21, 1857.	G. Wurdemann..	26.00	41.00	12.00	Iris brown.........
8692	....	........do.........	....	........do.........	27.50	44.00	13.00	....do.............
10372	♂	........do.........	January 17, 1858.	........do.........	26.50	41.50	12.00	....do.............
10373	♀	........do.........	February 2, 1858.	....	25.75	40.00	12.00	....do.............

Family ARDEIDAE.

Cʜ.—Bill conical, acuminate, compressed, and acute; the edges usually nicked at the end; the frontal feathers generally extending beyond the nostrils. Tarsi scutellate anteriorly; the middle toe connected to the outer by a basal web. Claws acute; the edge of the middle one serrated or pectinated on its inner edge.

The family is a well marked one, and is generally distributed throughout the globe, embracing a great number of species, a large proportion of them American. Bonaparte assigns to it but a single sub-family *Ardeinae*, making *Cancroma, Scopus,* and *Euripya* types of separate families.

The following schedule will illustrate the principal characters of the genera belonging to the territories of the United States. The measurements of the species of each section will be found under the head of its first genus.

Synopsis of genera.

A. Aʀᴅᴇᴀᴇ.—Bill much longer than the head, acute, rather slender proportionately. Legs very long and slender; tarsus much longer than middle toe; anteriorly broadly scutellate to the base. Outer lateral toe always decidedly longer than inner. Tibiae lengthened, always bare for the lower third or half. Body moderately compressed. Neck very long, usually well eathered all round. Tail of twelve stiffened feathers.

Middle of back with elongated plumes, their fibrillae distant.

Dᴇᴍɪᴇɢʀᴇᴛᴛᴀ.—Plumes straight, fastigiate, depending, and elongated. Feathers of the head and entire neck lanceolate, narrow, and well defined, (in this differing from all our other genera.) Toes very short; the lateral not more than half the tarsus, (a character entirely peculiar to this genus.)

Gᴀʀᴢᴇᴛᴛᴀ.—Plumes reaching about to the tail, recurved at the end; the fibrillae horizontal, but not fastigiate. A full occipital crest, and lower part of the throat with similar plumose feathers; the fibrillae fastigiate. Color white.

Hᴇʀᴏᴅɪᴀꜱ.—Plumes reaching beyond the tail, straight, fastigiate, depending. Head perfectly smooth.

Back without elongated plumes. Scapulars usually elongated.

Aʀᴅᴇᴀ.—Occiput with greatly lengthened feathers, reaching far beyond the occipital crest. Scapulars equal to the tertials.

Aᴜᴅᴜʙᴏɴɪᴀ.—Head without much lengthened feathers. Scapulars scarcely elongated.

Fʟᴏʀɪᴅᴀ.—Head with occipital feathers moderately elongated; the webs decompounded; those of lower throat, lanceolate. Scapulars longer than the tail. Lower outline of bill nearly straight.

B. Bᴏᴛᴀᴜʀᴇᴀᴇ.—Bill rather slender, acute. Culmen very gently curved, gonys ascending. Tibia feathered nearly to the joint. Tarsi short, less than middle toe, broadly scutellate anteriorly. Claws long, acute. Inner lateral toe longest. Tail of ten very soft feathers. Body much compressed. Neck short; bare inferiorly behind. No crests nor plumes.

Aʀᴅᴇᴛᴛᴀ.—Size very small. Plumage compact, lustrous. Back unicolor.

Bᴏᴛᴀᴜʀᴜꜱ.[1]—Size large. Plumage dull, loose, much spotted and streaked.

[1] I cannot find any important feature of form by which to separate these two genera.

660   U. S. P. R. R. EXP. AND SURVEYS—ZOOLOGY—GENERAL REPORT.

C. NYCTICORACEAE.—Bill thick and stout, scarcely longer than head.   Upper outlinede curved from base.   Legs short, stout.   Tarsi stout, short, nearly as long or a littlelonger than the middle teo ; the scutellation with a tendency to become hexagonal anteriorly .Lateral toes nearly equal, outer rather the longer.   Claws short, much curved.   Lower fourth of tibia bare. Head with much elongated occipital feathers.   No dorsal plumes.   Neck short ; bare inferiorly behind.   Tail of twelve stiff feathers.

> BUTORIDES.—Bill small, rather slender, gently curved.   Gonys straight, but ascending.   Tarsus shorter than middle toe.   No very long occipital plumes.
>
> NYCTIARDEA.—Large.   Bill very stout ; lower outline straight ; gonys slightly concave.   Tarsus about equal to middle toe.   Occiput with an elongated plume. Scapulars not longer than the tertials.
>
> NYCTHERODIUS.—Large.   Bill stoutest and shortest of North American herons ; inferior outline convex and curving as much as the superior.   Tarsus decidedly longer than the middle toe.   Occiput with several much elongated feathers. Scapulars reaching the tip of tail.

DEMIEGRETTA, Blyth.

Demiegretta, "BLYTH, 184-," perhaps described in Catalogue of Calcutta Museum, 280.   Type *Ardea jugularis*, Blyth. *Herodias*, BONAPARTE, Consp. II, 1855, 120.   Not of Boie, which has *Ardea egretta* for type.

CH.—Bill narrow, slender ; both outlines rather concave to the terminal half, then uniformly convex.   Tarsi very long, broadly scutellate ; toes very short ; the middle scarcely more than half the tarsus ; outer longest.   Claws much curved, very short and blunt.

Back of neck well feathered.   Head with a full occipital crest of elongated lanceolate feathers ; the tip of all the neck feathers similar, as well as those on the lower part of the throat.   Back with free fastigiate plumes longer than the tail.

This genus is one of the most strongly marked among the entire family of herons, and in some respects exhibits a near approach to the cranes.   The well defined lanceolate feathers and the short toes are quite peculiar features.

There are three species belonging to the United States, which may be readily distinguished as follows :

Plumage pure white.   Bill flesh colored at the base, the terminal half abruptly black...*D. pealeii*

Head and neck (even on the throat) uniform reddish brown tinged with lilac.   Body generally grayish blue, paler beneath...*D. rufa.*

Head, neck, and exposed upper parts slaty blue.   Chin and central line of throat, with the under parts generally and rump, white..*D. ludoviciana.*

I cannot determine satisfactorily what this genus should be called.   It is not *Herodias*, as stated by Bonaparte, since Boie's name was based upon the *Ardea egretta* of Linnaeus, and consequently anticipates *Egretta* of Bonaparte.   The only name I can find which has any reference to the group is *Demiegretta* of Blyth, with his *Ardea jugularis*[1] as the type.   I therefore adopt it, but with a strong suspicion that the American birds, with *Ardea ludoviciana* as type, are entitled to a new generic appellation, for which *Hydranassa* would be exceedingly appropriate.

[1] *Ardea jugularis*, BLYTH, Notes on the Fauna of Nicobar Islands, Jour. As. Soc. XV, 1846, 376.—*Herodias concolor*, BON. Conspectus, II, 1855, 121.

Comparative measurements of Ardeae.

Catal. No.	Species.	Locality.	Sex and age.	Length.	Stretch of wings.	Wing.	Tail.	Tarsus.	Middle toe.	Its claw alone.	Bare part of tibia.	Height of bill at base.	Bill above.	Along gape.	Specimen measured.
2721	Demiegretta pealii	Eastern U. S.	....	30.30	....	13.50	4.66	5.70	3.30	0.45	3 86	0.63	4.02	4.90	Skin....
1988	......do	......do	....	29.30	....	13.00	5.06	4.84	3.16	0.46	3.38	0.76	3.80	4.90	Skin....
4146	Demiegretta rufa.... ..	Matamoras				12.50	5.20	5.42	3.26	0.50	3.40	0.69	3 50	4.54	Skin....
1978	Demiegretta ludoviciana	Eastern U. S.	....	28.00	....	10.70	3.70	3.86	3.02	0.46	4.74	0.60	4.04	4.64	Skin....
8581	....do	Cape Florida	♂			10.26	3.60	4.00	3.22	0.52	2.66	0.60	3.94	4.50	Skin....
do.	......do	......do		25.50	37.00	10.50									Fresh...
1226	Garzetta candidissima ..	Eastern U. S.	....	24.00	....	10.20	4.00	3.93	2.90	0.44	3.62	0.54	3.14	3.60	Skin....
4274	......do	Calcasieu Pass, La..	....	20.80	....	9.60	3.70	3.08	2.64	0.39	2.10	0.47	2.94	3.54	Skin....
4145	......do	Cadereita, Mex	♂			10.00	4.12	3.46	2.60	....	2.34	0.49	3.06	3.42	Skin....
do.	......do	......do	..	27.25	36.00	10.12									Fresh...
8067	......do	Tamaulipas	....	26.00		10.60	4 44	3.86	2.72	0.46	2.78	0.62	3.38	3.84	Skin....
9469	.... do	Sacramento Valley ...	♂	23.00		10.70	3.80	3.76	2.74	0.43	2.54	0.54	3.25	3.64	Skin....
2735	Herodias egretta	Eastern U. S.		41.00	....	15.50	6.50						4.70	5.60	Skin....
9299	......do	Prairie Mer Rouge,La..	....	33.00		14.00	5.92	5.35	4.05	0.63	3.64	0.70	4.28	5.28	Skin....
10323	......do	Eastern U. S.	....			14.80	6.34	5.70	4.20	0.50	3.70	0.66	4.25	5.20	Skin....
5108	......do	Indianola,Texas	....	14.70		14.70	6.50	6.00	4.20	0.62	4.50	0.79	4.70	5.20	Skin....
do.	......do	......do	....	39.00	57.00	16.00	?								Fresh...
9298	......do	Prairie Mer Rouge,La..	....	33.30		14.20	6.04	6.00	4.50	0.64	4.00	0.86	4.50	5.25	Skin....
5107	......do	Texas	....			14.00	6.00	5.50	4.10	0.60	3.60	0.70	4.10	5.00	Skin....
10324	......do	Texas				15.20	6.20	6.30	4.50	0.62	4.42	0.76	4.34	5.46	Skin....
5775	......do	Kansas	....	33.50	....	15.00	6.00	5.85	4.65	0.65	4.20	0.86	4.25	5.30	Skin....
8066	...lo	California?	....			15.70	7.00	6.10	4.70	0.62	4.06	0.82	4.40	5.54	Skin....
9070	Herodias var. californica	San Diego, Cal	....	43.00		17.00	6.30	6.70	4.80	0.62	4.40	0.80	4.55	5.71	Skin....
do.	......do	......do	....	43.00	60.00	17.00									Fresh...
4610	......do	.... do.	....			16.50	6.20	6.25	4.90	0.69	4.34	0.83	5.00	6.00	Skin....
4524	Ardea herodias	Cape Flattery, W. T...	....	43.70		19.30	8.73	5.86	4.20	0.80	3.50	1.10	4.87	6.10	Skin....
9475	......do	Fort Steilacoom,W.T.	....	45.80		20.20	9.00	6.87	4.84	0.72	4.50	1.17	5.52	7.00	Skin....
9472	......do	Sacramento Valley...	♂	42.20		18.60	7.58	7.06	4.90	0.71	4.28	1.14	5.50	7.15	Skin....
4143	......do	Fort Brown, Texas ...	....			17.40	7.29	6.14	4.72	0.64	4.39	1.10	5.26	6.31	Skin....
do.	......do	......do	....	42.00	65.00	18.00									Fresh...
1677	......do	Carlisle, Penn.... ...	○♀			18.30	6.84	6.23	4.52	0.56	3.52	1.00	5.95	6.09	Skin....
do.	......do..	......do	....	43.00	70.00	18.50									Fresh...
9476	......do...	Mimbres to Rio Grande				19.20	7.60	6.57	5.00	0.66	4.36	1.14	5.46	7.02	Skin....
8065	......do	Mexico	....	39.50		17.60	7.20	5.96	4.13	0.53	3.36	1.00	4.36	5.70	Skin....
8690	Ardea wurdemannii....	South Florida	♂	*49.00		20.70	7.40	7.94	5.66	0.90	5.36	1.24	6.48	8.14	Skin....
9479	......do	......do	....			19.70	7.92	9.10	5.60	0.74	6.22	1.25	6.16	7.50	Skin....
6539	......do	Indian Key, Fla......	○♂					7.70	5.20	0.61	4.60	1.18	5.20	6.00	Skin....
6540	Audubonia occidentalis	Indian Key, Fla......	♂	41.00		19.50	8.00	8.80	5.62	0.74	5.88	1.26	6.50	8.00	Skin....
1985	......do	Florida	....			18.00		6.80	5.04	0.70	4.32	1.19	5.50	7.10	Skin....
3040	Florida coerulea	Liberty county, Ga...	♂			11.00	4.58	3.52	3.00	0.50	2.48	0.62	3.00	3.42	Skin....
do.	......do	......do ...	....	22.00	36.00	12.00									Fresh...
4554	......do	Florida	....	21.50		11.00	4.42	3.80	3.12	0.49	2.65	0.63	3.00	3.60	Skin....
8680	......do	Indian Key	♂	19.80		10.50	4.34	3.80	3.04	0.50	2.62	0.54	2.74	3.36	Skin....
do.	......do	..... do		19.50	39.50	11.00									Fresh....

* About.

DEMIEGRETTA PEALII, Baird.

Peale's Egret.

Ardea pealii, Bonap. Syn. 1828, 304.—Ib. Am. Orn. IV, 1833, 96; pl. xxvi, f. 1.—Ib. Oss. Cuv. 100.—Nuttall, Man. II, 1834, 49.

Egretta pealii, Gambel, Pr. A. N. Sc. IV, 1848, 127.

Sp. Ch.—Color pure white. Terminal half of bill black. Length about 30 inches; wing, 13; tarsus, 5.70; bill above, 4 inches.

Hab.—Seacoast of South Florida.

Bill, with the culmen concave along the middle; the gonys convex, and rising from the angle of the same; both culmen and gonys quite convex towards the end. Legs lengthened; the tibia bare for about half its length; the middle toe short, about three-fifths the tarsus; the outer lateral toe about one-half. The middle anterior claw short, stout, and blunt; the pectination reduced to a few obsolete notches. Occiput with a crest of long lanceolate firm feathers, shorter than the bill, and similar shaped ones on the whole neck, much elongated on the lower part of the throat; the pennules lax and free only at the base of the feathers. Back with long fastigiate, nearly straight, plumes, with the fibrillae elongated and distant, reaching the length of the tail beyond it.

Color pure white. Bill flesh-colored, the terminal half abruptly black. Legs black in the dried specimen; said to be dark olive green in life; the soles greenish yellow.

List of specimens.

Catalogue number.	Sex and age.	Locality.	Whence obtained.
2721	♂	Florida.............................	S. F. Baird.............................
1988		....do.............................	......do.............................

DEMIEGRETTA RUFA, Baird.

Reddish Egret.

Ardea rufa, BODDAERT, Tabl. Pl. Enl. 1784.
Ardea rufescens, GMELIN, Syst. Nat. I, 1788, 628.—LATHAM, Ind. Orn. II, 1790, 694.—WAGLER, Syst. Av. 1827; *Ardea* No. 13.—AUD. Orn. Biog. III, 1835, 411 : V, 604 ; pl. 256.—IB. Syn. 1839.—IB. Birds Amer. VI, 1843, 139 ; pl. 371.
Egretta rufescens, BONAP. List, 1838.
Herodias rufescens, BONAP. Conspectus, II, 1855, 125.—GUNDLACH, Caban. Jour. IV, 1856, 341.
Aigrette rousse, BUFFON, Ois. VIII, 378.—Pl. Enl. 902.
Reddish Egret, PENNANT, II, 447.

SP. CH.—Body grayish blue; paler beneath. Head and neck all round uniform reddish brown, or rufous chestnut, without white on the throat. Bill black on the terminal third. Young similar, but duller. Length, about 30 inches; wing, 12.50 ; tarsus, 5.72 ; bill above, 3.50.

Hab.—Coast of South Florida and Gulf of Mexico to mouth of Rio Grande. Cuba, Gundlach.

Middle toe about two-fifths the tarsus; outer lateral toe more than half the tarsus; inner, about half this length. Tibia bare for about one-half. Pectinations quite distinct. Bill compressed; the outlines excavated, but becoming considerably convex at the tip. General external form that of *H. pealeii*.

"Bill black on its terminal third; the rest, and the bare space on the head, pale flesh color. Iris white. Legs and feet ultramarine blue; the scutellae brownish black, as are the claws. Feathers of the head and neck all round light reddish brown, tinged with lilac, the tips fading into brownish white. Back and wings dull grayish blue, the long feathers of the train yellowish towards the tips; all the lower parts grayish blue, paler than that of the upper."—*Audubon.*

Without an adult of this species before me, I copy the description of its colors from Mr. Audubon. A young bird has the plumage generally plumbeous gray; the coverts, the throat, and the head tinged with reddish; the back slightly glossed with the same. There is only a rudimentary occipital crest, and no dorsal one whatever. The differences in color from the adult are chiefly in the duller blue of the body, and the absence of the decided reddish of the neck. The bill is black at the end and reddish at the base.

Audubon and, latterly, Bonaparte, have united the *H. pealeii* and *rufa* into one, considering the former as the two-years stage of the latter, and, as such, capable of reproduction. I agree with Dr. Gambel in considering them to be distinct, as the immature *H. rufescens* is now well known as described above. Judging from the specimens before me, the *pealeii* has shorter toes and longer tarsi than the other.

List of specimens.

Catalogue number.	Sex and age.	Locality.	Whence obtained.	Collected by—
4146	○	Matamoras, Texas..........	Lieut. Couch..............	Dr. Berlandier ....

DEMIEGRETTA LUDOVICIANA, Baird.

Louisiana Heron.

Ardea ludoviciana, WILSON, Am. Orn. VIII, 1814, 13; pl. xvi, f. 1, (not of Linnaeus, which is *Butorides virescens*.)—
    BON. Obs. Wils. 1825, No. 192.—NUTTALL, Man. II, 1834, 51.—AUD. Orn. Biog. III, 1835,
    136 : V, 605; pl. 217.—IB. Syn. 266.—IB. Birds Amer. VI, 1843, 156; pl. 373.
Egretta ludoviciana, BONAP. List, 1838.
Ardea leucogaster, ORD ed. Wilson, VIII, 125, 13.—? WAGLER, Syst. Av. 1827, No. 14.
Egretta ruficollis, GOSSE, Birds Jam. 1847, 338.
Herodias ruficollis, CAB. Cab. Jour. IV, 1856, 342.
Herodias leucoprymna, "LICHT." BONAP. Consp. II, Jan. 1855, 124.

SP. CH.—Slaty blue on head, neck, and exposed portion of body above; lower back, rump, under parts, longest occipital feathers and the middle line of the throat, white; occiput, nape, and neck behind, purplish. Bill brownish black above and at tip. Legs yellowish green. Young with the blue of head and neck replaced by purplish rufous, blotched with blue.

Length, 25; wing, 10.50; tarsus, 4; bill above, 4.

Hab.—Coast of South Atlantic and Gulf States.

Bill very slender and much attenuated, as long as the tarsus; the upper and lower outlines nearly straight, or slightly concave to near the tip, when they become gently convex. Legs rather short; middle toe about three-fourths the tarsus; inner lateral toe decidedly more than half the tarsus. Head with an elongated occipital crest, the longest feather the length of the toes; the feathers composing it as well as those covering the neck all round, and the upper part of the back, are lanceolate, acute, and well defined in their outlines. The lower part of the back, with a plumose train of feathers with the fibrillae distant, elongated, fastigiate, and nearly straight, or curving gently downwards. In the specimen before me this train is a little longer than the tail, but, according to Mr. Audubon, it becomes sometimes lengthened to such a degree as to sweep the ground.

The prevailing color of this species on the head, neck, wing, tail, and exposed portion of the body above, is slaty blue; the occiput, nape, and lower part of neck, (except inferiorly,) purplish. The six or eight longest feathers of the occipital crest, the chin, and central line of the throat, and the entire body, white, except the interscapular region. The white of the lower back and rump is concealed by the train, the feathers of which have concealed white at the base, and are of light brownish, tinged with purple.

The white of the throat is much concealed in its middle and inferior portion by blue edges of the feathers, and in places is spotted with purplish.

The bill in life is said to be brownish black above and on the sides below towards the point; the rest yellow, as is the space round the eye. The iris bright red. Feet light yellowish green; the anterior scutellae dusky.

A young bird differs in having the blue of the head and neck replaced by purplish rufous, blotched with blue; the wing coverts edged with the same rufous. Most of the bill appears to be yellow; the upper mandible dusky; the tip black.

There is no occasion to change Wilson's name for this bird, on account of its having been employed by Linnaeus. The white *Ardea ludoviciana* is a synonym of *Butorides virescens*, a bird of very different genus.

List of specimens.

Catal. No.	Sex & age.	Locality.	Whence obtained.	Length.	Stretch of wings.	Wing.	Remarks.
8681	♂	Cape Florida......................	G. Wurdemann..............	25.50	37.00	10.50	Upper mandible greenish, with black end-Lower part brownish. Iris light yellow.
1978	......	Florida...........................	S. F. Baird..............	......	......	......	....
10326	○♀	Georgia..........................	Prof. Jos. Leconte	24.20	36.00	9.50	....
10327	○♂	......do..........................	......do......................	25.00	37.00	10.00	....

GARZETTA, Bonaparte.

Garzetta, BONAP. Consp. II, 1855, 118.   Type *Ardea garzetta,* L. (whether of Kaup, 1829 ?)

CH.—Bill slender; outlines nearly straight to near the tip, when they are about equally convex. Middle toe more than half the tarsus. Tarsi broadly scutellate anteriorly. Tibia denuded for about one half. Outer toe longest. Head with a full occipital crest of feathers having the webs decomposed, hair-like; feathers of lower part of throat similar. Middle of back with long plumes reaching to the tail, recurving at tip. These plumes and the crest apparently permanent. Lower part of neck behind, bare of feathers. Colors, pure white in all ages.

Of this genus but a single well-established species is found in the United States, a Chilian one, (possibly occurring in California,) *Ardea thula* of Molina, (Hist. Nat. Chilé, 207,) is larger; the tarsi shorter; the bill yellow at the base instead of black.

This genus is called *Garzetta* by Bonaparte, after Kaup of 1829. I have not the work of Kaup at hand to know what species is his type, but suspect it to be *Ardea alba,* L. Without Macgillivray's British Birds before me, I am unable to say whether his *Erodius* belongs to this genus or to *Herodias.*

GARZETTA CANDIDISSIMA, Bonap.

Snowy Heron.

Ardea nivea, JACQUIN, Beit. 1784, 18. Not of S. G. Gmelin of prior date, and same genus.—LATHAM, Ind. II, 1790,
696, (in part.)—LICHT. Verz. 1823, No. 795.

Ardea candidissima, GMELIN, Syst. Nat. I, 1788, 633.—WILSON, Am. Orn. VII, 1813, 120; pl. 62.—BON. Obs.
Wils. 1825, No. 194.—IB. Syn. 1828, 305.—WAGLER, Syst. Av. 1827, *Ardea*, No. 11.—NUTT.
Man. II, 1834, 49.—AUD. Orn. Biog. III, 1835, 317: V, 1839, 606; pl. 242.—IB. Syn. 269.—
IB. Birds Amer. VI, 1843, 163.

Egretta candidissima, BONAP. List, 1838.—GOSSE, Birds Jam. 1847, 336.

Herodias candidissima, GRAY, Genera.—GUNDLACH, Cab. Jour. IV, 1856, 342.

Garzetta candidissima, BONAP. Consp. 1855, 119.

Ardea carolinensis, ORD. ed. Wilson, VII, 1825, 125.

Snowy heron, LATHAM.

SP. CH.—Occiput much crested. Dorsal plumes reaching to the end of the tail. Colors pure white. Bill black; the
base yellow. Legs black. Length, 24; wing, 10.20; tarsus, 3.80; bill above, 3.15.

Hab.—Coast of Middle and Gulf States, and across to California.

Bill compressed; culmen slightly concave in the basal two-thirds; terminally more convex
than the gonys. Middle toe, three-fourths the tarsus. Tibia bare for nearly one-half. Occiput
with a full crest of loosely fibred feathers as long as the bill; the feathers on the lower part of
the throat somewhat similar. The middle of the back with a series of plumes, with the fibrillae
distant and lengthened; the plumes recurved at tip, where the fibrillae of opposite sides are
horizontal, but approximated together in a vertical plane. They reach nearly to the tip of the
tail, sometimes beyond it.

Bill black, yellow at the base, including the loral region and around the eye, as also a larger
basal portion of the lower mandible. Leg black; the lower part of the tarsus behind and the
toes yellow. Color of plumage throughout pure white.

A specimen from California, 9469, has the occipital crest much elongated, considerably
longer than the bill; the other plumes also more developed.

This species differs from the *Garzetta egretta*, Bon., of the Old World, in having the bill shorter
than the tarsus, instead of equal. The crest in *egretta* is much smaller and less developed.

Most authors quote Jacquin for the name *candidissima* of this species. A reference to this
work shows, however, that he used the word *nivea*, already pre-occupied for the *Ardea garzetta*.

List of specimens.

Catal. No.	Sex.	Locality.	When collected.	Whence obtained.	Orig'l No.	Collected by—	Length.	Stretch of wings.	Wing.	Remarks.
1226	......	Eastern U. States..	....	S. F. Baird.....	......	....	....	....	....	....
4275	......	Calcasieu Pass, La.	1854.........	G. Würdemann.	......	....	....	....	....	....
4276	......	......do............	....do........	......do.......	......	....	....	....	....	....
4274	......	......do............	....do....	...... do......	......	....	....	....	....	....
8067	......	Tamaulipas........	Feb. 13,1837	John Gould....	......	....	....	....	....	....
4145	♂	Cadereita, Mex	April, 1853...	D. N. Couch ...	136	....	27.25	36.00	10.25	Eyes yellow, bill black. Feet yellowish black.
9469	.....	Sacramento Valley.	....	Lt. Williamson.	....	Dr.Heermann	....	....	....	....
......	......	Fort Tejon........	....	J. X. de Vesey.	......	....	....	....	....	....

July 24, 1858.

84 b

HERODIAS, Boie.

Herodias, BOIE, Isis, 1822, 559. Type *Ardea egretta*. Not of Bonap. 1855.

Egretta, BONAP. Saggio di una dist. Met. 1831. Type *Ardea egretta*.

CH.—Color white. Bill quite slender. Culmen nearly straight ; more convex terminally than the gonys. Middle toe more than half the tarsus. Tibia bare for one-half. Outer toe longest. Claws moderate, considerably curved. Tarsus broadly scutellate anteriorly. Head smooth. Back in breeding season with a series of fastigiate plumes longer than the tail, and curving gently downwards. Tail of twelve broad stiffened feathers. Back of neck well feathered. Colors pure white at all times.

The white heron from southern California is much larger than that from the eastern States, and possibly distinct.

HERODIAS EGRETTA, Gray.

White Heron.

Ardea egretta, GMELIN, I, 1788, 629.—LATH. Ind. Orn. II, 1790, 694, (not of other older European writers.)—
WILSON, Am. Orn. VII, 1813, 106 ; pl. vi.—WAGLER, Syst. Av. 1827 ; *Ardea* sp. 7.—BONAP. OSS. Cuv. 97.—NUTTALL, Man. II, 1834, 47.—AUD. Orn. Biog. IV, 1838, 600 ; pl. 386.—IB. Syn. 265.—
IB. Birds Amer. VI, 1843, 132 ; pl. 370.

Herodias egretta, GRAY, Genera.—GUNDLACH, Cab. Jour. IV, 1856, 341.

Ardea leuce, "ILLIGER," LICHT. Verz. 1823, sp. 793.

Egretta leuce, BONAP. (Saggio, 1831 ?) List, 1838.

Herodias leuce, BREHM, Handbuch, 1831, 585.

Ardea alba, BONAP. Obs. Wilson, 1825, No. 189.—IB. Syn. 304.   (Not of Linnaeus.)

Great egret, PENNANT, II, 446.—LATHAM.

SP. CH.—Head smooth ; bill yellowish to the tip ; feet black. Color pure white. Length, 39 inches ; wing, 15.50 ; tarsus, 5.70 ; bill above, 4.70.

Hab.—Southern portions of the United States ; straggling to Massachusetts.

Bill, with the culmen and gonys about equally curved, the commissure slightly concave near the tip. Legs slender, elongated ; middle toe about three-fourths the tarsus. Tibia bare for about half its length. Head without a crest ; the feathers lying close. Lower part of the back, in the breeding season, with a series of elongated feathers, with stiffened shafts, the plumulae distant and elongated. These feathers are gently pendent (not recurved) and extend beyond the tail by about its length ; their total length is nearly three times that of the tail. The feathers of the lower part of the neck but little elongated.

Color entirely white ; feet black ; bill yellowish, dusky above, (in 9298.) According to Audubon, the entire bill and the iris are yellow.

This species appears to differ from the European *E. alba* in lacking a black tip to the bill, which is five inches long, not six ; the tarsus is about six inches long, instead of eight.

List of specimens.

Catal. No.	Locality.	Whence obtained.	Collected by—
2735	Eastern United States	S. F. Baird	
9298	Prairie Mer Rouge, La	Jas. Fairie	
5892	do	do	
5775	Kansas	Lieut Bryan	W. S. Wood
5107	Texas	Capt. Pope	

HERODIAS EGRETTA, var. CALIFORNICA, Baird.

Сн.—Pure white. Larger than *H. egretta*. Length, 43 inches ; wing, 17 ; tarsus, 6.70 ; bill, 5.

Hab.—Coast of southern California, and perhaps the Rio Grande of Texas.

This bird is very similar to *Herodias egretta*, but is considerably larger ; the tibiae are bare for half their length. The feathers of the back are not fully grown out, so that I can make no comparison in this respect, but the scapulars are more elongated and plume-like than in the other species, and there is a tendency to the same along the belly. The bill appears of a more brilliant yellow, dusky only near the tip above.

It is possible that this may be only a variety of the *H. egretta*, but the size is so much greater as almost to warrant its specific separation.

List of specimens.

Catal. No.	Locality.	When collected.	Whence obtained.	Length.	Stretch of wings.	Wing.	Remarks.
9470	San Diego, Cal....................	....	A. Cassidy........	....	....	....	Bill and gums yellow. Legs black.........
4610	......do........	........:......	Major Emory......	....	....	....	....
8066	California..	....	John Gould........	....	....	....	....
5108 ?	Indianola?....................	Feb. 20, 1855.	Capt. Pope.........	39.00	57.00	16.00	....

ARDEA, Linn.

Ardea, LINN. Syst. Nat. I, 1735. Type *A. cinerea.*

Сн.—Bill very thick ; culmen nearly straight ; gonys ascending, its tip more convex than that of culmen. Middle toe more than half the tarsus ; tibia bare for nearly or quite one-half. Claws short, much curved ; outer toe longest. Tarsus broadly scutellate anteriorly.

Occiput with a few elongated occipital feathers. Scapulars elongate lanceolate ; as long as the secondaries. No dorsal plumes. Tail of twelve broad stiffened feathers. Back of neck well feathered. Size very large. Colors plumbeous ; streaked beneath.

The two North American species of the genus as restricted, are distinguished as follows :

Common characters.—Above bluish ash ; the primaries and outer secondaries blackish plumbeous. Head white and black. Middle of throat white, streaked with black and rufous. Edge of the wing and the tibia rufous.

Bill, 5.50. Tarsus, 6.50. Middle toe two-thirds the tarsus. Tibia bare for about one-third. Under parts, except crissum, black ; the middle of the belly broadly streaked with white. Neck light cinnamon brownish. Head, with the crest black ; the forehead white..*A. herodias.*

Bill, 6.50. Tarsus, 9. Middle toe not two-thirds the tarsus. Tibia bare for nearly half. Under parts white ; the feathers of the sides of breast and belly streaked black and white. Neck ashy. Head, with the crest white ; the forehead streaked with blackish...*A. würdemannii.*

ARDEA HERODIAS, Linnaeus.

Great Blue Heron, or Crane.

Ardea herodias, LINN. Syst. Nat. I, 1766, 237, No. 15.—GM. I, 1788, 630.—LATHAM, Ind. Orn. II, 1790, 692.—
WILSON, Am. Orn. VIII, 1814, 28; pl. lxv.—BON. Obs. 1825, No. 188.—WAGLER, Syst. Av. 1827;
Ardea, No. 1.—NUTT. Man. II, 1834, 42.—AUD. Orn. Biog. III, 1835, 87 : V, 599; pl. 211.—IB.
Syn. 1839.—IB. Birds Amer. VI, 1843, 122; pl. 369.—BP. Consp. II, 1855, 112.—GUNDL. Cab.
Jour. IV, 1856, 340.

Ardea hudsonias, LINN. Syst. Nat. I, 1766, 238, No. 18.—GMELIN, I, 1788, 631.

Ardea virginiana cristata and *Ardea freti hudsonis,* BRISSON.

Large crested heron, CATESBY, Car. App. pl. x.

Ash-colored heron, EDWARDS.—*Great heron* and *Red-shouldered heron,* PENNANT, LATHAM.

SP. CH.—Lower third of tibia bare. Above bluish ash; edges of wing and the tibia rufous. Neck cinnamon brown. Head
lblack, with a white frontal patch. Body beneath black, broadly streaked on the belly with white. Crissum white Middle
ine of throat white, streaked with black and rufous. Length, 42 inches; wing, 18.50; tarsus about 6.50; bill about 5.50.

Hab.—Throughout the entire territory of the United States; West Indies.

Bill lengthened, compressed, nearly straight to the terminal third, when there is a very
gentle convexity of the culmen and a greater of the gonys. Tibia bare for more than one-third.
Middle toe two-thirds the length of the tarsus. Outer lateral toe longer than the inner. Feathers
of the crown elongated, acute; the occiput with two long feathers as long as the bill. Scapular
feathers elongated, acutely lanceolated.

Adult.—Bill yellow dusky at the base and greenish above. The forehead and central part of
the crown are white, encircled laterally and behind by black, of which color is the occipital
crest and its two elongated feathers. The neck is of a light smoky cinnamon brown, with
perhaps a tinge of purple; the chin and throat whitish; the feathers along the central line of
the throat to the breast white, streaked with black, and also with reddish brown, except on the
elongated feathers of the breast. The body may be described as bluish ash above and on the
sides. The under parts, including the tuft of feathers on each side the breast and the belly to
the white crissum, are sooty black, much varied along the middle line with white. The tibia
and the edge of the wing are rufous. The quills are black, becoming more plumbeous internally
until the innermost secondaries are ashy, like the back. The elongated tips of the scapular
feathers have a whitish shade. The tail is of a bluish slate color. According to Mr. Audubon,
the bill in life is yellow; dusky green above; loral and orbital spaces light green; iris yellow;
feet olivaceous, paler above the tibio-tarsal joint. Claws black.

Young.—The upper mandible is blackish. The lower yellow, except along the commissure.
The head above is entirely dusky, without the much elongated occipital feathers. The breast
is grayish, streaked with white and light brown, but without any pure black patches. The back
is without the elongated scapular feathers. In still younger specimens the coverts are all margined with rufous, which becomes lighter at the tip. The rufous of the tibia is much lighter.

Specimens vary considerably in size as well as in shade of plumage. Washington Territory
skins are considerably darker and larger than more southern ones on the west coast. I have
before me no adult spring birds from the east.

A specimen from Mexico is smaller, but otherwise apparently similar. This appears to
correspond somewhat to the *Ardea lessoni* of Wagler, his specimen perhaps being immature,
with the whole head above still blackish.

List of specimens.

Catal. No.	Sex & age.	Locality.	When collected.	Whence obtained.	Orig'l No.	Collected by—	Length.	Stretch of wings.	Wing.	Remarks.
1677	♂♀	Carlisle, Pa..........	Aug. 16,1844	S. F. Baird......	......	....	43.00	70.00	18.50	....
4430	.....	Quasquiton, Iowa....	....	E. C. Bidwell....						....
5454	♂	Near Big Sioux......	May, 1856 ...	Lieut. Warren. ..	......	Dr. Hayden	49.00	73.00	20.00	....
9474	. .....	Texas...............	1853.........	Major Emory....		A. Schott......	....	....		
4143	......	Brownsville, Texas..	April 22,1853	Capt. S. Van Vliet	......	....	42.00	65.00	18.00	Eyes yellow..............
4144	......	Tamaulipas..........	....	Lieut. Couch....		....	....		.....	Bill black ; gums yellow ; iris yellow ; feet black.
5114	......	Pecos, Texas........	June 10,1855	Capt. Pope.......	96	....	42.00	61.00	17.50	....
5115	......	Doña Ana, N. Mex...	Jan. 5,1856	......do.........	173	....	40.50	64.00	18.00	....
9473	......	Mimbres to Rio Grande	....	Dr. Henry	......		....			
9477	......	Boca Grande, Mex...	Mar., 1855...	Major Emory....	......	Dr. Kennerly..	....			
9472	.....	Sacramento Valley...	....	Lieut.Williamson.			....	.. ..		
4523	......	San Francisco......					.....	....	.....	
9478	......	Bodega, Cal........	Dec. 5,1854	Lt. Trowbridge..	......	T. A. Szabo....	....			
9480	......	Shoalwater Bay, W.T.	....	Gov. Stevens....	......	Dr. Cooper.....	....	......		
9475	......	Fort Steilacoom.....		......do..... ...	......	Dr. Suckley...	....			
4578	......	........do............	Feb. 8,1856	Dr.Suckley......	222		....			
4524	......	Cape Flattery.......	....	Lt. Trowbridge...	......		....			
8065	......	Mexico.............	....	John Gould......	......		....			

ARDEA WÜRDEMANNII, Baird.

Florida Heron.

Sp. Ch.—Lower half of tibia bare. Above bluish ash. Edge of wing and the tibiae rufous. Middle of throat white, streaked with black and rufous. Neck ash-colored. Head white, with a patch in the forehead black. Under parts white ; the feathers on the sides of breast and belly streaked with black. Length about 49.00 ; wing, 20.75 ; tarsus, 8.00 (or more) ; bill above, 6.50. *Hab.*—South Florida.

Tarsi elongated. Tibia bare for half its length. Middle toe not one-third the tarsus. External form, otherwise, as in *A. herodias.*

Bill in the dried specimen greenish yellow ; dusky above. Entire head all round, including the occipital crest, snowy white ; the elongated feathers apparently not fully grown, but also white. Feathers of the forehead margined laterally with black. Neck ash color, with a shade of violet. The feathers of the middle line of the throat white, and streaked with dark plumbeous from a point distant the length of the culmen from the base of the bill. These feathers on the throat, likewise, have a wash of rufous. The upper parts generally are bluish gray, the elongated scapulars much paler. The under parts generally are white ; the feathers on the sides of the breast are bluish black, streaked centrally with white ; those of the sides of the body streaked on one side with the same. The sides of the body are like the back. The edge of the wing and the tibiae are purplish rufous, with a violet shade ; the portion of the former from the carpal joint to the quills, nearly white, with spots of the rufous. The greater coverts near the edge of the wing are streaked obscurely with whitish, and tinged with rufous. The primaries are dark hoary blackish plumbeous ; the outer secondaries still darker, but becoming lighter towards the back.

This species is somewhat similar to the *A. herodias,* but is much larger ; the bill and tarsus at least an inch longer. The tibia is bare for a greater distance. The head is entirely white, with the forehead streaked with black, exactly the reverse of the other, which has the head black above, the forehead white.   The under parts are almost entirely white, the sides of the breast and body streaked with black, instead of having nearly the whole belly black, streaked with white in the middle ; the sides of breast pure black.   The neck is not cinnamon brownish, but ashy. The upper parts are of much the same shade with *Ardea herodias*, No. 9472.

A young bird, supposed to belong to the same species, but without any indication of locality, differs from the adult much, as does that of the *A. herodias.*

This species is readily distinguished from *Ardea cocoi* by the head being white above, not black ; the tibia rufous, not white ; the belly mostly white, not black; the neck bluish ash, not white. It has much the same size and proportions with the *Ardea occidentalis*, and, in some respects, might almost be considered a cross between this species and *herodias.*

In presenting to the scientific world the most magnificent species of heron known to inhabit the United States, and one presumed to have been hitherto undescribed, I take much pleasure in giving to it the name of Mr. Gustavus Würdemann, of the United States Coast Survey, as a slight token of acknowledgment for what he has done towards bringing to light the novelties of our southern coast.   It is not too much to say that no one, for years, has been instrumental in adding so many species of birds to our southern fauna as Mr. Würdemann ; no less than nine previously unrecorded species having already been collected by him in Louisiana and Florida, besides very many new fishes and invertebrates.

List of specimens.

Catal. No.	Sex.	Locality.	Whence obtained.	Length.	Stretch of wings.	Wing.
9479	......	Florida ...... --------------------	G. Würdemann --------------------	--------	--------	19. 70
8690	♂	....do------------------------------	------.do----------------------------	--------	--------	-------
6539	......	Indian Key, Florida----------------	------.do--------------------------	49. 00	70. 00	20. 00

AUDUBONIA, Bonap.

Audubonia, BONAP. Conspectus, II, 1855, 113.   Type *Ardea occidentalis*, Aud.

CH.—Similar to *Ardea.*   Color white.   No very long occipital feathers, nor much elongated scapulars.

It is very questionable whether this bird can be considered as entitled to separate generic rank, the differences from *Ardea* consisting only in a less extent of the feathers of head and scapulars, as well as in the white color.

AUDUBONIA OCCIDENTALIS, Bonap.

Great White Heron.

Ardea occidentalis, AUD. Orn. Biog. III, 1835, 542: V, 596; pl. 281.—IB. Syn. 1839, 264.—IB. Birds Amer. VI, 1843, 110 ; pl. 368.—BON. List, 1838.—GUNDLACH, Caban. Journ. IV, 1856, 341. *Audubonia occidentalis*, BONAP. Consp. 1855, 115.

SP. CH.—Bill very stout.   Middle toe about two-thirds the tarsus.   Tibia bare for nearly one-half.   Feathers of occiput lengthened, but no conspicuous crest, except perhaps in the adult.   Scapulars not elongated.   Color pure white.   Length about 45 inches ; wing, 19.50; tarsus, 8.80 ; bill above, '6.50.

Hab.—South Florida and Cuba.

According to Mr. Audubon, the bill in life is yellow; the upper mandible greenish at the base; the loral space yellowish green; the orbital light blue. Iris bright yellow. Tibia and hind part of tarsus yellow; fore part of tibia and toes olivaceous, the sides of the latter greenish yellow; claws light brown. The young are smaller, the feathers of occiput and lower part of throat less elongated.

List of specimens.

Catal. No	Sex.	Locality.	When collected.	Whence obtained.	Collected by—
6840	♂	Indian Key, Florida	March 18, ——	G. Würdemann	
1985		Florida		S. F. Baird	J. J. Audubon

FLORIDA, Baird.

Ch.—Bill slender, acute; upper outline curving gently from near the base; lower straight, or even concave. Tarsi short; toes long; lateral more than half the tarsus; outer toe longest. A full occipital crest; the feathers composing it, and those of the neck generally, with the webs decomposed, only lanceolate on the lower part of the throat. No dorsal plumes, but the scapulars elongated, lanceolate, and reaching beyond the tail. Back of neck bare inferiorly. Neck rather short. Color blue.

This genus differs from *Herodias* in the bill, which is convex above, straight below, and very acute. The legs are shorter, the toes and claws longer and slenderer. The peculiar lanceolate character of the feathers of the neck is wanting, as also the dorsal plumes.

FLORIDA CAERULEA, Baird.

Blue Heron.

Ardea caerulea, Linn. Syst. Nat. I, 1766, 239.—Gm. I, 1788, 631.—Lath. Ind. II, 1790, 689.—Wilson, Am. Orn.
VII, 1813, 117; pl. lxii.—Ord's ed. 122.—Bon. Obs. Wils. 1825, 187.—Aud. Orn. Biog. IV, 1838,
58; pl. 307.—Ib. Syn. 266.—Ib. Birds Amer. VI, 1843, 148; pl. 372.
Ardea (Botaurus) caerulea, Bon. Syn. 1828, 300.—Nutt. Man. II, 1834, 58.
Egretta caerulea, Bon. List, 1838.—Gosse, Birds Jam. 1847, 338.
Herodias caerulea, Gray, Genera.—Ib. Bon. Consp. II, 1855, 123.—Gundl. Cab. Jour. IV, 1856, 343.
? *Ardea cyanopus*, Gmelin, Syst. Nat. I, 1788, 644.
Ardea caerulescens, ? Latham, Ind. Orn. II, 1790, 689.—Licht. Verz. 1823, 77.—Wagler, Syst. Av. 1827, *Ardea*,
No. 15.
" *Ardea plumbea*, Brown, Nat. Hist. Jam."
" *Ardea chalybea*, Stephens."
? *Egretta nivea*, Gosse, Birds Jam. 1847, 334. Young?

Sp. Ch.—Slate blue; head and neck bluish purple all round; bill blue; legs black. Young white, sometimes spotted with blue. Length, 22 inches; wing, 11; tarsus, 3.80; bill above, 3.
Hab.—South Atlantic and Gulf coast to Mexico.

Bill slender, compressed. Culmen rather concave in the basal half; the terminal gently convex. Gonys nearly straight, in marked contrast with the culmen. Toes slender and lengthened; middle nearly as long as the tarsus; inner or shortest lateral considerably more than half the tarsus; tibia bare for nearly half. Top of the head moderately crested, becoming longer on the occiput and nape; the feathers composing it with the fibrillae free and blended, as is the case in the feathers of the neck generally and the back. Scapulars greatly elongated, lanceolate, and reaching nearly its length beyond the tip of the tail, each feather well defined and the webs not decomposed.

The body generally in the adult is slaty blue; the head and neck glossed with bluish purple; the concealed portions of the feathers purplish brownish red. There is no trace of white on the throat. The bill in life is said to be ultramarine blue at the base, shaded into black towards the point; the bare space between it and the eye, as well as the edges of the eyelids, ultramarine. The iris pale yellow; the legs, tarsi, and toes, black.

The young bird is pure white; the head smooth, and the feathers without the decomposed webs. The scapulars are not elongated. The iris is white; the bill light blue, blackish at the end; the skin around the eyes and the base of the bill light yellow; the legs light green.

Birds changing show a confused patching of white and blue.

The young bird in white dress is much like the *Garzetta candidissima*, but is without any of the plumes or crests of the latter species, and almost always shows here and there a trace of blue, instead of being pure white. The middle toe is much longer. The feet are entirely greenish to the claws (livid black in the dry skin) instead of having the toes yellowish, and the base of the bill is without the abruptly defined yellow portion.

According to Lichtenstein, "the *A. caerulea* of Linnaeus has the feathers of neck and occiput and the scapulars well defined and linear; the bill black; the legs brown, with yellow toes. Length, 18 inches; bill, 2.50; tarsus, 3. Hab.—Cayenne. The North American *A. caerulescens* has the same feathers with the fibres loose; the bill whitish at base; the legs and toes greenish. Length, 22 inches; bill, 3; tarsi, 4." The species he refers to first is evidently a true *Herodias*.

List of specimens.

Catal. No.	Sex.	Locality.	When collected.	Whence obtained.	Collected by—	Length.	Stretch of wings.	Wing.	Remarks.
3040	♂	Liberty county, Ga. . . .	Spring, 1846..	S. F. Baird.........	....	22.00	36.00	12.00	....
4554	.....	Florida...............	....	Mr. Glover.........	....	....	....	....	
8680	♂	Indian Key, Fla........	....	G. Würdemann.....	....	29.50	39.50	11.00	Eyes dark blue; iris whitish; legs and feet light green.
9300	....	Prairie Mer. Rouge, La.	....	Jas. Fairie.........	....	....	....	....	
9495	....	Lower Rio Grande, Tex.	....	Major Emory.......	A. Schott ..	....	....	....	

ARDETTA, Gray.

Ardetta, Gray, List of Genera, Appendix, 1842, 13. Type *Ardea minuta*, L.
Ardeola, Bonaparte, Syn. 1828. Type *Ardea exilis*, L. Not *Ardeola*, Boie, Isis, 1822.

Ch.—Bill slender, acute; both mandibles about equally curved. Legs very short; tarsi less than middle toe. Inner toe much longest. Claws long, acute. Tarsi broadly scutellate anteriorly.

Tail of ten feathers. Neck short. Body much compressed. Head smooth; the occipital feathers somewhat lengthened; the lower neck bare of feathers behind. No plumes. Plumage compact, lustrous; uniform above. Sexes differently colored.

This genus embraces the smallest known species of heron, and has representatives in all quarters of the globe.

Comparative measurements of Botaureae.

Catal. No.	Species.	Locality.	Sex.	Length.	Stretch of wings.	Wing.	Tail.	Tarsus.	Middle toe.	Its claw alone.	Bare part of tibia.	H'ght of bill at base.	Bill above.	Along gape.	Specimen measured.
1099	Ardetta exilis	Washington, D. C.	♂	11.30	....	4.56	1.70	1.60	1.87	0.40	0.54	0.34	1.82	2.16	Skin.....
1547	........do...........	Carlisle............	♀	11.00	......	4.84	1.80	1.50	1.88	0.42	0.52	0.32	1.74	2.24	Skin......
1547	....do...........	......do........	....	13.75	17.75	4.89	......	......	......	......	......	......	......	......	Fresh......
9485	........do...........	Near 32° latitude.........	....	11.40	......	5.00	1.86	1.70	1.94	0.40	0.56	0.36	1.91	2.38	Skin......
9486	........do...........	Sacramento Valley	♂	11.30	......	4.44	1.96	1.50	1.76	0.40	0.54	0.34	1.80	2.32	Skin......
1396	Botaurus lentiginosus	Carlisle, Pa.	♂	22.60	......	11.10	4.00	3.64	4.06	0.84	1.24	0.66	2.76	3.84	Skin......
1396	........do...........	......do........	....	26.50	42.00	11.75	......	......	......	......	......	......	......	......	Fresh......
766	........do...........	......do......	♀	......	......	10.10	3.36	3.30	3.74	0.70	1.14	0.66	2.72	3.70	Skin......
do.	.....do..,..........	......do........	....	24.00	38.00	10.25	......	......	......	......	......	......	......	......	Fresh......
8064	........do...........	Mexico.............	....	......	......	9.90	3.76	3.22	3.57	0.68	1.18	0.58	2.54	3.58	Skin......

ARDETTA EXILIS, Gray.

Least Bittern.

Ardea exilis, GMELIN, Syst. Nat. I, 1788, 648.—WILSON, Am. Orn. VIII, 1814, 37 ; pl. lxv.—WAGLER, Syst. Av. 1827 ; *Ardea*, No. 36 —AUD. Orn. Biog. III, 1835, 77 : V, 1839, 606 ; pl. 210.—IB. Syn. 263.—IB. Birds Amer. VI, 1843, 100 ; pl. 366.

Ardea (Ardeola) exilis, BON. Obs. Wils. 1825, No. 191 —IB. Syn. 308.—NUTTALL, Man. II, 1834, 66.

Ardeola exilis, BONAP. List, 1838.—IB. Consp. II, 1855, 134.—GOSSE, Birds Jam. 1847, 343.

Butor exilis, SW. Birds, II, 1837.

Ardetta exilis, GRAY, Gen. 1842.—CAB. Journ. IV, 1856, 345.

"*Ardetta punctata*, GRAY, List, Br. Mus. III, 83."—BONAP.

Minute bittern, LATHAM, Syn. III, I, 66.

SP. CH.—Head above and the back dark glossy green. Upper part of neck, shoulders, greater coverts, and outer webs of some tertials, purplish cinnamon. A brownish yellow scapular stripe. Female with the green of head and back replaced by purplish chestnut.

Length, 13.00 ; wing, 4.75 ; tarsus, 1.60 ; bill above, 1.75.

Hab.—Throughout the United States, from Atlantic to Pacific.

Tarsi rather shorter than the middle toe ; the anterior half embraced by a single series of scutellae and a second series behind, with no intermediate ones distinguishable in the dried specimen. Claws greatly lengthened and acute, the inner lateral extending further than the outer ; the lateral as long as the middle. The toes free almost to the base. Tibia feathered almost to the tarsal joint. Neck above bare, covered by the feathers of the side. Quills lengthened ; the second and third longest. Tail of ten very soft feathers. Head with the occipital feathers slightly elongated. No plumes or elongated feathers elsewhere.

Top of head, with the short crest, interscapular region, and scapulars, glossy dark green. The sides of head and neck, with lesser and middle coverts, brownish yellow ; the region bordering the green of the head, the upper part of the neck, the shoulders, and the greater coverts, dark purplish cinnamon, as are the outer webs of inner tertials, and spots at the ends of the quills and outer edge of first primary. Throat broadly whitish buff, as are the under parts generally ; this is sometimes continuous, sometimes in the form of obsolete streaks on a lighter ground. On the jugulum, and concealed by the broad elongated feathers of the throat, is a large spot, varied with black, dark purplish, cinnamon, and buff. There is a narrow brownish yellow scapular stripe in the green, which is usually more or less concealed. The bill is yellow, the ridge dusky towards the tip ; the legs appear to be greenish yellow.

July 26, 1858.

85 b

The female differs in having the green of the head and back replaced by purplish chestnut; the brownish yellow tints more hoary; the feathers of the throat with a narrow central dusky streak.

An allied species in South America, (*A. erythromelas*,) according to Bonaparte, has the back purplish chestnut, instead of dark green. The European *A. minuta* differs in being larger; the upper wing coverts milk white, not brownish yellow; the under wing coverts white, instead of olivaceous yellow.

List of specimens.

Catal. No.	Sex.	Locality.	When collected.	Whence obtained.	Length.	Stretch of wings.	Wing.
1546	♂	Carlisle, Pa.	May 18, 1844.	S. F. Baird.	13.56	17.64	4.88
1547	♀	....do.	..do.	........do.	13.75	17.75	4.88
1099	♂	Washington, D. C.	June, 1843.	........do.			
9485		Texas.		Capt. Pope.			
9484		Mimbres to Rio Grande.		Dr. Henry.			
9486	♂	Sacramento valley.		Lieut. Williamson.			

BOTAURUS, Stephens.

Botaurus, STEPHENS, Shaw's Gen. Zool. XI, II, 1819, 592.   Type *Ardea stellaris*, L.

CH.—Bill moderate, scarcely longer than the head. Bill outlines gently convex, gonys ascending. Tarsi very short, less than the middle toe; broadly scutellate. Inner lateral toe much longest. Claws all very long, acute, and nearly straight. Tail of ten feathers. No peculiar crest. Plumage loose, opaque, streaked. Sexes similar.

But one species of this genus is found within the limits of the United States.

BOTAURUS LENTIGINOSUS, Stephens.

Bittern; Stake-driver.

Ardea stellaris, Var. FORSTER, Phil. Trans. LXII, 1772, 410.
Ardea stellaris, Var. β, *Botaurus freti-hudsonis*, GMELIN, Syst. Nat. I, 1788, 635.
Ardea lentiginosa, MONTAGU, Orn. Dict. Suppl. 1813.—JENYNS, Man. 191.—AUD. Syn. 1839, 263.—IB. Birds Amer. VI, 1843, 94; pl. 365.—SW. F. Bor. Am. II, 1831, 374.
Botaurus lentiginosus, STEPH, Shaw's Gen. Zool. XI, 1819, 596.
Ardea (*Botaurus*) *lentiginosa*, NUTT. Man. II, 1834, 60.
Butor lentiginosus, JARDINE, Br. Birds, III, 147.
Ardea minor, WILSON, Am. Orn. VIII, 1814, 35; pl. lxv.—BON. Obs. 1825, 186.—AUD. Orn. Biog. IV, 1838, 296; pl. 337.
Botaurus minor, BONAP. List, 1838.—IB. Consp. II, 1855, 136.—GUNDLACH, Cab. Journ. IV, 1856, 346.
Ardea mokoho, VIEILLOT, Dict. —WAGLER, Syst. Av. *Ardea*, No. 29.

SP. CH.—Brownish yellow, finely mottled and varied with dark brown and brownish red. A broad black stripe on each side the neck, starting behind the ear. Length, 26.50; wing, 11.00; tarsus, 3.60; bill above, 2.75.
Hab.—Entire continent of North America.

Bill short, scarcely longer than the head. Gonys ascending, nearly straight. Culmen curved towards the tip. Tarsi short, less than the middle toe and claw, covered anteriorly for two-thirds the circumference by a single series of scutellae, and behind by a double series. Claws all lengthened, and nearly straight; hinder toe nearly equal to the outer lateral, which is shortest; the inner reaching beyond the base of the middle claw. Tail very short, of ten soft feathers. Lower part of neck bare above; this space partly concealed by the feathers of the sides. Head without any crest; the feathers of the lower throat greatly developed, and covering the jugulum.

General color brownish yellow, much and finely mottled and variegated with dark brown and brownish red. The top of the head and a small patch at the angle of the mouth, the tail feathers, the ends and edges of the secondary quills, the whole of the inner tertials, are reddish brown, or brownish cinnamon; the first mentioned duller, the others minutely dotted with dark brown. The wing coverts are brownish yellow, sprinkled with brown; the back and scapulars, with the dark brown more predominant. The feathers of the upper part of the back are dark cinnamon brown, edged with brownish yellow. The feathers of the throat and under parts, except the anal region and crissum, have a very broad central stripe of finely mottled yellowish and dusky, the latter color accumulated externally; the edges of the feathers buff. The sides of the neck are somewhat similar, but with an olivaceous tinge. There is a broad black stripe on each side the neck, starting near the ear and running back a short distance, curving upwards. The chin and upper part of the throat are white, with narrow central streaks. The primary quills are plumbeous dusky.

The bill in life is said to be yellowish green, the culmen brownish black. Feet yellowish green; claws brown. Iris, reddish yellow. There appears to be but little difference in the sexes and young.

There is little difference in specimens from different localities. There is a brownish olivaceous tinge in some from the Upper Missouri I have not noticed in others.

This species has been so frequently shot in Europe, especially in Ireland, as to entitle it to a place in the fauna of the Old World.

List of specimens.

Catal. No.	Sex.	Locality.	When collected.	Whence obtained.	Orig'l No.	Collected by—	Length.	Stretch of wings.	Wing.	Remarks.
1396	♂	Carlisle, Penn..........	April 29, 1844	S. F. Baird......	......	....	26.50	42.00	11.75	....
766	♀	......do...............	Sept. 29, 1842	......do.........	......	....	24.00	38.00	10.50	....
6905	....	Nelson river, H. B. T...	....	D. Gunn.........	......	....				
8911	♂	Sand Hills of Platte.....	Aug. 11, 1857	Lt. Warren......	......	Dr. Hayden	25.00	38.00	10.00	Iris yellow. ....
5455	....	Mouth of Vermilion river	May —, 1856	......do.........	......	......do.........	26.87	42.12	12.12	......do..............
5777	♀	Forks of Platte..........	July 15, 1856	Lt. Bryan	112	W. S. Wood....				
8788	....	North Fork Platte river.	Aug. 20, 1857	Wm. M. Magraw .	161	Dr. Cooper.....	27.00	41.00	11.50	Iris yellow; bill black and green; feet gray.
5776	....	Republican Forks, Platte	Oct. 7, 1856	Lt. Bryan........	......	W. S. Wood ...	22.00	33.00	....	....
9302	....	Indian river, Fla........	....	Dr. Wall.........	......	....				
4152	....	Matamoras, Mex.	....	Lt. Couch	......	....				
9466	....	San Francisco..........								
9467	....	Bodega, Cal....	Jan. —, 1855	Lt. Trowbridge...	......	T. Szabo.......				
9468	....	Fort Steilacoom	....	Dr. Suckley	......	....	24.75	31.50	....	....

BUTORIDES, Blyth.

Butorides, "BLYTH, 1849. Type *Ardea javanica*, Horsf."
Ocniscus, CABANIS, Journal für Orn. IV, 1856, 343. Type *Ardea virescens*, Lin.

CH.—Bill acute, rather longer than the head, gently curved from the base above ; gonys slightly ascending. Legs very short ; tarsi scarcely longer than the middle toe ; broadly scutellate anteriorly. Lateral toes nearly equal. Head with elongated feathers above and behind ; these are well defined, lanceolate, as are the interscapulars and scapulars ; the latter not exceeding the tertials. Neck short ; bare behind inferiorly. Tibia feathered nearly throughout. Tail of twelve feathers.

This genus is not represented in Europe, although species occur in Asia, Africa, Australia, and Oceanica. But one is found in the United States ; a second species belongs to South America, (*B. scapularis,*) distinguished most easily by the neck being ash-colored, instead of dark purplish chestnut.

Comparative measurements of Nycticoraceae.

Catal. No.	Species.	Locality.	Sex & age.	Length.	Stretch of wings.	Wing.	Tail.	Tarsus.	Middle toe.	Its claw alone.	Hind toe and claw.	Hind claw alone.	Bill above.	Along gape.	Specimen measured.
9491	Butoridea virescens....	Tulare valley, Cal.		15.00		7.50	2.76	2.05	2.10	0.34	1.00	0.44	2.10	2.94	Skin.....
7068	......do..............	Salt creek, K. T....				7.20	2.92	2.15	2.26	0.40	0.94	0.52	2.46	3.20	Skin.....
do.	......do...	......do....		18.25	21.00	7.50									Fresh ...
1126	......do...	Carlisle, Pa.......	o♂	15.50		7.50	2.88	2.00	2.12	0.32	0.86	0.46	2.14	2.70	Skin.....
298	......do.....	......do..........	♂	14.80		7.50	3.14	1.92	2.00	0.40	0.86	0.50	2.46	3.10	Skin.....
1670	Nycticorax americanus.	Philadelphia, Pa...		23.00		12.90	5.10	3.16	3.33	0.50	1.40	0.93	3.10	4.06	Skin.....
4148	......do...	Pesqueria, N. Leon	♀			13.50	5.20	3.14	3.26	0.54	1.30	0.88	2.88	3.76	Skin ...
do.	......do...	......do.........		31.75	49.50	12.75									Fresh ...
5564	......do...	Petaluma, Cal.....	♂	28.00		12.50	5.46	3.30	3.78	0.66	1.56	0.92	3.30	4.48	Skin.....
3041	Nycterodius violaceus..	Liberty co., Ga....	♂			12.00	5.20	3.72	2.88	0.40	2.19	0.88	2.78	3.28	Skin.....
do.	......do...	......do..........		23.40	40.50	12.20									Fresh ...
3836	......do...	Fort Brown, Texas.				11.70	5.00	3.70	2.72	0.44	1.92	0.89	2.78	3.42	Skin.....
do.	......do...	......do..........		40.50	23.00	10.00									Fresh ..

BUTORIDES VIRESCENS, Bonap.

Green Heron; Fly-up-the-creek.

Ardea virescens, LINN. Syst. Nat. I, 1766, 238.—GM. I, 1788, 635.—WILSON, Am. Orn. VII, 1813, 97 ; pl. lxi.— ORD's ed. p. 102.—BON. Obs. 1825, No. 190.—WAGLER, Syst. Av. 1827 ; *Ardea,* No. 36.—AUD. Orn. Biog. IV, 1838, 274 ; pl. 333.—IB. Syn. 264.—IB. Birds Amer. VI, 1843, 105 ; pl. 367.
Ardea (Botaurus) virescens, BON. Specchio Comp. No. 180.—IB. Syn. 307.—NUTT. II, 1834, 63.
Herodias virescens, BON. List, 1838.—GOSSE, Birds Jam. 1847, 340.
Egretta virescens, SWAINSON, 2¼ Centen. 1838. No. 156.
Butorides virescens, BONAP. Conspectus Av. II, 1855, 128.
Agamia virescens, REICHENB. Icones Avium.
Ocniscus virescens, CABANIS, Journ. IV, 1856, 343. Cuba.
"*Ardea chloroptera,* BODD." 1784. Gray.
Ardea ludoviciana, GMELIN, I, 1788, 630.
"*Ardea torquata,* MILL. Illust. pl. lx." Gray.
Green Heron, PENNANT, II, 447.

SP. CH.—Top of head and body above are glossy green ; the coverts edged with brownish yellow. Neck dark purplish chestnut. Chin and central line of throat white. Body beneath plumbeous ash. Length, 15.00 ; wing, 7.50 ; tarsus, 2.00 ; bill above, 2.40.

H*b.*—United States generally.

Bill stout ; culmen much compressed, gently convex towards the tip ; gonys ascending. Tarsi shorter than the middle toe, covered behind and on the sides with small hexagonal scales. Lateral toes about equal. Lower fourth only of tibia bare. Head with a crest of long, lanceolate, well defined feathers. Feathers of back and scapulars similar, the latter not reaching to the tip of the tail. Feathers of the neck broad, the webs somewhat decomposed. Top of the head, with the crest, and the entire upper parts, metallic glossy green, darkest on the head ; the coverts all edged narrowly with brownish yellow ; the shafts of scapulars and interscapulars whitish. The scapulars and interscapulars sometimes tinged with opaque plumbeous. Neck and long feathers covering the jugulum purplish chestnut ; the chin and central line of the throat white, streaked with dusky greenish. Under parts and sides of body plumbeous ash. Bill black above ; yellowish beneath. Feet greenish yellow.

Younger specimens lack the scapular development. The colors generally are duller. The under parts white, streaked with brown. The coverts more spotted.

As already stated, this species differs from *B. scapularis*, of Brazil, among other points, in having the neck purplish chestnut instead of ashy.

Gundlach[1] describes a species of *Butorides* from Cuba, (*B. brunnescens*,) which differs in having the tip of the lower mandible greenish white, the naked skin of face olive black, that around the eye yellowish green. The legs olive brown. The lesser wing coverts and small quills dark metallic green, with very slight rusty edges. The large quills without white. Lesser under wing coverts gray, with scarcely brownish border. Throat feathers yellowish brown ; dark gray at the base ; the feathers of the fore neck blackish, with green metallic lustre, with rusty tips and pale yellowish lateral edges. In *virescens* there are two stripes on the side of the head, one from the angle of the mouth, and one from the base of the lower mandible towards the ear, and between them a white stripe streaked with black ; of this latter stripe there is no trace in *brunnescens*.

I introduce this indication of what Cabanis considers a very good species, to call attention to it as being almost the only Cuban heron recorded by Gundlach not yet detected within our limits, and undoubtedly yet to be found in Florida.

List of specimens.

Catal. No.	Sex and age.	Locality.	When collected.	Whence obtained.	Orig. No.	Collected by—	Length.	Stretch of wings.	Wing.	Remarks.
1126	○♂	Carlisle..	July 18,1843	S. F. Baird						
298	♂	.....do...	April 17,1841	.....do...						
4926	....	Florida...		G. Würdemann...						
5891	....	Prairie Mer Rouge. ..		James Fairie						
4271	....	Calcasieu Pass, La....	1854...	G. Würdemann...						
4272	....	.....do...	1854...	.....do...						
7068	♂	Salt creek ..	May 28,1857	Lieut. Bryan...	101	W. S. Wood...	18.25	21.00	7.50	
8189	♂	Kansas river...	July 9,1857	Wm. N. Magraw. .	125	Dr. Cooper....	17.75	25.25	4.75	Iris yellow ; bill black and yel'w; feet yel'w.
4154	....	Brownsville, Texas...		Capt. Van Vliet....	20	....	17.50	25.50	7.00	
9487	♀	Rio Grande..	May 4,1852	Major Emory...		J. H. Clark...	19.00	28.00	8.00	
4153	♀	Rio Nasas, Durango...		Lieut. Couch...			19.50	28.12	7.75	Eyes and feet green ; bill yellow and slate.
9488	....	Eagle Pass, Texas...	June, 1852...	Major Emory...		A. Schott...				
9490	....	San Bois creek, Choctaw county.		Lieut. Whipple...		H.B.Möllhausen				
9489	....	Sacramento valley, Cal.		Lieut. Williamson.		Dr. Heermann .				
9491	....	Tulare valley...		.....do...						
	....	Fort Tejon, Cal...		J. Xantus de Vesey.						

[1] *Ardea brunnescens*, GUNDLACH, Lembeye, Av. Cuba, tab. xii.
Ocniscus brunnescens, CAB. Journal für Orn. IV, 1856, 344.

NYCTIARDEA, Swainson.

Nyctiardea, SWAINSON, Classif. Birds, II, 1837, 354. Type *Ardea nycticorax*, Lin.
Nycticorax, STEPHENS, Shaw's Gen. Zool. XI, xi, 1819, 608. Same type. Not of Moehring, 1752.

CH.—Bill very stout ; culmen curved from base; the lower outline straight, or a little concave. End of upper mandible gently decurved. Tarsi short, equal to the middle toe ; the scales more than usually hexagonal inferiorly. Outer lateral toe rather longer. No unusual development of feathers, excepting a long, straight occipital plume of three feathers, rolled together. Neck short ; moderately feathered behind.

The night herons, with a certain resemblance to the bittern, differ in the much stouter and more curved bill, the lower edge of which is straight, instead of rising at the end. The tarsus is equal to the middle toe, not shorter, and is covered anteriorly below by small hexagonal scales, instead of large transverse scutellae. The claws are much shorter and more curved. The tail has twelve feathers instead of ten.

NYCTIARDEA GARDENI, Baird.

Night Heron.

Ardea naevia, BODDAERT, Tabl. pl. enl. 939, 1784. Young. (Gray.)
Ardea gardeni, GMELIN, I, 1788, 644.
Nycticorax gardeni, " JARD." BONAP. Consp. II, 1855, 141.—GUNDL. Cab. Jour. IV, 1856, 346.
Ardea nycticorax, WILSON, Am. Orn. VII, 1813, 101 ; pl. lxi.—BON. Obs. Wils. 1825, No. 193.—AUD. Orn. Biog. III, 1835, 275 : V, 600 ; pl. 236.—IB. Syn. 261.—IB. Birds Amer. VI, 1843, 82 ; pl. 363.
Ardea (Botaurus) nycticorax, BONAP. Specchio Comp. 1827, No. 176.—IB. Syn. 1828, 306.
Ardea (Botaurus) discors, NUTT. Man. II, 1834, 54.
Nycticorax americanus, BONAP. List, 1838.—TSCHUDI, Fauna Per.—GOSSE, Birds Jam. 1847, 344.

SP. CH.—Head above and middle of back steel green. Wings and tail ashy blue. Under parts, forehead, and long occipital feathers white. Sides tinged with lilac. Length, about 25 inches ; wing, 12.50 ; tarsus, 3.15 ; bill above, 3.10.

Hab.—United States generally.

Bill very thick at the base, and tapering all the way to the tip. Culmen nearly straight for half its length, then considerably curved. Lower outline of bill nearly straight. Gonys proper slightly concave. Legs short, but stout. The tarsus equal to the middle toe ; covered throughout with hexagonal scales, the anterior largest, but those on the upper portion much larger, and going entirely across. Tibia bare for about one-fifth. Lateral toes nearly equal ; the outer rather longest. Claws small ; considerably curved. Tail short, of twelve broad, rather stiff feathers.

Head with the occipital feathers elongated, and with two or three very long, straight feathers (as long as the bill and head) springing from the occiput. These are rolled up so as to appear like a single cylindrical feather. Back of the neck covered with down, but not provided with long feathers. Interscapular feathers and scapulars elongated and lanceolate, the webs scarcely decomposed.

The upper part of the head, including the upper eyelids, the occipital crest, and the interscapular region and scapulars, dark lustrous steel green. The wings and tail are ashy blue. The under parts, the forehead, and the long occipital feathers are white, passing into pale ashy lilac on the sides and on the neck above ; this color, in fact, tinging nearly the whole under parts. The region along the base of the bill, however, is nearly pure, as are the tibia. The bill is black ; the loral space green ; the iris red ; the feet yellow ; the claws brown.

Specimens are sometimes nearly pure white beneath. In two from California the green feathers of the occiput extend further back on the nape, behind the insertion of the long white plume, instead of the hinder ones being inserted in line with this. The black tips to these plumes, mentioned by Bonaparte, I have never seen.

An immature bird differs in having the green of the back and head replaced by dull chocolate brown ; the coverts with spots of whitish ; the neck and under parts streaked with dusky. The quills have a chocolate red tinge, tipped with whitish. Still younger specimens have all the feathers above with terminal spots of whitish.

The American night heron is similar to the European *N. grisea*, but is larger, the bill stouter. The young birds have the quills with an apical white spot, not found in the European. (Bonaparte.)

Catal. No.	Sex and age.	Locality.	When collected.	Whence obtained.	Orig. No.	Collected by—	Length.	Stretch of wings.	Wing.	Remarks.
1670	....	Philadelphia............	....	S. F. Baird...... .	......	....	......	......	......	....
4270	O	Calcasieu Pass, La.......	1854........	G. Würdemann....	......	....	......	......	......	....
4269	....	......do......	1854........	......do............	......	....	......	......	......	....
4150	....	Brownsville, Texas......	April 27,1853	Capt. Van Vliet....	3	....	26.00	43.00	12.50	Eyes red.........
4151	O	......do...............	April 3,1853	......do............	29	....	25.00	44.00	12.50	....
4149	♂	Pesquieria Grande,N.Leon	May,1853....	Lieut. Couch.....	......	....	33.25	42.50	12.75	Eye crimson; bill blue and yellow.
4148	♀	......do............	...do......	......do.......	......	....	33.75	42.50	12.75	...do...........
5113	....	Texas.........	....	Capt. Pope	......	....	......	......	......	....
9889	O	San Diego............	....	Lieut. Ives........	......	H. B. Möllhausen.	......	......	....	....
9888	♀	...... do............	....	Dr. Hammond.....	......	....	......	......	......	....
5564	♂	Petaluma, Cal...........	June 18,1856	E. Samuels........	81	....	......	......	......	....

NYCTHERODIUS, Reich.

Nyctherodius, REICHENB. Naturl. Syst. Vögel, in Systema Avium, 1853, p. xvi. Type *Ardea violacea*, L.

Nycticorax, BOIE, Isis, 1826. Not of Stephens and Moehring.

CH.—Bill very thick and stout, both outlines much and about equally curved ; commissure nearly straight. Tarsi moderate ; the scales, except anteriorly above, strongly hexagonal ; middle toe considerably shorter than tarsus ; outer lateral rather the longer ; claws small, obtuse, much curved. Tail of twelve broad feathers. Head with the occipital feathers elongated ; a few much longer. Scapulars and interscapulars lanceolate, the latter reaching to end of tail.

NYCTHERODIUS VIOLACEUS, Reich.

Yellow-crowned Night Heron.

Ardea violacea, LINN. Syst. Nat. I, 1766, 238.—GMEL. I, 631.—LATH. Ind. II, 690.—WILSON, Am. Orn. VIII, 1814, 26 ; pl. lxv.—Bon. Obs. 1825, No. 196.—AUD. Orn. Biog. IV, 1838, 290 ; pl. 336.—IB. Syn. 262.—IB. Birds Amer. VI, 1843, 89 ; pl. 364.

Ardea (Botaurus) violacea, BONAP. Specchio, 1827, No. 177.—NUTT. Man. II, 1834, 52.

Nyctiardea violacea, SWAINSON, Birds, II, 1837, 354.

Nycticorax violaceus, BONAP.

Nyctherodius violaceus, REICHENB. Syst. Av. 1853, p. xvi.—BONAP. Conspectus, II, 1855, 142.—GUNDLACH, Cab. Jour. IV, 1856, 346.

Ardea jamaicensis, GMELIN, I, 1788, 625.

Ardea cayanensis, GMELIN, I, 1788, 626.

" *Ardea sexsetacea*, VIEILL. Dict."

" *Ardea callocephala*, WAGLER."

Yellow-crowned heron, PENNANT.

CH.—Neck and body uniform grayish plumbeous ; the head bluish black ; the hood and a broad patch on the side of the head yellowish white. Interscapular and scapular feathers dusky, edged with grayish plumbeous. Length, 24.00 ; wing, 12.00 ; tarsus, 3.70 ; bill above, 2.78. Hab.—South Atlantic and Gulf States ; South America.

Bill very short and stout ; not longer than the head.   Culmen gently curved from the base ; most so towards the tip; lower outline of bill straight to the culmen, then ascending in a gentle convexity, a little straighter than the culmen, but the two mandibles tapering about equally. Legs rather long ; the tarsus one and a quarter time the length of middle toe, covered with hexagonal scutellae, which in front and above are larger, and cover the anterior face.   The tibia are bare for about one-third their length.   The outer toe is rather longest ; the claws all short, small, and much curved.   The occipital feathers are elongated, and there are two linear lanceolate ones about as long as the head and body, but these are not rolled together.   The back of the neck is thinly covered with normal feathers.   The interscapular feathers are rather elongated and lanceolate ; the scapulars are much developed, linear, lanceolate ; the tips rounded, and reaching to the end of the tail ; the pennules decomposed for the terminal half. The tail is composed of twelve broad, rather stiff feathers.

The external form of this species is a good deal like that of *Nyctiardea gardeni*. The bill, however, is much thicker and shorter ; the commissure is straight, instead of concave with the end of upper mandible attenuated ; the gonys is ascending and convex, instead of horizontal and slightly concave ; the tips of both mandibles nearly equally pointed and tapering.   The tarsi are much longer and the toes shorter, so that the former are much longer than the middle toe, instead of shorter ; the claws are much smaller and more curved ; the tibia bare for a greater distance ; the reticulation of the lower part of the tarsus is more hexagonal and smaller. The scapular feathers are much more elongated.

The prevailing color of this species is a grayish plumbeous.   The head all round is bluish black ; the top of the head from the bill, including the longest occipital feathers, and a broad isolated patch from beneath the middle of the eye, yellowish white.   The feathers of the inter- scapular region coverts and scapulars are dusky, edged with grayish plumbeous ; the quills and tail plumbeous dusky.   The body generally and neck are uniform grayish plumbeous, lighter below.   The bill is black ; the legs yellow above, the lower portion black.

The young are dark greenish olivaceous above, the feathers streaked centrally, and spotted terminally with brownish yellow.   The under parts are whitish, streaked with brown.   The feathers of the head have the shafts extended into a whitish thread.   The whitish of the neck is strongly tinged with brownish yellow.

The young bird is readily distinguished from that of *Nyctiardea gardeni* by the dark greenish olive back, with numerous spots ; plumbeous, not chocolate colored, quills ; better defined streaks below, and, above all, by the generic differences in the bill and feet.

List of specimens.

Catal. No.	Sex.	Locality.	When collected.	Whence obtained.	Orig'l No.	Collected by—	Length.	Stretch of wings.	Wing.	Remarks.
3041	♂	Liberty co., Ga.....	1846.........	S. F. Baird	......	....	....	....	....	....
4268	......	Calcasieu Pass, La..	1854.........	G. Würdemann....	......	....	....	....	....	....
5109	......	Indianola..........	Mar. 23,1855	Capt. Pope	35	.. ..	28.00	38.00	12.50	Eyes red ; feet dark gray yellow ; bill dark green and yellow.
3836	.. ..	Fort Brown, Texas.	....	Capt. Van Vliet....	......	....	23.00	40.50	10.00	......do.........do ....
4147	.....	Matamoras	....	Lieut. Couch	......	....	....	....	....	....
9481	......	Rio Grande, Texas.	Oct. 13,1853	Major Emory......	......	A. Schott..	....	....	....	....
9482	......	Fort Smith.........	....	Lieut. Whipple	......	H. Müll- hausen.	....	....	....	....
1782	......	South America.....	....	S. F. Baird.........	......	....	....	....	....	....

Family TANTALIDAE.

Cн.—With naked spaces about the base of the very long, rounded, much attenuated, and decurved bill. Toes with a basal web, especially between the inner and middle ones.

Of the present family but two well marked genera occur within the limits of the United States, namely *Tantalus* and *Eudocimus*. *Falcinellus* is so little different from the latter as scarcely to be worthy of generic rank. Bonaparte divides the *Tantalidae* into several sub-families, which, with the North American genera, may be characterized as follows :

TANTALINAE.—Bill very much thickened at base, without any nasal groove. Nostrils opening directly in the substance of the bill, not surrounded by membrane. Legs lengthened, and covered with hexagonal scales.

TANTALUS.—Head bare of feathers.

GERONTICINAE.—Bill with a groove extending nearly to the tip. Legs with reticulated scales. Species confined to the old world and to South America.

IBINAE.—Bill rather slender at the base ; upper mandible grooved to the tip. Nostrils surrounded, except below, by membrane. Legs anteriorly with transverse scutellae.

IBIS.—Forehead bare of feathers ; claws curved ; plumage dull.

FALCINELLUS.—Forehead feathered ; claws straight ; plumage metallic.

I have been obliged to change Bonaparte's names of sub-families by calling his *Ibinae*, *Geronticinae*, and restoring the name of *Ibinae* to his *Eudociminae*. This is in consequence of the fact that *Ibis* of Moehring, 1752, has the *Tantalus ruber*, of Linnaeus, as type, and must be applied to the North American birds, so that *Eudocimus* becomes a synonym.

Bartram, in his Travels in Florida, (1791,) describes a *Tantalus pictus*, of which Barton publishes a figure, in Trans. Linn. Soc. London, XII, 1818, 24, pl. i, given him by Bartram, and there calls it *Tantalus ephouskyca*. It is difficult to say whether this be *Tantalus, Ibis* or *Aramus*. The coloration as described, however, differs materially from that of any known species of these genera.

Comparative measurements of Tantalidae.

Catal. No.	Species.	Locality.	Sex.	Length.	Wing.	Tail.	Tarsus.	Middle toe.	Its claw alone.	Bill above.	Along gape.	Specimen measured.
9497	Tantalus loculator...	Lower Rio Grande.........	......	....	18.50	7.00	7.10	4.70	0.56	8.30	7.90	Skin ......
2736	Ibis rubra................	South America	.....	28.50	10.90	4.50	3.50	3.20	0.50	6.80	6.50	Skin ......
9502	Ibis alba.......................	St. Simon's island, Ga......	......	....	11.20	5.02	3.76	3.22	0.53	7.00	6.60	Skin ......
1076	....do...........................	Liberty county, Ga.........	......	....	12.00	4.80	3.48	3.08	0.50	6.60	6.50	Skin ......
9500	....do...........................	Indian river, Fla...........	♀	....	10.10	4.50	3.04	2.72	0.44	5.10	5.90	Skin ......
do..	....do..	.........do.....	......	....	......	......	......	......	......	......	......	Fresh......
9503	Ibis ordii	Texas...............	......	20.50	10.00	4.06	3.28	2.80	0.56	4.35	4.30	Skin ......
9870	....do...........................	San Diego, Cal..............	......	....	9.90	4.12	3.44	2.90	0.56	4.30	4.30	Skin ......

July 29, 1858.

86 b

TANTALUS, Linnaeus.

Tantalus, LINNAEUS, Syst. Nat. ed. 10, 1758.   Type *Tantalus loculator*, L.

CH.—Bill very long, much thickened at the base and decurved at the tip. *Edges rather smooth. Nasal groove not continued beyond the nostrils, which are broad, pervious, and not surrounded by membrane. Head and neck entirely bare in the adult; the latter with the skin transversely rugose. Legs lengthened; tibia more than half bare, and with the tarsus, covered by small hexagonal scales. Outer lateral toe longer than inner; the toes connected at base by membrane.

Young with the head partly feathered.

TANTALUS LOCULATOR, Linn.

Wood Ibis; Colorado Turkey.

Tantalus loculator, LINN. I, 1766, 240.—GM. I, 667.—LATH. Ind. Orn. II, 702.—WILSON, Am. Orn. VIII, 1814,
39; pl. lxvi.—BON. Obs. Wils. 1825, No. 197.—IB. List, 1838.—IB. Consp. II, 1855, 149.—
WAGLER, Isis, 1831, 530.—NUTT. Man. II, 1834, 82.—AUD. Orn. Biog. III, 1835, 128; pl.
216.—IB. Syn. 1839, 258.—IB. Birds Amer. VI, 1843, 64; pl. 36.—GUNDLACH, Cab. Jour.
IV, 1856, 348.

? "*Ibis naudopoa*, VIEILLOT," Gray.

"*Tantalus plumicollis*, SPIX, Av. Bras. tab. lxxxv."

Wood pelican, CATESBY, Car. pl. lxxxi.

SP. CH.—*Adult.* Entirely white; tail and quills metallic blackish green, with purple reflections.

Young. Neck and head feathered as in *Ibis*.   Color duller than in adult; the downy feathers of neck dusky.

Length about 45 inches; wing, 18.50; bill, 8.50; tarsus, 7.10.

Hab.—South Atlantic and Gulf States, and across to the Colorado river; as far north as North Carolina and mouth of Ohio.

This well known species needs no especial comparisons to distinguish it from every other North American bird.   It is said to be abundant on the Colorado river, especially about Fort Yuma, and to be there called Colorado turkey.

List of specimens.

Catal. No.	Sex & age.	Locality.	When collected.	Whence obtained.	Collected by—
-----	♂	Florida ?	-----	S. F. Baird	J. J. Audubon
9496	-----	Maj. Brown's island, Rio Grande.	Oct. 23, 1853	Major Emory	A. Schott
9497	-----	Lower Rio Grande	---do----	----do----	----do----
4144	-----	Matamoras	-----	Lieut. Couch	-----
8068	-----	Mexico	Sept. —, 1836	John Gould	-----

IBIS, Moehring.

Ibis, MOEHRING, Genera Avium, 1758, 71.   Type *Tantalus ruber*, L., according to G. R. Gray.

CH.—Bill very long, moderately thickened at the base, and curving downwards to the tip. Nasal groove deeply impressed, extending to the end of the bill. Nostrils impervious, surrounded, except below, by membrane. Basal portion of cutting edges of bill with dull serrations in one species. Forehead and base of bill all round, extending behind the eyes and on the chin, bare, except in *I. ordii.* Tibia bare for half its length, covered with hexagonal scales; scales on the anterior part of the tarsus broad and transverse. Middle toe nearly as long as the tarsus; outer lateral longer; hinder elevated; toes connected at base by web.

Gray gives *Tantalus ruber*, L., as the type of Moehring's genus *Ibis*.   This author quotes Belon. l. 4, c. 9, and Seba, Thesaurus, I, tab. 62, f. 3.   The latter citation is said to refer to *Tantalus ruber;* of the former I can learn nothing.

The North American species are readily known by the red color of the first, the white body and red bill of the second, and the chestnut body and neck with metallic green, &c., on the back of the third. There is a considerable difference in the external form of the species, which has caused systematic writers to place them in different sub-genera as follows:

LEUCIBIS, Reich.—In *Ibis alba* the bill has obsolete serrations along the middle portion, directed forwards. The forehead is naked to above the middle of the eye, the feathers coming forward at about a rectangle to this point, but there are rudiments of feathers half an inch beyond, or to a point a little anterior to the eye. The whole chin and upper part of the throat are bare for about an inch behind the lower mandible. The bill from the forehead is as long as the tarsus and toes. The tarsi are transversely scutellate for the anterior half; covered with hexagonal scales behind. The toes are stout; the claws thickened, blunt, and much curved. The outer lateral claw reaches a little beyond the base of the middle. The inner anterior surface of the middle claw is extended downwards into a sharp cutting edge, but is not pectinated. The primaries are considerably longer than the secondaries and tertials.

The young bird has the head feathered almost as far forward as the commissure, leaving the region round and in front of the eye bare.

IBIS.—*Ibis rubra* has the bill without any serrations whatever. The feathers of the forehead come forward to a point anterior to the eye, and about three-tenths of an inch from the bill; the upper part of the throat is rather more bare than in *I. alba*. The bill is rather shorter than the tarsus and middle toe. The toes and tarsus much as in *I. alba*, but the outer lateral claw does not reach to the base of the middle. The middle claw has its inner face extended into a cutting edge, with indistinct, perhaps accidental, notches, but no pectination.

The primaries are considerably longer than the secondaries and tertials.

FALCINELLUS, Bechst.—*Ibis ordii* has the bill quite slender at the base, and about as long as the tarsus and half the middle toe. It is entirely destitute of serrations. The head is feathered above to the base of both mandibles, leaving bare only the space between the horny rami of under jaw and the region in front of and a little around the eye. The outer claw reaches a little beyond the base of the middle, which has the inner face extended into a cutting edge, but with no pectination, as stated by Bonaparte, but only an occasional accidental notching. The claws are slender and almost perfectly straight. The primaries are scarcely, if at all, longer than secondaries and tertials.

IBIS RUBRA, Vieillot.

Red or Scarlet Ibis; Pink Curlew.

Tantalus ruber, LINN. I, 1766, 241.—GMELIN, I, 1788, 651.—LATH. Ind. II, 1790, 703.—WILSON, Am. Orn. VIII, 1814, 41; pl. lxvi.
Ibis rubra, VIEILLOT, Dict.—WAGLER, Syst. Av. 1827; Ibis, No. 4.—NUTTALL, Man. II, 1834, 84.—BON. List, 1838.—AUD. Orn. Biog. V, 1839, 62; pl. 397.—IB. Syn. 257.—IB. Birds Amer. VI, 1845, 53; pl. 359.
Eudocimus ruber, WAGLER, Isis, 1832, 1232, (type).—BONAP. Consp. 1855, 157.—GUNDL. Cab. Jour. IV, 1856, 348.
? *Tantalus fuscus*, LINN. I, 1766, 242.—GMELIN, I, 651. Young.
? *Tantalus minutus*, LINN. Young.
"*Ibis leucopygia*, SPIX, Av. Bras. tab. lxxxviii. Young."

SP. CH.—*Adult*. Uniform and brilliant scarlet red; the tips of outer primaries black. *Young*. Ashy; darker above. Under parts and rump white.

Length, 28 inches; wing, 10.90; tarsus, 3.50; bill above, 6.80.

Hab.—South America and West Indies. Very rare or accidental in the United States.

The occurrence of this *Ibis* as a North American bird is very problematical, the instances in which it has been observed being very rare. Mr. Audubon saw it but once, when a flock of three passed high over his head in Louisiana.

Catal. No.	Locality.	Whence obtained.
2736	South America............	S. F. Baird ....
1967	......do...................	......do...................

IBIS ALBA, Vieillot.

White Curlew; White Ibis; Spanish Curlew.

Tantalus albus, LINN. Syst. Nat. I, 1766, 242.—GM. I, 651.—LATHAM, Ind. Orn. II, 1790, 705.—WILSON, Am.
Orn. VIII, 1814, 43 ; pl. lxvi.

Ibis alba, VIEILLOT, Dict.—ORD. ed. Wilson, VIII.—BON. Obs. 1825, 179.—IB. List, 1838.—NUTTALL, Man. II,
1834, 86.—AUD. Orn. Biog. III, 1835, 178 : V, 1839, 593 ; pl. 222.—IB. Syn. 257.—IB. Birds
Amer. VI, 1843, 54 ; pl. 360.

Eudocimus albus, WAGLER, Isis, 1832, 1232.—BONAP. Consp. II, 1855, 156.—GUNDLACH, Cab. Jour. IV, 1856, 348.
" *Paribis albus*, Is. GEOFFR.".

Tantalus coco, JACQUIN, Beit. 1784, 13.—GMELIN, I, 1788, 652.

" *? Ibis brevirostris*, PEALE."

White Ibis, PENNANT, LATHAM.—*White Curlew*, CATESBY.—*Brown Ibis*, PENN. LATH.

CH.—Anterior half of head bare ; the feathers not reaching, in the adult, further than the middle of the eye. Pure white ;
the tips of five outer primaries lustrous greenish black. Bill red ; the terminal half black ; in the young entirely red. Length,
25 inches ; wing, 11.25 ; tarsus, 3.75 ; bill, 7.

Hab.—South Atlantic and Gulf States ; straggling occasionally northward.

A young bird, (9501,) probably of this species, is olive brown above ; the rump and concealed
portion of the back, with the under parts white ; the head and neck brown, the feathers
streaked centrally with darker.   The head is feathered further forward ; the primaries, which
appear to be full grown, are shorter than the tertials ; the bill is much shorter than tarsus and
toes ; scarcely longer than in *I. ordii*, and without black tip.   A rather older specimen from
St. Simon's Island (9502) has the bill entirely yellow, without black tip or serrations.   The
plumage generally is white, with here and there the more immature brown color, as in the
quills, the edge of wings, streaks on the feathers of the neck, &c.   The face is feathered nearly
as far forward as in the glossy Ibis, the feathers extending anterior to the eye, and nearly to
the rami ; the orbital region bare.

Wagler, in Isis,[1] describes a white *Ibis* from Mexico, with the bill much longer and less
curved, and entirely red, instead of being tipped with black.

Catal. No.	Locality.	When collected.	Whence obtained.	Collected by—	Remarks.
1076	Liberty county, Ga.............	March, 1843	S. F. Baird	W. L. Jones	....
9502	St. Simon's island, Ga..........	....	J. P. Postell	....	....
9580	Indian river	....	G. Wurdemann....	....	Iris white.
9501	Brownsville, Tex..............	Oct. 25, 1853	Major Emory.......	A. Schott.........	....

[1] *Ibis longirostris*, WAGLER, Isis, 1829, 760.—IB. 1832, 1232.—GRAY, Gen. III, tab. 152.
Eudocimus longirostris, WAGLER, Isis, 1832, 1232.—BP. Consp. II, 1855, 157.

IBIS ORDII, Bonap.

Glossy Ibis.

?? *Tantalus mexicanus*, GMELIN, Syst. Nat. I, 1788, 652.

Tantalus mexicanus, ORD, J. A. N. Sc. I, 1817, 53.

Ibis falcinellus, BONAP. Obs. 1825, No. 199.—IB. Syn. 312.—IB. Am. Orn. IV, 1831, 23 ; pl. xxiii.—NUTTALL; Man. II, 1834, 88.—AUD. Orn. Biog IV, 1838, 608 ; pl. 387.—IB. Syn. 257.—IB. Birds Amer. VI, 1843, 50 ; pl. 358.

Ibis ordii, BONAP. List, 1838.

Falcinellus ordii, BONAP. Consp. II, 1855, 159.

? *Ibis guarauna*, WOODHOUSE, Sitgreaves' Exp. 1853, 98.

SP. CH.—Forehead feathered almost to the bill. Color chestnut ; the top of head and back metallic green, glossed with purple. Bill dusky ; the naked skin at base slate blue. Length, 20.50 inches ; wing, 10 ; tarsus, 3.30 ; bill above, 4.30.

Hab.—Found singly and at intervals over the whole United States.

General color, including the lesser wing coverts, opaque purplish orange chestnut brown. Top of head and nape, both sides of wing, (except the lesser coverts,) and the tail, metallic green, glossed variously with purple ; the interscapular region and anterior scapulars purple chestnut. The opaque feathers of the neck and head edged obscurely with dusky ; the bare skin of the head all round bordered by whitish. The bill is dusky in the skin ; in life it is said to be blackish ; the bare skin at the base slate blue. The feet grayish black.

Young specimens are similar, except that the head and neck are of an opaque dull greyish brown, the feathers more or less edged narrowly with whitish.

The synonomy of this species is in very great confusion, and it is difficult to say what name it should bear. Admitting it to be distinct from the European *Ibis falcinellus*, the earliest name for an American bird is *Tantalus guarauna*, of Linnaeus, which, however, is considered by Bonaparte to be distinct, and confined to South America. The *T. mexicanus* of Gmelin, referred to the same species by Bonaparte, seems to have as much claim to identity with the North American as with the more southern bird. The *T. chalcopterus* of Temminck belongs to the South American species. Setting aside *T. mexicanus* of Gmelin as too uncertain for the present case, the next name in order is the *ordi* of Bonaparte.

List of specimens.

Catal. No.	Sex.	Locality.	When collected.	Whence obtained.	Orig. No.	Collected by—	Length.	Stretch of wings.	Wing.	Remarks.
9503	......	Texas	....	Major Emory	.....	A. Schott	....	....	....	... .
4142	♀	Cadereita, Mex	April —, 1853	Lieut. Couch	......	....	24.00	34.00	10.25	Eyes crimson, bill slate.
5117	.....	Ojo del Cuerpo, N. M ..	Sept. 29, 1855	Capt. Pope.......	139	....	26.00	33.50	11.00	Eyes brown, bill black, gums reddish yellow, feet dark gray.
9506	♀	Frontera,RioGrande,Tex	....	Major Emory....	......	C. Wright.....	....	30.00	10.50	....
9504	......	Santa Cruza, Sonora..	June —, 1855	......do....	71	Dr. Kennerly....	....	....	....	....
		Fort Tejon, Cal.......	....	J. Xantus......	......	....	....	....	....	....
9505	......	San Francisco, Cal.....	Mar. 28, 1854	Lieut. Whipple ..	196	Kenn. and Möll..	22.00	36.00	16.00	....
8069	.....	Mexico..............	Sept. —, 1836	J. Gould....	......	....	....	....	....	....

Family PLATALEIDAE.

Cʜ.—Bill completely depressed, very broad, and widening at the rounded tip.

No more detailed description is needed to characterize the spoon-bills, of which seven or eight species are described by authors.

PLATALEA, L.

Platalea, Lɪɴɴ. Syst. Nat. 1735. Type *Platalea leucorodia*. (Gray.)

Cʜ.—Bill very broad, excessively depressed, and spatulate or greatly widened to the rounded tip; the mandibles in close apposition; the edges not lamellar. Head bald in the adult American species. Legs rather shorter than in typical herons; tibia and tarsi covered throughout with small hexagonal scales; the former bare for nearly one-half. Toes webbed at the base; the outer longer than the inner; the middle claw not pectinated. Middle toe nearly as long as the tarsus; hind toe rather long.

Comparative measurements.

Catal. No.	Species.	Locality.	Age.	Length.	Wing.	Tail.	Tarsus.	Middle toe.	Its claw.	Bil above.	Along gape.	Specimen measured.
2734	Platalea ajaja............	Florida....................	......	32.50	15.00	4.70	3.96	3.64	0.56	6.60	6.15	Skin ......
4273	......do.................	Cacasieu Pass, La.........	○	....	14.00	5.26	4.28	3.76	0.55	7.00	6.60	Skin ......

PLATALEA AJAJA, Linn.

Rosy Spoon-bill.

Platalea ajaja, Lɪɴɴ. I, 1766, 231.—Gᴍᴇʟɪɴ, I, 614.—Wɪʟsᴏɴ, Am. Orn. VII, 1813, 123; pl. lxii, (two years old.)— Bᴏɴ. Obs. 1825, No. 185.—Iʙ. Conspectus, II, 1855, 146.—Nᴜᴛᴛᴀʟʟ, Man. II, 1834, 79—Wᴀɢʟᴇʀ, Isis, 1831, 530.—Aᴜᴅ. Orn. Biog. IV, 1838, 188, pl. 131.—Iʙ. Syn.—Iʙ. Birds Amer. VI, 1843, 72; pl. 362.—Gᴜɴᴅʟᴀᴄʜ, Cab. Jour. IV, 1856, 347.

Platea incarnatá, Sʟᴏᴀɴ, Hist. Jam. II, 316.

Roseate spoon-bill, Lᴀᴛʜᴀᴍ.

Adult.—Head all round and nape naked. General color rosy red; paler anteriorly, and nearly white on the neck. Lesser wing coverts, with upper and lower tail coverts and lower part of throat, intense carmine. Tail feathers brownish ochre yellow. Naked skin of head yellowish green. Bill mostly greenish blue in life.

Younger with the head feathered, except around the base of the bill, and around and a little behind the eye. Similar in color, but the carmine wanting and the tail rosy.

Length, 30 inches; wing, 15; tarsus, 4; bill above, 7.

Hab.—South Atlantic and Gulf States.

List of specimens.

Catal. No.	Locality.	When collected.	Whence obtained.	Collected by—
......	Florida? -----------------	----------	S. F. Baird ----------------	J. J. Audubon ----------------
4273	Calcasieu pass, La ------------	1854	G. Wurdemann ----------------	----------------------------
9499	Lower Rio Grande, Tex..........	1853	Major Emory -----------------	A. Schott....................
9498	Rio Grande, Tex --------------	1843	----do----------------------	----do----------------------

Family PHOENICOPTERIDAE.

Cʜ.—Legs and neck excessively elongated. Bill with the edges lamellated or denticulated, and bent abruptly in the middle. Toes fully webbed.

The precise position of this remarkable family is a matter of some uncertainty, some authors placing it with the *Anseres*, on account of its webbed feet and lamellar bill, while others keep it in the *Grallae*. I am inclined to think that its affinities are more with the *Anseres* ; at least, it seems less out of place there than in the other sub-order. Should the statement to Mr. Audubon be correct, that the young betake themselves to the water immediately on breaking the shell, it will almost settle the question by placing it in the sub-class *Praecoces*, and, consequently, with the *Anseres*.

PHOENICOPTERUS, Linn.

Phoenicopterus, Lɪɴɴ. 1748. Type *Phoenicopterus ruber*, L. (Gray.)

Cʜ.—Neck and feet excessively lengthened. Bill duck-like, bent abruptly downward in the middle ; the opposed edges of both mandibles lamellar. Tibia denuded for the inferior two-thirds ; the anterior two-thirds of both tibia and tarsus enveloped by one series of broad scutellae ; the circumference completed by a smaller posterior series. Toes one-fourth the tarsus, connected as far as the claws by a thickened membrane. Claws short, broad, blunt. Hind toe very small, elevated ; sometimes wanting.

There is a soft skin at the base of the bill which extends around and behind the eye.

Comparative measurements.

Catal. No.	Species.	Locality.	Sex.	Length.	Stretch of wings.	Wing.	Tail.	Tarsus.	Middle toe.	Its claw.	Bill above.	Along gape.	Specimen measured.	Remarks.
8695	Phoenicopterus ruber ..	Indian Key, Fla..	♂	....	......	... ..	6.70	12.20	3.50	0.38	5.90	5.00	Skin	Moulting ..
do.	..........do............	......do........	......	48.00	66.00	16.50	....	....	....	....	....	......	Fresh ...	....
8697	..........do............	......do........	♂	....	......	......	6.30	12.20	3.30	0.38	5.70	5.00	Skin	Moulting ..
do.	..........do............	......do........	......	48.00	66.00	16.50	....	....	....	....	....	......	Fresh ...	....
8696	..........do............	......do... ...	♀	....	......	......	5.60	11.50	3.20	0.35	6.00	5.00	Skin ...	Moulting ..
do.	..........do............	......do........	......	42.00	64.50	15.50	......	....	....	....	......	......	Fresh ...	....

PHOENICOPTERUS RUBER, Linn.

Flamingo.

Phoenicopterus ruber, Lɪɴɴ. Syst. Nat. I, 1766, 230, (in part.)—Gᴍᴇʟɪɴ, I, 612.—Wɪʟsoɴ, Am. Orn. VIII, 1814, 45 ; pl. lxvi.—Bon. Obs. 1825, No. 236.—Iʙ. Am. Orn. III, 1828, 101.—Iʙ. List, 1838.—Iʙ. Consp. II, 1855, 145.—Nᴜᴛᴛᴀʟʟ, Man. II, 1834, 70.—Aᴜᴅ. Orn. Biog. V, 1839, 255 ; pl. 431.—Iʙ. Syn. 269.—Iʙ. Birds Amer. VI, 1843, 169, pl. 375.

Sᴘ. Cʜ.—Hind toe moderate. Size very large. Color bright scarlet red ; deepest on the wings. Quills black. Legs red. Bill yellow ; black from the bent portion. Length, 45 inches ; wing, 16.50 ; tarsus, 12 ; bill above, (along curve,) 5.90.

Hab.—Warmer parts of America. Rare on the Florida Keys.

List of specimens.

Catal. No.	Sex.	Locality.	When collected.	Whence obtained.	Length.	Stretch of wings.	Wing.	Remarks.
8697	♂	Indian Key, Fla.....	....	G. Wurdemann	48.00	66.00	16.50	Moulting....
8698	♂	......do...........	....	......do............	48.00	66.00	16.50	....do......
8696	♀	......do...........	....	......do............	42.00	64.50	15.30	....do......
8695	♂	......do...........	August 6, 1857	......do............	48.00	66.00	16.50	....do......

GRALLAE.

Cн.—Feathers of the head and neck extending over the entire cheeks to the bill. Bill, when much longer than head, slender at the base; sometimes thick and shorter than the head. Young running about and feeding themselves as soon as hatched.

The preceding characteristics indicate, in a general way, the characteristics of the *Grallae* as distinguished from the *Herodiones*. They are usually much smaller birds, and more especially inhabitants of the open sandy shore. Few or none of the species nest on trees or bushes, the eggs being generally laid in a cavity scooped out in the sand.

The sub-order is divided by Bonaparte into two tribes, *Cursores* and *Alectorides*, (by Burmeister into *Limicolae* and *Paludicolae*,) the first having the hind toe elevated, small, or wanting, the second having it lengthened and inserted on a level with the rest. Additional characters are as follows:

Limicolae.—Species living on the shore, and generally probing the ground or mud in search of food. Bill and legs generally lengthened and slender. Bill hard at tip, softer and more contracted at base. Anterior toes connected at base more or less by membranes, and with very short claws. Hind toe very short, elevated, or wanting. Wings long, pointed; outer primaries longest, and reaching to or beyond the tip of tail, which is stiff.

Paludicolae.—Species living in marshy places among the grass, feeding from the surface of the ground. Bill hard to its base, where it is not contracted. Toes cleft to the base, lengthened, with very long claws. Hind toe lengthened, and on same level with the rest. Wing short, rounded, not reaching the tip of the soft tail; outer primaries graduated.

Tribe LIMICOLAE.

Cн.—Birds living on the shore or in open places, usually small species, with rounded or depressed bodies, and slender bills of variable length, having a more or less distinct horny terminal portion, the remainder covered with soft skin, in which are situated the elongated, narrow, open, and distinct nostrils. The feathers of the head are small, and extend compactly to the base of the bill; they are similar in character to those of the neck and body. The wings are long, acute, and when folded reaching to or beyond the tip of the tail. The posterior or inner secondaries are generally as long as the outer primaries. The primaries are ten in number; the three outer longest and about equal. The tail is stiff, short, broad, and rounded or graduated; the feathers usually twelve, sometimes more. The legs are slender and delicate, but corresponding with the bill in proportions. A large portion of the tibia below is bare of feathers. The covering of the legs is parchment-like, not horny, generally divided anteriorly and behind into small half rings, laterally more in hexagons. The claws are delicate, sharp, and gently curved. The hind toe is very small, scarcely touching the ground; sometimes wanting. There is usually (except in *Calidris*, *Tringa*, &c.) a rather broad basal membrane between the outer and middle toes, sometimes between the inner and middle; this web occasionally extends toward the ends of the toes.

In the prececeding diagnosis, borrowed, like that of *Paludicolae*, from the admirable work of Burmeister, I have given the most prominent characters of this tribe. By Bonaparte it is divided into 1. *Otididae*; 2. *Charadrididae*; 3. *Glareolidae*; 4. *Thinocoridae*; 5. *Haematopo-didae*; 6. *Chionididae*; 7. *Dromadidae*; 8. *Recurvirostridae*; 9. *Phalaropodidae*; and 10. *Scolopacidae*. Of these, however, the 1st, 3d, 4th, 6th, and 7th have no representatives within our limits, leaving the remaining five to be defined as follows:

A. Nostrils reaching usually to the end of basal third or half of the commissure ; oval, short. Bill contracted about the nostrils, where the culmen is more or less indented. Nasal groove closed obtusely and abruptly, or shallowing out broadly to the end. Hind toe generally wanting ; neck short and thick.

CHARADRIDAE.—Bill rather cylindrical, as long as the head, or shorter ; the culmen much indented opposite the nostrils, the vaulted apex more or less swollen and rising, quite distinct from the membranous portion. Legs elevated ; hind toe rarely present, and then rudimentary ; the outer and middle toes more or less united by membrane.

HAEMATOPODIDAE.—Bill as long as the head, or twice as long, compressed ; culmen but little indented, and the bill not vaulted beyond the nostrils, which are quite basal.

B. Nostrils narrow and fissured, not reaching beyond the basal fourth of the commissure. The bill attenuated and linear beyond the nostrils, not compressed nor indented around them. The nasal groove running out into a narrow, acute channel to or beyond the middle of the jaw, just above the edge of the bill ; the forehead narrowed and depressed to the bill.

RECURVIROSTRIDAE.—Legs covered with hexagonal plates, becoming smaller behind. Anterior toes all connected more or less by membrane. Bill much lengthened and attenuated ; the groove along the side of the upper mandible not extending beyond the middle. Gums denticulated only at the base.

PHALAROPODIDAE.—Feathers of breast compact, duck-like. Legs with transverse scutellae before and behind. Toes to the tips with a lateral margin, more or less indented at the joints, the hinder with a feeble lobe. Bill equal to or longer than the head, the lateral groove extending nearly to the tip.

SCOLOPACIDAE.—Legs with transverse scutellae before and behind, as in the last family, (except in *Numenieae*.) Toes not margined broadly to the tips, with or without basal membrane ; hind toe generally present. Bill generally longer than the head, the groove extending beyond the middle.

The determinations and descriptions of the species of *Grallae* in the following pages, with their synonymy, have been prepared by Mr. John Cassin.

August 2, 1858.
87 b

Family CHARADRIDAE.

This family is divided by Bonaparte into the three sub-families *Oedicneminae*, *Charadrinae*, and *Cursorinae;* but as the first and last are not represented in North America, there is no occasion to present them here. They are readily distinguished from the *Charadrinae* by well marked characters.

The characters of the *Charadrinae* are sufficiently well expressed in the diagnosis of the family already given. The wings when folded reach beyond the tail. The head is very large, the neck short, and nearly as thick as the head. The bill in size and shape has, in some instances, quite a close resemblance to that of the doves. The legs, as a general rule, have no hind toe, except in *Squatarola*. The middle and outer toes are connected at the base by a membrane.

CHARADRIUS, Linnaeus.

Charadrius, LINN. Syst. Nat. 1735.   Type *C. pluvialis*, L.

CH.—Plumage yellowish gray, spotted.   Tail transversely banded.   No collar on neck.   Tarsi and lower thighs uniformly reticulated.   Color of legs bluish green.

CHARADRIUS VIRGINICUS, Borck.

Golden Plover; Bull-head.

Charadrius pluvialis, WILSON, Am. Orn. VII, 1813, 71 ; pl. lix.—Sw. F. Bor. Am. II, 1831, 623.—NUTTALL, Man. II, 1834, 16.—AUD. Orn. Biog. III, 1835, 623.   (Not of Linnaeus.)
Charadrius virginicus, " BORCKHAUSEN and BECHSTEIN." LICHT. Verz. Doubl. 1823, No. 729.
Charadrius virginicus, " BORKH. Mus. Berolin."—MEYEN, Nova Acta, K. L. C. Akad. XVI, Suppl. 1834, 106; pl. xviii.
Charadrius marmoratus, WAGLER, Syst. Av. 1827, No. 42.—AUD. Orn. Biog. V, 1839, 575 ; pl. 300.—IB. Syn. 222— IB. Birds Am. V, 1842, 203 ; pl. 316.
?*Charadrius pectoralis*, VIEILL. Nouv. Dict. XXVII, 1819, 145.
Charadrius xanthocheilus, JARD. Ill. Orn. II, pl. lxxxv.

FIGURES.—WILSON, Am. Orn. VII, pl. 59, fig. 5.—AUD. B. of Am. pl. 300, Oct. ed. V, pl. 316.—MEYEN, Nova Acta, XVI, Supp. pl. 18.

SP. CH.—Bill rather short, legs moderate, wings long, no hind toe, tarsus covered before and behind with small circular or hexagonal scales.   Upper parts brownish black, with numerous small circular and irregular spots of golden yellow, most numerous on the back and rump, and on the upper tail coverts, assuming the form of transverse bands, generally ; also with some spots of ashy white.   Entire under parts black, with a brownish or bronzed lustre, under tail coverts mixed or barred with white.   Forehead, border of the black of the neck, under tail coverts and tibiæ, white ; axillary feathers cinereous ; quills, dark brown ; middle portion of the shafts white, frequently extending slightly to the webs and forming longitudinal stripes on the shorter quills ; tail dark brown, with numerous irregular bands of ashy white, and frequently tinged with golden yellow ; bill, black ; legs, dark bluish brown.   *Younger.*—Under parts dull ashy, spotted with brownish on the neck and breast, frequently more or less mixed with black ; many spots of the upper parts dull ashy white ; other spots, especially on the rump, golden yellow.
Total length about 9½ inches ; wing, 7 ; tail, 2½ inches.

Hab. All of North America, South America, Northern Asia, Europe.

This bird, well known throughout the United States as the Bull-head, Field Plover, or Golden Plover, appears to be one of the species that inhabit, at various seasons, the entire continent of America; rearing its young in the north, and wandering at other seasons to the extreme southern regions, and visiting also other continents. It has been found occasionally in Europe, and bears a very strong resemblance to a species of that continent, *Charadrius pluvialis;* in fact, so close is the similarity that the color of the axillary feathers is the most ready distinction for recognition, white, in *C. pluvialis;* ashy, *C. virginicus.*

This species varies somewhat in the colors of its plumage, and it is rare to meet with specimens, in the middle or southern States of this republic, in the full plumage of the nuptial season or with the under parts pure black, though frequently spotted, and showing a tendency to that color. It is of common occurrence throughout the United States.

List of specimens.

Catal. No.	Sex.	Locality.	When collected.	Whence obtained.	Collected by—	Length.	Stretch of wings.	Wing.	Remarks.
1183	♂	Carlisle, Penn..........	Oct. 3, 1843	S. F. Baird.........	....	10.40	21.75	7.08	....
744	♂	.....do...............	Sept. 23, 1842	......do.............	....	10.75	22.75	6.75	....
745	♂	.....do........	......do......	......do............	....	10.25	22.25	7.00	....
1706	♂	.....do...............	Sept. 24, 1844	......do.............	....	10.72	23.00	7.33	....
10408	......	Union county, Ill	April 21......	N. W. University....	R. Kennicott...	....	....	....	....
8679	......	Hudson's bay..........	June 16......	John Gould..........	....	....	....	....	....
5425	♂	15 miles below Ft. Pierre	....	Lieut. Warren	Dr. Hayden....	10.50	22.25	7.00	Iris brown ....
5427	......	Nebraska.............	....	......do.............	.....do.........	10.75	22.00	7.00	....
5426	.....	Fort Berthold, Neb....	Sept. 16, 1856	......do.............	.....do.........	10.25	21.25	7.00	....
4551	......	Fort Pierre, Neb.......	Oct. 21, 1855	......do.............	.....do.........	....	....	....	....
6579	......	St. Mary's Mission, Rocky mountains.	Oct. 1, 1853	Gov. Stevens	Dr. Suckley....	9.75	21.75	9.25	....
6580	......	.. ..do.............	......do......	......do.............	.....do.........	.... ..	....	....	....
5090	......	Indianola, Texas.......	Mar. 15, 1856	Capt. Pope	....	....	....	....	....
4180	......	Tamaulipas, Mexico....	....	Lieut. Couch	....	....	....	....	Eyes dark brown; feet dark slate.
1834	♂	India...............	....	S. F. Baird...........	....	....	....	....	....
1853	......	France	....	......do.............	....	....	....	....	....

AEGIALITIS, B o i e .

Aegialitis, Boie, Isis, 1822, 558. Type *Charadrius hiaticula,* L.

Aegialites, Kaup, 1829.

Cн.—Plumage more or less uniform, without spots. Neck and head generally with dark bands. Front of the legs with plates arranged vertically, of which there are two or three in a transverse series.

This genus, as far as North America is concerned, is distinguished from *Charadrius* by the generally lighter color and greater uniformity of the plumage ; by the absence of continuous black on the belly, and by the presence of dusky bands on the neck or head ; the size is smaller. The tarsi, in most species, have the front plates larger and conspicuously different in this respect from the posterior ones.

Oxyechus, Reich.[1]

AEGIALITIS VOCIFERUS, (Linn.) Cassin.

Kill-deer.

Charadrius vociferus, Linn, Syst. Nat. I, 1766, 253—Wils Am. Orn. VII, 1813, 73; fig. pl. lix.—Nutt. Man. II, 22.—Aud. Orn. Biog. III, 1835, 191: V, 577; pl. 225 —Ib. Syn. 222.—Ib. Birds Am. V, 1842, 207, pl. 317.

A·gialtes vociferus, Bon. List, 1838.

Oxyechus vociferus, Reich. Syst. Av. 1853, pl. xviii.

Charadrius torquatus, Linn. Syst. Nat. I, 1766, 255.

Charadrius jamaicensis, Gm. I, 1788, 685.

Figures.—Catesby's Carolina, Birds, pl. 71.—Buff. Pl. Enl. 286 —Wilson's Am. Orn. VII, pl. 59, fig. 6.—Aud. B. of Am. pl. 225, oct. ed. V. pl. 317.

Sp. Ch.—Wings long, reaching to the end of the tail, which is also rather long. Head above and upper parts of body light brown with a greenish tinge, rump and upper tail coverts rufous, lighter on the latter. Front and lines over and under the eye, white, another band of black in front above the white band; stripe from the base of the bill towards the occiput, brownish black; ring encircling the neck and wide band on the breast, black; throat white, which color extends upwards around the neck; other under parts white. Quills brownish black with about half of their inner webs white, shorter primaries with a large spot of white on their outer webs, secondaries widely tipped or edged with white. Tail feathers pale rufous at base; the four middle, light olive brown tipped with white and with a wide subterminal band of black; lateral feathers widely tipped with white. Entire upper plumage frequently edged and tipped with rufous. Very young, have upper parts light gray with a longitudinal band on the head and back black; under parts white. Total length about 9½ inches, wing 6½; tail 3½ inches.

Hab.—North America to the Arctic regions, Mexico, South America.

From its peculiar note, the "Killdeer" is one of the few birds of our country known to all classes and ages of the people. It is common throughout North America, wandering apparently in the winter season into the southern division of this continent, and to the islands of both the Atlantic and Pacific oceans.

List of specimens.

Catal. No.	Sex and age.	Locality.	When collected.	Whence obtained.	Orig'l No.	Collected by—	Length.	Stretch of wings.	Wing.	Remarks.
1871	♂	Carlisle, Pa..........	April 7, 1844	S. F. Baird	.....	....	10.00	20.00	6.25	....
7601	....	Washington, D. C.....	....	Wm. Hutton......	.....	....	.....	.....	.....	
5429	....	Fort Pierre	....	Lt. Warren	.....	Dr. Hayden.....	9.50	20.00	6.75	....
9054	♂	Loup Fork............	....	......do........	.....	...do........	10.00	20.50	6.25	Iris brown; feet greenish; bill black.
9058	♀	......do...........	July 30, 1857	......do.......	.....	......do.........	10.75	20.50	7.00	......do.......
8188	♂	Shawnee river, K. T...	......do....	Wm. M. Magraw...	.....	Dr. Cooper	11.25	20.25	6.75	......do.......
C591	....	Cedar creek, Neb	June 24......	Lt. Warren	.....	Dr. Hayden......	9.75	18.75	6.50	....
4646	....	White river, Neb......	May 12, 1856	Col. Vaughan......	.....	......do..........	.....	.....	.....	
5428	♂	Mouth of Yellowstone..	....	Lt. Warren........	.....	......do........	10.00	21.25	6.87	....
5752	♂	Platte river, Neb.......	July 19, 1856	Lt. Bryan..........	122	W. S. Wood.......	.....	.....	.....	
5751	♂	Medicine Bow, Neb	Aug. 10, 1856	......do........	239	......do.........	.....	.....	.....	
5756	○ ○	Platte river, Neb.......	July 19, 1856	......do........	126	......do.........	.....	.....	.....	
5753	♀	Bryan's Fork, 115 miles W. of Fort Riley.	July 3, 1856	......do........	61	...... do.........	.....	.....	.....	
5755	○ ○ ♂	Laramie river..........	Aug. —, 1856	......do........	213	......do.........	.....	.....	.....	
3707	....	Salt Lake	Mar. —, 1850	Capt. Stansbury....	.....	....	.....	.....	.....	
5093	....	Permanent camp, N. M.	....	Capt. Pope	122	....	11.00	20.50	7.00	....
4181	♂	Near Matamoras, Mex..	....	Lt. Couch	.....	....	9.00	19.00	6.25	....
4958	....	Ft. Chadbourne, Tex...	....	Dr. Swift, U.S.A...	.....	A. Schott.........	.....	.....	.....	
6594	....	Eagle Pass, Tex.... ...	....	Maj. Emory........	.....	....	.....	.....	.....	
6590	....	Camp 121, N. M......	... .	Lt. Whipple........	.....	Kennerly & Möllhausen.	.....	.....	.....	
6583	....	Boca Grande, Mex.....	Mar. —, 1855	Maj. Emory........	36	Dr. Kennerly.....	.....	.....	.....	
6588	♂	Los Angelos Valley....	....	Lt. Williamson.....	.....	Dr. Heermann....	.....	.....	.....	
....	....	Fort Tejon, Cal.......	....	J. Xantus de Vesey.	.....	....	.....	.....	.....	
6586	....	San Francisco, Cal....	....	R. D. Cutts........	.....	....	.....	.....	.....	
6589	....	Bodega, Cal..........	Dec. —, 1854	Lt. Trowbridge	.....	T. A. Szabo.......	.....	.....	.....	
6587	....	Ft. Steilacoom, W. T...	....	Gov. Stevens	.....	Dr. Suckley.......	.....	.....	.....	
5985	....	......do...........	....	Dr. Cooper........	.....	....	.....	.....	.....	
6585	♂	......do...........	....	Dr. Suckley........	366	....	9.40	18.80	.....	
6592	....	......do...........	Dec. —, 1826	Gov. Stevens	8	Dr. Suckley	10.12	20.00	.....	

[1] *Oxyechus*, Reich. Syst. Av. 1853, Introd. xviii.

AEGIALITIS MONTANUS, (Towns.) Cassin.

Mountain Plover.

Charadrius montanus, Towns, J. A. N. Sc. VII, 1837, 192.—Ib. Narr. 1839 349.—Aud. Orn. Biog. IV, 1838, 362; pl. 350.—Ib. Syn. 223.—Ib. Birds Am. V, 1842, 213; pl. 318.

Aegialtes montanus, Bon. List, 1838.

Sp. Ch.—Forehead, stripe over the eye, and entire under parts, white, generally tinged with dull yellowish and ashy on the breast. Another band of black in front above the white band; back of the neck and sides dull brownish fulvous; other upper parts ashy brown, usually with many feathers edged and tipped with fulvous or rufous; upper tail coverts lighter. Quills dark brown with their shafts white, tail brown with a wide subterminal band of brownish black and tipped with white. Shorter primaries with a white space on their outer webs, forming a patch of white on the wing; under wing coverts and axillary feathers pure silky white. Bill black, legs yellow. Younger, without the black band in front, and with the white band tinged with dull yellow, entire upper parts with the feathers edged and tipped with dull ashy rufous. Total length, about 9 inches; wing, 6; tail, 3 inches.

Hab.—Western North America.

This bird is only known to inhabit the western countries of North America. Like other species of this group it migrates very probably into South America.

List of specimens.

Catalogue number.	Sex.	Locality.	When collected.	Whence obtained.	Orig. No.	Collected by—	Length.	Stretch of wings.
9043	......	Loup fork of Platte, Neb..	....	Lieut. Warren	......	Dr. Hayden.....	......	......
9044	......	........do..............	....	......do..........	......	......do.........	......	......
6596	......	Mouth of Milk river	....	Gov. Stevens	......	Dr. Suckley.....	......	......
5757	♂	North Platte	Aug. 12, 1856	Lieut. Bryan.......	251	W. S. Wood	8. 75	15. 50
7055	......	Pole creek, Neb.........	July 10, 1857	......do..........	267	......do.........	......	......
3709	......	Western Texas.........	....	J. W. Audubon ...	......	......	......	......
6595	......	Near 32° latitude	....	Capt. Pope........	......	......	......	......
6597	......	Mimbres to Rio Grande...	....	Dr. Henry........	......	......	......	......
6599	♂	Los Angeles	....	Lieut. Williamson.	......	Dr. Heermann ..	......	......
6598	♂	........do..............	....	......do..........	......	......do.........	......	......

Ochthodromus, Reich.[1]

AEGIALITIS WILSONIUS, (Ord.) Cassin.

Wilson's Plover.

Charadrius wilsonius, Ord, ed. Wilson's Orn. IX, 1825, 77; pl. lxxiii.—Nutt. Man. II, 1834, 21.—Aud. Orn. Biog. III, 1835, 73: V, 1839, 577; pl. 284.—Ib. Syn. 223.—Ib. Birds Am. V, 1842, 214; pl. 319.

Aegialtes wilsonius, Bon. List, 1838.

Octhodromus wilsonius, Reich. Syst. Av. Int. 1853, p. xviii.

Charadrius crassirostris, Spix, Av. Bras. II, 1825, 77; pl. xciv.

Figures.—Wilson, Am. Orn. IX, pl. 73, fig. 5.—Aud. B. of Am. pl. 219; oct. ed. V, pl. 319.

Sp. Ch.—Smaller than the preceding; bill rather long and robust. *Male.* Front and stripe over the eye and entire under

[1] *Ochthodromus*, Reich. Syst. Avium, p. xviii. Type *Charadrius wilsonius*, Ord. Smaller than *Aegialitis*. Bill longer and thicker. Tail short.

parts white. Front with a second band of black above the white band ; stripe from the base of the bill to the eye and wide transverse band on the breast, brownish black. Upper parts of head and body light ashy brown, with the feathers frequently edged and tipped with pale ashy. Back of the neck encircled with a ring of white, edged above with fine light reddish. Quills brown, with white shafts ; shorter coverts tipped with white ; outer feathers of the tail white, middle feathers dark brown. Bill black, legs yellow. *Female.* Without the band of black in front, and with the pectoral band dull reddish and light ashy brown.

Total length, 7¾ inches ; wing, 4½ ; tail, 2 inches.

Hab.—Middle and Southern States on the Atlantic, and the same coast of South America.

This plover is of frequent occurrence on the shores of the Atlantic, and is easily recognized by its stout and rather long bill and short tail. It migrates apparently into the southern division of this continent in the winter, and is undoubtedly the species described and figured by Spix as a bird of Brazil, as above cited.

List of specimens.

Catal. No.	Sex.	Locality.	When collected.	Whence obtained.	Collected by—	L'gth.	Stretch of wings.	Wing.
1144	♂	Cape May, N. J.	July 15, 1843	S. F. Baird	W. M. Baird	7. 50	14. 50	4. 80
1145	♀	do	July 17, 1843	do	do	7. 50	15. 50	4. 80

Aegialeus, Reichenbach.[1]

AEGIALITIS SEMIPALMATUS, (Bon.) Cab.

King Plover; Semipalmated Plover.

Charadrius semipalmatus, Bon. Obs. Wils. 1825, No. 219.—Ib. Syn. 1828, 296.—Ib. Am. Orn. IV, 1832, 92 ;
  pl. xxv.—Kaup, Isis, 1825, 1375 ; pl. xiv, (head and foot.)—Wagler, Syst. Av. 1827,
  No. 23.—Nuttall, Man. II, 24.—Sw. F. B. Am. II, 1831, 367.—Aud. Orn. Biog. IV,
  1838, 256 ; V, 579 ; pl. 330.—Ib. Syn. 224.—Ib. Birds Am. V, 1842, 218 ; pl. 320.
Aegialtes semipalmata, Bon. List, 1838.
Aegialitis semipalmatus, Cab. Cab. Journ. 1856, 425.
Aegialeus semipalmatus, Reich. Syst. Av. 1853, pl. xviii.
Tringa hiaticula, Wilson, Am. Orn. VII, 1813, 65 ; pl. lix.
Charadrius hiaticula, Ord, ed. Wils VII, 69.

Figures.—Wilson, Am. Orn. VII, pl. 59, fig. 3.—Aud. B. of Am. pl. 330 ; oct ed. V, pl. 320.—Bonap. Am. Orn. IV, pl. 25, fig. 4.

Sp. Ch.—Small, wings long, toes connected at base, especially the outer to the middle toe. Front, throat, ring around the neck, and entire under parts, white, a band of deep black across the breast, extending around the back of the neck below the white ring. Band from the base of the bill, under the eye, and wide frontal band above the white band, black. Upper parts light ashy brown, with a tinge of olive ; quills brownish black, with their shafts white in a middle portion, and occasionally a lanceolate white spot along the shafts of the shorter primaries ; shorter tertiaries edged with white ; lesser coverts tipped with white. Middle feathers of the tail ashy olive brown, with a wide subterminal band of brownish black, and narrowly tipped with white ; two outer tail feathers white, others intermediate, like the middle, but widely tipped with white. Bill orange yellow, tipped with black ; legs yellow. *Female* similar, but rather lighter colored. *Young* without the black band in front, and with the band across the breast ashy brown.

Total length, about 7 inches ; wing, 4¾ ; tail, 2¼ inches.

Hab.—The whole of temperate North America. Common on the Atlantic.

[1] *Aegialeus,* Reich. Syst. Av 185, p. xviii. Type *Charadrius semipalmatus,* Bon. Small, bill rather short. Tail and wings rather long.

This species considerably resembles *Hiaticula minor*, of Europe, and *H. torquata*, of the same continent also, with both of which it has been confounded. It is intermediate in size between the two, and, in fact, can only be distinguished from the former with some difficulty. It appears to inhabit the whole of North America.

List of specimens.

Catal. No.	Sex and age.	Locality.	When collected.	Whence obtained.	Collected by—	Length.	Stretch of wings.	Wing.	Remarks.
2379	○	Carlisle, Pa............	Aug. 16,1845	S. F. Baird........	....	......	......	......	....
2378	♂	......do..............	Aug. 16,1845	......do....	....	......	......	......	....
898	....	Coast of New Jersey ...	....	......do....	....	......	......	......	....
6602	....	Presidio, Cal....	May 4,1853	Lieut. Trowbridge..	....	8.00	15.00	7.50	....
5565	....	Petaluma, Cal.........	May 7,1856	E. Samuels........	....	7.25	13.40	5.00	....
6605	....	Shoalwater Bay	May 3,1854	Gov. Stevens......	Dr. Cooper	7.00	15.50	....	Iris brown, feet black ......
6437	....	Puget's Sound.....	....	A. Campbell........	Dr. Kennerly...	......	......	....	....

AEGIALITIS MELODUS, (Ord.) Cab.

Piping Plover.

Charadrius melodus, ORD, ed. WILS. VII, 1824, 71.—BON. Am. Orn. IV, 1832, 74 ; pl. xxiv.—NUTT. Man. II, 18.—AUD. Orn. Biog. III, 1835, 154 : V, 578 ; pl. 220.—IB. Birds Am. V, 142, 223 ; pl. 321.

Aegialtes melodus, BON. List, 1838.

Aegialitis melodus, CAB. Jour. 1856, 424.

Charadrius hiaticula, Var. WILS. Am. Orn. V, 1812, 30 ; pl. xxxvii.

Charadrius okeni, WAGLER, Syst. Av. 1827, No. 24.

FIGURES.—WILSON, Am. Orn. V, pl. 37, fig. 3.—BONAP. Am. Orn. IV, pl. 24, fig. 3.—AUD. B. of Am. pl. 220; oct. ed. V, pl. 321.

SP. CH.—About the size of the preceding ; bill short, strong. *Adult.* Forehead, ring around the back of the neck, and entire under parts, white, a band of black in front above the band of white ; band encircling the neck before and behind black, immediately below the ring of white on the neck behind. Head above and upper parts of body light brownish cinereous ; rump and upper tail coverts lighter, and often nearly white ; quills dark brown, with a large portion of their inner webs and shafts white ; shorter primaries with a large portion of their outer webs white ; tail at base white, and with the outer feathers white ; middle feathers with a wide subterminal band of brownish black, and tipped with white. Bill orange at base, tipped with black ; legs orange yellow. *Female.* Similar to the male, but with the dark colors lighter and less in extent. *Young.* No black band in front ; collar around the back of the neck ashy brown.

Total length, about 7 inches ; wing, 4½ ; tail, 2 inches.

Hab.—Eastern coast of North America. Nebraska, (Lieutenant Warren.) Louisiana, (Mr. G. Wurdemann.)

Specimens from the survey of Lt. Warren, collected by Dr. F. V. Hayden in the valley of the River Platte, are in plumage apparently perfectly mature, and one which has never been accurately described nor figured by any author. In these specimens the black ring around the neck is perfect in front, and very conspicuous in both males and females, though narrower and less distinct in the latter. Usually in specimens obtained on the Atlantic coast, the ring alluded to is interrupted in front and assumes the form of two large spots on the side of neck or upper part of the breast, in which plumage this bird has been described and figured by both Bonaparte and Audubon, as cited above. The figure by Wilson represents the more mature bird.

There are no specimens of this bird in the present collection from west of the Rocky mountains.

List of specimens.

Catal. No.	Sex.	Locality.	When collected.	Whence obtained.	Collected by—	Length.	Stretch of wings.	Wing.	Remarks.
1137	♂	Cape May, N. J........	July 13, 1843	S. F. Baird........	....	7.00	15.00	4.75	....
1138	♂	......do...............	July 14, 1843	......do......	....	6.88	14.50	4.75	....
557	....	New York..............	....	......do.,.....	....	. .....	....	....	....
4326	....	Calcasieu, La...	1854........	G. Wurdemann	....	.....	....	....	....
9028	♂	Loup fork of Platte	1857........	Lieut. Warren.. ...	Dr. Hayden..	7.50	15.75	4.87	Pupil black, iris dark brown..
9035	♂	......do...............	July 8......	...... do......	......do......	6.75	14.75	4.25	............do.... ....
9038	♀	......do...............	....do..	......do.......	......do......	6.50	14.50	4.50	............do.... ....
9039	♂	......do...............	....do...	......do........	......do......	7.50	15.12	4.60	....do............. ......
9034	♀	......do	....do....	......do..	......do......	7.25	15.25	4.75	............do........ .. ..

Leucopolius, Bonaparte.[1]

AEGIALITIS NIVOSA, Cassin.

Ch.—Small, belonging to the same group and somewhat resembling *Charadrius azarae* and *falklandicus* of authors. Bill straight, pointed, rather narrow ; wing moderate, first quill longest ; tail short ; legs moderate, rather slender.

Front, line over the eye, and entire under parts white ; subfrontal band black ; head above light brownish ashy, with a tinge of reddish yellow ; upper parts of body and wings light ashy brown, darker on the rump. Quills brownish black, with their shafts white ; some of the shorter primaries irregularly marked with white on their outer webs ; secondaries tipped with white, and some of the longer secondaries almost entirely white ; middle tail feathers brown, outer white ; bill dark ; legs light. A dark spot on each side of the breast, probably indicating a band across the breast in more mature plumage than the present specimen.

Total length about 6¼ inches ; wing, 3¾ ; tail, 1¼.

Hab.—Presidio (near San Francisco) California. (Lieut. W. P. Trowbridge.)

A single specimen of the bird now described is in Lieut. Trowbridge's collection from the coast of the Pacific, and appears to be a species not previously noticed by naturalists. It is of the same group subgenerically as *C. azarae* of South America, but is quite distinct from that or any other which has come under our notice. It is the first representative of the group to which it belongs yet discovered in the United States.

List of specimens.

Catal. No.	Locality.	When collected.	Whence obtained.
6600	Presidio, California ------------------	May 8, 1854------------	Lieut. Trowbridge ------------------

SQUATAROLA, Cuvier.

Squatarola, Cuvier, Règne Anim. I, 1817. Type *Tringa squatarola*, Linn.

Ch.—A rudimentary hind toe. Legs reticulated with elongated hexagons anteriorly, of which there are five or six in a transverse row ; fewer behind. First primary longest. Tail slightly rounded.

[1] *Leucopolius*, Bonap. Small ; bill shorter and more slender than in preceding ; wings and tail rather short.

SQUATAROLA HELVETICA, (Linn.) Cuv.

Black-bellied Plover.

Tringa helvetica, Linn. Syst. Nat. I, 1766, 250.

Squatarola helvetica, Cuv. R. A. 1817.

Charadrius helveticus, Licht. Verz. 1827, No. 728.—Aud. Orn. Biog. IV, 1838, 280 ; pl. 334.—Ib. Syn. 221.—Ib. Birds Amer. V, 1842, 199 ; pl. 315.

Tringa squatarola, Linn. Syst. Nat. I, 1766, 252.

Charadrius hypomelas, Pallas, Zoog. Ross. As. II, 1811, 138.

Charadrius pardela, Palla·, Zoog. Ross. As. II, 1811, 142.

Charadrius apricarius, Wilson, Am. Orn. VII, 1813, 41.

Squatarola cinerea, Cuv.

Squatarola wilsonii, Lichtenstein.

Figures.—Buffon, Pl. Enl. 853, 854, 923.—Wilson, Am. Orn. VII, pl. 57, fig. 4.—Aud. B. of Am. pl. 334 ; oct. ed. V, pl. 315.—Naumann, B. of Germany, pl. 178.—Gould, B. of Eur. IV, pl. 290.

Sp. Ch.—Bill and legs strong ; wings long ; a very small rudimentary hind toe. Around the base of the bill to the eyes, neck before and under parts of body, black ; upper white, nearly pure and unspotted on the forehead ; sides of the neck and rump tinged with ashy, and having irregular transverse bars of brownish black on the back, scapulars and wing coverts ; the brownish black frequently predominating on those parts, and the rump also frequently with transverse bars of the same. Lower part of the abdomen, tibia and under tail coverts, white. Quills brownish black, lighter on their inner webs, with a middle portion of their shafts white, and a narrow longitudinal stripe of white frequently on the shorter primaries and secondaries. Tail white, with transverse imperfect narrow bands of black. Bill and legs black. The black color of the under parts generally with a bronzed or coppery lustre, and presenting a scale-like appearance ; the brownish black of the upper parts with a greenish lustre. *Younger and winter plumage*. Entire upper parts dark brown, with circular and irregular small spots of white, and frequently of yellow, most numerous on the wing coverts ; upper tail coverts white. Under parts white, with short longitudinal lines and spots dark brownish cinereous on the neck and breast ; quills brownish black, with large longitudinal spots of white on their inner webs and also on the outer webs of the shorter primaries. *Young*. Upper parts lighter, and with the white spots more irregular or scarcely assuming a circular shape ; narrow lines on the neck and breast more numerous.

Total length about 11½ inches ; wing, 7½ ; tail, 3 inches.

Hab.—All of North America. The seacoasts of nearly all countries of the world.

This handsome plover is one of the most widely diffused of birds. It inhabits the seacoasts and districts on the borders of fresh or salt waters of all known countries within the temperate and tropical zones. The black parts of the plumage in this species, which are characteristic of the adult bird in spring, are more persistent than in *Ch. virginicus*, and much more frequently to be observed in specimens obtained in the middle and southern States.

This bird is the largest of the American species of this group.

We can find no characters distinguishing American specimens from those of any other country

August 3, 1858.

88 b

List of specimens.

Catal. No.	Sex.	Locality.	When collected.	Whence obtained.	Collected by—	Length.	Stretch of wings.	Wing.
1222	......	Philadelphia	....	S. F. Baird	....	....	....	....
546	......	New York	....	......do.........	....	....	....	....
10407	♂	Ft. Snelling, Min ..	....	Governor Stevens..	Dr. Suckley	12. 50	24. 25	9. 75
6578	......	......do.........	1853............	......do.........	......do.........	11. 50	24. 50	7. 25
5986	......	Shoalwater bay	....	......do.........	Dr. Cooper.......	....	....	....
2775	♂	Columbia river, O.T.	Oct. 21, 1836.	S. F. Baird.......	J. K. Townsend ...	....	....	....
6374	......	Ft. Steilacoom, W.T.	....	Governor Stevens..	Dr. Suckley.......	....	....	....
4241	......	San Francisco, Cal.	....	R. D. Cutts.......	....	....	....	....
6575	......	Bodega, Cal.......	Dec., 1854....	Lieut. Trowbridge.	T. A. Szabo.......	....	....	....
6577	......	San Diego, Cal	....	......do.........	......do.........	....	....	....

APHRIZA, Aud.

Aphriza, AUD. Orn. Biog. V, 1839. Type, *Tringa virgata*, Lath.

CH.—Bill shorter than the head. Nostrils elongated, and rather linear. Tarsi equal to the middle toe, (which is not united by membrane to lateral,) transversely scutellate anteriorly. Hind toe distinct. Tail even.

This genus, variously placed by authors, appears to be a true plover. Its hind toe and unarmed wing assimilate it to *Squatarola*, from which its short tarsi, free toes, and transverse scutellae in front of the tarsus readily distinguish it.

APHRIZA VIRGATA, (Gmelin.) Gray.

Surf Bird.

Tringa virgata, GMELIN, Syst. Nat. I, 1788, 674.—IB. Lath. Ind. II, 1790, 735.

Aphriza virgata, GRAY, Genera, III, 1847 : pl. cxlvii.

Tringa borealis, GM. Syst. Nat. I, 1788, 674.

Aphriza townsendi, AUD. Orn. Biog. V, 1839, 249; pl. 428.—IB. Syn. 226.—IB. Birds Am. V. 1842, 228; pl. 322.

SP CH.—Bill about as long as the head, rather thick at base; nostrils large, groove very distinct in the upper mandible; wings long; legs moderate; tail rather long. Entire upper parts dark brown, lighter on the wing coverts; head and neck with numerous spots and longitudinal stripes of dull white; upper tail coverts white. Quills brownish black, white at base; tips of greater coverts white; tail with its basal half white, terminated with brownish black. Under parts white, nearly pure on the abdomen, tinged with ashy on the neck and breast, and nearly every feather having a crescent or transverse stripe of brownish black. Bill brownish; under mandible yellow at base; legs dull green.

Total length about 10 inches; wing, 7; tail, 3.

Hab.—Pacific coast of North America? South America ; Sandwich Islands.

This is a bird long known as inhabiting the islands in the Pacific; but as entitled to a place in the North American fauna, resting entirely on the authority of the late Dr. Townsend, who is represented by Mr. Audubon as having obtained it at the mouth of the Columbia river. It is not contained in either of the collections made by the surveying parties.

Family HAEMATOPODIDAE.

The *Haematopodidae*, as characterized on a preceding page, includes but two North American genera—*Haematopus* and *Strepsilas*. *Aphriza*, by some placed with them, appear more properly to belong with the *Charadridae*.

The genera are readily distinguished as follows:

Haematopus.—Size large. Bill longer than the tarsus; much compressed. Hind toe wanting. Tarsus reticulated anteriorly. Middle and outer toes connected at base.

Strepsilas.—Size median. Bill shorter than the tarsus, which is scutellate anteriorly. Hind toe present. No basal membrane to the anterior toes.

HAEMATOPUS, Linn.

Haematopus, LINN. Syst. Nat. 1735. Type *H. ostralegus*, L.

CH.—Bill longer than the leg, twice as long as the head. Mandibles much compressed, sharp edged, and truncate at end Hind toe wanting. Legs reticulated, with five or six elongated plates in a transverse series. Meshes larger anteriorly. A basal membrane between middle and outer toes. Toes enlarged laterally by a thickened membrane. Tail even. First primary longest.

HAEMATOPUS PALLIATUS, Temm.

Oyster Catcher.

Haematopus palliatus, TEMM. Man. II, 1820, 532.—AUD. Orn. Biog. III, 1835, 181 : V, 580 ; pl. 223.—IB. Syn. 228.—IB. Birds Amer. V, 1842, 236 ; pl. 324.

Haematopus ostralegus, WILS. Am. Orn. VIII, 1814, 15 ; pl. lxiv. (Not of Linnaeus.)

Haematopus arcticus, JARD. ed. Wils. III, 1832, 35.

Haematopus hypoleucus, PALLAS, Zoog. Rosso-As. II, 1811, 129.

SP. CH.—Bill long, straight, flattened vertically ; wing long ; tail short ; legs moderate, rather robust ; toes margined ; outer and middle united at base. Head and neck brownish black, with a slight ashy tinge in very mature specimens. Upper parts of body light ashy brown, rather darker on the rump. Upper tail coverts and wide diagonal band across the wing white. Quills brownish black ; tail feathers at base white, with their terminating half brownish black. Under parts of body and under wing coverts white. Bill and edge of eyelids bright orange red. Legs pale reddish.

Total length, about 17½ inches ; wing, 10 ; tail, 4½ ; bill to gape, 3½ ; tarsus, 2¼ inches.

Hab.—Coast of the Atlantic ocean. States on the Pacific? Florida, (Dr. Wall.)

Between specimens obtained, in winter, in New Jersey, and European specimens stated to be also in the plumage of winter, there is certainly a very strong similarity, and, unfortunately, the comparisons of naturalists have apparently been made only from specimens of the two continents, representing plumages of quite different seasons. Were it not so, we suspect that there would be some difficulty in distinguishing the American *H. palliatus* from the European *H. ostralegus*.

There is no bird amongst the Waders at present the changes of the plumage of which may be studied with greater interest than the bird now before us. The only plumage known to us, and, as far as we can ascertain, to our cotemporaries, in American ornithology, is that described above, with the upper parts of the body light brown. By analogy with its near relative of Europe our bird has, however, very probably much darker plumage in summer, which, oddly enough, though at present unknown, appears to be figured by Wilson as cited above. The determining of the summer plumage of this bird is a problem of much interest.

We have no specimens from Western North America in the collections of the surveying expeditions.

List of specimens.

Catal. No.	Locality.	Whence obtained.
1206	New York	S. F. Baird
9301	Indian river, Florida	Dr. Wall, U. S. A

HAEMATOPUS NIGER, Pallas.

Bachman's Oyster Catcher.

Haematopus niger, PALLAS, Zoog. Rosso-Asiat. II, 1811, 131.
Haematopus bachmani, AUD. Orn. Biog. V, 1839, 245 ; pl. 427.—IB. Syn. 229.—IB. Birds Amer. V, 1842, 243 ; pl. 325.—TOWNSEND, Narr. 1839, 348.

SP. CH.—Rather smaller than the preceding ; bill rather more slender, wings long ; legs robust ; tarsi covered with ovate scales ; tail short. Head and neck brownish black, with a glaucous or ashy tinge in very adult specimens. All other parts of the plumage, above and below dark brown, rather darkest on the rump ; bill bright red ; legs pale reddish, nearly white.

Total length about 17 inches ; wing, 10½ ; tail, 4½ ; bill to gape, 3¼ ; tarsus, 2 inches.

Hab.—Western coast of the United States. Curile Islands, (Pallas.)

This bird appears to be restricted to the shores of western North America, and, according to Pallas, of northeastern Asia and the islands intermediate between the two continents. We have no doubt that the name given by the distinguished Russian naturalist just mentioned applies to the present species.

List of specimens.

Catal. No.	Sex.	Locality.	When collected.	Whence obtained.	Collected by—
10397	♀	Russian America	1845	S. F. Baird	Wossnessjensky
4625		San Miguel's island, Cal	June, 1856	Lieut. Trowbridge	

HAEMATOPUS ATER, Vieillot.

Haematopus ater, VIEILLOT, Galerie, II, 1825, 88 ; pl. ccxxx.
Haematopus niger, CUV. R. A. I, 1829, 504.
Haematopus townsendii, AUD. Orn. Biog. V, 1839, 247 ; pl. 427.—IB. Syn. 229.—IB. Birds Amer. V, 1842, 245 ; pl. 326.

FIGURES.—Voy. Uranie, Birds, pl. 34.

SP. CH.—Larger than either of the preceding ; bill straight, rather slender ; wings long ; legs shorter than in the preceding, very robust ; tarsi covered with small circular and hexagonal scales ; tail short. Entire plumage brownish black, lighter on the under parts of the body ; bill and eyelids bright red ; legs red. Total length about 18 inches ; wing, 10½ ; tail, 4½ ; bill to gape, 3¼ ; tarsus, 2 inches.

Hab.—Western coast of the United States? South America. Coast of Chili, (Lieut. Gilliss.)

It is not at all probable that this bird is entitled as yet to be regarded as belonging fauna of the United States, though so given by Mr. Audubon. It was described and figured by that distinguished ornithologist from specimens in Dr. Townsend's collection, which were, very probably, from Peru or Chili, where he collected on the route from Oregon to the United States. No one of the later observers and collectors have met with this bird at any locality in North America, and it ought very probably to be omitted from our ornithology. It is a well known species of South America.

This bird much resembles that immediately preceding, *H. niger*, Pallas, (which is *H. Bachmani*, Audubon,) but is constantly darker in color, and has the legs bright red. It is also slightly larger than either of the preceding. Excellent specimens of this species are in the National Museum, brought from Chile by Capt. Gilliss' U. S. Astronomical Expedition.

STREPSILAS, Illiger.

Strepsilas, ILLIGER, Prodromus, 1811. Type *Tringa interpres*, L.

CH.—Upper jaw with the culmen straight from the nasal groove to near the slightly upward bent tip; the bill tapering to a rather blunt point. No membrane between the anterior toes. Hind toe lengthened, touching the ground. Legs transversely scutellate anteriorly; reticulated laterally and behind. Tail rounded.

The nasal groove is very broad and shallow, obtuse anteriorly, and not extending beyond the middle of the bill. The lower edge of upper jaw ascends slightly from the middle to near the tip.

STREPSILAS INTERPRES, (Linn.) Ill.

Turnstone.

Tringa interpres, LINN. Syst. Nat. I, 1766, 248.—WILS. Am. Orn. VII, 1813, 32; pl. lvii.
Strepsilas interpres, ILLIGER, Prod. 1811, 263.—SW. F. Bor. Am. II, 1831, 371.—NUTT. II, 30.—AUD. Orn. Biog. IV, 1838, 31; pl. 304.—IB. Syn. 227.—IB. Birds Amer. V, 1842, 231; pl. 323.
Tringa morinella, LINN. I, 1766, 249. (Young.)
Strepsilas collaris, TEMM. Man. II, 553.
Charadrius cinclus, PALLAS.

FIGURES.—Buff. Pl. Enl. 856.—Vieill. Gal. II, pl. 237.—Wilson, Am. Orn. VII, pl. 57, fig. 1.—Aud. B. of Am. pl. 304; oct. ed. V, pl. 323.—Gould B. of Eur. pl. 318.

SP. CH.—Upper parts rather irregularly variegated with black, dark rufous and white. Head and neck above generally white, with numerous spots and stripes of brownish black on the crown and occiput; space in front of the eye white, usually surrounded with black; throat white, on each side of which is a stripe of black running from the base of the bill downwards and joining a large space of the same color (black) on the neck before and breast. Abdomen, under wing coverts, under tail coverts, back and rump, white. Quills brownish black, with their shafts white; tail white at base, with its terminal half brownish black, and tipped with white. Greater wing coverts widely tipped with white, forming a conspicuous oblique bar across the wing; bill black; legs orange. In winter the black of the upper parts is more apparent, and the rufous is of less extent and of lighter shade. Total length about 9 inches; wing, 6; tail, 2½ inches.

Hab.—Shores of the Atlantic and Pacific, throughout North America. One of the most widely diffused of birds, being found in nearly all parts of the world.

List of specimens.

Catal. No.	Sex.	Locality.	When collected.	Whence obtained.	Collected by—	Length.	Stretch of wings.	Wing.
10453	......	Cape May, N. J..........	....	J. K. Townsend...	....	....	......	.....
10452	......	.........do.........	....	.....do.........	....	....	......	.....
1692	......	Philadelphia............	1843.........	S. F. Baird.......	....	....	......	.....
4296	......	Calcasieu Pass, La.......	1854.........	G. Würdemann ...	....	....	......	.....
4187	......	Brownsville, Tex........	....	Capt. Van Vliet ...	....	9.00	18.00	6.00
4188	♂	Brazos Santiago, Tex.....	....	.......do.........	....	9.00	18.00	5.75
4189	♂	.........do............	....	.......do.........	....	9.50	19.25	6.25
1795	......	Vera Cruz, Mex..........	....	S. F. Baird.......	....	....	......	.....
6636	......	Shoalwater bay..........	May 17, 1854	Gov. Stevens.......	Dr. Cooper ...	....	......	.....

STREPSILAS MELANOCEPHALUS, Vigors.

Black Turnstone.

Strepsilas melanocephalus, VIGORS, Zool. Jour. IV, Jan. 1829, 356.—IB. Zool. Blossom, 1839, 29.—GAMBEL, J. A. N. Sc. 2d series, Aug. 1849, 220.

SP. CH.—About the size of and having the same general form as the preceding, but differing in color. Head, breast and upper parts of the body fuliginous brown, lighter on the breast, and with every feather having a darker centre ; back and wing coverts darker, frequently nearly black and with a greenish lustre ; lower part of back, rump, and upper tail coverts white, with a large spot of black on the upper coverts. Abdomen, under tail and under wing coverts white ; tips of greater wing coverts white, forming a band across the wing ; shorter tertiaries edged externally white. Bill black ; feet dark orange. Quills brownish black with their shafts white ; tail at base white, with its terminal half black, narrowly tipped with white.

Total length about 9 inches ; wing, 6 ; tail, 2½ inches.

Hab.—Western North America.

Though with various specimens before us in the present collection and from the Museum of the Philadelphia Academy, it is not without some misgivings that we admit this curious bird as a distinct species. It is of exactly the size and the same form as the preceding, and its only character is the prevalence of the dark color on the head, breast and upper parts, while several of the most reliable of the specific characters of the preceding are found also in the present bird. The lower part of the back and upper coverts of the tail and the abdomen are white in both, with the same large spot of black on the upper tail coverts. We find also in the museum of the Philadelphia Academy, a specimen from India, which is exactly this bird, and others apparently from Europe which approach it very nearly. The specimen from India came in the collection made by Capt. Boys, of the British army, and its locality is undoubted. This bird appears to be, however, only abundant in western North America.

List of specimens.

Catal. No.	Sex.	Locality.	When collected.	Whence obtained.	Orig'l No.	Remarks.
4624	....	San Miguel island, Cal....	January, 1856	Lieut. Trowbridge...	....	....
3946	♀	Monterey, Cal............	Aug. 16, 1847	W. Hutton....	....	Feet brown; iris hazel; bill black.
6667	....	Fort Steilacoom, Cal.....	1856..........	Dr. Buckley....	566	....
6666	....	.......do..............	Aug. 29, 1856	.......do.........	565	....
6665	....	.......do..............	.......do......	.......do.........		..........--....-.....

Family RECURVIROSTRIDAE.

The *Recurvirostridae*, in addition to the features already mentioned, are essentially char
acterized by the excessive length of the legs, with a very long, slender neck and slender
elongated bill. Of the several genera assigned the family, but two belong to the United
States, with the following features :

RECURVIROSTRA.—Hind toe present. Toes webbed to the claws. Bill recurved at tip.

HIMANTOPUS.—Hind toe wanting. A short web between middle and outer toes at base. Bill
straight.

RECURVIROSTRA, Linnaeus.

Recurvirostra, LINN. Syst. Nat. 1744. Type *R. avocetta*, L. (GRAY.)

CH.—Hind toe rudimentary ; anterior toes united to the claws by a much emarginated membrane. Bill depressed, extended
into a fine point, which is recurved. Tail covered by the wings.

RECURVIROSTRA AMERICANA, Gm.

American Avoset.

Recurvirostra americana, GM. Syst. Nat. I, 1788, 693.—WILS. Am. Orn. VII, 1813, 126.—SW. F. Bor. Am. II, 1831,
375.—NUTT. Man. II, 78.—AUD. Orn. Biog. IV, 1838, 168 ; pl. 318.—IB. Syn. 252.—IB.
Birds Amer. VI, 1843, 247 ; pl. 353.

Recurvirostra occidentalis, VIGORS, Zool. Jour. IV, 1829, 356.—IB. Zool. Blossom, 1839, 2⅜ ; pl. xii.—WAGLER, Isis,
1831, 520.—BAIRD, Zool. Stansbury, Salt Lake, 1852.—CASSIN, Illust. I, VIII, 1855,
232, pl. xl.

FIGURES.—Wilson, Am. Orn. VII, pl. 63, fig. 2. Aud. B. of Am. pl. 318 ; oct. ed. vi. pl. 353. Latham, Synopsis, V,
pl. 92. Leach, Zool. Misc. II, pl. 101. Voy. Blossom, Birds, pl. 12. Cassin, B. of Cal. and Texas, pl. 40. (Young.)

SP. CH.—Bill rather long, depressed ; wings long ; legs long ; tarsi compressed ; tail short. *Adult :* Head and neck pale
reddish brown, darker on the head and fading gradually into white. Back, wing coverts and quills black ; scapulars, tips of
greater wing coverts, rump and tail and entire under parts white, the last frequently tinged with reddish. Bill brownish black,
legs bluish. *Young :* very similar to the adult, but with the head and neck white, frequently tinged with ashy on the head and
neck behind. Total length, about 17 inches ; wing, 8½ to 9 ; tail, 3½ ; bill to gape, 3¾ ; tarsus, 3½ inches.

Hab.—All of temperate North America ; Florida (Mr. Würdemann.)

Appears to inhabit the whole of North America to the Arctic regions ; more abundant on the
western coast. In the present collection we find numerous specimens in all stages of plumage,
and have no doubt that *R. occidentalis*, Vigors, is the young bird as given above.

List of specimens.

Catal. No.	Sex.	Locality.	When collected.	Whence obtained.	Orig. No.	Collected by—	Length.	Stretch of wings.	Wing.	Remarks.
4260	......	Calcasieu Pass, La.	....	G. Würdemann.	......	....	......	....	......	....
4549	......	Platte river,bel.Ft.Laramie	Sept. 6, 1855	Lt. Warren	......	....	......	....	......	....
8772	♂	Flatte river	Aug. 19	Wm. Magraw	......	Dr. Cooper	16.50	29.25	9.00	....
8771	.. ...	...do..	...do..	...do.	......	...do.	15.25	29.00	8.75	....
6635	♂	Minnesota	July 20, 1853	Gov. Stevens	......	Dr. Suckley....	13.12	30.60	9.50	....
7064	♂	Laramie river, Neb	July 23	Lt. Bryan	318	W. S. Wood ...	....	....	......	....
7..02	♂	W. slope of Med. Bow ...	July 23, 1857	...do.	317	...do.	....	....	......	....
5446	♂	Yellowstone river	July 30, 1856	Lt. Warren	......	Dr. Hayden.	18.00	28.00	8.50	....
6633	......	Fort Thorn, N. M	....	Dr. Henry.	......	....	....	....	......	....
4174	♂	Brazos Santiago, Texas..	....	Capt. Van Vliet.	......	....	18.00	28.00	9.00	....
		Fort Tejon, Cal.	....	J.Xantus de Vesey	......	....	....	....	......	....
4980	......	Doña Ana, N. M.	....	Capt. Pope.	......	....	18.00	31.00	10.00	Eye dark, bill black, feet bluish green.
10410	......	Livermore's ranche	....	Lt. Williamson ..●....	......	....	....	....	......	....
4507	......	San Francisco	....	...do.	......	Dr. Newberry..	....	....	......	....
8071	......	Mexico	Sept. —, 1836	John Gould	......	....	....	....	......	....

HIMANTOPUS, Brisson.

Himantopus, Brisson, Orn. V, 1760, 33. Type *Charadrius himantopus*, L.

Сн.—Hind toe wanting. Middle and outer toes connected by a short basal web. Bill rounded, straight, higher than broad. Tail projecting beyond the wings.

HIMANTOPUS NIGRICOLLIS, Vieillot.

Black Necked Stilt.

Himantopus nigricollis, Vieill. Dict. X, 1817, 42.—Ib. Galerie, II, 1824, 85 ; pl. ccxxix.—Nutt. Man. II, 1834, 8.—
    Aud. Orn. Biog. IV, 1838, 247 ; pl. 328.—Ib. Syn. 1839, 253.—Ib. Birds Amer. VI, 1843,
    31 ; pl. 354.

Recurvirostra himantopus, Wils. Am. Orn. VII, 1813, 48 ; pl. lviii.

Himantopus mexicanus, Ord, ed Wils. VII, 1824, 52.—Wagler, Isis, 1831, §20.—Bon. List. 1838.

Himantopus brasiliensis, Brehm, Vögel Deutschl. 1831, 684.

Hypsibates nigricollis, Cab. Schomb. Reise.

Macrotarsus nigricollis, Gundl. Cab. Journ. 1856, 422.

Figures.—Wilson, Am. Orn. VII, pl. 58, fig. 2.—Aud. B. of Am. pl. 328 ; oct. ed. VI, pl. 354.

Sp. Сн.—Legs very long, slender ; wings long. Large space in front of the head, spot behind the eye and entire under parts white, frequently with a very pale reddish tinge ; head above, neck behind, back and wings, glossy black ; rump and tail white, the latter frequently tinged with ashy ; bill black ; legs red. Total length, about 14 inches ; wing, 8½ to 9 ; tail, 3 ; bill to gape, 3 ; tarsus, 4 inches.

Hab.—United States generally.

The only species apparently that inhabits the United States. Though a *H. mexicanus* is given by Bonaparte (Comp. List, p. 54) as distinct and inhabiting the southern parts of the republic ; it is yet very probably the same as the northern bird.

List of specimens.

Catal. No.	Sex.	Locality.	When collected.	Whence obtained.	Collected by—	Length.	Stretch of wings	Wing.	Remarks.
1154	♀	Cape May, N. J........	July 21,1843	S. F. Baird............	....	13.50	26.50	8.50	....
4265	......	Calcasieu Pass, La.....	1854.........	G. Würdemann........	....	....	....	....	....
6620	......	Fort Thorn............	....	Dr. Henry	....	....	....	....	....
4171	......	Brazos Santiago, Texas.	....	Capt. Van Vliet........	....	14.00	27.50	8.75	Eye dark blue........
......	......	Fort Tejon, Cal........	....	J. Xantus de Vesey	....	....	....	....	....
1829	♀	Vera Cruz, Mexico	....	S. F. Baird............	....	....	....	....	....
8072?	......	Guayaquil.	July 19,1839	John Gould......	Capt. Belcher......	....	... .	....	....

Family PHALAROPODIDAE.

The general characters of the *Phalaropodidae* have already been given on page 689. The original and single genus *Phalaropus* has been divided by systematists into three, with the following characters:

A. Bill slender, attenuated, rounded, longer than the head.

STEGANOPUS, Vieillot.[1]—Marginal membrane of toes nearly even.

LOBIPES, Cuv.[2]—Membrane of the toes scolloped at the joints.

B. Bill much depressed or flattened ; broader than high ; the apex lancet-shaped.

PHALAROPUS, Briss.[3]—Membrane of toes scolloped at the joints.

Steganopus, Vieillot.

PHALAROPUS WILSONII, Sab.

Wilson's Phalarope.

Phalaropus wilsonii, SAB. Zool. App. to Franklin's first journey to Polar seas, 1823, 691.—Sw. F. Bor. Am. II, 1831, 405 ; pl. lxix.—AUD. Orn. Biog.—IB. Birds Amer. V, 1842, 299 ; pl. 341.—GRAY's Genera III, pl. clviii.

Phalaropus (Holopodius) wilsonii, BON. Syn. 1828, 342.—IB. Am. Orn. IV, 1832, 59 ; pl. xxiv and xxv.

Phalaropus lobatus, WILSON, Am. Orn. IX, 1825, 72. (Not Linnaeus.)

Phalaropus frenatus, VIEILL. Gal. II, 1825, 178.

Phalaropus stenodactylus, WAGLER, Isis, 1831, 523.

Lobipes incanus, JARD. & SELBY, Ill. Orn. I, p. (No page nor date.)

Phaloropus fimbriatus, TEMM. Pl. Col. V, p. (No page.)

FIGURES.—Wilson, Am. Orn. IX, pl. 73, fig. 3.—Sw. and Rich. Faun. Bor. Am. Birds, pl. 69.—Vieill. Gal. II, pl. 271.—Temm. Pl. Col. 270.—Aud. B. of Am. pl. 254 ; oct. ed. V, pl. 341.

SP. CH.—Larger than either of the preceding. Bill slender, flattened ; wings long ; tail short ; legs moderate ; tarsus compressed ; plumage very compact. *Adult*. Head above and neck behind light ashy ; wide stripe behind the eye reddish black ; neck before, and wide stripe running upwards on to the back, bright reddish brown, darker on the sides of the neck. Back, wings, and tail, cinereous ; darkest on the wings, and mixed with reddish on the back ; rump and upper tail coverts white. Entire under parts white, (except the neck before, which is pale reddish.) Bill and legs black. *Young*. Entire upper parts cinereous, more or less mixed with dark brown ; under parts white, tinged with ashy, especially about the head and neck ; rump white. Total length, about 9½ inches ; wing,,5½ ; tail, 2¼ ; bill, 1½ ; tarsus, 1¼ inch.

Hab.—Entire temperate regions of North America ; New Mexico. (Dr. Henry.)

The only species that appears to be more especially American, though wandering into contiguous regions of the Old World. Very handsome in mature plumage, and apparently about equally distributed on the eastern and western coasts of the republic.

[1] *Steganopus*, VIEILL. Encycl. Meth. 1823. Type *Phalaropus lobatus*, Wils. *Holopodius*, Bon. Syn. 1828.

[2] *Lobipes*, CUV. R. Anim. 1817. Type *Tringa hyperborea*, L.

[3] *Phalaropus*, BRISS. Orn. 1760. Type *Tringa fulicaria*, L. *Crymophilus*, Vieill. 1816.

August 4, 1858.

89 b

List of specimens.

Catal. No.	Sex & age.	Locality.	When collected.	Whence obtained.	Collected by—	Length.	Stretch of wings.	Wing.	Remarks.
7058	○	St. Louis	May 6.1857	Lieut. Bryan............	W. S. Wood........	....	....	....	....
10393	♂	Dane county, Wis......	May 20,1855	S. F. Baird	Th. Kumlien	....	....	....	
4346	......	Racine, Wis...........	....	......do.	Dr. Hay..........	9.00	16.00	5.00	....
4879	♀	Council Bluffs..........	April 28......	Lieut. Warren.........	Dr. Hayden........	10.50	16 25	5.00	
4880	♀	......do...............	....	......do........	...... do.........	9.50	16.12	5.12	
4876	....	......do...............	April 28......	......do........	......do............	9.25	16.75	5.75	....
4878	♀	Omaha City, Neb.......	....do......	......do.............	......do...........	9.50	17.50	4.37	Eyes dark blue.......
4877	......	......do...............	....	......do........	......do...........	9.25	16.75	4.50	
5444	......	Medicine Hill..........	June 23,1856	......do......	...... do..........	....	....	....	
5445	♂	Medicine creek........	June 6......	......do........	......do...........	8.25	15.00	4.75	
6658	......	Fort Thorn, N. M......	....	Dr. Henry, U.S.A....	....	....	....	....	
8077	......	Mexico...............	Sept. —,1836	John Gould...	....	....	....	....	

Lobipes, Cuv.

PHALAROPUS HYPERBOREUS, (Linn.) Temm.

Northern Phalarope.

Tringa hyperborea, LINN. Syst. Nat. I, 1766, 249.

Lobipes hyperboreus, "CUV. R. A."—BON. List, 1838.—AUD. Syn. 1839, 240.—IB. Birds Amer. V, 1842, 295 ; pl. 340.

Phalaropus hyperboreus, TEMM. Man. II, 1820, 709.—AUD. Orn. Biog. III, 1835, 118 : V, 595 ; pl. 215.

Tringa lobata, LINN. Syst. Nat. I, 1766, 249.

Tringa fusca, GM. Syst. Nat. I, 1788, 675.

Phalaropus ruficollis, PALLAS, Zoog. Rosso-Asiat. II, 1811, 203.

Phalaropus cinerascens, PALLAS, Zoog. Rosso-Asiat. II, 1811, 204.

FIGURES.—Buff. Pl. Enl. 766.—Edwards, Birds, III, pl. 143, 46, 308.—Pallas, Zoog. II, pl. 62.—Bonap. Am. Orn. IV, pl. 25, fig. 2.—Aud. B. of Am. pl. 254 ; oct. ed. V, pl. 340.

SP. CH.—Bill short, straight, pointed ; wings long ; tail short ; legs short. *Adult.* Neck encircled with a ring of bright ferruginous, and a stripe of the same on each side ; head above and neck behind sooty ash ; back, wings, and tail, brownish black, paler on the rump, mixed with bright ferruginous on the back. Tips of greater wing coverts white. Sides and flanks ashy, frequently mixed with reddish ; throat, breast, and abdomen white ; bill and legs dark. *Young.* Entire upper parts brownish black ; many feathers edged and tipped with dull yellow and ashy ; under parts white ; tips of greater wing coverts white. Total length, about 7 inches ; wing, 4½ ; tail, 2¼ ; bill, 1 ; tarsus, ¾ inch.

Hab.—The whole of temperate North America, Europe, Japan, (Mr. Heine, Japan Exp.) San Francisco, California, (Mr. Cutts.)

A very widely diffused little species, and one of the handsomest and most graceful of the wading birds. Specimens from various parts of the world are precisely alike in specific characters.

List of specimens.

Catal. No.	Sex & Age.	Locality.	When collected.	Whence obtained.	Orig'l No.	Collected by—	Length.	Stretch of wings.	Wing.	Remarks.
709	♂	Carlisle, Pa............	Sept. 7, 1842	S. F. Baird....	......	....	7.50	13.50	....	....
2505	○	Perry county, Pa.......	Sept. 19, 1845	.....do......	......	....	8.00	13.50	4.50	
6663	....	Puget's Sound, W. T...	Aug. 29, 1856	Dr. Suckley...	570	....	7.50	13.00	....	
6662	....	Fort Steilacoom, W. T.	....	..... do	571	....	....	....	....	
1049	....	......do.............	....	..... do........	569	....	....	....	....	
6661	....	......do........	....	..... do........	568	....	8.50	14.50	4.60	
6656	♂	Shoalwater bay	May 9, 1854	Gov. Stevens...	72	Dr. Cooper.........	7.50	13.75	....	Iris brown ; feet light slate blue.
6657	....	......do...............	..do......	......do......	......	......do..........	8.00	14.00	....	
4242	......	San Francisco, Cal.....	....	R. D. Cutts	......	....	....	....	....	
6660	......	Presidio, Cal	....	Lt. Trowbridge	......	....	....	....	....	.. ..

Phalaropus, Brisson.

PHALAROPUS FULICARIUS, (Linn.) Bon.

Red Phalarope.

Tringa fulicaria, LINN. Syst. Nat. I, 1766, 249.

Phalaropus fulicarius, BON. Obs. Wils. 1825, 2ქ2.—IB. Syn. 1828, 341.—SWAINSON, F. Bor. Amer. II, 1831, 407.—
NUTT. Man. II, 236.—AUD. Orn. Biog. III, 1835, 404 ; pl. 255.—IB. Syn. 239.—IB. Birds
Amer. V, 1842, 291 ; pl. 339.

Tringa glacialis, GM. Syst. Nat. I, 1788, 675.

Phalaropus rufus, PALLAS, Zoog. Rosso-As. II, 1811, 205.

Phalaropus platyrhynchus, TEMM. Man. II, 712.

FIGURES.—Edwards, Birds, III, pl. 142.—Vieill. Gal. Ois. II, pl. 270.—Wilson, Am. Orn. IX, pl. 73, fig. 4.—Aud. B. of
Am. pl. 255 ; oct. ed. V, pl. 339.—Pallas, Zoog. Rosso-As. II, pl. 63.

SP. CH.—Bill strong, flattened, widened towards the end ; wings long ; tail short ; legs short ; plumage thick and compact,
like the swimming birds. *Adult.* Head above, space around the base of the bill, throat, and back, brownish black, feathers of
the last edged broadly with pale ochre yellow ; wings and tail ashy brown, paler on the wing coverts ; greater wing coverts
widely tipped with white ; stripe on the cheek white. Entire under parts deep brownish red, inclining to purple on the abdomen,
and with a glaucous cast in very mature specimens ; under wing coverts and axillaries pure white ; bill greenish yellow ; feet
dark bluish brown. *Young.* Entire upper parts light cinereous ; head above and wings darker, and mixed with blackish brown ;
head in front, and entire under parts white ; tips of greater wing coverts white. Total length, about 7½ inches ; wing, 5¼ ;
tail, 2¾ ; bill, 1 ; tarsus, ¾ inch.

Hab.—Entire temperate regions of North America ; Asia ; Europe.

List of specimens.

Catal. No	Locality.	When collected.	Whence obtained.	Orig. No.	Collected by—	Length.	Stretch of wings.	Remarks.
2001	United States.	Spring.	S. F. Baird					
489	New York	1841	do					
1245	California		do					
6655	Shoalwater bay, W. T.	Nov. 24, 1854	Gov. Stevens	114	Dr. Cooper	8.75	16.00	Iris dark brown, bill black and yellow.

Family SCOLOPACIDAE.

On a preceding page will be found the principal character of the *Scolopacidae* as distinguished from the *Charadridae*, *Haematopodidae*, *Recurvirostridae*, and *Phalaropodidae*. According to Bonaparte's arrangement, the *Scolopacidae* are divisible into two sub-families—*Scolopacinae* and *Tringinae;* the former with one tribe, *Scolopaceae;* the latter with four, *Tringinae*, *Totaneae*, *Limosinae*, and *Numeninae*. The arrangement of Keyserling and Blasius and of Burmeister, however, seems more natural in associating *Tringeae* with *Scolopaceae* under *Scolopacinae*. On this basis the two sub-families may be characterized as follows :

SCOLOPACINAE.—Bill covered with soft skin to the sensitive, vascular, thickened, or laterally expanded tip. Uncovered portion of tibia short. Body and legs rather stout. Neck rather short and stout. Toes generally cleft to the base, (not in *Macrorhamphus* and *Micropalama*, &c.) Gape of mouth very small, not extending beyond the base of culmen.

TOTANINAE.—Bill covered with soft skin towards the base ; the terminal portion hard, horny, and more or less attenuated. Body more slender. Legs and neck slender and lengthened. Toes generally with a basal web. Gape of mouth larger, always extending beyond base of culmen, (except in *Limosa*.)

Sub-Family SCOLOPACINAE.

CH.—Bill swollen at the end, and covered almost to the tip with a soft skin, the edges only of the rather vaulted tip horny. The end of the upper bill generally bent a little over the tip of lower. The jaw bone in typical genera finely porous, and perforated by vessels and nerves, imparting a high degree of sensibility to the bill, enabling it to find food in the mud. After death the end of bill is usually pitted. Legs rather stout ; the naked portion of the tibia much abbreviated. The hind toe well developed and generally present ; the toes usually without basal membrane, (except in *Macrorhamphus*, &c.)

Under the head of *Scolopacinae,* as at present defined, I range two tribes, with the following brief diagnoses :

A. SCOLOPACEAE.—Bill much longer than the head or than the naked leg ; the end of upper jaw thickened and bent over beyond the tip of lower. Roof of mouth not excavated to the tip. A longitudinal furrow along the culmen towards the end. External ear placed beneath or anterior to the eye. Tail banded ?

B. TRINGEAE.—Bill shorter than the naked leg, widened or rather spoon-shaped at the end, with the edges not bent over. Roof of mouth excavated to the tip. No groove along the culmen. Ear behind the eye. Tail without bands ?

Tribe SCOLOPACEAE.

The general characters of the *Scolopaceae* have already been given. The genera found in North America belonging here are as follows :

A. Toes cleft to the base. Tarsi shorter than middle toe.

PHILOHELA.—Tibia feathered to the lower joint. Wings short, much graduated ; the three outer primaries much attenuated.

GALLINAGO.—Lower part of tibia naked. Wings lengthened ; the outer primaries longest.

B. Toes united at the base. Tarsi longer than middle toe.

MACRORHAMPHUS.—Somewhat like *Gallinago*, but the middle and outer toes united to the first joint.

PHILOHELA, . R. Gray.

Philohela, GRAY, List of Genera, 1841. Type *Scolopax minor*, GM.
Rusticola, GRAY, Genera, 1840, not of Moehring, 1752.
Microptera, NUTTALL, Man. II, 1834, 192, not of Gravenhorst, 1802.

CH.—Body very full, and head, bill, and eyes very large. Tibia short, feathered to the joint. Toes cleft to base., Wings short, rounded. First three primaries very narrow and much attenuated ; the fourth and fifth equal and longest. Tarsi stout, shorter than the middle toe. Hind nail very short, conical, not extending beyond the toe. Tail of twelve feathers.

The present genus, embracing a single species, the American woodcock, is much like *Scolopax*, with the European woodcock as type, in color and external appearance. The most striking difference is seen in the wings, which are short, rounded ; the fourth and fifth primaries longest and the outer three attenuated, while in *Scolopax* the wings are long ; the first primary longest and more attenuated.

PHILOHELA MINOR, (Gmelin,) Gray.

American Woodcock.

Scolopax minor, GMELIN, Syst. Nat. I, 1788, 661.—WILS. Am. Orn. VI, 1812, 40 ; pl. 48.—AUD. Orn. Biog. IV, 1835, 474 ; pl. 268.—DOUGHTY's Cab. N. H. I, 1830, 158 ; pl. xiv.
Rusticola minor, VIEILLOT, " Analyse, 1816."—GAL. Ois. II, 112 ; pl. ccxlii.—NUTTALL, Man. II, 1834, 194.
Scolopax (Microptera) minor, NUTTALL, Man. II, 1834, 194.
Philohela minor, GRAY, List Genera, 1841.
Microptera americana, AUD. Syn 1839, 250.—IB. Birds Amer. VI, 1843, 15 ; pl. 352.

SP. CH.—Bill long, compressed, punctulated and corrugated near the end ; upper mandible longer than the under, and fitted to it at the tip ; wings moderate, three first quills very narrow ; tail short ; legs moderate ; eyes inserted unusually distant from the bill. Occiput with three transverse bands of black, alternating with three others of pale yellowish rufous ; upper parts of body variegated with pale ashy, rufous, or yellowish red of various shades, and black ; large space in front and throat reddish ashy ; line from the eye to the bill, and another on the neck below the eye, brownish black ; entire under parts pale rufous, brighter on the sides and under wing coverts. Quills ashy brown ; tail feathers brownish black, tipped with ashy, darker on the upper surface, paler and frequently white on the under ; bill light brown, paler and yellowish at base ; legs pale reddish. Total length about 11 inches ; wing, 5¼ ; tail, 2¼ ; bill, 2½ ; tarsus, 1¼ inches.
Hab.—Eastern North America.

List of specimens.

Catal. No.	Sex.	Locality.	When collected.	Whence obtained.	Collected by—	Length.	Stretch of wings.	Wing.	Remarks.
852	♂	Carlisle, Pa.............	Nov. 12, 1842	S. F. Baird.......	....	10.73	17.75	5.16	....
1307	♀	......do.................	Mar. 23, 1844	......do.........	....	14.75	19.00	5.08	....
1086	○♀	......do.................	June 30, 1843	......do..........	....	10.50	17.25	4.80	....
9040	♂	Loup Fork, Neb	July 18......	Lieut. Warren	Dr. Hayden..........	10.75	17.00	5.75	Iris brown ; pupil black.

GALLINAGO, Leach.

Gallinago, "LEACH, Catal. British Birds, 1816." GRAY. Type *Scolopax major*, L.

CH.—Lower portion of the tibia bare of feathers, scutellate before and behind, reticulated laterally like the tarsi. Nail of hind toe slender, extending beyond the toe. Bill depressed at the tip. Middle toe longer than tarsus. Tail with twelve to sixteen feathers.

The more slender body, longer legs, partly naked tibia, and other features, distinguish this genus from *Scolopax* or *Philohela*.

GALLINAGO WILSONII, (Temm.) Bon.

Wilson's Snipe; English Snipe.

Scolopax wilson'i, TEMM. Pl. Col. V, livraison LXVIII, about 1824. In text of *Scolopax gigantea.*—BON. Syn. 1828,
    330.—SWAINS. F. B. Am. II, 1831, 401.—NUTT. Man. II, 185.—AUD. Orn. Biog. III, 1835,
    322 : V, 1839, 583 ; pl. 243.—IB. Syn. 248.—IB. Birds Amer. V, 1842, 339 ; pl. 350.
Gallinago wilsonii, BONAP. List, 1838.
Scolopax gallinago, WILS. Am. Orn. VI, 1812, 18. Not of Linnaeus.
Scolopax brehmii, "KAUP," BON. Obs. Wils. 1825, No. 204. Not of Kaup.
Scolopax delicata, ORD, ed. Wils. IX, 1825, 218.
? *Scolopax drummondii*, SW. F. Bor. Am. II, 1831, 400.—AUD. Orn. Biog. V, 1839, 319.—IB. Syn. 249.—IB.
    Birds Amer. V.
? *Scolopax douglassii*, SW. F. Bor. Am. II, 1831, 400.
? *Scolopax leucurus*, SW. F. Bor. Am. II, 1831, 50.

SP. CH.—Bill long, compressed, flattened and slightly expanded towards the tip, pustulated in its terminal half ; wings rather long ; legs moderate ; tail short. Entire upper parts brownish black ; every feather spotted and widely edged with light rufous, yellowish brown or ashy white ; back and rump transversely barred and spotted with the same ; a line from the base of the bill over the top of the head. Throat and neck before, dull reddish ashy ; wing feather marked with dull brownish black ; other under parts white, with transverse bars of brownish black on the sides, axillary feathers and under wing coverts and under tail coverts ; quills brownish black ; outer edge of first primary white ; tail glossy brownish black, widely tipped with bright rufous, paler at the tip, and with a subterminal narrow band of black ; outer feathers of tail paler, frequently nearly white and barred with black throughout their length. Bill brown, yellowish at base and darker towards the end ; legs dark brown. Total length about 10½ inches ; wing, 5 ; tail, 2¼ ; bill, 2½ ; tarsus, 1¼ inch.

Hab.—Entire temperate regions of North America. California, (Mr. Szabo.)

With numerous specimens before us from western North America, as will be seen in the list appended below, and numerous others from various localities in the United States, we fail to perceive the characters of more than one species, and much suspect that neither of the species established by Mr. Swainson in Fauna Boreali Americana, as cited above, are valid or really distinct from our present bird. There is amongst them a great variety of *widths* of the outer tail feathers, and quite as great a variety also in their shades of color, so great, in fact, as to render it utterly impossible to entertain the idea of regarding either as a specific character, and, moreover, making the determining of these species quite inconvenient with so many specimens.

Two of those supposed species, *Scolopax drummondii* and *S. douglasii*, are described in the body of the work cited above, and one, *S. leucurus*, is added in the appendix. It is worth bearing in mind that Mr. Swainson was not acquainted with the common *S. wilsonii*, and only describes it doubtfully with the following remark: "A specimen of a snipe from Hudson's Bay, in the British Museum, possesses all the distinctive characters ascribed by the Prince of Musignano to his *Sc. wilsonii, of which we have seen no authenticated examples.*"

Our present opinion is that all the names above given are synonyms for the species now before us. All of their characters can be found in the extensive series of specimens now under examination, but without tempting us to suppose for one moment that they indicate specific distinctions.

For convenience of reference we insert the diagnoses of the three supposed species alluded to, from Fauna Boreali Americana, as above cited:

"*Scolopax drummondii.*—Tail of sixteen feathers, *the two outer pairs somewhat narrowed,* varied with black and white, the rest banded with ferruginous. Total length, 11 inches 6 lines; wing, 5 inches 3 lines; tail, 2 inches 10 lines; of bill, 2 inches 7 lines; of tarsus, 1 inch 3 lines."

"*Scolopax douglosii.*—Tail of sixteen feathers, *not narrowed,* all banded with ferruginous, except the outer pair, which are paler. Total length, $11\frac{1}{2}$ inches; of wing, 5 inches; of tarsus, 1 inch $3\frac{1}{2}$ lines; middle toe, 1 inch 2 lines; its nail, $3\frac{1}{2}$ lines."

"*Scolopax leucurus.*—Tail of sixteen feathers, the three lateral ones pure white, with 2–3 basal black bands on the outer web; belly transversely banded. Total length, 10 inches 6 lines; of wing, 5 inches 4 lines; of tail, 2 inches 2 lines; of bill, 2 inches 5 lines; of tarsus, 1 inch $4\frac{1}{2}$ lines."

List of specimens.

Catal. No.	Sex.	Locality.	When collected.	Whence obtained.	Orig'l No.	Collected by—	Length.	Stretch of wings.	Wing.	Remarks.
1340	♀	Carlisle, Pa............	April 9, 1844	S. F. Baird	......	....	11.25	17.75	5.40	....
1686	♀	.....do..............	Aug. 21, 1844	......do.........	......	....	11.32	17.50	5.50	....
10424	♀	Cape May, N. J........	April —, 1842	J. K. Townsend .	....	....	....	....	....	....
10425	♂	.....do..............	.....do......	......do.........	......	....	....	....	....	....
4548	....	Washington, D. C......	April 24, 1856	S. F. Baird	......	....	....	....	....	....
4874	.....	Mouth of Big Horn.....	....	Lt. Warren	......	Dr. Hayden....	11.00	16.50	5.25	....
9042	♀	Black Hills............	Sept 19, 1857	......do.........	......	.... .do........	10.25	17.00	5.00	Iris dark brown.........
9041	......	.....do..............		......do...... ...	......	......do.........	....	....	....	....
8230	....	Fort Laramie...........	Sept. 20, 1857	Wm. M. Magraw	212	Dr. Cooper.....	10.75	17.75	5.50	Iris brown, feet olive.....
4874	♀	Near Bald Island.......	April 24, 1856	Lt. Warren	......	....	11 00	16. 5	5.12	....
4183	♀	Brownsville, Texas	Feb. —, 1853	Lt. Couch	......	....	12.00	17.00	5.50	Eye dark b.own.........
4184	.....	.....do..............	Mar. —, 1853	......do.........	......	....	....	....	....	....
6614	....	Camp 123.............	Feb. 16, 1854	Lt. Whipple	....	Kenn. and Mllll.	......	....	....	....
3940	....	California..............	....	Dr. Heermann ...	......	....	10.50	18.75	....	....
6608	♂	Sacramento valley......		Lt. Williamson...	......	Dr. Heermann.	......	....	....	....
6610	.....	Bodega, Cal...........	Dec. —, 1854	Lt. Trowbridge ..	......	T. A. Szabo ...	......	....	....	....
6616	.....	San Francisco, Cal....		R. D. Cutts	......	....	......	....	....	....
6615	♂	Fort Dalles, O. T.....	Nov. 16......	Gov. Stevens ...	......	Dr. Suckley ...	......	....	....	....
6613	♀	Shoalwater bay........	Sept. 22, 1854	......do..........	......	Dr. Cooper.....	......	... .	....	Iris hazel, feet pale gray..
6606	.....	Fort Steilacoom, W. T..	....	......do.........	......	....	......	....	....	....
4403	.....	.....do..............		Dr. Suckley	......	....	......	....	....	....
6612	♂	.....do..............	May 13, 1856	......do...... ...	......	....	....	....	....	....

MACRORHAMPHUS, Leach.

Macrorhamphus, "LEACH. Catal. Brit. Birds, 1816," GRAY. Type *Scolopax grisea,* Gm.

CH.—General appearance of *Gallinago.* Tarsi longer than middle toe ; a short web between the base of outer and middle toe.

The membrane at the base of the toes will at once distinguish this genus from *Gallinago,* though there are other characters involved.

MACRORHAMPHUS GRISEUS, (Gmelin,) Leach.

Gray Snipe; Red-breasted Snipe.

Scolopax grisea, GMELIN, Syst. Nat. I, 1788, 658, No. 27.

Macrorhamphus griseus, "LEACH, Catal. Brit. Mus. 1816, 31."—STEPHENS, Shaw. Gen. Zool. XII, 1824, 61.—
    BON. Am. Orn. IV, 1332, 51; pl. xxiii.

Scolopax noveboracensis, GM. Syst. Nat. I, 1788, 658, No. 28.—WILSON, Am. Orn. VII, 1813, 45; pl. lviii.—SW.
    F. Bor. Am. II, 1831, 398.—AUD. Orn. Biog. IV, 1838, 288; pl. 339.—IB. Syn. 249.—
    IB. Birds Amer. VI, 1843, 10; pl. 351.

Scolopax leucophaea, VIEILLOT, Dict. III, 358, (2d ed.) Not of Latham.

SP. CH.—Rather smaller than the preceding; bill long, compressed, flattened and expanded towards the end, and in the same space punctulated and corrugated; wing rather long; shaft of first primary strong; tail short; legs rather long. *Adult.* Upper parts variegated with dark ashy, pale reddish and black, the latter predominating on the back; rump and upper tail coverts, white, the latter spotted and barred transversely with black. Under parts pale ferruginous red, with numerous points and circular spots of brownish black on the neck before, and transverse bands of the same on the sides and under tail coverts; axillary feathers and under wing coverts white, spotted and transversely barred with black. Quills brownish black; shaft of first primary white; tail brownish black, with numerous transverse bands of ashy white, and frequently tinged with ferruginous, especially on the two middle feathers; bill greenish black; legs dark greenish brown. *Younger.* Entire under parts dull white, strongly marked with dull ashy on the neck in front, and transverse bands of the same on the sides; axillary feathers and under wing coverts white, spotted with brownish black; upper parts lighter than in the adult. Total length about 10 inches; wing, 5¾; tail, 2¼; bill, 2¼; tarsus, 1¼ inch.

Hab.—Entire temperate regions of North America.

Quite a variable species in plumage, scarcely any two being exactly alike, except in very mature plumage, but always readily distinguished from the preceding by the white shaft of the first quill in the present bird. This bird is widely distributed, and is very similar to, if not identical with, the succeeding species.

In the list of specimens I give species of sizes varying between considerable extremes, reserving for *M. scolopaceus* only three, which are still larger than any of these.

List of specimens.

Catal. No.	Sex.	Locality.	When collected.	Whence obtained.	Orig'l No.	Collected by—	Length.	Stretch of wings.	Wing.	Remarks.
1703	♀	Carlisle, Pa...............	Sept. 12, 1844	S. F. Baird......	......	....	11.24	19.25	5.16	....
1671	♂	......do................	Aug. 12, 1844	......do..........	......	....	10.56	18.50	5.56	....
2675	......	New Jersey	1845	......do.....	.....	....	....	....	....	....
10447	......	Cape May, N. J.............	May —, 1842	J. K. Townsend..	.....	....	....	....	....	....
5769	♀	Rock creek...............	Sept. —, 1856	Lt. Bryan........	340	....	....	....	....	....
5096	......	Texas..................	....	Capt. Pope	......	....	....	....	....	....
4182	......	Fort Brown, Texas	Mar. 27, 1853	Capt. Van Vliet..	......	....	11.00	18.25	5.50	....
6644	......	Mimbres to Rio Grande	....	Dr. Henry........	.....	....	....	....	....	....
6647	♀	Espia, Mexico	Mar. 27, 1853	Maj. Emory	......	Dr. Kennerly	10.50	18.00	5.75	Eyes black ....
6609	♂	Sacramento Valley.......	....	Lt. Williamson...	......	....	....	....	....	....
6643	♀	Fort Steilacoom	May 5, 1856	Dr. Suckley......	371	....	11.75	19.00	....	....
6646	......	Port Townsend.........	August	......do..........	572	....	....	....	....	....

MACRORHAMPHUS SCOLOPACEUS, (Say,) Lawrence.

Limosa scolopaceus, SAY, Long's Exped. II, 1823, 170.

Macrorhamphus scolopaceus, (SAY,) LAWR. Ann. N. Y. Lyc. N. H. V, 1852, (Read Jan. 1849,) 4, pl. i.

Scolopax longirostris, BELL, Ann. N. Y. Lyc. V, 1852, (Read Oct. 9, 1848, and published soon after, but vol. dated 1852,) 3.

FIGURES.—Bonaparte, Am. Orn. IV, pl. 23, fig. 3. Annals, Lyceum N. Y. V, pl. 1.

Sp. Ch.—Rather larger than the preceding [species, and with the bill and tarsi disproportionately longer, but much resembling *M. griseus* in colors and general characters. Bill long, flattened and expanded towards the tip, where it is punctulated and corrugated ; wing rather long ; shaft of first primary very strong ; tail short ; legs rather long. Colors very similar to those of *M. griseus*, though perhaps with the upper parts more cinereous ; rump and upper tail coverts white, the latter spotted and transversely barred with black ; under parts pale ferruginous, with circular spots on the neck and transverse bars on the sides brownish black ; axillaries and under wing coverts white, barred and spotted with brownish black. *Young.* Ashy brown above, dull white beneath. Legs and bill dark brown. Total length, about $11\frac{1}{2}$ inches ; wing, $5\frac{3}{4}$; tail, $2\frac{1}{4}$ to $2\frac{1}{2}$; bill, $2\frac{3}{4}$ to 3 inches ; tarsus, $1\frac{1}{2}$ inches.

Hab.—Entire temperate regions of North America. Washington Territory, (Dr. Suckley.) New York, (Mr. J. G. Bell.)

The only characters which appear to be reliable are those pointed out by Mr. Lawrence, as above, which are the greater length of the bill and tarsi in the present species. It is, however, nearly related to that immediately preceding, and, for the present, with numerous specimens of both before us, we consider it but of doubtful validity as a species ; and its study is further complicated by the fact that it bears a striking resemblance to the rare European species supposed to be identical with the common bird of America, as will be seen in Gould's beautiful figure in "Birds of Europe," vol. IV, pl. 323. The latter seems to be a little larger than our common species.

List of specimens.

Catal. No.	Sex.	Locality.	When collected.	Whence obtained.	Length.	Stretch of wings.	Wing
4927	♂	St. John's river, Florida _____	_____	G. Würdemann_____	_____	_____	_____
4381	_____	Calcasieu Pass _____	1854	_____do_____	_____	_____	_____
4871	♂	Omaha City_____	April 28, 1856	Lieutenant Warren _____	10.50	19.50	5.75

Tribe **TRINGEAE.**

The variations in external form of *Tringeae* are very great, and have given occasion for the construction of almost as many genera as species. Many of these genera are, however, scarcely tenable, in many cases being scarcely indicative of more than specific characters.

In none of the North American species, as far as observed, is there any indication of transverse bands on the tail, as in *Scolopaceae* and *Totaneae.* The gape of mouth is much less than in the latter.

The following synopsis will serve to characterize the genera of *Tringeae* as adopted ; the numerous sections of those with fully cleft anterior toes and the hinder one present, being all considered as *Tringa,* under which genus the subdivisions will be found detailed.

A. Toes cleft to the base, or with a very rudimentary membrane, which does not extend to the first joint.

    Tringa.—Hind toe present.

    Calidris.—Hind toe wanting.

B. Toes with a decided basal membrane.

    Ereunetes.—Bill straight, as long as the head, but equal to the tarsus. A web connecting all the toes at base, and between middle and outer, extending to the second joint ; all the toes slightly margined to the extremity. Legs short. Tibia with hexagonal scales. Tail doubly emarginate. Body stout. Middle toe equal to the tarsus.

August 3, 1858.

MICROPALAMA.—Bill slightly curved, longer than the head, but equal to the tarsus. Bases of all the toes about equally webbed to a little beyond the first joint. Legs lengthened; tibia with transverse scutellae. Tail nearly even. Body slender. Middle toe not two-thirds the tarsus.

TRINGA, Linnaeus.

Tringa, LINNAEUS, Syst. Nat. 1735. Type *T. canutus*, L.

CH.—Size moderate or small. General form adapted to dwelling on the shores of both salt and fresh waters, and subsisting on minute or small animals, in pursuit of which they carefully examine and probe with their bills sandy or muddy deposits and growths of aquatic plants, rocks, or other localities. Flight rather rapid, but not very strong nor long continued. Bill moderate, or rather long; straight, or slightly curved towards the end, which is generally somewhat expanded and flattened; longitudinal grooves in both mandibles, distinct, and nearly the whole length of the bill; wings long, pointed; the first primary longest; tertiaries long; secondaries short, with their tips obliquely incised; tail short; legs moderate, or rather long, slender; the lower portion of the tibia naked, and with the tarsus covered in front and behind with transverse scales; hind toe very small; fore toes rather slender, with a membranous margin, scaly and flattened underneath, free at base.

This genus comprises a large number of species of all parts of the world, some of which are very extensively diffused, especially during the season of their southern or autumnal migration. Generally these birds are met with in flocks, frequenting every description of locality near water, and industriously searching for the minute animals on which they feed. The species of the United States are migratory, rearing their young in the north, and in autumn and winter extending to the confines of the republic and into South America. The colors of the spring and autumnal plumage are different in nearly all species, though that of the two sexes is very similar.

The following synopsis will serve to define the sub-genera:

A. Bill longer than the head or tarsus. Bare space of tibia not exceeding half the tarsus.

   1. Bill straight, much flattened, and widening towards the tip. Tarsus longer than middle toe and claw. Feathers of tibia reaching nearly to joint. Tail nearly even.
      TRINGA, Linn.

   2. Bill nearly straight, not widened at tip. Tarsus shorter than middle toe and claw. Feathers of tibia reaching to joint. Tail wedge-shaped.
      ARQUATELLA, Baird.

   3. Bill slightly decurved beyond the middle; very little widened at tip. Tarsus longer than middle toe and claw.
      EROLIA, Vieill.—Bill not depressed; with hard tip.
      SCHOENICLUS, Moehr.—Bill depressed; with rather soft tip.

B. Bill straight; not longer than the head. Bare space of tibia nearly two-thirds the tarsus. Jugulum conspicuously streaked in all seasons.

   1. Tarsus equal to the middle toe. Bill scarcely widened at end, except, perhaps, in *T. maculata*. Tail doubly emarginate, the central feather longest.
      ACTODROMAS, Kaup.

In further illustration of these sub-genera, the following remarks may appropriately be made:

Tringa.—The tips of the tibial feathers extend nearly to the joint; the really bare portion, however, is one half the length of tarsus. The toes are quite short, the middle one, with its claw, being scarcely more than two-thirds the tarsus. The claws are all short and blunt.

Arquatella.—The bill is nearly straight, and very slender at base; the gonys, however, is slightly concave. The feathers of the tibia extend over the joint; the portion without any feathers inserted is nearly half the tarsus. The tarsus is remarkably short, being scarcely equal to the middle toe without its claw. The claws are all short, blunt, and much curved. The tail is rather wedge-shaped. The body is full and compact, standing very low on the legs.

Schoeniclus.—The bare portion of the tibia is not quite half the tarsus. The bill is decidedly decurved from the middle and depressed at tip. The toes are short, but straight and acute. The difference from *Erolia* appears very slight.

Tringa, Linn.

TRINGA CANUTUS, Linn.

Gray Back; Robin Snipe.

Tringa canutus, Linn. Syst. Nat. I, 1766, 251.—Bon. List, 1838.
Tringa ferruginea, Brunnich, Orn. Bor. 1764, No. 186.
Tringa cinerea, Gmelin, Syst. Nat. I, 1788, 673.—Wilson, Am. Orn. VII, 1813, 36 ; pl. lvii.
? *Tringa australis*, Gm. I, 679.
Tringa islandica, Gm. Syst. Nat. I, 1788, 682.—Aud. Orn. Biog. IV, 1838, 130 ; pl. 315.—Ib. Syn. 232.—Ib. Birds Am. V, 1842, 254 ; pl. 328.
Tringa naevia and *grisea*, Gm. I, 681.
Tringa rufa, Wils. Am. Orn. VII, 1813, 57 ; pl. lvii.

Figures.—Buffon. Pl. Enl. 365, 366.—Edwards, Birds, pl. 276.—Wilson, Am. Orn. VII, pl. 57, figs. 2, 5.—Aud. B. of Am. pl. 315 ; oct. ed. V, pl. 328.—Gould, B. of Eur. IV, pl. 324.—Naumann, B. of Germany, pl. 183.

Sp. Ch.—Large ; bill straight, rather longer than the head, compressed, slightly enlarged at the tip ; upper mandible with the nasal groove extending to near the tip ; legs moderate ; tibia with its lower third part naked ; neck moderate ; wing long ; tail short. Toes free at base, flattened beneath, widely margined ; hind toe slender, small. Entire upper parts light gray, with lanceolate, linear, and irregular spots of black, and others of pale reddish ; rump and upper tail coverts white, with transverse narrow bands and crescent-shaped spots of black. Under parts light brownish red, paler in the middle of the abdomen ; under tail coverts, tibial feathers, flanks, axillary feathers, and under wing coverts white, generally with spots and transverse bars of brownish black. Quills brownish black, with their shafts white ; tail light brownish cinereous, (without spots or bars) ; all the feathers edged with white, and frequently with a second sub-edging of dark brown. Bill brownish black ; legs greenish black.

Young and winter plumage.—Upper parts brownish ashy, darker on the back, every feather having a sub-terminal edging of brownish black, and tipped with dull ashy white ; rump white, with crescents of black ; under parts dull ashy white, nearly pure on the abdomen, but with numerous longitudinal lines, and small spots of dark brown on the breast and neck ; sides with crescent-shaped and irregular spots of brownish black. An obscure line of dull white over and behind the eye. Total length, (from tip of bill to end of tail,) about 10 inches ; wing, $6\frac{1}{2}$; tail, $2\frac{1}{2}$; bill from gape, $1\frac{1}{2}$; tarsus, $1\frac{1}{4}$ inches. Female larger?

Hab.—Eastern North America ; Europe.

This is the largest of the sandpipers of the United States, and appears to be restricted to the shores of the Atlantic in this division of the continent of America. We have never seen it from the Pacific coast.

In the United States this bird is known as the red-breasted snipe, or sometimes as the gray-backed snipe, though we have never heard the name "Knot" applied to it, which appears to be a common appellation of the same species in Europe, and is given by American authors. This is one of the few species of birds which appears to be absolutely identical with a species of Europe, and is of very extensive diffusion over the world, especially in the season of southern migration.

This bird has received a variety of names, of which the very first appears to be that adopted at the head of this article.

List of specimens.

Catal. No.	Sex.	Locality.	When collected.	Whence obtained.
2677	......	New Jersey...............	1845..........	S. F. Baird ....
10445	♀	Cape May, N. J...........	May, 1842....	John K. Townsend.......
10444	♂	.......do.................	....do........	......do.................
4170	♂	Brazos, Santiago..........	....	Capt. Van Vliet ....

TRINGA COOPERI, B a i r d.

Sp. Ch.—Rather smaller than *T. canutus.* Bill straight ; longer than the tarsus, which exceeds the middle toe. Above gray ; the feathers of back with dark centres, and without abruptly light borders. Upper tail coverts white, each feather with V-shaped marks of black. Beneath clear white ; the breast and sides with small oval spots or streaks of black. Length, 9½ inches ; wing, 5.75 ; tail, 2.80 ; bill above, 1.23 ; tarsus, 1.14 ; middle toe and claw, 1.

Hab.—Long Island.

Bill straight, rather broad, and a little widened at the tip ; a little longer than the tarsi. Tarsus a little longer than the middle toe. Hind toe and claw well developed. Bare part of tibia a little more than half the tarsus ; just half the bill. Tail doubly emarginate, but the central feathers projecting but slightly. Upper parts ashy gray, this being the color of the borders ; the basal and central portion, however, is blackish, showing occasionally as a large spot. There are several scapular feathers which appear to be assuming a more perfect dress, and which are black, abruptly edged laterally with pale rusty, passing towards the tip into ashy. There is no rusty, however, on any other feathers. The head and neck are grayish, streaked with brown ; the chin whitish. The upper tail coverts are white, each one with a V-shaped mark of brown ; the rump feathers are brown, edged with whitish. The under parts are quite pure white, with a trace of reddish on the lower neck, but no indication of an ashy jugulum. The lower part of the neck, the jugulum, and the sides of the body, show elongated oval spots of brown, not much crowded, but very well defined. These blotches under the wings are rather V-shaped, but where exposed are only in the end of the feather. There are also a few streaks in the crissum.

The subject of the present description appears in many respects different from any *Tringa* described as North American. It approaches to *Actodromas maculata* and *bonapartii* in the short, straight bill and other peculiarities of form. It is rather larger than the former, the bill exceeding the tarsus, and the tarsus longer than the middle toe, instead of having bill, tarsus, and toes of about the same length. There is nothing of the ashy jugulum of *maculata,* nor the blackish central field of the rump and upper tail coverts. The spots on the sides are better defined, and, instead of being shaft lines, are oval spots.

It is much larger than *A. bonapartii,* which has the same proportions of bill as *A. maculata.*

The affinities after all, are, perhaps, closest to *Tringa canutus.* It is, however, smaller, the bill not so stout at the base. The legs are slenderer and longer, the bare part of tibia nearly two-thirds the tarsus, instead of not more than two-fifths. The hind toe is longer, and all the claws are lengthened and acute, instead of short and blunt. The differences in coloration between winter specimens consists in the greater distinctness of the spots on the sides and breast. Both have the upper tail coverts white, with V or U-shaped marks of black. The feathers of the back, however, lack that distinct whitish border with the dark line margining it inside, while *cánutus* is without the black or dark brown central areas in the scapulars and back.

The bird here described was shot on the 24th of May, 1833, on Raynor South, Long Island, by Mr. Wm. Cooper, and I take much pleasure in giving to it his name, as that of almost the only living member of the band of zealous ornithologists who years ago studied the birds of North America, especially of the Atlantic coast, with so much zeal and success. Of these Wilson, Say, Audubon, Bonaparte, and DeKay, have passed away, while Peale and Cooper still remain.

It is possible that this species may have been previously indicated under some of the names quoted as synonyms, such as *Tringa noveboracensis*, &c., although, from the brevity of the descriptions, it is impossible to determine this point satisfactorily.—S. F. B.

List of specimens.

Catal. Number.	Locality.	When collected.	Whence obtained.
5989	Raynor South, L. I.....................	May 24, 1833	Wm. Cooper..................

Arquatella, Baird.

TRINGA MARITIMA, Brünnich.

Purple Sandpiper.

Tringa maritima, BRUNNICH, Orn. Bor. 1764, 54.—BON. Am. Orn. III.—NUTT. Man. II, 115.—AUD. Orn. Biog. III, 1835, 558 ; pl. 284.—IB. Birds Amer. V, 1842, 261 ; pl. 330.

Pelidna maritima, BON. List. 1842.

? Tringa striata, LINN, Syst. I, 1766, 248.

Tringa nigricans, MONTAGU, Linn. Trans. IV, 1796, 40 ; pl. ii.

Tringa arquatella, PALLAS, Zoog. Rosso-As. II, 1811, 190.

FIGURES.—Aud B. of Am. pl. 284 ; oct. ed. V, pl. 330. Gould B. of Eur. IV, pl. 344. Naumann B. of Germ. pl. 188.

SP. CH.—Bill rather longer than the head, straight, compressed ; nasal groove long ; wings long ; tail short, rounded ; legs moderate ; toes free at base, flattened underneath and slightly margined ; hind toe small. Entire head and upper parts dark smoky brown, with a purple and violet tinge, strongest on the back and scapulars. Under parts from the breast white, generally with longitudinal spots of dark ashy. Wing coverts more or less edged and tipped with white ; quills brownish black, edged with white ; middle tail feathers brownish black, outer feathers lighter, with their shafts white ; axillaries and under wing coverts white. Bill yellow at base, dark at tip ; legs yellow. Total length about 8 to 9 inches ; wing 5 ; tail 2½ ; bill from gape, 1¼ ; tarsus, 1 inch.

Hab.—Eastern North America; Europe.

The purple sandpiper, though not an abundant species, is frequently met with on the shores of the Atlantic, where it is diffused throughout the extent of temperate North America. It is also a winter visitant to tropical and South America. American and European specimens appear absolutely identical.

List of specimens.

Catal. No.	No. of spec.	Locality.	When collected	Whence obtained.	Collected by—
519	1	New York------------	1842..........	S. F. Baird -----------	----------------------
10396	2	Philadelphia ------------	------------	------do--------------	A. Galbraith----------
8658	3	Key Biscayne, Fla ----------	------------	G. Würdemann --------	----------------------

Erolia, Vieillot.[1]

TRINGA SUBARQUATA, (Guld.) Temm.

Curlew Sandpiper.

Scolopax subarquata, GULDENSTAEDT, Nov. Comm. Petrop. XIX, 1775, 471 ; pl. xviii. Caspian sea.—GM. Syst. Nat.
    I, 1788, 658.

Tringa subarquata, TEMM. Man. II, 1820, 609.—NUTT. Man. II, 104.—AUD. Orn. Biog. III, 1835, 444 ; pl. 263.
    IB. Syn. 234.—IB. Birds Amer. V, 1842, 269 ; pl. 333.

" *Ancylocheilus subarquata*," KAUP, Europ. Thierw. 1829.

Pelidna subarquata, BON. List. 1838.

Erolia variegata, VIEILLOT, Anal. 1816, 69.

FIGURES. -Buff. Pl. Enl. 851.--Temm, Pl. Col. 510.—Aud. B. of Am. pl. 263 ; oct. ed. V, pl. 333.—Gould, B. of Eur. IV, pl
328.—Naumann, B. of Germ. pl. 185.

SP. CH.—Bill rather longer than the head, slender, compressed, slightly curved towards the tip, which is somewhat expanded ;
both mandibles grooved ; wing long, pointed ; tail short ; legs long, slender ; toes moderate, marginated and flattened underneath. Upper parts brownish black, nearly every feather edged and spotted with bright yellowish red, rump ashy brown, upper
coverts of the tail white, with transverse bands of brownish black ; wings ashy brown, shafts of primaries white. Under parts
fine dark yellowish rufous ; sides, axillaries and under tail coverts, white ; under surface of wing white ; tail pale brownish
ashy, with a greenish gloss ; bill and legs greenish brown.

Young.—Upper parts much more ashy, and with little of the red of the preceding ; under parts entirely dull white, tinged
with yellowish on the breast and sides. An obscure line over the eye, ashy white ; outer feathers of the tail, nearly white.

Total length, about 8¼ to 9 inches ; wing, 5 ; tail, 2½ ; bill from gape, 1¼ to 1½ ; tarsus, 1 to 1¼ inches.

Hab.—Atlantic coast of the United States, rare ; Europe ; Asia ; Africa.

The Curlew sandpiper is one of the rarest of the sandpipers known to inhabit the United States,
and may be looked upon, very properly, as a straggler only, from the Old World. It is very
extensively diffused throughout Europe, Asia, and Africa, from each of which continents we
find specimens in the collection of the Philadelphia Academy, apparently quite identical in
specific characters.

This bird is occasionally shot on the shores of the Atlantic, and very probably also occurs on
the Pacific, though no specimens are contained in the collections of the surveying parties.
Our friend, Mr. John G. Bell of New York, informs us of several instances of the capture of
this bird on the coast near New York, and it is accordingly included by Mr. Giraud in his
interesting and valuable work, "The Birds of Long Island."

In several American specimens now before us, including that figured by Mr. Audubon, which
is now in Professor Baird's collection, we find no peculiar characters. All the specimens that
we have examined appear to be identical, from whatever country.

List of specimens.

Catalogue No.	No. of spec.	Sex.	Locality.	Whence obtained.
2000	1	----------	United States (?).	S. F. Baird .....
9685	2	♀	Europe..........	Baron V. Müller .
9686	3	----------	....do..........	.......do.......

[1] *Erolia*, VIEILLOT, Analyse, 1816. Type *Scolopax subarquata*, GULD.

Schoeniclus, Moehring.[1]

TRINGA ALPINA, var. AMERICANA, Cass.

Red-backed Sandpiper.

Tringa alpina, Linn. Syst. Nat. I, 1766, 249.—Wilson Am. Orn. VII, 1813, 25; pl. lvi.—Sw. F. B. Am. II. 1831, 383.—Nutt. Man. II, 106.—Aud. Orn. Biog. III, 1835, 580; pl. 290.—Ib. Syn. 234.—Ib. Birds Amer. V, 1842, 266; pl. 332.
Tringa cinclus, Linn. Syst. Nat. I, 1766, 251.—Wils. Am. Orn. VII, 1813, 39; pl. lvii.
Pelidna cinclus, "Cuv." Bon. List. 1838.
Tringa ruficollis, Gm. I, 1788, 680.
Tringa variabilis, Meyer, Tasch. Deutsch. Vögel, II, 1810, 397.
? *Tringa schinzii*, Brehm, Lehrb. Europ. Vögel, II, 1824, 571. (Not of American writers.)
Pelidna schinzii, Brehm, Nat. Vög. Deutschl. 1831, 663.

Figures.—Buff. Pl. Enl. 852.—Gould B. of Eur. IV, pl. 329.—Naumann, B. of Germ. pl. 186.—Wilson, Am. Orn. VII, pl. 57, fig. 3; pl. 56, fig. 2.—Aud. B. of Am. pl. 290, oct. ed. V, pl. 332.

Sp. Ch.—Bill longer than the head, wide at base, curved, slightly widened and flattened towards the end; nasal groove and another groove in the under mandible long and very distinct; wings long; tail short, with the two middle feathers longest and pointed; legs rather long and slender, lower half of the tibia naked; toes moderate, free at base, flattened underneath and slightly marginated; claws much compressed, hind toe small. Upper parts yellowish red, mixed with ashy, and every feather having a lanceolate, ovate or narrow spot in the centre, most numerous on the back and rump. Front, sides of the head, and entire under parts, ashy white, nearly pure white on the abdomen and under tail coverts; a wide transverse band of black across the lower part of the breast; neck before and upper part of the breast with narrow longitudinal spots of brownish black. Under wing coverts and axillary feathers white; quills light ashy brown, darker on their outer edges, with their shafts white; tail feathers light ashy brown; middle feathers darker, outer nearly white. Bill and legs brownish black. Sexes alike.

Winter plumage.—Entire upper parts dark ashy, nearly black on the rump, and upper tail coverts; throat, abdomen, axillaries and under wing coverts, white; breast pale ashy, with longitudinal lines of dark brown.

Total length, 8 to 8½ inches; wing, 5; tail, 2¼; bill from gape, 1½; tarsus, 1 inch.

Hab.—Entire temperate regions of North America.

In its summer plumage this is the most handsome bird of the family of sandpipers, and is easily recognized by its wide black band across the under parts of the body. It is exceedingly abundant on the shores of the Atlantic.

We have not a sufficient number of European specimens of the true *T. alpina* of that continent for satisfactory comparison, especially as ornithologists mention differences in size at the same localities; but of eight specimens from Europe and Asia, now before us, not one ought to be considered as specifically the same as the American bird. The size is invariably smaller and the bill disproportionately shorter. In fact, we have little doubt that the bird inhabiting both the Atlantic and Pacific coasts of the republic is quite distinct and may be easily recognized.

[1] *Schoeniclus*, Moehring, Gen. Av. 1752. Type *Tringa cinclus*, L. Equal to *Pelidna*, Cuv.

List of specimens.

Catal. No.	Sex.	Locality.	When collected.	Whence obtained.	Orig. No.	Collected by—	Length.	Stretch of wings.	Wing.	Remarks.
2519	♂	Carlisle, Pa............	Oct. 13,1845	S. F. Baird.........	......	....	8.32	15.00	4.75	....
2518	♂	......do..............	......do....	......do..........	......	....	8.32	15.16	4.80	....
1052	♂	Cape May, N. J........	May —,1842	J. K. Townsend ...	......	....	9.00	15.80	5.00	....
10442	♀	........do..	......do....	......do..........	......	....	....	....	....	....
3941	......	California.............	....	Dr. Heermann.....	......	....	....	....	....	....
5566	♀	Petaluma, Cal	....	E. Samuels	......	....	...	....	....	....
4602	......	St. Helen's, O. T......	....	Dr. Suckley........	......	....	....	....	....	....
6675	.. ...	Shoalwater bay........	May 3,1854	Gov. Stevens......	68	Dr. Cooper	8.50	15.25	....	Iris brown; bill and feet black..........
6668	.....	....do...............	.. ..	......do..........	.....	......do..........	....	....	....	......do.........
6674	......	....do...............	Mar. 2,1854	......do..	54	......do..........	9.00	16.00	....	......do.........
6671	......	....do...............	May 3,1854	......do..........	68	......do..........	8.50	15.25	....	....
6669	......	Fort Steilacoom, W. T.	April —,1853	Dr. Suckley	......	....	....	....	....	....
4591	......	......do..............	Feb. 6,1856	......do..........	......	....	8.50	15.00	4.84	....
9540	......	Puget's Sound........	Nov. 30,1856	A. Campbell......	......	Dr. Kennerly....	....	....	....	....
9538	......	Simeahmoo bay.......	..... do.....	......do..........	......	......do..	8.25	13.50	4.50	....
9539	......	........do.	....	......do..........	......	......do..	....	....	....	....

Actodromas, Kaup.[1]

TRINGA MACULATA, Vieill.

Jack Snipe.

Tringa maculata, VIEILLOT, Nouv. Dict. XXXIV, 1819, 465.
Tringa pectoralis, SAY, Long's Exped. I, 1823, 171.—BON. Am. Orn. IV, 1832, 43; pl. xxiii.—NUTT. Man. II, 111.—
  AUD. Orn. Biog. III, 1835, 601: V,582; pl. 291.—IB. Syn.233.—IB. Birds Amer. V, 1842, 259; pl. 329
Tringa campestris, LICHT. Verz. 1823, 74, (not of Vieillot, 1819.)

FIGURES.—Bonap. Am. Orn. IV, pl. 23, fig. 2.—Aud. B. of Am. pl. 294; oct. ed. V, pl. 329.—Gould B. of Eur. IV, pl. 327.

SP. CH.—Bill rather longer than the head, compressed, slightly depressed and expanded at the tip; nasal groove long; wings long; legs rather long, tibia with nearly its lower half naked; toes free at base, flattened underneath and slightly margined; tail rather short; middle feathers pointed.   Entire upper parts brownish black; all the feathers edged and tipped with ashy and brownish red; rump and upper tail coverts black, some of the outer feathers of the latter edged with white. Line from the bill over the eye ashy white; throat, abdomen, under wing coverts, axillary feathers, and under tail coverts, white. Breast and neck before ashy white; all the feathers darker at base, and with partially concealed lanceolate or pointed spots of brownish black. Quills brownish black; shaft of first primary white, of others brown; secondaries tipped and edged with white; tertiaries edged with dull reddish yellow.   Bill and feet dark greenish black.   Total length about 9 inches; wing, 5¼; tail, 2½; bill to gape, 1⅓; tarsus, 1 inch.

Hab.—The entire coasts of North America; South America; Europe.

Of rather frequent occurrence on the coast of the Atlant.c, and rearing its young in the northern States of the Union.   In the present collection also are specimens from western North America, and in the Museum of the Philadelphia Academy we find numerous examples from various parts of South America.   This bird is easily recognized by its spotted breast and the light yellow of the basal portion of the bill.   We have no doubt that the description and name given by Vieillot, as above, apply to this species.

This species has been ascertained to breed abundantly in Wisconsin by Professor T. Kümlein, an energetic cultivator of zoological science, now resident in that State.   In the Museum of the Philadelphia Academy, specimens from various countries of South America are in the winter

[1] *Actodromas*, KAUP, Sk. Ent. Europ. Thierw. 1829. Type *Tringa minuta*, LEISLER.

and young plumage, and tend to demonstrate that the winter migration of this species extends over a large portion of the southern division of this continent.

List of specimens.

Catal. No.	Sex.	Locality.	When collected.	Whence obtained.	Orig. No.	Collected by—	Length.	Stretch of wings.	Wing.
1316	♂	Carlisle, Pa..............	Mar. 28, 1844	S. F. Baird............		....	9.32	18.50	5.32
1739	♂	......do................	Nov. 2, 1844	......do...........		....	9.32	17.75	5.56
1712	♀	......do................	Oct. 7......	......do...........		....	8.64	16.25	5.16
2513	....	......do................	Sept. 27, 1845	......do...........		....	9.50	17.80	5.55
2093	♀	......do..............	April 12, 1845	......do...........		....	8.56	16.75	5.25
7597	....	Washington, D. C............	....	Wm. Hutton............		....	....	....	....
10417	♂	Marion county, Ill..........	April 8......	N.W. University........		R. Kennicott............	....	....	....
9537	....	Simeahmoo bay	....	A. Campbell		Dr. Kennerly	....	....	....
4186	....	Tamaulipas, Mexico	....	Lt. Couch		....	8.50	17.00	5.75
6690	....	Puget's Sound.	....	Dr. Suckley............		....	....	....	....
6691	....	Fort Steilacoom, W. T.......	May 5, 1856	......do............	373	....	....	....	....
6693	....	......do................	....	......do............	563	....	....	....	....

TRINGA WILSONII, Nuttall.

Least Sandpiper.

Tringa pusilla, WILSON, Am. Orn. V, 1812, 32; pl. 37. Not of Linnaeus.—AUD. Orn. Biog. IV, 1838, 180; pl. 320.—IB. Syn. 237.—IB. Birds Am. V, 1842, 280; pl. 337.

Pelidna pusilla, BON. List, 1838.

? *Tringa minutilla*, VIEILLOT, Nouv. Dict. XXXIV, 1819, 466.

Tringa wilsonii, NUTTALL, Man. II, 1834, 121.

FIGURES.—Wilson, Am. Orn V, pl. 37, fig. 4.—Audubon's B. of Am. pl. 320, oct. ed. V, pl. 337.

SP. CH.—The smallest of all known species of this group found in North America. Bill about as long as the head, slightly curved towards the end, which is very slightly expanded; grooves in both mandibles to near the tip; wing long; tertiaries nearly as long as the primaries; tail short; middle feathers longest; outer feathers frequently longer than the intermediate; legs long; lower third of the tibia naked; toes long, slender, margined and flattened beneath; hind toe small. Upper parts with nearly every feather having a large central spot of brownish black, and widely margined with ashy and bright brownish red; rump and middle of the upper tail coverts black; outer coverts white spotted with black. Stripe over the eye, throat, and breast pale ashy white, with numerous small longitudinal spots of ashy brown; abdomen and under tail coverts white. Quills dark brown with the shafts of the primaries white; tertiaries edged with reddish. Middle feathers of the tail brownish black; outer feathers light ashy white. Under surface of wing light brownish ashy, with a large spot of white near the shoulder; axillary feathers white; bill and legs greenish brown, the latter frequently yellowish green. Total length from tip of bill to end of tail about 5¼ to 6 inches; wing, 3½ to 3¾; tail, 1¾; bill to gape, ¾; tarsus, ¾ inch.

Hab.—Entire temperate North America.

This little bird is apparently quite as abundant on the western as on the eastern coast of the republic. Specimens from western localities seem to be slightly larger, and perhaps a shade more ashy in color, but we can make out no specific distinction.

August 5, 1858.

List of specimens.

Catal. No.	Sex.	Locality.	When collected.	Whence obtained.	Orig'l No.	Collected by—	Length.	Stretch of wings.	Wing.	Remarks.
1675	♂	Carlisle, Pa	May 15	S. F. Baird.......	......	....	5.88	11.16	3.50	....
1509	♂	......do...............	....do.....	.....do........			5.80	11.16	3.50	....
1674	♂	......do...............	Aug. 12,1844	.....do........			6.00	11.25	3.56	....
1510	♀	......do...............	May 15.....	......do.......			6.16	11.80	3.80	....
1511	..	......do...............		.....do...			5.80	11.50	3.64	....
10443	♂	Cape May, N. J.......		.....do..		J. K. Townsend				
1179	......	Washington, D. C...		.....do.........						
10416	......	South Illinois.........		N. W. University		R. Kennicott..				
9046	♂	Loup fork, Platte		Lieut. Warren ...		Dr. Hayden...	5.75	10.84	3.50	Iris deep brown... ......
8801	......	Scott's Bluff, Neb...	Aug. 29	W. M. Magraw ..		Dr. Cooper...	5.84	11.12	3.50	
8789	......	North fork of Platte....	...do.....	.....do........		.....do......	6.00	11.36	3.75	Iris brown; bill and feet black.
6686	......	Texas......................		Capt. J. Pope.....						
5568	♂	Petaluma, Cal.........		E. Samuels......	766	....	5.08	10.00	3.48	
6679		Fort Steilacoom, W. T.	May 5......	Gov. Stevens.....	376	Dr. Suckley....				
6688	♂	......do.............		Dr. Suckley.....	375		5.54	11.36		
6681	......	......do.............		Gov. Stevens	89	Dr. Suckley...				.
6678	♂	......do.............		.....do.........	377	.....do......				.
6682	......	Puget's Sound.........	Aug. —,1856	Dr. Suckley	561	.....do......				....

TRINGA BONAPARTII, Schlegel.

Tringa schinzii, "Brehm," Bon. Syn. 1828, (not of Brehm.)—Ib. Am. Orn IV, 1832, 69; pl. lxix.—Sw. F. Bor. Am. II, 384.—Nutt. Man. II, 109.—Aud. Orn. Biog. III, 1835, 529; pl. 278.—Ib. Syn 236.—Ib. Birds Amer. V, 1842, 275; pl. 335.

Pelidna schinzii, Bon. Comp. List, 1838.

Tringa cinclus, var. Say, Long's Exped. 1823.

Tringa bonapartii, Schlegel, Rev. Crit. Ois. Eur. 1844, 89.

? Scolopax pusilla, Gm. Syst. I, 1788, 663.

Figures—Bonap. Am. Orn. IV, pl. 24, fig. 2.—Aud. B. of Am. pl. 278; oct. ed. V, pl 335.—Gould B. of Eur. IV, pl. 330.

Sp. Ch.—Smaller; bill slightly arched towards the tip, which is somewhat enlarged and flattened, about the length of the head; grooves in both mandibles long and narrow; wings long; secondary quills obliquely incised at the ends; tail rather longer than usual in this group, with the feathers broad; legs rather long and slender; toes free at base; hind toe very small. Upper parts light ashy brown, darker on the rump; nearly all the feathers with ovate or wide lanceolate central spots of brownish black, and many of them edged with bright yellowish red; upper tail coverts white. Under parts white, with numerous small spots of dark brown on the neck before, breast, and sides, somewhat disposed to form transverse bands on the last. Quills brownish black, darker at the tips; shaft of outer primary white, of others light brown; middle feathers of tail brownish black; outer feathers lighter and edged with ashy white; under wing coverts and axillaries white; bill and feet greenish black. Total length about 7 inches; wing, 4¾; tail, 2¼; bill, 1; tarsus rather less than an inch.

Hab.—North America, east of the Rocky mountains.

This is an abundant little sandpiper, sadly misnamed by American ornithologists. It is really very little like *Tringa schinzii,* Brehm, (figured in Naumann's Birds of Germany, pl. 187,) which is merely a smaller variety, or perhaps only smaller specimens of the common *Tringa alpina* of Europe and America.

This bird appears to be restricted to the countries east of the Rocky mountains.

List of specimens.

Catal. number.	Locality.	When collected.	Whence obtained.
3451	New York	1846	S. F. Baird
4869	Omaha City		Lieutenant Warren
5442	Yellowstone river		do
8800	Fort Kearney to Laramie	August, 1857	Dr. Cooper

CALIDRIS, Cuvier.

Calidris, CUVIER, Anat. Comp. V, in chart, 1805.   Type *Tringa arenaria*, L.

CH.—General characters of *Tringa*, but without hind toe. Bill straight, rather longer than the head and tarsus, widened somewhat or spoon-shaped at the end. Tail doubly emarginate. Toes short; middle one scarcely two-thirds the tarsus.

CALIDRIS ARENARIA, Illiger.

Sanderling.

Tringa arenaria, LINN. Syst. Nat. I, 1766, 251.—AUD. Orn. Biog.—IB. Birds Amer, V, 1842, 287 ; pl. 338.
Calidris arenaria, ILLIGER, Prod. 1811, 249.—Sw. F. B. Am. II, 366.—NUTT. Man. II, 1834, 4.
Charadrius calidris, LINN. Syst. Nat. I, 1766, 255.—WILS. Am. Orn. VII, 1813, 68 ; pl. lix.
Charadrius rubidus, GM. I, 1788, 688.—WILSON, Am. Orn. VII, 1813, 129 ; pl. lxiii.
Tringa tridactyla, PALLAS, Zoog. II, 1811, 198.
Calidris tringoides, VIEILLOT, Gal. II, 1825, 95.
Calidris americana, BREHM, Vögel Deutschl. 1831, 675.—IB. Naumannia, I, 1850, 69.

FIGURES.—Wilson, Am. Orn. VII, pl. 59, fig. 4, pl. 63, fig. 3.—Aud. B. of Am. pl. 230; oct. ed V, pl, 338.

SP. CH.—No hind toe; front toes moderate or rather long, flattened underneath; distinctly margined with a membrane. Bill rather longer than the head, straight, rather thick ; ridge of upper mandible flattened ; nasal groove deep and nearly as long as the upper mandible, not so distinct in the lower; both mandibles widened and flattened at the tip; aperture of the nostril large and covered with a membrane. Wing long; tail short, with the middle feathers longest; under coverts long as the tail; legs moderate; lower third of the tibia naked. Upper parts light ashy, with lanceolate, hastate, and ovate spots of brownish black on the top of the head, on the back, scapulars, and shorter quills; rump and upper tail coverts with fine transverse lines of black. Under parts pure white. Shoulders brownish black, without spots; quills brownish black with their shafts white and much paler on their inner webs ; greater wing coverts widely tipped with white; middle feathers of the tail ashy brown, edged with white ; outer feathers paler; bill and legs greenish black. Sexes alike.

In spring plumage the head, neck, and breast are tinged with pale yellowish red and spotted with dark brown; back and scapulars edged and tipped with yellowish red; rump and upper tail coverts ashy brown; under parts of the body pure white.

Total length, 7¾ to 8 inches; wing, 5; tail, 2; bill about 1 inch; tarsus about 1 inch.

Hab.—Entire temperate regions of North America, South America, Europe.

An abundant species on both the Atlantic and Pacific coasts of the republic, and extending its range in winter into South America. We can find no reliable distinction between the American and the European bird, though specimens differ quite materially in size and length of bill.

List of specimens.

Catal. No.	Sex.	Locality.	When collected.	Whence obtained.	Orig'l No.	Collected by—	Length.	Stretch of wings.	Wing.	Remarks.
1150	♀	Cape May, N. J.........	July 20,1843	S. F. l aird	......	....	7.75	15.00	5.08	....
1151	....	.........do........	.....do......	......do............	......	....	7.64	14.50	4.89	....
2374	....	Marietta, Pa.......	....	......do....	......	....	....	....	....	....
8459	....	Florida	....	G. Würdemann....	......	....	....	....	....	....
6683	....	Puget's Sound, W. T.....	Aug. 26,1856	Dr. Suckley	562	....	....	....	....	....
6680	....	Fort Steilacoom, W. T....	....	Gov. Stevens	40	Dr. Suckley....	... ...	....	....	....
9535	....	Simeahmoo, W. T......	Nov. 24,1857	A. Campbell.......	......	Dr. Kennerly..	....	....	....	....
6670	....	Shoalwater bay, W. T....	Mar. 2,1854	Gov. Stevens	......	Dr. Cooper.....	8.00	15.50	....	Iris brown ; bill and feet black.
6672	....	.........do.	.....do......	......do...........	......	.....do..........	8.00	15.50	....	....
1788	....	England....................	.. ..	S. F. Baird........	......	....	....	....	....	....

EREUNETES, Illiger.

Ereunetes, ILLIGER, Prodromus, 1811, 262.

Hemipalama, BONAP. Obs. Wils. 1825, No. 212. Type *Tringa semipalmata.* Not of Syn. 1828.

Heteropoda, NUTT. Man. II, 1834. Not of Latreille, 1804.

The genus *Ereunetes* of Illiger has for its type a species, called *E. petrificatus* by him, from Bahia, supposed to be identical with *Tringa semipalmata,* although the description, " smaller than *Actitis hypoleucus,* the colors similar," leaves much to be desired.

The bill of our species of *Ereunetes* is quite stout and considerably expanded, by which it is readily distinguished from *Actodromas wilsonii* independently of the semipalmated feet. The tarsus and middle toe are about equal ; the tibia denuded anteriorly for about two-thirds the length of tarsus. The basal membrane of toes is more scolloped out interiorly than exteriorly ; the notch externally not quite as deep as to the first joint, although the membrane extends beyond the second. There is a tendency to hexagonal sub-division in the bare portion of tibia anteriorly. The tail is doubly emarginate.

EREUNETES PETRIFICATUS, Ill.

Semipalmated Sandpiper.

? Tringa pusilla, LINN. Syst. Nat. I, 1766, 252.

Ereunetes petrificatus, ILLIGER, Prod. 1811,262. (Proved identical with *Tringa semipalmata,* Wils. by Cabanis.) from actual examination of original specimen in Berlin Mus.

Tringa semipalmata, WILSON, Am. Orn. VII, 1813, 131 ; pl. lxiii.—Sw. F. B. A. II, 381.—AUD. Orn. Biog. V, 1839, 111 ; pl. 408.—IB. Syn 236.—IB Birds Amer. V, 1842, 277 ; pl. 336.

Tringa (Hemipalama) semipalmata, BON. Obs. Wils 1825 ; No. 212.

Tringa (Heteropoda) semipalmata, NUTT Man. II, 1834, 136.

Heteropada semipalmata, BON. List, 1838.

Ereunetes semipalmatus, CAB. Schomburgk's Reise, III, 758.—BON. Comptes Rendus, XLIII, Sept. 1856.—CABANIS, Journ. Nov. 1856, 419. (Cuba.)

Tringa brevirostris, SPIX, Av. Bras. II, 1825, 76.

? Heteropoda mauri, BON. Comp. List, 1838.

Ereunetes mauri, GUNDL. Cab. Jour. 1856. 419.

Hemipalama minor, GUNDLACH, Lembeye, Av. Cuba.

FIGURES —Wilson, Am. Orn. VII, pl. 63, fig. 4.—Aud. B. of Am. pl. 405, oct. ed. V, pl. 336.—Spix, B. of Brazil, II, pl. 93.

Sp. Ch.—Smaller; bill about the length of the head ; rather thicker than usual in this group; both mandibles somewhat expanded and flattened at the tip, and minutely punctulated, as in the genera *Scolopax* and *Gallinago.* Wings long ; legs moderate, rather slender ; toes united at base by a membrane, which is large, between the outer and middle toes extending to the first joint; hind toe small ; tail short, with the middle feathers longest ; outer feathers frequently longer than the third, presenting a doubly emarginate character to the tail; under coverts nearly as long as the tail. Upper parts light brownish ashy, with lanceolate or ovate spots of brownish black in the middle of the feathers ; rump and upper tail coverts black. Front, band of the eye, and entire under parts, ashy white, with small spots on the breast of ashy brown ; quills brownish black, lighter on their inner webs, and with their shafts white ; middle feathers of the tail brownish black : outer feathers pale brownish ashy ; under wing coverts and axillaries white ; bill greenish black ; feet dark, the lower part of the tarsus and toes frequently tinged with yellow. Upper parts in summer mixed with light reddish. Total length, about 6½ inches ; wing, 3¾ ; tail, 1¾ ; bill from gape, ¾ ; tarsus, ¾ to 1 inch.

Hab —Entire temperate regions of North America, South America.

This abundant little species is singularly variable in the length of its bill, so much so, in fact, that a student with two specimens representing extremes in this particular would deem it quite impossible that they could be identical specifically. We have before us, however, inter- mediates of quite a variety of dimensions.

On shortness of bill as a character Prof. Gundlach founded his species *minor,* as above cited. The shortest billed specimen in the present collection is Mr. Kennicott's, from Illinois.

We have little doubt that this bird is the true *Tringa pusilla* of Linnaeus, as cited above, the proper locating of which name has puzzled naturalists not a little. This name is applied by Linnaeus to the bird described and figured by Brisson as above given, examination of whose figure will show that he was very careful in giving the toes united by membranes at base. This character exclusively characterizes the species before us, amongst all the smaller sandpipers of the continent of America, so far as our knowledge extends. Brisson describes, however, specimens from the island of Saint Domingo, from which, nor from any other island of the West Indies, we have never seen specimens.

Specimens of this bird from various parts of South America are in the museum of the Philadelphia Academy.

The *Heterepoda mauri* of Bonaparte appears to be merely a larger race of the present species.

List of specimens.

Catal. No.	Sex.	Locality.	When col- lected.	Whence obtained.	Orig'l No.	Collected by—	Length.	Stretch of wings.	Wing.	Remarks.
708	♀	Carlisle, Pa	Sept. 6, 1842	S. F. Baird						
1650		....do.	July 27, 1844	....do.			6.56	12.25	3.80	
1139	♀	Cape May, N. J	July 14, 1843	....do.			5.64	10.87	3.56	
10415		South Illinois		N. W. University		R. Kennicott				
4870		Bijou Hill	May 14, 1856	Lieut. Warren		Dr. Hayden				
9045	♀	Loup fork of Platte		....do.		....do.	6.00	12.25	4.00	
9047	♀	....do.		....do.		....do.	6.60	12.25	3.75	
9048	♀	....do.	July 8.	....do.		....do.				
8446		Puget's Sound, W. T.		A. Campbell		Dr. Kennerly	6.00	11.50	3.25	
8444	♀	....do.		....do.		....do.	6.00	11.12	5.60	
6677		Shoalwater bay	May 3.	Gov. Stevens	69	Dr. Cooper	7.50	12.50		Iris brown ; bill and feet black.
6687		Presidio, Cal.		Lieut. Trowbridge						
5567	♂	Petaluma, Cal.		E. Samuels						

MICROPALAMA, Baird.

Hemipalama, Bon. Synopsis, 1828, 316.   Type *Tringa himantopus,* Bon.   Not of Bon. Obs. Wils. 1825, No. 212, which includes only *Tringa semipalmata,* Wilson.

The present genus, with a basal membrane to all the anterior toes, as in *Ereunetes,* has this a little more deeply emarginate ; the bill and legs much longer ; the former more curved.   The bare portion of tibia is covered before and behind by transverse scutellae, like the tarsus.   The tail is nearly even, with a single emargination.   The middle toe is not two-thirds the length of tarsus, and about equal to the bare portion of the tibia.   The bill is much pitted at the end in the dry skin.

In many respects this species approaches the snipe, and its true place is probably very near *Macrorhamphus.*   The legs, however, are much longer, and equal to the bill, instead of much shorter.

A reference to the original article on *Hemipalama,* by Bonaparte, in Obs. Wilson, 1825, will show that the genus was established for *Tringa semipalmata,* and, consequently, cannot be used for the present species.

MICROPALAMA HIMANTOPUS, (Bon.) Baird.

Stilt Sandpiper.

Tringa himantopus, Bon. Ann. N. Y. Lyc. II, Dec. 1826, 157.—Sw. F. B. Am. II, 1831, 380.—Aud. Orn. Biog. IV, 1838, 332 ; pl 344.—Ib. Syn. 235.—Ib. Birds Amer. V, 1842, 271 ; pl 334.

Tringa (Hemipalama) himantopus, Bonap. Specchio Comp. 1827, No. 187.—Ib. Syn 1828, 316.—Ib. Am. Orn. IV, 1832, 89 ; pl. xxv.—Nutt. Man. II, 138.

Hemipalama himantopus, Bon. List, 1838.

? Tringa douglassi, Swainson, F. B. A. II, 1831, 379 ; pl. lxvi.

Tringa (Hemipalama) audubonii, Nuttall, Man II, 1834, 140.   (Based on description of *Tringa himantopus,* in F. B. Am.)

Hemipalama multistriata, "Licht." G. R. Gray, Genera, III, 578.

Figures.—Sw. and Rich. Faun Bor. Am. II, pl. 66.—Aud. B. of Am. pl. 344, Oct. ed. V, pl. 334.—Bonap. Am. Orn. IV, pl. 25, fig. 3.

Sp. Ch.—Legs long, slender ; toes slender, united at base with webs, the outer of which is the larger ; hind toe small.   Bill long, somewhat arched, slender, much compressed, expanded, and flattened at the tip, which is minutely punctulated and corrugated ; wings long, pointed ; tail short ; middle feathers longest ; outer feathers frequently longer than the next ; under coverts long ; lower half of the tibia naked.   Upper parts brownish black, nearly all the feathers edged with ashy white and yellowish red ; narrow band from above the eye to the occiput bright brownish red, (inclosing the brownish black of the top of the head ; spot on the ears the same red ; rump and upper tail coverts white, with transverse narrow stripes and pointed spots of brownish black.   Under parts ashy white, tinged with pale reddish, with numerous longitudinal stripes of brownish black on the neck, and with transverse stripes of the same on the other under parts ; axillary feathers white ; under wing coverts ashy white ; bill and legs greenish black.

Young ? Very slight traces of the red on the ears and occiput ; line from the base of the bill over the eye white ; entire upper plumage paler and more tinged with ashy than in the preceding.   Entire under parts pale ashy white, tinged with dull yellow, and with small and obscure spots of dark brownish on the breast ; abdomen, and under tail coverts nearly pure white, (without the transverse stripes, as in the preceding plumage ;) rump and upper tail coverts white.

Total length, about 8½o 9 inches ; wing, 5¼ ; tail, 2¼ ; bill, 1¾ ; tarsus, 1¾ inches.

Hab.—Eastern North America.

This curious and very remarkable sandpiper appears to be restricted to the countries east of the Rocky mountains.   We have no doubt that all the above given names apply to one species, though amongst numerous specimens before us there are some differences in size and length of legs, but not sufficient for specific character.

List of specimens.

Catalogue number.	Locality.	Whence obtained.	Remarks.
8076	Arctic circle_____	Mr. John Gould_____	Supposed type of *Tringa douglassi* in F. B. A.___
_____	Red Fork of the Arkansas__	Dr. Woodhouse _____	_____
550	New York_____	S. F. Baird _____	_____

Sub–Family TOTANINAE.

Ch.—Bill as long as the head, or longer ; the basal portion covered with soft skin ; the terminal portion (generally at least half) horny, and more or less attenuated and pointed in *Totaneae* The lateral grooves of bill extending to the horny terminal portion. The gape of mouth extending behind the base of culmen. Toes generally connected by a basal membrane. The tail always with distinct transverse bars in North American species, except in *Heteroscelus.*

This sub-family appears to differ from most *Scolopacinae* in the less degree of sensitiveness in the tip of the bill, which is more horny, and not covered by soft skin well supplied with nerves. The toes are almost always connected at the base by a membrane, this being the rule and not the exception, as in *Scolopacinae.*

The following may be taken as an approximate indication of the divisions of this sub-family :

A. Tarsi covered anteriorly and posteriorly by transverse scutellae, except in *Heteroscelus ;* finely reticulated laterally. Bill nearly straight, or bent a little upwards.

TOTANEAE.—Bill nearly straight, about as long as the tarsus, attenuated. Bill not grooved for the terminal fourth. Gape of mouth extending beyond base of culmen.

LIMOSEAE.—Bill longer than the tarsus, curving slightly upwards towards the end, where it is thickened. Both mandibles grooved for nearly their whole length. Gape of mouth very short, not extending beyond the base of culmen.

B. Tarsi covered anteriorly only by transverse scutellae, reticulated laterally and behind. Bill curving considerably downwards from near the middle.

NUMENIEAE.—Lateral grooves not extending beyond the middle. Bill thickened at the tip ; longer than the tarsus.

The *Limoseae* and *Numenieae*, in many respects, the former especially, approach the *Scolopacinae*, and it would not be surprising if one or both were more properly placed in this sub-family, in more immediate connexion with *Macrorhamphus.*

Section TOTANEAE.

Ch.—Bill slender, straight, not exceeding the tarsus ; more or less attenuated for the terminal fourth, and pointed at the tip. Bill hard and horny for much of the terminal half ; the lateral grooves shallow. Toes anteriorly connected by membrane. Tail strongly barred, except in *Heteroscelus*, which also has the tarsus reticulated behind.

The *Totaneae* are distinguished from *Numenieae* by the transverse scutellae on the back of tarsus ; from the *Limoseae*, by the shorter and more deeply cleft bill. From *Tringeae* they may be known by the fact that the toes are almost always webbed at the base, although the web is usually confined to the outer toe, while in the rare instances where there is a web in *Tringeae* (*Ereunetes* and *Micropalama*) it extends to the inner also. The bill is much harder and stronger, more tapering and pointed, usually a little recurved, and without the papillose or pitted appearance of the other. It is seldom, if ever, expanded laterally near the tip. The difference in cleft of the mouth is very striking—this always extending behind the base of culmen, sometimes nearly to the eyes, instead of merely reaching to or even falling short of the beginning or base of culmen. This appears to indicate a radical difference in the character of food, the *Totaneae* being capable of feeding on hard substances of rather large size, while the food of *Tringeae* is softer, smaller, and sucked into the mouth, rather than taken in any other way. A strong mark of distinction for the North American species, at least, is seen in the conspicuous transverse bars of the tail in *Totaneae*, scarcely ever found in *Tringeae*, although occurring again in *Scolopaceae*. The single exception is seen in the genus *Heteroscelus*, in which the upper plumage is entirely uniform, without bars or spots anywhere. The tarsus is covered laterally and behind with hexagonal scales, somewhat as in *Strepsilas*, but they are more irregular.

Synopsis of genera.

A. Bill with the upper mandible grooved only for about basal half; rather longer than the head; commissure bent slightly upwards from the middle. Tarsi scutellate behind, with transverse scales.

   Both outer and inner toes webbed.

   SYMPHEMIA.—Bill very thick, recurved. Tarsus 1½ times the middle toe.

   Inner toe separated from middle nearly to base. Bill more slender.

   GLOTTIS.—Bill stouter and higher at base than in others of the section; more recurved. Legs green.

   GAMBETTA.—Legs lengthened; tarsus 1¼ times the middle toe. Legs yellow.

   RHYACHOPHILUS.—Legs short; tarsus equal to the middle toe.

B. Bill as in preceding; the nasal groove extending a little further forward. Commissure straight. Tarsus with polygonal small scales behind, (only present here among *Totaneae*.)

   HETEROSCELUS.—Bill much longer than the tarsus, which equals the middle toe. Legs short. Outer toe webbed.

C. Bill with the upper mandible grooved on the side for three-fourths or more its length; not longer than the head.

   Cleft of mouth extending but little beyond the base of culmen.

   TRINGOIDES.—Bill, tarsus, and middle toe about same length; legs short. Tail more than half the wings. Inner toe with very slight basal web.

   PHILOMACHUS.—Tarsus much longer than middle toe, which is longer than the bill. Legs lengthened. Tail not half the wings.

   Cleft of mouth extending nearly to eyes; the culmen two-thirds the commissure.

   ACTITURUS.—Feathers extending farther on upper jaw than lower. Interspace of rami not filled with feathers. Legs long; tarsus 1½ times middle toe. Outer toe much webbed at base; inner, with very slight web. Tail more than half the wing.

   TRYNGITES.—extending much farthest on lower jaw. Interspace of rami filled entirely with feathers. Legs short. Tarsus equal to middle toe; all the toes cleft to the base, or with a very short web. Tail not half the wing.

SYMPHEMIA, Rafinesque.

Symphemia, RAFINESQUE, Jour. de Phys. 1819.   Type *Scolopax semipalmata*, Gmelin.
Catoptrophorus, BONAP. Syn. 1828, 323.   Same type.

CH.—Bill compressed, very thick, the culmen rounded.   The lower mandible scarcely grooved ; the upper grooved to about the middle.   Culmen slightly convex : gonys ascending.   Bill cleft but little beyond base of culmen.   Feathers of sides of both mandibles falling short of the nostrils ; the lower rather further forward.   Chin feathers reaching to beginning of nostrils.   Bill longer than head ; about equal to tarsus, which is more than $1\frac{1}{2}$ times the middle toe.   Both toes webbed ; the emargination of inner web as far forward as the middle of basal joint of middle toe ; the outer reaching nearly to the end.   Base portion of tibia rather less than middle toe without claw.   Tail nearly even, or little rounded, not half the wings.

SYMPHEMIA SEMIPALMATA, (Gm.) Hartlaub.

Willet.

Scolopax semipalmatus, GMELIN, Syst. Nat. I, 1788, 659.—WILSON, Am. Orn. VII, 1813, 27 ; pl. lvi.

Totanus semipalmatus, TEMM. Man.—BON. Obs. 1825 ; No. 206.—SW. F. Bor. Am. II, 1831, 388 ; pl. lxvii.—AUD. Orn.
    Biog. III, 1835, 510 : V, 585 ; pl. 274.—IB. Birds Amer. V, 1842, 324 ; pl. 347.

" *Glottis semipalmatus*, NILSSON, Orn. Suec. 1817."

Totanus (Catoptrophorus) semipalmatus, BON. Syn. 1828, 328.—NUTT. Man. II, 1834, 144.

Symphemia semipalmata, HARTLAUB, Rev. Zool. 1845, 342.

? *Totanus speculiferus*, "CUV. R. A. 1817, 2d ed. I, 531."—PUCHERAN, Rev. et Mag. Zool. III, 1851, 569.

Totanus crassirostris, VIEILL. Nouv. Dict. VI, 1816, 406.

Symphemia atlantica, RAF. Journal de Phys. LXXXVIII, 1819, 417.

FIGURES.—Wilson, Am. Orn. VII, pl. 56, fig. 3.—Aud. B. of Am. pl. 274 ; oct. ed. V, pl. 347.—Rich. and Swains. Faun. Bor. Am. Birds, pl. 67.—Gould B. of Eur. IV, pl. 311.

SP. CH.—The largest American species of this genus.   Bill longer than the head, straight, rather thick and strong; groove in the upper mandible extending about half its length, in the lower mandible nearly obsolete; wings long; legs long, strong ; toes moderate. united at base by membranes, the larger of which unites the outer and middle toe ; hind toe small; tail short. *Adult*. Entire upper parts dark ash color, (without spots;) the shafts of the feathers brownish black; rump and upper tail coverts white.   Under parts white, tinged with ashy on the neck and sides; axillaries and under wing coverts brownish black ; primary quills white at base, and tipped with brownish black ; secondaries white, spotted with brownish black; tail ashy white, the two middle feathers strongly tinged with ashy; others spotted with dark ashy brown.   Bill dark bluish brown, lighter at base; legs light blue.   *Younger*. Entire plumage spotted, and transversely banded with brownish black.

Total length about 15 inches ; wing, $8\frac{1}{4}$; tail, $3\frac{1}{4}$; bill about $2\frac{1}{4}$; tarsus about $2\frac{1}{4}$ inches.

Hab.—Entire temperate regions of North America ; South America.

This large and handsome species is easily recognized, and is abundant on both the Atlantic and Pacific coasts of the republic.   There is very considerable difference of color between the adult and young birds ; but the white space on the wings is a character always present and easily distinguished.   It is the largest bird of this group inhabiting the United States.

The *Totanus speculiferus* of Cuvier, according to Pucheran, is very similar to the common willet, but stands higher, and has a longer bill; the feet are similar in both.   I have been unable to appreciate the validity of this distinction in the extensive series before me.

August 10, 1858.
    92 **b**

List of specimens.

Catal. No.	Sex.	Locality.	When collected.	Whence obtained.
1054	♂	Cape May, N. J	May, 1842	S. F. Baird
10155	♀	......do	......do	J. K. Townsend
4258	......	Calcasieu Pass, La	....	G. Würdemann
4259	......	......do	....	........do
5434	......	Medicine creek	....	Lieut. Warren
8998	......	....	....	........do
9818	......	Great Basin, Utah	....	Lieut. Beckwith
9822	......	San Pedro	....	Lieut. Williamson
9817	......	San Diego, Cal	....	Lieut. Trowbridge
9820	......	Bodega, Cal	....	........do
9818	......	Presidio, Cal	....	........do
6445	......	San Francisco, Cal	....	Dr. Suckley

GLOTTIS, Nilsson.

Glottis, Nilsson, Ornithol. Suec. 1817. Type *Scolopax glottis*, Linn. (Gray.)

Ch.—Similar to *Gambetta*. The bill high at base, where it is much compressed, with an upward bend about the middle. Legs green.

The genus *Glottis* differs very little from the American *Gambetta*, and all their species might very appropriately be combined in a single genus, *Glottis*.

GLOTTIS FLORIDANUS, Bon.

Florida Greenshank.

Totanus glottis, Aud. Orn. Biog. III, 1835, 483; pl. 269.—Ib. Syn. 244.—Ib. Birds Amer. V, 1842, 321; pl. 346.
Glottis floridanus, Bon. List, 1838, 51.

Sp Ch.—Very similar to *T. glottis* of Europe, but apparently rather smaller. Bill longer than the head, slender, and slightly curved upwards towards the end; wing rather long; legs long, rather stout; toes moderate, united at base, the larger membrane being between the outer and middle toes; that between the inner and middle toes very small; hind toe small. Entire upper parts dark ashy, on the head with lines of dark brown; wing feather of the scapulars and greater coverts edged with pale ashy white and with a sub-edging line of brownish black; tertiaries dark ashy, with imperfect transverse bars of black; back, rump, and upper tail coverts white, the last with transverse bars of brownish black. Tail white; two middle feathers and outer edges of others with lines of brown. Under parts white, tinged with ashy, and spotted with brown on the breast; under wing coverts and axillaries white. Bill greenish brown; legs dark green. Quills brownish black; shaft of first primary white. Total length about 11 inches; wing, 7; tail, 3; bill, 2¼; tarsus rather more than 2¼ inches.

Hab.—Florida, (Mr. Audubon)

With the original specimen of Mr. Audubon before us, it is not without some hesitation that we admit this bird as distinct from the common European species, *Totanus glottis;* but it appears to be smaller in all its parts than any one of numerous specimens from the old world in the museum of the Philadelphia Academy. The bill especially is slender and recurved.

This bird is only known to be entitled to a place in the North America fauna from the fact that it was obtained in Florida by Mr Audubon.

GAMBETTA, Kaup.

Gambetta, Kaup, Entw. Europ. Thierw. 1829.   Type *Scolopax calidris*, L. (Gray.)

Ch.—Bill much attenuated towards and tapering to the end, the extreme tip decurved, both culmen and gonys however, bent upwards from the middle; the lateral grooves of upper bill broad, shallow, and not extending to the middle; that of lower reaching about as far.   Feathers on side of both mandibles extend to about the same point, but fall short of nostrils; those on chin extend as far as middle of nostril.   Bill nearly as long as the tarsus, which is $1\frac{1}{2}$ times the length of middle toe.   Outer toe webbed to first joint; the inner web very short; bare portion of the tibia equal to the toes; tip of tail about opposite the middle of outstretched tarsi; legs yellow.

It is a question whether the American yellow legged sandpipers really belong to *Gambetta* or to *Glottis*.   They agree with the latter in the upward bend of the bill, and with the former in not having the legs green.

GAMBETTA MELANOLEUCA, (Gm.) Bon.

Tell Tale; Stone Snipe.

Scolopax melanoleucus, Gmelin, Syst. Nat. I, 1788, 659.

Totanus melanoleucus, Vieillot, Nouv. Dict. 1816.—Licht. Verz. 1823, No. 750.—Aud. Orn. Biog. IV, 1838, 68; pl. 308.

Gambetta melanoleuca, Bon. Comptes Rendus, Sept. 1856.

Scolopax vociferus, Wilson, Am. Orn. VII, 1813, 57; pl. lviii.

Totanus vociferus, Aud. Syn. 244.—Ib. Birds Amer. V, 1842, 316; pl. 345.

Totanus sasashew, Vieillot, Dict. 1816.

Sp. Ch.—Bill longer than the head, rather slender, curved towards the tip; wings rather long, first quill longest; tail short; neck and legs long; toes moderate, margined and flattened underneath, connected at base by membranes, the larger of which unites the outer and middle toe; hind toe small; claws short, blunt; grooves in both mandibles extending about half their length. Entire upper parts cinereous of various shades, dark in many specimens in full plumage, generally light with white lines on the head and neck and with spots and edgings of dull white on the other upper parts; lower back brownish black; rump and upper tail coverts white, generally with more or less imperfect transverse narrow bands of brownish black; under parts white, with longitudinal narrow stripes on the neck and transverse crescent lanceolate and sagittate spots and stripes on the breast and sides; abdomen pure white; quills brownish black with a purplish lustre, shaft of first primary white, secondaries and tertiaries tipped and with transverse bars and spots of ashy white; tail white, with transverse narrow bands of brownish black, wider and darker on the two middle feathers; bill brownish black, lighter at the base; legs yellow.

Total length, about 14 inches; wing, $7\frac{1}{2}$ to 8; tail, $3\frac{1}{4}$ to $3\frac{1}{2}$; bill, $2\frac{1}{4}$; tarsus, $2\frac{1}{2}$ inches.

Hab.—Entire temperate regions of North America; Mexico.

A large and handsome species, abundant throughout the United States.

List of specimens.

Catal. No.	Sex.	Locality.	When collected.	Whence obtained.	Collected by—	Length.	Stretch of wings.
201	------	Carlisle, Pa.--------------	Oct. 26, 1840	S. F. Baird ---------	--------------------	---------	---------
1301	♂	------do ----------------	Mar. 19, 1844	------do -	--------------------	---------	---------
301	♀	------do ----------------	April 20, 1841	------do -	--------------------	13.75	---------
10457	♂	Cape May, N. J ----------	May —, 1842	John K. Townsend---	--------------------	14.00	25.00
4860	------	St. Joseph's, Mo -------	--------------	Lieut. Warren ------	Dr. Hayden ------	---------	---------
5435	------	Fort Berthold, Neb -----	--------------	------do...---	--------------------	---------	---------
5760	------	Platte river, Neb -------	--------------	Lieut. Bryan--------	W. S. Wood ------	---------	---------
5759	------	Laramie river, Neb -----	--------------	------do...---	--------------------	---------	---------
6625	------	Eagle Pass, Texas -------	--------------	Major Emory--------	A. Schott ---- ------	---------	---------
6628	------	San Elizario, Texas -----	--------------	------do -	--------------------	---------	---------
4178	------	Brazos Santiago, Texas ---	--------------	Captain Van Vliet ---	--------------------	---------	---------
6627	-----	Mohave river, Cal ------	--------------	Lieut. Whipple------	Kenn. & Möll----	---------	---------
6631	------	San Diego, Cal ----------	--------------	Lieut. Trowbridge ---	--------------------	---------	---------
6623	------	Suisun valley, Cal-------	--------------	Lieut. Williamson ---	Dr. Heermann ------	---------	---------
6626	------	Presidio, Cal----------	--------------	------do...---	------do...---	---------	---------
6624	------	Shoalwater bay, W. T----	--------------	Gov. Stevens--------	Dr. Cooper ------	---------	---------
6629	------	Bitter Root river, W. T----	--------------	------do...---	Dr. Suckley ------	---------	---------
6630	------	Fort Steilacoom, W. T----	--------------	------do -	------do...---	---------	---------
4401	------	Puget's Sound----------	--------------	Dr. Suckley ----.---	--------------------	---------	---------

GAMBETTA FLAVIPES, (Gm.) Bon.

Yellow Legs.

Scolopax flavipes, GMELIN, Syst. Nat. I, 1788, 659.—WILSON, Am. Orn. VII, 1813, 55 ; pl. lviii.

Totanus flavipes, VIEILLOT, Nouv. Dict. VI, 1816, 400.—Sw. F. B. Am. II, 1831, 390.—AUD. Orn. Biog. III, 1835, 573: V, 586 ; pl. 228.—IB. Syn. 243.—IB. Birds Amer. V, 1842, 313 ; pl. 344.

Gambetta flavipes, BON. Comptes Rendus, Sept. 1856.

Totanus fuscocapillus, VIEILL. Nouv. Dict. VI, 1816, 400.

Totanus natator, VIEILL. Nouv. Dict. VI, 1816, 409.

SP. CH.—Bill rather longer than the head, straight, slender, compressed ; wing long, pointed ; tail short ; legs long, lower half of the tibia naked ; toes moderate, slender, margined, the outer and middle united at base ; rump and upper tail coverts white, the latter transversely barred with ashy brown ; other upper parts ashy, many feathers having large arrowheads and irregular spots of brownish black and edged with ashy white ; under parts white, with numerous longitudinal lines on the neck before, and arrowheads on the sides, of dark ashy brown ; axillaries and under wing coverts white, with bands of ashy brown, very indistinct in many specimens, but generally well defined ; quills brownish black ; tail ashy white with transverse bands of dark brown, middle feathers darker ; bill greenish black ; legs yellow.

Young. Entire upper plumage tinged with reddish brown, neck before with lines much less distinct and pale ashy.

Total length about 10 to 10½ inches ; wing, 6 to 6½ ; tail, 2½ ; bill, 1½ ; tarsus, 2 inches.

Hab.—Eastern North America ; western ?

One of the most abundant of the species of this group on the Atlantic slope of the United States. We have never seen this bird from South America, though numerous in the winter in Mexico and the states of Central America. It is very similar to the preceding, though smaller.

List of specimens.

Catal. No.	Sex.	Locality.	When collected.	Whence obtained.	Collected by—	Length.	Stretch of wing.	Wing.
1490	♂	Carlisle, Pa	May 8, 1844	S. F. Baird.............	....	10. 80	19. 75	6. 32
1489	♀	......do...........	......do......	......do..............	....	10. 56	19. 75	6. 40
717	....	......do...........	Sept. 9, 1842	......do..............	....	10. 50	19. 50	5. 50
......	....	Union county, Ill..	....	Northwestern University	R. Kennicott	....	....	......
5761	....	Platte river	....	Lt. Bryan.............	W. S. Wood	....	....	......
4861	....	Council Bluffs	....	Lt. Warren	Dr. Hayden.......	....	....	......
5098	....	Indianola, Texas...	....	Capt. Pope...........	....	....	....	......
4179	....	Fort Brown, Texas.	....	Lt. Couch	....	....	....	......

RHYACOPHILUS, Kaup.

Rhyacophilus, KAUP, Sk. Entw. Europ. Th. 1829. Type *Tringa glareola,* L. (Gray.)

CH.—Bill slender, but widening a little towards the end; lateral grooves of both mandibles extending to the middle of bill; nostril short; feathers on side of bill extending to about the same point and as far as beginning of nostrils; those of chin as far as their end; both mandibles curved upwards slightly from middle; legs short; bill about the length of tarsus, which is equal to middle toe;. bare portion of tibia about two-thirds the toes. Tail about opposite the middle of toes when outstretched.

RHYACOPHILUS SOLITARIUS, (Wils.) Bon.

Solitary Sandpiper.

Tringa ochropus, var. A. LATHAM, Ind. Orn. 1790.

Tringa solitaria, WILSON, Am. Orn. VII, 1813, 53; pl. lviii.

Totanus solitarius, AUD. Syn. 1839, 242.—IB. Birds Am. V, 1842, 309; pl. 343.

Totanus chloropygius, VIEILLOT, Nouv. Dict. VI, 1816, 401.—BON. Obs. 1825, No. 210.—Sw. F. B. Am. II, 1831, 393.— WAGLER, Isis, 1831, 521.—NUTTALL, II, 159.—AUD. Orn. Biog. III, 1835, 576: V, 583; pl. 289.— GOSSE, Birds Jam. 1847, 351.

Rhyncophilus chloropygius, BON. Comptes Rendus, Sept. 1856.

Totanus glareola, ORD, ed. Wils. VII, 1825, 57.

Totanus macroptera, SPIX, Av. Bras. II, 1825, 76; pl. xcii.

SP. CH.—Bill rather longer than the head, straight, slender, compressed; both mandibles with narrow grooves; wing long, pointed; tail medium or rather short, rounded; legs rather long, slender; lower half of the tibia naked; toes long, the outer united to the middle by a small membrane, flattened underneath, marginated. Upper parts greenish brown, with numerous small circular and irregular spots of ashy white; upper tail coverts darker. Under parts white; breast and neck before with numerous longitudinal lines of greenish brown; sides, axillaries, and under wing coverts white, with numerous transverse narrow bands of dark greenish brown; under tail coverts white, with a few transverse bands of dark brown. Quills brownish black, with a slight bronzed or reddish lustre on the primaries; two middle feathers of the tail greenish brown; other feathers of the tail pure white, with about five transverse bands of brownish black. Bill and legs dark greenish brown.

Total length, about 8 to 8½ inches; wing, 5; tail, 2¼; bill, 1¼; tarsus, 1¼ inches.

Hab.—Entire temperate regions of North America; Mexico.

Like the preceding, this bird is extensively diffused, specimens in the collections of the expeditions being from widely distant localities.

List of specimens.

Catal. No.	Sex.	Locality.	When collected.	Whence obtained.	Orig. No.	Collected by—	Length.	Stretch of wings.	Wing.	Remarks.
1382	♂	Carlisle, Pa.............	April 22, 1844	S. F. Baird		....	8.80	16.50	5.24	....
441	♂	....do........	Aug. 24, 1841	......do........						
1481	♀	......do.........	May 8, 1844	......do.........			8.64	16.40	5.32	
1178	♀	......do.........	Sept. 8, 1843	......do.........			8.50	16.00	5.30	
8992		Upper Missouri and Yellowstone rivers.		Lieut. Warren...........		Dr. Hayden....	9.00	17.00	5.25	Iris brown.....
4866	♀	Omaha City, Neb..........	April 28, 1856	......do....		....do....	9.00	17.00	5.60	
8993		Sand Hills, Neb	Aug. 8	......do....		....do....				
8994		......do.........	Aug. 10.	......do....		....do.....	8.00	16.25	5.12	
5438		Fort Union, Neb..........		......do....		....do.....	8.25	15.75	6.00	
5437		......do	July, 1856...	......do....		....do....				
8202		Little Blue river, K. T.	July 22, 1856	Wm. Magraw...........		Dr. Cooper ...	8.50	15.75	6.25	
5737		Pole creek, Neb..........	July 29, 1856	Lieut. Bryan...........		W. S. Wood ...				
5099		California Spring, Tex.....	April 29, 1855	Captain Pope			9.00	....	5.50	
10423		Fort Tejon, Cal............	....	J. Xantus de Vesey						
6648		Fort Steilacoom, W. T....	1856	Dr. Suckley.............	379					
6649		....do.........	May 6, 1856	Gov. Stevens		Dr. Suckley....	9.00	17.00	5.50	

HETEROSCELUS, Baird.

CH.—Bill longer than the head cr the tarsus, stout, much compressed. Commissure straight to near the tip, where it is gently decurved. The culmen is slightly concave about the middle. Nasal groove extending over the basal two-thirds of the bill. Mouth moderately cleft; gape extending nearly the length of the nostrils behind the base of culmen. Legs short. Tarsus about equal to middle toe, and about 2½ times the length of exposed tibia; covered anteriorly by narrow transverse scutellae, laterally and behind by hexagonal scales. Scales of tibia hexagonal. Outer and middle toe connected by a basal web as far as the first joint of the latter; a rudimentary web to the inner toe. Hind toe long; one-third the tarsus. Tail half the wings. Plumage perfectly uniform above, without spots or bands of any kind.

This very remarkable sandpiper differs, in the hexagonal scutellation of the tibia and on the posterior face of the tarsus, from any other of the *Totaneae*, and on this account should, with all propriety, be made the type of a distinct group. The bill is stronger than in any American Genus, except *Symphemia*, differing mainly from this in the straightness of the bill and greater amount of inflection of the edges. The nasal groove extends further forward, and the upper jaw is a little more decurved at the end. The gape is a little more deeply cleft. The legs, especially the tarsi, are much shorter; the inner toe only slightly webbed. The claws are short, stout, and unusually curved. The legs have a much roughened appearance.

HETEROSCELUS BREVIPES, (Vieill.) Baird.

Wandering Tatler.

Tringa glareola, PALLAS, Zoog. Ross.-As. II, 1811, 194.

Totanus brevipes, VIEILL. Nouv. Dict. VI, 1816, 410.—CASSIN, Pr. A. N. Sc. VIII, 1856, 40.

Scolopax undulata, FORSTER, Desc. An. 1844, 173.

Totanus oceanicus, LESSON, Comp. Buff. 1847, 244.

Totanus polynesiae, PEALE, Voy. Vincennes & Peacock, Birds, 1848, 237.

Totanus fuliginosus, GOULD, Voy. Beagle, Birds, 1841, 130.

? Totanus pulverulentus, MÜLLER, Verh. 1844, 153.

FIGURES.—PALLAS, Zoog. Ross.-As. II, pl. 60.—TEMM. & SCHLG. Faun. Japon. Birds, pl. 65?—GRAY, Genera, III, pl. 154?

SP. CH.—Rather larger than *T. flavipes*. Bill rather longer than the head; wings long; legs shorter than usual in this group;

toes moderate. Entire upper parts dark lead colored, uniform, and without white marks; under parts white, with more or less of dark cinereous or plumbeous on the sides and neck; under wing coverts white, spotted and barred with dark plumbeous. Quills dark brown; shaft of the first primary white on its upper surface; shafts of other primaries reddish brown on the upper surface, and white on their under surfaces. Tail dark lead colored, uniform with upper parts of body. Bill dark; feet greenish. *Younger.* Under parts white, transversely barred with dark ashy brown, especially on the sides and flanks. Throat and middle of abdomen white.

Total length about 10½ inches; wing, 6½; tail, 3¼; bill, 1½; tarsus, 1¼ inches.

Hab.—Washington Territory, (Dr. J. G. Cooper); islands in the Pacific; South America; northeastern Asia; Japan?

Easily distinguished from any other North American species by the uniform colors of its plumage. This species ranges over an immense extent of locality, embracing nearly all the islands of the Pacific ocean and its coasts from Russian America to Australia.

Several specimens of this interesting species are in the present collection, all of which were obtained in Washington Territory by Dr. J. G. Cooper. It has quite a profusion of names, a part of which are given above.

List of specimens.

Catal. No.	Locality.	Whence obtained.
4472	Shoalwater Bay, W. T...	Dr. Cooper ....
6697	........do............	....
....	........do............	....

TRINGOIDES, B o n a p .

Tringoides, BONAP. Saggio di una dist. etc. 1831. Type *Tringa hypoleucus,* Linn. (Gray.)

Actitis, BOIE, Isis, 1822, 566. Not of Illiger, Prodromus, 1811.

CH.—Upper mandible grooved to the terminal fourth; the bill tapering and rather acute. Cleft of mouth only moderate; the culmen about five-sixths the commissure. Feathers extending rather further on side of lower jaw than upper, the former reaching as far as the beginning of the nostrils; those of the chin to about their middle. Bill shorter than the head, straight, equal to the tarsus, which is of the length of middle toe and claw. Bare part of tibia half the tarsus. Outer toe webbed to first joint; inner cleft about to the base. Tail much rounded; more than half the wing.

TRINGOIDES MACULARIUS, (L i n n .) G r a y .

Spotted Sandpiper.

Tringa macularia, LINN. Syst. Nat. I, 1766, 249.—WILS. Am. Orn. VII, 1813, 60; pl. lix.

Totanus macularius, TEMMINCK, Man. II, 1820, 656.—BON Obs. Wils. 1825, No. 211.—NUTT. Man II, 1834, 162.— AUD. Orn. Biog. IV, 1838, 81; pl. 310.—IB. Syn. 242.—IB. Birds Amer. V, 1842, 303; pl. 342.

Actites macularius, BON. List, 1838.

Tringoides macularius, GRAY, genera.

FIGURES.—WILSON, Am. Orn. VII, pl. 59, fig. 1.—AUD. B. of Am. pl. 310, oct. ed. V, pl. 342.—GOULD, B. of Europe, IV, pl. 317.—NAUMANN, B. of Germ. pl. 195.

SP. CH.—Small; bill rather longer than the head, straight, slender; long grooves in both mandibles; wing rather long, pointed; tail medium, rounded; legs rather long; lower third of the tibia naked; toes long, margined, and flattened underneath; outer connected with the middle toe by a large membrane; inner very slightly connected to the middle toe. Upper parts brownish olive green, with a somewhat metallic or bronzed lustre, and with numerous longitudinal lines, and sagittate, lanceolate, and irregular spots of brownish black, having the same lustre. Line over the eye and entire under parts white, with numerous circular and oval spots of brownish black, smaller on the throat, largest on the abdomen. Quills brown, with a green lustre ; primaries slightly tipped with white, and having a white spot on their inner edges; secondaries white at their bases, and tipped with white ; middle feathers of the tail same green as other upper parts ; outer tipped with white, and with irregular bars of brownish black. Bill yellowish green, tipped with brown; feet reddish yellow.

Young less bronzed above, and under parts white, without spots.

Total length, 7½ to 8 inches ; wing, 4½ ; tail, 2 ; bill, 1 ; tarsus, rather less than 1 inch.

Hab.—Entire temperate North America ; Oregon. Europe.

Diffused throughout the United States, resorting, in the winter season, to the southern confines of the republic, and extending its range into Mexico and Central America. This little bird has so frequently been noticed in Europe that it is now given as a species of that continent by nearly all late authorities.

List of specimens.

Catal. No.	Sex & age.	Locality.	When collected.	Whence obtained.	Orig. No.	Collected by—	Length.	Stretch of wings.	Wing.	Remarks.
1504	♂	Carlisle, Pa..........	May 10, 1844	S. F. Baird......		....	7.72	13.40	4.32	....
1512	♂	......do...........	May 15, 1844	..... do		....	7.50	13.40	4.24	....
1620	○	..... do.............	July 9, 1844	...... do.........		....				
10422	♀	Cape May, N. J.......	....	Jno. K. Townsend		....				
7059	....	St. Louis	May 13, 1857	Lt. Bryan......	81	W. S. Wood...				
6535	♀	Indian Key, Fla.......		G. Würdemann...		....				
6534	♀	.... do.............		...... do........		....				
7484		Rockport, Ohio.......		J. P. Kirtland....		....				
10420	♀	South Illinois..........		N. W. University.		R. Kennicott ..	....			
8995	....	Loup Fork...........	July 6.....	Lt. Warren......		Dr. Hayden....	6 50	12.25	3.75	Iris dark brown ....
5439	♀	Knife river	Sept. 12.....	......do.........		.......do........	7.12	12.75	3.25	....
5440	♂	Mouth of Powder river.	....	...... do.........		.......do........	7.00	12.50	3.75	....
5100		Permanent Camp, N. M.	Aug. 20, 1855	Capt. Pope	121	....	8.00	13.00	4.00	....
10419	....	Fort Tejon, Cal.......		J.Xantus de Vesey		....	6.50	13.00		....
6639	♂	Sacramento valley.....	....	Lt. Williamson...		Dr. Heermann .	....			
4400	♂	Fort Dalles, O. T	May 25......	Dr. Suckley	177	....	7.50	12.60	4.75	....
6640	....	Shoalwater bay..... .	June 8, 1854	Gov. Stevens....	78	Dr. Cooper.....	7.12	13.25	....	Bill yellow and black...
8443	....	Puget's Sound	....	A. Campbell.....		Dr. Kennerly ..				
5988	....	tcilacoom, W. T .	....	Dr. Cooper.......		....				

PHILOMACHUS, Moehring.

Philomachus, Moehring, Genera Avium, 1752, 76. Type *Tringa pugnax*, L.
Machetes, Cuvier, R. Amer. 1817.

Ch.—Bill nearly straight; as long as the head or the outer toe. Groove of bill extending nearly to the tip. Bill depressed, broad to the tip, which is scarcely expanded. Gape extending a little further back than the culmen : the feathers of lower mandibles extending rather further forward than those of upper; those of chin still further. Legs slender; tarsus 1¼ times as long as middle toe, 1½ times the length of bare tibia. A basal web connecting the outer and middle toes to the first joint of the former; inner toe cleft to base. Tail rather long; distinctly barred.

This genus, usually placed among *Tringeae*, appears to have most affinity with the present section, and in a measure to connect *Tringoides* and *Actiturus*. The bill is more depressed, and rather broader to the end than usual ; but it appears hard and firm, and with little or none of the spoon-shaped expansion at the end. The greater cleft of the mouth, the half webbing of the toes, the bars on the tail, the lengthened tarsi, &c., all seem to indicate the propriety of placing it with *Totaneae*.

PHILOMACHUS PUGNAX, (Linn.) Gray.

Ruff.

Tringa pugnax, LINN. Syst. Nat. I, 1766, 247.

Machetes pugnax, CUV.—BON. List, 1838.

Tringa (Machetes) pugnax, NUTTALL, Man. II, 1834, 131.

Philomachus pugnax, GRAY, Genera.—LAWRENCE, Ann. N. Y. Lyc. V, June, 1852, 220. Long Island .

SP. CH.—Above varied with black, rufous, and gray, the scapulars and tertials exhibiting these colors in oblique bands. Beneath white, varied on the jugulum and throat. Primaries dark brown, with greenish reflection above; the inner webs finely mottled towards the base. Outer three tail feathers plain, the remainder transversely barred. Bill brown; sides of rump white; legs yellow. Male in spring dress with the feathers of the neck greatly developed into a ruff; the face covered with reddish papillae.

Length, about 10 inches; wing, 6.40; tail, 2.60; bill, 1.25; tarsus, 1.75; middle toe and claw, 1.40.

Hab.—Northern Europe and Asia. Accidental on Long Island.

The ruff has been so frequently killed on Long Island as to entitle it to a place among descriptions of North American birds, although it cannot be said to belong to our fauna. It is a very curious species, conspicuous for the combats among the males during the breeding season. At this time the feathers of the neck are greatly elongated, forming a kind of cape or ruff, and the face is beset with papillae.

The ruff is about the size of the Bartram's tatler or field plover, which it otherwise resembles somewhat in color. It has the same mottling of the inner webs of primaries as in *Tryngites rufescens*, though not to so great an extent, this feature not being found in any other North American *Totaneae*, though seen in *Limosa*.

ACTITURUS, Bonap.

Bartramia, LESSON, Traité d'Orn. 1831. Preoccupied in Botany.

Actiturus, BONAP. Saggio, etc., 1831. Type *Tringa bartramia*, WILS.

Euliga, NUTT. Man. II, 1834.

CH.—Upper mandible grooved laterally to within the terminal fourth, the lower not quite so far. Culmen concave to near the tip, where it is slightly decurved; gonys straight. Mouth deeply cleft, almost as far back as the anterior canthus. The culmen only about two-thirds the commissure, shorter than the head or tarsus, and about equal to middle toe without claw. Feathers extending much further forward on the upper jaw than on the lower, although those of chin reach nearly to end of nostrils. Tarsus 1½ times middle toe and claw; the bare part of tibia not quite equal to the middle toe above; outer toe united at base as far as first joint; web of inner toe very basal. Tail long, graduated, more than half the wings.

ACTITURUS BARTRAMIUS, (Wils.) Bon.

Bartram's Sandpiper; Field Plover.

Tringa bartramia, WILSON, Am. Orn. VII, 1813, 63 ; pl. lix.—AUD. Syn. 1839, 231.—IB. Birds Amer. V, 1842, 248; pl. 327.

Totanus bartramius, BON. Obs. Wils. 1825, No. 209.—SWAINSON, F. Bor. Am. II, 1831, 391.—AUD. Orn. Biog. IV, 1838, 24 ; pl. 303.

" *Actiturus bartramius*, BON. Saggio, 1831."—IB. List, 1838, 51.

Tringa (Euliga) bartramia, NUTT. Man. II, 1834, 168.

Tringoides bartramius, GRAY, Genera.

" *Tringa longicauda*, NILSSON.—BECHST. Vögel Deutschl.—NAUMANN, Nachträge ; pl. xxxviii." (Dates unknown.)

Totanus campestris, VIEILL. Nouv. Dict. XXXIV, 1819, 454.

? *Totanus melanopygius*, VIEILLOT, Nouv. Dict.

Totanus variegatus, VIEILLOT. " Nouv. Dict. 2d ed. VI, 317."—IB. Galerie II, 1825, 107 ; pl. 239.

Bartramia laticauda, LESSON, Traité d'Orn. 1831, 553

August 11, 1858.

FIGURES.—NAUMANN, B. of Germany, pl. 196.—GOULD, B. of Eur. IV, pl. 313.—WILSON, Am. Orn. VII, pl. 59, fig. 2.—AUD. B. of Am. pl. 303 ; oct. ed. V, pl. 327.

SP. CH.—Bill about as long as the head, rather wide and flattened at base, curved at the tip ; nostril with a large membrane ; nasal groove long ; wing long ; tail long for this group ; legs moderate or rather long ; lower half of the tibia naked ; toes moderate, the outer and middle toe united by a membrane, inner and middle free to the base, hind toe small. General color of the upper parts brownish black, with a greenish lustre, and with the feathers edged with ashy white and yellowish, the latter especially on the wing coverts ; lower part of the back, rump, and upper tail coverts, brownish black ; lateral coverts of the tail yellowish white, with arrow-heads and irregular spots of black. Wide stripe over the eye and entire under parts very pale yellowish white, nearly pure white on the abdomen ; neck before with numerous longitudinal lines of brownish black ; breast and sides with waved and pointed transverse narrow bands of the same ; axillary feathers and under wing coverts pure white, with numerous nearly regular transverse narrow bands of black. Quills brownish black, with numerous transverse bands of white on their inner webs, very conspicuous on the under surface of the wing ; shaft of first primary white. Middle feathers of the tail same greenish brown as the back, with irregular and imperfect transverse bands of black ; outer feathers pale reddish yellow, edged and tipped with white, and with several irregular transverse bands and a large sub-terminal arrow-head of black. Bill greenish yellow, with the under mandible more clear yellow towards its base, tip brownish black ; legs light yellow ; toes darker. Total length, about 12 inches ; wing, 6½ ; tail, 3½ ; bill,

Hab.—Eastern North America, South America, Europe.

Everywhere in the interior of the States on the Atlantic this is the most abundant and best known species of this group. Unlike nearly all others, this bird prefers plains and cultivated fields, and is one of the species which has not decreased in numbers on account of the extension of cultivation and the settlement of the country. On the contrary it appears to be quite at home in the farm lands, and rears its young in the fields of grass and grain in the most populous rural districts of the country. It is, in a considerable measure, a favorite with the people and seldom molested.

This species is extensively diffused, and though at home in the northern division of this continent, wanders over nearly the whole of South America. It is well described by Azara as a bird of Paraguay. We have never seen this bird from west of the Rocky mountains.

The generic name *Bartramia*, Lesson, Traité d'Orn. I, p. 553, (1831,) is that having priority of all others proposed for this species, and is a just compliment to one of the most liberal and accomplished of the earlier American naturalists. This name is, however, previously used in botany, and probably ought not to be again employed in zoology, though we confess to being strongly inclined to adopt it, notwithstanding, following in that respect the example of Mr. Gray, of the British Museum, in his Catalogue of the Genera and Sub-genera of Birds, p. 117, (1855.)

List of specimens.

Catal. No.	Sex & age.	Locality.	When collected.	Whence obtained.	Orig. No.	Collected by—	Length.	Stretch of wings.	Wing.	Remarks.
2291	♂	Carlisle, Pa...............	May 20, 1845	S. F. Baird	.....	....	11.00	21.25	6.56	....
1116	♀	......do...............	July 15, 1843	......do......	.....	....	12.00	21.50	6.40	....
6536	....	Indian Key, Fla...........	....	G. Wurdemann ..	.....	....	.....	.....	.....	....
8185	♂	Shawnee Mission, K. T..	July 4, 1857	Wm. M. Magraw.	121	Dr. Cooper	11.75	21.00	7.00	Iris brown, bill bl'k & yellow, feet green.
7095	♀	Republican river........	June 15, 1857	Lieut. Bryan.....	5	W. S. Wood...	.....	.....	.....	....
4868	♀	Loup Fork...............	....	Lieut. Warren...	.....	Dr. Hayden....	.....	.....	.....	....
4629		Fort Pierre.........	April 26, 1855	Col. Vaughan....	.....	......do	13.00	22.00	7.50	....
4633		Fort Union, Neb.	July —, 1855	......do..........	.....	......do	.....	.....	.....	....
5432	♂	Medicine Hill............	....	Lieut. Warren...	.....	......do	12.00	22.00	6.75	....
8988	♀	Loup Fork...............	July 7	......do..........	.....	......do	12.75	23.75	6.00	....
8891	♂	......do...............	July 21......	......do..........	.....	......do	12.00	23.00	6.25	....
8990	....	Platte river.............	July 7......	......do..........	.....	......do	12.25	22.50	6.50	Iris dark brown......
8989	♀	......do...............	......do..........	......do..........	.....	......do	12.50	22.00	6.25	......do ....
7097	○ ○	Elk creek, Med. Bow mts.	Aug. 4, 1857	Lieut. Bryan.....	91	W. S. Wood...	.....	.....	.....	....

TRYNGITES, Cabanis

Tringites, CAB. Journ. für. Orn. 1856, 418. Type *Tringa rufescens*, VIEILL.

CH.—Upper mandible grooved to about the terminal fourth ; the lower not quite so far. Culmen and gonys about straight. Mouth deeply cleft more than half way to the eye ; the culmen about two-thirds the commissure. Culmen much shorter than the head, and about equal to middle toe without claw. Tarsus about 1⅕ as long as middle toe and claw. Bare part of tibia decidedly shorter than middle toe without claw. Toes cleft to the base, with only a very rudimentary web. Upper jaw feathered to the nostrils ; the side of the lower and beneath feathered much further, or to the end of the nostrils ; the interspace of the rami entirely filled. Tail somewhat graduated, not half the wing.

It is possible that the genus *Prosobonia* of Bonaparte, 1853, may be identical with *Tryngites* of Cabanis, as based on *Tringa leucoptera* of Gmelin, I, 678 ; but until this is proved to be the case, it may be best to take the last mentioned name as a certainty. It is a little remarkable that Bonaparte makes no mention whatever of *Tringa rufescens* in his Catalogue in Comptes Rendus, Sept. 1856.

TRYNGITES RUFESCENS, (Vieill.) Cab.

Buff-breasted Sandpiper.

Tringa rufescens, VIEILLOT, Nouv. Dict. XXXIX, 1819, 470. (Louisiana.)—IB. Galerie Ois. II, 1825, 105; pl. 238.— NUTT. Man. II, 1834, 113.—AUD. Orn. Biog. III, 1835, 451 ; pl. 265.—IB. Syn. 235.—IB. Birds Amer. V, 1842, 264 ; pl. 331.—BON. List, 1838.—JARD. Br. Birds III, 235, (Am. sp.)—YARRELL, Trans. Linn. Soc. XVI, 109 ; pl. ii, European sp.

? *Actidurus naevius*, HEERMANN, Pr. Acad. N. S. Phil. VII, 1854, 179. (Texas.)

FIGURES.—Trans. Linn. Soc. London, XVI, pl. 2.—GOULD, B. of Eur. IV, pl. 326.—AUD. B. of Am. pl. 265 ; oct. ed. V, pl. 331.—VIEILL. Gal. II, pl. 238.

SP. CH.—Bill about the length of the head, straight, compressed, narrow at the point ; nasal groove long ; wings very long ; first quill longest ; tertiaries rather shorter ; tail moderate or longer than usual in this group ; legs rather long ; lower third of the tibia naked ; toes free at base, flattened underneath, and slightly margined ; hind toe small. Upper parts pale and dull ashy brown with a yellowish tinge ; every feather with a large central, lanceolate, crescent-shaped, or oblong spot of black, frequently with a glossy green tinge, especially on the back and shorter tertiaries. Under parts light yellowish red, or pale fawn color ; many feathers tipped with black, and paler on the flanks and abdomen, on the breast with partially concealed small spots of black ; axillary feathers white. Quills with their outer webs light brown, inner webs ashy white marbled with black and narrowly tipped with white ; middle tail feathers brownish black ; outer feathers lighter, with transverse waved lines of black, and tipped with white ; bill greenish black ; legs greenish yellow. Total length, 7½ to 8 inches ; wing, 5½ ; tail, 3 ; bill, from gape, 1 ; tarsus, 1¼ inches.

Hab.— All of North America, South America, Europe.

This is a little bird of rather peculiar style of form, and of remarkable and handsome plumage. Its relationship appears to be to the preceding well known species. Both this and the preceding bird more habitually frequent plains and other dry localities than any of the true sandpipers.

This bird is distributed throughout the continent of America. Specimens in the present collection are the first ever brought from west of the Rocky mountains.

In the collection of the Philadelphia Academy we find numerous specimens of this bird from various countries of Central and South America, in which it appears to be more especially at home than in North America or Europe. It is easily distinguished from all other known American species by the handsome mottling of the primaries, very conspicuous and characteristic on their inner webs. The intimate relationship of the present bird to that immediately preceding was first pointed out by Dr. Heermann in the Proceedings of the Philadelphia Academy, as above cited.

In suggesting the close relationship of this bird to the sub-genus *Prosobonia* of the Prince Bonaparte, we are guided mainly by Professor Schlegel's beautiful figure of *Tringa leucoptera*, Gmelin, on which it is founded, and also by specimens before us of *Tringa brevirostris*, Peale, which evidently is of the same group. Both the species here mentioned are from islands in the Pacific ocean.

Dr. Heermann's type specimen of his *Actidurus naevius* differs somewhat from the ordinary plumage, in the much coarser mottling of the primary quills.

Catal. No.	Locality.	When collected.	Whence obtained.	Collected by—
582	New York	1841	S. F. Baird	
4458	Cape Flattery, W. T.		Lt. Trowbridge	
6694	San Antonio, Texas		Lt. Parke	Dr. Heermann
6693	Shoalwater bay		Gov. I. I. Stevens	Dr. Cooper

Section LIMOSEAE.

LIMOSA, Brisson.

Limosa, BRISSON, Orn. 1760. Type *Scolopax limosa*, L.

CH.—Bill lengthened, exceeding the tarsus, slender, and curving gently upwards; grooved to near the tip; the tip not attenuated, but pointed; the lower almost as long as the upper. Culmen without any furrow. Tarsus with transverse scutellae before and behind, reticulated laterally. A short basal membrane between the middle and outer toes. Tail short, even.

Bill much longer than head, nearly equalling tarsi and toes together; curving gently upwards from the base, where it is elevated and compressed, depressed, however, at the end. The grooves on sides of bill and beneath extend nearly to the tip; the tip of the upper mandible is thickened, and extends a little beyond the lower. The gape is slight, not extending beyond the base of culmen; the feathers on the side of the bill reach forward to about the same point, those on the chin a little further. Tarsus more than $1\frac{1}{2}$ times the toes, twice the bare part of tibia. Hind toe lengthened. Outer toe webbed as far as end of first joint, inner toe with only a short basal web. Tail short, even, two-fifths the wings.

In some respects the bill of this genus resembles that of *Macrorhamphus*, the chief apparent difference being the upward curve of the one and its straightness in the other.

LIMOSA FEDOA, (Linn.) Ord.

Marbled Godwit.

Scolopax fedoa, LINN. Syst. Nat. 10th ed, I, 1758, 146 : 12th ed. I, 1766, 244.—WILS. Am. Orn. VII, 1813, 30; pl. lvi
Limosa fedoa, ORD. ed. Wils. VII, 1825.—BON. Obs. 1825, No. 202.—IB. List, 1838.—SW. F. B. A. II, 1831, 395.—
        NUTT. Man. II, 1834, 173.—AUD. Orn. Biog. III, 1835, 287 : V, 590; pl. 238.—IB. Syn. 246.—IB.
        Birds Am. V, 1842, 331; pl. 348.
"*Limicula fedoa*, VIEILLOT."
Scolopax marmorata, LATH. Ind. II, 1790, 720.
Limicula marmorata, VIEILL. Nouv. Dict.—IB. Gal. II, 1825, 115; pl. 243.
Limosa americana, STEPHENS, Shaw's Zool.
"*Limosa adspersa*, LICHT."

Figures.—Wilson Am. Orn. VII, pl. 56, fig. 1.—Aud. B. of Am. pl. 238; oct. ed. V, pl. 348.—Edwards' Birds, III, pl. 137.—Vieill. Gal. des Ois. II, pl. 243.

Sp. Ch.—Bill long, curved upwards; both mandibles grooved; wings long; tail short; legs long; tibia with its lower half naked; toes rather short, margined and flattened underneath; the outer and middle toes united by a rather large membrane. Entire upper parts variegated with brownish black and pale reddish, the former disposed in irregular and confluent bands, and the latter in spots and imperfect bands; in many specimens the black color predominating on the back, and the pale red on the rump and upper tail coverts. Under parts pale rufous, with transverse lines of brownish black on the breast and sides; under wing coverts and axillaries darker rufous; outer webs of primaries dark brown, inner webs light rufous; secondaries light rufous; tail light rufous, with transverse bars of brownish black. Bill pale yellowish, red at base, brownish black at the end; legs ashy black. Total length about 18 inches; wing, 9; tail, 3½; bill, 4 to 5; tarsus, 3 inches.

Hab.—Entire temperate regions of North America ; South America.

A large and handsome shore bird, well known to sportsmen as the godwit, and a great favorite for shooting. From the collections of the surveying expeditions it appears to be equally abundant in the interior and on the Pacific as on the eastern coast of the United States.

List of specimens.

Catal. No.	Sex.	Locality.	Whence obtained.	Collected by—
1205	♂	New York	S. F. Baird	
545		do	do	
4499		Cape Flattery, W. T.	Lieut. Trowbridge	
9833		Shoalwater bay	Gov. I. I. Stevens	Dr. Cooper
9839		Bodega, California	Lieut. Trowbridge	
6446		San Francisco	Dr. Geo. Suckley	
5450		Fort Union, Nebraska	Lieut. Warren	Dr. Hayden
4884		Kanesville, Nebraska	do	
4172		Brazos Santiago, Texas	Captain Van Vliet	
6439		Indian Key, Florida	G. Würdemann	

LIMOSA HUDSONICA, (L a t h.) S w.

Hudsonian Godwit.

? Scolopax lapponica, var, β. Gmelin, Syst. Nat. I, 1788.—Forster.

Scolopax hudsonica, Latham, Ind. Orn. II, 1790, 720.

Limosa hudsonica, Sw. F. B. A. II, 1831, 396.—Nuttall, Man. II, 1834, 175.—Aud. Orn. Biog. III, 1835, 426: V, 592; pl. 258.—Ib. Syn. 247.—Ib. Birds Amer. V, 1842, 335 ; pl. 349.

Limosa melanura, Bon. Specchio, 1827, No. 204.

Limosa aegocephala, Bon. Syn. 1828, 327.

? Limosa edwardsii, Sw. F. B. A. II, 1831.

Figures.—Edwards' Birds, III, pl. 138.—Aud. B. of Am. pl. 258; oct. ed. V, pl. 349.

Sp. Ch.—Smaller than the preceding. Bill longer than the head ; both mandibles grooved, slightly recurved; wings long; legs moderate; membrane uniting the outer and middle toe large. *Adult.* Upper parts brownish black, with spots and transverse bars of pale reddish on the back; rump brownish black; upper tail coverts white; wing coverts and shorter quills dark cinereous; primaries brownish black. Under parts yellowish red, with transverse bars of brownish black on the breast and sides and under tail coverts, and frequently with the feathers on the abdomen widely tipped with white; tail black, with the base white, and narrowly tipped with white. Under wing coverts and axillary feathers black; shafts of primaries white; bill pale yellowish at base; tip brownish black; legs bluish brown. *Younger.* Head and upper parts cinereous, irregularly marked on the top of the head and on the back with brownish black; stripe before and over the eye white; under parts dull yellowish white; under wing coverts and axillaries black; rump black; upper tail coverts white; tail black; base and tip white; bill yellow, tipped with brownish black; legs dark brown.

Total length about 15 inches; wing, 8; tail, 3; bill, 2¾ to 3½; tarsus, 2½ inches.

Hab.—Northern and eastern North America; New Jersey, (Mr. A. Galbraith.)

Much smaller than the preceding, and easily distinguished by its white rump and black tail at all ages, and when adult by the red color of the under parts of the body. It appears to be abundant in the northern regions of this continent, but is of rare occurrence in the United States, though occasionally met with in the winter. We have never seen it from the western shores of the republic.

This species is allied to the European *L. melanura*, but differs in having the axillars and under coverts dark brown instead of white; the neck brownish gray instead of chestnut.

List of specimens.

Catal. No.	Locality.	Collected by—
546	New York............	S. F. Baird ....
8074	Arctic America.......	Jno. Gould ....

Section NUMENIEAE.

NUMENIUS, Linnaeus.

Numenius, Linnaeus, Syst. Nat. 1746. Type *Scolopax arquata*, Linn.

Ch.—Legs covered anteriorly with transverse scutellae, laterally and behind with small hexagonal scales. Bill very long, exceeding the tibia, and curved downwards for the terminal half; the culmen rounded. Tip of bill expanded laterally and club-shaped. Grooves of bill not reaching beyond the middle. Tertials as long as primaries.

Bill variable in length, always longer than tarsus, sometimes exceeding tarsus and toes. It is nearly straight at the base, then decurving quite rapidly to the tip, where the upper mandible is thickened downwards beyond and over the lower. Lateral grooves occupying only the basal half or third of the bill; under mandible not grooved beneath. Cleft of mouth extending but little beyond the base of culmen. Feathers of head extending about the same distance on both mandibles; those of chin to opposite the anterior extremity of the nostrils. Tarsi nearly twice as long as middle toe, rather more than twice the bare part of tibia. It is covered behind by hexagonal scales larger than the lateral ones. Outer toe webbed for its basal joint; inner for half this distance. Tail short, nearly even, not quite half the wings. Tertials as long as the primaries.

Of the genus *Numenius* several species are found in North America, none of them occurring in the Old World, as is the case with so many of the *Tringeae*.

Numenius, Linn.

NUMENIUS LONGIROSTRIS, Wilson.

Long-billed Curlew.

Scolopax arquata, var. β. GMELIN, I, 1788, 656.

Numenius arquata, var. B. LATHAM, Ind. II, 1790, 710.

Numenius longirostris, WILSON, Am. Orn. VIII, 1814, 24; pl. lxiv.—BON. Obs. 1825, No. 200.—SW. F. B. A. II, 1831 376.—NUTT. Man. II, 1834, 88.—AUD. Orn. Biog. III, 1835, 240 : V, 587; pl. 231.—IB. Birds Am. VI, 1843, 35; pl. 355.

" *Numenius melanopus*, VIEILLOT, Nouv. Dict."

Numenius rufus, VIEILLOT, Galerie, II, 1825, 118; pl. 245.

" *Numenius brasiliensis*, WIED."

? *Numenius occidentalis*, WOODHOUSE, Pr. A. N. Sc. VI, Nov. 1852, 194.—IB. Sitgreaves' Expl. Zuñi & Col. 1853, 98; pl. vi

SP. CH.—The largest American species of this genus. Bill very long, much curved; upper mandible longer than the under somewhat knobbed at the tip; wing rather long; legs moderate; toes united at base. Entire upper parts pale rufous, tinged with ashy; every feather with transverse and confluent bands of brownish black, most numerous and predominating on the back and scapulars; secondary quills, under wing coverts, and axillaries, bright rufous; primaries with their outer webs brownish black and their inner webs rufous, with transverse bands of black. Under parts pale rufous, with longitudinal lines of black on the neck and sides; tail rufous, tinged with ashy, transversely barred with brownish black. Bill brownish black; base of under mandible reddish yellow; legs bluish brown. Specimens vary to some extent in the shade of the rufous color of the plumage, and very much in the length of the bill. The rufous color is probably more distinct in the young. Total length about 25 inches; wing, 10 to 11 ; tail, 4; bill, 5 to 8; tarsus, 2¼ inches.

Hab.—The entire temperate regions of North America.

Numerous specimens in the collection of the expeditions attest the abundance of this fine bird throughout every part of the United States.

This bird appears to vary in size quite materially, and in the length of bill in different specimens, so much so as to be quite perplexing. In fact, the bills of scarcely any two specimens are of the same length. In color, also, there is considerable variety, but the species can readily be distinguished.

There are in the present collection specimens which are undoubtedly *N. occidentalis*, Woodhouse, as above cited, and it is not without doubts that we do not at present give it as a distinct species. The clear rufous of the plumage and the shorter bill, as given by Dr. Woodhouse, are present in these specimens, and, without a series of intermediate specimens, would appear to be quite conclusive characters specifically. In the present collection, however, almost any length of bill can be produced, and the rufous color is very probably characteristic of young age. It is quite possible, though, that more than one species may yet be determined.

List of specimens.[1]

Catal. No.	Locality.	When collected.	Whence obtained.
462	New York	1841	S. F. Baird

[1] The list of specimens from the collections of the exploring expeditions having been mislaid, is not given here.

Phaeopus, Cuv.

NUMENIUS HUDSONICUS, Latham.

Short-billed or Hudsonian Curlew.

Scolopax borealis, GMELIN, Syst. Nat. I, 1788, 654. (Not of Forster, 1772.)—WILSON, Am. Orn. VII, 1813, 22; pl. lvi.

Numenius borealis, ORD, ed. Wils VII, 1825. Not of Latham.

Numenius hudsonicus, LATHAM, Ind. Orn. II, 1790, 712.—BON. Obs. 1825, No. 201.—SW. F. B. Am. II, 1831, 377.—
NUTT. Man. II, 1834, 97.—AUD. Orn. Biog. III, 1835, 233 : V, 589; pl. 237.—IB. Syn. 254.—
IB. Birds Am. VI, 1843, 42 ; pl. 356.

Numenius melanopus, VIEILLOT, in part.

Numenius rufus, VIEILLOT, Gal. II, 1825, 118; pl. 245. (Mixed with *longirostris*.)

?Numenius intermedius, NUTT. Man. II, 1834, 100.

SP. CH.—Smaller than the preceding. Bill about twice the length of the head; wings long; tail short; legs moderate. Head above brownish black, with a longitudinal band ; other upper parts brownish black, tinged with ashy, spotted with dull yellowish white, and lighter on the rump. Under parts dull yellowish white, with longitudinal narrow stripes of blackish brown on the neck and breast; under wing coverts and axillaries pale ashy rufous, transversely barred with black ; quills brownish black, with transverse bars of pale rufous on the inner webs; tail brownish black, with transverse bars of pale ashy brown. Bill brownish black ; base of lower mandible reddish yellow ; legs greenish brown. Specimens vary in the shade of the lighter colors of the plumage and in the length of the bill. Total length about 18 inches; wing, 9; tail, 4; bill 3 to 4; tarsus, 2¼ inches.

Hab.—Atlantic and Pacific coasts of North America ; California, (Mr. Cassidy.)

Smaller, and with the colors different from the preceding. This bird is represented as abundant in the northern regions of this continent, but is much less frequent in the United States than the preceding.

A *Numenius rufiventris* is described by Vigors[1] from the west coast of America, which is closely related to the present species, if not the same.

List of specimens.

Catal. No.	Sex.	Locality.	When collected.	Whence obtained.
1229		Atlantic coast		S. F. Baird
10458	♂	Cape May, New Jersey	May, 1842	J. K. Townsend
9823		Presidio, California		Lt. Trowbridge

NUMENIUS BOREALIS, (Forst.) Latham.

Esquimaux Curlew.

Scolopax borealis, FORSTER, Phil. Trans. LXII, 1772, 411; Albany Fort.

Numenius borealis, LATHAM, Ind. Orn. II, 1790, 712.—BON. Syn. 1828, 314 —IB. List, 1838.—SW. F. B. A. II, 1831,
378; pl lxv.—NUTT. Man. II, 1834, 100 —AUD. Orn. Biog. III, 1835, 69: V, 590; pl. 208.—
IB. Syn. 255.—IB. Birds Amer. VI, 1843, 45; pl. 357.

Numenius brevirostris, LICHT. Verz. 1823, No. 774.

" *Numenius hemirhynchus*, TEMM."

FIGURES.—Aud. B. of Am. pl. 208; oct. ed. VI, pl. 357.—Rich. and Swains. Faun. Bor. Am. Birds, pl. 65.—Temm. Pl. Col·
V, pl. 381.

[1] Zool. Journal, IV, Jan. 1829, 356.—IB. Zool. of Blossom, 1839, 28.

Sp. Ch.—Much smaller than either of the preceding, but resembling *N. hudsonicus* in color. Bill rather longer than the head, slender; wings long; tail short: legs mo lerate. Entire upper parts brownish black, spotted with dull yellowish rufous; quills brownish black, uniform on both webs, without bars on either; under wing coverts and axillaries light rufous, with transverse stripes of brownish black. Under parts dull white, tinged with rufous, with longitudinal narrow stripes of brownish black on the neck and breast, and transverse stripes of the same on the sides and under tail coverts; tail ashy brown, with transverse bands of brownish black; bill brownish black; base of under mandible yellow; legs greenish brown. Total length about 13½ inches; wing, 8¼; tail, 3; bill, 2¼ to 2½; tarsus 1¾ inches.

Hab.—Eastern and northern North America.

This small and interesting curlew is merely a bird of passage in the United States, to be met with in the spring and autumn. It is easily distinguished from either of the preceding by its small size and its comparatively short and weak bill. We have never seen it from the western countries of the United States.

List of specimens.

Catal. No.	Locality.	When collected.	Whence obtained.	Collected by—
10398	New York		S. F. Baird	
	Upper Missouri	1841	Lieut. Warren	Dr. Hayden
4881	do		do	do
6572	do		do	do
6573	Texas		Captain Pope	

Tribe **PALUDICOLAE.**

Ch.—Species living in marshes, with elevated bodies, much compressed laterally; usually with longer necks than most snipe, with moderately long, strong, and stout bills also much compressed and covered at tip by a horny investment; the remaining portion membranous, with elongated nasal furrow, and narrow, more or less perforate, nostrils. The lores are feathered uniformly as in the *Limicolae;* the rest of the plumage without the spotting of the snipes. Wings rather short, more rounded than pointed, and when folded do not reach beyond the short, soft and feeble tail; in fact, seldom to its base. The outer two or three primaries generally abbreviated. The toes are very long, cleft to the base, thin, and generally with very long claws; the same is the case with the hind toe, which is not only much longer than in the *Limicolae*, but is generally inserted more nearly on the same level with the anterior ones, touching the ground for most of its extent.

The species pick up their food on the surface, and do not probe the soft mud in search of it.

The North American species of this tribe are few in number, though very abundant in individuals. Their habit of close concealment among the reeds and grass of marshy places, renders them very difficult of detection, except when their abodes are more or less submerged.

The *Paludicolae*, or *Alectorides*, are divided by Bonaparte into four families, *Palamedeidae*, *Parridae*, *Rallidae*, and *Ocydromidae*. Of these the *Rallidae* only are represented within the limits of the United States. Of Bonaparte's two sub-families, *Prosoboninae* and *Rallinae*, the former with a single species, *Prosobonia leucoptera*, (*Tringa leucoptera*, Gmelin,) of the Pacific islands, is, by Gray, referred to *Totaneae*. The *Rallinae* thus remaining may be sub-divided into the following sections and genera:

August 12, 1858.
94 b

A. *Ralleae.*—Forehead feathered to the base of bill ; culmen parting the frontal feathers for a short distance only, and in an angle.

RALLUS.—Bill slender, longer than the head ; nasal groove extending beyond the middle of the bill ; the elongated nostrils within the basal third of the commissure.   Hind toe about one-third the tarsus.

PORZANA.—Bill thick, about equal to or shorter than the head ; culmen straight, or a little depressed near the nostrils ; gonys ascending.   Nostrils reaching beyond the middle of the commissure.   Hind toe about half the tarsus.

B. *Fuliceae.*—Base of the bill extended on the forehead for a greater or less distance, as a naked, flattened, and rounded or quadrate plate.

GALLINULA.—Toes without marginal lobes ; the lateral membrane very slightly developed. Nostrils linear.

PORPHYRULA.—Somewhat similar to *Gallinula.*   Nostrils small, nearly circular.

FULICA.—Toes with a well developed marginal membrane, which is incised at the joints into a series of semicircular lobes.

The genera *Heliornis*, which has usually been ranged with the *Totipalmi*, is, by Burmeister and Reichenbach, placed near *Fulica.*   A species, *H. surinamensis*, is said to have been occasionally seen in the United States.

As in the *Limicolae* the following account of the *Paludicolae* has been prepared by Mr. John Cassin.

Sub–Family RALLINAE.

RALLUS, Linnaeus.

Rallus, LINNAEUS, Systema Naturae.

CH.—Bill longer than the head, rather slender, compressed ; upper mandible slightly curved ; nostrils in a long groove, and with a large membrane ; wings short ; tertiary quills long, frequently longer than the primaries ; tail very short ; legs moderate ; tarsus shorter than the middle toe, and covered on all sides with transverse scales ; toes long and rather slender ; inner toe rather shorter than the outer ; hind toe short and weak.

This genus contains about twenty species, inhabiting all the temperate countries of the world, and very similar in their habits and frequently in appearance.   Their long toes enable them to run over and climb amongst aquatic plants with great facility.

RALLUS ELEGANS, Aud.

King Rail; Marsh Hen.

Rallus elegans, AUD. Orn. Biog. III, 1835, 27 ; pl. 203.—IB. Syn. 215.—IB. Birds Am. V, 1842, 160 ; pl. 309.— GUNDLACH, Cab. Jour. 1856, 427.

Rallus crepitans, WILS. Am. Orn. VII, 1813 ; pl. lxii, f. 2.   (Not the description.)

SP. CH.—The largest species of the United States.   Upper parts olive brown, with longitudinal stripes of brownish black, most numerous on the back ; line from the base of the bill over the eye dull orange yellow ; space before and behind the eye brownish cinereous.   Throat and lower eyelid white ; neck before and breast bright rufous chestnut ; sides and abdomen, and under tail coverts, with transverse bands of brownish black and white, the dark bands being the wider ; tibiae dull yellowish white, with spots and transverse bars of ashy brown.   Upper wing coverts reddish chestnut ; under wing coverts black, with transverse lines of white.   Sexes alike.   Total length, (from tip of bill to end of tail,) about 17 inches ; wing 6½ ; tail 3 inches.

Hab.—Middle and southern States on the Atlantic ocean ; California, (Dr. Suckley.)

This is the largest species of rail found in North America, and is one of the most handsome birds of this genus. It is found for much the greater part in fresh waters, and inhabits the entire country on the Atlantic from New Jersey to Florida, very probably extending also over the vast intermediate regions to the Pacific in the same latitude. The only specimens from California, or other country on the Pacific, that we have ever seen, are in the present collection.

List of specimens.

Catal. No.	Sex.	Locality.	When collected.	Whence obtained.	Orig. No.	Collected by—	Length.	Stretch of wings.	Wing.	Remarks.
2674	....	New Jersey......	....	S. F. Baird.......	......	....	......	....	....	....
1113	♂	Washington, D. C	July 7,1843	....do	.. ...	Wm. M. Baird.	17.00	22.00	6.75	....
4322	....	Calcasieu Pass, La........	1854.........	G. Würdemann ..	......	....	....	....	....	....
5087	....	Indianola.................	Mar. —,1855	Capt. Pope	......	....	13.50	19.00	6.00	Eyes brown, feet gray, bill dark...........
7055	♂	St. Louis.................	May 6,1854	Lieut. Bryan	1	W. S. Wood..	....	....	....	....
6444	....	San Francisco....	Mar. —,1857	Dr. Suckley	603	....	....	....	....	....
4512	......	......do	....	Lieut. Williamson	......	Dr. Newberry	....	....	....	....

RALLUS CREPITANS, G m.

Clapper Rail; Mud Hen.

? ? *Rallus longirostris*, BODDAERT, Tabl. Pl. enl. 1784 ; pl. 849.

Rallus crepitans, GM. Syst. Nat. I, 1788, 713.—WILS. Am. Orn. VII, 1813, 112, (not the plate.)—BON. Obs. Wils. 1825 ; pl. 228.—AUD. Orn. Biog. III, 1835, 331 : V, 570 ; pl. 214.—IB. Syn. 215.—IB. Birds Am. V, 1842, 165 ; pl. 310.—CAB. Jour. 1856, 427.

FIGURES.—WILSON, Am. Orn VII, pl. 62, fig. 2.—AUD. B. of Am., pl. 204 ; oct. ed. V, pl. 310.—BUFFON, Pl. Enl. 849?

SP. CH.—Smaller than the preceding. Upper parts light ashy olive, with longitudinal stripes of brownish black, most numerous on the back ; a line of dull yellowish white from the base of the bill over the eye ; space before and behind the eye ashy. Throat and under eyelid white ; neck before, and breast, pale reddish yellow, or tawny tinged with bluish ashy on the breast ; sides, abdomen, under tail coverts, and tibiae, with transverse bands of brownish black and white, the former being the wider. Upper wing coverts brownish olive ; under wing coverts black, with transverse lines of white. Total length, (to end of tail,) about 14 inches ; wing, $5\frac{1}{2}$; tail $2\frac{1}{2}$ inches.

Hab.—Middle and southern coast of the States on the Atlantic ocean ; South America.

Rather smaller than the preceding, but when in mature plumage considerably resembling it in colors. Specimens generally, however, have a faded or bleached appearance, and it is, in fact, rather unusual to meet with those that have not this character.

This bird is more an inhabitant of the seacoast than the preceding, and is abundant from New Jersey to Florida, and southwardly on the shores of South America. The proper name of this species is, very probably, *Rallus longirostris*, as above described and figured. Specimens before us, from the coast of Guiana, seem quite identical with others from New Jersey.

List of specimens.

Catal. No.	Sex and age.	Locality.	When collected.	Whence obtained.	Remarks.
1055	♀	Cape May, N. J --------------	May, 1842....	S. F. Baird -----------------	Eye hazel ------
10459	♀	------do.----------------------	-----do--------	J. K. Townsend-------------	----------------
2673	○ ○	------do.----------------------	-----do--------	------do - ----------------	----------------

RALLUS VIRGINIANUS, Linn.

Virginia Rail.

Rallus virginianus, LINN. Syst. Nat. I, 1766, 263, (may possibly refer to autumnal *Porzana carolina*.)—WILS. Am.
Orn. VII, 1813, 109 ; pl. lxii, f. 1.—BON. Obs. Wils. 1825 ; No. 210.—NUTT. Man. II, 1834,
205.—AUD. Orn. Biog. III, 1835, 41 : V, 573 ; pl. 205.—IB. Syn. 216.—IB. Birds Am. V, 1842,
174 ; pl. 311.—CAB. Jour. 1856, 427.

Rallus aquaticus, var. A. LATH. Ind. Orn. II, 1790.

Rallus limicola, VIEILL.

" *Rallus rythi hynchos*, VIEILL." Gray.

FIGURES.—EDWARDS' Birds, VI, pl. 279.—WILSON, Am. Orn. VII, pl. 62, fig. 1.—AUD. B. of Am. pl. 205 ; oct. ed. V,
pl. 311.

SP. CH.—Much smaller than either of the preceding, but resembling them in form, and resembling also *R. elegans* in colors.
Upper parts olive brown, with longitudinal stripes of brownish black ; line from base of bill over the eye reddish white. Throat
white ; neck before, and breast, bright rufous ; abdomen and under tail coverts with transverse bands of black and white, the
former being the wider. Upper wing coverts bright rufous chestnut ; under wing coverts black, with transverse lines of white.
Total length, (from tip of bill to end of tail,) about 7½ inches ; wing, 4 ; tail, 1½ inches.

Hab.—The entire temperate regions of North America ; New Mexico, (Dr. T. C. Henry ;) California, (Mr. R. D. Cutts ;)
Oregon, (Dr. Geo. Suckley.)

Quite frequent in the States on the Atlantic, and now brought, for the first time, from west
of the Rocky mountains. This little bird bears a singular resemblance to *Rallus elegans* in
form and colors, and is one of the instances in which size is a specific and distinctive character.

This species is found along the margins of the bays and rivers on the Atlantic, migrating
southward in the autumn, and is remarkable for quickness of movement and swiftness of foot,
running on the ground with great facility. It ranges northward into the British possessions.

List of specimens.

Catal. No.	Sex.	Locality.	When collected.	Whence obtained.	Orig. No.	Collected by—	Length.	Stretch of wings.	Wing.
1647	♂	Carlisle, Pa................	July 27,1844	S. F. Baird		....	10.00	14.25	4.16
2520	♂	.....do	Oct. 13,1845	......do		....	10.00	14.25	4.50
418	♂	.....do	May 22,1841	......do	....	....	9.25	14.00	....
7057	♂	St. Louis	May 6,1857	Lieut. Bryan............	3	W. S. Wood.........	....	....	....
6652	....	Near 32° L	....	Capt. Pope		Dr. Henry	....	....	....
6654	....	Sonora............	....	Maj. Emory	72	Dr. Kennerly	....	....	....
6653	....	San Francisco, Cal.............	....	R. D. Cutts		....	....	....	....
5999	....	Port Townsend, Puget's Sound...	1857.........	Dr. Suckley............		....	....	....	....
4450	... .	Cape Flattery, W. T.............	....	Lt. Williamson...........	......	....	... ...	....	....

PORZANA, Vieillot.

Porzana, VIEILLOT, Analyse, p. 61, (1816,) 61. Type *Rallus porzana*, L.

CH.—Bill shorter than the head, compressed, straight ; nostrils in a wide groove, with a large membrane ; wings moderate ;
primaries longer than tertiaries ; tail short ; tarsus about the length of the middle toe ; toes long ; inner toe slightly shorter
than the outer. General form compressed and slender ; legs rather robust.

Contains about twenty species, generally inhabiting temperate regions, inhabiting marshes
and borders of rivers. In the spring and autumn several species migrate in large numbers.

Porzana, Vieillot.

PORZANA CAROLINA.

Sora; Common Rail; Ortolan.

Rallus carolinus, LINN. Syst. Nat. I, 1766, 363.—DOUGHTY's Cab. N. H. 1, 1830, 206; pl. xviii.—AUD. Orn. Biog. III, 1835, 251 : V, 572 ; pl. 233.

Gallinula carolina, LATH. Ind. II, 1790, 711.

Rallus (Crex) carolinus, BON. Obs. Wils. 1825, No. 230.—NUTT. Man. II, 1834, 209.

Porzana carolina, ———?—CAB. Jour. 1856, 428.

Ortygometra carolina, BON. List, 1838.—AUD. Syn. 1839, 213.—IB. Birds Amer. V, 1842, 145 ; pl. 306.—GOSSE, Birds Jam. 1847, 371.

Rallus stolidus and *melanops*, VIEILL.

FIGURES.—EDWARDS' Birds, III, pl. 144.—WILSON, Am. Orn. VI, pl. 48, fig. 1.—AUD. B. of Am. pl. 233 ; oct. ed. V, pl. 306.

SP. CH.—Space around the base of the bill, extending downwards on the neck before and over the top of the head, black. *Male*. Upper parts greenish brown, with longitudinal bands of black, and many feathers having narrow stripes of white on their edges. Behind the eye, sides of the neck, and the breast, fine bluish ashy, with circular spots and transverse bands of white on the breast ; middle of the abdomen and under tail coverts white; sides and flanks with transverse bands of brownish black and white. Bill greenish yellow ; legs dark green. Female similar, but duller in colors. *Young*. Without black at the base of the bill or on the neck ; throat dull white ; breast dull yellowish ashy ; upper parts tinged with dull yellow.

Total length about 8½ inches ; wing, 4¼ ; tail, 2 inches.

Hab.—Entire temperate regions of North America.

The most abundant and most universally known bird of its genus inhabiting the United States, and everywhere known as "the rail." It is especially numerous along the creeks and rivers on the Atlantic during the autumnal migration, when excursions for obtaining it are a favorite amusement of our gunners and sportsmen.

This bird appears to inhabit the entire temperate regions of North America. Specimens in the present collection from California are precisely identical with others from the banks of the Delaware river.

List of specimens.

Catal. No.	Sex.	Locality.	When collected.	Whence obtained.	Orig. No.	Collected by—	Length.	Stretch of wings	Wing.	Remarks.
2421	♂	Carlisle, Pa..........	Aug. 30, 1845	S. F. Baird..........	......	....	9.64	14.25	4.32	....
1697	♀	......do..............	Aug. 16, 1844	......do.............	......	....	8.64	13.25	4.32	....
1649	♂	......do..............	July 27, 1844	......do.............	......	....	8.75	13.75	4.32	....
10461	♂	Cape May, N. J......	May —, 1842	J. K. Townsend......	......	....	......	......	......	....
6533	......	Tortugas, Fla........	....	G. Würdemann	......	....	......	......	......	....
6950	......	Red River, H. B. Terr.	....	D. Gunn	......	....	......	......	......	....
4875	......	Yancton Camp	1856.........	Lieut. Warren........	......	Dr. Hayden....	8.50	14.25	4.75	Eyes dark red, pupil blk.
4555	......	Colorado river, Cal...	....	Maj. Emory..........	41	A. Schott......	......	......	......	....
4901	......	San Diego, Cal.......	....	Dr. Hammond........	......	....	8.75	13.50	4.00	....

Creciscus, Cabanis.

PORZANA JAMAICENSIS.

Little Black Rail.

Rallus jamaicensis, GMELIN, Syst. Nat. I, 1788, 718.—AUD. Orn. Biog. IV, 1838, 359 ; pl. 349.

Ortygometra jamaicensis, STEPHENS.—BON. List, 1838.—AUD. Syn. 1839, 214.—IB. Birds Amer. V, 1842, 157; pl. 308.

Porzana jamaicensis, ———?

Creciscus jamaicensis, CABANIS, Jour. 1856, 428. (" Genus distinguished from *Porzana* by shorter toes.")

FIGURES.—EDWARDS' Birds, VI, pl. 278.—AUD. B. of Am. pl. 349 ; oct. ed. V, pl. 308.

SP. CH.—Smaller than the preceding, and is the smallest North American species of this family. *Adult.* Head and entire under parts dark bluish ashy, or nearly slate color ; darker and nearly black on the top of the head ; abdomen and under tail coverts with transverse bands of white.   Neck behind and upper part of back dark reddish chestnut ; other upper parts brownish black, with circular spots and irregular transverse stripes of white. Quills brownish black, with small spots of white ; tail nearly the same colors. *Very young.* Entirely bluish black.

Total length (from tip of bill to end of tail) about 5 inches ; wing, 3¼ ; tail, 1½ inches.

Hab.—Middle and southern States on the Atlantic ocean.

One of the most uncommon of North American birds, and highly prized by naturalists and collectors.   It is, however, apparently more abundant in the West Indies.

Coturnicops, B o n a p .

PORZANA NOVEBORACENSIS.

Yellow Rail.

Fulica noveboracensis, GMELIN, Syst. Nat. I, 1788, 701.

Gallinula noveboracensis, LATHAM, Ind. Orn. II, 1790, 771.

Ortygometra noveboracensis, STEPHENS, Shaw's Zool. XII, 1824.—BON. List, 1838.—AUD. Syn. 1839, 213.—IB. Birds Am. V, 1842, 152 ; pl. 307.

Rallus (Crex) noveboracensis, BON. Specchio Comp. 1827, 212.—IB. Am. Orn. IV, 1832, 136 ; pl. xxvii.—NUTT. Man. II, 1834, 215.

Rallus noveboracensis, SW. F. B. Am. II, 1831, 402.—AUD. Orn. Biog. IV, 1838, 251 ; pl. 329.

Porzana noveboracensis, ——— ?

Coturnicops noveboracensis, BON. 1854.

Perdix hudsonica, LATH. Ind. Orn. II, 1790, 655.

Rallus ruficollis, VIEILL. Nouv. Dict. 2d ed. XXVIII, 556.—IB. Gal. II, 1825, 168 ; pl. 266.

FIGURES.—VIEILL. Gal. II, pl. 266.—AUD. B. of Am. pl. 329 ; oct. ed. V, pl. 307.

SP. CH.—Entire upper parts ochre yellow, with longitudinal wide stripes of brownish black and transverse narrow stripes of white.   Neck and breast reddish ochre yellow ; many feathers tipped with brown ; middle of abdomen white ; flanks and ventral region with wide transverse bands of dark reddish brown and narrow bands of white ; under tail coverts rufous, with small spots of white ; under wing coverts white. Total length (from tip of bill to end of tail) about 6 inches ; wing, 3¼ ; tail, 1¾ inches.

Hab.—Eastern North America.

A very handsome little bird, reminding one of a young chicken in its general appearance. It is of rather unusual occurrence on the shores of fresh and salt waters in the eastern States of the republic.

List of specimens.

Catal. No.	Locality	When collected.	Whence obtained.	Length.	Stretch of wings.	Wing.
10394	Carlisle, Pa		S. F. Baird			
1722	....do	Oct. 16, 1844	......do	7. 24	13. 50	3. 80
1090	Philadelphia	Spring of 1843	......do			

CREX PRATENSIS, Bechstein.

Corn-Crake.

Rallus crex, LINN. Syst. Nat. I, 1766, 261.—DEGLAND, Orn. Europ. II, 1849, 266
Gallinula crex, LATHAM, Ind. Orn. II, 1790, 766.
Crex pratensis, BECHST. Gemein. Naturg. Deutsch. IV, 470.—CASSIN, Pr. A. N. Sc. VII, Jan. 1855, 265. (New
    Jersey.)

SP. CH.—Feathers above blackish brown, with brownish yellow edges, and without white spots. Quills and upper wing coverts brownish red ; under wing coverts rust red. Bill shorter than the head, conical, elevated at the base. Wings reaching nearly to the end of the tail. Outer primary edged externally with yellowish white ; flanks and beneath the tail banded with rufous and whitish.

Length about ten inches.

Hab.—Europe ; Greenland. Accidental on the Atlantic coast of the United States.

The well known corn-crake of Europe has, on several occasions, been found on the eastern coast of the United States, and is, therefore, entitled to mention here. It appears to be a constant summer visitor to Greenland, from which country it is probable that stragglers reach the United States.

FULICA, Linnaeus.

Fulica, LINN. Syst. Nat. 1735. Type *Fulica atra*, L.

CH.—Bill shorter than the head, straight, strong, compressed, and advancing into the feathers of the forehead, where it frequently forms a wide and somewhat projecting frontal plate ; nostrils in a groove, with a large membrane near the middle of the bill. Wings rather short, second and third quills usually longest ; tail very short ; tarsus robust, shorter than the middle toe, with very distinct transverse scales ; toes long, each toe having semicircular lobes, larger on the inner side of the toe ; hind toe rather long, lobed.

A very peculiar group, containing about ten or twelve species, all of which are of dark slate color, and which considerably resemble each other.

FULICA AMERICANA, Gmelin.

Coot ; Poule d'eau ; Mud Hen.

Fulica americana, GM, Syst. Nat. I, 1788, 704.—BON. Obs. Wils. 1825, No. 234.—AUD. Orn. Biog. III, 1835, 291 : V,
    568 ; pl. 239.—IB. Syn. 212.—IB. Birds Amer. VI, 1842, 138 ; pl. 305.—HARTLAUB, Cab.
    Jour. I, Extraheft für 1853, 1854, 75 ; 87.
Fulica wilsonii, STEPHENS, Shaw's Zool. XII, 1824, 236.—BREHM, Vög. Deutschl. 1831, 711.
Fulica atra, WILS. Am. Orn. IX, 1825, 61 ; pl. lxxiii.
? *Fulica leucopyga*, WAGLER, Isis, 1831, 518. Mexico.

SP. CH.—Head and neck glossy black, with a tinge of ashy ; under tail coverts white. Entire other plumage dark bluish cinereous or slate color, with a tinge of olive on the back and darker on the rump. Edge of wing at shoulder and edge of first primary white ; secondary quills tipped with white ; rump frequently tinged with brownish. Bill very pale yellow or nearly white, with a transverse band of brownish black near the end; tip white ; legs dull grayish green. Female similar, but with the tints lighter. Young like the adult, but with the under parts lighter ; abdomen frequently ashy white ; back and rump dark olive brown ; head and neck lighter.

Total length about 14 inches ; wing, 7 ; tail, 2 inches.

Hab.—Entire temperate regions of North America.

This species is readily distinguishable from the European *F. atra* by the white on the crissum and wings, the red frontal plate, &c.

List of specimens.

Catal. No.	Sex.	Locality.	When collected.	Whence obtained.	Orig'l No.	Collected by—	Length.	Stretch of wings.	Wing.	Remarks.
1729	♂	Carlisle, Pa..........	Oct. 26	S. F. Baird........	......	....	16.00	28.00	8.00	....
1707	♂	......do............	Sept. 30, 1844	.... do...........	......	....	15.25	27.25	8.16	....
1216	♀	Michigan..........	June, 1841...	.... do...........	......	....	....	....	......	....
......	......	Racine, Wis...............	....	N. W. University.	......	R .Kennicott ..	....	....	......	....
8907	♂	Loup Fork of Platte.... .	July 5, 1857	Lieut. Warren....	......	Dr. Hayden....	15.00	27.25	7.75	....
8906	♀	Upper Missouri	July 20, 1857	.... do...........	......	... do..........	14.25	28.25	7.25	Iris red, pupil black.....
4176	......	Brownsville, Texas	....	Lieut. Couch	......	....	15.50	28.00	8.00	.... do...... do ....
5088	......	Delaware creek, N. Mex..	Mar. 24, 1856	Capt. Pope ..,...	......	....	....	....	......	....
6621	......	Espia, Mexico............	Mar., 1855 ...	Maj. Emory......	46	Dr. Kennerly ..	....	....	......	....
4558	......	Colorado river, Cal.......	....	.... do...........	11	.... do........	....	....	......	....
......	......	Fort Tejon, Cal...........	....	J. Xantus de Vesey	......	....	....	....	......	....
4557	......	San Pasqual, Cal.........	....	Maj. Emory......	4	A. Schott......	....	....	......	....
9984	......	Great Salt Lake City	Mar., 1854...	Lieut. Beckwith...	......	Mr. Snyder....	....	....	......	....
9982	......	Presidio, Cal.............	Aug. 5, 1853	Lieut. Trowbridge	......	T. A. Szabo....	....	....	......	....
9986	......	Bodega, Cal.....	Jan., 1855....	... do...........	......	....	....	....	......	....
9989	......	Lake Elizabeth	....	Lieut. Williamson	......	....	....	....	......	....

GALLINULA, Brisson.

Gallinula, BRISSON, Orn. VI, 1760, 3. Type *Fulica chloropus,* L.

The gallinules are readily distinguished from the coots by the absence of the lobes of skin margining the toes. There is a very slight membrane, but this is scarcely appreciable in the dried skin.

The purple gallinule by Burmeister is placed in another family (*Parridae*) from the common gallinule, (*G. galeata,*) and by Bonaparte in a different section, *Porphyrioneae.* They seem, at any rate, well entitled to generic separation, although, for our present purposes, they may be combined under *Gallinula.* The most prominent character of the purple gallinule, or *Porphyrula,* consists in the thicker bill and nearly circular, instead of elongated or linear nostrils, although other distinctions might readily be adduced.

Gallinula, Brisson.

GALLINULA GALEATA, (Licht.) Bon.

Florida Gallinule.

Crex galeata, LICHT. Verz. 1823, 80, No. 826. San Paulo.

Gallinula galeata, BON. Am. Orn. IV, 1832, 128 ; pl xxvii.—IB. List, 1838.—NUTT. Man. II, 1834, 221.—GOSSE, Birds Jam. 1847, 381.—CAB. Journ. 1856, 428.

Gallinula chloropus, BONAP. Syn. 1828, 336.—AUD. Orn. Biog. III, 1835, 330 ; pl. 244.—IB. Birds Amer. V, 1842, 132 ; pl. 304.

SP. CH.—Frontal plate large, obovate, terminating square on the top of the head ; bill shorter than the head, rather thick, compressed ; wing rather long ; tail short ; legs moderate ; toes and claws long, robust. Head, neck, and entire under parts dark bluish cinereous, frequently nearly black on the head and neck, and generally lighter on the abdomen ; a few feathers on the flanks widely edged with white ; edge of wing at the shoulder and outer edge of first primary quill white ; shorter under tail coverts black, longer white. Upper parts brownish olive, darker on the rump ; quills dark brown ; tail brownish black ; frontal plate and bill bright red, tipped with yellow ; tibia with a bright red space on the bare portion next to the feathers ; lower portion of tibia, tarsus, and toes yellowish green.

Total length about 12¼ inches ; wing, 6¾ ; tail, 3 ; bill, 1¼ ; tarsus, 1¾ inches.

Hab.—Southern countries of North America, Louisiana, Florida, Texas, South America. Accidental in middle and northern States.

Abundant in the southern States, and occasionally occurring on the coasts of New Jersey and New York. This species much resembles the Gallinule of Europe, (*G. chloropus,*) and other species of the Old World, which appear to be mainly distinguishable from each other by the shape and size of the frontal plates which characterize all the species of this genus. This is said to be quadrate in our bird instead of acute. The toes also are longer.

Catal. No.	Sex.	Locality.	When collected.	Whence obtained.	Nature of specimen.
452	......	Carlisle, Pa...............	October 18, 1841	S. F. Baird..............	....
204	......	......do.................	May 14, 1840	......do.................	Head, wing, and leg.....
1204	.. ♀ ..	Michigan...............	Spring, 1841	......do.................	....
9824	......	Lake Elizabeth..........	....	Lieut. Williamson......	....
9825	......	San Pedro..............	....	Major Emory............	....

Porphyrula, Blyth.

GALLINULA MARTINICA, (Linn.) Lath.

Purple Gallinule.

Fulica martinica, Linn. Syst. Nat. 1766, 259.
Gallinula martinica, Latham, Ind. Orn. II, 1790, 769.—Bon. Obs. Wils. 1825, No. 231.—Nutt. Man. II, 221.— Aud. Orn. Biog. IV, 1838, 37 ; pl. 305.—Ib. Syn. 210.—Ib. Birds Amer. V, 1842, 128 ; pl. 303.
Crex martinica, Licht. Verz. 1823, 79.
Porphyrio martinica, Gosse, Birds Jam. 1847, 377.—Cab. Jour. 1856, 429.
Fulica martinicensis, Jacquin, Beit. 1784, 12 ; pl. iii.—Gmelin, Syst. Nat. I, 1788, 700.
Ionornis martinicensis, Reich. Syst. Av. 1853, p. xxi.
Fulica flavirostris, Gm. Syst. Nat. I, 1788, 699.
Porphyrio tavoua, Vieill. Gal. II, 1825, 170.
Porphyrio cyanicollis, Vieill.
Gallinula porphyrio, Wils. Am. Orn. IX, 1824, 69 ; pl. lxxiii.
Porphyrio americanus, Sw. Class. Birds, II, 1837, 357.
Martinico gallinule, Lath. Syn. III, i, 255 ; pl. lxxxiii.

Sp. Ch.—Frontal plate large, obovate ; bill about as long as the head, thick, compressed ; wings long ; tail short ; legs long, robust ; toes and claws long. Head and entire under parts fine bluish purple, darker and sometimes nearly black on the abdomen and tibiae ; lower tail coverts white ; sides and under wing coverts bluish green. Upper parts of body dark olive green, tinged with brown on the back and rump ; quills and tail feathers brownish black, edged with green on the outer webs of the feathers ; bill bright red, tipped with yellow ; frontal plate blue ; legs yellow.

Total length, about 12½ inches ; wing, 7 ; tail, 3 ; bill, 1¼ ; tarsus, 2¼ inches.

Hab.—Southern States of North America, Louisiana, Florida. Accidental in the middle and northern United States. Western ?

This very handsome bird is of frequent occurrence on the coasts of the southern States of this republic and in South America. It is occasionally met with as far north as New Jersey, and more rarely in New York and Massachusetts. We have never seen a specimen from the coasts of the Pacific.

Catalogue No.	Locality.	Whence obtained.	Collected by—
1827	Surinam	S. F. Baird.................	Dr. Calhoun...

ORDER VI.

NATATORES.

Ch.—Toes connected by membrane to the claws ; the feet fitted for swimming. Lower part of tibia usually feathered to near the joint, which is bare. Hind toe, however, usually elevated, and rather small, except in *Pelecanidae*. Fitted for an aquatic life, swimming and diving freely. Rump with well developed oil glands.

The order *Natatores*, as characterized above, embraces a large number of species of very varied forms, all more or less aquatic in their habits. A character common to all consists in the presence of a membrane between the toes, usually extending to the claws. This membrane, when found in the *Grallatores*, is confined more or less to the basal joint, unless *Phoenicopterus* be an exception. This genus has been variously placed in both orders, and it is still a question where it really belongs. The internal anatomy resembles that of the *Natatores*, as well as the lamellated bill and fully webbed toes ; the external form, however, as well as habits, bring it nearer the *Grallatores*.

With the exception of *Phoenicopterus*, if it really belong here, the legs of the *Natatores* are generally rather short, and with the tibia more covered with feathers inferiorly than in *Gralla-tores*. They are inserted rather far back, so that, when standing erect, the body of the bird is generally nearly upright. The tibia are buried to a considerable extent in the muscles of the trunk, which are much developed.

The order *Natatores* of most authors has been divided by Bonaparte into two—the *Gaviae* and the *Anseres ;* the former embracing species which rear their young in nests, and belong to the sub-class *Altrices ;* while the latter are *Praecoces*, the young procuring food for themselves almost from birth. There are no single external characters by which to distinguish these two orders or sub-orders, as I shall make them in the present report.

Gaviae.—Bill without lamellae, and more or less entire. Feet with the toes all connected by one continuous membrane ; or the hind toe free, with the anterior continuously webbed.

Anseres.—Bill with transverse lamellae along the edges. Hind toe free.

The *Anseres* of Bonaparte, as first established by him, included the *Urinatores*, (of the opposite page,) but he subsequently transferred them to the *Gaviae*.

ANSERES.

If we adopt the arrangement given by Bonaparte in the Comptes Rendus for October, 1853, Vol. XXXVII, the *Anseres* will be composed chiefly of species with the mandibles lamellated along the edges, nearly perpendicularly to the margins. Where there is no such lamellar condition of the bill, the legs are short and placed far back ; the wings very short, concave, and much rounded, sometimes very rudimentary ; the tail is sometimes nearly wanting.

There would then be three principal sections or tribes of the *Anseres* characterisable as follows :

A. *Lamellirostres.*—Bill, with transverse lamellae along the edges ; depressed.

    ANATIDAE.[1]—Bill with the commissure nearly straight. Bill covered with a soft skin, ending in a hard, horny nail. Legs rather short ; the tibia feathered nearly to the joint.

B. *Urinatores.*—Wings short, concave, rounded, but fitted for use in flight. Tail short or wanting. Bill with a horny covering ; usually compressed.

    ALCIDAE.—Hind toe wanting ; claws compressed. Bill compressed.

    COLYMBIDAE.—Hind toe with a conspicuous lobe. Anterior toes connected by a full membrane. Lores feathered. Tail distinct.

    PODICIPIDAE.—Hind toe with conspicuous lobe. Toes bordered laterally by a broad continuous membrane, but not connected across except at base. Lores naked. Tail rudimentary or wanting.

C. *Ptilopteri.*—Wings rudimentary, without projecting quills. Hind toe very small, anterior ; attached to the side of the tarsus. Legs entirely imbedded in the rump.

Of the *Ptilopteri*, with its single family *Spheniscidae*, embracing the different species of penguins, there are no representatives on the coast of North America.

As already remarked, however, Bonaparte subsequently confined the *Anseres* to the *Lamellirostres*, transferring the *Urinatores* to the *Gaviae.* He also made a separate order of the *Ptilopteri.* This modified arrangement has accordingly been adopted in the present report.

---

[1] If *Phoenicopteridae* be placed in the *Natatores*, it will come under *Lamellirostres*, with the following diagnosis compared with *Anatidae.*

Phoenicopteridae.—Commissure bent abruptly in the middle nearly at a right angle. Bill without nail. Legs excessively lengthened ; tibia bare for half its length.

Family ANATIDAE.

Cɴ.—The two jaws with transverse lamellae, alternating and fitting in each other. Upper mandible ending in an obtuse, rounded nail. A groove running along both jaws to the nail. The feathers of the forehead extend forward on the culmen in a rounded or acute outline ; those on the side of lower jaw and on the chin extend forward in a similar manner. Commissure straight. Legs short.

The *Anatidae*, or the family of the ducks, are universally distributed throughout the globe, and embrace an unusual proportion of species inhabiting both the Old and New World. The sub-families are all represented in North America, and a large number of the genera also. The sub-families are as follows :

A. The teeth of the bill directed downwards, the lamellae composing one series only on the edge of the upper jaw. The rami of the lower jaw separated. Bill broad ; depressed at the end.

    a. Tarsi reticulated, covered anteriorly with small hexagonal plates, gradually becoming smaller and rhomboidal laterally. Hind toe without free lobe.

        Cʏɢɴɪɴᴀᴇ.—Neck very long. Bill high at the base ; longer than the head ; of equal width to the rounded tip, with its narrow nail. Soft skin of bill generally extending to the eye. Tarsi shorter than the middle toe without claw.

        Aɴsᴇʀɪɴᴀᴇ.—Neck rather long. Bill high at base ; as long as or shorter than the head, narrowing to the tip, which is chiefly formed by the large nail. Region in front of the eye feathered. Tarsi longer than middle toe without claw.

    b. Legs with transverse plates or scutellae anteriorly, these becoming much smaller and more hexagonal laterally and behind. Tarsi generally shorter than middle toe without claw ; sometimes only half as long.

        Aɴᴀᴛɪɴᴀᴇ.—Hind toe without a broad membranous lobe attached. Tarsi not longer than the middle toe ; feet moderate.

        Fᴜʟɪɢᴜʟɪɴᴀᴇ.—Hind toe with a broad membranous lobe depending from its under surface. Feet large. Nail of bill superior, gently decurved. Tail rather soft ; the coverts well developed.

        Eʀɪsᴍᴀᴛᴜʀɪɴᴀᴇ.—Toes and feet as in the last. Nail of bill abruptly bent back from tip of bill, showing but little on upper surface of the latter. Tail feathers rigid, spinous, and almost entirely exposed ; the coverts much abbreviated.

B. Bill high at the base, much compressed. The lamellae directed backwards as serrations. The upper jaw with two series of teeth on each side ; the lower with one which fits between the others. The nail of the bill compressed, much curved, forming the tip of the bill. Edges of bill nearly parallel. Legs with transverse plates anteriorly.

        Mᴇʀɢɪɴᴀᴇ.—Characters as above.

Sub-Family CYGNINAE.

CYGNUS, Linnaeus.

Cygnus, LINNAEUS, Syst. Nat. 1735. Type *Anas olor*, Gmelin. (Gray.)

CH.—Neck very long. Bill longer than the head, (commissure longer than the tarsus,) the basal portion covered by a soft skin extending to the anterior half of the eye, the plane of the upper outline from eye to eye horizontal ; the lateral outline extending nearly straight to the commissure, or even sometimes widening slightly ; not half the width of the bill at tip. Nostrils situated in the middle portion of the bill. Lower portion of tibia bare ; the tarsus much shorter than the foot, much compressed, covered with hexagonal scales, which become smaller on the sides and behind. Hind toe small, much elevated ; the lobe narrow. Tail of 20 or more feathers, rounded, or wedge-shaped. Sexes similarly colored.

As North America possesses only one genus of *Cygninae*, I have combined the sub-family characters with the generic in the preceding diagnosis. By Wagler the peculiarities of the bill have been made the basis of sub-divisions of the old Linnaean genus *Cygnus*, as follows :

CYGNUS.—Bill with a swollen fleshy tubercle at the base of culmen. Teeth of the edge of bill projecting and visible from the side.

OLOR, Wagler.—No tubercle at the base of bill. Teeth of the edges of bill not projecting.

Other members of *Cygninae* are *Chenopis*, embracing the Australian black swan, and *Coscoroba*, a South American white species with feathered lores. The black-necked swan of South America belongs to the sub-genus *Cygnus*.

There are certain peculiarities of trachea and sternum which distinguish the genus and its species in a marked degree.

The two North American species of swan belong to *Olor* as restricted, with the following diagnoses :

Tail feathers 20. Bill as long as the head. The anterior end of nostrils considerably beyond the middle of commissure. Black naked skin at base of bill, with a reddish spot anterior to the eye..*C. americanus.*

Tail feathers 24. Bill longer than head. Anterior end of nostril opposite the middle of commissure. Skin at base of bill entirely black..*C. buccinator.*

Comparative measurements of species.

Catal. No.	Species.	Locality.	Sex.	Length.	Stretch of wings.	Wing.	Tail.	Tarsus.	Middle toe.	Its claw alone.	Bill above.	Along gape.	Specimen measured.
1197	Cygnus americanus....	Washington, D. C..	♀	....	....	21.50	7.20	4.06	5.40	0.74	4.20	3.72	Skin.....
do.	........do............	........do.........	......	55.50	84.00	21.75	....	....	....	....	....	......	Fresh....
9979	........do............	Near 32° L.........	......	54.00	....	22.00	8.68	4.12	5.90	0.90	4.20	3.86	Skin.....
9978	........do............	Salt Lake.........	......	... .	....	21.20	8.50	4.28	5.42	0.86	3.82	3.64	Skin.....
9980	........do............	........do.........	......	... .	....	22.00	8.50	4.32	5.58	0.74	4.02	3.60	Skin.....
9775	Cygnus buccinator	Puget's Sound......	......	....	....	24.70	9.62	4.92	6.44	0.84	4.56	4.22	Skin.....
9977	........do............	Pike Lake, Minn...	......	....	....	......	8.10	4.54	6.00	0.88	4.34	4.10	Skin.....
5470	........do............	Yellowstone........	♂	....	....	21.00	8.20	4.64	6.46	0.86	4.58	4.26	Skin.....
do.	........do	.... do..........	......	58.50	78.00	21.00	....	....	....	....	....	....	Fresh....

CYGNUS AMERICANUS, Sharpless.

American Swan.

? *Anas columbianus*, ORD, Guthrie's Geog. 2d Am. Ed. II, 1815, 319 ; based on Whistling Swan, Lewis & Clark, II, 192.

Cygnus americanus, SHARPLESS, Doughty's Cab. N. H. I, 1830, 185, pl, xvi.—IB. Am. Jour. Sc. XXII, 1831, 83 —
AUD. Orn. Biog. V, 1839, 133 ; pl. 411.—IB. Syn. 274.—Ib. Birds Amer. VI, 1843, 226 ; pl. 384·

Olor americanus, BONAP. Consp. Anser. Comptes Rendus, XLIII, Sept. 22, 1856.

Anas (Cygnus) cygnus, BON. Specchio Comp. 237.

Cygnus musicus, BONAP. Syn. 1827, 379.

Cygnus bewickii, Sw. F. Bor. Am. II, 1831, 224.

Cygnus ferus, NUTTALL, Man. II, 1834, 368.

SP. CH.—Bill as long as the head, broad, high at the base ; the feathers ending on the forehead in a semi-circular outline. Nostrils far forward, the anterior extremity considerably more forward than half the commissure. Tail of 20 feathers.

Adult pure white ; bill and legs black ; the former with an orange or yellowish spot in front of the eye. Less mature specimens with the head above tinged with reddish brown. Length, 55 inches ; wing, 22.00 ; tarsus, 4.25 ; bill above, 4.20.

Hab.—Continent of North America.

The common American swan is equally abundant on both sides of the continent, as well as throughout the interior. The young bird is brown, instead of white. The adult seldom, if ever, is without the yellow or orange space at the base of the bill, which is otherwise black.

List of specimens.

Catal. No.	Locality.	When collected.	Whence obtained.	Original No.	Collected by—
	Washington, D. C.		S. F. Baird		
9978	Salt Lake city		Lieut. Beckwith		
9979	Fort Thorn, N. M.		Dr. T. C. Henry		Dr. Henry
4543	Coast of California		Lieut. Trowbridge		
9981	Fort Vancouver, W. T	Dec., 1853	Gov. Stevens		Dr. Cooper
9976	Fort Steilacoom	Oct. 24, 1856	Dr. Suckley	582	

CYGNUS BUCCINATOR, Rich.

Trumpeter Swan.

Cygnus buccinator, RICH. F. Bor. Am. II, 1831, 464.—NUTTALL, Man. II, 1834, 370.—AUD. Orn. Biog. IV, 1838,
536 : V, 114 ; pl. 406 and pl. 376.—IB. Syn. 74.—IB. Birds. Amer. VI, 1843, 219 ; pl. 382,
383.—EYTON, Mon. Anat. 1838, 100.

Olor buccinator, WAGLER, Isis, 1832, 1234.—BON. Comptes Rendus, XLIII, Sept. 1856.

SP. CH.—Bill broad, longer than the head ; the feathers ending on the forehead in a semi-elliptical outline. The nostrils with the anterior extremity as far forward only as half the commissure. Tail of 24 feathers.

Adult pure white throughout, the bill and legs entirely black ; the bill without any red spot at the base. Less mature specimens with the head above tinged with reddish brown.

Length about 60 inches ; wing, 24.00 ; bill above, 4.50 ; tarsus, 4.60.

Hab.—Western America, from the Mississippi valley to the Pacific.

This large and powerful swan, doubtless, has special anatomical peculiarities of trachea, to distinguish it from *C. americanus*, as the note is much more sonorous. It is for this reason that it is called Trumpeter, in distinction from the other, or " Whistling Swan."

List of specimens.

Catal. No.	Sex.	Locality.	When collected.	Whence obtained.	Collected by—	Length.	Stretch of wings.	Wing.
9777?	......	Pike lake, Minn.......	1853..........	Gov. Stevens....	Dr. Suckley.....	....	....	....
5476	♂	Yellowstone river	Aug. 27, 1856.	Lieut. Warren....	Dr. Hayden......	58.50	76.00	21.00
9775	......	Puget's Sound..........	....	A. Campbell	Dr. Kennerly ...	....	....	....

Sub-Family ANSERINAE.

As already stated, the chief characters of the *Anserinae* are to be found in the elevated body, with the lengthened tibia and tarsus, fitting the species for a terrestrial life. They walk about much more than the other *Anatidae*, although equally able to swim. Their necks are shorter than those of the swans, but decidedly longer than in the ducks.

A common character, at least in most genera, is seen in the plates on the anterior portion of the tarsus, which, as in the swans, are small and hexagonal, becoming smaller behind. In the true ducks, the front of the tarsus is covered with transverse scutellae, the sides and behind, however, are reticulated.

The bill is generally rather short, and higher than broad at the base, in this differing from most ducks; it also tapers in most cases quite rapidly to the tip, which is constituted entirely by a large convex decurved nail. The foramen of the bill, in which the nostrils open, is very large, though mostly occupied by membrane. The tarsus is generally longer than the commissure or the middle toe without its claw. The cheeks are densely feathered to the bill.

The plumage is never very brilliant, white, black, and gray predominating. As in the swans, both sexes are colored alike, in this differing from the other *Anatidae*.

I differ from most authors in placing *Dendrocygna* in the present sub-family, rather than with the *Anatinae*. Its characters are, indeed, so peculiar as almost to warrant its forming the type of a separate sub-family. In the elevated base of the bill, with the large nail at the extremity, and the lengthened legs, with the hexagonal scales in front of the tarsus, there is certainly a much closer relationship to the geese than to the ducks.[1]

The North American genera of the *Auserinae*, as defined chiefly by Keyserling and Blasins, are as follows:

Ansereae.—Bill tapering to the tip; as long as the head. Nostrils reaching about to the middle of the commissure. Tibia bare near the lower end only.

ANSER.—Bill as long as the head ; mostly red or orange colored. The lamellae of upper mandible project below the edge as conical points. Nostrils opening behind the middle of the commissure, the anterior edge only reaching to this point. Tip of hind toe reaching the ground.

BERNICLA.—Bill shorter than the head ; black. Lamellae of upper jaw hidden by the margin of bill. Nasal apertures lying over the middle of the commissure, their anterior edge reaching beyond this point. Hind toe elevated ; rudimentary ; not touching the ground.

---

[1] Bonaparte, indeed, in his last schedule of *Anatidae*, Comptes Rendus, XLIII, September, 1856, places *Dendrocygna* with *Tadorna, Chenalopex,* &c , in a section *Tadorneae* of *Plectropteridae.*

DENDROCYGNEAE.—Bill longer than the head; nearly parallel as far as the tip. Nostrils decidedly posterior to the middle of the commissure. Lower part of tibia bare for a considerable extent.

DENDROCYGNA.—Lamellae of bill hidden by the edge. Hind toe lengthened, more than one-third the tarsus. Wings much rounded; first primary scarcely longer than the fourth.

ANS R, Linnaeus.

Anser, BRISSON, Orn. 1760. Type *Anas anser*, L.

Chen, BOIE, Isis, 1822. Type *Anas hyperborea*, Gm.

The characters of *Anser* have already been given in a preceding page with sufficient detail not to require additions here. As defined, however, it embraces two sections, differing in the following points :

CHEN.—Bill high at base, the upper angle advancing far on the forehead. Width of base of upper mandible more than half the commissure. Lower edge of upper mandible much arched; the teeth very prominent and large. Lower jaw very deep. Species *A. hyperboreus, caerulescens* ?

ANSER.—Bill not so much elevated at the base as in *Chen ;* the commissure less curved ; the teeth less prominent. Lower jaw not so deep. Species, *A. gambelii* and *frontalis*.

These characters apply pretty well to the American species, but European geese exhibit a very gradual transition between the two.

Comparative measurements of species.

Catal. No.	Species.	Locality.	Length.	Wing.	Tail.	Tarsus.	Middle toe.	Its claw alone.	Bill above.	Along gape.	Height of bill at base.	Width of bill at base.	Specimen measured.
1241	Anser hyperboreus.	....	*25.00	16.40	5.80	3.12	2.82	0.42	2.10	2.10	....	....	Skin......
1970	........do	Missouri river.	28.00	16.60	5.50	3.06	2.98	0.44	2.08	2.30	....	....	Skin......
1963	Anser gambelii.....	......do............	28.00	16.30	5.42	2.88	3.10	0.52	2.00	2.04	....	....	Skin. .....
10406	........do	Salt Lake	28.00	16.00	5.50	2.40	2.70	0.40	1.86	1.92	....	....	Skin.......
9953	Anser frontalis.	Fort Thorn, N. M..	26.00	16.75	5.10	2.92	3.00	0.40	1.96	2.12	0.96	0.90	Skin.......

* About.

ANSER HYPERBOREUS, Pallas.

Snow Goose.

Anser caerulescens, LINN. Syst. Nat. I, 1766, 198.—CASSIN, Pr. A. N. S. VIII, 1856, 12.

Anser hyperboreus, PALLAS, Spic. Zool. VI, 1767, 80, 25.—BON. Syn. 1828, 376.—SW. F. B. A. II, 1831, 467.—NUTT. Man. II, 344.—AUD. Orn, Biog. IV, 1833, 562; pl. 381.—IB. Syn. 273.—IB Birds Amer. VI, 1843, 212; pl. 381.—EYTON, Mon. Anat. 1839, 92.—CASSIN, Pr. A. N. S. VIII, 1856, 11.

Anas hyperborea, GM. I, 504.—WILS. Am. Orn. VIII, 1814, 76; pl. lxviii and lxix.

Anas nivalis, FORSTER, Phil. Trans. LXII, 1772, 413.

Tadorna nivea, BREHM, Vög. Deutschl. 1831, 854.

? *Anser albatus*, CASSIN, Pr. A. N. S. VIII, 1856, 41.

SP. CH.—*Adult*. Bill and legs red. Color pure white. Primary quills black towards the end, silvery bluish gray towards he base, where the shafts are white. The spurious quills are also bluish. Inside of wings, except primary quills, white. Immature birds have the head washed with rusty.

? Young. Head and upper part of neck white; lower part of neck to the wings dark brown, passing on the sides of body into a more ashy shade; rest of under parts, concealed portions of the back, rump, and upper coverts, white. The entire scapular and scapular region is ashy brown, each feather with faint reddish brown margin. The upper surface of the wing is of a clear silvery ash, but passing into dark brown on the ends of the quills. The coverts, secondaries, tertials, and scapulars, edged with white.

Length about 30 inches; wing, 16.40; tarsus, 3.12; commissure, 2.10.

Hab.—Whole of North America.

It is quite probable that, as Mr. Cassin suggests, the supposed young bird, as described above, is really distinct from the white bird, but in the absence of positive facts in the case I do not feel at liberty to separate the two, especially as Mr. Audubon asserts positively that a gray or bluish specimen in possession of Dr. Bachman became white.

I have not the means of testing the validity of Mr. Cassin's new *Anser albatus*, which is said to differ from the common species in smaller size, shorter bill, &c. In the very great variations of size and proportions in the geese I can scarcely believe that the grounds of distinction as announced are sufficient in the present case to make two species.

The name *caerulescens* has priority of date over *hyperboreus*, and if the species are the same should be used, but for the fact that the adult bird is not bluish, but white, thus conveying a false impression respecting it.

List of specimens.

Catal. No.	Locality.	Whence obtained.	Collected by—
	WHITE.		
1241	United States	S. F. Baird	
4527	San Francisco	Lieut. Williamson	Dr. Newberry
9968	Puget's Sound	Dr. Suckley	
10403	Northwest coast of America	United States Exploring Expedition	
	BLUISH.		
1970	Missouri river	S. F. Baird	J. J. Audubon

ANSER GAMBELII, Hartlaub.

White Fronted Goose; Laughing Goose.

Anser albifrons, Sw. F. B. A. II, 1831, 456. Not of Gmelin.—Nutt. Man. II, 346.—Aud. Orn. Biog. III, 1835, 568; pl. 280.—Ib. Syn. 272.—Ib. Birds Amer. VI, 1843, 209; pl. 380.

Anser gambelii, Hartlaub, Rev. et Mag. Zool. 1852, 7.

Sp. Ch.—Tail of sixteen feathers. Bill and legs red. Along sides of bill and forehead white, margined behind with blackish brown. Rest of head and neck grayish brown, becoming pale on the jugulum. Back bluish gray, the feathers anteriorly tipped with brown; the sides similarly colored. The breast and belly grayish white, blotched irregularly with black; the anal region, sides behind, and beneath the tail, with the upper coverts, white. The secondary quills and ends of primaries are dark brown; the remaining portion of primaries and the covert silvery ash. The shafts of quills white. Greater coverts edged with white. Tail feathers brown, tipped with white. Axillars and under surface of wings ashy plumbeous. Length 28 inches; wing, 16.30; tarsus, 2.88; commissure, 2.04.

Hab.—Whole of North America.

A specimen from New Mexico is smaller, with the nail of bill narrower. Another from El Paso (10463) has the under parts grayish, with only a trace of black in three or four feathers.

August 12, 1858.

96 b

The white forehead is very conspicuous. Another specimen goes to the opposite extreme in having the breast and belly continuously black, with only an occasional blotch of gray.

It is quite possible that this continent possesses two species of white fronted geese, but in the specimen before me I am unable to detect any constant differences of importance.

The difference between the European and American white fronted geese, according to Hartlaub, consists in the much larger bill of the latter. This in *A. gambelii* measures over two inches, instead of 1.50, as in *A. albifrons*.

List of specimens.

Catal. No.	Locality.	When collected.	Whence obtained.	Collected by—	Remarks.
4517	Washington, D. C		S. F. Baird		
1963	Missouri river		....do	J. J. Audubon	
10463	Frontera, Texas		Major Emory	J. H. Clark	
9967	Rio Grande		....do	A. Schott	
10406	Salt Lake		Captain Stansbury		
10405	California		United States Ex. Exp		
10462	Shoalwater bay	Nov., 1854	Governor Stevens	Dr. Cooper	Iris brown ; bill flesh color.

ANSER FRONTALIS, Baird.

Sp. Ch.—Bill apparently red; the nail blackish. The head and neck brown, darker above, and the space round the base of the bill much darker than elsewhere, instead of being white. The scapular region and wing coverts are purer and darker brown than the head, each feather edged with paler, excepting the lesser coverts, which are more ashy. The greater coverts are broadly tipped with whitish. The lower back, tail, primary, and secondary quills, are very dark brown; the tail narrowly tipped with white; the exposed portion of the primaries dark ashy. The sides of the rump, the upper and under tail coverts, and the region about the anus are whitish; the rest of the under parts are also whitish, each feather being brown and edged with this whitish color. The sides are continuously dark brown, but edged with the paler color of the head. The inside of wings and axillars are dark slate. Length about 26.00; wing, 16.75; tarsus, 2.92; commissure, 2.12.

Hab.—Interior of North America.

This goose is very similar to the common American white fronted goose in general appearance, the principal difference being the replacing of the white round the base of the bill by a brown, darker than that of the head, and the absence of black irregular blotches beneath, each feather having instead a dusky centre. The wings are precisely the same. The dusky nail of the bill instead of a white one appears to be characteristic.

I have not met with any indication of this goose in any American writer, and I am inclined to believe it a distinct and undescribed species. The young white fronted goose is said to have the white front indicated by a few white feathers; the under plumage plain gray. An *Anser temminckii* (*A. minutus*, Naum.) from Europe is much smaller than the European *albifrons*, with a dark nail, but the front is white. *Anser bruchii* of Brehm, (*A. medius* of Bruch,) likewise European, has the forehead uniform with the rest of the head, not darker; the breast is dusky; the nail of the bill is dark colored, as in the present bird ; the size appears smaller.

For the present, therefore, I have no other alternative but to impose a new name on the species, leaving the question of its relationship to be settled by fuller information respecting the American geese generally.

List of specimens.

Catal. Number.	Locality.	Whence obtained.
9957	Selkirk settlement............	R. Kennicott........ ....
9953	Fort Thorn......	Dr. Henry ....

BERNICLA, Stephens.

Bernicla, Stephens, Shaw's Gen. Zool. XII, ii, 1824, 45.   Type *Anas bernicla,* Linn.

Leucopareia, Reich. Syst. Avium, Int. 1853, pl. ix.   Type *Anser leucopsis,* Bech.

Ch.—Bill about as long as head or shorter; the commissure nearly straight; the teeth of upper mandible concealed, except perhaps at the base. Bill and legs black.

The American geese, with black bills and legs, exhibit very great variations in size; so much so, indeed, as to render it very difficult to distinguish them by this character alone.   The variation in the shade of plumage in the same species is likewise considerable.

Synopsis of species.

A. Leucoblepharon, Baird.—Head and neck black.   A large triangular patch behind the eye, usually broadly confluent with its fellow beneath, the upper angle truncate.   A few whitish feathers on lower eyelid.

Tail of eighteen feathers.

Bill elongated; as broad at the base as height of upper mandible.   Length of culmen equal to the head, and nearly two-thirds the tarsus, which is equal to the middle toe without its claw.   Under parts ashy brown, passing almost insensibly into white about anus.   No white ring on throat............*canadensis.*

Bill short; broader at the base than height of upper mandible.   Culmen shorter than head, about half the tarsus, which is longer than middle toe and claw.   Under parts dark brown, abruptly defined against white of the anal region.   A distinct white ring on lower throat.......................................*leucopareia.*

Tail of sixteen feathers.

Similar to *canadensis,* but much smaller...*hutchinsii.*

B. Bernicla, Steph.—Head, neck, and jugulum, black.   Middle of neck with a white crescent on each side.   Bill shorter than the head.

Crescents of neck distinct.   Upper parts brown, edged with paler.   Beneath grayish, sharply defined against the black of jugulum.......................*brenta.*

Crescents of neck confluent beneath.   Above uniform brown; belly nearly as black as jugulum..*nigricans.*

C. Leucopareia, Reich.—Head, neck, and jugulum, black.   Forehead, cheeks, and chin, white.

Feathers above ash color, terminated broadly with blackish and tipped with white.   Under parts nearly pure white......................................*leucopsis.*

Comparative measurements of species.

Catal. No.	Species.	Locality.	Sex.	Length.	Stretch of wings.	Wing.	Tail.	Tarsus.	Middle toe.	Its claw alone.	Bill above.	Along gape.	Height of bill at base.	Width of bill at base.	Specimen measured.
2128	Bernicla canadensis....	Carlisle, Pa	♂	....	....	17.75	6.68	3.10	3.50	0.50	1.84	2.10	......	......	Skin.....
do.	........do	......do	......	35.00	63.50	18.00	......	......	......	......	......	......			Fresh ...
10402	........do	Salt Lake	......	36.50	....	19.50	7.12	3 24	3.90	0.60	2.04	2.22	1.00	1.00	Fresh ...
10401	........do	......do	♂	36.50	....	19.10	7.10	3.26	3.62	0.52	2.20	2.30	1.02	1.02	Fresh ...
9960	........do	Bodega, Cal.......	about	37.00	....	17.75	6.70	3.31	3.60	0.44	1.92	2.01	1.00	1.00	Skin.....
9962	........do	......do	......	....	....	20.75	7.54	3.62	3.64	0.60	2.02	2.20	1.02	1.02	Skin.....
1192	........do	Potomac river	♀	36.00	....	18.00	6.84	3.16	3.22	0.40	2.00	2.30	1.02	1.02	Skin.....
do.	........do	......do	......	37.50	63.50	18.00	......	......	......	......	......	......			Fresh ...
5471	........do	Yellowstone.......	......	....	....	18.75	5.80	3.70	3.50	0.40	1.92	2.04	0.90	0.82	Skin.....
9961	........do	Frontera, Texas....	......	....	....	18.00	6.10	3.32	3.24	0.50	2.00	2.04	1.02	1.02	Skin.....
9954	........do	Rio Rita, N. M....	......	30.00	....	18.00	5.80	3.06	3.06	0.42	1.70	1.84	0.92	0.92	Skin.....
9554	........do	Simiahmoo bay.....	......	27.50	....	16.50	5.54	2.74	2.60	0.42	1.50	1.60	0.80	0.80	Skin.....
5994	Bernicla leucopareia...	Port Townsend	......	....	....	18.00	6.30	3.44	3.30	0.46	1.62	1.90	0.80	0.90	Skin.....
4529	Bernicla hutchinsii.....	San Francisco.....	......	....	....	15.50	6.20	2.74	2.64	0.48	1.44	1.50	0.74	0.74	Skin.....
	........do	Columbia river?....	......	30.00	....	15.80	5.60	2.70	2.50	0.44	1.62	1.76	.....	......	Skin.....
9956	........do	Red river, H. B. T.	......	....	....	13 60	4.66	2.70	2.50	0.34	1.36	1.42	0.70	0.64	Skin.....
2727	........do	Columbia river?....	......	30.00	....	15.80	5.60	2.70	2.50	0.44	1.62	1.76	.....	......	Skin.....
1199	Bernicla brenta.......	East'n shore of Md.	♀	22.00	....	12.84	4.60	2.26	2.25	0.33	1.32	1.40	.....	......	Skin.....
do.	........do	......do	......	23.50	45.50	12.75	......	......	......	......	......	......			Fresh ...
9965	Bernicla nigricans.....	Bodega, Cal	about	27.00	....	12.90	4.46	2.30	2.20	0.34	1.22	1.50	.....	......	Skin.....
9964	........do	......do	......	29.00	....	13.80	4.98	2.30	2.25	0.40	1.23	1.50	.....	......	Skin.....
1801	Bernicla leucopsis.....	Europe.............	......	28.20	....	17.00	4.14	2.76	2.42	0.36	1.40	1.40	.....	......	Skin.....

BERNICLA CANADENSIS, Boie.

Canada Goose.

Anas canadensis, LINN. Syst. Nat. I, 1766, 198.—FORSTER, Phil. Trans. LXII, 1772, 383.—WILS. Am. Orn. VIII, 1814, 52; pl. lvii.

Anser canadensis, VIEILL. Nouv. Dict.—Sw. & RICH. F. Bor. Am. II, 1831, 468.—NUTT. Man. II, 349.—AUD. Orn. Biog. III, 1835, 1: V, 607; pl. 201.—IB. Syn. 270.—IB. Birds Amer. VI, 1843, 178; pl. 376.

Cygnus canadensis, STEPH. Shaw's Zool. XII, II, 1824, 19.

Bernicla canadensis, BOIE, Isis, 1826, 921.

? Anser parvipes, CASSIN, Pr. A. N. Sc. VI, Oct. 1852, 188. (Vera Cruz.)

SP. CH.—Tail of eighteen feathers. Head, neck, bill, and feet, deep black. A large triangular patch of white on the cheeks behind the eye; the two of opposite sides broadly confluent beneath, but not extending to the rami of lower jaw; a few whitish feathers on lower eyelid. Upper parts brown, edged with paler. Under parts light, with a tinge of purple gray, sometimes a shade of smoky brown; the edges of the feathers paler; the color of the body of the feathers, though similar, becoming deeper on the sides, tibia, axillars, and inside of wings. The gray of the belly passes gradually into white on the anal region and under coverts; the upper tail coverts are pure white. The primary quills and rump are very dark blackish brown; the tail feathers are black. Length, 35; wing, 18; tarsus, 3.10; commissure, 2.10.

Hab.—Whole of North America. Accidental in Europe.

In comparing quite a large series of Canada geese together, I have found very great discrepancies in dimensions, as will be sufficiently evident from the table of measurements. I find almost every size between wide extremes, with great variations in size and proportions of the bill, as well as much difference in the shade and continuity of color. In several instances the bill is shorter than the head. At present I do not see the way clear to do else than consider them as one species, leaving it for further materials to decide the question.

One specimen, 9554, from Simiahmoo bay, is the smallest of all, and would be taken for *Bernicla hutchinsii*, but for the possession of eighteen tail feathers. In the yellowish color of the under parts, the small bill and feet, and in its diminutive size, it approaches very closely to the *Anser parvipes* of Cassin from Vera Cruz, and may possibly represent the same form or variety of *B. canadensis*, or even with it constitute a distinct species, which, however, I am scarcely inclined at present to admit.

List of specimens.

Catal. No.	Sex.	Locality.	When collected.	Whence obtained.	Collected by—	Length.	Stretch of wings.	Wing.
2128	♂	Carlisle, Penn		S. F. Baird		35.00	63.50	18.00
1192	♀	Potomac river, D. C.	Dec., 1843	......do......		37.50	63.50	18.00
9961		Frontera, Texas		Major Emory	J. H. Clark			
9954		Rio Rita, Laguna, N. M.	Nov., 1853	Lieut. Whipple	Kenn. & Möll.			
5471		Yellowstone		Lieut. Warren	Dr. Hayden			
10401	♂	Salt Lake		Capt. Stansbury				
9962		Bodega, Cal		Lieut. Trowbridge	T. A. Szabo			
9554		Simiahmoo bay	October 9	A. Campbell	Dr. Kennerly			

BERNICLA LEUCOPAREIA, Cassin.

Anser leucopareius, BRANDT, Bull Sc. Acad, St. Petersb. I, 1836, 37, (Aleutians.)—IB. Desc. et Icones Anim. Ross. Aves, fasc. I, 1836, 13; plate ii.
? *Bernicla leucopareia*, CASSIN, Ill. I, 1855, 272; pl. xlv.
Anser canadensis, PALLAS, Zoog. Rosso-As. II, 1811, 230.

SP. CH.—Tail of eighteen feathers; general appearance that of *A. canadensis*, but much darker; head and neck black, bounded inferiorly by a well defined half ring of white on the throat; a white patch on each cheek, the two confluent below, triangular on the sides and truncate above; the posterior outline perpendicular, the anterior sloping backwards behind the eye, almost exactly as in *A. canadensis*; there is a faint whitish patch on lower eyelids; upper parts dark wood brown, turning gradually into black on the rump, tail and primary quills, each brown feather of the fore back and wings with a rather paler edge. The under parts are very dark brown, as dark as the back of *A. canadensis*, paler along the middle of the belly, the sides as dark as the back; each feather has an obsolete margin of lighter; the region round anus is white, abruptly defined against the brown of the belly; the under and upper tail coverts are white; the bill is quite short, the culmen about half the tarsus, which is decidedly longer than the middle toe. Length about 35 inches; wing, 18; tarsus, 3.44; commissure, 1.90.

Hab.—West coast of America.

This species closely resembles the Canada goose, and, like it, has 18 tail feathers. It is a little smaller, however, and much darker, standing almost in the same relation to it that *B. nigricans* does to *B. brenta*. The belly is as dark as the back of *A. canadensis*, the color abruptly defined against the white about the anus. The white half ring round the neck is a conspicuous feature. The bill is proportionally shorter, the culmen being only half the length of tarsus, while the tarsus is longer, exceeding the middle toe, instead of being smaller by the length of the nail.

This species agrees very well in its peculiar proportions of bill and tarsus with *B. leucopareia* of Brandt, and quite well in color, excepting that in the latter, as described by Brandt, the white of the cheeks is more restricted to a crescent on each side behind the eye, the concavity anterior, instead of having a larger patch of more triangular shape, and confluent on the chin with its fellow. The chin, however, has a black peninsula, nearly an isthmus, and the strait is spotted with black. It is quite possible that cases might occur where the white would be divided into two patches, although this would be rare. The colors of the present bird are darker than as assigned to *leucopareia*, with less of the paler edging of feathers.

It is not to be denied, however, that the probabilities are very great that the present species is really distinct from *leucopareia* of Brandt, the form of the cheek spot being usually very constant in *Bernicla*. The great inferiority of size is also to be taken into account. Brandt's specimen measures 30 inches; the bill above 1.50; the wing, 16.00; the tail barely 6.00; the tarsus, 3.30; middle toe, 2.75; width of bill at base, .75. It was obtained in the Aleutian islands. Should the bird from Port Townsend be a different species, it may be appropriately called *Bernicla occidentalis*. The name might be taken from the white collar but for the possibility that this may not be always constant.

The bird described by Mr. Cassin as *B. leucopareia* agrees much more closely with Brandt's bird in size and coloration than the subject of the present article. The white patches on the cheek are smaller, and separated on the chin by a narrow longitudinal black band. The length is 23 inches and the wing 15. The figure indicates shorter toes and bill than in the Canada goose.

List of specimens.

Catal. No.	Locality.	When collected.	Collected by—
5994	Port Townsend, W. T....	1857.....	Dr. Suckley............

BERNICLA HUTCHINSII, Bonap.

Hutchins' Goose.

Anser hutchinsii, RICH. F. Bor. Am. II, 1831, 470.—NUTT. Man. II, 362.—AUD. Orn. Biog. III, 1835, 526; pl. 277.—IB. Syn. 271.—IB. Birds Am. VI, 1843, 198; pl. 377.

Bernicla hutchinsii, BON. List, 1838.

Anas bernicla, var. β RICH. App. Parry 2d voyage, I, 368.

SP. CH.—Precisely similar to *A. canadensis*, but smaller. Tail of 16 feathers. Tarsus longer than middle toe and claw.

Length, 30 inches; wing, 15.80; tarsus, 2.70; commissure, 1.76.

Hab.—Northern and western regions of North America.

In the specimens of Hutchins' goose before me I can detect no difference of form from the Canada goose, excepting in the smaller size and less number of tail feathers. The toes are rather shorter. In one supposed specimen from California the white cheek patches are separated inferiorly by black spottings.

There are some discrepancies in the accounts of Richardson and of Audubon respecting this goose. According to the former, it has 14 tail feathers, and the wing measures 14 inches. Mr. Audubon's specimen had 16 tail feathers, the wing measuring 16.75 inches. Of the skins enumerated in the accompanying table, No. 9956 agrees very closely with Richardson's account, although it is my impression that it had 16 tail feathers. No. 2727, on the other hand, from Mr. Audubon's collection, is much as described by him.

List of specimens.

Catal. No.	Locality.	When collected.	Whence obtained.	Orig. No.	Collected by—
9952	Fort Steilacoom ----------------	October 1 ---------	Dr. Suckley ---------	516	------------------
2727	Columbia river? ----------------	------------------	S. F. Baird ---------	--------	J. J. Audubon ----
4529	San Francisco --•--------------	------------------	Lt. Williamson------	--------	Dr. Newberry-----
9956	North Red river, Minnesota------	September, 1857---.	N. W. University----	--------	R. Kennicott -----

BERNICLA BRENTA, Steph.

Brant.

Anas bernicla, LINN. Syst. Nat. I, 1766, 198.—WILS. Am. Orn. VIII, 1814, 131 ; pl. lxxii.

Anser bernicla, BON. Syn. 1828, 378.—SW. F. B. A. II, 1831, 469.—NUTT. Man. II, 359.—AUD. Orn. Biog. V, 1831, 24, 610; pl. 391.—IB. Birds Amer. VI, 1843, 203 ; pl. 379.

Bernicla brenta, STEPH. Shaw's Zool. XII, II, 1824, 46.—BON. List, 1838.—EYTON, Mon. Anat. 1839, 85.

" *Anser torquata*, FRISCH."

Bernicla torquatus, BREHM, Nat. Vög. Deutsch. 1831, 848.

SP. CH.—Bill and feet, head, neck, and body anterior to the wings, primary quills, and tail black ; the secondary quills nearly black. On each side of the middle of the neck is a small white crescent, streaked with black. The lower eyelids with a very faint trace of white feathers. The black of the jugulum is abruptly defined against the bluish silvery gray of the remaining under parts, the feathers of which have the basal portions bluish gray ; the axillars and insides of the wings showing a darker tint of the same. The gray of the belly passes gradually into white behind, the tail being encircled all round and concealed by this color. The back and wing coverts are grayish blue, with slightly paler edges ; the rump is of a similar, but darker and more uniform blue. The secondaries have some concealed whitish on the inner webs towards the base. Length, 23.50 ; wing, 12 75 ; tarsus, 2.26 ; commissure, 1.40.

Hab.—Eastern or Atlantic coast of North America and Europe. Not yet observed on the Pacific side of the continent.

List of Specimens.

Catal. No.	Sex.	Locality.	Whence obtained.	Length.	Stretch of wings.	Wing.
1199	♀	Eastern shore of Maryland---------------	S. F. Baird -------------	23. 50	45. 50	12.75

BERNICLA NIGRICANS, Cassin.

Black Brant.

Anser nigricans, LAWRENCE, Ann. N. Y. Lyc. IV, 1846, 171 ; plate.

Bernicla nigricans, CASSIN, Ill. I, II, 1853, 52 ; pl. x.

SP. CH.—Head, neck, and body anterior to the wings deep black, passing into dark sooty plumbeous on the rest of the body ; this color beneath extending nearly to the anus, and above shading insensibly into the black of the rump. Middle of the throat with a white patch extending round on the sides, and somewhat streaked with black. No white on the eyelids. Sides of rump and of base of tail, with upper and under tail coverts concealing the tail, and space across the anus, white ; primary and secondary quills and tail black. Feathers on sides of body beneath wings like the belly, but with white tips. Length, 29 inches ; wing, 13.80 ; tarsus, 2.30 commissure, 1.50.

Hab.—Pacific coast of North America. Very rare on the Atlantic coast.

This species, with a general resemblance to the brant goose, is yet very distinctly marked. The bill, though of the same length, is much wider.   There is no conspicuous distinction between the black of neck and jugulum and the dark plumbeous brown of belly and back, the feathers of which have no lighter edges, but are perfectly uniform.   The white patches on the sides of the neck are confluent below, not separated.

List of specimens.

Catal. No.	Locality.	When collected.	Whence obtained.	Collected by—	Length.	Stretch of wings.	Wing.
9965	Bodega, Cal. ------------	Dec. 1845	Lieut. Trowbridge-------	T. A. Szabo-----	--------	--------	--------
5995	Port Townsend, W. T.----	----------	Dr. Suckley------------	----------------	23. 75	44. 75	12. 75

BERNICLA LEUCOPSIS.

Barnacle Goose.

Anas erythropus, LINN. I, 1766, 197.—GMELIN, I, 513.—DEGLAND, Orn. Europ. II, 1849, 402.

Bernicla erythropus, STEPH. Shaw's Zool. XII, 1824, 49.

Anser leucopsis, BECHSTEIN, Taschenbuch, II, 1810, 557.—BON. Syn. 1828, 377.—NUTT. Man. II, 1834, 353.—AUD. Orn. Biog. III, 1835, 609; pl. 296.—IB. Syn. 271.—IB. Birds Amer. VI, 1843, 200; pl. 378.

Bernicla leucopsis, ——— ?

SP. CH.—Forehead, cheeks, and under parts of the head white ; the side of bill narrowly bordered with black. Crown, nape, lower part of neck, jugulum, fore part of back, rump, and tail black. Feathers of interscapulars and wings silvery bluish gray, passing into black towards the end, but with the extreme tip whitish gray. Nostrils similarly marked, but without the pale tips. Under parts uniform bluish white, the feathers on the sides only showing a darker basal portion. Upper tail coverts and sides of the tail at the base white. Bill and legs black. Length, 28 ; wing, 17; tarsus, 2.76 ; commissure, 1.40.

Hab.—Europe. Very doubtful as an inhabitant of North America.

Although this species is abundant in Europe, its occurrence in North America is very doubtful, resting only on very insufficient evidence.

Catal. Number.	Locality.	Whence obtained.
1801	Europe --------------------------------	S. F. Baird------------------------------

CHLOEPHAGA CANAGICA, Bon.

Painted Goose.

Anas canagicus, SEWASTIANOFF, Nova Acta Acad. St. Petersb. XIII, 1800, 346 ; pl. x.

Anser canagicus, BRANDT, Bull, Sc. St. Pet. I, 1836, 37.—IB. Desc. et Icon. Anim. Ross. Aves, fasc. I, 1836, 7; pl. i

Chloephaga canagica, BON. Comptes Rendus, 1856.

Anser pictus, PALLAS, Zoog. Rosso-Asiat. II, 1811, 233.

Sp. Ch.—Body bluish gray. Quills with a black stripe anterior to the white tip. Head, nape, and tail white; throat black, dotted with white. Bill red, or yellowish edged with dusky; nail white.

Length, 26 inches; wing, 15 25; tail, 5.50; tarsus, 2.90; middle toe, 2.66; bill from front, 1.50.

Hab.—Aleutian islands.

I introduce a short notice of the *Chloephaga canagica* as a species belonging to our continent, and said to be quite common on the Aleutian islands. It will, doubtless, in time, be found on the northwest coast of the United States.

The genus *Chloephaga* was separated by Eyton, Mon. Anat. in 1838, from *Bernicla*, to accommodate species with a shorter bill and more convex culmen, the legs robust, the membrane of the toes scolloped out, the colors different from *Bernicla*.

DENDROCYGNA, Swainson.

Dendrocygna, Swainson, Class. Birds II, 1837, 365. Type *Anas arcuata*, Cuv.
Dendronessa, Wagler, Isis, 1832, 282. Not of Swainson, 1831.

Ch.—Bill much longer than the head; plane at the base above; high at base, the edges nearly parallel, or slightly con verging; the nail very large, much decurved, and projecting considerably anterior to the rest of the bill, of which it forms the tip. Nostrils small, oval, not reaching the middle of the commissure. Lamellae of bill low, not projecting below the edge of the bill. Neck and legs very long; the tibia bare for more than half the length of tarsus. The tarsus covered with large hexagonal scales on the anterior half, and with smaller ones on the posterior. Hind toe lengthened, more than one-third the tarsus. Feet very large. Wings broad and much rounded, the first quill shorter than the fourth.

Thus far but two species are well established as inhabiting the United States, confined chiefly to the Rio Grande and south California. There is strong reason to believe that a species occasionally visits the coast of Georgia and other southern Atlantic States from the West Indies, which, though possibly the *D. autumnalis*, is more probably *D. arborea*. The characters of the three species are as follows:

Head and neck grayish, inclining to brownish red on top of head. Fore part of body all round chocolate red. Posterior portion of body, with quills and under surface of body and wings, blackish brown. A white patch on wings. Bill and legs red...............*D. autumnalis*.

Neck dirty white; crown black. Fore part of body dark brown. Tail black. Under parts of body white, each feather barred with brown. Bill lead color; legs and feet black..*D. arborea*.

Head yellowish brown, darker on the crown; a black streak down the nape. Wings, tail, and rump black; the lesser coverts chocolate; under parts uniform pale cinnamon. Under and upper tail coverts white. Bill and legs bluish black ....*D. fulva*.

Comparative measurements of species.

Catal. No.	Species.	Locality.	Sex.	Length.	Stretch of wings.	Wing.	Tail.	Tarsus.	Middle toe.	Its claw alone.	Bill above.	Along gape.	Specimen measured.
10399	Dendrocygna fulva.......	Fort Tejon, Cal....	♂	18.50	....	9.10	3.16	2.20	3.18	0.50	1.58	2.18	Skin .....
	........do...............	........do...........	......	20.00	36.50	....	....	....	....	....	....	....	Fresh ....
2682	Dendrocygna autumnalis..	South America....	♂	....	....	9 40	3.00	2.16	2 76	0.46	1.87	2.14	Skin .....
9871	........do...............	Rio Grande, Texas	♂	....	....	10.00	3.60	2.26	3.10	0.50	2.06	2.20	Skin .....

August 17, 1858.
97 b

DENDROCYGNA AUTUMNALIS, Eyton.

Long-legged Duck.

Anas autumnalis, LINN. Syst. Nat. I, 1766, 205.

Dendronessa autumnalis, WAGLER, Isis, 1832, 282.

Dendrocygna autumnalis, EYTON, Mon Anat 1838 —LAWRENCE, Ann. N. Y. Lyc. V, May, 1851, 117.

SP CH.—Head grayish. Top of head, lower part of neck, jugulum, interscapulars, and scapulars, reddish chocolate. A narrow line down the nape, and the body generally, with wings and tail, black. Crissum and tibia white, spotted with black. A large white patch on the wings, composed of the greater wing coverts and the basal half of nearly all the primaries and secondaries. Bill and feet red.

Length, about 24 inches; wing, 10; tarsus, 2.26; commissure, 2.20.

Hab.—Valley of Rio Grande, Texas. Also in South America and West Indies?

Sides of head and neck gray, passing on the lower surface into whitish. Forehead grayish, passing on the crown into reddish brown, and on the nape and back of the neck into dark brown and black. Lower half of neck and anterior portion of body all round, including jugulum and fore back, dull chocolate red, lighter on the breast; the scapulars, interscapulars, and tertials, with the tips somewhat similar, but the body of the feather more olive brown. Lower part of back, rump, tail, the belly and sides, the entire inner surface of wing and axillars, with the quills, sooty brown, almost black, dullest on the belly; the crissum and tibia white, spotted with sooty. Lesser coverts yellowish olive, the greater with the outer webs of secondaries and primaries and spurious feathers, white, showing as a conspicuous patch. The first and second primaries, and outer spurious quills without, white. Bill yellowish or red, the nail black. Feet like the bill.

In a specimen apparently of the same species, but more mature, the top of the head from the bill is dull brownish red, and the back and scapulars are of the same color, the narrow black line down the nape very distinct. The jugulum and lower part of neck all round is, however, more yellowish, separating broadly the chestnut or chocolate red of the throat from that of the back. The belly is pure black; the tibia black, with only a few whitish specks.

List of specimens.

Catal. No.	Sex.	Locality.	When collected.	When obtained.	Collected by—
9871	♂	Isla los'Ayuntas, (Rio Grande) Texas.	Sept 8, 1853	Major Emory	A. Schott.............
9872	....	Texas	....	......do......	....do...... ....
2682	....	South America	...........,......	S F. Baird.............	....

DENDROCYGNA FULVA, Burm.

Anas fulva, GMELIN, Syst. Nat. I, 1788, 530.—LATH. Ind. Orn. II, 1790, 863.—STEPH. in Shaw's Gen. Zool. XII, 1819, 204.—BURM. Thiere Brasiliens, II, 1856, 435.

"Anas virgata, MAX. Reise nach. Bras. I, 322."

"Anas sinuata, LICHT." Bon.

"Anas bicolor, VIEILLOT," Bon.

"Anas collaris, MERREM," Bon.

Penelope mexicana, BR. Orn. VI, 1760, 390.

Sp. Ch.—Nail of bill bent down at a right angle. Frontal feathers advancing as an obtuse angle. Bill and legs bluish black. Body beneath and anteriorly, and sides, uniform pale cinnamon. The neck similar; the head above dark cinnamon; the nape with a black line. Lesser wing coverts chocolate; rest of wings, tail, and rump, black. Scapulars and fore part of back black, barred at the ends with cinnamon. Upper and under tail coverts white.

Length, 20; wing, 9.10; tarsus, 2.20; gape of bill, 2.18.

Hab.—Fort Tejon, California; and south into Brazil.

Feathers of forehead advancing on the bill as an obtuse angle. Nail of bill abruptly hooked, the posterior outline of the hook at a right angle with the commissure. Legs and feet very large and stout. First quill intermediate between 4 and 5. Tail much rounded.

Bill and legs entirely black. Prevailing colors, light yellowish brown, except on the lower back and wings. The head and neck are light yellowish brown; the top of head, and, to a certain extent the cheeks, glossed with dark cinnamon. The central line of the chin and throat is rather paler, becoming nearly white posteriorly, this white finely streaked with dark brown on the edge and bases of some of the feathers. There is a well defined black nuchal line extending down the whole neck from behind the occiput. The entire under parts, including the jugulum, sides, and tibia, are uniform light reddish cinnamon, paler on the central line, and becoming whitish about the anus, and on the tibiae and under tail coverts. There is not the faintest trace of streaks or bands, except very obsolete lines on the tibiae. The lesser wing coverts are reddish chocolate; the rest of the wings on both surfaces, the axillars, the tail feathers, the rump, and the hinder part of back, are uniform black. The scapulars are dark brown or black, with terminal bars of dark brownish yellow. The upper tail coverts are yellowish white.

I have found great difficulty in identifying this bird with any description of species accessible to me. It comes nearest to *D. fulva*. As given by Burmeister, however, this appears to be considerably smaller, according to the description, and all the feathers of the under parts are said to have a broad light streak along the shafts, bordered anteriorly by a black line. The account as given by Latham, Gmelin, and others, however, makes no reference to these lines. It is quite possible that there are really two species included in the synonymy, and that the present bird is the original *Anas fulva* of Gmelin, from Mexico.

I quote the names *sinuata*, *collaris*, and *bicolor* from Bonaparte, not having the opportunity at present to verify them.

List of specimens.

Catal. No.	Sex.	Locality.	Whence obtained.	Length.	Stretch of wing.
10399	♂	Fort Tejon, Cal Spring of 1858	L. J. X. de Vesey	20. 50	36. 50

Sub-Family ANATINAE.

The *Anatinae*, or river ducks, are easily known by their having the tarsi transversely scutellate anteriorly, and the membrane or lobe of the hind toe narrow and much restricted. The legs are longer than in *Fuligulinae*, but shorter than in the geese.

The differences in external form of the American river or fresh water ducks are very trifling, excepting in *Spatula*, and are scarcely of the generic value allotted them by ornithologists. The system of coloration would seem to furnish as reliable a basis for subdivisions as the form, and it is by this, in great measure, that the genera are determined.

All the North American river ducks agree in having the crissum black. In all, excepting *Querquedula*, there is a tendency to waved lines on the feathers of the flanks, most conspicuous in the mallard, gadwall, and green winged teal.

Synopsis of genera.

A. Bill rather longer than the foot; the sides nearly parallel; lamellae scarcely visible in the lateral profile, except in *Querquedula*. Tail about two-fifths the wing, except in *Dafila*.

ANAS.—Bill broad and the edges parallel; the width more than about one-third the lower edge. Tail two-fifths the wing.

DAFILA.—Bill narrow, widening somewhat to the tip. The width less than one-third the commissural or lower edge. Tail much pointed, three-fourths or more the wing.

NETTION.—Bill very narrow, the sides parallel; the width scarcely more than one-fourth the lower edge. Nail very narrow, the width one-fifth that of the bill; upper angle of the bill not reaching as far back as the beginning of its lower edge.

QUERQUEDULA.—Width of bill about one-third the length of lower edge, or rather more. The nail about one-third the width of bill. Upper angle of the side of the bill extending rather further back than the lower edge. Lamellae distinctly visible in the lateral profile.

B. Bill much longer than the foot, widening towards the end to double the breadth at the base.

SPATULA.—Lamellae much developed, projecting downwards much below the edge of the bill.

C. Bill not longer than the head, and shorter than the foot. The upper posterior angle on the side of the bill obtuse, and not extending backwards as far as the lower edge. Tail about two-fifths the wing.

CHAULELASMUS.—Bill as long as the head; the lower edge about as long as the outer toe, and longer than the tarsus. The lamellae distinctly visible below the edge of the bill

MARECA.—Bill shorter than the head; the lower edge about equal to the tarsus, and to the inner toe. The feathers at base of bill above extending across nearly in straight line.

D. Bill shorter than the head, and elevated at the base; the upper lateral angle extending backwards and upwards considerably behind the lower edge.

AIX.—Nail very large and much hooked, forming the tip of bill. Nostrils very large, the feathers of forehead reaching to the posterior edge. Tail half the wings.

Comparative measurements of species.

Catal. No.	Species.	Locality.	Sex.	Length.	Stretch of wings.	Wing.	Tail.	Tarsus.	Middle toe.	Its claw alone.	Bill above.	Along gape.	Specimen measured.
872	Anas boschas..........	Carlisle, Pa........	♂	20.30	....	10.82	4.06	1.70	2.36	0.36	2.10	2.50	Skin.....
do.	........do...............	......do............	......	22.75	37.00	11.00	....	....	....	....	....	....	Fresh....
873	........do...............	......do......... ...	♀	20.30	....	10.60	4.24	1.60	2.34	0.37	1.98	2.30	Skin.....
do.	........do...............	......do............	......	22.25	36.50	11.00	....	....	....	....	....	....	Fresh....
231	Anas obscura...........	......do............	♂	22 00	....	11 46	4.70	1.80	2.40	0.38	2.24	2.56	Skin.....
847	........do...............	......do............	♀	19.80	....	10.50	4.16	1.66	2.28	0.30	2.00	2.30	Skin.....
do.	........do...............	......do............	......	22.00	36.25	10.50	....	....	....	....	....	....	Fresh....
10332	Dafila acuta	......do............	♂	20.00	....	11.00	8.60	1.76	2.32	0.38	2.02	2.36	Skin.....
10333	........do...............	......do............	♀	18.90	....	9.70	4.62	1.60	2.08	0.40	1.76	2.10	Skin.....
9725	Nettion carolinensis...	Camp 118, Bill W. F.	♂	14.00	....	7.40	3.42	1.14	1.60	0.30	1.45	1.68	Skin.....
do.	........do...............	......do............	......	14.00	25.00	....	....	....	....	....	....	....	Fresh....
9728	......do...............	Boca Grande, Mex.	......	13.20	....	7.10	3.52	1.08	1.52	0.28	1.40	1.60	Skin.....
do.	Nettion crecca.........	..... do............	......	13.00	20.00	....	....	....	....	....	....	....	Fresh....
1200	Querquedula discors...	Michigan	♂	15.40	....	7 10	3.06	1.19	1.64	0.32	1.60	1.86	Skin.....
1201	........do......	......do............	♀	15.80	....	6.90	2.66	1.26	1.72	0.34	1.52	1.80	Skin.....
4458	Querquedula cyanoptera	San José, Cal......	♂	17.80	....	7.50	3.80	1.10	1.76	0.36	1.72	2.00	Skin.....
4459	........do...............	......do............	♀	16.20	....	7.20	3.52	1.21	1.70	0.31	1.66	1.90	Skin.....
925	Spatula clypeata.......	Carlisle, Pa.......	♂	18.50	....	9.70	3.80	1.38	2.18	0.40	2.68	3.02	Skin.....
do.	........do...............	......do............	......	20.00	32 25	9.50	....	....	....	....	....	....	Fresh....
2524	........do...............	......do	♀	19.30	....	9.20	3.94	1.41	2.00	0.37	2.58	2.94	Skin.....
do.	........do...............	......do............	......	20.25	31.75	9.50	....	....	....	....	....	....	Fresh....
1783	Spatula maculosa.......	South America	......	22.00	....	8.50	4.44	1.30	1.96	0.36	2.42	2.57	Skin.....
9788	Anas strepera..........	Bodega, Cal.......	♂	22.00	....	10.50	3.96	1.64	2.10	0.34	1.72	2.04	Skin.....
4560	........do	San José, Cal......	♀	19.20	....	10.10	4.20	1.46	2.10	0.34	1.72	2.00	Skin.....
1310	Mareca americana	Carlisle, Pa.......	♂	21.00	5	11.00	5.24	1.42	2.10	0.34	1.50	1.78	Skin.....
do.	........do...............	......do............	......	21.75	35.50	11.00	....	....	....	....	....	....	Fresh....
286	........do...............	......do............	♀	18.20	....	9.60	4.54	1.44	1.82	0.33	1.34	1.54	Skin.....
10376	Mareca penelope.......	... ..do............	♂	20.00	....	10.60	5.14	1.52	1.99	0.34	1.44	1.64	Skin.....
10331	Aix sponsa.............	......do............	♀	17.60	....	8.90	4.90	1 36	1.92	0.34	1.30	1.58	Skin.....
1732	........do...............	......do............	♂	18.00	....	9.20	4.50	1.40	1.90	0.32	1.36	1.54	Skin.....
do.	........do...............	......do............	......	19.00	29.50	9.58	....	....	....	....	....	... .	Fresh....

ANAS, Linnaeus.

Anas, LINNAEUS, Syst. Nat. 1735. Type *Anas boschas*, L. (Gray.)

CH —Bill longer than the head or the foot, broad, depressed ; the edges parallel to near the end, which is somewhat acute. Nail less than one-third the width of the bill. Nostrils reaching to end of the basal two-fifths of the commissure. Feathers of forehead, chin, and cheeks, reaching about the same point; upper angle of bill about in line with the lower. Tail pointed, about two-fifths the wing.

The genus *Anas* embraces very large species, among them the original of the domestic duck. The characters of the two North American species are as follows :

A. Ends of greater wing coverts white, tipped with black ; speculum purplish violet, terminated with black.

Head and neck green, succeeded by a white ring. Breast dark chestnut. Under parts and scapulars gray, finely undulated with dusky. Tail white, the coverts black..*A. boschas.*

B. Wing black, the speculum purplish violet, tipped with black.

Entirely dusky ; the head and neck brownish yellow, spotted with dark brown, which is uniform on the top of head and nape ; sides of nape with a greenish gloss. No white anywhere except on the axillars and inside of wing..............................*A. obscura.*

ANAS BOSCHAS, L.

Mallard ; Green Head.

Anas boschas, LINN. Syst. Nat. I, 1766, 205.—FORSTER, Phil. Trans. LXII, 1772, 383.—GMELIN, I, 538.—WILSON, Am. Orn. VIII, 1814, 112 ; pl. lxx.—BON. Obs. 1825, No. 256.—IB. List, 1838.—AUD. Orn. Biog. III, 1835, 164 ; pl. 221.—IB. Syn. 276.—IB. Birds Amer. VI, 1843, 236 ; pl. 385.—EYTON, Mon. Anat. 1838, 140.

Anas (Boschas) boschas, JENYNS, Man. 233.

Anas adunca, L. Syst. Nat. I, 1766, 206.—GM. I, 538 ; monstrous variety.

Anas domestica, GMELIN, I, 1788, 538.

Anas (Boschas) domestica, SW. F. Bor. Am. II, 1831, 442.—NUTTALL, Man. II, 1834, 378.

" *Anas bicolor,* DONOVAN, Br. Birds, IX ; pl. 212." (Supposed hybrid with *Cairina moschata,* or muscovy duck. Jenyns.)

" *Anas purpureo-viridis,* SCHINZ." (Supposed hybrid with *Cairina moschata.* Bonap.)

Anas maxima, GOSSE, Birds Jam. 1847. 399. (Supposed hybrid with *Cairina moschata*)

Fuligula viola, BELL, Annals N. Y. Lyceum, V, 1852, 219. New York. (Supposed hybrid with *Cairina moschata.*)

Anas glocitans, AUD ; pl. 338.

Anas breweri, AUD. Orn. Biog. IV, 1838, 302 ; pl. 338.—IB. Syn. 277.—IB. Bird's Amer. VI, 1843, 252 ; pl. 387.

Anas audubonii, BON. Geog. List, 1838. The three last names are based on the same specimen, supposed to be a hybrid between *Anas boschas* and *Chaulelasmus streperus,* possibly with *Aythya vallisneria.*

Mallard, PENNANT, Arctic Zool. II, 563.—Lath. Syn. III, II, 489.

SP. CH.—*Male.* Head and neck bright grass green, with violet gloss, the top of the head duller ; a white ring round the middle of the neck, below which and on the fore part and sides of the breast the color is dark brownish chestnut. Under parts and sides, with the scapulars, pale gray, very finely undulated with dusky ; the outer scapulars with a brownish tinge. Fore part of back reddish brown ; posterior more olivaceous. Crissum and upper tail coverts black, the latter with a blue gloss. Tail externally white ; wing coverts brownish gray, the greater coverts tipped first with white, and then more narrowly with black. Speculum purplish violet, terminated with black ; a recurved tuft of feathers on the rump.

Female with the wing exactly as on the male. The under parts plain whitish ochrey, each feather obscurely blotched with dusky. Head and neck similar, spotted and streaked with dusky ; the chin and throat above unspotted. Upper parts dark brown, the feathers broadly edged and banded with reddish brown parallel with the circumference.

Length of male, 23 ; wing, 11 ; tarsus, 1.70 ; commissure of bill, 2.50.

Hab.—Entire continent of North America and greater part of Old World.

A large duck, much exceeding the mallard in size, but quite similar in general appearance, is occasionally shot in the United States and in Europe, and described by the various names given in the synonomy. It is generally supposed to be a hybrid with the muscovy, *Cairina moschata,* although, from the constancy of its markings and the absence on the face of the peculiarities of the muscovy, it may be questioned whether, after all, it be not entitled to specific rank. The *Anas breweri* of Audubon is different from this form, and may, possibly, be a hybrid with the gadwall, as suggested by its describer.

This species is generally considered as identical with the barn-yard duck, and presents one of the few cases where the original is well known of a domesticated animal. A difference between the wild and tame mallard, according to Giraud, is to be found in the much broader, harder, and more horny feet of the latter.

List of specimens.

Catal. No.	Sex.	Locality.	When collected.	Whence obtained.	Orig'l No.	Collected by—	Length.	Stretch of wings.	Wing.
872	♂	Carlisle, Pa.....................	Nov. 25, 1842	S. F. Baird	......	....	22.75	37.00	11.00
873	♀	........do....................	......do......	......do..................	......	....	22.25	36.50	11.00
6897	♂	Selkirk Settlement, H. B. T	....	D. Gunn.................	......	....	......	......	......
6891	♀ ○	Nelson river, H. B. T	....	......do................	......	Jno. Isbister	......	......	......
9691	♂	Upper Mississippi and Yellowstone	....	Lieut. Warren	......	Dr. Hayden.............	......	......	......
9699	♂	Great Salt Lake City............	....	Lieut. Beckwith	......	....	......	......	......
9696	♂	Fort Thorn, New Mexico	....	Dr. Henry	......	....	......	......	......
5887	......	Fort Riley, K. T......	....	Hammond & Vesey......	......	....	......	......	......
9693	.....	Boca Grande, Mexico...	Mar. —, 1855	Major Emory............	30	Dr. Kennerly............	......	......	......
9697	♂	Bodega, Cal	Feb. —, 1855	Lieut. Trowbridge........	......	T. A. Szabo	......	......	......
9701	.....	Presidio, (near San Francisco) ..	July 6, 1853	......do...............	......	......do.................	......	......	......
9698	♂	Fort Steilacoom, W. T	....	Gov. Stevens	21	Dr. Suckley....... ...	......	......	......
9692	......	........do....................	Feb. 2, 1854	......do..................	31	......do	24.00	37.00	11.50

ANAS OBSCURA, Gm.

Black Duck; Dusky Duck.

Anas obscura, GM. Syst. Nat. I, 1788, 541.—LATH. Ind. II, 1790.—WILSON, Am. Orn. VIII, 1814, 141 ; pl. lxxii, f. 5.—IB. Ord's ed. VIII, 155.—BON. Obs. Wils. 1825, 260.—IB. Syn. 234.—AUD. Orn. Biog. IV, 1838, 15 ; pl. 302.—IB. Syn. 276.—IB. Birds Amer. VI, 1843, 244 ; pl. 386.—EYTON Mon. Anat. 1838, 140.

Anas (Boschas) obscura, NUTTALL, Man. II, 1834, 392.

Dusky Duck.—PENNANT, Arc. Zool. II, 564.—LATH. III, II, 545.

SP. CH.—Bill greenish ; feet red. Body generally blackish brown ; the feathers obscurely margined with reddish brown ; those anteriorly with a concealed V-shaped mark, more or less visible on the sides of the breast. Head and neck brownish yellow, spotted with black ; the top of head and nape dark brown, with a green gloss on the sides behind. Wings dull blackish, with a dull greenish gloss. Speculum violet, terminated with black. Inner tertials hoary gray towards tip. Axillars and inside of wing white. Tail of 18 feathers.

Female similar, but rather duller ; the light edges to the under feathers more conspicuous ; the sides of head without the greenish gloss. The speculum bluish, with less violet.

Length of male, 22 inches ; wing nearly 12 ; tarsus, 1.80 ; commissure, 2.56.

Hab.—Atlantic region of North America. Not yet detected on the Pacific, nor in Europe.

This is the most plainly marked as well as, perhaps, the largest of our river ducks, and excelled by none in the excellence of its flesh.

List of specimens.

Catal. No.	Sex.	Locality.	When collected.	Whence obtained.	Length.	Stretch of wings.	Wing.
231	♂	Carlisle, Penn..........	March 10, 1840.......	S. F. Baird	....	....	....
847	♀	......do.............	November 4, 1842....	......do...............	22.00	36.25	10.50

DAFILA, Leach.

Dafila, "LEACH," STEPHENS, Shaw's Gen. Zool. XII, 1824, 126. Type *Anas acuta.*

Phasianurus, WAGLER, Isis, 1832.

CH.--Bill long, narrow ; considerably longer than the foot ; nearly linear, but widening a little to the end, which is truncate, rounded. Nail small. Nostrils small, in the basal third of bill. Tail pointed ; the two middle feathers lengthened, so as nearly to equal the wings.

There is but one species of *Dafila* inhabiting the United States, the *D. acuta*, though the *D. urophasiana* is quoted as belonging to our western coast as well as that of South America. The *D. bahamensis*,[1] by some supposed to be the same with *D. urophasiana*, if really found in the Bahamas, in all probability extends its flight to our southern coast.

The characters of *Dafila acuta* are as follows:

Tail of 16 feathers. Head uniform brown. Neck and beneath plain white. Sides and fore part of back finely lined transversely with black and white. Wing coverts plain, terminated narrowly by reddish buff; then a purplish green speculum passing into black behind, and tipped with white. Scapulars and tertials streaked with black and hoary whitish.

DAFILA ACUTA, Jenyns.

Pintail; Sprigtail.

Anas acuta, LINN. Syst. Nat. I, 1766, 202.—GMELIN, I, 258.—WILSON, Am. Orn. VIII, 1814, f. 2; pl. lxviii.—
        BONAP. Obs. No. 258.—TEMM. Man. II, 838, (Europ. sp.)—AUD. Orn. Biog. III, 1835, 214 : V, 615;
        pl. 227.—IB. Syn. 279.—IB. Birds Amer. VI, 1843, 266; pl. 390.

Phasianurus acutus, WAGLER, Isis, 1832, 1235.

Anas (Dafila) acuta, JENYNS, Man. 1835, 232. Europ. sp.

Dafila acuta, BON. List, 1838.

Anas (Boschas) acuta, NUTTALL, Man. II, 1834, 386.

Anas caudacuta, (RAY,) Sw. F. Bor. Am. II, 1831, 441.

Dafila caudacuta, STEPHENS, Shaw's Zool. XII, II, 1824, 127.—JARD. Br. Birds, IV, 120.—EYTON, Mon. Anat.
        1838, 113. European.

Dafila longicauda, BREHM.

Pintail, PENNANT, Arc. Zool. II, 566.—LATH. Syn. III, II, 526.

Dafila acuta, var. *A. americana*, BON. Compt-s Rendus, XLIII, 1856.

SP. CH.—Tail of 16 feathers. Bill black above and laterally at the base; the sides and beneath blue. Head and upper part of neck uniform dark brown, glossed with green and purple behind. Inferior part of neck, breast, and under parts white; the white of neck passes up to the nape, separating the brown, and itself is divided dorsally by black, which, below, passes into the gray of the back. The back anteriorly and the sides are finely lined transversely with black and white. The wings are plain and bluish gray; the greater coverts with a terminal bar of purplish buff, below which is a greenish purple speculum, margined behind by black, and tipped with white. Longest tertials striped with silvery and greenish black. Scapulars black, edged with silvery; crissum and elongated tail feathers black; the former edged with white.

Female with only a trace of the markings of the wing; the green of the speculum brownish, with a few green spots. The feathers of the back are brown, with a broad U or V-shaped brownish yellow bar on each feather anteriorly. Sometimes those bars appear in the shape of broad transverse lines.

Length, 30 inches; wing, 11; tail, 8.60; tarsus, 1.75; commissure, 2.36.

Hab.—Whole of North America and Europe.

The young male is sometimes difficult to recognize when without the long tail, and with the markings those, in part, of both sexes.

---

[1] The following synonymy is assigned to *Anas urophasianus*, though it is most probable that *Anas bahamensis* is a distinct species:

DAFILA BAHAMENSIS.

Anas bahamensis, LINN. Syst. Nat. I, 1766, 199.

Paecilonetta bahamensis, EYTON, Mon. Anat. 1838, pl. 112.—GAY, Fauna Chilena.—CASSIN, Gilliss' Chile, II, 1855, 203.

Anas ilathera, BONN.

Anas urophasianus, VIGORS, Zool. Jour. IV, 1829, 357.—IB. Zool. of Blossom, 1839, 31; pl. xiv.

Dafila urophasianus, EYTON, Mon. Anat. 1838.

Phasianurus vigorsii, WAGLER, Isis, 1832, 1235.

List of specimens.

Catal. No.	Sex.	Locality.	When collected.	Whence obtained.	Orig. No.	Collected by—	Length.	Stretch of wings.	Wing.	Remarks.
10332	♂	Carlisle, Pa......... ...		S. F. Baird.......						....
10333	♀	......do............		......do.........						.
6896	♂	Nelson river, H. B. T...		D. Gunn		Jno. Isbister....				
8910	.....	Nebraska.............		Lt. Warren......		Dr. Hayden....				
5121	.....	Devil's river, Texas	May 4, 1855	Capt. Pope.......	68		19.50	30.00	10.00	Bill brown, edges yellow, eyes brown, gums yellow.
9769	♂	Texas.................	....	Maj. Emory		A. Schott.....				
5119	♂	Indianola.............	Feb. 13, 1855	Capt. Pope						
5120	♂	Ojo del Cuerpo	Mar. 9, 1856	......do.........	184	....	25.00	46.00	10.50	
5118	.....	Dona Aña, N. M.......	Feb. 10, 1856	......do.........	177	....	28.00	35.00	11.25	....
9773	.....	Mimbres to Rio Grande.	....	Dr. Henry						
9771	.....	Bodega, Cal............	Dec. —, 1854	Lt. Trowbridge..		T. A. Szabo ...				
4454	.....	San José, Cal...........		A. J. Grayson....						
9768	♂	Fort Vancouver, W. T .	Dec. 9, 1853	Gov. Stevens	27	Dr. Cooper	32.00	27.00	....	Bill and feet grayish, iris dark.
9770	.....	Fort Steilacoom........	Feb. 2, 1854	......do.........	26	......do........	18.50	24.25	8.00	
9767	♂	......do...............	April —, 1854	......do.........		......do........	28.00	37.00	10.50	....

NETTION, Kaup.

Nettion, Kaup, Entwick. 1829. Type *Anas crecca*, L. (Gray.)

Querquedula, Bonap. List, 1838. Not of Stephens, 1824.

Ch.—Bill unusually narrow, longer than the foot ; the sides parallel ; the upper lateral angle not extending back as far as the lower edge. Nail very narrow, linear, and about one-fifth as wide as the bill.

The European and American species of *Nettion* (*Querquedula*, of Bonaparte, Eyton, &c.) agree in having the head and neck chestnut, with a broad patch of green on the side of head ; the breast has rounded black spots ; the upper part and sides are finely waved transversely with black and grayish white ; the crissum is black, edged with creamy yellow ; the wing coverts are plain olive gray, the greater with a terminal bar of fulvous ; the speculum is green, edged externally and internally with black. The diagnoses are as follows :

A white crescent on the side, just anterior to the bend of the wing. Scapulars plain grayish brown...*N. carolinensis.*

No crescent on the sides ; longer scapulars, creamy white internally, velvet black externally. Light lines on the side of head more distinct...*N. crecca.*

NETTION CAROLINENSIS, Baird.

Green-winged Teal.

Anas carolinensis, Gmelin, Syst. Nat. I, 1788, 533—Aud. Syn. 1839, 281.—Ib Birds Amer. VI, 1843, 281 ; pl. 392. Reinhdt. Vid. Med. for 1853 (1854), 84 (Greenland.)

Querquedula carolinensis, Steph. Shaw's Gen. Zool. XII, 1824, 148.

Anas crecca, var. Forster, Phil. Trans, LXII, 1772, 383, 419.

Anas crecca, Wilson, Am. Orn. VIII, 1814, 101 ; pl. lxx.—Bon. Obs. No. 263.—Ib. Syn. 386.—Aud. Orn. Biog. III, 1853, 218 : V, 616 ; pl. 228.

Anas (Boschas) crecca, Sw. F. Bor. Am. II, 1831, 400.—Nuttall, Man. II, 1834, 400.

" *Anas sylvatica,* Vieillot."

American Teal, Pennant, II, 569.—Lath. Syn. III, ii, 554.

August 18, 1858.

98 b

Sp. Ch.—Head and neck all round chestnut ; chin black ; forehead dusky. Region round the eye, continued along the side of the head as a broad stripe, rich green, passing into a bluish black patch across the nape. Under parts white, the feathers of the jugulum with rounded black spots. Lower portion of neck all round, sides of breast and body, long feathers of flanks and scapulars beautifully and finely banded closely with black and grayish white. Outer webs of some scapulars, and of outer secondaries black, the latter tipped with white ; speculum broad and rich green ; wing coverts plain grayish brown, the greater coverts tipped with buff. A white crescent in front of the bend of the wing ; crissum black, with a triangular patch of buffy white on each side. Lower portion of the green stripe on each side of the head blackish, with a dull edge of whitish below.

Female with the wings as in the male. The under parts white, with hidden spots on the jugulum and lower neck ; above dark brown, the feathers edged with gray.

Length, 14 inches ; wing, 7.40 ; tarsus, 1.14 ; commissure, 1.68.

Hab.—Whole of North America ; accidental in Europe.

Males vary in having the under parts sometimes strongly tinged with ferruginous brown.

List of specimens.

Catal. No.	Sex.	Locality.	When collected.	Whence obtained.	Orig'l No.	Collected by—	Length.	Stretch of wings.	Wing.	Remarks.
3336	♂	Carlisle, Pa............	Mar. 20, 1847	S. F. Baird........	......	....	....	....	....	....
287	♀	......do................	April 10, 1841	......do........	......	....	....	....	....	....
207	♀	......do................	Oct. 31, 1840	......do........	......	....	13.50	21.00	6.75	....
5461	.....	Blackfoot country......	1855.........	Lt. Warren	......	Dr. Hayden......	....	....	....	....
5462	♀	Big Bend, Mo........	Oct. 10, 1856	......do........	......	......do........	14.00	21.50	6.50	....
6903	♂	Nelson river, H. B. T...	....	D. Gunn..... ...	......	Jno. Isbister...	....	....	....	....
9721	♂	Great Salt Lake City...	1854.........	Capt. Beckwith..	......	....	....	....	....	....
5122	......	Indianola.......	Feb. 14, 1855	Capt. Pope	14	....	....	....	....	Feet bright yellow,bill bl'k, iris red, gums yellow.
9734	♂	El Paso, Texas	....	Maj. Emory......	......	J. H. Clark	....	....	....	....
9722	♂	Rio Rito, Laguna, N. M.	Nov. 12, 1854	Lt. Whipple......	3	Kenn. and Müll.	....	....	....	....
9732	♀	......do................	Nov. —, 1854	......do........	2	......do........	....	....	....	....
4245	♂	Chihuahua	Oct. 16, 1854	J. Potts.........	......	....	....	....	....	....
9731	♀	Camp 118, B. W. Fork..	Feb. 10, 1854	Lt. Whipple.....	37	Kenn. and Müll.	12.50	20.00	... .	....
9720	♀	......do................	Feb. 8, 1854	......do........	77	......do........	13.00	21.00	... .	....
9728	.....	Boca Grande, Mexico..	Mar. —, 1858	Maj. Emory.......	31	Dr. Kennerly..	13.00	22.00	....	....
9724	.....	Bodega, Cal	Dec. —, 1854	Lt. Trowbridge..	......	T. A Szabo ...	....	....	....	....
9733	♂	Shoalwater bay, W. T..	....	Gov. Stevens	60	Dr. Cooper.....	15.00	24.50	....	Iris brown, bill and feet pale gray.
9730	♂	Fort Steilacoom........	Jan. 20, 1854	......do..........	19	Dr. Suckley....	....	....	....	....

NETTION CRECCA, Kaup.

English Teal.

Anas crecca, Linn. Syst. Nat. I, 1766, 204.—Gmelin, I, 1788, 532.—Temminck, Man. II, 846.
Querquedula crecca, Stephens, Shaw's Gen. Zool. XII, i, 1824, 146.
" *Nettion crecca*, Kaup, Entw. Europ. Thierw. 1829."

Sp. Ch.—Similar in size and general appearance to *Nettion carolinensis.* No white crescent in front of the bend of the wing ; the elongated scapulars black externally ; internally creamy white.

Hab.—Europe. Accidental on the eastern coast of the United States.

This species is exceedingly similar to the common green-wing teal, but is readily distinguishable on comparison. The lower border of the green on the side of the head, and a curved line running very near the anterior and superior outline of the side of the head, are quite distinctly whitish, instead of being merely obsoletely paler, as in the other. The transverse bands of the upper parts and sides are more sharply defined and rather more distant. The band at the end of the greater coverts is broader and whiter, that at the end of the lesser is narrower. The long scapulars are creamy white, with the outer edge broadly velvet black, the inner sometimes waved black and white, while in *carolinensis* these are plain grayish olive. There are other minor differences, but these will be sufficient to separate the two.

The specimen described was furnished by Mr. John G. Bell, and obtained by him in the New York market, where several others have from time to time been procured by him.

QUERQUEDULA, Stephens.

Querquedula, STEPHENS, Shaw's Gen. Zool. XII, II, 1824. Type *Anas querquedula*, Linn.
Cyanopterus, EYTON, Mon. Anat. 1838. (Not of Haliday.)
Pterocyanea, BONAP. List, 1842.

CH.—Bill narrow, lengthened, a little longer than the foot; widening a little to the end, which is obtusely rounded; the nail occupying about one-third the width; the lamellae visible in the lateral profile. The upper lateral angle at the base of bill extending rather further back than the lower edge.

The two species of this genus inhabiting the United States have the following common and special characters: Wing coverts and the outer webs of some scapulars bright blue; the greater coverts tipped with white. The axillars and middle of under surface of wings white. A grass green speculum just below the white of the coverts. Scapulars streaked with yellowish buff. Top of head and chin dusky. Crissum blackish. Female retains the blue and white of wing.

Head and neck plumbeous. A white crescent in front of the eye and a white patch on each side of the tail. Under parts purplish or violaceous, spotted with brown. Long feathers of flanks banded...*Q. discors.*

General color purplish chestnut, without white on head and tail; feathers of flanks uniform chestnut...*Q. cyanoptera.*

QUERQUEDULA DISCORS, Steph.

Blue-winged Teal.

Anas discors, LINN. Syst. I, 1766, 205.—GM. 1, 535.—WILSON, Am. Orn. VIII, 1814, 74; pl. lxviii.—BON. Obs. No. 262.—AUD. Orn. Biog. IV, 1838, 111; pl. 313.—IB. Syn, 1839, 282.—IB. Birds Amer. VI, 1843, 287; pl. 393.
Querquedula discors, STEPH. Shaw's Gen. Zool. XII, 1824, 149.
Anas (Boschas) discors, SW. F. Bor. Am. II, 1831, 444.—NUTTALL, Man. II, 1834, 397.
Cyanopterus discors, EYTON, Mon. Anat. 1838 —BON. List, 1838.—GOSSE, Birds Jam. 1847, 101.
Pterocyanea discors, BON. (?)—IB. Comptes Rendus, XLIII, 1856.
White-faced teal or *duck*, PENNANT, II, 568.—LATH. Syn. III, II, 502.

SP. CH.—*Male.* Head and neck above plumbeous grey; top of head black. A white crescent in front of the eye. Under parts from middle of the neck purplish gray, each feather with spots of black, which become more obsolete behind. Fore part of back with the feathers brown, with two undulating narrow bands of purplish gray. Feathers on the flanks banded with dark brown and purplish gray. Back behind and tail greenish brown; crissum black. Wing coverts and some of the outer webs of scapulars blue; other scapulars velvet black or green, streaked with pale reddish buff. Speculum glossy green; the outer greater wing coverts white, as are the axillars, the middle of under surface of the wing, and a patch on each side of the base of the tail. Bill black; feet flesh colored.

Female with the top of head brown, and the wing coverts blue and white, as in the male. Base of bill, except above, chin, and upper part of the throat, dirty yellowish white. Back brown, the feathers margined with paler; under parts whitish, with rounded obscure brown spots; the jugulum darker. Length of male, 16; wing, 7.10; tarsus, 1.20; commissure, 1.85.

Hab.—Eastern North America to Rocky mountains. Not yet found on the Pacific coast nor in Europe.

List of specimens.

Catal. No.	Sex.	Locality.	When collected.	Whence obtained.	Orig'l No.	Collected by—	Length.	Stretch of wings.	Wing.	Remarks.
4550	♂	Washington, D. C...........	April, 1856...	S. F. Baird	......	....	......	......	......	....
1200	♂	Michigan	....	......do......	......	Dr. Leib.......	......	......	......	....
1201	♀	Michigan	....	....do..... .▲..	......	....	......	......	......	....
8288	......	Independence, Mo..........	May 26,1857	Wm. M. Magraw.	1	Dr. Cooper.....	15.50	24.50	7.25	Iris brown, feet yellow and black.
9753	♂	Wild Rice river, Minn......	....	Gov. Stevens.......	......	Dr. Suckley....	......	......	......	....
5465	♂	Iowa river.............. ...	May 5,1856	Lieut. Warren...	......	Dr. Hayden....	......	......	......	....
5464	♀	Vermilion river...........	....	......do.......	......	.....do.......	......	......	......	....
5780	......	Pole creek, Neb	July 28,1856	Lieut. Bryan.....	172	W. S. Wood...	......	......	......	....
4637	.....	White river, Neb...........	May 10,1855	Col. A. Vaughan.	......	Dr. Hayden....	......	......	......	....
7071	♂	South Platte river..........	July 7,1857	Lieut. Bryan.....	......	W. S. Wood ..	......	......	......	....
4140	♂	New Leon, Mex...........	May, 1853....	Lieut. Couch ...	......	....	15.75	24.00	7.50	Feet black...........
4244	♀	Chihuahua.................	Oct. 16,1854	J. Potts..........	......	....	......	......	......	....
4243	♂	......do..............	......do.......	......do	......	....	......	......	......	....
5125	♂	Crossing of Pecos, N. M...	June 24,1855	Capt. Pope	102	....	17.00	25.50	8.00	Bill and eyes brown; gums and feet yellow.
9751	♀	Sabinitas, Rio Grande......	Sept. 25,1853	Maj. Emory......	......	A. Schott......	......	......	......	....
5130	♀	Pecos Crossing.............	May 27,1855	Capt. Pope	......	....	......	......	.. ...	....
9749	......	Mimbres to Rio Grande	....	Dr. Henry.......	......	....	......	......	......	....

QUERQUEDULA CYANOPTERA, Baird.

Red-breasted Teal.

Anas cyanoptera, VIEILLOT, Nouv. Dict. V, 1816, 104. Not of Temminck.

Querquedula cyanoptera, CASSIN, Illust. I, III, 1855, 84 ; pl. xv.

Anas rafflesii, KING, Zool. Jour. IV, 1828, 87 ; Suppl. pl. xxix.—CASSIN, Pr. A. N. Sc. IV, 1848, 195:

Pterocyanea rafflesii, BAIRD, Zool. Stansbury's Exp. Salt Lake, 1852, 322.

Pterocyanea caeruleata, ("LICHT.") GRAY, Genera, III, 1845.—LAWRENCE, Ann. N. Y. Lyc. V, 1852, 220.

Querquedula caeruleata, GAY, Fauna Chilena.

SP. CH.—*Male.* General color a rich dark purplish chestnut ; the top of the head, the chin, and middle of belly, tinged with brown. Crissum dark brown. Fore part of the back lighter, with two or three more or less interrupted concentric bars of dark brown. The feathers of rump and tail greenish brown ; the former edged with paler. Wing coverts and outer webs of some scapulars blue ; others dark velvet green, streaked centrally with yellowish buff. Edges of greater wing coverts white, as are the axillars and middle of wing beneath. Feathers of flanks uniform chestnut, without bands. Speculum metallic green.

Female with the top of the head dusky and the wing coverts blue, as in the male ; the speculum duller. The upper parts dark brown, with lighter edges to the feathers. The under parts are brownish yellow, with a strong tinge of purplish chestnut in the jugulum, the feathers with concealed spots of brown. The only feathers unspotted with brown on the head and neck are in small patches on each side of the base of the bill, and in the chin between the rami. There is an obscure dusky patch beneath the head.

Length, 17.80 ; wing, 7.50 ; tarsus, 1.15 ; commissure, 2.

Hab.—Rocky mountains to Pacific. Accidental in Louisiana. Spread over most of western South America.

The female of this species is very similar to that of the common blue-winged teal. It is, however, rather larger, and the bill decidedly longer. The unspotted whitish of the head is more restricted ; the under surface of the head not pure whitish, but each feather with a brownish spot, producing a dusky patch. There is almost always a decided purplish chestnut tinge in the jugulum. The tertials are more elongated.

SPATULA, Boie.

Spatula, Boie, Isis, 1822, 564. Type *Anas clypeata*, L.

Rhynchaspis, "Leach," Stephens, Shaw's Gen. Zool. XII, ii, 1824. Same type.

Ch.—Bill much longer than the head and spatulate, widening to the end, where it is twice as broad as at the base. Nail long and narrow. Lamellae of the upper mandible very close, delicate, and lengthened, projecting far below the lower edge. Tail acute, less than half the wing.

Of several species belonging to this genus, but one is found in the United States. Its essential characters are as follows :

Lesser and middle wing coverts and portion of tertials blue; cinerated portion of greater coverts brown, tipped with white; speculum grass green. Some of the tertials streaked with white.

Head and neck green ; breast, unspotted white ; underparts, purplish chestnut. Tail covert greenish. ....*S. clypeata*.

List of specimens.

Catal. No.	Sex.	Locality.	When collected.	Whence obtained.	Orig. No.	Collected by—	Length.	Stretch of wings.	Wing.	Remarks.
4409	♂	Fort Dalles, O. T.......	May 8, 1855	Dr. Suckley	169	....	16.87	25.25	7.75	Iris bright carmine.......
4410	♀	........do.............	May 17, 1853	......do.........	175	....	15.25	24.00	7.00	....
4459	♀	San José, Cal.........	....	A. J. Grayson ..	......	....	....	....	.....	....
4458	♂	........do.............	....	......do.........	......	....	....	....	.....	....
9741	♀	Sacramento valley.....	....	Lt. Williamson ..	......	Dr. Heermann.	....	....	....	....
9738	......	Tulare valley	....	......do.........	......	......do.......	....	....	....	....
		Fort Tejon, Cal.	....	J. X. de Vesey...	......	....	....	....	....	....
9750	......	Mohave river..........	Mar. 11, 1854	Lt. Whipple	......	Kenn & Moll....	....	.....	.....	....
9740	♂	Camp 123.............	Feb. 16, 1854	......do.........	166	......do.......	....	....	.....	Eyes yellow............
9739	♂	El Paso, Texas	....	Major Emory	......	J. H. Clark ...	16.00	25.00	7.40	Bill black, feet pale orange, iris yellow.
9746	......	Mimbres to Rio Grande.	....	Dr. Henry	....	....	....	....	.....	....
9743	......	Near 32° latitude	....	Captain Pope....	......	....	....	....	.....	....

SPATULA CLYPEATA, Boie.

Shoveller ; Spoonbill.

Anas clypeata, Linn, Syst. Nat. I, 1766, 200.—Gmelin, I, 518.—Lath. Ind. II, 1790, 856.—Wilson, Am. Orn. VIII, 1814 ; pl. lxvii.—Bon. Obs. 1825, No. 255.—Sw. F. Bor. Am. II, 1831, 439.—Aud. Orn. Biog. IV, 1838, 241 ; pl. 327.—Ib. Syn. 283.—Ib. Bird's Amer. VI, 1843, 293; pl. 394.

Spatula clypeata, Boie, Isis, 1822, 564.

Spathulea clypeata, Fleming.

Anas (Spathulea) clypeata, Nutt, Man. II, 1834, 373.

Rhynehaspsis clypeata, (Leach) Stephens, Shaw's Gen. Zool. XII, 1824, 115.—Bon. List, 1838.—Eyton, Mon. Anat. 1838, 134.

Anas rubens, Gmelin, Syst. Nat. I, 1788, 519.

Shoveller, Pennant, II, 557.—Lath. Syn. III, ii, 509.

Sp. Ch.—Head and neck green; fore part and sides of the breast, with greater portion of seapulars, and the sides of the base of the tail, white ; rest of under parts dull purplish chestnut ; crissum, rump, and upper tail coverts, black, the latter glossed with green. Wing coverts blue ; the posterior row brown in the concealed portion, and tipped with white ; longest tertials blue, streaked internally with white ; others velvet green, streaked centrally with white ; speculum grass green, edged very narrowly behind with black and then with white.

Female with the wing similar, but with the blue of coverts and scapulars less distinct Head and neck brownish yellow, spotted with dusky ; the belly with a decided chestnut tinge.

Length, 20.00 ; wing, 9.50 ; tarsus, 1.38 ; commissure, 3.02.

Hab.—Continent of North America ; abundant in Europe.

List of specimens.

Catal. No.	Sex.	Locality.	When collect-ed.	Whence obtained.	Orig'l No.	Collected by—	Extent.	Stretch of wing.	Wing.	Remarks.
925	♂	Carlisle, Pa..	April 20, 1840	S. F. Baird	.....	....	20.00	32.25	9.50	....
2524	♀	......do...............	Oct. 18, 1846	......do...........	......	.. ..	20.25	31.75	9.50	....
5452	♂	Ayoway river, Neb.....	May 5, 1856	Lt. Warren......	....	Dr. Hayden....	20.25	33.25	9.75	Eyes yellow.............
9760	....	Mimbres to Rio Grande.	....	Dr. Henry......	......	....	......	......	......	....
5124	♂	Dona Aña, N. M ...	Dec. 1, 1855	Capt. Pope	169	....	21.00	32.00	10.00	Bill light brown, iris yel-low, feet and gums dark.
4138	♀	New Leon, Mexico ...	....	Lt. Couch......	.....	....	......	......	......	Bill brown, feet yellow...
4908	♂	San Diego, Cal........	Mar. 20, 1856	Dr. Hammond..	.....	....	20.00	33.00	9.75	Iris light yellow..........
4455	......	San José, Cal..........	....	A. J. Grayson ...	......	....	......	......	......	....
9759	♂	Big Lagoon of desert ..	....	Lt. Williamson ..	......	Dr. Heermann..	......	......	......	....
9755	......	Bodega, Cal........ ...	Jan. —, 1558	Lt. Trowbridge.	....	T. A. Szabo....	......	......	......	....
4525	♂	San Francisco	Jan. 16, 1856	Dr. Suckley	......	....	......	......	.....	....

CHAULELASMUS, Gray.

Chauliodus, Sw. F. Bor. Am. 1831. Not of Bloch, 1801.

Chauliodes, EYTON, Mon. Anat. 1838. Not of Latreille, 1798.

Chaulelasmus, G. R. GRAY, 1838. Type *Anas strepera*, L.

The characters of this genus have been sufficiently indicated in the synopsis, on page 772. The diagnosis of the single species is as follows : ·

Head spotted ; lower throat, jugulum, back, and sides of body banded black and white ; rump and tail coverts black ; middle wing coverts chestnut, succeeded by black internally ; speculum white, bordered externally by black..*C. streperus*.

CHAULELASMUS STREPERUS, Gray.

Gadwall; Grey Duck.

Anas strepera, LINN. Syst. Nat., I, 1766, 200.—GMELIN, I, 520.—LATH., Ind. II, 1790, 849.—WILSON, Am. Orn. VIII, 1814, 120 ; pl. lxxi.—BON. Obs. 1825, No. 257.—AUD. Orn. Biog. IV, 1838, 353 ; pl. 348.—IB. Syn. 378.—IB. Birds Amer. VI, 1843, 254 ; pl. 388.—TEMMINCK, Man. II, 838. (European.)

Anas (Chauliodus) strepera, SWAINSON, F. Bor. Am. II, 1831, 440.

Anas (Boschas) strepera, NUTT. Man. II, 1834, 383.

Ktinorhynchus strepera, EYTON, Mon. Anat. 1838, 137.

Gadwall, or Gray, PENNANT, II, 575.—LATHAM.

"*Chaulelasmus streperus*, GRAY, 1838." Gray.

SP. CH.—*Male.* Head and neck brownish white, each feather spotted with dusky ; the top of head tinged with reddish. Lower part of neck, with fore part of breast and back, blackish, with concentric narrow bars of white, giving a scaled appearance to the feathers. Interscapular region, outermost scapulars, and sides of the body finely waved transversely with black and white. Middle wing coverts chestnut, the greater velvet black, succeeded by a pure white speculum, bordered externally by hoary gray, succeeded by black ; crissum and upper tail coverts black. Longest tertials hoary plumbeous gray. Innermost scapulars with a reddish tinge. Inside of wing and axillars pure white. Bill black.

Female with the bill dusky, edged with reddish. Wing somewhat like that of the male, but with the chestnut red more restricted.

Length, 22 ; wing, 10.50 ; tarsus, 1.64 ; commissure, 2.04.

Hab.—North America generally, and Europe.

A specimen of this bird from Illinois, otherwise similar, is entirely without chestnut red on the wing.

List of specimens.

Catal. No.	Sex.	Locality.	When collected.	Whence obtained.	Orig. No.	Collected by—	Length.	Stretch of wings.	Wing.
2739	......	Eastern United States..........	....	S. F. Baird..............	....	....	......	......	......
9790	♂	Rabbit river, Minn	....	Gov. Stevens	14	Dr. Suckley...............	......	......	......
9793	......	Tremont, Ill..............	June 22,1855	W. J. Shaw........	......	....	......	......	......
5132	......	Pecos, Texas	May 23,1855	Capt. Pope	......	....	......	......	......
9792	......	Mimbres to Rio Grande.........	....	Dr. Henry.............	......	....	......	......	......
9794	♂	Janos, Mex..............	April —, 1855	Major Emory	87	Dr. Kennerly............	19.50	34.50	10.50
4560	♀	San José, Cal..............	....	A. J. Grayson...........	......	....	......	......	......
9788	......	Bodega, Cal.	Feb. —,1855	Lieut. Trowbridge.. ...	......	T. A. Szabo.............	......	......	......
9796	♂	San Francisco, Cal..............	Mar. —,1854	Lieut. Whipple...........	......	....	......	......	......
9791	♂	Fort Steilacoom	Feb. —, 1854	Gov. Stevens.............	32	Dr. Suckley...............	......	......	......

MARECA, Stephens.

Mareca, STEPHENS, Shaw's Gen. Zool. XII, II, 1824, 130. Type *Anas penelope*, L.

Penelope, KAUP, 1829.

CH.—Bill shorter than the head, and equal to the inner toe claw. The sides parallel to near the end, which is rather obtusely pointed, the nail occupying the tip, and about one-third as broad as the bill. Bill rather high ; the upper lateral angle at the base not prominent, nor extending as far back as the lower edge. Tail pointed ; not half the wings.

The North American and European species of *Mareca* have the upper parts finely waved transversely with black and gray or reddish brown, the under parts, with the usual exceptions, snowy white. The top of the head is uniform white or cream color; the neck more or less spotted. The middle and greater coverts are white, the latter tipped with black. The speculum is green, encircled by black. The tertials are black on the outer web, edged with hoary white ; the entire outer web of one of them hoary. The characteristics of the species are as follows :

Head and neck grayish, the feathers of the former thickly spotted, of the latter banded with black. Top of head nearly white ; a broad and continuous patch of green around and behind the eye...*M. americana.*

Head and neck reddish brown or cinnamon, the feathers of the former slightly spotted with dusky, of the latter almost uniformly colored. Top of head cream colored ; only a faint trace of green around the eye, and a few spots behind it..*M. penelope.*

MARECA AMERICANA, Stephens.

Baldpate; American Widgeon.

Anas americana, GMELIN, Syst. Nat. I, 1788, 526.—LATH. Ind. II, 861.—WILSON, Am. Orn. VIII, 1814, 86; pl. lxix.—BON. Obs. No. 259.—AUD. Orn. Biog. IV, 1838, 337 ; pl. 345.—IB. Syn. 1839, 279.— IB. Birds Amer. VI, 1843, 259 ; pl. 389.

Mareca americana, STEPH. Shaw's Gen. Zool. XII, II, 1824, 135.—SW. F. Bor. Am. II, 1831, 445.—BON. List, 1838.—EYTON, Mon. Anat. 1838, 116.

Anas (Boschas) americana, Nuttall, Man. II, 1834, 389.

American widgeon, PENN. II, 567.

Sp. Ch.—*Male.* Tail of 14 feathers. Bill blue, the extreme base and tip black. Head and neck pale buff, or faint reddish yellow, each feather banded narrowly with blackish, so as to give the appearance of spots. The top of the head from the bill is pale unspotted creamy white; the sides of the head from around the eye to the nape, glossy green, the feathers however, with hidden spots, as described; chin uniform dusky. Forepart of breast and sides of body light brownish o chocolate red, each feather with obsolete grayish edge; rest of under parts pure white; the crissum abruptly black. The back, scapulars, and rump, finely waved transversely anteriorly with reddish and gray, posteriorly with purer gray, on a brown ground; a little of the same waving also on the sides. The lesser wing coverts are plain gray; the middle and greater are conspicuously white, the latter terminated by black, succeeded by a speculum, which is grass green at the base, and then velvet black. The tertials are black on the outer web, bordered narrowly by black, the outermost one hoary gray, externally edged with black. The tail is hoary brown. The upper coverts are black externally. The axillars are white.

The female has the head and neck somewhat similar, but spotted to the bill. Wings as in the male. The black of tertials replaced by brown; the gray of the lesser coverts extending slightly over the middle ones. Back and scapulars with rather broad and distant transverse bars of reddish white, each feather with two or three, interrupted along the shafts. These are much wider and more distant than in the male. Length, 21.75; wing, 11; tarsus 1.42; commissure, 1.80.

Hab.—Continent of North America. Accidental in Europe.

The blackish chin appears to be found only in very highly plumaged birds. The top of the head is sometimes pure white.

List of specimens.

Catal. No.	Sex and age.	Locality.	When collected.	Whence obtained.	Orig. No.	Collected by—	Length.	Stretch of wings.	Wing.	Remarks.
1310	♂	Carlisle, Pa....	Mar. 24, 1844	S. F. Baird.........	......	....	21.75	35.50	11.00	....
932	♂	......do...............	April 28, 1843	......do...........	......	....	20.00	33.50	10.25	....
286	♀	......do...............	April 10, 1841	......do...........	......	....	....	....	....	....
6895	♂	Nelson river, H. B. T..	....	D. Gunn............	......	John Isbister.....	....	....	....	....
5781	o♂	Platte river, K. T......	July 11, 1856	Lieut. Bryan....	92	W. S. Wood.....	....	....	....	....
5133	♂	Head of Delaware creek, N. M.	Mar. 24, 1856	Capt. Pope	186	....	21.00	34.50	11.25	Bill blue; tip dark; eyes dark brown; feet gray.
5453	....	Near Bijoux Hills...	Oct. 14, 1856	Lieut. Warren....	......	Dr. Hayden......	21.00	30.00	9.75	....
9713	♂	El Paso, Texas	....	Maj. Emory	......	J. H. Clark......	....	....	....	....
9704	....	Mimbres to Rio Grande.	....	Dr. Henry.........	......	....	....	....	....	....
9705	....	Western Texas.........	....	Capt. Pope	......	....	....	....	....	....
9706	....	Buca Grande, Mexico ..	Mar. —, 1855	Maj. Emory	28	Dr. Kennerly....	....	....	....	....
9715	....	San Diego, Cal.....	....	Lt. Trowbridge...	......	....	....	....	....	....
9717	....	Bodega, Cal.	Dec. —, 1854	......do...........	......	T. A. Szabo.	....	....	....	....
9716	....	Fort Steilacoom	....	Gov. Stevens......	......	Dr. Suckley	....	....	....	....

MARECA PENELOPE, Bon.

English Widgeon.

Anas penelope, Linn. Syst. Nat. I, 1766, 202.—Gm. I, 527.—Temm. Man. II, 840. European specimens. Giraud, Birds L. Island, 1843, 307, Am. sp.

Mareca penelope, Bon. List, 1838.

Mareca fistularis, Eyton, Mon. Anat. 1838, 118.

Sp. Ch.—Similar to *M. americana.* Head and neck reddish brown, without bars; a very small green patch round the eye. Length, 20; wing, 10.60; tarsus, 1.52; commissure, 1.64.

Hab.—Old World. Accidental on the Atlantic coast of United States. Greenland.

The European widgeon is so frequently shot along the Atlantic American coast as to be justly considered as belonging to our fauna, and not as a mere straggler. Every year a few specimens are found in the New York market, shot chiefly along the coast of Virginia, Carolina, and

Florida. The present description is based on a Florida skin, presented by Mr. Geo. N. Lawrence to the Smithsonian Institution.

It is hardly necessary to repeat the common characters of this species and the American Baldpate, the chief difference being in the head and neck. This is of a reddish brown or cinnamon color, not barred at all; the cheeks and chin with small spots of dusky. The forehead and crown are creamy white; the region near the base of the bill laterally quite similar, but spotted. The region immediately around the eye is greenish, most prominent on the posterior edge, but, except in the immediate vicinity of the orbit, there are only a few spots of green on the side of the head behind. The sides of the head below are paler cinnamon or chestnut than on the neck; the chin is blackish. I am unable to detect any other differences of importance. According to Mr. Lawrence, (Giraud, Birds L. Island, 309,) "the bill is much higher at the base, and without the black line where it joins the head; the nail black, with minute punctures. The frontal feathers extend on the bill a quarter of an inch, forming an acute angle, (not the case in ours;) the under wing coverts are ash gray intsead instead of white."

AIX, Boie.

Aix, BOIE, Isis, 1828, 329. Type *Anas galericulata*, L.

Dendronessa, SWAINSON, F. B. Am. 1831. Type, *Anas sponsa*, L.

CH.—Bill very high at the base, where the upper lateral angle runs back much behind the lower edge of the bill. Nostrils very large, and scarcely enveloped by membrane; the feathers of the forehead reaching to their posterior edge. Nail very large and much hooked, occupying the entire tip of bill. Lamellae depressed, broad, and distant. Bill, from feathers of forehead, shorter than the head, and equal to the tarsus. Head crested; claws short, much curved, and very sharp. Tail about half the wings, vaulted, cuneate, but truncate at the tip; the coverts nearly as long as the feathers.

This genus, embracing the most beautiful of American ducks, is very different from all our others, and almost entitled to rank as the type of a separate sub-family. A great peculiarity in *Anatinae* is the very large and much curved nail of the bill; which, in this respect, as well as in its height and narrowing to the tip, resembles that of the *Anserinae*. The second species of the genus is the celebrated mandarin duck of China, *A. galericulata*. The characters of *A. sponsa*, are as follows:

Head green, glossed laterally with purple. A line from the upper corner of the bill, one from behind the eye, and two bars on the side of the head confluent with the chin and upper part of throat, white; jugulum and sides of tail purple; under parts white, the sides yellowish, banded with black, and behind, subterminally, with white; speculum bluish green; primaries silver white externally, at the tip; back uniform, with various reflections.............. *A. sponsa*.

AIX SPONSA, Boie.

Summer Duck.

Anas sponsa, LINN. Syst. Nat. I, 1766, 207.—GM. I, 539.—LATH. Ind. II, 1790, 876.—WILSON, Am. Orn. VIII, 1814, 97; pl. lxx.—BON. Obs. No. 261.—AUD. Orn. Biog. III, 1835, 52: V, 618; pl. 206.—IB. Syn. 280.— IB. Birds Amer. VI, 1843, 271; pl. 391.

Aix sponsa, BOIE, Isis, 1828, 329.—EYTON, Mon. Anat 1838, 120.

Dendronessa sponsa, SW. F. Bor. Am. II, 1831, 446.

Anas (Boschas) sponsa, NUTTALL, Man. II, 1834, 394.

Summer duck, PENN. II, 562.

August 19, 1858.
99 b

Sp. Ch.—Head and crest metallic green to below the eyes ; the cheeks and a stripe from behind the eye purplish. A narrow short line from the upper angle of the bill along the side of the crown and through the crest, another on the upper eyelid, a stripe starting behind and below the eye, and running into the crest parallel with the first mentioned, the chin and upper part of the throat, sending a well defined branch up towards the eye and another towards the nape, snowy white. Lower neck and jugulum, and sides of the base of tail, rich purple ; the jugulum with triangular spots of white and a chestnut shade. Remaining under parts white, as is a crescent in front of the wing bordered behind by black. Sides yellowish gray, finely lined with black ; the long feathers of the flanks broadly black at the end, with a sub-terminal bar, and sometimes a tip of white. Back and neck above nearly uniform bronzed green and purple. Scapulars and innermost tertials velvet black, glossed on the inner webs with violet ; the latter with a white bar at the end. Greater coverts violet, succeeded by a greenish speculum, tipped with white. Primaries silvery white externally towards the end ; the tips internally violet and purple.

Female with the wings quite similar ; the back more purplish ; the sides of the head and neck ashy ; the region round the base of the bill, a patch through the eyes, and the chin, white. The purple of the jugulum replaced by brownish. The waved feathers on the sides wanting. Length, 19 inches ; wing, 9.50 ; tarsus, 1.40 ; commissure, 1.54.

Hab.—Continent of North America.

List of specimens.

Catal. No.	Sex.	Locality.	When collected.	Whence obtained.	Orig'l No.	Collected by—	Length.	Stretch of wings.	Wing.	Remarks.
1732	♂	Carlisle, Pa	Oct. 29,1844	S. F. Baird			19.00	29.50	9.56	
10331	♀	.....do....	....do.....	....do........						
5460	♂	Vermilion river		Lt. Warren		Dr. Hayden	17.87	29.00	8.87	Eyes red
5457	....	Heart river	Sept. 22,1856	......do.....		.....do.........				
5459	♀	Ioway R.	May 5,1856	......do.....		.....do........	18.25	29.50	9.25	
5458	♀	Nishnabtra	April 24,1856	......do.....		.....do........				
5456	♂	Vermilion river	May ?,1856	......do.....		.....do........	17.50	28.50	8.50	Eyes red
9775	......	Tulare valley, Cal.		Lt. Williamson		Dr. Heermann				
9776	♂	San Francisco	Feb. —,1854	Lt. Whipple		Kenn. & Möll	19.25	28.00		
4412	......	Fort Dalles, Oregon	Feb. —,1855	Dr. Suckley	156					
4363	♀	Puget's Sound	May —,1855	Mr. Geo. Gibbs						

Sub-Family FULIGULINAE.

The chief character of the *Fuligulinae*, as compared with the *Anatinae*, consists in the greatly developed lobe or membranous flap attached to or suspended from the inferior surface of the hind toe. The feet are usually enormously large, the tarsi short, the legs set far back, and the whole organization well fitted for swimming and diving. Many of the species live on or near the seacoast, although most of them straggle more or less through the interior of the countries they inhabit. The different North American forms may be arranged as follows :

A. Bill with the feathers of the forehead extending forward as a short obtuse angle, those of the sides as a crescent, giving rise to an acute basal process of the bill laterally and superiorly on each side, which extend back as far as the angle of the mouth. The feathers of the chin, cheeks, and forehead extending about opposite to the same point ; the former usually furthest.

a. Nail at the end of the bill small, narrow, and forming only a central part of the tip ; distinct.

FULIX.—Bill longer than the head and tarsus ; about equal to the inner toe and claw ; long, broad, and the sides parallel to the end, or widening. Nostrils in the basal two-fifths of the bill. Tail short, rounded, scarcely more than one-third the wing. Body black anterior to the shoulder and posterior to the tibia. Head and neck black or red. Sides and back mottled or waved with black and white. Axillars and inside of wing white.

AYTHYA.—Similar to the last. The bill longer and narrower, exceeding the inner toe ; the nostrils more anterior, close to the middle. Colors like the last, with reddish head.

BUCEPHALA.—Bill shorter than the head ; about equal to the tarsus ; compressed and somewhat tapering. Nostrils near the middle of the bill. Nail rather larger than in *Fuligula*. Tail longer and more pointed ; about half the wing. Head, neck, and back black ; the former with green or purple reflections. Under parts, including crissum, lower part of neck, scapulars, large patch on the wings, and cheeks, white. Axillars and inside of wing blackish.

b. Bill with the nail very broad, occupying the entire tip, and scarcely distinguishable by reason of its fusion with the rest of bill.

HISTRIONICUS.—Bill shorter than head or tarsus ; elevated at base ; narrowing rapidly. Nostrils reaching the middle of the bill. Tertials bent outwards. Bill with a membranous expansion overlapping its base. Color plumbeous ; the only white being in the form of spots or bands on the outer surface.

POLYSTICTA.—Bill somewhat similar, but broader at the tip and more truncate. Upper angle of base of bill not extending back as far as the lower. Feathers of head close set and velvety ; almost erect. Tertials much bent outwards. Body dusky ; lighter on the sides. Head, wings, and scapulars with much white. Inside of wing white. Head tinged with grass green.

B. Side of bill without any distinct acute angle at the base above, or, if present, it does not reach as far back as the angle of the mouth, the feathers extending forward, and further above than laterally, (so as to obliterate the angle more or less;) the lateral outline of feathers more or less oblique.

a. Bill without any peculiar gibbosity at the base.

HARELDA.—Bill shorter than the head, or than tarsus ; high, tapering to the tip, where the nail occupies the terminal portion. Nostrils linear, in the posterior half of the bill. No membrane at the end ; the feathers of head normal. Tail feathers excessively long and pointed ; equal to the wing. Color black and white. Breast and wings on both surfaces black ; the latter without any white ; rest of under parts, including crissum, white.

CAMPTOLAEMUS.—Bill broad and depressed ; the sides parallel to the end, which is bordered by a membranous skin. Nostrils in the basal third of bill. Feathers of cheeks stiffened. Tail short, rounded ; two-fifths the wing. Body and quills black ; rest of wings, head, and neck, white. A streak on top of head and a collar on neck black.

LAMPRONETTA.—Bill depressed, rather narrow ; longer than tarsus. Feathers of forehead extending on the culmen beyond the nostrils, and thence passing obliquely in a gentle curve to the angle of the mouth, across the posterior portion of the nasal groove. Tail short. Above white ; beneath black. A quadrilateral black outline round the eye ; occiput and nape green.

b. Bill much swollen or gibbous at the base ; then much depressed, and broad. Nail very large, forming the tip. Nostrils anterior to the middle of the bill.

OIDEMIA.—Feathers of forehead extending only to base of gibbosity ; those of side of head sloping gently forward. Nostrils linear, midway between feathers of forehead and tip of bill. Color entirely black.

PELIONETTA.—Feathers of forehead extending far forward ; nearly to end of the gibbosity, which is plain above ; those on the sides not beyond the angle of the mouth ; basal portion of bill swollen laterally. Nostrils large, rounded. Color black, with white patches on head.

MELANETTA.—Feathers of side of bill extending obliquely forward from the angle of the mouth as far as those above. Nostrils very open and sub-circular ; quite close to feathers around the base of bill. Nail very broad and truncate at the end. Colors black, with white patch on wing.

C. Bill narrow, compressed, tapering to the end. Feathers of forehead running forward in a long narrow point, and of cheeks extending along the lower edge of bill, so that the two strips embrace between them a linear portion of the bill, one half the length of culmen, and which extends back further than the lower edge of mandible.

SOMATERIA.—Nostrils situated beyond the middle of commissure. Nail very broad, thickened, and greatly overlapping tip of lower mandible. Tail short, rounded ; about two-fifths the wing.

In the arrangement of the sea ducks I have established three sections, which embrace species agreeing with each other more or less, although there are others of rather close alliance which are thereby separated. The more natural succession of the genera appears to be that of Bonaparte in Comptes Rendus, XLIII, Sept. 1856, nearly as follows :

FULIGULEAE.—*Fulix, Aythya.*

CLANGULEAE.—*Bucephala, Histrionicus, Harelda.*

OIDEMIEAE.—*Oidemia, Pelionetta, Melanetta.*

SOMATERIEAE.—*Polysticta, Lampronetta, Somateria.*

MICROPTEREAE.—*Camptolaemus.*

Where *Camptolaemus* should come is a matter of uncertainty, as it differs very much from all the other genera in the stiffened cheek feathers, the membranous expansion at the end of bill, the very large and unusually distant lamellae of the lower mandible, the broad, depressed bill, and other features. By Bonaparte it is placed with *Micropterus*, and *Hymenolaemus* among *Microptereae.*

The colors of the sea ducks furnish an excellent clue to their systematic arrangement, as shown by the following schedule :

Belly white.

Crissum and anal region black. Sides and back with waved feathers. Inside of wings and axillars white...*Fulix, Aythya.*

Crissum and anal region white. Inside of wing and axillars black...*Bucephala, Harelda.*

Belly dusky centrally ; reddish brown on the sides.

Prevailing color plumbeous, with white spots. No white inside of wings...*Histrionicus.*

Much white on head and wings. Inside of wings white..............................*Polysticta.*

Belly and under parts black. Inside of wings and axillars white.

Head, neck, and fore part of body white.............................*Somateria, Lampronetta.*

Head and neck white. The latter with a black collar............................*Camptolaemus.*

Body entirely black, with or without white patch on head or wing, including inside of wings.

No white whatever..*Oidemia.*

Wings with white patch.   Eyelids white..*Melanetta.*

Head above and nape with white patch...*Pelionetta.*

Comparative measurements of species.

Catal. No.	Species.	Locality.	Sex and age.	Length.	Stretch of wings.	Wing.	Tail.	Tarsus.	Middle toe.	Its claw alone.	Bill above.	Along gape.	Bill from feathers on sides.	Specimen measured.
1193	Fulix marila...............	Washington, D.C...	♂	18.00	... .	8.70	2.94	1.58	2.70	0.36	1.80	2.16	......	Skin.......
do..	......do...................	......do...........		20.00	32.50	9.00	.....	.....	.....	.....	.....	.....	......	Fresh......
2521	......do...................	Carlisle, Pa.........	♂	18.00	....	8.60	2.70	1.44	2.56	0.32	1.70	2.21	......	Skin.......
9546	..... do..................	Simiahmoo, W. T...	♀	....	....	8.60	3.20	1.40	2.64	0.32	1.74	2.14	......	Skin.......
1731	Fulix affinis	Carlisle, Pa.........	o ♂	16.30	....	7.80	2.60	1.34	2.27	0.28	1.62	1.94	......	Skin.......
do..	.....do................	......do...........		16.83	28.75	8.00	.....	.....	.....	.....	.....	.....	......	Fresh......
316	.....do...................	......do...........	♂	16.60	....	7.70	2.62	1.34	2.50	0.35	1.71	1.96	......	Skin.......
456	.....do...................	San José, Cal.....	♂	....	....	8.20	2.82	1.32	2.35	0.28	1.72	2.02	......	Skin.......
936	..... do.....	Carlisle, Pa.........	♀	15.20	....	7.60	2.38	1.40	2.34	0.34	1.50	1.78	......	Skin.......
do..	.....do...................	...do...........		16.25	28.00	7.41	.....	.....	.....	.....	.....	.....	......	Fresh......
598	Fulix collaris	...do............ ...	♂	17.60	....	7.80	2.90	1.28	2.40	0.32	1.96	2.10	......	Skin.......
do..	......do...................	.....do...........		18.25	29.00	8.00	.....	.....	.....	.....	.....	.....	......	Fresh......
1186	......do...................	......do...........	♀	16.50	....	7.50	2.50	1.20	2.14	0.30	1.58	1.80	......	Skin.......
do..	......do...................	......do...........		18.00	26.75	7.50	.....	.....	.....	.....	.....	.....	......	Fresh......
1330	Aythya americana...........	...do...........	♂	19.20	....	9.36	2.60	1.62	2.86	0.36	1.82	2.30	......	Skin.......
do..	......do...................	...do.		20.50	33.50	9.50	.....	.....	.....	.....	.....	.....	......	Fresh......
1727	......do..................	...do...........	♀	19.50	....	8.50	2.56	1.52	2.66	0.32	1.74	2.14	......	Skin.......
do..	......do...................	...do...........		19.50	31.50	8.75	.....	.....	.....	.....	.....	.....	......	Fresh......
9785	......do....................	Bodega, Cal.......		....	....	9.40	2.86	1 62	2.72	0.38	1.86	2.30	......	Skin.......
606	Aythya valisneria	Potomac river, D.C.	♂	20.10	....	9 36	3.00	1.70	3.00	0.36	2.76	2.64	......	Skin.......
10334	......do...................	......do...........	♂	20.80	....	9.10	3.20	1.70	2.82	0.32	2.76	2.68	......	Skin.......
9778	......do	Sacramento valley..	♂	21.20	....	9.60	2.88	1.74	3.10	0.40	2.90	2.76	......	Skin......
2793	Bucephala islandica........	Rocky mountains...	♂	9 50	....	9.50	3.80	1.58	2.80	0.40	1.26	1.80	1.60	Skin.......
224	Bucephala americana.......	Carlisle, Pa.........	♂	18.70	....	8.50	3.90	1.50	2.62	0.32	1.34	2.00	1.94	Skin.......
238	.....do...................	......do...........	♀	16.20	....	8.00	3.74	1.40	2.36	0.30	1.28	1.80	1.62	Skin.......
312	Bucephala albeola.........	...do...........	♂	14.90	....	6.66	3.90	1.24	2.20	0.30	1.08	1.44	1.22	Skin.......
1737	......do...................	...do...........	♀	13.00	....	6.30	3.08	1.14	2.00	0.25	1.02	1.40	1.18	Skin......
do..	......do...................	......do...........		13.25	22.25	6.32	.....	.....	.....	.....	.....	.....		Fresh......
1575	Histrionicus torquatus......	Boston, Mass	♂	17.40	....	7.70	4.68	1.48	2.20	0.26	1.00	1 54	1.20	Skin.......
8428	...... do................	Simiahmoo, W.T...	♀	14.30	....	7.60	3.58	1.40	2.04	0.26	1.04	1.46	1.30	Skin.......
4553	Harelda glacialis	Washington, D.C...	♂	20.70	....	8.90	8.00	1.38	2.22	0.32	1.10	1.62	......	Skin.......
do..	....do.................	......do...........		22.12	30.50	9.24	.....	.....	.....	.....	.....	.....	......	Fresh......
306	......do...................	Carlisle, Pa........	♀	15.50	....	8.36	3.20	1.28	2.06	0.24	1.06	1.50	......	Skin......
do..	......do...................	......do......		17.00	28.00	3.60	.....	.....	.....	.....	.....	.....	......	Fresh......
10197	Polysticta stelleri...........	Norway............	♂	18.10	....	8.00	3.84	1.48	2.14	0.28	1.40	1.82	1.58	Skin.......
10196	......do...................	......do...........	♀	17.00	....	8.40	3.90	1.40	2.23	0.30	1.46	1.80	1.62	Skin.......
1972	Camptolaemus labradoricus.	North Atlantic	♂	23.80	....	8.80	3.90	1.60	2.62	0.36	1.68	2.50	......	Skin.......
2733	......do...................	......do...	♂	22.20	....	8.50	3.60	1.52	2.36	0.22	1.64	2.36	......	Skin......
2722	Oidemia americana..........	......do...........	♂	23.80	....	9.20	4.54	1.78	3.00	0.39	1.76	2.14	1.86	Skin.......
904	......do....................	Potomac river, D.C.	♂?	17.30	....	9.00	3.36	1.66	2.80	0.30	1.60	2.10	1.78	Skin......
do..	......do...................	......do...........		19.00	33.00	9.00	.....	.....	.....	.....	.....	.....	......	Fresh......
4574	......do...................	Ft. Steilacoom, W.T.	♂	....	....	9.60	4.54	1.82	3.28	0.30	1.66	2.16	1.80	Skin.......
do..	......do...................	......do...........		21.50	36.25	9.75	.....	.....	.....	.....	.....	.....	......	Fresh......
913	Pelionetta perspicillata......	Philadelphia	♂	19.00	....	9.40	3.88	1.63	2.60	0.36	1.36	2.37	2.32	Skin......
1719	.....do...................	Carlisle, Pa...... ...	♀	17.50	....	8.60	3.24	1.58	2.55	0.30	1.44	2.23	1.97	Skin......
do..	.....do...................	......do...........		17.75	31.00	8.80	.....	.....	.....	.....	.....	.....	......	Fresh......
9553	.....do......	Simiahmoo........		21.00	....	9.50	4.20	1.62	2.66	0.36	1.40	2.60	2.60	Skin......
9860	Pelionetta trowbridgii......	San Diego...... ..	♂	22.00	....	9.80	3.46	1.80	2.86	0.36	1.56	2.72	2.56	Skin......
9852	Melanetta fusca...........	Shoalwater bay ...	♂	11.50	....	11.30	3.74	2.08	3.26	0.40	1.60	2.82	1.60	Skin......
do..	.....do...................	......do...........		21.50	38.00	....	.....	.....	.....	.....	.....	.....	......	Fresh......
905	.....do...................	Potomac river, D.C	♀	18.00	....	10.00	3.26	1.78	2.68	0.30	1.40	2.20	1.34	Skin......
do..	.....do...................	......do...........		19.75	36.00	10.16	.....	.....	.....	.....	.....	.....	......	Fresh......
1973	Somateria spectabilis.......	North Atlantic	♂	21.50	....	10.70	3.50	1.86	2.73	0.42	1.52	2.53	2.40	Skin......
480	Somateria mollissima......	......do...........	♂	26.20	... .	11.24	4.10	1.82	2.96	0.46	2.06	2.66	3.00	Skin.......

FULIX, Sundevall.

Fulix, SUNDEVALL, Kong. Vet. Ak. Hand. 1835, (as restricted.)
Fuligula of authors, but not of Stephens.
Marila, Bonaparte, not of Reichenbach.

CH.—Bill longer than the tarsus, and about equal to the head, and to the middle toe without the nail. Feathers of cheeks, chin and forehead advancing but slightly, and to about the same distance. Nostrils open, situated in the anterior portion of the basal two-fifths of the bill, not reaching the middle. Edges of bill about parallel, or widening to the tip ; profile gently concave to the nail, which is decurved. Nail not one-third the width of the bill, and forming only the central portion of its tip. Tarsus about half the middle toe and claw. Bill as long as the feet. Tail short, rounded, of 14 feathers. Head and neck black.

The name *Fuligula,* usually applied to this genus, cannot be employed, as it was based by Stephens (1824) upon the *Anas rufina* of Pallas, (not on *Anas cristata,* L., as given by Gray,) for which *Branta* had been proposed by Boie in 1822 ; but as this name is anticipated by Oken in 1815, *Fuligula* will precede *Callichen,* Brehm, 1830. *Marila* of Reichenbach, 1851, has for type *Anas ferina,* L., for which Boie also, in 1822, had proposed *Aythya.*

Fulix of Sundevall, (Kong. Sv. Vet. Ak. Hand. for 1835, 1836, 129,) assigned here by Gray, is merely used as a name for one group of the ducks with lobed hind toe, *Somateria,* his genera being *Somateria, Fulix,* and *Mergus.* Still, as he gives no type and names no species, it may be admissible to assign the name to a particular genus, and I shall therefore retain it for the present division. Should this be considered inadmissible, I would propose the name of *Nettarion* for the same genus.

The *Fuligula collaris* of North American species appears most to resemble the type. The common red head duck of the United States, *Aythya americana,* is excessively similar in general form, differing merely in having the legs a little further back and the feet proportionally longer, being, without the claw, longer than the bill, instead of nearly equal. The head and neck are red, instead of black.

SYNOPSIS OF SPECIES.

Common characters.—Head, neck and body anterior to the shoulders, tail, tail coverts, rump and lower part of back, black. Beneath white, finely waved with black behind and on the sides.

Bill blue, the nail black ; widening slightly to the tip, which is broad and much rounded. No collar on neck. Interscapulars and scapulars white, finely waved with black. Speculum white. Head, with a green gloss in all lights...*F. marila.*

Similar to preceding, but much smaller. Head with a purplish violet gloss. Sides of body less waved...*F. affinis.*

Bill with sides parallel, the tip more pointed; its color bluish black, with basal and subterminal bar of whitish. A chestnut collar round middle of neck. Back nearly plain greenish black. Speculum grayish plumbeous ....*F. collaris.*

FULIX MARILA, Baird.

Big Black-head; Scaup Duck.

Anas marila, LINN. Syst. Nat. I, 1766, 196.—GM. I, 1788, 509.—WILSON, Am. Orn. VIII, 1814, 84 ; pl. lxix.
Fuligula marila, STEPH. Shaw's Gen. Zool. Birds XII, II, 1824, 198.—?SW. F. Bor. Am. II, 1831, 456.—BON. List,
    1838 —AUD. Birds Am. VII, 1843, 355 ; pl. 498.—GIRAUD, Birds L. Island, 1844, 321. (*marila.*)
    EYTON, Mon. Anat. 156.
Aythya marila, BON. List Birds Europe, 1842.
" *Anas frenata,* SPARRMANN, Mus. Carlos. 1786." (Female.)
Marila frenata, BONAP. Comptes Rendus, XLIII, Sept. 1856.
Fuligula gesneri, (WILL.) JARDINE, Brit. Birds, IV, 138 ; pl. v.
Scaup duck, PENNANT, LATHAM.
Broad-bill ; Blue-bill ; Shuffler ; VULGO.

SP. CH.—Head and neck all round, jugulum and shoulders, lower part of back, tail, and coverts black ; the head with a gloss of dark green on the sides. Rest of under parts white ; feathers on the lower part of belly and on the sides, the long feathers of the flanks, the interscapulum, and the scapulars, white, waved in zigzag transversely with black. Greater and middle wing coverts similarly marked, but more finely and obscurely. Greater coverts towards the tip, and the tertials, greenish black ; the speculum is white, bordered behind by greenish black ; the white extending across the whole central portion of the secondaries . Outer primaries and tips of all brownish black ; inner ones pale gray ; the central line dusky. Axillars and middle of the inferior surface of the wing white. Bill blue ; the nail black. Legs plumbeous.

Female with the head brown ; the region all round the base of the bill white ; the undulations of black and white on the feathers wanting, or but faintly indicated above. Length, 20 ; wing, 9 ; tarsus, 1.58 ; commissure, 2.16.

Hab.—Whole of North America and Europe.

List of specimens.

Catal. No.	Sex.	Locality.	When collected.	Whence obtained.	Orig'l No.	Collected by—	Length.	Stretch of wings.	Wing.
2521	♀	Carlisle, Pa....................	Oct. 16,1845	S. F. Baird..............	......	....	18.75	31.50	8.75
1193	♂	Potomac river..................	Dec. —,1843	......do....	......	....	20.00	34.50	9.00
6889	♂	Selkirk Settlement, Red river...	....	D. Gunn..........	......	....	......	......	......
5136	....	Indianola..............	Feb. 20,1855	Capt. Pope	20	....	18.00	30.00	8.50
9867	....	San Diego, Cal.................	....	Lieut. Trowbridge.......	......	A. Cassidy..........	......	......	......
9863	....	San Francisco.................	....	Lieut. Williamson.......	......	Dr. Heermann..........	......	......	......
9866	....	Bodega, Cal.............:.....	Feb. —,1855	Lieut. Trowbridge.......	......	T. A. Szabo............	......	......	......
9865	♂	Fort Steilacoom..............	Jan. 20,1854	Gov. Stevens.............	20	Dr. Suckley	......	......	......
9549	....	Simiahmoo bay..............	Nov. 28......	A. Campbell..............	......	Dr. Kennerly.	......	......	......

FULIX AFFINIS, Baird.

Little Black-head; Blue-bill.

Anas marila, FORSTER, Phil. Trans. LXII, 1772, No. 44. (Not of Linn.)
Fuligula marila, AUD. Orn. Biog. III, 1835, 226 : V, 1839, 614 ; pl. 229.—IB. Syn. 286.—IB. Birds Amer. VI, 1843,
    316 ; pl. 397. (Not of Stephens.)
Fuligula affinis, EYTON, Mon. Anat. 1838, 157. (N. Am. sp.)—GOSSE, Birds Jamaica, 1847.
Marila affinis, BON. Comptes Rendus, XLIII, Sept. 1856.
Fuligula mariloides, VIGORS, Zool. Blossom, 1839, 31. (N. Am.) (Not of Yarrell, Brit. Birds.)
Fuligula minor, GIRAUD, Birds L. Island, 1844, 323.

SP. CH.—Bill blue ; the nail black. Head, neck, fore part of breast, and back anterior to the shoulder, lower part of back, tail and its coverts, black ; the head with violet purple reflections changing occasionally to green. The belly and sides, with axillars, and central portion of inner surfaces of wings, pure white. The lower part of the belly, near the anus, undulated finely with black spots. The interscapular region and scapulars white, with transverse zigzag bands or lines of black, these lines much further apart in the scapulars, which, consequently, are whiter. Wings blackish ; the lesser and middle coverts sprinkled with grayish. The speculum is white, edged behind by greenish black, the color, also, of the tertials.   The white of the speculum goes across the middle of the secondaries.

The female has the wing nearly similar ; the black replaced by brownish ; the region round the base of the bill whitish ; the marbling or mottling almost entirely wanting.

Length, 16.50 inches ; wing, 8 ; tarsus, 1.34 ; commissure, 1.94.

Hab.—Whole of North America. Accidental in Europe.

This species is exceedingly similar to the *F. marila*, but is much smaller. The gloss of the head is essentially purplish violet, occasionally changing to green, while that of the other is green throughout in all lights. The sides and long feathers of the flanks appear much less inclined to being banded with black, the best specimens showing only a slight obsolete sprinkling of brown scarcely appreciable. This may, however, vary in both. The scapulars seem to be more whitish in the small species, the black bands being fewer and more distant. The wings appear much the same, although, as far as I can judge from the skins, there is less whitish on the base of the primaries.

List of specimens.

Catal. No.	Sex.	Locality.	When collected.	Whence obtained.	Collected by—	Length.	Stretch of wings.	Wing.
1731	♂	Carlisle, Pa....................	Oct. 29,1844	S. F. Baird................	....	16.82	28.75	8.00
316	♂	.......do....................	April 28,1841	......do................	....	15.12	26.50	....
317	♀	.......do....................	April —,1841	....do................	....	16.25	28.00	7.40
936	♀	.......do....................	May 3,1843	......do................	....	....	....	....
6901	......	Nelson river, H. B. T...........	....	D. Gunn...............	Jno. Isbister...............	....	....	....
4456	......	San José, Cal............	....	A. J. Grayson.............	....	....	....	....
9869	......	San Francisco....................	....	Lieut. Whipple............	Kenn. & Müll..............	....	....	....

FULIX COLLARIS, Baird.

Ring-necked Duck.

Anas collaris, DONOVAN, British Birds, VI, 1809 ; pl. cxlvii.   (English sp.)

Fuligula collaris, BON. List, Birds Europe, 1842.

Marila collaris, BONAP. Comptes Rendus, XLIII, Sept. 1856.

Anas fuligula, WILS. Am. Orn. VIII, 1814, 66 ; pl. lxvi. Not of Linnaeus.

Anas (Fuligula) rufitorques, BON. J. A. N. Sc. Ph. III, 1824, 381.

Anas rufitorques, ORD, ed. Wils. VIII, 1825, 61.

Fuligula rufitorques, BON. Syn. 1828, 393.—IB. List, 1838.—SW. F. Bor. Am. II, 1831, 454.—NUTTALL, Man. II, 439.—AUD. Orn. Biog. III, 1835, 259 ; pl. 234.—IB. Syn. 287.—IB. Birds Amer. VI, 1843, 320 ; pl. 398.—EYTON, Mon. Anat. 1838, 158.—GOSSE, Birds Jam. 1847.

SP. CH.—Bill blackish, with a basal and subterminal bar of bluish white.   Head, neck, and body all round anterior to the shoulders, back, and tail coverts, black ; the head glossed with green above, on the sides with purplish violet ; the back with greenish. Middle of neck with a narrow chestnut ring, scarcely continuous above. Under parts, and a space immediately anterior to the shoulder, white. Space anterior to the black of crissum, and the sides, very finely waved with black ; the scapulars very slightly sprinkled with dots of grayish. Wings plain grayish brown ; the speculum, consisting of the terminal half of most secondaries, grayish plumbeous ; the innermost of them tipped with white. Point of chin white.

The female has the black replaced by brown ; the sides of the head and chin adjacent to the bill whitish ; a whitish ring ound the eye. Wing as in the male. The basal whitish bar of the bill appears to be wanting. Length, 18 ; wing, 8 ; tarsus, 1.28 ; commissure 2.10.

Hab.—Whole of North America. Accidental in Europe.

The bill of this species is more acutely pointed at the end than in *F. marila*.

List of specimens.

Catal. No.	Sex.	Locality.	When collected.	Whence obtained.	Orig'l No.	Collected by—	Length.	Stretch of wings.	Wing.
134	♂	Carlisle, Pa......................	Oct. 23, 1840	S. F. Baird..............	......	....	10.00	23.00	....
1186	♀	......do........................	Oct. 28, 1843	......do........	......	....	18.00	26.75	7.50
4516	♂	Washington, D. C..............	Mar. —, 1856	......do........	......	....	....	....	....
9870	.....	Boca Grande, Mexico...........	Mar. —, 1855	Major Emory..........	32	Dr. Kennerly.........	....	....	....
8429	......	Simiahmoo bay, W. T............	Sept. 14......	A. Campbell.............	32	......do........	....	....	....

AYTHYA, Boie.

Aythya, BOIE, Isis, 1822. Type *Anas ferina*, L.

CH.—Very similar to *Fuligula* in general characters of shape. The bill elongated, longer than the head, and about equal to the middle toe with the claw. The bill more slender in one species, the nail smaller and less decurved ; the bill higher at base and the upper outline nearly straight to beyond the end of the nostrils, which do not quite reach the middle of the bill. Colors similar to those of *Fuligula ;* the head and neck red. Tail of fourteen feathers.

I have based the generic characters of *Aythya* upon the *Anas vallisneria* of Wilson, the type *A. ferina* being much more like the *A. americana*. The latter would seem to come more naturally with *Fuligula*, (which see,) being combined with *vallisneria* chiefly on account of the great similarity in color. Still *A. vallisneria* is much like *Fuligula* in all points, except the bill, which is merely longer, narrower, higher at the base, and sloping. The nostrils are further forward, occupying the anterior portion of the posterior half of the bill. Should it be considered expedient, for these reasons, to establish for the canvas-back a new genus, the name of *Aristonetta* would be very appropriate, on account of the great superiority of its flesh as an article of food.

SYNOPSIS OF SPECIES.

Common characters.—Head and neck chestnut ; body anterior to shoulders, the rump, and tail coverts, black. Sides, scapulars, and interscapulars waved transversely with black and white. Speculum grayish blue, on the ends of the secondaries ; the innermost edged narrowly with black.

Bill broad, not longer than the head. Anterior extremity of nostril two-fifths the distance from upper corner of bill to the tip. No brown on the head. Black and white mottling on the back in equal amount.....................................*A. americana.*

Bill narrow, longer than the head ; anterior extremity of the nostril half the distance from upper corner of bill to the tip. Top of head and about base of bill dusky. White greatly predominating in the mottling of the back ; the black in dotted lines..*A. vallisneria.*

AYTHYA AMERICANA, Bon.

R

Anas ferina, WILSON, Am. Orn. VIII, 1814, 84 ; pl. lxx, (not of Linnaeus.)—DOUGHTY, Cab. N. H., II, 1832, 40 ; pl. iv
Anas (Fuligula) ferina, BONAP. Obs. Wils. 1825, No. 270.
Fuligula ferina, SW. F. Bor. Am. II, 1831, 452.—NUTTALL, Man. II, 1834, 434.—AUD. Orn. Biog. IV, 1835, 198 ; pl. 322.—IB. Birds Amer. VI, 1843, 311 ; pl. 396.

August 19, 1858.
100

Aythya erythrocephala, BONAP. List, 1838, (not of Brehm, 1831, which is European *A. ferina.*)—NEWBERRY, P. R.
Rep. VI, IV, 1857, 103.

Fuligula americana, EYTON, Mon. Anat. 1838, 155.—GOSSE, Birds Jam. 1847.

Nyroca americana, GRAY, Genera.

Aythya americana, BP. Comptes Rendus, XLIII, Sept. 1856.

SP. CH.—Bill as long as the head, broad, blue, the end black ; the region anterior to the nostrils dusky. Head, and neck
for more than half its length, brownish red, glossed above and behind with violaceous red. Rest of neck and body anterior to
the shoulders, lower part of back and tail coverts, black. Beneath white, sprinkled with gray and black anterior to the crissum ;
the sides, interscapulars, and scapulars finely lined with undulating black and white in nearly equal proportions, imparting a
general gray tint. Wing coverts bluish gray, finely sprinkled with whitish. The speculum, consisting of the ends of the
secondaries, hoary grayish blue, lightest externally, and the innermost narrowly edged externally with black. Basal portion of
inner primaries somewhat similar to the speculum. Tail of fourteen feathers.

Female with the head, neck, and fore part of body brownish ; the region round the base of the bill whitish. Length of male,
20.50 ; wing, 9.50 ; tarsus, 1.60 ; commissure, 2.30.

Hab.—Whole of North America.

This species, with a strong resemblance to the canvas-back, is readily distinguished by the
shorter, broader bill, absence of brown on the head, and a greater predominance of black in the
waved lines, this being equal in amount to the white, instead of much less. It is very similar
to the *A. ferina* of Europe, which, however, appears to have the bill more like that of the
canvas-back, *A. vallisneria.*

List of specimens.

Catal. No.	Sex and age.	Locality.	When collected.	Whence obtained.	Orig. No.	Collected by—	Length.	Stretch of wings.	Wing.	Remarks.
1330	♂	Carlisle, Pa...............	April 3, 1844	S. F. Baird		....	20.50	33.50	9.50	....
1185	○♂	......do....................	Oct. 23, 1843	.. ...do........		....	19.50	32.75	9.00	....
1727	♀	.... do....	......do.....	......do........		....	19.50	31.50	8.75	....
5135		Indianola, Texas	Feb. 14, 1855	Capt. Pope	17	....	15.50	24.50	7.50	Feet dark green, bill black, iris brown.
9786	....	Uncompagre river, Utah....	....	Capt. Beckwith..	26	Mr. Kreutzfeldt.	....	....	....	....
9787	♂	Salt Lake City	....	Lt. Beckwith .. .		.......do......	....	....	....	....
9784	♀	......do..............		......do.....		.......do.....	....	....	....	....
4621	....	Rio Grande...............	Feb. 7, 1855	Maj. Emory	45	A. Schott	....	....	....	....
9783	♂	San Diego, Cal		Lt. Trowbridge .		....	....	....	....	Eyes red ....
9785	....	Bodega, Cal	Feb. —, 1855	......do.....		....	....	....	....	....

AYTHYA VALLISNERIA, Bonap.

Canvas-back.

Anas vallisneria, WILSON, Am. Orn. VIII, 1814, 103 ; pl. lxx.—DOUGHTY's Cab. N. H. II, 1832, 36 ; pl. iv.

Fuligula vallisneria, STEPHENS, XII, 1824, 196.—BON. Syn. 1828, 392.—Sw. F. Bor. Am. II, 1831, 451.—
NUTTALL, Man. II, 430.

Aythya vallisneria, BON. List, 1838.—NEWBERRY, Rep. P. R. R. VI, IV, 1857, 103.

Anas vallisneriana, SABINE.

Fuligula vallisneriana, AUD. Orn. Biog. IV, 1838, 1 ; pl. 301.—IB. Syn. 1839.—IB. Birds. Amer. VI, 1843, 299 ; pl. 395.

Aristonetta vallisneria, BAIRD.

SP. CH.—Bill long, slender, and tapering. Head all round and neck chestnut ; the top of the head and region around the
base of the bill dusky brown Rest of neck, body anterior to the shoulders, back behind, rump and tail coverts, black. Under·
parts white ; the region anterior to the anus, the sides, the interscapulars and scapulars, white, finely dotted in transverse line,
with black, the white greatly predominating. Speculum bluish gray, lighter externally ; the innermost secondaries of the
speculum edged externally with black.

Female with the black and chestnut replaced by brown, the cheeks and chin lighter, and some tinged with dull rufous. Length, 20.10 ; wing, 9.30 ; tarsus, 1.70 ; commissure, 2.65.

Hab.—Whole of North America.

List of specimens.

Catal. No.	Sex.	Locality.	When collected.	Whence obtained.	Orig'l No.	Collected by—	Length.	Stretch of wings.	Wing.	Remarks.
606	♂	Potomac river, D. C....	Feb. —, 1842	S. F. Baird						
	♀	......do...		......do...						
5137	♂	Delaware creek, N. M..	Mar. 26, 1856	Capt. Pope	189		23.25	31.50	10.00	Bill black, iris red, feet dark gray.
9778	......	San Francisco		Lt. Williamson ..						
9780	......	Bodega, California.....	Jan. —, 1855	Lt. Trowbridge ..		T. A. Szabo....				
4414	......	Fort Dalles	.... .do......	Dr. Suckley	155					
9777	......	Fort Steilacoom	Jan. —, 1854	Gov. Stevens....		Dr. Suckley				

BUCEPHALA, Baird.

Clangula, FLEMING, Philos. Zool. 1828. Type *Anas clangula*, L. Not of 1822, which has *Anas glacialis* for type, according to G. R. Gray.

Glaucion, KAUP, Ent. Europ. Thierw. 1829. Not of Oken, 1816, Mollusca.

Bucephala, BAIRD. Type *Anas albeola*, L.

Ch.—Bill from feathers of forehead about equal to the tarsus and shorter than the head; high at the base; lateral outlines tapering to the tip, where the nail forms only the central portion, though rather large. Nostrils situated near the middle of the bill. Feathers of chin and forehead extending only moderately foreward a little further than those of cheeks. Tarsus rather more than half the foot. Tail moderately long, about half the wing, and somewhat pointed; of sixteen feathers.

The *B. americana* differs decidedly from the *B. albeola* in a stouter bill, with the nostrils in the posterior portion of the anterior half, instead of in the anterior portion of the posterior part.

As the genus *Clangula* of 1822 has *Anas glacialis* for type, according to Gray, it cannot be used for the present group. *Glaucion* of Kaup being pre-occupied, a new name appears to be required.

The following diagnoses will distinguish the species :

Common characters.—Head and upper part of neck dark colored, with varied reflections, usually of green, purple, or violet. Lower part of neck all round, under parts and sides, scapulars, middle and greater coverts, and many secondaries, white ; the scapulars edged externally with black ; upper parts generally black. Inside of wings and axillars sooty.

An oval patch of white in front of the eye and along the side of the bill, but not reaching its upper corner. White of wings continuous. Head with green reflections. Inside of wings and axillars entirely dusky.................................*B. americana*.

A triangular patch in front of the eye, applied against the entire base of the bill, and running up in a sharp point. White of wing coverts crossed by a black bar. Head glossed with violet reflections. Inside of wings and axillars pure sooty...*B. islandica*.

A broad white patch on each side the head, behind the eye, and confluent with its fellow on the nape. White of wings continuous. Head glossed anteriorly and behind with green ; between this, with purple violet. Under wing coverts and axillars tipped with white............................ ....*B. albeola*.

BUCEPHALA AMERICANA, Baird.

Golden Eye; Whistle Wing.

Anas clangula, FORSTER, Philos. Trans. LXII, 1772, 365.—WILSON, Am. Orn. VIII, 1814, 62; pl. lxvii.—DOUGHTY'S
Cab. N. H. I, 1830, 110; pl. x. Not of Linnaeus.

Fuligula (Clangula) clangula, BON. Syn. 1828, 393.—NUTT. Man. II, 441.

Fuligula clangula, AUD. Orn. Biog. IV, 1838, 318; pl. 342.—IB. Birds Amer. VI, 1843, 362; pl. 406.

Clangula vulgaris, Sw. F. Bor. Am. II, 1831, 456. Not of Fleming.

Clangula americana, BONAP. Comp. List, 1838.—EYTON, Mon. Anat. 1838, 167.

SP. CH.—Bill black. Head and upper part of neck glossy green; the under surface opaque velvety purplish black. An elliptical patch along the base of upper mandible anterior to the eye, lower part of neck, under parts generally, and sides, middle and greater wing coverts, the innermost secondaries (and tertials, except the innermost three or four) white. The white on the wing is in a continuous patch, although there is a concealed black bar on the bases of the greater coverts. The inner scapulars are white, margined externally with black, posteriorly, however, they are black, streaked centrally with white. The inner scapulars and tertials, and the whole back, rump, and lesser wing coverts are black; the primaries and tail black, with a hoary gloss. The under side of quills and lower greater coverts are plumbeous gray; the rest of the under wing and the axillars are sooty brown. The long white feathers of the flanks are edged superiorly with black.

Female with the head and neck above snuff brown, without white patch. White of wing less extended; the middle coverts only touched with white. There is a tendency to a black bar across the tips of the greater coverts. The white of the wing sometimes well defined.

Length, 18.75; wing, 8.50; tarsus 1.50; commissure, 2.

Hab.—Whole of North America.

List of specimens.

Catal. No.	Sex.	Locality.	When collected.	Whence obtained.	Orig. No.	Collected by—	Length.	Stretch of wings.	Wing.	Remarks.
224	♂	Carlisle, Pa.	Dec. 12, 1840	S. F. Baird						
1748	♂	.....do.	Nov. 15, 1844	......do.			19.00	31.75	9.00	
238	♀	.....do.	Feb. 1, 1841	......do.						
6898	♂	Nelson river, H. B. T.		D. Gunn		John Isbister.				
6899	♀	.....do.		......do.						
9798	...	Salt Lake City.		Capt. Beckwith.						
9799		Bodega, Cal.	Dec., 1854	Lieut. Trowbridge.		T. A. Szabo.				Iris yellow.
4517		San Francisco		Lieut. Williamson.		Dr. Heermann.				
9803		Fort Steilacoom		Gov. Stevens.		Dr. Suckley.	20.50	29.50	9.50	
9802	♀	.....do.	Feb. 15, 1854	......do.	35	......do.				
9800	♂	.....do.	April 1, 1854	......do.		......do.	23.00	29.00	9.75	

BUCEPHALA ISLANDICA, Baird.

Barrow's Golden Eye.

Anas islandica, GMELIN, Syst. Nat. I, 1788, 541.

Clangula islandica, BONAP. List Birds Europe, 1842.

Clangula barrowii, Sw. F. Bor. Am. II, 1831, 456; pl. lxx.—SWAINSON, Anim. in Men. 1838, 271.—BON. List, 1838.—EYTON, Mon. Anat. 1838, 165.

Fuligula (Clangula) barrowii, NUTTALL, Man. II, 444.

Clangula scapularis, BREHM & MEHLIS, Brehm Vögel Deutschl. July, 1831, 931.

Fuligula clangula, var. AUD. Orn. Biog. V, 1839, 105; pl. 403.—IB. Birds Amer. VI, 1843.

SP. CH.—Head and neck all round bluish violet, occasionally with green or purplish reflection; a large white patch anterior to the eye, occupying the entire side of the bill, and running up in a point on the forehead. Lower neck and under parts generally white; a narrow white patch on the middle wing coverts. The greater coverts black, tipped with white, which is continuous with the white secondaries, but separated from that on the middle coverts. Anterior scapulars white, edged externally with black ; the posterior ones black, with white central streak. Rest of upper parts black, as are the sides behind, and including the tibia. Long feathers of the flank white, tipped and edged above with black.

Length, 22.50 ; wing, 9.50 ; tarsus, 1.58 ; commissure, 1.80.

Hab.—Iceland and northern parts of America. In winter not rare on the St. Lawrence.

This species, supposed by Mr. Audubon to be identical with the common golden eye, is readily distinguished by its much greater size and different marks. The white patch along the base of the bill is triangular ; the anterior face applied against the whole side of the bill ; the posterior crescentic concave behind, and meeting the anterior in an acute angle running high up. (The other species has the spot truly oval, and elongated longitudinally, the white not reaching along to the upper corner of the bill.) The gloss of the head is bluish violet, not green. The white of the wing is divided by a black band, (the basal portion of greater coverts.) This appears to be owing to a less development of the white middle coverts, which do not cover the basal black of the greater coverts, instead of reaching to the white tips. The black of the lesser wing coverts overreaches more on the white of the middle one.

The specimen described, obtained by Mr. Audubon from Mr. Gould, appears to be the one upon which the species was based in the F. Bor. Americana.

Barrow's golden eye appears to be not rare on the St. Lawrence in winter, as I have seen several specimens in the Museums of Quebec and Montreal, which were supposed to be merely good representatives of the common golden eye.

List of specimens.

Catal. number	Sex.	Locality.	Whence obtained.	Original No.	Collected by—	Remarks.
2723	♂	Rocky Mountains......	S. F. Baird	3476	J. J. Audubon⁰..	Mounted ....

⁰ This is probably the original specimen described in F. Bor. Americana, and obtained from Mr. Gould by Mr. Audubon

BUCEPHALA ALBEOLA, Baird.

Butter Ball ; Dipper ; Buffle Head.

Anas albeola, Linn. Syst. Nat. I, 1766, 199 —Forster, Phil. Trans. LXII, 1772, 383.—Gmelin, I, 517.—Wilson, Am. Orn. VIII, 1814, 51 ; pl. lxvii.

Fuligula (Clangula) albeola, Bon. Syn. 1828, 394.—Nutt. Man II, 445.

Fuligula albeola, Aud. Orn Biog. IV, 1838, 217 ; pl. 325.—Ib. Syn. 1839, 293.—Ib. Birds Amer. VI, 1843, 369 ; pl. 408.

Clangula albeola (Jenyns,) Sw. F. Bor. Amer. II, 1831, 458.—Bon. List, 1838, 1842.—Eyton, Mon. Anat. 1838, 164.

Anas bucephala, Linn. Syst. Nat. I, 1766, 200, (male.)—Gmelin, I, 521.

Anas rustica, Linn. Syst. Nat. I, 1766, 201. (Female.)

Spirit duck ; Buffalo head ; Vulgo.

Sp. Ch.—*Male.* , Bill blue. Head and neck anteriorly dark colored ; the region in front of the eye and on the sides of the collar behind rich green ; this color shading into purplish on the upper and under surfaces of the head ; a broad patch on each side of the head from the posterior border of the eye, and meeting its fellow on the nape, the lower neck all round, under parts generally, wing coverts, (except the lesser,) and most of the secondaries, and the scapulars, white ; the latter narrowly edged externally with black. Rest of upper parts, except as described, black ; passing gradually on the upper tail coverts into pale gray. Axillars and under wing coverts sooty brown, more or less tipped with white.

Female with the entire head, neck, and upper parts almost black. An elongated patch behind and below the eye, (not reaching it.) The outer webs of some secondaries, and the under parts, white; the jugulum, sides, and anal region, plumbeous gray.

Length, 15; wing, 6.65; tarsus, 1.25; commissure, 1.44.

The nostrils of this species are more posterior than in the two others described.

The name buffle head is a corruption of buffalo head, under which name it is mentioned by Bartram, in 1791.

List of specimens.

Catal. No.	Sex.	Locality.	When collected.	Whence obtained.	Orig. No.	Collected by—	Length.	Extent.	Wing.
312	♂	Carlisle, Pa..........................	April 24, 1841	S. F. Baird	......	....	15.00	......	24.00
1737	♀	......do......	Nov. 2, 1844	......do........	......	....	13.50	22.25	6.32
6094	♂	Selkirk settlement, H. B. T.........	....	D. Gunn	......	....	......	......	......
6892		Nelson river, H. B. T..............	....	......do.....	......	John Isbister ..	......	......	......
4886	....	Colorado Laguna, N. M............	....	Maj. Emory	59	A. Schott......	......	......	......
9809	♂	St. Mary's Mission, Rocky Mountains	Dec. 18, 1853	Gov. Stevens...............	......	Dr. Suckley....	......	......	......
9813	....	Camp 119, Bill Williams' Fork, N. M.	Feb., 1854...	Lieut. Whipple	89	Kenn. & Möll.	11.00	21.00	7.50
9844	♀	Boca Grande, Mex............	Mar., 1855...	Maj. Emory	29	Dr. Kennerly ..	......	......	......
9816		Bodega, Cal.......................	Dec., 1854...	Lieut. Trowbridge............	......	T. A. Szabo....	......	......	......
9811	....	Presidio, near San Francisco, Cal...	....	......do.......	......	....	......	......	......
9805	....	Fort Steilacoom, W. T............	Mar., 1854...	Gov. Stevens...............	46	Dr. Suckley ...	15.00	25.00	7.50
9808	♂	..........do.....	....	......do........	3	......do.........	15.00	23.00	......
9815	......	.........do......	....	......do.......	40	......do.........	......	......	......

HISTRIONICUS, Lesson.

Histrionicus, LESSON, Man. d'Ornith. II, 1828, 415. Type *Anas histrionica*, L.

Clangula, STEPH. Shaw's Gen. Zool. XII, 1824. Not of Fleming, 1822.

Cosmonetta, KAUP, Entw. Europ. Thierw. 1829.

Phylaconetta, BRANDT, Mem. Ac. St. Pet. VI, 1849.

CH.—Bill very small; the culmen shorter than tarsus, tapering rapidly to the rounded tip, which is entirely occupied by the nail. Nostrils small, in the anterior portion of posterior half of bill; the centre about opposite the middle of commissure. A well marked angle at the postero-superior corner of the bill. The lateral outline concave behind, the feathers on forehead extending a little beyond it; those of chin not reaching further than those of the sides, and much posterior to the nostrils. Lateral outline of edge of bill nearly straight. A membranous lobe at the base of the bill. Tertials bent outward, so as to cross the edge of the wing. Tail more than half the wing; considerably pointed; of 14 feathers.

This genus differs from *Harelda* in the more compressed, attenuated, and tapering bill; the lateral outline straighter. The feathers of the sides of head and on chin do not extend so far forward. The tertials are bent outwards, and the tail, though pointed, lacks the elongation of the middle feathers. The coloration is entirely different. The two, however, might, with great propriety, be combined in the same genus.

The membranous lobe at the base of the bill is, as far as I know, peculiar among American ducks. This overhangs the basal portion of the commissure, and is an extension of the skin of the cheeks near the base of the bill.

The characters of the single species are as follows:

Bluish; the under parts mostly dull brownish. Two white spots on side of neck, two on wings, and one on each side of the root of tail. Scapulars and tertials in part white; secondaries with a violet blue speculum. Sides of crown, and of body behind, chestnut. Inside of wings and axillars dark brown..*H. torquatus.*

HISTRIONICUS TORQUATUS, Bonap.

Harlequin Duck.

Anas histrionica, LINN. Syst. Nat. ed. 10, I, 1758, 127; ed. 12th, I, 1766, 204.—FORSTER, Phil. Trans. LXII,
  1772, 383.—GMELIN, I, 534.—LATH. Ind. Orn. II, 1790, 849.—BRÜNNICH, Orn. Borealis, 1764,
  84.—WILSON, Am. Orn. VIII, 1814, 139; pl. lxxii.
Anas (Fuligula) histrionica, BON. Obs. Wils. 1825, No. 277.
Fuligula (Clangula) histrionica, BON. Syn. 1828, 394.—NUTTALL, Man. II, 448.
Fuligula histrionica, AUD. Orn. Biog. III, 1835, 612 : V, 1839, 617 ; pl. 297.—IB. Syn. 1839, 294.—IB. Birds Amer.
  VI, 1843, 374 ; pl. 409.
" *Cosmonetta histrionica*, KAUP."
Clangula histrionica, SWAINSON, F. Bor. Am. II, 1831, 489.—EYTON, Mon. Anat. 1838, 163.
Harelda histrionica, KEYS. & BLAS. Wirb. Europ. 1840.—BON. 2d list Eur. Birds, 1842.
Phylaconetta histrionica, BRANDT, Mem. Acad. St. Pet. Sc. Nat. VI, 1849, 9.
? *Anas minuta*, LINN. I, 1766, 204. Female.
Histrionicus torquatus, BONAP. Comptes Rendus, XLIII, Sept. 1856.
Harlequin Duck, PENNANT.

SP. CH.—*Male.* Head and neck all round dark blue. Jugulum, sides of breast, and upper parts, lighter blue, becoming
bluish black again on the tail coverts. The blue of breast passes insensibly into dark bluish brown behind. A broad stripe
along the top of head from the bill to the nape, and the tail feathers, black. A white patch along the entire side of the base
of bill anterior to the eye, and passing upwards and backwards so as to border the black of the crown, but replaced from above
the eye to the nape by chestnut. A round spot on the side of the occiput, an elongated one on the side of the neck, a collar
round the lower part of the neck, interrupted before and behind, and margined behind by dark blue, a transversely elongated
patch on each side the breast, and similarly margined, a round spot on the middle wing coverts, a transverse patch on the end
of the greater coverts, the scapulars in part, a broad streak on the outer web of tertials, and a spot on each side the rest of the
tail, white ; sides of body behind chestnut brown. Secondaries with a metallic speculum of purplish or violet blue. Inside
of wing, and axillars, dark brown.

Female with the head and body above, dark brown ; the chin more plumbeous ; the lower part of neck, breast, and under
parts generally, except the central region, (which is white,) duller and lighter brown ; a whitish patch in front of the eye, and
a rounded spot just behind the ear.

Length, 17.50 ; wing, 7.70 ; tarsus, 1.48 ; commissure, 1.54.

Hab.—Northern seacoast of northern hemisphere.

List of specimens.

Catal. No.	Sex.	Locality.	When collected.	Whence obtained.	Orig'l No.	Collected by—	Length.	Stretch of wings.
1575	♂	Boston		S. F. Baird		M. Kimball		
1576	♂	....do		....do				
		Port Townsend, W. T.	May —, 1856	Gov. Stevens		Dr. Suckley	17.50	27.00
9868		....do		Dr. McCurdy				
8428		Simiahmoo bay	Sept 19, 1856	A. Campbell	44	Dr. Kennerly		

HARELDA, Leach.

"*Harelda*, LEACH, 1816," Gray. Type *Anas glacialis*, L.

Clangula, FLEMING, Philos. Zool. 1822. Same type.

Pagonetta, KAUP, Europ. Thierw. 1829.

CH.—Bill shorter than the head and tarsus, tapering laterally to the end ; the nail very broad, occupying the entire tip. Lateral profile of lower edge of upper mandible straight to near the end, then rising suddenly to the prominent decurved nail. Nostrils large, in the posterior half of the bill, their centre about opposite the middle of the commissure. Tertials long, lanceolate, and straight. Tail pointed, of 14 feathers, the central feathers very long, equal to the wings. Bill with almost no posterior lateral upper angle ; the feathers of the sides advancing obliquely forwards. Feathers of chin reaching beyond the middle of the commissure, or almost to the anterior extremity of nostrils. Tail of 14 feathers.

The genus *Harelda*, of Leach, is stated by Gray to have been established in 1816, probably in the "Catalogue of British Museum." If not published until 1824, in Shaw's General Zoology, the name will be anticipated by *Clangula* of Fleming, 1822.

The characters of the single species are as follows :

Summer.—Blackish; the belly and sides whitish. Scapulars and lower part of back with rufous edgings. A grayish patch on the side of head, passing behind into whitish. No white spots, nor speculum. Inside of wing, and axillars, dark brown.

Winter.—Similar, but with the head, neck, and scapulars, whitish..................*H. glacialis.*

HARELDA GLACIALIS, Leach.

South Southerly; Old Wife; Long-tail.

Anas glacialis, LINN. Syst. Nat. I, 1766, 203.—FORSTER, Phil. Trans. LXII, 1772, 418.—GMELIN, I, 1788, 529.—WILSON, Am. Orn. VIII, 1814, 93, 96 ; pl. lxx.—SABINE, Linn. Trans. VII, 555.

Harelda glacialis, "LEACH."—STEPHENS, Shaw's Gen. Zool. XII, 1824, 175.—Sw. F. B. Am. II, 1831, 460.—BON. List, 1838.—EYTON, Mon. 1838, 162.—BRANDT, Mem. Ac. St. Pet. VI, 1849, 8.

Anas (Fuligula) glacialis, BON. Obs. Wils. 1825, 275.

Fuligula (Clangula) glacialis, BON. Syn. 1828, 395.

Fuligula (Harelda) glacialis, NUTT. Man. II, 1834, 453.

Fuligula glacialis, AUD. Orn. Biog. IV, 1838, 403 ; pl. 312.—IB. Syn. 1839, 295.—IB. Birds Amer. VI, 1843, 379 ; pl. 410.

Crymonessa glacialis, MACGIL. Man. II, 186.

Anas hyemalis, LINN. I, 1766, 202.—FORST. Phil. Tr. LXII, 1772, 418.—GMELIN, I, 529.

Anas miclonia, BODDAERT. (Gray.)

Anas leucocephalus, BECHST. (Gray.)

Anas brachyrhynchus, BESEKE. (Gray.)

Long-tailed Duck, PENNANT.

SP. CH.—*Male in summer*. Bill black, orange yellow towards the tip. Head, neck and breast, very dark blackish brown ; the head above, back, rump, and middle tail feathers, black. The whole side of the head from the bill and to behind the eyes and the sides of the body, pale bluish gray ; the portion of the cheek patch immediately around and behind the eye, with a longitudinal streak each side the occiput ; the under parts generally, and the more external tail feathers, white. Feathers on the fore part of the back, with the scapulars, broadly edged with light reddish brown ; under wing coverts and axillars, brownish chocolate. No white whatever on the wing.

Male in winter. Differs from summer dress in having the head and neck white to the jugulum and interscapular region. The gray of the cheeks persistent, and a broad patch of black on the sides of the neck behind this. The scapulars are pale pearl gray.

Female. Lacks the long points to the tail and scapulars. The head and neck dusky, with a whitish patch around the eye and on the sides of the neck behind.

Length, 20.75 ; wing, 8.90 ; tail, 8.00 ; tarsus, 1.38 ; commissure, 1.62.

Hab.—Along both coasts of North America. Europe.

List of specimens.

Catal. No.	Sex.	Locality.	When collected.	Whence obtained.	Collected by—	Length.	Stretch of wings	Wing.
335	○ ♂	Carlisle, Pa.	May 5, 1841	S. F. Baird.				
306	♀	......do	April 24, 1841	......do		17.00	28.00	
4553		Washington, D. C.	April —, 1856	Market		22.12	30.50	9.24
9843		New York		F. Ruhl				
4495		Shoalwater bay, W. T.	Jan. 8, 1855	Lt. Williamson	Dr. Cooper			
8430		Simiahmoo bay, W. T.	July —, 1857	A. Campbell	Dr. Kennerly			

POLYSTICTA, Eyton.

Polysticta, EYTON, British Birds, 1836. Type *Anas Stelleri*, Gm. Sufficiently different from *Polysticte*, Smith, 1835.

Stelleria, BONAP. Comp. List, 1838. Same type.

Macropus, NUTTALL, Man. II, 1834, 450. (Preoccupied.)

Eniconetta, GRAY, Genera, 1840.

CH —Bill quite similar to that of *Histrionicus*, but rather broader at the tip, which is more abruptly truncate, and with the nail less prominent. Scapulars slightly curved outwards ; tertials much more so. Tail pointed, about half the wing. Feathers of head and neck short, and velvet-like. Tail of 14 feathers.

This genus, in many respects, appears most like *Histrionicus;* the bill, however, is broader and more truncate ; the nail scarcely distinguishable. The feathers of the cheek extend rather more forwards, anteriorly. The feet are much smaller in proportion. The feathers of the head are much shorter, fuller, and more erect. The outward curvature of the tertials is much greater and more conspicuous, involving to some extent the scapulars. There is much resemblance in coloration to *Lampronetta* and *Somateria*.

POLYSTICTA STELLERI, Eyton.

Steller's Duck.

Anas stelleri, PALLAS, Spicil. Zool. VI, 1765, 80, 35 ; pl. v.—GMELIN, Syst. Nat. I, 1788, 518.

Fuligula (Clangula) stelleri, BON. Syn. 1828, 394.

Fuligula (Macropus) stelleri, NUTTALL, Man. II, 1834, 451.

Polysticta stelleri, EYTON, Mon. Anat. 1838, 150.—BRANDT, Mem. Acad. St. Pet.; Sc. Nat. VI, 1849, 7.

Eniconetta stelleri, GRAY, Genera.

Somateria stelleri, JARDINE, Br. Birds, IV, 173.

Harelda stelleri, KEYS. & BLAS. Wirb. Europ. 1840, 230.

Anas dispar, SPARRMANN, Mus. Carlson. 1786, tab. vii, viii.—GMELIN, Syst. Nat. I, 1788, 535.

Fuligula dispar, STEPHENS, Shaw's Gen. Zool. Birds, XII, 206; pl. ii.—AUD. Orn. Biog. V, 1839, 253; pl. 430.—IB. Syn. 293.—IB. Birds, Amer. VI, 1843, 368; pl. 407, (English Sp.)

Stelleria dispar, BON. List, 1838.

? *Anas berengii*, GMELIN, I, 1788. 508.

Anas occidua, BONN. Gray.)

Western Duck and Bering Duck. PENNANT.

SP. CH.—A large square black patch on the chin. Rest of head silvery white; the forehead and a broad band across the occiput dark pea green. Circle around the eye, with neck anteriorly as a narrow ring, and extending along the upper surface,

August 19, 1858.

101 b

glossy dark green, with violet blue reflections, passing behind into blue black, which extends along the middle of the back to the tail.   The body posterior to the tibial region is dull black, this including the crissum, and extending in a browner shade along the under surface to the jugulum.   Anterior to the tibia this brown is bordered laterally and anteriorly by reddish brown passing gradually into brownish buff, and then almost into white.   The greenish collar on the neck is bordered posteriorly by white, which widens along the sides of the cervical portion.   The wing coverts are white; the exposed portion of secondaries, tertials, and outer scapulars, are silvery white; the greater portion of outer webs violet blue, and terminated with white; the inner scapulars are black, streaked with white.   The under wing coverts are mostly white, as are the axillars; the sides of breast under the wings are white, with a large spot of greenish black.

The female is dusky throughout; the general tint reddish brown, but the belly and crissum blackish.   The feathers of the lower neck all round, jugulum, and fore part of back are banded with reddish brown and blackish; those of the head less conspicuously so.   The white of the upper surface of body and wings is restricted to the ends of greater coverts and of secondaries; the speculum is less brilliant.

Length, 18.00; wing, 8.00; tarsus, 1.50; commissure, 1.82.

Hab.—North Eastern Asia.   Accidental on northwest coast of America and in Europe.

The occurrence of this beautiful duck on our shores is a matter of much uncertainty, no specimens actually taken in North America having come to my knowledge.   It appears to inhabit northeastern Asia, especially Kamtschatka and the Kurile islands, and to extend thence into northern and western Europe.   It doubtless visits the northwest coast of America, where it is said by Bonaparte to be abundant; with what foundation I do not know.

The pair described was obtained in Norway by Mr. Wolley, the celebrated oologist, and presented to the Smithsonian Institution by the Norwich Museum, England.

List of specimens.

Catal. No.	Sex.	Locality.	When collected.	Whence obtained.	Collected by—
10197	♂	Norway -------------	-------------	Norwich Museum-------------	Mr. Wolley--------
10196	♀	----do-------------	March —, 1857	-------do-------------	-------do-----------

LAMPRONETTA, Brandt.

Lampronetta, BRANDT, Mém. Acad. St. Pet., 6th series; Sc. Nat. VI, 1849, (Pub. 1847?) 5.   Type *L. fischeri*, Brandt.

CH.—Bill but little elevated at the base, and rather narrowed; shorter than the head.   Nail moderate.   Lamellae not extending below the side of bill.   Feathers extending on the base of the bill, so as to pass beyond the nostrils on the culmen, and bounded by a straight line from this point to the angle of the mouth crossing the posterior portion of the nasal fossa.   Nostrils broad, open; situated above the middle of commissure.   Tertials curved outwards over the primaries.   Tail short, of 14 feathers.

The characters of this genus, as given by Brandt, indicate a form closely allied to *Polysticta* and *Somateria*.   From the former it differs in larger nasal fossae and the greater extension along the culmen of the feathers of the forehead, and the obliteration of the upper posterior angle of the bill.   The nail appears much less prominent than in *Somateria*, and the bill more depressed; if, however, the frontal processes of the base of the bill in *Somateria* were covered with feathers to a little beyond the nostrils, the resemblance would be very close.   There are also points of considerable affinity to both *Harelda* and *Camptolaemus*.

The single species is very similar to the eider and king duck.   Its character is as follows:

Back, wing coverts, tertials, and throat, white; under parts, rump, tail, and primaries, black. A large black circle or quadrangle round the eye; the back of the head and nape green..*L. fischeri*.

LAMPRONETTA FISCHERI, Brandt.

Spectacled Eider.

Lampronetta fischeri, BRANDT, Mém. Acad. St. Petersburg, 6th series; Sc. Nat. VI, 1849, 10, pl. 1 ♂. (Probably published in 1847.)

Arctonetta fischeri, GRAY, Pr. Zool. Soc. 1855, 212; pl. cviii, ♂, ♀, and young ♂.

SP. CH.—A large sub-circular or sub-quadrangular black outline around the eye, sending a short branch backwards; the space thus enclosed white tinged with reddish. Feathers about the base of bill tinged with greenish. The space between the black outlines above, their lower border, and the entire occiput and nape, green. Chin, throat, lower neck, fore part of back, wing coverts, tertials, and a patch each side of the rump, white. Under parts generally, rump, tail, and primary quills, black; bill yellow.

Female brown, with dull dusky blotches or bars. Chin and throat whitish. White eye patch of the male obscurely indicated. Length 21.20 inches; wing, 10 inches?; tarsus, 1.70; commissure, 2.20.

Hab.—Norton sound, Russian America, 63¼ N. L.

This fine duck is only known from the descriptions and figures of Brandt and Gray, mentioned above. All the specimens obtained were found at Norton Sound, Russian America, latitude 63½°, and doubtless in severe winters the species will be found on our own coast.

CAMPTOLAEMUS, Gray.

Kamptorhynchus, EYTON, Mon. Anat. 1838. Not of Cuvier. Type *Anas labradora*, GM.

Camptolaemus, GRAY, List Genera, 1841. Same type.

CH.—Bill broad, with the edges nearly parallel, but widening towards the tip, this expansion consisting of a tough membrane. Nostrils in the basal third of the bill as measured from the upper posterior angle. Feathers of cheek extending moderately forwards, convex anteriorly; those of chin reaching about as far. Bill nearly as long as the head, and considerably exceeding the tarsus. Feathers of cheeks stiffened and rigid. Tertials straight. Tail rather pointed.

The single species of this remarkable genus is almost entirely black and white in its colors.

CAMPTOLAEMUS LABRADORIUS, Gray.

Labrador Duck.

Anas labradoria, GMELIN, Syst. Nat. I, 1788, 557.—LATH. Ind. II, 1790, 859.

Anas labradora, WILSON, Am. Orn. VIII, 1814, 91; pl. lxix.

Anas (Fuligula) labradora, BON. Obs. Wils. 1825, No. 276.

Fuligula labradora, BON Syn. 1828, 391.—NUTT. Man. II, 428.—AUD. Orn. Biog. IV, 1838, 271; pl. 332.—IB. Syn. 288.—IB. Birds Am. VI, 1843, 329; pl. 400.

Rhynchaspis labradora, STEPHENS, Shaw's Zool. XII, 1824, 121.

Camptorhynchus labradorius, EYTON, Mon. Anat. 1838, 151.—BON. List.

Camptolaemus labradorius, GRAY, List Genera, 1841.

Fuligula grisea, LEIB, J. A. N. Sc. Phil. VIII, 1840, 170. Young.

Pied duck, PENN. II, 594.

SP. CH.—Bill black; yellowish along the base and a little in front of nostrils. Central line along the vertex, a ring around the lower part of the neck, extended broadly behind and above along the median line, and then continuous with the interscapular region, lower part of back and rump, with the entire under parts and sides, black. Head and neck, a half collar below the black ring, and the sides of the jugulum, scapulars, axillars, and entire wing on both sides, excepting the primaries, white; the primaries plumbeous black. The scapulars and tertials tinged with lead gray on some of the inner webs, the tertials externally margined narrowly with black.

Female entirely plumbeous gray; more dusky beneath. Wing without white on the upper coverts and scapulars; the tertials hoary plumbeous.

Length, 23.75; wing, 8.80; tarsus, 1.60; commissure, 2.50.

Hab.—Northeastern coast of North America.

List of specimens.

Catal. No.	Sex.	Locality.	Whence obtained.	Collected by—
1972	♂	North Atlantic_____	S. F. Baird _____	J. J. Audubon ___
2733	♀	_____do_____ ___	_____do_____	_____do_____

OIDEMIA, Fleming.

Oidemia, FLEMING, "Philos. Zool. 1822." Type *Anas nigra*, LINN.

CH.—Bill much swollen at base, the terminal portion much depressed and very broad. Nail broad, occupying the terminal portion of the bill. Nostrils situated anterior to the middle of the commissure. Feathers of the chin running forwards as far as the nostrils. Color black, with or without small patches of white.

The scoters or black sea ducks, although differing in the character of the bill to a certain extent, have yet so close a relationship that it may be questioned whether there is any foundation for generic divisions. For greater convenience in indicating these variations in the form of the bill, I shall at any rate consider the sections as sub-genera of *Oidemia*. The group *Oidemieae* of Bonaparte corresponds to *Oidemia* as characterized above.

A. Feathers extending forward in the forehead nearly to the posterior border of nostrils, and for nearly or quite half the length of the lateral edge of bill; nostrils broad and open.

MELANETTA, Boie.[1]—Feathers extending nearly as far forward on the sides of bill as above, leaving the edges only free from the base. Bill very broad; nail broad and almost truncate.

Male. Bill black at base and edges, red at tip; a small white patch around the eye and large white wing speculum. *Female* brown, with the white speculum on wing; sides of head whitish; bill black...........................*M. velvetina.*

PELIONETTA, Kaup.[2]—Feathers not extending on sides of bill at all. Nail pointed anteriorly. Colors black, with a triangular white patch on top of head and another on nape. Bill red, with a rounded black lateral spot at base.

Patch on top of head large, extending between posterior outline of eyes. Nostrils very open, rather obtuse anteriorly. Frontal feathers extending half the length of edge of bill, and to posterior border of nostrils..................*P. perspicillata.*

Patch on top of head much anterior to the eyes and very small. Frontal feathers extending for two-fifths the length of edge of bill, not as far as the nostrils, which are more linear and acute anteriorly than in the last.......*P. trowbridgii.*

B. Feathers of the forehead scarcely extending on the base of bill at all; the nostrils situated about midway between their anterior border and the tip of bill. Nail rather acute anteriorly.

OIDEMIA, Fleming.[3]—Color entirely black. Bill black on edges and end; swollen basal portion red..*O. americana.*

---

[1] *Melanitta*, BOIE, Isis, 1822.—*Maceranas*, LESSON, Man. II, 1828, 414. Type *Anas fusca*, LINN.
[2] *Pelionetta*, KAUP, Entw. Europ. Thierw. 1829. Type *Anas perspicillata*, L.
[3] *Oidemia*, FLEMING, Philos. Zool. 1822. Type *Anas nigra*, L.

A fifth species of *Oidemia*, probably a *Pelionetta*, if distinct, is mentioned at the end of the others as copied from the account of Herbert. If really *Pelionetta*, its diagnosis would be bill black; secondaries and eye patch white as in *Melanetta*.

MELANETTA VELVETINA, Baird.

Velvet Duck; White-winged Coot.

Anas fusca, WILSON, Am. Orn. VIII, 1814, 137 ; pl. lxxii. Not of Linnaeus.

Anas (Fuligula) fusca, BON. Obs. 1825, No. 266.

Fuligula (Oidemia) fusca, BON. Syn. 1828, 390.—NUTT. Man. II, 1834, 419.

Oidemia fusca, SW. F. Bor. Am. II, 1831, 449.

Fuligula fusca, AUD. Orn. Biog. III, 1835, 454 ; pl. 247.—IB. Syn. 1839, 280.—IB. Birds Amer. VI, 1843, 332 ; pl. 401.

Oidemia velvetina, CASSIN, Pr. A. N. Sc. V, Oct. 1850, 126.

Oidemia deglandii, BON. Rev. Crit. Orn. Degland, 1850, 108.—IB. Comptes Rendus, XXXVIII, 1854, Notes Orn. Delattre, 94.

Melanetta deglandii, BON. Comptes Rendus, XLIII, Sept. 1856.

Double macreuse d'Amerique, DEGLAND, Orn. Europ. II, 1849, 474.

SP. CH.—*Male.* Bill very broad, wider towards the tip than at the base ; feathers extending far along the side of the bill, and on the forehead, for nearly half the commissure, running in an obtuse point about as far forward as the lower corner of the outline of feathers on the side, both reaching nearly to the posterior border of the large, open, nearly rounded nostrils ; culmen horizontal a little beyond the frontal feathers, then abruptly bent downwards, nearly perpendicularly, to the much depressed, nearly horizontal portion ; a sharp indented ridge along the base of culmen, ending in a trihedral tubercle. Color black ; a white elongated patch around and a little behind the eye, and a large white speculum on the wing composed of white secondaries and tips of greater coverts ; bill black at base and lateral edges ; red elsewhere.

Female somewhat similar, but lighter beneath ; a large whitish patch on the side of the head behind the eye, but none around it ; wings with white speculum, somewhat as in the male ; bill also similar, but less swollen and elevated at base. Length, 21.50 inches ; wing, 11.30 ; tarsus, 2.08 ; commissure, 2.82.

Hab.—Along both coasts of North America, to the north.

The dates of publication of *Oidemia velvetina* of Cassin, and of *O. deglandii* of Bonaparte, are so near together as to render it difficult to say which should have priority. I have, however, taken Mr. Cassin's as being more in harmony with a common vernacular name.

The difference of the American Velvet Duck from the European *O. fusca* according to Degland, Ornith. Europ. (II, 474,) consists in the greater extension of the feathers of the forehead over the bill, causing it to appear shorter. The white spot of the lower eyelid is also much larger, and more triangular in shape.

List of specimens.

Catal. No.	Sex.	Locality.	When collected.	Whence obtained.	Orig'l No.	Collected by—	Length.	Stretch of wings.	Wing.	Remarks.
905	♀	Potomac river, D. C....	Dec. —, 1842	S. F. Baird		....	19.75	36.00	10.16	....
9851	......	Presidio,(near S. Fra'co)	....	Lt. Trowbridge ..		....	......	......	......	....
4519	......	San Francisco.........	....	Lt. Williamson..		....	......	......	......	....
9850	......	Bodega, Cal...........	Jan. —, 1855	Lt. Trowbridge...		T. A. Szabo...	......	......	......	....
9852	♂	Mouth of Columbia....	Mar. 2, 1854	Gov. Stevens	56	Dr. Cooper ...	21.50	38.00	......	Iris very pale gray, feet black and purple.
9853	♀	.......do......	Mar. 9, 1854	......do..........	59	......do........	21.25	38.00	......	Iris brown, bill and feet black and purple.
4405	♀	Puget's Sound, W. T ...	April 5, 1855	Dr. Suckley......	188	....	22.25	39.25	12.00	....
4573	......	Port Steilacoom........	Feb. 6, 1856	......do..........	214	....	......	......	......	Iris white...............
4575	.....	.......do......	....	......do..........	212	....	23.00	38.75	11.50	....
4576	♂	.......do...............	Feb. 1, 1850	..... do..........	211	....	22.50	39.00	11.50	....

PELIONETTA PERSPICILLATA, Kaup.

Surf Duck; Sea Coot.

Anas perspicillata, LINN. Syst. Nat. I, 1766, 201.—FORST. Phil. Trans. LXII, 1772, 383.—GMELIN, I, 524.—
  LATH. Ind. II, 1790, 847.—WILSON, Am. Orn. VIII, 1814, 49 ; pl. lxvii.
Melanitta perspicilla'a, BOIE, Isis, 1822, 564.—EYTON. Mon. Anat. 1838, 146.
Anas (Fuligula) perspicillata, BON. Obs. Wils. 1825, No. 265.
Fuligula (Oidemia) perspicillata, BON. Syn. 1828, 389.—NUTTALL, Man. II, 416.
Oidemia perspicillata, FLEMING, Philos. Zool. 1822?—SWAINSON, F. Bor. Am. II, 1831, 449.—MACGIL. Man. II, 181,
  Am. Sp.—BON. List, 1838.
" *Pelionetta perspicillata*, KAUP," REICH. Icones Av.—BONAP. Comptes Rendus, XLIII, Sept. 1856.
Fuligula perspicillata, AUD. Orn. Biog. IV, 1838, 161 ; pl. 317.—IB. Syn. 289.—IB. Birds Am. VI, 1843, 337 ;
  pl. 402.
  Black Duck, Pennant, II, 556.

SP. CH.—*Male.* Tail of 14 feathers. Bill but little longer than the head, the feathers extending forward half way from the base to the tip, and opposite the posterior border of the nostril ; the bill abruptly decurved or gibbous anterior to the end of the feathers ; nostrils open, nearly semicircular or stirrup shaped, the straight portion of the outline antero-inferior ; sides of bill swollen at the base so as to be further apart above than below.

Color, entirely black throughout, with a greenish lustre above, duller beneath ; a triangular white patch on the top of head, the base extending between the posterior outline of the eye and reaching forward to a point a little beyond the posterior line of the bill, the outlines rounded laterally and anteriorly ; the patch is separated from the eye by a narrow superciliary black space. There is a second triangular white patch beginning on the nape as a straight line the width of the other patch and running backwards for more than two inches. These triangular spaces are thus base to base.

Female. Bill as long as that of the male, but not swollen at the base, where the sides approach each other above ; the feathers of forehead do not extend one third the distance from base to tip of bill ; the middle of nostril not quite as far as the middle of the bill ; nostrils linear, acutely pointed anteriorly.

Color brown ; lighter on the neck. Sides and beneath the under surface of the body whitish. An obscure whitish patch at the base of the bill, and another on the side of the head behind the eyes.

Length of male, 19.00 ; wing, 9.40 ; tarsus, 1.63 ; commissure, 2.37.

Hab.—On and near seacoast of North America, quite far south in winter. Accidental in Europe.

List of specimens.

Catal. No.	Sex & age.	Locality.	When collected.	Whence obtained.	Orig. No.	Collected by—	Length.	Stretch of wings.	Wing.	Remarks.
913	♂	Philadelphia....................	....	S. F. Baird........	......	....	....	....	....	....
1719	○♀	Carlisle, Pa.................	Oct. 12,1844	......do.........	......	....	17.75	31.00	8.80	....
6904	......	Nelson river, H.B.T........	....	D. Gunn..........	......	Jno. Isbister.....	....	....	....	....
9856	......	Presidio, (near San Francisco)	....	Lt. Trowbridge...	......	T. A. Szabo.......	....	....	....	....
9858	......	...... do............	....	......do.........	......	......do..	....	....	....	....
9856	......	Bodega, Cal...............	Feb. —, 1855	......do.........	......	......do.........	....	....	....	White eye ring. ..
9862	♂	Shoalwater bay..........	April 28, 1854	Gov. Stevens. ..	66	Dr. Cooper......	20.00	33.00	....	Iris white........
9550	......	Mud bay, Puget's Sound, W.T.	Nov. 29, 1857	A. Campbell......	72	Dr. Kennerly.....	18.50	29.00	7.50	....
577	......	Fort Steilacoom, W.T........	....	Dr. Suckley.....	......	....	21.60	34.00	......	....
9553	......	Simiahmoo bay, W.T.........	Oct. 14......	A. Campbell......	56	Dr. Kennerly.....	....	....	....	....
9551	♂	......do.....	Nov. 30,1858	......do.........	......	......do.........	....	....	....	....

PELIONETTA TROWBRIDGII, Baird.

Long-billed Scoter.

SP. CH.—*Male.* Bill decidedly longer than the head, the frontal feathers extending over two-fifths its entire length from base to tip, and falling considerably behind the posterior border of the nostril. Nostrils open, but rather elongated and running out anteriorly in an acute point. Culmen sloping gently from the base and in a straight line with the forehead to the nail.

Color entirely black with a greenish gloss above ; a very small triangular white patch on the forehead reaching forward to the beginning of the bill, the posterior extremity considerably anterior to the eye ; a very broad triangular white patch on the nape, the feathers much longer and softer than elsewhere. Length 23.00 ; wing, 9.80 ; tarsus, 1.80 ; commissure, 2.72.

Hab.—Coast of southern California in winter.

This species is much like *O. perspicillata*, but is larger. The bill is more like that of the female *O. perspicillata* than of the male. It is longer and rather narrower, less swollen at the base. The frontal feathers do not extend so far forward, falling considerably behind the nostrils. The culmen is in a line with the forehead to the end of nostrils, instead of descending abruptly. The nostrils are narrower, more elongate and acute anteriorly. The white patch on the head is very much smaller and anterior to the eye, instead of coming back to the line of the posterior canthus. The nuchal patch is larger, broader, fuller and softer.

List of specimens.

Catal. No.	Sex.	Locality.	When collected.	Whence obtained.	Collected by—	Length.	Stretch of wings.	Wing.
9860	♂	San Diego, Cal.	1853	Lieut. Trowbridge.	A. Cassidy.	20.00	30.00	
9861	♂	....do.		....do.	....do.			
9859 ?	♀ ?	....do.		Lieut. Williamson.				

OIDEMIA AMERICANA, Swainson.

Scoter.

Anas nigra, WILSON, Am. Orn. VIII, 1814, 135; pl lxxii. Not of Linnaeus.

Anas (Fuligula) nigra, BON. Obs. Wilson, 1825, No. 267.

Fuligula (Oidemia) nigra, BON. Syn. 1828, 390.

Oidemia americana, SWAINSON, F. Bor. Am. II, 1831, 450.—BON. List, 1838.

Melanetta americana, EYTON, Mon. Anat. 1838, 144.

Fuligula americana, AUD. Orn. Biog. V, 1839, 117; pl. 408.—IB. Syn. 290.—IB. Birds Amer. VI, 1843, 343; pl. 403.

SP. CH.—*Male.* Tail of sixteen feathers. Bill much swollen on the basal third; the basal portion of culmen convex and rapidly descending ; the terminal portion of bill much depressed ; the anterior extremity of nostrils half way from the lateral or upper feathers at the base of bill to the tip. The swelling at base of bill divided by a furrow along the median line. The frontal feathers extend slightly forward in an obtuse point. Bill of female not very dissimilar, lacking the swelling at the base.

Color entirely black all over, without any white. Bill black along the edges and tip; the swollen basal portion red to beyond the nostrils.

Female. Brown; lighter on sides of head, throat, and under surface of body, where the feathers have each an obscure dusky spot.

Length, 23.80 ; wing, 9.20 ; tarsus, 1.78 ; commissure, 2.14.

Hab.—Seacoast of North America.

According to Degland, (Orn. Europ. II, 472,) the American scoter differs from the European in having the bill broader, the gibbosity less elevated, wider, and entirely orange from the frontal feathers to the nostrils : while in *A. nigra* the yellow begins only at the base of the tuberosity, surrounds the nostrils, and occupies only the centre of the middle portion of the bill. The basal protuberance, too, in the American bird is single, with a median sinuosity ; while in the European it is formed by two hemispheres, separated by a furrow.

List of specimens.

Catal. No.	Sex.	Locality.	When collected.	Whence obtained.	Length.	Stretch of wings.	Wing.
2722	♂	Atlantic coast, U. S...........	....	S. F. Baird	......	......	......
904	♀	Potomac river, D. C.	Dec. —, 1842	.......do...................	19.00	33.00	9.00
4574	....	Fort Steilacoom, W. T.	....	Dr. Suckley	21.50	36.25	9.75

OIDEMIA (PELIONETTA) BIMACULATA, Baird.

Huron Scoter.

Fuligula bimaculata, HERBERT, Field Sports U. S. 2d ed. II, 1848, 366. With wood-cut figure.

Sp. Ch.—Bill shorter than the head. Nostrils nearer to the tip than to the angle of the mandibles by nearly one-fifth. Feathers advancing on the top of the bill for about one-third its length.

Bill bluish black; iris brown; legs and feet dusky crimson. General color sooty black. Forehead, encroaching on the upper mandible, dull brownish black; chin, throat, and upper breast, dark cinereous gray. Belly and vent lighter than the breast, and more silvery. Under tail coverts and beneath the tail dark dingy gray. Under wing coverts dark cinereous gray. Secondaries snowy white. A dingy white patch anterior to the eye, and occupying the whole insertion of the upper mandible from the front downwards. Posterior and slightly inferior to the eye is a larger and brighter white spot, of an elongated and acute oval form running towards the nape. *Female* generally similar, but more dingy; more silvery gray beneath. Legs and feet dusky orange. Size less.

Length, 18.50; bill along gape, 2.20; from extremity of front to tip, 1.50; wing, 10.50; extent, 24.50; tarsus, 1.60; middle and outer toe, 2.90; inner toe, 2.50; weight, 2¼ pounds.

Hab.—Lake Huron and adjacent waters in fall and winter.

In the preceding description, condensed from the original account by Herbert, (Frank Forester,) will be found a notice of a scoter, supposed by him to be new. If the bird described were really an adult, there can be no question as to it being a fifth species of American *Oidemia*. The shape of bill is like that of *Pelionetta perspicillata*, but differs in being black throughout instead of red. The colors of body are more those of *Melanetta velvetina*, in the white secondaries, and white patch behind the eye, and in the absence of the white patches on top of head and on the nape of *P. perspicillata*.

The only reason to suspect immaturity is on account of the absence of the continuous and velvet black color all over the body, except where relieved by white, so characteristic of all adult males of the genus *Oidemia*. Still this would not explain the combination of the bill of *Pelionetta* with the colors of *Melanetta*, the former never having white secondaries. A hybrid between the two might possibly account for this union, but in the large number of specimens referred to by Herbert this is not likely to have been the case.

SOMATERIA, Leach.

Somateria, LEACH, in FLEMING's Philos. Zool. 1822. Type *Anas mollissima*, L.

Ch.—Bill much compressed, tapering to the tip; the nail enormously large, and forming the terminal portion of the bill, and much decurved. The feathers of forehead advancing forward in an acute long point, separating on each side a frontal extension or linear process, or the feathers of the cheek may be said to extend a considerable distance along the commissural edge of the bill. Nostrils situated anterior to the middle of the commissure. Tail rather pointed, but short; of 14 feathers.

In giving the two well known species of this genus, I add a third, recently described by G. R. Gray, from the northwest coast of North America.

Common characters.—Colors white and black; head with a gloss of emerald green; belly, rump, and tail, black.

White. Belly, rump, quills, and stripe on each side of head above eyes, black. Frontal process on each side nearly in line with culmen; rounded behind......................*S. mollissima.*

Similar to last; with a V-shaped black mark on chin......................................*S. V-nigra.*

Black. Body and neck anterior to shoulders, middle coverts, inside of wing, patch on each side the rump, white. Head above and nape bluish ash. Margin of frontal process and a V-shaped mark on chin black. Frontal process of bill on each side bent abruptly upwards, out of line with culmen, and sub-rectangular......................................*S. spectabilis.*

SOMATERIA MOLLISSIMA, Leach.

Eider Duck.

Anas mollissima, LINN. Syst. Nat. I, 1766, 198.—GMELIN, I, 514.—LATH. Ind. II, 1790, 845.—WILSON, Am. Orn. VIII, 1814, 122; pl. lxxi.

Somateria mollissima, LEACH, Fleming, Philos. Zool. 1822 ?—SWAINSON, F. Bor. Am. II, 1831, 448.—BON. List, 1838.— BRANDT, Mém. Ac. St. Pet. Sc. Nat. VI, 1849, 5.

Anas (Fuligula) mollissima, BON. Obs. Wils. 1825, 244.

Fuligula (Somateria) mollissima, BON. Syn. 1828, 388.—NUTT. Man. II, 1834, 407.

Platypus mollissimus, BREHM.

Fuligula mollissima, AUD. Orn. Biog. III, 1835, 344 : V, 611, pl. 246.—IB. Syn. 291.—IB. Birds Amer. VI, 1843, 349; pl. 405.

Anas cuthbertii, PALLAS.

Somateria St. cuthbertii, EYTON, Mon. Anat. 1838, 149.

Eider, or Cuthbert Duck, PENNANT.

SP. CH.—Tail of 14 feathers. Prevailing color white ; the under surface and sides of body, hinder part of back, rump, and tail, black. Wings white on both surfaces, except the quills, which are black. Narrow margin inferiorly of the frontal process of bill and the forehead violet black, this color bifurcating opposite the middle of the eye, and continued broadly on each side the head to the nape, the color extending a little below the eye ; the white below and behind the black glossed with transparent emerald green ; the interspace white. Length, 26; wing, 11.24; tarsus, 1.82 ; commissure, 2.53.

Hab.—Atlantic and Arctic coasts of northern hemisphere; Pacific coast N. A.?

There is a faint tinge of purplish cream color in the white, especially conspicuous on the breast and wings. The black of the back and belly is separated by white on the flanks.

The tertials have a slight outward bend, but much less than in *S. spectabilis*. The frontal process of the bill is elongated and rounded behind, and about in a line with the culmen.

List of specimens.

Catal. No.	Sex.	Locality.	Whence obtained.
480	♂	North Atlantic...........	S. F. Baird...........

August 20, 1858.

102 b

SOMATERIA V-NIGRA, Gray.

Pacific Eider.

Somateria V-nigra, GRAY, Pr. Zool. Soc. 1855, 212; pl. cvii. Kotzbue Sound, NW. coast of Am.

SP. CH.—Similar to *S. mollissima,* but larger, and with a V-shaped black mark on chin, as in *S. spectabilis.* The white longitudinal mark on the top of the head narrower than in *mollissima;* the black less rounded posteriorly. The bill of male is orange yellow, with white nail; of female dusky green. Feet brownish yellow.

Hab.—Kotzbue Sound, NW. coast of America.

The above description, (taken from G. R. Gray,) refers to a well marked species which appears to replace the common eider on our northwest coast. It is essentially an eider, in all respects, with the black V-shaped marks on the chin seen in the king duck. The female is brown, as in the eider.

SOMATERIA SPECTABILIS, Leach.

King Eider.

Anas spectabilis, LINN. Syst. Nat. I, 1766, 195.—GMELIN, I, 567.

Somateria spectabilis, LEACH, Flem. Philos. Zool. 1822?—SWAINS. F. Bor. Am. II,¦ 1831, 447.—BON. List. 1838.— EYTON, Mon. Anat. 1838, 148.—BRANDT, Mem. Ac. St. Pet. Sc. Nat. vi, Ser. VI, 1849, 5.

Fuligula (Somateria) spectabilis, BONAP. Syn. 1828, 389.—NUTTALL, Man. II, 1834, 414.

Fuligula spectabilis, AUD. Orn. Biog. III, 1835, 523; pl. 276.—IB. Syn. 1839.—IB. Birds Amer. VI, 1843, 347; pl. 404.

King Duck, PENNANT, II, 554.

SP. CH.—Body and wings black; the portion anterior to the shoulder joint, interscapular region in part, most of neck and throat, white; the jugulum with a creamy tinge. A narrow border to the frontal processes of the bill and their interspace. Small space round the eye and a V-shaped mark on the chin black. Top of head and nape bluish ash, slightly spotted with black. Midddle wing coverts, tips of secondaries, axillars, and most of under surface of wing, with a patch on each side of the rump, white. Sides of head glossed with transparent emerald green.

The scapulars have the black tinged with slate.

Length, 21.50; wing, 10,70; tarsus, 1.86; commissure, 2.53.

Hab.—Arctic regions of northern hemisphere. Pacific coast.?

I have not at hand the female of either this species or the eider. They differ in being chiefly brown.

The tertials in this species are bent outwards, so that the points project beyond the edge of the wing, about the middle of the outer primary. The frontal process of the bill is dilated and nearly quadrilateral; it is bent abruptly upwards, so as to be out of line with the culmen. The nostrils are large, oval, and open.

List of specimens.

Catal. No.	Sex.	Locality.	Whence obtained.
1973	♂	North Atlantic	S. F. Baird

Sub-Family ERISMATURINAE.

The most prominent character of the *Erismaturinae* is found in the very rigid tail feathers with the much abbreviated coverts, which leave the greater portion of the tail exposed.   There are peculiarities in the nail at the end of the bill in *Erismatura* not found in the other sub-families.

ERISMATURA, B o n a p.

Oxyura, BONAP. Syn. 1828.   Type *Anas rubida*.   Sufficiently distinct from *Oxyurus.?*   Type *Anas leucocephala*, Scop. *Erismatura*, BONAP. Saggio, etc., 1832.

CH.—Bill broad, rather high at the base, much depressed, and bent upwards.   Upper lateral angle of bill running back on the forehead some distance; farther than the lower edge of the bill.   Nostrils reaching to the middle of the bill, rather small. Portion of nail seen from above very narrow and linear; bent abruptly downwards and backwards at the tip so as to be invisible from the upper surface.   Tarsi very short, scarcely more than one-third the long feet.   Tail very stiff; of 18 feathers. The coverts above and below very much abbreviated, so as to expose the greater part of the tail.   The feathers narrow, linear.   The shafts very large, and channelled on the under surface near the base.   Wings very short, and incurved at the end.

Of this genus there are several species belonging to America, although but one is well established as an inhabitant of the United States.   Dr. Cabot, however, has recently announced the occurrence of the *E. dominica* on Lake Champlain.

Comparative measurements of species.

Catal. No.	Species.	Locality.	Sex.	Length.	Stretch of wings.	Wing.	Tail.	Tarsus.	Middle toe.	Its claw alone.	Bill above.	Along gape.	From lateral feathers.	Specimen measured.
315	Erismatura rubida	Carlisle, Pa...........	♂	16.00	....	5.80	3.64	1.26	2.52	0.36	1.62	1.80	1.86	Skin. ......
1184	........do....................	......do..............	♀	15.00	....	5.80	3.56	1.26	2.50	0.34	1.68	1.80	1.82	Skin........
do.	........do....................	......do..............	......	15.00	23.75	6.00	......	......	....	.....	....	......	......	Fresh.....

ERISMATURA RUBIDA, B o n a p.

Ruddy Duck.

Anas rubida, WILSON, Am. Orn. VIII, 1814, 128, 130 ; pl. lxxxi.

Anas (Fuligula) rubida, BON. Obs. Wils. 1825, 268.

Fuligula (Oxyura) rubida, BON. Syn. 1828, 390.

Fuligula (Gymnura) rubida, NUTTALL, Man. II, 1834, 426.

Fuligula rubida, Sw. F. Bor. Am. II, 1831, 455.—AUD. Orn. Biog. IV, 1838, 326 ; pl. 343.—IB. Syn. 288.—IB. Birds Am. VI, 1843, 324 ; pl. 399.

Erismatura rubida, BONAP. List, 1838.—EYTON, Mon. Anat. 1838, 171.

Anas jamaicensis, "LATH."—ORD, ed. Wilson, VIII, 1825, 138.

SP. CH.—Bill grayish blue.   Top of head and nape black.   Sides of head below the eyes, with the chin, pure opaque white. Lower part of neck all round, and the entire upper parts, with upper portion of sides, chestnut red.   Under parts generally lustrous grayish white, with an occasional brownish tinge ; crissum pure white ; wings brown, without speculum, finely and almost inappreciably sprinkled with gray ; tail nearly black.

Female with the entire upper parts dark brown ; the back and wing coverts finely sprinkled with grayish.   The under parts brownish white, tinged with greenish brown across the lower part of neck.   The brown of the head comes down below the level of the eye, and there is an obscure dusky stripe parallel with its lower outline, from the commissure.

Length, 16.00 ; wing, 5.80 ; tarsus, 1.26 ; commissure, 1.80.

Hab.—Whole of North America.   Abundant throughout the interior.

The continuity of the white of the under parts is interrupted by the occasional appearance of the basal brown of the feathers, owing to the shortness of the white tip, which thus gives rise to the appearance of dusky transverse bands.

Sometimes the females have the upper parts waved transversely with brownish yellow. Generally there is no white on the wings, but in one specimen from San Pasqual the secondaries and the greater tail coverts are narrowly tipped with white.

List of specimens.

Catal. No.	Sex.	Locality.	When collected.	Whence obtained.	Orig. No.	Collected by—	Length.	Stretch of wings.	Wing.	Remarks.
1184	......	Carlisle, Pa............	Oct. 26, 1843	S. F. Baird	......	....	15.00	23.75	6.00	....
315	......	......do.............	Oct. 27, 1843	......do.....	......	....	15.50	23.00	......	....
4551	♂	Washington, D. C......	April —, 1856	Market...........	228	....	......	......	......	....
5472	♀	Near mouth Platte river.	Oct. —, 1856	Lieut. Warren......	......	Dr. Hayden..	13.50	21.00	5.75	Iris very dark brown ....
4635	......	White river, Neb........	May —, 1855	Col. A. Vaughan..	......	......do......	......	......	......	....
8635	♀	100 m. east of Laramie..	Oct. 10, 1857	Wm. M. Magraw.	217	Dr. Cooper...	15.00	23.00	5.75	Iris brown, bill black, feet black.
5138	......	Crossing of Pecos, N. M.	Jan. 10, 1855	Capt. Pope	97	Dr. Kennerly..	......	......	......	....
9848	......	Janos, Mex............	April —, 1855	Maj. Emory......	65	Dr. Kennerly..	......	......	......	....
9847	......	San Pasqual, Cal.	Nov. 21, 1854	......do.........	10	A. Schott.....	......	......	......	....
4607	......	......do.........	....	......do.........	......	......do......	15.50	22.00	6.00	Eyes reddish brown, bill black, feet gray.
9846	......	Bodega, Cal............	Dec. —, 1854	Lieut. Trowbridge	......	T. A. Szabo..	......	......	......	....

Sub-Family MERGINAE.

Cн.—Bill very slender, narrow, compressed, terminated by a conspicuous nail. Edges much serrated, the serrations projecting. Tarsi much compressed ; the scales anteriorly large and transverse, becoming smaller and smaller on the sides and behind. Tail feathers 18 in North American species.

The *Merginae* or fishing ducks are represented in the United States by three well established species, placed by modern systematists in as many genera. Two of these, however, are so nearly alike that I prefer to consider them as the same ; the third is sufficiently distinct. The *Mergus albellus* of Europe is scarcely entitled to a place in our fauna.

The genera adopted may easily be recognized by the following characters :

MERGUS.—Most of bill red. Serrations acute, recurved. Tarsi two-thirds the length of middle toe. Head with a depressed crest.

LOPHODYTES.—Bill black. Serrations oblique. Tarsi half the middle toe. Head with an erect vertical crest.

Comparative measurements of species.

Catal. No.	Species.	Locality.	Sex.	Length.	Stretch of wings.	Wing.	Tail.	Tarsus.	Middle toe.	Its claw alone.	Bill above, from feathers.	Along gape.	Bill, from side.	Specimen measured.
1304	Mergus americanus........	Carlisle, Pa..........	♂	....	......	10.86	4.86	1.84	2.76	0.40	2.07	2.90	2.54	Skin.....
do.	........do.	......do............	......	26.50	38.25	11.00	......	......	......	......	......	......	......	Fresh....
879	........do....	......do............	♀	21.00	......	9.70	4.80	1.72	2.48	0.35	1.90	2.33	2.10	Skin....
do.	........do...............	......do............	......	23.25	33.50	9.75	......	......	......	......	......	......	......	Fresh....
311	Mergus serrator	......do............	♂	22.50	......	8.60	4.00	1.80	2.65	0.48	2.24	2.76	2.30	Skin....
do.	........do...............	......do............	......	23.25	33.00	......	......	......	......	......	......	......	......	Fresh....
8679	........do...............	Cape Florida.......	♀	......	......	9.10	3.96	1.74	2.56	0.36	2.18	2.56	2.34	Skin....
do.	........do	......do............	......	20.00	31.50	9.00	......	......	......	......	......	......	......	Fresh....
1311	Lophodytes cucullatus	Carlisle, Pa.........	♂	17.00	......	7.90	4.26	1.20	2.20	0.34	1.50	1.98	1.70	Skin....
do.	........do...............	......do............	......	17.50	26.25	7.32	......	......	......	......	......	......	......	Fresh....
1306	........do...............	......do............	♀	16.30	......	7.30	4.14	1.02	1.96	0.28	1.48	1.86	1 66	Skin....
do.	........do...............	......do............	......	17.50	25.00	7.40	......	......	......	......	......	......	......	Fresh...
209	........do...............	......do............	♀	15.10	......	7.10	4.12	1.20	2.06	0.32	1.43	1.76	1.60	Skin.....

MERGUS, Linnaeus.

Mergus, LINNAEUS, Syst. Nat. 1735. Type *M. castor*, L.

CH.—Bill longer than the head, mostly red ; serrations conical, acute, recurved. Crest occipital, pointed, or depressed. Tarsus about two-thirds the middle toe. Tail about half the length of wings.

The two North American species of this genus are very differently marked, though the females are quite similar. In external form they differ considerably from *Lophodytes cucullatus*, and to a less extent among themselves. The difference is chiefly in the position of the nostril, and the outline of the feathers at the base of the bill, as well as in the shape of the crest.

The species may be briefly characterized as follows:

Nostril near the middle of the bill ; the frontal feathers extending much beyond the lateral. Head without conspicuous crest. Head and neck green. Beneath salmon colored. Sides without transverse bars. Wing white from the extreme bend, crossed by one black bar.

M. americanus.

Nostril towards the base of bill. Lateral feathers extending beyond the frontal. Head with pointed occipital crest. Head and upper part of neck green ; jugulum light reddish brown, streaked with black ; feathers in front of elbow white, margined with black. Sides finely barred transversely with black. Edge of wing brown ; its white crossed by two black bars.

M. serrator.

MERGUS AMERICANUS, Cassin.

Goosander; Sheldrake; Fish Duck.

Mergus merganser, WILS. Am. Orn. VIII, 1814, 68 ; pl. lxviii. Not of Linnaeus.—BON. Obs. Wils. 1825, 248.— DOUGHTY, Cab. I, 1830, 109 ; pl. x.—SW. F. Bor. Am. II, 1831, 461.—NUTT. Man. II, 1834, 460.—AUD. Orn. Biog. IV, 1838, 261 ; pl. 331.—IB. Syn. 1839, 297.—IB. Birds Amer. VI, 1843, 387 ; pl. 411.

Mergus americanus, CASSIN, Pr. A. N. Sc. VI, 1853, 187.

Merganser castor, var. A. *americanus*, BON. Comptes Rendus XLIII, 1856.

SP. CH.—Feathers of the forehead extending on the bill in an acute angle for half the distance between those on the sides and the nostril ; outline of those on the sides nearly vertical and reaching but little beyond the beginning of lower edge of bill, but as far as those on the side of lower jaw. Nostril large, far forward, its middle opposite the middle of the commissure.

Male. Head without conspicuous crest. Head and neck green. Fore part of back black ; beneath salmon color. Wings mostly white, crossed by one band of black. Sides scarcely barred transversely.

Female. Head with a compressed occipital crest. Head and neck chestnut. Above ashy ; beneath salmon colored. White of greater coverts with a terminal bar of ashy, (sometimes wanting ;) the black of base of secondaries entirely concealed. Outer tertials ash.

Length, 26.50 ; wing, 11.00 ; tarsus, 1.84 ; commissure, 2.90.

Hab.--Whole of North America.

Head without conspicuous crest, though one is visible in life. Head and most of neck all round very dark green; rest of neck and the body generally, except the upper part, creamy white, deepening to salmon red beneath. Lower part of back, rump, and tail feathers, plumbeous. Fore part of back, interscapular region, and inner scapulars, black. Axillars, inside of wings, coverts, most of secondaries, and tertials, with the outer scapulars, creamy white; the greater coverts black at the base, forming a black bar and the tertials narrowly edged, externally, with the same.   The primaries and outer secondaries are black; the latter tipped with paler.

The female has a compressed occipital and nuchal crest; the head and neck chestnut brown; the chin yellowish white; the upper parts entirely bluish gray; the under parts like the male. The white on the wing is confined to the secondaries and the greater coverts, which are black at the base and brown at the end, producing a bar.   The tertials are entirely plumbeous.   The brown bar at the end of the greater coverts is sometimes wanting, leaving the speculum white.

According to Mr. Cassin the American "sheldrake," or goosander, differs from the European in having the prolonged feathers of the head almost restricted to the occiput and neck behind, while in the other species they begin almost at the base of the bill, and are erectile and crest-like.   On the greater wing coverts of the American bird there is always an exposed and conspicuous bar of black, which in the European is entirely concealed by the lesser coverts. Bonaparte says that the bill of the American species is shorter and thicker.

List of specimens.

Catal. No.	Sex.	Locality.	When collected.	Whence obtained.	Orig'l No.	Collected by—	Length.	Stretch of wings.	Wing.	Remarks.
1304	♂	Carlisle, Pa.............	Mar. 21, 1844	S. F. Baird.......	......	....	26.50	38.25	11.00	....
879	♀	......do...............	Nov. 25, 1842	......do..........	......	....	23.25	33.50	9.75	....
5473	......	Yellowstone river........	Aug. 16, 1856	Lt. Warren.....	......	Dr. Hayden....	....	....	....	....
5140	♀	Texas	Nov. 19, 1855	Capt. Pope	... ..	....	....	....	....	....
5139	......	Doña Ana, N. M.........	Nov. 17, 1855	......do..........	160	....	26.50	38.50	12.00	Feet red, bill red and black, eyes black.
9878	♀	St. Mary's Mission, R. mts.	Oct. 20, 1853	Gov. Stevens...	......	Dr. Suckley ...	....	....	....	....
9881	......	Boca Grande, Mexico....	Mar. —, 1855	Maj. Emory	33	Dr. Kennerly ..	....	....	....	....
9880	♂	Fort Vancouver.........	Dec. 9, 1853	Gov. Stevens....	......	Dr. Cooper.....	....	....	....	Bill and feet vermilion..
4413	......	Fort Dalles, O. T........	Jan. 7, 1855	Dr. Suckley......	155¼	....	....	....	....	....
9879	......	Puget's Sound	....	......do........	......	....	....	....	....	....
9877	......	Fort Steilacoom	April —, 1854	Gov. Stevens....	68	Dr. Suckley ...	....	....	....	....

MERGUS SERRATOR, Linn.

Red-breasted Merganser.

Mergus serrator, LINN. Syst. Nat. I, 1766, 208.—GM. I, 546.—WILSON, Am. Orn. VIII, 1814, 81; pl. lxix.—BON. Obs. 1825, No. 249.—SW. F. Bor. Am. II, 1831, 462.—NUTTALL, Man. II, 1834, 463.—EYTON, Mon. 1838, 175.—AUD. Orn. Biog. V, 1839, 92; pl. 401.—IB. Syn. 298.—IB. Birds Am. VI, 1843, 395; pl. 412.

Merganser serrator, STEPH. Shaw's Gen. Zool. XII, 1824, 165.—BON. List, 1838.

Mergus cristatus and *serratus*, BRÜNN. Orn. Bor. 1764, 23.

SP. CH.—Feathers of the forehead extending on the bill in a short obtuse angle, and falling far short of the end of those on the sides; the outline of the latter sloping rapidly forwards, and reaching halfway from the posterior end of the lower edge of bill to the nostrils, and far beyond those on the side of lower jaw.   Nostrils narrow, posterior; their posterior outline opposite the end of basal third of commissure.

Male. Head with conspicuous pointed occipital crest.   Head and upper part of neck, all around, dark green; under parts reddish white.   Jugulum reddish brown, streaked with black.   Sides conspicuously barred transversely with fine lines of black. Feathers anterior to wing, white, margined with black.   White of wing crossed by two bars of black.

Female. Head with compressed occipital crest; chestnut brown.   Body above ash; beneath reddish white.   The black at base of secondaries exposed; outer tertials white, edged with black.

Length, 23.25; wing, 8.60; tarsus, 1.80; commissure, 2.76.

Hab Whole o North America and Europe.

Head with an elongated slender occipital crest. Head and upper part of neck dark green, turning to black below and behind. Rest of neck and under parts generally cream white. Jugulum and sides of neck below light brownish red, streaked with black. Sides of body beneath wings sharply undulated transversely with white and black; the concealed portion of back mottled with black and gray. Feathers just before the bend of wing, white, margined sharply with black; the fore part of back, interscapulars, and inner long scapulars, with the primary quills, black. Wing coverts, secondaries, outer scapulars, and tertials, white; the wing showing two black bars across the base of the greater coverts and secondaries; the tertials edged externally with black.

Female with the head and neck above chestnut, tinged above with ashy; the upper parts bluish ash; the lower white. The white on the wing is confined to the ends of the greater coverts and of the secondaries; their basal portions black. There is no visible dark bar, as the coverts have none at their tips, and cover the basal black of the secondaries. The outer tertials are whitish, edged externally with black.

There is not the slightest difficulty in distinguishing the adult male birds of this species from *M. americanus*. The females likewise are very similar, but differ in the specific character of the bill. The colors are much the same. The greater coverts in *M. serrator* lack the terminal brown bar, while the black at the base of the secondaries is more extended, often showing externally, while in the other the dark bar is on the tips of the greater coverts; the basal black of the secondary quills more concealed. The outer tertials are mostly white, edged externally with black, instead of being plain bluish ash. The size is much less.

List of specimens.

Catal. No.	Sex.	Locality.	When collected.	Whence obtained.	Collected by—	Length.	Stretch of wings.	Wing.	Remarks.
311	♂	Carlisle, Pa..............	April 24, 1841	S. F. Baird.........	....	23.25	33.00	....	....
8679	♂	Cape Florida.............	Nov. 16, 1857	G. Würdermann....	....	20.00	31.50	9.00	Yellow iris ....
6902	....	Nelson river, H.B.T......	....	D. Gunn...........	....	....	....	....	....
9883	....	San Diego, Cal...........	....	Lt. Trowbridge.....	....	....	....	....	....
9885	....	......do................	....	......do	A. Cassidy........	....	....	....	....
9882	♂	San Francisco............	. ...	Lt. Williamson.....	Dr. Newberry	....	....	....	....
9887	....	Bodega, Cal.............	Mar. —, 1855	Lt. Trowbridge.....	F. A. Szabo........	....	....	....	Eye rings rose red......
9884	.. ...	Puget's Sound	....	....	....	....	....	....	....

LOPHODYTES, Reich.

Lophodytes, Reich. Syst. Av. 1852, p. ix.

Ch.—Bill shorter than the head, black. Serrations compressed, low, short, inserted obliquely on the edge of bill; the point truncated, and not recurved nor acute. Tail more than half the wings. Tarsi short; half the feet. Head with a much compressed, vertical, circular, and erect crest.

But a single species of this genus is known to naturalists.

LOPHODYTES CUCULLATUS, Reich.

Hooded Merganser.

Mergus cucullatus, LINN. Syst. Nat. I, 1766, 207.—GMELIN, I, 544.—WILSON, Am. Orn. VIII, 79; pl. lxix.—BON. Obs
No. 251.—SW. F. Bor. Am. II, 1831, 463.—NUTTALL, Man. II, 465.—AUD. Orn. Biog. III, 1835, 246 :
V, 619; pl. 233.—IB. Syn. 299.—IB. Birds Amer. VI, 1843, 402; pl. 413.—EYTON, Mon. Anat. 177.

Merganser cucullatus, BONAP. List, 1838.

Lophodytes cucullatus, REICH. Systema Avium, 1852, p. ix.—BONAP. Comptes Rendus, XLIII, 1856.

Round-crested Duck, CATESBY, Carol.

Hooded Merganser, PENNANT.

SP. CH.—Head with an elongated, compressed, semicircular crest. Anterior extremity of nostril reaching not quite as far as the
middle of commissure. Frontal feathers extending nearly as far as half the distance from lateral feathers to nostril; the latter
much beyond the feathers on side of lower mandible. Bill shorter than head.

Male. Bill black. Head, neck, and back black; under parts and centre of crest white. Sides chestnut brown, barred with
black. White anterior to the wing, crossed by two black crescents. Lesser coverts gray; white speculum with a basal and
median black bar; black tertials streaked centrally with white.

Female with a shorter and more pointed crest. The head and neck reddish brown; the back without pure black; the sides
without transverse bars; the white of wings less extended.

Length, 17.50; wing, 7.90; tarsus, 1.20; commissure, 1.98.

Hab.—Whole of North America.

The black border of the crest is about a quarter of an inch deep, the central portion snowy
white. The lower part of back and rump are dark brown. The greater coverts and secondaries
are black, tipped with white; the black showing at the base of both as two bars. The middle
coverts are ashy gray. The white of secondaries is confined to the outer webs. The axillars
and inside of wing are white.

The female has a much smaller crest, more like that of the female of the other species. The
head, neck, and jugulum are grayish chestnut brown; the back and top of head dark brown;
the chin whitish; the under parts purer white. The wing is somewhat similar; the white
more restricted, especially on the tertials; the middle coverts dark brown. The bill appears to
be blackish above, and reddish below.

Some specimens, perhaps young males in female plumage, have the reddish feathers of the
crest passing into whitish at the tips.

List of specimens.

Catal. No.	Sex.	Locality.	When collected.	Whence obtained.	Orig'l No.	Collected by—	Length.	Wing.	Remarks.
5475	♂	Yellowstone river	July 24	Lieut. Warren		Dr. Hayden			
5941		Doña Ana, New Mexico	Nov. 21,1855	Capt. Pope	164		19.00	8.00	Bill brown, iris yellow, feet gray.
9875		Fort Thorn		Dr. Henry					
9876	♀	Fort Steilacoom		Gov. Stevens	2	Dr. Suckley			
9874	♂	......do	Feb. 2,1854	......do	28	......do			
9873		......do		......do	48	......do			

MERGELLUS ALBELLUS, Selby.

Smew.

Mergus albellus, LINN. I, 1766, 209.—WILSON, Am. Orn. VIII, 1814, 126; pl. lxxi. (European sp. ?) —BON. Obs. Wils. 1825, 250.—NUTTALL, Man. II, 1834, 467.—AUD. Orn. Biog. IV, 1838, 350; pl. 347. (Female figured from Am. specimen; male from European.)—IB. Syn. 1839.—IB. Birds Amer. VI, 1843, 408; pl. 414.

Mergellus albellus, SELBY, Brit. Orn. 1840.

Mergus minutus, LINN. 1, 1766, 209, No. 6. Young.

Mergus albulus and pannonicus, SCOPOLI.

Mergus stellatus, BRÜNN. Orn. Bor. 98.

SP. CH.—Tail of 16 feathers. Bill shorter than the inner toe. General color white. Region round eye, patch on each side the nape, half collar on each side the lower neck, middle of back, tail, and wings black; the scapulars, middle wing coverts, tertials, and tips of greater coverts and secondaries white.

Female with head reddish brown.

Length, 17.50 inches; wing, 7.75; tarsus, 1.15; commissure, 1.60.

Hab.—Northern parts of Old World. Very accidental in America.

I introduce a brief diagnosis of this species, the existence of which in America is based upon a female bird found at New Orleans by Mr. Audubon. No one else has ever met with it, and this single straggler (in respect to which Mr. Audubon may have even been mistaken) can hardly warrant its being considered an American bird.

Wilson, in speaking of the abundance of the Smew in the northern United States, probably had the butterball, *Bucephala albeola*, in view.

August 20, 1858.

103 b

GAVIAE.

In the table, on page 594, taken from Bonaparte's system of 1853, the *Gaviae* are made to consist of the *Totipalmi* and *Longipennes;* the *Anseres* of *Lamellirostres, Urinatores,* and *Ptilopteri.* Subsequently the *Urinatores,* or *Brachypteri,* were removed by that author to the *Gaviae,* and the *Ptilopteri,* or *Impennes,* raised to the rank of a separate order. How far this modified arrangement agrees better with the author's primary idea of *Altrices* and *Praecoces* I am unable to speak; if some of the *Brachypteri* are known to rear their young in nests, the majority are supposed to conduct them to the water as soon as hatched. Be the circumstances, in this respect, as they may, the later arrangement of the orders and sub-orders seems the more natural, and I therefore adopt it in the present case.

As already stated, the chief characteristic of the *Gaviae* is to be found in the entire absence of lamellae within the edges of the bill. The wings are either conspicuously lengthened, as in the *Longipennes;* or they are quite short, the hinder toe connected to the anterior by a membrane, (*Totipalmi,*) or free, (*Urinatores.*) In all, the toes are well webbed, although the web is sometimes split. The young in most *Longipennes,* at least, are born helpless, and reared for a certain time in the nests.

The sub-order was originally divided by Bonaparte, as stated, into two tribes, *Totipalmi* and *Longipennes,* to which he subsequently added the *Urinatores.* Their characters are as follows:

A. *Totipalmi.*—Hind toe connected with the inner by a membrane, and more or less lateral or anterior. Bill generally longer than the head, and usually with a sharp curved nail at the end; sometimes without it. Nasal aperture an elongated narrow slit; sometimes scarcely visible. Face and throat usually somewhat naked.

    PELECANIDAE.—Upper jaw with a hooked, decurved, and acute nail at the tip. Edges of the bill even, without serrations. Throat naked, with an extensible pouch.

        PELECANINAE.—Tarsus and throat naked. Tail broad, rounded.

        TACHYPETINAE.—Tarsus feathered. Wings and tail excessively lengthened; the latter deeply forked.

    PLOTIDAE.—Bill straight, notched or serrated on the edges, with a slightly curved nail, or none. Face and chin partly naked. Tail rounded, or cuneate; rather long.

    PHAETONIDAE.—Bill without nail, slightly curved; edges scarcely serrated. Head entirely feathered. Tail with the middle feathers excessively lengthened.

B. *Longipennes.*—Hind toe disconnected from the lateral, small; the anterior toes webbed to the claws. Wings lengthened, acute; the first primary generally as long as the second. Bill without serrations. No naked spaces about the head.

PROCELLARIDAE.—Nail only of hind toe projecting. Nasal apertures circular, opening in projecting tubes. Bill with a much decurved nail at tip. Outer toe as long as the middle. Legs reticulated in front.

LARIDAE.—Hind toe free when present. Nasal apertures linear, opening laterally ; not at all tubular. Bill without nail except in *Lestris*. Outer toe shorter than the middle. Legs scutellate transversely in front.

C. *Brachypteri.*—Wings and tail short, the latter sometimes wanting. Hind toe free, or wanting. Legs very far backwards. Entirely aquatic, and for the most part capturing the food beneath the water.

COLYMBIDAE.—Hind toe distinct, with a broad hanging lobe. The membrane of toes entire, or divided. Claws nail-like, flattened. Mostly inhabit fresh waters of all countries.

ALCIDAE.—Hind toe wanting. Claws compressed. Entirely marine, and chiefly arctic.

In a strictly natural arrangement the *Totipalmi* should, perhaps, precede the *Longipennes*. In order, however, to facilitate the passage of the present report through the press, the latter tribe has been made to begin the sub-order, as the manuscript belonging to it was first ready for the printer. For a similar reason the *Anseres* come before the *Gaviae*, although most authors place them last.

The determinations and descriptions of the *Gaviae* have been prepared and furnished by Mr. George N. Lawrence, with the exception of the *Alcidae*, which are from the pen of Mr. John Cassin.

Tribe **LONGIPENNES.**[1]

Family PROCELLARIDAE. The Petrels.

Ch.—Bill more or less lengthened, compressed, and deeply grooved, appearing to be 'ormed of several distinct parts; the tip s strong, much hooked, and acute; the nostrils open from distinct tubes, either single or double, and are situated at the base of the upper mandible.

All the birds embraced in this family are strictly oceanic, some of the smaller species only being observed in bays near the ocean during or after a storm. They vary greatly in size, some being quite diminutive, while others are equal in dimensions to the largest known birds of flight.

Two sub-families, namely, *Diomedeinae* and *Procellarinae*, constitute this family, the distinguishing characters of which are as follows:

Diomedeinae.—Bill very strong, curved, and acute at the end; nostrils short, tubular, and situated on the sides of the upper mandible near the base.

Procellarinae.—Bill more or less strong, curved at the end, and pointed; nostrils tubular, situated on the culmen, near the base, and opening forwards.

Sub-Family DIOMEDEINAE.—The Albatrosses.

Ch.—These birds have powerful bills, much curved, and pointed at the end; the nostrils resemble short pipes, and are situated on each side of the upper mandible, near the base of the lateral groove; feet large and webbed.

They possess great extent of wing, and, consequently, very enduring powers of flight. But one genus is comprised in this sub-family.

DIOMEDEA, Linnaeus.

Diomedea, Linn. Syst. Nat. 1758. Type *D. exulans*, L.

Ch.—Bill rather longer than the head, compressed, with the end much curved, and the point acute; upper mandible deeply grooved on the sides for its entire length; nostrils near the base of the upper mandible, separate, tubular, and prominent; wings very long and narrow, the second quill the longest; tail rather short; legs strong, the tarsi shorter than the middle toe; interdigital membrane full; hind toe wanting; claws short and obtuse.

All the species are of large dimensions; they are most abundant in the Southern and Pacific Oceans, and are particularly numerous in the neighborhood of the Cape of Good Hope and Cape Horn. In the Pacific some species are found in quite high northern latitudes. Their food consists principally of fish, of which they are most voracious eaters.

[1] Prepared by Mr. George N. Lawrence, of New York.

There are four species in this genus which are stated to frequent the Pacific coast of the United States ; the following are their characteristics :

Very large; bill yellow ; upper plumage white, with transverse black lines ; under plumage white ; tail of medium size and rounded, dull plumbeous............*D. exulans.*

Large ; bill pale reddish yellow ; upper and under plumage white ; tail short, white, with the tip dark brown...*D. brachyura.*

Large ; bill black, culmen yellow ; upper plumage dark brown, rump and under parts white ; tail of medium size, lead colored...................... ....*D. chlororhynchus.*

Large ; bill black, with a yellow suture on the sides of the under mandible ; entire plumage fuliginous ; tail long and cuneate, blackish brown................. *D. fuliginosa.*

Diomedea, Linn.[1]

DIOMEDEA EXULANS, Linnaeus.

The Wandering Albatross.

Diomedea exulans, LINN Syst. Nat. I, 1766, 214.—BON. Syn. 1828, No. 314.—NUTT. Man. II, 1834, 340.

Diomedea spadicea, GMELIN. Young.

Diomedea albatrus, PALLAS.

FIGURE.—Pl. enl. ccxxxvii.

SP. CH.—Upper part of the head cinereous ; upper plumage white, with narrow transverse lines of black on the back and wing coverts ; quill feathers black ; tail dull lead color and rounded in form ; below white ; bill yellow ; tarsi and feet flesh color.

Length, 44 inches ; wing, 24 ; tail, 9 ; bill, 7 ; tarsus, $4\frac{1}{2}$.

The young birds are dusky brown, more or less mixed with white according to age.

Hab.—Pacific ocean. Specimens in the government collection from the south Pacific.

This species appears to differ much in size ; the dimensions given by writers vary from 3 to 4 feet in length, and in alar extent from 10 to 17. The measurements given are from a specimen in my collection.

Bonaparte speaks of this species as being "rare and accidental on the coasts of the middle States." According to Latham, they abound in the North Pacific, in summer, in the vicinity of the Kurile Islands, being attracted to these regions by the abundance of food ; they are voracious feeders and are lean on their arrival, but soon become very fat.

There is not, to my knowledge, any well authenticated instance of this bird having been procured off the coast of any part of our territory ; but being described by several writers as a North American species I have included it. It is possible that this species has been confounded with some others by the older authors, and that probably *D. brachyura,* which greatly resembles it in plumage, but is smaller, and abundant off the northwest coast, has been mistaken for it.

List of specimens.

Locality.	Whence and how obtained.	Original No.	Collected by—	Length.	Wing.
Pacific....................	George N. Lawrence	1010	J. Boston............	44. 00	24. 00

[1] Bill broad. Tail short.

Phoebastria, Reich.[1]

DIOMEDEA BRACHYURA, Temminck.

The Short-tailed Albatross.

Diomedea brachyura, Temm. Pl. col. v, about 1828.—Cassin, Ill. I, 1855, 289 pl. l. Adult.
Diomedea nigripes, Aud. Orn. Biog. V, 1839, 327.—Ib. Birds Am. VII, 1842, 198.—Cass. Ills. I, 1854, 210 ; pl. xxxv. (Young.)
? *Diomedea chiriensis*, Temm.
? *Diomedea epomophora*, Lesson.

Sp. Ch.—*Adult*. Head and neck white, tinged with pale yellow ; primaries, tips of secondaries and tertiaries, upper edge of the wing and greater wing coverts brownish black ; tail white, tipped with dark brown ; back and entire under plumage pure white ; bill pale reddish yellow ; legs flesh color.

Length, 33 inches ; alar extent, 84 ; wing, 20 ; tail, $5\frac{1}{2}$; bill, 5 ; tarsus, $3\frac{1}{4}$.

The young are ashy brown, lighter on the abdomen; for some distance around the base of the bill, and a space below the eye, grayish white ; bill dusky ; tarsi and feet black.

Hab.—North Pacific ; coasts of California and Oregon.

There are four specimens of the young in the collection.

In Mr. Cassin's Illustrations of the Birds of California, &c , (referred to above,) is given a quite full history of the habits and changes of plumage of this species, taken from Peale's volume on the Birds of the Exploring Expedition of the Vincennes and Peacock.

It seems to be an abundant species in the North Pacific, but most of the specimens obtained are young and in the plumage in which it is described by Mr. Audubon as *D. nigripes*. In adult plumage it resembles *D. exulans*, but is smaller and distinguished from it by its shorter tail.

Audubon gives 36 inches as the length, but the measurements given above are those of a young specimen in my cabinet taken when in a fresh state. They no doubt vary much in size as in some of the other species.

List of specimens.

Catal. No.	Sex	Locality.	When collected.	Whence obtained.	Orig. No.	Collected by—	Length.	Stretch of wings.	Wings.
9901	♂	Coast of California		Lieut. Williamson		Dr. Heermann			
9902		Shoalwater bay		Dr. Cooper					
9903		Pacific coast	April 5, 1856	Dr. Suckley	303				
		do		Geo. N. Lawrence	1011	J. Boston	33.00	84.00	20.00

Thalassarche, Reich.[2]

DIOMEDEA CHLORORHYNCHUS, Gmelin.

The Yellow-nosed Albatross.

Diomedea chlororhynchos, Gmel. Syst. Nat. I, 1788, 568.—Aud. Orn. Biog. V, '1839, 326.—Ib. Birds Am. VII, 1844, 196.
" *Diomedea chrysostoma*, Forster."
" *Diomedea presaga*, Brandt."

[1] Bill broad. Tail excessively short.
[2] Bill compressed. Tail moderate.

Figures.—Pl. col. 468.

Sp. Ch.—Head and neck grayish ash ; space between the bill and the eye, and around the latter, grayish black, a white line on the hind part of the lower eyelid ; back and wing coverts dark brownish ash, lightest on the back ; rump and upper tail coverts pure white ; primaries brownish black, having the edge of the inner webs dark ash, except near the end ; shafts of the primaries white at the base, but gradually changing to brown at the end ; secondaries dark brownish ash, with the basal parts of the inner webs ash gray ; tail plumbeous gray, with the base and shafts white : breast, abdomen, and under tail coverts white; bill black, having the ridge of the upper mandible yellow quite to the point ; lower part of under mandible also yellow ; legs and feet yellow.

Length about 36 inches ; wing, 22 ; tail 9 ; bill 4½ ; tarsus 3¼.

Hab.—Pacific ocean ; coast of Oregon.

One specimen in the collection from off the mouth of Columbia river.

The most striking characteristics of this species are its pure white rump and lead colored tail, and the yellow culmen of bill.

List of specimens.

Catal. No.	Locality.	Whence obtained.	O. ig. No.	Collected by—	Wings.
2726	Columbia river...............	S. F. Baird	....	J. K. Townsend	....
....	Pacific coast	Geo N. Lawrence	1012	....	22. 00

Phoebetria, Reich.[1]

DIOMEDEA FULIGINOSA, Gmelin.

The Sooty Albatross.

Diomedea fuliginosa, Gmel. Syst. Nat. I, 1788, 568.
" *Diomedea antarctica,* Banks."
" *Diomedea palpebrata,* Forster."
Diomidae fusca, Aud. Orn. Biog. V, 1839, 116.—Ib. Birds Am. VII, 1844, 200 ; pl. ccccliv.

Figures.—Pl. Col. 469.

Sp. Ch.—The general color of the plumage is sooty brown, darkest on the head ; the quill feathers and tail blackish brown, the shafts of both conspicuously white ; the tail cuneate ; bill black, with a deep, yellow lateral groove on the under mandible ; tarsi and feet yellow ; the eyelids are bordered with pure white, except for a small portion of the anterior part.

Length, 34 inches ; wing, 21 ; tail, 11 ; bill, 4¾ ; tarsus, 3.

Hab.—Pacific coasts of California and Oregon.

Readily distinguished from all the other species by its dark colored plumage, the white border to the eye, and the cuneate form of its tail.

List of specimens.

Catal. No.	Locality.	Whence obtained.	Orig. No.	Collected by—	Wings.
2718	Coast of Oregon	S. F. Baird	....	J. K. Townsend	....
....	Pacific	Geo. N. Lawrence	1013	....	20. 00

[1] Bill short, compressed, deeply sulcate ; tail elongated, cuneate.

Sub–Family PROCELLARINAE.—The true Petrels.

CH.—The bill more or less strong, compressed, tip much hooked and pointed ; the nostrils tubular to a greater or less extent, and situated on the basal part of the culmen. Generally of medium or small size, wandering in their habits, and capable of sustaining themselves on wing for a great length of time.

In this sub-family there are five genera which belong to North America, with the following characters :

1. PROCELLARIA.—Bill rather stout, strong, curved at the end ; lower mandible with a lateral groove ; nostrils covered by an elevated sheath, opening forwards, divided by a thin septum, and situated near the base of the culmen ; tarsi strong and rather short.
2. DAPTION.—Bill short, broad, compressed near the tip which is curved and acute ; nostrils at the base of the culmen, opening forwards, and covered with a flattened sheath ; tarsi slender.
3. THALLASSIDROMA.—Bill short and slender; nostrils situated at the base of the culmen, tubular and prominent ; tarsi slender and very long.
4. FREGETTA.—Bill small ; nasal tubes short and recurved, situated at the base of the culmen ; tarsi long, toes strong, nails flattened.
5. PUFFINUS.—Bill long, rather slender ; nostrils at the base of the culmen, covered with a sheath, which is elevated at the opening, where the apertures are separate ; tarsi rather long and compressed.

PROCELLARIA, Linnaeus.

Procellaria, LINN. Syst. Nat. 1746.

CH.—Bill rather short, strong, somewhat compressed near the tip, which is much curved and acute ; nostrils tubular, of different lengths, opening forwards and divided by a thin septum ; lower mandible grooved laterally and with the tip much arched ; wings long and pointed, first quill the longest ; tail rounded or cuneate ; tarsi strong and rather short ; toes long and united by a full web ; in place of the hind toe a triangular claw or spur.

They are found mostly in the higher latitudes, are strictly marine, seldom visiting the neighborhood of the shore.   They feed on fish, and the flesh and blubber of cetaceous animals. They are rapid in their manner of flying, and graceful in their movements.

Five species belong to North America, which may be characterized thus:

Large ; bill dark yellow ; nasal case long ; back and wings brown, mottled with dull white ; under plumage white ; legs and feet dusky yellow....................*P. gigantea.*

Middle size ; bill yellow ; back and wings pale grayish blue ; below white ; legs and feet flesh color...*P. glacialis.*

Middle size ; bill yellow ; nasal case with the ridge carinate ; back and wings light greyish blue ; under parts white ; legs and feet yellow...........................*P. pacifica.*

Middle size ; bill yellow, with the nasal case and tips of both mandibles black ; back and wings greyish blue ; below white ; legs and feet yellow..............*P. tenuirostris.*

Of rather small size ; bill black ; back and wings dark brown ; under plumage white ; tarsi and base of feet pale yellow ; terminal two-thirds of feet blackish brown ....*P. meridionalis.*

Ossifragus, Homb. & Jacq.

PROCELLARIA GIGANTEA, Gmelin.

The Gigantic Fulmar.

Procellaria gigantea, Gm. Syst. Nat. I, 1788, 563.—Aud. Orn. Biog. V, 1849, 330.—Ib. Birds Am. VII, 1844, 202.—
Nutt. Man. II, 1835, 329.
Ossifraga gigantea, Reich.—Bon. Cons. Avium, II, 1855, 186.
" *Procellaria ossifraga*, Forst."

Sp. Ch.—Upper plumage pale brown mottled with dusky white; wing coverts, quill feathers and tail, plain dusky brown; fore part of the neck, breast and belly, white; bill deep yellow; legs and feet dusky yellow.

The above is the adult plumage; the specimen procured by Dr. Townsend off the mouth of Columbia river, formerly belonging to Mr. Audubon, now in the cabinet of Prof. Baird, is of a pretty uniform dusky brown, lighter on the under plumage; bill yellow; legs and feet yellowish.

The dimensions of this specimen are as follows : length, 36 inches; wing, 20 ; bill, 4 ; length of nasal case, $1\frac{10}{12}$; tarsus, $3\frac{1}{2}$; outer toe and claw, $5\frac{1}{4}$.

Hab.—Pacific ocean, off Columbia river.

This is the largest species of the true petrels ; it measures seven feet in alar extent. They frequent the northwest coast only in spring and summer.

List of specimens.

Catal. No.	Locality.	Whence obtained.	Collected by—	Length.	Wings.
2743	Coast of Oregon	S. F. Baird	J. K. Townsend	37.00	20.00

Fulmarus, Leach.

PROCELLARIA GLACIALIS, Linnaeus.

The Fulmar Petrel.

Procellaria glacialis, Linn. Syst. Nat. I, 1766, 213.—Bon. Syn. 1828, No. 310.—Nutt. Man. II, 1834, 331.—Aud. Orn. Biog. III, 1835, 446.—Ib. Birds Am. VII, 1844, 204 ; pl. ccclv.
Fulmarus glacialis, Stephens, Shaw's Zool.—Bon. Cons. Avium, II, 1855, 187.
Procellaria glacialis, var. *A. audubonii*, Bon. Consp. Av. II, 1855, 187.
" *Procellaria hiemalis*, Brehm."

Sp. Ch.—*Adult.* Back and wings pale grayish blue ; primary quills and their coverts blackish brown ; tail pale bluish white ; head and neck white ; the throat slightly tinged with yellow ; before the eye and extending a little over it is a small black spot ; under plumage pure white ; bill yellow ; iris yellow ; tarsi and feet pale flesh colored.

Length of male, 20 inches ; wing, 13 ; tail, $4\frac{1}{4}$; bill, $1\frac{10}{12}$; tarsus, 2.

Female similar to the male and differing but little in size, being rather smaller.

Hab.—Northern Atlantic.

In form this species is rather robust ; the wings long and pointed ; tail short and rounded, of fourteen feathers ; bill short and very strong, the unguis much decurved and very acute ; the upper outline of the nasal tubes is concave, with the ridge flattened.

August 23, 1858.

104 b

These birds abound in the North Atlantic ocean, also in the large bays and straits; they are constant attendants upon the whalers, and when the process of cutting up a whale commences they assemble in immense numbers, and are so greedy and fearless, at such times, as to approach within a few yards of the men engaged in the work.

List of specimens.

Locality.	Whence obtained.	Original No.
North Atlantic	George N. Lawrence	1014

PROCELLARIA PACIFICA, Audubon.

The Pacific Fulmar.

Procellaria pacifica, Aud. Orn. Biog. V, 1839, 331.—Ib. Birds Am. VII, 1844, 208.
Fulmarus glacialis, var. C. *pacifica*, Bon. Consp. II, 1855, 187.

Sp. Ch.—*Adult.* Back and wings light grayish blue; the feathers largely terminating with brownish gray; primaries and coverts blackish brown tinged with gray; tail brownish gray, white at the base; head, neck, and under plumage, pure white; bill, tarsi and feet, yellow.

Length, 18 inches; wing, 12¾; tail, 4¾; bill, 1¾; tarsus, 1¹¹⁄₁₂.

Young of a uniform brownish gray; a dark spot before the eye; primaries brownish black; bill and legs yellow.

Hab.—Pacific coast of North America.

The type specimens are now in the cabinet of Prof. Baird, by whom they have been transmitted to me for examination.

Differs but little in form and size from the Atlantic bird, but the bill is rather smaller, with the unguis narrower and much weaker; the nasal case differs in having its ridge distinctly carinate, and its upper outline straight. Bonaparte considers it as merely a variety of the *P. glacialis.*

List of specimens.

Catal. No.	Locality.	Whence obtained.	Collected by—	Wings.
2750	Pacific	S. F. Baird	J. J. Audubon	12.50
2751	do	do	do	12.25

Thalassoica, Reich.

PROCELLARIA TENUIROSTRIS, Audubon.

The Slender-billed Fulmar.

Procellaria tenuirostris, Aud. Orn. Biog. V, 1839, 333.—Ib. Birds Amer. VII, 1844, 210.
Thalassoica glacialoides, var. *b. tenuirostris*, Bon. Consp. II, 1855, 192.

Sp. Ch.—*Adult.* Back and wings clear grayish blue; tail of the same color, but rather lighter; primaries brownish black on phe outer webs and on the inner at the end, remainder of inner webs white; secondaries dark bluish gray on the outer web and ture white on the inner; front, top, and sides of the head, neck in front, and under plumage, white; sides under the wing dusky ; there is a blackish spot in front of the eye ; the hind neck is grayish blue, of a lighter shade than the back ; bill yellow, except the nasal case and the ends of both mandibles, which parts are black ; tarsi and feet yellow.

Length, 18½ inches ; wing, 13 ; tail, 5 ; bill, 2₁₃ ; tarsus, 1⅛.

Hab.—Pacific coast ; Columbia river.

Resembling the two preceding species, but quite distinct; the bill is longer and more slender; the nasal case has its ridge a little concave and somewhat carinate ; the black markings on the bill and the white inner webs of the quill feathers are very distinguishing features.

In the color of its upper plumage, with that of the wings, and its rather narrow elongated bill, it makes a near approach to the gulls.

List of specimens.

Catal. No.	Locality.	Whence obtained.	Original No.	Collected by—	Length.	Wing.
2032	Pacific	S. F. Baird		J. K. Townsend (type)	18.00	13.50
	do	George N. Lawrence	1015			

Aestrelata, Bon.

PROCELLARIA MERIDIONALIS, Lawrence.

The Tropical Fulmar.

Procellaria meridionalis, Lawr. Ann. Lyc. Nat. Hist. N. Y. IV, 1848, 475.—Ib. V, June, 1852, 220; pl. xv.
Fulmarus meridionalis, Bon. Comptes Rendus tab. *Gaviarum,* 1855.
?,*Procellaria hæsitata,* Kuhl, Beitr. zur Zool. 1820, 142, vol. V.
? *Procellaria hasitata,* Temm. Pl. col. 416.—Newton, Zoologist, 1852, 3691.
?" *Aestrelata diabolica,* L'Herminier, Pl. col. 416."—Bon. Cons. Av. II, 1855, 188.

Sp. Ch.—Front white, marked with narrow waved lines and small spots of pale brown ; top and sides of head and occiput dark brown ; hind neck light brown, the white on the sides of the neck almost meeting on its lower part ; upper part of the back dark ash, this color extending for some distance on the breast ; lower part of back and wing coverts blackish brown ; primaries blackish brown ; secondaries dark brown at the end, with the base white ; upper tail coverts white ; tail brownish black, with the basal part white for one-third its length ; sides of the neck and entire under plumage pure white ; the dark feathers of the back extend down on the sides near the insertion of the tail ; lower tail coverts white, tipped with ash ; bill black ; tarsi pale yellow ; webs and toes yellow at the base for one-third their length, remainder blackish brown. Form not robust ; bill short ; tail graduated ; an acute spur in place of a hind toe.

Length, 16 inches ; alar extent, 39 inches ; wing, 12 ; tail, 5 , bill, 1½ ; tarsus, 1½.

Hab.—Atlantic coast, from Florida to New York.

The figure given in the "Zoologist" has the front rising rapidly from the bill an dthe forehead very prominent ; this character is therein alluded to very particularly as existing in the mounted specimen precisely as in the fresh bird. My specimen differs entirely in this particular, the top of the head being quite flat, its outline receding regularly from the bill to the hind part of the head ; but this may be owingto the manner of mounting. In the "Zoologist" two bands are stated to be on the wings ; these are not apparent in my bird. Otherwise, in form, size, and distribution of color they are much alike, and possibly my species may be the same as *diabolica,* (which name has precedence given to it by Bonaparte over the other synonyms,) but as it differs in the characters above stated, I feel justified in leaving it for the present as distinct.

List of specimens.

Locality.	Whence obtained.	Original No.
Florida coast ------ -------	George N. Lawrence -----	1016
Coast of New York. ------	------do--------------	--------

DAPTION, Stephens.

Daption, STEPH. Shaw's Gen. Zool. XIII, 1825, 239.   Type *Procellaria capensis*, L.

CH.—Bill short, broad at the base, compressed near the tip, which is curved and acute, but rather weak ; nostrils on the base of the culmen, and depressed ; wings rather moderate, first quill longest ; tail short and rounded; tarsi of moderate length and rather slender ; anterior toes long and united by a full web; a short spur, rather obtuse, in place of the hind toe.   In form quite robust.

This genus is founded on a single species.

DAPTION CAPENSIS, Stephens.

The Pintado Petrel; The Cape Pigeon.

Procellaria capensis, LINN. Syst. Nat. I, 1766, 213.—LAWR. Ann. Lyc. Nat. Hist. N. Y. VI, 1853, 6.

Daption capensis, STEPHENS, Shaw's Gen. Zool. XIII, 1825.—BON. Cons. Avium, II, 1855, 188.

SP. CH.—Upper part and sides of the head, and hind neck plumbeous black ; back, rump, and upper tail coverts white, each feather terminating with a plumbeous black mark, giving a mottled appearance to the upper plumage ; smaller wing coverts plumbeous black, tipped with brown ; larger wing coverts white, margined with plumbeous black ; primaries black on the outer webs and white on the inner, except near the end where they are dark ash ; secondaries white, with dark tips ; tail white, with a broad terminal band of plumbeous black ; lower parts white ; bill black ; tarsi and feet brown ; the toes marked with yellow. Length, 15 inches ; wing, 10¾ ; tail, 4½ ; bill, 1⅜ ; tarsus, 1⅜.

Hab.—Off the coast of California.

One specimen in the collection from the southern seas.   Specimen in my cabinet from the California coast.

List of specimens.

Catal. No.	Locality.	Whence obtained.	Original No.	Length.	Wing.
9971	South Pacific-------- ------- ----------	------------------------------------	--------	15.00	10.75
--------	Pacific coast of the United States----------	George N. Lawrence--------------	1017	--------	--------

THALASSIDROMA, Vigors.

Thalassidroma, VIGORS, Zool. Jour. 1825.

CH.—Bill shorter than the head, slender and weak, the tip curved and acute, the sides compressed and moderately grooved ; nostrils at the base of the culmen, tubular and prominent ; wings long and narrow, the second quill longest ; tail forked or emarginate ; legs slender and very long ; tibia bare for a considerable space ; anterior toes rather short and slender, united by an indented web ; a short spur in place of the hind toe.

This genus is composed of the smallest members of the petrel family; they are also the most diminutive of web-footed birds, but yet they are able to contend with the strongest gales, and on such occasions appear to be particularly active and numerous. While hovering near the water, for the purpose of securing their food, they project their feet in such a manner as to give them the appearance of running on its surface.

The species embraced in this genus may be arranged in the following manner:

Plumage wholly bluish gray; tail much forked; legs and feet brown. Type of *Oceanodroma*, Bonap...*T. furcata*.

Upper part of back gray, lower part ash gray; collar around hind neck and under parts white; tail forked...*T. hornbyi*.

Plumage sooty brown; rump white; tail forked; tarsi and feet black...........*T. leachii*.

Plumage dark sooty brown; rump white; tail slightly emarginate; tarsi and feet black, with the basal two-thirds of the interdigital webs yellow.........................*T. wilsoni*.

Plumage grayish black above, sooty brown below; rump white; tail a little rounded; tarsi and feet black..*T. pelagica*.

Upper plumage entirely black, below sooty black; tail deeply forked; legs and feet black...*T. melania*.

Oceanodroma, Reich.

THALASSIDROMA FURCATA, Gould.

The Fork-tailed Petrel.

Procellaria furcata, GM. Syst. Nat. I, 1788, 561.—LATH. Ind. II, 825.

Thalassidroma furcata, GOULD, Voy. Sulph. Birds, 1844, 50; pl. xxxiii.—CASSIN, Birds of Cal. & Tex. I, 1855, 274; pl. xlvii.

Oceanodroma furcata, BON. Cons. Avium, II, 1855, 194.

" *Thalassidroma cinerea*, GOULD." Bon.

Procellaria orientalis, PALLAS, Zoog. Rosso-Asiat. II, 1811, 315.

" *Thalassidroma orientalis*, GRAY." Bon.

Oceanodroma orientalis, REICH.

SP. CH.—Entire plumage light bluish gray, paler on the forehead, the abdomen, and under tail coverts; dusky around the eye; greater wing coverts and secondaries with grayish white margins; quills and tail brownish, the latter with the external web of the outer feather white; bill black; feet brown.

Length, about 8 inches; wing, 6; tail, $3\frac{3}{4}$; bill, $\frac{3}{4}$; tarsus, $\frac{7}{8}$.

Hab.—Coasts of Oregon and Russian America.

Specimens in Mus. Acad. Nat. Sc., Philadelphia.

THALASSIDROMA HORNBYI, Gray.

Hornby's Petrel.

Thalassidroma hornbyi, G. R. GRAY, Pr. Zool. Soc. 1853, 62.

Oceanodroma hornbyi, BON. Cons. Avium, 1855, 195.

SP. CH.—"Front, cheeks, throat, collar round the hind part of the neck, breast and abdomen, pure white; crown, hind head, a broad band in front of neck, bend of wing and lesser wing coverts, sooty grey; upper part of back gray; lower part of back and tail ashy gray; greater wing coverts brownish gray; tertiaries and quills deep black.

"Total length, $8\frac{1}{4}''$; bill from gape, $10\frac{1}{2}'''$, from front, $8\frac{1}{2}'''$; tail (outer feather,) $3\frac{3}{4}''$; tarsus, $1''$; middle toe, $1''$."

Hab.—Northwest coast of America.

The above is a copy of Mr. Gray's description of this species; he states that "in form it agrees best with *Thal. furcata*, but the coloration differs much in several particulars."

Thalassidroma, Vigors.

THALASSIDROMA LEACHII, Bon.

Leach's Petrel.

Procellaria leachii, Temm. Man. II, 1820, 812.
Thalassidroma leachii, Bon. Syn. 1828, No. 309.—Ib. Consp. II, 1855, 193.—Nutt. Man. II, 1834, 326.—Aud. Orn. Biog. III, 1835, 434.—Ib. Birds Am. VII, 1844, 219 ; pl. cccclix.
Procellaria bullockii, Flem. Br. Anim. 1828, 136, No. 219.—Vigors
? " *Procellaria leucorrhoa*, Vieillot." Bon.

Sp. Ch.—The plumage generally is sooty brown, darker on the crown ; primaries and tail brownish black ; wing coverts and inner secondaries ashy gray ; rump, feathers of the sides adjoining it, and outer lower tail coverts, white ; bill black ; iris dark brown ; tarsi and feet black.
Length, 8 inches ; wing, 6½ ; tail, 3 ; bill, ⅔ ; tarsus 1.
The female differs only in being rather smaller.
Hab.—Atlantic coast from Massachusetts to Baffin's Bay.

This is larger than Wilson's petrel, and has a much stronger bill ; it may be readily known from it by its forked tail, and the interdigital webs being entirely black.

List of specimens.

Locality.	Whence obtained.	Original No.
Coast of New York..............	George N. Lawrence	1018
Atlantic coast..................	S. F. Baird.................	....
Washington, D. C..............	....do......................	....

THALASSIDROMA MELANIA, Bonaparte.

The Black Stormy Petrel.

Procellaria melania, Bon. Comptes Rendus, Ac. Sc. XXVIII, 1854, 662.
Thalassidroma melania, Bon. Cons. Av. II, 1855, 196.
" ? *Procellaria fuliginosa*, Lath. Not of Kuhl." Bon.
" ? *Procellaria scapulata*, Brandt."

Sp. Ch.—Entire upper plumage black ; wing coverts wholly black ; below fuliginous ; wings long ; tail short, but deeply forked.
Hab.—Coast of California.

It somewhat resembles *Thal. leachii*, but is distinguished from this as well as all its congeners by the absence of white on the rump, crissum, and on the wing coverts.

Oceanites, Keys. & Blas.[1]

THALASSIDROMA WILSONI, Bonaparte.

Wilson's Stormy Petrel.

Procellaria pelagica, Wils. Am. Orn. VII, 1808, 90 ; pl. lx.

Procellaria " oceanica, Kuhl, Beitr. Zool. 1820 ; pl. x, f. 1." Gray.

Thalassidroma wilsoni, Bon. Syn. 1828, No. 308.—Nutt. Man. II, 1834, 324.—Aud. Orn. Biog. III, 1835, 486 ;
V, 1839, 645.—Ib. Birds Am. VII, 1844, 223 ; pl. cccclx.

Oceanites wilsoni, Bon. Cons. Avium, II, 1855, 199.

Sp. Ch.—The general color of the plumage is dark sooty brown ; primaries and tail blackish brown, the latter white at the
base ; some of the outer secondaries and the secondary coverts grayish ash, ending with grayish white ; rump, sides of the
abdomen and exterior lower tail coverts, white ; bill black ; iris dark brown ; tarsi and feet black, with the webs yellow except
at the margin.

Length, 7¼ inches ; wing, 6 ; tail, ⅔ ; bill, $\frac{7}{10}$; tarsus, 1⅜.

Hab.—Off the Atlantic coast from the Gulf of Mexico to Baffins' Bay.

This species is somewhat smaller than *T. leachii*, and more delicate in form, the bill is much
weaker ; it may readily be distinguished by the greater proportion of white on the under tail
coverts and on the sides at the base of the tail, together with its much longer tarsi and yellow
webs ; tail nearly even.

List of specimens.

Locality.	Whence obtained.	Original number.
Coast of New York	Geo. N. Lawrence	1019
Do	do	1022
Atlantic ocean	S. F. Baird	

Procellaria, Linn.

THALASSIDROMA PELAGICA, Vigors.

The Stormy Petrel; Mother Carey's Chicken.

Procellaria pelagica, Linn. Syst. Nat. I, 1766, 212.—Bon. Consp. Av. II, 1855, 196.

Thalassidroma pelagica, Vigors, Zool. Jour. II, 1825, 405.—Bonap. Syn. 1828, Append. Note 27, No. 3.—Nutt.
Man. II, 1834, 327.—Aud. Orn. Biog. IV, 1838, 310.—Ib. Birds Am. VII, 1844, 228 ;
pl. cccclxi.

" *Procellaria melanonyx*, Nilsson."

" *Procellaria melitensis*, Schembri."

" *Procellaria tenuirostris, minor, ferroensis, et albifasciata*, Brehm."

Sp. Ch.—Upper plumage grayish black, tinged with brown ; quill feathers black ; the secondary coverts are margined
towards the end, externally, and at the tip, with grayish white ; a band of white crosses the rump ; upper tail coverts white at
the base, but broadly ending with black ; tail black with the basal part white for a short distance ; under parts sooty brown ;
lower tail coverts white at the base ; axillar feathers and some of the under wing coverts white at the end ; bill black ; iris
dark brown ; tarsi and feet black.

Length, 5¾ inches ; wing, 5 ; tail, 2¼ ; bill, $\frac{7}{10}$; tarsus, ⅞.

Hab.—Atlantic ocean, banks of Newfoundland.

[1] Claws acute.

This is the smallest of the genus, has the white rump band conspicuous, the tail slightly rounded, and the interdigital webs black.

FREGETTA, Bonaparte.

Fregetta, Bon. Cons. Av. II, 1855, 197.   Type *Procellaria tropica*, Gould.

Ch.—Bill small ; nasal tube short and recurved ; wings very much lengthened ; tail subtruncated ; tarsi very long ; toes muscular for their entire length ; claws small and depressed.   Colors, sooty, more or less varied with white.

The depressed form of the claws will at once distinguish this genus from *Thallassidroma*. But one species of this genus is found on our coast.

FREGETTA LAWRENCII, Bonaparte.

The Black and White Stormy Petrel.

Thalassidroma fregetta, Lawr. Ann. Lyc. Nat. Hist. N. Y. V, 1851, 117.
Fregetta lawrencii, Bon. Cons. Av. II, 1855, 198.

Sp. Ch.—Head and wings black ; neck, breast and back, dark plumbeous, or dull bluish ash ; wing coverts brown ; the tail white at the base, with the terminal half and the two central feathers black ; abdomen, inside covering of wings, and rump, white ; bill and legs black.   Tail even ; claws flattened and of an ovate form.

Length, about 8 inches ; wing, 6 ; tail, 3 ; tarsus, 1¾ .

Hab.—Florida coast.

Prince Bonaparte has conferred my name on the above bird, which I had described as *Thal. fregetta*.   The specimen from which my description was taken was presented to the Academy of Nat. Sciences, Philadelphia ; on a recent visit there I wished to compare it anew with Mr. Gould's specimens of *Thal. fregetta*, but it could not be found at the time.   I have, therefore, concluded to let it stand as named by Prince Bonaparte.

PUFFINUS, Brisson.

Puffinus, Briss. Ornithologie, 1760.   Type *Procellaria puffinus*, L.

Ch.—Bill about as long as the head, rather slender, compressed near the end and obliquely grooved on the sides, the tip curved, strong and acute, the lower mandible grooved laterally on the sides ; nostrils basal, with two distinct openings ; wings very long and pointed, first quill the longest ; tail rather short and rounded ; tarsi as long as the middle toe and compressed ; toes long and united by a full web ; a straight claw or spur in place of the hind toe.

These birds are of medium size, and are endowed in a remarkable degree with great powers of flight.   They swim lightly and gracefully, and while seeking their food have the habit (like the small petrels) of patting the surface of the water with their feet.

The following diagnosis will serve to distinguish the five species of this genus, found in North America :

Upper plumage brownish ash, under parts grayish white ; bill yellowish green, tips brownish black ; tail brownish black, graduated ; tarsi and feet yellow ; hind part of tarsi and outer toe brown..*P. major*.

Upper plumage sooty brown, under pale dingy brown ; bill black ; tail blackish brown, graduated ; legs and feet black...*P. fuliginosus*.

Upper plumage black, under surface white; bill brownish black; tail black, rounded; legs and feet dull orange; the hind part of tibia, the outer toe and part of the next, dark brown; webs pale...*P. anglorum.*

Upper plumage black, lower parts white; bill pale blue black at tip; tail black, short and rounded; tarsi and toes on the outside bluish black, on the inside and webs pale yellowish flesh color...*P. obscurus.*

Upper plumage lead colored gray, below white; bill yellowish, with the culmen and groove on the under mandible black; tail brownish black, graduated; tarsi and feet yellow, having the hind part of tarsi and outer toes brown. Type of *Priofinus*, Homb. et Jacq..*P. cinereus.*

Ardenna, Reich.

PUFFINUS MAJOR, (Faber.)

The Greater Shearwater.

Procellaria puffinus, LINN. Syst. Nat. I, 1766, 213.
Procellaria major, FABER, Prod. Isl. Orn. 1822, 56.
Puffinus major, BON. Cons. Avium. 1855, 203.
Puffinus cinereus, BON. Syn. 1828, No. 311.—NUTT. Man. II, 1834, 334.—AUD. Orn. Biog. III, 1835, 555.—IB. Birds Am. VII, 1 44, 212; pl. ccclvi.

SP. CH.—*Adult.* Head above, cheeks, occiput, a narrow line on the nape and upper part of back, brownish ash, paler on the hind neck; feathers of the back with lighter margins; lower part of back dark brown; upper tail coverts of the same color, terminating broadly with grayish white; primaries and tail brownish black, the former white on the basal part of the inner webs; secondaries and tertiaries dark brown, the secondaries white on their inner webs nearly to the end; wing coverts ashy brown with lighter margins; under plumage pure white, the neck nearly encircled with white; sides of the neck anterior to the bend of the wings marked with waving lines of pale ash; some distinct spots on the side of the breast and sides of the body at the junction of the tail brownish ash; lower tail coverts dark ash, with light gray edgings; bill yellowish green, the tip$_s$ brownish black; iris brown; tarsi and feet livid yellow, with the outer toe and the hind part of the tarsus brownish; claws yellowish. Length about 20 inches; wing, 13¼; tail, 5; bill, 2¼; tarsus, 2¼; middle toe and nail, 2⅞.

Hab.—Atlantic ocean. Florida coast to the Gulf of St. Lawrence.

This species has been described by most ornithological writers as the *P. cinereus* of Gmelin. It is quite abundant off our northern coast, and may be known from *P. anglorum* by its larger size and the light brown color of its upper plumage.

List of specimens.

Catal. No.	Locality.	Whence obtained.	Original No.	Collected by—
2025	Atlantic ocean	S. F. Baird	....	J. J. Audubon ..
.....	Atlantic coast of New York.	Geo. N. Lawrence .	1021	....

August 23, 1858.

105 **b**

Nectris, Bon.

PUFFINUS FULIGINOSUS, Strickland.

The Sooty Shearwater.

Puffinus fuliginosus, STRICK. Proc. Zool. Soc. 1832, 129.
Nectris fuliginosus, BON. Cons. Av. II, 1856, 201.
Puffinus cinereus, DEKAY, Nat. Hist. State N. Y., Birds, 1844, 287; pl. cxxxvi, fig. 298.—BON. Comptes Rendus,
        XLIII, 1856.

SP. CH.—The entire upper plumage is sooty brown ; wings and tail blackish brown ; under plumage pale brown ; bill and legs black. Bill more slender than that of *P. major*. Length, 18 inches; wing, 12 ; bill along ridge, $1\frac{7}{12}$; from rictus, $2\frac{1}{2}$; tarsus, $2\frac{1}{4}$; middle toe, $2\frac{1}{2}$.

Hab.—Atlantic coast of the northern States. Banks of Newfoundland.

Specimens in the cabinet of the Lyceum of Nat. History, N. Y.

I have always been impressed with the opinion that this bird was not the young of *P. major*, but a distinct species.

Bonaparte, in Comptes Rendus, referred to above, states that M. Hardy, ornithologist of Dieppe, has compared a large number of specimens of *P. major* and *P. fuliginosus* of both sexes from the banks of Newfoundland, and is satisfied that there can be no doubt of their being specifically distinct. He says that being completely convinced of this, he has accordingly separated them.

Puffinus, Linn.

PUFFINUS ANGLORUM, Temm.

The Mank's Shearwater.

" *Procellaria puffinus*, LINN., not of other authors."—BON.
Procellaria anglorum, TEMM. Man. II, 1820, 806.
Puffinus anglorum, RAY, Synops. 1713, 134.—TEMM. Man. IV, 509.—BONAP. Syn. 1828, No. 312.—NUTT. Man. II,
        1834, 336.—AUD. Orn. Biog. III, 1835, 604.—IB. Birds Am. VII, 1844, 214 ; pl. cccclvii.—
        BON. Cons. Avium, 1855, 203.
" *Puffinus arcticus*, FABER."

SP. CH.—Entire upper plumage, wings, tail, and the tibial feathers, black ; primaries and secondaries black on the outer webs, dark ash on the inner; under parts white, sides of the neck and breast transversely barred with ash; bill brownish black; iris dark brown; tarsi and feet dull orange, with the hind part of tibia, the outer toe, and a portion of the next toe, dark brown; webs pale yellow ; claws brownish black. Length, 15 inches ; wing, $9\frac{3}{4}$; tail, $3\frac{1}{2}$; bill, $1\frac{2}{3}$; tarsus, $1\frac{10}{12}$; middle toe and claw, $2\frac{5}{12}$.

Hab.—Coast of New Jersey to Labrador.

The above description is from a specimen belonging to Professor Baird, from Mr. Audubon's collection. Said by Audubon to be " not uncommon off the coast of Maine during summer." Much smaller than *P. major*, with the bill quite slender and the upper plumage black.

List of specimens.

Catal. No.	Locality..	Whence obtained.	Collected by—
2725	Atlantic ocean	S. F. Baird............	J. J. Audubon ......

PUFFINUS OBSCURUS, Latham.

The Dusky Shearwater.

Procellaria obscura, GM. Syst. Nat. I, 1788, 559.

Puffinus obscurus, LATH. Ind. Orn. II, 1790, 828.—BONAP. Syn. 1828, No. 313.—IB. Consp. II, 1856, 204.—NUTT. Man. II, 1835, 337.—AUD. Orn. Biog. III, 1835, 620.—IB. Birds Am. VII, 1844, 216; pl. cccclviii.

" *Puffinus l'herminieri*, LESSON."

SP. CH.—Upper part of head, back, and wings, black ; tail black ; under plumage white ; bill light blue, black at the end ; iris bluish black ; outside of tarsus and toes bluish black, inside and webs pale yellowish flesh color ; claws black. Length, 11 inches ; wing, $7\frac{5}{8}$; bill, $1\frac{3}{10}$; tarsus, $1\frac{1}{2}$.

Hab.—Southern coast of the United States ; Gulf of Mexico.

Specimen in Museum of Lyceum of Natural History, New York.

In color it much resembles *P. anglorum*, but its very small size will distinguish it from that and the other American species.

Adamastor, Bonap.

PUFFINUS CINEREUS, Gmelin.

The Cinereous Petrel.

Procellaria cinerea, GM. Syst. Nat. I, 1788, 563.

Procellaria melanura, BONN. Encyc. Meth.

Procellaria hæsitata, FORST. Descr. An. Licht. 1844.

" *Procellaria hæsitata*, KUHL." Gould B. of Aust. pl. xlvii.

Puffinus hæsitata, LAWR. Ann. Lyc. Nat. Hist. N. Y. VI, 1853, 5.

Adamastor typus, BON. Cons. Av. II, 1855, 187.

SP. CH.—Sides of the head and entire upper plumage plumbeous gray, rather darker on the head ; wing coverts dark bluish ash, (in my specimen margined with umber brown ;) primaries grayish black on the outer webs and ends of the inner ; rest of the inner webs light brownish ash, becoming whitish at the base ; secondaries and tertiaries brownish ash ; inner lining of wings and axillary feathers ashy brown ; tail brownish black ; throat and sides of the neck pale cinereous ; under plumage white ; lower tail coverts ashy brown ; upper mandible black along the ridge, the sides and hooked end yellowish white ; under mandible dusky yellow, with the lateral grooves black ; tarsi and feet yellow, with the exception of the hind part of the tarsi and outer toes, which are brown ; claws yellow with dusky tips ; a short and strong spur in place of the hind toe. Rather more robust in form than the other species of *Puffinus* ; bill also stronger, tail rounded, the two central feathers a little projecting.

Length of skin, 19 inches ; wing, $13\frac{1}{4}$; bill, $2\frac{1}{4}$; tail, 5 ; tarsus, $2\frac{1}{2}$; outer toe and claw, 3.

Hab.—Pacific ocean, off the California coast.

When I described this species in the Annals Lyc. Nat. Hist., referred to above, I was at a loss for its true specific name, and do not feel fully assured that I am right in now affixing to it Gmelin's name of *cinereus*.

Mr. Gould states that it is very similar to *cinereus*, and Mr. Newton (Zoologist, 1852) considers Mr. Gould's *hæsitata* to be Gmelin's species. Bonaparte has made it the type of a new genus, viz: *Adamastor*, and in Cons. Avium names it *A. typus*. In the same work, under *Puffinus kuhlii*, Boie," he says that *Proc. cinerea*, Gm., is certainly the same as his *Adam. typus*; if such be the fact, Gmelin's name must be restored ; and if it does not belong in

Puffinus, the genus *Priofinus*, Homb. et Jacq., for which this species is given as the type, will have priority.   It would, therefore, appear to have the best claim to Gmelin's name, which has been more generally applied to *P. major*, Faber.

List of specimens.

Locality.	Whence obtained.	Original number.
California coast	Geo. N. Lawrence....	1022

Family LARIDAE. The Gulls.

Ch.—Bill generally shorter than the head, straight at the base, and more or less curved at the end. Nostrils linear. Head ovate; neck short; body rather full and compact; wings long and pointed; legs of moderate length, strong, and covered anteriorly with transverse scales; feet fully webbed, the hind toe small and elevated.

Birds of this family frequent the shores of the ocean, but often wander to great distances from land; they are incapable of diving, but swim buoyantly. Their food consists principally of fish and crustacea, but some of the larger species feed occasionally on the flesh of cetaceous animals, and devour the young and eggs of some species of sea birds.

The family of *Laridae* is divisible into four sub-families, with the following characters:

LESTRIDINAE.—Basal half of upper jaw with a horny covering, distinct from the tip, and under which the nostrils open considerably beyond the middle of the bill. Bill abruptly and much decurved at the tip. Tail cuneate. Body full, stout.

LARINAE.—Covering of the bill continuous. Anterior extremity of nostrils generally reaching to the middle of the bill. Culmen considerably decurved towards the tip. Body robust. Tail generally even.

STERNINAE.—Covering of bill continuous. Nostrils opening in the basal third of the bill. Culmen gently curved to the tip of the lengthened and attenuated bill. Body rather slender. Wing lengthened. Tail usually deeply forked.

RHYNCHOPINAE.—Bill excessively compressed, like the blade of a knife. Lower jaw much longer than the upper; the point obtuse. Body slender; tail forked.

Sub-Family LESTRIDINAE.—The Skua Gulls; the Jagers.

Ch.—Bill strong and much curved at the end, the base covered with a membranous cere. Wings lengthened. Tail cuneate, with the two central feathers projecting.

These hardy birds inhabit the high latitudes of both hemispheres. There are four Arctic species found both in Europe and North America. They are piratical in their habits, appearing to derive their subsistence mainly from the labors of others. They chase and harrass various species of gulls, compelling them to disgorge a portion of their food, which they dart after and seize before it reaches the water.

Bonaparte, in his conspectus of *Laridae,* admits two genera of *Lestridinae,* with the following characters:

STERCORARIUS, Vieill.—Bill and feet robust. Tarsi shorter than middle toe. Median tail feathers broadly rounded at tip; not much longer than the others. Size large. Species *S. catarractes.*

LESTRIS, Ill.—Bill and feet slender; tarsus not longer than middle toe. Tail feathers much elongated. Size moderate. Species *L. pomarinus, parasiticus, cepphus.*

I shall, however, consider both under a single genus, *Stercorarius.*

STERCORARIUS, Brisson.

Stercorarius, Briss. Ornithologie, 1760.

CH.—Bill rather strong ; the culmen straight and covered at the base with a smooth cere, the end curved. Nostrils linear and more open anteriorly. Wings pointed ; first quill longest. Tail of moderate length ; the two middle feathers elongated. Tarsi strong, and covered with prominent scales ; claws sharp and much curved. Feet fully webbed ; hind toe short and but little elevated.

Of this genus there are four species inhabiting North America equally with Europe, as follows :

Very compact in form ; color entirely dark ; bill very strong ; central tail feathers projecting but little beyond the others, and not at all pointed ....*S. catarractes.*

Upper plumage dark ; light underneath ; central tail feathers exceeding the others about two inches, and of a uniform width to the end ....*S. pomarinus.*

Upper plumage dark ; under light ; central tail feathers extending about three inches beyond the others, not varying much in width until near the end, when they rapidly become narrower to the point.....................................,..*S. parasiticus.*

Dark colored above ; under plumage light ; middle tail feathers projecting about eight inches beyond the others, and gradually tapering to a fine point...................................*S. cepphus.*

STERCORARIUS CATARRACTES, Temm.

The Common Skua.

Larus catarractes, LINN. Syst. Nat. I, 1766, 226.
Stercorarius catarractes, TEMM. Man. d'Orn. II, 1820, 792.—LAWR. Am. Lyc. N. Y. VI, 1853, 7.—BON. Consp. II, 1856, 206.
Lestris catarractes, BONAP. Synop. 1826, No. 304.—NUTT. Man. II, 1834, 312.
Catarracta skua, BRÜNN. Orn. Bor.

SP. CH.—The plumage of the upper surface is dark brown, having the feathers tipped with gray ; wings chocolate brown, with their shafts and basal parts white ; tail dark brown, white at the base ; under plumage dark grayish brown ; bill black, with a tinge of dull blue ; legs and feet black. The central tail feathers extend one inch beyond the others. Length, 22 inches ; wing, 15 inches ; bill, 2½ ; tarsus, 2¾ ; tail, 5¾.

Hab.—Coast of California.

This species has been rarely obtained in the United States. It may easily be distinguished from all others of the genus by its very robust form, the dark color of the adult, and the conspicuous white mark on the wing. There is a specimen in my possession obtained off the coast of California.

STERCORARIUS POMARINUS, Temminck.

The Pomarine Skua.

Lestris pomarinus, TEMM. Man. d'Orn. II, 1815, 514.—BONAP. Synop. 1826, No. 305.—RICH. & SW. F. B. A. II, 1831, 429.—NUTT. Man. II, 1834, 315.—AUD. Birds Amer. VII, 1844, 186 ; pl. ccccli.—BON. Consp. II, 1856, 207.
Stercorarius pomarinus, TEMM. Man. d'Orn. II, 1820, 793.

Sᴘ. Cʜ.—*Adult.* Front, crown of the head, back, wings, and tail blackish brown ; sides and back part of the neck bright yellow ; throat and entire under plumage white, with a band of brown spots extending across the upper part of the breast ; sides and lower tail coverts barred with brown. Shafts of quills and tail feathers white ; bill greenish olive, black at the tip ; legs and feet black. The middle tail feathers extend beyond the others for about two inches. They are rounded at the end, and of a uniform breadth throughout. Length, 20 inches ; wing, 14 ; tail, 8 to 9 ; bill, 1¾ ; tarsus, 2.

Hab.—Labrador ; as far south as New York in winter. One specimen taken in summer at Harrisburg, Pa.

Young birds have the plumage of the upper parts blackish brown ; of the lower grayish brown, with the feathers of the abdomen and lower tail coverts margined with dull ferruginous. Tarsi and base of the toes and webs yellow.

List of specimens.

Catal. No.	Locality.	When collected.	Whence obtained.	Collected by—
1275	Harrisburg, Pa.	Summer	S. F. Baird	
2755	Atlantic		do	J. J. Audubon

STERCORARIUS PARASITICUS, Temminck.

The Arctic Skua.

Larus parasiticus, Lɪɴɴ. Syst. Nat. I, 1756, 226.

Stercorarius parasiticus, Tᴇᴍᴍ. Man. d'Orn. II, 1820, 796.

Lestris parasiticus, Bᴏɴᴀᴘ. Synop. 1828, No. 307.—Iʙ. Conspectus, II, 1856, 208.

Lestris richardsonii, Sᴡᴀɪɴ. F. B. A. II, 1831, 433 ; pl. lxxiii.—Nᴜᴛᴛ. Man. II, 1834, 319.—Aᴜᴅ. Birds Amer. VII, 1844, 190 ; pl. cccclii.

Sᴘ. Cʜ.—*Adult.* Upper part of the head blackish brown ; nape and sides of the neck yellowish white ; remainder of upper plumage blackish brown ; wings and tail darker ; shafts of the primaries white ; under plumage white ; bill bluish at the base, black at the point ; tarsi and feet black. The central tail feathers extend beyond the others about three inches ; they taper slightly, varying but little in breadth until near the end, where they are abruptly accuminated, differing in this particular from all the other species. Length, 20 to 22 inches ; wing, 13½ ; tail, 8½ ; bill, 1₁⁴₂ ; tarsi, 1¾.

Hab.—Arctic America ; breeds in the Barren Grounds ; coast of the United States from New York northward.

List of specimens.

Catal. No.	Locality.	Whence obtained.	Collected by—
2752	Atlantic ocean	S. F Baird	J. J. Audubon
9970	Long Island	do	
2754	Boston	do	J. Kimball
2062	do	do	T. M. Brewer
	New York	Geo. N. Lawrence	

STERCORARIUS CEPPHUS, (Brünnich.)

Buffon's Skua.

Catharacta cepphus, BRÜNN. Orn. Bor. 1764, 36.
Lestris cepphus, KEYS. & BLAS. 1840.—BON. Cons. Av. II, 1856, 209.
Lestris buffonii, BOIE, Isis, 1822, 562.—BONAP. Synop. 1826, No. 306.
Lestris parasitica, RICH. & SW. F. B. A. II, 1831, 430.—AUD. Birds Amer. VII, 1844, 192 ; pl. ccccliii.
Arctic Bird, EDWARDS, Birds, pl. cxlviii.

SP. CH.—*Adult*. Space between the eye and bill, top of the head and nape black ; cheeks and sides of the neck yellowish
white ; back and wings blackish gray ; quills and tail black ; the shafts white, except near their tips ; under plumage white ;
breast tinged with pale yellow ; flanks and lower tail coverts brownish gray ; bill dull flesh color, dark at the tip ; feet black ;
tarsi yellow in front. The two middle tail feathers are six or eight inches longer than the others, and taper gradually to a fine
point. Length, about 20 inches ; wing, 12 ; tail, 10 to 12 ; bill, $1\frac{5}{12}$; tarsi, $1\frac{7}{12}$.

Hab.—Arctic seacoasts of America ; Baffin's Bay.

There are no specimens of any of the genus *Stercorarius* in the collection, but in the private
cabinet of Prof. Baird are specimens of the three last species. These he has kindly sent me
for examination. They are the more interesting from the fact of being Mr. Audubon's type
specimens of the three species described by him, although in assigning names to two of them I
have been compelled to differ from him.

List of specimens.

Catal. No.	Sex and age.	Locality.	Whence obtained.
2062	Adult	Boston	S. F. Baird

Sub-Family LARINAE.—The Gulls.

CH.— Bill differing considerably in strength and form ; generally straight, with the sides compressed ; the culmen straight
at the base, with the end curved ; nostrils lateral and oblong ; wings long and pointed ; tail usually even ; in two or three cases
pointed or forked ; tarsi rather strong ; fore toes united by a web ; hind toe short and elevated.

These birds vary much in size, some being quite small, while others rank among the largest
of marine birds. They are not peculiar to any region, but are found abundantly over the
world. They congregate in large numbers on the sand bars at the entrance of inlets and large
bays. In winter they migrate in search of food, frequenting harbors and ascending rivers.

This sub-family has been subdivided into many genera by different writers, in some cases
the distinction being based mostly upon the color of the wings or back. Prince Bonaparte and
M. Bruch, who have both specially studied this family, differ very much in the generic
arrangement. G. R. Gray, in his Genera of Birds, does not approve of so great a subdivision,
and has retained most of the large species under the old genus *Larus*, which accords with my
own views.

Eight well marked genera, however, included in this sub-family, are found in the United States.

1. LARUS.—Of large and medium size; bill strong and hooked at tip; mantle generally light colored; head white; tail nearly even.

2. BLASIPUS.—Of middle size; bill long and rather slender; head white; rest of plumage dark; tail slightly emarginate.

3. CHROICOCEPHALUS.—Size medium and rather small; bill moderate or slender; the head enveloped in summer with a dark colored hood; tail generally even.

4. RISSA.—Medium size; bill long and rather strong; colors light; hind toe short or rudimental; tail even.

5. PAGOPHILA.—Of middle size; bill short and very strong; mantle light; tarsi rather short; webs indented.

6. RHODOSTETHIA.—Small in size; bill short and rather slender; mantle pale; neck encircled with a black collar; tail uniform.

7. CREAGRUS.—Medium size; bill very strong and much curved; mantle grayish white; tail deeply forked.

8. XEMA.—Of small size; bill short and rather slender; mantle bluish gray; tail moderate and forked.

LARUS, Linnaeus.

Larus, LINN. Syst. Nat. 1735.

CH.—Bill strong and laterally compressed; the culmen straight at the base and curved at the end; nostrils lateral and linear, placed near the centre of the bill; wings pointed; first quill longest; tail even; tarsi nearly the length of the middle toe; feet with a full web; hind toe elevated. The largest of the family are found in this genus; none very small.

There are several well marked groups in this genus, but not sufficiently different for generic distinction. They may be arranged in the following manner:

A. LEUCUS, Bp.—Large and powerful in form; the upper plumage very light in color; primary quills white, or of the same color as the back.

Mantle grayish blue; primaries white at the end for a considerable space. ....*L. glaucus.*

Mantle greyish blue; primaries of the same color as the back, except the tips, which are white..*L. glaucescens.*

Mantle pale grayish blue; primaries of the same color at the base, terminating largely with white..*L. leucopterus.*

Mantle grayish blue; primaries ash gray; the tips marked with a rounded white spot..*L. chalcopterus.*

B. DOMINICANUS, Bruch.—Large; the upper plumage dark slate color; primaries black near the end; tips white ....*L. marinus.*

C. LAROIDES, Brehm.—Large; the mantle pearl or bluish gray; primaries marked near the end with a black band; tips white.

Mantle pale bluish gray; primaries black near the end, with the tips white...*L. argentatus.*

Mantle bluish gray; primaries crossed near the end with black; tips white.

L. californicus.

Mantle dark bluish gray; primaries black near the end, with the tips white.

L. occidentalis.

August 25, 1858.
106 **b**

Mantle pale bluish gray ; primaries marked near their ends with black, the tips being white ; bill yellowish green crossed with a black band. (Pr. Bonaparte puts this species in *Larus*.)...*L. delawarensis*.

Mantle light pearl blue ; primaries black near their ends, with white tips ; bill rather small and slender..*L. suckleyi*.

LARUS GLAUCUS, Brünnich.

The Glaucous Gull; The Burgomaster.

Larus glaucus, BRÜNN. Orn. Bor. 1764, 44.—BONAP. Synop. 1828, No. 302.—RICH. & SW. F. B. A. II, 1831, 416.—
    NUTT. Man. II, 1834, 306.—AUD. Birds Amer. VII, 1844, 170 ; pl. ccccxlix.

Laroides glaucus, BRUCH, Cab. Journ. 1855, 281.

Leucus glaucus, BONAP. Cons. Av. II, 1856, 215.

" *Larus consul*, BOIE."

" *Larus glacialis*, MACGILL "

SP. CH.—*Adult*. The head, neck, rump, tail, and entire under plumage pure white ; the back and wings are of a light bluish gray ; the edge of the wing, the ends of the first primaries, and the shafts and tips of the others white. Bill gamboge yellow, with a spot of reddish orange near the end of the lower mandible ; irides light yellow ; legs and feet flesh color.

Length, 30 inches ; alar extent, 60 ; wing, from flexure, 19½ ; tail, 8¾ ; tarsus 2¹¹₁₆ ; bill, along the ridge, 2¾.

Hab.—Arctic seas ; Labrador ; New York in winter, rarely.

Individuals appear to vary considerably from the above measurements, some being much smaller ; but Capt. Sabine found one example to measure 32 inches, with an extent of wing of 65 inches ; its tarsus was 3½ inches in length, and its bill 4 inches.

The young have the upper plumage pale yellowish white, mottled with very pale brown ; breast and abdomen gray ; tail white, irregularly spotted with pale brown ; bill yellow for two-thirds its length and terminating with blackish brown.

LARUS GLAUCESCENS, Lichtenstein.

The Glaucous-winged Gull.

" *Laroides glaucescens*, LICHT." BRUCH, Rev. Lar. in Cab. Jour. 1855, 281.

Leucus glaucescens, BON. Cons. Av. II, 1856, 216.

" *Laroides glaucopterus*, KITTL." BRUCH, Rev. Lar. in Cab. Jour. 1855, 281.

? *Larus brachyrhynchus*, GOULD.

SP. CH.—*Adult*. Head and neck white, streaked with gray ; under surface, rump, and tail pure white ; back and wings light pearl blue (same shade as in *L. argentatus ;*) the primaries are of the same color, but rather darker, with well defined white tips ; on the first quill the white extends on the tip for about two inches and is crossed by a bar of the same color as the primaries ; iris white ; bill yellow, with an orange red spot on the angle of the lower mandible ; legs and feet flesh color.

Length, 27¾ inches ; wing, 16½ ; tail, 7¼ ; bill along ridge, 2⅜, deep at base, 11-16, at angle, 12-16 ; tarsi, 2 9-16 ; middle toe and claw, 2⅝.

Young mottled with grayish white and cinereous ; the quills and tail bluish ash ; bill black, in some specimens yellowish at base ; legs and feet dusky flesh color.

Hab.—Northwest coast of North America.

In the collection are a number of specimens of this fine gull, from quite young to fully adult ; it is nearly equal in size to *L. glaucus,* but with a less powerful bill and more slender tarsi.

I have not seen the original description of *L. glaucescens,* the locality of which is Kamtschatka, but the description of it by Bruch in his "Revision der Gattung *Larus,* Linn." in Cabanis

Journal für Ornith. Juli, 1855, p. 281, applies so well to the adult specimens before me, that I have no doubt of their being the same. His account, in which no measurements are given, is very concise and is as follows :

"Resembling *L. glaucus* altogether, with the exception of the wing feathers, which in this species are ashy gray with round white spots on the points."

He puts *L. glaucopterus*, Kittlitz, as a synonym, but gives no references where to find the descriptions of either author.

The omission to make references to the original descriptions of species prevails throughout Dr. Bruch's very valuable monograph ; it would have added much to its usefulness if this had been done when citing authorities.

List of specimens.

Catal. No.	Sex.	Locality.	When collected.	Whence obtained.	Orig. No.	Collected by—	Length.	Stretch of wings.	Wing.	Remarks.
6462	♂	Puget's Sound..........	Feb. 4, 1856	....	215	Dr. Suckley..	25.00	54.00	17.25	....
	♂	......do.............	....	....	559	....	26.00	....	17.50	....
4527	♂	Washington Territory.	....	....	154	Dr. Suckley ..	23.00	....	15.75	....
6452	♀	Fort Steilacoom, W. T.	Dec. 26, 1856	Gov. Stevens..	7	....do	24.00	52.00	15.50	....
6457	♂	......do...............	Dec. 20, 1850	......do	6	....do	26.00	58.00	17.00	....
6453	......	Shoalwater Bay, W. T..	Oct. 13, 1854	......do	......	Dr. Cooper ..	24.50	51.50	15.50	Iris grayish yellow ; bill blue ; feet flesh color.
6458	......	......do...........	May 3, 1852	......do	67	....do	....	....	....	Iris white ; bill yellow and red.
6461	......	......do	Mar. —, 1854	......do	......	....do	22.50	52.00	15.00	Iris dark brown ; bill and feet gray.
6460	......	Bodega, Cal............	Dec. —, 1854	Lt. Trowbridge.	......	T. A. Szabo..	27.75	....	16.50	....

LARUS LEUCOPTERUS, Faber.

The White-winged Gull.

Larus leucopterus, FABER, Prodr. Isl. Orn. 1820, 91.—BONAP. Syn. 1828, No. 301.—RICH. & SW. F. B. A. II, 1831, 418.—NUTT. Man. II, 1834, 305.—AUD. Birds Amer. VII, 1844, 159 ; pl. ccccxlvii.

Laroides leucopterus, BRUCH, Cab. Journ. 1855, 281.

Leucus leucopterus, BON. Cons. Av. II, 1856, 217.

"*Larus islandicus*, EDMONSTON."

Larus glaucoides, TEMM.

SP. CH.—*Adult*. Back and wings pale bluish gray ; the terminal part of the quills and their shafts, as well as the rest of the plumage pure white ; bill bright yellow, with an orange red spot on the lower mandible towards the end ; legs and feet pale flesh color.

Length, 26 inches ; wing, 17½ ; tail, 6½ ; bill about 2 ; tarsi, 2¼.

Hab.—Arctic seas, Baffin's Bay, Labrador.

LARUS CHALCOPTERUS, Lawrence.

The Gray-winged Gull.

"*Laroides chalcopterus*, LICHT." BRUCH, Rev. Lar. in Cab. Jour. 1855, 282.

Leucus chalcopterus, BON. Cons. Av. II, 1856, 216.

The only notice of this species I have met with is in Bruch's Monograph of Gulls, referred to above ; his description is as follows :

"Resembles very much *L. leucopterus*, except in the wing feathers, which are ash gray with round white spotted points ; the young are dark gray like *L. glaucopterus*."

Hab.—"American coast of Behring's Straits and Greenland."

LARUS MARINUS, Linnaeus.

The Great Black-backed Gull.

Larus marinus, Linn. Syst. Nat. I, 1766, 225.—Bonap. Syn. 1828, No. 303 —Nutt. Man. II, 1834, 308.—Aud. Birds Am. VII, 1844, 172 : pl ccccl.
Dominicanus marinus, Bruch, Cab. Jour. 1855, 280.—Bon. Cons. Av. II, 1856, 213.

Sp. Ch —*Adult*. The head, neck, entire under plumage, upper tail coverts, and tail are pure white ; the back and wings are of a dark slate color ; the primaries are deep black, largely tipped with white, as are the extremities of most of the quills ; the bill is gamboge yellow, with an orange red spot near the end of the lower mandible ; legs and feet pale yellow.

Length about 30 inches ; wing, 20 ; tail, 9 ; bill, 2 10-12 ; tarsus, 3 2-12.

Young Head, rump, and under plumage grayish white with streaks of light brown ; back and wings mottled with brownish ash and grayish white ; primaries blackish brown, having the tips edged with white ; tail white, spotted with brown and having a broad subterminal band of the same color ; bill brownish black, yellowish at the base ; legs and feet yellow.

Hab.—North Atlantic, Labrador ; as far south as Florida in winter.

LARUS ARGENTATUS, Brünnich.

The Herring Gull; The Silvery Gull.

Larus argentatus, Brünn. Orn. Bor. 1764, 44.—Bonap. Syn. 1828, No. 300.—Nutt. Man. II, 1834, 304.—Aud. Birds Am. VII, 1844, 163 ; pl. ccccxlviii.
Laroides argentatus, Bruch, Cab. Jour. 1855, 282.—Bon. Cons. Av. II, 1856, 218.
Laroides argentatoides, Rich. F. B. A. II, 1831, 417.

Sp. Ch.—*Adult*. Head, neck, under parts, rump, and tail, pure white ; back and wings light pearl blue ; the first six primaries are marked towards their ends with black, which begins on the first at about half its length from the end, and is rapidly lessened on the others until it becomes only a sub-terminal bar on the sixth ; the primaries all tipped with white ; on the first quill it is about an inch and a half in extent, crossed near the end with a black bar, on the second quill there is a round white spot on the inner web near the end ; secondaries and tertiaries broadly ending with white ; bill bright yellow, with an orange red spot near the end of the lower mandible ; l gs and feet flesh colored.

Length of male, 23 inches ; wing, 18 ; tail, 7½ ; bill along ridge, 2½ ; depth at angle, $\frac{13}{16}$; tarsus, 2½. Female a little smaller than the male, but similar in plumage.

Young mottled with light grayish brown and dull white; primaries blackish brown; bill brownish black, yellowish at the base.

Hab.— Atlantic coast from Texas to Newfoundland ; western States ; Ohio and Mississippi rivers.

L. argentatoides, Richardson, is made a distinct species by both Bruch and Bonaparte. Bruch describes it as differing from *L. argentatus* "merely by its paler gull blue."

Bonaparte (Cons. Av. II, 1856, 218) makes it the bird described by American writers, and says, "distinct from *L. argentatus*, with the back paler, smaller, 20 inches in length, tarsi 2 inches."

I have specimens of the species herein described as *L. argentatus*, which vary in size from 22 to over 26 inches, but cannot discover sufficient characteristic differences to form two species.

There is great variation in the size of different individuals in the gull family, so much so that it would not be safe to make dimensions a guide for specific distinction.

Mr. McGillivray, in his "History of British Birds," under *L. argentatus*, notices this great disparity in size, and remarks upon the probable identity of the European and American bird as follows: "Having carefully examined specimens from various parts of North America, I find them clearly to belong to the same species."

List of specimens.

Catal. No.	Sex.	Locality.	When collected.	Whence obtained.	Orig. No.	Collected by—	Length.	Stretch of wings.	Wing.
4355	♂	Washington, D. C..	Jan. 31, 1855.	Market		S. G. Brown	23. 00	59. 00	18. 00
4356	♀	------do	---do---	--do		----do	22. 50	59. 00	16. 50
6926		Nelson river, H. B.		Dr Gunn		Jno. Isbister	26. 00		17. 00
------	♂	Coast New York		Cab. J. N. Lawrence.	982		26. 00		16. 50
------	♀	------do		---do	983		23. 00		16. 10

LARUS OCCIDENTALIS, Audubon.

The Western Gull.

Larus occidentalis, Aud. Orn. Biog. V, 1839, 320.—Aud. Birds Am. VII, 1844, 161.
Laroides occidentalis, Bruch, Cab. Jour. 1855, 282.—Bon. Cons. Av. II, 1856, 219.

Sp. Ch.—*Adult.* The head, neck, rump, tail, and under plumage, pure white ; the back and wings grayish blue, many shades darker than in *L. argentatus;* the first six primaries are black towards their ends, extending on the first for about half its length, and lessening on the others, until on the sixth it is reduced to a narrow sub-terminal bar ; the tips of all are white, on the first the white is an inch and a half in extent, and crossed near the end with black ; secondaries and tertiaries with broad white tips ; iris gray ; bill deep yellow, with a bright orange red spot on the angle of the lower mandible ; legs and feet flesh color.

Young mottled with lead colored brown, grayish white, and brownish ash, lighter on the lower parts ; primaries blackish brown ; bill brownish black, dull yellow at base ; legs and feet brownish flesh color.

Length, 25 inches ; wing, 17 ; tail, 7 ; bill, 2½ ; depth at angle, ⅞ ; tarsus, 2⅞.

Hab.—Northwest coast of North America.

There are numerous specimens of all ages of this well marked species in the collection ; it is easily distinguished from *L. argentatus* by its darker colored mantle. A striking characteristic in the young of this species is its very stout bill, which, though much shorter than in the adult, has comparatively great depth at the angle.

Mr. Audubon's original specimens of this species are now in the private cabinet of Professor S. F. Baird.

List of specimens.

Catal. No.	Sex.	Locality.	When collected.	Whence obtained.	Orig'l No.	Collected by—	Length	Stretch of wings.	Wing.	Remarks.
		Oregon		Cab. G. N. Lawrence.	984					
4493	O	Shoalwater Bay..	Dec. 6, 1854	Lieut. Williamson		Dr. Cooper ..	23.00	54.00	15.25	Eye dark brown ; feet brownish flesh color.
4510		------do	Jan. 6, 1855	------do		----do	21.50	52.50	15.50	Eye gray ; feet black ; bill yellow.
6451		------do	Oct. 30, 1854	Gov. Stevens	108	---do	24.00	55.00	16.00	Iris gray ; yellow bill ; feet flesh color.
6455		Bodega, Cal	Dec. —, 1854	Lieut. Trowbridge....		T. A. Szabo .	23.00		15.75	
6463		Presidio, Cal	Ap'l 25, 1853	------do		----do	22.00		15.26	
6464		.... do		------do			25.00		17.00	
6465		------do		------do			25.00		16.00	
6474	O	------do	May 4, 1853	------do			23.00		15.00	
6459	O	San Diego, Cal		------do			22.50		14 50	
6454		------do		------do		A. Cassidy...	24.00		16.00	

LARUS CALIFORNICUS, Lawrence.

The California Gull.

Larus californicus, Lawr. Ann. Lyc. N. H. N. Y. VI, 1854, 79.
Laroides californicus, Bon. Cons. Av. II, 1856, 220.

Sp. Ch.—*Adult.* The head, neck, under plumage, rump, and tail, pure white ; back and wings pearl blue, darker than in L. argentatus, but not so dark as in L. occidentalis; the six outer primaries are marked with black towards their ends, extending on the first for about two-thirds its length, and becoming less on the others, until on the sixth it consists only of a sub-terminal bar ; the tips of all are white, on the exterior quill the white extends about two inches, and is crossed near the end by a black bar ; the secondaries and tertiaries terminate with white; iris hazel ; bill yellow ; basal part of the upper mandible greenish gray for two-thirds its length ; a blackish band crosses both mandibles near their ends, it is darker in color on the lower mandible, where it is bordered with orange ; tarsus and feet flesh color.

Length, 22½ inches ; wing, 16½ ; tail, 7 ; bill, 2 ; depth at angle, 10-16 ; tarsus, 2⅜ ; middle toe and nail, 2¼.

There are three specimens of this gull in the collection ; one, of which the above are the measurements, differs only from my original specimen in the three outer primaries not having white tips, the first having a white spot near the end, and the tail being marked with an interrupted sub-terminal black band, an evidence that it is not fully adult.

The two other specimens are smaller, (probably females ;) they appear to be in mature plumage, and have the end of the first primary white for an extent of two inches ; there is a white spot on the second primary about one inch inside of the white tip, in other respects like my specimen.

They measure in length 20 inches ; wing, 15¼ ; tail, 6 ; bill, 1¾ ; depth at angle, $\frac{9}{16}$; tarsus, 2⅛ ; middle toe and nail, 2⅛.

Hob.—West coast of North America.

Among various specimens of gulls sent me by Professor Baird from his private cabinet for examination, I find two examples of the above species ; these were brought by Dr. Townsend from the Pacific, and were labelled by him L. argentatus.

List of specimens.

Catal. No.	Locality.	When collected.	Whence obtained.	Orig. No.	Collected by—	Length.	Stretch of wings.	Wing.	Remarks.
	California............	....	Cab. G. N. Lawrence..	985	....	20.00	....	15.25	....
4508	San Francisco	....	Lieut. Williamson.....	......	Dr. Newberry ..	20.00	....	15.25	....
4509	Shoalwater Bay........	Feb. 9, 1855	....	......	Dr. Cooper	20.00	49.00	15.25	Eyes dark brown; bill grayish.
6456	......do...............	Oct. 5, 1854	Gov. Stevens	102	....do..	22.50	55.00	16.00	Iris hazel ; bill pale gray ; feet flesh color.
2771	Columbia river	Oct. 22, 1836	S. F. Baird	......	J. K. Townsend	....	....	......	....
2772	......do...............	Oct. 6, 1836	......do	......	....do	....	....	......	....

LARUS DELAWARENSIS, Ord.

The Ring-billed Gull.

Larus delawarensis, Ord, Guth. Geog. 2nd Am. Ed. II, 1815, 319.
Larus canus, Bon. Syn. 1828, No. 296.—Rich. & Sw. F. Bor. Am. II, 1831, 420.
Larus brachyrhynchus, Rich. & Sw. F. Bor. Am. II, 1831, 422, (not of Gould.)
Larus zonorhynchus, Rich. & Sw. F. B. Am. II, 1831, 422.—Nutt. Man. II, 1834, 300.—Aud. Birds Am. VII, 1844, 152 ; pl. ccccxlvi.—Bon. Cons. Av. II, 1856, 224.
Gavina zonorhynchus, Bruch, Cab. Jour. 1855, 282.

Sp. Ch.—*Adult*. The head, neck, under parts and tail are pure white ; back and wings very light pearl blue ; first and second primaries black for two-thirds of their length towards the end, the three next quills have the black much less in extent, and on the sixth it is reduced to a sub-terminal bar, the first quill is black at the end, above which is a broad white band, the second quill is black to the tip, with a white spot on the inner web an inch and a half from the end, the other primaries tipped with white ; secondaries and tertiaries ending in white ; iris yellow ; bill crossed near the end with a blackish brown band, between which and the base it is greenish yellow, the tip is yellow ; tarsi and feet greenish yellow.

Length, about 20 inches ; wing, 15 ; tail, 6 ; bill, 1⅝ ; depth at angle, ½ ; tarsus, 2¼.

Young. On the upper plumage mottled with blackish brown and gray ; beneath grayish white, with light brown spots ; primaries black ; tail white, with a sub-terminal black band ; bill black, with the base yellow.

Hab.—Arctic America ; Texas to Labrador ; western rivers ; northwest coast.

No bird possessing the peculiar character of Mr. Ord's "*delawarensis*," also named "The Toothed-bill Gull," has been met with since the time of his description, nor has his species been identified with any other. His account of its measurements and coloraticn agrees precisely with the adult *L. zonorhynchus*, the only character to reconcile is the toothed bill ; this I consider as a possible malformation, or probably an accidental toothing, caused by its being worn in some particular mode of feeding.

It is, of course, difficult to establish certainly the identity of Mr. Ord's species with the present, but I am strongly of the opinion that they are the same, for the reasons given above, and also from the fact of no others having been obtained. As all our species are abundant, if this was really distinct, it surely could not have so long escaped observation.

Feeling, therefore, quite confident that Mr. Ord's species can be no other than the one now described, I have given his name priority.

Below I have given Mr. Ord's description.

"Length, 19½ inches ; extent, 46 ; upper mandible with four indentations or blunt teeth, lower with three; corner of mouth and eyelids bright vermilion; head, neck, tail, and beneath, pure white ; wings, back and scapulars, blue ash. Weight, 19 ounces."

I have appended to this, and also to the account of several other species, extracts from some original notes made by Dr. Suckley in Washington Territory.

Note by Dr. Suckley.—"This gull is quite common on Puget's Sound in winter. It seems to be subject to great changes in color of plumage, feet and bill, at different ages. The habits of this bird have been so well described by Nuttall and others, that I have scarcely anything to add. On Puget's Sound, during the cool months, this species is found abundantly on the marshes and flats at the mouths of the different rivers emptying into the Sound. When an individual is wounded, like other gulls, his comrades hover over and circle around the victim, as if impelled by motives of curiosity or compassion ; at this time frequently the others can be rapidly brought down by the same gunner with his undischarged barrels. But the occasion must be quickly seized, because the sympathizing birds which at first are bewitched, as it were, by the accident to their companion, soon lose the charm, and, becoming more wary, enlarge their circles, and ascending higher and higher soon place themselves out of shot range."

List of specimens.

Catal. No.	Sex.	Locality.	When collected.	Whence obtained.	Orig. No.	Collected by—	Length.	Stretch of wings.	Wing.	Remarks.
......		Coast of New Jersey...	....	Cab. G. N. Lawrence	986	....	....	....	......	....
	♀	Laramie river, N. T....	July 23, 1857	Lieut. Bryan.......	316	W. S. Wood...	....	....	......	....
8908	......	Nebraska Territory.....	....	Lieut. Warren......	......	Dr. Hayden....	....	....	......	....
6466	......	Fort Thorn, N. M......	....	Capt. Pope	......	Dr. Henry	17.50	....	14.50	....
4161	......	Brazos, Texas.........	Mar. 27, 1853	Capt. Van Vliet....	......	....	19.00	47.00	15.00	Eyes yellow ....
9541	......	Puget's Sound.........	Oct. 22, 1857	A. Campbell	53	Dr. Kennerly ..	....	....	......	....

LARUS SUCKLEYI, Lawrence.

Suckley's Gull.

Larus suckleyi, LAWR. Ann. Lyc. N. H. N. Y. VI, 1858, 264.

SP. CH.—*Adult*. Head, neck, under plumage and tail, pure white ; back and wings clear pearl blue ; ends of the primaries black, occupying about half the length of the first and decreasing to the seventh, on which it consists only of a sub-terminal spot ; the first primary has a white spot over both webs an inch and a half in extent inside the tip, the second has a similar mark of white, but less in extent ; the tips of the first and second primaries are black, but of all the others white ; the secondaries and tertiaries largely marked with white at their ends ; bill dusky yellowish green, except on the ridge of the upper mandible, forward of the nostrils, and on the angle of the lower mandible, which parts are orange yellow ; tips of both mandibles pale yellow ; legs and feet greenish yellow.

Length, 17½ inches ; alar extent, 43¼ ; wing, 13¾ ; tail, 5½ ; bill, 1 5-16 ; tarsi, 1⅝.

Young. Mottled with grayish white and dark ash ; wings and tail dark brown, the latter ashy white at the base and tip ; bill flesh color for half its length from the base, terminating with black ; legs and feet flesh color.

Hab.—Pacific coast ; Puget's Sound.

Four specimens are in the collection.

List of specimens.

Catal. No.	Age.	Locality.	When collected.	Whence obtained.	Orig'l No.	Collected by—	Length.	Stretch of wings.	Wing.	Remarks.
4571	.....	Puget's Sound	Feb. 4, 1856	....	217	Dr. Suckley ...	17.50	43.25	13.75	....
8435	......	......do.............	Sept. —, 1857	A. Campb'll......	.....	Dr. Kennerly ..	17.00	....	14.00	....
6472	O	Fort Steilacoom......	Dec. 26, 1854	Gov. Stevens.....	8	Dr. Suckley....	17.25	44.50	13.25	....
6476	O	Shoalwater bay	Oct. 13, 1854	......do..........	105	Dr. Cooper.....	16.00	41.50	12.75	Iris hazel; bill flesh color, black tips; feet flesh color.

BLASIPUS, Bonaparte.

Blasipus, BON. 1852.

CH.—Bill long and rather slender ; general color dusky ; of medium size.

Bonaparte enumerates three species under this genus, only one of which inhabits our coast ; in my opinion he has improperly placed *"belcheri"* and *"fuliginosus"* (closely allied species, if not identical with the above,) in a different genus, viz : *Leucophaeus*, the type of which is *"haematorhynchus,"* a species having the bill very robust.

BLASIPUS HEERMANNI, Bon.

The White-headed Gull.

Larus heermanni, CASS. Proc. Acad. N. Soc. Phil. VI, 1852, 187.—IB. Ills. I, 1853, 28 ; pl. v.
Adelarus heermanni, BRUCH, Cab. Jour. 1855, 279.
Blasipus heermanni, BON. Cons. Av. II, 1856, 211.

SP. CH.—*Adult*. " Bill red, both mandibles tipped with black ; feet and legs dark ; head white, which color gradually blends into an ashy lead color, enveloping the entire body above and below, darker on the back and wings and paler on the abdomen. Secondary quills tipped with white, forming an oblique bar when the wings are folded. Superior coverts of the tail very pale cinereous, nearly white. Quills and tail feathers brownish black, all of the latter narrowly tipped with white. Shafts of the two first primaries white on the inferior surface of the wing."

" Total length, about 17½ inches ; wing, 13½ ; tail, 5½ ; bill from angle to tip of upper mandible, 2¼ inches."

" *Young*. Smaller ; total length, about 16 inches ; wing, 13 ; tail, 5 inches. Entire plumage brown, darker on the head and paler on the under surface of the body ; quills and tail feathers brownish black, the latter narrowly tipped with white."

Hab.—Coast of California.

The above are Mr. Cassin's descriptions of the adult and young.

In the collection are seven specimens which I consider to be identical with the above species; one agrees very closely with Mr. Cassin's description of the young; none of the others have the head white, but in most of them this color exists on the throat and is developing itself on the head in such a manner as to leave no doubt that it would have become white eventually; the neck is of a clear ash; the upper tail coverts are of a pearl gray color; tail rather broadly tipped with white.

In this plumage they agree very well with *L. belcheri*, Vigors[1]; the measurements given by Vigors are as follows: length, 21 inches; wing, 11; tail, 6; bill, 2; tarsi, 2. The specimens in the collection range in length from 18 to 21 inches; wings, about 14; tail, 5½ to 6; bill, 2; tarsi, 2. Differing from the dimensions of *Belcheri* only in the length of the wing, which I am satisfied is an error, as a wing of 11 inches for a gull measuring 21 in length is out of all proportion.

They also answer very well to the description of *L. fuliginosus*, Gould, which is thus given in the Zool. of the Voy. of the Beagle, Birds, p. 141:

"The whole of the plumage deep leaden gray; the upper and under tail coverts being lightest; bill red at the base, black at the tip; feet black."

"Length, 16½ inches; wing, 13½; tail, 6; tarsi, 2⅛; bill, 2¾," (probably from gape.)

I incline to the opinion that the three names refer to the same bird, Mr. Cassin describing it in perfect plumage as *L. heermanni*. If this proves to be the case, Vigors' name of *Belcheri* will have priority.

Note by Dr. Suckley.—"*Larus belcheri*. Two gulls supposed by me to belong to this species, were obtained in the Straits of Fuca, near Whidby's Island, W. T. Both of these gulls had red bills. The species does not seem to be fond of feeding on the shores and bare flats, like the *L. zonorhynchus* and other species, but is almost always found on kelp beds floating in deep water some distance from the shore. In these situations both my specimens were shot. These gulls, when being skinned, emitted a very rank disagreeable odor, much stronger and more unpleasant than that of *L. zonorhynchus*."

List of specimens.

Catal. No.	Age.	Locality.	When collected.	Whence obtained.	Orig'l No.	Collected by—	Length.	Stretch of wings.	Wing.	Remarks.
6150	......	Puget's Sound......	Aug. 26, 1856	Dr. Suckley........	556	....	19.75	44.50	....	....
6449	......	......do............	......do......	......do...........	557	....	18.50	......	....	....
	......	Shoalwater bay....	Sept. 8, 1854	Gov. Stevens	89	Dr. Cooper...	21.00	42.50	....	Bill carmine and black; iris brownish gray.
	......	..... do..........	....	......do.........	......	......do......	20.00	......	....	....
6447	o	Bodega, Cal........	Dec. —, 1851	Lieut. Trowbridge...	......	T. Szabo.....	19.00	......	13.25	....
6448	......	San Diego, Cal.....	....	......do...........	......	.. ..	21.00	43.00	14.00	Bill dark red; legs black......
6475	......	......do..........	....	Lieut. Williamson.	......	....	....	....	....	....
	......	Mazatlan, Mexico..	....	Col. Abert........	......	......	....	....	....	....

[1] *Larus belcheri*, Vɪɢ. Zool. Jour. IV, 1829, 358.—Iʙ. Zool. Blossom, 1839, 39.

August 27, 1858.

107 b

CHROICOCEPHALUS, Eyton.

Chroicocephalus, EYTON, Cat. Brit. Birds, 1836.

CH.—Bill moderate, rather slender, much compressed ; upper mandible straight at base, more or less curved at the end; nostrils lateral and longitudinal ; wings long, narrow, and pointed ; tail moderate, usually even ; tarsi rather slender ; feet webbed ; hind toe small and elevated.

These gulls are of medium or small size ; in their spring attire the head is clothed with a dark colored hood, but in winter it becomes white, with a dusky spot behind the ear. These birds are very handsome, the dark and light colors of their plumage forming a beautiful contrast.

The species of this genus are beautiful birds, and readily known by the dark colored hood or cowl which envelopes the head in summer. Five species are enumerated as belonging to the United States, but the occurrence of *minutus* may be considered as accidental. They may be known by the following characters :

Mantle and wings grayish blue ; hood blackish lead gray ; narrow white lines on the upper and lower eyelids..*C. atricilla.*

Mantle and wings dark bluish gray ; hood plumbeous black, eyelids white..*C. franklinii.*

Mantle and wings ash blue ; hood plumbeous black ; an oval white spot over the eye and one on the lower eyelid...*C. cucullatus.*

Mantle and wings light grayish blue ; hood grayish black ; a white band divided by a narrow black line surrounds the posterior part of the eye..................*C. philadelphia.*

Mantle and wings pale bluish gray ; hood black ; behind the eye a white crescent.........
C. minutus.

CHROICOCEPHALUS ATRICILLÁ, (Linnaeus.)

The Laughing Gull.

Larus atricilla, LINN. Syst. Nat. I, 1766, 225.—BONAP. Syn. 1828, No. 294.—NUTT. Man. II, 1834, 291.—AUD. Birds Am. VII, 1844, 136 ; pl. ccccxliii.
Larus ridibundus, WILS. IX, 1824, 89 ; pl. lxxiv.
Atricilla catesbyi, BRUCH, Cab. Jour. 1855, 287.

SP. CH.—*Adult.* Head and upper part of neck blackish lead gray, extending lower in front ; upper and lower eyelids white posteriorly ; lower part of neck, entire under plumage, rump, and tail pure white ; in spring a beautiful roseate tint exists on the breast and abdomen ; back and wings grayish lead color ; the first six primaries are black, beginning on the first at about two-thirds of its length from the point and regularly becoming less on the others until on the sixth it is reduced to two spots near the end ; tips in some specimens white, and in others black to their points ; bill and inside of the mouth dark carmine ; iris bluish black ; legs and feet deep red. In winter the head becomes white, intermixed on the crown and hind neck with brownish gray.

Length, 17 inches ; wing, 13 ; tail, 5 ; bill, $1\frac{3}{4}$; tarsus, 2 inches.

Hab.—Texas to Massachusetts.

List of specimens.

Catal. No.	Sex.	Locality.	When collected.	Whence obtained.	Orig. No.	Length.	Stretch of wings.	Wing.	Remarks.
	....	Coast New York........	....	Cab. G. N. Lawrence	988	....	....	....	....
6541	♂	Key Biscayne, Fla.......	April 7......	G. Würdemann....	......	....	....	....	Pupil, feet, and bill (?) dark blue; eyes with hazel ring.
6473	♂	Indian river, Fla........	....	......do...........	.... .	16.50	39.50	12.50	Bill dark purple.............................
4929	♀	St. John's river, Fla......	....	......do...........	......	....	....	13.00	....
4318	....	Calcasieu Pass, La.......	1856........	......do...........	......	....	....	13.00	....
4319	....	....do........	1854........	......do...........	......	16.00	....	13.00	....
5642	....	Indianola, Texas.........	Mar. 27,1855	Capt. J. Pope......	38	17.00	40.50	13.25	Bill and gums red, eyes dark, feet dark gray.
4162	....	Brazos, Texas......	Mar. 26,1853	Capt. Van Vliet....	14	16.50	39.50	13.00	Eyes black...............................

CHROICOCEPHALUS FRANKLINII, Bruch.

Franklin's Rosy Gull.

Larus franklinii, Rich. F. B. A. II, 1831, 424; pl. lxxi.—Nutt. Man. II, 1834, 293.—Aud. Birds Am. VII, 1844, 145, (not figured.)

Chroicocephalus franklinii, Bruch, Cab. Jour. 1855, 289.

Sp. Ch.—*Adult.* Head and upper part of neck black, with a plumbeous hue on the fore part of the neck extending a little lower than it does behind; both eyelids white, except in front; lower part of neck, under plumage, rump, and tail white; the under surface and interior lining of the wings deeply tinged with peach-blossom red; back and wings dark bluish gray; the outer web of the first primary is black nearly to the end, the inner web of the first and both webs of the four next are crossed with a subterminal black band about two inches wide on the outer and lessening to a half inch on the fifth; all the quill feathers end with white, on the first primary it is about one inch in extent; shafts of all the primaries and the inner web of the first white, the other primaries are the same color as the back, except on the inner edge of the inner web and immediately adjoining the black bar, where they are white; bill and legs vermilion.

Length, 15 inches; wing, 12; tail, 4½; bill, 1¼; tarsus, 1⅜.

Hab.—Missouri river; interior of fur countries.

There are four specimens of this beautiful and well marked species in the collection, two of them in perfect plumage, in which a delicate roseate tint on the neck and under surface is very apparent. It is easily distinguished from *C. atricilla* by its much darker hood and the very differently colored primaries.

List of specimens.

Catal. No.	Sex and age.	Locality.	When collected.	Whence obtained.	Collected by—	Length.	Stretch of wings.	Wing.	Remarks.
4897	♂	Kanesville, Neb........	April 28, 1856	Lieut. Warren.....	Dr. Hayden....	15.00	38.12	12.00	Eyes black...............
5784	♀	Platte river............	July 14, 1856	Lieut. Bryan.......	W. S. Wood....	....	....	....	....
5790	○	Fort Pierre, Neb.......	....	Dr. Evans	... .	....	....	....	....

CHROICOCEPHALUS CUCULLATUS, Lichtenstein.

The Hooded Gull.

" *Chroicocephalus cucullatus*, Licht." Bruch, Rev. Lar. in Cab. Jour. 1855, 290.

Sp. Ch.—*Adult.* Hood plumbeous black, with an oval white spot over the eye and another on the hind part of the lower eyelid, both extending backward; the entire neck, upper tail coverts, and under plumage pure white; back and wings ash blue, about the shade of *franklinii*; primaries bluish ash, the first black on the outer web and for one quarter its length on the inner at the end: the second, third, fourth, and fifth also crossed with black towards their ends, decreasing behind ; on the sixth a nar-row bar of black; the tips of all white, occupying most space on the sixth and lessening in extent to the first, where it becomes a mere edging ; the remaining primaries, the secondaries, and tertiaries terminate largely with white ; the shafts of the three outer primaries are blackish brown ; the three lateral tail feathers are white, the others light pearl blue, deepest in color on the two central ones ; bill deep carmine, crossed near the end with black, tip dull yellow ; legs and feet red.

Length of skin about 13 inches ; wing, 11⅛ ; tail, 4 ; bill, 1¼, depth at base 6-16, at angle 5-16 ; tarsus 1½ ; middle toe and claw, 1½.

Young. Differs from the adult in having the forehead grayish white, crown, occiput, and sides of the head blackish brown, the white eye spots as in the adult ; the lesser wing coverts brownish ash, the primaries much darker, the inner ones tipped with white ; secondaries and tertiaries with dark brown centres and ending with white ; tail crossed with a subterminal band of brownish black.

Length of skin, 13½ inches ; wing, 11 ; tail, 4 ; bill, 1⅛ ; tarsus, 1⅜.

Hab.—Panama ; coast of Louisiana.

Two specimens are in the collection ; the adult is in fine plumage, and was obtained in Louisiana by Mr. G. Wurdemann, the first instance of its occurrence within the limits of the United States. This example agreeing so well with Bruch's description of *cucullatus,* cited above, I have referred it to that species. Mr. Bruch considers *L. pipixcan,* Wagler, to be the same as *cucullatus,* but in Wagler's description nothing is said of the white eye spots, which are a very conspicuous character.

List of specimens.

Catal. No.	Sex & Age.	Locality.	When collected.	Whence obtained.	Point of bill to end of tail.	Wing from carpal joint.
4320	------	Calcasieu Pass, Louisiana .	1854...............	G. Wurdemann.	13. 00	11. 12
4522	○	Panama	Dec. 28, 1855......	Dr. Suckley...............	13. 50	11. 00

CHROICOCEPHALUS PHILADELPHIA, Lawrence.

Bonaparte's Gull.

Sterna philadelphia, Ord, Guthrie's Geog. 2d Am. ed. II, 1815, 319.
Larus capistratus, Bonap. Syn. 1828, No. 293.
Larus bonapartei, Rich. & Sw. F. B. A. II, 1831, 425 ; pl. lxxii.—Nutt. Man. II, 1834, 294.—Aud. Birds Am. VII, 1844, 131 ; pl. ccccxlii.
Chroicocephalus bonapartei, Bruch, Cab. Jour. 1855, 292.

Sp. Ch.—*Adult.* Head and upper part of neck grayish black, this color extending rather lower on the throat than on the neck behind ; lower part of neck, under plumage, rump, and tail white ; back and wings clear bluish gray ; first primary black on the outer web ; inner web of the first primary, both webs of the second, and the outer web of the third white ; the inner web of the third and all the other primaries are of the same color as the back ; the six outer primaries have their ends black for the extent of about an inch on the central ones, but less on the first and sixth, they are all slightly tipped with white ; shoulders, anterior borders of the wings, and outer webs of the primary coverts white ; bill deep black ; inside of mouth carmine ; iris hazel ; legs and feet orange with a reddish tinge.

Length, 14½ inches ; wing, 10½ ; tail, 4¼ ; bill, 1⅛ ; tarsus, 1 5-16.

Hab.—Texas to Nova Scotia, Mississippi river, fur countries, Pacific coast of North America.

The young have the head white, intermixed on the occiput and hind neck with dark gray ; a round spot of dark plumbeous behind the eye ; the smaller wing coverts brown ; the outer webs of several of the primaries and a subterminal band on the tail black.

There are eleven specimens in the collection.

The specific name of "*bonapartei,*" under which this species has been so long known, in my opinion, must give place to that of Ord, cited above; he also designates it as the "Banded-tail Tern." To determine what species was described under the above name (if it was not distinct) has long been considered a problem which it was very desirable to solve; it agrees in every particular with specimens of the young of *bonapartei*, now under examination. Mr. Ord's description is as follows:

"Beneath pure white; above blue ash; below the auriculars a patch of dark slate; tail white, short, almost even, crossed by a dark brown band; a line of brown from the shoulder of the wing to the tertials. Weight full five ounces."

The slender and tern-like form of the bill probably induced Mr. Ord to put it in *Sterna*.

Note by Dr. Suckley.—"Abundant on Puget's Sound, in the neighborhood of which I obtained several specimens. This species is the only gull commonly eaten by the Nisqually Indians. I broiled one of these birds and found it about equal, in gastronomic qualities, to the *Rallus crepitans.*"

List of specimens.

Catal. No.	Sex.	Locality.	When collected.	Whence obtained.	Orig'l No.	Collected by—	Length.	Stretch of wings.	Wing.	Remarks.
.....	.....	Coast New York......	....	Cab. G. N. Lawrence.	991	....	....	....	....	....
6927	.....	Nelson river, H. B. T.	....	D. Gunn.............	.....	Jno. Isbister...	....	....	....	....
7934	♂	Arctic America......	....	J. Gould...........	32	....	....	....	....	....
7393	.....	California ,.......	....	....do..........	.....	....	....	....	....	....
6467	.....	San Diego, Cal......	....	Lt. Trowbridge......	.....	....	14.00	32.00	10.00	Eyes bl'k, legs yellow.
6468	.....	Presidio, Cal........	....	....do..........	.....	....	....	....	....	....
5569	♀	Petaluma, Cal........	....	E. Samuels.........	139	....	13.00	....	10.25	....
6469	.....	Puget's Sound, W. T...	Aug. —, 1856	Dr. Suckley.........	558	....	14.50	30.00	9.25	....
.....	.....	......do..........	....	......do...........	.....	....	14.00	....	10.00	....
8432	♀	......do..........	Sept. —, 1857	A. Campbell....	.....	Dr. Kennerly ..	....	....	....	....
8434	.....	......do..........	Aug. 30, 1857	......do........	.....	....do.........	....	....	....	....
8438	♀	......do..........	....do......	......do........	.....	....do.........	12.00	27.00	9.50	....

CHROICOCEPHALUS MINUTUS, Bruch.

The Little Gull.

Larus minutus, PALLAS, Reise, III, 702.—BONAP. Syn. 1828, No. 292.—RICH. & Sw. F. B. A. II, 1831, 426.—NUTT. Man. II, 1834, 289.

Chroicocephalus minutus, BRUCH, Cab. Jour. 1855, 290.

SP. CH.—*Adult.* Head and upper part of the neck black; a white crescent behind the eyes; part of the lower neck and under plumage roseate white; rump and tail pure white; back and wings of a pure and very pale bluish gray; primaries and secondaries ash gray tipped with white; bill deep lake red; iris dark brown; legs and feet carmine. Length, about 11½ inches.

Hab.—Arctic America? Europe.

There is no specimen in the collection from North America, although a fine series from Europe has been presented to the Smithsonian Institution by the Norwich Museum, England.

RISSA, Leach.

Rissa, LEACH, Steph. Gen. Zool. XIII, 1825, 180. Type *Larus tridactylus*, L.

CH.—Bill rather long, strong, and much compressed; culmen straight at base, curved from the nostrils to the tip; nostrils lateral and longitudinal; wings long and pointed; tail even; tarsi rather short; toes slender and united by a full web; hind toe rudimentary or very small.

These birds mostly inhabit the north.   They assemble in flocks, and are most graceful birds on the wing.   They possess great powers of flight, being able to contend with the strongest gale.   Medium in size.

Three species belonging to this genus are found in the United States.   They may be distinguished as below :

Mantle light pearl gray ; bill moderate, pale greenish yellow ; tarsi moderate ; hind toe rudimental..*R. tridactylus.*

Mantle light pearl blue; bill rather long ; greenish at the base, with the point yellow ; hind toe short; more developed than in the above species..............*R. septentrionalis.*

Mantle pale leaden gray ; bill short and strong, bright yellow ; hind toe short.*R. nivea.*

RISSA TRIDACTYLUS, Bonap.

The Kittiwake Gull.

Larus tridactylus, LINN. Syst. Nat. I, 1766, 224.—BONAP. Syn. 1828, No. 297.—RICH. & SW. II, 1831, 423.— NUTT. Man. II, 1834, 298.—AUD. Birds Am. VII, 1844, 146 ; pl. ccccxliv.
Rissa tridactylus, BON. List, 1838.—IS. Cons. Av. II, 1856, 225.—BRUCH, Cab. Jour. 1855, 284.
Larus rissa, BRÜNN. Orn. Bor. 1764.

SP. CH.—*Adult.* Head, neck, entire under plumage, rump, and tail white ; back and wings light bluish gray ; the ends of the five outer primaries and the outer web of the first black ; the fourth and fifth have small white tips ; bill greenish yellow ; iris reddish brown ; legs and feet brownish black with a green tinge.

Young. The head is white, marked on the hind head and neck with bluish gray ; a spot of the same color over the ears ; a narrow crescent of black in front of the eye.   Wings and shoulders marked with black ; primaries black.   Tail white, with a sub-terminal black band.   Bill black ; rest of the plumage same as in the adult.

Length, about 17 inches ; wing, 12 ; tail, 5¾ ; bill, 1½ ; tarsus, 1⅜.

Hab.—Fur countries ; Labrador ; southern coast in winter.

RISSA SEPTENTRIONALIS, Lawrence.

The North Pacific Kittiwake.

Rissa septentrionalis, LAWR. Ann. Lyc. N. Hist. N. Y. VI, 1858, 265.

SP. CH.—*Adult.* Head, neck, under surface, and tail pure white.   Back and wings light pearl blue ; first primary black for about half its length from the end ; a white spot one and a half inches in length crosses both webs near the end, which is black ; second primary black for about one third its length ; also with a white spot (but smaller) inside the black tip ; the next five primaries are black at their ends, with white tips ; the black decreases inwards, existing as a spot only on the seventh ; basal part of the primaries bluish ash, becoming white where it joins the black ends, except on the first and second ; secondaries and tertiaries ending with white ; bill dusky green at the base for two-thirds its length ; remainder yellow, which deepens to orange on the ridge of the upper mandible and angle of the lower ; legs and feet yellowish green.   Length, 17¼ inches ; wing, 13½ tail, 5¾ ; bill, 1⅜ ; tarsus, 1⅜.

Hab.—Pacific coast of North America ; Puget's Sound.

Two specimens are in the collection.

List of specimens.

Catal. No.	Locality.	When collected.	Whence obtained.	Orig. No.	Point of bill to end of tail.	Wing from carpal joint.
6470	Near Puget's Sound, W. T. ..	July 30, 1856...	Dr. Suckley............	520	16. 50	13. 50
4471	........do................	......do..........	......do..............	519	17. 25	13. 50

RISSA BREVIROSTRIS, B´r a n d t .

The Short-billed Kittiwake.

" *Rissa brevirostris*, BRANDT," BRUCH, Rev. Lar. in Cab. Jour. 1858, 285.

SP. CH.—Resembles *R. tridactyla* very much, both in structure and figure, but with the hind toe better formed ; bill yellow ; feet coral red.

Hab.—Northwest coast of North America.

No specimen in the collection.

The above is the substance of Bruch's description of this species. The type specimen he saw at St. Petersburg.

Bonaparte (Consp. Av. II, 1857, 226) puts the name of this species as a synonym to *brachyrhyncha*, Gould, which he says is not *L. niveus*, Pall., and puts the latter species in *Larus*, differing from Bruch, and also G. R. Gray, who consider *L. niveus*, Pall., and *L. brachyrhyncha*, Gould, as identical. Bonaparte further differs from Bruch in making a new species, viz., *Rissa kotzebui*, of " *R. niveus*, Pall., and *brachyrhyncha*, Gould,".No. 36 of Bruch's Monograph. These writers also vary materially in their views regarding other species ; but, as Mr. Bruch has made this family of birds his especial study, with apparently good opportunities for forming his opinions, I have chosen to follow him in enumerating the species now described as distinct.

RISSA NIVEA, B r u c h .

The Yellow-billed Gull.

Larus niveus, PALL. Zoogr. II, 1811, 320 ; pl. lxxiv.

Rissa nivea, BRUCH, Cab. Jour. 1855, 285.

? Larus brachyrhynchus, GOULD, Pro. Zool. Soc. July, 1843.—IB. Voy. Sulph. Birds, pl. xxxiv.

SP. CH.—*Adult.* Head, neck, all the under surface, rump, upper and under tail coverts, and tail, pure white ; back and wings, including the primaries, gray, passing into white at the tips of the scapulars, secondaries, and all but the first five primaries, which are thus marked ; the outer primary has its external web and three inches of the tip of the inner web deep black ; the next primary is tipped with black for three inches and a half on its outer, and two inches and a half on its inner web, and has a very minute speck of gray at the extreme tip ; the third primary is tipped with black for two inches, and has a small spot of gray at the extremity ; the fourth is tipped with black for an inch and a quarter, and has a larger spot of gray at the extremity than the third ; and the fifth is crossed by an irregular band of black near the tip three-quarters of an inch wide, the extremity being gray, fading into white on the margin of the inner web ; bill primrose yellow ; feet orange yellow.

Total length, 14 inches ; bill, $1\frac{1}{2}$; wing, $12\frac{1}{4}$; tail, $5\frac{1}{4}$; tarsi, $1\frac{1}{6}$.

Hab.—Russian America.

The above is Mr. Gould's account in the Zoology of the Voyage of the Sulphur.

No specimen in the collection.

PAGOPHILA, K a u p .

Pagophila, KAUP, Nat. Syst. der Eur. Thier. 1829.

CH.—Bill short and stout, compressed ; the upper mandible straight at base, curved at the end ; nostrils linear and lateral ; wings long and pointed ; tail moderate and even ; tarsi strong and rather short ; toes strong, united by an indented web ; hind toe short.

Found only in high northern latitudes, generally far out at sea; their food consists mostly of the flesh and blubber of cetaceous animals.

But two species known, which are mainly remarkable for the purity and whiteness of their plumage. They inhabit the Arctic regions, and are of medium size.

Plumage entirely white; bill bright yellow, dusky at the base; tarsi moderate.
P. eburneus.

Plumage more purely white than in the above species; bill short, yellow, with the point orange; tarsi short..*P. brachytarsi.*

PAGOPHILA EBURNEA, Kaup.

The Ivory Gull.

Larus eburneus, GMEL. Syst. Nat. I, 1788, 596.—BONAP. Syn. 1828, No. 297.—RICH. & SW. F. B. A. II, 1831, 419.—
NUTT. Man. II, 1834, 301.—AUD. Birds Am. VII, 1844, 150; pl. ccccxlv.
Pagophila eburnea, "KAUP," BRUCH, Cab. Jour. 1855, 286.—BON. Cons. Av. II, 1856, 230.
Larus candidus, FARR. Fauna Groenl. 67.
Gavia nivea, BREHM.

SP. CH.—*Adult.* The entire plumage is pure white; bill bright yellow, dusky at the base; margins of the eyelids vermilion; iris brown; legs and feet black. Length about 19 inches; wing, 13½; tail, 6¼; bill, 1 5-12; tarsus, 1 7-12.
Hab.—Coasts of Arctic America, Labrador, Newfoundland.

There are no specimens of this species in the collection.

In the cabinet of my friend J. P. Giraud, jr., esq., are two fine specimens, which originally belonged to Mr. Audubon.

PAGOPHILA BRACHYTARSI, Hollböll.

The Short-legged Gull.

" *Pagophila brachytarsi,* HOLLB." BRUCH, Rev. Lar. in Cab. J. 1855, 287.
" *Pagophila niveus,* BREHM," BONAP. Cons. Av. II, 1856, 230.

Bruch says of this species, " resembles *P. eburnea* in all its parts, but is smaller; the wings extend two lines beyond the tail."

Bonaparte makes it identical with *L. niveus,* Brehm., to which he gives precedence, and describes it as similar to *P. eburnea,* but whiter and handsomer; as being larger than that species, and having a shorter bill, which is yellow, with the point orange.

Hab.—Greenland.

There are no specimens in the collection.

RHODOSTETHIA, Macgillivray.

Rhodostethia, MACGILL. Man. of Orn. II, 1842.

CH.—Bill short and slender; upper mandible straight for half its length, then slightly curved to the tip, which is very narrow; prominence on the lower mandible small; wings long and pointed; tail wedge-shaped; tarsi rather strong; toes united by a full web, hind small and elevated.

But a single species in this genus, found in the Arctic regions; its most striking characteristic is the cuneate form of the tail.

RHODOSTETHIA ROSEA, Bonap.

The Wedge-tailed

Larus roseus, JARD. & SELBY, Ills. of Orn. ——, pl. xiv.
295.—AUD. Birds Am. VII, 1844, 130.
Rhodostethia rosea, BRUCH, Cab. Jour. 1855, 278.—BON. Cons. Av. II, 1856, 230.
Larus rossii, RICH. Parry 2d Voy. App. 1825, 359.—RICH. & SW. F. B. A. II, 1831, 427.—NUTT. Man. II, 1834,

Sp. Ch.—" *Color*. Scapulars, interscapulars, and both surfaces of the wings, clear pearl gray ; outer web of the first quill blackish brown to its tip, which is gray ; tips of the scapulars and lesser quills whitish ; some small feathers near the eye and a collar round the middle of the neck pitch black ; rest of the plumage white. The neck above and the whole under plumage deeply tinged with peach-blossom red in recent specimens. Bill black ; its rictus and the edges of the eyelids reddish orange. Legs and feet vermilion red ; nails blackish."

" Length, 14 inches ; wing, 10½ ; tail, 5½ ; bill, ¾ ; tarsus, 1.1-12."

Described as above in the Fauna Boreala-Americana.

Hab.—Arctic seas.

No specimens are in the collection.

CREAGRUS, Bonaparte.

Creagrus, Bon. 1854.

Ch.—Bill strong and much curved ; tail strong and very deeply forked.

But one species in this genus, from the coast of California ; it is remarkable for its deeply forked tail, an unusual form among the gulls.

CREAGRUS FURCATUS, Neboux.

The Swallow-tailed Gull.

Mouette a queue fourchue, Neboux, Rev. Zool. 1840, 290.

Larus furcatus, Neb. Voy. Venus, Zool. pl. x.

Creagrus furcatus, Bruch, Cab. Jour. 1855, 292.

Sp. Ch.—*Adult*. Head and nearly all of the neck grayish brown ; two small rounded white spots, embracing symmetrically the base of the upper mandible ; mantle grayish white ; breast, abdomen, and under wing coverts, white ; wings extend beyond the tail ; primaries black on their outer and inner edges ; the smaller wing coverts white ; the greater slate color bordered with white ; tail very much forked and white ; the two outer tail feathers much longer than is usual in this class of birds ; bill very much bent, black at the base and white at the extremity ; iris red ; eyelids orange ; tarsi and feet red ; claws black.

Total length, 60 centimetres.

Hab.—California

No specimen in the collection.

XEMA, Leach.

Xema, Leach, Linn. Trans. XII, 1818.

Ch.—Bill short, rather slender and compressed ; upper mandible straight at the base, curved at the end ; nostrils lateral and linear ; wings lengthened and pointed ; tail forked ; tarsi rather strong ; toes united by a full web ; hind toe short.

This genus has but one species, which inhabits the Arctic regions, seldom coming far to the south. Small in size.

XEMA SABINII, Sabine.

The Fork-tailed Gull.

Larus sabinii, J. Sabine, Lin. Trans. XII, 1818, 520 ; pl. xxix.—Rich. & Sw. F. B. A. II, 1831, 428 —Nutt. Man. II, 1834, 296.—Aud. Birds Am. VII, 1844, 127 ; pl. ccccxli.

Xema sabinii, Bruch, Cab. Jour. 1855, 292.

Sp. Ch.—*Adult*. Head and upper part of neck blackish gray, terminated below by a ring of deep black ; the rest of the neck, under plumage, the upper tail coverts, and the tail, pure white ; the back and upper surface of the wings bluish gray ; the edge of the wing from the flexure black ; the first five primaries black, with their tips white ; secondaries largely tipped with white ; bill black at base for more than half its length, then yellow to the point ; interior and angles of the mouth and edges of eyelids vermilion ; feet black.

Length, 13¼ inches ; wing, 11 ; tail, 5 ; bill, 1 ; tarsus, 1.4-12.

Hab.—Nova Scotia, northward ; Arctic seas.

There are no specimens in the collection.

August 27, 1858.

108 **b**

Sub–Family STERNINAE.—The Terns.

Ch.—Bill rather long, usually slender, straight, sometimes with the upper mandible curved at the tip, which is acutely pointed; nostrils linear and pervious; wings elongated; primaries long and pointed, secondaries of moderate length; tail rather long and in most species forked; tarsi slender; anterior toes have their webs emarginate, hind toe small; claws moderate, curved and acute.

These birds are mostly found on the seacoast and neighboring bays, occasionally on rivers and lakes; they assemble in large numbers on the sand bars and points at the mouth of inlets, are much on the wing, and are remarkable for their buoyant and easy flight. Their food consists of small fishes and crustacea, which they obtain by hovering over and suddenly darting down upon; although they thus seize their prey while in the water, they only occasionally swim or rest upon its surface.

This sub-family has been much subdivided into genera, but, as in the case of *Larinae*, I have adopted the views of Mr. G. R. Gray and retained most of the species in *Sterna*. This reduces the genera found in the United States to three, which may be characterized as follows:

1. STERNA.—Bill rather long; nostrils basal, with the frontal feathers extending up to them; tail forked; interdigital webs emarginate.
2. HYDROCHELIDON.—Bill rather short; frontal feathers reaching nearly to the nostrils, which are basal; tail emarginate; interdigital webs deeply indented.
3. ANOUS.—Bill longer than the head; the nostrils situated far forward of the frontal feathers; tail graduated; interdigital webs full.

STERNA, Linnaeus.

Sterna, Linn. Syst. Nat. 1748.

Ch.—Bill more or less strong, about the length of the head, the upper mandible slightly curved to the tip, which is narrow and acute, the lower straight, with the junction of the crura about the middle; the nostrils lateral and linear, with the frontal feathers extending to the opening; wings long, primaries narrow and tapering, the outer quill longest; tail rather long and more or less forked; tarsi short; toes small and slender, with the webs emarginate; hind toe short; claws slightly arched and acute.

This genus is abundant in species, which vary much in size, but may readily be distinguished by the following diagnoses:

Bill short and stout, entirely black; mantle pale bluish gray; under parts white; tail not deeply forked; legs and feet black. Type of *Gelochelidon*, Bp..............*S. aranea.*

Bill large and very strong, vermilion; mantle pale bluish ash; under plumage white; tail moderately forked; legs and feet black. Type of *Hydroprogne*, Kaup..*S. caspia.*

Bill large and strong, deep red; mantle bluish gray; beneath white; tail forked; legs and feet black..*S. regia.*

Bill long, but rather slender, deep red; mantle bluish gray; under surface cream color; tail deeply forked; legs and feet black...*S. elegans.*

Bill moderate, black, with the point yellow; mantle light pearl blue; lower parts white; tail deeply forked; legs and feet black. *Thallasseus* of Boie...............*S. acuflavida.*

Bill moderate, black, yellow at the point and base of lower mandible; mantle light pearl blue; below white; tail deeply forked; legs and feet orange yellow.........*S. havellii.*

Bill moderate, black, with the base and point yellow; mantle light bluish gray; under parts of the same color; tail deeply forked; legs and feet orange yellow...*S. trudeaui.*

Bill long and rather strong, black; mantle deep black; under plumage white; tail very deeply forked; legs and feet black..*S. fuliginosa.*

Bill slender, coral red, black near the end, tip yellow; mantle light grayish blue; beneath pearl gray; tail deeply forked; the outer web of the lateral feather blackish gray; legs and feet coral red..*S. wilsoni.*

Bill slender, deep carmine; mantle light grayish blue; under plumage bluish gray; tail very deeply forked; legs and feet crimson...*S. macrura.*

Bill rather slender, orange yellow at base, black near the point, which is pale yellow; mantle bluish gray; below white; tail deeply forked; the outer web of exterior feather white; legs and feet scarlet...*S. forsteri.*

Bill slender, brownish black, orange at base; mantle pale bluish gray; under plumage white, with a roseate tinge; tail very deeply forked; legs and feet vermilion.
S. paradisea.

Bill slender, carmine; mantle bluish gray; under surface white; tail deeply forked; legs and feet orange...*S. pikei.*

Bill small and slender, pale orange yellow; mantle bluish gray; below white; tail forked; legs and feet pale orange red...*S. frenata.*

STERNA ARANEA, Wilson.

The Marsh Tern.

Sterna aranea, WILS. Am. Orn. VIII, 1814, 143; pl. lxxii.—BONAP. Syn. 1828, No. 285.
Sterna anglica, NUTT. Man. II, 1834, 269.—AUD. Orn. Biog. V, 1839, 127.—IB. Birds Am. VII, 1844, 81; pl. ccccxxx.

SP. CH.—*Adult.* Upper part of the head, occiput and sides of the head upon a line with the lower eyelid, black; back and wings light bluish gray; primaries hoary on the outer webs and ashy gray on the inner, becoming lighter towards the base; tail same color as the back, but paler and with the outer feather nearly white; a line at the base of the upper mandible, neck in front and entire under plumage, pure white; bill deep black; iris brown; legs and feet black.

Length, 13¾ inches; wings in extent, 34, from flexure 10½; tail, 4; bill, 1⅜; tarsus, 1.

Hab.—Coast of the United States as far north as Connecticut.

Specimen in my cabinet.

STERNA CASPIA, Pallas.

The Caspian Tern.

Sterna caspia, PALL. Nov. Com. Petr. XIV, 582.—LAWR. Ann. Lyc. N. Y. V, 1851, 37.

SP. CH.—*Adult.* Forehead, crown, sides of the head, and occiput black, glossed with green; this color extends below the eye, under which is a narrow white line; back and wings light bluish ash; the six outer primaries dark slate grey on their inner webs; quill shafts strong and white; tail and its upper coverts grayish white; neck and entire under plumage pure white; bill and inside of mouth bright vermilion; legs and feet black. Bill very stout. Tail not deeply forked.

In the young the back, wing coverts, and tail are mottled and barred with blackish brown.

Length, 21½ inches; extent of wings, 51; from flexture, 16¾; bill from base, 2⅞; depth at base, ⅞; tarsus, 1¾; middle toe and claw, 1¾; tail, 6.

Hab.—Coast of New Jersey northward.

Specimens of adult and young are in my cabinet, obtained on the south shore of Long Island.

STERNA REGIA, Gambel.

The Royal Tern.

Sterna cayana, BONAP. Syn. 1828, No. 284.—NUTT. Man. II, 1834, 268.—AUD. Orn. Biog. III, 1835, 505: V, 639.—IB. Birds Am. VII, 1844, 76; pl. ccccxxix.
Sterna regia, GAMB. Proc. Ac. Nat. Sc. Phil. IV, 1848, 128.
Thalasseus regius, GAMB. Jour. Ac. Nat. Sc. Phil. I, 1849, 228.

Sp. Ch.—*Adult.* Front, crown, and long occipital feathers greenish black ; back and wings light bluish gray ; primaries hoary black on their outer webs, and on their inner next the shaft ; remaining part of inner webs white ; tail pearl white ; entire under surface pure white ; bill deep red ; iris dark brown ; legs and feet black.   Length, 21 inches ; wing, 15 ; tail, 7½ ; bill, 2¾ ; depth at base, $\frac{11}{16}$; tarsus, 1¼ ; middle toe and claw, 1⅓.

Hab.—Atlantic coast of the southern and middle States and California.

There are three specimens in the collection.

List of specimens.

Catal. No.	Locality.	When collected.	Whence obtained.	Orig. No.	Collected by—	Length.	Stretch of wings.	Wing.
------	Florida	------	Cab. G. N. Lawrence.	1000				
------	New York	------	------do	999				
4314	Calcasieu Pass, La	1854	G. Wurdemann	------	------	21. 00	------	15. 00
6477	Presidio, Cal	------	Lieut Trowbridge	------	------	21. 00	------	15. 00
6478	San Diego, Cal	1853	------do	153	A. Cassidy	21. 00	42. 00	15. 00

STERNA ELEGANS, Gambel.

The Elegant Tern.

Sterna elegans, Gamb. Proc. Ac. Nat. Sc. Phil. IV, 1848, 129.

Thallasseus elegans, Gamb. Journ. Ac. Nat. Sc. Phil. 2d series, I, 1849, 228.

Sp. Ch.—*Adult male.* " This elegant species differs from *Sterna regia*, not only in proportions, but in the delicate hue of the under parts, which are of a satiny cream color when living, but faded very much in the dried specimen.

" The bill is of the same color as in the *regia*, and as long, but much more slender ; the prominent angle beneath half an inch further from the point, and the depth at base two-tenths of an inch less. Wings two and a half inches shorter, but of the same color in every respect. Legs pure black ; the tarsus nearly as long as in the former, but the toes much shorter. Tail long, pure white, and deeply forked ; whole top of head from the bill pure white, extending into an ample flowing crest, as in the former species, (*S. regia.*)

" I procured this species on the Pacific coast of Mexico, particularly at Mazatlan, at the mouth of the Gulf of California."

"Length, 17 inches ; wing, 12½ ; outer tail feathers, $6\frac{8}{10}$; tarsus, $1\frac{1}{10}$; bill, bright red along the ridge, $2\frac{6}{10}$; depth at commencement of feathers, $\frac{6}{10}$; symphisis to point beneath, 1½ inches."

This species being an inhabitant of the coast of South California, I have included it among our birds, as it undoubtedly must frequent that of North California also. The description is taken from Gambel.

STERNA ACUFLAVIDA, Cabot.

Cabot's Tern.

Sterna cantiaca, Nutt. Man. II, 1834, 276.—Aud. Orn. Biog. III, 1835, 531.—Ib. Birds Am. VII, 1844, 87 ; pl. ccccxxxi.

Sterna acuflavida, Cabot, Proc. Bost. Soc. N. H. II, 1847, 257.

Sp. Ch.—*Adult.* Upper part of the head, occiput, and hind neck deep black ; back and wings light pearl blue ; four outer primaries blackish gray on their outer webs, and on the inner adjoining the shaft ; remainder of inner web white ; sides of the head below the eye, neck, entire under plumage, rump, and tail white ; bill black, with the tip yellow for one fourth its length ; iris brown ; legs and feet black. Length, 15½ inches ; wing, 11 ; tail, 5½ ; bill, 2⅜ ; tarsus, 1.

Hab.—Texas to Florida.

Specimen in my cabinet, and in that of Smithsonian Institution, from Texas.

STERNA HAVELLII, Audubon.

Havell's Tern.

Sterna havellii, Aud. Orn. Biog. V, 1839, 122.—Ib. Birds Am. VII, 1844, 103 ; pl. cccxxxiv.

Sp. Ch.—*Adult in winter.* Fore part of the head, crown, rump, and entire under surface white ; surrounding the eye and extending for about one inch behind it is a line of plumbeous black ; back and wings light pearl blue ; primaries dusky gray, except on the inner part of the inner web, where they are grayish white, having a portion of their margins grayish black ; edge of the wing and under wing coverts white ; tail of the same color as the back, but of a lighter shade ; bill black, yellow at the point for about one-fifth its length, and brownish yellow at the base of the lower mandible ; iris brown ; legs and feet orange yellow.

Length, 13¼ inches ; wing, 10½ ; tail, 4¾ ; bill, 1⅜ ; tarsus, 15-16.

Hab.—Texas to South Carolina.

Specimens in my cabinet.

STERNA TRUDEAUII, Audubon.

Trudeau's Tern.

Sterna trudeauii, Aud. Orn. Biog. V, 1839, 125.—Ib. Birds Am. VII, 1844, 105; pl. ccccxxxv.

Sp. Ch.—*Adult in winter.* Front, crown, sides of the head below the eye, and throat, white ; a line of dark plumbeous surrounds the eye and extends behind it for about one inch; back, wings, and under plumage, light bluish gray ; rump white ; tail same color as the back, but lighter ; first primary dusky gray on the outer web and on the inner next the shaft, the other primaries hoary on these parts, remainder of the inner webs grayish white, margined on the inner edge with blackish gray, most so on the inner quills ; bend of the wing and under wing coverts white ; bill yellow at the base for about one-third its length, then black with the point for about one quarter the entire length of the bill yellow ; iris brown ; legs and feet orange yellow.

Length, 15 inches ; wing, 10½ ; tail, 5½ ; bill 1 9-16 ; tarsus, 1.

Hab.—Coasts of New Jersey and Long Island.

Described from a specimen belonging to J. P. Giraud, esq.

I have never seen either this species or *S. havellii* in summer plumage ; they are both closely allied to *S. acuflavida.*

STERNA FULIGINOSA, Gmelin.

The Sooty Tern.

Sterna fuliginosa, Gmel. Syst. Nat. I, 1788, 605.—Wils. Am. Orn. VIII, 1814, 145 ; pl. lxxii.—Bonap. Syn. 1828, No. 290.—Nutt. Man. II, 1834, 284.—Aud. Orn. Biog. III, 1835, 263 : V, 1839, 641.—Ib. Birds Am. VII, 1844, 90 ; pl. ccccxxxii.

Sp. Ch —*Adult.* Forehead white ; lores, upper part of the head, hind neck, back, and wings, deep black ; tail black, except the outer and the basal half of the inner web of the outside feathers, which are white ; sides of the head, edges of the wings, and entire under surface, white ; bill black ; iris chestnut ; legs and feet black.

Length, 16½ inches ; wing, 11¾ ; tail, 7¼ ; bill, 1¾ ; tarsus, 15-16.

Hab.—Texas to Florida.

Specimens in my cabinet and in that of Smithsonian Institution.

STERNA WILSONI, Bonaparte.

Wilson's Tern.

Sterna hirundo, Wils. Am. Orn. VII, 1813, 76 ; pl. lx.—Bonap. Syn. 1828, No. 286.—Nutt. Man. II, 1834, 271.— Aud. Orn. Biog. IV, 1838, 74.—Ib. Birds Am. VII, 1844, 97 ; pl. ccccxxxiii.

Sterna wilsoni, Bonap. Comp. List, 1838, 61.

Sp. Ch.—*Adult.* Upper part of the head and hind neck deep black, tinged with brown on the front part of the head ; back and wings light grayish blue ; first primary with the outer web black, on the inner web grayish black next the shaft, this color increasing in extent towards the end, where it covers the entire web for about one inch, rest of inner web white ; the next five primaries are hoary on their outer webs and blackish gray on the inner next the shaft, occupying the entire web at the end, margin of the inner webs white ; central tail feathers very pale bluish gray, the others white on the inner webs and dusky gray on the outer webs, deepening in color from the central feathers until it becomes blackish gray on the lateral ones ; sides of the head, throat, rump, and under tail coverts, white; breast and abdomen clear pearl gray ; bill coral red, black near the end with the tip yellow ; iris hazel ; legs and feet coral red, not so dark as the bill ; claws brownish black.

Length, 14¾ ; wing, 10¾ ; tail, 5¾ ; bill, 1⅜ ; tarsus, ¾.

Hab.—Texas to Labrador.

Four specimens in the collection.

List of specimens.

Catal. No.	Sex.	Locality.	When collected.	Whence obtained.	Orig. No.	Length.	Stretch of wings.	Wings.
4359	♀	Beesley's point, N. J.	Aug., 1854	S. F. Baird		13.00	30.50	10.37
4360		do	do	do		14.75	30.00	10.75
4361	♀	do	do	do		13.00	28.25	10.12
6928		Nelson river, H. B. T.		D. Gunn				
		Coast New York		Cab G. N. Lawrence	1005			

STERNA MACRURA, Naumann.

The Arctic Tern.

Sterna macroura, Naum. Isis, 1819, 1847.

   Sterna arctica, Temm. Man. d'Orn. II, 1820, 742.—Bonap. Syn. 1828, No. 287.—Sw. & Rich. F. B. A. II, 1831, 414.—Nutt. Man. II, 1834, 275—Aud. Orn. Biog. III, 1835, 366.—Ib. Birds Am. VII, 1844, 107 ; pl. ccccxxiv.

Sp. Ch.—*Adult.* Upper part of the head and hind neck black ; back and wings light grayish blue ; first primary deep black on the outer web, dusky gray on the inner next the shaft, and over the entire web at the end, inner margin of inner web white ; the next five primaries are bluish gray on the outer web and on the inner web next the shaft, this color extending over the entire web at the end, where it is blackish gray on the inner margin, the remaining part of inner web white ; central tail feathers and inner webs of the others white, the outer web of the outer tail feather blackish gray, the outer webs of the two next pale bluish gray ; rump, sides of the head, and under tail coverts, white ; under plumage bluish gray, of a lighter shade than the back ; bill deep carmine ; iris brown ; legs and feet dark crimson.

Length, 14½ ; wing, 10½ ; tail, 6½ ; bill, 1 2-16 ; tarsus, ⅝.

Hab —Coast of the New England States to Arctic seas ; fur countries.

Specimens in my cabinet and that of Prof. Baird.

Dr. H. Bryant (Proc. Bost. Soc. of Nat. H. vol. VI, p. 120,) speaks of finding this species on the coast of Nova Scotia, breeding in large numbers and apart from any other kinds. He also gives comparative measurements, and points out the differences between it and its near ally *S. wilsoni.*

STERNA FORSTERI, Nuttall.

Forster's Tern.

Sterna hirundo, Sw. & Rich. F. B. A. II, 1831, 412.

Sterna forsteri, Nutt. Man. II, 1834, 274.   (Note.)—Lawr. Annals N. Y. Lyceum, V, 1852, 222.

Sp. Cн.—*Adult.* Upper part, and sides of the head to a line just below the eye, and hind neck, black ; back and wings bluish gray ; primaries grayish white on the outer webs, and dusky gray on the inner next the shaft, and over the entire web at the end, darker on the inner margin, the remaining portion of inner webs white ; tail bluish gray, except the outer web of the outer tail feather which is white, the inner web of this feather blackish gray for about two inches from the end ; rump white with a slight tinge of pale bluish gray ; sides of the head, throat, and entire under surface, white; in the dried specimens the bill is orange yellow at the base, black near the end, with the tip pale yellow ; legs and feet scarlet.

Length of skin 14 inches ; wing, 10½ ; tail, 6 ; bill, 1½ ; tarsus, ⅞.

Hab.—Louisiana to Florida ; New York, fur countries, and California.

Three specimens are in the collection.

It is distinguished from *S. wilsoni* by having the outer web of the exterior tail feather white, and the end of the inner web dusky gray, the reverse of *wilsoni ;* the tarsi are also uniformly longer, as in five specimens now before me.

List of specimens.

Catal. No.	Sex.	Locality.	When collected.	Whence obtained.	Orig. No.	Length.	Stretch of wings.	Wing.
------	------	Coast New York	------	Cab. of G. N. Lawrence	1010	13. 00	29. 25	9. 75
4928	♀	St. John's river, Fla	------	G. Würdemann	------	13. 00	------	10. 25
4317	------	Calcasieu Pass, La	1854	------do	------	14. 00	------	10. 50
9973	------	Sacramento valley	------	Lieut. Williamson	------	------	------	------
------	------	California	------	Cab. G. N. Lawrence	1009	------	------	------

STERNA PARADISEA, Brünnich.

The Roseate Tern.

Sterna paradisea, Brünn. Orn. Bor 1764, 46.
Sterna dougallii, Nutt Man. II, 1834, 278.—Aud. Orn. Biog. III, 1835, 296.—Ib. Birds. Am. VII, 1844, 112 ; pl. ccccxxxvii.

Sp. Cн.—*Adult.* Upper part of the head and long occipital feathers deep black ; hind neck white ; back and wings pale bluish gray ; first primary blackish gray on the outer web and on the inner next the shaft ; the other primaries bluish gray, the second and third dusky gray near the shaft ; all the primaries white on the inner part of their inner webs ; secondaries and tertiaries edged with white ; tail very light pearl gray ; entire under plumage white, with a beautiful roseate tinge ; bill brownish black, orange at the base ; iris brown ; legs and feet vermilion.

Length, 16 inches ; wing, 9½ ; tail, 8 ; bill, 1½ ; tarsus, 13-16.

Hab.—Florida to New York.

Specimens in my cabinet and that of Prof. Baird.

STERNA PIKEI, Lawrence.

The Slender-billed Tern.

Sterna pikei, Lawr. Annals N. Y. Lyceum, VII, 1853, 3.

Sp. Cн.—*Adult.* Front white speckled with dark gray ; crown and occiput black ; back and wings bluish gray ; smaller wing coverts dark plumbeous ; outer web of the first primary brownish black, inner web next the shaft dusky gray, with the inner margin white ; the other primaries are dark bluish gray on the outer webs and on the inner next the shaft, also at the end of the inner web ; inner webs of all the tail feathers white, the outer webs of the long lateral tail feathers grayish black with the tip white, outer webs of the others very pale gray ; throat, upper tail coverts and whole under plumage, white ; bill dark brown tinged with dark red (probably deep carmine in the living bird) ; legs and feet orange.

Length, 13 inches ; wing, 9 ; tail, 5½ ; bill, 1⅛ ; tarsus, ½.

Hab.—Coast of California.

One specimen in my cabinet.

STERNA FRENATA, Gambel.

The Least Tern.

Sterna minuta, WILS. Am. Orn. VII, 1813, 80 ; pl. lx.—BONAP. Syn. 1828, No. 288.—AUD. Orn Biog. IV, 1838, 175 —IB. Birds Am. VII, 1844, 119 ; pl. ccccxxxix.
Sterna argentea, NUTT. Man. II, 1834, 280.
Sterna frenata, GAMB. Proc. Acad. Sci. Phil. IV, 1848, 128.

SP. CH.—*Adult*. On the forehead is a triangular white spot extending to the eye ; crown, occiput, and a line from the eye to the upper mandible, deep black ; entire upper plumage and wings clear bluish gray ; first two primaries, with the outer web and half the inner next the shaft, grayish black, ends of the same color, inner margins white, the shafts of these two quills are black ; the other primaries same color as the back, with the inner margins white ; tail same color as the back except the outer margin of the exterior feather, and the inner webs of the others at the base, where they are white ; entire under plumage silvery white ; bill pale orange yellow ; iris hazel ; legs and feet light orange red.

Length, 8¾ inches ; wing, 6¾ ; tail, 3½ ; bill, 1⅛ ; tarsus, 9-16.

Hab.—Texas to Labrador ; western rivers.

Four specimens in the collection.

List of specimens.

Catal. No.	Sex.	Locality.	When collected.	Whence obtained.	Orig'l No.	Collected by—	Length.	Stretch of wings.	Wing.	Remarks.
		Coast New York.......		Cab. G. N. Lawrence.	1016					
4315		Calcasieu Pass, La.....	1854.........	G. Würdemann			7.50		6.50	
9005	♂	Platte river............	July 10, 1857	Lieut. Warren		Dr. Hayden....				
9007	♂	Loup Fork.............	1857.........	......do............		......do.........	6.75	19.25	6.25	Iris light blue, pupil black............
8999	♀	Yellowstone.	July 2, 1857	......do............		......do.........	8.50	19.00	7.50	Iris dark brown......

HYDROCHELIDON, Boie.

Hydrochelidon, BOIE, Isis, 1822, 563.

CH.—Bill rather short, strong, the upper mandible curving slightly to the tip ; nostrils basal, lateral, and longitudinal, the frontal feathers reaching nearly to the opening ; wings very long and pointed ; tail moderate and emarginate ; legs short ; the anterior toes slender, with the webs deeply indented ; hind toe small ; claws slender and acute.

We have but a single species to represent this genus, which much resembles and is very closely allied to the European *S. nigra*.

They frequent the salt water bays as well as the inland rivers and lakes. Late in the summer I have noticed them in compact flocks flying rapidly forward in the manner of some species of *Tringa*.

HYDROCHELIDON PLUMBEA, (Wilson.)

The Short-tailed Tern.

Sterna plumbea, WILS. Am. Orn. VII, 1813, 83 ; pl. lx. (Young.)
Sterna nigra, BONAP. Syn. 1828, No. 289.—SW. & RICH. F. B. A. II, 1831, 415.—NUTT. Man. II, 1834, 282.— AUD. Orn. Biog. III, 1835, 535 : V, 1839, 642.—IB. Birds Am. VII, 1844, 116 ; pl. ccccxxxviii.
" *Sterna surinamensis*, GM."—BONAP. Cons. Gav. Syst. Comp. Rend. XLI, 1855.

SP. CH.—*Adult*. Head, neck, breast, sides and abdomen, black ; lower tail coverts white ; under covering of wings ashy gray ; back and wings dark plumbeous gray ; the first four primaries grayish black, with their shafts white ; bend of the wing edged with white ; tail same color as the back ; bill brownish black ; iris brown ; legs and feet reddish brown.

Length, 9½ inches ; wing, 8½ ; tail, 3½ ; bill, 1⅛ ; tarsus, ⅝.

Young. Back, wings and tail, light plumbeous, with the feathers of the back margined with brown ; top of the head and around the eyes brownish black ; front and under plumage white ; tail short and but slightly forked.

Hab.—Texas to the New England States, Mississippi river and tributaries, fur countries.

There are several fine specimens in the collection.

List of specimens.

Catal. No.	Sex.	Locality.	When collected.	Whence obtained.	Orig'l No.	Collected by—	Length.	Stretch of wings.	Wing.	Remarks.
......	....	Coast New York.......	....	Cab. G. N. Lawrence.	1018	....	......	......	......	....
7073	♀	St. Louis...............	May 15, 1857	Lt. F. T. Bryan......	86	W. S. Wood...	......	......	....	....
7074	♀	......do	May 13, 1857	......do.....	76	.....do	......	......	... .	...............,....
7075	......	......do	......do......	......do........	......	.....do	......	......	......	....
7076	......	......do	....	......do.............	92	.....do	......	......	......	....
9023	♂	Loup Fork	Aug. 8, 1857	Lieut. Warren...........	......	Dr. Hayden	10 25	23.75	8.25	Iris hazel brown ....
9972	♀	Illinois	May 16, 1857	R. Kennicott.........	......	....	......	......	... ...	....

ANOUS, Leach.

Anous, "LEACH," STEPH. SHAW's Gen. Zool. XIII, 1825, 139.

CH.—Bill longer than the head and strong ; the upper mandible curving gradually to the tip, which is rather acute, the angle on the lower mandible quite prominent ; nostrils lateral and longitudinal ; wings very long and pointed, first quill longest ; tail long and graduated ; tarsi rather short and slender ; toes long and united by a full web ; the hind toe long and slender ; claws slender, arched and acute.

These are tropical birds, are much at sea and often seen at great distances from land ; but one species is found off our coast.

ANOUS STOLIDUS, Leach.

The Noddy Tern.

Sterna stolida, LINN. Syst. Nat. I, 1766, 227.—BONAP. Syn. 1825, No. 291.—NUTT. Man. II, 1834, 285.—AUD. Orn. Biog. III, 1835, 516 : V, 1839, 642.—IB. Birds Am. VII, 1842, 123 ; pl. ccccxl.

Anous stolida, LEACH.

SP. CH.—*Adult.* Front part of the head grayish white ; a black spot over and before the eye ; the remainder of the plumage sooty brown, except the primaries and tail, which are brownish black ; bill black ; iris brown ; legs and feet of a dull brownish red ; the webs dusky.

Length, 15 inches ; wing, 10½ ; tail, 5¼ ; bill, 1⅝ ; tarsus, ⅞.

Hab.—Texas to Florida.

Specimens in my cabinet and that of Prof. Baird.

Sub–Family RHYNCHOPINAE.

CH.—The mandibles are of very unequal length, the upper being much shorter and grooved to receive the edge of the lower , from the base their sides are suddenly compressed to the end ; wings very long and narrow ; tail forked and of moderate length ; tarsi a little longer than the middle toe ; anterior united by an indented web.

These birds abound most in the tropics ; they frequent the large bays and the inlets connecting them with the ocean ; their principal food is fish, which they obtain by skimming close to the surface of the water, into which they dip the lower mandible, suddenly closing it into the upper when it comes in contact with their desired prey. They have a peculiar undulating mode of flying. They are said rarely, if ever, to swim or rest upon the water, although possessing webbed feet.

August 31, 1858.

109 b

RHYNCHOPS, Linnaeus.

Rynchops, LINN. Syst. Nat. 1756.

CH.—Bill very broad at the base, from whence it becomes suddenly compressed for its entire length ; upper mandible considerably shorter than the lower and curving gradually to the tip, which is pointed, it is narrowly grooved underneath ; the lower mandible is straight and truncated, much more compressed than the upper, and having the cutting edge very sharp to admit of its being received in the groove of the upper mandible ; nostrils basal, oblong and lateral ; wings much elongated, first quill longest ; tail forked ; tarsi longer than the middle toe ; toes rather short, united by an indented web ; hind toe rather elevated ; claws much curved and acute.

But one species of this very peculiar genus is found on our southern coast.

They are stated by Audubon to be nocturnal in their habits, resting during the day upon sand bars.

RHYNCHOPS NIGRA, Linnaeus.

The Black Skimmer.

Rynchops nigra, LINN. Syst. Nat. I, 1766, 228.—WILS. Am. Orn. VII, 1813, 85 ; pl. lx.—BONAP. Syn. 1828, No. 283.—NUTT. Man. II, 1834, 264.—AUD. Orn. Biog. IV, 1838, 203.—IB. Birds Am. VII, 1843, 67 ; pl. cccccxxxiii.

SP. CH.—*Adult.* Front as far as the eye, throat and under plumage, white ; crown, hind neck, wings and back, deep brownish black ; primaries black, with the four inner ones white on their inner webs and tips ; secondaries broadly tipped with white ; central tail feathers dark brown, the others mostly white, some of them light brown on their inner webs ; bill carmine for about half its length, then black to the end ; iris hazel ; tarsi and feet red.

Length of male, about 19 inches ; wing, 14½ ; tail, 5 ; lower mandible, 4½, upper, 3⅛ ; tarsi, 1¼.

Female smaller.

Hab.—From Texas to New Jersey.

Specimens in my cabinet and that of Smithsonian Institution.

Tribe **TOTIPALMI.**[1]

Ch.—Bill long, rather broad at the base ; tip hooked and acute, the edges not serrated. Nostrils either wanting or hardly perceptible. Wings rather long ; tarsi short and stout. Toes long and all joined together by broad webs. Face and throat generally naked, the latter capable of being more or less extended in the form of a membranous sac or pouch.

Four families, the diagnostic characters of which are given below, are comprised in this strongly marked tribe, all well represented in North America. The arrangement of these families, and of their sub-divisions as here adopted, is a little different from that of Bonaparte, given on page 818.

1. Pelecanidae.—Head crested ; bill long, much depressed ; tip hooked and acute ; nostrils scarcely perceptible ; sub-maxillary pouch capable of very great extension ; tail short and rounded.

2. Sulidae.—Head without crest ; bill moderate in length, stout, straight, compressed on the sides, decurved at point, but not hooked ; nostrils indistinct ; gular sac very small ; tail rather long and wedge-shaped.

3. Tachypetidae.—Head crested ; bill long, rather slender, strong, much curved at the point, and very acute ; nostrils quite small ; gular sac rather extensive ; tail very long and deeply forked ; tarsi partly feathered.

4. Phalacrocoracidae.—Head generally with crests ; bill moderate, rather slender, unguis much curved ; nostrils in the adult obliterated ; gular sac moderate ; tail graduated, of moderate length, with the shafts very strong.

[1] Prepared by Mr. George N. Lawrence, of New York.

Family PELECANIDAE.

Cʜ.—Bill long, with the culmen depressed, unguis hooked and acute. Nostrils situated in lateral grooves and hardly perceptible. Wings long and pointed. Tail rather short. Toes long, and all four connected by webs. Underneath the lower
mandible, and connected with the throat, is a membranous sac or pouch, which may be exceedingly distended.

Bonaparte, in his Conspectus Avium, vol. II, divides this family into the genera *Pelecanus*,
Cyrtopelecanus and *Onocrotalus*, our two, species being included by him in the last two. I have,
however, thought best to retain them in the old genus *Pelecanus*.

PELECANUS, Linnaeus.

Pelecanus, Lɪɴɴ. Syst. Nat. 1735. Type *P. onocrotalus*.

Cʜ.—Bill very long, nearly straight, and very much depressed ; the tip strong, curved, and acute. Upper mandible with an
elevated ridge convex at the base, but gradually becoming flat towards the end ; lower broader at base than the upper.
Nostrils basal, lateral, linear, situated in the grooves adjoining the ridge, and scarcely perceptible. Wings moderate, the
secondaries not differing much in length from the primaries ; second quill longest. Tail short, broad, and rounded. Tarsi
short and stout, covered with reticulated scales. Toes situated on the same plane, and all connected by broad webs ; middle toe
the longest. A loose membranous skin occupies a large space on the throat, extending to the end of the lower mandible, and
capable of great expansion.

The birds of this genus are all of large dimensions, and species are found in all parts of the
world. They inhabit rivers and lakes equally as well as sea-coasts. Their flight is heavy and not
elevated. When resting on the water or on sand bars, after feeding, they are not difficult of
approach.

Two species belonging to this genus are found in the United States, which may be known by
the following characters :

Bill yellow, with a bony prominence on the upper mandible ; naked space in the region of the
eye yellow ; occipital crest yellow ; gular pouch yellow ; prevailing color white ; tail of 24
feathers... *P. erythrorhynchus*.

Bill greyish white, marked with dusky ; no prominence on the bill ; naked space between
bill and eye blue ; occipital crest light chestnut red ; gular pouch dark ; colors generally dark ;
tail of 22 feathers.. *P. fuscus*.

Cyrtopelicanus, Reich.

PELECANUS ERYTHRORHYNCHUS, Gmelin.

Rough-billed Pelican.

Pelecanus erythrorhynchus, Gᴍ. Syst. Nat. 1788, 571.
Pelecanus trachyrhynchus, Lᴀᴛʜ. Ind. Orn. II, 1790, 884.—Bᴏɴ. Comp. List, 1838, 60.—Gʀᴀʏ, Gen. of Birds, 1845,309.
Cyrtopelicanus trachyrhynchus, Bᴏɴ. Cons Av. II, 1855, 163.
Pelecanus onocrotalus, Bᴏɴ. Syn. 1828, No. 351.—Rɪᴄʜ. and Sw. F. Bor. Am. 11, 1831, 472·—Nᴜᴛᴛ. Nan. 11, 1834, 471.
Pelecanus americanus, Aᴜᴅ. Orn. Biog. IV, 1838, 88.—Iʙ. Syn. 1839.—Iʙ. Birds Am. VII, 1844, 20 ; pl. ccccxxii.
? *Pelecanus molinae*, Bᴘ. Comp. Rend. XXXVIII, 1854.—Iʙ. Notes sur Coll. Delattre, 1854, 91.
Rough-billed Pelican, Lᴀᴛʜ. Syn. VI, 1785, 586.

Sᴘ. Cʜ.—Head with a yellow occipital crest ; bill yellow, sub-maxillary pouch very large ; general color white ; primaries
black, second the longest ; legs and feet very strong

Adult male.—The general plumage is pure white ; in the breeding season, with a roseate tinge ; the crest and elongated feathers on the breast pale yellow ; the alula, primary coverts and primaries black, the shafts of the latter white for the greater part of their length, being brownish black at the end ; the outer secondaries black, the inner more or less white, the shafts of all white underneath. Bill yellow, with the edges and unguis reddish ; upper mandible high at the base, but becoming gradually flattened to the end ; on the ridge, just beyond the middle of the bill, is a thin elevated bony process about one inch high, and extending towards the end for three or four inches ; lower mandible broad at the base, with the cruta separated nearly to the point ; underneath the lower mandible, beginning at the junction of the cruta, and extending down the neck for about eight inches, is a large membranous sac or pouch, capable of great expansion ; it is of the same color as the bill ; bare space around the eye bright yellow ; iris white ; legs and feet yellow ; claws yellowish brown.

The female differs in not having the bony projection on the upper mandible.

Total length, 70 inches ; wing, 24.50 ; bill, 13.50 ; tarsi, 4.75 ; tail, 7.

Hab.—Throughout the United States, rare on the coasts of the Middle and Northern States. ur countries up to the 61st parallel. Specimens are in the collection from various sections, a number from the Pacific coast. There is no observable difference between them and eastern specimens.

This species breeds in the fur countries, generally selecting inaccessible places in the neighborhood of waterfalls. They also inhabit throughout the Rocky mountains and in California. In winter they are very abundant on our southern coast from Texas to Florida.

They remain inactive on sand bars most of the day, procuring their food about sunrise and again just before sunset. They swim buoyantly, and while feeding are very active in their movements ; on such occasions they do not dive, but secure their food by thrusting the head under water, but not keeping it below the surface for any length of time. Mr. Audubon states that their usual food consists of fish of rather a small size.

In the breeding season the color of the bill, bare space around the eye, the pouch, the legs and feet are much heightened in color, becoming reddish orange.

The peculiar bony process on the ridge of the upper mandible appears to be used for the purpose of defence when combatting with their rivals ; in some old individuals it is much abraded and worn, apparently caused by many and severe contests.

Both Gray and Bonaparte adopt Latham's name of "*trachyrhynchus*" for this species, certainly a very appropriate one ; but Gmelin having previously called it "*erythrorhynchus*," according to the law of priority, his name should take precedence.

List of specimens.

Catal. No.	Sex.	Locality.	When collected.	Whence obtained.	Orig. No.	Collected by—	Stretch of wings.	Wing.
------	----	Texas-------------	1853	Maj. Emory --------	------	A. Schott ------	------	22.00
9947	♀	Rio Grande, Tex ------	1853	------do-------	------	------do-------	------	--------
------	♀	Gulf of Mexico-------	-------------	Cab.of G. N. Lawrence	1022	T. T. Bruzon----	------	23.00
4439	♂	Quasquiton, Io-------	-------------	Dr. E. C. Bidwell ---	------	-------------	------	--------
2719	♂	Eastern U. S.-------	-------------	S. F. Baird -------	------	J. J. Audubon--	70.00	24.50
9951	♂	San Diego, Cal-------	-------------	Lt. Trowbridge------	------	A. Cassidy------	------	25.50
4523	♂	San Francisco, Cal-----	Jan. 10, 1856	Dr. Suckley -------	------	-------------	------	--------
9949	----	Pacific coast -------	Jan., 1855	Lt. Trowbridge------	------	T. A. Szabo-----	------	23.00
9950	♀	Bodega, Cal ---------	-------------	------do-------	------	------do-------	------	24.50
9948	♂	Sacramento valley-----	-------------	Lt. Williamson------	------	Dr. Heermann--	------	--------

Onocrotalus, Wagler.

PELECANUS FUSCUS, Linnaeus.

Brown Pelican.

Pelecanus fuscus, LINN. Syst. Nat. 1766, 215.—BON. Syn. 1828, No. 352.—NUTT. Man. II, 1834, 476.—AUD. Orn. Biog. III, 1835, 376 ; V, 1839, 212.— IB. Syn. 1839.—IB. Birds Am. VII, 1844, 32 ; pl. ccccxxiii and ccccxxiv.

Leptopelicanus fuscus, REICH. Syst. Av. 1850 ; pl. lxx.

Onocrotalus fuscus, BON. Cons. Av. II, 1855, 163.

SP. CH.—Head with a short occipital crest of light reddish brown ; bill greyish white, more or less dusky, and marked with pale carmine spots ; a large pouch appended to the under mandible ; below the color is very dark ash, above hoary ; second primary longest ; legs stout.

Adult male. Head white, except on the fore part, where it is yellow ; sides of the neck adjoining the pouch white ; hind part of neck and lower part in front dark chestnut brown, the short crest pale reddish brown ; back and wings greyish ash, with dusky margins, the former color prevailing on the larger wing coverts and scapulars ; primaries brownish black, secondaries dark ashy brown, with their outer margins greyish white ; shafts of the primaries white until near the end, when they become black ; tail greyish ash, with the shafts of the feathers white for one-half their length ; terminal half black ; under plumage dark brownish ash, with the sides of the body from the neck for its entire length, marked with narrow longitudinal white lines ; on the lower part of the neck is a small patch of pale yellow ; bill greyish white, tinged with brown and intermixed with spots of pale carmine ; the lower mandible blackish at the end, and having underneath a large pouch similar in character to that of the preceding species, but of a greenish black color, with the ridges formed by the wrinkles paler ; bare skin surrounding the eye deep blue ; iris white, the eyelids pink ; legs and feet black.

The plumage of the fully adult female is similar in color to that of the male ; the feathers of the head are rather rigid, not downy as in the male.

In the young the plumage generally is of a dusky brown.

Length of male, 56 inches ; wing, 22 ; bill, 13.50 ; tarsi, 3 ; tail, 6.50.

Hab.—From Texas to North Carolina ; California coast.

The brown pelican is a permanent resident of our southern coast and the shores of the Gulf of Mexico, also of California. Their nests are placed on trees, and also on the ground. Its general habits are much like those of the preceding species, but their mode of procuring food is quite different ; they dart upon their prey from on wing, frequently immersing the whole body, but immediately rising on wing, dart down again and again until hunger is allayed.

According to Mr. Audubon, its ordinary food consists of fishes of rather a small size, not often taking any longer than its bill ; attached to specimen No. 9959 is a note by Mr. Cassidy, stating that he has seen a fish weighing 2½ pounds taken from the pouch of one of this species.

List of specimens.

Catal. No.	Sex.	Locality.	Whence obtained.	Orig. No.	Collected by—	Wing.
1960	....	Florida	S. F. Baird	....	J. J. Audubon	....
....	♀	Gulf of Mexico..............	Cab. of G. N. Lawrence.	1023	T. T. Bruzon...........	20. 50
....	....	......do................	......do...............	1024	....	....
9959	....	San Diego, Cal.............	A. Cassidy.............	....	....	....
4526	♀	San Francisco, Cal...........	Lt. Williamson........	....	Dr. Heermann	21. 00
9958	♂	Bay of San Francisco, Cal......	......do...............	....	Dr. Newberry..........	22. 00

Family SULIDAE.

`CH —Bill rather long, straight, sides compressed, very strong, tapering to the point, which is a little decurved; nostrils hardly observable; wings very long; tail long and cuneate; toes long and all joined by full webs; gular sac moderate.

Prince Bonaparte has placed our Booby Gannet in the genus *Dysporus*, Ill., but I have not considered there was sufficient generic distinction to separate it from *S. bassana*, and have, therefore, admitted but one genus as existing in North America under this sub-family.

SULA, Brisson.

Sula, BRISS. Ornith. 1760. Type *Pelecanus bassanus.*

CH.—Bill rather longer than the head, straight, stout at the base, with the sides compressed, grooved near the tip, which is a little curved, the cutting edges serrated irregularly; nostrils basal and scarcely perceptible; wings lengthened; tail rather long and much graduated; tarsi short and stout; toes long and joined together by full webs; claws moderate, the middle one serrated; gular sac rather moderate.

These birds usually frequent almost inaccessible rocky islands, where they congregate in great numbers during the season of reproduction, at other times migrating along the coast. Their flight is rapid, powerful, and long continued.

The two species of this genus which are found in North America may be thus distinguished :
Bill bluish grey; naked skin around the eye and on the throat blackish blue; plumage white, with the primaries brownish black...*S. bassana.*
Bill bright yellow; bare space around the eye and on the throat yellow; head, neck, and upper plumage brown; breast and abdomen white..*F. fiber.*

SULA, Brisson.
SULA BASSANA, (Linnaeus.)
Common Gannet; Solan Goose.

Pelecanus bassanus, LINN. Syst Nat. 1766, 217.
Sula bassana, BRISS. Orn. 1760.—BON. Synop. 1828, No. 359.—IB. Cons. Av. II, 1855, 165.—NUTT. Man. II, 1834, 495.— AUD. Orn. Biog. IV, 1838, 222.—IB. Syn.. 1839, 311.—IB. Bird's Am. VII, 1844, 44; pl. ccccxxv.
Dysporus bassanus, Ill. Prodr. 1811, 279.
Sula americana, BON. Comp. List, 1838, 60.

SP. CH.—General color of the plumage white; bill bluish grey; bare space around the eye and on the throat blackish blue; primaries brownish black, first longest.

Adult. The color of the plumage generally is white, the head and hind neck being of a fine buff yellow; alula and primaries brownish black; shafts white for about two-thirds their length from the base, thence gradually becoming dark brown; bill pale bluish grey, greenish at the base, the lines on the upper mandible blackish blue; bare space in the region of the eye, and down the centre of the throat, blackish blue; iris white; tarsi, toes and their webs, blackish brown; the lines of scutellae on the tarsi and toes green; claws bluish white.

Length, 38 inches; wing, 19.50; bill, 4; tarsi, 2.25; tail, 10.

The female resembles the male, but is rather smaller.

The young have the head, neck, and upper plumage dark brown, each feather terminating with a triangular white spot; under plumage greyish white, the feathers broadly margined with greyish brown.

Hab —Atlantic coast, from Labrador to the Gulf of Mexico.

The Gannet breeds in almost incredible numbers on some of the rocky islands near the coast of Labrador. When the breeding season is over, it wanders as far south as the Gulf of Mexico. Its mode of flight is powerful, and at times graceful. Its food consists of fish, principally herrings; these are obtained by plunging from on high, often remaining under water for a minute or more at a time.

List of specimens.

Locality.	Whence obtained.	Orig. No.	Collected by—	Stretch of wings.	Wing.
Coast of New York	Cab. of Geo. N. Lawrence	1025	J. Akhurst............	38.00	19.25
Atlantic ocean	S. F. Baird	....	J. J. Audubon	....	....

Dysporus, Illiger.

SULA FIBER, (Linnaeus.)

Booby Gannet.

Pelecanus fiber, Linn Syst. Nat. 1766, 218.

Pelecanus sula, Linn. Syst. Nat. I, 1766, 218, 7.

Dysporus sula, Illiger, Prod. 1811, 279.—Bon Cons. Av. II, 1855, 164.

Sula brasiliensis, Spix, Av. Bras. 1824, tab. 107.

Sula fusca, Vieill. Gal. des Ois. 1825, tab. 277.—Bon Syn. 1828, No. 360.—Nutt. Man. II, 1834, 500.—Aud Orn. Biog. III, 1835, 63.—Ib. Syn. 1839, 311.—Ib Bird's Am. VII, 1844, 57; pl. ccccxxvi.

Sp Ch.—Head, neck, and upper plumage brown; breast and abdomen white; bill and naked part around the eye and on the the throat yellow; wings brown; first and second primary equal and longest.

Adult. Head, entire neck, back, wings, and tail dusky brown; under plumage and lower tail coverts pure white; bill bright yellow, flesh colored towards the end; naked space around the base of the bill yellow; iris white; tarsi and feet, with their webs, pale yellow; claws white.

Length, 31 inches; wing, 16.50; bill, 3.90; tarsi, 1.70; tail, 8.50.

The female is similar in plumage to the male, but smaller.

The young are of an uniform greyish brown, the lower parts being rather lighter; the bill dusky; the tarsi and feet dull yellow.

Hab.—Gulf of Mexico. Atlantic coast from Georgia southward.

The Booby Gannet is found only on our southern coast, where they collect at their breeding places in large numbers; their nests are built on low trees or bushes. Their method of procuring food is similar to that of the common species.

List of specimens.

Locality.	Whence obtained.	Orig. No.	Collected by—	Stretch of wings.	Wing.
Florida	S. F. Baird................	....	J. J. Audubon	30.00	15.00
Do	Cab. of G. N. Lawrence...... ...	1026	......do...............	....	....

Family TACHYPETIDAE.

Cн.—Bill very long, strong, hooked at the end, and acute; the culmen depressed and concave; nostrils basal, placed in the lateral grooves, and scarcely observable; wings exceedingly lengthened; tail long and much forked; tarsi very short; toes long, with the connecting webs deeply indented; throat bare, and capable of being much distended.

This family embraces but one genus.

TACHYPETES, Vieillot.

Tachypetes, VIEILL. Analyse, 1816.

Cн.—Bill long, broad at the base, the culmen concave, the unguis much hooked and very acute, the sides grooved and compressed; nostrils basal, linear, and hardly visible; wings very long and pointed, first two primaries longest; tail lengthened and deeply forked; tarsi very short, strong, compressed, and feathered for half their length; toes long and all united by webs; claws curved and rather small, gular sac extending nearly to the end of the lower mandible, and admitting of considerable expansion.

The tropical regions are the principal resort of this genus: they assemble in large numbers in the breeding season, placing their nests on trees, rocks, or on the ground; they wander to very great distances from land, their power of wing being almost unequalled; they contend against the severest gales apparently without effort.

TACHYPETES AQUILUS, Vieillot.

Frigate Pelican; Man-of-war Bird.

Tachypetes aquilus, VIEILL Gal. des Ois. 1825 tab. 274.—Bon. Syn. 1828, No. 358.—IB. Cons. Av. II, 1855, 166.— *Pelecanus aquilus*, LINN. Syst. Nat. 1766, 216.

NUTT. Man. II, 1834, 491 —AUD. Orn. Biog. III, 1835, 495 : V, 1839, 634.—IB. Syn. 1839, 307.—IB. Birds Am. VII, 1844, 10; pl. ccccxxi.—GAMB. Jour. Acad. Nat. Sci. Phil. 2d Ser. I, 1849, 227.

Attagen aquila, GRAY, Gen. of Birds, 1845.

SP. CH.—Plumage brownish black; bill long, with the unguis much curved; wings much lengthened, tail long and forked. *Adult.* Entire plumage brownish black, with changeable reflections of green and purple; primaries black; outer secondaries black on their outer webs, and amber brown on their inner, of which color are the inner secondaries; tail dark brown, with the shafts white on the under side; bill pale purplish blue, white in the middle, with the tips dusky; inside of mouth carmine; bare loral space purplish blue; iris dark brown; gular sac orange; feet reddish above, orange underneath.

Total length, 41 inches; wing, 25; bill, 5.50; tarsi, .80; tail, 18.

The female differs in having the sides of the neck and a broad space on the breast white, the feathers of the back not so lustrous as those of the male, and the wings and tail more tinged with brown.

Hab.—Texas to Florida; California.

The Florida keys are the principal resort of this species on our coast; here they congregate in large numbers at their breeding stations, several nests being frequently placed upon one tree. As might be supposed from their great depth of wing, they possess great power of flight, not being excelled by any other bird. They are tyrannical in their habits, harassing the terns and smaller gulls, robbing them of their food, causing them to drop or disgorge it, which they descend after with great rapidity, and recover it before it reaches the water; they also prey upon flying fish, and pick up floating substances in the manner of gulls; the young

Sept. 20, 1858.

110 b

of other species are devoured by them when left unprotected. They do not dive, but rest lightly upon the water, and rise easily from its surface.

A second species of *Tachypetes, T. palmerstonii,* is admitted by some authors and denied by others.

List of specimens.

Sex.	Locality.	Whence obtained.	Orig. No.	Collected by—	Stretch of wings.	Wing.
--------	Florida	G. Würdemann	--------	--------	--------	--------
♂	....do....	Cab. G. N. Lawrence...	1027	J. J. Audubon	38.00	25.00
♀	....do....		1028	......do		

Family PHALACROCORACIDAE.

Cʜ.—Bill rather moderate, culmen concave, tip much hooked and acute ; nostrils not perceptible ; wings moderate and pointed ; tail rather short and rounded ; tarsi short ; toes long and all joined by full webs ; gular sac capable of considerable expansion.

I have included all the Cormorants inhabiting our territory in the genus *Graculus.* They are placed in several genera by Prince Bonaparte, as may be seen by the synonymy given with each species.

GRACULUS, Linnaeus.

Graculus, Lɪɴɴ. Syst. Nat. 1735. Type *Pelecanus carbo,* L.

Cʜ.—Bill rather slender, of moderate length, with the culmen concave, hooked at the tip, the sides compressed and grooved ; nostrils not visible in the adult ; wings moderately long and pointed, second and third primaries longest ; tail moderate and graduated at the end ; tarsi short and much compressed ; toes long and full webbed ; a leathery pouch at the base of the lower mandible, which can be much distended.

These birds exist abundantly in all parts of the globe. They are mostly found on the sea-coast, breeding on rocky ledges difficult of access, and also on trees. They are exceedingly expert in catching fish, being very active in the water, and capable of remaining under its surface for a great length of time.

The following characters will distinguish the eight species of this genus inhabiting North America :

Bluish black ; bill strong ; gular sac yellow, the lower margin encircled by white feathers ; the gular sac is divided through the centre longitudinally by a line of white feathers, which extends for a short distance beyond the base of the lower mandible between the crura ; shafts of tail and quill feathers greyish blue at base, becoming black at the end ; feathers of the hind neck elongated ....*G. carbo.*

Dark green ; gular sac orange ; on the neck long filamentous straw colored feathers ; a patch of white on each side above the thighs ; shafts of tail feathers white.............*G. perspicillatus.*

Shining greenish black ; bill short, strong, and rugose ; a line of white feathers over the eye, prolonged behind, and curling downwards... *G. cincinnatus.*

Greenish black ; bill strong ; gular sac orange ; a large tuft of feathers on each side the crown ; shafts of tail feathers black...*G. dilophus.*

Greenish black ; bill rather strong ; gular sac orange, its lower part of a rounded form, the same as in " *dilophus ;*" crests consisting of a line of feathers on each side the crown, and curving downwards ; shafts of tail feathers black..*G. floridanus.*

Purplish black ; bill moderate ; gular sac dull orange, margined with pure white, its lower margin forming an arched line across the throat ; long white linear feathers on the neck ; shafts of tail feathers black..*G. mexicanus.*

Deep green ; bill moderately strong ; gular sac blue, encircled with a broad band of brownish drab or fawn colored feathers ; from the lower margin of the gular sac the feathers project for a short distance towards the bill ; very long, narrow, stiff white feathers on the neck and upper part of back ; shafts of tail feathers black..*G. penicillatus.*

Dark green ; neck and sides violet blue ; bill slender ; gular sac orange, feathers extending upwards upon it from its lower margin half way to the bill ; slender white feathers on the neck and sides ; shafts of tail feathers black...*G. violaceus.*

Phalacrocorax, Brisson.

GRACULUS CARBO, Gray.

Common Cormorant.

Pelecanus carbo, LINN. Syst. Nat. I, 1766, 216.

Phalacrocorax carbo, BON. Syn. 1828, No. 353.—IB. var. *macrorhynchus,* Cons. Av. II, 1855, 168.—NUTT. Man. II, 1834, 479.—AUD. Orn. Biog. III, 1835, 458.—IB. Syn. 1839, 302.—IB. Birds Am. VI, 1843, 412 ; pl. ccccxv.

Graculus carbo, GRAY, Gen. of Birds, 1845.

Phalacrocorax americanus, REICH. Syst. Av. 1850, t. 47.

" Phalacrocorax macrorhynchus, Cuv." BON. Comptes Rend. XLII, 1856, 766.

SP. CH.—Bluish black ; feathers on middle of occiput and hind neck elongated ; gular sac yellow, at the base of which is a broad band of white ; linear feathers on the head and neck white ; a patch of white on the sides ; third primary longest ; tail of fourteen feathers.

Adult. Plumage in general black, glossed with greenish blue ; the feathers of the upper part and sides of the back and wing coverts are dark ash, with bronzed reflections, and bordered with greenish black ; primaries and tail feathers greyish black, secondaries greyish brown ; bare space around the eye dull olive, under the eye red ; the gular sac yellow, encircling the lower part of which is a broad band of white ; numerous linear filamentous white feathers are distributed over the head and neck ; on the side over the thigh is a patch of elongated linear white feathers ; upper mandible greyish black, with the edges yellowish white, lower dusky yellowish white at the base ; iris bluish green ; eyelids with dusky margins ; tarsi, feet, and claws greyish black.

Length, 37 inches ; wing, 14 ; bill, 3.50 ; tail, 6.50 ; tarsus, 2.25 ; outer toe and claw, 4.25 ; inner, 2.90 ; hind, 1.90. The female resembles the male, but is smaller.

Hab.—Labrador, and along the coast as far south as New Jersey in winter.

The bill is strong and powerful, the ridge is smooth, but the sides of both mandibles are rugose.

These birds are abundant on the coast of Labrador, where large numbers assemble for the purpose of reproduction, forming their nests upon the inaccessible ledges of rocky cliffs.

Their mode of flight is swift and strong. Their food is obtained by diving and pursuing it beneath the surface, where they make rapid progress by the aid of their wings.

List of specimens.

Locality.	Whence obtained.	Orig. No.	Collected by—	Stretch of wings.	Wing.
Atlantic coast, U. S..............	Cab. G. N. Lawrence............	1029	J. J. Audubon	40.00	14.00

GRACULUS PERSPICILLATUS, Lawr.

Pallas' Cormorant.

Phalacrocorax perspicillatus, Pall. Zoog. Rosso–As. II, 1811, 305.—Gould, Zool. Voy. Sulph. 1844, 49; pl. xxxii.—
Bon. Cons. Av. II, 1855, 167.—Ib. Comptes Rendus, XLIII, Sep. 1856.
"Pelecanus urile? Lath." Gould. Zool. Voy. Sulph, 1844, 49.
Graculus urile, Reich. Syst. Av. 1850, t. 65.
Phalacrocorax urile, Bonap. Comptes Rendus, XLII, Ap. 1856, 766.

Sp. Ch.—Dark green; on the face and upper part of the neck are long narrow hair-like feathers of a straw color; gular sack orange; a large white mark on each side near the leg.

Adult. "Face and crest rich deep shining purple; neck deep greenish blue; the face and the upper part of the neck ornamented with some thinly dispersed, long, narrow hair-like straw-colored feathers; body above and beneath deep glossy green; scapularies and wings deep purple, primaries and tail black, the latter with white shafts; on each side of the abdomen, at the insertion of the leg, a large patch of white; bill blackish hair-color, lighter at the tip; naked part of the throat, corners of the mouth, and naked skin of the coverts apparently rich orange."

" Total length, 36 inches; bill, 4; tail, 9; tarsi, 3."

"*Hab.*—Russian America."

"Nearly allied to, if not identical with, but differs from the *Pelecanus urile* of Latham in its much larger size, and in the ornamental plumes being dispersed over face and sides of the neck, instead of on the front of the latter only."

There are no specimens of this species in the collection.

The above is Mr. Gould's account of this species, taken from the Zoology of the Voyage of the Sulphur.

There appears to be some doubt whether this may not be the Red-faced Cormorant of Pennant and Latham, ("*Pel. urile,* Gmelin.") Gray puts it under *P. urile,* Gm., with a question, and Bonaparte at one time also considered it to be that species, but finally concluded it was distinct.

GRACULUS CINCINNATUS, Gray.

The Tufted Cormorant.

Carbo cincinnatus, Brandt, Bull. Sc. Ac. Imp. Pet. III, 1837, 55.
Graculus cincinnatus, Gray, Gen. of Birds, 1845.
Phalacrocorax cincinnatus, Bon. Cons. Av. II, 1855, 168.—Ib. Comptes Rendus, XLII, 1856, 766.

Sp. Ch.—Silky black, glossed with shining green; superciliary feathers white, prolonged behind and curled downwards.

Adult. Head, neck, back, and entire under plumage silky black, glossed with green; wing-coverts dull brownish grey, margined with black; tail shining black; over the eye is a line formed of white feathers, the hinder ones greatly elongated, radiating singly, rather stiff, curled backward and downward; bill stout, horny, and very rugose; feet black.

Length, about 36 inches.

Hab.—Northwest coast, Sitka.

I have never had an opportunity of examining a specimen of this species.

Graculus, Bonap.

GRACULUS DILOPHUS, Gray.

Double-crested Cormorant.

Pelecanus (Carbo) dilophus, Sw. Faun. Bor. Am. II, 1831, 473.
Phalacrocorax dilophus, Nutt. Man. II, 1834, 483.—Bon. Comp. List, 1838, 60.—Aud. Orn. Biog. III, 1835, 420: V.
1839, 628.—Ib. Syn. 1839, 302.—Ib. Birds Am. VI, 1843, 423; pl. ccccxvi.
Graculus dilophus, Gray, Gen. of Birds, 1845.—Bon. Cons. Av. II, 1855, 172.—Ib. Comptes Rendus, XLII, 1856, 766.
Carbo dilophus, Gamb. Jour. Acad. Nat. Sc. Phil. 2d Ser. I, 1849, 227.

Sp. Ch.—Greenish black; behind each eye a recurved crest of loose feathers; gular sac orange; second quill longest; tail of twelve feathers.

Adult. The plumage of the head, neck, lower part of the back and entire under surface is greenish black, the feathers of the upper part of the back, the wing-coverts, the scapularies and tertiaries, greyish brown or dark ash, the margins of which are greenish black; primaries blackish-brown, lighter on the inner webs; the secondaries dark greyish brown; tail black, as are also the shafts; running from the bill over the eye is a line of white filamentous feathers, there are also a few of the same character sparsely distributed over the neck; behind each eye is a tuft of rather long slender feathers, erect and curving forwards; bare space in the region of the eye, and gular sac orange; upper mandible blackish brown, with the edges yellowish; lower yellow, marked irregular with dusky; iris bright green; legs, feet, and claws black, claw of the middle toe pectinated.

Length, 33 inches; wing, 13; tail, 6.75; bill, 2.85; tarsus, 3.50; outer toe and claw, 4; inner, 2.50; hind, 1.75.

Hab.—Atlantic coast from Labrador to Carolina; fur countries; Pacific coast from Washington Territory to California.

Numerous specimens are in the collection, mostly from the Pacific coast, from which point none are fully adult, most having the greyish under plumage of the young, the bills being yellow.

Ph. lenconotus and Ph. lencumus Aud. Orn. Biog. III, 1835, 334, are thought by both Gray and Bonaparte to be the young of this species.

The bill is strong, in the adult the culmen is smooth, the sides of both mandibles are crossed with slight prominences of a curved or scale-like form, pretty regularly distributed about a quarter of an inch apart from the base to the unguis.

This species resorts in large numbers to the low islands off the coast of Labrador, which are their breeding stations; they construct their nests on the surface of the rocks, not on the shelves of precipices.

I once witnessed a large migrating flight of these birds to the south, along our seacoast; they passed in great flocks, which succeeded each other frequently during the entire day; each flock formed a widely extended front, the individuals being side by side; their mode of flight was by alternate flapping of the wings, and their sailing for a short distance, the effect of which was peculiar and striking.

List of specimens.

Catal. No.	Sex.	Locality.	When collected.	Whence obtained.	Orig. No.	Collected by—	Stretch of wings	Wing.
2745	....	Atlantic coast.........	....	S. F. Baird..........	......	J. J. Audubon	....	12.00
2744	....	......do.........	....	......do.........	......	......do.........	....	13.00
....	....	Coast of New York	....	George N. Lawrence .	1030	....	....	12.00
....	....	Atlantic coast.........	....	......do.........	1031	J. J. Audubon	....	12.50
4438	....	Quasquiton, Iowa......	....	Dr. E. C. Bidwell...	......	....	....	12.00
9893	....	San Francisco, Cal.....	....	Lt. Trowbridge......	......	....	....	12.50
4503	....	......do.........	....	Dr. Newberry......	......	....	....	12.00
5571	♀	Petaluma, Cal...........	Feb. 1856	E. Samuels	......	....	....	12.00
9894	....	Bodega, Cal...........	Dec. 1854	Lt. Trowbridge......	......	T. A. Szabo......	....	12.00
9896	....	Shoalwater bay, W. T...	Oct. 5, 1854	Gov. Stevens.........	......	Dr. Cooper......	....	13.50
4577	....	Steilacoom, Puget Sound	Feb. 6, 1856	Dr. Suckley.........	216	....	50.50	14.00

GRACULUS FLORIDANUS, Bon.

Florida Cormorant.

Phalacrocorax floridanus, Aud. Orn. Biog. III, 1835, 387 : V, 1839, 632.—Ib. Syn. 1839, 303.—Ib. Birds Am. VI, 1843, 430 ; pl. ccccxvii.
Graculus floridanus, Bon. Cons. Av. II, 1855, 172.—Ib. Comptes Rendus, XLII, 1856, 766.
Phalacrocorax brasiliensis, Bon. Comp. List, 1838, 60.
Graculus dilophus, Gray, Genera of Birds, 1845.

Sp. Ch.—Greenish black ; behind each eye a narrow line of elongated feathers ; gular sac orange ; second primary longest ; tail of twelve feathers.

Adult. Head, neck, lower part of back, and under plumage, greenish black ; feathers of the back, wing coverts, scapularies, and tertiaries, ashy brown, tinged with purple, having their margins greenish black ; primaries blackish brown, the inner webs lighter ; secondaries dark brown ; tail and shafts of the feathers brownish black ; a crest of lengthened feathers extends in a line behind each eye backwards, and curving downwards ; bare skin near the eye and gular sac orange ; upper mandible black, along the basal margins blue, lower blue variegated with white spots ; iris light green, margins of the eyelids light blue, spotted with white ; tarsi, feet, and claws greyish black.

Length, 29.75 ; wing, 11.75 ; tail, 6 ; bill, 2.40 ; tarsus, 215 ; outer toe and claw, 3.75 ; inner, 2.25 ; hind, 1.50.

Hab.—Along the coast from Texas to Florida ; Mississippi river.

Rather smaller than *dilophus*, but in plumage much resembling it, the colors of the back and wings are ashy brown, in *dilophus* greyish, the sides of the bill are rough in the same manner as in that species.

The Florida cormorant is solely an inhabitant of the southern portion of the United States, not proceeding further to the north than Carolina. They congregate in thousands on the Florida keys at the season of reproduction, placing their nests on the mangrove bushes, many being established on the same tree.

They are expert divers and fly with great rapidity.

List of specimens.

Catalogue number.	Locality.	Whence obtained.	Original number.	Collected by—	Wings.
2002	Florida	S. F. Baird		J. J. Audubon	11.50
	do	Cab. Geo. N. Lawrence	1032	do	11.25

GRACULUS MEXICANUS, Bon.

Mexican Cormorant.

Carbo mexicanus, Brandt, Bull. Sc. Ac. Imp. Pet III, 1837, 56.
Graculus mexicanus, Bon. Cons. Av. II, 1855, 175.
Phalacrocorax lacustris, Gundlach's MSS.
" *Phalacrocorax resplendens*, Lembeye, Aves de Cuba, (Adult.)"
" *Phalacrocorax townsendi*, Lembeye, Aves de Cuba, (Young.)"

Sp. Ch.—Purplish black ; sides of the neck ornamented with white linear feathers, gular sac brownish orange.

Adult. Head, neck, lower part of the back, smaller wing coverts, and under plumage, glossy black, in a strong light having a tinge of bluish purple ; imbricate feathers of the upper part of the back and wings are of a clear brownish gray, with their margins and shafts glossy black ; primaries blackish brown, the other quills brownish grey ; tail and shafts black ; a line of small white spots runs from the upper mandible over and beyond the eye ; scattered over the sides of the neck are rather long filamentous feathers of pure white ; gular sac brownish orange, bordered narrowly with pure white ; the gular sac is wide, at the lower part of which, on each side, the bare skin descends for a short distance down the neck, gradually coming to a point, thereby giving an arcuate form to the lower margin of the pouch ; bill brownish horn color, the lower mandible marked with yellow spots ; iris pale green ; legs and feet black.

Length, 27, (skin) ; wing, 10 ; tail, 6.50 ; bill, 2.10 ; tarsus, 1.90 ; outer toe and claw, 3.10.

The young are dark brown, with the neck and breast brownish grey ; the bill yellow, with the ridge dusky.

Hab.—Texas, on the Rio Grande ; Cuba.

Of this species, new to our fauna, there are seven specimens in the collection, three nearly adult ; they are all from the Rio Grande. I have two fully adult specimens in my cabinet, one from eastern Mexico, the other from Cuba. The bill is of moderate length, rather stout, with the culmen smooth, and the sides crossed with ridges, in the same manner as in *dilophus* and *floridanus.*

Mr. Gundlach writes that it is abundant on the fresh water lakes and rivers of Cuba, also on the sea-shore ; it breeds in August ; the nests are placed on trees resembling those of *G. floridanus.*

Mr. Gray appears to have had some doubt of *G. mexicanus*, Brandt, being a valid species, as in his Genera of Birds he places it under *dilophus*, where he also puts *floridanus*, Aud. The bird above described has strong and decided characters, and agrees very well with Brandt's description of *G. mexicanus.*

List of specimens.

Catal. No.	Sex.	Locality.	When collected.	Whence obtained.	Orig. No.	Length.	Stretch of wing.	Wing.	Remarks.
-------	----	Cuba ---------	---------	Cab Geo. N. Lawrence	1034	-------	-------	-------	---------------
-------	----	Gulf of Mexico --	---------	--------do-------	1033	-------	-------	-------	---------------
3834	----	Brazos, Texas ----	Feb., 1853	Capt Van Vliet -----	-------	-------	-------	9.75	---------------
3833	----	Fort Brown, Texas	---- -----	--------do---------	-------	26.50	36.00	10.00	Eyes green -----
4191	♀	Brownsville, Texas	---------	--------do---------	-------	26.00	36.00	10.00	Eyes grass green.
9897	----	Fort Thorn, N. M.	---------	Dr. Henry---------	-------	-------	-------	-------	---------------
9895	----	-------------------	---------	--------do---------	-------	-------	-------	9.75	---------------
9899	----	-------------------	---------	--------do---------	-------	-------	-------	10.50	---------------

Urile, Bonap.
GRACULUS PENICILLATUS, Gray.
Brandt's Cormorant.

Carbo penicillatus, BRANDT, Bull. Sc. Ac. Imp. Pet. III, 1837, 55.—GAMB. Jour. Acad. Nat. Sc. Philad. 2d ser. I, 1849, 227.

Phalacrocorax penicillatus, HEERM. Proc. Phil. Acad. VII, 1854, 178.

Urile penicillatus, BON. Cons. Av. II, 1855, 175.

Graculus penicillatus, GRAY, Gen. III, 1845, 668—BON. Comptes Rendus, XLII, 1856, 766

Phalacrocorax townsendi, AUD. Orn. Biog. V, 1839, 149.—IB. Syn. 1839, 304.—IB. Birds Am. VI, 1843, 438; pl. cccxviii.

SP. CH.—Dark green ; long hair-like feathers of the neck and back white ; gular sac blue, below which is a gorgelet of dark fawn color.

Adult. Head and neck of a fine bluish black color ; back, rump, and under plumage of a very deep rich green, in certain positions inclining to bluish green ; imbricate feathers of the back and wings of a dull bronzed brownish green, very narrowly margined with black ; primaries and inner webs of the other quills blackish brown, the outer webs brownish green ; tail and shafts black ; sides of the neck and the upper part of the back on each side have numerous white, narrow, stiff, hair-like feathers, which extend beyond the other feathers from 2 to 2½ inches ; gular sac blue, encircling the base of which is a broad band of dark fawn color, the feathers of this gorgelet extend upward from the lower margin of the gular sac for ¾ of an inch and come to a point ; bill brownish, lighter at base of lower mandible ; legs and feet black.

Length, about 28 inches ; wing, 10½ ; tail, 5.25 ; bill, 2.90 ; tarsus, 2.40 ; outer toe and claw, 4 ; inner, 2.15 ; hind, 1.50.

These are the measurements of No. 4501.

Hab.—West coast of North America.

No. 9892 is larger, the wing measuring 12 inches ; the bill, 3 ; the tail, 5.50.

Young. Head, neck, back, and wings blackish brown, the feathers of the back and wings with greyish brown margins ; under plumage dull rusty brown, the middle of the abdomen greyish ; gorgelet fawn color as in the adult. This is the plumage of one of the original specimens of Mr. Audubon's "*townsendi,*" (now in the cabinet of Professor Baird.) The fawn colored gorgelet which extends in a point on the lower part of the gular sac, together with the form and character of the bill, agreeing with the specimens of the adult under examination, in my opinion, are satisfactory evidence of its being this species.

The true position of "*townsendi*" heretofore has been one of much uncertainty. Gray, in Gen. of Birds, places it under "*dilophus*" as the young, as does also Gambel in Jour. Phil. Acad. Bonaparte, in Cons. Avium, puts it with a question, as a synonym of "*Gr. brasilianus,* Gm.,*" but in Comptes Rendus has it under "*dilophus.*"

The form of the gular sac, and whether entirely bare or encroached upon by the feathers of the throat, are points which appear to have been generally overlooked in describing the different species of cormorants. I consider these features strong characters, that will materially aid in determining species when not in mature plumage, as maybe instanced in the above case.

The bill is of moderate strength, and entirely smooth both on the sides and ridge.

List of specimens.

Catal. No.	Sex and age.	Locality.	When collected.	Whence obtained.	Orig'l No.	Collected by—	Wings.	Remarks.
2742	♂ ○	Cape Disappointment, Columbia river	Oct. 8, 1836	S. F. Baird		J. K. Townsend.		Irides dark hazel.
		California		Cab. G. N. Lawrence	1037		10.75	
9892		San Francisco, Cal.		Lt. Trowbridge			12.00	
4501		Farrallon islands, Cal.		Lt. Williamson		Dr. Heermann	10.50	

GRACULUS VIOLACEUS, G r a y .

Violet Green Cormorant.

Pelecanus violaceus, GM. Syst. Nat. I, 1788, 575.

Graculus violaceus, GRAY, Gen. of Birds, 1845.—BON. Comptes Rendus, XLII, 1856, 766.

Phalacrocorax resplendens, AUD. Orn. Biog. V, 1839, 148.—IB. Syn. 1839, 304.—IB. Birds Am. VI, 1843, 430 ; pl. ccccxix.

Urile bicristatus, BON. Cons. Av. II, 1855, 175.

SP. CH.—Violet green ; narrow white feathers are sparingly distributed on the sides of the neck, and hind part and sides of the body ; gular sac orange.

Adult. Crown and sides of the head dark bluish green, gradually blending with the beautiful violet blue of the hind head and entire neck ; back, rump, wings, and under plumage of a rich deep green ; axillars, sides under the wings, and thighs violet blue ; smaller wing coverts violet ; primaries brownish black, as are the other quills on their inner webs ; tail and shafts black ; the entire plumage very lustrous and silky in appearance ; dispersed over the neck and on the sides of the body near the thighs are numerous short white piliform feathers which expand at the end in the form of a small brush ; gular sac and bare space about the eye orange; feathers of the throat extend upon the lower part of the gular sac for about half its length, and terminate in a point ; upper mandible blackish brown, lower dusky yellow ; legs and feet black.

Length, 28 inches ; alar extent, 41 ; wing, 10.50 ; tail, 6.25 ; bill, 2 ; tarsus, 1.90 , outer toe and claw, 3.75.

Hab.—Western coast of North America. California, Washington Territory.

Sept. 23, 1858.

111 b

Three adult specimens of this handsome species are in the collection.

The bill is slender, smooth on the culmen and sides ; the feathers of the wings and back are without the dark margins so characteristic of most of the species.

Bonaparte makes *bicristatus*, Pall., to be the same as the above species, whereas Gray puts *bicristatus*, Pall., as the synonym to *P. urile*, Gmelin.

List of specimens.

Catal. No.	Locality.	When collected.	Whence obtained.	Orig'l No.	Collected by—	Length.	Stretch of wings.	Wings.
2004	Cape Disappointment, W. T.	----------	S. F. Baird ----------	------	J. K. Townsend -----	28.50	40.00	10.50
4502	------do----------do----	----------	Dr. Cooper----------	------	----------------------	27.00	------	9.75
------	Orcas island, W. T.--------	Feb., 1858	A. Campbell --------	100	Dr. Kennerly--------	28.00	41.00	10.50

Family PLOTIDAE.

Cʜ.—Bill long, straight, a slight curvature at the end, the edges serrated ; nostrils small ; wings long ; tail long and rounded, narrow at base ; tarsi short and strong ; toes united by full webs ; face and throat bare, the latter with an extensible sac.

Sub-Family PLOTINAE.

Cʜ.—Bill long, slender, nearly straight and sharp at the point ; nostrils very small; wings rather long ; tail long, widening at the end ; tarsi stout and very short ; toes long, connected by full webs ; claws strong and curved ; gular sac rather moderate.

Only a single genus is comprised in this sub-family, containing but four recorded species, one peculiar to America, and one each to Africa, Asia, and Australia.

PLOTUS, Linnaeus.

Plotus, Lɪɴɴ. Syst. Nat. 1766. Type *P. anhinga.*

Cʜ.—Bill about twice the length of the head, very slender and pointed, with the sides compressed ; nostrils scarcely visible ; wings moderately long, third primary longest ; tail long, narrow at the base but becoming broader at the end, which is rounded, the shafts very strong ; tarsi short and very stout ; toes long and united by full webs ; claws strong, curved, and acute, the middle one pectinated ; gular sac capable of considerable distention ; neck very long and slender.

The species of this genus inhabit the warm regions of the Old World, and also of America. They assemble in communities on the shores of inland lakes, on rivers, and submerged swamps, placing their nests on trees ; they are exceedingly watchful and difficult to approach, are very expert in swimming and diving.

PLOTUS ANHINGA, Linnaeus.

Darter ; Snake Bird ; Water Turkey.

Plotus anhinga, Lɪɴɴ. Syst. Nat. 1766, 580.—Bᴏɴ. Syn. 1828, No. 362.—Iʙ. Cons. Av. II, 1855, 180.—Aᴜᴅ. Orn. Biog. IV, 1838, 136 —Iʙ. Syn. 1839, 306 —Iʙ. Birds Am. VI, 1843, 443 ; pl. ccccxx.—Nᴜᴛᴛ. Man. II, 1834, 507.
Plotus melanogaster, Wɪʟs. Am. Orn. IX, 1824, 79 & 82 ; pl. lxxiv.

Sᴘ. Cʜ.—Greenish black ; a broad band of gray over the wings ; bill long, slender, and pointed ; tail long, increasing in width at the end.

Adult male. Head, neck, back, and entire under plumage glossy greenish black ; on each side of the upper part of the back is a broad band extending downwards, composed of spots of a greyish white color ; they are quite small on the upper part, but become larger and elongated lower down ; the scapularies and tertiaries are long and lanceolate in shape ; they are black, but largely striped longitudinally with greyish white ; the smaller wing coverts are black at the base, terminating with greyish white ; the larger coverts are almost entirely of this color, having a narrow margin of black on a portion only of their inner webs, this forms a conspicuous broad band over the wings ; primaries and secondaries black ; tail black, with a terminal margin of brownish ash, paler at the end ; the two central feathers are crimped on their outer webs for their entire length—this peculiar character exists also on some of the tertiary feathers ; on the sides and back of the neck are numerous elongated filamentous feathers of a dark ash color ; bare space in the region of the eye bluish green ; gular pouch orange ; upper mandible dull olive, with the edges yellow ; lower yellow, the edges and tip dusky green ; iris bright carmine ; tarsi and toes dusky olive in front ; behind and the webs yellow ; claws brownish black.

Length, about 35 inches ; wing, 14 ; tail, 11 ; bill, 3.25 ; tarsus, 1.35.

The female has the upper part of the head, neck behind, and upper part of back brown ; neck underneath and breast of a light fawn color, margined with reddish brown where it joins the black of the abdomen ; elongated ash colored feathers on the neck very few ; in other respects resembling the male.

Hab.—Southern States from Florida to Carolina ; Texas.

The American Darter resides throughout the year in the Southern States, not ranging higher to the north than Carolina, even in summer. It frequents mostly the inland lakes and secluded bayous, never visiting the sea-shore. They fly with great rapidity, and are unexcelled in swimming and diving ; they procure their food much in the same manner as cormorants do. Their nests are constructed on trees or bushes, always over the water.

The Surinam Darter (*Heliornis surinamensis*, Gm.,) is noticed by Bonaparte and Nuttall as accidental on our southern coast. Its occurrence must be exceedingly rare, as no instance has ever come to my knowledge of one being obtained ; I do not therefore consider it entitled to a place in our Fauna ; but a short description of it may not be amiss.

It is a small and very beautiful species, being in length only 12 inches, the wing $5\frac{3}{4}$ inches. Above it is dark umber brown ; the primaries reddish brown ; tail blackish brown, margined narrowly with white ; upper part of head and hind part of neck jet black ; a white stripe runs from behind the eye along the side of the head towards the occiput ; a broad line of light chestnut red begins under the eye and runs half way down the side of the neck, then succeeds a line of black, which continues for the other half ; between the black of the lower part of the neck and that of the hind neck is a line of pure white ; throat and neck in front white ; breast and abdomen white, the former tinged with pale rufous ; sides of the body brownish ash ; bill orange red ; feet yellow, barred with black.

List of specimens.

Catal. No.	Sex and age.	Locality.	Whence obtained.	Original No.	Wings.
--------	♂	South Carolina----------------------	Cab. George N. Lawrence----------	1035	13. 25
--------	♀	------do------------------------------	----------do----------------------	1036	13. 25
--------	--------	South Atlantic coast------------------	S. F. Baird------------------------	--------	--------
9898	♀	Fort Thorn, New Mexico----------------	Dr. Henry------------------------	--------	--------

Family PHAETONIDAE.

Cʜ.—Bill long, broad at the base, and the upper outline gradually curving to the point, edges slightly serrated; nostrils pervious; wings long; tail with the central feathers extremely elongated; tarsi short and strong; toes joined by full webs; no bare space on the face or throat.

Sub Family PHAETONINAE.

Cʜ.—Bill rather long, with the base broad, the sides compressed and point acute, outline of the upper mandible curving to the tip; nostrils basal, linear and open; wings long and pointed; tail graduated, the two central feathers exceedingly elongated; tarsi short; toes long and connected together by full webs.

There is but one genus under this sub-family which belongs to North America.

PHAETON, Linnaeus.

Phaeton, LINN. S. N. 1756. Type *P. aethereus*.

Cʜ.—Bill about the length of the head, strong, broad at the base, compressed, the culmen curved to the tip, which is pointed; nostrils lateral, basal, and pervious, situated in a short groove near the ridge; wings long and pointed, the first primary longest; tail graduated, the two middle feathers extremely lengthened and narrow; tarsi short and stout; toes rather long, all connected together by full webs; claws small, curved and rather acute.

These birds frequent the warm parallels of the tropics, and are generally noticed far from and; at their breeding places they assemble in considerable numbers. They are excellent swimmers, and have enduring power of wing; flying fishes afford them an abundant supply of food: these are seized as they emerge from the sea for their short flight above its surface.

PHAETON FLAVIROSTRIS, Brandt.

Yellow-billed Tropic Bird.

Lepturus candidus, BRISS. Orn. VI, 1760, 485.—BON. Comptes Rendus, XLII, 1856, 767.
Phaeton candidus, GRAY, Gen. of Birds, 1847; pl. clxxxiii.
Phaeton aethereus, BON. Syn. 1828, No. 361.—IB. Cons. Av II, 1855, 183.—NUTT. Man. II, 1834, 503.—AUD. Orn. Biog. III, 1835, 442.—IB. Syn. 1839, 312.—IB. Birds Am. VII, 1844, 64; pl. ccccxxvii.
Phaeton flavirostris, BRANDT, Bull. Sc. Acad. Imp. St. Pet. I, 1837, 349.—SCLATER, Proc. Zool. Soc. Lond. 1856, 144.
The Tropic Bird, EDWARDS, Nat. Hist. of Birds, 1749; pl. cxlix.

Sᴘ. Cʜ.—White; wings banded with black; first five primaries black on the outer webs; shafts of long middle tail feathers black to near the end, where they are white.

Adult. General plumage of the body white, with a satiny gloss, and tinged on the head, back, and wings with cream color; there is rather a broad mark of black in the form of a crescent before the eye, extending over it in a line, and along the side of the head as far as the occiput; a band of black extends over the wings, beginning near the flexure and crossing about the middle of the coverts, where it is rather narrow, but occupying a large space on the base of the secondaries, and most of the terminal portion of the tertiaries and scapularies; the first five primaries are black on the outer webs and a portion of the inner next the shaft, remaining part of inner webs and tips of outer white; the sixth primary has the outer web black at the base; the tail is white, the elongated central feathers with a tinge of pale salmon color; the shafts of all the tail feathers are black nearly to the end, terminal portion white, as are all the shafts on the under side; the long hypochndriacal feathers are broadly marked down their centres with greyish black; bill orange red; iris brown; tarsus, hind toe, and outer basal edge of inner toe yellow, remaining part of foot black.

Length, 30 inches; wing, 11; tail, 18½; bill, 2.05; tarsus, .90.

Hab.—Florida coast.

The above description is taken from a very perfect specimen obtained on the south side of

Cuba. It is without doubt the species described and figured by Audubon, and which recent writers refer to the *"candidus"* of Brisson, (*flavirostris* of Brandt.)

In a monograph of the *Phaetonidae*, given by Professor F. Brandt in the Bulletin of the St. Petersburg Academy, he says Gmelin, Latham, and others have confounded the two species *aethereus*, Linn., and *candidus*, Briss.

The above bird agrees with the description of *"candidus"* as given by Brandt, differing only in having the six outer primaries marked with black instead of four ; six is the number stated by Edwards, whose figure agrees with the present species. The black markings on the primaries probably vary with age, as in many species of gulls.

Mr. Sclater, in Zool. Proc., (as above,) adopts Brandt's name of *"flavirostris,"* for the reason that "Brisson was no binomalist, and has no claim to bestow specific names in a binominal system."

I have another specimen, apparently of this species, purchased some years since from a dealer, the locality from which it was obtained being unknown. The black markings are distributed much the same as in the specimen from Cuba, but the black is confined to the four outer primaries, not crossing the shaft of the fourth, and on the fifth a very narrow margining of black on each side of the shaft near the base; the black is much further removed from the tips also. The prevailing color, instead of being white, is of a fine deep salmon, of a very uniform shade throughout ; the hypochondrical feathers are striped with greyish black, of which color are the upper tail coverts for about half their length at the base ; the bill is dusky greenish olive at the base of the upper mandible and sides of the lower, the remainder pale yellow; the toes are all yellow at the base. The length is 32 inches; the wing 11¼.

In the above plumage it agrees with a figure of this species given by Reichenbach, Syst. Av. pl. 30, taken from a specimen in the Dresden Museum.

List of specimens.

Locality.	Whence obtained.	Original No.	Collected by—	Length.	Wings.
Cuba	Cab. George N. Lawrence	1038	J. Gundlach	30. 00	11. 00

Tribe **BRACHYPTERI.**

Family C O L Y M B I D A E .[1]

Ch.—Bill more or less long and compressed ; the nostrils are linear or rounded, and situated in a lateral groove ; tail rudimentary or short ; tarsi much compressed ; anterior toes long, with the interdigital membrane more or less full, the outer longest ; hind toe short, free, with a hanging lobe ; claws broad, depressed, buried in the body.

The species are remarkable for their powers of swimming and diving; their ease and gracefulness on the water is in strong contrast with their awkwardness on land.

The following are the characters of the two sub-families, *Colymbinae* and *Podicipinae:*

COLYMBINAE.—Bill long, rather strong, much compressed, with the point acute ; nostrils basal, linear ; tarsi much compressed ; toes long and webs full ; tail short ; lores feathered.

PODICIPINAE.—Bill generally long and rather slender, compressed and pointed ; nostrils situated in a groove, oblong and narrow ; tarsi compressed; toes long and broadly lobed ; tail wanting, or very rudimentary ; lores naked.

Sub-Family **COLYMBINAE.**—The Divers proper.

Ch.—Bill about the length of the head, rather stout, much compressed, and acute ; nostrils basal, linear and pervious ; wings of medium size, narrow and pointed, first quill the longest, reaching far beyond the scapulars ; tail short and rounded ; tarsi very much compressed ; entire tarsi and base of toes reticulated ; toes long, the anterior ones united by regular webs, the claw of the middle twice as long as broad ; hind toe short, edged with a narrow membrane.

These birds excel all others in their rapidity of diving, and the great progress they are able to make under water. Only one genus in this sub-family is recognised by authors.

COLYMBUS, L i n n a e u s.

Colymbus, LINN. Syst. Nat. 1735. Type *C. arcticus.*

As the character of the sub-family include those of the single genus *Colymbus*, it is not necessary to repeat them.

They are abundant during summer in the high northern latitudes, both on the seacoast and on inland lakes; in winter they migrate to the south. They are solitary in their habits, keen sighted, and very difficult of approach; their flight is strong, rapid, and direct.

The species of this genus have the following characters :

Bill strong, compressed, nearly straight, a groove on the under mandible, continued from the junction of the crura to near the point; head and neck dark bluish green, a small patch of white feathers on the throat in front, also a larger one on each side of the neck...*C. glacialis.*

Bill rather strong, much like that of the above species, but smaller and without the groove underneath ; head and neck bluish grey, a large space of purplish black on the front part of the neck ....*C. arcticus.*

Bill not so strong as in either of the above named species. Adult plumage not known ....*C. pacificus.*

Bill straight and slender; head and neck clear light bluish grey, hind neck marked with white and greenish black, on the fore part of the neck is a large patch of dark reddish brown...*C. septentrionalis.*

[1] Prepared by Mr. George N. Lawrence, of New York.

COLYMBUS TORQUATUS, Brünnich.

The Great Northern Diver; The Loon.

Colymbus torquatus, Brünn. Orn. Bor. 1764, 134.

Colymbus glacialis, Linn. Syst. Nat. I, 1766, 221.—Forster, Phil. Trans. LXII, 1772, 383.—Wils. Am. Orn. IX, 1824, 84, pl. lxxiv.—Bonap. Syn. 1828, No. 368 —Rich. & Sw. F. B. Am. II, 1831, 474.— Nutt. Man. II, 1834, 513.—Aud. Orn. Biog. IV, 1838, 43, pl. 306.—Ib. Birds, Am. VII, 1844, 282; pl. cccclxxvi.

Colymbus immer, Linn. Syst. Nat. I, 1766, 222. (Young of year.)

Sp. Ch.—Bill compressed, strong and tapering, outline of upper mandible nearly straight, very slightly curved ; the lower mandible has a groove underneath, running from the junction of the crura towards the point; the tail consists of twenty feathers.

Adult.—The head and neck are dark bluish green, the upper part and sides of the head glossed with purple ; there is a small transverse mark on the throat, composed of white feathers of a quill like form, distinct from each other and placed longitudinally on each side of the neck ; lower down are larger patches of white, of the same peculiar form, and running in the same direction ; these almost meet behind, and in front are about one inch apart ; the effect of these pure white feathers, relieved by the dark color of the neck, is very beautiful ; the upper plumage and wing coverts are deep glossy black, beautifully marked with pure white spots placed in regular transverse rows, slightly curving downwards ; these spots, on the upper part of the back, are small and nearly round, but as they descend lower on the back increase in size and become quadrangular in form, being largest on the scapularies ; on the lower part of the back, upper tail coverts and sides (which are black,) the spots are small and round ; the sides of the neck, near the shoulder, are beautifully lineated with black and white ; the primaries, secondaries and tail brownish black ; the under surface glossy white, with a narrow band of dusky feathers crossing the lower part of the abdomen, and marked with small white spots ; lower tail coverts blackish brown, tipped with white ; bill black ; iris deep bright red ; tarsi and feet greyish blue externally, tinged on the inside with pale yellowish red ; webs brownish black ; claws back.

Length, 31 inches ; wing, 14 ; tarsus, 3¼ ; bill, 3 ; height at base, 1.

Young.—The plumage above is greyish black, the feathers of the back margined with greyish white, the under plumage pure white, bill yellowish with the ridge of the upper mandible dusky.

Hab —Very generally distributed ; it is abundant on the Atlantic coast, in the lakes of the interior and the fur countries Specimens are in the collection from the Pacific coast and from New Mexico.

There are two specimens in adult plumage, and a head of a young individual from the Pacific coast; two of the young from New Mexico. Individuals vary considerably in size, some measuring 36 inches in length.

Catal. No.	Sex.	Locality.	When collected.	Whence obtained.	Orig'l No.	Collected by—	Length.	Stretch of wings.	Wing.	Remarks.
1550	♂	Carlisle, Pa..........	May 18,1844	S. F. Baird	......	....	31.50	54.00	14.00	....
2161	♀	......do...............	Apr 26,1845	......do	......	....	31.00	56.00	14.50	....
......	......	Coast of New Jersey......	....	Cab. of Geo. N. Lawrence.	962	....	....	....	....	....
9916	......	Fort Thorn, N. M	....	Dr. T. C. Henry..	......	....	....	....	13 00	....
4516	,	Shoalwater bay.......	....	Gov. Stevens......	......	Dr. Cooper	30.00	....	....	Color of iris blood red, feet blue...............
4580	......	Steilacoom, W. T...	....	Dr. Suckley	......	Dr. Potts	31.00	....	14.50	....
9920	......	......do..................	....	...... do	575	....	....	....	14.00	....

COLYMBUS ARCTICUS, Linnaeus.

The Black-throated Diver.

Colymbus arcticus, Linn. Syst. Nat. I, 1766, 221.—Bonap. Syn. 1828, No. 369.—Rich. and Sw. F. B. A. II, 1831, 475.—Nutt. Man. II, 1834, 517.—Aud. Orn. Biog. IV, 1838, 345.—Ib. Birds Am. VII, 1844, 295; pl. cccclxxvii.—Gray Genera, III, 630; pl. clxxi.

Sᴘ. Cʜ.—*Adult.* Head and hind neck bluish grey, darker on the front and sides of the head; upper plumage glossy black, tinged with green; on the upper part of the back are two bands of transverse white bars, running longitudinally, formed by the tips of the feathers; the scapulars, with the exception of the outer, are similarly marked with transverse rows of large white spots, quadrangular in form; wing coverts black, marked with round white spots near the end; quill feathers blackish brown, with the outer margin grey, and paler on the inner webs; tail blackish brown; the fore port of the neck is purplish black for an extent of about six inches, terminating in an angle at the lower end; the upper part of this dark marking is crossed by a narrow band of white linear feathers; sides of the neck blackish brown, longitudinally streaked with linear white feathers, on the lower part of the neck is a broad space similarly marked; under plumage pure white, with the exception of a dusky longitudinal band on the sides under the wings; bill black; iris deep bright red; tarsi and feet greyish blue externally, pale flesh color on the inside; claws dusky, yellowish at the base.

Length, about 28 inches; wing, 12¼; tail, 2¾; bill, 2½; tarsus, 3 1-12; height of bill at base, ¾.

The plumage of the young, according to Mr. Audubon, is as follows:

"The bill is light bluish grey, dusky along the ridge; the iris brown; the feet more dusky. The upper part of the head and the hind neck are dark greyish brown; the sides of the head dark greyish white, minutely streaked with brown. The upper parts have a reticulated or scaly appearance, the feathers being brownish black, with broad bluish grey margins; the rump dull brownish grey. The primaries and their coverts are brownish black; the secondaries and tail feathers dusky, margined with grey. The fore part of the neck is greyish white, minutely and faintly dotted with brown, its sides below streaked with the same; the lower parts, including the under surface of the wing, pure white; the sides of the body and rump, with part of the lower-tail coverts, dusky, edged with bluish grey."

Hab.—According to Audubon, "the young range throughout the interior and along the coast as far as Texas, in autumn and winter; Columbia river. Breeds in high latitudes"

Specimens from Europe in the museum of the Phil. Academy.

I have never been so fortunate as to meet with an American specimen of this bird.

Mr. Audubon states that the young are quite abundant, but that in its adult state it is seldom obtained within the limits of the United States.

Richardson says, it is common on the shores of Hudson's Bay, but is rarely seen in the interior.

The locality of Columbia river, given by Audubon for this species, he states, was taken from Townsend's list of birds observed on the Columbia river. This appears to be an error, as I have examined his list given in the Proc. of the Phil. Acad.; also the one in his narrative, but do not find it enumerated.

COLYMBUS PACIFICUS, L a w r e n c e.

The Pacific Diver.

Sᴘ. Cʜ.—*Young.* Head above and hind part of neck dark bluish grey; back, wing coverts, and scapulars blackish brown, margined with greyish white, most conspicuous on the latter; primaries black: secondaries dark brown, with the ends of their inner webs margined with white; under lining of wings and axillars white; tail blackish brown, tipped with white; under plumage white; sides dark brown, the feathers with grey edgings; a dusky band on the lower part of the abdomen, at the base of the tail; lower tail coverts white, with brownish ends; the upper mandible is dark brown above, sides yellowish at the base for half its length, bluish white at the end; under mandible, with the basal half, yellow, the remaining half bluish white; tarsi and feet are externally reddish brown, (in the dried specimens,) yellowish internally; claws yellow, with dusky margins.

Length of one specimen, (No. 9924,) 25 inches; wing, 11¼; tail, 2; bill, 2½; tarsus, 2¾.

No. 9921, measures in length, 24 inches; wing, 10¼; tail, 2; bill, 2; tarsus, 2½; outer toe, 3½.

Hab.—Coast of California; Puget's Sound.

The two specimens in the collection are from the Pacific coast, and it is with some hesitation I have ventured to describe them as new. They are near allies, and may possibly be the young of "*C. arcticus,*" but they appear much smaller, and do not differ materially in size from "*C. septentrionalis;*" the bill is but little larger than that of the latter species, but is differently shaped, more of the form of that of "*C. arcticus;*" it is, however, comparatively slender. Upon

Sept. 23, 1858.

112 b

an examination of specimens of *C. arcticus*, in the Museum of the Phil. Acad., I found a fully adult individual; also one approaching maturity. These were precisely alike as regarded the form of their bills; there was also a specimen of a young bird labelled "*C. arcticus*," but, having no locality marked upon it, it came with the Rivoli collection, and was originally from that of the Duchess de Berri; the bill was weak and slender compared with the two other specimens, and the whole appearance of the bird quite different. I could not, therefore, reconcile them as being the same; the young specimen in the Phil. Acad. was exactly like the species now described, and may have come from the Pacific.

Richardson Fauna Bor. Am., vol. II, p. 475, describes the young of "*C. arcticus*," as "closely resembling those of '*C. glacialis*,' but may be distinguished by their inferior size, a slight curvature of the upper mandible, and the want of a groove on the under one, which is not thickened in the middle."

The above described specimens bear very little resemblance to "*C. glacialis*," which strengthens my opinion in thinking them distinct from *C. arcticus*. The true position of the Pacific species can only be surely settled by obtaining it in adult plumage.

Catal. No.	Locality.	Whence obtained.	Length.	Wing.
9921	San Diego, Cal	Lieut. Trowbridge	24. 00	10. 25
9924	Puget's Sound	Dr. Suckley.	25. 00	11. 25

COLYMBUS SEPTENTRIONALIS, Linn.

The Red-throated Diver.

Colymbus septentrionalis, Linn S. N. I, 1766, 220.—Bonap. Syn. 1828, 370.—Rich. and Sw. F. B. A. II, 1831, 476.— Nutt. Man. II, 1834, 519.—Aud. Orn. Biog. III, 1838, 20: V, 1839, 625.—Ib Birds Am. VII, 1844, 299; pl. cccclxxviii.

Colymbus lumme, Brünn. Orn. Bor. 1764, 132.

Colymbus stellatus, Brünn. Orn. Bor. 1764, 130.

Colymbus striatus, Gm. I, 1788, 556 (young.)

Colymbus borealis, Lath. Ind. Orn. II, 1790, 802 (young.)

Sp. Ch.—*Adult*. Front, sides of the head, upper part of the throat, and sides of the neck, clear bluish gray; upper part of the head of the same color, intermixed with blackish spots; the hind neck streaked longitudinally with white on a greenish black ground, the white feathers being raised above the others. On the fore part of the neck is a large longitudinal patch of deep reddish brown. Upper plumage brownish black, slightly tinged with green, and on the upper part of the back and lower part and sides of the neck streaked and mottled with white. Wings and tail brownish black; under plumage pure white, with a band across the hind part of the abdomen, and the lower tail coverts brownish gray; bill bluish black; iris bright red; tarsi and feet brownish black externally, on the inside pale flesh color; claws yellowish at the base, dusky at the end.

Length, 27 inches; wing, 11½; tail, 2½; bill, 2¼: tarsus, 2¾.

Young. Upper part of the head and hind neck dull gray, streaked with grayish white; back and wings blackish gray, profusely marked with oval shaped white spots, there being two on each feather, smallest on the upper part of the back and largest on the tertiaries; quill feathers and tail blackish brown, the latter edged with white; sides of the neck white, speckled minutely with gray; under plumage silky white, crossed on the lower part of the abdomen by a dusky band; bill bluish gray, dusky on the ridge and flesh colored at the base.

Hab.—During the winter as far south as Maryland; inhabits as far north as the Arctic seas; found also on the Pacific coast.

Two specimens are in the collection from the western side of the continent, and present no marked differences from those of the Atlantic coast. No. 9923 is in the anomalous dress of an albino, being white, with the exception of light brownish ash markings on the wings and lower part of the back.

In this species there is great variation in the size of different individuals. The upper mandible is straight; under, with the angle, very long, and sloping upwards to the point, giving a recurved appearance to the bill, which is quite slender in form.

Catal. No.	Locality.	Whence obtained.	Orig. No.	Collected by —	Length.	Stretch of wings.	Wing.	Remarks.
9966	Atlantic coast.......	S. F. Baird	......	J. J. Audubon.	25.00	....	11.50	....
473	.........do...........	......do...............	......	....do......	....	....	....	....
......	Coast of N. York....	Cab. of Geo. N. Lawrence.	963	....	....	....	....	....
......	.........do...........	......do...............	964	....	....	....	10.50	....
9922	San Diego, Cal	Lieut. Williamson	......	Dr. Heermann.	....	....	10.50	....
9923	Port Townsend, W. T.	Dr. Suckley...............	......	G. Gibbs	24.10	40.00	10.00	Eyes reddish hazel.

Sub-Family PODICIPINAE.—The Grebes.

Cн.—Bill generally long, compressed on the sides, and pointed; lores usually naked; nostrils placed in a groove, oblong and narrow. Wings short, the second quill longest, shorter than the scapulars The tail is represented by a tuft of downy feathers; tarsi much compressed and rather short; toes long, the outer longest, broadly and evenly lobed, most so on the inner side; claws short, broad and obtuse; tarsi with plates on the sides, in front with a single, behind with a double longitudinal series of projecting scales. Toes and their lobes plated above.

The plumage is very soft, and on the under surface silky. They are remarkably active on the water, and when alarmed remain below the surface, exposing only the bill.

The species of the genus vary considerably in form, giving rise to almost as many genera. Of these, however, I shall adopt only the two following:

1. PODICEPS.—Bill long and slender; the head ornamented with ruffs and crests in spring; hind toe broadly lobed.

2. PODILYMBUS.—Bill short, rather strong, and much compressed on the sides; without ornamental ruffs; hind toe moderately lobed.

PODICEPS, Latham.

Podiceps, Lath. Ind. Ornith. 1790, 780. Type *Colymbus cristatus, L.*

Cн.—Bill long, slender, tapering, and pointed; nostrils situated in a groove, small, linear, and pervious; wings short and narrow, second primary a little the longest, emarginate near the ends; tail a tuft of loose feathers; tarsi short, much compressed, the edges covered with small scutellae and the sides with broad transverse scutellae; toes long, the outer longest, flattened, with the sides lobed, the most on the inner side, and at the base united by webs; hind toe short and broadly lobed claws small, depressed, and obtuse.

These birds mostly frequent the fresh water rivers and interior lakes, but they are also found near the sea-coast. They are very expert swimmers, but make progress with great difficulty on land; their flight is rapid and direct. In the breeding season the head is ornamented with ruffs and elongated tufts, which disappear when they assume their winter garb.

The species of this genus vary much in size. The characters given below will serve to define them.

A. Culmen as long as tarsus ; more than half the middle toe with its nail.

Medium size; bill rather long and strong, black, yellow at the base, with the tip pale ; upper part of head and hind neck black, a white line under the eye ; throat ash gray ; fore part and sides of the neck brownish red ; ruffs and crests very short. Type of *Pedeaithyia*, Kaup...*P. griseigena*.

Rather large ; bill rather long and strong ; blackish brown tinged with carmine ; upper part of head and crests dark brown ; ruffs brownish red ending with brownish black ; throat white ; neck adjoining the ruffs brownish red ; upper edge of the wing white ; ruffs full and crests long. *Podiceps*, Lath...*P. cristatus*.

Very large; bill long and slender, dusky black, with the cutting edges and tips yellow ; loral space gray ; summer plumage not known ....*P. occidentalis*.

Rather large ; bill long and slender, yellow, with the ridge of the upper mandible black ; a line of white between the eye and the base of the bill ; summer plumage unknown ....*P. clarkii*.

B. Culmen about half as long as the tarsus ; not more than half the middle toe and nail.

Small ; bill short and weak, bluish black, yellow at the tip ; upper part of head, cheeks, throat and ruffs black ; occipital tufts yellowish red ; loral space carmine ; ruffs and crests very full. Type of *Dytes*, Kaup...*P. cornutus*.

Small ; bill short and slender, dark brown, yellow at base of lower mandible, tip light horn color ; has only been observed in winter plumage..................... *P. californicus*.

Small ; bill short, black tinged with blue ; head deep black ; tufts orange at base, yellowish at the end ; throat and fore part of neck black ; ear tufts long. Type of *Proctopus*, Kaup.. *P. auritus*.

PODICEPS GRISEIGENA, Gray.

The Red-necked Grebe.

Columbus griseigena, Bodd. Tab. des Pl. Enl. 1783, 55.

Podiceps subcristatus, Jacquin, Beit. 1784, 37. ; pl. xviii.—Gm. I, 1788, 590.

Columbus parotis, Sparrmann, Mus. Carlos. pl. ix.

Columbus rubricollis, Gm. Syst. Nat. I. 1788, 592.

Podiceps rubricollis, Lath. Ind. Orn. II, 1790, 783.—Bon. Syn. 1828, No. 365.—Rich. and Sw. F. B. A. II, 1831, 411.—Nutt, Man. II, 1834, 253.—Aud. Orn Biog. III, 1835, 617 : V, 1839, 620.—Ib. Birds Am. VII, 1844, 312; pl. cccclxxx.

Columbus cucullatus, Pallas, Zoog. II, 1811, 355.

Columbus naevius, Pall. ib. 356.

Columbus holbölli, Reinh. Vidensk. Meddel. 1853.

Sp. Ch.—*Adult.* Upper plumage blackish brown, with the upper part of the head and hind neck black ; primaries ashy brown, secondaries mostly white, a few of the inner ones dark ash ; cheeks and throat ash gray ; a white line extends from the lower mandible under and beyond the eye ; fore part and sides of the neck rich brownish red ; lower parts silvery white, with the sides dusky ; bill black, paler at the end and bright yellow at the base ; iris carmine ; tarsi and feet externally greenish black, internally yellow.

Length about 18 inches; wing, 7 ; bill, 1¾ ; tarsi, 2.

Young. The upper plumage is blackish brown, darker on the head ; throat and abdomen white ; sides of the head and fore part of neck brownish ash ; abdomen silky white ; sides dark brownish ash ; bill bright yellow.

Hab.—Fur countries and in the Atlantic States, as far south as Pennsylvania, in winter.

A very fine specimen, in full summer plumage, is in the collection from the Selkirk Settlement, H. B. T., which measures 19½ inches in length ; wing, 7¾ ; bill, 1⅞.

This grebe is of a stouter form and with a shorter neck than *P. cristatus ;* the occipital crest is short, and the ruffs on the sides of the head very slight.

The American bird has been separated from the Red-necked Grebe of Europe by Reinhardt, under the name of *holbölli*, principally on account of its being somewhat larger. On comparing specimens obtained here with European specimens of "*rubricollis*," ours appear somewhat larger, and generally with a longer bill; but in this family individuals vary much in size. The bills of the specimens of "*rubricollis*" from Europe measured 1¼ inches; in ours they ranged from 1⅝ to 2 inches.

Writers differ as to their being specifically distinct, and as I am not able to make out satisfactorily that they are so, shall for the present consider them the same.

List of specimens.

Catal. No.	Locality.	When collected.	Whence obtained.	Orig. No.	Collected by—	Length.	Wing.
	Coast of New York ------	1841--------	S. F. Baird -----------	466	J. J. Audubon.	--------	--------
	Do -----------	-------------	Cab. of Geo. N. Lawrence.	966	-------------	--------	--------
	Coast of New Jersey ----	-------------	----------do----------	965	-------------	--------	--------
10400	Selkirk Settlement, H. B T	Spring dress --	Donald Gunn ----------	-------------------		19.50	7.75

PODICEPS CRISTATUS, Lath.

The Crested Grebe.

Colymbus cristatus, Linn. Syst. Nat. I, 1766, 222.
Podiceps cristatus, Lath. Ind. Orn. 1790.—Rich. & Sw. F. B. A. II, 1831, 410 —Nutt. Man. II, 1834, 250.—Aud. Orn. Biog. III, 1835, 595; pl. 292 —Ib. Birds Am. VII, 1844, 308; pl. cccclxxix.
Colymbus urinator, Linn. Syst. Nat. I, 1766, 223.

Sp. Ch.—*Adult.* Front, upper part of the head, and long occipital tufts dark umber brown, the base of the tufts brownish red; the ruff is bright brownish red on the upper portion immediately under the tufts and anteriorly, on the hind part brownish black; upper plumage dark umber brown; humeral feathers white; primaries umber brown; secondaries mostly white; throat and sides of the head white; fore part and sides of the neck adjoining the ruff brownish red; under plumage silvery white; sides dusky, tinged with reddish brown; bill blackish brown, tinged with carmine; bare loral space dusky green; iris bright carmine; tarsi and feet greenish black externally, greenish yellow internally; webs greyish blue.

Length, 23½ inches; wing, 7¾; bill, 2¹⁄₁₆; tarsus, 2½.

Young. Upper part of head dark brown; hind neck brownish grey; back and wings brownish black; humeral feathers white; primaries dark umber brown on the outer webs, paler on the inner; lower parts silvery white, sides brown; upper mandible brownish black, pale at the end and yellow on the sides at the base; lower mandible yellow with the sides dusky.

Hab.—Atlantic States from Nova Scotia southward; Texas in winter; fur countries, Pacific side of the continent; Washington Territory.

Two specimens of the young are in the collection from Shoalwater bay, W. T. These have larger and stronger bills than the adult bird sent me by Prof. Baird from his cabinet, and of two adult specimens in my collection, in one specimen, No. 4499, measuring 2½ inches along the ridge, the adult having it but 2¹⁄₁₆, (the measure given by Audubon is 2 inches); the outline of the lower mandible from the angle to the point is concave, whereas in the adult it is a little rounding, but they have one of the strongest characteristics of this species, the white humeral feathers. It may, possibly, be a closely allied, but distinct species. This can only be satisfactorily determined by obtaining it in spring plumage.

Both the above specimens were obtained by Dr. J. G. Cooper, and if future research should prove it to be distinct, I propose for it the specific name of *cooperi*, in honor of its discoverer.

List of specimens.

Catal. No.	Locality.	Whence obtained.	Orig. No.	Collected by—	Length.	Wing.
1958	Atlantic coast	S. F. Baird		J. J. Audubon	23. 50	7. 75
	do	Cab. of Geo. N. Lawrence.	967			
	do	do	968			
4499	Shoalwater bay	Gov. I. I. Stevens		Dr. Cooper	23. 00	7. 75
4500	do	do		do	21. 00	7 50

PODICEPS OCCIDENTALIS, Lawrence.

The Western Grebe.

Sp. Ch.—*Winter.* Upper part of the head and nape fuliginous black ; back and wing coverts greyish black, the feathers margined with grey ; primaries light ashy brown, darker at the end and white at base ; secondaries white, marked with ash on the outer webs ; in some specimens the middle secondaries are pure white ; space between the bill and the eye grey ; throat, sides of the neck, and entire under plumage silvery white ; sides marked with greyish black ; bill dusky, appearing nearly black in the dried specimens, except on the cutting edges and at the end, where it is yellow ; iris orange ; tarsi and feet appear to have been greyish black externally and flesh color internally.

Length, 29 inches ; extent of wings, 36 ; wing from carpal joint, $8\frac{3}{4}$; bill, 3 ; tarsus, 3.

Hab.—Pacific coast from Washington Territory to California.

There are six specimens in the collection, differing considerably in size, which I consider as being specifically the same. They vary in length from 24 to 29 inches. Three of them measure, respectively, 27, 28, and 29 inches. In the above account I have given the dimensions of the largest one, as they were taken from the specimen while fresh. It is very superior in size to *P. cristatus*, and, judging from analogy, it is fair to infer that in its nuptial attire it makes a grand display. In this plumage its acquisition is very desirable.

The bill is quite different from that of "*cristatus*," being much longer, straighter, and relatively narrower. In some of the specimens it is quite slender.

On one of the specimens was a label with the MS. name of "*occidentalis*," which, being a very suitable one, I have adopted.

This is the largest known species of this genus, and its discovery is one of the important scientific results of connecting natural history explorations with the government expeditions.

Specimen No. 9544 resembles "*clarkii*" rather more than the others, not differing much from it in size and the color of the back ; but, having the bill dark colored, and being grey (not white) between the eye and the bill, I have labelled it as belonging to this species.

List of specimens.

Catal. No.	Locality.	When collected.	Whence obtained.	Orig. No.	Collected by—	Length.	Stretch of wing.	Wing.	Remarks.
9927	Bodega, Cal.	Feb. 1855	Lt. Trowbridge			24. 00		7. 50	
4497	Shoalwater bay		Gov. Stevens		Dr. Cooper	28. 00		8. 50	
4498 B	do		do		do				
9925[1]	Ft Steilacoom,W.T.	Apl. 21, '56	Dr. Suckley	320		29. 00	36. 00	8. 36	Irids,flame r'd.
9928	do		Gov. Stevens	500	Dr. Suckley				Irids, orange.
9544	Puget's Sound	Oct. 12, '57	A Campbell		Dr. Kennerly			7. 50	
9926	do	Oct. 10, '56	Dr. Suckley			27. 00		8. 00	

[1] Bill dusky green above, greenish yellow on sides ; outside of feet and tarsi dusky green, inside pale dingy greenish yellow. Bill to angle of mouth 3.75 ; tarsus, 3.50.

PODICEPS CLARKII, Lawrence.

Clark's Grebe.

Sp. Ch.—*Winter*. Upper part of the head and hind neck plumbeous black ; back and wing coverts blackish grey, with a plumbeous hue ; feathers with lighter margins ; primaries ash at the end for one-third their length, basal two-thirds white ; secondaries white, with the outer edges of the outer webs ash ; a line of white extends from the base of the upper mandible to the eye ; fore part and sides of the neck, with the whole under surface, pure silky white ; the bill is yellow, except the ridge of the upper mandible, including and on a line with the nostrils, where it is black ; iris red ; tarsi and feet greyish black externally, and flesh colored internally in the dried specimens.

Length, 22 inches ; wing, 7¼ ; bill, 2¼ ; tarsus, 2¾.

Hab.—California and New Mexico.

Three specimens are in the collection. It is a near ally of "*P. occidentalis,*" but, I think, quite distinct. In general appearance and color they somewhat resemble each other, but this species is smaller, has the bill differently colored, and a conspicuous white mark before the eye. The bill differs in shape from that of *occidentalis* ; the upper mandible being slightly recurved (nearly straight), and the outline of the under curving up to it. In "*occidentalis*" the outline of the lower mandible from the angle to the point is straight.

All the species of this family resemble each other very much in the coloring of their winter dress, consequently such species as approach each other in size are somewhat difficult to be distinguished, the most reliable character being the form of the bill. This applies to the preceding species and the one now described ; also to *P. cornutus* and *P. californicus.*

As is is well known, the distinguishing characteristics are the ruffs and crests with which the head is ornamented in the breeding season.

List of specimens.

Catal. No.	Locality.	Whence obtained.	Collected by—	Length.	Stretch of wing.	Win	Remarks.
9930	Chihuahua, Mexico	Major Emory.........	J. H. Clark_____	22.00	28.50	7.00	Iris, red...
9931	Santa Barbara, Cal........	Lieut. Williamson ...	Dr. Heermann			7.25	....
4498	San Pablo bay, Cal......	......do.............	Dr. Newberry.......	22.00	....	7.25	....

PODICEPS CORNUTUS, Lath.

The Horned Grebe.

Colymbus cornutus, Gm. Syst. Nat I, 1788, 591.

Podiceps cornutus, Lath. Ind. Orn. II, 1790, 783.—Bon. Syn. 1828, No. 366.—Rich. & Sw. F. B. A. II, 1831, 411. Nutt. Man. II, 1834, 254.—Aud. Orn. Biog. III, 1835, 429 : V, 1839, 623.—In Birds Am. VII, 1844, 316 ; pl. cccclxxxi.

Colymbus obscurus, Gm. I, 592.

Colymbus caspicus, Gm. I, 593.

Colymbus nigricans, Scop. Ann. I, 101.

?Podiceps arcticus, Boie, Tagebuch.

Sp. Ch.—*Adult*. Upper part of the head, cheeks, throat, and ruff, glossy black ; a broad band running from the bill over the eyes, and the elongated occipital tufts behind them yellowish red, deepest in color adjoining the bill ; upper surface brownish black, the feathers margined with grey ; primaries brownish ash, secondaries mostly white, some of the outer ones dark ash ; the fore neck and upper part of the breast bright chestnut red, sides of the same color, intermixed with dusky; abdomen silky white; bill bluish black, yellow at the tip; loral space bright carmine; iris carmine, with an inner circle of white; tarsi and feet dusky grey externally, dull yellow internally, and on both edges of the tarsus.

Length about 14 inches; wing, 5¾; bill, 1; tarsi 1¾.

Young. The whole upper plumage greyish black, darkest on the head, feathers of the back with grey margins; throat, sides of the head, a broad space on the sides of the neck, nearly meeting behind, breast and abdomen silvery white; sides and lower part of abdomen dusky.

Hab.—Generally distributed, specimens being in the collection from the Atlantic States, the interior ones and the Pacific coast.

List of specimens.

Catal. No.	Sex.	Locality.	When collected.	Whence obtained.	Orig'l No.	Collected by—	Length.	Stretch of wings.	Wing.	Remarks.
6489	......	Washington, D. C.	May, 1857	Market	......	....	....	....	5.50	
6490	......	....	...... do......	...... do......	......	....	....	....	5.75	
299	♀	Carlisle, Pa.......	....	Cab. of G. N. Law-	......	....	... .	....	......	
		New York.........	....	rence.	969					
	....	...... do	....	...... do..........	970	... .	....	....	......	
3753	♂	Grosse Isle, Mich..	Apr. 31,1852	Rev. C. Fox.......	......	....	....	....	5.75	Iris scarlet.
9969	......	Red river of North..	....	N. Y. University...	......	R. Kennicott,	....	....	......	
6925	......	Nelson's river, H. R. B. T.	....	Donald Gunn......	......	Jno. Isbister...	....	....	5.75	
9939	......	Shoalwater bay, W. T.	Oct., 1854	Gov. Stevens	100	Dr. Cooper	13.50	24.00	......	Iris carmine; bill bluish above, flesh color below; feet black and greenish white.
9934	......	...... do	....	...... do	......	....	....	... .	5.75	
4592	......	Steilacoom, W. T..	Feb. 6,1856	Dr. Suckley	220	....	....	....	......	
9937	......	...... do	Oct. 10,1856	...... do	584	Dr. Suckley ..	....	....	......	
9936	......	Port Townsend, W. T.	....	...... do	......	....	....	....	5.75	
9543	......	Simiahmoo bay,W. T.	....	A. Campbell.......	86	Dr. Kennerly ..	12.50	17.00	5.50	
8436	......	Puget's Sound.....	Sep. 25,1857	......do	......	......do	....	....	......	

PODICEPS CALIFORNICUS, Heermann.

The California Grebe.

Podiceps californicus, Heerm. Proc. Acad. N. Sc. Phil., VII, 1854, 179.

Sp. Ch — *Winter Plumage.* The entire upper plumage is blackish brown, nearly black on the head; primaries brownish ash, some of the inner ones tipped with white; secondaries white, with their basal portions dark ash; under parts silky white, the neck in front light ash, and the sides and lower part of abdomen brownish ash; under lining of the wings white; bill dark brown, the base of the lower mandible yellowish, and its tip light horn color; iris yellowish grey; tarsi and feet externally dark green, on the inside yellow.

Length 12 inches; wing, 5; bill, ⅞; tarsus, 1½.

Hab.—California, head waters of Missouri river.

Numerous specimens are in the collection, all in winter plumage; in its spring dress it has not yet been obtained. It resembles "*P. cornutus*" in its winter garb, but is smaller, and the bill somewhat differently shaped.

Dr. Heermann speaks of it as being abundant in California on the inland fresh water ponds, and on the sea shore.

A very small species, *P. dominicus*, (Linn.) will, without doubt, be found to inhabit our southern border. A specimen in the Philadelphia Academy was obtained by Dr. Gamble on the Gulf of California, and I have specimens from eastern Mexico and Cuba. It measures but 9 inches total length ; the wing, $3\frac{5}{8}$; the upper parts are brownish black, the greater part of the secondaries and the inner edges of the primaries white ; cheeks and throat blackish ash grey ; breast and abdomen white, mottled with ashy brown.

List of specimens.

Catal. No.	Sex and age.	Locality	When collected.	Whence obtained.	By whom collected.	Length.	Stretch of wings	Wings.	Remarks.
9938	......	San Diego, Cal......	....	Lt. Trowbridge.	....	13. 50	......	5. 00	....
4628	......	San Miguel, Cal......	January, 1856	......do......	....	......	......	5. 00	....
9942	......	San Pedro, Cal......	....	Lt. Williamson .	Dr. Heermann.	......	......	5. 00	....
9940	......	San Francisco, Cal...	....	Lt. Trowbridge .	....	......	......	5. 50	....
4465	......	......do............	....	Lt. Williamson .	Dr. Newberry.	10. 50	......	5. 12	....
9935	......	Bitter Root river, R.. mountains......	....	Gov. Stevens...	Dr. Suckley...	......	......	5. 25	....
5477	......	Snake river, Neb......	Sept. 17, 1856	Lt. Warren.....	Dr. Hayden. ..	12. 00	21. 25	4. 50	Iris gray......
5476	♂	Fort Berthold, Neb...	......do.....	......do......	.....do......	12. 50	22. 00	5. 00	....do.......

PODICEPS AURITUS, Latham.

The Eared Grebe.

Colymbus auritus, Linn. S. N. I, 1766, 222.

Podiceps auritus, Lath. Ind. Orn. 1790, 781.—Aud. Orn. Biog. V, 1839, 108; pl. 404.—Ib. Birds Am. VII, 1844, 322; pl. cccclxxxii.—Nutt. Man. II, 1834, 256.

Sp. Ch.—*Adult.* "Bill black, tinged with blue. Iris blood red. Feet dusky grey externally, greenish grey on the inner side. The tufts on the sides of the head are orange, anteriorly more yellow, posteriorly red ; the head and upper part of the neck are deep black ; the rest of the upper parts brownish black, the wings greyish brown, with a broad patch of white, the secondary quills being of that color. The throat, fore part and sides of the neck are dull black, its lower part with some spots of the same; the rest of the lower parts glossy silvery white, excepting the sides of the body and rump, which are light red."

" Length 13 inches; wing, $5.\frac{3}{12}$; bill, $\frac{11}{12}$; tarsus $1\frac{6}{12}$."

Mr. Audubon being the first to introduce this species into our fauna, I have copied his description, which was taken from specimens lent him by the Earl of Derby, said to have come from North America. There are no American specimens in any of the collections in this country, but as it is common in the north of Europe, it may occasionally visit Arctic America by the way of Greenland, where many European species are recorded as being found, that have not yet been observed on our continent.

PODILYMBUS, Lesson.

Podilymbus, Less. Traite d'Ornith. 1831. 595. Type, *Colymbus podiceps*, L.

Ch.—Bill shorter than the head, snout much compressed ; the culmen much curved to the tip, which is acute ; nostrils situated in the anterior part of a broad groove, oval and pervious ; wings short, second quill longest, the outer quills emarginate at the end ; tail a tuft of downy feathers ; tarsi short, and very much compressed ; anterior toes long, flattened, the outer longest, and broadly margined, the inner sides the most, hind toe short and moderately lobed ; claws small, depressed, oblong and obtuse.

Oct. 12, 1858.

113 b

But two species are enumerated in this genus, one inhabiting South and the other North America. They do not appear to go very far north, but are distributed pretty generally over the temperate parts of the continent, prefering the fresh water streams and lakes.

When alarmed by the approach of any person, they have a peculiar habit of sinking gradually in the water, the bill being the last to disappear; this is accomplished so slowly that no disturbance of the water takes place.

The head is not adorned with ruffs or tufts.

PODILYMBUS PODICEPS, Lawrence.

The Pied-Bill Grebe.

Colymbus podiceps, LINN. S. N. 1766, 223.

Colymbus ludovicianus, GM. I. 592.

Podiceps carolinensis, LATH. Ind. Orn. II, 1790, 785.—BONAP. Syn. 1828. No. 367.—RICH. & SW. F. B. A. II, 1831, 412.—NUTT. Man. II, 1834, 259.—AUD. Orn. Biog. III, 1835, 359: V, 1839, 624.—IB. Birds Am. VII, 1844, 324; pl. cccclxxxiii.

Sylbeocyclus carolinensis, BON. Comp. List, 1838, 64.

? *Podiceps brevirostris*, GRAY, Genera, III; pl. clxxii.

Podilymbus lineatus, HEERMANN, Proc. Acad. N. S. Phil. VII, 1854, 179.

SP. CH.—*Adult.* Upper plumage very dark brown; primaries dark ash; secondaries ash on the outer webs and white on the inner; bill pale blue, dusky on the ridge of the upper mandible, both mandibles crossed with a broad black band, including the nostrils; chin and throat marked with a conspicuous black patch nearly two inches in extent; cheeks and sides of the neck brownish grey; lower part of the neck, upper part of the breast, and the sides, dull rusty brown, spotted and rather indistinctly barred with brownish black; lower part of breast and abdomen greyish white, mottled with dusky spots; iris, brown; tarsi and feet, greyish black.

Length, 14 inches; wing, 5¼; bill, ⅞; tarsus, 1½.

Young. The throat is white and the bill without the transverse black band, the under plumage more silvery white; in other respects the same as the adult. Some specimens, probably the birds of the year, have whitish lines on the sides of the head. I have compared a specimen in this plumage with Dr. Heermann's type of *P. lineatus*, and found them precisely alike.

Hab.—Atlantic States generally. Texas and New Mexico. California and Oregon.

There are six specimens in the collection in different stages of plumage, besides a chick, just hatched, which is probably of this species; in this the color is black, having several whitish lines running the entire length of the body; two pure white stripes from each side of the head, and meeting above the bill, separated by a black line; some white stripes on the sides of the neck, and some bright rufous spots on the occiput; the bill is black, tipped with pure white.

As in the allied genera, there is a great disparity in the size of individuals. This species may be easily recognized by the short and stout form of the bill; and in mature plumage, by the black patch on the throat, and the transverse band on the bill.

List of specimens.

Catal. No.	Sex.	Locality.	When collected.	Whence obtained.	Orig. No.	Collected by—	Length.	Stretch of wings.	Wing.	Remarks.
775	♀	Carlisle, Pa........	....	S. F. Baird......	......	....	....	....	.....	
1710	♀	......do.................	Oct., 1844	..... do...........	......	....	12.50	....	......	
695	♂	Potomac river, D. C....	....	......do...........	......	....	......	....	......	
......	......	New York...,..........	....	Cab. George N. Lawrence.	971	....	......	....	......	
......	......	... ..do...............	....	......do...........	972	....	......	....	.....	
......	......	......do...............	....	......do...........	973	....	......	....	......	
4426	......	Quasquiton, Iowa	....	Dr. Bidwell......	......	....	12.00	22.00	5.00	Eyes black.
5143	......	Doña Aña, N. M.......	Nov. 20, 1855	Capt. Pope.......	162	....	13.50	22.00	5.00	Bill brown; eyes black; feet dark gray; gums pale blue.
9943	......	Bodega, Cal............	Dec., 1854	Lt. Trowbridge...	......	....	......	....	......	
4501	......	Steilacoom, W. T......	....	Gov. Stevens	......	.. ..	......	....	......	
9945	......	......do...............	Jan. 15, 1854	......do...........	......	Dr. Suckley.	14.00	....	......	
9946	......	......do...............	....	......do...........	.....	....	....	....	......	

Family ALCIDAE.[1]

Ch.—Bill without lamellae along the edges; usually shorter than the head, compressed, and pointed. Anterior toes connected fully by a continuous membrane; hind toe usually entirely wanting; the outer as large as the middle; the claws higher than broad. Legs inserted far back. Wings short, concave.

The *Alcidae* are readily distinguished from the *Colymbidae* by the absence of hind toe, the continuous webbing of the toes, the compressed claws, and other characters. The species are all exclusively marine, usually arctic, only coming southward in winter. Owing to their boreal residence they are little known, and several species doubtless yet remain to be discovered.

The present article embraces descriptions of nearly all the known species, including several scarcely known as inhabitants of North America. They may be arranged under the following sub-families, after Keyserling and Blasius.

Alcinae.—Bill compressed to the very tip; in the middle several times higher than wide, the ridge and keel sharp or acute. Both jaws in the typical forms, with transverse ridges and furrows in the middle, the base of the upper generally with a well marked swelling.

Urinae.—Bill moderately compressed only, with the ridge and keel obtuse and rounded, and without transverse ridges and grooves, or basal swelling.

It may be proper to state that the arrangement adopted for the *Alcidae* is essentially that of Bonaparte's *Conspectus Gaviarum* in Comptes Rendus, XLII, 1856.

Sub-Family ALCINAE.

The preceding diagnosis will express the characters of the sub-family sufficiently for our present purpose; it is composed of two sections: one, *Alceae*, including *Alca*, with its sub-divisions; the other, *Phalerideae*, embracing *Mormon*, *Phaleris*, and the other curious forms from the Arctic seas, with crests of curved feathers on the head.

ALCA, Linn.

Alca, Linnaeus, Syst. Nat. 1758.

Ch.— General form short, broad, and strong; wings short; tail short. Bill about as long as the head, feathered at base, much flattened laterally, wider, and somewhat hooked at the end; upper mandible with oblique transverse grooves. Wings short and feeble; tail short, pointed; legs and feet short and strong; toes fully webbed.

Chenalopex, Moehring.[2]

ALCA IMPENNIS, Linnaeus.

The Great Auk.

Alca impennis, Linn. Syst. Nat. I, 1766, 210.—Bon. Syn. 1828, 432. Note.—Aud. Orn. Biog. IV, 1838, 316.— Figures.—Buffon, Pl. Enl 367.—Edwards, Birds, III, pl. 147.—Gould, B. of Eur. VII, pl. 400.—Aud. B. of Am. pl. 341; Oct. ed. VII, pl 465.—Naumann, B. of Germ. pl. 337.

Sp. Ch.—Size large, general form stout; head large; bill rather long, curved, flattened laterally; upper mandible composed of two parts, the first of which is narrow, smooth, the terminal part with about six to eight or ten curved transverse grooves; under mandible with about ten nearly straight transverse grooves; both mandibles densely covered at base with short velvet-like feathers. The lateral feathers of upper jaw falling far short of the middle of the commissure and of the end of the feathers of lower jaw. Wings rudimental, not admitting of flight; tail short; legs and feet short, very robust.

[1] Prepared by Mr. John Cassin of Philadelphia.
[2] Wings rudimental, adapted to swimming only, and not to flight, not reaching to the rump.

A large ovate spot of white in front of each eye. Head and entire upper parts brownish black, darker on the back, and clearer brown on the head ; greater coverts of the wings narrowly tipped with white; under wing coverts ashy ; entire under parts white, which color extends to a point on the neck in front ; bill black, with the grooves in both mandibles white ; feet dark. Total length about 30 inches ; wing, 5½ ; tail, 3 ; bill from tip to gape, 4 inches.

Hab.—Northeastern coast of America, and Arctic seas. Newfoundland. (Mr. Audubon.)

The largest of the family *Alcidae* inhabiting the northern regions, and remarkable as the only species not possessing the power of flight, approximating in that respect to the penguins of the southern hemisphere. This bird appears to be of rather rare occurrence, and is highly valued by collectors and naturalists. We have never seen an American specimen. That figured by Mr. Audubon, and obtained on the banks of Newfoundland, is now in the cabinet of Mr. J. P. Giraud, jr. This and one in the collection of the Philadelphia Academy of Natural Sciences are all known to exist in any American museum.

Utamania, Leach.[1]

ALCA TORDA, Linnaeus.

The Razor-billed Auk.

Alca torda, LINN. Syst. Nat. I, 1753, 130.—IB. I, 1766, 210.—BON. Syn. 1828, 431.—AUD. Orn. Biog. III, 1835, 112 : V, 428 ; pl. 214.—IB. Syn. 345.
Utamania torda, " LEACH," STEPHENS, in Shaw's Zool. XIII, 1826.
Alca pica, LINN. Syst. Nat. I, p. 210, (1766.)
Alca unisulcata, BRÜNNICH, Orn. Bor. 1764, 25.
Alca balthica, BRÜNN. Orn. Bor. 1764, 28.

FIGURES.—BUFFON, Pl. Enl. 1003. 1004.—EDWARDS, Birds, VII, pl. 358.—GOULD, B. of Eur. IV, pl. 401.—NAUMANN, B. of Germ. pl. 336.—AUD. B. of Am. pl. 214 ; Oct. ed. VII, pl. 466.

SP. CH.—Much smaller than the preceding ; general form short and heavy ; bill rather long, densely feathered at base, flattened laterally ; upper mandible with three to five curved transverse grooves ; under mandible with three or four transverse grooves. Feathers on side of upper jaw reaching far beyond the middle of the commissure, and nearly as far as those of the lower jaw. Wing moderate, pointed ; tail short, graduated, with the middle feathers longest and pointed ; legs short, strong.

A narrow but very distinct line of white on each side from the base of the upper mandible to the eye. Head and entire upper parts brownish black, more clearly brown on the throat and neck in front, and darker on the back ; secondary quills narrowly tipped with white ; entire under parts white. Bill black, with a single transverse band of white on both mandibles ; feet black. Total length about 17 inches ; wing, 8 to 8½ ; tail, 3½ ; bill to gape, 2¼ inches.

Hab.—Northeastern coast of America; Newfoundland; Labrador, and south in winter to New Jersey; also, Arctic regions of Old World.

This well known species is very abundant on the northeastern coasts of North America, and appears to be quite identical with the bird of the northern regions of the Old World. It wanders southwardly in the winter, and is occasionally noticed on the coasts of the middle States on the Atlantic. This bird may always be recognized by the conspicuous white line in front of the eye, which is present in all ages and stages of plumage.

MORMON, Illiger.

Mormon, ILLIGER, Prodromus, 1811, 283.

CH.—General form short and heavy, and adapted to swimming and diving with great facility, and to limited power of flight. Bill short, entirely horny, much flattened laterally, and nearly as high as long; measured on the side obliquely rugose and laminated; a portion at the base punctulated; nostril in the edge of and in the second lamina of the upper mandible. Wing moderate or rather weak, first quill usually longest; tail short; legs short; toes, three only, directed forwards, rather long, fully webbed; claws large, curved. Plumage very compact.

[1] Wings moderately developed, admitting of flight, reaching the tail.

This genus contains three or four species only, easily distinguished from all other sea birds by their high compressed bills, usually brightly colored, and with the general heavy form, presenting a peculiar and somewhat grotesque appearance. These birds inhabit high northern latitudes, descending more southwardly in the winter season, and nearly all the species are well known to navigators and travellers under the name of puffins. The bill in this genus is uniformly corneous, and not composed of two parts of different texture, as is usual in birds.

Lunda. Pallas.

MORMON CIRRHATA, (Pallas.)

The Tufted Puffin.

Alca cirrhata, PALLAS, Spicilegia Zoologica, pt. V, p. 7, (1769.)—GM. Syst. I, 1788, 553.

Mormon cirrhatus, BON. Syn, 1828, 429.—AUD. Orn. Biog. III, 599; pl. 293.—IB. Syn. 343.

FIGURES.—BUFF. Pl. Enl. 761.—PALLAS, Spic. Zool. pl. I and V.—VIEILL. Gal. II, pl. 299.—AUD. B. of Am. pl. 249, Oct. ed. VII, pl. 462.

SP. CH.—The largest species of this genus, general form short and stout, head large, bill much flattened laterally, entirely horny, upper mandible composed of three parts or lamina, the first of which, next to the frontal feathers, is narrow, and covered with minute spots, the second smooth, with the apertures of the nostrils inserted at its lower edges, and with an elevated sub-cylindrical process on its upper edge or the culmen of the bill; third with two or three transverse curved grooves, and somewhat hooked at the tip; under mandible smooth. Head with two crests of elongated pendent feathers from behind the eyes; wings rather short, tail short, legs and feet strong, claws sharp.

Two first parts of the bill yellowish green, terminal part and under mandible reddish yellow or orange, the under mandible greenish at base. Crests pale yellow, plumage around the base of the bill, including the eyes, white. All other parts of the plumage brownish black, darker on the head and back, legs bright orange red.

Total length about 15 inches; wing, 8; tail, 3 inches.

Hab.—Western coast of America. Oregon, (Dr. Suckley,) California, (Dr. Heermann,) accidental on the coast of Maine, (Mr. Audubon.)

One of the most abundant species of this family on the coasts of western and northwestern America. It is easily recognized by the pendent crest-like feathers on each side of the head.

List of specimens.

Catal. No.	Sex.	Locality.	When collected.	Whence obtained.	Collected by—
10692	♂	Russian America	1845	S. F. Baird	H. E. Strickland
8092		N. W. coast		John Gould	
4370		Puget's Sound	May, 1855	Dr. George Suckley	
3943		California		Dr. A. L. Heermann	

Fraercula,† Briss.

MORMON CORNICULATA, Naumann.

Mormon corniculata, NAUMANN, Isis, 1821, p. 782, (N. America.)

Mormon glacialis, AUD. Orn. Biog. III, 1835, 599; pl. 293.

FIGURES.—NAUMANN, Isis, 1821, pl. 7, fig. 3, 4.—GRAY, Gen. of B. III, pl. 174.—AUD. B. of Am. pl. 293. Oct. ed. VII, pl. 463.—GOULD, B. of Eur. V, pl. 404.

SP. CH.—An elevated, sharp, spine-like process over each eye, longer and sharper than in any other species, under the eye a transverse process of the same description.

Smaller than the preceding, general form stout, head large, bill large, much flattened laterally, entirely corneous, upper mandible composed of two parts, the first of which at the base is narrow, and covered with minute spots, terminal portion with a ridge at its base, and two or three curved descending grooves near the end, under mandible smooth at base, and with about three grooves near its end   Wing rather short and weak, tail short, legs and feet strong.

Throat black, uniting with the same color of the upper parts of the body.   Large space on each side of the head and entire under parts, from the throat white, frequently tinged with ashy about the eyes.   Entire upper parts (and throat) brownish black, darker and frequently clear black on the back.   Head above frequently dark ashy, separated by a well defined line from the black of the other upper parts; bill and feet orange yellow.   Sides under the wings ashy black.

Total length about 12½ inches; wing, 7½, tail, 2¾ inches.

Hab.—Northwestern coast of America and adjacent coast of Asia.   Kamtschatka, (Mus. Acad. Philad.)

Strongly marked by its black throat and the prominent horn over the eye.   This is plainly the species figured by Audubon and Gould, and seems to be different from the succeeding, *M. glacialis.*

List of specimens.

Catal. No.	Locality.	Whence obtained.	Orig'l No.	Collected by—
1984	North Atlantic	S. F. Baird	V. 288	J. J. Audubon
10694	Sea of Ochotsk	Capt. F. Rodgers, U. S. N.		W. Stimpson

MORMON GLACIALIS, Leach.

Mormon glacialis, LEACH, STEPHENS, Shaw's Zool. XIII, 1826, p. 40.

FIGURES.—NAUMANN, Isis, 1821, pl. VII, fig. 2.

SP. CH.—An elevated, short and blunt process over each eye, and under it a narrow transverse process.   About the size of the preceding; general form stout; head large; bill much flattened laterally, entirely horny; upper mandible composed of two parts, the first at the base narrow; and covered with minute spots or granulations, terminal part with two or three curved grooves in its middle, and not so near the end as in the species immediately preceding; under mandible with grooves corresponding to those of the upper; bill rather longer, and not so wide laterally as in the preceding species, (*M. corniculata.*)   Wings moderate, rather weak; tail short; legs strong.

Throat white or pale ashy, large space on the sides of the head and under parts white, frequently tinged with ashy on the former.   Entire upper parts brownish black, darker on the back, and extending into a ring around the neck in front; head above frequently ashy brown; bill and legs orange yellow, the former frequently dull greenish at base.

Total length about 12½ inches; wing, 6½ to 7; tail, 2¼ inches.

Hab.—Northern and eastern coasts of America, Northern Europe.

Possibly the young of the preceding, and only differing from it in having the throat white or light ashy, and a short obtuse horn over the eye.   The specimens of this bird that we have seen are from Greenland and northern Europe.

MORMON ARCTICA, (Linnaeus,) Illiger.

Alca arctica, LINN. Syst. Nat. I, (1766,) p. 211.

Mormon arctica, ILLIGER, Prod. 1811.—AUD. O n Biog. III, 105.

?? *Alca labradoria,* GM. Syst. Nat. I, p. 550, (1788.)

Mormon fratercula, TEMM.. Man. II, 933.

FIGURES.—BUFF. Pl. Enl. 275.—NAUMAN, Isis, 1821, pl. 7, fig. 5, 6, 7, B. of Germ., pl. 335. -GOULD, B. of Eur. V, pl. 403.—AUD. B. of Am. pl. 213, Oct. ed. VII, pl. 464.

SP. CH.—Smaller than either of the preceding, but much resembling the two last species in form and color.   A short, blunt process over each eye, and a narrow transverse process under it; bill much flattened laterally, horny; upper mandible composed of two parts, that at the base narrow, and covered with minute spots or granulations, terminal part with about four curved grooves; under mandible with grooves corresponding to those of the upper. Wing moderate, or rather weak; tail short; legs robust.

Throat white, or pale ashy; large space on each side of the head, and under parts white, frequently tinged with ashy on the ormer. Upper parts and ring around the neck in front brownish black, darker on the back; head above frequently ashy brown; bill and legs orange yellow, the former frequently dull greenish at base.

Total length about 11½, wing 6½, tail 2¼ inches.

Hab.—Northeastern coast of America, descending southwardly in the winter. Northern Europe.

This species, quite distinct and easily recognized, appears to be restricted to the North Atlantic coasts of America and Europe. It is smaller than either of the preceding.

List of specimens.

Catal. No.	Locality.	Whence obtained.	Collected by—
1983	North Atlantic	S. F. Baird	J. J. Audubon
2731	......do	......do	......do

SAGMATORRHINA, Bonap.

Sagmatorrhina, BONAPARTE, Proc. Zool. Soc. London, 1851, p. 202.

CH.—Bill twice as long as high; upper mandible straight at the base, furnished with a very large cere, incurved at the point, the lower mandible suddenly ascending beyond the middle, and forming an obtuse angle; nostrils linear, marginal.—(Bonaparte, as above.)

SAGMATORRHINA LABRADORIA, (Gmelin,) Cassin.

Alca labradoria, GM. Syst. Nat. I, 1788, 550.

Sagmatorrhina lathami, BONAP. Proc. Zool. Soc. London, 1851, p. 202; pl. xliv.

SP. CH.—"The largest (of this group), blackish, beneath pale fuliginous; bill and feet red, cere and palms black. Length 16 inches; bill 2 inches long, 1 inch high, ⅚ wide at the base, ⅜ in the middle; wing 7½ inches; tail 3½ inches; tarsi 1¼ inches; the longest toe 2⅜ inches"—(Bonaparte, Proc. Zool. Soc. London, 1851, p. 202.)

Hab.—Northwestern coast of America.

This bird is stated by the Prince Bonaparte to be an inhabitant of the Arctic regions of northwestern America, and he regards it as the largest of the group of which *Phaleris* is the type. The specimen described by him is in the British Museum.

This species has never come under our notice, though we are not without a suspicion that it is intimately related to *Ceratorhyncha monocerata,* and possibly the same. According to Bonaparte, this bird is also the same as *Alca labradoria,* Gmelin, which renders it necessary to adopt that name for it, unless it can be demonstrated that such name implies a geographical error, very dangerous to presume on in an Arctic species.

CERORHINA, Bonap.

Cerorhina, BONAP. Syn. 1828. Type *C. occidentalis.*

Ceratorhyncha, BONAPARTE, Comp. List. 1838, 66.

Chimerina, ESCHSCHOLTZ, Zool. At. 1829.

CH.—General form short and heavy; wings rather long; tail short; legs and feet large and strong; tarsi short. Bill rather long, much flattened laterally; upper mandible usually with an upright horny appendage at its base, which is flattened and obtuse at the end; angle of under mandible very distinct and generally with a groove across it, giving the appearance of an additional part directly on the point of the angle.

CERORHINA MONOCERATA, (Pallas,) Cassin.

The Horn-billed Guillemot.

Alca monocerata, PALLAS, Zoog. Rosso-Asiat. II, 1811, 362.

Phaleris cerorhyncha, BONAP. Zool. Jour. III, 1827, 53.

Cerorhyncha occidentalis, BONAP. Ann. Lyc. N. Y. II, 1828, 428.

Ceratorhyncha occidentalis, BONAP. Comp. List, 1838, 66.—AUD. Orn. Biog. V, 1839, 104; pl. 402.

Chimerina cornuta, ESCHSCH. Zool. Atlas, III, 1829, 2; pl. xii.

" *Cerorhina orientalis*, BONAP." BRANDT, Bull. Acad. St. Petersburg, I, 1837, 345.

FIGURES.—ESCHSCHOLTZ, Zool. Atlas, pl. 12.—AUD. B. of Am. pl. 402, fig. 5, oct. ed. VII, pl. 471.

SP. CH.—Bill rather large, flattened laterally; upper mandible with an upright horny appendage at its base, the top or termination of which is frequently broken or worn off; angle of under mandible very distinct, and having the appearance of being a distinct piece; wings moderate, pointed; tail short, rounded; legs short, robust. Head and entire upper parts dark fuliginous; lighter and tinged with ashy on the throat and neck in front; darker and nearly black on the back and rump. A line of long yellowish white feathers over and behind the eye and another from the corner of the mouth. Under parts of body white; under wing coverts and sides ashy brown; bill dark orange; legs light colored.

Total length about 15 to $15\frac{1}{2}$ inches; wing, $7\frac{1}{4}$; tail, $2\frac{1}{4}$; bill to gape, 2 inches.

Hab.—Northwestern and western coasts of America; northeastern Asia; Japan, (Com. Perry's Expedition.)

This bird, though formerly regarded as very rare, and highly prized by naturalists and collectors, is now frequently brought in the collections of expeditions and travellers, and is apparently of quite usual occurrence on the western coast of North America. It is easily distinguished by the short upright horn at the base of the upper mandible, which, in the majority of specimens, is broken or worn off at the tip or end, leaving a hollow upright tube, which we have known persons to mistake for this bird's nostril. This upright horn is not, however, present in all specimens, and may be dependent for its growth or greater development on season or sex. In a very fine specimen now before us, obtained by Mr. William Heine in the island of Jesso, during the voyage of the United States Japan Expedition, there is not a vestage of this appendage. This specimen is labelled as a female, and is alluded to by us in our account of the birds collected by the Japan Expedition, in Vol. II of the Report of Commodore Perry.

The descriptions of this bird by the Prince Bonaparte, which have been relied on by American naturalists, are very defective, and no measurements whatever are given. This circumstance, in connexion with the fact that this bird has been little known to naturalists, has been the cause of some confusion and difficulty in determining this species. Even the Prince Bonaparte himself seems to have retained but an indistinct recollection of it, when he states that his *Sagmatorhina lathami* is one-third larger.—(Proc. Zool. Soc. London, 1851, p. 202.) The fact is, there is very little difference in the size of the two species, if such they are, though *Sagmatorhina* appears to be slightly larger, the Prince Bonaparte giving its total length as 16 inches in the description, as cited above. Audubon gives the total length of the present bird as $15\frac{1}{2}$ inches, which is very nearly the measurement of the skins now before us, though variously distorted. We regard it as by no means impossible that *Sagmatorhina* is the young of the present species.

List of specimens.

Catal. No.	Locality.	When collected.	Whence obtained.	Collected by—	Remarks.
3945	California.		Dr. Heermann		
10698	Hakodadi, Japan.	May, 1854.	Com. M. C. Perry, U. S. N.	Wm. Heine.	Eye pale yellow
10699	do	do	do	do	

Oct. 15, 1858.

CERORHINA SUCKLEYI, Cassin.

Sp. Ch.—Smaller than the preceding, and with the bill much more narrow laterally; plumage darker. Bill shorter than the head; upper mandible curved towards the end, without distinct basal knobs; under mandible with the angle very distinct; bill rather widened at the base, compressed towards the end; wings short; tail very short. Entire upper parts brownish black, darker and nearly clear black on the head and back. Throat, neck, and upper part of breast dark cinereous; lower part of breast and abdomen white; sides and under wing coverts cinereous; bill light at base, dark at the end; feet dark yellow.

Total length about 12½ inches; wing, 6½ inches; tail, 1¾ inch.

Hab.—Steilacoom, Puget's Sound, (Dr. Geo. Suckley.)

This species is smaller than the preceding and darker in color, especially on the upper surface of the head and body. The bill also is much more slender. The only specimen that we have ever seen is in the collection made by Dr. George Suckley, U. S. A., whose name we have taken the liberty of applying to it, as a slight testimonial to his great zeal and ability as a naturalist and scientific traveller.

According to Dr. Suckley, this species is said by the Indians to be not uncommon on Puget's Sound. He further states that in life the membrane at the base of the upper mandible is grayish dusky, the knob (!) slightly more greyish. The middle of both mandibles dingy orange, their tips dusky. Iris pale hazel. Under surface of toes bluish white, darker about the articulations; nails black.

List of specimens.

Catal. No.	Locality.	When collected.	Whence obtained.	Orig'l No.	Length.	Stretch of wings.	Wing.	Remarks.
4579	Fort Steilacoom, W. T...	January 8, 1856.	Dr. Geo Suckley.	221	13.75	24.00	6.75	Iris hazel.....

PHALERIS, Temminck.

? Simorhynchus, Merrem, 1819. Type, *Alca cristatella*.
Phaleris, Temminck, 1820. Same type.

Ch.—General form, short and robust. Head rather large and frequently with a crest of narrow feathers curved forwards. Bill short, compressed, with the commissure more or less curved. Aperture of the nostrils large, and with the base generally covered with short, velvety feathers. Wings moderate, pointed. Tail short; legs moderate; tarsi compressed, covered with minute circular or oval scales; feet with three toes fully webbed, (no hind toe;) claws moderate, rather short and blunt. Contains several species, amongst which are the smallest of the water birds.

Simorhynchus, Merrem.

PHALERIS CRISTATELLA, (Pallas,) Bonap.

Crested Auk.

Alca cristatella, Pallas, Spic. Zool. V, 1769, 18.—Gm. I, 1788, 552.
Phaleris cristatella, Bon. List, 1838. Not of Temminck.
Phaleris superciliosa, Bonap. Comp. List. 1838, 66.
" *Phaleris superciliata*, Bonap." (Name on Audubon's plate 402.)
Uria dubia, Pallas, Zoog. Rosso-Asiat. II, 371, plate 87?

Figures.—Pallas, Spic. Zool. pt. V, pl. 3.—Ib. Zoog. Rosso-Asiat. pl. 86.—Aud. B. of Am. pl. 402; Oct. ed. VII, pl. 467.

Sp. Ch.—With a crest of narrow feathers, curved forwards in front ; base of bill with horny appendages, especially at the corners of the mouth ; a line of narrow pendent hair-like feathers from behind the eye, white ; bill and appendages rich orange; lighter and nearly white at the tip. Head and upper parts of body brownish black ; crest black ; under parts dark cinereous ; under wing coverts cinereous ; feet dark greenish. *Younger.* No crest ; appendages of bill much smaller than in adult.

Total length about 8½ inches ; wing, 5½ inches ; tail, 1½ inches.

Hab.—Northwestern America; Aleutian Islands, (Pallas;) Kamtschatka, (Mus. Acad. Philad.;) Russian America ; Behring's Straits; Japan, (Perry's Expedition.)

This species is the largest of the genus, and is easily recognized by the curious horny appendages of the bill, which, at the base of the upper mandible, assume an upright, somewhat spoonlike form, and at the base of the lower mandible are semicircular and projecting. The bill and appendages are rich orange red at base, lighter and nearly yellow at its point. This is undoubtedly the species figured by Audubon, as above cited, though by several authors his plates are erroneously cited for the species immediately succeeding.

One specimen and several *heads* of specimens in the National Museum are labelled as from Russian America ; others now before us, including six from the Museum of the Philadelphia Academy, are labelled as from Behring's Straits and Kamtschatka. They are very uniform in the form and colors of the bill and colors of the plumage. One only is without the ornamental crest, and is evidently a young bird.

List of specimens.

Catal. No.	Sex.	Locality.	When collected.	Whence obtained.	Collected by—
9974	♂	Russian America	1845	S. F. Baird	H. E. Strickland
8096		N. W. coast of America		John Gould	
		Simoda, Japan		Com. M. C. Perry	W. Heine
		Bay of Yedo, Japan		do	do

Tylorhamphus, Brandt.

PHALERIS TETRACULA, (Pallas,) Stephens.

Alca tetracula, Pallas, Spic. Zool. V, 1769, 23.—Gm. I, 552.
Phaleris tetracula, Stephens, Shaw's Zool.
Dusky Auk, Pennant, II, 515.

Figures.—Pallas, Spic. Zool. pt. V, pl. 4.—Ib. Zoog. Rosso-Asiat. pl. 88.

Sp. Ch.—General form and color much like the preceding, but apparently rather smaller and with the bill simple, without appendages. Head with a crest of slender feathers in front, curved forwards. Bill simple, compressed ; commissure slightly curving upwards ; wing long ; tail short. Entire upper parts brownish black or fuliginous ; darker on the back ; a spot of white below the eye and a few long hair-like white feathers behind the eye. Under parts [dark cinereous ; lighter on the abdomen. Under wing coverts light cinereous ; bill dark ; feet greenish ; crest black.

Total length about 8¼ inches ; wing, 5½ inches; tail, 1½ inches.

Hab.—Northwestern coast of America ; Unalaschka, (Pallas ;) Kamtschatka, (Acad. Philad.)

We find in the Museum of the Philadelphia Academy one specimen only which appears to be this species. It is a very plain species, with a short crest, and in the present specimen easily distinguished by the white spot under the eye.

Though we regard this bird at present as a distinct species, we consider it as quite possible that it is a stage of plumage of the preceding *P. cristatella*, though entirely without the appendages of the bill so conspicuous in the latter.   Its bill tip is darker colored, and altogether our specimen agrees quite well with the description and figure of Pallas, cited above.

PHALERIS CAMTSCHATICUS, (Lepechin,) Cassin.

Alca camtschatica, LEPECHIN, Nov. Act. Acad. St. Petersburg, XII, 1801, 369.
Uria mystacea, PALLAS, Zoog. Rosso-Asiat. II, 1811, 372.
Mormon superciliosa, LICHT. Verz. 1823, 89.
Phaleris superciliosa, BON. List, 1838.
Phaleris cristatellus, TEMM. Pl. Col. V, pl. 200.

FIGURES.—Nov. Act. Acad. St. Petersburg, XII, pl. 8.—TEMM. Pl. Col. 200.—VIEILL. Gal. II, pl. 297.—PALLAS, Zoog. Rosso-Asiat. II, pl. 89.

SP. CH.—Smaller than either of the preceding.   Bill short, nearly simple ; commissure slightly curved; culmen ridged ; a crest of very slender feathers in front, curved forwards ; angle of upper mandible very distinct ; wing moderate, pointed ; tail short.   Numerous white slender feathers at the base of the upper mandible and in a line from the corners of the mouth on the neck ; long and pendent on the latter.   Entire upper parts dark brown ; under parts light cinereous ; paler and nearly white on the abdomen.   Bill orange red ; feet greenish brown ; crest black ; a few of the longer posterior feathers white.

Total length about 7½ inches ; wing, 4½ inches ; tail, 1¼ inches.

Hab.—Northwestern coast of America, (Mr. John Gould ;) Kamtschatka, (Lepechin ;) Unalashka, (Pallas.)

Of this species we have only seen a single head in the National Museum, to which it was presented by the eminent naturalist Mr. John Gould, of London.   Fortunately the skin and plumage are carefully preserved, showing, of course, the form and colors, which are precisely as given in Temminck's plate, as above cited, except that a few of the posterior feathers of the crest are white, as represented in Lepechin's plate, also cited above.   It appears to be one of the handsomest of these birds, and is most assuredly distinct from any other species.

The feathers of the crest in this species are more slender than in any other.   The present specimen is labelled as from the Northwest Coast of America.

Catal. No.	Locality.	Whence obtained.	Nature of specimen.
8098	Northwest coast of America	John Gould	Head ......

Ciceronia,[1] Reichenbach.
PHALERIS MICROCEROS, Brandt.
The Little Auk.

Phaleris microceros, BRANDT, Bull. Acad. St. Petersburg, I, 1837, 346.
Phaleris nodirostra, BONAP. Comp. List, 1838, 66.—AUD. Orn. Biog. V, 101, pl. 402.
? Alca pygmaea, GM. Syst. Nat. II, 1788, 554.

FIGURES.—AUD. B. of Am. pl. 402.—IB. oct. ed. pl. 468.

SP. CH.—Smaller than the preceding, not crested ; bill short, compressed, with a small elevated appendage or caruncle at base of upper mandible ; commissure nearly straight ; upper mandible curved and notched at the tip ; wing moderate ; tail short.   Bill orange red, with its base and elevated caruncle dark bluish ; numerous white hair-like feathers on the forehead, and others below the eye.   Entire upper parts brownish black, darker on the back ; cheeks and chin ashy brown ; under parts white, with numerous large spots of dark brown, especially on the breast ; throat pure white ; under wing coverts white ; feet greenish brown.

Total length about 6½ inches ; wing, 4 ; tail, 1¼ inches.

Hab.—Northwestern coast of America, (Mr. John Gould ;) Behring's Straits ; Kamtschatka, (Mus. Acad. Philada.)

[1]The smallest of sea birds.   General character of the preceding, but with the head not crested.

This handsome little species is easily recognized by its short elevated caruncle at the base of the bill and its small size, though larger than the succeeding. The figure of Mr. Audubon cited above is very accurate, and represents the adult bird, though the young differs in no material character. In all the specimens the under parts are spotted as described above, except the throat, which is pure white. It appears to be abundant on the coasts of northwestern America and northeastern Asia.

It is possible that the pigmy auk of Pennant, which is *Alca pygmaea*, Gmelin, may be the young of this species, but it is more probable, judging from the descriptions of Latham and Gmelin, that several small species have been confounded under this name. Latham describes his bird as having the bill: "the top is ridged, but on the sides of the ridge is considerably depressed, *as in the duck*," which is a character of no species which has come under our notice.

List of specimens.

Catal. No.	Locality.	Whence obtained.
8094	Northwest coast of America	John Gould

PHALERIS PUSILLA, Pallas.

The Least Auk.

Uria pusilla, PALLAS, Zoog. Ross.-Asiat. II, 1811, 373.

FIGURES.—PALLAS, Zoog. Ross.-Asiat. II, pl. 90.

SP. CH.—Smaller than either of the preceding. Head rather large ; bill short, slightly curved upwards towards the tip, without appendages ; a longitudinal groove in the under mandible ; wing moderate, second quill slightly longest ; tail short, truncate or even at the end ; legs and feet rather large. Entire upper parts black, lustrous on the head above and back. Scapular feathers ashy white, giving the appearance of two white spots on the upper view of the bird ; secondary quills tipped with white ; a spot of white over the eye ; a few hair-like feathers in front white, and a few of the same kind behind the eye. Entire under parts white, with some narrow transverse lines of dark ashy on the sides. Bill black ; edges of both mandibles at base, and tip of under mandible yellow ; legs dark. Narrow space on the throat at the base of the under mandible and cheeks dark brownish cinereous.

Total length about 5½ inches ; wing, 3½ ; tail, 1 inch.

Hab.—Northwestern coast of America? Semiavine Straits, (Nat. Mus. from Capt. Rodger's North Pacific Exploring Expedition.) Kamtschatka, (Pallas.)

This interesting little species is the bird described by Pallas as above, and is altogether distinct from the preceding. It is probably the very smallest of the sea birds, and is easily distinguished by the clear black of its upper plumage and pure white of the under parts, with the additional prominent character of having white scapulars.

The only specimens that we have ever seen of this bird are in the National Museum, and are part of the very extensive zoological collection made by the North Pacific Exploring and Surveying Expedition in command of Capt. John Rodgers, United States navy.

List of specimens.

Catalogue No.	Locality.	Whence obtained.	Collected by—
	Seniavine Straits	Captain J. Rodgers, United States navy	W. Stimpson

PTYCHORHAMPHUS, Brandt.

Ptychorhamphus, BRANDT, Bull. Acad. St. Petersburg, II, 1837.

CH.—Small. General form short and heavy; head rather large. Bill short, straight, conical, pointed; under mandible with one curved longitudinal groove from the base; upper mandible with two or three grooves of the same description; membrane of the nostril large; angle of the gonys very distinct. Wings moderate, pointed, first quill longest; tail very short; legs moderate, compressed, covered with very small circular and hexagonal scales.

This genus embraces the present species only.

PTYCHORHAMPHUS ALEUTICUS, (Pallas,) Brandt.

Uria aleutica, PALLAS, Zoog. Rosso-Asiat. II, p. 370, (1811)
Ptycho hamphus aleuticus, BRANDT, 1837.
Mergulus cassinii, GAMBEL, Proc. Acad. Philad. II, 1845, 266.—IB. J. A. N. S. 2d series, II, 1850; pl. vi.

SP. CH—Small. General form short and heavy; bill conical, pointed; wing moderate; tail short; legs and feet moderate; tarsi compressed. Bill brownish black, with a conspicuous spot of yellow at the base of the under mandible. Head above and entire upper parts dark fuliginous, nearly black on the back and top of the head, tinged with ashy on the rump. Throat and sides of the neck light ashy; other under parts white; a longitudinal stripe on the sides from the breast to the tibia dark ashy brown; under tail coverts white; feet dark.

Total length about 8 inches; wing, 4¾; tail, 1½ inches.

Hab.—Western and northwestern coast of America; California, (Dr. Gambel.)

This quite peculiar little bird is well figured in the Journal of the Philadelphia Academy, as above cited, and is occasionally brought in collections from the western coasts of the United States. It was first added to our fauna by the late Dr. William Gambel, as above, but is undoubtedly the bird described by Pallas in Zoographia Rosso-Asiatica.

List of specimens.

Catalogue No.	Locality.	Whence obtained.
8097	Northwest coast of America...	John Gould..........

OMBRIA, Eschscholtz.

? *Phaleris*, TEMMINCK, Man. 1820.
Ombria, ESCHSCHOLTZ, Zool. Atlas, pt. IV, p. 3, (1831.)

CH.—General form short and robust; head moderate. Bill short, much compressed; upper mandible with the culmen very distinct, and its cutting edge curved upwards; under mandible much curved upwards; nearly falcate in its terminal half; membrane of the nostril large, corneous; a short longitudinal groove at base of the under mandible. Wings moderate, pointed; tail short; legs short, strong; tarsus flattened laterally, covered with minute circular and oval scales; feet with three toes only, fully webbed; claws rather long. Contains one species only.

OMBRIA PSITTACULA, (Pallas,) Eschscholtz.

Alca psittacula, PALLAS, Spic. Zool. pt. V, 1769, 13.
Phaleris psittacula, STEPHENS, XIII, I, 1826, 44.
Ombria psittacula, ESCHSCHOLTZ, Zool. Atlas, IV, 1831, 3.

FIGURES.—ESCHSCHOLTZ, Zool. Atlas, pl. 17.—PALLAS, Spic. Zool. pl. 2.—Zoog. Rosso-Asiat. pl. 84.—LATH. Gen. Hist. X, pl. 170, fig. 2.

SP. CH.—A line of long hair-like feathers from under the eye, extending longitudinally on the side of the neck, white. Head and entire upper parts brownish black, slightly mixed with white on the throat; breast mottled with dark brown and white.

Under parts of body from the breast white ; sides under the wings spotted with ashy brown ; tibiae ashy brown ; under wing coverts dark ashy brown. Bill reddish orange, darker at base ; feet dark greenish.

Total length about 9 inches ; wing, 5¾ ; tail, 1½ inches.

Hab.—Northwestern coast of America ; Kurile islands ; Kamtschatka, (Pallas.)

The very singular bill of this bird strongly characterizes it, and seems to attain a maximum of oddity amongst the queer bills of this family of birds. The whole affair looks as if it might be a nose of wax badly pinched and jerked upwards, especially to the disadvantage of the under mandible.

Though nearly related to *Phaleris*, it is quite probable that the stronger relationship of this curious bird is to the genus *Mormon*. It appears to be not uncommon on the northwest coast of America.

List of specimens.

Catalogue No.	Locality.	Whence obtained.	Nature of specimen.
8099	Northwest coast of America---	John Gould----------	Head -----------
8100	------do----------do--------	------do-------------	Skin ---- --------

Sub-Family URINAE.

URIA, Moehring.

Uria, MOEHRING, Av. Gen., 1752. Type, *Colymbus grylle*, L.

CH.—General form short and robust. Head moderate, bill rather long, straight, somewhat compressed, pointed, angle of the under mandible distinct ; nostrils in a groove at base of upper mandible, the membrane of which is covered with short velvet-like feathers. Wings short, pointed ; tail short ; legs short and robust ; tarsus shorter than the middle toe, compressed, toes rather long, fully webbed ; claws rather strong, curved.

The size in this genus varies considerably, but is never large, and all the species present a general similarity of dark and white colors. There are not more than seven species, all of which inhabit high northern latitudes, migrating more southwardly.

According to Keyserling and Blasius the two sub-genera of *Uria* are characterized as follows :

URIA, Moehring.—Upper jaw near the tip entire, and without groove. Culmen not more than half the keel. Adult colors black, with patches only of white.

CATARACTES, Moehring.—End of upper jaw with a lateral furrow running into a notch behind the tip. Culmen or ridge more than half the keel. Dark above, with lines or stripes of white. Much white beneath.

Uria, Moehring.

URIA GRYLLE, (Linnaeus,) Latham.

The Guillemot.

Alca grylle, LINN. Syst. Nat. I, 1758, 130.

Colymbus grylle, LINN. Syst. Nat. I, 1766, p. 220.

Uria grylle, LATHAM, Ind. Orn. II, 1790, 797.—BON. Syn. 1828, 423.—AUD. Orn. Biog. III, 1835, 148; V, 627: pl. 219

Uria grylloides, BRÜNNICH, Orn. Bor. p. 28, (1764.)

Uria balthica and *groenlandica*, BRÜNNICH, Orn. Bor. p. 28, (1764.)

Uria scapularis, STEPHENS, Shaw, Gen. Zool. XII, p. 250, (1824.)

Cepphus lacteola, PALLAS, Spicil. V, 33.

FIGURES.—Edwards, Birds I, pl. 50.—VIEILLOT, Gal. II, pl. 294.—AUD. B. of Am. pl. 219, oct. ed. VII, pl. 474.—GOULD B. Eur. IV, pl. 399.—NAUMANN B. of Germ. pl. 330.

SP. CH.—Bill straight, pointed ; wing rather short, weak ; first quill longest ; tail short. A large oval transverse space on the wing, white, which is also the color of the under wing coverts and axillary feathers, outer edge of the wing and shoulder brownish black. All other parts of the plumage brownish black, with a greenish tinge and darker on the back. Bill black, feet red. Younger and winter plumage, under parts, neck and rump white ; head above and back dark brown ; large space of white on the wing, as in summer.

Total length about 13 inches; wing, 6½ ; tail, 2 inches.

Hab.—Northeastern coast of America, Greenland, (Dr. E. K. Kane ;) South, in winter, to New Jersey. Behring's Straits, Captain Rodgers.

Very abundant on the northeastern coasts and islands of America, and also in the northern latitudes of Europe. This bird is very easily recognized by its black plumage and large white space on the wing.

A single specimen is in the collection before me, collected by the expedition of Captain Rodgers on Herald island, inside of Behring's Straits.

URIA COLUMBA, (Pallas,) Cassin.

The Western Guillemot.

Cepphus columba, PALLAS, Zoog. Rosso-Asiat. II, p. 348, (1811.)

Uria mandtii, LICHT. Verz. p. 88, (1823) ?

" *Uria mandtii*, LICHT. Mus. Dresd." REICH. Vollst. Naturg. Schwimmv. pl. 4, fig. 47.

FIGURES.—Voy. Vincennes and Peacock, Birds, pl. 38, fig. 1.

SP. CH.—Rather larger than the preceding, bill larger and stronger. White space on the wing, divided by a band of brownish black running diagonally from the edge of the wing ; under wing coverts dark ashy, frequently tipped with white ; axillary feathers ashy brown. All other parts of the plumage brownish black, with a greenish lustre, and frequently tinged with ashy on the back. Bill black, feet red. *Younger and winter plumage.* Upper parts brownish black ; under parts white, generally more or less spotted with dark brown ; white space on the wing as in summer, but frequently less distinct.

Total length about 13¼ inches.

Hab.—Western and northwestern coast of America. Kamtschatka, (North Pacific Surveying and Exploring Expedition, Captain Rodgers, United States navy.)

Much resembling the preceding, but easily distinguished by the white space on the wing, being divided into two parts, as described above. This bird appears to be exclusively an inhabitant of the North Pacific ocean, and rears its young as far south as Puget's Sound. In the fine collection made by Dr. George Suckley, United States army, are young birds scarcely feathered, which were obtained at that locality.

List of specimens.

Catal. No.	Sex and age.	Locality.	When collected.	Whence obtained.	Orig. No.	Collected by—	Length.	Stretch of wing.	Win .
4407	♂	Fort Steilacoom, W. T	1855	Dr. Geo. Suckley	186		13.25	24.25	7.50
9907	♂	..........do	August 8, 1856	........do	524		14.25	24.25	7.00
9909	......	..........do	.......do	........do	560				
9910	○	..........do		... ...do	119				
9906		Farrallones, Cal		Lieut. Williamson		Dr. Heermann			

URIA CARBO, (Pallas.)

Cepphus carbo, PALLAS, Zoog. Rosso-Asiat. II, 1811, 350.

FIGURES.—PALLAS, Zoog. Rosso-Asiat. pl. 79.—REICHENBACH, Vollst. Naturg. Aves, pl. 375, fig. 2937.

S P. CH.—Larger than either of the preceding; bill rather long, compressed; wing moderate. Space around and behind the eye, white. All other parts of the plumage brownish black, rather paler than in either of the preceding, and more tinged with ashy on the under parts, and at the base of the bill; under wing coverts and axillaries dark ashy brown; some of the former tipped with white; bill bluish black; feet red.

Total length about 14½ inches; wing, 7½; tail, 3 inches.

Hab.—Aleutian Islands, (Pallas;) Kamtschatka, (Mus. Acad. Philad.;) Northwestern coast of America.

This singular and little known bird, though resembling both of the preceding in form and general appearance, can be recognized without difficulty by the white space around the eye and clear black of the wings. It is represented by Pallas to be an inhabitant of the Aleutian Islands, but the only specimens that have come under our notice are in the Museum of the Philadelphia Academy, and are from Kamtschatka.

Cataractes, Moehring.

URIA LOMVIA, Brünnich.

The Foolish Guillemot; The Murre.

Uria lomvia, BRÜNNICH, Orn. Bor. 1764, 27.
Uria svarbag, BRÜNNICH, Orn. Bor. 1764, 27.
Columbus troile, LINN, Syst. Nat. I, 1766, 220.
Columbus minor, GM. Syst. Nat. I, 1788, 585.

FIGURES.—BUFF. Pl. Enl. 903.—GOULD, B. of Eur. IV, pl. 396.—NAUMANN, B. of Germ. pl. 331.

SP. CH.—Bill rather long, pointed, compressed; from the lateral feathers longer than the tarsus or than the inner toe and claw. A narrow line under and behind the eye dark brown; head above and entire other upper parts brownish black; sides of the head and entire under parts white; sides of the body under the wing with transverse stripes of ashy brown; under wing coverts white, secondary quills tipped with white. Bill blackish brown, paler at base. Tarsi and feet dark greenish brown. Summer plumage, with the entire hind and upper parts of body, dark sooty brown; under parts white. Head and orbital region dusky, without white stripes.

Total length about 15 inches; wing, 7½ inches; tail, 2 inches.

Hab.—Northern coasts of America; Northern Europe and Asia.

This is the bird regarded as the true *Uria troile* of Linnaeus by a majority of late European authors, and is figured as such on Mr. Gould's Birds of Europe, cited above. It is the next species, however, which is given by Mr. Audubon under this name.

Authors are by no means unanimous in the opinion that the present species and that immediately succeeding are really distinct; and, in fact, doubts are expressed by very accomplished and reliable naturalists, amongst which is Mr. Gould, in Birds of Europe, who figures both the supposed species. We have no doubt that this bird inhabits the northern regions of this continent, though we have never seen an American specimen.

Oct. 15, 1858.

115 b

URIA RINGVIA, Brünnich.

Murre.

Uria ringvia, Brünn. Orn. Bor. 1764, 28.
Uria lachrymans, La Pylaie.
Uria leucopthalmos, Faber, Isis, 1824, p. 146.
Uria leucopsis, Brehm.
? Uria alga, Brünn. Orn. Bor. 1764, 28.
Uria troile, Bon. Syn. 1728, 424.—Aud. Orn. Biog. III, 1835, 142; pl. 218.

Figures.—Gould, B. of Eur. IV, pl. 397.—Audubon, B. of Am. pl. 218.—Ib. oct. ed. VII, pl. 473.—Naumann, B. of Germ. pl. 332.

Sp. Ch.—About the size of or rather larger than the preceding. Bill rather long, pointed, compressed; from the lateral feathers longer than the tarsus or than the inner toe and claw. Wings rather short; tail very short. A narrow line of white encircling and running backwards behind the eye and over the ear. Head and entire upper parts dark brown, with a tinge of ashy. Under parts white; sides with transverse stripes of ashy brown; under wing coverts white; bill black; feet greenish black. Winter plumage, with the throat and all other under parts, white. The white line behind the eye frequently wanting, and different in length in specimens.

Total length about 17 inches; wing, 7½ to 8 inches; tail, 2 inches.

Hab.—Northern America; Northern Europe and Asia.

Easily distinguished by the line of white behind the eye, which is, however, not always present in specimens, as stated above. This is one of the most common birds of the higher northern latitudes on both sides of the continent. Specimens in the present collection are from California.

List of specimens.

Catal. No.	Locality.	When collected.	Whence obtained.	Collected by—
3944	California		Dr. Heermann	
9905	Bodega, Cal	February, 1855	Lieut. Trowbridge	
	Atlantic ocean		S. F. Baird	J. J. Audubon

URIA ARRA, (Pallas.)

Thick-billed Guillemot.

Cepphus arra, Pallas, Zoog. Rosso-Asiat. II, 1811, 347.
Uria brünnichii, Sabine, Trans. Linn. Soc. London, XII, p. 539.—Bon. Syn. 1828, 424.—Aud. Orn. Biog. III, 1835, 336; pl. 345.
Uria francsii, Leach, Trans. Linn. Soc. London, XII, p. 588.
Uria troile, Brünnich, Orn. Bor. 1764, 103. (Not of Linnaeus.)

Figures.—Audubon, B. of Am. pl. 345; oct. ed. VII, pl. 472.—Gould, B. of Eur. IV, pl. 398.—Naumann, B. of Germ. pl. 333.

Sp. Ch.—Much resembling the preceding in form and colors, but with the bill shorter. About the size of *U. ringvia*. Bill moderate or rather short; curved at the tip, compressed; the distance from lateral feathers to tip less than the tarsus, but longer than inner toe and nail. Wing rather short; tail very short; tarsi strong. Head and entire upper parts brownish black; under parts white; tips of secondaries white; sides, under the wings, with transverse stripes of ashy brown; bill black; legs and feet greenish brown; no white stripe or circle about the eye. Winter and immature plumage, with the throat, (and other under parts,) white.

Total length about 17 inches; wing, 7½ inches; tail, 2 inches.

Hab.—Northern America; Northern Europe and Asia; coast of New Jersey, (Mus. Acad. Philad.)

This is the most frequent species of this group on the coast of the Middle and Northern States on the Atlantic, and occurs nearly every winter as far south as the coast of New Jersey. It differs from either of the preceding in having the bill much shorter and wider, and is not difficult to recognize by its short and rather wide bill, though of the same colors of plumage as the preceding.

List of specimens.

Locality.	Whence obtained.
Atlantic ocean	S. F. Baird ....
Herald island, Arctic ocean...........	Capt. J. Rodgers, U. S. N........

BRACHYRHAMPHUS, Brandt.

Brachyrhamphus, BRANDT, Bull. Acad. St. Petersburg II, 1837, 345.   Type, *Colymbus marmoratus*, Gm.

CH.—Small; general form short, broad, and very robust.   Head rather large; wings moderate; tail short.   Bill short, densely covered with feathers at base, compressed.   Upper mandible curved; lower mandible grooved at base.   Wings pointed, first quill longest.   Tail very short; legs moderate; tarsi compressed; feet 'rather small.   A group containing several species of beautiful little sea birds inhabiting the North Pacific ocean.

Apobapton, Brandt.[1]

BRACHYRAMPHUS MARMORATUS, (Gmelin,) Brandt.

Colymbus marmoratus, GMELIN, Syst. Nat. I, 1788, 583.
Uria marmorata, LATH. Ind. Orn. II, 1790, 799.—BON. Syn. 1828, 423.
Cepphus perdix, PALLAS, Zoog. Rosso-Asiat. II, 1811, 351.
Uria brevirostris, VIGORS, Zool. Jour. IV, 1828, 357.
Uria townsendii, AUD. Orn. Biog. V, 1839, 251, pl. 430.—TOWNSEND, Narrative, 1839, 352.
Marbled Guillemot, PENNANT; LATHAM.

FIGURES.—LATH. Gen. Syn. VI, pl. 96.—PENNANT, Arc. Zool. II, pl. 22.—AUD. B. of Am. pl. 430; oct. ed. VII, pl. 475.

SP. CH.—Small; bill slender, distinctly notched near the end; frontal feathers advancing upon it to near half its length' Wings short; tail very short; legs and feet short and weak.   Entire upper parts brownish black, tinged with ashy on the back. Scapular feathers white, forming two conspicuous spots on each side of the back; ring around the back of the neck white. Under parts white; under wing coverts dark ashy brown; longitudinal stripes on the side ashy brown; bill black; feet yellow.

Younger. Upper parts brownish black, with the feathers tipped and edged with dull reddish; under parts spotted and marbled with brownish black and white.

Total length about 10 inches; wing, 5 inches; tail, 1½ inches.

Hab.—Western and northwestern coasts of America ; California, (Mr. Geo. Davidson;) Washington Territory, (Dr. Cooper.)

A beautiful little sea bird, apparently abundant on the western coast of the United States, and probably constantly resident in the latitude of Puget's Sound.   In Dr. Cooper's collection are young birds evidently in the plumage of the year, and with the under parts mottled, as above described, and as described and figured by Latham, as above cited.

Bill rather slender, size smaller than in the succeeding sub-genus.

List of specimens.

Catal. No.	Sex.	Locality.	When collected.	Whence obtained.	Orig. No.	Collected by—	Length.	Stretch of wings.	Wing.	Remarks.
4489	......	Cape Flattery, W. T..	....	Lieut. Trowbridge...	......	....	....	....	....	
9552	......	Puget's Sound.......	Nov. 28, 1857	A. Campbell..........	......	Dr. Kennerly ..	10.50	17.75	5.38	
9912	......	........do	....	Dr. Suckley	......	....	....	....	....	
9914	......	Fort Steilacoom	Mar. —, 1854	Gov. Stevens	52	Dr. Cooper	....	....	....	
5984	♂	........do	Mar. 13, 1855	......do	......	......do........	9.75	17.75	....	Iris hazel; bill black; feet pale flesh color; webs bluish.
9913	......	Shoalwater bay......	Sept. 12, 1854	......do	93	......do........	8.00	16.25	....	Iris grayish; bill black; feet pale gray; webs black.

Synthliboramphus, Brandt.[1]

BRACHYRAMPHUS ANTIQUUS, Gmelin.

The Ancient Auk; The Grey-headed Auk.

Alca antiqua, Gm. Syst. Nat. I, 1788, 554.
Uria antiqua, Aud. Orn. Biog. V, 1839, 100; pl. 402.
Uria senicula, Pallas, Zoog. Rosso-Asiat. II, 1811, 367.
Mergulus cirrhocephalus, Vigors, Voy. Blossom, Orn. p. 32, (1839.)

Figures.—Aud. B. of Am. pl. 402, fig. 12; oct. ed. VII, pl. 470.—Temm. & Schleg. Faun. Jap. Aves, pl. 80.

Sp. Ch.—Small; bill wider and more flattened laterally than in the preceding, notched and curved towards the point. Wing moderate; tail very short; legs and feet moderate. Throat and head above black. A longitudinal stripe of narrow white feathers on each side above and behind the eye; another wide stripe of white on the neck below the eye, uniting with the white of the under parts of the body; back and rump light ashy. Under parts white, with a transverse wide stripe of brownish black on the sides below the closed wings. Under wing coverts white; quills and tail brownish black. Numerous lines of white on the neck behind and on the shoulders; bill yellow, with the culmen dark brown; feet yellow. *Younger*, with the upper parts obscurely tinged and striped with dull reddish, and the under parts with dark brown.

Total length, about 9½ to 10 inches; wing, 5½ inches; tail, 1½ inches.

Hab.—Northwestern coast of America.

Another very handsome sea bird inhabiting the North Pacific, but apparently not so abundant as the preceding. It is easily distinguished by its larger size and the white stripes on each side of the head.

BRACHYRAMPHUS TEMMINCKII, Brandt.

Brachyramphus temminckii, Brandt, Bull. Acad. St. Petersburg, II, 1837, 346.
Uria umizusume, Temm. Faun. Jap. Aves, p. 123.

Figures.—Temm. Pl. Col. pl. 579.—Temm. & Schleg. Faun. Jap. Aves, pl. 79.

Sp. Ch.—Small; bill rather lengthened and slender, a crest of long erectile feathers in front; wings rather short; tail short, rounded; legs and feet short and rather weak. Crest feathers black; longitudinal stripes on the top of the head, throat, back of the neck, and longitudinal wide stripe on the sides throughout the length of the body, brownish black. Back, wing coverts, and rump light cinereous; quills and tail brownish black. Wide stripes over each eye, uniting on the occiput, white. Entire under parts white; under wing coverts white; bill and feet light colored; culmen dark brown. *Female and winter plumage?*—No crest; head above brownish black; throat ashy brown; stripe on the sides ashy, frequently with circular spots of white.

Total length about 9½ inches; wing, 5¼; tail, 1½ inch.

Hab.—Northwestern coast of America; northern Asia; Japan, (Nat. Mus., from Perry's Expedition.)

Bill wide laterally, compressed; size larger than the preceding.

Rather smaller than the preceding, and in adult plumage readily distinguished by its crest of long elevated feathers. We have in the present collection young birds only, all of which are from Washington Territory. Adult specimens in the National Museum are from Japan.

In addition to the preceding three species of this genus, of which numerous specimens are now before us, three other species are described by Mr. Brandt in his very valuable Monograph of the *Alcidae*, in the Bulletin of the Academy of St. Petersburg, II, p. 345, (1837.) Never having seen either of those species, we can only transcribe the descriptions by the distinguished author just mentioned. According to Bonaparte, they belong to *Apobapton*.

List of specimens.

Catal. No.	Sex.	Locality.	When collected.	Whence obtained.	Orig. No	Collected by—	Length.	Stretch of wings.	Remarks.
8095	----	Northwest Coast Am .	----------	J. Gould----------	----	----------	--------	--------	--------
5987	♂	Port Gamble, W. T ..	March 16	Dr. J. G. Cooper---	----	----------	10.75	18.25	Bill, flesh color ; irids, black; feet, pale blue------
9911	----	Shoalwater bay------	Nov.25,'54	------do----------	113	----------	10.50	18.25	----------------
10677	♂	Simoda, Japan--------	May, 1854	Com. Perry, U. S. N.	----	Wm. Heine	--------	--------	--------
10696	♀	Yedo bay, Japan-----	Feb. 1854	------do----------	----	----do----	--------	--------	--------

BRACHYRAMPHUS WRANGELII, Brandt.

Brachyramphus wrangelii, BRANDT, Bull. Acad. St. Petersburg, II, 1837, 344.

SP. CH.—"Rostrum capitis dimidii circiter longitudine. Caput supra, nucha et dorsum e nigricante grisea. Alae et cauda nigrae. Reliquae partes, nec non stria longitudinalis supra alam albae. Tarsi digito medio breviores. Longitudino a rostri apice ad caudae apicem, 9½". Patria Insulae Aleuticae."

Bill about half the length of the head. Head above, neck behind, and back, blackish gray ; wings and tail black ; other parts and a stripe on the wing white. Tarsus shorter than the middle toe. Length from the tip of the bill to the end of the tail, 9½ inches. Inhabits the Aleutian Islands.

BRACHYRAMPHUS BRACHYPTERUS, Brandt.

Brachyramphus brachypterus, BRANDT, Bull. Acad. St. Petersburg, II, 1837, 344.
" *Uria brachyptera*, KITTL. MSS."—BRANDT, as above.

SP. CH.—"Supra cinerea, alis caudaeque nigricantibus. Collum subtus et in lateribus, pectus et abdomen alba. Rostrum capitis dimidii circiter longitudine. Tarsi digito medio longiores. Longitudino a rostri apice ad caudae apicem 9". Patria Unalaschka."

Above cinereous ; wings and tail blackish ; neck beneath and on its sides, breast, and abdomen white. Bill about half the length of the head ; tarsus longer than the middle toe ; length from the tip of the bill to the end of the tail, 9 inches. Inhabits Unalaschka.

BRACHYRAMPHUS KITTLITZII, Brandt.

Brachyramphus kittlitzii, BRANDT, Bull. Acad. St. Petersburg, II, 1837, 344.

SP. CH.—"Supra cinerea nigricante et pallide e fusco-flavescente undulata et submaculata. Subtus alba, sub-fuscescente tenuissime lavata, nigro et quidem in pectore frequentius undulata. Alae e cinerascente et fusco nigrae. Rostrum brevissimum, capitis longitudinus tertiam partem circiter adaequans. Tarsi digito medio breviores. Longitudo a rostri apice ad caudae apicem 9". Patria Kamtschatka."

Above cinereous, undulated, and somewhat spotted with blackish and pale yellowish brown. Beneath white, faintly tinged with brownish, and undulated on the breast with black ; wings ashy and brownish black. Bill very short, about one-third the length of the head ; tarsus shorter than the middle toe. Length from the tip of the bill to the end of the tail, 9 inches. Inhabits Kamtschatka.

MERGULUS, Ray.

Mergulus, RAY, Synopsis Avium, 1713, 125.

CH.—Small; general form short and heavy, head rather large. Bill short, thick ; upper mandible curved, slightly lobed on its edge ; membrane of the rounded nostril large ; wings moderate or rather short, pointed ; first quill longest ; tail short ; feet rather short.

MERGULUS ALLE, Linnaeus.

The Little Auk; The Sea Dove; Dovekie.

Alca alle, LINN. Syst. Nat. I, 1766, 211.
Mergulus alle, VIEILLOT, " Anal, 1816."— IB. Galerie, II, 1825, 237.—AUD. Syn. 347.
Uria alle, TEMMINCK, Man. II, 928.—BON. Obs. Wils. 1826, No. 238.—AUD. Orn. Bor. IV, 1838, 304 ; pl. 339.
Mergulus melanoleucus, RAY, Syn. Av. p. 125.
Alca candida, BRÜNN. Orn. Bor. 1764, 26.
Alca alce, GMELIN, Syst. Nat. I, 1788, 354.

FIGURES.—EDWARDS, Birds, II, pl. 91.—BUFFON, Pl. Enl. 917.—VIEILLOT, Gal. II, pl. 295.—WILSON, Am. Orn. IX, pl. 74, fig. 5.—AUD. B. of Am. pl. 339, oct. ed. VII, pl. 469.—GOULD, B. of Eur. IV, pl. 402.—NAUMANN, B. of Germ. pl. 334.

SP. CH.—Small ; head, breast, and entire upper parts brownish black, inclining to fuliginous on the head and breast; under parts from the breast white. A narrow line of white over the eye ; secondaries tipped with white ; scapulars edged with white ; under wing coverts dark ashy ; flanks with longitudinal stripes of brownish black ; bill black ; feet pale reddish ; webs of toes dark. Winter plumage and young with the throat (and other under parts) white, extending somewhat on the sides of the neck.

Total length about $7\frac{1}{2}$ inches ; wing, $4\frac{1}{2}$; tail, $1\frac{1}{4}$ inch.

Hab.—Northeastern coast of America ; northern Europe ; New Jersey, (Mus. Acad. Philad.;) Nova Scotia, (Nat. Mus. Washington.)

One of the most abundant of the sea birds of northern America and Europe, straying south in the winter occasionally to the coasts of the Middle States. We have never seen it from the northern Pacific, though it appears to be an inhabitant of the entire Arctic circle.

List of specimens.

Locality.	Whence obtained.	Nature of specimen
Halifax, N. S	J. K. Willis	Mounted

NOTE TO ALCIDAE.

In order to facilitate the comprehension of the genera of *Alcidae*, as given above, we present the following synopsis of Brandt's paper, in the "Bulletin Scientifique, publié par l'Acad. Imp. des Sciences de St. Petersbourg," II, 1837, 344, which has served, with some modification, as the basis of our article on the subject :

I. PTERORHINES.—Nostrils covered more or less with short feathers.
1. ALCA, Briss.—Bill transversely sulcate, compressed ; lateral profile oval. Species, *A. torda, impennis.*
2. URIA, Brünn.—Bill not sulcate, sub-conical, compressed, about equal to the head. Nostrils entirely covered above with feathers. ·Feet stouter.
   Lomvia.—Bill higher and broader. Species, *U. troile, brunnichi, ringvia.*
   Grylle.—Bill narrower, sub-conical. Species, *U. grylle, mandtii, carbo.*
3. BRACHYRHAMPHUS, Brandt.—Bill much shorter than the head, hooked at tip, compressed laterally. Nostrils half covered by feathers. Feet weaker.
   Apobapton, Brandt.—Bill less elevated, more narrow. Species, *B. marmoratus, wrangelii, brachypterus, kittlitzii.*
   Synthliborhamphus, Brandt.—Bill short, high, lateral outline almost oval. Species, *B. antiquus, temminckii.*
4. MERGULUS, Ray.—Species, *M. melanoleucus.*
II. GYMNORHINES.—Nostrils not covered by feathers.
5. PTYCHORHAMPHUS, Brandt.—Bill conical, sub-acute, moderately elongated. Basal part of maxilla covered above with narrow, transverse, cutaneous folds. Species, *P. aleuticus.*
6. PHALERIS, Temm.—Bill short, almost triangular. Maxilla without appendix at base, hooked at tip. Upper edge of mandible straight, or nearly so. Species, *P. tetracula, dubia, pygmaea, microceros, camtschatica.*
7. TYLORHAMPHUS, Brandt.—Maxilla at the base with a tubercle near the angle of the mouth. Upper margin of mandible emarginate. Species, *T. cristatellus.*
8. OMBRIA, Esch.—Bill much compressed and elevated, lateral outline almost oval. Maxilla emarginated beneath the tip ; mandible with the tip acute and directed upwards, falciform. Species, *O. psittacula.*
9. CERORHINA, Bon.—Bill compressed, elevated, lateral outline almost oval. Maxilla hooked, with a compressed horn on the basal part of ridge. Mandible hooked, the tip directed downwards. Species, *C. orientalis, (occidentalis.)*

10. FRATERCULA, Briss.—Bill very high, much compressed, lateral outline oval ; the tip with parallel transverse grooves.   Ceroma tumid, thickened.

Ceratoblepharum, Brandt.—A horny triangular appendage above the upper eyelid. Grooves at tip of bill arched backwards.   An elongated furrow in the plumage from the eyes to the nape.   Species, *F. arctica, corniculata.*

Gymnoblepharum, Brandt.—No horny appendage to the upper eyelid.   Grooves of bill arched forwards.   An elongated tuft of feathers occupying the place of the groove in the preceding sub-genus.   Species, *F. cirrhata.*

APPENDIX A.

ADDITIONAL REMARKS ON NORTH AMERICAN BIRDS

Additional materials having been received while the preceding report was passing through the press, I am enabled to make some important corrections and additions in reference to the number of species, as well as to their synonymy and localities. These are based chiefly on collections received at quite a late period, made by Mr. J. Xantus de Vesey, at Fort Tejon, California, Dr. W. W. Anderson, U. S. A., at Cantonment Burgwyn, N. M., and Mr. C. Drexler, at Fort Bridger, Utah. A special list of Mr. Drexler's whole collection is added. Sheets of the report, as printed, were sent to Mr. P. L. Sclater, of London; and some valuable criticisms received from him have also been embodied herein.

FALCO NIGRICEPS, Cassin, p. 8.—An erroneous measurement of Dr. Cooper's specimen, 8501, should read,—length, 17.25; extent, 39.50.

SYRNIUM NEBULOSUM, Gray, p. 56.—Fort Tejon, J. Xantus de Vesey.

NYCTALE ACADICA, Bon., p. 58.—Fort Tejon, J. Xantus de Vesey.

PICUS HARRISII, Aud., p. 87.—A specimen from Fort Bridger has the middle wing coverts unusually spotted with white. It belongs to the variety with pure white belly. The same may also be said of a specimen of *P. gairdneri*. A skin of *P. harrisii*, from Cantonment Burgwyn, has a reddish yellow patch in the crown.

SPHYRAPICUS NUCHALIS, Baird, p. 103.—In the article on *S. varius*, p. 103, reference is made to a supposed curious variety of the latter species with black curved band bordering the red of crown posteriorly, and succeeded by a nuchal crescent of red instead of soiled brownish white. A large number of specimens brought in by Mr. Drexler (about twenty) show further differences, in the fact that the female has a red throat like the male, instead of white, the extreme angle of the chin only being more or less white, which, with other peculiarities, entitle it to the rank of a distinct species. The characters are as follows :

Similar to *S. varius*. Under parts whitish, only faintly tinged with yellow. Black stripe from side of lower jaw not extending back to that of breast, but cut off by the extension of the red of throat to the lateral white stripe ; outer webs of secondaries almost entirely black. Tail feathers almost entirely black except the inner webs of the innermost, which are white banded with black, the others occasionally edged slightly with yellowish ; red of crown margined behind by black, this succeeded by a half collar or crescent of red curving forwards to the eye and becoming white on the sides of head. Female with the throat red, the chin more or less white.

Other differences might be indicated, but what I have mentioned is quite sufficient to establish a distinction of species. The specimens from Laramie Peak, collected by Lieutenant Warren, those of Dr. Henry, from Fort Thorn, and probably all from the Rocky mountains, belong to

Oct. 18, 1858.

the new species, which doubtless replaces *P. varius.* It is probably resident about Fort Bridger, specimens having been obtained in June.

LAMPORNIS MANGO, Sw., p. 130.—Mr. Sclater thinks that if any *Lampornis* occurs in Florida, it is most probably *L. porphyrula,* found in Jamaica, the *L. mango* belonging more to South America. The specimen described, however, is from Brazil, and a true *L. mango.*

SELASPHORUS PLATYCERCUS, Gould, p. 135.—Numerous specimens of this species have lately been received from Cantonment Burgwyn, N. M. (Dr. W. W. Anderson), and Fort Bridger, showing it to be a common bird of the Rocky mountains, and probably ranging far north. The female lacks the red throat and the green of the sides, which, with the crissum, are tinged with reddish, as in *S. rufus,* from which it differs in the absence of this color on the bases of the rump feathers. The tail is rounded, the lateral feathers wider than in *S. rufus,* broadly tipped with white. All are strongly edged and tinged towards the base with brownish red, less conspicuously than in *S. rufus.*

NEPHOECETES NIGER, Baird, p. 142.—Additional specimens of this species were collected in the spring of 1858, at Simiahmoo bay, where it was found by Dr. Kennerly to be quite abundant.

CHORDEILES HENRYI, Cassin, p. 153.—A large collection of *Chordeiles* (about 50 specimens) made at Fort Bridger by Mr. Drexler, shows constant differences from eastern specimens, entitling the Rocky mountain bird probably to specific rank. It is much lighter, greyer, and more generally mottled above, the back and scapulars varied with pale rufous. The white patch on the wing is nearer the carpus. The under parts are lighter, the black bars narrower. The greater under wing coverts are conspicuously instead of obsoletely barred with whitish.

MILVULUS TYRANNUS, Bon. p. 168.—According to Mr. Sclater this species reaches as far north as Vera Cruz.

TYRANNUS VOCIFERANS, Sw., p. 174.—West of Fort Laramie. C. Drexler.

EMPIDONAX OBSCURUS, Baird, p. 200.—Many specimens of this species were collected at Fort Bridger by Mr. Drexler. Some of these are more ashy above and less olivaceous than in 7234, the whitish bands on wing narrower, and very little yellowish beneath. There appear to be two types among Mr. Drexler's specimens, one with the bill longer, straighter on the edges, and with the lower mandible yellow, only tipped with black, instead of being uniformly brownish. I have not, however, time at present to pursue the investigation further for the purpose of ascertaining whether there are really two species.

The species was also found at Fort Yuma by Lt. Ives's expedition.

? TURDUS SILENS, Sw., p. 213.—In a series of thrushes referable to *T. nanus,* collected at Fort Bridger by Mr. Drexler, is a specimen much larger than the rest, or even than *T. pallasii,* and agreeing more nearly with No. 7950, considered identical with *T. silens* of Swainson. The length is $7\frac{1}{2}$ inches; the wing 4.25; the tail 3.60; the tarsus 1.30. The type of coloration is that of *T. nanus,* in a more olivaceous green of the upper parts anteriorly than in *T. pallasii.*

TURDUS FUSCESCENS, Steph., p. 214.—Specimens from Fort Bridger have the spots a little darker than in Carlisle skins, but scarcely enough so to have them referable to *T. ustulatus.*

SIALIA.—Mr. Sclater has a new species from Guatemala, *S. albiventris.*

HYDROBATA MEXICANA, Baird, p. 229.—Fort Tejon. J. Xantus de Vesey.

PARULA MEXICANA, Bon., p. 237.—Mr. Sclater writes that the oldest name of this species is *superciliosa.* (*Conirostrum superciliosum,* Hartlaub.)

AEGITHINA LEUCOPTERA, Vieill., p. 305.—According to Mr. Sclater, this is an *Iora* from East Indies; probably *I. scapularis.*

GEOTHLYPIS TRICHAS, Cab., p. 241.—A specimen from Fort Bridger has the light band margining the black of forehead posteriorly, extended over nearly the whole crown, and of a whiter shade than usual. This is scarcely indicative of a specific difference unless it should prove to be constant in western specimens, which does not appear to be the case.

GEOTHLYPIS MACGILLIVRAYI, Baird, p. 244.—Fort Tejon. J. Xantus de Vesey. Fort Laramie and Fort Bridger.

HELMINTHOPHAGA RUFICAPILLA, Baird, p. 256.—Fort Tejon. J. Xantus de Vesey.

DENDROICA TOWNSENDII, Baird, p. 269. Cantonment Burgwyn, N. M. Dr. W. W. Anderson.

DENDROICA NIGRESCENS, Baird, p. 270.—According to Mr. Sclater, the *Sylvia halseii* of Giraud is the female of this species. It is found at Oaxaca. Mr. de Vesey has collected it at Fort Tejon.

PYRANGA RUBRA, Vieill., p. 300.—A curious variety of this species, shot near Niles, Michigan, probably a male, has been furnished for examination by Dr. Sager, of Ann Arbor. It has the wing and tail black, as usual; but all the rest of the plumage is saffron yellow, instead of olive green above and yellowish beneath, as in the young male generally. There is a slight resemblance to *P. ludoviciana;* but the yellow is not pure lemon color, but has an orange shade, and the yellowish bands of the wings and the red of head are wanting.

HIRUNDO LUNIFRONS, Say, p. 309.—Mr. Sclater considers the *H. melanogaster* of Swainson (*Petrochelidon swainsonii*, Sclater) as quite distinct, and more allied to *H. fulva.*

PROGNE, ————?—A *Progne* collected by Mr. Würdemann at Cape Florida, May 18, 1858 (No. 10368), has the following characters:

Tail deeply forked (depth .80 of an inch). First quill rather shorter than second. Bill very broad. Above glassy steel blue and purple, as in *P. purpurea;* under parts dark smoky brown, passing on the belly into dull whitish. Under coverts whitish at base, passing into mottled brown to the tip. Length, before skinning, 7.50; extent, 15; wing, 5.50.

This skin differs from any specimens before me of *P. purpurea* in rather smaller size and the differently colored under plumage. The dark tail coverts separate it from *P. dominicensis* and *chalybea.* It may, after all, however, be nothing more than a peculiar stage of plumage of *P. purpurea.*

AMPELIS GARRULUS, Linn. p. 317. Mr. Drexler saw "millions" of this species while in the winter camp of the South Pass wagon road party, at the head of Powder river, Nebraska. Every tree for miles was filled with them, the flock rivalling that of the wild pigeon in its size.

CICHLOPSIS NITENS, Bd. p. 320.—Mr. Sclater writes that the type of *Cichlopsis* (*Turdus leucogonys* of Berlin Museum) is very different from *Ptilogonys nitens*, Sw. He proposes for the latter the generic name of *Phainopepla*, Sclater.

MYIADESTES TOWNSENDII, Cab., p. 321.—Mr. Sclater is decided as to the difference of *M. obscurus.*

COLLYRIO BOREALIS, Baird, p. 324.—A male shrike in good spring plumage, collected at Fort Bridger, differs from a Pennsylvania specimen, killed in November, in rather larger size, clearer grey above, and nearly white upper tail coverts.

HARPORHYNCHUS CRISSALIS, Henry, p. 351.—This name was erroneously printed in the Proceedings of the Philadelphia Academy as *T. dorsalis.* The page was afterwards cancelled and reprinted.

A second specimen has been collected at Fort Yuma by Lieutenant Ives's party.

TROGLODYTES HYEMALIS, Vieill., p. 369.—Fort Tejon. J. Xantus de Vesey.

CERTHIA MEXICANA, Gloger, p. 373.—Additional specimens from the west all show a much longer bill than eastern ones, tending to substantiate the existence of a second species.

PARUS SEPTENTRIONALIS, Harris, p. 389.—Specimens from Fort Bridger, like all others from the Rocky mountains, show an unusual amount of white on the quills and tail, almost enough to constitute them distinct species.

PARUS MERIDIONALIS, Sclater, p. 392.—The specimen described is not one of the types, as stated ; these are in the British and Paris Museums.

PAROIDES FLAVICEPS, Baird, p. 400.—Fort Yuma.

Family DACNIDIDAE.—The discovery of *Certhiola flaveola*, on Indian Key, Florida, by Mr. Würdemann, where it appears to be not rare, adds not only a species but a family (*Dacnididae*) to the fauna of the United States. The genus has the following characters :

Certhiola.[1]—Bill nearly as long as the head, as high as broad at base, elongated, conical, very acute, and gently decurved from base to tip. Culmen uniformly convex ; gonys concave. No bristles at base of bill. Tail rounded, rather shorter than the wings. Tarsi longer than middle toe. Primaries, nine.

Certhiola flaveola, Sund.[2]—First primary about equal to sixth. Body above black ; chin, throat, and sides, ash grey ; belly, edge of wing, and rump, yellow. A white stripe from upper mandible over the eye as far as nape, and a black one below it from the commissure, through and below the eye. Outer webs of primaries white at base, forming a patch ; all narrowly edged with grey towards the tip. Crissum white ; tail feathers black tipped with white, diminishing in amount from the outer feather inwards. Iris light blue ; bill and feet black. Length, 4.75 ; extent, 7.75 ; wing, 2.50. No. 10367. Indian Key, January 31, 1858.

This species appears subject to considerable variation, the throat being sometimes much darker. Several allied species appear to exist, but this is probably the typical *Certhia flaveola* of Linnaeus.

The genus *Certhiola* belongs to the family *Dacnididae*, characterized among *Oscines*, with a very few others, by the divided tongue. This in *Certhiola* has the branches bristle-like, divided at the ends into pencils. There are but nine primaries, as in *Sylvicolidae*. Other genera of the sub-family are *Conirostrum*, *Dacnis*, *Coereba*, and *Diglossa*.

CHRYSOMITRIS PINUS.—Spring specimens from Fort Bridger and Fort Tejon differ from spring specimens from Carlisle in having the streaks on the sides and belly darker and broader.

CURVIROSTRA AMERICANA, Wils., p. 426.—There seems to be a general tendency in the western cross-bills from the Rocky mountains and the Pacific slope to have larger bills than the eastern, thus referring them to the *Loxia mexicana* of Strickland.

LOXIA MEXICANA, Strickland, p. 427, is described in his review of *Monographie des Loxiens* by Bonaparte and Schlegel, Jardine's Contributions to Ornithology, 1851, 43. "Colors as in *L. americana.* Length, 6.2 ; wing, 3.9 ; bill to base, .8 ; depth of bill at base, .4. *Hab.* Near city of Mexico."

JUNCO CANICEPS, Baird, p. 468.—A large collection of *Junco* from Fort Bridger embraces a number of *J. caniceps*, agreeing generally with the description given. One specimen, however, is remarkable in having the sides reddish as in *oregonus*, although with the dorsal features of *caniceps*. There is, however, a trace of reddish on the wing coverts, which assimilates it further to *oregonus*. I have little doubt that it is a hybrid between the two species.

---

[1] *Certhiola*, SUNDEVALL, 1835.

Certhia flaveola, LINN. Syst. Nat. I, 1766.

Certhiola flaveola, "SUNDEVALL, 1835."—GOSSE, Birds Jam. 1847, 84.—IB. Illustrations, 1849, pl. xvi.—REICHENBACH, Icones, fig. 3825

The essential characters of *J. caniceps* consist in the reddish bill, with slight black tip, the well marked rufous confined strictly to the middle of the back, and not extending on the wing coverts at all. The head and neck all round are grey or ash, this color extending on the sides, leaving the middle of belly only white, as in the *J. hyemalis*, from which the red back distinguishes it. It shares the red bill with *hyemalis* and *oregonus*, both *J. cinereus* and *dorsalis* having the upper mandible black, the lower yellow.

Poospiza bilineata, Sclater, p. 470.—Big Cañon of Colorado. Lieut. Ives—H. B. Möllhausen.

Peucaea ruficeps, Baird, p. 486.—Fort Tejon. J. Xantus de Vesey.

Passerella schistacea, Baird, p. 490.—Eleven specimens from Fort Bridger, while generally resembling those from Fort Tejon, differ in a much smaller bill, as in the type from the head waters of Platte. Should this character be considered as specific, the bird of Fort Tejon may be called *P. megarhynchus.*

Quiscalus baritus, Vieill., p. 556.—This species was found to be very abundant on Indian Key, Florida, by Mr. Wurdemann, in the spring of 1858.

Picicorvus columbianus, Bon., p. 573.—Cantonment Burgwyn, New Mexico, Dr. Anderson. Fort Tejon, J. Xantus de Vesey.

Cyanura macrolophus, Baird, p. 582.—Cantonment Burgwyn, New Mexico, Dr. Anderson.

Cyanocitta woodhousii, Baird, p. 585.—Cantonment Burgwyn, New Mexico, Dr. Anderson.

Bonasa umbellus, var. umbelloides, p. 630.—Mr. Drexler collected a variety of the ruffed grouse in the winter camp, in November, corresponding with what Douglas calls *T. umbelloides.* Its chief peculiarity lies in the bluish grey, which replaces the reddish yellow which prevails in the common species. I am unable to distinguish any other features of importance indicative of specific differences, although it may be that such exist. Douglas's specimens were obtained in the valleys of the Rocky mountains, on the sources of the Pearl river, Linn. (Trans. XVI, 1833, 148.)

Gambetta melanoleuca, Bon., p. 731.—Among Mr. Drexler's specimens from Fort Bridger is a skin which differs in having the legs of a more greenish tint than in eastern ones. The basal web of the toes is greater. The entire rump is banded two, three, or four times on each feather. The under part and sides are more conspicuously banded than in eastern birds.

Tryngites rufescens, Cab., p. 739.—This species is not omitted by Bonaparte in his list published in Comptes Rendus, as stated in page 739, but is given by him under *Actiturus.*

Anser hyperboreus, p. 760.—From a recent examination of geese in the collection of the Philadelphia Academy, in company with Mr. Cassin, I am now satisfied as to the correctness of his separation of *caerulescens* as a distinct species, the young *hyperboreus* being quite different. It is also very probable that *A. albatus,* his smaller snow goose, is distinct from *hyperboreus.*

Bernicla leucopareia, Cassin, p. 765.—The specimen in the Philadelphia Academy figured by Mr. Cassin agrees very closely with Brandt's type in small size, pale breast, and black chin, separating the white cheek patches into two. In some respects the specimen I describe resembles *A. parvipes,* Cassin, as to feet and size, but differs in dark abdomen and white collar below the black neck.

Erismatura dominica, p. 811.—According to Dr. Cabot, Proceedings Boston Soc. Nat. History, VI, August, 1858, 375, a full plumaged male was shot at Alberg Springs, Missisquoi bay, Lake Champlain, on the 26th of September, 1857, and is now in the cabinet of the Boston Society of Natural History. The *E. dominica* is ferruginous above, the head black anteriorly, the speculum white. Length 13½ inches.

APPENDIX B.

BIRDS FOUND AT FORT BRIDGER, UTAH.

A large collection of birds made at Camp Scott, Fort Bridger, Utah, by Mr. C. Drexler, in April, May, and June, of 1858, was received too late to have its specimens assigned to their proper places in the present report. The interest attaching to so excellent an illustration of the ornithology of the central Rocky mountains is such as to induce me to give a complete list in this place, especially as this will tend to throw much light upon the geographical distribution of our western species. A striking feature of the collection is the entire absence of many birds otherwise found both on the plains of Nebraska and on the Pacific slope, as well as the presence of many species previously noticed only on the southern borders of New Mexico and the table lands of Mexico, as *Selasphorus platycercus, Empidonax obscurus, Tyrannus vociferans, Turdus pallasii* var. *silens,* &c.

Fort Bridger is situated on the Black fork of Green river, a tributary of the Colorado of the west, about lat. 41° 20', long. 110° 30', and is said to be at an altitude of about 7,000 feet above the sea. There is much level land to the north and east of the fort, and mountains at no great distance on the south and west, covered with pines. Mr. Drexler was unable to visit these, or he would doubtless have added many species of jays, woodpeckers, and other birds to his list. The open land about the fort is covered chiefly with low cottonwood.

Mr. Drexler was engaged in 1857 as assistant to Dr. Cooper, the surgeon of the South Pass Wagon Road expedition, under Wm. M. F. Magraw, Esq. When the party was partly broken up in September, 1857, Mr. Drexler remained with it and spent the winter in Mr. Magraw's camp on the sources of Wind river, Neb. In March he went to Fort Bridger, where the forces of tho United States, under General A. S. Johnston, United States army, had passed the winter, and there commenced his collections. In this work he received most essential and indispensable aid from General Johnston, by whose direction every facility was afforded him in his scientific operations.

A few species, not obtained at Fort Bridger, have their particular locality attached.

LIST OF BIRDS COLLECTED.

Tinnunculus sparverius.
Accipiter mexicanus.
        fuscus.
Buteo bairdii. (West of Fort Laramie, September 26, 1857.)
        montanus.
Pandion carolinus.
Bubo virginianus.
Picus harrisii.
        gairdneri.
Sphyrapicus nuchalis.
Melanerpes torquatus. (West of Ft. Laramie.)
        erythrocephalus.   do.

Colaptes mexicanus.
Chordeiles henryi. (Abundant.)
Selasphorus platycercus. (Abundant.)
Ceryle alcyon.
Tyrannus carolinensis.
        vociferans. (West of Fort Laramie Sept. 8, 1857.)
        verticalis.
Contopus borealis.
        richardsonii.
Empidonax obscurus. (Abundant.)
        minimus.
        pusillus.

Turdus fuscescens.
    nanus.
    silens?
    swainsonii.
    migratorius.
Sialia arctica. (Very common.)
Regulus calendula.
Hydrobata mexicana. (Common.)
Anthus ludovicianus.
Geothlypis trichas.
        macgillivrayi. (Very common.)
Helminthophaga celata.
? Seiurus noveboracensis.
Dendroica audubonii. (Very common.)
    aestiva.   do.
Myiodioctes pusillus.   do.
Setophaga ruticilla.
Pyranga ludoviciana. (Abundant.)
Hirundo horreorum.
    lunifrons. (Very common.)
    bicolor.
    thalassina. (Very common.)
Cotyle serripennis.
Ampelis garrulus.
Myiadestes townsendii. (Common.)
Collyrio borealis.
Vireo olivaceus.
    solitarius.
    gilvus.
Mimus carolinensis. (Common.)
Oreoscoptes montanus.
Salpinctes obsoletus.
Troglodytes parkmanni.
Sitta canadensis.
    aculeata.
Parus septentrionalis.
Eremophila cornuta.
Chrysomitris pinus.
Curvirostra americana.
Plectrophanes lapponica. (1857, Ft. Laramie.)
? Passerculus alaudinus. (Common.)
Pooecetes gramineus.
Zonotrichia leucophrys. (Very abundant.)

Zonotrichia gambelii. (Not very abundant.)
Junco caniceps. (Rather common.)
    oregonus. (Very abundant.)
Poospiza belli. (Very abundant.)
Spizella monticola.
    socialis.
    breweri. (Not rare.)
Melospiza melodia.
    lincolni.
Passerella schistacea. (Very common.)
Guiraca melanocephala. (Very common.)
Pipilo arcticus.
    chlorurus. (Common.)
Dolichonyx oryzivorus.
Molothrus pecoris.
Agelaius phoeniceus? ♀.
Sturnella neglecta.
Icterus bullockii.
Scolecophagus cyanocephalus. (Very common.)
Quiscalus versicolor. (Rare.)
Corvus carnivorus.
Picicorvus columbianus.
Pica hudsonica.
Zenaidura carolinensis.
Centrocercus urophasianus.
Bonasa umbelloides. (Winter camp.)
Grus canadensis.
Nyctiardea gardeni. (Platte.)
Ibis ordii.
Aegalitis vociferus.
    montanus. (Not rare.)
Recurvirostra americana. (Grey neck.)
Phalaropus wilsonii.
Gallinago wilsonii.
Ereunetes petrificatus.
Tringa wilsonii.
Gambetta melanoleuca.
Symphemia semipalmata.
Tringoides macularius.
Porzana carolina.
Fulica americana.
Querquedula cyanoptera.
Bernicla canadensis.

Fort Bridger species.. 104
Others.. 6
        Total.. 110

APPENDIX C.

LIST OF AUTHORITIES REFERRED TO IN THE PRECEDING REPORT.

In the present appendix I have endeavored to furnish as complete a list as possible of the articles and works quoted in the preceding pages. This I have not been able to do from personal examination to so great an extent as in respect to the mammals, many titles, for want of time, being copied from Engelmann's Bibliotheca Historico-Naturalis, although the works were actually in the libraries of the Smithsonian Institution and of the Philadelphia Academy of Natural Sciences.

The list is not given as a complete bibliography of ornithology, but only of works necessary to a proper understanding of the North American species; and even in this connexion many titles on the generalities of the subject have been omitted as not actually referred to. The enumeration of particular papers on ornithology, entering into the question of synonymy, as published in the United States, is believed to be pretty full.

A few titles quoted in the last hundred pages of the report will not be found in the list, as this was made up before the concluding manuscript of the volume was prepared.

LIST OF AUTHORITIES.

AGASSIZ, L.—Nomenclator zoologicus continens nomina systematica generum animalium tam viventium quam fossilium secundum ordinem alphabeticum disposita, adjectis auctoribus libris in quibus reperiuntur, etc. Auctore L. AGASSIZ. Fasciculus II continens Aves, et Fasciculus XII continens Indicem universalem. Soloduri, 1842 and 1847.

AGASSIZ, L.—See BOSTON, Society of Nat. Hist : Proceedings.

AMERICAN JOURNAL of Science.—See New Haven.

AMSTERDAM.—G e n o o t s c h a p "N a t u r a a r t i s m a g i s t r a" : Bijdragen tot de Dierkunde. Folio. I, I, 1848, et seq.

      WESTERMAN, G. F.—Beschrijving van twee nieuwe Soorten van Meezer. I, III, 1851, 15. (*Lophophanes woll-weberi* and *Psaltria personata*.)

AUDUBON, J. J.—Ornithological Biography ; or an account of the habits of the birds of the United States of America, accompanied by descriptions of the objects represented in the work entitled "The Birds of America." By JOHN JAMES AUDUBON. 5 vols. 8vo. Edinburg. Adam & Charles Black. I, 1831 ; II, 1834 ; III, 1835 ; IV, 1838 ; V, 1839. (This is the text or descriptive portion of the work in folio entitled "Birds of America.")

AUDUBON.—The birds of America, from original drawings, (made during a residence of 25 years in the United States and their territories.) By JOHN JAMES AUDUBON. Folio. London. 1827–1838. (This work was originally published in 87 parts, but subsequently bound in five volumes. It constitutes the atlas to the "Ornithological Biography," and its plates are quoted in that work. Vol. I, dated 1827-30, contains plates 1–100 ; II, 1831–1834, plates 101–200 ; III, 1834–5, plates 201–300 ; IV, 1835–1838, plates 301–435.)

AUDUBON.—A synopsis of the birds of North America. By J. J. AUDUBON. 8vo. Edinburg. Adam & Charles Black. 1839. (This work serves as a general systematic index to the "Ornithological Biography," but embraces a very few species not found in the latter, among them *Carduelis stanleyi*. The genera adopted, however, are very different.)

AUDUBON.—Birds of America, from drawings made in the United States and their territories. By JOHN JAMES AUDUBON. 7 vols. 8vo. New York, J. J. Audubon. Philadelphia, J. B. Chevalier. I, 1840 ; II, III, 1841 ; IV, V, 1842 ; VI, 1843 ; VII, 1844. (This work is a reissue of the "Ornithological Biography," with the species arranged systematically, and under the same names as in the "Synopsis." The plates are reduced by the camera lucida from those in the large folio "Birds of America " The Appendix to vol. VII contains a few species previously unpublished by the author, chiefly collected during a trip to the mouth of the Yellowstone in 1843.)

AUDUBON.—See LONDON, Loudon's Magazine, I, 1828, 115 ;—NEW YORK, Lyceum Nat. Hist.

BACHMAN, Rev. J.—See NEW HAVEN, Am. Jour. Science.

BAIRD, S. F.—See PHILADELPHIA, Academy of Natural Sciences ;—NEW HAVEN, American Journal of Science ;—GETTYSBURG, Pa , Literary Record and Journal ;—NEW YORK, Lyceum of Natural History ;—STANSBURY, Salt Lake Exped.

BAIRD, WM. M. & S. F.—See NEW HAVEN, Am. Jour. Sc ;—PHILADELPHIA, Academy of Nat. Sciences.

BARRERE, P.—Ornithologiae specimen novum ; sive series avium in Ruscinone, Pyrenaeis montibus, atque in Gallia aequinoxiali observatarum, in classes, genera et species, nova methodo digesta. 4to. Perpignan, 1745.

BARTON.—Fragments of the Natural History of Pennsylvania. By Benjamin Smith Barton, M. D. Part First : Philadelphia, 1799. Folio. (No more published. Consists chiefly of lists of birds of Pennsylvania, with dates of migration.)

BARTON, M. D., BENJ. SMITH.—See LONDON, Linnaean Society.

BARTRAM, JOHN.—Travels through North and South Carolina, Georgia, East and West Florida, etc. 8vo. Phila. 1791.

BARTRAM.—Reisen durch nord und sud Carolina, etc. Aus dem englischen. Mit erläuternden Anmerkungen, von C. A. W. Zimmermann. 8vo. Berlin. 1793. (Forming vol. X of " Magazin von merkwürdigen neuen Reisebeschreibungen, etc.") (Translation of preceding.)

BEAGLE, Zoology of.—See DARWIN.

BECHSTEIN, J. M.—Gemeinnützige Naturgeschichte Deutschlands, nach allen drei Reichen. 4 vols. 8vo. Leipzig. 1789, 1795. (Vols. II–IV on birds. 1791–1795. Several subsequent editions published.)

117 b

BELL, JNO. G.—See NEW YORK, Lyceum of Nat. Hist.

BENNETT, E. T.—The gardens and menagerie of the Zoological Society delineated. 2 vols. 8vo. II, Birds. London, 1835.

BERLIN.—Archiv für Naturgeschichte. Gegrundet von A. F. A. Wiegmann. Fortgesetzt von Erichson und Troschel.

 CABANIS.—Ornithologische Notizen. Von J. Cabanis. No. I, 1847, I, 202 ; No. II, Ib. 308.

  CABANIS.—Über die in Obercalifornien beobachteten Vögel. Von William Gambel. Mit Bemerkungen von J. Cabanis. 1848. I, 82.

BERLIN.—K. Akademie der Wissenschaften: Abhandlungen. 4to.

 LICHTENSTEIN.—Beitrag zur ornithologischen Fauna von Californien nebst Bemerkungen über die Artkennzeichen der Pelikane und über einige Vögel von den Sandwich-Inseln. Gelesen Juni 1837. Aus dem Jahre 1838, 1839, 417. (Falco (Buteo) ferrugineus, Strix frontalis, (new species.)

 MÜLLER, JOHANNES.—Ueber die bisher unbekannten typische Verschiedenheiten der Stimmorgane der Passerinen. Jahrg, 1845, 1847, 321.

BLACKWALL.—Researches in Zoology. London. 8vo.

BLASCHKE.—"Dissertatio inauguralis sistens topographiam medicam portus novarchangelcensis. St. Petersburg. 1842." (Quoted from Baer & Helmersen, who state that it contains a list of the birds of Russian America, prepared by Brandt.)

BLOSSOM, Zoology of.—The zoology of Captain Beechey's voyage : compiled from the collections and notes made by Captain Beechey, the officers and naturalists of the expedition, during a voyage to the Pacific and Behring's Straits, performed in his Majesty's ship Blossom, under the command of Captain F. W. BEECHEY in the years 1825–'28. 4to. London. 1839. (Birds by N. A. VIGORS.)

BODDAERT.—Table des planches enluminées d'histoire naturelle de M. d'Aubenton avec les denominations de MM. de Buffon, Brisson, Edwards, Linnaeus et Latham, precedé d'une notice des principaux ouvrages zoologiques enluminées. Par M. BODDAERT, Med. Doct. ancien conseiller de la ville de Flessingue, &c. Utrecht, 1783. (A manuscript copy of this very rare work is in the library of the Philadelphia Academy.

BOLLE.—See CASSEL.

BOLOGNA.—Annali delle scienze naturale.

 BONAPARTE.—Catalogo Metod. VIII, II. See BONAPARTE.

BONAPARTE.—American Ornithology, or the Natural History of the birds inhabiting the United States, not given by Wilson. With figures drawn, colored, and engraved from nature. By CHARLES LUCIEN BONAPARTE. Vol. 1, 1825 ; II, III, 1828 ; IV, 1833. 4 vols. 4to. New York.

BONAPARTE.—Observations on the nomenclature of Wilson's Ornithology. By CHARLES LUCIEN BONAPARTE. 8vo. Philadelphia. 1826. (Reprinted without paging from Journal of Philadelphia Academy of Natural Sciences, which see.)

BONAPARTE, C. L.—Specchio comparativo della ornitologia di Roma e di Filadelfia. 8vo. Pisa. Nistri, 1827.—Supplemento alla specchio comparativo, etc., 1832.

BONAPARTE, C. L.—Sulla seconda edizione del regno animali del Barone Cuvier, osservazione. 8vo. Bologna, Marsigli, 1830.

BONAPARTE, C. L.—Saggio di una distribuzione metodica degli animale vertebrati a sangue fredo. 8vo. Roma, Boulzaler, 1831, 1832. (Contains monographs of Numenius, Scolopax, &c.)

BONAPARTE, C. L.—A geographical and comparative list of the birds of Europe and North America. By C. L. BONAPARTE. 8vo. London, Van Voorst, 1838.

BONAPARTE, C. L.—Catalogo metodico degli Uccelli Europei. Di C. L. BONAPARTE. 8vo. Bologna, Marsigli, 1842. (Extracted from Annali delle Scienze Naturali di Bologna, VIII, II.)

BONAPARTE—Revue critique de l' ornithologie Européenne de M. le Docteur Degland, (de Lille.) Par CHARLES LUCIEN BONAPARTE. Lettre a M. De Sely's Longchamps. 12mo. Bruxelles, 1850.

BONAPARTE.—Conspectus generum Avium, auctore Carolo Luciano Bonaparte. 8vo. Lugduni Batavorum. Tom. I, 1850 ; Tom. II, 1857. (The signatures of tome I are all separately dated, from —— to Nov., 1850, and those of II from Oct., 1854, to May, 1856 ; the work breaking off abruptly in the account of the gulls.

BONAPARTE, C. L.—See PARIS, Ateneo Italiano : Academie des Sciences : Annales des Sc. Nat. : Comptes Rendus : Revue et Magazin de Zoologie ;—LONDON, Zoological Journal : Zoological Society ;—PHILADELPHIA, Academy of Natural Sciences : American Philosophical Society ;—NEW YORK, Lyceum of Natural History.

BONAPARTE, C. L.—Additional articles by Bonaparte, not quoted in the present volume, are to be found in Annali di Scienze Naturale, di Bologna 1838, on Trogon paradiseus, and Agrilorhinus sittaceus ; on birds of Bogota, in Atti della Riunione degli scienziati Italiani, in Milano, 1844 ; on Falco eleonorae, in ditto, of Turin ; on Querquedula angustirostris, and new European birds, in ditto, of Florence ; on rectifications of European Ornithology, in ditto, of Lucca, etc.

BONAPARTE ET SCHLEGEL.—Monographie des Loxiens, par CH. L. BONAPARTE et H. SCHLEGEL. 4to. Leiden et Düsseldorf, 1850.

Boston.—American Academy of Arts and Sciences: Memoirs. 4to.

NUTTALL, THOS.—Remarks and inquiries concerning the birds of Massachusetts. New series, I, 1833, 91.

Boston.—Boston Society of Natural History: Boston Journal of Natural History, containing papers and communications read to the Boston Society of Natural History. 8vo. Vol. I, 1834—1837, *et seq.*

BREWER, T. M.- Remarks on the position assumed by George Ord, esq., in relation to the Cow Blackbird, in Loudon's Magazine for 1836. I. IV, May, 1837, 418.

BREWER, T. M.—Some additions to the catalogue of the birds of Massachusetts in Prof. Hitchcock's report, etc. I, 1837, 435.

BREWER, M. D., THOMAS M.—A few ornithological facts gathered in a hasty trip through portions of New Brunswick and Nova Scotia, in June, 1850. VI, April, 1852, 297.

BREWER, M. D., THOMAS M.—Notice of the egg of *Thalassidroma leachii*, with descriptions of the eggs of *Procellaria bulwerii, Procellaria obscura*, and *Puffinus major.* VI, 1852, 308.

CABOT, JR., SAMUEL.—Observations on the plumage of the red and mottled owls. (*Strix asio.*) II, I, February, 1838, 126.

CABOT, JR., M. D., SAMUEL.—Observations on the character and habits of the ocillated turkey. (*Meleagris occellata.*—CUV.) IV, September, 1842, 246. (Gives 18 feathers to the tail, and says there is no pectoral tuft.)

CABOT, JR., M. D, SAMUEL.—Description and habits of some of the birds of Yucatan. IV, January, 1844, 460. Further account of the same. V, Jan., 1845, 90.

CABOT, JR., M. D., SAMUEL.—Description of *Pyranga roseogularis.* V, June, 1846, 416.

CABOT, JR., M. D., SAMUEL.—The dodo (*Didus ineptus,*) a rasorial and not a rapacious bird. V, Dec., 1847, 490.

GUNDLACH, JOHN.—Description of five new species of birds, and other notes of Cuban species. VI, April, 1842, 313. (*Muscicapa sagrae, lembeyii, Orpheus saturninus, Corvus minutus, Columba caniceps.*)

PEABODY, REV. W. B. O —A report on the birds of Massachusetts, made to the legislature in the session of 1838-'39. III, January, 1840, 65. (Same as that in the State report.)

Boston.—Society of Natural History, Continued: Proceedings of the Boston Society of Natural History. Vol. I, 1841 to 1844, *et seq.*

AGASSIZ.—Observations on the structure of the foot in the embryo of birds. By Prof. AGASSIZ. III, May 3, 1848, 42.

BREWER.—Facts tending to clear up the confusion and errors in the history of the Hermit Thrush, (*Turdus solitarius.*) By Dr. BREWER. I, July 17, 1844, 170.

BREWER.—Observations on the appearance of the Cliff Swallow, (*Hirundo lunifrons,*) giving data of its appearance in New England. By Dr. T. M. BREWER. IV, Nov. 17, 1852, 270.

BREWER.—List of birds found both in Europe and America, sometimes confounded from close resemblances. By T. M. BREWER. IV, April 6, 1853, 324.

BRYANT.—Remarks on the Sandhill Crane. By Dr. BRYANT. IV, Feb. 3, 1853, 303.

CABOT.—Remarks on the *Meleagris ocellata.* By Dr. CABOT. I, July 6, 1842, 73.

CABOT.—Observations on the birds common to Central America and the United States, with a memoir on the Paraguay Guan, or *Phasianus motmot.* By Dr. CABOT. I, July 20, 1842, 76.

CABOT.—Remarks on the wild turkey. By Dr. CABOT. I, August 17, 1842, 80.

CABOT.—Remarks on a species of *Ortyx* discovered by him in Yucatan, (*Ortyx nigrogularis.*) By Dr. CABOT. I, Nov. 1, 1843, 151,

CABOT.—Remarks on birds from Yucatan, which he regarded as new. (*Corvus vociferus, Oriolus musicus, Momotus yucatensis.*) By Dr. SAMUEL CABOT. I, November 15, 1843, 155.

CABOT.—Descriptions of three new species of woodpecker from Yucatan. *Picus dubius, P. parvus, P. yucatanensis.* By Dr. CABOT. I, January 3, 1844, 164.

CABOT.—Observations concerning the supposed identity of *Anas penelope* and *Anas americana,* the European and American widgeons. By Dr CABOT. II, March 18, 1846, 118.

CABOT.—Remarks on the *Tetrao cupido.* By Dr. CABOT. II, March 18, 1846, 120.

CABOT.—Description of a specimen of *Pyranga.* By Dr. CABOT. (*Pyranga roseo-gularis.*) II, December 2, 1846, 187.

CABOT.—Comparison between *Sterna cantiaca* of Europe and *Sturna acuflavida,* nobis, hitherto considered identical with *S. cantiaca.* By Dr. S. CABOT. II, November 17, 1847, 257.

CABOT —Description of a new species of wren, under the name of *Troglodytes albinucha.* By Dr. S. CABOT. II, November 17, 1847, 257.

CABOT.—Statement of the comparative measurements of the American and European oyster catcher.   By Dr. S. CABOT.   III, July 7, 1848, 43.

CABOT.—Observations upon the recent appearance in New England of *Ibis guarauna*.   By Dr. CABOT.   III, June 19, 1850, 313.

CABOT, jr., Dr. S —On the occurrence of *Erismatura dominica* at Alberg Springs, Lake Champlain, September 26, 1857.   VI, May, 1858, 375.

BOURCIER.—See LYONS ;—PARIS, Revue Zoologique, 1839, 294.

BOURCIER ET MULSANT.— See LYONS.

BRANDT.—Descriptiones et icones animalium Rossicorum novorum vel minus rite cognitorum.—Auctore J. F. Brandt.—Aves, fasc. 1.   4to.   Petropoli.   1836.

BRANDT.—See BLASCHKE ;—ST. PETERSBURG.

BREHM, C. L.—Lehrbuch der Naturgeschichte aller europ. Vögel. 2 Theile.   8vo.   Jena, Schmid, 1823.

BREHM, C. L.—Handbuch der Naturgeschichte aller Vögel Deutschlands, worin nach den sorgfältigsten Untersuchungen und den genauesten Beobachtungen mehr als 900 einheimische Vögel-Gattungen zur Begrundung einer ganz neuen Ansicht und Behandlung ihrer Naturgeschichte vollständig beschrieben sind.   8vo.   Ilmenau, 1831.

BREHM, C. L.--See CASSEL, Cabanis Journal.

BREWER, Dr. T. M.—See BOSTON, Society of Nat. Hist.: Proc. and Journal ;—NEW HAVEN, Am. Jour. Sc. ;—WASHINGTON, Smithsonian Institution.

BREWER, ed. Wilson —See WILSON.

BRISSON, M. J.—Ornithologia, sive synopsis methodica sistens avium divisionem in ordines, sectiones, genera, species, ipsarum varietates.   Cum accurata cujusque speciei descriptione, citationibus auctorum de iis tractantum, nominibus eis ab ipsis et nationibus impositis, nominibusque vulgaribus.   6 vols. 4to. et supplementum.   Paris, 1760.

BRISSON, M. J.—Ornithologia, etc.   2 vols.   8vo.   Lugduni-Batavorum, 1763.   (This is the Latin text of the preceding work reprinted separately.   A second edition was published in 4to at Paris, 1788.)

BROWNE, PATRICK.—The civil and natural history of Jamaica, in III parts, with fifty copper plates.   Folio.   London, 1756.—Second edition with complete Linnaean index and a map of Jamaica.   London, 1789.

BRUCH.—See CASSEL.

BRÜNNICH, M. T.—Ornithologia borealis, sistens collectionem avium ex omnibus imperio danico subjectis provinciis insulisque borealibus Hafniae factam, etc.   8vo.   Hafniae, 1764.

BRYANT, Dr. H.—See BOSTON, Society of Nat. Hist.: Proceedings.

BUFFON.—Histoire naturelle des oiseaux.   Par Geo. Louis Leclerc compte de Buffon, de Montbeillard, (et l'abbe Bexon.)   10 vols.   4to.   Avec 1008 Pl. color.   Paris 1770–86.   (The plates were published separately, under the title of Planches enluminées.)

BUFFON ET D'AUBENTON.—Figurarum avium coloratarum nomina systematica collegit H. Kuhl.   Edidit praefatione et indicibus auxit T. Van Swinderen.   4to.   Groningen, Oomkens, 1820.

BURMEISTER.—Systematische Uebersicht der Thiere Brasiliens, welche während einer Reise durch die Provinzen von Rio de Janeiro und Minas Geraes gesammelt oder beobachtet wurden von Dr. Heermann Burmeister, Prof., etc.   Zweiter Theil. Vögel, I, II.   8vo.   Berlin, G. Reimer, 1856.

BURMEISTER, H.—See NITZSCH.

CABOT, Dr. S.—See BOSTON, Society of Nat. Hist.: Proceedings and Journal.

CABANIS.—Museum Heineanum.   Verzeichniss der ornithologischen Sammlung des Oberamtmann Ferdinand Heine, auf Gut St. Burchard vor Halberstadt.   Mit kritischen Anmerkungen und Beschreibung der neuen Arten, systematisch bearbeitet von Dr. JEAN CABANIS.   I Theil. die Singvögel (*Oscines*) enthaltend.   Halberstadt, 8vo.   1850–'51.   (This work appears to have been published a few signatures at a time, the first of which had the date of publication attached.)

CABANIS, Dr. J.—See CASSEL, Journal für Ornithologie ;—SCHOMBURGK'S Reise ;—TSCHUDI, Fauna Peruana ;—BERLIN, Wiegmann's Archiv.

CASSEL.—Journal für Ornithologie.   Ein Centralorgan für die gesammnten Ornithologie, zugleich Organ der deutschen Ornithologen Gesellschaft.   Herausgegeben von Dr. JEAN CABANIS.   8vo.   Cassel.   Vol. I, 1853, *et seq*.

BOLLE.—Der californische Condor, *Sarcorhamphus californianus*.   Von Dr. CARL BOLLE.   V, 1857, 50.   (Translation of article of A. S. Taylor, of Monterey, Cal., in "Zoologist," 1855.

BREHM.—Der grosse Würger (*Lanius excubitor L.*) und einige seiner Verwandten.   Von Pastor CH. L. BREHM.   II, 1854, 143.   (Notice of *Lanius ludovicianus and mexicanus*.)

BRUCH.—Monographische Ubersicht der Gattung *Larus*.   Von Dr. BRUCH.   I, 1853, 96.

BRUCH.—Revision der gattung *Larus*, Lin. Von Notar L. BRUCH. III, 1855, 273. Nachtrag, V, 1857, 23. Zweiter Nachtrag, V, 1857, 113.

CABANIS.—See GUNDLACH.

GÄTKE.—Der Weg der nordamericanische Vögel nach Europa. Von HEINRICH GÄTKE. IV, 1856, 70.

GUNDLACH.—Dr. J. GUNDLACH's Beiträge zur Ornithologie Cuba's. Nach Mittheilungen an Hrn. Bez. Dir. Sezekorn. Von Herausgeber, Dr. J. CABANIS. II, 1854, Erinnerungschrift, lxxvii. First article. Succeeding ones in III, 1855, 465 ; IV, 1856, 1, 97, 337, 417 ; V, 1857, 225.

HARTLAUB.—Revision der Gattung *Fulica*. Von Dr. G. HARTLAUB. I, 1853, Extraheft, 1854, 73.

HARTLAUB.—Beiträge zur exotische Ornithologie. Von Dr. G. HARTLAUB. II, 1854, 409. (Notices of N. American *Cuculidae.*

HARTLAUB.—Ueber *Tetrao falcipennis.* Nov. sp. Von Dr. G. HARTLAUB. III, Jan 1855, 39.

HARTLAUB —Beiträge zur exotischen Ornithologie. Von Dr. G. HARTLAUB. III, 1855, 97. (Notice of. *Fulica americana.*

HARTLAUB.—Ueber *Grus hoyanus*, Dudl. Von Dr. G. HARTLAUB. III, 1855, 317.

HARTLAUB.—Index zu PUCHERAN's "Etudes sur les types peu connus du Musée de Paris," in GUERIN's Revue et Magazin de Zoologie. Von Dr. G. HARTLAUB. III, 1855, 417.

MALHERBE.—Nouvelles espèces de Picidae, par M. ALFRED MALHERBE. II, 1854, 171. (*Picus nataliae.*)

MÖSCHLER.—Notiz zur Ornithologie Grönlands. Von H. F. MÖSCHLER. IV, 1856, 335.

MÜLLER.—Einige Notizen über die Vögel des hochsten Nordens von Amerika. Von Baron Dr. J. W. VON MÜLLER. IV, 1856, 304.

MÜLLER.—Notizen über einige Ornithologen, Sammler, und wissenschaftlische Anstalten in den vereinigten Staaten. Von Baron Dr. J. W. VON MÜLLER. IV, 1856, 306.

REICHENBACH.—Aufzählung der Colibris oder Trochilideen ; ihre Verwandtschaft und Synonymik. Von Hofr. Dr. LUDW. REICHENBACH. I, Extraheft, 1853, 1854. (Besondere Beilage.)

REINHARDT.—Eemerkungen zur Ornithclogie Grönlands, von J. REINHARDT, Uebersetzt von Dr. GLOGER. III, 1854, 423.

SUNDEVALL.—Ueber die Flügel der Vögel. Von. C. J. SUNDEVALL. III, 1855, 118. (Translated from Kongl. Vet. Akademiens Handlingar, 1843, 303.)

THIENEMANN.—Ueber die von Dr. GUNDLACH eingesendeten Eier und Nester cubanischer Vögel. Von Dr. F. A. L. THIENEMANN, in Dresden. V. 1857, 145.

WIED.—Ueber den nordamerikanischen rothköpfigen Urubu, (*Cathartes aura.*) Von MAX PRINZ von WIED. IV, 1856, 119.

WIED.—Ueber die nordamerikanische Elster, (*Pica hudsonica.*) Von MAX PRINZ von WIED. IV, 1856, 197.

WIED.—Ueber den Papagei von Nord America. *Psittacus* (*Conurus*) *carolinensis* Lin. Von MAX PRINZ von WIED. V, 1857, 97.

WIED.—Verzeichniss der Vögel welche auf einer Reise in Nord America beobachtet wurden. Von MAX PRINZ von WIED. VI, 1858, 1 *et seq.*

CASSIN, JOHN.—Illustrations of the birds of California, Texas, Oregon, British and Russian America. Intended to contain descriptions and figures of all North American birds not given by former American authors, and a general synopsis of North American ornithology. By JOHN CASSIN. 8vo. (First series.) 1853–1855. Philadelphia. J. B. LIPPINCOTT & Co. 1856. (Fifty plates of unfigured species. Published in ten numbers.)

CASSIN, J.—See GILLISS, U. S. Naval Ast. Exp ;—PHILADELPHIA, Academy of Nat. Sciences ;—NEW YORK, United States Magazine ;—PERRY, Japan Expd.;—WILKES, U. S. Ex. Expd.

CATESBY, MARK.—The natural history of Carolina, Florida, and the Bahama islands. 2 volumes, folio, and appendix. London, 1731, 1743, 1748. New edition, by GEO. EDWARDS. London, 1754. Third edition, revised by EDWARDS, with Linnæan index of the animals and plants. 2 vols. London, 1771.

CLAYTON, P.—See LONDON, Philosophical Transactions.

CLINTON, DEWITT.—See NEW YORK, Lyceum Nat. Hist.

COLLIE.—See LONDON, Zool. Soc. Proceedings Comm. Sc. and Correspondence.

COPENHAGEN.—Naturhistorisk Tidskrift udgivet af H. KRÖYER. 8vo. 1837, *et seq.* See also KJÖBENHAVN.

COUCH, LIEUT. D. N.—See PHILADELPHIA, Acad. Nat. Sciences : Proceedings.

COX, J. C.—See LONDON, Zool. Soc. : Proceedings.

CUVIER, GEO.—Tableau élémentaire de l'histoire naturelle des animaux. Paris, Bailliere, 1798.

CUVIER, GEO.—Leçons d'anatomie comparée recueilles et publiées sous ses yeux, par G. DUMERIL et G. L. DUVERNOY. 5 vols. 8vo. Paris, 1800, 1805.

Cuvier, Geo.—Le règne animal, distribue d'apres son organisation, pour servir de base à l'histoire naturelle des animaux et d'introduction a l'anatomie comparée. 4 vols. 8vo. Paris, 1817.

Darwin, C —The zoology of the voyage of H. M. S. Beagle, under the command of Captain Fitzroy, during the years 1832 and 1836. Edited and superintended by Charles Darwin. 1840–'44.

Gould, J.—Birds, by John Gould. With a notice of their habits and ranges, by Charles Darwin.

Daudin, F. M.—Traité élémentaire et complet d'ornithologie, ou histoire naturelle des oiseaux. 2 vols. 4to. Paris, 1799, 1800.

Degland.—Ornithologie européenne ou catalogue analytique et raisonné des oiseaux observès en Europe. Par C. D. Degland. 2 vols. 8vo. Paris et Lille, 1849.

De la Llave.—See Mexico, Registro trimestre.

Desmarest, A. G.—Histoire naturelle des tangaras, des manakins et des todiers, etc. 2 vols., folio. Paris, 1805.

Des Murs, O.—Iconographie ornithologique, etc. 4to. Paris, 1845, et seq.

Deville.—See Paris, Revue et Magasin, 1852.

Donovan, Ed.—Natural history of British birds. A selection of the most rare, beautiful, and interesting birds which inhabit this country. 11 vols. 8vo. London, 1794, 1818.

Donovan.—See London, Naturalists' Repository.

Doughty, J. & T.—A Cabinet of Natural History and American rural sports. 3 vols, 4to. Philadelphia, 1830–33.

Douglas, David.—See London, Linnæan Society : Zoological Journal.

Dubus, B.—Esquisses ornithologiques : descriptions et figures d'oiseaux nouveaux ou peu connues. 4to. Bruxelles, 1845, et seq.

Dubus, B —See Bruxelles, Academie : Bulletin XIV, 1847, 104 ; XXII, 1.

Dudley, W.—See Philadelphia, Academy of Natural Sciences.

Duméril, A. M. C.—Zoologie analytique, ou méthode naturelle de classification des animaux, rendue plus facile a l'aide de tableaux synoptiques. 8vo. Paris, 1806.

Dumont.—See Paris : Dictionnaire des Sciences Naturelles.

Dupetit-Thouars.—Voyage autour du monde sur la frégate la Venus pendant les années 1836, 1837. Text in 8vo., atlas in folio. (The atlas of Zoology was published in 18—. The volume on Zoology of Vertebrata, in 8vo., did not appear until 1855. The Ornithological portion was prepared by MM. H. Prevost and O. Des Murs.)

Edwards, Geo.—A natural history of uncommon birds, and of some other rare and non-described animals, &c. In 4 parts, 4to. London, 1743–'51.

Edwards, Geo.—Gleanings of natural history, exhibiting figures of quadrupeds, birds, insects, plants, &c. 3 parts, 4to. London, 1758–'60–'64.

Edwards, Geo. and Catesby.—Sammlung verschied. ausländ. und seltener Vögel, worinnen ein jeder derselben nicht nur aufs Genaueste beschrieben, sondern auch in einer richtigen und sauber illum. Abbildungen vorgestellet wird. Nach dem engl. Von J. M. Seligmann. 9 vols., folio. Nürnberg, 1749—'76.

Eydoux, Zool. of Favorite.—See Laplace.

Eyton, T. C.—A history of the rarer British birds, containing descriptions of all the species discovered since the time of Bewick. 8vo. London : Longman & Co. ; 1836.

Eyton, T. C.—A monograph of the Anatidæ or duck tribe, including the geese and swans. 4to. London : Longman & Co. ; 1838.

Faber, Fr.—Prodromus der isländ. Ornithologie, oder Geschichte der Vögel Islands. 8vo. Kopenhagen, 1822.

Fabricius, O.—Fauna Groenlandiae, systematice sistens animalia Groenlandiae occidentalis hactenus indagata, &c. 8vo. Hafniæ et Lipsiae, 1780.

Feuillee, L.—Journal des observation physiques, mathematiques, et botaniques, faites par l'ordre du roi sur les côtes orientales de l'Amerique meridionale, et dans les Indes occidentales, depuis l'année 1707, jusques en 1712. 3 vols. 4to. Paris, 1714, 25.

Fleming, J.—A History of British Animals, exhibiting the descriptive characters and systematical arrangement of the genera and species of quadrupeds, birds, reptiles, fishes, mollusca, and radiata of the United Kingdom, &c. 8vo. Edinburg, 1828.

Fleming, J.—Philosophy of Zoology ; or a general view of the structure, functions, and classification of animals. 2 vols. 8vo. Edinburg, 1822.

Forster, J. R.—A catalogue of the animals of North America, &c. Pamphlet, 8vo. London, 1771.

Forster, J. R.—See London, Royal Society : Philosophical Transactions, LXII, 1772.

FORSTER, J. R.—Descriptiones animalium in itinere ad maris Australis terras, per annos 1772–74, suscepto observatorum, edidit H. LICHTENSTEIN. 8vo. Berlin, 1844.

FOX, CHAS.—See NEW HAVEN, Am. Jour. Sc.

FRANKFORT A. M.—Senckenbergische Gesellschaft: Museum Senckenbergianum.

RÜPPELL, E.—Ueber eine neue Gattung von Vögeln die mit *Corvus* verwandt sind, in den mexicanischen Provinzen lebend. (*Psilorhinus mexicanus*.) II, 1837, 187.

GÄTKE, H.—See CASSEL, Journal für Orn.

GAMBEL, W.—See PHILADELPHIA, Acad. Nat. Sciences: Proceedings and Journal.

GAY, CLAUDE.—Historia fisica y politica de Chile segun documentas adquiredos en esta republica durante doze años de residencia en ella. 8vo. Atlas in folio. Zoologia, 5 vols. I, 1847 ; II, 1848. (Containing birds.)

GETTYSBURG.—Linnaean Association of Pennsylvania College: The literary record and journal of, etc. 8vo.

BAIRD, S. F.—Catalogue of birds found in the neighborhood of Carlisle, Cumberland county, Penn. I. XII. Oct., 1845, 249.

GILLIS, U. S. N., Lt. J. M.—The U. S. Naval Astronomical Expedition to the Southern Hemisphere. 6 vols, 4to. Wash-ington. (Vol. 2 containing the Natural History published in 1855.)

CASSIN, JOHN.—(Report on the) birds (of Chile.) p. 172.

GIRAUD, JR., J. P.—A description of sixteen new species of North American birds, described in the annals of the New York Lyceum of Natural History. By JACOB P. GIRAUD, jr. Collected in Texas in 1838. Folio., New York, 1841. (These species were not published in the annals of the Lyceum. They were probably collected some distance, at least, south of the Rio Grande, the present southern boundary of Texas)

GIRAUD.— The birds of Long Island. By J. P. GIRAUD, jr. 8vo. New York, 1844.

GIRAUD, J. P.—See NEW YORK, Lyceum Nat. Hist.

GLOGER, C. L.—Vollständ. Handbuch der Naturgeschichte der Vögel Europas, mit besond. Rücksicht auf Deutschland. Erster Theil, die deutschen Landvögel enthaltend. 6 Hefte. 8vo. Breslau, 1834.

GLOGER.—See CASSEL, Journal für Ornithol.

GMELIN, J. F.—Systema naturæ, etc. ed. XIII, 1788–1793.—See LINNAEUS.

GMELIN, SAM. GEO.—Reise durch Russland zur Untersuchung der drey Natur-Reiche. Mit einer Vorrede herausgegeben von Pallas. 4 Theile, 4to. St. Petersburg, kais. Acad. der Wissenschaften, 1770–1774.

GOSSE.—The birds of Jamaica. By PHILIP HENRY GOSSE. 8vo. London, 1847.

GOSSE, PHILIP HENRY.—Illustrations of the birds of Jamaica. 8vo. London, 1849.

GOULD, J.—The birds of Europe. In 5 vols., comprising 449 beautifully colored figures, with descriptive letter-press. Imp. folio. London, 1832–1837.

GOULD, J.—A monograph of the *Trogonidae*, or family of Trogons: 36 species. Three parts in one vol., folio, with descrip. tive letter-press. London, 1838.

GOULD, J.—Icones avium, or figures and descriptions of new and interesting species of birds from various parts of the globe Parts I, II. Folio. London, 1837.

GOULD, J.—A monograph of the *Odontophorinae* or partridges of America. Folio. London, 1850.

GOULD, J.—A monograph of the *Trochilidae* or Humming birds. Folio. Part I, Jan., 1850, *et seq.*

GOULD, JOHN.—See LONDON, Zool. Soc. Proc. Comm. Sc. and Proceedings ;—DARWIN.

GRAY, G. R.—The genera of birds, comprising their generic characters, a notice of the habits of each genus, and an extensive list of species referred to their several genera. By GEORGE ROBERT GRAY, F. L. S. Illustrated by DAVID WILLIAM MITCHELL, B. A., F. L. S. 3 vols. Folio. London, 1844–49.

GRAY, G. R.—A list of the genera of birds, with their synonyms, and an indication of the typical species of each genus. By GEORGE ROBERT GRAY. Second edition, revised, augmented, and accompanied with an index. 8vo. London, 1841. With an appendix, 1842. (First edition published in 1840.)

GRAY, G. R.—Catalogue of the genera and sub-genera of birds contained in the British Museum. By GEORGE ROBERT GRAY. 16mo. London, 1855. (In series of British Museum catalogues)

GRAY, G. R.—See LONDON, Zool. Soc.: Proceedings.

GREEN, JACOB.—See NEW HAVEN, Am. Jour. Sc.

GUNDLACH, Dr. J. Birds of Cuba.—See CASSEL, Cabanis Journal für Ornithologie ;—NEW YORK, Lyceum of Natural History ;—BOSTON, Society of Natural History ;—LEMBEYE, Aves de la isla de Cuba.

GUTHRIE'S Geog.—A universal geography, or a view of the present state of the known world. Originally compiled by WILLIAM GUTHRIE, Esq., the astronomical part by JAMES FERGUSON. Second American edition. 2 vols. 8vo. Philadelphia, 1815. (This edition contains a list of North American birds by George Ord.)

HALDEMAN, S. S.—See PHILADELHIA, Acad. Nat. Sciences : Proceedings.

HARRIS, Ed.—See PHILADELPHIA, Acad. Nat. Sciences : Proceedings.

HARTLAUB.—See CASSEL;—PARIS, Rev. Zool.

HAYMOND, R —See PHILADELPHIA, Acad. Nat. Sciences : Proceedings.

HEERMANN, Dr. A. L —See PHILADELPHIA, Academy of Nat. Sciences.

HENRY, M. D , T. C.—See PHILADELPHIA, Acad. Nat. Sciences : Proceedings.

HERBERT.—Frank Forester's Field Sports of the United States and British Provinces of North America. By HENRY WILLIAM
HERBERT. Sixth edition, 2 volumes, 8vo. New York. (There is no date given for this edition, but the copyright is
entered 1848. The article on *Fuligula bimaculata*, from a note in II, 112, seems to have been added to the third
edition.)

H LL, R.—See LONDON, Zool. Soc.: Proceedings.

HOLBÖLL, CARL —Ornithologischer Beitrag zur Fauna Grönlands, von CARL HOLBÖLL. Ubersetzt und mit einem Anhang
versehen ; von J. H. Paulsen. 8vo. Leipsic, 1846.

HOY, Dr. P. R.—See MADISON, Wisconsin State Ag. Trans.;—PHILADELPHIA, Acad. Nat. Sciences.

HUMPHREYS.—Museum Calonnianum, Specification of the various articles which compose the magnificent Museum of
Natural History collected by M. De Calonne in France, and lately his property. Consisting of an assemblage of the most
beautiful and rare subjects in Entomology, Conchology, Ornithology, Mineralogy, &c. London, May 1, 1797. Sold by
George Humphrey, dealer in shells, minerals, &c., No. 4, Leicester street, Leicester square. Price 3s. 6d., corrected. (Contains first use of name *Sylvicola* for a genus of shells.)

HUTCHINGS' California Magazine.—See SAN FRANCISCO.

ILLIGER.—Caroli Illigeri D. Prodromus systematis mammalium et avium, additis terminis zoographicis utriusque classis,
eorumque versione germanica. 12mo. Berlin, 1811. (Introduction dated April, 1811)

ILLINOIS STATE Ag. Soc.—See SPRINGFILD.

JACQUIN.—Beiträge zur Geschichte der Vögel. Herausg, von J. F. E. von Jacquin. 4to. Wien, 1784.

JAMESON, ed. Wilson.—See WILSON and BONAPARTE.

JARDINE, Sir W.—The Naturalist's Library, conducted by Sir Wm. Jardine. 40 vols. 12mo. London and Edinburg,
1834-1843.

    JARDINE, Sir Wm.—Humming Birds. Ornithology, Vol. I, II. 1833.

    JARDINE, Sir Wm.—Gallinaceous bids. 2 vols. Ornithology. Vol. III, IV. 1834.

    JARDINE, Sir Wm.—History of birds of Great Britain and Ireland. By Sir Wm. JARDINE, I, 1837 : II, 1839, II,
1842, IV, 1843. Vols, 20, 24, 34, 40, of the series.

    SELBY, P. J.—Natural History of *Columbidae*. (Pigeons.) By P. J. SELBY. 1 vol. (Vol. 9 of the series.)

    SWAINSON, W.—History of fly-catchers : their natural arrangement and relations. 1 vol. (No. 21.) 1838.
Vol. 10 of Ornithological series.

JARDINE's ed. Wilson.—See WILSON.

JARDINE (WILL.) & SELBY, (P. J.)—Illustrations of Ornithology. Vols. I–III. 4to. Edinburg, 1825–1839. Vol. IV.
New series. 1843.

JENYNS, Rev. L.—A manual of British vertebrate animals, or descriptions of all the animals belonging to the classes Mammalia, Aves, Reptilia, and Pisces, which have been hitherto observed in the British Islands, etc. 8vo. Cambridge, 1835.

JONES, M. D., W. L.—See NEW YORK, Lyceum Nat. Hist.

JOURNAL FÜR ORNITHOLOGIE.—See CASSEL.

JOURNAL DE PHYSIQUE.—See PARIS.

KALM, PETER.—En resa til Nord America. 3 Deele. 8vo. Stockholm, 1753, 1756, 1761. (A German translation published 1754-1764.)

KAUP, J. J.—Skizzirte Entwickelungs—Geschichte u. natürl. System der europ. Thierwelt. 1 Theil, welcher die
Vögelsäugthiere u. Vögel, nebst Andeutung der Entstehung der letztern aus Amphibien enthält. 8vo. Darmstadt, 1829.

KAUP, Dr.—See LONDON, Zool. Soc.: Proceedings.

KENNERLY, Dr. C. B —See PHILADELPHIA, Acad. Nat. Sciences : Proceedings.

KENNICOTT, R.—See SPRINGFIELD, Ill. State Agric. Soc.: Transactions.

KEYSERLING & BLASIUS —Die Wirbelthiere Europas von A. Graf KEYSERLING und Professor J. H. BLASIUS. Erstes Buch :
die unterscheidenden Charactere. 8vo. Braunschweig, 1840. (Introduction dated October, 1839.)

KING, Capt. Phillip Parker.—See LONDON, Zoological Journal, IV, 1828.

KIRTLAND, M. D., J. P.—See OHIO, Geological Survey;—NEW HAVEN, Am. Jour. Sc.

KITTLITZ, F. H. von.—Kupfertafeln zur Naturgeschichte der Vögel, I-III. 8vo. Frankfort-a-M. 1832, 1833.

KJÖBENHAVN.—Naturhistoriske Forening: Videnskabelige Meddelelser für Aaret, 1853. 8vo. 1854.

REINHARDT.—Notitser til Grönlands Ornithologie, af J. REINHARDT. (Read Dec. 21, 1853,) III and IV, 69.

KOCH.—See BERLIN, Wiegmann's Archiv, 1836.

KÖRNER, M.—Skandinaviska Foglar tecknade efter naturen lithografierade, tryckte och utgifne af M. KÖRNER. 1–9 Häftet. 4to. Lund., 1839-1843.

KRÖYER, Tidskrift.—See COPENHAGEN.

KUHL, H.—Beiträge zur Zoologie und vergleichende Anatomie. 4to. Frankfort-a-M. 1820.

KUHL, H.—Conspectus psittacorum cum specierum definitionibus, synonymis et circa patriam singularum naturalem adversariis, adjecto indice museorum, etc. 4to. Bologna, 1820. (Extracted from the Nova Acta Acad. Leop. Carol. X.)

KUHL.—See BUFFON.

LAFRESNAYE.—See PARIS, Revue Zoologique.

LAPLACE.—Voyage autour du monde par les mers de l'Inde et de Chine, exécuté sur la corvette de S. M. la Favorite. Tome V, Histoire Naturelle, 8vo. Paris, 1839. Zoologie par F. EYDOUX.

LATHAM, J.—A natural history or general synopsis of birds, 6 vols.; supplement, 2 vols; Index ornithologicus, 2 vols.; 10 vols. 4to. London, 1781–1802. (A second edition, published in 11 vols., 1821–1828, under title of General History of Birds, etc.

LATHAM, J.—Index ornithologicus, sive systema ornithologiae, etc. 2 vols. 4to. London, 1790. Supplement, 1802.

LATHAM, J.—Index to the general history of birds. 4to. 1828.

LATHAM, J.—Systema ornithologiae, sive index ornithologicus complectens avium divisiones in ordines, etc., curis et opera Elizii Johanneau. 12 mo. Paris, 1809.

LAWRENCE, GEO. N.—See NEW YORK, Lyceum Nat. Hist.

LEACH, WM. E.—Systematic catalogue of the specimens of the indigenous mammalia and birds that are preserved in the British Museum, with their localities and authorities, etc. 4to. London, 1816.

LEACH, W. E.—See LONDON, Zoological Miscellany.

LECONTE, JOHN—See PHILADELPHIA, Acad Nat. Sciences: Proceedings.

LEIB, Dr. GEO. C.—See PHILADELPHIA, Acad. Nat. Sciences: Journal.

LEIPZIG.—Isis von Oken. 4to. Brockhaus.

  BOIE, F.—Ueber Classification insonderheit der europäischen Vögel. 1822, 545.

  BOIE, F.—Generalübersicht der ornithologischen Ordnungen, Familien und Gattungen. 1826, 969.

  BOIE, F.—Bemerkungen über mehrere neue Vögelgattungen. 1828, 312.

  BOIE, F.—Ueber Species und einige ornithologesche Familien und Sippen. 1831, 538.

  KAUP, J.—Saurothera mexicana, eine neue Art aus Mexico. 1832, 991.

  STREUBEL, A. B.—Die Cypseliden des Berliner Museums. 1848, 348. (Pseudoprocne, 357.)

  WAGLER, J.—Beiträge und Bemerkungen zu dem ersten Bande seines Systema avium. 1829, 505, 645, 736.

  WAGLER, J.—Revisio generis Penelope. 1830, 1109.

  WAGLER, J.—Einige Mittheilungen über Thiere Mexicos. 1831, 510. (Aves, 515.)

  WAGLER, J.—Mittheilungen über einige merkwürdige Thiere. 1832, 275.

  WAGLER, J.—Neue Sippen und Gattungen der Säugthiere und Vögel. 1832, 1218. (Vögel, 1221.)

LEMBEYE, J.—Aves de la isla de Cuba. Par JUAN LEMBEYE. 8vo. Habana, 1850. (Plates taken chiefly from Audubon.)

LESSON, R. P.—Manuel d'Ornithologie ou description des genres et des principales espèces d'oiseaux. 2 vols. 18mo. Paris, 1829.

LESSON, R. P.—Traité d'ornithologie ou description des oiseaux réunis dans les principales collections de France. 2 vols 8vo. Paris, 1831.

LESSON, R. P.—Histoire naturelle des colibris, etc. 1 vol. 8vo. Paris, 1831, 32.

LESSON, R. P.—Les trochilidés, ou les colibris et les oiseaux-mouches, etc. 1 vol. 8vo. Paris, 1832, 33.

LESSON, R P.—See PARIS, Ann. du Mus. 1835, 121.

LEWIS & CLARK.—History of the expedition under the command of Captains Lewis and Clark to the sources of the Missouri; thence across the Rocky mountains, and down the River Columbia to the Pacific ocean. Performed during the years 1804, '5, '6, by order of the government of the United States. 2 vols. 8vo. Philadelphia, 1814.

LINNAEUS, C.—Systema naturae, sive regna tria naturae systematice proposita per classes, ordines, genera, et species. Editio I. Folio. Lugduno-Batav. 1735. IDEM. ed. VI, 1748, Holmiae. IDEM. ed. X, Holmiae, 1758. IDEM. ed. XII, 1766o (The last edition is the one usually quoted,)

LINNAEUS, C.—Fauna Suecica sistens animalia Sueciae regni, etc. 8vo. Stockholm, 1746.

LINNAEUS, C.—See STOCKHOLM, Kongliga Vetenskaps Akademien.

LINSLEY, REV. J. H.—See NEW HAVEN, Ct. Am. Jour. Sc.

LICHTENSTEIN, H.—Verzeichniss der Doubletten des Zoolog. Museums der königl. Universität zu Berlin, nebst Beschreibungen vieler bisher unbekannten Arten von Säugthieren, Vögeln, Amphibien, und Fischen. 4to. Berlin, 1823.

(LICHTENSTEIN.)—Nomenclator avium musei zoologici berolinensis. 8vo. Berlin, 1854. (Supposed to have been prepared by Lichtenstein and Cabanis.)

LICHTENSTEIN, Dr. H.—"DEPPE und SCHIEDE, Preisverzeichniss, 1831?" (A pamphlet sale catalogue of certain collections in Mexico made by the above parties, and quoted by Richardson. I have never been able to ascertain whether it contains descriptions to accompany the numerous new names mentioned in it.)

LICHTENSTEIN, H.—See BERLIN, Akademie der Wissenschaften : Abhandlungen, 1839.

LONDON.—Annals and Magazine of Natural History, including Zoology, Botany, and Geology, etc. Conducted by Sir W. JARDINE, etc. 8vo.

SCLATER, P. L.—Description of a new species of Woodpecker discovered by Mr. THOMAS BRIDGES in Northern California. III Series, I, Feb. 1858, 127.

STRICKLAND, H. E.—On Cyanocitta, a proposed new genus of Garrulinae, and on C. superciliosa, a new species of blue Jay, hitherto confounded with C. ultramarina, Bon. XV, April, 1845, 260. Further notice respecting the same, May, 1845, 342.

LONDON.—British Association for the Advancement of Science: Report of the meetings. 8vo.

RICHARDSON, J.—Report on North American Zoology. Report of the sixth meeting, held 1836. London, 1837, 121.

LONDON.—Linnaean Society: Transactions. 4to. Vol. 1, et seq.

BARTON, M. D., BENJAMIN SMITH.—Some account of the Tantalus ephouskyca, a rare American bird. XII, 1818, 24, with plate.

DOUGLAS, DAVID.—Observations on some species of the genera Tetrao and Ortyx, natives of North America, with descriptions of four new species of the former and two of the latter. XVI, 1829, 133.

MONTAGU, GEO.—Descriptions of three rare species of British birds. IV, 1798, 35. (Tringa nigricans.)

SABINE, Capt. ED.—A memoir on the birds of Greenland, with descriptions and notes on the species observed in the late voyage of discovery in Davis' Straits and Baffin's Bay. XII, 1818, 527. New species, Uria brünnichii, (p. 538,) Larus argentatus. (The Uria brünnichii, named by Leach, U francsii, on p. 588.)

SABINE, Jos.—An account of a new species of gull lately discovered on the west coast of Greenland. XII, 1818, 520, with plate. (Larus sabini.)

YARRELL, WM.—Description of a species of Tringa killed in Cambridgeshire, new to England and to Europe. XVI, 1829, 109. (T. rufescens.)

LONDON.—The London Magazine of Natural History and Journal of Zoology, Botany, Mineralogy, Geology, and Meteorology. Conducted by J. C. LOUDON, etc. 8vo.

AUDUBON, JOHN JAMES.--Notes on the bird of Washington, Falco washingtoniana, or great American Sea Eagle, with fig., I, July 1828, 115.

LONDON.—The Naturalists' Repository or Monthly Miscellany of Exotic Natural History, exhibiting rare and beautiful specimens of foreign birds, insects, shells, quadrupeds, fishes, and marine productions ; especially such new subjects as have not hitherto been figured. By EDWARD DONOVAN. 5 vols. 8vo. London, 1823-'27.

LONDON.—The Philosophical Magazine or Annals of Chemistry, Mathematics, Astronomy, Natural History, and General Science. By RICHARD TAYLOR and RICHARD PHILLIPS, London. 8vo. I, Jan.—June, 1827.

SWAINSON.—A Synopsis of the Birds discovered in Mexico. By W. BULLOCK and Mr. WM. BULLOCK, jr. Vol I. (New and united series of the Philosophical Magazine and Annals of Philosophy.) May, 1827, 364, Nos. 1—37, and June, 1827, 433, Nos. 37—101.

LONDON.--The Quarterly Journal of Science, Literature, and the Arts. London. 8vo.

SWAINSON.--On the Tyrant Shrikes of America. By WILLIAM SWAINSON, esq., XX, Jan., 1826, 267.

LONDON.—Royal Society: Philosophical Transactions of the Royal Society of London.

CLAYTON, JOHN.—Letter to the Royal Society, giving a further account of the soil and other observables of Virginia ; of the birds. XVII, 1693, 988

FORSTER, J. R.—An account of the birds sent from Hudson's Bay, with observations relative to their natural history. LXII, 1772, 382.

PENNANT, THOS.—An account of the Turkey. Communicated by JOSEPH BANKS, esq. LXXI, 1781, 67.

LONDON.—The Zoological Journal. Conducted by THOMAS BELL, J. G. CHILDREN, J. DE CARLE SOWERBY, and G. B. SOWERBY. 4 vols. 8vo. Vol. I, 1825, et seq.

BONAPARTE, C. L.—Supplement to the genera of North American birds, and to the synopsis of the species found within the territory of the United States. III, January, 1827, 49.

BONAPARTE, C. L.—An account of four species of Stormy Petrel, (Thalassidroma.) By CHARLES LUCIEN BONAPARTE. III, January, 1827, 89.

BONAPARTE, C. L.—Notice of a nondescript species of Grouse from North America. By CHARLES L. BONAPARTE. July, 1827. III, 212.

DOUGLAS, DAVID.—Observations on the *Vultier californianus* of Shaw. IV, January, 1829, 328.

KING, Capt. PHILLIP PARKER —Extracts of a letter addressed by Capt. Phillip Parker King, R. N., to N. A. Vigors, on the animals of the Straits of Magellan. (Part 2.) IV, July, 1828, 91. (*Anas rafflesii*—a plate of the species in tab. xxix, supplement.)

SWAINSON, WILLIAM —On several groups and forms in ornithology not hitherto defined. By WILLIAM SWAINSON. 1827. III, 158, 343.

LONDON.—LEACH, W. E.—Zoological Miscellany ; being descriptions of new or interesting animals, (conducted by W. E. Leach,) illustrated with colored figures drawn from nature by R. P. Nodder. 3 vols. 8vo. London, 1814–1817.

LONDON.—Z o o l o g i c a l S o c i e t y : Proceedings of the Committee of Science and Correspondence. 2 vols. 8vo. 1831, 1832. (These precede the regular series of Proceedings of the Society commencing in 1833.)

COLLIE, A., esq —On the Pouch of the Frigate Bird (*Tachypetes aquilus*.) By A. COLLIE. April 26, 1831. Proceedings of Committee of Science and Correspondence, I, 62.

GOULD, JOHN.—On a new species of Woodpecker (*Picus imperialis*) from California. By JOHN GOULD. July 24, 1832. Proceedings of Committee of Science and Correspondence, II, 139.

OWEN, R.—On the anatomy of the Gannet, (*Sula bassana*.) By R. OWEN, esq. June 14, 1831. Proceedings of Committee of Science and Correspondence, I, 90.

OWEN, R.—On the anatomy of the Flamingo, (*Phoenicopterus ruber*.) August 28, 1832. Proceedings of Committee of Science and Correspondence, II, 141.

RICHARDSON, J.—Birds and mammalia collected during the last Arctic Land Expedition under Sir John Franklin. By J. RICHARDSON, M. D. September 27, 1831. Proceedings of Committee of Science and Correspondence, I, 132.

VIGORS, N. A.—Characters of several new species of birds collected by Mr. Cuming in Chili and Mexico. By N. A. VIGORS. January 10, 1832. Proceedings of Committee of Science and Correspondence, II, 3.

YARRELL, W.—On the specific identity of the *Gardenian* and Night Herons (*Ardea gardeni* and *nycticorax*.) By W. YARRELL. January, 1831. Proceedings of Committee of Science and Correspondence, I, 27.

YARRELL, W.—On the occurrence of several North American birds in England (*Anas sponsa, Anas occidua,* and *Alauda alpestris*.) By W. YARRELL. February 8, 1831. Proceedings of Committee of Science and Correspondence, I, 35.

YARRELL, W.—On a hybrid bred by the Society between a Muscovy Drake (*Anas moschata*) and a Common Duck, (*Anas boschas*.) By W. YARRELL. May 8, 1832. Proceedings of Committee of Science and Correspondence, II, 100.

LONDON.—Z o o l o g i c a l S o c i e t y, continued : Proceedings of the Zoological Society of London. Vol. I. 1833, *et seq.*

BONAPARTE.—Description of new or interesting birds from South America and Mexico. By C. L. BONAPARTE. November 14, 1837. V. 108.

BONAPARTE.—On the Garruline Birds or Jays ; with descriptions of new species. By Prince CHARLES LUCIEN BONAPARTE. April 9, 1850. XVIII, 79.

BONAPARTE.—On the largest known species of Phaleridine Bird. By Prince CHARLES LUCIEN BONAPARTE. July 22, 1851. XIX, 201. (*Sagmatorinus lathami.*)

COX.—Notice of a living Mocking-bird (*Turdus polyglottus*.) By J. C. Cox, esq. October 22, 1833. I, 114.

FRASER, L.—Description of three new species of birds. By L. FRASER. February 24, 1844. XII, 37. (*Lagopus ferrugineus*, from Mexico.)

GOULD.—On a collection of birds from North America presented by Mr. Folliot. By JOHN GOULD. February 25, 1834. II, 14.

GOULD.—On several species of birds allied to the European Wren, with characters of new species. By JOHN GOULD. October 11, 1836. IV, 88.

GOULD.—On a new species of *Ortyx* from California (*Ortyx plumifera*) from the collection of the late Mr. David Douglas, and a new species of the genus *Podargus* from Java. By JOHN GOULD April 11, 1837. V, 42.

GOULD.—On the characters of new birds in the Society's collection. By JOHN GOULD. July 25, 1837. V, 79.

GOULD, JOHN.—On the genus *Anous*. By JOHN GOULD, Oct. 14, 1845. XIII, 103.

GOULD.—On six new species of humming birds. By JOHN GOULD, June 25, 1850. XVIII, 162.

GOULD, J.—On a new turkey, (*Meleagris mexicana*.) By JOHN GOULD, April 8, 1856. XXIV, 61.

GOULD, J.—Descriptions of three new and very beautiful species of birds from Guatemala and from the Island of Lombock. By JOHN GOULD, April 28, 1857. XXV, 64.

GOULD, JOHN.—Observations on his visit to the United States of America, with description of a new species of *Ceriornis* found in the collection of Dr. Cabot, of Boston, United States. By JOHN GOULD, July 14, 1857. XXV, 166.

GRAY, G. R.—On a new species of *Thalassidroma*. By GEORGE ROBERT GRAY, (*Thalassidroma hornbyi*,) May 10, 1853. XXI, 62.

GRAY, G. R.—On a new species of *Somateria*, and the female of *Lampronetta fischeri*. By G. R. GRAY, November 27, 1855. XXIII, 211.

HILL.—Letter relating to the nests of the birds of Jamaica. By R. HILL, September 14, 1841. IX, 69.

KAUP.—Descriptions of some new birds in the museum of the Earl of Derby. By Dr. KAUP, February 11, 1851. XIX, 39.

SALLÉ, AUGUSTE.—Liste des oiseaux rapportes et observes dans la Republique Dominicaine (ancienne partie Espagnole de l'Île St. Domingue ou d'Haiti,) par M. A. Sallé, pendent son voyage de 1849 a 1851. By AUGUSTE M. SALLÉ, November 10, 1857. XXV, 230.

SCLATER, LUTLEY PHILIP.— On the genus *Culicivora* of Swainson and its component species. By PHILIP LUTLEY SCLATER, January 9, 1855. XXIII, 11.

SCLATER, LUTLEY PHILIP.—Note on sixteen species of Texan birds named by Mr. Giraud, of New York, in 1841. By PHILIP LUTLEY SCLATER, March 27, 1855. XXIII, 49.

SCLATER, LUTLEY PHILIP.—Note on the Zoological Appendix to the Report of the United States Naval Astronomical Expedition to the Southern Hemisphere, and on the geographic range and distribution of the Tanagrine Genera *Calliste* and *Euphonia*. By PHILIP LUTLEY SCLATER, February 12, 1846. XXIV, 18.

SCLATER, LUTLEY PHILIP.—Note on (*Psaltria flaviceps*) a third American species of the Parine genus *Psaltria*. By PHILIP LUTLEY SCLATER, March 11, 1856. XXIV, 37.

SCLATER, LUTLEY PHILIP.—Synopsis Avium Tanagrinarum. A descriptive catalogue of the known species of Tanagers. By PHILIP LUTLEY SCLATER, April 8, 1856. XXIV, 64, 108, 230.

SCLATER, LUTLEY PHILIP.—On the species of the American genus *Parra*. By PHILIP LUTLEY SCLATER, July 8, 1856. XXIV, 282.

SCLATER, LUTLEY PHILIP.—Catalogue of the birds collected by M. Auguste Sallé in Southern Mexico, with descriptions of new species. By PHILIP LUTLEY SCLATER, July 8, 1856. XXIV, 283.

SCLATER, PHILIP L.—Notes on the birds in the museum of the Academy of Natural Sciences of Philadelphia, and other collections in the United States. By PHILIP LUTLEY SCLATER, January 13, 1857. XXV, 1.

SCLATER, PHILIP.—Review of the species of the South American sub-family *Tityrinae*. By PHILIP SCLATER, April 18, 1857. XXV, 67.

SCLATER, PHILIP.—On *Parus meridionalis*, and some other species mentioned in the catalogue of birds collected by M. Sallé in Southern Mexico. By PHILIP LUTLEY SCLATER, May 12, 1857. XXV, 81.

SCLATER, PHILIP.—List of birds collected by Mr. Thomas Bridges, corr. mem., in the valley of San Jose, California. By PHILIP LUTLEY SCLATER, June 9, 1857. XXV, 125.

SCLATER, PHILIP.—List of additional species of Mexican birds obtained by M. Auguste Sallé from the environs of Jalapa and San Andres Tuxtla. By PHILIP LUTLEY SCLATER, July 14. 1857. XXV, 201.

SCLATER, PHILIP.—On a collection of birds made by Signor Matteo Botteri in the vicinity of Orizaba, in Southern Mexico. By PHILIP LUTLEY SCLATER. July 28, 1857. XXV, 210.

SCLATER, PHILIP.—On a collection of birds received by M. Sallé from Southern Mexico. By PHILIP LUTLEY SCLATER. Nov. 10, 1857. XXV, 226.

SCLATER, PHILIP.—Notes on Californian birds, by Thomas Bridges, corr. mem. Communicated with remarks by PHILIP LUTLEY SCLATER. Jan. 12, 1858. XXVI, 1.

SCLATER, PHILIP.—Notes on some birds from Southern Mexico. By PHILIP LUTLEY SCLATER. Feb. 23, 1858. XXVI, 95.

VIGORS.—On a collection of skins of birds from California. By N. A. VIGORS, esq. June 11, 1833. I, 65.

LONDON.—The Zoologist, a popular miscellany of Natural History. Conducted by Ed. Newman. 8vo.

NEWTON, ALFRED.—Some account of a petrel killed at Southacre, Norfolk, X, Dec., 1852. 3691. (*Procellaria haesitata*.)

LONG's Exped.—Account of an expedition from Pittsburg to the Rocky mountains, performed in the years 1819 and '20, under the command of Major Stephen H. Long. Compiled by Edwin James. 2 vols. 8vo. Philadelphia, 1823. (Zoological articles by Thos. Say.)

Lyon.—Société Royale d'Agriculture, Histoire Naturelle et Arts utiles de Lyon: Annales des sciences physiques et naturelles, d'agriculture et d'industrie, publiées par la société, etc. 8vo. Tome I, 1838, *et seq.*

Bourcier, Jules.—Description et figures de trois espèces nouvelles d'oiseaux-mouches. III, March, 1840. (*Ornysmya costae.* Pl. ii.)

Bourcier et Mulsant.—Description de vingt espèces d'oiseaux-mouches. IX, 1846, 312. '(*Trochilus alexandri,* p. 330, Sierra Madre, Mex.)

M'Call, Col. Geo. A.—See Philadelphia, Acad. Nat. Sciences : Proceedings.

M'Cown, Capt. J. P.—See New York, Lyceum of Nat. Hist.

M'Culloh.—See Boston, Society of Natural History : Journal.

Macgillivray, W.—A manual of British ornithology, etc. 2 vols. 8vo. London, 1840.

Madison, Wisc.—Wisconsin State Agricultural Society: Transactions. 8vo. Vol. I, 1852.

Hoy, M. D., P. R.—Notes on the ornithology of Wisconsin. II, 1853, 341. (This is a reissue, with additions, of the list of birds of Wisconsin by Dr. Hoy, in Proceedings of Phila. Acad. Nat. Sciences, and makes mention of 287 species.)

Malherbe, E.—See Metz, Academie : Mémoires ;—Paris, Revue Zoologique, 1849, 93 ; 1852, 553 ;—Cassel, Cabanis Journal für Ornithologie.

Massachusetts.—Reports on the fishes, reptiles, and birds of Massachusetts. 8vo. Boston, 1839. (Birds, p. 255, by Wm. B. O. Peabody.

Maximilian, Prinz von Wied.—Reise in das innere Nord America, in den Jahren 1832 bis 1834. 2 vols. 4to. Coblentz I, 1839 ; II, 1841. (See also under Wied.)

Maximilian, Prinz von Wied.—Beiträge zur Naturgeschichte von Brasilien. III, Vögel. i, 1830. ii, 1831.

Merrem, Blas.—Beyträge zur besond. Geschichte der Vögel, gesammlet. 4to. Leipsig, 1786, 1787.

Mexico.—Registro trimestre ó colleccion de memorias de historia, literatura, ciencias y artes. Por una sociedad de literatos. 8vo. Tomo I. Mexico, 1832. Tomo II, 1833.

De la Llave.—Memoria sobre el quetzaltototl, género nuevo de aves. I. i, Jan., 1832, 43. (*Pharomacrus mocinno.*)

De la Llave.—Sobre tres especies nuevas del género *Tetrao.* I. ii, April, 1832, 141. (*Tetrao marmorata, cristata,* and *guttata*)

Meyen, J. F.—See Breslau, K. L. C. Acad. nova acta. XVI, Suppl., 1.

Meyer, B. und J. Wolf.—Taschenbuch der deutschen Vögelkunde, oder kurze Beschreibungen aller Vögel Deutschlands. 2 vols. 8vo. Frankfort-a-M. 1809, 1810.

Michener, Dr. E.—See Philadelphia, Acad. Nat. Sciences : Journal.

Mitchell, D. W.—See Gray, Genera of Birds.

Moehring.—Avium genera. Auctore Paulo Henrico Gerardo Moehringio. 8vo. Aurica, 1752.

Möschler.—See Cassel.

Molina, G. J.—Saggio sulla storia naturale del Chili. 8vo. Bologna, 1782.

Montagu.—See London, Linnaean Society Transactions : IV, 1796, 40.

Montagu, Geo.—Ornithological dictionary, or alphabetical synopsis of British Birds. 2 vols. 8vo. London, 1802. Supplement, 1813. Second edition, edited by James Rennie. 8vo. London, 1831.

Morton, Dr. S. G.—See New Haven, Am. Jour. Sc.

Muller, Johannes.—See Berlin, Akad. der Wissench.

Muller, Ur. J. W. von.—See Cassel.

Naumann, J. A.—Naturgeschichte der Vögel Deutschlands, etc. 12 vols. 8vo. and Supplement. Leipzig, 1822-1847.

Naumannia.—See Stuttgart.

New York.—Lyceum of Natural History: Annals of the Lyceum of Natural History of New York. 8vo. vol. I, 1824, New York ; II, 1828 ; III, 1828-1836; IV, 1848 ; V, 1852 ; VI, 1853-1858.

Audubon.—Note on the *Hirundo fulva.* By John J. Audubon. Read August 9, 1824, I, 163.

Audubon.—Facts and observations connected with the permanent residence of swallows in the United States. By John J. Audubon. Read Aug. 11, 1824, I, 166.

Baird.—Description of a new species of *Sylvicola.* By S. F. Baird. (*Sylvicola kirtlandii.*) Read Jan. 12, 1852, V, 215.

Bell.—Observations on the *Limosa scolopacea* of Say. By John Bell. Read October 9, 1848, V, 1.

New York—Continued.

BELL.—On the *Pipilo oregonus*, as distinguished from the *Pipilo arcticus* of Swainson. By JOHN BELL. Read November 27, 1848, V, 6.

BELL.—Description of a new species of the genus *Fuligula*. By JOHN BELL. (*Fuligula viola.*) Read Aug. 30, 1851, V, 219.

BONAPARTE.—The genera of North American birds and a synopsis of the species found within the territory of the United States; systematically arranged in orders and families. By CHARLES L. BONAPARTE. Read Jan. 24, 1826, II, 7, and 293. (These articles on genera of North American birds have been published separately in a single volume; dated 1828. This is the edition quoted in the present volume, under the head of *Synopsis.* The memoir was read Jan. 1826, but the volume does not appear to have been published until 1828, its date.)

BONAPARTE.—Further additions to the Ornithology of the United States and Observations of the Nomenclature of certain species. By CHARLES L. BONAPARTE. Read Nov. 6, 1826, II, 154.

CLINTON.—On the *Hirundo fulva* of VIEILLOT, with some general remarks on the birds of this genus. By DEWITT CLINTON. Read August 9, 1824, I, 156.

GIRAUD.—Description of a new species of *Helinai.* By J. P. GIRAUD, jr. Read October 8,1850, V, 40.

GUNDLACH, M. D., JOHN.—Description of a new species of bird of the genus *Sylvicola.* 8vo. VI, v, Oct. 1855, 161. (*S. pityophila.*)

GUNDLACH.—Notes on some Cuban Birds, with descriptions of three new species. By JOHN GUNDLACH. Feb. 1858, VII, 1.

JONES.—Description of a New Species of Woodpecker, (*Picus lecentei.*) By WILLIAM L. JONES, M. D. Read March 13, 1847, IV, 489.

LAWRENCE.—Description of a New Species of *Anser.* By GEORGE N. LAWRENCE. (*Anser nigricans.*) Read March 16, 1846, IV, 171.

LAWRENCE.—Description of a New Species of *Procellaria.* By GEORGE N. LAWRENCE. (*Procellaria meridionalis.*) Read Feb. 18, 1847, IV, 475.

LAWRENCE.—Observations on Mr. BELL's paper on *Limosa scolapacea.* By GEORGE N.LAWRENCE. Read Jan. 7, 1849, V, 4.

LAWRENCE.—Description of *Mimus melanopterus.* By GEORGE N. LAWRENCE. Read April 16, 1849, V, 35.

LAWRENCE.—On the occurrence of the Caspian Tern (*Sylochelidon caspius*) in North America. By GEORGE N. LAWRENCE. Read May 6, 1850, V, 37.

LAWRENCE.—Description of a new species of *Tyrannus.* By GEORGE N. LAWRENCE, (*Tyrannus cassinii.*) Read June 3, 1850, V, 39.

LAWRENCE.—Descriptions of new species of birds of the genera *Conirostrum, Embernagra* and *Xanthornus,* together with a list of other species not heretofore noticed as being found within the limits of the United States. By GEORGE N. LAWRENCE. Read April 28, 1851, V, 112.

LAWRENCE.—Additions to North American Ornithology. By GEORGE N. LAWRENCE. Read April 28, 1851, V, 117.

LAWRENCE.—Descriptions of new species of birds of the genera *Toxostoma, Tyrannula, Plectrophanes.* By GEORGE N. LAWRENCE. (*Toxostoma lecontii, Tyrannula cinerascens, Plectrophanes McCownii.*) Read September 8, 1851, V, 121.

LAWRENCE.—Additions to North American Ornithology. By GEORGE N. LAWRENCE. Read September 8, 1851, V, 123—VI, 1853-'4.

LAWRENCE.—Ornithological Notes. By GEORGE N. LAWRENCE. Read April 24, 1852, V, 220—No. 2, VI, I, 1853-'7.

LAWRENCE.—Description of a new species of bird of the genus *Larus.* By GEORGE N. LAWRENCE. (*Larus californicus.*) Read March 7, 1854, VI, 79. Other new species, 1858.

LAWRENCE.—Description of seven new species of humming birds. By GEORGE N. LAWRENCE. Read February 8, 1858, VI, 258.

LAWRENCE.—Descriptions of new species of birds of the genera *Chordeiles* and *Polioptila.* By GEORGE N. LAWRENCE. Read December 22, 1856, VI, 165.

LAWRENCE.—Descriptions of new species of birds of the genera *Ortyx, Sterna,* and *Icteria.* By GEORGE N. LAWRENCE. (*Ortyx texanus, Sterna pikei, Icteria longicauda.*) Read February 14, 1853, VI, May, 1853, 1.

LAWRENCE.—Description of a new species of humming bird of the genus *Mellisuga,* with a note on *Trochilus aquila.* By GEORGE N. LAWRENCE. Read April 2, 1855.

LAWRENCE.—Observations on the paper of Mr. Gundlach. By GEORGE N. LAWRENCE. February, 1858, VI.

LAWRENCE.—Description of two new species of gulls in the Smithsonian Institution, at Washington, (*Larus suckleyi* and *Rissa septentrionalis.* By GEORGE N. LAWRENCE. Read February, 1858, VI, 264.

New York—Continued.

McCown.—Facts and observations from notes taken when in Texas. By Captain J. P. McCown, U. S. A. Read March 28, 1853, VI, 9.

Ward —Notice of the appearance of the pine grosbeak, (*Pyrrhula enucleator*,) in the environs of New York. By James F. Ward. Read December 19, 1836, IV, 49.

New York.—United States Magazine. 8vo. J. M. Emerson & Co.

Cassin, John.—Ornithology of the United States and British and Russian America. III, 1856, 18, 109, 205, 481 ; IV, 1857, 10. (Not continued beyond the *Raptores*.)

New York.—The American Monthly Magazine and Critical Review. 4 vols. 8vo. New York.

Rafinesque, C. S.—Further account of discoveries in natural history in the western States. IV, November, 1818, 39. (*Rimamphus.*)

New York.— Natural History of New York. 4to.

Dekay, James E.—Zoology of New York, or the New York Fauna, etc. Part II, Birds. Albany. 1844.

New Haven.—The American Journal of Science and Arts. (Vol. I under a little different title.) Conducted first by Benjamin Silliman, then by Benjamin Silliman & B. Silliman, Jr., and then by Silliman & Dana. 8vo. Vol. I. 1819, *et seq.*

Bachman, Rev. J.—On the migration of the birds of North America XXX, 1836, 81.

Baird, Wm. M. and S. F.—List of birds found in the vicinity of Carlisle, Cumberland county, Penn., about Lat. 40° 12′ N., Lon. 77° 11′ W. By Wm. M. and Spencer F. Baird. XLVI, Jan.–March, 1844, 261. (201 species.)

Baird, Wm. and S. F.—Description of two species, supposed to be new, of the genus *Tyrannula*, (Swainson,) found in Cumberland county, Penn. By Wm. M. and S. F. Baird, of Carlisle, Penn. (*Tyrannula flaviventris* and *minima.*)

Brewer, Dr. T. M.—Habits of *Hirundo fulva*, XXXVIII, 1840, 392.

Fox, Charles —Notice of some American birds. By Charles Fox, of Durham, England. XXIX, 1836, 291.

Green, Prof. Jacob.—*Falco leucocephalus*, Bald Eagle. IV, 1822, 89.

Green, Jacob.—Fragments relating to the history of animals, IV, 1822, 309.

Kirtland, Dr. J. P.—Fragments of Natural History. No. II. Ornithology. XL, 1841, 19.

Linsley, Rev. James H.—A catalogue of the birds of Connecticut, arranged according to their natural families. XLIV, 1843, 249. (302 species.)

Morton, Dr. S. G.—Hybridity in animals considered in reference to the question of the unity of the human species. Part II, birds ; 2d series III, 1847, 203.

Sharpless, John T., M. D.—Description of the American wild swan, proving it to be a new species. *Cygnus americanus.* XXII, July, 1832, 83. (With plate of sternum.)

Steel, Dr. J. W.—(Notes in reference to the cliff swallow. *Hirundo lunifrons.*) XIX, 1831, 356. (Noticed them in Maine in 1800.)

Woodruff, Samuel.—Notice of a barn swallow. XIX, 1831, 172. (*Hirundo lunifrons.*)

Newberry, Dr. J. S.—See Washington, War Department : Pacific R. R. Report, Vol. VI, Part IV. Zoology of routes in Oregon and California, explored by parties under the command Lieut. R. S. Williamson.

Newton, Alfred.—See London, Zoologist.

Nilsson, S.—Ornithologia suecica. 2 parts. 8vo. Copenhagen, 1817, 1821.

Nitzsch, C. L.—Pterylographia Avium. 4to. Halle, 1833.

Nitzsch, C. L.—System der Pterylographie. Nach seinem handschriftl. aufbewahrten Untersuchungen verfasst, (etc.,) von Herm. Burmeister. 4to. Halle, 1840.

Nomenclator Avium.—See Lichtenstein.

Nuttall.—A Manual of the ornithology of the United States and of Canada. By Thomas Nuttall. The land birds. 12mo. Boston, 1832. Second edition, with additions, 1840. (The second edition embraces all of Townsend's species and those described by Mr. Audubon in his Ornithological Biography.)

Nuttall.—A Manual of the ornithology of the United States and of Canada. By Thomas Nuttall. The water birds. 12mo. Boston, 1834.

Nuttall, Thomas.—See Boston, American Academy of Arts and Sciences : Memoirs I, 1833.

Ohio, Geological survey of.—Second annual report on the geological survey of Ohio. 8vo. Columbus, 1838. (Catalogue of birds by J. P. Kirtland, M. D.)

D'Orbigny.—See Ramon de la Sagra.

Owen, R.—See London, Zool. Soc.: Proc. Comm. Sc.

Ord.—See Guthrie's Geography;—Philadelphia, Acad. Nat. Sciences: Journal.

Pacific R. R. Report.—See Washington, War Department.

Pallas, P. S.—Zoographia Rosso-Asiatica, etc.   3 vols. 4to.   St. Petersburg, 1811.   (This work, though printed in 1811, does not appear to have been issued until 1831.   The plates have been issued separately, under the title of Icones ad Zoographiam Rosso-Assiaticam.   Fasc I–VII.   1834, *et seq.*)

Pallas, P. S.—Icones ad Zoographiam Rosso-Assiaticam.—See Pallas, Zoographia.

Pallas, P. S.—Reisen durch verschied. Provinzen des Russ. Reichs in den Jahren, 1768–1774.   3 vols. 4to.   St Petersburg, 1771, 1773, 1776.

Pallas, P. S.—See St. Petersburg, Acad. Imp. des Sc.: Novi Commentarii.   XIV, 582.

Paris.--Académie des Sciences: Comptes rendus hebdomadaires des séances de l'Académie des Sciences, etc. 4to.

Bonaparte, C. L.—Nouvelles espèces ornithologiques.   Prem. Partie, Perroquets.   XXX, 1850, 131.   Ib., 291, Accipitres.

Bonaparte, C. L.—Notes sur les Trochilidés.   XXX, 1850, 379.

Bonaparte, C. L.--Sur plusieurs genres nouveaux de passereaux.   XXXI, Sept. 16, 1850, 423.   (*Hesperiphona*.)

Bonaparte, C. L.--Sur deux espèces nouvelles de *Paridae*.   XXXI, Sept. 30, 1850.   (*Psaltriparus personatus, Lophophanes wollweberi*.)

Bonaparte, C. L.—Note sur plusieurs familles naturelles d'oiseaux, et descriptions d'espèces nouvelles.   XXXI, Oct. 21, 1850, 561.

Bonaparte, C. L.—Note sur les Tangaras, leurs affinités et descriptions d'espèces nouvelles.   XXXII, Jan., 1851, 76.

Bonaparte, C. L.—Notes sur les collections rapportées en 1853 par M. A. Delattre de son voyage en California et dans le Nicaragua.   XXXVII, Nov. 28, 1853.   Ib., Dec. 5, 1853, 827, (from *Pica nuttalli*.)   Ib., Dec. 19, 1853, 913, (from *Chrysometris lawrencii*.)   Ib., XXXVIII, Jan. 2, 1854, 1, (from *Chanteurs subulirostres*.)   Ib., Jan. 16, 1854, 53, (from *Troglodytides*.)   Ib., Feb. 6, 1854, 258, (from *Coereba cyanea*.)   Ib., Feb. 27, 1854, 365, (from *Chanteurs dentirostres*.)   Ib., March 20, 1854, 533, (from *Vanga*.)   Ib., April 3, 1854, 650, (from *Progne purpurea* to end)

Bonaparte, C. L.—Classification ornithologique par series.   XXXVII, Oct. 31, 1853, 641.

Bonaparte, C. L.—Coup d'oeil sur l'ordre des pigeons.   XXXIX, 1854, 869, 1072, 1102.   Ib., XL, 1855, 15, 96, 205.

Bonaparte, C. L.—Tableaux synoptiques de l'ordre des Herons.   XL, April 2, 1855, 718.

Bonaparte, C. L.—Notices ornithologiques.   XLI, Aug., 1855, 247, (on pigeons and *Colymbus*.)

Bonaparte, C. L.—(Remarks on the "Catalogue of Genera and Subgenera of Birds," by Geo. R. Gray; and Notices of Species observed in different Museums of Europe.) XLI, 1855, 649.   (No title was given of this article.)

Bonaparte, C. L.—Espèces nouvelles d'oiseaux d'Asie et d'Amerique, et tableaux paralléliques des Pélagiens ou Gaviae.   XLII, April 28, 1856, 764.

Bonaparte, C. L.--Tableaux parallélique de l'ordre des Gallinacés.   XLII, 1856, 874.   Ib., Notes sur les tableaux des Gallinacés, 953.   (Contains descriptions of the new species of the tableaux.)

Bonaparte, C. L.—Excursions dans les divers musées d'Allemagne, de Hollande, et de Belgique, et tableaux paralléliques de l'ordre des Echassiers.   XLIII, Aug. 25, 1856, 410.   Ib., 571.   Ib., 593.

Bonaparte, C. L.--Ornithologie fossile servant d'introduction au tableau comparatif des Ineptes et des Autruches.   XLIII, 1856, 775.   (Refers to N. American ornithichnites.)

Bonaparte, C. L.—Additions et corrections au coup d'oeil sur l'ordre des Pigeons, et à la partie correspondante du Conspectus Avium.   XLIII, 1856, 833.   Ib , 942.

Bonaparte, C. L.—Additions et corrections aux tableaux paralléliques de l'ordre des Herons et des Pelagiens ou Gavies, et a la partie correspondante, deja publiée du Conspectus Avium.   XLIII, Nov., 1856, 990.

Bonaparte, C. L.—Additions et Corrections aux tableaux paralléliques de la deuxième sous-classe des oiseaux, *Praecoces* ou *Autophages*.   XLIII, Dec. 1, 1856, 1017.

Bonaparte, C. L.—Tableau des genres des Gallinacés disposés en séries paralléles.   XLV, Sept. 28, 1857, 425.   (A posthumous incomplete memoir.)

Paris.—Annales des Sciences Naturelles comprenant la Zoologie, la Botanique, etc.   Redigées pour la Zoologie par M. Milne Edwards : pour la botanique par MM. Ad. Brogniart et J. Decaisne.   Quatrième serie.   Zoologie.   Tome 1, 1854, *et seq.*

Bonaparte, C. L.—Conspectus Systematis Ornithologie.   1854.   (This general arrangement is a few weeks subsequent to that of Comptes Rendus, 1854, and makes important changes.   It enumerates all the families, (131), genera, (2,100), and sub-genera of birds.   The sum total of species estimated is 8,300.)

PARIS.—Dictionnaire Classique d'Histoire Naturelle, par une société de naturalistes. (AUDOUIN, DRAPIEZ, etc.) 17 vols. 8vo. Paris, 1822–'31.

PARIS.—Dictionnaire des sciences naturelles, dans lequel on traite méthodiquement de differentes êtres de la nature, etc. (Rédigés par FRÉD. CUVIER.) 60 vols. 8vo. Paris et Strasbourg, 1816—1830. (Ornithological articles, by DUMONT.)

PARIS.—Encyclopédie Méthodique, ou par ordre de matière, par une société de gens de lettres. Histoire Naturelle, 10 Tom. en 20 Pt. et 17 vols. de pl. 4to. Paris, 1782, 92, et seq.

BONNATERRE—Tableau encyclopédique et méthodique. Ornithologie. Par l'ABBE BONNATERRE, 1790.

VIEILLOT.—Oiseaux, 1820.

PARIS.—Journal de physique, de chemie, et d'histoire naturelle. 4to. (Edited by BLAINVILLE from 1815—1820.)

RAFINESQUE, C. S.—Prodrome de 70 Nouveaux genres d'animaux découverts dans l'interieur des Etats-Unis d'Amerique durant l'annee, 1818. LXXXVIII, June 1819, 417. (Rimamphus, Helmitheros, Symphemia.)

PARIS.—Nouveau Dictionnaire d'Histoire Naturelle appliquée aux Arts, à l'Agriculture, à l'Economie rurale et domestique, à la Médicine, etc. Par une société de naturalistes et d'agriculteurs. 2d edition, 36 vols. 8vo. Paris, 1816—1819. (The articles on Ornithology in this edition are by VIEILLOT. The first edition, 24 vols. 1802—1804, probably contains nothing by him.)

PARIS.—Revue Zoologique par la Société Cuvierienne, Association Universelle pour l'Avancement de la Zoologie, de l'Anatomie Comparée et de la Palaeontologie, Journal Mensuel. Publiée sous la direction de M. F. E. GUÉRIN-MENEVILLE. 8vo. Vol. I, 1838, etc.

BOURCIER, JULES.—Description de quelques espèces nouvelles d'oiseaux mouches, 1839, Oct. 294. (Ornymya costal, California.)

PARIS.—Revue et Magasin de Zoologie, pure et appliquée, etc. Par M. F. E. GUERIN-MENEVILLE et avec la collaboration scientifique de M. AD. FOCILLON. 8vo. Tome I, 1849, et seq.

BONAPARTE, C. L.—Monographie des Laniens. 1853, July, 292 ; Oct. 433.

BONAPARTE, C. L.—Tableau des Perroquets. 1854, March, 145.

BONAPARTE, C. L.—Tableau des Oiseaux mouches. 1854, May, 248.

BONAPARTE, C. L.—Tableau des Oiseaux de Proie. 1854, Oct. 530.

BONAPARTE, C. L.—Notes sur les Larides. 1855, Jan. 12.

DEVILLE, E.—Observations faites en Amerique sur les moeurs de differentes espèces d'oiseaux mouches, etc. 1852, May, 209. (Notice of *Trochilus calubris.* The author was connected with Castelnau's expedition.)

MALHERBE, ALFRED.—Description de nouvelles espèces de *Picidæ.* 1852, Dec., 551. (*Geopicus chrysoides.*)

PEABODY, Rev. W. B. O.—See BOSTON, Soc. Nat. Hist.: Journal.

PEABODY, birds of Mass.—See MASSACHUSETTS.

PEALE, T. R.—See WILKES, United States exploring expedition.

PENNANT, THOS.—Arctic Zoology. First edition. 3 vols. 4to. 1784–87. Second edition. 2 vols. 4to. London, 1792.

PHILADELPHIA.—A c a d e m y o f Natural Sciences: Journal of the Academy of Natural Sciences of Philadelphia. First series, I–VIII, in octavo, 1817–1842. Second series in large quarto.

BONAPARTE.—An account of four species of stormy petrel. By CHARLES BONAPARTE. Read January 13, 1824. III, II. January 1824, 227.

BONAPARTE.—On a new species of duck, described by Wilson as the same with the *Anas fuligula* of Europe. By CHARLES BONAPARTE. Read April 6, 1824. III, II, April 27, 1824, 381. (*Anas rufitorques.*)

BONAPARTE.—Description of ten species of South American birds. By CHARLES BONAPARTE. Read April 19, 1825. IV, II, May 1825, 370. (*Monasa fusca*, BP.; *Picus rubricollis*, GM., var.; *Dendrocolaptes angustirostris*, VIEILL.; *Fringilla flaveola*, LINN.; *Tanagra flava*, GM.; *Muscicapa violenta*, BON.; *Muscicapa taenioptera*, BON.; *Muscicapa pullata*, BON.; *Caprimulgus semitorquatus*, GMEL.; *Rallus nigricans*, VIEILL.)

BONAPARTE.—Descriptions of two new species of Mexican birds. By CHARLES BONAPARTE. Read April 25, 1825. IV, II, May 1825, 387. (*Garrulus ultramarinus*, BON.; *Cassicus melanicturus*, BON.)

BONAPARTE.—Observations on the nomenclature of Wilson's ornithology. By CHARLES BONAPARTE. Read March 9, 1824. III, II, pp. 340–352. Published April 5, 1824, (including Nos. 1–21 of Wilson's list in Vol. VI, American ornithology.)—IB. pp 353–371, April 27, (Nos. 22–58).—Continuation of the same read March 23, 1824. IV, I, pp. 25–32, July, 1824, (Nos. 59–79.)—IB. pp. 33–66, August, 1824, (Nos. 70–112.)—IB. pp. 163–200, November, 1824, (Nos. 113–67.)—IB. IIV, II, pp. 251–277, (read November 23, 1824,) published February, 1825, (Nos. 168–184, with review of preceding numbers.)—IB. V, I, July, 1825, pp. 57–64, (Nos. 185–194.)—IB. August, 1825, pp. 65–106, (Nos. 195–227.)

BONAPARTE.—Additions to the ornithology of the United States. By CHARLES BONAPARTE. Read May 10, 1825, V, I, June, 1852, 26. (Species collected in Florida by Titian Peale. *Falco melanopterus: Sylvia palmarum ; Columba leucocephala ; C. zenaida*, BON., (n. s.); *Rallus giganteus*, BON., (n. s.); *Aramus scolopaceus; Sterna cayana.*)

PHILADELPHIA—Continued—

BONAPARTE.—Notes to the paper entitled descriptions of ten species of South American birds. By CHARLES BONAPARTE. Read July 12, 1825. V, I, November, 1825, 137.

BONAPARTE.—On the distinction of two species of *Icterus*, hitherto confounded under the specific name of *icterecephalus*. By CHARLES BONAPARTE. Read February 28, 1826. V, II, February, 1826, 222. (*Icterus xanthocepha lus*, BON.; *Icterus icterocephalus*, Daudin.)

BONAPARTE.—Description of a new species of South American *Fringilla*. By CHARLES BONAPARTE. Read March 1, 1825. IV, II, April, 1825, 350. (*Fringilla xanthoroa*, Rio Janeiro.)

CASSIN.—Monograph of the birds comprising the genera *Hydropsalis*, Wagler, and *Antrostomus*, Nuttall. By JOHN CASSIN. Second series. II, II, January, 1852, 113.

CASSIN.—Description of new species of birds of the genera *Melanerpes*, Swainson, and *Lanius*, Linnaeus. By JOHN CASSIN. Second series. II, III, January, 1853, 257.

CASSIN.—Descriptions of new species of birds of the genus *Spermestes*, Sw. Second series. III, I, May, 1855, 69.

CASSIN.—Descriptions of new species of *Psittacidæ*. Second series. III, II, December, 1855, 153.

GAMBEL.—Remarks on the birds observed in Upper California, with descriptions of new species. By WM. GAMBEL. 2d series, I, I, December, 1847, 25, and I, III, August, 1849, 215.

GAMBEL.—Description of a new species of *Mergulus*, Ray, from the coast of California. By WM. GAMBEL, M. D. 2d series, II. I. November, 1850, 55.

HEERMANN.—Notes on the birds of California observed during a residence of three years in that country. By A. L. HEERMANN, M. D. 2d series, II, III, January, 1853, 259.

LEIB.—Description of a new species of *Fuligula*. By GEO. C. LEIB, M. D. Read January 7, 1840, VIII, I, 1840 170. (*Fuligula grisea*, *F. labradora*.)

LEIB.—Description of the nest and eggs of the *Fulica americana* and *Anas discors*. By GEORGE C. LEIB, M. D. Read November 16, 1841, VIII, II, 1842, 203.

MICHENER.—A few facts in relation to the identity of the red and mottled owls, &c. By EZRA MICHENER, M. D. Read July 3, 1838, VIII, I, 1839, 53.

ORD.—Observations on the genus *Gracula*, of Latham. By GEORGE ORD. Read May 19, 1818 ; I, II, May, 1818, 253. *Gracula quiscala*, (*major*,) and *barita* (*versicolor*.)

ORD.—An account of the Florida jay, of Bartram. By GEORGE ORD. Read May 26, 1826 ; I, II, August, 1818, 345. (*Garrulus caerulescens*.)

ORD.—An account of an American species of the genus *Tantalus*, or Ibis. By GEORGE ORD. Read July 8, 1817, (*Tantalus mexicanus*,) I, No. IV, August 1817, 53.

TOWNSEND.—Description of twelve new species of birds, chiefly from the vicinity of the Columbia river. By JOHN KIRK TOWNSEND. VII, II. Read November 15, 1836 ; VII, I, 1837, 187. (*Siala occidentalis, Fringilla oregona, F. bicolor, Plectrophanes ornata, Parus rufescens, P. minimus, Sylvia occidentalis, S. nigrescens, S. audubonii, S. townsendii, Orpheus montanus, Charadrius montanus.*) With an appendix, p. 193, containing a list of birds from the Columbia river. Prepared by the Ornithological Committee of the Philadelphia Academy of Natural Sciences.

TRUDEAU.—Description of a new species of woodpecker. By JAMES TRUDEAU, M. D. Read June 27, 1837, 404. (*Picus audubonii*.)

TOWNSEND.—Description of a new species of *Cypcelus*, from the Columbia river. By JOHN K. TOWNSEND. Read March 3, 1839 ; VIII, I, 1839, 148, (*C. vauxii*.)

TOWNSEND.—Description of a new species of *Sylvia*, from the Columbia river. By JOHN K. TOWNSEND. Read April 2, 1839 ; VIII, I, 1839, 149. (*S. tolmoei*.)—Note on *Sylvia tolmoei*, p. 159. Read September 10, 1839.

TOWNSEND.—List of birds inhabiting the regions of the Rocky Mountains, the Territory of Oregon, and the northwest coast of America. By JOHN K. TOWNSEND. VIII, I, 1839(?), 151. Read September 10, 1839.

TRUDEAU.—Description of the white-winged tanager. (*Pyranga leucoptera*.) Read June 4, 1839 ; VIII, I, 160.

PHILADELPHIA—Academy of Natural Sciences, Continued: Proceedings of the Academy of Natural Sciences, of Philadelphia. I–IX, 1840–'58.

BAIRD, WM. M. and S. F.—Descriptions of two species, supposed to be new, of the genus *Tyrannula*, Swainson, found in Cumberland county, Pennsylvania. By WILLIAM M. and SPENCER F. BAIRD, Carlisle, Pennsylvania. (*T. flaviventris* and *minima*.) I, July, 1843, 283.

BAIRD.—Descriptions of new birds, collected between Albuquerque, New Mexico, and San Francisco, California, during the winter of 1853–'54, by Dr. C. B. R. Kennerly and H. B. Möllhausen, naturalists, attached to the survey of the Pacific railroad route, under Lieutenant A. W. Whipple. (*Cypselus melanoleucus, Oulicivora plumbea*,

Psaltria plumbea, Cyanocitta macrolopha, Carpodacus cassinii, Zonotrichia fallax, Pipilo mesoleucus, Centurus uropygialis.) VII, June, 1854, 118.

CASSIN.—On the occurrence of *Srix nyctea*, during the winter of 1843–'44, in the vicinity of Philadelphia. By JOHN CASSIN. II, March, 1844, 19.

CASSIN.—Description of a new vulture in the Museum of the Academy of Natural Sciences, of Philadelphia. (*Cathartes burrovianus*.) By JOHN CASSIN. II, March, 1845, 212.

CASSIN.—Note on an instinct probably possessed by the herons. (*Ardea.*) By JOHN CASSIN. III, December, 1846, 135.

CASSIN.—Description of a new rapacious bird in the Museum of the Academy of Natural Sciences, of Philadelphia. (*Cymindis wilsonii.*) By JOHN CASSIN. III, April, 1847, 199.

CASSIN.—Description of a new *Buceros*, and a notice of *Buceros elatus*, both of which are in the collection of the Academy of Natural Sciences of Philadelphia. By JOHN CASSIN. III, December 1847, 330.

CASSIN.—Descriptions of three new species of *Icterus*, (Briss,) specimens of which are in the Museum of the Academy of Natural Sciences of Philadelphia. By JOHN CASSIN. (*Icterus maculi-alatus, Icterus auricapillus, Icterus giraudii.*) III, December, 1847, 332.

CASSIN.—Descriptions of the new species of the genus *Cyanocorax*, of which specimens are in the collection of the Academy of Natural Sciences of Philadelphia. By JOHN CASSIN. IV, Feb., 1848, 26.

CASSIN.—Descriptions of new species of birds of the genera *Vidua, Euplectus, Pyrenestes,* and *Pitylus;* specimens of which are in the collection of the Academy of Natural Sciences of Philadelphia. By JOHN CASSIN. IV, June, 1848, 65.

CASSIN.—Description of a new *Tanagra* in the collection of the Academy of Natural Sciences of Philadelphia. By JOHN CASSIN. IV, Oct., 1848, 85.

CASSIN.—Catalogue of birds collected by Mr. William S. Pease during the march of the army of the United States from Vera Cruz to the city of Mexico. By JOHN CASSIN. IV, Oct., 1848, 87.

CASSIN.—Descriptions of owls presumed to be undescribed; specimens of which are in the collection of the Academy of Natural Sciences of Philadelphia. By JOHN CASSIN. IV, Dec., 1848. 121.

CASSIN.—Descriptions of new species of the genera *Nyctale* and *Sycobius;* specimens of which are in the collection of the Academy of Natural Sciences of Philadelphia. By JOHN CASSIN. IV, Feb., 1849, 157.

CASSIN.—Notes of the examination of the family *Vulturidae*, in the collection of the Academy of Natural Sciences of Philadelphia. By JOHN CASSIN. IV, Feb., 1849, 158.

CASSIN.—Remarks on a specimen of *Anas rafflesii* from Louisiana. By JOHN CASSIN. IV, Aug , 1849, 195.

CASSIN.—Description of new species of birds of the family *Caprimulgidae;* specimens of which are in the collection of the Academy of Natural Sciences of Philadelphia. By JOHN CASSIN. IV, Oct., 1849, 236.

CASSIN.—Descriptions of new species of birds, specimens of which are in the collection of the Academy of Natural Sciences of Philadelphia. By JOHN CASSIN. V, June, 1850, 56.

CASSIN.—Descriptions of new species of birds of the genera *Paradisea, Pastor,* and *Buceros*, and a proposition to rename others of the genera *Alcyon* and *Hirundo*. By JOHN CASSIN. V, Aug , 1850, 67.

CASSIN.—Descriptions of new species of birds of the genera *Parus, Emberiza, Carduelis, Myiothera, Leuzonerpes;* specimens of which are in the collection of the Academy of Natural Sciences of Philadelphia. By JOHN CASSIN. V, Oct., 1850, 103.

CASSIN.—Notice of an American species of duck hitherto regarded as identical with the *Oidemia fusca*, (*Oidemia velvetina*.) By JOHN CASSIN. V, Dec., 1850, 126.

CASSIN.—Sketch of the birds composing the genera *Vireo* and *Vireosylvia*, with a list of the previously known, and descriptions of three new species, (*Vireo huttoni*, and *Vireosylvia flavoviridis*, and *philadelphica*.) By JOHN CASSIN. V, Feb., 1851, 149.

CASSIN.—Descriptions of new species of birds of the genera *Galbula* and *Bucco*, specimens of which are in the collection of the Academy of Natural Sciences of Philadelphia. By JOHN CASSIN. V, Feb., 1851, 154.

CASSIN.—Notes of an examination of the birds composing the family *Caprimulgidae*, in the collection of the Academy of Natural Sciences of Philadelphia. By John CASSIN. V, April, 1851, 175.

CASSIN.—Notes on specimens of *Ephialtes naevia* and *E. asio*. By JOHN CASSIN. V, Aug., 1851, 236.

CASSIN.—Descriptions of new species of birds of the family *Laniadae*, specimens of which are in the collection of the Academy of Natural Sciences of Philadelphia. By JOHN CASSIN. V, Aug. 1851, 244.

Philadelphia—Continued—

 Cassin.—Descriptions of birds of the genera *Laniarius, Dicrurus, Graucalus, Manacus,* and *Picus,* specimens of which are in the collection of the Academy of Natural Sciences of Philadelphia. By John Cassin. V, December, 1852, 347.

 Cassin.—Descriptions of new species of *Hirundinidae* and *Psittacidae,* specimens of which are in the collection of the Academy of Natural Sciences of Philadelphia. By John Cassin. V, June, 1853, 369.

 Cassin.—Synopsis of the species of *Falconidae* which inhabit America north of Mexico, with descriptions of new species. By John Cassin. VI, Dec., 1853, 451.

 Cassin.—Remarks on birds from the arctic regions, presented by Dr. Kane. VI, June 1852, 107.

 Cassin.—Description of new species of birds, specimens of which are in the collection of the Academy of Natural Sciences of Philadelphia. By John Cassin. VI, Oct., 1852, 184.

 Cassin.—Remarks on the appearance of *Loxia leucoptera,* in great numbers in the vicinity of Philadelphia. VIII, Dec., 1854, 203.

 Cassin.—Remarks on *Crex pratensis,* a specimen of which was obtained from Salem, New Jersey. VII, Jan., 1855, 265.

 Cassin.—List of pigeons of the genus *Carpophaga,* in the collections of the Academy of Natural Sciences of Philadelphia, and of the United States Exploring Expedition, Washington ; with descriptions and notices of new and little known species. By John Cassin. VII, Dec., 1854, 227.

 Cassin.—Notes on North American Falconidae, with descriptions of new species, (*Buteo calurus, elegans* and *oxypterus.*) By John Cassin. VII, Feb., 1855, 277.

 Cassin.—Reference to several species of geese and other birds from the Falkland Islands, alluded to in a letter of Capt. Burnsee. By John Cassin. VII, April, 1855, 289.

 Cassin.—Descriptions of new species of birds from Western Africa, in the collection of the Academy of Natural Sciences, Philadelphia. By John Cassin. VII, April, 1855, 324.

 Cassin.—Notices of some new and little known birds in the collection of the United States Exploring Expedition, and the collection of the Academy of Natural Sciences of Philadelphia. By John Cassin. VII, Dec. 1855, 438.

 Cassin.—Notes on North American birds in the collection of the Academy of Natural Sciences, Philadelphia, and National Museum, Washington. By John Cassin. VIII, Feb. 1856, 89.

 Cassin.—Descriptions of new species of African birds in the Museum of the Academy of Natural Sciences, of Philadelphia. Collected by Mr. P. B. Du Chaillu in Equatorial Africa. By John Cassin. VIII, Aug. 1856, 156.

 Cassin.—Descriptions and notes on birds of the collection of the Academy of Natural Sciences of Philadelphia, and in the National Museum, Washington. By John Cassin. VIII, Oct. 1856, 253.

 Cassin.—Catalogue of birds collected at Cape Lopez, Western Africa, by Mr. P. B. Du Chaillu, in 1856, with notes and descriptions of new species. By John Cassin. VIII, Dec. 1856, 316.

 Cassin.—Notes on the North American species of *Archibuteo* and *Lanius,* and description of a new species of toucan, of the genus *Selenidera.* By John Cassin. IX, Dec. 1857, 211.

 Cassin.—Catalogue of the *Vulturidae* in the collection of the Academy of Natural Sciences of Philadelphia. By John Cassin.

 Cassin.—Catalogue of the *Hirundinidae* in the collection of the Academy of Natural Sciences of Philadelphia. By John Cassin.

 Cassin.—Catalogue of the *Strigidae* in the collection of the Academy of Natural Sciences of Philadelphia. By John Cassin.

 Cassin.—Catalogue of the *Halcyonidae* in the collection of the Academy of Natural Sciences of Philadelphia. By John Cassin. Nov. 1, 1852.

 Couch, Lt. D. N.—Descriptions of new birds of northern Mexico. VII, April, 1854, 66.

 Dudley, W.—Description of a species of crane found in Wisconsin, presumed to be new. VII, April, 1854, 64, (*Grus hoyanus.*)

 Gambel.—Descriptions of some new and rare birds of the Rocky Mountains and California. By Wm. Gambel. (*Picus nuttalii, Parus montanus, Fringilla blandingiana. Lophortyx gambelii.*) I, April, 1843, 258.

 Gambel.—Descriptions of new and little known birds, collected in Upper California. By Wm. Gambel. II, Aug. 1845, 263.

 Gambel.—Remarks on the birds observed in Upper California. By William Gambel. *Accipitres,* IV, April, 1846, 44 ; *Passeres,* III, Oct. 1846, 110 ; III, Feb. 1847, 154; April, 200.

 Gambel.—On an albino specimen of *Muscicapa virens* from Liberty county, Georgia, and a specimen of woodpecker, *Picus pubescens,* but probably a new species. By Wm. Gambel. III, Oct. 1847, 278.

PHILADELPHIA—Continued—

GAMBEL.—Observations upon several birds recently collected by Dr. Heermann, (*Rosthramus hamatus, Vireo longi-rostris, Ardea pealii.*) By WM. GAMBEL. IV, Aug. 1848, 74.

GAMBEL.—Description of a new Mexican quail, (*Ortyx thoracicus.*) By WM. GAMBEL. IV, Aug. 1848, 77.

GAMBEL.—Contributions to American Ornithology. By WM. GAMBEL. IV, December, 1848, 126.

HALDEMAN.—Facts in Ornithology. By S. S. HALDEMAN. I, July, 1841, 54.

HARRIS.—On *Cymindis hamatus.* By EDWARD HARRIS. II, May, 1844, 65.

HARRIS.—Description of a new species of *Parus (Parus septentrionalis)* from Missouri. By EDWARD HARRIS. II, Dec. 1845, 300.

HAYMOND.—Birds of southeastern Indiana. By RUFUS HAYMOND, M. D. VIII, November, 1856, 286.

HEERMANN.—Catalogue of the Oological collection in the Academy of Natural Sciences of Philadelphia. By A. L. HEERMANN, M. D. March 1, 1853.

HEERMANN.—Additions to North American Ornithology, with descriptions of new species of the genera *Actidurus, Podiceps, Podylymbus.* By A. L. HEERMANN, M. D. VII, October, 1854, 177.

HENRY.—Notes derived from observations made on the birds of New Mexico during the years 1853 and 1854. By T. CHARLTON HENRY, M. D., U. S. A. VIII, April, 1855, 306.

HENRY.—Description of a new *Toxostoma* and *Junco,* from Fort Thorn, New Mexico, (*Toxostoma crissalis, Junco dorsalis.*) By Dr. T. CHARLTON HENRY, U. S. A. X, May, 1858, 116.

HOY.—Description of two new species of owls, presumed to be new, which inhabit the State of Wisconsin. (*Nyctale kirtlandii, Bubo subarcticus.*) By P. R. HOY, M. D. V, December, 1852, 210.

HOY.—Notes on the ornithology of Wisconsin. By P. R. HOY, M. D. VI, March, 1853, 304; Aug., 381; Oct., 425.

KENNERLY.—Description of a new species of *Cypselus,* collected on the Northwestern Boundary Survey, A. Campbell, esq., commissioner. (*Cypselus borealis.*) By C. B. R. KENNERLY, M. D. IX, November, 1857, 202.

LECONTE, JOHN.—Notices of American animals formerly known but now forgotten or lost. By JOHN LECONTE. VIII, Jan., 1854, 8.

LECONTE, JOHN.—Observations on the wild turkey or *Gallopavo sylvestris.* By JOHN LECONTE. IX, Sept., 1857, 179.

LEIB.—Description of nest and eggs of the *Fulica americana.* By GEO. C. LEIB, M. D. I, November, 1841, 124.

McCALL.—Description of a supposed new species of *Columba,* inhabiting Mexico, with some account of the habits of the *Geococcyx viaticus,* Wagler. By GEO. A. McCALL. (*Columba solitaria,*) Wagler. III, July, 1847, 238.

McCALL.—Notes on Mexican birds heretofore not fully described. By GEORGE A. McCALL. IV, May, 1849, 63.

McCALL.—Remarks on the habits, &c., of birds met with in Western Texas, between San Antonio and the Rio Grande, and in New Mexico, with descriptions of several species believed to have been hitherto undescribed. By GEO. A. McCALL. (*Cyanocorax cassinii, Carpodacus obscurus.*) V, June, 1850, 213.

READ.—Catalogue of the birds of Northern Ohio. By M. C. READ. VI, August, 1853, 395.

SCLATER.—Description of a new species of Tanager of the genus *Saltator.* By PHILIP L. SCLATER. VIII, November, 1856, 261.

SCLATER.—Characters of an apparently undescribed bird belonging to the genus *Campylorhynchus,* with remarks upon other species of the same group. By PHILIP LUTLEY SCLATER. VIII, November, 1856, 263.

VESEY.—Descriptions of two new species of birds from the vicinity of Fort Tejon, California. (*Tyrannula hammondii, Vireo cassinii.*) By JOHN XANTUS DE VESEY. X, May, 1858, 117.

WOODHOUSE.—Descriptions of new species of birds of the genera *Vireo* and *Zonotrichia.* (*Vireo atricapilla, Zonotrichia Cassinii.*) By S. W. WOODHOUSE, M. D. VI, April, 1852, 60.

WOODHOUSE.—Description of a new species of *Ectopistes.* (*Ectopistes marginella.*) By S. W. WOODHOUSE, M. D. VI, June, 1852, 104.

WOODHOUSE.—Description of a new snow finch of the genus *Struthus.* (*Struthus caniceps.*) By S. W. WOODHOUSE, M. D. VI, December, 1852, 202.

PHILADELPHIA.—M a c l u r i a n L y c e u m o f N a t u r a l H i s t o r y : Contributions of, 1828. 8.

BONAPARTE, C. L.—List of birds of United States. (I cannot give the exact title, not having the work before me.)

PHILADELPHIA.—A m e r i c a n P h i l o s o p h i c a l S o c i e t y : Transactions. 4to.

BONAPARTE, C. L.—General observations on the birds of the genus *Tetrao,* with a synopsis of the species hitherto known. Read June 20, 1828. New series, III, 1830, 382.

ORD, GEORGE.—Some account of the moulting of birds. New series. III, 1830, 292.

PLANCHES ENLUMINÉES.—See BUFFON.

PRATTEN, H.—See SPRINGFIELD, Ill. State Ag. Soc.: Transactions.

PREVOST and DES MURS.—See DUPETIT-THOUARS, Venus.

PUCHERAN.—See PARIS, Revue Zoologique, I, 103.

PUTNAM, F. W.—See SALEM, Essex Institute : Proceedings.

RAFINESQUE, C. S.—See NEW YORK, American Monthly Magazine ;—PARIS, Journal de Physique.

RAMON DE LA SAGRA.—Histoire physique, politique, et naturelle de l'ile de Cuba, etc. Ornithologie par A. D'ORBIGNY. Text, 8vo, 1839. Plates in folio.

RAY, J.—Synopsis methodica avium et piscium, opus posthumium, etc. 8vo. London, 1713.

READ, M. C.—See PHILADELPHIA, Acad. Nat. Sciences : Proceedings.

REICHENBACH, L.—Avium Systema Naturale. Das natürliche System der Vögel mit hundert Tafeln grösstentheils Original-Abbildungen der bis jetzt entdeckten fast zwölfhundert typischen Formen. Vorlaufer einer Iconographie der Arten der Vögel aller Welttheile welche nachdem bereits fast dreitausend Abbilddungen erschienen sind, ununterbrochen fortgesetzt wird von L. REICHENBACH, Director am k. Zoolog. Museum in Dresden, &c. Erschienen sind Taf. I–LI den 1 December, 1849. Taf. LII–LXI den 1 März, 1850. Taf. LXXII–LXXXVI den 1 Juni, 1850. Taf. LXXXVII den 1 August, 1850. Dresden und Leipzig, 1850, etc.

REICHENBACH, L.—Handbuch der speciellen Ornithologie, beschreibender Text zu der vollständigsten Kupfersammlung der Vögel aller Welttheile von Dr. LUDWIG REICHENBACH. Dresden und Leipzig, 1851, et seq.

REICHENBACH.—Deutschlands Fauna, oder praktisch-gemeinnützige Naturgeschichte der Thiere des Inlandes, etc. 2 Theil, gr. 8vo, 1842. Vol. II, Vögel.

REICHENBACH.—See CASSEL, Journal für Ornithologie.

REICHENBACH, L.—Trochilinarum enumeratio ex affinitate naturali reciproca prima ducta provisoria. 8vo. Leipzig. J. Hofmeister, 1855. (This is subsequent to the list in Cabani's Journal.)

REINHARDT, etc.—Naturhistoriske Bidrag til en Beskrivelse af Grönland, af J. REINHARDT, J. C. SCHIÖDTE, O. A. L. MÖRCH, C. F. LÜTKEN, J. LANGE, H. RINK. 8vo. Kiobenhavn, 1857. Reprinted from "Grönland geographisk og statistisk beskrevet:" by H. RINK.

REINHARDT.—See CASSEL, Journal für Orn.

RENNIE, J.—See MONTAGU, Ornithological Dictionary.

RICHARDSON, J.—See SWAINSON & RICHARDSON, F. Bor. Am ;—LONDON, British Association : Zool. Society : Proceedings Comm. Sc.

RÜPPELL.—See FRANKFURT-a-M. Senckenbergische Gesellschaft, Mus. Senck. 1837, 188.

SABINE, Capt. ED.—See LONDON, Linnæan Society.

SABINE, Jos.—See LONDON, Linnæan Society.

SALEM.—Essex Institute: Proceedings. 8vo. I, 1848–1856, 2.

SALEM.—Essex Institute: Proceedings. 8vo. I, 1848–1856, 2.

PUTNAM, F. W.—Catalogue of birds of Essex county, Mass. I, 1856, 201. (245 species.)

SALLÉ, A.—See LONDON, Zool. Soc.: Proceedings.

SAN FRANCISCO.—Hutchings' California Magazine. 8vo. Vol. 1. 1856, et seq.

ST. PETERSBURG.—Académie Imperiale des Sciences: Novi Commentarii, etc. 4to.

GUELDENSTAEDT, A. I.—Sex avium descriptiones. XIX, 1775, 463. (Scolopax subarquata, p. 471 ; tab. xviii,)

PALLAS, P. S.—Descriptiones quadrupedem et avium anno 1769 observatarum. XIV, 1770, 548. (Sterna caspia.)

ST. PETERSBURG.—Acad. Imp. des Sciences, continued : Nova Acta Academiae, etc. 4to.

SAWASTIANOFF.—Description d'une nouvelle espèce de canard et d'une variété de l'huitrier. XIII, 1802, 346. (Anas canagica)

ST. PETERSBURG.—Acad. Imp. des Sc., continued : Bulletin Scientifique publié par l'Acad., etc.

BRANDT.—Note sur l'Anser canadensis, et sur l'Anser pictus de la Zoographie de Pallas. (lu avril 8, 1836.) I, 1836, 37. (Names Anser leucopareius.)

BRANDT, J. F.—Beiträge zur Kenntniss der Ruderfüssige Schwimmvögel, etc. II, 1837, 305. (Extract from memoir.)

BRANDT, J. F.—Rapport sur une monographie de la famille des Alcadées. II, 1837, 344. (Contains the characters of genera and subgenera.)

BRANDT.—Note sur les charactères des espèces du genre Phaeton II, 1837, 349. (P. flavirostris.)

BRANDT, J. F.—Observations sur plusieurs espèces nouvelles du genre Carbo ou Phalacrocorax, etc, III, 1838, 53.

St. Petersburg.—Academie Imperiale des Sciences: Memoires. Sixiéme série. Sciences Naturelles. Tome VI, 1849.

    Brandt.—*Fuligulam (Lampronettam) fischeri,* novam avium rossicarum speciem praemissis observationibus ad Fuligularum generis sectionum et subgenerum quorundam characteres et affinitates spectantibus descripsit J. F. Brandt. Read, Dec. 11, 1846. (The title page of the volume is dated 1849, although the memoir was probably published in a separate form in 1847.)

Say, Thos.—See Long's Expedition.

Schomburgk, R.—Reisen in britisch-Guiana in den Jahren 1840–1844, etc. 8vo. Vol. III, with special title of "Versuch einer Fauna und Flora von britisch-Guiana, Leipzig, 1848. Ornithology by Cabanis.

Sclater, P. L.—See London, Annals and Magazine of Natural History, February, 1858 ; Zoological Society ;—Philadelphia, Academy of Natural Sciences.

Selby, P. J.—Illustrations of British ornithology. 2 vols., folio. Edinburgh, 1821–1834.

Selby, P. J.—See Jardine, Naturalist's Library.

Seligmann.—See Edwards' Sammlung.

Sewastianoff.—See St. Petersburg, Acad. Imp. des Sciences: Nova Acta.

Sharpless, M. D., John T.—See New Haven, Am. Jour. Sc.

Shaw, Geo.—General Zoology, or Systematic Natural History, with plates from the first authorities and most select specimens. Continued by Stephens. 14 vols., 8vo., in 22 parts. Vols. 7–14, Aves, 1809–1826. (The ornithological portion edited and prepared, from vol. IX, 1815, by James Francis Stephens.)

Shaw, Geo. and Nodder, (F. P.)—Vivarium Naturae, or the Naturalist's Miscellany. 24 vols., 8vo., with 1068 plates. London, 1789–1813.

Siebold, P. T.—Fauna Japonica, etc. Conjunctis studiis C. J. Temminck et H. Schlegel pro vertebratis, etc. Folio. Aves, 1845.

Silliman's Journal.—See New Haven.

Sitgreaves, Captain L.—Report of an expedition down the Zuñi and Colorado rivers. By Captain L. Sitgreaves, Corps of Topographical Engineers. Accompanied by maps, sketches, views, and illustrations. Washington, D. C. 8vo. 1853. Birds by S. W. Woodhouse, M. D., naturalist and surgeon of the expedition.

Smithsonian Institution.—See Washington.

Sparrman, A.—Museum Carlsonianum, in quo novas et selectas aves, coloribus ad vivum, brevique descriptione illustratas. Fasc. I.–IV. Folio. Holmiae, 1786–9.

Spix, J. B.—Avium species novae, quas in itinere per Brasiliam annis 1817-20, collegit et descripsit. 2 vols., folio. 1825–26.

Springfield, Illinois.—Illinois State Agricultural Society: Transactions of, etc. 8vo. I, 1855, *et seq.*

    Kennicott, Robt.—Catalogue of animals observed in Cook county, Illinois. I, 1855, 577. (Includes the birds.)

    Pratten, Henry.—Catalogue of the birds of (South) Illinois. I, 1855, 598.

Steel, Dr. J. W.—See New Haven, Am. Jour. Sc.

Strickland.—Ornithological Synonyms. By the late Hugh Edwin Strickland. Edited by Mrs. Hugh E. Strickland and Sir W. Jardine. Vol. I. Accipitres. 8vo. London, 1855.

Strickland, H. E.—See London, Annals and Magazine.

Stockholm.—Kongliga Svenska Vetenskaps Akademien: Handlingar. 8vo.

    Sundevall.—Ornithologiskt System : af C. J. Sundevall. For Ar 1835, 1836, 43.

Stockholm.—Kongliga Svenska Vetenskaps Akademien: Ofversgit af Vet. Ak. Förhandlingar. 8vo.

    Sundevall, Prof.—Foglar fran Nord-östra Afrika. VII, v. 1850, 125. (Description of *Aegithalus flaviceps,* from America ; p. 129.)

Stuttgart.—Naumannia, Archiv für die Ornithologie, etc. Herausgegeben von Ed. Baldamus. 8vo. I. 1850–1.

    Bonaparte, C. L.—Notes sur les Larides. IV, 209.

    Bonaparte, C. L.—Tabellarische Uebersicht und Conspectus Geographicus der Papageien. VI, 383.

    Brehm, C. L.—Das Genus *Calidris.* I, ii. 1850, 66.

    Brehm, C. L.—Ueber der Kreuzschnabel (*Crucirostra.*) III, 1853, 241.

    Gerhardt, Alex.—Etwas über den Vögelgesang im südlich Nord Amerika. III, 1853, 37.

    Gerhardt, Alex.—Die Jagdbaren Vögel der Vereinigten Staaten von Nord Amerika. III. 1853, 378.

    Gerhardt, Alex.—Skizzen aus dem Vogelleben Nord Amerika's. IV, 1854, 192.

    Gerhardt, Alex.—Ueber die Lebensweise der Vögel Nord Amerika's (Georgia.) V, 1855, 380, 458 : VI, 1856, 1.

    Gerhardt, Alex.—Verzeichniss der Vögel des Staats Georgia, nach White. V, 1855, 382.

    Hartlaub, Dr. G.—Ueber neue Nord Amerikanische Gänse, II, i, 1852, 2.

HARTLAUB, Dr. G.—Ueber *Grus americanus* und *canadensis.* II, I, 1852, 2.

HARTLAUB, Dr. G.—Ueber einige neue oder weniger bekannte Vögel Nord Amerika's. II, II, 1852, 50.

SCHLEGEL, Prof. H.—Verzeichniss der mir bekannten Arten der Falken. V, 1855, 251.

ZANDER, H.—Ueber die europäischen Pieper. IV, 1854, I. (Notice of *Anthus pennsylvanicus.*)

ZUCHOLD, E. A.—Bericht üeber die am Obersee (Lake Superior) gesammelten und beobachten Vögel, von J. E. CABOT. II, III, 1854, 64. (Translated from Agassiz Lake Superior.)

SUNDEVALL.—See STOCKHOLM, Kongliga Svenska Vetenskaps Akademien: Handlingar. 1835, 1843. Ofversigt.—CASSEL, Journal für Ornithologie.

SWAINSON, WILLIAM, & RICHARDSON, J.—Fauna Boreali-Americana, or the Zoology of the northern parts of British America; containing descriptions of the objects of natural history collected on the late northern land expeditions under command of Captain Sir John Franklin, R. N. Part second, the birds, by WILLIAM SWAINSON, esq., F. R. S., F. L. S., and JOHN RICHAR-SON, M. D., F. R. S., F. L. S., surgeon and naturalist to the expedition. London, 4to. 1831.

SWAINSON.—On the natural history and classification of birds. By WILLIAM SWAINSON. 2 vols. 12mo. London, 1837. (Forming a portion of the series of Lardner's Cabinet Cyclopedia.)

SWAINSON.—Animals in menageries. By WM. SWAINSON. 12mo. London, 1838. (Part III of the work is entitled "Two centenaries and a quarter of Birds, either new or hitherto imperfectly described." This had been prepared to form part of the volumes on classification of birds.)

SWAINSON.—Zoological Illustrations, or original figures and descriptions of new, rare, or otherwise interesting animals, etc. 1st Series, 3 vols. 8vo., 1820–23.; 2d Series, 3 vols. 8vo., 1829–1833. London.

SWAINSON.—See JARDINE, Naturalist Library ;—LONDON, Zoological Journal ; Philosophical Magazine ; Journal of Royal Institution.

TEMMINCK.—Nouveau recueil de planches colorees d'oiseaux, pour servir de suite et de complement aux planches en-luminées de Buffon. Publié par C. J. Temminck et Meiffren Laugier, Baron de Chartrouse, d'après les dessins de Nic. Huet, fils et Prêtre. 102 Livr. 4to. Paris, 1820–39.

TEMMINCK, C. J.—Histoire Naturelle des Pigeons et des Gallinacées, accompagnée avec pl. anatomiques. 3 vols. 8vo. Amsterdam, 1813–15.

TEMMINCK, C. J.—Manuel d'Ornithologie, ou tableau systematique des oiseaux qui se trouvent en Europe, etc. 4 vols. 8vo. Paris, 1820, 35, 39, 40. Amsterdam, 1815.

TEMMINCK ET SCHLEGEL, Fauna Japonica.—See SIEBOLD.

THIENEMANN.—See CASSEL.

THOMPSON, ZADOCK.—History of Vermont, natural, civil, and statistical. In three parts, with a new map of the State. 8vo. Burlington, 1842. (Chap. VIII on the Birds of Vermont, p. 56.)

TOWNSEND, J. K —Narrative of a Journey across the Rocky Mountains to the Columbia River, and a visit to the Sandwich Islands, Chili, etc., with a scientific appendix. 8vo. Philadelphia, 1839.

TOWNSEND, J. K.—Ornithology of the United States. The descriptive part by J. K. TOWNSEND. The drawings from nature by French artists. 8vo. Philadelphia. J. B. Chevalier, (about 1839.) (This was apparently only a specimen number.)

TOWNSEND, J. K.—Ornithology of the United States of North America, or descriptions of the birds inhabiting the States and Territories of the Union, with an accurate figure of each drawn from nature. Edited by JOHN K. TOWNSEND. 8vo. Vol. 1. Philadelphia : J. B. Chevalier, 1849.

(Of this volume and work only the first number of 12 pp. and 4 plates (*Cathartes* 3 species and *Polyborus*) was published. It was then superseded by the work of Mr. Audubon, in 8vo.)

TOWNSEND, J. K.—See PHILADELPHIA, Acad. Nat. Sciences : Journal.

TRUDEAU, Dr —See PHILADELPHIA, Acad. Nat. Sciences : Journal.

TSCHUDI, J. J.—Untersuchungen über die Fauna Peruana auf einer Reise in Peru während der Jahre 1838–1842. 4to. St. Gallen, 1844–46.

UNITED STATES EX. EX.—See WILKES.

VENUS, Zool. of.—See DUPETIT-THOUARS.

VIEILLOT, L. P.—Histoire Naturelle des Oiseaux de l'Amerique septentrionale, depuis Saint Dominique jusqu'a la Baie de Hudson, etc. 2 vols. folio. Paris, 1807.

VIEILLOT, L. P.—Galérie des Oiseaux du Cabinet d'Histoire Naturelle du Jardin du Roi, etc. 2 vols. 4to. Paris, 1820–26.

(The edition quoted in some parts of the present volume bears date of 1834, probably a mere reprint of the title. The edition in the library of Phila. Acad. is dated 1825.)

VIEILLOT, L. P.—Analyse d'une Nouvelle ornithologie elementaire. 8vo. Paris, 1816.

VIEILLOT.—See PARIS, Nouveau Dictionnaire.

VIGORS, N. A.—See LONDON, Zool. Soc : Proc. Comm. Sc. and Proceedings ; BLOSSOM.

DE VESEY, J. XANTUS.—See PHILADELPHIA, Academy of Nat. Sciences.

WARD, JAMES F.—See NEW YORK, Lyceum Nat. Hist.

WASHINGTON.—Smithsonian Institution: Smithsonian Contributions to Knowledge. 4to.

> BREWER.—North American Oology. By THOMAS M. BREWER, M.D. Part 1, *Raptores* and *Fissirostres,* June, 1857. (To appear in vol. XI.)

WASHINGTON.—War Department: Report of explorations and surveys to ascertain the most practicable and economical route for a railroad from the Mississippi river to the Pacific ocean. Made under the direction of the Secretary of War in 1854-'55, according to acts of Congress of March 3, 1853, May 31, 1854, and August 5, 1854. Ordered 33d Congress, 2d session ; Executive Document (Senate) No 78. 8 vols. 4to., published up to 1858. Washington.

Vol. I, 1855, contains : Report of the Secretary of War ; examination of the reports of the several routes explored ; railway memoranda ; letter of Major General Thomas S. Jesup ; and report of Governor I. I. Stevens of route near the 47th and 49th parallels of north latitude.

Vol. II, 1855, contains : Report of Lieutenant E. G. Beckwith, 3d artillery, upon the route near the 38th and 39th parallels, and that near the 41st parallel ; report of a reconnaissance from Puget Sound to the Mississippi river, by F. W. Lander ; report of Brevet Captain J. Pope, Topographical Engineers, upon the eastern portion of the route near the 32d parallel, lying between the Red river and the Rio Grande ; report of Lieutenant J. G. Parke, Topographical Engineers, upon that portion of the 32d parallel lying between the Rio Grande and Pimos villages on the Gila ; extract from report made of a military reconnaissance made by Lieutenant Colonel W. H. Emory, U. S. A., of the portion of the route near the 32d parallel lying between the mouths of the San Pedro and Gila rivers.

Vols. III and IV, 1856, contain : Report of Lieutenant A. W. Whipple, Topographical Engineers, of the route near the 35th parallel. Of this report Part VI, in Vol. IV, consists of the report on the zoology of the expedition by C. B. R. Kennerly, M. D.

Vol. V, 1856, contains the report of Lieutenant R. S. Williamson, Topographical Engineers, upon the routes in California to connect with the routes near the 35th and 32d parallels.

Vol. VI, 1857, contains the report by Lieutenant Henry L. Abbott, Topographical Engineers, upon the routes in Oregon and California explored by parties under the command of Lieutenant R. S. Williamson, Topographical Engineers, in 1855. Part IV of this report includes one upon the zoology of the route by J. S. Newberry, M. D.

Vol. VII, 1857, contains report of Lieutenant John G. Parke, Topographical Engineers, upon the routes in California to connect with the routes near the 35th and 32d parallels, and upon that portion of the route near the 32d parallel lying between the Rio Grande and Pimos villages of the Gila ; also the conclusion of the official review of the reports upon explorations and surveys for railroad routes from the Mississippi river to the Pacific ocean.

Vol. VIII, 1857, contains : General report upon the zoology of the several Pacific Railroad routes. Part I, Mammals, by S. F. Baird. Vols. IX and X will contain the remainder of the natural history.

WIED, MAX. Prinz von.—See CASSEL : Journal für Orn.

WILKES, Capt. C.—United States Exploring Expedition.

> PEALE, T. R.—Report of the Mammalia and Birds of the U. S. Exploring Expedition under Capt. WILKES. 4to. 1848.

WILSON, ALEXANDER.—American Ornithology, or the natural history of the birds of the United States. 9 vols. 4to. Philadelphia. I, 1808 ; II, 1810 ; III, IV, 1811 ; V, VI, 1812 ; VII, 1813 ; VIII, 1814 ; IX, 1814. (Completed under the editorship of GEORGE ORD.)

WILSON, ORD's ed. of.—American Ornithology, or the natural history of the birds of the United States. Illustrated with plates, engraved and colored, from original drawings taken from nature. By ALEXANDER WILSON. With a sketch of the authors life by GEORGE ORD, F. L. S. 3 vols. 8vo. text, and one of plates in folio. Published by Collins & Co., New York, and Harrison Hall, Philadelphia. I, II, 1828 ; III, 1829.

WILSON, (Alex.)—American Ornithology, or the natural history of the birds of the United States. By ALEXANDER WILSON and CHARLES LUCIAN BONAPARTE. Edited, with notes and additions, by R. JAMESON. 4 vols. 18mo. Edinburg, 1831.

WILSON.—American Ornithology, or the natural history of the birds of the United States. By ALEXANDER WILSON ; with a continuation by CHARLES LUCIAN BONAPARTE, Prince of Musignano. The illustrative notes and life of Wilson by Sir WM. JARDINE, Bart. 3 vols. 8vo. London and Edinburg, 1832.

WILSON.—Wilson's American Ornithology, with notes by JARDINE ; to which is added a synopsis of American birds, including those described by Bonaparte, Audubon, Nuttall, and Richardson. By T. M. BREWER. 8vo. Boston, 1840.

> (Several editions of this work, with later dates, have been issued in New York from the original stereotype plates.)

120 b

ALPHABETICAL INDEX.

I. SYSTEMATIC INDEX OF COMMON NAMES.

121 b

ALPHABETICAL INDEX.

II. SYSTEMATIC INDEX OF SCIENTIFIC NAMES.[1]

[1] The names adopted are given in *italic*, the others are synonyms. The first reference after italicized names is to the page where the name is used as a heading.

125

THE BIRDS

OF

NORTH AMERICA;

THE DESCRIPTIONS OF SPECIES BASED CHIEFLY ON THE COLLECTIONS

IN THE

MUSEUM OF THE SMITHSONIAN INSTITUTION.

BY

SPENCER F. BAIRD,

ASSISTANT SECRETARY OF THE SMITHSONIAN INSTITUTION,

WITH THE CO-OPERATION OF

JOHN CASSIN,

OF THE ACADEMY OF NATURAL SCIENCES OF PHILADELPHIA.

AND

GEORGE N. LAWRENCE,

OF THE LYCEUM OF NATURAL HISTORY OF NEW YORK.

With an Atlas of One Hundred Plates.

ATLAS.

PHILADELPHIA: J. B. LIPPINCOTT & CO.

1860.

SALEM: NATURALIST'S BOOK AGENCY.

1870.

PREFACE.

THE present Atlas has been prepared for the two-fold purpose of completing the series of illustrations of the Birds of North America, and to give accurate and easily recognized figures of the numerous hitherto unknown birds described in the first volume. It contains figures of all birds inhabiting the United States which have not been given by former American authors, in connection with whose works it continues and concludes, as far as possible, to the present time the pictorial representation of all North American birds. In the accompanying volume of text will be found descriptions of all the known birds of the United States; their arrangement in the genera and families of modern zoologists; their geographical distribution; and, it is believed, everything necessary to a complete and thorough knowledge of this favorite department of the natural history of our country.

In 1843 the distinguished ornithologist, Mr. Audubon, brought to a completion the second and last edition of his great work on the Birds of North America, in which are given faithful and accurate representations of nearly five hundred species. This elaborate work included all the birds known to that celebrated author as inhabiting the continent of America north of Mexico.

In 1853 Mr. Cassin commenced the publication of a work entitled "Illustrations of the Birds of California, Texas, Oregon, and British and Russian America: intended to contain descriptions and figures of all North American birds not given by former American authors, and a general synopsis of North American Ornithology." Philadelphia: J. B. Lippincott & Co. The first series, containing plates of fifty species not given by Audubon, was completed in 1855, and has not been extended, having been superseded by the present work.

Many of the birds of the United States, not included in the works of the preceding or other American authors, having been collected by the several parties for the Survey of a Railroad Route to the Pacific Ocean, and of the Boundary between the United States and Mexico, as mentioned in the preface to volume I. of this work, they were figured in the reports of these expeditions published by Congress under the direction of the War and Interior Departments. All of these birds appear in the present volume, but, in almost every instance, redrawn from better and more characteristic specimens. Of the one hundred plates, however, of this volume, about one-half appear for the first time, having been prepared expressly for the present work. Many of the latter represent birds of Eastern North America.

As already stated, the work of Mr. Audubon contains figures of somewhat less than five hundred species of North American birds; that of Mr. Cassin contains fifty species. In the present volume will be found one hundred and forty-eight species, nearly all of which are now represented for the first time in any work on American ornithology. The three works together include illustrations of very nearly all the known birds of North America. A few species only are wanting, chiefly of Russian America and other remote localities, of which no specimens are preserved in American museums. All are carefully described, however, in the preceding volume.

The original specimens of a large majority of the species figured in the present volume are in the museum of the Smithsonian Institution, and have been described and figured by permission of the Secretary. The collections of the Academy of Natural Sciences of Philadelphia, and of the Boston Natural History Society, have also furnished valuable and interesting types for the same purpose, kindly placed at our disposal.

EXPLANATION OF PLATES.[*]

[*] Where not otherwise mentioned, the specimens figured are to be considered as in the museum of the Smithsonian Institution, and the numbers refer to the Smithsonian record of birds. The original of each figure is indicated as far as can now be ascertained.

* The figures in parenthesis refer to the numbers of the plates in the Mexican Boundary series.

* *Syrnium occidentale* XANTUS. — Proceedings Phila. Acad. Nat. Sciences, 1859, 193.

SP. CHAR. — A little smaller than *S. nebulosum*; general color liver brown, the feathers barred everywhere, even on the flanks. Axillars and under wing and tail coverts banded transversely with white, the bands towards and on the head are contracted into rounded spots.

General appearance that of *S. nebulosum*. Prevailing color light liver brown, each short feather with two transverse bars of white, the basal one tinged with rufous yellow; the subterminal pure white and not generally extending to the edges of the feathers. These bars have a marginal suffusion of brown darker than the ground color. On the top of the head and neck the subterminal bar exhibits a tendency to contraction into rounded or cordate spots, and in other places to a median interruption along the shaft. On the scapulars, axillars, and other elongated feathers there are several white bars. The facial disk is grayish, obscurely barred with brown; the posterior margin of the ear is uniform liver brown, then becoming banded with white. The longest quills and tail feathers show about 7 to 9 clouded transverse light bars, one of these at the end of the feather; the bars on the inner and outer margins are quite white, especially towards the base of the feather, elsewhere they are mottled yellowish brown or brownish yellow; the legs are dirty yellowish, with obscure and rather transverse mottlings of brown. The bill is greenish yellow; the iris gamboge; the claws horn color; the toes are thickly feathered to within two scutellæ of the base of the claws. The fourth quill is longest, the fifth and then the third a little shorter, the second between the sixth and seventh; the first rather shorter than the eighth.

Length of male 18 inches; extent 40; wing 13; tail 8¼; tarsus about 2.

This species, with a general resemblance to the *Syrnium nebulosum*, is of rather smaller size, and readily distinguished by the entire absence of any of the longitudinal brown stripes so conspicuous on the belly, flanks, and lower tail coverts of the latter species; these regions being barred transversely with white and brown. The white bars on the feathers are much less continuous and regular, and on the neck and head are restricted to rounded spots instead of forming regular zones. The under wing coverts are banded transversely instead of being uniform yellowish white. The bill is less pure yellow.

A single specimen (original number 1858) was collected at Fort Tejon, March 6, 1858.

* *Helminthophaga Virginiae* BAIRD. — Similar in general appearance to *H. ruficapilla*. Top and sides of head, back and wings light ashy plumbeous, with an almost imperceptible wash of olivaceous green; quills and tail feathers brown, edged with pure ashy plumbeous; the latter indistinctly and narrowly margined with whitish internally and at the end. Rump and upper and lower tail coverts bright yellow (with a greenish tint above) in vivid contrast to the rest of the body. Crown with a concealed patch of orange brown. Rest of under parts brownish white with indications of yellow along the median region (perhaps entirely yellow when mature). Inside of wings and axillars whitish. A white ring around the eye. Length 5 inches; extent 7¼; wing 2¼. No. 10719. Fort Burgwyn, N. M. Collected by Dr. W. W. Anderson, U. S. A.

* *Ibis guarauna* SHAW. — This species differs from *Ibis Ordii*, in longer legs, and an entire absence of chestnut red, which is replaced by bronzed green.   No specimens in the Smithsonian collection show any gloss on the head and neck.

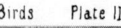

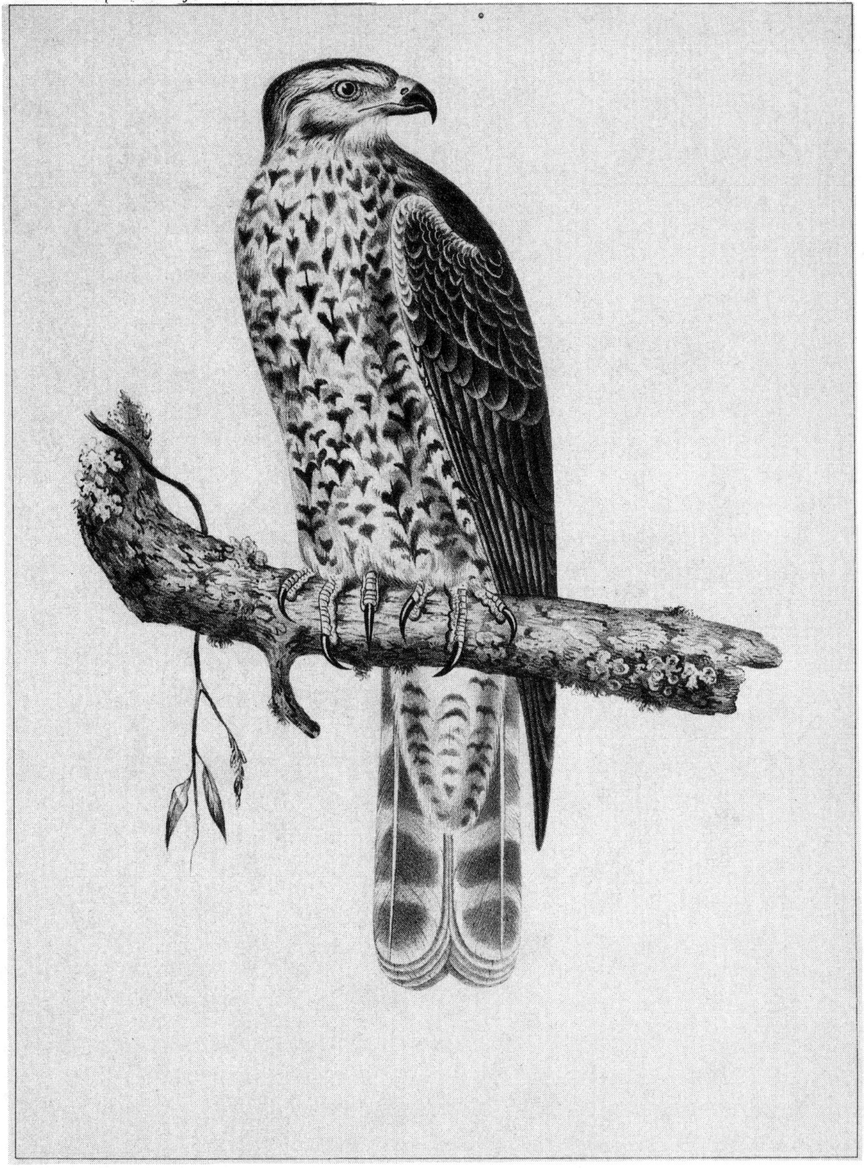

Fig. 2.

Fig. 1

Bowen & Cº Lith.& Col. Philada.

1. PASSERCULUS ALAUDINUS.　2. PEUCAEA CASSINII.

Pl. V

MYIARCHUS MEXICANUS

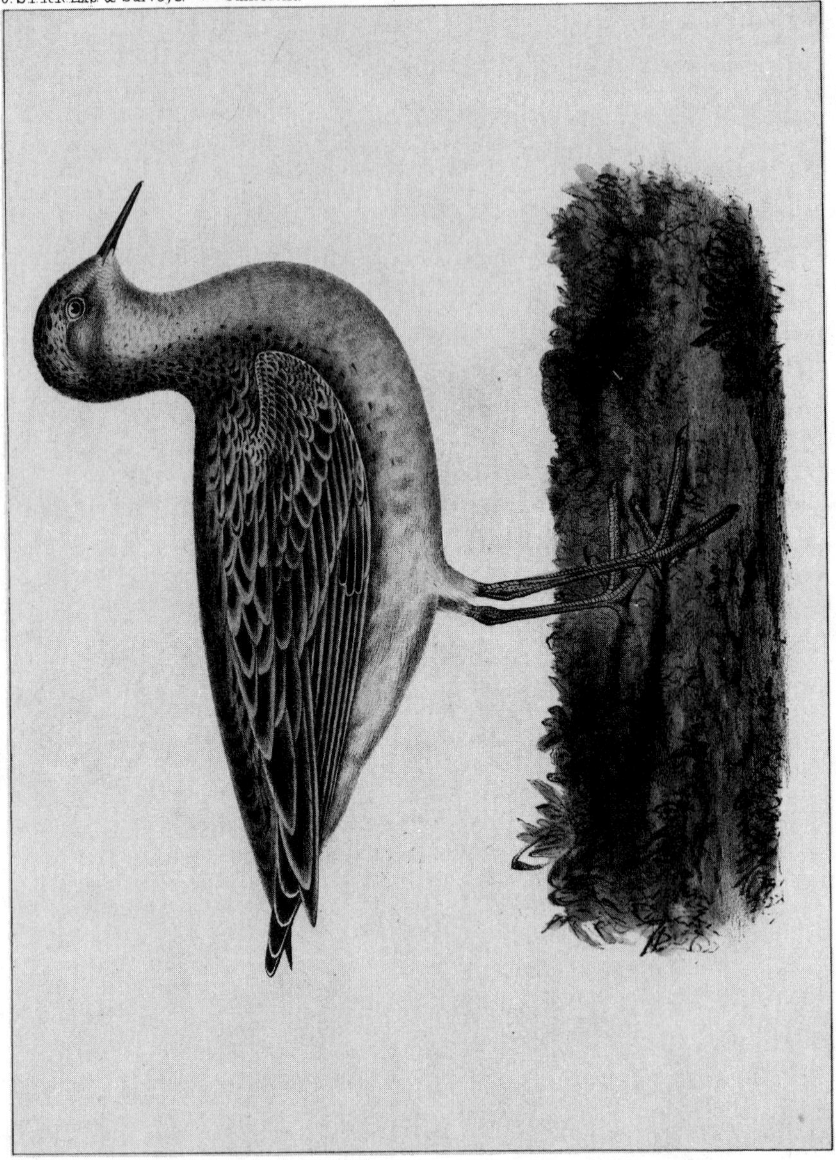

STREPSILAS MELANOCEPHALA.

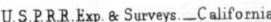

PHALACROCORAX PENICILLATUS.

Plate XI

Bowen & Cº Lith & Col. Philada.

BUTEO SWAINSONII.

Bowen & co lith & col. Philada.

BUTEO CALURUS.

I. BUTEO FULIGINOSUS. 2. B. OXYPTERUS.

BUTEO COOPERII.

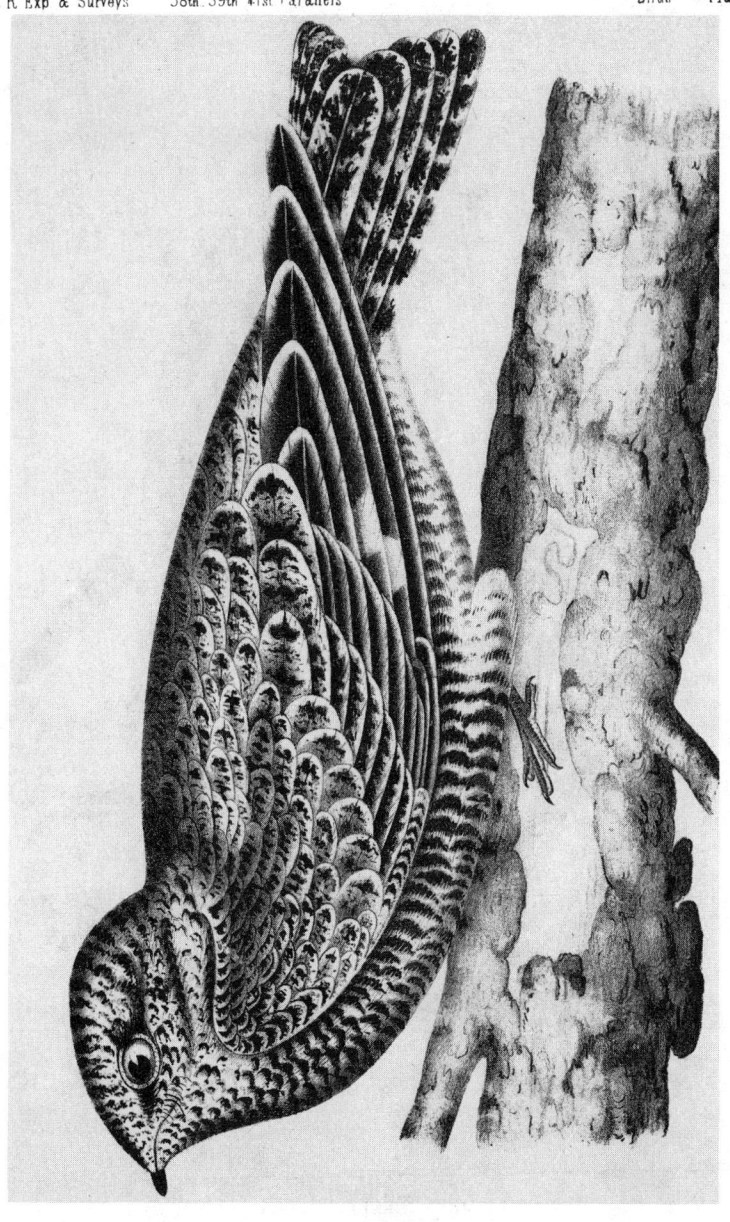

Bowen & Cº Lith & Col. Philada

1. PANYPTILA MELANOLEUCA. 2. CHAETURA VAUXII.

Bowen & Cº Lith. & Col. Philada

ATTHIS COSTAE.

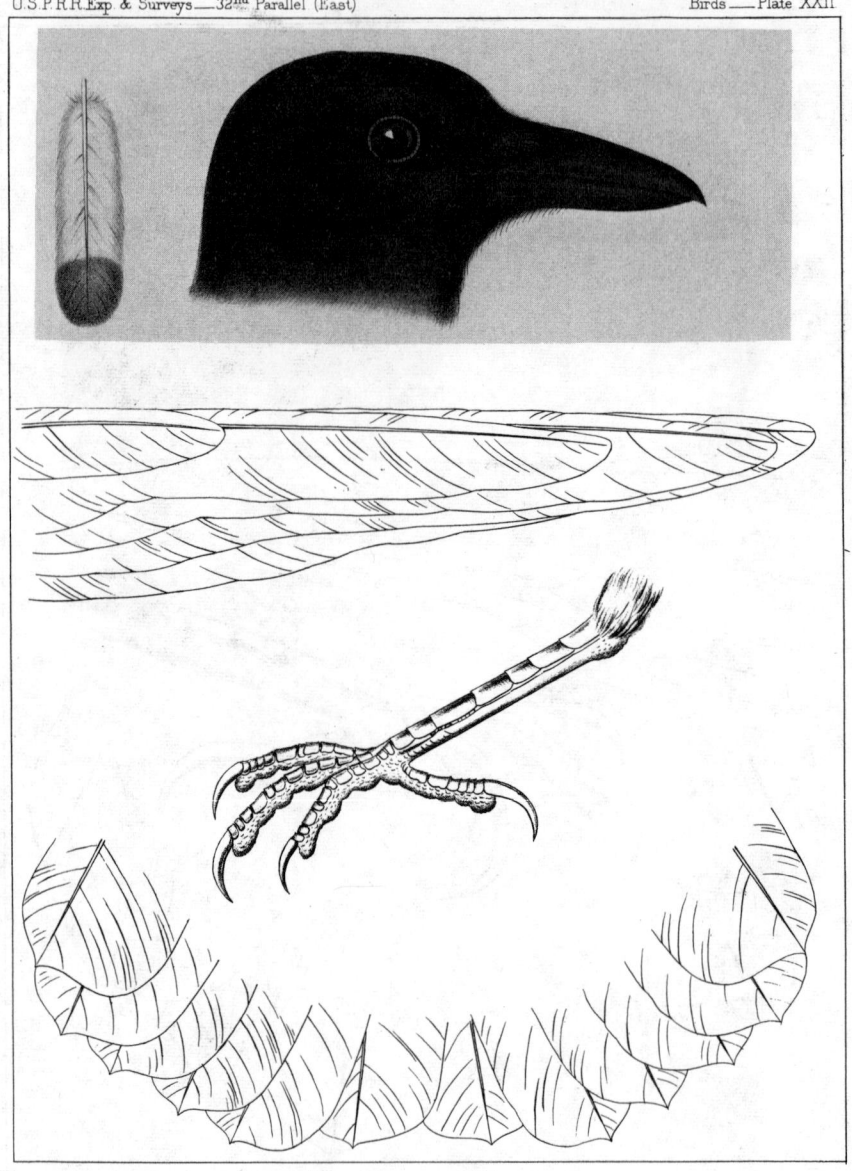

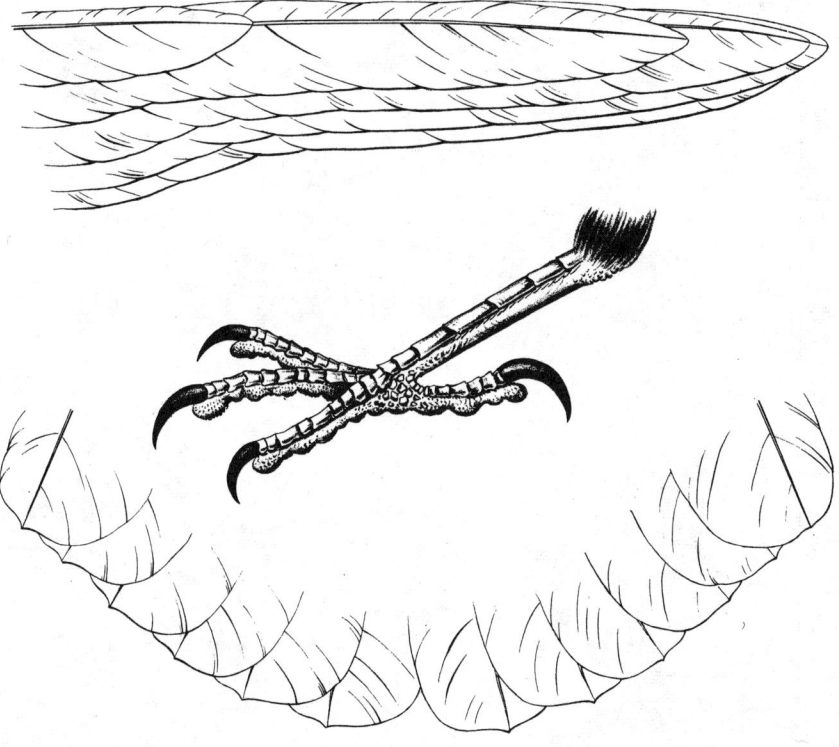

CORVUS AMERICANUS.

CORVUS CAURINUS.

Plate XXV.

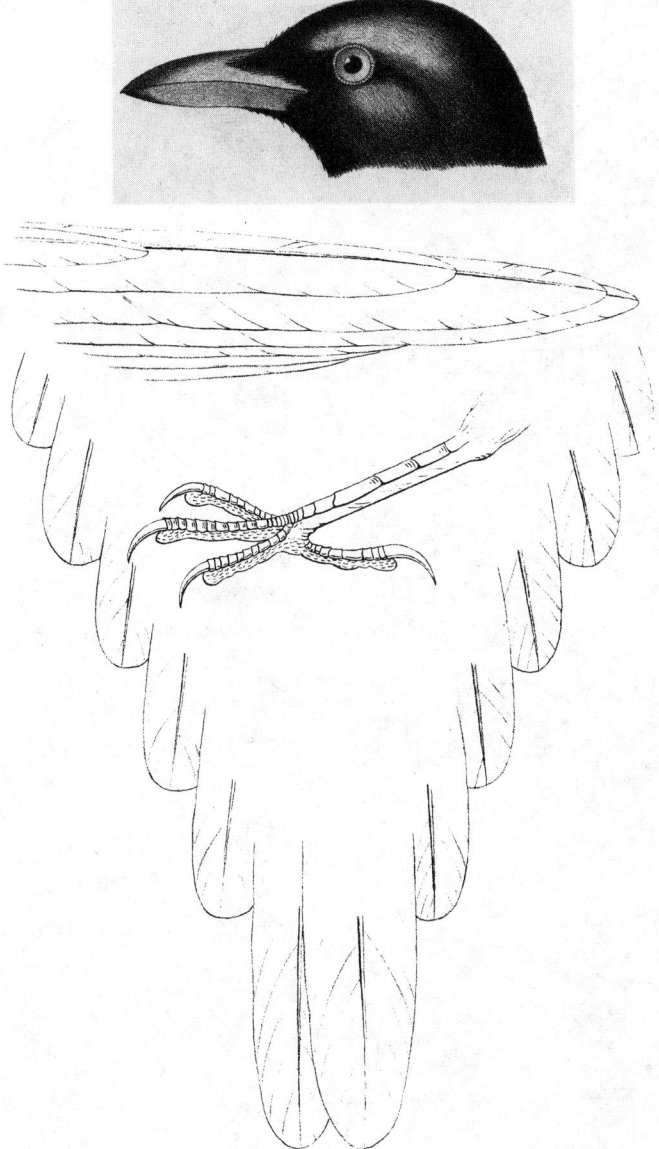

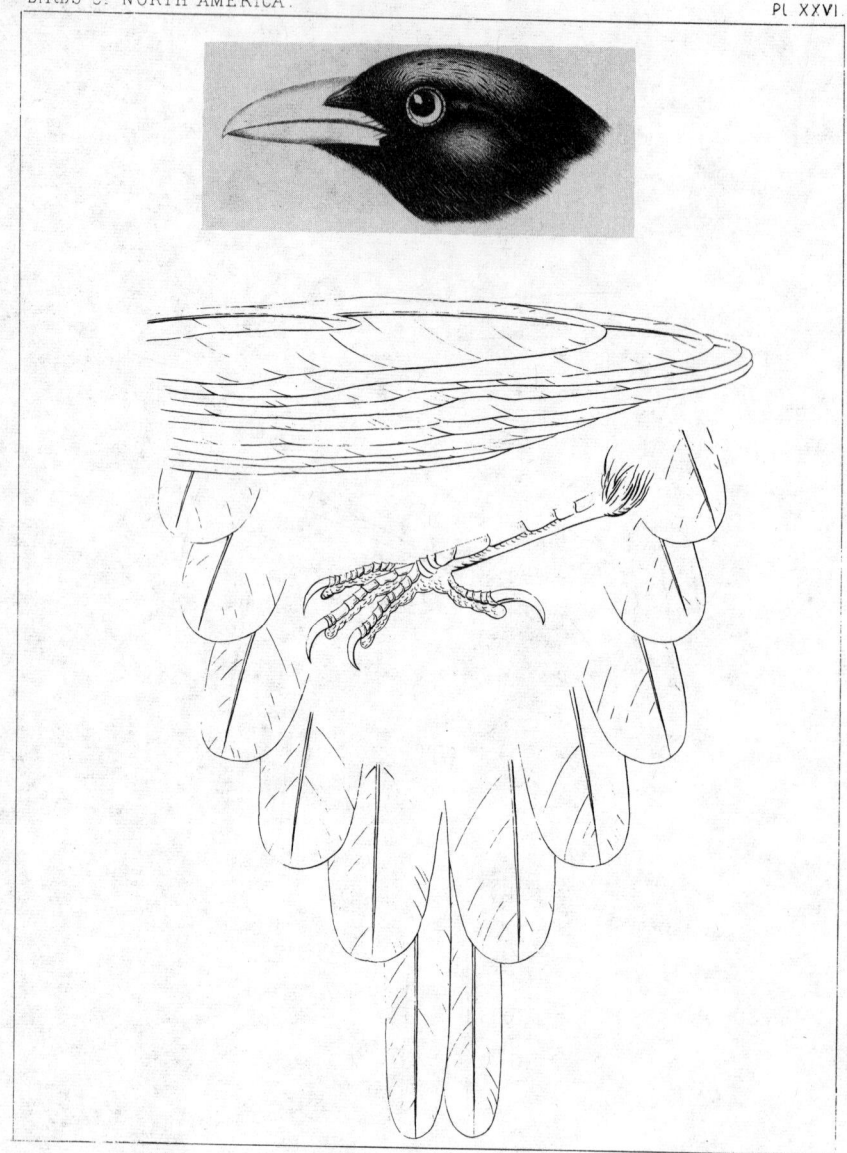

Bowen & Co. lith. & col. Philada.

PICA NUTTALLII.

Plate XXVII

Bowen & Cº Lith & Col Philada

1. CARPODACUS CASSINII 2. MELOSPIZA FALLAX.

1. JUNCO DORSALIS.   2. PASSERCULUS SANDWICHENSIS.

PIPILO ABERTII.

QUISCALUS BARITUS.

Bowen & Co lith & col Philad.

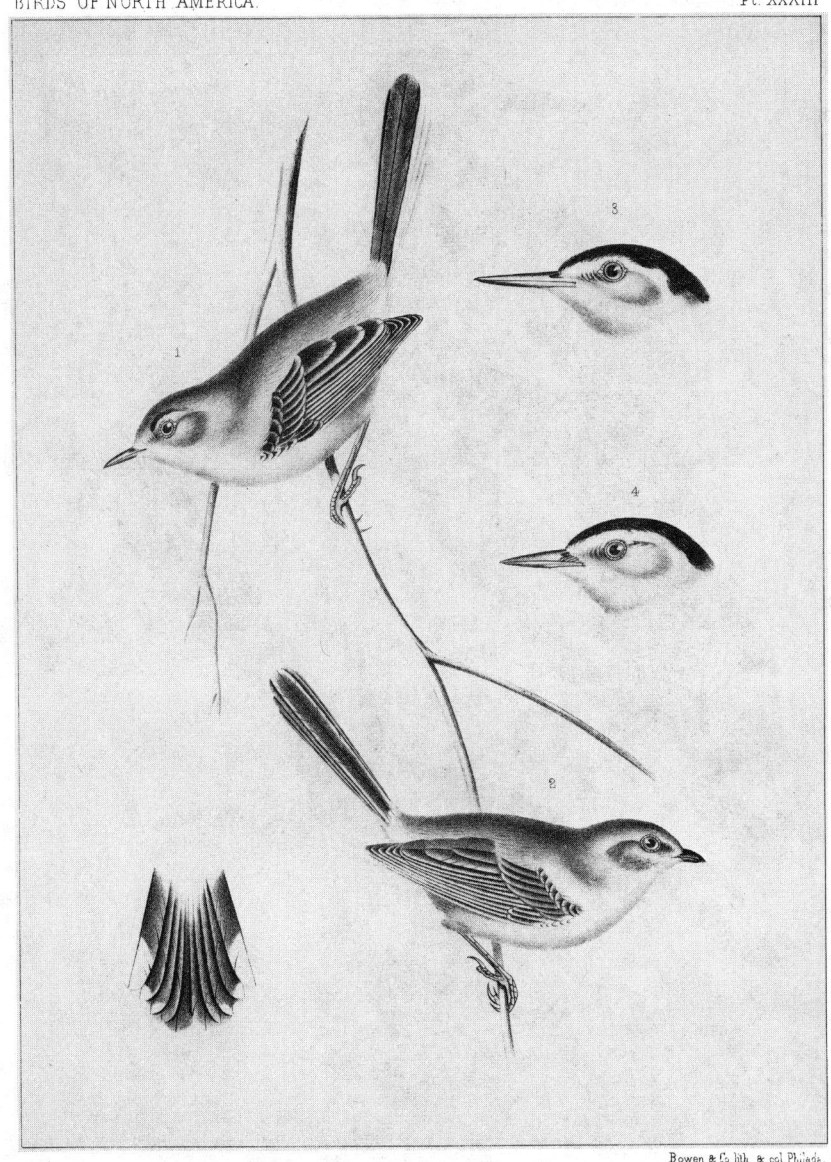

Bowen & Co. lith. & col Philada.

1. POLIOPTILA PLUMBEA. 2. PSALTRIPARUS PLUMBEUS.
3. SITTA ACULEATA. 4. SITTA CAROLINENSIS.

2

1

Bowen & Co. Lith & col. Philada.

SPHYRAPICUS NUCHALIS. 1. Male. 2. Female.

Bowen & Co. Lith. & Col. Philada.

CENTURUS UROPYGIALIS.